DICTIONARY OF
MISSION
THEOLOGY

DICTIONARY OF
MISSION
THEOLOGY

EVANGELICAL FOUNDATIONS

Editor:
John Corrie
Tutor in Mission and Ethics, Trinity College, Bristol

Consulting editors:
J. Samuel Escobar
Professor Emeritus of Missiology,
Palmer Theological Seminary, Wynnewood, USA;
Professor, Theological Seminary of the Baptist Union of Spain, Madrid

Wilbert R. Shenk
Senior Professor of Mission History and Contemporary Culture,
Fuller Theological Seminary, Pasadena, USA

Regional advisers:
Rosemary M. Dowsett
International Conference and Training Minister, OMF International

Roy Musasiwa
Principal, Domboshawa Theological College, Zimbabwe

K. Rajendran
General Secretary, India Missions Association, Hyderabad, India

Kang-San Tan
Head of Mission Studies, Redcliffe College, Gloucester

Inter-Varsity Press, Nottingham, England
InterVarsity Press, Downers Grove, Illinois, USA

INTER-VARSITY PRESS
Norton Street, Nottingham NG7 3HR England
Email: ivp@ivpbooks.com
Website: www.ivpbooks.com

First published 2007
Reprinted in paperback format 2013

British Library Cataloguing in Publication Data
A catalogue record for this book is available from the British Library.

ISBN: 978-1-84474-590-6

Set in 9.25/10.5pt Sabon
Typeset in Great Britain by CRB Associates, Potterhanworth, Lincolnshire
Printed in Great Britain by Ashford Colour Press Ltd., Gosport, Hampshire

Inter-Varsity Press is closely linked with the Universities and Colleges Christian Fellowship, a student movement connecting Christian Unions in universities and colleges throughout Great Britain, and a member movement of the International Fellowship of Evangelical Students. Website: *www.uccf.org.uk*

CONTENTS

ABBREVIATIONS AND CROSS-REFERENCES

1. Books and journals

EMQ	*Evangelical Missions Quarterly*
IBMR	*International Bulletin of Missionary Research*
IJFM	*International Journal of Frontier Missions*
IRM	*International Review of Mission*
JETS	*Journal of the Evangelical Theological Society*
JSNTSup	*Journal for the Study of the New Testament* Supplement Series
JSOTSup	*Journal for the Study of the Old Testament* Supplement Series
NICNT	New International Commentary on the New Testament
NovT	*Novum Testamentum*

2. Organizations

AAR	American Academy of Religion
CMS	Church Mission Society
CTBI	Churches Together in Britain and Ireland
IDSA	Institute for Defence Studies and Analyses
IINDEF	Instituto Internacional de Evangelización a Fondo
IMF	International Monetary Fund
MARC	Missions Advanced Research and Communications Center
USPG	United Society for the Propagation of the Gospel
WCC	World Council of Churches
WEA	World Evangelical Alliance
WTO	World Trade Organisation

3. Biblical books

Gen., Exod., Lev., Num., Deut., Josh., Judg., Ruth, 1 & 2 Sam., 1 & 2 Kgs, 1 & 2 Chr., Ezra, Neh., Esth., Job, Ps. (Pss.), Prov., Eccl., Song, Isa., Jer., Lam., Ezek., Dan., Hos., Joel, Amos, Obad., Jon., Mic., Nah., Hab., Zeph., Hag., Zech., Mal.

Matt., Mark, Luke, John, Acts, Rom., 1 & 2 Cor., Gal., Eph., Phil., Col., 1 & 2 Thess., 1 & 2 Tim., Titus, Philm., Heb., Jas, 1 & 2 Pet., 1, 2 & 3 John, Jude, Rev.

4. General abbreviations

ad loc.	at the place
c.	about, approximately
cf.	compare
ch(s).	chapter(s)
ed(s).	editor(s)
edn	edition
e.g.	for example
esp.	especially
est.	established
ET	English translation
et al.	and others

etc.	and so on
f., ff.	and the following
idem	the same author
i.e.	that is to say
KJV	King James Version
loc. cit.	in the place already quoted
n.	note
n.d.	no date
NIV	New International Version
no.	number
NRSV	New Revised Standard Version
n.s.	new series
NT	New Testament
OT	Old Testament
p(p).	page(s)
repr.	reprinted
RSV	Revised Standard Version
sic	thus
trans.	translated, translation
viz	namely
vol(s).	volume(s)

5. Cross-references

An asterisk before a word indicates that an article on that subject is included in the dictionary. Please note that the form of the asterisked word will not always be identical to the article title.

LIST OF CONTRIBUTORS

To the best of the editors' knowledge, this information was correct at the time of publication.

Martin N Accad, DPhil, MPhil, Academic Dean and Director, Institute of Middle East Studies, Arab Baptist Theological Seminary, Lebanon

Adetokunbo A Adelekan, PhD, MDiv, MA, MPhil, BA, Senior Pastor, Mount Olivet Tabernacle Baptist Church, Philadelphia, USA; Assistant Professor of Theology and Ethics, Palmer Theological Seminary, Wynnewood, USA; Instructor of Ethics and the Humanities, the W E B Dubois Summer Institute, Princeton University, USA

Clare M Amos, MA, Director of Theological Studies, Anglican Communion, London

Allan H Anderson, BTh(Hons), MTh, DTh, Professor of Global Pentecostal Studies, University of Birmingham

J Kwabena Asamoah-Gyadu, BA, MPhil, PhD, Associate Professor, African Christianity, Trinity Theological Seminary, Gegon, Ghana; Schiotz Visiting Professor of African Christianity, Luther Seminary, St Paul, USA

Victor R Atta-Baffoe, PhD, Dean, St Nicholas Seminary, Cape Coast, Ghana

Mariano Avila-Arteaga, PhD, Professor of New Testament, Calvin Theological Seminary, Grand Rapids, USA

Armand Barus, BEng, MDiv, PhD, Dean of Studies, Cipanas Theological College, Indonesia

Warren R Beattie PhD, BSc, BD, MSc, Director of Mission Research, OMF International; Adjunct Lecturer, Discipleship Training Centre, Singapore

Paul Joshua Bhakiaraj, MTheol, Commended Worker from the Brethren Assemblies; Director, Mylapore Institute for Indigenous Studies, India

J Roger Bowen, MA, formerly General Secretary, Crosslinks, London

Daniel R Brewster, DMiss, Asia Director for Child Advocacy, Compassion International

Colin O Buchanan, MA, DD, formerly Bishop of Woolwich

H Fernando Bullon, PhD, MSc, Post.Doc. Theology & Development, Professor of Mission, Ethics and Development, Universidad Evangélica de las Américas, Costa Rica

David G Burnett, BSc, PhD, MA, Visiting Professor in Anthropology, Chengdu, China

Barbara H Burns, BSN, DMiss, Academic Dean, Escola de Missoes Transculturais da Missao JUVEP, Joao Pessoa, Brazil

Victoria H Calver, BA, MA, Strategic Development Manager, Global Connections, London

Juan Carlos Carrasco, MTh, Director, Instituto de Formación Bíblico-teológica, Buenos Aires, Argentina

M Daniel Carroll (Rodas), BA, ThM, PhD, Earl S. Kalland Chair of Old Testament, Denver Seminary, USA; Adjunct Professor, El Seminario Teológico Centroamericano, Guatemala City, Guatemala

Tereso C Casiño, PhD, ThD, MDiv, BTh, Chair, Department of Systematic Theology, and Professor of Systematic Theology and Intercultural Studies/Missiology, Torch Trinity Graduate School of Theology, South Korea

Daniel J S Chae, BA, BA, PhD, Executive Director, MV Doulos, Germany; Research Fellow, Asian Center for Theological Studies and Missions, Seoul, South Korea

Alex D Chiang Nicolini, Bachelor in Sociology, Preacher, Lima, Peru

Emily J Choge, PhD, Lecturer, Nairobi Evangelical Graduate School of Theology; Lecturer, St Paul's United Theological College, Limuru, Kenya

Derek R Christensen, BA, BD, TheolM(Hons), Lecturer/Distance Co-ordinator, Carey Baptist College, Auckland, New Zealand

How Chuang Chua, BSc, MA, MDiv, ThM, Missionary, OMF International

David Claydon, BEc, DipEd, BD, DMin, MACE, formerly Federal Secretary, Church Missionary Society Australia, and International Director of the Lausanne Committee for World Evangelization

Paul P Cornelius, BA, BDiv, ThM, PhD, Principal, Hindustan Bible Institute and College, Chennai, India

John Corrie, MTh, PhD, Tutor in Mission and Ethics, Trinity College, Bristol

Samuel Cueva, BTh, MA, Founder and President, 'Mission for the Third Millennium'; Member, Latin American Core Group, Global Connections; Pastor, Iglesia Misionera Evangelica, London

Timothy J Dakin, BA(Hons), MTh, General Secretary, Church Mission Society, London

Monodeep Daniel, BA, BD, DipTh, BEd, MA, MTh, Chief Functionary, Delhi Brotherhood Society; Presbyter in Charge, St James Church, Delhi, India

Andrew P Davey, BA, DThM, National Adviser on Community and Urban Affairs, Church of England, London

Paul John Davies, PhD, MA, Postgraduate Programme Leader, All Nations Christian College, Ware

Levi T DeCarvalho, PhD, BLitt, MA, Research Co-ordinator, COMIBAM International; Training Co-ordinator, Latin American Centre for World Mission, USA

Richard H Dowsett, MA, International Conference and Training Minister, OMF International

Rosemary M Dowsett, BA, International Conference and Training Minister, OMF International

Tormod Engelsviken, Cand. Theol., PhD, Professor of Missiology, MF-Norwegian School of Theology, Oslo, Norway

J Samuel Escobar, MA, PhD, Professor Emeritus of Missiology, Palmer Theological Seminary, Wynnewood, USA; Professor, Theological Seminary of the Baptist Union of Spain, Madrid

David R J Evans, MA, Assistant Priest, Stourdene Group of Churches; Honorary Assistant Bishop of Coventry

Joyce E Winifred Every-Clayton, BA(Hons), BD(Hons), MTh, ThD, Professor of Church History, Recife Baptist and Recife Congregational Seminaries, Brazil

Keith Ferdinando, MA, BA, PhD, Lecturer and Principal, Faculté de Théologie Evangélique au Rwanda; Theological Education Consultant, Africa Inland Mission

Alexandre Brasil Carvalho da Fonseca, Doctor in Sociology, Master in Sociology, Professor, Federal University of Rio de Janeiro, Brazil

Joseph D Galgalo, BD, PhD, Head of Department of Divinity, St Paul's United Theological College, Limuru, Kenya

Chad N Gandiya, DPhil, MA, BTh, Desk Officer, Africa and the Indian Ocean, London

Laurel Gasque, BA, MEd, Team Leader, Religious and Theological Students' Fellowship, IVCF of Canada

Martin F Goldsmith, MA, Associate Lecturer, All Nations Christian College, Ware; travelling minister

Jules F P Gomes, BA, BD, MTh, PhD, Chaplain, The Old Royal Naval College, Greenwich, and Trinity College of Music

Rollin G Grams, BA, MTS, PhD, Research Tutor, Oxford Centre for Mission Studies; Lecturer, International Baptist Theological Seminary, Prague, Czech Republic

Jehu J Hanciles, PhD, MTh, BA, Associate Professor of Mission History and Globalization, School of Intercultural Studies, Fuller Theological Seminary, Pasadena, USA

Richard S Harvey, BA, MA, PhD candidate, Hebrew Bible and Jewish Studies, All Nations Christian College, Ware

Roger E Hedlund, BA, MA, DMissiology, PhD, Director of the Dictionary of South Asian Christianity Project, Mylapore Institute for Indigenous Studies, Chennai, India

Rolf Hille, DTheol, MPhil, Rector, Albrecht-Bengel-Haus, Tübingen, Germany

Hwa Yung, BSc, BD, MTh, DMiss, Bishop, The Methodist Church in Malaysia

Jonathan C Ingleby, MA, BD, DipEd, PhD, formerly Head of Mission Studies, Redcliffe College, Gloucester

William L Isley, Jr, PhD, AM, MDiv, BA, Professor, Universidad Internacional Cristiana ESEPA, Costa Rica; Pastor, Lighthouse Community Fellowship, EFCA, Kenosha, USA

Hermann Jansen, PhD, BTh, Director, Cross-Cultural Training Center and Northern Development Center, Thailand

Samuel Jayakumar, BD, MA, MTh, PhD, formerly Principal and Professor of Missions and Ministry, Madras Theological Seminary and College, India

Paul Yonggap Jeong, PhD, ThM, MDiv, BA, International Director, Vision for the Kingdom; Adjunct Professor, Fuller Theological Seminary, Pasadena, USA

Todd M Johnson, MA, PhD, Research Fellow, Gordon-Conwell Theological College, South Hamilton, USA

Jan A B Jongeneel, DrTh, Drs Jur, Professor of Missiology, Utrecht University, The Netherlands

Joshua Kalapati, MA, MTh, PhD, Reader, Department of Philosophy, Madras Christian College, Chennai, India

Ogbu U Kalu, BA (Hons), MA, PhD, MDiv, DD, Henry Winters Luce Professor of World Christianity, McCormick Theological Seminary, Chicago, USA

Joe M Kapolyo, BA, MTh, MA, Lead Minister, Edmonton Baptist Church, London

Kirsteen J Kim, BSc, PGCE, CDRS, MA, PhD, Tutor and Mission Programme Co-ordinator, United College of the Ascension, Birmingham

Sebastian C H Kim, PhD, Professor of Theology and Public Life, York St John University, York

J Andrew Kirk, BD, BA, MPhil, formerly Senior Lecturer in the Theology of Mission, University of Birmingham

Heinrich Klassen, MTh, DTh, MDiv, Pastor, Mennonite Church, Bielefeld, Germany

John A Kumar, BE, MA, PhD, Faculty in Religious Studies, South Asia Institute of Advanced Christian Studies, Bangalore, India

Peter Kuzmič, DTh, Founding President, Evandeoski Teološki Fakultet, Osijek, Croatia; Eva B and Paul E Toms Distinguished Professor of World Missions and European Studies, Gordon-Conwell Theological Seminary, South Hamilton, USA

David Tai-Woong Lee, BS, MDiv, DMiss, Director, Global Missionary Training Center, Korea; Chairman, Global Missionary Fellowship

R A Lidório, BA, MA, PhD, Team Leader, WEC Amazon Field; Church Planter and Consultant, WEC Mission; Presbyterian Pastor, Brazil

Richard D Love II, BA, MA, ThM, MA, DMin, PhD, International Director, Frontiers, Hemel Hempstead

Scot McKnight, BA, MA, PhD, Karl A. Olsson Professor in Religious Studies, North Park University, Chicago, USA

Imbumi Makuku
Details unavailable

Joseph A Manickam, East Asia Director, Mennonite Central Committee, Akron, USA

Colin A Marsh, PhD, Ecumenical Development Officer, Birmingham Churches Together

Pablo Mauger, MS, BA, Professor of Cross-Cultural Ministry and Director, Cross-Cultural Ministry Center, Costa Rica

Fernando Mendez-Moratalla, PhD, BD, New Testament Lecturer, Baptist Theological Seminary of Spain, Madrid; Baptist Minister, Barrio Del Pilar Baptist Church, Madrid, Spain

Eliya V Mohol, BD, MTh, PhD, Assistant Professor of Old Testament, Union Biblical Seminary, Pune, India

Sudhakar Mondithoka, MSc, MEd, MA, formerly Executive Director, RZIM Life Focus Society, and Executive Trustee, RZIM Educational Trust, India

A Scott Moreau, BS, MDiv, DMiss, Chair, Intercultural Studies, Wheaton College, USA; Editor, *Evangelical Missions Quarterly*

Salim J Munayer, PhD, MMiss, Dean of Academics, Bethlehem Bible College, Israel; Director and Founder, Musalaha Ministry of Reconciliation, Israel

Roy Musasiwa, BA, BEd, MTh, PhD, Principal, Domboshawa Theological College, Zimbabwe

Sampson S Ndoga, BTh, LTh, MA, Associate Programme Director, Africa Leadership and Management Academy; Senior Pastor of Emerald Hill Community Church, Harare, Zimbabwe

Z N Nthamburi, BA, MTh, PhD, Professor of Church History, Kenyatta University, Nairobi, Kenya

Rachel M Nunn, BA, MBBS, General Practitioner, Swansea

Stan W Nussbaum, BA, MA, MDiv, DTh, Staff Missiologist, GMI Research Services, Colorado Springs, USA

Nnamdi Emmanuel Omeire, PhD, MA, BA, DipTh, DipJr, AFES, Senior Lecturer and Head, Department of Interreligious and Mission Studies, St Paul's University College, Awka, and Archdeacon in the Diocese of Awka, Nigeria

Lalsangkima Pachuau, BA, BD, ThM, PhD, Associate Professor of History and Theology of Mission, Asbury Theological Seminary, Wilmore, USA

Catharine R F Padilla, AB, MA, Tutor, Centro de Estudies Teológicos Interdisciplinaries, Buenos Aires, Argentina

C René Padilla, BA, MA, PhD, DD, Director, Ediciones Kairós, Argentina

Augustine Pagolu, BD, MTh, PhD, Lecturer in Old Testament, Biblical Hebrew and Hermeneutics, Biblical Graduate School of Theology, Singapore

Ruben E Paredes, BA, MA, PhD, MDiv, Director, Orlando E. Costas Mission School of CEMAA, Lima, Peru

Joon-Sik Park, PhD, MDiv, BA, E Stanley Jones Associate Professor of World Evangelism, Methodist Theological School in Ohio, Delaware, USA

Jun Gyu Park, MDiv, ThM, PhD, Senior Pastor, Korean Friends Community Church, California, USA

Parush R Parushev, PhD, Pro-Rektor/ Academic Dean, Senior Lecturer in Theology, Course Leader of Postgraduate PhD MPhil Studies, and Director of the Institute for Systematic Studies of Contextual Theologies, International Baptist Theological Seminary Prague, Czech Republic

David B Pass, BA, MA, PhD, Founder/ Director, PassWord International, South Africa

Richard V Peace, BE, MDiv, PhD, Robert Boyd Munger Professor of Evangelism and Spiritual Formation, Fuller Theological Seminary, Pasadena, USA

Katharina Penner, MDiv, Lecturer in Biblical Studies and Applied Theology and Head Librarian, International Baptist Theological Seminary, Prague, Czech Republic

Peter F Penner, MDiv, MTh, ThD, Department Head of Biblical Studies and Director of the Mission and Evangelism Institute, International Baptist Theological Seminary, Prague, Czech Republic

R Howard Peskett, MA, Scholars Director, Langham Partnership, UK and Ireland

Ray J Porter, MA, MPhil, FRAS, Director of World Mission Studies, Oak Hill Theological College, London

P Solomon Raj, BSc, BD, MS(Ed), PhD, formerly Lecturer, Selly Oak Colleges, Birmingham

K Rajendran, Doctor of Missiology, General Secretary, India Missions Association, Hyderabad, India

Vinoth K Ramachandra, PhD, BSc, DIC, Secretary for Dialogue and Social Engagement (Asia), International Fellowship of Evangelical Students

Fyodor Raychynets, BTh, MTh, research student, International Baptist Theological Seminary, Prague, Czech Republic, and University of Wales; President, Christian Baptist Church, Bosnia and Herzegovina; Academic Dean, Bible Institute of CBCBiH, Sarajevo, Bosnia and Herzegovina

Hans Walter H Ritter, Dipl.Ing, Wirtschaftswissenschaften, MTh, National Director, OMF, Germany.

Dana L Robert, BA, PhD, Truman Collins Professor of World Christianity and History of Mission, Boston University School of Theology, USA

Richard A Robinson, MDiv, PhD, Senior Researcher, Jews for Jesus, San Francisco, USA

Cristian G Romocea, MA, PhD, Visiting Lecturer, Evangelical Theological Seminary, Osijek, Croatia

Sidney H Rooy, AB, BD, STM, DTh, Professor Emeritus of Church and Mission History, Instituto Superior Evangélico De Estudios Teológicos, Buenos Aires, Argentina

Catherine R Ross, BA, MA, BD, CDRS, DipTchg, PhD, Mission Interchange Advisor, CMS Britain, London

Vanmelitharayıl J Samkutty, BSc, BD, MTh, PCHE, PhD, Dean of Undergraduate Studies and Tutor in New Testament Studies and Greek, All Nations Christian College, Ware

J Norberto Saracco, PhD, President (FIET) International Faculty of Theological Studies; Pastor, Iglesia Buenos Nueuos, Buenos Aires, Argentina

Ivan M Satyavrata, BTh, BD, ThM, PhD, Senior Pastor, The Assembly of God Church, Kolkata, India

Thomas P Schirrmacher, Dr.Theol, Dr.Phil, PhD, President, Martin Bucer Seminary, Bonn, Germany; Professor of Missions and World Religions, Professor of the Sociology of Religions, State University of Oradea, Rumania

Lindy Scott, PhD, MDiv, MA, BA, Full Professor of Spanish and Latin American Studies, Whitworth University, Spokane, USA

Peter L Senkbeil, PhD, MA, BA, Associate Provost and Professor of Theatre, Concordia University, Irvine, USA

Calvin E Shenk, MS in Ed, PhD, Professor Emeritus of Religion, Eastern Mennonite University, Harrisonburg, USA

Wilbert R Shenk, BA, MA, PhD, Senior Professor of Mission History and Contemporary Culture, Fuller Theological Seminary, Pasadena, USA

David E Singh, BSc, BD, MTh, PhD, Research Tutor, Oxford Centre for Mission Studies

Juan Stam, MA, DTheol, formerly Professor of Theology and Hermeneutics, National University of Costa Rica

Simon M Steer, PhD, MDiv, BA(Hons), Principal, Redcliffe College, Gloucester

Pervaiz Sultan, BSc, MDiv, PhD, Principal of St Thomas' Theological College, Church of Pakistan, Karachi

Kang-San Tan, Master of Christian Studies (OT), DMin, Head of Mission Studies, Redcliffe College, Gloucester

Sunny Boon-Sang Tan, MTheol, ThD, Academic Dean of Malaysia Baptist Theological Seminary, Penang, Malaysia

James A Tebbe, BA, MDiv, MA, PhD, Vice-President, Missions, InterVarsity Christian Fellowship/USA, Madison, USA

Antonia L Van der Meer, BA, MTh, DMiss, Principal, Missions School, Evangelical Missions Center, Brazil; President, Association of Brazilian Tentmakers; co-leader, Brazilian Member Care Association

Michael S Vasanthakumar, BTh, MA, MPhil, DMin, Director, Tamil Bible Research Centre, London

Pius Wakatama, BA, MA, formerly Regional Director (Southern Africa), International Bible Society

Andrew Walls, OBE, MA, BLitt, DD, FSAScot, Honorary Professor, University of Edinburgh; formerly Director, Centre for the Study of Christianity in the Non-Western World

Roland S Werner, PhD, Senior Pastor Christus-Treff Marburg; Chairman, Christival 2008

Paul D A Weston, MA, MPhil, PhD, Tutor in Mission Studies and Homiletics, Ridley Hall, Cambridge

Keith J White, MA, MPhil, PhD, Director, Mill Grove; Chair, Child Theology Movement; Associate Lecturer, Spurgeon's College, London; Associate Lecturer, Malaysian Baptist Theological Seminary

Paulus S Widjaja, PhD, Director, Center for the Study and Promotion of Peace, Duta Wacana Christian University, Yogyakarta, Indonesia

Alfonso Wieland, BA, DipSoc, Executive Director, Paz y Esperanza, Peru

Wong Siew Li, Bachelor of Commerce, Masters in Christian Studies, Editor and Writer, Kairos Research Centre, Malaysia

Christopher J H Wright, MA, PhD, International Director, Langham Partnership International, London

Amos Yong, PhD, Associate Research Professor of Theology, Regent University School of Divinity, Virginia Beach, USA

INTRODUCTION

World Christianity and its associated mission are going through unprecedented change and development as the centre of gravity of the faith shifts ever further 'south'. Mission 'from everywhere to everywhere' challenges many traditional models of mission, and new contexts raise new questions for theologies that have hitherto seemed universal truths. Evangelicals need a mission theology with a sufficiently broad agenda, which both engages with these contexts and their perspectives, while also holding on to foundational truths and scriptural boundaries. In doing this, they need to listen to each other as they share their different perspectives. This dictionary documents a very wide range of voices from many different contexts, who have contributed to the task of charting the parameters of a missiology that will provide foundations for evangelical mission thinking and practice in any and every context.

Aims

In seeking to achieve this ambitious goal, the aims of the book can be summarized under three themes:

The integration of theology and mission

In recent years, the integral nature of the relationship between theology and mission has been increasingly recognized as mission has risen up the theological agenda worldwide. It is acknowledged that missiology should not be seen merely as an outpost of theological investigation, compartmentalized in the curriculum and tacked on alongside biblical theology, hermeneutics, ecclesiology and so on. It is rather that all theology is intrinsically missiological since it concerns the God of mission and the mission of God. This means that all theological categories are inherently missiological and all missionary categories are profoundly theological. This way of thinking theologically about mission

at the same time as thinking missiologically about theology has highlighted the Western theological problem of a failure of integration that arises from an enlightenment preoccupation with categorization. Too often Western theology has been done with no attempt to relate it to mission, and mission done with no attempt to think through the theological implications. Thankfully many are now recognizing the need to bring together theology and mission, so that those doing mission are thinking theologically about what they are doing, and those doing theology are thinking missiologically about what they are saying.

This book therefore sets out to encourage us all on that journey of integration. It aims to highlight and explore the missiological implications of a wide range of Christian doctrines and theologies, thereby creating a theology of mission that will serve as a reference book, resource and textbook for all those in any and every context, who are, or intend to be, involved in God's mission in the world. This aim represents a movement from theology to praxis: how mission arises out of theology, or how we think missiologically about theological categories and their implications for mission. Conversely, but complementarily, it will aim to explore the theological dimensions of mission engagement in as many of its aspects as possible. This is a movement from praxis to theology: how theological resources have relevance to missiological issues, or how we think theologically about mission. The basic assumption is that both movements are equally important; they are distinct, though related, exercises; so our aim is to show how theology and mission are integrally related to one another.

This exercise involves creative theological and missiological thinking. Contributors have been invited not simply to reproduce what others have said, nor to summarize themes in a way that can be found in other dictionaries and textbooks, but rather to explore the themes in such a way as to make an original contribution to current thinking. The focus is on exploring and understanding the intrinsic relationship between theology and missiology, and in this sense this dictionary is distinctive, especially within the evangelical world.

The view of mission that emerges from this exercise may be challenging to some of our evangelical traditional thinking about mission. The model of mission as 'integral mission', or 'wholistic mission', becomes inevitably predominant as the logical and necessary outcome of the integration of theology and mission. If mission arises out of the whole purpose of God for humanity, creation and ultimately the whole cosmos, then it is this universal mission of God which defines the scope of our involvement in it. If God in his mission is concerned with the transformation of the whole of reality, then he calls us to participate with him in that all-encompassing vision. Nothing is therefore ruled out of missiological consideration, be it the arts, ecology, HIV/AIDS, human rights, gender issues … the agenda is universal. But in each case the theme is seen in the context of the whole scope of God's salvation purposes so that our practice of mission in each place and project integrates evangelism, liberation, healing and justice. The articles here set out to explore this dynamic and its practical implications.

The contextualization of theology and mission

If mission is about universal themes of God's mission, it is also about the particularity of that mission in specific contexts. Just as all mission is intrinsically theological, it is also intrinsically contextual, as indeed is the exercise of theological reflection. This results in a triangular relationship between mission, theology and context. The growth of 'Majority World' Christianity has not only brought the priority of mission to our attention, it has also lifted contextualization up the theological agenda and obliged us to think contextually about mission. This book therefore sets out to reflect this reality by documenting a majority contribution from theologians and missiologists from different world contexts. Contributions from Majority World thinkers

therefore form 60% of the articles in this book, so that we can truly say that we have a 'majority contribution from the Majority World'. In this way the book aims towards a faithful reflection of the paradigm shift that has occurred in mission in recent years. These writers have been encouraged to reflect on their own contexts as they work on a theology of mission that both engages with it and transcends it. Some of them are exciting new voices in the field of missiology who are making a significant impact in their own contexts, often in practical ministries alongside their theological reflection. At the same time we recognize that Western missiologists have an ongoing and considerable contribution to make to mission theology, and many of their leading thinkers are well represented here.

This contextual view of mission is therefore a second distinctive feature of this book. It may also be seen as another challenge for evangelicals who have often been suspicious of contextualization, and preferred to think solely in terms of the universal truths of a supracultural gospel. But if each context is seen as enriching rather than undermining those universal truths, we may be more willing to welcome and affirm perspectives not our own, but which are necessary if the gospel is to engage meaningfully with the realities of each context.

The evangelical foundations of theology and mission

The sub-heading of 'evangelical foundations' is intended to convey a third aim of this book: an attempt to chart the contours of an evangelical missiology which both has its roots in cherished and recognized evangelical categories and also seeks to move evangelical mission thinking on beyond those categories. There is plenty here that will be recognizably 'evangelical': a respect for the priority of the biblical text as the authoritative source of theological and missiological thinking; a thoroughgoing trinitarian view of mission; an affirmation of the centrality and uniqueness of Jesus Christ at the heart of God's mission purposes; a confirmation of the importance of evangelism and the making of disciples of Jesus as the focus of our mission mandate; and the gospel call to all peoples and nations to come in repentance and faith to worship the one true and living God revealed in Scripture. But in recent years the boundaries of evangelical thinking have been stretching somewhat to include such themes as the importance of dialogue, the affirmation of humanity within a more developed creation theology, the conversation with cultures within which God's Spirit is at work, the appreciation of liberation as a category of salvation, the inclusion in the church's mission of reconciliation, social justice and political engagement, to name but a few areas that have not traditionally engaged much evangelical attention.

This book therefore seeks to set out some of the parameters for evangelical mission thinking in these relatively new areas. There is a wide range and variety of missiological thinking taking place that comes under what might be called an 'evangelical' umbrella. But our aim has been to reflect evangelical thinking as it is broadly and generously understood. We recognize that in some places finer theological distinctions are less relevant than in other contexts. But when theology is done in context, this will always produce fresh insights that invite new ways of thinking for other perspectives, and this will inevitably challenge some who may have previously maintained a mainly monocultural perspective. We may sometimes be breaking new ground in the evangelical theology of mission, and some may find this challenging. As evangelicals we will always maintain our concern for right doctrine, but we will also recognize the theological challenges that arise from new frontier situations that oblige us to face hard questions.

Scope

Dictionaries always have to be comprehensive within defined parameters, and our parameters have been carefully drawn to complement other dictionaries whilst making a distinctive contribution, as outlined above, to mission thinking. We have focused our perspective on the relevant dimensions of mission theology, rather than attempting comprehensive and exhaustive treatments of each theme. The choice of entries is necessarily selective, since descriptive material of famous people, missionaries, theologians or missiologists, other faiths, philosophies and world-views, and the historical dimensions of mission is readily available elsewhere. What is said is demonstrably grounded in the Scriptures, with a careful use of biblical material that articulates how the Bible provides a rich resource for mission thinking and how fresh contemporary approaches can yield new insights that remain faithful to the biblical witness as a whole.

Articles explore, where appropriate, the apologetic dimension; and how themes relate to mission in a multifaith context is discussed within the scope of relevant articles. The range of themes is sufficiently broad to fulfil our aim of providing an adequate foundation for evangelical missiology. It will be the ministry of others to build on the beginnings made here.

Readership

It is envisaged that the book will be read and used by church leaders, missionaries, students of mission and those involved in the teaching and practice of mission worldwide, and that it will be accessible to a non-specialist readership. The articles have scholarly integrity without being narrowly focused or esoteric. It will be a book that will be useful in any and every context in which mission is learnt and practised, which means that those who represent a range of contexts will see that many of their issues are recognized and explored. It will stimulate discussion, and specific articles will provide the basis for seminars and discussion groups in many different contexts of learning and practice. In this way, it is hoped that the book will have a wide relevance and distribution, and set a new benchmark for evangelical theological thinking about mission.

John Corrie
Editor

Accommodation/adaptation

Accommodation developed as a simple and early form of contextualization. Its practitioners had no expectation that the context itself would contribute anything to how the gospel might be either understood or expressed. It was simply a case of adapting the presentation of a given and unchanging gospel to the sensibilities and preferences of the context as a passive recipient of universal truths. It was accepted that local churches planted among different peoples can, and indeed must, worship God in forms that are meaningful to them, but it did not include the right to develop a local Christian theology in response to local questions and needs.

History of the terminology

David Bosch observed that the Protestant missionary movement was so linked to *colonialism that it effectively exported Western *culture alongside the gospel, even though it was understood that, 'to expedite the conversion process, some adjustments were necessary. The strategy ... was called adaptation or accommodation (in Roman Catholicism) or indigenization (in Protestantism) ... [but] it was often limited to accidental matters ... Accommodation never included modifying the "prefabricated" Western theology ...' So, while Western Christianity in its missionary outreach had some understanding about the need to allow people to use some elements of their culture, this was seen as a special concession, 'only a matter of *method*, of *form* rather than *content* ...' (*Transforming Mission*, pp. 448–449). Bosch, Luzbetak, and Hesselgrave and Rommen all use accommodation and adaptation as interchangeable words.

Because the expansion of the church was closely related to colonial assumptions, this limited understanding prevailed for over two centuries. It was only after the Second World War that Western churches started to realize that Third World churches, as they were called, needed to develop autonomously. Gradually, some permission, even liberty, for self-theologizing was granted. In fact, in several African countries, this understanding only came after independence when the missionaries were forced to leave. Simultaneously, local churches started to grow more rapidly, and both missionaries and churches began to learn the need to develop more respect for local culture and leadership (see *African theology, *Latin American theology, *Asian theology).

Practising accommodation

It has always been considered important to adapt *worship to local needs, although it is surprising how little accommodation took place when liturgies, vestments and hymns were transplanted wholesale by the missionary movement. But unless people are allowed to develop their own forms of worship, they can never understand that God accepts their lives and worship as they are. Communities in Africa, for example, become electrified and intensely joyful when singing their own songs in their own rhythms.

Adaptation is also required of mission practitioners themselves, first to a new language and lifestyle, and then accommodating their own ideas to the needs, challenges and sufferings of local people. For example, Westerners have largely failed to respond to the need for Africans to learn to deal with spiritual traditional healers, who were the only ones who knew how to deal with (what they saw as) traditional diseases caused by witchcraft (see *Healing). Elisha's response to Naaman, who wanted to believe in Israel's God, but had a very limited understanding of a 'correct' theology, can help us learn patience when sharing the gospel with people from cultures with very little understanding of biblical concepts (2 Kgs 5:1–19).

My greatest difficulty, while serving in Angola for ten years, was to understand how to relate to local concepts and practices of leadership. I learned that only *the* leader can take a decision, whatever the urgency of a need, and that in the Angolan context it was better to wait than to respond. I also learned that contesting the opinion of a leader publicly was considered a lack of respect. Eventually I learned to adapt, and instead of publicly speaking out my opinion or insight, I would seek an appropriate time to share it with an Angolan leader and let him present it to the others if and when he thought it appropriate.

I also discovered, after three and a half years in Angola, that many Christians still seek traditional spiritual healers for several kinds of diseases, believing that Western medicine is unable to deal with typical African problems. After interviews and study I started giving lectures about the problem, to which there was always a very enthusiastic response: 'Finally someone is speaking about these things and listening to us.'

Moving on from accommodation

The word 'contextualization' was first coined in the early 1970s in circles connected to the Theological Education Fund, but only recently has the essentially contextual nature of the Christian faith been recognized, the whole period from 1800 to 1950 having been marked in both Protestant and Catholic mission circles by an absence of contextualization. Christian theology, it was thought, had been definitively defined in the West and as such was universally valid: a contextual theology, on the other hand, implies ongoing dialogue between text and context.

All forms of contextualization, however, can fall prey to *syncretism. The best judges of what is appropriate adaptation of the Christian message and lifestyle will be local Christians, once they have access to God's word. A mission partner may judge innocent habits as idolatrous (e.g. the sprinkling of goat's blood on a deceased person to prevent putrefaction of the corpse), but not discern when apparently innocent habits may have idolatrous connotations for the local people (e.g. the use of magician-type tricks from a toy box to entertain children from a context of witchcraft). Adaptation should not make light of sinful practices.

Many still hold to the view that mere accommodation is an adequate level of contextualization, but by so doing they retain a patronizing and controlling stake in the search for engagement. Appropriate contextualization broadens, deepens and develops accommodation/adaptation by taking the whole context seriously in all its cultural, social and political complexity. It enters into serious dialogue with the context about the content as well as the form of the gospel. It defines better the kind of attitude needed to plant thriving local churches among all peoples and cultures.

See also CONTEXTUALIZATION, INCULTURATION.

Bibliography

R. Allen, *Missionary Methods, St Paul's or Ours?* (Grand Rapids: Eerdmans, 1993); D. Bosch, *Transforming Mission: Paradigm Shifts in Theology of Mission* (Maryknoll: Orbis Books, 1991); D. Hesselgrave and E. Rommen, *Contextualization: Meanings, Methods and Models* (Leicester: Apollos, 1990); G. Hunsberger, 'Accommodation', in S. Moreau (ed.), *Evangelical Dictionary of World Missions* (Grand Rapids: Baker Books, 2000); L. J. Luzbetak, *The Church and Cultures* (Maryknoll: Orbis Books, 1990).

T. VAN DER MEER

ADVOCACY, see APOLOGETICS

African Christology

It is often claimed that Western missionaries imposed on Africans a culturally 'Western-ized' Christ. The 'white Christ' as presented to the Africans was, in African eyes, a Christ fashioned in the image of the *colonialists. In response, African theologies usually begin Christological discourses from the premises of African realities. The approach typically betrays a polemical tendency in an attempt to break away from Euro-centric theological and philosophical frameworks. John Pobee expresses a common sentiment when he writes: 'African Christology is impossible without African anthropology' and 'Christ-ology in Africa cannot exist meaningfully without the social context' (*Toward an African Theology*, pp. 15, 17). Such background has deeply influenced the inspiration, method and content of African Christology. The critical tools employed by the African theologians in this regard are mainly social-cultural analysis, where African socio-economic conditions, historical-contextual realities, and presenting Christ using parallels and analogies from African world-views, provide a hermeneutical framework.

Approaches

There are two major approaches within African Christologies: inculturation and *liberation. Even then, the main motive of inculturation (i.e. to elucidate Christ from within the culture, by use of culturally relevant categories) leads to the more general 'contextual approach'. There are various sub-categories within this general approach. But all the categories engage with the African context, perhaps out of a theological sense of duty, and espouse functional or existential Christology: who is Christ for me.

The *inculturation* approaches generally interpret biblical Christological images in the light of similar African cultural categories. Nyamiti explains that 'most writers start from the African reality in order to see how this reality can be utilized to present Christian teaching on Christ in an African way' (in R. Gibellini [ed.], *Paths of African Theology*, p. 65). African themes include 'ancestor, chief, elder-brother, healer, hero, life, initiation, name and so forth' (ibid, p. 65). Nyamiti elsewhere refers to this method as 'a thematic approach', and describes it as 'the one most frequently used' (in R. Schreiter [ed.], *Faces of Jesus in Africa*, p. 4).

Then, to explain Christ in relevant terms, the inculturationists must identify 'elements of *African traditional religion and culture, such as ancestrology, chieftaincy, sacrifice, healing anthropology, the concept of the family and so forth' (E. Martey, *African Theology, Inculturation or Liberation*, p. 81). These are supposedly to provide building blocks for a Christology that is authentically African. How to do this, it seems, is not an easy matter. Wisdom is called for to discern and rightly identify what should be used, but more so how to apply the chosen element(s) in a theologically fruitful way. Nyamiti recognizes this challenge and offers some suggestions. He explains that a 'comparative approach' requires 'creative interpretation', which involves among other things identification and application of parallels and differences between cultural themes and 'Christian mystery' (in Gibellini, *Paths of African Theology*, pp. 70–71). In this regard Nyamiti makes some recommendations that he thinks are imperative. He insists that 'Christian mysteries' should not be treated in isolation, but themes, such as ecclesiology or Trinity, be interpreted one in the light of the other. He also recommends that the approach must incorporate a strong pastoral element or clarify the functional aspect of the inculturation enterprise, as well as engaging with theologies from all contexts and time, and not least, attend to the important task of metaphysical inquiry.

Nyamiti, despite identifying 'liberation Christology' as a distinctive approach, criticizes the proponents of this method as lacking in originality. He contends that, 'the African socio-cultural situation possesses an almost inexhaustible number of potentialities that can be actualized in original and authentically African liberation Christologies', and laments that 'few, if any, of the African liberation Christologists have availed themselves of these potentialities to any appreciable extent' (in Gibellini, *Paths of African Theology*, p. 71). We could point out that the approach also lacks substantial engagement with the actual subject of Christology – Jesus Christ – except for emphasizing his social action as a man. Efforts in the right direction are beginning to be made by theologians, especially those from South Africa, and women theologians, who find the model of Jesus-the-liberator greatly appealing.

Some missiological challenges

African theologians have sought to 'Africanize' Christ for the practical missiological purpose of communicating Christ effectively. In the process much seems to be lost, not only due to the inadequate theological premises employed, but also due to the inadequate linguistic and conceptual frameworks that are chosen for Christological elaboration. The basic Christological question: 'who is Christ?' has always been raised but quickly passed over. Attention has been focused on a more intimate question: 'who is Christ *for me*?' or 'how do I relate to Christ?' Often, the inquiry hardly proceeds beyond this existential concern. The images suggested, being exclusively anthropological, also fall short of pointing beyond the humanity of Christ to his divinity.

However, African theologians have not always uncritically applied these images. Kibongi, for example, using the traditional healer model for Christ, concludes that the idea only partially points to Christ, the true and ultimate healer, in whom the aspirations of the African search for wholeness find fulfilment. Cécé Kolié argues that 'to proclaim Jesus as the Great Healer calls for a great deal of explaining to the millions who starve in the Sahel, [and] to victims of injustice and corruption' (in Schreiter, *Faces of Jesus*, pp. 128–150). The image loses its relevance when seen against such a backdrop. Sawyer, dismissing Paul de Fueter's suggestion of presenting 'Christ-as-chief', gives four cogent reasons why the title is unsuitable: chiefs have limited power, corruptibility, inaccessibility and unsociability. He concludes that 'chieftainship is unsuited to the person of Christ' (*Creative Evangelism*, pp. 72–73). Pobee similarly notes that beside these negative connotations, the image also far more stresses the glorious picture of the exalted Christ than the cross, and may therefore be misleading. Parratt, pointing out the limitations of the 'Christ-the-liberator' model, observes that it fails 'to come to grips adequately with the problem of human sin and guilt' (*Reinventing Christianity*, pp. 87–88). This is true for almost all other images. Raymond Moloney, for example, observes that, 'The ancestor ... is clearly a human being, and his promotion to a state of nearness to God suggests ... adoptionism rather than full divinity' (in *Theological Studies* 48, p. 510). We must add that nothing less than divine can fully deal with human sin and the need for salvation. The proponents of ancestor-Christology also often forget that the fellowship with the ancestors is not something often desired, and that the 'shadowy existence' (ibid.) of the ancestors is more fearsome than assuring. The significance attached to the ancestors also varies from one African society to another.

These images are 'culture-specific' and are therefore limited to their particular contexts. They lack the kind of translatability that biblical or the Judeo-Christian models have achieved over the centuries. The cultural particularities of the categories, therefore, limit their usefulness outside the 'donor' culture. Most cultural models 'would at best represent points of contact within a very limited area only, and could thus not provide a very firm basis for an African – as opposed to a purely local – Christology' (Parratt, *Reinventing Christianity*, p. 80). This parochiality makes the images unhelpful for the communication of the universality of Jesus Christ, and also potentially problematic for a theology that seeks to actualize one redeemed family of God, a reconstituted new humanity.

The models also generally take for granted central Christological concerns such as incarnation or resurrection. What happens, for example, to the atoning aspect of Christ's mission? Unless Christology takes in its stride these central concerns, and stands out as being primarily trinitarian, then there is a danger of reducing Christian faith to a shallow spiritualism. The liberation models as advanced by many African theologians easily lose sight of an adequate soteriology that attends equally to both spiritual and physical needs. They easily settle for ideology or situational praxis, and often fail to convey salvation in its 'holistic' sense.

Conclusions

Christ does not need to be black in order to identify with Africans. But context-specific understandings of Christ need not claim universal validity to have meaning within their own context, so long as they are faithful to the person of Christ as he is revealed in Scripture. Christ is able to reveal an identity which both resonates with the context and is faithful to who he is. Christ is as he is in himself and will remain so. We can relate to him as we are in our own context and name him in our own tongue, but we cannot fashion him to be to us what he cannot be to others.

So there is no single Christological method to be used as a criterion to judge the different approaches within the study of African Christology. However, Christ the subject of Christology must be allowed himself to set the criterion within which the different approaches should formulate their understanding of him, and against which their soundness can be judged. While African Christologies must be lauded for their emphasis on the need for *contextualization and relevance, they must guard against the danger of sacrificing the faithful transmission of the 'criterion' at the altar of communicability.

See also AFRICAN THEOLOGY, CHRISTOLOGY, INCULTURATION.

Bibliography

R. Gibellini (ed.), *Paths of African Theology* (Maryknoll: Orbis Books, 1994); E. Martey, *African Theology: Inculturation or Liberation* (Maryknoll: Orbis Books, 1995); R. Moloney, 'African Christology', *Theological Studies* 48, 1987, pp. 505–515; J. Parratt, *Reinventing Christianity* (Grand Rapids: Eerdmans, 1995); J. Pobee, *Toward an African Theology* (Nashville: Abingdon Press, 1979); J. Pobee, *Exploring Afro-Christology* (New York: Peter Lang, 1992); H. Sawyer, *Creative Evangelism* (London: Lutterworth Press, 1968); R. Schreiter (ed.), *Faces of Jesus in Africa* (Maryknoll: Orbis Books, 2000).

J. D. GALGALO

African initiated churches

Estimated in 2001 at 78 million adherents, African initiated churches, or AICs, (including 'neo-*Pentecostals' as explained below) were a significant part of the astonishing conversion of a continent in the twentieth century. In virtually every respect these churches founded by Africans rather than missionaries were years if not decades ahead of Western missiological debates and buzzwords. While Western missionaries dreamed of planting 'self-supporting, self-governing, self-propagating' churches, these Africans actually did it. They *contextualized and inculturated the gospel before the books on those subjects were written and without reading them after they were. They were 'churches of the poor' before that phrase was coined. They have long been the 'missional churches' that today's avant-garde missiologists are trying to invent.

Above all, AICs have understood 'the gospel of the kingdom' much better than most other churches and even most missiologists. Though they have seldom used the term 'kingdom' to express it, the concept of the arriving kingdom is the key to AIC life and witness as well as to its helpful, though often unspoken, critique of common Western approaches to mission.

The fundamental contribution of AICs to missiology was that they converted the gospel witness from past and future to present. Western missionaries brought a message of some things the God of Israel had done through Jesus many generations ago in a place unimaginably far away, and some other things he will do in the future after we die. By contrast, the founders of AICs announced some good news – that same God of Israel is doing some things right now right here in Africa. He is sending visions, calling prophets, empowering healers, thundering out to Africans, 'Here I am! Here I am!' His 'kingdom', that is, his 'liberating control' (J. Verkuyl,

Contemporary Missiology: An Introduction, translating the Greek, *basileia*) or his 'overwhelming kingly aura and influence' is appearing in Africa, transforming everything as it comes (cf. Mark 1:15; Luke 4:16–21).

This highly contextualized newsflash was 'missionary' to the core, that is, it had to be told and retold. It whipped across the African landscape like wildfire, destroying the basis of white religious imperialism. If the Christian gospel was essentially about the past, then the whites were needed as its messengers and interpreters. But if the gospel was equally about God's personal arrival today in a powerful, unmediated way in the lives of God-chosen Africans, who needed the whites to explain it? In fact, how could the whites interpret a type of God-arrival they apparently had not experienced? The experts on the subject of welcoming the King to Africa would have to be Africans. Many of these King-welcomers became legends in their own time: William Wade Harris in Cote d'Ivoire (1915), Kimbangu in the Congo (1921), Babalola in Nigeria (1930), Jehu-Appiah in Ghana (1924), Legkhanyane in South Africa (1925), Maranke in Zimbabwe (1932), Kivuli in Kenya (1942). But thousands of other unknowns received their own call dreams and founded their own churches that met in homes, under trees, by roadsides – peppering the whole of Africa today with locally owned, locally controlled congregations and denominations. For example, Oduro describes an illiterate, non-Christian market lady in Nigeria in 1947 receiving a mysterious two-word message in a vision ('Matthew Ten'), a tiny kingdom seed that grew to become the Christ Holy Church with over 900 congregations today.

The leaders of AICs, whether legendary or unknown, usually carry the paradox of inculturation within their own conversion experiences. In one sense they have a completely new experience of the Holy Spirit of God, often unexpected and sometimes unwelcome because it demands a rejection of all idols, fetishes, magic and spirits. It pulls them into a new biblical orbit. At the same time, the experience is not anti-African. It does not overthrow African culture and values. Instead it opens the almost unheard-of opportunity to become a Christian without turning white.

Each Spirit-called person has to work

through the inculturation paradox and lead his or her followers through it, which causes immense variety among AICs and some hot theological debates between them (see *African theology). For example, in southern Africa some AICs theologically justify the practice of animal sacrifice with reference to Leviticus 1 – 3, saying they are performing an appropriate form of thanksgiving to God, unrelated to the sin and guilt offerings of Leviticus 4 – 5. Other AICs insist that Jesus' sacrifice has terminated all animal sacrifices. Traditional drums are another example, used in worship by many churches but rejected by a significant minority.

Besides its theological impact, the AIC experience of the kingdom has had huge liberating impact in the political and social realms, such as:

Colonial oppression: the same news which marginalized white religious authority also tended to lend theological and moral support to the African struggle against *colonialism. Confident of being God-called, AIC leaders could face, expose and outlast colonial powers.

Oppression of women: the news that God sends visions and healing power to women as well as men rocked the patriarchal structures of many African cultures.

Tribalism: quite incredibly the presence and activity of the Holy Spirit was able to unite newly urbanized people across ethnic lines into genuine congregations (not mere aggregations like many Western churches).

Urban struggles: today in these Spirit-centred groups, AIC members both discover and construct their new life in Christ in a community that provides dignity, healing, encouragement and connections. Literacy is not required; communication is.

All four of these aspects of the AICs' liberating impact occurred with very little money to promote them and even less foreign expertise to assist them, a fact that puts huge question marks over all dollar-dependent missiology.

In spite of all their missiological breakthroughs, churches based on a founder's experience of God's kingly intervention in his or her life are not without their problems, especially if that personal experience is seen as a substitute for Bible study, the wider Christian community, and church history. The AICs who have isolated themselves from those influences have run into four typical problems: fragmentation, fossilization, syncretism and messianism. If people other than the founder receive a call or spiritual empowerment similar to his or hers, they may split the church, especially if other divisive undercurrents are already present (extremely common). On the other hand, the founder's experience may be idolized and clung to as a substitute for such experiences by people today instead of a model and inspiration for them (somewhat common). The founder may reduce the faith to a new technique for acquiring spiritual power, which is the 'health and wealth' *syncretism (quite widespread) or drift into heretical, even bizarre, theology, which is syncretism with African culture (not nearly as common as many outsiders suppose). The founder may even see himself as a messiah replacing Jesus (quite rare).

Today the two major types of African initiated churches are the 'classic AICs' and the 'neo-Pentecostal AICs'. Most of the academic literature has focused on the classic AICs, which have often been called 'African independent churches' or 'African indigenous churches'. They tended to be culturally pro-African when the mission establishment was culturally anti-African. The neo-Pentecostal AICs have mushroomed in the last twenty years, especially among young, upwardly mobile, English-speaking Africans in urban areas. These new AICs are often highly enamoured with the modern Western lifestyle and have some connection with a Western preacher or Bible school, but they do not officially represent that person or institution in Africa nor are they controlled by him/her/it. Like the classic AICs, they are African initiatives, or as they would say, God's initiatives through Africans. Many of the neo-Pentecostal AICs do not regard the classic AICs as Christian groups. It is too early to tell how the tensions between the two camps will play out.

Missiologically AICs have had a massive significance throughout Africa. A Nigerian neo-Pentecostal congregation has a building that seats just over 50,000 (on plastic chairs) – filled weekly. The Zion Christian Church in South Africa alone has between 10 and 15% of the country's population, and its peace stance very probably was a significant factor in preventing a national bloodbath when apartheid ended.

The Organization of African Instituted Churches (P.O. Box 21736, Nairobi, Kenya; founded c. 1978) is the widest association of AICs. Large national associations also exist in Nigeria, South Africa and Zimbabwe. Rather than trying to wish them away, shun them or shut them down because they are not in our group (cf. Mark 9:38–40), other Christians need to engage both types of AICs for our own missiological benefit as well as theirs. One thinks of the disciples of John whom Paul met in Ephesus. They were following the gospel to the extent they had heard it, but they needed some explanation so they could more completely experience the kingdom and carry the witness (Acts 19:1–6). Perhaps the AICs are the disciples of John today. Or perhaps the rest of us are those disciples, and the AICs are Paul, bringing us the message and the power of the kingdom.

Bibliography

A. Anderson, *African Reformation: African Initiated Christianity in the 20th Century* (Trenton, NJ: Africa World Press, 2001); G. Cuthbertson, H. Pretorius and D. Robert (eds.), *Frontiers of African Christianity: Essays in Honour of Inus Daneel* (Pretoria: University of South Africa, 2003); F. Githieya, 'Freedom in the Spirit', *Scholars Press, AAR Academy Series*, 94, 1997; P. Johnstone and J. Mandryk, *Operation World* (Carlisle: Paternoster, 2001); T. Oduro, *Christ Holy Church International (1947–2002): The Challenges of Christian Proclamation in a Nigerian Cultural Context* (Luther Seminary, Minneapolis, PhD dissertation, 2004); J. Verkuyl, *Contemporary Missiology: An Introduction* (Grand Rapids Michigan: Eerdmans Publishing Co., 1978); C. P. Wagner and J. Thompson (eds.), *Out of Africa: How the Spiritual Explosion among Nigerians is Impacting the World* (Ventura, California: Regal Books, 2003); <http://www.artsweb.bham.ac.uk/aanderson>; <http://www.bu.edu/sth/cgcm>; <http://www.celestialchurch.com>; <http://www.geocities.com/Athens/Parthenon/8409/aic.htm>.

S. NUSSBAUM

African theology

Put simply, African theology is Christian theology written in the African context. It seeks to express Christian faith in African thought forms and idioms. It is born out of the African experience, taking as its point of departure African culture, history, and the biblical experience, which is interpreted within the African *world-view.

African theology is not an attempt to write an exclusive theology only applicable in Africa. It seeks to make a contribution to ecumenical theological discourse by offering a sufficiently broad theology, while reflecting a genuinely African understanding of the Christian faith. While claiming to be distinctly African, it is crucial that it reflects an understanding of the Christian faith which speaks to all human experience of fear, uncertainty, sickness, evil powers, foreign domination, poverty and all that distorts human life.

African theology encompasses a broad spectrum of thought patterns as the theological response of many different African communities with varying theological and ecclesiastical traditions. Despite this qualification, it is safe to speak of an African theology, which represents most African Christians within their ideological, cultural and religious moulds.

African theology emerged almost at the same time as African nations were being liberated from *colonialism. Most of the leaders of liberation movements were Christians who had gone through missionary institutions. Some of these leaders were even seminarians (e.g. Senghor and Nkrumah). There was very close affinity between liberation movements in Africa and African theology, which was triggered by a book by Placide Temples, a Belgian missionary based in Congo, entitled *Bantu Philosophy*, a serious study of African traditional religion in relation to Christianity. Temples believed that a genuine and careful study of African traditional religion would make it plausible to evangelize African peoples without doing harm to their cultural heritage.

The founding of the All Africa Conference of Churches in 1963 also contributed to the quest for African theology. Its first theological consultation in 1966 had the objective of mapping out African theology by drawing from grassroot movements, African traditional beliefs and cosmologies. The consultation culminated in the publication, *Biblical Revelation and African Beliefs*.

During the next theological consultation in 1971, the sources of African theology were identified as being the Bible, black identity and the African religious heritage. Out of the Ecumenical Dialogue of Third World Theologians in Ghana in 1977 came *African Theology en Route*. Since then many books and articles have explored the theological thread that connects the Christian faith and African traditional religions.

African theology responds to the challenges of contemporary African experience in a holistic way. *Globalization has challenged African theology to accommodate others who might not physically live on the African continent but who share the same cultural identity. Religion being the essence of life in Africa, great care must be taken to avoid creating a false dichotomy between the sacred and the profane. African theology therefore puts emphasis on holistic salvation for the community, person and whole creation. It still needs to engage more fully with issues such as human sexuality, cloning, abortion and *ecology.

The concept of God in African theology cannot be clearly understood without reference to *worship. African theology recognizes that the best way to know God is through worship and thanksgiving, rather than through speculative reflection. African theology therefore places great importance on various forms of worship, which include dance, song, lyrics, prayer and symbolic objects. A theological emphasis on *liturgical transformation in Africa has revolutionized *music and dance to the extent that African tunes and lyrics have often taken over from Western music.

Some key theologians

John Mbiti identifies three areas of African theology: written, oral and symbolic. The first area is for the privileged few who have had a theological orientation. The second category is done by ordinary people through songs, sermons, prayers and poetry. The third category is expressed in *art, *drama, symbols, rituals and dance. Mbiti tries to draw parallels between the biblical and African worldviews. According to Mbiti, African theology should seek to interpret Christ to Africans in a way that feels at home and in a language they can understand. He observes that

African theology and *black theology emerge from different historical and contemporary situations.

John Pobee strongly feels that African theology is an attempt at liberation from the North Atlantic captivity of Christianity, as a type of *liberation theology. Its two main sources are the Bible and African religions. Pobee believes that African culture should not be regarded as a past event; rather, it is what is happening here and now. He draws attention to the multiplicity of different cultures in Africa. While African traditional religion may be called natural or general *revelation, Jesus Christ remains the special revelation.

Aylward Shorter attempts to show how African theology must grow out of a dialogue between Christianity and theologies of African traditional religion. In order to be Africanized, theology then must include reflection on African belief systems.

Kwesi Dickson identifies the contribution which African culture can make to understanding the atonement. Kwesi suggests that the African regards death in a positive way and sees it as the fulfilment of the earthly life and a gateway to ancestorhood. Some Western theology puts the *cross in the shadow of the *resurrection, thus overshadowing its significance. To the African, death binds up relationships in society and revitalizes the living. It underscores the importance of community life, through Christ who is the perfect *ancestor.

Charles Nyamiti, taking his cue from Pobee, argues that the Christian faith has much to learn from the understanding of God found in African religions. While recognizing that there are negative features in African culture, such as superstition, magic and belief in the world of spirits, he feels that there are also positive features. He recognizes the rich symbolism applied to God in African cultures, particularly singling out the symbol of motherhood of God. He also argues for the ancestorship of Christ, thus bestowing upon Christ eternal ancestorship.

Benezet Bujo advances this concept further by calling Christ our 'Proto-Ancestor'. Just as African ancestors have done, Christ as our ancestor has handed down his experiences of death and resurrection and has become for us 'Ancestor par excellence'. Bujo advocates an African theology that can speak of God in human terms and describe him in terms drawn from human experience.

Desmond Tutu tries to set out the differences in approach between black and African theology. He observes that while black theology is a part of African theology, in a more limited sense African theology denotes a concern to relate Christian faith to African culture. He stresses the value of the African heritage as a medium through which Christian faith can be anchored in African communities. While black theology arises from the context of racism, suffering and exploitation and therefore becomes a liberation theology, African theology often fails to do this, hence its limitation. He asserts that in the past the African Christian has suffered from 'religious schizophrenia', paying lip service to Christianity while repressing his African-ness. He calls upon African theology to recover its prophetic calling through radical spiritual decolonization.

Jesse Mugambi sees the task of African theology to liberate Africans from all that hinders them from living a fully human life. To be truly African, Mugambi asserts that Christianity must be incarnated in Africa and speak out of the African context. Mugambi calls for a theology of reconstruction in order to engage with the idea of globalization. He suggests that we should move from enculturation and liberation in order to engage in a more proactive and innovative way concepts such as democracy, *human rights, nation building and economics. This he feels will propel African theological discourse into the twenty-first century.

Lamin Sanneh, while seeing the importance of exorcizing the phantom of foreignness, is convinced that it is the translatability of the gospel that made a breakthrough in the evangelization of Africa. African Christians and theologians must allow the gospel to speak to the African situation. He mounts a passionate argument in defence of both African Christianity and the twentieth-century missionary enterprise. Sanneh would wish to see an engagement of African theology with grassroots people using local languages that people can easily understand.

Mercy Oduyoye, a fervent and most articulate woman theologian, would like to challenge male theologians to listen to the voice of female theologians. This challenge is directed at both patriarchal African theology and patriarchal African cultures. She calls African women 'religions' chief clients', while they continue to be marginalized in the church and in theological circles. She appeals for a more gendered African theology.

Women theologians, through the circle of concerned African women theologians, are raising uncomfortable but pertinent questions that confront androcentric bias. They are challenging the image of the church in Africa in the midst of practices that are oppressive to women. They feel that theology must combat such practices as bride wealth, child marriages, clitoridectomy and widowhood rites. They have also raised issues concerning globalization, which they have associated with paternalism and domination. They perceive it as a smokescreen for a dominant culture to absorb and dominate the rest. According to Oduyoye, African theology must be liberative, coming from the trinitarian God of love, in order to empower women to overcome all evil forces that continue to dehumanize them even within the church. Until more recently African male theologians have not been sensitive to *gender issues. Theology was assumed to be objective and genetic and did not need to be gender sensitive. African theology needs to concern itself with the hegemony of male androcentrism as the main source of denigration and marginalization of women. This requires a cultural hermeneutic, since culture is dynamic, and at times open to abuse. More than ever before, African theology must acknowledge the role of gender in theology and endeavour to eliminate its debilitating effect.

The agenda for mission

African theology needs to encourage indigenous responses to the message of the gospel and to translate and make alive the message of Christ in a contemporary African setting. Seen from the perspective of salvation, African theology becomes a message of *transformation for both the individual and the community. Liberation in this sense means the creation of just instruments that advocate for equality, thus eliminating the fundamental sin of alienation.

African theology tries to liberate itself from Western static and abstract forms of theological reflection. It endeavours to be acculturated in the lives of people through the use of traditional symbols, imagery, poetry, dance and other forms of liturgical expression. As a theology of liberation, African theology takes the condition of the poor and the oppressed seriously by offering God's response to issues of poverty and oppression. It engages the Bible as central, a living book that proclaims the gospel of liberty, at the same time engaging many social and theological issues of our day, such as ethnicism, governance, the HIV/*AIDS pandemic and homosexuality. Most African theology has rejected the practice of homosexuality as being incompatible with biblical teaching, while encouraging a sympathetic dialogue. It takes the view that it is mission and faith in Jesus as Lord that gives birth to theology.

For theology to be relevant in Africa, reciprocity of acculturation and *inculturation must be acknowledged. It has been argued that Christian theology cannot be African without acculturation, nor can African theology be Christian without inculturation. African theology must also tackle marriage-related issues such as levirate marriages, *polygamy and the care for widows and widowers, as well as African ancestors, particularly the place of ancestor veneration in the African church. Traditional African ritual needs to be studied in some depth since *African instituted churches have taken these rituals into their church worship. African theology needs to critically examine the place of traditional specialists such as priests, prophets, healers and religious leaders, since they are the ones who make the history of African traditional societies both sacred and religious. The richness of African religious thought and practice can be enhanced by a deeper reflection on their lives and practices.

African theology thus takes its point of departure from the existential situation of African peoples. It takes the Bible seriously as the inspired word of God, while seriously engaging the African cultural heritage. The ultimate purpose of such theology is to make the gospel meaningful and authentic in the concrete life and thought of African people.

See also AFRICAN CHRISTOLOGY, AFRICAN TRADITIONAL RELIGONS.

Bibliography

K. Appiah-Kubi and S. Torres (eds.), *African Theology en Route* (Maryknoll: Orbis Books, 1979); K. Bediako, *Jesus in Africa: The Christian Gospel in African History and Experience* (Carlisle: Paternoster, 2000); B. Bujo, *African Theology in its Social Context*, trans. J. O'Donohue (Nairobi: Pauline Publications, 1992); K. A. Dickson and P. Ellingworth (eds.), *Biblical Revelation and African Beliefs* (London: Lutterworth Press, 1969); K. A. Dickson and P. Ellingworth (eds.), *Theology in Africa* (Maryknoll: Orbis Books, 1984); J. Gatu, *Joyfully Christian, Truly African* (Nairobi: Acton Publishers, 2006); R. Gibellini (ed.), *Paths of African Theology* (Maryknoll: Orbis Books, 1994); J. Mbiti, *Bible and Theology in African Christianity* (Nairobi: Oxford University Press, 1986); J. Mugambi (ed.), *The Church and Reconstruction of Africa: Theological Considerations* (Nairobi: All Africa Conference of Churches, 1997); Z. Nthamburi, *The African Church at the Crossroads: Strategy for Indigenization* (Nairobi: Uzima Press, 1995); C. Nyamiti, *Christ as Our Ancestor: Christology from an African Perspective* (Zimbabwe: Given, 1984); M. A. Oduyoye and R. A. Musimbi Kanyoro (eds.), *The Will to Arise: Women, Tradition and the Church in Africa* (Maryknoll: Orbis Books, 1992); J. S. Pobee, *Towards an African Theology* (Nashville: Abingdon, 1979); L. Sanneh, *Translating the Message: The Missionary Impact on Culture* (Maryknoll: Orbis Books, 1989); A. Shorter, *African Culture and Christianity* (Maryknoll: Orbis Books, 1977); D. Tutu, 'Black Theology and African Theology: Soul Mates or Antagonists', *Journal of Religious Thought* 33, 1975.

Z. NTHAMBURI

African traditional religion

Discussion of theology and mission in the African perspective must begin with the African context – a context which is located in time and space, and which sets the parameters for valid and relevant theological and missiological reflection. Since African traditional religion has shaped African spirituality so significantly for centuries, we need criteria to guide us in evaluating its elements and practices, so that present-day mission can engage with it in faithfulness to the Christian tradition. Neither blanket dismissal of African traditional religion as 'pagan', nor uncritical acceptance, will serve mission well.

One criterion relates to the way in which past ideas, values and practices have functioned to endorse, or undermine, Christian revelation in Scripture and tradition. This will determine whether or not, and in what ways, those traditional cultural values can play any meaningful and effective roles in attaining the goals and visions of our present cross-cultural mission encounter.

Cultural realities

Religion in African society is an unquestioned cultural reality. It is an integral expression of the African cultural background, and as such, determines the thoughts and actions of the educated professional in modern cities and towns as well as the peasant farmer in the village. Religion permeates every aspect of African life, so that any dichotomy between religious and socio-political concerns is false.

It is equally true to note that contemporary Africa is a society of mixed religions with three major religious traditions: African traditional religion, Christianity and Islam. Although Christianity and Islam have thrived at the expense of African traditional religion, nonetheless, the underlying philosophy and *world-view of traditional religion and *culture have by no means declined. Thus, despite an accelerated movement toward Islam and Christianity, the world-view and philosophy of traditional religion and culture is still crucial in contemporary African societies.

One such example is the institution of funerals among the Akans of Ghana. Owing to all sorts of beliefs about the supposed career of the spirits of departed relatives, the mourning of the dead takes the form of elaborate time-consuming social ceremonies. For instance, in addition to the burial ceremony, there is an eighth day funeral celebration at which customary rites are performed. There is also a fortieth day celebration. As if that is not enough, there is also a first anniversary celebration. All this involves considerable expense.

What happens these days is that in addition to all the traditional and customary celebration at funerals, there is also a neo-Christian memorial and thanksgiving service, and sometimes a requiem service. This is an attempt to Christianize the traditional practices without removing them altogether. This is again followed by extended and expensive refreshments from the bereaved family.

Given what happens on the ground, it is significant to note that in as much as people have embraced Christianity, it has not meant the *exchange* of traditional beliefs and practices for Christian people. If there has been any development, it is rather an *amalgamation* of both. Unfortunately, this *syncretism sometimes creates confusion and complicates issues for the Christian community.

These practical issues raise the need for critical evaluation of Christian mission in contemporary African society. Christian theologians cannot afford to ignore such evaluation in mission theology. Both the theologian and missiologist must see African traditional religion and Christianity as two contrary, but not necessarily contradictory, religious traditions; different, but not incompatible. The encounter between Christian faith and African socio-religiosity and culture need not be in terms of either-or, but can be in terms of both-and, provided that the resulting creative partnership is faithful to Christian revelation.

It is true to say that there are many and formidable differences between the Christian and African views of God, humanity and the world. It is equally true that one marvels at the many areas of similarity. These indicate that ultimately both traditions derive from a common belief in a Supreme Being which both call 'God'. So, what are some of the characteristics of this Supreme Being in African traditional religion that can be vessels for conceptualizing and interpreting the Christian *God?

A typical view is that he is the Creator. Several myths of creation abound. Without a Creator God nothing holds together or has any meaning. It is God, *Borebore*, who fashioned the universe (*bo adze*), who called being into being. This has many resonances with the story of Genesis 1, and with a universal intuition that the universe, all in it and all that happens in it, has a Designer and Maker. Both Christianity and African traditional religion affirm that the universe came into being out of God's love and purpose.

The assumptions common to both traditions about God include that: (1) God is real and concrete, and not a philosophically abstract God; (2) God is the absolute Lord of the universe, who keeps the universe going at all levels, even when delegating authority to spirit powers (since only God can give life to created beings, including human beings); (3) God is one. However, in African traditional religion there are several deities and divinities, and this contrasts with the distinctively Christian *trinitarian view of God, which affirms that only the three persons of the Godhead can properly be deified as divine. Although Christianity does have its spiritual powers, they are created by God and always under his authority, and this means that they cannot be appealed to, since all Christian prayer and worship is directed to God.

Since both Christianity and African traditional religion believe it is the One God, without whom there is no existence, who continues to redeem and sustain the world, theologically such understanding indicates that cross-cultural mission can begin with a positive approach to African traditional religion. This is in line with St Paul's approach at Athens in Acts 17. It is important to remember, however, that theological reflection based on such assumptions but which is divorced from ethical demands would have little relevance in traditional society. The goal of the process is to help fashion an African Christianity that is at the same time true to African traditional values *and* faithful to the Christian theological heritage. This is one of the greatest and most urgent services that mission theology could possibly render to the African cause and also to the cause of global Christianity today.

Conclusion

Cross-cultural mission has one common objective, namely to enable traditional cultures to preserve their individual cultural identity while also being incorporated as part of the Christian community, which will promote their human development. It demands an in-depth knowledge of both the African reality and the Christian heritage. This is a demanding task and yet it is rewarding. On the personal level, it leads to integration and harmony in human life. Thus, people no longer need to live two lives: a Christian life

in public, and an African traditional life in private. On the social level, it restores to people their sense of cultural pride and identity, and on the universal level, it gives them a sense of responsibility and belonging to the universal church. When this happens, the African church can share with the universal church the riches of the Christian faith that are specifically theirs and receive from it the riches that they lack.

Given what has been said, one comes to the conclusion that for African Christianity to be fully African and truly Christian is not an option among many but an imperative, which should be embraced with courage. Though its challenges are great and enormous, the fact still remains that its rewards promise to be greater for the mission of the church.

See also AFRICAN CHRISTOLOGY, AFRICAN THEOLOGY, CONTEXTUALIZATION.

Bibliography
K. A. Appiah, *In My Father's House: Africa in the Philosophy of Culture* (New York: Oxford University Press, 1992); K. Bediako, *Theology and Identity: The Impact of Culture upon Christian Thought in the Second Century and in Modern Africa* (Oxford: Oxford Regnum Books, 1992); B. Bujo, *African Theology in its Social Context* (Maryknoll: Orbis Books, 1992); E. C. Eze (ed.), *African Philosophy: An Anthology* (Oxford: Blackwell Publishing, 1998); R. B. Fisher, *West African Religious Traditions: Focus on the Akan of Ghana* (Maryknoll: Orbis Books, 1998); P. Gifford, *African Christianity: Its Public Role* (Bloomington: Indiana University Press, 1998); K. Gyekye, *African Cultural Values: An Introduction* (Philadelphia/Accra: Sankofa Publishing Company, 1996); G. H. Muzorewa, *An African Theology of Mission* (Lewiston: Edwin Mellen Press, 1991); K. Wiredu, *Philosophy and an African Culture* (Cambridge: Cambridge University Press, 1980).

V. Atta-Baffoe

AIDS

The chilling reality of the HIV/AIDS pandemic is that in 2006 between 36 and 40 million people were infected with HIV and the infection rate continued to rise. Over 15.2 million children were orphaned by AIDS and 95% of the people infected were in developing countries.

The devastating impact of HIV/AIDS on individuals, families, communities and nations across the world, especially in the developing world, has serious implications for the mission of the church. The pandemic is forcing the church both to rethink its priorities and to reshape its missionary engagement in a world so overwhelmed by the disease. The church's response calls for a significant paradigm shift in its understanding of mission, a necessary change if it is to engage meaningfully with these new realities worldwide.

Heated controversy surrounds the debate about the origin of AIDS. While it may be important to know from where AIDS originated, especially for scientists' efforts to develop a vaccine against HIV and effective treatments in the future, a word of caution needs to be sounded. There is a very real danger that the debate may be used to apportion blame for the disease to particular groups, nationalities, individuals or certain lifestyles. This is damaging and very unhelpful in our efforts to raise awareness, and in our strenuous efforts to contain the spread of the virus.

In sub-Saharan Africa, currently the most affected region of the world, there is no individual, family, community or nation that has not been touched. Church ministers are spending a large part of their time conducting funerals and burying those who have succumbed to AIDS. Grandparents, who should be taken care of, are bringing up grandchildren or great grandchildren whose parents have died because of AIDS, with almost no resources for this task. The children may also be HIV positive. There are many households that are now headed by children. The meagre resources of many poor nations are not enough to care for those living with the disease. The HIV/AIDS pandemic therefore raises a number of mission issues for the church.

Some mission issues
Holistic mission
The church's mission in this context must be holistic. It must minister to the total needs of total people – their spiritual, physical and psychosocial needs. The church is one of the few institutions with the advantage of being rooted in local structures and linked to the cultural and social environment of the people. It is present in all communities and therefore, it is in a unique position to minister holistically to people. Healing is needed in every dimension of the lives of those infected. This means that counselling, family support, care of children, education, and supervised medication provision must be in place alongside the spiritual guidance, prayer and biblical witness to God's love in Christ which the church offers.

Theological questions
Mission and theology in this context raise questions for ecclesiology: what does it mean to be the 'body of Christ' if the church is infected and affected by HIV/AIDS or living with the pandemic? What does it mean to say, 'If one part suffers, every part suffers with it' (1 Cor. 12:26) or, if one has AIDS, we all have AIDS? The virus has infected our body. Furthermore, how is the gospel to be proclaimed in such a context? Perhaps it is more appropriate to speak in terms of *witness rather than *proclamation; so how can we witness to the love of God through Jesus Christ in a context ravaged by HIV/AIDS?

For Jesus the two important commandments of loving God and loving our neighbour are inseparable (Matt. 22:34–40). 'To love God is to share in God's unconditional love for humankind' (K. R. Ross, *Missiology* XXXII, pp. 337–348). At the beginning of the epidemic many Christians regarded AIDS as God's punishment for sin, especially the perceived sins of homosexuality and promiscuity. This assumption raised further deeper theological problems regarding God, who this view implied to be vengeful, selective and cruel. However, the reasoning behind this assumption was flawed because many of those suffering were children, women and men, Christians and non-Christians, who were not homosexuals or promiscuous but had been infected through non-sexual means. HIV/AIDS once again highlighted the problem of suffering, and the meaning and importance of compassion for those infected and affected. God's first movement is the grace of unconditional love, and that should therefore be the church's first response.

Poverty

Poverty (see *Poor) and HIV/AIDS are inextricably linked. While poverty does not cause HIV/AIDS, it certainly makes people more vulnerable to infection. It facilitates transmission, makes treatment unaffordable, accelerates death from AIDS-related illnesses, and multiplies the social impact of the pandemic.

It comes as no surprise that about 95% of people infected with HIV are in developing countries. Christian mission needs to address the issue of poverty seriously in this context. In doing so, it cannot avoid linking HIV/AIDS with a crisis of conscience, caused when the church has complacently sat and watched the obscene gap between those who have and those who do not have drive the pandemic, both at the local and international levels.

Other underlying factors together with poverty that facilitate the rapid spread of HIV include: ignorance about HIV/AIDS; *gender inequality; cultural issues relating to sex, condoms, death and mourning practices, circumcision and some traditional treatment practices; and wars and displacement of people.

Coalitions with non-Christian organizations

HIV/AIDS is no respecter of people's faith. Christians and non-Christians, as well as people of other faiths and no faith at all, have been infected and affected. Responses have come from all quarters, and have of necessity lent themselves to forging alliances and making coalitions with at times unexpected partners. Mission engagement in this context requires great humility and a willingness to listen to others and to join forces when shared action is required.

Other mission issues to be taken seriously include the legal, ethical, justice and advocacy issues relating to the rights of those infected. This agenda raises the questions of access to scarce medicines, employment, housing, discrimination/exclusion, use of experimental drugs, relationships, and so on, which are all part of the integrated mission response.

It is also important to see that healing in the widest possible sense leads us to affirming the strong linkage between mission, healing and *reconciliation. The preaching of the gospel, through Christian witness, in communities ravaged by the disease, needs to address the issues we have identified. This will contribute towards the healing of individuals, families and communities. A church that takes mission seriously in any context, if it is to be a healing and reconciling church, cannot avoid getting involved in these issues, but especially when they are located in communities devastated by HIV/AIDS.

See also HEALING/HEALTH.

Bibliography
M. W. Dube, 'Theological Challenges: Proclaiming the Fullness of Life in the HIV/AIDS and Global Economic Era', *IRM* XCI, 2002, pp. 535–549; E. Kamaara, 'Stigmatization of Persons Living with HIV/AIDS in Africa: Pastoral Challenges', *African Ecclesial Review (AFER)* 46, 2004, pp. 35–54; P. Marshall, 'Toward a Theology of HIV/AIDS', *Evangelical Review of Theology* 29, 2005, pp. 131–148; G. M. Nguru, 'The Scourge of HIV/AIDS in Africa and the Church's Response', *Transformation* 20, 2003, pp. 245–249; R. Nicolson, *God in AIDS? A Theological Enquiry* (London: SCM Press, 1996); F. Nwaigbo, 'The HIV/AIDS Pandemic: A Crucial Task for the Church in Africa', *African Ecclesial Review* 46, 2004, pp. 2–22; P. Okaalet, 'The Role of Faith-Based Organizations in the Fight Against HIV and AIDS in Africa', *Transformation* 19, 2002, pp. 274–278; K. R. Ross, 'The HIV/AIDS Pandemic: What Is at Stake for Christian Mission?' *Missiology* XXXII, 2004, pp. 337–348.

C. GANDIYA

Aims of mission

The aims of Christian mission are derived from Scripture, Jesus and the apostolic era, although they have also been influenced by historical context.

In today's global world, some say that there should be no need for the church to be involved in cross-cultural mission since there are now Christians on every continent, and such mission activity can be offensive to the local culture. Today's *pluralistic context also raises the question of whether devout followers of other divinities can be accepted in heaven, if they have been committed to what revelation they have received. This undermines the necessity of mission. Another disincentive for active mission is that those living in a community committed to a local religion are likely to cause a major upset if they turn away from the faith commitment of their community and follow Jesus.

However, *God, the creator of this world, has made known to us that there is only one God; that he calls all people to be *reconciled to him; and that this is made possible only through his Son Jesus *Christ. Jesus prepared his disciples to be bearers of this unique message. He sent them into the world and instructed them to 'go and make disciples of all nations', baptizing and teaching all who respond in faith (Matt. 28:18–20). Christ enabled them to be bearers of this message through the gift and presence of his *Holy Spirit. So there is a consistently strong call on the people of God, who have benefited from the knowledge of God's covenant love, to go and make that love known to others.

The aim of mission is, therefore, to make known God's *revelation about himself and that reconciliation is available through Christ's sacrificial death. One outcome of preaching this message is that its hearers, in the power of the Holy Spirit, turn to Christ. Another outcome is for those hearers to realize that they have been enslaved by other values, and that there is need for a radical change in orientation, which Jesus called repentance. He made this clear in announcing the coming of the *kingdom of God, which would signify his sovereign rule of those who accepted his reign, and would have a transforming impact in the community (Matt. 4:17; Mark 1:14–15; Luke 4:18–19, 43). Thus the aim of accepting Jesus as Saviour and Lord is a change of heart, a reorientation of values and a desire to promote kingdom values in each community. For this to happen there is the need to *disciple new believers, teaching them God's values and his desire for them to reflect the character of Christ, as well as how to promote those values by their actions in society. A significant dimension of this is to demonstrate that God cares for all people, since Jesus demonstrated the arrival of the kingdom by works of mercy and power. Both the OT and Jesus' acts of mercy make it

clear that a new relationship with God brings with it the responsibility to work for justice and to care for those in need.

In the early period of Pietistic thinking, rooted in their understanding of the reign of God, mission was seen as a ministry both to the soul and to the body (see *Holistic mission), with the result that mission included care for the destitute, health and education. Part of the aim of this was to promote 'civilization' of pagan peoples alongside Christianization. However, a century later, under the influence of the Enlightenment, a dualistic approach emerged, separating the sacred and the secular, and reducing the aims of mission either to proclamation or to what became known as the *social gospel*. Some focused so exclusively on confronting the social and economic issues of the day, that the aim of merely changing society overtook the more biblical aim of personal transformation of all who accept Christ, who then transform society by their new lives.

John Calvin was committed to the doctrine of the reign of God, and viewed the calling of the church as extending Christ's reign on earth; he saw the need to declare in words the message of salvation, yet also to reflect in deeds God's mercy and grace. Despite the influence of this on the Protestant understanding of mission, the divide between a spiritual and a social gospel persisted. Vigorous debate continued until the 1974 Lausanne Congress, whose covenant statement reinstated holistic mission as a biblical aim (paragraph 5). The biblical duty of men and women, and thus the aim of mission, is to proclaim the good news of the kingdom and to be responsible to care for God's creation. The Christian's faith should be exhibited in good works and in denouncing evil, and the Christian's God-given love for others should be manifested in a longing to articulate the whole gospel in the power of the Holy Spirit.

The apostles planted churches in each place and instructed these new Christian communities in what it meant to be transformed by Christ (Rom. 12:1–2) as *Christ's ambassadors* (2 Cor. 5:20) and *God's fellow workers* (2 Cor. 6:1) responsible for sharing the good news of the kingdom of God. Communities of Christians could in themselves be demonstrators of kingdom values, and signs and instruments of the kingdom.

These NT models have therefore given rise to various aims of mission.

Discipleship

Making disciples of the kingdom is a central aim of mission, and involves equipping those who will proclaim the gospel, teach God's word, plant churches, care for those in need and bring glory to God in every dimension of life. However, for those living in situations antagonistic to the gospel, conversion can lead to division in the home or the local community, and *persecution for new Christians. Jesus warned the disciples that the world would hate them just as it had hated him (John 15:18–25) and so we know that in discipling believers we need also to prepare them for persecution. The threat of disruption to the community or of persecution, however, cannot be a valid reason for not making known a truth which has eternal consequences.

Dialogue

The World Council of Churches regarded inter-religious *dialogue as one way to communicate with non-Christian religions. This approach recognized and respected their historical-religious context and saw the building of relationships as essential to effective mission. However, it is important that those in dialogue hold to their own positions while being willing to better understand the position held by the other. Dialogue does not remove the call of Christ on his people to make known his *salvific purposes to all the world. Dialogue can be the context for this, although it can take an adversarial and defensive form. Alternatively, it may take the form of reducing the differences between the gospel message and other religions, thereby eliminating the challenge of the cross. At its best, dialogue may be a stepping stone to a contextually sensitive witness.

Presence

Taking up one of the themes in the OT, the promoters (e.g. F. Hahn, M. A. C. Warren) of this concept refer to the prophets and their calling to the children of Israel to live out God's values in such a way that their faith commitment and their lifestyle would be a beacon to the surrounding nations. Others have recognized the danger that a *presence theology on its own can result in Christian passivity, as if it is sufficient simply to be there in any particular context. Both in OT times, and clearly in the apostolic church, the call is actively to communicate God's grace, whilst at the same time living a transformed life, which is itself a witness. However, a *presence* theology on its own results in a mission aim of passivity.

Socio-political action

One benefit of the presence approach is to strengthen awareness of the context in which the church is present, and this includes its socio-political dimension. Although the gospel is relevant to all people whatever their cultural heritage, missionaries need to be more aware of how much they are conveying their own cultural and political values along with the gospel. There may be motifs in the local culture which can be used to explain the gospel message, but there is also the need for sensitivity to the socio-political context, which puts some people groups in a very sensitive and debilitating situation. This has taken leaders in these communities back to Isaiah 61 and Christ's declaration to the synagogue that he had come to liberate prisoners and the oppressed (Luke 4:16–21). Mission therefore cannot avoid engagement with this dimension of the context.

Transforming world-view

All mission activity needs an awareness of the *world-view, the ways of thinking and acting, the language, and the socio-religious structure of the recipient community. This not only ensures meaningful communication, it also enables Christians to critique what they are conveying to ensure that God's word and not their own inherited culture is being taught as the core of the biblical message. The aim is therefore not merely to convert individuals but to transform their world-view in line with the gospel. The process of crossing cultural-linguist boundaries can sharpen missionary understanding of the presence of the kingdom, challenge their own world-view, and clarify the way they apply biblical truth to the radical changing of cultural values.

Missio Dei

During the past hundred years other aims of mission have been promoted. One of these centres on the Willingen theme of the *missio Dei*. Mission is ultimately God's mission. He is the one who sent his Son into the world and who sends us into the world. Sometimes this concept has modified mission aims simply to seeing what God is already doing in the world and going with it, which can rob mission of the call actively to proclaim the gospel to all people. However, a useful outcome of this theme has been an emphasis on the trinitarian nature of God. Reference to the Trinity can be a reminder of the role of the Holy Spirit in mission (sending, gathering and sanctifying the Christian community). It can also highlight the communion we have in Christ and thus provide a clearer basis for understanding the role of the church which the Triune God sends out in mission. The combined influence of these themes can be to see the mission role of church-planting in terms of the work of the Holy Spirit rather than as an institutional exercise.

Current challenges

One challenging attack on mission in recent decades has been the position that non-Christian religions do not need the gospel, since they have sufficient elements of truth in them because Christ is not without a witness in every religious context. This view can change the aim of mission to (1) establishing that other religions simply need to add God as revealed in Christ to what they already believe (a 'better than thou' position); or (2) articulating that all divinities are expressions of the Creator God ('fulfilment of pagan religions' position); or (3) all divinities are ways to a relationship with the eternal Creator God (a pluralistic position). Whichever outcome, the great commission is set aside and the motivation that 'Christ's love constrains us' (2 Cor. 5:14, KJV) has been lost.

Another current challenging attack on mission is the *postmodern way of discounting the possibility of absolute truth, promoting scepticism about history and about meaning gained from history, and denying the possibility of a metanarrative. Mission must aim to engage with this world-view and not simply reject it. An apologetic approach will include the importance of experiencing God through a Christ-centred spirituality, which is best witnessed to in the lives of Christians. The postmodern attitude to truth does not diminish the aims of mission, which need to affirm that God does exist and he does enable us to be reconciled with him. Human beings also need a renewed humanity, and Christians need to demonstrate this truth in their own relationship with God and the consequent nature of their relationship with others.

Mission therefore cannot be said to have a single aim, unless it is to bring glory to God and to see representatives of all peoples and nations gathered around his throne in worship. On the way to this climactic purpose God calls his people to mission in all its rich dimensions, which themselves reflect the glorious riches of the gospel and the transforming power of Christ in all the world.

Bibliography

D. J. Bosch, *Transforming Mission* (Maryknoll: Orbis Books, 1991); A. F. Glasser and D. A. McGavran, *Contemporary Theologies of Mission* (Grand Rapids: Baker Book House, 1983); R. Hille (ed.), 'The Uniqueness of Christ in a Postmodern World', *Lausanne Occasional Paper* 31, 2005, <http://www.lausanne.org>; J. A. Kirk, *What is Mission?* (London: Darton, Longman and Todd, 1999); A. J. Köstenberger and P. T. O'Brien, *Salvation to the Ends of the Earth* (Downers Grove: InterVarsity Press; Leicester: Apollos, 2001); P. T. O'Brien, *Gospel and Mission in the Writings of Paul* (Carlisle: Paternoster, 1995).

D. CLAYDON

ALTERNATIVE SPIRITUALITIES, see NEW RELIGIOUS MOVEMENTS

Ancestors

Ancestors may be understood as biological forefathers/mothers. In Africa they include tribal chiefs and priests. In many ancient cultures, including Israel's popular cult, dead relatives, rulers and important people were honoured by the living by caring for them, consulting them on important matters, or propitiating them through sacrifice, ritual and magic. Today Hindus, Buddhists, Confucians, Shinto worshippers and Catholic Christians honour their dead relatives, saints, national heroes, or rulers by setting up images or pictures, lighting candles, burning incense, praying to or for them, and placing food or flowers on their graves.

Nonetheless, the terms used for one or more of the practices representing the care, consulting, placating or venerating the dead range from 'worship' and 'homage', to 'veneration' and 'remembrance'. The issue is not with the words we use but what we mean by them. Some use the term 'ancestor worship', and explain that by 'worship' they actually mean 'homage' or 'reverence'. This is confusing to say the least, because the term 'worship' is reserved in most cultures for gods and 'deified humans'. In recent times the word 'veneration' has become an accepted term in missiology to represent honour and respect to the dead.

Ancestral worship is widespread in Asia, Africa and Oceania. Although varied in certain details, the beliefs and practices associated with it present major issues for Christian mission. The cult is based on a universal belief that a non-material part of humans continues to exist after death; their spirits are interested in the affairs of the living, and possess powers to affect the course of events for the welfare of the family or clan by helping them in wars and protecting them from harm and evil. Therefore they demand to be consulted by their living relatives on important family/clan matters, to be respected, honoured and worshipped through sacrifices and other appropriate rituals. But if such services are neglected they may turn hostile and bring sickness, storms, calamities or other misfortunes. Therefore each culture has developed their own rituals and forms of respect, honour and worship to their ancestors.

Forms of ancestor worship

In ancient Rome ancestor worship was part of *family religion. In Chinese culture it undergirds important religious, social and ethical functions. This is based on the notion of filiality, with the aim of perpetuating the family name for future generations, and giving due glory to parents. Typically this involves worshipping the spirits of the deceased at the family altar at home and at grave sites. Worship at the ancestral tomb involves cleaning grave sites, offering food sacrifices, and placing paper money on them indicating that it is sent for their use.

With slight variations, ancestor worship in Japan represents similar beliefs and practices as in Chinese culture, focusing once again on grave sites (*bosan*), and family altars. It is said

that religion for Japanese people is instinctively 'ancestor worship'. Originally based on the Japanese family system, ancestor worship strongly undergirds their beliefs: first, death does not separate the living from the dead as they co-exist for mutual help. Secondly, it undergirds human relationships and forms the foundation of society. Its implications embrace family ties, community relations and eventually national solidarity. Furthermore, ancestor worship binds people to the imperial family, when family ancestors are placed within the family tree of the imperial gods. Interestingly, Buddhism in Japan has adopted ancestor worship. Today, the primary purpose of more than 90% of their active temples in Japan is to perform funeral rites and ancestor worship. And Buddhist leaders see this as essential to their survival: 'We don't have to despise funeral Buddhism, for we would lose out unless we should seek in this funeral Buddhism the truth of Japanese religion' (C. Shibata, in *Christian Alternatives to Ancestor Practices*, p. 257).

In Hinduism, food offerings (*pindas* or *shraddha* at ceremonies) made to the dead between the tenth and twelfth day after death and thereafter annually, form part of the life-cycle rites (*samskaras*). They are meant to help the departing spirit (*preta*) with transmigration. There is no idea of the dead becoming gods or worshipping their spirits, although the funeral rites before the body is cremated ensure that the deceased will not remain in this world as a ghost (*bhuta*) and trouble the living, but pass on to its next destination.

In Melanesia, individual and communal rituals are performed to honour the ancestral spirits and to seek their help. Since gods, demons, land-spirits (*maslai*) and other natural forces are also believed to interfere in their affairs, most of their seasonal rituals are directed to appease those spirits in order to be protected from harm and be blessed in their farming. But there is no evidence of family altars for ancestors, nor the idea of co-existence of the living and the dead as among the Chinese or Japanese. For the Polynesians, however, the creative powers (*mana*) that bring life and prosperity to the living come from the gods, but through the mediation of ancestors (traditionally tribal chiefs and priests) who have special access to the gods.

Therefore both the gods and the ancestors are invoked at the shrines through ritual feasts, dance, and offerings (including human sacrifice, only of enemies) so that the living may enjoy peace and prosperity. Belief in a mythical homeland of the dead (*Hawaiki*) where the ancestral spirits rest is popular, but there is no worship of them as among the Chinese or Japanese.

As for Africa, ancestor veneration is almost universally practised by its 742 different tribes. With some variations their beliefs and practices come very close to the Chinese. Although totemic spirits are invoked as guardians of tribes and clans, ancestral spirits are the chief patrons of the clan and family. Spirits of the chiefs and eminent personalities are invoked on behalf of the larger social groupings. The chief is often regarded as a 'living ancestor' ruling on behalf of his predecessors and to ensure a regular ancestral cult. Ancestors in general are considered to be mediators between the Supreme Being and living relatives, providing their needs and receiving worship on his behalf. Therefore the chief aim of their rituals is to please their ancestors and live in harmony with them. Offerings take the form mainly of foodstuffs or libation at the grave sites (Tanzania) or in the tomb houses (East African lake kingdoms), or on ancestral altars (Nigeria), or before the king and his golden stool (kingdom of Ashanthi, Ghana) as recognition of their powerful role in human affairs, while misfortunes are attributed to a failure of offerings in proper form or in due time.

Critical issues
Obligation
The 'obligation' of the living for the dead is for their ongoing protection and blessing. Apart from being a traditional belief, this has no ethical or moral sanction in Africa and the Pacific, where the Supreme Being remained the sole benefactor, and the ancestors, being only mediators, played a secondary role. These ancestral practices did not pose a big challenge for mission when Christ was introduced as the Mediator. The issue is more complicated in Chinese, Korean and Japanese cultures where ancestor worship is linked to filial piety and moral obligation to the state. For the Chinese this is the best thing you could do for your parents.

In Japanese culture, ancestor worship carries the implications of gratefulness to the ancestors for the benevolence (*on*) bestowed on them, which must be repaid through the virtue of filial piety (*ko*). Thus the ancestors and their descendants are linked together in a circle of obligation. This is developed into a principle of preserving the 'family system' (*ie*), which is viewed as an everlasting entity, consisting of the past (the dead), the present (the living), and the future (the not-yet-born) being united to transcend life and death.

Communion
The idea of 'communion' or 'continued relationship' between the living and the dead probably answers the universal quest for permanence and eternity. Most rituals are based on the belief that some sort of spirit survives the body after death. However, the focus of the rituals is the growth and continuity of this spirit with the living. In Japanese culture this idea is syncretized with Buddhist traditions.

Continuity
There is a fundamental 'continuity between the human and the divine', which in turn is based on the Buddhist belief in cosmic oneness or monism, which is one of its major pillars. In other words ancestors are entitled to be worshipped as much as anything else. So there is no denial of worship in ancestral rites without violating this assumption. Here is an inevitable conflict between ancestor worship and the Christian faith, when there is a fundamental discontinuity between the Creator and the created and no amount of ritual can bridge this gap. In this sense the African and Pacific cultures allow certain transcendence to the Supreme Being, leaving other deities and the ancestors as mediators and facilitators of his grace. No wonder that both Christian and Muslim faiths, both monotheistic, had phenomenal success among these cultures.

Challenges to mission
Christian missionaries reacted negatively wherever they went, as if every form of ancestor worship was un-Christian. Such views effectively shut the door of the church for most of the people, while the gospel was grossly misunderstood as anti-culture and anti-family among the majority of the

educated, especially in India, Japan and China where traditional religions had endorsed those practices as having religious and ethical functions in society.

Now the question is how did, or how should, Christian missions respond to the challenges of ancestral practices? Christian (Roman Catholic) response to ancestor worship in China oscillated between acceptance (Nestorian Christians during the Tang dynasty; Jesuits [Matteo Ricci] in the sixteenth century), rejection (Dominicans and Franciscans in the seventeenth century), and acceptance again in the twentieth century (1939). Catholic rejection of the practice in the seventeenth century angered the then Emperor Kang Shi of the Ching dynasty who decreed a ban on all Christian missions, which remained effective until the communist takeover of China.

Protestants also rejected the practice in China to begin with (1807), but themselves were divided over the issue. Finally, evangelicals under the leadership of Hudson Taylor won the battle over the issue, but most of the educated Chinese remained unresponsive to the gospel. Thereafter, the evangelicals were not even open to discuss the issue until the communist takeover. However, many Christian leaders today think that there cannot be a single choice between acceptance or rejection, but there is a need for indigenization and transformation of cultural practices. There is much room for this as long as ceremonies remain honouring and remembering but not worshipping the dead. Various biblical texts suggest that 'mourning', 'caring', 'honouring', and 'remembering' the dead is not breaching the first commandment. On the other hand, they probably imply a fulfilment of obligations underlying the fifth commandment, although this is not clearly stated (cf. Num. 25:2 with Ps. 106:28; Deut. 26:14).

The NT transformed funeral customs with the truth of the resurrection, where mourning gives way to songs of hope of resurrection, because death is not a loss but gain, passing not to nothingness but to eternal life. Their funeral practices like washing and anointing the body with perfumes, wrapping it in linen, and lighting candles around it express these beliefs. The corpse is no longer polluting, as Christians would kiss the body as a sign of love and honour for the person. Worship of the dead is no longer necessary because they neither become gods, nor are they malevolent, but they wait for the *resurrection of all when God reorders everything under the rule of Christ the Risen One.

Bibliography
J.-M. Berentsen, 'Ancestor Worship in Missiological Perspective', in Bong Rin Ro (ed.), *Christian Alternatives to Ancestor Practices* (Seoul: Word of Life/ATA, 1985); Chow Lien-Hwa, 'Christian Response to Chinese Filial Piety in Chinese Classical Literature', in *Christian Alternatives*; G. Elder, 'Responses of the Thai-Chinese Churches to the Ancestor Problem', in *Christian Alternatives*; P. S. Johnston, *Shades of Sheol: Death and Afterlife in the Old Testament* (Leicester; Downers Grove: Apollos, 2002); T. J. Lewis, *Cults of the Dead in Ancient Israel and Ugarit* (Atlanta: Scholars, 1989); R. E. Reimer *et al.*, 'Ancestor Worship', in S. W. Sunquist (ed.), *A Dictionary of Asian Christianity* (Grand Rapids; Cambridge: Eerdmans, 2000); C. Shibata, 'Some Problematic Aspects of Japanese Ancestor Worship', in *Christian Alternatives*; K. Spronk, *Beatific Afterlife in Ancient Israel and in the Ancient Near East* (Neukirchen-Vluyn: Neukirchener, 1986).

A. PAGOLU

Anthropology

It is difficult to give an agreed date for when anthropology emerged as a discipline, but one important event was the publication of Edward Tylor's classic book *Primitive Culture* in 1871. He presented a founding definition of culture as 'that complex whole which includes knowledge, belief, art, morals, law, custom, and any other capabilities and habits acquired by man as a member of society'.

It was, however, in the USA that a young German scholar named Franz Boas (1858–1942) commenced the study of the Inuit (Eskimos) of Baffin Island. He showed that their way of life was not determined solely by the environment as was previously believed, and should not be dismissed as merely primitive. He went on to study the many tribes of the North-West Coast Indians, and saw here again a sophisticated society. As a result he set about recording every aspect of their way of life that he thought was fast disappearing through the encroachment of the Europeans. He also made an important distinction between 'race' as a biological category and 'culture' as a way of life that is learned. This led him to argue that no culture was inherently superior to another, a teaching that became known as 'cultural relativism'. Boas was rightly named 'the father of American anthropology', and his students read like the who's-who of the subject in the USA: Margaret Mead, Ruth Benedict and Alfred Kroeber.

At the same time in the UK, Malinowski (1884–1942), a Polish academic, was making his mark. He had made a field study of the Trobriand Islanders of the Pacific. This was later considered to be the first example of fieldwork in the sense of an anthropologist living with the people and recording every aspect of their lives. Out of his studies Malinowski developed the theory known as 'functionalism', which essentially taught that every aspect of culture fulfils a function in meeting biological and sociological needs. In 1939, Malinowski went on a lecture tour of the USA, with the result that functionalism came to provide a theoretical foundation to the ideas of Boas and his students. Meanwhile, in Britain the ideas of Radcliffe-Brown became popular among anthropologists. His theory of 'Structural Functionalism' emphasized enduring institutions from which individuals derive rights and obligations.

It was, however, the writings of Boas and his followers that had an influence on missionaries and Bible translators (see *Language/Linguistics/Translation). The Summer Institute of Linguistics (SIL) and Wycliffe Bible Translators realized that an understanding of culture was of comparable importance to that of language. Eugene Nida's book *Customs and Culture* became standard reading for missionary candidates in the 1950s. Associated with Nida was a core of other scholars, William A. Smalley, William D. Reyburn and Jacob A. Loewen, who with others founded the journal *Practical Anthropology* in 1952. The journal was finally taken over by a new journal called *Missiology* in 1972 with Alan R. Tippett as editor.

The next major advance of anthropology into mission circles came through the writings of Donald McGavran, who in 1961 started the School of World Mission of Fuller Theological Seminary. Alan R. Tippet joined the school, which added greater anthropological sophistication. Later, they were joined by Charles H. Kraft and Paul G. Hiebert.

Anthropology was not welcomed by all Christians. One area of criticism was whether it was correct to apply a secular social science to the work of God and whether this would deprecate the work of the Holy Spirit in mission. The international Lausanne conference of 1974 tended to reassure most that this was not a danger. There was however one major issue for Christians which was the notion of 'cultural relativism'.

Boas had argued that any part of a culture must be viewed in its particular context rather than from the viewpoint of an external observer. Thus, no culture possessed a set of absolute standards by which all other cultures can be judged. Nida argued that all cultures are equally valid, but all subject to God's law. The outcome was an important statement in the Lausanne Covenant of 1974:

Culture must always be tested and judged by Scripture. Because man is God's creature, some of his culture is rich in beauty and goodness. Because he has fallen, all of it is tainted with sin and some of it is demonic. The Gospel does not presuppose the superiority of any culture to another, but evaluates all cultures according to its own criteria of truth and righteousness, and insists on moral absolutes in every culture.

It was the functionalist form of anthropological theory that had the greatest impact on missionary thinking, but it had its limitations. Boas had thought of the North American Indians in terms of 'tribes', each with their own discrete cultures. McGavran used this notion and spoke of 'homogeneous units', a term that was later changed to 'peoples', and later still 'people groups'. The model assumes that each culture is a discrete, bounded, homogeneous and self-contained unit. With adequate information it should therefore be possible to draw maps of the world identifying the various people groups, and design suitable mission strategies for each.

From this model developed the concept of *indigeneity. Earlier missionaries had struggled with the question of what should be the form of the new emerging missionary churches. In the nineteenth century, Henry Venn and Rufus Anderson had spoken of the need of a three-self church: self-supporting, self-governing and self-propagating. Indigeneity went further in suggesting that the indigenous local culture should have an impact on all aspects of church life: theology, liturgy, style of leadership, architecture, music, etc.

An associated idea was that of finding 'functional substitutes' for significant local customs that Christians felt unacceptable to their new faith. Tippett was an early advocate of this approach and argued that offensive rituals be replaced by wholesome Christian activities that served the same function. Reference was often made to Pope Gregory and his instruction to Augustine as he was sent to evangelize the Angles. If there was a sound heathen temple, it was not to be destroyed but cleansed and used for Christian purposes. In practice, although the concept is potentially valuable, it is not easy to find truly functional equivalents.

Although missionaries adopted the functionalist form of anthropology, they were not always aware that theory in anthropology was moving on. The restricted model of functionalism was found wanting. In the 1950s, the famous Oxford anthropologist E. E. Evans-Pritchard presented the case that culture cannot be regarded as static, but it must be seen within a historical context. In the 1960s, the structuralist ideas of the French scholar Claude Levi-Strauss influenced many in Europe, and this teaching was advocated in the English-speaking world by Edmund Leach. Structuralism saw culture not as an objective outward form to be studied, but more like a language to be learned.

It was however in the 1980s that *post-modern theory began to influence the discipline, with the ideas of deconstruction, authority and power. In European anthropology, it was the radical views of Foucault that had a major influence. Foucault advocated the importance of 'the author', who in writing exercises a power over the subject described. Edward Said wrote his classic text *Orientalism* that revealed the inherent assumptions of the Western writers in their portrayal of the Orient. Mundembi, in *Invention of Africa*, wrote about the impact of colonialists, missionaries and anthropologists in the creation of the notion of 'Africa'.

Anthropological concepts and methods have greatly helped missionaries and influenced missiology as a discipline. However, anthropology has essentially been seen as a tool for evangelism – a tool to increase the efficiency of the task. Sadly, there has been little engagement with postmodern anthropological approaches.

See also CULTURE.

Bibliography
A. Barnard, *History and Theory in Anthropology* (Cambridge: Cambridge University Press, 2000); R. Layton, *An Introduction to Theory in Anthropology* (Cambridge: Cambridge University Press, 1997); C. Taber, *The World is Too Much With Us* (Macon: Mercer, 1991).

D. BURNETT

Apologetics

The term is derived from the Greek *apologia*, meaning 'words (spoken) on behalf of'. It is normally used as a technical expression for the systematic defence and promotion of Christian faith, explaining and justifying beliefs and actions. It reflects the biblical command: 'always be ready to make your defence (*apologia*) to anyone who demands from you an account of the hope that is in you' (1 Pet. 3:15, NRSV). Unfortunately, in English the word is ambiguous, for its more normal meaning (apology/apologize) is to admit a mistake or error, a quite different sense from that intended in the Christian context.

For this reason, it may be preferable to use another word, such as *advocacy*, indicating the recommendation and promotion of a course of action or the defence of a person or cause. This range of meanings adequately covers the significance of the word in its sense of testimony and vindication. It calls to mind a legal context. Both the prosecution and defence prepare a brief and argue a case. They are based on rational processes and appeal to evidence, able to stand up to cross-examination and deal satisfactorily with alternative explanations. In the Christian context, the method can be used proactively, by exposing the weaknesses and contradictions of other belief systems – for example, naturalistic philosophies, the humanist basis for ethics or non-theistic religions – or defensively, by demonstrating the poverty of arguments used to refute the Christian faith.

Epistemological considerations

In Christian apologetics the objects of discussion are statements that possess truth-value. Truth is understood to refer to the accurate representative function of language and the exact correspondence between a statement and the reality to which it refers. Thus, apologetics concerns the advocacy of a reality independent of human thought about it. It is not about a language-game, in which statements are 'true' only in so far as they obey the grammatical rules of a particular system of belief. Nor are we discussing 'emotivism', in which convictions that appear to denote an objective reality, simply refer to inner desires. In neither of these cases would it be either desirable or possible to engage in apologetics, for there would be no common ground on which a meaningful dialogue or debate could proceed.

The purpose of apologetics is to secure a conviction; to persuade an observer of the validity of one's case. The most appropriate metaphor, therefore, is that of the law court. The objective is to convince the jury (or judge) to agree with one's arguments. Proceedings follow the method known as *inference to the best explanation*. The function of the court (in criminal cases) is to establish, beyond reasonable doubt, the truth or falsity of a charge brought against an individual or corporate body of having infringed the law. The court is seeking to establish the best explanation of all the evidence germane to the case. It sifts through a number of possible alternative explanations, showing ultimately which one does most justice to the relevant information.

Inference to the best explanation in action is a method for deciding between alternative theories that claim to give an account of reality as a whole. Thus, for example, a Christian would argue that it is impossible to explain human existence and experience on the basis of a self-generating, purely material world. Naturalism is not a plausible explanation of reality, if all the evidence is taken into account.

Rational processes are an important part of apologetics. Reason, however, is not the final arbiter of truth, but an instrument to measure the cogency of arguments and the correct use of evidence. It employs the laws of logic, such as the principle of non-contradiction. Thus, for instance, an explanation for the diversity of religious beliefs that argued that they all represent the same ultimate reality would be fallacious, because the same cannot be denoted by contradictory ideas and conflicting beliefs.

Issues in apologetics

Non-Christians raise a number of serious objections to Christian claims to know the truth about life and the universe. They fall into two categories. First, there are the moral and intellectual problems inherent in its system of belief. Obviously, the existence of innocent suffering and depraved cruelty, as evinced by Ivan in Dostoyevsky's novel, *The Brothers Karamazov*, or by Elie Wiesel in his account of Auschwitz in *Night*, appears to refute the existence of a God who is simultaneously all-powerful and absolutely good. This is reinforced by God's alleged severity and lack of mercy towards his opponents, according to some biblical passages. There are also alleged difficulties in the Bible, such as supposed errors of historical fact, untrue statements, contradictions and implausible fables. In contemporary thought, Christians are often accused of denying in practice their own beliefs, for example by justifying war, refusing to forgive or suppressing natural rights by discriminating against certain lifestyle choices. It is generally believed today that theistic proofs for the existence of God, the ontological, cosmological, teleological and moral arguments, are unsound, because they fail to demonstrate their claims.

Secondly, non-Christians argue that there are better explanations for belief than the ones adduced by Christians. Belief in an objective, divine presence, for example, can be explained by recourse to basic human needs. In different ways, human beings project their desires and existential predicaments outwards from themselves and invent an all-wise, all-powerful, supreme Being who solves life's dilemmas, whether practical or metaphysical. Human beings, as Feuerbach argued, create a Being who represents the fullness of all that they lack. Religion, as Marx proposed, is a compensation for the injustices of existence. It is a defence against fear of the unknown. It is a way of coping with traumas suffered as a child. In these senses, theistic belief is always the symptom of a malady.

Ever since the onslaught on faith in the eighteenth-century Age of Enlightenment, many thinkers have dismissed the supposed existence of God as an unnecessary hypothesis. God was postulated increasingly as a theory to account for gaps in knowledge; once knowledge expanded, God became redundant. The classic example of this principle is the neo-Darwinian theory of evolution. Simultaneously, the theory appears to give a comprehensive, empirical explanation of the emergence of life on earth, without the supernatural intervention of God, and to undermine the argument from design for God's existence.

Finally, the *postmodern emphasis on the historical and cultural contingency of belief systems and ethical norms, and the experience of different religions claiming an insight into ultimate truth, makes the assertion of one faith to know uniquely the way of salvation seem arrogant and absurd. Exclusive claims by Christianity seem to imply that God is unfair, harsh and intolerant.

On the other side, Christians raise fundamental questions about life, which they are convinced other belief systems cannot answer adequately. If evolutionary theory is the only conceivable alternative to a theistic account of origins, it must explain satisfactorily the source of human self-consciousness. The ability to know oneself as a person strongly suggests a personal, rather than impersonal, beginning to human life. Naturalistic theories of the world and non-theistic religions give explanations of existence that fail to satisfy human experience.

The universal search for the meaning of existence, and the reason why anything exists rather than nothing, points to a purposeful universe instead of an accidental and random one. Moreover, it would be impossible to make sense of the success of the natural sciences, if the existence of everything were a matter of pure chance. According to the *anthropic* principle, the possibility that the supremely complex and yet exceptionally

well-regulated natural order could be the outcome of wholly unintended, fortuitous processes is statistically so minute that the theory can be discarded as an explanation. Science itself points to the strong probability that the universe is the result of intelligent design.

In the area of moral philosophy, the justification of theories of right and wrong, good and evil, seem to require a transcendent reference point. The notion of human rights, for example, raises a fundamental question about their derivation. They seem to depend on a belief in the equal dignity and worth of every human being. Such a belief, however, cannot simply be affirmed as self-evident. Without a coherent account of what it means to be human, rights cannot be stated as intrinsic. *The Universal Declaration of Human Rights*, that speaks of the 'inherent dignity and of the equal and inalienable rights of all members of the human family' (Preamble), and affirms that 'all human beings are born free and equal in dignity and rights' (Article 1), assumes a foundation that only a theistic account of the universe can supply.

Evolutionary theory, for example, that postulates selection and mutation on the basis of the survival of the fittest, contradicts the notion of equal rights. Ethics is only possible on the basis of an altruism that negates the unequal struggle for survival, as if the theory of evolution were not true. As Kant recognized, moral action presupposes freedom of the will, eternal life and the coincidence of virtue and happiness. He was forced to conclude that the truly moral life required the postulation of God. However, if God is presumed merely to guarantee that actions are truly ethical, we are back with another version of the projection theory. God has to exist in reality and possess the characteristics of absolute justice and goodness, if there is to be a proper foundation for distinguishing between right and wrong.

Lastly, contemporary secular societies are intrinsically unable to say what constitutes a genuinely rich quality of life. The inclusion of 'the pursuit of happiness' into the *Declaration of the Rights of Man* might appear to suggest a basic motive for living. However, it is notoriously problematic to give any satisfactory definition of happiness. The plurality of views has been seized upon by commercial interests and turned into an infinite variety of goods and services designed to secure happiness. The result is to convert quality into quantity and to make the notion of human progress unintelligible. Quality of life (good or bad) is dependent on a fundamental understanding of what it means to be human. Contemporary, secular versions tend to be superficial and banal. The Christian understanding of 'abundant life' is often in sharp contrast to the trivial pursuits of contemporary consumerism. There is a responsibility to proclaim and show that a bountiful life greatly exceeds the shallow search for the modern equivalent of 'bread and circuses'.

Biblical examples of apologetics in action
In the book of Acts, on several occasions (e.g. Acts 17:2–4; 19:8–10) the Greek word, *dialogesthai* (to dialogue), is used of Paul's activity in seeking to persuade the members of the synagogue to believe in Jesus. Other phrases are also used of Paul's debates with both Jews and Gentiles in which he seeks to convince them of the truth of the gospel: thus, 'reason with' (Acts 17:17), 'dispute' (Acts 17:18), 'teach' (Acts 17:19), 'bear witness' (Acts 18:5), 'refute' (Acts 18:28). Perhaps the two best examples of Paul's apologetic strategy are the debate with the Epicurean and Stoic philosophers in the Areopagus in Athens and the daily discussions he held in the lecture hall of Tyrannus in Ephesus.

The anonymous letter to the Hebrews is also an excellent example of apologetics. The author argues that Christ's work of salvation fully achieves what the animal sacrifices commanded in the OT law only hint at. The readers comprised a Christian group tempted, as a result of persecution, to return to the security of the old religion. The author persuades them that this would be gross folly, given that Jesus Christ alone perfectly atones for human sin and opens the way into God's presence. By implication, the discussion can be applied to any religion or philosophy that offers an alternative way of salvation to that given in Christ. Arguing from 'inference to the best explanation', the letter is interpreted to demonstrate that Jesus Christ is in every way God's answer to all human needs, and accomplishes what no other system of faith can.

Christian views on apologetics
There is a vigorous debate among Christians concerning the aptness and value of apologetics as part of Christian mission. It continues a spirited discussion that has divided Christians down the ages, reflecting the relative weight given to the mind and the will in coming to *faith. Is belief a prerequisite of rational understanding or is faith partly the fruit of reason? How much is faith engendered solely by listening to the gospel, taking the truth-claims largely on trust? How much should the message's reliability be verified prior to believing?

There are two major schools of thought in answer to these questions. There are some (Barth is the most famous example) who do not believe that the gospel can be tested by human reason. According to this view, there is no *independent* ground, outside of a faith-commitment, from which it is possible to judge the truthfulness of God's revelation. Thus, failure to believe would not demonstrate intellectual inadequacy but rather a prior attitude of unbelief. The story of Jesus is essentially self-authenticating. Others, however, (including Brunner in his dispute with Barth) believe that the rational sifting of evidence has to be allowed, even encouraged, as a prelude to the act of faith. Part of the disagreement concerns the way in which sin is said to have affected reason. The first group believe that reason has been so corrupted that the things of God cannot be apprehended rightly by human thought-processes; God's (special) revelation is warranted only as a direct divine communication. The second group believe that, granted an awareness of preconceptions, the reality of God can be established by rational deliberation on the basis of persuasive evidence; God's (general) revelation is available in part to the discerning intelligence.

Although the second approach, often referred to as *natural theology, has a long tradition in Christian thinking, some claim that it concedes too much to post-Enlightenment rationalism and is powerless as an apologetic in the face of determined scepticism. Others suspect that the contemporary postmodern distrust of reason and exaltation of the affections makes rational apologetic strategies dubious. Nevertheless, granted that God desires to make known his plan of salvation to every human being, but without forcibly overcoming an unwillingness to believe, and that God uses human testimony to communicate the truth of his word, an apologetic that appeals to both special and general revelation seems to be appropriate.

Apologetics and mission

Notwithstanding the theoretical differences of opinion noted above, Christians of different traditions have sought both to defend and commend Christian faith in diverse contexts as a part of the call to mission. Thus, taking a few examples from the recent past, Schaeffer has advocated the rationality of Christian faith as a comprehensive answer to questions about human existence. Newbigin argues that the narrative of the gospel solves the post-Enlightenment dilemma concerning the divorce between so-called 'public' facts and 'private' values. Cragg has sought to demonstrate that the Qur'an should be read to show that Jesus Christ truly answers the Muslim's deepest longing to know the will of God. Gutiérrez promotes the view that God's liberating presence in the world is aimed at transforming structures of oppression and injustice as well as individual human hearts and minds. Yoder has advocated strategies of non-violence as the only appropriate Christian response to conflict. Other Christians have used contemporary literature, music, the visual arts and cinema as means of illustrating the dilemmas of a world seeking to live without God and of uncovering secret longings for a 'salvation' that comes from beyond human devising. Christians seek to respond to the alleged conflict between science and faith, by showing the total implausibility of an impersonal universe, the result of blind chance.

In this, and other ways, Christians engage in apologetics, as did the early 'Apologists', in order to respond to genuine doubts about the faith, to remove philosophical, cultural and moral objections to Christian believing, to show the advantages Christianity possesses over rival religious and humanist faiths and to manifest the benefits of faith in Jesus Christ. In these ways, apologetics is a significant part of what has been called 'mission to culture', relating the gospel message to societies' world-views, political, economic and legal structures, moral values, customs, traditions, art-forms and language. Without apologetics, Christian mission lacks a cutting edge in the unending contest for the allegiance of peoples' hearts, minds and wills.

Bibliography

E. E. Brunner, *Revelation and Reason: The Christian Doctrine of Faith and Knowledge* (Philadelphia: Westminster, 1946); P. Copan and P. K. Moser, *The Rationality of Theism* (London: Routledge, 2003); K. Cragg, *Muhammad and the Christian: A Question of Response* (London: Darton, Longman and Todd, 1984); W. L. Craig and J. P. Moreland (eds.), *Naturalism: A Critical Analysis* (London: Routledge, 2000); G. Gutiérrez, *Essential Writings*, ed. J. B. Nickoloff (Maryknoll: Orbis Books, 1996); J. A. Kirk, *The Future of Reason, Science and Faith: Following Modernity and Postmodernity* (Aldershot: Ashgate Publishing, 2007); J. A. Kirk and K. J. Vanhoozer, *To Stake a Claim: Mission and the Western Crisis of Knowledge* (Maryknoll: Orbis Books, 1999); C. S. Lewis, *God in the Dock: Essays on Theology and Ethics* (Grand Rapids: Eerdmans, 1970); A. McGrath, *The Foundations of Dialogue in Science and Religion* (Oxford: Blackwell, 1998); L. Newbigin, *Truth to Tell: The Gospel as Public Truth* (Grand Rapids: Eerdmans, 1991); A. Plantinga, *Warranted Christian Belief* (Oxford: Oxford University Press, 2000); V. Ramachandra, *Faith in Conflict? Christian Integrity in a Multicultural World* (Leicester: IVP, 1999); F. Schaeffer, *He Is There and He Is Not Silent* (London: Hodder and Stoughton, 1972); R. Trigg, *Rationality and Religion: Does Faith Need Reason?* (Oxford: Blackwell, 1998); K. Ward, *God, Chance and Necessity* (Oxford: One World, 1996); J. H. Yoder, *The Original Revolution: Essays on Christian Pacifism* (Scottdale: Herald Press, 1972).

J. A. KIRK

Art

Although the term 'art' can be broadly applied to include *music and literature, its usage here will refer principally, though not exclusively, to the visual arts. Scripture affirms the making of art, even as it prohibits the making of images for use in pagan worship or idolatry

(Exod. 20:4). Any good gift of God (intellect, wealth, sexuality, art) may become idolatrous; but all of God's good gifts, including art, can and should be sanctified and used in his service.

Scripture states that the Spirit of God filled Bezalel with intelligence, knowledge and skill to make artistic designs in metals, stone and wood for the tabernacle. He also had a colleague, Oholiab, suggesting that collaboration in artistic endeavours is good (in distinct contrast to modern notions of the artist as a lonely, tormented, misunderstood, impractical, and perhaps somewhat insane, genius). Furthermore, their work was centred in the community, and they had many gifted volunteers who worked with them in their task (Exod. 31:1–11; 35:30 – 36:5). With this background, we find that Jewish art has a tradition from the conquest of Canaan to contemporary art at odds with the popular perception of Jewish iconoclasm.

Christian art varies extremely in function, style, content and quality, and may or may not be made by professing Christians, but it exhibits explicitly or tacitly a Christian perspective. The term 'Christian art' is not a useless or indefensible label as some have argued, but descriptive of its content (mainly biblical) and in many instances its intent; and it is important to maintain this terminology in order to converse broadly across academic disciplines.

Christian art pre-dates the Peace of the Church (AD 313) and the Athanasian witness to the NT canon (AD 367) and has continued to the present. In parts of Africa (Egypt, Ethiopia) and Asia (Armenia) there is a venerable tradition of Christian art, and there are signs of its burgeoning in many parts of sub-Saharan Africa as well as being renewed in the Western world today.

Christianity has always amazingly adapted to any context and learnt to speak the vernacular languages. This has had implications for its art. There has not been one normative style as with Islam. Early Christian artists gradually transformed both the style and themes of the Greco-Roman art they received, so that between the third and sixth centuries the entire pantheon of gods and mythological heroes of the ancient world was replaced by the central image of Jesus Christ and the saints that lasted in the West until relatively recently

and is still not completely extinct. The implications for Christian mission of this powerful example of the proclamation of the gospel and radical transformation of culture by visual means have as yet been barely reflected on.

Monasticism, mission and art have often partnered. The Rule of St Benedict (c. 540) evidences the contribution that artists/artisans made and urges them to humility rather than conceit because of their skills. St Francis has been called the father of Italian art. In 1493 Franciscans built the first church in the Americas in Haiti. Dominicans did not lag behind, producing such renowned artists as Fra Angelico (c. 1400–55) and Fra Bartolommeo (c. 1472–1517), who became a monk through the influence of the fiery reformer, Savonarola (1452–98).

The missionary spirit of the Franciscans laid a foundation for the Jesuits. Art for the latter became an intentional evangelistic strategy as they fanned out to Asia, Africa and South America with trunks filled with *objets d'art*, that already had absorbed numerous European visual vernaculars, to use to impart their message. They were also willing to make significant artistic accommodations in order to communicate *contextually in vastly different cultures, arguably creating the first truly global visual currency for cultural exchange. The visualizing techniques of Ignatius Loyola's *Spiritual Exercises* (c. 1523) had profound influence on artists such as P. P. Rubens (1577–1640) and Gianlorenzo Bernini (1598–1680) and in the general shaping of Baroque art and architecture in Europe, Asia and Latin America. The art which the conquistadores took to Latin America from Spain in the sixteenth century, especially their depictions of the suffering Christ of the crucifix, significantly shaped the Catholic spirituality which the indigenous peoples adopted. In turn some artists learnt to contextualize Christ as distinctly native.

For the Orthodox, icons, formed with animal, vegetable and mineral matter taken from the world of God's creation, proclaimed in colour the same gospel in a universal language of art and beauty that which was spoken and written. Alaskan Orthodoxy has been particularly adept in expressing Aleutian indigenousness in its icons.

Protestant missions by and large have been word-centred, with music being the art form of choice. There have been, however, adventurous exceptions. For example, in 1883, the Church Missionary Society built a church in Peshawar in the Punjab, All Saints Memorial Church, described for its constituency as 'a remarkable building in a Saracenic style, designed to adapt a Christian place of worship to Oriental ideas'. Increasingly Protestants have been more open to the use of art in worship and outreach. The Protestant church in Bali is a notable example of the contextualization of faith and worship by means not only of indigenous art and architecture, but also music and dance.

If theology can inform art, art forms can radically direct theological understanding and missional engagement. The Gwandara-wará (Hausa for 'a people who prefer to dance') of Nigeria for centuries resisted both Muslim and Christian conversion, finding repugnant the legalistic strictures they perceived in both religions because they preferred to dance! They relented, however, about thirty years ago, and embraced Christianity when African missionaries of the Evangelical Missionary Society (an agency of the Evangelical Church of West Africa) decided to dance the gospel to them. Through rhythm and movement, applying the art language of the heart of these people, they further instructed them in some detail regarding doctrine, especially creation and redemption.

The way in which the visual depiction of the gospel shapes how Christianity is understood can be illustrated by the frequent representation of Christ as white, reinforcing a Western Christology as normative. Christ has even been famously depicted as Che Guevara as a way of communicating his revolutionary potential.

Missiological thinking and research regarding the artistic expression of Christianity as it is spread around the world is still in its infancy. Pioneers of this work for the non-Western world are: Cardinal Celso Costantini (1876–1958), Arno Lehmann (1901–84), John Francis Butler (1927–98) and Andrew F. Walls (1928–) The whole range of international Christian art, East and West, North and South is in need of a taxonomy in order to distinguish it, without separating its multiple functions (liturgical, ecclesiastical, missional, professional and personal), with an understanding of its historical development and contemporary application. Art as an important document for the study of the history of mission as well as doctrine is still largely underdeveloped.

The issues and implications of art for mission are manifold. The question of when a work of art is religiously syncretistic or simply contextualizing the faith remains to be explored. The idea that art is a luxury that we can well live without is refuted by the enormous amount of art made in Second World War concentration camps and by the poorest peoples of the world as well as by the irresistible need of believers of all kinds in all parts of the world to create art. These instances demonstrate art to be a necessity for our humanity and an expression that human beings are made in the image of God, who is Creator and ultimate artist. Associations of Christian artists transcending denominations are growing around the globe, also suggesting that the communal spirit of Bezelal and Oholiab is still alive.

There is rich evidence from Scripture (e.g. Paul in Athens, Acts 17:16–34) and the practice of the church, that art aids in propagating the faith by appealing to imagination as well as cognition, thus enabling a community of faith not only to communicate in a culturally relevant way, but also indwell salvation history. Jacques Maritain called art, 'the John the Baptist of the heart, preparing its affections for Christ'. Art is perhaps God's greatest gift to mortals to convey implicitly, multivalently and powerfully across diverse cultures and circumstances (rather than merely explicitly, and as a consequence reductively) his truth, love and grace.

Bibliography

G. A. Bailey, *Art on the Jesuit Missions in Asia and Latin America, 1542–1773* (Toronto: University of Toronto Press, 1999); J. F. Butler, *Christianity in Asia and America After A.D. 1500* (Leiden: E. J. Brill, 1979); L. Gasque, 'Voices of the New Heartland: Christian Art in Asia, Africa and Latin America', *Radix* 23, 1995, pp. 8–11, 26–28; L. Gasque, 'The Christian Stake in the Arts: Toward a Missiology of Western Culture', *Evangelical Review of Theology* 24, 2000, pp. 257–277; A. Lehmann, *Christian Art in Africa and Asia* (St Louis: Concordia Publishing, 1969); T. F. Mathews, *The Clash of*

Gods: A Reinterpretation of Early Christian Art (Princeton: Princeton University Press, 1993); M. Oleksa, *Orthodox Alaska: A Theology of Mission* (Crestwood: St Vladimir's Seminary Press, 1992); A. F. Walls, 'The Western Discovery of Non-Western Christian Art', in *The Missionary Movement in Christian History: Studies in the Transmission of Faith* (Maryknoll: Orbis Books; Edinburgh: T. & T. Clark, 1996); A. Wessels, *Images of Jesus* (Eerdmans, 1990).

L. GASQUE

Asian theology

Put simply, Asian theology is an Asian appropriation and expression of the gospel. This, of course, begs the question, 'What is Asian?' For the realities of Asia are indeed complex. The continent comprises some thirty-five countries with a combined population of nearly four billion. It is no surprise then to find on this huge land mass a mesmerizing diversity of cultures and languages. Asia is home to some of the world's oldest civilizations, hence their great literary traditions. Practically all the world religions claim an Asian origin: Confucianism, Taoism, Buddhism, Hinduism, Sikhism, Islam, and of course, Christianity. Traditional Asian religiosity is counterbalanced by an unprecedented postwar modernization that has created glaring disparities in income and education levels. Many are drawn to the cities, such that today six of the ten largest cities in the world are in Asia. At the same time, many places, notably the myriad villages and small towns, continue to be plagued by poverty, unemployment and illiteracy. Such are the diverse Asian contexts in which theology finds itself and to which it seeks to address.

In the light of the historical, socio-cultural, political and economic complexities that characterize Asia, it is impossible to construct a single overarching or unifying Asian theology. In reality there are as many Asian theolog*ies* as there are local Asian contexts. Asian theology as such is therefore an abstraction. But the term is not an unhelpful one, for it can be used to refer to all or any of the theological processes and products that arise from the multifarious contexts of Asia.

As a subject of formal theological inquiry Asian theology is of fairly recent origin, in all probability arising from the *con-textualization debates of the 1970s. That notwithstanding, theological reflection has already gone on for a long time. It is not often well appreciated, but Asian Christianity has a long and venerable history, as evidenced in Samuel Hugh Moffett's magisterial two-volume work, *A History of Christianity in Asia*. As early as the second century, a thriving Christian church was founded in Edessa in eastern Syria. There the theological debates concerning the trinitarian nature of God and the divinity of Christ took on a rather different philosophical course from that of the Roman churches. Bardaisan (c. 154–222), for instance, sought ways to express the Christian faith using prevailing cultural categories, describing the Trinity as the Father, the Word of Thought (the Son), and the Mother of Life (the Holy Spirit). Indeed from the time of the earliest missionary activity in Asia, Asian Christians have consistently sought to appropriate the biblical message in their own cultural terms.

Asian theology, like all indigenous theologies, is contingent on the vernacular principle. Though much of early Christian theology was penned in Latin and Greek, and the most widely published theology today is in English, German and French, strictly speaking, there is no linguistic privileging in theology. Even today, despite the theological predominance of the European languages, Asian Christians are continuing their theological and missiological reflection in their own tongue. The output of Asian theological writings over the centuries has been prodigious, to say the least. John England and others edited a three-volume bibliographic research guide entitled *Asian Christian Theologies*, which added up to more than 2,000 pages. This massive compilation contains references to theological materials from some twenty countries in Asia, spanning more than a millennium all the way back to the seventh century. The resources cited are not only in the Western languages, but also in the original languages. Unfortunately, most of these vernacular works have yet to be translated into English or any of the other world languages, thus making it still rather difficult for Asian theology to exert any meaningful influence on the global church. Perhaps it is time for Western theologians to learn the Asian languages in order to mine the theological insights in Asian writings that have remained hidden from the Western church for too long.

In terms of literary style, it is noted that unlike the discursive and propositional mode in which Western theology is largely written, Asian theological language tends to be parabolic, metaphorical, allegorical and narrative. In terms of approach and content, contemporary Asian theologies can broadly be classified into four types: (1) doctrinal; (2) existential; (3) religious; and (4) socio-political.

The first consists of those theological attempts to articulate the classical doctrines of the Christian faith from a distinctively Asian perspective, often using a single cultural theme. One of the most celebrated of such theologies is the 'pain of God' theology, in which Japanese theologian Kazô Kitamori explicates the atonement through the motif of pain. According to Kitamori, 'God who must sentence sinners to death fought with God who wishes to love them. The fact that this fighting God is not two different gods but the same God causes his pain' (*Theology of the Pain of God*, p. 21). More recently, another Japanese theologian, Nozomu Miyahira, constructed a Japanese theological interpretation of the Trinity using the Japanese theme of harmony between human beings. Miyahira's new trinitarian formula is 'three betweennesses and one concord'.

The second group of Asian theologies is characterized by an *accommodative attempt to make theological sense of the existential realities of everyday life. Theologians in this camp emphasize that theology has a necessary missiological orientation. Reflecting on his years of missionary service in Thailand, Kosuke Koyama developed his water buffalo theology, in which he employs vivid images of common sights and sounds to talk about the Christian life. For Koyama, theology cannot be abstracted and separated from life itself. And so, for instance, he understands God's revelation not only in the 'history-event' of freeing captives from prison (Isa. 42:7), but also in the 'nature-occurrence' of the monsoon season. Of course, nature must not only be understood naturally, but appropriated theologically. Koyama writes, 'The rain is theologized, historicized, and becomes more than just drops of water from heaven. It is God's rain. It is God's monsoon' (*Water*

Buffalo Theology, p. 29). In his third-eye theology, Taiwanese native Choan-Seng Song suggests that what theologians need today is a 'third eye', 'a power of perception and insight that enables them to grasp the meaning under the surface of things and phenomena' (*Third-Eye Theology*, p. xiii). This, according to Song, can only be acquired when theology is done not propositionally, but reflectively, using the resources of Asian folklore and mythology.

Third, there are those Asian theologians who interpret the Christian faith through the grid of Asian religions. Roman Catholic theologian Raimundo Panikkar, for instance, claims the presence of the 'unknown Christ' at the very centre of Hinduism. Another Indian theologian, Stanley Joseph Samartha, insists that in a religiously plural world there are many religious paths to Christ, all of which are theologically legitimate. A Hindu therefore is expected to respond to Christ as a Hindu. The title of Samartha's theological treatise on Christology is rather telling of his position: *One Christ – Many Religions*. The problem with Pannikkar, Samartha, and other theologians who take a religious pluralist approach is that it invariably leads to a *syncretism in which the authority of the Bible is compromised and the uniqueness of Christ dissolved without a trace. Sri Lankan evangelical theologian Vinoth Ramachandra argues that the uniqueness and decisiveness of what God has done for us in the historical and incarnate Christ simply cannot be compromised by any cultural or religious agenda. The encounter between biblical Christianity and the world religions surely constitutes one of the greatest missiological challenges today, and Asian evangelicals are only beginning to realize that they are situated in one of the best contexts to explore this issue.

In the final category are socio-political theologies that aim at the liberation of the oppressed. The *minjung theology (literally, theology of the masses) developed in South Korea in the late 1970s seeks to provide biblical justification for the struggle of the common people for freedom from the political and economic domination of the ruling class, not unlike the liberation theology of Latin America. In the 1980s, *Dalit Christians (those outside the traditional caste system of Indian society, hence considered ritually impure by those within it) explored theological means to redress problems of grave injustice and oppression and effect reconciliation between Dalit Christians and high caste Christians. The result is an emergent Dalit theology. There is also a growing literature on Asian *feminist theology that seeks to address issues of patriarchy, violence against women, women's spirituality and sexuality.

The comment is often made that the main proponents of contemporary Asian theology are non-evangelicals. While some evangelicals see the need to do theology in context, many are afraid of the ever-lurking danger of syncretism that seems to characterize much of Asian theology today. Perhaps this has to do with the radical separation of church and state posited by many Western evangelical missionaries, such that the relevance of the gospel becomes almost wholly other-worldly. Yet it is also true, paradoxically, that the fear of syncretism and the unwavering stance concerning the uniqueness of Christ on the part of most Asian evangelicals have generated a remarkable commitment to world missions. South Korea, currently the second largest provider of missionaries in the world after the United States, is a case in point. Asian evangelicals, not least Korean missionaries, however, are beginning to realize the dire need of a mission theology that proclaims the uniqueness of Christ relevantly, sensitively, and intelligibly in the various missiological contexts.

Evangelicals rightly insist that theology must begin with biblical revelation. But theology must also relate to lived existential realities lest it lose its missiological cutting edge. In the case of Asia, theology must minimally engage religious and cultural traditions, deal with the thorny issue of the ancestors and ancestral rites, grapple with the question of the cultural identity of Asian Christians, address the socio-economic realities of affluence and poverty, and tackle the prevailing problems of violence and suffering. Today one would hardly dispute the necessity of theologizing in context. The missiological challenge facing evangelical theologians in Asia is to facilitate the process by which theology adapts its form and language to the multireligious and multicultural milieus it finds itself in, without compromising the central biblical message of God's salvific revelation in Jesus Christ.

Bibliography

J. C. England, J. Kuttianimattathil, J. M. Prior, L. A. Quintos, D. S. Kwang-sun and J. Wickeri (eds.), *Asian Christian Theologies: A Research Guide to Authors, Movements, Sources*, Vols. 1–3 (Maryknoll: Orbis Books, 2002–04); Yong-Bock Kim (ed.), *Minjung Theology* (Singapore: CCA, 1981); K. Kitamori, *Theology of the Pain of God* (Eugene: Wipf and Stock, 2005); K. Koyama, *Water Buffalo Theology* (Maryknoll: Orbis Books, rev. edn 1999); Pui-Lan Kwok, *Introducing Asian Feminist Theology* (Cleveland: Pilgrim Press, 2000); N. Miyahira, *Towards a Theology of the Concord of God: A Japanese Perspective on the Trinity* (Carlisle: Paternoster, 2000); S. H. Moffett, *A History of Christianity in Asia*, Vols. I–II (Maryknoll: Orbis Books, 1998, 2005); R. Panikkar, *The Unknown Christ of Hinduism* (London: Darton, Longman & Todd, rev. edn 1981); V. Ramachandra, *The Recovery of Mission: Beyond the Pluralist Paradigm* (Grand Rapids: Eerdmans, 1996); S. J. Samartha, *One Christ – Many Religions: Toward a Revised Christology* (Maryknoll: Orbis Books, 1991); Choan-Seng Song, *Third-Eye Theology* (Maryknoll: Orbis Books, rev. edn 1979); J. C. B. Webster, *The Dalit Christians: A History* (Delhi: ISPCK, 1992).

How Chuang Chua

ATONEMENT, see CROSS

Authority

Authority, power, and dominion are words which provoke various reactions today. The powerless, marginalized and poor think of them as inaccessible, while the powerful and rich enjoy them. Authority for many people is associated with despotic and unbridled power that rules over people and against their will, or as a subversive, sophisticated manipulation that is directed not for the service and benefit of all, but for the achievement of selfish ambitions for those who are in power. Such a controversial notion of authority, be it political or religious, raises serious questions for the church and its mission in the world today. How should the church use the authority granted to it by God for mission in the world? What alternative understanding of authority does the church have to offer to the world in the light of the formative story of Christ, who is the head over every power and authority (cf. Col. 2:9–10), in whom God's authority is incarnated and exercised in his mission of the kingdom?

To answer these questions we can turn to Jesus' mission of the *kingdom as a paradigm which singles out some of the aspects of authority embodied and enacted in Jesus. In this way we will see how divine authority was manifested in Jesus, which in turn will help us to define what authority is all about, and how it ought to be applied by the church in its life and mission.

Authority: Jesus' mission of the kingdom

Jesus' ministry of the kingdom in the Gospels indicates that his understanding and attitude to authority was as controversial and ambiguous as it is today. His teaching and ministry were recognized as having unprecedented authority and power (Matt. 7:29; 9:33). Yet, when Jesus is questioned by the religious leaders 'by what authority are you doing these things?', he prefers to remain enigmatic (Mark 11:27–33; Matt. 21:23–27). Jesus' authority is recognized and embraced by sinners and all sorts of dubious people, but publicly rejected by the religious authorities. They even see Beelzebul behind his mission (Mark 3:22–27; Matt. 12:22–24). Jesus' authority is intimidating to the religious and political establishment, and yet comforting to sinners, outcasts, the powerless, and poor.

Controversy over Jesus' divine authority has to do with two seemingly contradictory aspects of authority: leadership and servanthood. If for religious leaders God's authority is about triumphal reign, for Jesus it is about serving people in need. Reign and servanthood are not contradictory, however, but integral dimensions of authority. If authority loses one of these two components, it loses its authenticity. It is in danger of being misused. Jesus' example explicitly demonstrates that such a balance of leadership and servanthood is not only possible, but essential for the authentic manifestation of what God's authority means.

Before defining authority let us outline some of the aspects of such an integrated view of authority embodied and enacted in Jesus.

It is the authority of integrity. The proclaimed divine reign and its presence are incarnated in authentic action in Jesus' ministry. Jesus demonstrates a harmony between proclamation of the promised kingdom and its implementation. What Jesus proclaims he fulfils, and because he is true to his word his authority is respected.

The authority enacted by Jesus is not restrictive but creative; it aims to set people free so that the divine likeness of humanity can be fully realized. Kingdom authority prefers to offer people the choice of obedience rather than imposed moral obligations, thereby creating a context in which responsible moral formation and growth become possible.

The authority of Jesus is recognized, discerned and responded to voluntarily. 'To be under authority is not to be subject to domination by an alien will, but to be required to become a responsive agent' (D. R. Shell, in *New Dictionary of Christian Ethics and Pastoral Theology*, p. 179). This kind of authority does not violate the rights and freedom of humanity but respects their value, dignity and right to choose. Authority is given to a leader by those who choose to be led. It implies that good remains to be good until it chooses as such voluntarily. An imposed good ceases to be good and becomes a necessary evil.

The submissive aspect of authority is explicitly manifested in Jesus' ministry. Being fully aware of the source and nature of his authority, Jesus voluntarily submits his right and power to God's will and salvific purpose (e.g. Mark 14:32–42; John 19:1–16). It is the right and power to become vulnerable in order to save vulnerable humanity. Salvation of human life is more important than a given authority for a mission.

Strictly speaking, authority in Jesus' mission of the kingdom means an ability to proclaim God's will and fulfil it: to be able to do what God would do, to be passionate about the things God is passionate about. This authority is not only about extraordinary miracles but also about the alternative and transformative politics of compassion, mercy and love.

Authority: church and its mission

Jesus' understanding of authority, integrating leadership and servanthood, is to be the paradigm for the church and mission agencies as communities of Christ's faithful disciples (cf. Eph. 5:1; 1 Thess. 1:6; 1 Pet. 2:21; 3 John 3). Just as Jesus' authority is exercised for his kingdom mission, so the church receives his authority for its mission. The mission of the church is not merely an activity, it is its *raison d'être*, justifying its existence: to proclaim the lordship of Christ, and be a living witness to the principles and means by which his lordship was accomplished through his death and resurrection (Matt. 28:19–20). The church's servanthood witnesses to the Servant King.

This servanthood is manifested whenever foreign churches or missions respect the authority of national churches, operating only in response to their invitation, giving them responsibility to make decisions, submitting to their leadership, and offering genuine partnership in mission.

So authority is granted to the church to empower and enable it to implement God's servant mission. The church, however, must be aware of the source, meaning and limitations of its authority in order to use it properly and not misuse it. The church is commissioned to proclaim God's will with authority in the world, 'but need not single out authority as one of her teachings' (W. J. McClendon, *Doctrine: Systematic Theology* 2, p. 456). Through its visible presence and tangible witness, what it does must be consistent with what it preaches, otherwise it loses respect and therefore authority.

Too often the church is seen as imposing moral obligations and limitations in society, whereas it could use its authority to promote an alternative lifestyle in which morality becomes an easy yoke, a light burden and a desirable goal (Matt. 11:28–30); demanding but liberating, in which service is not duty but a voluntary manifestation of God's love and care for the world.

The authority of the church is neither unbridled rule nor sacerdotal power, but responsible leadership through humble service. Such an understanding of authority is indeed a disturbing alternative, particularly in some non-Western contexts where authority is often associated culturally with chiefdom, patronage, and male domination of households and communities. This can easily become a tyrannical authority, ruling over people against their will, or a subversive

sophisticated manipulation to gain the selfish ambitions of those who are in power.

The authority of servanthood can be used to offer an alterative vision of society in opposition to the way cultures believe society should be structured. It rejects self-glorification and engages social and political challenges. This is a prophetic role in society, and a destabilizing presence for worldly authorities. The authority of the church gives it the ability in its mission to win rights for those with no rights, to use power for the powerless, to bring freedom for the enslaved, to be a voice for the voiceless, and to embrace the excluded. It is not enough for the church to be *concerned* about social and economic injustice, violation of human rights and religious freedom, but it ought to use its authority actively to *transform* the world for the value, dignity and freedom of humanity. Such is its mission, for which its authority is given.

See also POWER, WEAKNESS.

Bibliography

D. J. Bosch, *Transforming Mission: Paradigm Shift in Theology of Mission* (Maryknoll: Orbis Books, 2001); S. Hauerwas, *A Community of Character: Toward a Constructive Christian Social Ethic* (Notre Dame: University of Notre Dame Press, 1981); S. Hauerwas, *The Peaceble Kingdom: A Primer in Christian Ethic* (Notre Dame: University of Notre Dame Press, 1983); W. J. McClendon, *Doctrine: Systematic Theology*, Vol. 2 (Nashville: Abingdon Press, 1994); D. R. Shell, 'Authority', in D. J. Atkinson, D. F. Field, A. Holmes and O. O'Donovan (eds.), *New Dictionary of Christian Ethics and Pastoral Theology* (Leicester: IVP, 1995); G. S. Shogren, 'Authority and Power', in J. B. Green, S. McKnight, and I. H. Marshall (eds.), *Dictionary of Jesus and the Gospels* (Leicester: IVP, 1991); N. G. Wright, *Free Church, Free State: The Positive Baptist Vision* (Carlisle: Paternoster, 2005).

F. RAYCHYNETS

AWAKENING, see REVIVAL/RENEWAL

Black consciousness

The Negro is a sort of seventh son, born with a veil and gifted with second sight in this American world, a world which yields him no true self-consciousness, but only lets him see himself through the revelation of the other world. (W. E. B. Du Bois, *The Souls of Black Folk* [New York: Bantam Books, 1989])

Black double consciousness is a condition arising from the experience common to the majority of black people, by which they see themselves and the world through the eyes of white people. Many black people's existence has been dominated by the experience of living in white-oriented and white-dominated societies which impute inferiority to non-whiteness. White people in general historically have often shown little or no real regard or respect for black people as fellow human beings (e.g. the slave trade, colonialism, segregation, apartheid, etc.). In part this phenomenon has created problems of identity not only for African Americans, where the problem was most acute, but for many black people all over the world who have had significant contact with white people. In recent history the phenomenon has been seen most clearly in America and apartheid South Africa. Regretfully, the Christian church has often acquiesced instead of opposing the attitudes of the majority in those societies.

Black people have suffered discrimination and segregation. They have had to accept inferior economic, social, leadership, cultural and educational status. Every sphere of life has been affected, including jobs, equal opportunities or lack of them. Many black people have felt dehumanized, dissocialized, depersonalized and disempowered. In the African American experience, oppression, deprivation, exclusion, alienation and rejection were, and in some places continue to be, daily realities, even in the church. It is hard, perhaps even impossible, for people living under these conditions to make any significant contribution to the overall pattern of church growth. These are issues which mission alongside and amongst black people must take into account.

*Black theology is a protest movement that married political aspirations to Christian longings for a freer and better environment. It is unfortunate that the form of black theology's political commitments has undermined its potential for good within the black

communities. But in its favour black theology has at least encouraged black Christians to appropriate from the Bible and the Christian faith a healthy self-esteem; a new way of looking at themselves. This promises to open up a new future filled with hope for the masses of oppressed people. Black theology sought to empower black people and to release them from passively expecting either political freedom, or indeed a sense of self-worth and human dignity, from the hands of white people. Black people needed to grasp such freedom and dignity for themselves.

The task of mission theology is not just cognitive and informative but transformative. Black theology insisted, and rightly so, that a meaningful theology or missiology must take seriously and be informed by the experiences of the oppressed. Such a theology must be articulated primarily by the black people themselves or their representatives who have a deep empathy and understanding of their plight. This kind of mission theology, far from being 'a non-Western theology' is indeed true missiology. It must present God as a God of the oppressed; the one who hears the 'outcry' of the oppressed languishing under the injustices perpetrated by the 'arrogant, overfed and unconcerned' (Ezek. 16:49–52). The exodus experience took seriously the plight of the underclass in Egypt and God demonstrated his power in liberating them. Mission theology like all true theologies must empower the disempowered; in this case promote a faith that is actively pro-human (whether black or white). When Israel turned oppressor (Ezek. 16) God punished her and sent her into exile.

Foster and Smith suggest that the debilitating black 'double-consciousness' must give way to a reunited third consciousness of a Christian African American with a clear sense of self in Christ. This new consciousness has practical implications. One of the finest examples is the articulation of the *ubuntu theology practised by Desmond Tutu and demonstrated in the Truth and Reconciliation Commission in South Africa, in which both oppressor and oppressed found release from the destructive forces that had hitherto bound them in mutual hatred. There were Christians on both sides of the divide!

The implications for mission all over the world, and especially in the Western world, are clear. Mission theology must tackle *racism, *tribalism, superiority and inferiority complexes; it must reject them as having no place in the church of Jesus Christ. God called Abraham to be a blessing to all peoples of the world (Gen. 12:3b). Paul demonstrated clearly that Jesus died to break down the social barriers that created disunity (Eph. 2:14–16). He attacked the Corinthian Christians for their divisions based on social classes (1 Cor. 1:10, 20–31), he taught that the experience of God eliminated social barriers and promoted unity (Gal. 3:28–29; Eph. 4:1–6; Phil. 2:1–4). If mission theology is to be effective, it must be embraced by individual people who refuse to conform to the prevailing social cultural norms and instead seek to be truly counter-cultural by gospel standards. It is no secret that by and large the growth of the Black Majority churches in Britain today is both evidence of and a reaction to the perceived or real racism of the mainline white Anglo-Saxon denominations. The polarization is growing at an alarming rate. While in general the leadership and character of the British church lie firmly in white hands, the membership is increasingly becoming more mixed. Church attendance, and maybe even membership, in London is about 56% non-white compared to 12% nationwide.

The church deserves a mission theology that will speak unequivocally, with clarity and leadership, into the growing rift between northern and southern forms of Christianity, the widening gap between white and black churches, and many more situations in which human social sensibilities become insurmountable barriers to freedom and fellowship.

Bibliography
M. Battle, *Reconciliation: The Ubuntu Theology of Desmond Tutu* (Cleveland: Pilgrim Press, 1997); C. R. Foster and F. Smith, *Black Religious Experience* (Nashville: Abingdon Press, 2003); D. J. Hays, *From Every People and Nation, A Biblical Theology of Race* (Leicester: Apollos, 2003); P. Jenkins, *The Next Christendom* (Maryknoll: Orbis Books, 2001); G. Usry and C. S. Keener, *Black Man's Religion* (Downers Grove: InterVarsity Press, 1996).

J. KAPOLYO

Black theology

Black theology is a theological movement that seeks to address the experience of African Americans in the light of God's revelation in history. It insists that God is working within history on behalf of the oppressed, structuring their liberation and salvation, which are viewed as inextricably bound together (Exod. 3:7–8; 14:1–31; Isa. 51:10; Luke 4:18–21).

Historically, African American Christians have sought to develop religious meaning and moral stamina in response to their marginalized status in North America. Black theology, as a school of formal academic thought, emerged as both affirmation and negation of the many church movements that have emerged from this prolonged struggle. At its inception, the aim of black theology was to invest theological wisdom into the 'Black Power' movement of the 1960s, which it deemed a vital and vigorous, yet unfinished, campaign. It also functioned to rehabilitate the fractured self-image that has been part of the experience of black people in the modern world. Both black power and black theology proposed that *racism was a primal constituent of the historical and systematic development of the modern world and its thought systems, and as such infected it indelibly, producing devastating outcomes. Hence, the black theologian interprets God's activity in the world in light of the everyday struggles of the oppressed, en route to upholding their full humanity in the eyes of God.

The character of black theology
As a species of the wider field of liberation theology, black theology rests upon the premises that social, political and cultural elements affect theological reflection, and that all theology is human speech about God. God-talk is an intractably human venture that always reflects human aspirations and is expressed through historical situations. Thus its assertions are culturally conditioned; in other words, they are influenced by where one lives, how one lives and how one wishes to live. And although God, the subject of theology, carries universal weight and is a central norm for many religious traditions, God-talk itself reflects the prejudices and

preoccupations, desires and defences of a particular person, community or culture. Black theology, then, is 'engaged' theology, unashamed about its privileging of the experience of the oppressed, unapologetic about its task to alleviate human misery, and unrelenting about its quest to let 'suffering speak'.

The distinguishing features of black theology include a critique of what are seen as white supremacist values, visions and viewpoints; a struggle against exclusionary conceptions of the biblical witness and church practice; a disapproval of the cults of materialism and individualism in black churches in the US and beyond; a recognition of the sinful nature of all human aspirations and affairs; a critical retrieval of black peoples' beliefs and modes of being in the world that lead to wholesome selves and relationships; and a serious quest to affirm the full humanity of neglected peoples within the global community. Black theology has also functioned to rehabilitate the fractured self-image that has been part of the experience of black people in the modern world.

While black theology has expanded and enabled mainstream academic approaches to theological reflection and informed the worldwide struggle for human redemption, there are certain forms of black theology that tend to reductionism and relativism in the search for truth. This is primarily because these versions have tended to view God's revelation almost solely in terms of the liberation of the oppressed. Such simplistic readings of the scriptural witness often construe oppression in limited ways, either by making the oppressed have a 'corner' on the meaning of liberation, by defining liberation in limited ways (i.e. economic or political), or by ignoring its own central claim that all God-talk, including that of black theology, is done in the light of the cross of Christ and the demands of the gospel. These more vulgar forms of black theology function more to buttress and provide ideological justifications of a political programme or social crusade than illumine the divine truth of God's word.

Global black theology in the USA and South Africa

In more recent years, we have witnessed what has come to be known as the 'second wave' of black theology. Younger (and increasingly female) voices have emerged to grapple with the silences and limitations of the 'first wave' of black theology and to wrestle with the new social and moral challenges of situations brought on by *globalization, postmodernity and international conflict. They have extended the black theology project to include sexism, economic exploitation, and radical individualism while engaging in a critical mining of African and African American cultural elements as sources of theological reflection. In short, black theology has become increasingly inter-disciplinary and international in character. Hence, the scope of black theology has shifted from a near exclusive focus on racial oppression in North America to a broader analysis of how racial, *gender and market forces work to create large pockets of suffering around the globe.

Black theology has also undergone a certain degree of historical divergence along the axis of culture and custom. Its liberationist motifs and cultural impulses have been sources of political change and social reconstruction in Africa, Europe, Latin America and Asia. In this sense, the 'story' of black theology closely resembles that of other 'travelling' schools (in this case we mean the transcontinental, politico-cultural theologies) such as liberation theology in Latin America, womanist and *feminist theologies in the United States and *minjung theology in Asia (Korea).

Its most potent global version is probably found in South Africa where it has been central to anti-apartheid peace efforts. Similarities abound between what has come to be known as 'Black Theology USA' (BTUSA) and 'Black Theology South Africa' (BTSA). The two branches engage in a critical re-appropriation of the exodus narrative as a model for the church, one that places a premium on a compassionate God who acts in history as the architect and finisher of a nation's moral pilgrimage towards spiritual and social freedom. Moreover, both branches affirm a critical appreciation of indigenous cultures and experiences as sources of theological reflection. Not surprisingly, in South Africa, women theologians have objected to the dominance of the many male voices of the movement. Thus, both programmes must be viewed as a self-conscious crusade to eliminate various kinds of oppression.

Black theology and missiology

The idea of *culture has been a central emphasis of black theology in the several stages of its development in the US and around the world. Missiologists have also taken culture seriously, especially as it relates to the adaptation of the *gospel. Thus both black theologians and missiologists can learn from and support each other. A common tenet of many in both camps is the realization that God's will is expressed through the sinews of culture, within the religious consciousness of a community. This, of course, means that, while the *church is a primary locus of God's liberative activity, and the *cross is the ultimate reference point of God's love, covenantal operations extend beyond the formal, public structures of the church. God's activity is revealed in areas of society where it is least expected or less discernible, bearing witness to the biblical conviction that God's will cannot be circumscribed by the people of God or any other human agency, especially as it relates to the freedom of the oppressed.

Four points may be made on the creative relationship between black theology and missiology:

1. The witness of black theology invites those who seek to be agents of God's kingdom to view sin not solely as the domain of the private individual, but as situated within the complex social, historical and economic structures that define society. Black theologians affirm that *sin is public and private, institutional and individual. Hence, missiologists, church planters and social ethicists are called to 'engage' historical/structural realities in their efforts to be effective agents of grace in a world that is undergoing compressed complexity on all levels of private and social life. Manifestations of personal salvation must be complemented by sincere and practical efforts at social rehabilitation and communal regeneration in order for mission work to be meaningful.

2. Various black theologies accent and affirm the conviction of most missiologists that the gospel message can be mediated and/or obviated through complex processes involving varieties of *inculturation or acculturation. In this sense, culture, the permanent terrain of all missions activity, must always be seen as both contradictory and conducive space, thus a theatre that requires multiple perspectives and approaches to the work of evangelism. Black theologians and missiologists both need to continue to explore the complexities and ambiguities involved in the complex interplay between the sacred and the secular, between traditionalist and modern modes of being in the world and between the spiritual plane and material plane, especially as they bear upon the identity to non-Western and traditional communities.

3. The 'gift' of black theology and missiology may be found in their interdisciplinarity. To advance the reign of God, they must continue to engage in sober examination of the ways in which current global economic practices create worldwide suffering, and also in dismantling sin on the way to transformation; ministering to the 'least of these' by allowing marginal and invisible people to become subjects and not objects of history.

4. With regard to church planting and evangelism, the teachings of black theology invite missionaries to greater cultural self-awareness and even self-sacrifice. How may certain cultural elements of the missionary help or hinder the attempt of the reception of God's message in this particular context? What about the socio-religious history of the receiving culture that may render them open or closed to certain expressions or manifestations of the gospel? How do social structures, cultural practices and political systems combine? How does the social location of the agent and the audience affect the sharing and hearing of the gospel?

Conclusion

The witness of black theology is a critical source of both creativity and caution for those seeking to fulfil the great commission. As a field whose understanding of the church is born out of its view of who Christ was in relation to the oppressed and what he did for them (i.e. a Christology of liberation), black theology challenges the global church to bear witness to the widespread suffering, misery and invisibility that characterizes our present historical moment.

See also EXODUS, LIBERATION.

Bibliography

J. H. Cone, *A Black Theology of Liberation* (Maryknoll: Orbis Books, 1990); J. Grant,

White Women's Christ, Black Women's Jesus: Feminist Christology and Womanist Response (Atlanta: Scholars Press, 1989); D. N. Hopkins, *Black Theology USA and South Africa: Politics, Culture and Liberation* (Maryknoll: Orbis Books, 1989); D. N. Hopkins, *Shoes That Fit Our Feet* (Maryknoll: Orbis Books, 1993); C. West, *Prophesy Deliverance!: An Afro-American Revolutionary Christianity* (Philadelphia: Westminster John Knox Press, 2002); G. Wilmore and J. H. Cone (eds.), *Black Theology: A Documentary History* (Maryknoll: Orbis Books, 1979).

A. ADELEKAN

BLESSING, see PROSPERITY THEOLOGY

Buddhist relations

In relating the Christian message to Buddhist contexts, Christians have frequently encountered considerable objections and formidable obstacles, more challenging than in other religious contexts, for the fact that the fundamental tenets of Buddhism are so greatly different. Buddhism denies some of the central Christian concepts such as God, the human soul and eternal life. To the Buddhist mind these have always been not only incomprehensible illusions but non-existing entities or imaginary absurdities. While Buddhist tenets are based on human consciousness and apprehension, Christian doctrines have their foundation in the supernatural revelation of God. According to Buddhism, *nibbana* (deliverance from the ongoing endless cycles of births and deaths, the ultimate goal to which Buddhist morality is directed) is achievable purely by human self-effort, whereas Christianity sees all people as sinners who cannot do anything for their salvation apart from the grace of God. Even the ultimate objectives of both religions do not reach towards the same destination: in Buddhism people are striving to become free of an endless cycle of birth and death, whereas Christianity offers permanent eternal life to believers.

This article will confine itself to analysing some Christian contextual approaches in relating apologetically with Theravada Buddhists and will summarize some missiological propositions for a positive engagement.

The traditional Christian missionary approach

Traditional Christian missiology, which consisted of direct gospel presentation with the sole intention of conversion, often in the past simply condemned non-Christian religions and cultures, and even sometimes demonized them. The missionaries of the colonial era, influenced and motivated by Enlightenment rationalism and evangelical revivalism, saw the expansion of European *colonization during the nineteenth century as divine providence in paving the way for mission. Many saw an opportunity to remove the perceived darkness and idolatry of non-Christian religions and replace their sinful cultural practices with 'civilization' and Christian truth, a form of culture-Christianity which often associated the gospel with Western values. Hence they condemned Buddhism as 'false, absurd, blasphemous, dangerous, and a gigantic system of error'.

Some missionaries of that era utilized rational arguments to defend Christianity and denounce Buddhism, an example of which is William Paley's *A View of the Evidences of Christianity* (published in 1794), which became a major resource for many nineteenth-century missionaries. However, this rationalist, confrontational approach did not achieve the desired aims amongst Buddhists. In the face of missionary criticism, Buddhists were able to defend their religion, and went to the extent of showing that Buddhism was authentic and superior to Christianity.

Since Buddhism denies the existence of God, Christian theism is an incomprehensible illusion to the Buddhist mind. In fact, Buddhism cannot think of a 'god' to whom it can refer as Creator, Lord, Saviour, who could be described as eternal, omniscient, omnipotent and so on. In Buddhist thinking, the Buddha, and all enlightened individuals, are superior to the gods, and the ultimate objective of the gods is to arrive at this higher state. Hence, instead of men seeking gods, in Buddhism it is the gods who seek the Buddha and the enlightened individuals. Consequently, the gods are not objects of prayer and sacrifices, but they are a part of the world of *samsara* (the continuous cycle of birth and death), and occupy a lower position to the Buddha and other enlightened individuals.

In such contexts, Christian theism does not have much positive appreciation, and is susceptible to misunderstandings. Even using the simple and typical gospel text John 3:16 has difficulties in communicating the Christian message to the Buddhists. 'In the phrase *"God so loved the world"* the word "God" could refer to several things to the Buddhists but not the Christian God. Further, since all desires, good or bad, are bad according to Buddhism and they presuppose relationships and attachments, God loving the world will appear to the Buddhists like a god or a person prior to the enlightenment. Finally, believing, or trusting is also in total contrast to the Buddhist way of salvation' (J. R. Davis, *Poles Apart: Contextualizing the Gospel in Asia*, pp. 10-11).

Since traditional Christian missiology begins with God, Buddhists find it difficult to comprehend its fundamental message, for the simple reason that their mind is not ready to accept a theistic framework. Hence the starting point of Christian missiology in Buddhist contexts should begin where Buddhism has its own starting point. In this respect, Lynn de Silva has made a commendable attempt. He pointed out that 'Asian Christian theology should begin where Buddhism begins' by taking the Buddha's discovery of the three fundamental characteristics of the human predicament, *anicca* (impermanence), *anatta* (soullessness or selflessness) and *dukkha* (unsatisfactoriness or suffering) as the proper starting point. So Christian missiology should begin its apologetic with the desperate human condition, rather than the existence of God or salvation in Jesus Christ.

Employing Buddhist terms in the Christian message

The missionaries of the colonial era not only had a theistic foundation for their missiology, they also expressed Christianity in Western terms and concepts, which failed to convince the Buddhist mind. Therefore, in recent times, some have employed Buddhist terms in relating the Christian message to Buddhists. Even some earlier missionaries began to recognize this necessity. For instance M. Ricci (1552–1610), an early missionary to China, recognized the need to meet Chinese culture at the religious and philosophical level. Likewise, upon their arrival in India, William Carey

and his colleagues saw that they must understand not only the language but also the thought world of those to whom they preached the gospel.

However, relating to Buddhists by employing their religious terms has its limitations, since they understand them according to their own contexts and meanings. For instance, Christians may think it is helpful to use the term 'rebirth' instead of 'regeneration' when conversing with a Buddhist, assuming that 'rebirth' will convey the concept of regeneration. But Buddhists will not comprehend the Christian concept of regeneration from the term 'rebirth' without detailed explanation, since 'rebirth' will naturally relate in their minds to the endless cycle of births and deaths. Furthermore, the Buddhist doctrine of rebirth is different from the Hindu understanding of *reincarnation which implies the transmigration of a soul and its material rebirth, since Buddhism denies the existence of a soul. Rebirth is a result of karma, which teaches that we reap in future lives what we sow in this life, which for Buddhists explains the inequalities of life. If terms can be misunderstood, it is better to avoid them. However, if Buddhists have become familiar with some typical Christian terms through constant usage, adopting Buddhist words can also cause unnecessary confusion. Buddhists have sometimes accused Christians of deceiving people by using alternative religious terminology. It is vital therefore to use Buddhist terminology with great care.

Expressing Christian truth in Buddhist concepts

Some have gone a step further in using Buddhist philosophical concepts to express Christian truth. Many use the Buddhist concept of *pattidana* (transference of merit) to explain the Christian gospel. Even though this concept was developed within the Mahayana tradition, it is practised in Theravada societies in South East Asia as well. Early Mahayana Buddhists came to believe in a process of transference of merit, through which practitioners, especially a Buddha or a Bodhisattava, could apply merit to persons less advanced on the path. Using the framework of transference of merit, Christians can explain the concept of the imputation of Christ's righteousness to believers, and the transference of the consequences of sin onto Christ in his crucifixion. Finding such concepts in Buddhism and expressing Christian truth within such a conceptual framework, can make the gospel relevant and more understandable to the Buddhist mind.

Lynn de Silva has attempted to explain the concept of God to Buddhists through their cardinal doctrine of *anatta* (soullessness). In Buddhist philosophy *anatta* means there is nothing called self/soul or any unchanging or eternal abiding substance in human beings. Even though Buddhism denies the existence of God, as Lynn de Silva has pointed out, the concept of *anatta* necessitates such a belief. This is because Buddhism, while denying the self (this is the crux of *anatta*), teaches that man must depend on himself for his own deliverance. For de Silva this is 'one of the deepest dilemmas in Buddhism'. So he asks, 'What is the self that denies the self and at the same time asserts that it alone can save the self?' Buddhism asserts that people have the power to achieve the goal of *nibbana* purely by self-effort, so 'to deny the self and to affirm self-sufficiency is a contradiction'.

According to de Silva, it is the Bible that takes the doctrine of *anatta* seriously and points out the inability of human beings to save themselves: 'it can be shown that the Bible takes what is implied in the doctrine of *anatta* more seriously than Buddhism does, for the biblical teaching is that man is nothing by himself and can do nothing by himself about his salvation' (*International Review of Missions* LVII, pp. 450–451). The doctrine of *anatta* therefore points to the truth that man is in need of saving grace. De Silva positively affirms: 'it is in relation to the unconditioned (God) that the full depth and significance of *anatta* can be understood.' (*Emergent Theology in the Context of Buddhism*, p. 58). In other words, in the light of *anatta* God becomes indispensable. Thus by emphasizing *anatta* de Silva makes an attempt to convince Buddhists of the necessity of divine help in attaining the ultimate goal.

Dialogue with Buddhists

Some Christian missiologists in more recent times have developed a dialogical approach in relating to Buddhists. In contemporary Sri Lanka Aloysius Pieris has contributed much to the Buddhist-Christian *dialogue. Concluding that existing Asian Christologies 'are all out of place in Asia', Pieris insisted that Asian Christian theology as well as the church must be baptized in the 'Jordan of Asian religions' and crucified in the 'Calvary of Asian poverty'. By this dictum Pieris made an appeal to Christians to give up the colonial identity of their theologies and submit them to the judgment of other non-Christian soteriologies and socialism.

In recent times, however, rejecting syncretism and synthesis as violations of the unique identity of each religion, he has ventured to develop a mutual relationship between Buddhists and Christians to learn from and edify each other. Depicting this process as 'symbiosis', Pieris remarks that in such an engagement people of one religion expose themselves to another religion and in the process learn more about what is significant and unique in their own tradition through the judgments and witness of the other. Evangelical Christians may reject such a proposal, but Christians can and should learn about their own faith and enrich their spirituality by such encounters with Buddhists and vice versa. Nevertheless, Christianity is not just a learning process, since intrinsic to Christ's call to mission is the fundamental obligation to proclaim his unique salvation to all peoples and religious traditions.

Dialogue with Buddhists often takes place only amongst philosophically minded people, which does not involve the ordinary people of other faiths. Further, in many of the Theravada Buddhist countries, there is a paradox between philosophical and practical Buddhism. While philosophical Buddhism rejects theistic notions of religion, practical Buddhism has a tendency to absorb other religious deities. In fact, the Buddhist assertion of the non-theistic character of their religion is intended mainly to emphasize the unacceptability of Christian theism. Buddhists generally avoid asking for worldly blessings from Buddha, but they do go to the gods and other cultic rituals for such blessings, which contradicts their canonical teachings.

Buddhists find that they need the gods for their day-to-day practical life, since they cannot live with philosophical explanations alone. Hence, they worship the gods while trying to obtain *nibbana* through Buddha's eight-fold path. But rituals and ceremonies are the predominant features of the contemporary Buddhist world. This clearly indicates their need for a god, or a supernatural being, who could help them with their numerous problems pertaining to their lives. It is at this point that Christians could point out the power and even the divinity of Jesus Christ, although the Buddhist view of Christ is a major obstacle since he is not regarded with any respect in many Buddhist contexts. To raise the status of Jesus Christ in the minds of Buddhists is therefore a major task of mission.

The book of Ecclesiastes as a bridge

The present author has used Ecclesiastes as a bridge in relating the Christian message to Buddhists. This OT wisdom literature deals with a subject familiar to Buddhists, even though it proposes a different solution to the human predicament. The Buddha and Qoheleth (author of Ecclesiastes) have employed similar methodologies to analyse human existence and propose solutions to its predicament. The Buddha explained the Four Noble Truths after his enlightenment in consequence of his intense meditation on human life which he had personally experienced, observed, and analysed. Likewise, Qoheleth's insights are based on his own personal experiences and observations. Hence both have discovered similar facts about human life, but analysed and proposed solutions differently according to their religious and cultural contexts. Since the Buddha has denied the existence of God and the human soul, his doctrines do not have any reference to these concepts. Qoheleth, however, due to his Hebraic religious background, does put his thinking into a theistic framework. Nevertheless, Buddhists can appreciate and comprehend Qoheleth's writings, due to their familiarity with the similar analysis of the Buddha. Hence it is possible to use the book of Ecclesiastes to help Buddhists in their spiritual quest.

The growth of Western Buddhism

Buddhism has shown remarkable ability to adapt itself to Western thought and to offer its 'spirituality' as an attractive alternative for Westerners influenced by postmodernism but searching for enlightenment. In 1990 there were some 5,000 Buddhists in Britain, and by 1997 this had risen to 50,000. Many have claimed that meditation and personal disciplines have given them a path to inner wholeness and peace in the midst of a noisy and stressful Western culture. The Buddhist rituals present an attractive symbolism for Westerners who have rejected traditional Christian liturgies. Some mix and match elements of various Buddhist traditions to create their own 'spirituality'. This challenge for Western mission has been explored by David Burnett, but requires much more attention from missiologists as Eastern spiritualities grow in influence in the pluralistic milieu of the West.

Bibliography

D. Burnett, *The Spirit of Buddhism* (Crowborough: Monarch, 1996); J. R. Davis (ed.), *Poles Apart: Contextualizing the Gospel in Asia* (Bangalore: Bangalore Book Trust, 1998); L. De Silva, 'Good News of Salvation to the Buddhists', *International Review of Missions* LVII, 1968; L. De Silva, *Emergent Theology in the Context of Buddhism* (Colombo: Ecumenical Institute for Study and Dialogue, 1979); L. De Silva, 'Emergent Theology in a Buddhist Context', in D. J. Elwood (ed.), *Asian Christian Theology: Emerging Themes* (Philadelphia: Westminster Press, 1990); A. Pieris, 'Does Christ Have a Place in Asia? A Panoramic View', in L. Boff and V. Elizondo (ed.), *Any Room for Christ in Asia?* (London: SCM Press; Maryknoll: Orbis Books, 1993); M. S. Vasanthakumar, 'An Exploration of the Book of Ecclesiastes in the Light of Buddha's Four Noble Truths', in D. Lim and S. Spaulding (eds.), *Sharing Jesus Holistically with the Buddhist World* (Pasadena: William Carey Library, 2005).

M. S. VASANTHAKUMAR

Caste

The English word 'caste' derives from the Portuguese word *casta*, which denotes purity. While the origin of the Indian caste system is uncertain, historians who have studied ancient Tamil literature contend that, at the first stage, the primitive Tamils (or Dravidians) were divided into five settled tribes or clans according to natural geographical divisions such as *kurinchi* or hill regions, *pali* or barren regions, *marutham* or cultivable land, *mullai* or pastoral land, and *neythal* or coastal region. People who lived in these regions were known as *vettuvars* or hunters, *maravas* or warriors, *ulavars* or peasants, *aayars* or cowherds, and *paradavars* or fishermen respectively. It is maintained that these people of different regions doing different jobs maintained kinship and brotherhood.

Historians say that, in the next stage, prior to the introduction of caste (a religious system of purity and pollution), the Dravidians/Tamils were divided into four groups on the basis of their profession and not on the basis of caste. The four divisions were (1) *Anthanar*, the priests; (2) *Arasar*, the kings; (3) *Vanier*, the traders; and (4) *Vellalars*, the cultivators. The present caste names give some clue to this former system of grouping people according to their professions as agriculturalists, politicians, traders and religious people.

For the most part the nineteenth-century European missionaries had a keen understanding of caste. For them caste was not merely religious, nor merely political, but a mixture of both. They maintained that caste cannot be allowed among believers and it must be continually warned against, as a thing worthy of abolition.

However, caste in rural India was an endogamous clan or formal 'tribal unit' (*kudi, kulam*) – ethnic groups that had existed since the very earliest period and would not break all of a sudden and as easily as missionaries expected. While the discriminations could be challenged and even abolished, the distinctions cannot easily be rooted out. For even today the government of India asks every person's caste on joining educational institutions or government jobs.

Nevertheless, for the outcastes their caste is a socio-economic political oppression equal to Egyptian bondage. The tyrannies of the cast oppressions have caused outcastes to respond to the gospel of Christ. Recent historical investigations have demonstrated that conversion to Christ liberated the outcastes from oppressive culture, customs and behaviour. This is critically important for the further involvement of the church in India in the liberation of the poor and the oppressed who are victims of the Indian caste system.

Theological resources for a missiological approach are found in creation theology, in Christ's example, in God's concern for the outcast, and in the new identity which Christians receive in Christ. Creation theology reminds us that all human beings share a common humanity as the basis of all relationships. Christ frequently subverted and challenged the social categorizations of his day. There are numerous expressions of God's compassion and sense of justice for the poor and marginalized in Scripture. And the 'new creation' by which Christians find a new identity and find themselves 'all one in Christ Jesus' restores equal worth and dignity to those who are regarded as outcasts by society. All of these resources provide Christians with ample justification for challenging caste divisions in the context of mission. In Christ there is reconciliation and the free exercise of spiritual gifts, irrespective of social class. The church therefore is called to embody this new community and abolish all distinctions which categorize people into social hierarchies.

However, many Indian scholars, especially theologians, have still not explored the process through which the outcaste (now *Dalit) Christians were awakened to their consciousness, especially through Christian discipline and character formation with the assistance of their local pastors. In fact, in the Brahminical Hindu society where the ritual status of purity/pollution is held in high esteem, caste mobility is often related to refinement of customs and behaviour.

Moreover, recent studies show that mere change of religion does not change caste. It is conceded that caste often infiltrates into the church from a society dominated and even preoccupied by caste. Therefore, Indian society as a whole has also been responsible for the socio-economic suppression of the outcaste people, including Christians. Churches, however, must avoid being identified with one caste or another.

Even so, scholars have demonstrated that conversion to Christ has minimized caste disadvantage among the outcaste believers. The development of new opinions and attitudes about themselves and others provided them with self-esteem and self-worth. They got rid of the stigma of being classified as untouchables. Their attitude towards life became positive. This paved the way for spatial mobility, which in turn resulted in social mobility.

In India, although Christian conversion did not abolish caste, there was a new relationship among the outcastes as well as between outcastes and the uppercastes. Such community living reduced frequent inter- and intra-community quarrels and feuds, and fostered peace, harmony and brotherhood among the mutually hostile and mutually untouchable outcaste communities. The outcastes' communitarian way of life was often a challenge to the existing social order. Above all, the gospel continues to aid the outcastes to cross the pollution line and be integrated into the mainstream of Indian society.

Bibliography

D. B. Forrester, *Caste and Christianity: Attitudes and Policies on Caste of Anglo-Saxon Protestant Missions in India* (London: Curzon Press, 1980); G. Houghton, *The Impoverishment of Dependency: The History of the Protestant Church in Madras, 1870–1930* (Madras: CLS, 1983); S. Jayakumar, *Dalit Consciousness and Christian Conversion: Historical Resources for a Contemporary Debate* (Oxford: Regnum and Delhi: ISPCK, 1999); D. Kooiman, *Conversion and Social Equality in India* (Delhi: Manohar, 1989); D. D. Kosambi, *The Culture and the Civilisation of the Ancient India* (New Delhi: Vikas Publishing House, 1977); R. Kothari (ed.), *Caste in Indian Politics* (Delhi: Orient Longman, 1970); S. Manickam, *The Social Settings of Christian Conversion in South India* (Weisbaden: Franz Steiner Verlag, 1979); S. Manickam, *Slavery in the Tamil Country* (Madras: CLS, 1982).

S. JAYAKUMAR

Charismatic movements

The term 'charismatic movement' is derived from *charismata*, the Greek word for the gifts and extraordinary graces experienced by the presence and power of the *Holy Spirit. Thus, when revivals occurred in Wales (1904), North and South Korea (1904–7), Mukti and Calcutta, India (1905–10), Azusa Street California (1906–7), and West Africa (1910), they emphasized the anointing of the Holy Spirit that resulted in repentance, confession and manifestation of *charismata*. These movements revitalized many churches, but also birthed a number of denominations. This raises the contentious matter of *definition* because of the wide range of those who give much space to the activities of the Holy Spirit. Some remain as revival movements; others consolidate into denominations; or others mix much of the indigenous religion and lose a clear Christian identity. The *World Christian Encyclopedia* (2001) claims that there are half a billion charismatic Christians in the world, but it restricts the term to those who reject the 'cessationist' theories and exercise the gifts within mainline churches. Apart from their emphasis on the gifts and manifestations of the Spirit, charismatics share with most evangelicals the call for a conversion experience of repentance and faith; focus on a close walk and imitation of Christ; an acceptance of the Bible as the word of God; and a belief in eternal life in the presence of God after death.

Many charismatic movements began before the Second World War, but quickly ran out of steam; then a new wave exploded in many parts of the world between 1960 and 1970. A global perspective is important: in the Western world, the house church movement arose in the late 1960s and spawned a plethora of independent groups. But throughout Africa and Asia, charismatic movements had proliferated from the turn of the twentieth century. Universally significant was a charismatic spirituality among young people that challenged the traditionalism of the mainline denominations from the 1970s.

The enormous plethora of different kinds of charismatic movements worldwide compels regional documentation of origins, style of manifestation, provenance and explanation. Statistical data abound but some query the sources, accuracy, inconsistent categories and divergence from national census figures. All accept that charismatic movements catalyzed the enormous missionary growth of Christianity in sub-Saharan Africa, the hostile terrain of the Maghrib, and amidst the hostility of the Orthodox Churches of Egypt and Ethiopia. In Latin America, it fuelled the Protestant challenge against Roman Catholic dominance. In Asia, it ensured Christian survival in terrains challenged by Buddhism (South Korea and Myanmar), Hinduism (India), and vigorous Islam in Eastern Europe. In North America, it influenced the so-called 'Third Wave' movement among evangelicals.

The character of Christianity in the Global

South is generally very charismatic. Such groups have revitalized the traditional evangelical emphasis on church growth; they re-evangelize communities by deploying modern media; they have clear doctrinal affirmations unhindered by the cultural issues of the Western world; they use a 'hermeneutic of trust' that brings the immediacy of the biblical message into everyday life; and their strategy mobilizes all sectors of the Christian population to serve as evangelists with a degree of commitment akin to the story of the early church. In mission they counter the Western Enlightenment world-view by exploring the 'fit' or resonance between the biblical and indigenous world-views, instead of condemning or ignoring these powers as Western missionaries did. They understand the Christian life in terms of spiritual warfare that names, engages and unmasks the powers in human communities, and this strategy has catalyzed a new phase of missionary impulse worldwide. In fact, charismatic-driven groups are at the heart of the world mission movement, deploying the highest number of missionaries globally.

As growth occurs within communities, the roots of charismatic spirituality relate dynamically to the cultural soil of the *context and give rise to a reinterpretation of the gospel. The *instrumentalist* explanation sociologists have for the growth of southern Christianity argues that poverty, failed economies and the pressure of modernity drives people to church. They profile a spirituality that comes from global cultural flows into non-Western communities, and these serve as handmaids of fundamentalist Christian groups – indeed, as 'extensions of American electronic church' from the 1980s. Against this view the class composition of the membership is broad, and many countries are less implicated in global technology. Many charismatic groups are indigenous and do not owe their origin to outside influences. Alternatively the *religious market* explanation emphasizes competition, tendency to schism, internal competition, clientele/consumer membership, recycling through 'sheep stealing' from historic churches, and the benefits of population growth. However, this model misrepresents the character of living faith groups, the power of the gospel, and how culture contact occurs. It diminishes indigenous

initiative, local agency, and the patterns of appropriating the gospel. It ignores south-south connections and the nature of religious conversion. It focuses on churches as institutions and not as the gathered people of God.

A better explanation comes from combining *cultural* and *religious* discourse to analyse how people deploy the element of transcendence in religious experience as a tool for coping with everyday life. The pneumatic resources of the gospel answer questions raised within the interiors of pre-industrial maps of the universe. Charismatic spirituality connects with these world-views, which were innately charismatic and filled with the interventions of spiritual forces in human lives. Charismatic movements 'set to work' the message of the translated gospel as it voyages into new cultural contexts. Their distinctive message, values, beliefs and organizational structure deploy pneumatic resources which enable a re-invention of the self and the journey of life, offering coping mechanisms for daily life, and producing expressions of imagination in arts and aesthetics. The *prosperity gospel, which is sometimes a significant dimension of these movements, also finds resonance with indigenous spirituality and rituals, with its emphasis on faith strategies which oblige spiritual forces to work in our favour. Charismatic movements also enlarge the space for women and youth, who were hindered by patriarchal church institutions. They bring new pace, direction and scale to communicating the gospel, inventing new models of mass evangelism, and mobilizing human and material resources. They challenge traditional views of doctrine, liturgy, polity and ethics: their dominant ethical challenge is to holy living and faithful discipleship; the polity reclaims the priesthood of all believers; and the liturgy recovers the joy of celebration.

However, their anti-intellectual approach and their scrambling of strategies for ministerial formation are causes of concern for many evangelicals. Also authority structures are sometimes oppressive, unable to be challenged, and very hierarchical; others, by decentralizing control, open the gates for 'wolves in sheep's clothing', which gives rise to heretical teaching. There is a great need, therefore, for discernment, with criteria for distinguishing the spirits, solid biblical teaching, and wise, shared leadership. Submission to Christ as Lord, respect for the authority of Scripture, and the centrality of the cross will all be marks of an authentic charismatic congregation.

For charismatic movements in the Global South, most poignant is the re-entry of religion into the public space through a theology of engagement that contests the boundaries of the private and public, the separation of church and state, and the secularist attack on biblical morality. This is not usually radical politically: covertly, they aim to change historical events and redeem the public space through prayer and on their knees; overtly, they advocate godly policies and support public officials who share their views. Opponents allege discontinuity from the history and heritage of the church and some elements of banality and superficiality in the pre-eminent 'hermeneutics of trust'. But no one can deny that charismatic movements hold the cutting edge of Christian mission in every context in the twentieth century.

See also PENTECOSTALISM.

Bibliography
A. Anderson, *An Introduction to Pentecostalism* (Cambridge: Cambridge University Press, 2004); A. Anderson and E. Tang (eds.), *Asian and Pentecostal: The Charismatic Face of Christianity* (Oxford: Regnum, 2004); M. Berg and P. Pretiz, *Spontaneous Combination: Grassroots Christianity, Latin American Style* (Pasadena, CA: William Carey Library, 1996); R. Culpepper, *Evaluating the Charismatic Movement: A Theological and Biblical Appraisal* (Valley Forge PA: Judson Press, 1977); O. U. Kalu, 'Pentecostal-Charismatic Reshaping of African Religious Landscape in the 1990s', *Mission Studies* 20, 2003, pp. 84–111; O. U. Kalu, 'Preserving a Worldview: Pentecostalism in the African Maps of the Universe', *Pneuma* 24, 2004, pp. 110–137; V.-M. Kärkkäinen, *Pneumatology: The Holy Spirit in Ecumenical, International and Contextual Perspective* (Grand Rapids: Baker Books, 2002); C. N. Omenyo, *Pentecost Outside Pentecostalism: A Study of the Development of Charismatic Renewal in the Mainline Churches in Ghana* (Zoetermeer: Uitgeverij Boekecentrum, 2002);

J.-J. Suurmond, *Word and Spirit at Play: Towards A Charismatic Theology* (London: SCM Press, 1994).

O. U. KALU

Children

There is a misconception among some Christians that the Bible says very little about children. However, to read Scripture *with the child in the midst* leads us to conclude that children are one of the main ways God chooses to speak to us. Not only are children present and visible, they are at the very heart of mission.

Children and childhood in the OT
The stories surrounding Isaac, Ishmael, Joseph, Moses and Miriam, Samuel, the young servant girl (2 Kgs 5), David, Josiah and Jeremiah are a few of the significant representatives of children in the OT.

Children are a sign of God's blessing in the OT, and yet they are the first to suffer when sin, deceit, war and famine affect a tribe or city (e.g. Ps. 106:37–38; Jer. 31; Lam. 1, 2, 4; Joel 3:3; Amos 2; Zeph. 1, etc.).

Four important child-related themes in the OT provide a context in which these references to children are set:

God's relationship with his people. In Deuteronomy 8 God disciplines *as a father* those whom he has chosen. In Psalm 27 a child may be abandoned by father and mother, but not by God, the heavenly Father (cf. Ps. 103). The mother/child relationship is also used to characterize the bond between God and his people (Ps. 131; Isa. 66:13).

Children are ordained and designed to praise God and his glory. This is their nature and purpose (e.g. Ps. 8:2). They are not just consumers or future adults, but worshippers of the Creator God. Astonishingly, they even have a special role in silencing the enemies of God.

The future kingdom has children as children, at its heart. In Isaiah 11, the messianic kingdom is vividly portrayed as a safe environment in which children can play and where they have responsibilities in the new creation.

The focus of God's promise of salvation is not a warrior king, a wise rabbi, or a high priest, but a child. This is the crowning role for a child. In the midst of a bleak and hopeless situation for Israel, God gives them the sign of Emmanuel (Isa. 7:14; 9:6).

The NT and children

In the NT there are many incidents involving children in the life of Jesus: the daughter of the Canaanite woman (Matt. 15; Mark 7); the boy with a demon (Matt. 17:14–18; par.); the official's son at Capernaum (John 4); Jairus' daughter (Luke 10:40–56; par.); the son of the widow at Nain (Luke 7); and the boy who offered Jesus the five loaves and two fish (John 6). Jesus has a heart for children and they are drawn to him.

As in the OT, Jesus includes children in his teaching and mission. In fact, he is our example, for he is shown 'confounding' the religious elders as a young twelve-year-old boy (Luke 2:46–47).

Three aspects of the Gospels call for particular attention when we have *a child in the midst*.

The incarnation. Matthew quotes Isaiah (Isa. 7:14; cf. Luke 2:12). God has chosen to enter the world *as a baby*. How radical: the fullness of the creator God in a tiny child! A baby is small, weak, dependent and vulnerable, lacks education and training and language. God is teaching us to find him in little children.

The kingdom of God. Jesus teaches surprisingly that greatness is to become like little children, the only way to enter the kingdom (Matt. 18:1–4). The kingdom belongs to such as the child. Children help us with the great paradox of the meaning of the kingdom as both 'already' and also 'not yet'; for children are both fully human (now) and also not fully developed (not yet).

New birth. This will mean letting go of all adult, culturally-laden preconceptions to start all over again in Christ, just as a baby is starting life for the first time (John 3:1–15).

In Romans and Galatians we are adopted into God's family and enabled to know God as 'Abba'. We are to live as children of the light (Eph. 5:8). One of the favourite descriptions of the followers of Jesus is as 'dear children' (1 Cor. 4:14; Gal. 4:19; 1 John).

Children at the heart of mission

In recent missions practice, much attention has been given both to 'people groups' and to the '10/40 window'. Some missiologists, borrowing from these helpful constructs, have begun to give attention to children as a 'people group'. In this light, children are an enormous, often needy and neglected 'people group'. However, they are also the most receptive.

Some missiologists also now refer to the '4/14 window' – that is, the people between the ages of four and fourteen. Research shows that a large majority of people in the USA who make a decision for Christ, do so between the ages of four and fourteen, or at least before the age of eighteen. This same receptiveness exists in every culture. The reality of the 4/14 window means that any serious mission strategies will include careful, appropriate efforts to reach children and young people.

Children as agents *for* mission

But our missiological interest in children is not only because they are most receptive. They are also often very effective instruments and agents *for* mission. God often uses them when adults and the adult world have become corrupt, and deaf to his calling. In the story of the 'little maid' (KJV) who served the leprous Naaman's wife (2 Kgs 5:2), it is a little girl who recalls the prophet of God in Israel, and who encourages her mistress to send Naaman to see him, after which he can say: 'Now I know . . .' (v. 15, NIV).

Children have tremendous spiritual capacity

Children can hear and obey God from a very young age. The Bible shows that God has a very high regard for their ability to understand the faith and to participate in his redemption activities.

They are an integral part of the visual and dramatic worship in the OT. Children were included in the covenant so that they too would learn to fear the Lord (Deut. 31:12). Neither the Passover, nor other rituals (e.g. Josh. 4), can begin until a child asks what it means (Exod. 12). When the Law is read out (Ezra 10), children are part of the crowd (cf. Josh. 8:35; Neh. 12:43).

In the NT, Jesus rebukes the teachers for questioning the children's worship and their recognition of himself (Matt. 21:16). Then he praises God that he had revealed truths to little children (Matt. 11:25).

So children can both *understand* truth and

be its *channels* and *instruments*. Whenever a child is mentioned, God is often doing something important: when God needed great courage to kill Goliath, he chose the young boy David; when he needed to speak hard truths to Eli and his sons, he chose Samuel; when he needed great vision he chose the eight-year-old Josiah to be king; when he needed great generosity he chose a child willing to share his loaves and fishes.

The rediscovery of children in mission
Reading Scripture, therefore, with the child in the midst reveals both the presence and significance of children. It suggests that by viewing mission as an adult-orientated pursuit and underestimating the importance and the contribution of children in the mission of God, we may be ignoring the most fruitful mission field.

See also FAMILY.

K. J. WHITE AND D. BREWSTER

CHRIST, DEATH OF, see CROSS

Christ/Christology

Christology and culture: The problem of an alien Jesus
Jesus came from the Middle East. Culturally, therefore, Jesus' Palestinian background is more Asian than Western in outlook and values. But why is Christianity viewed as a Western religion by the majority of the non-Western world? One reason could be that the Christian *gospel was propagated predominantly by Western missionaries. They went with a deep love for Christ, and national Christians are grateful to God for the sacrifices they made. But did they faithfully *deliver* Jesus to the people in Asia, Africa and Latin America or did they *distort* him and his message by presenting a 'Western' Christ?

Why is an alien Jesus a serious missiological issue? First, if Jesus is presented in Western dress, Christianity will remain categorized as a foreign religion to the majority of Muslim, Buddhist and Hindu peoples. Christianity will not take root in the hearts, minds and aspirations of subsequent generations of non-Western believers. Secondly, newer mission movements from Asia, Africa and Latin America face the same danger as past Western

missionaries in their tendency to present their own cultural images of Jesus. History repeats itself when these newer mission movements impose a Jesus alien to local contexts. The problem of an alien Jesus has to do with the many portraits of Jesus communicated through cultural accretions, with minimal contextualization, resulting in Jesus being viewed by a majority culture as alien and foreign to the local people. Although the incarnate Christ is able to enter into all cultures, and therefore is at home in all cultures, successive attempts in the history of Christian transmission have exhibited a tendency toward monolithic portrayals of Christ.

Evangelicals have traditionally adopted such a single focus on Christ by emphasizing the birth, death and resurrection of Jesus; only in recent years have most taken the incarnation and life of Jesus seriously. This made it possible to ignore Jesus' cultural context and see him as a Christ 'from above'. But this had its consequences for mission: the humanity of Jesus was underplayed and an uncontextualized 'spiritual gospel' was proclaimed. It also resulted in a privatized Christ who was not seen as relevant to the public arena of social and political concerns. Those who have emphasized this latter engagement have adopted a Christology 'from below', and have sometimes gone in the other direction of understating or ignoring the transcendent, divine, creator Christ. Western portrayals are largely 'from above', whereas Christologies from the Majority World have been 'from below', with a Christ who identifies with us in our humanity and suffering.

This article surveys recent writings in NT Christology and argues that the dominant Christologies have been primarily a construct of Western categories and have failed to do justice to the wholeness of the Christian gospel and the global nature of Christian communities. The future of Christological discourse will need to be supplemented by a more balanced and complete portrait of Jesus from a global perspective. Such a portrait will involve the integration of a biblical portrait of Jesus with local Christologies from diverse Christian witnesses in mission situations.

NT Christology
The OT is an important place to begin Christology as it provided inspiration for the first

Christians in formulating their view of Jesus. The OT Messsianic expectations of the promised Prophet, Priest and King were foundational for their view of Christ, whom the early disciples then recognized and proclaimed as Lord. Clearly, the NT is our primary source for understanding Jesus, and Howard Marshall's *The Origins of New Testament Christology* is a good introduction. A thoroughly evangelical Christology works and flourishes only from these foundations of canonical revelation, so that scriptural primacy and authority becomes paramount as a basis and criterion for evaluating contextual formulations of Christ.

In addition to the issue of *source*, evangelical perspectives of Jesus locate the *central claims of Jesus* as the promised Messiah within the broad sweep of God's *salvation purposes in human history. Wolfhart Pannenberg argues that the identity and person of Christ are to be known through the total impact of his work: 'A separation between Christology and soteriology is not possible, because in general the soteriological interest, the interest in salvation, in the *beneficia Christi*, is what causes us to ask about the figure of Jesus' (quoted in A. E. McGrath, *Christian Theology: An Introduction*, p. 271).

The historical Jesus
The 'new quest' for the historical Jesus has been revived by the 'Jesus Seminar' and popularized, among others, by Marcus Borg, E. P. Sanders and Dominic Crossan. A good survey is Marcus Borg's *Jesus in Contemporary Scholarship*, claiming a major renaissance in North American Jesus studies. These studies spawned new directions in NT Christology, shifting from eschatological and apocalyptic interests to an increasing awareness of the significance of the social-political world of Jesus. Critical studies have been offered by more conservative scholars such as N. T. Wright, Ben Witherington and Markus Bockmuehl.

Given the dominance of Western portraits of Jesus, non-Western attempts in developing contextual Christologies will benefit from historical studies which explore Jesus' place within his first-century Jewish world. New portraits of Jesus in non-Western contexts can take advantage of these historical-biblical studies, but should avoid being subjected to minimalist formulations of Western Christologies, some of which have been heavily influenced by Enlightenment scepticism. A major development arising from these historical quests is that 'Son of God' does not always refer to Jesus' divinity and 'Son of Man' can refer to his humanity. However, as a Christological title, 'Son of God' often refers to Jesus' belonging to God (without always implying ontological divinity), and 'Son of Man' was often used by Jesus to demonstrate his divine authority from God (over the Sabbath etc.), rather than referring primarily to his humanity. These discussions will challenge traditional Christian readings of Jesus, while promising new insights into Jesus as personified wisdom, and as the eschatological prophet.

Another challenge comes from Borg's *Jesus: A New Vision*, which adopts a cross-cultural typology, using cultural anthropology and the psychology of religion to understand Jesus as a holy man and sage. Evangelism, in Borg's perspective, is not so much aiming at conversion, but inviting a different way of wisdom living, as found in Jesus the wisdom teacher, which radically and subversively challenges conventional secular and religious wisdoms. Evangelism for him is about living in a Spirit relationship with Jesus and belonging to a community of social radicalism, not just a religious, insular community.

Christology reconstructed from a global perspective
Jaroslav Pelikan surveys images of Jesus from the first to the twentieth century, describing how people in different ages understood the significance of Jesus for their period of history. Rather than chronologically, Colin Greene explores Christology through changing cultural paradigms in the West. Veli-Matti Kärkkäinen charts new directions by drawing together many examples from different parts of the world ('global Christology') and diverse Christian traditions ('ecumenical Christology'). In addition, Kärkkäinen discusses new attempts in process Jesusology, feminist Christology, and postmodern Christology. With the growth of Christianity in the non-Western world, African theologians such as Kwame Bediako and John Mbiti are developing 'Christologies from below', while Diane Stinton offers a fine survey of key

theologians contributing new conceptions of Christ from African perspectives. R. S. Sugirtharajah edited a collection of essays reflecting Christological constructions arising from contextual concerns from Asia, particularly attempts to relate Christ with Buddha or Krishna, and issues arising from religious pluralism.

Andrew Walls observed that 'our [Western] existing theologies of church and state were carved out of the experience of Western Christendom, and were never meant to deal with anything as complicated as the networks of political and economic structures that will characterise the twenty-first century' (A. F. Walls, *The Cross-Cultural Process in Christian History*, p. 113). Walls went on to argue that African and Asian Christianities have more experience than Western Christianity in dealing with the issues of suffering, ethnic and religious identities, problems of corruption, power struggles, principalities and spirit worship. This makes them better placed to be agents of social transformation in society; for example in China, where Christian thinkers should be encouraged to understand and engage with real social issues, and to see Christ related dynamically to local Chinese cultures. Local communities in Asia must be encouraged to see Christ through Japanese eyes, Chinese eyes, Filipino eyes and Indonesian eyes. Such diverse images and interpretations of an Asian Jesus will not only offer deep and rich understandings of an indigenized Jesus, but also serve to counteract the image of Christianity as a Western religion. For example, 'The Christ We Share' is a CD resource jointly produced by CMS and USPG which presents portraits of Jesus through the eyes of Christian artists from Africa, Asia and Latin America. The lack of such indigenous resources points to a tremendous need for similar work in each local culture.

Constructing local Christologies

Christology as an academic discipline cannot be divorced from the mission task of the church to present Jesus in all the fullness of his person and work. What is the significance of Jesus for people coming from Muslim, Buddhist, traditional religious and secular backgrounds? How can missionaries preach a faithful and biblical portrait of Jesus that is both true to his Jewish roots and dynamically related to the hearts and minds of *plural and intercultural societies? How can we facilitate the acceptance, construction and growth of contextual Christologies? These are the kind of questions that drive non-Western Christian communities.

Foreign interpreters of Jesus entering into non-Christian contexts need to be self-critical of themselves and their own interpretive frameworks, lest they perpetuate the portrait of an alien Jesus to these communities. Academic disciplines and good mission training will endeavour to develop such critical lenses and attitudes. Christian training centres, whether in local churches or institutions of training, need to study non-Christian religions on their own terms. Today, 'Who do people say that I am?' is still a valid starting point for Christological trajectories. Whenever Christian workers enter into new Buddhist cultures, for example, they are not presenting Jesus to empty minds. Instead, they will encounter existing portraits of Jesus commonly held by local peoples. Some of these portraits are cultural misunderstandings (e.g. that Jesus is a Westerner), while others are derived from non-Christian teachings or scriptures (e.g. Jesus as a mere prophet in the Qur'an or an avatar of Krishna). The Jesus of the Bible must find his significance and meaning within these non-Christian beliefs and misunderstandings. Therefore, missionaries need to learn how to address these socio-religious misunderstandings of who Jesus is. Notable in this direction is Paul J. Griffiths who introduces portraits of Jesus from Muslim, Hindu and Buddhist perceptions.

In the final analysis, these local perspectives of Jesus need to be shown to be consistent with the Jesus of the Scriptures, and be able to stand alongside historical images of Jesus articulated in historic Christian communities. The Black or African Jesus cannot be so inculturated in African soils to the extent that he is unrecognizable from the Jesus found in the Bible or apostolic Christology. Therefore, efforts to present Christ as, for example, an incarnation of Buddha will cause more confusion than clarity for Buddhists; or equating Jesus as the Brahman for Hindus needs careful thought in explaining those continuities and discontinuities between the Christ of the Bible and the Brahman in Hinduism. To guard against *syncretism, Christology reconstructed in mission contexts needs both the Scriptures as well as historic Christian communities as boundary markers and conversation partners respectively. Evangelicals in new communities will need to learn how to translate the Jesus of the Gospels as 'word made flesh' in their new missional contexts.

Therefore, in order to construct authentic images of Jesus, we need to engage with three contexts: the Scriptures, local cultures, and portraits of Jesus across the centuries. Foreigners offering *etic* (outsider's) perspectives can be involved in this joint enterprise alongside local believers offering *emic* (insider's) perspectives. We need practitioners as well as missiologists; Buddhist scholars as well as Bible scholars; Western and Eastern perspectives. Each group is valued for its distinctive contribution because no one group can fully represent the Christ of Scripture, the Christ in the history of gospel transmission, and the Christ who is related to diverse nations and cultures.

Mission Christology in Mark's Gospel

This section will give a brief indication of the kind of exercise that is required, using Mark's Gospel as a mission document. A missional Christology for the future will focus on the Gospel writers as witnesses and unique interpreters of Jesus' life and ministry within their own distinct communities. This makes it possible to explore Jesus' call to discipleship and the challenge to confess him as Lord within diverse cultures and contexts.

Mark's Gospel used to be treated as an abridged version of Matthew rather than studied on its own terms. But instead of attempting to harmonize the synoptics, recent scholarship considers each Gospel writer as a distinctive 'theologian and interpreter' of Jesus' ministry. Mark seeks to testify to the lordship of Christ, but he does this, not by constructing a systematic theology, but by following Jesus with a 'journey' motif from Galilee to Jerusalem. Answering the Christological question 'who am I?' therefore becomes a process of discovery within the context in which Jesus lives and moves. Galilee is primarily a place of receptivity (Mark 3:7–12) while Jerusalem is a place moving toward opposition and suffering (9:33 – 16:20). The call to discipleship and

following Jesus is thus placed firmly in Jesus' missionary contexts of suffering, sacrifice and preaching the kingdom of God.

Instead of focusing on titles of Jesus, or on ideas of his humanity or divinity, Mark draws his readers to Christ by reflecting on his missionary journey in terms of the challenges of discipleship (taking up the cross), and the call of mission (walking in Jesus' way). As Jesus moves from Galilee to Jerusalem, the disciples' failure to understand Jesus' ministry and the cross increases. The disciples fail to understand Jesus' parables and teachings (4:33–34; 7:17–18; 9:32); they refuse to feed the five thousand (6:30–44); each seeks to be the greatest (9:33–37; 10:35–45); they send the little children away (10:13–16). In chapter 14, Mark arranges three successive failures of the disciples (three of Jesus' closest disciples' falling asleep in Jesus' hour of need, Judas' betrayal of Jesus, and Peter's denial of Jesus three times). These failures are contrasted with the faith of the little people, the Syro-Phoenician woman, the blind and the outcasts. Mark ends his Gospel abruptly on the note of 'failure' (16:8). But in God's sovereignty, failure is not an end but a back door to success (16:9–20). The key to overcoming failure is to encounter the risen Lord and put faith in him (16:20).

Evangelical Christology will always need to emphasize the lordship of Christ. But in missional perspective this confession cannot be verbalized merely by individuals in the privacy of their churches, but is to be discovered and lived out in *public-plural spaces*. Contextually, our answer to the question of who Jesus is cannot be completely disconnected from the questions about Jesus commonly held by our Muslim and Buddhist neighbours. Likewise, Christian portraits of Jesus should emerge from the sufferings and heart struggles of the contemporary world rather than merely as a restatement of Christian creeds. This will then penetrate into the depths of Christian worship and discipleship where loyalty to Christ is not confined to safe religious boundaries.

The apostle Paul has these multiple dimensions of Christ's lordship in mind when he proclaims that Jesus Christ is 'the firstborn over all creation. For in him all things were created: things in heaven and on earth, visible and invisible, whether thrones or powers or rulers or authorities; all things have been created through him and for him' (Col. 1:15–16). Faithful Christology therefore cannot be done in isolation, but only through a missionary engagement with this whole creation context of the diverse world in which God has placed us. Christology and mission need each other.

See also ASIAN THEOLOGY, AFRICAN THEOLOGY, CULTURE, INCULTURATION, LATIN AMERICAN THEOLOGY.

Bibliography
M. Bockmuehl, *This Jesus: Martyr, Lord, Messiah* (Edinburgh: T. & T. Clark, 1994); M. J. Borg, *Jesus: A New Vision* (San Francisco: Harper San Francisco, 1987); M. J. Borg, *Jesus in Contemporary Scholarship* (Harrisburgh: Trinity Press International, 1994); C. Greene, *Christology in Cultural Perspective* (Carlisle: Paternoster Press, 2003); P. Griffiths, *Christianity Through Non-Christian Eyes* (Maryknoll: Orbis Books, 1990); V.-M. Kärkkäinen, *Christology: A Global Introduction* (Grand Rapids: Baker Academic, 2003); H. Marshall, *The Origins of New Testament Christology* (Leicester: IVP, 1976); A. E. McGrath, *Christian Theology: An Introduction* (Oxford: Blackwell, 1993); J. Pelikan, *Jesus Through the Centuries* (London: HarperCollins, 1987); D. Stinton, *Jesus of Africa: Voices of Contemporary African Christology* (Maryknoll: Orbis Books, 2004); R. S. Sugirtharajah (ed.), *Asian Faces of Jesus* (Maryknoll: Orbis Books, 1999); A. F. Walls, *The Cross-Cultural Process in Christian History* (London: Continuum, 2002); A. Wessels, *Images of Jesus* (Grand Rapids: Eerdmans, 1990); B. Witherington, *The Christology of Jesus* (Minneapolis: Fortress, 1990); N. T. Wright, *Jesus and the Victory of God* (Minneapolis: Fortress, 1996).

KANG-SAN TAN

CHRISTIAN LIFE, see DISCIPLESHIP
CHURCH AND STATE, see POLITICS/STATE

Church/ecclesiology

There are several reasons why the understanding of the church in mission (missional ecclesiology) is a topic of great importance and increasing interest:

The historically unprecedented growth of the church, especially in the non-Western world, and the shift of the centre of gravity of the church from the North to the South, draw attention to the worldwide expansion of the church.

Through the various movements of ecumenism and cooperation, both conciliar and evangelical, and aided by increasing globalization and internationalization in general, churches have come into closer contact with each other and become aware of the various societal and cultural contexts in which the church exists. Thus the relationship between the global and the local aspect of being church is becoming increasingly relevant.

There are a growing number of new models of the church making claims that challenge the historical forms and understandings of its identity.

Most importantly, the church played a crucial role in the NT and the formative years of the Christian movement, and the church needs to reflect anew on its own nature and mission in the light of twenty-first century contexts that in many respects resemble those of the early church.

In light of this, one may ask: What are the necessary and lasting elements in the nature and mission of the church, and how can they be a criterion for evaluating the church? Is there a common identity, a real continuity through the centuries, regardless of shifting cultures and contexts? How may the nature and mission of the church be realized in different historical contexts?

In answering these questions the main focus should not be the organization of the church or the characteristics of the national or denominational churches, but the local church, the 'church here with us', and the universal, global church in the world. Both a local and a global perspective is necessary in missional ecclesiology. It can be argued that the local church is the essential unit of mission. This derives from the most basic form of its identity given by Jesus: 'where two or three come together in my name' (Matt. 18:20), which is sufficient to constitute a 'church'.

Biblical and theological themes
The most frequent Greek term used for church

in the NT is *ekklēsia* (114 places). It may denote a congregation, a local church or church in a home (1 Cor. 1:2; Philm. 2); or it may denote the total sum of all local churches, the whole universal church (Matt. 16:18). The term *ekklēsia* is probably derived from the Greek verb for call, *kaleo*. The church is the community of those who are called by God to be his people (cf. Acts 2:39). It is the same verb that is being used for the call to God and the call to mission. God calls people to himself and sends them out into the world. This is seen in Jesus' call of the first disciples in Matthew 4:19: 'Come, follow me, and I will send you out to fish for people', in the call of the apostle Paul (Acts 26:14–16), and in the call of every believer (1 Thess. 1:6–8). It is not possible to be a disciple of Jesus and belong to his church without also being called to mission.

The church was the result of a mission that initially was directed towards Jews but later included Gentiles and encompassed 'all nations'. It was also an invitation to be incorporated in the church as the people of God. The church consisted of those who responded in repentance and faith and were included in the church through baptism (Acts 2:38–41).

The historical beginning of the church is the group of *disciples whom *Jesus called to follow him and later sent out as his witnesses (Matt. 4:18–22; 10:5). Jesus renewed the sending of the disciples after his death and resurrection, giving them the great commission. This universal commission is expressed or assumed in all the Gospels and Acts, in various forms (Matt. 28:18–20; Mark 16:15–18; Luke 24:46–49; John 20:21–23; Acts 1:8). The commission is accompanied by promises that the risen Jesus himself will be with the church until the end of the age (Matt. 28:20), and that the *Holy Spirit will be given to equip and empower it for mission (John 20:22–23; Luke 24:49; Acts 1:8).

As the people of God, belonging to his *kingdom, the church is called to live in loving communion with God. It is a pilgrim people on the way through this world towards the final goal of the church, which is perfect communion with *God 'face to face', and to serve and worship him forever in his new creation (Rev. 7:9–17; 21:1–5; Rom. 8:22–23). This means that the church is always on the way towards the form God wants it to be.

As the people of God, the church is a sign and an instrument of *salvation. To accomplish this task the church is sent by God into the world. In this sense the church is missional by nature. This sending or mission, often called *'*missio Dei*', is God's mission to totally transform all of reality. In its mission the church not only calls individuals to faith but it also plants new congregations, transformed and transforming communities of people who have come to faith (*plantatio ecclesiae*). The growth and multiplication of the church is thus one of the main goals of mission.

In its mission the church has primarily a ministry of *witness through the proclamation of the *gospel in various forms (Gk: *martyria*, Acts 1:8), through the loving communion of the people of God with one another (Gk: *koinonia*), through various forms of humble service towards other members of the body of Christ and towards the world (Gk: *diakonia*), and through prayer and *worship of God (Gk: *leitourgia*). It may also include the demonstration of the gospel by God through accompanying supernatural signs (Gk: *semeia*, signs, Rom. 15:19; Acts 14:3).

The 'priestly' nature of the people of God in conveying salvation to the world is most succinctly expressed in 1 Peter 2:9, where to 'declare the praises [or great works] of him who called you out of darkness' belongs to the very reason why the church is a 'chosen people, a royal *priesthood … God's special possession'. Based on this text and others it is right to speak of the 'priesthood of all believers' or a 'general priesthood'. It would be equally right to speak of a general missionary obligation or the 'mission of all believers' who are baptized into Christ.

The theological reason why the sending of the church is not an external or accidental attribute but belongs to the nature of the church, to its very essence, is not to be found only in the command and commission of Jesus. It has an even deeper foundation in the very God to whom the church belongs, in the nature of the *Triune God, and his eternal salvation-historical purpose. God is a missionary God, a sending God, who down through human history has sent his word and his servants to the fallen world with a message of salvation finally accomplished and revealed in his Son Jesus Christ. The sending of the church is derived from the Father's sending of the Son, and accompanied by the sending of the Spirit: 'He breathed on them and said, "Receive the Holy Spirit."' Through this mission in the Spirit forgiveness of sins will be conveyed (John 20:22–23). The church is constituted on the day of Pentecost as the *eschatological people of God, consisting of both Jesus-believing Jews and Gentiles. The promise of God to Israel is not cancelled but will be fulfilled through faith in Jesus Christ. In this salvation-historical perspective the church is the people of the Father, the Son and the Holy Spirit.

There are various images and metaphors used in the New Testament to characterize the church and bring out its nature and mission. Common for most of them are that they emphasize the relationship between the church and one or all of the persons of the Triune God, the growth of the church, and how the church is made up of people who are brought together in unity.

The expressions 'people of God', 'children of God', 'family of God', 'temple of God', 'church of God', are all used to characterize various aspects of the church's relationship to God, often seen as the heavenly father. The relation to Jesus Christ is brought out by terms such as 'disciples' and 'Christians' (Acts 11:26). The church as the body of Christ (1 Cor. 12:12–13; Rom. 12:5) emphasizes both the unity between the church and Christ as well as the growth and the charismatic character of the church. In the body of Christ each member has the Spirit as the eschatological gift of salvation and is equipped by the Spirit with special gifts (Greek: *charismata*) aimed at ministry (1 Pet. 4:10) and the building up of the body. The gifts are given to the church for the benefit of the church and its mission (1 Cor. 12:7; Eph. 4:11–13, 16). The church is a temple where God's Spirit dwells (1 Cor. 3:16; 6:19).

Historical perspectives

The ancient church during its first four centuries was not very occupied with ecclesiology or mission as theological themes. Yet the church could be characterized as a minority church with no political or worldly power,

existing in a religiously and culturally pluralistic world in which it gave witness. It was a martyr church, often despised and persecuted, yet it was always a missional church on the way to new people with the good news. The sending out of apostles or missionaries by the church (*missiones ecclesiae*) which started in Antioch (Acts 13:1–4) was continued through the ministry of itinerant evangelists and prophets, as well as by ordinary Christians bringing the gospel to new places. This mission history shows that the missionary nature of the church is not only a theological proposition, but also an empirical fact, rooted in a mission history which is not tied to certain political, cultural or economic conditions and contexts, but takes place in various situations and through all history.

From the time of the Roman Emperor Constantine in the fourth century up until modern times, and even today, the church, especially in the West, has often been allied with political power. This 'Constantinian period' with the idea of a *corpus Christianum* has in recent years come under attack as representing a distorted form of church contradicting the missional, prophetic nature of the church as seen in the Scriptures and the early church. While the folk church or state church system in the past has provided an opportunity to reach the whole people with the gospel, and thus can be given a certain missiological justification, it has been argued that due to increasing secularization, pluralization and a reductionist theology, it has become untenable and should be replaced by new forms of the church in mission. Most of the emerging churches in the South that form a majority within the global Christian church are at the same time minority churches in their own context, not representing the rich and powerful, but more often the poor, the powerless, and the marginalized.

The nature of the church

The nature of the church has been expressed theologically in the so-called attributes or characteristic marks of the church (*notae ecclesiae*). The church according to the Nicene Creed has four marks. It is one, holy, catholic and apostolic. All of these marks are essential for the mission of the church and may be interpreted in a missiological perspective.

The *unity* of the church is a theological

reality grounded in the one Triune God, the one faith, the one body, the one baptism and the one hope of the church. Yet unity is to be visibly realized and demonstrated in the life of the church as a strong testimony to the world (John 17:21). The church may appear in a variety of forms expressed as 'diversity in unity', but ecumenical endeavours are an obligation of the gospel. Evangelicals will emphasize that there are limits to diversity, and that visible unity in fellowship, work and witness is dependent upon sharing the same biblical faith (the Lausanne Covenant, para. 7).

The *holiness* of the church is an expression of the fact that the church is God's saved people set apart from the world. Its holiness is a divine gift due to the sanctifying work of Christ and the Holy Spirit (1 Cor. 1:30–31; Acts 20:28, 32). In this sense all Christians are saints (1 Cor. 1:2). The church is the *communio sanctorum*, the fellowship of holy people (cf. the Apostles' Creed). As a holy, loving people serving God and the needy, the church exerts an attraction on the world and invites people to give praise to God (Matt. 5:16), which makes holiness a vital dimension of the church's calling to mission.

The *catholicity* of the church means that it is universal, consisting of members from the whole world, from all peoples and cultures. In most of its history the church has been universal in its intention; in our time this universality is realized in an unprecedented way. The catholicity of the church may come to expression in 'the whole Church taking the whole gospel to the whole world' (cf. e.g. the Lausanne Covenant, para. 6).

The *apostolicity* of the church primarily means that the church is built on the faith and words of the apostles as expressed in the NT (Eph. 2:19–22). Some churches, such as the Roman Catholic, Orthodox and Anglican, have emphasized the office of the bishop as necessary for apostolicity, and developed the doctrine of 'apostolic succession' through laying on of hands. Other churches will claim that all churches that share the apostolic faith according to the biblical testimony also share in the apostolicity of the church.

The church is also apostolic because it is sent in mission and evangelism. 'Apostle' means a messenger, a 'sent one', being derived from the Greek *apostello* ('send'). As apostolic the church is also a missional church, sent to the world, and itself sending witnesses to the world with the gospel.

The true church?

The Protestant Reformation in the sixteenth century took up the questions of the marks of the church. The Lutheran church has in a classical way expressed its understanding of the church as the communion of saints (or believers), where the gospel is preached purely and the sacraments administered rightly (Augsburg Confession, art. 7). The church is seen as a fellowship of human beings, and not primarily as an institution. The church is visibly existing in this world, with God-given means of grace as characteristics or signs. The means of grace (the word and the sacraments) are in the Lutheran understanding so important because through them God creates faith and thus builds his church. The true church is, however, hidden in the sense that it is impossible to create an empirical, pure church consisting only of true believers, since many non-believers are mixed into the church in this world. The Reformed tradition has a similar understanding of the church but is occupied more than the Lutheran tradition with the structure of the church, its (four) offices, and church discipline as one of the marks of the church.

The so-called Radical Reformation or what is often today called the 'free church' or 'believers' church' movement emphasized separation of the church from the political powers. The church consisted of voluntary members who joined the church through personal conversion and 'believers' baptism'. This movement would also add more characteristics of the church, such as ethical holiness and church discipline, the mission and witness of all members, and brotherly love and service.

In revival movements of the eighteenth and nineteenth centuries, such as Pietism, Puritanism and Methodism, the spiritual and ecclesial ideals of the Reformation came closer to realization through the establishment of *ecclesiolae in ecclesia*, smaller fellowships of converted, believing Christians within the larger framework of state or folk churches. In these fellowships the priesthood of all believers in terms of new life (sanctification), Bible study, prayer, testimony, mission and even organization could be developed in a way that made these revival Christians an instrument of spiritual renewal and evangelical mission.

In the nineteenth century almost all Protestant churches in the West had their own mission work, with the express aim of establishing independent churches in all parts of the world. The principles of self-supporting, self-propagating and self-governing churches were seen by many as expressions and requirements of independence. Planting of churches often went hand in hand with attempts at spreading Western culture and civilization.

In the *Pentecostal and *charismatic movements of the twentieth century a special emphasis was placed on the work of the Holy Spirit in equipping the church and its members for ministry and mission through the experience of the baptism/fullness of the Spirit, with resulting empowerment and exercise of spiritual gifts (charismata), including speaking in tongues, prophecy and healing. They would insist that one of the marks of the church is that it is charismatic. In this connection miraculous 'signs' are seen as another mark of the true church in mission. By insisting that the missional church is charismatic, the Pentecostal/charismatic movements have significantly contributed to the recovery of a biblical missional ecclesiology.

Conclusion

Although there are certain marks and functions of the church that are necessary for its life and growth, no specific church structure or organization is prescribed as universally valid in the NT. Nevertheless, empirical studies of growing missional churches both in the North and the South tend to show certain common characteristic features of theology, spirituality and structure. They emphasize what may be called biblical, evangelical Christianity, often with a strong charismatic dimension, and with an integrated *holistic missional perspective on the nature and task of the church. The churches foster a missional spirituality and motivation, with close human relations through teaching, preaching and testimonies, through prayer and intercession, through social ministry, and personal care, through sacrificial giving and living, and through the ministries of the gifts of the Spirit. They also show the

importance of developing *contextually appropriate structures, forms of service and liturgy in order for the missionary task of the church to be fulfilled both locally and globally. 'Fresh expressions of the church' or 'emerging churches' are among the labels being used to characterize some new contextual forms of the church in mission: churches that draw on biblical principles, merge ancient and modern spirituality, exhibit great creativity and allow radical change in historical forms in order to enable the church for contextual mission in the twenty-first century.

Bibliography

E. Gibbs and R. K. Bolger, *Emerging Churches* (Grand Rapids: Baker Academic, 2005); D. L. Guder, *The Continuing Conversion of the Church* (Grand Rapids: Eerdmans, 2000); V.-M. Kärkkäinen, *An Introduction to Ecclesiology: Ecumenical, Historical and Global Perspectives* (Downers Grove: Inter-Varsity Press, 2002); H. Küng, *The Church* (London: Search Press, 1981); *Mission-Shaped Church: Church Planting and Fresh Expressions of the Church in a Changing Context* (London: Church House Publishing, 2004); J. G. Stackhouse, Jr (ed.), *Evangelical Ecclesiology: Reality or Illusion?* (Grand Rapids: Baker Academic, 2003); C. Van Gelder, *The Essence of the Church* (Grand Rapids: Baker Books, 2000); J. H. Yoder, *The Royal Priesthood. Essays Ecclesiological and Ecumenical*, ed. M. G. Cartwright (Scottdale: Herald Press, 1998).

T. ENGELSVIKEN

Church growth

The church grows both quantitatively in numbers (e.g. Acts 2:41) and qualitatively in understanding, relationships and action (e.g. Acts 2:42–47). For the most part, NT writers seem more concerned about the latter, whereas the term 'church growth' has in recent years focused particularly on the former, largely due to the influence of Donald McGavran who wrote, 'the student of church growth ... cares little whether a church is credible; he asks how much it has grown' (*Understanding Church Growth*, p. 159).

McGavran was in India in the 1930s when he asked why some churches were growing, and others were not. He concluded that missionaries should take more note of the *culture and *world-view of each distinct group of people. Converts should not be withdrawn from their community as 'islands of faith', but remain within it as 'bridges of God'. Thirty years later he founded the Church Growth Institute in the USA, which has greatly influenced evangelical mission strategy.

The Church Growth Movement (CGM) built on the insights of its missionary predecessors, especially Henry Venn, Rufus Anderson and Roland Allen, who wanted churches to be truly indigenous, not dependent on Western churches, but self-supporting, self-governing and self-propagating. Others who worked for the same ends, often in the teeth of missionary opposition, were John Nevius, Timothy Richard, Bruno Gutmann and W. V. Lucas.

CGM principles have been applied in a number of publications to distinct people-groups in a variety of locations. The merit of the CGM is its insistence that missions should (a) not set up permanent stations but move on; (b) never impose alien cultural or ethical patterns on local Christians; and (c) encourage new Christians to remain within their own culture both to affirm and to critique it and to set up churches which relate meaningfully to it. Thus it reflects patterns found in the NT. The CGM claims to be biblical and evangelical.

CGM principles

The Church Growth Movement affirms the following principles:

(1) The NT recognizes the priority of the 'evangelistic mandate'. Christians are obliged to work for justice, health, education and well-being for all people (the 'cultural mandate'), but such ministries are secondary to the call to proclaim and believe the *gospel. In other words, visible, numerical growth is the priority.

(2) The church must 'read the culture' of each people-group, using tools of sociology, psychology, statistics, communication and management theory, and so on, in order to communicate appropriately with each.

(3) People should be seen not as individuals but as group members, and are often expected to respond in groups (family, clan or tribe) and support one another.

(4) All baptized Christians should be witnesses to the gospel and use the gifts, which the Holy Spirit has given to all, within the church and in service outside.

(5) The church should focus its main effort on reaching those who show signs of being responsive to the gospel – while not entirely neglecting the unresponsive.

(6) Local churches should be '*homogeneous' (i.e. monocultural) if they are to be effective in evangelism, because people 'do not like to cross unnecessary cultural barriers to become Christians'.

(7) The church should use *management techniques to set relevant, measurable and achievable goals in its mission.

(8) Converts should not be faced with challenging ethical demands at an early stage. They are only 'learners'; the path to 'perfecting' them will come later as they are nurtured in Christ within their own cultural and Christian milieu. This two-stage process claims to be based on the distinction between 'discipling' and 'teaching' in Matthew 28:19–20.

In addition, there are two other principles commonly associated with the CGM: that every local church needs a dynamic leader who will take initiatives which others will readily follow; and that churches wishing to grow may need to 'leapfrog' local churches when these are lifeless or moribund, and make a fresh start by planting new churches.

Criticisms of the CGM

Some of the principles outlined above have been criticized along the following lines:

It is impossible to establish any priority in the ministry of Jesus and the apostolic church between the two mandates of evangelism and social action. Both ran concurrently, and reinforced each other.

It is impossible (especially for those outside the culture) to estimate people's level of response. The work of God's Spirit often takes the church by surprise.

A church that insists on being homogeneous denies its own nature and the gospel. Pagan associations in the Roman world tended to be homogeneous, but in the church social and racial barriers were broken down (1 Cor. 11:17–22; 12:13; Gal. 3:26–28). Heterogeneity was an essential mark of the church from the outset, and one of the main selling points of the gospel (Eph. 3:6). Migration and multi-cultural encounter (cf. Acts 8:4; 11:20) have been major causes of the church's expansion. Recent CGM writers seem to have dropped the homogeneous unit principle, although many churches still practise it.

Secular management techniques may at times prove helpful, but are never the key to church growth or health. The gospel itself is built not on human success or technique but on the apparent failure of the cross.

The church is characterized by certain given ethical requirements which potential new converts ought to be aware of and see reflected in its life from the outset.

Leaders must not only lead, but also listen to the wisdom which the Holy Spirit gives to lay people, not to pastors only (see principle 4).

Who decides when a local church is living or moribund? Ancient churches (e.g. the Orthodox churches of Russia or Ethiopia) may appear to Westerners to be stagnant, but are so bound up with the people's culture that new spiritual life is not possible without them. Many of the newer (e.g. *African Initiated) churches may appear unorthodox to traditional denominations, but may relate to local culture and reflect patterns found in the NT.

Two questions

First, why focus on numerical growth? NT writers give guidance on evangelism and church planting (Matt. 28:19; Rom. 15:18–20), but seem relatively uninterested in counting numbers. The reproduction of the church is promised, expected (Eph. 1:22–23) and described (Acts 6:7), to be sure, but it is more a divine activity growing out of ethical, doctrinal and spiritual purity than a human achievement. No simple formula can ensure numerical growth. Most hindrances to growth lie in weaknesses and failings within the church. This should be an encouragement, for it means Christians can do something about it, and change; they are not merely victims of the unresponsive surrounding cultures.

Second, why focus on the church, when Jesus focused on the knowledge of God and the life of his *kingdom? Focusing on the visible church (which, however, McGavran never did) has often perpetuated imported or outdated irrelevancies which have hindered growth.

Many missiologists feel that the social and managerial sciences have become so important in the CGM that they, not biblical theology, control the strategy of the church, even to the extent of inhibiting its growth in conformity to the pattern of Christ.

The CGM has been both defended and criticized. But much of the criticism calls for its principles to be modified, not abandoned. At its best, the CGM has crystallized the challenge of earlier missiologists for the application of the NT to mission. It has taught the church to recognize the three-cornered relationship between (a) traditional culture, (b) the message and example of the missionaries, and (c) the text of the Bible. The Bible operates 'as an independent source of criticism directed both against the Christianity of the missionaries and against the traditional culture of the tribe' (L. Newbigin, *The Open Secret*, p. 166).

The Church Growth Movement has given rise to other new movements, notably Church Planting, Power Evangelism and DAWN (Discipling a Whole Nation). In Britain it has been superseded by Healthy Churches UK, and the Anglican 'Fresh Expressions' movement, which focus on qualitative renewal through new ways of being church rather than on quantitative growth, which is seen as following naturally if the church is healthy. It is now generally accepted that the two kinds of growth should go together and should not be pursued in isolation.

See also CHURCH, CHURCH PLANTING.

Bibliography
R. Bowen, *So I Send You* (London: SPCK, 1996); R. Fung, *The Isaiah Vision: An Ecumenical Strategy for Congregational Evangelism* (Geneva: WCC, 1992); E. Gibbs, *I Believe in Church Growth* (London: Hodder, 1981); K. Hinton, *Growing Churches Singapore Style* (Singapore: OMF, 1985); R. Jackson, *The Road to Growth: Towards a Thriving Church* (London: Church House Publishing, 2005); D. McGravran, *Understanding Church Growth* (Grand Rapids: Eerdmans, rev. edn, 1980); L. Newbigin, *The Open Secret* (London: SPCK, 1978); W. Shenk, *Exploring Church Growth*

(Scottsdale: Herald, 1973); P. Wagner, *Church Growth and the Whole Gospel* (Bromley: MARC Europe, 1987).

R. BOWEN

Church planting

Church planting is normally associated with *evangelism, but carries a variety of meanings and concepts. According to Gailyn Van Rheenen it is 'initiating reproductive fellowships that reflect the kingdom of God in the world' (*Monthly Missiological Reflections*), but it is also linked with church nurturing, maturation and growth. Aubrey Malphurs defines church planting as a planned process of beginning and growing new local churches, which implies that it is (a) a process that involves planning; (b) an intentional activity; (c) it has to do with church multiplication and growth. Donald McGavran developed the study of *church growth, and later David Garrison presented the concept of church planting movements as a rapid, and even exponential, increase of indigenous churches, planted within a given people group or population segment. Patrick Johnstone, Luis Bush and others wanted to mobilize the world church to focus on church planting amongst people groups in less evangelized areas.

Missiology and theology
Foundations for church planting begin from the conviction that missiology and theology are not isolated fields of study but rather two sides of the same coin. David Hesselgrave, confirming the absence of theological foundation in church planting studies, asks, 'Of what lasting significance is the evangelical commitment to the authority of the Bible if biblical teachings do not explicitly shape our missiology?' (*Planting Churches Cross-Culturally*). Charles Van Engen stresses that the theology of mission needs to be a multi-disciplinary field that reads the Bible with missiological eyes and 'based on that reading, continually reexamines, reevaluates and re-directs the church's involvement in God's mission in God's world' (*Footprints of God*, p. 18).

In church planting we face three dangers if theology and missiology are not perceived as partners:

(1) to use God as an instrument to fulfil our purposes in church planting, instead of serving him by pursuing his plan on earth;

(2) to offer simplistic solutions for complex and ambiguous problems related to gospel communication, contextualization and church planting;

(3) to defend the view that there is only one biblical way to accomplish Jesus' commandment to take the gospel to the ends of the earth.

According to David Bosch, theology in the early days of the NT was practised in the context of mission in response to missiological questions, as church planters were spreading the gospel and nurturing the existing church. The apostle Paul is a classic example of that, as he was, at the same time, 'the most impressive theologian of Christianity and its greatest missionary' – to quote Augustus Nicodemus Lopes. St Paul's theology arose out of his mission and ministry, and his mission activity inspires us to reflect on God and his action in the world (Rom. 15). We begin therefore with the affirmation that church planting must have sound theological and *ecclesiological foundations.

A theological framework for church planting
Three theological values are particularly important:

Church planting is done in faithfulness to Scripture
The foundation of gospel communication should never be defined by what works, but rather by what is biblical (1 Thess. 1:5). In church planting, following what is biblical does not necessarily mean there will be greater results in terms of time-saving and numbers. Undergirding mission and church planting with sound biblical theology may require investment of time, patience and theological reflection, alongside national Christians. Stuart Murray explains that 'All church planters operate within theological frameworks, but often these are assumed rather than articulated and adopted uncritically rather than as the result of reflection' (*Church Planting: Laying Foundations*, p. 39).

Amongst progressive church planting movements today, non-biblical movements appear among the top ten in terms of numbers and influence. The Church of the Holy Spirit in Ghana, for example, is a church planting movement which is growing rapidly in the southern part of the country. A few years ago the founder declared himself to be the incarnation of the Holy Spirit on earth. But today this is a fast-growing movement, planting churches and spreading its influence throughout different parts of the country and beyond. In contrast, evangelicals are committed to God's mind and vision as revealed in Scripture, and not to human strategies of growth.

Church planting is done in dependence on God's power and desire to save

Although there is a great need for training we should not expect to fulfil our mission merely through carefully elaborated strategies and well-trained human resources. Nothing but God's power and activity can enable the church spiritually to accomplish his plan in a relevant way in today's world. Church planting is not merely a matter of marketing, methodology and strategy. It is first a spiritual matter, characterized by the power of God released through the unique and historical sacrifice of Christ and undertaken through the enabling of the Holy Spirit, who guides the church to pray, believe and work (John 14:15–18).

Church planting requires a clear understanding of the nature of the church and God's purposes for it (ecclesiology), so that the long-term objectives guide the short-term strategy and vision. In particular we hope to plant churches as communities:

- of redeemed people, birthed by God, and belonging to God (1 Cor. 1:1–2);
- of human, vulnerable people: men and women, parents, children, farmers and fishermen who live and breathe the gospel wherever they may be (Matt. 10);
- in the world, holy but not apart from it, not isolated or alienated (1 Cor. 6:12–20);
- without borders, so that they are therefore missionary by their very nature (Rom. 15:18–19);
- with a witness and a gospel that makes sense both in and out of the church building (John 14:26; 16:13–15);
- with the primary mission to glorify God (1 Cor. 6:20; Rom. 16:25–27).

Church planting is done through proclaiming the gospel

The 'praxis' of church planting begins by proclaiming the gospel, because the church is born where the word of God is powerfully at work. So *proclamation is the non-negotiable foundation of church planting. For many in mission today church planting itself has become the overriding focus of mission. But for Van Engen and Van Gelder the primary aim is making the gospel known and experienced for people in their own context, thereby creating disciples of Christ, rather than building a physical, ecclesiastical structure, which, although important, is for them a secondary matter. In any case in some contexts a visible church may not be possible or permissible, but that does not limit the growth of the *kingdom.

Missionaries may have good leadership, satellite communication, three-monthly reports and good pastoral care structures, but they may not be simply proclaiming the fullness of the gospel as the living word of God. Although proclamation involves both word and deed, social involvement, holistic ministry and cultural understanding can never substitute for clear verbal teaching, nor in themselves justify the presence of the church. Church planting envisages the creation of a viable, living and growing community which can itself be a powerful witness as a sign and instrument of the kingdom. A living church with a fresh experience of the Lord will be able in its turn to share the dynamic and powerful word of God through its life, words and witness (John 16:13–15).

Church planting and contextualization

Among the Gonja of Ghana we have a saying: 'The dogs of yesterday cannot catch the rabbits of today.' Culturally this means that new problems in the tribal society cannot be resolved with old solutions. From the missiological perspective it may help us to remember that in our fast, changing, globalized and postmodern world we need to pray for discernment in trying to catch new rabbits. This will require proclaiming a *contextualized gospel and planting a contextualized church.

David Bosch states that 'The gospel always comes to people in cultural robes. There is no such thing as a "pure" gospel, isolated from culture' (*Exploring Church Growth*, p. 218). George Hunsburger observes, 'no culture-free expression of the gospel exists, nor could it' (*Planting Churches Cross-Culturally*). Anthropology thus becomes a powerful tool for gospel communication, and cultural *anthropology and phenomeno-logy help the church to understand people and their culture with a view to proclaiming the gospel more effectively. The aim of cultural understanding and theological con-textualization is to plant indigenous churches whose members engage with the human and cultural questions of their own context and how these might be answered by a biblical theology. It is tempting to plant churches before doing the groundwork of cultural understanding, but this can result in churches that are poor at relating to their own contexts.

The churches that we plant need to be equipped to teach theology in a relevant, understandable and clear way to the people of their own culture. If we look at the African context, for example, we see that the de-Westernization that leads to true indigeneity of Christianity among some tribes can never be accomplished without a de-Westernized, but deeply biblical, theology that communi-cates God's mind and makes sense to Africans in their own land.

Although the gospel speaks supra-culturally to everyone in every culture in every age, the way to formulate the questions to which the gospel is the answer varies from culture to culture. For example, in the West, sickness is treated according to the presenting symptoms, which fit into a formalized under-standing of illness and medicine. In the animistic world-view, no action will be taken before they get an answer to 'why' the person is facing the problem, because knowing the source of the problem is the most important factor for dealing with it.

Alan Tippett stressed that 'when the indi-genous people of a community think of the Lord as their own, not a foreign Christ; when they do things as unto the Lord meeting the cultural needs around them, worshipping in patterns they understand; when their con-gregations function in participation in a body, which is structurally indigenous; then you have an indigenous Church' (*Introduc-tion to Missology*).

A brief historical perspective

When we consider the most common approaches to church planting in history, we may notice that after the Reformation in the sixteenth century Gisbertus Voetius in his *Politica Ecclesiastica* described a seven-fold purpose of the church's mission with a remarkable emphasis on personal evangelism and the training of leaders.

Later, Pietism emphasized individual sal-vation rather than church planting, although churches were planted with clear planning and intention by early Protestant missionaries such William Carey, William Ward and others. In the mid-nineteenth century the three-self formula of Henry Venn and Rufus Anderson guided the church towards self-governing, self-supporting and self-propagating churches. By the second half of the nineteenth century, denominational mission was well under way in terms of church planting and social action, combining evangelism with the building of hospitals and schools, and generating growth in all main denominational organizations. In the 1960s evangelicals began to recover this integrated approach to mission.

Hibbert notes that by the early 1980s there were three main streams with different emphases within church planting: McGravan and Winter emphasized evangelism and church multiplication; John Stott and others emphasized a *holistic approach to mission; and Samuel Escobar, René Padilla and others adopted a more radical focus on social justice.

Today there is a proliferation of church planting models: the Garrison church planting movement model, spiritual warfare model, meta model, Vineyard model, Willow Creek Seeker model, Ralph neighbour cell model, the purpose-driven church model, the Charles Brock itinerant church planter, the five-model approach to church planting and evaluation of Brian Woodford, and others. Although they have very different emphases most of them are defined by three main values: (a) intentional and planned church multi-plication; (b) quick incorporation of new believers into the church and church planting process; (c) emphasis on leadership training and self-governing communities.

Strategies and challenges for church planting in today's world

Anderson, explaining the three-self formula,

shows that the aim of evangelism with a view to church planting involves four stages: conversion of individuals; organizing converts into communities of local churches or cells; providing an able church leader for each community; and guiding the community to independence.

This makes church planting an ongoing dynamic process that brings with it a number of challenges. These challenges highlight the need for strategies that create mature and healthy churches with long-term viability.

The problem of the mother church model. A mother church tends to reproduce itself in its own image, without contextualization. Historical denominations have very often planted churches as exact replicas of their home church, reproducing a model that very often does not make sense for the people in a different place or culture. The danger is to spread an uncontextualized church model around the world.

So, the main framework for structuring a local church is the gospel and how it is understood by the recipient culture, not the identity of a mother church or the church planter's strengths and visions.

The problem of dependency. After a century discussing this issue, dependency remains one of the great issues in church planting. As a result of the mother church model many churches become dysfunctional. If the building maintenance, pastor's salary, instruments for worship, leadership courses, and so on, are built on mother-church templates, great conflict can result when local churches face the challenge to become self-supporting and self-governing. The question we should ask is not how many churches were planted in the past fifteen years, but how many of them remain and became independent communities.

There is also a tendency to create dependency on the charity of the mother church or church planters in meeting local social needs. A church planter should ask how the values of the gospel empower people to work for socially positive changes in the daily life of their own community. This draws education, health, dignity, clean water, rescue of relationships and sustainability into the mission responsibility of the newly planted church. But we should not wait to get a church building before helping local people to start a school if education is the main social need in

their community. The gospel should focus people on their real-life dreams and struggles, so that they in turn will create churches that take responsibility for their mission in their own contexts.

The problem of leadership training. Church growth is very often disassociated from leadership growth. The effects of dysfunctional leadership are immature churches and an open door for syncretism. Often church planters do not plan how to leave, but stay for too long; they do not invest a proportional time between evangelism and leadership training; and they do not address the main cultural problems in the context, leaving new believers to work this out as they go along, poorly prepared to face the issues.

Leadership training therefore begins as soon as the first believers appear. We should avoid making a difference between basic discipleship and training leaders, as discipleship should be the first step to identifying those who are natural leaders. To have a self-supporting and self-governing church we need to reproduce a structure compatible to its reality in terms of human and financial resources. The only input from outside should be the gospel. Leaders, finance, buildings and ongoing strategies should be generated from the inside by the efforts and initiative of the indigenous people themselves.

Conclusions

Drawing together what we have said we may conclude that:

Church planting is often associated with pragmatic methodology and field processes, leading to understanding and evaluating church planting on the basis of results rather than its theological foundation. Missiological decisions must be rooted in biblical theology, but unfortunately biblical theology can become less important than what works well and is pragmatically effective.

Some attempt to make church planting nothing more than a network of solutions to people's needs. This is a growing concern in our postmodern hedonistic world. It happens when church planters make decisions based purely on an anthropological understanding of needs rather than on theological criteria. In this case the culture and culturally related issues become determining factors. Vicedom affirms that only a deep biblical understanding of the nature of the church (Eph. 1:23) will enable church planters to make decisions and take action that is rooted in the *missio Dei* rather than the demands of culture.

A third and final observation has to do with understanding the very nature and mission of the church. Although we agree with Bosch that it is not the church of God that has a mission in the world, but the God of mission who has a church in the world, we need to clarify the intrinsic importance of the church in terms of its identity. When Dietrich Bonhoeffer wrote, 'The Church is the Church only when it exists for others', he was partially right. Its intrinsic value must also be recognized, because it is the result of the sacrifice of Jesus, and Jesus and the cross are at the heart of God's purposes. The identity of the church cannot be limited to mission. Worship, holiness, unity and fellowship are also important dimensions of the community of the body of Christ as it is built up and glorifies God (Eph. 3:10). Church planting therefore means planting a local church that reaches self-understanding as the fullness of the church of Christ in its local expression in the context in which God has placed it.

See also GOSPEL.

Bibliography
D. J. Bosch, 'The structure of mission: An exposition of Matthew 28:1–20', in W. R. Shenk (ed.), *Exploring Church Growth* (Grand Rapids: Eerdmans, 1983); D. Garrison, *Church Planting Movements* (Richmond: International Mission Board of the Southern Baptist Convention, 1999); D. Hesselgrave, *Planting Churches Cross-Culturally: A Guide to Home and Foreign Missions* (Grand Rapids: Eerdmans, 1980); R. Hibbert, 'A Survey and Evaluation of Contemporary Evangelical Theological Perspectives on Church Planting' (2005); P. G. Hiebert and E. M. Hiebert, *International Ministry: Planting Churches in Band, Tribal, Peasant, and Urban Societies* (Grand Rapids: Baker Book House, 1996); P. Johnstone, *The Church is Bigger Than You Think* (Fearn: Christian Focus, 1998); A. Malphurs, *Planting Growing Churches for the 21st Century* (Grand Rapids: Baker Books, 1998); D. McGavran, 'Reaching People Through New Congregations', in

D. McGavran and G. F. Hunter, III (eds.), *Church Growth Strategies That Work* (Nashville: Abingdon Press, 1980); S. Murray, *Church Planting: Laying Foundations* (Carlisle: Paternoster, 1998); A. Tippett, *Introduction to Missiology* (Pasadena: William Carey Library, 1987); C. Van Engen, *Footprints of God: A Narrative Theology of Mission* (Monrovia: World Vision Resources, 1999); G. Van Rheenen, *Monthly Missiological Reflections*, 2000 (Available from <http://www.missiology. org/mmr/mmr26.htm>); G. F. Vicedom, *The Mission of God*, trans. G. A. Thiele and D. Hilgrendorf (St Louis: Concordia, 1965); B. Woodford, *One Church, Many Churches: A Five-Model Approach to Church Planting and Evaluation*, DMis dissertation (Pasadena: Fuller Theological Seminary, 1997).

R. Lidório

Colonialism/postcolonialism

Colonialism refers to the occupation and possession of territory by which an empire or nation state attempts to establish a permanent outpost beyond its borders. Accordingly, the idea of colonialism usually has a civilizational component, not simply the occupation of territory, but also cultural and religious transformation. The almost universal use of the term as a pejorative refers not only to the use of force against indigenous peoples, but also the imposition of a 'foreign' world-view on them. Because the spread of world Christianity has largely taken place in the modern era, it has been difficult to disassociate it from colonial history. Further, whatever the reality, the missionary movement often described itself in 'colonial' language ('the spread of civilization', 'advance', 'progress', and the like), and the Bible was a frequent source of colonial cross-reference, particularly the ideas of a chosen people and the conquest of a promised land. Some have even seen Christianity as an inherently 'colonizing' religion.

From the point of view of mission practice there has been widespread criticism of the way in which Western missionaries imposed their own *cultural preferences in such matters as church order, family customs and styles of leadership, even including buildings and clothing. Missionaries thus fathered a 'colonial' mindset which disregarded the legitimate claims of the context and encouraged attitudes of paternalism and dependency. This danger was identified early on in the modern missionary movement (consider the attempts of leaders such as Henry Venn and Rufus Anderson to popularize self-governing, self-financing and self-propagating churches) but the problem persisted.

More positively, a number of contemporary scholars (e.g. Brian Stanley, Andrew Walls, Lamin Sanneh, Andrew Porter) have pointed out that the modern missionary movement often stood in a tense relationship with formal colonialism, particularly where it entailed the dispossession of peoples and the destruction of indigenous cultures. Also, some missionary activities, for example Bible translation, may have both unsettled and empowered local cultural traditions.

Colonialism continues to trouble the conscience of the West despite recent scholarly attempts to excuse its worst features. There is an awareness that there is still the possibility of a contined and even renewed attempt by the West to exert colonial power. This process (often called *neo-colonialism*) is, in the opinion of its critics, colonialism carried on by other, usually economic, means. It also refers to the way that national elites, inheritors of power through the independence movements, have sometimes also become inheritors of the colonial attitudes of their predecessors in power. The term 'neo-colonialism' clearly abandons the idea that colonialist practice is attached exclusively to land acquisition, but retains the themes of economic exploitation and colonization of world-views. Thus it becomes clear that Christian missiology still needs to address the issue of Western colonialism, and possibly also to re-examine its relationship with national leaders.

The term *postcolonialism* introduces an important new set of concepts into colonial discourse. While 'postcolonialism' as a descriptive term would seem to suggest that the era of colonialism is over, it rather means that our contemporary experience – for colonizers and colonized alike – is inevitably shaped by the colonial past. Postcolonialsm began as a literary theory which recognized that writers from the colonized nations had mastered and modified the languages that had been imposed on them, and were using them as instruments to express their own experience as colonized but also newly independent people. Authors from the Indian subcontinent writing in English (Salman Rushdie, Vikram Seth, Arundhati Roy) are the obvious, but not the only, examples. The discourse has more recently extended its range to historical studies of actual existing conditions under colonialism (see for example, Edward Said's master concept of 'Orientalism' and the series of case histories under *Subaltern Studies*). This includes an attempt at unearthing or even resurrecting the roles of those – 'natives', women, menials – whom the writers of 'colonial' history have forgotten. Postcolonialism also looks at the *continuing* way that traditional beliefs and practices are used as resistance resources to modernization and globalization, or alternatively where new practices continue to arise and challenge traditional ways. The discourse also has a special concern for the dispossessed of the Global South, especially where this entails both forced and voluntary migration. The story of migrancy, settlement, assimilation, resistance and of *diasporas* which keep alive their memories of 'home' also belong to postcolonialism. The celebration of subaltern resistance to colonialism through passive means and the embracing of the hybrid identity of the migrant have been criticized by *anti-colonialists* as a discourse which betrays the achievements of the national independence movements and masks the ongoing struggle against neo-colonialism.

A sensitive reading of postcolonialist discourse may suggest to missiologists that they have not done enough serious thinking about the way that the history of mission has been told or the way that identities have been formed and reformed by the colonial and postcolonial experiences. Further urgent theological reflection is needed on mission as a means of empowering the dispossessed (including those dispossessed by history) and on the new politics of identity which is a typical feature of a world refigured by the colonial experience.

Bibliography

A. Loomba, *Colonialism/Postcolonialism* (London: Routledge, 1998); A. Porter, *Religion versus Empire?* (Manchester: Manchester University Press, 2004); E. Said,

Orientalism (Harmondsworth: Penguin, new edn 2003); B. Stanley, *The Bible and the Flag* (Leicester: Apollos, 1990); A. Walls, *The Missionary Movement in Christian History* (Edinburgh: T. & T. Clark, 1996); R. J. Young, *Postcolonialism, An Historical Introduction* (Oxford: Blackwell, 2001).

J. INGLEBY

Community

A community is a historically and socially dynamic set of relationships, constantly evolving in its identity, and held together by 'principles of relationality'. It comes into being when a group of people who have something in common – nationality, religion, social class, ideals, or simply location – share their life together for a commonly agreed purpose. The communities are, thus, both people- and life-centred. In its widest sense one can speak of language communities, religious communities, professional communities, or even the 'international community'.

Because communities are principally cultural/social entities, they are usually held together by a common language, although sometimes there may be more than one language style represented in any such given community, and this can sometimes limit its effectiveness. However, commonly agreed and accepted means of communication, with a common vocabulary based on a common set of values, is essential to the developing life of a community. In addition to geo-cultural considerations, language goes a long way to determining and distinguishing one community from another, and a person can only be truly a member of a community if he/she can speak the language and actively live within the climate of a commonly agreed means of communication. This includes being able to express oneself adequately in the language stylistics of the community and to demonstrate ability in the use of language interiors such as proverbs, idioms and riddles, which are based on and determined by the culture. To know these factors means being accepted as a community 'insider'.

The community 'insider' could be figuratively referred to as a 'son of the soil', because of their profound identity with the socio-religious environment, social order, norms of behaviour, socio-religious values, and commonly accepted actions of the community.

African communities

In certain cultures, community is more important than individual identity. For example, the African understanding of relationships is different from the Western approach, which has clearly defined differentiations in family loyalties. In African cultures, however, all relatives are treated as 'brothers' or 'sisters'. I can be related to my first cousin because my father is his uncle, but by the cultural implication of this relatedness he is not just my cousin but my brother. Sister/brotherhood affords a more intimate relationship than cousinship in the context of an African sense of relationships within the community.

When, however, the relationship involves people crossing communities and cultures, it is called the 'inherent brotherhood/sisterhood' relatedness. The Igbo culture of Nigeria has a strong value system of relatedness, which encourages all people to embrace others as brothers/sisters, especially when they are outside their cultural areas or even abroad.

Another type of relationship for African communities involves the common heritage of both their living members and the spirit realm of their 'living dead'. Africans have an active community principle which binds together the living and the 'living dead' (all of the community who have died in the past).

This is why innovations such as conversion to a new faith are usually a community concern. For example, in the Igbo communities of Nigeria there is no room for individualism. The community is the custodian of the individual, who must go where the community goes. The Igbo 'we ethos' (communalism) is the ideal world-view, not 'I ... me' (individualism). So any distortion in one realm (of the living or the living dead) affects the other and causes disequilibrium in the community; therefore utmost care is exercised to uphold the traditions and ethical norms of the community. Offences committed against one another are committed against the whole community (of the living and the living dead), and by implication against God (*Chukwu*) who is the final reference point in the community scheme.

Community in Igboland is governed by its gods and ancestors or the spirit realm. So, the concept and practice of community joins together the physical and spirit realms of existence. The secular and the sacred, the natural and the supernatural represent a continuum. This unique African 'relationship' evokes 'wholesomeness, goodness, accommodation, purity and charity', and it implies undaunted fidelity to the community and the importance of immediate recompense, purification and rectification once wrong has been done. These are the 'principles of relationality', the fabric and life-blood that run through the veins of the community.

It is the duty of the community to ensure ethical and social compliance in order to advance its general welfare. Little wonder there exists in every community a multiplicity of institutions and rules for enforcing compliance to societal expectations. This enforcement may be positive (rewards conformity) or negative (punishes deviance). In Africa, negative sanctions are generally very severe because of the ultimate desire for the 'wholesomeness' of the community.

Community and mission

Human identity is bound up in relationships, and we are, therefore, impoverished if we do not belong to a community where we can be accepted and grow in self-understanding through others. We are whole people through whole communities, and therefore mission concerns the restoration of broken communities along with the healing of broken people.

A Christian view of community begins with the Genesis account of God's provision of human companionship because it was 'not good for the man to be alone' (Gen. 2:18). The biblical account moves from the companionship of two people to the families of Noah and Abraham, although these communities soon become fractured by sin. It is through Abraham and later the Exodus that another dimension is added: the covenant relationship through which God constitutes a whole nation as a community called a 'kingdom of priests and a holy nation' (Exod. 19:6), bound together by God's gracious commitment to them as his treasured possession.

It is this covenant community that is given the missionary mandate to be a 'light for the Gentiles', demonstrating what a community indwelt by God can be if they are truly servants of one another and the world (Isa. 49:1–6). This 'assembly' of desert people (Acts 7:38; *ekklēsia*: those called together) was the prototype of the *church community, the new covenant people of God, Christ's body, indwelt by the spirit. In them the community of trinitarian love was to be experienced and then shared with the world in mission. Their call becomes the call to join this community, the family of God, and discover the joy and fulfilment of being 'fellow-citizens with God's people' (Eph. 2:19), and heirs together of Christ's glory (Eph. 3:6).

Throughout the OT, Israel's contact with other nations was strictly limited lest their identity as a community should be compromised, because their election as the people of God (Deut. 4:20) had the purpose of being God's means of salvation for the nations, a purpose Israel could only fulfil in holiness (Lev. 19). Jesus builds on this by commissioning a new community of God's people, purified and equipped to continue his ministry as *witnesses to God's love as they obey Jesus' command to love one another (John 13:34–35).

But it was not sufficient reason to become witnesses just because they were commanded; there had also to be a conviction and an empowerment to witness. This was what happened at Pentecost, so that all that Jesus commanded could be fulfilled through the empowering of the Holy Spirit. It was this Pentecost experience that established the church as a community of believers in mission. As a united and empowered people the new community called 'the church' was to be distinct from both Roman and Jewish communities.

The NT church then became the new congregation of the people of God, not as individuals but as 'the body of Christ', whose primary calling was to be witnesses to the living Christ. So the Igbo 'we ethos' concept became a serious mission context and a veritable place to begin mission. When nationals took over from the white missionaries, this unity of purpose was the very focus of their calling in establishing Christianity in Igboland. And this is why Christianity there is as strong as the cultural community. There is rarely an institutionalized pagan in Igboland, except those who have made themselves pagan at heart.

It is natural, therefore, to think of mission

as forming communities of *grace, and of *salvation as bringing healing to fractured communities. Following the African paradigm already described we might say that mission is first of all about restored and reconciled communities, creating communities of faith by working together as community, and only secondarily is it about individual relationship with God – the very reverse of traditional Western thinking! Justice and holiness are important for the whole community, disequilibrium affects the whole body, everyone is accepted as a 'brother' or 'sister', all are bound together by the common language of God's word, and God's call is for them to witness together to his saving love. The mission of the church, therefore, is only as strong as the relationships which bind it together as a community; and as we do mission together, when the community is functioning properly, our combined service is much more powerful than what we can do individually.

See also CULTURE, FAMILY.

Bibliography
R. Bowen, *So I Send You: A Study Guide to Mission* (London: SPCK, 1996); P. C. Dike, 'Igbo Traditional Social Control and Sanctions', in *The 1986 Ahiajoku Lecture Colloquium* (Owerri: Ministry of Information and Culture, 1986); E. Isichie, *A History of Igbo People* (London: Macmillan Press, 1976); A. C. Krass, *Go and Make Disciples* (London: SPCK, 1974); W. O'Donovan, *Biblical Christianity in African Perspective* (Carlisle: Paternoster, 1995); O. Onwubiko, *African Thought, Religion and Culture* (Enugu: SNAAP Press, 1991); U. R. Onunwa, 'The Individual and Community in African Traditional Religion and Society', *The Mankind Quarterly* XXXIV, No. 3, Spring 1994, pp. 249–260.

N. E. OMEIRE

Contextualization

In outlining the theological foundations and missiological implications of contextualization, emphasis will be on African models. Christians need to familiarize themselves with such models especially because of the acknowledged shift in Christianity's centre of gravity to the non-Western world.

What is contextualization?
A conservative evangelical view of contextualization limits it to communicating the gospel message in a way that is both faithful to the Bible and meaningful to respondents in their respective *cultural and existential contexts. Charles Kraft puts forward a more radical evangelical understanding of contextualization. For him contextualization of theology is the activity of reinterpreting the gospel in new cultural contexts in ways dynamically equivalent to the way in which, for example, Paul translated it from Aramaic into Hellenistic thought patterns. The concept of 'dynamic equivalence' (see *Language/Translation) suggests a methodology radically different from the 'formal translation' of words and cultural forms from the Bible or the missionary culture into the forms of the receiving cultures. More recently, and going further than Kraft, Stephen Bevans has argued that contextualization is the understanding of the Christian faith in terms of a particular context, and is in fact the very essence of Christian theology. 'There is no such thing as "theology": there is only contextual theology' (*Models of Contextual Theology*, p. 3).

The difference in these three views lies in the understanding of the nature of the *gospel. If the gospel has an objective reality that lies outside any context, then its contextualization is limited only to the manner in which it is communicated. On the other hand, context can be seen as an essential part of the definition of the gospel itself, as Bevan argues.

The ensuing discussion will hopefully help readers to evaluate the relative merits of the above understandings of contextualization. What is clear for now is that the concept of contextualization is wider in scope than related concepts like indigenization and *inculturation, which tend to focus mainly on the relationship between the gospel and culture. Contextualization considers the relationship between the gospel and the totality of human experience arising from culture, nationality, history, geography, politics or economics.

Some Christians regard the notion of contextualization as being at best suspect. They regard it as a way of smuggling syncretism into the church in the guise of promoting relevance. The reality, however, is that contextualization is a biblical, theological and missiological imperative, not an optional pursuit for those interested in 'Third-World theologies'.

A biblical imperative

Bevans rightly points out that the different books that make up the Hebrew and Christian Scriptures have different 'theologies' because of the different contexts of the authors and the first recipients of the books and authors. Hence the Bible is situation-orientated rather than being a record of timeless, abstract systematic theology. However, while Bevans emphasizes the differences, he pays scant attention to the underlying similarities that have caused Christians to acknowledge the Bible as a unity transcending the diversity of its individual books. A more balanced view is that of Kraft, who calls the Bible an 'inspired classic casebook', meaning that the Bible is a series of time-tested and enduring case studies of how God interacts with human beings in different situations. Properly understood, the Bible is a record of contextualized revelation; a record of the way God interacted with humans in space-time history in the totality of their contexts. It follows, then, that to interpret the Bible properly we must first understand the context of the original hearers and readers.

A theological imperative

According to Kraft 'all theologising is culture-bound interpretation and communication of God's revelation' (*Christianity and Culture*, p. 291). There is no context-free theology. Kraft has convincingly argued that the traditional theologies that have originated from the West and are uncritically consumed by the rest of the world are in fact a product of Western culture and philosophy. These theologies are therefore neither exhaustive nor absolute, nor should they be regarded as standard theologies suited to every context.

Some have also understood contextualization as a process whereby ideas developed in one context (for example the West) can be applied in terms that make sense in another context. This methodology assumes that the receiving context has no contribution to the content of what is being communicated. This traditional understanding of contextualization has been heavily criticized by Nolan, one of the leading figures in the contextual theology that was part of the struggle against apartheid in South Africa.

Nolan describes the gospel as having both shape and content. The traditional understanding sees the content of the gospel as coming from outside while the present context gives local shape to the message. For Nolan it must be the other way round. 'You do not incarnate good news into a situation, good news arises out of a situation' (*God in South Africa*, p. 27). He argues that it is the shape of the gospel, the fact that it must be good news, that comes from the Bible. The situation in which the gospel is lived is what determines what is good news.

The problem with this kind of thinking is that it can relativize the gospel while absolutizing the context as the sole determinant of the content of the good news. What about the role of God in determining what is good news? The gospel must be relevant to the context in which it seeks to speak without being held captive to that context. This means theology is both context-defined and 'context-transcending'. Otherwise the dialogical nature of theology (see below) becomes impossible.

The African context

This may be illustrated from the various African theologies in their response to the history of domination, oppression and marginalization which has characterized Africa's contact with the West over the centuries. This history set the scene for the emergence of the quest for African identity in both the inculturation and the liberation theologies of Africa.

The early expression of inculturation theology was the *indigenization* theology typified by Idowu. Its *religious* thrust sought to rehabilitate African religious traditions by attempting to demonstrate their compatibility with the Christian faith. Its *cultural* thrust was the call to indigenize the church, including her structures and the whole Christian way of life so that Christianity is not perceived as a foreign religion or, worse still, an effective tool of Western imperialism. John Mbiti developed this inculturation theology further. For him Christianity is already an African religion and therefore does not need to be indigenized as if it were a foreign religion in the first place. He sees *African traditional religion as *praeparatio evangelica* and Christianity as fulfiller rather than destroyer of African traditions. The result is that true

Christianity, by its very nature, must bear the stamp of its context.

Being truly African and truly Christian is in fact the basis of the *translation theology* of Lamin Sanneh and Kwame Bediako. They argue that the universality and plurality of the Christian faith make it a linguistically and culturally translatable movement. Translation ensured that Christianity could legitimately be an African religion, hence the phenomenal growth of the church in Africa.

Bediako's hermeneutic of identity seeks to Africanize the Christian faith rather than merely Christianizing the African traditions. While earlier inculturation theologies sought a Christian way of reading Africa's past, Bediako now seeks an African way of reading Christian theology. He argues that if Hellenistic culture gave birth to Christological formulations like the Logos, African cultures can do the same. Hence he introduces such themes as Jesus as our 'Ancestor' and sole Mediator, fulfilling community expectations in a way that perfects what ancestral spirits previously did. This way of Africanizing Christianity shows that contextualization in Africa brings out aspects of the gospel that may be latent in the Bible and perhaps invisible in other cultural contexts.

The other main strand of African contextualization can be seen in the various *liberation theologies of Africa. For *black and African women theologies* the quest for identity and authenticity is inseparable from the struggle for liberation from different kinds of oppression and marginalization in such spheres as politics, economics, race and gender. These theologies adopt the underprivileged as their chief interlocutors. They then raise their historical *context* to a prime hermeneutical category for the purpose of achieving liberation. This necessitates that theology be a dialectic praxis going from action to reflection and vice versa. Some forms of liberation theology, however, absolutize the context to the extent of leaving the reality of God out of the equation. Mosala presents the most radical articulation of this view. For him the Bible is an ideological weapon of oppression by dominant classes, but which comes disguised as the 'Word of God'. The Bible is therefore only the word of human beings who are engaged in an inter-classist ideological struggle. The resulting relativism

arising from such theologizing means that no one interpretation of the Bible can claim legitimacy over another.

What is noteworthy, however, is that *African theology illustrates the critical importance of context in doing theology. It is the context of cultural marginalization that gave rise to inculturation theology, and the context of socio-political oppression that gave rise to various liberation theologies of Africa.

A missiological imperative

That contextualization is a missiological imperative can be seen in at least four ways.

Jesus modelled the incarnational ministry which for Christians represents the heart of contextualization. The opposite of Jesus' kind of incarnational ministry is the ethnocentric approach which imposes alien cultural forms on the receptors of the gospel message. African Instituted Churches arose as a reaction to this ethnocentrism, and so was the quest for identity in African theology discussed above.

Contextualization is an aid to gospel communication. Research has shown that in Zimbabwe many of those who rejected the gospel thought it was not being presented in ways that related to their felt needs. Gospel communication must therefore be *receptor-orientated*. Furthermore, once the gospel has taken root in any cultural context, the best contextualizers become the indigenous Christians themselves. Africans who communicate the gospel to fellow Africans do so in terms of a world-view that requires emphasizing the power of Jesus Christ over the power of all other spirits – a phenomenon commonly called 'power encounter'. The African cognitive process is generally concrete-relational, necessitating that gospel communicators clothe the gospel message in stories and life-experience sayings which are more relevant for Africans than abstract theologizing. For them the gospel will not just relate to a future heaven but will emphasize present blessings of the kingdom of God, such as the creation of an extended family in the form of the church.

Contextualization is a means of developing indigenous expressions of the gospel. This involves, among other things, the utilization of those aspects of the receptor culture that are in harmony with the fundamentals of the Christian faith so that the resulting church is truly Christian and also truly indigenous. One way to achieve this is the concept of *redemptive analogies*. In his book *Peace Child*, Don Richardson explains that the concept of 'redemptive analogies' was the key that opened the heart of the Sawi people of Irian Jaya to understand and accept the gospel. The local custom of offering a child to achieve peace between warring groups became the key the missionaries used to explain Jesus as the means of achieving peace between God and human beings.

Related to the concept of redemptive analogies is that of *functional substitutes*. This happens when a deeply rooted non-Christian cultural form is taken over and given new Christian content, meaning and purpose. The Bible and church history provide examples of pagan existing forms that were taken over and given new meanings and content in the service of God. They include the concept of covenant, the practice of sacrifice and the celebration of Christmas and Easter. In Zimbabwe and other African countries, the African Instituted Churches have boldly designed functional substitutes, some of which have been adopted by the mainline churches. Every critical function of African Traditional Religion has a substitute in those African Independent Churches. For example, prophets are the functional equivalent of spirit mediums. Faith healing takes the place of healing by traditional healers. Prayer services for rain take the place of traditional rain-making ceremonies. The consolation service (or *nyaradzo* in the Shona language of Zimbabwe) and memorial services become a substitute for the traditional after-burial ceremonies. This enables the followers of African Independent Churches to live holistic lives, thus avoiding the common phenomenon of African Christians having one foot in the church and another foot in African Traditional Religion.

Contextualization is a means of achieving holistic church growth. The debate between the *Church Growth Movement and Two-Thirds World radical discipleship thinkers like Padilla has given rise to a consensus that stresses qualitative multidimensional church growth. Contextualization of the gospel promotes qualitative numerical, organic, conceptual, and diaconal growth of the church. Take for example the qualitative diaconal growth – that service which the church renders to the surrounding community. This happens when the church ministers in ways that are relevant to the needs of the community. Some churches in sub-Sahara Africa have taken the HIV/AIDS pandemic as a serious challenge that has become an integral part of their ministry. This has helped to render the church both visible and relevant to the community.

Underlying some of the above missiological implications of contextualization is the concept of '*dynamic equivalence*'. This concept is important, for example, in cross-cultural Bible teaching. The cultural forms in which biblical messages are clothed are not part of the essential message to be reproduced in every culture. Otherwise the wearing of a veil and the washing of feet, for example, would become the unquestionable requirements of God every time and everywhere. It is therefore important to first ask what the essential meaning is behind any cultural form we find in the Bible. The next question is what forms are used in the receiving culture to convey the same meaning. Those are the forms which are considered to be dynamically equivalent to the forms as found in the Bible. Insisting on adherence to the literal forms in the Bible, or in the missionary culture, could in fact result in the distortion of the intended meanings.

The problematic feature of 'dynamic equivalence' is that it often suggests an endeavour limited to adapting the meaning of the gospel that is already predetermined and worked out from outside of the context. Yet in reality the dialogue between the *gospel* and the *context* will influence both. While some liberation theologians insist that the context changes the meaning of the gospel, evangelicals like René Padilla and Andrew Walls argue that context brings to light aspects of its meaning which may have hitherto remained hidden. When we see the gospel in context, different dimensions of it are revealed. This enriches its meaning, rather than changing it. Thus dynamic equivalence must go beyond clothing the old meaning in new forms. It must search for models and methods dynamically equivalent to those employed by Bible writers in an effort to articulate the gospel for different contexts. The Bible therefore becomes a casebook of these models and methods, a yardstick to help us in measuring our own progress and a tether which restrains us from going outside the 'range of allowable variation in interpretation and experience' (Kraft, *Christianity and Culture*, p. 192).

Criteria for healthy contextualization

Acknowledging the necessity of contextualization must not blind us to the fact that not all contextualization efforts are acceptable. Christianity always comes to any culture with a certain degree of intrusiveness and incompatibility to that culture; 'something totally indigenous would ... be no different than the rest of culture' (C. H. Kraft and T. N. Wisely, *Readings in Dynamic Indigeneity*, p. 88) and would therefore cease to be Christian. Therefore the following criteria, among others, must be applied in assessing the validity of any contextualization effort:

Contextualization must respect the authority of the Bible as the primary source of theology. Christians over the centuries have affirmed with St Paul that all Scripture is inspired by God, and is therefore our greatest authority in all matters of faith and conduct (2 Tim. 3:16). Our acknowledgment of the contextuality of the Bible is not incompatible with our conviction of its divine inspiration. Any theology that negates this conviction runs the risk of ceasing to be Christian. It is therefore necessary that any form of contextualization must be guided by the core of biblical doctrines as formulated and understood in the tradition of the church.

Contextualization must take account of church tradition as another source of theology. But just as the Bible books participate in the contexts in which and for which they were written, so too were the creeds developed in centuries of church history. When Christians recite the Nicene Creed and other creeds, they often do not realize the intense theological battles that conditioned their formulation. This should embolden us to formulate relevant theology for our different contexts, but without throwing away the wisdom contained in received traditions.

Contextualization must be dynamically relevant to the interlocutors. Interlocutors are the people with whom and for whom theology is formulated, and who therefore determine the type and content of the formulation. There should be freedom to find or create within receiving cultures new culture-specific forms that convey the intended meaning better than some of the forms in the biblical or in missionary cultures.

Contextualization must remain open-ended. No society is static. Anthropologists recognize that in each society there is an ongoing process of cultural evolution as one culture comes in contact with another and as cultures need change. The theologizing process must also evolve with culture. Otherwise there is a danger of focusing theology on past stages of culture and losing contact with the modern age (C. R. Taber, in *Readings in Dynamic Indigeneity*, p. 396). It follows from this that 'no contextualization can lay claim to authoritative finality' (D. J. Hesselgrave and E. Rommen, *Contextualization: Meanings, Methods, and Models*, p. 198). Contextualization must remain open-ended, recognizing its own provisionality.

Contextualization must be dialogical. Contextualized theology is both particularistic (emic) because it relates to a unique context, and universalistic (etic) because it shares with other emic theologies the same authoritative biblical revelation that must validate them all. Therefore although no one cultural formulation of the gospel must dominate others, there must be a dialogic element in all theologies enabling them to listen to and enrich one another. This dialogic element in contextualization ensures that the church remains one and universal.

Bibliography

K. Bediako, *Theology and Identity: The Impact of Culture upon Christian Thought in the Second Century and Modern Africa* (Edinburgh: University Press, 1992); K. Bediako, *Jesus in Africa: The Christian Gospel in African History and Experience* (Akropong-Akkuapem: Regnum, 2000); S. B. Bevans, *Models of Contextual Theology* (Maryknoll: Orbis Books, 2002); D. J. Bosch, *Transforming Mission: Paradigm Shifts in Theology of Mission* (Maryknoll: Orbis Books, 1991); D. J. Hesselgrave, *Communicating Christ Cross-culturally* (Grand Rapids: Zondervan, 1978); D. J. Hesselgrave and E. Rommen, *Contextualization: Meanings, Methods, and Models* (Leicester: Apollos, 1989); E. B. Idowu, *Towards an Indigenous Church* (London: Oxford University Press,

1965); C. H. Kraft, *Christianity and Culture: A Study in Dynamic Biblical Theologising in Cross-Cultural Perspective* (Maryknoll: Orbis Books, 1981); C. H. Kraft and T. N. Wisely (eds.), *Readings in Dynamic Indigeneity* (Pasadena: William Carey Library, 1979); J. S. Mbiti, *African Religions and Philosophy* (New York: Praeger, 1969); I. J. Mosala, *Biblical Hermeneutics and Black Theology in South Africa* (Grand Rapids: Eerdmans, 1989); R. Musasiwa, *Contextualisation of the Gospel in Zimbabwe*, MTh thesis (Sydney: Australian College of Theology, 1990); R. Musasiwa, *The Quest for Identity in African Theology as a Mission of Empowerment*, unpublished PhD thesis (Pietermaritzburg: University of Natal, 2002); A. Nolan, *God in South Africa: The Challenge of the Gospel* (Cape Town: David Philip, 1988); C. R. Padilla, *Mission Between the Times* (Grand Rapids: Eerdmans, 1985); D. Richardson, *Peace Child* (Rosemead: GL Publications, 1974); L. Sanneh, *Translating the Message: The Missionary Impact on Culture* (Maryknoll: Orbis Books, 1989); A. F. Walls, 'Africa and Christian identity', in W. Shenk (ed.), *Mission Focus: Current Issues* (Scottdale: Herald Press, 1980).

R. MUSASIWA

Conversion

Conversion is the work of God in a person both to reconcile that person to himself and to transform that person's life completely. As such, conversion can be studied from above (theologically) and from below (sociologically). Conversion is the process whereby God makes us fit to complete his design for the world for all eternity. Accordingly, the scope of conversion is more than (although it includes) 'personal forgiveness of sins', and extends to the entire process of God's work of transforming us so that we become what he wants us to be. This transformation is the goal of discipleship, which is the focus of the mission mandate of Matthew 28:19. Therefore, conversion, and its outcome in discipleship, lies at the heart of mission, because central to mission is God's design both for people and for the world.

Conversion 'from above'

Humans are made in the image of God (Gen. 1:26–27). However one understands 'image of God', that image was defaced by the fall when perfect reconciliation with God was broken through the choice made by Adam and Eve to rebel against God (Gen. 3). If we translate 'image' by the word 'icon' (the Greek equivalent of the Hebrew ṣelem), we can see that Genesis 3 reveals that the icon God made has cracked and no longer reflects the glory of God as it originally did. To re-establish the conditions of that reconciliation and to turn humans into glory-producing icons, God unites himself with Israel in a covenant, climaxing in the work of Christ, that is fundamentally familial and relational (Gen. 12; 15; 17; 22; Exod. 19 – 24; Mark 14:12–26; Acts 2).

The goal can be found in the eternal destiny of humanity. In eternity, people worship God and fellowship with one another. As Jesus taught his followers in the great commandment to love God and others (Mark 12:28–31), so 'heaven' is located where humans express their love of God in worship and praise, and love others perfectly (Matt. 8:11–12; 25:31–46). This vision finds its fulfilment in the 'New Jerusalem' of Revelation 21 (cf. Lev. 26:11–12).

If this is the theological 'story' of humans, then conversion is the process of transformation of cracked icons into glory-producing icons. By focusing on these two points – origins and eternity – the concept of conversion is given its proper theological context. In this context, the term 'conversion' embraces both 'becoming a *disciple' and 'being a disciple', both 'regeneration' and 'sanctification'.

There is a tendency to think of conversion exclusively in terms of Paul's dramatic experience (Acts 9; 22; 26), while the Peter paradigm provides another model of the transforming process. The human experiences of both sudden or gradual conversion fit within a biblical model of conversion, and even if some cannot give specific date and time, that experience does not obviate the importance of personal decision – it just does not dictate how that decision must occur. There is always the temptation in mission to manipulate an experience to fit a particular preferred model. Furthermore, a comprehensive biblical model of conversion recognizes that conversion can occur, at times (even if rarely), to a group, as can be seen in the conversion of the family of the Philippian gaoler (Acts 16:25–34), though it is effective only to the degree that individuals within that group genuinely experience conversion of the entire person.

'Mass conversion', so called, often generates more quantitative than qualitative discipleship.

Conversion 'from below'

Sociological analysis across cultures concludes that there are at least six 'dimensions' of conversion. While the work of conversion is wholly the result of God's grace, these dimensions can be clearly discerned. Each of them, though not chronological enough to be described accurately as 'steps', can be found in conversions in various cultures. We need to recognize the value of these dimensions without imposing them on humans as an assembly-line chronology of conversion.

Context. Each 'convert' has a context, for there are no 'generic' humans or Christians. The gospel may not change, but human cultures do. Each context shapes conversion: contexts involving one's social milieu, perceptions of the human selfhood, one's psychological and sociological health, as well as one's location in a social cycle or trend. Conversion in an Austrian post-Catholic, pluralistic society or in an American, southern Californian, Latin-American society, or in an Irani Sunni Muslim, anti-Western capitalism society will inevitably shape how the gospel is heard, how the gospel can be presented and how the individual will respond. Conversion even 'within' Christian contexts will show variations: some ease into conversion through parents and siblings and friends, while others show dramatic confrontations, deliberations and transformations. A theologically-informed understanding of 'context' will emphasize that a universal 'context' is that humans are 'cracked icons'. The human condition is thus a non-negotiable and universal feature of Christian mission theology.

Crisis. Conversion occurs as a result of some 'crisis', though conversion theorists (like L. R. Rambo) are the first to point out that not all 'crises' are dramatic (like Paul's or Luther's). Some 'crises' are unconscious and undetectable. A crisis is some human condition that precipitates the yearning for spiritual transformation. Studies show that a variety of crises can lead to conversion, including mystical experiences, near-death experiences, illnesses, political and social turbulence, along with the most common feature: a general dissatisfaction with life (made famous by Augustine, *Confessions*, 1.1). In a recent study it has been shown that some evangelicals convert to Roman Catholicism out of a gnawing need for certainty, history, unity and authority.

Quest. The most notable development in the scientific study of conversion has been the switch from seeing converts as 'passive' to 'active' in their own conversions. The older model led many to see conversion as manipulative, while the more recent model understands converts as actively questing for resolution to their own crises. The Willow Creek model of a 'seeker-friendly' church is in tune with recent conversion theory and can be utilized in a variety of cultural contexts and diverse ways. Humans 'quest' to resolve their spiritual crises in order to: (1) avoid pain (inner and outer), (2) find an intellectually satisfactory conceptual system or world-view, (3) settle relationships, and (4) encounter meaningful transcendence. Missionaries and pastors need to discover and provide structures that encourage 'questers' to find Christ from within each of these categories.

Encounter. Converts in one way or another 'encounter' Jesus Christ. Saul on the Damascus Road is the striking example (Acts 9). Whoever and whatever leads a potential convert to 'encounter' the gospel may be called an 'advocate'. Effective advocates develop a 'rhetoric' that shapes the gospel to the potential convert's own culture and use a variety of persuasive appeals, much like the apostle Paul saw it as his aim to 'persuade men' (2 Cor. 5:11). Three models of rhetoric are noteworthy in the New Testament: Jesus' exploitation of the image of 'kingdom', the apostle John's use of the expression 'life', and the apostle Paul's use of a set of metaphors to describe the gospel to his audiences: 'justification', 'reconciliation', 'redemption' or 'sanctification'.

Commitment. A convert, at some point and even if unconsciously done, 'commits' himself or herself to the truth of the gospel and to God in a personal manner. The commitment involves 'decision', 'surrender' and 'testimony'. Most converts sense a need to 'embody' their commitment in some sort of rite: baptism, 'walking forward', 'raising one's hand', or 'publicly testifying'. There are numerous books in the Western world recounting testimonies of faith; nevertheless there is a deep history of 'telling one's story' – beginning with the apostle Paul, moving through St Augustine, and into the modern world of such writers as diverse as V. S. Azariah, Michael Green, Roberta Bondi and Lauren Winner.

Consequences. Genuine conversion, because it is the work of God that is designed to transform 'cracked icons' into 'praising and fellowshipping icons', must make itself manifest in changes – affective, intellectual, ethical, and socio-political. Fundamentally, the consequence of conversion is the 'transformation of identity' – a person shifting from the self to God as the centre of gravity in one's life, shifting from love of self to love of God and others. A converted disciple can thus make with integrity the central affirmation of the Christian faith: Jesus is Lord!

See also SALVATION.

Bibliography

S. McKnight, *Turning to Jesus: The Sociology of Conversion in the Gospels* (Louisville, KY: Westminster John Knox, 2002); S. McKnight, 'From Wheaton to Rome: Why Evangelicals Become Roman Catholic', *JETS* 45, 2002, pp. 451–472; S. McKnight, 'Missions and Conversion Theory', *Mission Studies* 20, 2003, pp. 118–139; G. Poole, *Seeker Small Groups* (Grand Rapids: Zondervan, 2003); L. R. Rambo, *Understanding Religious Conversion* (New Haven, CT: Yale University Press, 1993).

S. McKNIGHT

Covenant

The word covenant expresses 'a relationship initiated by God, to which the body of people responds in faith' (Episcopal Church, USA). Other Christian denominations have similar definitions. The concept of covenant is fundamental to Jewish and Christian theology – indeed the closely related term 'testament' (which is an alternative translation for the Hebrew word *běrît*) is used to name the two halves of the Christian Bible. A covenant takes place when two (or more) individuals or groups pledge loyalty to each other in order to act together to achieve an end which would be impossible for one acting alone. It is thus intrinsically related to mission. The biblical understanding of covenant, however, is not as a contract between equals, but is based on the initiative and grace of God, who pledges himself to relationships, the continuance of which does not depend on human fidelity.

Old Testament

It is frequently suggested that the development of Israelite belief in a covenant between God and the nation or a specific individual (e.g. Abraham, David) was influenced by the widespread use of international treaties in the ancient world to regulate relationships between an imperial overlord and his vassals. However, whatever the original social and political background, the sense of a partnership with God, dependent upon God's *grace, which the concept of covenant expresses, means that it is a key concept for biblical thinking about mission. God graciously invites human beings to be partners with him, not simply for their own sakes, but in order to fulfil his greater purpose for the entire world; God's covenant partners become embodied recipients of his grace and therefore proclaim it through their very covenant relationship.

The covenant with Noah

The covenant God makes with Noah (Gen. 9:1–17) is the first explicit reference. Unlike later covenants it has a universal scope. The covenant is actually made between God and Noah and 'every living creature' (9:12, 15). Through this covenant God has committed himself to upholding creation; God invites Noah, and Noah's descendants (i.e. the whole of humanity) to be co-workers in ensuring the well-being of the earth. The covenant reminds us that there is an *ecological dimension to mission, which is echoed in recent statements (for example, the fifth mark of mission of the Anglican Communion speaks of striving 'to safeguard the integrity of creation and sustain and renew the life of the earth'). Later Jewish and Christian thinking also regarded the covenant with Noah as a counter-balance to the language of particularity which dominates much of the rest of the OT; when in Acts 15 the early church was debating the admission of Gentiles, the community seems to have drawn upon the provisions of Genesis 9:4–6 (see Acts 15:20) to justify and regulate this new step. The covenant with Noah is closely linked to humanity's privilege to have been created 'in the image of God' (Gen. 9:6). The implication of this is that there is a family likeness to all humanity. It is the as yet uncompleted task of mission to ensure that this is fully recognized.

The covenant with Abraham
This covenant (Gen. 15:7–21 and 17:1–27) is the most significant OT covenant from a missiological point of view. Through it God makes clear his intention to bless the world. The relationship between the covenant with Abraham and that with Noah reflects the biblical understanding that both particularity and *universality are important in God's mission. The establishment of the Abrahamic covenant is linked to key passages (e.g. Gen. 12:1–3; 22:18) which speak of Abraham's particular election, and the nations being blessed through him. However, clearly written into the fabric of this covenant is the assumption that its purpose is to enable God to engage with others beyond Abraham, his immediate covenant partner. Such outward movement is at the heart of mission. Abraham takes on the role of mediator between God and the rest of humanity. So the purpose of this covenant's particularity is ultimately universal blessing. 'In the end it is the world that turns out to be God's chosen people' (W. Brueggemann, *Isaiah 1 – 29*). This is not universalism, but it does prefigure John 3:16: 'God so loved the world . . . ' Beyond that, the covenant with Abraham is of fundamental importance for *Paul's theology (see e.g. Gal. 3:17) and underlies his commitment to mission to the Gentiles. God's choice of Abraham, and his later election of Israel, is not for their sake – it is a privilege with a great responsibility.

The covenant at Sinai
Comparing the covenant with Abraham with that made at Sinai (as described in Exod. 19 – 24, and as restated in Deuteronomy, esp. chs. 4 – 5), scholars increasingly view the Abrahamic covenant as fundamental to God's relationship with Israel, so that the Exodus/ Sinai events (including the Sinai covenant) come about because God has 'remembered' his covenant with Abraham (see e.g. Exod. 6:3–6). Additionally, the primary focus of the Sinai covenant relates to the well-being of Israel itself rather than wider humanity, with the key text: 'I will be your God, and you shall be my people.'

However, there are two missional aspects of this covenant to draw out. The first links the Sinai covenant to God's continuing presence with his people (see e.g. Exod. 25 – 40). This relationship between covenant and divine presence will become important in NT reworking of the covenant traditions: Jesus promises his disciples, as he commissions them, that he will be with them 'to the very end of the age' (Matt. 28:20). Secondly, the Sinai covenant makes clear the *ethical demands on Israel, and suggests that this is essential for mission. For example, Exodus 19:3–6 speaks of the need for Israel to be a 'holy nation', which then makes them a 'kingdom of priests': in other words, they have a priestly or mediatorial role vis-à-vis wider humanity. This is spelled out further in Deuteronomy 4:6–8, where Israel's obedience to God's covenant demands provides an example to the nations of God's own nature and character. Within the NT, 1 Peter draws on the language of Exodus to describe the Christian community as a 'royal priesthood, a holy nation', explicitly linking the ethical witness required by this role to their missionary task of proclaiming God's mighty acts (1 Pet. 2:9–10).

The covenant with David
Structurally, and perhaps historically, the covenant with David (2 Sam. 7) has close links with the Abrahamic covenant tradition. Both focus on the role of an individual to act as a mediator for a wider group: in the case of the Davidic covenant, this was originally King David and his successors. Traditionally, kings in the Ancient Middle East were considered to hold a mediatorial role between the 'gods' and the people they ruled, acting as the channel for divine blessings. The Davidic covenant adopts this traditional royal theology into the biblical covenant framework. So potentially there is a missional focus implicit in this covenant – through the king the divine purposes are fulfilled for a wider group, even though in its

original intention this group was restricted to Israel.

But the importance of the Davidic covenant model for the development of the messianic hope led ultimately to a much wider scope. Just as the Messiah would reign over all the earth, so too the people to whom he channelled divine blessings would not be restricted to Israel or Judah. A particularly creative use of the Davidic covenant tradition occurs in Isaiah 55:3–5 (often dated to the exile). Dealing with the problem of the apparent failure of the Davidic monarchy, the prophet suggests that the role of David has now been bestowed on the entire people – who in turn have royal privileges and responsibilities to act as a channel of divine blessing towards other nations. Thus the Davidic and Abrahamic covenant traditions (alluded to in Isa. 51:1–2) begin to coalesce.

The new covenant

The 'new covenant' language of Jeremiah (Jer. 31:31–34; cf. Ezek. 36:26) draws largely on the imagery of the Sinai covenant, but by 'internalizing' the covenant within individuals the prophets move towards enabling the covenant to have a universal scope, restricted neither to a particular time or place.

New Testament

All the OT covenant traditions have, to a greater or lesser degree, an open-ended quality about them, with a forward-looking focus, not completely inaugurated or fulfilled in their present. So the rich variety of OT covenant traditions provides the backcloth for the NT understanding of a covenant inaugurated through the life and death of Jesus *Christ (e.g. Matt. 26:28; Mark 14:24; Luke 22:20; 1 Cor. 11:25). This covenant can be understood as the renewal of the OT covenant traditions, a renewal which was only possible because the death of Jesus Christ took seriously the reality of sin and the need for forgiveness.

The early church quickly linked their understanding of the covenant brought about by Jesus to the Abrahamic and Davidic traditions as the context for their own mission. The very act of eating and drinking (an important part of many covenant-making ceremonies, see e.g. Gen. 26:30; Exod. 24:11), which is highlighted in the NT account, suggests that the human partners in this covenant (i.e. the first disciples) were committing themselves to being 'filled' with the body and Spirit of Christ the covenant mediator, and pledging themselves to carry out his goals. Indeed, such sharing of food and drink both acts as first-fruits of the messianic banquet and as a reminder that God's mission will not be fulfilled until all in our world are fed, both spiritually and physically.

Conclusion

The language of covenant holds together in creative tension the biblical themes of universality and particularity; of God's prevenient grace and God's ethical demands upon the people of his name; of God's transcendent sovereignty and the vulnerability he is willing to suffer in order to relate to human beings as his partners in his mission for our world. If covenant relationship is the mode of God's mission, he calls the church likewise to 'relational mission', which requires a generous, spontaneous and unconditional approach which 'speaks' and embodies grace, and invites others into relationship with him.

Bibliography

W. Brueggemann, *Isaiah 1 – 29* (Louisville: Westminster, John Knox Press, 1998); J. Chukwuma Okoye, *Israel and the Nations: A Mission Theology of the Old Testament* (Maryknoll, Orbis Books, 2006); J. A. Grant and A. I. Wilson (eds.), *The God of Covenant: Biblical, Theological and Contemporary Perspectives* (Leicester: Apollos, 2005); J. Sacks, *The Dignity of Difference: How to Avoid the Clash of Civilisations* (London: Continuum, 2002); T. Stuckey, *Into the Far Country: A Theology of Mission for an Age of Violence* (Methodist Publishing House, 2003).

C. AMOS

Creation/nature

The *God we confess is the creator of the heavens and the earth. We meet him both in the revelation to Israel and in Christ as the creator of the world. God the Creator and God the Redeemer are one. No room exists for a platonic dualism of matter and spirit, nor for the Gnostic notion that makes matter subject to a lesser divinity. Creation in itself is declared to be good. Though affected by human distortion, its reality is never rejected nor depreciated. Salvation recognizes creation's limitations and its need to be brought to a higher level in the fulfilment of its purpose. It yearns, as we do, for the perfection that redemption brings.

The Genesis creation accounts affirm God as the originator and caretaker of all that exists. The order and design make clear that structural coherence prevails, and chaos is overcome – even though to the human eye an element of randomness appears to be present. This does not mean, however, that there is to be no further creational activity nor progress. The commission for humankind to control and to tend the natural realm implies an openness to change and development within the existing reality. Human stewardship recognizes responsibility to the Creator for the fulfilment of nature's goals.

The Hebraic creation account is the beginning, not the ending, of a historical period. The fact of *sin and evil, immediately portrayed thereafter, calls for a divine providence to work for the overcoming of their effects. How this is carried out in all of creation becomes the overwhelming concern of the biblical message throughout both the Testaments.

In the OT story of the people of Israel, the references to creation occur in several ways. Perhaps best remembered are the numerous testimonies of the psalmists. There the history of God's saving acts for the people of Israel, whether in Egypt, the wilderness, or in Canaan, are recited together with the creative acts, in a paean of praise. Both serve to confirm the firm foundation of their faith in the divine redeemer (see Pss. 33; 74; 89; 95; 100; 136; 148).

In other Psalms, creation itself becomes the voice and dramatization of acclamation of its maker (Pss. 8; 19; 29; 104). It shows forth and reveals his glory so that his eternal power and the mystery of his divine being can be seen by all (Rom. 1:20). In this way creation itself is given a mission as witness to the greatness of God.

Isaiah 40 – 66 likewise brings the creative acts of God into confluence with the history of salvation as part of the redemptive story, and is especially loaded with creation language (bārā', 'āśâ, yāṣar, but also yāsad and kûn, all used as near synonyms). Yahweh is here proclaimed not only the Creator of heaven and earth (Isa. 40:21, 26, 28; 44:24; 45:9, 12, 18) and of what happens in creation (45:7–8); but also the Creator of redemptive action (41:18–20) and of Israel as his special servant people (43:1, 7, 15, 21; 44:2, 21, 24; 45:11; 46:4). Thus, references to God's special redemptive acts (using the verbal root gā'al – to redeem) are bonded with 'creation' language (41:14; 43:1, 14; 44:6, 22–24; 47:4; 48:20; 49:7, 26; cf. Pss. 95:6; 149:2; Hos. 8:14).

Other references to the God of creation and to his works accent the uniqueness and the once-for-all character of this happening. This, however, does not mean a closed, non-changing, and static universe. Rather, the creation is seen as a foundational reality that is ever dynamic and that progresses towards God's original intent and final purpose.

Several new dimensions are found in the NT. Central to the identity of Jesus as the *Christ are the four testimonies to him as the mediator of creation (John 1:1–5; 1 Cor. 8:6; Col. 1:15; Heb. 1:2, 10–12). This is the foundation for the bond between Christ as the creator of the world and the author of the 'new creation', the community which Paul calls the 'Israel of God' (Gal. 6:16). The new birth described by Paul (Eph. 4:22–24; Col. 3:10) becomes the sign and seal of the new creation already instituted by Christ. And, as James says, he gave us new birth that we might be 'a kind of firstfruits of all he created' (1:18).

Since all creation has been implicated with the disruptions and tensions of human history (2 Pet. 3:4–5), it 'groans' in eager expectation of liberation from its bondage which is to be accomplished through our redemption (Rom. 8:18–22). Here we have again the interlacing of creation and redemption as in the OT. This is confirmed by Christ's resurrection, which will usher in the fullness of the kingdom of God when all things created will be under his rule (1 Cor. 15:20–25; Eph. 1:20–23; Heb. 2:5–9).

These *eschatological promises reach their culmination in the new creation anticipated in the cosmic-renewal prophecies of latter Isaiah and described in Revelation 21 as the promised coming of the new heaven and the new earth. Here the word 'new' does not mean replace, but bears the meaning of restored, renovated, fulfilled, perfected, as the culmination of the history of salvation. To this grand finale of God's purpose and providence point the new covenant, the new mediator, the new birth, the new Israel, the new Jerusalem.

Creation and mission

Mission theology and practice are founded on creation as the ongoing activity of God, channelled through a humanity called to be his co-creator and agent for good.

Creation affirms the essential unity of humankind, made in the image of God. This fundamental unity is the basis for all mission as the first level of contact between people. Thus, we relate to people in mission first of all on the basis of their *humanity, not their sinfulness, or indeed any other characteristic such as race, creed, social class, gender, or nationality. Rather, humanity's common dependence upon the Creator and his continuing sovereignty provide the foundational relation for mission. As creatures and image-bearers all human beings share some awareness of God.

Creation integrates all beings as a whole and interdependent reality. Modern thought has through the Enlightenment accentuated individualism at the cost of communal mutuality. It taught that individuals have an enlightened reason which decides the value of the gospel individually. The missiology of individual conversion and salvation has been and is often atomistic and divisive. The goal of Christian mission is to form a community coherent with the character of creation.

Creation calls for a proactive care for all of life. All of life is webbed together. We are our brother's keeper. We are also creation's keeper. Humanity is not a *tertium quid* distinct from the Creator on the one hand and 'nature' (the rest of creation) on the other. Rather, humanity is indissolubly linked to and an integral part of the visible creation. Biblical mission proclaims that both creation and redemption spring from the same God, deal with the same realities, and are effected by the same 'Word'.

Creation continues towards its divine goal, which is to be conformed to the image of Christ (Gal. 4:19). The end of Christian mission is to create a humanity of self-giving love, such as Christ gave to us. The world is not a bunker nor a closed event, but a surprising and becoming reality in which there is room for signs and wonders. Small wonder that in response to the more intellectualized Western gospel, the mysterious and miraculous erupted in Latin America and much of the Majority World.

Creation becomes a dynamic partner with salvation history in the one indissoluble purpose of God. The missionary mandate of Matthew completes that of the creation mandate in Genesis. Together they call for the redemption of persons in community, the healing of all creation, the *reconciliation under Christ of all that exists, and the fulfilment of the universal promises for the new (restored, regenerated) heavens and earth. *Shalom* is the capstone of the mission task.

Creation came into being through the mediation of Christ. Only a cosmic Christology suffices to bring about the reconstitution of the universe (lit. to reconcile back again all things, 'whether things on earth or things in heaven', to a former state of harmony, Col. 1:20). The only authentic evangelism is one which is oriented by this radical and all-encompassing redemptive work of our Lord. Mission work which is centred only in the saving of souls, separation from the world, and preparation for heaven is an emaciated and unbiblical evangelism. This was done widely during the middle decades of the twentieth century in Latin America, though by the end of the century significant changes were taking place. Salvation challenges disciples to struggle to put all of creation under the lordship of Christ.

Creation achieves the fullness of its purpose in the *kingdom of God. Not the blind process of evolutionary accidents, not the exodus from historical reality into some sort of heavenly *nirvana*, not the passive resignation to chaotic forces, but the kingdom of God as the full realization of human life and all of creation. The NT recognition of the new birth, the transformation of human community and of the world, and the carrying out of the will of God on earth as it is done in heaven, all tend to the *eschaton*, God's future, when the goal of creation itself shall have been achieved.

See also ECOLOGY/ENVIRONMENT.

Bibliography

B. Anderson, *From Creation to New Creation* (Minneapolis: Fortress, 1994); H. Berkhof, *The Christian Faith* (Grand Rapids: Eerdmans, 1979); G. Daly, *Creation and Redemption* (Wilmington: Michael Glazier, 1989); W. A. Dyrness, *Let the Earth Rejoice: A Biblical Theology of Holistic Mission* (Westchester: Crossway, 1983); K. Koyama, 'New World – New Creation: Mission in Power and Faith', *Mission Studies* X, 1993, pp. 59–77; C. Millar, *The Gift of the World* (Edinburgh: T. & T. Clark, 2000); J. Reumann, *Creation and New Creation: The Past, Present and Future of God's Creative Activity* (Minneapolis: Augsburg, 1973); P. J. Robinson, 'Integrity of Creation and Christian Mission', *Missionalia* 19, 1991, pp. 144–153; M. Trigo, *Creation and History*, trans. R. R. Barr (Maryknoll: Orbis Books, 1991).

S. ROOY

Cross

Christian tradition sees the cross as the climax of a full and final revelation of God's love and justice demonstrated in Christ, and this makes every Christian community supremely a community of the cross. The theological dimensions of the cross have therefore great missiological significance for the life and ministry of the church.

Theology of the cross

St Paul was responsible for laying the foundations of a Christian interpretation of the cross. From the moment of his conversion, the revelation he received taught him the importance of the death of Jesus. No longer could the cross be a 'stumbling block' to his faith, but it was the 'power and wisdom of God' (1 Cor. 1:18–25). He saw the crucified Jesus as the exalted Messiah and confessed that this 'Jesus is Lord'. He realized that the death and resurrection of Jesus inaugurated the new messianic age and looked forward to the future coming of Christ in glory. From his background in Judaism he saw that the cross and *resurrection of Jesus were all 'according to the Scriptures' (1 Cor. 15:1–3), which spoke of those who hung on a tree as bearing the 'curse' of the Law (Deut. 21:23; Gal. 3:13).

Specifically, he recognized both the divine and human dimensions of the cross, seeing it first as the *action of God* (1 Cor. 1:18 – 2:5; Rom. 3:21–26; 5:6–8), a self-revelation, through which God's righteousness had been made known and the depth of his redeeming love made evident. But it also acted in relation to the *human situation*, as the means of *salvation from all the consequences of sin, not only for humanity, but ultimately for all of creation (Col. 1:20; Rom. 8:21). The repeated use of 'for' or 'on behalf of' (the Greek preposition *hyper*) focuses this salvific intention of the cross as a substitutionary atonement (Rom. 5:6, 8; Gal. 1:4; 4:20; 2 Cor. 5:14). Paul proclaimed that 'Christ died for our sins' (1 Cor. 15:3), that he was a 'propitiation' (Rom. 3:25 KJV; 'sacrifice of atonement' NRSV, NIV; 'expiation' RSV), that he became 'a curse for us' (Gal. 3:13), and that those 'who once were far away have been brought near by the blood of Christ' (Eph. 2:13). Furthermore, 'Christ was sacrificed once to take away the sins of many' (Heb. 9:28) and has become 'a new and living way' (Heb. 10:20) into God's presence. He is the one who 'bore our sins in his body on the cross' (1 Pet. 2:24).

Three principal soteriological images demonstrate how God acts with respect to human sinfulness: justification, redemption, and reconciliation. The church's mission points to the cross and flows from it, and so each of these words has important missiological implications.

Justification (dikaioō)

Paul uses justification as a legal metaphor, with the imagery of the court room. It speaks of how God demonstrates his justice by putting people right with himself. He does this by satisfying the demands of his own justice by imputing Christ's righteousness to those who are otherwise guilty and face judgment. This is a free act of grace, achieved through his self-sacrifice in Christ on the cross, which enables him to declare justified sinners free of the consequences of all their sin (Rom. 3:21–26).

Since the cross thus reveals that God achieves justice through a free act of sacrificial grace, the church must likewise work in its mission for this kind of liberating justice for individuals and communities. Through acts of sacrificial love it is called to set them free from the consequences of sin, both for a right relationship with God, and for deliverance from every dimension of oppression and suffering.

The cross and its justification are not only intended for individuals. From a human perspective the cross was a monumental act of injustice, but God took this on with the power of *love. The cross therefore confronts and challenges all injustice prophetically, that is to say by God's radical way of submissive love. So as the church confronts oppression and violence by proclaiming and living the gracious saving action of God in Christ, it participates in the fruits of the cross: justification, justice and restored righteousness.

Redemption (apolytrōsis)
Redemption is a slave metaphor, and speaks of the buying back of a slave or a war captive (Rom. 3:24; 1 Cor. 1:30). It means deliverance from captivity with the payment of a price. In Jesus' day it referred to the ransom sum of money paid for releasing a slave. Christ saw himself as giving his life a ransom for many (Mark 10:45). As the suffering servant, his was a costly sacrifice, the shameful and agonizing death of a Roman cross. St Paul therefore sees the death of Christ on the cross as the ultimate redemptive event, in which his blood becomes the purchase price to buy people back from their captivity to sin (Eph. 1:7; Heb. 9:12–14). NT redemption thus speaks of a substitutionary sacrifice as the price paid for forgiveness, demonstrating once again the totality of divine love and grace.

This redemptive love in Christ calls the church to offer redeeming grace that is prepared to pay a price as a suffering community to set others free. The redeeming power of Christ from sinful acts and evil powers must be demonstrated as well as proclaimed. The mission of the church is to work towards the *liberating and restoring processes of redeeming people from whatever enslaves them. It involves identification with their suffering, humiliation and pain, and sometimes loss and death.

Reconciliation (katallassō)
The cross speaks of reconciliation with God and with one another as communities in Christ (Eph. 2:16). Reconciliation is the bringing together of two parties separated by enmity with each other into a new relationship of peace and cooperation (Rom. 5:10; 2 Cor. 5:18–20). It removes the alienation, hostility and enmity that existed between them. Jesus dealt with the sin that separates mankind from God, 'making peace through his blood, shed on the cross' (Col. 1:20), and creating reconciled harmony and friendship between God and humanity. Reconciliation is effected by God, and since God takes the initiative in removing our hostility toward him, it is incumbent on us to take action to overcome the enmity that exists between us and others. In the Sermon on the Mount Jesus taught that reconciliation with one's brother was essential to genuine worship of God (Matt. 5:23–24). Also, the very purpose of Jesus' death on the cross is to create reconciled communities by breaking down the dividing wall of enmity and making them one in Christ (Eph. 2:14).

The church is commissioned in its mission to perform a ministry of reconciliation (2 Cor. 5:12–21). First, as the body of Christ, the church receives the command and power to be at peace with God and one another. It cannot have an effective ministry of reconciliation if it is divided within itself. Secondly, it is called to reconcile sinners with the healing and forgiving God. Thirdly, it has a practical role as an ambassador and peacemaker to restore relationships in divided communities; to bring together the colonized and colonizer, the oppressed and the oppressor, the rich and the poor, the black and the white, the vulnerable and the powerful. National and international missions and missionaries should have mutual and equal partnerships which demonstrate the reconciling power of Christ. Healing and forgiveness must be demonstrated, manifested and experienced at all levels. Only then can the holistic mission of the church be fulfilled in creating a new, liberated, reconciled and Spirit-filled community of God.

Historic views of the atonement
There are three main views of the reason why Jesus had to die on the cross. Briefly, they are based on Anselm's 'objective' view, Abelard's 'subjective' view and Aulén's 'classic' view. The 'objective' view is a forensic approach

which argues that human beings cannot meet the debt they owe because of their sin and that it has to be paid by God himself to satisfy the divine justice. God is therefore the object of Christ's atoning work, for it is to him that the reconciliation is made. The divine justice was met by Jesus by suffering the divine punishment on the cross. The 'subjective' view focuses on the cross as a demonstration of God's love, so intense and full that, as human beings respond in loving thankfulness, they are radically changed. The 'classic' or 'Christus victor' view sees the cross as the focus of a conflict between good and evil, and the death of Jesus achieves a victory over sin and Satan that sets human beings free from the power of death which operates through them. Each of these views is right in what they affirm and wrong in what they deny. Most commentators accept that it is necessary to bring together elements of all these views in order to have a complete and integrated understanding of the death of Christ.

In Western society most people do not take seriously the concept of sin either as an offence against God or even as a moral failure. But without these preunderstandings it is difficult to see the relevance of the death of Christ in relation to forgiveness for sin. In fact sin is much more than moral failure, it breaks the law of God which incurs his wrath. Sin carries its wages in terms of judgment, which makes it necessary to have a penal substitution which satisfies the demands of the law. This view is not without its critics, who argue that it depicts God as a cruel and dispassionate tyrant who inflicts punishment for sin, who is prepared to kill his own son to satisfy his harsh demands, and who then condemns to eternal damnation those who do not meet the condition of faith. Many evangelicals, however, regard the traditional view of substitutionary atonement as having strong biblical warrant, and would agree with Colin Greene when he says: 'Penal substitution has remained one of the distinguishing markers of the evangelical tradition, even though it is often asserted that such a punitive notion of substitution is both morally repugnant and incomprehensible to our contemporaries' (in *Atonement Today*, p. 231).

The point is that the atonement for sin provided by Christ's death had its origin in divine love. The anthem that continuously peals from the Bible is that 'God so loved the world that he gave his one and only Son' (John 3:16; see 1 John 4:9–10). This does not mean that God loves us because Christ died for us. Rather, Christ died for us because God loves us (e.g. Rom. 5:8). Because atonement issues from love, it is always seen as a divine gift, never as human achievement. Yet, divine love is not sentimental or merely emotional. It is a righteous love which blazes out against all that opposes God's will. The NT affirms that 'God is love' (1 John 4:8); it also affirms that 'our God is a consuming fire' (Heb. 12:29). Thus, the cross is a manifestation of God's gracious determination to save, even in the face of his wrath against sin. Failure to hold these two dimensions of the cross together results in misunderstanding the cross either as merely a harsh imposition of justice, or as nothing more than an inspiring example of sacrificial love.

Evangelical elder-statesman John Stott makes the point well when he says: 'We must never make Christ the object of God's punishment or God the object of Christ's persuasion, for both God and Christ were subjects not objects, taking the initiative together to save sinners. Whatever happened on the cross in terms of "God-forsakenness" was voluntarily accepted by both in the same holy love which made the atonement necessary' (*The Cross of Christ*, p. 150). Further, the biblical gospel of atonement is of God satisfying himself by substituting himself for us in Christ.

We have seen a variety of images and words used in the NT to illustrate the atonement and elucidate its meaning. However, no single image can convey the full extent of the significance of the cross-event. Its richness is only appreciated as each is given its due consideration, in which case they are seen as complementary and mutually reinforcing.

Mission and atonement
The obedience of Christ
The NT makes clear that Christ's death is the climax of his perfect obedience. He became 'obedient to death – even death on a cross' (Phil. 2:8). 'Son though he was, he learned obedience from what he suffered' (Heb. 5:8). Romans 5:12–19 contrasts Christ's obedience with Adam's disobedience. His sinless obedience qualified him to be the perfect sacrifice for sin (Heb. 5:8–10). Mission is a life of

obedience, whatever the cost. Christ calls us to take up our cross and follow him. This means bringing our lives into obedient service to his mission, and leaving God to work out the consequences. He does not call us to be successful; indeed, in human terms the cross can be interpreted as *weakness and failure. The history of mission is full of examples of obedient service that did not yield much fruit in visible terms until, perhaps, much later on. The mission call is to make disciples whose distinguishing mark is obedience to Christ.

The self-denial of Christ

The cross demonstrates an offering of *self-denial and self-sacrifice* which is God's way of doing mission. There is a necessary *kenosis*, a self-emptying, which takes us through *incarnation into death and only then on to resurrection (Phil. 2:5–11, cf. John 12:23–24; 20:21). Identification with the lowly and the marginalized, and feeling and understanding the pain and suffering of the weak and the downtrodden must be an integral part of the incarnational model of today's mission, through which we learn to die to ourselves, and can then bring others with us into the new life of Christ.

This is costly. The sacrificial imagery of the cross expresses the costliness of Christ's atoning work. It is a continual reminder that divine love has assumed the shape of the cross. But it is a sacrifice freely given and never demanded. So while mission is obedience, it is also the free and glad response of those who offer their lives unconditionally and unreservedly.

The suffering of Christ

Evangelicals have not traditionally focused much on the cross as an example of suffering, perhaps because of the fear that it may detract from the centrality of penal substitution. It has been liberation theologians who have seen the cross as Christ identifying with the suffering of the world, and therefore giving inspiration and hope to those who see themselves sharing in his suffering. In this case it is not the suffering of the church which is in view, but the suffering of those amongst whom we serve in mission. A full appreciation of this dimension of the cross leads to a compassionate mission which takes the suffering of the world seriously.

The forgiveness of Christ

Among the many aspects of the mission of the church, prominent must be the proclamation and practice of *forgiveness* manifested on the cross. Forgiveness is a universal human need. It has both divine and human dimensions. From the divine relationship, it proceeds from pure grace freely given, not as a one-off event but as the ongoing gift of God without which our lives as Christians would be out of joint and remaining in guilt. In terms of a human dimension, forgiveness is that act and attitude toward those who have wronged us which restores relationships and fellowship. The forgiven life is the forgiving life, such that human forgiveness reflects our experience and understanding of divine forgiveness. Jesus powerfully demonstrated this teaching on the cross, when he asked for forgiveness for his executioners (Luke 23:34). Paul reminded the church at Ephesus of both the grounds of their forgiveness and the basis on which they must forgive one another (Eph. 4:32). For example, it was this love of Christ that enabled the Australian missionary Gladys Staines to forgive those who burned her husband Graham Staines alive, along with their two sons, in Orissa, India in 23 January 1999. That in itself is a powerful witness to the cross. Forgiving and loving the enemies of the gospel brings transformation and healing in communities. This is particularly important where there is conflict between faith communities. But it has to come as a freely offered gift of grace. It cannot be demanded, imposed or surrounded with conditions. That is why, if someone finds it hard to forgive, they should not be condemned by others.

We conclude that the cross is at the heart of mission. Its atoning sacrifice enables the church to exercise transforming power in its total mission, making new, liberating and empowering others as a Spirit-filled community, bringing justice, healing, reconciliation, restoration and forgiveness, and proclaiming the redeeming grace of Christ through its incarnational and prophetic ministry.

See also CHRIST/CHRISTOLOGY, GOD.

Bibliography

S. Chalke and A. Mann, *The Lost Message of Jesus* (Grand Rapids: Zondervan, 2003); C. Greene, 'Is the Message of the Cross

Good News for the Twentieth Century?', in J. Goldingay (ed.), *Atonement Today* (London: SPCK, 1995); L. Morris, *The Apostolic Preaching of the Gospel* (London: Tyndale Press, 1965); L. Morris, *The Cross in the New Testament* (Exeter: Paternoster Press, 1976); J. R. W. Stott, *The Cross of Christ* (Leicester: IVP, 1989); V. Taylor, *The Atonement in the New Testament Teaching* (London: The Epworth Press, 1940).

V. J. SAMKUTTY

CULTS, see NEW RELIGIOUS MOVEMENTS

Culture

Origins and development of the concept

Our contemporary understanding of culture has its roots in the nineteenth-century European ideas of the 'cultured person' and the civilized society. *Kultur* in Germany originally referred to the cultivation of progress made in the technological, economic and material spheres of human life, and to the efflorescence of spirit (*Geist*) and the development (*Ausbildung*) of a society's intellectual, moral and spiritual capacities. The latter understanding gained in prominence when the Englishman Matthew Arnold (1822–88) defined the study of culture in 1869 as the study of the pursuit of perfection in beauty and intelligence, especially the inward conditions of the mind and spirit of a people, as represented in its religion, philosophy and art.

The emerging discipline of *anthropology toward the end of the nineteenth century combined these meanings so that the concept of culture came to include material (technological), social (customs), and ideational (world-view, language, symbols and religion) dimensions. This classical definition produced, by the mid-twentieth century, almost 300 proposed variations of the term among anthropologists and other theorists of culture. Yet because most anthropologists worked within an Enlightenment and evolutionary framework, a number of general features consistently appeared.

First, culture itself was a human universal, found in all human societies no matter how 'primitive' or advanced; yet whether or not there were any universal cultural specifics remained debated. Second, a diversity of fairly discrete and self-contained cultures existed, each more or less integrated with and connected to its own social group. Third, cultures were conceived of as entire ways of life, providing and conserving patterns and values that guide human behaviour. Fourth, cultures were emergent from social consensus and convention; as such, they are products of human creativity and not subject to strict causal laws. Fifth, cultures were best managed by their most successful and influential members, even if they can be understood by outsiders who take the time to ensure that their cultural descriptions are recognized by its insiders. Sixth, cultures are historically contingent: the artefacts through which they are embodied and the symbols through which they are expressed, while fairly stable when cultures are isolated, may change during periods of cross-cultural contact. Last but not least, religiousness was most often approached through psychological or sociological perspectives, and either connected to cultural 'primitivism' or set off as having only minimal cultural significance.

During the last half of the twentieth century, however, anthropological perspectives have shifted, in part with changing political situations. Classical Anglo-American anthropology emerged during the period when America's national self-understanding was founded on the metaphor of the 'melting pot'. Defined as a single unified society consisting of mixed cultural traits drawn from diverse traditions, this modernist model privileged cultural homogeneity and accentuated cultural assimilation. More recently, however, the Marxist model of class conflict has been retrieved to argue that the assimilationist agenda is an instrument of modernist oppression that hides existing social conflicts by creating false impressions of cultural unity. This response has opened up the possibility for the emergence of a 'postmodern multiculturalism' with its emphasis on cultural difference and differentiation.

The study of culture has shifted accordingly. Anthropologists have begun looking at culture more and more as complex 'webs of signification' (C. Geertz, *The Interpretation of Cultures*) to be interpreted, rather than as objective facts and artefacts to be described. In-depth ethnographic analysis helps us to begin decoding cultural symbolic forms in order to understand cultural meanings. In this *postmodern framework, the role of religion is central rather than marginal. As a complex system of actions and meanings, religious beliefs and practices are interrelated to other socio-cultural processes, and thereby contribute essentially to a culture's morals, aesthetics and cosmology (world-view). Anthropologists now study entire religious-cultural-social-economic-political-semiotic systems, illuminating how their patterns provide not only descriptive accounts for understanding reality but also normative models for behavioural imitation.

Contemporary postmodern criticisms of modern understandings of culture are more clearly understood against this background. Cultures are now emphasized as more dynamic rather than stable; as internally fragmented rather than internally consistent wholes; as formed through social argumentation rather than ordered by social consensus; as loosely defined and relational rather than sharply defined and self-contained; as informed essentially by religious beliefs and practices rather than only accidentally so. Whereas classical perspectives recognized the challenge of cultural relativism associated with the view of cultures as stable and self-contained, postmodern perspectives confront as never before the challenge of ethical relativism associated with the plurality of social-cultural-religious systems.

Classical missions and theologies of culture

Theologians and, especially, missionaries have also wrestled with the concept of culture over the last two centuries. Not surprisingly, missionary attitudes, strategies and practices were crucially shaped by their understandings of the concept of culture, which were in turn culturally embedded. Hence European ideas of culture clearly informed missions in the nineteenth century: 'natives' were 'uncivilized' and their technological underdevelopment was understood as resulting from their lack of intellectual, moral and spiritual maturity. They were therefore in need of missionaries to illuminate their sinful state and 'primitive' cultural conditions. Hence, missionaries were as much conduits of Western culture as of the gospel.

Later, classical anthropological views of culture also impacted missionary perspectives.

Positively, the idea of cultures as bounded and stable systems helped missionaries see foreign cultures with their own integrity. Further, the notion of cultures as entire ways of life led many missionaries to recognize that they themselves needed to be sympathetic participants in the culture of those they were attempting to evangelize. Finally, the understanding that cultures were best managed by their most successful and influential members led to the further development of the 'indigenous church' concept which emphasized the need for mission churches to be governed, supported, and propagated by national or indigenous workers. On the negative side, however, the emphasis on cultural stability and discreteness blinded missionaries to the dynamics of intra- and cross-cultural interactions. In addition, that religion was thought to be only accidental to culture rendered missionaries oblivious to the (Western) cultural dimension of their own faith on the one hand, while misleading them to ignore or dismiss the religious beliefs and practices of those who were being evangelized on the other. Undergirding this perception was the Christian understanding of the gospel as universal and as transcendent above all cultures, including their own. Attempts to communicate the gospel in the language and symbols of the indigenous culture struggled in part because of the cultural embeddedness of the gospel, and because the missionaries' understanding of it was not factored in.

Certainly the way in which the theological question was posed concerning the relationship between Christianity and culture contributed to this problematic situation. H. Richard Niebuhr's classic *Christ and Culture* assumed an understanding of the gospel as separate from culture. Defining the latter in terms of human achievements and social arrangements involving the world of values, Niebuhr's five-fold typology outlined the various ways in which the gospel related to culture. 'Christ against culture' identified how the gospel resisted cultural trends and realities (e.g. the radical Reformers); 'Christ above culture' pointed to how the gospel elevated and purified cultural realities (e.g. the medieval Thomistic synthesis); 'Christ and culture in paradox' illuminated the tensions of being in but not of the world (the Lutheran two kingdoms); 'Christ the transformer of culture' suggested the gospel as the transcendental principle of social critique and reformation (e.g. Calvin's Geneva); and 'Christ of culture' signified an accommodation or assimilation of gospel and culture (e.g. modernist liberalism). Of the many questions that have been raised regarding Niebuhr's typology, the most incisive remains that of whether it is right to think about Christ and culture as wholly distinct entities.

One alternative to Niebuhr's typology has been to view religion and culture as distinct but inseparable realities. The challenge here, however, is how to articulate the relationship and yet preserve the differences. For example, is religion the substantive or depth dimension of culture and culture the form of religion, or is culture the 'incarnation' of the religion of a people? While either case suggests that culture is inseparable from and actually emergent from a religious foundation, there is always a risk in these formulations of either reducing culture to religion, or confusing religion with its cultural manifestations. Perhaps one way forward is the kind of neo-Thomistic doctrine of nature being elevated by grace which informed the pre-Vatican II Catholic understanding of culture.

Vatican II developed a more positive view of culture by acknowledging that in the process of entering into communion with all cultures, the Christian faith can enrich both itself and the cultures themselves (*Gaudium et Spes* §58). Along with the vernacularization of the mass and other reforms instituted by the council, this has encouraged respect for and valuation of indigenous and local contributions to Catholic beliefs and practices. The dominant form of Roman Catholic missiology today thus emphasizes an inculturation model that is dialogical (defining evangelistic proclamation as a form of dialogue) and praxis oriented (directed to social justice concerns).

Toward an evangelical theology of culture

Evangelicals engaged with these matters have recognized that an uncritical embracing of certain schools of anthropology has been problematic for missionary anthropology, even as they have appreciated but not been satisfied with the theologies of culture proposed by mainline Protestant and Roman Catholic theologies. Anthropological models, while helpful, need to be measured by the biblical traditions. In turning to the Bible, however, it is realized that there is no equivalent word for 'culture' in either the OT or NT. Yet it has also become clear that the revelation of God occurred not in spite of but through the various cultural realities of the ancient Mediterranean world. The biblical narratives of God's self-revelation were made possible through the cultures of ancient Ur, Chaldea and Canaan as they shaped the identity of Abraham and his descendents; through the culture of ancient Egypt, as it informed the self-understanding of the Israelites during their 400-year stay; through the insights of the various Ancient Near Eastern cultures, as incorporated into the wisdom literature; through the cultural ideas and practices of the Babylonians, Medes and Persians, as assimilated during the exilic and post-exilic periods; and through the cultural milieu of the Hellenistic world, into which Jesus was born, and within which the early church emerged.

Yet on the other hand, that God chose to use these cultural realities for revelatory purposes does not mean that all aspects of all cultures are somehow divinely sanctioned. Because evangelicals emphasize the fallen human condition and see culture as tainted by sin, human cultures have more often than not distorted divine revelation in response to it. Thus there is not only the destruction of the Canaanites that was ordered in the conquest, but there are also the prophetic warnings against cultural accommodation. In the NT, the people of God are said to be in the world but are admonished about not being of the world (cf. John 17:15–16), and Christians are encouraged to be vigilant against being conformed to the world even as they are to be transformed by the gospel (e.g. Rom. 12:2). To be sure, the early Christian idea of 'the world' cannot be simply equated with our understanding of culture since the former is used by the NT writers to call attention to the idolatrous and pagan systems that remain antithetical to the gospel. Yet it is also surely the case that cultural systems can be co-opted by worldly structures and agendas in ways that oppose the gospel message.

Within this biblical framework, a distinctive evangelical theology of culture can be sketched which sees divine revelation as supracultural (transcultural) but yet mediated in and through culture. This means that we need to distinguish the supraculturally relevant principles, ideas, and messages from the cultural elements. Some of the biblical guidelines which help us to discern the one from the other include the OT's acceptance of slavery followed by the NT's emphasis on the dignity and freedom of believers in Christ; the OT's acceptance of polygamy followed by the NT's rejection of such practices; the clarification of Jesus regarding what Moses said versus how he (Jesus) fulfilled rather than abolished the Mosaic law; and the patriarchal culture of Hellenism that is redeemed by the Pauline principle of males and females being one in Christ (e.g. Gal. 3:28). Revelation therefore has both a subjective dimension associated with human/cultural reception and an objective dimension which is transcultural. Because of the complex dynamics of cultural formation and the interconnectedness between culture and religion, the gospel transforms culture both by destroying some and preserving and purifying other of its forms. The primary challenge that remains for evangelical theologies of culture is whether or not this distinction between supracultural revelation and cultural mediation requires ever increasingly abstractions of the particularities of the biblical content in order to attain the revelatory principles or ideas, since sufficiently abstract principles or ideas can be filled in with almost any content whatsoever. The consistent evangelical response is that any new articulation of the gospel has to be measured by the scriptural norm.

These developments in the evangelical theology of culture signal a shift from the modernist framework exemplified in Niebuhr's dualistic understanding of Christianity and culture, to a postmodernist holism emphasizing the interrelatedness of gospel and culture. Separating Christ and culture results in the incapacity to recognize the historical particularity of the incarnation: Christ is not an abstract principle, but comes fully embodied and inculturated as a first-century Mediterranean Jewish male. The 'people of God' has also always been historically concrete and, hence, internally diverse. Certainly 'Israel' was particularly located in relationship to the land of Canaan; but she was also shaped by socio-economic, political-territorial, ideological-religious, and cultural interrelations with her neighbours. On the day of Pentecost, the outpouring of the Holy Spirit allowed the presentation of good news to those from every tribe, tongue and nation. The resulting new people of God, the church, is therefore from the beginning multi-linguistic, multi-cultural, multi-ethnic and multi-national.

Toward an evangelical theology of mission in a postmodern world

The task today, then, is to conduct various 'two-culture dialogues' between the biblical cultures and the wide range of contemporary cultures. Here, the 'dynamic equivalence' model of biblical translation has functioned as a missiological principle. Similar to how Bible translators attempt to find linguistic and conceptual equivalents between the core meanings of the gospel and the receiving language, so also do missionaries and church planters attempt to find formal equivalents between early Christian ideas and the receiving culture. There is the recognition that biblical translation is controlled by the translator, whereas the contextualization of the gospel is not similarly controlled by the missionary, so the analogy does break down. But what if native speakers of a language are deployed not only in biblical translation but also in missionary work? This blurring of missionary and missionized represents the complex interrelationship between gospel and culture already seen in the pages of Scripture.

In this sense, evangelicals participate in the postmodern paradigm that rejects the modernist emphasis on homogeneity or uniformity and opt instead for a unity-in-diversity model. All cultures and religious traditions arise piecemeal in the various contexts of actual historical encounter among and between particular groups of people. Hence, there is neither simple accommodation nor opposition/rejection in the Christianity-culture dynamic, but always some sort of interaction through which both Christianity and culture appear. On the one hand, Christianity comes always culturally (in)formed; on the other hand, Christianity has also acted as a transformative force on cultural realities. Yet the emergence of world Christianity over the last few centuries can be attributed in part to the 'incarnational' and 'pentecostal' dynamic at the heart of Christian faith: its capacity to enter into and be carried by the diversity of cultures. Whereas modernity had defined 'difference' negatively (versus consensus, which was valued), in the postmodern context Christian diversity is applauded as a strength (rather than lamented as a weakness).

Contemporary evangelical missiological strategies have therefore emphasized both 'inter-culturality' and 'translatability'. The former denies that Christian understandings of culture should be framed by the discourses of modernity (i.e. by a Western science that dichotomizes fact and value, and a Western politics that dichotomizes the sacred and the secular), and proposes instead to explain culture in terms of the gospel rather than vice versa. The way forward is to recognize that the gospel is not owned by any particular cultural expression (hence, for example, there are four gospels, not one), and to open up modern Western understandings of the gospel to non-Western critical perspectives. Multi- and inter-cultural readings of the biblical story are therefore essential for illuminating and correcting any particular interpretation of the Bible. Of course, while the cross symbolizes the discontinuity between gospel and culture, incarnation and resurrection affirm some kind of continuity; hence, God both judges and accepts culture, and this requires that we struggle with the tension between simple rejection and simple affirmation of any cultural perspective.

The emphasis on 'translatability' provides additional biblical, theological and missiological warrant for various postmodern approaches to cultural diversity. Here, the linguistic, ethnic, and cultural pluralism of the day of Pentecost is not only intrinsic to Christian faith but also propels the perennial translation of the apostolic gospel. Thus several historical paradigms of cultural translation have followed: Hellenization (during the Patristic period); Latinization (exemplified chiefly in the longevity of Jerome's Vulgate); Westernization (in Europe and North America after the Reformation); and indigenization and vernacularization (today). In fact, the translation of the gospel into vernacular languages has led to the preservation and even renewal of indigenous cultures threatened most recently by the processes of globalization. 'Translatability', however, is not only descriptive of Christian diversification, but is also normative in functioning as a built-in safeguard against cultural idolatry. Culturally exclusivist versions of Christian faith, the argument goes, are increasingly implausible.

These developments have led to a shift in evangelical missiological strategy from 'indigenization' to 'contextualization'. Whereas indigenization is more culturally focused, views culture more statically as self-contained, begins with the form of the gospel and works to the accidents of context, and emphasizes the missionary's role, contextualization includes ecological, social, political and economic conditions, views culture more dynamically as interactive, begins with the forms of context which must be understood before Christian faith can be 'good news', and emphasizes local Christian responsibilities. A more holistic view of culture and of the mission of the church is thus increasingly recognized.

But what about the criticism that this celebration of holism and multiculturalism is itself framed by the discourses of postmodernism? To recognize the legitimacy of this question is itself a sign that any Christian theology (in this case, theology of culture) of necessity wrestles with the forces of history, situated as it is between the biblical and eschatological revelations of God. Post-postmodern theories will surely supplant present understandings, but this is not problematic for evangelicals who acknowledge their own limited and finite cultural perspectives through a glass dimly, who submit to the lordship of Christ, and who attempt to follow the Spirit who leads the people of God into all truth.

See also INCULTURATION.

Bibliography

T. S. Eliot, *Notes Toward the Definition of Culture* (New York: Harcourt, Brace and Company, 1949); C. Geertz, *The Interpretation of Cultures* (New York: Basic Books, 1973); J. González, *Out of Every Tribe and Nation: Christian Theology at the Ethnic Roundtable* (Nashville: Abingdon Press, 1992); C. H. Kraft, *Christianity in Culture: A Study in Dynamic Biblical Theologizing in Cross-cultural Perspective* (Maryknoll: Orbis Books, 1979); A. L. Kroeber and

C. Kluckholn, *Culture: A Critical Review of Concepts and Definitions* (New York: Vintage, 1963); J. A. Loewen, *The Bible in Cross-cultural Perspective* (Pasadena, CA: William Carey Library, 2000); L. J. Luzbetak, *The Church and Cultures: New Perspectives in Missiological Anthropology* (Maryknoll: Orbis Books, 1988); J. Maritain, *Religion and Culture, Essays in Order 1*, trans. J. F. Scanlan (New York: Sheed & Ward, 1931); L. Newbigin, *Foolishness to the Greeks: The Gospel and Western Culture* (Grand Rapids: Eerdmans, 1986); E. A. Nida, *Religion Across Cultures: A Study in the Communication of the Christian Faith* (Pasadena, CA: William Carey Library, 1968); H. R. Niebuhr, *Christ and Culture* (New York: Harper & Brothers, 1951); L. Sanneh, *Translating the Message: The Missionary Impact on Culture* (Maryknoll: Orbis Books, 1989); G. Stassen, D. M. Yeager and J. H. Yoder, *Authentic Transformation: A New Vision of Christ and Culture* (Nashville: Abingdon, 1996); C. R. Taber, *The World is Too Much with Us: 'Culture' in Modern Protestant Missions* (Macon, GA: Mercer University Press, 1991); K. Tanner, *Theories of Culture: A New Agenda for Theology* (Minneapolis: Augsburg Fortress, 1997); P. Tillich, *Theology of Culture*, ed. R. C. Kimball (Oxford: Oxford University Press, 1959).

A. YONG

Dalits

The Indian context

'Dalits' are specific to India. Therefore in order to address the issues of Dalit mission relevantly, the Indian context needs to be properly grasped. The 200 million (approximately) people who describe themselves as 'dalit' are those who have lived for centuries as outcasts, outside the village bounds. They have therefore no access to clean water, schools, or security, and their living areas are stacked with rubbish heaps and stinking channels that make them unhygienic places to live.

Society forces Dalits to acknowledge, accept and affirm certain notions:

(1) Dalits are polluted and are polluting because of their birth and work, as prescribed by the *dharma*: toiling in the fields of higher caste people, sweeping their streets, removing carcasses, cleaning latrines, and doing filthy, menial and other unclean tasks. They are relegated to life outside the boundaries of civilized human society as untouchables, unapproachable and useable. Due to the principle of fixity it is not possible to change one's caste.

(2) Dalits have no rights that are normally applicable to those within the bounds of human and civil society. Being outsiders they have no right to protest, demand, defy or defer.

(3) Dalits, therefore, have no right to priesthood, books or learning, no right to rule, defend or protect, no right of culture, leisure, space or hobbies.

Missiology needs to address the sad fact that Dalits have come to accept and internalize the notion of being polluted and polluting, and consequently their outcaste status of not belonging to civilized society. This has reduced them to 'no people', as they believe that they have been born under such conditions due to their own faults, which they must have committed in some previous life. Not surprisingly, many would go on further to believe that the more severe the conditions against them the greater chance they stand for a higher caste in the next life. Consequently their acceptance of servile work under humiliating, oppressive, degrading and exploitative conditions has been justified, and in some cases even considered a privilege to bear!

The issue of dignity is directly related to this. Despite a good education, better economic status and high position in the public service sector a Dalit will, nevertheless, always remain an outcaste.

Statistics

Out of 170 or 200 million Dalits, 80% live in rural areas, where they are under great pressure from ancestral oppressive customs of caste. Of these, 70% are landless labourers working in the fields of landlords, and 80% live under the poverty line, which indicates that Dalits are not paid the legally prescribed minimum wages.

Amartya Sen estimated that in India 5% of wealthy people have the advantage of having 20% of the national wealth at their disposal; 25% of the people have only 5% of this available for their needs. According to the

1991 census, 77% of Dalits, who constitute 16% of the total population of India, are landless, while 87% of the landowning Dalits are marginal landowners having two, or less than one, hectors of land. Mission strategies must take into consideration the fact that increasing national income will not improve the socio-economic condition of Dalits. It will only help to concentrate more wealth into the hands of the rich minority. However, a fair distribution of fertile and productive land could reduce the disparity between the poor Dalit and rich high-caste people.

Dalits and poverty

These statistical details reveal the fact that there is a direct relationship between Dalits and poverty. The social and customary practices in India have caused Dalits to starve, to become vulnerable to disease and insecurity, both physical and psychological, and to a higher risk of death. This is a direct result of Dalits being denied access to water, skill development, ownership of land, the means of production, availability of capital, and possession of political power. It is not surprising that this has bred psychological disorders, powerlessness, hopelessness, surrender and paranoia. This has led to a culture of silence amongst Dalits, which is how it is for all oppressed peoples in all cultures.

The plight of Dalit women

The plight of Dalit women should be taken with utmost seriousness in all mission concerns. They are thrice oppressed due to caste, class and *gender. Theirs is an unheard cry.

Given this context, Dalit missiology needs to explore the whole area of a Dalit woman's survival ability. How does she relate to the myths, stories and songs that help to sustain Dalit life and vigour? How do women subvert patriarchy and dominant cultural customs? Dalit mission will need to interconnect with these dimensions, adapting them in the light of the liberating good news of Jesus Christ. The reading of the Bible for women will have to be done by women themselves. Our missiological aim will have to be to help Dalit women regain a sense of value of their own bodies and sexuality, because their bodies have been humiliated. Along with this their children will also be a strong concern for mission. The strong bond of a mother with her children has direct consequences for body, mind and spirit.

Origins and meanings

The biblical root for Dalit is *dall*. It is a verb indicating to hang down, to be languid, weakened, low, feeble. It underscores the condition of specific groups of people. Its adjectival form *dal* has in English been simply translated as low, weak or poor. The NRSV renders the feminine plural constructed from *dalat* and *dalot* 'the poorest people of the land' and 'the poorest of the people'.

Inspiration and direction for dalit mission could be highlighted by the noun '*dala*'. This has a root meaning of 'to split', but can also mean 'a petal', and so can indicate the process of unfolding itself. From the perspective of the Dalit struggle for identity, dignity and freedom, aiming to usher in an egalitarian and just civil society against poverty, casteism, corruption, communalism and saffronization (i.e. the move towards a 'traditional' Hindu society), the growing assertion of Dalit people can be identified with the word *dala*. So Dalits are like petals unfolding their innovative powers to usher in a just and righteous society.

This biblical insight is of immense significance for mission related to Dalits, in view of the fact that the living standard of Dalits has not improved in India's post-independence era. Most of them remain landless, and the magnitude of poverty, illiteracy and unemployment is very great among Dalits. In extreme cases there are reports of humiliation and brutality, including the forced consumption of human excreta and cheap liquor, parading Dalit women naked, as well as rape, murder and burning of houses.

The significant point is that *dal* or *dalot* people, besides being economically and physically poor and weak, are psychologically impaired to the extent of becoming helpless. Unfortunately the English term 'poor' is too simple to rightly recover this deeper dimension of 'dalit'. Dalit mission would therefore engage not only with socio-economic alleviation or political emancipation, but also with the 'de-conditioning' and proper reconstruction of the Dalit psyche involving Dalit consciousness and identity. This entails enabling Dalits to explore new spiritual frameworks for setting free their inner selves from the mental complexities of inferiority, anxiety, guilt and shame.

The word *dalit* deeply resonates with another Hebrew word, '*ănāwîm*, which stands for all those who are bent ('*ānâ*) due to economic backwardness, social marginalization, mental sickness or physical handicap. *Anawim* are all those who are not merely economically deprived but who also are socially marginalized. It regards the socio-economic injustice as neither natural nor willed by God. It is regarded as an artificial condition imposed by the structures of society that need to be rejected outright. Furthermore, the exodus, along with the prophetic material and the Nazareth manifesto of Christ (Luke 4:18–21), is inspirational and corrective for Dalit missiologists. Living stories, besides the Bible, also have a very strong role to play in constructing Dalit mission theology.

What is God calling the Dalits to do?
Mission imperatives

Where is Dalit missiology? Alas, Dalit Christians have yet to begin reflection on this subject from their perspective. Presently there is no material exclusively available on this theme. However, missiological perspectives can be gleaned from the present Dalit theological literature. In this mass of literature one way to understand mission from a Dalit perspective is to perceive it as their answer, in and through Jesus the Messiah, to the stirrings of God's Spirit who is deeply involved with the painful suffering of the Dalit people and their salvation. No one else but Dalits can participate in this mission of God, because only Dalits have experienced God in the suffering which is unique to them.

It should also be kept in mind that Dalits have been deeply hurt by discrimination against them within the churches. For centuries they have been forced to sit separately from other Christians in church buildings, receive communion after higher caste Christians, and have separate grounds for burial. Dalit mission therefore will only be relevant when it takes the Dalit protest seriously both within the church as well as in the society at large. Furthermore, Dalit mission has to have a three-pronged approach. First, to *proclaim the gospel* of forgiveness, freedom and new life to all the Dalit people in every village. This involves rejecting as false both the world-view

of *karmasamsara* (successive rebirths based on karma), as well as the hierarchical society based on a caste system which claims divine origins. It involves Dalits as children of God receiving the forgiveness, freedom and dignity that God gives through Jesus as a gift of grace to all those who trust him.

Teaching will need to be related to the present Dalit realities. For instance, Dalit Christians will have to understand that the reason for their suffering in India today is due to structural discrimination that denies a Dalit Christian the privilege to be legally regarded as Dalit, which in turn leaves them with no recourse to police protection when they suffer atrocities due to their Dalit origins. Thus a Dalit who is a Christian believer is more vulnerable than they were before they were converted. Similarly, Dalit Christians suffer from other disadvantages common to all Dalits, but they have no recourse to legal compensation or preference, as they are not considered oppressed any more, in spite of the fact that conversion failed to bring about social emancipation, economic alleviation and educational progress in many Christian communities of Dalit origin. Literacy is very low among the Dalits and so literacy projects are imperative to enable people to read their Bible.

Secondly, to *live the gospel* by working hard to create solidarity among the diverse groups of Dalits both at the global and local levels. Living the gospel means nothing else but spirituality, which is related to what we should be as Dalit followers of Jesus. Missiologists must deal with the issue of Dalit identity and consciousness. This would mean encouraging Dalits to meet for study sessions to hear and to become aware of their roots contextually in Indian society and salvifically in Jesus Christ their Saviour.

In the light of the gospel the Dalits need to imbibe in their lifestyle the elements of graciousness and generosity. The aim should be to enable Dalits to repent when they adopt attitudes of laziness, callousness, inferiority, irresponsibility or complacency. Living the gospel entails a deep faith that through Dalit emancipation, oppressor castists will also be set free. At the same time living the gospel will provide the necessary support for psychological disorders arising from anxiety and frustration.

Thirdly, to *apply the gospel* with the hope of establishing justice and righteousness by demolishing the hierarchy of oppressive caste and all its atrocities and graded inequality, aiming towards the ideals of equality and generosity as enshrined in the kingdom of God. In the Indian context this takes concrete shape in the struggle of Dalit Christians to gain their equal right in the legal provisions of Reservation. Dalits know that there is no emancipation for them without destroying the whole caste system. For this reason alone Dalit identity marks itself as caste-free. A *bhangi* (sweeper) would not need to scavenge but could find alternative work. This possibility challenges caste-graded inequality, offering dignity and worth to an individual; but it also implies a consistent effort to educate and train Dalit children and youth in alternative employment skills.

Mission will have to consider a holistic approach which addresses all these needs. The programmes will be community-based due to the nature of Dalit mission, which will be for Dalits and by Dalits. This, however, does not exclude the possibility of networking with all Christians in solidarity with Dalits. Also, mission enablers will have to seriously address the psychological and pathological conditions of shame, emotional trauma and the wounded psyche of Dalits, due to endless enduring of traumatic suffering. The healing of these internal wounds would involve transforming strategies at many levels by respect, positive affirmation, worship and celebration to enable their dignity and human rights to flourish. The empowering of Dalits in all these ways involves the unwavering proclamation of God's coming kingdom of justice and peace.

Evangelical critique of Dalit theology

If Dalit mission is to be taken seriously, then a critique from an evangelical perspective is important. First, Dalits are not saved or reconciled to God by virtue of their being oppressed. Secondly, not everything associated with Dalits needs to be accepted and accommodated, but in the light of the gospel they need to be liberated from all superstitions and world-views that re-enforce their bondage. Thirdly, Dalit mission is not limited to social and economic improvement, but has to do with emancipation of hearts and minds

resulting from a firm faith that in Christ they are worthy children of God.

Dalit churches should be founded on sound biblical teaching, yet incorporating the cultural elements of language, lyrics, dress, buildings, interior decor, symbols and so on. Biblical reflection should be from among the people and their experience of suffering and rejection. This does not entail falling in line with a specific Western approach, but it is to be hoped that Western churches would eventually recognize the genuineness of these Dalit churches in coming years, and extend the hand of fellowship to them.

See also CASTE; POOR/POVERTY.

Bibliography

M. Grey, *The Unheard Scream* (Noida, India: VODI, Academy Press, 2004); D. Haslam, *Caste Out* (London: CTBI, 1999); H. Johannes, *Exodus of the Broken People* (New Delhi: Netphen KAIROS India, 2000); J. Massey, *Towards Dalit Hermeneutics* (Delhi: ISPCK, 1994); J. Massey, *Current Challenges and the Church's Response* (New Delhi: NICR Publication, 1998); J. C. B. Webster, *Religion and Dalit Liberation* (Delhi: Manohar, 2002).

M. DANIEL

Democracy

Democracy means government by the people for the people. It makes government accountable by giving its citizens ultimate control of those ruling them, either directly or indirectly through elected representatives. It is accountable to values and truths that transcend regimes or parties; it protects and values the individuals and institutions that form the society; and it is an open-ended process that does not claim to provide all the answers to society's problems, but allows space for open debate and self-criticism. Its vision inspires hope for a society in which all people are truly equal, free and just, and yet where difference is respected, social responsibility prevails and the gulf between rich and poor is overcome.

The historical relationship between democracy and Christianity

The relationship between Christianity and

democracy has fluctuated historically, sometimes ambiguous and even hostile. Often democracy was not necessarily compatible with historical churches (Roman Catholic and Eastern Orthodox) which espoused tendencies toward hierarchy and absolutism. However, Christianity has often embraced the democratic values of freedom, individual conscience, and human rights as compatible with the gospel, arguing that fundamental principles inherent in democracy can be traced back to the Christian tradition as it unfolded over centuries. These include, among others, the egalitarian communal experience of the early church as a model for modern emphases on social equality. The notion of subsidiarity and common good are said to have developed amidst the interaction between medieval Christianity and Aristotelian political philosophy. Also, concepts like the individual's dignity, human rights, freedom of conscience or religious tolerance may be traced back to the radical Reformation, English non-conformity and North American liberal Protestantism.

The dawn of the European Enlightenment and the French Revolution brought a major change of perspective. Because the thrust of the French Revolution was anticlerical and sometimes anti-Christian in character, European democracy became a political expression of secularism and atheism. This was different from Britain where the nonconformists were supporters of democratic governance; and the United States, where Christianity was formative to the constitution of the new American republic. Nevertheless, in the European countries under Catholic, Orthodox and mainline Protestant Christianity, the nineteenth-century state churches tended to eschew democracy, as it was perceived to undermine their role as the moral guardians of the nation.

During the twentieth century, having experienced the failure of the Fascist, Nazi and Communist totalitarianisms, churches began to develop a new appreciation for democracy. On the political scene, the defeat of Germany in war was recognized as a victory for democracy, and led to the establishment of democratic governments in most of the defeated countries as well as across countries formerly under colonial rule. By the 1990s, the collapse of the Eastern bloc brought about the transition of many formerly communist countries to democratic forms of governance. Passive sufferers or active militants against totalitarian regimes, churches became supporters of democratization. The examples of South Africa and the role of the ecumenical church in the Truth and Reconciliation Commission, or the role played by the Catholic church in Poland or by evangelical churches in Eastern Europe, have shown that they can make a crucial contribution to democracy.

Liberal democracies in particular have offered a political form of organization that Christians have welcomed. A form of representative democracy where the political power of the government is moderated by a constitution that protects the rights and freedoms of individuals and minorities, democracy ensures a moral basis for respect and fairness for all, tolerating and protecting those spheres within which people find meaning for their lives. Unlike totalitarian forms of government, liberal democracy seeks to affirm the protection of all human rights – personal, civil, political, economic and social. Churches support democracy because it sustains the freedom for religious faith and practice, which entails, for example, freedom to believe, to worship, to teach, to evangelize, to collaborate in works of mercy, and to witness to the public good.

Evangelicals and democracy

Evangelical churches in particular relate to democracy mainly in terms of *their own* religious equality and freedom, often with little regard for the democratic process in its entirety. This is true of the Latin American context, where the struggle for religious equality was carried out with a dual purpose: to gain freedom of action in the religious sphere, and to secure equality of treatment in the public sphere. An emphasis on ethnicity and national identity is more often found in the context of evangelical missions in Africa, parts of Asia and Eastern Europe. In Eastern Europe, evangelical mission emphasized religious equality in the context of dominant churches such as Catholic and Orthodox, which attempted to limit their 'sectarian' activities. Under Communism, evangelicals existed as dissident religious denominations, and remained strong in spite of a very controlled freedom of propagation. The political changes in the early nineties opened the door for an evangelical attempt to gain equality of civil status with the dominant church and equal space in the public sphere. The search for equal treatment from government and the law as the majority religion of the country often sums up the reason for evangelical presence in politics. However, their support for laws and policies that benefit larger denominations like themselves, but are utterly discriminatory against unrecognized religious minorities (Seventh-Day Adventists, Jehovah's Witnesses, Greek Catholics, etc.), is indicative of a deficient understanding of religious freedom.

Nevertheless, a commitment to religious plurality and equality ensures a democratic culture and helps overcome the hegemonic tendencies of the state churches. Evangelical churches offer a free social space, a new personality and responsible participation in, and solidarity with, the civil community. Evangelical mission has an important role in moralizing democracy by means of the Christian message, which brings about values and virtues first in individuals and then in civil society. Evangelicals can revitalize civil society through their support of voluntary associations, which intrinsically promote plurality and democracy. In most countries from Central and Eastern Europe that have joined or are in the process of joining the European Union, the contribution that these religious bodies can bring is crucial to developing a pluralist mentality which is suitable for an international community that cuts across religious and ethnic boundaries and liberates societies from xenophobia, national extremism and religious domination.

Evangelical churches in the countries from the Eastern bloc have been less influential in helping the process of *transition* to democracy as they are to the process of *consolidating* that democracy. Major social and political changes undergone by Romanian society over the fifteen years of transition from totalitarianism have found evangelicals retreating to a soul-saving mandate with no regard for the surrounding society. With their foreign originating roots, evangelicals were accepted with difficulty at the dialogue table in a context characterized by the rise of nationalism with ethnicity closely linked to religious identity. As in other places in Eastern Europe,

being a Romanian meant being Orthodox, just as being a Croat meant being Catholic. However, particularly because of the freedom evangelical churches enjoy from nationalist tendencies that are prevailing in the historical churches, they can become an essential asset to developing a pluralist mentality suitable for a democratic society.

Responsibilities for the church's mission

Reinhold Niebuhr wrote: 'Man's capacity for justice makes democracy possible, but man's inclination to injustice makes democracy necessary.' Liberal democracy can stress the importance of human freedom to the detriment of social responsibility. Churches' support for democracy therefore should be critical and prophetical in character, stressing the need for a society in which individual needs and rights are not pursued at the expense of the community. There are limitations in any democratic system, whose utopian vision will never be fulfilled and realized by a human form of government. The church is pledged to the growth of the *kingdom of God proclaimed by Jesus Christ, and consequently maintains a critical distance from all the governments of the world and from any social, political or economic order.

In transitional societies, religious commitment often leads to intolerance towards others, reinforcing social and political divisions. The church should promote a culture of tolerance, respect and mutual understanding, first among Christians and then in relation to other religious communities. This is crucial in parts of the world like the Middle East where democratization is often perceived as a Western cultural imposition. These attempts at bringing a Western form of democracy must take into account the cultural differences that exist between Western countries and the Arab states. For newly founded constitutional governments to survive and for democracy to succeed in the Arab states, there is a need not just for effective checks and balances, a free press and independent judiciary – which may take a long time to evolve – but also for dialogue between Muslim and religious minorities.

Democracy is a human form of political organization which does not determine or define Christian freedom. The freedom of the church is derived from faithfulness to God's justice and the implications this has to the prophetic witness to human justice and equity. Only in exercising this freedom is the church contributing and supporting the establishment or the consolidation of the democratic social order.

See also POLITICS/STATE.

Bibliography
J. W. De Gruchy, *Christianity and Democracy: A Theology for a Just World Order* (Cambridge: Cambridge University Press, 1995); J. W. De Gruchy, 'Democracy' in P. Scott and W. T. Cavanaugh (eds.), *The Blackwell Companion to Political Theology* (Oxford: Blackwell Publishing Ltd, 2004); P. Freston, *Evangelicals and Politics in Asia, Africa and Latin America* (Cambridge: Cambridge University Press, 2001); R. Plant, *Politics, Theology and History* (Cambridge: Cambridge University Press, 2001); C. Villa-Vicencio, *A Theology of Reconstruction: Nation-building and Human Rights* (Cambridge: Cambridge University Press, 1992).

C. ROMOCEA

DEMONS, see SPIRITUAL WARFARE

Development

Development is applied mainly to socio-cultural and economic processes, although it is also commonly used in psychology or biophysics. There has been much criticism of the inadequacy and limitations of the term to describe or represent appropriate social situations. However, it seems that the term still appears frequently, as no other 'graceful' one has been discovered to replace it; this is, perhaps, because of its great capacity to represent dynamics, processes, and comparative situations in organic/social bodies or entities.

In the last fifty years there has been a wide spectrum of secular research and study, resulting in the interdisciplinary area of 'Development Studies', which integrates perspectives from the sciences (natural and social), humanities and arts. Perspectives on development can be global/macro (including integrated studies of society) or partial/micro (communal, local or sectoral – economic, political, educational, agricultural, rural, urban, etc.). Here we adopt a global focus with a panoramic and integrated view. We will try to synthesize ideas coming from up-to-date debates, before we connect with Christian mission and theological reflection.

Secular and technical perspectives on development: a brief history
The concept and its origin
The classical discourse on development as promoting welfare in poor regions, countries or localities had its origins in Western countries during the late 1940s and was institutionalized in the 1950s and 1960s. This discourse on development included security issues in the context of the Cold War, and viewed global poverty (see *Poor) and 'underdevelopment' as a threat to the liberal world order. An interdisciplinary field of studies emerged, containing a set of theoretical cores with development economics as the leading discipline of the group.

Main orientations up to the 1980s
The most important theoretical schools on the hermeneutics of development until the 1980s have been: modernization, structuralism, dependency and 'alternative development', all normatively concerned with the specific problem of national development in the so-called 'Third World'.

In *modernization theory*, lack of development was defined in terms of differences between rich and poor nations. Development implied the bridging of the gap by the less developed countries imitating and gradually assuming the qualities of the developed; state-led investment, technology and education were critical factors.

For *structuralism*, a certain amount of intervention was considered necessary, due to institutional conditions which made growth in the poor areas less automatic than it was assumed to be in the so-called developed countries. From the late 1960s modernization theory and structuralism were confronted by the Latin American *dependencia* school (a neo-Marxist interpretation), which, together with the more global *world system theory*, articulated the weak structural position of Third World countries in the world system. The 'dependentists' asked for radical transformation, emphasizing more 'autonomy' by 'delinking' their economies from the world market.

In contrast, the *alternative development* school tried to emphasize some features which appeared across history in successful civilizations, as counterpoints to the modernist view. They suggested development should arise from within the context and be need-oriented, self-reliant, ecologically sound and based on structural transformation. These emphases were proposed to improve the real conditions of people who usually were excluded in the mainstream discourse. Along with elevating environmental consciousness a cousin of *alternative development* appeared called *sustainable development*, affecting every policy and understood as the way to fulfil present human needs without endangering the lives and opportunities of future generations.

Paradigm changes in the last two decades

Recent understanding of development has changed in many aspects, except in its normative concern for the emancipation of the underprivileged from inequality, poverty and domination. In the last twenty years, the most important changes in development studies can in fact be traced to a crisis of two main paradigms:

(1) The nation-state and the political and scientific confidence in this to realize progress; against this emphasis was put on *globalization and the dismantling of the state.

(2) The Enlightenment concepts of progress and the 'makeability' of society; against this emphasis was put on the postmodern critique of the 'grand narrative'.

Beginning in the1980s and deepening in the 1990s, *globalization*, as influenced by neo-liberal economic policies, became the new word for mainstream development. 'Globalization' as a development ideology implies the growth of a world market, increasingly penetrating and dominating 'national' economies. In contrast with the interventionist bias of former schools, the globalists consider that too much government is a big systematic mistake. Good governance is then defined as less government. Development aid has been reduced to a civil form of intervention by a complex of humanitarian agencies.

Postmodern theory, which dominates cultural studies, is deconstructing and relativizing development theory, which was after all a child of the Enlightenment. This makes the whole concept of 'development' rather meaningless. As a result the so-called '*post-development*' current has emerged in which the concept of 'development' itself is rejected because it is seen as the 'new religion' of the West; it is the imposition of science as power; it means cultural westernisation and homogenization; it brings environmental destruction; and in reality it does not work. But 'development' is rejected not merely on account of its results but because of its intentions, its world-view and mindset. The economic mindset implies a reductionist view of existence: it is said that 'it is not the fail ure of development which has to be feared, but its success'! Additionally, as development has operated as a discourse of power/knowledge to construct the hierarchical relationship between the First World and the Third World, it is said that 'the dream of development must be over, what is required is not more "development", but a different regime of truth and perception'. It is relationships of power/knowledge that are themselves constitutive of global inequality. Thus, in relation to culture and identity, the North Atlantic development thinking involving catching up and imitation must be abandoned in favour of an inclusive, liberating process, in which different world-views are included and constitute a dialogical process. This new emphasis on culture may constitute the greatest challenge to rethinking development.

The development predicament: the disjunction between theory and practice

In spite of their limitations, each theory has contributed in some way to a better understanding. None has a monopoly on 'truth', and none wholly excludes the others. Some consider that in the context of the dialogical climate opened by postmodernism itself, the differences are more of perspective, emphases and value judgment. However, what is really needed is to reinforce the link between theory and practice adequately; between grand theory, intermediate theory and baseline frameworks. The critical problem of 'implementation' of development policy requires a system where theory and practice form an inseparable unit, dynamically adapted to the degree of social development of the society whose political contradictions are seen to be resolved.

Mission and development
Theology, ethics and development
'Development' as a human endeavour with the purpose of personal, communal, national or international transformation falls into the sphere of social *ethics, which concerns social structures based on a particular world-view. Therefore, a biblical theology of development presupposes a biblical world-view about the cosmos, life and history, and, in contrast with secular perspectives on development, will also include the spiritual dimension (see *Culture).

Christian social ethics is therefore critical reflection on the social praxis of faith. It is founded on Scripture, and takes into account the history and tradition of the church and the particular historical situations in which the people of God exist. Mission, theology and development are then inseparable from a biblical perspective on communal and public life as it is reflected in economics, politics, education and social welfare, arts or religion. Scriptural values come from a world-view that includes a holistic perspective of human life, from the creation narratives to the eschatological vision of new creation. It is all interpreted now from the viewpoint of the gospel, which is the redemptive purpose of God for all creation in Jesus Christ. Practically, Christian ethical reflection articulates God's kingdom values in human history as a contribution to transformation and the common welfare of society, until the second coming of the Lord.

The creation narratives explain the nature of the physical world and of human life, its sustainability and responsibilities at the physical and biological level. The social nature of humanity points to the relational and corporative nature of human existence. If we add to those intrinsic characteristics the special faculties such as reason, freedom, moral responsibility and spirituality, then clearly 'social responsibility' is a matter of the substance of human existence, and therefore an unavoidable dimension of Christian ethics. This should prevent dichotomous arguments between social commitment on the one hand and Christian life, ethics and mission on the other. There is no arbitrary distinction between social ethics and mission, as if ethics were merely a consequence of mission. We cannot separate mission from the cultural mandate of creation, since the latter reinforces the substantiality of social responsibility and development as integral to a Christian perspective on life and therefore on mission in the world.

A biblical theology of development also acknowledges the reality of evil, and an imperfect and sinful humanity needing holistic transformation. The fall brought with it social evil, with both human and supernatural powers operating to destroy creation, social fabric and human integrities. To take seriously the reality of sin and its consequences in society implies a commitment to transformation from God's perspective. Therefore, the transformative action of God in the world affirms that Christian ethics is based on divine grace, which counteracts the consequences of the fall. Active Christian ethics corresponds to the action of the grace of God. God's grace precedes Christian ethics. So Christian social actions are expressions based on the grace of God.

Continuing in this vein, God expresses his grace best through his immeasurable love. Thus, Christian ethics is based in love and this should be the generator of Christian development. This attitude should involve all human work and efforts as the Earth's stewards and developers of culture and social life. For this reason, God's grace is also expressed categorically in justice, his justice. The God of love and justification is the same God who has established justice as a cornerstone of his throne and demands justice. We have the commandment to do justice and struggle for justice, especially on behalf of the oppressed. Justice in society is fundamental for peace, true welfare and progress. This goes to the heart of the kingdom of God, his rule and purpose in history, without which a biblical perspective of society and its transformation cannot be understood.

The church is then the community of the *kingdom, the alternative community with an eschatological nature which embraces and incarnates kingdom values as well as being instrumental in God's strategy for promoting his kingdom in this world. Christian development necessarily implies the active participation of the Christian community with a true eschatological perspective which does not promote escapism, but commitment with kingdom values in history, here and now.

However, the grace of God is not only

channelled through the Christian community, since the sovereign purposes of God in history transcend the institutional church. The common grace of God continues operating through all his creatures. Therefore, although we need a specific Christian theological and ethical focus for 'Christian' development, we must take into account technical knowledge coming from specialized disciplines such as development studies. Indeed, knowledge in every field is part of our cultural mandate and comes from the common grace of God. Thus, it is impossible not to recognize that every main development theory, and also experiences coming from non-Christian societies, have in some way contributed to illuminate part of the problem of poverty, inequality and human indignity. The question is how we use all these contributions in a carefully evaluated and sifted, integrative and constructive manner to reflect kingdom values.

Important trends from the 1950s onwards
There are those who acknowledge the special contribution of Louis Lebret from within the Catholic tradition, who advocated a 'human economics' against a reductionist view of mere economic growth. Human factors were essential, and more important than economic factors. 'To *have* more' needed to harmonize with 'to *be* more'. Authentic development should be holistic, promoting all people and the whole person. Also, with J. M. Aubert, development should be *unified* (including all humanity), and *in solidarity* with others. From an ethical-theological point of view, development also implies *salvation*. In the 1970s, the Latin American theology of liberation criticized the idea of development as overburdened with ambiguities and contradictions. An alternative framework proposed a global, creative, biblical approach, open to a transcendent process of social change: *liberation*. Problematic for many was their use of neo-Marxist theory when interpreting social problems and implementing social change.

On the Protestant side, the ecumenical movement has been very near to Catholic thinking, with parallel developments and contributions, especially between the 1960s to 1980s. Evangelicalism had to overcome the 'great reversal' which had arisen out of the fundamentalist-modernist controversy and had reversed a long missionary tradition of including social welfare as a dimension of mission. A process of clarification started in the late fifties, which reached a covenanted theological climax at the International Congress on Evangelization at Lausanne (1974). Social ethics and the social responsibility of the church were welcomed again as an expression of Christian mission. At Wheaton in 1983 a new term and concept emerged: '*transformation*', to be understood by evangelicals as a holistic perspective, following Catholics and ecumenical perspectives. It is now recognized that social sciences and related disciplines help us understand what is at stake when we talk of 'social transformation' and its connectedness with holistic spirituality. However, due to the atomistic nature of Protestantism and evangelicalism, a spectrum of understandings and modalities of projection exist when assuming 'social responsibility' as part of the mission of the church – from those with a mere philanthropic and paternalist approach to those involved in the struggles for justice, human rights and hard confrontation with power structures.

Conclusions
Christian development will seek integration at every level. Integrating theory and practice is a common problem for Christian life and mission. Theorists and practitioners need to recognize that development involves the permanent and eternal relationship between humanity and our natural and social environment. So even with sound theological frameworks, the elements of success, risk, failure and future possibilities, as well as limitations and new problems, must be considered as natural outcomes of the process. Therefore, we must evolve a less triumphalist approach to theorizing and policy making, *a priori* and *a posteriori* of the practice of development, which will in turn be the source for new theoretical and practical elaborations.

Christian service in the practice of development will try honestly to search for truth and wisdom to better serve and love our neighbour, and will therefore take seriously the lessons that can be learnt from the historical dynamic between theory and practice.

Christians can agree with many of the insights of experienced developmentalists:

there were errors, false starts and dead ends in recent decades; however, not all difficulties are the result of past mistakes. Deficiencies often lie with human attitudes, social institutions and political power structures, more than or as well as, with scarcities of productive inputs and their convenient allocation. As a 'second generation' of problems arises we may feel the hopelessness of all our endeavours. Realistically there are no simple remedies or solutions readily transferable between places and periods. Often only a concerted, properly phased, integrated approach from several directions yields results. But a Christian perspective is one of hope and new beginnings, living within the tension between the 'now' and the 'not yet' of the kingdom, and reaching forward to the full realization of our humanity in Christ.

In the case of Latin America the challenge for the evangelical church is to implement a truly holistic mission. This implies integrating the work of evangelization and church growth with a consistent discipleship which understands Christian social ethics, and also a sacrificial and thoughtful service which confronts the vast social problems, especially the extended poverty and acute inequality. Evangelicals are only around 12% of the continent's population, but growth needs to be qualitative as well as quantitative to be a force for transformation as an authentic Christianity. Even where evangelical growth is up to 30%, as in Guatamala, it seems that very little of this is happening. Also a thoughtful, informed and intelligent action is needed which understands the technical nature of social, economic and cultural transformations. When evangelicals occasionally occupy public positions, no meaningful contribution is given. Finally, the social impact of evangelicals cannot happen unless they understand the ethical imperative of unified action. As it is, there is an atomized Protestant spectrum which needs a strong coordinating will to pull it together. These efforts should extend to other sectors of Christianity and society, so that they can be effective in developing the quality of life of Latin Americans, in line with kingdom values.

Bibliography

J. K. Black, *Development in Theory and Practice: Paradigms and Paradoxes* (Boulder, CO: Westview Press, 1999); J. Brohman, *Popular Development: Rethinking the Theory and Practice of Development* (Oxford: Blackwell, 1996); S. Corbridge (ed.), *Development Studies: A Reader* (London: Arnold, 1995); M. P. Cowen and R. W. Shenton, *Doctrines of Development* (London & New York: Routledge, 1996); E. J. Elliston, *Christian Relief and Development* (Dallas: Word Publishing, 1989); S. Mott, *Biblical Ethics and Social Change* (Oxford: Oxford University Press, 1985); R. Padilla and C. Sugden, *How Evangelicals Endorsed Social Responsibility* (Nottingham: Grove Books Ltd, 1985); V. Samuel and C. Sugden (eds.), *Mission as Transformation: A Theology of the Whole Gospel* (Carlisle: Regnum, 1999); S. Schech and J. Haggis, *Development: A Cultural Studies Reader* (Oxford: Blackwell, 2002); R. Sider (ed.), *Evangelicals and Development: Towards a Theology of Social Change* (Exeter: Paternoster Press, 1981); D. Vandana and R. B. Potter (eds.), *The Companion to Development Studies* (London: Arnold, 2002).

H. F. BULLON

DEVIL, see SPIRITUAL WARFARE

Dialogue

The need for dialogue

Dialogue can be defined as a conversation which proceeds both from a commitment to one's own faith and an openness with genuine respect to that of others. Openness and respect do not presuppose agreement, or a search for a compromise, but do mean the willingness to listen. Recognition of another religious tradition as a 'faith' does not imply an equivalence or an acceptance of validity. But dialogue does involve a desire to understand those of another faith better and learn from one another, an attitude that leads to an ongoing reflection on one's own faith and practice. It also promotes mutual knowledge and friendship that leads to the correction of prejudices toward others. It is a relatively recent paradigm in the field of mission theology and has especially come to the fore within ecumenism as discussion on religious plurality has developed.

The need for dialogue with people of other faiths arises from the fact that increasingly we live in multi-religious societies, and different religious traditions must coexist in harmony. People of different religious traditions face the common problems of contemporary society, such as conflicts, injustice, spiritual deprivation, ecological crisis, moral and ethical dehumanization, and they also encounter the common challenge of secularism and modern and postmodern criticisms of religion. Dialogue is recognition of the need for religions to cooperate to face these difficulties. Furthermore, people of faith have a shared search for the answers to questions such as the meaning of life, salvation, religious truth, and life beyond the physical realm. Dialogue is also an attempt to help one another in our religious quests, while acknowledging that each religious tradition has its own historical development, takes different approaches to questions, and provides different answers.

Models of dialogue
Dialogue as the context for witness
Evangelical perspectives on dialogue have been well represented by John Stott in his book, *Christian Mission in the Modern World*. He represented evangelical concerns about an ambiguity in the relationship between dialogue, as understood in the ecumenical movement, and evangelism. He argued that dialogue can be understood as a vital aspect of Christian mission as long as, first, it is understood in line with the primary task of Christian *witness to the people of other faiths and, second, in relation to the first, that it is understood that, because of Christian conviction, total openness to the other religions is incompatible with the Christian gospel. He also raised objection to *proclamation being portrayed as the result of pride (with dialogue therefore preferred as a humble approach), insisting that proclamation can be done with humility. He further questioned whether people who hold strong convictions can approach others with an attitude of total openness without compromising their own integrity as Christians. Though Stott agreed on the importance of dialogue as a mark of authenticity, humility, integrity and sensitivity, he insisted it was in the context of Christian witness that dialogue should be understood, and this is an approach generally accepted amongst many evangelicals.

Dialogue as theological discourse
Theology of dialogue has been developed particularly from the multi-religious context of the Indian subcontinent, where religion has sometimes provoked violent clashes between different communities. E. Stanley Jones, a well-known Methodist missionary to India, explored the idea of a round table conference where people of different faiths could gather to share their own religious experiences without confronting each other or trying to persuade others to change their convictions. In his book, *The Christ of the Indian Road*, Jones stressed that Christians presented a Christ to India who is not a Western import but was there in India before them. He said that the aim of his mission was 'to produce Christlike character' not to Westernize India, and he discerned a regeneration of Indian life through an, as yet unrecognized, experience of Christ. For him, dialogue with people of other faiths was a vital component of this discernment of Christ already present in India and he therefore saw dialogue as the metaphor for theological discourse.

Dialogue as a mutual search for truth
Drawing on his own experience as an Indian, Stanley Samartha developed the concept of dialogue further in the World Council of Churches. He defined it as an attempt to understand ourselves in relation to the spiritual heritage of the faith of our neighbours. His theology is based in his understanding that God's covenant with Israel, and also Christ's incarnation, demonstrate the dialogical relationship between God and his people. A natural expansion of this understanding is that the relationship between different religious communities should be a form of mutual dialogue, rather than confrontation. Samartha draws his theology from the Indian multi-religious setting, from Indian philosophical approaches of finding truth by consensus, and from an attitude of acknowledging others as partners on the way rather than imposing one's own truth claims onto others. In his approach, mutual respect should take place in community, creating a 'community of communities'. He also suggested that dialogue among world religions was an opportunity to work together to discover new dimensions of religious truths.

From an evangelical perspective, Vinoth Ramachandra criticized Samartha's approach as relativistic and accused him of being too ready to negotiate away the distinctive claims of Christianity. Nevertheless, this idea of mutual search for the truth was taken up by the WCC and became a major plank of ecumenical mission theology, as explained in the document *Guidelines on Dialogue with People of Living Faiths and Ideologies*. Warning that religious communities may often become exclusive and absolutize their own religious and cultural identity, this document promoted dialogue in the spirit of reconciliation and hope provided by Christ. *Ecumenical Considerations for Dialogue and Relations with People of Other Religions* takes account of the recent development of fundamentalism. It insists that dialogue not only reconciles conflicting communities, but also prevents religion becoming the source of tension between communities in the first place.

Dialogue as a way of living together

Faced with a vast diversity of religious and cultural communities in the Indian context and the problem of communal conflicts, some Indian theologians have developed a pragmatic approach of living together alongside the philosophical approach of searching for truth and goodness together. Because of criticism of dialogue as an intellectual exercise – too academic and artificial – they now recognize that dialogue can be a grass-roots activity of ordinary people who share their religious stories and celebrations with one another. Whether or not it is possible for fellow citizens of different religions to reach agreement on ultimate questions, it is still necessary to work together on the socio-cultural, political and economic problems that arise in living together. Lesslie Newbigin, for example, argued that Christians should be willing to engage in projects in society which are in line with a Christian understanding of God's purpose in history, and that true dialogue occurs in this 'shared commitment' to the world. Some theologians may regard plurality as a blessing rather than an obstacle to harmony, and see active engagement in dialogue with neighbours of other faiths, with respect, as part and parcel of, if not essential to, any religious life.

Dialogue and mission

The question of dialogue remains entwined with how we view other faiths. Engaging in dialogue with people of other faiths requires the theological presupposition that 'God has not left himself without witness' in all cultures and their religious traditions. If 'all truth is God's truth' then there is something of that truth, however distorted, in all human witness to divine revelation. Much evangelical discussion has concentrated on this prior question of the relation between religions and truth, and here opinion is divided. Harold Netland, on the one hand, states that religious diversity is a result of the fall and of sin, and therefore follows Hendrik Kraemer in denying the benefit of any religion, and hence of inter-religious dialogue. Amos Yong, on the other hand, argues from the event of Pentecost that diversity is part of God's intention for humankind, and that it may be possible to identify the signs of the Spirit in other religions. Yong is therefore open to what Christians may receive from those of other faiths, while also striving to maintain an evangelical theology.

If other religions have received a revelation of God in any respect, there is a further question of whether or not there may be salvation in other religions. Lesslie Newbigin rejected the notion of other religions as vehicles of salvation, affirmed the uniqueness of God's work in Jesus Christ, and yet insisted on the need for dialogue, conducted with humility and yet with 'confidence in the Gospel'. David Bosch argued that there is a paradox between the universal saving intention of God and the necessity of the Christian message being proclaimed. He believed dialogue cannot be conducted with a completely 'open mind' because, in Christ, the way to salvation has been manifested for Christians. Witnessing to this conviction is part and parcel of dialogue. But Christians cannot presume to know the mind of God fully, therefore dialogue should be conducted, not with the attitude of a judge or lawyer, but of a witness in the spirit of 'bold humility'. There is therefore a tension in Christian mission, which Bosch and others recognize, between dialogue and proclamation, which may best be described as 'commitment to one's faith and openness to that of others'.

The Lausanne Covenant (1974) rejected dialogue, if it 'implies that Christ speaks equally through all religions and ideologies', but dialogue does not necessarily imply this. Dialogue is a theological paradigm which has made a significant contribution to the practical life of religious communities in general and in mission theology in particular. It is also an important theological tool to be employed in contemporary multi-religious societies. Calling for authentic dialogue is not an optional extra but a necessary concept to be explored creatively, and yet critically, by Christians who are engaged in mission.

Bibliography

D. Bosch, *Transforming Mission* (Maryknoll: Orbis Books, 1991); E. S. Jones, *The Christ of the Indian Road* (Whitefish: Kessinger Publishing Co., 2005 [1925]); H. Kraemer, *The Christian Message in a Non-Christian World* (New York: Harper, 1938); H. Netland, *Encountering Religious Pluralism: The Challenge to Christian Faith and Mission* (Downers Grove: InterVarsity Press, 2001); L. Newbigin, *The Gospel in a Pluralist Society* (Grand Rapids: Eerdmans, 1989); V. Ramachandra, *The Recovery of Mission: Beyond the Pluralist Paradigm* (Carlisle: Paternoster, 1996); S. Samartha, *Courage for Dialogue: Ecumenical Issues in Inter-Religious Relationships* (Maryknoll: Orbis Books, 1981); J. R. W. Stott, *Christian Mission in the Modern World* (Leicester: IVP, 1975); WCC, *Guidelines on Dialogue with People of Living Faiths and Ideologies* (Geneva: WCC, 1979); WCC, *My Neighbour's Faith – and Mine: Theological Discoveries through Interfaith Dialogue* (Geneva: WCC, 1986); WCC, *Ecumenical Considerations for Dialogue and Relations with People of Other Religions* (Geneva: WCC, 2001); A. Yong, *Beyond the Impasse: Toward a Pneumatological Theology of Religions* (Grand Rapids: Baker Academic, 2003).

S. C. H. KIM

Disciple

If they are to follow Jesus' teaching, each generation of disciples must continue the work of mission, balancing the need to testify to the kingdom of God in their own context, with the need to make disciples in the wider world.

Jesus and his disciples

Jesus' role as teacher (rabbi), is shaped by his own self-understanding, the OT background and the first-century world of Judaism. The title 'disciple' was applied to the twelve, whose call was an important dimension of their identity, but it was also used of those who travelled and associated with Jesus. The disciples of Jesus have certain distinctives: they are witnesses to Jesus and his resurrection, not simply 'custodians of insight'; they have authority from Jesus; and as they look forward to his coming again, they are prepared to share in his suffering. Discipleship is seen as a calling and a commitment for life – it involves more than simply a conversion experience of belief and faith in Jesus Christ.

The Gospels stress Jesus' relationship to his disciples and their interaction with him, as a critical starting-point for mission (e.g. Mark 3:14) (see *NT perspectives on mission). A relationship with Jesus is a vital aspect of discipleship and must be nurtured and cultivated both for Christian maturity and the development of an authentic witness.

Matthew's Gospel

David Bosch sees Matthew's Gospel, in particular, as important for its portrayal of 'mission as disciple-making' (*Transforming Mission*, pp. 36–41, 56–83). The idea that disciples are to take righteousness seriously is expressed in the Sermon on the Mount (Matt. 5 – 7) and is sustained throughout the Gospel. The centrality of Jesus' preaching of the gospel of the *kingdom frames this discourse (Matt. 4:23; 9:35); it recurs elsewhere (particularly in Matt. 13, 18 – 19, 21 – 24) and it highlights the 'inherent universal and missionary character of the kingdom ministry of Jesus'.

The great commission

The command to 'make disciples' of all nations is the principal imperative verb in Matthew 28:18–20, and provides the link between the first disciples and future disciples: 'the followers of the earthly Jesus have to make others into what they themselves are: disciples' (Bosch, *Transforming Mission*, p. 74). This commission is therefore a pivotal passage connecting discipleship and mission, although it needs to be read in the context of the whole of Matthew, where there are many elements of discipleship which relate Christian life to society. It is in the context of this depiction of 'costly discipleship' that disciples of Jesus are to continue to make disciples of others. This process will not be limited to Jewish people, but will spread out to embrace people of all nations.

Disciples in the church and society

What this means today can be illustrated from Asian contexts. The Centre for the Study of Christianity in Asia (CSCA) in Singapore has a legitimate concern for a spirituality that is appropriate for Asia and for disciples who have established a genuine Asian Christian identity.

Living in multi-cultural and pluralistic societies, disciples in Asia need to be sure of their identity as followers of Jesus so that they are able to recognize kingdom values and to dialogue with the many different discourses of 'Asian values'. Sometimes concern is expressed that this is not always happening and that 'the pressures of the context have subverted the discipleship of the church' (V. Samuel, *The Meaning and Cost of Discipleship*, p. 66). There is a desire that churches see discipleship as integral to Christian life and that the disciples of Jesus show that kingdom values are applicable to present-day societies by living out those values. Without such an understanding of discipleship, there is a concern that evangelism and mission will spread a gospel which is diminished and which will fail to address the spiritual and social needs of contemporary Asia.

During the International Congress on World Evangelization (ICOWE) at Lausanne in 1974, the tension between authentic Christian discipleship and the expansion of the church surfaced in other regions of the world. McGavran stressed the importance and priority of evangelization and discipling of the nations with an emphasis on church multiplication. By contrast, Latin American theologians such as Padilla and Escobar were concerned to show that the quality of Christian life demonstrated by disciples of Jesus is a *prerequisite* for authentic evangelism. The ICOWE statement on radical discipleship and the subsequent writings of its adherents in the 1980s show that this tension between social presence and evangelization continues

to be an issue for disciples of Jesus engaging in mission in the modern world.

In Asia, writers such as Maggay write about the 'politics of discipleship'. The possibility that 'discipleship is a dance of death' is a reminder of what the cost of discipleship can be for those who seek to promote justice (M. Maggay, *Transforming Society*, pp. 12, 40, 79). For Maggay, the role of the local church is not to specialize in these activities but to focus on 'nurturing disciples' through the traditional activities of word and sacrament and sharing the gospel through communities. Disciples of Jesus can be involved in the shaping of civil society through their vocational expertise, and in this way disciples can participate in shaping the world of work and the global marketplace with kingdom values.

The importance of the disciple's relationship with Jesus and his or her experience of the cross and resurrection is highlighted by Ramachandra. The lifestyle of Jesus himself is a model for disciples in its 'vulnerability'. By drawing on Johannine perspectives on discipleship (John 12:23–26; 17; 20:21–23), Ramachandra shows that because disciples of Jesus are 'not of this world' they are capable of risking all in the cause of Jesus' service. Jesus' focus on 'two principles of dying and loving', rather than specific strategies or methods of mission, remains as an enduring challenge. Disciples need to take seriously Jesus' desire that his followers make disciples and impart '*all* that I have commanded you'. Superficial notions of evangelism and conversion are to be discouraged and discipleship is to be envisaged as a kingdom lifestyle.

Disciples in the wider world

Each Christian community must present and live out an authentic version of Christian discipleship in its own context as well as being concerned with the wider world. Such a vision of discipleship is presented in Luke–Acts. The disciples of Jesus are told 'You will be my witnesses in Jerusalem, and in all Judea and Samaria, and to the ends of the earth' (Acts 1:8). This is a reminder that discipleship takes place between the local and the global. All disciples are called to be faithful in their own contexts living out the good news of the kingdom. At the same time, the global church must grapple with the issue of making disciples of all nations. This theme concludes Matthew's Gospel and a similar thread runs throughout Luke's writing: disciples of Jesus are 'witnesses' and will share the gospel 'to all nations' (Luke 24:45–49); it continues through the testimony of the risen Jesus (Acts 1:8), the example of the church in Antioch (Acts 13), Paul's preaching of the kingdom (Acts 19:8) and his arrival in Rome (Acts 28:14).

The idea of disciples who are *witnesses in the sense of 'messengers' needs to be maintained in today's global church. In the emerging context of world Christianity we need disciples who combine exemplary spirituality and social engagement with being witnesses to the ends of the earth. The rise of Majority World missionary movements offers the possibility of new cross-cultural models of discipleship that will be an inspiration to the whole global church.

Bibliography

D. Bosch, *Transforming Mission* (New York: Orbis Books, 1992); D. Douglas (ed.), *Let the Earth Hear His Voice* (Minneapolis, MI: World Wide Publications, 1975); M. Maggay, *Transforming Society* (Oxford: Regnum Lynx, 1994); V. Ramachandra, *Recovery of Mission* (Delhi: ISPCK, 1996); V. Samuel, *The Meaning and Cost of Discipleship* (Bombay: Bombay Urban Industrial League for Development and Exeter: Paternoster Press, 1981); M. J. Wilkins, 'Disciples' and 'Discipleship' in J. Green and S. McKnight (eds.), *Dictionary of Jesus and the Gospels* (Leciester: IVP, 1992).

W. R. BEATTIE

DISPENSATIONALISM, see
ESCHATOLOGY
DIVINE–HUMAN ENCOUNTER, see
REVELATION

Drama/theatre

In the church's long and complicated relationship with the theatre, some Christians have argued that it is inherently sinful, or that it is so prone to distortion that it is best avoided altogether; others have presented plays based on stories and themes from the Scriptures with the intention of evangelizing the lost or discipling the faithful.

Although theatre is not mentioned directly in the Bible, Scripture affirms the making of all kinds of *art, including the performing arts. Creativity is the first revealed attribute of God (Gen. 1), and human beings, created in God's image, are thus creative as well. Adam's first task, the naming of the animals, involves symbolic communication, the core of all art-making. The OT describes dance, poetry, storytelling, vocal and instrumental *music among the ancient Hebrews and records that God instructed Isaiah (ch. 20), Ezekiel (ch. 4) and Hosea (chs. 1–3) to do things that closely resemble contemporary performance art. In the NT, storytelling in the form of parables was indispensable to Jesus' earthly ministry (Matt. 13:34) (see *Narrative).

Theatre and religious ritual are closely intertwined in both Christian and non-Christian traditions. The Abydos Passion Play (c. 2500 BC) recounts the death and resurrection of the Egyptian god Osiris, and classical Greek theatre (fifth century BC) was performed in conjunction with rituals honouring the god Dionysus. The medieval Christian church helped revive European scripted drama in the form of tropes performed in worship services and, later, mystery plays associated with the festival of Corpus Christi. Many Asian theatrical forms, including Japanese Noh and Indian kathakali, combine music, dance, storytelling and religious ritual elements. In the late twentieth century, avant-garde theatre companies in the US and Europe developed experimental productions that fused religious and secular ritual elements with political and social commentary.

At various times in church history, Christians have embraced theatre and explored its possibilities in mission and discipleship. In addition to tropes and mystery plays, medieval Christians also produced miracle plays that depicted events in the lives of saints, passion plays that focused on the suffering and death of Jesus, and morality plays that presented allegories of sin, repentance and grace. By the late 1500s, Spanish missionaries were producing traditional religious plays (*autos sacramentales*) in North America (sometimes in the languages of local natives) as a missionary outreach.

In the late nineteenth century, Roman Catholic and Protestant congregations in the

US and the UK began producing religious plays in worship services, Sunday schools and parish halls. Authors such as T. S. Eliot, Graham Greene and Christopher Fry wrote religious plays that were produced in London's West End and on Broadway in the 1940s and 1950s. In the 1970s, London and Broadway productions of *Jesus Christ Superstar* and *Godspell* generated controversy among some Christians but encouraged others to explore theatre. In the UK and North America, Christians founded professional theatres, many of which are still running today. By the 1990s, many US churches were developing drama programmes similar to the one at Willow Creek Community Church, which presented short sketches as sermon introductions and produced occasional full-length plays as local mission outreach.

Critics have ascribed a variety of purposes to theatre, beginning with Aristotle's theory that tragedy produces a catharsis by purging audience members through fear and pity and Horace's theory that the twofold purpose of dramatic poetry is to instruct and delight. Until the nineteenth century, virtually all theories of drama included an element of moral education or transformation; the concept of 'art for art's sake' is a relatively late development first associated with Romanticism.

As it fulfils such purposes, theatre works differently from most other forms of oral communication. Like the other fine arts, theatre is non-discursive; it conveys meaning through a rich combination of symbols, images, allusions and narrative structures. It combines aural and visual elements (including human speech and movement) in the enactment of a story that presents multiple levels of meaning simultaneously. Thus interpreting a play involves ambiguities that are typically absent from interpreting a speech or a sermon. Unlike a parable that typically has one key point of comparison, a play may admit multiple (sometimes conflicting) interpretations. Theatre tells moving stories, creates powerful images and depicts intense conflicts, but it is not always well suited to conveying large amounts of information in a clear and unambiguous manner.

As a result, Christians accustomed to worship, preaching and teaching organized around logical and rhetorical structures may be more uncomfortable with theatre (especially in the context of worship) than Christians accustomed to worship, preaching and teaching that draw on a more symbolic, story-based aesthetic approach. This may explain why until recently, the Roman Catholic and 'high church' worship traditions have been more comfortable with theatre than the 'low church' and evangelical Protestant worship traditions. However, as evangelicals have embraced the use of contemporary music and media in worship, they have also begun to explore the uses of live theatre and other dramatic media for evangelism and discipleship. Furthermore, as the focus of Western culture has shifted from the written word to the visual image – as we put down our books and turn to film, television and the Internet – Christians have seen theatre, with its strong visual orientation, as a means of engaging that culture. For Christians doing mission work in non-Western cultures in which orality still predominates, or in cultures that are moving directly from the oral to the visual without bothering to stop at the literary, theatre's emphasis on visual storytelling also provides intriguing possibilities.

Christians have often struggled to capitalize on such opportunities, for two main reasons. First, since theatre both reflects and comments upon the culture that produces it, a play's story, acting styles and visual elements are all closely tied to a specific culture's mores, values, behaviours and material aspects. Those who want to make effective theatre must understand and master a culture's dominant modes of artistic expression. Christians have sometimes shied away from serious arts training, either because they regard it as a frivolous pursuit when souls are dying, or because they fear that moral contamination will result from such close contact with certain aspects of that culture. On the other hand, viewing creativity as God-given suggests that art-making is anything but frivolous. Furthermore, acknowledging that sin arises from within our rebellious hearts and embracing the power of the gospel to transform such hearts opens the possibility that Christians need not fear unduly such contact with the culture in which they, after all, inevitably participate.

Second, Christians have sometimes regarded theatre in a purely utilitarian sense – a tool to communicate scriptural truths – without considering the implications of theatre's non-discursive nature or learning to use it effectively. As a result, Christians have sometimes scorned professionalism as worldly or regarded it as unimportant as long as the message gets through, failing to consider that non-Christian audiences attuned to theatrical excellence will judge drama first precisely on such grounds. Audiences used to stage and screen dramas enacted with wit, depth, nuance and attention to detail may reject or ignore more simplistic productions, regardless of the truth-claims of their content. Because the consequences of poor theatre are less evident than, say, poor medicine or poor engineering, such mistakes are not always easily recognized, much less readily corrected. However, the God who accepted Abel's first-fruits sacrifice calls Christians to excellence, including excellence in the arts.

It is worth noting that according to Scripture, Jesus frequently told parables without explaining them, saying to his audiences, 'Whoever has ears to hear, let them hear.' Christians who are willing to tell stories theatrically and trust audiences' abilities to grasp artistic nuance, allusion and wit may find exciting new ways of expressing eternal truths. With these concepts in mind, Christians can examine a wide variety of plays for their spiritual content. They can produce plays in a wide variety of theatrical styles as they seek to create theatre that reveals truths about God and the world to audiences of Christians and non-Christians.

Bibliography

H. Adams (ed.), *Critical Theory Since Plato* (San Diego: Harcourt Brace Jovanovich, 1971); P. Senkbeil, *Faith in Theatre: Professional Theatres Run by Christians in the United States and Canada and Their Strategies for Faith-Art Integration*, PhD dissertation (Evanston: Northwestern University, 1995); E. Wilson and A. Goldfarb, *Living Theatre: A History* (Boston: McGraw-Hill, [4]2004).

P. SENKBEIL

Ecology/environment

Is it time for humanity to be de-centred as the focus of mission? Do we need to repent of the anthropocentric bias of much missiology and recapture the radically inclusive biblical emphasis upon God's mission toward the whole cosmos? These are questions prompted by the engagement of theologians and mission practitioners with contemporary issues of environmental degradation and ecological sensitivity. The growing awareness over the last several decades of major environmental challenges, such as ozone depletion, global warming, deforestation, bio-diversity loss, water and air pollution, has prompted a quest for a holistic understanding of mission relevant to the contemporary ecological crisis. Such an understanding needs to include a commitment to sustainable relationships between human beings and the non-human creation. A transformation of our understanding of this relationship is an aspect of our discipleship.

The global nature of many of the environmental challenges adds further missiological relevance: these are issues that cross national boundaries, connecting countries and people groups. In this way they raise awareness of our interconnectedness as human beings inhabiting the same planet, as well as our dependence upon and influence over the non-human creation. Indeed, it could be argued that 'ecology' is the most interconnected word in the English language, referring to the relations of organisms to one another and to their surroundings.

God's commitment to the integrity of these relationships is made abundantly clear in the first two chapters of Genesis. They emphasize the inextricable links between the human and non-human creation and view the whole as 'good'. A biblical doctrine of creation that can properly inform missiology emphasizes that the whole of creation reflects God's glory and, as such, must be honoured and treated with respect. Humanity, while sharing all kinds of commonalities with the non-human creation, is distinguished from it and given a particular responsibility for creation care, a crucial component of what it means to be created in 'the image of God' (Gen. 1:26–27).

While some have accused Christianity of being responsible for environmental degradation as a result of the abuse of the principle of human dominion over the rest of creation (Gen. 1:28), the verse needs to be interpreted in conjunction with Genesis 2:15 which combines legitimate development of the earth's resources with nurture and conservation. Thus the contemporary concept of 'sustainable development' can be seen to be biblically rooted.

This emphasis upon creation care as a fundamental element of God's calling upon human beings is reiterated elsewhere in the Pentateuch. Many biblical laws relate to the responsible treatment of animals, trees, vegetation and the land itself (e.g. Exod. 23:4–5, 10–11; Deut. 22:6–7; 25:4; 25:13–15). Both Sabbath and *jubilee provisions (Lev. 25) affect the non-human creation as well as human beings, while the story of Noah and the ark has been called 'the original endangered species act'. It is highly significant that the first biblical covenant (Gen. 9:8–17) is with every living creature and the text repeatedly emphasizes the inclusive nature of God's commitment to his creation. Similarly, later biblical texts that look forward to the Messianic age depict a peaceable kingdom in which all creatures will dwell together (e.g. Isa. 65:17–25).

Beyond particular biblical texts, it is important to relate the essential framework of Christian theology and missiology to our understanding of environmental issues. We properly begin with the doctrine of the *Trinity in which God is understood as an interdependent 'ecology of persons'. As such, God is the root and pattern of all mutually supporting and interconnecting processes. If the doctrine of the Trinity and creation are our starting points, the doctrine of the fall provides the proper framework in which to assess the root causes of environmental degradation. One important aspect of human sin is failure in our stewardship of creation. Rebellion against God is manifested in terms of over-consumption and the exploitation of natural resources, with insufficient attention being given to just patterns of distribution and the well-being of future generations. The gospel, therefore, calls us to repent of all the ways in which we have failed to cherish and care for God's creation.

We also need to 'green' our understanding of the person and work of Christ. The doctrines of incarnation, salvation and resurrection all have vital environmental resonances. The *incarnation expresses God's commitment to creation and emphasizes that matter matters. In his own life, Jesus acknowledged and celebrated the non-human creation, while the resurrection confirms God's commitment to the physical realm and points forward to a renewed creation. It is also true that the non-human creation is involved in the judgment of God (indicated for example in the withering of the fig tree, Mark 11:12–24, and the destruction of the swine, Mark 5:1–13), and this militates against any sacralizing of creation. In broad terms, however, Christian eschatology needs to stress not the destruction of the present order, as has so often been the case, but rather its restoration to wholeness (Rom. 8:19–23). Even those passages (notably 2 Pet. 3:7–13) that have frequently been taken to indicate future destruction of the earth, can persuasively be interpreted in terms of purification, renewal and transformation. Given this reading, creation care is a living out in the present of God's ultimate purpose of cosmic reconciliation.

Perhaps at the heart of the matter lies the doctrine of *salvation. We urgently need to avoid a reductionist view of salvation, by supplementing the dimension of human individual relationship with God with a comprehensive biblical vision of renewed harmony and justice between people and the rest of the created order (Eph. 1:9–10; Col. 1:15–20).

This theological framework provides the foundation for a properly *holistic or integral understanding of mission that emphasizes the interdependence between people and their social and physical contexts. Although the environmental component of mission should not be viewed as a new phenomenon (St Francis, Calvin and Wesley are three examples among many in the Western tradition who promoted creation care), it has become significantly more prominent in recent decades.

Within the ecumenical community, since the 1970s the World Council of Churches has organized a series of conferences on the theme of 'Justice, Peace and the Integrity of Creation'. Although some evangelicals have been concerned about perceived pantheistic tendencies and the radical political agenda of these conferences, they have undeniably contributed to the growing profile of environmental issues within the global church. Within the evangelical community notable developments have included the creation in 1979 of the

Au Sable Institute in Michigan, USA (subsequently extended to other centres in the USA, Canada, India and Kenya), which has had an influential educational and advocacy role, and the Evangelical Declaration on the Care of Creation (1994) signed by hundreds of church leaders throughout the world.

In terms of praxis, missionary earth-keeping includes education, advocacy, field work and conservation, and community development initiatives that combine economic development and environmental conservation with opportunities for evangelism. Valuable case studies from Africa, Asia and Latin America are provided by De Witt and Prance. One particularly successful example of environmental mission is A Rocha, founded in 1983 in Portugal and now working in over fifteen countries across five continents. A Rocha projects combine science and research with practical conservation and environmental education. There is a strong cross-cultural and communal dimension to the ministry, providing natural evangelistic opportunities. Numerous other examples of environmental mission around the world are evangelistically effective, demonstrating to an increasingly environmentally aware generation the relevance of the Christian gospel to every aspect of life.

While there is growing recognition of the validity and value of missionary earth-keeping, it remains something of a Cinderella within the mission community. Many evangelical Christians still need to be persuaded that creation care, in its various dimensions of conservation, education, lifestyle choices, and advocacy, is an important component of Christian witness and worship. That task needs to be undertaken urgently, for the sake of the gospel and for the sake of the world.

See also CREATION/NATURE.

Bibliography
R. J. Berry (ed.), *The Care of Creation: Focusing Concern and Action* (Leicester: IVP, 2000); S. Bouma-Prediger, *For the Beauty of the Earth: A Christian Vision for Creation Care* (Grand Rapids: Baker Academic, 2001); M. L. Daneel, *African Earthkeepers: Wholistic Interfaith Mission* (Maryknoll: Orbis Books, 2001); C. DeWitt

and G. T. Prance (eds.), *Missionary Earth-keeping* (Macon: Mercer University Press, 1992); R. B. Fowler, *The Greening of Protestant Thought* (Chapel Hill: University of North Carolina Press, 1995); K. Gnanakan, *God's World: A Theology of the Environment* (London: SPCK, 1999); D. G. Hallman (ed.), *Ecotheology: Voices from South and North* (Maryknoll: Orbis Books, 1994); B. R. Hill, *Christian Faith and the Environment: Making Vital Connections* (Maryknoll: Orbis Books, 1998); A Rocha: Christians in conservation <http://www.en.arocha.org>; Evangelical Environmental Network and 'Creation Care' Magazine <http://www. creationcare.org>; the John Ray Initiative <http://www.jri.org.uk>; United Nations Environment Programme <http://www.unep. org>.

S. STEER

ELECTION, see COVENANT

Eschatology

In the Gospel of Mark Jesus begins his public ministry announcing, 'The time has come ... The kingdom of God has come near' (Mark 1:15; cf. Matt. 4:17). Eschatology is concerned with the way God is acting in the world to fulfil the divine plan of *salvation. The OT prophets proclaimed God's redemptive purposes and emphasized that these purposes would be realized at some point in the future through the work of the Messiah. The advent of Jesus the Messiah marked a new stage in salvation history. In the NT eschatology and mission are closely linked (cf. Matt. 28:18–20), for mission is concerned with *witness to the reign of God, the climax of which will be the universal recognition that Jesus Christ is Lord (Phil. 2:11). The relation between mission and eschatology is therefore integral.

Salvation history in OT and NT
Christian mission is rooted in the Triune God, and therefore in God's sending of himself in Christ to fulfil his plan of salvation. This plan is enacted in trinitarian stages throughout *history as it moves towards its eschatological goal. Therefore, history, faith and world mission can only be understood teleologically, that is, from a linear view of history leading to

its climax in the new heaven and the new earth in which all things are brought into harmony under the lordship of Christ (Eph. 1:10; Col. 1:20).

In the OT God's historical relationship with his people, and his eschatological purposes, are at the heart of the covenant with Abraham (Gen. 12:1–3). The proclamation of the prophets points to God's eschatological purpose that includes all the nations. World mission cannot be divorced from the OT salvation history and eschatology of the people of Israel, and therefore must be understood and carried out in this larger perspective. Paul confirms this in Romans 9 – 11.

In his ministry Jesus engages with both the prophetic and apocalyptic dimensions of OT eschatology, both as he embodies its fulfilment and as he constructs a vision of the future promises of God. By fulfilling OT prophecy he becomes the foundation of the *gospel, which is proclaimed through mission to the nations. Only when all peoples of the world have heard the gospel will Jesus return (cf. Matt. 24:14). Each of the four Gospels reaches its climax with the call to mission.

Jesus' present lordship ensures that the goal of mission will be fulfilled, and his total authority is the presupposition and assurance of the great commission. His authority is seen both in his headship of the church and as King and Judge of the world. Thus, the great commission is not merely an assignment for the church but also a promise and a sure prophecy. World mission occurs in the interim between Pentecost and the glorious return of Christ. During this time Jesus himself takes ultimate responsibility for discipling the nations, for he says, 'I will build my church, and the gates of death [Hades] will not overcome it' (Matt. 16:18). History, therefore, is moving toward the grand climax foretold in Revelation when people of all languages and cultures belonging to the numberless congregation of the redeemed are gathered together before God (Rev. 5:9–10; cf. Rev. 7:9; 10:11; 14:6).

The parable of the wheat and the weeds (Matt. 13:24–30, 36–43) warns us that during this interim period evil will flourish along with the growth of the *kingdom. The weeds, however, can only last until the wheat has ripened. Although evil continues, God is building his church among all nations as mission advances. So long as this programme of mission and the gathering of God's people continues, final *judgment of the world is stalled. Paul and the apostles understood their ministry as both the fulfilment of prophecy (as 'realized eschatology') and encouragement to anticipate the completion of God's eschatological promises.

Millennial views and mission history

Since the apostolic period eschatology has been interpreted variously. Speculation about the future has generally been based on theories of the millennium. It is clear that the *present* socio-political context influences the way the *future* is interpreted. Millennial hopes have played an important role in inspiring mission movements in history. In the twelfth century new eschatological hope inspired an important mission thrust. Eschatological impulses motivated the Crusades. Columbus's understanding of biblical prophecy impelled him to sail to America. Conversely the Lutheran Reformation did not lead to world mission because Luther expected the imminent end of the world; he believed the great commission was fulfilled and denied any millennial views.

In the modern period evangelicals have interpreted the millennium according to four theories. Each theory has played a role in mission and church history. (1) *Amillennialism* anticipates no literal millennial kingdom; instead there will be a continuous and unbroken line of history between Pentecost and the parousia. This was the dominant view from Augustine until the seventeenth century. This view encourages a holistic view of mission as ongoing transformation. (2) *Postmillennialism* was influential in the seventeenth and eighteenth centuries and was identified especially with the Puritan tradition. It teaches that Christ will return following the millennial kingdom. During this period the church will grow; justice, peace and righteousness will prevail, climaxing in the return of Christ at the parousia. Mission anticipates the coming of the kingdom in this world. (3) *Historical (or classical) premillennialism* became prominent in the nineteenth century. It argues for a future, literal, earthly millennial kingdom where Christ will reign after his return. Meanwhile the church will grow but the world will deteriorate. Since Christ's return is imminent, the Christian duty is to win as many people as possible before Christ returns. Mission should focus on vigorous personal evangelism and church growth rather than working to overcome the injustice and evil of this world. (4) *Dispensational premillennialism* starts with premillennialism, but strictly separates between Israel and the church, that is, between OT and NT; and it insists that during the millennium Israel will be saved and rule the earth. John Nelson Darby, an early Brethren leader, formulated dispensationalism in the 1820s with its pessimistic attitude toward the possibility of improving the world in this dispensation.

These simple designations of a-, post-, and pre- emphasize the chronological relationship between the millennial kingdom and Christ's return. But each is reductionist, failing to capture the full measure of biblical eschatology. The focus ought to be on the nature of the kingdom of God and the means of its expansion. These positions reflect different understandings of history and the world, be it optimistic or pessimistic, and views of the church's strategy in fulfilling her mission.

Klaus Fiedler has made a helpful classification of Protestant mission societies of the nineteenth and twentieth centuries. 'Classical' mission societies were a fruit of the Evangelical Awakening whose roots can be traced largely to the Reformed theology represented by Jonathan Edwards. They tended to be a- or postmillennial. William Carey's Baptist Mission Society (1792) was a leading example. Many of these societies later became denominational agencies. 'Post-classical' missions emerged a generation later from several sources, including the Brethren movement. Hudson Taylor, a Methodist, and the China Inland Mission (1865) came to symbolize 'faith missions'. The 'Post-classical' missions were generally dispensationalist or premillennialist.

Enthusiasm for mission through postmillennialism

Gustav Warneck, the 'father' of German missiology, whilst considering the influence of eschatology on Reformed mission, discovered evidence that Lutheran eschatology actually hindered mission up to the rise of Pietism in the eighteenth century. Among Protestants enthusiasm for world mission was stimulated by the influences of an optimistic amillennialism and emerging postmillennialism. However, Charles L. Chaney sees significance in Calvin's view of the progress of the kingdom of God, in his eschatology, and in his belief in the personal responsibility of the individual Christian towards God's word. Here lie the roots of the Calvinists' later missionary fervour, when Calvinist, mostly Puritan, pastors who had emigrated to America from England preached the gospel to the Indians. As many studies have shown, postmillennialism was the mother of Anglo-Saxon missions. This is true for Anglicans, Presbyterians and Congregationalists, as well as for Calvinist Baptists such as William Carey.

The Postmillennialism of the 18C played an important role in the development of Anglo-American missions. In the light of chiliastic expectations, British and American revival movements were considered the first signs of a great wave soon to engulf the whole world. Not only [Jonathan] Edwards, but also English (Isaac Watts, Philip Doddridge) and Scottish (John Williston, John Erskine) theologians related Postmillennial eschatology with revival and with the missionary idea – a combination which gave rise to the growth of organized missionary activity at the end of the century. Carey, for example, was strongly influenced by the Postmillennial view of a universal Kingdom of God. (R. J. Bauckham, in *New Dictionary of Theology*, p. 429).

This postmillennial eschatological view generated great optimism that world mission would succeed in reaching all the nations, and it established a close connection between the spreading of the gospel and the betterment of the world. Social and educational efforts became an integral part of world mission. As Jesus was not expected to return immediately, missions made considerable long-term investments in health, educational systems, including Christian universities, and political involvement: the campaign against slavery, William Carey's fight against the caste system, missionary opposition to the burning of widows, and protection of indigenous peoples.

Premillennialism: from opposition to mission to enthusiasm

The growth of premillennialism in the nineteenth century led to increasing conflict with postmillennial ideas that critics believed were becoming accommodated to modern thought. For some, premillennialism was an argument against hopes of evangelistic success. Dispensationalist J. N. Darby expressed his premillennial view of mission in an 1840 lecture in Geneva: 'I am afraid that many a cherished feeling, dear to the children of God, has been shocked this evening; I mean their hope that the gospel will spread by itself over the whole earth during the actual dispensation.' The influential Pietist professor of systematic theology in Tübingen, Johann Tobias Beck (1804–78), opposed the work of the Basel Mission, and the spreading evangelical world mission movement in general, asserting that Jesus must first return and mission would be carried out following the millennium.

However, in the second half of the nineteenth century opinion on the relationship between premillennialism and mission changed. The emerging faith mission movement identified strongly with premillennialism and, in many cases, dispensationalism. The principal idea was that reaching all the nations would hasten the coming of Jesus. Faith missions grew steadily and premillennial dispensationalism became the major force in Protestant missions in the twentieth century.

Premillennialism, especially of the dispensationalist variety, changed the character of world mission. It was indifferent or even opposed to social action. The great commission was interpreted as being concerned only with the salvation of the soul. Long-term investments in human well-being were said to divert missionary efforts from the highest priority: preaching the gospel so that souls might be saved. It is difficult to reconcile premillennialism's underlying philosophy with Christian social responsibility. The world is expected to grow worse and worse and there is little or no hope of improving or reforming it by any human effort. This means that, for evangelical Christians with a premillenial orientation, their negative world-view inclines them to a low engagement with social, political and cultural affairs.

Each of the millennial theories led to reductionism. Certain dimensions of the gospel were emphasized while others were obscured.

Recovery of biblical eschatology

Eschatology was at a low ebb throughout the nineteenth century. In the twentieth century, two world wars shattered the illusion of unlimited human progress associated with modernity. At the same time new currents in biblical studies emerged. Biblical realism called for the recovery of eschatology. Whereas eschatology played no role at the World Missionary Conference at Edinburgh in 1910, the International Missionary Council sponsored theological studies such as Hendrik Kraemer's 1938 *The Christian Message in a Non-Christian World* that emphasized the importance of eschatology. NT scholar Oscar Cullmann insisted there is no mission without eschatology. Missiologist Walter Freytag held that *basileia*, or the reign of God, is the substance and goal of mission.

The recovery of eschatology required the retrieval of a theology of the kingdom of God. This calls for a full-orbed gospel. In 1964 George Eldon Ladd published *The Presence of the Future: An Eschatology of Biblical Realism*. Ladd said that 'Jesus' message of the Kingdom of God is the announcement by word and deed that God is acting and manifesting dynamically his redemptive will in history' (p. 178). In Jesus the kingdom has been introduced but it has not yet been consummated. God's people yearn for Christ's return when the kingdom will be realized fully. The kingdom of God comes to us as a gift. It is God who initiates and, finally, brings all things to completion. The kingdom and the church must not be collapsed into one reality. The kingdom always stands in judgment over the church. It is the privilege of the faith community to witness to the kingdom – nothing more and nothing less. But this vision of a comprehensive eschatology has not yet been fully developed. Bosch observed that, 'In every Christian tradition and in every continent we are still in the midst of a movement to reformulate a theology of mission in the light of an authentic eschatology' (D. J. Bosch, *Transforming Mission*, p. 508).

Evangelical theology of mission has evolved since the 1960s. The Wheaton and Berlin congresses in 1966 both recognized that the integrity of Christian evangelization and mission depended on witness to the *whole* gospel. Formulations and theories that resulted in only a partial gospel must be rejected. The Congress on World Evangelization held at Lausanne, Switzerland in 1974 marked a turning point in evangelical missiology and eschatology. The Lausanne Movement's Theology Commission sponsored a series of consultations that have challenged traditional evangelical world missions to reclaim a commitment to a whole gospel that embraces every dimension of human need.

Conclusion

This article has demonstrated the importance of eschatology for our view of mission. If the way we engage in mission is largely determined by how we understand its goal, then lack of clarity and conviction in our eschatology will cause confusion and loss of incentive for mission. Admittedly, it is not easy to be faithful to Scripture in this area, since the texts, especially in Revelation, are susceptible to a wide range of interpretation. What is clear in the NT is the consistent promise of the return of Christ, which is itself a powerful incentive for holiness, obedience and faithfulness to the mission mandate. If the 'last days' are understood as applying to the whole period between Pentecost and the parousia, then this should give a sense of urgency to our obedience to the *missio Dei* as well as the desire to see the whole world brought into the purposes of God for its transformation and renewal.

Bibliography

R. J. Bauckham, 'Millennium', in S. B. Ferguson *et al.* (eds.), *New Dictionary of Theology* (Leicester: IVP, 1988); D. J. Bosch, *Transforming Mission* (Maryknoll: Orbis Books, 1991); C. L. Chaney, *The Birth of Missions in America* (Pasadena: William Carey Library, 1976); J. A. de Jong, *As the Waters Cover the Sea: Millennial Expectations in the Rise of Anglo-American Missions, 1640–1810* (Kampen: J. H. Kok, 1970); K. Fiedler, *The Story of Faith Missions* (Oxford: Regnum Books, 1994); G. E. Ladd, *The Presence of the Future: An Eschatology of Biblical Realism* (Grand Rapids: Eerdmans, 1964); T. Schirrmacher, *Be Keen to Get Going: William Carey's Theology* (Hamburg: RVB, 2001); T. Schirrmacher, 'Post-millennialism' in A. Scott Moreau (ed.), *Evangelical Dictionary of World Missions* (Grand Rapids: Baker Books; Carlisle: Paternoster Press, 2000).

T. SCHIRRMACHER

ETERNAL LIFE, see HEAVEN/ETERNAL LIFE

Ethics

Approaching ethics

This article presupposes that the Christian mission is the witness of God's people to the character and work of God. Christian ethics in the context of mission is thus the Christian community's *embodiment* and *performance* of the biblical narrative as a *witness about God for the world.

Ethics has to do with how we understand, develop and practise the good life. Different approaches to ethics arise as the 'good life' is defined with reference to one or more of the following: a person's (or community's) character, motivation and empowering; laws, principles, and communal obligations that clarify one's duty to act in certain ways; the consequences, goals or outcomes of actions; and the specific context (time, place, culture).

Christian ethical approaches depend on the authoritative status one gives to Scripture, tradition, reason, and experience and on one's interpretation and use of Scripture.

Such considerations lead to different views on moral guidance, acceptable means, moral motivation, empowerment, and the content of an ethic. Roman Catholic ethics has traditionally determined moral obligations and goals from natural law – what is true for all as creatures created by God. For Immanuel Kant, any moral action should be that which all are obliged to do regardless of context (his 'categorical imperative', e.g. never lie or treat people as means). Utilitarians (Jeremy Bentham, John Stuart Mill) argue that one should pursue the goal of 'the greatest good for the greatest number of people'. But such universal approaches to ethics have come under attack in the last fifty years. Situation ethics (what one ought to do depends on the situation one is in) is contextual and opposes universal ethics, but it remains modernistic in its emphasis on the *individual* making *decisions* in *quandary* situations. It is also *reductionistic*, being based on a single principle, such as 'do the loving thing'. The Anabaptist emphasis on the Sermon on the Mount and character of Jesus has focused Christian ethics on the virtues of character and practices of kingdom disciples.

Over the past thirty years, universal ethics has been challenged by philosophers such as Alisdair MacIntyre, postliberal theologians such as George Lindbeck, biblical scholars such as Hays, and Christian ethicists such as Yoder, McClendon, Hauerwas, Stassen and Gushee. For them, different traditions are shaped by different narratives that give rise to different moral visions of the good life, and so the definition of virtuous character will also differ. Interest in contextualization in mission studies is likely to favour non-universal ethics. African Catholic ethicist Bujo emphasizes context and community in ethical decision-making.

Ethics, mission and intercultural studies

Someone who combines intercultural studies with a narrative, virtue and communitarian approach to ethics is Bernard Adeney in his book *Strange Virtues*. He explores how individual, social and cosmic values, priorities, virtues and vices are variously construed in different cultures. For example, regarding family structure and authority, an egalitarian *culture will value equality, independence and self-determination, will see individual rights and personal freedom as priorities, will understand independence and competitiveness as virtues but fragmentation and selfishness as vices. A hierarchical culture will value honour and loyalty, see duty, security and harmony as priorities, understand respect for the other, obedience, self-control and loyalty as virtues, but oppression as a vice. Here ethics and etiquette overlap. One culture's bribe is another culture's gift. The same vice might be construed differently: Westerners see adultery as falsehood; Africans see it as theft. Recognizing the cultural context takes one a long way towards an appreciative and relational dialogue with the different ethics of a foreign culture or non-Christian religion. What assists Christians in this dialogue is that, no matter how much the cultural differences, the same biblical narratives give rise to a shared (for Christians) moral vision.

Ethics, mission and contextual theology

Abstract principles such as 'liberation', 'justice' and 'love' mean very different things within different narratives and so are easily co-opted by *contextual theologians for their own agenda. But seeing how such principles are *embodied* in a community's practices, web of beliefs, and so on, in Scripture will make such co-opting difficult. It will require entering the cultural-linguistic world of the Scriptures just as much as mission scholars speak of entering the cultural-linguistic world of a people.

For narrative, character and communitarian ethicists, embodiment entails:

(1) Understanding how the concrete ethic of the people of Israel, or the NT community, relates to their moral vision;

(2) bringing this moral vision into sharper focus by seeing how Jesus embodied it;

(3) imaginatively placing oneself and one's community within this embodied moral vision by letting it shape our loyalties, trusts, interests, passions, way of seeing, basic convictions, and way of reasoning;

(4) by analogy (rather than abstraction), embodying this biblical tradition in our life today.

Ethics, mission and the church in the world

Stanley Hauerwas has argued that the church does not *have* but *is* a social ethic. John Howard Yoder wrote of the need for a hermeneutic of 'peoplehood', a mission of incarnation as the church views itself not from a position of power ('Christendom') but as a minority active in service. The character of a kingdom community becomes its primary mission. For the people of Israel God's demand for the holiness of the community was integral to their mission witness to the nations, and the church likewise is called to reflect the character of God to the world. Thus the church's outward focus in its mission shapes a uniquely Christian ethic, and conversely its ethic gives shape to its mission practice. The world mission and community ethic of God's people are both present in the great commission (Matt. 28:18–20). The work of discerning the church's mission ethic should emphasize biblical interpretation: Scripture's narratives, community convictions and practices entail both a mission and moral way of being in the world. Wright, Stassen and Gushee, and Bauckham provide excellent beginnings towards this project.

In relation to *development ethics in mission, Myers offers a narrative and biblical ethics approach that involves 'spiritual transformation', exemplary witness, a people rather than growth-centred approach, and a transformative community engaged in social transformation. A 'holistic approach' in mission is now widely accepted. Yet the question remains, 'To what extent does a holistic gospel involve the church in social transformation?' Are 'nation building' or 'human rights' on the church's agenda, especially if this means adopting a particular economic or ideological position, a diminished ecclesial role, or a universal ethics argument?

Tradition, narrative and community

The modernist approach works from principles, reason and proof, and translates in Christian terms into simply abstracting ethical principles directly from the scriptural text. An alternative approach can reason not *from* but *towards* first principles, and will see itself as belief seeking understanding. This will begin with the narratives from the texts of its tradition and focus on embodying those narratives in its own community, as well as evaluating the tradition's good and bad performances through history. This is not a purely contextual approach, since a tradition can both live by its own narrative and make claims about reality and truth beyond itself.

Thus the 'tradition inquiry' approach to mission ethics suggested here will be more narrative than anthropological, more communal than contextual, more interested in biblical mission narratives than a single theological theme (liberation, reconciliation), more concerned with *interpreting* the biblical narrative than *reflecting* upon it after praxis, more interested in exploring mission and ethics in the community's historical vision, convictions and practices, and more interested in developing churches of moral and mission discourse and practice. A tradition inquiry will identify different versions of Christian mission and ethics, evaluate ideal and actual performances within those traditions, and engage in a critical discussion between the various Christian traditions (Anabaptist, holiness, Pentecostal, Reformed, Catholic, Orthodox, Lutheran, etc.).

The challenge in mission, therefore, is whether the gospel will be practised institutionally (government, agencies, denominations), operationally (addressing the issue non-formally: prayer, evangelism, emergency aid) and/or communally (forming an intentional community, e.g. the Jerusalem church in Acts living out a vision of kingdom community). Mission understood as the church's witness to God's character calls for a biblically formed community that embodies the Christian story in its vision, virtues and practices.

Bibliography

B. T. Adeney, *Strange Virtues: Ethics in a Multicultural World* (Leicester: Apollos, 1995); R. Bauckham, *Bible and Mission: Christian Witness in a Postmodern World* (Carlisle: Paternoster Press; Grand Rapids, MI: Baker Book House, 2003); B. Bujo, *Foundations of an African Ethic: Beyond the Universal Claims of Western Morality* (New York: Crossroad Pub. Co., 2001); S. Hauerwas, *The Peaceable Kingdom: A Primer in Christian Ethics* (Notre Dame, IL: University of Notre Dame, 1983); R. B. Hays, *The Moral Vision of the New Testament: A Contemporary Introduction to New Testament Ethics* (San Francisco: Harper Collins, 1996); A. MacIntyre, *Three Rival Versions of Moral Enquiry: Encyclopaedia, Genealogy, and Tradition* (Notre Dame, IL: University of Notre Dame, 1990); J. W. McClendon, Jr, *Systematic Theology: Ethics* (Nashville: Abingdon, 1986); B. Myers, *Walking With the Poor: Principles and Practices of Transformational Development* (Maryknoll, NY: Orbis Books, 1999); G. Stassen and D. Gushee, *Kingdom Ethics: Following Jesus in Contemporary Context* (Downers Grove, IL: InterVarsity Press, 2003); C. J. H. Wright, *Old Testament Ethics for the People of God* (Leicester: IVP, 2004); J. H. Yoder, *The Priestly Kingdom: Social Ethics as Gospel* (Notre Dame, IL: University of Notre Dame, 1985).

R. G. GRAMS

Ethnicity/ethnocentrism

Issues surrounding ethnic identity and ethnic groups today have become so prevalent that they cannot be ignored either in the practice or the theology of mission. What one author calls 'the resilience of the *ethnie*' (M. Featherstone, *Global Culture: Nationalism, Globalization and Modernity*, p. 10) today is a major challenge to missionaries and missiologists. Issues such as cultural self-assertion (or ethnic assertion) and cultural conflicts (often termed 'ethnic conflicts') are burning contemporary issues missiology must address from different angles.

Definition

Although the Greek *ethnos* translates the Latin *natio*, the English terms 'ethnic group' and 'nation' (or 'ethnicity' and 'nationality') are not used as synonyms nor considered equivalent. The noun 'ethnicity' in English came into use only during the second half of the twentieth century. However, what the term refers to, in relation to cultural identity and kinship, are as old as human society itself. Because of the absence of a proper noun to translate the Greek *ethnos* in English, it is becoming common to use the French *ethnie* among scholars.

In contemporary discussion, the definition of an ethnic group by Max Weber remains the cornerstone. Weber defined ethnic groups as 'those human groups that entertain a subjective belief in their common descent because of similarities of physical type or of customs or both, or because of memories of colonization and migration; this belief must be important for the propagation of group formation; conversely, it does not matter whether or not an objective blood relationship exists' (in *The Ethnicity Reader: Nationalism, Multiculturalism and Migration*, pp. 18–19). Taking the various factors into consideration and following Weber, Hutchinson and Smith came to a comprehensive definition of *ethnie* as 'a named human population with myths of common ancestry, shared historical memories, one or more elements of common culture, a link with a homeland and a sense of solidarity among at least some of its members' (J. Hutchinson and A. D. Smith, *Ethnicity*, p. 6). The main weakness of this definition is its confinement of common ancestry into myths, especially since 'myth', in the way the authors use the term, is seen as opposite to a 'fact', giving *ethnie* a sense of fictive kinship. The common ancestry or kinship need not be a myth, but can be a fact whether provable or not.

Indisputably, ethnicity has to do with the culture or cultural-consciousness of a group. But whether the consciousness is a given or a construct is an issue debated by scholars. Furthermore, cultural changes have come about through intercultural interactions which can be politically engineered. The two main contesting positions are often termed *primordialists* and *instrumentalists* or *constructivists*. Whereas primordialists contend that ethnic or national identities are reflections of primordial identities, the latter group argues that they are social and political constructions as means to mobilize groups for particular or political ends. The two opinions need not be set in contention, but seen as important and different aspects of the nature and origin of ethnies. In the rich variety of ethnies, both primordial ties and political motives have their place in the rise or revival of ethnicity. While some groups have more durable ethnies, others dissolve more easily and transform into new ethnies.

Whether nationalism and ethnicity are modern phenomena constructed out of political necessity or just that they are the modern faces of primordial entity, they are founded on, to use Weber's words, 'a subjective belief in' the people's 'common descent'. Every individual or group has multiple identities. Consciously or subconsciously, either because of the felt need or because of the strength of the tradition, one category of identity (or a set of categories) is opted for (either consciously or subconsciously) as one's identifying mark over others. But to discount *ethnie* as 'optional identity' and thus trivialize it, either for the purpose of assimilating minority ethnic groups into larger groups or as a way of curbing its destructive potential, is to underestimate its political force. Such trivialization or marginalization, done either to dominate or absorb ethnic minorities, often provokes ethnic groups into conflict.

Contemporary use

Although ethnicity can play, and has played, positive and significant roles, its destructive potential has been seen in the former Yugoslavia, Sri Lanka or Rwanda, which all bring to mind the ravaging consequences of the abuse of ethnicity. Through widespread reports of such sad events in recent history, the term ethnicity is attached to terms like 'ethnic cleansing' and 'ethnic conflicts' in popular ideas and understanding. As against the expectation of the liberals of the nineteenth century, modernity has not expunged *ethnies*. Instead, *ethnie* has played new and significant political roles in modern bureaucratic nation-states and capitalism. As a source of empowerment for the dominated minorities, or as a way of competing for political and economic power, ethnicity provides the basis for conflicts over the distribution of power and resources. Ethnic identity assertions for political gain have reaped much conflict and violence in our world today, demanding Christian witness in ways not known before. This witness must begin from the basic truth that in Christ Christians have received a primary identity as children of God which relativizes all other identities, undermining the absoluteness of ethnic identity for which some are willing to die and to kill. However, due in part to massive migrations around the world, the challenge is rampant and worldwide. As a way of peaceful co-existence among different *ethnies*, the pluralistic attempt to promote 'multiculturalism' has been popularized to replace earlier symbolic ideals such as the 'melting pot'.

Missiological approaches

Two prevalent theological approaches may be highlighted as representative current missiological models. The first of these is *interculturality*. Rightly so, many relate Christian mission to cross-cultural ministry. But to limit Christian mission to cross-cultural activities impoverishes mission theologically. Nevertheless the *gospel as God's good news revealed in Jesus Christ is communicated to us in cultural forms through which we understand and communicate it to each other. Through intercultural interactions themselves, cultural boundaries are redrawn and new cultural forms are emerging. We crisscross cultural lines to articulate the gospel meaningfully to ourselves and to each other. Since there is no one culture above another culture in this enterprise, the crossing is not a one-way activity, but multiple.

As the gospel is now carried and communicated from everywhere to everywhere, from every culture to every culture, mutuality among cultures or *ethnies* built on the

meekness of Christ is the essence of intercultural witness to the gospel. Since there is 'neither Jew nor Greek', but all are one in Christ, no ethnic group has intrinsic superiority over any other. This spirit of mutuality in Christ in the intercultural communication of the gospel provides the theological basis for a meaningful witness to the gospel in the context of ethnic division, competition and violence.

Closely related to the intercultural model is the second missiological model, reconciliation. The biblical message of reconciliation is the most powerful weapon to withstand emotive ethnic violence and conflict. Reconciliation is a term Paul uses in connection with a change of relationship. It is a change from wrong relation to right relation. God's gift of reconciliation calls and empowers Christians to be reconciled with God (2 Cor. 5:18–19), with other people or *ethnies* (Eph. 2:11–16) and with the entire creation (Col. 1:20). Our present concern is with the second, which is appropriately named 'the reconciliation of peoples' by Baum and Wells (in *The Reconciliation of Peoples: Challenge to the Churches*). The reconciliation of peoples (represented in the Bible by Jews and Gentiles) is built on reconciliation with God in Christ. Through his death, Christ has broken down the dividing wall between peoples, put to death the hostility among them, reconciled them to God, and created them as one new humanity. The new common identity which people of different *ethnies* share in Christ is both the basis as well as the product of reconciliation.

Conclusion

The resurgence of *ethnies* in the contemporary world is both a blessing and a curse. While it helps to empower dominated people by giving them a sense of identity and dignity, it also makes groups selfish and arouses their desire to dominate others. Ethnic identity assertions may positively promote diversity of cultures and enrich the cultural landscape, but the emotive and arrogant nature of identity assertion often defeats such positive potential ends. A missiology characterized by God's reconciling grace and a theology of intercultural mutuality are powerful tools of Christian mission to address the intensifying conflicts among *ethnies* in the world.

See also CULTURE, RECONCILIATION.

Bibliography
G. Baum and H. Wells (eds.), *The Reconciliation of Peoples: Challenge to the Churches* (Geneva: WCC Publication and Maryknoll: Orbis Books, 1997); M. Featherstone (ed.), *Global Culture: Nationalism, Globalization and Modernity* (London, Newbury Park, New Delhi: Sage Publications, 1990); N. Glazer and D. P. Moynihan (eds.), *Ethnicity: Theory and Practice* (Cambridge and London: Harvard University Press, 1975); M. Guibernau and J. Rex (eds.), *The Ethnicity Reader: Nationalism, Multiculturalism and Migration* (Cambridge: Polity Press, 1997); J. Hutchinson and A. D. Smith (eds.), *Ethnicity* (Oxford Readers, Oxford and New York: Oxford University Press); L. Pachuau, *Ethnic Identity and Christianity: A Sociohistorical and Missiological Study of Christianity in Northeast India with Special Reference to Mizoram*, Studies in the Intercultural History of Christianity, Vol. 129 (Frankfurt: Peter Lang, 2002); F. X. Scheuerer, *Interculturality: A Challenge for the Mission of the Church* (Bangalore: Asian Trading Corporation, 2001); R. J. Schreiter, *Reconciliation: Mission and Ministry in a Changing World Order* (Maryknoll: Orbis Books, 1992).

L. PACHUAU

Evangelism

Evangelism sits at the very heart of mission. In fact, there is a considerable literature that explores the connections (differences and commonalities) between 'mission' on the one hand and 'evangelism' on the other hand. Still, within the evangelical world, evangelism has been a prime motivation for mission: presenting the *gospel by word, deed and presence so that men and women around the world might come to know *Jesus as the Messiah who is the Son of God (to use Markan categories). Donald McGavran states: 'Theologically mission was evangelism by every means possible' ('What is Mission?', p. 17).

Perhaps the most helpful way to distinguish between mission and evangelism is to understand mission as the broader category. 'Mission denotes the total task God has set the church for the salvation of the world ...

Mission is the church sent into the world, to love, to serve, to preach, to teach, to heal, to liberate' (D. Bosch, *Transforming Mission*). Thus evangelism is but one dimension of the total task of mission – though it can be argued that evangelism is the very heart of mission.

As such, the ministry of evangelism needs to be defined carefully so that its special task is not lost within the wider demands of mission. When everything we do as the church is considered 'mission', then it is easy to mute, avoid, forget about, or fail to engage in evangelism. Evangelism has always been a challenging calling. Especially in this postmodern world, to call men and women to follow the way of Jesus is threatening. ('Why his way? Why not other ways?') The church has a history of avoiding the ministry of evangelism.

The definition of evangelism
The word *evangelism* (or its more ecumenical equivalent 'evangelization') is derived from the Greek verb *euangelizō/euangelizesthai*. The core meaning of this verb is to proclaim the good news that the *kingdom (reign) of God has come near in the person and work of Jesus, the response to which is *repentance and *faith (Mark 1:15). The content of the message of the early church became known as *to euangelion*, the good news. In Luke 4:16–21, using a passage from Isaiah, Jesus describes the good news as coming to the poor, bringing release to the captives, sight to the blind, and freedom to the oppressed. He identifies himself as the one anointed to bring this good news. In 1 Corinthians 15:1–11 Paul tells us that the good news focuses on the death (for our sins), burial, and (especially) the *resurrection of Jesus from the dead.

Two closely related words to *euangelizō/euangelizesthai* (virtually synonymous, in fact) are *kēryssein* and *martyrein*. *Kēryssein* means to proclaim (as by a herald). The focus of this word is on those who do the proclaiming and the content of that proclamation (Rom. 16:25). *Martyrein* is a legal term meaning *witness to the facts, vouching for their truth (Luke 24:48). At the heart of the cluster of words that are related to evangelism (Barrett identifies some forty-two NT Greek words that overlap in meaning around the word *euangelizō*) is the idea that there is a task to which the church is called, namely that of communicating a particular message (the gospel) about a particular person (Jesus) in a particular context (the redeeming/ *reconciling/restoring work of God in the world). To evangelize is to 'preach, bring, tell, proclaim, announce, declare' the good news. (These are the six major words that have been used to get at the meaning of *euangelizō*.)

Having said this, it must be added that it is not at all easy to pin down a definition of the work of evangelism or the content of the gospel that will capture a full and nuanced understanding. In fact, as Barrett has pointed out in his exhaustive survey, definitions of evangelism abound. In English there are over 300 different definitions of 'evangelize', employing over 700 synonyms. In light of this fact it is not possible to offer a single, all-comprehensive definition. Rather, I propose to highlight several definitions that have resonated with a wide audience.

A classic definition of evangelism (by dint of its wide usage and frequent quotation), was offered in the 1918 Church of England Report of the Archbishops' Committee:

'To evangelise is so to present Christ Jesus in the power of the Holy Spirit, that men [and women] shall come to put their trust in God through Him, to accept Him as their Saviour, and serve Him as their King in the fellowship of His Church.'

The power of this definition (in addition to the beauty of its language) is the trinitarian emphasis, the focus on Jesus, with language emphasizing his salvific work ('Saviour') and his ongoing role in the life of the believer ('King'), the use of the word 'trust' to capture the NT sense of 'believe', the call to conscious commitment ('accept Him'), the inclusion of the need to continue following Jesus ('serve Him'), and the communal, as against individualistic, setting ('the fellowship of His Church'). As such this definition serves as a reliable guide for those seeking to engage in the ministry of evangelism.

Consultations on evangelism

However, over the years new issues emerged in terms of the definition of evangelism, motivated in part by the plethora of consultations on evangelism that have taken place from the 1970s through to the most recent Lausanne Committee for World Evangelization Forum in Thailand (2004) and the World Council of Churches Conference on World Mission and Evangelism in Athens in 2005. On the conciliar ecumenical side of things, concern was expressed that there be a wholistic understanding of mission and evangelism: 'the "whole church" brings the "whole Gospel" to the "whole world" '. It also insists that such evangelism be 'comprehensive – involving both word and deed'.

Rethinking evangelism within the evangelical movement was fuelled by a series of consultations and conferences sponsored by the Lausanne Committee for World Evangelization (LCWE). This group was initiated and led by Dr Billy Graham and associates, so right from the beginning evangelism has been at the centre of the agenda. One of the most significant documents produced by LCWE is the so-called Lausanne Covenant. Penned in large part by John R. W. Stott, an evangelical Anglican, the Lausanne Covenant includes a masterful definition of evangelism; one which builds upon the Archbishops' definition and responds to issues raised both in conciliar and evangelical circles in the 1960s and 1970s.

'To evangelise is to spread the good news that Jesus Christ died for our sins and was raised from the dead according to the Scriptures (1 Cor. 15:3–4), and that as the reigning Lord he now offers the forgiveness of sins (Acts 2:32–39) and the liberating gift of the Spirit to all who repent and believe (John 20:22). Our Christian presence in the world is indispensable to evangelism, and so is that kind of dialogue whose purpose is to listen sensitively in order to understand. But evangelism in itself is the proclamation of the historical biblical Christ as Saviour (1 Cor. 1:23; 2 Cor. 4:5) and Lord, with a view to persuading people to come to him personally and so be reconciled to God (2 Cor. 5:11, 20). In issuing the gospel invitation we have no liberty to conceal the cost of *discipleship (Luke 14:25–33). Jesus still calls all who would follow him to deny themselves, take up their cross (Mark 8:34), and identify themselves with his new community. The results of evangelism include obedience to Christ, incorporation into his

Church (Acts 2:40, 47) and responsible service in the world (Mark 10:43–45).'

This definition is more comprehensive than the 1918 Archbishops' definition. It shows the influence of church growth thinking by identifying the three aspects of the process of evangelism as *presence, *proclamation and persuasion. (J. I. Packer and other Reform scholars would omit persuasion from this list.) It includes a call to link the invitation to follow Jesus to a call to discipleship, responding to the charge that evangelicals made conversion merely a matter of 'easy believism'. Finally, there is a strong call to community (over against individualism), obedience (so that lifestyle is included in conversion), and service in the world (alluding to the social justice element of the gospel). The issue of social justice is discussed more fully in the Lausanne Covenant in the section following this statement on the nature of evangelism.

The Lausanne Covenant was updated fifteen years later at Lausanne II in Manila (1989) responding to issues of postmodernism and the challenge of AD 2000 for world evangelization. In the twenty-one affirmations that open the document there is language that incorporates conciliar ecumenical insights from the left and language that incorporates charismatic thinking from the right. Thus there is an emphasis on *peace and justice, *culture, *spiritual warfare, and the role of the *Holy Spirit in evangelism. So indeed at this point in history there is an interesting conjunction of the best thinking about evangelism in the evangelical world and in the conciliar ecumenical world, while the Roman Catholic world draws upon some of this Protestant reflection as it struggles to make sense of the postmodern world.

Evangelistic method
Following the Second World War the evangelical movement in America blossomed and with it the evangelistic enterprise. From an emphasis on mass evangelism in the 1950s (with Billy Graham as the key figure) to visitation evangelism in the 1960s (evangelism explosion), to church growth (Fuller Theological Seminary) in the 1970s, to church planting in the 1980s, to seeker-sensitive churches in the 1990s, to 'belonging before believing' in the 2000s (e.g. the Alpha

programme out of Holy Trinity Brompton in London), so the techniques of evangelism shifted in an ever-changing cultural environment. On the run-up to AD 2000 numerous plans were developed to reach the world with the message of Christ.

These evangelistic efforts have been exported to the Majority World. In Korea, for example, following its spectacular hundred-year growth-spurt, American methodologies were adopted (in particular church growth methods) in order to jump-start the growth of the church, which plateaued and then declined slightly in the mid-90s. In sub-Saharan Africa, mass evangelism resulted in vigorous church growth. But both in Africa and Brazil these efforts began to take on a charismatic 'health and wealth' orientation, which invited people to Jesus and promised immediate reward.

Postmodern evangelism
The advent of a postmodern mindset called into question much of what might be labelled 'the technology of evangelism', developed in large part in the United States since the Second World War. For example, Christian witness became stereotyped as a three-part process beginning with an abbreviated story of one's conversion, followed by a plan of salvation (such as 'The Four Spiritual Laws' of Campus Crusade for Christ), and ending with a challenge to accept Jesus then and there. But was conversion to Jesus merely a matter of 'asking Jesus into your heart' or 'making Jesus your Lord and Saviour'? Did a transaction with God take place upon praying 'the sinner's prayer'? What about the call to discipleship? Where was the kingdom of God in all this? What about the belonging, believing and behaving of the early church?

There have been various responses to the challenges of postmodernism. For example, in his nuanced theology of evangelism entitled The Logic of Evangelism, William Abraham argues that the kingdom of God must be kept at the centre of the gospel and that evangelism can be re-conceptualized as 'that set of intentional activities which is governed by the goal of initiating people into the kingdom of God for the first time'. He identifies six aspects of this initiating activity: conversion, baptism, morality (the rule of life as found in the great commandment), the creed (Christian world-view), spiritual gifts and spiritual disciplines.

Robert Webber responds to postmodernism by calling for what he calls ancient-future evangelism. This is evangelism that is rooted in the biblical and classical tradition of the church (in particular the writings of the church fathers and mothers), which is open to the community-based, story-driven, media savvy postmodern world that is opening before us.

The *gospel in our culture* movement, building upon the work of British theologian Bishop Lesslie Newbigin, calls us to recognize that Christendom is a thing of the past, at least in the West. No longer are church and state one. The state predominates and the church has been pushed to the margins of society – even though the church may not yet recognize this fact. But this new state of affairs is not necessarily bad. When Christendom prevailed, the church was often compromised. Now our challenge is to evangelize a secular, materialist state and this begins with recognition that the gospel stands over against the culture of consumption. 'The gospel is not just a message to be proclaimed; it is the form of our participation in what God is doing in and for the world' (J. Brownson *et al.*, *StormFront: The Good News of God*). The good news of Jesus is missional: it is not simply what the church does. Mission is rooted in the initiative of God as God seeks to restore and heal creation. In this context, evangelism is the call to receive and enter into the reign of God by repentance and faith as apprentices to Jesus. *Conversion becomes a change of social identity, the acquisition of a new conceptual language, and a paradigm shift whereby one aligns with a new community and a finds a new story (about God's redemptive activity in Jesus) that brings meaning to life.

With this recognition of the church as missional, the role of the community is newly emphasized. The so-called emerging church is one example. This is the name given to alternative communities, often with an under 35-year-old membership, that seek 'to be God's people 24/7'. Often small in number, these communities embrace the neighbourhood in which they are located, seeking to serve it. Evangelism is a matter of 'blessing' others in tangible ways and inviting them to participate in the church community in ways small and large, as one is able, with the hope that over

time the life, death and resurrection of Jesus will move to the centre of each person's horizon. Creative ways of outreach are being suggested in various parts of the English-speaking world where postmodernism is most evident. This includes 'contemplative evangelism' in which seekers and the curious are invited to engage in spiritual activities such as silent retreats, liturgical services, spiritual direction, Ignatian small groups, spiritual journaling and autobiography, and prayer experiences so as to encounter God directly in an interpretive environment that incarnates the presence of Jesus.

Interestingly, in this postmodern era evangelism and mission are once again connected. Evangelism is understood to be inherently wholistic. There is no divide between evangelism and social justice. To come to Christ is come to him and his community, the church, which is engaged in God's redemptive mission to the world. This is a healthy sign.

Bibliography

W. Abraham, *The Logic of Evangelism* (Grand Rapids: Eerdmans, 1989); D. Barrett, *Evangelize! A Historical Survey of the Concept* (Birmingham: New Hope, 1987); D. Bosch, *Transforming Mission* (Maryknoll: Orbis Books, 1991); J. Brownson, I. Dietterich, B. Harvey and C. West, *StormFront: The Good News of God* (Grand Rapids: Eerdmans, 2003); M. Frost and A. Hirsch, *The Shaping of Things to Come* (New South Wales: Strand Publisher, 2003); A. Glasser and D. McGavran, 'What is Mission?', *Contemporary Theologies of Mission* (Grand Rapids, MI: Baker Book House, 1983); M. Green, *Evangelism in the Early Church* (Grand Rapids: Eerdmans, 1970); B. Kallenberg, *Live to Tell: Evangelism for a Postmodern Age* (Grand Rapids: Brazos Press, 2002); *Mission-Shaped Church* (London: Church House Publishing, 2004); J. Scherer and S. Bevans (eds.), *New Directions in Mission and Evangelization 1: Basic Statements, 1974–1991* (Maryknoll: Orbis Books, 1992); J. Scherer and S. Bevans (eds.), *New Directions in Mission and Evangelization 2: Theological Foundations* (Maryknoll: Orbis Books, 1994); R. Webber, *Ancient-Future Evangelism* (Grand Rapids: Baker Books, 2003).

R. PEACE

Exodus

The enduring impact of the exodus

The exodus historically has captured the imagination of those who suffer injustice and who, like the ancient Israelites, long for freedom. Groups that have undertaken actual physical migrations believed their own experience of journeying to a promised land to be analogous to the exodus. The crossing of the Atlantic by the pilgrims to the New World (1621), the Great Trek of the Boers in South Africa (1835–42), and the journey soon after of Mormons under Brigham Young to what is now the state of Utah in the United States were interpreted in this light.

Other movements have appealed to the exodus as a model for a militant politics. Here the correspondences are felt to lie in the experience of oppression and the effort to overturn the socio-political situation, often under the leadership of a contemporary Moses figure. In the mid-seventeenth century the exodus was used to encourage Puritan involvement in the English Civil War and the establishment of Cromwell's Commonwealth. A century later it was preached from evangelical pulpits in the run-up to the American Revolution to rally opposition to the British crown. During the early years of the United States religious leaders connected the exodus with national identity: the nascent republic was like Israel, the recipient of the blessing of God with a calling to be a light to the world.

The exodus has played a significant role in African-American religion. Ironically, while the white majority saw in this theme definitive proof of God's good hand, slaves likened their cruel exploitation within that supposed land of freedom to the affliction of the Israelites in Egypt. The motif was incorporated into 'Negro' spirituals to picture release from bondage in this life and in heaven after death and was a theological underpinning for slave insurrections in the Antebellum South. Many equated the Emancipation Proclamation of 1863 and the ratification in 1865 of the Thirteenth Amendment (which formally freed all slaves) as fulfilments of the exodus dream. The Civil Rights movement of the 1950s and 1960s found inspiration in the exodus as well. The Reverend Dr Martin Luther King, Jr on several occasions presented himself as another Moses and their efforts as part of the ongoing saga of participating in that story (see *Black Consciousness).

South African and Black Liberation theologians have made extensive use of the exodus. From Latin America Gutiérrez has argued that the demand for *liberation transcends the particular historical experience of Israel; it is paradigmatic of the actions of God and should lead Christians to effect change. Croatto holds that the exodus event has a 'reservoir of meaning' that can be appropriated afresh by modern movements of liberation. Interestingly, not all are as sanguine about the liberating potential of the exodus. For some Palestinian Christians, who witness how the text has been used by Zionism, the exodus, along with the conquest narrative, is oppressive. Based on critical theories that hypothesize that the exodus account went through a series of redactions, a few liberationists believe that its liberating impulse was gradually weakened with each additional layer that expanded on the original tradition of a peasant revolt.

The exodus in Scripture and Christian mission

The influence of the exodus across historical and geographical contexts and theological traditions is patent. For those who accept the full authority of the Bible, the crucial question is 'What might the biblical text warrant for Christian mission today?'

Redemption and social responsibility

Through the exodus Yahweh wrought the redemption of Israel. This event established a special relationship between God and his people at corporate and individual levels. The nation as a whole, families, and each individual, celebrated this deliverance at the feasts of Passover and Tabernacles. The personal spiritual aspect of this redemption was enacted in the offering of sacrifices for sin and fellowship with God and is evident in prayers that utilize exodus imagery (e.g. Pss. 77; 78). Exodus typology in fact pervades the Gospels. Jesus' self-sacrifice is called a 'departure' (Luke 9:31; Gk *exodos*). It offers freedom from slavery to sin, the demonic, disease and death. Paul writes that believers are redeemed from bondage to sin through the sacrifice of the Passover lamb (Rom. 6 – 8; 1 Cor. 5:7).

The exodus also was the response of

a gracious God to physical suffering. He heard the anguished cry of his people and honoured the patriarchal covenant by freeing Israel from Pharaoh's grip (Exod. 2:23–25; 3:7–8; 6:1–8). His very name is connected to this deliverance (Exod. 3:13–17). This redemption was the foundation of the Law, which was designed to create an ethical community different from the oppressive system under Pharaoh (Exod. 19:3–6; Deut. 6:13–25). It subverted the socio-economic and political arrogance of Egypt and was to motivate Israel to be merciful to those in need: the poor, widows, orphans and aliens (Exod. 22:21–27; 23:6–9; Lev. 19:33–36; Deut. 10:14–22). The Sabbath day ethic (Deut. 5:12–15) and legislation for the unfortunate, such as the sabbatical year (Deut. 15:12–18) and the jubilee (Lev. 25), also appealed to the exodus. In other words, with election came responsibility (Amos 3:1–2). This connection between redemption and active social concern is clear in the life of Jesus and in the rest of the NT (Acts 2; 4; 6; Rom. 12 – 15; Jas).

The redemption of God has a personal spiritual component. Christian mission cannot ignore the centrality of the forgiveness of sin and the promise of eternal life accomplished at the cross of Christ. Just as importantly, the exodus demonstrates that God is compassionate and that he insists that his people be, too. Mission, therefore, also has a social dimension that should find expression in concrete strategies on behalf of the powerless – at the very least within the alternative community that confesses his name. It will not do to dichotomize the personal from the social, the spiritual from the ethical. All are inseparable aspects of an integrated, *holistic mission.

Divine involvement in history

The opening survey is a sample of how the exodus has been appropriated for good or ill by diverse movements. There is no denying its power, but an evaluation of this sort of typological hermeneutic lies beyond the purview of this essay. A careful reading of the biblical text suggests some caution in its use. To begin with, for Israel, the exodus was a singular event. It marked the miraculous birth of the nation. It was paradigmatic in that it substantiated that God would act in history,

but that did not mean that Yahweh would necessarily work in like manner again. The return from the exile is described in Isaiah as a second exodus (Isa. 43:16–20; 51:9–11; 52:10–12), but this, too, is seen as a unique event. Freedom from bondage was not always forthcoming; sometimes defeat came as the judgment of God himself. Even in Egypt Israel suffered for a time, and in its history it would be subject in turn to the Assyrian, Babylonian, and Persian Empires. In times of national distress the prophets called for lament to implore Yahweh to come to their aid, but divine intervention was contingent on confession (Jer. 9; Joel 1 – 2). To sin against Yahweh would lead to exile, the reversal of the exodus.

The particularity of Israel confirmed at the exodus (Amos 3:1–2), however, in no way negates God's participation in the history of other peoples (Amos 9:7). These interventions often are moral judgments. Yahweh hears the cry of victims of injustice (Gen. 4:10); he is creator of rich and poor alike (Prov. 14:31; 17:5; 22:2). The exodus narrative graphically exposes the self-destructive pretence of any socio-political system or ideology that denies the sovereignty of God and violates his moral law. He punishes cruelty in warfare (Amos 1:3 – 2:3), oppressive tyrants (Isa. 10:12–34; 13 – 14; Nah.), and corrupt economic powers (Ezek. 26 – 28). But God also will be as merciful to the most violent of nations who turn to him as he was to the people of the exodus (Jon. 3:7 – 4:2; cf. Exod. 34:6).

The exodus teaches that mission is inseparable from historical realities and social processes, even as it challenges every unjust social construct. Some have rightly warned of the propensity of some liberationists to misread the role of the people of God in the exodus event itself and to reduce as well the relevance of the exodus to the political, while ignoring how the NT utilizes the theme; they also have wisely pointed out, however, the opposite tendency among others to limit its significance to spiritual salvation. God does have a deep concern for human suffering. The trajectory of the exodus motif in Scripture in fact underscores God's commitment to justice, but it does not delineate a specific course of action – whether for God or his people. The pilgrimage of the redeemed is to live as a community that strives to incarnate and responsibly promote God's moral demands at every level, trusting that he will intervene as he wills until the final redemption.

Bibliography

N. S. Ateek, *Justice, and Only Justice: A Palestinian Theology of Liberation* (Maryknoll, NY: Orbis Books, 1989); W. Brueggemann, *Theology of the Old Testament: Testimony, Dispute, Advocacy* (Minneapolis: Fortress, 1997); J. H. Cone, *A Black Theology of Liberation* (Maryknoll, NY: Orbis Books, 1990); J. S. Croatto, *Exodus: A Hermeneutic of Freedom* (Maryknoll, NY: Orbis Books, 1981); G. Gutiérrez, *A Theology of Liberation: History, Politics, and Salvation* (Maryknoll, NY: Orbis Books, ²1988); A. Kirk, *Liberation Theology: An Evangelical View from the Third World* (Atlanta, GA: John Knox, 1979); D. W. Kling, *The Bible in History: How the Texts have Shaped the Times* (Oxford: Oxford University Press, 2004); E. A. C. Núñez, *Liberation Theology* (Chicago: Moody, 1985); J. Pixley, *Exodus: A Liberation Perspective* (Maryknoll, NY: Orbis Books, 1987); W. M. Swartley, *Israel's Scripture Traditions and the Synoptic Gospels: Story Shaping Story* (Peabody, MA: Hendrickson, 1994); B. Van Iersel and A. Weiler (eds.), *Exodus: A Lasting Paradigm* (Edinburgh: T. & T. Clark, 1987); M. Walzer, *Exodus and Revolution* (New York: Basic Books, 1985); G. O. West, *Biblical Hermeneutics of Liberation: Modes of Reading the Bible in the South African Context* (Pietermaritzburg: Cluster; Maryknoll, NY: Orbis Books, rev. edn. 1995); J. H. Yoder, 'Withdrawal and Diaspora: The Two Faces of Liberation', in D. S. Schipani (ed.), *Freedom and Discipleship: Liberation Theology in an Anabaptist Perspective* (Maryknoll, NY: Orbis Books, 1989).

M. D. CARROLL R.

Faith

This article explores faith through the three main dimensions of its past, present and future orientation. There is the faith that looks back to *Christ's death and resurrection and trusts that these events are the means of being put right with God and receiving new life in Christ (e.g. Rom. 3:22, 26; 5:1; Acts 16:31). Belief in these events has been historically expressed in statements of faith. There is the faith that trusts *God for his presence, strength and guidance to live the Christian life in the present (e.g. Luke 17:5–6; Acts 16:5; 2 Cor. 1:24; Jas 1:2–3). Then there is faith that believes God for his promises of future hope and glory (e.g. 2 Tim. 4:7–8; Heb. 11:1–38; 12:1–3). These dimensions are inseparable and integral to each other.

Christian faith is essentially in God himself and has good grounds for its confidence because of who God is and how he has revealed himself in Jesus Christ. Nevertheless, faith is a conviction about what cannot be seen or proved; and it is in those times when God's purposes and will are not clear that faith comes into its own as an abiding assurance of the love of God in spite of all evidence to the contrary.

The three dimensions of faith are all present in authentic mission. Dependent faith is necessary for mission because mission is God's mission, the *missio Dei*. It is based on what God has done in and through Christ, what he is doing through his *Spirit, and what he will do to draw humanity into his trinitarian glory. The *church in its mission proclaims the events of faith, nurtures people in the *discipleship of faith, and encourages Christians to exercise the hope of faith.

Faith in mission is frequently associated with obedience, because faithful response to God's call to participate in his mission requires his people to trust in him to guide and strengthen them for the task. Faith operates at the point where human resource is not available. If the church trusts in its own genius it may have a mission, but it will not be God's mission. God looks for faith as dependence on him and submission to his will in those who would be his servants. So Abraham, one of the first chosen by God through whom to work out his mission purposes, needed a faith relationship with God, in order to enter into all that God had planned for him and through him for all the nations. All the men and women of faith since then have shown similar qualities, and in spite of their humanity, God has chosen to use them and bless others through them.

Faith and missionaries

Missionary biographies frequently highlight

the faith of those who made great sacrifices in their obedience to the call of God. Because mission calls Christians to cross boundaries, cultural, religious and personal, it takes them out of their 'comfort zones' and obliges them to trust God for their work and their very lives. Mission, because it is the central component of discipleship, requires the willingness to take up the cross and share in Christ's sufferings. Many missionaries, past and present, have done this quite literally in laying down their lives as they fulfilled the call of God. However, sometimes biographies have become hagiographies, which have exalted missionaries as super-human, faith-filled heroes whose level of super-spirituality leaves the rest of God's people with a great sense of inadequacy. The reality is that God has often worked through those who were humanly speaking most *weak and unqualified.

Many mission agencies (see *Mission Societies) of the nineteenth and twentieth centuries were so committed to the principle of faith that they were called 'faith missions', which meant trusting God to provide for them without actively soliciting support or advertising their needs. Equally importantly, they were interdenominational, independent, 'non-church' missions. They had a strong vision for 'reaching the unreached' and in pursuit of this they were committed to mission as *evangelism. They looked back for their inspiration to Hudson Taylor, who founded the China Inland Mission in 1865, widely regarded as the first true 'faith mission'. There are many agencies today who work on the same principles, believing that if God has called so he will faithfully provide for and bless the task he has entrusted to them. Other agencies have different approaches to the way by which they fund mission, and many actively seek support for their work. It is generally accepted that all of these ways have their own legitimacy, and asking for specific support for specific needs may be simply seen as another way of exercising faith.

The 'faith principle', however, can be abused. Those who 'live by faith' can claim, overtly or implicitly, that their kind of mission with its apparently fully committed faith is more blessed by God than those who conduct mission through more conventional means. Sometimes missions have been set up as a way of doing mission in a supposedly better way than others. There is a temptation to claim results for great faith, as if faith of itself gives the authority to command blessing from God. Some agencies and missionaries have been criticized for 'lack of faith', and that is sometimes presumed to be the cause of their failure of 'success', usually measured numerically. Suffering, lack of healing, poor response, financial difficulties – these are all sometimes wrongly attributed to weak or absent faith. But God must always be sovereign in his mission, to bless or withhold blessing as he chooses. That he does work his purposes out through human beings is more a testimony to his grace than to their faith. Faith is essentially a relationship of dependence, not a quantifiable quality which can be used or abused as a way of manipulating God into action.

Faith and mission

As well as on an individual level, the church corporately requires faith for its mission. To be called by God to work for his *kingdom in the world requires faith that building relationships across cultural and religious boundaries, and freely demonstrating the love of God in all situations of need, will in God's time bear fruit for his kingdom. Mission is as much the sowing of seeds as the reaping of a harvest. Prophetic proclamation also requires faith to speak against injustice, and to confront the principalities and powers at work in the world, since this will always generate opposition.

Mission is difficult in a *pluralistic context, not least because Christian 'faith' has a problem establishing its unique and distinctive credentials. Faith has meaning only in relation to its object: it has to be faith in something or someone. The authenticity of 'faith' therefore is determined by the genuineness and reliability of its object. Some pluralists speak of 'other faiths' as if they all have equal authenticity merely for the fact that they exhibit faith, the important thing being for people to have faith irrespective of its object or content. Some claim that the ultimate object of all faiths is the same 'God'. Christian faith, however, looks back to the concrete truths of the revelation made to humanity by the God and Father of Jesus Christ. The *cross and *resurrection as the source of salvation is therefore at the heart of what the church preaches in its mission. Christian mission can only witness to the Triune God who has been revealed in the life and teaching of Jesus Christ of Nazareth, who alone is the source of true faith.

This kind of committed belief or trust is inimical to a postmodern world that has lost confidence in the possibility of objective knowledge and is therefore reluctant to commit to anything. Faith is ridiculed as belief in fairies at the bottom of the garden. It is said that faith in the past can only be an interpretation, faith in the present is merely experiential, and faith in the future is wishful thinking. The church in its mission in this context must therefore work to restore the authenticity of faith at each of these three levels: there are good grounds for faith in what God has done, there are genuine experiences of God today, and because God's promises can be trusted the future for those who believe in him is assured. So we can conclude that mission is required for faith and faith is required for mission.

Bibliography

J. A. Carpenter and W. R. Shenk (eds.), *Earthen Vessels: American Evangelicals and Foreign Missions* (Grand Rapids: Eerdmans, 1990); K. Fiedler, *The Story of Faith Missions* (Oxford: Regnum Lynx, 1994).

J. CORRIE

FAITH MOVEMENT, see PROSPERITY THEOLOGY

Family

The family is one of the oldest human societal institutions. This article will limit itself to brief consideration of the family of biblical times, of the NT church as the family of faith, and of the implications of this for the missional dimension of the family.

Biblical dimensions

Biblical families are multi-generational social units of those who have blood ties and live together in a common household. Included are also servants, foreigners, travellers, widows and orphans. The household head had the responsibility to protect, assist, discipline and sustain the family as well as fulfil his priestly function toward family members, especially the children. Each member of the family was to work for the good of the whole

group, and to accept responsibility for all of its aspects, so as not to bring shame on the family. There is a strong emphasis on including the whole family in spirituality and in religious festivals, especially the Sabbath, in the OT. In the NT whole households are brought to faith in Christ. While individualistic Western culture may not consider such an approach necessary today, in the majority of the world's cultures social cohesion depends on strong family and extended family relationships. So it is more effective to introduce the gospel to whole families and not primarily to individuals, and to bring whole families into the new community of faith. This will help, for example, believers from a Muslim background to remain steadfast in their faith and not to feel as if they are bringing shame onto their family.

Church dimensions

The NT church community is described as the new spiritual family, or family of God. This may have its roots in Jesus: when his family visit him (Matt. 12:46–50), he declares those who do God's will to be his 'real' family. The Lord's Prayer also unites all believers into one family under God as father. When asked about the reward of leaving one's house and family for the sake of the gospel, Jesus promises that his followers will in return receive homes, mothers, brothers, sisters and children (Mark 10:30), a new family of faith to care and be responsible for. Although continuing to live in nuclear or extended families, the church today is called to create a new community that includes people of different standing and provides a spiritual family for them: singles, one- and two-parent families, divorced persons, those whose biological relatives do not belong to the faith, children and adults from broken and distorted families. Humans are created for community (Gen. 2:18) and will be able to fulfil their God-given purpose best through being integrated into a community.

We need to be careful, at least in the West, in using the image of family for the church, not to discourage singles or people less integrated into a biological family while, on the other hand, promoting communal fellowship, belonging and support in the church, values that have traditionally been described by the image of family.

Mission dimensions

While much has been said from a sociological point of view about the purpose of the family in society, Paul perceives marriage and single-ness as gifts from God (1 Cor. 7:7). Spiritual gifts are always given for the purpose of mission: serving one another, for the benefit of the whole church, for God's glory. Whilst many Christian singles more consciously accept their standing as a calling and often dedicate their lives to the mission work of the kingdom, families in their busyness often fall for exactly that which Paul warns about, namely 'the affairs of this world'. A Christian family, however, can never be a goal in itself and must overcome the self-sufficiency and the idolatrous (Western) focus on the happiness of its members. It must be concerned 'about the Lord's affairs' (1 Cor. 7:32–35), and how to work together as a family for the kingdom.

Having the privilege of a safe and em-powering home base, family members are better equipped to join God's mission in the church and beyond it. *Children are included in this calling and are sensitively helped to grow naturally into the larger community and accept appropriate responsibilities. The biblical perspective that God relates to whole families leads us to conclude that when God calls Christians into mission, there is a corresponding call on their whole family. When Abram obeyed God's call, his family went with him (Gen. 12:5). This means including children in taking big deci-sions to leave home for life in a different cultural context.

Positively children often receive a great deal by being brought up in a culture different from their own, from acquiring language skills to awareness of global issues. However it must be admitted that orientation to mis-sion poses great challenges for a family and puts many strains on its members. Children especially will need to receive special atten-tion, for example, when dealing with cross-cultural issues, when trying to find their own place in the ministry, when confronted with time restraints of their parents. Nevertheless, a focus on mission will help them to create intentional communities that expand beyond the nuclear family; and to fulfil in creative ways the greatest commandment of seeing and loving one's neighbour(s).

Bibliography

S. C. Barton (ed.), *The Family in Theological Perspective* (Edinburgh: T. & T. Clark, 1996); P. C. Blum, 'Who Defines Family? Mennonite Reflection on Family and Sociology of Know-ledge', *Conrad Grebel Review* 19, 2001, pp. 68–82; A. Destro and M. Pesce, 'Fathers and Householders in the Jesus Movement: The Perspective of the Gospel of Luke', *Bib-lical Interpretation* 11, 2003, pp. 211–238; S. K. Gallagher, *Evangelical Identity and Gendered Family Life* (Rutgers, NJ: Rutgers University Press, 2003); D. R. Garland, *Family Ministry: A Comprehensive Guide* (Downers Grove: InterVarsity Press, 1999); E. E. Johnson, 'Apocalyptic Family Values', *Interpretation* 56, 2002, pp. 34–44.

K. PENNER

Feminism

Feminism should really be called feminisms. It is still an evolving phenomenon and there are different kinds of feminisms. Feminism from the Two-Thirds World or Majority World is different from feminism in the West, or from *mujerista* feminism (Hispanic), or from womanism (black American). In general feminism has gone through several stages, or waves, from being an equal rights movement to an intellectual discourse that appreciates and affirms difference and particularity.

Historical perspective

The eighteenth century saw a significant change in the way women were portrayed in religious discourse. The traditional emphasis on Eve as temptress gave way to seeing women as the virtuous sustainers and repos-itories of religious values in a way that was not true of men. Evangelical religion began to offer a clear definition of separate spheres. The men's sphere was in the public arena of work and business while women occupied the private sphere of home and hearth. A woman's task was to contribute daily and hourly to the comfort of all those around her in the domestic circle. She was to shape and improve the manners and behaviour of men by her example and she was to model the human mind in its early stages of growth. This was commonly known as 'the angel in the house' phenomenon.

For evangelicals in the nineteenth century

there was a spiritual equality but a functional and social subordination of women. Women were active in the abolitionist, temperance and suffrage movements both in the UK and the USA. During this period the Pentecostal and Wesleyan movements accepted women into positions of leadership. Women were serving overseas as missionaries – in fact by 1900 forty-one of the ninety-four mission boards in the USA were women's boards, supported by and sending only women missionaries. R. Pierce Beaver's book on women in mission, *American Protestant Women in World Mission: A History of the First Feminist Movement in North America* (Grand Rapids: Eerdmans, 1980) argues that these women, by involving only women, were among the first feminists. Unfortunately the existence of these boards was shortlived and by the early twentieth century they had merged and integrated with the general boards, almost certainly to the detriment of the involvement of American women in mission.

Evangelical women in the abolitionist movement realized that *liberation is an overarching theme in Scripture and that this should equally apply to the role and place of women in society. The Female Anti-Slavery Society, founded in 1833 in the USA, made a natural connection between the oppression of slavery and the subordination of women. Women such as the Grimke sisters (Sarah, 1792–1893 and Angelina, 1805–79) along with the well-known black woman, Sojourner Truth (Belle Baumfree, 1797–1883, famous for her 'Ain't I a Woman' speech), not only strongly condemned the evils of slavery but also promoted the right of women to speak publicly in churches against it. Galatians 3:28 became a hermeneutical key by which to interpret Scripture. Although many evangelical and secular women were active in promoting equality for women in the nineteenth century, women were still underrepresented in all areas in both church and society and patriarchy was still the prevailing world-view.

Contemporary feminism

Feminism today is a complex phenomenon. Twentieth-century secular feminism arose in the post-war period. Women had worked at men's jobs during two world wars and birth control meant that women now had more choices. Twentieth-century Marxism also influenced feminism. In a capitalist culture they saw white males as controlling the means of production in the public sphere and devaluing the private sphere which was still predominantly the sphere of women. Feminist issues are not experienced in the same way by all women. Women of colour have been critical of white women for universalizing their experience as common to all women. Social location and attention to difference are vital. Black American feminist bell hooks claims that much feminist theory has come from privileged women who live at the centre and that we must include the voices of those from the margins. Women from various parts of the world are also bringing insights from feminist analysis to bear on the ecological crisis. They call for an end to all forms of oppression, especially the exploitation of creation. So the feminist agenda has widened to include not just the social, political and economic equality of women with men, but also the fundamental re-imagination of humanity and creation.

Feminist theology

Feminism and feminist theology are concerned with exposing and dealing with patriarchy. Patriarchy is the male bias that is found in all spheres of life such as language, institutions, the workplace, family traditions, cultural structures and practices. Feminists expose patriarchy that oppresses and excludes women overtly or covertly not only from the public sphere, but also from exercising their full humanity. In our world women are the poorest and the most oppressed by any indicators; in terms of health, education, economics, abuse and violence, whether by individuals or by social structures. In every country of the world men earn more pay for less work. It is estimated that women do 62% of the world's work hours, yet own only 1% of the world's property. Women form 75% of all sick people, 70% of all the poor, 66% of all illiterates and 80% of all refugees.

Feminist theology deals with issues such as these and asks why there is such systemic injustice against women. It critiques theology as having been done by men and for men, and as validating only men's experience, thereby ignoring the concerns and experience of half of humanity. Feminist theologians approach the Bible with new lenses and new questions, noticing women where they have previously been obscured, and offering alternatives to previously male-dominated biblical hermeneutics. They critique exclusively male images of God, an association of female sexuality with original sin, exclusive language and imagery in liturgy and worship, the hierarchical and male structures of the church, and they are open to a variety of understandings of the cross. Feminist theology is deeply rooted in women's experience, is marked by commitment and engagement and is focused on personal and social transformation. It has an experiential and experimental quality to it, which can be seen in its language, style, poems, prayers, liturgies and art.

In its most extreme form, feminist theology has become post-Christian, moving beyond any doctrinal core of belief, or authoritative word. At times it can suffer from reductionism by allowing gender to drive its theology and allowing context and experience to override Scripture. This makes feminist theology problematic for many evangelicals. According to Sally Gallagher's most recent work, the majority of evangelicals in USA still believe in gendered roles in church and family.

Leading feminist theologians in the West are women such as Elisabeth Schuessler-Fiorenza, Rosemary Radford Ruether, Letty Russell, Phyllis Trible, Sally McFague and Nancy Hardesty. Evangelical feminists include Elaine Storkey, Mary Stewart van Leeuwen, Rebecca Merrill Groothuis, Elouise Renich-Fraser and Marianne Meye-Thompson. Some of these women are involved in 'Christians for Biblical Equality' (see bibliography), a significant organization which believes that the Bible, properly interpreted, teaches the fundamental equality of men and women of all ethnicities and all economic classes, based on the teachings of Scripture as reflected in Galatians 3:28. Theologians such as Mary Daly and Daphne Hanson have left the church and invoked a post-Christian response to the systemic injustice against women.

Feminist theology in the Two-Thirds World has emerged from interaction with Western feminists and from their own contexts. Women in the Two-Thirds World may suffer from a triple oppression: poverty, racism and sexism. Feminist theologians in the

Two-Thirds World want to decide for themselves what feminist theology will be for them in their contexts. They claim that it is not for First-World women nor for Third-World men to set the agenda for them. Some common themes in feminist theology from the Two-Thirds World are: a sharing of the depth of oppression, suffering and struggle; a new vision worked out in the context of a renewed church community; empowerment to change their circumstances and liberation.

Some of the leading feminist theologians from the Two-Thirds World include Musa Dube (Botswana), Elsa Tamez (Mexico), Ivone Gebara (Brazil), Virginia Fabella (Philippines), Marianne Katoppo (Indonesia), Mercy Amba Oduyoye (Ghana), Philomena Mwaura and Anne Nasimiyu-Wasike (Kenya).

Finally, as we live and work in a world where women are among the suffering and the most oppressed, feminist theology can provide insights into why there is still this systemic injustice and why women are still discriminated against everywhere in the world. It can also offer suggestions as to how, in the practice of mission, we make both church and society more akin to the biblical vision of Galatians 3:28.

See also GENDER ISSUES, WOMEN IN MISSION.

Bibliography
M. L. Bendroth, *Fundamentalism and Gender 1875 to the Present* (New Haven: Yale University Press, 1993); A. Clifford, *Introducing Feminist Theology* (Maryknoll: Orbis Books, 2001); S. K. Gallagher, *Evangelical Identity and Gendered Family Life* (New Brunswick: Rutgers University Press, 2003); I. Gebara, *Out of the Depths: Women's Experience of Evil and Salvation* (Minneapolis: Fortress, 2002); R. M. Groothuis, *Women Caught in the Conflict: The Culture War Between Traditionalism and Feminism* (Grand Rapids: Baker, 1994); N. Hoggard Creegan and C. Pohl, *Living on the Boundaries: Evangelical Women, Feminism and the Theological Academy* (Downers Grove: InterVarsity Press, 2005); U. King (ed.), *Feminist Theology from the Third World* (London: SPCK, 1994); C. C. Kroeger and M. J. Evans (eds.), *The IVP Women's Bible Commentary* (Downers Grove: InterVarsity Press, 2002);

M. Oduyoye, *Daughters of Anowa: African Women and Patriarchy* (Maryknoll: Orbis Books, 1995); R. R. Ruether, *Women and Redemption: A Theological History* (Minneapolis: Fortress, 1998); E. Storkey with M. Hebblewaite, *Conversations on Christian Feminism: Speaking Heart to Heart* (London: HarperCollins, 1999); Christians for Biblical Equality, <http://www.cbeinternational.org>.

C. Ross

Folk religion

People groups everywhere have their own versions of standard or official beliefs and practices. How to deal with such popular understandings and lifestyles is crucial in cross-cultural mission. Before we shun such popular beliefs and practices as unbiblical and useless we should consider how the Bible reports on and deals with them. The Lord confronts people groups as well as individuals, both inside and outside the church, in ways that are instructive to us.

Definition

Simply put, folk religion has to do with popular beliefs and practices that become an accepted and unquestioned element in a people's concepts and behaviour regarding any sphere of life for which they may need extra help, regardless of the official religious system to which they may subscribe. Issues such as disease, spiritual instability, relational problems, economic hardship, or mere greed, lust, pride, vendetta feelings, and so on, are fertile ground for the insertion or perpetuation of folk beliefs and practices. In the Western world, for one, astrology has never lost its appeal; on the other hand, *shamanism and its many varieties, such as *witchcraft and the occult, have never been stronger, and people invest time and money in acquiring personal benefits from the specialists, great and small.

The great religions of the world have their own folk versions. It is one thing to discuss Buddhism with a Buddhist scholar; it is quite another to dialogue with a faithful Buddhist who is untrained in theological matters. The same can be said of Christianity. When Western-minded missionaries shun folk beliefs and practices as mere superstition, they may be liable to present a message which is less than biblical and largely irrelevant to their audience.

People everywhere encounter problems that technology, however advanced, cannot handle. When institutional religion cannot cope with seemingly insoluble cases, folk religion may look like a natural outlet. Time-honoured solutions to common problems are transmitted from person to person, often in critical situations of life. Alternatively, a willingness to experiment with novel solutions depends largely on the seriousness of the problem, especially when familiar time-honoured solutions have proven ineffective. An added factor in such openness has to do with the attitude of the change advocate, which is a role often played by cross-cultural workers. If such workers propose the truth and power of the gospel in *culture-specific ways, the receptors of the message may experiment with the novelty. Such seems to have been the case of Paul in places such as Corinth, Ephesus, Philippi, Athens and Malta (Acts 14, 16, 17 and 28). When the message did not follow cultural traditions, as in Lystra (Acts 14), the results were confusing at best. However, we should note that such openness is vital if people are to experience the Christian way.

Persistence

Power is the key issue. Questions such as whence the *power comes are secondary, in many cases, to issues of whether it works or not in a given crisis. Power encounters, however, are not the sole and determining factor in turning people to the God of the Bible (1 Kgs 17). As Charles Kraft has advocated, power, truth and allegiance constitute a balanced set of encounters people need to engage in order to decide whether to adopt the Christian faith and grow in it. A polarization between a rationalistic form of Christianity, on the one hand, and an ecstatic view of the gospel, on the other, is therefore unscriptural and misplaced.

Here are some features that a missionary must take into account regarding folk religion:

It is resilient. It withstands all forms of opposition, from inside and outside, including the missionary. Although typically the missionary ignores (literally), shuns and condemns all forms of folk religion and its practices and practitioners, folk religion has a way of surviving through difficult times.

It is effective. Only those features of folk religion that work are preserved over time.

It thrives through cultural adaptation. People adopt those beliefs and practices that help them find solutions in critical situations, often without regard for their religious or cultural origin.

It is non-formal in structure and transmission. In order to survive alongside sophisticated religious systems, folk religion is not complicated when it comes to its intrinsic structures and ways of transmission, which facilitates its perpetuation and adaptability.

*It survives in *narrative form.* Stories have a way of consolidating a people's world-view; they strengthen their beliefs and practices vis-à-vis competing systems, such as those introduced typically by missionaries.

Folk religion and mission

In Latin America, responses to folk religion have been diverse. The Roman Catholic Church has long given up obliterating those aspects of folk religion that have proven stubbornly resilient through time. Today, the official church co-exists peacefully with the worship of popular saints, African deities and indigenous spirits, and their corresponding practices. The recent canonization of the Mexican saint Diego is a case in point. Since during the 'conquest' there was no clear strategy for Christianizing the slaves arriving from the coasts of Africa, on the one hand, and the indigenous populations (with honourable exceptions) on the other, Latin American (folk) versions of the Roman Catholic Church have carved a niche for themselves.

The later arrival of conservative Protestantism did little to abort the survival of folk religion throughout the continent. Since early Protestantism did not enjoy the political freedom and power it had in Reformed Europe, it survived as an isolated belief system, often with a foreignness of its own, which could aspire only to peaceful co-existence with the nominal Catholic majority. The Protestant evangelistic message adapted accordingly, becoming strongly heaven-centred, with an outright condemnation of all things political, earthly and heathen. However, with the recent arrival of Pentecostalism and its openness to the spirit world, which resonates with folk beliefs everywhere, the face of the evangelical church in Latin America has changed dramatically. The truth, however, is that vestiges of folk religion, in various degrees, can be found among the many religious groups of the continent.

A biblical and missiological critique

Can God reveal himself through folk religion? That is a question many missiologists and theologians are carefully considering. Jonah 1 is instructive at this point.

The sailors believe that the gods are accessible to humans and are liable to display compassion on their behalf. They also believe that actions in the visible world have consequences in the invisible world, since both are intertwined and interdependent. It is their strong conviction that human beings are responsible for their actions and that is the reason why something has to be done to Jonah so that natural order can be restored. (Note that 'natural order' depends on the right relationship between people and their gods.) The highlight of the sailors' belief is that one person's obedience can benefit many, just as one person's disobedience (Jonah's) brought harm to many (all on board the boat). Clearly, those sailors have many ideas which are consistent with biblical revelation. However, some corrections are in order and God sees to it that they occur. By means of *truth (Jonah's speech) and power (the calming of the storm), God draws the sailors to himself. In the end, they learn that God is above all gods, his truth is above all human understanding, he alone is compassionate and merciful, and he is a just and righteous God. They learn above all that God demands allegiance to him above all gods, and the sailors comply by praying to him, fearing him in their hearts and making a pledge of allegiance (through sacrifices) to the God of Jonah. We note thus that God uses folk beliefs and practices as ways to draw people to himself just as he used an imperfect servant to communicate biblical truth to people at the point of their need.

We learn from this that, instead of shunning folk religion: God can use it to bring people to himself; God's servants must be willing to communicate his truth and power to people in need; God corrects people's ideas about him in ways that they can understand; and beyond communicating his truth and displaying his power, God expects and demands personal and collective allegiance to him above all other forms of allegiance. Biblical texts on God's similar dealings with folk religion include such characters as Pharaoh (Gen. 12, 41), Melchizedech (Gen. 14), Naaman (2 Kgs 5), Nebuchadnezzar (Dan. 1 – 6) and the Magi from the East (Matt. 2), not to mention Jesus' own ministry with his people (Luke 24:36–49). Shunning folk religion as useless to God, therefore, has no biblical basis. What is needed for an effective mission response is a Bible-based strategy that glorifies God and affirms the ways in which he wants to draw people everywhere to himself.

See also WORLD-VIEW.

Bibliography
G. Cook (ed.), *New Face of the Church in Latin America* (Maryknoll: Orbis Books, 1999); L. DeCarvalho, *The Shaman and the Missionary: Worldview Construction among the Terena*, PhD thesis (Pasadena: Fuller Seminary, 1999); P. G. Hiebert, *Cultural Anthropology* (Grand Rapids: Baker, 1983); C. H. Kraft, 'What Kinds of Encounters Do We Need in Christian Witness?', *EMQ* 27, 1991, pp. 258–265; A. F. C. Wallace, 'Revitalization Movements', *American Anthropologist* 58, 1956, pp. 264–281.
L. DeCarvalho

FORGIVENESS, see RECONCILIATION
FUTURE, see ESCHATOLOGY, HOPE

Gender issues

Gender issues are ignored in most textbooks of missiology. This fact reflects the general exclusion of women from ecclesiological concerns. In Paul Hiebert's threefold categorization of mission thought into evangelistic, ecclesiocentric and kingdom-centric types, women's mission activity has typically fallen either into personal evangelistic work, or kingdom-centric forms of social outreach. Excluded from ordination throughout most of history, women have offered little ecclesiological reflection on what has been seen as the male domain of church-planting, ordination and church organization. A barrier to gendered mission theology has been the assumption that women's mission work is

'auxiliary' to that of men; women have engaged in much mission practice but little mission reflection.

Nevertheless, mission service has long been the major venue for women's ministry. Women accompanied Jesus and the disciples, providing them support (Luke 8:1–3). The Samaritan woman was the first indigenous evangelist who shared the news that Jesus was the Messiah (John 4). The women at the tomb were the first witnesses to the resurrection. The only female called a 'disciple' in the NT was Tabitha, the leader of widows, whom Peter raised from the dead (Acts 9:36–42). Groups of widows were the prototype for orders of celibate virgins and deaconesses, who in early centuries served the church in social outreach to the sick and the poor, and in the care of female catechists. Individual women had prominent roles in the NT: Priscilla was a house church leader and teacher of theology (Acts 18). Yet despite the biblical role models of female leadership, formal women's mission leadership was largely suppressed by Roman Catholic rules of cloister from the Middle Ages until the eighteenth century.

In the 1700s, starting with the Moravians, missionaries went out in mixed-gender communities. Unmarried women were gathered into 'choirs' that focused on working with women and girls. Married women were partners with their husbands. The presence of women, both married and unmarried, created a distinctly Protestant model of mission that deviated from the traditional Catholic model of the celibate male. During the early 1800s, justifications for women's mission activity spread throughout Protestantism, based on the assumption that gender-separate societies required separate women's work. Missionary women became the chief missionaries among women, in particular as teachers and home-based evangelists. In the 1810s, the earliest American women missionaries staked the legitimacy of their mission work on Matthew's version of the great commission (KJV), arguing that women may not have been sent to 'preach', but were sent to 'teach'.

Under the slogan 'Woman's Work for Woman', women in Great Britain and the United States founded separate women's missionary societies to evangelize women and girls who could not be reached by men. In the 1850s, British missionary wives publicized the existence of 'hidden' women locked in harems, zenanas and women's quarters. Mission promoters argued that homes were the opening wedge for the conversion of entire societies, and that only women could reach other women. In addition to home visitation, missionary women founded girls' schools as a major locus of their evangelistic efforts. Beginning in 1869, women became missionary doctors because female physicians were needed to treat women in gender-separate societies, and Jesus' own work as a healer justified medical missions. Both personal evangelistic work, and kingdom-centred social outreach, including schools, hospitals, orphanages and social services, became the hallmark of gender-based missions. Female mission theorists like Helen Barrett Montgomery argued that Christianity was the key to elevating the role of women around the world, because Christianity was the only 'gender-neutral' religion whose founder treated women as equal human beings, rather than making special rules to enforce their inferior social status. Social activism against female infanticide, sex slavery, foot-binding, child marriage and other gender-based inequalities were a natural outgrowth of women's participation in missions. By the early twentieth century, in many circles the number of Protestant missionary women outnumbered missionary men by two to one.

As with Protestant women, the assumption of complementarian gender ideologies meant that Catholic women worked predominantly with women and children. By 1923, 13,000 Western sisters and innumerable indigenous sisters were staffing educational and social service missions throughout the world. After Vatican II loosened restrictions, and ecclesiological focus shifted to the church as the 'people of God', many Catholic sisters left missionary convents and moved by twos into poor communities, exchanging institutional ministries for 'accompanying the poor' in their struggles for social liberation.

Despite the substantial contributions of women to Christian mission, the mid-twentieth century saw a decline in gender-based mission theories. The dismissal of separate women's work as 'old fashioned' meant in practice the gradual reduction of women's freedom and priorities in missions. In denominations where women are not allowed to preach, the adoption of proclamation evangelism as the sole definition of mission has reduced the opportunities of missionary women. Groups such as the Christian and Missionary Alliance and Southern Baptist Convention that in early years prided themselves on their pioneer unmarried female missionaries, by the year 2000 had officially downgraded their status. Although exceptional women sustained strong ministries of Bible translation, pastoral education, and even church planting, gender virtually disappeared as a major category for missiological analysis among twentieth-century evangelicals.

Recovery of gendered mission theory

In the 1990s, historical research into the work of missionary women began emphasizing the importance of gender analysis in mission theory. A few groups like World Vision called for its renewal, with a strategic focus on the health and well-being of the 'girl child'. The growth of Christianity in the Majority World is connected with strong women's leadership in evangelistic movements like Chinese house churches, African healing ministries, and Latin American Pentecostalism. Anthropological studies reveal that Christianity is predominantly female, with women vastly outnumbering men in virtually every sector of the growing world church. These realities beg for a recovery of gender analysis in mission theory. How and why are women becoming Christians in greater numbers than men? In what ways are women's missional activities distinctive?

One major venue for renewed gender-based reflection is the 'Christian home'. In conservative Muslim societies, outreach to women focuses on hospitality and home visitation as a way to reach women who are not allowed to speak to men, or to mingle freely in public. Christianizing the home remains a major priority for Mothers' Unions, a common organization in many African denominations. Inspired by biblical models of Mary the mother of Jesus, Tabitha the leader of widows, and Mary Magdalene the witness to the resurrection, Mothers' Unions promote monogamous marriage, support the sick and needy, conduct evangelistic campaigns among women, and give girls biblically based teaching about the need for chastity in singleness, and well-ordered households in marriage. Mothers' organizations are the backbone of African Christianity in the twenty-first century.

*Healing remains an important priority for gender-based mission theory. The experience of being healed of both physical and relational problems is a major attraction to Christianity for women. As women pour into Pentecostal churches in Latin America, and into house churches in China, they testify to the healing power of the gospel. Missiological attention to the themes of healing and female empowerment have become urgent priorities in parts of Africa where HIV/AIDS is devastating the women of child-bearing age, and thus risking the very future of the church. In Eastern Europe and South-East Asia, the proliferation of sex trafficking has created a population of millions of exploited women and children in need of healing and reconciliation.

The equality of men and women in the gospel lays a foundation for challenging social practices that discriminate against women, who remain disproportionately the victims of poverty, violence, illiteracy and war. Perhaps the most complex gender issue to be faced in missions today is the disjunction between women's freedom and liberation in Jesus Christ, and the denial of their gifts of leadership in mission structures themselves. Even as they spread the gospel message of good news, missionary women experience frustration and disappointment under male leadership when the work of teaching, healing and hospitality is considered auxiliary and expendable rather than central to the evangelistic task. Gender analysis in mission thought is especially important when missionaries from egalitarian societies enter gender-separate cultures, and vice-versa. At its best, attention to gender issues in mission preserves the biblical, holistic, relational and person-centred dimensions of sound missionary practice.

See also FAMILY, WOMEN IN MISSION.

Bibliography
M. Kraft, *Frontline Women: Negotiating Crosscultural Issues in Ministry* (Pasadena, CA: William Carey Library, 2004); H. B. Montgomery, *Western Women in Eastern Lands* (Macmillan, 1910); J. Olson, *One Ministry, Many Roles: Deacons and Deaconesses through the Centuries* (St Louis, MO: Concordia, 1992); D. L. Robert, *American Women in Mission: A Social History of their Thought and Practice* (Marcon, GA: Mercer University Press, 1997); D. L. Robert (ed.), *Gospel Bearers, Gender Barriers: Missionary Women in the Twentieth Century* (Maryknoll, NY; Orbis Books, 2002); R. Tucker, *Guardians of the Great Commission* (Grand Rapids: Academie Books, 1988).

D. L. ROBERT

GENERAL REVELATION, see REVELATION

Globalization

There is no single accepted definition of globalization. Many would agree, though, that it has to do with the increasingly interconnected nature of the economic, political and cultural lives of peoples around the world. Various global processes (at root, technological) uproot human activities from local contexts and re-attach them in complex ways in other contexts. Economic globalization refers to the political project to create a single global market in which all barriers to trade and capital flows are removed. The convergence of global capitalism, a multipolar political world and technological innovation has led to the emergence of a global civil society, alongside the nation-state system, comprising transnational actors of different kinds and with varying degrees of global influence.

However, the novelty of this phenomenon should not be exaggerated. While the intensity, scope and pace of globalization has increased in recent decades, nations, empires and cultures have always interacted and influenced each other through the movement of commodities, peoples and ideas. For example, the Silk Road was, for many centuries, the equivalent of an 'information superhighway' as well as a trade-route connecting Europe and Asia. Seizing on the novel possibilities of printing and mass communication in the nineteenth century, but also responding to Christian evangelism, Islam, Hinduism and Buddhism began to reconfigure themselves as 'world religions', competing for converts, borrowing extensively from the Christian West, but also reinterpreting their own theological and cultural traditions.

However, the new technologies that lie at the root of globalizing processes have made possible the more rapid exchange of ideas and information around the world. The Internet and television have the potential to mobilize protest movements across nation-state boundaries, thus holding national states responsible for human rights violations and environmental catastrophes. To this extent, the emergence of a global information society is a powerful democratizing force.

On the other hand, the growth of a handful of giant multinational media corporations means that unelected business tycoons wield enormous political influence and thus determine for the rest of the world what counts as 'news'. The relentless marketing of brand names around the world means that more and more young people watch the same news, wear the same clothes and follow the same cultural icons. The loss of individual expression and of cultural diversity raises serious missiological, as well as political, challenges.

It can be argued, though, that many who are at the receiving end of globalizing processes are not passive, docile absorbers but are selective in their responses. Novel hybrids of the foreign and the local emerge in an unpredictable pattern of cultural and political responses. Roland Robertson, one of the founders of cultural globalization research, has proposed replacing the concept of cultural globalization with that of 'glocalization' – a combination of the words 'global' and 'local'. Global symbols acquire new local meanings, and local meanings are expressed as globally significant.

Positively, globalization has the potential to encourage genuine dialogue across *cultures. In the presence of the 'other', things that used to be taken for granted are now open to question. Even where traditions assert themselves in the face of perceived external threat, loyalty to traditional ways of life and thought has to be put on a new footing.

However, given the huge inequalities of economic power between cultures, the tendency is for the more powerful cultural images, icons and practices to dominate the less powerful in a largely one-way traffic. So,

while Americans and Europeans enjoy the best cuisine from Asia in their restaurants, most Asians have access only to American fast-food chains. The dominance of English as a world language, and the control of scientific and technological research by a relatively small number of nations, means that authentic cross-cultural interaction rarely happens. Thus the master-narrative of globalization represents a false universalism. Local culture and place are commodified; and the local and particular are prized only because of their novelty.

Globalizing processes both corrode inherited cultural and personal identities and, at the same time, stimulate the creation and revitalization of particular identities as a way of gaining more power or influence in this new global order. Hence the resurgence of ethnic and religious nationalisms all over the world. With the spread of global communications, the radicalization of some Islamist groups, and the rise of a free-floating transnational army of fighters ('jihadis'), conflict in one part of the 'Muslim world', with its specific local causes and character, is immediately presented and utilized as part of conflict in another region. The globalization of local conflict serves powerful propaganda purposes.

The Indian and Chinese diasporas today are significant carriers of cultural and religious globalization (see *Migration), especially as professionals and business entrepreneurs have replaced the cheap migrant labour of the nineteenth and early twentieth centuries. The movement of forms of Hinduism and Buddhism round the world through the efforts of travelling gurus and monks is an important event in recent times that has taken place alongside the emigration of South Asians and South Asian culture. At the heart of European and North American cities, 'Third World' cultures, as well as varied expressions of the global church, have taken root.

Mission historians have drawn attention to the southwards shift of the centre of gravity of the Christian world in the postcolonial era. Although this phenomenon is only marginally related to the technological and economic globalization described above, the global nature of Christianity and Christian missions has profound consequences for the church's response to globalization and for its missionary understanding and practice today.

Two brief examples will suffice:

First, many of the world's *poor are Christians, particularly in sub-Saharan Africa, South Asia and parts of Latin America. Unfair trading practices (e.g. huge agricultural subsidies, tariffs on imports, trade-related property rights) on the part of the US and the EU, and the privatization of public natural resources by multinational companies threaten to lock their societies into chronic poverty. At the same time poor nations disproportionately bear the costs of economic globalization – financial instability, tax evasion and the theft of public funds by corrupt politicians and businessmen (aided by the international banking system), migration of professional elites to the West, and the undermining of nascent democratic institutions.

What is the responsibility of rich Christians in ensuring that the poor have access to all that they themselves take for granted? A prophetic challenge is necessary, through word and action, to a global economic regime that encourages greed, wastefulness and exploitation. If globalization is to work for people and not just for profits, then Christians must press for banking transparency, limits on the power of corporations, and more democratic accountability on the part of international institutions such as the World Bank, the IMF and WTO. Thus the challenge of globalization is fundamentally ethical and political. Faithfulness to God's mission of justice and peace requires the global church to respond to that challenge collectively and through its individual members.

Secondly, Christian missionary outreach can no longer be mono-cultural and monodenominational if it is to be both credible and effective. Moreover, there is a great need to develop local theologies and missionary practices that receive from all that is best in other cultures, while being relevant to one's own. The church has always had a global history, but this has rarely been reflected in typical theological college curricula. We now have a 'hermeneutical community' that is global in scope and character, so we can test the local expressions of Christian faith against one another, thus manifesting the true catholicity of the body of Christ. The way we become truly global Christians is not by organizing more 'mission trips' but by seriously engaging with the *local* as members of a *global* community that has redefined our identities and interests.

Bibliography

Z. Bauman, *Globalization: The Human Consequences* (Cambridge: Polity Press, 1998); U. Beck, *What is Globalization?* trans. P. Camiller (Cambridge: Polity Press, 2000); J. Bhagwati, *In Defense of Globalization* (Oxford: Oxford University Press, 2004); P. Heslam (ed.), *Globalization and the Good* (London: SPCK, 2004); W. Hutton and A. Giddens (eds.), *On the Edge: Living with Global Capitalism* (London: Vintage, 2001); V. Ramachandra, 'Global Society: Challenges for Christian Mission', *Anvil* 21, 2004, pp. 9–21; Joseph Stiglitz, *Globalization and its Discontents* (London: Penguin, 2002).

V. RAMACHANDRA

God

The Christian faith confesses that God is the one who has revealed himself to be Father, Son and Holy Spirit. The means of this revelation are his gracious acts of creation and redemption, which are related and interpreted in Scripture, God's written *revelation. This understanding of God is profoundly related to mission, as can be seen in theology's method and task, the character of God and the nature and task of the Christian mission.

Theology's method and task

Theological method is not prior to theological content given through revelation. Classical Indian and Greek philosophical speculation about God has generally started with a worldview based upon a spirit-matter dichotomy. The result is a negative theological method (*via negativa*) in which matter is seen as illusory or less real, and so the philosopher proceeds by denying all material characteristics to the divine. The Christian world-view is monotheistic and thus contends that the fundamental distinction is not between spirit and matter but between the Creator and his creation. The Creator transcends the space-time limitations of creation and is thus enabled to relate to all of creation and to reveal himself to and within, or by means of, his creation. He reveals himself both through the created structures of existence (natural revelation) and through specific historical acts such as the election of Israel, the prophetic word, the life, death and resurrection of his Son, Jesus of Nazareth, and the coming of the Holy Spirit at Pentecost (special revelation). Thus methodologically the Christian doctrine of God must be built biblically upon God's revelation of himself in creation and redemption because this is the only way he can be known. Such a methodology relates the doctrine of God inseparably to mission, because the foundation of theology is the God who goes forth in gracious love in his mission to redeem the world he created.

The task of theology is to follow this missionary God in the way that he has revealed by the sending of his Son and Spirit, the way of loving *witness and service. Specifically, theology's task is directed both toward the church and the *world. Because God has chosen his people to live in loving obedience to him as his witnesses, theology concerns itself with expounding God's revelation in order to affirm, correct and equip the church to carry out its mission. Theology is also called to witness to the world by listening compassionately to its cry and faithfully relating God's revelation to its needs. It does this because the God whom it knows and serves is the God who created the world and answered mankind's need in the incarnation of Jesus Christ and the outpouring of his Spirit. In doing this, the theologian does not stand apart from the church or the world, but rather speaks as a member of God's people and as one who has been created to glorify God but still participates as a sinner in the neediness, ambiguity and struggles of a fallen world. Thus through prayer, meditation and trials the theologian follows the missionary God who has chosen to dwell in the midst of his people so that together they go forth to seek and to save the lost. In following God, theology not only nurtures mission, but also its own understanding of God is nurtured by mission as it discovers previously unrealized treasures in God's revelation when it confronts new challenges in its witness to the world.

God's character and acts

Because God's character is known only by his revelation, our exposition of it must start with his revelatory acts in creation and redemption interpreted by Scripture. Furthermore, since the Trinity is the Christian doctrine of God, these attributes must be understood in a trinitarian fashion.

The uniqueness of God as Creator and Redeemer

The Bible opens with the declaration that in the beginning God created the heavens and the earth (Gen. 1:1) and consummates the story of redemption with the creation of a new heaven and earth (Rev. 21:1). The implication of this is that God's creative and redemptive works are not two separate works but one. God's original purposes for *creation are fulfilled in redemption. It also means that the creator God is the same redeemer God. Both of these points are fundamental to the Christian mission through which we participate with God in his mission and thereby embrace every dimension of his purposes.

Traditionally Christian theology has understood creation to mean that God created the universe out of nothing (*creatio ex nihilo*). While not explicitly affirmed in Scripture, this understanding of creation rightly develops the creation theologies of Isaiah (44:24) and Job (38:4), which assert God's unlimited freedom and sovereignty in his actions. He alone is the creator. There is no other god but the Lord (Deut. 4:39; Isa. 45:18). Just as strongly God is proclaimed as the only Saviour or Redeemer (Isa. 44:6; 45:5–6, 14–15, 21). As sole Creator and Redeemer he has universal authority (Isa. 45:11–12). To him alone are *worship and service due (Exod. 20:2–6). For this reason God is said to be jealous (Deut. 4:24; 5:9), not in the fallen human sense of an insecure and selfish lover, but rather in the sense of being the only one deserving of complete devotion and who alone is the source of humankind's and creation's final good. It is to this God alone that we witness in mission.

God's unique universal authority is the justification of the *universal scope of the Christian mission. Its scope is universal first because it is for all nations. All nations will come to the Lord (Isa. 2:2; Zech. 14:16). Jesus in the great commission justifies sending his disciples to all nations, because as the risen Lord he has received God's universal authority (Matt. 28:16–20) and at the end of the age he will be recognized as the universal lord (Phil. 2:9–11). The universal scope of the

Christian mission for human *culture was demonstrated at Pentecost (Acts 2:1–11). The fact that the Spirit enabled people from all nations to hear the proclamation of the *gospel in their own tongue demonstrates that the gospel is intended to transform not only individuals but cultures as well. *Contextualization of the gospel is itself a redemptive event.

The scope of mission is also universal because it addresses all of created reality. God as the sole Creator proclaimed his completed creation very good, including man and woman as his image, who, as his image, had a positive role to play in fulfilling God's creation purposes (Gen. 1:26–31). They were to fill the earth and rule over it by developing and protecting it as God's stewards (Gen. 2:15; Ps. 8) and establishing a community of love (Gen. 2:18–25). As outlined by Paul in Romans 5 – 8, the Christian mission proclaims the restoration of God's image in Christ the second Adam (Rom. 5:12–21; 8:28–30), by means of the Spirit (Rom. 8:2–17), so that mankind will again worship and obey the one true God (Rom. 12:1–2). The fragmentation of individual and corporate human life is healed through service to the one and only God (Rom. 15:1–6).

As such the gospel becomes the charter of human freedom (Gal. 5:1; Jas 1:25). The good news is that our God reigns (Isa. 52:7). His sovereignty limits all demonic and human pretensions to dominance over others. 'You shall have no other gods before me' liberates people from slavery to lesser powers, including their own selves. Since there is one God, there is also one gospel for mankind. There is not one gospel for Jew and another for Gentile, for slave or free, for man or woman (Gal. 3:28; Col. 3:11). Thus the uniqueness of Christ as Creator is the charter of human unity and *reconciliation, and the mission of the church is to display that unity in reconciled love under God's rule (Eph. 2:11–22). In this unity of love the church is to reflect the eternal pattern of the perfect love of the Triune God (John 17:20–23). Finally, the gospel is the charter of the *creation's liberation, as it waits for the redemption of God's people (Rom. 8:18–25). The mission of the church is to proclaim this hope and to live in a manner that demonstrates God's original calling upon humanity to develop and care for his creation as faithful stewards (see *Ecology/environment). As such the mission of the church points toward God's final purpose to unite all things in Christ (Eph. 1:10), based upon the reconciliation of heaven and earth in the cross (Col. 1:20).

Nevertheless, the Scriptures do not permit a doctrine of universal salvation. Philippians 2:11 in particular admits only of a final recognition of the lordship of Christ by all beings irrespective of their being saved or not through his cross.

God's presence, power and knowledge

God's uniqueness as Creator and Redeemer has significant consequences for how he relates to his creation; that is, how his presence, power and knowledge operate in the world. These are typically dealt with under the three divine attributes of omnipresence, omnipotence and omniscience. It would be wise to distinguish two types of understanding of these attributes. The first is ontological and seeks to explain these attributes from the perspective of God's nature as the one divine being. The second is redemptive and describes God's attributes as he is seen to act in *salvation and *judgment. The redemptive type is clearly the dominant interest of Scripture, but properly understood, the ontological type as an implication of God's role as Creator does not contradict the redemptive and is supportive of it.

God is everywhere present in the totality of his person. He fills heaven and earth (Jer. 23:24), not as gas or liquid fill a container, but as their personally present transcendent Creator. As such he is able to be near and not far from us (Acts 17:27–28). God is the Almighty. As creator he brought all things into existence and by his power maintains them, even those human beings who oppose him (Matt. 5:45). Not only is the opposing power of 'the kings of the earth' laughably weak in comparison to God's power (Ps. 2), but nothing good or evil falls outside of the realm of his sovereign will and all will be used to accomplish his purposes (Rom. 8:28). God knows all things. He is not limited by the temporal nature of events but declares their end from their beginning (Isa. 46:10). So intimately acquainted is he with his creation that he knows when every sparrow falls, numbers the hairs of our heads (Matt.

10:29–30) and penetrates into the secrets of the human heart and its intentions (1 Chr. 28:9). Psalm 139 brings together these themes, recognizing that they wonderfully transcend human comprehension and so call for a response of worshipful awe and of prayer for deliverance.

Redemption increases the wonder of God's transcendent presence, power and knowledge in his election of Israel. He who dwells in the heavens has placed his name in Jerusalem (1 Kgs 8:27–29) and is with Israel only (Isa. 45:14) (see *Zion). He who knows all things out of all the nations knows only Israel (Amos 3:2) and the All-Powerful fights for his people (Josh. 10:14). The other side of this particularity is the necessity of human response. Election carries responsibilities: God's election is to result in mission. God has elected his people to declare his glory among the nations (Ps. 96:3). Their mission is to follow only him, the missionary God who goes forth to judge the world with righteousness (Ps. 98:9), a righteousness that he has already executed in their midst (Ps. 99:4). On the other hand, the God who is with his people does not accompany them when they follow other gods (Deut. 31:17). He no longer delivers them nor knows them as his people according to Hosea's denunciation of faithless Israel (Hos. 1:2–9). This redemptive understanding of God's relation to his creation speaks in terms of approval, blessing and empowerment for mission or their opposites, signifying that their ontological reality does not guarantee God's redemptive action.

This tension between ontological reality and redemptive action continues in the new covenant. Jesus is Emmanuel, God with us (Matt. 1:23), and through the empowering presence of his Spirit accompanies the church on its mission to the nations (Matt. 28:20; Acts 1:8). Once again God's action calls for human response. As the universal Lord, he commands all men everywhere to *repent (Acts 17:30) and to believe in order to be saved (Rom. 10:9). Such affirmations cast doubt upon universalistic schemes of salvation based solely upon God's ontological presence. The fact that the Creator is everywhere present does not automatically result in salvation. Nor do they support a concept of mission that identifies God's action with historical processes, whether in favour of global

democracy or revolutionary socialist movements of '*liberation'. Just as clearly, they negate a strictly institutionally based ecclesiastical redemption in which the *sacraments operate salvifically irrespective of believing human response. The risen Lord does not know all who confess him to be Lord (Matt. 7:21–23), and God's servants can grieve and quench his Spirit (Eph. 4:30; 1 Thess. 5:19). Nevertheless, in the *cross tension becomes paradox as God's power is revealed in *weakness and his wisdom in folly (1 Cor. 1:17–30). The paradox is the identity of the crucified Lord with the presently resurrected Lord who will come again. This is the true God whom Christians worship, proclaim and serve, and it is he, the crucified resurrected Lord, who has sent them forth in mission (Matt. 28:16–20), and set the pattern for that mission in his person and work until he returns in glory (John 20:19–23).

This revealed pattern has several implications for mission. First, since Christ's food was to do the Father's will (John 4:34) by seeking and saving the lost and serving and giving his life as a ransom for the many (Luke 19:10; Mark 10:45), so the church's mission is to submit to the Father's sovereign will, which is true freedom and justice (1 Pet. 2:16). The church is present by serving a suffering and sinful world because her missionary God was present in Christ in the same way (John 17:18). Second, in serving the world for the Lord's sake and in his way the church's mission will often collide with the world's agenda because the latter seeks an autonomous freedom and justice apart from God (John 17:14). And, just as the master suffered, so do his disciples (John 15:20) (see *Martyrdom).

Third, the church is to exhibit by its internal relations God's way of life-giving sacrifice and liberating service by not lording it over one another (Luke 22:25–27). Fourth, the relationship between mission and *power and knowledge needs to be biblically based. Clearly the use of military force under the sign of the cross as an instrument of mission should be rejected (Luke 22:49–51). Nevertheless, there should be no exaltation of weakness and ignorance in and of themselves. Even a cursory glance at Acts demonstrates that the Spirit of God Almighty performs signs and wonders through his witnesses as he did through Jesus, and the history of missions shows that *healing, exorcism and miraculous provision have been used to bring people to genuine faith. Nevertheless, more fundamentally these signs and wonders are related to the message of forgiveness as evidence of the breaking in of the eschatological *kingdom of God (Matt. 12:28). They point forward to the resurrection of the body and the renewal of all creation as the hope of mission and heart of its message. Additionally, although missionary strategy, which uses the insights of the social sciences, is valuable, its findings must always arise out of theological reflection, which seeks to plummet the depths of the wisdom revealed in the folly of the cross.

God's holy love

Essential to the church's mission is living and proclaiming that God is holy (Lev. 19:2) and that God is *love (1 John 4:8). Unfortunately the gospel is often presented as if these divine characteristics were in conflict. Holiness is seen as hard, judgmental and rejecting; love soft, forgiving and accepting. It thus presents two gods, rather than the one God who is both. Scripturally, God's holiness describes his transcendence and thus his purity. Through Hosea, God announces that he will not execute his wrath 'for I am God, and not a human being – the Holy One among you' (Hos. 11:9). The incarnate Son of God, conceived by the Holy Spirit, dwells in the midst of a sinful people to save them and is driven by the Spirit to confront the devil (Matt. 1:20–21; Mark 1:12–13). In like manner he sends his disciples into the world with the Spirit to administer the forgiveness of sins (John 20:21–23). The contents of the command to be filled with the Holy Spirit are defined by a life of love lived within human institutions and by confronting demonic abuse of them (Eph. 5:18 – 6:20). God has chosen to be in the world in the way of holy love. The church's love is perfected by being in this world as God is in it (1 John 4:17) and its mission cannot be carried out apart from this being in the world out of love for God and neighbour. 'Whoever lives in love lives in God, and God in them' (1 John 4:16).

The nature and task of the Christian mission

The nature and task of the Christian mission are determined by the character of our God. It finds its origin in his loving character that freely reaches out to create and redeem and is oriented toward the end that he has for all creation, which is to make the creation a fit habitation for his holy presence. Thus its nature is best defined as the *missio Dei* (mission of God). Its scope is as universal as is the sovereignty of its Lord that extends to all nations and to all aspects of his creation. Its primary task is to follow the missionary God who has set the pattern for mission in Jesus Christ, the way, and accompanies his people in the Spirit, who also empowers them. It follows God by means of loving service to and in the world by living and proclaiming that there is no salvation, no life or truth apart from the God who has revealed himself to be Father, Son and Holy Spirit.

See also CHRIST/CHRISTOLOGY, HOLY SPIRIT, TRINITY.

Bibliography

C. E. Gunton, *Act & Being: Towards a Theology of the Divine Attributes* (Grand Rapids: Eerdmans, 2002); J. Mackay, *A Preface to Christian Theology* (New York: Macmillan, 1941); R. H. Nash, *The Concept of God* (Grand Rapids: Zondervan, 1983); L. Newbigin, *The Open Secret: Sketches for a Missionary Theology* (Grand Rapids: Eerdmans, rev. edn, 1995); W. C. Placher, *The Domestication of Transcendence* (Louisville: John Knox, 1996); G. F. Vicedom, *The Mission of God: An Introduction to a Theology of Mission* (St Louis: Concordia, 1965).

W. L. ISLEY, JR

Gospel

The meaning of the gospel

The word 'gospel' (*euangelion* in Greek) is used over seventy-five times in the NT, with the sense of good news. In Mark 1 it is good news of the coming of God's kingdom: the two expressions – gospel and *kingdom of God – are indeed very close in meaning. But it is at the same time good news of Jesus Christ, for the great herald of the gospel is also its content, the one in whom God fulfils OT promise and expectation.

The irreducible, non-negotiable content of the gospel is this unique historical event of

God's coming in Christ to redeem and restore his lost and disordered creation. Its focus is the incarnation, life, death, resurrection, ascension, cosmic enthronement and final return of the Son of God. It is therefore appropriate that NT narratives of his ministry should themselves later be termed 'Gospels', for they tell the story that is itself good news. Indeed, Mark's Gospel opens with the words, 'the beginning of the gospel about Jesus Christ, the Son of God' (NIV). Nevertheless, the good news is not mere narrative but also 'the power of God for salvation' (Rom. 1:16). The expression underlines its sovereign and transformative character. Its source is God alone: it is pure gift. Messengers may announce it, but can contribute nothing to it. Indeed, any attempt to combine it with human effort undermines its essential nature. The gospel is God come in power through the eternal Son and eschatological Spirit, to recreate humanity and cosmos.

Exploring the gospel

The gospel is variously identified as good news of God's grace, of peace, of *salvation, and of the glory of Christ (Acts 20:24; Eph. 6:15; 1:13; 2 Cor. 4:4). It has a profuse, multidimensional character, and embraces the entire created cosmos in its scope (Eph. 1:10; Col. 1:20). This is a crucial point in view of the frequent tendency to highlight one aspect to the comparative neglect or total exclusion of others, thus losing the gospel's comprehensive richness.

Good news of reconciliation

At the most fundamental level the gospel is good news that in Christ God has overcome humanity's estrangement from himself caused by *sin, which – with the exception of the angelic rebellion – is the source of every other aspect of human and cosmic alienation. Thus, it is profoundly theocentric: all else that the gospel promises flows from the one focal point of *reconciliation with the creator. The gospel declares that on the cross Jesus Christ, the perfect and climactic sacrifice, took human sin and all its consequences upon himself, achieving for his people a complete pardon, justification and reconciliation. The good news is that rebels are redeemed from condemnation, and become children of God and heirs of all the blessings of salvation.

Good news of deliverance

The gospel is news not only of objective liberation from the guilt and judgment of sin, but also of subjective deliverance from the enslavement that it inflicts as an existential power. Believers are raised with Christ to a new life communicated by the *Holy Spirit. He makes salvation a reality in their experience, effecting an inner spiritual and moral transformation. Consequently God's image in human beings, defaced by sin but never eradicated, is progressively restored in the likeness of Christ, himself the image of God. Those who are in Christ are a new creation; they have been born again.

Good news of restored community

Western conceptions of the gospel have tended to emphasize its individual dimension while losing sight of the communal, but the latter is critical. The Genesis account of primeval human rebellion against God is rapidly followed by references to breakdown in the closest of human relationships: sin fractures human community. However, the gospel announces a salvation that is 'in Christ', known through solidarity with him, and all who are *in* him constitute together a new humanity.

To be saved, then, is to be baptized by the Spirit into his body (1 Cor. 12:13): the church is no appendix to the gospel, nor a merely human association, nor a purely instrumental means of encouraging spiritual growth. It is fundamental to the identity of believers – what they have become by divine act, and now *are*. Thus, while sin destroys relationships and tends towards the disintegration of society, the good news is of community restored in Christ. It is particularly significant that the most deeply rooted sources of division – gender, ethnicity, social class – are transcended in the body of Christ. As both promise and command, the new humanity is to be characterized by that love which God displayed in achieving its redemption; it is this that should identify believers as Christ's true disciples, and children of the Father's one family. This is good news in a warring world.

Good news to the poor

It means too that the gospel is good news to the *poor (Luke 4:18). The tendency to honour the rich and despise the poor is as marked in the modern world as in that of the NT, but it is evidence of false values (cf. Jas 2:1–7). The gospel takes no account of economic distinctions, and the poor suffer no disadvantage in accessing God's grace in Christ. So Mary's song proclaims the radical reversal of social status that God accomplishes (Luke 1:51–53), and Luke records that those who first heard the good news of Jesus' birth were shepherds from the lowest strata of society. The significance of this is compellingly demonstrated in a world where most believers are indeed the poor, on whom the gospel confers a dignity habitually denied them.

Attempts to translate this into present socio-economic reality take diverse forms. *Liberation theology looks to an overturning of political and socio-economic structures in the pursuit of equality and the ending of injustice. However, it tends to lose the uniqueness of God's work in Christ, and to subsume salvation into purely historical and socio-economic processes. The gospel is not *primarily* about social transformation. This is not, however, to deny its socially radical character, for by its very nature it challenges every unjust status quo and calls for engagement on behalf of the oppressed. The poor are welcomed into communities of the redeemed where they are valued as people and not despised as poor. And, by refusing to submit to the world's distorted values, such communities testify actively against oppression, pursue righteousness in the wider society, and witness to an approaching definitive liberation. Moreover, the redemption of individual human beings – in terms of world-view, values and lifestyle – contains transformative potential for every dimension of their lives.

Good news for creation

The gospel addresses humanity's physical *environment. In consequence of Adam's rebellion, Genesis speaks of the curse inflicted on an earth that was created 'very good'. This, it may be argued, has entailed a multiplicity of physical ills: sickness, accident, hunger, natural catastrophe, death, and the rest. The present dimension of good news may be harder to distinguish at this level. However, in Jesus' ministry it is expressed in the healing of the sick, blind and lame, the feeding of the hungry, even the resurrection of the dead and

subjugation of recalcitrant natural forces. Such occurrences are not without parallel as the gospel has advanced in later generations. And at a less obviously miraculous level, the renewal of minds through the gospel, the restoration of responsible, beneficent human stewardship over the earth, and liberation from fatalism and every false ideology, all enhance life and reduce pain.

Good news of victory

The gospel is good news too of Christ's victory over Satan and every evil force, including *witchcraft and sorcery. NT references to 'spiritual forces of darkness in the heavenly realms' have often been neglected in Western articulations of the gospel (see *Spiritual warfare). Attempts to identify them with, for example, human power structures or the ethos that animates them, while at times perceptive, reflect also the influence of a rationalistic world-view on exegesis, and forfeit a distinctive feature of the NT witness.

However, for much of the world, as for Jews and Greeks in the NT era, such notions resonate with terrifying meaning. The NT suggests that Satan's power is rooted in human rebellion against God: in defying God men and women fell unwittingly under the sway of evil powers. Thus Satan is parasitic: human sin enthrones him as 'prince of this world' and 'god of this age' (John 12:31; 14:30; 16:11; 2 Cor. 4:4), rather than the possession of any legitimate authority, which also explains why Scripture presents him as the accuser (Job 1 – 2; Zech. 3:1; Rev. 12:10). Therefore, by redeeming people from sin, Christ equally delivers them from the grip of demonic tyranny. He disarms the 'powers and authorities' by cancelling the certificate of indebtedness that testified against humanity (Col. 2:13–15). This underlines the fact that the gospel is a seamless unity, while affirming also its multi-faceted nature. Redemption from sin and from Satan are integrally related: the fact of pardon brings with it, as its inseparable consequence, deliverance from demonic powers.

The gospel in eschatological tension

Every aspect of the gospel is an announcement of future as well as present good news: actual experience of salvation is not yet complete, but carries the promise of future fulfilment (see

*Eschatology). There is an ambiguity to the gospel, which demands that the hearers hope in an as yet invisible realization of the divine promise. Christians walk by faith rather than sight, believing that Christ's resurrection is the first-fruit and guarantee of that of his people, and of the renewal of all creation. And so they struggle still with sin; they face Satan as a defeated but still venomously active enemy; their churches are often mired in schism, error and moral failure; and all the while creation groans, sickness and catastrophe continue, and bodies decay and die. Nevertheless, the certain hope of a complete deliverance from sin, of the elimination of Satan's kingdom, of physical resurrection and a renewed creation, motivates their pursuit of God's kingdom in the present (1 Cor. 15:58).

However, maintaining the tension between the realized and unrealized aspects of the good news is vital to its integrity and credibility. Paul's first Corinthian epistle is in part a polemic against an over-realized understanding, expressed at times in irony: 'Already you have all you want! Already you have become rich! You have begun to reign...' (4:8). The, somewhat widespread, offer of a gospel promising present health and wealth is fraudulent (see *Prosperity gospel), supported neither by the NT nor by the experience of the church through the ages. It is also desperately cruel to announce good news in such terms to the poor, as it leads quickly and inevitably to disillusionment.

The gospel in missiological perspective

As may already be clear, the notion of the gospel has emphatic and multiple missiological implications. What follows traces a few of them in only the briefest fashion.

Gospel and proclamation

First and most fundamental, gospel and mission are indivisible. Good news must be declared; otherwise, it is not news, let alone good. The notion of gospel contains the imperative of *proclamation, made explicit in Peter's words, 'We cannot help speaking about what we have seen and heard' (Acts 4:20). Similarly, Matthew's gospel closes with the 'great commission': mission is the final and only possible response to the preceding narrative. Paul's logic in Romans 10:12–15 demands the same conclusion: the gospel must be proclaimed to men and women: 'how beautiful are the feet of those who bring good news!'

Gospel and universality

Moreover, it is good news for all. The universal thrust present throughout Scripture finds full expression in the NT. It is pre-eminently apparent in Paul's mission and writings, for 'Is he not the God of the Gentiles too?' (Rom. 3:29). Nor is it merely a question of geographic extension, but also of social, ethnic and gender inclusiveness, embracing every class and condition of humankind. The Acts of the apostles shows the difficulty with which this crucial dimension of the gospel was understood and embraced in the context of Jewish ethnic and religious particularism. All equally need God's good news, and all may equally benefit from it, for he shows no favouritism. The gospel is for the world.

Gospel and culture

The gospel is, however, to be announced in *culturally appropriate ways. Paul's proclamation in the synagogue of Pisidian Antioch is strikingly different from that before the Areopagus in Athens, both in form and substance. The hearers' world-view shapes the way in which the gospel is grasped, even determining what counts as good news. Gospel messengers need therefore to be sensitive to the cultural contexts into which they speak. In some contexts particular articulations of it may not sound like good news at all, unless they are carefully qualified, such as proclaiming the necessity of new birth to those longing to escape the endless reincarnations of *samsara*. On the other hand, adherents of primal religions may find the message of Christ's conquest of the powers more potent than that of forgiveness from sin, suggesting that the communication should begin there. Similarly, in situations where ethnic hatred has brought devastating violence and destruction, the gospel may first need to be heard as good news of restored community in Christ, through whom ethnic divisions are transcended. The greatest challenge facing the twenty-first-century Western church is that of articulating the gospel in ways that are culturally relevant to post-Christian generations.

There is, nonetheless, a tension between the universal and the particular. The gospel is not infinitely malleable, and cannot without fatal loss be reduced to whatever constitutes good news in a given culture. That would be the route to cultural relativism, removing its unique and universal quality (Gal. 1:8). The noetic effects of sin mean that lost humanity is blind to the true nature of its plight, seeing it variously in terms of material deprivation, false consciousness, craving and desire, and so on, while missing the fundamentally theo-centric focus at the heart of the biblical narrative. Consequently, the biblical definition of the human dilemma must be communicated if the good news is ever to be rightly understood; otherwise expressed, the gospel tells us the questions as well as the answers. Indeed, if it is to retain its integrity and take root in the hearers' minds, a vital element of gospel proclamation will be a reshaping of world-view so that it can be rightly understood. For this reason storying is increasingly adopted as a particularly effective approach to gospel communication, since it sets the central events of Jesus' life, death and resurrection in the context of the biblical storyline as a whole, so that their meaning can be properly grasped.

Gospel and life

It is vital that the gospel be visible in the lives and works of the believing community and of the human messengers. The heralds do not only declare good news, but they must also *be* good news: gospel living and gospel proclaim-ing are inseparable. By being a community of acceptance and grace, of compassion and service, of reconciliation and healing, and by pursuing righteousness in social relationships and environmental stewardship, God's people demonstrate the gospel in act. They must be salt and light in society, a radical witness to another way. The challenge they face in every place and time is to resist the pressure to conform to the surrounding culture, at which point the gospel is muted and those who should be heralds simply reflect society's values back to itself, thereby ceasing to be messengers of good news at all.

Conclusion: receiving the gospel

The gospel of Jesus Christ is the greatest good news – for all people, of every condition, in every time and place, and for every dimension of their lives. It demands expression in word and act, and impels the mission of the church

as a matter of the utmost priority. However, it has an imperative as well as an indicative mode: to be experienced, it must be received. Jesus called for repentance and belief in the gospel, and only those who receive it truly benefit from it. Certainly its growth within a society is good news for the society as a whole, for it brings blessings that are shared by all, even though many may reject it. However, it spreads only as people hear *and* receive it; and they alone come to know, now and eternally, 'what God has prepared for those who love him'.

See also CHRIST, CONVERSION, GOD.

Bibliography

H. Blocher, '*Agnus Victor*: The Atonement as Victory and Vicarious Punishment', in J. G. Stackhouse, Jr (ed.), *What Does it Mean To Be Saved?* (Grand Rapids: Baker, 2002); T. Chester, *Good News to the Poor: Sharing the Gospel through Social Involvement* (Leicester: IVP, 2004); G. Goldsworthy, *Gospel and Kingdom: A Christian Inter-pretation of the Old Testament* (Exeter: Paternoster, 1981); D. J. Hesselgrave, *Com-municating Christ Cross-Culturally* (Grand Rapids: Zondervan, 1978); C. E. Hill and F. A. James III (eds.), *The Glory of the Atonement* (Downers Grove: InterVarsity Press, 2004); J. R. W. Stott, *The Cross of Christ* (Leicester: IVP, 1986).

K. FERDINANDO

Grace

Grace is God's unmerited and freely bestowed favour towards sinful humanity. It is a unique attribute of God, and speaks of his initiative in choosing to reveal himself and to act in *love for human beings before they have even given him a thought (Rom. 5:8). It is therefore an unprovoked gift, and not dependent upon any incentive or offering. It is unlimited in its lavish generosity and reaches its fullness in the person of Jesus Christ, from whom humanity has received 'grace upon grace' (John 1:16; Eph. 1:6–8).

Grace is therefore the means by which human beings can be saved ('by grace, through faith', Eph. 2:8), and beyond that it is freely given to enable Christians to do God's will and fulfil their calling (Eph. 4:7–13).

Some Reformers argued that sovereign grace operates alongside election, acting as 'irresistible grace' on behalf of those chosen by the foreknowledge of God. Others have argued that grace has always to be received by *faith, which gives to human beings some responsibility for experiencing its efficacious saving power. Either way *salvation is a gift that cannot be earned or merited, and therefore human beings need God's prevenient initiative of grace, by which he does all that is necessary to deliver them from the guilt and consequences of sin.

Grace in Scripture

From the earliest pages of Scripture we learn that it is at the heart of God's nature to be gracious and compassionate (Exod. 34:6–7), and therefore grace forms a primary characteristic of his *missio Dei as he works out his saving purposes. This means that in mission God is always ahead of the church; whatever happens to extend his *kingdom begins with his initiative and is fulfilled by his grace. This is particularly evident in Acts where the church's mission grows by the grace of God, sometimes through individuals (Stephen, Acts 6:8; Paul, 15:40–41) and sometimes corporately experienced (11:23; 14:23). The 'word of grace' is identified with the gospel (13:43; 20:24).

St Paul recognized in his own experience that he had been saved by grace, and it was grace that had not only given him the calling to be an apostle but had also sustained him in fulfilling that calling (Rom. 1:5; 12:3; 1 Cor. 3:10, etc.). In fact the Christian life from beginning to end was an experience of grace, making him the person he was and energizing his mission (e.g. 1 Cor. 15:10). It was his experience of grace that gave him such a sense of both gratitude and obligation, seen as an indebtedness to Christ, which was in turn a powerful motivation for his mission (e.g. Rom. 1:14; 2 Cor. 5:11). The church's mission likewise flows out of gratitude and indebtedness to Christ, which implies conversely that an inadequate appreciation of all that Christ has done will disempower its mission.

Grace in mission

The church therefore is always responding in its mission to what God has already done and is already doing, and it can claim no merit or privileges of its own which make its mission any more successful. God in fact sometimes acts independently of the church or missionary involvement in revealing himself by his grace to those who are open to receive it; although it is his normal way of working to commission the church and individual Christians as the means of fulfilling his mission purposes in the world as signs and instruments of his kingdom.

Mission is therefore both initiated and sustained by grace. This becomes particularly important in a place of suffering in which God's grace is found to be all-sufficient in providing strength to endure it and his power comes into its own in human *weakness (2 Cor. 12:7–10). St Paul's discovery of this truth enabled him to endure the hardships of his mission. A recognition of inadequacy for the mission entrusted to Christians may well be the key to their strength; and can in turn give them compassion for others in their weakness and suffering so that their demonstration of the love and grace of God becomes authentic.

Indeed, it is only by grace that the church achieves anything in its mission, and it is well that Christians recognize their weakness and dependence on God in order to give them the due humility that they need. A lack of dependence on God's grace conversely can lead to arrogance and triumphalism with all its attendant ungracious evangelism and judgmental selectivity. This was a favourite theme for David Bosch, who sees in Luke–Acts a 'paean of praise to the incomparable grace of God lavished upon sinners' (*Transforming Mission*, pp. 107–108). The task of mission is entrusted to very fallible human beings who do nothing in their own power but only by the grace of God. For Bosch Christians 'are not really called to accomplish anything, only to point to what God has done and is doing, to give testimony to what they have seen and heard and touched' (*Mission*, p. 116). This led Bosch to his now famous injunction to 'bold humility and humble boldness' (*Mission*, p. 489).

God's grace is also indiscriminate and often works in favour of those who are least qualified to receive it. The equivalent Hebrew word (ḥēn) in the OT speaks of the stronger coming by voluntary decision to the help of the weaker, so that the latter 'find favour' in their eyes (e.g. Gen. 32:5; 47:25), an experience that is sometimes seen as 'salvation'. Liberation theologians have argued that the poor are privileged receivers of God's grace, since they are disempowered by their poverty and in no position to claim any blessing for themselves. However, St Paul makes it clear that all humanity is under God's judgment, that no one has any righteousness of their own and therefore that all are equally in need of God's grace (Rom. 3:21–24). There is no prior judgment made by God of the worthiness or readiness of a person on whom he chooses to bestow his grace; that is the point about grace – it is freely and sovereignly given.

The church in mission as it participates in the *missio Dei* is therefore likewise called to emulate God's love by being freely and generously indiscriminate in the way it reaches out to all human beings. No prior judgments should be made on the grounds of ethnicity, sexuality, morality, social status or any other criteria about a person's worthiness to receive the gospel and its holistic blessings. Indeed, by demonstrating in their mission the lavish generosity of God's undeserved love, Christians make a powerful witness to the reality and possibility of grace. An example of this at work amongst Muslims is offered by Steve Bell.

Grace, however, as Bonhoeffer famously reminded us, is freely offered but is not 'cheap grace' (*The Cost of Discipleship*, p. 35ff.). It is not received simply in order to allow human beings to go on sinning. It is a grace of forgiveness which at the same time demands *repentance and holiness of life. It is grace which flows from a cross. So 'living by grace' does not mean abusing it, as if grace gives humanity permission for self-indulgence (Rom. 6:1–14). Mission therefore is also about *discipleship, through which Christians learn how to take up their cross and follow Christ. This means to appropriate and appreciate the grace of God, living in its lavish and joyful freedom, and at the same time accepting the responsibilities of those to whom much is given to honour and glorify the giver.

Grace is a distinctive characteristic of the Christian faith and a unique attribute of the God of Jesus Christ. But given that, there have been different emphasises on its importance. Protestantism has often seemed more concerned about faith, whereas Catholic theology has a strong element of grace, which can become universalistic. Evangelicalism, however, has sometimes exhibited what Philip Yancey called 'ungrace', with a legalism and dogmatism which means that the world does not always associate grace with evangelical Christian mission. Yancey's plea is that the church might become a 'nourishing culture' of God's grace, which means that it will demonstrate and offer grace to a world desperate to experience it. Evangelical mission will then be known as generous, compassionate, welcoming and in every sense gracious.

See also GOD.

Bibliography
S. Bell, *Grace for Muslims?* (Milton Keynes: Authentic Books, 2007); D. Bonhoeffer, *The Cost of Discipleship* (New York, Macmillan, 1963); D. J. Bosch, *Transforming Mission* (Maryknoll: Orbis Books, 1991); H. H. Esser in C. Brown (ed.), *New International Dictionary of New Testament Theology*, vol. 2 (Grand Rapids: Zondervan), pp. 115ff.; P. D. Yancey, *What's So Amazing About Grace?* (Grand Rapids: Zondervan, 1997).

J. CORRIE

Health/healing

Healing and mission
Healing refers to recovery from any kind of ill-health, bringing the restoration of physical, mental and spiritual wholeness. In the Christian context, *prayer for God's intervention in the crisis of illness has always been an integral part of mission. Healing was certainly central to the ministry of Jesus, whose missionary mandate to his disciples gave them the authority to 'heal and cast out demons' (Luke 9:1–2; 10:9; cf. Mark 16:15–18). The provision of scientific medical facilities as an integral dimension of mission has always been one of the most effective means of Christian missionary service. This has been especially so in the Third World and primal cultures where poverty, deprivation and economic under development lead to all kinds of vulnerabilities and detract from healthy living. However, healing in the context of mission is broader than the provision of scientific medical care in the form of medicines, hospitals, clinics and

medical personnel trained in the diagnosis of disease. Health and healing, especially in primal cultures, has had to take cognizance of world-views that attribute crises in general and sicknesses in particular to supernatural forces. This means dealing with health issues against the backdrop of belief in curses, activities of principalities and powers including demons, *witches, the evil eye, and the effects of personal and communal sins. In such cases confessions, prayer, exorcism and deliverance are commonly employed. This article argues that to restore the sick and afflicted to health and wholeness these methods need to be incorporated in the church's mission strategy, along with discernment, and together with conventional medical practice. All healing comes from God as a gift of his sovereign grace, and is to be received with thanksgiving, whether it comes through medicine or prayer, or a combination of both.

Healing and Scripture

The Scriptures generally support a holistic world-view of health/healing in which sickness appears to encapsulate more than physiological disabilities. In the OT the people of Israel experienced the healing presence of God in their journey through the wilderness, not just in the healing of physical diseases but also in the provision of material things: water, bread and clothing that made for human sustenance. God was their healer in every sense (Exod. 15:26–27; 23:25–26), and obedience to him would protect Israel from the diseases that had plagued the Egyptians. In the OT there was often a direct link made between *sin and sickness, in which case God's forgiveness and restoration were sought either for victims or even whole communities (e.g. Isa. 57:17–19). However, later in their history the link between sin and sickness was questioned, especially in the book of Job. Good men suffered, and sometimes sinners went free; so clearly not all sickness was attributable to sin. This view was confirmed by Jesus in the case of the man born blind, when he dismissed that view as inapplicable, and placed the emphasis on healing in the context of his mission as showing the glory of God (John 9:1–3).

In the NT healing appeared as an inseparable part of the ministry of *Jesus. He interpreted the effectiveness of his healing and exorcist ministry as an indication of the coming of the kingdom of God into the world. Sometimes this involved a direct confrontation with the powers of evil, establishing a close relationship between healing and exorcism/deliverance (e.g. Mark 1:29–34) (see *Spiritual Warfare). On one occasion Satan had kept 'a daughter of Abraham' bound with a bent back for eighteen years (Luke 13:10–17). Sin, demons or evil spirits, such as in the case of the boy with an epileptic fit (Matt. 17:18), were all seen as contributory sources of sickness for which Jesus' healing power was required. This understanding of causation recalls St Paul's reference to 'a thorn in my flesh' (2 Cor. 12:7–9) as 'a messenger of Satan'. James 5:14–18, however, which suggests a healing formula for the early church, leaves open the possibility that sickness may, or may not, be the direct result of sin requiring confession and forgiveness.

Thus the Gospels reveal the missionary mandate that Jesus Christ bequeathed to the church as not simply the command to preach but also the authority to heal and to cast out demons. Like Jesus, the apostles incorporated healing as an important part of Christian mission in the early church (Acts 3:1–10; 5:15; 19:11–12).

Healing and salvation

The evidence from the Bible, especially the ministry of Jesus, which sets the agenda for Christian mission, is that Christian intervention in human history is one that brings holistic *salvation: sight to the blind, deliverance to the oppressed and possessed, and release for the captives (Luke 4:18–19). Jesus frequently tells those he has healed: 'your faith has "saved" you' (e.g. Matt. 9:22; Luke 18:42; Gk: sōzein. It is possible to find eighteen occasions in the gospels when this verb is used with reference to healing). Healing and salvation are therefore related because salvation in the biblical context is a rescue function experienced as deliverance, release, redemption, payment of debt, resolution of disputes, vindication in the courts, restoration of life and recovery from illnesses. In Christian thought such salvation, encapsulating health and healing, originates from God.

God's salvation, which is an amalgam of physical and spiritual well-being, is therefore concerned with the conditions in which people live in this world, as well as with their physical, mental, and spiritual health. The church, as God's instrument of healing, brings restoration of health and comfort to the sick through visitation, prayer, words of encouragement, confession of sin, and anointing with oil. This is because sickness leads to alienation, and when health is restored, 'salvation' or 'abundant life' comes to people for which they bring thanks to God (Ps. 116).

The role of *faith in both healing and salvation has been controversial. Some give it a pivotal role, and make healing dependent on the presence of faith, so that blessing received is in direct proportion to the amount of faith a person has. The problem with this is dealing with the guilt and sense of failure of faith experienced by those who do not receive healing in the way they expected. It is preferable therefore to see healing and salvation as a gift of God's grace, and while faith needs to be present as trust in God's goodness and willingness to receive, the nature of God's response to prayer is always left in his hands.

Implications for mission

The implications of a broad view of health and wholeness for Christian mission are enormous. Christian missions in primal societies of the Third World for example have been most successful when healing has been made an integral part of the gospel message. In many poverty-stricken Third World countries, like those of Africa in particular, mission without some attention to the physical health needs of people is often meaningless.

Healing is therefore important for mission in indigenous cultures for two reasons.

First, primal cultures have a holistic view of life, particularly of the human person. The spirit, the soul and the flesh constitute an integral human whole, so physical and spiritual healing are inseparable. Sickness affecting the body may well be seen as being the result of personal or communal sin, or the activities of evil powers. However, there may sometimes be inappropriate attributing of sickness to sin or evil powers, and great discernment is needed. The phenomenon of holistic healing within indigenous *worldviews has generated a number of prophetic and healing ministries dedicated to deliverance. In some cases this has led to one-sided interpretations of certain diseases such as

HIV/AIDS, tuberculosis and epileptic fits, seeing them as 'spiritual sickness' with its stigmatization and improper counselling. Inappropriate attempts at deliverance have sometimes led to serious psychological damage.

Second, as a result of the strong belief in mystical causality associated with primal cultures, answers to problems, particularly of ill health and supernatural disturbances, are sought within a religious context. Christian healing centres are expected to provide spiritual contexts within which these effects of sickness and disease can be dealt with. The ministry of healing must take seriously worldviews of mystical causality where ill health is attributed to supernatural agents, though it can never endorse them uncritically, and it can never assume that there is always some demon or other behind every sickness.

On the whole, the historic Western mission denominations have often dismissed supernatural causes of ill health as psychological delusions in the minds of non-literate peoples. They often completely rejected indigenous beliefs as mere superstition (see *Folk Religion). The provision of health centres and clinics with sophisticated equipment for treating all kinds of diseases has been welcomed and essential, but these have not been considered sufficient in dealing with sicknesses which have a supernatural dimension. It is therefore not surprising that the independent indigenous Pentecostal/charismatic churches of Africa, for example, have usually emerged in response to the lack of these kinds of healing ministries in older denominations. They take primal world-views concerning supernatural powers and mystical causalities into consideration, and make strong cases for the provision of appropriate Christian contexts for bringing healing to those being troubled by sin, witches, demons and curses.

In this vein, the word 'deliverance' has in non-Western Christian contexts come to encapsulate being freed from all afflictions preventing people and communities from experiencing the abundance of life promised by Christ. The combinations of techniques, including the laying on of hands, prayers, fasting, counselling and rituals of exorcism and deliverance through which total transformation may be experienced, affirms health/healing as integral to Christian mission.

See also HOLISTIC MISSION.

Bibliography
S. Davies, *Jesus the Healer: Possession, Trance, and the Origins of Christianity* (London: SCM, 1995); D. Duncan, *Health and Healing: A Ministry to Wholeness* (Edinburgh: St Andrew Press, 1988); M. Kelsey, *Healing and Christianity: A Classic Study* (Minneapolis: Augsburg, 1995); F. MacNutt, *Healing* (London: Hodder and Stoughton, 1996); J. C. Thomas, *The Devil, Disease and Deliverance* (Sheffield: Sheffield Academic Press, 1998); K. Warrington, *Jesus the Healer: Paradigm or Unique Phenomenon* (Carlisle: Paternoster, 2000); J. Wimber with K. Springer, *Power Healing* (London: Hodder and Stoughton, 1986).

K. ASAMOAH-GYADU

Heaven/eternal life

In the wake of painful disagreements among Christians in the nineteenth and twentieth centuries, and perhaps more influenced than we know by secularism and materialism, many contemporary Western Christians are nervous of talking much about heaven. Observing some to be overly confident about the timetable, and very prescriptive about what heaven is, how and when we shall arrive there, they over-react by being too tentative altogether.

Not so our missionary forebears of the nineteenth century, whose writings pulse with joyful certainty that heaven is very near to us, and is the sure destination of all believers, a place and state of utter bliss in the immediate presence of the Lord. And not so for many Christians in the Majority World, whose ancestral cultures attune them to the nearness and reality of the unseen world.

The Bible speaks of heaven in different ways. It is what is above and beyond the earth (e.g. Gen. 1:1; Ps. 19:1), bearing testimony to the glory of God. It is the eternal dwelling place of God (e.g. Deut. 26:15; Matt. 6:9). Sometimes, as in Matthew's use of 'the kingdom of heaven', it can mean God himself. Most commonly, biblical usage denotes heaven as a place, and it is this place to which our resurrected bodies will be raised.

The believer already 'has' eternal life (e.g. John 3:16; Col. 3:1), the gift of the regenerating Spirit through the cross-work of the Son, which brings 'life in all its fullness'. Heaven is the eternal dimension of that promise. But what we now experience is only a foretaste of what is to come, a glimpse of heaven which one day we shall see and experience completely. In heaven believers joyfully see God face to face, delight in wondering perfected worship, and experience a quality of life we can only dimly imagine in the here and now. There will be no sin, no suffering, no tears, no death, no hunger or want, but absolute perfection and absolute fulfilment. Heaven is described as a city, a new Jerusalem, within which the whole community lives together in loving peace. Meanwhile, we live with the sure hope of a glorious life after death, which takes away the sting and victory of mortality.

Heaven and the religions

Every culture and every religion develops some way of dealing with death, and what – if anything – is believed to lie beyond it; but the Christian teaching of heaven and of eternal life is distinct from all others. For instance, Hinduism teaches loss rather than fulfilment of personal identity at death, and probable reincarnation in another earthly form.

Buddhists seek to make merit as the grounds on which their future fate will be determined. There is no continuity of personal identity after death, and the ultimate goal is to achieve a state of non-being, a complete detachment from suffering and desire. Since there is no belief in a personal God, who creates and redeems, there is absolutely no concept of heaven and a joyous future in God's presence.

Islam shares a Christian belief in life after death, and a distinct heaven and *hell. However, heaven is attained not through a Saviour but through meritorious good works, and for most Muslims there is no assurance that God will look kindly upon them at death. Heaven is a place of beauty and sensual pleasure, especially for men, but God will be distant.

Most primal religionists have no concept of life after death apart from the dead as spirits troubling the living and needing to be appeased.

Heaven and mission

Some mission theologies preach a gospel which encourages believers to invest all their expectations in future glory; this world is only seen as somewhere to escape from. Mission may be strongly individualistic and locate salvation entirely in the perfecting of a person's relationship with God. Incarnational mission theologies look for the fulfilling of the promise of 'eternal life' in the transformation of life on earth. This creates a world-affirming missiology which is communitarian, since it is concerned about how the gospel transforms society.

Between these models of mission there are varying degrees of commitment to the 'now' or the 'not yet' of the promise of eternal life, with most evangelicals traditionally veering towards the 'not yet' end of the spectrum; though charismatic theologies look very much for blessing, complete healing and full salvation now. However, contrary to some erroneous teaching associated with the *prosperity gospel, full deliverance from the impact of the *fall will only come in heaven. Nonetheless, this life and this world are valuable in God's sight, and mission must be concerned about this life – challenging injustice, caring for the poor, and so on – as well as the next.

In the post-Christian, secular Western world, as well as among the world's religions, a humble but firm Christian testimony that is this-life affirming but also points to the reality of heaven and of eternal life with Christ, far stronger than death, is very powerful.

Bibliography

R. Chia, *Hope for the World: A Christian Vision of the Last Things* (Downers Grove: InterVarsity Press; Leicester: IVP, 2005); P. S. Johnston, *Shades of Sheol: Death and After-life in the Old Testament* (Leicester: Apollos, 2002); B. Milne, *The Message of Heaven and Hell* (Leicester: IVP, 2002).

R. DOWSETT

Hell/judgment

Belief in divine judgment is not unique to Christianity. Islam and Judaism share that sense of accountability to the Creator. And even the Buddhist doctrine of *karma*, though without reference to God, carries the conviction that 'as you sow so you will reap'. However, the Christian doctrine of judgment differs from that of most popular religion.

Common belief holds that human behaviour is evaluated at judgment, with many accepted by God on the grounds that they were more good than bad. People are acceptable on the grounds of relative goodness, human effort and religious observance. In contrast, Christianity teaches that God's standard at judgment is perfection, and that none can reach the standard: every mouth is stopped in shame and embarrassment. So the Christian obligation to world mission is based in significant part upon the perilous condition of humanity (Rom. 1:14–18; 3:9–11, 19–20).

When Jesus was crucified, he stood in the place of condemned humankind. Thus the *gospel announces that there is no condemnation for those who are in Christ Jesus. Such *salvation is an undeserved, free gift from God and is to be found only in *Christ. On the basis that Christ died for all, some have argued for *universalism* – that all will ultimately be saved. There are evangelical Bible scholars who suggest that the vast majority of humankind, though not all, will eventually find salvation. The key issue is whether or not overt knowledge of and commitment to Christ is necessary for salvation (or to escape judgment). Many expect salvation for seekers who were never told the gospel, for infants and those who are brain damaged. But Scripture is largely silent on these issues. No one can state assuredly that there is salvation beyond the church. What is certain is the church's obligation to take the gospel to people everywhere, to presume that *evangelism is essential if people are to be saved.

Traditionally in Christian thinking, the judgment of God results in unbelievers being consigned to hell, a position sometimes referred to as *eternalism*. Deep concern about people suffering appallingly there motivated John Wesley to preach wherever he had opportunity. Hudson Taylor hurried to China when barely qualified, burdened that multitudes there were headed hopelessly for hell. Concepts of terrible punishment in the next life are not unique to Christianity. Islam and Hinduism have pictured its horrors quite as vividly as Christian artists like Bruegel. Fear of judgment and punishment is widespread if not universal.

Unique to Christianity is the tension between God's holiness in judgment and his compassionate *love. While some Islamic theologians speak of God's indifference at judgment as the unmoved, impassive One, the Scriptures speak of his grief, shown most poignantly in Jesus weeping over unresponsive Jerusalem. The Japanese theologian Kazo Kitamori, whose theology revolved around the concept of the pain of God, helped many troubled people to explain the mind of God in relation to the nuclear tragedy of Hiroshima and Nagasaki. The compassionate concern of God about the consequences of sin is central to the gospel. It is also an important antidote to careless teaching about human lostness.

Although the majority of Christians through history have, as *eternalists*, believed that hell is a place of endless torment, others, troubled by the apparent injustice of the same punishment for all, have argued that hell is a place of eternal consequences rather than of endless pain. There is no way out of hell, but those punished there are eventually destroyed, a position called *annihilationism* or *conditional immortality*. This terrible, but 'fairer' idea of hell has released some to preach judgment with integrity. While nineteenth- and twentieth-century evangelical missionaries were often more holistic in their work than many would credit, their concern about people's eternal future made evangelism and church planting paramount. Contemporary Western culture, with its denial of a meta-narrative and deep relativism, has largely rejected any concept of accountability to the Creator. As part of such societies, many Christians have come to believe that few apart from war criminals and paedophiles are deserving of hell. In such a context it is hardly surprising that few Christians, even those in theological training, are committed to in-depth, lifelong evangelism.

In dialogue with other faiths, it is important to recognize their openness to concepts of judgment and hell. Disasters like the 2004 tsunami were explained by some Muslim teachers as the judgment of God. While such concepts are not alien to the Bible (Gen. 6; Amos 1), few Christians have been prepared to explain disasters with reference to the wrath of God. But they would do well to reflect on the gospel as a message of hope for those who feel themselves alienated from God. Evangelists in Buddhist communities may build on people's concern about the consequences of the way they have lived,

without confirming their belief that karma will be worked out in reincarnation. The felt needs of other faiths may be answered by the gospel. But the way they explain that feeling and its consequences may be contrary to the gospel. Other faiths provide both bridges and barriers for Christian mission, not least in fears of hell and judgment.

Bibliography

ACUTE, *The Nature of Hell. A report by the Evangelical Alliance Commission on Unity and Truth among Evangelicals* (ACUTE) (Paternoster: Carlisle, 2000); P. Cotterell, *Mission and Meaninglessness* (London: SPCK, 1990); W. V. Crockett and J. G. Sigountos (eds.), *Through No Fault of Their Own? The Fate of Those Who Have Never Heard* (Grand Rapids: Baker Books, 1991); D. Dowsett, *God, That's Not Fair* (Authentic: Milton Keynes, 2006); E. W. Fudge and R. A. Peterson, *Two Views of Hell: A Biblical and Theological Dialogue* (Downers Grove: InterVarsity Press, 2000); C. Moucarry, *The Search for Forgiveness: Pardon and Punishment in Islam and Christianity* (Leicester: IVP, 2004); C. H. Pinnock: *A Wideness in God's Mercy: The Finality of Jesus Christ in a World of Religions* (Grand Rapids: Zondervan, 1992); D. Strange, *The Possibility of Salvation Among the Unevangelised* (Paternoster: Carlisle, 2002); J. Wenham, *Facing Hell: An Autobiography 1913–1996* (Paternoster: Carlisle, 1998).

D. DOWSETT

Hindu relations

'Hindu relations' is about mission in a Hindu context and how evangelicals can speak of the uniqueness of Christ 'from below'. The focus here is on contemporary mission thinking and not on the historical development of the theme under discussion.

Hindus and Hinduism

This is a brief description of the main beliefs of Hindus and not a discussion of what Hindus believe. The Hindu population consists of a hierarchy of various *caste groups that form the majority of India, as well as those that have migrated from India to other parts of the world. In the fifth century BC the Persians, deriving the word *Hindu* from the Indian word *Sindhu* for the river Indus, called Hindus by that name, identifying them as the people of the land of the Indus. During their long, unbroken history, which can be traced back in some manner over five millennia according to some scholars, the Hindus were influenced by various religions and they absorbed foreign elements that contributed to their religious expression in a wide variety of beliefs and practices. The religion of the Hindus is a hugely variegated series of facts and it does not refer to the entity 'Hinduism' that the West tried to create. Some high caste would like to extend as definition to all Hindus what applied to their community, such as 'those who believe in the Vedas' or 'those who follow the way (*dharma*) of the four classes (*varnas*)' (the *varnas* are Brahmin, Kshatriya, Vaisnava and Shudra), and the four stages of life (*ashramas*) (the *ashramas* are *brahmacharya, grhastha, vanaprastha* and *sanyasa*). However, there are groups such as the *Dalits, the Lingayats and Vaishnavas who do not subscribe to this definition. Therefore it is important these days not to club people together who do not perceive themselves as being Hindu. The expression Hindu-Christian relations accordingly needs modification to accommodate the increasing self-perception of people.

The religious texts, both in Sanskrit of the high caste and in the vernacular of others, basically define what people do rather than what they think. Consequently, far more uniformity of behaviour than of belief is found among castes, although they share very few practices or beliefs. Almost all castes observe a few usages: reverence for Brahmans; marriage within the caste (*jati*) in the hope of producing male heirs; belief in *dharma*, which is doing one's duty in accordance with their caste affiliation; belief in *karma*, which is that one's actions in this life determine rebirth into a caste, or salvation, *moksha*, that is the end of rebirths. Most caste groups worship Shiva, Rama and Krishna, both believed to be forms of Vishnu, and Devi, the goddess, but they also worship hundreds of additional minor deities peculiar to a particular village or even to a particular family. No doctrinal or ecclesiastical hierarchy exists in Hinduism, but the intricate hierarchy of the social system, which is inseparable from the religion, places each person within the whole.

Historical perspectives
The beginning of the Christian era
Christian-Hindu relationships could be said to have had their beginning in the first century AD with the arrival of Thomas, one of the twelve apostles, in India. He is said to have received a vision commissioning him to preach the gospel in India and landed on the east coast of India. His ministry is said to have resulted in establishing some of the earliest churches in India that survive till today. However, his actions are said to have caused offence to some of the high caste Hindus that resulted in them spearing him to death. The first Christian community in India adapted Hindu cultural aspects into its lifestyle from their local context. It was affiliated to the eastern Christian tradition, to the Syrian Orthodox church. The Hindus therefore came in contact with the eastern Christians from outside initially and then soon were faced with some of their own becoming Christians. Survival of this community to date is a testimony to the tolerance shown by most Hindus initially and later on. Hence, evangelism in India, acceptance of its message, persecution of Christians and tolerance of them, all has pre-colonial history in India. Hindu-Christian relations right from the start have been a mixture of responses. Some Hindus became Christians, some staunch high-caste groups opposed them, while most Hindus showed tolerance.

The colonial era
In AD 1600 the Christians who followed the moguls into India marked another milestone in Christian-Hindu relationships. The Roman Catholic Portuguese were first to report on the Syrian Christians of Kerala, who were already there. They noted that those people were 'Christian in religion but Indian or Hindu in their culture'. They were right in this diagnosis but hasty in their treatment and conclusion that everything Indian had a pagan Hindu component to it and hence was alien to the Western Christianity that they sought to propagate. The Portuguese occupation in India included propagation of religion. This was done forcibly, which resulted in the formation of nominal Christian communities initially, which has for a long time been used by Hindus as a description for all things Christian until recently. Early foreign missionaries who served in India from the sixteenth century

onwards began to interact with the religious and cultural aspects of Hindus. Francis Xavier, Robert de Nobili and the Frenchman Abbé J. A. Dubois (1765–1848) are all examples of this. The Roman Catholic Christians had responses from Hindus similar to that in the first century. Some became Christians, some opposed, resulting in Christians being killed, and most tolerated the Christians. The converts even after the end of 1800 had assimilated a large measure of Hindu practices. This was facilitated by the Roman Catholic missions generally adopting the caste system for their converts. The Christians were faced with the problem of distinguishing between a harmless social custom, an unavoidable cultural difference and something that destroys the church's unity in Christ. During this period attempts to Indianize the church had already begun.

With the sixteenth-century Reformation the Protestant church began in the West. The Protestant mission in India began in the seventeenth century with Bartholomaeus Zieganbalg (1682–1719), a Lutheran from Germany who went to Tranquebar, South India.

Nineteenth and twentieth centuries: the British rule
The British Empire began its regime from the beginning of the nineteenth century. The latter half of the nineteenth century was a period of intense missionary activity under the British regime. Colonial and missionary projects went on in parallel, especially in the domains of education and linguistics. Many British authorities felt special moral and religious convictions that influenced social change in India in the areas such as child marriage, widow burning, and education for women and lower caste.

Hence the arrival of Vasco da Gama in India marked not only the beginning of the colonial era but also of European missionary activity. Hindus in the rest of India, unlike in the first century, for the first time came in contact with culturally diverse Christians from the West and later were faced with some of their own becoming Christians, following the diverse practices of the Western Christians. They viewed European Christians as strangers ruling them and their fellow Christian countrymen with suspicion.

The Indian Christians themselves were very diverse in culture, language and denominational and Western affiliations. They in various measures retained some of their pre-Christian Hindu practices. Out of these observances, caste affiliations played a major role and the church in India is riddled with problems related to it.

Mogul invasion had resulted in many forced conversions to Islam and destruction of many temples in the north. Many Hindus felt this action was repeated in the beginning of the colonial era by the Christian powers in the south. The political domination, combined with forced conversions by two different religious groups from the West, produced considerable resistance from high caste Hindus, which was already evident from the first century. The ripple effect of the discontent of the reactionary groups reached their zenith with the coming to power of a Hindu-backed government in the recent years, when opposition to non-Hindu groups was on the increase and many state governments banned forced conversions.

Indian independence
Indian independence marked another milestone in the Christian-Hindu relationship. The secular state of India banned missionaries to India and the Indian church began to shoulder the responsibility of missions. The formation of the Church of South India and the Church of North India also marked the unification of some of the churches, while the American Methodists and Baptist and other independent churches began to grow without joining the unified churches. During the seventies under the Indian leadership of the churches, national cultural particularism received a greater attention. In this context the Church History Association of India published in six volumes a history of Christianity in India from the point of view of Indian Christians. The aim in all this, scholars suggest, was to undo the ties of Indian Christianity with the West and to change the perception that Christianity is a foreign body in India.

The current state of relations
This varies from region to region. Among Hindus in more recent times, the popularity of numerous self-proclaimed Indian religious

gurus has grown. Sai Baba, who proclaims himself to be an *avatar* of Shiva in South India, attracts a large following from middle-class groups and also a following from the West. Some gurus of various types have migrated to Europe and the United States, and have inspired large followings. One such following is the Hare Krishna sect founded by Bhaktivedanta.

In recent years in India, with the coming of the Bharatiya Janatha Party (BJP) and its coalition to power, some Hindu groups' relations with people of other faiths certainly deteriorated, with various Hindu reforms imposed on the nation and with local incidents of attacks and counterattacks by some fervent Hindus on people of other faiths. But it also brought people together. For example, a Christian police officer joined the ruling coalition, which changed the character of the coalition from being chiefly Hindu. Many Hindu groups that had not worked closely with other Hindu groups came together. Similarly, Christian denominations and other religious groups consolidated their identity. It was during the coalition rule that a good number of Dalits converted to Buddhism.

Now that the BJP has gone, things are changing. For instance, one of the coalition politicians defeated in recent elections is said to have had a change of heart when that person learnt that the limit on religious freedom imposed by the coalition was not popular with the middle class and the poor and hence the defeat. At a popular level Hindus have generally been accommodative of other faiths.

Mission strategy: many approaches

There are many evangelical and non-evangelical sympathetic approaches expressed in literary works, intercultural dialogues, indigenizing Christian rituals and worship, healing meetings, health, education and community development services. These modes of approaches have their place in building relationships with the Hindus and should not be dispensed with for that reason.

Hindu-Christian dialogue

One dimension of mission in the Hindu-Christian relational context is *dialogue. Sometimes it goes under the banner of 'inter-faith dialogue'. However, the initiative in

these has always been from the Christians. Inter-faith dialogues are welcomed both by evangelicals and non-evangelicals. The Hindu-Christian dialogue has occupied the interest of many Christians in progressive Protestant and Catholic circles in India since 1960 and influenced global discussion and practice.

The topics of such dialogues have included issues in Hindu-Christian relations, joint heritage, harmony and human integration, Sankara's monism compared with Thomas à Kempis and the like. Based on varying degrees of complexity of formal dialogues, scholars group them into at least four kinds: 'discursive', 'secular', 'interior' and 'existential'. Theologians, depending on their understanding of religion in general and Hinduism in particular, accept dialogue in any or a combination of those modes, although with conditions. For example Lesslie Newbigin accepted the first two of those dialogue modes but displayed reluctance and even resistance to its other forms.

Scholars note 'discursive dialogue' as the least complex form of formal Hindu-Christian dialogue. In this form the emphasis is on conversation that seeks clarity of understanding, sometimes as a shared quest. Scholars suggest this results in understanding in both groups about the other and it might also lead to a search for truth together. Some theologians accept the first of these intentions but not the latter.

'Secular dialogue', also known as 'practical dialogue', 'the social approach' to dialogue and 'dialogue through collaborative action', according to scholars, 'intends principally to facilitate a joint approach to social and other problems in the "secular" realm'. Some theologians are only in broad agreement with holding such dialogues. Scholars have also noted that there are novel situations in such 'secular dialogue' where there are 'no prepared positions'. Recently, in the political sphere, 'secular dialogue' was used to enhance Hindu-Christian relations during the BJP-coalition regime. While Christians held on to the view that it was for communal harmony, the participating Hindu groups viewed it with scepticism and regarded it as an attempt to convert them to Christianity.

'Interior dialogue' is 'interior' or 'inner' dialogue as prior preparations of Christians and the Christian community for the 'external' encounter of actual dialogue with Hindus. These are said to be more demanding forms of the practice of dialogue, which have come to be called dialogue in its interior and existential forms. Again not all theologians are interested in this.

'Existential' dialogue is said to be the most comprehensive, complex and demanding form of the Christian-Hindu encounter. This is also called 'religious' and 'spiritual' dialogue because of special emphasis laid on religious experiences in such dialogue. In this form individuality, freedom and authenticity are given importance in the encounter. Since this form of encounter can happen only when there is a shared belief, a common search for truth and participation in a common religious experience, evangelical theologians find this type of dialogue unacceptable. For them, this type goes against the grain of the biblical message of the gospel and against their commitment to the commands of the Lord Jesus Christ. However, from within this framework and engagement in this form of dialogue, a fruitful self-examination in the light of the experiences of people from other religions can come about.

Many contemporary advocates of Hindu-Christian dialogue suggest three conditions for successful endeavours: a willing acceptance of religious pluralism, sympathetic understanding and the suspension of evaluative judgment about the faith of the other. Again many theologians warm to the idea of sympathetic understanding and not to the other two.

What is the best approach to dialogue?
For some Hindus who actively participate in such 'inter-religious dialogue', the axiom, 'Not to argue and win but to learn and to inform', seems to serve as the first principle. This principle has been acceptable to both Hindu and Christian participants of dialogues. This demands that both groups stand their ground, which means that Christians ought to uphold their Christian commitment uncompromisingly. Recently a Hindu who has been involved in dialogues and is sympathetic to Christians noted that the unity of Christians is of prime concern for meaningful interaction. Hence the dialogue context points to Jesus' vision of the unity of his disciples as a witness of the church. In the light of

this Mahatma Gandhi's words that if all the Christians were like Jesus, Indians would no longer be Hindu, is very pertinent in the present context and presents a challenge to the church in India.

An alternative approach
The focus on the *family is an interesting and important dimension of mission amongst Hindus. 'The nuclear family' among all other relationships forms the core model to the Hindus. A Hindu individual is bound to his family and to his wide family such as *kula* or *gotra*. Whatever the caste group the family is the core model relationship. This social model also has religious significance to the Hindus. Usually amidst many deities, they have a deity affiliated to each family. They use the family model to understand divine-human relationships. The 'deity-devotee relationships' and 'family relationships' inter-define relationships for the Hindus. The Hindu scriptures underline the family as important and seek to uphold family values.

Missionary endeavours by churches and mission agencies using an evangelical and holistic approach, the many instances of inter-caste marriages, inter-religious, intercultural marriages where one of the spouses is a committed Christian leading their other half and family to faith in Christ, the many instances of committed individuals planting churches among a select group of people have all been successful generally. The main feature of such instances has been chiefly evangelical, related to church planting and following mostly a web method along family lines, that is, reaching joint families as a whole through the family members. An example of this is the Tirunelveli evangelical Christians. By choice Jesus Christ becomes their personal and family deity. Lessons from this could benefit those developing a familial model for church planting work among the Hindus. One such model is the 'Family and Mission-orientation In Laying Young-churches' (FAMILY) method, using family relations as the chief channels to share the gospel with a definite aim of planting a church as a result.

Bibliography
J. L. Brockington, *The Sacred Thread: Hinduism in its Continuity and Diversity* (Edinburgh: Edinburgh University Press,

[2]1996); F. X. Clooney, *Hindu God, Christian God: How Reason Helps Break Down the Boundaries Between Religions* (Oxford: Oxford University Press, 2001); C. G. Dempsey, *Kerala Christian Sainthood: Collisions of Culture and Worldview in South India* (Oxford: Oxford University Press, 2001); C. B. Firth, *An Introduction to Indian Church History* (Delhi: ISPCK, 2003); C. J. Fuller, *The Camphor Flame* (Princeton, NJ: Princeton University, 1992); K. Knott, *Hinduism: A Very Short Introduction* (Oxford: Oxford University Press, 1998); B. Robinson, *Lesslie Newbigin and Hindu-Christian Dialogue: A Decided Ambivalence* (Christchurch: Bible College of New Zealand, 2001); D. Packiamuthu and S. Packiamuthu (eds.), *Tirunelveli's Evangelical Christians* (Bangalore: SAIACS Press, 2003); World Council of Churches, 'Statement from Hindu-Christian consultation held in Varanasi, India, 23–26 October 1997', <http://www.wcc-coe.org/wcc/what/interreligious/cd31–05.html>; C. Wright, *Thinking Clearly About the Uniqueness of Christ* (London: The Evangelical Alliance and Cape Town: SCB Publishers Ltd, 1997).

J. A. KUMAR

History

The church participates in God's mission as his saving purposes unfold through history, which gives the church's mission an inescapably historical frame of reference. The first part of this article outlines a distinctively Christian understanding of history as the basis for considering in the second part some aspects of the relationship between history and mission, which the church cannot ignore if it is to be faithful to the *missio Dei* as it works out its missionary calling in the contemporary world.

Elements in a Christian understanding of history

Christian faith accords value to history as the sphere of God's saving activity. Some of the important religious traditions of the world present the historical process as part of the burden of the human condition, a reflection of the endless cycle of rebirth. Salvation in these traditions belongs to a timeless realm outside history. In Christian understanding, however, salvation takes place in history, by means of historical events. History thus holds value as the theatre in which the process of *salvation takes place. That process took thousands of years to reach its climax, and has occupied many centuries since.

The incarnation of the divine Son is an event historically locatable. The *incarnation which brings salvation about is an event in the sense that it can be located geographically in a specific area and at least approximately dated. There are time markers relating to contemporary events (e.g. Luke 2:1); the early statement of faith known as the Apostles' Creed stresses that the death of Jesus was under Pontius Pilate.

The Christ event is anchored in the history of Israel. The climactic event of the incarnation occurs after millennia of preparation, featuring the coming into existence of the nation of Israel and its subsequent history. Jesus was born a Jew, and his very title, Messiah or Christ, can be understood only in the light of the history of Israel. The history of Israel as the people of God acts as a demonstration model of God's dealings with humanity.

The history of Israel becomes an adoptive history for the church as the people of God. After the incarnation the historical process of salvation widens in order to introduce 'the nations', that is, those outside Israel, into the people of God. Those who recognized as Lord the Messiah of Israel entered Israel (according to Paul, they were grafted in: Rom. 11:17), but without becoming Jews. Thus Abraham, the ancestor of Israel, is seen by Paul as the archetypal Christian. A single historical process links 'the [Israelite] fathers', receiving God's message partially and episodically through the prophets, and the Christian believers of 'these times' who receive that message in its fullness and completeness in the divine Son (Heb. 1:1–4). Abraham's journey of faith only reaches its goal with the coming to faith of multitudes many centuries later (Heb. 11:40)

History is teleological, directed by the Creator of the universe towards the undisputed reign of Christ (1 Cor. 15:25; Eph. 1:10); a reign defined in prophetic tradition in terms of the messianic attributes of justice, equity and peace. This evidently relates not only to humanity, but to the whole cosmos ('all things in heaven and on earth'); it is the renewal of the creation by its author and redeemer, and represents the goal of God's mission.

Progress towards this designated end is periodically marked by *climactic events* of permanent significance occurring at a confluence of specific conditions. The exodus that brought Israel into existence as a nation, and the Babylonian exile and return which mark the re-formation of the nation, were such landmark events. The coming of Jesus ('when the set time had fully come', Gal. 4:4) is the determinative event. Similar language is used of the final summing up ('when the times reach their fulfilment', Eph. 1:10).

Teleological history is concerned with salvation. 'Powers and authorities' have vitiated the cosmos since the fall; Christ broke their grip with his cross and resurrection (Col. 2:15). This turns the whole of history into salvation history. Much of biblical history is specifically about the people of God. But salvation history is not to be equated with their story, which takes place within a wider world history that is equally under God's direction and is equally directed to the salvation of the cosmos in the kingdom of God. Sennacherib and Cyrus, unbeknown to themselves, are servants of the Lord of Hosts; Melchizedek and Balaam, though not of Israel, receive the word of God. The orbit of God's mission is universal.

Christian history is cross-generational. The writer to the Hebrews asserts the continuity between the historic revelation to the fathers 'through the prophets' and that 'to us by his Son' (Heb. 1:2). Equally, he sees the Christians of his day as organically connected with the 'fathers' of old Israel. Thus he says that Abraham and other faith-full people have not yet received what was promised to them; they will not be made complete without us (Heb. 11:39–40). Abraham's story is thus not complete in itself; its conclusion and fulfilment come many centuries afterwards, through people for whom Abraham was a remote and even an adoptive ancestor.

If all later believers are to be included in the 'us' of the Hebrews passage, we meet another aspect of the value added to history in Christian thinking. Just as Abraham's story is not complete in itself, so likewise no part of Christian history. The history of salvation is a single story, requiring for its fulfilment the totality of the generations. The people of God belong to one another across time as much as across space.

Christian history is global, serial and cross-cultural. Christian history over the past two millennia does not encourage the idea of the triumphant, irresistible progress of mission, and certainly not permanent possession. It suggests rather recession following advance, and advance following recession. Christianity has often faded in areas once thought of as its heartlands, with churches withering at the centre to find new life at or beyond the margins. The faith has always been global in principle, despite some recent centuries when it appeared essentially European. In the seventh century there was a Christian presence across the Eurasian landmass from the Atlantic to the Chinese capital; in the twentieth and twenty-first centuries the presence has been literally worldwide. Leading, pattern-giving churches have arisen, Jerusalem in the first century being the first; they have faded, sometimes disappeared – and been replaced in Christian leadership by other churches elsewhere. There was a time when the leadership belonged undoubtedly to Europe, and Europeans took the lead in propagating it. A worldwide expansion of the faith followed, but simultaneously with a rapid decline in Europe, Christianity is now in process of becoming a predominantly non-Western religion, making Christian history and mission of necessity multicultural.

Salvation history operates at different levels of the universe. The gospel of the kingdom of God is good news at every level of a fallen universe. The history of this gospel is not the same as the history of the church. That aspect of salvation history that records the history of the people of God properly takes account of the growth of the church in response to the gospel; but that growth cannot be established by statistical criteria alone. Salvation comes not from the church, but from the kingdom of God, and the church is not the kingdom. But in its mission it should be a sign of the kingdom (though historically it has often been a countersign); and its preaching and reflection of the kingdom in mission may produce developments in society that reflect the saving work of God though they bring no expansion of the church.

Some chapters in the historiography of mission

Christian reflection on history has taken many forms over the centuries. What follows is a small and almost random selection of those most obviously relevant to Christian mission.

God in the pre-Christian past

Second- and third-century Gentile Christian converts encountered historical problems about their faith that Jewish believers had never known. The Scriptures clearly indicated God's revelatory activity in the history of Israel; had there been no parallel activity in the history of other nations? That there were corrupt, indeed demonic, elements in contemporary Hellenistic culture was evident; but were there not also developments which pointed to Christ? How should one think of the death of Socrates, condemned on the very charges often levelled against Christians? Christian thinkers from Justin Martyr onwards developed a critique of pre-Christian antiquity which posited among all the corruption the activity of the pre-incarnate Logos, active in the creation of the universe and the light that lightens everyone.

Clement of Alexandria went further; there was a divine activity within Greek philosophy parallel to that represented by the law in Israel, 'a schoolmaster to Christ'. In the twentieth century, missionary thinkers facing the issue of high truth in Asian religious traditions revisited these early writers; and Kwame Bediako has demonstrated how twentieth-century African theologians met a similar issue about the divine activity in pre-Christian Africa, and answered it in an analogous fashion.

Church-wide or empire-wide?

In the early centuries, Christianity spread, not only within the Roman Empire, but beyond it. The first major historian of the church, Eusebius of Caesarea (d. 339), was aware of this, as his *Ecclesiastical History* makes plain. He was also aware that the accession of Constantine had opened a new era for the church. The end of persecution and the imperial favour shown to the church encouraged the growth of Christianity within the Empire, and eventually a collapse of organized paganism which Christian commentators depicted as a cosmic event. But these developments led emperors increasingly to aim at doctrinal consensus within the Empire on matters that equally affected Christians outside the Empire.

In the pre-Constantinian era Christians had thought of a single church in the Roman and Persian Empires, and in territories beyond either; by the sixth century the church had divided along linguistic and cultural lines. Differences in Christology were cited for the separation of Greek- and Latin-speaking churches from those speaking Syriac or Coptic. The division proved to be permanent, and prepared the way for a further split, absolute by the eleventh century, between Latin-speaking Christians of Western Europe and their Greek-speaking neighbours. The paradigm of Ephesians faded from sight; Christianity operated from now on in blocks identified by language and culture, with each block conscious of its own history and with little consciousness of the others.

Nations defined by the gospel

Following the fall of the Western Roman Empire, many of the European peoples designated by the Romans 'barbarians' adopted the Christian faith en masse. This process eventually issued in Western Christendom: contiguous territory from the Atlantic to the Carpathians where the Christian faith was universally professed and regarded as the basis of society. Developments in history writing resulted. One was the production of histories of peoples who had had no literacy until they adopted Christianity.

The conversion to the faith becomes the central theme of these histories; and these 'nations' thus find a Christian identity, and one that links them with antiquity, both Roman and biblical. Gregory of Tours on the Franks and Bede on the English are examples of this activity. Bede also had a role in a still more significant historiographical development: the practice of recognizing the incarnation as the pivotal event in history, and dating all other events BC or AD.

The Protestant Reformation and the non-Western world

The Reformation period produced much revisionist historical writing from both sides of the religious divide. Generally speaking, Catholics were quicker than Protestants to see the significance of the non-Western world that contemporary maritime developments were bringing within reach; Protestants long tended to identify the propagation of the gospel with the Reformation struggle.

The Puritan settlements in America brought the first major change; the sense of a new era arising from the presence of gospel churches in the 'wilderness' where Satan's rule had hitherto been unchallenged. Puritan thought also reflected on the strange limitation of the true faith to a geographically circumscribed sector of humanity. And Puritan *eschatology, largely inherited by their evangelical successors, expected a great outpouring of the Spirit in the last days, when the earth would be full of the knowledge of God as the waters covered the sea. Evangelistic success or revival sometimes encouraged the idea that this dawn was at hand; in that conviction Jonathan Edwards, in the mid-eighteenth century, called for a universal 'concert of prayer' for the extension of Christ's kingdom.

The idea was a powerful stimulus to the early Protestant missionary movement; it also had a historiographical effect in the appearance of histories of the propagation of the gospel. One of the earliest was Robert Millar's *History of the Propagation of Christianity* (Edinburgh 1723); one of the best known the historical section of William Carey's *Enquiry* (Leicester 1792).

Effects of the missionary movement from the West

The adoption of missions by most branches of the Western church, and the developing encounter of the Christian message (in a form heavily acculturated by centuries of European history), produced many developments in historical understanding – not all of them pointing in the same direction. A revised eschatology, stressing a premillennial return of the Lord, not so much as a development in history as a bolt from outside it, became influential among evangelicals and other radical Christians who were the backbone of the missionary movement. Its first effect was to stimulate missions to the Jews, and to create a new interest in their future, which laid the foundations of Christian Zionism. Its subsequent effect was to act as a powerful spur – as the older, very different eschatology had been – to missionary enterprise. It was especially formative for the 'faith missions'

that followed in the wake of the China Inland Mission, with the expectation of the Lord's return giving urgency to the proclamation of the gospel where Christ was not known.

Engagement with the thought of other religious traditions renewed the stress on the historical character of the person and events that bring salvation. Missionary concerns took Christian thinkers into Asian history at a new depth, and the new discipline of history of religions emerged. The missionary challenge did much to open up Christian thinking about history.

Ecumenical history

In the twentieth century the Christian church assumed a different shape, culturally and demographically, from that geographically circumscribed Western manifestation that the Puritans had known. Phenomenal growth in Africa and some parts of Asia, deep recession in Europe and many other parts of the Western world, and a truly global Christian presence, meant that traditional models of church history were outdated. The first substantial truly global Christian history during the century came from the American scholar K. S. Latourette, whose *History of the Expansion of Christanity* appeared in seven volumes between 1938 and 1945. Latourette's scheme was based on a pattern of advance and recession, with each recession the prelude to a greater advance; and his understanding of expansion was threefold, the statistical growth of the church, the signs of the kingdom and the transforming influence on society. He wrote before much fundamental research had been done on the modern – or for that matter the ancient – Christianity of Africa and Asia. That work, which is ongoing, and the work of synthesis making use of its discoveries, are likely to transform Christian historiography and its relationship to mission in the twenty-first century.

See also CHURCH, GOSPEL, KINGDOM OF GOD.

Bibliography

O. Cullmann, *Christ and Time: The Primitive Christian Conception of Time and History* (London: SCM, ³1962); R. E. Frykenberg, *History and Belief: The Foundations of*

Historical Understanding (Grand Rapids: Eerdmans, 1996); W. R. Hutchison and H. Lehmann (eds.), *Many Are Chosen: Divine Election and Western Nationalism* (Minneapolis: Fortress Press, 1994); A. Van Leeuwen, *Christianity in World History: The Meeting of the Faiths of East and West* (London: Edinburgh House Press, 1964); A. F. Walls, *The Missionary Movement in Christian History* (Maryknoll: Orbis Books, 1996); A. F. Walls, *The Cross-Cultural Process in Christian History* (Maryknoll: Orbis Books, 2002).

A. F. WALLS

Holistic mission

Establishing the principle

That the church is by nature missionary is hardly contested. But what does that mean? How is the mission of the church defined? What is included in mission? In a way, the adjective *holistic* only intends to correct a one-sided understanding of mission that majors on either the vertical or the horizontal dimension of mission.

The aspiration for a more comprehensive view of mission became evident in evangelical circles as early as the Wheaton Congress of 1966. Then it grew consistently throughout the years to such an extent that by the time of the International Congress on World Evangelization (Lausanne, 1974) the statement could be made in paragraph 5 of the Lausanne Covenant that 'Although reconciliation with man is not reconciliation with God, nor is social action evangelism, nor is political liberation salvation, nevertheless we affirm that evangelism and socio-political involvement are both part of our Christian duty' (J. R. W. Stott, *Making Christ Known: Historic Mission Documents from the Lausanne Movement 1974–1989*, p. 24).

Such a statement makes clear that, as Rodger C. Bassham has pointed out, the Lausanne Congress 'produced some marked changes in evangelical *mission theology ... through broadening the focus of the Congress from evangelism to mission' (*Mission Theology: 1948–1975 Years of Worldwide Creative Tension*, p. 231). These changes are well illustrated by the 'change of mind' that John Stott experienced between the Berlin Congress (1966) and the Lausanne Congress.

In his opening address on 'The Biblical Basis of Evangelism' at the memorable 1974 Congress, Stott claimed that 'the mission of the church arises from the mission of God' and should, therefore, follow the incarnational model of Jesus Christ. On that basis, he argued that 'mission ... describes everything the church is sent into the world to do', as those who are sent by Jesus Christ even as the Son was sent by the Father, that is 'to identify with others as he identified with us' and to serve as 'he gave himself in selfless service for others'.

The affirmation that the actual commission itself must be understood to include social as well as evangelistic responsibility seems to suggest a real integration of the vertical and the horizontal dimensions of mission, which is at the very heart of *holistic* mission. This approach, however, did not become part and parcel of the Lausanne Covenant, which in paragraph 6 qualified paragraph 5 by stating that 'the church's mission of sacrificial service evangelism is primary', thus supporting the two-mandate approach to mission-evangelism *and* social action. In contrast, the holistic approach was forcefully expressed by the so-called Radical Discipleship group, an *ad hoc* group of about four hundred participants who met spontaneously during the Congress. Their document on 'Theological Implications of Radical Discipleship', which may be regarded as the first worldwide evangelical statement on holistic mission, affirms, among other things, that 'There is no biblical dichotomy between the Word spoken and the Word made flesh in the lives of God's people. Men will look as they listen and what they see must be at one with what they hear.' This definition of holistic mission, as including what the church is, what the church does, and what the church says, can hardly be improved.

It must be said, however, that after the Lausanne Congress the holistic approach to mission was very much under pressure in conservative evangelical circles. But in spite of much resistance the position expressed by the Radical Discipleship group in 1974 was echoed in various important documents drafted in the eighties, including the statement 'Transformation: The Church in Response to Human Need', which summarized the conclusions of the consultation on this topic held in Wheaton, Illinois, in June 1983, sponsored by the World Evangelical Fellowship.

After the Wheaton '83 Statement, as a result of the amazing paradigmatic shift in the concept of mission which had taken place during the previous decade, the moment for the *practice* of holistic mission had arrived. Many observers of this phenomenon interpreted it as a wonderful recovery of the social dimensions of the gospel and the mission of the church. Hundreds of Christian faith-based organizations were now engaged in integral mission. It has been claimed that the so-called parachurch organizations, special-purpose groups or voluntary societies grew more than a hundredfold in the twentieth century. Today there are approximately 100,000 of these organizations. Heavily dependent on volunteer help, they have become a very important faith-based means through which the people of God, regardless of race, social class, or gender, participate in kingdom work all over the world.

An outstanding illustration of the process of change in perspective which took place especially after the Lausanne Congress is the formation of the Micah Network, whose first international conference was held in Oxford, England, in the aftermath of the terrorist attacks of 11 September, 2001. The Micah Network has grown into a worldwide group of more than 200 evangelical Christian relief, development and justice agencies. At the Oxford meeting Micah adopted, as a matter of practicality in network communication, a distinctive term to refer to the biblical model of mission that it advocates, namely, *integral mission*, which is understood as pointing to 'the proclamation and demonstration of the gospel', not as separate but as distinctive yet inseparable aspects of the Christian mission.

The biblical basis for holistic mission

For a proper integration of the various constituent elements of the church's mission at least three approaches are possible.

The purpose of God

The first approach takes as its starting point the purpose of God, which embraces the whole of *creation. The biblical message of *salvation points towards 'a new heavens and a new earth', and that means that we cannot view salvation as separated from creation. The purpose of salvation is not merely an endless life of individual souls in heaven, but the transformation of the totality of creation, including humankind, to the glory of God. A person's conversion to Christ is the eruption of the new creation into this world: it transforms the person, in anticipation of the end time, in a wonderful display of God's *eschatological purpose to make all things new.

This way of looking at conversion has important consequences for evangelism. The purpose of the proclamation of the good news of Jesus Christ is not to change people into religious individuals who cut themselves off from the world in order to enjoy the benefits of their salvation. Rather, the purpose of evangelism is to constitute communities that confess Jesus Christ as the Lord of the totality of life, and live in the light of that confession; communities that not only talk about God's love but also demonstrate it in concrete terms, through good works which God prepared in advance for them to do (Eph. 2:10).

The unity of human beings

The view that the *human being is a unity of body, soul and spirit, which are inseparable, is taken for granted in both the OT and NT, and has been confirmed by modern science. Because a human being is a unity, one cannot properly help a person by taking care of his or her needs of one type (e.g. the need of God's forgiveness, a spiritual need) but leaving completely aside his or her needs of another type (e.g. material or bodily needs). James acknowledges this in linking faith with action (Jas 2:15–17).

From this perspective, holistic mission is mission oriented towards the meeting of basic human needs, including the need of God, but also the need of food, love, housing, clothes, physical and mental health, and a sense of human dignity. Furthermore, this approach takes into account that people are spiritual, social and bodily beings, made to live in relationship with God, with their neighbours, and with God's creation. Consequently, it presupposes that it is not enough to take care of the spiritual well-being of an individual without any regard for his or her personal relationships and position in society and in the world. As Jesus saw it, *love for God is inseparable from love for neighbour (Matt. 22:40). To talk about 'holistic mission', therefore, is to talk about mission oriented towards the formation of God-fearing persons who see themselves as stewards of creation and do not live for themselves but for others; persons who are willing to fulfil their God-given vocation in the world and to receive and to give love; persons who 'hunger and thirst for righteousness' and who are 'peacemakers' (Matt. 5:6, 9).

The reduction of the Christian mission to the oral communication of a message of otherworldly salvation grows out of a misunderstanding of God's purpose and of the nature of human beings. It is assumed that God wants to 'save souls' rather than 'to reconcile to himself all things, whether things on earth or things in heaven' (Col. 1:20); that the human being only needs to be reconciled to God rather than to experience fullness of life. In the final analysis, this is a reduction related to ideas taken from Greek philosophy, not from Scripture.

Mission is faithful to Scripture only to the extent to which it is holistic. In other words, it is faithful when it crosses frontiers (not just geographic but also cultural, racial, economic, social, political, etc.) with the intention of transforming human life in all its dimensions, according to God's purpose, and of enabling human beings to enjoy the abundant life that God wants to give to them and that Jesus Christ came to share with them. The mission of the church is multifaceted because it depends on the mission of God (see *Missio Dei), which includes the whole of creation and the totality of human life.

The 'Christ-event'

The third approach takes as its starting point the 'Christ-Event', including *Christ's life and ministry, his death on the cross, his resurrection, and his exaltation. Each of these events points towards integral mission as the means whereby the church continues Jesus' mission throughout history, and whereby the redemptive work of Jesus takes effect under present circumstances:

The life and ministry of Jesus: Jesus' life established the foundations for the definition of what it means to love God above all things and to love one's neighbour as oneself. His earthly life and ministry in this way came to be the model for the life and mission of the church. If that is the case, the proclamation of good news to the poor, the preaching of freedom for captives, of the recovery of sight for the blind, and the liberation of the oppressed is a basic criterion by which to assess how far the mission of today's church is really the continuation of the mission of Jesus of Nazareth.

The cross: The mission of the church provides the link between the death of Jesus and the appropriation of the justice of God through justification by *faith. As Paul states, the work of reconciliation contains two closely related aspects: reconciliation with God and the ministry of reconciliation (2 Cor. 5:18–19). This has its cost, however, both in terms of sacrificial surrender for the sake of others – a self-giving which reproduces that of Jesus Christ – and also in terms of suffering for the sake of the gospel. The church is not truly the church unless it is, according to Bonhoeffer's description, 'the Church for others', in which the image of 'the man for others' – the man who 'did not come to be served, but to serve, and to give his life as a ransom for many' (Mark 10:45) – is reproduced.

Also on the cross Christ broke down the wall of separation between Jew and Gentile, thus producing a new humanity, one body (Eph. 2:14–16). The church therefore provides a glimpse of this new humanity by demonstrating, both in its life and in its message, this reconciliation with God and between individuals and groups.

Jesus' resurrection: The fulfilment of God's plan for the life and mission of the church relies on one incomparable resource, the power with which God raised Jesus from the dead (Eph. 1:19–20). The risen Christ is the first-fruits of the great harvest, a new humanity. By his *resurrection he has introduced into history a principle of life which guarantees not only the survival of the soul for all eternity, but also the permanent validation of all that the church does through the power of the Spirit for the cause of Jesus Christ, that is, the cause of love and justice. The cause of Jesus Christ is the only cause that has a future. So it makes sense to pray, 'Your kingdom come, your will be done, on earth as it is in heaven', and to strive that the power of the resurrection may become manifest in the here and now, and in every sphere of human life and in the whole of creation.

Jesus' exaltation: The close relationship that exists between the present dimension of the kingdom of God and the presence of the Holy Spirit who works in history to make the mission of the church possible, is clearly seen in Jesus' view of the combination of factors involved in salvation history after his ascension, expressed in Acts 1:7–8. We will explore these factors in the next sections.

Mission in the light of the ascension

In the coming mission in Acts, the church occupies a vital place, but not the church alone: it is the church in the power of the Spirit. The mission is no mere human project. It is the result of Jesus' mission being extended in history, an extension made possible by the action of the Holy Spirit. As such it is brought to fruition, not only by what the witnesses to Jesus *say*, but also by what they *are* and *do*.

Pentecost follows immediately upon the ascension and is inseparable from it. With the exaltation of Jesus as Lord and Messiah (Acts 2:36), and the coming of the *Holy Spirit at Pentecost, a new era has been inaugurated in salvation history: the era of the Spirit, which is at the same time the era of the exalted Jesus, and the era of the church and her mission to make disciples in the power of the Spirit.

Jesus' promise to his apostles that he would be with them 'always, to the very end of the age' in their mission (Matt. 28:20) is fulfilled through the presence of the Spirit and the word, the combination that made possible the existence of the church and the success of her mission.

Acts 2:41–47 clearly shows that the result of the Pentecost experience is no ghetto church, devoted to cultivating individualistic religion in an exclusive, separatist church. On the contrary, it is a community of the Spirit, a community that becomes a centre of attraction, 'enjoying the favour of all the people' (v. 47), because it incarnates the values of the kingdom of God and affirms, by what it is, by what it does, and by what it says, that Jesus Christ has been exalted as Lord over every aspect of life, including economics. It is a missionary community which preaches reconciliation with God and the restoration of all creation by the power of the Spirit. It is a community which provides a glimpse of the birth of a new humanity, and in which can be seen, albeit 'only a reflection as in a mirror' (1 Cor. 13:12), the fulfilment of God's plan for all humankind.

'Kingdom mission' points beyond the community of faith to the crucified King who has been exalted and reigns 'until he has put all his enemies under his feet' (1 Cor. 15:25). The kingdom of God provides the framework within which faith acts in love, a love that is translated into action on behalf of the needy. Holistic mission is the means through which the glory of the kingdom of God is announced and concretely manifested in history in anticipation of the end by the power of the Spirit. Consequently, the first condition for the church to become an agent of transformation in its own community is to see herself as nothing more (and nothing less!) than a witness to the kingdom that has come and is yet to come.

The role of the local church

An important deficiency in evangelical theology has been an ecclesiology rooted in biblical revelation, often relegated to a secondary question. Consequently what takes priority is the institutional church, regulated by human traditions and preoccupied with the achievement of secondary objectives such as its *quantitative* growth, to the detriment of its *qualitative* growth.

Also practical consequences relate to the way the local church perceives its mission. If mission is not holistic or if mission is seen as a peripheral matter, the minimal condition for the church to fulfil its purpose is missing and the church becomes a religious club with no positive impact on its neighbourhood. As the *Micah Declaration on Integral Mission* puts it,

> God by his grace has given local churches the task of integral mission [proclaiming and demonstrating the gospel]. The future of integral mission is in planting and enabling local churches to transform the communities of which they are part. Churches as caring and inclusive communities are at the heart of what it means to do integral mission. (*Justice, Mercy and Humility*, p. 21)

The meaning of 'caring and inclusive communities' needs to be spelled out in practical terms if the church is going to be recognized in its own neighbourhood as more than a religious institution concerned above all for its own self-preservation. The first condition for the local church to break down the barriers with its neighbourhood is to engage with it, without ulterior motives, in the search for solutions to felt needs. Such an engagement requires a humble recognition that the reality that counts for the large majority of people is not the reality of the kingdom of God but the reality of daily-life problems that make them feel powerless, helpless, and terribly vulnerable.

If that is the case, a top priority for the church that cares is to enable people to articulate their needs, to analyse them, and to reflect on them. Inquiring what people would like to see changed, what major needs they see in their area, what services they use and what services they lack, and so on, can prevent the church from jumping in with its own agenda. It can also help the church to begin developing meaningful links with the community.

The knowledge of the community based on serious conversation with the people who participate in it is the starting point for the kind of action that goes beyond paternalistic poverty relief and helps people to help themselves. Without this kind of empowerment, there is no solution to the underlying problems affecting many, especially the poor, namely, the lack of sense of human dignity oftentimes expressed in terms of marred identities and distorted vocations. Each church is called to be a transformation centre that enables people to change their self-perception by seeing themselves as human beings created in the image of God and called to participate in the accomplishment of God's purpose.

Not every church, however, is fit to become involved in holistic mission. According to the Apostles' Creed, the church is 'one, holy, catholic and apostolic'. Traditionally, these are the essential marks, *signa* (signs) or *notae* (characteristics) of the church. Experience makes evident that these characteristics have to be supplemented by others if the church is to be a true agent of transformation in its own context. We suggest the following:

(1) *Commitment to Jesus Christ as the Lord of all humankind and the whole creation:* There are many secular service agencies that do very good work among the poor. There is,

however, one unique thing that Christians can give the poor, namely their witness to Jesus Christ as the Lord of all humankind and the whole creation – the witness that gives meaning to our own struggle for justice and peace. Faithfulness to the King of kings and Lord of lords is not to be measured in terms of big church buildings full of people, but in terms of faith communities that are making *disciples who are learning to obey all that Jesus Christ taught.

(2) *Commitment to one another:* Individualism is inimical to holistic mission because it requires that church members experience integral growth in Christ (Eph. 4:16). The church is a faithful witness to the extent to which she becomes a community of love in which people accept one another just as Christ accepted them. When love becomes visible in the church community, outsiders are given ears to hear about the love of God and eyes to see its reality (Acts 2:47).

(3) *Commitment to the world as the object of God's love:* In full agreement with Jesus, Paul took it for granted that Christians are 'not of this world' but are sent 'into the world' to witness to God's transforming truth and love (1 Cor. 5:10; John 17:14–18). Such an attitude of openness to 'people of this world' prevents the church from becoming a religious sect or club. It impels the church to look for ways to work in partnership with her neighbourhood in improving the quality of life on both a personal and a community level. The church fulfils her vocation as 'light of the world' not merely by preaching the gospel, but by letting her light shine through 'good deeds' – works that point towards *shalom* (well-being for all and by all) and at the same time show the reality of God's love for his world and move people to praise the Father in heaven (Matt. 5:16).

(4) *Commitment to the priesthood of all believers:* The church as 'a royal priesthood' (1 Pet. 2:9) is a community of priests called to exercise their *priesthood in sacrificial practical action (Heb. 13:15–16). The church is faithful to its priestly call to the extent to which she combines the sacrifice of praise with the sacrifice of good deeds that alleviate human suffering. Holistic mission thus becomes a priestly service in which the whole church, not just a sector of it, is involved (Heb. 10:24).

(5) *Commitment to leadership defined in terms of service:* Holistic mission cannot become a reality unless church leaders heed Peter's exhortation to his fellow elders to become servant leaders (1 Pet. 5:2–3). It is only possible whenever it is fully recognized that the church as a whole is called to witness to the crucified Messiah through humble service that seeks no other reward than that of pleasing the Giver of every good gift. The role of the leaders in this context is to serve by enabling others to develop and to use their own gifts (Eph. 4:12). They are faithful to their vocation to the extent to which they are able to release others for service.

(6) *Commitment to flexible church structures:* Effective holistic mission is not dependent on good structures and organization, but on the Spirit of God. That is true. But if is true that good structures and organization do not guarantee success in mission, it is also true that bad structures and organization lead to failure. Holistic mission, therefore, requires a careful assessment of the ways in which such matters as the planning, organizing, implementing, and evaluating of the service projects, whether in word or in deed, are functioning in reality.

Conclusion

It is now widely accepted that the church's mission is intrinsically holistic or 'integral'. Word and deed must work together to complement one another. Their separation results both in impoverished evangelism and inadequate commitment to compassionate service. The church proclaims the love of God through what it says, does, and is.

See also CHURCH/ECCLESIOLOGY, EVANGELISM, INCARNATION, KINGDOM OF GOD, RECONCILIATION.

Bibliography

R. C. Bassham, *Mission Theology: 1948– 1975 Years of Worldwide Creative Tension: Ecumenical, Evangelical, and Roman Catholic* (Pasadena: William Carey Library, 1979); T. Chester (ed.), *Justice, Mercy and Humility: Integral Mission and the Poor* (Carlisle: Paternoster, 2002); O. E. Costas, *Christ Outside the Gate: Mission Beyond Christendom* (Maryknoll: Orbis Books, 1982); J. D. Douglas (ed.), *Let the Earth Hear His Voice: International Congress on World Evangelization, Lausanne, Switzerland* (Minneapolis: World Wide Publications, 1975); N. Goodall (ed.), *The Uppsala 68 Report* (Geneva: WCC, 1968); V. Samuel and C. Sugden (eds.), *The Church in Response to Human Need* (Grand Rapids: Wm. B. Eerdmans, 1987); J. R. W. Stott, *Christian Mission in the Modern World* (Downers Grove: Inter-Varsity Press, 1975); J. R. W. Stott (ed.), *Making Christ Known: Historic Mission Documents from the Lausanne Movement 1974–1989* (Carlisle: Paternoster, 1996); W. K. Willmer, J. D. Schmidt and M. Smith, *The Prospering Parachurch: Enlarging the Boundaries of God's Kingdom* (San Francisco: Jossey-Bass Publishers, 1998).

C. R. PADILLA

Holy Spirit

The theology of the Holy Spirit and theology of mission are intimately linked. Pentecost, when the Holy Spirit was poured out on believers, was simultaneously the birth of the church – the fellowship of the Spirit – and the beginning of Christian mission in the power of the Spirit. Not only is mission characteristic of the Spirit but the **missio Dei* (mission of God) may also be said to be the movement of the Spirit in the world. The Holy Spirit (or Holy Ghost in the KJV) is the Spirit of God or the Spirit of the Lord, that is, the sovereign presence and activity of God in the world. Jesus Christ was conceived, led, anointed and raised by the Holy Spirit, after which he bestowed the Spirit on his disciples. Since then, the Holy Spirit has been recognized as the Spirit of Christ, who is the means by which human beings can experience God and know the truth, and who indwells and empowers the community of believers. The Holy Spirit is understood to be the third person of the Trinity, co-equal with God the Father and God the Son and in eternal relationship with them. In the Nicene Creed, the Spirit is described as 'the Lord and Giver of Life' because by the Spirit's creative power God brings birth and life to everything.

The Holy Spirit in Scripture

In Scripture the Hebrew word (*rûaḥ*), translated 'spirit' (*pneuma* in Greek), means 'blowing', as in wind or breath, and came to mean divine power. The Spirit is involved in the initial act of creation (Gen. 1:2) and is also the breath of God that constituted Adam a living soul (Gen. 2:7; the word *nĕšāmâ* used here is virtually equivalent to *rûaḥ*, as shown by e.g. Job 27:3; Gen. 2:17). In the OT, the Spirit is given to leaders to empower them for particular tasks (Num. 11:17; 27:18; Judg. 13:25; 1 Sam. 16:13–14). The Spirit inspires poetry and song but is most closely associated with the prophets, who spoke the word of the Lord by the power of the Spirit (2 Kgs 2:15; Isa. 61:1; cf. Luke 4:18). The Gospel writers take up the prophetic expectation of a new era of the Spirit (e.g. Joel 2:28–29). In Luke's Gospel the incarnation is seen to take place within the mission of God through the Holy Spirit from the annunciation of the birth of Jesus (1:35) onwards. After Jesus' resurrection, he commanded his disciples to wait for the promised Spirit, who would empower them to 'be my witnesses in Jerusalem, and in all Judea and Samaria, and to the ends of the earth' (Luke 24:49; Acts 1:8). This promise of the Spirit of mission was fulfilled when the Spirit came upon the disciples at Pentecost as a wind and fire (Acts 2:1–4). According to John's Gospel, the Spirit brings about new birth (3:5) and is also described as truth (4:23–24; 14:17; 15:26; 16:13). Several chapters (14 – 16) are devoted to the Paraclete (or Counsellor, Advocate or Comforter), who is the Spirit (14:17). When the resurrected Jesus sent his disciples in mission, he breathed his Holy Spirit into them, which gave them power to forgive sins (20:21–23). For the apostle Paul, the new life made possible by the death and resurrection of the Lord Jesus Christ is lived 'in the Spirit' (Rom. 8:2, 5; Gal. 4:6–7) and so the Spirit is an earnest or foretaste of the life to come (Rom. 8:23; 2 Cor. 1:22; 5:5; Eph. 1:13–14), giving a variety of gifts to individuals to build up the whole body of Christ and cause the church to grow (1 Cor. 12:4–11; Rom. 12:6–8). The Spirit is the Spirit of love (Rom. 5:5; 15:30; 1 Cor. 13; Phil. 2:1).

The theology of the Spirit

In Western theology (Catholic and Protestant), the study of the Holy Spirit (pneumatology) has been neglected until recently. Without the agreement of the Eastern (Orthodox)

churches, the Western church added the phrase 'and the Son' (*filioque*) to the line of the Nicene Creed which states that the Spirit 'proceeds from the Father'. This later became indicative of the way in which Western Christians tended to see the sending (mission) of the Spirit as a consequence of or sequel to the sending of the Son. Catholic and Protestant theologians understood the Holy Spirit primarily as the means of applying the salvation achieved by Christ to the church (Catholic) or to the human heart (Protestant). In Catholic theology, pneumatology was taken over by the doctrine of grace and issues surrounding the mass, confession, the church as institution, the priesthood and the Virgin Mary. Protestants repudiated the association of the Spirit with the Catholic hierarchy and with the uniqueness of Mary. They concentrated instead on the illuminating role of the Spirit in the interpretation of Scripture and the sanctifying role of the Spirit in the life of the believer. Pneumatology was therefore implicit in other Protestant doctrines, such as sovereignty (Puritans), inspiration of Scripture (Reformed churches), grace (Methodists), holiness (holiness churches), light (Quakers), baptism (Baptists) and empowerment (Pentecostals).

Whereas in the West, pneumatology was consequent upon Christology, Eastern Orthodox theology, following Irenaeus, thought of the Son and the Spirit as 'two hands of the Father' and saw them as having two distinct (not separate) and complementary roles in God's economy. Following the Church Fathers, Orthodox theologians recognize the Spirit as Co-creator. The revival of interest in the third person of the Trinity in twentieth-century Western theology was partly due to encounter with Orthodox thought. Other important factors have been the expression of the life of the Spirit in the *Pentecostal-*charismatic movement; the empowerment experienced in the spiritual struggle for liberation and freedom from oppression; and the new possibilities offered by the fluid nature of the Spirit's personality for being church and for affirming what is good and true in human cultures (inculturation).

The agent of mission

Commenting on Luke's Gospel, David Bosch shows that the Spirit is by nature missionary and that the mission of the church is a participation in the ongoing mission of the Spirit of God. He concludes that the Spirit initiates, guides and empowers Christian missionary activity. Lesslie Newbigin gave his *theology of mission a trinitarian basis by describing mission as 'bearing the witness of the Spirit'. He showed how, biblically, the Spirit 'leads the way' in mission, 'the church is witness insofar as it follows obediently where the Spirit leads', and so mission remains 'the mission of the Spirit' (*The Open Secret: An Introduction to the Theology of Mission*, pp. 56–65). Christians agree that 'The Spirit is the agent of mission, convicting of sin, righteousness, and judgment' (World Evangelical Alliance Missions Commission, *The Iguassu Affirmation* [1999]; cf. the papal encyclical *Redemptoris Missio* 1990, paragraph 21). However, Christians differ over the scope of the Spirit's presence and activity in the world.

In *The Go-Between God*, a reflection on 'the Holy Spirit and the Christian Mission', mission leader John V. Taylor suggested that the role of the Holy Spirit in the world goes beyond explicitly Christian missionary activity to bring about communion in the form of relationship with God, love between human beings or the integrity of the creation itself. For Taylor, the mission of the Spirit encompasses all creative and up-building activities, including art, prayer and right living, but finds its focus in Jesus Christ in whom is the fullness of the Spirit. In *I Believe in the Holy Spirit*, fellow British evangelical, Michael Green questioned whether the Spirit should be conceived as involved in the continuous and ongoing processes of creation. While not completely dismissing the idea, Green sensed a danger that the life-giving work of the Spirit could be confused with nature mysticism or pantheism. This debate about the wideness of the Spirit's involvement in the world is a crucial one. It can be restated as a question about the connection between *pneuma* and *rûah*, between the spirit poured out at Pentecost and the spirit of life in the OT, and therefore between Christians, their fellow human beings and the rest of the created order.

Some biblical scholars such as Eduard Schweizer and C. F. D. Moule have so emphasized the discontinuity between *pneuma* and *rûah* as to deny that the Holy Spirit has a role in creation. It is true that there is no clear passage in the NT in which the Spirit of God appears as working in the entire creation; however, the OT references to the involvement of the Spirit in creation and the role of the Spirit in bestowing life (see Gen. 1:2; 2:7; Pss. 33:6; 104:30; Job 33:4; Ezek. 37:1–14, etc.) are implicit in the NT. Furthermore, the sovereignty of the Spirit, who comes from God, is affirmed in the NT: the Spirit blows where s/he wills (John 3:8) and is poured out on Jew and Gentile alike (Acts 11:15–17). The distinctive stance of the NT is that the Spirit of God, who is present and active in the world, is focused in and inseparable from Jesus Christ and concentrated in – but not necessarily limited to – his followers who live in the Spirit.

The Spirit in the world

The issue raised above has implications not only for the scope of mission activity but also for its nature and its approach. It is biblical testimony and the experience of mission that God's Spirit goes before us: 'Conviction of sin, faith in Christ, new birth and Christian growth are all [the Holy Spirit's] work' (Lausanne Covenant §14). Therefore, recognition of the activity of the Spirit of God beyond the boundaries of the believer's heart and the Christian church is implicit in all mission theology. Moreover, many missionaries have been challenged by their discovery that God's good gifts are not limited to Christians. Because all human beings are made in God's image and enlivened by God's Spirit (Gen. 1:27; 2:7), despite sin, there are signs of the life of the Spirit within us: for example in our cultures (cf. Lausanne Covenant §10), in indigenous faith (Matt. 8:10; Acts 17:22–23), in our natural actions (Ruth 1:16–17; cf. Luke 10:29–37).

Some theologians from the Majority World, such as José Comblin, Stanley Samartha and Justin Ukpong, have seen pneumatology as a way forward beyond the negative portrayal of their traditional cultures and practices by some missionaries and rejection of their histories in favour of a salvation-history that appears coextensive with the history of the Judeo-Christian West. They wish to affirm that 'God has not left himself without testimony' (Acts 14:17) and has been present among them before the encounter with Christian mission. At the Canberra Assembly of the

World Council of Churches (1991), Chung Hyun Kyung went further in asserting the presence and activity of the Spirit in the whole creation without necessary reference to Jesus Christ and the Christian church, based on the description of the Spirit groaning in sympathy with the whole of creation as it waits to be set free (Rom. 8:18–27). This view was condemned by the Orthodox present at the Assembly as syncretism, repudiated by evangelicals as misrepresenting biblical revelation, and generally criticized as contrary to Christian belief in the Trinity. The creation theology of the Spirit developed by Jürgen Moltmann is more carefully constructed to avoid these dangers. While affirming the mission of the Spirit to bring life to all, Moltmann also stressed the role of the church in this ministry to the whole created order.

Mission in the Spirit

If the Spirit is the agent of mission, then mission begins when Christians seek to discern the movement of the Spirit in the world and participate in it. Furthermore, since the Spirit is sovereign, mission in the Spirit implies an attitude of openness to recognize the presence and activity of the Spirit wherever the Spirit blows. From a pneumatological perspective, mission consists in affirming whatever is true, honourable, just, pure, lovely, gracious, excellent and praiseworthy, wherever encountered (Phil. 4:8), and at the same time exercising discernment in order to distinguish evil and be led by the Spirit into all truth (John 16:13). In this way mission takes place not only 'by the Spirit' but also 'in the Spirit' as we bear witness, develop gifts and bring forth spiritual fruit.

There are three main biblical criteria for discerning the Holy Spirit: the confession of Jesus as Lord (1 John 4:2); the evidence of the fruit of the Spirit (Gal. 5:22); and the practice of the gifts of the Spirit given to the body of Christ (1 Cor 12:4–11; Rom. 12:6–8). All of these are signs of the Spirit and point toward the incarnate Son of God, who is the embodiment of the Spirit. Discernment is difficult because Christian confession is not necessarily a guarantee of the right Spirit (Matt. 7:21–22); nor are good works alone the work of the Spirit (Rom 7:6); nor is exercise of any particular gift incontrovertible proof of the Spirit's presence (1 Cor. 13:1–3). However, God gives the church the spiritual gift of discernment (1 Cor. 12:10). Discernment proceeds through the study of God's word, heartfelt knowledge of Jesus Christ, and discussion with one another (Luke 24:31–32).

In the early twentieth century, Roland Allen compared modern missionary methods unfavourably with those of St Paul, and identified a lack of awareness of or trust in the work of the Holy Spirit in their converts as the reason for inflexibility and paternalism on the part of Western missionaries. He argued that Paul's mission was done out of the Spirit of love rather than the letter of the commandment. Allen drew attention to the spirituality of mission, which he regarded as more important than achieving mission goals. If mission takes place 'in the Spirit', then it is not only important to do the job but also to do it in a way that expresses the Spirit of Christ. Aggressive and arrogant attitudes are not compatible with the mission of the Spirit that is the ministry of reconciliation, of which we are ambassadors (2 Cor. 3:6, 8; 5:18), motivated by Christ's love (5:14), not commending ourselves but Christ, in sincerity and humility (5:12; 2:17; 4:7).

The Spirit and cultures

The way the Holy Spirit is understood is bound to be influenced by the meaning of 'spirit' in any particular cultural-linguistic context. Scientific materialism has little place for thinking about the Spirit, except as coterminous with the human mind. The renewal of interest in the theology of the Holy Spirit in the West has gone along with a revival of interest in spirituality. In India, the background of fascination with spiritualities of all kinds and a pervasive awareness of one universal Spirit, has led to pneumatology becoming the cornerstone of Indian Christian theology. In North America, Amos Yong has sought to develop a Pentecostal-charismatic theology of spiritual discernment that also reflects his background in Chinese folk Buddhism in which there is a prevailing tradition of belief in the many spirits. These varied pre-understandings of 'spirit' greatly enrich pneumatological reflection. They also raise questions for biblical scholars about the NT background meaning of *pneuma*, the answers to which will further enhance our understanding of the biblical text.

See also CHRIST, GOD, INCULTURATION.

Bibliography
R. Allen, *Missionary Methods: St. Paul's or Ours?* (Grand Rapids: Eerdmans; 1962 [1912]); D. J. Bosch, *Transforming Mission: Paradigm Shifts in Theology of Mission* (Maryknoll, NY: Orbis Books, 1991); E. Castro (ed.), *To the Wind of God's Spirit: Reflections on the Canberra Theme* (Geneva: World Council of Churches, 1990); J. Comblin, *The Holy Spirit and Liberation* (Tunbridge Wells: Burns & Oates, 1989); M. Green, *I Believe in the Holy Spirit* (London: Hodder & Stoughton, 1985); K. Kim, *Mission in the Spirit: The Holy Spirit in Indian Christian Theologies* (Delhi: ISPCK, 2003); M. Kinnamon (ed.), *Signs of the Spirit*. Official Report of the Seventh Assembly of the WCC, Canberra, 1991 (Geneva: World Council of Churches, 1991); J. Moltmann, trans. M. Kohl, *The Spirit of Life: A Universal Affirmation* (London: SCM Press; 1992); L. Newbigin, *The Open Secret: An Introduction to the Theology of Mission* (Grand Rapids, MI: Wm B. Eerdmans, rev. edn 1995); J. V. Taylor, *The Go-Between God: The Holy Spirit and the Christian Mission* (London: SCM Press, 1972); A. Yong, *Discerning the Spirit(s): A Pentecostal-Charismatic Contribution to Christian Theology of Religions* (Sheffield: Sheffield Academic Press, 2000).

K. KIM

Homogeneous unit

Homogeneous units are social groups with a strong sense of membership identity and interaction. The so-called homogeneous unit principle originated in the missiology of Donald A. McGavran, adapting a sociological-anthropological concept for missionary methodology and missiological research. As defined by McGavran, 'The *homogeneous unit* is simply a section of society in which all the members have some characteristic in common' (*Understanding Church Growth*, p. 85). Typical examples include kinship groups, castes and tribes. Kinship groups are basic to human cultures. In contrast to Western individualism, 'Relationships to kinsmen take precedence over other social bonds in much of the world' (P. G. Hiebert, *Cultural Anthropology*, p. 221). Kinship gives identity and meaning, hence the importance of family and extended family relationships in most societies. Kinship functions to provide security, legal aid, marriage regulations, and social and religious observances. McGavran urged the study of homogeneous units to understand *church growth patterns and dynamics of resistance and response. The identification of responsive groups for evangelization came to be known as the homogeneous unit principle.

McGavran's missiology was honed in the crucible of rural India with its multiple castes, each of which 'believes itself to be a separate people and scrupulously keeps its intimate life to itself' (*The Bridges of God*, p. 41). This being so, 'The great obstacles to conversion are social, not theological' (McGavran, *Understanding Church Growth*, p. 191). It follows that evangelization can best proceed along the lines of family, social and cultural relationships. Much of the population in Asia and Africa live in contexts where group loyalty is demanded, hence the importance of group conversions, what McGavran called 'people movements'. In such conversion movements members of a homogeneous unit make a joint commitment to follow Jesus Christ and join together into churches with a homogeneous identity – which in turn are successful at evangelism and continue to grow easily.

McGravan's classic *Bridges of God* argues that the NT church grew through a series of people movements among the Jews, among Jewish proselytes, and among the Greeks. From these beginnings the faith multiplied among related communities around the Mediterranean world. It can be demonstrated that historically from the first century onward the church has grown through group conversions.

Awareness that *conversion can take place in a group setting, in which all the members participate in a personal act of faith, runs counter to the individualistic assumptions characteristic of Western missionaries, but has given fresh insight for contemporary mission strategy. Focusing on the importance of homogeneous units is also helpful for understanding the diversity of human responses.

Nevertheless, the homogeneous unit principle has been severely criticized for its optimistic over-dependence on *anthropology and the social sciences, and for a shallow biblical hermeneutic. Indeed, some have said that the homogeneous unit principle has no biblical foundation, since NT churches witnessed to the power of the gospel to unite people *across* cultural and *ethnic divisions (Eph. 2:11–22), rather than nurturing homogeneous response and development. A biblical *ecclesiology envisages a church in which there is 'neither Jew nor Gentile' (Gal. 3:28), so that all ethnic and cultural differences are relativized by our oneness in Christ. Others have been concerned that the homogeneous unit principle approach might result in churches with a weak social ethic and which fail to counteract the evils in society, or which fail to nurture converts.

Nevertheless, churches with strong homogeneous ethnic identities have established themselves in many major cities of the world as effective ways of evangelizing and drawing together people who might otherwise feel their identity threatened in today's multicultural urbanization. Nigerian, Korean, Chinese, Ghanaian churches, and many similar, are amongst the fastest growing in the Western world. They have shown how the homogeneous unit principle works well for *evangelization, especially in cultures in which group conversion is normal. Further, they have the potential for a mission engagement with other ethnic groups and indigenous people, in which they share the vibrancy and dynamic of their corporate life, and receive much in return. Some mono-ethnic churches in India, for example, are heavily involved in missionary outreach, sending and support.

McGavran saw the homogeneous unit principle as a tool for evangelization in the non-Christian world, especially amongst *unreached peoples, and it was derived from scrutiny of scores of conversion movements around the world. It is not therefore a Western concept, but emerged from the crucible of India and the Hindu world as an important way to communicate the gospel among Hindu-Buddhist-Islamic-tribal peoples. In fact, McGavran considered homogeneous unit principles optional, a possible methodology; a major point missed by critics. The homogeneous unit principle is therefore first a sociological-anthropological category, not primarily theological, and McGavran's deeper theological concern was the continuing validity and necessity of mission as evangelization. This constituted a theological protest against an excessive secularization of the gospel by those of his time who no longer believed in the lostness of humankind and the need for conversion. In actuality McGavran was a social radical who believed in Christianization as the surest path to social transformation.

Bibliography

O. E. Costas, *The Church and Its Mission: A Shattering Critique from the Third World* (Wheaton: Tyndale House, 1974); P. G. Hiebert, *Cultural Anthropology* (Philadelphia: J. B. Lippincott, 1976); Lausanne Committee for World Evangelization, 'The Pasadena Consultation – Homogeneous Unit Principle', *Lausanne Occasional Papers* 1, 1978; D. A. McGavran, *The Bridges of God: A Study in the Strategy of Mission* (New York: Friendship Press, 1955); D. A. McGavran, *Understanding Church Growth* (Grand Rapids: Eerdmans, 1970); C. R. Padilla, 'The Unity of the Church and the Homogeneous Unit Principle', in W. R. Shenk (ed.), *The Challenge of Church Growth: A Symposium* (Scottdale: Herald Press, 1973); J. W. Pickett, A. L. Warnshuis, G. H. Singh and D. A. McGavran, *Church Growth and Group Conversion* (Lucknow: Lucknow Publishing House, 1962); R. L. Ramseyer, 'Anthropological Perspectives on Church Growth Theory' in *The Challenge of Church Growth: A Symposium*; W. R. Shenk (ed.), *The Challenge of Church Growth: A Symposium* (Scottdale: Herald Press, 1973).

R. E. HEDLUND

Hope

Hope is a central motif and a strong motivator in the missiological self-understanding and missionary practice of the church. Eschatological hope is rooted in the *resurrection of Jesus and is thus an integral part of the proclamation of the gospel as good news.

Through this proclamation the church engages with the hopes and fears expressed in the human context of its mission. Generally speaking, human hope is the expectation of some future good. Humans are creatures of suffering, guilt and death, and they appear to overcome despair, anxiety and resignation best when they have an object of hope. In most cultures and languages the word hope signifies a simple desire for a different or better future. At the heart of all human thirst for meaning and purpose of life is a latent search for hope. In the classical tradition of Christian thought and spirituality, hope is a theological virtue bestowed by God, which along with faith and love orientates human persons toward an improved present and ultimately perfect union with God.

Mission proclaims a gospel in which hope and *faith are closely linked, for hope depends on faith and expresses its forward-looking aspect, for 'faith is being sure of what we hope for and certain of what we do not see' (Heb. 11:1). Both are grounded in the character of the trustworthy *God. Hope is a believing response to God's promises yet to be fulfilled and is therefore faith oriented toward the future – the 'future tense of faith'. That future is not to be conceived purely in terms of chronology as that time which has not yet arrived. It is a distortion of scriptural teaching to think in terms of a sharp separation between the present (history) and the future (eschatology), as if the *eschaton* was a strange future reality which is totally unrelated to our present history. A biblical understanding of *history also does not allow us either to confine God to a pure and remote transcendent dwelling, or to consign his activity to past events. It is equally wrong to see him simply immanent within the processes of history and present developments. God the creator, sustainer and redeemer of the universe and humanity is also God of the future and therefore 'God of hope'. He is presently involved with and in our world in terms of accomplishing his purposes in history and especially through the church, his own eschatological missional community of faith, love and hope.

The centre of gravity of Christian faith lies not in the events that come at the end of history, but in the events that have already taken place within history – in the incarnation, death and resurrection of *Jesus and in the outpouring of the *Holy Spirit. The decisive event of redemptive history has already taken place and the end-point has been predetermined by the mid-point. The future tense is therefore predicated on the past perfect tense

of God's mission in Christ. Christians have a hope because they have a memory. They celebrate what Christ has accomplished by his death and resurrection as the culmination of his first coming and joyfully anticipate his assured second coming, 'the blessed hope – the appearing of the glory of our great God and Saviour, Jesus Christ' (Titus 2:11–13). The 'already-fulfilled' and the 'not-yet-completed' aspects of the kingdom of God lead to the conclusion that in the NT teaching there is both a realized and a future eschatology.

The mission of the church therefore reflects both dimensions of the kingdom. It speaks of a hope that is not static but a very dynamic concept, for it speaks of confident and eager expectation and trust coupled with anticipatory living and hopeful actions that at least partially express in the present the vision and values of the hoped for future. Our anticipation of the future kingdom of God is also a call to proleptic participation on the journey toward that future, and should determine the way we live in the present.

Christian hope is opposed to all fatalism and does not lead to a passive attitude of waiting for the hereafter, but to a transformative and missional engagement in the present world. Genuine Christian hope engenders ethical living in the present. Christian *ethics should be an ethics of change that goes beyond individual repentance. It must also be extended to the areas of social relationships and societal structures. Christians can initiate some significant changes in the world as they faithfully proclaim and courageously practise the universally valid values of the kingdom of God. It is regretful that much fundamentalist and semi-evangelical eschatology with its other-worldly distortions and groundless apocalyptic speculation about the 'end times' consumes much time and energy needed for transformative mission in our broken world. Its reduced understanding of salvation as rescuing souls for heaven treats hope as an escape clause and results in socially passive communities and defective ethics of acceptance of the status quo.

The future makes demands on our living in the present, since God's eschatological kingdom is a radical critique of the present state of things in the world. Christian hope expressed in mission disturbs the present by its refusal to accept the status quo in all realms of human existence. Proleptic living is a hope-shaped lifestyle by faith that takes the promises and commands of God equally seriously and honours Christ by implementing them in the present. Christian eschatological hope relativizes this world and the present historical realities by pointing to the future perfect rule of Christ when justice and peace will be completely actualized. This hope therefore frees us from all this-worldly national and political idolatries, ideological servitudes, religious perfectionisms and utopian schemes.

In terms of personal and communal mission spirituality, hope is a source of joy and strength which sustains and encourages Christians in the midst of life's difficult circumstances. It enables patient waiting when faced with unjust suffering and persecution. Patience and perseverance in these contexts have to do with fortitude and wisdom and must be distinguished from indifference or lack of sensitivity. This is especially evident in references to hope in 1 Peter, a letter written to Gentile converts who lived in a society hostile to their faith. In such contexts, persevering in hope implies the ethical obligation of holy living in a manner that does not satisfy selfish human desires but pleases the One who has graciously provided the ground of hope available (1 Pet. 1:3, 13–16). At other times hope fills followers of 'Christ Jesus our hope' (1 Tim. 1:1) with a holy discontent over present circumstances and empowers them for prophetic words and transformative actions.

In their missional encounter with the world followers of Christ must 'always be prepared to give an answer to everyone one who asks you to give the reason for the hope that you have' (1 Pet. 3:15). Central to this message is that death does not have a final word for believers, since the death and resurrection of Jesus and the expectation of his glorious return assure for them eternal fellowship with him which sets them apart from 'the rest [of humankind], who have no hope' (1 Thess. 4:13). The Gentiles who do not know Christ are 'foreigners to the covenants of the promise, without hope and without God in the world' (Eph. 2:11–12). To the spiritually lost and morally confused humanity Christians respond with a Christocentric message of life and hope.

Christian hope generates a model of mission in which there is neither this-worldly utopianism nor other-worldly detachment. Amidst and contrary to secular and religious fears and frenzies about present and future, Christians do creatively participate in God's transformative mission in our world as agents of the kingdom already-arrived and live in a watchful expectation of the king(dom) to come in power and glory. These two dimensions of our participation in actualizing provisional (penultimate) hopes and our anticipation of the ultimate hope are best expressed when we pray: 'your kingdom come, your will be done on earth as it is in heaven.'

See also ESCHATOLOGY, GOSPEL, KINGDOM OF GOD.

Bibliography
R. Bauckham and T. Hart, *Hope Against Hope* (Grand Rapids: Eerdmans, 1999); R. Chia, *Hope for the World* (Leicester: IVP, 2006); P. Kuzmič, 'Eschatology and Ethics' in V. Samuel and C. Sugden (eds.), *Mission as Transformation* (Oxford: Regnum Press, 1999); G. Tinder, *The Fabric of Hope* (Atlanta, GA: Scholars Press, 1999).
P. KUZMIČ

Hospitality

Hospitality in both biblical and African traditions is not just about entertaining family and friends; it also concerns the 'other', the stranger, the outsider, the foreigner. In most of the African languages the same word is used for both stranger and guest: the Kiswahili word for both is *mgeni*, and among the Nandi in Kenya the word *toot* is used. To show how hospitality was built into the structure of life of the Kipsigis people in Kenya, Chepkwony tells us that whenever a meal was prepared, it was normal to set aside one portion, known as *kimyet ab lakwa* (lit. the food for a child), so that if a stranger showed up after an evening meal there would be something to offer. It is also a normal practice in most African homes to prepare more food than required because there is the expectation that a stranger will show up.

Christians have a rich biblical heritage of hospitality as mission. The Hebrew Scriptures do not have a word for the concept of hospitality but the practice is evident through-out the whole OT. For ancient Israel, it was one of the central pillars of their identity and mission as the people of God. Abraham, who is considered the father of the nation and also of the faithful, is lifted up as the prime practitioner of hospitality. Christians are urged not only to emulate Abraham's example of faith (Heb. 11:11–17), but also his practice of hospitality (Heb. 13:2).

The NT word most closely associated with hospitality is *xenos*, which means literally stranger, foreigner or even enemy. The one who receives visitors is said to be *philoxenos* 'a lover of strangers' or practising the virtue of *philoxenia*. Hospitality played a significant role in the life and mission of Jesus and his disciples. Jesus enjoyed hospitality in several homes during his mission, such as the home of Lazarus and his two sisters (Luke 10:38–42) and that of Simon the leper (Matt. 26:6–13). He also practised hospitality when he fed the five thousand and when he welcomed sinners, prostitutes and tax collectors. His free inter-action with outcasts shows how he broke the barriers of table fellowship, demonstrating vividly the radical message of hospitality. He also instructed his disciples to depend on the hospitality of their hosts when he sent them out on mission (Matt. 10:1–13; Luke 9:1–6; 10:1–7).

Jesus' teaching about the final judgment shows that hospitality is what mission is about, by saying that those who welcomed 'the least of these' will be received into the kingdom: 'Come, you who are blessed by my Father; take your inheritance, the kingdom prepared for you since the foundation of the world. For ... I was a stranger and you invited me in ...' (Matt. 25:34–35).

It is clear from the epistles that both church leaders and members were expected to show hospitality (Rom. 12:13; 1 Tim. 3:2; 5:9–10; Titus 1:8; Heb. 13:2; 1 Pet. 4:9; 2 John 10–11; 3 John 10). In this way the gospel was spread not just by word of mouth but also through vibrant relationship as people interacted in their homes. In order to regulate the practice of hospitality the *Didache* gave the following instruction: 'But let everyone who cometh in the name of the Lord be received, and then when you have tested him you shall have understanding on the right and the left. If the comer is a traveler assist him as you are able,

but he shall not stay with you for more than two days or three days if necessary.'

Hospitality in our world is on the decline. The prevalence of walls and gated communities is evidence of this. It is also clear that our world has become violent and insecure so we really struggle whether to obey the biblical command or be concerned about our own safety and comfort. In African urban areas the practice has also been abused and over-stretched through the overdependence of relatives on a few working individuals. The answers are not straightforward, but we need to grapple with how to uphold the practice and yet at the same time be vigilant. Pohl shows us that throughout the history of the church the practice gradually became institu-tionalized, and so lost its radical meaning of reaching out to those on the margins of society and the disconnected in this world. We need to recover the essence of this virtue so that it can be practised within the Christian church as well as in public life. The violent conditions in our world should not deter us from showing hospitality to those who need it the most. These include the homeless, the poor, orphans, widows, *refugees, those suffering from incurable diseases such as HIV/*AIDS and those who live on the margins of society. Pohl describes them as 'those who are discon-nected from basic relationships that give a secure place in the world' (C. D. Pohl, *Making Room: Recovering Hospitality as a Christian Tradition*, p. 13).

Hospitality as mission in the church is a practice that is potentially subversive, upset-ting the status quo, and full of risks. It is about giving those who have been displaced a legit-imate place to be and belong. It breaks the vicious circle that makes people continually vulnerable and perpetually dependent on handouts. Rightfully applied, this practice can be a tool for empowerment, restoration and transformation for those who have been excluded. In recovering this concept, espe-cially in the public arena of the nation and the church, we are also recovering our rich biblical heritage, enshrined in church history and attested in traditional societies all over the world. One Kiswahili proverb (almost similar to the instruction of the *Didache*, which can be used to regulate our practice of hospitality) is *Mgeni siku ya kwanza, siku ya pili mpatie jembe*. It literally means 'one is a guest only for two days; on the third day give him/her a hoe to dig'. It shows that a guest should participate in the life of the people and not be a burden. Such is the wisdom that we need in our complex world where insecurities thrive and people are not sure how to respond to strangers. It is also important to note that hospitality should be practised in the context of community, so that individual responses are not overwhelmed by enormous needs.

The mystery and joy of hospitality brings great gifts to the hosts as well as to the recipient. The host becomes the guest and the guest becomes the host as the gifts of God's church are shared. In hospitality people are emulating the great giver, God, 'who did not spare his own Son, but gave him up' (Rom. 8:32). The practice will help to heal divisions, hostilities and distinctions in our world that occur due to ethnic, racial, class and gender differences, for the sake of expansion of the *kingdom. A practical example of how this has been applied with great results is the 'Alpha' course programme. Before discussions people are first invited to share the hospitality of the host. Likewise in modern short- and long-term mission work there is the acknowledgment that mission is two-way, a giving and receiving. Thus, hospitality is that fundamental attitude of openness towards one's fellow human beings as those made in the image of God. It is best practised by those who have experienced God's free grace and will freely give in kind and in word to enrich others so in the process lives are also transformed.

Bibliography

E. J. Choge, *I was a Stranger and You Welcomed Me ... Jesus' Teaching on Hospitality with Special Reference to Matthew 25:32–46*, unpublished MTh thesis (Nairobi: Nairobi Evangelical Graduate School of Theology, 1997); E. J. Choge, 'Hospitality in Africa', in T. Adeyemo (ed.), *Africa Bible Commentary* (Nairobi: WordAlive Publishers, 2006); J. Koenig, *New Testament Hospitality: Partnership with Strangers as Promise and Mission* (Philadelphia: Fortress Press, 1985); A. G. Oden (ed.), *And You Welcomed Me: A Sourcebook on Hospitality in Early Christianity* (Nashville: Abingdon, 2001); T. W. Ogletree, *Hospitality to the Stranger: Dimensions of Moral Understanding* (Philadelphia: Fortress Press, 1985); C. D. Pohl, *Making Room: Recovering Hospitality as a Christian Tradition* (Grand Rapids: Eerdmanns, 1999); C. D. Pohl, 'Biblical Issues in Mission and Migration', *Missiology* XXXI, 2003, pp. 4–15.

E. J. CHOGE

HUMANENESS, see *UBUNTU*

Human/humanity

The Christian view

The Christian view of humanity begins with the *Trinity. God invested the whole of his trinitarian personhood in creating human beings in his own image (Gen. 1:26–27). The expression 'Let *us* make...' clearly indicates the corporate determination of the Godhead. It is from the Father that the human family derives its identity (Eph. 3:14–15); it is in the Son, through whom all things were created (John 1:3) that true humanity is revealed (Heb. 2:17); and it is from the Spirit that human beings receive the breath of life (Gen. 2:7). God put the whole of himself into humanity as the pinnacle of his creation.

A human being therefore is made in the image of God as an integrated, whole person. The image of God lies in the 'whole complexity of being human, the diversities and distinctivenesses of what it is to be a human being in this world' (*The Message of Genesis 1 – 11*, p. 36). Most modern writers shy away from a crude Greek dualistic view of human beings in which the image of God is attributed to the soul and not the body. It is the whole human being that bears the image of God.

It is helpful to think of the image of God as God-given capacities (formal) that enable human beings to function in particular ways (material). The formal capacities include the ability to relate, rationality and creativity. The material capacities include competence to exercise loving stewardship of the earth, to make moral decisions, and above all to love (both God and other human beings). These capacities enable all humanity to reflect the image of God to a greater or lesser extent.

This positive view of humanity is where relationships in mission must begin. It enables us to meet people first of all on the basis of what we have in common, and not what differentiates us. Meeting people first on the basis of a common humanity created in God's image is an affirming and non-judgmental basis for mutual relationship which forms the context for trustful witness.

However, humanity, in spite of exalted status as bearer of the image of God, is flawed by *sin, which is part of the very fabric of human nature. For most people and under normal circumstances, sin does not show itself in outwardly sinful behaviour. But when human spirits are stirred by the winds of violent emotion then such base passions as rage, spite, greed, lust, jealousy, malice, cruelty and revenge easily manifest themselves. The Bible traces sin back to the rebellion of the prime ancestors of all human beings: Adam and Eve in the Garden of Eden (Gen. 3). Since then all humanity has inherited as it were 'the sinful gene', which pervades all human thought and activity and works as a dehumanizing force in individuals and communities.

In Adam's case, the result was a demeaning sense of pollution, shame and guilt. This experience drove a wedge between God and humanity so that human beings no longer desired the presence of their Creator. The only remedy was ultimately to be found in the sacrificial death of Jesus Christ. Through the *cross the possibility of a new humanity becomes real because sin and all its consequences is dealt with. This paves the way for full communion between God and humanity as well as harmony between all human beings. This is God's purpose for humanity and therefore the goal of mission. It puts 'humanization', as the restoration of humanity in all its glory, at the heart of mission.

The significance of a theology of humanity for mission

This theological formulation is significant for mission for many reasons:

(1) If all human beings are created by God and entrusted with certain obligations on earth (Gen. 1:26–28; cf. Acts 17:26–28), then all human beings are addressable by God. This distinguishes human beings from the rest of creation, and is the basis for the universality of the *gospel.

(2) All human beings are accountable to God. This universal moral obligation is the foundation of biblical *ethics. This means that all human beings have the moral capacity to understand the gospel when it speaks of the need to repent of wrongdoing (Acts 17:30).

(3) Every human being is of great value to God and deserves to be treated with dignity and respect. This is the basis for mission without discrimination.

(4) Humanity is made for relationships (Gen. 1:27; cf. 2:18). As God exists in a community of love, perfect harmony and unity of purpose and action, so he made human beings as essentially social people. Individual human isolationism, even in penal contexts, is therefore destructive of our essential humanity.

David Atkinson reinforces this last point in a Western context by saying, 'One of the disastrous consequences of the Enlightenment philosophy ... was the concentration on the individual as the centre of rational self-consciousness. The end of that road is the misery of the Me-generation' (*The Message of Genesis 1 – 11*, p. 68). Cartesian dualism led to the isolation of the individual from society and the separation of facts from values, mind from body, reason from emotion, subject from object and consequently, communion between human beings, horizontally or vertically, has become a casualty. Community is fragmented and fractured, so that even when people share the same roof, they may have very little to do with each other in their lives. Neighbourhoods, especially in the Western world, are generally a collection of houses inhabited by people who do not know each other and care little for one another. That human beings were made for community is more appreciated in other contexts. As the Africans would say: true *ubuntu* ('humaneness') is only possible among *abantu* ('common humanity'). Because people need vital relationships within family, community, society and culture, the restoration of relationships must be at the heart of mission.

The scope of mission

A biblical anthropology has already highlighted important missiological implications. Three especially can be highlighted.

First, because creation is good and positive (Ps. 111:2; cf. 19:1–6), human qualities, gifts and creativity should be our delight, the focus of our study (Ps. 145:5), and valued (though not as the object) in our worship. If mission makes the mistake of focusing exclusively upon the 'soul', it is selling people short on God's purposes for them. Mission must confront everything that dehumanizes people, even as it works for a transformed humanity in harmony with others and with the earth. It is significant that God has eternal plans for both human beings and the earth (Rom. 8:18–23). God's invitation to exercise careful stewardship, not exploitation, of the earth is not just for the sake of the earth, but also for humanity. He gives humanity work, economic activity and creativity as creation ordinances. The earth's resources must be utilized in an atmosphere of justice and concern both for all people and the whole environment, and this draws *ecology and its effect on humanity into the scope of mission.

Second, all human beings, individually and collectively, must be given an opportunity to hear God's words addressed to them and to make a response. The vision of mission is universal to all nations (Matt. 28:18–20; John 20:21). But 'nations' represent territories, histories, and shared cultures, mental and relational processes by which decisions are made. All these aspects of what is meant by 'nations' need to be brought under the authority of Jesus, and therefore this task is integral to the outworking of mission. Mission confronts historical, cultural and social dislocations and seeks to bring national structures into obedient discipleship to the kingdom of God.

Third, in spite of all the failures of human experience the Bible holds out the promise of a future humanity in perfect harmony with God, itself, and the environment. God will dwell permanently with his people (Rev. 21:3–4). There is an ultimate *transformation from that which is perishable to the imperishable, corrupt to incorruptible, mortal to immortality, and material or natural to spiritual (1 Cor. 15:42–44, 50–54). The eternal worship of God draws in all of creation (Rev. 4:6–11; 7:11; cf. Ezek. 1:6, 10), and gives humanity a 'living hope', whose reality is guaranteed through the resurrection of Jesus Christ (1 Pet. 1:3). This provides mission with its ultimate goal and gives meaning to all that we do on this earth for the coming of the kingdom.

See also CULTURE, HOLISTIC MISSION.

Bibliography
D. Atkinson, *The Message of Genesis 1 – 11* (Downers Grove: InterVarsity Press; Leicester: IVP, 1990); I. Barbour, *Nature, Human Nature and God* (London: SPCK, 2002); F. W. Bridger, 'Humanity', in D. J. Atkinson and D. H. Field (eds.), *New Dictionary of Christian Ethics and Pastoral Theology* (-Leicester: IVP, 1995); D. J. A. Clines, 'Image of God in Man', *Tyndale Bulletin* 19, 1968, p. 72; J. M Kapolyo, *The Human Condition* (Leicester: IVP, 2005); L. Stevenson, *Theories of Human Nature* (Oxford: Oxford University Press, 1974).

J. KAPOLYO

Human rights

The Bible does not speak directly about 'human rights' as they are understood today, and some Christians therefore claim that it is not necessary to engage in the defence and promotion of human rights as a dimension of the church's mission. Nevertheless, the OT has many laws and commandments that serve as prohibitions to certain acts which deprive others of justice or dignity, and it sets high ethical demands for the treatment of individuals and communities. God is especially concerned that human beings should build individual and social relationships that are just, free of corruption, and bear witness to his own justice and righteousness (e.g. Ps. 15). The OT witnesses to a God who rescues those who are oppressed and dehumanized through injustice, and his mission in its fullest sense aims to restore humanity wherever it is fractured or abused by others (e.g. Ps. 10:12–18). The expectation is that God's people will be a 'light to the nations' by the standards of justice and human value that they reflect in their individual and corporate commitment to setting captives free (Isa. 42:6).

Although principles of justice should be applied to making human rights possible for everyone, in the OT God demands especially that we act justly towards the widow, the fatherless, the alien and the *poor; that is, to those who have less possibilities of validating their rights (Deut. 24:17–22; Ps. 82:3–4). This is because God has a special care for the poor and needy (e.g. Pss. 35:10; 140:12). Even when declarations and pacts on human rights state that we all, including poor people, have the same rights and duties, in practice such rights are not implemented. People in better economic positions or positions of power have more opportunities to enforce and exercise their rights. This means that the church in its mission must pay particular attention to those who are the weakest and most vulnerable members of society.

Most human rights, taken as we understand them, have some biblical basis. To take a simple example, the commandment 'do not kill' stands for the current position on the right to life that God gives to every human being. The biblical concept of human dignity is based on the creation of human beings in the image of God (Gen. 1:27; cf. Gen. 9:5–6). To God, all humans are valued the same 'without distinction of any kind, such as race, color, sex, language, religion, political or other opinion, national or social origin, property, birth or other status' (Article 2, Universal Declaration on Human Rights).

The commandment to act justly (Mic. 6:8) is a foundation text for work in human rights. The OT consistently witnesses to God's care for individuals who are justly treated. In the NT Jesus identified with those who were marginalized and had no rights, and supremely in his trial and crucifixion shared the suffering of those who suffer injustice. But he spoke of a *kingdom which would signal God's ultimate authority over all things on earth as it is in heaven (Matt. 6:10). This means that all issues that involve the restoration of humanity, according to God's intention, are important to the establishing of the kingdom. That kingdom has already come in the person of Jesus, but it is also a promise and, as such, it implies hope for those who do not experience its just and gentle rule. So for the church to apply the principles of human rights in its mission is not to follow a 'secular religion', but to make basic commitments emerging directly from core Christian beliefs. It follows that evangelism which ignores human rights abuses in the context of its activity lacks both authority and credibility.

Human rights and society

Human rights can be considered under two aspects, which protect both corporate and individual rights: (1) as a universal judicial tool protecting and guaranteeing life and the whole development of people and their communities; (2) as an ethical agreement aimed at protecting the dignity of human beings by empowering them before the state, other people, power groups, and so on. With regard to this second dimension, biblical material which speaks of respect for life and the promotion of human dignity can help us to build bridges between the Christian and judicial perspectives.

The Universal Declaration of Human Rights was adopted in 1948. It constituted a normative framework of fundamental freedoms and rights related to human dignity and worth. Since this Declaration, the implications of human rights have been developed and, at present, there are a significant number of international agreements: on civil and political rights, the rights of the child, on racial and gender discrimination, torture, and so on. Other conventions are being prepared, such as the Universal Declaration of Indigenous Peoples' Rights.

The UN has regularly confirmed the universal, indivisible nature and interdependence of individual and social rights, as well as civil and political rights. Human rights have usually been considered to be limited to the civil and political level, while economic, social and cultural rights have been difficult to deal with in the courts. There has also been an important discussion about whether civil/individual rights or social/collective rights are the most important. This discussion took place within the cold war framework where the two ideological concepts of the so-called socialist and capitalist worlds were opposed. However, it is not possible to divide these categories of rights, since they are strongly connected and interdependent. For example, an individual's guarantee of freedom without the guarantee of access to health or education would raise critical questions about the kind of freedoms that a state claims to protect. Conversely, keeping the right to health with restrictions to individual freedom would weaken society and the state in the long term.

To have laws establishing rights is no guarantee of these rights being implemented. It is necessary to have social and political mechanisms in place that ensure these rights are protected. However, without normative frameworks guaranteeing rights, people can be at the mercy of arbitrary governments who may use and abuse the laws as they wish.

Human rights and Christian responsibility

The Bible gives Christians a clear responsibility to make sure that laws on human rights are not empty and insignificant. It is sometimes indeed necessary to *demand* that state authorities should respect and protect rights, even though we are all called to enforce rights in all areas of our influence (i.e. domestic and multinational companies, trade unions, political parties, national and international NGOs, financial institutions, churches and civil society).

So how can we make human rights and justice a more important dimension of the missionary task? We must first make every effort to re-discover and teach exactly what the Bible does say regarding justice and the implications of God's kingdom for our world today. This will include consideration of the meaning of 'justice' in its many dimensions. The next step is to encourage Christians to bear witness to justice and its role in church life, worship, praise, prayer and discipleship. A primary task for local churches is to help in shaping responsible citizens who are aware of their rights, who exercise them, and who carry out their civil duties faithfully. In poor countries where large sections of the population are considered second-class citizens, it is important for churches to develop educational tools that inform people of their rights and encourage good citizenship. In rich countries, where individualism and indifference are a problem, the church in its mission must open believers' eyes to the realities of injustice and generate compassion and commitment to acting on behalf of those suffering through the terrible events that happen not only in their country, but in poor countries across the world. In summary, it will involve encouraging Christians to take responsibility for demanding justice and human dignity rights on behalf of others as well as themselves.

A second missional task is for the church to be active both in helping to bring into existence laws protecting human rights, and then in working to ensure that they are fulfilled by everyone, beginning with state authorities. This can only be done effectively by setting up specialist agencies which have the necessary expertise and networks to promote these objectives in the name of Christ. Here there is room for para-church ministries, as in the case of *Paz y Esperanza* (Peace and Hope) in Peru. Peace and Hope has worked alongside other organizations to promote social and environmental rights, the rights of indigenous communities and people imprisoned unfairly. There is also a place for specialized organizations providing legal assistance in situations where justice is almost non-existent for those who are powerless and lack resources. An important aspect of the work is human rights education and conflict-prevention, among other issues.

The enforcement of rights also sometimes implies *political action*. It is clear that human rights are frequently violated by governments around the world. Dictatorial governments make it almost impossible to secure state protection for these rights. In order to ensure human rights are respected, it is necessary to draw on various strategies, namely advocacy, IEC (information, education and communication), organizing and strengthening civil society and pleading international pressure (governmental and non-governmental entities).

Because Christians share in a common humanity, they are able to join with others of different religious traditions in certain contexts to defend human rights. However, many Christians especially suffer abuse, persecution, torture and imprisonment through violation of basic human rights, and they look to their brothers and sisters worldwide to stand alongside them. Agencies such as Christian Solidarity Worldwide play an important role in this area. When one part of the universal body of Christ suffers, all suffer, and therefore all share the responsibility to defend and support them not only in prayer but in active advocacy to protect their human rights to life, justice, and freedom. It is this global commitment which must characterize the mission of the global church.

See also HUMAN/HUMANITY.

Bibliography

J. Moltmann, *On Human Dignity* (Philadelphia: Fortress, 1984); J. W. Montgomery, *Human Rights and Human Dignity: An Apologetic for the Transcendent Perspective* (Grand Rapids: Zondervan, 1986); S. Plant, 'Freedom as Development: Christian Mission and the Definition of Human Wellbeing', <http://www.martynmission.cam.ac.uk/cplant. html>; United Nations, *Universal Declaration on Human Rights*, <http://www.un.org/ Overview/rights.html>; D. L. Whiteman (ed.), 'Missionaries, Anthropologists and Human Rights', *Missiology* 24, 1996.

A. WIELAND

Humility

'Humility' is a word rarely immediately associated with Christian mission, except in connection with unusual iconic figures such as Mother Teresa of Calcutta. On the contrary, critics and opponents of Christian mission would charge that it is arrogant to try to change people's religion, or to make exclusive claims for the Christian God. How can we hold together strong biblical conviction and humility of life and praxis, both of which are biblically non-negotiable?

There are few cultures in the world where humility – the state of being humble – is regarded as an unqualified virtue. It may be expected of others towards oneself, especially if they are considered to be socially inferior. In some cultures, it may be expected of women towards men, but not of men towards women. But as a universal virtue? No!

On the contrary, in many cultures humility, especially in men and in leaders in society, is regarded as evidence of weakness to be despised, and so is a strongly negative value. This should not surprise us, because the desire to dominate others is described in Genesis 3:16 as a direct consequence of the fall. Both OT and NT condemn as sin pride and domineering over others, and affirm humility and mutual submission – their opposite – as an aspect of godliness. So, wherever in the world we may be, humility is almost always counter-cultural. For the Christian, humility is to be an attitude of mind, springing from a conviction of heart, which expresses itself in a way of life affecting all relationships and all evaluation of oneself (Rom. 12:3; Phil. 2:3).

Paul's great Christological hymn in Philippians 2:5–11 shows us the ultimate model for humility. The Lord Jesus Christ, 'being in very nature God, did not consider equality with God something to be grasped, but made himself nothing, taking the very nature of a servant ... he humbled himself ... to death ... on a cross'. Because the Son voluntarily humbled himself, the Father was able in due time to exalt him to heaven's highest honour and glory. Jesus washed his disciples' feet (John 13:1–17) as a vivid example of humility.

Both James (Jas 4:6) and Peter (1 Pet. 5:5) quote Proverbs 3:34: 'God opposes the proud but gives grace to the humble.' Humility is not natural in our fallenness, but we are urged to wrap ourselves in it as deliberately as putting on our clothes each morning if we are to experience God's grace. Pride is a declaration of self-sufficiency, and thus rebellion against God and denial of our creatureliness. Humility is a recognition of and evidence of our dependence on God, and only so can we receive his grace. How crucial then is humility, whatever our culture may say about it!

Some *cultures, including many Western ones, especially those that have been or are 'world powers', are arrogant about human ability. In church or mission circles, that may lead to confident plans that 'if we do this or that, in this way, we can win the world for Christ in that number of years'. Humility requires us to plan wisely but very humbly, recognizing that only God can create true spiritual life, and he does not do it to human orders. Our planning, strategizing and activity must be bathed in prayer, with willingness to respond to God's redirecting; and we will live in the consciousness of the limitations of human effort – it is God who builds his kingdom, not ourselves.

Some cultures have strongly authoritarian patterns of leadership. Church and mission must resist this, however hard it is to do so, and embrace instead the pattern Christ taught us of servant leadership (see, for example, Matt. 20:25–28). Some cultures concentrate power in the hands of men, others produce women who despise and manipulate men: church and mission must model mutual submission, respect and humility between people of both *genders. In some cultures, older people do not apologize or explain themselves to younger ones; but humility requires that we are courteous to all, old and young alike, and that we do not consider ourselves better than others on the basis of age, rank, education or leadership role. The church is to demonstrate transformed relationships, where former categories have no place.

Some cultures are strongly ethnocentric:

church and mission must model commitment to the multi-cultural family-ness of God's people, with humble acknowledgment of the fallenness of our own cultures (that doesn't mean there's nothing good at all to affirm and delight in!) and of the same mixture of good and bad in other cultures. In mission, humility will mean that as God builds his global church, the role of expatriate missionaries (of any nationality, not just Westerners) will change to partnership with, or service under, national believers. Conversely, expatriates will not be rejected just because they are not nationals: there is mutual enrichment in working together, complementing one another's gifts and experiences. 'Older churches' need the humility to learn from Christians, including theologians, from 'newer churches', with increasing multi-directional flow of people and writings and ideas. This includes the humility to learn from those theologizing out of unfamiliar contexts and perhaps in unfamiliar formats, as the Spirit incarnates the word in new settings. 'Newer churches' need the humility not to condemn 'older churches' for flaws in past mission activity, acknowledging the blessing under God as well as the mistakes, and recognizing that all believers everywhere are fallen as well as redeemed.

Humility does not mean that Christians should not contend for the truth, resist error (for example, the lie that all religions lead to God), and seek godliness however countercultural that may be. It does mean, though, that we will do these things with grace and gentleness, and with a humble spirit.

Bibliography

B. T. Adeney, *Strange Virtues: Ethics in a Multicultural World* (Leicester: Apollos, 1995); D. Gitari, *In Season and out of Season* (Oxford: Regnum, 1996); D. W. Smith, *Against the Stream* (Leicester: IVP, 2003).

R. DOWSETT

IDENTIFICATION, IDENTITY, see ETHNICITY/ETHNOCENTRISM, TRIBALISM

Incarnation

Theological meaning

Incarnation literally means 'in the flesh'. It refers to the historic act whereby the eternal Son of God, the second person of the *Trinity, without ceasing to be God, took upon himself our human nature and became fully human. This was not a temporary persona, a disguise or a mask; it was an irreversible union of the divine and the human. In his life *Christ was fully *God and fully man; in his death 'the crucified God' was revealed in his suffering humanity as he reconciled the world to himself; and in his resurrection Christ took his transformed humanity with him into eternal glory (John 1:14; Rom. 1:3; 5:8; 8:3; Gal. 4:4; Eph. 2:15; Phil. 2:7–8; Col. 1:19–20, 22; 1 Tim. 3:16; 1 John 4:2; 2 John 7; Rev. 5:6–9).

In the incarnation of the eternal Word all false dualisms between the material and spiritual, visible and invisible, human and divine, temporal and eternal, this-worldly and other-worldly, finite and infinite, were dissolved in the totally integrated person of Christ. It was not that the divine and the human existed side by side: the divine was revealed as human, and humanity was seen to be divine. This had to be so for God's revelation to be complete: when the Word became flesh, God revealed himself as a person and spoke to us in the fullest possible way in human terms (Heb. 1:2). It also had to be so for God's redemption to be complete: he fully identified with us in our humanity in order to redeem us and transform us into his glory (Heb. 2:14). The incarnation is the ultimate expression of the immanence of the transcendent Creator God, who, without ceasing to be holy, entered into the sinful world to make human beings holy and to enable them to participate in his glory.

Alongside the ontological dimension of the incarnation is the identification of Christ with the *human condition and *culture. St John speaks of God 'pitching his tent' and dwelling among us (John 1:14). Christ's title, Immanuel (God with us) also signifies this. In his incarnate state Christ identified with all kinds of people and was called a 'friend of tax collectors and "sinners"' (Matt. 11:19; Mark 2:15–17). He crossed all social barriers, welcomed all and shunned none. For example, he spoke with a Samaritan woman (John 4:1–26), touched lepers (Mark 1:41) and welcomed children (Matt. 19:13–15). But no one, including his enemies, could find any sin in him (Matt. 26:59–60; John 8:46). Although he identified in the most intimate manner, his character was in no way compromised. This was identification without the loss of identity.

The incarnation was therefore the most spectacular instance of cultural identification in human history. The Son of God did not stay in the safe immunity of heaven, remote from human sin, suffering and tragedy. As he entered the world, in his *kenosis* (self-emptying), he laid aside the divine status that was his by right, and humbled himself to serve. He took our nature, lived our life, endured our temptations, experienced our sorrows, felt our hurts, bore our sins and died our death. He never stayed aloof from the people he might have been expected to avoid. He made friends with the dropouts and outcasts of society and touched the untouchables. In India it would be like a Brahmin or some higher caste person going to *Dalits or Harijans and living among them. Jesus could not have become more one with us than he did. It was the total identification of love; and this must have a direct bearing on the way we do mission.

Incarnation as a model for mission

The Johannine version of Jesus' mission commission 'as the Father has sent me, I am sending you' (John 20:21; cf. 17:18) could simply have reference to the fact of his sending: 'The Father sent me, so now I am sending you.' Many however have seen in the 'as' a deeper equivalence between the way Jesus was sent by the Father and the way he sends his disciples. It is of course true that the incarnation is a unique historical and theological event which we cannot hope to emulate. As we enter another's world we cannot take on another identity in the fully integrated way Jesus did. Perhaps it would be blasphemous to suggest that we should try. Some have therefore said that the incarnation as a model of mission is misleading and even dangerous. But the apostles encouraged Christians to imitate Christ as a way of identifying with him, and so they did draw inspiration from the manner of Jesus' coming, not least at the level of attitude (Phil. 2:1–11; Eph. 5:1–2; 2 Cor. 5:7–9).

Therefore, incarnation as a principle can serve as a model for our missionary engagement of the world, for Jesus sends us into the world in the manner in which he was sent. This has a number of implications. We

should, like Jesus, identify ourselves with the people of a receiving culture without losing our own integrity or compromising our Christian convictions, values and standards. 'To the Jews I became like a Jew ... to the weak I became weak' was Paul's way of identifying with those he wanted to win (1 Cor. 9:20–23). But because Jesus retained his divine nature in coming to earth it means that we need not lose our original cultural or personal identity: we need to be ourselves.

However, in laying aside his status and not holding on to the privileges which were his, we are challenged to put aside the status and privileges we have enjoyed. Leaders must step aside in order to allow others to lead, the rich must leave their possessions behind in order to live alongside those they have come to serve, the powerful must learn the power of *weakness and vulnerability. In relating to another culture we need to penetrate the world of their thinking (as we strive to understand their misunderstandings of the gospel), the world of their feelings (as we try to empathize with their pain), and the world of their living (as we sense the humiliation of their social situation, whether poverty, homelessness, loneliness, unemployment or discrimination on the basis of caste or race). We should identify ourselves as much as we are able at the physical, emotional, intellectual, social, cultural and practical levels. The more we are able to do this the more genuine will be our relationship with other people and cultures, and therefore the more effective our communication of the gospel. In our service we will be able to be alongside people in their suffering, working together to restore their dignity, not doing things for them but with them.

This incarnation principle was applied by the early missionaries who came to India. They sat cross-legged on the floor, ate rice or roti and curry with their hands, used charcoal to clean their teeth, learned and talked to people in their language, wore native dresses and sandals, and were thus able to enter into the lifestyle and lives of the people and communicate with them. They studied the customs, traditions and beliefs of the people and learned how to connect with them. Paul had spent time studying and understanding the secular culture of Athens and was able to quote their poets in his Mars Hill address (Acts 17:28). We too need to study and learn to enter into the thought world of the people that we are trying to reach, because they live in a totally different thought world and belief system from our own (see *World-view).

The incarnation principle applies differently in different contexts. Most obviously it applies to primary evangelism alongside practical service amongst *unreached peoples where the national church is small or struggling. In such places incarnational missionaries from outside the culture are needed for any kind of effective mission engagement with the context. However, as mission has diversified in more recent years, the focus in many places has shifted to *partnership with an already established national church. Understanding, listening and identifying are still important for communication, but in this case we are happier to accept our cultural differences and may indeed celebrate our diversity as something mutually enriching. The disciples came to profound self-understanding through seeing themselves in relation to a Jesus who was so radically different to them (e.g. Peter's 'Go away from me, Lord; I am a sinful man!' Luke 5:8). In a situation of partnership mission is two-way: each partner is learning and growing together. So for mission partners to identify with the local culture does not mean that they need to try to become as much as possible like their national counterparts.

Christians may even share a cultural identity at a certain level with those they wish to reach, and with whom they may live and work on a daily basis, but there are many ways in which they will need to enter into the thinking and belief systems of those around them. In India, where religion abounds, and there are relatively few Christians, most people think that all religions are ultimately the same or that they are like different routes to the same destiny, so that exclusive Christian claims betray intolerance and narrow-mindedness. *Syncretism, relativism and pluralism seem to govern the thinking of many. They have no problem in accepting Jesus as one of the many ways to God or one of the *avatars* (a bodily manifestation of a higher being). Belief in *karma* and reincarnation leads to salvation by works and the belief that they have many lives to attain *moksha* (liberation from the cycle of birth and death). In this context it is absolutely

vital for Christians to learn how to find ways into the values, beliefs, hearts, and thought patterns of those who need to hear the gospel. They must find bridges into the others' frame of reference, otherwise communication is not possible. This underlines the critical importance of apologetics: 'We should be praying and working hard for a whole new generation of Christian thinkers and apologists who will dedicate their God-given minds to Christ, enter sympathetically into their counterparts' dilemmas, unmask false ideologies, and present the gospel of Jesus Christ in such a way that he is seen to offer what other religious systems cannot, because he and he alone can fulfil our deepest human aspirations' (J. R. W. Stott, *The Contemporary Christian*, p. 360).

Incarnation in the Indian context
Incarnation is therefore about the embodiment of God's love at a community level as well as an individual level. In India and Asia there is a strong sense of community with close bonds. One of the challenges people face in responding to the gospel is the fear of losing family and community. Disowning and excommunicating people who put their faith in Christ is common in India. If they see an attractive, alternative community into which they could go, then they could overcome this challenge. A genuine Christian community which embodies truth, love and unity, for which Jesus prayed (John 13:34–35; 17:20–23), will give people confidence to join it. We must embody our acknowledgment of the reality of God in the manner in which we live and this entails participation in community – living in fellowship with God and others.

Incarnation means the visible, concrete presence of spiritual truth: the Word made flesh. One of the reasons why Christianity has not had the kind of influence it should have had on India is that the Christian '*proclamation' has not been backed up well enough by Christian '*presence'. This is what Lesslie Newbigin meant when he described the church as the 'hermeneutic of the gospel' – the gospel can be understood through the lives of its followers, individually and corporately. This requires individually distinctive Christian lives to be present in the world (Titus 2:9). It requires communities of love and transformed relationships so that the world will know that we are his disciples (John 13:34-35).

A young woman came to know Christ from a Hindu family. She faced much opposition and social pressure to conform to their patterns, but she stood her ground. The real test came at the time of marriage, because she wanted to marry a Christian. Her family told her that if she married someone from another community they would ostracize her. Her brother-in-law threatened to divorce her sister. When she refused to yield, they forced her to leave the home. But she was able to stand in this trying situation, because one Christian family stood with her throughout this process, received her into their home, mobilized the Christian community and took care of all the arrangements. Many young women have not been able to withstand the social pressure because there were no Christians willing to take the risk of standing with them.

In India caste and class divide people in a class-oriented and stratified society. It is believed that some are superior and others are inferior because people are created unequally. Caste is one force that keeps Hinduism strong and growing. Incarnation affirms the value of all humanity: each human being is equally valuable before God, because he sent his Son to identify with every human being and to die for all who will identify with him in his death for them. This brings everyone redeemed by him into one family where cultural and human divisions are broken down and there is no room for discrimination. But unfortunately in India casteism continues to divide people even in the church. This serious indictment counts against the witness and mission of the church.

Finally, incarnation has important implications for 'critical contextualization', which means applying God's truth in a culturally relevant and sensitive manner and yet without compromising its meaning. Here again the incarnation is our model. The eternal truths we communicate must take flesh in human languages and cultures. Just as Christ chose to live in a particular time and setting, so we must 'incarnate' our ministry in the contexts of the people we serve. Jesus exemplifies this embodiment and communication of universal truths. The stories, figures of speech, words and analogies that he used in different contexts were particular to those contexts and they immediately resonated with his listeners. He was 'incarnating' the truth about God, giving its meaning life and reality. For example, in our predominantly Hindu context in India we can use the concept of *avatar* in presenting the gospel to Hindu friends. Introducing Christ as the unique or perfect Avatar helps people to move from the known to the unknown. St John uses *theos* for God and *logos* for Jesus Christ. These terms had their distinctively Greek meanings. But the evangelist gives specifically Christian content to these terms, transforming them in the service of the truth. In the same way, Christians in India can use the term *avatar*, familiar to the vast majority of Indians, as a way of introducing Christ.

But there is the danger that the recipients will interpret the gospel with categories, meanings or associations with which they are familiar, but which lead them to draw completely wrong conclusions. There has therefore been considerable debate over the use of the term 'avatar' for the incarnation of Christ. Some have been concerned about possible misunderstanding, while others have been uncritical in their use of the term in their commitment to contextualization. It is important to present Christ as the perfection of the concept of avatar, demonstrating how Christ is different from the avatar and how he transcends familiar associations. There are fundamental dissimilarities between incarnation and the avatar, so it is vital to ensure that the full truth of Christ as the only God-incarnate is communicated to eliminate all possible dangers of syncretism, misinterpretation and distortion. We can do this confidently and build bridges to our Hindu friends, because the idea of God coming down to where man is or appearing in human history as a man is common between Hinduism and Christianity.

Conclusions

The incarnation of Christ is a unique historical and theological truth. But as the manner in which God chose to send his Son, the incarnation principle still serves as a model for cross-cultural identification and immersion. It brings a human dimension to mission; it communicates the gospel through a person who demonstrates the love of God, sometimes without words; it identifies with people in their suffering; it speaks their language; it leaves the preoccupations of its former life behind; it contextualizes God's love; it embodies the truth so that people can experience it as well as understand it; it serves with people not against them or above them. Mission without incarnation is evangelism without humanity.

See also CONTEXTUALIZATION, INCULTURATION.

Bibliography

M. J. Erickson, *The Word Became Flesh: A Contemporary Incarnational Christology* (Grand Rapids: Baker Books, 1991); R. E. Hedlund and P. J. Bhakiaraj, *Missiology for the 21st Century: South Asian Perspectives* (Delhi: ISPCK & MIIS, 2004); K. P. Kuruvilla, *The Word Became Flesh: A Christological Paradigm for Doing Theology in India* (Delhi: ISPCK, 2002); H. Peskett and V. Ramachandra, *The Message of Mission* (Leicester: IVP, 2003); V. Ramachandra, *The Recovery of Mission* (Delhi: ISPCK, 1999); C. Ratendas, *Incarnation and Contextual Communication* (Tiruvalla: Christava Sahitya Samithy, 2000); J. R. W. Stott, *The Contemporary Christian* (Leicester: IVP, 1992); W. D. Taylor (ed.), *Global Missiology for the 21st Century* (Grand Rapids: Baker Academic, 2000); V. Thampu, *Rediscovering Mission* (New Delhi: TRACI, 1995); H. Yung, *Mangoes or Bananas?* (Oxford: Regnum Books International, 1997).

S. MONDITHOKA

Inculturation

The dimensions of inculturation

Inculturation describes how the Christian faith interacts with a culture by influencing its people's understanding of the *gospel and the way in which it is practised and shared within that particular culture. The objective of inculturation is to enable the gospel message to be readily understood, accepted and lived out in the thought-forms of the culture as it is expressed in its vocabulary, art forms and imagery.

The encounter of faith with culture is both incarnational and confrontational. In so far as the gospel 'finds a home' in the culture such

that it is experienced and understood through particular and recognizable cultural clothing with which its people readily identify, the *incarnational principle is at work. This is sometimes referred to as 'enculturation'. However, the gospel also confronts culture with a truth which challenges its thought forms and *world-view and seeks to transform it, and this is the other dimension of inculturation. Andrew Walls has described this tension as 'the indigenising principle of incarnation and the "pilgrim" principle of transformation and change' (in *New Directions in Mission and Evangelism*, pp. 17–28).

From its beginning the gospel has been expressed in cultural idioms: first Jewish and then Greek, and in many other cultural forms as it moved across the world. There is thus no culturally neutral form of the gospel, as both Newbigin and Walls have pointed out. Missionaries may have once imagined that they had a wholly supracultural gospel to impart, but their own understanding of it was already inculturated; so inculturation was not merely what happened when the gospel travelled from the Western world to Asian and African cultures. In its worst form this resulted in the impartation of what became known as 'culture Christianity' – a form of the gospel so much clothed in the characteristics of the missionary culture that indigenous Christians were asked to accept this form of the gospel uncritically, rejecting their own culture in favour of what the missionary brought to them. Westerners assumed that certain characteristics were intrinsic to the gospel, for example its rationalism, individualism, manners, material blessings, and forms of prayer and praise; whereas these were to a greater or lesser extent culturally determined. Missionaries thus adopted an arrogant form of inculturation, by which the gospel was exported and transplanted with little effort to inculturate it afresh. This was a cultural imposition, and made it very difficult for indigenous Christians subsequently to inculturate the gospel back in their own culture again.

It is not that the gospel does not have supracultural truths, since it is rooted in God who is above all things and all cultures. But inculturation is about the manner in which those truths are expressed, which can itself throw light on their meaning. The process of inculturation is always happening when the gospel encounters a new culture. The gospel however is not reducible to its cultural dimensions, meaning that all cultures should be able to recognize its truth and respond to it, and all cultures must be subject to it. The missionaries used a 'radical replacement' approach, whereas a model of 'continuity and discontinuity' might be a better way of inculturating the gospel (W. R. Shenk, *International Bulletin of Mission* 25, p. 100). In fact, it is the element of continuity which helps us to recognize the 'core' of the gospel which applies to all cultures, since these truths have been commonly recognized by the church throughout history. A universally recognizable truth has the capacity to be translatable, relevant and accessible to the people of any culture, so that there is no cultural context in which this essential, universal gospel cannot take root.

It is also possible to distinguish inculturation and 'contextualization', even though they both invoke the incarnational principle. Contextualization engages the gospel with the whole context, including its social and political dimensions, whereas inculturation, although a form of contextualization, focuses on the cultural clothing which the gospel takes on in a particular context. Lesslie Newbigin suggested contextualization as an alternative word to avoid some of the difficulties of inculturation. For him contextualization related to the questions people ask not so much about the past as about their future. This process is different in different cultures.

Cultures are highly layered, so a complex dynamic of inculturation goes on within cultures and subcultures, with specific applications in certain subcultures that are not appropriate to others. For example, 'fishers of men' is a new expression which Christ used with the fishermen of Galilee, and they identified with it readily. But this expression does not appear anywhere else in the NT to describe evangelism. In India this expression suggests negative images like the hook, the bait and the hide-away basket, which is quite different from its original connotation and therefore unhelpful in an Indian context.

Inculturation in the Bible

The God of the Bible has always spoken to people through their contemporary cultures. Biblical characters understood the message of God in their own cultural context and shared that message and passed it on in their particular cultural idiom. In the OT God used cultural images, language and concepts when he spoke through the prophets. The word pictures of the OT are culturally oriented and familiar to the people of their time. The parables of Jesus are simply truths about the kingdom expressed in the cultural language and thought forms of his time.

From the Hebrew religion the Jerusalem Christians adopted temple imagery, and gave some of its feasts and festivals a new name and a new significance. Christ often spoke in familiar Jewish and OT categories as he 'incarnated' his teaching. St Paul used Greek imagery when he preached the gospel in a Hellenist context: fighting a good fight, running the race, winning the crown which does not fade away. As images from Greek culture they powerfully communicate what he wanted to convey. For a Jewish audience Paul adopted and reinterpreted concepts such as covenant and circumcision. This process of adaptation by a host culture which brings to light new meanings has always been considered a natural and necessary process for the gospel.

When the good news of Jesus Christ went to every land and culture, it became embedded in those cultures. It demonstrated what Andrew Walls has described as the 'infinite translatability of Christian faith', (*The Missionary Movement in Christian History*, p. 22). Commenting on the process of inculturation in the NT, Newbigin says 'the variety of Christologies actually to be found in the NT is part of the fundamental witness. It points to the destination of the Gospel in all cultures of mankind.' Newbigin also reminds us of a theology of Asian and African cultures which he calls the Third World theology: 'There is also another kind of third world theology, namely, that which is being continuously produced in the languages of the (receptor) churches in the form of preaching, catechesis, song story and drama. The volume of this material is very great but it is rarely translated into the languages of Europe, yet it represents the real fruit of the day by day struggle of the Christians of these lands to interpret the gospel to their contemporaries' (*The Gospel in a Pluralist Society*, pp. 154–155).

Inculturation today

Inculturation today takes place through indigenous forms of liturgy, hymns and worship; ways of life and witness, and thought forms and theologies. In speaking of Christology we can say that there is one Christ and many Christologies. For example, a convert to Christianity from Hinduism may talk about Christ as 'guru'. To a Western theological mind the word 'guru' is not equivalent to words like 'Lord', 'Saviour' or 'Christ'. But we should not forget that these words, namely Lord (*Kurios*), Saviour (*Yehoshua*) or Christ (*Christos* the anointed), originated within Greek, Hebrew and Roman languages and cultures. It is possible to identify many hundreds of names (attributes) for Christ in a wide variety of languages and cultures. So to a Hindu convert 'guru' does not just mean a teacher (equivalent to a rabbi for a Jew); his guru is the one who leads him from ignorance into knowledge, from darkness into light, and so on. This is clearly the influence of culture on the expression and understanding of faith.

It is tempting to see the faith only through the lenses of our own culture, and we need to have a wider vision of how our faith is experienced and expressed in other cultures. Sometimes, however, we have the reverse problem, when the gospel is mediated through the missionary culture and we fail to inculturate it for ourselves. In India for example, Christians must speak in the idioms of the land if they want to share their faith with people of the great religion (*sanathana dharma*) of Hinduism. For too long the Christian church in India has spoken a strange language in trying to bring the gospel to its people. Its creeds are carbon copies of Western products, its liturgies have specific historic contexts that people in India do not know, the clerical robes and symbols are very strange and do not mean anything to the average person, and Indian Christians speak most of the time in a strange language. Someone has joked that the Indian church has not contributed even one decent heresy to the universal church.

Inculturation involves taking risks. It is a creative and dynamic process in which it is often difficult to discern the boundaries, so it is important to have a critical and discerning approach. There is the danger of a *syncretism which welcomes inculturation hesitatingly. But it can be an enrichment of the gospel, since it brings to light aspects of its truth which may have remained hidden in other cultural contexts. It can facilitate evangelism and bring the gospel alive to a particular culture. But many times the line between religion and culture is very thin and in trying to adopt cultural idioms to express Christian faith, or use a cultural practice to experience that faith, it is difficult to know where to draw the line. Great Christian missionaries like Robert de Nobili in the eighteenth century faced the problem of adoption and adaptation in seeking to express the Christian faith in Hindu forms. He determined to become as much a Hindu as possible in dress and lifestyle. He did not want the converts to adapt Latin or Portuguese names, so he gave them Tamil names. He also 'Christianized' the local harvest festival of Pongal and other symbols. Some may judge him to have crossed too far over the line.

So this problem is not new. In the Indian context M. M. Thomas has spoken of the possibility of a 'Christ-centred syncretism'. In recent years Victor Premsagar, the one time moderator of the Church of South India, discussed this problem. He described how the people of God, the Israelites, had to walk the difficult path of selection and variation as they faced the then existing religions, at the same time keeping their identity as the chosen race of the God whom they knew. The OT is the story of their frequent failure to achieve this. Sometimes institutional Christianity has accepted uncritically the patriarchal, male-dominated assumptions of the surrounding culture, and it is only through the influence of cultural changes which have recognized women that a gospel which affirms women has emerged. In this case cultural change has brought to light an important dimension of the gospel which was previously suppressed.

Often inculturation is unconscious, as the gospel takes on certain characteristics because of the way we express it in our own culture, whether we are aware of it or not. It is helpful to distinguish this from conscious inculturation, which is a more deliberate attempt to express the gospel in relevant cultural clothing as a means of communicating it more effectively. In this respect it is an essential tool of mission engagement, for unless the good news of Christ is reincarnated in every cultural context it will not be seen and experienced as good news.

See also CULTURE,
CONTEXTUALIZATION.

Bibliography
G. A. Arbuckle, *Earthing the Gospel: An Inculturation Handbook for the Pastoral Worker* (Maryknoll: Orbis Books, 1990); L. F. Gispert-Sauch, *Christianity in India* (London: Penguin/Viking, 2004); L. Newbigin, 'Mission in the 1980s', *Occasional Bulletin of Missionary Research* 4, 1980; L. Newbigin, *The Gospel in a Pluralist Society* (Grand Rapids: Eerdmans, 1989); S. Raj, *A Christian Volk Religion in India* (Bangalore: Peterlang Verlag, ²2004); L. Sanneh, *Translating the Message: The Missionary Impact on Culture* (Maryknoll: Orbis Books, 1989); J. A. Scherer and S. B. Bevans, *New Directions in Mission and Evangelism 3: Faith and Culture* (Maryknoll: Orbis Books, 1999); W. R. Shenk, 'Recasting the Theology of Mission', *International Bulletin of Mission* 25, 2001; A. Shorter, *Towards a Theology of Inculturation* (Maryknoll: Orbis Books, 1988); A. F. Walls, *The Missionary Movement in Christian History* (Maryknoll: Orbis Books, 1996).

P. S. RAJ

Indian theology

A rich and lengthy tradition holds that Christianity came to India in the first century AD through the apostle Thomas. Ever since those early days Christian presence has been shaped by the gospel and culture, both of these missionaries and Indians themselves.

With the coming of the Portuguese, Germans and British many centuries later, however, the popular image of Christianity was that of a Western religion and Indian Christians as those who possessed shallow roots in Indian culture. This abiding image has been seen as a theft of identity, motivating the forging of an identity simultaneously Indian and Christian. Constructing an Indian Christian theology may be seen as one dimension of that larger quest, which seeks to contextualize the gospel and forge an indigenous integrity to ecclesial practice, funding missionary efforts and situating societal presence.

Early attempts

Disturbed that Christianity was associated with meat-eaters, alcoholics and morally loose folk, Jesuits Thomas Stephens (1549–1619) and Roberto Nobili (1577–1656) sought to disentangle it from the base connotations of a *farangi margam*, or a foreign path, and raise it to the high ideals Indians held dear. Stephens produced *Krista Purana* in Marathi, and Nobili, who became a *sannayasi* (renouncer), produced *Gnanopadesam* in Tamil. Similar foundations were laid by Bartholomeus Ziegenbalg (1683–1719), William Carey (1761–1834) and Henry Martyn (1781–1812), who translated the Bible into Tamil, about thirty languages and dialects, and Urdu respectively. These pioneers thus initiated a cultural renaissance and rendered the vernacular a vehicle for divine truth. That in turn became a mine for nascent Indian Christian theology, shaping concepts and growing vocabulary. Modes such as hymnody, preaching, poetry, art and indigenous forms of communication and devotion represent no less a significant strand in the development of Indian Christian theology than the more explicit and formal style.

Direct stimulus for formal theology came from Ram Mohan Roy (1722–1833) and Keshub Chandra Sen (1838–84). In *The Precepts of Jesus*, Roy expressed admiration for Christ's ethical teaching. However, in his *Appeals to the Christian Public* he found Jesus' divine sonship, and the doctrines of the Trinity and atonement unpalatable. Sen came closer to orthodox Christian teaching, though the Western trappings of Christianity were anathema to him. One of Sen's key ideas in *Jesus Christ: Europe and Asia* was that Jesus was Asian. This 'Asiatic Christ' elicited a reflective and devout response, including the launch of the 'Church of the New Dispensation', with its Christian-type rites of initiation and communion. The dialogue these pioneers initiated thus came to serve as a framework for Indian Christian theology.

Contribution of Indian Christian theologians

On becoming a disciple of Christ, Nehemiah (Nilakanta Shastri) Goreh (1825–95), an authority on Sanskrit and ardent defender of Hinduism, engaged Brahmo Samaj leaders, who, he felt, adopted theism only because of their exposure to the gospel. The next logical step was to accept Christ as the unique incarnation of the one God, a move for which they were uniquely prepared through notions like *ananyabhakti* (devotedness), *avatara* (incarnation) and *namrata* (humility). 'Providence has certainly prepared us, the Hindus, to receive Christianity, in a way which, it seems to me, no other nation – excepting the Jews of course – has been prepared.'

However, acutely aware of Christianity's conflation with *colonialism, Goreh demonstrated that Christianity was well suited for India. In his *A Rational Refutation of the Hindu Philosophical Systems*; *Christianity not of Man but of God*; *Proofs of the Divinity of Our Lord*, Goreh stressed that: 'No one should call it a foreign religion, and yet if any people have a greater right to call it theirs than other people they are the Asiatics.' Goreh is significant because his theology was shaped by his evangelistic vision. Additionally, in mounting an intellectual response to Hinduism, he pioneered what came to be called the *jnana marga*, or the 'way of knowledge' approach in Indian Christian theology.

Brahmabandhab Upadhyay (1861–1907), a prolific journalist and a leader in the nationalist movement, was a thinker of similar ilk. Born a Brahmin, and later a member of the Brahmo Samaj, Upadhyay was deeply acquainted with Hinduism. He felt that: 'Indian soil is humid and its humidity will make the ever-new Christian Revelation put forth newer harmonies and newer beauties ... The Hindu mind and heart, coming under the dominion of the One, Holy, Apostolic and Catholic Church, will sing a new canticle which will fill the earth with sweetness from end to end.'

Upadhyay sought to sing this new canticle by reconciling 'pure Hinduism and pure Christianity': 'Indian thought can be made just as useful to Christianity as Greek thought has been to Europe ... The truths of the Hindu philosopher must be baptised and used as stepping stones to the Catholic faith ... The European clothes of the Catholic religion should be laid aside as soon as possible. It must assume the Hindu garment which will make it acceptable to the people of India. This change can be only be effected by Indian Missionary orders who preach the sacred Faith in the language of the Vedanta.'

His exposition of the doctrine of the Trinity employing the concept of *sacchiananda* (being – intelligence – bliss) was one attempt, as was his doctrine of creation employing the concept of *maya* (illusion). The worship and mission of the church thus provided the framework for his significant contribution to Indian Christian theology.

A second approach may be referred to as the *bhakti marga* or 'way of devotion', of which one prominent exponent was Sadhu Sundar Singh (1889–1929). At an early age Singh exhibited deep spiritual yearnings but resented Christianity. It was not until he had a personal vision of Christ that he found fulfilment and became a *sadhu* (ascetic). Thereafter frequent mystical encounters with Christ funded a deep devotional ardour. Alongside the Scriptures he placed *anubhava*, or experience, as authoritative. 'I do not believe because I have read about Him in the Bible. I saw Him and experienced Him and know Him in my daily experience.'

Singh travelled widely as an evangelist and wrote various books: *At the Master's Feet*, *Reality and Religion*, *The Cross is Heaven* and *The Real Pearl*. His teaching was couched in a uniquely Indian idiom and shot through with 'pictures' drawn from that milieu. He considered that Hinduism had been digging channels for centuries but Christ is the water to flow through them. This combination of reverence for Indian tradition and devotion to Christ characterized Singh's Christocentric theology. Singh thus allowed Jesus to sit on an Indian mat and enthrall the hearts and minds of the people.

One such a person was A. J. Appasamy (1891–1975), who later became a Church of South India bishop. Brought up in Tamil Nadu, Appasamy was personally and academically conversant with the *bhakti* tradition. In *The Mysticism of the Fourth Gospel in its Relation to the Hindu Bhakti Literature* he developed a deep dialogue with *bhakti*, followed by *Christianity as Bhakti Marga* and *What is Moksa?*. Appasamy spoke of the Christian life as one of ardent devotion to Christ and union with God. Though the goal of *bhakti* was ultimate oneness with God and for *moksa*, immersion in the divine soul, for the Christian salvation is not absorption but faith – union with Christ. The Christ who says, 'abide in me' calls us to find in him meaning and fulfilment. He is our pattern for life. Just as Jesus enjoyed union with God the Father, we may enjoy *moksa* (liberation/

salvation) through *bhakti*. This love for God, he stressed, however, cannot be pursued in isolation from neighbours. As demonstrated in the cross, both are integrally conjoined. *Moksa* 'is a continuous contact with Reality, personally conscious and radiant with joy. It is like the life of Jesus with God ... It is a personal experience which, however, in its highest reaches transcends the personal. It is a corporate experience, man mingling with his fellowmen in order to attain the heights of God's love.'

A further coalescence between social and spiritual dimensions was forged in the third approach: *karma marga*, or 'way of action', of which M. M. Thomas (1916–96) was one prominent advocate. In *The Acknowledged Christ of the Indian Renaissance* Thomas argued that evident amongst early pioneers like Ram Mohan Roy and others was the Christian gospel at work. This gospel-initiated renaissance was indeed an acknowledgment of Christ. If Christ was working within history, the church's responsibility, Thomas averred, was to engage in a dialogue with society that would facilitate establishment of a common and open culture that would further such an end.

If, as in *Salvation and Humanisation*, Thomas taught salvation was the restoration of lost humanity, then Christians were 'to risk Christ for Christ's sake'. Dialogue with secular society was necessary, for it was in such a context that the church could work for the humanization of the oppressed and the provision of justice. 'Herein lies the mission of the church. It is to participate in the movements of human liberation of our time in such a way as to witness to Jesus Christ as the sources, the judge and the redeemer of humanity spirituality.'

Samuel Rayan (1920–), a Jesuit, similarly pursued spirituality that was open to wider reality and expressed in liberative action. In his *Breath of Fire: The Holy Spirit – Heart of the Christian Gospel* he affirmed that at the root of the experience of the early church and indeed the world at large, was the Spirit at work: 'To be spiritual is to be open and responsive to the reality of the earth, of history, of life, of people, of the Spirit.' The *shakti* or goddess tradition within Indian thought, which reveres female deities, appealed to Rayan, who held that since the

walls of the church do not exhaust the realm of her operation, our calling is to recognize her activity within the whole cosmos. We are called to join her action in the world, as her 'team-mates'. Our spirituality for mission therefore ought to be characterized by 'openness to the missionary dimensions of creatures, cultures and religions and in "response-able" dialogue with concrete given realities.' Inter-religious dialogue enables one discern this *shakti*, and thus contributes to a liberation of society, even of ecology. In *Come Holy Spirit* Rayan suggested that a life directed by the Spirit will not entertain on the one hand the dichotomy of contemplation and action and on the other of 'Christian' and 'other', rather it will be one that seeks to align with icons of the Spirit within the world in the liberation that she is working out.

In addition to themes of contextualization and liberation, inter-religious dialogue has also attracted considerable attention. In his *The Unbound Christ of Hinduism*, Stanley Samartha clarified that India did not entertain a distaste for Christ, but rather produced its own mature response. However, this attachment to Christ, he discovered, did not entail an affiliation with the church. Consequently he stressed dialogue with other religious traditions. In the light of such dialogue his *One Christ – Many Religions: Toward a Revised Christology* urged that Christocentricism, as the church's norm for the world, was to give way to theocentricism. 'This Mystery, the Truth of the Truth (*Satyasya Satyam*) is the transcendent Centre that remains always beyond and greater than apprehensions of it, even in the sum total of those apprehensions.' Since religions were only frail human responses to mystery, they are not exhaustive apprehensions of truth, but as only partial visions of a larger whole. If Christians are privy only to a limited glimpse of reality and are called to love their neighbours, 'an ontological equation of Jesus Christ and God would scarcely allow any serious discussion with neighbours of other faiths or with secular humanism ... To make exclusive claims for our particular tradition is not the best way to love our neighbour as ourselves.'

Contemporary evangelical contributions

Attending to a similar task of establishing a theology of religions in his *The Pluralistic*

Predicament, Ken Gnanakan differed radically from Samartha. He clarified that while the fact of plurality was neither new for the Bible nor for Indian Christians, as a theological stance it acquired force recently. This was partly due to the Western guilt complex for colonialism's misdemeanours. Gnanakan argued instead, that while colonialism's models are to be discarded, 'we do not need to compromise biblical claims ... what we need is the sensitivity to harmonise these claims with the spirit of love and service that Jesus Christ would have us demonstrate.'

Gnanakan suggests that active engagement with the world in the spirit of Christ has no substitute: 'A greater degree of human commonality will need to be restored in order to build a relationship from within which the message of Jesus Christ can be demonstrated.'

So rather than sacrifice Christian convictions at the altar of communal harmony, Gnanakan preferred Christian service as one way of dialogue. For his part he forged creative collaborations, particularly for the care of the environment; his *God's World: A Biblical Theology of the Environment* perhaps represents his most mature reflections.

Despite their insistence on taking traditional south Asian religions seriously and their disavowal of Western theology's hold, in *The Recovery of Mission* Vinoth Ramachandra eloquently demonstrated that radical theological proposals tabled by Samartha, Aloysius Pieris and Raimundo Panikkar were indebted more to liberal post-Kantian notions than they cared to admit. In contrast Ramachandra, in seeking to engage with south Asian religions and modernity which indelibly shapes the contemporary world, stressed that 'the normativeness and ultimacy of Jesus Christ in God's salvific dealings with his word, far from being an arbitrary and repressive doctrine, is intrinsic to Christian praxis and self-understanding, then and now.'

To best explicate the significance of Jesus in a context where religious pluralism was becoming alarmingly prescriptive, a 'gospel praxis', characterized by a 'gospel humanity', a 'gospel integrity' and a 'gospel radicalness' was called for. A gospel lifestyle, he stressed, would both affirm the particularity of the gospel in a world of many faiths, and empower its concrete embodiment in a quest for justice in a world where the homogenizing power of globalization and other forms of enslavement are potent.

As the above demonstrates, the roots of Indian Christian theology lie in the attempt to express what it means to be a follower of Jesus Christ in the south Asian context, characterized by urgent political, religious and socio-economic factors. That is to say, mission forms the soil in which Indian Christian theology blossomed and bloomed. Consequently Indian Christian theology has [always] been a missionary theology at heart. Doubtless for some theologians context determined its content, issuing in some radical revision of theology; for evangelically oriented scholars, though their response to context was no less determinative, their stress on biblical teaching allowed them to remain gospel-centred. Evangelical proposals of Indian Christian theology have established that faithfulness to the gospel can be maintained while integral presence and action in the world pursued. This contextually sensitive yet biblically faithful approach in turn has funded impressive efforts in mission throughout the region. The role of the south Asian church in the shifting centre of gravity of world Christianity to the southern hemisphere is adequate proof of that.

Challenges ahead

While evangelicals have contributed significantly, yet some challenges remain. One is to develop contextual methods for in-depth study of the Scriptures. For the most part scholars have hitherto focused on select theological themes, perhaps at the expense of a comprehensive biblical analysis. The challenge is to engage contextually with the whole corpus of Scripture for the missional task of the church. A second challenge is to expand the remit of Indian Christian theology so as to attend to the spiritual formation of Indian Christians. Astute proposals that have and are being tabled are to be seen as more than intellectual answers alone. The need is to recognize that at the heart of the theological enterprise lies spirituality, both of the scholar and the masses.

This leads to the third challenge of ensuring that Indian Christian theology serves all the people, rather than an elite cadre alone. Even though *Dalit theology has sought to fill such a lacunae, an evangelical theology 'of', 'for' and 'by' the people is yet to emerge. A fourth challenge is to harness the vitality of growing movements to Christ for theological and missiological reflection. The potential for the experience of the people to inform and shape theology may be unsettling for conventional modes of theology, yet it appears rather promising for the future of theology and the mission of the church.

See also ASIAN THEOLOGY; HINDU RELATIONS.

Bibliography
R. Boyd, *An Introduction to Indian Christian Theology* (Delhi: ISPCK, 1975, 1998); J. Parappally, *Theologizing in Context: Statements of the Indian Theological Association* (Bangalore: Dharmaram Publications, 2002); V. Ramachandra, *The Recovery of Mission: Beyond the Pluralist Paradigm* (Carlisle: Paternoster Press, 1996); R. S. Sugirtharajah and C. Hargreaves (eds.), *Readings in Indian Christian Theology* (London: SPCK, 1993); S. Sumitra, *Christian Theologies from an Indian Perspective* (Bangalore: TBT, 1995); F. Wilfred, *Beyond Settled Foundations: The Journey of Indian Theology* (Madras: University of Madras, 1993).

P. J. BHAKIARAJ

INDIGENIZATION, see ACCOMMODATION/ADAPTATION

Indigenous peoples

The scope of this article, although restricted to Latin America, will find resonance in other parts of the world where indigenous peoples live. By 'indigenous peoples' we refer to the original peoples who have lived in the Americas for thousands of years prior to the arrival of the Europeans at the end of the fifteenth century. The descendants of these peoples are still very significant, not only in numbers, but especially as a vigorous cultural expression, in spite of five centuries of exploitation and ethnocentric treatment by outsiders. The missiological implication of this is the need for a *holistic approach to mission that includes indigenous peoples in the call to faith in Jesus Christ as Lord and Saviour. But it will also involve the struggle for justice, defence of their human rights, and the promotion of their holistic development that includes the whole of their beings and their cultures. This involves the church in the debate about indigenous peoples' right to have their lands and a degree of socio-political autonomy and real access to socio-political power in their respective countries.

It is estimated that there are over forty million indigenous peoples in the Americas as part of around 400 distinct ethnic groups who have their own languages, customs, social structures and cultures. They constitute between 30% to over 50% of the population of Guatemala, Ecuador, Peru and Bolivia. They are scattered throughout the Americas, in the Amazon basin and its rivers, as well as in the Andes and major cities. Until recent years it was thought that these populations were dying out and losing their ethnic identity by being absorbed into the dominant Hispanic and Portuguese populations. However, this is only partially true. The bigger picture is that in the last twenty years they have experienced an ethnic revitalization and have also gained political clout to the point of having been influential in the resignation of presidents and government ministers in several countries of Latin America, examples being Ecuador and Bolivia.

The political independence of most Latin American countries from Spain and Portugal did not translate into significant socio-political benefits for the indigenous peoples. Conditions for them continued the same, and in some cases worsened. In a sense, they still await their *liberation, and have become conscious that unless they themselves take the initiative and leadership to claim their basic human rights as full citizens in their own countries, non-indigenous peoples will not willingly share power with them. As a result we have a confrontation between the indigenous peoples and the non-indigenous ruling elites that are not willing to share the power they already hold. An example of the dynamic, dialectical nature of today's socio-cultural reality in the continent of the Americas is the revival of Indian cultures and political movements such as the Quichuas in Ecuador and their counterparts in Bolivia and Peru. The Indian movement in Ecuador was fundamental in the removal from office of two presidents: Jamild Mahuad de Witt and Gustavo Novoa. Similarly in Bolivia, former president Lozada was forced to resign from office. In Peru the Aymara population in Puno at the time of writing has been appraising and has toppled local authorities; they are claiming not only the attention of the state but also the possibility of establishing their own nation and real access to political power. The apparent non-resistant and passive Aymara have 'awakened' and are clamouring for justice. Furthermore, in early 2006 the indigenous leader Evo Morales was elected president of Bolivia with a nationalistic and indigenous political platform that will significantly affect the Bolivian peoples. The globalized states of Latin America have to learn to deal with the affirmation and revitalization of local ethnicities and cultures. The Christian church has a tremendous challenge in this area.

The evangelization of Indian peoples in the Americas has followed at least two main forms:

(1) Forced imposition of the Christian faith by which the outward appearance of Indian religious expression is Roman Catholic. However, upon closer examination their worldview continues to be essentially the original one.

(2) Selective incorporation of Christian Roman Catholic elements, particularly in their rituals, as well as a pantheon of deities, which are a mixture of Indian as well as Roman Catholic elements. The cult of the Christian saints, for both men and women, is widespread. Many indigenous deities have taken on Christian names, including Jesus Christ and the Virgin Mary.

Indian cultures have been discriminated against throughout the Americas. When indigenous peoples accepted Christianity, they were told, consciously or unconsciously, that their cultures were inferior or not good enough to express the Christian faith. An alternative to this traditional, patronizing way of thinking sees culture as the space where God is actively involved in affirming all that is good and that does not contradict the gospel; on the other hand where God is also transforming all that is sinful and demonic in the culture. Indigenous cultures are thus neither idealized nor suppressed.

The integrity of mission recognizes culture as the vehicle used by God to interact with humans as well as the vehicle to carry out his mission in this world. Culture is also the vehicle in which humans can realize themselves as well as render homage and worship God. Therefore as part of creation, we can see in cultures the evidence of God's love, presence and dynamic involvement. Therefore Indian cultures are the space where indigenous peoples who follow the Lord Jesus Christ should, without losing their integrity, strive to feel at home. On the other hand Christians have the challenge under the guidance of the Holy Spirit and the word of God to transform all that is evil in their cultures.

Christians in Latin America, particularly evangelical Christians, need to re-evaluate their view and relationship with our Indian cultures so that they can affirm and welcome all that is good and positive in those cultures. This has begun to happen in several population sectors such as the Pentecostal, as well as amongst Indian evangelical peoples.

Among evangelicals, until recently, the 'Christ against culture' attitude has been the norm; Indian peoples were told that unless they forsook their Indian cultural ways such as dancing, music and instruments, they could not be truly Christians. For many years they could not worship God in their own music, with their own instruments, in their own language. They were denied basic aspects of their cultural expression. In the last twenty-five years this has considerably changed. Several evangelical Indian movements have risen up throughout the Americas and have begun to revalue and rescue their own language and culture to express and live out their Christian faith. This has particularly been true in the Andean areas of Ecuador, Peru and Bolivia. The translation of Scripture into indigenous languages has been a significant factor in their affirmation and growth. A new indigenous leadership has been emerging which is in need of *contextual theological training that will be able to continue to lead the indigenous churches, responding to the spiritual and socio-economic needs of millions of their peoples, who yearn for full freedom and abundant life in Jesus Christ.

Indigenous people have great contributions to make to the universal church, particularly in expressing practical solidarity with other needy human beings; also in their relationship to creation and the integration of the sacred and secular. An ecological sensitivity and integration of the whole of life are practical contributions and consequences of indigenous people's holistic view of the gospel and mission.

See also CULTURE.

Bibliography

E. Galeano, *Open Veins of Latin America: Five Centuries of the Pillage of a Continent*, trans. C. Belfrage (New York: Monthly Review Press, 1973); L. Hanke, *The Spanish Struggle for Justice in the Conquest of America* (Philadelphia: University of Pennsylvania Press, 1959); W. Mangin (ed.), *Peasants in Cities: Readings in the Anthropology of Urbanization* (Boston: Houghton Mifflin, 1970); E. A. Nida, 'The Roman Catholic, Communist, and Protestant Approach to Social Structure', *Practical Anthropology* 4, 1957, pp. 29–219; R. E. Paredes Alfaro, 'The Protestant Movement in Ecuador and Peru: A Comparative Socio-Anthropological Study of the Establishment and Diffusion of Protestantism in Two Central Highland Regions', PhD dissertation (Los Angeles: University of California, 1980); R. E. Paredes Alfaro, 'Peace and Hope for Peru: Living in the aftermath of Shining Path', *Latin America Evangelist* 81, 2001, pp. 12–13; R. E. Paredes Alfaro, 'Popular Religiosity: A Protestant Perspective', *Missiology, an International Review* 20, 1992; R. E. Paredes Alfaro, 'Peruvian Protestant Missionaries and the Struggle for Human Rights 1980–1993', *Transformation: An International Evangelical Dialogue on Mission and Ethics* 13, 1996, pp. 1–7; P. L. Van Den Berghe, *Class and Ethnicity in Peru* (Leiden; E. J. Brill, 1974).

R. PAREDES

INDIGENOUS THEOLOGY, see AFRICAN CHRISTOLOGY, AFRICAN THEOLOGY, ASIAN THEOLOGY, INDIAN THEOLOGY, LATIN AMERICAN THEOLOGY, MINJUNG THEOLOGY
INTEGRAL MISSION, see HOLISTIC MISSION
JERUSALEM, see ZION

Jewish mission

Christian mission to the Jewish people, though ultimately rooted in the OT and in the ministry of Jesus, properly commenced after Pentecost. The mission of the OT prophets was to call their own people to return to God. In Jesus' mission, the promises made to the Jewish people of the expected *kingdom are fulfilled: God had remembered his *covenant and come to redeem his people (Luke 1:68).

After Pentecost, *evangelism initially took place among the Jewish people. In Romans 1:16 Paul says he made mission among Jewish people his priority. Despite his call as apostle to the Gentiles, Paul's regular practice was to visit the synagogues in each town he visited, even following rejection in a previous city. Romans 11:11 perhaps even suggests that Gentiles will evangelize Jews, a reversal of Israel's call to be a light to the nations.

Theologizing about Jewish missions has largely centred on three areas: (1) the validity of Jewish mission, that is, whether Jewish people need to hear and respond to the gospel; (2) the nature of the Jewish people, that is, whether and to what extent they remain the 'people of God'; and (3) methods and argumentation (apologetics). Perhaps because the first two seem to be perennial questions, Jewish missions theology has not yet sufficiently gone on to explore other areas.

In this first part of the twenty-first century, there are particular challenges in theology and practice that affect bringing the gospel to Jews, as well as nurturing their spiritual life. Theology and practice are of course mutually interrelated, but it will be helpful to explore their particular challenges separately.

Key theological challenges

The validity of Jewish mission was largely established in the past, but recent trends have again pushed the question to the forefront in both mainstream and evangelical circles. Dual covenant theology is rooted in the thought of Jewish philosopher Franz Rosenzweig (1886–1929) and postulates a separate divine covenant for Jews and non-Jews. This renders Jewish evangelism unnecessary. It also meshes nicely with certain types of pluralistic and postmodern trends, for which Jewish, and indeed any, evangelism is inappropriate. Recently, Mark Kinzer has advocated for a 'postmissionary Messianic Judaism', influenced by Karl Rahner's 'anonymous Christian' theory, and by Karl Barth's ideas about the solidarity of Jesus with his people. Kinzer postulates that Jesus has had a 'hidden presence' among the Jewish people during the past two millennia – which again seems to make Jewish evangelism unnecessary. It can no longer be taken for granted that the evangelical world, let alone others, sees Jewish mission as a proper enterprise.

A second issue concerns the nature of the Jewish people and their role in God's plan. Among evangelicals, this discussion has tended to divide along the lines of dispensationalism and Reformed theology. Historically, however, there have been voices from both sides affirming the uniqueness of the Jewish people within the present plan of God. Among all theological streams there has also been the divide of supersessionist and non-supersessionist theology. (Supersessionism views the church as in some way supplanting the Jewish people, though within supersessionism there is a spectrum of positions.) In North America, at any rate, these discussions have tended to work out in a neglect of Jewish missions in the Reformed churches compared to the more vigorous advocacy on the part of Baptist, charismatic, and dispensational churches – a pattern that obscures a stronger Reformed presence in Jewish missions in earlier times.

A third major area concerns the way the Holocaust, anti-Semitism, and the State of Israel have impacted on the mission to Jewish people. Reflection on these issues has led some to assert the particularity of the Jewish people in a way that again makes Jewish evangelism to be inappropriate and unnecessary. For example, the history of anti-Semitism and the complicity of many churches in the Holocaust implies to some that the church has spent its capital as far as Jewish people are concerned. Therefore, it is concluded, efforts ought to be put into support for Israel and the Jewish people instead of – note the false dichotomy – evangelization.

Key practical issues

One significant question, with a long history in Jewish missions, is that of the relationship of Jewish believers in Jesus to the Law of Moses, including its ritual and ceremonial aspects. Vigorous discussions have taken place on whether Jewish believers in Jesus can even *voluntarily* observe aspects of the law for reasons of witness or personal identity. More recently, though at present a distinctly minority view, appeal has been made to apostolic practice and the ongoing covenant with the Jewish people to argue that there is a divine mandate for Jewish believers in Jesus to observe the Law of Moses. Complicating matters is the fact that Jewish culture is rooted in both the OT and in post-biblical traditions.

A second major practical area also has a history of discussion among the Jewish missions. This concerns the spectrum of rejection by the Jewish community (on one end) and acceptance (on the other). (By 'acceptance' is meant first, willingness to consider Jewish believers in Jesus as Jewish and part of the Jewish community, and second, willingness to seriously interact over the *gospel message.) Here questions arise as to what are the marks of an effective Jewish mission, and what should our stance be vis-à-vis the Jewish community. Scripture offers us the complementary models of acceptance/social change/ *dialogue along with rejection/resistance/ confrontation. Serious study of these two models has not yet been attempted in Jewish missions, and there has developed a polarization among those who see one axis or the other as primary. This is not simply a theoretical discussion; it affects (1) how the Jewish community views Jewish believers in Jesus, and (2) how Jewish believers in Jesus view the Jewish community.

As to how the Jewish community views Jewish believers in Jesus, the official stance of the Jewish community is to condemn Jewish missions (and Jewish believers in Jesus as 'not really' Jewish, 'deceitful' and so on). Thus, 'counter-missionary' organizations exist whose *raison d'être* is to dissuade Jews and often others, from considering the gospel. At the opposite extreme, Jewish scholars such as Dan Cohn-Sherbok wish to give Jewish believers in Jesus a place at the Jewish table, within an overall pluralistic model.

As far as how Jewish believers in Jesus view the Jewish community, acceptance of one of the two models as primary has led some to distance themselves altogether from traditional Jewish missions and to postulate a 'postmissionary Messianic Judaism'. In this thinking, the Jewish community rather than the church becomes the primary place of social life for the Jewish believer in Jesus – a rather non-evangelical and so far distinctly minority view. Others, aligning along the opposite pole, tend to see rejection, at least at the larger community level, as the apostolic norm and an accurate reflection of the experience of Jewish believers in Jesus. There is clearly room to offer an integrated theology on this matter.

A third major issue is that of ecclesiology and concerns the worshipping community. Apart from the minority view just described (in which the Jewish community becomes the primary social location for Jewish believers in Jesus), debate has generally centred on whether Jewish believers in Jesus ought to worship in churches, or in 'messianic congregations' – which in theory incorporate Jewish ethnicity, religious practices, and a larger number of Jewish members than found in traditional churches. Points of discussion have included whether Jewish believers in Jesus *must* worship in such a setting; whether messianic congregations are better vehicles for evangelism than traditional Jewish mission agencies; whether churches provide an adequate vehicle for maintaining Jewishness over successive generations; and the viability of the entire project, for statistically there is a preponderance of Gentiles within most messianic congregations. The questions are part of the larger ones of '*homogeneous unit groups' or the more recent discussions of *ethnicity. At any rate, to date the majority of Jewish believers in Jesus – for any number of reasons – have joined churches rather than messianic congregations.

The shape of Jewish evangelism today

Jewish mission today recognizes the vast changes that have taken place in the Jewish community in the past decades. Today's Jewish community is largely non-traditional and secular; has undergone dramatic demographic shifts; has seen the establishment of the State of Israel (home now to some 5 million out of a total of 14 million Jews); and an intermarriage rate of around 50%. Despite these sea changes, a constant remains, which is that despite openness to secularism, Buddhism, and much else, for large swaths of the Jewish community, Jesus remains the big 'No'. For all their diversity, assimilation and intermarriage, Jews tend to see themselves as distinct from the non-Jewish world, and to see acceptance (even consideration) of the gospel as tantamount to abandonment of one's identity and people. In light of Romans 9 – 11 this is not entirely unexpected, as Paul speaks of a hardening in part of the Jewish people in this present age. In fact, Paul makes reference to a remnant of those who believe, and refers us back to a similar situation in the time of Elijah, thereby bringing the discussion round again to the roots of Jewish mission theology in the OT.

Jewish mission is therefore most helpfully seen in terms of God's dealing with particular Jewish people rather than as a 'people movement'. This remains true even where mission work among Jews in, for example, Ukraine and Russia, reveals a greater openness than elsewhere. To that end, not only mission agencies but individuals have a part to play, dialoguing with Jewish friends and, as openings arise, telling the story of their own journey.

Bibliography

Y. Ariel, *Evangelizing the Chosen People: Mission to the Jews in America, 1880–2000* (Chapel Hill: University of North Carolina Press, 2000); M. Kinzer, *Postmissionary Messianic Judaism: Redefining Christian Engagement with the Jewish People* (Grand Rapids: Brazos, 2005); T. Zaretksy (ed.), 'Jewish Evangelism: A Call to the Church', Occasional Paper No. 60 (Lausanne Committee for World Evangelization, 2005). At <http://community.gospelcom.net/lcwe/assets/LOP60_IG31.pdf>; *Mishkan: A Forum on the Gospel and the Jewish People*, at http://www.caspari.com/mishkan>; *Digital Jewish Missions History Project*, <http://www.lcje.net/history>.

R. ROBINSON

Jubilee

Jubilee legislation in the OT

Christians have always wrestled with the questions of *if* and *how* OT law might be relevant for life and ministry. This is a crucial issue in the consideration of the appropriation of the jubilee for Christian mission.

From the beginning, the existence of Israel is set in a universal missional context. The call of Abram comes against the backdrop of the fall and the spread of *sin (Gen. 3 – 11). Yahweh ordains that he and his descendants be the divine instruments of blessing to 'all the families of the earth' (Gen. 12:1–3). The blessing entails spiritual relationship with God and the enjoyment of the material provisions of his good creation. The giving of the Law must be understood within this framework. Israel was to be a holy, priestly kingdom among the nations (Exod. 19:1–6); the economic and socio-political structures established by God's decrees were to be a paradigm of the values that God requires of all peoples (Deut. 4:5–8; cf. Isa. 2:2–4). Ideally, the law and the society it generated were to be a means by which Israel could bless the world. The nation was to exemplify for that time and place the kind of life that pleases God.

The law attended to the needy in various ways. These directives, based on the character of Yahweh and the redemption at the *exodus, were designed to preserve the stability of Israel's families within its land tenure system and to prevent the accumulation of riches by the powerful at the expense of the defenceless. For example, there was to be provision made for the *poor at harvest (Deut. 24:19–22) and by the collection of a triennial tithe (Deut. 14:28–29). The jubilee was one of three humanitarian laws that followed sabbatical (or seven) patterns. The Sabbath day afforded rest for labourers (Deut. 5:12–15); slaves were to be freed and debts remitted during the Sabbath year (Lev. 25:1–7; Deut. 15:1–18). The jubilee was to occur every fifty years, after seven Sabbath years, and be proclaimed on the Day of Atonement (Lev. 25:8–10). Leviticus 25 portrays a family's progressive descent into destitution: selling the family land (vv. 25–28), receiving interest-free loans through the good graces of others (vv. 35–38), and finally selling themselves into debt-slavery (vv. 39–55). By eliminating debt and restoring their property, the jubilee gave a family the opportunity to be self-sustaining and to recover its dignity as productive members of society. In the Ancient Near East kings sometimes decreed exoneration from debts for political motives, but the jubilee was unique as an ethical call. Yahweh was the owner of all the land and was no cruel patron (v. 23). He had graciously redeemed his people from slavery at the exodus; hence, the nation was to be generous to its poor (vv. 38, 42, 55).

There is no record of the jubilee ever being implemented. It stipulated no sanctions, appealing solely to the conscience of the people. On two separate occasions debts were forgiven (Jer. 34; Neh. 5), but these were exceptional proclamations. The hope for jubilee was pushed into the eschatological future with the promise of a messianic jubilee on an international stage. The entire nation would be restored after its devastation and be served by those peoples that had mistreated them (Isa. 61; cf. T. Levi 17–18: 11Q Melch).

Jesus and the jubilee

Jesus quotes the passage from Isaiah in the synagogue at Nazareth (Luke 4:16–21; cf. 7:18–23). He announces that the messianic jubilee was being fulfilled in his person and makes clear that it is programmatic for his ministry. Jesus, however, turns Israel's nationalistic aspirations on their head. The Jews longed for the day when the Gentiles would attend them, but Jesus announces that it would be the Gentiles who would properly respond to God, not the chosen nation (Luke 4:22–30)! The messianic jubilee is for all peoples.

Jesus' calling in large measure was to bring 'good news' to the marginalized. With his *kingdom comes the reversal of usual social and economic arrangements. The poor are blessed; they are to be invited to banquets to which they are normally excluded and are rewarded for a life of suffering (Luke 6:20–22; 14:1–24; 16:19–31). Those of social standing, however, are challenged to evaluate their priorities and lifestyle (Luke 12:13–21; 18:18–23, par.; 19:1–10). The messianic jubilee also expands deliverance into new dimensions: freedom from sin (Luke 1:77; 7:47–50, par.) and disease (Luke 5:17–26, 7:17–23, par.).

Early Christians grasped the importance of the jubilee principle, which now was grounded in a greater *redemption. The book of Acts recounts their efforts to organize care for the disadvantaged of the church, whether those close by (2:42–47; 4:32 – 5:16; 6:1–7) or far away (24:17; cf. Rom. 15:25–28; 1 Cor. 16:1–4; 2 Cor. 8 – 9). There is no dearth of injunctions in the epistles to provide for the poor, widows and orphans (Rom.

12:13; Gal. 2:10; 1 Tim. 5:3–16; Jas 1:27 – 2:10). Of course, the ministry of the churches also involved the proclamation of the forgiveness of sin, healing the sick (Acts 5:15–16; 28:8–9; Jas 5:14–15), and the release of the demon-possessed (Acts 19:11–20).

Jubilee and mission

The jubilee theme informs Christian mission in several ways. First, it underscores the fact that the people of God, as those who have experienced divine grace, have social obligations to the less fortunate among them. Both OT and NT believing communities put mechanisms into place to help those in need and to restrain unjust hoarding of *wealth. To do otherwise violates fundamental aspects of their identity and vocation. Lifestyle issues, moral values and faith commitments are thus intimately intertwined. The consistent biblical teaching on these matters demonstrates that the *ethical call of the jubilee remains a constant in the will of God. At the same time, the messianic jubilee extends into the spiritual realm. The connection with the Day of Atonement in the OT and the *cross in the NT underscore that the jubilee is rooted ultimately in redemption. It will not do, therefore, to reduce mission to either the material or the spiritual. Both realities are essential, integral parts of *holistic mission.

Although some might argue to the contrary, the socio-economic implications of the jubilee cannot be limited to the church. As pointed out earlier, the breadth of its application is evident in both the paradigmatic nature of OT law and the worldwide reach of the messianic jubilee. Throughout the Bible moral obligations begin within the family and extend outward in ever-widening circles. The same principle holds here. This interplay between the particular (people of God) and the universal (humankind in general) can function in at least two ways. On the one hand, what is done within Christian communities can serve as a small-scale model of socio-economic solidarity and concern and, therefore, also as a testimony to those outside the church of the life-changing power of the gospel in every dimension of human existence. On the other hand, the jubilee mandate should propel Christians to penetrate personal, ecclesial and social spheres with the fullness of the reality of what has been wrought in Christ.

Said another way, the gracious acts of God yield 'imperatives of redemption'. In the confidence of the empowerment of the Spirit and inspired by biblical precedent and the life of Jesus and the early church, the people of God should work, even with those of other persuasions, towards seeing his moral demands embodied in practical initiatives and formal legislation – those 'structures of grace' commensurate with the common good and appropriate to any given context.

The term 'jubilee' appears in the names of Christian ministries worldwide that actively work at peacemaking or with marginalized groups, such as the poor, refugees and prisoners. In Latin America and elsewhere missiological insights from the jubilee inform those who seek socio-economic systemic change to bring relief to the disenfranchised and socially excluded. In a world challenged by the potentially dehumanizing and even idolatrous effects of some aspects of economic and cultural globalization, Christians need a solid biblical-theological basis to guide them in the task of fulfilling a constructive role in safeguarding fundamental values of life. The jubilee is a reminder of the responsibility under God of establishing avenues that allow opportunities for the unfortunate to regain financial stability and live with a new sense of dignity and hope. Fittingly, the jubilee has captured the imagination of several international cooperative ventures, not always strictly Christian, which campaign to reduce debt at an international level – that is, the enormous paralyzing foreign debt of developing countries – and advocate for a more equitable world market (e.g. Jubilee South; Jubilee Research, formerly Jubilee 2000).

Bibliography

J. S. Bergsma, *The Jubilee from Leviticus to Qumran: A History of Interpretation*, VT Sup 115 (Leiden: Brill, 2007); M. D. Carroll R., 'Wealth and Poverty', in D. W. Baker and T. D. Alexander (eds.), *Dictionary of the Old Testament: The Pentateuch* (Downers Grove: InterVarsity Press, 2003); R. Kinsler and G. Kinsler, *The Biblical Jubilee and the Struggle for Life* (Maryknoll: Orbis Books, 1999); R. H. Lowery, *Sabbath and Jubilee* (St Louis: Chalice, 2000); W. E. Pilgrim, *Good News to the Poor: Wealth and Poverty in Luke–Acts* (Minneapolis: Augsburg, 1981);

S. Ringe, *Jesus, Liberation, and the Biblical Jubilee: Images for Ethics and Christology* (Philadelphia: Fortress, 1985); J. Rogerson, *Theory and Practice in Old Testament Ethics* in M. D. Carroll R. (ed.), *JSOTSup* 405 (London: T. & T. Clark, 2004); R. J. Sider, *Rich Christians in an Age of Hunger* (Dallas: Word, rev. edn., 1990); H. Ucko (ed.), *The Jubilee Challenge: Utopia or Possibility: Jewish and Christian Insights* (Geneva: WCC, 1997); C. J. H. Wright, *Old Testament Ethics and the People of God* (Downers Grove: InterVarsity Press, 2004); J. H. Yoder, *The Politics of Jesus: Vicit Agnus Noster* (Grand Rapids: Eerdmans; Carlisle: Paternoster, ²1994).

M. D. CARROLL R.

JUDGMENT, see HELL/JUDGMENT

JUSTICE, see DEVELOPMENT, HOLISTIC MISSION, HUMAN RIGHTS, LIBERATION, POOR/POVERTY

Kingdom of God

The focus of this article will be on the significance of the kingdom of God for the theology and practice of mission. This will require a summary of the meaning of the term from a biblical and theological perspective, but the emphasis will be on the dimensions of the kingdom of God and how these have influenced mission thinking and practice.

The meaning of the kingdom

There is a consensus, now well established amongst scholars, that Jesus used the term 'kingdom' to refer to God's saving and transforming reign, proclaimed and prophetically promised throughout the OT (e.g. 2 Sam. 7; Pss. 2; 24; 99; Isa. 49:1–7; Zech. 9:9–10), but which had invaded the present in himself and his ministry (e.g. Mark 1:15; Matt. 11:1–15; Luke 4:21). In the OT God reigns over, and for, all the nations (e.g. Isa. 2:2; Pss. 22:26–31; 47), giving the theme a universal, missiological reference. Jesus, however, radically transformed the phrase, retaining the associations with apocalyptic, prophetic and wisdom usage, but giving it a unique reference to himself and his mission (e.g. Matt. 12:28). The kingdom of God would reach its fulfilment in the *eschatological new age, the consummation of history in which all creation

would acknowledge and experience the reign of God, often associated by Jesus with the coming of the Son of Man (e.g. Matt. 16:27–28; 25:31–46; Mark 13). So the kingdom of God is the 'presence of the future', an 'eschatology in process of realization', or 'God reigning in strength' to fulfil his purposes (Matt. 6:10). The emphasis is not upon spatial identity, but on the dynamic and active rule of God to establish his will and sovereignty over all things (Phil. 2:6–11; Rev. 11:15–17). There is something mysterious about the kingdom of God, and yet it can be seen and experienced (e.g. Mark 4:26–32; Matt. 10:7–8). It has values which its disciples are expected to live by (e.g. Matt. 5:3–10). It is both 'now' and 'not yet': 'now' because already revealed in the life and ministry of Jesus, it can be 'entered into', and it continues as a present experience in the ministry of the church in the power of the Spirit (e.g. John 3:3–8; Acts 8:9–13); 'not yet' because the 'old age' is not yet totally displaced, God's sovereignty is not yet universally acknowledged, and his reign of justice and peace remains to be experienced in its fullness (e.g. 1 Cor. 15:24–28; Rom. 8:14–25; Eph. 1:9–10). This duality of present and future experience has many implications for mission (see below).

The kingdom of God is manifested through each of the three persons of the Trinity. It is the kingdom of the Father because it belongs to him (Luke 12:32). He brings people by *grace into repentant relationship with himself, he calls them to reflect his character in every dimension of life, he invites them to participate in his authority and victory, and he welcomes them into his family, a community of disciples of the kingdom who experience his reigning presence in their midst (Matt. 16:18–19; Eph. 1:15–23; 5:1–5). God's saving reign is characterized by grace (e.g. Titus 2:11–14; 3:4–7; Col. 1:12–13). It follows that grace must characterize our gospel and all our mission; and that whatever is accomplished in mission is only by God's sovereign grace. Note also that the goal of mission is the coming of the kingdom, not the planting of the church. The kingdom of God is also the kingdom of the Son because it is proclaimed and demonstrated in his ministry of word and power, which sets people free from every oppression. It is good news for the '*poor', which includes all those who for whatever reason do not experience God's justice and peace (e.g. Matt. 11:4–6; 22:1–14; Luke 4:18–19; 16:19–31). This gives Christian mission its agenda. It is the kingdom of the Spirit because the Spirit is the dynamic power by which God fulfils his purposes (Luke 4:18; Acts 10:38; 1 Cor. 12:1–11). The Spirit is the decisive mark of the new age, equipping Jesus for his messianic ministry of healing and teaching, and enabling the church to continue the agenda of the kingdom (John 20:21–22; Rom. 14:17; 1 Cor. 4:20; Rev. 1:5–6). The Spirit is the Spirit of mission, and without his dynamic power and gifts the church's mission will be ineffective.

The dimensions of the kingdom

God's sovereign reign is experienced through a number of dimensions of the kingdom of God which have to be held together in tension with one another. It is both present and future, individual and corporate, heavenly and earthly. It involves both God's gracious action and the human responsibility of submission and obedience; both power and suffering, grace and judgment, the cross and resurrection, the supernatural and the ordinary. Any attempt to reduce it to one or other of these dimensions will impoverish our understanding of the fullness of God's purposes and lead to a deficient view of mission. God's mission (*missio Dei*) is to reign over the whole of reality, so that all creation will be ultimately reconciled to his sovereignty (Eph. 1:9–10; Col. 1:20; Rom. 8:21). This is his mission first and foremost, in which we are invited to participate. These several dimensions of the kingdom of God overlap to a considerable degree. However, an emphasis on one or other dimension leads to models of mission with differing, and often unbalanced, goals and priorities.

The kingdom as a personal spiritual experience

There is a long and hallowed evangelical tradition of interpreting the kingdom as God's reign in the heart and life of the individual who acknowledges Jesus as Lord. To 'enter' the kingdom is to come through repentance and faith into personal relationship with God through Jesus Christ. 'The kingdom of God is within you' (Luke 17:21, NIV) is a key text for this view, even though most scholars prefer the translation 'among you', giving the phrase a corporate rather than individual reference. This view sees the teaching of the kingdom as primarily about the personal ethics of *discipleship. This gives rise to a view of mission as the discipling of individuals, in which the gospel is a personal invitation to faith, and those who accept it are taught how to live in relationship with God as Father in the power of the Spirit. This model has good scriptural precedent, not least in Jesus' great commission to 'go and make disciples' (Matt. 28:19), and in the many references to the personal challenge of the kingdom. The kingdom does require personal repentance, faith and obedience, and there is plenty in Jesus' teaching about personal ethics. On this view, whatever structures of church are created, their goal is individual discipleship by obedience and conformity to the will of God. This view teaches us that it is not sufficient in mission to gain converts or plant churches if we are not 'making disciples'.

The kingdom as a future hope

The focus here is on the promise of eternal life and future glory. The kingdom is the 'new heaven and the new earth', an apocalyptic expectation which gives hope of future deliverance to those who are oppressed. There is a final cosmic reconciliation to look forward to, ushered in by the coming again of the Lord Jesus Christ, and this experience will completely eclipse this earthly life with all its misery. This view generates any number of approaches, some of them highly speculative, to what will happen in the 'end times', and it calls us to be prepared for what is to come. Sometimes there is a strong emphasis on judgment alongside future salvation. This view gives rise to a view of mission as the saving of as many souls as possible before it is too late. It sees the church as a lifeboat, pulling in any who will respond and giving them protection and preparation for future glory. This model also has scriptural precedent, not least because the apocalyptic expectations of an 'age to come' was the prevailing view at the time of Jesus, and we have seen how Jesus sometimes endorsed that view. But again mission is seen primarily to individuals so that they might escape the coming judgment. There is no hope envisaged for this world and its created order, since it will all be burnt up and completely replaced (as in 2 Pet. 3:10–13). Positively, this view reminds us that the fullness of the kingdom is always future, so no church or movement can claim to embody it.

The kingdom as a new social order

Rather than justice and peace being a future hope, this view sees them as a present possibility as God's kingdom comes and his will is 'done on earth as it is in heaven' (Matt. 6:10). Every transformation of the old order, every manifestation of justice, every turning upside down of the values of this world, is a manifestation of God's reigning power. Transformation and transfiguration become key words. Liberation theologians sought to root the reality of the kingdom in history, seeing it as 'the cosmic-human divine realization of God's historical purposes'. It is a vision of a new society, which is good news to the poor and offers them the transformation of their existing circumstances. It offers 'life in all its fullness'. On this view mission brings humanization, transformed economic and political structures, *liberation for the oppressed. It is a view strongly promoted by the ecumenical movement, and supported by evangelicals who have a strong sense of social justice. Sometimes there is a focus on the love and compassion of the kingdom of God as motives for social change, as distinct from its justice. This model sometimes seems to bypass the church, though at its best sees the church as a sign and instrument of the kingdom, in so far as it conforms to God's liberative project on behalf of the poor and marginalized. This view sometimes makes use of the Hebrew concept of 'shalom', expressing the harmony and coherence of a human society ordered in line with God's will.

The ideal of a new society can take several forms. It can be seen as an earthly utopia, often premillennial in its vision of a transformed society. It can be a theocratic kingdom, similar to the notion of 'Christendom', in which politics and church work together to promote and safeguard the kingdom. It can be seen as a subversive kingdom in which social structures are organized as counter-cultural, and Christians are encouraged to live out the radical character of the kingdom of God in a way that challenges the prevailing values. Again, all of these approaches have some biblical support, though it is often pointed out that Jesus did not have a programme as such for the radical restructuring of society. But his Lukan manifesto was radical enough (Luke 4:18–19), and had profound political and social implications, based as it was in the *jubilee principle of the 'year of the Lord's favour' (Lev. 25:8–13). We have seen how he saw himself fulfilling the OT vision of the King who reflects the character of God's kingship by ensuring justice and intervening on behalf of the weak and oppressed. There is a continuity here of promise and fulfilment, which Jesus would have intended and expected his disciples to follow through into their mission (e.g. John 20:21; Luke 24:45–49).

The kingdom as the church

Under the influence of Augustine this was the dominant view of medieval Christianity in the West right through the Middle Ages up to the Reformation. It was the view that predominated within Roman Catholicism up to Vatican II (1962–65), where it was acknowledged that the kingdom can find expression beyond the church and can be experienced in churches other than Catholic. There is now a consensus that the church is not the kingdom, since God is free to exercise his sovereign will in the world and its history independently of the church. However, this view of the kingdom of God leads to models of mission which make the church their focus, including movements for church growth and church planting. These movements often see little or no role for the kingdom of God in society, politics or creation. For many, their sole aim is to plant churches. Some see the destiny of history as dependent upon what happens to the church: when the church is prepared as the bride of Christ, then Christ can come again and claim it for himself. Some see Christ as exercising his authority as king through the church and its leadership, which gives leaders and ministers the priestly, or sometimes apostolic, role of representing Christ for the people and mediating his authority over them. This is not just a Catholic view, it is also seen in some charismatic and neopentecostal ecclesiologies. The relationship of the church to the kingdom is difficult to identify biblically, although Jesus intended his disciples to continue the characteristic ministries of the kingdom of preaching, teaching, service, healing and casting out demons, so the church becomes a community of the kingdom by being the central, but not the only, means through which God exercises his kingly rule in the world.

The kingdom as a manifestation of power

This view sees the kingdom as God's way of confronting and destroying all the powers of evil. It sees Jesus' deliverance ministry as a central manifestation of this (Matt. 12:25–28). Some who hold this view see the world as a battleground between the kingdom of God and the kingdom of Satan, and so all the resources of *spiritual warfare are required to establish decisively God's reign on earth. The model of mission becomes one of prayer ministry for deliverance and healing, the expectation of signs and wonders accompanying the preached word, and manifestations and miracles which act to convince and convict unbelievers. This again has scriptural precedent (e.g. Acts 2:43; 4:30; 6:8; 14:3; etc.) though the preaching of the word was not always accompanied by signs and wonders in Acts, and we need great discernment in judging the genuineness of manifestations (e.g. Matt. 24:24; 2 Thess. 2:9; cf. John 4:48; Luke 16:31; Matt. 16:4).

The kingdom and mission

We have seen how there is no dimension of the kingdom which does not have its implications for mission. There is no dimension of mission for which the kingdom of God does not have some relevance. All of the above perspectives are focusing on some truth about the kingdom, yet none of them is adequate in itself, otherwise God's mission is reduced to one dimension or the other, and the creative tension between its polarities is lost. We must therefore conclude that justice can only be given to this range of perspectives with a model of mission that is holistic, inclusive and integrated. These dimensions of the kingdom work together to fulfil God's will. Mission must likewise seek the fullness of God's kingdom by practising its dimensions in relation to one another, and not in isolation. So manifestations of power must go hand in hand with compassion, social justice and discipleship, or they are dangerously unbalanced. Mission through healing must go hand in hand with the acceptance of the 'not yet' of the kingdom which obliges us to accept the reality of suffering. Church planting must go hand in hand with concern for the wider social context in which we are working. Evangelism must not be divorced from social justice, since that also witnesses to God's compassionate grace. Kingdom salvation is reconciliation with God, with others and with creation. We recognize tensions inherent in this approach, and it is easier to resolve them by opting for one side or the other, but by so doing we reduce the meaning of the kingdom and have an impoverished mission practice. Mission is always done in the tension between the 'now' and the 'not yet', but that gives it its dynamic, forward moving, provisional and creative character. The kingdom becomes 'the goal of messianic mission'.

There is the question of whether the kingdom of God is known only where Jesus is consciously acknowledged as Lord. In this case examples of social justice or restoration are not seen in themselves as manifestations of the kingdom. The kingdom and Jesus cannot be separated. Others would say that if the kingdom 'comes' wherever God's will is done, then every example of the fulfilling of his will manifests its presence. God's mission is to transform every dimension of reality, sometimes independently of the church and Christian presence, since that is his sovereign privilege. We must not set limits to the grace of God.

The kingdom of God also challenges the world-views of each context and culture. In the Western context of relativism and pluralism in which there are only fragmented truths and personal perspectives, it presents an overarching vision of an integrated world which has a coherent pattern of meaning. It offers a justice, righteousness and peace which restores integrity to creation. It invites dynamic change in the hope of a transformed world. Many of its parables have striking modern relevance. Evangelism must proclaim these possibilities, and not simply offer personal hope of a place in heaven, otherwise new Christians may not see how their story fits into the wider unfolding of God's purposes for the world. Thus the kingdom also challenges Western individualism and a faith based solely on personal need.

The kingdom of God also presents us with a challenge to our mission amongst those of other faiths when it calls for repentance and faith in Jesus Christ and acknowledgment of him as Lord and King. It recognizes that 'every knee shall bow and every tongue confess' (Phil. 2:10–11) and it calls all nations to submit to God's kingly rule in Christ. But we have seen how it is a mysterious and secret work of the Spirit that sometimes happens where we least expect it, so we must not think that we can circumscribe what God is doing in the world, or deny God his sovereign right to reveal himself in all kinds of ways to those of other faiths; he does not leave himself without witness in every context (Acts 14:17). People of other faiths and none sometimes turn to Christ without any obvious missionary influence.

The kingdom of God must be associated with the cross as well as the resurrection and the glory of Jesus. This prevents Christians from both triumphalism and defeatism in mission. Disciples of the kingdom are called to 'take up their cross' and follow Christ the 'Servant King' in a life of service and love, identifying with the human frailty and suffering of the world. But they also have hope of a future glory and victory in which all that is opposed to God will be defeated. Christians need to keep an open mind as to how God will do that, and in mission they must be careful not to force the issue by 'bringing in the kingdom' in militaristic style, or forcing people to 'enter the kingdom' by inducement, false promises, or aggressive proselytism.

Because the kingdom is much bigger than our own church's experience of it, we must work with its manifestation in other Christian churches, and this calls us to ecumenical cooperation wherever possible. Too often in mission Christians are setting up their own version of the kingdom with complete disregard for others.

Here then are some of the main missiological implications of kingdom theology, rich in its associations, broad in its focus, holistic as it calls us into integrated mission. Christian mission is as broad and as deep as God's purposes for all humanity and all creation.

See also CHRIST, GOD, HOLY SPIRIT, SALVATION.

Bibliography

P. R. Clifford, *The Reality of the Kingdom* (Grand Rapids, MI: Eerdmans, 1996); A. Glasser *et al.*, *Announcing the Kingdom: The Story of God's Mission in the Bible* (Grand Rapids, MI: Baker, 2003); K. R. Gnanakan, *Kingdom Concerns* (Bangalore: Theological Book Trust, 1989); R. Kew and C. Okorocha, *Vision Bearers: Dynamic Evangelism in the 21st Century* (Harrisberg, PA: Morehouse Publishing, 1996); C. R. Padilla, *Mission Between the Times: Essays on the Kingdom* (Grand Rapids, MI: Eerdmans, 1985); V. Samuel and C. Sugden (eds.), *Mission as Transformation* (Oxford: Regnum, 1999); W. R. Shenk (ed.), *The Transfiguration of Mission* (Scottdale: Herald Press, 1993).

J. CORRIE

LAITY, ROLE OF, see MARKETPLACE THEOLOGY, PRIESTHOOD, TENTMAKING

Language/linguistics/translation

According to Genesis 11, there was a time when the world spoke a single language. The multiplicity of languages and the scattering of humanity all over the world were the result of divine judgment on human pride and presumption. Language, as everything else in the created order, is subject to the influence of *sin. Nevertheless, God saw fit to use language as the primary vehicle of divine revelation. It is not insignificant that God spoke the whole creation into being. Conversely, language is the principal means by which humans hear God through his word and respond to him in praise and prayer. On the day of Pentecost people gathered from different nations and praised God in their respective languages. This seems to be a reversal of the Tower of Babel, except that there was no divine impulse toward a common language. According to Revelation 5 and 7, the great diversity of language will be preserved even in heaven. Despite their dubious origins, it is clear that all languages are God's gifts to the different peoples of the world.

Compared with animal communication systems, language as a uniquely human phenomenon is distinguished by three properties: arbitrariness, creativity and displacement. By arbitrariness is meant the absence of a necessary relation between a linguistic form and the meaning it carries. For example, other than conventional agreement, there is no compelling reason why English speakers should call a canine animal 'dog', rather than, say, 'kog'. Next, displacement allows language users to symbolize objects, events and concepts which are not immediately present in time and space. Thus we can talk about things outside our immediate environment or even things that have only an imaginary existence. Displacement enables humans to handle generalizations and abstractions, and manipulate concepts such as truth, infinity, multiplication, and so on. Third, creativity, or productivity, is evidenced by the fact that human speakers can, without conscious effort, generate and understand an infinite number of grammatically well-formed utterances from a finite set of linguistic symbols. This is why there are word dictionaries but not sentence dictionaries. In the realm of human cognitive endeavour, linguistic creativity enables humans to bridge between the common and the extraordinary, the familiar and the extremely unfamiliar. For example, although there are no ready-made words for all the discoveries and inventions of cyber technology, we are able to use the linguistic resources at our disposal in novel ways, and we do so successfully.

The linguistic properties of arbitrariness, displacement and creativity are intrinsically tied up with the symbolic nature of language. Because language functions essentially in the symbolic mode, it is possible to talk about God and matters of ultimate concern. However, any discourse about God must respect his uniqueness and mystery. A linguistic form of divine transcendence necessitates 'speaking at the edges of language and straining its limits' (P. van Buren, *The Edges of Language*, p. 115). It is no coincidence then that religious language is largely metaphorical, rather than propositional, in nature. The missiological implication is obvious: for the gospel to be intelligibly presented, one must creatively draw from the resources of the recipients' language that relate to the metaphorical, such as allegories, parables, proverbs and similes.

There is a common fallacy that some languages are highly developed while others are primitive or inferior. Research has shown that every human language, without exception, is a highly complex system of codes and rules. Moreover, every language is unique. Some languages are more closely related to each other than to others, although the syntactic and semantic relationships between any two languages are never isomorphic. For instance, it is hard, and often impossible, to find an exact word in another language that carries the same specific meaning, with all its inherent nuances, as a word in one's own language. The lack of an exact conceptual equivalence between languages has to do with the relationship between language and thought. Subsequent research following the pioneering work of American linguist Edward Sapir and his student Benjamin Lee Whorf in the 1930s has shown that language does exert a substantial (though not total) influence in predisposing speakers of that language toward adopting a particular *world-view. If language A has a word for a particular concept, then that word makes it easier for speakers of language A to refer to that concept than speakers of language B, who lack such a word and are forced to use a circumlocution. Moreover, it is easier for speakers of language A to perceive instances of that concept. Conversely, and more obviously, the *culture of a people is mirrored in their language.

The intrinsic and intricate relationship between language and thought bears profound missiological implications for language learning. Too many missionaries mistakenly believe that it is enough just to know the grammatical rules of usage. 'Linguistic competence' (Noam Chomsky) is necessary but not sufficient. The famous Chomskyan sentence 'Colourless green ideas sleep furiously' is perfectly grammatical, but clearly it carries little semantic and communicative value. Besides rules of usage, the speaker needs to have what Dell Hymes calls 'communicative competence', in other words, knowledge of the rules of use. These, according to William Labov, are 'rules for appropriate selection of speakers, the interrelations of speaker, addressee, audience, topic, channel, and setting; and the ways in which the speakers draw upon the resources of their language to perform certain functions' (*Sociolinguistic Patterns*, p. 184). Missionaries learning Japanese, for instance, not only have to learn correct Japanese grammar, but also work hard to learn the appropriate use of the complex honorific system. The point can never be overemphasized that language is not simply a syntactic set of codes, but a form of socio-cultural behaviour – perhaps its most basic form. In application, language learning cannot be divorced from cultural learning. Indeed learning a language well enough to preach the gospel in ways that are culturally intelligible demands much time and effort.

Although every language is unique, universals exist in all languages by virtue of common human experience. Notwithstanding the difficulty in translating between languages, linguists have yet to find two languages that are not mutually translatable. Indeed it is always possible to translate between any two languages, provided one is willing to use some degree of circumlocution. One, however, often hears the assertion that 'something is always lost in translation'. Although in most cases the core meaning is preserved, subtle nuances are often lost in the translation process. These nuances might be linguistically transmittable, but their translation would involve the loss of verbal economy, especially with lengthy circumlocution. Indeed all translators are faced with the inescapable tension between how much to lose in terms of meaning and how much to sacrifice in terms of verbal economy.

Andrew Walls speaks of the 'infinite cultural translatability' of the Christian faith. The implication is that it is also infinitely linguistically translatable. In other words, the gospel can be coded in any language. While an exact translation between languages is not possible, an adequate translation is.

The effective translation of the biblical message is predicated on the proper understanding of language in linguistic rather than philological terms. What this means is that the pragmatic and semantic functions of a language are primary, and their focus should always precede the choice of words to be used in translation. Missiologically this entails a good working knowledge of not only the grammatical and syntactic rules of the language, but also of the way speakers use their language to organize and make sense of the world. The translator is also mindful that language does not only serve the singular function of transmitting information and

aiding understanding, but that it involves the expression of thought and feelings in ways that are culturally acceptable. In other words, language is not all cognitive, but also affective. And so, as in language learning, translation requires not only a high level of linguistic competence, but also sound communicative and cultural competence.

The word of God was originally given in three human languages, namely, Hebrew, Aramaic and Greek. These languages are no more sacred than any other language. Kevin Vanhoozer rightly describes the Bible as 'overdetermined in meaning' (in *Modern Reformation* 8:4 p. 27). This means that divine revelation is much larger and richer than the capacity of any finite language to contain it. Consequently when the biblical message is translated into another language, whatever loss is incurred in subtle shades of meaning is always compensated by gains in fresh theological insights. A case in point is the translation of the Greek word *logos* in John 1 into Chinese as *dao*, an ancient Chinese word referring to that transcendent and ineffable principle which animates all phenomena in the universe. While *dao* and *logos* are not conceptually identical, it can be argued that the former enriches the theological meaning of the latter. The theological validity of local words used in translation, however, must be properly assessed. Criteria for assessment must be drawn from two sources: the biblical canon and the global ecclesiastical community. In sum, all translation must pass the rigorous tests of canonicity and catholicity.

The main objective of Bible translation is to make available and understandable the word of God to all people of the world in their mother tongue. Translation as such is theologically grounded in the *incarnation, when God as a human being was 'embedded' in a *particular* culture and spoke a *particular* language. Not that God became a human being only so that he could speak to us in words. Rather, the incarnation principle refers to the total and *particular* embodiment of the divine Word. In biblical translation, the gospel is not merely grammatically translated, but it is theologically incarnated within a particular language.

Translation as an act of incarnation is oriented toward the recipients of the biblical message, and draws therefore from the linguistic resources of the recipients' language. Where necessary, it seeks to make explicit in that language what is implicitly understood or taken for granted in the biblical text in order to facilitate correct understanding. For instance, careful thought should be given to translating 'daily bread' in the Lord's Prayer in a culture where bread is hardly eaten, or to the expression 'holy kiss' (1 Thess. 5:26) in many cultures where the act of kissing carries serious moral overtones.

In sum, translation is aimed at preserving original authorial intent, so that today's hearers (or readers) can experience as much as possible the same cognitive and affective impact as the original hearers (or readers), and respond with the same existential commitment. Since no two languages are isomorphic, or conceptually equivalent, a literal translation of the biblical text would only render it unintelligible. On the other extreme, a translation which is too free stands the risk of either adding to or subtracting from the authorial intent. We need a *contextualization model that takes into account such things as the rich literary genres of the Bible, the content behind the message form, the reader's cultural biases and presuppositions, and so on.

The same principles apply when preaching the gospel in another language. Here missionaries should especially be concerned about the use of language since they are communicating truths of ultimate importance. The resources in the recipients' language should be explored from the outset, and utilized to explain and translate concepts such as 'God' or 'sin' in a way which conveys the biblical intent. Missionaries often make the mistake of looking for a theological word for sin in the culture, only to be disillusioned that it does not exist. Even in the Bible, sin is expressed through a variety of common, everyday words. Every language has words pertaining to wrongdoing, uncleanness, brokenness and the like, and these words can be a starting point for biblical teaching on sin. Since language is never static, as the gospel spreads through a culture, the semantic range of some of these words will be modified, or extended to include a biblical or theological dimension that was originally missing. One important implication of the Sapir-Whorf Hypothesis is not often appreciated: linguistic change does

bring about cultural change. But this is a process that takes time and requires a persevering intentionality.

The missionary moves in two, if not three, linguistic-cultural worlds – his or her own world, the biblical world, and the world of the recipients' language. These three worlds may be very different, but they are never totally mutually exclusive. The overlaps between them can be profitably utilized as a common platform for gospel proclamation, moving from the culturally familiar to the unfamiliar. Also, inherent in each world is a set of cultural presuppositions that the missionary will do well to explicate and understand, especially his or her own. Therefore, preaching and translation are best done in partnership with local Christian leaders. From the outset, missionaries should emphasize that people learn to read the biblical text for themselves, in their own language. Ultimately the coding of the gospel in any language, in a way that is linguistically accurate, communicatively appropriate, and biblically sound, is done best by the speakers of that language.

Bibliography

J. B. Carol (ed.), *Language, Thought, and Reality: Selected Writings of Benjamin Lee Whorf* (Cambridge: MIT Press, 1956); N. Chomsky, *Aspects of the Theory of Syntax* (Cambridge: MIT Press, 1965); R. Fowler, *Understanding Language: An Introduction to Linguistics* (London: Routledge and Kegan Paul, 1974); J. J. Gumperz and D. Hymes (eds.), *Directions in Sociolinguistics: The Ethnography of Communication* (New York: Holt, Rinehart and Winston, 1972); C. Kraft, *Christianity in Culture: A Study in Biblical Theologizing in Cross-Cultural Perspective* (Maryknoll: Orbis Books, rev. edn, 2005); W. Labov, *Sociolinguistic Patterns* (Philadelphia: University of Pennsylvania Press, 1973); J. M. Soskice, *Metaphor and Religious Language* (Oxford: Oxford University Press, 1985); P. van Buren, *The Edges of Language* (New York: Macmillan, 1972); K. Vanhoozer, '"But That's Your Interpretation": Realism, Reading, and Reformation', *Modern Reformation* 8:4, 1999, pp. 21–28; A. Walls, *The Missionary Movement in Christian History: Studies in the Transmission of Faith* (Maryknoll: Orbis Books, 1996).

HOW CHUANG CHUA

Latin American theology

The Iberian conquest of Latin America during the sixteenth century was carried on with a purported missionary intention for which there was an elaborate theology of mission. That theology followed Aquinas's reasoning, and justified war against the natives of the Americas as a means to subject them in order to evangelize them. Catholic Liberation theologian Gustavo Gutiérrez (b. 1928) has followed the long development of such theology in his book *Las Casas* (1993), which also records the theological controversy underlying the opposition of the Dominican missionary Bartolomé de las Casas (1474–1566) to the theology of war as a missionary method, that which prevailed in the end. The Catholic Church transplanted to the Americas limited itself to reproducing the scholastic theology brought from Spain and Portugal.

Protestant mission theology

The Protestant missionary presence began in the first decades of the nineteenth century. Protestant churches saw themselves as evangelizing communities in a territory where Catholicism was imposed by force but no true evangelization had taken place. Scottish missionary John Alexander Mackay (1889–1983) provided the first systematic theological effort with his classic book *The Other Spanish Christ* (1933), in which he developed a three-fold agenda. He analysed the spiritual condition of Latin America as a Christianized continent in which there was basically a docetic type of Christianity; he posed the question of the legitimacy of Protestant missionary activity in a Catholic continent; and he sought to find points of contact in the contemporary cultural situation of Latin America that could connect with the gospel that Protestantism was preaching. Mackay was influential in the meeting of the International Missionary Council in Jerusalem (1928), in which the legitimacy and validity of Protestant missionary work in Latin America was acknowledged by the ecumenical movement.

Towards a Latin American Protestant theology

The next theological effort involved Latin American Protestant thinkers from the older historic denominations. Significant among them were two Mexicans, Congregationalist Alberto Rembao (1865–1962) and Methodist Gonzalo Báez Camargo (1899–1983), both of whom developed a Latin American reading of the Protestant heritage. True to their evangelical origins they kept the vision of the continent as missionary territory where evangelism was of the essence of the life of the church, but they also emphasized the agenda of social transformation that was urgently required as evidence of the transformation that followed logically from the gospel and the Protestant experience. Rembao and Báez Camargo were also active and successful in a continuous dialogue with Latin American culture.

Social analysis of the church was applied critically to their own Methodist tradition by the three Latin Americans who entered into the global theological dialogue within the World Council of Churches (WCC): José Míguez Bonino from Argentina, the only Latin American Protestant observer present during the Vatican II Council; Emilio Castro from Uruguay who became director of the Commission on World Mission and Evangelism of the WCC; and Mortimer Arias, a bishop of the Methodist Church in Bolivia. They represent a generation of thinkers rooted in the Wesleyan theology of their church, trained in Europe and the United States and conversant with American and European theologies, especially the work of Karl Barth. These theologians kept their reflection closely related to their participation in the daily life of their churches.

A new generation of Latin American theologians came to the fore in the 1960s in the wake of the social tensions generated by the Cuban revolution (1959) and its aftermath. Social awareness and a dialogue with Moltmann, Bonhoeffer, Mannheim, Marcuse and Marx characterized the thought of Brazilian Presbyterian Rubem Alves (b. 1933) who published *A Theology of Human Hope* in 1969. In both method and subjects of study, Alves and other Protestants involved in the 'Church and Society Movement' (in Spanish ISAL) were an antecedent of liberation theologies that were developing within Catholicism, but they progressively detached themselves from the Protestant churches and their conviction that evangelism is the essence of the mission of the church. Alves rather emphasized the role of religion in relation to the social struggles, in which theology would be an 'instrument for liberation' rather than 'opiate for the people'. This theological method included the use of Marxist analysis to understand social dynamics as well as the role of the church; and a new reading of biblical themes such as liberation and hope.

Catholic liberation theologies

The social turbulence of the 1960s was also the setting for the development of liberation theologies, the first original theological reflection within Catholicism in Latin America. The movement involved a new generation of priests and foreign missionaries who, having embarked in pastoral work among the poor, became social activists on their behalf. They were influential in the Latin American Conference of Bishops of Medellín (Colombia, 1968) in which officially the church decided to take 'an option for the poor', a new social and political alignment acknowledging that traditionally the church had been allied to the rich and powerful, the military and authoritarian governments. For Gustavo Gutiérrez, whose theological work was recognized in Medellín and entered in the official message of the conference, the social struggles of those days were the 'irruption of the poor in history' who wanted to become actors of their own social and political liberation. Thus, from its experience of immersion among the poor, the church was learning to read the word of God and historical events with the eyes of the poor. The Christian duty was to cooperate with political projects aimed at the destruction of that old order built during centuries of dependence and oppression and now in its capitalistic phase. The way ahead was a form of liberation that would come by the use of Marxist social analysis and the organization of people for revolution. The presupposition was the Marxist tenet that history moves towards socialism. Revolution was the way to liberation, and Christians were called to take part in that revolution. For Gutiérrez, liberation theology was to be defined as the reflection of Christians on this new historical praxis, in light of God's word. This theology represented a new understanding of the being, the message and the pastoral work of the church.

Towards an evangelical theology of holistic mission

The decade of the 1960s was also a time of intensive evangelistic work in the more conservative sector of Latin American Protestantism that had developed significantly after the Second World War. In this sector, evangelistic zeal was not always accompanied by social sensitivity and contextual awareness. A step ahead came from Argentinean missionary and evangelist R. Kenneth Strachan, who represented a self-critical reflection. His book *The Inescapable Calling* (1968) is an effort to forge a theology of mission that is rooted in evangelical conviction and practice but attentive to the great amount of biblical and theological work on mission theology coming from the International Missionary Council and the WCC. Best known as the leader and thinker of the movement 'Evangelism in Depth' that had a strong influence among evangelicals around the world in the 1960s and 1970s, Strachan contextualized the ideas of Roland Allen and Lesslie Newbigin and insisted that in order to accomplish its mission, the divided Protestantism in Latin America needed a renewal of ecclesiology that would be open to the Holy Spirit, paying more attention to the unity of the church and social awareness. The ideas of Allen were also influential in the development of a Pentecostal missiology by Melvin Hodges on the basis of his missionary experience in Latin America.

A new generation of evangelical thinkers gathered in the Latin American Theological Fraternity that was founded in 1970. It was formed by evangelicals active in evangelism and involved in the search for answers to the questions of a theology of mission within the Latin American context. They found unacceptable the ecumenical theology shaped by a mood that reflected the uncertainties and the fatigue of a declining Protestantism in Europe as well as Catholic liberation theology, heavily dependant on the assumption that Latin America was 'a Christian continent'. Evangelical theologians became engaged in the development of a *contextual theology, whose 'aim was to offer a new open-ended reading of Scripture with a hermeneutic in which the biblical text and the historical situation become mutually engaged in a dialogue whose purpose is to place the Church under the Lordship of Jesus Christ in its particular context' (C. R. Padilla, 'Biblical Foundations: A Latin American Study', *Evangelical Review of Theology* 7, p. 86).

Hermeneutics became a key field for debate because liberation theologies reflected the biblical renewal within Catholicism after Vatican II. Fresh reading of the Bible within the social crisis of the 1960s in Latin America brought the rediscovery of some aspects of the biblical message that had remained obscure, unknown or even purposefully forgotten. It became necessary to acknowledge that themes such as justice, poverty (see *Poor), oppression and liberation are not accidental departures from the great lines of biblical teaching. They are teachings which cannot be separated from the core of God's self revelation through Jesus Christ, intrinsic to other themes such as revelation, relationship with God, repentance and the nature of Christian life. Understanding of every point of biblical teaching requires adequate regard to the wholeness of the message. As the *exodus became a favoured motif for liberation theologies, the method of social analysis used to understand the social condition of Latin America was also used to understand the biblical story of the exodus as an historical event. The contention of evangelical theologians was that to adopt a Marxist reading of the exodus is to push the biblical view into the mould of the Marxist version of the Enlightenment. The Bible had to be read on its own terms and not forced into an ideological straitjacket.

Orlando Costas, C. René Padilla and Samuel Escobar made significant theological contributions to the 1974 Lausanne Congress of Evangelism and the covenant that it issued. The Lausanne movement after 1974 came to accept that there is a new global missionary situation which includes growing and vigorous churches in the Two-Thirds World. This made possible a new reading of Scripture as a communal exercise involving the multicultural and international fellowship of believers around the planet. Latin American evangelicals also contributed to the discussions about 'Gospel and Culture' in the 1978 conference sponsored by the Lausanne movement in Willowbank. An evangelical consensus emerged with the conviction that there was an urgent need to develop a fresh reading of the Bible as a dynamic interplay between the text and the interpreters. This was incorporated in the *Willowbank Report* (<http://www.lausanne.org/Brix?pageID=14322>), which sets an agenda for evangelical mission theology: 'Today's readers cannot come to the text in a personal vacuum, and should not try to ... As we address Scripture, Scripture addresses us. We find that our culturally conditioned presuppositions are being challenged and our questions corrected. In fact, we are compelled to reformulate our previous questions and to ask fresh ones. So the living interaction proceeds.'

A missiological Christology

The course followed by evangelical theological reflection in Latin America may be summarized as the development of a missiological *Christology, starting with the proposal of Mackay in *The Other Spanish Christ*. In this evangelical exploration a unique distinctive that has been constantly clarified and stressed is its evangelistic thrust: 'Theology enables evangelization to transmit the faith with integrity by clarifying and organizing its content, analyzing its context and critically evaluating its communication. Evangelization enables theology to be an effective servant of the faith by relating its message to the deepest spiritual needs of humankind' (O. E. Costas, *Liberating News: A Theology of Contextual Evangelization*, p. 1). In fact the Latin American Congresses of Evangelism (CLADE) have been the platform for theological reflection, from the first in Bogotá (1969), to the fourth in Quito (2000). This emphasis makes evangelical theologizing different from the forms of Protestant theology that stem from churches that are not concerned with evangelization and from the Catholic approach in which the sacramental presence of the Roman Catholic Church in Latin America is taken as the basis for assuming that the population is already Christian. Evangelical theology has also developed a consistent clarification and debate against the theological assumptions – not always explicit – of *managerial missiology.

Historian and theologian Justo L. González used a study of the Johannine material in the NT as a way of calling evangelicals to become aware of the kind of docetic Christology into which they had fallen, that was proving sterile, especially in relation to social ethics. It was an effort to develop a social ethics that would use a Christological paradigm as a foundation, and a contextual interpretation of Christology as a way to figure out the nature and mission of the church. González urged evangelicals to reject the view that sees mission as no more than that of saving souls for a future life, as docetic; equally they should reject the view of those who imagine that their action in society and in history is going to establish the kingdom of God, since this can be seen as ebionite. He deepened the analysis of Christological themes, working from the concerns of the Hispanic context in the United States, and he concludes, 'In the last analysis, what docetism denied was not only the reality of the incarnation and the suffering of Jesus but the very nature of a God whose greatest victory is achieved through suffering and whose clearest revelation is in the cross' (*Mañana Christian Theology from a Hispanic Perspective*, p. 143). Docetism among evangelicals could be traced back to the negative effect of post-Second World War independent missionaries from North America, who were heavily influenced by dispensationalism, the mentality of the Cold War with its suspicion about social change, and the delayed effects of the liberal-fundamentalist debates.

The Latin American missionary involvement in other parts of the world has brought a need to rediscover and expound the concrete actions of Jesus as they were reported by the evangelists so that they may be grasped, contemplated and understood as the shaping patterns for contemporary discipleship and missionary activity, a challenging task that Mortimer Arias describes as recovering 'the subversive memory of Jesus' for evangelization (*Announcing the Reign of God*, p. 12). This theological task goes to the wealth of biblical data that lies behind the creedal systematizations in which 'the Christian message was cast into philosophical categories, and the historical dimension of revelation was completely overshadowed by dogma' (C. R. Padilla and M. L. Branson, *Conflict and Context: Hermeneutics in the Americas*, p. 81). Padilla's work may be appreciated in his book *Mission Between the*

Times (1985). Emilio A. Núñez acknowledges the fact that Latin American evangelicals received an Anglo-Saxon Christology that was the result of the liberal-fundamentalist debate: 'We were presented with a divine-human Christ in the theological formula; but in practice he was far removed from the stage of this world, aloof to our social problems' (*Liberation Theology*, p. 236). Costas chose Jesus' pattern of a missionary effort starting from Galilee, from the margins, as a significant pattern for the Hispanic minorities in the USA and for Latin Americans at a global level. Valdir Steuernagel has shown the renewed relevance of historical models of missionary obedience patterned after Jesus.

A Christological discernment
The significant growth of *Pentecostalism has brought the work of the *Holy Spirit and the relationship of Word and Spirit to the agenda of evangelical theology. Pentecostal theologians Norberto Saracco from Argentina and Ricardo Gondim from Brazil are among those that have worked at articulating a self-critical reflection that looks to Christology as the basis for discernment in evaluating the Pentecostal experience. The memory of Jesus and the centrality of the kingdom of God in his teachings are to enrich the traditional evangelical soteriology of popular Protestantism. They will also provide guidelines for the evangelistic and pastoral tasks of the church as well as for the social and political participation of believers at a time of social transitions. At the beginning of the twenty-first century in Latin America, postmodern culture and the rise of so-called post-denominational megachurches pose the question of how the work of the Spirit is to be distinguished from what could be a manipulative purely human enterprise. Latin American evangelical thinkers continue their theological task with a strong Christological foundation and frame. What comes from the Spirit will transform human lives and create living communities, modelling them after the pattern of Christ.

See also LIBERATION.

Bibliography
M. Arias, *Announcing the Reign of God. Evangelization and the Subversive Memory of Jesus* (Philadelphia: Fortress Press, 1984);

M. Arias and A. Johnson, *The Great Commission: Biblical Models for Evangelism* (Nashville: Abingdon Press, 1992); E. Castro, *Amidst Revolution* (Belfast: Christian Journals Limited, 1975); O. E. Costas, *Theology of the Crossroads in Contemporary Latin America* (Amsterdam: Rodopi, 1976); O. E. Costas, *Liberating News: A Theology of Contextual Evangelization* (Grand Rapids: Eerdmans, 1989); S. Escobar, *Changing Tides: Latin America and World Mission Today* (Maryknoll: Orbis Books, 2003); J. L. González, *Mañana Christian Theology from a Hispanic Perspective* (Nashville: Abingdon Press, 1990); G. Gutiérrez, 'The Irruption of the Poor in Latin America', in S. Torres and J. Eagleson (eds.), *The Challenge of Basic Christian Communities* (Maryknoll: Orbis Books, 1982); G. Gutiérrez, *Las Casas: In Search of the Poor of Jesus Christ* (Maryknoll: Orbis Books, 1992); J. Míguez, *Doing Theology in a Revolutionary Situation* (Philadelphia: Fortress Press, 1975); J. Míguez, *Towards a Christian Political Ethics* (London: SCM Press, 1983); J. Míguez, *Faces of Latin American Protestantism* (Grand Rapids: Eerdmans, 1997); E. A. Núñez, *Liberation Theology* (Chicago: Moody Press, 1985); C. R. Padilla, *Mission Between the Times: Essays on the Kingdom* (Grand Rapids: Eerdmans, 1985); C. R. Padilla and M. L. Branson (eds.), *Conflict and Context: Hermeneutics in the Americas* (Grand Rapids: Eerdmans, 1986); D. Schipani (ed.), *Freedom and Discipleship* (Maryknoll: Orbis Books, 1989); V. Steuernagel, 'The Theology of Mission in Relation to Social Responsibility within the Lausanne Movement', PhD dissertation (Chicago: Lutheran School of Theology, 1988).

S. ESCOBAR

Liberation

The word 'liberation' is one of the ways by which Scripture refers to the mighty acts of God to free his people from every dimension of oppression. It begins with the *exodus, through which God liberated the people of Israel from exploitation and oppression, brought them into a new relationship with himself, and gave them the Promised Land in faithful fulfilment of his covenant with the patriarchs.

The exodus was so significant for Israel, and for the early church, that it became paradigmatic for God's saving action throughout history. Thus, for example, the return from exile (Isa. 40) and the coming of the Messiah in Luke (ch. 1) are described in terms evocative of the exodus.

Theologies of liberation which emerged from *Latin America in the 1960s and 70s, (predominantly among Roman Catholic progressive theologians, but also among Protestants and evangelicals) drew inspiration from the exodus story, and concluded that the God of the Bible is a God of justice who has a 'preferential option for the poor'.

The 'foundational experience' of Latin America

Liberation theologies in Latin America emerged from the 'foundational experience' of inhumane and demeaning poverty which is the result of centuries of institutionalized injustice. In the daily experience of that reality, progressive Catholicism (CELAM 1968 and the Basic Ecclesial Communities) and Protestantism (the movement *Iglesia y Sociedad en Amèrica Latina, ISAL [Church and Society in Latin America]*), faced an agonizing experience of self-criticism in the decade of the 1960s. They discovered that their churches had become the ideological allies of foreign and national forces; they had supported the political and social 'status quo', and they had failed to take the side of the poor against forces which created and sustained dependence, inequality and injustice for the vast majority. But this traumatic experience created the need for a post-*colonial, politically engaged understanding of the Christian gospel, committed to a praxis of social transformation with those for whom poverty meant death.

Liberation theologians taught that theology is always done in a historical context, from a social location, and in response to issues and challenges coming from that context. Thus, they asked: 'what is the meaning of faith in a context of extreme poverty, political oppression, and economic injustice?' and concluded that traditional Roman Catholic and Protestant theologies did not answer or even address those issues. Accordingly, liberation theologians developed a new way of doing theology in which social sciences became one of the main tools to articulate their thinking. What was needed was an 'orthopraxis', which would become a new way of doing theology, beginning with a commitment to change the context. Theology became a second step, a reflection on praxis in the light of God's word. This led also to a new way of being church, built by the poor and with the poor, from the ground up rather than as the traditional hierarchical 'top-down' approach.

Similar developments emerged in other contexts in which other kinds of oppression were the starting point. In the USA, for example, *racial* and *gender* discriminations gave rise to significant searches for liberation and a rich theological reflection. The methodology of liberation theology has established itself as a widely accepted approach to any context of oppression.

Finding a solution

Everyone agrees that the millions in poverty must be set free from their misery. The controversial question is *how* to achieve it. Historically, there have been many socio-economic models supported by their legitimating theologies and ideologies. In Latin America during the 60s and 70s, inspired by the Cuban revolution, many sought revolution as a way of solving the abysmal social differences and injustices. Some liberation theologians, in concrete situations, opted for this approach.

Today, armed revolutions are no longer an option (at least for the poor) and the moral force of non-violent resistance by millions of people in all the world (for example, demonstrations during the meetings of the G8) has gained some significant ground in the search for a more just and human world in which there is room for everybody. (The ONE movement, the Millennium Challenge, and the Micah Challenge are instances of these determined efforts to transform the world.)

Others proposed welfare reforms to the present socio-economic structures. But such measures have had no lasting results. Many of Latin America's governments and ruling elites in recent years have accepted the neoliberalism of free-market economics; they have submitted to World Bank and IMF-imposed limits on social spending, privatized state enterprises, and encouraged foreign investment. Many analysts see this as having created an increasing gap between rich and poor, a decline in the middle classes, and growing misery for the majority. However, in recent years countries like Brazil are looking for a combination of free-market economics (which is impossible to avoid in a globalized economy) with a socialized economy that takes seriously its responsibility towards the disenfranchised.

Evangelical responses

In general, evangelicals in Latin America rejected liberation theology as unbiblical. Others welcomed it as a radical way of affirming that 'faith without works is dead'. In general, however, evangelicals maintained a conservative political attitude towards social realities. As one scholar said: 'Liberation theologians opted for the poor, but the poor opted for Pentecostalism.' Accordingly, a world-denying theology prevented many from responding to the crisis that the continent suffered during those traumatic decades. Many remained unrelated and indifferent to social realities, and concentrated on the verbal communication of a reduced, spiritualized version of the gospel. Some did make efforts to alleviate the miseries of the poor, but often these were paternalistic and charity-based approaches which worked *for* the poor but not *with* the poor.

Most conservative evangelicals opted for a model of mission which seeks to convert and transform individuals who will, in turn, transform society. This continues to be a preferred model for many. Yet, in spite of explosive evangelical growth, extreme poverty, corruption, violence and drug trafficking, far from being reduced, have increased dramatically in Latin America. It seems that the growing presence of evangelicals has left these terrible realities largely untouched.

Some evangelicals, conscious of their social influence due to their growing numbers, even entered into politics, attempting to bring Christ to the centres of power. But for some, their naivety, the corrupting influence of power, and ethical compromises marred their testimony and good reputation. (Notable negative examples in the 1980s and 1990s are the two 'evangelical' presidents of Guatemala, the role of evangelical pastors in Chile during the days of Pinochet, the manipulation of the evangelicals' vote for Fujimori in

Peru, and the corruption of many pastors and leaders who were members of the Brazilian Constitutional Assembly in 1986.)

A middle-ground evangelical position came to be represented by the biblical-theological and *missiological* reflection under the general rubric of *misión integral* (integrated or *holistic mission), a theology that has been pioneered by the Latin American Theological Fraternity. This theology takes seriously the socio-economic and political challenges of Latin America and attempts to transform churches and communities in conformity to the values and principles of God's kingdom. Related to this, and the Lausanne movement, there has been an increase in holistic mission projects and many forms of service to the poor and the struggle for justice.

The contemporary challenge for liberation

We live in an age full of tensions and contradictions; of cruel fears and renewed hopes; of extreme riches in the hands of very few, and appalling misery shared by millions; of heartless corporate greed, and the human solidarity of forgotten communities; of a dominant ideology that values profit over people; and the stubborn insistence of multitudes for a world free of all forms of terror, violence and misery. In her book *L'Horreur Économique*, Viviane Forrester describes 'the brutal mutation that our civilization is suffering: from exploitation to exclusion and from exclusion to elimination' (p. 20, Spanish edition). It is a time in which human beings are valued merely in terms of profit, and as a result feel disempowered by alienating and dehumanizing forces.

This era, characterized especially by economic *globalization, confronts the church with unavoidable questions. What will it mean to be the church in a world in which profit is much more important than people? How can the church give an effective counter-testimony of God's love, rather than give blessing and legitimization (often by its silence) to political leaders who work against the values of the kingdom? How can the church act in a world where the cure for AIDS is within our economic reach and yet, in the rich nations, politicians use their economic resources in militaristic projects, and the population spends millions on diets, gyms for body culture, cosmetics and junk food? What

biblically responsible actions should characterize the churches of rich contexts in which consumerism, environmental pollution and self-interest govern their policies? Liberation is not just for the disenfranchised; it also offers deliverance for those who are so poor that they have nothing except their money.

The contemporary face of evangelical liberation

In recent years there has been an evangelical search for a theology of mission which engages with this context. Its starting point is to face the challenges of the concrete realities of its context, wherever injustice and oppression prevail. An evangelical holistic theology insists on having its reference point in the authority of God's revelation in the Scriptures and in Christ. Therefore, it affirms the lordship of Jesus Christ over every dimension of life in the created order (Matt. 28:16–20; Eph. 1:20–23). It elevates the supreme dignity of *all human beings* due to their creation in the image of God (Gen. 1:28; Ps. 8). It celebrates the victory of Christ over all evil and demonic structures (Col. 1:15–20). It rejoices in his resurrection and ascension in which Jesus was declared Lord of everything and head of the new humanity and all creation (Eph. 1:10). He is the maker of reconciliation and peace. He brings *shalom* to his creation, through us (Eph. 2:11–22; 2 Cor. 5).

These truths, universal in scope, point to a comprehensive salvation by which God purposes to transform and liberate every dimension of life and reality. Therefore, the church, as a community of disciples of Christ, takes up the cross and fulfils God's liberating mission in at least three main ways:

(1) *By fulfilling its calling as the first fruits of God's new humanity in Christ* (Eph. 2:11–22; 4:13–15, 23–24) and living a lifestyle of self-sacrificial love and service to others (Matt. 20:25–28; John 13:12–17; Eph. 5:1–2, 21). The church is God's new society marked by mutual love and service (Eph. 5:1–2). But it will be very difficult for the church to respond to Jesus' call to obedient discipleship today if it becomes obsessed with its own well-being, numerical growth and, in some cases, even survival.

(2) *By developing a comprehensive code of ethics* that works out in tangible justice for all human life regardless of colour, nationality or

religion and is based on the radical values of God's kingdom (*justice, joy and shalom,* Matt. 6:33; Rom. 14:17). This is much more than personal ethics. It will include a serious commitment to protect God's creation; a practical compassion for strangers and refugees that expresses itself in a love that welcomes (*philoxenia*) and cares in concrete and tangible ways for the 'other' (Matt. 25:31–46); a sacrificial ministry of reconciliation which recreates relationships with God (2 Cor. 5:18–19), with our enemies (Matt. 5:38–48; Eph. 2:11–22), and with creation (Col. 1:19–20).

(3) *By adopting a prophetic role and critique in relation to its social and political context.* This will require leaders to be well informed in their reading of social reality; to be aware of the many ways in which societies are manipulated by media and how consent is manufactured by those who control news; to be liberated from ideologies so that they may be free to act responsibly as moral conscience, the salt of the earth and the light of the world.

See also ETHICS, JUSTICE, POOR/ POVERTY.

Bibliography
M. Arias, *Announcing the Reign of God: Evangelization and the Subversive Memory of Jesus* (Philadelphia: Fortress Press, 1984); O. E. Costas, *Liberating News: A Theology of Contextual Evangelization* (Grand Rapids: Eerdmans, 1989); I. Ellacurìa and J. Sobrino, *Mysterium Liberationis* (Maryknoll: Orbis Books, 1993); S. Escobar, *Liberation Themes in Reformational Perspective* (Sioux Center: Dordt College Press, 1989); V. Forrester, *The Economic Horror* (Cambridge: Polity Press; Blackwell, 1999); E. Galeano, *The Open Veins of Latin America* (New York: Review Press, 1973); G. Gutiérrez, *A Theology of Liberation* (Maryknoll: Orbis Books, rev. edn, 1988); J. Míguez, *Doing Theology in a Revolutionary Situation* (Philadelphia: Fortress, 1975); J. P. Miranda, *Marx and the Bible* (Maryknoll: Orbis Books, 1974); C. R. Padilla (ed.), *The New Face of Evangelicalism* (Downers Grove: InterVarsity Press, 1976); C. R. Padilla and T. Yamamori (eds.), *Serving With the Poor in Latin America* (Monrovia: MARC, 1997); J. E. Stiglitz, *Globalization and its Discontents* (New York: Norton, 2002).

M. AVILA

Liturgy

Origins
'Liturgy' derives from the Greek noun *leitourgia,* which had a background in classical times of service to the state, but came in NT times to mean 'service' in both a social and a religious sense. Thus Epaphroditus (Phil. 2:30) completes a 'service' to Paul, but the verb *leitourgountes* in Acts 13:2 clearly implies a form of group worship activity. In history the term has come to mean a fixed form or order of worship, often characterizing a particular church, as in phrases like 'the Anglican liturgy'.

The origins of liturgy lie in a combination of God's *revelation and human psychology. In the Pentateuch, God gives the most detailed instructions about the ritual of the sacrificial system. Clearly, the NT church is delivered from both the OT system, and also the legalism which readily attached to it. But Christians had rites (or ordinances) to perform, not least baptism and the Lord's Supper; they had songs to sing or poems to recite, both from the inherited psalter and from their own composition; they had forms of greeting and blessing each other, of praising and petitioning God, and of affirming their credal convictions. They had teaching roles which were fulfilled in part by repeating the teachings of Jesus. They had an immediate rhythm of treating the first day of the week as the time for meeting, and, deriving from Judaism, they began to develop a sense of annual cycles as well as weekly ones. In due course, and perhaps in one generation, the psychological security given by repetition meant that worship developed an 'order'. It is the tracing of that 'order' that we call 'liturgy'.

However, the use of the term should not be interpreted as necessarily meaning a wholly pre-scribed (literally 'written in advance') order. Its very apostolic and post-apostolic origins suggest considerable liberty retained within it. A rigid, inflexible development, such as has sometimes occurred, is neither necessary, nor desirable, nor integral to the use of the term. Thus, over the years, orders of worship which include options of prayers on the one hand or room for extemporary provision on the other, have appeared in different denominations across the globe – but are still appropriately called liturgies. Even those who often have appeared most distrustful of the alleged straitjacketing of worship in written forms have their own settled (but often undeclared) orders of Sunday worship, with recognized patterns of use for songs and hymnody, and familiar acclamatory and responsive words.

Reasons for liturgy

Opposition to fixed forms has sprung from both a fear of formalism and a concern lest there be a quenching of the Spirit, although the problem may well lie in the abuse of liturgy rather than in the liturgy itself. Defendants of fixed liturgies justify them in the following ways:

- they provide for a known, standard, doctrinal content which embraces the whole gospel, not allowing it to shrink or become diluted;
- they provide for full congregational participation;
- they guarantee some objectivity in the choice of the contents of worship; thus, for instance, ensuring that confession is included, and the needs of the nation and the world are included in prayer;
- they help people to know where they are in the movement of the worship;
- they focus worshippers on God rather than on the worship leader;
- they become memorable and thus impact people's lives outside of worship times;
- they give the people of God a life-changing grasp of both doctrine and ethics, so that through the liturgy their faith is both formed and informed.

Liturgy and mission

The relation of liturgy to mission emerges from this analysis. The key question is: to what extent is worship an *evangelistic opportunity? If Christian corporate worship is first a gathering of *believers*, its liturgy will have an overtly credal basis and content, which may not be seen as appropriate for outsiders. For this reason in Western post-Christian society many congregations drop a formal liturgical structure in favour of what is seen as a more enticing quality to their worship. This may not be without results if and when it is of genuinely high quality and irresistible. Yet, in the light of the NT, providing a lively and relevant worship experience is not of itself a direct strategy for mission. Thus the 'evangelistic service', or the 'seeker service', if they take no credal standpoint as agreed at the outset, are untypical of Christian liturgy. They may be justified as having a particular use in particular contexts, but they can never provide a liturgical norm. In short, liturgy cannot be seen as a direct act of evangelistic mission, and the primary purpose of worship remains to build up believers corporately and individually in their relationship with God.

The principles behind this assertion are seen in 1 Corinthians 14 (for all that the assembly in Corinth may still lack some 'decency and good order' [v. 40]!). The rigorous criteria Paul is setting out relate to how the conduct of worship may 'build up' the body of Christ. The primary point is how they may truly 'hear' each other, and benefit by hearing. The possible effect upon an unbeliever provides an additional argument, but it is clearly secondary in importance. Primarily, believers have to follow their distinctive agenda, whether or not unbelievers show up. If the worship is truly 'Spirit-filled' and glorifies God, unbelievers may be convicted whether there is a liturgy or not. Paul's main concern is for good order, so that God's word may be heard. Underneath the principles of 1 Corinthians 14 there is, no doubt, also the Pauline requirement that the words which formed prayer, praise and exhortation should express true doctrine, forming believers in their faith, and that has guided the compilers of liturgy (including hymn books) down the generations.

Here then is the indirect relationship to the church's mission. The church gathers to 'form' God's people for their mission. That mission will include not only a personal *discipleship (with a readiness for witness), but also service to the community, concern for the worldwide church, transformation of society's structures, and stewardship of the environment. And, once the all-inclusive nature of mission has been grasped, then this mission will in turn impact the liturgy. The liturgy will indeed have a Christian doctrinal core, but if it merely expresses credal correctness, without reference to the context of the people and their calling to mission, then it becomes a kind of Gnosticism.

To be rooted in the lives of Christians, worship will be *culturally adapted to the particular contexts: expressed in the language and ceremonial of the people, incorporating existing customs (and music and architecture) where they are not inimical to the gospel. This is sometimes characterized as following an '*incarnational principle' and gives rise to contextual liturgies. The application of this is obvious. For the convert (or prospective convert) the offence of the cross should be the only offence; to have to change cultures over and above what is distinctive to being Christian is indeed an obstacle none should be expected to face. People should be able to worship in forms and words that are culturally resonant.

But, rightly conducted and understood, liturgy is the point where the Christian faith of the last 2,000 years penetrates the lives of worshippers in ways that bring them into relevant discipleship. The liturgy will ideally include news and information, prayer, giving, sharing of needs, organizing care (cf. Acts 6:1–6), commissioning of people for tasks, and a host of other ways of addressing the church's mission. This in turn means that it cannot be simply read from an inherited book, and the need of skilled leadership of a dynamic congregational event is correspondingly increased. Liturgy should never become a polished art form, so detached from life outside that even the most profound words of obedience, self-sacrifice and discipleship can enter the ear or run off the tongue without apparently touching the heart, emotions or will. In both the *givenness* of received forms, and the art of *relating* them to the present church and world, the fuel is there, ready to blaze when the fire of the Spirit ignites it. And, ideally, the liturgy of corporate worship will impact not only individual discipleship but also the corporate mission of the people as they gather in order to be sent out.

See also SACRAMENT, WORSHIP.

Bibliography

A. Chupungco, *Liturgical Inculturation: Sacramentals, Religiosity, Catechesis* (Collegeville: Liturgical Press, 1992); M. Earey

and C. Headley, *Mission and Liturgical Worship* (Cambridge: Worship Series 170, Grove, 2002); A. Kreider, *Worship and Evangelism in Pre-Christendom* (Cambridge: Acuin/GROW Joint Liturgical Studies 32, Grove, 1995); T. Stratford, *Liturgy and Urban Mission* (Cambridge: Worship Series, 173, Grove, 2002).

C. O. BUCHANAN

Love

'*The first and greatest commandment.*' Jesus' statement of the essence of OT law and of the ethical ideals he has set for his own followers is recorded by Matthew, Mark and Luke, and summarized in one word: 'love' (Matt. 22:37; Mark 12:30–31; Luke 10:27). Love for God and neighbour is the essence of the new lifestyle of the kingdom, the *ethic of Jesus. In Paul's words, it is 'the fulfilment of the law' (Rom. 13:8–10).

The command to love is firmly rooted in the OT in the person and character of the God of love and grace (Deut. 6:5; 10:12; Lev. 19:18; Josh. 22:5). Time and again God communicated to his people his 'grace-love', love that gives in spite of the condition or reaction of those loved. Time and again the people rejected God's offer of forgiveness and restoration, and persisted in their idolatry and godlessness. God knew the reality of rejected love, but never stopped loving, even in times in which that love was expressed in terms of judgment and punishment.

God's love in action challenges his people to conform their lives to his standard, to love him in return, and to love their neighbours. To love God implies obedience to his commands, wholehearted service, and perseverance in his ways. This love is much deeper than any feeling and involves the commitment of the whole person – mind, soul, will, time, dedication, action and sacrifice – to please the one who is loved. Love for God and love for one's neighbour as a concrete expression of that love permeate OT teaching, and apparently were already linked in Jewish ethical reflection in Jesus' day (Luke 10:27).

Love is the outworking of the relationship of the believer with the Triune God. When we respond to God's grace with faith and love, we come in touch with the heart of the Father who 'so loved the world that he gave his one and only Son ... to save the world through him' (John 3:16–17; 1 John 4:7–21; Rom. 5:8). Here we begin to comprehend the significance of true love, love that does not depend on the loveliness of the ones loved, love that can never be earned or deserved, love that is willing to sacrifice its own rights for the good of others, love that suffers for the benefit of the one loved. In response to God's love, the Christian church loves and demonstrates that love in commitment to serve God and to cooperate in God's great redemptive project for the world, more concerned for God's glory than with simply enjoying the benefits of personal salvation (Eph. 1).

In the person of Jesus Christ, Christians find the supreme example and model of self-sacrificing, redeeming love (Mark 10:45; 1 John 3:16). Jesus gave a practical demonstration of love in action as humble service to others (John 13:1–35), explained his approaching betrayal and his self-sacrifice in death for their sake, and gave his followers his 'new command': to model his love for them in their relationship (13:34). The quality of newness in this mutual love that Jesus enjoins on the fledgling Christian community is found in his model, expressed in the words 'as I have loved you' – a love that holds nothing back as it gives of itself to bring positive good to others. This also became an important part of Christian discipleship and teaching (1 John 4:19–21; 2 Cor. 8:9), and is the outstanding characteristic of the Christian community (John 13:35).

For Jesus, the principal contender for a person's love and loyalty, capable of usurping God's place as the object of love, is material wealth, mammon (Matt. 6:19–24). Love for God and the love of material wealth are mutually exclusive.

Paul, like Jesus (John 14 – 16), attributes the capacity for love and obedience in the life of the Christian to the presence and activity of the Holy Spirit (Rom. 5:5; Gal. 5:22; cf. Col. 3:12–14). It is clear that only on the basis of conversion, new life in Christ, and the presence of the Spirit is a person able to follow Jesus' example and live out a life of love. Living and serving in love are never considered a means of salvation nor of merit with God, nor a motive for boasting. Rather, they are the result of a relationship with the Triune God.

'The greatest commandment' and the great commission. The implications of the biblical teaching on love for Christian ethics are often pointed out, but it is necessary to go one step further and see the implications of the practice of love in the mission of the church.

Matthew's 'great commission' (Matt. 28:18–20) has frequently been cited as the primary call to the church to become involved in mission, often with emphasis on the 'go' to the neglect of the principal mandate, 'make disciples'. The missionary task could be defined as 'making *disciples who make disciples', and calls every follower of Jesus Christ to serve in a worldwide movement that cooperates with God in the realization of God's purpose for the world. This process begins with the proclamation of the gospel and evangelization ('baptizing them...') and includes instruction, mentoring or apprenticeship ('teaching them to obey...'). The goal of the missionary responsibility of the church is 'incarnational discipleship' [Stassen and Gushee, p. 58], the formation of disciples who are committed to live out everything that Jesus had instructed his first disciples as summarized in 'the first and greatest commandment': to love God and love their neighbours, to incarnate that love in humbly sharing the good news of the kingdom and serving people in their need for material sustenance, for justice, for hope, for peace..., and in the formation of other disciples in the obedience of love.

In his parable of the good Samaritan (Luke 10:25–37), Jesus illustrated the meaning of grace, love and compassion for one's neighbour. Love does not ask 'Who is my neighbour?' but rather 'Who needs me to be a good neighbour?' Who needs to hear the liberating news of the gospel? Who is in need of forgiveness? Who is suffering from the lack of food? Who is suffering the injustice of the system? Who needs our help? What can I do? This is what Micah refers to as 'to act justly and to love mercy...' (Mic. 6:8).

The Christian mission finds its *motivation* in God's love revealed in his great redemptive plan for the world and the love revealed by Christ in his sacrificial death and his resurrection (2 Cor. 5:14). As the church shares God's perspective on a lost world, and experiences salvation, reconciliation and restoration in Christ, it is called to become

God's agent of reconciliation, his ambassadors in an alien society (2 Cor. 5:11 – 6:2).

The love of Christ is the *model* for the Christian mission: Christ's disciples are sent out as he was sent by the Father (John 20:21), to incarnate the whole gospel, to meet human needs (salvation, healing, hope, justice), and to communicate God's love to a suffering world, even to the point of death. His concern for people, his non-judgmental acceptance of those rejected by society, his gracious concern for rich and poor – these qualities of Christ's love should characterize his representatives.

The *method* of Christian mission is the expression of love, as it unites evangelization and social action, meeting spiritual need and alleviating physical suffering. Mission encompasses both, for the church is sent as Jesus was sent (Luke 4:18): to preach good news to the poor, to bring deliverance and freedom, to heal – to love as Jesus loved. As some missionaries from Latin America to the people of Muslim countries have discovered, mission does not depend on being free to conduct an evangelistic crusade in the largest stadium in town; mission is sharing the gospel of God's love in humble, sacrificial service to the sick, the handicapped, the poor and the marginalized, in Jesus' name. Love, then, becomes the *motivation*, the *model* and the *method* of the holistic, integral mission of the church.

See also CHRIST, HOLISTIC MISSION, INCARNATION.

C. DE PADILLA

Magic

Magic is the manipulation of supernatural powers for one's own perceived good. While the precise rituals and forms vary from culture to culture, what remains uniform is an underlying belief in spirits (often fear of spirits) and the conviction that they can be harnessed and controlled.

A missiological analysis of magic involves three perspectives: the phenomenological (how magic finds expression in culture), the functional (how it operates in culture), and the biblical (how Scripture addresses magic).

J. Dudley Woodberry specifies six ways in which magic finds expression in culture – illustrating with folk Islamic practices. There are *powers* (beings, such as demons or jinn; or forces such as mana). There are *power people* (imams and shamans) and *power objects* (charms and amulets). There are *power places* (Mecca, saints' tombs), *power times* (Muhammad's birthday, the night of power during Ramadan, the pilgrimage), and *power rituals* (prayers and incantations often using portions of the Qur'an). These six categories provide a helpful taxonomy for cross-cultural workers to analyse magic among their people.

Magic provides four functions. *Productive magic* is the pursuit of prosperity, fertility, and success. *Protective magic* seeks supernatural resources in order to overcome evil spirits and forces. *Destructive magic* uses spells and incantations to control or harm others. *Divination* seeks to learn about the future through supernatural beings or through natural phenomena such as astrology and numerology.

A functional perspective of magic equips the cross-cultural worker to appreciate some of the motivations of those practising magic. Christian believers similarly long for blessing and seek protection. Moreover, there is a desire in the heart of God's people to know God's will and to discern the future. Finally, the motivation for justice or a sense of righteous anger has some similarities to destructive magic.

Strong prohibitions against magic are scattered throughout the OT (Exod. 22:18; Lev. 19:26, 31; 20:6, 27; Deut. 18:9–15; Isa. 8:19–20; cf. 2 Kgs 17:17; Mic. 5:12). The NT describes the practice of magic as a 'work of the flesh' and warns that those who practise such things will not inherit the kingdom of God (Gal. 5:20–21). Revelation 21:8 says that those practising magic will face judgment.

Perhaps the most relevant teaching on magic in the Bible is found in Acts. Luke has carefully crafted his narrative to equip the church to confront magic in power-oriented societies. He intentionally selects four key stories (Acts 8:4–24; 13:4–12; 16:16–18; 19:8–41) in order to: (1) clarify the difference between magic and miracle, contrasting Satan-inspired magic with Holy Spirit-empowered miracle. (Magic is based on formulas and manipulation, having its source in Satan, while miracle is based on faith and supplication, having its source in God.); (2) equip the church for *spiritual warfare against the forces of darkness most focally expressed in magic; and (3) demonstrate the supernatural confirmation of the gospel through signs and wonders in pioneer missions.

Paul's ministry at Ephesus (Acts 19:8–41) provides the most detailed example of how to minister to people from a magical background. Ephesus was a renowned centre of the magical arts, famous for its amulets and magical incantations known as the 'Ephesian letters' (probably similar to the books burned in 19:18–19). The worship of Artemis was also permeated with magical practices.

Paul's approach to magic reflects a multi-faceted strategy. First, Paul taught the Scripture comprehensively (Acts 19:8–10; 20:25, 27), centring his message on the kingdom of God (19:8; 20:25). This emphasis on the kingdom would have clarified the differences between the kingdom of God and the kingdom of Satan, thus highlighting the distinction between miracle and magic. Secondly, Paul engaged in signs and wonders. 'God was performing extraordinary miracles by the hands of Paul' (19:11). Finally, Paul demanded true repentance and faith (20:21).

The new believers in Ephesus had begun to follow Jesus while maintaining adherence to their old magic practices. They held to this dual allegiance until the failed attempt of the Jewish exorcists to cast out demons in Jesus name (19:13–19). After that dramatic event, many of those who 'had believed' (*pepisteu-koton*, a perfect participle), confessed and disclosed their practices. They renounced their demonic practices, destroying their charms, amulets and magical paraphernalia.

Paul's follow-up letter to the Ephesians also provides a magnificent example of how the gospel is contextualized to power-oriented societies. Ephesians has the highest concentration of power terminology of all Paul's letters and provides the most comprehensive teaching on spiritual warfare in the NT. Moreover, Paul explicitly shows how the gospel relates to those from a magical background. Missionary engagement with magic must combine the wisdom to recognize its reality with the confidence to confront it with the conviction of the victory of Jesus over all spiritual powers.

The *resurrection and enthronement of Christ were a central part of the early church's proclamation (Acts 2:33; Rom. 8:34; Heb.

1:3; 1 Pet. 3:22). Paul makes an explicit link between this proclamation and Christ's present exaltation over the powers of darkness (Eph. 1:20–23). He underscores the unrivalled authority of Christ's rule: 'He has been raised and seated far above all rule and authority and power and dominion and every name that is named.' Christ is not just above all the powers of darkness. He is far above them. The word translated 'far above', *hyper-anō*, magnifies the power gap between the exalted Christ and demonic powers. This use of spatial language symbolizes Christ's transcendence and authority over all inimical spirits. This means that there is no place for a dualistic model of conflict between the kingdom of God and the kingdom of Satan as if the battle were conducted on equal terms.

After describing how the power of God is demonstrated in the resurrection of Christ (Eph. 1:19–23), Paul then shows how this same resurrection power works in the believer in his classic exposition of the gospel of grace (Eph. 2:1–10). We have been made alive together with Christ, raised up with Christ, and seated with Christ in the heavenly places (Eph. 2:5–6). In other words, a central element of salvation is our participation in Christ's rule over the powers of darkness, and this affirmation must form a principal dimension of missionary proclamation.

According to Ephesians, dominion over the powers of darkness is due to our union with Christ in his resurrection and exaltation, based on grace, appropriated by faith. Thus, Paul highlights two important differences between Christian power and magical power. Christian power is based on relationship (union with Christ by grace), whereas magical power stresses ritual. Magicians manipulate spirits through formulas. Followers of Christ have dominion over spirits through faith.

Bibliography

C. E. Arnold, *Ephesians: Power and Magic: The Concept of Power in Ephesians in Light of its Historical Setting* (Grand Rapids: Baker, 1992); C. E. Arnold, 'Magic', in G. F. Hawthorne and R. P. Martin (eds.), *Dictionary of Paul and His Letters* (Downers Grove: InterVarsity Press; Leicester: IVP, 1993); R. Love, *Muslims, Magic and the Kingdom of God* (Pasadena, CA: William Carey Library, 2003); J. D. Woodberry, 'The Relevance of Power Ministries for Folk Muslims', in C. P. Wagner and F. Douglas Pennoyer (ed.), *Wrestling with Dark Angels* (Ventura: Regal Books, 1990).

R. LOVE

Managerial missiology

As any human enterprise, the practice of Christian mission is an activity that must be conducted according to some basic organizational principles. The concept of management presently current in mission practice is the result of a way of reading such principles in Scripture and the development of the science of management, especially in industrialized societies. For instance, evangelicals have tended to see Nehemiah as a model of leadership and management. In the list of seven gifts for the edification of the church that Paul offers in Romans 12:6–8, the Greek term *metadidous* has been translated as 'leader'. It is one of the four charismata that serve the holistic mission of the church, and that, according to Cranfield, 'most probably have to do with the practical assistance of those who are, in one way or another, especially in need of help and sympathy' (C. E. B. Cranfield, *The Epistle to the Romans* [Edinburgh: T. & T. Clark, 1979], p. 628).

The term managerial missiology refers to a trend within evangelical missiology that emphasizes the management of mission practice. It developed in North America during the last third of the twentieth century. It came from a cluster of institutions connected to the *Church Growth school and movements such as AD 2000 and Beyond. It is an effort to reduce Christian mission to a manageable enterprise.

Every characteristic of this missiological trend becomes understandable when perceived within the frame of that avowed quantifying intention. Concepts such as 'people-groups', '*unreached peoples', '*homogeneous units', '10–40 window', 'adopt a people' and 'territorial spirits' (see *Spiritual warfare), express both a strong sense of urgency and an effort to use every available instrument to make the task possible. One way of achieving manageability is precisely to reduce reality to an understandable picture, and then to project missionary action as a response to 'a problem' that has been described in quantitative form.

Missionary action is thus reduced to a linear task that is unfolded into logical steps to be followed in a process of management by objectives. Movements that express this trend proliferated as the end of the twentieth century approached, proposing strategies that used the year 2000 as a date to complete evangelization.

The use of statistical information in order to visualize the missionary task or to motivate missionaries is not something new in the history of missions. It was used in William Carey's famous *Enquiry* as well as in preparation for some of the great missionary conferences of the twentieth century. Statistical information was compiled in order to communicate the nature of the missionary effort that was required, and promote a sense of urgency about it. Within managerial missiology, statistical analysis was used first as a way of measuring the effect of missionary action, in an effort to reduce the lack of clarity that surrounded it and a certain fuzziness in the traditional way of defining and evaluating it. The call for measuring was a key component of the necessary process of evaluation required by the missionary enterprise at the middle of the twentieth century. A clarification of goals and plans was called for in view of biblical imperatives.

The negative aspect of this approach was that such evaluative methodology was at the service of a concept of mission narrowly defined as the numerical growth of the church. Donald McGavran was the champion of this position, presenting it in contrast to more inclusive definitions of mission that were dominant especially in the conciliar ecumenical movement. In one of his last articles McGavran posed the dilemma very clearly: 'In short, is mission primarily evangelism, or is it primarily all efforts to improve human existence?' ('Missiology Faces the Lion', *Missiology* 17, p. 338). His choice is clearly on the side of evangelism, and just evangelism.

However, anyone who has engaged in mission in the Majority World, or among the poor in developed nations, knows that the neat distinction established by McGavran is artificial. It was good for debate against exaggerations in the conciliar movement, but it does not function in practice. Mission many times starts by a diaconal and transformative presence, long before there is an opportunity to share the gospel verbally and call people to follow Christ. In missionary work there are some aspects that cannot be reduced to statistics, but this missiological approach gave predominance to that which can be reduced to a statistical chart. Some acts of verbal communication of the gospel, such as distribution of the printed page, hours of broadcasting through radio or TV, massive gatherings for evangelism, or groups of new believers organized into churches, are all activities that can be counted and registered. It is more difficult to measure the time, energy and sacrifice involved in leadership training, personal discipleship or theological creativity, all of them necessary for new churches. Charles Taber proved that the theological presuppositions of the Church Growth school are a 'narrowed-down version of the evangelical hermeneutic and theology' (C. R. Taber, 'Contextualization', in *Exploring Church Growth*, p. 119).

A second aspect related to its reductionist theological foundation is that as the missionary effort is reduced to numerical growth, anything that would hinder it has to be eliminated or postponed. If the struggle for obedience to God in *holistic mission involves costly participation in the processes of social transformation, it is simply eliminated. The slow process of development of a *contextual theology for a young church tends to be considered inefficient and costly, and it is easy to substitute it for pre-packaged theologies translated from English, German or Korean. Efficient educational techniques like 'extension' have been developed within the frame of church growth, but there has not been much success in the production of contextual textbooks.

A third note is the unbalanced pragmatic approach to the task, which de-emphasizes theological questions, takes for granted the existence of adequate content, and consequently majors in method. This anti-theological bias has been the distinctive note of some of Ralph Winter's writings. It is the kind of process that demands a closed view of the world and in which the tough questions are not asked because they cannot be reduced to a linear management by objectives process. This system cannot live with paradox or mystery, and it has no theological or pastoral resources to cope with the suffering and

*persecution involved many times in mission, because it is geared to provide methodologies for a guaranteed success. Only categories such as paradox, mystery, suffering and failure can help us to grasp something of the depth of the spiritual battle involved in mission. In this way an important aspect of the history of missions is either silenced or underestimated because it does not fit the mathematical categories of so-called 'church growth'.

A fourth aspect of managerial missiology is the strong influence of American functionalist social sciences. The structural-functional model of cultural *anthropology is based on a static view of the world for which, as Taber says, ' "Cultural givens" take on permanence and rigidity; it suggests that whatever is endures. This cannot help but undermine the hope of transformation which is central to the Gospel' (Taber, in *Exploring Church Growth*, p. 119). Peruvian missiologist Tito Paredes has developed this critical point, showing how the way in which managerial missiologists read Scripture is affected by this socially conservative approach.

Proponents of Church Growth who entered into a global dialogue after Lausanne 1974 have worked critically to develop the best of its insights. On the other hand, Harvie Conn suggested that McGavran's evolution and self-correction have not been always adequately noticed or followed by his students and defenders. As an insider in the movement Arthur Glasser provided a brief and clarifying evaluative chronicle, showing how concepts such as 'homogeneous units' were abandoned. Some anthropologists that were related to the early phase of the church growth movement, especially Alan Tippet, Charles Kraft and Paul Hiebert, worked patiently on a clarification of methodologies from the social sciences as they are applied to missiological work, especially the communication process. Missiologist Charles Van Engen has worked systematically in an effort to incorporate key concerns from the managerial approach, such as 'yearning for numerical growth', into a full-fledged evangelical theology of the church in mission.

Bibliography
J. Engel and W. Dyrness, *Changing the Mind of Missions: Where Have We Gone Wrong?* (Downers Grove: InterVarsity Press, 2000); A. F. Glasser, 'Church Growth at Fuller',

Missiology 14, pp. 401–420; P. G. Hiebert, *Anthropological Insights for Missionaries* (Grand Rapids: Baker, 1986); C. Kraft, *Christianity in Culture* (Maryknoll: Orbis Books, 1979); C. R. Padilla, *Mission Between the Times* (Grand Rapids: Eerdmans, 1985); T. Paredes, *El Evangelio: Un Tesoro en Vasijas de Barro* (Buenos Aires: Kairos, 2000); W. R. Shenk (ed.), *Exploring Church Growth* (Grand Rapids: Eerdmans, 1983); A. R. Tippet, *Introduction to Missiology* (Pasadena: William Carey Library, 1987); C. Van Engen, *God's Missionary People: Rethinking the Purpose of the Local Church* (Grand Rapids: Baker, 1991).

S. ESCOBAR

Marketplace theology

The 'marketplace' is a metaphor for the everyday places where people gather to look for what they need for life, and where stalls are set up offering them many alternatives. Marketplace theology encourages Christians to engage with this context of work and daily life in society, and to get involved where people are living their everyday lives.

In presenting the *gospel as the only true option among many alternatives, Christians must first be willing to take their place among these competing voices and earn their right to be heard. They are called to live committed Christian lives in the world of work and social interaction in which they spend most of their time. Lesslie Newbigin argues that as Christians flesh out godly values in the course of daily living in the world, they provoke curiosity in non-believers and prompt them to ask questions for which the gospel is the only answer. Their lives provide a natural and accessible context for sharing Christ.

The dynamic nature of the marketplace requires that the church undertakes this task 'boldly and imaginatively', and in ways that are understandable for the generation it addresses. Only then will non-Christians be able to see the gospel as an attractive alternative. In order to be able to do this, Christians need theological resources to engage with the issues that ordinary people have, to see the value of their work to God, and to have a confident Christian witness in the world of economics and cultural/social interaction.

Theological framework

The importance of the *witness of ordinary Christians in the context of their homes, places of work and communities in which they live is clearly attested to in the Scriptures (e.g. Matt. 5:13–16; Rom. 12:1–2; Eph. 4:12; Col. 3:23; 1 Cor. 10:31).

Due to the influence of dualistic Greek thinking, and as the church became more institutionalized and professionalized, the role and contribution of the laity to the church's mission post-NT was downplayed. Luther revived it in the sixteenth century with the doctrine of the 'priesthood of all believers', asking Christians to embrace whatever station in life they found themselves in as their vocation. Calvin went a step further in saying that each Christian has a specific vocation and each should try to discover what their calling is. Both tried to break down the church/society divide as to how Christians viewed work. Despite what the Reformers did, many sections of the church today still live with this false dichotomy.

Traditionally, theology has been done by scholars and the clergy for the academy and the church. Marketplace theology, however, is done by all of God's people for all of life, focusing more on the ordinary lives of the laity outside the church walls from Mondays to Saturdays. It encourages them to reflect on a theology of work based on the 'creation commission' of God (Gen. 1:26–28). If we emphasize the reconciling work of the Son or the transforming work of the Spirit while neglecting the creating work of the Father, lay people fail to see the significance of their work in the world and the different roles they play at home and in the community in the light of God's *trinitarian purposes. At best, they regard these merely as contexts for evangelism and nothing more. Christians must be taught that they are also called to 'administer the earth' as good stewards (i.e. act to care for the world through the work that they do), and that this is in itself a powerful witness (see also *Ecology/environment).

Such an understanding of God and of our calling challenges a common view that some aspects of life are more sacred than others when, in fact, Christ is Lord of all (Col. 1:15–20). We must do away with this false dichotomy and reclaim all of life as belonging to

God. That means that rather than focus all our talents, time and energy on what we do together on a Sunday, we ought to see Sunday as a time when we equip, commission and empower God's people to bring the rule and witness of Christ to wherever each one is called during the rest of the week (Eph. 4:11–16).

Marketplace theology therefore encompasses both the cultural mandate (Gen. 1:26–28) and the evangelistic mandate (Matt. 28:18–20), each seen as complementary dimensions of the church's one mission. Some conservative missiologists have argued that the cultural mandate is not 'mission', which they see as primarily *evangelistic. To this, proponents of marketplace theology would argue that the cultural mandate has been renewed in Christ through his central role in creation, and it is therefore the ongoing responsibility of the church's mission.

Missiological importance

The Lausanne Manila Manifesto states, 'God is calling the whole church to take the whole gospel to the whole world.' The task of world evangelization can only be completed if the entire church, both clergy and laity, is mobilized to live committed Christian lives and proclaim Christ through presence, word and deed wherever they are called.

In a post-colonial era of new nation states and growing nationalism, missionary involvement can be either impossible or ambiguous, whereas a mobilized laity can live the gospel everyday in their local communities. In this respect, Christians in the marketplace and *tentmakers play a crucial role in fulfilling the church's mission in the new world order. In a number of Asian countries, mission-minded Christians with relevant marketplace skills or resources can find opportunities to do this under special programmes that offer residency to foreigners by way of business or direct investments, or retirement schemes.

Especially in Muslim-majority countries where strict local laws exist to prohibit evangelism, as well as in other restrictive environments such as in some communist countries, the presence of Christian believers who live and work among the people as colleagues, friends and neighbours is crucial. Though they cannot *speak* the gospel, they can live it and they can share their personal stories especially in response to queries from those with whom they have built a relationship. In the most difficult of such environments, the mere presence of Christians living faithful Christian lives may be the only witness to the gospel such non-Christians will ever encounter.

The importance of marketplace theology is particularly acute in the twenty-first century due to the context we live in. In the global inter-connected world where people are constantly being bombarded by messages, words alone may be insufficient. More convincingly, people need to see the power of a transformed life and the love of a transformed community in all the complexities of daily living. Benjamin Barber in *Jihad vs McWorld* identifies globalism/market economy and radicalism/tribalism as the two main forces shaping the world today. Both forces are potentially dehumanizing in their own ways. Marketplace theology can provide a 'third way' that addresses the human hunger that fuels both forces.

In materialistic market societies, Christians often have to pay a price in one form or another for refusing to go along with company policies that place profits over employee welfare, good ethical practices and environmental concerns. These same difficulties, however, also offer opportunities for Christians to denounce the temporal nature of wealth vis-à-vis the certain promises of the gospel.

A growing movement

In the last thirty years or so, there has been a growing awareness regarding the role of the laity and the importance of marketplace theology. Hendrik Kraemer's *A Theology of the Laity* is a key, influential work in this area. Those at the forefront of this movement include Robert Banks, R. Paul Stevens and Peter Hammond. A number of institutions of learning have also attempted to incorporate marketplace emphasis into their courses. These include Regent College (Canada), Gordon-Conwell Theological Seminary (USA), London Institute for Contemporary Christianity (UK) and Macquarie Christian Studies Institute (Australia). At the same time, a number of parachurch and professional groups have also been formed to support Christian witness in the marketplace. Growing alongside and out of the marketplace movement are sub-groups such as tentmakers and those engaged in business as mission.

The movement has seen encouraging growth led by individuals and parachurch groups. There is also a growing amount of literature written in this area. The main encouragement for accelerated growth, however, must come from church leaders whose teaching and practice will equip and encourage the role of the laity. Though some training institutions have incorporated marketplace theology into their curricula, many more need to do so to influence a whole new generation of clergy who understands the importance of marketplace theology. Perhaps by its nature, even the adoption of marketplace theology will have to start with the laity and not the clergy.

See also HOLISTIC MISSION, PRESENCE, WORLD.

Bibliography
R. Banks, *All the Business of Life* (Sutherland: Albatross Books, 1989); B. R. Barber, *Jihad vs McWorld: How Globalism and Tribalism Are Reshaping the World* (New York: Ballantine, 1996); M. Greene, *Thank God It's Monday: Ministry in the Workplace* (London: Scripture Union, 1994); O. Guinness, *The Call: Finding and Fulfilling the Central Purpose of Your Life* (Dallas: Word, 1999); L. Hardy, *The Fabric of This World: Inquiries into Calling, Career Choice and the Design of Human Work* (Grand Rapids: Eerdmans, 1990); T. Liu, G. Preece and Wong Siew Li, 'Lausanne Occasional Paper No. 40: Marketplace Ministry' in D. Clayton (ed.), *A New Vision, A New Heart, A Renewed Call*, Vol. 1 (Pasadena: William Carey Library, 2005); L. Newbigin, *The Gospel in a Pluralist Society* (Grand Rapids: Eerdmans, 1996); G. Preece, *Changing Work Values: A Christian Response* (Melbourne: Acorn Press, 1995); D. Sherman and W. Hendricks, *Your Work Matters to God* (Colorado Springs: NavPress, 1992); R. P. Stevens, *The Other Six Days* (Grand Rapids: Eerdmans, 1999).

SIEW LI WONG

Martyrdom

Throughout Christian history, across all traditions of Christianity, and in every part of the world, some 70 million Christians have been murdered for their faith and hence are called martyrs. This number continues to grow as, on average, over 400 new martyrs are being killed every day. This quantitative aspect of martyrdom is not peripheral to understanding the theological or missiological meaning of martyrdom. Unfortunately, many Christians are under the false impression that Christian martyrdom is a rare occurrence reserved for only a few highly spiritual individuals. This brief article will illustrate why this is not the case and what the theological implications of ubiquitous martyrdom might be.

Origin of the word 'martyr'
The English word 'martyr' is derived from the Greek *martys*, which carries the meaning 'witness' in English. In New Testament usage, it meant 'a witness to the resurrection of Christ'. This witness resulted so frequently in death that by the end of the first century *martys* had come to mean a Christian who witnessed to Christ *by his or her death*. This enlarged meaning has become the accepted norm throughout church history.

Definition of terms
For a quantitative analysis of martyrdom, Christian martyrs are defined as 'believers in Christ who have lost their lives prematurely, in situations of witness, as a result of human hostility'. This definition has five essential elements which can be stated as follows:

(1) *'Believers in Christ.'* These individuals include the entire Christian community of Roman Catholics, Orthodox, Protestants, Anglicans, marginal Christians and independents. In AD 2005, over two billion individuals match this description, and since the time of Christ over 8.3 billion have believed in Christ.

(2) *'Lost their lives.'* The definition is restricted to Christians actually put to death, for whatever reason.

(3) *'Prematurely.'* Martyrdom is sudden, abrupt, unexpected, unwanted.

(4) *'In situations of witness.'* 'Witness' in this definition does not mean only public testimony or proclamation concerning the risen Christ. It refers to the entire lifestyle and way of life of the Christian believer, whether or not he or she is actively proclaiming at the time of being killed.

(5) '*As a result of human hostility.*' This excludes deaths through accidents, crashes, earthquakes and other 'acts of God', illnesses, or other causes of death, however tragic.

Martyrdom not exclusively an early Christian phenomenon

In the early church the idea developed that it was not enough to be called a Christian, one had to show some proof. That proof was normally some kind of verbal acknowledgement of identification with Christ, starting with the confession 'Jesus is Lord'. T. Baumeister writes: 'Dying because one is a Christian is the action par excellence in which the disciple who is called to this confirms his or her faith by following the example of Jesus' suffering and through action is able once again to become a word with power to speak to others' (Metz and Schillebeeckx, p. 4). Eventually confessors were distinguished from martyrs.

Martyrdom is a consistent feature of church history. The rate of martyrdom across the world throughout the ages has been a remarkably constant 0.8%; that is, one out of every 120 Christians in the past has been martyred, or in the future is likely to so be.

Why are there martyrs?

According to Latin American theologian Leonardo Boff there are two reasons: Christians prefer to sacrifice their lives rather than to be unfaithful to their convictions and, those that reject proclamation persecute, torture and kill. Over half of the seventy million Christian martyrs were killed in the twentieth century alone, and over twenty million were martyred in Soviet prison camps. Even though state-ruling powers (atheists and others) are responsible for most martyrs, sometimes Christians themselves (in the broadest sense of the word) have been the persecutors, responsible for martyring 5.5 million other Christians! Table 1 summarizes the proportion of martyrs in each Christian tradition. It reveals that over half of all martyrs have been Orthodox Christians. One partial explanation for this is the vast anti-Christian empires throughout history centred in Eastern Europe and Central Asia. Nonetheless, all Christian traditions have suffered martyrdom.

Table 1. Confessions of martyrs, totals from AD 33–2005

Tradition	Martyrs
Orthodox	43,000,000
Russian Orthodox	25,000,000
East Syrians (Nestorians)	12,800,000
Ukrainian Orthodox	4,000,000
Gregorians (Armenian Apostolic)	1,200,000
Roman Catholic	12,200,000
Catholics (before AD 1000)	900,000
Independents	3,500,000
Protestants	3,200,000
Anglicans	1,100,000
Marginal Christians	7,000
Other and background martyrs	7,000,000
Total all martyrs	**70,000,000**

A theology of martyrdom

Josef Ton, persecuted as a Christian in Romania, developed a theology of martyrdom that is centred on God's purpose for human history. He writes, 'God revealed to us that suffering and self-sacrifice are His specific methods for tackling the problems of rebellion, of evil, and of the sin of mankind.' Looking to the example of Jesus and the apostles, Ton outlines two major purposes of martyrdom: as instruments by which God achieves his purposes in history and by which he shapes and forms the character of Christians who suffer and die. Under the first purpose we understand that three things are achieved: (1) the triumph of God's truth: unbelievers' eyes opened by the manner of death (Mark 15:39); (2) the defeat of Satan: those formerly in bondage are brought into life (Rev. 15:2–4); (3) the glory of God: voluntary suffering reflects God's love and power (2 Cor. 4:7–12). Under the second purpose Christians are made perfect as Christ was made perfect through suffering and even death (Heb. 2:10).

Martyrdom and church growth?

'The blood of the martyrs is the seed of the church' was famously stated by Tertullian, a third-century lawyer who in his investigation of Christian martyrdom was converted to Christianity. In assessing the impact of the martyrdom situations listed above it is not possible to make a definitive statement about the relationship between martyrdom and the growth of the church. We do know for certain that the purges of Stalin did not result in the extinction of Christianity in the Soviet Union. In fact, the church there today is enjoying a renaissance. Another contemporary example is the church in China. In 1949 there were only one million Christians. Fifty years of antireligious Communist rule produced some 1.2 million martyrs. The result: explosive church growth to today's one hundred million believers. Today major martyrdom situations continue in Sudan, Indonesia, Nigeria, and other hot spots around the globe.

But one can equally point to the decline of Christianity in Central Asia under the Mongols and later under Tamerlane. This did not lead to further church growth, but rather to the disappearance of one of Christianity's most vibrant missionary traditions – the Church of the East.

This evidence fits into earlier observations that martyrdom is an instrument used by God for his purposes. One cannot presuppose what these purposes might be. As a phenomenon, martyrdom does seem to have the effect of impressing unbelievers with the faith and courage of those being killed. In that sense, even without church growth, martyrdom can be said to bring glory to God's name.

The future of martyrdom

We might be tempted to believe that mankind will gradually grow out of its violent nature and that, perhaps one hundred years in the future, will no longer be killing others, for whatever reason. However, this is not likely to be the case. The future almost certainly holds more martyrdom situations and the names of individual martyrs are likely to continue mounting year after year at the same shocking rate of over 160,000 a year.

See also PERSECUTION.

Bibliography

D. Barrett and T. M. Johnson, *World Christian Trends* (Pasadena, CA: William Carey Library, 2001); T. Baumeister, *Martyr Invictus* (Münster: Regensburg, 1972); B. Chenu *et al. Livre des Martyrs Chrétiens* (Paris: Éditions du Centurion, 1988); P. Marshall with L. Gilbert, *Their Blood Cries Out: The Untold Story of Persecution Against Christians in the Modern World* (Dallas: Word Publishing, 1997); J. Metz and E. Schillebeeckx (eds.), *Martyrdom Today* (Edinburgh: T. & T. Clark, 1983); J. Ton, *Suffering, Martyrdom, and Rewards in Heaven* (Lanham, MD: Rowman & Littlefield, 1997); D. Wood (ed.), *Martyrs and Martyrologies* (Oxford: Blackwell, 1993); <http://www.worldchristiandatabase.org>.

T. M. JOHNSON

Messianic Judaism

Messianic Judaism is a Jewish form of Christianity and a Christian form of Judaism, a form of cultural, religious and theological expression adopted in recent years by an increasing number of Jewish people worldwide who believe in Yeshua (Jesus) as the promised Messiah. Messianic Judaism finds its expression in Messianic congregations and synagogues, and in the individual lifestyle of Messianic Jews, who combine Jewish identity with belief in Jesus.

There are some 150,000 Jewish believers in Jesus worldwide, according to conservative estimates. More than 100,000 are in the USA, approximately 5,000 in Israel, the remainder being found throughout the approximately 14 million worldwide Jewish population. There are over 200 Messianic groups in the USA, and over eighty in Israel. Whilst they are not uniform in their beliefs and expression, the majority adhere to orthodox Christian beliefs on the uniqueness and deity of Christ, the Trinity, the authority of Scripture, and so on, whilst expressing their beliefs in a Jewish cultural and religious context which affirms the continuing election of Israel (the Jewish people) and the ongoing purposes of God for his people.

There have always been Jewish believers in Jesus, from the time of the early church. These 'followers of the way' or Nazarenes were known and accepted by the Church Fathers (Jerome, Justin Martyr, Epiphanius), but as Judaism and Christianity emerged as separate ways in the fourth century, it became increasingly unacceptable to ecclesiastical and rabbinic authorities to allow the legitimacy of Jewish expressions of faith in Christ. Excluded from the synagogue for their belief in the Trinity and divinity of Christ, and anathematized by the church for continued practice of Jewish customs, they were known as Ebionites ('the poor ones') and suspected of legalism and an adoptionist Christology.

Small groups of Jewish Christians continued in the East, and Jewish converts to Christianity were afforded protection in the midst of an anti-semitic European church by institutions such as the Domus Conversorum (House of Converts), which was maintained by royal patronage. But it was not until the modern missionary movement and an interest in mission to the Jewish people that a community of testimony of Jewish Christians re-appeared.

In 1809 Joseph Samuel Christian Frey, son of a rabbi from Posen, Hungary, encouraged the formation of the London Society for the Promotion of Christianity Among the Jews, which became the Church's Ministry Among the Jewish People (CMJ). Encouraged by CMJ and other Jewish missions, the growing number of 'Hebrew Christians', as they called themselves, formed their own Prayer Union (1866), British (1888) and International Alliances (1925), and developed their own liturgies and Hebrew Christian churches in Europe, Palestine and the USA. By the end of the nineteenth century it was estimated on the basis of baptismal statistics that over a million Jewish people had become Christians, many for reasons of assimilation and emancipation from the ghettos into European society with access to commerce, education and secular society. Nevertheless, a recognizable number, such as Alfred Edersheim, Adolph Saphir, Augustus Neander and Bishop Samuel Schereschewsky wished to retain aspects of their Jewish identity alongside faith in Christ and were both a blessing to the church and a testimony to their people.

After the Second World War, the Holocaust, and the establishment of the State of Israel, Jewish believers in Jesus from a new generation were concerned to rediscover their *ethnic roots and express their faith from a Jewish perspective. In the wake of the Jesus movement of the 1970s, 'Jews for Jesus' moved from a slogan used on the streets of San Francisco to an organization of Jewish missionaries to their people. At the same time, the Messianic Jewish Alliance of America encouraged the establishment of Messianic congregations and synagogues. In Israel a new generation of native-born Israelis ('sabras') were finding the Messiah, and

starting Hebrew-speaking congregations. At the beginning of the twenty-first century an international network of Messianic groups exists, expressing denominational, theological and cultural diversity, but united in belief in Yeshua.

Messianic Jews, to varying degrees, observe the Sabbath, keep kosher food laws, circumcise their sons, and celebrate the Jewish festivals, seeing Jesus and the church in Acts as their model and example. They celebrate Passover, showing how Yeshua came as the Passover Lamb, and practise baptism, linking to the Jewish *mikveh* (ritual bath). They *worship with their own liturgies, based on the synagogue service, with readings from the Torah and NT. Pointing to Paul's teaching in Romans 9 – 11 and his practice on his missionary journeys, their hermeneutic of Scripture repudiates traditional Christian anti-Judaism ('the Jews killed Christ') and supersessionism (the church replaces Israel as the 'new Israel'), arguing for forms of Torah observance that testify to the presence of the believing remnant in the midst of unbelieving Israel as a witness to the Messiah.

Messianic Jewish theology has developed in the light of its Protestant evangelical background and its engagement with Jewish concerns. The doctrinal statements of Messianic Jewish organizations are uniformly orthodox, but are often expressed in Jewish rather than Hellenistic thought forms, and are more closely linked to Jewish concepts and readings of Scripture. Many Messianic Jews are influenced by the charismatic movement, although an increasing number are opting for more formal styles of worship using the resources of the Jewish prayer book, and standard liturgical features such as the wearing of the prayer shawl (*tallit*) and the use of Torah-scrolls.

Most Messianic Jews are premilliennial (but not necessarily dispensationalists) in their *eschatology, seeing God's purposes for Israel being played out with various degrees of linkage to the present political events in the Middle East. Many advocate *aliyah* (immigration to Israel) for Messianic Jews, although the majority of Messianic Jews live in the diaspora. A growing number are concerned for reconciliation ministry with their Arab Christian neighbours.

Messianic Jewish theology is a theology

constructed in dialectic with Judaism and Christianity, refined in discussion between reflective practitioners engaged with Messianic Judaism, and developed into a new theological tradition based on the twin epistemic priorities of the continuing election of the Jewish people and the recognition of Jesus as the risen Messiah and incarnate Son of God.

Its key concerns are the nature and functions of the Messiah, the role of the Torah, and the place of Israel in the purposes of God. Its ongoing fashioning of Messianic Jewish identity, self-definition and expression in lifecycle and liturgy are the visible manifestation and practical application of its theological activity. Messianic Jewish theology is thus theoretical and theological reflection that arises from the faith and practice of Messianic Judaism. It is a theology of Jewish identity linked to belief in Jesus as Messiah.

It is a type of theology (both dogmatic and speculative) that is eclectic in its form and contents, covering relevant aspects of Jewish and Christian thought, theology and praxis. It is arranged according to the key issues and topics that concern the contemporary Messianic movement. It is articulated in bilingual modes, speaking to both Jewish and Christian publics, combining the two modes of discourse of Jewish and Christian thought, but challenging, renewing and redefining them to form a coherent synthesis of meaning around the revelation of the Messiahship of Jesus and the Jewishness of this belief.

Missiological implications

The Messianic movement represents for missiologists a classic example of *contextualization and ethnotheological formation. As the movement matures, it provides an object lesson of the challenges and possibilities of mission in a gospel-resistant culture with 2,000 years of misperception of the Christian message. Some Messianic Jews would advocate Messianic congregations as the most effective missionary tool, but this is not borne out by the evidence of the majority of Jewish believers in Jesus, who come to faith through the witness of their Christian friends in mainstream churches. The *homogeneous unit principle does not precisely apply, as Jews are far from being a homogeneous unit, yet the solidarity that Jewish believers in Jesus

recognize does promote the need for an ethnic church which remains connected to the majority of the Jewish people who do not yet believe in Jesus.

Some would argue that all Jewish believers in Jesus should remain (or become) Torah-observant, or they will be lost to their people, but this view also has not been accepted by the majority of Messianic Jews, who are happy in their membership of the universal church. They see their freedom in the Messiah as allowing them to choose how much they identify with different forms of Judaism and Jewish identity.

In terms of witness, Messianic Jews vary in their styles and strategy. A small number, often 'secret believers', retain active membership in non-Messianic synagogues, but this option is not typical. Others are highly visible in high-profile witness on the streets in major cities, stalls at New Age festivals in Israel, and meeting Israeli tourists on the hippy trail in India. Others prefer a less overt engagement within the Jewish community through joining communal organizations, and through day-to-day contact with friends and family. A growing number of Messianic Jews recognize their missionary calling to be a 'light to the nations' and a blessing to the whole church, and seek ways to educate and challenge the church as to the riches of its heritage and the Jewish roots of its faith.

See also JEWISH MISSION.

Bibliography

Y. Ariel, *Evangelizing the Chosen People: Mission to the Jews in America, 1880–2000* (Chapel Hill: University of North Carolina Press, 2000); D. Cohn-Sherbok, *Messianic Judaism* (London: Cassell, 2000); D. Cohn-Sherbok (ed.), *Voices of Messianic Judaism: Confronting Critical Issues Facing a Maturing Movement* (Baltimore: Lederer Books, 2001); D. Juster, *Jewish Roots: A Foundation of Biblical Theology for Messianic Judaism* (Rockville: Davar Pubishing, 1986, 1992); M. Kinzer, *Postmissionary Messianic Judaism: Redefining Christian Engagement with the Jewish People* (Grand Rapids: Brazos, 2005); R. Robinson, *The Messianic Movement: A Fieldguide for Evangelical Christians* (San Francisco: Purple Pomegranate Productions, 2006); D. H. Stern, *Messianic Jewish*

Manifesto (Clarksville: Jewish New Testament Publications, 1991).

R. HARVEY

Migration

Human migration is a fact of history. People have been on the move from the earliest times and their movements often involved great distances. In cultural terms, the impact and implications of such movements can be profound; not least because when people move they carry their ideas, beliefs, and religious practices with them. Within a wide range of possible modes of interaction and reactions, migrant movement has the capacity not only to foster cultural diversity but also to significantly alter demographic, economic and social structures. Not surprisingly, migration is integral to the processes of *globalization, including the emergence of the so-called world religions. The case of Christianity is particularly compelling, which is why inattentiveness to this migrant factor in much missiological reflection is curious. (In what follows, the term 'migration' is used in the broadest sense as descriptive of different forms of transience involving degrees of choice and compulsion.)

Christianity is a migratory religion, and migration movements have historically been a functional element in its expansion. To start with, the Bible depicts every known form of migration. One scholar rightly suggests that the book of Genesis might almost readily have been named the book of 'migrations'. In the ancient world, it has to be said, the unpredictability and precariousness of normal existence (including occurrences of famine and natural disasters) made migration the norm and permanent settlement the exception. Even so, the link between mobility and divine purposes in the biblical record is striking and figurative of Yahweh's intimate involvement in human affairs.

Throughout the OT, God's plan of salvation and redemptive action repeatedly unfold within the trauma and travail of displacement, uprootedness and migration. Those whom God chose and commissioned were for the most part individuals and communities in whose lives migration or displacement featured prominently. The OT patriarchs (and matriarchs) were frequently migrants (Gen. 12:1–4, 10–16; 26:3; 28:10–15; 26:1). Abraham, the quintessential migrant, models the profound integration of mobility, spiritual pilgrimage and the unfolding of divine intentions. The 'forced' migration of Joseph set the stage for the emergence of the Hebrews as a captive people whose exodus and subsequent wanderings became an archetypal biblical metaphor of God's people as a mobile community of faith guided by his promises. Taken as a whole, migration remained an overarching motif of the OT story.

Migration was also integral to 'missionary' action. In truth, the people of Israel remained impervious to the missionary implications of their chosen-ness. But, as the books of Daniel and Esther clearly demonstrate, enforced mobility and exile necessitated missionary encounters (cf. Dan. 2:26–30; Esth. 2:5–11; 8:11–17). Dispersal not only evoked overwhelming homeland memories and a renewed sense of religious identity (Ps. 137), but also afforded possibilities of faithful witness and religious representation that cast the God of Israel as the God of all humanity. Similarly, exile and displacement informed the sweeping gaze of major prophets who proclaimed both God's judgment on the nations (Jer. 46 – 51) and God's universal plan of salvation (Isa. 56:1–8).

In the NT the intersection of migration and mission is further extended and capsulated in the establishment of the church, the new Israel which, not unlike the old, comprised 'foreigners and exiles' (1 Pet. 2:11). From the outset, the spread of the gospel was linked to migrant movement and networks. The inception of the Gentile mission involved the actions of unnamed migrant refugees in Antioch – who as emigrants were perhaps more disposed to preach the message of salvation to other outsiders (Acts 11:19–20). And, in the centuries which immediately followed, the faith spread mainly through kinship and commercial networks, migrant movements (some stimulated by persecution), and other forms of mobility.

In the thousand years from 500 to 1500, vast movements of peoples on the Eurasian landmass were critical to the Christian conversion of Western European peoples. And the emergence of Christian communities across Asia and in South Arabia owed much to the vast network of trade routes by land

and sea which acted as outlets for Christian migrant movement. The end of this thousand-year period also witnessed the beginning of that momentous expansion of Europeans from the heartlands of Christianity to other parts of the world. From about 1800 to 1914 – the great ('long') century of Western missionary enterprise – up to 60 million Europeans left for the Americas, Oceania, and East and South Africa. In effect, the most remarkable of all migrations in known human history coincided with the greatest Christian missionary expansion to date. The net impact transformed the face of global Christianity.

It is now a commonplace that more than two-thirds of Christians in the world reside in the southern continents – an epochal development which signifies the emergence of Christianity as a non-Western religion. This transformation, which dates to the closing decades of the twentieth century, coincides with two historic trends: first, the massive escalation in the volume and velocity of inter-national migrations – by 2005 there were an estimated 191 million international migrants (one out of every 34 persons) in the world; second, the momentous reversal in the direction of global migratory flows – now primarily south to north (and east to west) where it was once predominantly north to south. Migrant movement from less developed countries (in the South) to highly developed countries (in the North) constitutes a dominant element in these trends. By 2000, more than 70% of immigrants arriving in the United States, the United Kingdom, Germany and Canada were from the non-Western world.

Once again migration and mission are powerfully linked. Precisely because the heart-lands of global Christianity are now in the South, contemporary South-North migrations form the tap-root of a major non-Western missionary movement. Among the swelling tide of guest workers, students, labour migrants, asylum seekers, political and economic refugees, and family members of previous migrants, are innumerable Christians, each one a missionary in some sense. In Europe, where the largest church is African-founded and led, African Christians alone are thought to number in excess of three million. In the US, where Hispanic, Korean and Chinese congregations have prolifer-ated vigorously, the religious landscape looks less and less Western. Through migrant movements, Christian missionary activities are criss-crossing the globe, mainly as part of invisible, unstructured, transnational networks.

Against this backdrop, Western missionary initiatives are of diminishing significance. Indeed, the growing presence of non-Western immigrants and immigrant churches impli-cates the largely post-Christian West as a new frontier of global Christian expansion. For Christians and churches in wealthy, securaliz-ing Western societies, this new reality requires radical adjustments in outlook, missiological understanding and witness. Often objects of propaganda and widespread hostility, the new immigrants are among the most vulnerable and exploited. Their presence reminds the church not only of the challenges of globaliza-tion but also of the centrality of hospitality (concern and care for the alien) as a biblical mandate. It is a curious understanding of mission which sanctions significant expend-iture on *short-term mission trips to distant lands but ignores vulnerable populations down the street. The presence of the new immigrants also portends far-reaching trans-formations within Western societies, notably in the area of religious diversity. Here too, the church is presented with unprecedented challenges in terms of its witness and self-understanding. Paradoxically, it is in this novel status of marginality – being divested of a longstanding position of domination and privilege – that the church in the West may yet experience the efficacy of that core scriptural motif: of the people of God as strangers and pilgrims.

Meanwhile, the emergence of the non-Western missionary movement in conjunction with global migratory flows represents a major turning point in the history of Chris-tianity. Never before has the course of mission ary movement been this multi-directional, disparate and global. Prominent features associated with the Western missionary project are largely absent: including the entrenched territorial (and one-directional) structure of missions, the instrumentality of para-church mission societies, the complic-ated relationship with colonial dominance, and the projection of cultural superiority. In particular, the new South-North mission-ary movement involves both individual and institutional initiatives (predominantly the former). It is church-based, self-evidently *incarnational in its witness; it closely exemplifies NT patterns in its dependence on individual inventiveness, emphasis on spiritual power, use of house churches, reliance on *tentmaking ministries, and disconnection from empire.

The full extent to which this non-Western missionary movement will break new ground in its vision, strategies, and even choice of missionary text, remains to be seen. Once more, migration is intimately linked with inscrutable divine purposes and, most important, remains critical to the future of the faith.

See also TWO-THIRDS WORLD MISSION MOVEMENTS.

Bibliography

S. Castles and M. J. Miller, *The Age of Migration: International Population Movements in the Modern World* (New York: The Guilford Press, ²1998); J. J. Hanciles, 'Mission and Migration: Some Implications for the Twenty-first Century Church', *International Bulletin of Missionary Research* 27, 2003, pp. 146–153; K. Latourette, *The Thousand Years of Uncertainty*, vol. 2 (Grand Rapids, MI: Zondervan, 1970 [1938]); M. Spellman, *The Global Community: Migration and the Making of the Modern World* (Gloucestershire, England: Sutton Publishing Limited, 2002); A. F. Walls, 'Mission and Migration: The Diaspora Factor in Christian History', *Journal of African Christian Thought* 5, 2002, pp. 3–11; United Nations, *Trends in Total Migrant Stock: The 2005 Revision* (United Nations Publication, 2006).

J. J. HANCILES

Ministry

The word 'ministry' comes from the Latin *ministerium*, which means 'office' or 'service'. Most secular dictionaries give the first definition of 'ministry' as a branch of government. A 'minister' is the person through which that function of government (ministry) is carried out. While the religious meaning of ministry, as in 'clergy', is secondary in dictionaries today, it has the longer history. Ministry was only first used as a term in British government

in 1916. The Latin root and secular designation are mentioned here in order to provide a broader starting point for a reflective understanding of ministry in the context of mission.

Although the word 'ministry' is widely used in church and mission circles, its assumed meaning often varies significantly. Historically, for Christians, the word has referred to the office of the ordained clergy (as above). Some groups even today continue to insist that it is only the ordained clergy that can do ministry in the context of mission. For example, the Assemblies of God, which is highly missional and one of the fastest growing denominations in the world, is among some 350 different exhibitors at the triennial 20,000-student Urbana Mission Convention. Recently, though, response from students has decreased, and a significant reason for this may be because the AOG requires ordination for their missionaries. Similarly, in large parts of the Korean church, being ordained is an important, if not essential, part of being a missionary. Only relatively recently have some Korean mission groups provided a model for ministry in the context of mission that does not assume ordination. This is a smaller but fast-growing part of the Korean mission force. This view of ministry can mean that missionaries are seen as specialists, people set apart from the rest of the body of Christ, so that the laity do not see themselves as missionaries.

What is the difference between ministry and mission, or are they equivalent? Does every Christian have a ministry but not every Christian a calling to mission? Ministry is often seen in relation to the life of the church and what goes on within Christian communities, whereas mission is what happens when the church goes out into the world. But as the church does that, it will need the ministries it has nurtured within it. So, for example, the gifts of the *Holy Spirit, while they are primarily for building up the body of Christ, are also available for mission. Ministry as serving one another is transferred into service to the world. So ministry and mission certainly need each other, even though they are not quite equivalent.

For the Western evangelical church today, the predominant model of mission is church planting, so the churches see ministry in that context, and value the ministries which serve that goal. At the other end of the continuum, 'ministry' in mission can be understood as anything a Christian does that glorifies God. For example, 'being the hands and feet of Jesus' is a common expression used in North America as part of the growing term 'missions'. For them a very popular quote is from St Francis of Assisi, 'Preach the gospel always and if necessary use words.' In each of these instances the focus is on service rather than proclamation or the end product of a planted church. Much of the younger generation's intense interest in mission focuses on issues of justice and social concern. The International Justice Mission and more recently a student-led start-up movement 'Acting on AIDS' would insist their social activism is 'ministry in mission'.

A biblical view of ministry in mission can help us bring these streams together. Ministry is best understood as service which reflects the nature and purposes of *God. In the context of mission, *Jesus' servant life and work on earth is the foundation of our own ministry cross-culturally. In his life, proclamation of the *kingdom of God was seamlessly integrated with his service, friendship, training and death for sin. All that he did was a movement towards the kingdom. As the risen Christ, he breathed on the disciples the Holy Spirit and gave them the commission, 'As the Father has sent me, I am sending you' (John 20:21).

Ministry is therefore best seen as *integrated* or *holistic* ministry. Whether demonstrating God's love in meeting physical and social needs or sharing the good news message while calling people to love and repentance in all areas of life, our activities in ministry should be indivisible and work together towards a whole reflection of God's character and purpose.

As individual believers, however, we are each limited and finite, with distinctive gifts. At any point in time we can only minister with one aspect of the way Jesus touched people. The biblical teaching on natural and spiritual gifts tells us that separately gifted persons and local churches make up the body of Christ on earth, all parts needing each other (Eph. 4:1–16). Truly integrated ministry is therefore what the church of Jesus Christ *as a whole* does. Thus, integrated ministry happens as the 'whole church takes the whole gospel to the whole world'.

Because ministry is not just activity or assigned tasks, the entire life of a Christian is involved: attitudes, lifestyle, relational patterns and behaviour. If these areas are conforming to Jesus Christ through the Holy Spirit, then holistic, integrated ministry is possible. NT ministry is *transformational*, affecting all areas of life and community until they are marked by the righteousness, justice, love, and holiness of Jesus (2 Cor. 3:18).

Our ministry is motivated and guided by Christ's own *love for a world that is ravaged by sin (2 Cor. 5:14–21). In the same way that we have been the recipients of God's great love within our own souls, and responded to his grace to us personally, we long that others also know Christ's freedom. This call to ministry enables us to put aside our personal comfort and ambitions, persevere in difficulties, and find fulfilment in seeking God's kingdom above everything else (Matt. 6:33).

Personal and corporate integrity is vital for ministry. To reflect God's character, who we say we are must be congruent with our own inner lives, continually bringing our inclination towards deception and all areas of sin to the cross of Jesus. As we depend on the Holy Spirit, we are guided, empowered and equipped for ministry that glorifies him. Transformational ministry begins with the minister's own life and social circles.

Cross-cultural ministers of the gospel will be on guard against the real temptation to use deceptive means to accomplish righteous ends. Even in problematic situations, social programmes are not used as 'cover' or 'platforms' to accomplish the 'real work' of evangelism and church planting. Projects seek to do what they say they will do, in the name and love of Jesus Christ (2 Cor. 4:2). Lives of simplicity, identification with host culture, sacrifice and humility are as important to our message as our proclamation and acts of kindness (Phil. 2:1–16). We resist all categorizing of ministries and ranking some as more important than others, because this goes against the biblical teaching on gifts/ministries of the Spirit in 1 Corinthians 12. The mandate to 'make disciples' encompasses the entire scope of evangelism, reconciliation, restoration, meeting needs and countering the effects of sin in the world, planting churches, training individuals and multiplying cross-cultural witness.

See also CHURCH PLANTING, DISCIPLE.

Bibliography

R. S. Anderson, *The Shape of Practical Theology: Empowering Ministry with Theological Praxis* (Downers Grove: InterVarsity Press, 2001); C. V. Gelder, *The Essence of the Church* (Grand Rapids: Baker, 2000); D. B. Kraybill, *The Upside-Down Kingdom* (Scottdale: Herald Press, 1990); J. Tiller, 'Ministry' in S. B. Ferguson and D. F. Wright (eds.), *New Dictionary of Theology* (Downers Grove: InterVarsity Press, 1988).

J. TEBBE

Minjung theology

Minjung theology is a Korean theology, which grew out of the particular experience of South Korean people in the political and social struggles for justice in the 1970s; it affirms Korean culture and history as the context in which a proper Korean theology is to be done. It has been an effort 'to provide a framework of political theology which takes into consideration the socio-economic and political history of Korea and the socio-political biography of the Christian koinonia in Korea' (D. Kwang-Sun Suh, *Minjung Theology*, ed. CTC-CCA, p. 17).

Minjung as the subject of history

'Minjung' is a Korean word, which may be translated as the 'mass of the people' or just the 'people'. Minjung theologians have been unwilling to define the term too sharply since they believe that minjung is a living, dynamic reality able to interpret its own existence. Commonly, the minjung has referred to those who are politically oppressed, economically exploited, sociologically marginalized, and culturally despised. It is, however, differentiated from the Marxist proletariat. While the proletariat is confined to socio-economic determination and thus to the internal logic of history, the minjung has an intrinsic transcendental dimension beyond the present history. It is also inclusive of all who are oppressed, whether due to gender, race, or ethnicity, and it is not limited to the socio-economically poor. Minjung theology calls for the understanding of the minjung as the subject of and prominent reality in history. History is not to be seen from the point of view of the ruling power but as the process in which the minjung are awakened to and gradually obtain their subjecthood through their struggles against oppressive powers and structures.

A theology of 'han'

The minjung are to seek their own liberation and salvation in the process of reclaiming their identity as the subject of history. According to minjung theologians, the most important element in the political consciousness of the minjung is *han*, which denotes both a personal and a collective feeling of unresolved resentment at the heart of the social biography of the Korean minjung, against unjustifiable suffering. Thus, *han* 'is the language of the minjung and signifies the reality of their experience. If one does not hear the sigh of *han* of the minjung, one cannot hear the voice of Christ knocking on our doors' (Nam-Dong Suh). Yet, *han* is not simply a feeling of defeat or resignation; it entails a critical social consciousness of and a growing sense of resistance against the status quo. Out of accumulated and unresolved *han* could erupt a revolution, which could be violent and destructive. According to minjung theologians, the church is to be a comforter to help heal the *han*, stop the vicious cycle of violence, and transform it into a constructive energy for social change.

Confluence of two stories

Two essential reference points for minjung theology are the biblical story and the story of the minjung; to do minjung theology means to interweave both stories. While biblical texts are carefully explored with a view to their socio-economic backdrops, the socio-cultural biography of the minjung is appreciatively studied at the same time. An underlying belief is that God has been operative in and through the minjung's history and culture, and that the minjung carry an epistemological privilege to interpret the history from God's perspective. Therefore, 'the task for Korean *minjung* theology is to testify that in the mission of God in Korea there is a confluence of the *minjung* tradition in Christianity and the Korean *minjung* tradition' (Nam-Dong Suh). What distinguishes minjung theology from *liberation theology is its strong affirmation of the people's cultural heritage, which includes mask dance, *pansori* (one-person opera), and folk tales and songs. On the one hand, the identity and reality of the minjung are known through their social biography in which both their sufferings and hopes are expressed through story-telling; minjung theology is faithfully to hear and articulately to tell the stories of the minjung from their side and their perspective. Thus, 'the Korean tradition of resistance and revolution, with its unique vitality under the incredibly negative circumstances prevailing here,' stated Catholic poet Chi-Ha Kim, 'are precious materials for a new form of human liberation,' since they represent the story of the minjung's struggle. On the other hand, the stories of the *exodus and Jesus – whose existence was concretely embodied in the minjung – are also the stories of the minjung, and serve as pivotal paradigms for understanding the total witness of the Bible.

Future of minjung theology

Minjung theology contributed to Korean Christianity by vehemently calling for the church to renew its prophetic mission to enhance human rights and to ensure justice, even at the price of its own security, against the military dictatorship and unjust economic system in the 1970s and 1980s. Minjung theology is a creative contextual theology that has discovered the minjung as agents and bearers of mission. It keenly recognizes the value of their socio-cultural-political biography as central to constructing a living theology, claiming that 'the people of the kingdom are the *minjung*'. However, such an exclusive focus on the minjung tends to blur or even erase the distinction between the minjung and the church in its ecclesiology, turning the minjung, a sociological category, into a theological one. In its hermeneutical efforts to interweave the two stories, minjung theology could put the socio-cultural-political context of the minjung on a par with Scripture to the point that it would be difficult to hear the word of God as a possible judgment against all human experience, even against that of the minjung.

Minjung theology began as a theological exercise among intellectuals and educated groups. Whether it has become a theology among and by the minjung is still a troubling question for minjung theology. Without a grass-roots movement like 'base communities', it has not been successful in developing itself as an organic theology. At the beginning of the twenty-first century, South Korea has become a democratic country, and its national economy has grown remarkably, with the labour movement becoming a major force. Faced with a challenge to identify a new horizon of vision and hope, a crucial and urgent question to be addressed by minjung theology is who now the minjung are; it is called to provide alternative narratives and images for future.

Most Korean evangelicals have held a sharply critical view of minjung theology, in particular, of its hermeneutical method and *ecclesiology. Yet, it is questionable whether they have fully recognized that minjung theology in part arose in protest against the indifference and inability in evangelical churches to confront systemic injustice. Korean evangelical Christianity's apolitical stance and insensitivity to issues of social justice has in fact curbed its prophetic mission. If minjung theology has erred on the side of identifying salvation exclusively with freedom from political, social and economic oppression, Korean evangelical theology has erred on the side of keeping salvation overly individualistic and isolating it from the social and political realities of the day. One of the challenges of minjung theology to evangelical churches would be that their theology and practice of mission become more integral and historically relevant, overcoming the dichotomy between evangelism and social justice, and being in solidarity with the poor and marginalized.

Bibliography

Commission on Theological Concerns of the Christian Conference of Asia (CTC-CCA) (ed.), *Minjung Theology: People as the Subjects of History* (Maryknoll: Orbis Books, 1983); J. C. England, J. Kuttiaimattathil, J. M. Prior, L. A. Quintos, D. Suh Kwang-sun and J. Wickeri (eds.), *Asian Christian Theologies, vol. 3: Northeast Asia* (Maryknoll: Orbis Books, 2004); *International Review of Mission* 74, 1985; J. Y. Lee (ed.), *An Emerging Theology in World Perspective: Commentary on Korean Minjung Theology* (Mystic: Twenty-Third Publications, 1988); M. R. Mullins and R. F. Young (eds.), *Perspectives on Christianity in Korea and*

Japan: The Gospel and Culture in East Asia (Lewiston: Edwin Mellen Press, 1995); D. Kwang-Sun Suh, *The Korean Minjung in Korea* (Hong Kong: CTC-CCA, 1991).

JOON-SIK PARK

Miracles

A miracle is an unexpected and unexplained event, in which God reveals himself as the gracious redeemer of humanity. This has three dimensions: *surprise*, **revelation* and **salvation*. The Greek word-groups *thauma* (to behold, to watch, to adore), *sēmeion* (signs, clues) and *teras* (miraculous signs, miracles) serve as helpful clues in helping us to interpret miracles in mission.

Miracles involve the faith to be *surprised* by *God! In this respect, the Bible plays down the view of miracles as demonstrations, which could render faith superfluous; rather they are given to awaken and strengthen faith. Already in the OT miracles are not phenomena as such, but events that draw human beings into an encounter with God.

Miracles *reveal something about God* and his purposes, which bring glory to him and provide clues to who he is and how he acts. Their primary purpose therefore is not in relation to the people involved, but as a way of enhancing God's self-revelation.

Miracles are set in the context of *salvation* and are gifts of *grace which set people free from whatever oppresses them. They are neither reproducible nor to be provoked by human beings, since they are, by definition, exclusively located in God's sphere of control and will. This means that any scientific approach to verify the possibility and existence of miracles inherently fails.

Five general missional views

The key question is whether miracles should be expected to accompany the preaching of the gospel as a normal occurrence, and therefore whether they are necessary to its effectiveness. In what sense do they confirm the truth of the gospel?

In mission there is a spectrum of positions of at least five views (with some overlapping of categories):

(1) Those with a progressive or liberal theological persuasion blur the distinction between the 'natural' and 'supernatural'. They prefer to see God as active in all of life, rather than expecting him to intervene occasionally in dramatic 'supernatural' fashion as a 'God of the gaps'. They do not see miracles as necessary for effective mission, and would not look for or pray for dramatic *healing. They see the progress of medical science leading inevitably to a better understanding of Jesus' ministry of healing and signalling an advance over the traditional claims about NT miracles.

(2) Certain theologically conservative missionaries affirm the integrity of the biblical miracles, but do not believe in their prolongation after the period of the early church, even though they believe that God answers prayer and acts sovereignly in human affairs. For them, miracles were events of revelation for the apostolic age. They would also believe therefore that miracles are not necessary for the effectiveness of the gospel, since the word of God conveys truth with its own integrity and power.

(3) Other evangelicals compare the first-time proclamation of the gospel in a context where Christ is unknown to the experience of the first-century church. Miracles therefore have their place in primary evangelism by confirming the message of salvation, and as a revelation of God, especially in cultures where the miraculous is expected and the supernatural is part of life. However, they see little role for on-going miracles after the successful introduction of Christianity to that context.

(4) Evangelicals of a more radical persuasion allow for the continuation of miracles and extraordinary spiritual manifestations, but within limits. Miracles are seen as unusual, and although they may confirm the truth of the gospel and serve as a sign of God's power, they are not seen as necessary to accompany the preaching of the gospel.

(5) In this category the full restoration of miracles and spiritual gifts is anticipated as an important dimension of mission. Going one step further than those in the fourth category, these missionaries pray for the sick and trust God for their own healing, and expect miracles to serve as a witness of God's power before unbelievers. Healing is immediately available to every believer by the exercise of faith in the atoning work of Jesus *Christ (Isa. 53:4–5; Matt. 8:17). In addition, they believe

in intercessory prayer for spiritual victory in the cosmic realm to bind the power of satanic forces that resist the successful evangelization of the nations, so *spiritual warfare becomes an important dimension of healing and evangelism.

Miracles and mission

Although there are examples of miraculous signs accompanying the preaching of the gospel in Acts (e.g. 4:29–30; 5:12–16; 8:6; 9:32–35, 42; 14:3), there are also examples of successful preaching where the miraculous is not mentioned (e.g. Acts 8:26–39; 11:20–21; 13:48; 14:1, 21). It can hardly be said therefore that miracles are necessary to effective evangelism, though they can provide a 'power encounter' which unlocks unbelief and makes a person receptive to the truth. However, the presence of miracles in themselves does not guarantee a response to Christ, even if they are verifiable, since the strict materialist, who deprecates not only the existence of God, but also any non-material existence, may only conclude that what has happened are unexplainable events which could be explained scientifically if we had the knowledge or technology.

So miracles will not convince someone who does not want to believe. But they are able to deeply move those who are honestly seeking God. That is like the bouquet of flowers which a husband buys for his wife after a conflict: if she is not willing to believe that he is genuinely sorry, the flowers will probably not convince her! However, if she is ready to forgive and is looking for a sign of remorse, a bouquet of flowers will be an unambiguous sign which will release reconciliation. Likewise, the miracles of God are not corrections by a forgetful God, but instead a proof of love to those who are looking for a sign of God's love.

Some question whether the scale or quality of miracles experienced in the ministry of Jesus, and to an extent in Acts, can possibly be reproduced today. The ministry of Jesus is clearly unique, although in sending the disciples out in mission he expected them to do what he was doing in healing and casting out demons, and the expectation of the early church was that these events would accompany their mission as signs of the presence of the *kingdom (cf. Rom. 15:19).

Thus miracles have the character of a sign. They do not stand by themselves, but are designed to focus our eyes upon God and his marvellous personhood. This becomes specifically clear in Jesus' miracles: the blind receive their sight, the lame walk, lepers are cleansed, and the deaf hear (Matt. 11:5), Jesus heals diseases and afflictions of any kind (Matt. 9:35), doing this both because he had compassion on their suffering and wanted their physical well-being, but also because he wanted them to know God and find full salvation.

Most scholars accept that the gifts of the Spirit, of which the performing of miracles is one (1 Cor. 12:10), are given to build up the church in every age, and therefore should be welcomed when they are sovereignly given. They serve as signs of the coming kingdom to remind us that there is no limit to the power of God, that he chooses a rich variety of ways through which to bring salvation, and that he is active to fulfil the purposes of his mission in the world.

See also HOLY SPIRIT.

Bibliography

C. Brown, *Miracles and the Critical Mind* (Grand Rapids: Eerdmans, 1984); N. Geisler, 'Miracles and Modern Scientific Thought' (Truth Journal: <http://www.leaderu.com/truth/1truth19>); C. J. Humphreys, *Miracles of Exodus* (San Francisco: Harper, 2003); G. B. McGee, 'Miracles and Mission Revisited', *IBMR* 25, 2001, p. 146; C. S. Lewis, *Miracles: A Preliminary Study* (New York: Macmillan, 1947); C. F. D. Moule (ed.), *Miracles: Cambridge Studies in their Philosophy and History* (London: Mowbray 1966); G. Twelftree, *Jesus the Miracle Worker: A Historical and Theological Study* (Leicester: IVP, 1999); K. L. Woodward, *The Book of Miracles* (New York: Simon & Schuster, 2000).

H. KLASSEN

Missio Dei

The Latin term *missio Dei* ('mission of God') came to common parlance especially among theologians of mission as a reference to the Christian theological understanding of mission which seeks to ground Christian missionary theory and practice in the missionary activity of the Triune God. Since the middle of the twentieth century, this understanding of Christian mission as *missio Dei* has enjoyed such a popularity that it has come to be recognized almost as a theological consensus. Based on the sending of one divine Person by another in the doctrine of the Trinity, the idea of missionary formation and practice came to be related to the church's participation in the activity of divine sending into the world. The process of formulating the missionary understanding of the doctrine of the Trinity and its missiological implication is succinctly articulated by David Bosch as follows: 'The classical doctrine on the *missio Dei* as God the Father sending the Son, and God the Father and the Son sending the Spirit was expanded to include yet another "movement": Father, Son, and Holy Spirit sending the Church into the world' (*Transforming Mission: Paradigm Shifts in Theology of Mission*, p. 390).

Karl Barth and other continental theologians, including Karl Hartenstein, are credited with the genesis of this theological understanding of mission. While he came closest to identifying the idea of mission as *missio Dei* in his paper presented at the Brandenburg Missionary Conference in 1932, Barth's theology in general served as the impetus for the development of the *missio Dei* concept. Although the term *missio Dei* was not used, the idea of deriving the Christian missionary impulse from the very nature of God was made in the Willingen conference of the International Missionary Council in 1952. In affirming the theological basis of mission, the conference stated: 'the missionary obligation of which we are a part has its source in the Triune God Himself.' The same sectional report, dealing with the theological basis of mission, concluded: 'There is no participation in Christ without participation in His mission to the world.' The Willingen conference came to be recognized as the first instance of publicly affirming this theological concept.

Karl Hartenstein, who had articulated a similar idea two decades earlier, appears to have been the first to utilize the term *missio Dei*. In his report on the Willingen conference, he wrote, 'The mission is not only obedience to a word of the Lord, it is not only the

commitment to the gathering of the congregation; it is participation in the sending of the Son, in the *missio Dei*, with the inclusive aim of establishing the lordship of Christ over the whole redeemed creation' (G. F. Vicedom, *The Mission of God: An Introduction to the Theology of Mission*, p. 5). However, no full-fledged articulation of mission as *missio Dei* was made until George Vicedom's book of the same name.

The emergence of the concept and the manner of its appearance are explained historically by some as the outcome of the new quest for the theological foundation of the missionary practice of the church. The twentieth century was a century of revolutionary change, which also brought a major crisis in the thoughts and practice of mission. For its own continued existence based on rational support, the enterprise of mission demanded a theological basis and rational justification. The concept of *missio Dei* emerged in the middle of the twentieth century as the most decisive response, as well as the most significant theme, for the development of the theology of mission. Until this period, wrote American missiologist James Scherer, 'the study of the "theology of mission" in today's sense hardly existed' (*Gospel, Church, & Kingdom: Comparative Studies in World Mission Theology*, p. 35). The concept of *missio Dei* served as the corrective to the Christendom notion of Western mission of the past centuries and gave impetus to a new and unifying thought in mission. It provided a rationally acceptable and theologically founded conception of mission. With the divine mystery at its centre, it has an open-endedness, leaving room for creative theological exploration of the divine purpose in the world. It calls for new ways of doing mission which are both theologically justified and practically challenging. The emphasis on the singularity of mission – that there is only one mission, namely God's mission – has important implications. It serves as a significant theological basis for the unity of the churches and the church's action. Symbolically, the name of the most historic ecumenical mission journal changed from *International Review of Missions* to *International Review of Mission*.

Because of the broadening of the notion of mission, reservations have been raised. At the practical level, the concept is accompanied by ambiguities and difficulties. Two issues in particular are at stake. The limitless broadening of mission leads to the loss of its cutting edge. Stephen Neill has rightly cautioned us, 'If everything is mission, nothing is mission.' Secondly, identification of God's work in secular history as God's mission questions the role of the *church. Lesslie Newbigin informs us that even the Willingen conference 'wrestled with the question of the relation between God's work in the mission of his Church and his work in the secular history' (*The Relevance of Trinitarian Doctrine for Today's Mission*, p. 23).

Since Willingen, two major competing approaches and interpretations have emerged. While one understands mission as God's evangelizing work in the world through the church, the other conceives *missio Dei* as God's activity in the secular world over and beyond the church. The first approach maintains the church as the principal vehicle of God's mission, while the latter affirms the world as the locus of God's mission and reduces the church's place 'even to the point that it excluded the Church's involvement' (Bosch, *Transforming Mission*, p. 392). Tension between church-centred and world-centred understandings of God's mission are manifested in various forms. Voices heard quite clearly in ecumenism from the 1960s endorsing the latter have tended to identify *missio Dei* with the good works and service done by all. God is at work through everything that is good. This ecumenical development has been welcomed as well as criticized in enormously broadening the concept of *missio Dei*. Some critics have observed that this unrestrained broadening has led to a loss of the uniqueness of *Christ as the central message and means of practising Christian mission. When taken to its extreme, the agenda for social justice, for instance, led to the demotion of the theme of Christ's justification.

A controversial pluralistic theology, which surfaced as a major theological theme in the 1980s, also loosely identified itself with the concept of *missio Dei*. Radical pluralists relegate the uniqueness of Christ for the sake of a theocentric theology through which they seek to affirm the revelation and saving power of God in other religious traditions. Such a theology of *missio Dei*, which gives little or no place to Christ, has drawn strong objections from evangelical missiologists. Seeing this as an 'abuse' of the concept, some suspect *missio Dei* as a merely liberal theology, but then they fail to appreciate the depth and significance of the concept. In the history of missionary thought, *missio dei* has played both deepening and corrective roles. It places the theology of mission at the heart of Christian theology by upholding the missionary nature of the Triune God from which it seeks to draw the theological basis and meaning of the church's mission. It is not the church that has a mission, it is God's mission that has a church. Mission is wherever God is at work fulfilling his missionary purposes. The strong corrective element in the concept has helped to relinquish mission from the ownership of the Western churches and to make it a truly worldwide phenomenon.

See also GOD, MISSION THEOLOGY, TRINITY.

Bibliography

D. J. Bosch, *Transforming Mission: Paradigm Shifts in Theology of Mission* (Maryknoll: Orbis Books, 1991); N. Goodall (ed.), *Missions Under the Cross: Addresses Delivered at the Enlarged Meeting of the Committee of the International Missionary Council at Willingen in Germany, 1952* (London: Edinburgh House Press, 1953); L. Newbigin, *The Relevance of Trinitarian Doctrine for Today's Mission* (London: Edinburgh House Press, 1963); H. H. Rosin, '*Missio Dei': An Examination of the Origin, Contents and Function of the Term in Protestant Missiological Discussion* (Leiden: Interuniversity Institute for Missiological and Ecumenical Research, Department of Missiology, 1972); J. A. Scherer, *Gospel, Church, & Kingdom: Comparative Studies in World Mission Theology* (Minneapolis: Augsburg Publishing House, 1987); N. E. Thomas (ed.), *Classic Texts in Mission and World Christianity* (Maryknoll: Orbis Books, 1995); G. F. Vicedom, *The Mission of God: An Introduction to the Theology of Mission*, transl. G. A. Thiele and D. Hilgendorf (St Louis: Concordia Publishing House, 1965 [1958]).

L. PACHUAU

Mission societies

Mission societies exist to facilitate Christian mission movements. To meet the exploding growth of missionary vision in the Majority World in recent years, hundreds of such voluntary mission societies have been established worldwide. This article outlines some historical dimensions of the rise of Protestant *Western* mission societies; it explores their mission strategy, and then considers some contemporary challenges for all such agencies of mission. An exploration of the significance of Western mission societies can open the door to a deeper understanding of the Western church, for example: 'It is of no small importance that the rise of the modern western Christian missions coincided with the demise of western *territorial* Christendom' (D. Irvin, in *Mission Studies*, p. 197, my emphasis). Under four headings this article offers a framework for reflection on this relationship.

Beginnings: the ultimate significance of Jesus
Mission societies first began in the seventeenth century, but were to flourish in the nineteenth century in Europe and then again in the twentieth in North America. They emerged across the denominations: Anglican, Baptist, Congregational, Lutheran, Presbyterian, and so on. By the beginning of the eighteenth century there were already a hundred mission societies. By the middle of the twentieth century they had penetrated every continent, sharing the Protestant perspective on the gospel.

It would be wrong, however, to see mission societies from a purely organizational, pragmatic perspective, as if they were *just* parachurch delivery systems for 'overseas' mission programmes on behalf of the church, or merely efficient mechanisms for church expansion. A more appreciative historical approach to the Western context comes from mission historians like Andrew Walls, who suggest that in an eighteenth-century context, without denial, complicity or endorsement in the European Enlightenment or in imperial expansion, the modern missionary movement was made possible by three things:

(1) A spirituality that encouraged mission volunteers to engage in evangelistic outreach – locally and then 'overseas' – so that others might share the ultimate significance of Jesus. This was also a practical spirituality that encouraged personal holiness and social justice (e.g. the abolition of slavery). (2) Lay people prepared to band together to pray and support those willing to share the gospel 'abroad'. (3) The practical and logistical opportunities made possible by modern communications (A. Walls, *The Cross-Cultural Process in Christian History*, ch. 11).

It has not been widely recognized, either by the sending or receiving contexts, that these three developments were the last flourish, but also the radical transformation, of a European Christianity we call 'Christendom'. Histories of *colonialism, and of the institutions of the churches sponsoring the mission societies, have dominated the interpretation of the *motivation for mission and of the reception of the gospel in other cultures. But in the new mission era what was obscured can now be clearly seen: a new 'Ephesian moment'; that first coming together at Ephesus of Jewish and Hellenistic cultures in discovering the greater significance of Jesus, has come again. This time there are now innumerable cultures brought together in the body of Christ, and therefore, in the context of *globalization, the ultimate significance of Jesus is revealed afresh (*The Cross-Cultural Process*, ch. 4).

A three-fold strategy
The three-fold strategy that emerged to characterize the work of the mission societies still stands as a major landmark in the understanding of Christian mission. The three elements of this mission strategy, that are integrated but interact separately, include the following.

First, a commitment to the permanent priority of *evangelism* that rests on the theological vision of a world interpreted by the ultimate significance of the person and work of *Jesus.

Second, the importance of planting and growing the *church* as an expression of what it means to follow Jesus in each culture and context.

Third, a practical out-working, through social transformation and individual conversion, of what following Jesus means in terms of morality, justice and social *development*.

This three-fold strategy, the height, breadth and depth of Christian mission, emerged only as the missionary movement engaged with different cultural contexts within the pre- and post-imperial period. In other words, this was not a linear theory-to-practice strategy. Rather, it emerged by experimentation, and through the interchange of mission work, as the mission societies discovered the greater significance of Jesus, grounding and shaping mission. This means that mission history is vitally important: *it is the narrative of how the gospel has been interpreted and expressed in different *cultures*. Local reception and mission motivation have steadily been integrated into mission history; these are differently interpreted, but the global spread of gospel, church and *transformation cannot be denied.

The challenge
The challenges which mission societies face in the twenty-first century include three major developments in mission: cultural, church-based and *holistic.

There is now a globalized context for how communication about religion, economics and politics works. It is therefore not possible to establish a simple mono-cultural context for promoting an authentically ethnic and contextual response to traditional Christian belief – the gospel of Jesus' ultimate significance has become everybody's gospel. This applies to Western Christians as well, who now find themselves in a cross-cultural relationship with their past as they follow Jesus in a multi-faith Western context.

In this new era of multiple communication systems about the main aspects of life, there are therefore innumerable cultures in the church each expressing their commitment to Jesus in different ways, and impacting on each other. It is thus not surprising that people are asking about the nature of the church. Western mission societies are therefore having to think again, not just about their traditional 'mission field' contexts, which have changed, but about 'home' contexts. In the latter there are experiments with alternative or fresh expressions of church which, in ethos, are similar to the pioneering churches planted by the Western mission societies in their earlier cross-cultural outreach.

The threefold approach to mission has been 'bought out and broken up'. Development agencies and proselytizing missions have moved in and, in specializing in one aspect of the threefold approach, have divided what should be kept together and emphasized just one aspect of mission. This leaves the mission societies facing a double challenge of secularization and 'hijacking', and also means that they are left with the challenging second aspect of mission – the church! Mission societies (and their histories) are important because they keep together the three aspects of mission, and do this as a *voluntary expression of a normative Christian commitment to mission* (J. V. Taylor, *For All the World*, ch. 5).

Given these changes, and the rise of non-religious voluntary civil society, is it time to reassess mission societies and acknowledge a 'disjunction between the era for which these organizations were designed and the emerging new phase' (W. R. Shenk, *Changing Frontiers of Mission*, p. 178)? Perhaps the relief and development agencies, spun off from mission societies, religious orders and churches as specialist or secularizing agencies, are the true inheritors of what mission societies stand for, expressing the appropriate form of mission today? Yet the paradox, that mission societies are not only the last flourish of Christendom but also the subversion of the Western territorial church, leaves the possibility that they still contain the seeds of the future of mission, sustaining a wide range of mission networks and relationships.

Responses
So what place do mission societies have today? What priorities do they embody that contribute to contemporary mission? What might be the key factors uniting such a world-wide movement?

First, there is a common commitment to interpret the world from the constants of a *Christian theological vision*. God's mission of redemption and re-creation, revealed uniquely through Jesus and by the particular work of the Spirit, interprets all time and place, and provides a Christian orientation for humanity and culture. God as the 'beyond in our midst', the 'native and stranger in every context' creates a new world for all. This theological vision is held in conversation with those of other faiths or no faith.

Second, mission societies, in keeping together the threefold aspect of mission, still provide an *analogy of God's mission* (see *missio Dei*) in which there is a resistance to secularizing or to specializing each aspect of mission. They are still committed to evangelism centred on the tradition of Jesus' lordship, to creating Christian community, and to communicating and enabling holistic transformation. Nevertheless, there are new forms of mission, such as business-as-mission, emerging church and environmental and social transformation initiatives.

A third factor is that mission societies have become aware of their own contribution as being themselves faith communities: they are *trans-local vocational mission communities and networks*. Their way of life is therefore not a specialist Christian interest, but something reflecting the core of Christian identity. They invite all Christians into participation for the sake of God's world mission.

Conclusion

With the breakdown of Western territorial Christianity, initiated partly by mission societies, we are moving into a new period of mission. 'The territorial "from-to" idea that underlay the older missionary movement has to give way to a concept much more like that of the Christians within the Roman Empire in the second and third centuries: parallel presences in different circles and different levels each seeking to penetrate within and beyond its circle' (A. Walls, in *The Missionary Movement in Christian History*, p. 258). In this era the mission societies, as communities who make mission connections between different levels and diverse circles, have an ongoing role and strategic significance in sharing the ultimate significance of Jesus in all contexts and cultures.

See also TWO-THIRDS WORLD MISSION MOVEMENTS, WOMEN IN MISSION.

Bibliography

G. H. Anderson, R. Coote, N. Horner and J. Phillips, *Mission Legacies: Biographical Studies of Leaders of the Modern Missionary Movement* (Maryknoll: Orbis Books, 1998); S. B. Bevans and R. P. Schroeder, *Constants in Context: A Theology of Mission for Today* (Maryknoll: Orbis Books, 2004); J. Cox, 'Master Narratives of Imperial Missions', in J. S. Scott and G. Griffiths (eds.), *Mixed Messages: Materiality, Textuality, Missions* (New York: Palgrave Macmillan, 2005);

D. Irvin, 'Ecumenical Dislodgings' in *Mission Studies*, vol. 22 No. 2, pp. 187–206 (Leiden: Brill 2005); A. Porter, *Religion versus Empire: British Protestant Missionaries and Overseas Expansion, 1700–1914* (Manchester: Manchester University Press, 2004); W. R. Shenk, *Changing Frontiers of Mission* (Maryknoll: Orbis Books, 1999); R. Schreiter, *The New Catholicity: Theology between the Global and the Local* (Maryknoll: Orbis Books, 1997); B. Stanley, *The Bible and the Flag: Protestant and Imperialism in the Nineteenth and Twentieth Centuries* (Leicester: Apollos, 1990); J. V. Taylor, *For All the World* (London: Hodder & Stoughton, 1966); A. Walls, 'Missionary Societies and the Fortunate Subversion of the Church' and 'The Old Age of the Missionary Movement', in *The Missionary Movement in Christian History: Studies in the Transmission of Faith* (Edinburgh: T. & T. Clark, 1996); A. Walls, *The Cross-Cultural Process in Christian History* (Edinburgh: T. & T. Clark, 2002).

T. DAKIN

Mission theology in the twentieth century

Terminology and discipline

In the second part of the nineteenth century Gustav Warneck, the founding father of mission studies as an academic discipline, repeatedly used the term 'mission theology'. After a while it became popular and replaced the older term 'theory of mission'.

'Mission theology' is the normative part of mission studies or missiology, as distinct from 'mission philosophy' and 'mission science' which are its empirical dimensions. Whereas the philosophy and science of mission can be developed by both Christians and non-Christians, only Christians are equipped to do mission theology, because committed Christian belief is the *conditio sine qua non* for doing mission studies in a normative way.

Johannes C. Hoekendijk at Utrecht made another distinction, between 'mission theology' and 'missionary theology'. He saw the former as that theological discipline in the field of systematic and practical theology which deals with the who, how, what, where and when of missions; it is strictly the 'theology of mission'. 'Missionary *theology*', however, was viewed as the whole of systematic and practical theology seen from a missionary viewpoint. Consequently the latter is broader and less specific than the former. Thus the whole theology of the apostle *Paul can be regarded as 'missionary' ('missionary theology'), although merely some parts of his letters explicitly deal with 'mission' ('mission theology'). This dictionary is looking at mission and theology from both directions, but this article focuses mainly on mission theology, or the theology of mission.

Finally, the theology of mission(s) must be distinguished from the theology of religions. As an academic discipline the former is older than the latter (which evolved from the 1960s), although the latter is broader. From one point of view, mission theology can be regarded as a branch of the theology of (Christian and non-Christian) religion. Alternatively, Christian missions produce their own view of non-Christian religions, so that the Christian theology of mission becomes the mother of the Christian theology of religions. In other words, Christian mission can be dealt with in the framework of the theology of religion (the dominant viewpoint among pluralist scholars) or conversely, religions can also be worked out in the framework of Christian mission (cf. the publications of the Dutch lay theologian Hendrik Kraemer).

A brief historical perspective

It is outside the scope of this article to give an in-depth survey of the history of Protestant mission theology. However, this history can be traced back to the Pietists, the Moravians, and William Carey in the eighteenth century. Nevertheless, it only started to flourish after the world missionary conferences of Edinburgh 1910, Jerusalem 1928 and Tambaram 1938. The first decades after the Second World War are described by Roger Bassham as a period of 'worldwide creative tension' between ecumenical, evangelical and Roman Catholic theologies of mission, and this tension was set to continue through the following decades. At the same time both *Pentecostal mission theology and also non-Western theologies began to flourish. The former can be traced back to the Azusa Street revival of 1906. The latter is preceded by the contributions to Edinburgh 1910 of such

men as Vedanayagam S. Azariah (India), Chyeng Ching Yi (China), and Tasuku Harada (Japan).

Mission theology can be subdivided in various ways. In this article the classical division of Christian theology into four areas is used. Consequently biblical, historical, systematic and practical mission theology are identified and reviewed.

Biblical mission theology

Although the apostle Paul is widely regarded as the first mission theologian, he was a disciple of Jesus *Christ, the one who both was sent and has sent. Moreover, the divine-human mission and ministry of Jesus Christ cannot be understood properly unless the missions of Moses, the Hebrew prophets and Israel as 'light to the nations' (Isa. 42:6; 49:6) are taken into account. Thus there is continuity and unity in the biblical theology of mission.

Biblical mission theology investigates the use and meaning of the verb *šālaḥ* and the noun *šālîaḥ* in the Hebrew Bible, and the verbs *pempein* and *apostellein* and the nouns *apostole* and *apostolos* in the NT. The biblical scholar Karl H. Rengstorf regarded *šālîaḥ* as the technical term for 'the sending of a messenger with a special task; the messenger does not have to be named. In other words, the emphasis rests on the fact of sending in conjunction with the one who sends, not on the one who is sent' (in *Theological Dictionary of the New Testament*, p. 400). The 'one who sends' is the one sovereign *God, identified as JHWH in the OT and the Lord Jesus Christ in the NT. The message of the prophets in the OT to Israel, and that of the apostles and evangelists in the NT to Israel and non-Israel (Hebrew: *goiim*), is therefore always God's message, never their own message.

Some biblical scholars distinguish between missionary Bible books (Ruth, Deutero-Isaiah, Jonah, Acts) and other Bible books, as well as between missionary Bible chapters (Pss. 67; 87; Matt. 10, par.; Matt. 28, par.) and other Bible chapters. But other biblical scholars regard the whole Bible as a missionary book. Hugh Martin is an early supporter of the latter view: 'The Bible is a missionary book, not because it contains isolated texts with a missionary flavour, but because the main line of argument that binds together all its volumes is the exposition, the unfolding, and the gradual execution of a missionary purpose' (*The Kingdom Without Frontiers*, p. IX).

The 'execution of a missionary purpose' in the Bible has various aspects. A basic one is that the people of Israel moved away from the cyclical view of time and history common in the surrounding nations, to develop a radically theocentric linear view. They rejected polytheism and worshipped the one god of history: JHWH created the world *ex nihilo* in the beginning (Gen. 1), called Abraham out of cyclical Ur of the Chaldeans (Gen. 12:1–12) and Israel out of cyclical Egypt (Exod.), went on to unfold his purpose to the Hebrew prophets and in Jesus Christ, and promised to bring the history of Israel and the *goyim* to fulfilment at the end of the times. The foundational events of the *exodus and the *resurrection are viewed as unrepeatable and irreversible. Consequently the Bible rejects *goyim* belief in the eternal cycle of birth, death, and rebirth (*reincarnation), endless in time. It understands history as unidirectional, via a unique process of *sacrifice and atonement, *repentance and *renewal, *reconciliation and *liberation in history, and via the return of the Messiah/Christ in power and glory (*parousia*) and the final *judgment at the end of the times, moving towards a new heaven and a new earth. The achievement of God's purpose (*telos*) at the end of the times, promised to Israel, includes the *goyim* (Matt. 28:19). It is through Jesus Christ, the Christian mission and the church that the OT's linear view of time and history became globally recognized. The person and work of Jesus Christ revealed to Israel and the *goyim* 'the meaning of history' (H. Berkhof, *Christ the Meaning of History*).

However, the path to the end of the times in Scripture is not strewn with roses: the people of God will not only experience revivals, *healing and other miracles, but also exile, *persecution and *martyrdom. Sacrifice goes with forgiveness, humility, *love, righteousness and stewardship as the lifestyle of the pilgrims to Zion.

Since the classical 1962 study of Johannes Blauw, *The Missionary Nature of the Church: A Survey of the Biblical Theology of Mission*, which is based upon the concept of universality ('all nations') versus particularity, other theological surveys and analyses of missions in the Bible have been published that deal with mission either in the whole Bible, or merely in the OT, in the NT, and in specific Bible books such as the letters of the apostle Paul.

Historical mission theology

Historical mission theology starts chronologically more or less where biblical mission theology ends (around the end of the first century of the Christian era). At the same time, it views biblical mission theology as normative for understanding human history and mission. Systematic theologians compare the link between biblical and historical mission theology with the connection between Scripture and tradition.

In the course of the two millennia after the incarnation, suffering, death, resurrection and ascension of Jesus Christ, Jewish Christian (or Messianic Jewish), Eastern Orthodox, Roman Catholic, Anglican, Lutheran, Reformed, Mennonite, Moravian, Methodist, Baptist, Evangelical, Pentecostal, post-denominational, and many more, missions have been established, each in their own way applying biblical and traditional insights. David J. Bosch's widely used study, *Transforming Mission* distinguished six paradigm shifts in the course of history: post-NT, the missionary paradigms of the Eastern (Orthodox) Church, the Roman Catholic Church in the Middle Ages, the Protestant Reformation, the Enlightenment era, and the contemporary ecumenical era. In this regard, Bosch largely followed Hans Küng's survey of the history of Christian theology. The main problem of Bosch's *opus magnum* is that it applied Küng's *internal* Christian distinction and outline to the *external* relations of Christianity to non-Christian religions, *world-views, and ideologies. The consequence is a narrow perspective, minimalizing analysis of missionary engagement with other religious traditions or non-Christian movements. Third millennium evangelical mission theology has to have a much broader framework and perspective than Bosch. The really fundamental paradigm shifts in world history are people's past and present moving away from or moving towards Socrates, the Buddha, Lao-Tse, Muhammad, Enlightenment philosophers,

Marx, the gurus of New Religious Movements, and so on, and it is with these movements that evangelical mission theology must engage.

So historical mission theology primarily reflects upon humanity's acceptance or rejection of the linear view of time implied in the OT and NT: world history as having a beginning and an end. This biblical view is accepted, but at the same time changed, by Islam as religion, by evolutionism (big bang theory) as world-view, and by marxism-leninism-maoism as ideology. It is rejected not only by the primal religions and Hinduism, Buddhism, Taoism and other cyclical Asian religions, but also, in the West, by theosophy, anthroposophy, most new religious movements, and the New Age Movement. So Christian mission in a cyclical world-view context must be quite different from Christian mission in a linear context; just as mission in the context of primal religions with an oral tradition has proved to be different from mission in the context of religions, world-views and ideologies with normative texts.

Historical mission theology also reflects upon humanity's acceptance or rejection of Jesus Christ as God's ultimate revelation of purpose in human history. It reflects on the fact that Jesus is more widely known than merely in Christianity; his name is not only mentioned in the Qur'an, but also in many publications outside the realm of the linear world-view. For instance, several *Hindus referred to Jesus Christ as one of the great avatars (next to Rama, Krishna and the Buddha). The crucial mission question is: how to interpret such references to Jesus Christ? On the one hand, fulfilment theologians, such as John N. Farquhar in India, have regarded them as preparation for the gospel (*praeparatio evangelica*): Jesus Christ provides the fulfilment of the highest aspirations and aims of Hinduism and other religions, world-views and ideologies. On the other hand, orthodox Christians have judged these views only negatively; in every context they insist that there is 'no other name given under heaven by which we must be saved' (Acts 4:12).

Historical mission theology is less developed than biblical theology. Western scholars, challenged by their interaction with the adherents of non-Christian religions and world-views, have wrestled with questions of the providence of God in history. Contemporary non-Western scholars in this field, such as Kwame Bediako and Lamin Sanneh, have sought to reinterpret mission history in relation to their own religious and secular contexts. In the West, after the publication of his seven volume *History of the Expansion of Christianity*, Kenneth S. Latourette pointed to 'the advance and recession' of Christian missions in world history, concluding that the path of Jesus Christ as 'the unquenchable light' had broadened over the centuries. In a 1959 article Bishop Lesslie Newbigin understood Jesus Christ not only as the centre of world history, but also as the one who holds the whole of history in his 'grip'. Through Jesus Christ, world history is being propelled toward its ultimate goal, through tribulation and conflict to the final consummation in which the judgment and the mercy of God, as set forth in the cross, are conclusively worked out. And Arend Th. van Leeuwen pleaded for an 'ecumenical theology of history' which would unmask false Christs and false prophets. For the present author, historical mission theology also needs to reflect upon the way in which the idea of a 'Christian era' challenges secular views of history, creating signs which point to the full realization of God's *telos* at the end of the times.

Systematic mission theology

Systematic mission theology is rooted in biblical and historical mission theology. It seeks to develop a 'doctrine' of mission and its identity and purpose in context. The first Protestant theologian who did this was Gisbertus Voetius (founder of Utrecht University in 1636). He based mission primarily on God's decree of predestination. This Calvinistic doctrine did not however make Voetius passive: missions were needed to achieve God's *telos* in history; they aim at (1) *conversion, (2) the *planting of churches, and (3) the glorification and manifestation of divine *grace. In the centuries after Voetius other purposes have been added, including Christianization of cultures, justice for the poor, peace building, and care for the *environment/ecology.

Theocentrism, Christocentrism, and/or

pneumatocentrism (see *Holy Spirit) are characteristics of most 'systems' of mission theology. Kraemer's classic work, *The Christian Message in a Non-Christian World*, is especially marked by radical theo- and Christocentrism: in the world of non-Christian religions, world-views and ideologies, God's revelation in Jesus Christ is viewed as the decisive and exclusive disclosure of 'the mystery of [God's] will' (Eph. 1:9). In Kraemer's own words: 'Not the mystery of [God's] being or essence is revealed, because that remains God's exclusive domain, but his redemptive will towards mankind. God's saving will, ... manifest in divine action, is what is revealed ... Therefore it is quite natural that the God who wills and acts is the God who commands, and that the appropriate correlate to the divine command is human obedience' (p. 73). *Missio Dei* (a term introduced by the German theologian Karl W. Hartenstein) and *missio Christi* can be regarded as the *alpha* of systematic mission theology. The subjection to, and adoration of the God of Israel, the Father of Jesus Christ – *soli Deo gloria* – by all human beings is then its *omega*. The pneumatocentrism of the Pentecostal movement and the charismatic renewal supplements Kraemer's theo- and Christocentrism in mission and mission studies.

Additionally systematic mission theology is shaped by anthropocentrism, soteriocentrism and ecclesiocentrism. Mission is anthropocentric because of the covenant relationship between God and humanity since creation. Evangelical theology, until recent years, has not had a strong doctrine of *creation and *humanity, preferring to focus its primary concern on mission and salvation. The 1974 Lausanne Covenant stated: 'Jesus Christ is the only mediator between God and man ... To proclaim Jesus as "the Saviour of the world" is not to affirm that all men are either automatically or ultimately saved, still less to affirm that all religions offer salvation in Christ' (para. 3). This statement implicitly challenged the perspective of salvation as humanization which dominated the 1973 World Missionary Conference of the WCC in Bangkok: 'Salvation today'. Ecclesiocentrism (seen in Roman Catholic missiology and the *Church Growth school), which focuses on offices (ordination), ministries (episcopacy, priesthood, laity), *sacraments (baptism, Eucharist) and growth,

is widely disputed. It is not favoured by Pietists, with their personalized approach; but neither is it supported by the growing group of missiologists who regard the *kingdom of God as more important than the *church as a body. In the context of non-Christian belief-systems, systematic mission theology must rethink and, if possible, restore the balance between polarities: in the all-embracing framework of the *missio Dei* (with its trinitarian perspective), attention should be paid to both *missio hominum* (universality) and *missio ecclesiae* (particularity); to both eternal and present salvation; to both the individual and the covenant/communion of saints; and to both the church as institution and as God's kingdom. These relationships need to be held in creative tension with one another.

*Eschatology is not an appendix of systematic mission theology but a core issue. In 'the last days' (the period since the cross and the resurrection of Jesus Christ) systematic mission theologies must clarify how the Triune God directs humanity to its *telos* at the end of the times.

After Kraemer's pre-war *opus magnum* many missiologists have published theologies of mission, theologies of evangelism, theologies of evangelization and theologies of the apostolate. But hardly any had the deep insight and broad knowledge of Kraemer. Nevertheless, outstanding studies by Stephen C. Neill, Kenneth Cragg and George R. Sumner paved the way for drafting a new comprehensive *Christian message in a non-Christian world*.

Practical mission theology

Practical missionary theology reflects upon putting the 'theory' of missions into 'practice'. It includes not only well-known themes such as educational missions and medical missions, but also teaching and preaching, *worship, pastoral care, missionary service and encounter.

The first crucial practical issue is the preparation of mission partners as people: their vocation, *training, theological education, language abilities, and views on the aims and motives of mission. Many evangelicals are trained for evangelism, church planting and *spiritual warfare, whereas ecumenical missionaries have focused on how to create social justice, welfare, non-violence and reconciliation. In recent years however there has been a more '*holistic' training for evangelicals, involving 'heads, hearts and hands'. They have recognized that love has to be the hallmark of mission, both for people in their human need (e.g. HIV/AIDS patients) and spiritual need, whether they are 'reached' or '*unreached' peoples at home or abroad.

This relates theologically to the relation between word and deed. Over against ecumenicals such as Hoekendijk, evangelicals have emphasized the primacy of evangelism, strongly influenced by evangelists such as Billy Graham: 'I am convinced if the church went back to its main task of ... getting people converted to Christ, it would have a far greater impact on the social, moral and psychological needs of men than any other thing it could possibly do. Some of the greatest movements of history have come about as result of men being converted to Christ' (in *In Word and Deed*, p. 234). It could be argued that the abolition of slavery is a good example of Graham's conviction.

Closely related is the issue of how mission relates to political and social issues, requiring *presence, *dialogue, *development, human rights and the struggle for religious freedom among others. In a world of great tensions between religious traditions, inter-religious dialogue, interfaith dialogue, or 'dialogue with peoples of living faiths' (WCC's terminology) must be high up the agenda. Most evangelicals have traditionally affirmed dialogue as certainly a duty, but never replacing the missionary task of proclaiming Jesus Christ as 'the way, the truth and the life' (John 14:6). Many, however, have recognized that mission does not have to choose between dialogue or evangelism. For example, in the religiously plural setting of the Roman Empire, John's Gospel combined dialogue (involving creative use of the Greek concept of the *logos*) with proclamation of the Word become flesh in the exclusive revelation of the Word of Christ.

The relationship of mission to social realities obliges it to engage with the context in which it is practised. '*Contextualization' (cf. contextual theologies) was and is discussed under related headings: *accommodation, acculturation, adaptation, assimilation, association, communication, *inculturation, indigenization. Robert J. Schreiter's *Con-structing Local Theologies* has proved an excellent guide to the study of the contextuality of Christian missions.

This however raises the issue of *syncretism. The attempted accommodation of elements of non-Christian belief-systems with the Christian faith can be seen both in non-Western and Western contexts. Over against Kraemer, who thought of syncretism as 'illegitimate', M. M. Thomas (India) pleaded for a 'Christ-centred syncretism', which recognized the possibility and even necessity of Jesus Christ taking form in different cultures and reforming them from within. This shift in WCC thinking (from Kraemer to Thomas, and beyond from Thomas to Stanley J. Samartha and Wesley Ariarajah) was not acceptable to most evangelicals. They declared in the Lausanne Covenant: 'We reject as derogatory to Christ and the gospel every kind of syncretism and dialogue which implies that Jesus Christ speaks equally through all religions and ideologies' (para. 3).

Finally, practical mission theology identifies and relates to groups of people (*ethnic groups, tribals, *migrants, *refugees, youth, women – involving *feminism and *gender issues); categories of missionary work (rural mission, *urban mission, industrial mission); and mission *management (methods, strategies, priorities, mass media, fund-raising, etc.). A few practical mission theologians reflect on non-Christian practices (such as ancestor worship, astrology, yoga, magic, *witchcraft, spirit possession and voodoo).

The agenda for evangelical mission theology must include the missionary character of non-Christian religions (the *jihad* of Muslims, Ramakrishna mission, the radiation of the Dalai Lama); world-views (such as humanism and secularism); and ideologies (the propaganda of nationalism and communism); and the way they challenge both Christianity and society at large.

There are more missionary publications in the field of practical theology than in biblical, historical and systematic theology, but there is no comprehensive survey of practical mission theology. Encyclopedias are useful introductory guides in this broad field.

Final observations

The famous words of John R. Mott, leading figure in the International Missionary Council

(1921–61), 'Before "give" and before "go" comes "pray". This is the divine order', are still relevant. They eminently set the classical phrase, 'pray and work (*ora et labora*)' in a missionary setting.

It is no longer the case that the West is the subject and the non-Western world the object of the missionary enterprise. All Christians and all churches are now seen as responsible for 'taking the whole Gospel to the whole world' (Lausanne II in Manila, 1989). In an increasingly complex world the missionary task becomes greater. At the same time, each new generation can more easily share the responsibility, since there are now more mission agencies and missionaries than ever before in history.

In the contemporary situation both unity and diversity are needed for effective mission (Eph. 4:3–6). Diversity in the body of Christ today is a blessing, so long as it does not endanger fundamental unity. Mission is enriched by different churches and Christian communities (ashrams in Asia, *African Initiated Churches in sub-Saharan Africa and base communities in Latin America), different types of mission (holistic mission, faith missions, etc.), different types of *evangelism (*power evangelism, *presence evangelism, etc.) and different types of theology (*African, *Asian, *Black, *Dalit, *Indian, *Minjung, *Latin American theologies).

Mission 'at the crossroads' or 'in a pluralist world' engages every dimension of life: private life (sex, marriage, family, work, leisure, *money, tax) as well as public life (culture, politics, socio-economic activities); nothing can be left outside the dominion of God in Christ. And it must use all available means: literature, *art, *drama, theatre, *music.

The immense missionary task in the coming century in a pluralist, multicultural and globalized world, may be more complex. But its focus remains, as it has always done, on the challenge to all religions (including *African traditional religions and *folk religion), all world-views (including modernism and *postmodernism) and all ideologies (including racism, capitalism and neo-colonialism) to recognize the truth of Israel's affirmation: 'The LORD (JHWH) is our God, the LORD (JHWH) alone' (Deut. 6:4) and its extension in and through the church: 'Jesus is the Messiah/Christ' (Mark 8:29, par.).

Bibliography

Association of Professors of Missions, *The Theology of the World Apostolate: Common Ground for Protestant-Catholic Consideration*, held at Eastern Baptist Theological Seminary, Philadelphia, 1964 (N.p., 1964); R. C. Bassham, *Mission Theology: 1948–1975, Years of Creative Tension, Ecumenical, Evangelical and Roman Catholic* (Pasadena, William Carey Library, 1979); K. Bediako, *Christianity in Africa: The Renewal of a Non-Western Religion* (Edinburgh: Edinburgh University Press, 1995); H. Berkhof, *Christ the Meaning of History* (London: SCM Press, 1966); J. Blauw, *The Missionary Nature of the Church: A Survey of the Biblical Theology of Mission* (New York: McGraw-Hill, 1962); D. J. Bosch, *Transforming Mission: Paradigm Shifts in Theology of Mission* (Maryknoll, Orbis Books, 1991); O. E. Costas, *Theology of the Crossroads in Contemporary Latin America: Missiology in Mainline Protestantism: 1969–1974* (Amsterdam: Rodopi, 1976); K. Cragg, *The Christ and the Faiths: Theology in Cross-Reference* (London: SPCK, 1985); D. S. Gilliland, *Pauline Theology and Mission Practice* (Grand Rapids: Eerdmans, 1983); A. F. Glasser and D. A. McGavran, *Contemporary Theologies of Mission* (Grand Rapids: Baker Book House, 1985); J. A. B. Jongeneel, 'The Missiology of Gisbertus Voetius: The First Protestant Theology of Missions', *Calvin Theological Journal* 26, 1991, pp. 47–79; J. A. B. Jongeneel, *Philosophy, Science and Theology of Mission in the 19th and 20th Centuries: A Missiological Encyclopedia*, 2 vols. (Frankfurt am Main: Lang, 1995–1997; repr. in Bangalore: Centre for Contemporary Christianity, 2006); J. A. B. Jongeneel, 'Is Missiology an Academic Discipline?' *Exchange* 27, 1998, pp. 208–221; W. C. Kaiser Jr, *Mission in the Old Testament: Israel as a Light to the Nations* (Grand Rapids: Baker Books, 2000); J. A. Kirk, *What is Mission: Theological Explorations* (London: Darton, Longman, Todd, 1999); R. Kolb, *Speaking the Gospel Today: A Theology for Evangelism* (St Louis: Concordia Publishing House, 1984); H. Kraemer, *The Christian Message in a Non-Christian World* (London: Edinburgh House Press, 1938); W. J. Larkin Jr and J. F. Williams (eds.), *Mission in the New Testament: An Evangelical Approach* (Maryknoll, NY: Orbis Books,

1998); K. S. Latourette, *A History of the Expansion of Christianity*, 7 vols. (Exeter, Devon: Paternoster Press, 1971 [1937–45]); K. S. Latourette, *The Unquenchable Light* (London: Eyre, Spottiswoode, 1948); H. Lindsell, *An Evangelical Theology of Missions* (Grand Rapids: Zondervan, 1970); H. Martin, *The Kingdom Without Frontiers: The Witness of the Bible to the Missionary Purpose of God* (London: Student Christian Movement, 1927); A. S. Moreau (ed.), *Evangelical Dictionary of World Missions* (Grand Rapids: Baker Books, 2000); K. Müller, *Mission Theology: An Introduction* (Nettetal: Steyler Verlag, 1987); K. Müller, T. Sundermeier, S. B. Bevans and R. H. Bliese (eds.), *Dictionary of Missions: Theology, History, Perspectives* (Maryknoll, NY: Orbis Books, 1997); S. C. Neill, *Christian Faith and Other Faiths: The Christian Dialogue with Other Religions* (London: Oxford University Press, 1965); J. E. L. Newbigin, 'The Gathering up of History in Christ', in C. C. West and D. M. Paton (eds.), *The Missionary Church in East and West* (London: SCM Press, 1959); J. E. L. Newbigin, *The Open Secret: An Introduction to the Theology of Mission* (Grand Rapids: Eerdmans, 1995); B. J. Nicholls (ed.), *In Word and Deed: Evangelism and Social Responsibility* (Exeter, Devon: Paternoster Press, 1985); A. H. Oussoren, *William Carey: His Missionary Principles* (Leiden, Sythoff, 1945); P. A. Pomerville, *The Third Force in Missions: A Pentecostal Contribution to Contemporary Mission Theology* (Peabody: Hendrickson, 1985); V. Ramachandra, *The Recovery of Mission: Beyond the Pluralist Paradigm* (Grand Rapids: Eerdmans, 1997); K. H. Rengstorf, '*Apostello* and *pempo* in the LXX (OT) and Judaism', in G. Kittel (ed.), *Theological Dictionary of the New Testament*, vol. 1 (Grand Rapids: Eerdmans, 1964); L. Sanneh, *Encountering the West: Christianity and the Global Cultural Process* (Maryknoll, NY: Orbis Books, 1993); R. J. Schreiter, *Constructing Local Theologies* (Maryknoll, NY: Orbis Books, 1993); D. Senior and C. Stuhlmüller, *The Biblical Foundations for Mission* (Grand Rapids: Eerdmans, 1983); G. R. Sumner, *The First and the Last: The Claim of Jesus Christ and the Claims of Other Religious Traditions* (Grand Rapids: Eerdmans, 2004); C. Van Engen, *Mission on the Way: Issues in Mission Theology* (Grand Rapids: Baker Books, 1996); A. T. Van Leeuwen, *Christianity in World History: The Meeting of the Faiths of East and West* (London: Edinburgh House Press, 1965).

J. A. B. JONGENEEL

Money

Although the topic of money receives extensive mention in the Bible, it has been neglected in many missiological circles. More recently as church leaders in the Two-Thirds World have insisted on the recovery of a more *holistic gospel, the role that money and economics play in missions has received more attention and has become more controversial.

It can be argued that money has been a blessed instrument used by God to extend the gospel of Jesus Christ. Church history seems to back up that claim. The efficiency and material success of Western economies greatly facilitated international missions in the nineteenth and twentieth centuries by enabling churches to send missionaries to Africa, Asia and Latin America. Most churches in the Global South owe at least some of their growth to the role of Christian wealth from the West. Today many Christian relief agencies are making effective use of money in partnership with local churches to bring well-targeted and well-costed *development projects.

Nevertheless, many Third World church leaders argue that the transfer of wealth has been a mixed blessing. Sometimes it has created issues of power and control, when those who have the money want to direct how the money is spent, and trust and responsibility are not handed over to the local church. Sometimes money has been spent unilaterally and inappropriately, when the local church would have preferred to focus on other needs. Sometimes it has resulted in an unhealthy dependency on foreign support. Sometimes issues of the misuse or mishandling of money, where there has been a failure of accountability, have created tensions on both sides.

The gospel itself issues warnings about wealth, which are relevant for both rich and poor. Although money in itself is morally neutral, John the Baptist preached a repentance which required changes in how people acquired or utilized money and possessions (Luke 3:7–14). Jesus recognized that the idolatry of money was a serious problem in his day (the rich young ruler, parable of the seeds, the money-loving Pharisees). Although materialism is a major problem in today's world, many presentations of the gospel (e.g. the Four Spiritual Laws, Evangelism Explosion, Peace with God, etc.) ignore these economic dimensions of repentance. As a consequence, conversions tend to be dichotomized and superficial, and result in church life that is frequently shallow and individualistic. It has been said that the last place to be converted is a person's pocket.

The most extensive and pertinent passage regarding mission and money is 2 Corinthians 8 – 9. Just like today, the first century witnessed great disparities between the haves and the have-nots. The Jewish Christians in Jerusalem were very poor, whereas some believers in Corinth (and in some other locations) were fairly well off. Paul spent most of his third 'missionary' journey, not on planting new churches, but rather on organizing a collection from the Gentile Christians for the believers in Jerusalem. Paul mentioned the collection in 1 Corinthians (16:1–4). The Corinthians responded with enthusiastic words, but their subsequent actions lagged. So Paul dedicated two entire chapters to rekindling the project among them. It was not merely a good 'social' project. Paul understood the collection as a work of grace (2 Cor. 8:7), just like the *grace demonstrated in the ministry of Jesus (v. 9). Paul tried to motivate the Corinthians' giving by even describing the incarnation in economic terms: 'For you know the grace of our Lord Jesus Christ, that though he was rich, yet for your sake he became poor, so that you through his poverty might become rich.' Paul's economic goal for this project was that there might be 'equality' (v. 13, and then repeated again in v. 14), and his overarching goal was reconciliation between Jewish and Gentile Christians. The fact that the apostle appeals to the sacrificial example of the Macedonian churches, the enthusiasm of Titus, the OT reference to the manna in the desert, and most importantly, to the incarnation of our Lord, all suggest that this Pauline project has universal application and cannot be relegated to a unique, culturally specific, first-century experiment. The universal challenge is to

open-hearted generosity, and disparities in wealth can be opportunities for genuine partnership and liberating support. But Canadian missiologist Jonathan Bonk forcefully argues that the 'relative affluence and security of our Western missionaries frequently constitutes a serious obstacle to the furtherance of the Gospel'. If missionaries are living in relative affluence amongst those they serve, this can raise serious tensions for the local churches.

*Globalization and disparate economic systems have created additional problems for the mission of the church. What do you do if you are a gifted pastor in the Third World, and you are invited to become the regional representative for an international Christian organization at a salary three or four times your previous one? Or perhaps you are invited to move to Germany, England, or the USA, to pastor there because there are not enough ministers in the West? The enticement of a larger salary draws away some of the best and brightest church leaders.

The fact that 30,000 children needlessly die every day due to poverty and sickness demands a response of love from a church faithful to Jesus Christ. The year 2000 provided the church with a special opportunity to deal with worldwide poverty. The *jubilee legislation (Lev. 25) was picked up, as churches in the Two-Thirds World, together with a large coalition of Christian organizations and churches worldwide, including the Pope, urged the wealthiest countries to forgive the foreign debt of the poorest countries. Many Western economies were obliged to respond by initiating a programme of debt relief. But however good such campaigns are, they need to be supplemented by sustained pressure on financial institutions and governments to bring greater justice into the ways in which trade systems, money markets and international capital flows operate.

Latin American theologian René Padilla argues that our contemporary ecological crisis and socioeconomical inequalities are both consequences of a world economical system that favours the few at the expense of the many. He urges a return to the jubilee principles of *ecology and freedom (Lev. 25:1–12), justice and peace (Lev. 25:13–23), and solidarity with the poor expressed through legislation that dealt with loans, property and slavery (Lev. 25:23–55). According to Padilla, allowing the 'invisible hand of the free market' to decide unilaterally the fate of billions would be sub-Christian and therefore must be improved by biblical action similar to jubilee legislation. The benefits of free-market economics are vigorously debated by Christian economists on both sides. One hopeful trend around the world is the growth in 'ethical investment' as some companies recognise the moral dimension of how they use their money. Another encouraging sign is the emergence of 'Business as Mission' enterprises. Christian entrepreneurs are using their business expertise to create jobs, make useful products and serve their neighbours. They emphasize that if business methods are guided by the 'quadruple bottom line: spiritual, economical, social and environmental transformation', then the kingdom of God will be advanced.

The question of 'value for money' is raised in mission, especially in relation to '*short-term missions'. From North America it is common that from $20,000 to $50,000 can be spent on a single trip. The sending churches value them because they produce 'maturity' and a larger 'vision for the world' in their youth, some of whom go back into long-term mission as a result. Local churches are often especially grateful for the practical support that is offered, and there are reports of mutual benefit. However, some host churches suggest that it would be a better stewardship of resources if the money could be spent to support national workers or local projects instead of on the large transportation costs of a 'short-term missions' trip.

Many ethical issues in missiology (like massive immigration) have arisen because of the disparate salaries in countries that are increasingly tied together through globalized markets. The minimum wage on the US side of the US/Mexican border is about $50 a day; on the Mexican side it is $5 a day. In Honduras it is about $3 a day, and in China and India, it is even lower. According to neo-liberal economic theory, if capital freely flows into these areas, 'all ships will rise', that is, everyone will benefit. Nevertheless, the results of the last two decades have not always borne this out. Although some in the Two-Thirds World have been able to escape poverty, others argue that in many countries there is a growing disparity between the rich and the poor, with a shrinking middle class and an overall increase in absolute poverty.

In light of the tremendous human needs in the world, the church has an agenda that is an important dimension of its mission responsibility: to enter vigorously into the *ethical debate about the role of money and macro-economics; to employ well-qualified Christian economists to rigorously analyse economic systems according to biblical criteria; to challenge governments, financial institutions and economists in line with a strong prophetic tradition of concern for social and economic justice; to think afresh about missionary life-style; and to encourage mission agencies to re-examine what genuine financial partnership will mean.

See also POOR/POVERTY, WEALTH.

Bibliography
J. J. Bonk, *Missions and Money: Affluence as a Western Missionary Problem* (Maryknoll: Orbis Books, 1991); R. J. Sider, *Rich Christians in an Age of Hunger* (Nashville: W. Publishing Group, 20th anniv. edn, 2005); J. Stiglitz, *Globalization and its Discontents* (W. W. Norton & Company, 2003); World Council of Churches, *Christian Faith and the World Economy Today,* (Geneva: WCC Publications, 1993).

L. SCOTT

Moratorium

The idea of a moratorium on mission activity became a controversial issue in the 1970s. It referred to the voluntary halting of foreign missionary activities, usually in certain Third World contexts where churches were well established, to allow them to be independent within their own cultural contexts. It could be a temporary or a permanent moratorium, depending on the context.

The issue arose because many foreign missionary organizations and denominations successfully evangelized areas and organized churches, but continued to exist side-by-side with them and often retained control over them. This created conflict as it was difficult to establish workable church/mission relationships.

Indigenous churches claimed that instead of assisting national churches to grow, missionaries were now retarding their growth through their paternalism and dependence, which hindered the churches from becoming self-governing, self-supporting and self-propagating. Churches relied on the founding missionary organizations for everything, instead of relying on the Holy Spirit.

In frustration some national church leaders came up with the idea of a moratorium on foreign missionaries. They pointed to the example of *Paul who, as soon as he founded a church, appointed local leaders to take over from him and he went to work elsewhere. He returned once in a while to see how the new churches were doing; he also wrote letters to strengthen them through teaching and exhortation; but he avoided a dependency-syndrome.

In his book, *Independence for the Third World Church*, this author wrote, 'In Africa we have missions which have been working in a particular country for fifty years or more. Up to now some of them have not transferred leadership to the nationals. This is unscriptural and is becoming more and more intolerable to national Christians' (P. Wakatama).

In Africa the idea of moratorium was spearheaded by John Gatu, head of the Presbyterian Church in East Africa. He believed that the presence of foreign missionaries had become a hindrance to the growth of the African Church. In 1973 at the WCC conference in Bangkok on 'Salvation Today', he suggested that there be a moratorium on foreign missionaries to Africa for at least five years, so that Africans could take charge of their own church affairs.

In 1974 at the meeting of the All Africa Conference of Churches this idea was adopted as a reasonable suggestion. Some churches, mostly belonging to the ecumenical movement, started to scale down the number of missionaries going to places where churches were well established.

Many evangelical church leaders, both in the sending and receiving countries, rejected the idea of a blanket moratorium on theological grounds. They maintained that the biblical imperative of the great commission to make disciples of all nations applies until the end of the age (Matt. 28:19–20), and

therefore that any suggestion of a moratorium would be against this.

Today moratorium is still an issue, though not as contentious as it was in the 1970s. There has been a new era of '*partnership' in mission which has been mutually respectful and enriching. Missions and churches have generally accepted that there are sometimes valid reasons for a moratorium, but they are not agreed on the solutions. In Africa, although political *colonialism is a thing of the past and the spirit of independence permeates its societies, neo-colonial attitudes of paternalism sometimes persist within mission organizations. As a result, national churches have become more militant against the controlling relationships between them and the foreign mission organizations which founded them. In some cases national churches have acrimoniously cut off relationships with the founding missionary organizations and are now working independently. In Zimbabwe the acrimony was so bad that the church and the mission organization ended up in a court of law, fighting over property. Up to this day reconciliation has not been possible. In such cases the gospel is compromised because of open competition between the church and mission agencies. Sometimes church members are recruited to work for the mission's foreign supported service ministries, and form new congregations in competition with existing churches.

Because such problems still exist, churches and mission organizations, internationally, continue in the process of working out mutually acceptable and biblical church-mission relationships. This is sending them back to the fundamental theological question: 'what is mission?' In 1983 the World Evangelical Fellowship convened the international Wheaton conference on 'Nature and Mission of the Church'. Papers presented dealt with major issues in mission, including church mission relationships and organizational structures. The final comprehensive report is still relevant today. It said, 'The worldwide moving of God's Spirit has seen multitudes ushered into the Kingdom, the creation of numerous churches and the launching of thousands of missionaries from these churches in the *Two Thirds World. God's Spirit is challenging not only the form of our present mission structures, but also the way we engage in mission. Present forms need to be reassessed as to their relevance to today's world. Current practices of missions need to be reconsidered in the light of newly formed churches.' This continual, critical, reassessment of mission structures and practice must be built into all mission agency thinking, so that they have the wisdom and humility to withdraw strategically to allow local leadership and church structures to mature into independent and dynamic missional communities.

Bibliography

D. E. Clark, *The Third World and Mission* (Waco: Word Books, 1971); H. Kane, *Winds of Change in the Christian Mission* (Chicago: Moody Press, 1973); *Evangelical Missions Quarterly* 26, No. 2, April 1990; 'The Lausanne Covenant' in J. D. Douglas (ed.), *Let the Earth Hear His Voice* (World Wide Publications, Minnesota, 1975); P. Sookhdeo (ed.), *New Frontiers in Mission* (Grand Rapids: Baker Book House; Exeter: Paternoster Press, 1987); P. Wakatama, *Independence for the Third World Church* (Downers Grove: InterVarsity Press, 1976); World Council of Churches, *Salvation Today* (Geneva: WCC, 1973).

P. WAKATAMA

Motives for mission

Motives play a crucial role in God's mission. Therefore, this article attempts to find a workable definition for motives. It then describes how motives, both biblical and historical, have influenced God's mission in the past and today, and concludes with comments on how motives may be transformed today.

Definition and categorization of motives

Psychology generally understands a motive to be an inner driving force, triggered by some underlying need. In most cases, an inner deficiency (basic need to live, need for security, need to be respected and loved) is presupposed, which triggers the respective motive, leading to the corresponding behaviour. Some authors do recognize a wider motivation, originating from 'meta-needs', which have their origin outside of someone's inherent needs. A biblical world-view supports this, since it suggests that human beings who are made in God's image can be motivated by the desire to please him and glorify him, motives which go beyond their own inner desires, and may overrule them.

Motives for God's mission can thus be defined as inner driving forces which respond to God's revealed will ('pure' motives), rather than arising out of human desires ('impure' motives); although nearly always there will be a mixture of human and godly motivation.

Most authors differ in their categorization of motives for mission. Some distinguish between 'pure' and 'impure' motives (J. Verkuyl, *Contemporary Missiology*), some between 'fundamental', 'secondary' and 'defective' motives (G. Van Reenen, *Missions: Biblical Foundations and Contemporary Strategies*). Others categorize into specific motives derived from Scripture, for example, doxological, soteriological, antagonistic and eschatological motives (P. Beyerhaus, *Er sandte sein Wort*).

Motives for mission in the Bible

In both the OT and the NT, it is always God who is the author of mission (*Missio Dei*). By grace, human beings are called and sent to minister alongside God in his mission. Christlike servants derive not only their sending, but also their motives for going, from him who sent them (John 20:21), which means that their motives must correspond with those of Christ and God.

God's motives

God's dealings with creation as sovereign creator reveal a 'creational motive' which leads him to create all things for his good pleasure, sustaining and blessing his creation out of his own delight. This is closely related to God's love, which guides all his dealings with human beings (the 'agape motive'). Arising from this is God's desire to redeem his creation by sacrificial love in the death of Christ on the cross (the 'soteriological motive'). His desire that the whole universe should worship him alone may be referred to as the 'doxological motive'. This is accompanied by the righteous anger of God against everything that usurps his power (the 'antagonistic motive'). Finally, God plans to bring everything under the headship of Christ, indicating a final motivation which is eschatological (the 'eschatological motive').

Human motives

The Bible speaks very honestly about the mixed motives of God's servants in mission. Selfish ambitions (e.g. Phil. 1) are contrasted with motives after God's own heart (e.g. 2 Cor. 5). This ambivalence has continued throughout the history of the church. Nevertheless, the six motives of God are represented at different times in history in the human motives seen in the church and its mission.

Motives for mission in history

Different motives for mission marked different epochs of church history. According to Bosch (*Transforming Mission*), Christians of the first centuries were motivated primarily by the love motive derived from God's 'agape' love (John 3:16; 2 Cor. 5:14). After Constantine and the joining of church and state, this changed as the growing power and influence of the church became the dominant motive. In spite of the fact that the Reformation lacked motivation for mission, the rediscovery of justification by grace through faith alone triggered mission in the Anabaptist movement. At the beginning of the Enlightenment era, Christianity increasingly diversified, resulting in a similar diversity of motives for mission. Whereas the Pietists concentrated on a strongly individualistic form of the 'agape motive', liberals pushed for a social interpretation of love. During the great missionary awakening of the nineteenth century, the possibility that mission could hasten the return of Christ awakened the eschatological motive. To this were added romantic motives, and then later on the motive of compensation for the damage done to indigenous peoples through the colonial experience.

In the modern and early postmodern era, biblical motives partly turned back on themselves. The 'agape motive', for example, which motivated the first Christians toward mission, sometimes developed either into individualism, which overemphasized a spirituality of separatism, or into an inclusivism with an overemphasis on accommodation with the world. Both extremes prevented mission from being truly holistic. After the sobering experience of two world wars, mission plummeted into a deep crisis. For the evangelicals, at least, it was only towards the beginning of the seventies that mission began to recover. It became evident that this crisis was also, in essence, a crisis of mission motivation. Even around the turn of the century, the three leading streams representing evangelical mission, the Lausanne movement, the AD 2000 and Beyond Movement, and Mission Commission of the World Evangelical Alliance, were spurred on by many different, mixed motives. So motives such as the glory of God ('doxological motive'), love ('agape motive'), the desire that the whole world be blessed ('creational motive'), obedience to the great commission, and the salvation history motive, were mingled with less pure motives relating to the size of the task, the success of human strategies, faith in the methods used and the achievability of the goal. It is clear that throughout mission history, human motives have never been completely 'pure', even if some would have liked to believe otherwise.

Motives for mission today

Predominant evangelical motives today include the love of God for his world ('agape motive'), the need for the world to be saved ('soteriological motive'), the desire to bless the created world ('creational motive'), as well as the desire to see God honoured and glorified in all the earth ('doxological motive'). None of these are, of course, exclusive; each Christian experiences some combination of them (and others), albeit in different proportions. But an increasing number of young people worldwide are motivated fervently by the glory of God, and many are boldly exploring new avenues in mission and passionately serving the disadvantaged. Their motives are sometimes mixed with a sense of adventure, the desire to see the world, or the motive of gaining experience in another culture. None of these are wrong in themselves, unless they become the only or main motive for going. The important thing is that that there is a growing alignment of their motives for mission with God's motives.

Transforming motives for mission

This side of the resurrection, all servants of God will be governed by mixed motives. But how can 'impure' motives gradually be transformed for today's generation? In order to be 'transformed into his image' (2 Cor. 3:18), there is no substitute for spending time with God, and giving time to observing and learning from spiritual role models found in Scripture and in contemporary mission.

Today's church must identify those factors in mission, such as outdated structures, boring worship or traditional leadership styles, that can create stumbling blocks and result in de-motivation for the current generation. Leaders who seek to motivate must begin with the integrity and authenticity of their own relationship with God, as young people today very easily see through false motivation. Young Christians who are taught a deep understanding of who God is and how his purposes relate dynamically to their lives as disciples will become more like Jesus, and will naturally capture a vision for mission which motivates them powerfully to make great sacrifices in responding to the call to serve God and others.

Bibliography
P. Beyerhaus, *Er sandte sein Wort* (Wuppertal: Brockhaus, 1996); D. J. Bosch, *Transforming Mission: Paradigm Shifts in Theology of Missions* (Maryknoll: Orbis Books, 1991); H. Dürr, 'Die Reinigung der Missions-Motive', *Evangelisches Missions-Magazin* 1, 1951, pp. 2–10; A. H. Maslow, *Motivation and Personality* (New York: Harper & Row, 1970); H. W. Ritter, *Motive zur Welt-mission* (Wiedenest, 2003); G. Van Rheenen, *Missions: Biblical Foundations and Contemporary Strategies* (Grand Rapids: Zondervan, 1996); J. Verkuyl, *Contemporary Missiology* (Grand Rapids, MI: Eerdmans, 1978); P. G. Zimbardo, *Psychology and Life* (Gleview, Boston, London: Scott, Foresman and Co., 1988).

H. W. RITTER

Music

Missiological orientation
I begin this article with an assertion: 'Music is one of the social practices which God uses to enable and inspire the church to fulfil its mission.'

1. To find out why this is so, we need to look at the life and mission of the church. A concise summary of the NT church is found in Acts 2:42: 'They devoted themselves to the apostles' teaching and to the fellowship, to the breaking of bread and to prayer.' I see in these verses three distinctive collective social actions which God uses in cooperation with human beings to fulfil the mission of the church: kerygmatic actions (the proclamation of the word); koinoniac actions (the upbuilding of the community); and leitourgic actions (the addressing of God). These three basic action types empowered by the Spirit result in many different social practices like, for example, preaching, teaching, participating in fellowship, breaking of bread and praying. It is through these practices which build up the church that the church fulfils its mission.

Elsewhere in the NT it becomes evident that song and music-making are social practices which can perform kerygmatic, koinoniac and leitourgic functions. In this way, music is clearly a means by which the church fulfils its life and mission. Colossians 3:16 (and Eph. 5:18–20), for example, is the musical equivalent of Acts 2:42: 'Let the word of Christ dwell in your midst richly with all wisdom teaching and admonishing one another with psalms, hymns, songs spiritual with grace/gratitude singing with your hearts to God' (trans. by Gordon Fee, 1994). Here we have the kerygmatic function ('teaching and admonishing'), the koinoniac function ('one another') and the leitourgic function ('singing with your hearts to God'). Colossians 3:16 concentrates on the content of our song ('the word of Christ') whereas the parallel passage in Ephesians 5:18–20 emphasizes the means of our song ('be filled with the Spirit').

2. Music also facilitates the emergence of both social and personal identity. This is why disagreements over music in the church (or anywhere else for that matter) can provoke such hostility. Ingrid Byerly in her article on the role of music in late-apartheid South Africa speaks of it as mirror, mediator and prophet (*Ethnomusicology* 42, pp. 1–44). Music can be used to retrieve identity ('mirror'), express identity ('mediator') or preserve identity ('prophet') (p. 8). It is music's powerful role as a mediator between social and personal identity through its ability to express emotion which makes it such a significant social practice in Christian mission. Jonathan Edwards maintained, correctly I believe, that 'True Religion, in great part, consists in Holy Affections' (*The Religious Affections*, p. 23). Music's role in this process of forming 'holy affections', especially

through congregational song, is of unparalleled importance: 'And the duty of singing praises to God seems to be appointed wholly to excite and express religious affections' (*The Religious Affections*, p. 44). This is music's mission within the larger mission of the church: to stimulate kerygmatic, koinoniac and leitourgic affections, thus enhancing Christian identity.

Theological orientation

Since music is a medium through which truth about God is expressed, it is a theological category. The people of God learn their theology in part through the songs and hymns they sing. It is vital therefore that music and hymnology faithfully convey the 'whole counsel of God' and lead worshippers into a fuller appreciation of God. The agreement of song lyrics with the principles of God's word is therefore crucial, since as we saw in Colossians 3:16 and Ephesians 5, the task of the singer/songwriter/musician is to let the word of Christ dwell richly in our hearts (note the affective dimension) by means of the Spirit. Word and Spirit should thereby happily co-exist in a biblical theology of church song.

It is routinely said that music is a gift from God. It is more accurate to say that the capacity to make music is a gift and a task from God. This gift and task is part of a much larger capacity, the capacity God has given human beings to create culture. There are three components to this 'cultural mandate': subduing/ruling creation (Gen. 1:28) (management); working and taking care of creation (Gen. 2:15) (development); and naming living creatures (Gen. 2:19–20) (symbolizing). God creates a space, as it were, in this world for humanity to fill by managing, developing and symbolizing. That 'space' is culture: structures made by humanity for the good of humanity. Sound was used by God (Gen. 1:3) to create the world – humanity now has the gift and the task of managing it, developing it and using it to symbolize other things for the good of humanity. This is what we call music. The fall makes it difficult for humans to fulfil this cultural mandate, but it has never been rescinded by God. After the fall music's role adds to a preservational role as the history of redemption proper begins. Music therefore has a creational role (cultural mandate), a preservational role (to cause us to look for

God) and a redemptive role (music becomes from earliest times in the Bible a means to proclaim God's saving power, e.g. Miriam's song after the exodus from Egypt, Exod. 15:1–21).

The role of music in mission can therefore be summarized as: (a) a way of connecting: music is one way of contextualizing the gospel in a form that resonates with the hearers, which means that mission needs to be eager to use indigenous music where possible; (b) a way of moving: as we have observed music appeals to the emotions and can act as a powerful advocate of the gospel, where a purely intellectual approach may be resisted; (c) a way of inspiring: songs and hymns of mission strengthen Christian resolve and help us to prioritize mission. It could be said that there are not enough songs and hymns about mission, and that as a result mission is not a priority for many churches, or it is poorly understood.

A missional theology of music calls the church to create kerygmatic, koinoniac and leitourgic music and to honour the creational, preservational, and redemptive aspects of music. In so doing it fulfils the mission of the church.

See also WORSHIP.

Bibliography

M. Archer, *Being Human* (Cambridge: Cambridge University Press, 2000); H. S. Becker, 'Art as Collective Action', *American Sociological Review* 39, 1974, pp. 767–776; I. Byerly, 'Mirror, Mediator and Prophet', *Ethnomusicology* 42, 1998, pp. 1–44; J. Edwards, *The Religious Affections* (Edinburgh: Banner of Truth Trust, 1961 [1746]); D. B. Pass, *Music and the Church* 2nd edn (Johannesburg: Password, 2005).

D. B. PASS

Muslim relations

In terms of the broad picture, Christian mission among Muslims appears to represent a tiny fraction of the total work, as most missionaries to Muslim contexts cannot openly act as 'missionaries'. It is therefore nearly impossible to assess the full extent and intensity of mission among Muslims today. In any case, if the success were to be gauged in terms of numbers, the mission among Muslims would perhaps not be counted as significant, despite suggestions from certain quarters that an organized native and expatriate Christian mission among Muslims is on the increase.

Both Christianity and Islam have been, and are, missionary faiths. Whilst some approaches from the past continue, Christian mission has experienced a sea change, reflected in the variety of ways in which mission among Muslims is experimentally expressed.

Historically, Christians living in the majority Islamic contexts generally exhibited greater respect for the Islamic tradition in that they seriously sought to make sense of their faith in relation to it. Part of it had to do with their minority status and part to their natural empathy stemming from the shared culture and history. It has been argued, on the other hand, that many missionaries representing Western mission organizations and churches of the colonial era did not show the same degree of respect for Islam and Muslims, owing mainly to the anthropological and religious convictions of their time. Even today, it is argued, the same attitudes continue as the new global 'empire' is conducive to the spread of missionaries, who are seen often to be working in the wake of global conflicts and local intra-Islamic fissures caused by ethnic, economic, theological, sociological inequalities.

Judging from the information available, a large number of resources are being engaged for the preparation of the mission worker from the West, not least in North America. Information on this is available openly, and thus it is not surprising that most Muslims in the South believe America is 'Christian' and is not just spreading its economic and cultural influences around the globe, but is also spreading Christianity on the back of it. In addition, there is a host of books seeking to help and encourage missionaries and their families working among Muslims. Others show increasing evidence of local workers engaging in mission among their own people groups and places inaccessible to Westerners and Western mission agencies supporting these indigenous movements.

Mission and ethnic groups

Christians often 'competed' with Muslim missionaries in focusing on ethnic minorities and not directly on converting traditional Muslims. For instance, Francis Xavier came to Malaya in 1545. He believed Christians could scotch the spread of Islam if they outdid Muslims in converting the native Indonesians to Christianity. Muslim majority states like Indonesia, Malaysia and Brunei are evidence of the fact that Muslim efforts at converting the nationals outstripped Christians. Christians succeeded largely in those regions where Muslims had not yet penetrated. The Catholic Christianity in the Philippines is the legacy of sixteenth-century Spain. Christian missionaries converted 85% of the native folk-religious peoples, making the Philippines the only Christian nation in Asia. But Christianity never made headway in the south because of the presence of Islam. This region has remained virtually sealed to Christian mission, although Muslim jihad against some Christian communities and the government continues. The growth of Christianity in regions now under the Malaysian flag occurred mainly among the tribes of Kayan, Kenyah, Penans and Sekapans. Likewise, the Borneo Evangelical Mission succeeded among the Orang Ulu in Saravak, a people untouched by Islam.

Following this model from the past history of mission, Christians appear to continue in their focus on Muslims who define themselves primarily in terms of their ethnic/tribal identities and, hence, seem to exist on the margins of traditional Islam. Many mission experts working in or for Islamic contexts use insights from socio-anthropological analyses in developing an approach to Islam/Muslims. One of the theories about intra- and inter-religious 'contact zones' suggests that theological and cultural similarities between groups/sub-groups within/across religions encourage contact and crossing-over. This has, in certain quarters of Christian mission enterprise, led to the belief that 'becoming like the Muslims will reach the Muslims'. This involves living and dressing like Muslims; acquiring a vocabulary, forms of worship and creedal formulae akin to the Islamic creed (e.g. 'there is no God but God, and Isa is his Messiah' in place of 'there is no God but Allah and Muhammad is his Prophet'). Part of the reason for this approach may also be to protect themselves from potential threats from Muslims. Nowhere in the Islamic world has this approach been refined as perfectly as in Indonesia. Several sub-approaches have been outlined, which range from use of indigenous languages (C2), through Christ-centred communities using local language and cultural forms (C3), communities using biblically permissible cultural and Islamic forms (C4), Christ-centred communities of messianic Muslims (C5), to Christ-centred communities of secret believers (C6). Arguably, these approaches are set against the clearly unacceptable C1 model where Christians and churches exist as separate communities, aloof from the local culture and languages. While C1–C4 models can be empirically examined, C5–C6 models serve as mere conceptual frameworks of the Christian theology of Islam in majority Muslim contexts (at least until some empirical means of verifying these comes to light).

These groups represent a repeat of the original mission opportunities afforded by the *folk religions of Asia where Christian and Muslim missions competed to seek converts among the natives. *Ethnic identities are said to be stronger than the assumed historical religious (Christian or Islamic) identities. Christian mission among these often receives a justification on grounds that these people need 'liberation' from different sorts of bondages. Being on the margins of Islam, these groups live relatively independently of the norm. They represent, therefore, a challenge to Muslim efforts for their Islamization on the one hand and, on the other, an opportunity to Christian missionaries to seek converts among those weakly linked to their adopted normative religion, Islam. Christian missionaries see them as relatively easy targets of mission, whereas Muslim missionaries perceive them as the objects of Islamization (incorporation within 'the centre of Islam').

In India, a majority Hindu country, Christian missionaries have traditionally focused on the people groups on the margins of society and not on mainstream Hindus and Muslims. For instance, mission work has largely been done along the tribal belts, among low and backward classes and marginal or conflict-ridden Muslim groups such as the refugees from Bangladesh. Given the democratic climate and a secular constitution of India, this work is understandably more overt than it is in Nepal, Bangladesh, Pakistan or Afghanistan. Unlike American Islam, which is said to be growing among black American Christians, in India the conversions from Islam to Christianity or vice versa have undoubtedly been miniscule. A greater number of conversions to these religions take place as a consequence of social protests of the marginal groups against the hegemony of the Hindu caste system.

Public debates and polemics

Whilst Christians are known for antithetical polemics against Islam and Muslims, they are also known for encouraging honest public debates, a precursor of the theology of dialogue and mission as reconciliation. For example, in thirteenth to fourteenth century West Asia, Francis of Assisi and Raymond Lull acted ahead of their times in largely thinking of Muslims as a highly sophisticated people capable of reasonable theological debates, without the fear of losing their lives. Muslim majority states for their part, both in the Middle East and also in the Indian sub-continent, in fact encouraged such open public debates. For instance, the Mughals, especially Emperor Akbar, encouraged Christian priests to hold serious debates right at the very centre of political and state power, the courts. In terms of the number of converts their contribution to mission cannot be deemed as successful. In eighteenth and nineteenth century Asia, Henry Martyn, William Carey, Leighton Pennell and Karl Pfander differed little from St Francis and Lull in their approach to mission among Muslims. In order to aid debates with Muslims, Martyn and Carey helped translate the Bible into Arabic, Urdu, Hindustani, Bengali, Persian and other languages but, despite this, remained largely unsuccessful in gaining significant numbers of converts among Muslims. But the times had changed. Thus, for example, Karl Pfander's famous debate with a Muslim Ulema in the mid-nineteenth century was not the same as Lull's debate or St Francis' debate, since the British and not the Muslims were the paramount power.

In line with this past, there are perhaps only a handful of mission organizations who continue the legacy of classical polemicists. The difference is that these organizations are less personality based as they seek to equip a broad spectrum of native Christians to 'rescue fellow native Muslims from Islam'. Attention is being paid to training indigenous missionaries in the art or science of polemics as an approach to mission among Muslims, not just because they are culturally and linguistically closer to the target groups, but also for pragmatic concerns, including the cost of mission enterprise.

Exceptions exist. The *Answering Islam* website goes by the subtitle 'a Christian-Muslim Dialogue'. However, its content appears to betray a polemical intent: 'America, Muslims and torture', 'Who was the Crucified One?', 'Isa, the Muslim's Jesus', 'Which roots?', 'The Islamic agenda and its blueprints', 'Does Islam promote peace?' The site also gives rebuttals to the polemics of well-known Islamic speakers. It presents the outlines of Christianity; responds to Muslim questions on the issue of the corruption of the Bible; lists names of Muslims all over the world who converted to Christianity and why they chose Christianity over Islam; gives an evaluation of Muslim claims about the Qur'an and Muhammad. It also has sections on women; Christians living under Muslim rule; Islam and terrorism; and providing answers to the favourite questions of Muslims against Christianity. The *Debate Site* lists the various debate topics between Christians and Muslims relating to history, politics, society, science, theology, and the specific issues to do with contradictions in the Bible, issues of suffering, miracles, and so on. This is a Christian website, but it encourages Muslims to engage with Christian writings on the site.

Dialogue and reconciliation

A development over Lull's and St Francis' approach is in the modern emphasis on dialogue. This recognizes seriously that there are devout Muslims living honorably and truthfully to their apprehension of the light, though the approach does not adopt 'uncritical acquiescence'. Affirmation of the truth of the gospel and loyalty to Jesus Christ need not be compromised, but not necessarily promoted in confrontational terms of the absoluteness of Christianity in relation to Islam. This kind of dialogue is not mere sophisticated polemics, and emphasis is laid on 'inter-faith fraternization' and 'understanding' of the other.

Dialogue takes place at different levels. Local clergy meet and seek to work together at common problems in their communities. At the international level the Archbishop of Canterbury, for example, holds annual seminars with leading Muslim scholars called 'Building Bridges'. The Henry Martyn Institute (HMI) (formerly 'of Islamic Studies') in Hyderabad, India has held debates for many years. Sam Bhajjan's era as director was characterized by HMI's subscription to dialogue as the mission of Christians among Muslims. When Andreas D'Souza took over as director the dialogue process was, and continues to be, characterized by the evolution and formalization of dialogue to the idea of *reconciliation as the goal of Christian mission among Muslims. The context for this transformation was actual inter-faith violence and conflict.

Christians in this conflict saw themselves as the harbingers of peace and harmony. The *cross was seen as the means of absorbing religiously-motivated hatred and violence and as a means of healing and effecting friendships in practical ways. The Anabaptist tradition which affirms peaceable public conversations and deeds was also tested in contexts of violence and conflict. The 'compulsion of Christ's love' was understood to be the main motive for this approach. It sought to overcome the bipolar responses of Christians to the challenge of Islam: aggressive combativeness/absolute exclusivism or acquiescence/absolute relativism. Personal contact, genuine friendships and relational Christianity were emphasized. This is also the approach adopted by Salim Munayer's Musalaha ministry in Jerusalem. The central fact of Jesus' *sacrifice is not merely seen as a doctrine but as a powerful example of the way conflicts can be resolved, violence checked and reconciliation effected.

Holistic mission

Mission understood *holistically (integrating social action and proclamation of the good news) underlines the bulk of mission work done in, at least, the poorer and conflict-ridden states of Asia today. In extreme circumstances of war or conflict, charity often follows close on its heels. In terms of Christian-Muslim relations on a global level, Huntington's cultural analysis (seeing an intrinsic conflict between Christianity and Islam as a 'clash of civilizations') does underline the West's rationale for interventionism to achieve 'liberation', 'democracy' and 'freedom'. But many non-Western scholars have pointed out that this war of liberation is increasingly being seen by Muslims as a war of Christianity against Islam; the overflowing of charity and Christian humanitarian agencies in such contexts contributes to the common perception that 'conflicts are initiated so that that charity can aid Christian witness'.

This view needs to be balanced. Western interventions in Islamic lands cannot be simplistically twinned with Christians' motivation. The majority of Christians genuinely mean well and wish to be holistic in their approach, in line with their rethinking of the gospel in terms of the poor. In most Islamic countries, Christians can engage with Muslims not as 'missionaries' but as teachers, doctors, social workers, and relief or development/aid workers and so on. Today there is a greater recognition of the broader faith-based approach to *development. Christians are not alone in providing healthcare, education, and so on. For this reason, partnerships are being considered, especially at the grass-roots level, between faith-inspired initiatives to meet immediate needs of people affected by political, ethnic, racial and natural violence and calamities.

Leisure and lifestyle Christianity

In the West, where businesses supporting leisure are huge, some have found new ways of reaching out to people by combining leisure with work. The Mission Beyond Tours seeks to 'refresh and challenge people's lives through the provision of personally enriching quality adventures in the forum of God's glorious creation'. There is a single objective in the activities of this group: to facilitate the refreshment of 'Christian fellowship through adventure and fun within creation'. It does this through a range of outdoor activities. The Ministry Group Travel programme of Travel Management Inc. also organizes tours to special locations like Israel, Egypt, Rome, Greece and the Aegean with a view to refreshing people's faith in combination with leisure. This group also encourages the mission groups to combine the objective of 'refreshing and challenging' people's lives with the objective of interfacing with people of other faiths in what may be seen as a 'quick-fix mission'.

These outings are designed to combine the pleasure of a holiday, adventure and the impulse for mission. For instance, the 'South-east Asia bike ministry team' ($3,900) leads bikers through the mountains of South-East Asia offering 'prayers for the land and the people', 'low-key evangelism' and 'building relationships with local Muslims'.

This approach involves the expectation that, since Muslims already know Jesus as the Messiah of the Qur'an, it is up to them to choose to enquire more of the Jesus of the gospel if they are attracted by the life of the Christian. It distinguishes the compulsion to believe in Jesus being the Son of God from living like Jesus. An empirical example of living Christianly comes from Bangladesh (85% Muslim); a Catholic mission in Bangladesh proposes this as an alternative to approaches of the Baptists and SDAs (Seventh Day Adventists) that are allegedly conflicting, and culturally and religiously insensitive.

This approach supports examples of Christians living sacrificially among marginal and minority groups. The theological impulses for these experiments are complex, but at the heart of it is the belief in an all-embracing Abrahamic spirituality including both Christianity and Islam by the common grace of God. This can be a basis for a dialogue of life and living together. The idea, however, is liable to be carried further into the more inclusive position of supposing that there are resources for life within the Qur'anic world-view that fulfil the law and become an alternate means of 'salvific intimacy' with God.

Conclusion

Historically, Christians have seen Islam in divergent ways, eliciting equally divergent responses from them. Generally, Christians living among Muslims showed greater respect and continuity with Islam even as theological factors dominated their mutual relationship. Western Christianity's response, however, ranged from polemics to conflict and war. The seeds of disjunction between Western and Eastern Christianity also affected the way that Western Christianity perceived itself vis-à-vis Islam and continue in some respects to characterize their relations even today.

Because both religions make absolute claims to truth, polemics as an approach continues, although appearing to lessen in intensity and extent among Christians. Increasingly, many mainstream Christian groups recognize the need for reconciliation and bridge-building, especially in the context of growing fundamentalism and violence.

In terms of the number of converts, Christian mission has historically never been successful, and perhaps for this reason a lot of effort has gone into thinking and experimenting with different approaches. Whilst an accurate assessment of the number of converts might be near to impossible, a measure of the extent and intensity of mission can be gauged by the current Christian interest and engagement with Islam all over the world. It is this sense of experimentation that propels a proportion of Christian mission enterprise to engage a significant degree of creativity in conceiving a variety of possible ways for doing mission.

See also DIALOGUE.

Bibliography

M. I. Beaumont, *Christology in Dialogue with Muslims* (Carlisle: Regnum 2005); K. Cragg, *Muhammad and the Christian: A Question of Response* (London: Darton, Longman and Todd; Maryknoll: Orbis Books, 1984); K. Cragg, *The Christ and the Faiths: Theology in Cross-Reference* (London: SPCK, 1986); D. D'Souza, *Evangelism, Dialogue, Reconciliation: The Transformative Journey of the Henry Martyn Institute* (Hyderabad, Henry Martyn Institute, 1998); B. D. Kateregga and D. W. Shenk, *Islam and Christianity: A Muslim and a Christian in Dialogue* (Grand Rapids: Eerdmans 1981); P. Parshall, *Bridges to Islam: A Christian Perspective on Folk Islam* (Grand Rapids: Baker Book House, 1983); P. G. Riddell, *Christians and Muslims: Pressures and Potential in a Post 9/11 World* (Leicester: IVP, 2004); D. Shenk, *Journeys of the Muslim Nation and the Christian Church: Exploring the Mission of Two Communities* (Scottdale: Herald Press, 2003); D. E. Singh (ed.), *Jesus and the Cross: Reflections of Christians from Islamic Contexts* (2007); W. M. Watt, *Islam and Christianity Today: A Contribution to Dialogue* (London: Routledge & Kegan Paul, 1983); D. Woodberry (ed.), *Muslims and Christians on the Emmaus Road* (Monrovia: MARC 1989).

Answering Islam, <http://answering-islam. org>; Muslim-Christian Debate website, <http://debate.org.uk>; Travel Management Inc. < http://www.travelmgmt.com/missions/ missions.asp>.

D. E. SINGH

Narrative

Narrative theology

In recent years a stream of theology has reacted against a rationalistic and conceptual approach to biblical hermeneutics and to theology. Influenced by Richard Niebuhr's *The Meaning of Revelation*, theologians like Paul Ricoeur, Hans Frei, Stephen Crites, Stanley Hauerwas and James Gustafson have developed the concept of narrative theology. They have emphasized the significance of narrative for the understanding of humanity in general as well as the more particular issues of theology and biblical interpretation. Hauerwas and David Burrell have further related narrative approaches to the issue of ethics, debating the relation of story to more rationalist approaches. Johannes Metz has led the way in applying narrative to biblical interpretation.

This hermeneutic method has been further applied to specific narrative studies of biblical books. A variety of new commentaries have been published with particular reference to a fresh understanding of the gospels, but also of other books of the Bible. The narrative approach to biblical understanding reacts specifically against a more systematized theological basis for hermeneutics, noting the central role of the actual stories of the Bible. In this context it should be noted that the Bible does not present its readers with a systematic theology. And indeed no such thorough systematic theology issued from the Christian church until Thomas Aquinas' *Summa Theologica*.

Narrative theologians note that the OT faith of the Hebrews was not normally codified in systematic or rationalistic concepts, but rather in the stories of the patriarchs and of the Passover, *exodus and giving of the Torah on Sinai. Israel's faith centred on the story of her liberation from slavery in Egypt, God's saving work on her behalf. And still today the story of these events forms the basis for Jewish faith.

Halakah and haggadah

Jewish teaching has traditionally consisted of two basic forms. *Halakah* contains direct legal teaching which has no direct narrative content. But *haggadah* includes stories which may be historical accounts or they may be parabolic or pictorial. Likewise, truth may be conveyed through dramatic actions, such as prophets hiding things in the ground until they rot or lying on their side for a long time (see Jer. 13; Ezek. 4). In Jewish tradition the greatest form of *haggadah* is found in the actions of the liturgy for Passover. For Christians too our teaching may consist of non-narrative halachic and conceptual communication or it may equally come through the narrative form of pictorial teaching. In the NT the Gospels and the book of Acts do not merely contain history, as used to be commonly taught. Their telling of the story of Jesus and of the early church also has definite theological purposes. And the epistles contain within their more halachic teaching examples of haggadah (e.g. Paul's use of the Abraham narrative, James' pictorial references to the tongue or a ship's rudder).

While narrative theology reacts against what is seen as an over-emphasis on the conceptual and systematic, it may be argued that narrative theologians have swung the pendulum too far in tending to reject more halachic forms of teaching. True biblical hermeneutics must include both the haggadic and the halachic.

Storytelling in proclamation

Influenced perhaps not only by the development of narrative theology, but also by our historical context of *New Age and *postmodernism, storytelling has gained influence in the practice of Christian mission. Some of us already came to understand the significance of storytelling back in the 1960s because of the realization that systematic and conceptual forms of preaching and teaching failed to relate to traditional Asian or African societies. In more recent years much has been written about communicating the gospel through stories.

Every society has ancient traditional myths or stories which are commonly taught to children and generally loved. These often include animal stories. Thus in Indonesia stories abound concerning a small mousedeer known as Sang Kancil. Such stories can be utilized in slightly amended form to communicate Christian truth. In earlier years the Jungle Doctor stories of Paul White were much used not only in their East African background, but also with adaptation in other parts of the world. More recently the Japanese theologian Kosuke Koyama has used pictorial forms of teaching in his books.

The author of this article developed the use of NT parables adapted for a Muslim audience. Questioning people's *niyyah* (intention or motive), the parable of two men going to the mosque for prayer or two men giving their *zakat* (alms) could distinguish between a true motive of gratitude to God or a false motive of desire to be seen by others. Kenneth Bailey in his books has also shown how to use a NT parable for communication of the good news of Jesus Christ.

Different cultures have different forms of storytelling. Thus Jewish stories often have a sudden unexpected twist at the end which shocks or amazes the listener. On the other hand, Korean stories tend to be much longer and the conclusion with its moral lesson may be clearly perceived long before the end. Both to understand the significance of a story and in order to be able to communicate effectively by stories, one needs to appreciate the form of narrative used in any particular context.

See also CULTURE, WORLD-VIEW.

Bibliography

K. Bailey, *Poet and Peasant, and Through Peasant Eyes* (Grand Rapids: Eerdmans, 1983); T. Dennis, *Lo and Behold! The Power of Old Testament Storytelling* (London, SPCK, 1991); H. Frei, *Theology and Narrative – Selected Essays* (Oxford: Oxford University Press, 1993); S. Hauerwas, R. Bondi and D. Burrell, *Truthfulness and Tragedy: Further Investigations in Christian Ethics* (Notre Dame: University of Notre Dame Press 1977); S. Hauerwas and L. G. Jones (eds.), *Why Narrative? Readings in Narrative Theology* (Grand Rapids: Eerdmans, 1989); K. Koyama, *Mount Fuji and Mount Sinai* (London: SCM 1984); H. R. Niebuhr, *The Meaning of Revelation* (Louisville: Westminster John Knox Press, 2006 [1941]); G. Sauter and J. Barton,

Revelation and Story (Aldershot: Ashgate 2000).

M. GOLDSMITH

New Age

Identifying the New Age

The New Age movement is a diverse and complex phenomenon which has evolved over the last few decades against various cultural, geographic and religious backgrounds. It can be distinguished from *new religious movements by its unstructured, non-institutional and diffuse characteristics, although it is a 'movement' in the sense that it is constantly changing and evolving. Its enormous diversity defies definition, and its manifestations and beliefs often appear paradoxical.

The New Age is especially widespread in the Western context of fragmented religious and philosophical pluralism, where it has thrived on the search for alternative spiritualities and lifestyles. Having seen the human spirit as trapped in a Western cultural heritage of critical scientific thinking rooted in the Enlightenment and institutionalized religion, New Age has offered people new choices for happiness, enlightenment and personal transformation. Many of its manifestations have either originated in or been influenced by the Eastern religions and sects such as Hinduism, Buddhism, Taoism, Shamanism, neopaganism and Spiritism. Some of the prominent underlying beliefs of the New Age have included pantheism, monism, mysticism, occultism and esoterism, karma and reincarnation, yoga and alternative therapies, the latent divinity of both humans and nature, futuristic visions, holistic development of the individual, and vegetarianism.

New Age diversity makes it difficult to identify a set of coherent beliefs. Belief patterns change in tune with the fast-paced developments on the world stage. Many characteristically hold that humans are essentially good, so human dislocation does not arise from objective guilt or sin against a holy God. The human self must be a new starting point, with its 'divine', or potentially divine, nature. Each person has within them a spiritual core with which they need to re-connect through a journey inwards in order to find their true self. This is a personal journey with a self-constructed spiritual path to the Higher Self.

Many believe in monism, the essential unity of all reality, and therefore in the 'divine' nature of 'Mother Earth', the source of all life. The secret is to re-tune to the spiritual powers that are there in nature. Others have strongly Gnostic, dualistic origins, especially in the notions of a metaphysical imprisonment of the spirit, the construction of elaborate mythologies, and beliefs in 'other worlds' where salvation can be found.

The attractions of the New Age

What attracts people, literally in millions today, to these new spiritualities? Some reasons may be as follows:

- A clear disenchantment with traditional, organized religions and their eschatological tones.
- The charisma of the Indian gurus, Zen masters, or 'Christian' prophets, who preach alternative visions and spiritualities.
- Social unrest and disillusionment with wars, combined with scientific and technological developments.
- The emergence of the secular, *postmodern spirit, which celebrates individuality, independence of thought and life, and relativity of truth, knowledge and morals.
- The birth of psychological theories which speak of optimizing human potential within.
- The urge to experience instant spirituality through sex, drugs or mysticism.
- A fascination for, and encounters with, 'extra-terrestrials', which create the desire to control, subdue or even please natural, cosmic forces, thus lending strength to astrology.
- Alternative therapies, which promise holistic health and well-being.
- Mind-control techniques, through yogic meditation and breath control, and body control through practices like vegetarianism.
- A utopian zeal to change the present state of affairs and create a new world community and order, where peace and harmony prevail for ever.

All these reasons are a pointer to the fact that we are living in a world where 'pick and mix' spirituality is an instant, irresistible attraction. Thanks to the process of *globalization, information as digital bytes disseminates thick and fast, and people are not content with living with the old and well-trodden paths of spirituality. There is an attraction in innovating and experimenting with 'alternative', 'postmodern' spiritualities.

In a country like India, with its all-encompassing philosophies and religions, New Age ideas are not out of place, nor do they attract any special attention, because these have always been, broadly speaking, part and parcel of the Hindu world-view. Therefore it is all the more easy for any scholarly person with an Indian background to propagate New Age philosophy. The greatest strength of India is its in-built toleration. Down the ages, unlike in the West, there has hardly been any heresy-hunting or proscription of 'alien' ideas. No one in Indian society needs any sanction to develop his or her own philosophies and integrate them into the Indian tradition. Counter philosophies from Muslims, Christians and Sikhs emphasize the supremacy of reason and rationality, the imperfections and even sinfulness of humanity, the ultimate reality being the 'wholly other', and the need for God's grace and salvation. However, New Age gurus are to be found in abundance in India.

Some New Agers trace their philosophical origins to an enlightened founder, guru or master who has a particular focus and a special methodology to attain what he or she believes to be the essence and the ultimate goal of life: if it is transcendental meditation for Mahesh Yogi, and Krishna consciousness for Prabhupada, it is tantric sex for Rajneesh. Today we have New Age gurus like Deepak Chopra articulating the ageless mind and the wonders of *ayurveda*, and Sri Sri Ravi Shankar discoursing on the 'art of living'. However, ideas drawn from Eastern philosophies are often sifted and refashioned in the West to such an extent that they bear little relation to the original.

Missiological response

Scholarly studies in the last few decades clearly range from extreme counter apologetics to approaches which embrace New Age thinking uncritically. It is wise for those in mission to avoid the two extremes of either reviling the New Agers in harsh language, or embracing them, using their own methods to win them over. What is needed today in the face of such variegated phenomena, with an ever-evolving plethora of belief patterns, is culture-specific, context-specific and belief-specific Christian responses. Therefore any blanket description of them or any single response will not be adequate, since there is no single world-view to which a general response can be made. Some Christian responses, for example, give too much weight to the presence of occult dimensions and imagine that a spiritual warfare approach is sufficient. It is important also to distinguish the seriously philosophical from the popular, technique-based, alternative therapies of the lifestyle gurus.

Another problem is that rational criticism is ineffective in speaking to those who are looking to transcend conventional Western rationalism, and for whom paradoxes are often accommodated in the search for experiences and therapies that work. Many also see institutional Christianity as part of the problem, not part of the solution, so Christian truth has to be approached from a different direction by engaging the undogmatic, experiential and 'spiritual' aspirations of New Age thinking. This will involve a more intuitional, emotional and relational approach that brings Christian truth into play tangentially rather than confrontationally.

Biblical models to engage the followers of new religions have been developed. For a good example of the above approach, much is made of St Paul when he engaged the Athenians (Acts 17:16–31). Here Paul reasons with the philosophers of the day by beginning with the 'unknown god' of their own spiritual search. He takes the risk of building on what seem to be universalist ideas of One 'in whom we live and move and have our being'. He does not condemn these alien beliefs outright, but displays great sensitivity and understanding. But he does go on to show that God is other than the material world as the Creator of all, who cannot be turned into a mere idol. Their approach may have had something going for it, but it was a blind alley. To redirect their thinking he moves from natural to revealed theology, explaining that however strange peoples' beliefs may be, all humans are created by God. Humans need to realize that their problem is their sinful nature and to look to God for a new beginning through repentance. He gives them a view of history which does not go in endless cycles, but would come to an end one day, when each person will have to face judgment. Finally, his *Christology is uncompromising: Jesus Christ, as the risen Lord, is the only standard to judge every belief pattern and every believing community.

The church has some lessons to learn from these new spiritualities and their phenomenal attraction and growth, if it can take the time to listen and understand. Some disturbing questions need to be raised: Why are some Christian believers disenchanted with organized Christianity? What can the church do differently to meet the longings of New Agers? What doctrinal beliefs and worship patterns alienate people? How could the various churches/denominations come together to engage the New Agers collectively, rather than individually? What strategies should missionaries adopt, and what training should they undergo in order to engage New Agers for Christ? These questions form the basis for more developed missiological response.

See also RELIGIOUS PLURALISM, WORLD-VIEW.

Bibliography
R. Clifford and P. Johnson, *Sacred Quest* (Farnham: Albatross, 1995); J. Drane, *What is the New Age Still Saying to the Church?* (London: Harper Collins, 1999); J. Enroth (ed.), *A Guide To New Religious Movements* (Downers Grove: InterVarsity Press, 2005); D. Groothuis, *Unmasking the New Age* (Downers Grove: InterVarsity Press, 1986); W. J. Hanegraaf, *New Age Religion and Western Culture* (New York: State University of New York, 1998 [1996]); V. Mangalwadi, *The World of Gurus* (Landour: Good Books, 1987); V. Mangalwadi, *When the New Age Gets Old: Looking for a Greater Spirituality* (Downers Grove: InterVarsity Press, 1992); J. Newport, *The New Age Movement and the Biblical Worldview* (Grand Rapids: Eerdmans, 1998); C. Partridge (ed.), *Encyclopaedia of New Religions: New Religious Movements, Sects and Alternative Spiritualities* (Oxford: Lion, 2004).

J. KALAPATI

New religious movements

The problem in the study of *new* religious movements is that there is hardly anything 'new' under the sun. Each 'new' movement recalls ideas and practices that had existed or still exist in other parts of the world, especially those grounded in a universalist utopian ideal. Some scholars, therefore, prefer to talk about new religious *consciousness*.

At different points in history, religious and social forces have produced reactions against dominant religious and secular institutions. The missiologist recognizes both the potentials and challenges, because the Protestant Reformation arose from a new religious consciousness! Newness challenges what exists; the concern is that some new religious forms harbour unwholesome spirits that challenge Christian orthodoxy. But the unique claims of Christianity will always be challenged by religious pluralism and the counter-claims of other faith perspectives.

For example, the Western world felt the impact of the 'flower children' and their counterculture in the 1960s, forcing Christianity to rearticulate itself differently in the face of the decline in the belief in a personal God, a new self-awareness, and a new spiritual quest and sensitivity. But new religious consciousness also appeared among indigenous communities in the Americas, Asia, Africa, Pacific and Oceania, and First Nation Indians. There are common denominators and wide differences based on contexts and time. So, we shall treat new religious movements differently, first focusing on those that emerged from the encounter between indigenous religions and world religions.

New religious movements in indigenous cultures and religions
Changes can occur within indigenous religions because their sustaining *world-views are elastic. However, significant new religious movements have also arisen from interactions with world religions: Christianity, Hinduism, Buddhism and Islam. In this encounter the new religious movements were catalysed by an exchange of images, symbols and ideas; by exploring lines of resonance; by the muscular creativity of religious entrepreneurs; or as a way of adjusting to more powerful and universal religions and cultures. Some have no

written sacred texts; some founders left journals, or had their oral testimonies transcribed. These became canonical sacred texts.

Essentially, new religious movements depend on oral traditions enshrined in accounts of an origin, the founder's call, divine revelations, visions or revealed texts, symbols, rituals, and colours. These oral traditions may contain new forms of old myths, or wisdom sayings that would later form the bases for songs and hymn books, as became the case among the Xhosa of South Africa and Maori of New Zealand. For instance, when Ntsikana died in the autumn of 1821, his poetic epigrams, rich in Xhosa idiom and symbolic forms, became hymns that appeared in the Wesleyan *Book of Songs*, published in Grahamstown in 1835. Some of the traditions contained a hostile perception of the intruding outsiders, and dire predictions of a new age of colonization that would attack the indigenous culture and religion.

Origins and characteristics

Many social scientists explain new religious movements either as products of social change, when indigenous structures respond to external change agents, or as economic responses to deprivation. Cargo cults are seen as an irrational search for wealth. For some, they are covert protest movements to *colonialism; or manifest cases of neurosis and crisis. Historians pay attention to biographies of leaders who reshaped the religious landscape, while others see them as charlatans. Phenomenological method in the study of religions examines the interior of the phenomenon, suspending judgment so as to search for its specific features and inner spirituality. This has produced conclusions that some of the new religious movements, like the *African Initiated Churches, have used indigenous 'maps' of the universe to generate new versions of Christianity. The creativity consists in constructing a set of beliefs: in invisible spiritual forces, especially malevolent spiritual powers; in the efficacy of ritual action, and the construction of ritual space as the foundation for contact between this world and God in the heavenly realm; in how revelation (dream, vision, prophecy) functions; and in what ritual symbols and traditions about the founders mean. Prayer replaces divination for controlling malevolent spiritual forces.

Missiologists express two subtle perspectives: they distinguish between movements that originated from mission churches (and still retain the centrality of the Bible, albeit *inculturated), and the home-grown movements tapping into unwholesome spirits and compromising the gospel. The label '*syncretism' is now seen by many as pejorative and ambiguous. New religious movements should be studied as a 'spiritual mapping' of broad religious landscapes that seek to identify the spirits at the gates of communities. This should enhance evangelical strategies by identifying the points at which new religious movements distort orthodox interpretations of the faith, and by clarifying the ways in which the gospel can both resonate with and confront their world-view. Exploring the differences sends us back to our core beliefs in *revelation, *Christology and the true nature of redemption.

Historians of religions focus on the new revelations about life, the supernatural, the divinity of the leader, the attitude to indigenous religions, and the remarkable missionary zeal to propagate the new spiritualities. Many new religious movements focus on healing (mental and physical) and the availability of blessings and prosperity. They search for meaning amidst rapid social changes and invasive religious systems and world-views, and they search for spiritual power. A number of new religious movements start from urban contexts, transcend old ethnic groupings, constitute a 'place for belonging', and offer safe, trans-ethnic networks in the midst of anomie, stress, and competition. Others remain localized ethnic responses to modernity. The polities vary widely from loosely decentralized to highly structured, enclosed, centralized, communal, hierarchical power structures. Uniforms, titles and colours denote roles and status. The gender construction among some enlarges administrative roles while using indigenous prohibitions, such as menstrual taboos, to limit access to ritual authority. Others reinforce the patriarchy ideology that permeates Jewish, Victorian and indigenous cultures.

Historical examples

A number of new religious movements emerged from encounters with Iberian Catholicism, whose cultic symbols and practices fascinated the communities in southern and central America from 1530. In Africa, examples include the Antonian movement started by a Congolese young woman, Vita Kimpa, who had been baptized as Beatrice before she claimed that St Anthony possessed her during the Easter of 1704. She was deeply disturbed by the wars caused among her people by competing European slavers. Roman Catholic missionaries beheaded her as a heretic. Similarly, as the Portuguese presence waned around Cape Coast (on the Atlantic seaboard) in the eighteenth century, a cult known as *Nana Antonia* emerged as a hybrid of indigenous religion and Iberian Catholic symbols.

The nineteenth century was particularly fertile in nurturing new religions because of social suffering and stress in the encounter with more destructive religions and cultures: in the United States, some were founded among the First Nation communities in Seneca, and Narragansett of Rhode Island. In the Caribbean, the Peyote cults, the Native Baptist Church, Jamaica, jostled with Pocomania, Revival Zion, Bedwardism, Rastafarians and Convince. Old African religions survived in Santeria, Shango and Candobra. In the twentieth century, the Pai Marire and Ringatu in New Zealand had identical character with some cargo cults in Melanesia, and over one hundred cults that emerged from shamanism among the Koreans and Japanese. There were two main reasons for the rise of these movements: creative religious genius, combined with a search to make sense of new conditions. They decoded the missionary message by linking the traditional with the new religions. Many signalled resistance to the new order. In the inter-war years, a plethora of African Indigenous Churches exploded all over the continent, named *Zionists* in southern and central Africa, *Abaroho* (drunk in the spirit) in eastern Africa, and *Aladura* (people of prayer) in western Africa.

Some reflected nationalism in unsettled times, others reworked the missionary message, and many responded to *racism by creating indigenous religious alternatives. It is possible to distinguish between those that tend more towards the indigenous religion (nativistic), those that attempt to reinvent the old by borrowing symbols from the new (revivalistic), and those that focus on acquisition of power through occult practices (vitalistic).

Issues for mission

A missiological issue is the quality of the mix when Christianity is appropriated from out of the context of traditional religions. The question is whether the new faith is modelled with borrowed elements (neo-pagan); or whether the emergent form rejects both the local and invading religions by creating a composite religion (synthetist). A number of the new religious movements perceived large swaths of resonance between indigenous cultures and the Jewish traditions found in the OT. They practised the rites and prohibitions in the Torah and rejected Christological doctrines. The religions of pre-industrial societies tended to be charismatic, recognizing the presence of spirits. These new religious movements emphasized the role of the Holy Spirit and wanted the new to perform better the goals of the old religion. In some cases, a messianic charismatic figure emerged claiming to be one or the other of the Trinity, or a millennarian apostle of a new dispensation. These challenged those missionary-founded churches that deployed cessationism to reject the charismatic gifts.

New religious movements represent an innate religious quest in the human nature; they are indigenous religious initiatives which both appropriate world religions and contest their core beliefs and boundaries. They breed at the interface of religion and culture and create pluralistic religious landscapes that challenge co-existence. They represent both a missiological challenge and an opportunity by obliging Christians to re-examine and clarify the nature of authority, the importance of tradition, the theology of revelation, the role of spiritual power, and the uniqueness of Christ.

New religious movements in modern Western societies

Many identical issues are raised in the study of new religious movements in modern Western societies. Some originate as sects within the world religions, or reinvent old religious forms driven underground by the Enlightenment world-view and industrialization. Others react against the heritage built on Judeo-Christianity in the heydays of 'Christendom'. They are alternative, non-conventional, fresh religious expressions that contest the dominant religions and their secular implications. Immigration and the proliferation of alternative religious movements have reshaped the religious landscape in modern Europe and North America. Some argue that they pose enormous security problems.

A new religious landscape

The numbers and varieties reflect changes in social values and political trends. New religious movements have benefited from an increasingly liberal climate of religious tolerance and freedom, the separation of church and state, the assertion of individual rights, and the emergence of pluralistic ideology. With the faster decline of Christianity in Europe than in the USA and Canada, alternative religions grew by about two-thirds more in Europe than in the USA.

Some scholars argue that the Parliament of World Religions in Chicago in 1893 unleashed a religious force that linked the East and West, and catalysed an influx of eastern religions. This force intensified when immigration policies in the period 1960–80 opened the West further to enthralling contacts with eastern migrants and their religions, coinciding with the youthful protests against the Vietnamese war that nurtured a culture of protest in the 1960s. The 'hippies' and 'flower children' preferred to make love rather than war, and indulged in drugs, psychedelic spiritualities, and the practice of religious communalism led by gurus, swamis and millennialist prophets. A creative, religious enthusiasm occurred in the 1970s all over the world that widened choices in the enlarged religious market. Opponents brand thousands of new religious movements as 'cults'.

Typology

The typology is complex: some are counter-cultural movements seeking for alternative lifestyles or promoting a political agenda; others focus on personal growth, while some revitalize or reinterpret a world religion. Broad categories include:

- Sects within world religions that reinterpret the faith and are considered as deviations from the mainline faith (e.g. Mormonism, Deists, Swedenborgians, Chasid Judaism, Sufism, and Reformed Buddhism).
- Spiritualists (e.g. National Spiritualist Association of Churches).
- Metaphysical, new science religions, psychic groups (e.g. International New Thought Alliance, Christian Science, Moonies).
- Eastern religions characterized by intense meditational practice, vegetarianism, pacifism, celibacy and various types of yoga.
- Ritual magic (high and low, and ceremonial).
- Ancient wisdom (e.g. Rosicrucianism, Theosophy, *New Age).
- Witchcraft (e.g. satanism, earth goddess, wicca).

In each type, there are internal variations that nonetheless share a common thought world of ideas, similar lifestyle, predictable behaviour patterns and heritage traceable to a common root. Until the turn of the twentieth century these alternative religions were indigenous to the Western world. However, the influx of eastern religions widened the scope. Statistics indicate that the three fastest growing types are the psychic, eastern religions and the magical. When the church types consolidated, the cutting edge shifted to communal and new thought/new age religions. It was estimated in 1990 that there were over a thousand sects in the USA.

The first category refers to groups that deviated from orthodoxy but still function within the broad scope of a major religious type. Thus Mormons use the collected revelations of Joseph Smith alongside their own version of the Bible. Sect typology has become ambiguous. For instance, the Mormons have consolidated, fragmented into different genres, and launched into a vibrant global mission. Others, especially communal family subtypes, built on a literal reading of the Bible, such as Shakers, Hutterites and the Farm and the Church of Armageddon, have been battered by modernity into small colonies. The Children of God community grew imperceptibly into prominence when they conflicted with state authorities.

A Christian missiological reading would place the categories of the metaphysical and spiritualist groups together as transcendental, soulish religions that believe in tapping the power in the human psyche and strengthening the intellect, will and human emotions for solving the problems of everyday life in a competitive world. One example of this is Christian Science.

Spiritualism delves into the reality of the soul force beyond the veil of death. Spiritualism attempts to use 'scientific' evidence of life after death to connect with the dead through mediums and channels, and especially with 'masters' or teachers or 'spiritual contacts', who assist in unravelling the questions of human destiny for the living. Spiritualism exists in every human religion and culture. During the psychedelic 1960s, new forms proliferated, including astrology, UFOs, reincarnation, efficacious meditations, personal angels and astral travel.

Missiological engagement

In the West many new religious movements are small enough to be ignored by the institutional churches, and even the larger manifestations are only studied by individuals or theologians with a specialist interest. However, there is a combined effect of a significant movement towards alternative spiritualities which the Western church has recognized that it cannot ignore. Since mission always works both ways, changing the church even as it seeks to change society, this has resulted in a re-evaluation: why do people reject institutional and traditional forms of religion? What do they find in the new religious movements, apart from the newness itself, which they do not find in the church? In Britain, 'fresh expressions' of church are trying to provide a worship space and quality of communal life which is radically different from the institutional forms and seeks to resonate with some of the characteristics of the new religious movements: spiritual reality, flexibility of expression, space and freedom in worship, social engagement, and creative ways of relating to God.

The Western church is poorly equipped for the spiritual discernment needed of the 'spirits' operating in a post-Christian West, in spite of the influence of the charismatic movement. The boundaries are often blurred, and some Christians see no problem in being involved in yoga, alternative therapies, or meditation practices. A missiology of discipleship would equip Christians for a more discerning and engaged understanding of new religious movements. Many of their manifestations have been seen before in other contexts, so Christians need not be taken by surprise by the latest development if they are equipped to 'see through' to where a movement is coming from.

New religious movements also exploit the Western confusion with the nature of *truth, since experience is valued over objectivity, and personal truth over corporate belief. Many now recognize that it is not enough for the church simply to repeat the traditional formulas, as if they are self-evident; a missiological engagement will take this context seriously, recognize that truth works at different levels, and adopt a critical realism towards its own affirmations.

New religious movements will continue to proliferate and many will come and go. The extent and complexity of the phenomenon is enormous. The missionary church will recognize that new religious movements form a significant component of the context in which it does its mission, and their approach takes root in the consciousness and culture of those to whom it seeks to relate the gospel.

Bibliography

S. Ellis and G. ter Haar, *Worlds of Power: Religious Thought and Political Practice in Africa* (New York: Oxford University Press, 2004); C. Y. Glock and R. N. Bellah (eds.), *The New Religious Consciousness* (Berkeley: University of California Press, 1976); P. C. Lucas and T. Robbins (eds.), *New Religious Movements in the Twenty-First Century: Legal, Political and Social Challenges in Global Perspective* (New York: Routledge, 2004); B. Wilson and J. Cresswell (eds.), *New Religious Movements: Challenge and Response* (New York: Routledge, 1999).

O. U. KALU

New Testament perspectives on mission

Christian mission in the NT is both unique and distinctive. The new, unique element is Jesus Christ, and the distinctiveness of mission is the call to people of all nations to become his disciples.

Missionary nature of the NT

The NT concept of mission is not unrelated to that of the Old, as Chris Wright has argued in his article on *OT mission. They are not identical, but there is both continuity and discontinuity. In the OT, Yahweh, though Lord of the earth, establishes his primary relationship with the people of Israel, not however for their own sake, but so that they may be a 'light to the nations'. Nevertheless, with a few exceptions (such as Jonah), this does not translate into a missionary impulse to reach out to the nations. But in the NT the universality of the *gospel and its missionary character become explicit and fulfilled. There is now no difference between Jew and non-Jew (Rom. 2:11; 3:9; Gal. 3:28).

Some have discerned a distinction between the centripetal mission of the OT (the nations are invited into Zion to discover God's saving grace), and the centrifugal mission of the NT (the church takes God's saving grace out to the nations). Certainly although the OT does reveal the salvific will of *God and his mission purposes for the nations, the universal implementation of this comes through the unique mission of Jesus. Yet Jesus, in giving to the church the command to 'disciple all nations', affirms the missionary intentions of key OT texts such as the promise to Abraham (Gen. 12:3) and Isaiah's 'great commission' passage (Isa. 49:6). Biblical mission therefore makes Jesus and his directive to the church the central focus. In fact NT texts are intrinsically missiological since they arise out of a church in mission mode and are intended to strengthen that church in its mission. As Lesslie Newbigin states, 'The mission of the church is in fact the church's obedient participation in that action of the Spirit by which the confession of Jesus as Lord becomes the authentic confession of ever new peoples, each in its own tongue' (*The Open Secret*, p. 22).

Mission in the Synoptic Gospels

The high points in Jesus' mission are three 'sending moments': his sending of the Twelve (Matt. 10; Mark 6:7–13; Luke 9:1–6), his deployment of the seventy (Luke 10:1–24), and his commissioning of the church (Matt. 28:19; Luke 24:44–49; John 20:21). Jesus' handing of his mission to the apostles is the culmination of teaching and actions which

have laid the foundations for the universality of the gospel.

Mission in Mark

Mark provides his *Christological basis for the Christian mission by presenting Jesus' life and ministry in a dynamic story format, culminating in the cross and resurrection.

It has been suggested that Mark's narrative is based on Peter's sermon at the house of Cornelius (Acts 10), and is therefore kerygmatic. The author is thought to be the same Mark who went on missionary journeys with the apostles (Acts 13; 15). Perhaps Mark himself was a Gentile Christian and therefore highly interested in the Gentile mission. He quickly shows how Jesus' fame spread beyond Galilee and attracts Gentiles as well as Jews (Mark 3:7–8). Jesus soon enters Gentile territory (Mark 5:1–20), he repudiates Pharisaic Judaism (Mark 7:1–13) and returns to minister in Gentile country (Mark 7:24–25). The main point of the cleansing of the temple concerns the house of prayer for all nations (Mark 11:17). Mark emphasizes the acceptance of the Gentiles (12:9) and the Gentile mission (13:10). The tearing of the temple curtain and the confession of the Gentile centurion (Mark 15:38–39) is the climax of the passion story. The gospel must be preached, these events told, to all people everywhere.

Mission in Matthew

Matthew's narrative begins with the story of Mary and Joseph. The human side of the *incarnation is significant for his Christology. The genealogy includes four women whose marriages contained elements of scandal – Tamar, Rahab, Ruth, Bathsheba. Mary shares their vulnerability. The incarnation takes place in a context of risk. The Bethlehem massacre (2:16–18) intrudes. Brutal infanticide seems alien to our reading of the Christmas story. Yet in contemporary Asia and the West, as in first-century Palestine in which the incarnation took place, similar violence is a tragic reality and part of the human story. A Christology 'from below' begins from the human story of Jesus. Throughout history the church has preferred a Christology 'from above' in which the incarnation is clearly the action of God. Matthew's Christology 'from above' is qualified by the human elements in the story. The scandal of the incarnation is its humanness. Scandal follows, from beginning to end – the scandal of his birth, a refugee in Egypt, his life in Nazareth, criminal death ... God's mission to humanity takes place in a context of scandal and risk.

Matthew's theology resolves the apparent contradictions between a mission to Jews and the Gentile mission. In the Jewish story of the Syro-Phoenician woman, Jesus, despite the objections of his disciples, receives the woman's request and commends her faith (15:21–28; cf. Mark 7:24–30). Inclusion of this event indicates acceptance of the Gentile mission. Matthew sought to persuade the Jew; but he did not exclude the Gentile.

The parables of Matthew 13 and their exposition depict the course of events related to the missionary spread of the good news. The text assumes that before the close of the age all nations will have been confronted with the gospel (Matt. 24:14).

Matthew's great commission (28:18–20) is the most elaborate rendition in the NT and appears to reflect the text of Isaiah 49:6. Events in Matthew's narrative are synchronized to the commission, which gives coherence and meaning to the entire composition.

Mission in Luke

Luke alone of the Gospel writers sets his account within the context of world history (cf. 1:5; 2:1–4; 3:1–2). Luke is neither a Jew nor an eyewitness follower of Jesus. He is a Gentile convert, the product of mission as well as an early participant in the church's mission.

Luke begins his account of Jesus' public ministry with the famous 'Nazareth Manifesto' (4:16–21), which Jesus reads from the prophet Isaiah (61:1–2). In applying this Scripture to himself (Luke 4:21), Jesus delineates his own mission in terms of the poor, the marginalized, the handicapped and the powerless (4:18). Compassion is the hallmark of the Christian mission.

Jesus at Nazareth inaugurates the day of God's mercy to the Gentiles as well as to the poor and oppressed. The Sidonian widow and Naaman the Syrian (4:26–27) are harbingers of a future Gentile response. Not surprisingly the Romans and other 'sinners' receive sympathetic treatment by Luke. Luke's purpose is to show the acceptance of the Gentiles in God's kingdom and plan. Luke's 'orderly account' (1:3) is addressed to a representative of the Greek world (1:1–3). It is written from the background of participation in the missionary expansion of the church (cf. Acts 16:10–15; 20:6; 21:1; 27:1 – 28:1).

The third Gospel together with the book of Acts should be regarded as a two-volume history of Christian origins, written by a participant-observer in the Gentile mission.

Mission in the fourth Gospel and the Johannine epistles

The prologue to John's Gospel is profoundly missiological. John's utilization of the Greek *logos* concept is a brilliant example of *contextualization. The *logos* has affinity to the Hindu idea of *dharma* and ultimate reality. But Jesus is not an *avatar* (a mythical descent of deity in temporary form). The incarnation is an event, historical and permanent. 'The resurrection of Jesus was not a casting off of the human and the resumption of the divine nature. The human is the manifestation and vehicle of the divine, both in the earthly life of Jesus and in his glorified humanity' (H. Peskett and V. Ramachandra, *The Message of Mission: The Glory of Christ in All Time and Space*, p. 75).

The distinctive incarnational Christology of the fourth Gospel continues throughout the narrative. David Ball argues that the 'I am' sayings of Jesus in the fourth Gospel refer to similar sayings in Isaiah spoken in a pluralistic context and which thus identify Jesus with the God of the OT. Identifying himself with the forgiving action of God, and applying to himself language reserved for God, Jesus claims for himself the very nature of God. In John's Christology, 'Jesus is unique not because of what God has done through him as a man but because he himself is divine' (D. M. Ball, in *One God, One Lord in a World of Religious Pluralism*, p. 64).

The incarnation is inconceivable in Islam. But the *cross, the *resurrection and the incarnation are integral to the gospel. 'The incarnation speaks of a God who *is* entangled with our world, who immerses himself in our tragic history, who embraces our humanity with all its vulnerability, pain and confusion' (Peskett and Ramachandra, *The Message of Mission*, p. 86). Incarnational Christology presents a challenge to dialogue with Islam, and is problematic to pluralists such as Hick and Samartha who reject the historicity of the fourth Gospel. John's portrayal of Jesus contradicts the viewpoint of the pluralists.

The Johannine epistles have much in common with the fourth Gospel. First John presents a high Christology. Its missionary purpose is specific: Christ is 'the expiation for ... the sins of the whole world' (2:2).

In the fourth Gospel mission has been defined as 'sending' (John 20:21). The first epistle points beyond the sending to its outcome: the formation of fellowships of new *disciples.

John stresses the *koinonia* of the NT church: fellowship 'with us' and 'with the Father' (1 John 1:3). Converts need a point of reference. Whatever it may be called, there will always be need for such groups. The church's mission involves creation of contextual Christ-centred fellowships, local cultural incarnations of the Christian faith. Such a church will have a high Christology (2:22–23), a passion for truth (2:21) and for holiness (1:8–10; 2:1); it will practise love in action (4:7–8, 11–12, 19–21), animated by Christian hope (3:1–3; cf. 2:28), in the assurance of Christ's victory over sin and death (5:4–5, 11–14). We may dispose of the foreign shape of the church, but we cannot dispense with the fellowship of Christians, which is basic to the NT concept of the church and its mission.

Christian mission takes place in a marketplace of monistic religions, theistic cults, spirit manifestations and secular humanism. It is a world not unlike that in which John addressed the early Christians. In each context the question is how best to communicate the message of Jesus Christ. Holding fast to its confession of Christ, the church can affirm values found in every human reality which are consistent with the kingdom. This is important in the multi-religious context in which the church carries out its mission in Asia and indeed in most of the world today. The hallmark of John's writings is 'love'. The incarnation itself is the embodiment of love, conceptualized by John as the Father's love for humanity. In like manner the Christian mission is to model compassionate, redeeming love.

Consistently therefore throughout the NT, Jesus is the essential core of gospel proclamation.

Pentecost and mission

Pentecost! Here again is something old and something new: the OT feast of harvest is the occasion for the advent of the *Holy Spirit. At the same time the NT church is instituted and its mission inaugurated.

The Pentecost event, and its importance for mission, has been anticipated by the fourth Gospel (John 15:26–27). The Holy Spirit arouses faith, brings people to turn from their sins and receive forgiveness, and empowers and enables the people of God for witness.

The Holy Spirit comes at Pentecost in fulfilment of the promise of Jesus (John 14:26; 16:7; Acts 1:5) and the prophets (Joel 2:28–29; Acts 2:16). The event is accompanied by signs reminiscent of 'the original theophany on Sinai which was commemorated by the Jewish feast of Pentecost' (J. Dupont, *The Salvation of the Gentiles*, p. 40). But there is something more than signs here. These happenings signify the inauguration of the evangelizing mission of the church among all nations, which is to proceed throughout the 'last days' of the dispensation of the Holy Spirit between the ascension and the second coming of Christ.

The worldwide missionary spread of the gospel begins from Pentecost; and as the church becomes obedient to the missionary command, the natural outcome is the expansion of the church.

The conversion of Gentiles raises new theological questions concerning the shape of the church as the new movement progresses beyond the Jerusalem Jewish context. We see churches taking shape in a variety of cultures.

Mission and culture

Mission takes place in a world of *cultures. The book of Acts shows the progression of the gospel from the 'Jewish' Jews of Jerusalem into the Judean countryside, then to the Samaritans and to the Hellenized Jews, and from the latter to the Gentiles at Antioch, and finally to the multiple cultures of the Roman Empire and the world.

The first stage takes place in Jerusalem (Acts 1:8), the centre of Jewish culture and orthodoxy. The church at Jerusalem reflects the strict cultural and religious traditions of this exclusive Hebrew community (Acts 6:1). Questions of pollution (Acts 10:28; 11:2–3), dietary restrictions (Acts 10:13–14), circumcision (Acts 15:1), and ritual purification (Acts 21:24) are all important to a people whose life has been regulated by Mosaic legislation (Acts 21:20); so it is not easy for this community to be a missionary people.

The second stage, witness 'in all Judaea and Samaria', is carried out primarily by Hellenized Jewish converts driven out of Jerusalem (Acts 8:1). The martyrdom of Stephen, the Hellenist deacon and evangelist, is a crucial event (Acts 6:8; 7:57–60), beginning a period of transition. The election of Hellenists in the Jerusalem church (Acts 6), the conversion of the Samaritans and the Ethiopian eunuch (Acts 8), and Saul's conversion (Acts 9) denote the change. The Hellenists are the bridge. But the key event is the conversion of the Gentile Cornelius (Acts 10). The revelation that 'God does not show favouritism but accepts those from every nation who fear him and do what is right' (Acts 10:34–35) is revolutionary. God has no favourites! The Christian faith can freely move beyond the confines of Judaism. The Pentecostal signs are therefore repeated when Cornelius and his household received the Holy Spirit (Acts 10:44–48).

The third stage, 'to the uttermost parts of the earth', brings into view all the diverse cultures and varieties of the human race, as is most evident in the mission of Paul.

The mission of Paul

Paul's missiology is clearly Christological. The starting point is his encounter with the living Christ. In Jesus the Messiah the final age has come, and *Paul is commissioned to announce salvation to the Gentiles.

Theologically, Paul recognizes the Gentiles as heirs of the promise of God (Eph 2:11; 3:1). Paul reasons from the OT that the way is open for anyone to be a child of God through Jesus Christ (Gal. 3:7). God's promise to bless all nations through Abraham (Gen. 3:7; Gal. 3:8) is fulfilled in Jesus Christ (Gal. 3:14). Therefore, anyone who belongs to Jesus Christ is a child of Abraham and heir of the promise (Gal. 3:26, 29).

Paul communicates Jesus Christ through his lifestyle, work and activity as well as by preaching. His methodology accommodates his audience. His approach to the Jewish synagogue community is through the OT Scriptures (Acts 13:16–43). At Athens, on Mars Hill, he establishes points of contact from local culture, religion and philosophy (Acts 17) in order to relate Christ to the Athenians' quest for the God they do not know. Among the animists at Ephesus the gospel is communicated in terms of miraculous signs, healing and deliverance from evil spirits (Acts 19:11–12). In each case Paul begins where his hearers are. By entering into their frame of reference he is able effectively to advocate the gospel.

Mission is carried out in a world dominated by rebellious powers which impede the advance of the gospel. But by his death and resurrection Christ has disarmed the powers (1 Cor. 15:24). Paul perceives his mission in terms of a rescue operation which is to turn the Gentiles 'from darkness to light and from the power of Satan to God' (Acts 26:18).

Mission to the end of time

The general epistles give further indicators of the development of theology in the mission of Christ in a non-Christian world. The epistle to the Hebrews ties everything to Christ and his perfect sacrifice. This has great significance in any society with a sacrificial or priesthood system. James provides a theology of social action and justice, of poverty and equality, of suffering and healing. The Mosaic demands for social righteousness (Deut. 10:12–20; 14:29; 15:1, 4, 11; 16:18–20; 24:17–22) are the substance of true religion (Jas 1:27) and of mission.

Peter stresses the priestly function of the people of God among the nations (1 Pet. 2:12). The church is called to represent God among the peoples of the world and bring the nations to faith (1 Pet. 2:9–10).

Finally Revelation gives a vision of the end. The struggles of new churches are set against a background of a hostile environment, including persecution. Against a backdrop of cosmic contest between good and evil, Revelation presents a cosmic Christology. The Christian mission entails proclamation of the victory of Christ over cosmic evil (Rev. 14:6), anticipating a universal acclamation of the Redeemer 'from every tribe and language and people and nation' (5:9–10, 13).

We are given a vision of hope for the created world, a new heaven and new earth (Rev. 21:1). The Lord himself is the light of the eternal city (21:23). In the restored paradise the tree of life reappears with leaves 'for the healing of the nations' (22:2).

The redeemed will enjoy the glories of the new world. But there is another sobering aspect: some are outside of Christ and outside of eternal life (22:14–15). This fact should impel us to mission. There is hope. God's judgment is tempered with mercy. The Bible ends with a warning and an invitation to come and find mercy. The appeal is urgent. Christ is returning (Rev. 22:20). His coming will terminate the mission and consummate the kingdom. This certainty motivates the church's mission in anticipation of that day.

See also KINGDOM OF GOD.

Bibliography

D. M. Ball, ' "My Lord and My God": The Implication of "I Am" Sayings for Religious Pluralism', in A. D. Clarke and B. W. Winter (eds.), *One God, One Lord in a World of Religious Pluralism* (Cambridge: Tyndale House, 1991); J. Dupont, *The Salvation of the Gentiles*, trans. J. Keating (New York: Paulist, 1979); F. Hahn, *Mission in the New Testament* (London: SCM, 1965); R. E. Hedlund, *God and the Nations: A Biblical Theology of Mission in the Asian Context* (Delhi: ISPCK, 2002); S. Karotemprel (ed.), *Following Christ in Mission: A Foundational Course in Missiology* (Bombay: Pauline Publications, 1965); G. E. Ladd, *A Theology of the New Testament* (Grand Rapids: Eerdmans, 1974); W. J. Larkin Jr and J. F. Williams (eds.), *Mission in the New Testament: An Evangelical Approach* (Maryknoll: Orbis Books, 1998); L. Newbigin, *The Open Secret* (Grand Rapids: Eerdmans, 1978); H. Peskett and V. Ramachandra, *The Message of Mission: The Glory of Christ in All Time and Space* (Downers Grove: Inter-Varsity; Leicester: IVP, 2003); D. Senior and C. Stuhlmueller, *The Biblical Foundations for Mission* (Maryknoll: Orbis Books, 1983).

R. E. HEDLUND

Old Testament perspectives on mission

Reading Israel's Scriptures for mission

Mission is often thought of as a NT and post NT phenomenon. Is it possible to read the OT

also as a missional text? The clearest justification for doing so is that Jesus himself told his disciples to read it that way. In Luke 24 he twice surveys the whole canon of OT Scripture and claims that 'this is what is written': both that the Messiah would come, suffer, die and rise again; and that repentance and forgiveness of sins would be preached in his name to the nations (vv. 45–47). The first claim reads Scripture messianically; the second reads Scripture missiologically – and Jesus urges this double hermeneutical strategy on those who read the OT in conscious relation to himself.

Starting in this way with Jesus' theocentric and teleological use of the Scripture (i.e. that the Scriptures reveal the 'whole will of God') also reminds us that handling the Bible in relation to mission is not merely a matter of identifying themes within it that justify and shape *our* engagement in mission. For behind all human mission stands the mission of God. And the Bible itself (including of course the OT) is a dimension of the mission of God. The whole canon of Scripture is a missional phenomenon in the sense that it witnesses to the self-giving movement of this *God, in *revelation and redemption, towards his creation and towards us, human beings made in God's own image, but wayward and rebellious. The writings, which now comprise our Bible, are themselves the product of, and witness to, the ultimate mission of God for the redemption of humanity and creation.

Furthermore, the processes by which these texts came to be written were often profoundly missional in nature. Many of them emerged out of events, or struggles, or crises, or conflicts, in which the people of God engaged with the constantly changing and challenging task of articulating and living out their understanding of God's revelation and redemptive action in the world. Sometimes these were struggles internal to the people of God themselves; sometimes they were highly polemical struggles with competing religious claims and world-views that surrounded them. Biblical texts often have their origin in some issue, need, controversy or threat, which the people of God needed to address in the context of their mission. The text in itself is a product of mission in action.

This is easily seen in the NT. Most of *Paul's letters were written in the heat of his missionary efforts: wrestling with the theological basis of the inclusion of the Gentiles; affirming the need for Jew and Gentile to accept one another in Christ and in the church; tackling the baffling range of new problems that assailed young churches as the gospel took root in the world of Greek polytheism; confronting incipient heresies with clear affirmations of the supremacy and sufficiency of Jesus Christ, and so on. Similarly, the Gospels were written to explain the significance of the good news about Jesus of Nazareth, especially his death and resurrection. Confidence in these things was essential to the missionary task of the expanding church.

But also, in the case of the OT we can see that many of these texts emerged out of the engagement of Israel with the surrounding world in the light of the God they knew in their history and in covenantal relationship. People produced texts in relation to what they believed God had done, was doing, or would do, in their world. The Torah records the exodus as an act of YHWH that comprehensively confronted and defeated the power of Pharaoh and all his rival claims to deity and allegiance. It presents a theology of *creation that stands in sharp contrast to the polytheistic creation myths of Mesopotamia. The historical narratives portray the long and sorry story of Israel's struggle with the culture and religion of Canaan, a struggle reflected also in the pre-exilic prophets. Exilic and post-exilic texts emerge out of the task that the small remnant community of Israel faced to define their continuing identity as a community of faith in successive empires of varying hostility or tolerance. Wisdom texts interact with international wisdom traditions in the surrounding cultures, but do so with staunch monotheistic disinfectant. And in worship and prophecy, Israelites reflect on the relationship between their God, YHWH, and the rest of the nations – sometimes negatively, sometimes positively – and on the nature of their own role as Yahweh's elect priesthood in their midst.

This observation that the canon of Scripture, including the OT, is missional in its origin (in the purpose of God), and in its formation (in the multiple contexts of *cultural engagement), means that so-called *'contextualization' is not something we add

to 'the real meaning' of biblical texts, but is intrinsic to them. The task of re-contextualizing the word of God is a missional project that has its basis in Scripture itself and has been part of the mission of God's people all through the centuries of their existence. The finality of the canon refers to the completion of God's work of revelation and redemption, not to a foreclosure on the necessary continuation of the *inculturated witness to that completed work in every culture.

In short, a missional hermeneutic proceeds from the assumption that the whole Bible renders to us the story of God's mission through God's people in their engagement with God's world for the sake of God's purpose for the whole of God's creation.

What follows is a brief survey of some of the key OT themes which undergird this understanding of mission. This is not a search for odd verses of the OT that might say something relevant to our narrowed concept of sending missionaries, but rather a sketch of some of the great trajectories of Israel's understanding of their God and of God's mission through Israel for all the nations. We are not concerned about how the OT gives incidental support to what we already do, but about the theology that undergirds the whole worldview that Christian mission presupposes.

We survey briefly the missiological implications of four major pillars of OT faith: monotheism, election, *ethics and *eschatology.

The uniqueness of Israel's God

Israel made remarkable affirmations about Yahweh, affirmations which had a polemical edge in their own context and still stand as distinctive claims. Among them was the monotheistic declaration that Yahweh alone is God and there is no other (e.g. Deut. 4:35, 39). As sole deity, it is Yahweh, therefore, who owns the world and runs the world (Deut. 10:14, 27; Ps. 24:1; Jer. 27:1–12; 1 Chr. 29:11). This ultimately means the radical displacement of all other rival gods and that Yahweh must be acknowledged as God over the whole earth and all nations (e.g. Ps. 96; Jer. 10:1–16; Isa. 43:9–13; 44:6–20). The impact of these claims is felt in such widely varying contexts as the struggle against idolatry, the language of *worship, and the response to other nations, both in their own contemporary international history, and in eschatological vision.

There is no doubt that the strength of the OT affirmations about the uniqueness and universality of Yahweh as God underlie, and indeed provide, some of the vocabulary for the NT affirmations about the uniqueness and universality of *Jesus (cf. Phil. 2:9–11, based on Isa. 45:23; and 1 Cor. 8:5–6, based on Deut. 6:4). It is also noteworthy that these early Christian affirmations were equally polemical in their own historical context as those of ancient Israel, and in turn provided the primary rationale and motivation for Christian mission. We are dealing here with the missiological implications of biblical monotheism. If Yahweh alone is God and if Jesus alone is Lord, and if it is God's will (as it manifestly is in the Bible) that these truths be known throughout the whole creation, then there is a missional mandate intrinsic to such convictions (see *Evangelism).

A fully biblical understanding of the universality and uniqueness of Yahweh and of Jesus Christ stands in the frontline of a missional response to the relativism at the heart of religious pluralism and some forms of postmodernist philosophy.

The purpose of Israel's election

The OT begins on the stage of universal history. After the accounts of creation we read the story of God's dealings with fallen humanity and the problem and challenge of the world of the nations (Gen. 1 – 11). After the stories of the flood and of the Tower of Babel, could there be any future for the nations in relation to God? Or would *judgment have to be God's final word?

The story of Abraham, beginning in Genesis 12, gives a clear answer. God's declared commitment is that he intends to bring blessing to the nations, 'all peoples on earth will be blessed through you' (Gen. 12:3). Repeated five times in Genesis alone, this key affirmation is the foundation of biblical mission, inasmuch as it declares the mission of God. The Creator God's mission is nothing less than blessing the nations of humanity. So fundamental is this divine agenda that Paul defines the Genesis declaration as 'the gospel in advance' (Gal. 3:8). And the concluding vision of the whole Bible signifies the fulfilment of the Abrahamic promise, as people from every nation, tribe,

language and people are gathered among the redeemed in the new creation (Rev. 7:9). The gospel and mission both begin in Genesis, then, and both are located in the redemptive intention of the Creator to bless the nations. Mission is God's address to the problem of fractured humanity and is universal in its ultimate goal and scope.

The same Genesis texts which affirm the *universality* of God's mission to bless the nations also, and with equal strength, affirm the *particularity* of God's election of Abraham and his descendants to be the vehicle of that mission. The election of Israel is one of the most fundamental pillars of the biblical world-view, and of Israel's historical sense of identity. It is vital to insist that although the belief in their election could be (and was) distorted into a narrow doctrine of national superiority, that move was resisted in Israel's own literature (e.g. Deut. 7:7–10). The affirmation is that Yahweh, the God who had chosen Israel, was also the creator, owner and Lord of the whole world (Deut. 10:14–17, cf. Exod. 19:4–6). That is, Yahweh was not just 'their God', he was God of all (as Paul insists in Rom. 4). Yahweh had chosen Israel in relation to his purpose for the world, not just for Israel. The election of Israel was not tantamount to a rejection of the nations, but explicitly for their ultimate benefit. Election is not an exclusive privilege but an inclusive responsibility. If we might paraphrase John, 'God so loved the world that he chose Israel'.

Thus, rather than asking if Israel itself 'had a mission', in the sense of being 'sent' anywhere (anachronistically injecting our 'sending missionaries' paradigm again), we need to see the missional nature of Israel's existence in relation to the mission of God in the world. Israel's mission was to *be* something, not to go somewhere. This perspective is clearly focused in the person of the Servant of Yahweh in Isaiah 40 – 55, who both embodies the election of Israel (identical things are said about Israel and the Servant), and also is charged with the mission (like Israel's) of bringing the blessing of Yahweh's justice, salvation and glory to the ends of the earth.

The life of Israel in the world

Our main concern here is ethical, and it is the missiological dimension of Israel's *holiness*.

Israel was called to be distinctive from the surrounding world in ways that were not merely religious but also ethical. In Genesis 18:19 this is expressed as the very purpose of Israel's election in relation to God's promise to bless the nations. In stark contrast to the world of Sodom and Gomorrah, Yahweh says of Abraham: 'I have chosen him, so that he will direct his children and his household after him to keep the way of the LORD by doing what is right and just, so that the LORD will bring about for Abraham what he has promised him.' This verse, in a remarkably tight syntax, binds together election, ethics and mission as three interlocking aspects of God's purpose. His choice of Abraham is for the sake of his promise (to bless the nations); but the accomplishment of God's mission demands the ethical obedience of God's community – the fulcrum in the middle of the verse.

In Exodus 19:4–6 Israel's ethical distinctiveness is also linked to their identity and role as a priestly and holy people in the midst of the nations. As Yahweh's *priesthood*, Israel would be the means by which God would be known to the nations and the means of bringing the nations to God (performing a function analogous to the role of Israel's own priests between God and the rest of the people). As a *holy* people, they would be ethically (as well as ritually) distinctive from the practices of surrounding nations. The moral and practical dimensions of such holy distinctiveness are spelled out in Leviticus 18 – 19. Such visibility would be a matter of observation and comment among the nations, and that expectation in itself was a strong motivation for keeping the law (Deut. 4:6–8). The question of Israel's ethical obedience or ethical failure was not merely a matter between themselves and Yahweh, but was of major significance in relation to Yahweh's agenda for the nations (cf. Jer. 4:1–2). And that means that OT ethics is inseparably linked to God's mission as the OT declares it.

This missiological perspective on OT ethics seems to me a fruitful approach to the age-old hermeneutical debate over whether and how the moral teaching given to Israel in the OT (especially the law), has any authority or relevance to Christians. If the law was given in order to shape Israel to be what they were called to be (a light to the nations, a holy

priesthood), then it has a paradigmatic relevance to those who, in Christ, have inherited the same role in relation to the nations. In the Old as well as the New Testament, the ethical demand on those who claim to be God's people is determined by the mission with which they have been entrusted. There is no biblical mission without biblical ethics.

The scope of Israel's vision of the future
Israel saw the nations (including themselves) as being subject to the sovereign rule of God in history – whether in judgment or in mercy (cf. Jer. 18:1–10; Jonah). But Israel also thought of the nations as 'spectators' of all God's dealings with Israel – whether positively or negatively. That is, whether on the receiving end of God's deliverance, or of the blows of his judgment, Israel lived on an open stage and the nations would draw their conclusions (Exod. 15:13–16; Deut. 9:28; Ezek. 36:16–23).

Eventually, however, and in a rather mysterious way, the nations could be portrayed as the beneficiaries of all that God had done in and for Israel, and even invited to rejoice, applaud and praise Yahweh the God of Israel (Pss. 47; 67; 1 Kgs 8:41–43). And, most remarkable of all, Israel came to entertain the eschatological vision that there would be those of the nations who would not merely be *joined to* Israel, but would come to be *identified as* Israel, with the same names, privileges and responsibilities before God (Ps. 47:9; Isa. 19:19–25; 56:2–8; 66:19–21; Zech. 2:10–11; Amos 9:11–12).

These texts are quite breathtaking in their universal scope. This is the dimension of Israel's prophetic heritage that most profoundly influenced the theological explanation and motivation of the Gentile mission in the NT. It certainly underlies James's interpretation of the Christ-event and the success of the Gentile mission in Acts 15:16–18 (quoting Amos 9:12). And it likewise inspired Paul's efforts as a practitioner and theologian of mission (e.g. Rom. 15:7–16; Eph. 2:11 – 3:6). And it provided the theological shape for the Gospels, all of which conclude with their various forms of the great commission – the sending of Jesus' disciples into the world of nations.

And finally, we cannot omit the even wider vision that not only the nations, but also the whole creation will be included in God's purposes of redemption. For this God of Israel, of the nations, and of the world, declares himself to be creating a new heavens and a new earth, with redeemed humanity living in safety, harmony and environmental peace within a renewed creation. Again, this is a portrait enthusiastically endorsed in the NT (Ps. 96:11–13; Isa. 65:17–25; Rom. 8:18–21; 2 Pet. 3:13; Rev. 21:1–5), and so not only sustains our hope today, but also enables us to see Christian concern and action in relation to the *environment and care of creation as an essential part of our holistic biblical mission.

See also *MISSIO DEI*.

Bibliography

R. Bauckham, *The Bible and Mission: Christian Mission in a Postmodern World* (Carlisle: Paternoster, 2003); D. Filbeck, *Yes, God of the Gentiles Too: The Missionary Message of the Old Testament* (Wheaton: Billy Graham Centre, Wheaton College, 1994); W. C. Kaiser, Jr, *Mission in the Old Testament: Israel as a Light to the Nations* (Grand Rapids: Baker, 2000); A. J. Köstenberger and P. T. O'Brien, *Salvation to the Ends of the Earth: A Biblical Theology of Mission* (Leicester: Apollos, 2001); H. Peskett and V. Ramachandra, *The Message of Mission* (Leicester: IVP, 2003); E. J. Schnabel, 'Israel, the People of God, and the Nations', *Journal of the Evangelical Theological Society* 45, 2002, pp. 35–57; C. J. H. Wright, *Knowing Jesus through the Old Testament* (Oxford: Monarch, ²2005); C. J. H. Wright, 'Mission as a Matrix for Hermeneutics and Biblical Theology', in Craig Bartholomew, M. Healy, K. Moller and R. Parry (eds.), *Out of Egypt: Biblical Theology and Biblical Interpretation* (Carlisle: Paternoster and Grand Rapids: Zondervan, 2004); C. J. H. Wright, *The Mission of God: Unlocking the Bible's Grand Narrative* (Downers Grove: InterVarsity Press; Leicester: IVP, 2006).

C. J. H. WRIGHT

Partnership

Partnership speaks of a new relationship between the 'South' and the 'North' in terms of mutual covenant and reciprocal cooperation. Today, partnership can be described as 'South to South' as well as 'South to North'.

However, in today's *globalized world, partnership must be seen as 'from everywhere to everywhere' with no sense of inferiority nor superiority, but with all cultures united in the same purpose of God's *kingdom.

A missiological imperative

The northern hemisphere did not have any proper vision of real partnership until the protest of the Indian Bishop Azariah in the Edinburgh Congress of 1910. He claimed that the North did not practise a proper biblical theology of partnership, since power and control were totally in their hands. In the 1940s, the 'Whitby Declaration', with help from Anglican Bishop Stephen Neill, was instrumental in rethinking a new theology of partnership. The word came to be used in a wider sense, to fully include the southern hemisphere, and this thinking developed during the 1970s within the evangelical movement with the participation of some Majority World missiologists such as Orlando Costas, Samuel Escobar and René Padilla. Events that stimulated this missiological thinking from the South were Lausanne 1974; Pattaya Congress 1981; Mission for the Third Millennium movement 1985; and COMIBAM 1987.

Historically, it was generally acknowledged that modern mission had developed as one-way traffic from North to South. *Theologically*, the radical change of hermeneutical horizons meant the rethinking of partnership not in terms of master-servant, or older-younger, but in terms of *koinonia*, mutuality, interdependency, companionship, and so on. *Ecclesiologically*, it was recognized that, biblically speaking, the local *church should be the main agent of mission, out of which the various missionary structures are empowered. *Missiologically*, mission had been understood in terms of 'sending churches' and 'receiving churches'; but after the international mission conference of Whitby (Canada, 1947) this idea moved towards 'Partners in Obedience'. This change came about by demand from the South rather than from any real desire for change from the North. But the South's clamour was idealistic rather than pragmatic, since at first the South was unable to develop models of transnational mission. Today that has changed, and the main movements of mission are now South-North and South-South.

Partnership embodies the theological idea of a 'covenant' in which two or more persons agree to participate in a determined vision, action, purpose, target and methodology strategy, in order to accomplish one or more tasks in cooperation. The one church of God around the world should act as a united partner in God's mission, the *Missio Dei*. Partnership means that every church in Christ must be a church in mission united to the others in respect and love. Real partnership in mission should avoid and prevent competition. Christ's command to preach the gospel to all the world can only be done by all churches uniting all their strengths and resources.

The NT word *koinonia* is the nearest biblical word to partnership. Andrew Kirk identifies four aspects of biblical partnership: sharing in common projects; sharing of gifts; sharing in suffering; and sharing of material resources. However, this new theology of partnership must also include four more: sharing more in praying for others (2 Cor. 9:14) and sharing more of our resources (2 Cor. 9:8–10), which generates, third, praise and thanksgiving to God (2 Cor. 9:12–13), since, fourth, sharing with others is the expression of obedience to the gospel of Christ (2 Cor. 9:13).

The qualities needed for partnership to work include: *mutual trust* and *respect* where both partners can give and receive with no sense of inferiority or superiority; *transparency* through clear explanations of what are our mutual goals; *openness* in understanding each other culturally, theologically and missiologically; *patience* in learning from one another and from God; *stability* through the formation of long-term relationships; *vision* which is worked out together and jointly owned; *spiritual maturity* through supporting one another in word and deed, which draws on humility and confidence in God; *friendship*, which takes time, and needs a 'chemistry that comes from heaven'; and *identification* and solidarity which generate commitment to share with those who require support in mission.

So real partnership is a persevering and permanent relationship of mutual commitment and dialogue through which words, jointly understood and affirmed, are put into practice. It begins, though, with what we have in our hands, and the willingness to give what we have unconditionally. However, that cannot be understood only, or mainly, in terms of finance. Our abilities, talents, professions, time, experience, knowledge of other languages, voluntarism, and so on, all help us to put into practice this new theology of partnership.

Mission cannot be developed in isolation. Mission in the third millennium should be an 'interdependence-mission', where the agenda, decisions, influences of financial power and cultural differences are worked on together so that both partners can give unconditional support to the plans that emerge.

Many issues remain to be resolved. Some see 'partnership' as an old-fashioned movement; some prefer 'networking cooperation' which implies less dependence on more formal structures; some develop 'independence movements' which try to find their own space as a result of the tensions with Western missiology. Sometimes influence remains in the hands of Western missiology, as money clearly implies power. Positively, *cultural variety is also generating new paradigms of doing mission in multicultural teams that are revitalizing it across the six continents. No one can deny these days that the agenda and decisions for the mission task must be made with the participation of Third-World missiologists. Partnership must be seen to work as a covenant of friendship and mutual cooperation of unconditional relationship.

A missiological model

How can partnership work in practice? Our story is one example. Two Peruvian missionaries, Samuel and Noemi Cueva, were sent, with their two young children, by the Iglesia Misionera Evangelica (IME) of Huancayo Peru, to plant a church among the Spanish-speaking people in London where there are more than 300,000 Latins. The partner for the London project has been the Anglican Church of St James's Muswell Hill, whose vicar is the Rev. Alex Ross.

The IME Latin American model of mission is local church based, with a non-denominational mission structure called Misión IME Internacional. Its missionaries have to provide their own financial support. The sending church supports with 10% of the budget and the difference is covered through relatives, friends and 'friend-churches'. St James's should be included as a 'friend-church'.

St James's church has provided support for this partnership through a *building* for the Spanish-speaking church free of rent; providing pastoral *spiritual support* and friendship from the staff; by giving a small but regular *financial* gift; *practically* by helping to buy a building for the IME church in Lima, Peru and making a 'Christmas appeal' for them.

IME has supported St James's through *motivating* the British church in providing a vision for global mission; *sending* short-term mission teams for experience in Peru every two years; *strengthening* the prayer meeting services every Friday at 6 am; *being part* of the staff team involved in the new 5 pm service and participation in other services; *supporting* the World Mission Group.

Both sides say that it has been a great model of partnership, involving honesty, maturity in ministry, friendship and giving unconditionally, all of which have generated the success.

This model is 'local church to local church'; it has its own missiological tensions, but in general it has worked successfully. There are now many such partnerships with British churches. Other models involve partnerships of mission societies, or mission societies with denominations, denominations with denominations and so on. There is now a substantial mission theology of partnership which provides solid foundations for genuine and mutual participation between interdenominational and intercultural teams. There is no going back.

Bibliography

L. Bauerochse, *Learning to Live Together* (Geneva: WCC Publications, 2001); D. Bosch, *Transforming Mission* (Maryknoll: Orbis Books, 2001); K. Clements, *Faith On the Frontier* (Geneva: T. & T. Clark/WCC Publications, 1999); S. Cueva (ed.), *Misión para el Tercer Milenio* (Barcelona: CLIE, 2005); A. Kirk, *What is Mission?* (London: Darton, Longman and Todd Ltd, 1999); L. E. Koyes, *The Last Age of Missions: A Study of Third World Mission Societies* (Pasadena, CA: William Carey Library, 1983); S. N. Stephen, *Creative Tension* (London: Edinburgh House Press, 1959); J. R. W. Stott, *Making Christ Known: Historic Mission Documents from the Lausanne Movement 1974–1989* (London: Paternoster Press, 1996); US Center for World Mission, *Mission Frontiers: Profiles in Partnership* 28:3, 2006, pp. 12–16; W. Ustorf, *Christianized Africa – De-Christianized Europe? Missionary Inquiries into the Polycentric Epoch of Christian History* (Seoul: Tyrannus Press, 1992); G. Van Rheenen, *Biblical Foundations and Contemporary Strategies* (Grand Rapids: Zondervan, 1996); J. Verkuyl, *Contemporary Missiology, An Introduction* (Grand Rapids: Eerdmans, 1978); R. D. Winter and S. C. Hawthorne (eds.), *Perspectives on the World Christian Movement* (Pasadena: William Carey Library, 1992).

S. CUEVA

Paul

Paul was the first true missionary theologian. His mission was carried out through his theological convictions, and his theology was formulated and developed through dialogue with the churches he had planted. Understanding Paul as a missionary therefore gives us the key to understanding him and his theology.

Although this correlation was noted, for example, by G. B. Stevens (1892) and M. Kähler (1908), the missionary dimension of his theology has hardly been recognized. Since the 1950s, however, there has emerged a paradigm shift among biblical scholars in understanding Paul both as a missionary and a theologian. It was J. Munck who emphasized this most by asserting, 'All Paul's work as a thinker arises from his missionary activity, and its object is missionary work ... His theology arises from his work as apostle and directly serves that work' (*Paul and the Salvation of Mankind*, p. 67).

Munck's view was soon supported by O. Cullmann, K. Stendahl and E. P. Sanders. In his study on Romans, N. A. Dahl also advocated the need for integrating Paul's theology and mission, for 'his theology and his missionary activity were inseparable from one another' (*Studies in Paul: Theology for the Early Christian Mission*, pp. 70, 88, 97). M. Hengel put it more precisely: 'In them [the epistles] Paul develops his theological ideas as a *missionary*; i.e. the *Sitz im Leben* of Pauline theology is the apostle's mission ... Paul ... becomes the first Christian "theologian" because he is a missionary; that is, his theology is "mission theology" in the comprehensive sense' (*Between Jesus and Paul: Studies in the Earliest History of Christianity*, pp. 49–53). In more recent years this line of understanding has produced some significant studies on the correlation between Paul's mission and his theology.

Paul's self-awareness of his apostleship

Such a correlation is based on Paul's own understanding of himself. He was fully aware that he had been called to preach the *gospel of Jesus *Christ to the Gentiles. He was also keenly aware that the mystery of God which had been hidden for all generations had now been revealed and entrusted to him. He travelled far and wide to preach the gospel and as a result saw great success in establishing churches.

His self-awareness of being an apostle to the Gentiles was best expressed in Romans 15:15–16. Here he made it clear that he received *grace from God to become a minister to the Gentiles with the priestly duty of proclaiming the gospel. What Paul wrote to the Romans would prove his true apostleship to the Gentiles. Furthermore, such self-awareness prompted him to defend his gospel when it was under attack. He did not hesitate to rebuke even Peter when the truth of the gospel was undermined.

It is also to be noted that 'Paul the writer' achieved a more permanent role as the apostle to the Gentiles than 'Paul the missionary' could ever do during his lifetime. What he wrote in Romans, for example, fulfils a permanent apostolate, since it provides the fundamental theological foundation for the legitimacy of the *salvation of the Gentiles and the mission to them. In Romans his self-awareness of apostleship to the Gentiles influenced its content and tone. So he argued for the equality of Jew and Gentile in sinfulness (Rom. 1:18 – 3:20), in justification (3:21 – 4:25), in their new status (5:1 – 8:39) and in the plan of God (9:1 – 11:36). He wrote Romans *as* apostle to the Gentiles. Paul's strong determination to fulfil his calling is a challenging example for the calling to mission of every generation.

Paul's missionary message

If Paul was fully conscious that his first and foremost responsibility was to preach the gospel, what was the main content of his preaching and teaching? In his pioneering, benchmark work on Paul's missionary methods, Roland Allen summed up the elements and characteristics of Paul's missionary preaching almost entirely from Acts. However, more recent scholars, such as C. H. Dodd, H. Conzelmann and J. D. G. Dunn, have regarded the speeches attributed to him in Acts as secondary material at best, and have therefore attempted to reconstruct the core of Paul's missionary preaching from his letters. One cannot be certain, however, whether what they have rediscovered is the core of Paul's *missionary* preaching, or the message developed later in the course of defending and expounding his earlier proclamation.

Following C. Bussmann, D. Senior identifies three themes as Paul's initial missionary preaching. (1) Paul urged the Gentiles to 'turn to God from idols to serve the living and true God' (1 Thess. 1:9–10; Rom. 1:18–32). Such '*conversion' to bring total transformation through Jesus Christ was the goal of Paul's preaching. (2) 'Knowing God' or 'being known by God' was another motif of Paul's preaching, which reflects the emphasis on salvation (Gal. 4:8–9). (3) Paul proclaimed the death and *resurrection of Jesus as God's definitive act of salvation.

Whilst these are still valid methodologies, we propose to reconstruct Paul's initial missionary preaching by paying attention to *a reminder formula*. These reminders are, in most cases, very briefly formulated, yet they provide us with *Paul's own testimony* to what he actually preached and taught during his missionary endeavour. At least three themes are repeatedly 'reminded'.

The death and resurrection of Christ

Perhaps the most outstanding example is in 1 Corinthians 15:1–2a: 'Now, brothers and sisters, I want to remind you of the gospel I preached to you...' Here Paul reminds the Corinthians that he preached Christ's death, burial and resurrection as fulfilment of the Scriptures. Earlier he reminded them that he preached Christ and him crucified (1 Cor. 1:23; 2:1–2; cf. 15:15, 20). He also reminds the Galatians of his message of the *cross.

Furthermore, his declaration that his only boast is in the cross reaffirms that he had preached the cross there (Gal. 3:1; 6:14; 1 Cor. 2:2).

To the Romans Paul is now writing the gospel which he intended to preach in person. Here he declares that two vital elements for saving faith are belief in the resurrection of Jesus and confession of the lordship of Christ (Rom. 10:9; 14:9). The death, resurrection and exaltation of Jesus form the essential core of his preaching, and he preached the same message during his work in other cities. Paul also reminds the Colossians of the gospel they had heard and which had been universally proclaimed (Col. 1:21-23). The death and resurrection of Christ must therefore always be at the heart of missionary proclamation.

The parousia of Christ

Paul's message of resurrection naturally led him to speak of the parousia of Christ (see *Eschatology), for example during his missionary preaching in Thessalonica (1 Thess. 1:10; cf. 4:16; 5:2; 2 Thess. 1:7). As a result they had waited for God's Son from heaven (1 Thess. 1:10). In the course of his reinforced teaching, Paul explicitly reminds the perplexed Thessalonians, by asking: 'Don't you remember that when I was with you I used to tell you these things?' (2 Thess. 2:5). This reminder is intended to exhort confused believers 'to hold fast to the teachings we [previously] passed on' (2 Thess. 2:15). The teaching of the parousia always gives missionary proclamation a sense of urgency.

Godly life in Christ

Paul writes, 'we instructed you how to live in order to please God', and urges them simply by saying, 'do this more and more. For you know what instructions we gave you' (1 Thess. 4:1-2, 9-10). He also recalls his earlier warning: 'We have told you and warned you before' to avoid sexual immorality, and to live a quiet and diligent life (1 Thess. 4:3, 6b, 11). He reminds them of his own lifestyle as an example (1 Thess. 2:5-12; 2 Thess. 3:6-10). Paul clearly recalls the Corinthians, too, by saying, 'I already gave you a warning [about orderly Christian life] *when I was with you*' (2 Cor. 13:2, emphasis added). The apostle had a set of teachings concerning the Christian manner of life, which '[he taught] everywhere in every church' (1 Cor. 4:17, cf. 7:17-19). Such was the case in Galatia and in Philippi (Gal. 5:19-21; Phil. 3:17-19). It is significant to note that to the Romans and the Colossians (whom he did not teach in person), Paul wrote in detail about godly living in harmony with fellow-believers (Rom. 12-15; Col. 3). *Ethics must always be an integral dimension of missionary preaching, since holiness has always served as a faithful witness to the gospel.

Paul's exhortation to evangelism

Paul dedicated himself to the task of testifying to the gospel. Paul was a bold, highly effective *evangelist in his words and lifestyle. It is somewhat surprising, however, that nowhere does Paul explicitly exhort his converts and churches to preach the gospel. This omission does not mean that Paul did not intend his churches to take responsibility for continuing the evangelistic work that he had started. Neither does it necessarily mean that Paul intended his churches to be 'missionary by their very nature' (i.e. by their godly lifestyle), *rather than* missionary by their very action (i.e. by their active missionary outreach). O'Brien's conclusion, that Paul certainly intended his churches to get involved in actively sharing their faith, still requires an answer to his own question, 'Why is so little written in the Pauline letters about the need for Christians to evangelize?'

Most of Paul's letters address the specific situations of the churches by providing answers to the questions raised by them or by expounding his earlier teaching. There is no hint in his letters, however, that his churches lacked evangelistic zeal. Rather, they were praised for doing well in their witnessing and loving lifestyle (Rom. 1:8; Gal. 5:7; Col. 1:6; 1 Thess. 1:8; 4:9-10), and this may be one of the reasons why Paul did not need to exhort them specifically to share their faith.

Another possible reason for the omission is that during his initial missionary work Paul had already instructed his converts to share their faith, and, since they are doing well he sees no need to write about it again. With this regard, it is interesting to note that a more explicit exhortation to witness is given to the churches which Paul did not found himself, namely the churches in Colossae and in Rome. Colossians 4:5-6 is the only passage that P. Bowers accepts as Paul exhorting his converts to witness. But he qualifies this by saying, 'It is a ministry of attraction and responsiveness rather than one of deliberate outreach and active solicitation. ... it is a stationary rather than a mobile witness' (in *JSNT* 44, p. 101).

However, by their ministry of attraction they are to take initiative for every evangelistic opportunity: 'Be wise in the way you act towards outsiders; make the most of every opportunity. Let your conversation [with outsiders] be always full of grace, seasoned with salt, so that you may know how to answer everyone' (Col. 4:5–6; so also 1 Pet. 3:15). Paul expects that the moral excellence of Christians would inevitably cause non-believers to ask questions, and so he tells his converts to be ready and pro-active, making the most of every opportunity for *witness to Christ. For Paul, godly lifestyle is crucial for Christian witness (Phil. 1:27; 2 Tim 2:22–26). Once again therefore we see Paul's emphasis on ethics as evangelistically oriented.

Furthermore, the explicit exhortation for 'mobile witness' is also given, and this time to the church in Rome. Paul makes it plain that people must hear the gospel in order to believe and must call on the name of the Lord to be saved. He then rhetorically challenges the importance of sending, going and preaching for evangelistic outreach (Rom. 10:14–15). More specifically, Paul urges Timothy to 'do the work of an evangelist' (2 Tim. 4:5). Timothy was solemnly charged to 'preach the word; be prepared in season and out of season' (2 Tim. 4:2). Paul also expresses his prayers for Philemon: 'you may be active in sharing your faith' (Philm. 6, NIV). It is clear that Paul intended his churches in turn to focus themselves upon ongoing mission. He taught them through his own example as an evangelist. He encouraged them to become 'missionary' both by their godly lifestyle and by their active outreach.

Paul's mission strategy

Paul preached the gospel to both Jews and Gentiles, but his primary interest was to 'bring in' the Gentiles. He worked with his co-workers as a team. Often the delegates of the churches became Paul's partners in the gospel. He aimed to reach 'the regions beyond' (2 Cor. 10:15–16). Even after preaching from Jerusalem to Illyricum, he still planned to visit Rome and Spain. However, as D. Senior notes, 'Paul apparently focused on provincial centres that had not yet been evangelized, leaving to the communities themselves and perhaps to other apostolic workers the task of dealing with their non-Christian neighbours' (*The Biblical Foundation for Mission*, p. 184). He pressed on to preach in the areas where Christ was not known (Rom. 10:14; 15:20–21).

However, despite his primary focus on the Gentiles, Paul always wanted to reach his own people. His strategy was to provoke the Jews to jealousy through his mission to the Gentiles. Furthermore, he was deeply concerned about the unity between the Jewish and the Gentile Christian communities. The collection from the Gentile churches for the believers in Jerusalem was a means to affirm and strengthen their unity and commitment to one another.

Next he brought the converts together as a church and appointed leaders to look after it. He then expected them to take responsibility for it, and did not allow them to become dependent upon him. The church was to be a sign of the presence of Christ and an instrument of fulfilling God's purposes. In evangelism, conversion is not enough; converts must be put together as a church for their mutual and ongoing growth.

Furthermore, Paul was concerned for the health of the churches, their establishment in faith in Christ, their godly life and unity in brotherly love. Thus he constantly prayed for them, sent his representatives, and wrote them letters to help them to grow strong in Christ as individual believers and as churches. Paul was committed to provide pastoral care to his converts. By his own example he authenticated what he taught. Yet he did not depend on financial support from his converts, but he worked hard to support himself and his team.

As Senior has rightly pointed out, 'Paul's missionary strategy and style directly related to his mission theology' (*The Biblical Foundation for Mission*, p. 185). It is important for modern missionaries, too, to do their mission work rooted in theological understanding, and for theologians to do their theology integrated with its mission perspective. Paul wrote his letters *in* mission and *for* mission; therefore, without grasping his missionary perspective, it is impossible adequately to understand either him or his theology.

Bibliography

R. Allen, *Missionary Methods: Paul's or Ours?* (Grand Rapids: Eerdmans, 1962 [1912]); D. Bosch, *Transforming Mission: Paradigm Shifts in Theology of Mission* (New York: Orbis Books, 1991); P. Bowers, 'Church and Mission in Paul', *JSNT* 44, 1991, pp. 89–111; P. Bowers, 'Mission', in G. F. Hawthorne and R. P. Martin (eds.), *Dictionary of Paul and his Letters* (Downers Grove: InterVarsity Press; Leicester: IVP, 1993); D. J. S. Chae, *Paul as Apostle to the Gentiles: His Apostolic Self-Awareness and its Influence on the Soteriological Argument in Romans* (Carlisle: Paternoster, 1997); O. Cullmann, 'Eschatology and Missions in the New Testament', trans. O. Wyon, in G. H. Anderson (ed.), *The Theology of the Christian Mission* (London: SCM, 1961 [1956]); N. A. Dahl, 'The Missionary Theology in the Epistle to the Romans' [1956], in N. A. Dahl, *Studies in Paul: Theology for the Early Christian Mission* (Minneapolis: Augsburg, 1977); F. Hahn, *Mission in the New Testament* (London: SCM, 1965); M. Hengel, *Between Jesus and Paul: Studies in the Earliest History of Christianity*, trans. J. Bowden (London: SCM, 1983); A. J. Hultgren, *Paul's Gospel and Mission: The Outlook from his Letter to the Romans* (Philadelphia: Fortress, 1985); A. J. Köstenberger and P. T. O'Brien, *Salvation to the Ends of the Earth: A Biblical Theology of Mission* (Leicester: Apollos, 2001); J. Munck, *Paul and the Salvation of Mankind*, trans. F. Clarke (Atlanta: John Knox Press, 1959); P. T. O'Brien, *Gospel and Mission in the Writings of Paul: An Exegetical and Theological Analysis* (Grand Rapids: Baker; Carlisle: Paternoster, 1995); D. Senior and C. Stuhlmueller, *The Biblical Foundation for Mission* (London: SCM, 1983).

D. CHAE

Peace

Peace can be understood from various perspectives.

Negatively, peace exists where *there is no war or overt conflict*. This is a very narrow understanding, however, and can hinder us from seeing the hidden structural dimensions of peace. We might be satisfied in thinking that peace has prevailed simply because there is no war or overt conflict.

Positively, peace is where *there is* something specific that *supports* peace. Hence peace exists where people can live with dignity, or where there is a just social structure that sets people free from oppression (explicit or hidden). It is not enough that there is no war or overt conflict; as long as things that support peace do not exist, it can only mean that peace has not yet prevailed.

Another approach to peace is to focus on what constitutes the *violence* (individual, institutional or cultural/systemic), or to focus on the dynamic and mechanism of *conflict* and how it can be transformed creatively and non-violently.

The biblical peace, however, is all that and even more. In the OT, 'peace' (*shalom*) appears about 235 times, and its meaning is very wide-ranging. Sometimes it is used in relation to the condition or well-being of a person (Gen. 29:6; 43:23; 1 Sam. 29:7), a group of people (Jer. 15:5), animals (Gen. 37:14), and even war (2 Sam. 11:7). But sometimes it is used in a more serious context such as in relation to worship, laws, politics, and so on (Num. 6:24–26; Lev. 26:6).

OT 'shalom' refers to physical *well-being and material prosperity*, alongside the absence of the threat of war, disease or famine (Gen. 37:14; Jer. 33:6, 9; Eccl. 3:8; 1 Sam. 7:14). It also refers to *just relationships* between people and nations. It points to a social order and harmony where there is no economic gap, injustices, social-political oppression or exclusion of other human beings in any form (Isa. 32:16–17; 54:13–14; 57:18–21; 1 Kgs 5:12; see also 1 Sam. 7:14). A person whose life is oriented toward peace does not pursue her or his own interests, but cares for others, whoever they are (Ps. 34:14; Jer. 29:7). Peace even refers to the *moral integrity* of a person where there is straightforwardness, and no deceit, fault or blame (Ps. 34:13–14).

In the NT, the word 'peace' (*eirēnē*), which appears over 100 times, brings yet another nuance. It is related to *God and the good news from God*. It is from here that we get the proclamation of God as 'the God of peace' (Rom. 15:33; 16:20; 1 Cor. 14:33; 2 Cor. 13:11; Phil. 4:9; 1 Thess. 5:23; Heb. 13:20). Jesus is proclaimed as 'the Lord of peace' (2 Thess. 3:16). Peace is also connected to the Holy Spirit (Rom. 8:6). Out of this confession, Christians are asked to proclaim 'the gospel of peace' (Eph. 6:15).

The NT concept of peace fulfils and transforms that of the OT. It does not simply replace the OT understanding with the Greek or Roman concept. The Greeks understood peace as a peace of mind, an inner harmony that results in emotional stability, a personal inner tranquility. The Romans understood peace as a state of law and order where there is a balance of competing self-interest between power groups maintained by military force. The NT is distinctive, retaining the range of OT understanding, while introducing the new dimension of fulfilment by Jesus of the OT messianic peace, and in the way peace takes shape in the church as the messianic community.

Jesus does not bring peace through righteous vengeance or domination of former enemies, but rather through *suffering and death (Eph. 2:13–22). It is through the *cross that Jesus reconciles former enemies and creates one community that worships one Lord. Messianic peace is thus brought about by Jesus both through the *reconciliation of former enemies at the social level and by the provision of common access to God. The NT concept is therefore both deconstructive and constructive. It breaks down barriers between human beings, bringing reconciliation between Jews and Gentiles, men and women, masters and slaves, rich and poor. It is the enmity, not the enemies, that should be eliminated.

Constructively, peace creates a new community and constructs a new social relationship between former enemies, and between them and God; there is a whole new creation (2 Cor. 5:17). Peace is not therefore confined only to the forgiveness of past sin and guilt, since a new creation also has a social dimension. These dimensions cannot be separated. Marlin E. Miller has correctly pointed out, 'The message of peace means that through no merit of our own, we are in Christ reconciled to our enemies and called to participate in the social realities of a new community where old structures of personal, social, and economic hostility are replaced by those of reconciliation' (*Theology for the Church*, p. 11).

Biblical peace is thus related to the *spiritual*, *moral*, *physical* and *relational* dimensions of human beings. It is a comprehensive understanding that integrates the material and the spiritual, the individual and the communal, the religious and the social-political. All this is what Peter refers to as the gospel of peace preached by Jesus (Acts 10:36).

Peace and mission

What does all this mean concretely for the mission of the church? First, we must learn a *discerning theological orientation* both towards the inner life of any individual human being as well as the social-political dimensions of each context. Our gospel proclamation includes the messianic peace and reconciliation addressed both to the broken souls and to hostile and unjust situations. Our mission to a given context is only completed when all the dimensions of peace mentioned earlier have prevailed. Where there is need for human reconciliation, the mission of the church must engage in efforts for peace, even as it invites people to experience peace with God, to be reconciled with the one and only true source of peace. The church should be at the forefront of building and modelling relationships across divided communities, seeking to discern together what God's will is, and confronting attitudes that divide people from one another.

Secondly, through mission we create *disciples who have a *radical Christ-like life*. Created in God's image everyone has the divine capability to be creative, enabling us to participate in God's empowering grace to live out Jesus' way of peace. But because we are human, we need the discipline to seek peace and pursue it. We should not in our mission proclaim a gospel of pure grace, devoid of *ethical demands. This may make some people think building peace is hard work. So we need to understand peace witness as a continuum, beginning from peace with God, moving into peace with ourselves, our families, our churches, those of other faiths, work colleagues, at national and international level, and, most challengingly, with our enemies. Each Christian will be at a different point on the continuum, and must be encouraged to move on through it.

Mission therefore involves *the empowerment of individuals* and *the empowerment of the structures*. In our discipleship programmes, how can we shape the character of individual Christians through social practices in the church so that they become peace-builders wherever and whenever they are? For example, cathecisms for new church members or Sunday School material can be evaluated for their adequacy in equipping disciples to live out Jesus' way of peace and to have the knowledge and skills necessary for peacebuilding.

Likewise with *worship, we need to evaluate whether reconciliation and peace are central in our worship. How can we celebrate peace and reconciliation? How can we build into worship prayers for peace and opportunities for fasting? Could we plan a pilgrimage for peace in places that have been torn apart by violent conflicts and wars, through which the church could witness to the community around it that it is serious about reconciliation?

Pastors and leaders will need the knowledge and skills for non-violent conflict transformation. They need time to struggle together with biblical texts related to peace; they need to work together to design curricula for peace education in the church, Christian schools and other places. Church members can thus be trained for peacebuilding inside and outside the church, so that they learn how to function as mediators and reconcilers.

All this and more, however, cannot be done without adequate structures. Therefore we need to evaluate how our churches are structured for mission. Alongside organizations for youth, women and so on, there need to be structures for educating and training church members for peacebuilding, seen as a dimension of mission.

Bibliography

C. N. Kraus, *The Community of the Spirit: How the Church Is in the World* (Scottdale and Waterloo, Ontario: Herald Press, rev. edn, 1993); A. Kreider, E. Kreider and P. Widjaja, *A Culture of Peace: God's Vision for the Church* (Intercourse: Good Books, 2005); U. Mauser, *The Gospel of Peace: A Scriptural Message For Today's World* (Louisville: Westminster/John Knox Press, 1992); M. E. Miller, *Theology for the Church* (Elkhart: Institute of Mennonite Studies, 1997); J. H. Yoder, *Politics of Jesus* (Grand Rapids: Eerdmans, ²1994); J. H. Yoder (ed.), *The Royal Priesthood: Essays Ecclesiological and Ecumenical* (Grand Rapids: Eerdmans, 1994); P. B. Yoder, *Shalom: The Bible's Word for Salvation, Justice, and Peace* (Newton: Faith and Life Press, 1987); P. B. Yoder and W. Swartley (eds.), *The Meaning of Peace: Biblical Studies* (Louisville: Westminster/John Knox Press, 1992).

P. S. WIDJAJA

Pentecostalism

Much of the dramatic church growth in the twentieth century has taken place in Pentecostal and independent Pentecostal-like churches, especially since the 1980s including the 'neo-pentecostal' and 'neo-charismatic' churches. The forms of Christianity in the Majority World have been profoundly affected by several factors, including the desire to have a more contextual and *culturally relevant form of Christianity, the rise of nationalism, a reaction to what are perceived as *colonial forms of Christianity, and the burgeoning Pentecostal and *charismatic renewal. The renewal has affected all Christian denominations with its practices and teaching, so that it is difficult today to draw lines between what is 'Pentecostal' and what is not. The globalization of charismatic Christianity in recent years has created remarkable similarities in different cultural contexts, only differing in outward, more superficial forms. Six discernible features of this renewal and how they affect mission theology are outlined here.

Pneumatocentric mission

Pentecostals place primary emphasis on being 'sent by the *Spirit' and depend more on what is described as the Spirit's 'leading' than on formal structures. Missionaries are doing that job because the Spirit directed them to do it, often through some spiritual revelation like a prophecy, a dream or a vision, and even through an audible voice perceived to be that of God. In 1908, American Pentecostal leader Roswell Flower wrote, 'When the Holy Spirit comes into our hearts, the missionary spirit comes in with it; they are inseparable. ... Carrying the gospel to hungry souls in this and other lands is but a natural result' (G. B. McGee, 'Pentecostals and their Various Strategies for Mission', p. 206). The first Pentecostal missionaries got on with the job in a hurry, believing that the time was short and the second coming of Christ (see *Eschatology) was near. Reflection about the task was not as important as action in evangelism. Their mission theology was that of an action-oriented missions movement, and Pentecostals have only recently begun to formulate a distinctive Pentecostal mission theology.

The Holy Spirit poured out at Pentecost is a missionary Spirit, the church full of the Spirit is a missionary community, and the church's witness is the release of an inward dynamic. But it was not only a collective experience of the Spirit; the individual experience that each Christian had with the Holy Spirit was also the key to the expansion of the church. The centrality of the Spirit in mission has been a consistent theme in Pentecostal studies. The Pentecostal movement from its commencement was a missionary movement, made possible by the Spirit's empowerment. The experience of Pentecost in Acts 2 becomes a 'normative paradigm for every Christian to preach the gospel'; and 'Luke's primary and pervasive interest is the work of the Holy Spirit in initiating, empowering and directing the church in its eschatological worldwide mission' (J. M. Penney, *The Missionary Emphasis of Lukan Pneumatology*, pp. 11, 15).

Although Pentecostal missions may be described correctly as 'pneumatocentric' in emphasis, this should not be construed as an overemphasis. Most Pentecostals have a decidedly Christocentric emphasis in their proclamation and witness. The Spirit bears witness to the presence of *Christ in the life of the missionary, and the message proclaimed by the power of the Spirit is of the crucified and resurrected Jesus Christ who sends gifts of ministry to humanity.

Dynamic mission praxis

Pentecostals believe that the coming of the Spirit brings an ability to do 'signs and wonders' in the name of Jesus Christ to accompany and authenticate the gospel message. The role of signs and wonders, particularly that of *healing and miracles, is prominent in Pentecostal mission. Pentecostals see the role of healing as good news for the poor and afflicted. Divine healing is an evangelistic door-opener for Pentecostals, and signs and wonders are the 'evangelistic means

whereby the message of the kingdom is actualized in "person-centred" deliverance' (L. G. McClung, 'Spontaneous Strategy of the Spirit', p. 74). This 'power from on high' is the 'radical strategy in missions', which 'new paradigm' has impacted Pentecostal and charismatic movements in their mission endeavours (G. B. McGee, 'Power from on High', pp. 317, 324). At the beginning of the twentieth century, there was an expectation in many evangelical circles that signs and wonders would accompany an outpouring of the Spirit. Pentecostal missionaries and healing evangelists expected miracles to accompany their evangelism and 'prioritized seeking for spectacular displays of celestial power-signs and wonders, healing, and deliverance from sinful habits and satanic bondage' ('Power from on High', p. 329). The signs and wonders promoted by independent evangelists have led to the rapid growth of Pentecostal churches in many parts of the world, although they have seldom been without controversy. Some evangelistic ministries lead to the self-aggrandizement and financial gain of the preacher, often at the expense of those who have very little at all to give. This is particularly crass when the health-and-wealth preachers of today proclaim that the poor will become rich if they give to the church (see *Prosperity Gospel). Nevertheless, Pentecostalism has attracted the poor all over the world, despite this ambiguous relationship.

In many cultures of the world, healing has been a major attraction for Pentecostalism. In these cultures, the religious specialist or 'person of God' has power to heal the sick and ward off evil spirits and sorcery. This holistic function, which does not separate physical from spiritual, is restored, and people see Pentecostalism as a powerful religion to meet human needs. The central role given to healing is probably no longer a prominent feature of Western Pentecostalism, but in the Majority World, the problems of disease and evil affect the whole community and are not relegated to a private domain for individual pastoral care. These communities were, to a large extent, health-orientated communities and in their traditional religions, rituals for healing and protection are prominent. Pentecostals declared a message that reclaimed the biblical traditions of healing and protection from evil; they demonstrated the practical effects of these traditions, and by so doing became heralds of a Christianity that was meaningful. But sadly, this message of power became in some instances an occasion for the exploitation of those who were at their weakest.

Central missiological thrust

From its beginning, Pentecostalism was characterized by an emphasis on evangelistic outreach, and it places *evangelism as its highest priority. For Pentecostals, evangelism meant to go out and reach the 'lost' for Christ in the power of the Spirit. The Azusa Street revival (1906–08) resulted in a category of ordinary but called people fanning out to every corner of the globe within a remarkably short space of time. These missionaries were mostly untrained and inexperienced. Their only qualification was the baptism in the Spirit and a divine call, their motivation was to evangelize the world before the imminent coming of Christ, and so evangelism was more important than education or 'civilization'. Reports filtering back to the West to garnish newsletters would be full of optimistic and triumphalistic accounts of how many people were converted, healed and Spirit-baptized, seldom mentioning any difficulties encountered or the inevitable cultural blunders made. Saayman has observed that most Pentecostal movements 'came into being as missionary institutions' and their work was 'not the result of some clearly thought out theological decision, and so policy and methods were formed mostly in the crucible of missionary praxis' ('Some Reflections on the Development of the Pentecostal Model in South Africa', p. 42). Pentecostal missionaries often have a sense of special calling and divine destiny, thrusting them out in the face of stiff opposition to steadfastly propagate their message.

Pentecostal evangelism was geared towards *church planting, a central feature of all mission activity. Pentecostal churches were missionary by nature and the dichotomy between church and mission that so long plagued other churches did not exist. This central missiological thrust was clearly a strong point in Pentecostalism and central to its existence. Thriving Pentecostal 'indigenous' churches were established in many parts of the world without the help of any foreign missionaries. These churches were founded in unprecedented and innovative mission initiatives, motivated by a compelling need to preach and even more significantly, to *experience* a new message of the power of the Spirit. The effectiveness of Pentecostal mission in the Majority World was based on this unique message, which was both the motivation for the thousands of grass-roots emissaries and their source of attraction. All the widely differing Pentecostal movements have important common features: they proclaim and celebrate a *salvation (or 'healing') that encompasses all of life's experiences and afflictions, and offer an empowerment which provides a sense of dignity and a coping mechanism for life. Their mission was to share this all-embracing message with as many people as possible, and to accomplish this, Pentecostal evangelists went far and wide.

Unfortunately, the emphasis on self-propagation through evangelism and church growth through signs and wonders has sometimes resulted in Pentecostals being inward looking and seemingly unconcerned or oblivious to serious issues in the socio-political contexts, especially where there were oppressive governments. However, Pentecostals are beginning to recognize the social implications of the gospel and this failure in their mission strategy. It is also a characteristic of most forms of Pentecostal evangelism that the *proclamation becomes a one-way affair, without sufficient consideration being given to the religious experience of the people to whom the gospel is proclaimed. The result is those innumerable opportunities to connect the Christian message with the world with which the convert is most familiar are lost, and the Christianity that results remains rather foreign.

Contextualization of leadership

Although missionaries from the West went out to the Majority World in independent and denominational Pentecostal missions, the overwhelming majority of Pentecostal missionaries have been national people sent by the Spirit, often without formal training. This is a fundamental historical difference between Pentecostal and 'mainline' missions. In Pentecostal practice, the Holy Spirit is given to every believer without preconditions. One of the results of this was that 'it ensured that a rigid dividing line between "clergy" and "laity" and between men and women did not develop early on in Pentecostal churches' and even more significantly, 'there was little resistance to the ordination of indigenous pastors and evangelists to bear the brunt of the pastoral upbuilding of the congregations and their evangelistic outreach' ('Some Reflections', p. 43). This was one of the reasons for the rapid transition from 'foreign' to 'indigenous' church that took place in many Pentecostal missions.

Leaders tended to come from the lower and uneducated strata of society, and were trained in apprentice-type *training where their charismatic leadership abilities were encouraged. Pentecostal missions are quick to raise up national leaders who are financially self-supporting, and therefore the new churches are nationalized much more quickly than older mission churches had been. The pioneering work in this regard of the Assemblies of God missiologist Melvin Hodges and his widely influential book *The Indigenous Church* (1953) not only emphasized creating 'indigenous churches', but also stressed church planting. The influence of Hodges on Western Pentecostal missions contributed towards the establishment of theological training institutes ('Bible schools') and in-service training structures throughout the world, and resulted in the much more rapid growth of Pentecostal churches. Hodges articulated what had always been at the heart of Pentecostal growth in different cultural contexts. He said that the aim of all mission activity was to build an 'indigenous New Testament church' that followed 'New Testament methods'. He emphasized that the church itself (and not the evangelist) is 'God's agent for evangelism' (M. L. Hodges, *The Indigenous Church*, pp. 12, 22), and that the role of the cross-cultural missionary was to ensure that a church became self-governing, self-supporting and self-propagating. The foundation for this to happen was the Holy Spirit.

For churches to become really contextual, however, attaining 'three selfhood' does not guarantee that contextualization unless the 'three selfs' are no longer patterned on foreign forms of being church, and unless those churches are grounded in the thought patterns and symbolism of popular culture.

Mobilization in mission

The remarkable growth of Pentecostal movements in the twentieth century cannot be isolated from the fact that these are often 'people movements', a massive turning of different people to Christianity from other religions on an unprecedented scale, set in motion by a multitude of factors for which Western missions were unprepared. Charismatic leaders tapped into this phenomenon, and became catalysts in what has been called (in the African context) a 'primary movement of mass conversion' (A. Hastings, *The Church in Africa 1450–1950*, pp. 530–531). Throughout the world, these early initiators were followed by a new generation of missionaries, learning from, and to some extent patterning their mission on, those who had gone before. The use of women with charismatic gifts was widespread throughout the Pentecostal movement. This resulted in a much higher proportion of *women in Pentecostal ministry than in any other form of Christianity at the time. This accorded well with the prominence of women in many pre-Christian religious rituals, contrasting again with the prevailing practice of older churches which barred women from entering the ministry or even from taking any part in public worship.

The proliferation of Pentecostalism would not have taken place without the tireless efforts of a vast number of ordinary and virtually now unknown women and men. These networked across regional and even national boundaries, proclaiming the same message they had heard others proclaim which had sufficiently altered their lives to make it worth sharing wherever they went. Most forms of Pentecostalism teach that every member is a minister and should be involved in mission and evangelism wherever they find themselves. Although increasing institutionalization often causes a reappearance of the clergy/laity divide, the mass involvement of the laity in the Pentecostal movement was one of the reasons for its success.

A contextual liturgy

The style of freedom in the Spirit that characterizes Pentecostal *liturgy has contributed to the appeal of the movement in many different contexts. This spontaneous liturgy, which is mainly oral and narrative with an emphasis on a direct experience of God through his Spirit, results in the possibility of ordinary people being lifted out of their mundane daily experiences into a new realm of ecstasy, aided by the emphases on speaking in tongues, loud and emotional simultaneous prayer and joyful singing, clapping, raising hands and dancing in the presence of God – all common Pentecostal liturgical accoutrements. These practices made Pentecostal worship easily assimilated into different contexts, especially where a sense of divine immediacy was taken for granted, and they contrasted sharply with rationalistic and written liturgies presided over by a clergyman that was the main feature of most other forms of Christianity. Furthermore, this was available for everyone, and the involvement of the laity became the most important feature of Pentecostal worship, again contrasting with the dominant role played by the priest or minister in older churches. Pentecostalism's emphasis on freedom in the Spirit rendered it inherently flexible in different cultural and social contexts. All this made the transplanting of its central tenets in the Majority World more easily assimilated.

Pentecostalism emphasized an immediate personal experience of God's power by his Spirit, it was more intuitive and emotional, and it recognized charismatic leadership and national church patterns wherever they arose. Preaching a message that promised solutions for present felt needs like sickness and the fear of evil spirits, Pentecostal preachers (who were most often local people) were heeded and their 'full gospel' readily accepted. Churches were rapidly planted in different cultures, and each culture took on its own particular expression of Pentecostalism. Throughout the world, Pentecostal movements create new voluntary organizations, often multi-ethnic, to replace traditional kinship groups. Many Pentecostal churches have programmes for recruiting new members that transcend national and ethnic divisions, and this belief in the movement's universality and message for the whole world is a radical departure from ethnically based traditional religions.

Pentecostals proclaim a pragmatic gospel and seek to address practical needs like sickness, poverty (see *Poor), unemployment, loneliness, evil spirits and sorcery. In varying degrees, Pentecostals in their many and varied forms, and precisely because of their inherent flexibility, attain a contextual character which enables them to offer answers to some of the fundamental questions asked by people. A sympathetic approach to local life and culture and the retention of certain indigenous religious practices are undoubtedly major reasons for their attraction, especially for those overwhelmed by urbanization with its transition from a personal rural society to an impersonal urban one. At the same time, these Pentecostals confront old views by declaring what they are convinced is a more powerful protection against *witchcraft and a more effective healing from sickness than either the existing churches or the traditional rituals had offered. Healing, guidance, protection from evil, and success and prosperity are some of the practical benefits offered to faithful members of Pentecostal and charismatic churches. All this does not say that Pentecostals provide all the right answers, a pattern to be emulated in all respects, nor to say that they have nothing to learn from other Christians. But the enormous and unparalleled contribution made by Pentecostals independently has altered the face of world Christianity irrevocably and has enriched the universal church in its ongoing task of proclaiming the gospel of Christ by proclamation and demonstration.

See also CONTEXTUALIZATION.

Bibliography
A. Anderson, *An Introduction to Pentecostalism: Global Charismatic Christianity* (Cambridge: Cambridge University Press, 2004); A. Anderson, *Spreading Fires: The Missionary Nature of Early Pentecostalism* (London: SCM, 2007); S. M. Burgess and E. van der Maas, *New International Dictionary of Pentecostal and Charismatic Movements* (Grand Rapids: Zondervan, 2003); A. Hastings, *The Church in Africa 1450–1950* (Oxford: Clarendon, 1994); M. L. Hodges, *The Indigenous Church* (Springfield: Gospel Publishing House, 1953); D. Jacobsen, *Thinking in the Spirit: Theologies of the Early Pentecostal Movement* (Bloomington: Indiana University Press, 2003); L. G. McClung, Jr, 'Spontaneous Strategy of the Spirit: Pentecostal Missionary

Practices' in L. G. McClung, Jr (ed.), *Azusa Street and Beyond: Pentecostal Missions and Church Growth in the Twentieth Century* (South Plainfield, NJ: Logos, 1986); G. B. McGee, 'Pentecostals and their Various Strategies for Global Mission: A Historical Assessment', in M. A. Dempster, B. D. Klaus and D. Petersen (eds.), *Called and Empowered: Global Mission in Pentecostal Perspective*, pp. 203–224 (Peabody: Hendrickson, 1991); G. B. McGee, 'Power from on High: A Historical Perspective on the Radical Strategy in Missions', in Wonsuk Ma and R. P. Menzies (eds.), *Pentecostalism in Context* (Sheffield: Sheffield Academic Press, 1997); J. M. Penney, *The Missionary Emphasis on Lukan Pneumatology* (Sheffield: Sheffield Academic Press, 1997); P. A. Pomerville, *The Third Force in Missions* (Peabody: Hendrickson, 1985); W. A. Saayman, 'Some Reflections on the Development of the Pentecostal Mission Model in South Africa', *Missionalia* 21:1 (1993); A. Yong, *The Spirit Poured Out On All Flesh: Pentecostalism and the Possibility of Global Theology* (Grand Rapids: Baker Academic, 2005).

A. ANDERSON

Persecution

Persecution has often been related to the growth and mission of the church. Tertullian's famous words: 'The blood of the martyrs is a seed of the Church' (*Apologia* 50:12), forewarns the Roman emperors that their opposition will only enlarge the church. Jesus, when warning his disciples of future persecution, had prophesied that it would turn them into his witnesses (Luke 21:12–13). Paul shows clearly that his imprisonment and suffering do not hinder the gospel but further it (Phil. 1:12–26).

And indeed, the first organized persecution of the first congregation in Jerusalem only led to the dispersal of Christians into the whole Roman Empire and the beginning of Christian mission to the Gentiles. The first Gentiles were converted in Antioch, not by the apostles but by 'normal' Christians who had fled Jerusalem (Acts 7:54 – 8:8). The International Congress on World Evangelization Lausanne (1974) noted: 'Persecution is a storm that is permitted to scatter the seed of the Word, disperse the sower and reaper over many fields. It is God's way of extending his kingdom.'

So persecution often accompanies mission, for 'Missions lead to martyrdom, and martyrdom becomes missions' (Hans von Campenhausen in his study of the early church: 'Das Martyrium in der Mission', p. 71). Jesus warned his disciples that they were going out as sheep into the midst of wolves (Matt. 10:16; Luke 10:3). The universal spread of Christ's church has always been accompanied with the blood of the martyrs, and world mission is 'mission beneath the cross'.

Johan Candelin rightly observed, however, that persecution does not always produce church growth, although persecution increases because some of the fastest growing churches in the world exist in countries without religious liberty (in *Persecution of Christians Today*, pp. 16–17). According to Candelin, 300 million evangelicals worldwide live with the threat of physical persecution and the vast majority belong to fast-growing evangelical communities, such as in China.

The collapse of international communism and the fall of many dictators may have resulted in a decrease in direct persecution in some places. However, the expansion of Islamic fundamentalism, the growth of political Hinduism and the rise of new dictatorships in Africa are all global factors giving rise to new growth in attacks on Christian churches and individuals.

Mission to persecutors

Following OT tradition (e.g. Job 31:29; 42:8–9), the NT exhorts us to pray for God's grace for persecutors and to give testimony to them (Matt. 5:44; Luke 6:27–28; 1 Cor. 4:12). The most impressive testimony is Jesus' prayer that God will have mercy on his persecutors (Luke 23:34). The first Christian martyr, Stephen, prayed similarly (Acts 7:60). Both requests were heard, for some of the persecutors were later converted (the Roman officer in Luke 23:47; Paul in Acts 9:1–18). Church history contains many descriptions of dying Christians, such as Polycarp, who pray for those tormenting them.

The modern church has its own examples. In 1913, the Indonesian evangelist, Petrus Octavianus, described a missionary in the Toradya area in Southern Celebes. Five tribe members wanted to kill him, but permitted him to pray first. He prayed aloud that they would be saved. Three of the murderers were banned to Java, were converted in prison and returned to Toradya, where they founded a church which later (1971) became the fourth largest church in Indonesia with over 200,000 members. Let us also not forget the five missionaries shot to death by the Aucas in Equador in the 1960s. Several of the murderers later became pillars of the Aucan church.

Many who began as persecutors of Christians have later become believers themselves. The best known is, of course, Paul, who frequently referred to his former persecution of the church (1 Cor. 15:9; Gal. 1:13, 23–24; Phil. 3:6; 1 Tim. 1:13. See also Acts 9:4–5; 22:4, 7–8; 26:11–15).

Jesus, mission and persecution

To speak of Jesus is to speak of mission, but at the same time to speak of suffering and persecution. The prediction of his death accompanies his whole earthly ministry (e.g. Matt. 16:21; 17:22–23; 20:28; 26:2). The details of the passion narratives take up the longest sections of the Gospels. Paul consistently presented Jesus as the archetypal martyr and as an example for all Christians, so it is not surprising that the early church's documents on martyrdom considered Jesus to be the prototype of the martyr.

Jesus is the actual object of all persecution. For this reason, Jesus asks Saul, 'Saul, Saul, why do you persecute *me*?' (Acts 9:4; 22:7; 26:14), and identifies himself as, '…Jesus whom you persecute' (Acts 9:5; 22:8; 26:15). The true reason for Christians' suffering is Christ, since it is the focus on him which justifies the opposition: 'The clearer the Church recognizes Christ and testifies of Him, the more certainly it will encounter the contradiction, the confrontation and the hatred of the Antichrist' (Martin Luther). Jesus himself frequently reminded the disciples that they would be persecuted for his sake while preaching the gospel (e.g. Matt. 10:22; 16:25; Luke 21:12).

Without the offence of the cross there would be no mission but also no persecution (Gal. 5:11). Paul accuses his opponents of being circumcised only to escape persecution (Gal. 6:12, 14). The 'word of the cross' is 'foolishness' to unbelievers (1 Cor. 1:18), an impediment to the Jews and nonsense to the Gentiles (1 Cor. 1:23), but the centre of salvation history (1 Cor. 1:23; cf. 2:2). The message of the cross is thus the glory of the gospel as well as its foolishness (1 Cor. 1:17–25; Gal. 6:11–14).

The Holy Spirit, the real missionary, and persecution

Without the *Holy Spirit, all mission is futile and comes to nothing. But since mission and persecution are closely related, the Holy Spirit also plays a vital role in the experience of persecution. He is 'the Comforter' (John 14:16, 26), and gives Christians the strength to endure persecution, even to rejoice in the most difficult conditions (1 Pet. 4:14). The Spirit of Glory, which had rested on the Messiah (Isa. 11:2), brings his glory to those who seem to have lost all glory, such as Stephen, whom Luke describes as being 'full of the Holy Spirit' (Acts 7:55) during his defence and his execution, as he saw the glory of God in heaven.

Jesus promises wisdom to the persecuted when they stand before their judges and have to give testimony, and the Holy Spirit will give them what to say (Luke 21:12–15; Matt. 10:19–20). William Carl Weinrich notes that Jesus seldom spoke of the Holy Spirit's function, but when he did so, frequently described him as helper and comforter in persecution (Matt. 10:17–20; Mark 13:9–11; Luke 21:12–19). No wonder Paul attributes his endurance to the Holy Spirit (2 Cor. 6:6; Phil. 1:19; 1 Thess. 1:6–7). The early church was constantly aware that only the Spirit of God could provide the persecuted with wisdom and strength to endure.

No automatic blessing from persecution

Nowhere are Christians encouraged to seek persecution or martyrdom. This is in contrast to those who justify self-destruction (e.g. suicide bombers) on religious grounds. Neither does persecution automatically lead to church growth or to a purer, stronger faith. The experience of the German church under the Third Reich and under communism, for example, has led to neither a more intense reflection about persecution nor to revival or church growth. Even when persecution is fruitful, however, its results are never automatic, but always due to God's sovereign grace.

Jesus' parable of the sower (Matt. 13:3–8, 20–22) identifies wealth and egotism as just as dangerous to faith as persecution and pressure. Western Christians tend to glorify persecution, and believers under persecution tend to glorify liberty and wealth. The faith of the one suffers under persecution and pressure, the faith of the other is suffocated by worldly concerns and the deceit of wealth. Also in the West persecution comes in many forms and is much wider than physical abuse. Thus Christians are persecuted at work for upholding Christian values, and Christians who take a stand against secularism are exposing themselves to ridicule and abuse. The church is called to help and support such Christians, as well as those suffering more obvious physical opposition.

It is an unfortunate fact of ecclesiastical history that persecution can also engender conflict and division between Christians. An appropriate, if terrifying, modern example occurred in Korea, when the Japanese rulers (1910–45) required all Koreans to kowtow to Shinto shrines in order to honour the Japanese emperor and the sun goddess. After long resistance, in 1937 and 1938, most Christian groups surrendered to the increasingly intolerable coercion, but were strongly divided (particularly the Presbyterians) on the significance of the required ceremony; was it a religious rite or merely a cultural formality? Sixty years later, the issue remains unresolved and the breach is still evident, even though the original problem is long gone.

Christians persecuting Christians

Prophets and true believers have always been persecuted by institutional religious authorities. Israel itself persecuted the OT prophets, as well as Jesus and the apostles. Jesus compared the spiritual leaders of his day with those who had murdered the OT prophets (Matt. 5:10–12; 23:29–34; Luke 11:49; 13:34; 21:12; John 5:16. See also Stephen in Acts 7:52; Peter in Acts 2:23; and Paul in I Thess. 2:14–15; Gal. 4:29).

Christians today also persecute both fellow Christians and others. We need only remember the forced conversions in the Middle Ages, the colonization of Latin America,

the Crusades, the oppression of heretics, the Inquisition and the Jewish pogroms. Ever since the fourth century, the term 'martyr' has been expanded to include Christians killed by other 'orthodox' Christians. Throughout history, denominations have produced collections of martyr histories from their own traditions, whilst at the same time denying the ugly truth that all denominations also persecuted Christians of other persuasions.

The fact that Christians themselves are martyred in the name of the Christian God, as dreadful as it is, is not foreign to Scripture. The holy books of no other religion depict their followers so negatively as the Bible does the people of Israel and Christians. This honest and sometimes severe self-criticism is integral to both Judaism and Christianity, in contrast to other religions.

The state, politics and persecution

We must avoid defining persecution in merely pious terms, since it can arise when Christians take certain ethical or political positions. Recent Catholic theology, particularly liberation theology, sometimes has applied martyr terminology to political martyrs and resistance fighters. It is quite proper that persecution sometimes has a concrete political aspect, especially when criticism of rulers initiates the persecution. There is a long tradition of political critique giving rise to persecution, from the OT prophets to people such as Athanasius, Thomas à Becket, Dietrich Bonhoeffer, Martin Luther King and Archbishop Oscar Romero. Christians are normally loyal citizens, who seek the welfare of their state, country and people, but whenever the State tries to force them to dishonour God, and especially seeks to suppress their mission, they must obey God rather than man (Acts 5:29; 4:19).

It is, of course, difficult to conjecture in advance to what extent we can cooperate with governments during periods of persecution, and when we must begin to resist. In world mission this question has to be decided anew by Christians in each context. We certainly need a new evaluation of the possibility of breaking state laws and resisting the powers for the sake of the gospel. Peter and the apostles preached the gospel in spite of the state's prohibition (Acts 4:19–20; 5:29) and were frequently arrested and punished as a result (Acts 12:1–3). In the face of Roman opposition, Christians referred to Jesus as lord (Gk *kyrios*) and king (in opposition to an imperial edict, Acts 17:6–7; 4:12). They followed OT examples (e.g. Daniel in Dan. 6; priests in 2 Chr. 26:18; the Egyptian midwives in Exod. 1:15–20; Rahab in Josh. 2). Rather than condemning their dishonesty, the NT presents them as role models of faith (Heb. 11:31; Jas 2:25). Note that these examples do not concern only idolatry or recantation of the gospel, but any infringement of God's law (murder, etc.). Such resistance assumes, however, that the state has required us to transgress against God's law.

There has never been a persecution solely on religious grounds, since there is always a confusing blend of religious concerns with cultural and social problems. Political, national, economic and personal motives may also play a role. In Revelation, hatred for the church is augmented by political and economic issues. Another example is the Ephesian craftsmen who instigated a riot, because they considered Paul's mission work a threat to their welfare (Acts 19:23–29). In Acts 16, Paul and Silas were imprisoned after exorcising a fortune-telling demon out of a slave girl, because her owners were angry at the loss of their profit (Acts 16:16–24).

There is actually no difference between those 'persecuted because of their faith' and those persecuted for their 'active support of justice'. In Revelation, the anti-Christian government (the Beast) oppresses the saints ... 'they that keep the commandments of God, and the faith of Jesus' (Rev. 14:12, KJV; cf. 12:17). Both obedience to principles of justice and truth, as well as loyalty to Jesus, equally attract hatred. And as world mission is a primary commandment (Matt. 28:18–20) and includes teaching all aspects of God's commandments (Matt. 28:20), oppressors may name social or ethical issues as the reason for their opposition, but the real reason is our faithfulness to the mission mandate. Christians know the true reason for persecution: the world hates them as it hates their Lord (John 15:18–25), and therefore persecution will always be closely associated with missionary obedience.

See also MARTYRDOM.

Bibliography
Bong Rin Ro, 'Need for a Theology of Suffering', *Asia Theological News* 14, 1988, pp. 2–3; H. von Campenhausen, 'Das Martyrium in der Mission' pp. 71–85 in H. Frohnes (ed.), *Die Alte Kirche* (Kaiser: München, 1974); J. Candelin, 'Persecution of Christians Today', *Persecution of Christians Today: Christian Life in African, Asian, Near East and Latin American Countries* (Berlin: Konrad-Adenauer-Stiftung, 1999); Chua Wee Hian, F. S. Khair-Ullah and S. Sahu, 'Evangelism in the Hard Places of the World', in J. D. Douglas (ed.), *Let the Earth Hear His Voice: International Congress on World Evangelization Lausanne, Switzerland* (Minneapolis: World Wide Publications, 1975); M. E. Gómez, *Fire against Fire: Christian Ministry Face-to-Face with Persecution* (Minneapolis: Augsburg Publications, 1990); P. A. Marshall, *Their Blood Cries Out: The Untold Story of Persecution against Christians in the Modern World* (Dallas: Word, 1997); J. S. Pobee, *Persecution and Martyrdom in the Theology of Paul* (Sheffield: JSNTSup, 1985); *Preparing Believers for Suffering and Persecution: A Manual for Christian Workers* (Bulawayo: Hope, c. 1979); T. Schirrmacher. *The Persecution of Christians Concerns Us All: Towards a Theology of Martyrdom* (Bonn: VKW, 2001); T. Schirrmacher and M. Klingberg (eds.), *Märtyrer: Das Jahrbuch zur Christenverfolgung Heute* [yearbook] (Bonn: VKW, 2000–2007); N. Shea, *In The Lion's Den: A Shocking Account of Persecution and Martyrdom of Christians Today and How We Should Respond* (Nashville, TN: Broadman & Holman, 1997).

T. SCHIRRMACHER

Politics/state

The historic relationship between mission and politics has echoed the ambivalence that seems to be found in the biblical literature. Mission leaders have often been controlled more by events than theological principles. Scriptural texts have been used to justify both political activity and total passivity. There will always be a conflict between the assertion that Jesus has authority over all nations, and the reality of interacting as Christians with any particular nation.

The emerging church of the NT had a political identity from the beginning. Preaching as Messiah a man who was crucified on the orders of a Roman procurator gave nascent Christianity a suspect nature in Roman colonies (e.g. Acts 16:21). Paul urged the Roman Christians to give obedience to the state (Rom. 13:1–7), but Peter set forth the principle that we should obey God rather than man when confronted with the opposition of the Jewish leaders (Acts 4:19–20). Whilst in most of the NT the Roman Empire was seen as neutral and occasionally benign towards the emerging Christian church (e.g. Gallio in Acts 18), the book of Revelation reflects the growing claims of the emperor cult which challenged the assertion that Jesus is Lord of all.

With the acceptance of Christianity by the Emperor Constantine in the fourth century the balance shifted towards working with the state. In due course the church assumed political power. Mission then became focused on partnership with the state and securing the agreement of political leaders. The entry of Christianity into any new state was often pursued from the top down in the expectation that the principle *cuius regio, eius religio* (whose King, their religion) would apply. In Anglo-Saxon England there was a practice of exporting princesses from Christian kingdoms as wives for pagan kings in the expectation of their conversion. Moffett in his *History of Christianity in Asia* has commented that one reason for the failure of Christianity to become the religion of the Chinese Empire was because no emperor ever professed the faith. This experience of the religious choice of the ruler determining at least the opportunity of the conversion of his subjects, continued to be the norm until after the Reformation. The continental Reformation was governed by the religious choices of German princes. The long period in which the will of the ruler was identified with the reign of Christ had the positive effect of opening up whole nations to hear the gospel. The negative aspect was the adopting of political values and methods into the life of the church and the equating of spiritual warfare with political warfare, which was what happened during the Crusades.

Luther, however, against the secular and religious claims of the papacy, separated the activity of the left hand of God through earthly government from his right hand through the gospel of salvation. He also looked forward to seeing changed hearts resulting from the establishment of reformed churches by godly princes. In the English Reformation there was an expectation that the political will would enable gospel preaching throughout the parish system, leading to true conversions. With the second Reformation the emphasis shifted from the unity of the state under one Christian ruler to the individual hearts and beliefs of the people. The fight for liberty from unjust rulers was conjoined with a desire for religious liberty. That was especially seen in the Commonwealth period in England and the early American settlers.

Missionary activity from Catholics through the Counter-Reformation continued to focus on the conversion of rulers and the baptizing of their subjects. Jesuit work in China and Japan was connected with the imperial courts, and they expected to see their work grow on a foundation of acceptance of their missionaries as emissaries of Western civilization, as well as of faith. Even though Protestant missionary activity did not target rulers in the same way, the association of missionary work with the advance of Western civilization continued. This was in part because the opportunity to bring the gospel into foreign nations was associated with the advance of Western political power. Andrew Porter has argued that missionaries were not co-workers with colonizers, but even the most apolitical missionary often made his or her entry to a country because of the progress of Western political power. There was a general assumption that the progress of Western civilization would be congenial to the advance of the gospel. This was particularly so when the only permitted missionaries were chaplains to the colonial authorities, as in the Dutch East Indies.

The rise of Western Protestant interdenominational missions in the nineteenth century coincided with the shift of *eschatological belief from post-millennialism to pre-millennialism. This had a great effect on the relationship between politics and mission. Whereas post-millennialists expected the world to grow better in every way before the coming of Christ and political activity to be part of bringing in the kingdom of Christ, the effect of pre-millennialism was very different. The belief that suffering and difficulty would increase before Christ comes again; that the coming of Christ was very near; that the chief calling was to preach the gospel and save individuals, meant that political activity was seen as either unnecessary or a distraction from the main task of evangelism. There was occasional political engagement, as in the involvement of the China Inland Mission in opposition to the opium trade. Not only did the missionaries avoid any overt political activity, but they also taught the churches they established to be apolitical. The desire for peace and security for the growth of the church could lead to the acceptance of political injustices and a lack of true discipleship in political issues. This was especially so if the governments of the sending countries supported corrupt regimes, or quietude was thought essential to preserve visas for gospel proclamation. However, the championing of the oppressed and marginalized by missionaries sometimes gave rise to political action to defend them.

The adoption by the World Council of Churches of a theology of mission that concentrated more on the political *liberation of countries and peoples than on freedom from individual sin and judgment brought a stronger negative reaction from evangelical Christians to political involvement. Evangelicals would not agree with the WCC statement that 'The liberation movement led by Mao Tse-tung falls within what Christians understand as God's saving work in history.' However, the events in China are an indication that the God of faith is also the Lord of history, since through the persecution started by Mao the church in China has grown. Christians may have had no part in the arranging of the political situation in China, but they can see that God has so ordered it that the church might grow. God is not bound by any one political situation. In Indonesia it was the apparent overthrow of communism that led to the growth of the church.

The leaders of churches founded by missionary activity have often been ready to take a part in the political process. In the Philippines evangelical Christians joined in the protests that brought the downfall of Marcos. In Sarawak, an evangelical church released one of its pastors to stand for parliament.

In Malaysia, evangelical Christians have engaged as co-belligerents with other non-Muslim groups to protect the church's status. In South Africa some Christian churches were active in the post-Apartheid situation, and in particular the Truth and Reconciliation Commission was built upon Christian principles. However, where the church has failed to engage with its own political context, opting for a gospel that is disengaged from the world, the result can be disastrous, the events in Rwanda in 1994 being a classic example. Many churches have accepted that as communities still in this world it is vital for them to take a role in the political process of their countries both as individual Christians and as institutions. What was not deemed appropriate for the missionaries, either because of their nationality or calling, has become an important part of the ministry and mission of the local church.

See also COLONIALISM.

Bibliography
E. L. Frizen and W. Coggins (eds.), *Christ and Caesar in Christian Missions* (Pasadena: William Carey Library, 1979); S. Moffett, *A History of Christianity in Asia*, 2 vols. (Maryknoll: Orbis Books, 1998, 2005); I. Murray, *The Puritan Hope: Revival and the Interpretation of Prophecy* (London: Banner of Truth Trust, 1971); S. Neill, *Colonialism and Christian Missions* (London: Lutterworth Press, 1966); S. Neill, *Salvation Tomorrow: The Originality of Jesus Christ and the World's Religions* (London: Lutterworth Press, 1976); O. O'Donovan, *The Desire of Nations: Rediscovering the Roots of Political Theology* (Cambridge: Cambridge University Press, 1996); A. Porter, *Religion versus Empire? British Protestant Missionaries and Overseas Expansion 1700–1914* (Manchester: Manchester University Press, 2004); B. Stanley, *The Bible and the Flag: Protestant Missions and British Imperialism in the Nineteenth and Twentieth Centuries* (Leicester: Apollos, 1990).

R. PORTER

Polygamy

The term polygamy is a generic term, which refers to any plural union. It could be polygyny (one husband with several wives) or poly-andry (one wife with several husbands). In our usage here it refers to a husband who has more than one wife.

Polygamy is seen as an actual form of marriage in contemporary African society. While Christians may view polygamy to be a problem, within the African traditional setting it is merely another form of family life. To a Muslim, polygamy is not a problem so long as one does not go beyond the lawful limit of four wives. The provision is, however, hedged with the basic demand that a man who takes more than one wife must ensure that he treats them all equally. In both Islam and *African traditional religion, however, while polygamy may be a common practice it is not the norm of family life. Most marriages in tropical Africa are monogamous, and only a minority in any given community find poly-gamous unions functional and necessary for their existence. It is certainly conditional upon the ability to take care of the family, and a strong character to maintain peace and harmony between wives.

Historical perspective

With the advent of Christianity in Africa, polygamy was portrayed as an impediment to a Christian marriage. Some of the poly-gamous families were required to transform themselves to monogamous status soon after conversion. This meant that a part of the family would be neglected when additional wives were divorced or separated. Many were deprived Christian sacraments as a result of their polygamous status. Since monogamy was the norm of a Christian marriage, the church could not recognize polygamous unions as marriages. In some instances the church grudgingly accepted the first wife as having been canonically married; all other subsequent wives were deemed to be living in adulterous relationships and were sup-posed to be set aside after conversion. Most churches now recognize the importance of keeping the family intact and would concede that those who accept Christianity when they are already in a polygamous marriage should be admitted to membership. Only those who contract other marriages later are normally put under discipline.

The practice of polygamy is so deeply intertwined with African culture historically that the church has found it difficult if not impossible to extricate itself from its social implications. The Anglican Church in Kenya was able to recognize this quite early and conceded that it was not possible to redeem the individual's attitude to marriage quite apart from that of the entire community.

Christian viewpoints

Christians in Africa have traditionally upheld monogamy as a higher and purer form of marriage, which conformed to the biblical demand. They have believed it to be the only form of marriage acceptable to God. With reference to Pauline exhortations where a church official has to be the husband of one wife and married only once, this is interpreted to mean that every Christian ought to have only one partner as part of the divine plan (Matt. 19:1-6).

In the NT the question of polygamy is not dealt with, and all texts which deal with marriage refer to the relationship of one man and one woman. It is, however, generally assumed that 'one flesh' means one partner, implying that monogamy was the ideal and that love as understood in the NT ought to lead to monogamous marriage.

Some argue that toleration by the Chris-tian community of polygamous families would demonstrate Christ's teachings on love. Preference for monogamy should not give anyone a licence to blindly condemn poly-gamy. It can be argued that since baptism is a means of grace, as is received through faith in God, it should not be denied anyone who desires it. Faith demands sacramental expres-sion and no individual who confesses faith should be denied this means of grace. It is their hope that the church in Africa would find ways and means of admitting faithful poly-gamous families to communion and accord them all the privileges of church membership. Some families found their faith in Jesus Christ while they were already in a polygamous situation, hence, this appeal for sympathetic consideration.

While polygamy has at times been treated as a sin comparable to adultery, positively it has been grudgingly regarded by many as an inferior form of marriage, at times tolerated but not accepted by Christians. Some have adopted the more moderate position of seeing both monogamy and polygamy as forms of marriage, which can be functional in different circumstances. This position, however, is not supported by any biblical evidence and has not been popular with mainline theologians.

Genesis 2:24 points to the mystery of marriage which can only be understood by those who have a special relationship with Christ. In the NT this is the mystery of Christ and his bride the church. The man-woman relationship in marriage is expected to follow this spiritual union between Christ and his church. In essence all marriage in a Christian context is intended to approximate such a spiritual union. While as Africans we do not want to deny our past, we should not also glorify the past. As we know it, polygamy cannot foster the kind of relationship, which is both exclusive, loving and sacrificial (Eph. 5:21–33); while every form of marriage relationship can be abused, it is difficult to see how polygamy can exemplify sound Christian living.

The social context
In a patriarchal society, polygamy helped to stabilize family life by ensuring divorce was curtailed. In situations of conflict between communities, the leader tried to cement relationships by contracting marriages from rival communities to ensure equilibrium and tranquillity. A contemporary example is King Mswati of Swaziland who contracts marriages every year as a way of strengthening his bonds with his community. However, polygamy should not be seen as a desire for unrestricted sexual satisfaction, nor just a question of prestige. Historically some of the major causes of polygamy were barrenness, lack of a male offspring in a predominantly patriarchal society, and a desire to ensure all women were married. In an African society a married woman is more respected and likely to be given greater responsibilities than an unmarried one. For many women, sterility can lead to psychological trauma. In many instances it was the first wife who gave her husband consent to contract another marriage. The larger family unit had to be consulted before marriage took place. Unfortunately, due to creeping individualism, this is no longer the case. Marriages can now be contracted without due regard to how other family members would be affected by such decisions.

Generally, the possession of some wealth was a necessary prerequisite for polygamy. Bride-wealth was normally demanded by each bride's family in addition to the general upkeep of several wives and numerous children. Among the nomadic communities, polygamy was more of an asset rather than a liability due to increase of the labour force. In such situations it made much more sense to have had many hands doing the work, notwithstanding the fact that there were also many mouths to feed as well. Where families relied on wage employment, particularly in towns, it was not rare to find that co-wives were left in charge of farms in the rural setting in order to provide extra income for the family as well as being a means of food security.

Women's perspective
Polygamy is mainly a male institution and with growing education women are becoming more independent and less willing to be in a polygamous union. Enlightened women are demanding a greater degree of spousal companionship. Christian women in particular would settle for nothing less than a monogamous marriage. Educated women today would prefer divorce to polygamy due to economic, social and religious considerations. Many women who are capable of providing for themselves would shun polygamy and would wish to be in a stable monogamous union or even remain single.

Amba Oduyoye observes that both men and women need to re-examine Christian and cultural traditions and confront those aspects that tend to justify the domestication of women. She contends that polygamy is one such tradition that depicts male superiority. Nasimiyu Wasike, another female theologian, is even more emphatic. She calls polygamy the enslavement of some human persons and an institution in our tradition that is not only oppressive but dehumanizing.

Some church responses
Some of the *African instituted churches have reclaimed some of the traditional and somewhat archaic social structures of African communities, including polygamy. These churches have tended to become a creative response to the breakdown of traditional African society, providing security and order in the midst of disintegrating social norms.

They genuinely consider their position as an authentic indigenous response to OT teaching, and an attempt to correct the foreignness of the practices of the Christian church in Africa. While the NT evidence may not support this inclination, and while the ideal Christian marriage must be monogamous, we can understand their concern for including those that might be excluded by mainline Christian churches.

Mainline African churches have lived with the problem of plural marriage ever since they were founded by the missionaries. They may have a clearly defined line of discipline on the matter but they are still unable to offer any substantial pastoral help to their members, and are often not facing up to the problem, or providing any answers. This results in plural marriage continuing among church members which only serves to exclude them from participating in Holy Communion. Some are perpetually put under church discipline but continue to participate in the life of the church. Independent (indigenous) churches do not seem to see a problem, as many of them arrive at a more pragmatic solution between being a Christian as well as being African. It is not surprising that some members of the emerging indigenous charismatic churches are ex-Roman Catholics, ex-Methodists, ex-Presbyterians or ex-Anglicans.

With pastoral sensitivity the church should present monogamy as the normative ideal but at the same time be patient with those who find themselves in plural marriage.

Conclusion

We can, therefore, safely state that the teaching of the NT affirms monogamy as God's plan for marriage. It gives it a firm context for the expression of love between a man and a woman and forms a perfect foundation for a Christian family. A social system that creates superiority of man over woman and limits the freedom of the individual is incompatible with the Spirit of the gospel, contradicting God's ideal of equality of persons. Polygamy is not only a social and economic system but a reflection of man's image in relation to the woman. It is a manifestation of male chauvinism and a reflection of a male superiority complex. It is a contradiction of the biblical message that woman and man were created as equal partners by divine plan.

See also FAMILY, GENDER ISSUES.

Bibliography
K. Bediako, *Christianity in Africa: The Renewal of a Non-Western Religion* (Edinburgh: Edinburgh University Press, 1995); T. Berglund, in T. D. Verryn (ed.), *Church and Marriage in Modern Africa* (Johannesburg: Laverna, 1975); B. Bujo, *The Ethical Dimensions of Community* (Nairobi: Pauline Publications, 1998); Church of the Province of Kenya, *Rabai to Mumias: A Short History of the Church of the Province of Kenya 1844–1994* (Nairobi: Uzima Press, 1994); E. Hillman, *Polygamy Reconsidered* (Maryknoll: Orbis Books, 1975); B. Kisembo, L. Magesa and A. Shorter, *African Christian Marriage* (London and Dublin: Chapman, 1977); J. Mbiti, *Love and Marriage in Africa* (London: Longman, 1973); S. M. Musawi, *Western Civilization Through Muslim Eyes* (Teheran: Sadr Publishing House, 1977); M. A. Oduyoye, *Hearing and Knowing: Theological Reflections on Christianity in Africa* (Nairobi: Action Press, 2000); M. A. Oduyoye and M. Kanyoro, *The Will to Arise: Women, Tradition and the Church in Africa* (Maryknoll: Orbis Books, 1995); M. Perlman, *Toro Marriage*, PhD thesis (Oxford: Oxford University, 1963); R. Schreiter, *Constructing Local Theologies* (Maryknoll: Orbis Books, 1986); H. Turner, *Religious Innovations in Africa* (Boston: G. K. Hall, 1979).

Z. NTHAMBURI

Poor/poverty

Poverty is a socio-economic condition of deprivation and powerlessness which affects individuals and communities at several levels, and it constitutes an important mission issue for the church. The church has a divine imperative to show solidarity with the poor, not least because Jesus Christ endorsed the law and the prophets which had highlighted Yahweh's commitment to social justice. Then the missionary mandate of Christ for the church was to make disciples who would follow what he taught about love for the neighbour, which must include showing compassion for all people, including our enemies, in their poverty. Therefore the church's commitment to the poor is realized in commitment to their total well-being, in restoring their dignity, and in helping them to meet their basic human needs.

A significant cause of poverty is exploitation of the vulnerability of the poor and the weak by those with resources and *power. The powerlessness of poverty means an inability to control economic and social decision-making, putting the poor at the mercy of influential forces over which they have no say. Unemployment amongst the poor is high, and sometimes they have to accept menial or sub-grade work for very low or nominal wages, or find creative ways to make a living from their own resources. As with any other social evil, poverty has certain causes at different levels of society, and this raises the need for the church to take a prophetic stand to address this and other related issues of social justice as a dimension of its mission to the world.

Biblical social concern

Social concern for the poor in the land and the causes and effects of their poverty is a key issue in both OT and NT. The plethora of words for the condition of the poor shows that the writers of the Bible were much concerned for the restoration of the poor in society. In the NT, the Greek word, *penes* (linked with *ponos*) means 'burden' or 'trouble', and refers to someone of limited means who has to do manual work for a living. *Ptochos*, on the other hand, refers to a person who is poor enough to be a beggar and cannot sustain themselves without help. In the OT the Hebrew equivalent of the Greek *ptochoi* is *miskēn* (according to the latest OT writings) and refers to the one who is dependent, or socially low (e.g. Eccl. 4:13; 9:15), and the Greek *ptocheia* is rendered by *miskēnût*, poverty (e.g. Deut. 8:9).

Old Testament

In the context of God's rich blessings in the Promised Land, the children of Israel were told that there ought not to be any poor among them (Deut. 15:4). At the same time the Bible affirms the human reality that there will always be the poor in the world, therefore Israel was commanded to be open-handed towards those within Israel, and others in the land, who were poor (Deut. 15:11).

Poverty was described as a condition of impoverishment when someone was unable to support themselves (Lev. 25:35). The social structure in the early days of Israel meant that slaves were of the lowest social status, then the hired landless labourers, and then the land owners and the privileged. Slavery and landlessness were key causes of poverty, although the *permanent* sale of land and *permanent* slavery were both prohibited (Lev. 25:23, 42). The *jubilee year was therefore appointed to cancel debts owed by the poor, and to free land that had been sold by the poor so as to return it to its original owner. The resourceful were warned not to lend money at interest or to sell food to the poor at a profit, and all the Israelites were warned not to take advantage of their fellow brothers and sisters, but rather to fear the Lord (Lev. 25:17). All these laws were designed not only to protect the poor but also to provide adequately for them.

God is seen throughout the OT as having concern for the poor (e.g. Ps. 113:7). Israel's redemption from the slavery of Egypt by the mighty hand of God became for them a visible proof that God was on the side of all the afflicted who become prey to the exploitation which causes poverty. Micah, Amos and Isaiah among the prophets were much concerned for *peace and justice and the maintenance of social concern within Israel and Judah, as well as among the surrounding nations. Amos specifically highlighted the case of the poor and their oppression by the rich of his time (5:11–12), and raised the importance of social concern. Micah was much concerned for justice in Israel (Mic. 3:8), and Isaiah looked at the global context of his time (Isa. 2:2–4) and promoted the cause of international peace to eradicate poverty, linking this with God as restorer of his blessings (Isa. 25:4–8; 28:12). Christian missiologists maintain that the OT law insists that poverty must be addressed, and redressed in mission, whatever its causes may be.

New Testament

The NT was written against the backdrop of the Judaism of the first century and intertestamental period. The first century included years of famine and hardship, compounded by Roman and Herodian taxes. On top of that the Jewish law prescribed the tithe, which could amount to from 17% to 23%

of a household's gross income. Some commentators see this as a dimension to the background of Jesus' call to the 'heavy laden' to come to him for rest (Matt. 11:28).

Christ's concern for every kind of poverty is demonstrated by the place he gave them in his beatitudes and parables. Luke begins with the blessedness of the poor (Luke 6:20), those who are humbled by circumstances, which Matthew qualifies with *hoi ptochoi tō pneumati* ('poor in spirit'), indicating a concern for poverty that arises as a result of discipleship (Matt. 5:3; cf. Ps. 34:17–18). Many see Christ's *holistic mission and ministry for the poor and the oppressed (e.g. Luke 4:18–20; Matt. 4:23) as a model for the way in which the church must show practical solidarity with them.

Many parables of Jesus also indicate clear solidarity with the poor, and challenge those who perpetuate poverty. The rich man and Lazarus (Luke 16:19–31), and the rich fool (Luke 12:13–21) highlight Jesus' concern for the poor and his rejection of materialistic wealth accumulation. Jesus draws attention to the generosity of the poor widow (Mark 12:41–44), and also sees social action as an important qualification for entering God's kingdom. Correspondingly, indifference towards the poor can be a reason for exclusion from the *kingdom and coming under God's *judgment. (Matt. 25:31–46).

The first Christians consciously committed themselves to one another in a spirit of sharing resources with those in need (Acts 2:45; 4:32). They also addressed the welfare of the poor widows among them, and appointed seven deacons to look after their concerns (Acts 6:1–6). The missionary zeal for the poor by the disciples and the apostle Paul is on record (Gal. 2:10). Giving from out of plenty so that there should be equality (Corinthian principle, 2 Cor. 8:13), and giving from out of poverty (Macedonian principle, 2 Cor. 8) promoted the privilege of sharing and cheerful giving (2 Cor. 9:7). There is a debate about whether the social concern of the early Christians was restricted to their own people, although it is unthinkable that in a time of famine, which gave rise to the collection for which Paul devoted so much energy, the Christians would not also be concerned to maintain a good witness amongst their neighbours by sharing their resources.

Definitions and concepts

Secular socio-political perspectives of poverty analyse the causes in terms of class distinctions between those who own the forces of production and labour; the unequal distribution of authority; or that poverty is linked with the 'market situation': the more power someone has to influence market forces, the more resourceful they become.

Sociologists place poverty at three major levels: *absolute poverty*, when the basic human needs of food, shelter and health are not met and people fall below a designated 'poverty line'; *relative poverty*, when poverty is measured in relation to the expectations of a particular group of people; and *subjective poverty*, which describes whether an individual or group feels poor. They conclude that poverty is a manifestation of underdevelopment caused by alienation of groups from development activity, and call for application of workable remedies based on scientifically tested knowledge.

Christian missiologists, along with social scientists, believe that poverty has no single cause, be it backwardness, injustice, exploitation, corruption, market forces, or natural conditions. There are powerful and complex structural and global economic and trade issues which usually work against the poor. There are some general causes of poverty, as, for example, *feudalism* in the case of the subcontinent of India and Pakistan; extensively *rural societies* where there is considerable long-term underinvestment, which applies to most of Africa, Asia and Latin America; *urbanization* as cities become overwhelmed by migration; as well as issues such as *peace and justice* and *over-population*. Some factors are both causes and effects of poverty, as for example unemployment and population growth. Just as there is no single cause of poverty so there is no single remedy.

Theological and missiological discourses

Christian missiologists address poverty from different perspectives, though there is much overlap in these categories.

Conservative evangelicals for the most part link poverty and other social evils to the human sinful condition: if poverty is a consequence of individual *sin (although not necessarily the sin of the poor themselves), the focus of mission must be upon personal salvation and *conversion, which changes individuals who then change society. Verbal proclamation of the gospel thus takes primacy over social responsibility. To tackle poverty many prefer charitable giving rather than challenging social structures. This can result in a 'top-down' approach to development. They take a passive attitude towards the world and focus more on Christ's return and his coming kingdom as the only real remedy to the world's problems. The Lausanne Covenant (1974) and Manifesto (1989) broadened evangelical commitment to social responsibility. They affirmed that God is both the Creator and Judge of all humans and therefore Christians should share God's concern both for justice and *reconciliation throughout society, and for the liberation of men and women from every kind of oppression. They encouraged Christians to integrate words and deeds in the way that Jesus did.

Pragmatic evangelical missiologists come mostly from the conservative tradition, but emphasize practical commitment to the poor as central to Christian mission. They combine proclamation with social action, taking them as two inseparable dimensions of mission, much as the two blades of a pair of scissors. They have endorsed documents like Wheaton '83 and the themes of *'transformation' and 'Church's response to human need'. They do not emphasize evangelism as a separate theme, because they see it as an integral part of the whole Christian response to human need. Indeed, only through spreading the gospel can the most basic needs of human beings be met. Their preference is for a 'bottom-up' approach to development which begins with the needs of the community and seeks to empower people to organize themselves to take responsibility for tackling poverty in their own contexts.

Ecumenical missiologists see poverty in the context of exploitative socio-political and religious structures. Anything which oppresses the poor is to be opposed and condemned. In this case the mission approach is incarnational and experiential because it is enacted in solidarity with the poor and underprivileged. The cause of Christian social action has been championed by *liberation theologians and the World Council of Churches, who have argued that if social responsibility is not interpreted in the context

of the common life of humanity then this is a denial of the incarnation of God's love.

Catholic Christians see the church's mission as following in the footsteps of the Lord Jesus, which means evangelization through the presence of the church amongst the poor. Evangelization in this case encourages people to find salvation through the church, to return to the commitments of baptism, and to accept the way of personal poverty and obedience, of service and self-sacrifice even to death. This approach does not attempt to tackle structural causes of poverty, but it does take its adherents into practical solidarity with the poor in the spirit of sacramental service of the church as part of a collegiate activity. Mother Teresa of Calcutta is the most famous Catholic example of practical care and service to the poor.

Poverty eradication and Christian involvement

There has been a huge global response to the problem of poverty in recent years, prompting campaigns for economic justice and debt relief such as 'Jubilee 2000' and 'Make Poverty History', in which many evangelical Christians have been very involved. These campaigns have been partly successful in persuading the IMF to cancel or reduce debt for many of the world's poorest countries. However, there is a long way to go before global trading structures, market forces, debt conditions and the way that multinational companies operate can be changed sufficiently to make a lasting historical change.

Poverty is challenged today by religious and secular groups together. Christian churches have engaged in practical dialogues with agencies like World Bank, IMP and UNDP. Recent dialogue and consultations have highlighted that the World Bank is recognizing the importance of factors other than finance and economics, and the churches, having focused on relationships, are now realizing that finances and economics are areas they must engage with. These dialogues have identified that mission is both dedicated to fighting poverty by raising income and promoting empowerment, security and opportunity, and also that the spiritual dimension of life is an essential component of development.

Christians should encourage the mega-development agencies like the World Bank and the UNO in their commitment to eradicating extreme poverty and hunger; achieving universal primary education; promoting *gender equality and empowering women; reducing child mortality; improving maternal health; combating HIV/AIDS, malaria and other diseases; ensuring *environmental sustainability; and developing a global partnership for development.

There is general agreement that the church's understanding of poverty should include religious, *family, ethical, and cultural dimensions. Simply providing handouts to meet material poverty is a very limited response. For example, by including issues of gender equality in its mission, the church can increase awareness about injustices against women, offer empowerment programmes and gender training for both men and women. This can release much energy and human resource for local development.

Central to the common ground is the fight against extreme global poverty. For example, at the local level in Pakistan, as part of their mission, churches have run small loan schemes, educational and community health work in some areas, and land redemption to help farmers get their land back from money lenders. In other areas some have been fighting against diseases and oppression of all kinds by including a charismatic healing approach. Poverty alleviation is to do with developmental educational commitment as a dimension of mission theology, and churches all over the world can learn how to do this from one another.

Conclusion: the call to a theology of development and social change

So in order to address poverty at a local and global level, the church needs to develop and adopt a theology of development that clearly leads to social change based on biblical principles of Christ-like servanthood. One of the problems of world poverty in any context is exploitation. For example, church leadership in a situation like Pakistan has a central role to define and relate to social issues theologically. First, mission to the poor cannot be diminished there in any form, and saving souls must include social action. The church in Pakistan has a record of contributing to nation building and helping and identifying the poor. But it needs to improve its unity in mission and its broader understanding of a theology of development. The majority of Pakistani Christians are among the poorest of the poor, therefore the church in Pakistan has the potential to implement social change based on its own first-hand experience of poverty. The vision must be for poverty to be eradicated. It cannot be eradicated in isolation, it needs to be addressed ecumenically and internationally, joining hands with others with a mission commitment to fight it together.

See also DEVELOPMENT, MONEY/ ECONOMICS, WEALTH.

Bibliography

D. Belshaw and R. Calderisi (eds.), *Faith in Development* (Oxford: Regnum Books, 2001); C. Brown (ed.), *The New International Dictionary of New Testament Theology, Vol. 2* (Exeter: Paternoster, 1986); T. Chester, *Awakening to a World of Need* (Leicester: IVP, 1993); A. Flannery (ed.), *Vatican Council II, The Conciliar and Post Conciliar Documents* (Dublin: Dominican Publications, rev. edn, 1987); N. Goodall, *The Uppsala Report* (Geneva: WCC, 1968); M. Haralambos, *Sociology: Themes and Perspectives* (London: Bell & Hyman, 1985); D. Hughes, *God of the Poor* (Carlisle: Authentic Media, 1998); V. Samuel and C. Sugden, *Mission as Transformation* (Oxford: Regnum Books, 1999); V. Samuel and C. Sugden (eds.), *The Church in Response to Human Need* (Oxford: Regnum Books, 1987); R. Sider, *Evangelism and Social Action* (London: Hodder & Stoughton, 1993); P. Sultan, *Church and Development* (Karachi: FACT Publications; Oxford: Regnum Books, 2000); C. J. H. Wright, *Old Testament Ethics for the People of God* (Leicester: IVP, 2004).

P. SULTAN

POSTMILLENNIALISM, see ESCHATOLOGY

Postmodernity

Many people claim that during the second half of the twentieth century, the cultural mood of the Western world shifted significantly. Whereas, for the past two hundred years, the intellectual, social and moral ideals of the eighteenth-century Enlightenment – described as 'modernity' – moulded the fabric of Western societies, now convictions about the meaning and goal of human life have altered fundamentally. 'Postmodernity', called by François Lyotard a 'condition' of post-industrial society, is simultaneously a cultural theory, a social ideology and a philosophical thesis.

As its name implies, the notion depends on the existence of a coherent concept of modernity. As generally understood, 'modernity' refers to a particular understanding of social history. The scientific revolution of the seventeenth century combined with an emerging confidence in the power of rational thought. This inaugurated a new stage of critical development in human self-awareness by liberating people from arbitrary tradition and futile superstition, and enabling them to solve moral and technical problems. Modernity stands for a progressive realization of the innate human capacity for self-reliance.

Postmodernity/postmodernism was a term originally applied to an architectural style. In contrast to the rigid conformity, rational predictability and mass construction of modern architecture, the postmodern alternative was, in the words of Robert Venturi, 'hybrid', 'compromising', 'distorted', 'ambiguous', 'perverse' and 'messy', Postmodernity refers to a cluster of beliefs that has affected all aspects of culture: visual art, the cinema, the media, literature, music, lifestyles, politics, even science and technology. However, its most systematic expression comes as a movement in philosophy. It builds on the post-structural rejection of the inherent stability of language and other human systems and institutions. It represents a mood of disillusionment with the 'brave new world' of implicit trust in science to solve most human problems, such as disease, reproductive incapacities, genetic failings, poverty and environmental destruction, and in technological advance to deliver a society of ever-increasing convenience. It symbolizes a sceptical attitude towards the alleged expertise of the cultured, professional elite educated in the standard intellectual procedures of the Western academic system. It has developed a sophisticated critique of the notion of universally valid norms in areas such as mental health, education, punishment and the economy.

Characteristics

In its attitude towards historical development, postmodernity is critical of all simple notions of progress, especially the unfolding of some vital force inherent within evolving human social life. Famously, it is 'incredulous towards all meta-narratives', understanding these to be comprehensive, all-inclusive descriptions and explanations of human existence from a religious, social-scientific or philosophical viewpoint. It rejects post-Hegelian dialectical discourse, both Marxist and neo-liberal, that pretends that human history can be understood in terms of the successive resolution of social conflicts, and its outcome predicted. It believes that the 'discovery' of certain 'laws of history' that explain the dynamic of social systems are, at best, undemonstrated hypotheses and, at worst, mechanisms of social control that allow self-proclaimed pundits to eliminate alternative views. In other words, it renounces the pretensions of certain theories to possess universal validity as no more than claims to social and political domination.

In contrast to these comprehensive and globalizing theories about human existence, postmodernity proposes a reading of history always bound by limited, context-specific, fallible, and therefore constantly revisable, perspectives. Human beings and societies are mainly the result of haphazard processes operating through time. They are not determined by intrinsic and eternal principles such as justice, reason, the class struggle or market forces. Human history is not fixed. There are no immutable processes. There is no pre-ordained goal.

In its attitude to the notion of truth, postmodernity tends to dismiss the possibility of language representing accurately and invariably a given reality, external to human perception and desire. This makes it anti-realist. It also denies that we can possess any certain, wholly objective and dispassionate knowledge of entities completely external to the observing subject. This makes it anti-foundational. The only world we can know is that which we ourselves shape by our own, internal apprehension of what lies beyond our mental processes. Truth, in the celebrated phrase of Richard Rorty, amounts to what can be defended in normal conversation against alternative views. It is whatever conforms to the social conventions of the moment.

Postmodernity asserts that no statement or belief is safe from contradiction. There is, therefore, no self-evident, undeniable, error-free basis for asserting something to be true. All we can expect is a certain consistency in our beliefs within a community of tradition we find meaningful. There is no way of deciding between traditions. Truth, therefore, is essentially pluralist. Both the definition and discernment of truth is pragmatic. The truth of a belief, moral conviction or course of action is determined by its consequences for the person or community that asserts it. Truth-claims are no more than a declaration of the beneficial results of believing. Truth is deeply and irreversibly relative to time and circumstances.

In its attitude to social existence, post-modernity delights in difference. In line with its deep suspicion of a culturally imposed, rational uniformity, it proposes the inviolable right of minority groups to deviate from the norms of the majority. The French phil-osopher, Jacques Derrida, has attacked the long-established principle in Western thought of reasoning by means of antithesis. He argues that, depending on which sector of society is currently shaping its thought-structures, certain beliefs become privileged and their opposites dismissed. He is motivated by a desire to undermine the control which an invariable set of definitions gives to those who manipulate language in the interests of some ideology. The intention is to release those parts of human experience and society which, hitherto, have been suppressed – for example, the emotional over against the rational, the bodily in place of the mental, the female principle as a counterweight to the male. In other words, the strategy is to allow 'the Other' (the excluded opposite) to unsettle the 'essences' and 'certainties' of 'normal' society, in order to rehabilitate those ideas and institutions which have been marginal-ized or eliminated from the mainstream of social engagement.

Outcomes

There are a number of significant conse-quences of this shift in cultural mood. In keeping with the rejection of the priority given to the rational dimension of human life, post-modernity has encouraged people to explore their emotions, to be in contact with their deepest feelings, even to discover a 'spiritual' aspect of their being. Existence is more varied and richer than the mind and intellectual pursuits. The inner self of sensations, affec-tions, sentiments, instincts and intuitions has become a neglected part of human life. The tendency in modernity to emphasize those aspects of the world that can be demonstrated by standardized rational procedures has led to a diminished and impoverished experience. This move to rediscover the whole person is often referred to as being in touch with the 'feminine' side of human nature. This includes a re-emphasis on the human body as an integral part of each person, not merely a medium to express the dispositions of the mind and the will.

There is a new consciousness of the indis-pensable link existing between human life and the whole of nature. Modernity has tended to justify the exploitation of the environment in the interests of economic growth and an ever-expanding standard of living. It implies that the material world is always available to satisfy human desires for increasing comfort and innovation. The industrialized world has acted as if nature held an inexhaustible supply of primary materials to be converted into goods for human pleasure. Postmodernity, supported by the compelling evidence of ecological breakdown, draws attention to the arrogance that such an aggressive and pre-sumptuous attitude to natural resources implies. Again it is a manifestation of the dominance of the rational and the masculine in human existence.

As a result, postmodernity tends to be highly critical of the way in which the whole of life has become subservient to the drive of global capitalism for expanding markets and increasing profits, with the consequent mobil-ity of capital, internationalization of labour and assertive commercial advertising. Such a push for growth irreparably damages the very ecosystem on which economic life depends, and therefore becomes self-defeating. It also represents the insolence of unaccountable and unregulated power, such a feature of the post-Enlightenment world. Moreover, along with international capital comes the tendency to *globalize Western culture, either suppressing other cultures or co-opting them for profit.

Postmodernity seeks to redress the balance by promoting 'multiculturalism'. This is another manifestation of respect for the 'other'. What makes life truly human is diversity, variety and multiplicity, even contradiction. It is essential that the cultures of minorities, particularly those of immigrant populations, should not be lost, either by being absorbed into the host culture or overtaken by a uniform culture promoted by economic interests. Multiculturalism is a tool for resisting the tendency to consider that the latest promotion is the best and everything else old-fashioned, primitive or anachronistic.

In all kinds of art forms, postmodernity tends to promote a certain anarchy. Starting from the premise that objective standards of good and bad in aesthetic matters do not exist, only changing tastes, art becomes whatever anyone is prepared to accept. There has been a determined effort to break down artificial boundaries between so-called 'high art' and 'popular art'. Elitism must be repudiated, if art is to become accessible to all social and cultural groups. Contemporary, postmodern art is simultaneously ironic towards pretensions of power and satirical in relation to the fragmentation and dysfunction of modern life. It parodies the banality and emptiness of consumer-culture and assimilates the absurdity and meaninglessness of scientific 'progress' for its own sake.

Assessment

From the standpoint of the history of culture, postmodernity displays a transitory shift in people's perception of what is important in life. From one perspective, it represents a justified reaction against overconfidence in the ability of humans to comprehend and manage life through empirical knowledge and rational thought. It is a critical response to the brash belief that advances in technology and the rational, bureaucratic management of social life can solve human problems. From another perspective, it is an intellectual echo of significant changes that have taken place in the business world: for example, the uncertainty caused in recent times by unstable and unreliable patterns of employment and the unpredictable and volatile fluctuations of stock markets. It highlights the transition from a seemingly rational approach to economic management to the apparently irrational forces and decisions that shape contemporary economic life.

As a move in the history of philosophy, it seeks to attack traditional ideas. People like Rorty have spoken eloquently of the end of philosophy. It appears to favour the local, the anti-establishment, the contradictory, the ephemeral and the sensual in thought processes. It exalts the Dionysian principle of desire over the Apollonian principle of order. It is reminiscent of other attempts to discredit the predominance of empirical method or rational logic in human discourse, such as the Romantic movement of the late eighteenth and early nineteenth centuries and Existentialism in the middle of the twentieth century.

In spite of the impression that postmodernity is counter-cultural, against tradition and contentious, it is, paradoxically, socially and culturally conservative. Its commitment to questioning all values, its incredulity towards universally valid truth-claims and its belief that reality is historically and culturally constructed (and therefore changeable), means that it is unable to offer any secure, durable norms of critical judgment. If all beliefs are necessarily relative to particular historical circumstances and geographical contexts, there are no independent standards for evaluating right and wrong ways of living. To be coherent to its own principles, postmodernity must allow an unlimited degree of tolerance to all views and opinions.

Its weakness as a genuinely critical principle springs from confusing methodological suspicion with a properly founded social analysis. As a result, it is powerless to offer a legitimate critique of existing states of affairs. It looks paradoxically as if postmodernity is the cultural offspring of the consumer culture of late capitalism: freedom of choice in the market place is the supreme value and tolerance of other people's lifestyle choices is the social equivalent.

The missiological relevance

If Christian mission is concerned with the encounter between the gospel of Jesus Christ and human communities, it is important to discern whether the beliefs of those communities are favourable or unsympathetic to the gospel. Some Christians claim that the postmodern condition has raised afresh the question of a spiritual dimension to human nature. People affected by Western culture are open again to listen to a message that emphasizes the significance of a reality beyond the material. At the same time, however, postmodernity is intrinsically pluralist and relativist in its attitude to all beliefs, so the Christian claim that the life, death and resurrection of Jesus Christ alone interprets and gives meaning to human existence will be treated with incomprehension.

A strong emphasis on the pragmatic value of beliefs means that a postmodern generation will only respect a faith devoid of self-interest. However, because postmodernity's elevation of tolerance and non-discrimination into a supreme ethical code conflicts with the Christian faith's claim to be based on the unique revelation of God's truth, the gospel will likely be heard as a message of self-justification, prejudice and narrow-mindedness.

Postmodernity has launched a devastating onslaught against all self-legitimizing traditions, seen largely as negative forces for controlling and manipulating unsuspecting and credulous people. Hence, postmodernity has been uncompromising in exposing the various attempts to rationalize gender inequalities and hierarchical structures, and sanction traditions as defences against change. A church in mission should be sensitive to this postmodern challenge, by being willing to adopt new models of community life that express gender equality and non-authoritarian patterns of leadership. At the same time, human communities do not live without traditions. As each new generation is dependent on guidelines from the past, the question, for which postmodernity hardly has a coherent answer, is by what criteria the goodness, or otherwise, of particular traditions are to be judged.

In the theological field in recent years there has been a strong tendency to criticize the alleged false influence of modernity on faith. This is understood as an overemphasis on rationalistic expressions of orthodoxy couched in terms of propositional statements. In contrast, Christians influenced by postmodern considerations wish to stress the primacy of personal relationships, story (or narrative) and orthopraxis. This contemporary expression of theology is also referred to

as 'post-foundational'. By this is meant abandoning attempts to give the Christian faith a universally valid, rational basis (see *Apologetics), which should command the assent of all right-thinking people. Much is made of the priority of faith over reason, as in the phrase, 'I believe in order to understand' (*credo ut intelligam*). Christian believing then becomes more a matter of intuitive experience than a sober exploration of evidence for truth-claims.

Sweeping Christian criticisms of modernity tend to forget that the scientific enterprise was born in an age permeated by a theistic *worldview. Most of the sixteenth and seventeenth centuries' pioneers of the sciences believed in the external world as a gift of God showing forth his glory and power, and in reason as the divinely endowed tool for exploring its meaning and functioning. The problem with modernity is not in the use of reason and the empirical sciences, but in their misuse, when the gifts become divorced from the Giver. Postmodern theology runs the grave risk of opening up the way to an anti-realist view of religion, in which the only reference point for belief is the language of a particular community. Such a stance would discredit truth-claims, warrant the equal validity of all (religious) beliefs and nullify the church's unique vocation to communicate to the whole world God's saving action in Christ alone.

Bibliography

R. Bauckham, *Bible and Mission: Christian Witness in a Postmodern World* (Carlisle: Paternoster Press, 2003); Z. Bauman, *Postmodernity and its Discontents* (Cambridge: Polity Press, 1997); H. Bertens, *The Idea of the Postmodern: A History* (London: Routledge, 1995); D. Bosch, *Believing in the Future* (Harrisburg: Trinity Press International, 1995); L. Cahoone (ed.), *From Modernism to Postmodernism: An Anthology* (Oxford: Blackwell, 1996); J. A. Kirk, *The Future of Reason, Science and Faith: Following Modernity and Postmodernity* (Aldershot: Ashgate Publishing, 2007); N. C. Kraus, *An Intrusive Gospel? Christian Mission in the Postmodern World* (Leicester: Apollos, 2001); D. Lyon, *Postmodernity* (Buckingham: Open University Press, 1994); J. R. Middleton and B. J. Walsh, *Truth is Stranger Than It Used to Be: Biblical Faith in a Postmodern*

Age (London: SPCK, 1995); P. Sedgwick, *Descartes to Derrida: An Introduction to European Philosophy* (Oxford: Blackwell, 2001); S. Sim (ed.), *The Icon Critical Dictionary of Postmodern Thought* (Cambridge: Icon Books, 1998); D. Smith, *Mission after Christendom* (London: Darton, Longman and Todd, 2003); A. Thiselton, *Interpreting God and the Postmodern Self: On Meaning, Manipulation and Promise* (Edinburgh: T. & T. Clark, 1995).

J. A. KIRK

Power

What is 'power'?

Power denotes the ability to perform an action or achieve an objective. Having power involves possessing the means to act and being able to decide how and when something will happen. Thus power bestows the ability to make decisions and can be used to maintain control over people or situations. Those who are powerless have no control over their lives since the decisions which affect them are made by others. Power is associated with authority but is not the same, since it is possible to have a position of authority but no power to make decisions, which is very weak; and conversely someone may have a lot of power, but no authority to use it, which is very dangerous. God relativizes all human power, since he is all powerful (omnipotent) and all power emanates from him, though in his sovereignty he may choose not use it.

Sociologically, therefore, power can be understood primarily as a constitutive element of social relations. Every relationship is a means for power to be exercised and as such bears profound implications for the practice of Christian mission. In each context we need to ask: what power relationships are operating? who has the power to make decisions? Who is in control of the resources and the initiative? What power does the national church have?

Power exercised with authority implies on the one hand the ability to issue an order or command and, on the other hand, a demand of obedience, with the strength to enforce it. Thus power can bestow hegemony, which arises precisely when there is, on the side of the person who commands, a relationship of dominion. This represents power *over*

others, a typically secular view of power; whereas Christianity speaks radically differently of power *for and with* others: the power that serves and does not dominate or manipulate others (1 Pet. 5:2–3). It is this power that is available for mission.

God's power
The power that empowers

For the first Christians, the Spirit of God was the source of power, through whom the power of God could be released to perform his will. The *Holy Spirit is the presence of God who bestows power, the presence that empowers. God gives his power away, he entrusts it to us for our mission. Such is the idea conveyed by Acts 1:8, where the power of the Spirit is shown as the power of mission, the driving force of the testimony of a new *kingdom. This missionary kingdom has the *spiritual* dimension of the changing lives and values of its citizens; it is *global* as it includes all peoples and races; and it has a *gradual* enactment, starting from the centre and spreading over time and space across the earth.

NT Christianity has a distinct posture in relation to power and its exercise. The notion of power as service (Mark 10:35–45) – the power of *love – which rejects the abuse of power through domination, is what distinguishes the biblical teaching, and gains greater scope when considered alongside the two commandments of non-violence and love for enemies (Matt. 5:38–48; Luke 6:27–37). This power works silently, without the use of coercion, and is given and received, mutually affirmed and shared. In imitation of God Christians are encouraged to let go of whatever power they have, and to release it to empower others. This can work in economic and political dimensions, but also in social, ideological and cultural spheres. This legitimate use of power has to be the central objective for human beings, both in their family relations, between spouses or in relation to children, and in the sphere of organizations, political or religious.

The power of weakness

Power in God's perpective also involves the 'power of weakness', supremely demonstrated by Christ on the *cross, which implies the ability of weakness to achieve something which human strength could not do. Mission as service, exercised in and through weakness, can be a very powerful thing. Much can be learned of this theme from the experiences of popular Bible reading amongst *poor and needy people groups in Latin America. It is precisely in human weakness that the redemptive work of Christ was carried out (Phil. 2:6–11), and through this we understand the nature of the power that God wishes us to experience. This is a power that means giving yourself up unconditionally on behalf of the other, and that has manifested itself on a broad spectrum, ranging from the experience of liberation theology to the practice of Pentecostal groups, and even to varied experiences of significant and positive political influence in Africa, where Christianity fulfilled a central role in promoting 'the desacralisation of authority and power in history' (K. Bediako, *Christianity in Africa: The Renewal of a Non-Western Religion*, p. 234).

God uses human weakness, and it is through this weakness that his strength is shown (2 Cor. 13:4). By understanding and practising this concept of power in our homes, neighbourhoods, churches and organizations we will be showing society at large that a different collective dynamic is possible. However, as well as light (as an *example*), we are also called to act as salt (as a *stimulant*); that is as *anticipators* of a kingdom whose coming we cry out for and whose realization we seek through the communication of its word and its praxis.

The power for victory

We live in the midst of 'fallen powers', structures that were created to serve us but which became our lords and guardians. In this sense and with the hope of the coming kingdom, the church in its mission is challenged to act for justice and peace (Mic. 5:5; 6:8), seeking to live out the power of service in a shared and democratic way that may genuinely 'give a chance and a voice to the forgotten, the humiliated and the excluded'. This challenges oppressive worldly power. The church is motivated by *Christ who, 'having disarmed the powers and authorities, made a public spectacle of them, triumphing over them by the cross' (Col. 2:15). It is also conscious that the power of the kingdom is a gift to be received and not something to be grasped, something which in Christ associated itself with the powerless, the socially marginalized: women, lepers, tax-collectors and Samaritans, among others.

It is in the daily living of mission that the church faces the issue of spiritual conflict. The power given by God enables Christians to counter Satan's attacks, through the victory of Christ (Heb. 2:14). Power that is victorious is exerted in obedience and submission to the God of the cross. This understanding must pervade the exercise of so-called *'spiritual warfare', which, in several contexts, has drifted towards the exercise of dazzling power. This kind of power does not conform to the kind of power we have described, being nothing more than a methodological toolkit built out of a search for efficacy.

The core of Christian mission is the conservation and rescue of human life, its liberation and *salvation, and its power lies in humble love through self-denial. This recognizes that the enemy of mission is the devil (as well as the flesh and the world), and gaining victory is not a matter of techniques and methods, but is rooted in the transforming power of relationships.

Power in the service of mission

The church should never seek power for its own sake. Some large churches have power that seems to have very little to do with the cross, manipulated for their own prosperity and pride. God always challenges our human use of power: 'God chose the weak things of the world, to shame the strong' (1 Cor. 1:27). The great mass of faithful Christians in various sub-equatorial countries are powerless have-nots; often small religious communities, forgotten in their societies and in the world, but nevertheless having a personal and spiritual dignity that rejoices in the love and presence of God. They form communities of mutual support that offer real possibilities of empowerment, possibilities that are generally not predicted by the academic manuals, but that find their origin in the power of the Holy Spirit: 'Not by might, nor by power, but by my Spirit' (Zech. 4:6).

In other places mission today has powerful resources at its disposal, especially in technology. This has shifted the balance of power to the places where these resources are freely and cheaply available. Mission practitioners need to evaluate carefully the role of the electronic media in establishing new kinds of power relationships through which new forms of dominance and '*colonialism' can be exercised. How can the powerful resources of today's world be placed at the service of others? The power of service comes from God, the only source of power, who releases it for his mission, the goal of which is to give power and glory back to him; even as we pray: 'for yours is the kingdom and the power and the glory' (Matt. 6:13).

See also WEAKNESS.

Bibliography
K. Bediako, *Christianity in Africa: The Renewal of a Non-Western Religion* (Edinburgh: Edinburgh University Press; Maryknoll: Orbis Books, 1995); C. Boff, 'Teologia do poder (teses)', in M. H. Arrochelas (ed.), *A igreja e o exercício do poder* (Rio de Janeiro: ISER, 1992); J. M. Bonino, *Poder del evangelio y poder político* (Buenos Aires: Kairos Ediciones, 1999); L. J. Dietrich (ed.), *Ser é poder* (São Paulo: Paulus & CEBI, 2002); S. Escobar, *et al.* (eds.), *Poder y misión: debate sobre la guerra espiritual en América Latina* (San José: IINDEF, 1997); T. Engelsviken and S. Moreau (eds.), *Spiritual Conflict In Today's Mission: A Report from the Consultation on 'Deliver Us from Evil' August 2000 Nairobi, Kenya* (Monrovia: Lausanne Committee for World Evangelization, 2001); G. Fee, *God's Empowering Presence: The Holy Spirit in the Letters of Paul* (Peabody: Hendrickson, 1994); D. Petersen, *Not by Might nor by Power: A Pentecostal Theology of Social Concern in Latin America* (Oxford: Regnum Books, 1996); V. Ramachandra, *Gods That Fail* (Carlisle: Paternoster, 1996); N. Saracco, 'Deus nos tem dado espírito de poder!', in V. Steuernagel (ed.), *CLADE III: No princípio era o verbo – todo o evangelho* (Curitiba: Encontro Publicações, 1994); J. R. W. Stott, *The Message of Acts* (Leicester: IVP, 1990); J. H. Yoder, *The Politics of Jesus* (Grand Rapids: Eerdmans, 1972).

A. B. FONSECA

Power evangelism

Power evangelism is associated with John Wimber (1934–97), founder and international director of the Association of Vineyard Churches. To use Wimber's own words, power evangelism is 'spontaneous, Spirit-inspired, empowered presentation of the gospel ... which is preceded and undergirded by supernatural demonstration of God's presence' (*Power Evangelism: Equipping the Saints*, p. 46). This concept was developed mainly out of his observation that evangelism as practised in the West lacked the evident power visible in the NT. Michael Horton echoes these sentiments by restating that 'the proponents of power evangelism insist that the Western world-view of rationalism and materialism have so prejudiced men and women against the supernatural that this bias must be abandoned' (in *Power Religion*, p. 70). Some attribute this bias to the influence of secularism.

On the other hand, Wimber's impressions resonated from his studies of *church growth strategies at the Charles E. Fuller Institute of Evangelism from 1974–78. It was under the tutelage of C. Peter Wagner that Wimber's philosophy became solidly formalized. During this period, his analysis of various statistical data revealed rapid growth within *Pentecostal and *charismatic churches (which are deeply rooted in the concept of direct guidance as a firm conviction) compared to other circles. This phenomenon was attributed, almost single-handedly, to the miraculous power of God at work. Following that discovery came the coining of the premise that the supernatural, as in signs and wonders, is an indispensable element in the communication of gospel truth.

Wimber was also influenced by George Eldon Ladd. Although not a proponent of charismatic theology, Ladd's understanding of the 'kingdom of God' is associated with the preaching of the gospel and the central task of evangelism. Wimber's interpretation of Ladd is interesting as he comments:

'As I read George Ladd's books and reread the Gospels, I realised that at the very heart of the Gospel lies the *kingdom of God and the power for effective evangelism and discipleship related directly to our understanding of and experiencing the kingdom today. This revelation remains the most significant spiritual experience since my conversion in 1963, because thereafter I exposed the practical implications of the presence of the kingdom' (*Kingdom Come*, pp. 7–8).

The practical implications of power evangelism resulted in Wimber's thesis that the presentation of the *gospel is, or should be, initiated by the *Holy Spirit in terms of a specific place, time, person or group, as distinct from indiscriminately spreading the message or depending on a pre-programmed message. His book has examples where evangelistic opportunities occurred through what was patently supernatural knowledge of a specific reality in a previously unknown person's life. This 'power encounter' would be the basis for a gospel presentation which would almost invariably lead to a faith commitment. Wimber saw Philip's encounter with the Ethiopian eunuch in Acts 8:26–40 as a good biblical example of such a 'power encounter'.

Although power evangelism cannot be single-handedly attributed to Wimber's success, which led to some 450 congregations in the United States alone and another 250 abroad by the time of his death, it is imperative, however, that the *power premise be acknowledged. Maybe the most appreciated aspect of Wimber's contribution is his quest for re-living biblical reality in our time. According to Armstrong, Wimber cannot be accused of insincerity. Moreover, Wimber's concerns reappear in much contemporary mission. A recent example is found in an article on hindrances to church planting in North America where J. D. Payne agonizes over the phenomenal growth of churches in South East Asia, which is almost unheard of in his context. He suggests among other causative factors for the lack of growth that there is a theological deficit in the understanding of the nature and power of the Holy Spirit amongst the churches of his own context.

However, a number of theologians are particularly concerned about the quest for power in contemporary society, a preoccupation that could potentially replace the unique authority of the gospel. Three contributors to *Power Religion*, a collection of essays, namely Armstrong, Carson and Boice, express reservations about Wimber, although they acknowledge that his views should be taken seriously. Among other things, Armstrong appreciates the placing of no limit on God's power and freedom which emerges from Wimber's orientation. Carson observes that 'there can be little doubt that the Vineyard leaders believe they are bringing genuine integration back into Christian life. The West is so rationalistic, so enslaved by the prevailing scientism, that it leaves no place for the power of God' (D. A. Carson, in *Power Religion*, p. 114). Boice surmises that power evangelism is against what we could call 'programmatic evangelism' and calls for reconsideration of the power of the Word and Spirit.

The reality on the ground is that the charismatic/Pentecostal movement continues to realize rapid growth globally, which James describes as 'phenomenal, dramatic, explosive, unprecedented and uncontrolled', considering that this movement did not exist prior to 1901 (G. L. James, *Missionalia* 33, p. 115). Although this reality cannot be wholly attributed to power evangelism, it is interesting that it was out of a similar setting that Wimber's thesis developed. N. Ripken observes that 'Pentecost is more than a one-time event [but] a catalyst by which the Holy Spirit takes scattered believers, multiplies them and gathers them into a community' (in *Evangelical Missions Quarterly* 39, p. 149). This then brings us back to Wimber's view of the kingdom of God which in practice makes all things whole.

In response to Wimber's power evangelism, first, while we can agree that all evangelism is aided by the supernatural power of the Holy Spirit (John 16:8–9; Acts 1:8), it is a sovereign work of the Holy Spirit to convict a person of sin and provoke faith in Christ. This clarification is significant in guarding us against an over-preoccupation with power and associated *miracles. It also keeps us from elevating certain individuals to the unassailable position of being sole 'conduits of divine power', as expressed by Van Rheenen, wrestling with the essence of divine power, and how God uses us as mediators of his power.

Secondly, the word of God in evangelism must be central. Some have questioned Wimber's credentials on this point. On centre stage are words of knowledge, spiritual phenomena and *healings. Armstrong also observes Wimber's 'failure to offer any definition of the evangel' (i.e. the gospel message) in the book *Power Evangelism*. Wimber's preoccupation with other means of salvation seems patent in the titles of his publications, *Power Healing* and *Power Points*.

Thirdly, miraculous signs and wonders are not necessarily evidence or confirmation of God's presence or power, particularly in these last days (Matt. 7:21–23; 24:24–25). Carson cautions about the possibility of the miraculous outside of the heritage of God. By the same token, rapid growth does not necessarily imply God's blessing; indeed, sometimes the opposite may just be true. On the contrary, while miraculous signs are sometimes associated with belief in Christ (John 20:30; 21:25), there seems to be an element of authenticity in those who believe apart from the miraculous (John 8:45–47; 20:29). In fact Christ himself associates the search for miraculous signs with wickedness in Luke 11:28–32, perhaps to refute the unbelief that resisted his teaching as sufficient validation of his authenticity.

Fourthly, Wimber could be said to use Scripture to *justify* his findings, rather than allowing it to be the *determinant*. In fact Wimber goes on to claim that God is above his word and thus not limited by it. Anderson suggests this places importance on 'experience and practice' rather than orthodox teaching. This undermines an understanding of what is normative in faith, and raises the question of the reliability of experience.

Most commentators have concluded that 'power encounters' are not indispensible for effective evangelism. God brings people to faith in Christ in a rich variety of ways, sometimes through 'encounters' that are completely independent of missionary involvement. However, Wimber and others have drawn attention to a dimension of the Holy Spirit which cannot be ignored. Carson offers a conciliatory view when he writes that this 'does not mean that Wimber thinks a miracle should take place every time someone is converted, or in every instance where there is evangelism, but that in the sweep of our evangelism signs and wonders must find a place or the gospel we preach is defective, robbed of its power. Signs and wonders have an apologetic function in evangelism' (in *Power Religion*, p. 90). It is not necessary to agree completely with Wimber to acknowledge his sincerity. Perhaps to a degree his approach explains the phenomenal growth of the church in Africa, Asia and South America, as distinct from the West where rationalism and materialism are deep seated.

See also EVANGELISM.

Bibliography
A. Anderson, 'The Mission Initiatives of African Pentecostals in Continental Perspective', *Missionalia* 28, 2000, pp. 83–98; J. H. Armstrong, 'In Search of Spiritual Power', in M. S. Horton (ed.), *Power Religion: The Selling Out of the Evangelical Church?* (Chicago: Moody Press, 1992); J. M. Boice, 'A Better Way: The Power of the Word and Spirit', in *Power Religion*; D. A. Carson, 'The Purpose of Signs and Wonders in the New Testament' in *Power Religion*; M. S. Horton, 'Introduction: What this Book is and is Not', in *Power Religion*; G. L. James, 'Charismacity: The Prevalence of the Pentecostal/Charismatic Church in the City', *Missionalia* 33, 2005, pp. 111–124; G. E. Ladd, 'The Gospel of the Kingdom', in R. D. Winter and S. C. Hawthorne (eds.), *Perpectives on the World Christian Movement: A Reader* (Pasadena: William Carey Library, 1992); F. Möller, 'Pentecostal Theology', in S. Maimela and A. König (eds.), *Initiation into Theology: The Rich Variety of Theology and Hermeneutics* (Pretoria: J. L. van Schaick, 1998); J. D. Payne, 'Problems Hindering North American Church Planting Movements', *Evangelical Missions Quarterly* 39, 2003, pp. 220–228; N. Ripken, 'The Two Sides of Pentecost', *Evangelical Missions Quarterly* 39, 2003, pp. 148–150; G. Van Rheenen, 'A Theology of Power', *Evangelical Missionary Quarterly* 41, 2005, pp. 32–38; J. Wimber and K. Springer, *Power Evangelism: Equipping the Saints* (San Francisco: Harper and Row 1985/92); J. Wimber and K. Springer, *Power Healing* (San Francisco: Harper and Row, 1986); J. Wimber, *Kingdom Come* (Ann Arbor: Servant Publications, 1988); J. Wimber and K. Springer, *Power Points* (San Francisco: Harper and Row, 1991).

S. NDOGA

Praxis/orthopraxis

Praxis is a technical expression that owes its theological use to the seminal ideas propagated by German theologians and philosophers known as the Frankfurt School (started in the 1920s). Such free thinkers as Eric Fromm, Max Horkheimer, Wilhelm Reich and Herbert Marcuse affirmed that reality is not what it should be; strategies for change should be grounded on a critical view of reality ('social critical theory') as an anticipation of and a means toward a freer, more just society. Paulo Freire's educational insights, which were strongly influenced by Marxist ideology, also helped shape the use of praxis as a theological/missiological method. For Freire, work equals praxis, whereas action without reflection is activism and reflection without action is verbalism. The term has been closely associated with *liberation theology, which originated in Latin America.

Praxis has become an exercise in which action and reflection are used as tools to understand and transform reality in ways that reflect the values of God's kingdom. In theological circles, praxis is Bible-dependent, regardless of whether action or reflection comes first. Since no one comes to the Bible with a clean slate, all theologies mirror the theologian's context in one way or another. The critical issue is whether the Bible is the parameter whereby all action and reflection are instructed and corrected. This is what constitutes orthopraxis: action-and-reflection which ultimately glorifies God and contributes to his redeeming purposes, as exemplified in Jesus' ministry on earth.

Praxis can be seen as a way of 'doing' theology, a hermeneutic tool, a perspective on reality and a missiological approach applied to cross-cultural issues. These dimensions help us understand its uses as well as its limitations.

Praxis as a way of doing theology

Perhaps the basic concern of the praxis theologians has been the virtual dissociation between word and deed ('proclamation and action') predominant in the traditional ministry of the church, particularly in (but by no means limited to) its Roman Catholic branch.

Contextual theology merges the two questions of *proclamation and *presence into one: 'doing the will of God' (Matt. 6:10; 7:21) in 'doing the truth' (1 John 1:6). Doctrine and Christian living, faith and life, 'orthodoxy' and 'orthopraxis' cannot be separated, held in balance or even considered apart from each other. If I tell the truth apart

from love and piety, I am not 'doing the truth' at all – and subsequently I am not telling the truth, according to Scripture.

Although liberation theologians have been correctly criticized for their dependence on Marxist ideas, it can be said that humanity as the image of God (*imago dei*) cannot exclude its man as worker (*homo laborans*) component. When God created humanity, he gave them a concrete mandate to be productive and creative, which implied the use of God-given physical as well as metaphysical capacities which are reflective of that image, even after the fall. Therefore, a dissociation of labour and the human spirit is mistaken, since God linked the human means of production to a correct worship of his deity (cf. the story of Cain and Abel, Gen. 4). The physical and the spirit world are inextricably connected; thus, economic activity is just as spiritual as the worship of God, a concept which is conspicuously present throughout Scripture.

Praxis as a hermeneutic tool

A new way of doing theology requires a new hermeneutic, which, in the case of liberation theology, has meant that *doing* is pivotal for such correct understanding. Praxis is seen as a first act. In this sense, liberation theology has challenged the traditional Western way of doing theology which put theological reflection first. But liberation theology claimed that this contributed to the distant dialogue between academia and the average church member, not to mention the agonizing process of transposing foreign theological models in cross-cultural contexts.

Evangelicals, in particular, have been pressed to rethink their hermeneutic in view of the rediscovered dynamic between action-and-reflection which is present in the biblical account of the ministry of Jesus and the apostles. The weakness of the standard praxis approach to hermeneutics, however, has been its prioritization of praxis to the detriment of a Christ-centred view of Scripture. The basic tenets of the faith have succumbed to the immediacy of human reality. The imperative of liberation became the hermenetical key. Ironically, the liberation ideal which sustained this praxiological approach has produced subservience to a Marxist economic model that has proven deficient, notably in its incapacity to elevate the human condition as intended. Nonetheless, the praxiological dimension of theology has forced us all to a 'reflective commitment *in* praxis' (H. M. Conn, *Eternal Word and Changing Worlds: Theology, Anthropology and Mission in Trialogue*, p. 233) instead of the usual evangelical response that merely reflected *about* that praxis. How to prioritize Scripture in a praxis exercise is the hermeneutic question we all should ask ourselves.

Praxis as epistemology

Because of its pervasiveness, the praxis method has gone all the way from an approach to reality to a model of that same reality. Although they attempt to distance themselves from modernity and its rational stance on history and historical change, advocates of the standard praxis approach have tended to negate or dismiss the spiritual dimension that permeates the forces of history. A biblical view which sees a confluence of human and non-human agencies, which includes satanic forces as well as God's sovereign presence-and-action in, through and above human history, is usually beyond their scope. Sin and evil are treated as part and fabric of human-made structures rather than an interchange between these structures and metaphysical realities.

The 'challenge of rationality' posed by modern thought (especially after Descartes and Kant) has led liberation theologians to question the authority basis of institutional Christianity and conceive a new 'positive theology' that deconstructs ecclesiastical dogma (speculative theology) in view of contextual factors. More important than believing what we always have believed, so they say, it is necessary to discover what we should believe in order to change human history for the better – which reflects Marxist influences.

Praxis as a missiological approach

'Missiology is fundamentally a praxiological phenomenon. It is a critical reflection that takes place in the praxis of mission' (O. Costas, *Theology of the Crossroads in Contemporary Latin America: Missiology in Mainline Protestantism, 1969–1974*, p. 8). That is to say, 'missional action always occurs in a context' (C. W. Van Engen, *Mission on the Way: Issues in Mission Theology*, p. 25).

A praxiological missiology consists in reading and rereading Scripture in light of the biblical *contexts, the interpreter's context and the audience's context, while seeking ways of applying rediscovered biblical truths to the target context. As Van Engen says:

Missiology helps us understand that not only the reflection, but profoundly the action as well, is part of a theology-on-the-way that seeks to discover how the church may participate in God's mission in God's world. The action is itself theological, and serves to inform the reflection, which in turn interprets, evaluates, critiques, and projects new understanding in the transformed action. Thus the interweaving of reflection and action in a constantly spiralling pilgrimage offer a transformation of all aspects of our missiological engagement with our various contexts. (*Mission on the Way*, p. 100)

Application

Latin American critics of both traditional and liberation models of doing theology have yet to produce a concrete, autochthonous alternative. Their discourse is often limited to discussions about the presence of the church in the world. Their gospel, reduced to a dual discourse on proposition and social action (mind and body), leaves the spiritual dimension almost untouched – which can be taken as a neo-modernist message within a neo-modernist paradigm. A more biblical approach would embrace all three dimensions which encompassed Jesus' praxis: body, mind and spirit.

Jesus' praxis is exemplified in his Sermon on the Mount. His reflection is centred on Scripture and his actions promote God's glory on earth. Jesus' concern is for the correct interpretation and application of God's *word (Matt. 5:17–20) to all spheres of life, great and small, issues of the heart as well as issues of outward behaviour. Jesus challenges the mistaken values of his time and corrects them according to the spirit of the law, by word and deed – which is the core of orthopraxis. Thus he sets forth a perfect model of what Christian praxis should be.

Issues such as suffering and persecution for his sake (Matt. 5:11–12), lawsuits and reconciliation (5:21–26; 5:38–42), family life (5:27–32), the true nature of agape love (5:43–48), personal and social justice (6:1–4), caring for the poor and God's true riches (6:2–4, 19–21, 25–34), spiritual exercises (6:5–18), the deceitful nature of the human heart (6:22–23; 7:1–5), modelling human relationships after God's mercy (7:7–12), external versus temporal values (7:13–14), true leaders and the fruit of their hearts (7:15–20), are contemplated in Jesus' praxis exercise. Our lives should be built on his principles and practices (Matt. 7:21–27). What ultimately counts in our praxis is whether we have done God's will on earth (7:21–23).

Bibliography

S. B. Bevans, *Models of Contextual Theology* (Maryknoll: Orbis Books, 1992); L. Boff, *The Path to Hope*, transl. P. Berryman (Maryknoll: Orbis Books, 1993); H. M. Conn, *Eternal Word and Changing Worlds: Theology, Anthropology and Mission in Trialogue* (Phillipsburg: P & R, 1984); O. Costas, *Theology of the Crossroads in Contemporary Latin America: Missiology in Mainline Protestantism, 1969–1974* (Amsterdam: Rodopi, 1976); L. DeCarvalho, 'What's Wrong with the Label "Managerial Missiology?"', *IJFM* 18, 2001, pp. 141–146; P. Freire, *Pedagogy of the Oppressed* (New York: Continuum Books, 1993); W. Taylor (ed.), *Global Missiology for the 21st Century* (Grand Rapids: Baker Books, 2000); C. E. Van Engen, *Mission on the Way: Issues in Mission Theology* (Grand Rapids: Baker Books, 1999).

L. DeCarvalho

Prayer

Partnership in mission

The sovereign action of God in fulfilling his mission in his way in the world is dynamically linked with the involvement of his people through intercessory prayer. Jesus links the harvest of the kingdom with the need to send out workers to reap it (Luke 10:2). Of course there is the command to 'go'; but with it there is also the command to 'pray'.

God's sovereignty is not abrogated by his own decision to give his people a real and vital role in partnership with him. He could have planned his mission without us, but he chose to include us. From Abraham in Genesis 15, through Jonah and on to the apostolic band in Acts 1 and Acts 13 at the beginning of Paul's first journey, the communication of God's will through prayer was the decisive initiative for mission. Constant prayer characterized the apostolic band between the ascension of Jesus and the Holy Spirit's empowering for mission at Pentecost (e.g. Acts 1:14).

This shared partnership is not of course between equals. Prayer makes the initial link, tuning human ears to God's wavelength, focusing human eyes on God's vision, so that human feet move at God's calling and timing, and go to the planned destination. The divine encounter with Isaiah shows this pattern of partnership grounded in prayer (Isa. 6:8). Prayer is God's ordained means of preparing us to take up our role of 'junior partnership' in mission with him. Theologically, therefore, prayer is intrinsically missiological, since it is a dynamic engagement with the God of mission.

Spiritual direction

Because the *missio Dei* is God's, he directs it. He uses the willing and the unwilling. Jonah provides an excellent example of a very unwilling human partner, who thoroughly disapproved of the ethnic inclusivity of God's intentions. Jonah did everything possible to avoid involvement in God's purposes for Baghdad (Nineveh). His story epitomizes the unwilling mission partner. Keen to dictate his own terms, Jonah had to learn a very hard way that mission is a thoroughly universal and all-inclusive activity. He struggled with God in prayer, but at the end of his story we leave him angry with God, though successful as an evangelist. We are not told that his basic attitude to the revelation of God's compassion had changed. He did not weep over Baghdad as Jesus wept over Jerusalem. He did not see death as the macabre shepherd of the multitudes without the gospel. But God in his grace and mercy used this reluctant and recalcitrant disciple in his mission purposes.

Spiritual direction through prayer continued in the movement of the mission from Jerusalem to the heart of the Roman Empire in Acts. The first missionary journey was launched out of corporate prayer as Barnabas and Saul were set apart for the work to which God had called them (Acts 13:2). The further direction of God's mission was eventually clarified through prolonged spiritual struggle. Paul and his companions were prevented from preaching in Asia and Bithynia by the Spirit of Jesus. Then the Macedonian vision led them across to Greece. Later in Acts 18:10, God clearly indicated to Paul that he was to spend considerable time in Corinth. At each stage God used prayer to clarify the nature, scope and timetable of his mission, as well as its planned geographical extension.

Later still, Paul's desire to travel to Rome and indeed on to Spain was conditioned by constant prayer (Rom. 1:10). He comments that he had planned many times to travel to Rome, 'but I have been prevented from doing so until now'. As he discusses his future itinerary across Europe, he urges those in Rome to pray (Rom. 15:23–33). In both passages Paul submits his planned pastoral and evangelistic journeys to Rome and Spain to the will of God, accepting his timing and planning. Prayer is therefore the key to effective mission: indeed, closer adherence to the overarching strategy and timing of the *missio Dei* through the listening ear of human mission partners in prayer could have reduced wasted effort in many mission enterprises.

The challenge of collaborating with the God of mission involves also a spiritual power struggle behind the scenes. Jesus came to destroy the works of the devil (1 John 3:8), and Paul sees the triumph of the cross in the disarming of the powers (Col. 2:15). This struggle is not fought with worldly weapons but with those which have divine power to demolish strongholds (2 Cor. 10:4). Many Pentecostal and charismatic churches and agencies have made prayer their main mission strategy by linking it with *spiritual warfare and focusing prayer on 'spiritual strongholds' in an area, or making 'prayer walks'. The biblical basis for some of this activity is controversial; nevertheless the importance of engaging the spiritual battle to push back the forces of evil, and to see God's kingdom come so that the gospel flourishes, is one of Paul's own strategies (Eph. 6:10–20).

We pray for the coming of the kingdom (Matt. 6:10; cf. Matt. 3:2). It is significant that the NT ends with the divine declaration of God's own return to the world and the human prayer, 'Amen. Come, Lord Jesus' (Rev. 22:20). Prayer, power, preaching and the parousia all belong together.

Holy attraction

It is striking that the content of much of the intercessory prayer material recorded in the NT has to do with the process of sanctification of God's chosen people. Paul was not always praying that the churches around the Mediterranean would be more outward looking, develop five-year evangelistic plans and move from maintenance to mission! But he was always praying that converted men and women would become increasingly holy and, by so becoming, adorn the doctrine of the gospel, providing thereby a magnetic and attractive power to draw people to Christ (e.g. Col. 1:9–14). It is the transformation of the lives of Christian converts that is the most powerful witness in society and the best propaganda for mission.

Similarly Paul's intercessory prayers focus on the converts' working faith, love-inspired labour and hope-filled endurance (1 Thess. 1:3), which all have significant consequences for mission (v. 10). Holiness of life with a transformed lifestyle spreads the gospel message and promotes mission. If the life speaks louder than the lips, then more intercession for holiness is needed for effective mission.

The Queen of Sheba had her breath taken away by her experience of the wisdom of Solomon and the magnificence of the Jerusalem temple. Men and women worldwide wait to be confronted by the transformed lives of God's saints by the Holy Spirit. Praying for holiness means praying to be attractive visual aids in the cause of the *missio Dei* in the world. Intercessory prayer and worldwide mission are umbilically linked.

Bibliography

D. Coggan, *The Prayers of the New Testament* (London: Hodder and Stoughton, 1967); J. Jeremias, *The Prayers of Jesus* (London: SCM, 1967); W. D. Taylor (ed.), *Global Missiology for the 21st Century: The Iguassu Dialogue* (Grand Rapids: Baker, 2000).

D. R. J. EVANS

PREACHING, see PROCLAMATION

Presence

For evangelicals, verbal proclamation has traditionally been an indispensable dimension of mission. The idea that simply 'being present' is a sufficient witness to a particular context has been favoured more by Catholic and ecumenical missiologists. For Roman Catholics, presence has a sacramental significance, whilst for ecumenicals it serves as a more acceptable alternative to overt proclamation, which may be seen as too aggressive.

In recent years there has been confusion concerning the meaning of a theology of presence. Some regard presence as mainly silence or significant service. Others have contrasted presence, proclamation and persuasion; they criticize presence because it so often fails to be concerned with making disciples. It has been misused by both proponents and opponents, and there is need for a more adequate evangelical understanding of presence theology which can restore wholeness to mission.

The theology of presence begins with the presence of God. God is present and active in history, and he invites us to participate in that presence. Christians are called to live among the nations in ways that embody the healing and renewing presence of God. Rather than emphasizing laws that have to be obeyed or doctrines that need to be learned, presence emphasizes divine presence through personal encounter. Jesus in his *incarnation embodied the presence of God in the world, and so being present as Jesus was present is to express solidarity, self-emptying and sacrifice for others. Presence means to live transparently in the world by living alongside people in non-paternalistic or non-patronizing ways. Sometimes, Jesus' silence raised curiosity, stimulated questions and invited response. In some situations it is more Christlike to be silent than to speak, especially when Christian witness is experienced as harshness and aggressiveness.

Presence in mission is therefore God-centred and people-centred. It follows Jesus in sharing people's lives, living by alternative values, and so emphasizing transforming relationships in contrast to the pursuit of power. Presence models Jesus' powerlessness and vulnerable lifestyle. Jesus' presence was powerful, but it was not the power of imposition; it was the power of demonstration. Presence attracts others into transformed lives and relationships when words are often misunderstood, and therefore ineffective. It follows Jesus in its concern for the entire person, witnessing to a love and openness in contrast to aggressive imposition of convictions upon others.

Presence connects with Jesus' teaching about the influence of salt, light and leaven (Matt. 5:13–14); it has an intrinsic value as an 'active' influence which incorporates both being and doing. It is about visualization before verbalization. We can see how it attracted the attention of others as the Jewish community in Acts 2 drew seekers to itself. They saw themselves as 'a royal priesthood, a holy nation' (1 Pet. 2:9) and a community which spread the fragrance of God (2 Cor. 2:14). Energized by the Holy Spirit and prayer, presence demonstrated the life of the people of God among and for others. When Christians model a community of reconciliation and peace, their presence is a 'missionary presence'. Although presence is foundational to other forms of witness, it is also witness in itself. It is not merely pre-evangelism, and mission is not only defined by word and deed.

Max Warren, general secretary of the Church Mission Society from 1942 to 1963, is credited with emphasizing presence in missiological thought and literature. He was editor of a series of books called the Christian Presence Series. Writing at the end of the 1950s and 1960s, the closing years of the colonial period, he argued that the present moment of history offered fresh opportunity for demonstrating the gospel. People needed to discover new and deeper dimensions of the gospel. At the time many were reacting against Western domination and saw Christian faith as inherently Western.

Warren argued that Christians should seize this new opportunity to be free from the burden and responsibility of Western power. He hoped that Christianity could overcome Asian and African accusations of the Western character of Christianity and reclaim its true character so that it could provide a spiritual home for all people. In the light of the renaissance of traditional religions, he believed that Christian presence among other religions was necessary to find the way between coexistence and aggressive attack.

Christian presence therefore focuses on relationships in witness. The presence of Christ in our lives transforms our relationships. Those to whom we witness are not enemies to be conquered but friends to be won. We cannot share faith when we are afraid or intolerant of those to whom we witness. One of the most successful ways to break down walls of suspicion is to meet the person on the other side of the wall. Bridges need to be built rather than walls. Suspicion is lived away, not talked away.

Witness by presence is important for those churches that live and work in situations where mission in the traditional sense is not permitted. In such situations overt witness is seriously limited and a witness by life is crucial. If we are not present as Christians we have opted for absence. The decision to be present should not be based upon the amount of freedom permitted. Lack of freedom might even help to illuminate the gospel as Christians are forced to give more attention to the quality of their presence. Powerlessness has its own potency.

The presence of Christians can either reinforce or detract from witness. Where the language of the church is a foreign language in religious or ideological contexts, it is vitally important that Christians give attention to the quality of their presence. Christian presence demonstrates the gospel and helps people understand its deeper dimensions.

Christian witness therefore is not imposition. Jesus stands at the door and knocks. Our life must commend faith rather than coerce faith. Presence cultivates empathy rather than judgment. The Christian task in mission is to beam light, build bridges of understanding and model Christian presence with patience.

See also CONTEXTUALIZATION.

Bibliography
G. Appleton, *On the Eightfold Path: Christian Presence Amid Buddhism* (London: SCM Press, 1961); Bertha Beachy, 'The Somali Journey: Presence and Patience', in Krabill *et al.*, *Anabaptists Meeting Muslims* (Scottdale: Herald Press, 2005); K. Cragg, *Sandals at the Mosque: Christian Presence Amid Islam* (New York: Oxford University Press, 1959); D. Entz, 'Incarnational Witness among the Samoghos of Burkina Faso', in Krabill *et al.*, *Anabaptists Meeting Muslims*; M. Jarrett-Kerr, *The Secular Promise: Christian Presence Amid Contemporary Humanism* (London: SCM Press, 1964); J. R. Krabill, D. W. Shenk and L. Stutzman (eds.), *Anabaptists Meeting Muslims: A Calling for Presence in the Way of Christ* (Scottdale, PA: Herald Press, 2005); W. Sawatsky, 'Response: Historical Perspectives', in Krabill *et al.*, *Anabaptists Meeting Muslims*; C. E. Shenk, *A Relevant Theology of Presence* (Elkhart, IN: Mission Focus pamphlet, 1982); C. E. Shenk, 'A Theology of Presence and Patience', in Krabill *et al.*, *Anabaptists Meeting Muslims*; J. V. Taylor, *The Primal Vision: Christian Presence Amid African Religion* (Philadelphia: Fortress Press, 1963).

C. E. SHENK

Priesthood

Biblical background
Priesthood was at the centre of the Israelite faith community. The first responsibility of Levites and priests was to serve the whole Israelite community, not only in liturgical roles but also as leaders and prophetic speakers. The latter role was taken over by the prophets during the monarchy, so that *liturgy and ministry on behalf of all Israel, mediation between *God and Israel, intercession, and leadership in worship and teaching were the main priestly roles. The priesthood was responsible for keeping Israel in line with God's will and the regulations of the covenant. But very often they degraded the office to formal performance of cultic rituals without providing spiritual leadership.

Priests and Levites are not very visible in the Gospels, since they were rarely involved in events around Jesus (see, however, Elizabeth and Zechariah in Luke 1). Sometimes we see them as delegates. They are found in Jesus' miracle stories when, after healing and cleansing, people were sent to priests for inspection. However, we also find confrontational statements by Jesus against the chief priests and Sadducees, who comprised the ruling class and the privileged priestly group. After the resurrection, some priests joined the Messianic movement (Acts 6:7), a famous example being Barnabas, a Levite (Acts 4:36).

In a collective sense, Israel as God's people

was called as a servant to the nations, with a corporate priestly role on their behalf. This view was reinterpreted in the NT with reference to the church as a corporate 'royal priesthood' with a missionary role of declaring his praises to the world (1 Pet. 2:1–10). This 'priesthood of all believers' meant that holiness and intercession became important dimensions of missionary calling.

Historical perspective

Some historic Christian churches picked up the OT notion of priesthood with a cultic intermediary role similar to that in the OT. In the early Middle Ages, the role of priests was also to educate communities, celebrate church liturgy, and to serve as mediators between God and the people. The church and the priest stood at the centre of social life and were usually located at the centre of villages and towns. In the Western church, the Reformation challenged these ideas, and the Enlightenment further reduced and limited the social role of priests as society became gradually more secular.

However, historically priests had also at least three other roles: (1) teaching and preserving the Christian faith; (2) living in and demonstrating an intentional community; and (3) being missionaries. Before the time of Gutenberg, it was primarily the role of priests and monks to preserve historical documents, such as Bible texts and other Christian writings, by copying them. Their diligence preserved Christian and non-Christian texts of the past for our access today. Priestly or monastic communities were not inward-looking: they had at their centre the spiritual renewal of society. From these communities many moved out to start new communities, and in this way propagated the gospel in Europe, Siberia, Asia, Alaska, India and America. They planted new churches, reached out to distant lands, and inspired later Protestant and evangelical missionaries.

Priesthood and mission

At the time of the Reformation, radical Reformers, or Anabaptists, insisted on widening the concept of priesthood, seeking to reconnect with the NT view of the 'priesthood of all believers'. Anabaptists, and later the Free Church tradition, understood that each and every member in the Christian community is a priest, a member of the 'holy and royal priesthood' on behalf of the world. Supremely this responsibility meant service, to God and all people, and involved a threefold mission:

(1) *Responsibility to God*: praising and worshipping him, interceding for individuals, governments, the needy, *praying for the world that cannot pray for itself, and serving God in many other ways (leitourgia).

(2) *Responsibility to the church*: community building, *discipleship and education, as well as attending to the needs of the community through a variety of servant ministries (diakonia).

(3) *Responsibility to society(s)*: *witnessing (martyria) through communal and individual living as part of the society, proclaiming the good news (kerygma), responding to the needs of the immediate society and to global needs in the world (diakonia) and with this, inviting and building a community of the kingdom. Priests also have a prophetic voice in society to remind each other, the faith community and the surrounding society of the moral standards God the Creator and Sustainer has set for all. They have the responsibility for on-going dialogue between different groups, continuing the ministry of Christ Jesus, the High Priest, in bridging and *reconciliation (2 Cor. 5:18, 21), building a healing community of forgiven and forgiving individuals, keeping it open to those who are outside of it.

The priesthood of all believers widens the spectrum and quality of the responsibilities of every Christian, individually and corporately. Even though this concept is, with some variations, also widely accepted in historic churches, it still remains in tension with some ecclesial, hierarchical structures, especially in the differences between lay and ordained ministries. Their tensions are also present in the missional responsibilities of the church, which are often seen to belong to special missionaries or ministries. This sets them apart from the majority in the church, who then fail to accept their own priestly role as missionaries, or cannot see that the church *as the church* has a missionary calling. Positively, as we work through this tension and see the post-Christendom church being a visible, witnessing community in society, non-ordained members will accept their place in God's mission through the church. When the church adopts in its fullness the 'priesthood of all believers' model, gifts will be fully shared and the church will be effective in its calling to serve in the spirit of a priestly servant in the mission of God to the world.

Bibliography

P. Beasley-Murray, 'The Ministry of All and the Leadership of Some: A Baptist Perspective', in P. Beasley-Murray (ed.), *Anyone For Ordination?* (London: Monarch, 1993); C. Bulley, *The Priesthood of Some Believers: Developments From the General to the Special Priesthood in the Christian Literature of the First Three Centuries* (Carlisle: Paternoster, 2000); T. George, 'The Priesthood of All Believers', in P. A. Basden and D. S. Dockery (eds.), *The People of God: Essays on the Believers' Church* (Nashville: Broadman Press, 1991); M. Grossman, 'Priesthood as Authority: Interpretive Competition in First-Century Judaism and Christianity', in J. R. Davila (ed.), *Dead Sea Scrolls as Background to Postbiblical Judaism and Early Christianity* (Leiden: Brill, 2003); H. H. Hobbs, *You Are Chosen: The Priesthood of All Believers* (New York: HarperCollins, 1990); V.-M. Kärkkäinen, *An Introduction to Ecclesiology: Ecumenical, Historical & Global Perspectives* (Downers Grove: InterVarsity Press, 2002); B. Leonard, *Priesthood of All Believers* (Nashville: The Historical Commission of the Southern Baptist Convention, 1989); M. Rodriguez, *The Priesthood of All Believers: 1st Century Church Life in the 21st Century* (Delta: Rebuilders, 2004); E. Schweizer, 'The Priesthood of All Believers: 1 Peter 2:1–10', in M. J. Wilkins and T. Paige (eds.), *Worship, Theology and Ministry in the Early Church: Essays in Honour of Ralph P. Martin* (Sheffield: JSNT Supp., 1992); W. B. Shurden (ed.), *Priesthood of All Believers* (Macon: Smyth & Helwys, 1993); S. K. Wood (ed.), *Ordering the Baptismal Priesthood: Theologies of Lay and Ordained Ministry* (Collegeville, MN: Liturgical Press, 2003); N. G. Wright, 'Inclusive Representation: Towards a Doctrine of Christian Ministry', *Baptist Quarterly* 39, 2001, pp. 159–174.

P. PENNER

PRIMAL RELIGION, see AFRICAN TRADITIONAL RELIGION

Proclamation

Proclamation, and its associated preaching ministry, has always been a priority in mission for the majority of evangelicals. This finds inspiration from the Lukan version of Jesus' commission to his disciples, which envisages *repentance and forgiveness *preached* in his name to all nations (Luke 24:47; cf. Mark 16:15). However, in more recent years a broader understanding of what proclamation involves has developed, with the recognition that the gospel must be conveyed in word and deed, and that what we do can 'speak' more loudly than what we say. St Francis of Assisi famously said: 'Preach constantly, and use words if you must.' In fact words can never be separated from actions, example, Christian *presence and testimony. Action without words is dumb, and words without action are empty. Words interpret deeds even as deeds validate words, so that the gospel needs to be conveyed in an integrated way to be effective. The Word became flesh, conveying God's truth in human, visual, concrete and relational dimensions, all of which worked together with what Jesus actually said verbally.

However, at least in the West, there is also the challenge of effective communication in an age when visual media are overtaking verbal and written media as the preferred mode of conveying understanding. There is decreasing tolerance for long monologues; preaching has to be more creative; and how the church 'speaks' to the world has to be re-examined. This article will suggest that there is still a vital place for 'prophetic proclamation' at the heart of mission, based on the conviction that God speaks today and the world needs to listen.

Definitions

In the OT to 'proclaim' comes from the semantic root *qārā'*, which means 'to attract someone's attention, by use of the voice, so as to be able to contact them'. Depending on the context it is also translated as to call, to shout, to name, to invoke, to announce. 'Proclaim' is used for official decrees. It is an announcement of something important to which everyone should listen.

In the NT there are more than 30 Greek terms which are translated 'to proclaim' or 'proclamation'. The most common is the verb *keryssein* (71 times) and its substantive *kerygma* (9 times). *Kerygma* is used in the context of the announcement of a herald. The herald was a person of integrity and character, who was at the service of the king or the state in order to make public proclamations. He only said what the king wanted to be known. To add or take away words would be considered a betrayal.

Theologically the proclamation of the gospel arises from the desire of the living God to reveal himself and communicate to fallen humanity his invitation of saving grace. At its height, this self-revelation is given in Scripture through the most direct means of human communication: a person who speaks. The word 'proclamation' therefore refers primarily to the *verbal* dimension of *evangelism. The proclamation of the gospel is about open and public communication, oral transmission, or direct and explicit declaration of the saving activity of God. It is an inescapable dimension of evangelism, as it was for the early church in Acts, because however powerful a witness deeds, holy life and actions might be, they can never be sufficiently transparent to provide a reasoned explanation of what the message of salvation is about. There are numerous texts in the NT which link preaching and proclaiming with the gospel.

Biblical perspectives
Prophetic proclamation
Judaism was a religion of the word, and the announcement of the message of salvation was characteristic of biblical faith from the messages of Moses to the visions of Daniel. A wide range of preaching, teaching and proclamation can be observed throughout the OT.

The prophetic tradition elaborated a refined theology of the word, which 'came to' the prophets directly and was proclaimed with characteristic directness: 'Thus says the Lord...'. The word of God was seen as a creator and so inevitably fruitful (Ps. 33:6; Isa. 55:9–11). The power of the word was experienced with such personal force that it communicated to Israel the saving power of God: a God who does not keep silent nor is far away, but who speaks truth to his people (e.g. Isa. 45:19; Jer. 23:29). The prophets were

God's heralds, declaring his justice and the future hope of salvation and speaking out against the sins of the people and their leaders. Their message came to Israel as a cutting critique backed up with prophetic signs. It was not an abstract proclamation of eternal truths which bore no relation to reality, but it had direct application to the social reality of their time.

The prophetic message was a spontaneous but coherent message given under the direct inspiration of the Holy Spirit and given as an announcement of what God wanted to say which spoke directly into a given context. This can be distinguished from the teaching ministry of the Aaronic and Levitical priesthoods, whose responsibility was to explain the Law (e.g. Lev. 10:11; 2 Chr. 17:9), and encourage the people to obey it.

Messianic proclamation
Preaching occupied a central place in Jesus' understanding of his messianic mission (e.g. Mark 1:38; Matt. 9:35; Luke 4:43). A large proportion of his ministry was dedicated to preaching and teaching. His message was directed to the will of his hearers, inviting them to make a concrete decision: to follow him and submit themselves to the will of God.

Jesus was not afraid to be confrontational. His prophetic proclamations, in the fullness and power of the Spirit, involve a raised voice in sharp criticism against the exclusivist and hypocritical posture of religious leaders. Hypocrisy consists in the absence of good works, however correct the words. Jesus warns of the danger of focusing on words, and ignoring actions (e.g. Matt. 23:3). In contrast Jesus' words and actions are completely complementary and mutually affirming.

Apostolic proclamation
The apostles had some training and experience in preaching before they were finally commissioned for their mission (Mark 3:14; Matt. 10:7; Luke 9:6; 10:1–16). But a significant change would take place in their message after the ascension. They would continue proclaiming the presence of the *kingdom, but in a distinct sense. The announcement of the kingdom was replaced by a focus on *Christ himself, the King of the kingdom. In

this way the apostles proclaimed the kingdom more clearly as a decision about the King. To preach Christ is to preach about the kingdom, and so Christ, and especially his death and resurrection, became the focus of all their preaching (e.g. 1 Cor. 2:2). The apostles gave priority to this ministry of preaching and did not allow it to be taken over by other important dimensions of mission (Acts 6).

For the apostles proclamation was no cold repetition of merely interesting truths. There was a sense of compulsion which gripped them as they proclaimed the gospel, constrained by the conviction that God himself was making his appeal through them and in essence demanding a decision of repentance and faith (e.g. 2 Cor. 5:11 – 6:2).

Paul made the proclamation of Christ the main goal of his life. He lived under an irresistible impulse which drove him to proclaim the gospel on every possible occasion. Paul understood that the proclamation of the gospel was the way designated by God for sinners to hear about the Saviour and turn to him for *salvation (Rom. 10:14; 1 Cor. 1:17; 9:16). He referred to the passion which dominated his life as the 'foolishness' of preaching (1 Cor. 1:21). The announcement of a crucified Messiah was contradictory and absurd to the brilliant Jewish and Greek intellectuals (1 Cor. 1:23). But the scandal of the *cross was the way chosen by God to transmit his power and wisdom to the world (1 Cor. 1:24).

In 1 Corinthians 2:1–5 Paul makes a distinction between the Christian message in its form and content and Greek wisdom and rhetoric, which fascinated the Christians at Corinth. Paul distanced himself from the Sophists and itinerant orators who were so popular in the ancient world. Paul wanted to make it clear that the power of his message did not come from philosophical rationalism nor from his ability to speak. He refused to use brilliant rhetoric as a vehicle to communicate the gospel, because he wanted the power of his words to come uniquely and exclusively from the Spirit of God.

Gordon Fee sums up Paul's concern in the following words: 'What [Paul] is rejecting is not preaching, nor even persuasive preaching; rather, it is the real danger in all preaching – self-reliance. The danger always lies in letting the form and content get in the way of what should be the single concern: the gospel proclaimed through human weakness but accompanied by the powerful work of the Spirit.' (*The First Epistle to the Corinthians*, pp. 96–97.)

Preaching today
Modern proclamation
The Protestant Reformation developed a systematic and detailed expository style as it cherished each word of Scripture. Modernity, with its Enlightenment focus on the power of reason, built on this to encourage a highly rational form of preaching. Preachers who have inherited this tradition have recovered the central importance of the word of God for the worship and life of the Christian community, and expounded and applied the Scriptures directly. Because of them today's Protestant liturgical celebrations cannot take place without a central place given to the preaching of the word.

However, the need to be an exegete and to have academic training became indispensable to be a preacher. The modern preacher was expected to be a good apologist and to know how to articulate the biblical message in a way which resonated with contemporary thinking. Moving the body and the expression of emotion as the message was delivered was not encouraged. A highly structured, systematic and intellectual approach led to long and complex sermons in which the prophetic element was all but buried.

The prophetic dimension, however, was recovered under the influence of the evangelical revivals of the eighteenth century which gave rise to the dynamic and powerful preaching of George Whitefield, Jonathan Edwards, John Wesley and many others. They announced the gospel in a way which convicted their hearers, even while it retained its roots in reasoned application of scriptural truth. They were not afraid of emotional appeal which aimed directly at the hearts of their hearers. Proclamation can never merely appeal to the mind, but must always appeal at the same time to the will.

Pentecostal proclamation
The appearance of Pentecostal preachers at the beginning of the twentieth century in the context of the great marginal areas of the urban cities of the Third World brought

with it a new form of communication. Their tremendous ability to construct images with words resonated with many within a culture of poverty, who considered mere eloquence more appropriate for audiences who could read. The spontaneity and informality of their communication came from their unshakeable confidence in the Spirit of God. The use of the body made it an instrument of their teaching, such that their words seem to come out of every pore of their skin and not just their lips.

The Pentecostal preacher does not read his sermon but specializes in direct communication during which his eyes never leave his audience, except perhaps to read a text from the Bible. The force with which the truths are proclaimed makes it almost unnecessary to explain them. Their innate ability to tell stories, and share living testimonies of the transforming power of God, allows them to deliver a very effective message. The best forms of Pentecostal preaching combine this passion and directness with words deeply rooted in Scripture which bring the text alive and help people to engage hearts, minds and wills with what God is saying.

Postmodern proclamation
When the gospel arrived in the media of mass communication, above all television, the post-modern preacher appeared. He had roots in Pentecostal preaching, which originally flour-ished amongst the poor and uneducated as a way of making the truth of the gospel directly relevant to their lives. The media preacher, however, while keeping the element of 'popularity', cleverly turns the gospel into something that also appeals to a wide audi-ence. He is very familiar with marketing strategies and knows how to 'sell' the gospel too. He is an expert at manipulating the cul-ture of the 'show' and the spectacle, which he uses deliberately to capture the attention of a wide range of viewers. He fits the profile of a postmodern man who listens with his eyes and thinks with his heart. He constructs a message which is not only to be heard, but above all to be seen and experienced. The use of up-to-date audio-visual technology and contemporary music is exploited to the full in order to attract people, above all a great number of young people.

Much experimental preaching is going on in churches today using visual, dramatic, poetic and video-generated means as ways of proclaiming truth to a visual culture. All these are valid so long as the truth of the gospel is faithfully communicated such that people 'hear' what God is saying and it engages their minds as well as their interest.

Proclamation and contextualization: God speaks today

The God who reveals himself in the Judeo-Christian Scriptures is a God who speaks, and this is attested from Genesis 1:3: 'and God said...', through to Hebrews 1:1: 'God, having spoken...'. The proclamation of the gospel therefore is God continuing to speak to the world through the church. This is prophetic in the sense that God speaks through Christian proclamation in a way that is relevant and authoritative and commands attention.

It is particularly important in the Latin American context to emphasize that when God speaks he does not do so in an abstract or unhistorical way. God speaks in the midst of concrete and specific realities, definite historical contexts. It is there that the phrase is born: 'God speaks today.' We find a NT example in Luke 3:1-2, where the writer specifies the political, social, economic and religious context in which God spoke through John the Baptist. It follows that if we want God to speak today we need to be familiar with today's context in which people live, and understand their reality, in order to enlighten them with a gospel which resonates with their real lives.

This means that we need to have an answer to liberation theology's question: what does it mean to proclaim the gospel as 'good news to the poor' in a context of misery and poverty, in a world marked by profound inequalities and injustices? Those who preach and pro-claim must relate the gospel to these realities and confront difficult questions: how should we announce Jesus Christ as Lord of life in the midst of a culture of death which reigns from legal abortion clinics to the hidden torture chambers of the intelligence services of modern states? How can we preach Jesus Christ as Lord of Creation in the midst of the perverse destruction of our environ-ment, driven by insatiable economic greed? How can we share the gospel of peace and reconciliation in the midst of national conflicts and international wars?

Proclamation and mission

We conclude that the proclamation of the gospel should not be equated directly either with evangelism or with mission. Both are broader in scope than verbal proclamation. The biblical message of salvation was transmitted by the religious leaders of Israel and the early church through a whole series of means, including the spoken word, prophetic symbolic actions, and the witness of a community faithful to God.

The church evangelizes both through what it does and says. The proclamation of the gospel shares with evangelism the objective of aligning people and communities with the purposes of God. But to 'proclaim' has a more limited sense than to evangelize.

Mission denotes the totality of the work with which the church is sent by God for the salvation of the world. So mission is much more than evangelism, just as to evangelize is much more that the verbal proclamation. So we conclude that the proclamation of the gospel should not be made equivalent either to evangelism or mission.

However, the clear and unambiguous verbal proclamation of the gospel is an essential dimension of mission. It is not an element or component that can be isolated or made independent of the rest, or treated as automatically present in other dimensions of mission. For this reason the announcement of the gospel can never be divorced from the practice of justice. In this way prophetic words combine with prophetic actions.

See also GOSPEL.

Bibliography

R. J. Allen, B. S. Blaisdell and S. B. Johnston, *Theology for Preaching: Authority, Truth and Knowledge of God in a Postmodern Ethos* (Nashville: Abingdon Press, 1997); W. Brueggemann, *Finally Comes the Poet: Daring Speech for Proclamation* (Philadelphia: Augsberg/Fortress, 1989); G. D. Fee, *The First Epistle to the Corinthians* (Grand Rapids: Eerdmans, 1987); G. Johnston, *Preaching to a Postmodern World* (Leicester: IVP, 2001); C. A. Loscalzo, *Apologetic Preaching: Proclaiming Christ to a Postmodern World* (Downers Grove: IVP, 2000); J. R. W. Stott, *I Believe in Preaching* (London: Hodder and Stoughton, 1982).

A. CHIANG

Prophecy

Prophecy is a function of Christian mission because it reinforces the *proclamation and truth of the gospel. It is one way through which *God declares his will, usually applying gospel truth to particular people in specific contexts. The OT prophets declared God's mind on particular matters to his people. The prophetic inspiration was usually described in terms of 'the hand of the Lord' falling upon the prophets (1 Kgs 18:46; 2 Kgs 3:15; Jer. 15:17; Ezek. 1:3); the Spirit of God 'resting' on the prophet (Num. 11:25–26); or 'clothing' the prophet (Judg. 6:34). The oldest Hebrew expression for inspired individuals who mediate divine communication was 'seer', one who was considered to have received privileged access to the mind of God. Thus the OT prophet was first and foremost a person of the Spirit with access to the 'counsel' of God, usually through revelations, dreams or visions (e.g. Isa. 6; Ezek. 1; 8 – 11; cf. 2 Pet. 1:21). On occasion a prophetic message would be communicated through physical symbolic acts to demonstrate the message.

OT prophets were therefore charismatic persons, inspired by the *Spirit, who proclaimed the word under compulsion from God. Jeremiah and Amos, for instance, speak clearly of the experience of divine compulsion under which they prophesied (Amos 3:8). In Jeremiah's case, he speaks of the word of God being in his heart 'like a fire, a fire shut up in my bones' and that cannot be held in (Jer. 20:9). The message of the later prophets often centred on public pronouncements on moral issues, and impending activities of God in salvation or judgment. Thus God mediated his dealings with his people through his prophets.

However, Jeremiah and other classical prophets, who were simply passing on God's word, need to be distinguished from the earlier ecstatic prophets who appeared during the time of Samuel (1 Sam. 10), and who operated through possession, worship and ritual, a form more vulnerable to abuse, as in the case of Saul. Worse still, those who prophesied out of selfish glory and ambitions were dismissed as 'false prophets' (Jer. 23).

Some have taken the OT prophetic ministry as paradigmatic for contemporary prophetic ministries. Others see the NT gift of prophecy as something different, and certainly not revelatory in the same way. Also NT prophecy needs to be corporately discerned, lest an individual claim authority for themselves which no one is allowed to challenge. However, in the context of Christian mission the essence of prophecy is that God still speaks today. He speaks through spontaneous declarations, sometimes during worship or prayer, but also through the preaching of his word. Prophecy is listed by St Paul as one of the gifts of the Spirit in 1 Corinthians 12:10, gifts given to the church to equip it for its mission. Paul takes a democratic view of the gift of prophecy. On the one hand, it is seen as a special gift given to some (Eph. 4:11), but all believers are also encouraged to desire the gift and to prophesy (1 Cor. 14:1, 5, 39; Moses also expressed the wish that all might have the ability to prophesy, Num. 11:24–30). In other words, if mission is the reason for the existence of the church and prophecy is a gift for mission, then the church is called to declare God's mind in ways that speak to existential situations today.

Paul identifies three main reasons why prophecy is important (1 Cor. 14:3): edification, exhortation and comfort. Most relevantly, prophecy could serve as a means of challenging unbelievers, who, when they witness the manifestation of this gift might recognize the presence of God, be convicted of sin, and end up joining the worshipping community (1 Cor. 14:24–25). To this end, there is a clear relationship between prophecy and mission, and indeed Jesus himself, the Lord of Christian mission, is presented in the gospels as a 'prophet' (Luke 7:16; 24:19; Matt. 21:11; John 4:19).

The element of prophecy as a means of communicating what God wants to say (and occasionally the prediction of future events) has been sustained. In many churches, prophecy is a cherished part of worship. It has acquired a central and even broader meaning in contemporary *Pentecostal movements to include 'spirit-filled' expository preaching that addresses specific conditions in the lives of people. African Pentecostal churches thus introduced the use of prophecy as a valid element in Christian ministry. In African traditions where people are given to seeking answers to their problems from traditional shrines, the incorporation of prophecy into the indigenous Pentecostalism has never been seen as an aberration. It is usual for individuals and communities to visit the traditional priest or priestess who through spirit possession reveals personal and communal destinies and prescribes remedies as directed by the gods. However, Christian prophecy must be distinguished from pagan ritualistic manifestations (which are more akin to the OT ecstatic prophets), since it is not 'worked up' in a frenzy of possession; the Spirit always respects the personality of the prophet, and the gift must be corporately discerned before it is accepted. But the prophetic ministry has proved very popular among ordinary Christians in Africa, who find in it an alternative to traditional divination.

The church in its mission in every context is called to continue the prophetic ministry of Jesus. In a world of great injustice, sin and moral relativism, the missionary situation confronting the church is no different from biblical times. Prophecy is an essential gift of the Spirit for mission, enabling the church to speak with conviction to the world. Some follow John Wimber in seeing prophecy as a means of 'power encounter' (see *Power evangelism). Unfortunately, of all the pneumatic aspects of the Christian faith, prophecy is often least associated with mission. Yet mission has to do with communicating or mediating God's presence relevantly to people, and prophecy, in its very broad sense, is an important way in which God still speaks to and through his people.

See also REVELATION, WORD.

Bibliography

D. Aune, *Prophecy in Early Christianity and the Ancient Mediterranean World* (Grand Rapids: Eerdmans, 1983); C. G. Bata, *Prophetism in Ghana: A Study of Some 'Spiritual' Churches* (London: SCM, 1962); J. Blenkinsopp, *A History of Prophecy in Israel: From the Settlement in the Land to the Hellenistic Period* (Philadelphia: Westminster, 1983); J. D. G. Dunn, *Jesus and the*

Spirit (Philadelphia: Westminster, 1975); M. Hengel, *The Charismatic Figure and His Followers* (New York: Crossroad, 1981); D. Hill, *New Testament Prophecy* (Atlanta: John Knox, 1979); I. M. Lewis, *Ecstatic Religion* (London: Routledge, 1989); J. Lindblom, *Prophecy in Ancient Israel* (Oxford: Basil Blackwell, 1962).

K. ASAMOAH-GYADU

Proselytism

Biblical perspective

The term originates from the Greek word used in the Septuagint to translate the Hebrew word *gēr* (foreigner), and describes those who were brought into the midst of the Israelite community from outside of it. The OT differentiates *nokrî*, one who may live in the midst of the Israelite community for a short period of time, from *gēr*, one who settles in the community. So *proselytos* was used in a sociological sense, bringing with it not only responsibilities, such as keeping the Sabbath, but also privileges and rights which were protected by the Israelite community (Exod. 23:9, 12).

To proselytize, therefore, was to bring representatives of other nations into the community of God, an effective way of fulfilling God's mission for Israel to be a light among the nations, though not the only way. According to Rabbinic texts, a proselyte was someone who had received baptism and brought sacrifices to the Temple; males also had to be circumcised. Only then was integration into the Israelite community possible, as in the case of a *proselytos* participating in a *pesaḥ* feast (Exod. 12:48). The temple played an important role in this witness to all nations from the time of Solomon to the NT (1 Kgs 8:41–43; the Herodian temple had a place for Gentiles). Intensive mission activities outside Palestine developed during the Greco-Roman period. Jesus speaks of these Pharisaic mission activities in Matthew 23:15. However, his denouncement was not directed against proselytizing activities as such, but against the aggressive manner in which the proselyte was initiated.

Having developed out of a Jewish context, the early church at first attracted Jewish converts, who still thought of Gentiles as outsiders needing to be proselytized. But as the church contextualized the gospel in the Gentile social and cultural milieu, it encouraged them to keep their cultural roots while at the same time belonging to the new community. They therefore became fully accepted members of the Christian church and so lost their status as 'proselytes'. The word soon lost its significance.

Historical perspective

The term 'proselytism' reappeared in the eighteenth century but now with a somewhat negative connotation. It referred to those who were persuaded to change their religious allegiance and to move from membership of one religious group to another. A more intensive discussion on proselytism was initiated during the second half of the twentieth century at the WCC, Vatican II and Lausanne conferences on mission when it became associated with aggressive evangelism. The agreement on 'Common Witness and Proselytism' between the WCC and the Roman Catholic Church came out of these discussions.

This particular document was also supported by evangelicals, as it defined proselytism as: (1) whenever our *motives* are unworthy (when our concern is for our glory rather than God's); (2) whenever our *methods* are unworthy (when we resort to any kind of 'physical coercion, moral constraint, or psychological pressure'); and (3) whenever our *message* is unworthy (whenever we deliberately misrepresent other people's beliefs).

The World Evangelical Alliance, together with the Lausanne movement, reinforced criticism of proselytism, describing it as an 'unworthy witness' and questioning the motives of those who call such practice evangelism or mission. Evangelism was seen not as 'fishing in the neighbour's pond' but as sharing the good news of the gospel with un-churched people, without exerting pressure and manipulating people, but rather respecting their right to make a free, individual decision of faith.

Contemporary perspective

Since the dramatic changes in Central and Eastern Europe the controversy on proselytism has entered a new phase. The Eastern Orthodox Church feels threatened by Protestant evangelicals and even more by the Roman Catholic Church. The presence of their missionaries in the so-called canonical Orthodox lands is threatening, and the sending of humanitarian aid is perceived as inducement to conversion and therefore interpreted as proselytism. Some of the activities in the name of evangelism were, in fact, unworthy witness, and true witnesses of Christ kept their distance from such practices. On the other hand, we need to differentiate between 'proselytism', when active members of another Christian tradition are manipulatively seduced into a different faith community, and legitimate 'evangelism', by which people are invited to a committed faith who may have very little link with a church as nominal believers, or who live within the canonical territory of a church but are clearly separated from any Christian tradition. Practising mission in a context in which one Christian tradition predominates requires *dialogue and mutual understanding in order to maintain peace and a faithful Christian witness.

Aggressive proselytism reflects a sectarian understanding of 'us' and 'them' between churches or denominations. It separates the body of Christ and works against the Holy Spirit. In particular it is Christian cults and sects that claim exclusivity of salvation and purity of doctrine who very often proselytize, since they see everyone else as 'outsiders'. True evangelism respects a person's right to refuse to accept Christ or change their religious allegiance, it engages sensitively with their own context, and it does not use manipulative techniques. All churches and Christian groups need to appreciate and affirm the wider context of variety in the body of Christ beyond their own boundaries. At the same time part of the mission of the Christian church is to protect those belonging to Christ from the aggressive proselytism of sectarian religion with its corrupted faith.

See also EVANGELISM, WITNESS.

Bibliography
I. Bria, 'Evangelism, Proselytism, and Religious Freedom in Romania: An Orthodox Point of View', *Journal of Ecumenical Studies* 36, 1999, pp. 163–183; *Common Witness and Proselytism*, a Study Document of the Joint Working Group between the Roman Catholic Church and the World Council of Churches, Information Service, 14, 1971; M. Elliott, 'Evangelism and Proselytism in Russia: Synonyms or Antonyms?' *International Bulletin of Missionary Research* 25, 2001, pp. 72–75; *International Bulletin of Missionary Research*, 20/1, 1996; V.-M. Kärkkäinen, 'Proselytism and Church Relations: Theological Issues Facing Older and Younger Churches', *Ecumenical Review* 52, 2000, pp. 379–390; J. Matthey and A. D. Falconer (eds.), 'Ecclesiology and Mission (I)', *International Review of Mission* 90, 2001, pp. 227–357; R. J. Schreiter, 'Changes in Roman Catholic Attitudes Toward Proselytism and Mission', in M. E. Marty and F. E. Greenspahn (eds.), *Pushing the Faith* (New York: Crossroad, 1988); M. Volf, 'Fishing in the Neighbor's Pond : Mission and Proselytism in Eastern Europe', *International Bulletin of Missionary Research* 20, 1996, pp. 26–31; P. Walters, 'Missions in Russian and Russian Orthodox Territories', *Religion, State & Society* 25, 1997, pp. 307–392; J. Witte, Jr and M. Bourdeaux, *Proselytism and Orthodoxy in Russia: The New War For Souls* (Maryknoll: Orbis Books, 1999); J. Witte, Jr and R. C. Martin, *Sharing the Book: Religious Perspectives on the Rights and Wrongs of Proselytism* (Maryknoll: Orbis Books, 1999); <http://www.worldevangelical.org/news_prosetylism_28oct03.html>.

P. PENNER

Prosperity theology

The prosperity gospel or, prosperity theology, is a theological current that states that if certain principles are followed, the expiatory work of Christ guarantees to all who believe, divine healing, the riches of this world, and happiness without suffering. This movement originated in the USA in the early twentieth century, and has developed greatly throughout the world, in spite of being considered heretical by a number of Christian churches.

Precursors

Prosperity theology is one of the expressions of the so-called 'Faith Movement', whose main exponents have been E. W. Kenyon (1867–1948), Kenneth Hagin (1917–2003), and Kenneth Copeland (1936–).

E. W. Kenyon was ordained a Methodist and later founded several churches linked to the Baptists. He maintained good relationships with the pioneers of the Pentecostal movement, even though he rejected some of their main doctrines. He came in touch with ideas related to the so-called 'New Thought' and Christian Science. According to the teachings of these movements, a positive thought and a positive verbal declaration could create health and wealth, while a negative attitude and declaration could lead to poverty and illness. Kenyon was fully convinced that his teachings would create a new human race, which would not be affected by demons, nor by illnesses or poverty.

Kenneth Hagin, who during his childhood and adolescence was severely ill, had several revelations and visions from which he extracted teachings for his ministry. Hagin said the principles that made faith operative were believing with all your heart, confessing with your mouth what you believe, and receiving what you have confessed. Hagin came into contact with Kenyon's writings and incorporated some of his teachings into his own.

Kenneth Copeland is the successor of Hagin in the leadership of the faith movement. His teachings are broadcast mainly through the TV programme *Believer's Voice of Victory*, which reaches over 500 stations around the world.

Prosperity theology has been supplemented and reinforced by the 'positive thought' current. At the roots of positive thought are the ideas of William James, the ideologue of American pragmatism. One of James's most important contributions was the need to believe to achieve results. Norman Vincent Peale Christianized and popularized James's ideas and quoted them often. In his book, *The Power of Positive Thinking*, quoting James, Peale said, 'Your belief will help create the fact' (p. 14). Positive thought would attract riches, success, health and happiness. Currently, the prosperity gospel is a worldwide phenomenon with similar manifestations in the most diverse of contexts.

Main doctrines

The prosperity gospel goes under several names: 'Wealth, health, and happiness gospel', 'name it and claim it gospel', 'success gospel', and 'positive confession theology'. It is based theologically on what its theologians call spiritual 'principles' or 'laws' that function inexorably, such as the laws ruling the universe. Just as God made the laws governing creation (e.g. the law of gravity), these laws function naturally, without implying a divine action each time they operate.

These principles or laws operate when we exercise faith. Copeland said, 'There are certain laws that govern prosperity revealed by God in His Word. Faith makes them function' (*The Laws of Prosperity*, p. 10). To understand what prosperity theology proposes we must understand the relationship between these two key elements: spiritual laws or principles, and faith.

The law of blessing. This law is based on God's covenant with Abraham. According to prosperity theologians, the main reason for the covenant God made with Abraham was to bless him materially. In this case, Christians, as spiritual sons of Abraham, are heirs of the blessings of the covenant. Copeland said that since the covenant has been established and prosperity is a provision of that covenant, we must be aware of the fact that prosperity belongs to us now. Christians must affirm that prosperity is God's will, because he wants us to prosper in all areas of life. The best homes, the best cars, the best clothes, are our inheritance. Possessions and riches are not so much a show of opulence as of a successful Christian life.

The law of sowing and reaping. According to the interpretation prosperity theology makes of Mark 10:29–30, we will receive from God a hundred times what we put in his hands. Whoever puts into practice this law would practically enter into a cycle of endless wealth. Osteen mentions the testimony of a young rich Saudi Arabian who was in the habit of calling the poorest people to learn of their needs and then providing for these needs. According to Osteen, this would be the reason this man maintains a flourishing business. Osteen concludes, 'I doubt this man is a Christian, but the principles of living are spiritual principles. They work regardless of nationality, skin color, or religion' (J. Osteen, *Your Best Life Now: 7 Steps to Living at Your Full Potential*, p. 229).

The law of faith. In 'faith movements', faith operates by itself, just as a natural law. This is what is called *faith in faith*. Kenyon and his followers translate the text of Mark 11:22 in a special way. Instead of the commonly accepted translation 'Have faith in God', they translate it as 'Have the faith of God'. Faith is the faith of God. That is, there would be a faith originating in God which is, for example, the faith that operated when God created everything out of nothing. This faith is activated, as happened in creation, when we name what we want to achieve. For example, God said, 'Let there be light' and there was light (Gen. 1:3). Just as God created the universe through his word, God's work today also is done when we activate his power through the word. The act of faith would be to dare to pronounce what we want, with the certainty that the things we name will become a reality. In faith movements, prayer is not a plea to God but a voice of command that calls things into existence.

The law of the proclaimed word. The formula is 'proclaim to have'. Hagin said, 'You can have what you say' (*Having Faith in Your Faith*). The text which is most used to back this idea is Mark 11:23–24. According to this interpretation, the force of faith is released by words. It is not sufficient to believe something in the heart, but for something to become real it is necessary to confess it. The development of this faith formula implies that when we confess something negative, this also becomes a reality. That is, we live according to what we say. Some say that there are people who cannot come out of poverty because they only talk about their debts: their negative words are actually creating debt.

The expiatory work of Christ. In faith movements, both divine healing and material prosperity have been provided by Christ in his redeeming work on the cross. In Christ's death God put our sins, illnesses, sorrows, pains and poverties onto Jesus. According to this, we have been redeemed from the curse of poverty and illness.

An appraisal of the prosperity gospel

As we have pointed out, the prosperity gospel is one of the emphases of twentieth-century faith movements. These movements have contributed significantly in keeping alive faith in the power of God in the context of rationalism and modernity. They have also contributed, from their view of faith, to mitigate much human suffering. We could say that with their focus on the supernatural and their emphasis on a life willing to enjoy material benefits they got ahead of post-modernity. Or, maybe, they contributed to prepare the religious matrix for it.

There are, however, biblical interpretations, theological developments, and ethical positions that raise serious objections to this movement. Passages such as Mark 10:30, 11:22 and 11:23–24 are key to the prosperity gospel, and interpreted by forcing their arguments on the translation. For example, the hundredfold reward promised by Jesus in Mark 10:30 is not a formula for personal enrichment but a show of God's love toward those who have left all for his cause. Even so, the same passage clarifies explicitly that these blessings will not preclude adversity. To be consistent with the literal hermeneutics of the passage, as stated by the prosperity gospel, together with promises of a hundred houses, we would have to mention a hundred times more tribulations! Regarding the translation of Mark 11:22 *'echete pistis theou'* as 'have the faith of God': (1) it does not respond to the interpretation of analogous passages (Ps. 2:34; 2 Thess. 2:13; Rom. 3:22, 26; Phil. 3:9); (2) there is no indication in the Bible that faith can be attributed to God, since those having or lacking faith are always human beings; and (3) this passage is an exhortation by Jesus to have faith and it makes no sense in this context to speak of a faith of God. Finally, in Mark 11:23–24 the emphasis is put on faith, and not in the audible expression of what we want to achieve. It is not the words that have power in themselves.

The theological argument that gives autonomy to the so-called spiritual laws or principles also lacks support from the word of God. Blessing always results from fulfilment or lack of fulfilment of covenants, God's sovereignty or, since Jesus, his pure grace.

In the prosperity gospel there is a foundational problem stemming from its origins and that runs through its theology and practice – everything is centred in the human being and his or her attitudes, not in God and his grace. According to this gospel, God meant to bless us, and through the expiatory work of Jesus Christ everything remains at our disposal. What we are capable of having will depend on our will, the words we say, the faith we have, or the spiritual laws we activate. In his last book, *Your Best Life Now*, Joel Osteen proposes seven steps for a full life. Some of them are: develop a healthy self-image, discover the power of words, and choose to be happy. This invitation to live a life of success and happiness rests on the personal decision each one must make for this to become reality. That is, if we want it to be, it will be.

But we must remember that it is not human beings who can manipulate the blessings of God, nor do these operate independently of his sovereignty. Regardless of how much faith we have or the conviction with which we pronounce our expectations, we must always be willing to listen, like Paul, to the answer of the sovereign God: 'My grace is sufficient for you' (2 Cor. 12:9).

Missiological implications

Either because of the good things it promises, the prosperity of those teaching it, or because it manages to revitalize faith in people, the prosperity gospel is today one of the theological currents having the greatest impact on evangelical churches and the preaching of the gospel worldwide.

Those opposing the prosperity gospel say that some of its teachings come from metaphysical cults, that their leaders get rich by exploiting the faith of people, or, as we have pointed out, it casts aside essential values of faith such as integrity, justice, or the value of suffering. We can affirm this is so in many cases, but to remain with the simplistic accusation of its weaknesses and errors does not help us understand a phenomenon as global and complex as this. Though born in the USA and containing elements of American culture (individualism, achievements through personal effort, the idea of success linked to economic prosperity), what happens in different countries is not a copy of this model. The teachings of the prosperity gospel act as a trigger from which each context develops its own features. Clearly, this 'gospel' is 'good news' for millions.

Of course, success and support from the masses is not a criterion for truth, nor is failure and isolation. We must recognize that the prosperity gospel appeals especially to social classes who have possibilities of advancement; that is, lower middle classes with expectations of progress and higher middle classes who wish to increase their resources. Impoverished lower classes tend to go to faith movements that emphasize divine healing or miracles. Higher classes prefer experiences with mystical emphases or of spiritual self-satisfaction. It is interesting to note the advance of the prosperity gospel in countries of South East Asia that are in economic expansion, the so-called 'Asian Tigers'. The same happens in Latin America, Africa, and Eastern Europe. All these contexts share in common the impact of the expansion of neo-liberal economic models, creating an illusion of global economic development.

The prosperity gospel has made a break with ideas of resignation common to all religions, both in their theologies as well as in their practices. Around the middle of the last century the Presbyterian theologian John Mackay noted how the suffering Christ brought by the Spaniards to Latin America marked Christianity in these lands. Catholic celebrations in Latin America are full of gestures of pain, suffering and flagellation. The same happens with religious images. Native peoples and slaves assimilated these elements and were able to identify their pain with that of Christ on the cross. But they were unable to overcome this stage, since they lacked the triumphant Christ of resurrection. Would this be one of the keys to understand why Latin American peoples massively abandon their Catholic faith and join churches whose theologies identify with faith movements? If so, Christian churches have today the task of recovering a sense of the cross which does not appear in the prosperity gospel, without falling into a gospel of resignation.

The *cross cannot be absent. The cross reminds us that in the 'not yet' of the kingdom, suffering, illness, pain, poverty and even martyrdom are present. These are enemies defeated and yet to be defeated. We cannot ignore the influence of the ideology of postmodernity, prevalent even in pre-modern societies, such as some in Latin America. This ideology attempts to trivialize suffering. But a gospel, such as that of prosperity, that promises a life which ignores these realities becomes a false gospel.

Jesus cared for the poor. How can we be supportive of the poor in our mission from a truly liberating perspective? The 'gospel' for the poor is not in itself how to be happy in the midst of poverty, but must tackle the question of how to overcome poverty. Poverty in itself is not a virtue; at least, poor people never live it as such. This has been a culpable vision of poverty from those who have more. Nor is it a curse, as the prosperity gospel teaches. In this theology, poverty as such has no structural, economic or political cause. It is a curse from which we have been freed by the sacrifice of Christ, and we only need to appropriate that truth and live according to it. The poor remain then trapped by this tension that the church has not always been able to solve – accept their condition as a virtue or add to the pain of poverty the guilt of not knowing how to break free from it.

The prosperity gospel proposes responses from faith to the human drama in a biblical language, with a contemporary image, consistent with the life philosophy of postmodernity. At the same time, it is a scandal when it focuses blessings on material things, showing Christ as Mammon, the god of riches, and his church in opulence, contrary to the values of humility, sacrifice and abnegation which characterize the kingdom of God.

See also FAITH, HEALING/HEALTH, POVERTY.

Bibliography
J. E. Barnhart, 'Prosperity Gospel: A New Folk Theology', in R. Abelman and S. M. Hoover (eds.), Religious Television (Norwood: Ablex Publishing Corporation, 1990); B. Barron, The Health and Wealth Gospel (Downers Grove: InterVarsity Press, 1987); C. Capps, How to Have Faith in Your Faith (Tulsa: Harrison House, 1986); K. Copeland, The Laws of Prosperity (Fort Worth: K. Copeland Publications, 1974); G. Fee, The Disease of the Health and Wealth Gospels (Costa Mesa: The Word for Today, 1979); K. Hagin, Having Faith in Your Faith (Tulsa: Faith Library, 1980); S. Hunt, 'Winning Ways: Globalization and the Impact of the Health and Wealth Gospel', Journal of Contemporary Religion 15, 2000; D. W. Jones, 'The Bankruptcy of the Prosperity Gospel: An Exercise in Biblical and Theological Ethics', Faith and Mission 16, 1998, pp. 79–87; E. W. Kenyon, The Blood Covenant (Seattle: Kenyon's Gospel Publishing Society, 1969); D. R. McConnell, A Different Gospel (Peabody: Hendrickson Publisher, updated edn 1995); J. Osteen, Your Best Life Now: 7 Steps to Living at Your Full Potential (New York: Warner Faith, 2004); N. V. Peale, The Power of Positive Thinking (New York: Prentice Hall, 1952); A. Perriman (ed.), Faith, Health and Prosperity (London: Paternoster Press, 2003).

J. N. SARACCO

Racism

Race and racism

Racism originates in the modern social construct of race. This construct classifies people according to certain racial characteristics such as skin colour or group identity. Racism is then the prejudicial use of the race construct using attitudes, words or actions which denigrate others on the basis of a generalization about their race (e.g. 'white people are imperialists; black people are lazy; Indians are ignorant', etc.). Race crosses ethnic, class or national differences, with the result that racism is often confused with other social constructs such as ethnocentrism, classism, or nationalism. Many sociologists today largely understand racism through social, as distinct from biological, definitions. Racism remains the most powerful product of the race construct, for it goes to the heart of human identity and relationships.

Theologically, racism corrupts God's deliberate creation of phenotypical diversity, which allows for the affirmation of difference and individual identity. God intends us to rejoice in our God-given identity, which includes our skin colour, and he wants us to be affirmed in who we are. However, the modern construct of race was birthed from human sinfulness. Sin distorts God's truth (Gen. 3:1–7), and so racism distorts human identity, marring human relationships and leading to human separation (Eph. 4:25). God intended humans to live in unity with himself and with others (Gen. 2:18; Eph. 2:14). But the modern construct of race was shaped to categorize and separate people; as the construct evolved this purpose did not change, so that today race constructs continue to divide humanity. Race as it is constructed assumes a corporate identity God did not intend and therefore works against his mission purposes as the antithesis of his missional call.

Characteristics of racism

Racism exists at three primary integrative levels.

Racism is institutional

We have affirmed that diversity is depicted in all God's creation, and racial diversity among humans in itself is an expression of this creative nature of God. However, history is full of examples of the ways in which human sin has institutionalized a racial corruption of God's good creation. For example, during the sixteenth century Western Enlightenment era, philosophical, theological and scientific theories converged to create the myth of white superiority over members of other races. These assumptions misused God's original intention for racial diversity since they classified and ranked humans according to their race. With modernity in full swing, race served as a basis for how institutional power and privilege was set up in favour of white supremacy. The Western missionary movement of the era was not necessarily exempt from this history and often served to reinforce the myth of race as a viable indicator of human assessment for leadership roles within institutions.

Though sometimes overt, today's institutional racism often works beneath the surface through unconscious attitudes. It can be found in the prejudicial nature of institutions where any race retains control over policy and programme. Police, employers, and even the church have all been accused of institutional racism. Systems and structures are created and maintained around values, assumptions and allegiances of the racial group with institutional power. As institutions evolve and replicate, institutional racism continues to empower and give privilege to members of that group. Though all forms of racism impair the missional mandate of God, the clandestine nature of institutional racism can be the most damaging, for it silently mutates the human infrastructure of community which serves as the human tool for interpreting God's kingdom on earth.

Racism is communal

Communal racism presents itself when group membership and group identity become the racial criteria for assumed rights of inclusivity or exclusivity, attitudes which stand in opposition to God's intention for community (Col. 3:10–11). Such determination is often made with little or restrictive interpersonal relationship between individuals, and it is maintained by assuming that a person's race determines their communal status. A person can therefore be excluded from a group on the basis of their racial identity. For example, in some churches people have been made to feel unwelcome, or even turned away, because they do not fit the criteria of racial identity which the community has constructed for itself.

When an assumed commonality – whether intentional or not – is race, communal racism has overridden God's intention for a missional community, for it rests on presumed relationships. Similar communities, though not specific to race, existed during biblical times and were at the heart of Paul's concern. He constructed reconciling bridges between Jewish and Gentile communities (1 Cor. 9:19–23). Ultimately, God's people are called to live as integrated missional communities that challenge the ways in which communal racism is sustained.

Racism is personal

At this level, racism is expressed through self-assumptions of racial superiority or racial inferiority regarding self and others. The use of personal racism denies the biblical truth that all humans are equally created in the image of God – an image beyond race (Gen. 1:26–27). It also denies the truth that God's people in the Bible are representative of inter-racial/inter-ethnic unity (Gen. 38:2, 6; 41:45; Exod. 2:16–21; Num. 12:1–2; Josh. 2:11–12; 2 Sam. 15:19–21; Jer. 38:7–13; Acts 10; Luke 13:29; Rev. 5:9). Personal racism is most insidious when racial assumptions are formed in the absence of relationships. Mission as discipleship will teach Christians to recognize their own tendencies to racial prejudice and to confront them in the power of the Spirit.

Racism, mission and the church

With an eye toward racism, mission can be defined as the proclamation of God's good news toward the recovery of human relationships marred by race (Matt. 5:24; 2 Cor. 5:18). Repentance and conversion with regard to race is returning to God's original intention for human relationship leading towards a new identity in Christ that transcends racial difference and neutralizes its power to separate. Followers of Christ are called to redefine identities and relationships in line with Christ and the missional agenda of Christ's kingdom. This does not deny racial identity, but it does relativize it in the light of Christ. The claiming of this new identity is a movement toward recognizing human identity through Christ, not only for oneself but also for others (2 Cor. 5:15).

A common thread holding these many voices together is therefore that of *identity*; race contributes to identity. Race-based identities are used to name social status for self and others, thereby fuelling disparity between racial groups. Though race-based identity can provide the means to confront and thereby deconstruct institutional racism, race is unable to provide a constructive identity to the individual, who is unique. Human uniqueness, however, can be found in personal stories each person carries, which can both stand alone and be fully integrated with the larger narrative. Aspects of one's story can be inherited, freshly created, or co-opted into a larger story. Such stories can exist at the personal level, family level, communal level and the institutional level. Regardless of the level, how each person approaches a particular story is unique on the one hand yet exists in concert with other stories. Each story is entangled with multiple stories and thereby coexists in a larger narrative. Mission therefore includes the recovery of individual and corporate stories. Evangelism should build relationships of trust through which people can be encouraged to connect their story with the story of the gospel, and then with the stories of others. Race can work against this by denying a person her or his unique story, and presupposes that one can know the other without knowing his or her story. Race can hide one's true self and seeks to create an identity for each without the vulnerability of entering into a relationship.

Conclusions

The race construct is today's virus and racism is its symptom. Just as a human body can become infected with a virus, God's body, the church, can be infected with the virus of the race construct. The symptom of this virus is witnessed through race-based relationships, which serve to divide the church. Relationships based on racial indicators do not have the capacity to unite God's creation. Racism is the symptom, and any social project seeking to dismantle racism must address the misconstrued concept of race. The cure for racism rests in the eradication of the virus – the eradication of the construct of race itself.

There is no magic pill to eradicate the virus. The journey toward racial healing is long and hard, full of missteps, brokenness, repentance and forgiveness. Yet a key to eradicating the race construct virus is to infuse it with a new Christ-centred identity through wholistic relationships – relationships based on story sharing. Stories shed light on both people's uniqueness and commonalities. Stories provide the basis for relationships out of which programmes and projects can flow. Stories allow each person to claim her or his place in God's missional narrative. As God's missional agents, Christians are called to seek Christ-centred identity and relationships, which lead to holy unity. Such unity is the hope the church has to offer a broken world seeking racial healing.

See also ETHNICITY/ETHNOCENTRISM, HUMAN/HUMANITY.

Bibliography
M. Battle, *Reconciliation: The Ubuntu Theology of Desmond Tutu* (Cleveland, OH: Pilgrim Press, 1997); G. Bhattacharyya, J. Gabriel and S. Small, *Race and Power: Global Racism in the Twenty-First Century* (London, New York: Routledge, 2002); A. Montagu, *Man's Most Dangerous Myth: The Fallacy of Race* (Walnut Creek, CA: AltaMira Press, 1997); J. Solomos and L. Back, *Theories of Race and Racism: A Reader* (London: Routledge, 2000).

J. MANICKAM

Reconciliation

Reconciliation is a word that is needed in our world today, which is hurting from many rifts and estrangements, ranging from domestic violence and inner-city strife, to ethnic tensions leading to civil wars, terrorist activities and protracted conflicts between nations such as the war between the US and Iraq. Thus reconciliation, which springs largely from a religious context, has gained political attention. Interestingly, this NT word came out of a secular usage, namely 'making peace after a time of war'. It is a word that goes to the heart of interpersonal conflicts, seeking to unmask the causes as well as provide radical solutions to the problem of broken relationships.

Paul is the principal resource for the concept of reconciliation. Some form of 'katallassein' or 'katallagē' occurs thirteen times in his writings. This is derived from the word allasō, which means 'exchange, alter or change'. Paul uses the word in three ways: first the restoration of relationships between human beings and God (Rom. 5:11; 2 Cor. 5:18–19); second, reconciliation between two estranged groups, the Jews and the Gentiles (Eph. 2:11–20); and third, cosmic restoration (Col. 1:15–22) or the eschatological consummation when *God will reconcile all things through Christ. The primary agent of reconciliation is the *Triune God. The Father conceives the plan, the Son executes it through his death and resurrection and the Holy Spirit convicts the world of the need for it and effects this through the church, called to be the minister of reconciliation (2 Cor. 5:18–20).

The word reconciliation is not used at all in the Hebrew Scriptures, though it is implied in the concept of atonement. However, the whole biblical narrative depicts the mission of a reconciling God reaching out to estranged humanity. The story of creation shows that God created human beings at peace with God, with one another and with the environment. But the fall (see *Sin/the fall) brought estrangement at all three levels; human beings were removed from the presence of God, and there was a rift between the first two human beings. This was immediately followed by the first homicide (Gen. 4:1–12). The ground was also cursed and human beings had to bring forth food through hard labour and sweat.

That God initiates reconciliation is evident throughout the whole OT. The call and mission of Abraham and the people of Israel is to demonstrate to the world what it means to live in a restored relationship with God, with one another and with creation. The elaborate sacrificial system not only regulated relations with God but also just relations with neighbours, particularly the poor, the stranger, the widow and the orphan (Lev. 18–

19), and the land was also supposed to enjoy Sabbath rest (Lev. 25–26).

However, 'God was reconciling the world to himself in Christ' (2 Cor. 5:19). The enmity of the world was removed through the exchange of Christ's sacrifice (Col. 1:21). The centrality of Christ's death on the *cross as the agent of reconciliation cannot be overemphasized. Violence robs us of our humanity. It is only the violence of the cross that completely deals the blow to the violence of estrangement in order to restore human beings, first into relationship with God and then into relationship with others.

Though the death of Jesus was the climax of the reconciliation process, he demonstrated through his life and teachings that he had come to confront the powers and structures that were keeping people estranged from God and from one another. By cleansing the temple he clashed head on with the Jewish political and religious authorities (Matt. 21:12–17), as he revealed the corruption of a system that had alienated the outsiders and the poor. The temple had become a means for exploitation rather than an avenue for bringing people to God. His radically inclusive table fellowship confounded the elaborate ritual system that excluded sinners, the outcasts and the women. He ate and interacted with 'the least of these', showing that he was the reconciler par excellence. In the parables of the lost coin, the lost sheep and the lost son (Luke 15) he shows a God who relentlessly pursues the estranged ones till he brings them back to the fold.

The life of the early church demonstrates that restoration of human relationships is a fundamental mission of the church. During Pentecost, language, which had been a barrier, was transformed by the Holy Spirit so that everyone could hear others praising God in their own language (Acts 2:11). Economic barriers were broken down as people sold their possessions and shared equally (Acts 2:42–47; 4:32–37). Ethnic divisions were dealt with when the gospel was preached to the Gentiles and the early Christians confronted their prejudices, as demonstrated by the story of Cornelius (Acts 10). Paul is the apostle to the Gentiles par excellence who challenged racial, economic and gender differences (Gal. 3:28). These early Christians anticipated the vision of the book of Revelation of a community from 'every tribe and language and people and nation' (Rev. 5:9–11) before the throne of the Lamb praising God.

However, history shows that the church has at times faltered and many times failed in its mission of reconciliation. Outwardly it has sometimes sided with the powers of oppression to exploit people instead of being the agent of good news of reconciliation. Inwardly, it has been torn by schisms and distressed by heresies. During *colonial times in Africa we note that 'the flag followed the cross', implying that the relationship of some missionaries to Africans prepared the latter for subjugation by the colonial powers; many times the missionaries sided with the colonial masters. One popular African saying is '*Gutiri ngurani ya Mubia na Muthungu*', meaning 'there is no difference between the colonial administrator and the missionary'. However, the biblical message of a reconciling God got through, and Bible translation became a powerful tool of transformation as many oppressed people all over the world took inspiration from the Bible. They not only overthrew the colonial masters but were liberated from sin and alienation from God and were reconciled with their brothers and sisters. An example is the East Africa Revival group who risked their lives in protecting the 'brother and sister' from another tribe during the fight for independence in Kenya.

In view of this we ask: what role does the church have as a minister of reconciliation in situations where it has been silent, or, worse still, where it has been part of the oppressive system? Does it have a credible voice to speak on behalf of those who have been oppressed? Robert Schreiter says that the church has 'an abstract right to the ministry of reconciliation', by virtue of its connection with the Master, but 'historically' it might forfeit that right in circumstances where it has been part of the problem (R. J. Schreiter, *Reconciliation: Mission and Ministry in a Changing Social Order*, p. 64). In such a situation the mission of the church is to regain some of its legitimacy through repentance, by seeking reconciliation within itself and reconciliation with victims in the society which it did not heed. Though it is rare to see this happen it carries a powerful message. Examples of this are the apologies of the United Church of Canada to the Native peoples of Canada in 1988, and the Southern Baptist Church's acceptance of their participation in slavery in the US.

Furthermore, in order to avoid bringing more hurt, the church needs to understand what reconciliation is *not*. It is not a hasty peace of letting bygones be bygones, nor is it an avoidance of the consequences of past crimes, or a human conflict management strategy. First and foremost, it is a process that begins with those who have been hurt. The Bible shows God as the subject of reconciliation, which implies it is only those who have been hurt that can extend reconciliation. 'Reconciliation and forgiveness must come from the side of those who have suffered violence' (Schreiter, *Reconciliation*, p. 20). This process is not easy. It can only come through the power of God's grace bringing healing in the lives of those who have been hurt, empowering them to extend forgiveness to the perpetrators.

In the South African Truth and Reconciliation Commission, Archbishop Tutu recounts the moving episodes of those who after hearing gruesome stories were able to forgive: 'You encounter people who having suffered grievously should by right have been riddled with bitterness and a lust for revenge and retribution. But they are different' (R. Helmick and R. Petersen, *Forgiveness and Reconciliation*, p. xi). Another example is the late Ugandan Anglican Bishop Festo Kivengere, who having gone through much suffering wrote a book entitled *I love Idi Amin*.

In conclusion, the mission of the church as the 'minister of reconciliation' in a world that is riddled with violence on every side is to recover its biblical identity and calling to be a counter-cultural community transcending ethnic, gender, racial and economic barriers.

Bibliography

J. W. De Gruchy, *Reconciliation: Restoring Justice* (Minneapolis: Fortress Press, 2002); C. P. DeYoung, *Reconciliation: Our Greatest Challenge: Our Only Hope* (Valley Forge: Judson Press, 1997); C. E. Gunton, *The Theology of Reconciliation* (London: T. & T. Clark, 2003); R. Helmick and R. Petersen (eds.), *Forgiveness and Reconciliation* (Philadelphia: Templeton, 2001); S. G. Hines and C. P. DeYoung, *Beyond the Rhetoric:*

Reconciliation as a Way of Life (Valley Forge: Judson Press, 2000); R. J. Schreiter, *Reconciliation: Mission and Ministry in a Changing Social Order* (Maryknoll: Orbis Books, 2002); M. Volf, *Exclusion and Embrace: A Theological Exploration of Identity, Otherness and Reconciliation* (Nashville: Abingdon, 1996); W. Wink, *When the Powers Fall: Reconciliation in the Healing of the Nations* (Minneapolis, Fortress Press, 1998).

E. CHOGE

REDEMPTION, see SALVATION
REFORMATION, see REVIVAL/RENEWAL

Refugees

The definition of the word 'refugee' has been the subject of much discussion. The UN definition, arising out of the Second World War experience, reads:

> Any person who, owing to a well-founded fear of being persecuted for reasons of race, religion, nationality, membership of a particular social group or political opinion, is outside the country of his nationality and is unable or, owing to such fear, unwilling to avail himself of the protection of that country, or who, not having a nationality, is outside the country of his former habitual residence, is unable or, owing to such fear, is unwilling to return to it.

This definition is seen by many as narrow, because it excludes those who are internally displaced and also those who move from their countries due to natural catastrophes or economic crisis. Christian organizations have tended to define the term to include many categories of displaced people, both internal and external. Interestingly, the United Nations High Commission for Refugees (UNHCR) extended its protection and concern in 2006 to include not only refugees but also asylum seekers, internally displaced persons and others. A 2006 report estimated 33 million refugees and internally displaced people in the world today. Faced with this kind of crisis one needs to ask: what is the role of the church's mission towards such people?

Over the years, Africa has hosted the greatest number of refugees and internally displaced persons. Kenya, for example has hosted refugees from the 1970s, but the numbers increased to over 500,000 in the 1990s due to the influx of peoples from Somalia, Ethiopia, Sudan, Rwanda, Burundi, Democratic Republic of Congo and Uganda. In 1992 there were about ten refugee camps but these camps were consolidated to two, namely Dadaab and Kakuma.

The response to this problem by individual churches and Christians has not been encouraging. I suggest two reasons for this. First, it has been perceived that the responsibility lies in the hands of huge organizations led by UNHCR, who work closely with other UN bodies such as the World Food Program (WFP), and also Christian organizations such as Lutheran World Federation (LWF), Jesuit Refugee Services (JRS), World Vision, All Africa Conference of Churches (AACC), and the National Christian Council of Kenya (NCCK). Individual Christians and local churches have thought that this was not their work, and have thus neglected it. Secondly, I suggest that Christians in Kenya, indeed all Christians, do not understand their own true identity as refugees and pilgrims, otherwise they would be ready to respond to refugees more positively.

Life for refugees in the camps is very dismal. They depend on handouts from these huge organizations. They suffer every kind of alienation and deprivation, including loss of homeland, loved ones and sometimes even life. They are vulnerable people and this is the reason behind God's concern and clear biblical instructions on how we should treat strangers and refugees. The people of Israel who lived as aliens in the land of Egypt and later in Babylon enshrined within their constitution and mission the care of refugees (Lev. 19:33–34). Throughout the OT people are repeatedly commanded by God to care for those who are strangers; they were to be treated with respect, dignity and equality, like fellow citizens or blood brothers or sisters. Provision was made for those who had been forced from their homes due to war, famine and economic hardships (Lev. 25; Isa. 16:1–4; Ezek. 47:21–23).

The presence of refugees in our communities is a great opportunity for Christians to practise their first prime duty of *hospitality as mission*. When they meet the needs of the refugees for security, food, shelter, clothes, they are fulfilling the mission of Christ. It is clear in the parable of the sheep and the goats that those who are received into the kingdom are those to whom Jesus says, 'I was a stranger and you invited me in' (Matt. 25:35). Christians are also enjoined to live as 'foreigners and exiles'(1 Pet. 1:17; 2:11). The life of a refugee thus provides Christians all over the world with a living paradigm of what it means to live as aliens, exiles and pilgrims in this world. The heroes and heroines of faith are described in the book of Hebrews as 'foreigners and strangers' (Heb. 11:13).

Jesus was a pilgrim par excellence. He was a refugee in Africa when his parents had to flee Herod's sword in his childhood (Matt. 2:13). In his mission on earth he described himself as one who did not have a place to lay his head (Luke 9:58), and yet he made the greatest impact on earth. Following Jesus, the refugees and Kenyan Christians at Kakuma Refugee Camp, in a cooperative effort, have taken their situation seriously as a great opportunity for mission. Through the vision of one refugee pastor, the Kakuma Interdenominational School of Mission (KISOM) was founded in 2001. The presence of over 80,000 refugees in one camp from eight countries in Africa was a good catalyst to propel Christians to evangelize and disciple these people, so that they could be a witness for Jesus Christ wherever they went.

In a world that is wrecked by many conflicts causing displacements both internally and externally, the response by many governments has been the tightening of immigration rules and the closing of borders, the building of walls, as well as increased cases of xenophobia. It is the responsibility of Christians to know that mission includes guiding their governments to institute humane policies with regard to influx of populations and asylum seekers. They should join hands with organizations that offer help to immigrants in their countries and not leave it to huge impersonal organizations to do the work. An example is the Refugee Highway Network, a cooperative effort of Christians in Europe (www. refugee-highway.net). At the same time Christians in the West should advise their governments, who have sometimes been the source of the

wars that have caused displacements, to discourage the proliferation of firearms in the world and to promote *human rights, while working for peaceful solutions in conflict situations.

In places that have huge refugee populations in camps, attempts should be made to give these people lasting solutions by integrating them with the local population, so that they are not left to perpetually depend on handouts. Refugees have many gifts to bring and they need the opportunity to know they are making a contribution to life. Among the refugees at Kakuma camp in Kenya there were those who were pastors reaching out as missionaries to the host community, the Turkana. Refugee and immigrant Christians in Europe and America are revitalizing and bringing life to churches that were dying. Above all, when all Christians embrace their identity as refugees and pilgrims they will care for fellow pilgrims along the way and 'pray and seek the welfare of the city' (cf. Jer. 29:7) they are in, while en route to their eternal homeland.

See also MIGRATION.

Bibliography
E. J. Choge, *An Ethic for Refugees: The Pilgrim Motif in Hebrews and the Refugee Problem in Kenya*, PhD thesis (Pasadena: Fuller Theological Seminary, 2004); E. J. Choge, 'The Role of Religious Organizations in Promoting Peace Education Among Refugees and their Neighbours: A Case Study of Kakuma Refugee Camp', *Maarifa: A Journal of Humanities and Social Sciences* 1, 2005, pp. 42–49; E. G. Ferris, *Beyond Borders: Refugees, Migrants and Human Rights in the Post-Cold War Era* (Geneva: WCC Publications, 1993); M. N. Getui and P. Kayandogo (eds.), *From Violence to Peace: A Challenge for African Christianity* (Nairobi: Acton Publishers, 1999); P. Kayandogo, 'Who is My Neighbour? A Christian Response to the Refugees and the Displaced in Africa', in J. N. K. Mugambi and A. Nasimiyu Wasike (eds.), *Moral and Ethical Issues of African Christianity: Exploratory Essays in Moral Theology* (Nairobi: Initiatives Publishers, 1992); C. Musekura, 'Refugees', in T. Adeyemo (ed.), *The African Bible Commentary* (Nairobi: Word Alive

Publishers, 2006); C. D. Pohl and B. Donley *Responding to Refugees: Christian Reflections on Global Crisis*, World Relief and Crossroads Monograph Series on Faith and Public Policy, No. 28 (2000); US Committee for Refugees and Immigrants, *World Refugee Survey* 2006, <http://www.refugees.org/article.aspx?id=1565&subm=19&ssm=29&area=Investigate>; <http://www.refugeehighway.net>.

E. J. CHOGE

Reincarnation

Reincarnation, or rebirth, is the belief that after physical death the soul of a person is reborn into another existence with a different human or animal body, as a spirit, ghost or deity.

Faith in an afterlife is found in tribal animism, Hinduism and Buddhism, as well as in Greek and Egyptian religions. Neoplatonism was the first philosophical system which had a concept of reincarnation similar to Hinduism, in which a being with one body transmigrates into another according to the demands of the inexorable law of karma (destiny or fate). What is reincarnated in Hinduism is the impersonal self or *atman*. Karma is a basic pillar of this doctrine and motivates people to gain merit through good works in the hope of a better future life.

In Buddhism rebirth is also believed to occur according to one's karma (e.g. that a person who has killed an animal may be reborn as such an animal and suffer the same fate). The human realm is regarded as the most precious to be reborn into, since it includes the possibility of freeing oneself from the cycle of reincarnation, which is seen as the cause of all suffering. From Hinduism this concept entered various schools of Buddhism and Chinese Taoism, and into the Western world.

In *Theravada Buddhism* rebirth is believed to occur on several planes, from existences as gods to existences in hells. Any individual may have wandered over many ages from rebirth to rebirth. To claim that one will enter Nirvana after this life may sound like blasphemy, since only Buddha is thought to have gained Nirvana. However, in *Mahayana Buddhism* any dedicated person may be able to reach Nirvana after death.

Reincarnation in *Tibetan* or *Tantric Buddhism* has the distinguishing feature that the soul of a leading monk or Dalai Lama never vanishes but returns after death into a newly born male child. Tantric practitioners may replace the high moral standards of Mahayana Buddhism through radical amoral behaviour, hoping that by reversing the classical Buddhist values into the opposite, they may gain enlightenment within this life.

In recent years there has been an increasing interest worldwide in the concept of rebirth, with the hope of entering into a better life after death. In the West this is all part of the search for alternative spiritualities, and many look to Buddhism and Hinduism as sources of inspiration. However, most Westerners, having rejected the concept of hell, cannot entertain the possibility of being born into many hells. Nevertheless, the idea of rebirth to something better becomes attractive.

A missiological engagement with reincarnation must begin with the biblical truth that *human beings are individually and uniquely created in the image of God, distinguishing them clearly from all other created beings, and giving to each person their own distinctive features (Gen. 1:24–27). This unique individual human identity is permanent and non-transferable, so it is not possible to be reborn as anything else or anyone else. This highlights the importance of beginning gospel preaching from the doctrine of *creation.

It is true that God gives each person responsibility for their life and future, making them accountable for their actions. Destiny is not just fate or determinism. Good deeds have good consequences, although not as a way of earning salvation. God commended the Roman centurion Cornelius for his devotion and generosity, but it was still necessary for him to turn to Christ and receive the Holy Spirit to enjoy fullness of life (Acts 10). From a Christian perspective, consequences for our actions, good or bad, are experienced in this life as well as the next.

Jesus taught the need for a spiritual new birth during one's lifetime (John 3), which would lead into the experience of 'eternal life', which is a natural extension and intensification of the new life of Christ into *resurrection (e.g. John 6:54). Never once in the teaching of Jesus is there any hint of a rebirth of souls into other bodies or beings after death. The vague hope of reincarnation into a better existence in some distant future is replaced by a new, unique and permanent relationship with God through Jesus Christ. The comprehensive power of *salvation through Jesus Christ in this time and age gives all believers the certain hope of eternal glory, which is very different from the uncertainties of reincarnation (1 Pet. 1:3–5). On the other hand the gospel also makes it clear that God has appointed for each person a unique time to die, and after that comes their *judgment and eternal destiny (Heb. 9:27). This gospel also gives the assurance of a life in communion with others who have trusted God and are in glory already.

However, a presentation of the gospel that focuses on the forgiveness of past sins and an endless afterlife alone does not catch the interest and imagination of those who believe deeply in reincarnation. They need to see the full implications of the death, resurrection and ascension of Christ, and the possibilities of the power of the Spirit of Christ in us, all of which gives the promise of the authentic life of the new creation. Paul spoke of dramatic and lasting change experienced in the life of the early Christians (2 Cor. 5:17). Such changed lives have a powerful and authentic testimony to present-day people who believe in reincarnation.

See also NEW AGE, NEW RELIGIOUS MOVEMENTS.

Bibliography
M. E. Spiro, *Buddhism and Society* (New York: Harper Paperbacks 1970); V. and V. Trimondi, *Im Schatten des Dalai Lama* (Düsseldorf: Patmos Verlag, 1999), *In the Shadow of the Dalai Lama*, trans. M. Penny, <http://www.iivs.de/~iivso1311/SDLE/Index.htm>; E. Valea, *Reincarnation, Its meaning and consequences*, <http://www.comparativereligion.com/reincarnation.html>.

H. JANSEN

RELATIONALITY, RELATIONSHIPS, see COMMUNITY

Religious pluralism

The plurality of religions and *cultures has always been an integral feature of the human race. However, the twin forces of modernization and *globalization have helped give rise to a phenomenon that is distinctively modern, both in terms of the cultural diversity experienced by societies today, and the contemporary response to this reality within the global cultural environment. Globalization has resulted in unprecedented proximity to one another of people of different religions and cultures. The cultural 'other' has thus become less alien and unfamiliar, resulting in increased acceptance of difference. The growing irenic attitude to cultural diversity and *postmodern scepticism towards absolute truth-claims have been the main impulses for the rise of the modern phenomenon of pluralism.

The term 'pluralism' generally describes the perspective that all religions, more or less, offer equally valid ways of leading people to God. In its descriptive sense it denotes the socio-cultural reality of religious diversity, more properly designated 'plurality'. Its normative use implies the acceptance of an egalitarian and democratized view of religions that affirms a rough parity among them concerning truth and salvation. Pluralism in this sense is a distinctive way of thinking about religious plurality that celebrates diversity of religious experience and expression as good and healthy. It maintains that no one tradition can be normative for all, and is sceptical of claims that any particular religious tradition has special access to truth about God.

It is in this ideological sense that pluralism raises crucial questions concerning the nature and purpose of Christian mission. The Christian gospel has elements of both *universality and particularity at its core. On one hand it maintains that all humans are sinners in need of redemption by God's grace, and that God desires the salvation of all irrespective of ethnicity, culture or religion. On the other hand it affirms that God's salvation comes to us through a particular person, Jesus Christ, the absolutely unique incarnation of God, who took upon himself the sins of the world, and sinful human beings are restored to a proper relationship with their Creator based on their *faith response to the truth revealed in Jesus *Christ.

This understanding of the *gospel is regarded by pluralists as intellectually untenable and morally repugnant in today's world.

In recent decades, a significant number of Christian theologians have rejected the idea that what God has revealed in Jesus Christ of his nature and purpose is universally normative. For them, God alone is absolute and all religions are relative. Christians must recognize as real God's self-disclosure in the lives of neighbours of other faiths and in the secular struggles of mankind. Hence, while the Christian faith is 'true' and legitimate for Christians, other religions can be equally 'true' and legitimate for others. The widespread influence of this view upon popular culture today may be observed among the entertainment and media elite, and in many centres of university education.

While the issues raised by religious pluralism impinge upon almost every major area of theology, we focus our concern on three critical questions which seem to strike at the heart of Christian faith and mission.

The first point at which the pluralist view challenges historic Christianity is its claim to have privileged access to divine revelation. Evangelical Christians regard the sixty-six books of the Bible as divinely revealed and possessing exclusive divine authority. Pluralists question this claim, insisting that the presence of divine revelation in other religions requires that the sacred scriptures of other religions also be considered the word of God. There are several passages in the Bible that point to a general revelation among Gentiles (Rom. 1:18–23; 2:12–16; Acts 14:15–17; 17:24–30; John 1). A growing number of evangelicals view this general revelation (reflected in conscience, creation, providence and history) as a basis for recognizing the presence of elements of truth in other religions, without thereby regarding them as revealed religions or ascribing to them salvific sufficiency.

The question of Jesus, his particularity and universality, is undoubtedly the central issue in the pluralism debate. The bedrock of historic Christianity is the claim that Jesus of Nazareth was not simply a great religious and moral teacher in first-century Palestine, but the decisive self-revelation of the eternal Creator God. Pluralists regard this claim as arrogant, imperialistic and an insurmountable obstacle to what they consider an absolute – the movement towards human unity and world peace. They accordingly advocate a renewed search for a revised, alternative Christology in which Jesus is in effect regarded as qualitatively the same as any other great religious figure.

Thirdly, pluralism regards the various religious traditions as representing many different paths leading to the same ultimate goal. No one religion can claim salvation/liberation as exclusive to its own tradition: all the world religions are legitimate paths to God. They represent different contexts within which men and women experience salvation/liberation. In actual fact we observe that the different religions do not merely offer different ways of achieving salvation, they offer different salvations. All the routes to salvation cannot be equally legitimate when the goals are so radically different.

The ideology of pluralism is thus rejected by evangelical Christians today as biblically indefensible, historically weak, theologically inadequate and logically untenable. Biblical evidence for pluralism is hard to come by, hence, rarely, if ever, do pluralists attempt to offer biblical justification for their position. Similarly, since pluralism is a relatively recent theological trend, it has little historical support. Theological criticisms of pluralism rest principally on the arbitrary theological criteria employed in reductionist reinterpretations of religious beliefs, the mutually incompatible claims among various religions and inevitably substandard Christology. The logical objection essentially exposes the inconsistency inherent in the pluralist insistence that there is no privileged religious tradition, even as pluralism itself occupies the high ground and employs tradition-specific criteria in evaluating religious beliefs.

The church's present response to the issue of pluralism will have direct bearing on the future of historic Christianity and mission. The decisiveness or finality of Christ remains a core affirmation of evangelical Christianity. This does not, however, preclude the possibility of a true knowledge of God and points of contact within non-Christian religions. The critical theological challenge facing the church today is the need to articulate its understanding of the decisive significance of Christ in relation to the other great religions of the world in a way that acknowledges the possibility of truth and grace outside the church.

The church's evangelistic mandate requires her to announce the arrival of the kingdom decisively in Christ, to share the story of what God has done in the birth, life, death and resurrection of Jesus of Nazareth. The church is also obligated to discern and celebrate truth and goodness wherever it may be found, and to work for peace, justice and equality with people of all faiths or no faith. There is no a priori reason why the claim of Christianity – or any other faith or ideology – to have access to universal truth, should be regarded as imperialistic or arrogant, unless it asserts this claim coercively, denying the same privilege to others. Our mission is essentially fulfilling our stewardship of the story of the saving love of God in Christ: a story that must be told with profound respect for the other person's faith and experience, and in humble awe of the undisclosed depths of the Majesty of the universe.

See also NEW AGE, NEW RELIGIOUS MOVEMENTS.

Bibliography

G. D'Costa, *The Meeting of Religions and the Trinity* (Edinburgh: T. & T. Clark, 2000); G. D'Costa (ed.), *Christian Uniqueness Reconsidered: The Myth of a Pluralistic Theology of Religions* (Maryknoll: Orbis Books, 1990); J. Hick and P. Knitter (eds.), *The Myth of Christian Uniqueness: Towards a Pluralistic Theology of Religions* (New York: Orbis Books, 1987); V.-M. Kärkkäinen, *An Introduction to the Theology of Religions* (Downers Grove: InterVarsity Press, 2003); G. R. McDermott, *Can Evangelicals Learn from World Religions? Jesus, Revelation and Religious Traditions* (Downers Grove: InterVarsity Press, 2000); H. Netland, *Encountering Religious Pluralism: The Challenge to Christian Faith and Mission* (Downers Grove: InterVarsity Press, 2001).

I. SATYAVRATA

Repentance

Repentance is a frequent theme in both OT and NT. In the OT, two words are commonly translated repentance: *nāḥam* and *sub*. *Nāḥam* is used primarily of God, who, in the face of sin and evil must respond in judgment, but who delights to 'change' to love and mercy when people recognize that they have sinned, call out to God for forgiveness and commit themselves to live under God's rightful authority. See for example Jeremiah 26, with its repeated plea that God longs to 'relent and not bring the promised disaster' (vv. 3, 13, 19); or the story of Jonah, where God treats the Ninevites with compassion and mercy instead of the destruction he had threatened, in response to their turning from evil (Jonah *passim*, but especially 3:10). *Sub* is used for people coming to their senses, changing direction from rebellion to obedience, and returning to live as God created us to live, under his lordship and sheltered by his mercy. God repeatedly sends his messengers to plead with people 'to return and live' (e.g. the whole theme of Hosea).

In the NT, repentance is most usually expressed through forms of the verb *metanoein*, 'to change one's mind'. This is not simply mental assent or a formula of words, but radical transformation of world-view to embrace Christ as Lord, a new mindset devoted to faith and obedience, sorrow for past rebellion and present sin, and a life turned round to 'love the Lord your God with all your heart and with all your soul and with all your strength' (Deut. 6:5). Repentance and faith are two sides of one coin, and in Acts the apostles sometimes urge people to repent (e.g. Acts 2:38; 17:30) and sometimes to believe (e.g. Acts 16:31); both are the gift of God (e.g. Acts 5:31; 2 Tim. 2:25–26). Paul describes the renewing of one's mind as an ongoing process (e.g. Rom. 12:1–2); it is in this sense that repentance is not only a hallmark of true regeneration and *conversion, but also the evidence of authentic discipleship. As we follow Jesus, the Holy Spirit will continue to convict us of more and more areas of our lives – both beliefs and behaviour – that need to be changed, and empower that change to happen. For this reason, repentance is to be a continuous experience.

While repentance is to affect the whole personality, and is to be progressive and life-long, the starting point may be different for different people, or in different cultures. For Paul, confidence in privilege of birth, race and religious diligence had to be replaced by humble dependence on the grace and mercy of God (Phil. 3:3–11). Further, the community he had been intent on destroying now had to become the family he would die to serve. For some of the Ephesians, repentance began with renouncing the occult and burning their scrolls of magic (Acts 19:17–20). For the Thessalonians, the starting point was turning from idols to serve the living and true God, looking in expectant faith for Jesus' return (1 Thess. 1:9–10). For the dying thief, repentance came right at the last moments of his life (Luke 23:39–43). There are many other examples in Scripture.

In the same way, the evidence of genuine repentance may appear differently in different cultures today. The Hindu or Buddhist who comes to true faith in Jesus will stop going to the temple to make offerings. The animist will cut off his spirit strings, and no longer be in bondage to the spirits or participate in spirit practices. The secular humanist will change his mind about the material world being the only reality, and about human capacity to control it; his world-view will now revolve around God as Creator, Saviour and Judge, and the reality of the unseen and of eternity. Thus, disciple making, and the appeal to repentance, needs to be sensitively *contextualized.

Repentance may be very costly. While some cultures regard religious belief as a private matter, and there is little hostility provided it remains that way, other cultures strongly identify with a non-Christian religion and regard Christian conversion as betrayal. Some cultures are so deeply interwoven with dominant religious beliefs at every level of life that Christians face extreme difficulty: for example, most Thai would say that it is not possible to be authentically Thai except as a Buddhist, and every part of everyday life is threaded through with Buddhist and animist observance. The Buddhist or animist who turns to follow Christ will often then be blamed for any 'bad luck', sickness or death in the community, and will find it hard to withstand pressure to go back to his former ways. He may lose his job, and be unwelcome in his home. In some cases, as with some Muslims who become believers, his life may be at risk.

It is then understandable that in such circumstances there is a great incentive to be a secret believer. In particular, there may be unwillingness to be baptized, which is often seen (by both Christians and those of other faiths) as an outward declaration of transfer of allegiance to Jesus Christ. In recent years, there has been considerable discussion (and considerable disagreement) about whether true believers in Jesus can continue to go to the mosque or temple, praying in their hearts to Jesus rather than Allah or the gods, and still outwardly conform to many rites of their former faith, or whether genuine repentance must show itself in clear separation from those practices. In some cultures and traditions, churches do not practise baptism immediately upon profession of faith, as seems the normal pattern of the NT church, but require a probationary period to prove genuineness of repentance and a clear grasp of gospel fundamentals.

In recent years there has also been growing attention to the need for conversion of worldview at the deepest levels. It is arguable that the Rwanda genocide highlighted the fact that the East Africa revival dealt with superficial levels of personal piety and behaviour, but did not challenge to repentance at the far deeper levels of ethnic hatred. In the West, Christians may need to repent of living as practical materialists, and of greed.

The Lord Jesus taught that it is easier to see sin in others than in ourselves (Matt. 7:1–5). In the global church, we need to help one another identify the areas where our repentance is shallow and incomplete.

Bibliography

B. Bradshaw, *Change Across Cultures* (Grand Rapids: Baker Academic, 2002); J. D. G. Dunn, 'Repentance', in *The Illustrated Bible Dictionary* (Leicester: IVP, revised edn 1994); D. Willard, *Renovation of the Heart* (Leicester: IVP, 2002).

R. DOWSETT

Resurrection

The NT affirms the fact of the resurrection of Christ and its central importance for Christian *faith (1 Cor. 15:12–19). The risen Christ revealed a transformed humanity, able to walk, talk and eat (Luke 24:15–49; John 20:15; 21:4–13), yet his resurrected body was freed from all the limitations of mortal flesh (Luke 24:31, 36; John 20:19) and no longer subject to death (1 Cor. 15:42–44, 51–54). Various NT authors also insist that the resurrected Christ is the 'firstfruits' (guarantee and prefiguration) of the final resurrection of all believers (1 Cor. 15:20–23; Col. 1:18; John 5:28–29; Rev. 1:5). As he was in his resurrection, so shall we be in ours.

Christian hope does not promise to turn humans into bodyless angels, but to take redeemed sinners and give them a renewed and heightened humanity. The resurrected Jesus was never mistaken for an angel: Mary took him for a gardener (John 20:15); the pilgrims en route to Emmaus saw in him only an uninformed foreigner (Luke 24:18); the disciples-turned-fishermen thought he was one more fisherman by the shore (John 21:4, 7, 12). When they reached the shore with their massive haul of fish, Jesus was already preparing their breakfast (John 21:9). The resurrected Jesus was so human, he could converse playfully with the disciples who did not recognize him (Luke 24:17–24).

The purpose of *salvation and the ultimate goal of mission is to turn imperfect people, all more or less dehumanized by sin, into fully and richly renewed human persons set free from sin. The resurrection should mean that all those who come within the scope of the mission of the church begin an ongoing transforming process of humanization which is perfected only in God's new creation. Unfortunately, some Christian groups around the world actually give a dehumanizing witness. Sociological studies, for example, show higher rates of racial prejudice in religious circles (especially conservative and evangelical) than for the society in general. In Latin America, where the gospel usually arrived as a predominantly negative message (anti-Catholic, and later anti-socialist and anti-ecumenical), this dehumanizing effect is frequently visible.

The resurrection highlights the crucial importance of the physical body for Christian faith and mission. If the only purpose of evangelism were to get souls to heaven, both the return of Christ and the resurrection of the body would be entirely superfluous. But God has created us as an integral unity of body and soul; God's own Son became flesh and lived in a physical body identical with our own; and God's final goal is fully realized only when believers, with resurrected bodies, live together on a new earth in the *shalom* of a transformed community, the New Jerusalem.

Thus understood, the resurrection is a call for integral mission to integral persons, who have the full range of human need: physical, social, and spiritual (see *Holistic mission).

The resurrection is God's triumphant affirmation of life, face to face with the reality of death. The *Logos* 'in whom was life' (John 1:4) came that we might have life and have it more abundantly (John 10:10). He shared our human condition and, 'found in appearance as a human being' (Phil. 2:8), lived life fully in mortal flesh like our own, and then demonstrated in all its riches resurrected fullness of life. Therefore Christian mission must be mission in the service of life, both physical and spiritual, both temporal and eternal. This has broad implications for such aspects of mission as medical and health ministries, education, poverty (see *Poor), *HIV/AIDS and attitudes toward war.

Latin America is a battlefront of conflict between the forces of death and the forces of life. The Bishops' Conference in Medellín, Colombia (1968), described this continent as 'conceived in iniquity', and its status-quo 'normalcy' as a state of mortal sin. Statistics vary, but all of them show totally unpardonable levels of poverty and extremely unequal distribution of wealth. In many countries, children die every day of hunger or lack of minimal medical attention. Peruvian theologian Gustavo Gutiérrez has very well identified one of the crucial problems for Christian mission in Latin America as 'how to explain to a black, poverty-ridden widow in the *favelas* of Sao Paulo, Brazil, that God really loves her'.

The resurrection of Christ transformed forever the meaning of death. By his own death and victorious resurrection, Christ transformed death from fatality into liberty (John 10:17–21), from defeat into victory (1 Cor. 15:57), from loss into gain (Phil. 1:21), and from an ending into a new beginning (Rev. 21:1, 5). Christ himself transformed death into life abundant. At the heart of the message and mission of the church should be the faith expressed by the parting words of Dietrich Bonhoeffer: 'This is the end, for me the beginning.' In one of his last sermons, Martin Luther declared, 'the world tells me that in the midst of life, I am dying; God replies: No! In the midst of death, you live!' In the age-long struggle between the forces of death and of life, the church must be the greatest and strongest ally of life over against death, in the name of God the *Creator vitae*.

Death has many agents in Latin America, often in high places and sometimes within the church itself. The history of this continent, from one perspective, can be seen as the history of its bloody dictators, who (with their soldiers and police) have tortured dissidents, murdered them and often mutilated their corpses, as well as raping women at will. Those governments have almost invariably favoured the rich aristocracy at the expense of the poor, thus causing more death. And some 'Christians' have often massively supported those governments. All such conduct is a flagrant offence against the resurrection of the body which God has promised us.

Quite incredibly, the church is called to carry out this difficult mission in the power of Christ's resurrection. In a truly astounding affirmation, replete with superlatives and emphatic synonyms, Paul states that the 'incomparably great power' and 'mighty strength' by which God raised Jesus from the dead, now works actively in us who believe (Eph. 1:19–22), who are the living body of the resurrected Christ. The very same power by which God raised Jesus from the dead, has also 'resurrected' us from our spiritual death to newness of life in Christ (Eph. 2:1, Greek) and will one day clothe us in perfected, resurrected bodies. The power of the resurrection is already working efficaciously in the life and mission of the church as God's redeemed people. This effective working of resurrection begins as each believer seeks, like Paul, to die with Christ and thereby share, here and now, the power of his resurrection (Phil. 3:10–11).

Because our Lord has risen, Christian mission must be resoundingly affirmative, in Christ who is God's 'Yes' and God's 'Amen' (2 Cor. 1:20). The church of the crucified and resurrected Christ was never called to specialize in negatives, in sour tones and minor keys. The redeemed community knows that after the resurrection, it is impossible not to *hope; the community of the resurrected Lord 'cannot not hope'. With such a people, hope is an incurable habit and a way of life. A vital part of the mission of the church is to radiate hope contagiously, especially where it is most difficult to hope at all. The church is called to embody and proclaim the greatest message of hope there ever was, because her Lord has conquered death.

See also CHRIST, INCARNATION.

Bibliography

S. T. Davis, *Risen Indeed* (Grand Rapids: Eerdmans, 1993); G. Gutiérrez, *El Dios de la Vida* (Lima, Perú: CEP, 1982); G. E. Ladd, *I Believe in the Resurrection of Jesus* (Grand Rapids: Eerdmans, 1975); R. Longenecker (ed.), *Life in the Face of Death: The Resurrection Message of the New Testament* (Grand Rapids, Eerdmans, 1998); N. T. Wright, *The Resurrection of the Son of God* (Minneapolis: Fortress Press, 2003).

J. STAM

Revelation

The biblical doctrine of revelation touches all aspects of God's activities in relation to creation and the lives of human beings. Revelation will be expounded on the basis of its missiological relevance as it applies to current mission theology and practice.

Missiological perspective of biblical revelation

Revelation refers to all God's initiatives, activities and modes in disclosing and communicating his redemptive will to human beings. Revelation establishes God's distinction from and relation to creation and all living creatures. God's initiative to reach out to human beings is decidedly missiological: he makes himself known so that he can be known. He reveals his very self, not merely truth about himself, thus making possible a relationship with himself into which he desires to draw all of creation.

Even prior to the actual creation of the cosmos, God's missionary plan was already in place. After creation, especially in the aftermath of the disobedience of the progenitor of the human race, God's redemptive will has been consistently articulated, disclosed, and communicated throughout the course of human history.

Revelation as divine-human encounter

Biblical revelation essentially speaks of divine-human encounter; in other words,

God taking the initiative to communicate himself to humanity, and human beings either acknowledging or rejecting the divine initiative. This framework stresses the missionary aspects of revelation in terms of *phases*, with the Triune God unveiling his redemptive will as *extensive* (preparatory), *intensive* (personal) and *supreme* (ultimate). Revelation is creative, dynamic, and progressive; it builds around what God discloses (*content*), how God reveals (*modes*), to whom God reveals his nature and redemptive will (*recipients*), and when God reveals his redemptive love (*timing*).

Extensive revelation

The first phase of divine-human encounter occurs within the arena of *extensive* revelation (sometimes called 'general revelation') that includes the structuring and disclosing of God's redemptive truth in nature, history and human conscience. Extensive revelation displays God's 'invisible qualities', which the apostle Paul qualifies as 'eternal power and divine nature' (Rom. 1:20). Human disobedience distorts this revelation by replacing God with idols and worshipping the creation (materialism) rather than the Creator (Rom. 1:25). Universal in scope, extensive revelation depicts God as the 'the mystery of the world' (Eberhard Jungel) or the *mysterium tremendum* (Rudolf Otto), thereby limiting humanity's grasp of redemptive love on a personal level. Nonetheless, God ensures that fallen humanity would have a glimpse – albeit limited – of divine *love, holiness, and justice, all of which are universally available and accessible to all persons at all times. Extensive revelation offers human beings some degree of knowledge of divine truth, although the general view is that this is essentially remedial and bears no salvific currency. In relation to missions, extensive revelation becomes *preparatory* for and *introductory* to a deeper encounter with God. It underscores the universality of God's presence, the *universality of the reality of human need for *salvation, and the theological necessity of global missions.

Intensive revelation

The second phase of divine-human encounter takes place on the canvas of *intensive* revelation (sometimes called 'special revelation').

Its main function is to enable those under *extensive* revelation to establish a personal redemptive relationship with God. It functions through the modes of history, divine speech, Scripture, dreams and visions. On history as a mode of revelation, Millard Erickson (*Christian Theology*) notes three forms: (1) G. Ernest Wright's revelation *in* history that holds biblical narratives as authoritative, a recital of historical events confessed by the people of Israel (OT) and the Christian church (NT); (2) neo-orthodoxy's revelation *through* history that considers historical events as a dynamic process that reports a personal encounter (i.e. 'direct coming' to a person) between God and humans (Exod. 3; Isa. 6); and (3) W. Pannenberg's revelation *as* history that stresses God's action in history in that the events actually were and are revelation of himself.

Another modality is *divine speech* (e.g. Jer. 18:1), either as 'audible speech' (e.g. God talking to Moses or Peter), 'inaudible speech' (a muted, inward hearing of God's message, dream or vision), or a 'concursive inspiration' (combines revelation and inspiration, as in the case of biblical writers).

Next is the *Scripture* – revelation in *written* form – which comprises a 'historical dialogue' that God made with Israel and specific persons (e.g. Adam and Eve, Moses, Jacob, David, Solomon, prophets, apostles). Scripture provides human beings opportunities to know God *propositionally*, and, consequently, under the conviction of the Spirit of God, to encounter God *personally* (Gal. 3:11, 19; Jas 1:21–25). Intensive revelation also manifests in *dreams* and *visions*, which continue to play a prominent role in today's missionary work, especially among Islamic communities and areas hostile to the gospel.

Supreme revelation

The third phase of divine-human encounter arises within the framework of *supreme* revelation. In this case God himself is revealed in his fullness as *Trinity in and through *Christ. Shortly before his ascension, the risen Lord mandated his disciples to 'go and make disciples of all nations, baptising them in the name of the Father and of the Son and of the Holy Spirit, and teaching them to obey everything I have commanded you' (Matt. 28:19–20). The great commission sets the stage for a *deeper* encounter between human beings and the missionary God, and, for new believers, a growing relationship with the Triune God through *discipleship. Discipleship means therefore to grow in faith and knowledge of God, and to increase in knowledge and experience of the activities of God the Father, the Son and the Holy Spirit.

Trinitarian revelation. Biblical revelation portrays God as one with distinct yet co-equal, co-eternal and co-existent persons: Father, Son, *Holy Spirit. Crucial to the fulfilment of the missionary task of the church (*missio Ecclesia*) is the trinitarian participation in the planning, executing and sustaining of God's redemptive work (**missio Dei*). Trinitarian revelation dispels any notion of an ontological existence of gods in world religions as legitimate centres of spiritual devotion and orientation of life.

Incarnational revelation. At the heart of *supreme* revelation is the *incarnation of Christ. In the Gospels, God the Father makes a personal introduction of the Son at his baptism (Matt. 3:17; Mark 1:11; Luke 3:22). God the Son then introduces the Father in many instances, especially in his *Abba* utterances (Matt. 6:9–15; esp. John 17). Christ's character, life and ministry best articulate God's commitment to unveil his redemptive will in concrete historical terms; his miracles, death and *resurrection are 'redemptive history' in its most condensed form. God, in the personality, character, attitudes and ministry of Jesus, showed that he was actually living among men and women. Viewed missiologically, Christ's incarnation demands the incarnational ministry (*contextualized forms and methods) and *witness (local actualization of the gospel) of the church in the world. Incarnational revelation paves the way for human beings to experience divine love and forgiveness in symbols they understand. Because God 'translates' himself into human form, 'written revelation' (Scripture) requires *translation in the available language of local cultures. Incarnation makes possible the 'infinite translatability of the gospel'. People need not learn Hebrew or Aramaic or Greek in order to understand God's love and offer of salvation. Missionaries who painstakingly translate the Scripture into people's local languages do so according to the example of Christ's incarnational revelation (Phil. 2:5–11).

Dynamic revelation. God does not stop revealing himself at the ascension of the Risen Christ, but carries on in the dynamic operations of his Spirit in the world. The Holy Spirit guarantees that the disclosures and communication of God's saving plan continue through his convincing, enabling, indwelling, empowering, abiding and sustaining presence. The Spirit of God works preveniently (John Wesley) in the hearts of sinners even before the actual exercise of faith and experience of new birth. Gospel communicators simply follow the 'trails' of the Sprit of God in their evangelistic efforts because the Holy Spirit constantly works prior to any human efforts (John 16:7–15). Dynamic revelation warrants God's acts before, during and after the experience of spiritual birth. Through the Holy Spirit's dynamic revelatory work, God's persistent engagement with the world is guaranteed. The Holy Spirit preserves the intent, authority, power and validity of all revelations – especially the Scripture (2 Tim. 3:16; 2 Pet. 1:20–21; 1 Cor. 2:13) – that have taken place under extensive and intensive revelations. Discernment, however, is needed for 'revelation' given through prophetic utterance. Dynamic revelation need not undermine the truth that Scripture is a full and final revelation of God's purposes of salvation, but as such it carries an authority to which all subsequent claims of God's voice must be consistent.

Missiological implications of revelation

Relevant missiological implications emerge from the perspectives of God who is self-articulating, self-disclosing and self-communicating.

God's disclosures to the nations

Universal accessibility to divine truth explains the existence of religions and religious systems. God's judgment of those who have never heard the gospel in the full and formal sense is made possible because divine truth is accessible universally. Human beings 'knew God' but have since 'exchanged the truth for a lie', abandoned 'the knowledge of God', and ignored their knowledge of 'God's righteous decree' (Rom. 1:18–32). They have suppressed the truth that made them responsible for their rejection of God. The fact that Yahweh discloses himself to the nations means he is not a local or tribal God confined solely to the boundaries of Israel. God is at work to make himself known outside the geographical territories of the covenant people (Jonah), and he does not leave himself without witness (Acts 14:17).

God's disclosures in other religious contexts

Two major issues regarding God's disclosures in other religious environments have divided Christians around the world: the validity of truth-claims outside the Judeo-Christian tradition and the final destiny of those who die without the awareness of the gospel or Christ. Within Christian circles, there is no universal consensus.

Major categories that have played prominently over the years are 'pluralism,' 'inclusivism' and 'exclusivism', although in recent years these categories have been recognized as being inadequate to account for the range and complexity of views held. *Pluralism* views the revelation of the incarnation of Jesus Christ as a myth, claiming that Christ is not the unique Saviour or mediator, as other religions also have equally legitimate means of salvation and spiritual mediators. A Christ-centred notion of salvation is invalid as world religions offer alternative vehicles for achieving spiritual salvation and eternal liberation. Emphasizing the experiential, pluralists take a positive view of world religions and cultures and put the burden of salvation on human responsibility based on their response to the real, the higher being, or the ultimate. The pluralistic framework of salvation surrenders any notion of special or intensive revelation, yet partially holds on to the spiritual benefits of extensive revelation. Opportunities for salvation exist even to those who do not hear the gospel because general revelation bears inherent saving capability; saving truth and the natural means to obtain it has been embedded in creation, history and the conscience of humanity.

Taking a middle view, *inclusivism* acknowledges the integrity of the revelation of Jesus Christ, but accommodates the validity of extra-biblical revelations as long as they do not diametrically oppose biblical revelation. General revelation bears salvific currency, although the value of special revelation of the incarnation of Christ remains relevant. Here partial salvation found through extensive revelation combines with the experience of salvation on a personal level one experiences under intensive revelation.

Exclusivism rejects the validity of 'truth-claims' in world religions in view of the consistent witness of the Scripture (Isa. 44:6; Rev. 1:8; 1 Tim. 2:5; Acts 4:12) and the direct claims Jesus makes of himself (John 10; 14:6). Internal biblical evidences strongly support Christ's unique lordship and his life-giving sacrifice at Calvary (1 Tim. 2:5–6). Stressing the 'faith factor', proponents of 'salvation-in-Christ-alone' reject any proposal of experiencing eternal life under the auspices of world religions. Those who have not heard of the gospel and the Scripture would not therefore be able to experience consciously salvation in Christ.

Rejecting the validity of truth-claims based on natural theology, Donald Bloesch proposes a 'theology of creation' that seeks to analyse nature and conscience in light of God's self-revelation in Jesus Christ, thereby viewing the world as created and loved by God, destined for redemption, and the theatre of God's glory. Human beings should not seek God in nature but rather view nature in the light of God's revelation in Jesus Christ. Bloesch claims that adherents of world religions end up in idolatry as they construct God 'out of human reason and experience'. Revelation is basically an event of God speaking and humans hearing. 'Other lights' and 'other revelations' in nature and history are not new or different revelations but are 'echoes' or 'reverberations' of God's one revelation in Christ, which may clarify and illumine what God has done for believers in Christ in view of the incarnation. Bloesch is open to the idea of a 'hidden Christ' in world religions and cultures, although Christ 'will invariably be misunderstood and confused with the idols of human imagination'. He sees God's self-revelation in Christ as standing in judgment over all religions, including institutional Christian faith. True religion exists, but only as it is constantly reformed and purified by the holy grace of God in Jesus Christ. Christian religion must avoid proclaiming its superiority over other religions, but rather submits its inadequacies and ambiguities to the judgment of Christ so that it can present an authentic witness to the gospel for the world.

In recent years, *accessibilism* has been gaining ground among missiological circles, courtesy of Terrence Tiessen's work, *Who Can Be Saved?*. Borrowing William Craig's terminology, Tiessen argues for the exclusiveness of Jesus Christ as God's means of salvation. He sees no parallel in other religions to the covenantal relationships God established with Israel first and later the church in implementing the redemptive plan. However, the uniqueness of these agents does not rule out any hope regarding the possibility of salvation experience among people who lack access to the gospel. Accordingly, adherents of non-biblical religions may obtain salvation according to 'God's middle knowledge', according to which God knows how people would have responded to Christ given the opportunity.

Other perspectives include: (1) *ecclesiocentrism*, which considers the church and gospel proclamation are essential to God's work of salvation, arguing that salvation becomes accessible only to those who hear the gospel, especially among 'competent adults'; (2) *agnosticism*, whose proponents 'do not know for sure that God has means by which to save people who do not hear about Christ', but affirming that in the Scripture none of the unevangelized are saved; (3) *religious instrumentalism*, which holds that God has raised other religions as his instruments in salvation, thereby ruling out the exclusive claim of Christ as the mediator and only Saviour; and (4) *relativism*, which concedes the universal accessibility of salvation through various religions as part of God's programme. Like their pluralist counterparts, relativists hold that all extra-biblical religions are 'more or less equally true' and legitimate paths to spiritual salvation.

God's continuing engagement in the world

Biblical revelation operates progressively, not in terms of gradual evolutionary development, but in experiencing God's disclosure of himself that builds upon earlier divine disclosures, accentuating its complementary and supplementary nature rather than contradicting previous occurrences of God's communication (Mal. 3:6; Matt. 5:17–18). Centuries of missionary work attest to God's

continuing engagement in the world. Modern science may have stifled the contemporary understanding of the continuing activity of the living God, since the modern form of deism holds that he does not intervene in the world, if he exists at all. This has been especially a Western problem; but other parts of the world where manifestations of the Spirit of the living God have been experienced, identified and reported, indicate otherwise. Adherents of world religions (e.g. Islamic and Hindu traditions) who have reportedly come to Christ through dream-encounters, reinforce biblical claims that 'God speaks', sometimes in the strangest of ways. His gracious and free self-disclosure cannot be limited. In areas where spiritual conflicts and warfare are more evident, the continuing revelation of God is a crucial category in interpreting what is going on.

These are some of the ways in which mission and revelation are inextricably bound together: it is not possible to have a biblical theology of mission without an equally rigorous and thoroughly worked out theology of revelation. The revelatory nature of the missionary God is the foundational framework of missions.

See also GOD.

Bibliography

G. C. Berkouwer, *General Revelation* (Grand Rapids: Eerdmans, 1955); B. Demarest, *General Revelation: Historical Views and Contemporary Issues* (Grand Rapids: Zondervan, 1982); A. Dulles, *Models of Revelation* (Garden City: Image Books, 1985); M. J. Erickson, 'Knowing God', in *Christian Theology* (Grand Rapids: Baker Books, 1998); F. H. Henry (ed.), *Revelation and the Bible* (Grand Rapids: Baker Book House, 1958); T. Meadowcroft, 'Between Authorial Intent and Indeterminacy: The Incarnation as an Invitation to Human-Divine Discourse', *Scottish Journal of Theology* 58, 2005, pp. 199–218; L. Morris, *I Believe in Revelation* (London: Hodder & Stoughton, 1976); R. Swinburne, *Revelation: From Metaphor to Analogy* (New York: Oxford University Press, 1992); T. Tiessen, *Who can be Saved?* (Downers Grove: InterVarsity Press, 2004); T. F. Torrance, 'A Realist Interpretation of God's Self-Revelation', in *Reality and Evangelical Theology: The Realism of Christian Revelation* (Downers Grove: Inter-Varsity Press, 1999); N. Wolterstorff, *Divine Discourse: Philosophical Reflections on the Claim that God Speaks* (New York: Cambridge University Press, 1995).

T. C. CASIÑO

Revival/renewal

All religions go through cycles of remarkable growth and creativity followed by normalization of worship and daily practice. Eventually this leads to loss of vitality and decline that may be arrested by new processes of revitalization. A religion survives and thrives to the extent it effectively engages its changing socio-cultural environment in the light of its original revelation.

The OT records the changing fortunes of the people of God over many generations. Israelite history moves between two poles: fidelity to the covenant with Yahweh on the one hand, and acceptance of the worship of the idols of their neighbours on the other. In seasons of spiritual decline and faithlessness, the voice of the prophet would be heard pleading with the people of Israel to repent of their sins and return to covenant faithfulness with God (e.g. Isa. 65; Hos. 6:1–3; Joel 2:12–17). The Christian church has historically followed a similar cyclical pattern: spiritual vitality alternating with decline and barrenness.

Religious revitalization is a complex process that can take many forms. Renewal in the Roman Catholic tradition is different from evangelical Protestant revivalism that has developed since the seventeenth century. Although the Protestant modern mission movement is a direct fruit of the Pietist-Evangelical revivals of the seventeenth and eighteenth centuries, revivalism has not become institutionalized ecclesiastically in Asia, Africa and Oceania in the same way as in the West. However, although modern revivalism has largely begun as an Anglo-American Protestant phenomenon, it can be found in most cultural contexts of the world, and often as an indigenous movement.

To avoid reductionism, revival and renewal dare not be treated only as a matter of religion. Account must be taken of the total historical, religious, economic, political and social context. Religion does not develop in a vacuum or in isolation from the larger environment. Theories developed since 1950 have given us new tools for studying the multiple dimensions of such movements.

Definitions

Since the sixteenth century, *reformation, revival, awakening* and *renewal* have become technical terms for spiritual revitalization inspired by the Holy Spirit. The term *reformation* can be traced to the fifteenth century but it became associated with the Protestant Reformation in the sixteenth century. The term Puritan was used pejoratively in the sixteenth century against those reformers who wanted to purify the Church of England of vestiges of Roman Catholicism and bring it into line with Calvinist ideals. In the next century the term encompassed a variety of groups united in their opposition to the established (Anglican) church. Puritanism was the formative religious influence as European immigrants arrived in North America and began settling the continent, and Puritanism was the common well from which Presbyterians and Congregationalists drew as they established their churches in the American colonies. Especially in North America the *reforming* and *reviving* dynamic of Puritanism contributed to the emergence of the eighteenth-century Evangelical Revival.

The Pietist renewal movement emerged in Germany in the seventeenth century, first among Reformed churches and later among Lutherans. Pietism stressed a warm heartfelt piety, lay participation and the practical application of Christian faith in daily life. It became the seedbed of philanthropic and missionary activity. *Revival* was used as early as 1651 to describe any effort to restore vitality. In his history of New England religion, *Magnalia Christi Americana* (1702), the Puritan pastor in Boston, Cotton Mather, wrote of 'a notable revival of religion' in seventeenth-century New England.

The eighteenth-century movement associated with John and Charles Wesley, George Whitefield and Jonathan Edwards was called the *awakening* (1741). The preferred term in the nineteenth century was *revival* and *revivalism* (1815) and this spurred discussion of the phenomenology and methodology of revivals led by *revivalists* (1820). The

American evangelist, Charles G. Finney, a leading figure in the second Great Awakening, shaped the future of both the methodology ('new measures' that induced response), and the theology of modern revivals, as presented in his book *Lectures on Revivals* (1835).

After 1950, *renewal* was used to describe various initiatives to revitalize the church, and in the 1960s became associated especially with the *charismatic movement. 'Revival' and 'evangelism' have sometimes been used interchangeably. Historically, 'revival' and 'renewal' refer to the revitalization of adherents of a particular religion, although 'revival' has carried more of an expectation of large numbers of converts. Renewal has also been more associated with an on-going process of change, whereas revival has been used of more dramatic revitalization. Davies defines revival as: 'A sovereign outpouring of the Holy Spirit upon a group of Christians resulting in their spiritual reviving and quickening, and issuing in the awakening of spiritual concern in outsiders or formal church members' (R. Davies, *I Will Pour Out My Spirit*).

However, Christians have not been agreed as to the relationship between revival/revivalism and evangelism. For Roman Catholics and European Protestants *evangelism* means engendering vital faith in members of the church that were hitherto nominal adherents. In Anglo-American usage *evangelism* has meant to share the Christian message with people who have not yet heard or accepted. Dwight L. Moody, prominent evangelist from 1875 to 1899, realized that revivalism was not effective in reaching people with no prior allegiance to the church, but did not find an effective way to cross this barrier. Similarly, the most influential evangelist in the twentieth century, Billy Graham, found his primary audience among people who already were Christian or had a Christian background.

Social theories of revitalization

In 1956 anthropologist Anthony F. C. Wallace put forward his theory of religious revitalization. He suggested that the underlying process present in all movements of change could be described as 'revitalization'. Wallace cited cases, starting with the birth of Christianity in the Mediterranean world, from many parts of the world and over the span of the past two millennia. He canvassed a range of religions. 'A revitalization movement is defined as a deliberate, organized, conscious effort by members of a society to construct a more satisfying culture. Revitalization is ... a special kind of culture change phenomenon'. Wallace sought to demonstrate that revitalization movements differ from the typical process of cultural change that evolves over long periods of time. Revitalization starts with an abrupt shift that sets a new course. Wallace argued that 'all organized religions are relics of old revitalization movements'.

Historians and social scientists have further developed this theory by drawing on the work of another anthropologist, Victor Turner, who introduced the concept of ritual process. In a series of studies of religious renewal movements in American history, William G. McLoughlin has also applied revitalization theory. The process can be conceptualized in terms of three stages. The first stage is reached when ordinary people in a social group conduct their lives in ways that deviate so sharply from traditional standards that a 'crisis of legitimacy' ensues. This is followed by a second stage, a 'period of cultural distortion', a sense that the institutions of society, including the church, no longer function effectively. This triggers a crisis. In the third stage, 'the awakening' brings resolution when a new and clarified *world-view emerges: fundamental values are restated, institutional forms adjusted and appropriate behavioural standards established. The result is a revitalized, restored and dynamic culture.

Impact of revivals

Revival or revitalization movements have played a decisive role in shaping the Christian movement since the seventeenth century. The revival impulse was felt across the ecclesiastical spectrum. This can be demonstrated in terms of several developments. In late seventeenth century Germany, Pietist leader A. G. Francke evangelized across Germany, pioneered a range of social services, and contributed to the founding of the modern mission movement. At the same time in the American colonies, pastors such as Solomon Stoddard, grandfather to Jonathan Edwards, were concerned to lead their congregations in spiritual renewal. The Dutch Reformed pastor

Theodore J. Freylinghuysen, who had come under the influence of Pietism, settled in northern New Jersey and in 1725 began itinerating among the churches preaching a revival message. The following year Presbyterian pastor William Tennent started training ministers to preach a message of personal faith based on repentance of sin. These developments were precursors to the Great Awakening a decade later.

The modern mission movement that began after 1790 is a direct fruit of the Pietist-Evangelical Awakening; and subsequent waves of revival, on all continents, spurred new evangelistic and missionary activity. In 1800 less than 15% of all Christians were found outside the West, but by 2000 more than 60% of all Christian adherents were in Asia, Africa and Latin America. During the first Great Awakening evangelicals began to wrestle with ethical issues such as slavery. Evangelicals led the anti-slavery movement. In Great Britain evangelicals reshaped public policy with regard to prisons, child labour laws, and education. In the United States Charles G. Finney was an abolitionist and supported women's rights. The impact of the East African Revival, starting in 1929, helped overcome inter-racial tensions. Its revival message spread to other continents. All these movements demonstrate how genuine revival brings social change to the world as well as spiritual renewal to the church.

In contrast to revivalism prior to 1850, with its emphasis on personal *and* social transformation, increasingly revivalism came to be understood in terms of personal salvation. An important exception to this is the Salvation Army. William and Catherine Booth, Methodists drawn to holiness teaching, opened a rescue mission in the slums of East London in 1865 that was renamed the Salvation Army in 1878. The Booths combined emphasis on personal conversion and social uplift in a ministry to the whole person. But generally the ethos of revivalism after 1850 was marked by a focus on the call to personal conversion.

The evangelical movement has long been associated with commitment to 'continuous revival' and renewal. After 1850, this took new forms that came from the holiness movement. William Boardman came under the influence of the writings of Finney and Asa Mahan so that he and his wife experienced 'rest of heart in Jesus for sanctification'. Boardman published *The Higher Christian Life* in 1859, a book that had wide influence throughout the English-speaking world. Others helped spread the teaching on the 'second blessing' or sanctification. In 1873–74 Dwight L. Moody and Ira D. Sankey led evangelistic campaigns in Great Britain that helped set the stage for what became the Keswick Convention. American holiness teachers, Hannah Whitall Smith and Robert Pearsall Smith, spent 1874 teaching about holiness throughout Great Britain.

Many revivals look back to the first great outpouring of the Holy Spirit upon the church at Pentecost in Acts 2. Many see this as paradigmatic, even though as a defining moment in history it has to be taken as a unique event. However, the rise of Pentecostalism in 1901 is the most important revitalization movement of the past century. In contrast to revivalism that has remained primarily a Western phenomenon, the Pentecostal movement has found indigenous form throughout the world. By 2000 more than 500 million Pentecostals, of many varieties and indigenous to a wide range of cultures, were found around the globe. They also represented the fastest growing Christian stream. It has often been pointed out that the Pentecostal movement arose among the lower classes, people with meagre education and living in poverty, who found no place in the established churches.

Evaluating revival and renewal movements

Religious movements typically challenge and disrupt the status quo. Revivals do not simply restore forms and patterns but introduce new varieties of religious experience, thereby updating and recontextualizing a religion. Revival and renewal movements have often drawn strong criticism. They have been charged with engendering unhealthy emotionalism or bizarre behaviour.

What revitalization movements have in common is that people who were religiously lukewarm become fervent, change their behaviour and become active participants. Yet church leaders have sometimes been the sharpest critics. In the eighteenth century, Jonathan Edwards admitted that many people were alarmed by the effects of the Evangelical

Awakening due to manifestations 'such as persons crying out aloud, shrieking, being put into great agonies of body, and deprived of their bodily strength, and the like'. Yet he defended these happenings, saying that these were people he knew well and he could vouch for their integrity and emotional stability. In his book, *The Distinguishing Marks of a Work of the Spirit of God* (1741), Edwards identified five criteria by which to evaluate the authenticity of a movement: (1) it exalted Jesus Christ; (2) the kingdom of Satan was attacked; (3) the Scriptures were honoured; (4) the movement promoted sound doctrine; and (5) love for God and other people was being demonstrated. Edwards emphasized that authentic revival was the work of God alone, a sovereign outpouring of the Spirit that could not be manufactured or manipulated by human intervention.

By contrast, a century later Charles G. Finney, reflecting the increased emphasis on the autonomous self of modern culture, held that revival is the human response to the divine. In his *Lectures on Revivals of Religion* (1835), Finney's manual on how to conduct a revival, he said: '[A revival] presupposes that the church is sunk down in a backslidden state, and a revival consists in the return of the church from her backslidings, and in the conversion of sinners ... A revival is nothing else than a new beginning of obedience to God.' Finney pioneered the use of modern techniques that would produce the greatest possible number of responses.

Revivalists have continued to follow Finney's lead, adapting to each new stage of technology and appropriating it for their work. First radio and then television made possible much larger audiences than were possible with other forms of mass evangelism. The very term 'televangelist' points to the fact that revivalism has sought to exploit the full range of communications technology to carry on this ministry. But critics have pointed out that the medium inevitably shapes the message. Producing programmes for television is costly. Whereas the earliest televized evangelistic programmes featured a standard church service, by the 1970s enterprising televangelists adopted the talk show or entertainment mode.

Several reasons have been suggested as to why most revivals peter out and do not meet long-term expectations. The emphasis on emotional response is often accompanied by a corresponding lack of solid biblical teaching. There is often a focus on one or two charismatic leaders on whom too much may depend, and when they move on, or fail, the movement is not self-sustaining. Promises of healing or prosperity made in the context of revivalism can raise unrealistic expectations, and disillusionment can set in. Revival can create a 'band-wagon' effect with certain phenomena, which people jump on as a supposed means of greater blessing, only to find that the phenomena are not sustainable and life soon returns to normal. Finally, if revivals are 'in-house' experiences, there is a lack of social engagement which brings no benefit to society and therefore no long term difference is experienced. For example charismatic renewal in Britain since the 1970s has had a significant impact on a number of churches and denominations, but it could not be said to have made a difference socially or politically.

Three observations can be made about the challenge of evaluating religious renewal movements. In the first place, perhaps because all such movements have generated controversy, objective evaluation has seldom been carried out. Second, evaluations by participants in a movement have typically focused on the number of people attracted to the movement or the 'conversions'. Little attention has been given to such questions as the theological content of an evangelist's message or whether long-lasting results could be demonstrated on the quality of church life and witness in society. A third observation is that a theory such as *revitalization* establishes a framework for examining the multiple aspects of revival, renewal and revitalization movements. This will allow for a study of the historical, phenomenological, theological, ecclesiological, sociological, and psychological dimensions of a particular movement.

Revival/renewal and mission are linked by the work of the Holy Spirit who is the Spirit of mission. Revitalization movements may be evaluated according to their fruit in terms of renewed commitment to mission, since the anointing of the Holy Spirit in the Bible is intended for missionary impetus and dedication to service (e.g. Isa. 61:1–2; Acts 1:8). The effectiveness of mission, however, does not rely on extraordinary outpourings of the Spirit, and people do not have to receive remarkable and emotional experiences to be convinced of the truth of the gospel. Nevertheless, St Paul prayed for ongoing renewal for the early church believers (e.g. Eph. 3:14–21), and there is no doubt, as we have shown from the history of the missionary movement, that revival can be a significant influence on mission commitment.

See also HOLY SPIRIT, EVANGELISM, PENTECOSTALISM.

Bibliography

D. Bebbington, *Evangelicalism in Modern Britain* (London: Routledge, 1989); R. Davies, *I Will Pour Out My Spirit* (New York: Monarch, 1992); R. F. Lovelace, *Dynamics of Spiritual Life: An Evangelical Theology of Renewal* (Downers Grove: Inter-Varsity Press, 1979); W. G. McLoughlin, *Revivals, Awakenings, and Reform* (Chicago: University of Chicago Press, 1978); J. E. Orr, *The Second Evangelical Awakening in America* (London: Marshall, Morgan & Scott, 1952); P. E. Pierson, *Emerging Streams of Church and Mission* (Pattaya: Forum for World Evangelization, 2004); P. Scharpff, *History of Evangelism* (Grand Rapids: Eerdmans, 1966).

W. R. SHENK

Sacraments

Sacraments are outward and visible signs of inward, spiritual grace. They 'ratify the gifts which the divine liberality has bestowed on us' (Calvin). They are 'means of *grace', ways through which God bestows blessing. The two 'dominical' sacraments are baptism and the Lord's Supper. Some Christians add matrimony, ordination, extreme unction, confirmation and penance, which are certainly sacramental but not specifically prescribed by Jesus. Foot-washing (John 13:14–15) and the use of water, oil or hands in healing (Mark 16:18) have also been regarded as sacraments given by Jesus. The church has been seen by some as the fundamental sacrament, or pledge, of God's coming kingdom.

Human beings can scarcely communicate without using signs (see Gen. 9:12–13; Isa. 8:3; Ezek. 4:1; Rom. 1:20). A sacrament does what the word of God does, but tangibly and visibly. It both signifies divine things, and stimulates and strengthens *faith in those who participate. It is like a flag which signifies a nation's identity; it is only a piece of cloth, but when it is raised it has the power to foster loyalty and passion in those who identify with it.

Baptism

This is the sacrament most obviously relevant to mission. The church baptizes new believers. All baptisms done in water and in the trinitarian name are normally recognized by all Christian churches, whoever actually performs the rite. Baptism has, however, given rise to many disputes which are relevant to mission theology:

(1) *Should the church baptize young children of believing parents?* This immense debate cannot be summarized here, but it is worth noticing that those who live in tightly-knit communities (e.g. Judaism, African clans) may be more likely to answer 'yes' than those whose lifestyle is more individualistic (Acts 16:33). See (7) below.

(2) *Is immersion necessary?* Even if we answer 'no' to this much-disputed question, it remains essential that the form of baptism should at least symbolize dying and rising again in conformity with *Christ (Rom. 6:3). Some ancient baptisteries had steps leading into a shallow pool, to symbolize dying and rising.

(3) *Should a convert be baptized immediately on profession of faith or after a long period of instruction as a catechumen?* Some churches delay baptism until the convert can read the Bible or has shown commitment to a new way of life, so as to guard against superficial discipleship; others follow the NT pattern of linking baptism (which ratifies the grace of God to the believer) as closely as possible to the initial response of faith (Acts 8:38; 10:47; Gal. 3:26–27; Col. 2:12). The point to be safeguarded is that baptism signifies not the faith of the believer but the grace of *God. It is first of all a movement from God to us.

(4) *Is baptism essential for every believer?* Most churches answer 'yes', since it is commanded by Jesus (Matt. 28:19; Acts 2:38), but many converts, wishing to remain loyal to their own communities, decide not to be

baptized or join a church. Some are Muslims (e.g. the Isawa of northern Nigeria) or Hindus (e.g. Jesu bhakta of Tamil Nadu). To help such people remain within their own community and to witness to Christ from within, several solutions have been proposed, such as delaying baptism until a group of catechumens can be assembled; baptizing secretly; allowing self-baptism; or using a local initiation ceremony, which can be seen as baptism in meaning but not in form. This issue has been much debated, notably by M. M. Thomas and L. Newbigin in India. (See *Church growth, second paragraph.)

(5) *Baptism, as far as possible, should not be presented as a strange ritual.* It can, with caution, be administered to a group of, say, adolescent believers within the context of their own local initiatory rites, since peoples throughout the world regard water as a symbol of life-giving power.

(6) *Baptism signifies complete initiation into Christ.* All the baptized are 'in Christ' and set apart as his witnesses and representatives. They are in principle ordained through baptism for his service (1 Pet. 2:5), and 1 Corinthians 1:14–16 may suggest that the first Christians to be baptized in a new place should, because they are local people, be responsible for the baptism of subsequent converts.

(7) *Should the church expect to baptize individuals one by one, or in corporate groups of believers?* Both forms are found in the NT, but perhaps the second is more common (Acts 16:15; 1 Cor. 1:16). Vincent Donovan, working among the Masai in Tanzania, one day told the chief which individuals he thought had shown mature enough faith to qualify for baptism. The chief rebuked him: 'We always do things together; why are you trying to break us up? You said you were bringing good news. When we say "We believe", that is what we mean.' So they were all baptized in a group.

The Lord's Supper

Different church traditions favour different names for the Lord's Supper: Holy Communion, the Mass, the Eucharist, the Breaking of Bread. Whatever name is used, it brings us to the heart of the church's life. Many suppose that its purpose is to comfort and strengthen believers and has little to do with mission (i.e. being sent out into the world). In response, let us consider three aspects, past, present and future. It 'recalls a past event, the passion of Christ, indicates the effect of Christ's passion in us, i.e. grace, and foretells the glory that is to come' (Aquinas). They all have major implications for mission.

Present

The Lord's Supper continues the table fellowship with Jesus which his disciples enjoyed with him, until the last, sorrowful occasion in the Upper Room. But he came to eat with them again and changed their sorrow into joy. They continued to rejoice after his final departure (Acts 2:46–47). Exuberant joy in the powerful presence of Jesus and his spiritual gifts at work among us should be a feature of every Eucharist (which simply means 'thanksgiving'). Gathering at the table of Jesus signifies the united life and fellowship of his disciples. As they receive God's grace by faith they are strengthened and renewed and sent out in the power of the Spirit to serve God in mission.

But mission in practice has shown that the Eucharist need not be as exclusive as the church has often made it. In the community of Madurai jail in India, where the sacrament was celebrated regularly from 1976 to 1986, it was impossible to admit Christians but refuse Hindus, so the table was opened to all. The result was a steady stream of requests for baptism. The table was literally a means of grace precisely because it was inclusive, not exclusive. It had become like Jesus' table fellowship with outcasts, at which the religious leaders of his day took such offence. However the degree to which the Lord's table should be 'open' continues to be a point of dispute amongst Christians.

Past

It is also a solemn memorial of Jesus' death, as Paul needed to remind the Corinthians, who were overdoing the party aspect (1 Cor. 11:17–34). Like the Jewish Passover, it brings a sacrifice offered in history into our present experience as we hear, see, touch, taste and believe, both as individual believers and as a community. It is a dramatic movement of grace from God to human beings who are thankful recipients. It therefore '*proclaims' (1 Cor. 11:26), or vividly 're-enacts' the gospel story. To receive the body and blood of Christ in this symbolic action may be an appropriate way for anyone to make a personal response to the gospel of repentance and faith. And re-enacting the past event reminds us that Jesus was unjustly killed, and commits us as participants to oppose all injustice and political oppression.

Future

It looks forward to the coming of the *kingdom of God, which Jesus often described as a banquet (Luke 14:16). Believers feel the pain and frustration of having 'not yet' arrived, but the Eucharist, just like the presence of the Holy Spirit, is a pledge, given to them now, of all that is promised to them in the future kingdom (Luke 22:16, 19–20). Christians, by taking part in it, commit themselves to work for justice, the renewal of *creation and the well-being of all people, which is God's will for the world now and will be realized in his coming kingdom. This is where the Corinthian Christians were failing, by allowing the rich to enjoy luxurious food and the poor to go hungry – a big enough disgrace to deserve the judgment of God (1 Cor. 11:20–32). Christians are obliged to challenge the gross inequalities they see around them and model compassion and justice in their community life, as Jesus did in teaching, healing and feeding the crowds (John 6). This is why this sacrament, properly understood, is not a comfortable, domestic rite, but subversive and revolutionary – not least in the lives of Christians.

The NT gives no indication that the Lord's Supper is a mysterious, secret ritual. Its relevance and importance reach beyond the event itself, proclaiming the giving of Jesus' body and blood for the life of the world. Jesus made ordinary food and drink signs of the gospel which is freely offered to all – and told us to do the same. Every local church should ask itself therefore whether these three aspects of the Lord's Supper are reflected in its life and worship, and whether and how its theology and practice of the sacraments are furthering its mission in the world.

See also CHURCH.

Bibliography

T. Balasuriya, *The Eucharist and Human Liberation* (London: SCM, 1979); R. Bowen, *So I Send You* (London: SPCK, 1996); T. Gorringe, *Sign of Love: Reflections on the Eucharist* (London: SPCK, 1997); M. Green, *Baptism: Its Purpose, Practice and Power* (London: Hodder, 1987); H. Marshall, *Last Supper and Lord's Supper* (Exeter: Paternoster, 1980); E. Schlink, *The Doctrine of Baptism* (St Louis: Concordia, 1969); P. Ward (ed.), *Mass Culture: Eucharist and Mission in a Post-Modern World* (Oxford: Bible Reading Fellowhip, 1999).

R. BOWEN

Sacrifice

Sacrifice is a universal phenomenon known from the time of at least the Neolithic period. By sacrifice we mean objects, living or inanimate, involving blood or bloodless, which are set apart and offered to gods, spirits, demons or ancestors as propitiation, thanksgiving, supplication, or invocation of blessing and fruitfulness. In this sense sacrifice is widely attested among nomadic shepherds in both Asia and Africa and among food-growing people, from primitive tuber-cultivators down to the most highly developed rice-growing cultures of Japan and China.

Our concern here is: how much of a challenge to the Christian gospel is the idea of sacrifice in different cultures of the world? What, then, is the value of such understanding for mission? Although many ancient religions no longer exist, nor can their rituals be traced directly in today's religious traditions, some form of their practices is still prevalent among most *cultures of the world. While some of them are derived from a major religion native to their culture, others are simply traditional customs and practices adapted to, or surviving, those religions. In many cultures Christianity has faced, or is still facing, its toughest challenge on both these fronts.

Sacrifice in the world's religious traditions

Sacrifice is so extensive and varied that space does not permit a full discussion. Here we offer three examples.

Greek religion was influenced by the invading Indo-European religion, and the combination resulted in both bloodless sacrifice of food and drink, and blood sacrifice of animals. On the other hand, Roman religion before it was influenced by the Greeks was largely agrarian, following an agricultural year, although in its pre-Roman culture animal sacrifice of pigs, cattle and sheep, along with divination, were included.

Among the food-growing cultures of Africa, sacrifice is rarely made to the Supreme God, though they believe in such a being, but is largely directed to the lesser gods and spirits, and also to the *ancestors who are not considered as gods but as the 'living dead' who still form part of the family, and who are consulted as mediators to the Supreme Being. In West Africa (Yoruba land) where gods and spirits are organized loosely under the headship of the Supreme Being, as in the Hindu pantheon, sacrifices and prayers are made only to the lesser gods who are in charge of divination (Orunnula), fate (Esu, the trickster spirit who manipulates the divine fate), creation (Obatala), and war (Ogun). Below these are the powerful gods and spirits of lakes, woods and mountains, and the ancestral spirits who come in this category remain relatively unimportant.

While official Islam approves of no sacrifice (Qur'an, surah 22:38), pre-Islamic blood sacrifice continues, especially as part of the pilgrimage ritual at Mount Arafat near Mecca, as well as on the tenth day of the month, Dhu al-Hijjah, throughout the Islamic world. They are interpreted as a commemoration of Abraham's sacrifice, and as almsgiving as part of it is shared with the poor. Similarly, both bloodless and blood sacrifice forms part of popular Islam throughout the world.

Sacrifice in the Judeo-Christian tradition

The primary sources in the Bible are the so-called priestly texts of Leviticus, Exodus 25 – 40, and Numbers 5 – 10, 15, 28 – 29. The rituals associated with the sacrifice are described in minute detail as to the type of animals required at each occasion, the place of slaughter and the distribution, consumption or disposal of their various parts.

The main purpose of a clear prescription of each type of sacrifice and a detailed description of how it must be offered, is to teach Israel that their God is holy, and sinful human beings cannot approach him except on his terms. Thus the five major sacrifices were meant to achieve, first and foremost, propitiation/expiation ('burnt offering'), and

then favour ('cereal offering'), communion with God ('peace offering'), cleansing ('purification offering'), and communion with fellow humans ('guilt offering').

However, Israel is not to presume on these benefits as automatic, as obedience and humility toward God and justice and equality toward fellow humans are considered more important than sacrifices (1 Sam. 15:22–23; Isa. 1:11–17; Amos 5:21–25; Mic. 6:8). A subsidiary purpose of these sacrifices may be to wean Israel from idolatry where sacrificial banquets and drunken orgies are commonplace and the motivation behind them is to appease an angry god or to bribe him in order to receive favours. But the God of Israel is not to be approached in this way, and he is not like other gods. He has no physical form and needs no food (Exod. 20:4–6; 1 Sam. 2:28; Isa. 40:18–25; Ps. 50:7–15). His people's relationship with him is established on the basis of grace, and the *covenant is sustained by his faithfulness to its promises and not on their ability or willingness to bring offerings to him. The purpose behind the sacrifice is interpreted in the NT as a reminder of the seriousness of their sin before a holy God and not as a remedy in itself (Heb. 10:3).

The NT presents Jesus as the Lamb of God (John 1:29; cf. 1 Cor. 5:7), and his death is a substitutionary offering for sinners (Mark 10:45; cf. Isa. 53). The 'Eucharist' is commemoration of that sacrifice, and Jesus' redemptive activity is explained in sacrificial language (Rom. 3:24–25; Gal. 3:13; Eph. 5:2; 1 John 2:1–2; Rev. 1:5), so that the OT's sacrificial system was entirely subsumed and superseded in and through the death of Christ on the *cross (Heb. 9:11–28; 10:1–4). The idea of sacrifice is reinterpreted and transformed with a radically different meaning. Christians now offer themselves and everything they do – missions, praise and prayer, giving and receiving – as a 'spiritual sacrifice' (Rom. 12:1; Phil. 4:18; Heb. 13:15–16; 1 Pet. 2:5; Rev. 8:3–4). While they cannot atone, they belong properly to the age of the Holy Spirit (John 4:23–24). For Paul, presenting the gospel to the Gentiles is a priestly service and the converts are as 'offerings' to God (Rom. 15:16). But at the same time they involved an ultimate sacrifice of discipleship for Paul (Phil. 2:17; 2 Tim. 4:6), and in a different way for all disciples.

Sacrifice in the context of mission

In contexts in which sacrifices are considered essential for maintaining the human relationship with the spirit world, a radical change of world-view is required to be set free from this dependence. This may require time and determination: Christians in these contexts sometimes secretly practise rituals or consult the gods alongside their Christian devotions. It does not help simply to ignore or reject as pagan the sacrificial rites which are deeply embedded in the culture, otherwise we will not remove the strong presumption that humans must sacrifice *something* in order to appease God/a god.

A missiological engagement begins with discussion and recognition of the similarities and differences with the OT sacrificial system, which points to a God who is to be approached very differently from all other so-called gods. He is a God of both absolute *grace and utter holiness. Only when people understand who God is, will they see the futility of sacrifices. In the light of this, the uniqueness of Jesus' sacrifice can be understood: it is a grace-filled God-given provision in which God himself, in Christ, satisfies the demands of his own holiness. Here there is nothing that humans can bring as an offering of atonement; they are simply asked to identify with the one who was crucified and accept him dying in their place. Christ's sacrifice is thus 'once for all', and can never be repeated, which is why the Eucharist cannot be a re-enactment of the sacrifice of Christ (Heb. 9:25–26).

In secular contexts, there is nevertheless an understanding of sacrificial *love, in which a person gives even their life for someone else. Here it will be more helpful to approach the sacrifice of Christ first as an act of love, and the understanding of substitutionary atonement will come later.

The call to personal sacrifice is central to the gospel, not as an appeasement but as a response to God's love. Jesus challenges his disciples to take up their cross and follow him – an invitation to death! Mission history is full of innumerable itinerant preachers, evangelists, missionaries and pastors who forsook many things that were otherwise legitimate, such as loved ones, personal ambitions, comfortable lifestyle, properties, fame and familiar cultures, knowing that all this was well worth the trouble for the salvation of those who are still outside Christ. Many have sacrificed their lives in mission service. In fact many felt that their sacrifice was no sacrifice at all. This was well stated by the missionary martyr Jim Elliot: 'He is no fool who gives what he cannot keep to gain what he cannot lose.' Similarly, Hudson Taylor: 'What we give up for Christ we gain. What we keep back for ourselves is our real loss.'

Bibliography

G. A. Anderson, *Sacrifices and Offerings in Ancient Israel: Studies in their Social and Political Importance* (Atlanta: Scholars Press, 1987); J. van Baal, 'Offering, Sacrifice and Gift', *Numen* 23, 1976, pp. 161–178; R. T. Beckwith, *Sacrifice in the Bible* (Carlisle: Paternoster, 1995); J. Ching, *Chinese Religions* (Maryknoll: Orbis Books, 1993); J. Henninger, 'Sacrifice', in *Encyclopedia of Religion*, 12, pp. 544–557; J. R. Hinnells, *A New Handbook of Living Religions* (London: Penguin, 1998); E. O. James, 'Aspects of Sacrifice in the OT', *ExpTim* 50, 1938–39, pp. 151–155; J. Milgrom, *Leviticus 1 – 16. Anchor Bible* (New York: Doubleday, 1991); J. Quaegebeur (ed.), *Ritual and Sacrifice in the Ancient Near East* (Leuven: Peeters, 1993); L. G. Thompson, *Chinese Religion: An Introduction* (Belmont: Wadsworth, [4]1989).

A. PAGOLU

Salvation

Approaching salvation

Salvation and the related concepts of redemption, deliverance, rescue and *liberation (*peace, tranquillity and justice) have strong religious and missiological connotations. Religiosity belongs to our human 'hardware', and salvation is a fundamental concern of all humankind.

Salvation is the central theme of biblical revelation, and Christian missionary witness is guided by the salvific vision of *Christ. In our pluralistic world, Christians share the commonality of humanity struggling to secure its fragile existence, but the question they face is how to witness to other faiths of the salvific 'uniqueness of Jesus' (Wright) with complete loyalty to 'the incomparable Christ' (Stott).

This article considers that Christian mission is a holistic and embodied witness about the fullness of God's presence in and for the world. It assumes that Christians are entrusted with a vision that calls them forth to bear witness to the 'better' (cf. Heb. 11:40), and indeed complete, salvation by living in the way of Christ. Thus, Christians should be willing to listen attentively to other religions' soteriological claims, discuss them seriously and be prepared to show how they fit into, or diverge from, the biblical account of the redemption of humanity.

Salvation is a rescuing from some real or potential peril. Something is wrong with a person or with humanity and needs to be made right. The helplessness of humans in the face of atrocious evil, oppressive power structures, grievous situations and other such predicaments necessitates a solution. Salvation presupposes that there is someone to be saved, a threat they need to be rescued from, and some way in which they can be saved from it. Salvation is a comprehensive term for all the benefits that are graciously bestowed on humans by a benevolent deity or supernatural powers. Salvation extends the vision of the meaning of life beyond the mundane experience of temporal life into the realm beyond death.

Christians differ in the way they conceptualize salvation, which in turn determines their approach to mission. Those who see salvation as primarily the restoration of an individual relationship with God make personal *evangelism their main model of mission (mostly evangelical). Some see the teaching of doctrinal truths as the prime focus of mission (Protestant). Some see salvation as mediated through the church (Catholic, Orthodox). Others see the gospel embodied in transformed individuals and communal living (free church). Still others think more in terms of common humanity (ecumenical, environmentalist), social justice (social activist) or the transformation of all of social reality (liberationist). In fact our view of salvation is probably the most critical determinant in deciding on our approach to mission. In recent years there has been general recognition that all these dimensions of salvation have their own validity, and that salvation is a comprehensive term which includes them all and brings deliverance from every dimension of the consequences of evil, be it personal sin, sickness and/or social injustice.

Salvation in world religions

A religious tradition's way of unpacking the meaning of salvation reflects on that tradition's anthropological concerns. To understand the need for salvation and what it means to be saved presumes an understanding of what it means to be *human. The presupposition is that salvation requires a rescuing of humanity from all that dehumanizes it. Thus, salvation for every religious tradition is at the heart of their mission, and may be understood either as a specific mandate to actively share a universal salvific message, or as a witness to a better way of life and to a deeper existential meaning of one moral tradition over against the others.

Monotheistic religions relate salvation to the activity of an omnipotent deity. *God is conceived as having sovereignty over all creation. The world exists by divine permission. In Abrahamic theisms, God is completely sovereign over the created world and the source of morality. God defines the course of history and its end. God's will is discernible through prophetic visions of humanity's eschatological future. People have knowingly and freely acted against God's will. Sin is as much individual as it is social and institutional. Thus, there is a need for restored relationships and *reconciliation with God. In Christianity reconciliation is achieved if God's gracious pardon meets humankind's willing response of repentance and *faith.

Salvation in monotheistic traditions is essentially about the restoration of communion with God and the enabling of deeper participation in the life of God. This is usually achieved through works of merit which earn divine favour. Christians, however, insist that salvation through sheer self-effort, unaffected by God's grace, is impossible. Salvation does require that a person sincerely repents of his or her sins. It is also conditional on that person actively seeking God's mercy and making every effort to flourish in and with a community that lives in God's presence. But Christian salvation is distinctive in that it comes from God by his *grace as a gift which cannot be earned.

Non-monotheistic traditions divide along the lines of primal (tribal) religions of traditional societies (e.g. African and Asian) and religions drawing inspiration from formative sacred scriptures (e.g. Buddhism, Jainism and traditional Hinduism). The former perceive that there is little or no difference between divinity and nature, which is the source of life. Nature is permeated with vital divine forces (*mana* or spirits) both good and evil. A person's destiny is indissoluble from that of the tribe. The goal of life is to participate fully in present communal living while facing the past. To attain salvation, persons (and their tribes) hearken back to the 'golden past' in order to reunite with the ancestors and ultimately to the sources of life by preserving the integrity and harmony of the hierarchy of traditional living.

Non-monotheistic religions with scriptural texts consider a particular sort of ignorance to be the basic problem of humanity. The ignorance in question involves having false beliefs about the nature of persons and their divine cosmic environment, which is the essence of all phenomena both good and evil. The aim of meditative practices is the achievement of an esoteric religious experience of enlightenment in which calm and bliss are accompanied by an understanding of the true nature of reality. Salvific practices enable a person to develop attitudes and disciplines of cessation of individual existence by becoming absorbed into the cosmic (*moksha* in Hinduism) and escaping from personal suffering into eternal peace (via *nirvana* as in Buddhism). Absorption into the universal is the essence of human existence. Different traditions give very different accounts of what is the actual nature of the divine environment (pantheism in Hindu *Brahman*, or Buddhist substance-less universal state of non-being). Whatever this understanding, the cessation into the divine is one's sole responsibility. Ultimate religious truth is learned by an individual enlightenment experience.

Being a derivative of religious soteriology, notions of salvation in enlightenment humanism (e.g. classical Marxism), tend to be reinterpretations of one or another religious conception (e.g. the notion of the kingdom of God with justice and peace). The motivation for achieving salvation is entirely dependent on the human's initiative and works.

It is important for mission practice to understand these different approaches to salvation, avoiding the assumption that the gospel can simply be applied indiscriminately as if each context understands salvation in similar terms. If Christian mission does not address people's specific concerns, they will not 'hear' the gospel, and may not consider the 'salvation' that is offered to them as relevant.

Judeo-Christian soteriological themes

Jewish and Christian theisms are rooted in the biblical narrative recording experiential and revelatory encounters between God and humanity. In the holy Scriptures of Jews and Christians, God's gracious self-disclosure takes place in creation and in history (including personal stories of biblical characters) and will lead the creation to its ultimate purpose of a 'new heaven and a new earth' in accordance with God's intention to rescue everything from the consequences of sin. God permeates the beginning, the end and everything in between in the story of the creation and human life.

Salvation, as understood in the sacred texts of ancient Jewish and early Christian traditions, is to experience the *shalom* of God's presence or liberation from oppression, exile, injustice, torment by evil spirits, and rescue from death, tragedy, evil and suffering. It can refer to the state of blessedness of an individual after death, usually envisioning eternal life in a spiritual realm beyond the limitations and fragility of the known physical world. It is also an expectation of newness or transformation of the individual, the community and the created world order at the end of history in which the dead are resurrected, and life is restored to the perfect harmony of God's original intent.

The vehicle of salvation, both of individuals and of nations, is a God-chosen and renewed God-centred community of faith in voluntary *covenant with God and in covenant among the community's members to follow God's commandments. It is an alternative community to other communities with different faiths, in order to be a light among all peoples, a blessing to all nations, and to offer healing to all peoples. Being 'grafted into' (Rom. 11:24) the salvation story of Jewish people, Christians share with contemporary Jews the beginning, the unfolding and the messianic expectations of the story's ending. They differ considerably in their understanding of the *eschatological closure of history and the means of overcoming alienation from God.

Christians accept Jesus as the promised Messiah, the Son of God, and his saving work is the focus of their mission. God vindicated Jesus' unjust and yet atoning suffering by raising him from the dead and thereby endorsing his messianic mission of bringing *healing, justice and peace into the world. In the cross of Jesus, Christian faith sees God's self-giving love redeeming desperate humanity's sin and rebellion, both individually and corporately, and offering forgiveness.

Christianity is a religion of the crucified and *resurrected Messiah. In Jesus the Christ a cosmic transformation has happened: God and humanity are reconciled. We cannot come to God, so God has come to us. Salvation is firmly secured only in and through Jesus – God's Messiah. While the spiritual encounter with the risen Lord is formative, salvation is not an esoteric experience of autonomous individuals. Neither is salvation a set of ideas, but a relationship with a living person and a process of transformation fostered by this relationship, which reaches beyond and through Christians to the whole world.

Christian traditions have different emphases on the past, present and future dimensions of salvation. Some see salvation as primarily past tense, to do with Christ's finished work on the cross. Mission applies this to a restored personal relationship with God. Those who think in terms of salvation as on-going transformation will focus their mission more on *discipleship and the need for continuous renewal and growing in faith. Those who see salvation eschatologically will try to get as many saved as possible before the second coming. No one Christian tradition is exclusively one or the other; the emphasis, however, is a strong determinant of their approach to mission. Sharing the good news of Christ in a world saturated with a plethora of religious beliefs is a challenge and an opportunity for *witness and *dialogue.

Missiological implications

The Christian missionary perspective raises a serious question: If salvation in Christian terms is seen in relation to the uniqueness and centrality of Christ, what are the implications of this for other religious traditions which might work for their salvation independently of whether they have heard of Christ or the gospel? In other words, if salvation is by God's grace, does that make it possible for God to save those who have never heard of Christ? Why mission? Or is salvation only through an explicit faith in Christ? This is perhaps the most burning question of our time and Christians must deal candidly with it.

One way to frame these questions is to ask: Who will be saved? There have been multiple attempts to find the Christian answer depending on one's understanding of the nature of God and human nature. They can be positioned in three distinctive groupings from the point of view of their salvific value:

(1) Only Christianity offers true salvation; there is no salvific value in any other religion, and salvation in Christ is indispensable (exclusivist, absolutist).

(2) All religions have legitimate salvific insights and they will find their ultimate fulfilment in the cosmic salvation of Christianity (fulfilment, evolutionist, universalist).

(3) All great religions are equally sufficient for salvation and Christianity is not the definitive norm (relativist, pluralist).

While these three perspectives are shared across denominational borders, exclusivism has been the dominant perspective of Western Christianity and contemporary evangelicalism. Fulfilment is the position popular largely in the liberal and ecumenical Protestant, post-Vatican II Catholic and Orthodox Christian circles. Relativism is a philosophical theological position rather than an ecclesial perspective.

In recent times these distinctions have become less definite, with some evangelicals answering the question with a more mixed approach. While a matter of continuing debate, the question as it stands bears the stamp of modern Enlightenment preoccupation with speculative theologizing. It refers solely to something that happens to an individual after death and suggests that people join a religion in order to be beneficiaries of salvation by subscribing to a set of dogmas, rites and institutions. 'Such an ahistorical, [individualistic] and otherworldly perception of salvation is spurious' (D. Bosch, *Transforming Mission: Paradigm Shifts in Theology of Mission*, p. 488) It also betrays a human pretence of knowing the mysteries of God (*contra* Rom. 11:33–34).

Another way of framing the same question is: how should Christians witness, and to what? While agreeing on the uniqueness and unsurpassability of Jesus' salvific claims, Christian theological responses to other religions' salvific claims cannot be merely dismissive, and can only remain agnostic as to their eternal value. Christian theists must admit that 'the line between God's work of common and special grace is not something that [they] are well able to discern' (T. L. Tiessen, *Who Can Be Saved? Reassessing Salvation in Christ and World Religions*, p. 384).

Thus, the practice of Christian mission is characterized by creative tension between openness for dialogue with other faiths and firm convictions that God has decisively wrought salvation for all in and through Jesus Christ. Mission is best done as a witness to the new quality of life that comes in Christ. There is an indispensable Christological perspective on soteriology. And yet, salvation in Christ is 'in the context of human society en route to a whole and healed world' (Bosch, *Transforming Mission*, p. 399) In the light of the gospel, salvation is not so much concerned with a person going to heaven as it is about God 'redeeming the whole earth' (J. G. Stackhouse, *What Does It Mean to Be Saved? Broadening Evangelical Horizons of Salvation*, p. 10).

Christian mission testifies to the holistic message of salvation that if anyone is united to Christ, following his vision and engaging in practising his deeds, a world-shattering conversion and alteration of human conditions will occur: 'a new creation' (2 Cor. 5:17) will come into being. This results in a personal relationship with God that is constituted in the context of a Spirit-led community of fellow pilgrims on the salvific journey and is extended to the whole creation. Thus, even now in the present a foretaste of the salvation expected at the end times may be savoured. To be credible, the message has to be an embodied witness to Christ's way of salvation (Acts 16:17) and to him as 'the truth and the life' (John 14:6) to people of other living faiths. The church is the 'hermeneutic of the gospel' (Newbigin). Salvation in Christ is a matter of identity not of superiority.

Considering the points of contact between Christianity and other religions in the field of ethics, it can be argued that *ethics is the theological grammar of missionary valuation and missionary engagement with the soteriological claims of any religion in a pluralistic and global world. As with Abrahamic faiths in general, Christianity highlights the coherence of correct beliefs and authentic behaviour. By emphasizing the integrity of individual and communal moral living of persons created in the image of God, the reality and the goodness of the creation (see *Ecology/environment), *jubilee for the oppressed, care and responsibility for the peaceable and prosperous future of humanity, Christians are well situated to press on towards higher ethical standards in their missionary witness, particularly by the embrace of the radical ethical vision of the *kingdom of God.

Christian communities have a holistic 'three-stranded' (McClendon) way of relating their message of salvation to the inspirations of the surrounding cultures. Recognizing the sovereignty of God over all life, they can constructively and positively engage with the explicit and hidden religious depths within cultures by providing a way to fulfil human longings. Being informed by the gospel story, they are in a position to help cultures to rightly see themselves in the light of a prophetic critique of any culture's social deformity, illusions and self-deceit. By embodying and not merely proclaiming Christ's kingdom vision, a gospel-formed Christian community can be a sign of a whole new world of social relations and a catalyst of change in the surrounding community.

See also GOSPEL, HOLISTIC MISSION.

Bibliography
D. J. Bosch, *Transforming Mission: Paradigm Shifts in Theology of Mission* (Maryknoll: Orbis Books, 1993); B. J. Kallenberg, *Live to Tell: Evangelism for a Postmodern Age* (Grand Rapids: Brazos Press, 2002); J. W. McClendon, Jr, *Systematic Theology*, 3 vols. (Nashville: Abingdon Press, 1994–2002 [1986]); L. Newbigin, *The Gospel in a Pluralist Society* (Grand Rapids: Eerdmans, 1991); R. A. Parry and C. H. Partridge (eds.), *Universal Salvation? The Current Debate* (Grand Rapids: Eerdmans, 2003); D. W. Shenk, *Global Gods: Exploring the Role of Religions in Modern Societies* (Scottdale: Harold Press, 1995); J. G. Stackhouse, Jr

(ed.), *What Does It Mean to Be Saved? Broadening Evangelical Horizons of Salvation* (Grand Rapids: Baker Academics, 2002); J. R. W. Stott, *The Incomparable Christ* (Downers Grove: InterVarsity Press, 2001); T. L. Tiessen, *Who Can Be Saved? Reassessing Salvation in Christ and World Religions*, (Downers Grove: InterVarsity Press; Leicester: IVP, 2004); C. J. H. Wright, *The Uniqueness of Jesus* (Mill Hill: Monarch Books, 2001 [1997]).

P. R. PARUSHEV

Samaritan mission

What is the significance of the Lukan portrait of the Samaritan mission for the theology and practice of today's mission? This study focuses on Luke–Acts, as only these books contain material about the Samaritans: a narrative on Jesus' sending of messengers into Samaria (Luke 9:51–56), a parable of the compassionate Samaritan (10:25–37), a miracle of the grateful Samaritan (17:11–19) and an extensive account of the evangelization of Samaria (Acts 8:4–25). Also, in Acts, Samaria is mentioned at important points at 1:8, 8:1, 9:31 and 15:3.

The socio-religious setting

The Samaritans, up to and including the NT period, were a people who struggled to find their status and identity in the midst of colonial, political and religious oppression. The available sources are often ambiguous and ambivalent in their portrayal of the Samaritans' socio-religious and ethnic identity. Samaritans are variously described in Josephus and other Jewish sources: 'Cuthaeans', 'Shechemites', 'Sidonians', 'those on Gerizim' and the 'foolish people that dwell in Shechem'. All these are an attempt to show symbolically that the Samaritans were not true Israelites but syncretists, outcasts, apostates and idolaters and of pagan origin; thus the association is derogatory. 2 Kings 17:24–41 speaks of them negatively as always compromising their worship of Yahweh with idolatry. It would not be surprising therefore if, in view of their ambiguous and questionable status and ethnic identity, doubts were cast on the legitimacy of Samaritan mission and later on that of the Samaritan Christians themselves.

Jesus and the Samaritans

Matthew has the mission prohibition to all Gentiles, including Samaritans: 'Do not go among the Gentiles or enter any town of the Samaritans' (Matt. 10:5b). This seems anti-Samaritan, implying that the Samaritans could never belong to the 'house of Israel', although it needs to be seen in the context of Jesus' priority on Jewish mission at this stage in his ministry. John is more pro-Samaritan, as Jesus has a mission to them and he wins a large crowd (John 4). Luke shows an even more positive affinity towards them. Jesus himself takes the initiative to go through Samaria. He does not bring any charge against the Samaritans when they fail to receive him and his messengers (Luke 9:52, 55), nor are they allowed to be the victims of the disciples' fire of destruction. They are treated favourably by Jesus, in contrast to the criticism directed towards his disciples. The parable of the compassionate Samaritan overturns the popular prejudice against Samaritans and exhorts Jews to be neighbours to anyone in need, just like the merciful Samaritan (10:36–37).

If love of the neighbour is to act beyond one's own religious and racial boundaries, then Luke not only defends the action of the merciful Samaritan (in contrast to the inaction of the priest and the Levite), but also the Samaritan's status as part of Israel in fulfilling the *love command of the Law. It may be that Luke intends to show that the Jews must learn from the action of their enemies, the Samaritans, what love of neighbour means. Likewise, Jesus commends the one Samaritan who was healed of leprosy and who came back to thank Jesus (Luke 17:18–19). The Samaritan, though a foreigner, becomes the sharer of true faith and worship, and thereby Luke defends his action and his new experience of salvation. Luke encourages an affinity towards Samaritans and challenges his readers to follow their example.

Mission to the Samaritans in Acts

Philip, who proclaimed the gospel to the Samaritans in Acts, appears as a relatively minor figure (Acts 6:5) to carry out a major and difficult stage in preaching to the marginalized Samaritans. Luke describes Philip's success in the Samaritan mission, and his introduction of Philip as one 'full of the Spirit and wisdom' (6:3) equates him with leading figures of the Scripture. Philip's ministry involves preaching, healing, exorcism, and the manifestation of the kingdom of God in Samaria. Luke wants to show that Philip is an authentic figure like other leading figures of the Scripture, and that the Samaritan mission is legitimate and no lesser in result than the ministry of Jesus and the Jerusalem mission conducted by the apostles.

Theology of Samaritan mission

The Samaritan mission of Philip in Acts 8 might be seen as contradicting Matthew 10:5b, at least in the early church context; and similarly Jesus' sending of the messengers into a Samaritan village in Luke 9:52. But in the context of the universal call to mission in Matthew 28:19 and Acts 1:8, the church moves from the focused mission of Jesus to the universalistic dimension of mission. The centrifugal mission out from Jerusalem in Acts 1:8 finds its fulfilment in the activity of Philip with regard to Samaria. The following aspects of mission derive from this:

First, the 'Samaritans' of today vary according to context. In a broad sense, they are the marginalized in society, the *poor and the weak or even the colonized. In the Indian context, they are the '*dalits', the broken and the oppressed, the untouchables who find themselves in the lowest of the class and caste system, the voiceless who sometimes suffer in silence. God is interested in defending their cause, using their godly examples as paradigms for Christian behaviour, and making them heirs of his *kingdom. The mission of the church is to come out of its comfort zone and break through the boundaries of culture, class, caste, colour, religion and society. More than that, however, 'Samaritans' are also in a special way mediators of gospel truth and examples of genuine compassionate faith. It is often not what we give to the poor and the marginalized that is significant, but what we receive from them.

Second, the mission to the Samaritans was not initially apostolic but Hellenistic. It was not started by any of the apostles, but by Philip, one of the Seven who was chosen to 'wait on tables'. Though there were many others who were exiled with Philip, he was the 'first significant foreign missionary' beyond the borders of Judea. In the case of the Gentile mission, it was Peter who took the initiative, after it was ratified by his heavenly vision. In the case of the Samaritans, it was neither an apostle who started the work, nor was there any heavenly or supernatural vision to ratify the mission. It is not always the leaders of mission who have significant roles to play in the *missio Dei, but ordinary servants of God who can have key roles in his purposes. The account of the mission in Acts 8:4–25 indicates that it is not by specially commissioned apostles alone that mission can be accomplished, but by those who are 'full of the Spirit and wisdom' (6:3) and are prepared to carry out his commission.

Third, Philip, or his Hellenist group, did not seem to share the popular hostility of the Jews towards the Samaritans. None of the Jerusalem-based apostles went to evangelize the Samaritans. Apart from other reasons, whatever they may be, their natural enmity towards the land and the people of Samaria (cf. Luke 9:54) would have probably discouraged them from being engaged in a proper Samaritan mission. The great commission and the experience of Pentecost apparently failed to transform the thinking of the Twelve to include Samaritans in their mission vision. Racial or religious antagonism towards people who have different religious practices and ideology has absolutely no place in modern mission.

Bibliography

J. Adna and H. Kvalbein (eds.), *The Mission of the Early Church to Jews and Gentiles* (Tübingen: Mohr Siebeck, 2000); S. Cunningham, 'Through Many Tribulations': The Theology of Persecution in Luke–Acts (Sheffield: Sheffield Academic Press, 1997); C. F. Evans, *Saint Luke* (London: SCM, 1990); I. H. Marshall, *The Gospel According to Luke* (Exeter: Paternoster, 1978); J. D. Purvis, 'The Fourth Gospel and the Samaritans', NovT 17, 1975, pp. 161–198; V. J. Samkutty, *The Samaritan Mission in Acts* (London: T. & T. Clark, 2006); R. C. Tannehill, *Luke* (Nashville: Abingdon Press, 1996); J. Zangenberg, '"Open Your Eyes and Look at the Fields": Contacts between Christians and Samaria According to the Gospel of John', in V. Morabito *et al.* (eds.), *Samaritan Researches, vol. V: Proceedings of the*

Congress of the SES 1996/1997 (University of Sydney: Mandelbaum Publishing, 2000).

V. J. SAMKUTTY

SATAN, see SPIRITUAL WARFARE

Shamanism

The word shamanism 'comes to us, through Russian, from the Tungusic *saman*' (M. Eliade, *Shamanism: Archaic Techniques of Ecstasy*, p. 4). 'In all Tungus languages this term refers to persons of both sexes who have mastered spirits, who at their will can introduce these spirits into themselves and use their power over the spirits in their own interests, particularly helping other people, who suffer from the spirits' (S. M. Shirokogoroff, *Psychomental Complex of the Tungus*, p. 269). Identifying shamanism with the 'technique of ecstasy', Mircea Eliade explains that 'the shaman specializes in a trance during which his soul is believed to leave his body and ascend to the sky or descend to the underworld' (*Shamanism*, pp. 4–5). Michael Harner defines a shaman as 'a man or woman who enters an altered state of consciousness, at will, to contact and utilize an ordinarily hidden reality in order to acquire knowledge, power, and to help other persons' (*The Way of the Shaman*, p. 20). In short, shamanism is a family of traditions seeking to solve human problems by interactions with the spirits through the shaman acting as mediator.

Shamanism in Korea

As 'Korea's earliest and only indigenous religion', shamanism has exercised 'a profound influence on the development of Korean attitudes and practices' (Pyong-Choon Hahm, *Shamanism: The Spirit World of Korea*, p. 60). Pervasive as *folk religion down through history, shamanism has become rooted in Korean cultural soil. The main purpose of the shamanic ritual, *kut*, performed by the shaman, *mudang*, is 'a resolution of real problems through supernatural power' (Tae-gon Kim, in *Shamanism: Past and Present*, p. 281). Indeed, Korean shamanism is based on a strong reality-focused, fortune-seeking secularism, which has made it possible not just to survive the challenge of imported religions such as Buddhism, Confucianism, Taoism and Christianity but, in a real sense, rather to shamanize them. In the case of Protestantism, for instance, it is well known that the blessing-centred faith of the Korean church, which in effect has created mass appeal, has its cultural root in a shamanic religiosity.

Both inside and outside the church, shamanism in Korea is increasingly popularized in line with the worldwide trend towards a shamanic renaissance in the name of neo-shamanism closely associated with the *New Age. More significantly, the manipulation of the spirit world for prosperity is increasingly driven by materialism. No longer trusting institutionalized religious authorities, and so with less commitment to them, many people accept shamanism as part of personal life, as they pursue worldly fortunes through more instant and tangible mystic experiences.

Shamanism and the Bible

Clearly, the Bible strictly prohibits any kind of shamanic practices among the people of God. The Israelites were not to let anyone be found among them 'who sacrifices their son or daughter in the fire, who practises divination or sorcery, interprets omens, engages in witchcraft, or casts spells, or who is a medium or spiritist or who consults the dead' (Deut. 18:10–11). However, shamanic activities never disappeared in Israel. Saul visited a shaman to call the dead Samuel in order to solve his pressing question (1 Sam. 28). Manasseh provoked God to anger by his affirmation of shamanic practices (2 Kgs 21:6; 2 Chr. 33:6). Finally, God had to judge Israel, partly because of their adherence to pagan shamanism (Isa. 2:6).

In the NT, Jesus' miracles were considered by some Jews to result from his close connection with the spirits (Matt. 12:24; Luke 11:15). Jesus explained that he drove out demons by the *Spirit of God (Matt. 12:28). Due to his oneness with the Spirit, Jesus has often been identified as a shaman or mystic, a spirit-possessed healer, who had shamanic experiences of communion with the divine in a variety of non-ordinary states of consciousness. However, Jesus never manipulated spiritual powers for his own ends, and he always made himself accountable to his Father, not operating merely on his own authority. Also his aim was to set people free, not to bring them into slavish reliance on techniques or rituals for success.

Shamanism and mission

These observations imply two important facts with regard to the relation of shamanism to the Christian community. First, some Christians have deviated from the faith by seeking help from shamanism outside the church. Secondly, more seriously, there has been distortion of faith by creating a shamanism *inside* the church which portrays Jesus and/or ecclesiastical leaders as shamanic mediators. These two phenomena have been clearly observed among Korean churches, and they have deprived them of ecclesial integrity and social credibility.

In this respect, the first urgent mission of the church today is to practise de-shamanization, eliminating shamanic dimensions from Christian faith and life. The church must restore its authentic identity by discarding religiously *syncretistic and culturally accommodated impurities. The church being the church, in faithfulness to its origins in God's purposes, is the strongest way for it to do mission. Secondly, the church needs to encounter shamanism with missional dialogue rather than simply to despise it and drive it out as a primitive superstition, which is what most early missionaries in Korea did, with their civilizing, imperialistic mindset.

Christians can tell shamanists that there is only one God, who is both Lord and Creator, whom all human beings are to obey in love, not to manipulate for earthly benefits, which actually come from him, not as a result of functional rituals but as gifts of relational communion. Lastly, the church must be able to witness to a distinctive, even contrasting, way of life based on biblical values, sufficiently different from shamanic secularism that people in the world cannot but recognize it as a true and alternative community.

Bibliography

M. J. Borg, 'Jesus Before and After Easter: Jewish Mystic and Christian Messiah', in Marcus J. Borg and N. T. Wright (eds.), *Meaning of Jesus: Two Visions* (San Francisco: Harper, 2000); S. L. Davis, *Jesus the Healer: Possession, Trance, and the Origins of Christianity* (London: Continuum, 1995); M. Eliade, *Shamanism: Archaic Techniques of Ecstasy* (New York: Pantheon, 1964); Pyong-Choon Hahm, 'Shamanism and the Korean World-View', in R. Guisso and Chai-shin Yu (eds.), *Shamanism: The Spirit World of Korea* (Berkeley, CA: Asian Humanities Press, 1988); M. Harner, *The Way of the Shaman* (San Francisco: Harper, ³1990); Tae-gon Kim, 'The Realities of Korean Shamanism', in M. Hoppal and O. J. von Sadovszky (eds.), *Shamanism: Past and Present. Part I* (Budapest: Hungarian Academy of Sciences, 1989); S. M. Shirokogoroff, *Psychomental Complex of the Tungus* (London: Kegan Paul, Trench and Trubner, 1935).

JUN GYU PARK

Short-term mission

Short-term mission is a phenomenon particularly of the twenty-first century. The ease of travel and the desire to get involved combine to enable large numbers of people to cross cultural boundaries to serve the world church. This means that local churches are more aware of what is happening within the worldwide body of Christ.

There are many definitions of what constitutes short-term mission. They can include individuals and teams, those serving from two weeks to two years, and people involved in specific activities for a particular time frame in their local area, another part of the country or overseas. Short-term mission trips can encompass a breadth of age groups in the church but are particularly popular among college students, Christian professionals with specialized abilities such as medical training, couples without children and those who are retired. Activities range from building work to street evangelism and everything in between. Trips are organized by mission agencies, individuals or local churches.

Terms like 'exposure trips' (lasting a few weeks) and 'gap years' (usually three months to one-year programmes) have been used for clarification. However these are not universally used. This means that short-term mission continues to include activities that are very diverse both in purpose and nature.

Given this breadth and the diversity of benefits and challenges related to short-term mission, this article will briefly consider three areas.

The place of short-term mission in an understanding of mission

There have been those who have questioned whether short-term mission is actually 'mission tourism'. This argument needs to be considered in the light of a definition of mission because particular definitions can lead to different conclusions as to the length of time required. For example, the degree to which mission is about *contextualization and *incarnation, questions the ability of those entering a situation for short periods of time to know a culture and build adequate relationships. However, there are brief mission trips outlined in the NT, like Jesus sending out the seventy in Luke 10:1–24, or Paul's journeys to plant churches and encourage newly established churches, outlined in the epistles. These passages suggest that mission can be short-term and can be effective in spreading the gospel; although it is hermeneutically debatable whether they can be interpreted paradigmatically for every generation.

Within this discussion, there are questions as to whether the nature of mission can be described as long or short-term. These time-related definitions may not fit a concept of the *missio Dei* that will only be complete on Christ's return. It could be that such time-related expressions are more a reflection of culture than biblical truth. Thus short-term mission may be a reflection of a time-focused culture and embody a mentality that expects immediate results and instant solutions. This can be positive where it injects a sense of urgency into the missionary task, yet may result in disillusionment and cultural insensitivity where the cultural context is not understood.

There are questions as to how short-term mission activities can be understood in the context of a call to mission. This has led to discussions as to whether short-term trips lead to long-term service. Concern has been raised about an 'anti-long-term' sentiment in current mission practice, and the impact of the redefinition of the term 'missionary' to include all Christians, thereby reducing an understanding of the specific challenges that those serving cross-culturally face. However, recent research appears to reflect a correlation between short-term mission trips and longer-term service. There is anecdotal evidence to suggest that hands-on experience during a short-term mission trip encourages people into full-time missionary service. However, the debate continues, as there is not currently sufficient statistical data to be conclusive.

Short-term mission and the church

Where short-term mission trips are organized by parachurch organizations, there are challenges to the sense of ownership and relationship both with the home church of the people going on the trip and the local church(es) receiving them. This is important in providing a context of consistency and ongoing ministry both in the life of the participant and the people that they ministered to in the other context. The short-termers can develop a belief that those that they are going to serve have little to offer. Yet the church of Christ is interdependent, and mutual edification is key for its health, no matter where the short-term team is called to minister.

This may enable short-term mission programmes to play a broader role in demonstrating the unity of the church, while pointing to the task that is still ahead of the church as it spreads the gospel. One example is an annual mission trip to Tanzania that combines church members from the USA, Kenya and Tanzania. Such activity is a physical demonstration of the body of Christ and the unity expressed in John 17.

Short-term mission trips have increasingly become an avenue for introducing Christians to a taste of what mission is all about. They have helped raise local church interest in other parts of the world and so increased the support for world mission. However, concern has been expressed about the cost of short-term mission trips and the way that money which could have been used to support local people or mission agency activity, is spent on airfares. Yet, the challenge of stewardship is one that affects all areas of the mission task and is not exclusive to short-term mission. The cultural differences that are encountered and the realization that the gospel is supracultural makes tangible the fact that the church is indeed universal and has one Lord and Saviour, Jesus Christ.

Good practice in running short-term mission programmes

Lastly, there are a number of practical challenges in short-term mission. These include whether the team is under national or foreign leadership; the type of food and standards of hygiene; ministering in cultures that are technologically worlds apart; accountability and financial administration; cultural differences and different worship styles. Other difficulties can arise when short-term workers participate in activities that the nationals can best do left to themselves; the attitudes of and relationship between long-term, short-term and national workers that can lead to tensions or even antagonism; and the significant workload required to prepare, organize and implement these trips that can take staff and time away from other ministry. Some of these are dependent on how a trip is organized and managed.

Concern about this has led to codes of good practice being developed in the UK, Canada and USA. These seek to outline the need for appropriate publicity, orientation, pastoral care and debriefing as key elements in the organization of trips. One development in the area of codes has been made by Global Connections (the UK network for world mission) who revised their code in 2005 to make it more applicable to churches.

The issues raised in this article are not all exclusive to short-term mission but may be more apparent when activity is limited to short periods of time. It is important that all involved in mission, short or long-term, are prepared to serve in honesty, openness, and accountability before the Lord and each other.

Bibliography

M. Allen, 'Mission Tourism,' <http://www.faithworks.com / archives / mission_tourism.htm>; C. M. Brown, 'Field Statement on the Short-term Mission Phenomenon: Contributing Factors and Current Debate,' <http://www.tiu.edu/tedsphd/ics_research/fieldstatements/STMFieldStatement.pdf>; R. Friesen, 'The Long-term Impact of Short-term Missions', in *Evangelical Missions Quarterly* 41, 2005, pp. 448–454; E. M. Givens, 'When are Short-Term Trips Terminal?', *World Pulse*, 12 March 2004, pp. 6–7; Global Connections Code of Best Practice in Short-term Mission, <http:www.globalconnections.co.uk/code.asp>; A. O'Sullivan, 'The Changes to Short-Term Mission Work,' *The Baptist Times*, 19 August 2004, pp. 8–9; D. Parrott, 'Managing the Short-Term Missions Explosion,' in *Evangelical Missions Quarterly*, 40, 2004, pp. 356–360; G. Schwartz, 'Maximising the Benefits of Short-Term Missions,' <http://www.wmausa.org/art-shortterm.htm>; A. Scott Moreau and M. O'Rear, 'Missions on the Web: All You Ever Wanted on Short-Term Missions', *Evangelical Missions Quarterly* 40, 2004, pp. 100–105.

I. MAKUKU AND V. CALVER

SIGNS AND WONDERS, see MIRACLES

Sin/the fall

Sin is the transgression of *God's will which constitutes rebellion against him and an offence to his holiness. It is both action and principle: as such it corrupts the human heart, causes human beings to 'fall short' of God's glory, and separates them from his presence. Central to God's mission, therefore, is the defeat and removal of sin in all of its dimensions and all of its consequences.

God's saving purposes, culminating in the life, death and resurrection of his Son Jesus, are focused in a recreation and transformation of all that has been marred by sin. The cross of Christ deals with sin in all of its manifestations both personal and cosmic. How sin is understood, and relatedly, how God's purposes of salvation are interpreted, are therefore pivotal for the theology and practice of mission.

Sin in biblical perspective

Sin entered the world, and thereby corrupted the human nature of all humanity, through the one man, Adam, whose sin was disobedience of the clear command of God (Rom. 5:12; Ps. 51:5; 1 John 3:4). The consequence was banishment from the Garden of Eden, and therefore from companionship and intimacy with God, resulting in spiritual death (Isa. 59:2; Rom. 6:23). Thereafter its corrosive influence affected the whole of the created order, since creation shared the consequences of the sin of Adam as its representative (Rom. 8:19–22). The relationships between God and humanity, God and creation, and humanity and creation, were all fractured as a result. God's mission therefore set about bringing reconciliation into all three dimensions of these broken relationships, so that ultimately all of *creation would be set free from the consequences of sin (Rev. 21:4; Col. 1:20).

The biblical concept of sin recognizes the

universality of sin, claiming that all human beings have sinned and stand condemned before the righteous God whom they have sinned against (Rom. 3:12, 23; 1 John 1:8). Sin is thus both a human *condition* as well as a human *action*. Culture, religion, society, politics and economics are all infiltrated by its influence and therefore come under the *judgment of God, needing redemption if they are to serve God in righteousness and truth. Against sin there is no defence nor any room for excuse. Hence, St Paul in Romans represents the situation of 'universal sin' (all have sinned), as well as 'universal guilt' (all are guilty), and worst of all is 'universal silence' (every mouth shut in silence, Rom. 3:19). However, whilst sin corrupts human nature, it does not universally destroy the image of God in which human beings were created, allowing many dimensions of creativity, beauty, love and truth to shine in human life and culture (Acts 17:25–28).

Nor does sin have the last word in the biblical relationship between God the Creator and the created order. The last word is '*salvation'. As a guilty person is incapable of helping him or herself, God who is love takes the initiative to provide a 'universal Saviour' in Christ as the 'Second Adam' (Rom. 5:18). Thus, God revealed his plan to save a sinful, helpless and lost world from the guilt, influence and consequences of sin. In response sinful human beings are called to *repent of their moral guilt and sinful actions, and receive the freely offered grace of the forgiveness of sin and the gift of eternal salvation in Jesus *Christ (Rom. 6:23; Acts 17:30). The remedy of the *cross of Jesus thus deals with sin in all of its dimensions and manifestations and this is the central message of the mission of the church (2 Cor. 5:17–21).

Sin in cultural perspective

Since all cultures are affected by sin, none can be uncritically endorsed, just as none can be unthinkingly condemned. Cultures, however, understand sin and wrongdoing very differently, so when mission theology encounters culture with the gospel of redemption, in an African context for example, it must make a conscious effort to understand what sin means from an African cultural perspective.

To illustrate this we will use the Igbo idea of sin from eastern Nigeria, which can very well speak for other African societies. The African traditional *world-view agrees with the biblical understanding that uprightness was the original state of mankind and that sin constitutes both transgression and rebellion. The difference is, perhaps, against whom the transgression or rebellion is made.

In the Igbo world-view, the Supreme Being, God (*Chukwu*), created and established an ordered world. The Igbo believe, however, that, though sin is lawlessness and an act of rebellion, it is not against God but against the society or the community. Sin is neither original nor universal; it can be avoided, and a person who has not rebelled or transgressed any known law cannot be considered a 'sinner'. Human beings are not forever hopelessly trapped in the condition of sin. It is possible to walk sinless; hence, the Igbo proffer their sinlessness, and do not in doing so think they are deceiving themselves. As long as a person does not act contrary to the established moral order he or she has not committed any sin.

One person's sin, however, can affect a whole community and pollute society, as it was in the case of Achan (Josh. 7:10–26). Sin is an act that consists in *Iru ala*, or *Imeru ala*, which means an act that desecrates both people and the earth or community. To sin means, therefore, to go contrary to those acts regarded as *Nso ala* (abominable acts that are taboo). Mishaps can befall that community because its people have polluted the society and fallen out of favour with the spirit realm. As long as the spirit realm of the community remains unhappy, angry or uncomfortable with the living realm, there will be no peace. Sin consists in wrongdoing, not just in breaking abstract laws but also mainly in going contrary to the command of the spirit realm in the bond of filial and social relationship in the community. Society takes pre-eminence, and the 'I' is subsumed in the 'we'.

Sin in the Igbo world-view, and among Africans in general, is not, therefore, conceived as an act against God's holiness. The Igbo do not even worship God directly; how then can they offend One they do not worship directly? Sin constitutes, rather, an offence that brings shame or defilement, and renders the offender an 'outsider' in the eyes of the community. This introduces the prevalent 'shame culture', instead of a 'moral guilt culture' as is the case with the Western world. Someone refrains from wrongdoing, not because those things are wrong in themselves but because of the shame such action will bring on the one and his family in the society. Many cultures share this prevalence of 'shame' before 'guilt'.

Consequently, it is a serious offence in the Igbo world-view to refer to someone as *Onye ojoo* (a bad person), or *Onye uru* (an evil and iniquitous person), without convincingly showing what evil act the person has done or committed; or which law or laws the person has broken.

Sin in mission perspective

We have seen how a Western view of sin is guilt-centred, whereas the Igbo cultural theology focuses more on shame as its consequence. The gospel for a 'shame' culture such as this therefore needs to address this cultural perspective by emphasizing relational restoration through the reconciliation that is possible through the death of Christ. To begin with 'original sin' or the 'universal sin condition' is not a helpful starting point. God reconciles us both to himself and to others, and this is the angle on being put right with God that will resonate more readily than a focus on the guilt of transgression, a truth that may be received as faith and understanding grow.

Peace with God means first peace with others. Christ can also deal with the 'defilement' of sin, setting a person free from a sense of impurity in the eyes of others. While the Western concept of life is philosophical and rational, the African concept is primarily relational and this is the framework for the traditional African lifestyle and attitude to sin. If this is not properly and precisely understood, there will be a different and strange understanding of what we are being saved from. The Igbo, therefore, do not take it kindly when mission preaching maintains that one is 'a miserable offender' (Anglican 1662 Prayer Book). He may inquisitively ask you what he has done wrong, how and when? No wonder a popular Igbo proverb says that 'one who does not balance a pot on his head has nothing to break'.

In the Igbo culture, strained relationships can be straightened by pacifying the offended supersensible world through rituals or sacrifices. Such sins can also be removed by certain sanctions on the individual sinner or his entire family or by certain very difficult tasks; for instance, they could be asked to bring a basketful of certain ants as a gift to the spirits. Mission preaching must emphasize the once-for-all death of Christ, which removes the need for such repeated sacrifices or gifts, and that acceptance of his forgiveness is a liberating experience.

Africans are incurably religious. The gods and ancestors govern the Igbo as in all African societies, but strangely and paradoxically under the overall governance of *Chukwu* – the Supreme Creator God. The very fabric and blood that runs through the veins of society symbolizes 'wholesomeness', 'goodness', 'purity' and 'righteousness'. In the Igbo traditional community, 'the secular and the sacred, the natural and the supernatural represent a continuum; supernatural forces continually infringe on life, and must be propitiated by appropriate prayers and sacrifices'. In this religiosity, all aspects of life are reducible to religious influence since there is no dichotomy between the spiritual and the physical. Mission theology must be conscious of this in its encounter with this religious perspective.

There is a third level of sinful influence besides the individual and communal. Sin as an institutional, corporate principle has been recognized as corrupting organizations, governments, structures, and economic systems. This kind of 'structural sin' is not reducible to the sins of individuals, but characterizes the very identity and life of an institution as something endemic. Some have suggested that demonic powers have a role in controlling or influencing whole organizations. However, in attributing corruption to satanic powers we must be careful not to remove human responsibility, both corporate and individual. Liberation theologians especially identified a corporate dimension of sin in structures of poverty and injustice, or in 'institutional racism' for example. This led them to develop a model of mission and a view of the gospel that engaged with sin primarily at the structural level. It was not that the poor had sinned, but that they were the ones sinned against by the unjust systems of economic and political power that oppressed them.

Scripture sees people both as communities and as individuals: God dealt with nations as whole peoples, and Jesus confronted the corrupt religious institutions of his day. So the gospel does speak good news to corporate structures as well as to individuals. This gives the church responsibility in its mission to witness truth to whole communities and to engage prophetically with the endemic corruption and the moral decay of societies and institutions whose sinfulness is not attributable to any one person. If sin distorts all cultural assumptions and world-views, then it is at this level that mission must look for the transforming power of the gospel to set people free from every dimension of its influence.

See also CULTURE, RECONCILIATION.

Bibliography

U. L. Nwosu, *The Religious Factor in the History of West Africa* (Owerri: Vivian's Publishers, 1998); W. O'Donovan, *Biblical Christianity in African Perspective* (Carlisle: Paternoster, 1995); U. R. Onunwa, 'Encounter of Christianity with African Religiosity: A Critical Review from Eastern Nigeria', *JORAT* 1.1 (1993), pp. 32–43; O. A. Onwubiko, *African Thought, Religion and Culture* (Enugu: SNAAP Press, 1991); C. Osuji, *Foundations of Igbo Tradition and Culture* (Owerri: Opinion Research and Communications, 1998).

N. E. OMEIRE AND J. CORRIE

Slavery

The theme of slavery is a pivotal missiological motif in the Hebrew Bible. Israel's history as a nation and her encounter with Yahweh begins with the announcement of his mission manifesto to rescue and free the Hebrew slaves in Egypt (Exod. 3:7–10). This is a paradigm shift in the religious history of humankind and is novel and unique in its conception; divine agency is no longer controlled by the powerful and privileged, but is revealed at the service of those at the base of the social pyramid. The mission of God is envisaged as rescuing slaves and reconstituting them into the people of God. The grand operation of the deliverance of slaves – the *Exodus – becomes a paradigm that is then repeatedly flagged up from the settlement in Canaan down to the Babylonian exile and beyond, culminating in the death and resurrection of Christ – the 'new exodus'.

The historical core of Israel's creed is the remembrance and reaffirmation of redemption by Yahweh from the 'land of slavery' (cf. Exod. 13:3, 14; Deut. 7:8). The ethical core of Israel's legal corpus – the Decalogue – is prefaced with the fundamental description of Yahweh as the God who rescued the Israelites from the 'land of slavery' (Exod. 20:2; Deut. 5:6). Indeed, Israel's ethic is predicated on her previous existence as a nation of slaves (Deut. 5:15; 24:18). It is for this reason that Yahweh demands their exclusive allegiance (Exod. 20:3: Deut. 5:7). However, this is a mission that is not carried out exclusively by Yahweh, but delegated to the agency of Moses. Yahweh's mission of rescuing the Hebrew slaves now becomes Moses' mission (Exod. 3:7–10).

The NT writers inherited the Israelite affirmation of freedom from the tyranny of slavery under Pharaoh and transposed it into a new, liberating form of 'slavery' under the 'easy and light' yoke of Jesus Christ (Matt. 11:30). The historical reality of slavery is now used figuratively. It is in this sense that Paul urges Christian slaves to regard themselves as a freed person belonging to the Lord, just as 'those who were free when called are Christ's slaves' (1 Cor. 7:22), adding that they had been 'bought with a price' by God (7:23). For Paul, bondage to the law is 'slavery' (Gal. 4:24). Christians are cautioned against living as 'slaves to sin' and urged to become 'slaves to righteousness' (Rom. 6:6, 16–18). The 'spirit of slavery' is opposed to the 'spirit of sonship'. God's mission to the Israelite slaves in the Hebrew Bible broadens out as God's mission through Christ to the whole of humanity and indeed all creation labouring under the slavery of sin, corruption and death (John 8:34; Rom. 8:21; Heb. 2:15).

A number of difficulties arise when attempting to develop a theology of mission from the biblical witness, particularly from the OT. The primary Hebrew word for slave or servant ('ebed) occurs approximately 800 times in the OT. However, the terms used for 'slave' and 'slavery' ('ebed, 'ĕbôdâ) are ambiguous and have a wide semantic range – from slaves, servants and attendants to the king's courtiers, officials, ambassadors, advisors, and ministers. English translations usually translate 'ebed as 'slave' when used in a context of oppression, while using the word 'servant' in a non-oppressive context. This is not without its problems, as is seen for example in the King James Version, which uses the word 'servant' almost throughout without making any distinction between 'slave' and 'servant'. The root word in most Semitic languages can mean slave or worshipper. It is significant that the same word is used to denote the lowest possible status on the social ladder and the highest privilege of being God's servant. Nearly one third of the OT references to slavery are religious in nature, describing the individual or the nation as God's slave, and the same word is used to describe both worship and servitude. In this light, mission may be seen as the transposition of the status of 'slaves' from their oppressive servitude to another human being into the liberative service of God.

It is significant that the same word for slave is used to designate the 'servant of the Lord' in the servant songs of Isaiah (Isa. 42:1–4, etc.). Here the servant of Yahweh, displaying both corporate and individual features, is entrusted with the mission of Yahweh of bringing 'justice to the nations' (Isa. 42:1). In the NT, Jesus empties himself and takes the form of a slave (Phil. 2:7). Furthermore, the mission of Jesus is closely identified with the mission of the Isaianic 'servant of Yahweh'. Moreover, the Greek term *doulos* is used to designate those sent to continue the mission of God and Christ: apostles, Christian workers, and Christians in general.

A further problem arises from the sociological reality of slaves in the cultures contemporaneous with the OT and NT. Their situation is economically and socially broader than normally assumed, as much of slavery in these cultures entailed relationships that were non-obligatory, often temporary and not necessarily deemed socially inferior. Israelites were required to treat slaves from their own nation as those possessing certain well-defined rights. Israelite slaves were entitled to the Sabbath rest (Exod. 20:10; Deut. 5:14) and to participate in Israelite festivals (Exod. 12:44; Deut. 12:12, 18; 16:11, 14). Slaves were to be protected from physical abuse by their masters (Exod. 21:20–21, 26–27), and runaway slaves were to be given refuge (Deut. 23:15–16). Hebrew debt slaves were to be released after six years of service and adequately provided for (Exod. 21:2–4). Poverty-stricken citizens were to be treated like hired workers or temporary residents, not

as slaves (Lev. 25:39, 40, 53). The basis for the fair treatment of slaves was Israel's own past experience of slavery in Egypt (Deut. 5:15; 16:12; cf. Lev. 25:42; Neh. 5:5–9).

Historical perspective

In the Greco-Roman cultures slaves came to be regarded as possessions (Aeschines). Dio Chrysostom, a popular orator in the first century AD, defined slavery as the right to use another man at pleasure, like a piece of property or a domestic animal (XV.24). Slaves were not treated as well under Roman law. If a slave murdered his master all the slaves of the same household were required to be put to death (Tacitus, *Annals*, xii, xiii). The life of the slave was absolutely at the mercy of his owner (Juvenal, vi). It is not surprising that given the OT attitude to slavery a number of Church Fathers denounced the practice. Thus Clement of Alexandria declared that 'no man is a slave by nature' (*Paedagogos*, iii. 12).

Nevertheless, one must be careful not to read the situation and status of African slavery in the New World from the seventeenth to nineteen centuries back into biblical times and texts, since there were significant differences in the treatment of slaves. Slavery in the Greco-Roman world was not based on race; slaves were allowed to own property, to pursue an education and to assemble publicly; they were entrusted with responsible social functions; their religious and cultural traditions were the same as those of the freeborn; and the majority of urban and domestic slaves were often freed by the age of thirty.

Given the preferential option of the biblical writers in favour of slaves who had suffered oppression, it is not surprising that Christian mission historically was directed at the emancipation of those labouring under the yoke of dehumanization as non-persons, whether actually designated slaves as in the New World or those treated as untouchables by the *caste system in India. As a result of Christian influence, within two centuries after the death of Christ, reforms regarding the abolition of slavery were introduced in Rome. While a number of Christians and even missionary societies shamefully acquiesced and even owned slaves, often supporting it from an alleged biblical basis, a number of

Christian reformers and missionaries were at the forefront of the battle against slavery. The late eighteenth-century struggle for the abolition of the transatlantic slave trade was inspired largely by Quakers and evangelicals in England, noteworthy among them William Wilberforce, and resulted in the Abolition Act of 1807 prohibiting all British subjects from participating in the slave trade. Thomas Buxton, a British evangelical, continued the struggle by working for the abolition of West Indian slavery in 1833–34. In India, millions of untouchables, who were condemned to a lifetime of dehumanization by the caste system, a core tenet of Hinduism, embraced the new gospel brought to them by missionaries, which also gave them dignity and access to literacy and a new life.

Modern-day slavery

As Christians commemorate the bicentenary of the Abolition of Slavery Act in 2007, the church recognizes that slavery is not merely part of history, but lives on, not only in its legacies of racism, the destabilizing of African societies, and the continuing psychological trauma experienced by those whose ancestors were enslaved, but also with the reality that some of today's major banking, investment and insurance institutions have their foundations in the transatlantic trade. Although slavery has been abolished, it continues in other forms when people are sold like objects, or grossly underpaid for their 'slave labour'. It is estimated that there are around 27 million people who today are suffering some form of enslavement. A major dimension is the trafficking of women and children to the West for prostitution and sexual exploitation; other forms of slavery continue in today's world, including bonded labour, dehumanizing working conditions in 'sweat-shops' run by multinational companies, the exploitation of migrant workers, forced marriages, and untouchability.

In many countries, churches and mission agencies are challenging these modern forms of slavery through various means of advocacy and involvement. Since deliverance from slavery is a central dimension of the gospel, and freedom characterizes life in Christ, 'setting all free' from all forms of slavish oppression and exploitation must be at the heart of the mission of the church.

See also LIBERATION.

Bibliography

I. Chatterjee and R. M. Eaton, *Slavery and South Asian History* (Bloomington: Indiana University Press, 2007); I. A. H. Combes, *The Metaphor of Slavery in the Writings of the Early Church: From the New Testament to the Beginning of the Fifth Century* (Sheffield: Sheffield Academic Press, 1998); L. W. Cowie, *William Wilberforce, 1759–1833: A Bibliography* (London: Greenwood Press, 1992); C. Cox, *This Immoral Trade: Slavery in the 21st Century* (Oxford: Monarch, 2006); D. Goldenberg, *The Curse of Ham: Race and Slavery in Early Judaism, Christianity, and Islam* (Princeton: Princeton University Press, 2003); J. Pollock, *William Wilberforce* (London: Constable, 1977).

J. GOMES

SOUTH, MISSION FROM, see
TWO-THIRDS WORLD MISSIONARY
MOVEMENT

Sovereignty of God

The world rings with songs in hundreds of languages that celebrate the kingly rule of God, through Jesus Christ. Amongst the poor, the powerless, the persecuted, the victims of climate change or of civil war or unrest, this is often their first and last resort – songs of confidence, or prayers of desperation, arise expressing the faith and hope that on high there is One who rules over all things well, One who turns the hearts of kings and despots, One who can bring good out of evil, One who will eventually bring all things into subjection, when *Christ will be all in all. Christian mission proceeds with joy, patience, and sometimes despair, but always in the conviction (based on *faith, nourished by *hope and expressed in *love) that the church serves a living King whose *kingdom is steadily growing towards its final and magnificent unveiling at the end of time.

Believing that God rules is not something that can be proved by a chain of inductive reasoning. Natural disasters in the twentieth century killed more than 100 million people; and wars and other atrocities perhaps another 180 million. It does not appear obviously true that God 'works out everything in conformity with the purpose of his will' (Eph. 1:11). However, the Christian conviction is that 'Our God reigns'; that he is the Almighty, El Shaddai, the King of kings; that to him belong majesty, *power, dominion and authority; and that supreme power is focused in the historical life, teaching, death, *resurrection and ascension of the Lord Jesus Christ.

One of the earliest Christian confessions was 'Jesus is Lord', an extraordinary assertion about Jesus' divine nature, but also a subversive claim that could be extremely dangerous politically when Roman emperors were demanding the acclamation 'Caesar is Lord!' The same confession has caused trepidation in all sorts of totalitarian regimes ever since, where governments demand absolute, undivided loyalty. Authentic missionary zeal, however, must be based on the justifiable 'jealousy' of God to see his name glorified in all the earth, and must be distinguished from personal bigotry or paternalistic self-confidence.

The whole story of the Bible's missionary purpose could be summarized in terms of God's kingly rule. In the beginning he created all things by his word of command. Unlike other creation narratives the story of Genesis is not nationalistic; God is the creator of all humankind. He is greater than all earthly kings: greater than Pharaoh (Exod.); greater than the king of Assyria (Isa.); greater than the king of Babylon (Dan.). For this reason the Psalms call all the others to worship the One who reigns. But human beings rebelled against his rule and word, and this is the reason for the catastrophic state of human society, marked by fratricide, vengefulness, arrogance and disharmony. However, God will not be frustrated in his purpose to bless the whole world through the descendants of Abraham. The Israelites were called to be a society living under the law of God, and blessed with his glorious presence in their midst (Deut. 4:5–8). When the Israelites asked for a king so that they could be like the other surrounding nations, we read in 1 Samuel of the struggle to which this gave rise – they were warned that the characteristics of earthly kings were to take and take and take (1 Sam. 8). David and Solomon were given amazing promises, but on the whole the institution of kingship in Israel was a disappointment; hence the Psalms cast their hopes

into the future when there will arise a truly righteous king (Ps. 78), and when the nations will flock to Jerusalem to learn from the Lord (Isa. 2:3–4). The missionary vision of the Bible foresees not one nation ruling over another, but all nations bowed in homage at the 'name that is above every name', applied in the OT to Yahweh, and in the NT to Jesus (Phil. 2:9).

Although Jesus was born in humble circumstances, the wise men who came from the east to worship him asked about the 'king of the Jews' (Matt. 2:2). Ironically, this was the inscription that was nailed to the cross above Jesus' head (Matt. 27:37). From the beginning to the end of his life, Jesus' kingly work was a threat to human kings and governors. To people living under the yoke of an occupying power he spoke constantly and vividly of the 'rule of God', the 'rule of heaven', illustrating the values of his kingdom with everyday stories, whose meaning the careless could not capture. Jesus would not fulfil the hopes of nationalistic Jewish revolutionaries: he rode into Jerusalem on a donkey not on a stallion; in conversation with Pilate he did not deny that he was a king, but he insisted that his kingdom was not a this-worldly kingdom (John 18). Pilate's cowardice was revealed when he was threatened that if he released 'king Jesus' he was not Caesar's friend (John 19:12). But the preachers of Acts were adamant that the death of Jesus did not come about primarily because of human treachery, fear or cowardice, but 'by God's deliberate plan and foreknowledge' (Acts 2:23).

After the resurrection, Christ's great commission to his followers to make disciples among all peoples (Matt. 28:18–20) was premised on the claim that now he had all authority in heaven and on earth. The story of Acts reveals how, in obedience to this command, and with the enabling of the Holy Spirit, the lordship of Jesus was proclaimed throughout Asia Minor, Greece and right up to Rome itself. Paul (and the rest of the NT) did not use the *language* of 'kingship' very much, but his opponents understood well enough that he was proclaiming 'another king, one called Jesus' (Acts 17:7). No NT writer and no true Christian missionary ever preached a 'remembered Christ', as a figure of the past. Christian mission takes place in the quiet and persevering confidence that Jesus is a *living* Lord.

The story of the Bible ends amidst earthquake, fire and suffering with the vision of an innumerable multitude of saints singing songs to the One who sits on the throne (Rev. 7:9–10). Here is the ultimate goal of mission. In those early centuries when there were ten fierce outbreaks of persecution, and in many centuries and communities since then, especially the twentieth century, this vision has sustained suffering Christians who continue to hope that one day 'the kingdom of the world [will] become the kingdom of our Lord and of his Messiah, and he will reign for ever and ever' (Rev. 11:15).

So a conviction that the whole world is subject to God's powerful, just and gentle rule is profoundly influential for Christian life and mission in the world:

- It affects our attitude to the *created world and our natural *environment, for we are stewards, vice-gerents of an estate which we do not own but care for.
- It enables us to hold steadily on our way through titanic upheavals and struggles in national and international history.
- It assures us that he is in control of mission, so it is not our place to manipulate success or imagine that it is our responsibility to bring in the kingdom.
- It gives us our only hope of lasting success in *evangelization, for we know that underlying all our patient, thoughtful and enterprising efforts to preach the *gospel, it is God who calls, stirs, saves and keeps those who cast themselves upon his mercy.
- It gives us confidence to trust God for his final *judgment, releasing us from speculation about who may or may not be saved.
- It strengthens us for *spiritual warfare, for the one in whom we trust is not just King of Israel, King of the Jews, but Lord of all supernatural powers, good and bad.
- It challenges the church to recognize those who differ from us as subjects of the same Sovereign, and gives the church songs to sing through which their unity may be recognized and celebrated.

See also GOD.

Bibliography
J. Calvin, *Institutes of the Christian Religion*, trans. F. L. Battles, ed. J. T. McNeill, 2 vols. (London: SCM Press, 1961); D. A. Carson, *Divine Sovereignty and Human Responsibility: Biblical Perspectives in Tension* (Grand Rapids: Baker, 1994); J. I. Packer, *Evangelism and the Sovereignty of God* (Leicester: IVF, 1961); J. Piper, *God's Passion for His Glory: Living the Vision of Jonathan Edwards* (Wheaton: Crossway, 1998); R. S. Sproul, *Almighty Over All: Understanding the Sovereignty of God* (Grand Rapids: Baker, 1999).

H. PESKETT

Spiritual warfare/territorial spirits/demons

In biblical terms, spiritual warfare essentially encompasses Satan's rebellion against God and the manifestations of that rebellion in the created order. In practical terms it refers to the ongoing conflict between humanity and Satan framed in light of the kingdom of God.

Scriptural orientation
Spiritual warfare is cast as an ongoing conflict in creation. To understand this conflict, we must understand three sets of protagonists: *God and his hosts, Satan and his hosts, and *humanity.

The first set of protagonists is comprised of the Triune God and his angelic hosts. God himself is not actually a protagonist in the way his angels or humanity are, at least in the sense of directly warring against Satan. While it is certainly true that Satan opposes God, that Christ defeated Satan on the cross and that the Holy Spirit gifts and empowers Christians to stand against the enemies of God, we must remember that God is the Creator who brought Satan into being. Thus spiritual warfare is not a dualistic struggle, but rebellion of a creature against the Creator in which the outcome is already assured. On God's side there is also a host of angels who engage in direct spiritual warfare against God's enemies.

The second set of protagonists is Satan and the spiritual hosts that follow him. They are clearly portrayed in Scripture as actual beings and not simply metaphors or symbols of evil. Satan is the tempter, the inciter and accuser with a murderous and lying nature, who leads these beings in an attempt to establish a false kingdom that is a warped caricature of the kingdom of God. As creatures, even in their rebellion they can be used as an instrument of God's judgment or even training in righteousness for God's purposes.

The third set of protagonists is collectively known as humanity. Unlike Satan and his hosts, we are made in the image of God and have the ability to choose the side on which we will serve. As a result, humanity is split into two camps, though we must never usurp God's role in judging who is in which camp. Most simply described, one camp is comprised of those who follow Christ and the other of those who do not. While there are depths and complexities to this reality, and no human is in the place to make a judgment on another human, the fact of this bifurcation of humanity is clearly portrayed in Scripture. Each person can join forces with God through Christ in the power of the Holy Spirit and oppose Satan's rebellion, or may choose to continue the rebellion into which he or she was born.

Spiritual warfare, then, is most explicitly the struggles of these sets of spiritual hosts and humanity, all under the sovereign control of God. This conflict ranges from the more mundane (e.g. struggles with temptation) to the more exotic (e.g. demonic confrontations and angelic battles). This conflict plays out across multiple venues all through the created order. In addition to the direct encounters between humanity and the demonic, it also includes indirect battles such as struggles against crippling and deadly diseases, over the destruction of the environment, and against demonically-inspired dehumanizing political and ideological systems. Some Christians dangerously tend to reduce all the struggles in life to spiritual warfare. The result can be the demonization of those with whom we disagree or the recasting of everything in terms of proper techniques or methods. While certain theological, and cultural, orientations lend themselves more readily to these reductionisms, all of us are susceptible and must be alert to avoiding them. Pastoral care requires us to see people as whole people, and demonic influence in the wider context of human frailty and dislocation.

The biblical evidence offers no single spiritual warfare encounter as the model or exemplar to be used for all encounters. Our struggle is against spiritual powers, and as in any battle against living enemies, we are to be aware of their modus operandi. Thus, trying to reduce spiritual warfare to a particular set of methodologies or techniques is a mistake. The closest we come to a general frame for victory in spiritual warfare for Christians is found in Revelation 12:10–12, which indicates that Christians overcome Satan by (1) the blood of the Lamb (their genuine expression of faith in Christ), (2) their testimony (the way believers live for Christ and bear witness to the work of his grace in their lives), and (3) a lack of fear in the face of death.

Contemporary discussion

Western theological scholars are willing to wrestle with manifestations of evil, but tend to cast their discourse more in anthropological, sociological and psychological terms than as actual battles with the demonic. Many have been more comfortable with a view that assumes a bifurcated universe with God on one side, the material universe on the other and the whole 'middle realm' – the realm of angels and demons – excluded from discussion or interaction. Paul Hiebert identified this as 'the flaw of the excluded middle', resulting in what has been described as 'powerless Christianity'.

Western missionaries and missiologists who served in Majority World contexts were exposed to encounters with evil spirits as real beings. In many cases, the missionaries' materialistic outlook was challenged, and they returned to the Scriptures to examine the biblical perspective. Some remained critical while others reduced mission strategy to that of spiritual warfare. More recently voices from Majority World settings have joined in the academic discussion. For example, in 2000, the Lausanne Committee for World Evangelization sponsored a conference on spiritual warfare in Nairobi, Kenya, which brought together more than thirty theologians, academics, and practitioners from a variety of cultures and theological perspectives to wrestle with the missiological implications. The statement issued from the consultation identified common ground, issued warnings, noted areas of tension, and identified frontiers in which future work was needed.

Issues in context

Spiritual warfare takes place wherever humanity is found. No society or culture is exempt, and Satan is able to contextualize his strategies in the light of culture. As a result of the different cultural perspectives Christians bring to the task, it is not surprising that there are areas of significant tension in regard to spiritual warfare. Following the lead of the 2000 Lausanne consultation statement, we will briefly mention three.

First, the language used in spiritual warfare literature has tended to be excessive and triumphalistic. If our ultimate goal is not to boast in victories over Satan but to draw people to Christ, then Christians must beware of polemic language that demeans or belittles. We cannot use Satan's tactics to defeat him. There is a critical need to incorporate interdisciplinary approaches in our spiritual warfare methods. Reducing human experience exclusively either to demonic encounters or to psychological or social dimensions does not do justice to the full-orbed presentation of humanity in the Bible.

Then there are the twin problems of *syncretism and secularization. Those who tend to reduce life to spiritual warfare imagery accuse those who downplay the reality of the demonic of being secularists, while the latter accuse the former of being Christian animists. Both need to listen carefully to each other if discussion is to move forward; neither side accurately represents the full biblical picture. This tension is especially evident in the discussion on territorial spirits and spiritual mapping, in which one side trumpets identification and binding of territorial spirits as the key to world evangelization while the other condemns such practices as Christian magic. As the Majority World church continues to grow and gain a stronger voice in the global faith, all of these issues will be part of the ongoing discussion that will characterize the future of spiritual warfare thinking and practice.

See also CULTURE, KINGDOM OF GOD.

Bibliography

P. Hiebert, 'The Flaw of the Excluded Middle', *Missiology* 10, 1982, pp. 35–48; L. L. Johns and J. R. Krabill (eds.), *Even the Demons Submit: Continuing Jesus' Ministry of Deliverance* (Elkhart: Institute of Mennonite Studies, 2006); C. Kraft, *Confronting Powerless Christianity: Evangelicals and the Missing Dimension* (Grand Rapids: Chosen, 2002); M. Kraft, *Understanding Spiritual Power* (Eugene: Wipf and Stock Publishers, 1996); C. Lowe, *Territorial Spirits and World Evangelization: A Biblical, Historical, and Missiological Critique of Strategic-Level Spiritual Warfare* (Borough Green: OMF, 1998); A. S. Moreau, T. Adeyemo, D. G. Burnett, B. L. Myers and H. Yung (eds.), *Deliver Us from Evil* (World Vision International, 2002); A. S. Moreau 'Spiritual Warfare', in W. A. Elwell (ed.), *Evangelical Dictionary of Theology* (Grand Rapids: Baker Books, ²2001); J. Nevius, *Demon Possession* (Grand Rapids: Kregel, 1968); M. Reid, *Strategic Level Spiritual Warfare: A Modern Mythology?* (Fairfax, Virginia: Xulon Press, 2002); E. Rommen, *Spiritual Power and Missions: Raising the Issues* (Pasadena: William Carey Library, 1995); C. P. Wagner, *Defeating Dark Angels* (Ventura: Regal Books, 1990); C. P. Wagner, *What the Bible Says About Spiritual Warfare* (Ventura: Regal Books, 2002); W. Wink, *Engaging the Powers* (Minneapolis: Augsburg Fortress Publications, 1992); N. G. Wright, *A Theology of the Dark Side: Putting the Power of Evil in Its Place* (Downers Grove: InterVarsity Press, 2004).

A. S. MOREAU

Spirituality

Spirituality describes the God–human relationship and how it is mediated as an experiential relationship of the believer and *God. This experience of God, made real in the believer's life in Christ and enabled by the Holy Spirit, is the manifestation of the mystery of the Holy *Trinity. It is viewed as a transforming process of deepening intimacy, which at the same time renews relationships with others as a reflection of this mystery. Its connection with mission begins with the God of mission, who draws us into relationship with himself in order to engage us in participation with him in that mission. This is the source of a 'spirituality of mission' as an expression of that relationship with God which initiates and empowers mission commitment.

Spirituality as a transforming experience therefore has two causally related aspects: the relationship with God (theology), and the relationship with human beings (mission and ethics). The first explores the possibility of establishing a transforming relationship with a personal yet transcendent God. It is a biblical spirituality which, according to Sandra Schneiders, is 'a transformative process of personal and communal engagement with the biblical text' (in *Interpretation* vol. 56:2, p. 136). Because spirituality is related closely to the biblical text it has a theological dimension, which expounds the biblical witness to the ways in which God relates to humanity. This transforming relationship between humanity and God is actualized in human relationships, which, regardless of gender, social status or ethnic group, are deepened dynamically through reading the biblical text communally and contextually.

Relationship with God is integrated with, and reflected in, the relationship with other human beings and *creation. In other words, the vertical relationship determines the nature of the horizontal relationship. Spirituality therefore fuses theology, mission and ethics as a dynamic integrative language. The progressive movement of theology runs dynamically in line with the movement of mission and ethics. Spirituality attempts to transform words into contextual deeds. In short, being precedes doing, and both are bound together in any meaningful relationship with God. To know God is therefore characterized by acting justly and loving mercy (Mic. 6:8), and prayer is only of value when combined with defending the cause of the fatherless and the widow (Isa. 1:15–17).

The importance of an integrated spirituality of mission is also seen in the way in which the heart and the mind are often polarized. Christians in different contexts have all understood spirituality as nurturing the heart rather than the mind, primarily because the word is associated merely with the 'spiritual' dimension of the human being. Theological and historical exposition of the Bible is regarded as less 'spiritual' than spiritual practice because it touches the mind and not the heart. This, however, reduces the biblical messages to merely spiritual concepts. Spirituality is developed based on, for example, the concepts of love or church tradition, which are viewed as the quintessence of the Bible. These reduced spiritual concepts have tended to ignore the plurality and diversity of the Bible's messages and have viewed Christian spirituality as a branch of systematic theology, thereby divorcing it from mission and ethics. Spirituality should engage heart, mind and will in a dynamic exchange which results in an integration of action and reflection.

A spirituality of mission will also seek to integrate the Christian's relationship with God with his or her relationship with the world. For example, in the pluralistic *postmodern world, the understanding of spirituality must take into account this cultural reality. Many postmoderns are searching for a 'spirituality' through which they can connect with reality beyond the purely material. The church in its mission must be able to offer a way of relating to God which is multidimensional enough to engage both the postmodern context and the biblical text, without necessarily rejecting the richness of Christian traditions.

The plurality of the postmodern world and its understanding of human experience cannot be used as a norm when defining spirituality, since this would render spirituality as purely subjective. However, the possibility of exploring a multidimensional spirituality is underscored by the plurality and diversity of the contexts and experiences of God in the Bible. Furthermore, the contexts where the Bible is being interpreted today are not only diverse but also changing dynamically, necessitating varied responses to the text. In short, when the Bible is read contextually, the interpreted text shapes the personal and communal life and mission of the Christian in a postmodern world, and out of this process comes a multidimensional approach to spirituality which contemporary postmoderns can connect with.

Spirituality as the experience of divine and human relationships has other missiological implications. We have said that the Bible portrays who God is and what his works are, which in turn transforms who we are and what we do. The dominant colours of God's portrait in the Bible are *love and justice, which find clear expression in his work of *reconciliation. Reconciliation derives from and fuses love and justice; and the *cross as the final expression of God's love and justice points to a reconciling God. In other words, the word reconciliation captures God's essential nature as a missionary God. God in his mission forms a universal community which demonstrates to the fallen world what it means to live as reconciled persons, as God's new people, a demonstration which draws diverse people to the reconciling God.

This reconciled community also demonstrates to the broken world a new relationship to creation. Reconciliation is the central and eternal mission of God and must therefore be at the heart of a spirituality of mission, worked out as a ministry of reconciliation that reflects the love and justice of God. These qualities are expressed in a reconciling life, which infuses a reconciled person's words and deeds and gives shape to a spirituality of mission for a postmodern world.

Bibliography

P. Adam, *Hearing God's Words: Exploring Biblical Spirituality* (Downers Grove: InterVarsity Press; Leicester: Apollos, 2004); W. Au, *By Way of the Heart: Toward a Holistic Christian Spirituality* (New York: Paulist Press, 1989); S. C. Barton, *The Spirituality of the Gospels* (Peabody: Hendrickson, 1992); A. Barus, 'Meditasi Sebagai Pelatihan Spiritualitas', in E. P. Sembiring (ed.), *Dikembangkan Untuk Mengembangkan* (Jakarta: Sora Mido, 2004); A. Barus, 'Spiritualitas Biblika', *Setia* 1, 2004, pp. 69–83; A. Barus, 'John 2:12–25: A Narrative Reading', in F. Lozada and T. Thatcher (eds.), *New Currents through John: A Global Perspective* (Leiden: E. J. Brill, 2006); S. Chan, *Spiritual Theology: A Systematic Study of the Christian Life* (Downers Grove: InterVarsity Press, 1998); S. M. Schneiders, 'Biblical Spirituality', *Interpretation*, 56:2, 2007, pp. 133–142.

A. BARUS

STEWARDSHIP, OF CREATION, see CREATION
STEWARDSHIP, OF MONEY, see MONEY
STORYTELLING, see DRAMA/THEATRE, NARRATIVE
SUBALTERN STUDIES, see COLONIALISM/POSTCOLONIALISM
SUPERSESSIONISM, see JEWISH MISSION
SUSTAINABLE DEVELOPMENT, see DEVELOPMENT

Syncretism

Historical overview

The term 'syncretism' derives etymologically from the Greek *syn* (with) and *krasis* (mixture). Plutarch (45–125 BC) used it to reference the behaviour of Cretans who united over their differences in self-defence against attacking enemies. Much later, Erasmus (1466–1536) used the term to refer to the collaboration among scholars united by the classical tradition to overcome the emerging Catholic-Protestant divide. Similarly, in 1645 George Calixtus Helmstadt called for the syncretism or reconciliation of theological and ritual differences among Protestant denominations (against Rome). This came to be known as the 'syncretistic controversy' because of the political and ideological situation of mid-seventeenth century Christian Europe: on the one hand, the Peace of Westphalia (1648) both signalled the end of the Catholic Church's universally accepted authority and established the concept of toleration (which alone makes mixture possible); on the other hand, the rise of the nation-state and the emergence of denominationalism emphasized the distinctiveness of political and religious identities.

By the early twentieth century, anthropologists and other scholars in the humanities had come to define syncretism as the reinterpretation that takes place in any acculturating process involving an established people group that comes into prolonged contact with another (often expanding) culture. In this framework, the history of religions school advocated the thesis that all religions were the result of syncretistic processes. Manicheanism and Roman religion were prime examples, with the former fusing together various traditions, and the latter adopting the foreign cults of conquered peoples as a means of assimilation. Similarly, Israelite religion was understood to be a syncretism of Ancient Near Eastern cultures, and Christianity was seen as a syncretism of Jewish and Hellenistic traditions during the Patristic period. The fact that religious traditions arose out of cross-cultural processes suggested the possibility of a new, universal religious horizon emanating from the modern encounter of East and West facilitated by the colonial enterprise.

Kraemer's reaction against syncretism

It is against this background that Henrik Kraeme (1888–1965) defined syncretism as the illegitimate mixture of religious elements that cannot and should not be integrated. While Kraemer acknowledged syncretism in various respects to be a universal phenomenon, he suggested that indigenous and Asian traditions were more syncretistic, the former because of their pragmatic nature and the latter because of their relativistic, subjectivistic and monistic (in his estimation) orientation. In contrast, the three great Western monotheistic faiths – Judaism, Christianity and Islam – are fundamentally anti-syncretistic because their exclusivistic, objectivistic and dualistic commitments presume the existence of absolute norms that do not allow any incorporation of elements contrary to their core features. Given the Christian conviction regarding the unique and normative revelation of Christ, all other formulations of truth are to be judged by the biblical witness to Christ rather than harmonized toward a more universal religion for humankind. Because fallen humanity is naturally syncretistic, the diversity of religions represent mistaken human responses to divine revelation. Hence Christian missions must aim at conversion. Of course the gospel needs to be adapted to, and become rooted in, foreign cultures so as to be intelligible to others, but the substantive meaning of the biblical truths must be preserved so as to allow the possibility of a Christian 'confrontation' with other cultural-religious realities.

Postmodern perspectives

More recently, however, modern understandings of cultures and religions as static, self-contained, and internally coherent entities have given way to *postmodern perspectives of *cultures and religions as dynamic, interactive, and internally differentiated. From the perspective of the study of religion, this means that the concept of religion itself is recognized as a recent Western construct. From the perspective of postcolonial historiography, the missionized are increasingly recognized not as passive 'victims' but as active agents who have contributed to the process of interreligious and intercultural encounter. From the perspective of economic theory, the interaction of local, national and global processes

is seen as producing new religious movements and their marketable commodities.

Syncretism usually follows when any of the following conditions are present: 'points of contact' which encourage 'borrowing'; the availability of answers in another tradition to persisting questions; universal or 'portable' religious traditions assimilated by indigenous or 'local' traditions confronting rapid social change; the meeting of religious traditions under conditions of war, resulting in the defeated adopting the religion of the victors; and missionary endeavours, especially when missionaries see the missionized as being incomplete apart from evangelization. In this new postmodern paradigm, 'syncretism' calls attention to the primary processes of cultural and religious formation related to conquest, trade and migration.

More important, for postmoderns the idea of syncretism as a contamination of cultural and religious 'purity' is seen as part of a distinctively modern discourse (that includes other notions like nationalism, regionalism and ethnocentrism). They claim that this is used by religious elites in their attempts to conserve group identity and promote group solidarity and superiority. For them, syncretism is a process more likely to occur among marginalized groups seeking to assimilate, adjust and adapt to a foreign but stronger cultural force. Also, the postmodern perspective privileges marginalized perspectives. This means that syncretistic processes of renewal have actually become the norm against which non- or anti-syncretistic processes are evaluated. The reality, of course, is that if 'syncretism' is successful to the point of producing an established and working tradition, then it ceases to be 'syncretism', since practitioners of any faith, including their new religious elite, usually do not see their loyalties as divided.

Contemporary questions

This new situation raises a host of complex questions. Conceptually, does syncretism describe the end result of a mixture or the process of mixing? Does syncretism involve equal influences from two or more traditions, or can it involve unequal contributions involving one dominant (universal) tradition and one or more indigenous (local) traditions? How helpful is syncretism as a principally socio-anthropological category for understanding religious processes? What about the political dimension of syncretistic processes: who has the power to define when a mixture is a distortion of one or more traditions? What if syncretism is not merely a counter-cultural resistance strategy, but actually necessary for the survival of marginalized groups threatened by a domineering society (e.g. as in African slaves in the New World)?

From this, a second set of questions arises for mission theory and practice. How important are indigenous perspectives for naming and assessing syncretism? On the one hand, 'native' insiders will usually not identify a process as syncretistic, in part because many religious mergers result from unconscious processes. But on the other hand, outsiders may not recognize syncretistic processes either. In the case of the Arapaho (a Native American plains tribe) incorporation of the Flatpipe in the eucharistic meal, for example, outsiders may see this as a cultural element that enriches the Christian rite; insiders, however, see the pipe not merely as an instrument of veneration but as an object of it. But in the case of the demonization of all other Ewe deities in Ghana by missionaries (except for Mawu, redefined as 'God'), what was intended to combat syncretism resulted instead in a robust demonology among Ghanaian Christians which Western pastoral agents are now ill-equipped to deal with.

This raises, finally, theological questions. The Bible itself reveals the tensions posed by the changing nature of the concept of syncretism. On the one hand, for example, Colossian 'philosophy' can be seen as a syncretism of Phrygian and local folk beliefs/practices, Judaism and Christianity, in which case Paul's response was to present Christ's uniqueness and supremacy. On the other hand, there were also occasions when the peoples of God consciously appropriated existing religious ideas for their own purposes, such as when El's universal qualities of fatherhood and kingship were incorporated by Yahweh, or when notions like *logos* and *kyrios* were adopted from their Greco-Roman milieu and transformed theologically or ritually into a Christian framework. Is it legitimate syncretism when Christianity subordinates these 'foreign' elements for its own purposes, in contrast to illegitimate forms of

syncretism such as Gnosticism, which reverses this relationship and subordinates the Christ event to being an example of a more universal rule?

Conclusion

These matters caution against any abstract pronouncement regarding syncretism. Certainly evangelicals continue to insist that legitimate forms of syncretism always result in the enrichment of our understanding of the gospel and not in additions to its essential meaning. Yet, identifying syncretistic processes requires nothing less than prolonged attention to and engagement with the ever-changing historical, social and political dynamics of religious identities. Outsider and insider viewpoints should be considered, allowing dialogical perspectives to emerge and enable discernment. And this give-and-take is itself part of the process of religious transformation.

Bibliography

G. Aijmer (ed.), *Syncretism and the Commerce of Symbols* (Götenborg, Sweden: The Institute for Advanced Studies in Social Anthropology, 1995); C. E. Arnold, *The Colossian Syncretism: The Interface between Christianity and Folk Belief at Colossae* (Grand Rapids: Baker, 1996); G. D. Gort, H. M. Vroom, R. Fernhout and A. Wessels (eds.), *Dialogue and Syncretism: An Interdisciplinary Approach* (Amsterdam: Editions Rodopi; Grand Rapids: Eerdmans, 1989); S. M. Greenfield and A. Droogers (eds.), *Reinventing Religions: Syncretism and Transformation in Africa and the Americas* (Lanham: Rowman & Littlefield, 2001); S. S. Hartman (ed.), *Syncretism: Based on Papers read at the Symposium on Cultural Contact, Meeting of Religions, Syncretism held at Abo on the 8th–10th of September, 1966* (Stockholm and Uppsala: Almqvist & Wiksell, 1969); H. Kraemer, *Religion and the Christian Faith* (Philadelphia: Westminster, 1956); B. A. Pearson (ed.), *Religious Syncretism in Antiquity: Essays in Conversation with Geo Widengren* (Missoula, MT: Scholars Press, 1975); C. F. Starkloff, *A Theology of the In-between: The Value of Syncretic Process* (Milwaukee, WI: Marquette University Press, 2002); C. Stewart, and R. Shaw (eds.), *Syncretism/Anti-syncretism: The Politics of*

Religious Synthesis (New York and London: Routledge, 1994); W. A. Visser't Hooft, *No Other Name: The Choice between Syncretism and Christian Universalism* (Philadelphia: Westminster, 1963).

A. YONG

Tentmaking

Tentmaking draws its name from Acts 18:1–4 when Paul supported himself making tents alongside fellow tentmakers Priscilla and Aquila. It is a name oddly out of place today and yet attempts to find suitable alternatives have been unsuccessful. It remains a useful shorthand for people who use their study, business or employment across cultures in mission settings, as a platform from which to join with the work of the kingdom in that place. Lausanne 2 defined tentmaking as follows:

> Tentmakers are ... 'believers in all people groups who have a secular identity and who in response to God's call, proclaim Christ cross-culturally. Tentmakers witness with their whole lives and their jobs are integral to their work for the Kingdom of God.'

Key elements are secular identity, kingdom intention and a cross-cultural setting. Many are self-supporting but not all. Many engage in church planting, others in community ministries, small group leadership, church support, youth and children's work. While most operate in areas where there is no access for people with missionary visas, they can be found in every region of the world.

Biblical and theological roots

Although Acts 18:1–4 is the traditional source for a model of tentmaking, there are many other biblical examples where people exercised significant ministry while in their secular occupation. Abraham was a farmer (Gen. 13), Amos a sheep farmer and orchardist (Amos 7), and Joseph a shrewd prime minister (Gen. 47). In fact a minority of the people described in Scripture held religious posts. Perhaps more powerful as a basis for tentmaking than Acts 18 is Acts 8:1–4, where the ordinary Christians were scattered after the death of Stephen and 'preached the word wherever they went' (Acts 8:4). In Acts 11:19–21, we see the outcome of this as some shared the good news in Antioch, leading to the foundation of the church there.

In biblical terms, we find many people of faith who move out of their own setting and continue to exercise that faith in the new setting, without holding a formal religious post. Concepts such as the priesthood of all believers (1 Pet. 2:5, 9) and the ministry of all believers indicated in Ephesians 4:11–16, reinforce the notion that all of God's people can contribute to the work of the kingdom.

Theologically, there are several important themes emphasized over the last half-century that have helped shape the modern tentmaking movement.

One theme is a renewed lay theology, a reaction against a lay-clergy division that arose partly out of the contemplative-active categories of Augustine. We are all part of the *laos* (1 Pet. 2:10), the whole people of God, and the work of God belongs equally to all, including mission.

Another theme is work as the creation of God and we join with his creative activity in our own work. While work became a scene of misery in Genesis 3:17–19, it is now made new for those in Christ (2 Cor. 5:17). Work can be both mission in itself and a location where mission occurs.

There has been considerable work recently on the idea of call, once seen as necessary only for those called to pastoral ministry or career missions. Recent writers such as Paul Stevens have emphasized the fact that all of God's people are called to salvation, righteousness and service.

Others have reminded us that mission occurs where the people are who need it, rather than within the programmes and structures of the gathered church. The workplace is highly significant in this regard, and the workplace in a cross-cultural setting provides double mission benefits as both an entry point and an immediate witness point for tentmakers. This also fits the concept of *missio Dei*, joining with what God is already doing in all the structures of society around us. The emphasis on the missional church has also been helpful in reinforcing this approach.

The current movement

People have always served mission within the context of their travel or occupation. Others have supported mission by their work, and the Moravians and the Serampore Trio led by Carey are good examples. The recent focus on tentmaking really emerged after Christy Wilson worked as a teacher in Afghanistan from 1951 and helped found a church in Kabul. He wrote of his vision for tentmaking in *Today's Tentmakers* in 1979. Both the book and Christy Wilson's personal advocacy had profound impact on many, and the movement grew rapidly in USA during the 1970s and 1980s, gaining formal recognition at the Lausanne 2 Congress in 1989 in a tentmaker track. An international body, Tentmakers International Exchange, was formed soon after and through the 1990s, the movement gradually expanded. *World Christian Trends* in 2001 estimated some 150,000 people could be classed as tentmakers.

Note, however, that well before Christy Wilson wrote, a booklet published by the *Commission on Mission and World Evangelism* of WCC used the word 'tentmaking' probably for the first time in the modern era, and provided a strong case for the development of this form of ministry with solid biblical and theological support.

There are several reasons why the movement has grown so rapidly in the past fifty years. First, globalization provides not only rapid communication but an international job market with high demand for skills. It also means some countries provide huge numbers of migrant workers for industry and domestic work, a prime example being the thousands of Filipinos who work in the Middle East. Many of these are keen Christians and operate as tentmakers in that environment. Secondly, many countries are now closed to missionaries and so entry is only through employment, business or study. Some seventy countries are classed as 'restricted access' for traditional missions. Thirdly, new emphases in evangelical mission strategies have contributed, especially through the frontier mission movement which has emphasized a people-group focus. Fourthly, high financial demands for mission support have forced some to reconsider support levels and made self-support more attractive. Fifthly, growth of the marketplace movement or the faith at work movement has been significant, occurring over the same time-span. It has focused on the workplace as a locus of mission and

the work of the laity, all of which prepare for the cross-cultural form which we call tentmaking. Recent opportunities for international business development in the former Eastern bloc and in emerging Asian markets have led to the 'business as mission' form of tentmaking.

Some challenges for the future

Tentmaking faces major challenges. It struggles to be fully accepted by the missions community. There is as yet very little significant writing, tentmakers generally preferring action to reflection. *Training is a major need. Resources are limited and many attempt roles beyond their preparation. An area of major tension is that of integrity. Does the work itself have intrinsic value or does it aim simply to provide a means of entry into a closed access nation? Are the visas gained for genuine reasons and are the facts given to host governments true and transparent? The tentmaking world as a whole is eager to ensure the highest standards of integrity, especially as an increasing trend is in business as mission, setting up businesses that gain entry and allow for significant Christian impact. However, the movement is likely to keep growing as the international job market expands and mission remains in the heart of God's people.

Bibliography

Anon, 'A Tentmaking Ministry: The Church is a Missionary Community', *International Review of Missions* 52, 1963, pp. 47–59; J. D. Douglas (ed.), *Tentmakers Declarative Appeal Proclaim Christ Until He Comes* (Minneapolis: Worldwide Publishers, 1990); P. Lai, *Tentmaking: Business as Mission* (Waynesboro, GA: Authentic Media 2005); J. Lewis (ed.), *Working Your Way to the Nations* (Pasadena, CA: William Carey, 1993); S. Rundle and T. Steffen, *Great Commission Companies* (Downers Grove, IL: InterVarsity Press, 2003); P. Stevens, *The Other Six Days* (Grand Rapids, MI: Eerdmans, 1999); 'Tentmaking I', *International Journal of Frontier Missions* 14:3, 1997; 'Tentmaking II', *International Journal of Frontier Missions* 15:1, 1998; J. C. Wilson, *Today's Tentmakers* (Wheaton, IL: Tyndale House, 1979); T. Yamamori, *Penetrating Mission's Final Frontier* (Downers Grove,

IL: InterVarsity Press, 1993); <http://www.globalopps.org>.

D. CHRISTENSEN

Terrorism

In the book *Political Terrorism*, Jongman and Schmidt cite 109 different definitions of terrorism, compiled from leading academics in the field. From these definitions they find the following recurring elements in the definitions: violence and force; political motivation; generation of fear; emphasis on terror; threats; psychological effects and anticipated reactions; discrepancy between the targets and the victims; intentional, planned, systematic, organized action; and methods of combat, strategy, and tactics. Kshitij Prabha offers a definition that includes most of these aspects. Terrorism is 'an act or threat of an act of tactical violence by a group of trained individuals, having international linkage, to achieve a political objective. This group could be sponsored by non-state or state agencies' (in *Strategic Analysis* XXIV). It is important to add that the victims of terrorism are usually non-combatants used to send a message to those in power.

While most feel that they can recognize terrorism when they see it, experts have difficulty in creating and agreeing on a definition of terrorism that is universally accepted. Terrorism has been defined largely according to the political or socio-economic considerations and interests of those defining it. They have their own guidelines for who is a terrorist, which are grounded in their own politics. There are a number of questions to deal with in regards to terrorism: Who is a terrorist? What is the difference between terrorism and other forms of political violence or criminal acts? Are government terrorism and resistance terrorism the same phenomenon?

Terrorism existed well before the twentieth century, and various manifestations of it were present in ancient times when holy warriors would kill innocent civilians. The term originated in the time of the 'Reign of Terror' in eighteenth-century France, when leaders used terror to weed out 'traitors'. Since the Second World War it has been employed on a larger scale. The growth of terrorist activities is connected to technological innovations in modern weaponry, and advances in communications and mass media. In addition, there is often a religious aspect to terrorism. Most religious persuasions contain extremists who often use terrorist tactics to promote their religious and political agenda.

In the last half-century, terrorism was associated with specific regions of the world, for example the Middle East and Northern Ireland, and with certain ideological groups like the IRA, ETA, the Red Brigade or the Baader-Meinhof gang. Today it has developed an international scope and affects most of the world's population. Many people involved in mission are now operating under its shadow. The atrocity of 9/11 brought a paradigm shift in the world's experience and attitude towards terrorism, especially for the people of the USA. Due to the scale and tactics used on 9/11, and the way the US government responded, there has been an internationalization of the phenomenon, and the potential for worldwide terrorism has increased. However, many commentators see in a simple 'us/them' approach to a 'war on terror' the danger of creating a 'clash of civilizations' between the Christian West and the Muslim worlds, and that deeper divisions worldwide could only generate more terrorism.

The weaponry and methodology of terrorism is becoming increasingly sophisticated. The suicide bomber requires an extensive network and infrastructure in order to carry out and finance the attack. Another aspect of terrorism that is emerging is the potential use of weapons of mass destruction, or 'dirty bombs' such as nuclear, chemical, or biological warfare. Such weapons give terrorists the potential for causing damage on a large scale.

Christian response

Terrorism works with the moral assumption that the political ends justify a violent means. Terrorism attacks civil society, and uses fear and indiscriminant violence to terrorize civilians, in order to achieve political purposes, acquire power and air grievances. The use of terrorism is not an end in itself, but a means to an end.

The only moral and ethical response to terrorism is unreserved condemnation. From a Christian perspective, terrorism rejects the sanctity of life and the value of *humans as created in the image of God (Gen. 9:6). It defies the biblical commandment against murder, and has no regard for justice or *reconciliation (Exod. 20:13). In addition, it can be argued that terrorism is counter-productive. The violent means that terrorists employ cannot bring about a new healthy resolution to their grievances, since outcomes are never purely unrelated to means. Terrorism provokes further violence that continues the cycle of destruction, and can only create a situation that perpetuates the rule of force and violence to gain power and control.

Christian moral thought has always rejected the justification of indiscriminate violent actions by their effects. In some cases *liberation theology has been accused of allowing for violent methods to achieve a greater good or liberation. In general this is an unfair accusation and most liberation theologians have not offered justification for acts of terrorism.

In order to implement political or social change, the church must present alternatives to terrorism. The legitimate use of force is embodied in the principle of a 'just war,' developed since St Augustine. However, terrorism does not fall under the criteria for a just war because its victims are largely powerless and non-combatants. In the light of today's terrorism, the church urgently needs a reassessment of the concept of just war and other positions such as non-violence. The non-violent position advocated by the Anabaptists and Mennonites also needs to be explored in the church as a means of affecting social or political change.

The missiological implications
Individual
On a personal level, terrorism has an impact on an individual's sense of safety and can create a state of fear or paranoia that inhibits people from living a normal life. In the midst of threat Christians can have *peace and security, ways to deal with fear, assurance of God's faithfulness, and the promise of the resurrection that overcomes death (Ps. 91; 1 Cor. 15:19–54). This encourages them to seek refuge in God, and to encourage others to turn to him as a source of comfort in the face of fears.

Terrorism creates a cycle of hatred, anger, bitterness and desire for revenge. All human beings can be in danger of entering into this cycle in attitude and action. The Christian faith offers a way out of this cycle (1 John 4; Rom. 12:17). God will bring justice, and he declares repeatedly in Scripture that vengeance belongs to himself (Mic. 5:15; Lev. 19:18). Christ's death on the cross can also bring redemption from the self-destructive attitudes of hatred and bitterness (Eph. 2). Christians have a mandate to be active, not only in proclamation of the gospel, but also in fighting for social justice by legitimate means (Deut. 16:20; Mic. 6:8).

Community and church
Terrorism appeals to those who suffer injustices and to the disenfranchised. Economic hardship and political oppression create a breeding ground for terrorism. The work of the church is to win the minds and hearts of those who would turn to violence and to offer alternatives which address grievances and political problems. This is based in the biblical principles of reconciliation. Believers in many places (e.g. Northern Ireland, South Africa and Israel/Palestine) are building bridges across the divides. In sharp contrast to their societies, the church is working out what it means to love your enemies and understand the pain and grievances of those on the other side (Matt. 5:43–44; Rom. 12:15). The church can teach and model conflict-resolution methods in the community. It can bring effective examples of non-violent means of solving conflict, such as its involvement in the Truth and Reconciliation Commission in South Africa.

The church has the opportunity today to exercise a prophetic voice. But in order to do this, the church needs to be inclusive, to reach out and include those who are marginalized and without access to power. It has a responsibility to provide a welcoming community that meets the real needs of people (Matt. 25:44–46), which tends to the needs of the disempowered and which speaks out against social injustices. The work of the Christian Peacemaker Team in the Middle East is a strong example of Christians who take a non-violent role in monitoring and advocating human rights.

Another aspect of the church's response to terrorism is in developing relationships with other religious communities. The church needs to be involved in building bridges with other religious communities and working for a common response to terrorism. In this way religious militant groups can be corporately challenged, both on their use of violence as a means to achieve their ends and on the way they appeal to their religious tradition to justify their violence. All religions need reminding that their faith tradition offers alternatives to violence as a way to confront injustice. Mass media can be used to communicate these alternatives in the local languages, in a way that addresses specific grievances.

The church maintains the important role of representing and reflecting the identity of Christ among all communities. In a world where the political actions of Western countries are perceived as 'Christian' actions, the church must speak clearly to differentiate the message of the gospel from the agenda of the state. Many in the Muslim world perceive Western foreign policy as Christian and based on Christian principles, but the church needs to point out that the political actions of Western governments are not representative of the Christian faith.

Church and state
Many analysts have recognized that terrorism can be perpetrated by governments as well as by revolutionary organizations. The church needs to develop a refined social theology that can speak to all forms of unjust use of fear. In an age of weapons of mass destruction and suicide bombers, nations are compelled to defend themselves and maintain the balance of preserving civil rights. However, the rights of the individual can be trampled upon in the name of security against terrorism. The act of profiling or labelling communities can push individuals to anger and frustration. If the state is not itself following biblical principles of human rights or social justice, the church must be a prophetic voice to the state, and bring attention to the misuse of power. A historical example, when the institutional church failed miserably at this task, was its role in Nazi Germany. It was left to the minority 'confessing church' to stand up to what its government was doing. The church can be involved in taking local and international legal action against injustice, and must be active in balancing the

need for national security with democratic principles.

The state can use the premise of security and fighting terrorism to push other agendas. Protection from the threat of terrorism can be used as a tactic to manipulate public opinion and to violate human rights and religious freedom. The church has a responsibility to critique the messages of the media. Perceived threats of terrorism can blind us to the humanity of the other. We must be careful that our fears do not allow us to disenfranchise or demonize other people groups, and to foster attitudes and approaches that imperil the message of the gospel.

Bibliography
A. Jongman and A. Schmid, *Political Terrorism* (Piscataway: Transaction Books, 1988); K. Prabha, 'Defining Terrorism', *Strategic Analysis: A Monthly Journal of the IDSA*, XXIV, 2000; K. Prabha, 'Terrorism', in D. J. Atkinson and D. H. Field (eds.), *New Dictionary of Christian and Ethics and Pastoral Theology* (Downers Grove; Leicester: IVP, 1995).

S. J. MUNAYER

Theology of mission

Special attention will be given in this article to the methodology and contours of a missionary theology as well as theology's relationship to mission.

Historical perspective
The fact that the NT was 'consciously written within a missionary context', and responded to that context, is almost universally recognized today. In the NT there was no separation between theology and mission. It was the emergence of Christendom that led theology to lose its missionary character. By the eighteenth century, theology as a discipline had developed theoretical and practical aspects. It was either a scholarly discipline studying the observable world, or a practical discipline preparing religious functionaries. Schleiermacher developed a four-fold pattern for theology: biblical studies, systematic theology, church history and practical theology. The study of mission was placed within practical theology along with liturgy, ethics and church government; it was practical theology

for the church in 'foreign parts'. On one hand, mission was marginalized, becoming one option for study among many others, and on the other hand, mission became the application of Western biblical studies and systematic theology to 'the third world'.

Various attempts were made to find a place for mission studies in the house of theology. Some tried to make it an autonomous discipline with its own criteria and subject matter. These tended to adapt the already established four-fold pattern, dividing it into the biblical basis of mission, mission theory, history of mission and missionary strategy. Theology, for its part, was released from any obligation to reflect upon the church's missionary task. Theology, on the whole, was not affected by mission.

In the twentieth century, both historical and theological events changed the relationship of mission to theology. The end of Christendom, the rise of secularism, two world wars, and the growth of the church in the Majority World, led to the realization that the church was in a missionary context wherever it was placed. Britain and Germany were as much 'mission fields' as were Brunei and Gambia. If this was true then theology in Western countries must have a missionary agenda. In addition, the validity of mission itself was being questioned. The confidence of the Edinburgh Missionary Conference (1910), which asked *how* to do mission, was replaced by the tentative question of *what* is Christian mission. Moreover, the realization that the church is missionary by its very nature, the Dutch theology of the apostolate, and the development of the *Missio Dei concept, led to the need for a new model for the relationship between mission and theology.

Johannes H. Hoekendijk called for a shift from a theology of mission as a subsection of systematic and practical theology, to a mission theology. The theology of mission examines mission, as the subject of study, from a theological standpoint. A missionary theology is where mission is the locus of all theological reflection. In this sense: 'theology as a whole is related to the starting point and goal of the gospel's journey through the world and the problems encountered on that journey' (F. J. Verstraelen et al., Missiology: An Ecumenical Introduction).

The development of such a theology was advanced by the development of Latin American *liberation theology. Its emphasis on the priority of *praxis as a prerequisite of knowledge and its insistence upon theology as a process rather than a product began to construct a basis for methodology for missionary theology.

Development of missionary theologies

It is fruitful to analyse missionary theologies via their doctrinal motifs and via the context from which they emerge.

Ecclesiocentric theologies are strongest in the evangelical and Roman Catholic traditions. The *Church Growth School of Missiology has emphasized the *how* of the planting and growth of churches, focusing on barriers to conversion, methods of evangelism and strategies for structural growth. Roman Catholicism has emphasized apostolic succession and papal authority to highlight the central role of the church in mission. Vatican II and some subsequent encyclicals, such as *Evangelli Nuntiandi*, tended to relativize the role of the church, calling it a sign, sacrament and instrument of salvation, rather than the deposit of salvation. The ecumenical movement contains both *ecclesiocentric* tendencies (mainly influenced by Eastern Orthodox participation) and *anti-ecclesiocentric* (influenced by the 'Dutch Theology of the Apostolate').

Theologies that emphasize *God's action in building God's kingdom* as central to mission are strongest in the ecumenical movement. Inspired by the theology of Karl Barth, introduced by Karl Hartenstein at the IMC conference at Willengen (1952), and later popularized by Goerg Vicedom, *missio Dei* theologies emphasize that mission is primarily the work of God, not of the church. During the 1960s there were conflicting interpretations of this concept, some seeing the church as auxiliary to God's mission and others relegating the church to an almost negligible role. The concept was welcomed by various non-Western theologians such as D. T. Niles, as well as Western Conciliar theologians such as Johannes Heokendijk and Roman Catholics such as Frans Verstraelen.

Missio Dei theologies have led to missionary theologies of the *Trinity. Lesslie Newbigin and Jürgen Moltmann were two of the first, followed by others such as José Míguez Bonino, Leonardo Boff and Juan Luis Segundo. God is a missionary God, and so God's being as Trinity must also be missionary. The Trinity, therefore, becomes a model for missionary praxis of the *church.

These theologies can be analysed using various criteria:

From the perspective of *salvation-history theologies, God's mission is seen as the establishment of God's *kingdom on earth. God's action in the life of Israel and especially in the life, death and resurrection of Jesus Christ and his future return are the basis of missionary theology's reflection. Mission is both a preparation for, and a sign of, the end times. These theologies have been more important in Conciliar theology than in either evangelicalism or Roman Catholicism; René Padilla is an exception in the former, as are Karl Rahner and Ludwig Rütti in the latter. Oscar Cullman, however, made salvation history central to his theology, as have others such as David J. Bosch and Walter Freytag. Some Latin American theologians such as Emilio Castro and Jose Míguez Bonino have also developed this theme from a Latin American perspective.

All these theologies have a *context from which they emerge*. Among these one could mention theologies which emerge from a *context of oppression and injustice*. These include the *Latin American theologies of liberation; *black theologies emerging from South Africa or from the United States; *feminist and womanist theologies; *minjung theologies from Korea and even Palestinian liberation theologies.

Some theologies emerge from contexts of *religious pluralism*. These have traditionally been analysed using the categorization of pluralist, inclusivist and exclusivist theologies, although the usefulness of this approach has been questioned in recent years, since many theologies contain elements of each and cannot be described purely in terms of a single category. Broadly pluralist theologies from the Majority World include those from India such as the theology of Stanley Samartha and M. M. Thomas; Western pluralist theologies have been pioneered by Paul Knitter and John Hick. Inclusivist theologies include the development of a missiology for the Western world following the work of Lesslie Newbigin, and represented in North

America by the Gospel and Culture Network. Evangelical and generally more exclusivist missiologies from a pluralist context would include the work of Howard Netland, Ken Gnanakan and Ravi Zacharias.

Other missiologies have been the attempt to understand Christianity from the *cultural background* of a people. In Africa, the work of John Mbiti in relation to the African concept of time and Kwesi Dickson in regard to African Christologies has been vital. In Asia, Kazoh Kitamori was one of the first Japanese theologians, and Japanese theologian Kosume Koyama attempts to express the Christian faith from an Asian perspective (see *Asian theology). From India the emerging *Dalit theology not only is a response to oppression but also an effort to express the faith from a Dalit perspective.

Methodology for missionary theology

The most important theological issue in missionary theology is that of methodology: how do we develop a biblical, contextual missionary theology that takes both mission and theology seriously?

The point of departure for an evangelical missionary theology is the *revelation of God's mission purposes in the Scriptures. From this derive the call, the motivation and the commitment necessary for obedience, and the desire for the glory of God. Missionary obedience is a prerequisite for missionary theology, because missionary theology is not a neutral discipline. This does not mean that it does not achieve critical distance, but it does mean that it cannot be done from outside of the missionary task. This means that the context of missionary obedience comes immediately into play.

Analysis of the context of mission will help to identify the key questions and priorities to which mission must address itself; this is as true of the analysis of the external context of mission as the place of the Christian community within that context. This analysis must avail itself of such ancillary disciplines as historical investigation, ideological and sociological critique, as well as cultural and social anthropology. The theologians of liberation tended to use dialectical tools of analysis based in the 'masters of suspicion', whereas evangelicals have tended to rely upon cultural anthropology, and especially that stream influenced by Bronislaw Malinowski (1884–1942). Today, with the high level of cultural change, new tools, such as structuralist anthropology and semiotics, must be found and critically investigated.

In its analysis of the context, missionary theology must study planned and unplanned developments in the preaching, expression, and spread of the Christian gospel in diverse cultural contexts. Unplanned processes would include such things as the development of popular religion among the urban poor, the growth of popular *Pentecostalism or the expression of faith among the *African Initiated Churches (AICs). It must also study planned processes such as how the church was planted and developed among certain groups.

The contextual analysis and the questions which emerge from it can then be taken back to the Bible. This does not mean simply seeking for the biblical basis of mission, much less, justification for missionary activity. Missionary theology's reflection upon the church's mission in its context must be a living and fresh reading of God's salvific activity in Jesus Christ as it works out in Scripture. This should be a truly contextual reading of God's word, which takes place in the context of obedience; in the light of its own theological traditions and background (what it has received in tradition from church history – the living stream of the life of the church); and in fellowship with the Holy Spirit.

This then leads back to the concrete context of the mission of the church. A missionary theology must be active at this point as well. This is part of the theological task because theology is responsible for the practical outworkings of its theological reflections. Due to the fact that there are no straight lines from biblical reflection to missionary practice, a second moment of analysis is needed, without which theology either remains in the abstract or its practical outworkings become arbitrary. This analysis tries to establish valid outworkings within the context, in the light of the theological reflection. It also attempts to perceive the consequences of these actions. It is important to have strategies at this point. The theological nature of a missionary theology requires that faith become concrete in different contexts.

Consequences of a contextual missionary theology

There needs to be differentiation between *contextual and contextualized theologies. It is generally accepted that all theology is written from within a particular context, consciously or unconsciously responding to the needs of that context. That is, *all* theology is contextual, including Western biblical and systematic theologies. A missionary theology, however, is consciously contextualized, that is, it is aware of the context in which it is written and moreover consciously assumes that context. Thereby it exposes any ideological supposition that may have slipped into interpretation. It then intentionally reflects upon the being and mission of the church within that context, treating the issues of that context in the light of the word of God. It is theology done in the light of, and for the sake of, the missionary context. This would mean that a contextualized theology is indeed a missionary theology.

This leads to the fact that theological curricula need to be altered. The artificial division between courses on theology (usually meaning Western systematic theology) and contextual theology or contextualized theology (meaning theology done in the Majority World) should be abandoned. The ideological myth that Western theology is not 'contextual', and so is valid for all places and all times, must be discarded. Therefore, the theology of the Majority World church is not beholden to Western theology to give an account of its theology as if that theology were to be the *norma normans* of all theology.

Thirdly, it also means that churches planted in new contexts have both the right and the responsibility to do their theology from within their own contexts. The church must reflect upon the work of Christ from their perspective. They will take into account theological articulations from church history, but they will also re-read the work of Christ from their perspective. Theologically, the role of the missionary is to be a 'midwife' of the new church's theology, not giving birth to the new theological articulations but rather, accompanying the church in the process of theological reflection.

Fourthly, it will lead to diversity in theological articulations and expressions. It is clear that different contexts will bring about widely differing interests in the development of missionary theology. Europe and North America will have the responsibility to develop a post-colonialist missiology for its post-Christian world: how can non-colonialist and anti-colonialist theology break out from the straitjacket of *colonialist thinking? In addition, theological reflection upon issues of immigration, fair trade, global terrorism and global warming will require a new missionary approach.

Asia, Africa and Latin America, the traditionally colonized world, has the challenge of an emerging contextual missionary theology for the future. Emerging missionary movements, which have been reliant upon undigested First-World missiology, have the responsibility to develop a new missionary theology for their own contexts as well as for cross-cultural missionary theology.

Conclusion

Finally, theology needs to be aware of the danger of theological pluralism – the attitude that one missionary theology is as good as another and that there is no way of reconciling them. This threatens Christian unity; contextuality must be balanced by the universal recognition of the centrality and authority of Scripture. To admit the contextual nature of all theology should not deny the possibility of dialogue based on a common respect for Scripture, but should lead to mutual accountability in the areas of biblical hermeneutics, the understanding of tradition, and the interpretation of reality. So, for example, *African theology is accountable to Latin American theology, and vice versa; Western theology is both responsible to and responsible for Asian articulations.

In this way it is hoped that theology will be able to be done in its fully universal and missionary spirit (a catholic missionary theology); done in the unity and *koinonia* of the faith (an ecumenical missionary theology) and done in the preaching and living out of the gospel (an evangelical missionary theology).

Bibliography

G. H. Anderson, *The Theology of Christian Mission* (London: SCM Press, 1961); R. Bassham, *Mission Theology: 1948–1975 Years of Worldwide Creative Tension* (Pasadena: William Carey Library, 1979); S. B. Bevans, *Models of Contextual Theology* (Maryknoll: Orbis Books, 1992); S. B. Bevans and R. P. Schroeder, *Constants in Context: A Theology of Mission for Today* (Maryknoll: Orbis Books, 2004); D. J. Bosch, *Transforming Mission: Paradigm Shifts in Theology of Mission* (Maryknoll: Orbis Books, 1991); J. A. B. Jongeneel, *Philosophy, Science and Theology of Mission in the 19th and 20th Centuries, Parts 1 and 2* (Frankfurt; New York: Peter Lang, 1995, 1997); J. A. Kirk, *What is Mission? Theological Explorations* (London: Darton, Longman & Todd, 1999); S. Nussbaum, *A Reader's Guide to Transforming Mission* (Maryknoll: Orbis Books, 2005); J. M. Phillips and R. T. Coote, *Towards the 21st Century in Christian Mission* (Grand Rapids: Eerdmans, 1993); J. Verkuyl, *Contemporary Missiology: An Introduction* (Grand Rapids: Eerdmans, 1978); F. J. Verstraelen, A. Camps, L. A. Hoedemaker and M. R. Spindler, *Missiology: An Ecumenical Introduction* (Grand Rapids: Eerdmans, 1995).

P. DAVIES

Theology of religion

Categories of Christian theology as it relates to other religions have been traditionally grouped into a threefold typology of pluralism, inclusivism and exclusivism. These categories are now critiqued as having too sharp a distinction between them, and for their failure to take into account the complexities and nuances of difference between various proponents of religious encounter.

For example, some evangelicals will be exclusivist on the finality of Jesus for *salvation, but will be open to incorporating insights from other religions in relation to life and faith. On the basis that God has not left himself without witness (Acts 14:17), others affirm some degree of *revelation from God for other religious traditions which would enable those who have never heard of Christ to turn to him in faith. New models are still being proposed and debated with no real consensus in the evolving debate on the theology of religion; so the focus of this article will be to survey the writings of a selection of evangelical theologians.

Contemporary perspectives

A good introductory survey is offered by Veli-Matti Kärkkäinen. Recent evangelical positions involve inclusivists such as Clark Pinnock, John Sanders and Mark Heim, as well as particularists such as Gerald McDermott, Timothy Tennent, Ida Glaser and Terrence Tiessen. Even so, none of these are strict exclusivists. McDermott argues from Scripture and the writings of Jonathan Edwards that evangelicals can discover new insights by engaging with the teachings of other religions, so long as that encounter is shaped by a commitment to the Bible. It is clear from Scripture that God wants those outside the covenant community to know him, and God's people can learn much from those outside the Jewish and Christian contexts. For example McDermott discusses moral virtues in Confucianism, Buddhist thinking of 'no-self', and Islam's integration between religion and public life, all of which can be reshaped through biblical reflection. He distinguishes those who question the value of human culture from those who recognize God's 'common grace' working in and through all human culture, and who therefore respond positively to it.

Tennent likewise recognizes that religious conversations can no longer be entered into with Christians positioning themselves at the head of the table, controlling the agenda and the conclusions. Rather, Christians today need to sit at a round table and engage in dialogue. Tennent demonstrates what such roundtable discussions might look like through interactions with Hinduism, Buddhism and Islam. He lists two potential weaknesses in exclusivism: first, a failure to appreciate fully God's activity in the pre-Christian heart; and secondly, an unwillingness to engage honestly with the objections from non-Christian religions. Tennent presents himself as an 'engaged exclusivist', committed to the uniqueness of Christ but also more open toward what God reveals of himself through general revelation. For him, engaging the religions from a missiological perspective has to be a serious commitment.

Evangelicals such as Harold Netland, Amos Yong and Terrence Tiessen are exploring new models of engagement. Yong has pointed out that exclusivism is primarily a soteriological category, helpful for clarifying the question of the unevangelized, but not so adequate for developing a theology of non-Christian religions.

In dealing with the question of who can be saved, Tiessen proposed the following five categories:

(1) Ecclesiocentrism: salvation is coextensive with the church.

(2) Agnosticism: Scripture is silent on the issue of who can be saved.

(3) Accessibilism: hopeful (not simply agnostic) about the possibility of salvation beyond church boundaries. Non-Christians can be saved although non-Christian religions may not be regarded as instruments for salvation.

(4) Religious instrumentalism: God's salvation is available through non-Christian religions, a form of inclusivism.

(5) Relativism: many ways of salvation as part of God's divine programme.

Tiessen himself proposes accessibilism as a new position for engaging with non-Christian religions. He argues that early Church Fathers (Clement of Alexandria, Irenaeus), and writers such as Lesslie Newbigin and J. N. D. Anderson, affirm the uniqueness of Christ as the means of salvation while at the same time are more open to what God is doing among non-Christian religions.

Why traditional evangelical categories need contextual reformulation

A Christian theology of non-Christian religions will need to engage with non-Christian beliefs on their own terms. Comparing belief systems of religions within their scriptural and socio-religious contexts may reveal new languages and categories for engagement. To illustrate the complexities of inter-religious discourse, consider eight interconnected factors impacting the nature and dynamic of Christian-Muslim encounter in Malaysia:

(1) Theological differences between Islam and Christianity; (2) religious misunderstandings inherited from centuries of Christian-Muslim relations; (3) racial and cultural differences between Muslims and Christians; (4) social pressures within the Malay community against conversion; (5) legislative barriers hindering freedom of conversion, marriage, burial and religious practice; (6) political structures organized along racial lines; (7) economic deprivations for converts

(e.g. withdrawal of special privileges for housing, business, children's education); and (8) impact of global events such as Palestinian-Israeli conflicts, war on terror, and trade protectionism in Western countries.

The multi-dimensional realities of ethnicity, religion, socio-historical and political dimensions must be included in any adequate Christian theology of non-Christian religions. There is no such thing as a purely spiritual conversation. Where does one draw the line between culture and religion? Can Malay Christians, for example, follow Jesus while remaining in their culture? How do Christians develop a map for discerning the possibility of being a hybrid of Christian-Buddhist? To share these struggles is to appreciate that these are complex issues which require more reflection and dialogue among evangelical missiologists.

Hans Frei's typology

Hans Frei's model of five types of theology can help us to develop a more critical evaluation of approaches toward non-Christian religions. Frei based his analysis on Richard Niebuhr's typology: Christ against *culture, the Christ of culture, Christ above culture, Christ and culture in paradox, and Christ the transformer of culture.

Frei was frustrated with the lack of nuance between the different theological categories of pluralism and exclusivism, which led to an impasse in evangelical approaches to other religions. This made it easier for evangelicals to retreat into rejectionism or isolationism and not to move outside their theological boxes. But in an age of increased religious tensions, there is a danger of erecting more fences than bridges for inter-religious encounters. Rather than labelling various approaches as liberal, evangelical, catholic or confessional, it may be helpful to evaluate our approaches to people of other faiths through Hans Frei's typology.

Basically Frei posited two extreme and opposite ways in which Christianity relates to modernity, with three mediating points in between:

Type 1. At this polarity theology is developed from modern philosophy, based on Enlightenment thinking or on an agenda such as ecology, poverty or justice. Science, genetics, psychology, or some other discipline lend their authority to a theological frame of reference that is essentially pluralistic. Ironically, however, all perspectives are judged according to how well they fit this frame of reference, which can lead to selectivity and reductionism. In relation to religions, we may argue that whenever pluralistic approaches rely on concepts of tolerance, or the notion that all religions are essentially the same, they run the risk of lacking biblical or even distinctively Christian foundations.

Type 5 is at the other extreme polarity, and is an attempt to reproduce a scriptural world-view by recycling classical theology (Calvinist, Lutheran, Barthist, Wesleyan) or a denominational theological position (Catholic, Reformed, Pentecostal, Baptist), and to see all reality in those terms. The inerrant Scripture is the basis for encountering people of other faiths, ignoring any nuances in the real beliefs of other cultures. Any new attempts at formulating theological engagements with non-Christian religions are rejected. Western theological interpretations and categories are regarded as 'foundational' and as the basis for judging Islam, Buddhism and Hinduism. The best of Christianity is compared with the worst of other religions. The context is irrelevant and deep-seated belief systems are seldom addressed. Nominalism, legalism, fundamentalism and parochialism thrive in communities that operate within a Type 5 theological approach.

Type 2 Christian theology interacts positively with social sciences, management theories, psychology, non-Christian religious studies and so on, and applies all that to understanding Christianity and the relevance of the gospel for today. In some cases missiologists may allow specific agendas such as dialogue, holistic mission, justice, modernity or pluralism to become their integrative framework for engaging with people of other faiths, with the result that there is minimum engagement with Scripture.

Type 3 is in the middle because it refuses to allow any single agenda or framework to dominate the multi-perspectives needed for engaging with the social, cultural and religious worlds. It recognizes that there is no such thing as a purely religious encounter. For example, meaningful engagement with Islam must include an understanding of its distinctive sects, political structures, historical meanings, and economic realities of these concrete communities. This view does not come with a set of presuppositions or doctrines or projects, but sets up dialogues between Christians and people of other faiths. The key idea is correlation – 'the aim is to correlate issues raised by the Christian faith and practice with other approaches to those issues' (D. Ford, *Theology: A Very Short Introduction*, p. 24).

For example, to answer the question of possible correlations between Buddhists' vision for nirvana and enlightenment with the Christian vision of salvation requires a necessary engagement with Buddhists and in-depth study of religious meanings. Seeking correlation does not mean wholesale acceptance of another religious belief system, rather it recognizes the intricate balance between religion and culture and it seeks an authentic gospel in each social context. Intimate knowledge and careful study of other faiths give evangelicals a reliable position to make judgments, to come up with truth-validations, and to allow the Christian gospel's interaction with any contradictory truths.

Inclusivists such as Gavin D'Costa and Marcus Borg generally may be comfortable with this position, but so would accessibilists such as Terrence Tiessen, missiologist Lesslie Newbigin, Islamicist Kenneth Cragg or anthropologist Charles Kraft. These are examples of theologians who fit into this type 3 category. People who describe themselves as 'radical' or 'open' evangelicals, or those experimenting with new forms of communities will be most likely to be launching from this Type 3 base of mission theology. The key liberating fact is that they are not operating with a single meta-narrative, but have the capacity to engage with people in their contextual realities, believing that God is far bigger than their Christianity.

Type 4 tries to avoid the middle path of correlation by giving priority to the Christian narrative. It is 'faith seeking understanding', based on a prior commitment to Scripture and the gospel. Such faith-commitment does not exclude the need for dialogue. Instead, it seeks to find new ways of being believers in the midst of non-Christian cultures, while maintaining its roots and identities within historic Christian community. Mainstream

evangelicalism will be most comfortable with this position, with scholars such as Tennent and McDermott identifying with it.

The challenge of encountering non-Christian religions

Developments in mission thinking on non-Christian religions have not resulted in radical reformulation of mission practices in Asian and African contexts. The Christian community seems stuck between those who uncritically embrace relativistic values and those who vociferously resist any suggestions that they can learn anything from non-Christian religions. Among non-Western churches, particularly those who have suffered persecution from other religions, or those who have rejected spiritism and idolatry, learning from other faiths is viewed with suspicion, if not resisted as another form of syncretism. Increasing religious conflict, fears of serious debates over competing faith-claims, and growing fundamentalism between and within religions challenges evangelicals to revisit their positions on the value of non-Christian religions. The challenge is to move beyond the impasse, without surrendering evangelical affirmations and yet to live as the people of God in the midst of concrete social and political realities.

Other developments

Although the themes of salvation and revelation are critical, Christians in the minority amongst the world's religions struggle with other basic issues of identity and inter-religious relations: what does it mean to be a post-Muslim Christian, or a post-Buddhist Christian? How do we interpret our past religious-cultural practices? With our new-found faith, how do we relate and engage with people of other faiths?

In response, positive developments have taken place when Christian studies are undertaken to engage with specific beliefs of other religions. Ida Glaser and Chawkat Moucarry are two recent attempts at engaging Islam based on careful readings of the Qur'an and sensitive treatment of Islamic beliefs. A second set of contributions are context-specific studies which help Christians to understand other religions on their own terms rather than stereotyping all religions as evil: such scholars include David Burnett,

Paul J. Griffiths, Peter Riddell and Peter Cotterell.

Theology of the kingdom of God and Islam

As an example, it is possible to explore how the theology of the *kingdom of God may be used as a framework for engaging with people of other faiths and challenging their world-views. The kingdom is also a promising symbol for breaking the impasse within evangelicalism in exploring religious encounters. The encounter begins with the acknowledgment that Muslims, Jews and Christians share similar roots in monotheism, Judeo-Christian prophetic traditions and inter-religious civilizations. But Jesus' message of the kingdom in its context was an invitation to follow God's ways rather than the nationalistic aspirations of establishing a political Jewish kingdom. Rather than offering spiritual promises of heaven, his parables break open the Jewish world-view to the fact that the true people of God are not just Jews but also Gentiles. The parables act not merely as stories about the kingdom, but also as the very means for inviting Gentiles as well as Jews into the kingdom.

The miracles of Jesus are another tool that he uses for world-view transformation, because they act as signs of God's surprising inclusion of the poor and the lepers who exhibited faith in Jesus as the Messiah. As well as demonstrating Jesus' divinity, these miracles and healings are signs that God is vindicating Jesus' way of life and mission. When Muslims are invited to become followers of such a radical kingdom, they are invited to see faith and ethics embodied in a life witness that exceeds religious righteousness. They then discover that Christians are also people of a book. Religious encounter, in this way, cannot be achieved without long-term friendship, and living amongst Muslims where that 'righteousness' of faith can be demonstrated.

The kingdom of God becomes a mutual discovery that includes not just the religious but every aspect of life. It is like a pearl, precious and pursued by the merchant who is willing to surrender everything for the sake of possessing it. Over time, the signs of the kingdom present a coherent and consistent message, lived out in humble obedience of a follower of Isa Al-Masih, and that speaks powerfully and relevantly to Muslim mindsets.

The tripolar view of other religions

Evangelical Peter Beyerhaus proposed a tripolar view of non-Christian religions which takes into account three sources of all religions: humans and their cultures, God and the supernatural elements in all religions, and the works of the devil in all religions. On this view we take seriously the supernatural elements within all religions. There are powerful forces at work, 'principalities' that have brought people into slavery. These demonic forces are at work in both Christendom and non-Christian religions. Therefore, Christian encounter is not merely an exchange of reasoned arguments and theological debates.

Conclusion

Using Hans Frei's typology of Christian theology, this article has evaluated the spectrum of contemporary evangelical perspectives on the theology of religions. It has suggested that the extreme positions of Type 1 and 5 are untenable in formulating an adequate theology of religion. Conservative Christians tend to move between Type 5 and Type 4, with some fundamentalist groups operating mainly in Type 5. Within evangelical circles, missiologists and practitioners who place priority on cultural and religious understanding, whilst retaining a firm commitment to an exclusivist position, tend to operate in Type 4, whilst the innovative radicals and scholars of religions are mostly found within Type 3. An 'open evangelical' operates with personal commitment to the uniqueness of Christ, remains open to dialogue and to learning from other religious practitioners, but does not close off the possibility that God's saving purposes are at work within non-Christian religions. However, no theologian or missionary can be typecast in one category, nor is it impossible to move between categories. The value of Frei's model is to help us reflect on our particular way of thinking about inter-religious encounter, so that we can be self-critical about our own presuppositions and open to other perspectives.

See also AFRICAN TRADITIONAL RELIGION, BUDDHIST RELATIONS, HINDU RELATIONS, JEWISH MISSION,

MUSLIM RELATIONS, NEW RELIGIOUS MOVEMENTS.

Bibliography

H. Frei and G. Hunsburger, *Types of Christian Theology* (Yale: Yale University Press, 1992); I. Glaser, *The Bible and Other Faiths: Christianity's Responsibility in a World of Religions* (Leicester: IVP, 2005); S. M. Heim, *Salvations: Truth and Difference in Religion* (Maryknoll: Orbis Books, 1995); V.-M. Kärkkäinen, *An Introduction to the Theology of Religions: Biblical, Historical and Contemporary Perspectives* (Downers Grove: InterVarsity Press, 2003); P. F. Knitter, *Theologies of Religions* (Maryknoll: Orbis Books, 2003); G. R. McDermott, *Can Evangelicals Learn From World Religions?* (Downers Grove: InterVarsity Press, 2000); C. Moucarry, *Faith to Faith* (Leicester: IVP, 2001); H. Netland, *Encountering Religious Pluralism: The Challenge to Christian Faith and Mission* (Downers Grove: InterVarsity Press, 2001); R. Niebuhr, *Christ and Culture* (London: HarperCollins, rev. edn, 2001); T. C. Tennent, *Christianity at the Religious Roundtable* (Grand Rapids: Baker, 2002); T. L. Tiessen, *Who Can Be Saved? Reassessing Salvation in Christ and the World Religions* (Downers Grove: InterVarsity Press, 2004); A. Yong, *Beyond the Impasse: Toward a Pneumatological Theology of Religions* (Grand Rapids: Baker, 2003).

KANG-SAN TAN

Training missionaries

Adequate missionary training is essential to long-term permanence and in-depth contribution to the missionary outreach of the church. Jesus certainly thoroughly trained his disciples for mission. His was not a short-term academic course, but a transforming experience as the disciples accompanied him day by day, learning from his teaching, example and guidance in their own developing ministries. With the exception of James, church traditions and history reveal that they all eventually became cross-cultural missionaries.

People cross *cultures for different reasons and to perform different ministries. Their training must be as varied as their gifts and calling. Thankfully formal schooling is only one part of a far more extensive training programme, sovereignly directed through the candidate's family, school, church and life experiences.

However, a World Evangelical Alliance study demonstrates the importance for missionary retention of structures and intentional pre-service training. In newer and older sending countries alike, 'high retaining agencies expect twice as much theological training from their missionary candidates, on average, and three times as much formal missiological training as low retaining agencies' (D. Bloecher, in *Connections*, June 2004, p. 13).

Indeed, a lack of such training can result in people arriving in complex situations unequipped for cross-cultural understanding, living, communication or ministry, leaving them unable to cope or produce fruitful results. An earlier WEA study proves this. The study reveals that in older sending countries lack of training contributes to 2.7% of attrition. In newer sending countries it contributes to 4.5%. These figures seem small until other reasons directly connected to training are considered: lack of cultural adaptation, spiritual immaturity, character disorders, problems with national leaders and linguistic problems. Adding all these reasons together leads to 60.8% attrition in newer sending countries and 83.8% in older sending countries (B. Dipple in *Internationalizing Missionary Training: A Global Perspective*, p. 188).

What is missionary training?

A biblical framework

Models of in-depth pre-field and on-going missionary training can be found in the biblical accounts of Barnabas, Paul, Timothy and the disciples of Jesus.

Barnabas was an active, respected and giving member of the Jerusalem church from its beginning. He was an encourager, exercising his gift in a way especially significant when, with insight and courage, he accepted Saul and presented him before the apostolic leadership. So high was his recognized capacity for discernment that he was chosen for the task of evaluating a new church in Antioch which had, shockingly, included Gentiles. Only after years of fellowship in the exciting Jerusalem church did Barnabas become the leader of a new church, teaching and helping it to grow. His training had included learning the 'apostles' doctrine', being faithful in prayer, participating in provision of welfare, performing miracles and engaging in aggressive evangelistic outreach in dangerous Jerusalem. He was a humble man, willing to share leadership, and ready at a moment's notice to leave all and follow God's commission to the outside world. Christian maturation and ministry experience combined with a cross-cultural childhood in Cyprus were surely all preparation for the more difficult cross-cultural task in a Gentile world.

Paul was very well prepared before his commissioning in Acts 13:1–4. He had spent some time at least in the important and cultured Gentile city of Tarsus. He learned the Scriptures so successfully that he gained a seat at the feet of Gamaliel, the most respected rabbi of the time. He was certainly proven in his knowledge, life and ministry during his three years in the desert and up to ten subsequent years in Tarsus. Paul's training continued at Barnabas' side in the context of the Antioch church's dynamic, teaching and evangelistic community.

Timothy was also trained and proven before he was sent to Ephesus and other places. He studied the Scriptures from his childhood, grew up in a home with a cultural mix of a Gentile father and Jewish mother, was chosen to accompany Paul and his missionary team, and was recommended to the church in Philippi as a faithful and trusted servant (2:19–22).

These first missionaries had profound scriptural knowledge which they seriously applied in daily life. They were apprenticed in the church and in practical ministry. They had cross-cultural experience and sensitivity. They were not neophytes, just racing out to 'do God's will'. Under the power and direction of the Holy Spirit they knew how to evangelize people and plant new viable churches wherever they went.

The disciples of Jesus afford the greatest and clearest example for missionary training in the Bible. In a three-year period Jesus lived and worked with this group. His was a discipleship of the road, not from a pulpit, office or classroom. He did not simply tell people how to minister; he ministered among them and they along with him. Occasionally he sent them off by themselves and when they returned, he corrected, praised and enhanced their learning.

Jesus' training style was interactive, practical and deeply theological. He continually related his teaching and practice to the Scriptures and Israel's history. Jesus is the master model for what is called 'integrated training'. He had no dichotomies. He did not separate the social from the spiritual. Theory was totally applied in practice and practice based on theory. True theology had a missionary outcome and missiology never stood alone without its foundational theology. Character was as important as knowledge or capability. He repeatedly emphasized *humility and servant leadership (contrary to some programmes for training that can mistakenly give missionaries a sense of being able to meet cross-cultural ministry challenges because of intellectual preparation alone).

Missionaries need knowledge of what Jesus taught, wisdom in how to teach people of other cultures and, as so clearly and forcefully spoken by our Lord in his last minutes here on earth, the power of the Holy Spirit, the promise of Acts 1:8. The central goal in missionary training is to lead people to full obedience to God's will so that his name will be exalted in all the earth (Isa. 42:6–12; 2 Thess. 1:11–12).

The missionary's own cultural context

There is much debate about where training can be most effective. Some current models train people in the context where they will serve, either in church teams or in seminaries. They claim that the mission context itself is the best place to learn cross-cultural orientation, and where missionaries can learn from nationals. However, a strong case can be made for training in the missionary's own cultural context. Practices that import missiological curricula or send people to other countries for training often miss particular needs which arise within the missionary's own culture and personal background. Some candidates come with a lot of personal 'baggage' that needs to be sorted out before they set off anywhere! Candidates need good awareness of the strengths and weaknesses of their own culture so that they can enhance and apply positive cultural, psychological and character traits, and confront and diminish negative traits. All the classical missiological subjects need cultural awareness and application, and this can only be done appropriately in the missionary's own cultural context (see *Contextualization).

Taking these things into consideration requires flexibility about the time needed for missionary preparation. There are no time or curriculum formulas that can be passed from one country or culture to the next.

The realities of mission
Each missionary field and type of service holds its own challenges. Preparation must take at least the following factors into consideration:

Levels of cross-cultural distance in living and communication. Culture shock and communication stress occur on all levels of cultural distance. Anthropology, religious phenomenology, ethnological studies and methods of communication and contextualization reduce distance and enhance the well-being and effectiveness of the missionary.

Mission and ministry priorities. In pioneer situations the focus will be an integrated and *incarnational engagement with the context, which combines translation of the Bible, evangelism and church planting with medical and educational programmes. Where there are already churches with structures and leaders, missionaries will work in partnership fulfilling specific indicated needs. Many contexts will require teaching, mechanics, medicine, agriculture, piloting and generally aiding the mission and church organizations, without creating dependency or weakening the national Christians.

With the rise of '*short-term missionaries', the issue of training is in debate. How do we ensure that these young recruits do not mistake a few weeks or months in a new culture as the answer to the church's missionary responsibility? What kind of training do they need? How do we send 'short-termers' who will enhance missionary efforts and avoid mistakes that could jeopardize the career missionary's long years of work? Correct training is essential for good outcomes in short-term as well as long-term ministry.

Health, family and community safety. Depending on the field of service, medical and survival knowledge and care can help both impoverished communities and the missionary family.

Who does missionary training?
Missionary training is first of all sovereignly directed
The missionary's entire life is a preparation for his/her work. Family, school, church, friends and enemies and personal experiences of all kinds are instruments in God's plan for training, just as in the lives of Barnabas, Paul and Timothy. No school or church or agency should consider themselves the sole provider for training, even though each one is essential.

Training in church
Lifelong attitudes are formed as people participate in the local church. The church serves as a model for missionary work and life, imparts knowledge of all kinds, especially in regard to the nature of biblical truth, Christian life and service, community relationships and practical ministry development. A school can fulfil these requirements with difficulty, although it also is very important for specialization and maturation in areas where the church has no expertise. It is important, however, that churches take responsibility for their role in equipping Christian disciples for mission, and that they do not leave it solely to the agencies or formal schools.

Training in formal schools
At the present time there is a danger of fragmentation between theology and missiology. Theological training without missiology is a well-documented ongoing problem. Missiology without theology is a more recent phenomenon, but even more serious. Missionaries are in danger of creating a good-looking missiological curriculum, but when they arrive at their destination they find they have no biblical *content* in applying it. Jesus' great commission sends people to make disciples, teaching them to obey all that he taught. To do this the missionary not only needs to know *how* to teach the people in their language and culture, but *what* to teach. The key question must always be: how can we create a missionary training programme that is both biblically faithful and culturally relevant?

This means that the missions school must verify the level of biblical and theological knowledge each student has and how much he or she will need. All should be *growing* in Christian maturity, but also in their ability to integrate their theology and missiology.

A school's 'hidden' curriculum, or the informal programme of a school, teaches more than instructional classroom content. Relationships, administrative and leadership styles, monetary policies and didactic methods all have a tendency to be copied on the field.

Formal curricular content must also reflect Christian values. It is important that God's word and missiological studies be integrated, one constantly woven into the other, reflecting what should mark missionary life and work. One way to do this is to include a discussion of relevant biblical texts in all missiological subjects. Examples, case studies and issues relating to anthropology, contextualization, history, linguistics and practical areas are easily found in the Scriptures.

Another method of integration is to use the Bible as the foundation and structure for missiology, starting with the biblical text and relating missiological questions to a good exegesis and understanding of that text. I have found Ephesians to be especially relevant because it addresses cross-cultural problems, the essence of the gospel, the state of people without Christ, the natural functioning of the church, practical living and relationships, including the missionary team, and the need for spiritual awareness and power, culminating in a life of prayer and dependence on God. Students participate in their own learning by working on comprehension of the text in question, and then by applying the truths of that text to specific missiological issues and situations.

Training through mission agencies

The missionary sending agency also participates in missionary training. Some agencies have training programmes which bypass traditional seminaries. At least field orientation and introduction to the ethos and policies of the mission must be included. Ongoing training is very important for the missionary and should be provided for and encouraged by the agency, with the help of schools and churches. The first stages of training should lead to a desire and capacity for a continuous lifestyle learning process throughout the missionary's life.

A cooperative effort for missionary training

The churches, schools and agencies should communicate and plan together for missionary training. Biblical guidelines for life and practice, field necessities, ministry specifics, and agency ethos should all be taken together for well-rounded missionary formation. Too often each one operates separately, leading to fragmented and irrelevant pre-field and ongoing training.

Conclusion

After three years of the best Bible school possible, the disciples were told to wait for the Holy Spirit who would supernaturally empower them to be testimonies, spreading the gospel to needy peoples in the whole world. Missionary preparation is not complete if the students do not realize that they cannot depend on their 'training' or themselves for the effectiveness of what they do. The goal for missionary training must be the formation of men and women who, with humility, will exercise wisdom and spiritual power in bringing glory to God, show discernment and sensitivity in cross-cultural relationships, adopt an integrated approach to mission which manifests redeeming love to the peoples of the world, and learn how to make disciples of the nations by baptizing and teaching them to obey all that Jesus taught.

Bibliography

D. Bloecher, 'Good Agency Practices: Lessons from ReMAP II', in W. D. Taylor (ed.), *Connections: The Journal of the WEA Missions Commission*, June, 2004; A. B. Bruce, *The Training of the Twelve* (New York: Harper and Brothers Publishers, ²n.d.); B. H. Burns, 'Teaching Cross-Cultural Missions Based on Biblical Theology: Implications of Ephesians for the Brazilian Church', D.Miss. Project (Chicago: Trinity Evangelical Divinity School, 1987); H. M. Conn and S. F. Rowen, *Missions and Theological Education in World Perspective* (Farmington, MI: Associates of Urbanus, 1984); L. B. Ekstrôm, in B. H. Burns (ed.), *Journal of the Brazilian Association of Missions Teachers* (APMB) 5, 1997; R. W. Ferris (ed.), *Establishing Ministry Training: A Manual for Programme Developers* (Pasadena, CA: William Carey Library, 1995); E. S. Medeiros, 'Missiology as an Academic Discipline in Theological Education', DMiss dissertation (Jackson, MS:

Reformed Theological Seminary, 1992); W. D. Taylor (ed.) *Internationalizing Missionary Training: A Global Perspective* (Exeter: Paternoster Press, 1991); W. D. Taylor, *Too Valuable to Lose: Exploring the Causes and Cures of Missionary Attrition* (World Evangelical Fellowship Missions Commission, 1997); J. D. Woodberry, C. Van Engen and E. J. Elliston, (eds.), *Missiological Education for the 21st Century: The Book, the Circle and the Sandals* (Maryknoll: Orbis Books, 1996).

B. H. BURNS

Transformation

Transformation is a word that has found its way into mission terminology in recent years as a way of describing the radical and permanent change which the *gospel envisages for every dimension of life. As such it is personal, corporate and universal, and speaks of the hope of a new created order in conformity to the *kingdom of God. So when the gospel of Jesus Christ and the power of the Holy Spirit are present and active in people and in communities, the result is transformation.

In Romans 12:1–2, the apostle Paul calls Christians to a process of transformation and continual *renewal. Through this transforming growth Paul tells us that we are given the opportunity to discover, through individual and communal discernment, what the will of the Lord is for our lives personally and corporately. But he also warns of the danger of conformity to the way the world thinks and acts, and in the context of mission this is always a risk for every missionary. Transforming mission, therefore, will require a perceptive discernment based on a faithful vision of biblical teaching about the mission of the church. Our ways of thinking about mission may themselves need to be transformed, so that we ask afresh questions such as: what should be transformed and what not transformed? What is the difference between cultural characteristics and the true principles of Scripture? What do missionaries have to contribute to the practice and reflection of mission? What is the end result that is expected from mission?

Jesus Christ is Lord of all and of everything, and so transforming mission should be integral. Theological reductionism practised in the past gave rise to partial missionary strategies which affected the manner in which mission was done. We need missionary strategies which have a more integral vision of the task and which are aware of the transforming power of mission. Therefore, since the Lausanne Congress in 1974, and later on through particular Latin American Evangelical Congresses (CLADE), there has been a growing interest in articulating the theology and practice of *Mision Integral* ('integral mission'), which can produce concrete transformation reflecting the values of the kingdom of God.

We should expect that as Jesus Christ works in the lives of people, societies, and indeed all of creation, the outcome will be an integral transformation. As Latin American theologian René Padilla has said: 'The call of the gospel is a call to a total transformation that reflects God's purposes to redeem human life in all its dimensions.'

A related element is *repentance, since without the radical turn around which repentance demands, there can be no transformation. This is why the Bible gives the highest importance to repentance, with the intention to produce an integral transformation whose dimensions are personal, community, universal and continuous.

Personal transformation

The mission of the church is to make *disciples whose lives are being transformed through the work of the Holy Spirit (John 3:1–16; 2 Cor. 3:18). In mission strategy, personal transformation should be understood in relation to every dimension of life, so that we do not fall into an evangelistic reductionism which fails to address every personal need. If this happens, the missionary task is reduced to verbal proclamation and this 'discarnates' the gospel of Christ.

The apostle Paul puts it like this: 'Therefore, if anyone is in Christ, the new creation has come: the old has gone, the new is here!' (2 Cor. 5:17). In the original text the verbs indicate continuous process and so this encourages us to work for an ongoing approach so that discipleship and the resulting progress in transformation of people might be permanent. It challenges us to go out into mission with strategies that plan for continuity, or which set up processes of development over time for people and the church as a community of faith.

It is true that in his practice of mission, Jesus gave priority to the integral well-being of the life of the individual before that of the *culture and its characteristics. It is clear, however, from the rest of the NT that what God purposes for individuals is paradigmatic for the whole of creation (Rom. 8:20–21), and therefore personal transformation cannot be separated from the wider context of the community and creation.

The Bible is full of stories of dramatic personal transformation. For example, God's plan for Moses, an inadequate and uncertain man originally from an enslaved people, involved putting him first in Pharaoh's court so that he could receive training in Egyptian culture. Then God sent him into the desert for spiritual and theological training with his uncle Jethro; and finally, when he was ready, God called him to set free, and bring into being, the new community of Yahweh.

Community transformation

We then see a good example of corporate transformation in the experience of the people of Israel. Enslaved for generations in Egypt, they were without identity, without culture and without resources. Through God's intervention they were transformed into a community characterized by their relationship with him, with the beginnings of a Scripture, with land, and with resources. In every sense they became a new community.

In the NT there is a constant search for a process of transformation of the church. This is the way that texts such as 1 Corinthians 3, Romans 12 and Ephesians 4 describe it. Samuel Escobar expresses it in this way:

In the apostolic teaching about the life and mission of the church, a correlation between the fullness of Christian living and the complexity of integral mission can be established. This teaching sees the church as a community in process of continuous growth. It is a process of metamorphosis through which the Holy Spirit enables believers in Christ to be continually transformed in conformity to the image of Jesus Christ.

This means that church planting must plan for long-term growth of the church as a community of the kingdom.

Considerations for the future

In the twenty-first century the history and practice of mission still carries the baggage of experiences and paradigms worked out in the past, and is therefore still waiting for its own transformation. There is often resistance to changing our models of mission. But the process of globalization challenges a human tendency to uniformity and the resistance of people to a threatened loss of their identity. This tension is particularly present amongst Latin Americans, whose identity is so bound up with their history.

However, in the countries in which we serve the Lord in Latin America, we know that the church should be, and could be, a formidable agent of transformation of culture and society. The numerical growth of the faith communities gives us a unique opportunity, because in each town and village, even in the most isolated places, one can see that the 'evangelical church' is very present and active. In some countries they are a significant social and political presence. Nevertheless, if the quality of their Christian practice is very far from being that which the Lord hopes and expects for his church, they will not be effective transforming agents. If in our mission we can educate Christians to take their full place in society, and if the church conscientiously practises integral mission, the transforming potential could be truly powerful.

Latin American theologian René Padilla summarizes some basic characteristics that the church should have in order to produce this transforming impact on society:

It means that it has to be the Church in which God's Spirit is free to act so that in it the Word of God becomes flesh: a church which is making progress in its own transformation and the transformation of the community which it serves. More concretely, an integral church is a community of faith which gives priority to: (1) commitment to Jesus Christ as Lord of everything and everyone; (2) Christian discipleship as a missionary lifestyle to which the entire church and every member has been called; (3) the vision of the church as the community that confesses Jesus Christ as Lord and lives in the light of that confession in such a way that in it can be seen the inauguration of a new humanity; and (4) the use of gifts and ministries as instruments that the Spirit of God uses to prepare the Church and all its members to fulfil their vocation as God's co-workers in the world.

Mission and missionaries, therefore, are a powerful means of establishing and empowering churches so that they can transform the world. That is the vision, and that is therefore the ultimate goal of mission.

See also CONVERSION.

Bibliography

D. J. Bosch, *Transforming Mission: Paradigm Shifts in Theology of Mission* (Maryknoll: Orbis Books, 1991); D. J. Bosch, 'Reflections on Biblical Models of Mission', in J. M. Phillips & R. T. Coote (eds.), *Toward the 21st Century in Christian Mission* (Grand Rapids: Eerdmans, 1993); F. Hahn, *Mission in the New Testament* (London: SCM, 1965); C. R. Padilla (ed.), *Bases Bíblicas de la Misión: Perspectivas Latinoamericanas* (Buenos Aires: Nueva Creación, 1998); C. R. Padilla, *The Local Church, Agent of Transformation* (Buenos Aires: Kairos ediciones, 2004); B. Ramm, *The Theology of Evangelism* (Pasadena: Institute of Youth Ministries/ Fuller Theological Seminary, 1978); H. H. Rowley, *The Missionary Message of the OT* (London: Carey Press, 1944); H. Snyder, *La Comunidad del Rey* (Buenos Aires: Kairós ediciones, ²2005); J. Stam, 'Historia de la Salvación y Misión Integral', in V. Steuernagel (ed.), *La Misión de la Iglesia: Una Visión Panorámica* (San José: Visión Mundial, 1992); V. Steuernagel (ed.), *La Misión de la Iglesia: Una Visión Panorámica* (San José, Visión Mundial, 1992); S. Vinay and C. Sugden, *Mission as Transformation* (Oxford: Regnum Books International, 1999).

J. C. CARRASCO

Tribalism

Tribalism is both a social phenomenon as well as an ideology. In its traditional sense it refers to a social system in which human society is divided into groups, independent of each other. Each of these groups has its own recognizable cultural norms and commonalities which form the basis of its identity as a tribe. This is manifest in the basic and instinctive sense that human beings are divided into 'us' and 'them'. These divisions are based on traits acquired at birth or upbringing, race, language, religion, clan or caste membership. In its more recent manifestation, tribalism is one of two forces that is radically altering and reshaping the landscape of the world today. It is at once a reaction to, and the result of, pervasive *globalizing processes enhanced by technological advancement. It is an ideology that is representative of various groups seeking to reassert themselves.

Tribalism therefore is an effort to gain or regain identity in the face of globalizing or universalizing processes. It is similar to 'ethnification'. While local tribes in various parts of the world, untouched by technological advancement and modernity, have retained their ethnic and cultural identity, larger entities like countries have had to reconstruct their identities in the process of shaking off military and cultural imperialism. However, multiple ethnic and cultural groupings also have the ability to come together with an agreement to function under an overarching identity, as in the case of India. This does not negate the fact that even within such a larger entity, localized ethnic minorities have time and again sought independence. More recently, in India, religiously fundamental groups, using the process of selective memory, have sought to create a distinctive identity which creates a stronger distinction between 'us' and 'them'.

In recent understanding, tribalism is viewed as a reaction against globalizing forces, especially against the onslaught of cultural imperialism symbolized by the 'McWorld' or consumerist culture. Students of the globalization phenomenon view it as an ideology that fragments society. In this regard tribalism is fundamentally opposed to universalism, with parochial ethnic identity as its goal. While globalization does not respect boundaries, tribalism seeks to redraw national, religious and ethnic boundaries.

Positively, tribalism celebrates diversity. It finds value and identity in being different. It is here that local cultures and values find their voice and are appreciated. Negatively, tribalism promotes a double standard of morality where those on the inside are more deserving of better treatment than those outside. Such an attitude breeds violence. According to political analysts, in the new world order the real players are not nations but tribes, many of whom are at war with each other. Tribalism contains and exudes great power. It is an antagonistic world full of conflict where 'the strongest wins, and where honour and glory lie in fighting, even dying, in a noble cause' (J. Sacks, *Dignity of Difference*). Resurgent tribalism, therefore, is clearly one of the greatest dangers to, as well as the cause of, the fragmenting world we live in. Most often identity is constructed in contradistinction to the 'other', with fear being the operative word. At its very root is the fear that a lack of self-assertion will destroy a group's or individual's uniqueness.

This aspect has significant implications for the mission of the church across cultures and for ministry within its boundaries as well. There are at least two related implications of tribalism as it pertains to the church and its mission in the world, and both are related to the issue of identity.

First, we must address the question of denominationalism and the fact that it reflects a subtle form of tribalism. Denominationalism is a modern descriptor of an 'ancient and universal reality' and contains both positive and negative elements (S. Portaro, *Cross Currents*, p. 205). If pushed to its extreme, it can degenerate into sectarianism. Additionally, the need to maintain doctrinal identity often results in confusion on the part of the layperson or the non-Christian with regard to what the church is and where one's identity is found. A positive aspect, however, if one is open to it, is found in the balance that different emphases bring to our understanding and depth of reflection of the gospel, ministry, mission, biblical doctrine and theology. If denominational boundaries are treated as watertight compartments that should not be crossed, then one loses out on an overall development of one's personhood and how they are part of the larger picture.

Second, in relation to the missionary movement, if tribalism is concerned with the assertion of self-identity, the church, both in its global and local context, has critically to examine and arrive at a nuanced understanding of the basis of its own identity. From a historical angle Christian mission has been criticized for the lack of sensitivity that many times accompanied its expansion. An unintentional aspect that the missionary must guard against is the 'us/them' attitude that often characterizes such activity. The challenge is to be able to engage in God's mission while recognizing and celebrating our differences, but in a way that transcends the 'us/them' approach. The key is to remain appreciative of, or not be fearful of participating in, the host culture. This will ensure that cultures are not destroyed but preserved as an integral part of God's plan and purpose for humankind.

It is crucial that we understand that the Bible does not negate tribalism in its positive sense. Creation presumes diversity and differences. These are upheld as 'good' (Gen. 1 – 2). The variety of cultures and ethnicities help us towards a richer understanding of the Creator God. A key biblical premise, therefore, on which the mission of Christ's followers must rest, is that of respect for the diversity represented in other cultures and ethnic groups. The church, by its very nature, contains within itself both universal and particular elements. So while one part of her identity is found in universal interconnectedness, the other part is determined and shaped by her engagement with the local and particular context.

See also CASTE; CULTURE; ETHNICITY/ETHNOCETRISM.

Bibliography

B. R. Barber, *Jihad Vs. McWorld: How Tribalism and Globalism are Reshaping the World* (New York: Ballantine Books, 1996); S. Portaro, 'Whence Pluralism, Whither Denominationalism?' *Cross Currents* 50, 2000, pp. 203–210; J. Sacks, *Dignity of Difference* (London: Continuum, 2002); Robert Schreiter, *The New Catholicity: Theology Between the Global and the Local* (Maryknoll: Orbis Books, 1999).

P. CORNELIUS

Trinity

The affirmation of the present article is that the church's expression in and for the world should be modelled on God's triune expression of his own mission (*missio Dei*) in the world through history as reflected in the biblical witness. If mission is essentially God's mission, then the Trinity is foundational for the *theology of mission. It requires us to do mission in faithfulness to the fullness of God's triune purposes as they are worked out in history from creation through redemption to eschatology.

The Trinity as the foundation for mission

Mission is rooted in the sending activity of God as the continuing movement of his trinitarian life, from the Father who sends his Son into the world, through the sending of the Spirit, so that the church in turn can be sent into the world. Jürgen Moltmann related the Trinity to the mission of God: 'It is not the Church that has a mission of salvation to fulfil in the world; it is the mission of the Son and the Spirit through the Father that includes the Church' (*The Church in the Power of the Spirit*, p. 64). Similarly Johannes Verkuyl defined missiology as '... the study of the salvation activities of the Father, Son and Holy Spirit throughout the world, geared towards bringing the Kingdom of God into existence' (*Contemporary Missiology*, p. 5). In more recent years Carl Braaton has observed: 'To know the history of God's trinitarian activity in the messianic ministry of Jesus and the apostolic ministry of the Spirit is to know the starting point and the purpose of the Church' (*Missiology* XVIII, p. 415). John Stott affirms: 'Christian mission is rooted in the nature of God himself. The Bible reveals him as a missionary God (Father, Son and Holy Spirit), who creates a missionary people, and is working towards a missionary consummation' (*The Contemporary Christian: Applying God's Word to Today's World*, p. 325).

If how we understand the Trinity has direct implications for mission, the three main ways in which it is variously interpreted can give rise to different tendencies in mission:

(1) The 'immanent Trinity' emphasizes the being of God as he is in himself, who seeks to draw humanity into his eternal glory. In focusing on the transcendent unity of the three-in-one in triune majesty this view tends towards a monarchical approach, a Christology 'from above' and a world-denying spirituality. The *gospel emphasizes the promise of eternal life and mission concentrates on bringing people into personal relationship with God.

(2) The 'economic Trinity' emphasizes the history of God's unfolding revelation through his engagement with the world. It focuses on the distinctive roles of the three persons, and tends towards a dynamic, incarnational view of a God who reveals his identity through the historical development of his kingdom. Christology is 'from below' and spirituality is world-affirming. The gospel becomes good news of 'life in all its fullness' in this world, mission concentrates on historical/cultural engagement and personal/social transformation.

(3) The 'social Trinity' emphasizes the *love which flows between the three persons in community and is a primarily relational view of the Trinity as a committed community. It also sees love as intrinsic to the nature of God, so it shares much in common with the two previous models. The gospel offers us a share in the divine *koinonia*, which draws us both into the love of God and into fellowship with one another, so that as the church we experience the 'unity in diversity' of the trinitarian relationships. The goal of mission becomes the creation of such a community, in which there is freedom for one another and fellowship with one another in commitment to one another. In fact this can give mission an irresistible social dimension if we affirm that all human society should reflect the perfect community of the Trinity.

No-one of course views the Trinity in any of these ways exclusively, although historically evangelicals have tended to favour the 'immanent', ecumenicals the 'economic' and radical Catholics the 'social'. An 'immanent' view can become disengaged from the suffering and injustices of the world; an 'economic' view can lose transcendence and the 'hope of glory'; and the social view can lose touch with a personal relationship with God. In recent years, however, these distinctions have become less contested and a general recognition of the breadth of the Trinity has given rise to a broader and more integrated view of mission. The immanent Trinity is the economic Trinity is the social Trinity. There is a unity and continuity in all of God's work, from creation through redemption to final consummation, and therefore what he is doing in the world by his Spirit cannot be separated from who he is in himself and what he was doing in and through Christ. There is therefore no false distinction between theocentrism, christocentrism and ecclesio-centrism, and the God we speak of in Christian mission is not some vague 'other' or 'ultimate reality', but the God who revealed himself in Christ and is at work by his Spirit to establish his *kingdom.

Theologically to base our mission thinking on the Trinity is to give us an irresistibly integrated approach to mission. If we are truly trinitarian we cannot set evangelism, social justice and church unity over against one another. God puts the whole of himself into everything he does, so that his creative, redemptive and eschatological energy is channelled into a mission whose ultimate goal is the total transformation of the whole of reality.

Mission, evangelism and church planting

However, the traditional concepts of mission, *evangelism, and *church planting remain difficult to accept in today's pluralistic world. Polarization goes on: on the one hand, history has witnessed too many missionary movements that have walked hand in hand with 'triumphalist colonial-style arrogance'; on the other hand, our world is weighed down by an over-polite and considerate postmodernist relativism that continues to deconstruct all points of reference for many in the church, divesting them of any passion for mission. Both these positions are equally abusive of God's expansive *grace, although they are not new, having polarized the church's attitude towards other faiths for several centuries. But as the Middle East and Islam globally come to centre-stage of world interest, both in the realms of politics and missions, it is crucial that we be aware of such precedents and realities. For in such circumstances, how can the church still speak of mission, evangelism and church planting? Is it called to give up such concepts? Or are these so entrenched in the church's identity that it is a continuous reflection and redefinition which is required? This article suggests that these traditional concepts represent in fact, in their essence, the church's calling to express the reality of the Triune God in the world. 'Mission',

'evangelism' and 'church planting' are in fact pointers to the activity of the Trinity in the totality of its expression, and in order to demonstrate this, the article will borrow from Daniel Migliore's creative concepts about God as a *self-giving, other-affirming* and *community-forming* God.

This analysis is based on the observation that Jesus offered a teaching and way of life that is a supreme critique of 'institution-alized religion'. This point seems to be forgotten in much of what is written on mission. The expression 'institutionalized religion' is used here in its pejorative sense, as 'stratification' of religion, where adherents of a religion attempt to claim some arrogant, exclusive right to God within the confines of their own religious system.

There are what Miroslav Volf rightly calls 'institutional procedures' which come about 'through confessing Jesus Christ as Saviour and Lord, through baptism in the name of the triune God, through the Eucharist, which celebrates communion with the triune God and with one another' (*After Our Likeness: The Church as the Image of the Trinity*, p. 234). The question is not whether the church is an institution, but rather what kind of institution it is. If institutions are understood as 'stable structures of social interaction', then the Trinity can be regarded as an 'institution' to which the church is intended to correspond. The essence of this is relational, a stable, social organization as an expression of human life. Thus, it is still legitimate to affirm that Jesus was the supreme critic of 'institutionalized religion' in its negative sense, where the power of religious leadership is expressed as lordship rather than servanthood (Mark 10:42–43), and where mainline religion becomes elitist and the poor are marginalized. Jesus therefore remained within the fold of Judaism, but at the same time elevated himself above it, yet without ever wishing to establish a new 'religion' with all its systematized theology and institutional hierarchies. We will always need to affirm therefore that Jesus' message was supra-religious par excellence.

Mission as the Father's self-giving expression in and for the world

In essence, the position that one takes with regard to mission will reflect one's view of religions, and vice versa. This is exemplified in the approach of Perry Schmidt-Leukel, a pluralist who attempts to hold to a true 'pluralist' position while maintaining a trinitarian theology. But his emphasis is on the economic expression of the Trinity to the detriment of its immanence: the pluralist theologian, he maintains, will not 'pretend to possess a precise description of God's eternal being, but rather a testimony to how the divine presence came to human consciousness *in one section of human religious history*' (emphasis ours). Such a view is also articulated in a theologian like John Hick. Schmidt-Leukel claims that 'Christian mission that works with a trinitarian model like this [the pluralistic one] will not only rejoice in communicating the great experience of divine revelation in Christ, but will rejoice no less in discovering the spiritual richness of the other divine epiphanies, and it will not hesitate to give them due praise' (in *A Scandalous Prophet: The Way of Mission after Newbigin*, p. 64).

This approach becomes embarrassed by the gospel. But the main problem is that Schmidt-Leukel tends to develop his critical framework entirely within the confines of what we have called 'institutionalized religion', within which he sees religions relating to each other in either 'inclusivist', 'exclusivist' or 'pluralist' categories. Jesus however removed himself from these confines through his supra-religious mission.

This enables us to adopt a supra-religious, Christ-centred approach to religions which transcends the three simplistic categories above. We affirm that God's salvific plan was entirely focused on the Christ-event, but it is possible to maintain that God may use any of the humanly expressed institutional religious manifestations as means to fulfil his greater mission purposes. God offers himself to the world in his mission in and through Christ by his Spirit, thereby transcending human structures. This enables us to appreciate 'the spiritual richness of the other' humanly expressed 'divine epiphanies', including God's epiphany in the natural world through creation, while yet maintaining the crucial importance of proclaiming God's unique good news of Christ himself (rather than of Christianity). With this inspiration we can give ourselves to building (with other faiths)

meaningful relationships that provide bridges for the saving activity of God.

From this perspective, the activity that we call 'mission' was always the essence of the activity in which God is engaged towards our world. His self-giving is immanent within himself, but is expressed historically. It begins with God stepping out of his comfort zone and taking the risk to create all things outside of himself by the breath of his living Word. It reaches its climax in his self-giving at the historical event of Christ. The self-giving missionary activity of God is radical *contextualization at its best, such as even our most concerted contemporary efforts could never match. Our missionary work too, we learn, will be most effective if we understand that true contextualization and contextually-appropriate mission is not about the right technique, but about the giving of self.

The inexhaustible, key gospel verse of John 3:16 will never cease to inspire our thinking about God's immanent nature and economic expression in the world. It is God (the Father) who 'so loved the world that he gave his one and only Son'. In his position as source of the *incarnational mission, the Father is both 'sender' and 'sent'. The *missio Dei* is thus beautifully expressed as an act of self-giving.

Evangelism as the Son's other-affirming activity towards persons

The affirmation of persons is the fundamental characteristic of the ministry of Jesus in the Gospels. Though God's mission is an indiscriminate giving of self to the whole world while it is still steeped in sin, the *kerygmatic* ministry of Jesus seems to be more discriminate. Jesus, in the Gospels, shows little patience towards 'ritualistically righteous' religious leaders who should have known better than their hypocritical application and imposition of the law (Matt. 23:1–4). On the other hand, he displays enormous patience towards the 'ritualistically unclean', the outcasts living on the margins of society, the hopeless who could never possibly have experienced redemption outside his affirming grace.

The evangelical expression of evangelism has too often relied on the demonstration of a person's depravity as a launching pad to justify the proclamation of the gospel. However, if our message is truly gospel in its Greek sense of *euangelion*, then the good news to be proclaimed is that God offers affirming grace in Christ to people *as they are*, without pre-conditions or judgment of their social or spiritual status. The arrogance of some forms of evangelism has often been rightly perceived as egoistic and intolerant. If on the other hand evangelism is perceived and expressed as good news, then it is, as Kenneth Cragg puts it, 'the abeyance of mission (which) would be the supremely damnable egoism' (*The Call of the Minaret*, p. 167).

The Son, then, expresses the 'other-affirming' nature of an *evangelistic* God, who gives an extravagant divine invitation to humanity into relationship as 'sons' (children) of the Father and into brotherhood with himself. Here the relational dimension of the Trinity is fully experienced, and once again the institutional is bypassed. The Son's activity in the world is good news through and through, a passionate and limitless ex-pression of creative love for all who would receive it.

If we understood the full implication of Christ's calling for us to take the good news to the world in the same way that he brought it to us, there would be little need for our petty arguments about the orally proclaimed gospel versus a gospel of social action. Christ's proclamation as we have it in the written witnesses is not one that made choices between one technique of *proclamation or another. Rather, Christ's gospel is a fully released initiative of creative proclamation, ever seeking to add ways to express the divine love to humanity, rather than finding excuses to eliminate one or other means of expression. This is evangelism at its best!

Church planting as the Holy Spirit's community-forming work among Christ's followers

When a Muslim accepts the invitation to become a 'Christian' and join a 'church', he or she is often understood to be a traitor, a *murtad* (apostate), who has rejected an entire community with its culture, language, family ties, social structures, and traditions. In most cultures, including Western ones, traitors are to be put away or eliminated.

When Christians invite anyone to become a 'Christian', if they mean to invite them to become adherents of an institutional religious system, they will be entirely missing the point of Christ's supra-religious gospel. However, this reflects a deep inter-cultural misunder-standing between an *individualistic* culture that perceives religion and faith as a matter of personal preference and inclination, and a profoundly *communal* culture that perceives religion and faith as the main tenet of social, family and personal identity. As a result of this misunderstanding, the gospel which is preached is not the gospel which is heard. The tragedy of much of modern Protestant mission history is that it has failed to see that the power of the evangelical message and of biblical Christianity precisely lies in its calling to resist institutionalization.

Thus, evangelical mission should never impose 'form'. Instead, we suggest that it has to pay intentional attention to two funda-mental guidelines: (1) The preservation of an individual Christ-follower's witness within his/her community, and (2) the fostering of the emergence of a 'reproducible' model of a Christ-following believer.

The forming of a trinitarian community faithful to the social model of the Trinity is the end product of the Holy Spirit's work among followers of Christ. This is a total refocus on the church as represented by people, not by buildings or religious institu-tions and forms. This does not mean that the community will become some sort of formless reality, but by emphasizing 'witness' and 'reproducibility', the community in any set-ting will be able to acquire its own form that fits its context.

But beyond form, what is the *community* to preserve? Lesslie Newbigin's affirmation that 'the Church is not the source of the witness; rather, it is the locus of witness' places the emphasis in the right place: mission as the life of the church rather than its mere oral procla-mation or even the undertaking of some social workings. Whereas we tend to measure the success of our mission in terms of numbers of converts brought into the church, or in terms of the extent of our success in eradicat-ing social ills, Newbigin points out that 'by contrast St. Paul's criterion seems to be differ-ent. He can tell the Christians in Rome that he has completed his work in the whole vast region from Jerusalem to the Adriatic' (Rom. 15:23). He has, in his own words, 'fully preached the gospel' and left behind 'com-munities of men and women who believe the gospel and live by it. So his work as a missionary is done' (*The Gospel in a Pluralist Society*, pp. 120–121).

The church-planting activity of traditional approaches to mission, that have viewed their evangelistic work as primarily a *verbal* activity, has resulted in physical buildings that have come to define the identities of exclusivist communities with self-asserted legitimacies. The Holy Spirit's church-planting activity as we find it in the book of Acts, however, is an *adjective*. It is the adjective of inclusive invitation into the inclusive fellowship of the inclusive community of God's kingdom. This is no doubt one of the great lessons of Pentecost in Acts 2. Church planting Holy Spirit-style is synonymous with 'community forming'. Buildings cease to be an issue and so does any exclusivist symbol of self-definition.

Conclusion

There remains then for the Christ-following community to live out the Triune life of God in the world as a kind of divine curriculum that leads members of society to fulfilment in God. The Father's *self-giving grace* is experienced through *worship, bringing affective fulfilment to the believers and extending grace to the world. The Son's *other-affirming life-style* leads his followers into affirmative behaviour that is always open and inclusive of others, extending invitation into God's saving plan. The Holy Spirit's *community-forming work* will 'guide [the Christ-following community] into all the truth' (John 16:13), inspiring them with the cognitive knowledge that leads them further into growth as catalysts of social transformation and influence. And again as Newbigin puts it, 'where the Church is faithful to its Lord, there the powers of the kingdom are present and people begin to ask the question to which the gospel is the answer' (*The Gospel in a Pluralist Society*, p. 119). God, Father, Son and Holy Spirit, provides the affective, behavioural and cognitive sustenance to a community of Christ-followers who can then live out their incarnational existence in the world through *worship, witness* and *knowledge*. In this way both the root and the outcome of mission is faithful to the fullness of the Trinity in its essential, historical and relational dimensions.

See also CHRIST/CHRISTOLOGY, GOD, HOLY SPIRIT, *MISSIO DEI*.

Bibliography

C. A. Braaten, 'The Triune God: The Source and Model of Christian Unity and Mission', *Missiology* XVIII, 1990; K. Cragg, *The Call of the Minaret* (Oxford: Oxford University Press, ³2000); T. F. Foust *et al.* (eds.), *A Scandalous Prophet: The Way of Mission after Newbigin* (Grand Rapids: Eerdmans, 2002); D. Migliore, *Faith Seeking Understanding* (Grand Rapids, Eerdmans, 1991); J. Moltmann, *The Church in the Power of the Spirit* (London: SCM, 1977); J. Moltmann, *The Trinity and the Kingdom of God* (London: SCM, 1981); L. Newbigin, *The Gospel in a Pluralist Society* (Grand Rapids: Eerdmans, 1989); J. R. W. Stott, *The Contemporary Christian: Applying God's Word to Today's World* (Downers Grove: InterVarsity Press; Leicester: IVP, 1992); J. Verkuyl, *Contemporary Missiology* (Grand Rapids: Eerdmans, 1978); M. Volf, *After Our Likeness: The Church as the Image of the Trinity* (Grand Rapids: Eerdmans, 1998).

M. ACCAD AND J. CORRIE

Truth

'What is truth?' Pilate's question to Jesus recorded in John's Gospel (John 18:38) has found its echoes in every age, not least our own. Indeed, in the contemporary culture of the West it could be argued that the concept of truth has never been under greater threat. The cultural shifts that have brought this about raise profound challenges for the missionary enterprise, but they may also have opened up new opportunities for apologetic engagement. This article explores three contemporary trends that have contributed to the current crisis. Then in the light of a fresh look at the biblical material, it surveys and critiques some diverse contemporary responses before suggesting some missiological implications.

Subjectivism

The development of twentieth-century philosophical thought tended towards the belief that the only reliable source of knowledge about reality was to be found from *within* the individual rather than from outside. Paradoxically, this transition was one of the results of the so-called 'Enlightenment', whose central contention was that it was indeed possible for human beings to gain access to an objective and certain knowledge *outside* of the self. The writing of René Descartes (1596–1650) has been particularly important in this connection, seeking to provide the ultimate rational basis for such knowledge in the thinking self. But the Cartesian 'method' effectively helped to open the way to the contemporary critique of truth in general – and of religious truth in particular.

First, reason rather than revelation became established as the ultimate arbiter of truth-claims. But secondly, the central Cartesian principle (that nothing could be shown to be true unless the position from which such a judgment was made could not itself be doubted) came to be seen as an increasingly unstable foundation for truth. In fact, the possibility of an infinite regress opened up as each staging post in the quest for truth itself became questionable from another supposedly more secure foundation. Friedrich Nietzsche (1844–1900) saw the implications of these developments at the end of the nineteenth century, arguing that the methods of the Enlightenment (with their accompanying tendency towards grand 'unifying' ideas) were unable to make sense of the chaos and fragmentation of modern life, but would lead only to despair and even nihilism.

Representative of this newer culture are writers such as Michel Foucault (1926–84) and Jean-François Lyotard (1924–98). Both argue that what actually exists as an explanation of the world and its history is not one 'grand' narrative, but many lesser ones, none of which can claim to be true for everybody. 'Truth' functions merely at a localized level – whether in the 'power-discourses' of Foucault, or the 'language games' of Lyotard. Individual communities inhabit a unique set of narratives and sustain and create their own ideas of 'truth' in ways appropriate to their habits and mores. Truth is a meaningless concept outside of this local context. Such a reconstruction, at least in general terms, is one which has won adherents across many disciplines, not least amongst radical theologians. Don Cupitt, for example, argues that postmodernity is a 'flux of images and fictions', in which truth is a humanly manufactured concept, socially produced, and historically changing.

Pluralization

Hand in hand with this process has been the increasing impact of 'pluralization' on the culture of both modernity and postmodernity. On the one hand this term can simply describe the fact that in our contemporary world there is an increasing *plurality* of world-views on offer in the ideological marketplace which was inconceivable in earlier eras. Writers like Peter Berger have argued that this development has meant that religious affirmations are no longer regarded as public 'givens' but have become merely personal 'preferences', or lifestyle 'choices'. On the other hand, the term pluralization is also used to refer to a more fundamental *philosophy* of 'pluralism': a belief that in a world of plurality no single truth-claim can hold a privileged position. Sociologists of religion argue that in a multicultural context the nature and perception of religious truth changes dramatically. The truth-claims of the various world faiths tend to be relativized, either by those who argue that the disagreements between them are really only differing perceptions of one universal religious 'truth', or by those who argue that a plurality of beliefs increases the belief that we cannot really know the truth in an ultimate sense. Either way, 'pluralists' argue that no single religion can claim to be 'true' for all. All we can say is that there exists a number of disparate 'truths' out there, but truth as 'ultimate reality' is increasingly unknown and unknowable.

Spin

The corollary of Nietzsche's prediction that unifying frameworks of truth would break down is his assertion that versions of 'truth' would be sustained not by knowledge, but by power. Michel Foucault in particular has developed this idea, arguing that every society functions with its own 'regime' of truth (meaning those patterns of belief which it chooses to 'make true'). The process by which 'truth' is manufactured in this context is inevitably fuelled by the peculiarly contemporary concept of 'spin' – from the marketing of consumer goods through advertising to the dissemination of policies and values in the world of politics and public affairs. The world of 'spin' is in fact a characteristic example of the revolution in the approach to language which has run parallel to the demise of other traditional forms of foundationalism. For words themselves have lost their signifying power to reflect an objective and external reality and have instead become tools with which to create and sustain a plurality of sometimes competing 'truths'. In the words of Richard Rorty, 'anything can be made to look good or bad by being redescribed'. 'Truth' in this context is all about presentation and interpretation.

Biblical patterns of truth

All this is in marked contrast to the way in which truth is pictured in the Bible. The biblical writers (in contrast with Enlightenment thinking) rarely refer to the idea of 'truth' in abstract or impersonal terms, nor do they describe it (by contrast with much postmodern thinking) as being dependent upon local context, community or the subjective individual. Rather, though biblical truth is communicated and received in a variety of diverse cultural contexts, it always finds its central focus and authentication in the self-disclosure of the creator *God within history; supremely in the life, death and resurrection of Jesus.

Within this framework, biblical truth has to do both with the truthful revelation of the character of God in the course of redemptive history (Ps. 119:41–43; Dan. 8:12; 9:13), and also with the existential experience of that truth as it is lived out by believers in daily practice (Pss. 25:10; 111:7). So in the OT the word *'ĕmet* (the word which is most closely equivalent to the Gk *alētheia*) is used in the great majority of senses to refer not to some theoretical or abstract notion of truth, but rather to the truthful words and deeds of the God of Israel. What God says and does, both in promise and fulfilment, is described as being in full agreement with the truthful nature of his character and being (Num. 23:19; 1 Sam. 15:29; Pss. 111:8; 119:160). Moreover, the reliability of this disclosure is borne out by a people brought into relationship with God, who prove his trustworthiness through faithful response and humble witness in the course of their daily lives.

The NT picks up this theme of the divine revelation of truth as a correspondence between truthful words and deeds, and shows that it is most fully apparent in the incarnation,

death, resurrection and exaltation of Jesus *Christ. Here is the fulfilling and embodying of God's truth within history to which the OT points. This is characteristically summed up in Jesus' declaration that he is 'the way and the truth (*alētheia*) and the life' and that 'no-one comes to the Father except through me' (John 14:6).

Two aspects of this revelation are worth emphasizing. First, though the Bible contains many different means by which the truth of divine revelation is communicated and appropriated, all expressions of truth find their ultimate fulfilment and comprehensiveness in the person of Jesus Christ, the Creator God incarnate. He is therefore the ultimate 'personification' of all truth, truth which may be stated, witnessed to, and experienced by individuals and local communities, but whose truthfulness finally transcends each cultural context in which it is made known. Thus the Bible transcends the objective-subjective divide that has characterized many modern and postmodern approaches to the question of truth. For it describes the truth-as-it-is-in-Jesus as both personal and yet not subjective, as local and yet not localized, and as intimately relational and yet also cosmic and absolute. Secondly, as Wolfhart Pannenberg has pointed out, this revelation of the truth in Jesus prefigures within history the truthful outcome of *all* things at the end of time. Pannenberg wants to emphasize that any conception of truth must be both unified and comprehensive if it is to be truly real and biblical (thus avoiding the pitfalls of relativism and radical pluralism), but also to avoid the modernist tendency to describe truth as though it were an abstract concept detached from history. Truth is Christ-centred, and though the meaning of human history will fully emerge only at the end of time (when all things will be made known), the *clue* to the meaning of the whole has already been made known – ahead of time as it were – in the incarnation, death and resurrection of Jesus Christ.

Missionary implications

These cultural and biblical reflections should cause us to stop and think about how we respond missiologically. Certainly, the cultural transition from modernity to postmodernity has already spawned a number of different approaches to the question of how to relate the truth of the gospel to the culture in which we live. We can identify four broad possibilities.

First, radical pluralists argue that the concept of truth as traditionally understood is no longer relevant or viable in a postmodern climate, and that therefore mission is at best irrelevant or at worst offensive. Don Cupitt, for example, argues that the crucial feature of our postmodern contemporary culture is 'our growing incapacity ... to separate truth from fiction, the objectively real from the flux of human interpretations'. In this context, to speak of 'mission' is both futile and even offensive, for to ask people to consider the 'truth' of Christianity immediately implies the existence of an external 'truth-referent' on the basis of which you are asking them to believe.

A second approach builds on the work of writers like Hans Frei and George Lindbeck (associated with the 'New Yale' school), who argue that the cultural reaction against modernity means that we must be more nuanced in our attitude to cultural engagement. Characteristic of this style is George Lindbeck's 'intratextual' understanding of Christian doctrine, developed in his short but seminal book, *The Nature of Doctrine* (subtitled 'Religion and Theology in a Postliberal Age'). Given contemporary assumptions – particularly about the subjectivism of religion under modernity – Lindbeck argues that the function of religious language is not so much to propose truth-claims to outsiders, but to enable believers to understand and articulate how doctrine functions *within* the Christian community. In other words language is no longer able to carry the weight of *proclamation, but may help in self-description. The missiological implications of this approach are clear and serious. As religious languages are peculiar to the particular faith-communities in which they are used, their ability to transcend these boundaries is severely limited. It is impossible for outsiders to assess the 'reality' of a faith community unless they themselves become part of it, and so begin to share its particular language. As Lindbeck puts it, the 'intratextual' nature of religious language means that Christian truth is essentially 'untranslatable', for there is simply no common language in which such conversation can take place. Whatever the

strengths of this 'intratextual' approach for the study of doctrine, its missiological shortcomings are serious, with the church in danger of becoming sectarian.

A third approach takes the opposite view, arguing that if gospel truth is 'public' truth then the grounds upon which it is defended must also be fully 'public'. Broadly representative of this approach are those like David Tracy and John Cobb (of the new 'Chicago' school) who argue that Christians 'should argue the case (pro or con) on strictly public grounds that are open to all rational persons' (D. Tracy, *The Analogical Imagination*, p. 64). Personal faith or beliefs simply by themselves cannot serve as a basis on which to defend public claims to truth. Instead, 'some form of philosophical argument (usually either implicitly or explicitly metaphysical) will serve as the major warrant and support for all such claims'. This kind of approach tends to assume the existence of a common rationality as the prerequisite for the public defence of truth, and insists that the process by which this takes place is open to all. Missiologically, it is still much in fashion, particularly in some evidentialist styles of apologetics which are over-reliant upon an appeal to reason as the presupposition of Christian truth. In more overtly postmodern contexts, such strategies may quickly flounder, with detractors arguing that this approach is more indebted to Enlightenment assumptions about 'neutral' starting points and 'common' rationalities than to the Bible.

A final approach is represented by writers such as Lesslie Newbigin, whose attempt to address the missionary challenge of Western culture came to be associated with his description of the gospel as 'public truth'. Newbigin's approach occupies something of a middle ground between approaches two and three. On the one hand he disagrees strongly with the Enlightenment idea that there is some 'neutral' starting point from which to commend Christian truth. Christian apologetics cannot be 'public' in this sense. But he is also equally insistent that the Christian claim to know the truth is not to be reduced to some sectarian or privatized option (as some postmoderns would argue). His path through this apparent impasse is to insist that the Christian's grasp of the truth about God is ultimately personal – both in the sense that it is personally disclosed through Jesus Christ, and also in the sense that it is personally received by faith. By means of this revelation, Newbigin argues (in a way similar to Pannenberg) that Christians are brought into an understanding of the meaning of the human story as a whole by its disclosure in and through Jesus Christ within history. Christians therefore, whatever their cultural background, are brought into contact with ultimate truth, can begin to discover their place within the wider cosmic story, and are called to bear witness to this truth for the sake of the world as a whole.

For Newbigin, therefore, God's truth is 'public' not in the sense that it is grounded on some supposedly neutral philosophical foundation, but because it has been publicly revealed in the life, death and resurrection of Jesus Christ in a way that reveals the meaning of world history. Witness to this truth is therefore to be confident (knowing the one who reveals it), but also humble (since we will only fully know when all is fully made known at the end of history).

Conclusion

The cultural transition between modernity and 'post'-modernity in the West continues to highlight some critical questions about the nature of truth. The transition has been a serious one, highlighting a seismic shift between an Enlightenment ideal of truth as an objective and knowable 'commodity', and a postmodern rebuttal which protests that such truth is at best a subjective variable, and at worst an illusion. Navigating the contemporary cultural landscape will continue to be a demanding task for the would-be apologist, seeking biblical faithfulness on the one hand and cultural relevance on the other. But in the process of missiological reflection, the reality of cultural transition, in whatever context, can be a helpful catalyst to prompt more faithful and biblical forms of thought, speech and action.

Perhaps above all, Christians should ask themselves whether their confidence in the public defence of Christian truth is sufficiently Christological (and therefore sufficiently universal) to reflect the focus of the Bible's witness. Whatever else it is, the cultural confusion felt on the borderlands of modernity and postmodernity ought to provide a fresh impetus for missionary proclamation and engagement, for in Jesus Christ we find neither the false objectivity of a Descartes, nor the hopeless subjectivity of a Cupitt, but rather the offer of real and lasting truth through personal encounter. For 'this *is* eternal life', says Jesus 'that they may know you, the only true God, and Jesus Christ, whom you have sent' (John 17:3).

See also CULTURE, POSTMODERN, WORLD-VIEW.

Bibliography

P. L. Berger, *The Heretical Imperative: Contemporary Possibilities of Religious Affirmation* (London: Collins, 1980); P. G. Hiebert, *Missiological Implications of Epistemological Shifts: Affirming Truth in a Modern/Postmodern World* (Harrisburg: Trinity Press International, 1999); J. A. Kirk and K. J. Vanhoozer (eds.), *To Stake a Claim: Mission and the Western Crisis of Knowledge* (Maryknoll: Orbis Books, 1999); J. R. Middleton and B. J. Walsh, *Truth is Stranger than it Used to Be: Biblical Faith in a Postmodern Age* (London: SPCK, 1995); H. A. Netland, *Dissonant Voices: Religious Pluralism and the Question of Truth* (Grand Rapids: Eerdmans; Leicester: IVP, 1991); L. Newbigin, *Truth to Tell: The Gospel as Public Truth* (London: SPCK, 1991); L. Newbigin, *Truth and Authority in Modernity* (Valley Forge: Gracewing/Trinity Press International, 1996); W. Pannenberg, 'What is Truth?' in W. Pannenberg and G. H. Kehm (eds.), *Basic Questions in Theology* (London: SCM Press, 1971); A. C. Thiselton, 'Truth', in C. Brown (ed.), *New International Dictionary of New Testament Theology* (Exeter: Paternoster Press, 1978); D. Tracy, *The Analogical Imagination: Christian Theology and the Culture of Pluralism* (New York: Crossroad Publishing, 1981); D. Wells, *No Place for Truth; or, Whatever Happened to Evangelical Theology?* (Grand Rapids: Eerdmans; Leicester: IVP, 1993).

P. D. A. WESTON

Two-Thirds World missionary movement

The emergence of the missionary movement from the Two-Thirds World (TTWMM), sometimes called the 'non-Western missionary movement', was probably the most significant development in mission during the latter half of the twentieth century. It is sometimes called the 'mission from the South', the 'newer sending missions', the 'missions from the younger church', or more recently the 'mission from the Four-Fifths world'.

Prior to the 1900s the TTWMM was seldom heard of. With some notable exceptions, most missionary activity heard about was from the West to the non-Western world. By the 1970s the tide began to turn. Today, it is estimated that nearly half of the entire Christian missionary force consists of missionaries sent from the non-Western church, either as foreign or domestic missionaries. However, if one only counts foreign missionaries (that is those who are serving outside of their own country), Western missionaries still outnumber the Two-Thirds World missionaries. There are, however, factors to be considered such as the growth of the church in China, and other new, rapidly growing, sending bases such as Korea and Brazil. It is estimated that there is already a considerable number of missionaries sent by the Chinese house churches to various ethnic groups.

However, the trend in the last decade or so is to speak in terms of 'global mission', which better reflects the globalization of mission by which missionaries now go 'from everywhere to everywhere'.

Historical background

Surprisingly little has been written on the TTWMM. It was only in the latter half of the twentieth century that the world church, particularly in the West, began to notice what was happening. Harvie Conn, commenting on the number of TTWMM missionaries, aptly captured the scene when he noted that the '...figure indicates not so much growth though, as it does an increasing knowledge [of the non-Western missionaries] in the West of their existence' (IBMR, Oct 1986, p. 163).

By the early 1980s missiologists such as Ralph Winter and Herbert Kane estimated that there were 8,000 (Winter), or 6,000 (Kane) TTW missionaries. Even the conservative estimate at the time was 3,000. Some serious studies on the movement were made by such persons as James Wong et al., Marlin Nelson, Larry Keyes, Larry Pate, David

Barrett and Patrick Johnstone. The latest edition of the Operation World lists 95,428 non-Western missionaries, which is approximately 49% of the global mission force. (The calculation is mine as there are some discrepancies in the summary. New Zealand and Australia are added to the West, while the rest of Oceania is added to the TTW figures.) Meanwhile, the World Christian Encyclopedia (2001) gives somewhat different figures. It claims that there are still four times more Western missionaries (336,070) as compared to the non-Western missionaries (83,454).

A simple survey of world missionary conferences of the past century shows similar trends. At the 1910 Edinburgh conference, out of 1,200 participants, less than 2% of the delegates were from the non-Western world. By the time the International Congress on World Evangelization was held in 1974 at Lausanne, 50% of the speakers were from the non-Western world. TTW participation in the Global Consultation on World Evangelization increased to more than 60% in Seoul (1997) and Plethora, South Africa (2000).

Notable regional mission congresses have included the All Asia Mission Consultation, which was held in 1973 in Seoul, Korea; subsequent to this event the Asia Mission Association was formed in 1975 with fifty delegates from twelve Asian nations. When the historic 'Seoul Declaration' was read at the conclusion of the consultation there were no less than 8,000 enthusiastic participants. The COMIBAM (Ibero-American Missions Congress) movement, which began in 1984, held its first and second congresses in Latin America in 1988 and 1997 respectively, and its third in Spain in Granada in 2006, to mobilize the Ibero-American church for mission, and they have put the Latin American missionary movement permanently on the map. Today there are probably over 8,500 Latin missionaries, going within the continent as well as to the rest of the world.

In Africa there is the Association of Evangelicals of Africa and Madagascar, whose Commission of Evangelism and Missions is actively engaged in mission on a regional level. There are also some of the prominent national missionary movements such as the Nigerian Evangelical Mission Association

(NEMA), an arm of the Nigerian Evangelical Fellowship (NEF), and the Evangelical Missionary Society (EMS), which is the official missionary arm of the Evangelical Church of West Africa (ECWA).

The ecumenical movement in fact has been more aware of the TTWMM than evangelicals. If we analyse the various ecumenical mission conferences through the twentieth century, we see an emphasis on the whole world as a single mission field. After the integration in 1961 in New Delhi of the International Missionary Council (IMC) and World Council of Churches (WCC, founded in 1948), it was argued that 'the churches of the Third World began to play a dominant role in world mission'. By 1963, 'mission on six continents' was the perception of ecumenical missiologists, and the principle of mission as a shared responsibility was well established.

Characteristics of the TTWMM

The first and the most obvious characteristic is that the majority of missionaries serve within their own region. About 36% of Latin American missionaries work trans-continentally. Africa is very similar. According to the 1992 statistics, out of 2,180 missionaries affiliated with Nigerian Evangelical Mission Association (NEMA), only 177 worked out of their continent. Except for countries like Singapore, Hong Kong, Japan and Korea, most Asian missionaries are sent from one people group to another within their own country. India is a prime example. India has some 40,000 missionaries, but the majority is sent to cross-cultural situations within India. South Korea is in a unique situation. The country is largely monocultural and monolingual. As the sea on three fronts, and the border with North Korea surround it, its only option is to send people to other nations. It is estimated that the Korean church sends out missionaries to no less than 163 countries of the world.

This characteristic has at least two implications. First, TTW missionaries are now reaching out to many of the *unreached people groups within their own countries or continents previously inaccessible to conventional Western missionaries – or for that matter even to some of the TTW missionaries who need visas. Secondly, and relatedly, at the beginning of the twenty-first century there is an increasing recognition of the large number of unreached people groups scattered globally. In order to reach these people, mobility is vital, but generally speaking the TTWMM lacks the necessary transport capability; so they need the partnership of more mobile and flexible Western support.

The TTWMM usually does not have an unfavourable image inherited from a past *colonial history. Non-Western missionaries may have fewer barriers to face when going to countries once colonized by the West. The flip side of this is that they need to establish their own identity as a new brand of authentic missionaries. Missionaries are no longer considered a socially privileged class compared to the nationals. However, it is just as difficult for the non-Western missionary to find a new image as for the Western missionary to live with the stigma of colonialism. In the 1970s when non-Western missionaries first began to pour into mission fields once monopolized by the West, the nationals were somewhat ambivalent, as they were only used to Western missionaries. Now there is a new openness towards non-Western missionaries.

Most of the TTWMMs have much simpler missional structures compared to their Western counterparts. Often local churches act as the missional structure. In the West, it was mostly mission societies that took the initiative since the church was situated too far from the so-called overseas mission fields. It made sense to gather volunteers, form a society, and send missionaries through them. In the case of the TTWMM, their churches are usually located near to the mission context. For countries like Korea and Japan missionary societies work alongside denominational mission boards to send missionaries overseas. In the case of numerous Latin American, African and Asian churches the local churches play a vital role in missionary work. It is natural for local churches to provide structures in the absence of more sophisticated Western missionary organizations.

Mission is less costly for the TTWMM. To send someone from one cultural context to another in India, for example, is incomparably cheaper than for Western churches to send someone. Those who join an international missionary organization to travel out of their own country require much more financial support, even the non-Western missionaries. Nevertheless, mission is still much cheaper for non-Westerners.

There is a shift from traditional forms of mission to much more creative ways. For example, non-Western missionaries working in China operate green tea research groups, or run bakery shops, or find specialist jobs in marketable professions. In some countries being a student is a good way to establish a presence.

Non-Western missionaries on the whole are much more used to living in harsh environments. This is certainly an advantage, for most mission contexts are in underprivileged areas, and that is already the background of many non-Western missionaries.

However, there are areas of weakness that the TTWMM must overcome in order to develop as a healthy movement in the future. Appropriate infrastructures at home and in the mission context, improvement in pre-field *missionary training, developing a better financial support system, not to mention establishing holistic member care networks, are some of their urgent needs.

Key issues for the TTWMM

An appropriate *contextual missiology is needed. Otherwise *praxis without much theological basis may become the norm. Andrew Walls has commented that the TTWMM is facing a similar situation to the early church. The church has been born and global mission abounds; yet, except for the Western missiological textbooks, there is very little missiology written by Non-Western mission practitioners from their own context, particularly in English. TTWMM leaders have been formulating global missiology along with Western mission leaders through various international and regional mission conferences and consultations. Nevertheless, there is a need for more work to be done at the local level, by missiologists on their own. This then will be used as a stepping-stone for global and local interaction (glocalization), leading to the creation of a truly global missiology.

We need to broaden our horizons. It is sometimes still convenient to think separately in terms of the TTWMM and the Western mission movement. We must grasp a global and integrated view of mission. The church is one and there is only one mission, which means we should no longer do mission in isolation, but think in terms of the global church and the global mission movement.

We need new infrastructures for new contexts. Many modifications have been made from when mission was exclusively Western, and often the structures have become very sophisticated. Many Non-Western missionary organizations cannot afford to be elaborate, and simple modification of the Western model is often unsatisfactory. There need to be completely different wineskins to hold the new wine.

We need creative ways of arranging family care. For non-Western missionaries often it is not enough to care for the immediate family. With no adequate social care systems, often it falls to missionaries to cater for elderly parents. Missionary organizations must be creative and flexible in these situations. Some Asian missionaries can raise funds for parents as well as for themselves. Education is also a tremendous burden for non-Western missionaries. It is too costly to establish their own schools. Many end up sending their children to Western mission schools. A lack of field structure also has implications for member care. For these reasons most non-Western missionaries remain in their own region or country.

Adequate training is absolutely vital. After a WEA missionary training consultation in Manila in 1989, a number of new missionary training centres were established in Latin America, Africa and Asia. Nevertheless, training is still grossly inadequate. In Central Asia, with the demise of the former Soviet Union, missionary work began with non-Western missionaries, and ten years later many more are dedicating themselves to mission in that region. Nevertheless, training for them is still urgently needed, as it is also for the house church movement of China.

Partnership became the new trend in mission after the 1980s. For the TTWMM partnership is even more relevant. According to one study made in the late 1980s, only 5.6% of non-Western missionaries were sent through international mission organizations. For countries like Korea the percentage has risen remarkably in recent times. For Latin Americans, as much as 18% of missionaries were sent through international organizations. The number will steadily increase as more and more Western missionaries retire and restricted areas for them increase, particularly in the Islamic world. This points to an increasing need for partnerships between the non-Western missions.

Conclusion

Since the world church began to notice the TTWMM in the 1970s, the movement has grown in leaps and bounds. There are no simple explanations. It may be less of a surprise for God, for he expects all his people to be living in full obedience to his mission mandate, which is as much for the non-Western church as for westerners.

It was not simply that the West passed the baton to the non-West, although in some senses that is true; rather, the non-Western church simply obeyed the mission command given by the Triune God. It was God who brought worldwide revival in the 1970s and awakened his people scattered all over the world with a vision for the whole world. Today, there is a global church doing global mission in all six continents. Mission will never again be one-way traffic; from now on it will always be in every direction. The TTWMM is here to stay.

Bibliography

M. Jaffarian, 'Are There More Non-Western Missionaries than Western Missionaries?', *International Bulletin of Missionary Research*, 2004, pp. 131–132; P. Johnstone, *Operation World* and CD-ROM (Seoul, Korea: Joy Press, 2002); L. E. Keyes, *The Last Age of Missions: A Study of Third World Missionary Societies* (Pasadena: William Carey Library, 1983); T. Limpic (ed.), *Ibero-Amrican Missions Handbook 1997* (Acapulco, Mexico: COMIBAM 1997); M. Nelson, *How and Why of Third World Missions: An Asian Case Study* (Pasadena: William Carey Library, 1976); M. Nelson (ed.), *Readings in Third World Missions: A Collection of Essential Documents* (Pasadena: William Carey Library, 1976); L. D. Pate, *From Every People: A Handbook of Two-Thirds World Missions with Directory/History/Analysis* (Monrovia: MARC, 1989).

D. TAI WOONG LEE

Ubuntu

Ubuntu (humaneness) is a term used to describe part of the spiritual/philosophical basis of African societies, especially among the Bantu language groups of East, Central and Southern Africa. It is an element in a *world-view that understands the human being to be made of several essential elements, also including physical flesh, breath, vitality, heart (emotions), and head (intellect).

It tries to capture the essence of what it means to be human, finding expression in the Zulu maxim '*umuntu ngumuntu ngabantu*'. This can be translated as 'a person is a person through other persons'. It is a description of a strength of character demonstrated fundamentally through relationship: caring and sharing among the living and concern for the needy, and sometimes including respectful behaviour towards the dead ancestors (*amadlozi*). It is characterized by a desire to act for the felt common good of the society at large and by a consensus approach to decision-making. This can be a positive force that produces accountability and reciprocal responsibility within community.

However, using this way of defining 'humaneness' (through demonstrable characteristics), non-sentient people (e.g. handicapped) can be defined as non-people (*ekintu*), some of whom traditionally would have been killed at birth, or at least not fully counted as part of the community but hidden away within the homestead.

Ubuntu must be taken into account when undertaking any missiological endeavour, which should be grounded in relationship with local people. The importance of living out one's life within view of the community, and ideally, living within that community, cannot be overstated. Building socially reciprocal relationships with local people, apart from one's employment on any specific project, is hugely valuable – gaining a 'good name' for oneself is important and quickly known about throughout the extended community.

Due consideration must be given to the very real difficulty new converts face when their Christian faith and practice is contrary to their previous traditional religious practices or the expectations of the (highly respected) older members of their family or community. Many new believers find it especially difficult to resist community pressures to continue with ancestor-related activities, such as ceremonies to honour deceased family members.

As the birth of children 'increases' the community, it is generally welcomed, regardless of the marital state of the parents. Single women, therefore, are often pressurized to conceive before a marriage takes place. Childlessness, on the other hand, can be seen as a diminution of one's status in society, and thus a childless marriage is often put under significant pressure to dissolve by the local community.

Encouraging local church leaders (and their families) to be mentors is important to build up a repository of faith and orthopraxy amongst a community that can function itself as additional or alternative points of reference for Christians.

Ubuntu as a theological endeavour has been well described, predominantly in the work of Desmond Tutu, who brought this element of his Xhosa heritage to the fore in his mediatory role during the end of the apartheid era in South Africa.

Tutu's emphasis is that all human beings are: 'Persons of infinite value because they were created in the image of the triune God. Their value was intrinsic to them and did not depend on merely extraneous biological factors over which they had no ultimate control' (M. Battle, *Reconciliation: The Ubuntu Theology of Desmond Tutu*).

Reflecting on his work with the Truth and Reconciliation Commission in the aftermath of apartheid, he says:

'We are sisters and brothers of one another whether we like it or not, and each one of us is a precious individual. This does not depend on things such as ethnicity, gender, or political, social economic or educational status. Each person is not just to be respected but to be revered as one created in God's image. To treat anyone as if they were less than this ... is veritably blasphemous, for it is to spit in the face of God.' (D. Tutu, *No Future without Forgiveness*)

While Tutu would not endorse some aspects of the traditional understanding of *ubuntu* (such as the utilitarian dismissal of handicapped individuals' 'human' status), some evangelicals may feel his *ubuntu* theology fails to lay an appropriate emphasis on sin and personal salvation. It is possible for some community theologies to devalue the individual, and while a consensus approach can be a positive force, inherent within it is the potential to stifle innovation and to engender what can become an oppressive conformity.

However, evangelicals will also recognize that, in Scripture, God is seen relating to people through their communities as well as individually.

Tutu's *ubuntu* theology is a useful corrective hermeneutic for a Western soteriology that often focuses on the individual alone. It demands an appropriate elevation of societal ethics to a higher status within the church. It provides a reasoned argument for proceeding with social justice and liberation concerns as a divine imperative distinct from a primary political agenda. Indeed, concerning his contribution of his *ubuntu* theology, it has been said that 'more than any black theologian he has challenged the Christian community to participate in the process of liberation and reconciliation' (B. Goba, *Essays in Honour of Desmond Tutu*).

Very importantly, it enshrines the oppressors'/others' inalienable (if tarnished) status as one made in the image of God. There is much in this that would be of use in conflict situations, such as civil war, or in reconciliation processes worldwide.

See also AFRICAN THEOLOGY, AFRICAN TRADITIONAL RELIGON, HUMAN/HUMANITY.

Bibliography
M. Battle, *Reconciliation: The Ubuntu Theology of Desmond Tutu* (Cleveland: The Pilgrim Press, 1997); B. Goba, 'A Theological Tribute to Archbishop Tutu', in I. Mosala and B. Tlhagale (eds.), *Essays in Honour of Desmond Tutu* (London: Marshall Pickering, 1987); J. Kapolyo, *The Human Condition* (Leicester: IVP, 2005); D. Tutu, *No Future without Forgiveness* (London: Rider, 1999).

R. NUNN

Unity

Unity is a gift of *grace from *God and centres on a shared relationship with *Christ (Eph. 4:16). It emulates the aspiration of Jesus in John 17:21: that 'all of them may be one, Father, just as you are in me and I am in you'; this unity immediately has a specifically missional intent: 'that the world may believe' (v. 23). It witnesses to the oneness of the *Trinity and the intimacy that exists between Father, Son and Holy Spirit, and therefore glorifies God by demonstrating to the world the relational potential and reconciling power of being one in Christ. Unity and mission are therefore inseparable: unity without mission is inconceivable, but mission without unity is a failure of witness and a faithless denial of the trinitarian glory shared by Christians as the gift of God in Christ through the *Spirit.

Paul affirms that unity flows from the *cross of Christ, breaking down all human barriers, making peace and creating a new and reconciled identity through which all Christians have equal access to God in Christ (Eph. 2:14–18). There are therefore no privileged Christians in the body of Christ who can claim superiority of status over each other (Gal. 3:28; 1 Cor. 1:10–13). But Paul envisages two levels of unity: first, the ontological unity that Christians have in the Spirit, by virtue of the fact that all are called by one Lord into one baptism in Christ (Eph. 4:3). All who belong to Christ share this given unity, and they must make every effort to maintain it. Secondly, there is a confessional 'unity in the faith and in the knowledge of the Son of God', which Christians are working towards and which takes them eschatologically into the 'fulness of Christ' (Eph. 4:13). There is therefore a sense in which unity is both a present reality and a future goal. In Christ, Christians are already united with God, yet in reality Christian unity in the truth is not complete, so all are called to strive for it.

Seeking unity and working for *reconciliation is therefore part of the Christian calling, both for the sake of mission and for the glory of God. In recent mission history, unity came to the forefront as an issue at the end of the nineteenth century when many missionary leaders recognized that the disunity of the church and the overt competition between traditions was detrimental to the gospel. The divisions of churches in Europe and America were being exported to the southern continents. Following the 1910 Edinburgh World Missionary Conference, national councils of churches became established across the globe, and in 1948 the World Council of Churches (WCC) was inaugurated in Amsterdam with the goal of achieving the visible unity of the church. Today the WCC describes itself as 'a fellowship of churches which confess the Lord Jesus Christ as God and Saviour according to the scriptures'. Its latest conference in Brazil brought together 691 delegates from 348 member churches from over 100 countries, representing some 550 million Christians, predominantly from countries in Africa, Asia, the Caribbean, Latin America, the Middle East and the Pacific.

Following Edinburgh 1910, the International Missionary Council (IMC) continued to organize world mission conferences (Jerusalem 1928, Tambaram 1938, Whitby 1947, Willingen 1952 and Accra 1958). Increasingly, these gatherings enabled leaders from the southern continents to address issues of mission and evangelism in partnership with the Western missionary agencies. In 1961, the IMC was integrated into the WCC at its assembly in New Delhi and a Commission for World Mission and Evangelism was established.

However, the increasingly overt political and liberation agenda of the WCC concerned many evangelical leaders who thought that the social agenda was being adopted to the exclusion of more traditional approaches to evangelism. This was a motivating factor for holding the 1974 Lausanne International Congress on World Evangelization. Drawing over 2,300 evangelical leaders from 150 countries, it sought to define the necessity, responsibilities and goals of spreading the gospel. The covenant affirmed a commitment to unity: 'Evangelism also summons us to unity, because our oneness strengthens our witness, just as our disunity undermines our gospel of reconciliation.' Even so, evangelical participation in the ecumenical movement has often been less than enthusiastic, although some Anglicans, notably John Stott and Lesslie Newbigin, and a number of Pentecostals, have maintained an engaged and critical dialogue from within.

Positively Lausanne recognized that organizational unity may take many forms that do not necessarily lead to effective *evangelism. Consequently, other approaches or models of unity have emerged over the past fifty years. Predominant in the historic churches is the model of organic unity. Considerable bilateral and multilateral dialogue has been initiated between and amongst different Christian traditions and denominations. In some countries this has led to the formation of United Churches, for example, India, Pakistan, Bangladesh and Zambia. A weakness of this approach is the length of time that it takes to overcome doctrinal differences on key areas, most especially on sharing of bread and wine during communion (eucharist) and the mutual recognition of orders of ministry. Also fault lines often remain in newly established structures, and the human desire for power and influence undermines the unity that has been achieved. While some traditions find common ground and achieve reconciliation within the same visible church, new churches are springing up with a renewed vigour and concern to share the gospel.

Here, a second model of unity in action is evident. Participating together and sharing in evangelism and mission projects is itself an expression of Christian unity. In contrast with the painstakingly slow progress of the first model, this approach is practical and focuses on achieving work together for the *kingdom of God. It is possible this way to have a 'unity in diversity', which both affirms the importance of unity for the sake of mission and values the differences between churches as opportunities for enrichment. The key is relationships, without which there is no meaningful unity.

David Bosch's plea in Transforming Mission was for an 'ecumenical' paradigm for mission. He sought grounds for convergence focused on a model of mission which is integral, inclusive and dialogical, holding together different perspectives in 'creative tension'. Since then this aspiration has been increasingly undermined by a proliferation of evangelical denominations, many of them quite small, but each with their distinctive emphases, each striving for doctrinal purity and each possessive and separatist. Even within denominations bitter divisions over sexual ethics, church order, the role of women and the authority of Scripture drive Christians apart and motivate them to set up their own versions of the kingdom.

More recently 'networking' has become another mode of bringing Christians together in common cause. A younger generation of Christians is now less denominational in outlook and does not share the passions with

which the battles of the past have been fought over the details of doctrine or church order. Altogether more relaxed and relational they are happy to work together in the name of Christ with loyalties of tradition put to one side in their desire to serve the world. This local, relational, spontaneous unity is of course much easier than unity at the institutional level, but it has generated a powerful force for mission amongst teams, networks and alliances of people who come together as one in Christ across their ecclesial differences and find powerful unity in working together for the sake of the kingdom.

Furthermore, Christian solidarity with those who suffer has become increasingly important, so that in the face of persecution, poverty, hunger and death, doctrinal differences become irrelevant. If mission is at the heart of the identity of the church, it is therefore also the key to unity: with integral mission as the shared priority, all other differences are put into their proper perspective.

Bibliography

J. Briggs, M. A. Oduyoye and G. Tsetsis (eds.), A History of the Ecumenical Movement, Volume 3: 1968–2000 (Geneva: WCC, 2000); G. Goosen, Bringing Churches Together: A Popular Introduction to Ecumenism (Geneva: WCC, ²2001); N. Lossky et al. (eds.) Dictionary of the Ecumenical Movement (Geneva: WCC, ²2002); J. R. W. Stott (ed.), Making Christ Known: Historic Mission Documents from the Lausanne Movement 1974–1989 (Carlisle: Paternoster, 1996); WCC, You Are the Light of the World: Statements on Mission 1980–2005 (Geneva: WCC, 2005).

C. MARSH

Universalism/universality

Definition of terms

Universalism describes a concept of *eschatology which presumes that all human beings, without exception, will ultimately be brought into God's kingdom. According to this position, redemption attained through Christ is not only offered by grace to all, but is also ultimately imparted to all, regardless of the personal faith of the individual. The opposite soteriological position is the eschatological doctrine of dual judgment, or two destinies, that brings eternal life for believers and eternal condemnation for unbelievers. In the course of the history of theology diverse exegetical, dogmatic and philosophical arguments have been put forth for universal salvation, as well as for the conviction of dual judgment. Moreover, there is an abundance of modifying mediating approaches between the two contrary positions. Therefore, the topic of universalism presents a complex problem that warrants making careful distinctions.

By contrast, the *universality* of the biblical message of redemption is unchallenged in theology and missiology. Christ died on the cross for all humanity and his salvation must therefore also be offered universally to all people. The open question is, ultimately, whether or not the universality of salvation through Christ leads to universalism.

Missiological dimensions

The universality of the Triune God as the Creator, Redeemer, and Consummator of the whole world leads to the global dimension of the great commission. There is no reason to exclude any human being, any ethnic group, or any social class from hearing the good news of Jesus Christ. The church is, by her divine mission, a universal body. Compared with Judaism, for instance, which is restricted primarily to the Jewish people, or Hinduism, which is identified as a religion of the Indian people, the Christian gospel is a message for all peoples, and is not identified with any one culture. The *gospel, in itself, is the attractive news about God's unconditional love for all humanity, and this attractiveness is the main motivation for the worldwide proclamation of the gospel.

The Bible makes it very clear, however, that there is, as a consequence of the fall, a struggle within human nature between God and the powers of *sin and evil. We find the seriousness of this struggle in the passion of Christ when he is tempted to avoid a painful and shameful death on the cross. In this fight, Christ overcame Satan's power of temptation through his response of humble obedience to the Father. By contrast, in universalism, there is no necessity for a personal response of faith and acceptance of Christ. But the question of belief or unbelief is the continuation of the struggle within every human being. According to Scripture, everyone is called to repentance

by God (e.g. Acts 17:30), but universalism naively overlooks the seriousness of the human condition before God. The grave situation of the possibility of judgment gives the urgency to the missionary call of the church; but universalism effectively removes the obligation of mission by rendering it unnecessary.

Exegetical basis
Biblical references to dual judgment

Clear statements of two destinies are found in the OT (e.g. Dan. 12:2). These continue throughout the NT. Jesus warns against the danger of ending up in hell (Mark 9:43–48), and speaks of a wide and narrow way (Matt. 7:13–14). The abyss between the rich man in hell and the bliss of the poor man Lazarus is presented as insurmountable (Luke 16:26). This view finally culminates in the statements about the judgment of the nations (Matt. 25:41) and the final judgment in Revelation 20:14–15 and 21:8. Paul explicitly confirms this apocalyptic view in 2 Thessalonians 1:6–9. Universalist theologians, however, place against these few exemplary NT passages other biblical passages whose inner logic makes universal salvation at least theoretically possible.

NT texts implying universalism

There are texts which have fostered universalist teachings. But in each case this idea has to be read into these texts, and in terms of their clarity, they cannot be compared with the clear statements on the duality of judgment.

(1) *The nature of God:* Theological reasoning for universal salvation begins from two supporting attributes of God, namely, his omnipotence and *love. The proof-text for both lines of argument is the statement that God our Saviour 'wants all people to be saved and to come to a knowledge of the truth' (1 Tim. 2:4). It is argued that no human sin, and ultimately no power of evil, can resist the universal will of the Almighty God to save. Moreover, the loving God could not bear it if even only one of his creation was lost. Therefore, the eschatological new creation implies the *apokatastasis pantōn* (restoration of all things, or, universal reconciliation, cf. Eph. 1:10; Col. 1:20). The perfection of the kingdom of God brings all without exception into

the eternal and blessed fellowship with God, so that grace ultimately triumphs.

However, God in his omnipotence and love granted to humanity the dignity of choice and moral responsibility, and therefore he is also a God of justice for whom sin and evil must have consequences, which are as serious as death. It is in the death of Christ that the love and justice of God meet.

(2) *Christ confessed:* Universalists point out that, at the end of human history, Christ will be confessed and worshipped by all, even by all creatures (cf. Phil. 2:9–11; Rev. 5:13). To be totally consistent, this would also include Satan and all demons.

However, this understanding of a future acceptance of Christ as universal Lord does not necessarily imply a faithful, loving relationship with Jesus. Universal 'reconciliation' can be seen as the universal acknowledgment of God's kingly rule, which includes those who have nevertheless already rejected it and therefore sealed their own destiny (e.g. John 3:18).

(3) *Adam and Christ:* In the Adam-Christ typology (Rom. 5:12–21), *Paul sees redemption through Christ as a universal possibility which triumphs over the universal sin and death that came with Adam. Correspondingly the reconciliation of the world with God is completed objectively through Christ (2 Cor. 5:19).

However, in each of these passages there is a clear statement of personal responsibility, to *receive* God's grace (Rom. 5:17) and to *be reconciled* to God (2 Cor. 5:20), so Paul does not see salvation as automatic. This typology does not refer to a biological condition, but it refers to a spiritual reality.

(4) *God as 'all in all':* The eschatological unity of all things is focused in Christ as the goal of all of salvation history. As Alpha and Omega (Rev. 1:8), Christ is the fulfilment of the eternal plan of God (Eph. 1:9–10). The entire apocalyptic process, which began as new creation with the resurrection of Christ, is completed in the surrender of the Son to the Father 'so that God may be all in all' (1 Cor. 15:28). This definition of God's eschatological purpose plays a prominent role in the discussion of universalism.

However, Paul's statement that God may be 'all in all' is not understood in a Greek philosophical way as an ontological statement,

but, as the supreme finality of the Triune God.

(5) *After-death repentance?* A further missiological dimension arises with the question of if and to what extent people who were not able to hear the gospel during their lifetimes get the chance after their death to turn to Christ. 1 Peter 3:19, in saying that Jesus 'made proclamation to the imprisoned spirits', might lend support to this idea.

However, this difficult reference cannot be generalized to every deceased person. These verses refer only to the generation living at the time of Noah, although it is not clear why this statement is restricted to that single generation.

Missiological relevance
The urgency of proclamation
Christian mission starts from the absolute obligation and urgency of proclaiming the gospel, which is about an eschatological here and now which decides the destiny of peoples and nations (cf. Acts 17:30–31). The earthly existence of each individual is seen in the horizon of an eschatological decision of endless significance. Only through a relationship with Christ, based upon personal faith, is substitution *coram deo* possible. Biblically speaking, the reality of final judgment with the destinies of either salvation or lostness is unambiguous.

Because God calls each person before the judgment seat of Christ, this ultimacy puts evangelism as proclamation of the love of God freely offered in Christ at the top of the agenda for the church. This good news is to be proclaimed with joy; but also with sober realism in the light of the destiny of those who have consciously rejected God's saving grace.

Pastoral considerations
The good news is for every person, regardless of culture, race, nationality, and so on. But in view of the question of universalism, the picture is much more complex. This becomes particularly relevant for the pastoral care of those Christians who are troubled about the eternal destiny of their loved ones. There is comfort in the sovereignty of God and the power of grace. However, it is important to stress that we, as limited human beings, are not able to pronounce final judgment upon any human being. For, in an absolute sense,

we do not know what the relationship will ultimately be between God and any other human being. Therefore, it is prudent for a counsellor to point out that we should entrust the dead into God's gracious hands, knowing that he will judge justly and that his love never ceases. For even his wrath will be rooted in his character as the loving Father.

Summary
The universality of the gospel and its urgency is a fundamental basis for Christian mission. The idea of a universal general salvation for all creation is an ambiguous perspective which, on the one hand, is hinted at in Scripture and may have some pastoral relevance. On the other hand, universalism easily leads to consequences that jeopardize the relevance and urgency of mission and this understanding of universalism is, therefore, to be rejected on scriptural and missiological grounds.

See also HELL/JUDGMENT, PROCLAMATION, SALVATION.

Bibliography
R. J. Bauckham, 'Universalism: A Historical Survey', *Themelios* 4, 1979, pp. 48–54; D. Hilborn (ed.), 'The Nature of Hell', A Report by the Evangelical Alliance Commission on Unity and Truth among Evangelicals (ACUTE) (Carlisle: Paternoster Press, 2000); R. Parry and C. Partridge (eds.), *Universal Salvation? The Contemporary Debate* (Carlisle: Paternoster, 2003); D. Strange, *The Possibility of Salvation among the Unevangelised: An Analysis of Inclusivism in Recent Evangelical Theology* (Carlisle: Paternoster, 2002); T. L. Tiessen, *Who Can Be Saved? Reassessing Salvation in Christ and World Religions* (Downers Grove: InterVarsity Press; Leicester: Apollos, 2004); T. Whittemore, *The Modern History of Universalism: From the Era of the Reformation to the Present Time* (Whitefish: Kessinger Publishing, 2005); A. Wilford Hall, *Universalism Against Itself* (Whitefish: Kessinger Publishing, 2003).

R. HILLE

Unreached peoples

The concept of 'unreached peoples' has its origins in the OT in reference to the nations who were outside the covenant and worshipped their own gods. A prophetic expectation developed that the righteousness, justice, and light of God's kingdom would reach all of them through the mediation of God's servant Israel. In the apostolic period, Paul had a strong commitment to reaching those who had not yet heard the gospel, hoping that he would reach as far as Spain and the limits of the known world.

Discussion today focuses on who can be described as 'unreached'. In line with the geographical model of mission which prevailed in the eighteenth and nineteenth centuries, they were thought of as the most remote people, the pagans of the jungles, the remote and scattered peoples of inaccessible and mysterious places. This developed into recognition of the millions of adherents of other faiths who have never heard of Jesus Christ and never had an opportunity to respond to him. In more recent time, it has been recognized that there are millions even in the West who have never heard or heard only certain aspects of the gospel, and are therefore effectively 'unreached', even in places where the church has been well established for centuries.

Four periods of Protestant mission
In the experience of much of the colonized Two-Thirds world, the first era of mission can be described as the 'coastland missions', which got their name from the missionaries who landed in the coastal areas on the ships which were the main form of transportation in the eighteenth and nineteenth centuries. During this period missionaries established prominent mission stations in the coastal cities of the colonized world. Indeed, there was a general experience worldwide of churches planted in the coastal cities. One emphasis in this period was on the vision to take the gospel 'to the nations', which developed into the cross-cultural and cross-geographical nature of missions, a missionary task involving great sacrifice and dedication.

Later, in the early and mid nineteenth century, there was a second period known as 'inland missions' in which bold innovators set out from the shipping ports, to which missionary supplies were readily brought, and ventured inland, often at great sacrifice to their lives and families. But they pioneered new routes, and brought education and health along with the *gospel of God's love in Christ to previously unreached peoples.

During the third period, from around the mid twentieth century, the emphasis changed to a focus on 'people groups' or 'hidden peoples'. During this time of many political and cultural changes, national and religious identity became less clearly defined, and the geographical model of mission lost its potency. Each 'people group' was taken as a 'nation' (*ethne) representing a distinct people with a distinct culture or language, even if mixed politically.

The fourth period is represented by the modern mission movements of the Two-Thirds world, where the numbers of Christians and churches has begun to exceed that of Western nations. With this radical shift in the focus of mission, local and non-Western missionary movements have proliferated, often with a vision for the unreached peoples of their own nations. Mission has become 'from everywhere to everywhere'.

This period is well illustrated in the experience of Indian mission. Simultaneously, while the Two-Thirds world became more responsible for mission movements, India led the way in many mission endeavours, both within India and in sending missionaries to the rest of the world.

However, unlike some other Two-Thirds world movements, Indian churches and missions sent missionaries to culturally very different peoples *within India itself*, with all its diversity of people groups and languages. India as a nation consists of many 'nations', *ethne* or people groups, with distinct *cultures and languages, and the many volatile changes this brings pose a tremendous challenge which has given rise to many different mission visions and strategies. The hope is that the Indian Christian church will ultimately contribute to the nation as a whole, and transform it with a Christ-like ethos which brings economic and spiritual blessing.

Misconceptions in 'reaching the unreached'
Inherited ways
There were several different mission concepts, philosophies, and thought patterns from the previous Protestant missions which had unfortunate consequences for Indian mission thinking. Local people often regarded the Western missionaries as the only 'true missionaries', and associated them with the *colonial era, a way of thinking that can still be found in many churches. Thus some adopted romantic notions of mission to unreached peoples, regarding them as 'exotic' tribal peoples, the 'under-developed', or the ones who are denied justice. The unreached were considered pagans, and all or most of the local customs, including some good and neutral ones, were rejected as pagan and 'unspiritual'. Some confused the concepts of '*evangelization' and 'civilization'. It is also still a common belief that true mission must be cross-cultural and cross-geographical.

Deciding priorities
As Christians have developed their understanding of the concept of 'unreached peoples', this has influenced and guided the priorities for mission. Some identify the *Dalits (the untouchables), the 'tribals' or the oppressed poor as the most unreached. Others prefer to think of their priorities in terms of the 'least reached', or those who have had the least opportunity to hear the gospel. Others think in terms of those who are 'winnable', whilst still others focus on the strategy of reaching one person at a time. Some look beyond India to the 10/40 window and other areas least reached because they are most resistant. However, many mission organizations and churches began their 'outreach' in abstraction, without the total picture of India, Asia or the world. Thus, there have been struggles in relating to India as a whole nation. The challenges to *disciple *India* to follow Christ are greater than just addressing Dalits, the marginal, the tribals, the illiterate, the poor and other so-called 'unreached peoples'. The situation could similarly be attributed to the rest of the Two-Thirds world in some way or other.

Separated believers
New followers of Christ have often been taken from their local communities into traditional mission compound situations. This is part of the evangelical emphasis on 'holiness' which separates Christians from relationships with non-followers of Christ. In the areas of business, politics and cooperative public awareness programmes, this mentality discourages Christians from becoming active

members of public societies and clubs, with the consequence that new 'unreached people groups' are gradually created. Some do see the importance of placing Christians in the existing local bodies such as clubs, civic services and government employment, where they can exercise an influence of service to humanity. But Christians have often exacerbated the problem by creating structures parallel to government through Christian NGOs.

Specialist ministry

In general, there has been an over-emphasized tendency in the Christian world to think of ministry to unreached peoples as a specialist or privileged form of mission, implying that only the 'priests', the 'trained', the 'called' or those with recognized degrees, can do this kind of mission. This 'specialist' concept has, in many senses, crippled the imagination of lay people to be creatively involved in establishing living worship groups among all peoples. Lay people were expected merely to bear the financial burden. It is true that there are those called specifically to work with unreached peoples; nevertheless, if we hold to the principle that all God's people are missionaries, we need to recover the view that the whole church is called to witness in every context.

Confused terminology

Unreached peoples have no tradition of theological and missiological discourse to draw on, so when they become Christians there is confusion and ambiguity in the use of terminology such as 'evangelism', 'mission' and 'holistic gospel'. There is also the belief that Christian culture and traditions have to be preserved to be faithful to 'historic' Christianity.

Innovative communication

If we are stuck with the geographical model of mission we will fail to grasp the opportunities which the Internet and other visual and audio means offer for innovative communication to young people unreached by conventional means. This will involve training of like-minded bright young people. Increasingly the technology is available, but is the church ready to make use of it with innovative communication?

Missionary care

With the over-emphasis on 'unreached' or 'least reached peoples', the pastoral care of missionaries has been neglected, and this has affected the effectiveness and the future recruiting of others into mission.

The consequences and problems

There is no doubt that there has been much good work done for the poor, the downtrodden, the marginalized and their communities, as well as for the whole nation and for other nations. However, we need to look honestly at the negative effects of the above misconceptions if we are going to improve our ministry and mission to the nations of the world.

There has been slow progress in developing Christian *leadership* amongst newly converted local people. This is because the 'reached' communities continue to be dominated by cross-cultural missionaries who import their human and financial power into those communities.

They also bring a *denominational* orientation, transplanting churches in their own image and traditions, instead of developing an indigenous ecclesiology which relates to local customs, traditions and names. As a result, church practices and followers more resemble those of the imported denomination.

Christian and *mission practices* are also carried over, so that local people copy the same imported methodologies instead of developing creative ways of engaging their own cultures. This simply repeats the colonial model of mission from the past.

Because there were some good results for evangelism amongst those considered 'winnable', there was less determined effort among the seemingly 'difficult' people who did not turn to Christ in large numbers and as communities. Most mission therefore took place amongst 'responsive' peoples, which in India developed into a bias towards certain religious and ethnic groups.

Many faithful Christians resigned from their jobs to do what they considered as the more 'holy' work of mission, even though some were strategically placed in their work to reach people not reached by anyone else. This created a divide between 'secular' work and 'Christian' work. *Tentmaking was downplayed, and imaginative mission in places of employment was lost.

Looking to the future

It is quite clear from the above discussion that there is a need for all Christians and churches to think again about what mission is. This will require education, new role models, a reemphasis on tentmaking, rethinking about funding, and a building up of discipleship training. This is beginning to happen in many of the new missionary sending Two-Thirds world nations.

In relation specifically to 'unreached peoples' in this context a number of practical ways forward are proposed:

(1) We need to recognize that most unreached people become Christians in stages. Evangelism therefore must be aimed at moving people from one stage to the next, while respecting their personal freedom to follow Christ in their own time. Sometimes evangelism to unreached people has been too aggressive and result-orientated.

(2) We need to identify people who seem 'reached', but in fact are not in the sense that they understand the gospel. For example, many young people and educated middle class people in India can be considered 'unreached'. Christians need to be taught to recognize unreached people on their own doorsteps in their own cities, and abandon the myth that unreached people only live in the jungle!

(3) More tentmaking opportunities need to be developed within secular contexts, and these need to be supported by the whole church. In particular, people in secular and civil service jobs need to be encouraged in their pre-evangelism and presence evangelism.

(4) There will still be a need to recruit and train cross-cultural missionaries, who will sometimes go to remote places, if the people there really have not been reached by any other means. But this may need to get beyond the traditional categories of 'tribals', 'Dalits' or the 'marginalized'.

(5) Our experience in India has been that sometimes missionaries who are culturally similar to those to whom they go are less welcomed and accepted than those who are very different. For example, the middle- and upper-middle-class people will be more accessible to overseas 'secular' Christians who are themselves involved in business than the local

Indian Christian missionaries. So we need to think about who are the best people to relate to unreached people. It may not always be those who think they can relate to them culturally.

(6) Finally, it is vital to prepare and pass on church leadership to the local leaders as quickly as possible so that their churches and movements can be truly indigenous.

Conclusion

It is clear that we need a new understanding of 'unreached people', who they are and where they are, if our mission is going to be meaningful and relevant. The concept has generated too much idealism and unthinking mission in many parts of the world. It is not enough simply to 'reach' people with the gospel, as if once they have been reached the job has been done. At what point can we safely say that people have been 'reached'? The aim of mission must be to build and establish followers of Christ for the next generation, and that will mean that the gospel continues to reach into their hearts and lives with its transforming power. When God 'reaches' us, he desires to transform every dimension of our lives and communities.

See also HOMOGENEOUS UNIT.

Bibliography

G. David, *Communicating Christ Among Hindu Peoples* (Chennai: CBMTM Publications, 1998); N. David, 'The Birth of a MUF Group' in J. J. Ratna Kumar and K. Sunder Raj (eds.), *Mission and Vision: Who and What?* (Bangalore: MUT Publishers, 1996); R. E. Hedlund, *Evangelisation and Church Growth* (Madras: CGRC, 1992); D. Hicks, *Globalising Missions* (Miami: Unilit, 1994); L. J. Jayaprakash, *Evaluation of Indigenous Missions of India* (Madras: Church Growth Research Centre, 1987); S. D. Ponraj, *Tribals of India* (Madhupur: Institute of Multi-Cultural Studies, 1991); K. Rajendran, *Which Way Forward For Indian Missions?* (Bangalore: SAIACS Press, 1998); E. Sargunam (ed.), *Mission Mandate* (Madras: Mission India, 2000 [1992]); A. Shourie, *Missionaries in India* (New Delhi: ASA Publications, 1994); E. Sunder Raj, *The Confusion Called Conversion* (New Delhi: TRACI, 1986); R. D. Winter, 'The Task

Remaining: All Humanity in Mission Perspective' in R. Winter, S. Hawthorne *et al.* (eds.), *Perspectives on the World Christian Movement* (California: William Carey Library, 1981).

K. RAJENDRAN

Urban mission

At the beginning of the third millennium the world reached a symbolic point when over half the global population could be said to live in towns and cities. Cities with over ten million people are becoming commonplace. Elsewhere smaller settlements are exploding with rural *migrants. The urban poor now outnumber the rural poor in many countries of the south, their number doubling each decade. The world is now an urban place. Urbanization is a human phenomenon brought about by the movement of people in search of social and economic well-being. Those who move to the city find severe challenges, when expectations are not met, difficulties as strangers are encountered, and the way they understand their identity and belonging fades.

For many parts of the church the city seems to be a new experience. For example, African and South American cities are expanding at such a rate that the civil authorities struggle to construct a physical infrastructure or allocate resources. In parallel, the traditional church finds its assets and plant are tied up in rural areas, when instead there is a serious need to develop a pastoral infrastructure in the new urban areas, involving appropriate training and resources for lay and ordained leadership. Emergent and independent churches, however, often find they have the flexibility needed to plant themselves in transitional and informal urban areas.

In the global north, urban mission has traditionally concentrated on industrial and post-industrial areas, where decline and de-population have left community and church life weakened and impoverished.

The urban context is a critical arena of Christian mission, whatever stage of development or decline is found in the local context. Urban mission needs to be integral, or *holistic, as it encounters extensive material and spiritual hardship. With an abundance of people the issues faced by the church in the city are manifold: poverty (see *Poor), drugs,

micro-violence, youth, the place of migrants and *refugees, housing, spatial justice. Cities are contested arenas in which social, ethnic, religious and economic interests compete for space, status and power. This challenge was articulated by Spanish sociologist Manuel Castells when he wrote: 'The destiny of humanity is being played out in urban areas, in particular, in the great metropolises' (*Local and Global*, p. 3).

Biblical and historical background
The roots of Christian mission are found in the cosmopolitan port cities and colonies of the Roman Empire. Marginal people, slaves and women were attracted by a message that offered alternatives to patrician civic order. The first urban Christians lived resistively against the culture of the Empire by meeting needs, offering hospitality, and celebrating new possibilities of community. They created alternative assemblies (*ekklēsia*) and households (*oikos*), which were a direct challenge to, and imitation of, the building blocks of Roman civic life. Early on in its life, the church seems to have developed a cellular form based on *families and households (Rom. 16:5; 1 Cor. 16:19), gathering in small cells throughout a city and coming together for a specific occasion or ritual (1 Cor. 14:23). The courtyards or atriums of larger houses, as well as the *insulae* workshops of artisans (1 Cor. 16:19), are mentioned as meeting places where unusually diverse gatherings would congregate. The fellowship (*koinonia*) of the church's urban network was realized in a constant exchange of visitors and news, as well as material support for those who were facing difficulties. About the middle of the second century, *The Epistle to Diognetus* described Christians in the city as the soul present throughout the urban community. Not visibly different to their neighbours but 'they show forth the wonderful and confessedly stranger character of the constitution of their citizenship' (v. 4). A community life that challenged accepted social patterns often meant that persecution was severest in urban centres.

In the Christian cities of the West in the pre-industrial era, the church's mission found its expression in the civic and ritual life of community as lay fraternities and guilds practised charity, and monastic renewal movements developed holistic approaches to the proclamation and service of the gospel.

In the nineteenth century, rapid urbanization and industrialization in Europe and North America changed the size and social structure of the cities, drawing in migrants from rural areas and other countries. The failure of the churches to move with the population is well documented. Squalor and poverty became widespread as new urban dwellers fell victims to exploitation by industrialists and landlords. Responses came to be based around institutions and non-denominational groupings promoting welfare and mission such as the Settlements and City Missions. William Booth (a contemporary of Karl Marx) through the Salvation Army created new forms of evangelistic outreach and rehabilitation, while Methodism established itself in industrial communities with a strong emphasis on mutuality and holiness. The new urban communities provided rich soil for the missions of renewal groups within established churches, such as the Catholic missions and religious orders of the Anglican churches. Christians were present within proletarian movements for social and political change, playing significant roles in the founding of unions and socialist societies.

New contexts, new challenges

The closing years of the twentieth century saw a new awareness of the challenge of cities worldwide, accompanied by a recognition and utilization of increasing global connections between cities. Urban mission in both hemispheres has looked to integrated forms of outreach, promoting social justice and *environmental concerns, as part of human transformation. Evangelism and *church planting has been coupled creatively with community development and popular organizing. Peace making, mediation and reconciliation work has become critical as cultural differences become exaggerated, particularly in cities coming out of civil conflict. All this has involved Christians in analysis of the communities in which they live and work, and an understanding of the many cultures of the city. Missiological and theological training has created new awareness of how evangelism needs to be based on social analysis and the challenge to structural injustice.

New patterns of *discipling, church life and ministry have emerged in communities with few material resources, in spite of little history of confident local leadership. Migrant churches, often using a variety of languages and worship forms, are commonplace. Elsewhere, however, churches have come to replicate the divisions and exclusions that are systemic in urban communities. In many cities the churches are still concentrated in middle-class suburbs, isolated from the cities in which they are set, and often they fail to address issues of power and complicity. Similarly, megachurches (replicating the practices of retail malls) kill off local congregations through deliberate targeting of neighbourhoods and city regions. The practice of urban mission needs to be informed by a vision for the whole of the earthly city in all its contradictions and manifestations.

Theological issues
Analysis and training

In the past century the church's work in the poorest urban communities has characterized urban mission. While recognizing the missional imperative, recent mission practioners have emphasized the need to understand the whole urban system in relation to its global connectivity, as well as the local interconnections between what were designated as 'inner city areas' and more affluent suburbs. If *proclamation and discipling are to be effective, there is a need to question the dynamics that create and exclude poor and migrant communities. Casual use of theologies that reject the city as an arena for salvation has led to the failure of many to conceive their own complicity in a city's degeneration, disintegration and decline. *Presence and *witness need to be based on an awareness of the principles that sustain and strengthen common life, particularly in places where Christians are in a faith minority.

Incarnation

The missional imperative of the *incarnation has been critical in the theology of urban mission. People and places in which they live matter because God became flesh and lived in human society. To divide the sacred and the secular is to deny the incarnation; as one nineteenth-century slum missioner put it: 'I speak out and fight about the drains because

I believe in the Incarnation.' Incarnational mission involves a commitment to be part of the communities of the poor in which the transformation of lives becomes a real possibility. The gospel could be preached authentically to the poor only by those who share their space. Those who pursue an incarnational ministry should not dismiss the signs of God's presence already at work: Hispanic theologian Villafañe describes the Pentecostal churches of the barrios as a '...disturbing sign on the fringes of an unjust society...' (E. Villafañe, *Seek the Peace of the City*, p. 37), as it embodies the struggles and longings of the dispossessed, who are provoked and empowered by the Spirit.

Power
Some Christians have perceived urban mission in terms of *spiritual or spatial warfare, discerning malevolent spiritual forces which need to be confronted through various strategies to reclaim and exorcise the urban space (Eph. 1). Others, such as Walter Wink, would speak of confronting 'powers and principalities' embodied in socio-political forces which corrupt the potential of individuals and communities. Community organizing, based on the model of Saul Alinsky's Industrial Areas Foundation in Chicago, has become a vital analytical and practical tool in mission strategies for cities in both hemispheres. Linthicum, through his work with World Vision's Urban Advance, identifies five 'biblical tactics': accountability, confrontation, civil disobedience, negotiation and agitation, as effective organizing strategies for those who seek change.

The throng
It is within the emergent movements and struggles that some would find the potential of the city as an arena for justice and praise – *on earth as it is in heaven*. The tumult of the city is not the same as the primeval chaos of the planet desperate for a world of order, but it is a dynamic creative interaction through which human beings create community. Many regard Christian participation in movements of struggle for the coming kingdom as central to their calling in urban mission, because it is in the midst of the urban throng that worship and the sacraments can be offered, as acts of proclamation and solidarity

(Ps. 109:30). The city is literally 'praised open' by these defiant acts with a new vision of how the future must be different.

God's shalom community
Amidst change and divergence in our cities, the creation of innovative spaces for assembly, resistance and assessing possibility might be one way the church can offer itself. These are the spaces and communities where stories are told and futures imagined that will often deviate from the dominant narratives of globalizing cities. Those stories are seen and heard through acts of advocacy and support given to refugees and migrants or to fledgling grass-roots community organizations. Linthicum writes of the transformation possible as Christians seek 'God's shalom community by being involved in:

- empowerment of our people as we together confront political systems of oppression and greed
- equitable distribution of wealth so that there will be no poor among us
- relationship with God and each other through Jesus Christ.' (R. Linthicum, *Transforming Power*, p. 190).

Bibliography
M. Castells and J. Borja, *Local and Global: Management of Cities in the Information Age* (London: Earthscan, 1997); H. Conn, M. Ortiz and S. S. Baker (eds.), *The Urban Face of Mission* (Phillipsburg: P & R Publishing, 2002); A. Davey, *Urban Christianity and Global Order* (London: SPCK, 2001); A. Davey, 'In the Midst of the Throng: The Politics of Mission in Globalizing Cities' *Missionalia* 2005; M. Davis, *City of Slums* (New York, London: Verso, 2005); J. Eade and C. Mele, *Understanding the City* (Oxford: Blackwell, 2002); M. Gornik, *To Live in Peace* (Grand Rapids: Erdmanns, 2003); R. Jewett, *Paul: Apostle to America* (Louisville: WKJP, 1994); R. Linthicum, *Transforming Power* (Downers Grove: InterVarsity Press, 2004); A. Shorter, *Church in the African City* (Maryknoll: Orbis Books; London: Geoffrey Chapman, 1991); E. Villafañe, *Seek the Peace of the City* (Grand Rapids: Eerdmans, 1993); J. J. Vincent, *Starting All Over Again* (Geneva: WCC, 1981); J. J. Vincent, *Into the City* (London: Epworth,

1982); W. Wink, *The Powers That Be* (New York: Doubleday, 1999).

A. DAVEY

Values

The importance of values in cross-cultural ministry

Cross-cultural mission partners are prepared for eating strange creatures and language learning, but are sometimes less prepared for the deeper differences in culture. These typically take longer to be identified, but in the long run are more influential in finding bridges to communication and empathy across cultural differences. One such dimension of culture is its values, which are a measure of what the culture considers important to the quality and preservation of its shared existence.

Values express the principles which govern attitudes, behaviour and decision-making, whether individually or corporately. Cultural values arise from the world-view of a culture, which expresses how its people believe the world works. These values provide norms for the kind of behaviour which conforms to the world-view and reinforces it, so that life on an individual or social level can work in their favour. Cultural values are considered worth respecting to preserve what is important about a culture or society. All cultures have values, some of which may be unique to a culture and others that are shared. Sometimes they will endorse Christian values (e.g. *love, *truth, *peace, loyalty), and at other times they will challenge them (e.g. sexual freedom, consumerism, bribery). Values can be morally neutral, until they are interpreted and applied, in which case only then can they be endorsed or challenged from a Christian perspective. For example, the principle of human rights can be rightly affirmed if it is applied to injustices suffered, but not necessarily when it threatens other principles such as responsibility, personal freedom, or even life itself.

Values affect relationships. The Asian missionary to Latin America may feel her hosts lack respect if they are repeatedly interrupting her and speaking among themselves. Her Latin American counterparts may see her modest participation as lack of enthusiasm for discussing ministry strategy.

Similarly, an African Christian worker in northern Europe may find his local ministry partner cold and unwilling to offer help, while his European colleague may view his African brother as too concerned about what others think of him.

Crossing cultural boundaries in mission involves understanding the intangible values that members of a culture consider precious, in order to communicate with them at the heart level. Beyond sharing a cup of *chai* or coffee, they must learn to laugh and weep with their hosts over the same things that cause them to rejoice and mourn (see Rom. 12:15). As far as is possible this means learning to think and feel as they do, sharing their values, and at least empathizing, even if total identification is never completely possible.

Frameworks for understanding values of other cultures

It is possible to map the values of different cultures from their attitudes to work, time, relationships, *money, *authority, justice and so on. Some cultures are task orientated and others are people orientated, some plan ahead and others live spontaneously, some value efficient use of time and others use time to develop relationships. Whilst there is a danger of generalization, these frameworks are useful conceptual tools which help us to situate where we are in relation to others and help us to identify cultural differences.

Other broader value systems can be developed. How individualistic a culture is affects many specific values related to achievement, commitment and freedom; how power is handled influences views on equality and organization. It is important to identify preferences in styles of leadership and authority to understand how meetings are conducted. The relative importance a culture assigns to justice and honour permeates thought and behaviour in relationships with different social or racial groups.

A biblical/theological perspective

Because human beings are made in God's image (Gen. 1:26–27), they are able to possess, cherish and express God's communicable attributes. Values which express justice, love, faithfulness and mercy are universally articulated culturally in family, workplace, government and other institutions. Christians will therefore find many values in all cultures which they can affirm and endorse. Nevertheless, since all human beings and their cultures are fallen (Rom. 3:23; 5:12), collective values can arise out of greed, revenge, pride or other selfish, sinful motives.

Faith in Christ redeems individual and social values, enabling people more fully to live in conformity with godly virtues (e.g. 1 John 4:7–21) which are generated by the Holy Spirit (e.g. Gal. 5:22–23). Cultural values will therefore always be somewhat ambiguous. Is the value of individual freedom (found for example in some Western cultures) a biblical value? Yes, if it is about individual responsibility, but not if it reinforces self-centredness. How do we evaluate the authoritarianism found in some Asian cultures? Authority is to be valued, but not if it is misused to oppress. Thus, cultural values and mores may or may not reflect biblical, godly virtues.

Scripture gives us three perspectives on cultural values:

(1) *The contexts of the biblical cultures.* We must be faithful to the original biblical context from which values are derived in order to apply them appropriately first to our own cultural context, then open-mindedly to another, host culture. For example, the values of the people of Israel were influenced by their sense of collective identity, historical destiny and spiritual distinctiveness, all of which may be experienced differently in our contemporary contexts. Nevertheless, because they also derived from revelation of God's law, their values become paradigmatic for us today.

(2) *The biblical role of conscience.* Romans 2:15 indicates that God has engraved his law on every conscience, to confirm good and point out evil. All human beings therefore have a God-given inner resource for their values, although their sinfulness distorts the process and results in flawed values. However, human conscience is shaped both by universal moral standards and by culture. For example, Paul taught the culturally mixed NT church to respect the conscience of a neighbour with different values, taking as his example cross-cultural issues such as food offered to idols (1 Cor. 10:23–33; Rom. 14:13, 20–21; 15:2).

(3) *Biblical cross-cultural interactions, which serve as examples.* Abraham relocates from Ur to Canaan (Gen. 11:27 – 25:10), and

finds his values tested in a foreign context. Joseph oversees Egypt, then brings Israel there (Gen. 37 – 47), maintaining his godly values in a hostile environment. Israelites under Joshua chase out Canaanites with uncompromising values, while tolerating some (Josh. 1 – 12). Later however, Israel's interaction with the surrounding nations often leads to a compromise in their values.

Jesus ministers to a Samaritan woman (John 4), and other non-Jews (e.g. Mark 5:1–20; 7:24 – 8:9), and so breaks through previously unquestioned cultural values. The Spirit works through cultural diversity in Jerusalem (Acts 2), and the apostles eventually reach out across cultural boundaries (Acts 8:4–40; 9:32 – 28:31). The gospel brings a new set of values and priorities into every cultural context, so that sometimes values are endorsed and sometimes challenged.

Variations in Christian values

Not all Christians may share the same values, even though they share the same moral framework. Christians in different cultures may have conflicting but legitimate, even unique, values derived from the same biblical virtue. The love many Central Americans hold for their children is notably intense. But when a Central American family lives among hospitable West Africans, they may be surprised to find parents serving their guests the best food, while their own children go hungry. Both cultures have valid ways of expressing love, but the result can be cross-cultural misunderstanding.

A Westerner, commenting openly to a national East Asian co-worker on an aspect of his family life that she finds difficult to understand, can be surprised when her host conceals his true feelings to maintain his family's honour. Meanwhile, the Asian host may be appalled by what he sees as a direct assault on his loved one's character. Both value truth and love, and may desire to grow in Christ by 'speaking the truth in love', but their relative emphases on truth and love may cause conflict, the Westerner feeling that the Asian host disregards truth, while the host doubts the Westerner's sincerity because of her lack of love.

Misunderstandings often stem from fundamental differences in the values which underlie these interactions. Inclusive cultures encounter conflict with efficient, time-oriented peoples;

a person from a culture which values organization and careful planning might become frustrated with his relaxed mission partners who feel that over-planning will stifle the Spirit's work. At work underneath are more basic values derived from trust, love, faith, truth, productivity and security.

When conflict does result, the resolution can be complex. A culture of direct communicators may become suspicious of using mediators, while those who prefer an intermediary may be horrified to find their foreign friends requesting a face-to-face meeting. Guests to a culture must seek to handle conflict by national norms, where they are not expressly unbiblical.

Conclusion

Understanding cross-cultural values and how they are modelled biblically and socially should help to predict areas of conflict and promote healthy interaction, understanding and appreciation of the heart values of a host culture. Christians who embrace cultural values that reflect Christ's virtues can find themselves resonating easily with those seeking truth and values to live by. A set of shared values can be the basis for a relationship within which other values can be challenged. Christians who model with culturally appropriate sincerity those biblical virtues that challenge and even contradict local values will gain the respect that enables them to lead their hosts to the Source of all virtue. In this way values become important partners in the task of mission, and how they function must be appreciated for effective cross-cultural relationships.

See also CULTURE, WORLD-VIEW.

Bibliography
D. M. Crow, *Spiritual Authority Across Cultures: The Cultural Contours of Pneumatic Leadership – East and West*, PhD dissertation (Pasadena: Fuller Seminary School of World Mission, 2000); D. Elmer, *Cross-Cultural Conflict: Building Relationships for Effective Ministry* (Downers Grove: InterVarsity Press, 1993); G. Hofstede, *Cultures and Organizations: Software of the Mind* (New York: McGraw-Hill, 1997); R. D. Lewis, *When Cultures Collide* (London: Nicholas Brealey, 1999); S. G. Lingenfelter and M. K. Mayers, *Ministering Cross-Culturally* (Grand Rapids: Baker, ²2003); J. A. Louwen, *Culture and Human Values: Christian Intervention in Anthropological Perspective* (Pasadena: William Carey, 1975); L. L. Noble, *Naked and Not Ashamed: An Anthropological, Biblical, and Psychological Study of Shame* (Jackson: Jackson Printing, 1975); R. J. Priest, 'Missionary Eclectics: Conscience and Culture', *Missiology: An International Review* 22, 1994, pp. 291–315; B. Thomas, 'The Gospel for Shame Cultures', *Evangelical Missions Quarterly* 30, 1994, pp. 284–290; F. Trompenaars and C. Hampden-Turner, *Riding the Waves of Culture* (New York: McGraw-Hill, ²1998).

P. C. MAUGER

Weakness

The word 'weakness' in mission theology has powerful connotations best explained through the concept of 'mission from a position of weakness'. Because Jesus' mission for the *kingdom of God was ultimately accomplished from a position of weakness on the *cross, the kingdom mission of his church should also be practised from a position of weakness.

In the new era ushered in through the coming of the kingdom in the person and ministry of Jesus, the weakness of the cross was revealed to be the hidden character of that glorious kingdom. The weakness of the cross was actually the power of *God, a power that exposed and disarmed the power of darkness. Therefore, this weakness must accompany the church in her ministry.

Mission from a position of weakness is not weakness itself. Neither does it mean a weak mission, or a fruitless ministry. Since God has established the powerlessness of the cross as a way of demonstrating might and power in this new era, the church of Christ must understand that a position of weakness in faithfulness is mighty, and humility is powerful. The church should know that God uses his church in vulnerability to demonstrate his power and to reveal the true character of the gospel of God's kingdom.

Scriptural basis
The theme of 'mission from a position of weakness' runs right through Scripture.

Luke–Acts and 1 and 2 Corinthians especially address the concept.

In *Luke–Acts*, the Magnificat sets out a theological theme of reversal which overshadows the mood of the entire Gospel. The proud are brought down and the humble lifted up; the hungry are filled and the rich go away empty (Luke 1:51–53). The coming of God's reign causes the reversal to take place throughout the whole of human society. Luke describes the reversal by contrasting tax collectors and sinners to the self-righteous (e.g. 5:27–32; 7:31–35), the poor to the rich (e.g. 6:20–26; 7:18–23; 8:14), women to men (8:1–3), Gentles and Samaritans to Jews (e.g. 7:1–10; 9:51–56), widows to religious leaders (e.g. 7:11–17; 18:1–8), and children to the wise and learned (9:10–17; 46–50; 10:21–24).

This reversal extends into Acts. The word *diakonia* (service) is emphasized from the beginning (Acts 1:17, 25). Eventually two forms of service appear (6:1–4): *diakonia* (service) of the word, and to *diakonize* (serve) tables.

In *1 and 2 Corinthians*, Paul sets the weakness of the cross, of the messenger (Paul himself), and of the Corinthians, as the norm in the proclamation of the gospel of the kingdom (1 Cor. 1:18 – 2:5). Paul's emphasis on weakness is repeated in 2 Corinthians. He speaks of comfort through suffering (1:3–5), glory through shame (2:14 – 4:6), life through death (4:7–15), and riches through poverty (8:1–15). The theme of weakness reaches a crescendo in 2 Corinthians 12:1–10, with the theme of 'power made perfect through weakness'. From the very first chapter of 2 Corinthians, Paul has had an ongoing conflict with the Corinthians concerning the character of his apostleship and the gospel message itself. In saying that he received the truth about weakness from God himself (12:9), he claims authority for the character of the gospel that he proclaims, and also confirms that he is an apostle of weakness, not of personal power. There is a different kind of power at work in him, the power of the cross. This from a human perspective is weak, but Paul had to become weak for the sake of the Christ who was crucified.

The history of world mission

Understanding the history of world mission through the perspective of 'mission from a position of weakness' is critically important.

For instance, the conflation of church and state, that began with Constantine in the third century and resulted in the possession of worldly power by the church, marked a dramatic change in Christian mission. During his reign the institutional church first gained and used political power in spreading the gospel, moving into the centre stage of influence from the periphery where she had originally been.

This in itself may not have been a bad thing had not the church fallen for the temptation, as time went on, to abuse its power, impose its authority, baptize abuses of state power with its blessing, and seek to preserve the status quo in its own interests. The idea of 'Christendom' was established. And to those receiving the * gospel its very character became different from its humble origins on the periphery of society. For example, the gospel that the South American Indians received from their Spanish and Portuguese conquerors in the sixteenth century was a far cry from the one that the earliest Christians preached. While spreading this distorted gospel, the conquerors simultaneously inflicted massive, premature, and unjust death. It was amid this tragedy that Bartolome de Las Casas (1474–1566) and others stood against the oppression and cruelty of the conquistadores. These faithful few stayed true to mission from a position of weakness.

There are many more examples of mission from weakness throughout history. Among them are Frances of Assisi (1182?–1226) who stood against the Crusades in the Middle Ages, the Anabaptists in the sixteenth century, who were willing to die under the persecution of the more powerful religious groups, and the Celtic movement in the fourth century that was later absorbed into the Catholic Church, thus smothering the vitality of the movement.

Missiology

Mission from a position of weakness is not new. But because of an influential trend which focuses on the power needed to achieve certain goals and strategies in mission, the reality that God's power is manifested in weakness has been well buried in missiological thought and practice.

Lesslie Newbigin originally used the phrase

'mission from a position of weakness' in his book, *The Open Secret*. David Bosch, in his last speech in 1991, spoke on the 'vulnerability of mission'. Jürgen Moltmann, John Howard Yoder and Jacob Loewen are among those keenly aware of the importance of mission from weakness.

The practice of mission

Mission from a position of weakness may be practised in many ways in today's context:

(1) *Vulnerability*. 'By sharing one's weaknesses, struggles, temptations, failures, and even shames, one can connect with the hearts of the hearers, and any walls between the missionary and the hearers can be easily removed' (P. Y. Jeong, in PhD dissertation, p. 180). Being honest about their own weaknesses and failures enables mission agents to identify with those who are themselves vulnerable. They are seen as real people, and this differentiates them from their own professional idealism.

(2) *On the periphery*. By intentionally being with people on the periphery, and identifying themselves with people who are seen as sinners, as well as with women, widows, children, and the *poor, mission agents become weak, and find they have powerful opportunities for the gospel.

(3) *Humble boldness*. Glad acceptance of the weaknesses that accompany obedience to God, and recognition of the fact that they are ultimately following the footsteps of Christ crucified, leads mission agents to a new level of boldness; they know that God will use their weaknesses to manifest his power. In relating to those of other faiths they can have 'humble boldness and bold humility'.

(4) *Service*. Practising *diakonia* is imperative for both the internal structure and external mission activity of the church. The Christian paradox finds its climax in the achievement of victory by a Lamb who was slain. The Lamb calls his followers to 'take up their cross' (Mark 8:34), and even to accept defeat and powerlessness to remain faithful to the Lamb. But weakness becomes the channel God uses to manifest his power to fulfil his mission.

A missionary understanding of this theme will become even more crucial as we move into a new era of mission in which the abuse and corruption of political power are widespread, cynical self-interest predominates, social and religious divisions are growing, and peoples everywhere look for alternative ways of exercising power. The church can demonstrate that alternative through 'mission from a position of weakness'.

See also POWER.

Bibliography

D. Bosch, *The Vulnerability of Mission* (Birmingham: Selly Oak Colleges, 1991); P. Y. Jeong, 'Mission from a Position of Weakness and its Implications for the Korean Church', PhD dissertation, Fuller Theological Seminary, 2004; J. A. Loewen, *Culture and Human Value: Christian Intervention in Anthropological Perspective* (Pasadena: William Carey Library, 1975); J. Moltmann, *The Crucified God* (New York: Harper and Row, 1974); L. Newbigin, *The Open Secret* (Grand Rapids: Eerdmans, rev. edn, 1995); T. B. Savage, *Power through Weakness: Paul's Understanding of the Christian Ministry in 2 Corinthians* (Cambridge: Cambridge University Press, 1996); J. H. Yoder, *The Politics of Jesus* (Grand Rapids: Eerdmans, ²1994); J. H. Yoder, *For the Nations* (Grand Rapids: Eerdmans, 1997); J. H. Yoder, *The Royal Priesthood: Essays Ecclesiological and Ecumenical*, M. C. Cartwright (ed.) (Scottdale: Herald Press, 1998).

P. Y. JEONG

Wealth

In today's consumer-orientated world Jesus' teaching on wealth and mission comes across as either impossibly idealistic or profoundly liberating: 'Take nothing for the journey – no staff, no bag, no bread, no money, no extra shirt' (Luke 9:3). While Anthony of Egypt (c. AD 251–356) took Jesus' words literally, instructing his followers: 'Let none among us have even the yearning to possess', some nineteenth-century missionaries from among the wealthy maintained their lifestyle while abroad. Others chose poverty as a basic missionary principle: Moravian artisans, twenty-first-century Filipinos, Indian evangelists, Hudson Taylor's recruits, to name but a few.

Today the richest 1% of the world's population (about sixty million) has as much income as the poorest 57%. Contemporary mission takes place in a world of financial injustice, both individual and national – many of the most heavily indebted nations both needing and welcoming Christian mission, with its schools, HIV/AIDS clinics and feeding programmes.

In such contexts two questions loom large: How should mission be done? How should missionaries live? Answers must take into account the following general biblical principles.

Wealth in the Bible

Wealth is discussed in the OT, where one main word, 'ôṣār, is used. There are many words for poverty and oppression, as the OT world was like ours: a few wealthy, the majority poor. Even the wealthy in Israel were poor when compared to counterparts in Egypt or Babylon. The OT teaches that God is a generous Creator/Provider who cares about material needs; all are equal before God; to accumulate wealth at others' expense is sin and will be punished; wealth is to be shared as we care for the poor; the apparent security which wealth affords can lead to attitudes of independence in relation to God; wealthy and righteous are not synonyms; wealth should be a reward for labour and not a reward for unjust exploitation of others.

The NT builds on the OT, stressing God's care for the *poor, though not, in contrast to some modern interpretations, teaching that the poor are necessarily closer to God, or more loved by him. God's love in Christ extends to rich and poor alike.

Specific biblical guidelines

Exodus 16 (also 2 Cor. 8:13–15) describes how God sustained his people, giving each one enough food and a weekly rest, instead of surplus for some and around-the-clock labour for others. Often missionary practice has not respected this equality, and the growing disparity between Western and non-Western agencies and their staff is particularly evident as the internationalization of mission proceeds. The traditional model of the white, salaried, cross-cultural Western missionary is changing – it is simply too expensive. Furthermore, by 2025 over half of the world's full-time missionaries will come from the Two-Thirds World.

In *Daniel* the first serious temptation encountered by the young Jews in pagan Babylon illustrates the close relationship between wealth, power and idolatry: the huge 'image of gold' dominates Daniel 3. Although not to bow down before it was to face the fiery furnace, the Jews insisted that they would never abandon their worship of God, whether he saved them or not (vv. 16–18).

A few decades ago, teaching on *sacrifice, even on the ultimate sacrifice, death, in the cause of Christ, was common, alongside theologies of liberation and justice. Today's health and prosperity theology can hardly produce missionaries able to cope with the reality of a 'planet of slums' ever more resistant to the gospel and increasingly dangerous and uncomfortable.

Mark 6 is a sequence of events related to wealth: the poor carpenter heals the sick; the activities of his missionaries among the needy anger wealthy, powerful Herod; 5,000 hungry are fed. It is noteworthy that the needy crowd did have something to offer, that Jesus was able use their apparently insignificant seven items. Mission practitioners today need to remember that 'even the poor' have something to offer in spiritual gifts, human wisdom and creative talents. Failure to harness these can kill local initiative, create dependency, and, eventually, paternalism. Foreign money has been the death of many a national project, making it too big, too good – and completely unsustainable. Too much foreign money can weaken a national church for generations, especially when it is support for national pastors. As with Jesus, so today: seeking out the gifts of the poor and organizing an appropriate and respectful use of them takes time and effort.

At the same time, in India, for example, the poor themselves are the wealth of the church, comprising between 60% and 70% of its members. And more than 65% of all Indians live in slums. But the Friends Missionary Prayer Band (FMPB) does not accept Western money for its ministries, only for capital improvements. Support for their thousand workers is raised locally, but the humble FMPB annual budget is little more than the missionary giving of just one North American church. Such Indian missions, and also the growth of Pentecostal churches among the Latin American poor, are proof that mission is not dependent on wealth for success.

However, while a poor church can support its missionaries to a poor country, this is not possible when the receiving country is rich. This is the single most serious issue facing trans-national mission today. Partnership between rich and poor churches could be the answer, making ministry both possible and cheaper – but only if it is done with integrity, seeking the best for both sides. Otherwise the long-term cost will be higher, in the form of a weakened national church, with good leaders lured off to USA/Europe by temptingly large salaries.

Philippians 4 discusses financial aspects of partnership in mission, stressing that money given for God's work returns to God as an offering to him. It is God who controls it, and not the giver. The text also implies financial accountability, which both helps maintain trust and gives donors and receivers opportunity to rejoice in God's provision. There is nothing to suggest that either the contemporary 'donor nurture' culture or money-raising on the basis of emotional appeals to compassion (for glue-sniffing street children, for example) is biblical. The latter is inconsistent with biblical teaching about human dignity.

In partnership it can never be enough simply to advocate that the West gives the money, while the rest supplies the manpower. Nor is the solution to stop sending money! The present explosive growth of mission from Brazil demands partnership, as Brazilian leaders discover that there are aspects of their foreign missionary enterprise that may take generations for the local churches to finance – but there is no time to wait! Education for missionary children, pensions, health care and adequate pastoral oversight are expensive. Perhaps a solution could be an adaptation of the FMPB model, with Western money being used to finance such large expenditures, and Brazilian churches financing the ministries themselves. Even so, the generation of local funds is still a problem.

Ephesians 4:12, with its emphasis on all God's people, suggests that part of the answer to many of these problems may lie in a more voluntary concept of missionary work than has been common in the past. Or in giving more value to so-called *tentmaking, and to the preparation of missionaries who are able to earn their own wealth in the receiving country, and to live at the same level as those they wish to reach. Paul's example (Acts 20:33–35) shows how to avoid the trap of missionary affluence which isolates socially and strategically from the very people who must be reached.

See also MONEY/ECONOMICS.

Bibliography
D. Barrett, *Cosmos, Chaos and Gospel* (Birmingham, AL: New Hope, 1987); J. J. Bonk, *Missions and Money: Affluence as a Western Missionary Problem* (Maryknoll, NY: Orbis Books, 1991); V. Grigg, *Companion to the Poor* (Sutherland, NSW: Albatross Books, 1984); P. V. Martinson (ed.), *Mission at the Dawn of the 21st Century* (Minneapolis, MN: Kirk House Publishers, 1999); S. E. Wheeler, *Wealth as Peril and Obligation: The NT on Possessions* (Grand Rapids, MI: Eerdmans, 1995).

J. E. W. EVERY-CLAYTON

Witchcraft

Most peoples for most of history have held beliefs in witchcraft. The exact content of such beliefs is culture-specific, and they cannot be simply identified with Western notions of the witch. Indeed, use of the Western vocabulary of 'witchcraft' and 'sorcery' risks imposing an alien structure on patterns of belief that can be very different and also highly complex. Central to most notions of witchcraft is the idea that some human beings possess a capacity to injure others by non-empirical, occult means. However, it may also be understood as the deployment of occult power, often activated through engagement in anti-social acts like cannibalism (which is itself frequently conceived in psychic terms as the eating of a person's heart or soul) or incest, to gain desirable ends such as increased wealth. As societies have experienced 'modernization' in the post-colonial era, the notion of witchcraft has sometimes undergone a degree of transformation, and may be identified as the path to new forms of affluence or political power, and even to sporting success. In these circumstances it is viewed with ambivalence: it remains no doubt a terrifying and evil thing, but equally one that has much to offer. Paradoxically, it is also seen as a weapon utilized by the weak for the purpose of *equalizing* economic and political disparities.

Since Evans-Pritchard's work on Azande witchcraft belief, a distinction has often been made between witchcraft and sorcery: sorcery involves the employment of material objects, rites and incantations to achieve its ends, whereas witchcraft is an innate, perhaps even unconscious, capacity. While the distinction has proved useful, for many peoples notions of witchcraft and sorcery cannot be reduced to such a simple dichotomy, and there may indeed be a range of conceptions of malevolent occult activity.

Probably in most cultures the strength of witchcraft and sorcery belief lies in its explanatory power. Along with ancestor and spirit attack it is invoked to explain the incidence of suffering or, in some cases, of economic or political success. For certain peoples scarcely any misfortune or death can be explained apart from witchcraft. Nor do such beliefs necessarily disappear in the face of scientific, empirical explanations of sickness and accident. On the one hand, witchcraft may itself be seen as an empirical and normal phenomenon rather than an unnatural or supernatural one; some peoples believe in the existence of a material witchcraft 'substance' which is located in the witch's body. On the other hand, it might be accepted that empirical factors can explain *how* an event occurred, but it is witchcraft that explains *why*. Why here and now? And why to this person rather than that?

Societies with strong witchcraft beliefs defend themselves against witches. Apotropaic medicines might be acquired from traditional practitioners, some of which supposedly cause an attack to rebound on the aggressor. Ordeal is widely practised as a means of identifying a witch, who might then be expelled from society or executed. In some cultures there is the specialist role of witch-smeller, in others there are anti-witchcraft societies, and in the twentieth century witch-cleansing movements proliferated across much of Africa. Some modern states actually take judicial action against 'witches'. Witch-focused paranoia may at times take hold of a society, bringing immense suffering to the often large numbers accused.

Western anthropologists have tended to assume that witchcraft and sorcery are illusions. They explain the existence and tenacity of such beliefs in functionalist terms, focusing on their explanatory role, or the use made of them to articulate social strains, enforce social conformity, or project inner psychological struggles. Nor are such approaches necessarily invalid; nevertheless, at heart witchcraft belief is profoundly anti-functional and destructive of human relationships and society.

The Bible makes very little reference to witchcraft and sorcery. Magic arts of every sort are condemned, as in Deuteronomy 18:9–14, but their potential efficacy is not denied. Up to a point, the magicians of Egypt were able to match the works of Yahweh (Exod. 7:10–12, 22; 8:6–7, 18), while Ezekiel 13:17–23 seems to have some form of witchcraft in mind and assumes its power. The book of Revelation mentions sorcery several times, which may reflect its prevalence in the context to which the book was addressed; Ephesus in particular was well known as a centre of magic. Nevertheless, nowhere in the Bible are witchcraft or sorcery presented as significant sources of human suffering.

Furthermore, the Bible nowhere explicitly identifies the source of magic power. Some have suggested that it derives from neutral and purely human psychic abilities that may be turned to good or evil ends. Indeed, in the languages of some African peoples the term rendered into English as 'witchcraft' refers to a neutral power, the moral orientation of which depends on the possessor. However, this is not true of all ethnic groups, some of which believe that the witch has entered into some sort of relationship with a spirit. Moreover, there are biblical grounds for the view that the power behind all supernatural acts, other than those effected by the Holy Spirit or angels, is demonic. It may, for example, be implied in Paul's identification of the magician, Elymas, as 'a child of the devil' (Acts 13:10). Similarly, in Matthew 12:24–28, when Jesus and the Jerusalem rabbis debated the source of the power by which he drove out demons, both parties recognized only two possibilities – either it was Beelzebub (or Satan), or it was the Holy Spirit.

In view of the misery created by witchcraft belief, it is vital to confront it with a contextually relevant and solidly biblical response.

However, any such response must be carefully nuanced. On the one hand, in that the Bible does not deny its possibility, an approach which simply dismisses the very notion of witchcraft as superstition, may be reflecting a syncretistic fusion of Christianity with rationalistic naturalism. Moreover, for those convinced of the reality of occult aggression, it offers little comfort but rather tends to drive them back to traditional means of defence. On the other hand, responses which accept the total structure of local witchcraft beliefs at face value, thereby affirm a brutally destructive explanatory system which has little biblical support, and so fall into the trap of what has been termed 'missiological' syncretism.

Consequently, a biblical approach to witchcraft must, first, promote a renewed worldview, in which human fallenness replaces witchcraft as the underlying explanation of all human suffering, and God's sovereign rule replaces the anarchy of malevolent spirits and forces that dominates traditional thinking (Rom. 8:28). Second, it is crucial so to communicate the supremacy of the risen and enthroned Christ, that believers find their security in him. In Ephesians Paul insists on the pre-eminence of Christ's name over every other, the others being the spiritual power sources invoked in contemporary Ephesian magic. Therefore, having been raised and enthroned with Christ, Christians enjoy protection from every hostile power in him (1:19 – 2:6). Significantly, both here and in Colossians, Paul does not belittle his readers' fears but proclaims Christ as the definitive response to them. Third, there needs to be a recognition that Satan, and not the witch, is the real enemy of humanity. As such, he – the liar and father of lies (John 8:44) – fosters and exploits witchcraft paranoia in order to foment human violence and suffering, and thereby destroy human community. Finally, insofar as witchcraft fear and accusation breed in an atmosphere of interpersonal suspicion, envy and hostility, churches must proactively seek to become true communities of reconciliation, which function in turn as salt in the wider society. Traditionally it has often been the diviner's role to repair those breaches in human relationships that provoke allegations of witchcraft. It is now for Christian leadership to take that responsibility, and so to strive towards the practice of forbearance and forgiveness in their churches, that both the discourse and the use of witchcraft become unacceptable and redundant.

See also SPIRITUAL WARFARE.

Bibliography
E. E. Evans-Pritchard, *Witchcraft, Oracles and Magic among the Azande* (Oxford: Clarendon Press, 1976 [1937]); P. Geschiere, *The Modernity of Witchcraft: Politics and the Occult in Postcolonial Africa* (Charlottesville: University of Virginia Press, 1997); P. G. Hiebert, R. Daniel and T. Tiénou, *Understanding Folk Religion* (Grand Rapids: Baker, 1999); H. Hill, 'Witchcraft and the Gospel: Insights from Africa', *Missiology* XXIV, 1996, pp. 323–344; L. Mair, *Witchcraft* (London: World University Library, 1969); M. Marwick (ed.), *Witchcraft and Sorcery* (Harmondsworth: Penguin Books, 1990); E. G. Parrinder, *Witchcraft: European and African* (London: Faber & Faber, 1963).

K. FERDINANDO

Witness

Biblical and theological background

'Witness' is generally employed as a synonym for 'informant', 'spectator', or 'attestor', and as such is found in both law and religion. Both the Greek *martys* and the Hebrew *'ēd* carry the idea of someone possessing a first-hand knowledge of an event or a fact, and so able to report what is seen or heard. Ancient Israel's legal practice of holding court at the city gate was based on certain rules: (1) a witness's testimony was the primary method of proof; (2) a witness presented the material evidence for the case; (3) a false witness was heavily punished; (4) the minimum of two witnesses was needed to confirm a fact; (5) a witness could also be an advocate; and (6) a witness was obliged to testify.

When Jesus commissioned his disciples as 'witnesses' to the ends of the earth (Acts 1:8; cf. Luke 24:48), he put this obligation to testify at the heart of mission. They had seen and experienced events and heard truths to which they were called faithfully to witness. Supremely they were witnesses to the fact of the *resurrection (Acts 2:32). For St John a true testimony was critical to the authenticity of Jesus' gospel (John 21:24; 1 John 1:1–2), so the disciples must testify, not merely as observers but because they had been in relationship with him (John 15:27).

Hence, while witnesses are valuable as informants, the witness metaphor in the Bible is only fully understood in the context of the divine-human covenant relationship, the primary context in which *God's *revealed truth about himself is made known. Relation and revelation thus come together in the covenant. Its laws, intended to keep God's people in relation with himself, are described as a 'testimony' to the revealed character and will of God (Exod. 31:18). If the covenant is broken, witnesses are called before judgment is passed: Yahweh calls upon 'heaven and earth' (Deut. 4:26), 'the Book of the Law' (31:26), and the song of Moses (31:19, 21). The people themselves act as witnesses of their covenant commitment (Josh. 24:22, 27), and God himself can be called as witness (Gen. 31:50). Consistent with God's character, Jesus is described as both 'the Truth' and the 'faithful witness' (John 14:6; Rev. 1:5); and one of the Holy Spirit's main ministries is to testify (martyrēsei) to Jesus with the aim of convincing and convicting the world of the truth (John 15:26; 16:7–11).

So in their mission Christians are called to witness to the truth of what God has revealed of himself, which they have come to know through their relationship with him. Personal testimony should therefore primarily focus on God and what Christians have discovered to be true about him. But this can be costly, since the world is opposed to truth, and witnesses for Jesus can face *martyrdom (Gk martys, cf. Revelation 17:6).

Witness as a key concept in mission

Therefore, biblically and theologically, 'witness' is a key category for mission thinking and practice. Michael Green has described martyrein as 'one of the three great words used for proclaiming the Christian message' in the NT. However, witness has not always featured strongly in evangelical mission thinking. Among evangelicals, witness is commonly used interchangeably with *proclamation as the way of communicating the gospel, with the intention of conversion. Ecumenical missiologies, however, have often preferred to see witness as distinct from proclamation, since it conveys a less aggressive and confrontational mode of evangelism, more personal and relational. Witness can be as much in deed as in word, and there can be the silent witness of *presence and being, thereby avoiding approaches that are disrespectful of other people's beliefs and practices. Some evangelicals prefer categories such as 'warfare', 'targeting', 'strategy', and similar military metaphors which tend to run counter to a more relational mode of witness. All categories have some biblical support and also some limitations.

What are the implications for mission when 'witness' becomes a key category?

The practice of evangelism

Witness in relation to evangelism has three underlying assumptions: (1) that truth has the power to convict and convince, especially when made public, implying that witness must always be made to what is true; (2) that words are an essential means of conveying truth, pointing to the importance of verbal witness; (3) that *truth has its own integrity and therefore methods of coercion and manipulation are contrary to the nature of witness.

Truthful, verbal and sincere witness reflect the nature of God. That God always speaks the truth is never questioned in Scripture (e.g. Isa. 45:19). Secondly, he is a God who communicates to human beings in words they can understand and he calls them to reason with him (e.g. Isa. 1:18). Thirdly, words that are sincere have their origin in God (e.g. 2 Cor. 2:17).

Witness, of course, is not just verbal. Creation itself 'speaks' of God's glory without using words (Ps. 19:1–4). Nevertheless, when God comes to us in the person of Jesus, he speaks to us verbally of God's truth. If we accept that verbal witness is central to mission thinking and practices, our evangelism must be consistent with the above three assumptions. Regardless whether the evangelistic activity is carried out through preaching, proclamation, storytelling, dialogue or testimonial, each is based on the conviction that truth clearly communicated can challenge the hearers and lead them to an encounter with Jesus. This allows us to justify a wide range of word-based evangelistic interactions with non-believers, for example, through publications, inter-religious dialogues and teaching. Though wordless actions and unspoken conduct may also bear witness for Jesus, verbal explanation can prevent wordless actions and conduct from being inadequately or wrongly interpreted.

The scope of mission

However, God calls us to witness to him by the consistency of our lives as well as our words. Paul was able to testify to both holiness and sincerity in the apostolic witness (2 Cor. 1:12). What we are can speak so loudly that people may not hear what we say. A powerful witness is the combined effect of words and deeds (e.g. 1 John 2:3–6). God speaks to people in Scripture in a rich variety of ways; so we also must reflect the breadth of his creativity in the way that we witness.

But truthful witness is not just for outsiders: it challenges and renews the church. The scope of God's mission thus includes the church. God's people are prone to illusion and falsehood, and God sent his witnesses throughout history to call his people to return to the truth. God uses prophetic witnesses who speak the truth to call unfaithful believers to repentance. This can lead to *renewal and revival, and this in turn can cause believers to *become* enthusiastic witnesses with personal stories to tell about their Lord; their energies and resources will be re-channelled into mission. This cycle creates a dynamic witness, and not mere activism or pragmatism.

The context of mission

Since 'God has not left himself without witness' (Acts 14:17, KJV) in any context in the world, a strategic step in mission is to determine what or who these witnesses are, and then to build our own witness upon them. The question we ask in each context is: what is God already doing and in what ways has he gone ahead of us? Such a 'witness' could be a 'person-of-peace', or someone who is working for the values of the kingdom, even though they may not be aware of it. There may be a belief or a practice which witnesses to God's truth; or perhaps a crisis situation that causes people to seek after their Creator. There may have been a remarkable event which 'speaks' of God's presence and power. Any of these 'witnesses' can be a contact point for the gospel.

The mode of witness needs to be aware of the context in which it is spoken. In cultures in which truth is communicated through the telling of stories, witness as testimony will be a powerful way of helping people to relate their stories to the gospel story. In cultures in which propositional truth is important, witness as apologetic may be more appropriate. In a multi-faith context, witness as *dialogue will be relevant, whilst in places where any kind of public proclamation is difficult, witness to the power of God demonstrated in healing and transformed lives will carry its own power of persuasion.

Conclusion

Witness is a key word in relation to the *Holy Spirit, which is not surprising since he is the Spirit of mission (e.g. John 15:26; 1 John 5:6). It is the word of our testimony that is the final key to our victory once the mission of God is complete (Rev. 12:11). Witness therefore is not a passive word; even silent witness, as Jesus himself demonstrated in his trial, can be powerful. God calls us to faithful witness, and then asks us to trust him for the outcome.

See also EVANGELISM, GOSPEL.

Bibliography

J. M. Boice, *Witness and Revelation in the Gospel of John* (Grand Rapids: Zondervan, 1970); M. Green, *Evangelism in the Early Church* (London: Hodder & Stoughton Ltd, 1970); J.-P. Jossua, *The Condition of the Witness*, trans. J. Bowden (London: SWCM, 1985); P. Ricoeur, 'The Hermeneutics of Testimony', in D. Stewart and C. E. Reagan (trans.), *Essays on Biblical Interpretation* (Philadelphia: Fortress, 1980); A. A. Trites, *The New Testament Concept of Witness* (Cambridge, Cambridge University Press, 1977).

S. TAN

WOMEN, see FEMINISM, GENDER ISSUES

Women in mission

The role of women in mission has often been neglected. Even the reputable *A History of*

Christian Missions by Stephen Neill (1964) and David Bosch's magnum opus, *Transforming Mission* (1991), largely ignore the vital contribution of women in mission over the centuries. However, women have always been involved in mission since those first followers of Jesus discovered his empty tomb and rushed to give the other disciples the news. Women were active in the early church as deacons (for example, Phoebe) and teachers (for example, Priscilla). Some women remained widows so they could give their resources to the church. They, along with deaconesses and celibate women, cared for the sick and gave baptismal instruction to other women. Women were among the earliest Christian martyrs. By the mid 300s celibate women were an important part of the Christian community. After Constantine the church became more regimented and hierarchical, and women who exercised ministries of healing and education became confined to convents.

Reformation Protestants were not especially interested in cross-cultural mission with one notable exception – the Moravians. In the mid 1700s the Moravians sent *family groups as missionaries from Germany to the West Indies and elsewhere. Married women were missionary partners along with their husbands, and bands of single women were also part of the community. However, during the early decades of the modern missionary movement (usually associated with William Carey's mission to India in 1793) women were not allowed to be missionaries in their own right. They could go as wives of missionaries, and indeed male missionaries were often encouraged to marry. The wives served several purposes in the thinking of the male mission strategists. First, the existence of a wife generally signified the missionary had a peaceful intent. Secondly, she reduced her husband's temptation to sexual philandering. Finally, she provided an excellent role model of feminine behaviour and she could teach useful domestic skills to native women; together they could model the evangelical domesticity that was seen as a necessary part of a Christian home. Thus altruism and domesticity became the prevailing emphases for the wives. Dana Robert, who has written extensively on the place of the Christian home as a mission strategy for missionary wives, argues that by the 1830s domesticity had become for women the dominating discourse and that the object lesson of a civilized Christian home was seen as an essential mission strategy. This meant that married women were generally invisible, performing only in the private sphere, while their husbands were preaching, travelling and founding mission stations. No matter how capable and educated a wife might be, it was always assumed that men would undertake the publicly lauded role of mission leadership.

Despite this, many women became missionary wives precisely because they wanted to be missionaries and this was the only avenue open to them to pursue this vocation. Robert has ably documented this in her comprehensive study, *American Women in Mission: A Social History of Their Thought and Practice* (1996), where she relates stories of women who raged in frustration at the limits placed on their gender. She cites Ann Judson (née Hasseltine) as an example and quotes Harriet Lathrop, 'When I reflect on the multitudes of my fellow creatures who are perishing for lack of vision, and that I am living at ease, without aiding in the promulgation of the Gospel, I am almost ready to wish myself a man, that I might spend my life with the poor heathen.' Of course, many missionary wives were involved in work well beyond the domestic. They learnt the language, taught local women and girls, engaged in health work, Bible translation and even advocacy, wherever they saw injustice.

Not until the second half of the nineteenth century were single women accepted as missionaries in any significant numbers. This was due in part to the increased number of well-educated single women. Partly also, mission societies realized that their traditional strategies were not reaching women who were kept in separate quarters – in harems or zenanas in countries such as India and China. For this reason the Zenana Bible and Medical Mission was founded in Britain in 1852. The mission, now known as Interserve, employed female field staff only until as recently as 1952. Women's mission boards developed in the USA during the nineteenth century because existing American mission boards were reluctant to recruit and send single women. By the end of the nineteenth century nearly half of the mission-sending boards in the USA were women's boards, despite fears that this activity was masking the women's rights and suffrage movement. Women were on the move in mission, organizing and managing their own structures, sending women to be involved with women's issues. Women were raising financial support, interviewing candidates, corresponding with women overseas and educating their support base. Over three million women were involved, and by the early twentieth century this had become the largest women's movement in the USA. Unfortunately their existence was relatively short-lived. Male church and mission leaders suspected a different agenda and were unhappy that women's work in mission was being built up to the detriment of the general programme. They were concerned that the women's mission agencies always seemed to have enough finance while other agencies were struggling. This was partly due to large numbers of women volunteers, both at home and overseas, and to successful fundraising. The women succumbed to a variety of pressures: appeals to denominational loyalty; criticisms about duplication of resources and inefficiency; assurances that they would be represented in decision-making structures; and that their concerns would be acknowledged and served in the new 'integrated' structures. Most of the 'integration' took place in the 1920s. The demise of the women's mission organizations is a sad story: in 1922 the Presbyterian church took the decision to dissolve the Woman's Board of Foreign Missions without consulting either its membership or executive. Despite women's evident ability to maintain independent and separate structures, they had no laity rights in the churches and were forced to accept compromises which meant the eventual collapse of their organizations.

Today we witness the tragic legacy of this history. Women missionaries are often still invisible. At mission conferences and in mission journals it is usually the men who reflect on the work of mission while women's perspective can be unheard and unappreciated or confined to comments about family. This is despite there being an estimated twice the number of women missionaries as men. In the Western evangelical world of mission, there are very few women running either denominational or interdenominational mission agencies. Women are woefully underrepresented at the levels of determining policy and decision-making. Moreover, it seems that women may have even less opportunity now to be involved at these levels because of a reaction against secular feminism.

Thankfully, this is only part of the picture. We know that the heartlands of Christianity have moved and the centre of gravity has shifted south. There are now more Christians in the Two-Thirds (Majority) World than in the West, and more missionaries from the Majority World also. In many cases women seem to be preferential recipients of the gospel – perhaps because of the marginalization and alienation they experience in their own cultures. In China the house church movement has grown largely through the faithful work of the 'Bible women'; in Korea the gospel came first to the women because they were willing to read the Bible in the new simplified Korean script, while the men insisted on only reading it in Chinese. We are told that 70% of Christians in African indigenous churches are women, 80% of house church members in China are women, in Korea cell groups are mainly led by women, and in Latin America Protestant women join churches to encourage better family life while Roman Catholic women are active in the base Christian communities to improve social conditions for their families and communities. These women are particularly involved with caring for the sick and those dying from AIDS, running income-generating projects to pay school fees, caring for the orphans and the widows as well as running prayer meetings and preaching events. Women are engaged in all areas of mission service and their approach is generally holistic. For our work in the cause of the gospel to be most effective we need to acknowledge, in our structures, in our thinking, in our planning, that women, all over the world, are the majority participants in mission – as both givers and receivers.

See also GENDER ISSUES.

Bibliography

M. Adeney, 'Women in the World Christian Movement', *Crux* XXXVI, 2000, pp. 31–38; F. Bowie, D. Kirkwood and S. Ardener, *Women and Missions: Past and Present*

Anthropological and Historical Perspectives (Oxford: Berg, 1993); M. T. Huber and N. C. Lutkehaus (eds.), *Gendered Missions: Women and Men in Missionary Discourse and Practice* (Ann Arbor: University of Michigan Press, 1999); D. Robert, *American Women in Mission: A Social History of their Thought and Practice* (Macon, GA: Mercer University Press, 1996); D. Robert (ed.), *Gospel Bearers, Gender Barriers* (Maryknoll: Orbis Books, 2002); R. Tucker, *Guardians of the Great Commission* (Grand Rapids: Zondervan, 1988); 'Women and Mission', *International Review of Mission* 93, 2004; Women in Mission Study Group, <http://www.missionstudies.org>.

C. ROSS

Word

The Hebrew Bible offers different terms for word: *mar* and *dābār*, the most relevant being *dābār*. As a noun it can be translated as 'word', 'speech', while as a verb it is translated as 'to speak', 'to declare'. In the NT, the terms used are *logos* and *rema*, although *logos* is the most frequent.

Word in the Bible

'Word' relates first to the creating power of *God: God spoke, uttered his word, and it came to be (Gen. 1:3, etc.). This power of God is still evident in creation, which continues to obey God's word (Ps. 148:8; cf. Heb. 1:3). God's power is made evident through his active and dynamic word (Isa. 55:10–11), which is compared to 'a hammer that breaks a rock in pieces' (Jer. 23:29), indicating that God's word powerfully accomplishes that of which it speaks. Frequently 'word' refers to the way in which God reveals himself, as in 'the word of the Lord', a phrase which introduces many of the OT prophetic books (e.g. Jer. 1:2; Hos. 1:1, etc.). Similarly, prophetic writings have expressions such as 'thus says the Lord' or 'hear the word of God'. The church can thus be encouraged in its mission to believe that God's word which it proclaims has power within itself to fulfil God's purposes to convict and convert, and to reveal God without the need to manipulate or distort it.

The NT has continuity with the OT's understanding of word, both as the way in which God reveals himself (Luke 11:28; Rom. 9:6) and as God's dynamic power acting through *Jesus (Matt. 8:8, 16; Luke 4:36). There is a new dimension, however, in that the word itself becomes a living person in Jesus, who is also the incarnation of all OT wisdom traditions, embodying the creative and personal reality of God himself (John 1:14; cf. 1:3, 10). Christ himself is God's revealed Word (Heb 1:2). The word therefore becomes proclamation and action embodied in a person. Mission is thus essentially personal; the word is not just to be proclaimed verbally, it is embodied in people and churches who demonstrate it in their lives and their actions.

Furthermore, the word refers to the content of what Jesus and the early church proclaimed, understood as the *proclamation of the kingdom of God (Mark 4:14; Matt. 13:19; Luke 5:1; 11:28; John 5:37–38; Acts 4:31). The *gospel preached is the word of truth (Eph. 1:13) and life (Phil. 2:16; cf. John 6:68). Jesus Christ himself becomes the content of the word preached (1 Cor. 1:23; 15:12; 2 Cor. 1:19; 11:4; Phil. 1:15). Thus, the word is both the message Jesus came to bring and the message *about* him, which together form the scriptural witness. This proclaimed *logos* is the word of *truth, because he himself is the truth that liberates (John 17:17; 14:6; 8:32). In the words of a document produced by a group of evangelical Protestants and Catholics: 'in communion with the body of faithful Christians through the ages, we also affirm together that the entire teaching, worship, ministry, life, and mission of Christ's Church is to be held accountable to the final authority of Holy Scripture, which, for Evangelicals and Catholics alike, constitutes the word of God in written form (2 Tim. 3:15–17; 2 Pet. 1:21)' (C. Colson and R. J. Neuhaus, *Your Word Is Truth: A Project of Evangelicals and Catholics Together*, p. 3). Mission thus depends for its power on its faithfulness to the word of God, heard as God speaking through the Scriptures, and through its witness to his living Word in Christ.

Word and mission in a postmodern world

The understanding of society and reality is being transformed by a *postmodern world that faces Christian mission with a new perception of reality(-ies). Such a transformation affects basic assumptions in Christian mission. Postmodernity rejects the understanding of truth as an all-encompassing reality, and since there is no universal or final claim to truth, everything is relative. There is no place for metanarratives, that is, the use of stories that express and interpret an understanding of history and reality in universal terms. Such a universalistic approach to reality is seen as an expression of power leading to domination and oppression, under the supernatural disguise of faith. The emphasis on individualism, hedonism and indifference, which clash with the integral meaning of the kingdom of God, affects not only individuals but also the world, and directly challenges mission.

In this context Christian mission must resist the call to downplay its message of the universal significance of Jesus Christ for humanity through its fear of being considered disdainful or intolerant towards other positions. The litmus test of authentic mission is its ability to move beyond presenting the word of God as a conceptual reality, as a set of mere doctrinal principles to be imposed on all, to showing that it is a dynamic, living Word, representing the life-transforming love of God in a growingly sceptical society. The word is much more that the text itself, since God speaks and acts in a rich variety of ways. Mission should likewise be creative in the way it speaks in each context, sometimes through symbols, images, narrative or analogies. This creativity may be particularly important in a postmodern world in which experience often supersedes rationality and images replace texts as sources of truth.

Jesus Christ, the living Word, must continue to become flesh and embody powerful truth through the church in the world. In this way the power of the word will be removed from any notion of oppression and degradation of human dignity. The life-transforming power of the word of God gives people the opportunity to be fully part of Christ's reality (Eph. 1:13).

See also REVELATION.

Bibliography

J. Barton, *People of the Book? The Authority of the Bible in Christianity* (London: SPCK, 1989); R. Bauckham, *Bible and Mission: Christian Witness in a Postmodern World* (Carlisle: Paternoster and Grand Rapids: Baker, 2003); C. Colson and R. J. Neuhaus (eds.), *Your Word Is Truth: A Project of Evangelicals and Catholics Together* (Grand Rapids: Eerdmans, 2002); S. Escobar, 'Text and Context: The Word Through New Eyes', in *A Time for Mission: The Challenge for Global Christianity* (Leicester: IVP, 2003); C. R. Padilla (ed.), *Bases Bíblicas de la Misión. Perspectivas Latinoamericanas* (Buenos Aires: Nueva Creación and Grand Rapids: Eerdmans, 1998); D. Senior and C. Stuhlmueller, *The Biblical Foundations for Mission* (Maryknoll: Orbis Books, 1983).

F. MENDEZ-MORATALLA

World

Jesus explained his own presence and mission in the world as a movement motivated by God's *love for the world (John 3:16). His life and ministry thus embodied God's first movement of *grace towards the world. In sending his apostles in mission Jesus described the nature of their presence as those that were called to him 'from the world' and then sent back into the world where they were to be salt and light as they lived and proclaimed the *gospel. This twofold movement involved in mission is clearly expressed in the Lausanne Covenant (1974): 'We affirm our belief in the one eternal God, Creator and Lord of the world, Father, Son and Holy Spirit, who governs all things according to the purpose of his will. He has been calling out from the world a people for himself, and sending his people back into the world to be his servants and his witnesses...' (para. 1).

Missionary practice through the centuries has reflected intensely at some points the motivation as well as the tension implied in this twofold action of God's call and God's sending. Such was the case in the practice of the early missionaries as depicted in the book of Acts, in the development of the monastic movement which was the source of mission activity during a good part of the Middle and Modern Ages, and in the Protestant mission movement which was strongly influenced by the Pietistic revival in the eighteenth century. After the Second World War the development of young contextual churches in mission fields that experienced processes of social change, such as independence from colonial status and nation building, prompted urgent questions about the relationship between the church and the world. During the second part of the twentieth century, missiologists grappled with the nature of missionary practices that were polarized between those that proposed that mission should allow the world to set the agenda, and those that limited mission to the proclamation of an other-worldly salvation. As in the case of other missiological questions there has been a return to Scripture in order to grasp anew a balanced understanding of biblical teaching.

Four words are used in the NT to refer to the world. First, *gē*, which is a reference to the physical earth as the dwelling of human beings, created by God (Mark 13:31; Acts 4:24; Col. 1:16; Rev. 3:10; 20:8). Second, *oikoumenē*, the inhabited earth (Matt. 24:14; Luke 2:1; 4:5; 21:25; Acts 17:6; Heb. 1:6) that may denote either humanity living in a geographical extension or within an order such as the Roman Empire. Third, *kosmos*, the most frequent term in the NT that may evoke a spatial image (John 21:25), or that encompasses the totality of creation (John 1:10), denoting structure, order, system (1 Cor. 8:6). Fourth, *aiōn*, a term that refers to time periods such as an age or an era, with special reference to the transitory character of the world as it now stands (Matt. 13:22; 1 Cor. 1:20; 7:33).

The NT usage of all these terms is rooted in the OT view of reality as created by God and dependent on his continuous action, but it also conveys the notion that this created universe and the human race are fallen and under the influence of Satan, whom Jesus describes as the 'prince of this world' (John 12:31), but whose power is limited by God's authority (John 14:30). However, the world is the object of God's liberating purpose, which is made possible through the victory of Jesus Christ in the cross and the resurrection that has made him lord above all, and whose full dominion and kingship will be manifested at the end of the present age. It is in this confidence that the church goes out in mission that aims to transform the world.

In his contribution to the Lausanne Congress, René Padilla explored in depth the missiological significance of the different meanings of *kosmos* in the NT, especially in the Johannine and the Pauline writings. For Padilla, 'the most distinctive usage of cosmos in the NT is predominantly negative. It refers to humanity, but to humanity in open hostility to God: it is personified as the enemy of Jesus Christ and his followers' (*Mission Between the Times*, p. 5). This explains the rejection of Jesus by his own people (John 3:19; 15:18, 24; 1 John 3:1, 13), due to the influence of spiritual powers hostile to human beings and to God (1 John 5:19). Blindness to the gospel comes from the influence of Satan (2 Cor. 4:4), who works through the 'elemental spiritual forces' (Gal. 4:3, 9) and 'thrones or powers' (Rom. 8:38; Eph. 1:21; Col. 1:16).

In the contemporary situation this opposition of the world to God and Jesus Christ is expressed in an unjust, materialistic social order based on selfishness and in the corresponding ideologies that explain and justify it. 'The church of Jesus Christ is engaged in a spiritual conflict with the powers of evil entrenched in ideological structures that dehumanize man, conditioning him to make the absolute relative and the relative absolute' (Padilla, *Mission*, p. 53). Mission therefore must engage these structures and not simply seek to rescue individuals from the world.

It has been a characteristic of some theologies within the ecumenical movement to underplay this conflictual dimension with the world. Unfortunately much evangelical theology has applied the conflictual model to every meaning of 'world', thus adopting a too negative view of *culture and *creation, an isolationist attitude and a judgmental posture that has hindered an *incarnational approach to mission. In mission the church is always involved in the tension between being in the world but not of it, affirming what there is of beauty, truth and goodness, whilst also confronting its evil and sin in the name of Christ.

The evangelical missionary activism of the nineteenth and twentieth centuries emphasized the geographical dimension of the world, as well as the universal thrust of the gospel as a message for all humankind. But within the presuppositions of Christendom, and as a consequence of the influence of Western individualism and of theological debates between liberals and fundamentalists, the NT eschatological vision of a transforming world was lost. Even worse, much missionary activism reflected the conditioning of the consumer society. The necessary self-criticism was included in paragraph 12 of the Lausanne Covenant: 'At other times, desirous to ensure a response to the gospel, we have compromised our message, manipulated our hearers and become unduly preoccupied with statistics or even dishonest in our use of them. All this is worldly. The church must be in the world, the world must not be in the church.'

The blind acceptance of the spirit of the age was recognized as the worst form of worldliness. Padilla's emphasis was to recover a concept of mission that took seriously the cosmic dimension of the gospel: 'The aim of *evangelization is, therefore, to lead man not merely to a subjective experience of the future salvation of his soul but to a radical reorientation of his life, including his deliverance from slavery to the world and its powers on the one hand and his integration into God's purpose of placing all things under the rule of Christ on the other' (Padilla, Mission, p. 27). In this way Padilla expected mission to recover hope and direction and become world-transforming.

During the twentieth century, the development of the social sciences provided a more precise understanding of the world in its geographical, sociological and *anthropological dimensions. Missiology and missionary practice benefits from their insights, qualified by biblical criteria. This interaction has been studied by Charles Taber. From the recovery of a biblical perspective on the world, new missiological proposals have come, which include a theological critique of contemporary culture and a new mission agenda. It is the work of evangelical missiologists such as David Smith in the UK, Tom Sine in North America, and a group of writers from the Majority World gathered by Richard Tiplady, all of whom are developing the missiological seeds planted at Lausanne, which will enable the church to relate to the contemporary world in mission with compassion and confidence.

Bibliography
J. L. González, Mañana: Christian Theology from a Hispanic Perspective (Nashville: Abingdon Press, 1990); C. R. Padilla, Mission Between the Times (Grand Rapids: Eerdmans, 1985); T. Sine, Mustard Seed Versus McWorld: Reinventing Life and Faith

for the Future (Grand Rapids: Baker, 1999); D. W. Smith, Mission After Christendom (London: Darton, Longman and Todd, 2003); C. R. Taber, To Understand the World, To Save the World (Harrisburg: Trinity Press International, 2000); R. Tiplady (ed.), One World or Many? The Impact of Globalisation on Mission (Pasadena: William Carey Library, 2003).

S. ESCOBAR

World-view

The relevance of world-view to mission has gained increasing attention over the past half-century, especially with the realization that its neglect has been historically one of the major flaws in mission thinking. It is now generally accepted that our understanding of Scripture and faith, our mission practices and perceptions of reality, are all significantly shaped by our respective world-views.

Defining world-view
Charles H. Kraft asserted that in terms of 'the culturally structured assumptions, values, and commitments underlying a people's perception of reality ... a society structures such things as what its people are to believe, how they are to picture reality, and how and what they are to analyze. People interpret and react on this basis reflexively without thinking' (Christianity with Power: Your World-view and Your Experience of the Supernatural, p. 20). Our world-view shapes our values, gives order and meaning to life and death, provides us with a model of the world and guides us in the way that we should function within it. It teaches us how the world works. It shapes every aspect of our culture, whether religion, language, family life, art, education or economics, and is in turn shaped by it. World-views are 'universes' within which people live. Because world-view is so crucial to a person, any threat to it will be unconsciously resisted. As Paul G. Hiebert writes: 'The world-view incorporates assumptions about ... the "givens" of reality. Challenges to these assumptions threaten the very foundations of their world. People resist such challenges with deep emotion, for such questions threaten to destroy their understanding of reality' (Anthropological Reflections on Missiological Issues, p. 38).

Contrasting world-views in modern missions

World-views change and adapt in the process of historical development. The Western world-view largely shifted from the premodern to the modern and on to the *postmodern, each time retaining elements of the previous way of thinking. The premodern world-view is closely linked to animism, which sees the world controlled by a multiplicity of gods, belief in the spirit world and the miraculous, and superstitions of various kinds. Modernity on the other hand is largely controlled by a dualistic world-view, which is also naturalistic and mechanistic in its view of the physical world, wherein the supernatural is marginalized. This modern world-view is rooted in Greek dualism and Enlightenment thought. Postmodernity has rejected the rationalism and optimism of modernity in favour of a more fragmented, relativist and pluralist view of reality which has no overarching 'metanarrative' to hold it together.

The early incorporation of the Platonic body-soul distinction into Christian theology laid the foundation of a pervasive dualism within Western thought. The Chinese theologian, Carver Yu, suggests that the roots of Western dualism are traceable even further back to the pre-Socratic Greeks. The adoption of their view of reality as 'reality-in-itself', uncontaminated by anything other than itself, led to the idea that reality is made up of discrete self-subsistent things, with dynamic interaction and interpenetration of being categorically excluded in principle. This perception of the unrelatedness of the world underlies the dualistic model of reality in the Western mind.

Further, scholars like David Bosch noted that the empiricist trend initiated by Copernicus, Bacon, Hume and others, combined with the rationalism introduced by Descartes, produced a climate in which autonomous reason became the final criterion for truth. Reason replaced faith and revelation as the point of departure. This led to a radical anthropocentrism that increasingly had little room for God. The rise of modern science and the subject-object distinction by which Enlightenment thought operated led increasingly to the objectification of nature. This in turn paved the way for the introduction of direct causality as the means for understanding reality, thereby eliminating the category of purpose from science. The result was a mechanistic view of a closed universe, which supposedly could be explained fully by science, with no room left for the supernatural.

This led to what Hiebert describes as a two-tier view of reality in the modern Western mind. This perceives the world in terms of soul and body, spirit and matter, and sacred and secular. These dichotomies effectively split the world into two separate, almost ironclad and unrelated, parts, which Hiebert speaks of as the upper realm of high religion and lower realm of science. The former deals with spiritual and other-worldly matters, with belief in God and inner religious experience; the latter deals with this-worldly and secular matters which are governed by scientific laws within a closed universe. But there is no real interpenetration and interaction between the two tiers! Over time the lower realm assumed greater importance and the upper realm became increasingly irrelevant. This removed the place of the miraculous, prayer, angels or demons, and similar realities. Hence the modern world-view became increasingly naturalistic in seeking to understand the world without recourse to spiritual realities.

This contrasts sharply with the supernaturalistic and more holistic world-views generally found in non-Western cultures, which Hiebert describes as three-tier. Like the modern Western view of reality, it has an upper realm of high religion and a lower realm of science or folk science. But these are not distinct categories. Immediately below the upper religious realm, which deals with theological ideas and other-worldly matters, there is a middle tier in non-Western world-views. This is the realm of folk or low religion, which deals with local gods and goddesses, ancestral spirits, demons, astrology, magic and so on. These are not merely other-worldly realities, but interact directly with the physical world. Hence the physical world, that is the bottom tier, is not merely controlled mechanistically by impersonal forces and laws, as in the modern world-view. Rather it is a relational, not deterministic, world in which not only humans, but also animals, plants and inanimate objects are often thought to have personalities, wills and life.

Thus, unlike the modern Western two-tier world-view wherein the upper and lower realms are almost totally unrelated, typically, non-Western three-tier world-views are perceived as integrated and interrelated. Details may vary with different cultures, but some key elements are common to all. They are generally holistic, with spirit and matter and the sacred and secular seen as parts of an organic whole. The universe is open, with each part interpenetrating and interconnecting with every other. Within such a world, God and deities, angels and ancestral spirits, the devil and demons, astrology, charms, miracles and other supernatural elements interact freely with the empirical realities of the physical world.

Missiological implications

The differences in world-views have tremendous implications for mission. Western scholars in the twentieth century were largely domesticated by modernity's dualistic and naturalistic world-view. As a result much of Western mission theology accepted Enlightenment presuppositions and created dichotomies between evangelism and social action, evangelization and humanization. The material world was denied any share in the presence and activity of God, and *faith became a world-denying, purely spiritual exercise, with little relevance to society, culture or politics. Clearly this dichotomy was rooted in the dualistic separation of the spiritual and the material, a distinction which is alien to the *gospel. This unbiblical dichotomy was exported with Western mission and was often adopted by non-Western converts, who took on Westernized faith and theology, and denied a theological place to their own culture. However, there seems to be a growing convergence towards a biblical holism in mission theology in recent years, which recognizes a proper distinction between evangelism and social action, but nevertheless sees them as dimensions of an inseparable and integrated strategy. This is also resulting in emerging non-Western theologies with a very different perspective on the world.

Secondly, because the average Western - missionary does not have the middle tier in his or her world-view, he or she has little or no answers for questions posed from this realm. Consequently, much of Western theology is inadequate in its treatment of supernatural realities like demons, miracles and spiritual gifts. Hiebert refers to this as 'the flaw of the excluded middle' in the Western mindset. It is this that has often prevented the gospel, framed in Western terms, from penetrating fully the non-Western mind. Hiebert's analysis finds abundant support from the fact that where the gospel today is making most headway in the Two-Thirds World, it often assumes a *Pentecostal form, which takes seriously questions about the supernatural posed by the middle tier.

A third issue arises when non-Westerners with a three-tier world-view are converted without the questions posed by the middle tier being properly addressed by the gospel. Often the new Christian returns to the shaman or temple for answers to these questions. In other words, the failure to address the middle tier of such a person's world-view often results again in a conversion to a Western cultural Christianity, rather than a genuinely indigenous Christianity. This inevitably leads to a 'split-level' Christianity, wherein the rational belief level of the indigenous convert is Christianized, but the sub-rational level of consciousness remains decidedly pagan.

These problems have led some to incorporate a postmodern approach in their world-view and mission thinking. Postmodernism affirms a knowledge that is not merely objective, but relational, experiential and perspectival. It leads to creative, interactive and open-ended ways of doing mission. But clearly, to give reality meaning we need meta-narrative, not merely contextual perspective and open interpretation. The end result of postmodernism is an incoherent world where ultimately there is no possibility of knowing universal truths or ethical norms. Nevertheless, postmodernism has reintroduced the possibility of the spiritual dimension, which has led many into a new search for a meaningful spirituality, and this has given mission new opportunities for exploration and creative engagement with the culture.

The way forward

The above demonstrates that a proper understanding of world-views is crucial to mission thinking and practice. Some would like to have one single universal Christian world-view.

That, however, would not be possible, as every world-view is distinguished by different cultural characteristics. But we can affirm that Christians from different cultures should share some basic similarities in their respective world-views because of their common biblical faith. First, a Christian world-view should be defined by the fullness of God's revelation of himself and the universe in Scripture, including the whole supernatural dimension. Second, we must reject the Greek dualism that has plagued much of Christian thought for two millennia, resulting in the unbiblical dichotomization of body or soul, matter or spirit, and social action or evangelism. We need to recover a proper biblical vision of the world in integrated relationship. Finally, in contrast to postmodernism's total agnosticism and rejection of metanarratives, as well as the parallel tendency towards religious pluralism, our world-views need to affirm unambiguously the possibility of knowing truth, both about God and his universe, even if we concede that our knowledge is only partial and dimly perceived.

See also CULTURE.

Bibliography
D. Bosch, *Transforming Mission: Paradigm Shifts in Theology of Mission* (Maryknoll: Orbis Books, 1991); P. G. Hiebert, *Anthropological Reflections on Missiological Issues* (Grand Rapids: Baker, 1994); C. H. Kraft, *Christianity with Power: Your World-view and Your Experience of the Supernatural* (Ann Arbor: Servant, 1989); B. J. Walsh and J. R. Middleton, *The Transforming Vision: Shaping A Christian World-view* (Downers Grove: InterVarsity Press, 1984); C. Yu, *Being and Relation: A Theological Critique of Western Dualism and Individualism* (Edinburgh: Scottish Academic Press, 1987); H. Yung, 'A Systematic Theology that Recognizes the Demonic', in A. Scott Moreau *et al.* (eds.), *Deliver Us from Evil* (Monrovia: MARC, 2003).

H. YUNG

Worship

This article is structured in two parts – the first part gives an outline of a missional theology of worship, the second looks at some contextual factors with a few suggestions as to the light each part can shed on the other.

Outline of a missional theology of worship
These broad biblical principles are transcultural and valid for all time and every culture:

The trinitarian basis of worship
The Triune Godhead is the source, means and end of worship (Rom. 11:36). But, as Robert Taft reminds us, 'liturgy is not a thing but a meeting of persons' (*Beyond East and West*, p. 243). It is 'love responding to love' (J. Cornwall, *Let us Worship*, p. 59). This relationship, begun in a formal way at our conversion, is meant to be 'a never-ending, ever-increasing discovery of more and more of God's glory with greater and ever-greater joy in him' (J. Piper, *God's Passion for His Glory*, p. 37).

Yet each person of the Godhead plays a distinctive role in worship: The Father initiates our worship (John 4:23), the Son mediates it (Heb. 9:14) and the Spirit empowers it (Phil. 3:3). We worship by means of the Spirit, understanding worship here as the totality of a life offered up in service to God, which would obviously include 'public worship'.

What this focus on the trinitarian basis of worship can do for us is to relieve us of the ungodly drive to try to make worship 'happen'. Obviously, our active response to God is a necessity but our worship (thankfully!) is carried by the Father's initiative, offered through the mediation of Jesus and empowered by the Holy Spirit. Worship conducted in this way will inspire humble dependence on God in our mission, through which God invites all people to enter into and share in the glory of his trinitarian life. Mission is thus first an invitation to worship, and as such becomes an invitation to share in the climactic gathered worship of the nations around the throne of heaven in Revelation. This is the goal of mission and it is an act of universal worship.

The definition of worship
According to C. E. B. Cranfield's threefold definition the word 'worship' is used in three ways:

(1) to denote a particular element of what is generally referred to as worship, namely, adoration;

(2) to denote generally the public worship of the religious community gathered together and also the private religious exercises of the family and the individual; and

(3) in a still wider sense, 'to denote the whole life of the community or of the individual viewed as service of God' (quoted by Hilber, in *JETS*, 39, p. 177).

I will refer to these three aspects of worship as Worship I, Worship II and Worship III. All three can be verified in Scripture, through what I call the 'triangle of worship': worship as heart attitude, worship as the work of the people of God, and worship as Christian ethical action in the world.

The heart of worship (Worship I)

Without an individual who worships from the heart, no corporate worship would be possible (Col. 3:16; Eph. 5:19; Heb. 12:28–29). The internal attitudes for a 'heart of worship' include prayer (confession, petition and intercession) and praise (thanksgiving, praise and adoration). Mission is therefore an invitation to a change of heart.

The community of worship (Worship II)

As the early church began to absorb and express the significance of Jesus' death and resurrection as the Lamb of God (with the eventual transcending of temple liturgy and animal sacrifice) a radical 'spiritualization' of worship began. It most certainly did not mean the abolition of time, place and forms of worship. Peter likens Christians to living stones (1 Pet. 2:5). Notice the rich temple imagery used by Peter, signifying not the denigration of temple liturgy but its transcendent culmination, completion and perfecting in Christ (see also Heb. 13:15).

To talk of the 'spiritualization' of worship in the NT has absolutely nothing to do with worship that is privatized, unreal, vacuous or ephemeral. Rather, the worship enabled by the Spirit through the Son is to be seen as more radically real and life-changing than any other kind of worship. 'Forms of worship' are never abolished in the NT, but made subservient and relative to the explosive reality of new life in Christ.

The other radical NT insight into worship noticed by Alexander Schmemann is that 'Christianity was preached as a saving faith and not as a saving cult. In it the cult [forms of worship] was not an object of faith but its result' (A. Schmemann, *Introduction to Liturgical Theology*, p. 107). We cannot be saved by worship, not even Christian worship. We can only be saved by faith in the finished work of Christ. Worship is the result of salvation by faith and not its means. However, the context of worship can be the place where this is realized.

Worship in the NT – at least Worship II as defined by Cranfield – is therefore the public work of the community of believers, clearly involving cooperative, collective social action expressed in social practices. From this perspective mission becomes an invitation to belong to a worshipping community.

The lifestyle of worship (Worship III)

In Romans 12:1 Paul radicalizes, realizes, and spiritualizes worship. One's entire life from beginning to end, every thought, word, action and desire is to be offered to God – nothing is excluded (cf. 1 Cor. 10:31). Again we need to be reminded that 'spiritual' worship is not the denial of the real but its absolute restoration and recovery. Nothing in all reality is outside the worship of God who is reality.

The writer to the Hebrews also picks up on the 'earthiness' of spiritual worship as lifestyle and 'this-worldliness' when he pairs the sacrifice of praise with the sacrifice of doing good and sharing with others (Heb. 13:16). This sacrifice is as important and pleasing to God as is the sacrifice of praise. Public praise of God (Worship II) and the doing of good works (Worship III) are not the same thing but they are inseparably linked in the biblical writer's mind as different aspects of the same reality of worship (Worship II and Worship III still fall under the larger definition of worship). This is because they both spring from the motive of glorifying God and result in glory to God.

It is important to understand that Worship I, II and III actually form a cohesive, integrated unit under the generic name 'worship'. Worship I facilitates Worship II, and Worship II is the preparation for Worship III. Worship III is thus the concrete outworking of a mission heart and a mission community, and as we offer and present ourselves as a 'living sacrifice' (Rom. 12:1–2) through our service to the world, every dimension of a 'lifestyle of mission' can be offered to God as an act of worship.

The three-component model of Christian worship

Since Worship II is the public face of the church, it can be argued that it is the strongest context for the fulfilment of the mission of the church. Thomas Oden maintains that the strongest and surest medium for the transmission of the Christian faith is what we have called Worship II, liturgy and church practice.

It is these practices which we must look at in the light of Acts 2:42. Although Luke lists four elements in this verse I believe that there are three underlying functions which the Holy Spirit energizes in cooperation with united groups of believers:

(1) The kerygmatic function: all actions facilitating the proclamation of the gospel (e.g. the apostles' preaching).

(2) The koinoniac function: all actions which build the Christian community (e.g. fellowship and the breaking of bread).

(3) The leitourgic function: all actions which facilitate prayer and praise to God (e.g. prayer) (D. Pass, *Music and the Church*, p. 68).

It is through these practices inside and outside the walls of the church that the church fulfils its mission. Worship is therefore essential to mission: where the worship fails, the mission fails.

The current situation in worship worldwide

1. The *Pentecostal movement has had an immense impact on the worship of Christianity worldwide, I believe much larger than that of the liturgical movement. Within a short space of time much traditional worship has been entirely abandoned and what is left is under major pressure from a seemingly unstoppable global charismatic movement. The emerging pattern worldwide seems to be the structure discerned by Daniel Albrecht in his excellent research on the worship rites of Pentecostals:

A: Gathering/greeting rites
B: Rite of worship and praise
C: Rite of pastoral message
D: Rite of altar/response
E: Dispersing/farewell rites

We should expect these trends to continue and even accelerate. One striking example is that within less than a generation social practices like baptism and the Lord's Supper are rapidly becoming extinct in large sections of Christianity. In the Nairobi Statement on Worship and Culture released by the Lutheran World Federation in 1996, for example, a plea is made to member churches to 'recover the centrality of Baptism, Scripture with preaching, and the every-Sunday celebration of the Lord's supper' (C. Plantinga and S. Rozeboom, *Discerning the Spirits*, p. 66).

2. Globalization ensures that the commercialization and dissemination of largely Western and largely English worship music cover the globe from Sao Paolo to Sri Lanka. At the same time 'world music' is growing in popularity in the West.

3. Where do we go from here? How can we combine faithfulness to the gospel and the Bible while remaining flexible as the Christian movement expands into a multitude of different cultures and still needs to adequately *contextualize worship? Primarily we need a return to Scripture as the norm and content of our worship while at the same time being completely open to the Holy Spirit. It is possible to combine a strong commitment to both and it will become ever more necessary as the new millennium unfolds. Secondly, we need to develop a theology of worship which is biblically based but culturally relevant. It will be important also to look at current worship practices inherited from our past and instead of abandoning them in their current form try to distil their real meaning from Scripture and create new culturally relevant forms (C. Kraft, *Anthropology for Christian Witness*, pp. 132–147). I am thinking here particularly of two social practices central to Christian worship, baptism and the Lord's Supper, which fulfil what I have called the koinoniac function. Can the Christian church live without them or are we impoverished by their rapidly disappearing presence in the contemporary church?

Following a missiological approach would mean that new social practices would have to be invented, with new forms in new contexts, to carry biblical meanings by the power of the

Spirit. To do this we must begin with an adequate biblical interpretive framework: most Protestants look on the Lord's Supper in a purely 'symbolic' way (i.e. a minimized social practice). It is a 'pious memory exercise', but this is not adequate and does not do justice to its place in Scripture. Secondly, a biblical interpretative framework must be embodied in our religious practice and belief, in short, in our tradition. In the situation of a fast-growing Christianity powered by charismatic phenomena, the Lord's Supper has developed anomalies in this new context, producing negative effects: many Christians don't see why they should bother with it (G. Lindbeck, *The Nature of Doctrine*, p. 39).

Thirdly, the social practice of the Lord's Supper must be seen as belonging to the koinoniac function. Once we do that, the way is open for us to see that a 'privatized cocktail party' for individuals will never do justice to its essential koinoniac meaning: which means we must save the meaning, but change the form.

The centrality of Scripture to the process of renewal is thus reaffirmed: the Spirit that empowers the collective social actions by which the church fulfils its mission is the same Spirit which inspired the Scriptures and makes them come alive as the Word of God to us today. In this way we can read the Scriptures about the Lord's Supper with new eyes, as when Tom Driver suggests that 'the real presence of Christ is the spirit of Christ active and experienced in the ritual performance (T. Driver, *The Magic of Ritual*, p. 211).

There is a great need for new social practices which can enable the kerygmatic, koinoniac and leitourgic functions. The key to collective social action working in the church is first and foremost the Holy Spirit, but in conjunction with what Tuomela calls a shared we-attitude 'where the we-attitude must be a "primary" reason for the repeated activity [the social practice]' (Tuomela, p. 94). One is reminded of the believers gathered on the day of Pentecost 'all together in one place' (Acts 2:1).

The three modes of the church – kerygmatic, koinoniac and leitourgic – are thus an interlocking, independent and balanced mechanism of the Spirit which results in these outcomes: no kerygma, no koinonia; no koinonia, no leitourgia. First the gospel: a repentant and believing response to the reconciling love of God in conversion is an absolute necessity. This response creates a community unlike any other (Gal. 3:26–29). And unless that community is living in the light of the gospel, it will be, as it sadly often is, a corrupted *community. And a corrupted community cannot worship effectively: it can only fight about worship. From opposite ends of the Christian tradition we find evidence that this breakdown of community, the erosion of a 'shared we-attitude', is the greatest problem facing global Christianity in its mission and worship. From a Roman Catholic perspective, J. L. Segundo comments that it seems that 'our yearning and zeal for ritual reform and liturgical renewal is a superficial way of solving a much deeper problem. For it enables us to hide from the real problem: The problem of community' (quoted in Driver, *The Magic of Ritual*, p. 204). And a recent charismatic writer points to the same problem of community with different words: 'The most powerful hindrance to heavenly worship being experienced today is the general passivity of your typical congregation' (B. Sorge, *Following the River*, p. 63). We are passive because we have lost touch with the liberating power of the gospel which then leads to a breakdown in koinonia. No amount of 'top-down' liturgy or worship renewal can counter this lethargy in anything more than a superficial way. This is where missiological theory and practice must meet: where worship succeeds, the mission succeeds; where the mission succeeds, the worship succeeds.

Bibliography

D. Albrecht, *Rites in the Spirit* (Sheffield: Sheffield Academic Press, 1999); J. Cornwall, *Let Us Worship* (Plainfield: Bridge Publishing, 1983); T. Driver, *The Magic of Ritual* (San Francisco: HarperSanFrancisco, 1991); J. Hilber, 'Theology of Worship in Exodus 24', *JETS* 39, 1996, pp. 177–189; C. Kraft, *Anthropology for Christian Witness* (Maryknoll: Orbis Books, 1996); G. Lindbeck, *The Nature of Doctrine* (Philadelphia: Westminster, 1989); T. Oden, *The Living God*, vol. I (San Francisco: HarperCollins, 1987); D. Pass, *Music and the Church* (Johannesburg: Password, 2005); J. Piper, *God's Passion for His Glory* (Wheaton: Crossway, 1998); C. Plantinga and S. Rozeboom (eds.),

Discerning the Spirits (Grand Rapids: Eerdmans, 2003); A. Schmemann, *Introduction to Liturgical Theology* (Crestwood: St Vladimir's Seminary Press, 1996); B. Sorge, *Following the River* (Missouri: Oasis House, 2004); R. Taft, *Beyond East and West* (Rome: Pontifical Oriental Institute, [2]1997); R. Tuomela, *The Philosophy of Social Practices* (Cambridge: Cambridge University Press, 2002).

D. B. PASS

Youth culture

Identifying youth culture

After the Second World War Western countries saw the emergence of a phenomenon now identified as 'youth culture'. The word 'culture' here means the totality of cultural expressions of a certain group within a general population, in this case the young generation. In this sense, youth culture is a 'sub-culture', which shares some of the characteristics of the general culture, but also has its distinctive expressions. It is therefore a parallel culture to the prevailing adult culture, and in the West tries to be consciously separate and deliberately different as a way of exploring identity.

In many traditional societies, such as in Africa, elaborate 'rites of passage' ensure an organized transition from childhood to adulthood, often around the ages of fourteen to sixteen. In such societies where the livelihood of the extended family is dependent on the work of as many people as possible, children take on the responsibilities of adulthood very quickly and an extended period of intermediate youth is less likely than in the West. However, influenced by global culture and especially TV and the Internet, the phenomenon of 'youth culture', with common characteristics, is becoming worldwide as music, lifestyle and fashions become globalized. Thus, some speak of youth as the 'MTV generation', after the globally available popular music television channel.

In order to distinguish itself from the prevalent culture, youth culture employs certain 'semantic signs', with specific meanings which together form a whole semantic system, often only recognizable to themselves. These signs help young people to identify themselves with a certain group and to define their own philosophy. Important signs are seen in music, clothing styles, language (i.e. 'slang' or linguistic particularities), forms of bodily expressions such as dance (e.g. hip hop) and modes of movement, hair styles, and other modifications of the body, such as earrings, piercings and even 'branding'. Youth culture subdivides into many diverse sub-groups which use different semantic signs to differentiate themselves from each other. Each sub-culture presents itself as a complete entity with a defined set of such characteristics. However, there is still a lot of common ground and overlap amongst all these youth cultures.

Familiarity with these signs certainly makes it easier to communicate, although with confident love, acceptance and time, meaningful relationships can be established which transcend generational or cultural differences. However, the signs are always rapidly changing and adapting within different contexts, and every few years there is a new wave, a new trend or 'hype'. In addition, the cycle of re-invention of youth culture is seemingly accelerating. On the other hand, new expressions of youth culture also tend to 'quote' from former cultures, creating new and unique blends of innovative and repackaged images, forms, musical styles and other marks which constantly shape and re-shape the culture of the young generation. Sometimes this culture is driven by commercial interests and not by young people themselves.

Youth culture and the church

The church in the West has generally struggled to relate and respond to youth culture. Partly because the Western church has been too entrenched in Enlightenment thinking, youth culture moved on too quickly for it, leaving it way behind and perceived by young people as too institutional, anachronistic and boring. In recent years this has changed, as expressions of church have developed that resonate and engage with youth culture. Mission requires a process of *inculturation and translation with expressions of the *gospel which identify with the issues young people have and translate the faith into the framework of their cultural expressions. *Music is a particularly strong component of this identity, as also is informality, relationality, and the enhanced importance of images and shared experiences in preference to written texts. To be true to its original calling, the church must again and again overcome the cultural limitations of its own background and history and incarnate its message into each *culture. Too often the church has expected young people to adjust to church culture, instead of seeking to accept and reach them where and as they are.

In seeking to do this, Christians should seek local, regional and even global cooperation. Youth culture can be studied like all cultures, and creative ways of *evangelism and *discipleship have been developed and can be shared. Here mutual encouragement and learning can enhance our effectiveness and guide the church to be a true and always up-to-date and visionary witness to the unchanging gospel of our Lord Jesus Christ.

Practical missionary engagement

Despite strong regional differences (relating to young people in North America is very different even from Europe), some practices may be transferable and adaptable to other contexts. Models of good practice can be shared. In Marburg, Germany, a local youth network of several churches decided to participate in a nationwide evangelistic youth outreach which was transmitted from Berlin to over 800 venues via a special satellite signal. Instead of simply inviting young people to a central place for five nights in the traditional crusade manner, they decided to rent an empty shop and lived 'publicly' for ten days with ten young Christian boys and girls and several youth workers. The young people went to school in the mornings and wore T-shirts associated with 'ten days'. This attracted many young people to come by and spend the day with them, and a public and *holistic witness was established. The five more directly evangelistic nights were integrated with the communal experience, and as a result quite a number of unchurched young people came to faith. This shows how a relaxed, relational, community-based approach, far removed from the institutional and formal, can open a door to authentic witness, and this principle can be reproduced in any context.

In Cakovec, Croatia, a group of young people started a series of music events in a basement and called it 'Jesus goes Underground'. The unusual venue and music attracted many young people. In Europe

'youth churches', often run by young people themselves, have developed creative forms of worship and discipleship, and sometimes attract many hundreds of young people. They can serve as a half-way contact point with the institutional church, and ideally need to avoid exclusivity and instability through some measure of integration with a larger body of believers.

Many youth ministries involve inspiring social involvement, which channels the energy to change the world in practical ways. Others have involved young people in concerted prayer, for example the '24/7 global prayer movement' which inspires young people to pray in rotas around the clock; the answers to their prayers are an encouragement to faith.

Other examples show that relationships and openness to new cultural expressions are the key to engaging with youth culture. The Bible's truth must be brought to life by living, authentic people. That is more important to young people than technological gadgets or following the newest fad. Authenticity and openness, truth and integrity, are essential. Young people sniff hypocrisy immediately, and often find the church stuffy, impersonal and distanced. They long for real and close relationships, not only with their peers, but also with older mentors who take a genuine interest in them. Because many are confused, fearful and untrusting, coming from broken homes and sexually abusive relationships, sometimes trapped in a drug and alcohol culture, often with no moral framework to draw on, in a context of caring relationships they are open to moral guidance.

Thus, mission with young people must be a living and creative response to the changes in sociological, cultural and technological realities of today's world. This is a highly sacrificial ministry, requiring endless patience and often disappointment. It is a ministry for the long haul, which demonstrates a commitment not often seen in a culture of instant gratification. In the final analysis, truth, authenticity, relationships and practical love will be more important than methods and programmes.

Bibliography

D. Claydon (ed.), 'The 12/25 Challenge: Reaching the Youth Generation', Lausanne Occasional Paper 52, in A New Vision,

A New Heart, A Renewed Call, Vol. 2 (Pasadena: William Carey Library, 2005) or <http://www.lausanne.org>; D. Borgman, *When Kumbaya Is Not Enough: A Practical Theology for Youth Ministry* (Toronto: Hendrickson Publishers 1997); K. C. Dean, C. Clark and D. Rahn (eds.), *Starting Right: Thinking Theologically about Youth Ministry* (Grand Rapids: Zondervan/Youth Specialties, 2001); D. Lambert, *Teaching that Makes a Difference: How to Teach for Holistic Impact* (Grand Rapids: Zondervan/Youth Specialties, 2004); D. Robbins, *This Way to Youth Ministry: An Introduction to the Adventure* (Grand Rapids: Youth Specialties, 2004); M. H. Senter III, W. Black, C. Clark and M. Mel, *Four Views of Youth Ministry and the Church* (Grand Rapids: Zondervan/Youth Specialties, 2001); <http://www.youthspecialties.com>.

R. WERNER

Zion

Zion, the city of Jerusalem, has been historically the epicentre of God's mission to the nations. This role, however, has blurred due to contradictory identities Zion now seems to echo. Thinking of 'Zion' reminds us of the song, 'let us go to Zion', but also of the slogan 'Zion for Jews only'. How can this paradox be reconciled?

Definition

Zion means fortress, and refers to the temple mount, south-east of Jerusalem. By extension it came to refer to the city of Jerusalem, the Promised Land and the new creation. Metaphorically it refers to the people of Jerusalem and the believing community (i.e. the church worldwide). Believers are the children of Zion and Yahweh is their Father. Since he is king, Zion can be called his royal family.

Zion in the Bible

Scripture witnesses consistently to the pivotal role which Zion plays in the fulfilling of God's purposes for the nations. It is a focal point of God's presence and power both for Israel and for all nations.

Old Testament

Although the term 'Zion' is absent, movement towards the promised land is a prominent motif in the Pentateuch. Abraham visits the vicinity of Jerusalem. He receives blessings from Melchizedek, Jerusalem's priest-king and pays him a tithe (Gen. 14:18–20). Moses sings about Yahweh leading the Israelites to 'the mountain of your inheritance', which probably refers to Zion (Exod. 15:17). Mount Zion originally was the Jebusite temple mount, but was conquered by David (2 Sam. 5:6–9).

In the Prophets, the people and the city of Zion undergo both judgment and transformation. Zion becomes corrupt. Her land is deserted and people sent into exile. Hence Yahweh plans to restore and redeem Zion (Isa. 1:21, 27).

The 'transformation of Zion' is the theme of the book of Isaiah. God establishes transformed Zion as the refuge for the 'poor', the humble and the believing of the nations. On Mount Zion, he breaks down the barriers between Israel and the nations (Isa. 25).

The Psalms focus on the mount and the city of Jerusalem as symbols of *unity and *peace. The beauty, compactness, thrones and festivals of the city attract the nations. Similarly the mount is praised as being Yahweh's highest abode and throne where he fights and subdues the enemies. It is the centre from where rivers of paradise flow (Pss. 46 – 48; 76; 84; 87; 122).

New Testament

In the Gospels, Jesus keeps going to Jerusalem. It is where Jesus wants to die. His words 'Destroy this temple and I will raise it again in three days' (John 2:19) mean that his body has taken over the role of the temple. True worship will be offered neither on Mount Gerizim, nor on Mount Zion.

In Luke–Acts, the light of the gospel spreads out from Jerusalem through Samaria, through Antioch to the end of the world. The Ethiopian eunuch journeys to Jerusalem to worship (Luke 13:33–34; Acts 8:27).

In the letters, Zion brings Israel and the nations together. On this mountain, the Jews and Gentiles become one new entity and heirs together in the promises of God. It is the place where Jesus triumphs over forces of division and death and paves the way for unity between nations (2 Cor. 5:19; Col. 2:15). In Romans 9 – 11, Paul uses the Zion theme to deal with the issue of Jew-Gentile relationships: Jews stumbled over the stone set in Zion (Jesus the Messiah), but Gentiles in faith used it as a stepping stone to salvation (Rom. 9:33; 1 Pet. 2:6). In future Jews will also believe in Jesus and be joined again to the main tree. Jesus takes over and transfers the role of the temple to the body of believers (1 Cor. 3:16; 6:19). In this body, Jews and Gentiles become one new person.

In the books of Hebrews and Revelation, Mount Zion is the heavenly Jerusalem. It is where Jesus holds the great banquet inviting all for fellowship with the saints. It is from there he will rule for ever (Heb. 12:22–23; Rev. 14:1).

This brief review shows the central place that Zion, and therefore the people of God, occupies in God's saving purposes. However, this does not imply ecclesiocentrism, since it is God as Yahweh who is the real protagonist of history, and it is he who graciously chooses Zion as the place of his sovereignty. So it is God himself, and not the church, who is the true centre of gravity of mission.

The missiology of Zion

The missiology of Zion functions within the creative tension between the particularity and *universality of the revelation of God. Zion plays a role in God's mission of reaching out to all nations and bringing them into the citizenship of God's people.

Particularity refers to Yahweh's choice of Zion, through whom he sends a redeemer to fulfil his covenant and disclose his will in a given historical context. *Universality* points to Yahweh's purpose in choosing Zion for channelling salvation to all humanity. Particularity provides mission with theological motivation and methodology, while universality provides it with its goal: the blessing of all nations (Gen. 12:3). The interaction of the universal and the particular results in three characteristics of biblical mission: centripetality, centrifugality and citizenship.

Centripetal movement refers to the movement of the nations towards Zion. The light of Yahweh's teachings, shining through Zion, attracts the nations. They come, worship, and find acceptance and salvation (Isa. 56:3–8; 66:19–21).

Centrifugal movement is the movement of messengers away from Zion towards the nations. Yahweh sends messengers to bring in the dispersed Israelites and believing nations (Isa. 66:19).

Citizenship occurs when the nations go up to Zion. They pay tribute, and do menial jobs like building walls, feeding flocks, and dressing the vine (Isa. 60:5–10), which might indicate their subservient status. But the nations seem engaged, like the Israelites, in all, including priestly, work (Isa. 56:3–5; 66:19–21). Moreover, they make Zion their home, and claim it as their birthplace (Ps. 87:4–7). Their kings sit in assembly as equals with Israel (Ps. 47:9). This suggests that the nations are not inferior but they become equal citizens.

How theology informs the missiology of Zion

The Abrahamic covenant provides the plan for Zion's missiology

The Abrahamic *covenant provides the plan and goal of mission. Yahweh chooses the family of Abraham *from* and *for* the nations. The family of Abraham is chosen as a vehicle of blessing and is blessed first; and then through her, blessings reach all the families. Similarly, Yahweh chooses Zion as his family, and blesses her so that the blessings might reach all nations. Yahweh promises both Abraham and Zion protection, as a friend to their friends and foe to their foes (Gen. 12:2; Isa. 60:12). Abraham is asked to 'be a blessing'! Similarly, Zion is asked to 'arise and shine'; in other words, to show the light of her righteousness and be a blessing (Isa. 60:1).

The above plan shows that the particularity of Yahweh's choice of Zion is to achieve universality of blessings whereby all human families are benefited. Particularity is intended to lead to universality. The church is therefore constituted as the people of God precisely for universal mission.

The particularity of election and exaltation triggers centripetality

When David captures the fortress 'Zion', he brings into it the ark of the covenant. This signals Yahweh's choice of Zion as his abode. Thus the redeemer is sent to Zion to mediate the everlasting covenant (Isa. 59:21). Yahweh exalts Zion. He puts in her his word and spirit. He bestows upon her blessings: new relationship, name, offspring and protection – 'the nation or kingdom that will not serve you will perish' (Isa. 60:12). Thus he endows her with the splendour of his glory, which pulls nations towards Zion (Isa. 60:9; 55:5). With singing, the nations stream to Zion. They offer their wealth and allegiance to Yahweh. They hear his words and receive blessings. When the presence of God is seen in the church all cultures will be attracted to it.

The universality of the covenant triggers centrifugality

Through the covenant, Yahweh entrusts Zion, like Abraham, with the role of channelling the blessings to all nations. She is set as light and covenant to the nations, and must let her light shine outward (Isa. 42:6; 60:1). 'Light for the Gentiles [nations]' could be passive or active: the passive refers to setting an example of ethical and moral excellence; the active refers to 'sending missionaries' to the nations. Most opt for a passive interpretation, because 'setting an example' is emphasized; without it active missionary work would be futile. Nevertheless, there is ample evidence for active mission in the book of Isaiah.

Yahweh establishes Zion as his 'priests' and 'ministers' for mediating his blessings to the nations personally and actively (Isa. 61:6). The kinsman redeemer, who is sent, is the model for mission. Since Yahweh redeems Zion through righteousness, not allowing any evasion of justice, it is hinted that the redeemer takes Zion's punishment upon himself (Isa. 1:27); he thus accomplishes the work of redemption for all who repent in Zion (Isa. 59:20). Following the redeemer, evangelists are sent to Zion herself first, and then to all nations with good news of salvation. The nations are brought to Zion as faith offering and offspring (Isa. 40:9; 66:19).

The centrifugality thus leads to centripetality: the gathering and bringing of the nations to Zion. It is Yahweh, the great gatherer, who draws them in, to join the line of salvation along which the chosen people move (Isa. 56:8). The church is sent out in mission in order to gather others in.

The theology of realized eschatology triggers a change of status

The theology of realized *eschatology advocates living in tune with Yahweh's character in the light of the fast-approaching day of the

Lord. When the nations come into Zion, they enjoy equal freedom and a change of status. This can be traced to the divine oracle 'maintain justice and do what is right' (Isa. 56:1–8). This oracle lifts the ban on foreigners and eunuchs approaching the altar for serving Yahweh. The prophets and the Torah rest on justice and righteousness. By doing justice, one imitates Yahweh, who advocates solidarity with widows, orphans and foreigners (Mic. 6:8). The call to Zion, 'Arise and shine' echoes the call to Abraham: 'walk before me and be blameless' (Isa. 60:1; Gen. 17:1). Zion should so attune her behaviour to Yahweh that the light emerging from his instructions may shine through her outwards to the nations.

The oracle is rooted in the 'day of the LORD', that has arrived 'already but not yet', the day when Yahweh will even out injustice and inequality and bring foreigners and eunuchs into his house. The 'day of the LORD' signifies that King Yahweh would come as warrior-shepherd. He will fight and rescue the oppressed and marginalized faithful, leading them as sheep to the refreshing waters. In anticipation of that event, believing members of Zion community should direct their behaviour in line with Yahweh's character and develop a sense of accountability and excellence. Their new status as citizens causes the whole community to increase in perfection and exaltation, as Yahweh had promised to Israel (Deut. 26:19).

Peace and prosperity is tied to freedom and equality. The community where this happens can be called an open community. Isaiah envisages the church as Zion to be such a community, where irrespective of class, colour and gender, all are welcome to be equal members on the basis of the one criterion – *faith.

Contemporary Zion movements

Modern Zion, the actual city of Jerusalem, continues to be a hotchpotch of contentious issues, with three major monotheistic communities – Jews, Christians and Muslims – dwelling side by side and claiming stakes in the city. On the other hand, we see many micro-Zion communities emerging worldwide. First, we have the Zion movement within the Jewish communities worldwide. Redemption of and return to Zion is their common aspiration. So, they still pray 'may the Redeemer come to Zion' and greet 'next year in Jerusalem'. It is for this reason the Zion movement has embraced Jewish communities worldwide.

Secondly, we have Zion movements within the non-Jewish world. *Ama-Ziyoni*, an African Indigenous Church group, prays, 'Remember . . . this mount Zion wherein thou hast dwelt'. They sing the praises of local Mount Zion *Ekuphakameni*, 'the Elevated place which enlightens all nations', 'the city built on a mountain'.

The non-Zionic church traditions too have developed prayer mountains outside Africa. In South Korea, the best known prayer mount is of Yoido Full Gospel Church. It is in Jorimyeon in northern Gyeonggi province with facilities for 10,000 people. People pray for hours at a time, sitting or kneeling on the hard floor, and out in the open. The founders of the prayer mounts drew inspiration from the Zionic and indigenous South Korean tradition of mountain worship.

In India, many of these prayer mounts are in *ashrams*, where teacher and students live and learn, meditate and reflect together, particularly in the northern Himalayan and southern Sahyadri ranges. One such ashram is called *Sat-Tal*, established by Dr Stanley Jones. As in Africa, there are Zion Pentecostal and Apostolic churches throughout India. They are known for a simple lifestyle, fervent spirituality and fast growth.

The Zion communities listed above are not so much bonded by 'wanting to possess modern Zion', but by the ideals of purity and peace that Zion represents. They exude love for Jerusalem and loyalty to their respective Zion mounts and countries. The monotheistic groups that want to lay exclusive claims on the physical Jerusalem can learn lessons from these universal communities in emphasizing the ideals of Zion and not hankering after land in Jerusalem.

Implications for mission
Reaching out in humility
The particularity of election gives a special status to God's people. But it entails the dual responsibility of humbly channelling blessings to the nations and accountability to Yahweh. The church should never forget her particular identity as holy and gifted people, but she should cherish, preserve and sharpen it for efficient witness. Her humility and gratitude should be seen in her dialogue with, and witness to, the nations.

Mission with covenantal commitment
The universality of the covenant calls for deep commitment to the cause of mission: 'channelling God's blessings to humankind'. It encourages a kinsman-redeemer approach, entering into covenantal relationship, *incarnating into culture, and redeeming it from within.

The city of Jerusalem has served a historic and useful purpose in God's plan of salvation as a place of the death and resurrection of Jesus. It stands as a symbol of unity and peace among the nations. Though the monotheistic groups lay exclusive claim to her, Jerusalem equally belongs to the nations as their house of prayer. The kinship redeemer, Jesus, has died equally for other cities and wants us to seek their welfare and peace.

Love for the city and commitment towards its peace and prosperity are fundamental tenets that Zion theology offers to *urban missiology. One must become part of the city to know and understand her people.

Realized eschatology
Zion is established as a refuge for the 'poor' and the weak. Yahweh will come on his day and hold the church accountable for her duty of reaching out to the marginalized, orphans, widows, those whose sight and hearing are impaired, and other needy groups. Reaching out is not only a matter of social action and compassion; it means also to bring them into the fold of God's community and give equal opportunity and freedom of a new citizenship. The missiology of Zion forces us to be eschatologically oriented in our approach to others.

Conclusion
The missiology of Zion issues in centripetality, which turns into centrifugality and ends in the changed status of the 'poor'. These movements take place because of Yahweh's presence in Zion. Zion no longer only stands for the city of Jerusalem or the Jewish race. It also represents the believing community of Jews and Gentiles, across the whole earth. The believing community of Zion is confessional and egalitarian. Anyone, irrespective of

caste, class, colour, gender or ability, can, on the basis of faith, become a full and equal member.

Bibliography

A. Anderson, *Zion and Pentecost: The Spirituality and Experience of Pentecostal and Zionist/Apostolic Churches in South Africa* (Pretoria: University of South Africa Press, 2000); R. Hedlund and P. Bhakiaraj (eds.), *Missiology for the 21st Century: South Asian Perspective* (Delhi: ISPCK, 2004); S. B. Isenberg, *India's Bene Israel: A Comprehensive Inquiry and Sourcebook* (Bombay: Popular Prakashan, c. 1988); E. Jacob, *Theology of the Old Testament* (New York: Harper & Row, 1958); E. Mohol, 'Confessional Community of Isaiah 56–66: A New Paradigm for Mission' in *Missiology for the 21st Century*, pp. 24–42; M. Roth, 'Korea's Dynamic Christianity: Reflections on an Explosive Revival', in M. Roth (ed.), *Christian Commentary* (2002) <http://www.martinrothonline.com/MRCC 20.htm>; P. A. Smith, *Rhetoric and Redaction in Trito-Isaiah: The Structure, Growth and Authorship of Isaiah 56–66* (Leiden, 1995); B. Sundkler, *The World of Mission* (Grand Rapids: Eerdmans, 1965); B. Sundkler, *Zulu Zion and Some Swazi Zionists* (Oxford: Oxford University Press, 1985).

E. Mohol

INDEX OF NAMES

INDEX OF SUBJECTS

INDEX OF ARTICLES

7/24

Degree Course Offers

The only Comprehensive Guide on Entry to UK Universities and Colleges including the new UCAS Tariff

2002 entry
32nd edition

BRIAN HEAP

TROTMAN

Degree Course Offers 2002

In order to ensure that *Degree Course Offers* retains its reputation as the definitive guide for students wishing to study at UK universities, over 9,000 questionnaires are distributed, months of research and analysis undertaken, and painstaking data checking and proofing carried out.

We hope that you find this 32nd edition useful and would welcome your feedback as to how we can ensure the 33rd edition is even better.

Editorial and Publishing Team
Author Brian Heap
Compilation and Data Processing Dianah Ellis; Henry Ellis
Editorial and Production Amanda Williams, Editorial Director; Rachel Lockhart, Managing Editor; Francisca Perez, Production Manager
Advertising Sales Alistair Rogers, Advertising Manager; Jonathan Ball, Advertising Executive; Georgina Francis, Advertising Executive
(contact the team on 020 8486 1164 or email advertising@trotman.co.uk
Sales and Marketing Tom Lee, Director; Deborah Jones, Marketing Manager; Tracy Deadman, Sales & Distribution Co-ordinator.
Toby Trotman, Managing Director; Andy Fiennes Trotman, Chairman.

This 32nd edition published in 2001 in Great Britain by
Trotman and Company Limited
2 The Green, Richmond, Surrey TW9 1PL
© Brian Heap and Trotman and Company Limited

British Library Cataloguing in Publication Data
A catalogue record for this book is available from the British Library

ISBN 0 85660 615 4

Typeset by Florence Production Ltd,
Stoodleigh, Devon
Printed and bound in Great Britain
by Creative Print & Design (Wales) Ltd

UNIVERSITY COLLEGE
CHICHESTER

Here at University College Chichester, our results speak for themselves. We are in the top 26% of universities and colleges for student retention and successful degree completion, with an "efficiency" rating of 91%* against a national average of 85% for all universities. It doesn't stop there: the rate of employment for our graduates is also much higher than the national benchmark level.

What's more, we have a wide choice of undergraduate and postgraduate courses, and good inspection results are proof of their quality. Our Teaching Quality Assessment results have all achieved 20 out of 24 or higher, with two subjects (Media and Art) judged as excellent.

But they're not the only reasons why so many students choose to join us. We have a great reputation as a friendly place to study, a good social scene and two brilliant south coast campuses at Chichester and Bognor Regis.

So before you even start applying for university, start thinking about where you'll make the most of your potential.

For more information please telephone the Admissions office on 01243 816002 or Email: marketing@ucc.ac.uk ww.ucc.ac.uk

Please quote reference BHSG1.

*source: Performance indicators in Higher Education - 1996-97, 1997-98.
            Published by HEFCE, December 1999

The results don't stop when your course does.

CONTENTS

WIN £3,000!

PLUS 100 RUNNERS-UP PRIZES:
Copies of *Students' Money Matters* worth £10.99

WIN YOUR RENT!
Competition

Competition Entry Form

How To Enter

1 Please <u>underline</u> your answers clearly (a, b or c) for each of the three competition questions below.

2 Complete your name and address details overleaf.

3 Complete the questionnaire overleaf.

1 What is the maximum annual amount UK students attending a university in England or Wales will be asked to pay in tuition fees for the 2001/2002 academic year?

a. £500   b. £750   c. £1,075

2 How much is the average student (not living at home or London-based) expected to live-on during 2001/2002?

a. £3,815   b. £4,545   c. £5,545

3 What is the threshold annual salary graduates must be earning before they have to start paying back their student loans?

a. £8,000   b. £10,000   c. £12,000

Trotman publishing

WIN £3,000!

PLUS 100 RUNNERS-UP PRIZES:
Copies of Students' Money Matters worth £10.99

QUESTIONNAIRE

Name ....

Address ....

....

....

....

Postcode..

Telephone ....

Date of Birth ....

E-mail address ....

Where are you currently studying?
☐ School
☐ FE College
☐ HE College
☐ University
☐ Other..

What year are you in? ....

What subjects are you taking?

Subjects	Level	Predicted Grades
....	....	....
....	....	....
....	....	....
....	....	....
....	....	....
....	....	....

When will you be sitting your exams? ....

In which year would you like to start university? ....

Do you have internet access?
☐ at home   ☐ at school

Which subject areas are you considering studying at Higher Education?
☐ Art & Design
☐ Business
☐ Computer Studies
☐ Engineering
☐ Medicine/Healthcare
☐ Performing Arts
☐ Physical Sciences
☐ Other...

From which of the following information sources have you sought advice on entering Higher Education?
☐ UCAS Big Guide
☐ Degree Course Offers
☐ UCAS Handbook
☐ Student Book
☐ University/college literature/prospectuses
☐ The Complete Guides
☐ Other
☐ Internet
  If so which site? ....

Please photocopy this form and give to your friends

SEND COMPLETED FORMS TO: 'WIN YOUR RENT' COMPETITION, 2 THE GREEN, RICHMOND, SURREY TW9 1PL.

Data Protection: Your name and address will be held on a database and may be used to send you details of other selected products. If you do not wish to receive this information, please tick this box. ☐

Conditions of entry

1. Entry Forms with three correct answers will be entered into the Prize Draw. The Draw will be made on 1st September each year, and the winner and runners-up will be notified shortly after that date.

2. Prizes: The winner will receive a cheque for £3,000. 100 runners-up will receive copies of the 7th edition of Students' Money Matters (RRP £10.99; published May 2001).

3. All competition entrants must be students applying for 2002 entry to university or college, or current students who will still be studying for an undergraduate or postgraduate degree in 2002.

4. Only one entry is allowed per person.

5. No purchase necessary. Separate Entry Forms are available by sending an SAE to the address given above.

SPONSOR'S INTRODUCTION

Accenture is delighted to support this edition of *Degree Course Offers.*

Long established and highly regarded, *Degree Course Offers* has educated and guided generations of students through the selection process. It has grown significantly in response to huge changes in higher education over the past three decades, reflecting the wealth of opportunities in course and career choice.

With the introduction of both Curriculum 2000 in September last year as well as the new UCAS Tariff System which affects entrants to higher education from 2002 onwards, applicants need straightforward advice on choosing a university and course now more than ever. *Degree Course Offers*, now in its 32nd edition, embraces the changes taking place in higher education while remaining true to its fundamental principles – to provide a first-stop reference point for applicants, to encourage them to consider all their options and to ensure the best outcome for every student.

As one of the foremost global business and technology consulting organisations, Accenture's integrated approach helps put our clients at the leading edge of a changing business world. That's why we invest so much in continually developing the skills and potential of our people and offer a dynamic environment where you can build transferable skills through working in a team-based environment. In the emerging electronic economy, success means staying at the forefront of change. By joining Accenture, you'll help transform world-class organisations as they compete for leadership in the future.

Making progress in your education and your career is your responsibility; course choice is one of the important decisions you have to make. The opportunities available to you are limitless; it's up to you to find them and seize them.

Ben Johnston
Head of Graduate Recruitment, Accenture

AUTHOR'S ACKNOWLEDGEMENTS

I acknowledge gratefully the efforts of university and college registrars, schools liaison staff, faculty and departmental heads and admissions tutors in providing detailed information about their courses.

I should also like to thank the staff of the Universities and Colleges Admissions Service (UCAS) for providing me with up-to-date information. I am grateful to James Burnett of Mander Portman Woodward for information on the new medical schools, Kathryn McLean of the Scottish Further Education Unit and Rosemary Williamson of the Committee of Scottish Higher Education Principals for information on higher education in Scotland. My thanks are due also to the Higher Education Funding Council (England, Scotland and Wales) for permission to publish information relating to research ratings and teaching quality assessments. In addition, I would also like to express special thanks to the Higher Education Statistics Agency (HESA) for access to their Data Report and Reference Volume *First Destinations*, the Quality Assurance Agency for information on subject assessment reports, to Dr Judith Secker of the Engineering Council for information on the new Engineering regulations and to Professor Alan Smithers and Dr Pamela Robinson for permission to publish information from the Teacher Training Index. I should also like to thank those admissions tutors, teachers and their pupils who have sent me interview reports and other information which has provided useful supplementary data for the book.

Every effort has been made to maintain absolute accuracy in providing course information and to ensure that the entire book is as up-to-date as possible. However, changes are constantly taking place in higher education so it is important for readers to check carefully with prospectuses before submitting their applications.

I also wish to thank Dianah Ellis for her continuing editorial advice, and the many readers who have written to me about the problems they have encountered in choosing courses and places to study. Such information adds to a valuable store of knowledge which can be passed on, thereby creating a better understanding of mutual difficulties.

Finally, my thanks to Jane Heap of Putney High School (staff) for checking on course changes and also to my wife Rita for her administrative help (and patience!) through 32 years of publication.

Brian Heap
January 2001

University of
HUDDERSFIELD

School of Music and Humanities

The School of Music and Humanities has a well-established reputation for high quality teaching and research and a good record for graduate employment. Currently there are over 60 full-time staff and 1,600 full-time undergraduates in the School.

Varied, Vocationally-Oriented Courses

The School offers a wide range of degree courses within a flexible modular structure that enables students either to pursue single subject programmes or to combine two or more disciplines in joint programmes. Degrees are characterised by:

- a **friendly supportive teaching environment**,
- **high quality teaching** supported by an active research culture,
- a clear **vocational orientation** including work placements, work-related projects, skills development and careers modules,
- the opportunity to **study abroad** via the SOCRATES exchange programme.

Central Location

Huddersfield is a thriving 'University Town' located in pleasant countryside but with easy access to nearby Leeds and Manchester. The campus is close to the town centre and its shopping, sports and cultural facilities. **The cost of living in Huddersfield is relatively low** which enables students to enjoy extensive social activities both on and off campus. The University has a wide range of leisure and sporting clubs.

Excellent, affordable accommodation

The University has six halls of residence including the highly successful **Storthes Hall Student Village which provides excellent but reasonably priced accommodation**. The Village has its own mini-market, bars and sports and recreational facilities. The University gives preference to first-year students, but continuing students may also apply for university accommodation. In addition, there is a good supply of **affordable private accommodation** in the town. The University Accommodation Service inspects and rates all properties for safety.

Social Life

Huddersfield is particularly noted for its musical traditions: you can hear **everything from indie, jungle and jazz to classical, choral and the avant-garde**. The award winning McAlpine Stadium, as well as being the home of Huddersfield Town FC and the Huddersfield-Sheffield Giants RLFC, is a spectacular venue for top-flight concerts. The University itself hosts regular concerts and is the hub of the internationally-renowned Contemporary Music Festival. In addition, Huddersfield has established itself as the **"Poetry Capital" of England** with an active circle of local writers who can be heard in local clubs, pubs and theatres. The town hosts an increasingly important Women's Writing Festival. There is ample opportunity to watch or take part in a **wide range of sports**. As well as the University Sports Hall, there are well-equipped sports complexes at the Sports Centre, the Stadium and the Multi-Sport Centre.

MUSIC: ENGLISH: MEDIA: THEATRE: HISTORY: POLITICS:LANGUAGES
Further information: Web site: //www.hud.ac.uk/schools/music+humanities

ABOUT THIS BOOK

Choosing a career or course of study is not easy. There is much that applicants need to know in order to make decisions which are right for them as individuals, and each year they will spend a great deal of time exploring various options. One option is higher education, although entry to degree and diploma courses can be highly competitive and applicants need good advice on how to choose courses. Comprehensive and comparative information about selection policies and the range of courses, therefore, is an essential part of this process. To assist applicants, *Degree Course Offers* (now in its 32nd year) aims to provide a **first stop** reference for applicants choosing courses of higher education by providing information from official sources.

The new Curriculum 2000 arrangements started last September and the majority of schools and colleges now offer a range of study programmes covering GCE Advanced, Advanced Subsidiary and VCE Vocational Advanced and Advanced Subsidiary level subjects and, in some cases, Key Skills certificates. These new arrangements will affect applicants for entry to degree and diploma courses in 2002 when many universities and colleges adopt a new system of offers, using grades (as before) and/or a new points scale (the UCAS Tariff Points System). The offers arrangements are often wide-ranging in order both to suit the needs of individual applicants who are offering a range of qualifications and also to meet the needs of universities' subject departments and the requirements of their degree or diploma courses. It will be noted that these changes are reflected in the information appearing in the subject tables in **Chapter 5** and described in **Chapter 4**.

The offers information in the subject tables in **Chapter 5** has been supplied by universities and colleges to provide a first source of reference to the entry requirement for courses. **Since offers can vary and are subject to change, it is essential for applicants to refer to prospectuses and web sites to obtain full information.**

It must be stressed that the positioning of the institutions in each of the subject tables in **Chapter 5** must not necessarily be regarded as a reference to the quality of the course offered.

Details of the new offers arrangements appear on the inside fold of the back cover of this book and at the beginning of **Chapters 4** and **5**. Other qualifications, for example, the International Baccalaureate and other international qualifications, are not affected as yet by these new arrangements.

Degree Course Offers lists:

- a guide to offers for courses in grades and/or using the new UCAS tariff
- subject information
- course special features
- advice on how to complete Section 10 of the UCAS form – the Personal Statement
- opportunities for study and work experience abroad and advice for students
- types of questions faced by applicants at interview
- institutions accepting equivalent points scores, after A-levels
- institutions likely to accept applicants who marginally fail their offers

- top teaching universities
- top research universities
- reasons for rejection at interview
- information about vacancies in Clearing
- advice on taking a gap year
- new graduates' destinations.

The information in *Degree Course Offers* is updated each year from over 9000 questionnaires returned by admissions tutors. The information is collated between November and January of each academic year (for publication in the following spring) so providing up-to-date advice on admissions policies and details of new courses for the next application cycle starting in the following September.

The information and advice given covers all the stages of choosing courses and deciding on universities, and, importantly, the processes and steps to take if offers are not met in August. Used in conjunction with *Choosing Your Degree Course and University* (the companion title to *Degree Course Offers*) the student is taken through the entire guidance process for higher education. *Degree Course Offers 2002* once more, therefore, provides in a single volume a comprehensive survey of selection information and guidance for applicants at a time when they need it most.

Note Every effort is made to ensure accuracy throughout this book. It is important, however, that readers always check web sites and prospectuses carefully for any late changes in offers, admissions policies or courses, and contact admissions officers of their chosen institutions should queries arise.

Brian Heap
January 2001

SPONSORSHIP WITH THE ROYAL NAVY

Yes, the Royal Navy might pay you to continue your studies

Bursaries

You can apply for one of our Bursaries of £1,050 per year. This increases to £4,000 if you're studying engineering.

Engineering

With our Engineering Sponsorship Scheme you could receive £5,500 per year for engineering studies at Southampton University.

Cadetships

If you really impress us, you could gain one of our University Cadetships. This gives you a year's training with the Navy before beginning your degree course and be paid between £8.000 and £12,000 per year whilst you're at University.

Officers

And, don't forget, if you've got 2 or more A Levels you are eligible to apply to become an Officer in the Navy.

Interested?

Have a look at our website (**www.rnjobs.co.uk**) or call us on **0845 607 5555**. You can also call in at your local Armed Forces Careers Office (you'll find the address in the phone book under 'Naval Establishments') or write to us at FREEPOST ROYAL NAVY & ROYAL MARINES (no stamp is required).

ROYAL NAVY. THE TEAM WORKS

1 YOUR FIRST DECISIONS

HIGHER EDUCATION OR NOT?

Why do you want to go on to higher education? If you are taking GCE Advanced (AL), Advanced Subsidiary (AS) and VCE Vocational Advanced Level (VA) qualifications, this is an important question to ask. In 2000 over 430,000 students applied for full-time first degree and diploma courses in the United Kingdom, with some 320,000 obtaining places, but higher education is just one of two options you have. The other is employment, and perhaps it is important to note that higher education is not necessarily the best option for everyone. It is, however, one which is appropriate for many and therefore should not be rejected lightly.

Higher education is likely to open many doors and give you opportunities for work and leisure which otherwise you might not have. Also, very often and quite accidentally, it leads into careers you have not considered before.

Most courses in higher education lead to a degree or a diploma and for either you will have to make a *subject choice*. This can be difficult because the universities alone offer over 900 degree subjects and over 80,000 courses. You have two main options:

- choosing a course similar or the same as one (or more) of your examination subjects, or related to an interest outside the school curriculum, such as Anthropology, American Studies, Archaeology;
- choosing a course in preparation for a future career, for example, Medicine, Architecture, Engineering.

CHOOSING YOUR COURSE BY A- AND AS-LEVEL SUBJECTS

Deciding on your degree or diploma course by your GCE A-level subjects is a reasonably safe option. VCE Vocational A- and AS-levels, which have parity with GCE A- and AS-levels, are listed in **Choosing your Course by Career Interests** because of their relevance to specific careers and related courses. Already you are familiar with the subjects and what they involve, and you may well look forward to studying at least one of them to a much greater depth over the next few years. If the long-term career prospects concern you, don't worry – a degree course isn't necessarily a training for a job. If you are taking science subjects they can lead naturally on to a range of scientific careers although many scientists follow non-science careers, such as law and accountancy. If you are taking arts or social science subjects, remember that the training for most non-scientific careers can start once you have your degree. Finally, when choosing AS-level subjects, students may prefer to select subjects with a similar subject base, for example, four science subjects or four arts or humanities subjects. However, some institutions welcome one or even two contrasting subjects (for example, Bradford, Brunel, London (Imp), the London Medical Schools), providing the required A-level subjects are also offered. Subjects and policies are likely to vary depending on subject requirements for specific degree courses. (Information on graduate employment is given in many of the subject tables in **Chapter 5**.) But let's go a stage further.

These subjects do not stand on their own, in isolation. Each subject you are taking is one of a much larger family. Each has many similarities with subjects studied in degree and diploma courses which you might never have considered, so before you decide finally on taking a subject to degree level read through the following lists of GCE A-level subjects, each followed by examples of related degree courses. Here you will find some examples of degree courses with similarities to the subjects you might be taking. (These lists are also useful if you have to consider alternative courses after the examination results are published!)

Ancient History: Archaeology, Biblical Studies, Classics and Classical Civilisation, Greek, Latin, Middle and Near Eastern Studies.

Art and Design: Archaeology, Architecture, Communication Studies, Film Studies, Fine Art, Graphic Communication, History of Art, History of Design, Landscape Architecture, Media Studies, Photographic Art, Textile Design, Town and Country Planning, Typography.

Biology/Human Biology: Agricultural Sciences, Anatomy, Biochemistry, Biological Sciences, Botany, Dentistry, Dietetics, Ecology, Education, Fisheries Science, Food Science, Forestry, Genetics, Health and Life Sciences, Horticulture, Human Sciences, Life Sciences, Marine Biology, Medicine, Microbiology, Nursing Studies, Nutrition, Oceanography, Occupational Therapy, Optometry (Ophthalmic Optics), Pharmacology, Pharmacy, Physiology, Podiatry, Psychology, Radiography, Speech Science/Therapy, Veterinary Science, Wood Science, Zoology.

Chemistry: Agricultural Sciences, Animal Sciences, Bacteriology, Biochemistry, Biological Studies, Biotechnology, Botany, Brewing, Chemical Engineering, Chemical Physics, Colour Chemistry, Dentistry, Dietetics, Earth Sciences, Education, Food Science and Technology, Fuel and Energy Science, Genetics, Geochemistry, Geology, Glass Technology, Human Sciences, Materials Science, Marine Biology, Medicine, Microbiology, Natural Sciences, Paper Science, Pharmacology, Pharmacy, Physiology, Polymer Sciences, Textile Chemistry, Veterinary Science, Zoology.

Economics: Accountancy, Administration, Banking, Business Economics, Business Studies, Development Studies, Estate Management, Financial Services, Operational Research, Politics, Quantity Surveying, Social Studies, Statistics.

English: Drama, English Language and Literature, Journalism, Librarianship, Theatre Studies.

Environmental Sciences/Studies: Biological Sciences, Biology, Botany, Earth Science, Ecology, Fisheries Science, Forestry, Geography, Geology, Land Management, Marine Biology, Oceanography, Wood Sciences, Zoology.

Geography: Development Studies, Earth Sciences, Environmental Science, Estate Management, Forestry, Geography, Geology, Land Economy, Meteorology, Oceanography, Population Sciences, Surveying, Town Planning, Urban Studies.

Geology: Earth Sciences, Geochemistry, Geography, Geophysics, Mineral Sciences, Minerals Surveying, Mining, Oceanography, Petroleum Geology, Soil Science, Surveying.

Government and Politics: Development Studies, Economics, Government, Industrial Relations, International Politics, Law, Politics, Public Administration, Social Policy, Social Studies, Strategic Studies.

History: American Studies, International Relations, Law, Religious Studies.

Languages: Apart from French and German – and Spanish for some universities – it is not usually necessary to have completed an A-level language course before studying many languages (over 60) offered at degree level, for example, Chinese, Japanese, Scandinavian Studies.

Mathematics: Accountancy, Actuarial Mathematics, Aeronautical Engineering, Astrophysics, Building Science and Technology, Business Management, Chemical Engineering, Civil Engineering, Computational Science, Computer Systems Engineering, Control Systems Engineering, Cybernetics, Economics, Electrical/Electronic Technology, Engineering Science, Ergonomics, Geophysics, Management Science, Materials Science and Technology, Mechanical Engineering, Metallurgy, Meteorology, Mining Engineering, Naval Architecture, Nuclear Engineering, Operational Research, Physics, Quantity Surveying, Statistics, Systems Analysis, Telecommunications Engineering, Textile Engineering.

Media Studies: Advertising, Art and Design, Communication Studies, Film, Radio, Video and TV Studies, Journalism, Media Communication Systems, Media Production and Design, Photography, Publishing.

Physics: Aeronautical Engineering, Architecture, Astronomy, Astrophysics, Automotive Engineering, Biomedical Engineering, Biophysics, Building Science and Technology, Chemical Engineering, Civil Engineering, Chemical Engineering, Communications Engineering, Computer Science, Cybernetics, Education, Electrical/Electronic Engineering, Engineering Science, Ergonomics, Geophysics, Glass, Plastics and Rubber Technology, Instrument Physics, Materials Science, Marine Engineering, Mechanical Engineering, Meteorology, Mineral Sciences and Technology, Naval Architecture, Oceanography, Optometry (Ophthalmic Optics), Telecommunications Engineering, Textile Physics.

Religious Studies: Archaeology, Anthropology, Biblical Studies, Divinity, Psychology, Social Administration.

CHOOSING YOUR COURSE BY CAREER INTERESTS

An alternative strategy for deciding on the subject of your degree or diploma course is to relate it to your career interests or to your VCE A-level subjects. However, even though you may have set your mind on a particular career, it is important to remember that sometimes there are others which are very similar. The following lists give examples of career areas, some related Vocational A-level subjects and examples of possible relevant degree courses.

Accountancy: (Vocational A-level: Business) Actuarial Science, Banking, Business Studies, Economics, Financial Services, Management Science.

Actuarial work: (Vocational A-level: Business) Accountancy, Banking, Insurance.

Agriculture: (Vocational A-level: Science) Agriculture and Countryside Management, Agricultural Engineering, Agricultural Surveying, Animal Sciences, Biological Sciences, Botany, Ecology, Environmental Science, Estate Management, Forestry, Horticulture, Plant Science, Surveying.

Animal careers: (Vocational A-level: Science) Agricultural Sciences, Biological Sciences, Veterinary Science, Zoology.

Archaeology: (Vocational A-level: Science) Ancient History, Anthropology, Classical Civilisation and Classics, History of Art and Architecture.

Architecture: (Vocational A-level: Construction and the Built Environment) Building, Civil Engineering, Landscape Architecture, Quantity Surveying, Surveying, Town and Country Planning.

19-22 Charlotte Road, London EC2A 3SG
Tel: 020 7613 8600 Fax: 020 7613 8599
E-mail: enquiry@princes-foundation.org
Website www.princes-foundation.org

THE PRINCE'S
FOUNDATION

BROAD STUDY AREAS: ARCHITECTURE, FINE ART, TRADITIONAL ART.
Founded: 1992. **Main awards**: Foundation/LOCN validated certificate; **Site**: Shoreditch; **Access**: Old Street/Liverpool Street (underground), many buses. Academic features: Many student projects are 'live', undertaken in conjunction with planners, local councils and communities; students design and build a simple building. All staff are practising artists/architects. **Other learning facilities**: Well-equipped metal and wood workshops; darkroom and computer facilities, personal studio space. **Tuition fees**: Home students: £1,000; Overseas students: £5500.

WHAT'S IT LIKE: The Foundation Course is a challenging and stimulating course, which culminates with the whole group of students working as a team to build a building. The curricula of the first two terms provide the foundation to enable the final project to happen; it is broad ranging and an astonishing amount is achieved in a short space of time. Students learn art, design and craft skills which, combined with an understanding of architectural language provide a route into higher education or, in some cases, access to direct participation in the built environment. Students of diverse nationalities, various ages and a rich mix of past experience. The intensity of the course provides important skills and confidence boost for both those continuing in their education and those moving straight into practice.

Art: (Vocational A-levels: Art and Design, Media) Advertising, Architecture, Education (Art), Estate Management, Industrial Design, Landscape Architecture, Three Dimensional Design.

Astronomy: (Vocational A-level: Science) Astrophysics, Mathematics, Physics.

Audiology: (Vocational A-level: Health and Social Care) Nursing, Education of the Deaf.

Banking/Insurance: (Vocational A-levels: Business, Information and Communication Technology, Retail and Distributive Services) Accountancy, Business Studies, Economics, Financial Services.

Biology careers: (Vocational A-level: Science) Agricultural Sciences, Biochemistry, Botany, Ecology, Education, Environmental Health, Environmental Science, Genetics, Medicine, Microbiology, Pharmacy.

Book Publishing: (Vocational A-levels: Business, Media, Retail and Distributive Services) Advertising, Business Studies, Printing, Typographical Communication.

Brewing: (Vocational A-level: Science) Biochemistry, Chemistry, Food Science.

Broadcasting: (Vocational A-level: Media) Film and TV Studies, Journalism, Media Studies, Media and Communications Studies.

Building: (Vocational A-level: Construction and the Built Environment) Architecture, Building Services Engineering, Building Surveying, Civil Engineering, Estate Management, General Practice Surveying, Land Surveying, Quantity Surveying.

Business: (Vocational A-levels: Business, Retail and Distributive Services) Accountancy, Advertising, Banking, Economics, Estate Management, Hospitality Management, Housing Management, Industrial Relations, Insurance, Marketing, Operational Research, Public Relations, Transport Management, Tourism.

Cartography: (Vocational A-level: Science) Geographical Mapping Science, Geography, Land Surveying.

Catering: (Vocational A-level: Hospitality and Catering) Consumer Studies, Dietetics, Food Science, Hotel Management, Nutrition.

Chemistry careers: (Vocational A-level: Science) Agricultural Science, Biochemistry, Botany, Ceramics, Chemical Engineering, Colour Chemistry, Education, Geochemistry, Pharmacology, Pharmacy, all Technologies (for example, Dairy, Food, Paper, Plastics, Materials).

Computing: (Vocational A-level: Information and Communication Technology) Artificial Intelligence, Business Studies, Electronic Engineering, Mathematics, Microelectronics, Physics, Telecommunications.

Construction: (Vocational A-levels: Construction and the Built Environment, Engineering) Building, Civil Engineering, Construction Engineering and Management, Structural Engineering.

Dance: (Vocational A-level: Performing Arts) Drama, Movement Studies, Performance Arts, Physical Education, Theatre Studies.

Dentistry: (Vocational A-levels: Health and Social Care, Science) Biochemistry, Medicine, Nursing, Pharmacy.

Drama: (Vocational A-levels: Media, Performing Arts) Dance, Education, Movement Studies, Teaching, Theatre Management.

Education: (Vocational A-levels: Art and Design, Information and Communication Technology, Performing Arts, Science) Psychology, Social Work, Speech Science/Therapy, Youth Studies.

Engineering: (Vocational A-levels: Engineering, Manufacturing, Science) Engineering (for example, Chemical, Civil, Computing, Control, Electrical, Environmental), Food Process, Manufacturing, Mechanical, Microelectrics, Nuclear, Product Design, Software, Telecommunications), Geology and Geotechnics, Mathematics, Physics.

Estate Management: (Vocational A-level: Construction and the Built Environment) Architecture, Building, Civil Engineering, Economics, Forestry, Housing Studies, Landscape Architecture, Town and Country Planning.

Food and Accommodation: (Vocational A-levels: Hospitality and Catering, Leisure and Recreation) Dietetics, Home Economics, Hotel and Institutional Management, Housing Management, Nutrition.

Food Science and Technology: (Vocational A-level: Science) Biochemistry, Brewing, Chemistry, Dietetics, Home Economics, Nutrition.

Forestry: (Vocational A-level: Science) Biological Sciences, Botany, Ecology, Environmental Science, Wood Science.

Furniture Design: (Vocational A-level: Art and Design) Furniture Production, History of Art and Design, Three Dimensional Design, Timber Technology.

Geology: (Vocational A-level: Science) Chemistry, Earth Sciences, Engineering (Civil, Mining), Environmental Science, Geochemistry, Geography, Land Surveying, Quarrying.

Graphic Design: (Vocational A-levels: Art and Design, Media) Advertising, Photography, Printing.

Health and Safety: (Vocational A-levels: Health and Social Care, Science) Environmental Health, Health Sciences, Nursery Nursing. (See also **Medicine**.)

Horticulture: (Vocational A-level: Science) Agriculture, Botany, Landscape Architecture.

Hotel and Catering Administration: (Vocational A-levels: Business, Hospitality and Catering) Food Science, Food Technology, Institutional Management, Travel and Tourism.

Housing: (Vocational A-level: Construction and the Built Environment) Architecture, Estate Management, General Practice Surveying, Social Administration, Town and Country Planning.

Law: (Vocational A-levels: Business, Health and Social Care) Business Studies, Government and Politics, International History, Land Management.

Leisure and Recreation: (Vocational A-levels: Leisure and Recreation, Travel and Tourism) Dance, Drama, Music, Movement Studies, Physical Education, Theatre Studies, Travel and Tourism.

Librarianship: (Vocational A-level: Information and Communication Technology) Information Management, Information Sciences and Technology, Publishing.

Marketing: (Vocational A-levels: Business, Retail and Distributive Services, Travel and Tourism) Advertising, Business Studies, Operational Research, Population Sciences, Printing and Packaging, Travel and Tourism.

Materials Science/Metallurgy: (Vocational A-levels: Engineering, Science, Manufacturing) Chemistry, Engineering, Glass Science and Technology, Materials Technology, Mineral Exploitation, Physics, Polymer Science.

Mathematics careers: (Vocational A-levels: Engineering, Science) Accountancy, Actuarial Science, Banking, Business Studies, Computer Studies, Economics, Education, Engineering, Operational Research, Physics, Quantity Surveying.

Medicine: (Vocational A-levels: Health and Social Care, Science) Anatomy, Biochemistry, Biological Sciences, Dentistry, Genetics, Human Physiology, Medical Laboratory Sciences, Nursery Nursing, Nursing, Occupational Therapy, Orthoptics, Pharmacology, Pharmacy, Physiotherapy, Radiography, Speech Science/Therapy, Social Sciences.

Micro-electronics: (Vocational A-levels: Engineering, Information and Communication Technology, Science) Computer Studies, Electrical/Electronic Engineering.

Mining and Minerals careers: (Vocational A-levels: Engineering, Manufacturing, Science) Chemistry, Earth Sciences, Chemical Engineering, Environmental Sciences, Geology, Mining Engineering, Soil Science.

Music: (Vocational A-level: Performing Arts) Drama, Performance Arts, Theatre Studies.

Nautical careers: (Vocational A-levels: Engineering, Science) Marine Engineering, Naval Architecture, Nautical Studies, Oceanography, Offshore Engineering.

Naval Architecture: (Vocational A-levels: Engineering, Science) Maritime Studies, Marine Engineering, Offshore Engineering.

Nursing: (Vocational A-levels: Health and Social Care, Science) Anatomy, Applied Biology, Biochemistry, Biological Sciences, Biology, Dentistry, Education, Environmental Health and Community Studies, Health Studies, Human Biology, Medicine, Midwifery, Occupational Therapy, Orthoptics, Physiotherapy, Psychology, Podiatry, Radiography, Social Administration, Speech Therapy. (See also **Medicine**.)

Nutrition: (Vocational A-levels: Health and Social Care, Science) Dietetics, Food Science and Technology, Nursing.

Occupational Therapy: (Vocational A-levels: Health and Social Care, Science) Art, Nursing, Orthoptics, Physiotherapy, Psychology, Speech Science/Therapy.

Optometry (Ophthalmic Optics): (Vocational A-level: Science) Applied Physics, Orthoptics, Physics.

Photography/Film/TV: (Vocational A-level: Media) Communication Studies (some courses), Documentary Communications, Graphic Art, Media Studies.

Physical Education: (Vocational A-levels: Leisure and Recreation, Science) Leisure and Recreation Management, Sport and Recreational Studies, Sports Science.

Physiotherapy: (Vocational A-levels: Health and Social Care, Science) Chiropractic, Nursing, Orthoptics, Osteopathy, Physical Education.

Physics: (Vocational A-level: Science) Applied Physics, Astronomy, Astrophysics, Education, Engineering (Civil, Electrical, Mechanical), Medical Instrumentation, Optometry (Ophthalmic Optics).

Printing: (Vocational A-levels: Art and Design, Media) Advertising, Graphic Design, Typographic Design and Communication.

Production Technology: (Vocational A-levels: Engineering, Manufacturing, Science) Engineering (Mechanical, Manufacturing), Materials Science.

Property and Valuation Management: (Vocational A-level: Construction and the Built Environment) Architecture, Estate Management, Quantity Surveying, Urban Land Economics.

Psychology: (Vocational A-levels: Health and Social Care, Science) Applied Social Studies, Occupational Therapy, Psychology (Clinical, Developmental, Educational, Experimental, Occupational, Social), Social Work.

Public Administration: (Vocational A-level: Business) Applied Social Studies, Business Studies, Social Administration, Social Policy, Youth Studies.

Quantity Surveying: (Vocational A-level: Construction and the Built Environment) Accountancy, Architecture, Building, Civil Engineering, Surveying (Building, Land and Valuation).

Radiography: (Vocational A-levels: Health and Social Care, Science) Anatomy, Audiology, Biological Sciences, Medical Photography, Nursing, Orthoptics, Photography, Physiology, Physiotherapy.

Secretarial Work: (Vocational A-levels: Business, Information and Communication Technology) Bi-lingual Secretarial Studies, Business Studies.

Silversmithing/Jewellery: (Vocational A-level: Art and Design) Three Dimensional Design.

Social Work: (Vocational A-level: Health and Social Care) Anthropology, Journalism, Politics and Government, Public Administration, Religious Studies, Social Administration, Sociology, Town and Country Planning, Youth Studies.

Speech Science/Therapy: (Vocational A-levels: Health and Social Care, Science) Audiology, Education (Handicapped Children), Nursing, Occupational Therapy, Psychology, Radiography.

Statistics: (Vocational A-level: Information and Communication Technology) Business Studies, Economics, Mathematics, Operational Research, Population Sciences.

Technology: (Vocational A-levels: Engineering, Manufacturing, Science) Applied Chemistry, Chemistry, Food Science and Technology, Paper Science, Polymer Science, Timber Technology, Wood Science.

Textile Design: (Vocational A-level: Art and Design) Art, Clothing Studies, Fashion Design, Textile Management.

Theatre Design: (Vocational A-levels: Art and Design, Performing Arts) Drama, Interior Design, Leisure and Recreational Studies, Theatre Management, Theatre Studies.

Three Dimensional Design: (Vocational A-level: Art and Design) Architecture, Industrial Design, Interior Design, Theatre Design.

Town and Country Planning: (Vocational A-level: Construction and the Built Environment) Architecture, Environmental Science, Estate Management, Geography, Leisure and Recreational Management, Planning Studies, Population Sciences, Statistics, Transport Management.

Transport: (Vocational A-levels: Business, Retail and Distributive Services) Business Studies, Town and Country Planning.

WHY NOT
put a spring in
your step

why not a career in Chemical Engineering? check out the website at
www.whynotchemeng.com, speak to your teacher or call
01788 578214 for an information pack

KEY CHEMICAL ENGINEERING FACTS

#01   Trainer Sole

Trainer designers work with Chemical Engineers to make their vision a reality.

The soles are produced from polyurethane foam. Two chemicals are injected into a mould and the difference in reaction of those chemicals determines where the sole is hard or springy.

Chemical Engineers ensure the sole develops the right properties where they are needed and that no bubbles, cracks or other unwanted effects appear.

#02   Fabrics

It doesn't always help the worst offenders but Chemical Engineers can stop smelly feet!

They add special properties to the trainer fabric such as anti-microbial agents which prevent foot odour. If you still need to put your trainers in the wash they can also stop your trainers losing their colour by preventing the dyes from running.

IT'S A
bLAST
CHEMICAL ENGINEERING – THE SCIENCE OF SUCCESS

Come to the University
that leads not follows...

Leeds, one of the countries oldest and most respected universities
is merging with Bretton Hall, one of the best known institutions
for the Performing and Visual Arts, to provide an exciting range
of new degrees and opportunities at both campuses.

Taking a leading role in Acting, Applied Cultural Studies, Arts
Education, Arts Management, Creative Writing, Dance, Design,
Education, Fine Art, Music and Performance Design.

**For the full range of opportunities at the University of
Leeds from Astronomy to Zoology, visit our website at**
www.leeds.ac.uk
Tel 0113 233 3999

engineering
science
computing
business

ROYAL ACADEMY of ENGINEERING

By working in industry you can gain valuable experience and earn some money too..

expecting good grades?

Interested in

A real job with pay for a year between school and university?

Responsibility and challenges?

Management training?

The possibility of sponsorship?

 70% of Year in Industry students go on to gain a first or upper second degree.

We work with hundreds of top companies offering year long employment opportunities to the right people – it could be you!

Want to know more

Write to The Year in Industry, University of Manchester, Simon Building, Oxford Road, Manchester M13 9PL, or e-mail enquiries@yini.org.uk website www.yini.org.uk quoting ref DCO

The Year in Industry
Employment opportunities before university

Typography and Graphic Communication: (Vocational A-levels: Art and Design, Media) Graphic Design, Packaging, Printing, Publishing.

Veterinary Science: (Vocational A-level: Science) Agricultural Sciences, Agriculture, Animal Sciences, Medicine, Pharmacology, Pharmacy, Zoology.

COURSE TYPES AND DIFFERENCES

Courses in the same subject at different universities and colleges can vary considerably in content and in their subject requirements or preferences. It is important, therefore, to check the acceptability of your A/AS/VA and GCSE subjects (or equivalent) for your preferred courses.

When choosing courses, the first factor to consider is the course requirements. Certain A/AS/VA-levels may be stipulated and, in some cases, GCSE subjects. You will then need to decide on the type of course you want to follow. For example, a subject might be offered as a single-subject course (a single honours degree), or as a two-subject course (a joint honours degree), or as one of two, three or four subjects (a combined degree) or a major-minor degree (75 and 25 per cent of each subject respectively). Many universities and colleges of higher education have modularised their courses which means you can choose modules of different subjects, so 'building' your own course within specified 'pathways' with the help and approval of your course tutor. It also means that you are likely to be assessed after completing each module, rather than being assessed in your last year for all your previous years' learning.

Many institutions have introduced credit accumulation and transfer arrangements. This means that students can gain credit for modules or units of study they have successfully completed and these credits can be accumulated towards a certificate, diploma, first degree or postgraduate award.

In almost every course the options and modules offered include some which reflect the research interests of individual members of staff. In some courses subsidiary subjects are available as minor courses alongside a single honours course. In an increasing number of courses these additional subjects include a European language, the importance of which cannot be over-emphasised with the United Kingdom's membership of the European Union.

When choosing your course it is important to remember that one course is not better than another – it is just different. The best course for you is the one which best suits **you**. To give some indication of the variations between courses, their special features are described in the tables and more fully in *Choosing Your Degree Course and University* and in *The Best in University and* College *Courses* (see **Appendix 2 Booklist**).

After provisionally choosing your courses, read the prospectuses again carefully to be sure that you understand what is included in the three, four or more years of study. Each institution varies in its course content even though the course titles may be the same. Courses differ in several ways, for example, in their:

- subject/module options
- methods of assessment (eg unseen examinations, continuous assessment, project work, dissertations)
- contact time with tutors
- how they are taught (for example, frequency and size of lectures, seminars)

- practicals; field work requirements
- library, laboratory and studio facilities
- amount of free study time available.

These are useful points of comparison between courses in different institutions when you are making final course choices. Other important factors when comparing courses include the availability of opportunities for studying and working abroad during your course, and professional body accreditation of courses leading to certain professional careers (see **Appendix 1 Professional Associations**).

Once you have chosen your course subject(s) the next step is to find out about the universities and colleges offering courses in your subject area. **Chapter 2 Where to Study** provides information to help you do this.

2 WHERE TO STUDY

WHICH UNIVERSITY? WHICH COLLEGE?

How do you decide?

Since your main objective for going into higher education is to obtain a degree or diploma, your course choice must take priority over deciding on a particular university or college. You have three, four or five years of study ahead and you need to choose a subject which is going to keep you interested. Motivation, therefore, is the most important factor. It is well worth realising that every year a large number of students – some 18 per cent – drop out of their chosen course before the end of their first year because the course and university or college life is very different from what they expected.

Finding the university or college which is right for you means that you have to spend time finding out about the institutions offering your chosen courses and the best place to start is the prospectus. This research is important because another contributory cause for students' unhappiness or drop-out is insufficient knowledge about the location of the universities and colleges they select. Many applicants have little idea of where those institutions are or what their environment is really like, and the discovery on arrival can unsettle even the well-motivated!

Most applicants look for places or courses with good reputations but they should be very cautious in following this approach. The word 'reputation' suggests that one place or a specific course is better than another. It is true that some universities such as Oxford or Cambridge or London are 'well known', but this is no criterion of quality. Many applicants are concerned about employers' perceptions of their chosen university or college but it is likely that most employers are just as concerned with the quality of applicant and not necessarily with his or her place of study. Similarly, the quality of teaching is often regarded as important – which it is – although it is dangerous to assume that the most popular institutions have the best teachers! Universities vary widely in the attainment levels of the students they recruit, the types of teaching they offer and the research they do. However, they all have to meet minimum standards of quality in their teaching and research and are 'inspected' by the Quality Assurance Agency for Higher Education (QAA). Reports are published by the Higher Education Funding Councils and the QAA. Contact the QAA (Southgate House, Southgate Street, Gloucester GL1 1UB or Albert Chambers, 13 Bath Street, Glasgow G2 1HY) for a list of reports available and prices. Applicants should also see *The Best in University and* College *Courses* to check on the teaching and research quality assessments in their chosen subject (see **Appendix 2 Booklist**).

The main objective in choosing the right place, however, is for applicants to try to identify the 'character' of each institution in which they are interested. This 'character' is a mix of factors which will determine whether or not an institution is 'right' for you and these factors can be identified by answering the following questions:

- Where is the institution located?
- How far or close is it to home? (This is an increasingly important factor because of travel costs and their impact on your student loan.)
- What courses are on offer?

- How are studies organised?
- How many students are there?
- What leisure opportunities are there?
- What is the social life like?
- How much does it cost to live in halls of residence, or in private accommodation?
- How much does it cost to travel to the university or college from student accommodation?
- Are there any bursaries or scholarships for undergraduates in your subject area?
- How good are the study facilities – libraries, laboratories, computers, teaching equipment?

The best way to choose what and where to study is to start by reading prospectuses which provide detailed information about all aspects of courses and facilities for students in universities and colleges. Readers wanting to compare institutions and courses are advised to refer to *Choosing Your Degree Course and University* (see **Appendix 2 Booklist**) which provides information on individual subject areas and enables useful comparisons to be made between institutions offering the same course subjects.

The general rule for institution choice must be to regard universities and colleges as not better than the next, but different. Often your choice will be dictated by **location** (town, city, rural) or by **size** (large or small), by **distance** from home or by **travel** factors (particularly the ease or difficulty of reaching the university or college by public transport) and, of course, the availability of your preferred course.

After reading the prospectuses, visit some of the institutions which interest you. Many have Open Days and the dates of these are available from sixth form tutors, careers advisers and direct from the institutions concerned. Alternatively, applicants may write directly to the university or college and make arrangements for a personal visit.

Below are lists of universities, colleges, specialist colleges and further education colleges offering higher education degree and diploma courses. Also provided are contact details for further information. Because of changes which continually take place in higher education, for example, in the names of institutions, numbers and locations of campuses, readers should check web sites and prospectuses for up-to-date information.

DIRECTORY OF INSTITUTIONS

Section 1: Universities

Listed below are universities in the United Kingdom which offer degree and diploma courses at higher education level. Applications to these institutions are submitted through UCAS unless otherwise stated. (See the UCAS *Directory* and *University and College Entrance* for a full list of courses; see **Appendix 2 Booklist**).

Aberdeen: Location Two city sites; **Courses** Arts, Social Sciences, Divinity, Law, Medicine, Sciences, Mathematics, Agriculture and Forestry. *(The University of Aberdeen, Regent Walk, Aberdeen, Grampian, Scotland AB24 3FX. Tel 0122 427 3504; http://www.abdn.ac.uk)*

Abertay Dundee: Location City centre; **Courses** 23 subject areas in four schools – Social and Health Sciences, Computing, Accountancy, Law and Business Administration and Science and Engineering. *(University of Abertay Dundee, Bell Street, Dundee, Tayside, Scotland DD1 1HG. Tel 01382 308080; http://www.abertay.ac.uk)*

Aberystwyth: Location Hill site overlooking the town and bay; **Courses** Arts, Law, Sciences, Mathematics, Art, Drama, Agriculture, Economics and Social

Sciences. The College of Librarianship on a nearby campus offers a wide range of joint programmes. *(The University of Wales, Aberystwyth, Ceredigion, Wales SY23 2AX. Tel 01970 622021; http://www.aber.ac.uk)*

Anglia: Location Three main sites in Cambridge, Chelmsford, Brentwood; **Courses** BA, BSc, BEd and HND courses; check the prospectus. *(Anglia Polytechnic University, East Road, Cambridge CB1 1PT. Tel 01223 363271; http://anglia.ac.uk)*

Aston: Location Forty-acre green city-centre campus in Birmingham; **Courses** Single, Joint and Combined Honours degree courses in four schools: Engineering with Applied Science, Life and Health Sciences, Languages and European Studies, and Aston Business School. *(Aston University, Aston Triangle, Birmingham B4 7ET. Tel 0121 359 6313; http://www.aston.ac.uk)*

Bangor: Location Situated in a small city in an area of outstanding natural beauty between the mountains of Snowdonia and the shores of the Menai Strait; **Courses** Arts, Sciences, Theology, Nursing and Electronic/Computer Engineering. *(The University of Wales, Bangor, Gwynedd, Wales LL57 2DG. Tel 01248 351151; http://www.bangor.ac.uk)*

Bath: Location Purpose-built campus overlooking Bath; **Courses** Social Sciences, Engineering; Management; many sandwich courses. *(The University of Bath, Bath BA2 7AY. Tel 01225 826826; http://www.bath.ac.uk)*

Belfast (Queen's): Location Two sites two-three miles south of the city; **Courses** Agriculture, Arts, Law, Social Sciences, Engineering and Medicine. *(The Queen's University of Belfast, University Road, Belfast, Northern Ireland BT7 1NN. Tel 028 9033 5081; http://www.qub.ac.uk)*

Birmingham: Location Campus at Edgbaston two miles south of the city; **Courses** Arts, Social Sciences, Science, Engineering, Materials Science, Medicine and Dentistry. *(The University of Birmingham, Edgbaston, Birmingham B15 2TT. Tel 0121 414 3344; http://www.bham.ac.uk)*

Bournemouth: Location Two main sites, with the campus about two miles from the city centre; **Courses** A marked vocational emphasis, eg Art and Design, Marketing, Public Relations, Hotel Management, Nursing and Tourism Studies; HND courses are also offered; franchised courses available at associate colleges. Check the prospectus. *(Bournemouth University, Talbot Campus, Fern Barrow, Poole, Dorset BH12 5BB. Tel 01202 524111; http://www.bournemouth.ac.uk)*

Bradford: Location City centre; **Courses** Engineering and Physical Sciences, Health and Environmental Sciences, Social Sciences and Humanities and Modern Languages; sandwich courses are offered. *(The University of Bradford, Richmond Road, Bradford, West Yorkshire BD7 1DP. Tel 01274 233081; http://www.brad.ac.uk)*

Brighton: Location Four main sites, including Eastbourne (Sports Science, Hotel and Catering, Teaching and Podiatry); **Courses** Degrees and HND courses in Art, Accounting and Finance, Architecture, Construction, Design, Humanities, Education, Sport and Leisure, Surveying, Engineering and Environmental Studies, Health, Information Technology and Business; franchised courses available at associate colleges. Check the prospectus. *(University of Brighton, Mithras House, Lewes Road, Brighton BN2 4AT. Tel 01273 600900; http://www.bton.ac.uk)*

Bristol: Location Site close to city centre; **Courses** Arts, Science, Medicine, Engineering, Law and Social Sciences. *(The University, Bristol BS8 1TH. Tel 0117 928 9000; http://www.bris.ac.uk)*

Bristol UWE: Location Four campuses around Bristol and three regional centres with 17,000 full-time and sandwich students; **Courses** 12 faculties offering Degree and DipHE programmes covering Art, Built Environment, Business, Computing, Economics, Education, Engineering, Humanities, Languages, Law, Mathematics, Nursing, Science and Social Sciences. Most programmes are modular. *(University of the West of England, Frenchay Campus, Coldharbour*

Lane, Bristol BS16 1QY. Tel 0117 965 6261; http://www.uwe.ac.uk)

Brunel: Location Four self-contained campuses to the west of London: Uxbridge (main campus), Runnymede, Twickenham and Osterley; **Courses** Degrees offered by the Faculties of Arts, Professional Education, Science, Social Services and Technology. *(Brunel University, Uxbridge, Middlesex UB8 3PH. Tel 01895 203007; http://www.brunel.ac.uk)*

Buckingham: Location Two sites in restored historic buildings in the town of Buckingham; **Courses** Two-year (eight term) degree courses in Business, Law, Humanities and Sciences. UCAS and direct application; the university is independent of direct government funding and charges tuition fees (2001 fees were £2125 per term). However, generous scholarships are available, particularly for students from Buckinghamshire and the surrounding counties of Northamptonshire, Oxfordshire, Berkshire, Hertfordshire and Bedfordshire, which, together with the award from the Student Loan Company available to EU students, reduced the fees to £1000 per term in 2001. *(The University of Buckingham, Hunter Street, Buckingham MK18 1EG. Tel 01280 814080; http://www.buckingham.ac.uk)*

Cambridge: Location Colleges situated around the city centre; **Courses** 20 faculties offer a wide range of subjects. Students admitted to colleges, not to the University. Colleges New Hall and Newnham (women only); the following admit both men and women undergraduates: Christ's, Churchill, Clare, Corpus Christi, Downing, Emmanuel, Fitzwilliam, Girton, Gonville & Caius, Homerton, Jesus, King's, Magdalene, Pembroke, Peterhouse, Queens', Robinson, St Catharine's, St John's, Selwyn, Sidney Sussex, Trinity, Trinity Hall. Also Hughes Hall, Lucy Cavendish, St Edmunds and Wolfson (graduates and mature undergraduates). (Enquiries should be addressed to the *Tutor for Admissions, . . . College, Cambridge,* or to *Cambridge Intercollegiate Applications Office, Kellett Lodge, Tennis Court Road, Cambridge*

CB2 1QJ. Tel 01223 333308; http://www.cam.ac.uk; for details of courses at Homerton contact *The Registry, Homerton College, University of Cambridge, Hills Road, Cambridge CB2 2PH. Tel 01223 50711.)*

Cardiff: Location City centre; **Courses** Law, Business, Accounting, Engineering, Health and Life Sciences, Humanities, Social Studies and Theology. *(The University of Wales, Cardiff, PO Box 494, Cardiff, Wales CF1 3XQ. Tel 029 2087 4404; (prospectus requests 029 2087 4899); http://www.cf.ac.uk)*

Central England: Location Main campus two miles from city with six other sites around city centre; **Courses** Art and Design, Built Environment, Business, Computing, Engineering, Law, Health and Community Care. Franchised courses available at associate colleges. Check the prospectus. *(University of Central England in Birmingham, Perry Bar, Birmingham B42 2SU. Tel 0121 331 5000; http://www.uce.ac.uk)*

Central Lancashire: Location Town centre site; **Courses** Business, Social Studies, Tourism, Sciences and Law; HND courses offered. Franchised courses offered at associate colleges. Check the prospectus. *(University of Central Lancashire, Preston PR1 2HE. Tel 01772 201201; http://www.uclan.ac.uk)*

City: Location Small campus site in the City of London; **Courses** Business and Management, Computing, Law, Journalism, Speech Therapy, Nursing, Social Sciences and Engineering. *(City University, Northampton Square, London EC1V 0HB. Tel 020 7477 8000; http://www.city.ac.uk)*

Coventry: Location Purpose-built institution on a central site in Coventry; **Courses** Degree and HND courses in Applied Sciences, Built Environment, Business, Computing, Engineering, Law, Mathematics and Languages. Check the prospectus. *(Coventry University, Priory Street, Coventry CV1 5FB. Tel 024 7688 7688; http://www.coventry.ac.uk)*

Cranfield: Location Campus at Shrivenham; **Courses** Engineering and Applied Science and Defence Management. *(The Royal Military College of Science, Shrivenham, Swindon, Wiltshire SN6 8LA. Tel 01793 785496; http://www.shrivenham.cranfield.ac.uk)*

De Montfort: Location Ten sites, three near Leicester city centre, one in Milton Keynes, two in Bedford and four in Lincolnshire; **Courses** Degree and HND courses in Art and Design, Engineering, Law, Pharmacy, Sciences, Business Studies and Education. Check the prospectus. *(De Montfort University, Leicester, The Gateway, Leicester LE1 9BH. Tel 0116 255 1551; DMU Bedford: Tel 01234 351966; DMU Lincoln: Tel 01522 512912; DMU Milton Keynes: Tel 01908 695511; http://www.dmu.ac.uk)*

Derby: Location Five sites in Derby; **Courses** Education and Social Sciences, Art and Design, Business Studies, Engineering, Environmental and Applied Sciences, European and International Studies, Health and Community Studies, Mathematics and Computing; HND courses also offered. *(University of Derby, Kedleston Road, Derby DE22 1GB. Tel 01332 622222; http://www.derby.ac.uk)*

Dundee: Location City-centre precinct site; teaching hospital in suburbs; **Courses** Arts, Social Sciences, Art and Design, Architecture, Dentistry, Science and Engineering. *(The University, Dundee, Tayside, Scotland DD1 4HN. Tel 01382 344160; http://www.dundee.ac.uk)*

Durham: Location Colleges throughout the city. There are 12 colleges and two societies admitting undergraduates: Collingwood, Grey, Hatfield, St Aidan's, St Chad's, St Cuthbert's, St Hild/St Bede, St John's, St Mary's (women), Trevelyan, University, Van Mildert. Some courses are offered at the Stockton campus; **Courses** Arts, Social Sciences, Education, Law, Medicine (applications through Newcastle University), Engineering, European Studies and Environmental Studies. *(The University of Durham, Old Shire Hall, Durham DH1 3HP. Tel 0191 374 2000; http://www.dur.ac.uk)*

East Anglia: Location Campus site two miles from Norwich; **Courses** Arts, Law, Medicine, Science, Engineering, Accountancy and Computing. *(The University of East Anglia, Norwich NR4 7TJ. Tel 01603 456161; http://www.uea.ac.uk)*

East London: Location Three main campuses – Barking, Docklands and Stratford; **Courses** Degree and HND courses in Business, Social Studies, Engineering, Sciences, Law, Art and Design, and a wide range of combined degrees. *(University of East London, Barking Campus, Longbridge Road, Dagenham, Essex RM8 2AS. Tel 020 8223 2835; http://www.uel.ac.uk)*

Edinburgh: Location Three main sites in and around city centre; **Courses** Arts, Divinity, Education, Law, Medicine, Music, Social Science, Veterinary Medicine, Science, Engineering, Nursing and Commerce. *(The University, Old College, South Bridge, Edinburgh, Lothian, Scotland EH8 9YL. Tel 0131 650 1000; http://www.ed.ac.uk)*

Essex: Location Modern campus two miles east of Colchester; **Courses** Four schools of study cover Law, Humanities and Comparative Studies, Social Sciences and Science and Engineering. Courses also validated for East 15 Acting School at Loughton. *(The University of Essex, Wivenhoe Park, Colchester, Essex CO4 3SQ. Tel 01206 873666; http://www.essex.ac.uk)*

Exeter: Location Two sites in Exeter and one (Camborne School of Mines) in Cornwall; **Courses** Accountancy, Business, Economics, Law, Medicine (Peninsular Medical School – applications through Plymouth University), Social Sciences, Education, Engineering and Mining. *(University of Exeter, Northcote House, The Queen's Drive, Exeter, Devon EX4 4QJ. Tel 01392 263035; http://www.exeter.ac.uk)*

Glamorgan: Location Two sites in town centre; **Courses** Degree, diploma and HND courses are offered in Arts, Social Sciences, Art and Design, Business and Law. Franchised courses are offered by associate colleges some distance from Pontypridd. Check the prospectus. *(University of Glamorgan, Treforest, Pontypridd, Mid-Glamorgan, Wales CF37 1DL. Tel 01443 480480; http://www.glamorgan.ac.uk)*

Glasgow: Location A 14-acre site one mile from city centre; **Courses** Arts, Architecture, Divinity, Law, Engineering, Science and Social Sciences. *(The University, Glasgow, Strathclyde, Scotland G12 8QQ. Tel 0141 330 4575; http://www.gla.ac.uk)*

Glasgow Caledonian: Location Purpose-built campus close to city centre; **Courses** Degree and HND courses in Business, Nursing, Social Work, Social Sciences and Engineering. *(Glasgow Caledonian University, City Campus, Cowcaddens Road, Glasgow, Strathclyde, Scotland G4 0BA. Tel 0141 331 3000; http://www.gcal.ac.uk)*

Greenwich: Location Five main sites in East and South London and Kent; **Courses** Degree and HND courses in Architecture, Business, Engineering, Arts, Social Sciences, Law, Sciences and Education. Check the prospectus. *(University of Greenwich, Wellington Street, Woolwich, London SE18 6PF. Tel 020 8331 8590; http://www.gre.ac.uk)*

Heriot-Watt: Location Six miles west of central Edinburgh on a 370-acre site of wooded parkland around a small loch; Scottish Borders campus at Galashiels; **Courses** Science, Engineering, Economic and Social Studies, Environmental Studies and (in conjunction with Edinburgh College of Art) Art and Design. *(Heriot-Watt University, Edinburgh, Riccarton, Edinburgh, Lothian, Scotland EH14 4AS. Tel 0131 451 3376; http://www.hw.ac.uk)*

Hertfordshire: Location Four main campuses at Hatfield, Hertford, St Albans and Watford; **Courses** Art and Design, Business, Engineering, Health and Human Sciences, Humanities and Education, Information Services, Natural Sciences and Combined Studies. HND courses are also offered. Franchised courses are offered by associate colleges. Check the prospectus. *(University of Hertfordshire, College Lane, Hatfield, Hertfordshire AL10 9AB. Tel 01707 284800; http://www.hert.ac.uk)*

Highlands and Islands (UHI): Location A partnership of colleges placed throughout Scotland (see **Section 8**); **Courses** Arts, Culture and Heritage, Business and Leisure, Environmental and Natural Systems Sciences, Health and Social Studies and Information and Engineering Systems. Full-time undergraduate courses are provided by the following partner colleges (for addresses see **Section 8**): Highland Theological College, Inverness College, Lews Castle College, Lochaber College, Moray College, North Atlantic Fisheries College, North Highland College, Orkney College, Perth College, Sabhal Mor Ostaig, Scottish Association for Marine Science and Shetland College. Enquiries to the Executive Office. *(University of the Highlands and Islands (UHI), Caledonia House, 63 Academy Street, Inverness, Highland, Scotland IV1 1BB. Tel 01463 279000; http://www.uhi.ac.uk/admissions)*

Huddersfield: Location Two main sites in and near Huddersfield; **Courses** Offered in Arts, Business Studies, Architecture, Education, Engineering, Science and Law. HND courses are also offered. *(The University of Huddersfield, Queensgate, Huddersfield HD1 3DH. Tel 01484 422288; http://www.hud.ac.uk)*

Hull: Location Precinct three miles north of Hull; **Courses** Single and joint degrees in Arts, Music, Law, Accounting, Science and Engineering. *(The University of Hull, Admissions Office, Cottingham Road, Hull, East Yorkshire HU6 7RX. Tel 01482 466100; http://www.hull.ac.uk)*

Keele: Location Campus two miles from Newcastle-under-Lyme; **Courses** Social Studies, Physiotherapy, Medicine (applications through Manchester University), Sciences, Arts, Languages, Law and Computer Sciences. Many students follow two-subject courses. Some follow the Foundation course enabling a change of subject at end of the first year. *(The University of Keele, Keele, Staffordshire ST5 5BG. Tel 01782 621111; http://www.keele.ac.uk)*

Kent: Location A 300-acre campus overlooking Canterbury; **Courses** Computer Science, Electronic Engineering, Mathematics, Arts, Humanities, Natural Sciences, Business and Social Sciences. *(The University of Kent at Canterbury, Canterbury, Kent CT2 7NZ. Tel 01227 827272; http://www.ukc.ac.uk)*

Kingston: Location Four main sites in and around the riverside town of Kingston-upon-Thames; **Courses** Architecture, Art & Design, Maths, Science, Engineering, Computing, Business & Law, Humanities and Social Sciences. Franchised courses at associate colleges. Check the prospectus. *(Kingston University, Admissions Office, Cooper House, 40–46 Surbiton Road, Kingston-upon-Thames, Surrey KT1 2HX. Tel 020 8547 2000; http://www.kingston.ac.uk)*

Lampeter: Location Large site in the small country town; **Courses** Degree courses mainly in the Faculty of Arts including Languages, Computing, Management, Archaeology and Theology. *(The University of Wales, Lampeter, Ceredigion, Wales SA48 7ED. Tel 01570 422351; http://www.lampeter.ac.uk)*

Lancaster: Location Two hundred-acre parkland site three miles south of the city centre; **Courses** Accounting, Languages, Sciences, Art, Economics, Computer Science and Engineering. *(The University, Lancaster LA1 4YW. Tel 01524 65201; http://www.lancs.ac.uk)*

Leeds: Location Main site near city centre; **Courses** Arts, Social Studies, Law, Engineering, Sciences, Medicine, Dentistry, Radiography and Midwifery. *(The University of Leeds, Leeds LS2 9JT. Tel 0113 233 3999; http://www.leeds.ac.uk)*

Leeds Met: Location Three campuses in Leeds and Harrogate; **Courses** Almost all courses are vocational and lead to degrees, or in some cases HNDs, including Architecture, Business, Art and Design, Physical Education, Teaching, Engineering and Law. *(Leeds Metropolitan University, City Campus, Leeds LS1 3HE. Tel 0113 283 2600; http://www.lmu.ac.uk)*

Leicester: Location Compact site with modern buildings one mile south of the city; **Courses** Arts, Engineering, Sciences and Medicine. *(University of Leicester, University Road, Leicester LE1 7RH. Tel 0116 252 5281; http://www.le.ac.uk)*

Lincolnshire & Humberside: Location Four sites – one in Lincoln and three in and around Hull city centre; **Courses** Law, Health Studies, Social Sciences, Journalism, Psychology, Environmental Studies, Food Science, Accountancy, Languages, Engineering, Art and Design and Agriculture. Degree, DipHE and HND courses are offered. Franchised courses offered by associate colleges. Check the prospectus. *(University of Lincolnshire & Humberside, Humberside University Campus, Sutton House, Cottingham Road, Hull HU6 7RT. Tel 01482 440550; Lincoln University Campus, Brayford Pool, Lincoln LN6 7TS; http://www.lincoln.ac.uk)*

Liverpool: Location Compact site close to city centre; **Courses** Arts, Social Sciences, Medicine, Dentistry, Nursing, Engineering and Sciences. *(The University of Liverpool, Liverpool L69 3BX. Tel 0151 794 2000; http://www.liv.ac.uk)*

Liverpool John Moores: Location Four campuses within the city; **Courses** Business, Sciences, Art and Design, Architecture, Engineering and Education; HND courses also offered. Franchised courses offered by associate colleges. Check the prospectus. *(Liverpool John Moores University, Roscoe Court, 4 Rodney Street, Liverpool L1 2TZ. Tel 0151 231 5090/5091; http://www.livjm.ac.uk)*

London – Birkbeck (Birk): Location Central London; **Courses:** Degree courses are offered for 5000 mature part-time students. Evening teaching. A-level offers for places not made. *(Birkbeck College, University of London, Malet Street, London WC1E 7HX. Tel 020 7631 6270; http://www.bbk.ac.uk)*

London – British Institute in Paris:
Courses BA French Studies. *(The British Institute in Paris, University of London, Department of French Studies, 9–11 rue de Constantine, 75340 Paris Cedex 07. Tel 00331 4411 7383; http://www.bip.ion.ac.uk)*

London – Courtauld Institute of Art (Court): Location Central London; **Courses** History of Art. *(Courtauld Institute of Art, University of London, Somerset House, Strand, London WC2R 0RN. Tel 020 7848 2645; http://www.courtauld.ac.uk)*

London – Goldsmiths College (Gold): Location New Cross – 15-minute rail link with Charing Cross; **Courses** Art and Design, Arts, Psychology, Mathematics and Education. *(Goldsmiths College, University of London, Lewisham Way, New Cross, London SE14 6NW. Tel 020 7919 7282; http://www.gold.ac.uk)*

London – Heythrop College (Hey): Location Central London; **Courses** Theology, Philosophy. *(Heythrop College, University of London, Kensington Square, London W8 5HQ. Tel 020 7395 6600; http://www.heythrop.ac.uk)*

London – Imperial College of Science, Technology and Medicine (Imp): Location Precinct site in South Kensington, Medical School sites and a site near Ashford in Kent (originally London, Wye College); **Courses** Subject areas include Engineering, Sciences, Mining, Metallurgy, Medicine and Agriculture (Applied Natural Sciences). *(Imperial College of Science, Technology and Medicine, University of London, South Kensington, London SW7 2AZ. Tel 020 7594 8014; http://www.ic.ac.uk)*

London – King's College (King's): Location Central London; **Courses** Humanities, Science, Engineering, Education, Law, Medicine and Dentistry. *(Guy's, King's and St Thomas' Schools of Medicine and Dentistry, Hodgkin Building, Guy's Campus, London Bridge, London SE1 9RT. Tel 020 7848 6501; School of Biomedical Sciences, Academic Centre, Guy's Campus, London SE1 9RT. Tel 020 7848 6400; School of Health and Life Sciences, Programme Office, Franklin Wilkins Building, 150 Stamford Street, London SE1 8WA. Tel 020 7848 4190; School of Humanities: Tel 020 7836 5454; School of Law: Tel 020 7848 2503; School of Physical Sciences and Engineering: Tel 020 7873 2271; Florence Nightingale School of Nursing and Midwifery, James Clark Maxwell Building, 57 Waterloo Road, London SE1 8WA. Tel 020 7848 4698; King's College, University of London, Strand, London WC2R 2LS; http://www.kcl.ac.uk)*

London – Queen Mary College (QM): Location Campus college centrally located near the City and Docklands; **Courses** Arts, Social Studies, Informatics and Mathematical Sciences, Engineering, Law, Physical and Biological Sciences, Medicine and Dentistry. *(Queen Mary and Westfield College, University of London, Mile End Road, London E1 4NS. Tel 020 7882 5555; http://www.qmw.ac.uk)*

London – Royal Holloway (RH): Location Country campus close to Windsor and 30 minutes from central London; **Courses** Faculties of Science, Arts and Drama, Music and Social Sciences. *(Royal Holloway, University of London, Egham Hill, Egham, Surrey TW20 0EX. Tel 01784 434455; http://www.rhbnc.ac.uk)*

London – Royal Veterinary College (RVC): Location London and Potters Bar; **Courses** Veterinary Science; pre-clinical work takes place in Camden Town. *(Royal Veterinary College, University of London, Royal College Street, London NW1 0TU. Tel 020 7468 5000; http://www.rvc.ac.uk)*

London – St George's Hospital Medical School This is the only remaining 'stand-alone' medical school in London. Applications are submitted to St George's through UCAS and all applicants under serious consideration are interviewed. *(St George's Hospital Medical School, University of London, Cranmer Terrace, Tooting, London SW17 0RE. Tel 020 8725 5992; http://www.sghms.ac.uk)*

London – School of Economics and Political Science (LSE): Location Central London; **Courses** This is the leading institution for courses in Social Sciences in the UK, perhaps in the world. *(London School of Economics and Political Science, University of London, PO Box 13401, Houghton Street, London WC2A 2AS. Tel 020 7405 7686; http://www.lse.ac.uk)*

London – School of Oriental and African Studies (SOAS): Location Central London; **Courses** Oriental and African languages, Law and other studies. *(School of Oriental and African Studies, University of London, Thornhaugh Street, Russell Square, London WC1H 0XG. Tel 020 7637 2388; http://www.soas.ac.uk)*

London – School of Pharmacy: Location Central London; **Courses** Pharmacy. *(The School of Pharmacy, University of London, 29–39 Brunswick Square, London WC1N 1AX. Tel 020 7753 5831; http://www.ulsop.ac.uk)*

London – University College (UCL): Location Central London; **Courses** Arts, Built Environment, Law, Social Sciences, East European Studies, Fine Art and Medicine. *(University College London, University of London, Gower Street, London WC1E 6BT. Tel 020 7679 3000; http://www.ucl.ac.uk)*

London Guildhall: Location Six main sites in London; **Courses** Business, Social Studies, Art and Design; extensive modular scheme. HND courses offered. *(London Guildhall University, 133 Whitechapel High Street, London E1 7QA. Tel 020 7320 1616; http://www.lgu.ac.uk)*

Loughborough: Location Campus to the west of the town; **Courses** Drama, Social Sciences, Information Studies, Engineering, Industrial Design, Accounting, Business and Science. *(Loughborough University, Loughborough, Leicestershire LE11 3TU. Tel 01509 263171; http://www.lboro.ac.uk)*

Luton: Location Luton town centre and also a rural campus; **Courses** Degree, professional and diploma courses and a large number of HND courses in Art and Design, Business, Psychology, Social Sciences and a large number of combinations – see prospectus.

(University of Luton, Park Square, Luton, Bedfordshire LU1 3JU. Tel 01582 734111; http://www.luton.ac.uk)

Manchester: Location Campus site south of the city centre; **Courses** Arts, Modern Languages, Social Studies, Economics, Law, Architecture, Education, Science, Engineering, Medicine and Dentistry. *(The University of Manchester, Manchester M13 9PL. Tel 0161 275 2077; http://www.man.ac.uk)*

Manchester – The University of Manchester Institute of Science and Technology (UMIST): Location City centre; **Courses** Business, Languages, Engineering, Sciences and Technology. *(The University of Manchester Institute of Science and Technology, Sackville Street, Manchester M60 1QD. Tel 0161 236 3311; http://www.umist.ac.uk)*

Manchester Met: Location Seven main sites in and around the city and a campus in Cheshire; **Courses** Art and Design, Architecture, Business, Languages, Engineering, Law, Sciences and Education; also HND courses. *(The Manchester Metropolitan University, Oxford Street, Manchester M15 6BH. Tel 0161 247 2000; http://www.mmu.ac.uk)*

Middlesex: Location Six main sites, three minor and four hospital locations in north London and Middlesex; **Courses** Arts, Business, Performing Arts, Health Studies, Nursing, Social Sciences, Art and Design, Education and Law. *(Middlesex University, White Hart Lane, London N17 8HR. Tel 020 8411 5000; http://www.mdx.ac.uk)*

Napier: Location Seven main teaching sites to the south and west of the city centre and also at Melrose and Livingston; **Courses** Art and Design, Arts, Social Sciences, Engineering, Technology and Business; HND courses. *(Napier University, 219 Colinton Road, Edinburgh, Lothian, Scotland EH14 1DJ. Tel 0131 444 2266; http://www.napier.ac.uk)*

Newcastle: Location City centre precinct; **Courses** Agriculture, Biological Sciences, Art, Medicine, Dentistry, Architecture, Law, Engineering and Science. *(University of Newcastle upon Tyne, 6 Kensington*

Terrace, Newcastle upon Tyne NE1 7RU. Tel 0191 222 6138/8672; http://www.ncl.ac.uk)

North London: Location two main sites in Islington; **Courses** Degree and HND courses are offered in Architecture, Business, Art and Design, Law, Sciences, Mathematics and Environmental Studies. There is also an extensive Combined Honours scheme; franchised courses are offered by associate colleges. Check the prospectus. *(University of North London, 166–220 Holloway Road, London N7 8DB. Tel 020 7753 3355; http://www.unl.ac.uk)*

Northumbria: Location Main sites at Newcastle, Carlisle and Morpeth; **Courses** Degree and HND courses in Accountancy, Business, Languages, Social Sciences, Law, Art and Design, Engineering and Sciences. *(University of Northumbria at Newcastle, Ellison Place, Newcastle upon Tyne NE1 8ST. Tel 0191 227 4777; http://www.unn.ac.uk)*

Nottingham: Location Campus site in parkland west of the city and two other sites, one at Sutton Bonington ten miles south; **Courses** Arts, Social Sciences, Law, Science, Engineering, Medicine, Nursing and Agriculture. *(The University of Nottingham, University Park, Nottingham NG7 2RD. Tel 0115 951 6565; http://www.nottingham.ac.uk)*

Nottingham Trent: Location Three sites – one close to city centre and two four miles away; **Courses** Business, Art and Design, Engineering, Education and Sciences; also HND courses. Franchised courses are offered by associate colleges. Check the prospectus. *(The Nottingham Trent University, Burton Street, Nottingham NG1 4BU. Tel 0115 941 8418; http://www.ntu.ac.uk)*

Oxford: Location Colleges situated throughout the city; **Colleges** Balliol, Brasenose, Christ Church, Corpus Christi, Exeter, Hertford, Jesus, Keble, Lady Margaret Hall, Lincoln, Magdalen, Manchester (mature students only), Mansfield, Merton, New College, Oriel, Pembroke, Queen's, St Anne's, St Catherine's, St Edmund Hall, St Hilda's (women only), St Hugh's, St John's, St Peter's, Somerville, Trinity, University, Wadham, Worcester. Private Halls: Campion Hall (men only), Greyfriars, Regent's Park, St Benet's Hall; **Courses** Arts, Social Studies, Engineering, Materials Science, Sciences and Fine Art. (Enquiries should be addressed to *The Tutor for . . . Admissions, . . . College, Oxford,* or to *The Oxford Colleges Admissions Office, Wellington Square, Oxford OX1 2JD. Tel 01865 270207; http://www.oxford.ac.uk)*

Oxford Brookes: Location Three sites – main campus at Headington; **Courses** Modular courses in Business,Science and Engineering, Art, Nursing, Built Environment, Law and Social Sciences. *(Oxford Brookes University, Gypsy Lane, Headington, Oxford OX3 0BP. Tel 01865 483040; http://www.brookes.ac.uk)*

Paisley: Location Twenty-acre campus in the centre of Paisley, seven miles west of Glasgow and at Craigie campus at Ayr; **Courses** Technology, Science, Engineering, Computing, Surveying, Business Management, Social Studies and Education. *(University of Paisley, High Street, Paisley, Strathclyde, Scotland PA1 2BE. Tel 0141 848 3727; http://www.paisley.ac.uk)*

Plymouth: Location Four sites in Plymouth (main), Exeter, Exmouth and at the former Seale Hayne College; **Courses** Degree and HND courses in Agriculture, Business, Languages, Medicine (Peninsular Medical School – see also Exeter University), Sciences, Marine Studies, Social Studies and Art and Design. Franchised courses at associate colleges; check the prospectus. *(University of Plymouth, Drake Circus, Plymouth PL4 8AA. Tel 01752 232232; http://www.plym.ac.uk)*

Portsmouth: Location Two sites – campus near the city centre; **Courses** Portsmouth Business School, Faculty of the Environment, Faculty of Humanities and Social Sciences, Faculty of Science and Faculty of Technology. Franchised courses at associate colleges; check the prospectus. *(The University of Portsmouth, University House, Winston Churchill Avenue, Portsmouth PO1 2UP. Tel 023 9284 8484; http://www.port.ac.uk)*

Reading: Location A large parkland site south of the town; **Courses** Agriculture and Food, Letters and Social Sciences, Education and Community Studies, Art and Design, Law, Science and Urban Studies. *(The University of Reading, PO Box 217, Reading, Berkshire RG6 2AH. Tel 0118 987 5123; http://www.reading.ac.uk)*

Robert Gordon: Location Six sites in or near the centre of Aberdeen; **Courses** Business, Engineering, Sciences, Nursing, Pharmacy; HND courses also offered. *(The Robert Gordon University, Schoolhill, Aberdeen, Grampian, Scotland AB10 1FR. Tel 01224 262000; http://www.rgu.ac.uk)*

St Andrews: Location Small campus site in the town; **Courses** Arts, Social Sciences and a large number of Combined courses. *(The University of St Andrews, College Gate, St Andrews, Fife, Scotland KY16 9AJ. Tel 01334 462150; http://www.stand.ac.uk)*

Salford: Location Campus site close to Manchester city centre; **Courses** Art and Design, Business, Health Studies, Engineering, Environmental Studies, Media Studies and Sciences. *(The University of Salford, The Crescent, Salford M5 4WT. Tel 0161 295 5000; http://www.salford.ac.uk)*

Sheffield: Location Site one mile from the city centre; **Courses** Arts, Social Sciences, Law, Architecture, Sciences, Engineering, Medicine and Dentistry. *(The University of Sheffield, Western Bank, Sheffield, Yorkshire S10 2TN. Tel 0114 222 2000. Medical School; Tel 0114 271 2142; http://www.shef.ac.uk)*

Sheffield Hallam: Location Three sites near the city centre; **Courses** Business, Languages, Education, Art and Design, Engineering and Sciences; HND courses also offered. Franchised courses are offered by associate colleges; check the prospectus. *(Sheffield Hallam University, City Campus, Pond Street, Sheffield, Yorkshire S1 1WB. Tel 0114 225 5555; http://www.shu.ac.uk)*

South Bank: Location Two campuses in central south London; **Courses** Architecture, Languages, Business, Engineering, Sciences and Law. Franchised courses at associate colleges; check the prospectus. *(South Bank University, 103 Borough Road, London SE1 0AA. Tel 020 7815 7815; http://www.sbu.ac.uk)*

Southampton: Location Landscaped site two miles from the city centre; **Courses** Arts, Languages, Archaeology, Art and Design, Science, Engineering, European Studies, Medicine, Nursing and Law. The University of Southampton New College and Winchester School of Art are campuses of The University of Southampton. *(The University of Southampton, Highfield, Southampton SO17 1BJ. Tel 023 8059 5000; http://www.soton.ac.uk)*

Staffordshire: Location Sites in Stafford, Stoke-on-Trent and Lichfield; **Courses** Degree and HND courses are offered in Accountancy, Business, Media, Social Sciences, Art and Design, Engineering and Law. Franchised courses are offered by associate colleges; check the prospectus. *(Staffordshire University, College Road, Stoke-on-Trent, Staffordshire ST4 2DE. Tel 01782 294000; http://www.staffs.ac.uk)*

Stirling: Location A large scenic campus site two miles north of the town; **Courses** Arts, Social Sciences, Education, Languages, Film, Accountancy and Business. *(The University of Stirling, Stirling, Central Scotland FK9 4LA. Tel 01786 473171; http://www.stir.ac.uk)*

Strathclyde: Location Two campuses: the Anderson Campus in the centre of Glasgow, and the Jordanhill Campus, a 70-acre parkland site on the west side of the city; **Courses** Education, Business, Social Sciences, Law, Engineering and Science. *(The University of Strathclyde, 16 Richmond Street, Glasgow, Scotland G1 1XQ. Tel 0141 552 4400; http://www.strath.ac.uk)*

Sunderland: Location Three sites near city centre; **Courses** Art and Design, Computing, Education, Engineering,

Environment, Health Sciences and Business; HND courses also available. Franchised courses are offered by associate colleges; check the prospectus. *(University of Sunderland, Unit 4C, Technology Park, Chester Road, Sunderland, Tyne and Wear SR2 7PS. Tel 0191 515 3000; http://www.sunderland.ac.uk)*

Surrey: Location Hill site next to the Cathedral and close to the city centre; **Courses** Engineering, Materials Science, Music, Psychology and Sciences. *(The University of Surrey, Guildford, Surrey GU2 5XH. Tel 01483 300800; http://www.surrey.ac.uk)*

Surrey Roehampton: Location Based around four colleges (Digby Stuart, Froebel, Whitelands and Southlands); **Courses** Over 400 undergraduate degree programmes are offered on a modular system leading to BA, BSc, BMus or BA with Qualified Teacher Status degrees. *(The University of Surrey Roehampton, Roehampton Lane, London SW15 5PU. Tel 020 8392 3232; http://www.roehampton.ac.uk)*

Sussex: Location Campus site four miles north of Brighton; **Courses** Arts, Social Sciences, Law, Sciences, Engineering and Computing. *(University of Sussex, Sussex House, Falmer, Brighton, Sussex BN1 9RH. Tel 01273 678416; http://www.sussex.ac.uk)*

Swansea: Location Campus site west of the city; **Courses** Arts, Social Sciences, Languages, Humanities, Business, Law, Engineering, Health Care and Computer Science. *(University of Wales, Swansea, Singleton Park, Swansea, Wales SA2 8PP. Tel 01792 295784; http//www.swansea.ac.uk)*

Teesside: Location One site near to town centre; **Courses** Business, Computing, Art and Design, Mathematics, Social Sciences, Science and Technology; HND courses also available. Franchised courses are offered by associate colleges; check the prospectus. *(University of Teesside, Borough Road, Middlesbrough, Cleveland TS1 3BA. Tel 01642 385200; http://www.tees.ac.uk)*

Thames Valley: Location Sites at Ealing and Slough; **Courses** Degree and HND courses. A large number of Combined courses in Business, Arts, Social Sciences, Leisure, Media, Languages, Law and Music. *(Thames Valley University, St Mary's Road, Ealing, London W5 5RF. Tel 020 8579 5000; http://www.tvu.ac.uk)*

Ulster: Location Four campuses – Jordanstown, Belfast, Coleraine and Londonderry; **Courses** Business, Art and Design, Business and Management, Engineering, Informatics, Science, Social and Health Sciences and Education. *(University of Ulster, Coleraine, County Londonderry, Northern Ireland BT52 1SA. Tel 028 7032 4221; http://www.ulst.ac.uk)*

Cardiff: University of Wales College of Medicine (UWCM): Location Fifty-acre parkland site in Cardiff with University Hospital; **Courses** Medicine, Dentistry and Nursing. *(The University of Wales College of Medicine, Heath Park, Cardiff, Wales CF4 4XN. Tel 029 2074 2027; http://www.cf.ac.uk)*

Warwick: Location A large campus site outside Coventry; **Courses** Economics, Mathematics, Languages, Psychology, Engineering, Sciences Medicine (with Leicester University) and Law. *(The University of Warwick, Coventry, Warwickshire CV4 7AL. Tel 024 7652 3723; http://www.warwick.ac.uk)*

Westminster: Location Four campuses; three in the West End of London and one in Harrow; **Courses** Degree and HND courses in Architecture, Surveying, Engineering, Law, Art and Design, Biological and Health Sciences. *(University of Westminster, Metford House, 115 New Cavendish Street, London W1M 8JS. Tel 020 7911 5000; http://www.wmin.ac.uk)*

Wolverhampton: Location Four campuses plus three Nurse Training centres; **Courses** (modular) Art and Design, Business, Computing and IT, Education, Engineering, Health, Humanities, Languages, Law, Leisure, Midwifery, Nursing, Science, Social Science and Sports Studies. Franchised courses offered with associate colleges;

check the prospectus. *(The University of Wolverhampton, Wulfruna Street, Wolverhampton, West Midlands WV1 1SB. Tel 01902 321000; http://www.wlv.ac.uk)*

York: Location Campus east of the city; **Courses** Applied and Natural Sciences, Arts, Archaeology, Computer Science, Engineering, Mathematics, Politics, Economics, Philosophy and Social Sciences. *(The University of York, Heslington, York YO1 5DD. Tel 01904 433533; http://www.york.ac.uk)*

Section 2: University Colleges and Colleges and Institutes of Higher Education. These institutions are in the UCAS scheme for their courses. (See also specialist and other colleges in sections 3, 4, 5, 6 and 7.)

Changes are taking place in this higher education sector, with some colleges merging with, or becoming affiliated to, universities. Changes are also taking place in the further education sector to give more degree course opportunities. All this means that you can study for a degree or diploma in a wide range of colleges, and it is important that you read prospectuses and check web sites carefully and go to college open days to find out as much as you can about them and about their courses which interest you.

Aberystwyth: University Theological College and College of Welsh Independents King Street, Aberystwyth, Wales SY23 2LT. Tel 0970 624574.

Bath Spa University College Newton Park, Bath, Somerset BA2 9BN. Tel 01225 875875; http://www.bathspa.ac.uk

Bell College of Technology Almada Street, Hamilton, Lanarkshire, Scotland ML3 0JB. Tel 01698 283100; http://www.bell.ac.uk

Bishop Grosseteste College Newport, Lincoln LN1 3DY. Tel 01522 527347; http://www.bgc.ac.uk

Bolton Institute of Higher Education Deane Road, Bolton, Lancashire BL3 5AB. Tel 01204 528851; http://www.bolton.ac.uk

Bradford College Great Horton Road, Bradford, West Yorkshire BD7 1AY. Tel 01274 753111; http://www.bilk.ac.uk

Bretton Hall (merger prepared with University of Leeds for August 2001) West Bretton, Wakefield, West Yorkshire WF4 4LG. Tel 01924 830261; http://www.bretton.ac.uk

Buckinghamshire Chilterns University College Queen Alexandria Road, High Wycombe, Buckinghamshire HP11 2JZ. Tel 01494 522141; http://www.bcuc.ac.uk

Canterbury Christ Church University College North Holmes Road, Canterbury, Kent CT1 1QU. Tel 01227 782423; http://www.canterbury.ac.uk

Cardiff (University of Wales Institute – UWI) PO Box 377, Llandaff Campus, Western Avenue, Cardiff CF5 2SG. Tel 029 2041 6070. http://www.wyc.ac.uk

Cheltenham & Gloucester College of Higher Education PO Box 220, The Park, Cheltenham, Gloucestershire GL50 2QF. Tel 01242 532835; http://www.chelt.ac.uk

Chester, A College of the University of Liverpool Parkgate Road, Chester CH1 4BJ.Tel 01244 375444; http://www.chester.ac.uk

Chichester University College Bishop Otter Campus, College Lane, Chichester, West Sussex PO19 4PE. Tel 01243 816002; http://www.chiche.ac.uk

Colchester Institute Sheepen Road, Colchester, Essex CO3 3LL. Tel 01206 518000; http://www.colch-institute.ac.uk

Edge Hill College of Higher Education St Helen's Road, Ormskirk, Lancashire L39 4QP. Tel 01695 584274; http://www.edgehill.ac.uk

Harper Adams University College Newport, Shropshire TF10 8NB. Tel 01952 820280; http://www.harper-adam.ac.uk

King Alfred's Winchester Sparkford Road, Winchester, Hampshire SO22 4NR. Tel 01962 841515; http://www.wkac.ac.uk

Leeds, Trinity & All Saints College Brownberrie Lane, Horsforth, Leeds LS18 5HD. Tel 0113 283 7123; http://www.tasc.ac.uk

Liverpool Hope Hope Park, Liverpool L16 9JD. Tel 0151 291 3295; http://www.livhope.ac.uk

Newman College of Higher Education Genners Lane, Bartley Green, Birmingham, West Midlands B32 3NT. Tel 0121 476 1181; http://www.newman.ac.uk

Newport, University of Wales College PO Box 101, Newport, South Wales NP6 1YH. Tel 01633 432432; http://www.newport.ac.uk

North East Wales Institute of Higher Education Plas Coch, Mold Road, Wrexham, Clwyd, Wales LL11 2AW. Tel 01978 290666; http://www.newi.ac.uk

Northampton University College Park Campus, Boughton Green Road, Northampton NN2 7AL. Tel 01604 735500; http://www.northampton.ac.uk

Northern College of Education Aberdeen Campus, Hilton Place, Aberdeen, Scotland AB24 4FA. Tel 01224 283500; http://www.olcol.ac.uk (Mergers pending with Aberdeen and Dundee Universities.)

Oxford Westminster College This college is due to merge with Oxford Brookes University in July 2000.

Queen Margaret University College Clerwood Terrace, Edinburgh, Lothian, Scotland EH12 8TS. Tel 0131 317 3247; http://www.qmced.ac.uk

Ripon & York St John College Lord Mayor's Walk, York YO31 7EX. Tel 01904 656771; http://www.ucrysj.ac.uk

St Mark & St John College Derriford Road, Plymouth, Devon PL6 8BH. Tel 01752 636827; http://www.marjon.ac.uk

St Martin's College, Lancaster: Ambleside: Carlisle Lancaster, Cumbria LA1 3JD. Tel Lancaster 01524 384444; Ambleside 01539 430211; Clarence House, Fese Street, Carlisle, Cumbria CA1 2HH. Tel 01228 616235; http://www.ucsm.ac.uk

St Mary's College Waldegrave Road, Twickenham, Middlesex TW1 4SX. Tel 020 8240 4029; http://www.smuc.ac.uk

Southampton Institute East Park Terrace, Southampton, Hampshire SO14 0RT. Tel 023 8031 9000; http://www.solent.ac.uk

Stranmillis University College: A College of the Queen's University of Belfast Stranmillis Road, Belfast, Northern Ireland BT9 5DY. Tel 028 9038 1271; http://www.stran-mi.ac.uk

Suffolk College Ipswich, Suffolk IP4 1LT. Tel 01473 296369; http://www.suffolk.ac.uk

Surrey Institute of Art and Design, University College Falkner Road, Farnham, Surrey GU9 7DS. Tel 01252 892609; http://www.surrart.ac.uk

Swansea Institute of Higher Education Mount Pleasant Campus, Swansea, Wales SA1 6ED. Tel 01792 481000.

Trinity Carmarthen College Carmarthenshire, Wales SA31 3EP. Tel 01267 676767; http://www.trinity/cm.ac.uk

Warrington Collegiate Institute Padgate Campus, Crab Lane, Warrington, Cheshire WA2 0DB. Tel 01925 494494; http://www.warr.ac.uk

Worcester University College Henwick Grove, Worcester WR2 6AJ. Tel 01905 855111; http://www.worc.ac.uk

Section 3: Colleges of Agriculture and Horticulture (see also Section 2, 6, 7 and 8)

Some Colleges are in the UCAS scheme (as indicated) for some or all of their courses (see UCAS *Directory* for details). Apply direct to Colleges for courses outside UCAS.

Askham Bryan College Askham Bryan, York YO2 3FR. Tel 01904 772211; http://www.askham-bryan.ac.uk (UCAS)

Berkshire College of Agriculture Hall Place, Burchett's Green, Maidenhead, Berkshire SL6 6QR. Tel 01628 824444; http://www.berks-coll.ag.ac.uk

Bicton College of Agriculture East Budleigh, Budleigh Salterton, Devon EX9 7BY. Tel 01395 562300; http://www.eclipse.co.uk/bicton

Bishop Burton College Bishop Burton, York Road, Beverley, East Yorkshire HU17 8QG. Tel 01964 553000; http://www.bishopb-college.ac.uk (UCAS)

Cambridgeshire College of Agriculture and Horticulture Landbeach Road, Milton, Cambridgeshire CB4 6DB. Tel 01223 860701.

Cheshire College of Agriculture Reaseheath, Nantwich, Cheshire CW5 6DF. Tel 01270 625131; http://www.reaseheath.ac.uk

De Montfort University School of Agriculture and Horticulture Caythorpe Court, near Grantham, Lincolnshire NG32 3EP. Tel 01400 272521. (UCAS)

Durham College of Agriculture and Horticulture Houghall, Durham DH1 3SG. Tel 0191 386 1351.

Enniskillen College of Agriculture Levaghy, Enniskillen, Co Fermanagh, Northern Ireland BT74 4GF. Tel 01365 344853; http://www.enniskillen.ac.uk (UCAS)

Greenmount and Enniskillen Colleges Greenmount Road, Antrim, Co Antrim, Northern Ireland BT41 4PU. Tel 028 9442 6700; http://www.greenmount.ac.uk

Harper Adams University College Newport, Shropshire TF10 8NB. Tel 01952 820280; http://www.harper-adam.ac.uk (UCAS)

Lackham College Lacock, Chippenham, Wiltshire SN15 2NY. Tel 01249 466806.

Loughry College of Agriculture Cookstown, Co Tyrone, Northern Ireland BT80 9AA. Tel 028 9076 8107.

Myerscough College (affiliated to Central Lancashire University) Myerscough Hall, St Michael's Road, Bilsborrow, Preston, Lancashire PR3 0RY. Tel 01995 640611; http://www.myerscough.ac.uk

Newton Rigg Campus (Central Lancashire University) Newton Rigg, Penrith, Cumbria CA11 0AH. Tel 01768 863791; http://www.newtonrigg.ac.uk

Otley College, Otley, Ipswich, Suffolk IP6 9EY. Tel: 01473 785543; http://wwar.otleycollege.ac.uk

Pershore Group of Colleges (includes Pershore College, Hindlip College and Holme Lacy College) Avonbank, Pershore, Worcestershire WR10 3JP. Tel 01386 552443. http://www.pershore.ac.uk (UCAS)

Plumpton College, Ditchling Road, Plumpton, Nr. Lewes, East Sussex BN7 3AE. Tel 01273 890454.

Reaseheath College See **Cheshire College of Agriculture**.

Rodbaston College Rodbaston, Penkridge, Stafford ST19 5PH. Tel 01785 712209; http://www.rodbaston.ac.uk

Royal Agricultural College Cirencester, Gloucestershire GL7 6JS. Tel 01285 641404; http://www.royagcol.ac.uk (UCAS)

School of Agriculture & Food Science, The Queen's University of Belfast Newforge Lane, Belfast BT5 9PX. Tel 028 9025 5202; http://www.qub.ac.uk/ajs (UCAS)

Scottish Agricultural College The National College for Food, Land and Environmental Studies, Auchincruive, Ayr, Strathclyde, Scotland KA6 5HW. Tel 01292 525350; http://www.sac.ac.uk (UCAS)

Seale-Hayne Faculty of Agriculture, Food and Land Use (University of Plymouth) Newton Abbot, Devon TQ10 6HR. Tel 01626 325606; http://www.plymouth.asc.uk (UCAS)

Sparsholt College, Hampshire Sparsholt, Winchester, Hampshire SO21 2NF. Tel 01962 776441; http://www.sparsholt.ac.uk (UCAS)

Welsh College of Horticulture Northrop, Mold, Flintshire, Wales CH7 6AA. Tel 01352 841000; http://www.wcoh.ac.uk

Welsh Institute of Rural Studies
Llanbadarn Fawr, Aberystwyth, Ceredigion, Wales SY23 3AL. Tel 01970 624471.

Writtle College Lordship Lane, Writtle, Chelmsford, Essex CM1 3RR. Tel 01245 424200; http://www.writtle.ac.uk (UCAS)

Section 4: Colleges of Art

Many Colleges of Art are in UCAS for some or all of their courses (see the UCAS *Directory* for details). Some have now merged with universities – check with the UCAS *Directory* and prospectuses for details. Note that Art and Design courses are also offered by universities and higher and further colleges. Apply direct for courses outside UCAS.

Architectural Association (School of Architecture) The School offers RIBA Parts I and II and the AA Diploma, and has an international reputation. It is situated in Georgian houses in the centre of London. There are approximately 260 fee-paying students. Architectural Association School, 34 Bedford Square, London WC1B 3ES. Tel 020 7636 0974; http://www.arch-assoc.org.uk

Arts Institute of Bournemouth
Wallisdown Road, Poole, Dorset BH12 5HH. Tel 01202 533011 http://www.art-inst-bournemouth.ac.uk (UCAS)

Batley School of Art (Dewsbury College) Halifax Road, Dewsbury, West Yorkshire WF13 2AS. Tel 01924 451649. (UCAS)

Byam Shaw School of Art 2 Elthorp Road, Archway, London N19 4AG. Tel 020 7281 4111; http://www.byam-shaw.ac.uk

Camberwell College of Arts (The London Institute) Peckham Road, London SE5 8UF. Tel 020 7514 6300; http://www.camb.linst.ac.uk (UCAS)

Central Saint Martin's College of Art and Design (The London Institute) Southampton Row, London WC1B 4AP. Tel 020 7514 7000; http://www.csm.linst.ac.uk (UCAS)

Chelsea College of Art and Design (The London Institute) Manresa Road, London SW3 6LS. Tel 020 7514 7750; http://wwwchel.linst.ac.uk (UCAS)

City and Guilds of London Art School 124 Kennington Park Road, London SE11 4DJ. Tel 020 7735 2306; http://www.cityandguildsartschool.ac.uk

Cleveland College of Art and Design Green Lane, Linthorpe, Middlesbrough, Cleveland TS5 7RJ. Tel 01642 288888; http://www.ccad.ac.uk (UCAS)

Cumbria College of Art and Design Brampton Road, Carlisle, Cumbria CA3 9AY. Tel 01228 400300; http://www.cumbriacad.ac.uk (UCAS)

Dartington College of Arts Totnes, Devon TQ9 6EJ. Tel 01803 862224; http://www.dartington.ac.uk (UCAS)

Edinburgh College of Art (Heriot-Watt University) 74 Lauriston Place, Edinburgh, Lothian, Scotland EH3 9DF. Tel 0131 221 6000; http://www.eca.ac.uk

Falmouth College of Arts Woodlane, Falmouth, Cornwall TR11 4RH. Tel 01326 211077; http://www.falmouth.ac.uk (UCAS)

Glamorgan Centre for Art and Design Technology Glyntaff Road, Glyntaff, Pontypridd, Mid-Glamorgan, Wales CF37 4AT. Tel 01443 663312; http://www.glamorgan.ac.uk (UCAS)

Gray's School of Art (Robert Gordon University) School Hill, Aberdeen, Grampian, Scotland AB10 1FR. Tel 01224 262000; http://www.rgu.ac.uk

Heatherley School of Art Upcerne Road, London SW10 0SH. Tel 0207 351 4190; http://www.heatherley.org

Herefordshire College of Art and Design Folly Lane, Hereford HR1 1LT. Tel 01432 273359; http://www.hereford-art-col.ac.uk (UCAS)

Kent Institute of Art and Design Maidstone College, Oakwood Park, Oakwood Road, Maidstone, Kent MD16 8AG. Tel 01622 757286; http://www.kiad.ac.uk (UCAS)

Leeds College of Art and Design Jacob Kramer Building, Blenhelm Walk, Leeds LS2 9AQ. Tel 0113 202 8000; http://www.leed-art.ac.uk (UCAS)

London City and Guilds Art School 124 Kennington Park Road, London SE11 4DJ. Tel 020 7735 2306; http://www.cityandguildsartschool.ac.uk

London College of Fashion (The London Institute) 20 John Princes Street, London W1M 0BJ. Tel 020 7514 7400; http://www.lcf.linst.ac.uk (UCAS)

London College of Printing (The London Institute) Elephant and Castle, London SE1 6SB. Tel 020 7514 6500; http://www.lcp.linst.ac.uk

London Institute 65 Davies Street, London W1Y 2DA. Tel 020 7514 6000; http://www.linst.ac.uk (UCAS)

Norwich School of Art and Design St George Street, Norwich, Norfolk NR3 1BB. Tel 01603 610561; http://www.nsad.ac.uk (UCAS)

Oxfordshire School of Art and Design Broughton Road, Banbury, Oxfordshire OX16 9QA. Tel 01295 252221; http://www.northox.ac.uk (UCAS)

Plymouth College of Art and Design Tavistock Place, Plymouth, Devon PL4 8AT. Tel 01752 203434; http://www.pcad.plym.ac.uk (UCAS)

Ravensbourne College of Design and Communication Walden Road, Chislehurst, Kent BR7 5SN. Tel 020 8289 4900; http://www.rave.ac.uk (UCAS)

Reading College and School of Arts and Design Crescent Road, Reading, Berkshire RG1 5RQ. Tel 0118 967 5000; http://www.reading-**college**.ac.uk (UCAS)

Royal Academy Schools (Royal Academy of Arts) c/o Bellington Gardens, London W1V 0DS. Tel 020 7300 5650.

Royal College of Art Kensington Gore, London SW7 2EU. Tel 020 7590 4444; http://www.rca.ac.uk (Royal Charter; postgraduate only)

Sotheby's Institute 30 Oxford Street, London W1N 9FL. Tel 020 7323 5775; http://www.sotheby-instit.edu

Surrey Institute of Art and Design, University College Falkner Road, Farnham, Surrey GU9 7DS. Tel 01252 892610; http://www.surrat.ac.uk (UCAS)

Wimbledon School of Art Merton Hall Road, London SW19 3QA. Tel 020 8408 5000; http://www.wimbledon.ac.uk (UCAS)

Winchester School of Art (part of Southampton University) Park Avenue, Winchester, Hampshire SO23 8DL. Tel 023 8059 6918; http://www.soton.ac.uk/wsart

Section 5: Colleges of Dance, Drama, Music and Speech

Some Colleges are in the UCAS scheme (as indicated) for some or all of their courses (see *UCAS Handbook* for details). Apply direct to college for courses outside UCAS.

Arts Educational London Schools Drama Department, Cone Ripman House, 14 Bath Road, London W4 1LY. Tel 020 8994 9366.

Birmingham Conservatoire Paradise Place, Birmingham B3 3HG. Tel 0121 331 5901; http://www.uce.ac.uk

Birmingham School of Speech Training and Drama 45 Church Street, Edgbaston, Birmingham, West Midlands B15 3SW. Tel 0121 454 3424.

Bristol Old Vic Theatre School 1–2 Downside Road, Clifton, Bristol BS8 2XF. Tel 0117 973 3535.

Central School of Speech & Drama Embassy Theatre, 64 Eton Avenue, Swiss Cottage, London NW3 3HY. Tel 020 7722 8183. (UCAS)

Drama Centre, London 176 Prince of Wales Road, London NW5 3PT. Tel 020 7267 1177; http://wwwdcl.drama.ac.uk

East 15 Acting School Hatfields, Rectory Lane, Loughton, Essex IG10 3RY. Tel 020 8508 5983; http://wwweast15.ac.uk

Guildford School of Acting Millmead Terrace, Guildford, Surrey GU2 5AT. Tel 01483 560701; http://www.gsa.drama.ac.uk

MOUNTVIEW

Academy of Theatre Arts

President: Sir John Mills CBE
Founder Principal & Chief Executive:
Peter Coxhead LittD
Principal: Paul Clements MA Cert Ed

Mountview, one of the UK's leading academies of Theatre Arts, offers an extensive and stimulating training for those interested in pursuing a Performance, Directing or Technical Theatre career

BA (Hons) in Performance*
(Acting and Musical Theatre Options)
validated by the University of East Anglia

2 year BA (Hons) in Technical Theatre*
validated by Middlesex University

I year Postgraduate Courses
Acting & Musical Theatre · Directing · Technical Theatre
Accredited by the National Council for Drama Training

Performance and directing courses information
Tel: 020 8826 9216 Fax: 020 8829 0034
e-mail: acting@mountview.ac.uk

Technical theatre courses information
Tel: 020 8347 3616 Fax: 020 8348 1727
e-mail: techtheatre@mountview.ac.uk

Scholarship and Financial Assistance
may be available for full-time training

Part-time and summer courses available for adults and young people
Tel: 020 8826 9217 for further information

CDS MEMBER

Member of ELIA

Mountview is a registered charity and exists to provide
training and education in the theatre and related arts.

Guildhall School of Music and Drama
Silk Street, Barbican, London EC2Y 8DT.
Tel 020 7628 2571;
http://www.gmsd.ac.uk

Laban Centre for Movement and Dance
at University of London Goldsmiths
College, Lewisham Way, New Cross,
London SE14 6NW. Tel 020 8692 4070;
http://www.laban.ac.uk

Leeds College of Music 3 Quarry Hill,
Leeds, West Yorkshire LS2 7PD. Tel 0113
222 3400.

**Liverpool Institute of Performing Arts
(LIPA)** Mount Street, Liverpool L1 9HF.
Tel 0151 330 3232; http://www.lipa.ac.uk
(UCAS)

**London Academy of Music and
Dramatic Art** Tower House, 226 Cromwell
Road, London SW5 0SR. Tel 020 7373
9883; http://www.lamda.org.uk

London College of Music Thames Valley
University, 3 St Mary's Road, Ealing,
London W5 5RF. Tel 020 8231 2304;
http://www.tvu.ac.uk (UCAS)

Mountview Academy of Theatre Arts
104 Crouch Hill, London N8 9EA. Tel 020
8347 3616; http://www.mountview.ac.uk

**Northern College of Contemporary
Dance** 98 Chapeltown Road, Leeds
LS7 4BH. Tel 0113 219 3000;
http://www.nscd.ac.uk.

Rose Bruford College Lamorbey Park,
Burnt Oak Lane, Sidcup, Kent DA15 9DF.
Tel 020 8300 3024;
http://www.bruford.ac.uk (UCAS)

**Royal Academy of Dramatic Art
(RADA)** 18–22 Chenies Street,
London WC1E 7EX. Tel 020 7636 7076;
http://www.rada.org.uk

Royal Academy of Music Marylebone
Road, London NW1 5HT. Tel 020 7873
7373; http://www.ram.ac.uk

Royal Ballet School 155 Talgarth Road,
London W14 9DE. Tel 020 8748 6335.

Royal College of Music Prince Consort
Road, London SW7 2BS. Tel 020 7589
3643; http://www.rcm.ac.uk

Royal Northern College of Music
124 Oxford Road, Manchester M13 9RD.
Tel 0161 907 5200; http://www.rncm.ac.uk

**Royal Scottish Academy of Music and
Drama** 100 Renfrew Street, Glasgow,
Strathclyde, Scotland G2 3DB. Tel 0141
332 4101; http://www.rsamd.ac.uk

Trinity College of Music 11–13
Mandeville Place, London W1M 6AQ.
Tel 020 7935 5773; http://www.tcm.ac.uk

**Webber Douglas Academy of Dramatic
Art** 30–36 Clareville Street, London SW7
5AP. Tel 020 7370 4154.

Welsh College of Music and Drama
Castle Grounds, Cathays Park, Cardiff,
Wales CF10 3ER. Tel 029 2034 2854;
http://www.wcmd.ac.uk (UCAS)

Section 6: Other Colleges Offering Higher Education Courses in the UCAS Scheme

The following Colleges appear under
various subject headings in the Tables in
Chapter 5 and some are in the UCAS
scheme (shown in brackets) whilst others
collaborate with UCAS institutions for
some courses. They may also offer
higher education courses (for example,
Higher National Diploma courses) which
are outside the UCAS scheme (see also
Section 7). Contact Colleges for further
information.

Amersham & Wycombe College (now
part of **Buckinghamshire Chilterns
University College**, see Section 2)

Aylesbury College Oxford Road,
Aylesbury, Buckinghamshire HP21 8PD.
Tel 01296 588588;
http://www.aylesbury.ac.uk (UCAS)

Barking College Dagenham Road,
Romford, Essex RM7 0XU. Tel 01708
766841; http://www.barking-coll.ac.uk
(UCAS)

Barnet College Wood Street, Barnet,
Hertfordshire EN5 4AZ. Tel 020 8440
6321; http://www.barnet.ac.uk

Barnfield College Enterprise Way, Luton,
Bedfordshire LU3 4BU. Tel 01582 569500;
http://www.barnfield.ac.uk

Barnsley College Central Registry,
PO Box 266, Church Street, Barnsley,
South Yorkshire S70 2YW. Tel 01226
216171; http://www.barnsley.ac.uk
(UCAS)

Basford Hall College Stockhill Lane,
Nottingham NG6 0NB. Tel 0115 916 2001;
http://www.demon.co.uk/basford

Basingstoke College of Technology
Worting Road, Basingstoke, Hampshire
RG21 8TN. Tel 01256 306453. (UCAS)

Beverley College Longcroft Road,
Gallows Lane, Beverley, East Yorkshire
HU17 7DT. Tel 01482 868362;
http://www.beverleycollege.ac.uk

Bexley College Tower Road, Belvedere,
Kent DA17 6JA. Tel 01322 442331.

**Birmingham College of Food, Tourism
and Creative Studies** Summer Row,
Birmingham, West Midlands B3 1JB.
Tel 0121 604 1040;
http://www.bcftcs.ac.uk

Bishop Auckland College Woodhouse
Lane, Bishop Auckland, Durham DL14
6JZ. Tel 01388 443000;
http://www.bacoll.ac.uk

Bishop Burton College Bishop Burton,
York Road, Beverley, East Yorkshire
HU17 8QG. Tel 01964 553000;
http://www.bishopb-college.ac.uk

Blackburn College Feilden Street,
Blackburn, Lancashire BB2 1LH.
Tel 01254 551440;
http://www.blackburn.ac.uk (UCAS)

Blackpool and The Fylde College
Ashfield Road, Bispham, Blackpool,
Lancashire FY2 0HB. Tel 01253 352352;
http://www.blackpool.ac.uk (UCAS)

Boston College Skirbeck Road, Boston,
Lincolnshire PE21 6JF. Tel 01205 365701;
http://www.boston.ac.uk (UCAS)

**Bournemouth & Poole College of
Further Education** North Road, Poole,
Dorset BH14 0LS. Tel 01202 747600;
http://www.bournemouthandpoole
cfe.ac.uk

Bournville College Bristol Road South,
Northfield, Birmingham, West Midlands
B31 2AJ. Tel 0121 411 1414;
http://www.bournville.ac.uk

Brackenhurst College Brackenhurst,
Southwell, Nottinghamshire NG25 0QF.
Tel 01636 817000.

Braintree College Church Lane, Braintree,
Essex CM7 5SN. Tel 01376 321711;
http://www.braintree.ac.uk

Bridgwater College Bath Road,
Bridgwater, Somerset TA6 4PZ. Tel 01278
455464; http://www.bridgwater.ac.uk
(UCAS)

Brighton College of Technology Pelham
Street, Brighton, East Sussex BN1 4FA.
Tel 01273 667788;
http://www.bricoltech.ac.uk

Brinsbury College North Heath,
Pulborough, West Sussex RH20 1DL.
Tel 01798 877400.

**British College of Naturopathy and
Osteopathy** Lief House, 3 Sumpter Close,
120–122 Finchley Road, London NW3
5HR. Tel 020 7435 6464;
http://www.bcno.org.uk (UCAS)

British School of Osteopathy 275
Borough High Street, London SE1 1JE.
Tel 020 7407 0222; http://www.bso.ac.uk
(UCAS)

Brockenhurst College Lyndhurst Road,
Brockenhurst, Hampshire SO42 7ZE.
Tel 01590 625549; http://www.brock.ac.uk
(UCAS)

**Bromley College of Further and Higher
Education** Rookery Lane, Bromley, Kent
BR2 8HE. Tel 020 8295 7000;
http://www.bromley.ac.uk

Brooklands College Heath Road,
Weybridge, Surrey KT13 8TT. Tel 01932
797700; http://www.brooklands.ac.uk

Brooksby College Brooksby, Melton
Mowbray, Leicestershire LE14 2LJ. Tel
01664 434291; http://www.brooksby.ac.uk

Broomfield College Broomfield, Morley,
Ilkeston, Derbyshire DE7 6DN. Tel 01332
836605; http://www.broomfield.ac.uk

Broxtowe College High Road, Chilwell,
Beeston, Nottinghamshire NG9 4AH.
Tel 0115 917 5252;
http://www.broxtowe.ac.uk (UCAS)

Burnley College Shorey Bank, Ormerod
Road, Burnley, Lancashire BB11 2RX. Tel
01282 711200; http://www.burnley.ac.uk

Burton College Lichfield Street, Burton-upon-Trent, Staffordshire DE14 3RL. Tel 01283 494400; http://www.burton-college.ac.uk (UCAS)

Bury College Market Street, Bury, Lancashire BL9 0BG. Tel 0161 280 8280; http://www.burycollege.ac.uk

Cambridge Regional College Kings Hedges Road, Cambridge CB4 2QT. Tel 01223 418200; http://www.cambri.ac.uk

Cannington College Cannington, Bridgwater, Somerset TA5 2LS. Tel 01278 655123; http://www.cannington.ac.uk (UCAS)

Canterbury College New Dover Road, Canterbury, Kent CT1 3AJ. Tel 01227 811188; http://www.cant-col.ac.uk (UCAS)

Capel Manor College Bullsmore Lane, Enfield, Middlesex EN1 4RQ. Tel 020 8366 4442; http://www.capelmanorcollege.ac.uk (UCAS)

Carlisle College Victoria Place, Carlisle, Cumbria CA1 1HS. Tel 01228 819000; http://www.carlisle.ac.uk

Carmarthenshire College Graig Campus, Llanelli, Wales SA15 4DN. Tel 01554 748000; http://www.ccts.ac.uk (UCAS)

Carshalton College Nightingale Road, Carshalton, Surrey SM5 2EJ. Tel 020 8770 6800. (UCAS)

Chelmsford College Moulsham Street, Chelmsford, Essex CM2 0JQ. Tel 01245 265611; http://www.chelmcollege.u/net.com (UCAS)

Chesterfield College Infirmary Road, Chesterfield, Derbyshire S41 7NG. Tel 01246 500500. (UCAS)

Chichester College of Arts, Science and Technology Westgate Fields, Chichester, West Sussex PO19 1SB. Tel 01243 536196; http://www.chichester.ac.uk (UCAS)

Chippenham College (now Wiltshire College)

City & Islington College The Marlborough Building, 383 Holloway Road, London N7 0RN. Tel 020 7700 9200; http:/www.candi.ac.uk

City of Bath College Avon Street, Bath, Somerset BA1 1UP. Tel 01225 312191; http://www.citybathcoll.ac.uk

City College, Birmingham 47A George Street, Birmingham B3 1QA. Tel 0121 236 4725; http://www.citycol.ac.uk (UCAS)

City of Bristol College Brunel Centre, Ashley Down, Bristol BS7 9BU. Tel 0117 904 5000; http://www.cityofbristol.ac.uk (UCAS)

City College Manchester PO Box 40, Manchester M23 0DD. Tel 0161 957 1790; http://www.ccm.ac.uk (UCAS)

City of Sutherland College (Hylton Centre) North Hylton Road, Sunderland, Tyne and Wear SR5 5OB. Tel 0191 511 6201. (UCAS)

City of Westminster College Paddington Centre, London W2 1NB. Tel 020 7723 8826; http://www.cwc.ac.uk

Clarendon College, Nottingham Pelham Avenue, Mansfield Road, Nottingham NG5 1AL. Tel 0115 960 7201; http://www.clarendon.ac.uk

Coleg Menai Friddoedd Road, Bangor, Gwynedd LL57 2TP. Tel 01248 370125. (UCAS)

College of West Anglia Tennyson Avenue, King's Lynn, Norfolk PE30 2QW. Tel 01553 761144. (UCAS)

Cordwainers College (now part of the **London Institute**) 182 Mare Street, London E8 3RE. Tel 020 8985 0273; http://www.cordwainers.ac.uk (UCAS)

Cornwall College with Duchy College Pool, Redruth, Cornwall TR15 3RD. Tel 01209 611611; http://www.cornwall.ac.uk (UCAS)

Coventry Technical College The Butts, Coventry CV1 3GD. Tel 024 7652 6700; http://www.covcollege.ac.uk (UCAS)

Crawley College College Road, Crawley, West Sussex RH10 1NR. Tel 01293 442200; http://www.crawley-college.ac.uk (UCAS)

Crichton College of the University of Glasgow Cricton University Campus, Dumfries, Scotland DG1 4ZT. Tel 01387 244025; http://www.cc.gla.ac.uk

Croydon College Fairfield, Croydon CR9 1DX. Tel 020 8686 5700; http://www.croydon.ac.uk (UCAS)

Darlington College of Technology Cleveland Avenue, Darlington, Durham DL3 7BB. Tel 01325 503050; http://www.darlington.ac.uk (UCAS)

Dearne Valley College Manvers Park, Wath-upon-Dearne, Rotherham, South Yorkshire S63 7EW. Tel 01709 513101. (UCAS)

Derwentside College Park Road, Consett, Durham DH8 5EE. Tel 01207 585900; http://www.derwentside.ac.uk

Dewsbury College Halifax Road, Dewsbury, West Yorkshire WF13 2AS. Tel 01924 465916; http://www.dewsbury.ac.uk (UCAS)

Doncaster College Waterdale, Doncaster, South Yorkshire DN1 3EX. Tel 01302 553553; http://www.don.ac.uk (UCAS)

Dudley College of Technology The Broadway, Dudley, West Midlands DY1 4AS. Tel 01384 363277; http://www.dudleycol.ac.uk (UCAS)

Dunstable College Kingsway, Dunstable, Bedfordshire LU5 4HG. Tel 01582 477776; http://www.cablerl.net/duncol

East Devon College Bolham Road, Tiverton, Devon EX16 6SH. Tel 01884 235200; http://www.eastdevon.ac.uk

East Durham & Houghall Community College Burnhope Way Centre, Burnhope Way, Peterlee, Co. Durham SR8 1NV. Tel 0191 518 2000. (UCAS)

East Surrey College 127 Blackborough Road, Reigate, Surrey RH2 7DE. Tel 01737 766137. (UCAS)

East Yorkshire College St Mary's Walk, Bridlington, East Yorkshire YO16 7JW. Tel 01262 852000; http://www.east-york-coll.ac.uk

Eastbourne College of Art and Technology St Anne's Road, Eastbourne, East Sussex BN21 2UF. Tel 01323 644711; http://www.bcat.ac.uk

Eastleigh College Chestnut Avenue, Eastleigh, Hampshire SO50 5HT. Tel 023 8032 6326; http://www.eastleigh.ac.uk

Easton College Easton, Norwich, Norfolk NR9 5DX. Tel 01603 731200; http://www.easton-college.ac.uk (UCAS)

European Business School London Regent's College, Inner Circle, Regent's Park, London NW1 4NS. Tel 020 7487 7507; http://www.regents.ac.uk (UCAS)

European School of Osteopathy Boxley House, The Street, Boxley, Maidstone, Kent ME14 3DZ. Tel 01622 671558; http://www.eso.ac.uk (UCAS)

Exeter College Exeter Business School, Brittany House, New North Road, Exeter, Devon EX4 4EP. Tel 01392 205581; http://www.exe-col.ac.uk (UCAS)

Fareham College Bishopsfield Road, Fareham, Hampshire PO14 1NH. Tel 01329 815200; http://www.fareham.ac.uk (UCAS)

Farnborough College of Technology Boundary Road, Farnborough, Hampshire GU14 6SB. Tel 01252 407028; http://www.farn-ct.ac.uk (UCAS)

Filton College Filton Avenue, Filton, Bristol, Somerset BS12 7AT. Tel 0117 931 2121; http://www.filton-college.ac.uk

Franciscan Study Centre Giles Lane, Canterbury, Kent CT2 7NA. Tel 01227 769349.

Furness College Howard Street, Barrow-in-Furness, Cumbria LA14 1NB. Tel 01229 825017; http://www.furness.ac.uk

Gateshead College Durham Road, Gateshead, Tyne and Wear NE9 5BN. Tel 0191 490 0300; http://www.gateshead.ac.uk

Gloucestershire College of Arts and Technology Brunswick Road, Gloucester GL1 1HU. Tel 01452 426714; http://www.gloscat.ac.uk (UCAS)

Grantham College Stonebridge Road, Grantham, Lincolnshire NG31 9AP. Tel 01476 400200; http://www.grantham.ac.uk

Greenwich School of Management Meridian House, Royal Hill, Greenwich, London SE10 8RD. Tel 0208 516 7800; http://www.greenwich-college.ac.uk (UCAS)

Grimsby College Nuns Corner, Laceby Road, Grimsby, North East Lincolnshire DN34 5BQ. Tel 01472 311222; http://www.grimsby.ac.uk (UCAS)

Guildford College Stoke Park, Guildford, Surrey GU1 1EZ. Tel 01483 448500; http://www.guildford.ac.uk (UCAS)

Gyosei International College London Road, Reading, Berkshire RG1 5AQ. Tel 01189 310152; http://www.gyosei.ac.uk (UCAS)

Hadlow College Hadlow, Tonbridge, Kent TN11 0AL. Tel 01732 850551; http://www.hadlow.co.uk

Halesowen College Whittingham Road, Halesowen, West Midlands B63 3NA. Tel 0121 550 1451; http://www.halesowen.ac.uk (UCAS)

Halton College Kingsway, Widnes, Cheshire WA8 7QQ. Tel 0151 423 1391; http://www.haltoncollege.ac.uk (UCAS)

Hammersmith & West London College Gliddon Road, Barons Court, London W14 9BL. Tel 020 8741 1688; http://www.hwlc.ac.uk (UCAS)

Harlow College The High, Harlow, Essex CM20 3LT. Tel 01279 868000; http://www.harlow-college.ac.uk

Harrogate College Hornbeam Park, Harrogate, North Yorkshire HG2 8QT. Tel 01423 879466; http://www.harrogate.ac.uk

Hartpury College Hartpury House, Hartpury, Gloucestershire GL19 3BE. Tel 01452 700283; http://www.hartpury.ac.uk

Hastings College Archery Road, St Leonards-on-Sea, East Sussex TN38 0HX. Tel 01424 442222; http://www.hastings.ac.uk

Havering College of Further and Higher Education Ardleigh Green Road, Hornchurch, Essex RM11 2LL. Tel 01708 462801; http://www.havering-college.ac.uk (UCAS)

Hendon College Grahame Park Way, Colindale, London NW9 5RA. Tel 020 8200 8300; http://www.hendon.ac.uk (UCAS)

Henley College, Coventry Henley Road, Bell Green, Coventry, West Midlands CV2 1ED. Tel 024 7662 6300; http://www.henley-cov.ac.uk (UCAS)

Herefordshire College of Technology Folly Lane, Hereford HR1 1LS. Tel 01432 352235; http://www.hereford-tech.ac.uk (UCAS)

Hertford Regional College Scott's Road, Ware, Hertfordshire SG12 9JF. Tel 01920 465441; http://www.hertreg.ac.uk (UCAS)

High Peak College, University of Derbyshire Harpur Hill, Buxton, Derbyshire SK17 9JZ. Tel 01298 71100; http://www.highpeak.ac.uk

Highbury College, Portsmouth Dovercourt Road, Cosham, Portsmouth, Hampshire PO6 2SA. Tel 023 9231 3281. (UCAS)

Hillcroft College South Bank, Surbiton, Surrey KT6 6DF. Tel 020 8399 2688. (UCAS)

Holborn College 200 Greyhound Road, London W14 9RY. Tel 020 7385 3377; http://www.holborncollege.ac.uk

Holme Lacy College Holme Lacy, Hereford HR2 6LL. Tel 01432 870316. (see Section 3 Pershore Group of Colleges)

Hopwood Hall College Hopwood Campus, St Marys Gate, Rochdale Road, Middleton, Manchester M24 3XH. Tel 0161 643 7560; http://www.hopwood.ac.uk

Huddersfield Technical College New North Road, Huddersfield, West Yorkshire HD1 5NN. Tel 01484 536521; http://www.huddcoll.ac.uk (UCAS)

Hull College Queen's Gardens, Hull, East Yorkshire HU1 3DG. Tel 01482 329943; http://www.hull-college.ac.uk

Huntingdonshire Regional College
California Road, Huntingdon,
Cambridgeshire PE18 7BL. Tel 01480
379100; http://www.huntingdon.ac.uk

Isle of Wight College Medina Way,
Newport, Isle of Wight PO30 5TA.
Tel 01983 526631;
http://www.iwighttc.ac.uk (UCAS)

Kendal College Milnthorpe Road, Kendal,
Cumbria LA9 5AY. Tel 01539 724313;
http://www.kendal.ac.uk

Kidderminster College Hoo Road,
Kidderminster, Worcestershire DY10 1LX.
Tel 01562 820811. (UCAS)

Kingston College Kingston Hall Road,
Kingston upon Thames, Surrey KT1 2AQ.
Tel 020 8268 3011; http://www.kingston-college.co.uk

Kingston Maurward College Kingston
Maurward, Dorchester, Dorset DT2 8PY.
Tel 01305 215000; http://www.kmc.ac.uk

Kingsway College Gray's Inn Centre,
Sidmouth Street, London WC1H 8JB.
Tel 020 7306 5700;
http://www.kingsway.ac.uk

Kirkley Hall College Ponteland,
Northumberland NE20 0AQ.
Tel 01661 860808.

Lambeth College Brixton Centre,
56 Brixton Hill, London SE2 1QS.
Tel 020 7501 5000;
http://www.lambethcollege.ac.uk

Lancaster & Morecambe College
Morecambe Road, Lancaster, Lancashire
LA1 2TY. Tel 01524 66215. (UCAS)

Lansdowne College 40–44 Bark Place,
London W2 4AT. Tel 020 7616 4400;
http://www.cife.org.uk/lansdowne
(UCAS)

**Leek College of Further Education and
School of Art** Stockwell Street, Leek,
Staffordshire ST13 6DP. Tel 01538
398866; http://www.leek.ac.uk

Leicester College Freemen's Park
Campus, Aylestone Road, Leicester
LE2 7LW. Tel 0116 224 2000;
http://www.leicestercollege.ac.uk
(UCAS)

Leo Baeck College 80 East End Road,
London N3 2SY. Tel 020 8349 5600;
http://www.lbc.ac.uk

Lewisham College Lewisham Way,
London SE4 1UT. Tel 020 8692 0353;
http://www.lewisham.ac.uk (UCAS)

Liverpool Community College Bankfield
Centre, Bankfield Road, Liverpool
L13 0BQ. Tel 0151 252 3000;
http://www.liv-coll.ac.uk (UCAS)

Llandrillo College Llandudno Road,
Colwyn Bay, North Wales LL28 4HZ.
Tel 01492 542338;
http://www.llandrillo.ac.uk (UCAS)

Loughborough College Radmoor Road,
Loughborough, Leicestershire
LE11 3BT. Tel 01509 618375;
http://www.loucoll.ac.uk (UCAS)

Lowestoft College St Peter's Street,
Lowestoft, Suffolk NR32 2NB.
Tel 01502 583521;
http://www.lowestoft.ac.uk (UCAS)

Macclesfield College Park Lane,
Macclesfield, Cheshire SK11 8LF.
Tel 01625 41000. (UCAS)

Mackworth College, Derby Prince
Charles Avenue, Mackworth, Derby
DE22 4LR. Tel 01332 519951;
http://www.mackworth.ac.uk

**Manchester College of Arts and
Technology** City Centre Campus, Lower
Hardman Street, Manchester M3 3ER.
Tel 0161 953 5995;
http://www.mancat.ac.uk (UCAS)

**Matthew Boulton College of Further
and Higher Education** Sherlock Street,
Birmingham, West Midlands B5 7DB.
Tel 0121 446 4545;
http://www.matthew-boulton.ac.uk
(UCAS)

**Melton Mowbray College of Further
Education** Asfordby Road, Melton
Mowbray, Leicestershire LE13 0HJ.
Tel 01664 850850.

Merrist Wood College Merrist Wood,
Worplesden, Guildford, Surrey
GU3 3PE. Tel 01483 884000;
http://www.merristwood.ac.uk

Mid Cheshire College Hartford Campus, Chesterford Road, Northwich, Cheshire CW8 1LJ. Tel 01606 74444; http://www.midchesh.ac.uk (UCAS)

Mid-Kent College of Higher and Further Education Horsted Centre, Maidstone Road, Chatham, Kent ME5 9UQ. Tel 01634 830633; http://www.midkent.ac.uk

Middlesbrough College Roman Road, Linthorpe, Middlesbrough, Cleveland TS5 5PJ. Tel 01642 333333; http://www.mro.ac.uk

Milton Keynes College Chaffron Way Centre, Woughton Campus West, Leadenhall West, Milton Keynes, Buckinghamshire MK6 5LP. Tel 01908 684444; http://www.mkcollege.ac.uk

Neath Port Talbot College Dwr-y-Felin Road, Neath SA10 7RF. Tel 01639 648000. (UCAS)

Nescot Reigate Road, Ewell, Epsom, Surrey KT17 3DS. Tel 020 8394 1731.

New College, Durham Framwellgate Moor Centre, Durham DH1 5ES. Tel 0191 375 4210; http://www.newdur.ac.uk

New College Nottingham Pelham Avenue, Mansfield Road, Nottingham NG5 1AL. Tel 0115 960 7201. http://www.ncn.ac.uk/ncnfrontend.html (UCAS)

New College Swindon Helston Road, Park North, Swindon, Wiltshire SN3 2LA. Tel 01793 611470; http://www.newcollege.ac.uk

Newcastle College Rye Hill Campus, Scotswood Road, Newcastle upon Tyne NE4 7SA. Tel 0191 200 4000; http://www.ncl-coll.ac.uk (UCAS)

Newcastle under Lyme College Liverpool Road, Newcastle under Lyme, Staffordshire ST5 2DF. Tel 01782 715111; http://www.ncl-u-lyme.ac.uk (UCAS)

Newham College of Further Education East Ham Campus, High Street South, London E6 4ER. Tel 020 8257 4000; http://www.newham.ac.uk (UCAS)

North East Institute of Further and Higher Education Trostan Avenue, Ballymena, Nortern Ireland BT43 7BN. Tel 028 2565 2871; http://www.nei.ac.uk (UCAS)

North East Worcestershire College Peakman Street, Redditch, Worcestershire B98 8DW. Tel 01527 570020; http://www.ne-worcs.ac.uk (UCAS)

North Hertfordshire College Monkswood Way, Stevenage, Hertfordshire SG1 1LA. Tel 01462 424242; http://www.nhc.ac.uk

North Lincolnshire College Monks Road, Lincoln LN2 5HQ. Tel 01522 876000; http://www.nlincs-coll.ac.uk (UCAS)

North Lindsey College Kingsway, Scunthorpe, North Lincolnshire DN17 1AJ. Tel 01724 281111; http://www.northlindsey.ac.uk

North Nottinghamshire College Carlton Road, Worksop, Nottinghamshire S81 7HP. Tel 01909 473561; http://www.nnotts.col.ac.uk (UCAS)

North Oxfordshire College and School of Art Broughton Road, Banbury, Oxfordshire OX16 9QA. Tel 01295 252221; http://www.northox.ac.uk

North Shropshire College College Road, Oswestry, Shropshire SY11 2SA. Tel 01691 688000; http://www.n-shropshire.ac.uk

North Tyneside College Embleton Avenue, Wallsend, Tyne and Wear NE28 9NJ. Tel 0191 229 5000; http://www.ntyneside.ac.uk (UCAS)

North Warwickshire & Hinckley College Hinckley Road, Nuneaton, Warwickshire CV11 6BH. Tel 024 7624 3000. (UCAS)

Northbrook College, Sussex Littlehampton Road, Durrington, Worthing, West Sussex BN12 6NU. Tel 01903 606060; http://www.northbrook.ac.uk (UCAS)

Northern College of Education Hilton PLace, Aberdeen AB24 4FA. Tel 01224 283500; http://www.norcol.ac.uk (UCAS)

Northumberland College College Road, Ashington, Northumberland NE63 9RG. Tel 01670 841200; http://www.northland.ac.uk (UCAS)

Norton Radstock College South Hill Park, Radstock, Bath, Somerset BA3 3RW. Tel 01761 433161. (UCAS)

Norwich City College Ipswich Road, Norwich, Norfolk NR2 2LJ. Tel 01603 773136; http://www.ccn.ac.uk (UCAS)

Oaklands College Oaklands Campus, Hatfield Road, St Albans, Hertfordshire AL4 0JA. Tel 01727 737000; http://www.oaklands.ac.uk

Oldham College Rochdale Road, Oldham, Lancashire OL9 6AA. Tel 0161 785 4053; http://www.oldham.ac.uk (UCAS)

Otley College Otley, Ipswich, Suffolk IP6 9EY. Tel 01473 785543; http://www.otleycollege.ac.uk

Oxford College of Further Education Oxpens Road, Oxford OX1 1SA. Tel 01865 245871; http://www.oxfe.ac.uk/ocfe (UCAS)

Park Lane College Park Lane, Leeds, West Yorkshire LS3 1AA. Tel 0113 216 2400; http://www.parklanecoll.ac.uk (UCAS)

Pembrokeshire College Haverfordwest, Pembrokeshire SA61 1SZ. Tel 01437 765247; http://www.pembrokeshire.ac.uk (UCAS)

People's College, Nottingham Maid Marian Way, Nottingham NG1 6AB. Tel 0115 912 8581; http://www.peoples.ac.uk (UCAS)

Pershore Group of Colleges (includes Pershore College, Hindlip College and Holme Lacy College) Avonbank, Pershore, Worcestershire WR10 3JP. Tel 01386 552443; http://www.pershore.ac.uk (UCAS)

Peterborough Regional College Park Crescent, Peterborough, Lincolnshire PE1 4DZ. Tel 01733 767366; http://www.peterborough.ac.uk (UCAS)

Plumpton College Ditchling Road, Lewes, East Sussex BN7 3AE. Tel 01273 890454; http://www.plumpton.ac.uk

Plymouth College of Further Education King's Road, Devonport, Plymouth, Devon PL1 5QG. Tel 01752 305300; http://www.pcfe.plymouth.ac.uk

Reading College and School of Arts and Design Crescent Road, Reading, Berkshire RG1 5RQ. Tel 0118 967 5000; http://www.reading-college.ac.uk

Redcar & Cleveland College Corporation Road, Redcar, Cleveland TS10 1EZ. Tel 01642 473132; http://www.cleveland.ac.uk

Regents Business School London Regent's College, Inner Circle, Regent's Park, London NW1 4NS. Tel 020 7487 7654; http://www.regents.ac.uk (UCAS)

Richmond, The American International University in London Queens Road, Richmond, Surrey TW10 6PJ. Tel 020 8332 9000; http://www.richmond.ac.uk (UCAS)

Rodbaston College Rodbaston, Penkridge, Stafford ST19 5PH. Tel 01785 712209; http://www.rodbaston.ac.uk

Rotherham College of Arts and Technology Eastwood Lane, Rotherham, South Yorkshire S65 1EG. Tel 01709 362111; http://www.rotherham.ac.uk

Royal Academy Schools (Royal Academy of Arts) c/o Bellington Gardens, London W1V 0DS. Tel 020 7300 5650.

Rugby College of Further Education Lower Hillmorton Road, Rugby, Warwickshire CV21 3QS. Tel 01788 338800; http://www.rugbycoll.ac.uk

Runshaw College Langdale Road, Leyland, Lancashire PR5 2DQ. Tel 01772 622677; http://www.runshaw.ac.uk

Ruskin College Oxford Walton Street, Oxford OX1 2HE. Tel 01865 310713; http://www.ruskin.ac.uk (UCAS)

Rutland College Barleythorpe Road, Oakham, Rutland LE15 6QH. Tel 01572 722863. (UCAS)

Rycotewood College Priest End, Thame, Oxfordshire OX9 2AF. Tel 01844 212501; http://www.rycote.ac.uk (UCAS)

SAE Technology College United House, North Road, London N7 9DP. Tel 020 7609 2653; http://www.sae.edu (UCAS)

St Helens College Brook Street, St Helens, Merseyside WA10 1PZ. Tel 01744 733766; http://www.sthelens.mernet.org.uk (UCAS)

St Loye's School of Occupational Therapy Millbrook House, Millbrook Lane, Topsham Road, Exeter EX2 6ES. Tel 01392 219774; http://www.ex.ac.uk

Salford College Worsley Campus, Walkden Road, Worsley M28 7QD. Tel 0161 702 8272. (UCAS)

Salisbury College Southampton Road, Salisbury, Wiltshire SP1 2LW. Tel 01722 344344; http://www.salcol.com (UCAS)

Sandwell College Wednesbury Campus, Woden Road South, Wednesbury, West Midlands WS10 0PE. Tel 0121 556 6000; http://www.sandwell.ac.uk (UCAS)

SEEVIC College Runnymede Chase, Benfleet, Essex SS7 1TW. Tel 01268 756111; http://www.seevic-college.ac.uk

Sheffield College Central Admissions, Head Office, PO Box 345, Sheffield S2 2YY. Tel 0114 260 2600; http://www.sheffcol.ac.uk (UCAS)

Shrewsbury College of Arts and Technology London Road, Shrewsbury SY2 6PR. Tel 01743 342342; http://www.s-cat.ac.uk (UCAS)

Solihull College Blossomfield Road, Solihull, West Midlands B91 1SB. Tel 0121 678 7001; http://www.solihull.ac.uk (UCAS)

Somerset College of Arts and Technology Wellington Road, Taunton, Somerset TA1 5AX. Tel 01823 366366; http://www.somerset.ac.uk (UCAS)

Soundwell College St Stephens Road, Kingswood, Bristol BS16 4RL. Tel 0117 967 5101. (UCAS)

South Birmingham College Cole Bank Road, Hall Green, Birmingham, West Midlands B28 8ES. Tel 0121 694 5002; hhtp://www.sbirmc.ac.uk (UCAS)

South Cheshire College Dane Bank Avenue, Crewe, Cheshire CW2 8AB. Tel 01270 654654; http://www.s-cheshire.ac.uk (UCAS)

South Devon College Newton Road, Torquay, Devon TQ2 5BY. Tel 01803 406406; http://www.sdevon.ac.uk (UCAS)

South Downs College College Road, Waterlooville, Hampshire PO7 8AA. Tel 023 9279 7979; http://www.southdowns.ac.uk (UCAS)

South East Derbyshire College Field Road, Ilkeston, Derbyshire DE7 5RS. Tel 0115 849 2000; http://www.sedc.ac.uk

South East Essex College Carnarvon Road, Southend-on-Sea, Essex SS2 6LS. Tel 01702 220400; http://www.se-essex-college.ac.uk (UCAS)

South Kent College The Grange, Shorncliffe Road, Folkestone, Kent CT20 2NA. Tel 01303 858223.

South Nottingham College Greythorne Drive, West Bridgford, Nottingham NG2 7GA. Tel 0115 914 6400; http://www.south-nottingham.ac.uk (UCAS)

South Thames College Wandsworth High Street, London SW18 2PP. Tel 020 8918 7000; http://www.south-thames.ac.uk

South Trafford College Manchester Road, West Timperley, Altrincham, Cheshire WA14 5PQ. Tel 0161 952 4600; http://www.st.coll.ac.uk

South Tyneside College St George's Avenue, South Shields, Tyne and Wear NE34 6ET. Tel 0191 427 3500; http://www.stc.ac.uk (UCAS)

Southampton City College St Mary Street, Southampton, Hampshire SO14 1AR. Tel 023 8048 4848; http://www.southampton-city.ac.uk (UCAS)

Southport College Mornington Road, Southport, Merseyside PR9 0TT. Tel 01704 500606; http://www.southport.mernet.org.uk (UCAS)

Southwark College Surrey Docks Centre, Drummond Road, London SE16 4EE. Tel 020 7815 1526; http://www.southwark.ac.uk (UCAS)

Stafford College Earl Street, Stafford ST16 2QR. Tel 01785 223800; http://www.staffordcoll.ac.uk (UCAS)

Stamford College Drift Road, Stamford, Lincolnshire PE9 1XA. Tel 01780 848300; http://www.stamford.ac.uk (UCAS)

Stephenson College Bridge Road, Coalville, Leicestershire LE67 3PW. Tel 01530 836136; http://www.stephensoncoll.ac.uk (UCAS)

Stourbridge College Hagley Road, Stourbridge, Dudley, West Midlands DY8 1QU. Tel 01384 344344; http://www.stourbridge.ac.uk

Stockport College of Further and Higher Education Wellington Road South, Stockport, Greater Manchester SK1 3UQ. Tel 0161 958 3100; http://www.stockport.ac.uk (UCAS)

Stoke on Trent College School of Visual and Performing Arts, Burslem, Stoke on Trent, Staffordshire ST6 1JJ. Tel 01782 208208; http://www.stokecoll.ac.uk (UCAS)

Stratford-upon-Avon College The Willows North, Alcester Road, Stratford-upon-Avon, Warwickshire CV37 9QR. Tel 01789 266245; http://www.stratford-upon-avon.co.uk (UCAS)

Strode College Church Road, Street, Somerset BA16 0AB. Tel 01458 844400.

Strode's College High Street, Egham, Surrey TW20 9DR. Tel 01784 437506; http://www.strodes.ac.uk

Sutton Coldfield College Lichfield Road, Sutton Coldfield, West Midlands B74 2NW. Tel 0121 355 5671; http://www.sutcoll.ac.uk (UCAS)

Swansea College Tycoch Road, Swansea SA2 9EB. Tel 01792 284000. (UCAS)

Swindon College Regent Circus, Swindon, Wiltshire SN1 1PT. Tel 01793 498308; http://www.swindon-college.ac.uk (UCAS)

Tameside College Beaufort Road, Ashton-under-Lyne, Lancashire OL6 6NX. Tel 0161 908 6789; http://www.tamesidecollege.ac.uk (UCAS)

Tamworth & Lichfield College Croft Street, Upper Gungate, Tamworth, Staffordshire B79 8AE. Tel 01827 310202; http://www.tamworthandlichfield.ac.uk

Teesside Tertiary College Marton Campus, Marton Road, Middlesbrough, Cleveland TS4 3RZ. Tel 01642 275000; http://www.ttc.ac.uk

Telford College of Arts and Technology Haybridge Road, Wellington, Telford, Shropshire TF1 2NP. Tel 01952 642237; http://www.tcat.ac.uk

Thanet College Ramsgate Road, Broadstairs, Kent CT10 1PN. Tel 01843 605040; http://www.thanet.ac.uk

Thomas Danby College Roundhay Road, Leeds, West Yorkshire LS7 3BG. Tel 0113 249 4912.

Thurrock College Woodview, Grays, Essex RM16 2YR. Tel 01375 391199; http://www.thurrock.ac.uk

Tile Hill College of Further Education Tile Hill Lane, Coventry CV4 9SU. Tel 024 7669 4200; http://www.tilehill.ac.uk

Totton College Water Lane, Totton, Hampshire SO40 3ZX. Tel 023 8087 4874; http://www.totton.ac.uk (UCAS)

Tresham Institute St Mary's Road, Kettering, Northamptonshire NN15 7BS. Tel 01536 410252; http://www.tresham.ac.uk

Trowbridge College College Road, Trowbridge, Wiltshire BA15 0ES. Tel 01225 766241; http://www.trowcoll.ac.uk

Truro College College Road, Truro, Cornwall TR1 3XX. Tel 01872 264251.

Upper Bann Institute of Further and Higher Education Lurgan Campus, Kitchin Hill, Lurgan, Co. Armagh, Northern Ireland BT66 6AZ. Tel 01762 326135.

Uxbridge College Park Road, Uxbridge, Middlesex UB8 1NQ. Tel 01895 853333; http://www.uxbridge.ac.uk

Wakefield College Margaret Street, Wakefield, West Yorkshire WF1 2DH. Tel 01924 789200; http://www.wakcoll.ac.uk (UCAS)

Walford College Baschurch, Shrewsbury, Shropshire SY4 2HL. Tel 01939 260461; http://www.walford-college.ac.uk

Walsall College of Arts and Technology St Paul's Street, Walsall, West Midlands WS1 1XN. Tel 01922 657000; http://www.walsall.ac.uk (UCAS)

Waltham Forest College Forest Road, Waltham, London E17 4JB. Tel 020 8527 2311; http://www.waltham.ac.uk

Warwickshire College, Royal Leamington Spa and Moreton Morrell Warwick New Road, Leamington Spa, Warwickshire CV32 5JE. Tel 01926 318000; http://www.warkscol.ac.uk (UCAS)

West Cumbria College Park Lane, Workington, Cumbria CA14 2RW. Tel 01900 64331; http://www.wcc.ac.uk (UCAS)

West Herts College Hempstead Road, Watford, Hertfordshire WD1 3EZ. Tel 01923 812565; http://www.westherts.ac.uk (UCAS)

West Kent College Brook Street, Tonbridge, Kent TN9 2PW. Tel 01732 358101; http://www.westkent.ac.uk

West Nottinghamshire College Derby Road, Mansfield, Nottinghamshire NG18 5BH. Tel 01623 627191; http://www.westnotts.ac.uk (UCAS)

West Oxfordshire College Holloway Road, Witney, Oxfordshire OX8 7EE. Tel 01993 703464; http://www.oxfe.ac.uk

West Suffolk College Out Risbygate, Bury St Edmunds, Suffolk IP33 3RL. Tel 01284 701301; http://www.westsuffolk.ac.uk

West Thames College London Road, Isleworth, Middlesex TW7 4HS. Tel 020 8326 2000; http://www.west-thames.ac.uk (UCAS)

Westminster College 76 Vincent Square, London SW1P 2PD. Tel 020 7828 1222; http://www.westminster-cse.ac.uk (UCAS)

Weston College Knightstone Road, Weston-super-Mare, Somerset BS23 2AL. Tel 01934 411411; http://www.weston.ac.uk (UCAS)

Weymouth College Cranford Avenue, Weymouth, Dorset DT4 7LQ. Tel 01305 208808; http://www.weycoll.ac.uk (UCAS)

Wigan & Leigh College PO Box 53, Parsons Walk, Wigan WN1 1RS. Tel 01942 761601; http://www.wigan-leigh.ac.uk (UCAS)

Wigston College of Further Education Station Road, Wigston, Leicester LE18 2DW. Tel 0116 288 5051; http://www.wigston-college.ac.uk (UCAS)

Wiltshire College Cocklebury Road, Chippenham, Wiltshire SN15 3QD. Tel 01249 466800; http://www.wilts.coll.ac.uk

Wirral Metropolitan College Borough Road Campus, Birkenhead, Wirral, Merseyside L42 9QD. Tel 0151 551 7472; http://www.wmc.ac.uk (UCAS)

Worcester College of Technology Deansway, Worcester WR1 2JF. Tel 01905 725555; http://www.wortech.ac.uk (UCAS)

Wulfrun College Paget Road, Wolverhampton, West Midlands WV6 0DU. Tel 01902 317700; http://www.wulfrun.ac.uk

Yeovil College Holland Campus, Mudford Road, Yeovil, Somerset BA21 3DN. Tel 01935 443254; http://www.yeovil-college.ac.uk (UCAS)

York College of Further and Higher Education Tadcaster Road, York, North Yorkshire YO2 1UA. Tel 01904 770200. (UCAS)

Yorkshire Coast College of Further and Higher Education Lady Edith's Drive, Scarborough, North Yorkshire YO12 5RN. Tel 01723 372105; http://www.ycoastal.ac.uk (UCAS)

Ystrad Mynach College Twyn Road, Ystrad Mynach, Wales CF82 7NR. Tel 01443 816888. (UCAS)

Section 7: Further Education Colleges in England, Wales and Northern Ireland which offer Higher Education Courses not in the UCAS Scheme

Apply direct to Colleges for further information.

Abingdon College Northcourt Road, Abingdon, Oxon OX14 1NN. Tel 01235 555585; hhtp://www.abingdoncollege.ac.uk

Accrington & Rossendale College Sandy Lane, Accrington, Lancashire BB5 2AW. Tel 01254 389933.

Alton College Old Odiham Road, Alton, Hampshire GU34 2LX. Tel 01420 88118; http://www.altoncollege.ac.uk

Arnold & Carlton College Digby Avenue, Mapperley, Nottingham NG3 6DR. Tel 0115 952 0052; http://www.arnold-carlton.ac.uk

Bedford College Cauldwell Street, Bedford MK42 9AH. Tel 01234 345151; http://www.bedford.ac.uk

Bolton College Manchester Road Campus, Brampton Road, Bolton, Lancashire BL2 1ER. Tel 01204 531411.

Bracknell & Wokingham College Church Road, Bracknell, Berkshire RG12 1DJ. Tel 01344 420411; http://www.bracknell.ac.uk

Calderdale College Corporation Francis Street, Halifax, West Yorkshire HX1 3BR. Tel 01422 357357; http://www.calderdale.ac.uk

Cannock Chase Technical College The Green, Cannock, Staffordshire WS11 1UE. Tel 01543 462200; http://www.cannock.ac.uk

Carmel College Prescot Road, St Helens, Merseyside WA10 3AG. Tel 01744 22876; http://www.carmel.mernet.org.uk

College of North East London Tottenham Centre, High Road, London N15 4RU. Tel 020 8802 3111; http://www.conel.ac.uk

College of North West London Willesden Centre, Dudden Hill Lane, London NW10 2XD. Tel 020 8208 5000; http://www.cnwl.ac.uk

Craven College High Street, Skipton, North Yorkshire BD23 1JY. Tel 01756 791411; http://www.craven-college.ac.uk

Cricklade College Charlton Road, Andover, Hampshire SP10 1EJ. Tel 01264 363311; http://www.cricklade.ac.uk

Derby Tertiary College London Road, Derby DE24 8UG. Tel 01332 757570; http://www.derby-college.ac.uk

East Berkshire College Station Road, Langley, Slough, Berkshire SL3 8BY. Tel 01753 793000; http://www.eastberks.ac.uk

East Birmingham College Garrets Green Lane, Garrets Green, Birmingham, West Midlands B33 0TS. Tel 0121 743 4471; http://www.ebham.ac.uk

Enfield College 73 Hertford Road, Enfield, Middlesex EN3 5HA. Tel 020 8443 3434; http://www.enfield.ac.uk

Epping Forest College Borders Lane, Loughton, Essex IG10 3SA. Tel 020 8508 8311.

Great Yarmouth College Southtown, Great Yarmouth, Norfolk NR31 0ED. Tel 01493 655261.

Greenhill College, Harrow On The Hill Campus, Lowlands Road, Harrow, Middlesex HA1 3AQ. Tel 020 8869 8600; http://www.harrow.ac.uk

Hackney Community College Shoreditch Campus, Falkirk Street, London N1 6HQ. Tel 020 8985 8484; http://www.comm-coll.hackney.ac.uk

Havering College of Further and Higher Education Ardleigh Green Road, Hornchurch, Essex RM11 2NN. Tel 01708 455011; http://www.havering-college.ac.uk

Isle College Ramnoth Road, Wisbech, Cambridgeshire PE13 0HY. Tel 01945 582561; http://www.isle.ac.uk

Keighley College Cavendish Street, Keighley, West Yorkshire BD21 3DF. Tel 01535 618555; http://www.keighley.ac.uk

Knowsley Community College Rupert Road, Roby, Merseyside L36 9TD. Tel 0151 477 5700; http://www.kcc.mernet.org.uk

Leeds College of Building North Street, Leeds, West Yorkshire LS2 7QT. Tel 0113 222 6000; http://www.lcd.ac.uk

Leeds College of Technology Cookridge Street, Leeds, West Yorkshire LS2 8BL. Tel 0113 297 6300; http://www.leeds-lcot.ac.uk

Lewes Tertiary College Mountfield Road, Lewes, East Sussex BN7 2XH. Tel 01273 483188; http://www.lewescollege.ac.uk

Moulton College West Street, Moulton, Northamptonshire NN3 7RR. Tel 01604 491131; http://www.moulton.ac.uk

Nelson & Colne College Scotland Road, Nelson, Lancashire BB9 7YT. Tel 01282 440200; http://www.nelson.ac.uk

New College, Telford King Street, Wellington, Telford, Shropshire TF1 1NY. Tel 01952 641892.

Newbury College Oxford Road, Newbury, Berkshire RG14 1PQ. Tel 01635 37000/42824; http://www.newbury-college.ac.uk

Norfolk College Tennyson Avenue, King's Lynn, Norfolk PE30 2QW. Tel 01553 761144; http://www.col-westnorfolk.ac.uk

North Birmingham College Aldridge Road, Great Barr, Birmingham, West Midlands B44 8NE. Tel 0121 360 3543; http://www.northbham.ac.uk.ac.uk

Northampton College Booth Lane, Northampton NN3 3RF. Tel 01604 734567.

Northwest Institute of Further and Higher Education Strand Road, Londonderry, Northern Ireland BT48 7BY. Tel 028 9026 6711.

Orpington College of Further Education The Walnuts, Orpington, Kent BR6 0TE. Tel 01689 899700; http://www.orpington.ac.uk

Portsmouth College Tangier Road, Portsmouth, Hampshire PO3 6PZ. Tel 023 9266 7521; http://www.portsmouth-college.ac.uk

Queen Mary's College Cliddesden Road, Basingstoke, Hampshire RG21 3HF. Tel 01256 4175001; http://www.qmc.ac.uk

Richmond upon Thames College Egerton Road, Twickenham, Middlesex TW2 7SJ. Tel 020 8607 8000; http://www.richmond-utcoll.ac.uk

Ridge Danyers College Hibbert Lane, Marple, Stockport, Cheshire SK6 7PA. Tel 0161 427 7733; http://www.theridge.ac.uk

Royal Forest of Dean College Five Acres, Coleford, Gloucestershire GL16 7JT. Tel 01594 833416; http://www.rfdc.ac.uk

St Austell College Trevarthian Road, St Austell, Cornwall PL25 5BU. Tel 01726 67911; http://www.st-austell.ac.uk

Selby College Abbot's Road, Selby, North Yorkshire YO8 8AT. Tel 01757 211000; http://www.selbycollege.co.uk

Skelmersdale College Northway, Skelmersdale, Lancashire WN8 6LU. Tel 01695 728744.

Southgate College High Street, Southgate, London N14 6BS. Tel 020 8886 6521; http://www.southgate.ac.uk

Spelthorne College Church Road, Ashford, Surrey TW15 2XD. Tel 01784 248666; http://www.spelthorne.ac.uk

Stroud College of Further Education Stratford Road, Stroud, Gloucestershire GL5 4AH. Tel 01453 763424; http://www.stroudcollege.fsnet.co.uk

Walsall College of Arts and Technology St Paul's Street, Walsall, West Midlands WS1 1XN. Tel 01922 657000; http://www.walcat.ac.uk

Weald College Brookshill, Harrow Weald, Middlesex HA3 6RR. Tel 020 8420 8888; http://www.harrow.ac.uk

West Cheshire College The Handbridge Centre, Eaton Road, Handbridge, Chester CH4 7ER. Tel 01244 677677; http://www.west-cheshire.ac.uk

Wolverhampton College Westfield Road, Bilston, Wolverhampton, West Midlands WV14 6ER. Tel 01902 821000; http://www.wolverhamptoncollege.ac.uk

SECTION 8: Further Education Colleges in Scotland offering Higher Education Courses

The following Colleges appear under various subject headings in the tables in Chapter 5. Contact the Colleges direct for details of courses and method of application.

Aberdeen College Gallowgate Centre, Gallowgate, Aberdeen, Grampian AB25 1BN. Tel 01224 612000; http://www.abcol.ac.uk

Angus College of Further Education Keptie Road, Arbroath, Tayside DD11 3EA. Tel 01241 432600; http://www.angus.ac.uk

Anniesland College 112 Hatfield Drive, Glasgow, Strathclyde G12 0YE. Tel 0141 357 3969; http://www.anniesland.ac.uk

Argyll College West Bay, Dunoon, Argyll PA23 7HP. Tel 01369 707187; http://www.uhi.ac.uk/argyll.htm

Ayr College Dam Park, Ayr, Strathclyde KA8 0EU. Tel 01292 265184; http://www.ayrcoll.ac.uk

Banff & Buchan College of Further Education Henderson Road, Fraserburgh, Grampian AB43 9GA. Tel 01346 515777; http://www.banff-buchan.ac.uk

The Barony College Parkgate, Dumfries, Dumfries and Galloway DG1 3NE. Tel 01387 860251; http://www.barony.ac.uk

Borders College Melrose Road, Galashiels, Lothian TD1 2AF. Tel 01 896 757755.

Cambuslang College Hamilton Road, Cambuslang, Glasgow, Strathclyde G72 7NY. Tel 0141 641 6600; http://www.south-cambuslang-college.ac.uk

Cardonald College 690 Mosspark Drive, Glasgow, Strathclyde G52 3AY. Tel 0141 272 3333; http://www.cardonald.ac.uk

Central College of Commerce 300 Cathedral Street, Glasgow, Strathclyde G1 2TA. Tel 0141 552 3941; http://www.centralcollege.ac.uk

Clackmannan College of Further Education Branshill Road, Alloa FK10 3BT. Tel 01259 215121.

Clydebank College Kilbowie Road, Clydebank, Strathclyde G81 2AA. Tel 0141 952 7771; http://www.clydebank.ac.uk

Coatbridge College Kildonan Street, Coatbridge, Strathclyde ML5 3LS. Tel 01236 422316; http://www.coatbridge.ac.uk

Cumbernauld College Town Centre, Cumbernauld, Glasgow, Strathclyde G67 1HU. Tel 01236 731811; http://www.cumbernauld.ac.uk

Dumfries & Galloway College of Technology Heathhall, Dumfries, Dumfries and Galloway DG1 3QZ. Tel 01387 261261; http://www.dumgal.ac.uk

Dundee College Old Glamis Road, Dundee, Tayside DD3 8LE. Tel 01382 834834; http://www.dundeecoll.ac.uk

Edinburgh's Telford College Crewe Toll, Edinburgh, Lothian EH4 2NZ. Tel 0131 332 2491; http://www.ed-coll.ac.uk

Falkirk College of Further and Higher Education Grangemouth Road, Falkirk, Central FK2 9AD. Tel 01324 403000; http://www.falkirkcollege.ac.uk

Fife College of Further and Higher Education St Brycedale Avenue, Kirkcaldy, Fife KY1 1EX. Tel 01592 268591; http://www.fife.ac.uk

Glasgow Central College of Commerce 300 Cathedral Street, Glasgow, Strathclyde G1 2TA. Tel 0141 552 3941; http://www.centralcollege.ac.uk

Glasgow College of Building and Printing 60 North Hanover Street, Glasgow, Strathclyde G1 2BP. Tel 0141 332 9969; http://www.gcbp.ac.uk

Glasgow College of Food Technology 230 Cathedral Street, Glasgow, Strathclyde G1 2TG. Tel 0141 552 3751.

Glasgow College of Nautical Studies 21 Thistle Street, Glasgow, Strathclyde G5 9XB. Tel 0141 565 2525.

Glasgow School of Art 167 Renfrew Street, Glasgow, Strathclyde G3 6RQ. Tel 0141 353 4512; http://www.gsa.ac.uk

Glenrothes College Stenton Road, Glenrothes, Fife KY6 2RA. Tel 01592 772233.

Highland Theological College (UHI partner college – see Section 1) High Street, Dingwall IV15 9HA. Tel 01349 867600; http://www.ac.uk/htc.htm

Inverness College (UHI partner college – see Section 1) 3 Longman Road, Longman South, Inverness, Highland IV1 1SA. Tel 01463 236681; http://www.uhi.ac.uk/inverness

James Watt College of Further and Higher Education Finnart Street, Greenock, Strathclyde PA16 8HF. Tel 01475 724433; http://www.jameswatt.ac.uk

Jewel & Esk Valley College Eskbank Centre, Newbattle Road, Dalkeith, Lothian EH22 3AE. Tel 0131 660 1010; http://www.jevc.ac.uk

Kilmarnock College Holehouse Road, Kilmarnock, Strathclyde KA3 7AT. Tel 01563 523501; http://www.kilmarnock.ac.uk

Langside College 50 Prospect Hill Road, Glasgow, Strathclyde G42 9LB. Tel 0141 649 4991; http://www.perceus.langside.ac.uk

Lauder College Halbeath, Fife KY11 5DY. Tel 01383 845000; http://www.lauder.ac.uk

Lews Castle College (UHI partner college – see Section 1) Stornaway, Western Isles HS2 0XR. Tel 01851 703311; http://www.lews.uhi.ac.uk

Lochaber College (UHI partner college – see Section 1) An Aird, Fort William, Inverness, Highland PH33 6AN. Tel 01397 874000.

Moray College (UHI partner college – see Section 1) Moray Street, Elgin, Grampian IV30 1JJ. Tel 01343 554321; http://www.moray.ac.uk

North Atlantic Fisheries College (UHI partner college – see Section 1) Port Arthur, Scalloway, Shetland SE1 0UN. Tel 01595 880328; http://www.nafc.ac.uk

North Glasgow College 110 Flemington Street, Glasgow, Strathclyde G21 4BX. Tel 0141 558 9001; http://www.north-gla.ac.uk

North Highland College (UHI partner college – see Section 1; formerly Thurso College) Ormlie Road, Thurso, Highland KW14 7EE. Tel 01847 889000; http://www.uhi.ac.uk/thurso

Oatridge Agricultural College Ecclesmachan, Broxburn, Lothian EH52 6NH. Tel 01506 854387.

Orkney College (UHI partner college – see Section 1) Kirkwall, Orkney. Tel 01856 872839; http://www.uhi.ac/orkney.htm

Perth College (UHI partner college – see Section 1) Crieff Road, Perth, Tayside PH1 2NX. Tel 01738 621171; http://www.uhi.ac.uk/perth

Reid Kerr College Renfrew Road, Paisley, Strathclyde PA3 4DR. Tel 0141 581 2222; http://www.reidkerr.ac.uk

Sabhal Mor Ostaig (UHI partner college – see Section 1) Sleite, Isle of Skye IV44 8RQ. Tel 014761 844373; http://www.smo.uhi.ac.uk

Scottish Association for Marine Science (UHI partner college – see Section 1) PO Box 3, Oban, Argyll PA34 4AD. Tel 01631 562244; http://www.nerc-oban.ac.uk/dmll/uhi

Seafish Aquaculture (UHI partner college – see Section 1) Marine farming Unit, Ardtoe, Acharacle, Argyll, PH36 4LD. Tel 01967 431213; http://www.uhi.ac.uk/sfia.htm

Shetland College (UHI partner college – see Section 1) Gremista, Lerwick, Shetland SE1 0PX. Tel 01595 695514; http://www.uhi.ac.uk/shetland

Stevenson College Bankhead Avenue, Edinburgh, Lothian EH11 4DE. Tel 0131 535 4600; http://www.stevenson.ac.uk

Stow College, Glasgow 43 Shamrock Street, Glasgow, Strathclyde G4 9LD. Tel 0141 332 1786; http://www.stow.ac.uk

West Lothian College Marjoribanks Street, Bathgate, Lothian EH48 1QJ. Tel 01506 634300; http://www.west-lothian.ac.uk

3 APPLICATIONS AND SELECTION

APPLICATIONS FOR UNIVERSITY AND COLLEGE COURSES THROUGH UCAS

The Universities and Colleges Admissions Service (UCAS) deals with applications for admission to all full-time and sandwich first degree, Diploma of Higher Education and Higher National Diploma courses and some full-time Higher National Certificate courses in all United Kingdom universities (except the Open University), university colleges, colleges and institutes of higher education, specialist colleges and some further education colleges.

The UCAS procedures are designed to give applicants freedom to make responsible choices of course and institution, while giving universities and colleges freedom to select their own students, using whatever criteria and selection methods they favour. UCAS does not recruit on behalf of universities and colleges, nor does it advise applicants on their choice of courses although it does publish material which applicants may find useful. Educational considerations are the concern of applicants, in conjunction with their careers teachers, parents, other advisers and the universities and colleges themselves.

Entry requirements

Before applying to universities and colleges, applicants should check that by the time they plan to start their course they will have the required qualifications. Details of entry requirements are available direct from the universities and colleges.

Applicants will need to fulfil:

(i) the **general** entry requirements for degree or DipHE or HND or HNC courses
(ii) any **specific** requirements to enter a particular course, for example, study of a specified subject at A-level and AS-level of the Advanced GCE (A-level), Vocational A-level, Scottish Highers/Advanced Highers, GCSE, Scottish Standard Grades or Edexcel BTEC qualifications (for example, National Diploma, National Certificate). The course requirements are set out in prospectuses.

Potential applicants should ask the advice of teachers, careers advisers and university and college advisers before submitting their application.

The application process

Details of application procedures are set out in *How to Apply*, available from UCAS with the application form. Note that applications can also be made electronically using the Electronic Application System (EAS) software (contact your school or colleges advisers or UCAS for details). Course information is contained in the UCAS *Directory*. Applicants can get a copy of the *Directory*, application form, card and *How to Apply* from Distribution, UCAS, Rosehill, New Barn Lane, Cheltenham, Glos GL52 3LZ; (telephone 01242 223707; web site www.ucas.com/packreq/). The *Directory* and *How to Apply* are also available on-line and as a CD-ROM.

Applications for courses (excluding Art and Design (Route B) see below) should be submitted between 1 September and 15 January (or between 1 September and 15 October if you are including Oxford or Cambridge in your university choices or applying for Medicine, Dentistry or Veterinary Science) in the year before taking A/AS-levels or other examinations. You should send in your UCAS form as soon as possible after 1 September. Although UCAS forwards applications received from 16 January onwards to the universities or colleges concerned, admissions tutors will consider them only at their discretion.

The normal procedure is as follows:

1 You complete your UCAS application form in black ink – usually making up to six choices of institution and course – and hand it with your fee to your educational referee.

NB For Medicine, Dentistry or Veterinary Science you may only make four applications.

2 The referee completes the report and sends your form and fee to UCAS which then records your details.

3 UCAS acknowledges receipt of your form and sends you a personal application number and booklet explaining what will happen next.

4 UCAS sends reduced-size copies of your form to the universities/colleges you have named on the form.

5 Each university/college considers your application and subsequently informs UCAS of its decision. (Applicants may hear unofficially from the institutions.)

6 UCAS notifies applicants of the institutions' decisions.

7 If you have received at least one university/college offer, UCAS will send you – with your last decision – a statement of all your decisions in the scheme, a reply slip and an explanatory leaflet. You will be asked to reply to your offers as soon as possible, but you need not reply until you have attended Open Days or visits to which you have been invited. However, you must reply by the date given on the UCAS final decision letter.

If, before you have received all your decisions, you are **sure** of the offer you wish to accept, you may use the CNC slip in the booklet received from UCAS.

If you have firmly accepted a conditional offer (CF) you can also hold one additional offer (either conditional or unconditional) as an insurance (CI or UI). Normally the insurance offer would be one which specifies lower grades. A typical A-level applicant's record might read as follows:

Conditional offer – Firmly accepted (CF) – Grades BBC

Conditional offer – Insurance (CI) – Grades BCC

If your results are not as good as you had hoped and you cannot meet the conditions of the offer of the university/college you have firmly accepted but can fulfil the conditions of the insurance offer, you are committed to going to the insurance institution for the specified course.

If you do not inform UCAS of your firm acceptance of an offer and (if appropriate) your acceptance of an insurance offer, it will not be possible to hold the offers open and they will be declined by UCAS on your behalf.

If you leave any boxes blank on the Statement of Decisions reply slip UCAS will treat the offers concerned as declined and you will lose them. For example, if you have entered your firm acceptance but have not entered an insurance, UCAS will decline all your other offers and you will lose the opportunity to hold an insurance offer. Once you have replied to your offers, UCAS will send you a final statement of your replies and all the decisions made.

UCAS does not make decisions: it sends to you the decisions of the universities/colleges to which you have replied. It cannot change an institution's decision. If you need advice or more information, write direct to the institution.

8   The UCAS Clearing scheme operates from July to September. Its purpose is to try to match applicants without an offer with suitable courses where there are vacancies. Vacancy information is available via a variety of media systems, for example, the UCAS web site (http://www.ucas.com) and UK Course Discover (ECCTIS 2000) as well as *The Independent* and *The Independent on Sunday* newspapers. Details of these services and any other sources of vacancy information are given in a leaflet sent to all applicants when they become eligible for Clearing.

UCAS Timetable

1 September	UCAS begins accepting applications.
15 October	Deadline for applications to Oxford or Cambridge and courses leading to a professional qualification in Medicine, Dentistry and Veterinary Science to reach UCAS.
15 January	Deadline for all other applications to reach UCAS.
16 January to 30 June	Late applications received by UCAS are forwarded to the institutions for consideration at their discretion. Applications received after 30 June (Art and Design Route B after 12 June) are processed through the Clearing Scheme.
1 July to 20 September	UCAS will process applications through the Clearing Scheme.
Late July to early September	Confirmation of offers. UCAS tells you whether or not universities/colleges have confirmed conditional offers. If you are unsuccessful or did not receive any offers earlier in the year, you will be sent Clearing instructions automatically.
Throughout the second half of August and September	Remaining university/college places filled through Clearing (see below 'What To Do on Results Day – and After').

PLEASE NOTE:
- You are not required to reply to any university/college offers until you have received your last decision.
- Do not send a firm acceptance to more than one offer.
- Do not try to alter a firm acceptance.
- Send a Withdrawal slip to UCAS at once if you decide not to go to university/college this year.
- Remember to tell the institutions and UCAS if you change your address, or change your examination board, subjects or arrangements.

APPLICATIONS FOR ART AND DESIGN

Applications for Art and Design courses are submitted via one or both of two routes, which are of equal status.

Route A: Courses will normally be identified in a separate box in the UCAS *Directory*. Applicants may enter up to **six** choices and the closing date for receipt of applications at UCAS is 15 January. Applications will be considered simultaneously by the institutions listed.

Route B: Courses will be identified in a separate box in the UCAS *Directory* and by the prefix or suffix 'E' in the course code. Applicants may enter up to **three** choices and the closing date for receipt of applications at UCAS is 24 March. Applicants will be asked to indicate on an interview preference form the order in which they wish to be interviewed by the institutions to which they have applied through Route B. Applications will be considered in that order.

Applicants using Route B may previously have used three or more of their six available choices to apply through Route A.

APPLICATIONS FOR NURSING AND MIDWIFERY

Applications for entry to diploma-level nursing and midwifery courses at universities and colleges in England are handled by the Nursing and Midwifery Admissions Service (NMAS) at Rosehill, New Barn Lane, Cheltenham, Glos GL52 3LZ. For degree courses in Nursing and Midwifery you apply through UCAS in the usual way.

APPLICATIONS FOR SOCIAL WORK

Applications for courses should be made through UCAS. Details are available from the Social Work Admissions Service (SWAS) at Rosehill, New Barn Lane, Cheltenham, Glos GL52 3LZ.

THE APPLICATION FORM

Two important aspects of the UCAS application form concern Sections 3 and 10. In Section 3 all your university/college choices (a maximum of six) are to be listed in the order in which they are listed in the UCAS *Directory*, not in order of choice. Secondly, you should not mix your subjects. For example, in popular subject areas such as English, History, Medicine or Physiotherapy, it is safer to show total commitment by applying for all courses in the same subject and not to include second and/or third subject alternatives on the form.

A brief glance at the subject tables in **Chapter 5** will give you some idea of the popularity of various courses. In principle, institutions want the best applicants available, so if there are large numbers of applicants the offers made will be high. For Medicine, offers in terms of A-level grades usually reach BBB or higher, and for Veterinary Science AAB. Conversely, for the less popular subjects such as Chemistry or Mining Engineering, the offers are much lower – down to CC and even CD or equivalent points.

Similarly, some institutions are more popular (not better) than others. Again, this popularity can be judged easily in the tables in **Chapter 5**: the higher the offer, the more popular the institution. Quite often 'popular' universities are those located in attractive towns or cities such as Bristol, Exeter, Warwick, Bath or York. Alternatively, some institutions have established a good 'reputation' for various reasons, for example, Oxford, Cambridge and Durham. Conversely and unfortunately, some universities have confused applicants with unfamiliar names and no immediate identity as to their location, such as De Montfort (situated in Leicester, Milton Keynes, Lincoln and Bedford), Brunel (with campuses in West London) and Heriot-Watt (outside Edinburgh). More applicants would apply to these excellent institutions if their knowledge of geography were more extensive!

When you have chosen your courses and your institutions, look again at the offers the latter usually make and compare these with the grades projected by your teachers on your UCAS reference. *It is most important to maximise your chances of a place by choosing institutions which might make you a range of offers.* When all universities have considered your application form you can hold only two offers (one 'firm' and one 'insurance' offer) and naturally it is preferable for one to be lower than the other in case you do not achieve the offer grades or equivalent points for your first choice of university or college.

The other section of the UCAS form which deserves a lot of careful thought is Section 10 *(Personal Statement)*. How innocuous that sounds, yet it is the only part of the form where you can put in a personal bid for a place! In short, you are asked to give relevant background information about yourself, your interests and your choice of course and career (if you have a Record of Achievement you could use it as a guide).

Motivation to undertake your chosen course is very important. You can show this by giving details of any work experience and work shadowing you have done and of visits to places of historical interest (for history courses, for example). It is a good idea to begin your statement with such evidence explaining how your interest in your chosen subject has developed. In the subject tables in **Chapter 5** 'Planning Your UCAS Personal Statement', advice is given on what you might include in Section 10. You should also include various activities in which you have been involved in the last three or four years. Get your parents and other members of the family to refresh your memory – it is easy to forget something quite important. You might consider planning out this section in a series of sub-sections – and if you have a lot to say, be brief. The sub-sections can include:

School activities Are you a prefect, chairperson or treasurer of a society? Are you involved in supervisory duties of any kind? Are you in a school team? Which team? For how long? (Remember, teams mean any team: sports, chess, bridge, even business.)

Intellectual activities Have you attended any field or lecture courses in your main subjects? Where? When? Have you taken part in any school visits? Do you play in the school orchestra or have you taken part in a school drama production – on or off stage? Do you go to the theatre, art galleries or concerts?

Out-of-school activities This category might cover many of the topics above, but it could also include any community work you do, or Duke of Edinburgh Awards, the CCF, youth-hostelling, fell-walking etc. The countries you have visited might also be mentioned – for example, any exchange visits with friends living abroad.

Work experience Details of part-time, holiday or Saturday jobs could be included here, particularly if they have some connection with your chosen course. Some applicants plan ahead and arrange to visit firms and discuss career interests with various people who already work in the chosen field. For some courses such as Veterinary Science, work experience is essential, and it certainly helps for others, for example Medicine and Business courses.

Key Skills These cover numeracy, communication and information technology (the basics) and also advanced skills involving teamwork, problem solving and improving own learning. If you are not offering the Key Skills Certificate then evidence of your strengths in these areas may be mentioned in the school or college reference or you may include examples in your personal statement relating to your out-of-school activities. (See **Appendix 3 Key Skills Guide**.)

Finally, plan your UCAS form carefully. Take a photocopy of the form to use as a trial form and take a photocopy of your completed form to keep by you for reference if you are called for interview. Almost certainly you will be questioned on topics you have written on the form. Remember, also, to write or print legibly. Your form will be reproduced at UCAS and copies sent out to each university/college you have listed. As these copies will be only about two-thirds the size of the original it is important to present your information so that it can be easily read – type if necessary. Use black ink – not green or blue since these colours do not reproduce well. To assist the admissions tutor, use paragraphs and write between, not on the lines, preferably printing your statement. You may write short statements if you wish. It is not essential to write in prose except perhaps if you are applying for English or language courses in which case your statement will be judged grammatically!

Admissions tutors always stress the importance of the confidential report written by your head teacher or form tutors. Most schools and colleges will make some effort to find out why you want to apply for a particular course, but if they do not ask, do not take it for granted that they will know! Consequently, although you have the opportunity to write about your interests on the form, it is still a good idea to tell your teachers about them. Also, if you have to work at home under adverse conditions or if you suffer from any medical problem, your teachers must be told since these points should be mentioned on the report.

Deferred entry

Although application is usually made in the autumn of the year preceding the proposed year of entry, admissions tutors may be prepared to consider an application made two years before entry, so that the applicant can, perhaps, gain work experience or spend a period abroad. Policies on deferred entry may differ from department to department, and applicants should consult the Gap Year section of the tables in **Chapter 5**. Simply remember that there is no guarantee that you will get the grades you need or a place at the university of your first choice at the first attempt! If not, you may need to repeat A-levels and try again. It may be better not to apply for deferred entry until you are certain in August of your grades and your place.

ADMISSION TO CAMBRIDGE UNIVERSITY

The only major difference between the Cambridge admissions process and the normal UCAS arrangements is the date by which applications must be submitted. To allow early decisions for the benefit of other universities, the UCAS form and a Preliminary Application Form (PAF) must be submitted by October 15 at the latest: the UCAS form to Cheltenham and the PAF to Cambridge. This allows some interviewing to start in September, although the main batch of interviews takes place in

December. Examples of written work may be required prior to the interview and a short test may be set at the interview itself. This practice, however, varies between colleges. In January applicants receive either an offer conditional upon certain grades in examinations to be taken the following summer, or a rejection.

Conditional offers are made on the basis of school reports and interviews. The conditions set are grades to be obtained in examinations such as A-levels, Scottish Highers or the International Baccalaureate. Offers made by some Cambridge University colleges may also include Sixth Term Examination Papers (STEP) and the Medical and Veterinary Admissions Test (MVAT) (see below).

STEP examinations will take place in 2001 in June: information can be obtained from the STEP Office, OCR, Mill Wharf, Mill Street, Birmingham B6 4BU. Applicants for Medicine and Veterinary Medicine take the Medical and Veterinary Admissions Test instead of STEP and individual college written tests.

College Policies

All colleges which admit undergraduates will use the selection procedures described above. However, there will be some minor variations in policy between the various colleges, within each college and also between subjects. Further information about the policies of any particular college can be found in the *Cambridge Admissions Prospectus* and may also be obtained from the Admissions Tutor of the college con-cerned. No college operates a quota system for any subject except Medicine and Veterinary Medicine, where there are strict quotas for the whole University from which places are allocated to each college and for which a test (MVAT) must be taken.

The Medical and Veterinary Admissions Test (MVAT)

The Cambridge colleges have agreed that all candidates applying to Cambridge to read Medicine or Veterinary Medicine must take a written test. The Medical and Veterinary Admissions Test (MVAT) will be taken in schools and colleges before interview and will last for two hours. This test will supersede the use of STEP and individual college written tests for these subjects.

The test will be used to assess scientific aptitude, not fitness to practise medicine or veterinary medicine (which will continue to be assessed in other ways, including interview), and will focus on scientific abilities relevant to the study of medicine and veterinary medicine at Cambridge. It will not, in its first few years at least, be used to select for interview: all eligible candidates will normally still be invited for inter-view. The test is not to require special teaching or preparation, being intended to test ability and fundamental relevant understanding rather than advanced factual knowledge. This test will also provide a measure by which all candidates – pre- and post-A-level, mature, those from Scotland, Ireland and other European countries and those from further afield – can be judged, and will increase the transparency of the admissions process.

Selection of candidates will be based on a combination of GCSE and A-level (or equivalent) results or predictions, the school report, the written application, the results of the MVAT, and the interviews. As always, the process will take into account not just candidates' achievement so far, but their perceived potential for success in the Cambridge medical course. Schools/colleges may continue to use the Cambridge Special Access Scheme (CSAS) for candidates whose educational or personal background is particularly disadvantaged. (Details about the CSAS are available from the Intercollegiate Applications Office (CIAO) or on the web site below.)

Any further information about the MVAT will be posted on the Cambridge University web site at www.cam.ac.uk/cambuniv/undergrad. Some specimen test questions will be available during the summer on the web, and can be requested from the CIAO or any college admissions office.

Full details of the admissions procedures are contained in the current *Cambridge Admissions Prospectus*. Schools on the UCAS mailing list are invited to order copies in bulk from the Cambridge Intercollegiate Applications Office, Kellet Lodge, Tennis Court Road, Cambridge CB2 1QJ (web site: www.cam.ac.uk). Individuals can obtain copies from the same address or from the Admissions Office of any Cambridge college.

ADMISSION TO OXFORD UNIVERSITY

Application procedures to Oxford are similar to all other universities except that candidates applying to Oxford must submit a UCAS form and an Oxford Application Form by 15 October 2001 for those applying for entry in October 2002 or for deferred entry in October 2003, and admissions are carried out on a college basis. Candidates can name a college of preference but if they do not have a college in mind, they can make an open application. This means that they will be allocated a college through a computer program which takes account of their chosen course (and gender in the case of the one women-only college). Candidates will be allocated second and third preference colleges.

There are no separate or specific course requirements for individual courses at Oxford except for Medicine. All candidates are considered carefully on their individual merits. Tutors take into account a range of information from the candidate's application form including details of the academic record and the reference to assess a candidate's suitability and potential for his or her proposed course at Oxford. Candidates applying for some courses may be required to submit samples of marked school work by early November, and/or to take a short written test when they are in Oxford for interview. The majority of candidates applying to Oxford are invited for interview at the beginning of December and this is an integral part of the selection procedure. Candidates will be interviewed at their college of preference and also may be interviewed by other colleges. Colleges co-operate and pool candidates in order to ensure that the most able candidates are offered places. Successful candidates who have not completed their school-leaving examinations will be set conditional offers based on their forthcoming examinations such as A-levels, Scottish Highers, Advanced Highers, International Baccalaureate, European Baccalaureate and other European and overseas qualifications. Decisions are notified to candidates via UCAS by the end of January. Candidates are welcome to attend Open Days which are held at all of the colleges and a number of departments, usually during the summer term.

GENERAL SELECTION POLICIES

University and college departmental admissions tutors are responsible for selecting candidates, and the outline which follows provides information on the way in which candidates are selected for degree and diploma courses. There is little doubt that academic achievement and promise are the most important factors, although other subsidiary factors may be taken into consideration:

- Grades obtained at GCSE and AS-level examinations and the range of subjects studied may be considered. For **Chapter 5** some universities in some subject areas have indicated the levels they seek.
- Academic record of applicant throughout his or her school career, especially up to A/AS-levels and/or Vocational A-levels, Highers or other qualifications, and the choice of subjects.
- Time taken to obtain good grades at GCSE/Standard Grade and A/AS-level/Vocational A-levels/Highers/Advanced Highers.
- Forecast or the examination results at A/AS-level or Vocational A-level and head teacher's report.
- Applicant's intellectual development; evidence of ability and motivation to follow the chosen course.
- Applicant's range of interests, both in and out of school; aspects of character and personality.
- Vocational interests, knowledge and experience, particularly of applicants choosing vocational courses.
- If you are taking General Studies at A- or AS-level confirm with the admissions tutor that this is acceptable. Details of individual General Studies selection policies have been advised by some institutions and are shown next to the offers in **Chapter 5**.

AND FINALLY . . .

Before you send in your application:

CHECK that you have passes at Grade C or higher in the GCSE (or equivalent) subjects required for the course at the institutions to which you are applying. FAILURE TO HAVE THE RIGHT GCSE SUBJECTS OR THE RIGHT NUMBER OF GRADE C PASSES IN THE GCSE WILL RESULT IN A REJECTION.

CHECK that you are taking (or have taken) the A/AS-level or Vocational A-level (or equivalent) subjects required for the course at the institution to which you are applying. FAILURE TO BE TAKING OR HAVE TAKEN THE RIGHT A-LEVELS WILL ALSO RESULT IN A REJECTION.

CHECK that the GCE and VCE A-levels and other qualifications you are taking will be accepted for the course for which you are applying. Some subjects and institutions do not stipulate any specific A-levels, only that you are required to offer two or three subjects at A-level. In the view of some admissions tutors NOT ALL GCE A LEVELS CARRY THE SAME WEIGHT.

It should be noted that some similarities exist between certain GCE A-level subjects. If you are offering two GCE A-level subjects in any one group listed below you should contact your selected universities and colleges to confirm that both GCE A-level subjects are acceptable.

1. Ancient History
   Ancient History & Literature
   Classical Civilisation
   Classical Studies
   Latin with Roman History

2. Art
   History of Art

3. Biology
   Botany
   Environmental Science
   Social Biology

4. Biology
   Environmental Science
   Zoology

5. Business Studies
   Industrial Studies
6. Chemistry
   Physical Science
7. Communications Studies
   Media Studies
8. Craft Subjects
   Design
   Design & Technology
   Engineering Drawing
   Technical Drawing
   Graphical Communications
   Technology
9. Home Economics
   Economics & Political Studies
   Economics & Public Affairs
   Industrial Studies
10. Electronics
    Electronic Systems
11. Engineering Science
    Technology
12. Geography
    Economic Geography
    Environmental Science
13. Geology
    Environmental Science

14. Government & Politics
    Public Affairs
    Economics & Public Affairs
15. History
    Economic & Social History
16. Latin
    Latin with Roman History
17. Law
    Constitutional Law
18. Physics
    Physical Sciences
    Engineering Science
19. Theatre Studies
    Film Studies
20. Subjects in the following groups:

    (a) Pure Mathematics
        Pure Mathematics and
        Statistics

    (b) Mathematics
        Pure Mathematics and
        Statistics

    (c) Pure Mathematics and
        Statistics
        Statistics

INTERVIEWS

Fewer applicants are now interviewed than in the past but even if you are not called you should make an effort to visit your chosen universities and/or colleges before you accept any offer.

Interviews may be arranged simply to give you a chance to see the institution and the department and to meet the staff and students. Alternatively, interviews may be an important part of the selection procedure for specific courses such as Law, Medicine and for Teaching courses. If they are, you need to prepare yourself well.

Most interviews last approximately 20–30 minutes and you may be interviewed by more than one person. For practical subjects such as Music and Drama almost certainly you will be asked to perform, and for artistic subjects, to take examples of your work. For some courses you may have a written or other test in your interview (institutions setting tests are shown in each table in **Chapter 5** 'Selection Interviews').

How best can you prepare yourself?

Firstly, as one applicant advised, 'Go to the interview – at least you'll see the place'.

Secondly, on the question of dress, try to turn up looking smart (it may not matter, but it can't be wrong). Two previous applicants were more specific: 'Dress smartly but sensibly so you are comfortable for travelling and walking round the campus'.

More general advice was also important:

'Prepare well – interviewers are never impressed by applicants who only sit there with no willingness to take part.'

'Read up the prospectus and course details. Know how their course differs from any other you have applied for and be able to say why you prefer theirs.'

'They always ask if you have any questions to ask them: prepare some!'

Questions which you could ask might include the way in which internal examinations are assessed, the content of the course, and for vocational courses, contacts with industry, commerce or the professions, field work, work experience, teaching methods and accommodation. However, don't ask questions which are already answered in the prospectus!

These are only a few suggestions and other questions may come to mind during the interview which, above all, should be a two-way flow of information. It is also important to keep a copy of your UCAS form (especially Section 10) for reference since your interview will probably start with a question about something you have written.

Interviewers usually will want to know why you have chosen the subject and why you have chosen their particular institution. They will want to see how well-motivated you are, how much care you have taken in choosing your subject, how much you know about your subject, what books you have read. If you have chosen a vocational course they will want to find out how much you know about the career it leads to, and whether you have visited any places of work or had any work experience. If your chosen subject is also an A-level subject you will be asked about your course and the aspects of the course you like the most.

Try to relax. For some people interviews can be an ordeal; most interviewers know this and will make allowances. The following extract from the Oxford prospectus will give you some idea of what admissions tutors look for:

'Interviews serve various purposes, and no two groups of tutors will conduct them in the same way or give them exactly the same weight. Most tutors wish to discover whether a candidate has done more than absorb passively what he/she has been taught. They try to ascertain the nature and strength of candidates' intellectual interests and their capacity for independent development. They are also likely to ask about applicants' other interests outside their school curriculum. This is partly because between two candidates of equal academic merit, preference will be given to the one who has the livelier interests or activities, and partly because it is easier to learn about candidates when they talk on what interests them most.'

'Interviews are in no sense hostile interrogations. Those candidates who show themselves to be honest, thoughtful and unpretentious will be regarded more favourably than those who try to impress or take the view that it is safest to say as little as possible. We do not expect candidates to be invariably mature and judicious.'

In **Chapter 5** you will also find examples of questions which have been asked in recent years for which you might prepare, and non-academic reasons why applicants have been rejected!

WHAT TO DO ON RESULTS DAY – AND AFTER

BE AT HOME! Do not arrange to be away when your results are published. If you do not achieve the grades you require, you will need to follow an alternative course of action and make decisions which could affect your life during the next few years. Do not expect others to make these decisions for you.

If you achieve the grades or points which have been offered you will receive confirmation of a place, but this may take a few days to reach you. Once your place is confirmed contact the accommodation office at the university or college and inform them that you will need a place in a hall of residence or other accommodation.

If you achieve grades or points much higher than you expected – higher than the offer you have received – and you are already holding one or two places, you are not entitled to ignore these offers and try for a place at another 'better' university or college. If, however, you have decided definitely to change courses advise the university or college immediately.

If your grades or points are higher than you expected and you are not holding any offers you can telephone the admissions tutor at the universities and colleges which rejected you and request that they might reconsider you.

If you just miss your offers then telephone the universities and colleges to see if they can still offer you a place. ALWAYS HAVE YOUR UCAS REFERENCE NUMBER AVAILABLE WHEN YOU CALL. Their decisions may take a few days. You should check the universities and colleges in your order of preference. Your first choice must reject you before you contact your second choice.

If you have not applied to any university or college earlier in the year then you can apply through the Clearing Scheme in September. Check the tables in **Chapter 5** to identify which institutions normally make offers matching your results, then telephone the institution to see if they have any vacancies before completing your Clearing form.

If you learn finally that you do not have a place you will receive automatically a Clearing form to enable you to re-apply. Before you complete this form follow the instructions above.

If an institution has vacancies they will ask you for your grades. If they can consider you they will ask you for your Clearing form. You can only be considered by one institution at a time.

If you have to re-apply for a place:

(a) Check the vacancies report in the subject tables.

(b) Check the vacancies on the UCAS web site (www.ucas.com), in the national press and through your local careers office. If there are vacancies in your subject, check with the university or college that these vacancies have not been taken.

REMEMBER – There are many thousands of students just like you. Admissions tutors have a mammoth task checking how many students will be taking up their places since not all students whose grades match their offers finally decide to do so!

IF YOU HAVE AN OFFER AND THE RIGHT GRADES BUT ARE NOT ACCEPTING THAT OR AN ALTERNATIVE PLACE – TELL THE UNIVERSITY OR COLLEGE. Someone else is waiting for your place!

You may have to make many telephone calls to institutions before you are successful. It may even be late September before you know you have a place so BE PATIENT AND STAY CALM!

OVERSEAS APPLICANTS

The choice of a subject to study (from over 80,000 degree course options) and of a place for study (from more than 200 institutions) is a major task for students living in the United Kingdom. For overseas applicants it is even greater and the decisions which have to be made need much careful planning, preferably beginning two years before the starting date of the course.

Selection policies: The first reason for making early contact with your preferred institution is to check their requirements for your chosen subject and their selection policies for overseas applicants. For example, for all Art and some Architecture courses you will have to present a portfolio of work or a box of slides. For Music courses your application will often have to be accompanied by a tape recording you have made of your playing or singing, and in many cases a personal audition will be necessary. Attendance at an interview in this country is compulsory for some universities and some courses. At other institutions the interview may take place either in the United Kingdom or with a university or college representative in your own country.

The ability to speak and write good English: This is essential and many institutions require evidence of competence; for some you may have to send examples of your written work. At many institutions English classes are available, for example, Bangor, Cranfield, Leeds, Surrey, London (Royal Holloway), East Anglia Universities. Pre-entry language courses are offered by Brighton, Bath, Liverpool, Loughborough, Sheffield Hallam, Coventry and De Montfort Universities. Access and Foundation courses covering English language and other subjects are also available in many institutions.

Overseas student adviser: Most higher education institutions in the United Kingdom have an overseas student adviser who can advise you on all these points. They can also advise you on other factors you need to consider, such as passports, visas, entry certificates, evidence of financial support, medical certificates, medical insurance and the numbers of overseas students from your own country. All these details are very important and need to be considered at the same time as choosing your course and institutions.

The British Council: Finally, an excellent source of help, information and advice is your local office of the British Council. Their advisers can provide information on many of these points or put you in touch with those who can, and they can also help with information on fees, scholarship schemes (see also *University Scholarships and Awards* – in the **Appendix 2 Booklist**) and arrangements for English language tuition. If you have difficulty in finding the address of your local British Council office, get in touch with the British Council at 10 Spring Gardens, London SW1A 2BN.

MATURE APPLICANTS

(a) Check with your nearest university or college to determine the courses they can offer, for example degrees, diplomas, full-time, part-time.

(b) Some institutions will require examination passes in some subjects, others may not.

(c) An age limit may apply for some vocational courses, for example Medicine, Dentistry and Teaching.

(d) If entry requirements are an obstacle, intending students should approach their local careers service for information on Access, Open College, Gateway or Second Chance courses. These courses are fast-growing in number and popularity, offering adults an alternative route into higher education other than A-levels. These courses are usually developed jointly by colleges of further education and the local higher education institution. Check your local colleges.

(e) The demands of the course – how much time will be required for study? What are the assignments and the deadlines to be met? How will you be examined – unseen examinations, continuous assessment, practicals?

(f) The demands on finance – cost of the course – loan needed – loss of earnings – drop in income if changing to another career – travel requirements – accommodation – need to work part-time for income.

(g) The availability and suitability of the course – geographical location – competition for places – where it will lead – student support services, for example childcare, library, accommodation.

(h) What benefits will you derive? Fulfilment, transferable skills, social contacts, sense of achievement, enjoyment, self-esteem, career enhancement.

(i) Why would employers want to recruit you? Ability to adapt to the work scene, realistic and balanced approach, mature attitude to work.

(j) Why would employers not want to recruit you? Salary expectations, inability to fit in with younger colleagues, limited mobility. However, some employers particularly welcome older graduates: Civil Service, local authorities, Health Service, religious, charitable and voluntary organisations, teaching, social/probation work, careers work, housing.

HOW TO CALCULATE YOUR OFFERS

Units

One **GCE A**-level = 6 units
One **GCE AS**-level = 3 units
One **VCE Voc A**-level = 6 or 12 units
One **VCE Voc AS**-level = 3 units

Points

Vocational A-levels (12 units – double award)
Examples:

AA = 240pts	**BC** = 180pts	**DD** = 120pts
AB = 220pts	**CC** = 160pts	**DE** = 100pts
BB = 200pts	**CD** = 140pts	**EE** = 80pts etc

A-levels and 6 unit **Vocational A**-levels

A = 120pts	**C** = 80pts	**E** = 40pts
B = 100pts	**D** = 60pts	

AS-levels or **Vocational AS**-levels

a = 60pts	**c** = 40pts	**e** = 20pts
b = 50pts	**d** = 30pts	

Individual **Key Skill** unit scores

Level **4** = 30pts per unit
Level **3** = 20pts per unit
Level **2** = 10pts per unit

ABBREVIATIONS

A-level = **AL**
AS-level = **AS**
Vocational A-level = **VA**
A-level or Vocational
A-level grades = **A | B | C | D | E**
AS- or Vocational
AS-level grades = **a | b | c | d | e**
General Studies = **gs**
Units = **u**

An example of an offers line

Univ. name	Tariff pts	Units	ALs	ASs	VAs	Grades	Gen. st.	Course title
	200pts	15u	CCD or	CC + c or	VA 12u	BB	gs	

The grades and points totals shown in the tables should be regarded as the minimum levels to be achieved. The points totals to the left of the offers lines are for ease of reference only. Tariff points are not always used by institutions, check web sites.

4 INTRODUCTION TO THE SUBJECT TABLES

HOW TO READ THE TABLES

The subject tables in **Chapter 5** list degree subjects on offer in universities, university colleges, colleges and institutes of higher education, specialist colleges in the United Kingdom and some further education colleges. The names and abbreviations of degree courses vary widely, even in the same subject area, so if you have any problems locating your chosen course, check the index. Details of joint courses – for example, French and German – will appear in either subject table but not necessarily in both.

The tables are designed to provide you with information on how to choose your course, how applicants are selected, some of the important points to consider after the examination results are published and about gap years and graduate employment. This information has been provided by admissions tutors and will be of help to applicants submitting UCAS applications in 2001 for entry in 2002. **It must not be assumed that the offers and policies will apply to courses commencing in 2003 or thereafter**.

When selecting a degree course it is important to try to judge the points score and/or grades at A, AS and/or Vocational A-level you are capable of achieving and to compare them with the offers listed. Even though you might be capable of obtaining the right points and/or grades, there is no guarantee that you will be offered a place. Entry to degree courses is competitive and admissions tutors will consider other factors as well as your academic background.

Each table is planned to provide the following information:

Subject title and the special subject requirements/preferences: The requirements of each course may vary but the information provided is a guide to the subjects required at GCSE and A/AS-Levels. Additional subject requirements will also feature in some offers lines, as required by institutions. CHECK THE PROSPECTUSES AND WEB SITES before submitting your application. Remember – some universities stipulate **General Requirements** which apply to all courses offered in both science and arts subjects. **A-level:** Information is provided about institutions' required or preferred subjects at A-level for some courses listed in the table below. **AS-Level:** As for A-level. **GCSE:** This sub-section provides some details of subjects required. In addition information is also given on the grades **preferred** by institutions. For most degree courses four or five GCSE subjects at grades A to C would be the minimum requirement, often including English and mathematics to meet the professional requirements of certain career bodies.

Name of Institution: Universities and colleges offering degree courses are listed in order of level of points. The points levels shown, however, are only for ease of reference for the reader, since not all universities will be making offers using the UCAS tariff points system and not necessarily accepting equivalent points to the grades stipulated. In brackets after the titles of some universities, the names of their university colleges are given, for example, **London (King's)**, or a campus, for example, **De Montfort (Lincoln)**. After some college titles an abbreviation is given in brackets to indicate the type of college, for example **(CHE)**, **(UC)**, **(CAg)**, **(SAD)**, **(CT)**, **(CFHE)**: see **Institutional Abbreviations** at the end of this chapter. This is to help readers to differentiate between the types of colleges and to help them identify any special-isation it may have, for example art, agriculture.

Offers: The keynote this year is flexibility. Because of the range of qualifications being offered in schools throughout the UK, admissions tutors realise that each applicant must be considered individually depending on the qualifications being offered. The information on offers in the subject tables in **Chapter 5** is presented as a **first reference source** as to the approximate level required but they may be amended in the light of the qualifications offered by applicants. For entry in 2002 universities and colleges are at a transitional stage in framing their offers to cover a range of qualifications. These qualifications are part of the UCAS Tariff System which allocates points to the grades achieved for each qualification. The Tariff covers GCE Advanced (A-levels), Advanced Subsidiary (AS), the VCE Vocational A-level (formerly Advanced GNVQ) and the Vocational AS-Level, Key Skills certificates (with components in number, communication and IT) and free-standing units in mathe-matics. Scottish qualifications at Higher and Advanced Higher levels are also included in the Tariff. However, not all these qualifications will be included in the offers made. Whilst some universities will still require specific A-levels and in some cases AS subjects and grades to meet the requirements of their courses, others will stipulate UCAS Tariff points and the number of units to be achieved by candi-dates, calculated on the basis of the following:

Units

One GCE A-level = 6 units; one GCE AS-Level = 3 units; one VCE Vocational A-level = 12 or 6 units (depending on the syllabus taken); one VCE Vocational AS-Level = 3 units.

Points

Points are calculated as follows:

Vocational A-levels (12 units – double award): Examples: Grade AA=240 pts; AB=220 pts; BB=200 pts; BC=180 pts; CC=160 pts; CD=140 pts; DD=120 pts; DE=100 pts; EE=80 pts etc.

GCE and VCE A-levels (6 units): Grade A=120 pts; B=100 pts; C=80 pts; D=60 pts; E=40 pts.

GCE and VCE AS-Levels (3 units): Grade A=60 pts; B=50 pts; C=40 pts; D=30 pts; E=20 pts.

Key Skills: Level 4=30 pts per component; level 3=20 pts per component; level 2=10 pts per component. Key Skills Certificates – levels and points – will be stip-ulated by institutions should they form part of the offer, which is unlikely for entry in 2002. Applicants not offering the Key Skills Certificate should include evidence of key skills activities in their personal statement as admissions tutors will take this into account when considering your application (see **Appendix 3, Key Skills Preference Tables**).

Two AS-Levels and a six-unit Vocational A-level may generally be regarded as equivalent to one A-level. Similarly, Vocational A-level grades are equivalent to A-level grades.

The information provided by institutions this year (the first year of the new system) varies considerably and, in view of the wide range of alternative offers available within the the Tariff System and the offers published, the information given should be used as a first source of reference and comparision only. **Applicants must check prospectuses and websites for full details of all offers.** A table showing how to calculate offers appears at the beginning of this chapter, at the beginning of **Chapter 5** and on the inside fold of the back cover.

In each subject table institutions are listed in groups, representing similar levels of offers. To the left of each group the number of points shown either represents the grades or the tariff points required. Tariff points are not necessarily stipulated by every institution nor can it be assumed that grade offers can be substituted by points.

Depending on the details given by institutions, the offers lines aim to provide information as follows:

(a) The tariff points or range of tariff points stipulated (the range of tariff points may be higher than the grades indicated).
(b) The units (u) required.
(c) The specific grade or average grades required at A-level (AL) **or** at A-level plus AS subjects **and/or** Vocational A-levels.
(d) Whether or not General Studies is acceptable (gs or not gs).
(e) Abbreviated course titles (see Abbreviations at the end of this chapter).

Examples:

320 pts York – BBC+c **or** BB+ccc; gs; (Fr/Ger)

For the joint course in French and German, York requires grades of BBC (280 pts) at A-level plus AS-Level grade c (40 pts) **or** an alternative total of 320 points by way of BB (200 pts) at A-level plus AS-Level grades ccc (120 pts).

320 pts Bath – 18u ABB **or** VA12u+AL(maths); (not gs) (Comp Sci)

For Computer Science, Bath requires a minimum of 18 units and A-level grades at ABB (320 pts) **or** a 12 unit Vocational A-level (VA) plus A-level maths. The 12 unit VA grades and the maths grade to total at least 320 points.

260 pts Bristol UWE – 260–200 pts 18u pref/12u – ALs **or** ALs+ASs **or** VAs+/- ALs/ASs (min 80 pts AL maths); (MEng Mech Eng)

For Manufacturing Engineering, Bristol UWE requires a minimum of 12 units and 200 points and prefers 18 units and 260 points. This can be achieved by way of 3 A-levels (18 u) **or** 2 A-levels (12u) plus 2 AS-Levels (6u) **or** a 12 unit Vocational A-level plus an A-level (6u). For example, CCE **or** BD+ee **or** VA12u CD plus A-level grade D or 2 AS-Levels grades dd.

Advanced Extension (World Class) Tests

It is proposed that Advanced Extension (World Class) Tests will replace the Special Papers required by a small number of universities offering very competitive courses. As yet, no universities are intending to introduce these tests as a requirement for entry in 2002 and information is not yet available.

Course title: An abbreviated title of the course is listed following the offer. The abbreviation used (see **Course abbreviations**) is that which most closely refers to the course title shown in the UCAS *Directory*. In some cases, when a number of joint courses exist with a major subject, these may be shown as, for example, European Management at Lancaster – Euro Mgt with Fr/Ger/Ital/Span. Some courses are shown in the subject tables as awaiting validation. Before applying, students should check that these courses will run.

Alternative Offers:

EB offers: These are offers made to students taking the European Baccalaureate examination.

IB offers: These are made to applicants offering the International Baccalaureate. Assessment of all aspects of the IB curriculum is conducted both during and at the conclusion of the two-year programme. All subjects at both Higher and Subsidiary levels are marked on a 1–7 scale with up to 20% of the marks in a given subject awarded upon the basis of internal assessment. All students require a minimum of 24 points to qualify for the Diploma.

Irish offers: These offers are made to students taking the Irish Leaving Certificate.

Scottish Qualifications: Full details of entry to courses in Scotland are published annually in the *Entrance Guide to Higher Education in Scotland* by the Committee of Scottish Higher Education Principals (COSHEP), 141 West Nile Street, Glasgow G1 2RN. Scottish applicants are advised to contact admissions staff in universities and colleges in England, Wales and Northern Ireland regarding offers before submitting applications.

Overseas applicants: General information for overseas applicants is provided when available.

Choosing Your Course

This section provides information under the five headings below on different aspects of degree and diploma courses which is important for making informed course decisions. This section should be read in conjunction with **Chapter 1**.

Subject information: Advice is provided on the subject content and the priorities to be considered when choosing courses and similar alternative courses.

Special features: All institutions aim to maintain a high standard of scholarship and teaching. However, whilst many courses offered by universities are similar in content, this section identifies some of the special features which exist, such as course emphases, options, flexibility, which might be of special interest to potential applicants. These special features refer to single honours courses except where otherwise indicated by course abbreviations.

Top universities and colleges (Teaching Quality): The Quality Assurance Agency (QAA) provides information on quality ratings. These cover such features as the quality of teaching and learning, learning resources, development of transferable skills, curriculum, student progression and achievement, accessibility of staff, student support systems, non-completion rates and library and laboratory facilities. The institutions listed are those whose courses in the subject area have been assessed and have reached high standards in their teaching. Note that not all courses and institutions have been assessed. (For full details and extracts from reports, see *The Best in University and College Courses* in **Appendix 2, Booklist**.)

Top universities and colleges (Research): Details of Research Excellence Exercises undertaken in 1996 have been provided by the QAA. University courses listed have ratings of 4 and 5* on a scale of 1 (lowest) to 5* (highest). Some universities may not offer undergraduate courses in these subjects. The next Research Assessment Exercise is scheduled for 2001.

Study opportunities abroad: In recent years new initiatives have been introduced to enable undergraduates to study abroad, some schemes giving students opportunities to take part of their course in a European university. This section of the tables lists universities in some subject areas in which students study abroad for long or short periods.

Work opportunities abroad: This section lists universities which offer work opportunities links in which students may be attached to industrial, commercial and administrative organisations abroad. Some of these placements are optional.

Admissions Information

This section includes additional information under the following headings:

Number of applicants per place (approx): These figures show the approximate number of applicants initially applying for each place before any offers are made. It should be noted that any given number of applicants represents candidates who have also applied for up to six other university and college courses. **Foreign applicants:** Numbers of foreign (non-EU) applicants are shown in several tables, including **Medicine**, **Dentistry** and **Physiotherapy** where this information is available.

Planning your UCAS personal statement: Guidelines are provided on information which could be included in this section. In most cases applicants will be required to indicate why they wish to follow a particular course and if possible to provide positive evidence of their interest (see **Chapter 3**).

Selection interviews: Institutions are listed which normally use the interview as part of their selection procedure. Those institutions adopting the interview procedure will interview only a small proportion of applicants. Mature and Access students are often interviewed. (W) indicates that written work is required before interview; (T) indicates that tests are set at interview.

Examples of interview questions: These are examples of some of the interview questions faced by applicants during recent years, together with relevant comments from admissions tutors.

Reasons for rejection (non-academic): Academic ability is the major factor in the selection (or rejection) of applicants. In this section admissions tutors give non-academic reasons for rejecting applicants.

Gap Year Advice

General information is provided, together with any specific advice available from individual institutions. Most institutions are agreeable to students taking a gap year, but for some subjects (for example Mathematics) academic staff may advise against it. Check with the institutions.

Institutions willing to defer entry after A-levels: These institutions will allow you to defer your entry for a year. (NB: Some very popular universities with popular courses may have a limited quota of places for the following year. Check this before applying.)

After A-Levels Advice

This section provides information for helping you decide what to do after the examination results are published (see also **Chapter 3, What to do on Results Day – and after**). Details refer to the main subject named in each table unless otherwise stated in brackets.

Institutions which may accept the same points score after A-levels: Some candidates may not achieve the actual grades of the offer required, yet obtain grades with an equivalent points score (see above). The institutions listed in this section usually accept a points score equivalent to the original offer made after the publication of examination results. **(NB** With the demand for places at present, some of the institutions listed may change their policies after the results are known. Check with admissions tutors at the time of interview or when an offer is made to you.)

Institutions which may accept lower grades/points score after A-levels: Some universities and colleges are able to accept applicants whose grades or points are marginally lower than the offers originally made to them after the publication of the examination results. Applicants searching for a place are recommended to contact these institutions first.

Offers to applicants repeating A-levels: This sub–section gives details of whether offers to repeating applicants may be **higher, possibly higher** or the **same** as those offers made to first time applicants for single honours courses. It should be noted that circumstances may differ between candidates. Some will be repeating the same subjects taken in the previous year, while others may be taking different subjects. Offers will also be dictated by the level of grades achieved at the first sitting of the examinations.

Probable vacancies from June 2001 and in Clearing: Under this heading some information is provided about possible vacancies occurring from June and into Clearing. This may assist applicants not holding offers to assess their chances of a conditional offer before Clearing and of a possible place following the publication of examination results. It should be noted that the majority of vacancies advertised in Clearing are for combined or joint subject courses. Applicants should note the following:

- Some popular universities have one or two vacancies every year in competitive courses but do not advertise them in the official vacancy lists.
- Vacancies are **not** filled on a first–come, first–served basis, but on a 'first come with the highest grades' basis. Thereafter, as the start of the university year approaches, lower grades may become acceptable if vacancies remain unfilled – so keep trying!
- Even a day or two after the term has started, vacancies may occur since some applicants will fail to arrive to register for the course. At this stage late applicants can still be considered.

Remember If you were rejected by all your universities and have achieved good grades, contact them by telephone – they may be prepared to revise their decision. THIS APPLIES PARTICULARLY TO THE MEDICAL SCHOOLS.

New Graduate Destinations and Employment

The information in the tables has been provided by the Higher Education Statistics Agency (HESA) and is taken from their report *First Destinations of Students Leaving*

Higher Education Institutions 1998-1999. The report can be obtained from HESA, 18 Royal Crescent, Cheltenham, Glos GL50 3DA (price £30.00 inc postage and packing in the UK: please mention *Degree Course Offers* when ordering).

Details are given of the total number of graduates whose destinations have been recorded – not the total number who graduated in that subject. Employment figures relate to those in full-time permanent employment unless otherwise stated (short-term and unpaid employment figures are not included). The 'Unemployed' category refers to those students still seeking permanent employment six months after grad-uating. 'Further Study' includes research into a subject-related field, higher degrees, private study or, alternatively, a career training. The apparent discrepancy between the total numbers of graduates and their destinations represents those who did not seek employment, for example, travellers, overseas students returning home and those unable to work for health and other reasons.

INSTITUTIONAL ABBREVIATIONS USED IN THE TABLES

AI	– Arts Institute
AMD	– Academy of Music and Drama
CA	– College of Art(s)
CAD	– College of Art and Design
CAg	– College of Agriculture
CAgF	– College of Agriculture and Forestry
CAgH	– College of Agriculture and Horticulture
CAST	– College of Arts, Science and Technology
CAT	– College of Advanced Technology *or* Arts and Technology
CBP	– College of Building and Printing
CC	– College of Communication
CD	– College of Design
CDC	– College of Design and Communication
CFash	– College of Fashion
CFE	– College of Further Education
CFTCS	– College of Food, Tourism and Creative Studies
CGAS	– City and Guilds Art School
CHE	– College of Higher Education
CHFE	– College of Higher and Further Education
CHort	– College of Horticulture
CMus	– College of Music
CMus/Dr	– College of Music and Drama
Coll	– College
Cons	– Conservatoire (Birmingham)
Court	– Courtauld Institute (London University)
CSAD	– College and School of Art and Design
CSM	– Camborne School of Mines (Exeter University)
CT	– College of Technology
CTA	– College of Technology and Arts
Gold	– Goldsmiths' College (London University)
HCC	– Hotel Catering College (Portrush)
Hom	– Homerton College (Cambridge University)
Hey	– Heythrop College (London University)
HMS	– Hospital Medical School
IA	– Institute of Art

IAD	– Institute of Art and Design
IEd	– Institute of Education
IHCS	– Institute of Health Care Studies
IHE	– Institute of Higher Education
Imp	– Imperial College (London University)
Inst	– Institute
IT	– Institute of Technology
King's	– King's College (London University)
LIPA	– Liverpool Institute of Performing Arts
LSE	– School of Economics and Political Science (London University)
QMW	– Queen Mary and Westfield College (London University)
RAcMus	– Royal Academy of Music
RCMus	– Royal College of Music
Reg Coll	– Regional College
RH	– Royal Holloway College (London University)
RMCS	– Royal Military College of Science
RNCM	– Royal Northern College of Music
RVC	– Royal Veterinary College (London University)
SA	– School of Art
SAD	– School of Art and Design
SCE	– Scottish Certificate of Education
Sch	– School
Sch Sp/Dr	– School of Speech and Drama
SHCS	– School of Health Care Studies
SOAS	– School of Oriental and Asian Studies (London University)
SOT	– School of Occupational Therapy
SP	– School of Physiotherapy
TC	– Technical College
TerC	– Tertiary College
TrCMus	– Trinity College of Music
UC	– University College
UCL	– University College (London University)
UMIST	– University of Manchester Institute of Science and Technology
Univ	– University
UWCM	– University of Wales College of Medicine (Cardiff)
UWC	– University of Wales College
UWI	– University of Wales Institute
WCMD	– Welsh College of Music and Drama

COURSE ABBREVIATIONS USED IN THE TABLES

Aboricult	– Aboriculture	Admin	– Administration/ Administrative
Abrd	– Abroad		
Acc	– Accountancy/ Accounting	Adv	– Advertising
		Advnc	– Advanced
Accs	– Accessories	Advntr	– Adventure
Acoust	– Acoustical	Aero	– Aeronautical/ Aeronautics
Act	– Actuarial		
Actg	– Acting	Aerodyn	– Aerodynamics
Actvts	– Activities	Aeromech	– Aeromechanical
Add	– Additional	Aerosp	– Aerospace

Af	– Africa(n)		Bio Ins	– Bio Instrumentation
Affrs	– Affairs		Biol	– Biological/Biology
Agncy	– Agency		Biom	– Biometry
Agric	– Agriculture/Agricultural		Biomed	– Biomedical
Agrofor	– Agroforestry		Bio-org	– Bio-organic
Agron	– Agronomy		Bioproc	– Bioprocess
Air	– Aircraft		Biophys	– Biophysics
Am	– American		Biorg	– Biorganic
Amen	– Amenity		Biotech	– Biotechnology
Analys	– Analysis		Bld	– Build/Building
Analyt	– Analytical		Blt	– Built
Anat	– Anatomy/Anatomical		Bookbind	– Bookbinding
Anim	– Animal		Br	– British
Animat	– Animation		Braz	– Brazilian
Ant	– Antique		Brew	– Brewing
Anth	– Anthropology		Brit	– British
App	– Applied/Applications/		Broad	– Broadcast
	Applicable		Bty	– Beauty
Appr	– Appropriate		Bulg	– Bulgarian
Aqua	– Aquaculture/Aquatic		Bus	– Business
Arbc	– Arabic		Byz	– Byzantine
Arbor	– Arboriculture			
Arch	– Archaeology		Callig	– Calligraphy
Archit	– Architecture		CAMS	– Credit Accumulation
Artfcts	– Artefacts			Modular Scheme
Artif	– Artificial		Can	– Canada/Canadian
As	– Asian		Cap	– Capital
Ass	– Assessment		Carib	– Caribbean
Assoc	– Associated		Cart	– Cartography
Asst	– Asset		Cat	– Catering
Astro	– Astrophysics		Cell	– Cellular
Astron	– Astronomy		Celt	– Celtic
Atmos	– Atmospheric		Cent	– Century
Auc	– Auctioneering		Ceram	– Ceramics
Aud	– Audio		Cert	– Certificate
Aud Vid	– Audio Video		Ch Mgt	– Chain Management
Audtech	– Audiotechnology		Chat	– Chattels
Aus	– Australia(n)		Chc	– Choice
Auth	– Author/Authoring		Chch	– Church
Auto	– Automotive		Chem	– Chemistry
Autom	– Automated		Child	– Childhood/Children
Avion	– Avionics		Chin	– Chinese
			Chn	– Chain
Bd	– Based		Chng	– Change
Bhv	– Behaviourial		Chr	– Christian
Bib	– Biblical		Cits	– Cities
Bioarch	– Bioarchaeology		Civ	– Civilisation/Civil
Bioch	– Biochemistry/		Class	– Classical
	Biochemical		Clim	– Climatic
Biodiv	– Biodiversity		Clin	– Clinical
Bioelectron	– Bioelectronics		Cllct	– Collect/Collecting
Biogeosci	– Biogeoscience		Cloth	– Clothing

Cmnd	– Command	Def	– Defence
Cmpsn	– Composition	Defer	– Deferred Choice
Cmpste	– Composite	Deg	– Degree
Cmwlth	– Commonwealth	Des	– Design/Designer
Cnflct	– Conflict	Desr	– Desirable
Coach	– Coaching	Dev	– Development/
Cog	– Cognitive		Developmental
Col	– Colour	Diag	– Diagnostic
Comb	– Combined	Diet	– Dietetics
Combus	– Combustion	Dif	– Difficulties
Comm	– Communications	Dig	– Digital
Commer	– Commerce/Commercial	DipSW	– Diploma in Social
Commun	– Community		Work
Comp	– Computer/ised/-aided	Dir	– Direction/Director/
Compar	– Comparative		Directing
Complem	– Complementary	Dis	– Diseases
Comput	– Computational	Disab	– Disability
Con	– Context	Disas	– Disaster
Concur	– Concurrent	Discip	– Disciplinary
Cond	– Conductive (Education)	Diso	– Disorders
Cons	– Conservation	Disp	– Dispensing
Constr	– Construction	Dist	– Distribution
Consum	– Consumer	Distil	– Distillation/Distilling
Contr	– Control	Div	– Divinity
Contemp	– Contemporary	Dntl	– Dental
Conv	– Conveyancing	Doc	– Document/Documentary
Corp	– Corporation/ate	Dom	– Domestic/
Cos	– Cosmetic		Domesticated
Cosmo	– Cosmology	Dr	– Drama
Cost	– Costume	Drg	– Drawing
Couns	– Counselling	Dscrt	– Discrete
Country	– Countryside	Dvnc	– Deviance
Cr	– Care		
Craft	– Craft/smanship	Ecol	– Ecology/Ecological
Cre	– Care	Ecomet	– Econometrics
Crea	– Creative	Econ	– Economics
Crim	– Criminal/Criminology	Ecotech	– Ecotechnology
Crit	– Criticism/Critical	Ecotour	– Ecotourism
Cro	– Croatian	Edit	– Editorial
Crs	– Course	Educ	– Education
Crsn	– Corrosion	Educr	– Educare
Cstl	– Coastal	EFL	– English as a Foreign
Ctln	– Catalan		Language
Culn	– Culinary	Egypt	– Egyptian/Egyptology
Cult	– Culture/Cultural	Elec	– Electrical
Cxt	– Context	Electroacout	– Electroacoustics
Cyber	– Cybernetics/space	Electromech	– Electromechanical
Cz	– Czech	Electron	– Electronics
		Embr	– Embroidery
Dan	– Danish	Emp	– Employment
Decr	– Decorative/Decoration	Ener	– Energy
Decn	– Decision	Eng	– Engineering

Engl	– English	Frsty	– Forest/Forestry
Ent	– Enterprise	Ftbl	– Football
Enter	– Entertainment	Furn	– Furniture
Entre	– Entrepreneur/ Entrepreneurship	Fut	– Futures
Env	– Environment/ Environmental	Gam	– Gambling
		Gard	– Garden
Eqn	– Equine	Gem	– Gemmology
Equip	– Equipment	Genet	– Genetics
Ergon	– Ergonomics	Geochem	– Geochemistry
Est	– Estate	Geophys	– Geophysical
Eth	– Ethics	Georg	– Georgian
Eth-Leg	– Ethico-Legal	Geotech	– Geotechnics
Ethn	– Ethnic	Ger	– German/Germany
Ethnol	– Ethnology	Gk	– Greek
Ethnomus	– Ethnomusicology	Glf Crs	– Golf Course
EU	– European Union	Glob	– Global
Euro	– European	Gmnt	– Garment
Eval	– Evaluation	Gms	– Games
Evnt	– Event	Gndr	– Gender
Evol	– Evolution	Gnm	– Genome
Ex	– Executing	Gov	– Government
Exer	– Exercise	Graph	– Graphic
Exhib	– Exhibition	Grmnt	– Garment
Exp	– Export		
Explor	– Exploration	Hab	– Habitat
Expmt	– Experimental	Hard	– Hardware
Expnc	– Experience	Haz	– Hazard
Ext	– Extended	Heal	– Healing
		Heb	– Hebrew
Fac	– Faculty	Herb	– Herbal
Facil	– Facilities	Herit	– Heritage
Fam	– Family	Hisp	– Hispanic
Fash	– Fashion	Hist	– History
Fbr	– Fibre	Hlth	– Health
Fctn	– Fiction	HlthSC	– Health and Social Care
Fd	– Food		
Fdn	– Foundation	Hol	– Holistic
Fbr	– Fibre	Hom	– Homeopathic
Fin	– Finance	Homin	– Hominid
Finn	– Finnish	Horol	– Horology
Fish	– Fisheries	Hort	– Horticulture
Fit	– Fitness	Hosp	– Hospital
Fld	– Field	Hous	– Housing
F.maths	– Further Mathematics	HR	– Human Resources
Foot	– Footwear	Hspty	– Hospitality
For	– Foreign	Htl	– Hotel
Foren	– Forensic	Hum	– Human/Humanities
Foss	– Fossil(s)	Hung	– Hungarian
Fr	– French	Hydrog	– Hydrography
Frchd	– Franchised	Hydrol	– Hydrology
Frshwtr	– Freshwater	Hyg	– Hygiene

Iber	– Iberian	Las	– Laser
Ice	– Icelandic	Lat	– Latin
Id	– Ideas	Lcl	– Local
Illus	– Illustration	LD	– Learning Disabilities
Imag	– Imaging/Imaginative	Lea	– Leather
Imgntve	– Imaginative	Learn	– Learning
Immun	– Immunology	Leg	– Legal
Inc	– Including	Legis	– Legislative
Ind	– Industrial/Industry	Leis	– Leisure
Indep St	– Independent Study	Lib	– Library
Inet	– Internet	Lic	– Licensed
Inf	– Information	Lic de Geog	– Licence de Geographie
Infec	– Infectious/Infection	Lif	– Life/Lifestyle
Inform	– Informatics	Ling	– Linguistics
Innov	– Innovation	Lit	– Literature/Literary
Ins	– Instrument	Lnd	– Land
Inst	– Institution/al	Lndbd	– Land-based
InstIn	– Installation	Log	– Logistics
Instr	– Instumentation	Lsr	– Laser
Int	– International	Ltg	– Lighting
Intcult	– Intercultural	Lvstk	– Livestock
Integ	– Integrated		
Intel	– Intelligence	Mach	– Machine/ry
Inter	– Interior	Mait	– Maitrise Internationale
Interact	– Interactive	Mak	– Making
Interd	– Interdisciplinary	Manuf	– Manufacturing
Interp	– Interpretation	Map	– Map/Mapping
Intlctl	– Intellectual	Mar	– Marine
Intnet	– Internet	Marit	– Maritime
Intrmdl	– Intermodal	Mark	– Marketing
Inv	– Investment	Mat	– Materials
Invn	– Innovation	Mathem	– Mathematical
Invstg	– Investigating	Maths	– Mathematics
Is	– Issues	Mbl	– Mobile
Islam	– Islamic	Mdl	– Modelling
IT	– Information Technology	Measur	– Measurement
Ital	– Italian	Mecha	– Mechatronics
ITT	– Initial Teacher Training	Med	– Medicine/cal
		Medicin	– Medicinal
Jap	– Japanese	Mediev	– Medieval
Jewel	– Jewellery	Medit	– Mediterranean
Jrnl	– Journalism	Metal	– Metallurgy/Metallurgical
Juris	– Jurisprudence	Meteor	– Meteorology/
Just	– Justice		Meteorological
		Meth	– Methods
Kntwr	– Knitwear	Mgr	– Manager
Knwl	– Knowledge	Mgt	– Management/
Kor	– Korean		Managerial
		Microbiol	– Microbiology/ical
Lab	– Laboratory	Microcomp	– Microcomputer/ing
Land	– Landscape	Microelec	– Microelectronics
Lang	– Language	Midwif	– Midwifery

Min	– Mining		OR	– Operational Research
Miner	– Minerals		Org	– Organisation
Mkup	– Make-up		Orgnc	– Organic
Mltry	– Military		Orgnsms	– Organisms
Mndrn	– Mandarin		Orth	– Orthoptics
Mnstry	– Ministry		Orthot	– Orthotics
Mnswr	– Menswear		Oseas	– Overseas
Mntnce	– Maintenance		Ost	– Osteopathy
Mod	– Modular		Out	– Outdoor
Modl	– Modelling		Out Act	– Outdoor Activity
Model	– Modelmaking		Ovrs	– Overseas
Modn	– Modern			
Mol	– Molecular		P	– Primary
Monit	– Monitoring		Pacif	– Pacific
Mov	– Movement/Moving		Pack	– Packaging
Mtl	– Metal(s)		PActv	– Physical Activity
Mtlsmth	– Metalsmithing		Pal	– Palaeobiology
Mtrcycl	– Motorcycle		Palae	– Palaeoecology
Multid	– Multidisciplinary		Paramed	– Paramedical
Multim	– Multimedia		Parasit	– Parasitology
Mus	– Music/Musician		Parl	– Parliamentary
Musl	– Musical		Past	– Pastoral
Musm	– Museum		Pat	– Patent
			Path	– Pathology
N Am	– North America		Pathobiol	– Pathobiological
Neg	– Negotiated		Pathogen	– Pathogenesis
Nat	– Natural		Patt	– Pattern
Navig	– Navigation		Pblc	– Public
Nclr	– Nuclear		PE	– Physical Education
Net	– Network		Per	– Person
Neuro	– Neuroscience		Perf	– Performance
News	– Newspaper		Perfum	– Perfumery
NI	– Northern Ireland/		Pers	– Personnel
	Northern Irish		Persn	– Persian
Norw	– Norwegian		Petrol	– Petroleum
Nucl	– Nuclear		Pharm	– Pharmacy/
Nurs	– Nursing			Pharmaceutical
Nursy	– Nursery		Pharmacol	– Pharmacology
Nutr	– Nutrition		Phil	– Philosophy
			Philgy	– Philology
Obs	– Observational		Photo	– Photography/
Occ	– Occupational			Photographic
Ocean	– Oceanography		Photojrnl	– Photojournalism
Ofce	– Office		Phtmedia	– Photomedia
Off	– Offshore		Phys	– Physics
Offrd	– Off-road		Physio	– Physiotherapy
Op(s)	– Operation(s)		Physiol	– Physiology/
Oph	– Ophthamic			Physiological
Opt	– Optical		Physl	– Physical
Optn/s	– Optional/Options		Plan	– Planning
Optoel	– Optoelectronics		Planet	– Planetary
Optom	– Optometry		Plas	– Plastics

Plcg	– Policing	Recr	– Recreation
Plmt	– Placement	Rehab	– Rehabilitation
PMaths	– Pure Mathematics	Rel	– Relations
Pmed	– Paramedic(al)	Relgn	– Religion
Pntg	– Painting	Relig	– Religious
Pod	– Podiatry/Podiatric	Reltd	– Related
Pol	– Politics/Political/Policy	Reg	– Regional
Polh	– Polish	Regn	– Regeneration
Pollut	– Pollution	Rem Sens	– Remote Sensing
Poly	– Polymer	Ren	– Renaissance
Pop	– Population	Renew	– Renewable
Port	– Portuguese	Reqd	– Required
PPE	– Philosophy, Politics and	Res	– Resources
	Economics	Resid	– Residential
Ppr	– Paper	Resoln	– Resolution
PR	– Public Relations	Resp	– Response
Prac	– Practice/Practical	Restor	– Restoration
Prdcl	– Periodical	Rev	– Revenue
Precsn	– Precision	Rltd	– Related
Pref	– Preferable	Robot	– Robotics
Prem	– Premises	Rom	– Roman
Proc	– Process	Romn	– Romanian
Prod	– Production	Rsch	– Research
Prof	– Professional	Rstrnt	– Restaurant
Prog	– Programme	Rtl	– Retail/ing
Proj	– Project	Rts	– Rights
Prom	– Promotion	Rur	– Rural
Prop	– Property/ies	Russ	– Russian
Propul	– Propulsion		
Pros	– Prosthetics	S	– Secondary
Prot	– Protection	Sansk	– Sanskrit
Prt	– Print	Sat	– Satellite
Prtd	– Printed	Scand	– Scandinavian
Prtg	– Printing/Printmaking	Sci	– Science
Psy	– Psychology	Scot	– Scottish
Psybiol	– Psychobiology	Script	– Scriptwriting
Psysoc	– Psychosocial	Scrn	– Screen
Ptcl	– Particle	Sculp	– Sculpture
Pub	– Publishing	SE	– South East
Pwr	– Power	Sec	– Secretarial
Pwrcft	– Powercraft	Sect	– Sector
		Secur	– Security
Qntm	– Quantum	Serb Cro	– Serbo-Croat
QTS	– Qualified Teacher	Serv	– Services
	Status	Sfty	– Safety
Qual	– Quality	Sgnl	– Signal
Quant	– Quantity/Quantitative	Ship	– Shipping
		Simul	– Simulation
Rad	– Radio	Slov	– Slovak/Slovene
Radiog	– Radiography	Smtc	– Semitic
Rdtn	– Radiation	Snd	– Sound
Rec	– Recording	Soc	– Social

Sociol	– Sociology	Tnnl	– Tunnel/Tunnelling
Soft	– Software	Tns	– Tennis
Soty	– Society	Topog	– Topographical
Sov	– Soviet	Tour	– Tourism
Sp	– Speech	Tox	– Toxicology
Span	– Spanish	Tr	– Trade
Spat	– Spatial	Tr Stand	– Trading Standards
SPD	– Surface Pattern Design	Trad	– Traditional
Spec	– Special/isms	Trans	– Transport/
Spec Efcts	– Special Effects		Transportation
Sply	– Supply	Transl	– Translation
Spo	– Sports	Trav	– Travel
Srf	– Surf/Surfing	Trg	– Training
SR	– State Registration	Turk	– Turkish
SS	– Solid-state	Typo	– Typographical/
St	– Studies		Typography
St Reg	– State Registration		
Stats	– Statistics	Ukr	– Ukranian
Stg	– Stage	Undwtr	– Underwater
Stgs	– Settings	Unif	– Unified
Str	– Stringed	Urb	– Urban
Strat	– Strategic	USA	– United States of
Struct	– Structural		America
Surf	– Surface	Util	– Utilities
Surg	– Surgery	Val	– Valuation
Surv	– Surveying	Veh	– Vehicle
Sust	– Sustainability/	Vict	– Victorian
	Sustainable	Vid	– Video
Swed	– Swedish	Viet	– Vietnamese
		Virol	– Virology
3D	– Three-dimensional	Vrtl Rlty	– Virtual Reality
Tap	– Tapestry	Vib	– Vibration
Tax Rev	– Taxation and	Vis	– Visualisation/Visual
	Revenue	Voc	– Vocational
Teach	– Teaching	Vstr	– Visitor
Tech	– Technology/		
	Technician	Wat	– Water
Technol	– Technological	Wdlnd	– Woodland
Telecomm	– Telecommunications	Welf	– Welfare
Testmt	– Testament	Wldlf	– Wildlife
Tex	– Textiles	Writ	– Writing/Writer
Thea	– Theatre	Wrld	– World
Theol	– Theology	Wtr	– Water
Theor	– Theory/Theoretical		
Ther	– Therapeutic	Yth	– Youth
Thera	– Therapy		
Thrd	– Third	Zool	– Zoology
Tht	– Thought		

OTHER ABBREVIATIONS USED IN THE TABLES

AGNVQ	– Advanced General National Vocational Qualification	IB	– International Baccalaureate
Alt	– Alternative	int sci	– integrated science
Apprv	– Approved	Lond	– London
Ave	– Average	min	– minimum
biol	– biology	N/A	– Not applicable
BTEC	– Edexcel Foundation BTEC National Certificates and Diplomas	non-sci	– non-science
		P(s)	– Pass(es) in BTEC National Awards often preceded by the number required
chem	– chemistry		
comb sci	– combined sciences	phys	– physics
CSYS	– Certificate of Sixth Year Studies	phys sci	– physical science
		Prac	– Practical
D	– Distinction	Pref	– Preferred
Des Tech	– Design and Technology	psy	– psychology
Dip	– Diploma	Qualif	– Qualification
dsci	– double science	Rcmd	– Recommended
EB	– European Baccalaureate	Req	– Required
		sci	– science
FQ	– Further Qualifications	soc biol	– social biology
GCSE	– General Certificate of Secondary Education	soc sci	– social science
		Subsids (S)	– International Baccalaureate Subsidiary Level Examination
gs	– General Studies		
Highers (H)	– International Baccalaureate Higher Level Examination		
		T	– Test (at interview)
		u	– Units
HND	– Higher National Diploma	UHD	– University Higher Diploma
hum biol	– human biology	zool	– zoology
IA	– Individual Assessment	W	– Written work required before interview

HOW TO CALCULATE YOUR OFFERS

Units

One **GCE A**-level = 6 units
One **GCE AS**-level = 3 units
One **VCE Voc A**-level = 6 or 12 units
One **VCE Voc AS**-level = 3 units

Points

Vocational A-levels (12 units – double award)
Examples:

AA = 240pts	**BC** = 180pts	**DD** = 120pts
AB = 220pts	**CC** = 160pts	**DE** = 100pts
BB = 200pts	**CD** = 140pts	**EE** = 80pts etc

_A_-levels and 6 unit **_Vocational A_**-levels

A = 120pts	**C** = 80pts	**E** = 40pts
B = 100pts	**D** = 60pts	

AS-levels or **_Vocational AS_**-levels

a = 60pts	**c** = 40pts	**e** = 20pts
b = 50pts	**d** = 30pts	

Individual **Key Skill** unit scores

Level **4** = 30pts per unit
Level **3** = 20pts per unit
Level **2** = 10pts per unit

ABBREVIATIONS

A-level = **AL**
AS-level = **AS**
Vocational A-level = **VA**
A-level or Vocational
A-level grades = **A | B | C | D | E**
AS- or Vocational
AS-level grades = **a | b | c | d | e**
General Studies = **gs**
Units = **u**

An example of an offers line

Univ. name	Tariff pts	Units	ALs	ASs	VAs	Grades	Gen. st.	Course title
	200pts	15u	CCD or	CC + c or	VA 12u	BB	gs	

The grades and points totals shown in the tables should be regarded as the minimum levels to be achieved. The points totals to the left of the offers lines are for ease of reference only. Tariff points are not always used by institutions, check web sites.

5 SUBJECT TABLES

ACCOUNTANCY/ACCOUNTING (see also **Banking, Finance and Insurance**)

NB The information supplied by the universities and colleges this year varies considerably and the offers listed below should be used as a first source of reference only. Many institutions will accept combinations of Advanced (AL), Advanced Subsidiary (AS) and Vocational Advanced (VA) level qualifications to achieve the required points total, but applicants must check web sites and prospectuses for full details of all offers. Grades and points totals shown should be regarded as the minimum levels to be achieved, but offers may be adjusted downwards when results are known. The points totals shown to the left of the institutions are for ease of reference only. It must not be assumed that tariff points are always used by institutions or that they can be substituted for an offer in grades. The level of an offer is not necessarily indicative of the quality of a course. To calculate your offers see Chapter 4 and the inside fold of the back cover.

Special subject requirements/preferences: A-level: A-level mathematics preferred at some universities. **East Anglia** Mathematics preferred. **GCSE:** Mathematics essential for all courses. **Brighton, Birmingham, Dundee, East Anglia, Exeter** (also English), **Kingston, Lancaster, Leeds, Liverpool John Moores, Portsmouth, Sheffield, Sheffield Hallam, Warwick** Grade A or B (A-Level mathematics may be accepted in lieu). **Southampton** Grade B. **Bangor** Average grade B. **London (LSE)** Grades A and B. **Mid Kent (CHFE)** Five subjects at grade A or B. **Southampton** Good range of grade A and B. **Aberdeen, Dundee, Edinburgh, Glasgow** English, mathematics or science and a foreign language.

360 pts	**and above**
	Southampton – 370 pts 21u (inc 2ALs 220 pts); (not gs) (Acc/Fin; Acc/Econ)
340 pts	**Belfast (Queen's)** – AAB (Acc/Law)
320 pts	**Bath** – ABB/ABC (Bus Admin)
	Belfast (Queen's) – ABB (Acc/Fin)
	Birmingham – 320 pts – ABB or BB+2ASs (60 pts yr12 + 60 pts yr13); gs (not AL) (Acc/Fin)
	Birmingham – 320–300 pts – B(lang)BB or BB+2ASs (60 pts yr12 + 60 pts yr13); gs (not AL) (Acc/Fin Lang)
	Bristol – ABB–BBC (inc maths also Fr/Ger (GCSE Ital/Span) for lang course); (not gs) (Acc/Fin; Econ/Acc/Euro)
	Edinburgh – ABB (Acc/Law)
	Leeds – ABB or AB+bb; VAs (contact univ); (not gs) (Acc/Law)
	London (LSE) – ABB (Acc/Fin)
	Manchester – ABB/AA (Acc/Law)
	Newcastle – ABB (Acc/Law)
	Warwick – ABB (Acc/Fin)
	UMIST – ABB (Mgt (Acc Fin))
300 pts	**Aston** – BBB or ALs+ASs or VAs+/-ALs/ASs; gs (contact Admissions Tutor) (Acc Mgt)
	Bradford – 300 pts 12u; gs; (Acc/Fin)
	Brunel – 300–260 pts 2x6u – ALs or ALs+ASs or VAs+/-ALs/ASs; (Fin/Acc)
	Cardiff – BBB/AB (Econ/Fr)
	Cardiff – BBB–BBC (Acc; Acc/Mgt; Acc/Econ; Acc/Span)
	Edinburgh – BBB (Bus St/Acc; Econ/Acc)
	Exeter – 300 pts 18u – BBB or BB+bb or VA6u B+BB; (not gs) (Acc Fin/Euro)
	Glasgow – BBB (Accountancy courses)
	Hull – BBB (Acc; Int Acc)
	Keele – BBB–BBC (Finance courses)
	Lancaster – 300 pts approx (Acc/Fin)

Leeds – 18u – BB+B/2AS; (not gs) (Acc/Fin; Acc/Mgt)
Loughborough – BB+B/bb **or** VA12u BB+AL(B); (not gs) (Acc/Mgt)
Manchester – BBB–BBC (Accounting courses)
Nottingham – BBB/BB (Ind Econ/Acc)
Sheffield – BBB/AB (Acc/Fin Mgt courses)

280 pts **Aberdeen** – BBC (Accountancy courses)
City – BBC (Econ/Acc)
East Anglia – BBC (2ASs max); gs; (Acc Fin; Acc/Law; Acc/Mgt)
Hertfordshire – 280–240 pts 12u – ALs+ASs; gs; (Accounting courses)
Kent – 280 pts approx/AB (Accounting courses except under **260 pts**)
Newcastle – BBC (Accounting courses except under **320 pts**)
Reading – BBC (Accounting courses)
Strathclyde – BBC/AB (1st yr entry) BBB (2nd yr entry) (Accounting courses)
Ulster – BBC (Accounting)

260 pts **Bristol UWE** – 260–220 pts; (not gs) (Accounting joint courses)
Brunel – BCC (Accounting courses)
Durham – 260 pts (Bus Fin)
East Anglia – BCC (Econ/Acc)
Essex – 260 pts 21u – B(maths for Fin courses)C+AL/2ASs **or** VA12u+AL/ASs; (Accounting)
Heriot-Watt – 260 pts 18u – BCC; gs; (Acc/Fin courses)
Kent – 260 pts approx (Acc Fin/Ger)
Kingston – BCC–CCC (Acc/Fin)
Liverpool – 260 pts – ALs **or** ALs+ASs **or** VAs+/-ALs/ASs; (Acc; Acc/Comp Sci)
Loughborough – 260 pts approx (Acc/Fin courses)
Oxford Brookes – (Accounting courses – offer varies with subject comb)
Salford – BCC–CCC (Fin/Acc)
Stirling – BCC (Accountancy courses)

250 pts **Buckingham** – 250 pts 21u – 3ALs **or** 3ALs+AS; (Acc/Fin Mgt; Acc/Econ; Acc/Fr/Span)

240 pts **Aberystwyth** – 240 pts approx (Accounting courses)
Bangor – 240 pts; gs; (Acc/Fin) (Accounting courses)
Bournemouth – 240 pts – CCC; (Acc/Fin; Acc/Law)
Brighton – 240–220 pts approx (Acc/Fin; Acc/Law; Int Fin/Cap Mark St)
Dundee – CCC/AB (BAcc; BFin)
Glamorgan – 240–200 pts approx (Accounting courses except under **200 pts**; Comb courses)
Manchester Met – 240 pts approx – ALs **or** ALs+ASs **or** VAs+/-ALs/ASs (inc C Fr/Ger for Acc/Euro); (Acc/Fin courses)
Napier – CCC (Accounting courses)
Northumbria – 240 pts approx (Accounting)
Nottingham Trent – CCC (Acc/Fin)
Paisley – CCC/BB (Accounting)
Plymouth – 240–220 pts approx (Accounting courses)
Robert Gordon – CCC (Acc/Fin)
Sheffield Hallam – 240–200 pts approx (Accounting courses)
Staffordshire – 240 pts – CCC **or** CCC+AS(40 pts); gs; (Acc; Acc Bus/Law)
Sunderland – 240 pts approx (Acc/Bus)

220 pts **Bristol UWE** – 220–180 pts 12u – ALs **or** ALs+ASs **or** VAs+/-ALs/ASs; (not gs) (Acc/Fin)
Central England – 220 pts – 2ALs **or** ALs+ASs **or** VAs+/-ALs/ASs; gs; (Accountancy)
Central Lancashire – 220 pts 12u; gs; (Acc; Acc Fin St)
De Montfort (Leicester) – 220 pts 2x6u **or** 1x12u: ALs **or** ALs+ASs **or** VAs+/-ALs/ASs; (Acc/Fin; Acc courses)
Greenwich – 220–200 pts approx (Acc/Fin courses)
Huddersfield – 220 pts approx (Law/Acc; Mgt/Acc)
Kingston – 220 pts 2x6u; (Acc/Fin)
Middlesex – 220 pts approx (Accounting courses)

Portsmouth – 220 pts: ALs or ALs+ASs or VAs; gs; (Acc; Fin/Acc St)
Wolverhampton – 220 pts 12u – CCD/BB/AC/BCE or BC+c or VA12u BB; gs; (Accounting courses)
200 pts **Abertay Dundee** – 200 pts – CDD/BC (Accounting)
Central England – 200 pts – 2ALs or ALs+ASs or VAs+/-AL/ASs; gs; (Acc/Fin)
Central Lancashire – 200–180 pts 12u; gs; (Acc/Bus; Acc/Bus Inf Sys; Acc/Law; Acc/Mgt; Acc/Mark)
Derby – 200 pts 12u – CDD or CD+dd or VA12u CD; gs; (Acc)
Derby – 200 pts 12u – CDD or CD+dd or VA12u CD+AL(D); gs; (Mgt Acc)
Dundee – CDD (Acc Comb Hons courses)
East London – 200–180 pts approx (Acc/Fin)
Glamorgan – 200 pts approx (Int Acc; Acc/Fin)
Liverpool John Moores – 200 pts (inc 160 pts from ALs/VA6u); (Acc/Fin)
Luton – 200–180 pts approx (Accounting)
South Bank – 200–180 pts approx (Acc/Fin)
Sunderland – 200 pts approx (Acc/Econ)
190 pts **North London** – 190 pts (inc 2ALs 160 pts) or VAs; (Acc; Acc/Fin)
180 pts **Blackburn (Coll)** – 180 pts 12u – CDE/DDD/BC or A+a or CC+e or DD+dd or aaa or bbbd or VA6u C+AL; gs; (Acc/Fin)
Cardiff (UWI) – 180 pts (Bus Fin)
Central Lancashire – 180–160 pts 12u; gs; (Acc/Econ) (Acc Comb Hons)
Cheltenham & Glos (CHE) – 180–140 pts approx (Acc Fin Mgt courses)
Coventry – 180 pts approx (Accounting courses)
Glasgow Caledonian – BC (Accountancy courses)
Norwich City (Coll) – 180 pts approx (Acc/Fin)
Regents (Bus Sch London) – 180 pts approx (Int Fin/Acc)
South Bank – 180 pts approx (Acc/Fin Fdn)
South Bank – 180–160 pts (Prof Dip)
Southampton (Inst) – 180–160 pts approx (Accountancy courses)
Sunderland – 180 pts – 2ALs or ALs+ASs or VA12u+/-AL/ASs; gs; (Acc/Comp)
Swansea (IHE) – 180 pts approx (Accounting)
Teesside – 180 pts approx (Accounting courses)
Thames Valley – 180–140 pts approx (Accountancy courses)
160 pts **Anglia** – 160 pts 12u – 2ALs or VA12u CC; gs; (Acc/Fin Analys)
Bolton (IHE) – 160 pts approx (Accountancy courses)
East London – 160 pts approx (Acc/Fin)
Farnborough (CT) – 160 pts approx (Accounting)
Lincolnshire & Humberside – 160 pts (Accountancy)
London Guildhall – 160–140 pts approx (Accounting courses (Mod))
London Guildhall – CC (Acc/Fin)
Newport (UWCN) – 160–140 pts – ALs or ALs+ASs or VAs+/-ALs/ASs; (Acc/Fin; Acc/Leg St)
North East Wales (IHE) – 160–80 pts approx (Accounting courses)
Northampton (UC) – 160 pts approx (Acc Fin)
Paisley – 160 pts (Accounting courses)
140 pts **and below**
Buckinghamshire Chilterns (UC) – 140 pts approx (Bus/Fin)
Croydon (Coll) – 120 pts approx (Bus/Acc)
Derby – 140 pts 12u – CD or DE+ee or VAs+/-ALs/ASs; (Acc Comb)

Leeds Met – (contact university)

Diploma of Higher Education courses
160 pts Huddersfield; Napier (Univ Cert; Dip in Acc); Northumbria; Nottingham Trent; Salford; Ulster CDD.

Foundation courses
180 pts Brighton; Hertfordshire; Kingston; London Guildhall; Oxford Brookes (Dip Acc St); Sheffield Hallam; Westminster.
160 pts De Montfort; Norwich City (Coll).

140 pts Central England; Coventry; Derby; East London; Exeter (Coll); Glamorgan; Huddersfield; Liverpool John Moores (Bus St); Newport (UWCN); Northumbria; Norwich City (Coll); Nottingham Trent; Portsmouth.

80 pts Anglia; East London; Farnborough (CT); Greenwich; Lincolnshire & Humberside; Manchester Met; Middlesex; Mid Kent (CHFE); North London; Northampton (UC); Plymouth; Sandwell (Coll); Southampton (Inst); Staffordshire; Suffolk (Coll); Thames Valley.

Diploma and Certificate courses
180 pts Napier (Acc).
140 pts and below
Aberdeen (Coll); Abertay Dundee; Ayr (Coll); Bell (CT); Blackburn (Coll); Blackpool & Fylde (Coll); Bradford (Coll); Cheltenham & Glos (CHE); Clackmannan (CFE); Coventry; Croydon (Coll); De Montfort; Derby; East London; Exeter (Coll); Fife (CFHE); Glamorgan; Glasgow (CC); Inverness (Coll); London Guildhall; Luton; Mid Cheshire (Coll); Newport (UWCN); North London; Oxford Brookes; Plymouth (CFE); Reid Kerr (Coll); Salford; Sandwell (Coll); Southampton (Inst); Stevenson (Coll); Suffolk (Coll); Swansea (IHE); Thames Valley (ACCA course); UHI (Perth); Ulster DD; West Herts (Coll).

Alternative Offers:

IB offers: Aberdeen 32 pts; Aberystwyth 26 pts; Aston 31 pts; Bangor 30–24 pts; Belfast (Queen's) H766 S555; Birmingham 32 pts; Brighton 24 pts (4 pts in each of 6 subjects); Buckingham 26 pts; Cardiff 29 pts H665 + S level 15 pts; Central Lancashire 28 pts; Derby 24 pts; Dundee 29 pts; East Anglia 30 pts; Essex 28 pts 11 pts at H; Exeter 32 pts; Hertfordshire 28–26 pts; Hull 28 pts; Kent 30–28 pts; Lancaster 32 pts; Leeds 30 pts – 5 in maths; London (LSE) 38 pts; London Guildhall 28 pts 7 subjects, 24 pts 6 subjects; Luton 26 pts; Manchester Met H12 pts S12 pts; Newcastle 30–28 pts; North London H543 S65; Oxford Brookes 28 pts; Plymouth 26 pts; Salford 28 pts H13 pts; Sheffield H665; South Bank 24 pts; Southampton 32–30 pts inc 14/15 H; Staffordshire 24 pts; Stirling 33 pts Thames Valley 24 pts; Warwick 34–32 pts.

Irish offers: Aberdeen BBBB; Brighton BBCCC; Bristol UWE CCCC minimum; Central England BBBCC; East Anglia BBBBB; Heriot-Watt AAABC; Leeds AAB; London Guildhall CCCCC; Sheffield AABBB; Warwick AAABB.

Scottish Qualifications: Aberdeen BBBB; Abertay Dundee BBC; Dundee (BAcc) BBBBC or BBBB in 2 sittings, (Acc/Law) ABBBC; Edinburgh (Acc/Law) AAAAB, (Econ/Acc) ABBBC, (Bus St/Acc) BBBBB; Glasgow AABBB at 1 sitting, AAABBB at 2 sittings; Glasgow Caledonian BBBC; Heriot-Watt (Acc/Fin) ABBB; Napier BBCC; Paisley BCC/BBC inc Engl); Robert Gordon BBBC; Stirling BBBB (Acc), BBBC (Fin St); Strathclyde (Bus/Acc) AAABB.

Overseas applicants: Hull Living costs 30% lower than in London area.

CHOOSING YOUR COURSE (See also **Ch.1**)

> **Subject information:** All courses offer financial management and accountancy training. Students should note that a degree in Accountancy is not the only method of qualifying as an accountant. It is estimated that only about one in five entering the profession do so with an Accountancy degree. Other degree subjects for consideration include Actuarial Studies, Banking, Business Studies, Economics, and Quantity Surveying, all of which require the same attention to detail. Applicants should note that, as well as degree courses, many institutions offer Foundation courses which provide opportunities to move directly into degree courses.

Special features: Bristol UWE Strong vocational bias. **Greenwich** Alternative pathways in business studies. **Huddersfield** Opportunity to study in the Netherlands in year 2. **Kent**

Links with France and Germany. Placements in the UK, the Netherlands and USA. **London Guildhall** Pathway in Forensic Accountancy. **Napier** Strong vocational emphasis. **Portsmouth** Year abroad offered in France, Germany or Denmark with a European diploma. Taxation is now a feature on many courses including **Abertay Dundee, Belfast, East London, Kingston, London Guildhall** and **Robert Gordon**. *NOW CHECK PROSPECTUSES AND WEB SITES.*

Study opportunities abroad: Aston; Bangor; Birmingham; Brighton; Bristol UWE; Buckingham; Central England; Cheltenham & Glos (CHE); Cardiff; Dundee; Exeter; Glamorgan; Glasgow; Heriot-Watt; Huddersfield; Hull; Lancaster; Leeds; Lincolnshire & Humberside; Liverpool John Moores; London Guildhall; Loughborough; Manchester Met; Napier; North London; Norwich City (Coll); Oxford Brookes; Plymouth; Portsmouth; Robert Gordon; Sheffield Hallam; Stafford; Strathclyde; Sunderland; Teesside; Thames Valley.

Work opportunities abroad: Central England; De Montfort; Glamorgan; Lancaster; Leeds; Lincolnshire & Humberside; Napier; Nottingham Trent; Portsmouth; Robert Gordon; Salford; Sheffield Hallam; Staffordshire.

ADMISSIONS INFORMATION

Number of applicants per place (approx): Aberdeen 10; Abertay Dundee 7; Aberystwyth 5; Anglia 7; Bangor 35; Belfast (Queen's) 5; Birmingham 10; Bournemouth 6; Bristol UWE 17; Buckingham 6; Cardiff 12; Central England 7; Central Lancashire 15; Derby 5; Dundee 5; East Anglia 17; East London 11; Essex 7; Exeter 18; Glamorgan 4; Glasgow 10; Glasgow Caledonian 10; Hertfordshire 7; Heriot-Watt 7; Huddersfield 5; Hull 8; Kent 10; Kingston (Acc/Fin) 33; Lancaster 20; Leeds 25; Liverpool John Moores 12; London (LSE) 10; London Guildhall 20; Loughborough 12; Manchester (Fin) 1; Manchester Met (Acc/Fin) 10; Middlesex 12; Napier 11; Newcastle 15, (Acc/Law) 20; North London 7; Northumbria 10; Nottingham Trent 17; Oxford Brookes 9; Plymouth 10; Portsmouth 10; Robert Gordon 10; Salford 8; Sheffield 40; South Bank 7; Stirling 20; Strathclyde 10; Swansea (IHE) 3; Teesside 3, (Acc/Law) 1; Thames Valley 7; Ulster 10; Warwick 14.

Planning your UCAS personal statement (see Ch.4): On the UCAS form you should be able to demonstrate your knowledge of accountancy and to give details of any work experience or work shadowing undertaken. Discuss the differences between the types of work done by chartered and certified accountants and management and public finance accountants. Try to arrange meetings with accountants, or work shadowing or experience in accountants' offices, commercial or industrial firms, town halls, banks or insurance companies and describe the work you have done. Obtain information from the main accountancy professional bodies (see **Appendix 1**). Refer to current affairs which have stimulated your interest from articles in the *Financial Times*, the *Economist* or the business and financial sections of the weekend press. **South Bank** Full chronological history – no gaps.

Selection interviews (see Ch.4): Aberdeen (No); Aberystwyth; Bangor (No); Belfast (Queen's); Birmingham; Blackburn (Coll); Brighton (No); Bristol UWE (No); Buckingham; Cardiff (some); Central England; Central Lancashire (No); Cheltenham & Glos (CHE); De Montfort (No); Dundee (No); East Anglia (No); East London (T); Exeter (No); Farnborough (CT) (No); Glamorgan; Glasgow; Glasgow Caledonian (No); Greenwich (No); Heriot-Watt; Hertfordshire (No); Huddersfield (No); Hull (No); Kent (some); Kingston; Liverpool John Moores; London (LSE) (rarely); London Guildhall; Loughborough (No); Manchester (No); Manchester Met (No); Middlesex; Napier (No); Newcastle (No); Newport (UWCN) (No); North London; Northampton (UC); Northumbria; Norwich City (Coll) (No); Paisley (No); Portsmouth; Regents (Bus Sch London) (No); Robert Gordon (No); Salford (T for mature students); Sheffield (No); Sheffield Hallam; South Bank (W) (T); Southampton (No); Southampton (Inst); Staffordshire (No); Stirling (No); Sunderland (No); Teesside; Thames Valley; Ulster; Warwick.

Interview questions (see Ch.4): Be prepared to answer questions on why you have chosen the course, the qualities needed to be an accountant, and why you think you have these qualities! You should also be able to discuss any work experience and to describe the differences in the work of chartered, certified, public finance and management accountants.

Reasons for rejection (non-academic): Poor English. Lack of interest in the subject because they realise they have chosen the wrong course! No clear motivation. Course details not researched. **South Bank** Punctuality, neatness, enthusiasm and desire to come to South Bank not evident.

GAP YEAR ADVICE

Most institutions accept a gap year. **East London** Apply early; **Glasgow** It may interrupt the habit of study; **Heriot-Watt** Not recommended; **Newcastle** Make your plans clear on the UCAS application.

Institutions willing to defer entry after A-Levels: Abertay Dundee; Aberystwyth; Bangor; Birmingham; Blackburn (Coll); Bournemouth; Brighton; Brunel; Buckingham; Cardiff; Central England; Central Lancashire; De Montfort; Derby; Dundee; East Anglia (not for Acc/Euro); East London; Farnborough (CT); Glamorgan; Glasgow; Glasgow Caledonian; Heriot-Watt; Hertfordshire; Huddersfield; Hull; Kent; Kingston; Lancaster; Leeds; Lincolnshire & Humberside; Liverpool John Moores; London Guildhall; Luton; Manchester Met; Napier; Newcastle; Newport (UWCN); Northumbria; Paisley; Plymouth; Portsmouth; Regents (Bus Sch London); Robert Gordon; Salford; Sheffield Hallam; Southampton; Staffordshire; Sunderland; Swansea (IHE); Teesside; Thames Valley; Warwick.

AFTER RESULTS ADVICE

Institutions which may accept the same points score after A-Levels: Abertay Dundee; Aberdeen (No); Belfast (Queen's); Birmingham (No); Cardiff; Dundee; East Anglia; East London; Exeter; Glasgow; Glasgow Caledonian; Hull; Kingston; Lancaster; Leeds; London Guildhall; Loughborough (No); Middlesex; Newcastle (No); Northumbria; Oxford Brookes; Plymouth; Portsmouth; Robert Gordon; Salford; Sheffield (No); Sheffield Hallam; Staffordshire; Warwick (No).

Institutions which may accept lower grades/points score after A-Levels: Bangor; Birmingham (No); Brighton; Cardiff; Central England; De Montfort; Derby; Dundee; East Anglia; East London; Farnborough (CT); Glamorgan; Glasgow Caledonian; Heriot-Watt; Hertfordshire; Huddersfield; Hull (overseas students 16–14 pts); Kingston; Lancaster; Leeds; Liverpool John Moores; London Guildhall; Luton; Manchester Met; Napier; Newcastle; Newport (UWCN); Northumbria; Portsmouth; Robert Gordon; Salford; Sheffield; Sheffield Hallam; Southampton (Inst); Staffordshire; Sunderland; Swansea (IHE); Thames Valley; Warwick (possibly); Wolverhampton.

Offers to applicants repeating A-Levels: No offer made Belfast (Queen's), Lancaster (rare); **Higher** Brunel, Glasgow, Hull, Liverpool (Acc/Comp Sci), Manchester Met, North London, Plymouth, Sheffield, Warwick; **Possibly higher** Brighton, Bristol UWE, Central Lancashire, East Anglia, Leeds, Newcastle, Oxford Brookes, Sheffield Hallam; **Same** Bangor, Birmingham, Blackburn (Coll), Central England, De Montfort, Derby, Dundee, East London, Farnborough (CT), Heriot-Watt, Huddersfield, Lincolnshire & Humberside, Liverpool John Moores, Loughborough, Manchester, Napier, Newcastle, Newport (UWCN), Northumbria, Salford, Staffordshire, Thames Valley, Ulster.

Probable vacancies from June 2001 and in Clearing (see Ch.4): Places are very likely in this subject area. Last year over 60 universities advertised vacancies, with popular universities asking between 280 and 240 pts. Others will make lower offers.

NEW GRADUATE DESTINATIONS AND EMPLOYMENT (1999 HESA) (see **Ch.4**)

From a total of 2345 graduates, 1769 entered full-time employment, 217 followed courses of further study and 136 were believed to be unemployed. The majority of employed graduates entered financial work in business, manufacturing, property development and retailing.

ACTUARIAL SCIENCE/STUDIES

NB The information supplied by the universities and colleges this year varies considerably and the offers listed below should be used as a first source of reference only. Many institutions will accept combinations of Advanced (AL), Advanced Subsidiary (AS) and Vocational Advanced (VA) level qualifications to achieve the required points total, but applicants must check web sites and prospectuses for full details of all offers. Grades and points totals shown should be regarded as the minimum levels to be achieved, but offers may be adjusted downwards when results are known. The points totals shown to the left of the institutions are for ease of reference only. It must not be assumed that tariff points are always used by institutions or that they can be substituted for an offer in grades. The level of an offer is not necessarily indicative of the quality of a course. To calculate your offers see Chapter 4 and the inside fold of the back cover.

Special subject requirements/preferences: A-Level: Grade A or B mathematics usually required. **London (LSE)** Grade A/B **GCSE:** Most institutions require grade A or B in mathematics. **London (LSE)** Grades A and B. **Southampton** 50% passes at grade A or above in mathematics and science.

340 pts **London (LSE)** – AAB–ABB (Act Sci)
320 pts **City** – 3x6u – ABB **or** VAs (contact univ); (not gs) (Act Sci)
300 pts **Heriot-Watt** – 300 pts 18u – BBB; gs; (Act Maths)
 Kent – BBB/AB (Act Sci)
 Swansea – 300 pts 18u – BBB/AB (maths grade A/B) **or** ALs+ASs **or** VAs+/-
 ALs/ASs; (Act St)
280 pts **Southampton** – 280 pts approx (B maths) (Econ/Act St; Maths/Act St)

Alternative Offers:

IB offers: City 28 pts H665 inc maths H5; Heriot-Watt H665; Kent 32 pts H14 pts; London (LSE) 36 pts H766; Southampton 30 pts; Swansea 32 pts.

Irish offers: Heriot-Watt BBBBC.

Scottish Qualifications: Heriot-Watt AABB.

CHOOSING YOUR COURSE (See also **Ch.1**)

Subject information: Actuaries are problem-solvers. They tackle the uncertainty of future events using their skills in mathematics, probability and statistics. Their expertise is vital to the running of pension funds, life assurance societies, merchant banks and insurance companies. Actuaries are reputed to have one of the highest paid careers in finance, and so naturally the subject attracts a number of applicants! A strong mathematical background is required. Training as an actuary is extremely demanding and must not be under-estimated. An alternative route to actuarial work is a Mathematics degree. Other courses which might be considered are Accountancy, Business Studies, Banking, Insurance, Economics, Statistics, Mathematics and Applied Mathematics. See also **Accountancy** and **Banking, Finance & Insurance.**

Special features: City Placements in the UK and Canada. **Heriot-Watt** Study abroad for part of the course. **Swansea** Year 1 is common with other degree schemes in the Business field. *NOW CHECK PROSPECTUSES AND WEB SITES.*

Top universities and colleges (Research) (see Ch.4): Kent; London (LSE); Southampton.

Study opportunities abroad: City; Southampton; Swansea.

ADMISSIONS INFORMATION

Number of applicants per place (approx): City 6; Heriot-Watt 5; Kent 6; London (LSE) 6; Southampton 7; Swansea 9.

Planning your UCAS personal statement (see Ch.4): Demonstrate your knowledge of this career and its training, and mention any contacts you have made with an actuary. (See **Appendix 1** for contact details of professional associations for further information.) Any work experience or shadowing in insurance companies should be mentioned.

Selection interviews (see Ch.4): City (No); Heriot-Watt; Kent; Southampton; Swansea (influences level of offer, not used to accept or reject).

Interview questions (see Ch.4): In view of the demanding nature of the training, it is important to have spent some time discussing this career with an actuary in practice. Questions, therefore, may focus on the roles of the actuary and what qualities you have to succeed. You should also be ready to field questions about your mathematics course and the aspects of it you enjoy most.

Reasons for rejection (non-academic): Kent Poor language skills.

GAP YEAR ADVICE

Institutions willing to defer entry after A-Levels: Southampton.

AFTER RESULTS ADVICE

Institutions which may accept the same points score after A-Levels: City; Heriot-Watt; Kent; Southampton (No).

Offers to applicants repeating A-Levels: Higher City; **Same** Heriot-Watt, Southampton.

Probable vacancies from June 2001 and in Clearing (see Ch.4): Few vacancies are likely before Clearing and even then only one or two will be declared.

NEW GRADUATE DESTINATIONS AND EMPLOYMENT (1999 HESA) (see **Ch.4**)

No data available.

AFRICAN STUDIES

Special subject requirements/preferences: A-Level: Language/s at grade A or B may be required. **GCSE:** Grade A to C in mathematics.

NB The information supplied by the universities and colleges this year varies considerably and the offers listed below should be used as a first source of reference only. Many institutions will accept combinations of Advanced (AL), Advanced Subsidiary (AS) and Vocational Advanced (VA) level qualifications to achieve the required points total, but applicants must check web sites and prospectuses for full details of all offers. Grades and points totals shown should be regarded as the minimum levels to be achieved, but offers may be adjusted downwards when results are known. The points totals shown to the left of the institutions are for ease of reference only. It must not be assumed that tariff points are always used by institutions or that they can be substituted for an offer in grades. The level of an offer is not necessarily indicative of the quality of a course. To calculate your offers see Chapter 4 and the inside fold of the back cover.

300 pts	**Birmingham** – BBB (Af St; Af St/Anth)
	Sussex – BBB–BCC (Af As St)
280 pts	**London (King's)** – BBC + AS (or equiv) **or** BB+bbc (inc AL lang) or VAs considered; (Af; Port/Braz Relig St)
	London (SOAS) – 280–260 pts approx (Af St courses and languages)
240 pts	**North London** – 240 pts (Carib/Law)
160 pts	**North London** – 160 pts – 2x6u **or** VAs; (Carib Comb St)

Alternative Offers:

IB offers: Birmingham 33–30 pts; London (SOAS) 32–30 pts.

CHOOSING YOUR COURSE (See also **Ch.1**)

> **Subject information:** African Studies is often combined with Caribbean Studies and can involve geography, history, political science and sociology (refer also to these particular tables).

Special features: Birmingham Course covers anthropology, geography, sociology and the study of sub-Saharan Africa and West Africa. Four weeks spent in Year 2 in Ghana. **London (SOAS)** Different regional studies offered, for example Amharic Studies (Ethiopia), Hausa Studies (Nigeria), Swahili Studies (East Africa). **North London** Focus on Caribbean Studies. *NOW CHECK PROSPECTUSES AND WEB SITES.*

Top universities and colleges (Research) (see Ch.4): Birmingham; London (SOAS).

Study opportunities abroad: Birmingham; Sussex.

Work opportunities abroad: Birmingham.

ADMISSIONS INFORMATION

Number of applicants per place (approx): Birmingham 4; London (SOAS) 3.

Planning your UCAS personal statement (see Ch.4): Describe any visits you have made to African countries or why you wish to study this subject. Embassies in London may be able to provide information about the history, geography, politics, economics and the culture of the countries in which you are interested. Keep up-to-date with political developments in Africa. Discuss any aspects which interest you.

Interview questions (see Ch.4): These courses tend to specialise in various geographical regions of Africa. You could therefore be questioned on your choice of region and your awareness of some of the political and social problems which exist.

AFTER RESULTS ADVICE

Institutions which may accept the same points score after A-Levels: Birmingham; London (SOAS).

Probable vacancies from June 2001 and in Clearing (see Ch.4): From June onwards there are likely to be very few vacancies.

NEW GRADUATE DESTINATIONS AND EMPLOYMENT (1999 HESA) (see **Ch.4**)

From a total of 20 graduates, nine entered full-time employment (mainly business, some spending time working in Africa), four went on to further study and one was reported as unemployed.

AGRICULTURAL SCIENCES/AGRICULTURE (including **Agricultural Economics, Countryside Management, Rural Resources Management** and **Soil Science**; see also **Engineering (Agricultural), Landscape Architecture** and **Surveying**)

NB The information supplied by the universities and colleges this year varies considerably and the offers listed below should be used as a first source of reference only. Many institutions will accept combinations of Advanced (AL), Advanced Subsidiary (AS) and Vocational Advanced (VA) level qualifications to achieve the required points total, but applicants must check web sites and prospectuses for full details of all offers. Grades and points totals shown should be regarded as the minimum levels to be achieved, but offers may be adjusted downwards when results are known. The points totals shown to the left of the institutions are for ease of reference only. It must not be assumed that tariff points are always used by institutions or that they can be substituted for an offer in grades. The level of an offer is not necessarily indicative of the quality of a course. To calculate your offers see Chapter 4 and the inside fold of the back cover.

Special subject requirements/preferences: A-Level: Science subjects required; **Coventry** (Country Chng Mgt) Geography and economics preferred. **GCSE:** English and mathematics usually required. Practical experience for Agriculture required by **Aberystwyth, Bangor, Newcastle, Nottingham**.

NB: Many agricultural courses are run at agricultural colleges on separate sites not located at the university shown in the UCAS *Directory*.

280 pts **East Anglia** – BBC (Dev St/Nat Res)
Glasgow – BBC–CCC (Agric/Fd/Env Chem)
Harper Adams (UC) – 280–140 pts (Agri/Fd Mark courses; Agric courses; Country courses; Farm Mgt)
260 pts **London (Imp)** – 260 pts (App Nat Sci/Agric courses)
Newcastle – BCC (Agric (Bus Mgt); Country Mgt)
240 pts **Aberdeen** – CCC (Rur Dev)
Bangor – 240 pts (Agric/Bus Mgt; Mgt/Agric)
Bangor – CCC (Agrofor; Frst; Wrld Agric)
Belfast (Queen's) – CCC (Agric Sci)
Edinburgh – CCC (Forestry)
Reading – CCC (Agric; Crop Prot; Rur Env Sci)
Stirling – CCC (Cons Mgt)
220 pts **Aberdeen** – CCD (Agric Bus Mgt; Country Env Mgt; Frst Mgt; Organ Agric; Rur Bus Mgt)
Bangor – CCD (Frst/Frst Prod; Rur Res Mgt)
Coventry – 220 pts (Country Chng/Mgt)
Greenwich – 220 pts (Gard Des; Land Mgt)
Nottingham – CCD–BC; (not gs) (Agriculture)
Nottingham Trent – 220 pts (Cons Country Mgt)
Reading – CCD (Agric Bot; Agric Bus Mgt; Rur Res Mgt)
200 pts **Aberdeen** – CDD (Agric; Abor/Amen Frst)
Belfast (Queen's) – CDD/BC (Agric Tech; Agric; Agric Econ)
Bournemouth – 200–180 pts (Lndbd Ind)
De Montfort (Lincoln) – 200 pts (Rur Land Mgt)
Newcastle – CDD; (not gs) (Agric; Anim Prod Sci; Rur Res Mgt)
Scottish (CAg) – CDD (Rur Res Mgt)
180 pts **Aberystwyth** – 180 pts (Country Cons; Country Cons/Mgt; Country Recr/Tour; Rur Res Mgt; Agric/Bus St)
Cheltenham & Glos (CHE) – 180–140 pts (Rur Plan courses)
Chester (Coll) – 180 pts (Country/Env Mgt)
Derby – 180–140 pts (Cons Country Mgt)
Greenwich – 180 pts (Env Cons)
Royal (CAg) – 180 pts (Agric courses)
Wolverhampton – 180–140 pts (Plant/Crop Sci courses)
Writtle (Coll) – 180 pts (Agric/Sci)
160 pts **Aberystwyth** – 160 pts (Agric courses except under **180 pts**)
Bishop Burton (Coll) – 160 pts (Country Mgt courses)
Buckinghamshire Chilterns (UC) – 160–140 pts (Frst Prod Tech)
De Montfort (Lincoln) – 160 pts (Frsy; Land Ecol)
Plymouth – 160 pts (Wldf Cons; Agric/Env; Anim Prod)
Scottish (CAg) – CC (Agric; Country Mgt; Rur Recr/Tour Mgt)
Trinity Carmarthen (Coll) – 160–80 pts (Rur Env; Biodiv Cons)
Writtle (Coll) – 160 pts (Agric courses; Country Mgt; Rur Res Mgt; Spo Turf Sci/Mgt)
140 pts **Bristol UWE (Hartpury)** – 140 pts (Agric/Cons/Land Mgt)
De Montfort (Lincoln) – 140 pts (Agric (Crop Prod Prot))
120 pts **Sparsholt (Coll)** – DD (Fish Mgt; Agric Prod Mgt; Anim Mgt)
East Anglia – CD (Cons Mgt)
100 pts **Cannington (Coll)** – 100 pts ((Agric Mgt)

80 pts   Central Lancashire – 80 pts (Agric courses; Abor Urb Frst; Cons/Land Mgt; Frst/Wdlnd Mgt; Turfgrass Sci/Env Cons; Game Wldlf Mgt)

Diploma of Higher Education courses
UHI.

Higher National Diploma courses
120 pts   and below
Aberystwyth (Agric; Agric Bus; Country Mgt/Cons; Country Rec); Askham Bryan (Coll); Bangor; Barony (Coll) (Fish Farming); Bath; Bicton (Coll) (Agric; Country Mgt); Bishop Burton (CAg); Bournemouth; Bristol UWE (Hartpury); Broomfield (Coll); Capel Manor (Coll); Central Lancashire (Myerscough Coll) (Turf Sci/Golf Course Mgt; Aboricult; Agric), (Newton Rigg); Cheltenham & Glos (CHE) (Lnd Use); De Montfort; Derby (Country Mgt); Duchy (Coll); Glamorgan (Lnd Sci); Greenmount (CAgH); Hadlow (CAgH); Harper Adams (UC); Hartpury (Coll) can inc gs; Hertfordshire; Isle of Wight (Coll); Nottingham Trent; Oaklands (Coll); Pershore (Anim Cr); Plumpton (CAgH); Plymouth; Scottish (CAg) (Agric; Rur Res Mgt; Poultry Prod; Pig Ent Mgt); Sheffield Hallam; Sparsholt (Coll); Staffordshire (CAg); Sunderland 100 pts (Country Mgt); UHI (Barony Coll) (Fish Farming), (Perth Coll) (Country Recr/Cons Mgt); Warwick (CAg); Wiltshire (Coll); Writtle (Coll).

Other Diploma courses
**100 pts   **Royal (CAg) (Rur Est Mgt).

Alternative Offers:

IB offers: Aberystwyth 26 pts maths H4; Bangor 28 pts H555; Belfast (Queen's) H555 S555; Exeter 30 pts; Harper Adams (UC) 24 pts; Newcastle H654; Nottingham 24 pts (sci); Plymouth 24 pts; Reading 24 pts; Royal (CAg) 26 pts.

Irish offers: Aberdeen BBCC; Bangor CCC; Harper Adams (UC) CCCC; Nottingham CCCCC1; Plymouth CCC.

Scottish Qualifications: Aberdeen AAB or BBB, (other Agric courses) BBBC; Glasgow BBB or BBBB or ABB; Nottingham BBBB (first sitting); Scottish (CAg) (Agric) BCC; Stirling (Cons Sci) BBBC.

CHOOSING YOUR COURSE (See also **Ch.1**)

> **Subject information:** Farming, biochemical applications to plants and animals and agricultural surveying are just some of the specialisms within Agriculture courses. For some courses practical experience is required. There has also been a recent expansion in agri-business studies courses (see also **Appendix 1**). Other courses which could be considered are Animal Sciences, Biology, Biochemistry, Biological Science, Botany, Chemistry, Conservation Management, Crop Science, Ecology, Environmental Sciences, Estate Management, Food Science and Technology, Forestry, Horticulture, Land Surveying, Plant Science, Veterinary Science and Zoology.

Special features: Bangor The World Agriculture course covers both temperate and tropical agriculture. **Bournemouth** The Land-based Enterprise course includes retail aspects of agriculture and tourism. **Central Lancashire (Myerscough Coll)** Courses for Arboriculture and Turfgrass Science. **Royal (CAg)** Study abroad options. **Sparsholt (Coll)** Aquaculture and Fishery Management offered. Horticulture courses offered at **Askham Bryan (Coll), Bangor, Bristol UWE, Central Lancashire, London (Imp), Middlesex, Nottingham** Opportunity to carry out a major research project. **Plymouth, Royal (CAg), Scottish (CAg), Strathclyde, Worcester (UC).** Garden Design is available at **Central Lancashire, Cheltenham & Glos (CHE), Greenwich, Writtle (Coll).** *NOW CHECK PROSPECTUSES AND WEB SITES.*

Top universities and colleges (Teaching Quality) (see Ch.4): Aberystwyth; Belfast (Queen's); Harper Adams (UC); London (Imp); Newcastle; Nottingham; Plymouth (Seale Hayne); not all institutions assessed.

Top universities and colleges (Research) (see Ch.4): Aberdeen; Bangor; Belfast (Queen's); Leeds; Newcastle; Nottingham; Reading; Stirling.

Study opportunities abroad: (Check subjects with institutions) Aberdeen; Aberystwyth; Bangor; Belfast (Queen's); Cheltenham & Glos (CHE); De Montfort; Exeter; Harper Adams (UC); London (Imp); Newcastle; Nottingham; Plymouth; Reading; Royal (CAg); Scottish (CAg); Sheffield Hallam.

Work opportunities abroad: Aberystwyth; Aberdeen; Askham Bryan (Coll); Bangor; Bath; Cheltenham & Glos (CHE); Harper Adams (UC); Hertfordshire; London (Imp); Newcastle; Plymouth; Royal (CAg); Scottish (CAg); Writtle (Coll).

ADMISSIONS INFORMATION

Number of applicants per place (approx): Aberdeen 10; Aberystwyth (Agric) 8; Askham Bryan (Coll) 4; Bangor (World Agric) 5; Bournemouth 7; Buckingham 3; Cheltenham & Glos (CHE) 9; De Montfort 2; Harper Adams (UC) average 2; Newcastle 6; Nottingham 4; Plymouth 5; Reading 9; Royal (CAg) (Agric) 2; Scottish (CAg) (Rur Bus St) 3; Sheffield Hallam (Country Recr Mgt) 4; Trinity Carmarthen (Coll) 3; Wolverhampton 4; Writtle (Coll) 5.

Planning your UCAS personal statement (see Ch.4): First-hand farming experience is necessary for some courses and obviously important for all. Check prospectuses and web sites. Describe the work done. Experience of work with agricultural or food farms (production and laboratory work), garden centres, even with landscape architects, could be appropriate. Keep up-to-date with European agricultural and fishing policies and mention any interests you have in these areas. Read farming magazines and discuss any articles which have interested you. (See **Appendix 1** for contact details of relevant professional associations.)

Selection interviews (see Ch.4): Aberystwyth (No); Bangor (Agric) (No); Bath; Belfast (Queen's) (Agric); Bishop Burton (CAg); Bournemouth; Cheltenham & Glos (CHE); De Montfort (informal); Derby (some); Harper Adams (UC); Liverpool John Moores (No); Newcastle; Nottingham (depends on application); Plymouth; Royal (CAg); Scottish (CAg) (No); Swansea; Writtle (Coll) (No).

Interview questions (see Ch.4): Agriculture is in the news, especially in relation to the problems facing farmers today. You should be up-to-date with political and scientific issues concerning the farming community in general and how these problems might be resolved. You are likely to be questioned on your own farming background (if relevant) and your farming experience. Questions asked in the past have included: What special agricultural interests do you have? What types of farms have you worked on? Do you read any farming publications? If so, which? How long will an egg last before going bad? What is wrong with this tomato? (it had been frozen and defrosted.) Have you visited any agricultural shows in the past year?

Reasons for rejection (non-academic): Insufficient motivation. Too immature. Unlikely to integrate well. Lack of practical experience with crops or animals.

GAP YEAR ADVICE

Most institutions will accept a gap year, some insist upon it. **Aberystwyth** Try to work in a related area; **Harper Adams (UC)** Work experience on a farm recommended; **Newcastle** Keep a diary/photographs of anything done or seen relevant to the course; **Royal (CAg)** Strengthen language skills for the international courses and agriculture for the practical courses.

Institutions willing to defer entry after A-Levels: Aberystwyth; Bangor; Bournemouth; Central Lancashire (Myerscough Coll); Cheltenham & Glos (CHE); Harper Adams (UC); London (Imp) to gain relevant experience; Newcastle; Nottingham; Plymouth; Royal (CAg); Sheffield Hallam; Writtle (Coll).

AFTER RESULTS ADVICE

Institutions which may accept the same points score after A-Levels: Aberystwyth; Bangor; Bournemouth; Cheltenham & Glos (CHE); Lincolnshire & Humberside; Liverpool

John Moores; London (Imp); Newcastle; Nottingham; Plymouth; Royal (CAg); Scottish (CAg); Writtle (Coll).

Institutions which may accept lower grades/points score after A-Levels: Aberdeen; Aberystwyth; Bangor; Belfast (Queen's); Cheltenham & Glos (CHE); Essex; Harper Adams (UC); Liverpool John Moores; Nottingham; Plymouth; Royal (CAg); Scottish (CAg); Writtle (Coll).

Offers to applicants repeating A-Levels: Higher Newcastle (Agri-Bus Econ); **Possibly higher** Newcastle (Agric), Nottingham (Agric), Plymouth (Agric); **Same** Bangor (Agric), Cheltenham & Glos (CHE), Harper Adams (UC), Royal (CAg), Writtle (Coll).

Probable vacancies from June 2001 and in Clearing (see Ch. 4): Most universities and colleges are likely to have vacancies in this subject, many with offers of 200 pts or lower in both Agriculture and Agricultural Sciences. Vacancies are also likely in Crop Science and Countryside Management courses.

NEW GRADUATE DESTINATIONS AND EMPLOYMENT (HESA 1999) (see **Ch.4**)

Out of 1077 students who graduated in Agriculture, 690 entered full-time employment, 133 went on to further study and 56 were believed to be unemployed; 12 graduates in Agricultural Sciences entered full-time employment out of a total of 25. Nine went on to further study and none was reported to be unemployed.

AMERICAN STUDIES

NB The information supplied by the universities and colleges this year varies considerably and the offers listed below should be used as a first source of reference only. Many institutions will accept combinations of Advanced (AL), Advanced Subsidiary (AS) and Vocational Advanced (VA) level qualifications to achieve the required points total, but applicants must check web sites and prospectuses for full details of all offers. Grades and points totals shown should be regarded as the minimum levels to be achieved, but offers may be adjusted downwards when results are known. The points totals shown to the left of the institutions are for ease of reference only. It must not be assumed that tariff points are always used by institutions or that they can be substituted for an offer in grades. The level of an offer is not necessarily indicative of the quality of a course. To calculate your offers see Chapter 4 and the inside fold of the back cover.

Special subject requirements/preferences: A-Level: Hull History or English grade A or B. **Nottingham** English/history grade A/B. **Sheffield** English literature grade A/B, history grade B. **Aberystwyth, Belfast (Queen's), Hull, Kent, Leicester, Manchester, Reading, Warwick** History. **Nottingham** English, history, media studies or politics preferred. **GCSE: Dundee, Edinburgh** English, foreign language and mathematics and science. **East Anglia** English and history at grade A or B.

320 pts **Birmingham** – ABB (Am Can St)
   East Anglia – 320 pts 18u – ABB–BBB or AB+bb (VA6u as 3rd AL); (not gs) (Engl/Am Lit)
   Hull – ABB (Am St/Drama)
   Kent – 320 pts approx (Am St (Art/Film))
   London (King's) – ABB+AS (or equiv) (inc AL Engl/hist pref) **or** VA6u+ALs/ASs; (AM St courses)
   Manchester – ABB (Engl/Am Lit)
   Sheffield – ABB (Am St)
   UMIST – ABB (Am Bus St Int Mgt; Civ Eng/N Am St)
   Warwick – ABB (Engl Am Lit)
300 pts **Birmingham** – BBB (Am St courses except under **320 pts**)
   East Anglia – 300 pts 18u – BBB–BBC **or** AB+bc (VA6u as 3rd AL); (not gs) (Am St; Am Lit)

Edinburgh – BBB (Am St; Soc Sci (Can St))
Hull – BBB–BCC (Am St courses except under **320 pts**)
Lancaster – BBB–BBC (Am St – yr 2 in USA)
Leicester – 18u at AL – BBB **or** ALs+ASs **or** VA12u BB+AL(C); gs (AS only); (Am St – 4yr)
Nottingham – BBB–BBC or 3ALs+AS; (not gs) (Am St; Am St/Phil/Engl St/Hist)
Sussex – BBB (Am St (Hist); Am St (Soc St); Am St (Lit))
Swansea – 300 pts 18u – BBB–BBC/AB **or** ALs+ASs **or** VAs+/-ALs/ASs; (Am St courses)
Warwick – BBB (Compar Am St)

280 pts **Brunel** – 280–220 pts 2x6u – ALs **or** ALs+ASs **or** VAs+/-ALs/ASs; (Am St courses)
Essex – 280–260 pts 21u – BB+AL/2ASs **or** VA12u+AL **or** VA6u+2ALs; gs; (Am St)
Exeter – 280–240 pts approx (Theor Phys/N Am St)
Keele – BBC–BCC **or** equiv AS accepted; gs; (Am St courses)
Kent – BBC; gs; (Am St (Hist) & (Lit))
Lancaster – BBC–BCC (Am St courses except under **300 pts**)
Leicester – 18u at AL – BBC **or** ALs+ASs **or** VA12u BB+AL(C); gs (AS only); (Am St – 3yr)
London (King's) – BBC+AS (or equiv) **or** BB+bbc (inc B Span+Engl/hist) (US Lat Am St)
Manchester – BBB–BCC (Am St)
Reading – BBC (Am St)
UMIST – BBC (Civ Eng N Am St)

260 pts **Aberystwyth** – 260–200 pts – ALs (C Engl hist) **or** ALs+ASs (Am St)
Belfast (Queen's) – BCC (Am St)
Dundee – BCC/BB (Am St courses)
East Anglia – 260 pts 18u – BBC–BCC **or** BB+cc; VA6u as 3rd AL; (not gs) (Am Hist/Pol; Am Hist)
Kent – 260 pts approx (Br Am Pol St)
Liverpool John Moores – 260 pts 4ALs; 220 pts 3ALs; 160 pts 2ALs (pref inc Engl/hist/film st/media st/comm st) **or** VAs C+AL; (Am St)

240 pts **Ulster** – CCC (Am St/Modn St)
220 pts **Central Lancashire** – 220 pts 12u – CCD (inc hum/soc sci subj); gs; (Am St; Am St/Film)
Falmouth (CA) – 220 pts (Am St)
King Alfred's Winchester (Coll) – 220 pts 12u – 3ALs **or** 2ALs+ASs **or** VAs+/-ALs/ASs; (not gs) (Am St)
Lampeter – 220 pts approx (Am St courses)
Middlesex – 220–180 pts approx (Am St)
Plymouth – CCD–CDD (Am St courses)
Wolverhampton – 220–160 pts 12u – CDE/CC **or** CD+de **or** VA12u CC; gs; (Am St)

200 pts **Central Lancashire** – 200–180 pts 12u – gs; (Am St/Hist)
De Montfort (Leicester) – 200 pts – ALs **or** ALs+ASs **or** VAs+/-ALs/ASs; (not gs) (Am St courses)
Derby – 200 pts 12u – CDD **or** CD+dd **or** VA12u CD; gs; (Am St)
Glamorgan – 200–140 pts approx (Am St courses)
Sunderland – 200–180 pts approx (Am St Comb Hons)
Wolverhampton – 200–180 pts approx (Am St courses)

180 pts **Cheltenham & Glos (CHE)** – 180 pts (Am St courses)
Liverpool Hope (Coll) – 180 pts approx (Am St courses)
London Guildhall – 180 pts (Am St)
Ripon & York (Coll) – 180 pts approx (Am St courses)
Thames Valley – 180–140 pts approx (Am St courses)

160 pts **Canterbury Christ Church (UC)** – CC (Am St courses)
Manchester Met – CC (Am St courses)
Staffordshire – CC/180 pts approx (Am St courses)

140 pts   and below
Derby – 140 pts 12u – CD **or** DE+ee **or** VA12u CD; gs; (Am St Comb)
North London – (Carib St)
Northampton (UC) – DD (Am St courses)

Alternative Offers:

IB offers: Aberystwyth 30 pts H6 in history or English; Birmingham 33 pts; Brunel 32 pts: Central Lancashire 28 pts; Derby 14 pts; Essex 28 pts, H 11 pts; Exeter 30 pts; Hull 30 pts H66 in English and history; Keele 26 pts; Kent 32 pts, H 13 pts, Am St (Art/Film) 34 pts, Am St (Lit) (Hist) 30 pts; Lancaster 32–30 pts; Leicester 30 pts; Liverpool Hope (CHE) 28 pts; Northampton (UC) 24 pts; Ripon & York (Coll) 30 pts; Staffordshire 27 pts; Swansea 30 pts; Warwick 32 pts.

Irish offers: Keele BBBCC; Sheffield AABBB.

Scottish Qualifications: Dundee BBBC; Edinburgh BBBB.

CHOOSING YOUR COURSE (See also **Ch.1**)

Subject information: American literature and history with a year in the USA represent the core of most courses (variations are given below). Other courses which might be considered are English Literature, Government, History, International History, International Relations, Latin-American Relations, Spanish-American Studies and Politics.

Special features: Birmingham The course includes Canadian studies. **Derby** The American Studies modular scheme includes a semester in the USA. **Dundee** Students take English or History in year 1 and commence American studies in year 2 and post-war American society in year 3. **Exeter** The American and Commonwealth Arts course offers a placement in the US or Canada in year 3. **Glamorgan** A course in American Business Studies is offered. **Reading** The course is taught across four departments – English, Film and Drama, History and Politics. **Ripon & York (Coll)** Exchange scheme in USA. *NOW CHECK PROSPECTUSES AND WEB SITES.*

Top universities and colleges (Teaching Quality) (see Ch.4): Birmingham; Brunel; Central Lancashire; Derby; East Anglia; Hull; Keele; Kent; Liverpool John Moores; Middlesex; Nottingham; Reading; Ulster; Warwick; not all institutions assessed.

Top universities and colleges (Research) (see Ch.4): East Anglia; Keele; Liverpool; Nottingham; Sussex.

Study opportunities abroad: Most institutions make some arrangements for a period of study in USA or Canada (check with institution); Brunel; Canterbury Christ Church (UC); Derby; Dundee; East Anglia; Exeter; King Alfred's Winchester (Coll); Nottingham; Sheffield; Thames Valley; Warwick.

Work opportunities abroad: Brunel.

ADMISSIONS INFORMATION

Number of applicants per place (approx): Aberystwyth 19; Belfast (Queen's) 11; Birmingham 14; Brunel 6; Central Lancashire 15; Derby 3; East Anglia 25; Essex 6; Exeter 20; Hull 15; Keele 7; Kent 12; Lancaster 25; Leicester 20; Liverpool John Moores 3; Liverpool Hope (Coll) 12; Manchester 33; North London 2; Nottingham 20; Reading 9; Ripon & York (Coll) 4; Sheffield 30; Staffordshire 7; Sussex 12; Swansea 8; Warwick 14.

Planning your UCAS personal statement (see Ch.4): Visits to America should be described and any knowledge or interests you have of the history, politics and economics of the USA should be included on the UCAS form. The US Embassy in London may be a useful source of information. American magazines and newspapers are good reference sources and books written by Alistair Cooke (*America* – BBC publication) will also give a good insight to life in the USA. **Lampeter** Looks for interest in USA and Canada.

Selection interviews (see Ch.4): De Montfort (No); Dundee (No); East Anglia; Hull; Kent (some); King Alfred's Winchester (Coll); Lampeter; Leicester (No); Liverpool John Moores (No); Manchester (No); Nottingham (No); Ripon & York (Coll) (No); Staffordshire (some); Sunderland (No); Swansea (interview before offers are made); Warwick.

Interview questions (see Ch.4): Courses generally focus on history and literature so expect some questions on any American literature you have read and also on aspects of American history. Visits you have made to America (or Canada) and the conclusions you have reached about the people, culture and society in general may be discussed. Current political issues might also be raised, so keep up-to-date with the political scene.

Reasons for rejection (non-academic): If personal reasons prevent year of study in America. **Swansea** Lack of knowledge covering literature, history and politics.

GAP YEAR ADVICE

Most institutions accept a gap year; **Swansea** Useful to spend part of the year in the USA.

Institutions willing to defer entry after A-Levels: Aberystwyth (prefers deferred entry application); Birmingham; Central Lancashire; Derby; Dundee; Glamorgan; Hull; King Alfred's Winchester (Coll); Lancaster; Leicester; Liverpool John Moores; Nottingham; Ripon & York (Coll); Sheffield; Staffordshire; Sussex; Swansea; Thames Valley; Warwick.

AFTER RESULTS ADVICE

Institutions which may accept the same points score after A-Levels: Aberystwyth; Birmingham (No); Canterbury Christ Church (UC); Dundee; East Anglia; Essex; Exeter; Hull; Keele; Kent; Leicester (No); Liverpool Hope (Coll); Manchester (No); Nottingham (No); Ripon & York (Coll); Sheffield (No); Swansea; Warwick (No); Wolverhampton.

Institutions which may accept lower grades/points score after A-Levels: Aberystwyth; Brunel; Canterbury Christ Church (UC); Derby; Dundee; East Anglia (some); Exeter; Hull; Keele; King Alfred's Winchester (Coll); Leicester; Sheffield (No); Swansea; Warwick; Wolverhampton.

Offers to applicants repeating A-Levels: Higher Essex, Warwick; **Possibly higher** Nottingham; **Same** Derby, East Anglia (some), Hull.

Probable vacancies from June 2001 and in Clearing (see Ch.4): Vacancies almost certainly will be declared in this subject, many on joint courses. Popular universities could ask for 260 or 240 pts.

NEW GRADUATE DESTINATIONS AND EMPLOYMENT (1999 HESA) (see **Ch.4**)

Out of 519 graduates, 314 entered full-time employment (business being the most popular career), 78 entered further education and training, and 29 were reported to be unemployed.

ANATOMICAL SCIENCE/ANATOMY (see also **Physiology**)

NB The information supplied by the universities and colleges this year varies considerably and the offers listed below should be used as a first source of reference only. Many institutions will accept combinations of Advanced (AL), Advanced Subsidiary (AS) and Vocational Advanced (VA) level qualifications to achieve the required points total, but applicants must check web sites and prospectuses for full details of all offers. Grades and points totals shown should be regarded as the minimum levels to be achieved, but offers may be adjusted downwards when results are known. The points totals shown to the left of the institutions are for ease of reference only. It must not be assumed that tariff points are always used by institutions or that they can be substituted for an offer in grades. The level of an offer is not necessarily indicative of the quality of a course. To calculate your offers see Chapter 4 and the inside fold of the back cover.

Special subject requirements/preferences: A-Level: Chemistry plus two other science subjects usually required. **GCSE:** mathematics usually required. **Cambridge** Grade As in most subjects usually required.

360 pts and above
    Cambridge – Offers, mainly in grades, vary between colleges (Nat Sci (Anat))
300 pts **Bristol** – BBB (inc 2 sci); (not gs) (Anat Sci)
    London (UCL) – BBB–BBC **or** 3ALs+AS/VA; (Anat/Dev Biol)
    Sheffield – 300–280 pts approx (Anat/Cell Biol)
280 pts **Edinburgh** – BBC (Anat Sci)
    Glasgow – BBC–CCC/BB–BC (Anatomy)
    Manchester – BBC (Anat Sci courses)
260 pts **Cardiff** – BCC (Anat Sci)
    Leeds – BCC (Anat Sci)
    Liverpool – 260 pts – ALs **or** ALs+ASs **or** VAs+/-ALs/ASs; (Anat/Hum Biol)
240 pts **Belfast (Queen's)** – CCC/BB (Anatomy)
220 pts **Dundee** – 220 pts approx (Anat Sci; Anat/Physiol Sci)

Alternative Offers:

IB offers: Bristol 28 pts 2 sci at H; Dundee H554; London (UCL) 32 pts.

Irish offers: Sheffield BBBBB.

Scottish Qualifications: Dundee BBB or BBCC; Edinburgh BBBB; Glasgow BBBB or BBB.

CHOOSING YOUR COURSE (See also **Ch.1**)

> **Subject information:** Anatomical Science/Anatomy is a highly specialised scientific study covering the biological sciences and a variety of research techniques. The most appropriate alternative course is Biological Sciences in which anatomy may be included as an option, but Biology, Genetics, Microbiology and Physiology should also be considered. Anatomical Science is an excellent basis for careers in neuroscience, molecular endocrinology, oral biology or skeletal tissue research. See also under **Physiology**.

Special features: Bristol Anatomy occupies one third of the curriculum which also covers neurobiology, anthropology and computing. **Cambridge** One option fosuses on a training in research in medical science. **Glasgow** Practical work emphasised. **Manchester** The course covers biochemistry, cell biology, immunology and physiology. *NOW CHECK PROSPECTUSES AND WEB SITES.*

Top universities and colleges (Research) (see Ch.4): Cambridge; Dundee; Liverpool; London (UCL); Oxford.

Study opportunities abroad: Dundee; Manchester.

ADMISSIONS INFORMATION

Number of applicants per place (approx): Bristol 20; Cardiff 8; Liverpool 8; London (UCL) 11; Sheffield 7.

Planning your UCAS personal statement (see Ch.4): Give reasons for your interest in this subject (usually stemming from school work in biology). Read medical and other scientific journals and discuss any interest you may have in new developments in medicine related to anatomical science.

Selection interviews (see Ch.4): Bristol; Cambridge; Cardiff (No); Liverpool (No); London (UCL); Manchester; Sheffield (No).

Interview questions (see Ch.4): Questions are likely on your particular interests in biology and anatomy, why you wish to study the subject, and your future career intentions.

GAP YEAR ADVICE

Institutions willing to defer entry after A-Levels: Bristol; Cardiff; Dundee; London (UCL) (No); Manchester; Sheffield.

AFTER RESULTS ADVICE

Institutions which may accept the same points score after A-Levels: Bristol (No); Cardiff; Dundee; Liverpool; London (UCL) (No).

Offers to applicants repeating A-Levels: Higher Bristol, Dundee, Sheffield; **Possibly higher** Liverpool; **Same** London (UCL), Manchester.

Probable vacancies from June 2001 and in Clearing (see Ch.4): Most universities are likely to have vacancies in this subject. In Clearing offers are likely to range from 240–220 pts.

NEW GRADUATE DESTINATIONS AND EMPLOYMENT (1999 HESA) (see **Ch.4**)

Out of 969 graduates in Anatomy and Physiology, 371 went into full-time employment, 397 on to further study and 55 were believed to be unemployed.

ANIMAL SCIENCES (including **Equine Studies** and **Horse Studies**)

NB The information supplied by the universities and colleges this year varies considerably and the offers listed below should be used as a first source of reference only. Many institutions will accept combinations of Advanced (AL), Advanced Subsidiary (AS) and Vocational Advanced (VA) level qualifications to achieve the required points total, but applicants must check web sites and prospectuses for full details of all offers. Grades and points totals shown should be regarded as the minimum levels to be achieved, but offers may be adjusted downwards when results are known. The points totals shown to the left of the institutions are for ease of reference only. It must not be assumed that tariff points are always used by institutions or that they can be substituted for an offer in grades. The level of an offer is not necessarily indicative of the quality of a course. To calculate your offers see Chapter 4 and the inside fold of the back cover.

Special subject requirements/preferences: A-Level: Biology, chemistry required or preferred. **Harper Adams (UC)** Biology at grade C or above. **GCSE:** Mathematics usually required. **Newcastle** Biology or chemistry or biological sciences and mathematics grade A or B. **Aberdeen, St Andrews** English, mathematics or science and a foreign language required. **Cambridge** Grade A in most subjects preferred. **Other:** Check any weight limits on equitation modules. Practical farming experience could be an advantage.

360 pts **and above**
  Cambridge – Offers, mainly in grades, vary between colleges (Nat Sci)
320 pts **Bristol** – ABB–BBB (inc chem+sci); (not gs) (Eqn Sci)
  London (Imp) – ABB (Anim Sci)
300 pts **Bristol** – BBB (chem+sci) **or** BB+bbb (chem+biol/maths); (not gs) (Vet Pathogen)
280 pts **Glasgow** – BBC (Anim Biol)
  Leeds – BBC–BCC (Anim Nutr Physiol)
  St Andrews – BBC (Anim Biol)
260 pts **Lancaster** – BCC (Bioch/Anim Physiol)
  Leicester – BCC (Biol Sci (Physiol))
  London (Imp) – BCC (App Nat Sci/Eqn Sci courses)
  Nottingham – BCC–CCC; (not gs) (Anim Sci)
240 pts **Aberystwyth** – 240–200 pts – ALs **or** ALs+ASs **or** VAs+/-ALs/ASs; gs; (Anim Sci; Eqn Sci)
  Belfast (Queen's) – CCC (Anim Sci)

Newcastle – CCC (Anim Sci; Dom Anim Sci)
Reading – 240 pts approx (Anim Sci)
220 pts **Aberdeen** – CCD–CDD/BC (Anim Sci; Eqn Sci)
Bristol UWE (Hartpury) – 220 pts – ALs **or** ALs+ASs **or** VAs+/-ALs/ASs; gs; (Eqn Sci)
200 pts **Chester (Coll)** – 200 pts – ALs (180 pts inc C biol/chem/sci) **or** VAs (180 pts inc C sci)+AS; AS(20+ pts); (Anim Bhv/Welf; Anim Bhv)
Coventry – 200 pts approx (Eqn/Hum Spo Mgt)
Portsmouth – 200 pts (inc 2 sci subjs) – ALs **or** ALs+ASs **or** VAS; gs; (Anim Dev; Anim Hlth)
180 pts **Bishop Burton (CAg)** – 180 pts approx (Eqn Sci/Mgt)
Chester (Coll) – 180 pts approx (Eqn St)
De Montfort (Lincoln) – 180–160 pts inc 80 pts biol – ALs **or** ALs+ASs **or** VAs+/-ALs/ASs; (not gs) (Anim Sci; Anim Mgt/Welf; Eqn Sci)
East London – 180 pts (Anim Biol)
Manchester Met – 180 pts approx – ALs(inc sci (pref biol) for Eqn Sci) **or** ALs+ASs **or** VAs+/-ALs/ASs; (Anim Sci; Anim St; Eqn Spo Sci)
Nottingham Trent (Brackenhurst) – 180–160 pts approx (Eqn St)
Scottish (CAg) – 180 pts approx (App Plant/Anim Sci)
Wolverhampton – 180 pts – DDD/DDE/CC **or** CC+dd/ee **or** VA12u CC; gs; (Anim Biol)
Writtle (Coll) – 180 pts approx (Eqn St)
160 pts **Bishop Burton (CAg)** – 160 pts approx (Anim Sci Mgt)
Brinsbury (Coll) – 160 pts; gs; (Eqn Mgt; Anim Sci)
Bristol UWE (Hartpury) – 160 pts – ALs **or** ALs+ASs **or** VAs+/-ALs/ASs; gs; (Anim Sci)
Chichester (UC) – 160 pts 12u (inc C relevant subj); (Anim Mgt; Eqn Mgt)
Harper Adams (UC) – 160 pts 18u – CC (inc chem/biol) **or** CC+c **or** VAs+/-ALs/ASs; (not AL gs) (Anim Nutr; Anim Hlth)
Myerscough (Coll) – 160 pts approx (Eqn Sci courses; Anim Welf/Lvstk Prod)
Northampton (UC) – 160–140 pts (Eqn St)
Plymouth (Seale Hayne) – 160 pts approx (Anim Sci)
Royal (CAg) – 160 pts 12u – CC/CEE/DDE **or** DD+c **or** CE+c **or** VA CC; gs; (Anim Mgt; Eqn/Agric Mgt)
Writtle (Coll) – 160 pts approx (Eqn St/Bus Mgt)
140 pts **Harper Adams (UC)** – 140 pts 18u – CD **or** DE+e **or** VAs+/-ALs/ASs; gs; (Eqn Sci)
Liverpool John Moores – 140–120 pts (inc AL sci inmc geog): ALs **or** ALs+ASs; (Wldlf Cons)
Nescot – 140 pts approx (App Anim Sci)
Warwickshire (Coll) – 140–120 pts; (Eqn Sci/St courses)
120 pts **and below**
De Montfort (Lincoln) – 120 pts (inc 60 pts AL biol/life sci) **or** VA (60 pts)+AS; (Eqn Spo Sci/Stud Mgt)
Sparsholt (Coll) – 120 pts; gs; (Anim Mgt; Wldlf Mgt; Eqn St)
Suffolk (Coll) – 80 pts approx (Anim Sci Cons)
Wolverhampton – DD; gs; (Eqn St)

Higher National Diploma courses
120 pts **and below**
Bangor; Bath; Bishop Burton (CAg); Bristol UWE (Hartpury); Buckinghamshire Chilterns (UC); Central Lancashire (Newton Rigg); Chester (Coll); Chichester (UC) (Anim Mgt); De Montfort (Anim Sci); Dudley (CT) (Anim Mgt); Filton (Coll); Harper Adams (UC) (Anim Care); Moulton (Coll) (Anim Welf; Eqn St); Myerscough (Coll) (Anim Prod/Anim Nurs); North Highland (Coll) (Horse St); Park Lane (Coll) gs; Rodbaston (Coll) (Aqua/Fish); UHI; Wiltshire (Coll) (Anim Sci; Eqn Sci); Worcester (UC).

Horse/Equine Studies courses

Offered at Aberdeen (Coll); Aberystwyth; Bangor; Bath; Bicton (Coll) (Anim Care; Eqn St); Bishop Burton (CAg); Brackenhurst (Coll); Brighton; Bristol UWE (Hartpury) (Anim Sci/Eqn Sci); Buckinghamshire Chilterns (UC); Cannington (Coll); Central Lancashire; Cheltenham & Glos (CHE); Chichester (UC) (Eqn St); Cordwainers (Coll) (Saddlery Tech); Cornwall & Duchy (Coll); Coventry; De Montfort (weight limit 13st for Equitation); Enniskillen (CAg); Glamorgan; Harper Adams (UC) (Anim Care); Hertfordshire; Myerscough (Coll); Nescot; Northampton (UC); Nottingham Trent; Oaklands (Coll) (Anim Care); Plymouth (Seale Hayne) (Eqn Sci); Rodbaston (Coll) (Anim Care); St Helens (Coll); Sparsholt (Coll); Warwickshire (Coll); West Oxfordshire (Coll); UHI; Wolverhampton; Writtle (Coll).

Alternative Offers:

IB offers: Birmingham 30 pts; Coventry 28 pts; London (Imp) 25 pts H555; Nottingham 24 pts (sci); St Andrews 28 pts; York 32–30 pts H or L5 in biol or chem.

Irish offers: Nottingham CCCCC1;) St Andrews BBBC.

Scottish Qualifications: Aberdeen BBBC; Glasgow BBBB or BBB; Nottinghan BBBB (first sitting).

CHOOSING YOUR COURSE (See also **Ch.1**)

Subject information: A popular course choice for those without a place in Veterinary Science. It covers a biological study of animals, reproduction and nutrition. Equine Studies has also become popular in recent years, particularly at HND level. Apart from Veterinary Science, there are few other courses which directly relate to animals. Some Agriculture courses include farming with cattle. Check Agriculture courses for suitable alternative studies. NB: Some of the courses have been advertised as Veterinary Science courses in vacancy lists. Applicants should note that these degrees do **not** qualify the graduate to practise as a veterinary surgeon (see **Appendix 1** for contact details of relevant professional associations).

Special features: Aberdeen Core subjects include chemistry, biochemistry, biology and ecology. **Aberystwyth** Exchange programmes exist with Germany and Portugal. **Bristol** The university has an equine sports medical centre. **Bristol UWE (Hartpury)** Involvement in the practical handling of companion animals. **De Montfort** Equine Sports Science is offered. **Nottingham** a scientific programme covering nutrition, physiology and production science. Sandwich courses are offered at some universities eg **Nottingham Trent**. *NOW CHECK PROSPECTUSES AND WEB SITES.*

Top universities and colleges (Research) (see Ch.4): See under **Agricultural Sciences/Agriculture**.

Study opportunities abroad: Aberystwyth; Chester (Coll); Coventry; London (Imp); Newcastle; Nottingham; Plymouth (Anim Prod); Reading; Royal (CAg); St Andrews; York.

Work opportunities abroad: Aberystwyth; Chester (Coll); Coventry; Harper Adams (UC); Leeds; Plymouth (Anim Prod); Royal (CAg); Scottish (CAg); Sparsholt (Coll).

ADMISSIONS INFORMATION

Number of applicants per place (approx): Aberystwyth 6; Coventry 6; De Montfort 3; Harper Adams (UC) 5; Leeds 6; Liverpool 6; Newcastle 9 (all courses); Nottingham 6; Reading 10; Royal (CAg) 4; York 10.

Planning your UCAS personal statement (see Ch.4): Describe any work you have done with animals which generated your interest in this subject. Work experience in veterinary practices, on farms or with agricultural firms would be useful. Read agricultural/scientific journals for up-dates on animal nutrition or breeding. For Equine courses, details of practical experience in the horse industry (eg references, BHS examinations, Pony Club tests) should be included. **Coventry** Good equine background and commitment required. A clear, concise, well-structured statement – no waffle! **Leeds** Farm experience helpful but not a requirement. **St Andrews** Looks for reasons for choosing the course and evidence of interest, sport/extra-curricular activities and posts of responsibility.

Selection interviews (see Ch.4): Aberdeen (No); Aberystwyth (No); Bishop Burton (CAg) (No); Bristol; Cambridge; Harper Adams (UC); Leeds (No); London (Imp); Nescot (No); Newcastle; Nottingham (depends on application); Nottingham Trent (Brackenhurst) (No); Royal (CAg); Scottish (CAg); Suffolk (Coll); Writtle (Coll); York (some).

Interview questions (see Ch.4): Questions will be asked on your experience with animals and your reasons for wishing to follow this science-based subject. Other questions asked in recent years have included: What do your parents think about your choice of course? What are your views on battery hens and the transportation of veal calves? Outline the BSE crisis and European reactions.

Reasons for rejection (non-academic): Uncertainty as to why applicants chose the course. Too immature. Unlikely to integrate well.

GAP YEAR ADVICE

Most institutions accept a gap year. **Warwickshire (Coll)/Coventry** Experience of the equine industry useful. Gain riding experience during the gap year since this is not part of the course.

Institutions willing to defer entry after A-Levels: Aberystwyth; Chester (Coll); Coventry; Harper Adams (UC); Leeds; London (Imp); Newcastle; Nottingham; Nottingham Trent (Brackenhurst); Royal (CAg); St Andrews; Sparsholt (Coll); Writtle (Coll); York.

AFTER RESULTS ADVICE

Institutions which may accept the same points score after A-Levels: Aberdeen (No); Bristol; Chester (Coll); Leeds; London (Imp); Newcastle; Nottingham; Royal (CAg); St Andrews; Sparsholt (Coll).

Institutions which may accept lower grades/points score after A-Levels: Aberdeen; Aberystwyth; Chester (Coll); Harper Adams (UC); London (Imp); Newcastle; Nottingham; Royal (CAg); Sparsholt (Coll).

Offers to applicants repeating A-Levels: Higher St Andrews; **Possibly higher** Nottingham; **Same** Leeds, London (Imp), Royal (CAg).

Probable vacancies from June 2001 and in Clearing (see Ch.4): Vacancies are likely at many institutions from June onwards.

NEW GRADUATE DESTINATIONS AND EMPLOYMENT (1999 HESA) (see **Ch.4**)

No data available.

ANTHROPOLOGY (including Social Anthropology)

NB The information supplied by the universities and colleges this year varies consider-ably and the offers listed below should be used as a first source of reference only. Many institutions will accept combinations of Advanced (AL), Advanced Subsidiary (AS) and Vocational Advanced (VA) level qualifications to achieve the required points total, but applicants must check web sites and prospectuses for full details of all offers. Grades and points totals shown should be regarded as the minimum levels to be achieved, but offers may be adjusted downwards when results are known. The points totals shown to the left of the institutions are for ease of reference only. It must not be assumed that tariff points are always used by institutions or that they can be substituted for an offer in grades. The level of an offer is not necessarily indicative of the quality of a course. To calculate your offers see Chapter 4 and the inside fold of the back cover.

Special subject requirements/preferences: GCSE: Grade A–C in mathematics may be required. **Cambridge, Oxford** Grade A in most subjects preferred. **East London** Five–six subjects at grade A–C. **Edinburgh, St Andrews** English, mathematics or science and a foreign language. **Lampeter** Prefer six or more subjects at grade A or B. **London (LSE)** English, mathematics and biology at grade C.

360 pts	**and above**
	Cambridge – Offers, mainly in grades, vary between colleges (Arch/Anth) (See also **Archaeology**)
	Oxford – Offers vary between candidates (Arch/Anth)
340 pts	**Durham** – AAB (Nat Sci)
	Edinburgh – AAB (1 sitting); (not gs) (Soc Anth courses)
	London (UCL) – AAB–BBB **or** 3ALs+AS/VA; (Anthropology)
330 pts	**Southampton** – 330 pts 21u (inc 180 pts from 2ALs); (App Soc Sci (Anth))
	Southampton (New Coll) – 330 pts 12u – ALs **or** 2ALs (inc 180 pts)+ASs **or** VAs+/-ALs/ASs gs; (Anth Hum)
320 pts	**Durham** – ABB–BBB (Anth/Psy)
	Brunel – 320–280 pts 2x6u – ALs **or** ALs+ASs **or** VAs+/-ALs/ASs; (not gs) (Soc Anth courses)
	Manchester – ABB–BBB/AA–BB (Soc Anth)
300 pts	**Durham** – BBB–BBC (Anth courses except **320/240 pts**)
	Keele – BBB–BBC **or** equiv AS accepted; gs; (Soc Anth courses)
	Kent – 300 pts approx/AB (Soc Anth courses except under **260 pts**)
	Liverpool – 300–260 pts – ALs **or** ALs+ASs **or** VAs+/-ALs/ASs; (Hum Evol)
	London (LSE) – BBB (Anth; Anth/Law courses)
	London (UCL) – BBB–BBC **or** 3ALs+AS/VA; (Anth/Geog)
	Manchester – BBB–BBC (BA Econ Soc Anth)
	St Andrews – BBB (Soc Anth)
	Sussex – BBB (Soc Anth)
280 pts	**Aberdeen** – BBC (Anthropology)
	East Anglia – BBC/BB (Anthropology)
	Glasgow – BBC (Anth courses)
	Hull – BBC (Soc Anth/Anth courses)
	London (Gold) – BBC **or** 2ALs (inc B)+ASs; (not gs) (Anthropology)
	London (SOAS) – BBC/BB (Soc Anth courses)
	Swansea – 280 pts 18u – BBC–BCC/BB **or** ALs+ASs **or** VAs+/-ALs/ASs; (Soc Anth courses)
260 pts	**Belfast (Queen's)** – BCC (Anth courses)
	Kent – 260 pts approx/BB (Soc Anth/Ger/Fr)
	Oxford Brookes – BCC–CCD (Anthropology – offer varies with 2nd subject)
240 pts	**Durham (Stockton)** – CCC/BC (Anth – Hum Sci)
	Lincolnshire & Humberside – 240–160 pts (Soc Anth)
220 pts	**Lampeter** – 220 pts approx (Anth courses)
	Surrey Roehampton – 220 pts approx (inc 120 pts min from 2ALs) – ALs **or** ALs+ASs **or** VAs+/-ALs/ASs; (Anth; Biol Anth; Soc Anth)
180 pts	**East London** – 180 pts approx (Anth courses)
	Glamorgan – 180 pts approx (Anth courses)
160 pts	**Liverpool John Moores** – 160–120 pts (inc 80 pts biol) – ALs **or** ALs+ASs **or** VA6u+AL; (Biol Anth)

Alternative Offers:

IB offers: Durham H554; East Anglia 28 pts; Kent 28 pts; Lampeter 24 pts; London (LSE) 36 pts H666, (UCL) 30 pts; St Andrews 30 pts; Swansea 30 pts.

Scottish Qualifications: Aberdeen BBBB; Edinburgh ABBBC; Glasgow ABBB; St Andrews BBBB.

CHOOSING YOUR COURSE (See also **Ch.1**)

Subject information: Anthropology study will include some biology, some history and a study of the cultures, rituals and beliefs of humankind (ancient and modern) with extensions into art, kinship, family, religion, political and legal structures. Psychology, Sociology, Religious Studies, Archaeology and History of Art are also subjects that reflect the development of society and which could be considered as alternative courses of study.

Special features: Aberdeen The course covers the anthropology of religion, carnival, the environment and the anthropology of the North Atlantic. **Edinburgh** Social Anthropology focuses on ritual, family, marriage and the Third World or, alternatively, on environment, society and gender. **Glasgow** Societies in Melanesia, Africa, Australia, South America and Indonesia are studied. **Kent** The course covers biological, cultural and social processes underlying the human experience in non-industrial and industrial societies. **Lampeter** Topics include contemporary human society with an emphasis on the study of art and material culture including film and museum studies. **London (SOAS)** Ethnography of a selected area in Africa or Asia is the main focus of the course. **Manchester** Student exchanges take place within the European Union and a one-year placement can take place on VSO. **St Andrews** A particular emphasis on Africa, India and the Americas. *NOW CHECK PROSPECTUSES AND WEB SITES.*

Top universities and colleges (Teaching Quality) (see Ch.4): Brunel; Cambridge; Durham; Kent; London (LSE), (SOAS), (UCL); Manchester; Oxford; Oxford Brookes; Sussex; not all institutions assessed.

Top universities and colleges (Research) (see Ch.4): Belfast (Queen's); Brunel; Cambridge; Durham; Edinburgh; London (Gold), (LSE), (SOAS), (UCL); Manchester; Oxford; Oxford Brookes; St Andrews; Sussex.

Study opportunities abroad: Belfast (Queen's); Brunel; Edinburgh; London (Gold), (UCL); Manchester; Oxford Brookes; Surrey Roehampton; Sussex; Swansea.

ADMISSIONS INFORMATION

Number of applicants per place (approx): Belfast (Queen's) 10; Brunel 13; Durham 14; East London 2; Hull 11; Kent 6; London (Gold) 7, (LSE) (Anth) 8, (Anth/Law) 15, (SOAS) 8, (UCL) 3; Manchester 10; Oxford Brookes 8; Sussex 10; Swansea 6.

Planning your UCAS personal statement (see Ch.4): Give details of any overseas travel. Visit the museums of anthropology (for example, London, Cambridge) and describe any aspect of the subject which interests you (including books you have read) and how you have pursued this interest. Since this is not a school subject, you will need to convince the selectors of your knowledge and interest. **St Andrews** Reasons for choosing course. Evidence of interest, sporting/extra-curricular activities. Positions of responsibility.

Selection interviews (see Ch.4): Cambridge; Durham (some); Durham (Stockton) (W); East Anglia, Hull; Kent (No); London (Gold), (LSE) (some), (UCL) (mature students); Manchester; Oxford; Oxford Brookes; St Andrews (No); Surrey Roehampton (some); Swansea.

Interview questions (see Ch.4): This is a broad subject and questions will tend to emerge as a result of your interests in aspects of anthropology or social anthropology. Past questions have included: What stresses are there among the nomads of the North African desert? What is a society? What is speech? If you dug up a stone axe what could you learn from it? What are the values created by a capitalist society? Discuss the role of women since the beginning of this century.

Reasons for rejection (non-academic): Lack of commitment. Inability to deal with a more philosophical (less positivist) approach to knowledge.

GAP YEAR ADVICE

Institutions willing to defer entry after A-levels: Brunel; Durham; East London; Lampeter; London (Gold No), (UCL No); St Andrews; Sussex; Swansea.

AFTER RESULTS ADVICE

Institutions which may accept the same points score after A-Levels: Durham; Durham (Stockton); London (UCL) (No); Oxford Brookes.

Offers to applicants repeating A-Levels: Possibly higher Durham, Oxford Brookes; **Same** London (UCL), Manchester, Surrey Roehampton.

Probable vacancies from June 2001 and in Clearing (see Ch.4): Although universities may not have filled all their places by June, they are likely to withhold details until Clearing when the highest offers are likely to be in the 240–220 pts range.

NEW GRADUATE DESTINATIONS AND EMPLOYMENT (1999 HESA) (see **Ch.4**)

From 410 graduates, 214 obtained full-time employment, 70 chose to enter research and further training, and 30 were believed to be unemployed.

ARABIC (see also **Near & Middle East Studies**)

NB The information supplied by the universities and colleges this year varies considerably and the offers listed below should be used as a first source of reference only. Many institutions will accept combinations of Advanced (AL), Advanced Subsidiary (AS) and Vocational Advanced (VA) level qualifications to achieve the required points total, but applicants must check web sites and prospectuses for full details of all offers. Grades and points totals shown should be regarded as the minimum levels to be achieved, but offers may be adjusted downwards when results are known. The points totals shown to the left of the institutions are for ease of reference only. It must not be assumed that tariff points are always used by institutions or that they can be substituted for an offer in grades. The level of an offer is not necessarily indicative of the quality of a course. To calculate your offers see Chapter 4 and the inside fold of the back cover.

Special subject requirements/preferences: A-Level: A language may be preferred. **GCSE: Leeds** Grade A–C in a foreign language required, grade A in Arabic. **Cambridge, Oxford** Grade A in most subjects preferred. **Edinburgh** English, mathematics or science and a foreign language required.

360 pts and above
    Cambridge – Offers, mainly in grades, vary between colleges (Modn Arbc; Class Arbc)
    Oxford – Offers vary between candidates (Arabic courses)
340 pts **Edinburgh** – AAB–BBB (Arabic courses)
    St Andrews – AAB (Arabic courses)
300 pts **Manchester** – BBB–BBC (Mid E St; Mid E Langs/Compar Relig))
280 pts **Durham** – BBC/BB (Arabic courses)
    Exeter – 280 pts 18u – BBC **or** BB+cc **or** CC+aa **or** VA6u B+BC; gs; (Arabic; Arbc/Islam/St; Mid E St/Arbc)
    Glasgow – BBC (Islam St)
    Leeds – BBC/AB (Arbc St; Arbc/Islam St; Arbc/Engl/Fr/Ger/Gk Civ/Mgt St/Pol/Port/Span)
    London (SOAS) – BBC (Arabic courses)
    Salford – BBC (Arabic courses)
240 pts **Lampeter** – 240–220 pts approx (Islam St courses)
180 pts **Birmingham (Westhill)** – 180 pts (Islam St)
160 pts **Westminster** – CC (Arabic courses)

Alternative Offers:

IB offers: Exeter 30 pts; St Andrews 28 pts.

Scottish Qualifications: Edinburgh ABBB–BBBB; Glasgow BBBB; St Andrews BBBB.

CHOOSING YOUR COURSE (See also **Ch.1**)

Subject information: Linguists may wish to extend their interest into a different language form, although in this subject interests in the Middle Eastern cultures must also predominate. Such courses, however, should never be under-estimated as they involve considerable study. Alternative courses will depend on the student's preferences for other unusual languages or courses in Middle Eastern or African Studies, for example Archaeology, History.

Special features: Durham Arabic courses focus on Modern Arabic and the Modern Arab World with a wide range of options. **Edinburgh** Modern and Classical Arabic, Islamic history and Arabic literature. **Exeter** Compulsory year abroad in the Middle East. (Arbc/Islam St) Students spend year 2 in Egypt or Jordan. Course covers language and history (600–1258 AD). **Leeds** (Arbc St) Course concentrates on language as a tool for research, professional jobs and the media; year 2 is spent in Fez/Yemen. *NOW CHECK PROSPECTUSES AND WEB SITES.*

Top universities and colleges (Research) (see Ch.4): See under **African Studies**.

Study opportunities abroad: Durham; Leeds; St Andrews; Salford.

Work opportunities abroad: Leeds.

ADMISSIONS INFORMATION

Number of applicants per place (approx): Durham 3; Exeter 10; Leeds 2; Salford 5.

Planning your UCAS personal statement (see Ch.4): Describe any visits to, or your experience of living in, Arabic-speaking countries. Develop a knowledge of Middle Eastern cultures, history and politics and mention these topics in the UCAS form. Provide evidence of language-learning skills and experience. **Leeds** Knowledge of Arabic. **St Andrews** Reasons for choosing course and evidence of interest. Sporting/extra-curricular activities and positions of responsibility. **Salford** Experience of use and interest in foreign languages. Experience of foreign countries.

Selection interviews (see Ch.4): Cambridge; Durham; Edinburgh (No); Exeter (T); Leeds; Oxford; St Andrews (No).

Interview questions (see Ch.4): You will need to be able to justify your reasons for wishing to study Arabic and to discuss your interest in, and awareness of, cultural, social and political aspects of the Middle East.

GAP YEAR ADVICE

Institutions willing to defer entry after A-Levels: Leeds; St Andrews.

AFTER RESULTS ADVICE

Institutions which may accept the same points score after A-Levels: Durham; Exeter; Leeds (some); St Andrews (No).

Institutions which may accept lower grades/points score after A-Levels: Leeds; St Andrews.

Offers to applicants repeating A-Levels: Higher Leeds, St Andrews; **Same** Durham, Exeter.

Probable vacancies from June 2001 and in Clearing (see Ch.4): Few universities are likely to have vacancies from June, but one or two places probably will be available in Clearing.

NEW GRADUATE DESTINATIONS AND EMPLOYMENT (1999 HESA) (see **Ch.4**)

Of the 48 graduates who took courses in Middle Eastern Studies, 14 went on to further study, 22 entered full-time employment and five were believed to be unemployed.

ARCHAEOLOGY

NB The information supplied by the universities and colleges this year varies considerably and the offers listed below should be used as a first source of reference only. Many institutions will accept combinations of Advanced (AL), Advanced Subsidiary (AS) and Vocational Advanced (VA) level qualifications to achieve the required points total, but applicants must check web sites and prospectuses for full details of all offers. Grades and points totals shown should be regarded as the minimum levels to be achieved, but offers may be adjusted downwards when results are known. The points totals shown to the left of the institutions are for ease of reference only. It must not be assumed that tariff points are always used by institutions or that they can be substituted for an offer in grades. The level of an offer is not necessarily indicative of the quality of a course. To calculate your offers see Chapter 4 and the inside fold of the back cover.

Special subject requirements/preferences: A-Level: For BSc courses chemistry may be required. Latin or Greek may be required by some universities. **Cardiff** (Arch Cons) Chemistry preferred. **GCSE:** Mathematics or science usually required for BSc courses. **Bournemouth** CC or above in science plus English. **Edinburgh, Liverpool** Latin or Greek preferred. **Lampeter** Geography or related science. **Cambridge, Oxford** Grade A in most subjects preferred. **London (UCL)** Strong GCSE background.

360 pts **and above**
    Cambridge – Offers, mainly in grades, vary between colleges (Arch/Anth)
    Oxford – Offers vary between candidates (Arch/Anth)
340 pts **Durham** – AAB (Nat Sci (Arch); Arch/Hist)
    York – 340–300 pts 18–12u – BBC+c (Archaeology)
320 pts **Durham** – ABB–BCC (Arch courses)
300 pts **Birmingham** – BBB (Arch courses)
    Cardiff – BBB (Arch Cons)
    East Anglia – ABC–BBC/BB (Arch courses)
    Edinburgh – BBB (1 sitting); (not gs) (Arch; Arch/Soc Anth)
    Exeter – 300–260 pts 18u – BBB–BCC **or** BB+bb **or** BC+cc **or** VA6u B+BC;
        (not gs) (Arch; Arch/Euro St; Arch/Chem (inc AL chem)
    London (UCL) – BBB–BCC **or** 3ALs+AS/VA; (Arch courses)
    Liverpool – 300 pts: ALs **or** ALs+ASs **or** VAs+/-ALs/ASs; (Anc Hist/Arch; Arch;
        Egypt)
    Manchester – BBB–BBC (Archaeology)
    St Andrews – BBB (Arch courses)
    Sheffield – BBB–BBC (Arch courses)
    Warwick – BBB–BBC (Anc Hist/Class Arch)
280 pts **Birmingham** – BBC (Arch; Anc Hist/Arch)
    Bristol – BBC (inc sci for Arch/Geol); (not gs) (Arch; Arch/Geol)
    Exeter – BBC–BCC (Arch courses)
    Glasgow – BBC (Arch courses)
    Kent – 280–260 pts; gs; (Arch single/joint courses)
    London (King's) – BBC+AS **or** BB+bb+AS (inc AL/AS class civ/anc hist pref);
        (Class Arch)
    London (SOAS) – BBC–BCC/BB average (Arch courses)
    Newcastle – BBC–BCC/BB (Arch courses)
    Nottingham – BBC–CCC (Arch courses)
260 pts **Bangor** – BCC (Arch courses)
    Belfast (Queen's) – BCC (Arch courses)

Department of Archeological Sciences

The Department is committed to the discipline of archaeology, in particular in its integration with the natural sciences, and aims to maintain and enhance excellence in teaching and research. It has an international reputation for research and teaching.

In November 2000 the Department was rated Excellent in Teaching by the Quality Assurance Agency (QAA) for Higher Education.

The Department offers three course BSc Archaeological Sciences, BSc Archaeology and BSc Bio-archaeology. Students can take the course over three or four years, with the unique opportunity of a third year spent out 'on placement', with a professional body such as an excavation unit, museum, or research laboratory.

The Department has major field programmess in Pompeii, and at Old Scatness, Shetland.

Department of Archeological Sciences, University of Bradford, West Yorkshire BD7 1DP. Tel: 01274 233531.

Visit our Web Pages at
http://www.brad.ac.uk/acad/archsci/homepage

UNIVERSITY OF
BRADFORD

MAKING KNOWLEDGE WORK

Bradford – 260 pts 12u; gs; (Arch Sci (inc AL sci); Arch; Bioarch (AL biol))
Cardiff – BCC/BB (Arch courses except under **300 pts**)
Kent – 260–200 pts approx (Class/Arch St; Hist/Arch St)
Lampeter – 260/200–160 pts approx (Arch courses)
Leicester – BCC/BB (Arch courses)
Reading – BCC (Arch courses)
Southampton – BCC (Arch; Arch/Geog; Arch/Hist; Arch/Iber St)
240 pts **Aberdeen** – CCC (Scot Arch)
Edinburgh – CCC (Env Arch)
220 pts **Bournemouth** – 220 pts from 3ALs **or** 200–180 pts from 2ALs **or** VAs; (Archaeology)
King Alfred's Winchester (Coll) – 220 pts 12u: 3ALs **or** ALs (min 2 subjs)+ASs **or** VAs+/-AL/ASs; gs; (Arch; Arch Prac)
200 pts **Chester (Coll)** – ALs (160 pts inc C)+AS; **or** VAs (160 pts inc C)+AS; AS(40+ pts); gs; (Arch courses)
180 pts **East London** – 180 pts approx (Arch courses)
160 pts **Cumbria (CAD)** – 160 pts: CC **or** ASs (contact coll) **or** VA; (Archaeology)
Newport (UWCN) – 160–140 pts: ALs **or** ALs+ASs **or** VAs+/-ALs/ASs; (Arch; Arch Hum)
Northampton (UC) – 160–140 pts approx (Ind Arch courses)
Trinity Carmarthen (Coll) – CC–EE (Arch courses)

Higher National Diploma courses
120 pts Bournemouth (Prac Arch); Exeter; Somerset (CAT); Truro (Coll).

Alternative Offers:

IB offers: Bradford 28 pts; Bristol H655; Cardiff 28 pts; Edinburgh H655; Lampeter 28 pts; Leicester 28 pts; Liverpool 30 pts inc 5 and 6 in sciences; Newcastle 30 pts; Southampton 26 pts; Warwick 30 pts; York 28 pts.

Irish offers: Bradford BBBBC; Lampeter BBBCC; Liverpool BBCCC; Sheffield BBBB; Warwick BBBBC; York BBBC.

Scottish Qualifications: Aberdeen BBBB; Edinburgh BBBBC; Glasgow AAB or BBBB (MA), ABB or BBB or BBBB (BSc); St Andrews BBBB.

CHOOSING YOUR COURSE (See also **Ch.1**)

Subject information: It would be unusual for an applicant to pursue this degree course without having been involved in some basic field work. Studies can cover, for example, European, Greek, Roman and African archaeology. As alternatives, the following courses could also be considered: Ancient History, Anthropology, Classical Studies, Classics, Geology, History, History of Architecture, Art and Design, Medieval History, Prehistory and Social Anthropology.

Special features: Birmingham The course focuses on Ancient Greece, Rome, Egypt, Britain and European pre-history. **Bradford** There is a strong applied science element on the course which includes bioarchaeology, focusing on the human environment. **Bristol** The Ancient Mediterranean Studies course covers Iberia and the Middle East although there is extensive fieldwork in the UK and European sites. **Glasgow** The course has a commitment to English and Scottish archaeology up to 1000 AD and later to European and Mediterranean areas. **Liverpool** The course covers the ancient civilisations of the Eastern Mediterranean, Africa, Europe and the near East. **London (UCL)** Wide range of options available including prehistoric, Western Asiatic, Greek, Roman and medieval archaeology, Egyptology and conservation. **Newport (UWCN)** Archaeology plus 2 subjects in year 1; Archaeology then taken as a single honours subject in years 2 and 3. **Nottingham** Specialist studies include historical buildings, numismatics and mathematical and computer applications in archaeology. **Sheffield** Students bias their studies towards prehistoric, Roman or medieval archaeology. **Southampton** Wide range of options including the archaeology of food and drink to prehistoric studies. **York** One main course is taken each term on single themes covering Europe from the Bronze Age onwards. Opportunity to study a modern language. *NOW CHECK PROSPECTUSES AND WEB SITES.*

Top universities and colleges (Teaching Quality) (see Ch.4): Cardiff; Lampeter; not all institutions assessed.

Top universities and colleges (Research) (see Ch.4): Belfast (Queen's); Birmingham; Bradford; Bristol; Cambridge; Cardiff; Durham; Edinburgh; Glasgow; Leicester; Liverpool; London (UCL); Oxford; Reading; Sheffield; Southampton; York.

Study opportunities abroad: Chester (Coll); Durham; King Alfred's Winchester (Coll); Leicester; Nottingham; Sheffield; Southampton; York and most other universities.

Work opportunities abroad: Bradford.

ADMISSIONS INFORMATION

Number of applicants per place (approx): Bangor 6; Birmingham 11; Bournemouth 8; Bradford 4; Bristol 29; Cambridge 2.4; Cardiff 4; Durham 6; Lampeter 2; Leicester 15; London (UCL) 5; Newcastle 14; Nottingham 11; Oxford 2.8; Sheffield 5; Southampton 8; Trinity Carmarthen (Coll) 2; York 12.

Planning your UCAS personal statement (see Ch.4): First-hand experience of 'digs' and other field work should be described. The Council for British Archaeology (see **Appendix 1**) can provide information of where digs are taking place. Describe any interests in fossils and museum visits as well as details of any visits to current archaeological sites. Your local university archaeological department or central library will also provide information on contacts in your local area (each county council employs an archaeological officer). Since this is not a school subject, the selectors will be looking for good reasons for your choice of subject. **Bournemouth** Show willingness to participate in excavations. **Durham** Archaeological experience useful but not necessary. **Lampeter** Experience useful but not essential. **Southampton** Give evidence of practical experience (see also **Appendix 1**).

Selection interviews (see Ch.4): Bangor; Bournemouth (T for mature applicants); Bradford; Bristol (No); Cambridge (W); Cardiff (some); Cumbria (CAD (some); Durham (mature students); East Anglia; Edinburgh (No); Glasgow; King Alfred's Winchester (Coll) (No); Lampeter; London (UCL); Manchester (No); Newcastle; Newport (UWCN); Nottingham; Oxford (W – candidates will be given artifacts, maps and other material to interpret); Sheffield (some); Southampton (mature students); York (No).

Interview questions (see Ch.4): Questions will be asked relating to any experience you may have had in visiting archaeological sites or taking part in digs, for example: How would you interpret archaeological evidence, for example a pile of flints, coins? What is stratification? How would you date archaeological remains? What recent archaeological discoveries have been made? Is it archaeology's job to write world history? How did you become interested in archaeology? With which archaeological sites in the UK are you familiar?

Reasons for rejection (non-academic): (Mature students) Inability to cope with essay-writing and exams. **Bournemouth** Health and fitness important for excavations.

GAP YEAR ADVICE

Bournemouth Only apply for gap year after exam results are known. **Bradford** Travel. Get some experience in field archaeology.

Institutions willing to defer entry after A-Levels: Birmingham; Bradford; Bristol (No); Cardiff; Chester (Coll); King Alfred's Winchester (Coll); Lampeter; Leicester; London (UCL) (No); Manchester; Newcastle; Newport (UWCN); Nottingham; York (prefer not).

AFTER RESULTS ADVICE

Institutions which may accept the same points score after A-Levels: Birmingham; Bradford; Bristol; Cardiff; Durham; Lampeter; Leicester; Liverpool; London (UCL) (No); Manchester; Newcastle (No); Nottingham (No); Sheffield (No); York.

Institutions which may accept lower grades/points score after A-Levels: Birmingham; Bradford; Chester (Coll); Edinburgh; Glasgow; Kent; King Alfred's Winchester (Coll); Lampeter; Leicester; London (UCL); Newcastle (a few); Newport (UWCN); Sheffield (No); York.

Offers to applicants repeating A-Levels: Same Birmingham, Bradford, Chester (Coll), Durham, Lampeter, Leicester, London (UCL), Newport (UWCN), Sheffield.

Probable vacancies from June 2001 and in Clearing (see Ch.4): Several universities are likely to have vacancies in Clearing when popular universities could ask 260–220 pts.

NEW GRADUATE DESTINATIONS AND EMPLOYMENT (1999 HESA) (see **Ch.4**)

The records of 344 graduates show that 174 entered full-time employment, 80 went on to further study (research, teacher training, law) and 28 were believed to be unemployed.

ARCHITECTURE (including **Architectural Technology**; see also **Building**)

NB The information supplied by the universities and colleges this year varies considerably and the offers listed below should be used as a first source of reference only. Many institutions will accept combinations of Advanced (AL), Advanced Subsidiary (AS) and Vocational Advanced (VA) level qualifications to achieve the required points total, but applicants must check web sites and prospectuses for full details of all offers. Grades and points totals shown should be regarded as the minimum levels to be achieved, but offers may be adjusted downwards when results are known. The points totals shown to the left of the institutions are for ease of reference only. It must not be assumed that tariff points are always used by institutions or that they can be substituted for an offer in grades. The level of an offer is not necessarily indicative of the quality of a course. To calculate your offers see Chapter 4 and the inside fold of the back cover.

Special subject requirements/preferences: A-Level: One A-Level from mathematics or physics may be required. **Belfast (Queen's)** English and mathematics. **De Montfort** Engineering drawing not acceptable. **Edinburgh** Physics. **South Bank** Art or English or history. **Strathclyde** Mathematics or physics. **London (AA School)** Two subjects, one can be art, but art and mathematics preferred. **GCSE:** English in all cases required. **Bath** All subjects at grade A or B with mathematics at grade A, double science or A-level physics. **Cardiff** Physics or science preferred. Seven/eight subjects grade A–C, A/B for mathematics and English preferred. **East London, Greenwich, South Bank** Art or design. **Edinburgh** Mathematics, and a foreign language. **Glasgow** English, mathematics grade A or B. **Huddersfield** Six subjects above grade C. **Manchester Met** Seven subjects at grade A or B. **Newcastle** Mathematics grade A or B if not at A-Level. **Nottingham** Mathematics or physics. **Oxford Brookes** Science. **Robert Gordon** English and mathematics or science. **Strathclyde** Science.

360 pts **and above**
    Cambridge – Offers, mainly in grades, vary between colleges (Architecture)
320 pts **Edinburgh** – ABB (1 sitting); (not gs) (Archit; Archit Des; Archit Hist)
    Kingston – 320 pts (inc 280 pts from 3x6u); (not gs); portfolio; (Architecture)
    Sheffield – ABB (Architecture)
300 pts **Bath** – BBB (Archit St)
    Cardiff – BBB (Archit St)
    Glasgow – BBB–CCDF (Civ Eng/Arch)
    Liverpool – ABC–BBB (Architecture courses)

Newcastle – BBB; (not gs) (Archit St; Archit Hist Theor)
Nottingham – BBB (Archit; Archit St)
280 pts **Bristol UWE** – 280–220 pts 18u pref/12u – ALs **or** ALs+ASs **or** VAs+/-
ALs/ASs; (Archit/Plan)
London (AA School) – BBC (Architecture) (see **Special subject**
requirements/preferences)
London (UCL) – BBC **or** 3ALs+AS/VA; (Architecture)
Manchester – BBC–BCC (Architecture)
Plymouth – 280–240 pts (Architecture)
Strathclyde – BBC (Archit St; Archit St/Euro)
260 pts **Belfast (Queen's)** – BCC (Architecture)
Edinburgh (CA) – BCC (art des/Engl/sci pref); (Architecture)
Glasgow – BCC (Architecture)
Liverpool John Moores – BCC **or** ALs+ASs; (Archit St)
Sheffield – BCC (Archit courses except under **320 pts**)
Sheffield Hallam – 260 pts approx (Archit Env Des)
Ulster – BCC (Archit Tech Mgt)
240 pts **Brighton** – 240 pts approx (Architecture)
Central England – 240 pts 12u – BCD–CCC; (Architecture)
Central Lancashire – 240 pts 12u – gs; (Archit Tech)
De Montfort (Leicester) – 240 pts – ALs **or** ALs+ASs **or** VAs+/-ALs/ASs; gs;
(Archit; Archit Des Tech/Prod)
Dundee – CCC (Architecture)
East London – 240 pts approx (Architecture)
Leeds – CCC (Archit Eng)
Manchester Met – CCC **or** ALs+ASs **or** VAs+/-ALs/ASs; (Architecture)
Napier – CCC (Archit Tech)
North London – 240 pts 1x12u **or** 2x6u; portfolio; (Architecture)
Northumbria – 240 pts approx (Archit Des Mgt; Archit Env Des; Archit Urb Cons)
Portsmouth – 240 pts: ALs **or** ALs+ASs **or** VAs; (Architecture)
Oxford Brookes – 240 pts approx (Architecture)
Robert Gordon – CCC (Archit; Archit/Lang)
220 pts **Glasgow** – CCD (Civ Eng/Archit)
Greenwich – 220 pts approx (Architecture)
Huddersfield – 220–180 pts approx (Archit Comp Aid Tech)
Kent (IAD) – 220 pts approx (Architecture)
Luton – 220–180 pts approx (Architecture)
Sheffield Hallam – 220 pts approx (Archit Tech)
South East Essex (Coll) – 220–180 pts (Archit Tech)
Wolverhampton – 220 pts 12u – CCD/BB **or** CC+b **or** VA12u BB; gs; (Int
Archit Des; Archit Des Tech)
200 pts **Coventry** – 200 pts approx (Archit Tech)
Lincolnshire & Humberside – 200 pts (Architecture)
Luton – 200 pts (Archit Tech)
Nottingham Trent – 200–180 pts approx (Archit Tech)
Plymouth – 200 pts approx (Archit Tech Env)
Robert Gordon – 200–180 pts approx (Archit Tech)
180 pts **Anglia** – 180 pts 12u – 2ALs **or** VA12u BC; portfolio; gs; (Archit; Archit Tech)
Derby – 180 pts approx (Archit Des)
Huddersfield – 180 pts approx (Archit St)
Kent (IAD) – 180 pts approx (Int Archit)
North East Wales (IHE) – 180–120 pts approx (Archit Tech Des)
South Bank – 180 pts approx (Architecture)
Westminster – BC–CC (Architecture)
160 pts **Bell (CT)** – DDE/CD (Archit Tech)
Central England – 160 pts 12u – DDE/CC; (Archit Tech)
Derby – 160 pts approx (Archit Tech Innov; Archit Cons)
Lincolnshire & Humberside – 160 pts (Archit/Archit Tech)

140 pts **Liverpool John Moores** – 140 pts approx (Archit Tech Mgt)
Wolverhampton – 140 pts 12u – CD **or** DD+ee **or** VA12u CD; Archit Tech Innov; Archit Cons; Archit Des Comb)
120 pts **and below**
Bolton (IHE) – 120 pts approx (Archit Tech)
Glamorgan – (Archit Bld Cons)
Glasgow Caledonian – (Archit Tech)
Huddersfield – 120 pts 12u – DE **or** D+dd **or** VA12u+/-AL/ASs; gs; (Archit Comp Aid Tech)
Huddersfield – 40 pts approx (Archit Fdn)
Northampton (UC) – EE (Archit Tech)
South Bank – (Archit Fdn course)

Leeds Met – (contact university)

Higher National Diploma courses
100 pts **and below**
Anglia (Archit Tech); Bell (CT) (Archit Tech); Brighton (Archit Tech); Cardiff (UWI); Derby; Huddersfield; Mid Kent (CHFE); Nescot; North East Wales (IHE); Northumbria (Archit St Tech); Nottingham Trent (Archit Tech); Oxford Brookes (Westminster); Robert Gordon (Archit Tech); Swansea (IHE) (Archit Stained Glass); UHI (Archit Tech).

Alternative Offers:

IB offers: Bath 32 pts H655 inc 6 or 5 in maths; Brighton 30–24 pts inc 12 pts 3 Highers; Cardiff 32 pts; Central England 28 pts; De Montfort 30 pts; East London 28 pts; Glasgow 30 pts; Greenwich 24 pts inc 12 pts 3 Highers; Heriot-Watt 30 pts; Kingston 28 pts; London (UCL) 32 pts; Luton 26 pts; Newcastle 30 pts; Nottingham 32 pts H555 in maths/physics/art; Plymouth 30 pts; Portsmouth 28 pts; South Bank 24 pts.

Irish offers: Brighton BBBB; Dundee BBCC; East London BBCC; Robert Gordon BCCC; Sheffield BBBB.

Scottish Qualifications: Dundee BBBC; Edinburgh ABBBC; Glasgow BBBC; Greenwich BBB; Heriot-Watt BBBB; Napier BBCC; Robert Gordon BBCC; Strathclyde ABBB/BBBBC.

CHOOSING YOUR COURSE (See also **Ch.1**)

> **Subject information:** Institutions offering Architecture have very similar courses (some variations are given below). An awareness of the relationship between people and the built environment is necessary, plus the ability to create and to express oneself in terms of drawings, paintings etc. Most Architecture Schools will expect to see a portfolio of art work, particularly drawings of buildings or parts of buildings. Some work experience or work shadowing is advisable prior to submitting the UCAS form (see **Appendix 1** for details of relevant professional associations). Courses in Building, Building Surveying, Civil Engineering, Estate Management, Land Surveying, Landscape Architecture, Quantity Surveying, Town and Country Planning and Urban Studies might also be considered as alternatives to Architecture.

Special features: Bath Common first year for students studying architecture and civil engineering. **Liverpool John Moores** The course includes graphics, economics and philosophy. **London (UCL)** Course largely based on design projects. **Manchester Met** As in other universities, field trips abroad are compulsory (costing approximately £100–£150 each year). Exchanges take place in France, Germany, Italy and Spain. **Robert Gordon** Years 3 and 4 in a French/German speaking country. **Sheffield Hallam** The Architecture and Environmental Design degree (subject to approval) includes options in conservation studies and a European language. *NOW CHECK PROSPECTUSES AND WEB SITES.*

Top universities and colleges (Teaching Quality) (see Ch.4): Bath; Cambridge; Cardiff; East London; Glasgow (SA); Greenwich; Heriot-Watt; London (UCL); Newcastle; Nottingham; Sheffield; Strathclyde; York (MA course); not all institutions assessed.

Top universities and colleges (Research) (see Ch.4): Bath; Cambridge; Cardiff; London (UCL); Newcastle; Nottingham; Sheffield.

Study opportunities abroad: Bath; Brighton; Central England; De Montfort; Dundee; East London; Edinburgh; Glasgow: Heriot-Watt; Kent (IAD); Kingston; Lincolnshire & Humberside; Liverpool John Moores; London (UCL); Manchester; Manchester Met; Newcastle; Northumbria; Oxford Brookes; Portsmouth; Robert Gordon; Sheffield; South Bank; Strathclyde.

Work opportunities abroad: Dundee; Greenwich; Heriot-Watt; Kent (IAD); Lincolnshire & Humberside; Liverpool John Moores; London (AA School); Manchester Met; Robert Gordon.

ADMISSIONS INFORMATION

Number of applicants per place (approx): Bath 15; Belfast (Queen's) 9; Cambridge 6.1; Cardiff 10; Central England 14; De Montfort 6; Derby 5; Dundee 8; East London 10; Edinburgh 18; Glasgow 16; Greenwich 6; Heriot-Watt 12; Kent (IAD) 4; Kingston 10; Liverpool John Moores 16; London (AA School) 2, (UCL) 16; Manchester 20; Manchester Met 25; Newcastle 11; North London 13; Nottingham 30; Oxford Brookes 15; Plymouth 7; Portsmouth 5; Robert Gordon 8; Sheffield 20; South Bank 7; Strathclyde 10.

Planning your UCAS personal statement (see Ch.4): You should have visited both historical and modern architectural sites: describe your interests and indicate which buildings or architects impress you (including modern architects). Contact architects in your area and try to obtain work shadowing/experience in their practices. Describe any such work you have done. Develop a portfolio of drawings and sketches of buildings and parts of buildings (you will probably need this for your interview). Show evidence of your reading on the history of architecture in Britain and modern architecture throughout the world. Discuss your preferences among the work of leading 20th century world architects. **De Montfort** Evidence of work experience and an emphasis on free-hand pencil drawing. (See **Appendix 1 for professional bodies**.)

Selection interviews (see Ch.4): The majority of universities and colleges interview or inspect portfolios for Architecture and most require a portfolio of art work. Bath (No); Bradford; Brighton; Cambridge; Cardiff (some); Coventry; Derby; Edinburgh (W); Huddersfield (T); Kingston; London (AA School); London (UCL); Manchester (No); Napier (No); Newcastle; Nottingham; Portsmouth (No); Sheffield (No); South Bank (W); Wolverhampton (No).

Interview questions (see Ch.4): Most Architecture departments will expect to see evidence of your ability to draw; portfolios are often requested at interview and in some cases, drawing tests are set prior to the interview. You should have a real awareness of architecture with some knowledge of historical styles as well as examples of modern architecture. If you have some work experience then you will be asked to describe the work being done in the architect's office and any site visits you have made. Questions in the past have included the following: What is the role of the architect in society? Discuss one historic and one 20th century building you admire. Who is your favourite architect? What sort of buildings do you want to design? Do you like the university buildings? Do you read any architectural journals? What are your views on the Millennium Dome? **Cambridge (Robinson)** Candidates who have taken, or are going to take, an A-level should bring with them their portfolio of work (GCSE work is not required). All candidates, including those who are not taking A-level art, should bring photographs of any three-dimensional material. Those not taught art should bring a sketch book (for us to assess drawing abilities) and analytical drawings of a new and old (pre-1900) building and a natural and human-made artifact. We are interested to see any graphic work in any medium that you would like to show us – please do not feel you should restrict your samples to only those with architectural reference. All evidence of sketching ability is helpful to us. (NB: All colleges at Cambridge and other university departments of architecture will seek similar evidence.)

Reasons for rejection (non-academic): Weak evidence of creative skills. Folio of art work does not give sufficient evidence of design creativity. Insufficient evidence of interest in architecture. Unwillingness to try free-hand sketching.

GAP YEAR ADVICE

Students should take every opportunity to travel and study architecture abroad. Work experience in an architect's office strongly recommended.

Institutions willing to defer entry after A-Levels: Bath; Brighton; Cardiff; Central England; De Montfort; Derby; Dundee; East London; Glasgow (No); Greenwich; Heriot-Watt; Kent (IAD); Kingston; Lincolnshire & Humberside; London (AA School); London (UCL) (No); Luton; Manchester; Manchester Met (No); Newcastle; Nottingham; Nottingham Trent (Archit Tech); Plymouth; Portsmouth; Sheffield; South Bank (No); Westminster (Archit).

AFTER RESULTS ADVICE

Institutions which may accept the same points score after A-Levels: Bath (No); Belfast (Queen's) (No); Brighton; Cardiff; Dundee; Glasgow; Heriot-Watt; Liverpool John Moores (No); London (UCL (No); Manchester; Manchester Met; Newcastle (No); Nottingham (No); Plymouth; Robert Gordon; Sheffield (No); South Bank; Strathclyde; Westminster (perhaps).

Institutions which may accept lower grades/points score after A-Levels: Bath; Brighton; Cardiff; Central England; Derby; Dundee; East London; Glasgow; Heriot-Watt; Kent (IAD); Lincolnshire & Humberside; Liverpool John Moores; London (UCL); Manchester Met; Newcastle; Nottingham; Plymouth; Portsmouth; Robert Gordon; Sheffield (No); South Bank; Strathclyde; Westminster (perhaps).

Offers to applicants repeating A-Levels: Higher Huddersfield; **Possibly higher** Brighton, De Montfort, Glasgow, Newcastle; **Same** Bath, Belfast (Queen's), Central England, Derby, Greenwich, Heriot-Watt, Kent (IAD), Kingston, Liverpool John Moores, Manchester, Manchester Met; North London, Nottingham, Oxford Brookes, Robert Gordon, Sheffield, South Bank.

Probable vacancies from June 2001 and in Clearing (see Ch.4): A large number of universities had vacancies last year when the highest offers were in the 280–240 pts range.

NEW GRADUATE DESTINATIONS AND EMPLOYMENT (1999 HESA) (see **Ch.4**)

Out of a survey of 1049 graduates, 645 entered full-time employment, 228 went on to further research (142 undertaking professional training) and 31 were believed to be unemployed.

ART AND DESIGN (General) (including Animation, Arts Management, Biological Imaging, Community Arts, Creative Studies, Design Management, Design Studies, Imaging Technology, Multimedia Design and Technology, Visual Arts, Visual Communication; see also **Media Studies**)

NB The information supplied by the universities and colleges this year varies considerably and the offers listed below should be used as a first source of reference only. Many institutions will accept combinations of Advanced (AL), Advanced Subsidiary (AS) and Vocational Advanced (VA) level qualifications to achieve the required points total, but applicants must check web sites and prospectuses for full details of all offers. Grades and points totals shown should be regarded as the minimum levels to be achieved, but offers may be adjusted downwards when results are known. The points totals shown to

CARDIFF SCHOOL OF ART & DESIGN

UWIC

UNIVERSITY OF WALES INSTITUTE, CARDIFF
ATHROFA PRIFYSGOL CYMRU, CAERDYDD

Courses
offered throughout
2002/2003

MA Courses
Ceramics, Fine Art, Design: Interior Architecture

BA (Hons) Courses
Fine Art, Ceramics, Interior Architecture
Graphic Communication, Contemporary Textile Practice,
Art & Aesthetics,
Advanced Vocational Certificate of Education in
Art & Design, Foundation Course in Art & Design

SCHOOL OF PRODUCT & ENGINEERING DESIGN

BA (Hons) Courses
Product Design, Multimedia Product Design

BSc (Hons) Courses
Product Design (with electronics), Product Design (with
mechanics), Computer Aided Product Design

HND Courses
Product Design & Technology, Product Design,
Architectural Design & Technology

*A range of part-time courses in areas of Art, Design,
Engineering and Building Studies is also offered.*

For further information, please contact:
Student Recruitment & Admissions

Tel: 029 2041 6044
Fax: 029 2041 6286
email: uwicinfo@uwic.ac.uk

the left of the institutions are for ease of reference only. It must not be assumed that tariff points are always used by institutions or that they can be substituted for an offer in grades. The level of an offer is not necessarily indicative of the quality of a course. To calculate your offers see Chapter 4 and the inside fold of the back cover.

This table covers a range of subjects under the heading of Art and Design. Degree courses are grouped together in subject tables in the following categories: **Art and Design (General), Art and Design (Fashion), Art and Design (Fine Art), Art and Design (Graphic Design), Art and Design (History), Art and Design (Industrial/Product Design), Art and Design (Three Dimesional Design).** *Alternatively, refer to the index at the back of the book. It should be noted that degree courses in Photography, Printing/Packaging/Publishing, and Textiles are listed in their individual subject tables.*

Art and Design courses can be divided into two main groups:

(1) Courses for which two A-level passes and five GCSE subjects at grade C or above are required as a minimum qualification in universities, colleges and institutes of higher education. An interview is not necessarily required.

(2) Courses which include the more specialist practical art courses. Entry is normally by way of a portfolio inspection and often through a Foundation course in Art for which A-level passes may not be necessary if applicants have a minimum of five subjects at GCSE grade C or above. An interview is usually required for these courses (see **Chapter 3** for modes of entry).

Applicants for Art and Design courses may choose from three application pathways – **Route A, Route B** or **Route A and B**:

Route A: The closing date for applications is 15 December (applicants for Fine Art at Oxford must submit their applications by 15 October). Candidates may enter up to six choices in their order in the UCAS *Directory*. Portfolios must be available for inspection.

Route B: Applications are submitted between 1 January and 24 March. Interviewing and portfolio inspection may be necessary and applicants may indicate their interview preference on a separate form. You can list up to three choices in the order that they are listed in the in the UCAS *Directory*.

Route A and B: Candidates may apply through both routes in which case six choices may be named with a maximum of three choices through through Route B.

Special subject requirements/preferences: A Central Portfolio Inspection scheme operates for courses at **Aberystwyth, Edinburgh, Lancaster, Newcastle** and **Reading**. The scheme is administered by the University of Reading. Art and Design courses via Routes A and B are listed in the UCAS *Directory*. **Bournemouth** A-Level art and mathematics preferred. **Birmingham (Westhill), Welsh (CMus/Dr)** Three grade Cs inc Engl lang.

A portfolio of art work will be required for the following courses.

300 pts	**Bournemouth** – 300 pts from 3ALs (art+maths pref) – (BBB) **or** VA (Art & Des)+AL/AS (maths); (Comp Vis Animat)
	Bradford – 300–280 pts 12u; gs; (Comp Animat/Spec Efcts; Electron Imag/Media Comms; Media Tech/Prod; Interact Sys Vid Gms Des)
	Brunel – 300 pts 2x6u – ALs **or** ALs+ASs **or** VAs+/-ALs/ASs; (Multim Tech/Des)
	⎯ Reading – BBB (Art/Psy)
280 pts	**Central England** – 280 pts; gs; portfolio; (Vis Comm)
	De Montfort – 280 pts (Multim Des)
	Keele – BBC–BCC (Vis Arts courses)
	Manchester – BBC–BCC (Art Arch Anc Wrld)
	Reading – BBC (Art/Hist Art)
260 pts	**Lancaster** – BCC (Art courses; Crea Arts)
	London (UCL-Slade SA) – BCC **or** 3ALs+AS/VA; (Des/Ital)
	Reading – BCC (Art/Phil; Typo Graph Comm)
	Salford – 260–160 pts approx (Des St)

240 pts **Aberystwyth** – ALs+ASs; portfolio; gs; (Fine Art courses)
Brunel – 240–200 pts approx (Ind Des Tech)
Central England – 240 pts; gs; portfolio; (Mgt Des Comm; BA Art Des)
Central Lancashire – 240 pts approx (Web/Multim)
Derby – 240 pts 12u – CCC **or** CC+cc **or** VA12u AB; portfolio; (App Arts Fdn)
Greenwich – 240 pts approx (Multim Tech)
London (Gold) – CCC; portfolio (Des; Eco-Des)
Nottingham Trent – 240 pts approx (Des St; Multim Prod; Multim Tech; Des TV; Decr Arts)
Sheffield Hallam – 240 pts approx (Art Comb; Des Comb)
South Bank – CCC/CC (Arts Mgt)
Staffordshire – CCC **or** CCD+AS(40 pts) **or** VAs; gs; (Des Tech courses)
Surrey (IAD/UC) – 240–180 pts approx (Des Mgt)
220 pts **Blackburn (Coll)** – CCD (Integ Arts – Fine Art)
Bradford – 220 pts 12u; gs; (Vrtl Des/Innov)
Central England – 220 pts approx (Multim Tech)
Cheltenham & Glos (CHE) – 220–180 pts approx (Vis Arts/Engl; Vis Arts/Media Comm; Vis Arts/Psy; Vis Arts/Spo Exer Sci)
Greenwich – 220 pts approx (Arts Mgt; Arts Mgt/Lang)
Hertfordshire – 220 pts approx (Multim Tech)
Plymouth – CCD (Vis Arts Comb; Media Arts)
St Mark & St John (Coll) – 220 pts approx (Art Des/Media St; Art Des/Pub Rel; Art Des/Leis Tour St)
South East Essex (Coll) – 220–180 pts (Media Prod/Tech; Multim Tech)
Surrey (IAD/UC) – 220–180 pts approx (Des Mgt)
Teesside – 220 pts approx (Crea Vis; Des Mark)
Ulster – CCD (Tech Des)
200 pts **Bangor** – ALs **or** ALs+ASs **or** VAs+/-ALs/ASs; gs; (BEd Des Tech)
Bradford – 200–180 pts 12u; gs; (Fdn Electron Imag)
Central Lancashire – 200–180 pts 12u; gs; (Vis Cult/Film Media St)
Central Lancashire – 200–180 pts 12u – Art Fdn **or** AL art/des; gs; (Design courses)
Chester (Coll) – 200 pts approx (Art courses)
De Montfort (Leicester) – 200 pts – ALs **or** VAs+/-ALs/ASs (inc C); (Multim Des)
Glamorgan – 200–180 pts approx (Vis Arts courses; Des; Art Prac)
King Alfred's Winchester (Coll) – 200 pts approx (Des/Tech; Art courses)
Liverpool John Moores – 200 pts (inc ALs art/des pref); portfolio; (Multim Arts)
Reading – BB–EE (Art)
Robert Gordon – BB (Des Dig Media)
Salford – 200–120 pts approx (Vis Arts)
Wolverhampton – 200–160 pts 12u – DDD/CC **or** CD+d **or** VA12u CC+/-AL/ASs; gs; (Des St; Pblc Art)
Wolverhampton – 200–160 pts 12u – DDD/CDE/CC **or** DD+b **or** VA12u CC; gs; (200 pts 12u) (Des Tech)
Worcester (UC) – 200 pts approx (Art QTS)
180 pts **Blackpool & Fylde (Coll)** – 180 pts 12u; (Tech Inf Illus; Graph Des; Sci Nat Hist Illus)
Brighton – 180 pts approx (Des/Tech QTS)
Central Lancashire – 180–160 pts 12u; gs; (Vis Cult)
Cheltenham & Glos (CHE) – 180–140 pts approx (All Art courses except under **220 pts**)
Chichester (UC) – 180 pts approx (Art)
Coventry – 180 pts approx (Art – BTEC/Fdn route preferred)
Derby – 180 pts 12u – BC **or** DD+dd **or** VA12u BC; gs; (Vis Cult; Biol Imag; Prod Des; Arts Thera)
Glamorgan – 180 pts – 2ALs **or** 2ALs+2ASs; gs; (Des Vis Comm; Des Media)

Choosing your university and degree course?

... then why not contact **Brian Heap** the author of *Degree Course Offers* for a personal or telephone consultation for advice on ...

... choosing A-level subjects
... choosing degree or diploma courses
... choosing the right university or college
... completing your UCAS form
... preparing for interview
... deciding what to do in August if you haven't got the right A-levels
... lectures to schools, colleges and other groups

For details of services and consultation fees contact:
The Higher Education Advice and Planning Service
Phone or fax: 01386 859355

Greenwich – 180 pts approx (Des Tech)
Huddersfield – 180 pts 12u – 2ALs (inc A/B art+des) **or** VAs (160 pts)+C; (not gs); portfolio; (Crea Imag; Multim Des; Vrtl Rlty Des)
Liverpool Hope (Coll) – 180 pts approx (Art courses; Art Comb)
North East Wales (IHE) – 180–120 pts approx (Design)
Northampton (UC) – 180 pts approx (Vis Arts)
Nottingham Trent – 180 pts approx (Des Tech Educ)
Portsmouth – 180 pts – ALs **or** ALs+ASs **or** VAs; gs; portfolio; (Restor/Decr St; Art/Tech)
St Martin's (Coll) – CDE–DD (Art Des)
Salford – 180/180–160 pts approx inc non-art subject (Des St Comb Hons)
Staffordshire – 180 pts (inc 160 pts from 2ALs); gs; (Art/Des/Media)
Welsh (CMus/Dr) – 180 pts approx or good portfolio (Thea Des)
Westminster – 180 pts approx (Contemp Media Prac)

160 pts **Anglia** – 160 pts 12u – AE/BE/CC (CC for Art/Art Hist); gs; (Art Comb; Art/Art Hist; Mod Vis Cult; Vis Arts Mgt)
Birmingham (Westhill) – 160 pts 12u – ALs **or** C+ASs **or** VAs+/-ALs/ASs; gs; (Hum; Crea Arts)
Bishop Grosseteste (Coll) – CC (inc art) **or** C+c **or** VA12u CC; portfolio; (Art)
Blackpool & Fylde (Coll) – CC (Sci Nat Hist Illus; Des (Tech Inf Illus)
Canterbury Christ Church (UC) – CC (Art joint courses)
Cumbria (CAD) – 160 pts – CC **or** ASs (contact coll) **or** VA + portfolio; (Edit Des; Edit Photo; Des Perf; Des Crafts; Multim Des; Media Prod; Vis Arts)
De Montfort – 160 pts – ALs **or** ALs+ASs **or** VA (Art Des)+/-ALs/ASs; portfolio; (not gs) (Contemp Decr Crafts; Decr Artfcts; Des Mgt)
Hull (Scarborough) – 160 pts approx (Art Des QTS; Vis Art/Art Hist)
Leeds (Bretton Hall) – CC (Arts Educ)
London (Gold) – CC (Des Fdn)
London Guildhall – CC–CD (Des St; Restor/Cons)
Luton – 160 pts approx (Des courses)
Manchester Met (Crewe) – 160 pts 6u approx; (not gs) (2 subjs from Dance/Drama/Mus/Vis Arts/Writ)
Napier – CC (Graph Comm Mgt)
Newman (CHE) – CC (Art Des courses)
Newport (UWCN) – 160–140 pts approx (Art courses)
North London – 160 pts 2x6u **or** 1x12u; (Multim Tech)
Ripon & York (Coll) – CC–CD (Art/Des; Art/Engl Lit)
St Mark & St John (Coll) – 160 pts approx (Art Des)
Sheffield Hallam – 160 pts approx (Des Tech Comb)
Surrey Roehampton – 160 pts – ALs **or** ALs+ASs **or** VAs+/-ALs/ASs; (Art Pblc Space)
Swansea (IHE) – 160 pts approx (Art/Engl St)

140 pts **Bath Spa (UC)** – 140–120 pts 12u – CD **or** ALs+ASs **or** VA12u CD; (not gs) (Crea Arts; Des Tech Comb)
Bolton (IHE) – CD (Art Des courses; Vis Art courses)
Bradford (Coll) – 140 pts approx (Crea Thera St)
Central Lancashire – 140 pts approx (Des Manuf)
Edinburgh (CA) – 140 pts approx – 2ALs **or** AL+2ASs (inc Engl+art des); (Comb St Art/Des)
Liverpool John Moores – 140 pts 1x6u – ALs **or** ALs+ASs **or** VA12u **or** VA6u+AL; portfolio; (Innov Des)
Newport (UWCN) – 140–120 pts – ALs **or** ALs+ASs **or** VAs+/-ALs/ASs; portfolio; (Media/Vis Cult; Multim;; Des Tech courses)
Ripon & York (Coll) – CD (Des Tech/Mgt St)
Sunderland – 140 pts – 2ALs **or** ALs+ASs **or** VA12u+/-ALs/ASs; gs; BTEC accepted; (Arts Des; Electron Media Des; Illus/Des; Perf Arts St)

120 pts **Derby** – 120 pts 12u – 2ALs **or** VA12u (120 pts); gs; (Des Comb)
Manchester Met – 120 pts approx; (Interact Art)

Middlesex – DD (Des Tech; Vis Comm)
Swansea (IHE) – 120 pts approx (Pntg/Drg)
Worcester (UC) – 120 pts 12u – DD **or** ALs+ASs **or** VAs+/-ALs/ASs; gs; (Art Des)

100 pts **and below or other selection criteria (Foundation course, interview and portfolio inspection)**

Abertay Dundee (Comp Arts); Barnsley (Coll) (Comb); Bournemouth (AI) (Animat); Bradford (Art Des); Brighton (Vis Art/Thea); Cardiff (UWI) (Art); Carmarthenshire (CTA); Chichester (UC) (Art major; Art/Music/Dance; Commun); City College Manchester (CFE); City/London (SA) (Cons St); Cleveland (CAD) (Des Craft Enter); Colchester (Inst) (Des); Coventry (Art Craft St; Arts Prac); Cumbria (CAD) (Vis Arts; Des Crafts; Edit Des; Multimedia Des); De Montfort (Dec Crafts); Derby (Vis Comm; App Arts); Dundee (Animat; Drg/Pntg; Time-based Art); Edinburgh (CA) (Comb St Art/Des); Falkirk (CHFE) (Des); Hertfordshire (App Arts Pract); Huddersfield (Des Tech); Kent (IAD) (Time-based Art Comb; Vis Comm); Leeds (CAD) (Vis Comm); Liverpool Hope (Coll) (Des); Liverpool John Moores (Vis St courses); Liverpool (LIPA) (Perf Des; Art Des; Commun Arts); London (CGAS) (Cons); London (Gold) (Art); London Inst (Camberwell) (Vis Arts Cons), London Inst (Central Saint Martins), London Inst (Chelsea) (Pblc Art), London Inst (CP) (Retail Des); Lowestoft (Coll); Manchester Met (Des/Art/Dir; Contemp Crafts; Crea Arts; Interac Arts+A-Level); Nescot (Des/Tech; Imag Tech); North East Wales (IHE) (Animat; Des Mgt; Animat Comb; Des Crafts); Northern (Coll) (Ex Arts – check with admissions tutor); Norwich (SAD) (Cult St; Vis St); Nottingham Trent (Dec Arts); Plymouth (Multim; App Arts; Des/Ital); Portsmouth (Comm Des; Vis St); Ravensbourne (CDC) (Des courses); Reading (Art); Robert Gordon (Des Craft); St Helens (Coll) (Multim Prod); Salford (Vis Arts); Solihull (Coll) (Des Media); Southampton (Inst) (Des); Staffordshire (Des; Des Mgt; Fdn Art/Des; Hist Art); Suffolk (Coll) (Art Des courses); Surrey (IAD/UC) (Animat; Vis Comm); Teesside (Des Mkt; Vis); Ulster (Des; Art Des Comb; Vis Comm); Wiltshire (Coll) (Des).

Leeds Met – (contact university)

Diploma of Higher Education courses
80 pts **and below approx + portfolio**

Bath Spa (UC); Central (Sch Sp/Dr) (Des); Worcester (UC).

Higher National Diploma courses
180 pts **and below approx + portfolio**

Barking (Coll); Barnsley (Coll); Bolton (IHE); Bournemouth (AI) (Arts Admin); Bridgwater (Coll); Brighton; Cardiff (UWI); Carmarthenshire (Coll) (Des Crafts); Colchester (Inst); Craven (Coll); Cumbria (CAD); Glamorgan (CADT); Glasgow Caledonian (Med Illus); Glasgow (CBP) (Imag Med Illus); Gloucestershire (CAT) tel 01452 426500 for an informal interview; Hastings (Coll); Herefordshire (CAD); Hertfordshire; Leicester South Fields (Coll); Liverpool (CmC); Lowestoft (Coll); Mid Cheshire (Coll); Mid Glamorgan (CAD); Mid Warwickshire (Coll); Newcastle (Coll); North Warwickshire/Hinckley (Coll); North East Worcestershire (Coll); Oxfordshire (SAD); St Helens (Coll); Sheffield (Coll); Sheffield (Hallam); South Warwickshire (Coll); Southwark (Coll); Walsall (CA); Warrington (CI); Wigan & Leigh (Coll); Wirral Met (Coll); Wolverhampton.

Alternative Offers:

IB offers: Anglia 28 pts; Bristol 30 pts inc H6; Brunel 26–24 pts; Buckingham 24 pts; Dartington (CA) 26 pts; De Montfort (Comb) 30–26 pts; Glamorgan 24 pts; Plymouth 28 pts; Ripon & York (Coll) 30–27 pts; Staffordshire 24 pts; Surrey Roehampton 24 pts.

Irish offers: London Guildhall CCCCC.

Scottish Qualifications: Abertay Dundee (Comp Arts) AABB; Dundee CCC; Edinburgh (CA) (Fine Art) BBBB; Heriot-Watt CCC (Tex Des) BBC; Napier CCC; Robert Gordon BBCC.

CHOOSING YOUR COURSE (See also **Ch.1**)

Subject information: This is a wide field comprising many aspects of two-dimensional and three-dimensional work as well as art history. The well-motivated art student (almost twice as many females as males) with real ability will be a self-starter who never needs to be advised to choose this subject. (See **Appendix 1** for contact details of professional associations.) All practical art and design courses could also be considered, including Advertising, Architecture, Communications Studies, Film Studies, Media Studies and Landscape Architecture.

Special features: Bournemouth Design Management is offered with an emphasis on engineering. **Central Lancashire** A course in Creative Advertising is available. **Lincolnshire & Humberside** Phonic Art (art and sound) can be studied. **London (UCL Slade – SA)** The programme 'is taught by artists for the education of artists'. **London Guildhall** Restoration and conservation can be studied. **Plymouth** A course is offered with Italian with the third year in Rome, Milan or Urbino. **Salford** Digital 3D Design for the entertainment industry is available. **Sunderland** The Art and Desgin BA course offers 18 subjects: minimum of two and a maximum of four are taken in year 1 with two specialist subjects chosen in years 2 and 3. **Teesside** Design and Crafts for the entertainment industry covers film, theatre, television, heritage museum display and the leisure industries. NOW CHECK PROSPECTUSES AND WEB SITES.

Top universities and colleges (Teaching Quality) (see Ch.4): Cardiff (UWI); Derby; Manchester Met; Winchester (SA); see **Art & Design (Fine Art)**, **(Graphic Design)**, **(Industrial/Product Design)**, **(Three Dimensional Design)**; not all institutions assessed.

Top universities and colleges (Research) (see Ch.4): Bournemouth; Brighton; Brunel; Coventry; Dundee; London (Gold), (UCL); Middlesex; Oxfordshire (SAD); Reading; Sheffield; Southampton; Westminster; Wimbledon (SA); Ulster.

Study opportunities abroad: Bath Spa (UC); Blackpool & Fylde (Coll); Cheltenham & Glos (CHE); Chichester (UC); De Montfort; Derby; Dundee; East Anglia; Kent (IAD); Lancaster; Leeds (CAD); London (Inst); Manchester Met; Newcastle; Norwich (SAD); Nottingham Trent; Plymouth; Robert Gordon; South Bank; Staffordshire; Surrey Roehampton; Wolverhampton; Worcester (UC).

Work opportunities abroad: Aberystwyth; Blackpool & Fylde (Coll); Bristol; Brunel; De Montfort (Des Crafts); Napier; Suffolk (Coll).

ADMISSIONS INFORMATION

Number of applicants per place (approx): Aberystwyth 5; Bath Spa (UC) (Crea Art) 18; Birmingham 20; Birmingham (Westhill) 4; Bournemouth (Des Vis) 3, (Crea Adv Des) 3, (Comp Vis) 16; Brunel 14; Camberwell (SAC) 2; Canterbury Christ Church (UC) 3; Central Lancashire 4; Cheltenham & Glos (CHE) 8; Chichester (UC) 3; Cumbria (CAD) 5; Dartington (CA) 4; De Montfort (Vis Cult) 5, Des Mgt) 3, (Multim Des) 12; Derby 4; East Anglia 7; Glamorgan 7; Lancaster (Vis Arts) 15; Leeds (CAD) 5; London (Gold) 10; London Inst (Chelsea) 2; London (SOAS) 4; Manchester Met 10; Newman (CHE) (BEd) 5; Newcastle 23; Norwich (SAD) 3; Nottingham Trent (Des St) 13; Plymouth (Fine Art/Lang) 25; Portsmouth 20, (Art Des Media) 13; Ripon & York (Coll) 3; Robert Gordon 5; St Martin's (CHE) (Comb) 15, (QTS) 12; Sheffield Hallam 15; South Bank (Arts Mgt) 5; Southampton (Inst) 1; Staffordshire 7; Surrey Roehampton 4; Swansea (IHE) 5; Teesside 2; Welsh (CMus/Dr) 6; West Herts (Coll) 3.

Planning your UCAS personal statement (see Ch.4): Admissions tutors will look for a wide interest in aspects of art and design. Discuss the type of work and the range of media you have explored through your studies to date. Refer to visits to art galleries and museums and give your opinions of the styles of painting and sculpture, both historical and present-day. Mention art-related hobbies. **Aberystwyth** Looks for attendance at evening classes for art (if not at A-level), visits to galleries and related hobbies, for example reading, cinema, music, literature. **Coventry** What Foundation course/BTEC experience has been the most significant? Show the nature of your external involvement in art. Not interested in potted life-history or lists of irrelevant jobs. See also **Appendix 1**. See also under **Art and Design (Graphic Design)**.

Selection interviews (see Ch.4): Manchester (No); Staffordshire (Des/Tech) (No); most institutions will interview and require a portfolio of work.

Interview questions (see Ch.4): Your portfolio of work will be discussed. You should spend some time in organising this portfolio. Finished pieces of work should be mounted, titled and dated and a good selection of types of work in different media and sketch books should be included. Questions will vary, for example: How often do you visit art galleries and exhibitions? Discuss the last exhibition you visited. What are the the reactions of your parents to your choice of course and career? How do they link up with art? Do you feel that modern art has anything to contribute to society compared with earlier art? Is a brick a work of art? **Oxfordshire (SAD)** A drawing examination will be taken by all interviewed candidates (two drawings in pencil or pen and ink from a number of possible subjects).

Admissions tutors' advice: Show signs of life – no apathy! Be eager and enthusiastic.

Reasons for rejection (non-academic): (Des Mgt) Lack of enthusiasm for design issues or to acquire design skills. Poorly presented practical work. Lack of interest or enthusiasm in contemporary visual arts. Lack of knowledge and experience of the art and design industry.

GAP YEAR ADVICE

Travel and visits to art galleries and museums strongly recommended by many universities and colleges.

Institutions willing to defer entry after A-Levels: Aberystwyth (considered individually); Blackpool & Fylde (Coll); Birmingham; Bournemouth; Brighton; Brunel; Buckingham; Central Lancashire; Cheltenham & Glos (CHE); De Montfort; Derby; Dundee (No); Glamorgan; King Alfred's Winchester (Coll); Lancaster (No); Liverpool Hope (Coll); London (UCL – Slade SA); Luton; Manchester Met (No); Napier; Newcastle (No); Northampton (UC); Nottingham Trent; Plymouth; Sheffield Hallam (No); South Bank; Staffordshire; Surrey Roehampton; Swansea (IHE); Thames Valley; West Herts (Coll); Wolverhampton; York.

AFTER RESULTS ADVICE

Institutions which may accept the same points score after A-Levels: Bath Spa (UC) (No); Brighton; Derby; Glamorgan (No); Leeds (Bretton Hall); Newman (CHE); Ripon & York (Coll); South Bank; Staffordshire.

Institutions which may accept lower grades/points score after A-Levels: Aberystwyth; Blackpool & Fylde (Coll); Brunel; Cheltenham & Glos (CHE); De Montfort; East Anglia; Glasgow; Leeds; Liverpool Hope (Coll); Manchester Met; Napier; Northampton (UC); Salford; South Bank; Surrey Roehampton; Swansea (IHE).

Offers to applicants repeating A-Levels: Higher Brunel; **Possibly higher** Brighton, Essex; **Same** Aberystwyth, Blackpool & Fylde (Coll), Canterbury Christ Church (UC), Leeds, Leeds (Bretton Hall), Napier, Newcastle, Salford, Staffordshire.

Probable vacancies from June 2001 and in Clearing (see Ch.4): Vacancies are likely: contact institutions for further information.

NEW GRADUATE DESTINATIONS AND EMPLOYMENT (1999 HESA) (see **Ch.4**)

From a survey of 7492 graduates, 4125 entered full-time employment, 750 went on to further study and 693 were reported to be unemployed. These figures include Fashion, Design Studies and general Art and Design courses.

ART AND DESIGN (Fashion) (including Beauty Therapy, Fashion/Textile Design and Fashion Marketing; see also Textile Courses)

NB The information supplied by the universities and colleges this year varies considerably and the offers listed below should be used as a first source of reference only. Many institutions will accept combinations of Advanced (AL), Advanced Subsidiary (AS) and Vocational Advanced (VA) level qualifications to achieve the required points total, but applicants must check web sites and prospectuses for full details of all offers. Grades and points totals shown should be regarded as the minimum levels to be achieved, but offers may be adjusted downwards when results are known. The points totals shown to the left of the institutions are for ease of reference only. It must not be assumed that tariff points are always used by institutions or that they can be substituted for an offer in grades. The level of an offer is not necessarily indicative of the quality of a course. To calculate your offers see Chapter 4 and the inside fold of the back cover.

Special subject requirements/preferences: GCSE: Somerset (CAT) English and preferably a foreign language grade C or above. A Foundation Art course may be a condition of entry to some courses. Students may be interviewed and portfolios scrutinised. Applicants should note that for some of these courses, there are two application pathways (Routes A or B) or both. See the general notes under **Art and Design (General)** and **Chapter 3**; refer to the UCAS *Directory* for course details.

It should be noted that a good interview and portfolio of work will often be acceptable in lieu of the stipulated A-level grades.

280 pts **Central England** – 280 pts; gs; portfolio; (Tex Des)
240 pts **Central England** – 240 pts; gs; portfolio; (Fash Des)
    Nottingham Trent – 240 pts approx (Fash Tex Mgt; Fash Knit; Fash Mark Comm)
    Rose Bruford (Coll) – 240 pts approx (Cost Prod)
    Somerset (CAT) – 240 pts approx (Des (Fash) (Fash Tex) (Tex Surf Patt) (Surf Patt) (Tex))
    Surrey (IAD/UC) – 240 pts approx (Fash Prom Illus)
220 pts **Central Lancashire** – 220 pts 12u (inc AL art/des/photo/media/film st); gs; (Fash Prom St/AV Media St; Fash Prom St/Journal; Fash Prom St/Mark)
    South East Essex (Coll) – 220–180 pts (Fashion)
    Southampton (Inst) – 200 pts approx (Fashion)
200 pts **Central Lancashire** – 200–180 pts 12u (inc Fdn art or AL art/des); gs; (Fash Prom/Des)
    Liverpool John Moores – 200 pts (inc AL/VA art/des pref); (Fash/Tex Des)
    Wolverhampton – 200–160 pts 12u – DDD/CC **or** CD+d **or** VA (CC overall)+/- ALs/ASs; gs; (Des Int Tex)
180 pts **Huddersfield** – 12u – ALs **or** ALs+Ass **or** VAs+/-ALs/ASs; Fdn course pref; (Fash Manuf Mark Prom; Surf Patt)
    Manchester Met – 180 pts approx (Fash Des Tech; Embr)
160 pts **De Montfort** – 160 pts – ALs **or** ALs+ASs **or** VAs (Art Des)+/-ALs/ASs; portfolio; (Fash St; Fash Des; Contour Fash)
    Heriot-Watt (Scottish Borders) – CC (Tex Des Fash Des/Mark)
    Leeds (Bretton Hall) – CC–CD (Fash)
    London Inst (CFash) – CC minimum (Fash Mgt; Fash Comm/Prom; Cost Mk-up Perf Arts)
140 pts **Bath Spa (UC)** – 140 pts approx (Tex Des St/Art)
    Edinburgh (CA) – 140 pts approx: 2ALs **or** AL+2ASs (nc Engl+art des); (Fash; Perf Cost; Tex)
    Newport (UWCN) – 140–120 pts: ALs **or** ALs+ASs **or** VAs+/-ALs/ASs; portfolio; (Fash Des)
120 pts **Huddersfield** – ALs (inc C art) **or** VA12u (inc art); (MText; Tex Des; Crea Tex Crafts)

100 pts   and below or other relevant criteria (Foundation course, interview and port-folio inspection)

Bournemouth (AI) (Cost Scrn/Stage; Fash); Bristol UWE (Fash/Tex Des; Brighton (Fash Tex/Des courses); Buckinghamshire Chilterns (UC); Cleveland (CAD) (Int Tex/Surf Patt); Croydon (Coll) (Fash Bus); De Montfort (Fash St); Derby (Fash St); East London (Fash/Tex); Kent (IAD) (Fash Des; Euro Fash); Kingston; Leeds (CAD) (Cloth/Fash; Prtd Tex/Surf Patt Des); London (Gold) (Tex); London Inst (Central Saint Martins) (Fash; Tex Des); London Inst (CFash) (Des Tech Fash; Fash; Fash Mgt; Prod Dev); Loughborough (Tex); Manchester Met (Fash; Embr); Middlesex (Fash); Northbrook (Coll) (Mnswr Des); Northumbria (Fash; Fash Mark); Norwich (SAD) (Tex Art); Ravensbourne (CDC) (Fash/Tex); Reading (CSAD) (Fash); Salford (Fash Tex); Somerset (CAT) (Fash/Tex; Fash); Southampton (Winchester) (Fash; Tex Art; Tex Des); Southampton (Inst) (Fash; Tex); Staffordshire (Surf Patt); Stockport (CFHE); Surrey (IAD/UC) (Fash; Tex); Sutton Coldfield (Coll) (Fash/Tex); Westminster (Fash).

Diploma in Higher Education

Huddersfield (Tex Des); Salford.

Higher National Diploma courses (100 pts and below approx + portfolio)

Batley (SA); Birmingham City (Coll); Blackburn (Coll) (Tex Des); Bournemouth (Fash Tex); Bournemouth (AI) (Des (Fash/Fash Mark)); Carmarthenshire (Coll); Cleveland (CAD); Crawley (Coll) (Bty Thera inc gs); Croydon (Coll); Cumbria (CAD) (Tex; Fash/Tex); De Montfort; (Tex); Dewsbury (Coll); Doncaster (Coll); Dudley (CT) (Fash); Glasgow (CC) (Bty Thera); Gloucestershire (CAT) (Bty Thera); Kent (IAD); Lincolnshire & Humberside; Llandrillo (Coll); London Inst (CFash); Manchester Met; Mid Cheshire (Coll); Middlesex; Newcastle (Coll) (Tex); North Warwickshire/Hinckley (Coll); Northbrook (Coll) (Tex); Northampton (UC); Norwich (SAD) (Tex); Nottingham Trent, Oxfordshire (SAD); Plymouth (CAD); Portsmouth; Salford; Shrewsbury (CAT); Solihull (Coll) (Fash/Knit/Tex); South Downs (Coll) (Bty Thera); Southampton City (Coll) (Bty Thera); Southampton (Inst); Southwark (Coll); Stafford (Coll); Tameside (Coll); UHI (Bty Thera); York (CFHE); Yorkshire Coast (CFHE).

Alternative Offers:

Scottish Qualifications: Glasgow Caledonian BBC.

CHOOSING YOUR COURSE (See also **Ch.1**)

Subject information: Fashion is a popular subject with about half the applicants accepted on to courses. These specialised degree courses almost always follow Foundation Art courses. See also **Textile Courses** (Subject information). See also **Appendix 1**.

Special Features: Huddersfield Pathways in design, pattern cutting, garment construction, art history, marketing and promotion. **Kingston** Industrial links with top fashion design companies. **Ravensbourne (CDC)** 100 first-choice applicants for 34 places. Places cannot be held open for students taking a gap year. **Surrey (IAD/UC)** (Fash Prom) Work placement in fashion with a magazine, newspaper, television or public relations. **Westminster** Subsidiary subjects include business studies, fashion jewellery and knitwear design. International contacts with Italy. Industrial sponsorships. *NOW CHECK PROSPECTUSES AND WEB SITES.*

Top universities and colleges (Teaching Quality) (see Ch.4): Manchester Met; not all institutions assessed.

Top universities and colleges (Research) (see Ch.4): See under **Art and Design (General)**.

Study opportunities abroad: Bristol UWE; Central England; Leeds (CAD); Liverpool John Moores; London (Gold); London Inst (CFash); Manchester Met; Ravensbourne (CDC); Salford; Somerset (CAT).

Work opportunities abroad: Brighton; Central Lancashire; Leeds (CAD); Liverpool John Moores; Manchester Met; Nottingham Trent (Kntwr); Ravensbourne (CDC); Salford; Somerset (CAT); Westminster.

ADMISSIONS INFORMATION

Number of applicants per place (approx): Brighton 6; Bristol UWE 4; Central England 12; Central Lancashire 4; Cheltenham & Glos (CHE) 7; De Montfort 5; Derby (Tex Des) 2; Heriot-Watt (Scottish Borders) 6; Huddersfield 4, (Tex Des) 2; Kingston 5; Leeds (CAD) 4; Liverpool John Moores 6; London Inst (CFash) (Fash Mgt) 20, (Central St Martins) 5; London (Gold) 5; Loughborough (CA) 5; Manchester Met 3; Middlesex 5; Northumbria 8; Surrey (IAD/UC) 8, (Tex) 5; Wolverhampton 2.

Planning your UCAS personal statement (see Ch.4): An interest in this broad field may come through visits to exhibitions, department stores and through personal contacts, work experience, work (making and doing skills, if any, for example, pattern-cutting, sewing), work observation in textile firms, fashion houses, even the costume departments in theatres. These contacts and visits should be described in detail together with your knowledge of the types of fabrics and production processes. Give opinions on trends in haute couture, and show awareness of the work of others. Provide evidence of materials handling (see also **Appendix 1**). **London Inst (CFash)** (Fash Prom) Give details of written work (school magazine etc), work placement in media (journalism, broadcasting etc). See also under **Art and Design (Graphic Design)**.

Selection interviews (see Ch.4): Most institutions interview and require a portfolio of work. **Brighton** Application route B recommended for students on pre-degree courses.

Examples of interview questions (see Ch.4): Questions mostly originate from student's portfolio. **Oxfordshire (SAD)** A drawing examination is taken by all candidates who are interviewed (2 drawings in pencil or pen and ink).

Reasons for rejection (non-academic): Portfolio work not up to standard. Not enough research. Not articulate at interview. Lack of sense of humour and inflexibility. Narrow perspective. Lack of resourcefulness, self-motivation and organisation. Complacency, lack of verbal, written and self-presentation skills.

AFTER RESULTS ADVICE

Probable vacancies from June 2001 and in Clearing (see Ch.4): Vacancies almost certain – contact institutions.

NEW GRADUATE DESTINATIONS AND EMPLOYMENT (1999 HESA) (see **Ch.4**)

See under **Art and Design (General)**.

ART AND DESIGN (Fine Art) (including Printing, Printmaking and Sculpture) (see also **Art and Design (Graphic Design)**)

NB The information supplied by the universities and colleges this year varies considerably and the offers listed below should be used as a first source of reference only. Many institutions will accept combinations of Advanced (AL), Advanced Subsidiary (AS) and Vocational Advanced (VA) level qualifications to achieve the required points total, but applicants must check web sites and prospectuses for full details of all offers. Grades and points totals shown should be regarded as the minimum levels to be achieved, but offers may be adjusted downwards when results are known. The points totals shown to the left of the institutions are for ease of reference only. It must not be assumed that

tariff points are always used by institutions or that they can be substituted for an offer in grades. The level of an offer is not necessarily indicative of the quality of a course. To calculate your offers see Chapter 4 and the inside fold of the back cover.

Special subject requirements/preferences: None. Foundation Art courses may be required for entry to courses listed below. Students may be interviewed and portfolios scrutinised. Applicants should note that for these courses there are two application pathways (Routes A or B) or both. Read the general comments under **Art and Design (General)** and refer to the UCAS *Directory* for course details. **GCSE: Oxford** Usually grade As.

It should be noted that a good interview and portfolio of work will often be acceptable instead of the stipulated A-Level grades.

320 pts	**and above**
	Oxford – Offers vary between candidates (Fine Art)
	Oxford Brookes – ABB/BC (Fine Art/Law)
300 pts	**Exeter** – BBB–BBC (Fine Art courses)
280 pts	**Leeds** – BBC (Fine Art)
	Oxford Brookes – BBC/BC (Fine Art/Bus Admin Mgt; Fine Art/Psy)
260 pts	**Oxford Brookes** – BCC/BC (Fine Art; Fine Art/Acc; Fine Art/Anth; Fine Art/Hist; Fine Art/Mark; Fine Art/Sociol)
240 pts	**Aberystwyth** – ALs+ASs; portfolio; gs (Fine Art courses)
	Central England – 240 pts; gs; portfolio; (Fine Art)
	Derby – 240 pts 12u – CCC **or** CC+cc **or** VA12uAB; gs; portfolio; (BA Fine Art Fdn)
	Newcastle – CCC; portfolio; (Fine Art)
	Northumbria – 240 pts approx (Fine Art)
	Oxford Brookes – 240 pts approx (All Fine Art courses except under **320/280/260/220 pts** – offer varies with 2nd subject)
220 pts	**Lincolnshire & Humberside** – 220 pts; portfolio; (Fine Art)
	Oxford Brookes – AB–BC (Fine Art/Pol)
	South East Essex (Coll) – 220–160 pts (Fine Art)
200 pts	**Chester (Coll)** – 200 pts – ALs (180 pts inc C art subj)+AS **or** VAs (180 pts inc C art subj)+AS; AS(20 pts); portfolio; (Fine Art)
	East London – 200–120 pts approx (Fine Art)
	Liverpool John Moores – 200 pts (inc AL/VA art/des pref); portfolio; (Fine Art)
	Wolverhampton – 200–160 pts 12u – DDD/CC **or** CD+d **or** VAs CC+AL/ASs; gs; (Pntg; Sculp; Prtg; Fine Art/Soc Prac)
180 pts	**Chichester (UC)** – 180 pts approx + Fdn/portfolio (Fine Art)
	Derby – 180 pts approx (Fine Art Comb)
	Huddersfield – 180 pts approx (Fine Art/Drg Pntg)
160 pts	**Anglia** – 160 pts 12u – 2ALs (inc B art) **or** VA12u(art) CC; gs; Fdn Dip reqd; (Prtg; Prtg Comb)
	Canterbury Christ Church (UC) – CC (Fine Art joint courses)
	Chichester (UC) – 160 pts 12u (inc C art); (Fine Art)
	Cumbria (CAD) – 160 pts – CC **or** ASs (contact coll) **or** VA + portfolio; (Fine Art)
	De Montfort (Leicester/Lincoln) – 160 pts – ALs **or** VAs+/-ALs/ASs; (not gs) (Fine Art courses)
	Derby – 12u – VA12u CC; portfolio; (BA Fine Art)
	Leeds (Bretton Hall) – CC–CD (Fine Art (Prtg) (Pntg) (Sculp))
	London Guildhall – CC–CD (Fine Art Mod)
	Robert Gordon – CC (Fine Art)
140 pts	**Edinburgh (CA)** – 140 pts approx – 2ALs **or** AL+2ASs (inc Engl+art des); (Prtg; Pntg; Sculp) contact Edinburgh univ
	Hull (Scarborough) – CD (Fine Art)
	Newport (UWCN) – 140–120 pts – ALs **or** ALs+ASs **or** VAs+/-ALs/ASs; portfolio; (Fine Art; Contemp Media)

Oxfordshire (SAD) – 140 pts approx (Fine Art)
Sunderland – 140 pts – 2ALs **or** ALs+ASs **or** VA12u+/-AL/ASs; gs; BTEC accepted; (Fine Art)

80 pts **and below or other selection criteria (Foundation course, interview and portfolio inspection)**

Barnsley (Coll) (Fine Art); Bath Spa (UC) (Prtg; Sculp); Blackburn (Coll) (Fine Art); Bournemouth (AI); Bradford (Coll); Brighton (Pntg; Crit Fine Art; Sculp; Prtg); Bristol UWE (Fine Arts); Buckinghamshire Chilterns (UC); Byam Shaw (SA) (Fine Art); Camberwell (SAC); Central England; Central Lancashire (Fine Art); Cheltenham & Glos (CHE) (Prtg; Sculp); Cleveland (CAD) (Fine Art); Coventry (Fine Art); Croydon (Coll) (Prtg); De Montfort; Derby (Fine Art); Dundee (Prtg; Sculp); East London (Fine Art); Edinburgh (CA) (Pntg; Prtg; Sculp); Falmouth (CA) (Fine Art); Herefordshire (CAD) (Prtg); Hertfordshire (Ptg); Hull (Scarborough) (Fine Art); Kent (IAD) (Fine Art); Kingston (Fine Art); London (CGAS); London (Gold) (Fine Art), (UCL-Slade SA) (Fine Art); London Guildhall (Fine Art); London Inst (Central Saint Martins), (Chelsea) (Fine Art); Loughborough (Prtg; Pntg; Sculp; Hist Art); Manchester Met (Fine Art); Middlesex (Fine Art); North London; North Oxfordshire (Coll); Northampton (UC); Norwich (SAD) (Fine Art); Nottingham Trent (Fine Art); Oxfordshire (SAD); Plymouth (Fine Art); Portsmouth (Fine Art); Robert Gordon; Salford (Fine Art); Sheffield Hallam (Prtg; Ptg; Sculp); Solihull (Coll) (Fine Art); Southampton (Winchester) (Fine Art; Prtg; Pntg; Sculp); Southampton (Inst); Southport (Coll); (Fine Art); Staffordshire (Fine Art); Suffolk (Coll); Surrey (IAD/UC) (Fine Art); Swansea (IHE); UHI; Ulster (Fine Art); West Thames (Coll); Wiltshire (Coll); Wimbledon (SA) (Pntg; Sculp); Wirral Met (Coll) (Fine Art); Wolverhampton; gs (Pntg; Sculp).

Leeds Met – (contact university)

Diploma of Higher Education courses

City/London (SA) (Fine Art); UHI.

Higher National Diploma courses (100 pts and below approx + portfolio)

Blackpool & Fylde (Coll); Bournemouth (AI); Brighton; Carmarthenshire (Coll); Cumbria (CAD) (Fine Art); Doncaster (Coll); Dudley (CT) (Sculp); Filton (Coll); Gloucestershire (CAT); Mid Cheshire (Coll); Newcastle (Coll); Northbrook (Coll); Plymouth (CAD); Solihull (Coll); Somerset (CAT); Stafford (Coll); Sutton Coldfield (Coll); Tameside (Coll); UHI (Inverness/Moray) (Fine Art via DipHE, HNC); Warwickshire (Coll).

Overseas applicants: Good photographs or transparencies may be acceptable for applicants unable to attend for interview. Original work helpful.

CHOOSING YOUR COURSE (See also **Ch.1**)

> **Subject information:** Many of these courses are usually specialised studies in painting and are often preceded by a Foundation Art course. A study of the history of art provides a theoretical basis for study Fine Art careers and could be an appropriate alternative course in itself. (See also **Appendix 1**, Professional Associations.)

Special features: Falmouth (CA) Optional areas cover painting, printmaking and photographic media. **Staffordshire** A critical/theoretical course which includes a 'writing for mass media' course. **Wimbledon (SA)** Mixed media option (film, video, photography, illustration, performance). *NOW CHECK PROSPECTUSES AND WEB SITES.*

Top universities and colleges (Teaching Quality) (see Ch.4): Cardiff (UWI); not all institutions assessed.

Top universities and colleges (Research) (see Ch.4): See **Art and Design (General)**.

Study opportunities abroad: Bristol UWE; Cardiff (UWI); Central England; Cheltenham & Glos (CHE); Chester (Coll); Dundee; Huddersfield; Kent (IAD); Kingston; Liverpool John

Moores; London (Gold), (UCL-Slade SA); London Guildhall; London Inst (Chelsea); Loughborough; Manchester Met; Middlesex; Northumbria; Norwich (SAD); Nottingham Trent; Oxfordshire (SAD); Plymouth; Robert Gordon; Salford; Sheffield Hallam; Sunderland; Wimbledon (SA); Wirral Met (Coll); Wolverhampton.

Work opportunities abroad: Chester (Coll); Huddersfield; Kent (IAD); Norwich (SAD); Oxfordshire (SAD); Wirral Met (Coll).

ADMISSIONS INFORMATION

Number of applicants per place (approx): Bath Spa (UC) 10; Bristol UWE 3; Cardiff (UWI) 3; Central England 6; Central Lancashire 4; Cheltenham & Glos (CHE) 5; Cleveland (CAD) 2; Cumbria (CAD) 5; De Montfort 5; Derby 3; Dundee 4; Falmouth (CA) 5; Hertfordshire 6; Hull (Scarborough) 2; Kent (IAD) 2; Kingston 9; Lincolnshire & Humberside 4; Liverpool John Moores 3; London (Gold) 10, (UCL-Slade SA) 24; London Guildhall 11; London Inst (Chelsea) 5; Loughborough 4; Manchester Met 4; Middlesex 3; Newcastle 30; Northumbria 4; Norwich (SAD) 3; Nottingham Trent 3; Robert Gordon 5; Sheffield Hallam 4; Solihull (Coll) 4; Staffordshire 3; Wimbledon (SA) (Sculp) 3; Wirral Met (Coll) 3.

Admissions Tutors' advice: Brighton Application route B recommended for applicants on pre-degree courses.

Planning your UCAS personal statement (see Ch.4): Since this is a subject area which can be researched easily in art galleries, you should not only discuss your own style of work and your preferred subjects but also your opinions on various art forms, styles and periods. Keep up-to-date with public opinion on controversial issues. State your reasons for wishing to pursue a course in Fine Art. **London Inst (Chelsea)** Looks for visual and plastic skills, conceptual development. (See also **Appendix 1**, Professional Associations.) See also **Art and Design (Graphic Design)**.

Selection interviews (see Ch.4): Most institutions will interview and require a portfolio of work. **London Inst (Chelsea)** Interviews with portfolios and essays.

Examples of interview questions (see Ch.4): Questions asked on portfolio of work. Be prepared to answer questions on your stated opinions on your UCAS form and on controversial topics which are currently reported in the press.

AFTER RESULTS ADVICE

Probable vacancies from June 2001 and in Clearing (see Ch.4): Vacancies are likely – contact institution for further information.

NEW GRADUATE DESTINATIONS AND EMPLOYMENT (1999 HESA) (see **Ch.4**)

From a survey of 2285 graduates, 940 entered full-time employment, with about 50% going into various business careers. 480 into further study and 220 were understood to be unemployed.

✗ ART AND DESIGN (Graphic Design) (see also **Art and Design (General)**; including Animation, Calligraphy, Marketing Design, Medical Illustration, Printmaking (see also **Art and Design (Fine Art)**, Scientific Illustration, Technical Illustration and Typography (see also **Printing, Publishing & Packaging**))

NB The information supplied by the universities and colleges this year varies considerably and the offers listed below should be used as a first source of reference only. Many institutions will accept combinations of Advanced (AL), Advanced Subsidiary (AS) and Vocational Advanced (VA) level qualifications to achieve the required points total, but applicants must check web sites and prospectuses for full details of all offers. Grades and points totals shown should be regarded as the minimum levels to be achieved, but offers may be adjusted downwards when results are known. The points totals shown to

the left of the institutions are for ease of reference only. It must not be assumed that tariff points are always used by institutions or that they can be substituted for an offer in grades. The level of an offer is not necessarily indicative of the quality of a course. To calculate your offers see Chapter 4 and the inside fold of the back cover.

Special subject requirements/preferences: None. A Foundation Art course may be required for some courses listed below. Candidates may be interviewed and their portfolios of work scrutinised. Applicants should note that for these courses there are two application pathways (Routes A or B or both). Read the general comments under **Art and Design (General)** and refer to the UCAS *Directory* for course details.

It should be noted that a good interview and portfolio of work will often be acceptable in lieu of the stipulated A-Level grades.

260 pts   **Reading** – 260 pts approx (Typo Graph Comm)

240 pts   **Derby** – 240 pts 12u – CCC **or** CC+cc **or** VA12u AB; gs; portfolio; (Graph Des; Illus Fdn)

            Nottingham Trent – 240–220 pts approx (Graph Comm Mgt)

            Southampton (Inst) – 240 pts approx (Graph Des)

220 pts   **Lincolnshire & Humberside** – 220 pts; portfolio; (Graph Des; Animat; Illus)

            South East Essex (Coll) – 220–180 pts (Graphics)

200 pts   **Liverpool John Moores** – 200 pts (inc AL/VA art/des pref); portfolio; (Graph Des)

            Salford – 200–120 pts approx (Graph Des courses)

            Surrey Roehampton – 200–160 pts approx (Calligraphy)

180 pts   **Cheltenham & Glos (CHE)** – 180 pts approx + Fdn course (Prof Media)

            Glamorgan – 180 pts approx (Graph Des)

            Huddersfield – 180 pts approx (Mov Imag Des)

            Luton – 180 pts approx (Graph Des)

            Nottingham Trent – 180 pts approx (Graph Des)

            Swansea (IHE) – 180 pts approx (Illus; Graph Arts; Graph Des)

            Wolverhampton – 180–160 pts – DDD/CC **or** CD+d **or** VAs CC+/-ALs/ASs; gs; (Graph Comm; Illus)

160 pts   **Anglia** – 160 pts 12u – 2ALs (inc B art) **or** ALs (inc B art)+ASs **or** VA12u(art) CC; gs; Fdn course reqd; (Graph Des)

            Blackpool & Fylde (Coll) – 160 pts approx (Graph Des)

            Cumbria (CAD) – 160 pts – CC **or** ASs (contact coll) **or** VA + portfolio; (Graph Des)

            De Montfort (Lincoln) – 160 pts – ALs **or** VAs+/-ALs/ASs (inc C); (not gs) (Graph Des; Illus)

            Derby – 12u – VA12u CC; gs; portfolio; (BA Graph Des; Illus)

            Falmouth (CA) – CC (Graph/Comm courses; Graph Des; Illus)

            Leeds (Bretton Hall) – CC (Graph Des)

            Manchester Met – CC (Illus/Animat)

            Napier – CC (Graph Comm Mgt)

            Southampton (Inst) – 160 pts approx (Mark Des)

            Swansea (IHE) – 12u – VA12u CC; gs; portfolio; (Tech Graph)

140 pts   **Edinburgh (CA)** – 140 pts approx – 2ALs **or** AL+ASs (inc Engl+art des); (Graph; Animat; Illus; Photo)

            Newport (UWCN) – 140–120 pts – AL **or** ALs+ASs **or** VAs+/-ALs/ASs; portfolio; (Graphics)

            Sunderland – 140 pts (Illus)

100 pts   **and below or other selection criteria (Foundation course, interview and portfolio inspection)**

            Anglia; Barnsley (Coll) (Graph Des Comb); Bath Spa (UC) (Graph Des); Blackburn (Coll) (Graph Des); Blackpool & Fylde (Coll) (Sci Nat Hist Illus; Tech Inf Illus; Graph Des); Bournemouth (AI); Brighton (Graph Des; Illus); Bristol UWE (Graph Des; Illus); Buckinghamshire Chilterns (UC); Cardiff (UWI); Central Lancashire (Graph Des); Colchester (Inst) (Graph); Coventry (Graph Des); Croydon (Coll) (Graph Des);

Cumbria (CAD); Dundee (Graph Des; Illus); East London (Graph); Edinburgh (CA) (Graph; Animat; Illus; Photo); Falmouth (CA); Glamorgan; Glasgow Caledonian (App Graph Tech; Med Illus); Herefordshire (CAD) (Illus); Heriot-Watt; Hertford Regional (Coll) (Vis Comm – Graph Des); James Watt (CFHE) (Graph Des); Kent (IAD) (Graph Des; Illus); Kingston (Graph Des; Illus); Leeds (CAD) (Vis Comm); London Inst (Camberwell SA) (Graph Des, (Central Saint Martins) (Print Media; Graph Media); Loughborough (Graph; Illus); Lowestoft (Coll); Manchester Met (Graph Des; Illus Anim); Mid Cheshire (CFHE); Newport (UWCN) (Graph); North East Wales (IHE) (Animat; Graph; Graph Comb; Illus; Illus Comb); Northampton (UC); Northbrook (Coll); Northumbria (Illus; Graph Des); Norwich (SAD) (Graph Des); Oxfordshire (SAD) (Graph Des; Illus); Plymouth (Illus; Graph Des; Typo); Portsmouth (Illus); Ravensbourne (CDC) (Graph Des); Reading (CSAD); Salisbury (Coll); Solihull (Coll) (Graph Des); Southampton (Inst); Staffordshire (Electron Graph; Animat); Suffolk (Coll) (Illus; Graph Des); Surrey (IAD/UC); Surrey Roehampton (Callig/Bookbind); Swansea (IHE); Teesside (Graph Des); Warrington (CI); Westminster (Graph Inf Des; Illus); Wiltshire (Coll) (Graph Des courses).

Leeds Met – (contact university)

Higher National Diploma courses (100 pts and below approx + portfolio)

Barking (Coll); Barnsley (Coll); Batley (SA); Birmingham City (Coll); Blackburn (Coll); Bournemouth (AI) (Animat; Des/Nat Hist; Illus; Graph Des); Bradford (Coll); Buckinghamshire Chilterns (UC); Cardiff (UWI); Carmarthenshire (Coll); City Bristol (Coll); City of Manchester (Coll); Cleveland (CAD); Cumbria (CAD); De Montfort; Doncaster (Coll) (Adv Des); Dudley (CT); East Surrey (Coll) (Callig); Farnborough (CT); Filton (Coll); Glamorgan; Gloucester (CAT); Hastings (CAT); Hereford (Coll); Isle (Coll) (Illus); James Watt (CFHE); Kent (IAD); Kingston; Leicester (Coll); Lincolnshire & Humberside; London Inst (Central Saint Martins) (Typo); Loughborough; Lowestoft (Coll) (Graph Des; Illus); Luton; Mid Cheshire (CFHE); Newham (CHE); Newcastle (Coll) (Adv Des; Graph); North East Worcestershire (Coll); Northampton (UC); Norwich (SAD) (Graph Des); Northbrook (Coll); North East Wales (IHE) Oxfordshire (SAD); Perth (Coll); Plymouth (CAD) (Graph Des; Prnt Prod); Portsmouth; Reading (CSAD); Salford; Salisbury (Coll); Sandwell (Coll); Shrewsbury (CAT); Solihull (Coll); Somerset (CAT); Southampton (Inst) (Graph Des; Illus); Southwark (Coll); St Helens (Coll); Stockport (CFHE); Suffolk (Coll); Sutton Coldfield (Coll); UHI; Warrington (CI); West Herts (Coll); West Thames (Coll); Wigan & Leigh (Coll); Wiltshire (Coll); Wolverhampton; Worcester (CT); York (CFHE); Yorkshire Coast (CFHE).

Alternative Offers:

Scottish Qualifications: See **Art and Design (General)**.

Overseas applicants: De Montfort 12 examples of work on transparencies required.

CHOOSING YOUR COURSE (See also **Ch.1**)

> **Subject information:** Graphic Design is the most popular specialisation in the art field. In turn, this subject divides into such areas as advertising, art, audio-visual media, book design, illustration and photography, TV graphics. Most courses are almost always preceded by a Foundation Art course. Theoretical aspects of this subject can be studied in History of Art and Design courses. Graphics has also become a feature in some Computer Science and Media Studies courses.

Special features: Bath Spa (UC), Kingston, Lincolnshire & Humberside, Liverpool John Moores, Southampton (Inst) all include animation. **Anglia, Bath Spa (UC), Coventry, Kingston, Lincolnshire & Humberside** all include video studies. **Central Lancashire, Coventry, Kingston, Nottingham Trent, Plymouth** all include typography. **Napier** A management, not a graphic design course. *NOW CHECK PROSPECTUSES AND WEB SITES.*

Top universities and colleges (Teaching Quality) (see Ch.4): Dundee; Swansea (IHE); not all institutions assessed.

Study opportunities abroad: Anglia; Bath Spa (UC); Bournemouth (AI); Bristol UWE; Central England; Central Lancashire; De Montfort; Derby; Dundee; Kingston; Liverpool John Moores; London Inst (Central Saint Martins); Lincolnshire & Humberside; Northumbria; Norwich (SAD); Nottingham Trent; Oxfordshire (SAD); Plymouth; Ravensbourne (CDC); Surrey Roehampton; Teesside.

Work opportunities abroad: Blackburn (Coll); Derby; Liverpool John Moores; Northumbria; Teesside.

ADMISSIONS INFORMATION

Number of applicants per place (approx): Anglia 5; Bath Spa (UC) 8; Blackburn (Coll) 2; Bristol UWE 4; Central Lancashire 5; Colchester (Inst) 3; Coventry 6; Derby 5; Falmouth (CA) 2; Glamorgan 3; Hertfordshire 6; Kingston 8; Lincolnshire & Humberside 5; Liverpool John Moores 7; London Inst (Central Saint Martins) 4; Loughborough 5; Manchester Met 8; Middlesex 3; Napier 7; Norwich (SAD) 4; Northumbria 8; Nottingham Trent 6; Ravensbourne (CDC) 3; Solihull (Coll) 3; Surrey (IAD/UC) 8; Swansea (IHE) 10; Teesside 5; Wolverhampton 5.

Planning your UCAS personal statement (see Ch.4): Discuss your special interest in this field, and any commercial applications which have impressed you. Discuss the work you are enjoying at present and the range of media which you have explored. Interests in travel, architecture, the arts, literature, film, current affairs (see also **Appendix 1** for contact details of relevant professional associations). **London Inst (Central Saint Martins)** Personality is an important factor.

Selection interviews (see Ch.4): Most institutions will interview and require a portfolio of work. London Inst (Central Saint Martins) (T) (some); Nottingham Trent.

Examples of interview questions (see Ch.4): Discuss recent trends in graphic design from the points of view of methods and designers. Questions asked on applicant's portfolio of work.

Reasons for rejection (non-academic): Not enough work in portfolio. Inability to think imaginatively. Lack of interest in the arts in general. Lack of drive. Tutor's statement indicating problems. Poorly constructed personal statement.

AFTER RESULTS ADVICE

Probable vacancies from June 2001 and in Clearing (see Ch.4): Vacancies are likely – contact institutions for further information.

NEW GRADUATE DESTINATIONS AND EMPLOYMENT (1999 HESA) (see **Ch.4**)

See under **Art and Design (General)**.

ART AND DESIGN (Industrial/Product Design) (including Design, Footwear, Furniture Design, Garden Design, Interior Architecture, Interior Design, Modelmaking, Museum Design, Theatre Design and Transport Design)

NB The information supplied by the universities and colleges this year varies consider-ably and the offers listed below should be used as a first source of reference only. Many institutions will accept combinations of Advanced (AL), Advanced Subsidiary (AS) and Vocational Advanced (VA) level qualifications to achieve the required points total, but applicants must check web sites and prospectuses for full details of all offers. Grades and points totals shown should be regarded as the minimum levels to be achieved, but offers may be adjusted downwards when results are known. The points totals shown to the left of the institutions are for ease of reference only. It must not be assumed that

tariff points are always used by institutions or that they can be substituted for an offer in grades. The level of an offer is not necessarily indicative of the quality of a course. To calculate your offers see Chapter 4 and the inside fold of the back cover.

Special subject requirements/preferences: A-Level: Brighton (Prod Des) Mathematics/ science required. **Brunel** Mathematics and physics at A or AS-level. **Sheffield Hallam** Two subjects preferably from art, design, mathematics, physics, technology. **GCSE: Salford** Five subjects grade A/B. All institutions will assess the applicant's portfolio. Applicants should note that for these courses there are two application pathways (Route A or B or both). Read the general notes under **Art and Design (General)** and refer to the UCAS *Directory* for course details.

It should be noted that a good interview and portfolio of work will often be acceptable instead of the stipulated A-Level grades.

280 pts	**Central England** – 280 pts; gs; portfolio; (Thea Des; Inter Des; Ind Des; Furn Des)
	Strathclyde – BBC (Prod Des Eng)
260 pts	**Coventry** – 260 pts approx (Consum Prod Des)
	Loughborough – 260 pts 18u; (not gs) (Ind Des/Tech; Ind Des/Pack Tech)
240 pts	**Aston** – 240 pts 12u – CCC **or** VA12u BB+AL(B); (Prod Des courses)
	Bournemouth – 240 pts from 3ALs **or** 200 pts from 2ALs **or** VAs; (Comp Aid Prod Des courses)
	Brighton – 240 pts approx (Prod Des)
	Brunel – 240 pts 2x6u – Als **or** ALs+ASs **or** VAs+/-ALs/ASs; (Ind Des; Ind Des Eng; Prod Des; Ind Des Tech)
	Central Lancashire – 240 pts 12u (inc AL art or des/tech); gs; (Ind Des; Prod Des)
	Hertfordshire – 240 pts approx (Prod Des)
	Nottingham Trent – 240 pts approx (Furn/Prod Des)
	Robert Gordon – CCC (Inter Archit; Innov Mgt; Des Ind)
	Rose Bruford (Coll) – 240 pts approx (Thea Des)
220 pts	**Bournemouth** – 220 pts from 2–3ALs **or** VAs; (Prod Des courses)
	Bournemouth – 220 pts from 3ALs **or** 180 pts from 2ALs **or** VAs; (Inter Des)
	Bradford – 220 pts 12u; gs; (Vrtl Des Innov)
	Huddersfield – 220 pts approx (Instln Art Evnts)
	Salford – 220 pts approx (Prod Des)
	South East Essex (Coll) – 220–180 pts (Inter Archit)
200 pts	**Bradford** – 200 pts 12u; gs; (Mat Des Prod; Integ Ind Des)
	De Montfort – 200 pts – ALs **or** VAs+/-ALs/ASs (inc BC); (not gs) (Prod Des; Furn Des; Ind Des/Eng; Inter Des; Ftwr Des)
	Glasgow – CDD (Prod Des Eng)
	Liverpool John Moores – 200 pts (inc AL/VA art/des pref); portfolio; (Prod Des)
	Loughborough – 200 pts 18u; (not gs) (Ind Des/Tech Educ)
	Sheffield Hallam – BB (Ind Des (Prod))
180 pts	**East London** – 180 pts approx (Prod Des)
	Huddersfield – 180–160 pts approx (Ind Des; Prod Des; Inter Des; Trans Des)
	Luton – 180 pts approx (Inter Des; Prod Des)
	Napier – BC (Ind Des)
	Staffordshire – 180 pts approx (Prod Des Tech)
	Wolverhampton – 180–160 pts 12u – DDD/CC **or** CD+d **or** VA CC(overall)+/- AL/ASs; gs; (Comp Aid Ind Prod Des; Furn Des; Inter Des)
160 pts	**Buckinghamshire Chilterns (UC)** – CD (Furn; Inter Des)
	Coventry – 160 pts approx (Ind Prod Des Fdn)
	Lincolnshire & Humberside – 160 pts; portfolio; (Inter Des Musm/Exhib Des)
	Manchester (CAT) – CC (Furn Restor Cons; 3D Furn Des Mak)
	Middlesex – 160 pts approx (Prod Des; Des/Tech)

Napier – CC (Interd Des; Inter Archit)
Robert Gordon – CC–EE (Des Eng; Inter Archit)
Sheffield Hallam – CC (Pack Des)
South Bank – CC (Ind Des)
140 pts   **Central England** – 140–120 pts 12u – DEE/DD **or** DE+d **or** VA12u DD; gs;
(Comp Aid Prod Des)
Derby – 140 pts 12u – CD **or** DD+ee **or** VA12u CD; gs; (Prod Des courses;
Comb courses)
Edinburgh (CA) – 140 pts approx – 2ALs **or** AL+2ASs (inc (Engl+art des);
(Furn; Inter Des)
Sunderland – 140 pts (Model Des)
120 pts   **Manchester Met** – 120 pts approx (Ind Des; Inter Des)
80 pts   **and below or other selection criteria (Foundation course, interview and portfolio inspection)**
Anglia; Barking (Coll) (Prod Des); Basford Hall (Coll) (Furn); Bath Spa (UC) (Ceram); Bolton (IHE) (Cons Prod Des; Auto Prod Des; Ind Des Mgt; Electron Prod Des); Bournemouth (AI) (Model; Prod Des); Brighton (Inter Archit; 3D Prod); Cardiff (UWI) (Ind Des; Inter Archit); Central Lancashire (Inter Des); Central Sch (Sp/Dr) (Thea St); Colchester (Inst) (Prod Des); Cordwainers (Coll) (Foot Accs); Coventry (Consum Prod Des; Trans Des); Croydon (Coll) (Thea); Dundee (Inter Des); Edinburgh (CA) (Furn; Inter Des); Glasgow Caledonian (Inter Des); Heriot-Watt (Furn); Hertfordshire; James Watt (CFHE) (Inter Des); Kent (IAD) (Prod Des; Inter Des; Inter Archit); Kingston (Prod Furn Des; Inter Des); Leeds (CAD) (Inter Des); Liverpool Hope (Coll); Liverpool (LIPA) (Perf Des); London Guildhall (Furn; Inter Des); London Inst (Central Saint Martins) (Prod Des; Thea Des), (Chelsea) (Inter Des; Inter Des); Loughborough (Furn); Manchester (CAT) (Furn); Manchester Met (Crea St); Middlesex (Furn; Gard Des; Inter Des); Napier (Ind Archit); North East Worcestershire (Coll) (Thea); North London (Inter Des); Northumbria (Des Ind; Trans Des; Furn); Nottingham Trent (Inter Archit; Furn; Thea Des); Oxford Brookes (Comp Aid Prod Des); Paisley (Prod Des Dev); Plymouth (CAD) (Inter Des); Ravensbourne (CDC) (Furn Rltd Prod Des; Inter Des); Shrewsbury (CAT) (Furn; Inter Des); South Bank (Ind Des; Spo Prod Des; Prod Des Env); Southampton (Inst); Staffordshire (Prod Des Tech); Suffolk (Coll) (Model Des); Surrey (IAD/UC) (Inter Des); Teesside (Inter Archit Des; Ind Des); Welsh (CMD) (Thea Des); Wimbledon (SA) (Thea Des; Cost Des).

Leeds Met – (contact university)

Diploma in Higher Education
Huddersfield 160 pts (Prod Des).

Higher National Diploma courses (100 pts and below approx + portfolio)
Anglia; Barking (Coll) (Modelmaking); Basford Hall (Coll) (Furn); Bell (CT); Bishop Burton (CAg) (Inter Des); Bridgwater (Coll) (Furn Des); Bournemouth (AI) (Modelmaking); Buckinghamshire Chilterns (UC); Cardiff (UWI); Carmarthenshire (Coll); Central Sch (Sp/Dr); City of Bristol (CAD); Cordwainers (Coll), Cornwall (Coll); Croydon (Coll) (Thea St); Derby; Glamorgan; Huddersfield; James Watt (CFHE); Leeds (CAD); Leicester (Coll) (Foot); London Guildhall (Furn St); Newcastle (Coll) (Inter Archit); Northbrook (Coll) (Thea Des; Inter Des); Oxfordshire (SAD); Rycotewood (Coll) (Des Furn, Model); St Helens (Coll); Salford; Shrewsbury (Coll) (Furn); Somerset (CAT); South Bank; West Thames (Coll); Wiltshire (Coll) (Pack Des); Wolverhampton.

Alternative Offers:

IB offers: Anglia 24 pts; Brighton 25 pts; Brunel 26 pts; Central Lancashire 28 pts.

Irish offers: Brighton BBB.

Scottish Qualifications: See **Art and Design (General)**.

CHOOSING YOUR COURSE (See also **Ch.1**).

Subject information: These are product design courses (for example, the design of cars, telephones, cookers, radios) which are almost always preceded by a Foundation Art course. Furniture courses are the least popular specialisation. A similar approach is taken by way of craft design and technology (CDT) often through teacher training courses. A more technical emphasis will lead into Engineering and Materials Science courses, for example, Glass, Metal, Polymers. See also **Appendix 1**.

Special features: Brunel Covers design and technology including emphasis on high-tech aspects (electronics and mechanics). Leads to Qualified Teacher Status. **Central England** (Eng Prod Des) Optional schemes cover advanced manufacture, information technology, business management and a foreign language. **De Montfort** (Ind Des/Eng) Engineering with business and a language. **Derby** Students hold their own intellectual property rights to their design work on the course. **East London** Balance between engineering and product design. Product Design Foundation course offered. **Lincolnshire & Humberside** (Musm & Exhib Des) Covers communication, information, entertainment and education. **Wimbledon (SA)** The only specialised degree course in costume design. *NOW CHECK PROSPECTUSES AND WEB SITES.*

Top universities and colleges (Teaching Quality) (see Ch.4): Cardiff (UWI) (Inter Des); not all institutions assessed.

Top universities and colleges (Research) (see Ch.4): See under **Art and Design (General)**.

Study opportunities abroad: Huddersfield; Kent (IAD); Leeds (CAD); Manchester (CAT); Manchester Met; Ravensbourne (CDC); Salford; South Bank; Teesside.

Work opportunities abroad: Brunel; Coventry; Huddersfield; Leeds (CAD).

ADMISSIONS INFORMATION

Number of applicants per place (approx): Abertay Dundee 6; Bath Spa (UC) 4; Bolton (IHE) 1; Bournemouth 6; Brunel 4; Cardiff (UWI) 4; Central England 8; Central Lancashire 7; Central Sch (Sp/Dr) 5; Colchester (Inst) 4; Coventry 5; De Montfort 5; Derby 2; London Inst (Central Saint Martins) 2, (Chelsea) 2; Loughborough 9; Manchester Met 2; Middlesex (Inter Des) 4; Napier 6; Northumbria 4; Nottingham Trent 5; Salford 6; Sheffield 5; Shrewsbury (CAT) 6; Swansea (IHE) 3; Teesside 3; Wimbledon (SA) 3.

Planning your UCAS personal statement (see Ch.4): Your knowledge of design in all fields should be described, including any special interests you may have, for example domestic, rail, road and visits to exhibitions, motor shows. **School/College reference:** Tutors should make it clear that the applicant's knowledge, experience and attitude match the chosen course – not simply higher education in general. See also **Appendix 1**. **Derby** Basic computer knowledge useful. See also under **Art and Design (Graphic Design)**.

Selection interviews (see Ch.4): Most institutions will interview and require a portfolio of work. Hertfordshire (No); Kingston (Interview plus essay); Nottingham Trent.

Examples of interview questions (see Ch.4): Applicants' portfolios of art work form an important talking point throughout the interview. In what aspects of industrial design are you interested? Applicants should be able to discuss examples of current design and new developments in the field.

Reasons for rejection (non-academic): Not hungry enough! Mature students without formal qualifications may not be able to demonstrate the necessary mathematical or engineering skills. Poor quality and organisation of portfolio. Lack of interest. Inappropriate dress. Lack of enthusiasm. Insufficient portfolio work (eg exercises instead of projects).

GAP YEAR ADVICE

Coventry (No).

AFTER RESULTS ADVICE

Probable vacancies from June 2001 and in Clearing (see Ch.4): Vacancies are likely – contact institutions for further information.

NEW GRADUATE DESTINATIONS AND EMPLOYMENT (1999 HESA) (see **Ch.4**)

See under **Art and Design (General)**.

ART AND DESIGN (Three Dimensional Design) (including Bookbinding, Ceramics, Design/Crafts, Glassware, Jewellery, Metalwork, Silversmithing, Plastics and Woodwork)

NB The information supplied by the universities and colleges this year varies considerably and the offers listed below should be used as a first source of reference only. Many institutions will accept combinations of Advanced (AL), Advanced Subsidiary (AS) and Vocational Advanced (VA) level qualifications to achieve the required points total, but applicants must check web sites and prospectuses for full details of all offers. Grades and points totals shown should be regarded as the minimum levels to be achieved, but offers may be adjusted downwards when results are known. The points totals shown to the left of the institutions are for ease of reference only. It must not be assumed that tariff points are always used by institutions or that they can be substituted for an offer in grades. The level of an offer is not necessarily indicative of the quality of a course. To calculate your offers see Chapter 4 and the inside fold of the back cover.

Special subject requirements/preferences: None. Entry via Foundation Art course. Selection by interview and scrutiny of portfolio of student's work. Applicants for these courses should note that there are two application pathways (Routes A or B) or both. Read the general notes under **Art and Design (General)** and refer to the UCAS *Directory* for course details.

It should be noted that a good interview and portfolio of work will often be acceptable instead of the stipulated A-Level grades.

240 pts **Central England** – 240 pts; gs; portfolio; (Jewel/Silver; Ceram/Glass Des)
220 pts **Bradford** – 220 pts 12; gs; (Vrtl Des Innov)
200 pts **Bradford** – 200 pts 12u; gs; (Integ Ind Des)
Surrey Roehampton – 200–160 pts approx (Bookbinding)
Wolverhampton – 200–160 pts 12u – DDD/CC **or** CD+d **or** VAs CC+/-AL/ASs; gs; (Wood/Mtl/Plas/Ceram; Glass; Ceram)
180 pts **Swansea (IHE)** – 180 pts approx (Glass; Ceram)
160 pts **Buckinghamshire Chilterns (UC)** – CC (Ceram/Glass; 3D Multid Des)
De Montfort – 160 pts – ALs **or** ALs+ASs **or** VAs+/-ALs/ASs; (Mtlsmth/Jewel; Ceram/Glass)
Falmouth (CA) – CC (Ceram; 3D Des)
Leeds (Bretton Hall) – CC–CD (Ceramics)
140 pts **Edinburgh (CA)** – 140 pts approx – 2ALs **or** AL+2ASs (inc Engl+art des); (Ceram; Glass; Jewel; Tap)
Newport (UWCN) – 140–120 pts – ALs **or** ALs+ASs **or** VAs+/-AL/ASs; portfolio; (3D Des)
Sunderland – 140 pts – 2ALs **or** ALs+ASs **or** VA12u; gs; (Glass/Archit Glass; Ceram; Model/Des)
80 pts **and below or other selection criteria (Foundation course, interview and portfolio inspection)**
Bath Spa (UC) (Ceram); Bournemouth (AI) (Integ 3D Des); Brighton (3D Crafts); Bristol UWE; Canterbury Christ Church (UC) (Ceram); Cardiff (UWI) (Ceram); Central England (Gem); Central Lancashire (Surf Patt; Ceram; Glass; Furn; Jewel; Plas); Cleveland (CAD) (Des Crafts Enter Ind); Cordwainers (Coll) (Foot Des);

Croydon (Coll) (Des Crafts); Cumbria (CAD) (Des Crafts); Dundee (Ceram); Edinburgh (CA) (Ceram; Glass; Jewel; Tap); Herefordshire (CAD) (3D Des; Ceram); Hertford Regional (Coll) (3D Des); Hertfordshire (Model); Kent (IAD) (Ceram; Jewel; Model; Silver; Gold); London Guildhall (Jewel); London Inst (Camberwell) (Silver; Mtl; Ceram), (Central Saint Martins) (Ceram; Jewel); Loughborough (Coll) (Ceram; Jewel); Manchester Met (Ceram; Wood; Mtl; Crafts; 3D Des; Euro); Middlesex (3D Des; Ceram; Jewel; Mtl; Glass); North East Wales (IHE); (Glass; Ceram; Jewel; Mtl); North East Worcestershire (Coll) (Ceram); Northumbria (3D Des); Plymouth (CAD) (3D Des; Ceram; Glass; Mtl); Portsmouth (Art Des Media; 3D Des); Ravensbourne (CDC) (Furn Rltd Prod Des); Sheffield Hallam (Jewel; Mtl; Ceram); Staffordshire (Ceram; Des Crafts); Surrey (IAD/UC) (Ceram; Glass; Mtl); Swansea (IHE); Westminster (Ceram).

Leeds Met – (contact university)

Diploma in Higher Education + portfolio
Central Sch (Sp/Dr).

Higher National Diploma courses
140 pts Central England (Jewel; Silver; Horol; Gem)
100 pts and below approx + portfolio
Barking (Coll); Batley (SA); Bournemouth (AI); Brighton; Burnley (Coll) (Furn); Carmarthenshire (Coll); Central England; City of Bristol (Coll); City of Manchester (Coll); Cordwainers (Coll) (Foot/Accs); Cumbria (CAD); De Montfort; Dudley (CT) (Glass; Ceram; 3D Des); Glasgow (CC); Kent (IAD); Leicester (Coll); London Guildhall; Lowestoft (Coll); Newcastle (Coll); Northbrook (Coll); North Warwickshire/Hinckley (Coll); Oxfordshire (SAD) (Ceram; Jewel); Plymouth (CAD) (Mtl; Glass; Ceram); St Helens (Coll); Staffordshire; Suffolk (Coll); Sutton Coldfield (Coll); Swansea (IHE); Warwickshire (Coll) (3D Des); West Thames (Coll); Wigan & Leigh (Coll); York (CFHE).

CHOOSING YOUR COURSE (See also **Ch.1**)

Subject information: Foundation Art courses are normally required prior to specialised studies in this wide-ranging field of design which can range from architectural stained glass and stage design to silverware, jewellery and metalwork – the last two being the least popular. A more technical interest in these fields could lead to Architecture and Engineering courses. See also **Appendix 1**.

Special features: Kent (IAD) European exchange programme – language options in French, German or Italian. **London Inst (Central Saint Martins)** The only specialised jewellery course in the UK. *NOW CHECK PROSPECTUSES AND WEB SITES.*

Top universities and colleges (Teaching Quality) (see Ch.4): Cardiff (UWI) (Ceram); not all institutions assessed.

Study opportunities abroad: Central England; De Montfort; Kent (IAD); Kingston; Plymouth; Ravensbourne (CDC); Sunderland; Surrey Roehampton.

Work opportunities abroad: Kent (IAD); Manchester Met; Plymouth.

ADMISSIONS INFORMATION

Number of applicants per place (approx): Bath Spa (UC) 3; Brighton (Wood) 3; Bristol UWE (Ceram) 3; Central England (Thea) 8; De Montfort 3; London Inst (Camberwell) 2, (Ceram) 3, (Central Saint Martins) (Ceram) 2, (Jewel) 2; Loughborough (Furn) 1, (Ceram) 4, (Silver) 3; Manchester Met 5; Middlesex (3D Des) 4, (Jewel) 4; Ravensbourne (CDC) 110 first-choice applicants; Swansea (IHE) 3; Wolverhampton (Wood/Mtl/Plas) 4.

Planning your UCAS personal statement (see Ch.4): Practical work will have been carried out in this field already. Discuss the range of your work and your experience of different types of materials used. Compare your work to that of professional artists and designers and describe visits to museums, art galleries, exhibitions etc. See also **Art and Design (Graphic Design)**.

Selection interviews (see Ch.4): Most institutions will interview and require a portfolio of work.

Examples of interview questions (see Ch.4): Questions focus on the art work presented in the student's portfolio.

AFTER RESULTS ADVICE

Probable vacancies from June 2001 and in Clearing (see Ch.4): Vacancies are likely – contact institutions for further information.

NEW GRADUATE DESTINATIONS AND EMPLOYMENT (1999 HESA) (see **Ch.4**)

See **Art and Design (General)**.

ARTS (General/Combined/Humanities/Modular) (including Cultural Studies; see also Science)

NB The information supplied by the universities and colleges this year varies consider-ably and the offers listed below should be used as a first source of reference only. Many institutions will accept combinations of Advanced (AL), Advanced Subsidiary (AS) and Vocational Advanced (VA) level qualifications to achieve the required points total, but applicants must check web sites and prospectuses for full details of all offers. Grades and points totals shown should be regarded as the minimum levels to be achieved, but offers may be adjusted downwards when results are known. The points totals shown to the left of the institutions are for ease of reference only. It must not be assumed that tariff points are always used by institutions or that they can be substituted for an offer in grades. The level of an offer is not necessarily indicative of the quality of a course. To calculate your offers see Chapter 4 and the inside fold of the back cover.

Special subject requirements/preferences: A-level: Good grades in chosen subjects. **Chester (Coll)** A–C grades in main subjects. **GCSE: Aberdeen, Dundee, Edinburgh, Glasgow, St Andrews** English, mathematics or science and foreign language. **De Montfort** Seven/eight subjects at grades A–C.

The grades shown below are approximate since offers made in Combined, General and Humanities courses may vary, depending on the subjects chosen.

The offers listed below are average offers. Specific offers will vary depending on the popularity of the subjects in combination.

330 pts   **Southampton (New Coll)** – 330 pts 12u (inc 2ALs 180 pts); gs; (Hum)
320 pts   **Cardiff** – ABB/AA (Cult Crit)
          Kent – 320–260/240–220 pts approx (offer varies with subjs) (Fac of Hum courses)
          Leeds – ABB–BCC/AB–BC (Comb Hons – offer varies with subj)
          St Andrews – ABB–BBC (MA Fac of Arts courses – see also **Classics, Religious Studies** and indivl Lang courses)
300 pts   **Birmingham** – BBB–BBC (Hum Joint Hons)
          Durham – ABC (Comb St/Soc Sci)
          Durham – BBB (Comb St/Arts)
          Edinburgh – BBB (MA Gen)
          Lancaster – 300–280 pts (Cult Media Comm)
          Liverpool – 300–280 pts – ALs **or** ALs+ASs **or** VAs+/-ALs/ASs; (Arts Comb)
          Newcastle – BBB–ABC/AB–BB (Comb St inc Chin/Jap/Kor)
          Oxford Brookes – BBB–CCC (BA/BSc – offer varies with subj choice)

280 pts **Bristol UWE** – 280 pts approx (Cult/Media St)
           Glasgow – BBC/AA (Lib Arts; Gen Hum)
           Manchester – BBC–BCC (Comb St – Arts)
270 pts **Brunel** – 270–240 pts 2x6u – ALs **or** ALs+ASs **or** VAs+/-ALs/ASs; (Humanities)
260 pts **Belfast (Queen's)** – BCC (Cult St)
           Birmingham – BCC–BCD (General)
           Dundee – BCC/BB (Arts/Soc Sci)
           Essex – 260 pts 21u – BC+AL/2ASs; (Humanities)
           Leicester – BCC/BB (Comb Arts)
           Northumbria – 260–180 pts approx (Comb Hons – offer varies with subj)
           Swansea – BCC–CCC/BB (BSc Econ – deferred choice Joint Hons)
240 pts **Aberdeen** – CCC (Arts Soc Sci)
           Belfast (Queen's) – CCC/BB (Arts Comb)
           Bradford – CCC/BB (Interd Hum St)
           Heriot-Watt – 240 pts 18u – CCC; gs; (BA Comb St)
           Hertfordshire – 240–200 pts approx (Hum Mod)
           Nottingham Trent – 1x12u **or** 2x6u – 2ALs **or** AL+2ASs **or** VA12u; gs; (Contemp Arts)
           St Andrews – CCC (BSc General degrees)
           Sheffield Hallam – 240 pts approx (Comb Hons – offer varies with subjs)
           Strathclyde – CCC/BC (Arts/Soc Sci) BBD (2nd yr entry)
           Ulster – CCC (BA Comb St; Comb St/Hum)
           Westminster – 240 pts approx (Comb Hons)
220 pts **Anglia** – 220 pts approx (Comb Hons)
           De Montfort – 220 pts; (not gs) (Arts Hum; Comb Arts; Arts Mgt)
           Lampeter – 220–200 pts approx (Comb Hons; Relig Eth Soty)
           Manchester Met – CCD/CC (Hum/Soc St joint courses)
           Middlesex – 220–180 pts approx (Comb Hons)
           Nottingham Trent – 220 pts 1x12u **or** 2x6u – 2ALs **or** AL+2ASs **or** VA12u; gs; (Humanities)
           Nottingham Trent – ALs(120 pts min) **or** VAs(120 pts)+AL/ASs; (Comb St)
           Plymouth – CCD/BB (Comb Arts)
           St Mark & St John (Coll) – 220–180 pts (BA Hons)
           Staffordshire – 220–180 pts approx (Comb St)
           Wirral Met (Coll) – 220 pts approx (Comb St – Cult St)
200 pts **Bath Spa (UC)** – BB–EE (Comb Awards; Cult St)
           Canterbury Christ Church (UC) – 200 pts approx (Comb St)
           Chester (Coll) – 200 pts – ALs (180 pts inc C)+AS **or** VA (180 pts inc C)+AS; AS(up to 20 pts); gs; (Comb Arts)
           Derby – 200 pts approx (Arts Thera)
           Hertfordshire – 200 pts approx (Joint Hons)
           Huddersfield – 200 pts approx (Humanities)
           London Guildhall – BB–DD (Mod – offer varies with subj)
           Luton – 200 pts approx (Humanities)
           Manchester Met – CDD/CC **or** ALs+ASs **or** VAs+/-ALs/ASs; (Hum Soc St joint courses)
           Northampton (UC) – CDD/CC (Comb Hons)
           Staffordshire – 200 pts – CC **or** ALs+ASs **or** VAs+/-ALs/ASs; gs; (Cult St)
           Sussex – CCE (Cult St)
           Teesside – CDD (Cult St)
           Warrington (CI) – 200–180 pts approx (BA Comb St)
           Worcester (UC) – 200–140 pts approx (Comb St – depending on subj)
180 pts **Anglia** – 180 pts approx (Hum Arts Admin)
           Bolton (IHE) – 180–160 pts approx (Modular)
           Boston (Coll) – BC–CC (Comb; Hum)
           Bridgwater (Coll) – 180 pts approx (Cult St)
           Brighton – 180 pts approx (Hum; Cult Hist St)
           Central England – 180 pts approx (Arts St)

City (Coll) – 180 pts approx (Comb Arts)
Colchester (Inst) – 180 pts approx (Comb St; Hum)
Derby – 180–140 pts approx (Comb Hons)
East London – 180 pts approx (Cult St; Comb)
King Alfred's Winchester (Coll) – 180 pts approx (Comb St)
Liverpool Hope (Coll) – 180 pts approx (Cult St)
Oxford Brookes – DDD (BA QTS)
Peterborough (Coll) – 180 pts approx (Cult St)
Teesside – DDD (Hum)
Wolverhampton – 180 pts approx; gs; (Comb St; Hum – offer varies)

160 pts   **Birmingham (Westhill)** – CC (Hum)
Cheltenham & Glos (CHE) – 160 pts approx (Cult St)
Chichester (UC) – 160 pts (inc C); (Rel Arts)
Cumbria (CAD) – 160 pts – CC **or** ASs (contact coll) **or** VA; (Contemp Cult)
Doncaster (Coll) – 160 pts CC **or** ALs+ASs **or** VAs+/-AL/ASs; gs; (Comb St; Hum)
Glamorgan – CC average offer varies with subject (Comb Hons; Hum; Joint)
Greenwich – CC (Hum)
Grimsby (Coll) – 160 pts approx (Comb St)
Kingston – CC (Hist Ideas)
Leeds (Bretton Hall) – CC–EE (Engl; Soc St) (see **English**)
Manchester Met – CC (Cult St/Sociol)
Newman (CHE) – 160 pts – CC **or** VA12u CC(C chosen subj) gs; (BA joint courses; Hum)
Newport (UWCN) – 160–140 pts – ALs **or** ALs+ASs **or** VAs+/-ALs/ASs; (Humanities)
North East Wales (IHE) – 160 pts approx (Comb St)
North London – 160 pts 1x12u **or** 2x6u; (Crit Theor courses; Cult St; Hum Inf Tech; Arts Mgt)
Norwich City (Coll) – CC (Comb Arts)
Paisley – CC (Comb St)
Peterborough Reg (Coll) – 160–120 pts 12u – CC/DD **or** DE+c **or** VAs C/D+/-ALs/ASs; gs; (Comb St DipHE)
Peterborough Reg (Coll) – 160 pts 12u – CC/cccc **or** ALs+ASs; gs; (Comb St Cult St)
Ripon & York (Coll) – CC (Cult Crit St)
Sunderland – 160 pts; gs; (Joint Hons)
Surrey Roehampton – 160 pts 15u – ALs **or** ALs+ASs **or** VAs+/-ALs/ASs; (Hum; Cult St)
Thames Valley – 160–140 pts approx (Humanities)
Worcester (UC) – CC–EE varies with subjects (BA Mod)

140 pts   **and below**
Barnsley (Coll) – 100 pts – ALs **or** VA12u; (Humanities)
Bolton (IHE) – (Arts/Hum)
Bradford (Coll) – (Comb St)
Buckinghamshire Chilterns (UC) – (Arts/Soc – mature students part-time)
Coventry – (Mod St)
Greenwich – (Cult/Belief)
Huddersfield – (Humanities)
Hull (Scarborough) – 140 pts approx (Hum; Arts)
Leicester – (Hum – mature students only)
Lincolnshire & Humberside – (Lit/Hist St; Comb St)
Liverpool (LIPA) – (Perf Arts; Comm Arts)
Liverpool Hope (Coll) – (Comb St)
Plymouth (CAD) – (Cult Prac)
Queen Margaret (UC) – CD (Comb Hons)
St Mary's (Coll) – (Comb Hons)
Solihull (Coll) – (Cult St)

Somerset (CAT) – (Comb Arts)
Swansea (IHE) – (Comb St)
Trinity Carmarthen (CHE) – (Humanities)
UHI (Inverness/North Highland/Orkney/Shetland) – (Cult St via DipHE)
West Herts (Coll) – (Humanities)
Yeovil (Coll) – 120 pts approx (Comb St)

Leeds Met – (contact university)

Diploma of Higher Education courses
80 pts   Bangor; Barnsley (Coll); Bath Spa (UC); Bradford (Coll); Doncaster (Coll); East London; Edge Hill (CHE); King Alfred's Winchester (Coll); Lincolnshire & Humberside; London Guildhall; Manchester Met (Mod); Motherwell (Coll) (Arts Mgt); Northampton (UC); Oxford Brookes; Peterborough Reg (Coll); Plymouth; Trinity Carmarthen (CHE); UHI; Worcester (UC).

Alternative Offers:

IB offers: Aberdeen 30 pts; Belfast (Queen's) H555 S555; Bolton (IHE) 24 pts; Brunel 32 pts; Cardiff 32 pts; De Montfort 26 pts; Dundee 29 pts inc 15 pts in Highers; Durham 30 pts; Essex 28 pts; Glamorgan 24 pts; Glasgow 30 pts; Heriot-Watt 28 pts; Huddersfield 30 pts; King Alfred's Winchester (Coll) 24 pts; Leeds 28–30 pts; Leicester 28 pts; Manchester Met 28 pts; Newcastle 33 pts; Nottingham Trent 28 pts; Strathclyde 30–28 pts; Surrey Roehampton 30 pts; Warwick 30–28 pts.

Irish offers: Brighton BBBC; St Andrews BBBB; Warwick BBBC.

Scottish Qualifications: Aberdeen BBBB; Dundee BBBC; Edinburgh BBBB; Glasgow BBBB; Heriot-Watt BBBB; Paisley BBCC; Robert Gordon CCC; St Andrews BBBB; Strathclyde BBBB/BBBCC.

Overseas applicants: Oxford Brookes Special International Foundation Programme – details from institution.

CHOOSING YOUR COURSE (See also **Ch.1**)

> **Subject information:** Many different subjects are included in Arts courses which offer the student a wide choice and flexibility of study. At each institution the student normally chooses two or three subjects from a list of up to 80 (see below). Arts courses are, therefore, ideal for students with a range of interests in non-scientific areas who do not wish to commit themselves to a single subject course.

Special features: A large number of combined courses allow students to choose up to three or four or even five subjects in their first year. These include: **Aberdeen** (Arts) Specialisation in years 3 and 4. **Aberystwyth** Part 1 (year 1) 'Year of Discovery', Part 2 (years 3 and 4) single or joint courses chosen. **Bath Spa (UC)** (Comb St) Two subjects as either major, joint or minor combinations plus electives (including Japanese) in year 1. **Central Lancashire** (Comb Hons) Over 60 subjects offered; two or three chosen in year 1; two subjects chosen in years 2 and 3 as equal or major/minor options. **Cheltenham & Glos (CHE)** (Mod) Extensive subject choice of major/minor or joint course. **Colchester (Inst)** Choice of two main fields, but individual modules can be chosen from other fields. **De Montfort** (Comb Arts/Hum) Choice of three subjects from 12. (Mod) Two or three pathways in years 1 and 2; one subject chosen in year 3. **Derby** 58 subjects with major/minor or joint courses. **Durham** (Comb) Three subjects chosen in years 1, 2 and 3 from 16. **East London** (Comb Hons) 30 subjects, two main subjects as major/minor or joint courses. **Edge Hill (CHE)** (Mod) Three subjects chosen in year 1, then two as major/minor or joint combinations. **Edinburgh** (Arts) Four subjects taken in years 1 and 2. **Essex** (Arts) Four courses from 30 taken in the broad first year; degree choice in year 2. **Exeter** Modular course suitable for mature and part-time students. **Glamorgan** (Hum) Final course decisions made at end of year 1. **Glasgow** (Arts) Five subjects studied for two years. Honours course chosen in years 3 and 4. **Hertfordshire** (Comb St) Three subjects in year 1, two or three in year 2, two in year 3. **Keele** (Arts) Most students take two principal subjects and one subsidiary subject from humanities or social sciences. **Leicester** (Comb Arts) Three subjects chosen, two studied for three years, and a third studied for two years from 16 subjects. **Liverpool** (Comb Hons) Three or four subjects in year 1, then two in years 2 and 3. **London Guildhall** Students select three subjects from 37. Thereafter two are chosen for a joint degree or three for the combined degree. **Newcastle** (Comb St) Five subjects over three years, either two or three in each year chosen from arts, social sciences and sciences. **Northumbria** Three subjects are taken from a choice of nine groups, specialisation follows in years 2 and 3. **Nottingham Trent** (Cult Arts) Experiment and practice across the boundaries of visual art, performance, dance, new media and writing. (Hum) Twelve modules each year (six per semester), two main subjects from 13. Two-year course for mature students (23+). **Ripon & York (Coll)** (Comb) Four subjects in year 1 (two majors/two minors) then major/minor choice in year 3. **St Andrews** (Arts) Common General (3 year) or Hons (4 year) courses in years 1 and 2 (sometimes year 3) allows students to change courses. **Staffordshire** (Cult St) Strong focus on popular culture, options in media, literature, history of art and design, heritage and national identity, urban landscape. **Teesside** A choice is made from 39 major and 46 minor subjects. **Trinity Carmarthen (Coll)** (Hum) Three subjects in year 1 followed by major/minor choice. **Worcester (UC)** Joint or major/minor or triple subject options from 22 subjects. *NOW CHECK PROSPECTUSES AND WEB SITES.*

Study opportunities abroad: Aberdeen; Bath Spa (UC); Birmingham; Bristol UWE; Chester (Coll); De Montfort; Derby; Dundee; Glamorgan; Kent; Leicester; Lincolnshire & Humberside; Manchester; Manchester Met; Newcastle (see course requirements); St Andrews; St Mark & St John (Coll); Surrey Roehampton; Teesside; Thames Valley; Wolverhampton.

Work opportunities abroad: Chester (Coll); Derby; Dundee; Kent; Leicester; Thames Valley; Worcester (UC).

ADMISSIONS INFORMATION

Number of applicants per place (approx): Anglia 4; Bath Spa (UC) 8; Bolton (IHE) 7; Boston (Coll) 2; Bradford 7; Bristol UWE 16; Brunel 4; Cardiff (Cult Crit) 5; Central England 14; Central Lancashire 9; Chester (Coll) 10; Chichester (UC) 6; Colchester (Inst) 5; De Montfort 10, (Arts Mgt) 5; Derby 5; Dundee 13 average; Durham (Arts) 5, (Soc Sci) 9; East Anglia 12; East London 4; Glamorgan 5; Greenwich 5; Grimsby (Coll) 2; Hertfordshire 12; Heriot-Watt 3; Lancaster 20; Leeds 15; Leicester 11; Liverpool Hope (Coll) 8; Manchester Met (Hum/Soc St) 8, (Comb St) 12; Newman (Coll) 4; Newcastle 7; Newport (UWCN) 2; North East Wales (IHE) 2; North London 10; Northampton (UC) 8; Norwich City (Coll) 3; Nottingham Trent 5; Oxford Brookes 14; Plymouth 11; Portsmouth 10; Ripon & York (Coll) 3; St Mark & St John (Coll) 3; Sheffield Hallam 40; Staffordshire 9; Strathclyde 9; Suffolk (Coll) 7; Surrey Roehampton 4; Swansea 4; Swansea (IHE) 3; Teesside 8; Thames Valley 4; Trinity Carmarthen (Coll) 3; Wolverhampton 13; Worcester (UC) 12.

Planning your UCAS personal statement (see Ch.4): Refer to chosen subject tables. **Bradford** (Interd Hum St) Indications of interest in addressing academic work to contemporary issues. **De Montfort** (Arts Mgt) Show work experience in a related field. Demonstrate experience of teamwork/leadership. **Nottingham Trent** Refer to work experience, reasons for choice of subject, career ambitions.

Selection interviews (see Ch.4): Aberdeen; Anglia (T); Bath Spa (UC); Brighton; Bristol UWE; Brunel; Cardiff (No) (W); Central Lancashire (some); Cheltenham & Glos (CHE); Chester (Coll); Colchester (Inst) (T); De Montfort; Dundee; Durham (No); Glamorgan (No); Greenwich; Hertfordshire (No); Lancaster; Leicester (No); Lincolnshire & Humberside (T); Liverpool Hope (Coll); Manchester (No); Manchester Met; Newcastle (No); Newman (CHE) (No); North London; Northampton (UC); Nottingham Trent (No); Paisley (No); Ripon & York (Coll); St Mark & St John (Coll); St Mary's (Coll); Sheffield Hallam (No); Solihull (Coll) (W); Surrey Roehampton; Teesside; Trinity Carmarthen (CHE); Worcester (UC).

Interview questions (see Ch.4): Questions will focus on your chosen subjects. See under separate subject tables.

GAP YEAR ADVICE

Dundee Voluntary Service Overseas encouraged.

Institutions willing to defer entry after A-Levels: Aberdeen; Aston; Birmingham (Westhill); Bolton (IHE); Brighton; Brunel; Chester (Coll) Do not submit a deferred entry application; Colchester (Inst); De Montfort; Dundee; East London; Glamorgan; Heriot-Watt; Hertfordshire; King Alfred's Winchester (Coll); Lancaster; Leeds; Leicester; Lincolnshire & Humberside; London Guildhall; Manchester Met; Newman (CHE); Newcastle; Northampton (UC); Norwich City (Coll); Nottingham Trent; St Helens (Coll); Sheffield Hallam; Staffordshire; Surrey Roehampton; Swansea (IHE); Teesside; Wolverhampton.

AFTER RESULTS ADVICE

Institutions which may accept the same points score after A-Levels: Aberdeen; Anglia; Bath Spa (UC); Bolton (IHE); Brighton; Bristol UWE; Central Lancashire; Cheltenham & Glos (CHE); Chester (Coll) (No); Colchester (Inst); De Montfort; Derby; Dundee (No); Durham; East London; Glamorgan (No); Greenwich; Heriot-Watt; Hertfordshire; Huddersfield (No); Kingston; Lancaster; Leicester; Lincolnshire & Humberside; Liverpool (No); Liverpool Hope (Coll); Liverpool John Moores; Manchester; Manchester Met; Newcastle (varies); Newman (CHE); North London; Northampton (UC); Nottingham Trent; Portsmouth; Ripon & York (Coll); St Andrews (No); St Mark & St John (Coll); St Mary's (Coll); Sheffield Hallam; Strathclyde; Surrey Roehampton; Swansea (IHE); Teesside; Trinity Carmarthen (Coll) (No); Ulster; Wolverhampton; Worcester (UC) (varies).

Institutions which may accept lower grades/points scores after A-Levels: Aberdeen; Bolton (IHE); Brighton; Bristol UWE; Brunel; Chester (Coll); De Montfort; Durham; East London; Glamorgan; Heriot-Watt; Hertfordshire; Leicester; Manchester Met; Newman (CHE); Portsmouth; Ripon & York (Coll); St Andrews; Staffordshire; Strathclyde; Surrey Roehampton; Teesside.

Offers to applicants repeating A-Levels: Higher Glamorgan, Huddersfield, Manchester, Ripon & York (Coll), St Andrews; **Possibly higher** Bristol UWE, De Montfort, Leeds, Liverpool, Liverpool Hope (Coll), Newcastle, St Mary's (Coll), Surrey Roehampton, Teesside; **Same** Anglia, Bath Spa (UC), Birmingham, Bolton (IHE), Brunel, Cheltenham & Glos (CHE), Chester (Coll), Derby, De Montfort, Durham, Greenwich, Kingston, Leicester, Lincolnshire & Humberside; Manchester Met, Newman (CHE), North London, Northampton (UC), Portsmouth, Staffordshire, Swansea (IHE), Teesside, Wolverhampton, Worcester (UC).

Probable vacancies from June 2001 and in Clearing (see Ch.4): Vacancies are likely – contact institutions for further information.

NEW GRADUATE DESTINATIONS AND EMPLOYMENT (1999 HESA) (see **Ch.4**)

In a survey of 1862 graduates taking Combined or General Arts, 922 entered full-time employment, 437 went on to further study and 163 were believed to be unemployed.

ASIA-PACIFIC STUDIES (including **South East Asian Studies**; see also **Chinese** and **Japanese**)

NB The information supplied by the universities and colleges this year varies consider-
ably and the offers listed below should be used as a first source of reference only. Many
institutions will accept combinations of Advanced (AL), Advanced Subsidiary (AS) and
Vocational Advanced (VA) level qualifications to achieve the required points total, but
applicants must check web sites and prospectuses for full details of all offers. Grades
and points totals shown should be regarded as the minimum levels to be achieved, but
offers may be adjusted downwards when results are known. The points totals shown to
the left of the institutions are for ease of reference only. It must not be assumed that
tariff points are always used by institutions or that they can be substituted for an offer in
grades. The level of an offer is not necessarily indicative of the quality of a course. To
calculate your offers see Chapter 4 and the inside fold of the back cover.

Special subject requirements/preferences: GCSE: A language subject grade A–C. **Leeds** Seven/eight subjects at grades A and B. **London (SOAS)** For Vietnamese a good reading knowledge of French is required. **Sheffield** (E As St/Bus St) Grade B mathematics.

360 pts	**and above**
	Cambridge – Offers, mainly in grades, vary between colleges (Oriental St)
	Oxford – Offers vary between candidates (Oriental St)
320 pts	**Edinburgh** – ABB–BBB (Soc Anth/S As St; Sociol/S As St)
300 pts	**Durham** – 300 pts 18u – BBB; (not gs) (E As St courses)
	London (SOAS) – 300–260 pts approx (SE As Lang courses)
	Newcastle – BBB (Comb St (Kor) (Sansk) (Hindi) (E As St))
280 pts	**Hertfordshire** – 280–240 pts 1x12u **or** 2x6u – 2ALs **or** AL+2ASs **or** VA12u; gs; (As/Pacif Bus)
	Leeds – BBC (As/Pacif courses)
	London (UCL) – BBC (Af-As Lang)
	Sheffield – BBC (E As St/Bus St; Kor St/Econ)
	Sussex – BBC (Af As St)
260 pts	**Sheffield** – BCC (E As St)
240 pts	**Liverpool John Moores** – 240–180 pts – inc 2ALs **or** 2ALs+ASs **or** VAs+/- ALs/ASs; (As/Pacif St)
220 pts	**Central Lancashire** – 220 pts 12u (inc C lang); gs; (As/Pacif St)
200 pts	**Liverpool John Moores** – 200 pts (inc ALs); (Pacif-As St/Chin; Pacif-As St/Jap)
180 pts	**Hull** – BC (SE As St/Dutch St)
140 pts	**Bradford (Coll)** – 140 pts approx (S As Commun St)

Alternative Offers:

IB offers: Leeds 30 pts.

Scottish Qualifications: Edinburgh ABBBC.

Overseas applicants: Hull Living costs 30% lower than in London.

CHOOSING YOUR COURSE (See also **Ch.1**)

> **Subject information:** These courses focus on the study of the cultures and the languages of this region of the world, such as Burmese, Sanskrit, Vietnamese, Bengali, Marathi, Tamil and Urdu.

Special features: Hertfordshire Placement in Asia/Pacific region. **Hull** Topics covered in second and third years include history, politics, anthropology, defence, international relations, geography, economics and Malay language. **Leeds** Job opportunities in East Asia and Asia/Pacific region. Year abroad. **London (SOAS)** Seventeen South East Asian languages offered. **Sheffield** (E As St) Applications welcomed. (E As St/Bus St) Mature applicants welcomed). *NOW CHECK PROSPECTUSES AND WEB SITES.*

Top universities and colleges (Teaching Quality) (see Ch.4): Cambridge; Durham; London (SOAS); Oxford; not all institutions assessed.

Study opportunities abroad: Leeds; most universities.

ADMISSIONS INFORMATION

Number of applicants per place (approx): Hull (SE As Dutch St) 3; London (SOAS) (Thai St) 2, (Burm St) 1.

Planning your UCAS personal statement (see Ch.4): Connections with and visits to South and South East Asia should be mentioned. You should give some indication of what impressed you and your reasons for wishing to study these subjects. An awareness of the geography, culture and politics of the area also should be shown on the

UCAS form. **Leeds** Skills at learning a foreign language (if choosing a language course). Interest in current affairs of the region. Experience of travel. Self-discipline.

Examples of interview questions (see Ch.4): General questions are usually asked which relate to applicants' reasons for choosing a degree course in this subject area and to a background knowledge of the various cultures.

GAP YEAR ADVICE

Institutions willing to defer entry after A-Levels: Hull; Leeds.

AFTER RESULTS ADVICE

London (SOAS) Actual grades are required after A-Levels and interviews are held.

Institutions which may accept lower grades/points score after A-levels: Hull (overseas applicants 200–180 pts); Leeds.

Probable vacancies from June 2001 and in Clearing (see Ch.4): Several universities had vacancies last year from June onwards for Asian Studies. Offers are likely to range from 240–200 pts.

NEW GRADUATE DESTINATIONS AND EMPLOYMENT (1999 HESA) (see **Ch.4**)

Of 127 graduates surveyed, 72 went into full-time employment, 27 into further study and eight were unemployed.

ASTRONOMY/ASTROPHYSICS

NB The information supplied by the universities and colleges this year varies considerably and the offers listed below should be used as a first source of reference only. Many institutions will accept combinations of Advanced (AL), Advanced Subsidiary (AS) and Vocational Advanced (VA) level qualifications to achieve the required points total, but applicants must check web sites and prospectuses for full details of all offers. Grades and points totals shown should be regarded as the minimum levels to be achieved, but offers may be adjusted downwards when results are known. The points totals shown to the left of the institutions are for ease of reference only. It must not be assumed that tariff points are always used by institutions or that they can be substituted for an offer in grades. The level of an offer is not necessarily indicative of the quality of a course. To calculate your offers see Chapter 4 and the inside fold of the back cover.

Special subject requirements/preferences: A-Level: Mathematics and physics usually required for all courses. **GCSE: Edinburgh, Hertfordshire, St Andrews** English and a foreign language. **London (QM)** Average of grade B in all subjects.

360 pts	**and above**
	Cambridge – Offers, mainly in grades, vary between colleges (Nat Sci)
	London (UCL) – AAA–BBB **or** 3ALs+AS/VA; (Astron courses)
320 pts	**Liverpool** – 320 pts – ALs **or** ALs+ASs **or** VAs+/- ALs/ASs; (Astrophyics)
300 pts	**Bristol** – ABC (Phys/Astro)
	Hertfordshire – 300–200 pts 1x12u **or** 2x6u – 2ALs **or** AL+2ASs **or** VA12u+/- AL/ASs; gs; (Astron Mod)
	London (RH) – ABC–BBC (Astro courses)
	London (UCL) – BBB **or** 3ALs+AS/VA; (Astron; Astron/Phys; Astro)
	Surrey – BBB (Phys/Nucl Astro)
280 pts	**Belfast (Queen's)** – BBC–CCC (Astro courses)
	Cardiff – 280–240 pts approx (Astro courses)
	Durham – BBC (Phys/Astron)
	Liverpool John Moores – 280 pts inc ALs phys+maths B+AL(C); VAs (check univ); (MPhys: Phys/Astro)

London (QM) – 280–240 pts approx (MSci/BSc: Astron; Astro)
Manchester – BBC–BCC (Phys/Astro)
St Andrews – BBC–BCC (Astrophysics)
Southampton – BBC–BCC (Astron courses)
UMIST – BBC (Astron/Astro courses)
260 pts **Birmingham** – BCC (Phys/Astro)
Hertfordshire – 260–220 pts 1x12u **or** 2x6u – 2ALs **or** VA12u; gs; (Astronomy)
Keele – BCC–CCC **or** equiv AS accepted; gs; (Astro courses)
Lancaster – BCC (Phys/Cosmo)
Leeds – BCC (Astron courses)
Leicester – BCC (Astron/Astro courses)
Liverpool – 260 pts approx (Astro)
Liverpool John Moores – 260 pts inc ALs phys B/C+maths C/B+AL(C); VAs (check univ); (BSc: Phys/Astro)
London (King's) – 260 pts approx (Phys/Astro)
London (UCL) – BCC–CCC **or** 3ALs+AS/VA; (Earth Space Sci)
Newcastle – BCC/BB (Astron/Astro)
Portsmouth – 260 pts approx (Maths/Astro)
Sheffield – BCC (Astron courses)
Sussex – BCC–CCC (Astrophysics)
York – BCC (Phys/Astro)
240 pts **Edinburgh** – CCC/BB (Astrophysics)
Glasgow – CCC (Astron/Phys; Astron/Maths)
Hertfordshire – 240–200 pts 1x12u **or** 2x6u – 2ALs **or** AL+2ASs **or** VA12u; gs; (Astrophys courses)
Kent – BCD (Phys/Astro; Phys/Space Sci Sys)
220 pts **Aberystwyth** – 220–180 pts approx (Phys/Plan Space Phys; Earth Planet Space Sci)
Central Lancashire – 12u – CCD (inc maths+phys); gs; (Astron; Astrophys)
200 pts **Plymouth** – 200–180 pts approx (Astron courses)
180 pts **Central Lancashire** – 180–160 pts 12u (inc AL maths+phys); gs; (Astron/Comp; Astron/Mgt; Astron/Maths; Astron/Media Tech)
Glamorgan – 180 pts – CC **or** ALs+ASs; gs; (Astron Comb Hons)
160 pts **Staffordshire** – CC (Phys/Astro)

Alternative Offers:

IB offers: Birmingham 30 pts; Bristol 26 pts H55 (maths & phys); Cardiff Individual offers; Central Lancashire 26 pts; Hertfordshire 24 pts; Kent 26 pts, H 11 pts; London (QM) H777-H555, (UCL) 32 pts; Newcastle 30 pts H5 phys; St Andrews 28 pts.

Irish offers: Kent BBBCC.

Scottish Qualifications: Edinburgh BBBC; Glasgow BBBB; St Andrews BBBC.

CHOOSING YOUR COURSE (See also **Ch.1**)

> **Subject information:** Astronomy courses have a mathematics and physics emphasis. Applicants, however, should realise that subject-related careers on graduation are limited. Courses in Geophysics, Mathematics, Meteorology or Applied Physics could be suitable alternatives. Astrophysics courses involve both physics and astronomy and are more difficult than single honours courses in these subjects. See also **Appendix 1**.

Special features: Central Lancashire Practical observations are made with Britain's largest optical telescope. **Liverpool John Moores** Astrophysics is a collaborative venture between the university and Liverpool university and covers physics, mathematics and computing. **Southampton** The Physics and Astronomy course can be taken as a degree in both subjects or as two degrees in each subject. *NOW CHECK PROSPECTUSES AND WEB SITES.*

Top universities and colleges (Teaching Quality) (see Ch.4): Cambridge (Nat Sci); Hertfordshire; not all institutions assessed.

Top universities and colleges (Research) (see Ch.4): See **Physics**.

Study opportunities abroad: Birmingham; Bristol; Glasgow; Kent; Leeds; Leicester; Liverpool John Moores; London (QM); St Andrews; York.

ADMISSIONS INFORMATION

Number of applicants per place (approx): Bristol 9; Cardiff 6; Central Lancashire (Astro) 12; Hertfordshire 5; Leicester 12; London (QM) 6, (RH) 6, (UCL) 5; Newcastle 7.

Planning your UCAS personal statement (see Ch.4): Books and magazines on astronomy and astrophysics are an obvious source of interest which should be described on the UCAS form. A visit to the London Planetarium or observatories would also be important. See also **Appendix 1**.

Selection interviews (see Ch.4): Bristol; Hertfordshire (No); London (UCL); Newcastle.

Interview questions (see Ch.4): You will probably be questioned on your study of physics and the aspects of the subject which you enjoy the most. Questions in the past have included: Can you name a recent development in physics which will be important in the future? Describe a physics experiment, indicating any errors and exactly what it was intended to prove. Explain weightlessness. What is a black hole? What are the latest discoveries in space?

GAP YEAR ADVICE

Universities stress that it is important to keep up with your maths.

Institutions willing to defer entry after A-Levels: Birmingham; Central Lancashire; Kent; London (UCL); Newcastle; St Andrews.

AFTER RESULTS ADVICE

Institutions which may accept the same points score after A-Levels: Bristol; London (UCL) (No); Newcastle; St Andrews (No).

Offers to applicants repeating A-Levels: Higher St Andrews; **Same** London (UCL), Newcastle.

Probable vacancies from June 2001 and in Clearing (see Ch.4): A large number of course vacancies were declared last year in this subject, with offers made by popular universities in the 240–220 pts range.

NEW GRADUATE DESTINATIONS AND EMPLOYMENT (1999 HESA) (see **Ch.4**)

Out of 86 graduates, 31 entered full-time employment, 37 went on to further study and 10 were believed to be unemployed.

BANKING, FINANCE & INSURANCE (including **Financial Services**; see also **Accountancy/Accounting**)

NB The information supplied by the universities and colleges this year varies consider-ably and the offers listed below should be used as a first source of reference only. Many institutions will accept combinations of Advanced (AL), Advanced Subsidiary (AS) and Vocational Advanced (VA) level qualifications to achieve the required points total, but applicants must check web sites and prospectuses for full details of all offers. Grades and points totals shown should be regarded as the minimum levels to be achieved, but offers may be adjusted downwards when results are known. The points totals shown to the left of the institutions are for ease of reference only. It must not be assumed that

tariff points are always used by institutions or that they can be substituted for an offer in grades. The level of an offer is not necessarily indicative of the quality of a course. To calculate your offers see Chapter 4 and the inside fold of the back cover.

Special subject requirements/preferences: A-Level: Paisley English. **GCSE:** English and mathematics required. **Bangor** Average grade B. **Birmingham, Buckingham, De Montfort, East Anglia** and **Portsmouth** Grade B in mathematics. **City** Grade B in English and mathematics.

320 pts	**City** – 3x6u – ABB **or** VAs (contact univ); (not gs) (Bank/Int Fin; Invest Fin Risk Mgt; Real Est Fin Invest; Risk Analys Ins)
	Nottingham – ABB (Ind Econ/Ins)
	Reading – ABB (Int Sec Invest Bank)
300 pts	**Aston** – BBB (Acc Mgt)
	Belfast (Queen's) – BBB (Finance courses)
	Birmingham – BBB (Money Bank Fin; Money Bank Fin/Lang)
	Bradford – 300 pts 12u; gs; (Acc/Fin)
	Cardiff – BBB (Bank/Fin)
	East Anglia – 300–280 pts approx (Bus Fin Econ)
	Glasgow – BBB (Fin Leg St)
	Lancaster – BBB–BBC (Fin; Fin Econ)
	Leeds – 300–280 pts approx (Fin/Acc)
	Loughborough – 18u – BB+B/bb **or** VA12u BB+B/bb; (Bank/Fin Mgt)
	Manchester – BBB–BBC (Finance)
	Sheffield – 300 pts approx (Fin Mgt)
280 pts	**Durham** – 280 pts approx (Bus Fin)
	Essex – BBC (Maths/Fin)
	Heriot-Watt – BBC–BCC (Bus Fin)
	Oxford Brookes – BBC–BCC (Int Bank Fin)
	Reading – 280 pts approx (Invest Fin Prop)
260 pts	**Aberystwyth** – 260 pts approx (Finance courses)
	Bournemouth – 260 pts – BCC; (Tax/Law)
	Keele – BCC–CCC **or** equiv AS accepted; gs; (Finance courses)
	Stirling – BCC (Finance courses)
	Strathclyde – BCC (Maths Stats Fin)
250 pts	**Buckingham** – 250 pts 21u – 3ALs **or** 3ALs+AS; (Fin Serv)
240 pts	**Aberdeen** – CCC (Finance courses)
	Bangor – 240 pts – ALs **or** VAs+/-ALs/ASs; gs; (Bank/Fin; Bank/Acc)
	Bournemouth – 240 pts: CCC; (Fin Serv)
	Brighton – 240 pts approx (Int Fin Cap Mark St; Bus St/Fin)
	Dundee – CCC (Finance)
	Lincolnshire & Humberside – 240–160 pts (Finance courses)
	Manchester Met – 240 pts approx – ALs **or** AL+2ASs **or** VA12u; (Fin Serv)
	Northumbria – 240 pts approx (Fin Serv)
	Nottingham Trent – CCC/BB (Fin Serv/Econ)
	Paisley – CCC (Fin Serv)
	Robert Gordon – CCC (Acc/Fin)
	Westminster – 240 pts approx (Bus Fin)
220 pts	**Central Lancashire** – 220–200 pts approx (Fin Serv)
	De Montfort (Leicester) – 220 pts – inc 2ALs **or** VA12u+/-AL/ASs; (Finance)
	Greenwich – 220–200 pts approx (Fin Serv; Fin/Fin Inf Sys)
	Portsmouth – 220 pts – ALs **or** ALs+ASs **or** VAs; (Fin Serv; Int Fin Trade; Int Fin/e-bus)
	Staffordshire – CCD/BC (Int Fin/Bus)
	Wolverhampton – 220–200 pts approx (Fin St)
200 pts	**Central England** – 200 pts – 2ALs **or** ALs+ASs **or** VAs+/-ALs/ASs; gs; (Finance)
	Huddersfield – 200–180 pts approx (Fin Mgt/Econ)
	Middlesex – 200–180 pts approx (Money Bank Fin; Fin)

North London – 200 pts approx (Fin Serv Mgt; Math Sci; Fin Serv Mgt/App Psy)

Sheffield Hallam – 200 pts approx (Int Fin Leg St; Fin St Comb; Ins; Bank; Fin Serv)

180 pts **East London** – 180 pts approx (Fin Money Bank)

Glasgow Caledonian – BC (Fin Serv; Risk Mgt)

Heriot-Watt – CDE (Maths/Fin)

Regents (Bus Sch London) – DDD/CC (Int Fin/Acc)

Thames Valley – 180–140 pts approx (Fin minor)

160 pts **Abertay Dundee** – 160 pts – CD (Fin Serv)

Anglia – 160 pts 12u – 2ALs **or** VA12u CC; gs; (Fin Serv)

Cheltenham & Glos (CHE) – 160 pts approx (Fin Serv)

Glamorgan – 160 pts approx (Fin Inf Tech)

London Guildhall – 160–140 pts approx (Bank Fin Ins courses)

Napier – DDE (Fin Serv courses)

140 pts **and below**

Bradford (Coll) – 140 pts approx (Fin Serv)

Buckinghamshire Chilterns (UC) – (Fin courses)

Paisley – CD (Fin Serv)

Southampton (Inst) – 140 pts approx (Fin Serv)

Higher National Diploma courses
100 pts and below

Bell (CT); Blackpool & Fylde (Coll); Buckinghamshire Chilterns (UC); Cheltenham & Glos (CHE); De Montfort; Newport (UWC); Reading (CSAD); Salford; Stockport (CFHE); Suffolk (Coll); Teesside; Thames Valley; UHI; West Herts (Coll).

Alternative Offers:

IB offers: Aberystwyth 26 pts; Aston 31 pts; Bangor 30–32 pts inc H666; Birmingham 33 pts; Buckingham 26 pts; Cardiff 30 pts; Cheltenham & Glos (CHE) 26 pts; City (Bank/Int Fin) H666 S555.

Irish offers: Bangor AAABB

Scottish Qualifications: Aberdeen BBBB; Abertay Dundee BBC; Dundee BBBC; Glasgow BBBB; Glasgow Caledonian BBBC; Heriot-Watt BBBB; Napier BCCC; Paisley BBCC; Robert Gordon CCC; Stirling BBBC.

CHOOSING YOUR COURSE (See also **Ch.1**)

> **Subject information:** Financial Services courses provide a comprehensive view of the world of finance and normally cover banking, insurance, investment, building societies, international finance, accounting and economics. These courses will not necessarily provide graduates with full exemptions from Institute of Banking qualifications (see **Appendix 1**, Professional Associations). Major banks offer sponsorships for some of the specialised banking courses. Economics, Accountancy, Actuarial Studies, Business Studies and Financial Services courses could be appropriate alternatives.

Special features: Birmingham Money, Banking and Finance can be studied with modern languages. **Bournemouth** The third year of the Financial Services course is spent in work placement in the commercial sector. **Brighton** The degree in International Finance and Capital Markets (full-time or sandwich) is directly relevant to careers in stockbroking, portfolio management and corporate finance. **Buckingham** The Financial Services course commences in January, not in September. **Glasgow Caledonian** A course in Risk Management relates to insurance with topics involving fire, employee injury, pollution and computer fraud. **Portsmouth** Opportunities to study in France, Germany, Holland or Spain. **Stirling** Finance can be studied with 13 other subjects including Japanese. *NOW CHECK PROSPECTUSES AND WEB SITES.*

Top universities and colleges (Teaching Quality) (see Ch.4): Aberystwyth; City; not all institutions assessed.

Study opportunities abroad: Bangor; Birmingham; Central England; City; Portsmouth; Sheffield Hallam; Staffordshire.

Work opportunities abroad: Brighton; Central England; Cheltenham & Glos (CHE); City; Sheffield Hallam; Staffordshire.

ADMISSIONS INFORMATION

Number of applicants per place (approx): Aberystwyth 4; Bangor 30; Birmingham 18; Bristol UWE 4; Buckingham 4; Cardiff 10; Central England 13; Central Lancashire 6; City 10; Glamorgan 3; Loughborough 35; Middlesex 3; Portsmouth 4; Sheffield Hallam 4.

Planning your UCAS personal statement (see Ch.4): Relevant visits arranged through school or college should be described, together with the various types of work done or observed and any particular aspects of banking which interest you. **City** Sport, voluntary work, skills. See also **Appendix 1**, Professional Associations.

Selection interviews (see Ch.4): Bangor (No); Brighton (No); Buckingham (pref); Cardiff (No); Central Lancashire (No); City (No); Dundee (No); Greenwich (No); Huddersfield; Loughborough (No); Manchester (No); Manchester Met (No); Napier (No); Portsmouth (No); Regents (Bus Sch London) (No); Sheffield Hallam (No); Staffordshire (some).

Interview questions (see Ch.4): Banking involves both high street and merchant banks, so a knowledge of banking activities in general will be expected. Mergers might be discussed and also the role of the Bank of England in the economy.

Reasons for rejection (non-academic): Lack of interest. Poor English. Lacking in motivation and determination to complete the course.

GAP YEAR ADVICE

Cardiff Try to gain some experience in the finance sector; **City** Deferred entry preferred.

Institutions willing to defer entry after A-Levels: Bangor; Birmingham; Bournemouth; Brighton; Buckingham; Cardiff; Central England; Cheltenham & Glos (CHE) Work experience may give exemptions from placement year; City; London Guildhall; Luton; Manchester; Northumbria; Sheffield Hallam.

AFTER RESULTS ADVICE

Institutions which may accept the same points score after A-Levels: Bangor; Birmingham (some); Brighton; Bristol UWE; Cardiff; Cheltenham & Glos (CHE); City; London Guildhall; Loughborough; Napier; Portsmouth.

Institutions which may accept lower grades/points score after A-Levels: Bangor; Brighton; Cardiff; Cheltenham & Glos (CHE); London Guildhall; Napier; Sheffield Hallam.

Offers to applicants repeating A-Levels: Possibly higher Bangor; **Same** Birmingham, Central England, City, London Guildhall, Loughborough, Manchester, Napier, Northumbria.

Probable vacancies from June 2001 and in Clearing (see Ch.4): A wide selection of courses in this field are likely from June onwards for Banking, Insurance, Finance and Financial Services. Contact all institutions.

NEW GRADUATE DESTINATIONS AND EMPLOYMENT (1999 HESA) (see **Ch.4**)

(Financial Management) Out of 588 graduates surveyed, 436 were reported to be in full-time employment, 31 were understood to be unemployed, and 56 went on to further study.

BIOCHEMISTRY

NB The information supplied by the universities and colleges this year varies consider-ably and the offers listed below should be used as a first source of reference only. Many institutions will accept combinations of Advanced (AL), Advanced Subsidiary (AS) and Vocational Advanced (VA) level qualifications to achieve the required points total, but applicants must check web sites and prospectuses for full details of all offers. Grades and points totals shown should be regarded as the minimum levels to be achieved, but offers may be adjusted downwards when results are known. The points totals shown to the left of the institutions are for ease of reference only. It must not be assumed that tariff points are always used by institutions or that they can be substituted for an offer in grades. The level of an offer is not necessarily indicative of the quality of a course. To calculate your offers see Chapter 4 and the inside fold of the back cover.

Special subject requirements/preferences: A-Level: Chemistry, usually supported by another science subject; physics, mathematics or biology often preferred. **London (RH)** Biology strongly recommended. **GCSE: Bath** Approx five grade As, five grade Bs. **Birmingham** Eight subjects A*, A or B (minimum C in English/mathematics, grade B some sciences). **Bristol** Mostly grades A or B. **Cambridge, Oxford** Grade As in most subjects preferred. **Cardiff** Seven subjects grades A or B. **Kingston** Grade A or B in sciences. **Leeds** Nine to ten subjects A*, A or B including mathematics. **London (RH)** Minimum five As and Bs in sciences and mathematics. **Southampton** Grade C in maths. **Surrey** A cluster of A* and As creates a good impression. **Swansea** Mainly A/B grades especially in the sciences.

360 pts **and above**
    Cambridge – Offers, mainly in grades, vary between colleges (Nat Sci/Bioch)
    Nottingham – 18u – AAA/AAA+AS; (not gs); (Bioch/Genet)
    Oxford – Offers vary between candidates (Biochemistry)
350 pts **York** – 350–300 pts 21–18u – ABB/BBB/BBC or ALs+ASs or VAs (check with
    univ); gs; (Bioch courses)
340 pts **Bristol** – AAB–ABB (inc chem+sci); (not gs) (Bioch; Bioch/Med Bioch;
    Bioch/Mol Biol Biotech)
    London (Imp) – AAB (Bioch/Euro)
330 pts **Southampton** – 330 pts 21u (inc 200 pts 2AL sci subjs inc chem); (not gs)
    (Bioch courses)
320 pts **Bath** – 320 pts 18u – ABB or 320 pts(B chem) or VA12u+/-ALs/ASs; (not gs)
    (MBioch; Bioch; BSc Bioch)
    East Anglia – ABB (Bioch/USA)
    Liverpool – 320–280 pts – ALs or ALs+ASs or VAs+/-ALs/ASs; (Bioch; App
    Bioch)
    London (Imp) – ABB (Bioch; Bioch/Ind; Bioch/Mgt/Ind/Res; Bioch/Euro)
    London (UCL) – ABB–BBB or 3ALs+AS/VA; (Biochemistry)
300 pts **Durham** – B(biol)B(sci)+B/bb; (not gs) (Biochemistry)
    Leicester – BBB (Biol Chem USA)
    London (QM) – 300–250 pts – ALs or ALs+ASs or VAs+/-ALs/ASs;
    (Bioch/Microbiol; Bioch)
    Manchester – BBB (Med Bioch; Bioch; Bioch/Biotech; Bioch/Modn Lang)
    Salford – BBB–BBC/AA–AB (Bioch Sci/USA)
    Sussex – BBB (Bioch/N Am St)
280 pts **Cardiff** – BBC/AB (Bioch courses)
    East Anglia – BBC (Bioch/Euro)
    Edinburgh – BBC (Biochemistry)
    Glasgow – BBC–CCC (Bioch courses)
    Kent – 280–240 pts 21–18u – BBC–CCC or BC–CC+ASs; gs; (Biochemistry)
    Lancaster – BBC (Bioch/USA)
    Leeds – BBC (Joint Hons Bioch courses except under **240 pts**)
    Leicester – 18u – BBC or BB+ASs or VA12u+AL(B chem); gs; (Med Bioch;
    Bioch)

London (King's) – BBC+AS (or equiv) **or** BB+bc (inc B chem+sci) **or** VA12u BB+AL(C chem)+AS **or** VA6u+ALs/ASs; (Bioch; Med Bioch; Bioch/Immun; Bioch/Micro)

London (RH) – BBC–BCC **or** ALs+ASs **or** VAs+/-ALs/ASs; (Bioch courses)

Manchester – BBC (Bioch/Biotech; Bioch/Ind Exp; Med Bioch/Ind Exp)

Newcastle – BBC–BCC/BB (Biochemistry)

Nottingham – BBC–BCC (Bioch; Biol Chem)

Sheffield – BBC (Bioch courses)

Swansea – 280 pts 18u – BBC–BCC/AB–BB **or** ALs+ASs **or** VAs+/-ALs/ASs; (Biochemistry)

UMIST – BBC **or** BB+cc (inc AL chem+sci/maths); (not gs) (Bioch; Bioch/Ger; Bioch/Ind Exp; Bioch/Med Bioch; Biotech; Mol Biol)

Warwick – 280–260 pts approx (Biochemistry)

260 pts **Birmingham** – BCC (Bioch; Bioch/Biotech; Bioch/Mol Cell Biol; Med Bioch)

Durham – BCC–CCC (Mol Biol/Bioch)

East Anglia – BCC/AA–BB (Bioch Mol Biol; Bioch)

Exeter – BCC–CCC (Biol/Med Chem)

Hertfordshire – 260–200 pts 1x12u **or** 2x6u – 2ALs(biol or/with chem) **or** AL+2ASs **or** VA12u; gs; (Bioch courses)

Keele – BCC **or** equiv AS accepted; gs; (Bioch courses)

Lancaster – BCC (Bioch courses except under **280 pts**)

Leicester – BCC–CCC (Biol Chem)

Salford – BCC–CDD (Bioch Sci)

Surrey – BCC–BCD (Bioch courses)

Sussex – BCC (Bioch courses except under **300 pts**)

240 pts **Aberystwyth** – 240 pts 21u – CCC **or** CC+cc **or** VAs; gs; (Bioch; Med Bioch/Biotech)

Belfast (Queen's) – CCC/BB (Bioch)

Brunel – 240 pts 3x6u (inc biol/chem) – ALs **or** ALs+ASs **or** VAs+/-ALs/ASs; (Bioch; App Bioch; Med Bioch)

Central Lancashire – 240 pts 12u (inc AL sci); gs; (Bioch/Foren; Foren Sci courses)

Essex – 240 pts 21u – CC (inc chem+sci/maths)+AL/2ASs **or** VA12u CC+AL **or** VA6u+2ALs; gs; (Biochemistry)

Heriot-Watt – 240 pts 18u – CCC; gs; (Biochemistry)

Leeds – CCC (Bioch Fd Sci)

Oxford Brookes – CCC–DD (Biol Chem)

Reading – BCD–CCC (Bioch; Bioch/Physiol)

St Andrews – CCC (Biochemistry)

Staffordshire – 1x12u **or** 2x6u; gs; (Bioch courses)

Strathclyde – CCC (2nd yr entry) (Bioch; Bioch/Immun; Bioch/Pharmacol)

Surrey – CCC/BC (Bioch with Fdn Yr)

220 pts **Aberdeen** – CCD/BC (Bioch courses)

Bradford – 220 pts 12u (inc AL biol/chem); (Biochemistry)

Bristol UWE – 220–180 pts 12u – ALs **or** ALs+ASs (inc 6u sci/chem) **or** VAs+/-ALs/ASs (inc chem related subj); (App Bioch/Mol Biol)

Dundee – 220 pts approx (Bioch courses)

Luton – 220–180 pts approx (Bioch Mod)

Salford – CCD/BC (Bioch with Chem/Econ/Geog/Phys)

Stirling – CCD/BC (Biochemistry)

Ulster – CCD/BC (App Bioch Sci)

210 pts **Wolverhampton** – 210–160 pts 12u – DDD–DDE/CC **or** CC+dd-de **or** VA12u CC; gs; (Bioch courses)

200 pts **Central Lancashire** – 200–180 pts 12u (inc AL chem+biol); gs; (Bioch/Bus)

Nottingham – CDD (Nutr Bioch)

Portsmouth – 200 pts – ALs **or** ALs+ASs **or** VAs; gs; (Bioch; Bioch/Microbiol)

180 pts **Central Lancashire** – 180–160 pts 12u (inc AL chem+biol); gs; (Bioch/Fr/Ger)

Coventry – 180 pts approx (Bioch courses)
East London – 180 pts approx (Bioch; Med Bioch)
Greenwich – 180 pts (Biochemistry)
Kingston – 180 pts – 2x6u (inc 60 pts AL chem); (not gs) (Bioch; Med Bioch; Medicin Chem)
Liverpool John Moores – 180–120 pts (inc AL biol/chem); (App Bioch courses)
Northumbria – 180 pts approx (Chem/Bioch)
Nottingham Trent – 2ALs (inc biol+chem) **or** AL+2ASs **or** VA12u; (Bioch/Micro)
South Bank – 180 pts approx (Biochemistry)
Sunderland – 180 pts – 2ALs **or** ALs+ASs **or** VAs+/-ALs/ASs; gs; (Bioch/Mol Biol; Bioch Comb);

160 pts **Central Lancashire** – 160–140 pts 12u (inc AL chem+biol); gs; (Bioch courses except under **240/200/180 pts**)
Huddersfield – 160 pts 12u – 2ALs **or** AL+2ASs **or** VA12u; gs; (Biochemistry)
Manchester Met – 160 pts approx (Medicin Biol Chem)
Nottingham Trent – DDE/BD (Bioch/Microbiol)
Westminster – CC (Bioch/Microbiol)

120 pts **and below**
Nescot – DD (Biochemistry)
North London – 120 pts – 2ALs **or** VAs6u/12u; (Bioch courses)
Paisley – DD (Bioch/Immun; Bioch/Microbiol; App Bioch)
Stockport (CFHE) – EE (Biochemistry)

Higher National Diploma courses
Coventry; Hertfordshire; Truro (Coll); Wolverhampton.

Alternative Offers:

EB offers: Aberystwyth 70% in 2 named subjects; Bath 70%; Bradford 65%; Keele 60%; Sheffield 65%; UMIST 60%.

IB offers: Aberdeen 26 pts; Aberystwyth 28 pts + (minimum of 5 in each subject); Bath 24 pts or more inc 18 pts at Highers; Birmingham 30 pts; Bradford 24 pts; Bristol 32 pts inc 6 in Chemistry; Brunel 26 pts min inc 15 pts Highers; Cardiff 28 pts + H555; Dundee H554; Durham H665; East Anglia 28 pts; Essex 28 pts; Greenwich 24 pts; Heriot-Watt 28 pts; Keele 26 pts; Kent 25 pts, H 11 pts; Lancaster 32–30 pts; Leeds 26 pts H6 chem; London (RH) 28 pts, (UCL) 32 pts; Portsmouth 30–28 pts; Salford H555; South Bank 30–28 pts; Southampton H655; Surrey 28 pts; Swansea 28 pts; UMIST 30 pts H555; Warwick 30–28 pts; Wolverhampton 28 pts; York 28 pts H555.

Irish offers: Aberdeen BBCC/BCCC; Aberystwyth BBBCC; Bradford BBBB; Brunel BBCCC; Keele BBCCC; Sheffield BBBBB; UMIST ABBBBC; Warwick BBBBB.

Scottish Qualifications: Aberdeen BBBC; Dundee BBB/BBCC; Edinburgh BBBB; Glasgow ABB or BBBB or BBB; Heriot-Watt BBB; Paisley BBC; St Andrews BBCC; Stirling BBCC; Strathclyde BBC.

Overseas applicants: Durham No Foundation courses. **East Anglia** English courses for students.

CHOOSING YOUR COURSE (See also **Ch.1**)

Subject information: Many subjects can be covered in Biochemistry courses, such as medical biochemistry, plant and animal physiology, microbiology, biophysics. Check prospectuses and web sites carefully. Other alternative courses to Biochemistry are equally varied, for example, Agricultural Sciences, Agriculture, Biological Sciences, Botany, Brewing, Chemistry, Food Science, Genetics, Geochemistry, Geological Sciences, Medicine, Microbiology, Nutrition, Pharmacology and Pharmacy. See also **Appendix 1**.

Special features: Bath Placements can be arranged in Europe and the USA. **Bradford** Common course in years 1 and 2 followed by specialisation. **Manchester** Broad modular course in the School of Biological Sciences gives flexibility and a range of specialisms. **Newcastle** A common first year course with Genetics and Molecular Biology enables students to change courses at the end of the year. **North London** An emphasis on clinical and applied biochemistry in year 3. **Oxford** Part 2 includes a research project which may be done at one of several European universities. **Reading** A broad first year course leads to over 20 specialised options. **Warwick** Options in the final year include industrial biology, oncology, business and languages. Medical Biochemistry is offered as a specialism at several universities, for example **Aberystwyth, Bradford, Bristol, Brunel, Cardiff, East London, Glasgow, Leicester, London (RH), North London, Surrey, Warwick** and **Wolverhampton**. *NOW CHECK PROSPECTUSES AND WEB SITES.*

Top universities and colleges (Teaching Quality) (see Ch.4): Bath; Brunel; Essex; Huddersfield; Kent; Leicester; London (RH); Nottingham; Nottingham Trent (see also **Biology**); Southampton; not all institutions assessed.

Top universities and colleges (Research) (see Ch.4): Birmingham; Bristol; Cambridge; Dundee; Glasgow; Leeds; Leicester; London (Imp), (UCL); Manchester; Newcastle; Oxford.

Study opportunities abroad: Aberystwyth; Belfast (Queen's); Birmingham; Bradford; Brunel; Cardiff; Central Lancashire; Coventry; East Anglia; Glasgow; Greenwich; Kent; Kingston; Lancaster; Leeds; Leicester; London (Imp); Manchester; Nescot; Newcastle; Nottingham; Oxford; Reading; Salford; Sheffield; Staffordshire; Surrey; Swansea; UMIST; York.

Work opportunities abroad: Aberystwyth; Bath; Birmingham; Brunel; Greenwich; Kingston; Leeds; Liverpool John Moores; London (RH); Manchester; Nescot; North London; Staffordshire; Surrey; Swansea; Warwick; York.

ADMISSIONS INFORMATION

Number of applicants per place (approx): Aberystwyth 6; Bath 7; Birmingham 6; Bradford 7; Bristol 13; Brunel 5; Cardiff 9; Central Lancashire 9; Coventry 10; Dundee 8; Durham 6; East Anglia 10; East London 5; Edinburgh 8; Essex 5; Heriot-Watt 10; Keele 7; Kent 11; Lancaster 7; Leeds 10; Leicester (Med Bioch) 17; Liverpool John Moores 10; London (Imp) 6, (RH) 8, (UCL) 8; Manchester 13; Newcastle 7; Nottingham 14; Oxford 1.4; Salford 4; Sheffield 11; South Bank 5; Strathclyde 7; Surrey 10; Swansea 7; UMIST 7; Warwick 6; York 12.

Planning your UCAS personal statement (see Ch.4): Extend your knowledge of chemistry and biology beyond the exam syllabus by reading scientific journals. Focus on one or two aspects of biochemistry which interest you and mention these on the UCAS form. Attend scientific lectures (often arranged by universities on open days), find some work experience, and use these to show your understanding of what biochemistry is. Give evidence of your communication skills and time management. If relevant, explain the need to repeat A-levels or why you might wish to defer entry. Further information may be obtained from the Institute of Biology, the Royal Society of Chemistry (see **Appendix 1**), and from the Civil Service Commission (Schools Liaison). **St Andrews** Evidence of interest and reasons for choosing the course. Sport/extra-curricular activities, posts of responsibility. **Southampton** Evidence of work experience. See also **Appendix 1**.

Selection interviews (see Ch.4): Aberystwyth (No); Bath (50%); Birmingham (Clearing only); Bradford (informal – after offer); Bristol; Brunel; Cambridge; Cardiff (No); East Anglia; East London; Huddersfield (No); Keele (mature students only); Kent (No); Kingston; Leeds; Leicester (No); Liverpool John Moores (No); London (RH), (UCL); Manchester; Newcastle (No); North London (No); Nottingham (No); Nottingham Trent (No); Oxford; Paisley (No); Portsmouth (mature students only); Salford; Sheffield; South Bank; Southampton (No); Staffordshire (No); Surrey; Swansea; UMIST; Warwick; York (No).

Interview questions (see Ch.4): Questions should be expected on your study of chemistry and biology and your understanding of what a course in Biochemistry involves. In the past questions covering Mendel, genetics, RNA and DNA have also been asked.

Reasons for rejection (non-academic): Borderline grades plus poor motivation. Failure to turn up for interviews or answer correspondence. Inability to discuss subject. Not compatible with A-level predictions or references. **Birmingham** Lack of total commitment to Biochemistry, for example intention to transfer to Medicine without completing the course.

GAP YEAR ADVICE

Laboratory work in some form is recommended by many universities. **Bristol** Adequate chemistry revision necessary before starting the course; **Brunel** Think beforehand since this course offers experience outside the academic world.

Institutions willing to defer entry after A-Levels: Aberystwyth (contact the admissions tutor if you change your mind); Birmingham; Bradford; Bristol (No); Brunel; Cardiff; Central Lancashire; Coventry; Dundee; East Anglia; East London; Heriot-Watt; Huddersfield; Kingston; Lancaster; Leeds; Leicester; Liverpool John Moores; London (RH), (UCL) (No); Luton; Manchester; Nottingham; Portsmouth; Salford; Sheffield; Staffordshire; Surrey; Swansea; UMIST; Warwick; Wolverhampton; York.

AFTER RESULTS ADVICE

Institutions which may accept the same points score after A-Levels: Aberystwyth; Bath; Bradford; Bristol; Brunel; Cardiff; Central Lancashire; Coventry; Dundee; Durham; East Anglia; East London; Heriot-Watt; Hull; Keele; Kent; Kingston; Lancaster; Leeds (grade C chem); Leicester; Liverpool; London (RH), (UCL); Manchester; Newcastle; Nottingham (No); Nottingham Trent (No); Salford; Sheffield; Southampton; Staffordshire; Stirling (No); Strathclyde; Surrey; Swansea; UMIST; Warwick (No); Wolverhampton; York.

Institutions which may accept lower grades/points score after A-Levels: Aberdeen; Aberystwyth; Bath; Belfast (Queen's); Birmingham; Bradford; Bristol; Brunel; Cardiff; City; Coventry; Dundee; East Anglia; East London; Heriot-Watt; Hull; Keele; Kent; Lancaster; Leeds (chem grade as in offer); Leicester; Liverpool; Liverpool John Moores; London (RH), (UCL); Newcastle; Salford; Sheffield (No); Staffordshire; Surrey; Swansea; UMIST; Warwick; Wolverhampton; York.

Offers to applicants repeating A-Levels: Higher Durham (BCC), East Anglia, Leeds, Leicester, Nottingham (BBC or BCC), St Andrews, Strathclyde, Surrey, Warwick; **Possibly higher** Aberystwyth, Bath, Bristol, Brunel, Central Lancashire, Keele, Kent, Lancaster, Newcastle, York; **Same** Aston (Comb Hons), Birmingham, Bradford, Heriot-Watt, Hull, Liverpool, Liverpool John Moores, London (RH), (UCL), Salford, Sheffield, Staffordshire, Swansea, UMIST (C chem).

Probable vacancies from June 2001 and in Clearing (see Ch.4): It is worth contacting most universities for vacancy information since this is a serious shortfall subject. Offers rarely rose above 24 pts (now 300 pts) in Clearing last year and went down to 14 pts (now 200 pts). 'New' universities are likely to accept lower grades.

NEW GRADUATE DESTINATIONS AND EMPLOYMENT (1999 HESA) (see **Ch.4**)

Out of 1202 graduates, 475 went on to further study, 565 went into full-time employment and 65 were believed to be unemployed.

BIOLOGICAL SCIENCES (including **Biomedical Science, Ecology** and **Neurosciences**)

NB The information supplied by the universities and colleges this year varies considerably and the offers listed below should be used as a first source of reference only. Many institutions will accept combinations of Advanced (AL), Advanced Subsidiary (AS) and Vocational Advanced (VA) level qualifications to achieve the required points total, but applicants must check web sites and prospectuses for full details of all offers. Grades and points totals shown should be regarded as the minimum levels to be achieved, but offers may be adjusted downwards when results are known. The points totals shown to the left of the institutions are for ease of reference only. It must not be assumed that tariff points are always used by institutions or that they can be substituted for an offer in grades. The level of an offer is not necessarily indicative of the quality of a course. To calculate your offers see Chapter 4 and the inside fold of the back cover.

Special subject requirements/preferences: A-Level: Two or three subjects from mathematics/science; chemistry usually essential. **Birmingham** Two sciences from biology, chemistry, physics, mathematics. **Exeter** One science at A grade, chemistry desirable. **GCSE: Cambridge, Oxford** Grade As in most subjects preferred. **Birmingham** Grade B in five relevant subjects. **Leeds** Mainly grade As, minimum grade B in mathematics, science and English. **London (King's)** Grade C chemistry or combined science. **Nottingham** Grades A or B required for dual science or biology, chemistry, mathematics and English. **Swansea** Majority of A/B grades, especially in the sciences. **UMIST** (Biol/Comp Sci) Mathematics grade B or above. **York** The general requirement for a foreign language may be waived.

360 pts **and above**
    Cambridge – Offers, mainly in grades, vary between colleges (Nat Sci)
    Oxford – Offers vary between candidates (Science – Biol)
350 pts **York** – 350–300 pts 21–18u: ABB/BBB/BBC **or** ALs+ASs; gs; (Ecol)
340 pts **Cambridge (Hom)** – AAB–ABB (Biol Sci/Educ St BA)
330 pts **Southampton** – 330 pts 21u (inc 200 pts 2 sci ALs inc chem); (not gs) (Biomed Sci)
320 pts **East Anglia** – ABB (Ecol/USA; Biol Sci/USA)
    Liverpool – 320–280 pts – ALs **or** ALs+ASs **or** VAs+/-ALs/ASs; (Biol Sci; Biol Med Sci)
    London (UCL) – ABB–BBB **or** 3ALs+AS/VA; (Ecol; Immun)
300 pts **Birmingham** – BBB (Biol Sci/Euro)
    Bradford – 300 pts 12u (inc AL maths+sci); gs; (MEng Med Eng)
    Bristol – BBB (inc 2 sci); (not gs) (Neuroscience)
    Cardiff – BBB–BBC (Neuroscience)
    Durham – B(biol)B(sci)B/bb; (not gs) (Ecol; Biol Sci)
    East Anglia – BBB (Ecol/Euro)
    Edinburgh – BBB–BBC (Ecol; Immun; Neuro; Mol Biol; Virol; Biol Sci)
    Leeds – BBB (Med Sci)
    London (King's) – BBB+AS (or equiv) **or** ABC+AS **or** BB+bb (inc B chem/biol) **or** AC+ac+AS **or** VA12u BB+AL (B sci)+AS **or** VA6u+ALs/ASs; (not gs); (Biomed Sci)
    London (QM) – 300–250 pts – ALs **or** ALs+ASs **or** VAs+/-ALs/ASs; (Ecology)
    London (UCL) – BBB–BBC **or** 3ALs+AS/VA; (Neuro; Biomed Sci)
    Nottingham – 300 pts – BBB–BBC (biol, chem pref) **or** VAs by indiv assessment; (Neuroscience)
    Salford – BBB–CCC/AA–AB (Biol Sci/USA)
    Sheffield – 300 pts approx (Biomed Sci; Neuro)
290 pts **London (King's)** – 290–280 pts – BBC+AS (or equiv) **or** BB+cc (inc B biol+sci) **or** VA12u **or** VA6u+ALs/ASs; (Biol Sci courses; Immun)
280 pts **Birmingham** – BBC–BCC (Biol Sci courses except under **300 pts**; (Med Sci)
    Cambridge (Hom) – BBC–BCD (Biol Sci/Educ BEd)

Cardiff – BBC/AB (Ecol/Env Mgt)
East Anglia – BBC (Ecol; Biol Sci/Euro; Biol Sci/Defer)
Exeter – 280 pts 18u (inc AL biol+sci) – BBC **or** BB+cc **or** VA6u B+BC; (not gs) (Biol Sci; Biol/Med Chem)
Hull – 280 pts approx (Biomed Sci 4 yrs)
Kent – 280–240 pts 21–18u – BBC–CCC **or** BC–CC+ASs; gs; (Biol Sci)
Lancaster – BBC (Ecol/USA; MSc Biol Sci; Biol Sci/USA)
Leeds – BBC (Ecology)
Leicester – 18u – BBC **or** BB+2ASs **or** VA12u+/-AL/ASs; gs (at AL if only 2ALs offered); (Biol Sci)
London (King's) – BBC+AS **or** ABD+AS (or equiv) **or** BB+bc+AS **or** AC+bc+AS (inc C chem/biol **or** AS b) **or** VA12u BC+AL (B chem)+AS **or** VA6u+ALs/ASs; (Clin Sci)
London (RH) – BBC–BCC **or** ALs+ASs **or** VAs+/-ALs/ASs; gs; (Sci/Media (Biol Sci))
Manchester – BBC (Biomed Sci; Neuro courses)
Newcastle – BBC–CCC (Biol Sci courses)
Sheffield – BBC (Ecology)
Swansea – 280 pts 18u – BBC–BCC/AB–BB **or** ALs+ASs **or** VAs+/-ALs/ASs; (Biol Sci; Med Sci/Hum)
UMIST – 280 pts – BBC **or** BB+cc (inc AL biol or chem+sci/maths); (Biol Sci; Biol Sci/Ind Exp; Biol/Comp Sci)
Warwick – BBC (Biol Sci)
260 pts **Aberystwyth** – BCC–CCC (Biol Sci courses)
Bangor – 260 pts – ALs **or** ALs+ASs (inc biol 6u) (Ecology)
Bangor – 260 pts – ALs **or** ALs+ASs (inc biol 6u+chem 3u min); (Biomol Sci)
Bradford – 260 pts 12u (inc AL maths+sci); gs; (BEng Med Eng; Med Cyber)
De Montfort (Bedford) – 260 pts – ALs **or** ALs+ASs **or** VAs+/-ALs/ASs; (Ecol Sci)
Durham – BCC **or** ALs+ASs **or** VAs+/-ALs/ASs; (not gs) (Biomed Sci)
East Anglia – BCC/AA–BB (Ecol/Biol; Biol/Mgt; Biol Sci)
Keele – BCC **or** equiv AS accepted; gs; (Biomed Sci; Neuro Sci)
Lancaster – BCC/BB (Ecol; Biomed/Med Stats)
London (RH) – BCC (Ecol; Env Biol)
St Andrews – BCC (Neuroscience)
Salford – BCC–CDD/AB–BC (Biol Sci)
Surrey – 260 pts 18u – ALs **or** ALs+ASs **or** VAs (depends on subj)+/-ALs/ASs; (not gs) (Biol Sci courses)
Sussex – BCC (Ecol/Cons; Neuro)
Wolverhampton – 260 pts 18u – BCC **or** CCC+e **or** VA12u AA; (Biol Sci)
Wolverhampton – BCC **or** CCC+e **or** VA12u AA; gs; (Biol Biomed Sci)
240 pts **Aberdeen** – CCC–CCD/BC (Neuroscience)
Aberystwyth – CCC–CCD (Env Biol)
Anglia – 240 pts approx (Med Tech Dev)
Belfast (Queen's) – CCC/BB (Biol Sci)
Bradford – 240 pts 12u (inc AL sci); gs; (Pharm Mgt; Med Tech Spo)
Central Lancashire – 240 pts approx (Foren Sci)
Heriot-Watt – 240 pts 18u – CCC **or** ALs+ASs **or** VAs+/-ALs/ASs; gs; (Biol Sci; Brew Distil)
Lancaster – CCC/BC (Biol Sci/Biomed)
Liverpool John Moores – 240–180 pts (inc 2ALs from biol/chem/maths/phys); (Foren/Biomol Sci)
Manchester Met – 240–140 pts approx (Biol Sci Comb Hons – offer varies with subjs)
Newcastle – CCC/CC (Ecol Res Mgt)
Plymouth – 240 pts approx (Ecol courses)
Reading – CCC–BCD (Biol Sci; Mol Biol)
Sheffield – CCC (Biol Sci)

Staffordshire – 240 pts 1x12u **or** 2x6u (inc 80 pts biol/chem) **or** VA12u 160 pts; gs; (Foren Sci courses; Ecol)

Stirling – CCC/BC (Ecol; Frshwtr Sci – BBB 2nd yr entry)

Strathclyde – CCC–BCD (2nd yr entry) (Biol Sci; Biosci/Modl; Immun/Pharmacol; Immun/Microbiol)

Ulster – CCC (Biomed Sci; Clin Sci)

York – CCC (Ecol/Cons/Env)

220 pts **Bradford** – 220 pts 12u (inc AL biol/chem) (Biomed Sci; App Ecol/Cons (inc AL biol); Med Sys Eng (inc AL maths+sci))

Bristol UWE – 220–180 pts 12u (inc 6u sci) – ALs **or** ALs+ASs (chem 6u) **or** VAs+/-ALs/ASs (inc chem related subj); (Biomed Sci; App Biol Sci; Foren Sci)

Glasgow – CCD (Biol courses; Neuro)

Leicester – CCD (Sci Comb Hons)

Liverpool John Moores – 220–180 pts (inc AL biol+chem); (Biomed Sci)

Portsmouth – 220 pts – ALs **or** ALs+ASs **or** VAs; gs; (Biomed Sci; Biomol Sci; Gnm Sci)

Sunderland – 220 pts approx (Biomed Sci)

Surrey Roehampton – 220 pts approx (inc AL subjs inc biol sci) – ALs **or** ALs+ASs **or** VAs (inc sci)+/-ALs/ASs; (Biol Sci; Ecol Cons; Biomed Sci)

Ulster – CCD–CDD (Biol Sci)

Ulster – CCD (Biol Sci – Hons)

200 pts **Brighton** – 200 pts approx (Biol Sci; Biomed Sci; Hum Ecol; Biol/Geog; Biol/Chem)

Central Lancashire – 200 pts approx (Ecotourism)

Chester (Coll) – 200–180 pts – ALs (160 pts inc C biol/chem/hum biol)+AS **or** VA (160 pts inc C sci)+AS – AS(40 pts); (Biomed Sci)

De Montfort (Leicester) – ALs 180–160 pts (inc 2ALs with sci biol pref) **or** VA12u (sci) 200–180 pts; (Biol Sci courses; Biomed Sci courses)

Dundee – CDD/BC (App Env Biol)

Newcastle – CDD/BC (Env Sci/Agric Ecol)

Plymouth – 200–160 pts approx (Biol Sci)

Sheffield Hallam – 200 pts approx (Biomed Sci; Hum Biosci)

Sussex – 200 pts approx (Biomed Sci)

Warwick – CCE–CDE (C biol) (BA (QTS) Biol)

180 pts **Anglia** – 180 pts 12u – 2ALs (inc biol/chem) **or** VA12u BC; gs; (Foren Sci; Ecol)

Central Lancashire – 180–160 pts 12u (inc AL from biol/chem/env sci) – ALs **or** ALs+ASs **or** VAs+/-ALs/ASs; gs; (Biol Sci; Biomed Sci; Neuro)

Chester (Coll) – 180 pts approx (Biomed Sci)

Coventry – 180 pts approx (Biol Sci courses)

Glasgow Caledonian – DDD (Biomed Sci; App Biosci)

Heriot-Watt (Scottish Borders) – DDD (Biomed Mat; Biol Sci) CCC (2nd yr entry)

Kingston – 180 pts – 2x6u (inc 40 pts min chem/biol) **or** VA 180 pts; gs; (Biomed Sci)

Liverpool Hope (Coll) – 180–160 pts approx (App Biol courses)

Manchester Met – 180 pts approx (App Biol Sci 3yr programme; Biomed Sci)

Newman (CHE) – DDD/CC (BEd Biol Sci)

Northumbria – 180 pts (Biol Fd Sci)

Nottingham Trent – 2ALs (chem+biol) **or** AL+2ASs **or** VA12u; (Biomed Sci)

Oxford Brookes – DDD/CC (Ecol Joint Hons)

Sussex – DDD (Biol Sci)

Wolverhampton – 180–160 pts 12u – DDD–DDE/CC **or** CC+dd/ee **or** VA12u CC; gs; (Biol Sci Comb)

160 pts **Anglia** – 160–140 pts approx (Biol Sci)

Cardiff (UWI) – 160–140 pts approx (Biomed Sci)

Glamorgan – CC (inc chem+biol/maths/sci) (App Sci/Biol Sci; Foren Sci)

Greenwich – 160 pts approx (Biol Sci)
Hull (Scarborough) – 160 pts approx (Biol Sci QTS)
Lincolnshire & Humberside – 160 pts (Neuro; Foren Sci; Biomed Sci)
Scottish (CAg) – 160 pts – CC (inc biol/chem); (App Plant Anim Sci)
Sunderland – 160 pts – 2ALs **or** ALs+ASs **or** VAs+/-ALs/ASs; gs; (Biomed Sci; Ecol courses)
Westminster – CC (Biol Sci)

140 pts **Bath Spa (UC)** – CD–EE (Env Biol courses)
Colchester (Inst)/Essex – 140 pts (Biol Sci yr 1)
Derby – CD **or** DD+dd **or** VA12u CD **or** VA6u+/-ALs/ASs; gs; (Ecology)
Edge Hill (CHE) – CD (Biol Sci QTS)
Liverpool – 140 pts (inc 2ALs); (Fdn Biol Sci)
Liverpool John Moores – 140–100 pts (inc AL biol 60 pts) – ALs **or** ALs+ASs **or** VAs+/-ALs/ASs; (Fdn App Ecol)
Manchester Met – 140 pts approx (Biol Sci 4 yr prog – Fdn course)
Napier – CD (Biol Sci; Env Biol; Biomed Sci; App Biol Sci; Ecotour; Immun/Tox; Tox; Biosci)
Ripon & York (Coll) – CD (Bio QTS)
St Martin's (Coll) – DEE/DD (Biol Sci QTS)
Sunderland – 140 pts approx (Fdn Biomed Sci)
Sussex – 140 pts approx (Fdn Biol Sci)

120 pts **Bell (CT)** – DD (App Biol Sci)
North London – 120 pts – 2ALs **or** VA6u/12u; (Biol Sci courses; Biomed Sci; Foren Sci; Ecol)
Paisley – DD (Biomed Sci)

100 pts **and below**
Bromley (Coll) – 2ALs; gs; (Biomed Sci)
East London – 80 pts approx (Immun; Infec Dis; Biomed Sci)
Middlesex – (Biol Sci)
Nescot – EE (Biol Sci)
Northampton (UC) – DE (Hum Biol St – Comb Hons)
Robert Gordon – DE (Biosci/Biomed Sci; App Biosci/Chem; App Biosci/Mgt)
Staffordshire – EE (Ext Ecol)
Worcester (UC) – 80 pts 12u – EE **or** ALs+ASs **or** VAs+/-ALs/ASs; gs; (Biol Sci)

Leeds Met – (contact university)

Diploma of Higher Education courses
40 pts Abertay Dundee; Edge Hill (CHE)

Higher National Diploma courses
100 pts Abertay Dundee; Bell (CT); Bromley (Coll); Cardiff (UWI); Cornwall & Duchy (Coll); De Montfort; Fife (CFHE); Halton (Coll); Manchester Met; Myerscough (Coll); Napier; Nottingham Trent; Paisley; Robert Gordon; Sheffield Hallam; Stratford on Avon (Coll); Westminster (App Biol); Wolverhampton.

Alternative Offers:

EB offers: Newcastle 65%.

IB offers: Bangor 30 pts; Birmingham 30 pts H655; Bradford 24 pts; Brighton 26–25 pts; Durham H665; Durham (Stockton) 26 pts; East Anglia (Biol Sci Euro) 30 pts, (Ecol) 444, (Biol Sci) 28 pts inc 15 pts Highers, (Biol/USA) 32 pts inc 6 in relevant sciences; Essex 28 pts; Exeter 30 pts; Kent 25 pts, H 11 pts; Lancaster 28 pts; Leeds 28 pts, (Med Sci) 32 pts inc 15 pts H; Leicester 30 pts; London (UCL) 32 pts; Manchester Met 24 pts; Newcastle 30–28 pts, (Ecol Res Mgt) 27 pts; Plymouth 28–26 pts inc 15 pts from 3 science subjects; St Andrews 28 pts; St Martin's (Coll) 28 pts; Salford H555; Stirling BBCC; Surrey Roehampton 24 pts; Sussex 30 pts; Swansea 28 pts, (Biol Sci/Lang) 32 pts; Warwick 30–28 pts; Worcester (UC) 24 pts; York H555.

Irish offers: Bradford BBBBC; Brighton BBCC; London Guildhall CCCCC; Newcastle AABB; Sheffield BBBBB; Sunderland BCCC; Warwick BBBBB.

Scottish Qualifications: Glasgow Caledonian BBCC. See also under **Biology**.

CHOOSING YOUR COURSE (See also **Ch.1**)

> **Subject information:** Biological Sciences cross many subject areas, for example biochemistry, botany, ecology, zoology, microbiology, biotechnology, genetics, physiology. All these can be studied as degree courses in their own right. See also **Appendix 1**. See also **Biology**.

Special features: Bangor The School of Ocean Sciences offers courses in Oceanography, Ocean Science, Marine Biology and Marine Chemistry. **Birmingham** Six specialisms follow a common first and second year. **Bristol UWE** Sandwich courses with some placements in Europe, the USA and the Far East. **Coventry** Opportunity to study in Europe and to specialise in Biotechnology. **Durham** Biomedical Sciences is offered at the Stockton campus. **East Anglia** Courses also offered in Europe and North America. **Lancaster** Specialisms include the biology of lakes and rivers. **Lincolnshire & Humberside** Biomedical Sciences can be taken with Microbiology, Neuroscience or Health Studies. **Liverpool John Moores** Work placement either one year full-time or 130 hours in level 3. **Swansea** A four-year course is offered with French, German, Italian or Spanish and with a year abroad in the relevant country. NOW CHECK PROSPECTUSES AND WEB SITES.

Top universities and colleges (Teaching Quality) (see Ch.4): Bristol UWE; Durham; Heriot-Watt; Hull; Kent; Leicester; Liverpool John Moores; Napier; Nottingham Trent; Southampton; Surrey Roehampton; Wolverhampton; see also **Biology**; not all institutions assessed.

Top universities and colleges (Research) (see Ch.4): Bath; Birmingham; Bradford (Biomed Sci); Bristol; Cambridge; Durham; East Anglia; Edinburgh; Essex; Glasgow; Kent; Lancaster; Leeds; Leicester; Liverpool; London (Imp), (QM), (UCL); Manchester; Nottingham; Oxford; St Andrews; Sheffield; Sheffield Hallam (Biomed Sci); Southampton; Sussex; Ulster (Biomed Sci); UMIST; Warwick; York.

Study opportunities abroad: Aberdeen; Abertay Dundee; Anglia; Bangor; Birmingham; Bristol UWE; Chester (Coll); East Anglia; Hull; Kingston; Lancaster; Leeds; Leicester; Manchester Met; Napier; Nescot; Newcastle; North London; Oxford Brooks; Portsmouth; Robert Gordon; Salford; Surrey Roehampton; Sussex; Swansea; Ulster; Wolverhampton; Worcester (UC); York.

Work opportunities abroad: Chester (Coll); Hull; Kingston; Liverpool John Moores; Napier; North London; Oxford Brookes; Salford; Surrey Roehampton; Worcester (UC).

ADMISSIONS INFORMATION

Number of applicants per place (approx): Aberystwyth 10; Bangor 11; Birmingham 7, (Biol Sci) 9; Bradford 7; Bristol UWE 4; Cambridge (Hom) 4; Cardiff 8; Cardiff (UWI) 2; Durham 11; East Anglia (Biol/USA) 15, (Biol/Euro) 5, (Biol Sci) 15, (Biol Chem) 4; East London 5; Edinburgh 8; Essex 8; Greenwich 8; Heriot-Watt 10; Kingston 6; Lancaster (Biol Sci) 12; Leeds (Ecol) 5, (Med Sci) 25; Liverpool John Moores 3; London (QM) 8; Manchester 25; Manchester Met 5 average for all courses; Napier 8; Nescot 6; Newcastle (All courses) 14; Newman (CHE) 12; North London 7; Nottingham 11; Nottingham Trent 4; Oxford 1.9; Plymouth 8; Portsmouth (Biomed Sci) 5; Reading 8; Ripon & York (Coll) 12; St Martin's (Coll) 8; Salford 3; Stirling 7; Strathclyde 30; Surrey Roehampton 5; Swansea 10; Wolverhampton 17, (Biomed Sci) 4; Worcester (UC) 3.

Planning your UCAS personal statement (see Ch.4): Read scientific journals and try to extend your knowledge beyond the A-level syllabus. In your UCAS form discuss your special interests, for example, microbiology, genetics or zoology (read up thoroughly on your interests since questions could be asked at interview). (Botany) Visit botanical gardens. **De Montfort** Evidence of outgoing personality (sport, community work, part-time job). Statement of interest in a 'pure' science career is a *negative* factor. **Surrey** Voluntary attendance on courses, work experience, voluntary work, holiday jobs. See also **Appendix 1**. See also **Anatomy, Biochemistry, Pharmacology, Genetics, Microbiology, Zoology**.

Selection interviews (see Ch.4): Aberystwyth (No); Anglia (No); Bangor; Birmingham (No); Bristol UWE; Cambridge (Hom); Cardiff (No); De Montfort (No); Durham (Stockton) (No); East Anglia; Exeter (No); Essex; Greenwich; Huddersfield; Hull; Kent (some); Kingston (No); Leeds (No); Leicester (No); Liverpool Hope (Coll) (No); Liverpool John Moores (No); London (RH), (UCL); Manchester; Manchester Met (No); Newcastle; Newman (CHE); Nottingham; Nottingham Trent (No); Oxford (W); Oxford Brookes; Paisley (No); Plymouth; Portsmouth (No); St Andrews (No); Salford; Sheffield (No); Sheffield Hallam (No); Southampton (No); Staffordshire (No); Stirling; Strathclyde; Sunderland; Surrey Roehampton (No); Sussex; Swansea; Warwick; Wolverhampton (No); Worcester (UC) (No); York. **Oxford** Examples of written work are usually required. One could be a report of a practical investigation or project, the other could be an essay. Informal written exercises may be required of candidates during the interview. Candidates will be advised beforehand by the college. Candidates may be given a second interview if they fail to do themselves justice at their first choice college, with the second interview at a different college.

Interview questions (see Ch.4): You are likely to be asked about your main interests in biology and your choice of specialisation in the field of biological sciences or, for example, about the role of the microbiologist in industry. What do you understand by biotechnology or genetic engineering? Questions on field courses attended may also be asked. If you have a field course workbook, take it to interview.

GAP YEAR ADVICE

Lancaster Stay tuned to biology, chemistry, maths.

Institutions willing to defer entry after A-Levels: Bangor; Bell (CT) (No); Birmingham; Bradford; Brighton; Cardiff (by prior arrangement); De Montfort; Durham; East Anglia; East London; Heriot-Watt; Huddersfield; Hull; Kingston; Leeds; Leicester; Liverpool John Moores; London (UCL); Manchester; Manchester Met; Napier; Nescot; Newcastle; Northampton (UC); Nottingham; Nottingham Trent; Oxford Brookes; Plymouth (decide quickly!); Portsmouth; Robert Gordon; St Andrews; St Martin's (Coll); Salford; Sheffield; Surrey Roehampton; Sussex; Swansea; Warwick; Westminster; York.

AFTER RESULTS ADVICE

Institutions which may accept the same points score after A-Levels: Bangor; Birmingham; Bradford; Brighton; Bristol UWE; Brunel; Cardiff (Neuro); Chester (Coll); De Montfort; Durham; East Anglia; East London; Essex; Exeter; Greenwich; Heriot-Watt; Hull; Lancaster; Leicester; London (RH); Manchester Met; Napier; Nescot; Newcastle; Newman (CHE); Oxford Brookes; Plymouth (No); Portsmouth; Robert Gordon; St Andrews; Salford; Strathclyde; Surrey Roehampton; Swansea; Warwick; Wolverhampton; Worcester (UC) (No).

Institutions which may accept lower grades/point score after A-Levels: Bangor; Birmingham; Bradford; Brighton; Bristol UWE; Cambridge (Hom); Cardiff; Chester (Coll); De Montfort; Durham; East Anglia (not Biol/USA); East London; Essex; Exeter; Kingston; Leeds (Ecol); Leicester; Liverpool John Moores; London (RH); Napier; Nescot; Newcastle; Oxford Brookes; Plymouth; Portsmouth; Reading; Robert Gordon; St Andrews; Salford; Sheffield (No); Surrey Roehampton; Swansea; most other new universities and colleges.

Offers to applicants repeating A-Levels: Higher Bristol, Bristol UWE, Durham, East Anglia, Hull, Newcastle, St Andrews, Sheffield, Swansea; **Possibly higher** Cambridge (Hom), Essex, Lancaster, Leeds (Ecol), Manchester Met; **Same** Birmingham, Exeter, Heriot-Watt, Kingston, Leeds, Liverpool John Moores, London (RH), Napier, Oxford Brookes, Robert Gordon, Surrey Roehampton, Worcester (UC), York (or 2 pts higher).

Possible vacancies from June 2001 and in Clearing (see Ch.4): Most universities are likely to have vacancies in this subject. Some of the more popular universities probably will ask between 300 and 260 pts in Clearing but much lower grades will gain access to the 'new' universities. Last year several institutions advertised vacancies for Biomedical Sciences and Ecology.

NEW GRADUATE DESTINATIONS AND EMPLOYMENT (1999 HESA) (see **Ch.4**)

See **Biology, Botany, Genetics, Microbiology** and **Zoology**.

BIOLOGY (including **Applied, Human, Marine** and **Plant Biology, Biomedical Science, Ecology** and **Fishery Science**)

NB The information supplied by the universities and colleges this year varies considerably and the offers listed below should be used as a first source of reference only. Many institutions will accept combinations of Advanced (AL), Advanced Subsidiary (AS) and Vocational Advanced (VA) level qualifications to achieve the required points total, but applicants must check web sites and prospectuses for full details of all offers. Grades and points totals shown should be regarded as the minimum levels to be achieved, but offers may be adjusted downwards when results are known. The points totals shown to the left of the institutions are for ease of reference only. It must not be assumed that tariff points are always used by institutions or that they can be substituted for an offer in grades. The level of an offer is not necessarily indicative of the quality of a course. To calculate your offers see Chapter 4 and the inside fold of the back cover.

Special subject requirements/preferences: A-Level: Chemistry and another science, usually biology. **GCSE:** Mathematics and English stipulated in some cases. **Bangor** Five subjects grade A, grade C minimum in mathematics and English language. **Bristol** Reasonable balance of grade As. **Brunel** Grade B chemistry or combined sciences. **Cambridge, Oxford** Grade As in most subjects preferred. **London (QM)** Mathematics, chemistry grade A–C if not at A-Level. **Newcastle** (App Biol; Env Biol) Grade B in chemistry, mathematics or integrated science, if not offered at A-Level. **Surrey Roehampton** Grade A or B in double science, mathematics, English. **Swansea** Majority grade Bs or better.

360 pts	**and above**
	Cambridge – Offers, mainly in grades, vary between colleges (Nat Sci)
	Nottingham – AAA–BBB (Biol; Mol/Cell Biol)
	Oxford – Offers vary between candidates (Biology)
350 pts	**York** – 350–300 pts 21–18u: ABB/BBB/BBC **or** ALs+ASs **or** VAs (contact with univ); gs; (Biol courses; Mol Cell Biol courses)
330 pts	**Southampton** – 330 pts 21u (inc 200 pts in 2ALs inc biol/zool/bot/hum biol); (Biol courses)
320 pts	**Bristol** – ABB–BBB (inc biol+sci); (not gs) (Biol/Geog; Biol)
	Durham – ABB (Nat Sci)
	East Anglia – ABB–BBB (Biol/USA; Biol/Euro)
	Liverpool – 320–280 pts – ALs **or** ALs+ASs **or** VAs+/-ALs/ASs; (App Biol; Mar Biol; Mol Biol; App Mol Biol)
	London (Imp) – ABB (Biol courses)
	London (UCL) – ABB–BBC **or** 3ALs+AS/VA; (Biol; Cell Biol)
300 pts	**Bath** – 300 pts – BBB (inc B chem/biol) **or** VA12u+/-ALs/ASs; (not gs) (Mol Cell Biol; Biol; App Biol)
	Bradford – 300 pts 12u (inc AL maths+sci); gs; (MEng Med Eng)
	Cardiff – 300 pts approx (Biol courses; Neuro) (see also **280 pts**)
	Durham – B(biol)B(sci)+AL(B)/bb; (not gs) (Biol courses)
	Glasgow – BBB–CCC (Biol courses)
	Hertfordshire – 300–200 pts 1x12u **or** 2x6u; gs; (Hum Biol Comb Hons Mod)
	Leeds – BBB–BBC (Biology)

London (QM) – 300–250 pts – ALs or ALs+ASs or VAs+/-ALs/ASs; (Biol courses)
Sheffield – BBB (MChem Biol Chem; Mol Biol)
Sussex – BBB (Biol/N Am)
Warwick – BBB (Comput Biol)

280 pts **Aston** – 280–260 pts – 3ALs+ASs or VAs+/-ALs/ASs; gs; (App Hum Biol; Biol Comb Hons)
Birmingham – BBC–BCC (Biol Sci (Anim Biol; Env Biol)
Bristol – BBC (Biol/Geol)
Cardiff – BBC/BB (Med Mol Biol)
Edinburgh – BBC (Biol courses)
Exeter – 280 pts 18u (inc AL biol+geog) – BBC or BB+cc or VA6uB+BB; (not gs) (Biol/Geog)
Kent – 280–240 pts 21–18u – BBC–CCC or BC–CC+ASs; gs; (Mol Cell Biol)
Leeds – BBC (App Biol)
Leicester – 18u – BBC or BB+2ASs or VA12u+AL; gs (AL if only 2ALs offered); (Env Biol)
London (King's) – BBC+AS or ABD+AS or BB+bc+AS (inc C chem/biol or with AS b) or VA12u BC+AL(B)+AS or VA6u+ALs/ASs; (Biol courses; Mol Biophys)
London (RH) – 280 pts 18u – BBC–BCC or 2ALs+2ASs; (not gs) (Biol courses)
London (UCL) – BBC–BCC or 3ALs+AS/VA; (Palaeontology)
Manchester – BBC (Biol courses)
Newcastle – BBC–BCC/BB (Mar Biol)
St Andrews – BBC (Biol courses)
Sheffield – BBC (Biology)
Sussex – BBC–BCC (Biomol Sci)
Swansea – 280 pts 18u – BBC–BCC/AB–BB or ALs+ASs or VAs+/-ALs/ASs; (Biol courses)

260 pts **Bangor** – 260 pts – ALs or ALs+ASs (inc biol 6u); (Biol courses)
Birmingham – BCC (Biol Sci)
Bradford – 260 pts 12u (inc AL maths+sci); gs; (Med Cyber)
East Anglia – BCC–BCD/BB (Biol courses except under **320 pts**)
Hertfordshire – 260–220 pts 1x12u or 2x6u; gs; (App Biol; Mol Biol)
Hull (Scarborough) – 260–220 pts approx (Biol courses except under **160 pts**)
Keele – BCC or equiv AS accepted; gs; (Biol courses)
Loughborough – 260 pts 18u – ALs or ALs+ASs or VA12u+AL/2ASs; (not gs) (Hum Biol)
Newcastle – BCC/BB (Mol Biol)
Nottingham – BCC–CCC (2 sci ALs); (not gs) (App Biol; Env Biol)
Salford – BCC (Biol course)
Sheffield – 260–240 pts approx (Ecology)
Staffordshire – 260 pts approx/AB (Biol/Psy)
Surrey – BCC–CCC (Mol Biol)
Sussex – BCC (Ecol; Biol courses except under **300 pts**)
Wolverhampton – 260 pts 18u – BCC or CC+e or VA12u AA; gs; (Biol Comb Hons; Hum Biol Comb Hons)

240 pts **Aberdeen** – CCC–CCD/BC (Biol courses; Biomed Sci)
Aberystwyth – 240 pts 21u – CCC or CC+cc or VAs; gs; (Biol; Mar Biol; Env Biol)
Belfast (Queen's) – CCC/BB (Biol courses; Env Biol)
Bradford – 240 pts 12u (inc AL sci); gs; (Pharm Mgt)
Brunel – 240 pts 3x6u (inc biol/chem) – ALs or ALs+ASs or VAs+/-ALs/ASs; (Biol; App Biol; Cell Biol; Med Biol)
Cambridge (Hom) – BCD (Biol Educ) (See also **Education**)
Essex – 240 pts 21u – CC (inc biol+sci/maths)+AL/2ASs or VA12u CC+AL or VA6u+2ALs; gs; (Biol; Cell Mol Biol; Ecol Env Biol; Mar Frshwtr Biol)

Heriot-Watt – 240 pts 18u – CCC; gs; (Biol/Spo Sci; Mar Biotech)
Kingston – 240 pts approx (Biomed Sci; Biol/App Geol; App Biol/Geog; App Biol/Fr; App Biol/Chem; App Biol/App Phys)
Leeds – CCC (Biol/Food Sci)
Napier – CCC (Env Biol yr 2 entry)
Newcastle – CCC/BC (Biol; Env Biol courses)
Oxford Brookes – CCC–DD (offer varies with 2nd subj) (Biol courses)
Plymouth – CCC/BB (Biol courses)
Reading – CCC–BCD (Env Biol)
St Andrews – CCC (Biol Gen Hons)
South Bank – 240–220 pts (App Biol)
Staffordshire – 240 1x12u **or** 2x6u (inc 40 pts min biol); (not gs) (Biol courses)
UMIST – CCC (Biomed Mat Sci)

220 pts **Bradford** – 220 pts 12u; gs; (App Ecol/Cons(inc AL biol); Med Sys Eng (inc AL maths+sci); Biomed Sci (inc AL biol+chem))
Dundee – 220 pts approx (Biology)
Salford – CCD/BC (Biol/Chem; App Biol/Geog)
Staffordshire – 220–180 pts approx (App Ecol)
Stirling – CCD/BC (Biol courses)
Surrey Roehampton – 220 pts approx (inc 2AL subjs inc biol sci) – ALs **or** ALs+ASs **or** VAs (inc sci) +/-ALs/ASs; (Biol; Hum/Soc Biol)
Teesside – 220–180 pts approx (Hum Biol)

200 pts **Bradford** – 200 pts 12u (inc AL sci); gs; (Med Electron)
Bristol UWE – 200–160 pts 12u – ALs **or** ALs+ASs **or** VAs+/-ALs/ASs; (12u in biol+1 sci, can inc geog); (Env Biol; Biol/Chem/IT/Env Sci)
Chester (Coll) – 200 pts – ALs (180 pts inc C biol/sci)+AS **or** VAs (180 pts inc C biol/sci)+AS; AS (up to 20 pts); (Biol Comb Hons; App Biol)
Colchester (Inst) – CCE (Mar Biol; Ecol Env Biol)
De Montfort (Leicester) – ALs 180–160 pts (inc 2ALs with sci pref biol) **or** VA12u (sci) 200–180 pts; (Cell Biol; Env Biol; Cons Biol/Anim Bhv; Tox)
Derby – 200 pts 12u – CCE **or** CC+e **or** VA12u CC+AL (E); gs; (MSci Biol)
Durham (Stockton) – 200 pts approx (Biomed Sci)
Kingston – 200–180 pts approx (App Biol)
Manchester Met – 200–140 pts approx (Biol Comb Hons)
Newman (CHE) – 200–140 pts approx (Biol Sci/Soc App Psy/Engl/Educ St/Hist)
Nottingham Trent – CCE/BC (inc biol+chem) **or** ALs+ASs; (Biomol Analys)
Plymouth – 200–180 pts approx (Biol courses except under **240 pts**)
Portsmouth – 200 pts – ALs **or** ALs+ASs **or** VAs; gs; (Biol; Cell Biol; Env Biol; Foren Biol; Mol Biol; Pal)
Scottish (CAg) – CDD/CD (Aquaculture)
Sunderland – 200 pts approx (Biol Comb St)
Ulster – CDD/CC (Biol courses)
Worcester (UC) – 200 pts approx (Biol QTS)

180 pts **Abertay Dundee** – DDD (Biol courses; Ecol)
Brighton – 180 pts approx (Biol courses)
East London – 180–160 pts approx (Biol courses)
Glasgow Caledonian – DDD/CC (App Biosci)
Liverpool Hope (Coll) – 180–140 pts approx (Hum App Biol courses)
Liverpool John Moores – 180–120 pts (inc ALs biol+chem); (Mol Biol/Evol)
Manchester Met – 180 pts approx (Biomed Sci)
Northumbria – 180 pts approx (App Biol)
Norwich City (Coll) – 180 pts approx (Biol courses)
Nottingham Trent – DDD/CDE (inc biol+chem) **or** ALs+ASs **or** VAs+ALs/ASs; (App Biol; Biol; Env Biol; Biomed Sci)
Paisley – 180–40 pts approx (Biol courses)
Staffordshire – DDD (Biol courses)
Warwick – CDE/CC (Biol QTS)
Westminster – 180 pts approx (App Biol)

160 pts   **Anglia** – 160 pts approx (Imag Sci; Biomed Sci; Env Biol; Cell Mol Biol)
　　　　　Bath Spa (UC) – 160–120 pts – BD **or** VA12u BD; (not gs) (Env Biol Comb Hons)
　　　　　Edge Hill (CHE) – 160–140 pts approx (Biol courses)
　　　　　Glasgow Caledonian – DDE (App Biosci)
　　　　　Greenwich – 160 pts approx (Biol courses)
　　　　　Huddersfield – 160 pts 12u – 2ALs **or** AL+2ASs **or** VAs+/-ALs/ASs; gs; (Hum Biol; Mol Cell Biol)
　　　　　Hull (Scarborough) – 160 pts approx (Biol QTS; Cstl Mar Biol)
　　　　　Kingston – 160 pts 2x6u (inc 40 pts min biol); (not gs) (Biology)
　　　　　Lincolnshire & Humberside – 160 pts (App Biol; Hum Biol)
　　　　　Liverpool John Moores – 160–120 pts (inc 2ALs or equiv inc sci 80 pts) – ALs **or** ALs+ASs **or** VAs+/-ALs/ASs; (Palaeo/Evol)
　　　　　Liverpool John Moores – 160–140 pts (inc 2ALs biol+geog/geol at 80 pts) – ALs **or** ALs+ASs **or** VAs+/-ALs/ASs; (Biol/Geog)
　　　　　Liverpool John Moores – 160–120 pts (inc AL biol 80 pts) – ALs **or** ALs+ASs **or** VAs+/-ALs/ASs; (Biol/Anth)
　　　　　Luton – 160–120 pts approx (Biol courses)
　　　　　Norwich City (Coll) – 160 pts approx (Env Biol)
　　　　　Plymouth – 160 pts approx (Fisheries courses)
　　　　　Plymouth (Seale Hayne) – 160–140 pts approx (Food Biol)
　　　　　St Martin's (Coll) – CEE/DD (QTS)
　　　　　St Mary's (Coll) – 160 pts – CC–DD **or** ALs+ASs **or** VAs+/-ALs/ASs; gs; (Biol courses)
　　　　　South Bank – 160 pts approx/DD (Hum Biol Comb Hons)
140 pts   **Bell (CT)** – 140 pts (App Biol)
　　　　　Bolton (IHE) – CD (Biol courses)
　　　　　Cardiff (UWI) – CD (Biomed Sci)
　　　　　Derby – 140 pts 18u – CD **or** DD+dd **or** VA12u CD **or** VA6u C/D+AL (C/D); (Biol courses; Biol Comb)
　　　　　Liverpool John Moores – 140–100 pts (inc Al biol 80 pts) – ALs **or** ALs+ASs **or** VAs+/-ALs/ASs; (App Biol)
　　　　　Napier – CD (Biol courses)
　　　　　Nescot – 140 pts approx (Biol courses)
　　　　　Northampton (UC) – 140 pts approx (Biol courses)
　　　　　Nottingham Trent – 140 pts approx (Biol courses except under **160 pts**)
　　　　　Plymouth – 140 pts approx (Biol; Env Biol)
　　　　　Sheffield Hallam – 140 pts approx (Biomed Sci; App Biol Sci (via HND))
　　　　　Stockport (CFHE) – 140 pts approx (Biology)
　　　　　Strathclyde – CD (Mathem Biol)
　　　　　Suffolk (Coll) – 140 pts apoprox (App Biol courses)
　　　　　Thames Valley – 140 pts approx (Sci/App Biol)
　　　　　Trinity Carmarthen (Coll) – 140 pts approx (Biodiv/Cons)
　　　　　Worcester (UC) – 140 pts; gs; (Biol courses)
120 pts   **Bath Spa (UC)** – 120 pts 12u – DD **or** VA12u DD; (not gs) (Env Biol)
　　　　　North London – 120 pts – 2ALs **or** VA6u/12u; (Hum Biol; Hum Life Sci)
　　　　　Ulster – DD (App Biol)
100 pts   **and below**
　　　　　Bromley (Coll) – 2ALs; gs; (App Biol)
　　　　　Canterbury Christ Church (UC) – (Env Biol)
　　　　　Glamorgan – (Biol courses)
　　　　　Lincolnshire & Humberside – (Biol courses)
　　　　　North East Wales (IHE) – (Biol courses)
　　　　　Staffordshire – 80 pts 2x6u (inc 40 pts AL/AS biol); (Fdn App Biol)

　　　　　Leeds Met – (contact university)

Diploma of Higher Education courses
　80 pts   Bath Spa (UC); Chester (Coll); Hertfordshire; Luton; Oxford Brookes; Plymouth.

Higher National Diploma courses: (Applied Biology)
100 pts and below
Barony (Coll) (Fish Farming); Bell (CT); Bradford (Coll); Brighton; Brighton (CT); Bristol UWE; Bromley (CFHE); Cannington (Coll); Cardiff (UWI); Central Lancashire; Cornwall (Coll); Coventry; De Montfort; East London; Exeter; Glasgow Caledonian; Greenwich; Halton (Coll); Hertfordshire; Luton; Manchester Met; Nescot; North Down & Ards (IFHE); North East Wales (IHE); North London; Nottingham Trent; People's (Coll); Plymouth; Portsmouth; Sheffield Hallam; South Bank; Sparsholt (Coll); Staffordshire; Sunderland; Truro (Coll); Ulster; Westminster; Wolverhampton.

Alternative Offers:

EB offers: Bradford 65%; Keele 65%; Liverpool John Moores 60%; Newcastle 65%; Nottingham 60% (sci); Sheffield 65%.

IB offers: Aberdeen 26 pts; Aberystwyth 28 pts; Bangor 30–28 pts H665; Bath 30 pts; Bradford 24 pts H6/7 chem, biol, maths or physics; Bristol 32 pts inc H655; Brunel 26 pts H66 chem biol; Cardiff 30 pts; Central Lancashire 26 pts; De Montfort 24 pts; Essex 28 pts; Exeter 28 pts; Keele 26 pts; Lancaster 33 pts; Leeds 30–28 pts; Leicester 30 pts; Liverpool John Moores 24 pts; London (RH) 27 pts, (UCL) 32 pts; Newcastle 30 pts, (Mar Biol) 30 pts; Nottingham 24 pts (sci); Nottingham Trent 28 pts; Oxford Brookes 26 pts; Portsmouth 24 pts; Reading 30 pts; St Andrews 28 pts; Sheffield 30 pts; Southampton H655; Swansea 30–28 pts; York 32–30 pts inc 5 in biol/chem H or L.

Irish offers: Aberdeen BBCC/BCCCC; Aberystwyth BBBCC; Bangor BBCCC; Bradford CCCCD; Brighton CCC; Bristol overall 32 pts: H655 inc biol; Keele BBBCC; Liverpool John Moores CCC; London Guildhall CCCCC; Newcastle ABBB, (Mar Biol) BBBCC; Nottingham CCCCC1; St Andrews BBBC; Sheffield BBBBB; South Bank DDD; York BBBB.

Scottish Qualifications: Aberdeen BBBB; Abertay Dundee BBC; Bell (CT) CCC; Dundee BBCC; Edinburgh BBBB; Glasgow BBBB; Glasgow Caledonian BBCC; Heriot-Watt BBB; Napier BCC; Nottingham BBBB (first sitting); Paisley BBC; Robert Gordon BCC; St Andrews BBBB–BBBC; Scottish (CAg) BCCC/ABC; Stirling BBCC; Strathclyde BCC.

Overseas applicants: East Anglia English courses available for overseas students. **Heriot-Watt** No remedial courses available. **South Bank** Foundation courses in year 1.

CHOOSING YOUR COURSE (See also **Ch.1**)

Subject information: Biology courses are usually more specialised than Biological Sciences with such options as aquatic biology, human biology, animal and plant biology. Many of these options are also offered on Applied Biology courses. There are also several subjects closely related to Biology which are offered as degree subjects or specialisms and which could also be considered. These include Biochemistry, Botany, Environmental Studies, Biotechnology, Microbiology, Genetics, Anatomy, Physiology, Pharmacology and Pharmacy. See also **Appendix 1**.

Special features: Abertay Dundee The joint course in Biology and Chemistry includes work experience. **Anglia** Environmental Biology is offered with specialist programmes in toxicology, ecology and animal behaviour. **Belfast (Queen's)** A broad introductory course provides pathways in environmental biology, biological sciences, marine biology and plant biology. **Brighton** Courses are offered in Biogeography and Human Ecology. **Cardiff** A broad first year leads to degrees in Applied Biology, Biology, Biotechnology, Ecology, Environmental Management, Genetics, Microbiolgy or Zoology. **East Anglia** Opportunities to study in Europe and North America. **Huddersfield** Optional work placements. Final year options include immunology, medical biology, and DNA technology. **Nottingham** opportunity for major research project. **Portsmouth** Elective streams lead to named degrees in Cellular, Environmental or Population Biology. **Reading** Biology courses focus on animal and microbial sciences and plant sciences. *NOW CHECK PROSPECTUSES AND WEB SITES.*

Top universities and colleges (Teaching Quality) (see Ch.4): Aberdeen; Abertay Dundee; Aberystwyth; Aston; Bangor; Bath; Brunel; Derby; Dundee; Durham; Edinburgh; Essex; Exeter; Glasgow; Glasgow Caledonian; Heriot-Watt; Huddersfield; Kent; Liverpool John Moores; London (RH); Napier; Newcastle; Nottingham; Nottingham Trent; Paisley; St Andrews; St Mary's (Coll); Staffordshire; Stirling; Strathclyde; Swansea; not all institutions assessed.

Universities and colleges (Research) (see Ch.4): See under **Biological Sciences**.

Study opportunities abroad: Aberdeen; Aberystwyth; Bangor; Birmingham; Brunel; Cardiff; Central Lancashire; Chester (Coll); Derby; Dundee; East London; Greenwich; Hertfordshire; Hull; Kent; Kingston; Leeds; Leicester; Liverpool Hope (Coll); London (Imp), (King's), (QM); Manchester; Middlesex; Napier; Nescot; Newcastle; Nottingham; Nottingham Trent; Oxford Brookes; Plymouth; Portsmouth; Reading; St Andrews; Salford; Scottish (CAg); Sheffield; Sheffield Hallam; Staffordshire; Surrey Roehampton; Sussex; Swansea; Wolverhampton; York.

Work opportunities abroad: Bath; Bangor; Brunel; Chester (Coll); Derby; Greenwich; Leeds; Manchester; Napier; Newcastle; Scottish (CAg); Staffordshire; Ulster; Wolverhampton.

ADMISSIONS INFORMATION

Number of applicants per place (approx): Aberdeen 8; Abertay Dundee 2; Aberystwyth 8; Anglia 5; Aston 5; Bangor (Env Biol) 10, (Mar Biol) 13, (all other courses) 8; Bath 9; Birmingham 5; Bradford 7; Bristol 13; Brunel 5; Cardiff 8; Cardiff (UWI) 2; Central Lancashire 10; Chester (Coll) 11; Derby 10; Dundee 4; Durham 11; Edge Hill (CHE) 3; Exeter 6; Glamorgan 5; Glasgow Caledonian 9; Greenwich 5; Hertfordshire 4; Huddersfield 2; Hull 4; Hull (Scarborough) 2; Kent 10; Leeds 6; Leicester 15; Liverpool John Moores 11; London (Imp) 4; London (RH) 5; Loughborough 6; Luton 3; Manchester (Biol) 13, (Cell Biol) 6, (Env Biol) 16; Newcastle (Plant Biol) 4, (Mar Biol) 15, (App Biol) 9; Norwich City (Coll) 4; Nottingham 14; Nottingham Trent 8; Oxford Brookes 13; Portsmouth 3; St Martin's (Coll) 9; St Mary's (Coll) 2; Salford 3; Scottish (CAg) 3; Sheffield Hallam 8; South Bank 8; Staffordshire 3; Stirling 15; Surrey Roehampton 5; Sussex 4; Swansea 10 each course; Warwick (QTS) 20; York 11.

Planning your UCAS personal statement (see Ch.4): Bristol (Biol/Geog) Looks for experience in the ecological field. See also **Appendix 1**. See also **Biological Sciences**.

Selection interviews (see Ch.4): Aberystwyth (No); Aston; Bangor; Bath; Bath Spa (UC) (No); Birmingham; Bradford (informal, after offer); Brighton (No); Bristol (No); Bristol UWE (No); Brunel; Cambridge; Cardiff (No); Central Lancashire (No); Derby (No); Durham (No); East Anglia; East London (No); Essex; Exeter (No); Hertfordshire; Hull (No); Kent; Kingston; Leeds (No); Leicester (No); Liverpool Hope (Coll) (No); London (RH), (UCL); Manchester; Manchester Met (No); Nescot; Newcastle (Mar Biol) (not usually); Newman (CHE) (No); Norwich City (Coll) (No); Nottingham (depends on application); Nottingham Trent (No); Oxford (W) (T) see **Biological Sciences**; Oxford Brookes (No); Paisley (No); Portsmouth (No); St Andrews (No); St Mary's (Coll) (No); Salford; Scottish (CAg); Sheffield (No); Sheffield Hallam; Southampton; South Bank; Staffordshire (No); Stirling (No); Surrey; Surrey Roehampton; Swansea; Writtle (Coll); Warwick (BA QTS); York (some).

Interview questions (see Ch.4): Questions will focus on your studies in biology, on any work experience or any special interests you may have, for example: Is the computer like a brain and, if so, could it ever be taught to think? What do you think the role of the environmental biologist will be in the next 40–50 years? Have you any strong views on vivisection? You have a micro-organism in the blood: you want to make a culture – what conditions should be borne in mind? What is a pacemaker? What problems will a giraffe experience? How does water enter a flowering plant? Compare an egg and a potato. Discuss a family tree of human genotypes. (Fishery Science) Discuss fish farming in Britain today. Is there a future in the industry? What are the limitations? **Brunel** Ability to present ideas (fluently for those applying for sandwich courses).

Reasons for rejection (non-academic): Mainly academic. **Derby** (Biol Imag) Poor work in portfolio.

GAP YEAR ADVICE

Students are recommended to try to do something relevant to Biology.

Institutions willing to defer entry after A-Levels: Abertay Dundee; Aberystwyth; Anglia; Aston; Bangor; Bradford; Brighton; Bristol; Brunel; Canterbury Christ Church (UC); Cardiff (by prior arrangement); Central Lancashire; Chester (Coll); De Montfort; Derby; Edge Hill (CHE); Glamorgan (No); Heriot-Watt; Huddersfield; Hull; Kingston; Leeds; Leicester; Liverpool Hope (Coll); London (RH), (UCL) (No); Loughborough; Luton; Manchester; Manchester Met; Napier; Newcastle; North East Wales (IHE); North London; Norwich City (Coll); Nottingham; Oxford Brookes; Plymouth; Portsmouth; St Andrews; St Mary's (Coll); Salford (Not encouraged); Sheffield; Sheffield Hallam; Staffordshire; Surrey; Surrey Roehampton; Swansea; Warwick; Wolverhampton; York.

AFTER RESULTS ADVICE

Institutions which may accept the same points score after A-Levels: Abertay Dundee; Aberystwyth; Aston; Bangor; Bath; Bradford; Brighton; Bristol UWE; Brunel; Canterbury Christ Church (UC); Cardiff; Derby; Essex; Greenwich; Heriot-Watt; Hertfordshire; Humberside; Kent; Kingston; Leeds; Leicester (No); Liverpool John Moores; Loughborough; London (RH), (UCL) (No); Luton; Manchester Met; Napier; Nescot; Newcastle; North East Wales (IHE); Nottingham (No); Nottingham Trent; Oxford Brookes; Portsmouth; St Andrews (No); Sheffield (No); Sheffield Hallam; Southampton; Staffordshire; Stirling (No); Surrey; Surrey Roehampton; Swansea; Warwick (No); York (varies).

Institutions which may accept lower grades/points score after A-Levels: Aberdeen; Abertay Dundee; Bangor; Bath; Bradford (Biomed Sci); Brighton; Brunel; Canterbury Christ Church (UC); Cardiff; Chester (Coll); Derby; Durham; Edge Hill (CHE); Heriot-Watt; Hull; Hull (Scarborough); Humberside; Keele; Kingston; Leicester; Liverpool Hope (Coll); Liverpool John Moores; London (RH), (UCL); Loughborough; Manchester Met; Napier; Newcastle (not Mol Biol); North East Wales (IHE); Nottingham; Oxford Brookes; Portsmouth; St Andrews; Salford; Sheffield Hallam; Staffordshire; Surrey; Surrey Roehampton; Teesside; Warwick; York.

Offers to applicants repeating A-Levels: Higher Brunel, Cardiff, Dundee, East London, St Andrews, Strathclyde; **Possibly higher** Bath, Bradford, Durham, Leeds, Liverpool John Moores, London (RH), Nottingham, Portsmouth; **Same** Aston, Bangor, Bradford, Brunel, Chester (Coll), Derby, Heriot-Watt, Hull, Liverpool Hope (Coll), Liverpool John Moores, London (RH), (UCL), Loughborough, Luton, Manchester Met, Napier, Newcastle, Oxford Brookes, Sheffield, South Bank, Southampton, Staffordshire, Surrey Roehampton, Teesside, Ulster; York.

Probable vacancies from June 2001 and in Clearing (see Ch.4): Choose your university! Almost all are likely to have vacancies, with 220 pts as a probable highest grade you need for a place at one of the old universities. Vacancies in Fishery Sciences are also likely.

NEW GRADUATE DESTINATIONS AND EMPLOYMENT (1999 HESA) (see **Ch.4**)

Out of a total of 3145 graduates, 1508 entered full-time employment. Further study accounted for 945, and 186 were believed to be unemployed.

BIOTECHNOLOGY

NB The information supplied by the universities and colleges this year varies considerably and the offers listed below should be used as a first source of reference only. Many institutions will accept combinations of Advanced (AL), Advanced Subsidiary (AS) and Vocational Advanced (VA) level qualifications to achieve the required points total, but applicants must check web sites and prospectuses for full details of all offers. Grades and points totals shown should be regarded as the minimum levels to be achieved, but offers may be adjusted downwards when results are known. The points totals shown to

the left of the institutions are for ease of reference only. It must not be assumed that tariff points are always used by institutions or that they can be substituted for an offer in grades. The level of an offer is not necessarily indicative of the quality of a course. To calculate your offers see Chapter 4 and the inside fold of the back cover.

Special subject requirements/preferences: A-Level: Chemistry usually required; with two/three mathematics/science subjects. **GCSE:** Mathematics grade A–C. **Birmingham** Grade A*-B in five relevant subjects (grade B biology). **Leeds** Nine or ten subjects at grade A*, A or B.

340 pts London (Imp) – AAB–BBB (Biotech courses)
320 pts Liverpool – 320–280 pts – ALs **or** ALs+ASs **or** VAs+/-ALs/ASs; (Microbiol Biotech)
　　　　London (UCL) – ABB–BBB **or** 3ALs+AS/VA; (Biotech; Bioch Eng (Proc Biotech))
300 pts Birmingham – BBB (Biomed Eng)
　　　　Bradford – BBB (MEng Med Eng)
　　　　Sheffield – BBB–BCC (Med Sys Eng)
280 pts Birmingham – BBC–BCC (Biol Sci (Biotech))
　　　　Bradford – BBC (BEng Med Eng)
　　　　Cardiff – BBC/AB (Biotechnology)
　　　　Leeds – BBC pts (Biotechnology)
　　　　London (RH) – BBC–BCC **or** ALs+ASs **or** VAs+/-ALs/ASs; gs; (Bioch/Biotech)
　　　　Manchester – BBC (Microbiol/Biotech)
260 pts Hertfordshire – 260–220 pts 1x12u **or** 2x6u; gs; (Biotechnology)
　　　　Kent – BCC (Biochem/Biotech)
　　　　Nottingham – BCC–CCC (2 sci ALs); (not gs) (Biotechnology)
240 pts Heriot-Watt – 240 pts 18u – CCC; gs; (Mar Biotech)
　　　　Napier – CCC approx (App Biotech/Microbiol)
　　　　Reading – 240 pts (Biotechnology)
　　　　Strathclyde – BCD–CCC (Bioch/Biotech) (2nd yr entry)
　　　　Surrey – CCC/BC (Microbiol (Biotech))
　　　　Sussex – BCD (Mol Genet Biotech)
　　　　Ulster – CCC (Biomed Eng)
220 pts Aberdeen – CCD/BC (Biotech (App Mol Biol))
　　　　City – CCD/CC (Biomed Eng)
　　　　Luton – 220–180 pts approx (Biotech courses)
　　　　Ulster – CCD (Biotechnology)
200 pts De Montfort (Leicester) – ALs 180–160 pts (inc 2ALs + sci pref biol) **or** VA12u(sci) 200–180 pts; (Biotech/Gnm St)
　　　　Portsmouth – 200 pts – ALs **or** ALs+ASs **or** VAs; gs; (Biotech; Env Biotech)
180 pts Liverpool John Moores – 180–120 pts (inc 2ALs biol+chem) – ALs **or** ALs+ASs **or** VAs+/-ALs/ASs; (Biotechnology)
　　　　Oxford Brookes – 180–160 pts approx (Biotechnology)
　　　　Paisley – 180–80 pts approx (Biotechnology)
　　　　South Bank – 180–140 pts (Biotechnology)
　　　　Staffordshire – 180 pts approx (Med Eng)
　　　　Teesside – 180–160 pts approx (Biotechnology)
　　　　Wolverhampton – 180–160 pts 12u – DDD–DDE/CC **or** CC+dd/de **or** VA12u CC; gs; (Biotechnology)
160 pts Greenwich – 160 pts approx (Biotechnology)
140 pts Abertay Dundee – CD (inc biol/chem) (Biotech courses)
　　　　Liverpool John Moores – 140 pts 2x6u **or** 1x12u – ALs **or** ALs+ASs **or** VAs+/-ALs/ASs; (Med Tech)
　　　　Nescot – 140 pts approx (Biotechnology)
　　　　Westminster – CD (Biotechnology)
120 pts and below
　　　　Barnsley (Coll) – (Fdn Sci)
　　　　East London – 80 pts approx (Biotechnology)
　　　　Glasgow Caledonian – (Med Phys Tech)

Higher National Diploma courses

100 pts Anglia (Bio Instr); Bristol UWE; Halton (Coll); Scottish (CAg); Suffolk (Coll); Teesside; Truro (Coll); Wolverhampton.

Alternative Offers:

IB offers: Aberdeen 26 pts; Birmingham 30 pts; Cardiff 28 pts; City 27 pts; Leeds 26 pts + H6 chem; Nottingham 24 pts (sci); St Andrews 28 pts; South Bank 24 pts.

Irish offers: Aberdeen BBCC/BCCCC; Leeds BCC; Nottingham CCCCC1; St Andrews BBCC/BBB; Sheffield BBBBB; South Bank CCCC.

Scottish Qualificatios: Aberdeen BBBC; Abertay Dundee BCC; Napier BCC; Nottingham BBBB (first sitting); Paisley BBC; St Andrews BBCC/BBB; Strathclyde BBCC (1st yr entry).

CHOOSING YOUR COURSE (See also **Ch.1**)

Subject information: Biotechnology is an interdisciplinary subject which covers biochemistry, microbiology, genetics, chemical engineering, biophysics etc. Courses in these subjects should also be explored. See also **Appendix 1**.

Special features: Birmingham Biotechnology is offered as part of the degree in Biological Sciences or Biochemistry. **Leeds** The study focuses on the biotechnology of medicine, chemical engineering, genetics and industrial and environmental microbiology. **Luton** The Biotechnology degree covers techniques in medicine, agriculture and the food industry. **Nottingham** opportunity for a major research project. **Westminster** The course is biased towards medicine, food and agriculture. *NOW CHECK PROSPECTUSES AND WEB SITES*.

Top universties and colleges (Teaching Quality) (see Ch.4): Glasgow; Liverpool John Moores; not all institutions assessed.

Top universities and colleges (Research) (see Ch.4): Cambridge; Leeds; London (UCL); Nottingham; Surrey.

Study opportunities abroad: Birmingham; Leeds; London (Imp); Nottingham; Reading; Teesside.

Work opportunities abroad: Liverpool John Moores; South Bank; Teesside.

ADMISSIONS INFORMATION

Number of applicants per place (approx): Cardiff 4; East London 5; Leeds 7; London (Imp) 4, (UCL) 4; Reading 10; South Bank 5; Strathclyde 4; Teesside 3; Westminster 3.

Planning your UCAS personal statement (see Ch.4): See **Biological Sciences** and **Biochemistry**. See also **Appendix 1**.

Selection interviews (see Ch.4): Abertay Dundee (No); Cardiff (No); City (No); Leeds; Liverpool John Moores (No); Paisley (No); Portsmouth (No); Sheffield Hallam; South Bank; Staffordshire (No); Strathclyde; Surrey.

Interview questions (see Ch.4): See **Biology** and **Biological Sciences**.

GAP YEAR ADVICE

Teesside Apply as for direct entry but explain your plans at interview for deferred entry.

Institutions willing to defer entry after A-Levels: Birmingham; Cardiff (request deferment before A-levels); East London; Leeds; Liverpool John Moores; London (UCL) (No); Luton; Nottingham; Portsmouth; South Bank; Teesside; Westminster.

AFTER RESULTS ADVICE

Institutions which may accept the same points score after A-Levels: Birmingham; Cardiff; East London; Leeds; South Bank; Strathclyde (No); Teesside.

Institutions which may accept lower grades/points score after A-Levels: Cardiff; East London; Leeds; Nottingham; St Andrews; South Bank; Teesside.

Offers to applicants repeating A-Levels: Higher St Andrews; **Possibly higher** Nottingham; **Same** Leeds, South Bank.

Probable vacancies from June 2001 and in Clearing (see Ch.4): Many universities declared vacancies in Clearing last year and the most competitive universities asked for 320–300 pts.

NEW GRADUATE DESTINATIONS AND EMPLOYMENT (1999 HESA) (see **Ch.4**)

Out of a survey of 71 graduates, 27 entered full-time employment, 34 went into further study and two were believed to be unemployed.

BOTANY (including **Plant Science**; see also **Biology**)

NB The information supplied by the universities and colleges this year varies considerably and the offers listed below should be used as a first source of reference only. Many institutions will accept combinations of Advanced (AL), Advanced Subsidiary (AS) and Vocational Advanced (VA) level qualifications to achieve the required points total, but applicants must check web sites and prospectuses for full details of all offers. Grades and points totals shown should be regarded as the minimum levels to be achieved, but offers may be adjusted downwards when results are known. The points totals shown to the left of the institutions are for ease of reference only. It must not be assumed that tariff points are always used by institutions or that they can be substituted for an offer in grades. The level of an offer is not necessarily indicative of the quality of a course. To calculate your offers see Chapter 4 and the inside fold of the back cover.

Special subject requirements/preferences: A-Level: Two science subjects usually including biology and chemistry (physics and mathematics may be acceptable). **GCSE:** Mathematics if not offered at A-level. **Birmingham** Grade B in five relevant subjects. **Cambridge** Grade As in most subjects preferred.

360 pts and above
    Cambridge – Offers, mainly in grades, vary between colleges (Nat Sci (Plant Sci))
330 pts Southampton – 330 pts 21u (inc 200 pts in 2 subjs from biol, zool, bot, hum biol) (Plant Sci)
320 pts Bristol – ABB–BBB (inc biol+sci); (not gs) (Botany)
    Liverpool – 320–280 pts – ALs **or** ALs+ASs **or** VAs+/-ALs/ASs; (Plant Sci)
    London (Imp) – ABB (Plant Sci)
300 pts Durham – BB(B biol+sci)+B; (not gs) (Plant Sci)
280 pts Birmingham – BBC–BCC (Biol Sci (Plant Biol)
    Edinburgh – BBC (Plant Sci)
    Glasgow – BBC–CCC (Plant Sci)
    Leeds – BBC (Biol Plant)
    Leicester – 18u – BBC **or** BB+2ASs **or** VA12u+AL; gs (AL if only 2ALs offered); (Biol Sci (Plant Sci))
    London (RH) – BBC/BB (Botany courses)
    Manchester – BBC (Plant Sci courses)
    St Andrews – BBC (Plant Env Biol)
    Sheffield – 280 pts approx (B biol) (Plant Sci)
    Southampton – BBC (Plant Sci)
260 pts Bangor – 260 pts – ALs **or** ALs+ASs (inc biol 6u); (Plant Biol)
    East Anglia – BCC (Plant Biol)
    Nottingham – BCC–CCC (2 sci ALs); (not gs) (Plant Sci)
240 pts Aberystwyth – 240 pts 21u – CCC **or** CC+cc **or** VAs; gs; (Botany)
    Belfast (Queen's) – CCC/BB (Plant Sci)

London (RH) – CCC (Fdn Bot Sci)
Reading – 240 pts approx (Bot; Bot/Zool; Env Plant Sci)
220 pts Aberdeen – CCD/BC (Plant Sci; Plant Sci (Cell Mol); Plant Soil Sci)
Luton – 220–180 pts approx (Plant Biol courses)
200 pts Plymouth – 200–180 pts approx (Plant Sci)
Scottish (CAg) – CDD (App Plant/Anim Sci)
180 pts East London – 180 pts approx (Env Plant Sci)
Wolverhampton – 180–160 pts 12u – DDD–DDE/CC or CC+dd/de or VA12u
CC; (Plant Crop Sci)
160 pts Writtle (Coll) – 160 pts (App Plant Sci)
100 pts and below approx
Barnsley (Coll) – (Fdn Plant Sci)

Higher National Diploma courses
100 pts and below
Writtle (Coll)

Alternative Offers:

EB offers: Aberystwyth 70%; Nottingham 60% (sci); Sheffield 65%.

IB offers: Aberdeen 28 pts; Aberystwyth 28 pts and above; Bangor 28 pts; Belfast (Queen's) H555 S555; Birmingham 30 pts; Bristol 32 pts inc H665, 6 in biology; Durham 28 pts; Leeds 30–28 pts; Leicester 30 pts; London (RH) 25 pts; Nottingham 24 pts (sci); St Andrews 28 pts; Sheffield 30 pts.

Irish offers: Aberdeen BBCC/BCCCC; Aberystwyth BBBCC; London (RH) BBCCC; Nottingham CCCCC1; St Andrews BBCC/BBB; Sheffield BBBCC.

Scottish Qualifications: Aberdeen BBBC; Edinburgh ABBC or BBBB; Glasgow BBBB; Nottingham BBBB (first sitting); St Andrews BBBB.

CHOOSING YOUR COURSE (See also **Ch.1**)

Subject information: Botany is also sometimes referred to as Plant Sciences in which final year studies lead to specialised studies of plant physiology or broader areas of ecology or environmental aspects. Biological Science courses should also be checked since botany is often taken as a specialist subject in later years. Courses in Agriculture, Biochemistry, Food Science, Horticulture, Forestry and Landscape Architecture could also be of interest to botanists. See also **Appendix 1**.

Special features: Aberystwyth Years 2 and 3 courses include ecology, plant-soil relations, genetics and evolution of land flora, plant physiology and floral biology. Final course decisions can be delayed until start of year 2. Optional year in employment. **Bangor** Botany studied in year 2 with one subject from biochemistry, marine biology, mathematics, soil science, zoology. **Bristol** Course transfers possible in year 2 between Biology, Botany, Zoology and joint courses. Students have extensive course choice in final two years, selecting from many options. Course covers environmental studies, ecology, plant physiology, pollution studies. **East Anglia** Plant Biology programme includes courses in molecular biology, biochemistry, physiology, pathology, genetic manipulation of plants and ecology. **Edinburgh** Optional courses in years 3 and 4 include ecology, evolution, physiology. **Glasgow** Honours course focuses on plant physiology and biochemistry, the study of fungi (mycology) and ecology. **London (Imp)** Common first year offered, leading to degrees in Biology, Microbiology, Plant Science and Zoology. **London (RH)** Broad courses available with chance to specialise in applied plant biology (plant pathology, breeding and genetics) or botany and microbiology. **Nottingham** Opportunity to carry out major research project. **Reading** Botany plus two other subjects in terms 1 and 2. **St Andrews** Third year focuses on environments, population biology and adaptive physiology. **Sheffield** In year 2 botany combined with biochemistry, genetics, geography, geology, microbiology or zoology. **Southampton** Course is unitised. Biology, Botany and Zoology courses have common first year. *NOW CHECK PROSPECTUSES AND WEB SITES.*

Top universities and colleges (Research) (see Ch.4): Cambridge; Leicester; Nottingham; Oxford; Reading; see also **Biological Sciences**.

Study opportunities abroad: Bangor; Birmingham; Leicester; Nottingham; Sheffield.

Work opportunities abroad: Scottish (CAg).

ADMISSIONS INFORMATION

Number of applicants per place (approx): Aberystwyth 8; Bangor 4; Bristol 5; Edinburgh 6; Glasgow 4; Harper Adams (UC) 2; Leeds 2; London (RH) 3; Manchester (all courses) 4; Nottingham 5; Reading 3; Sheffield 5.

Planning your UCAS personal statement (see Ch.4): See **Biological Sciences**. See also **Appendix 1**.

Selection interviews (see Ch.4): Aberystwyth (No); Bristol (No); Cambridge; Durham (No); Leeds (No); Leicester (No); London (RH); Manchester; Nottingham (depends on application).

Interview questions (see Ch.4): You are likely to be questioned on your biology studies, your reasons for wishing to study Botany and your ideas about a possible future career. In the past questions have been asked about, for example Darwin's Theory of Evolution, photosynthesis and DNA.

GAP YEAR ADVICE

Institutions willing to defer entry after A-Levels: Birmingham; Bristol; Leeds; Luton; Nottingham; Plymouth; Sheffield; Swansea (discouraged).

AFTER RESULTS ADVICE

Institutions which may accept the same points score after A-Levels: Aberystwyth; Bangor; Birmingham; Bristol; Leeds; Leicester; London (RH); Manchester; Nottingham (not for joint courses); Sheffield (No).

Institutions which may accept lower grades/points scores after A-Levels: Aberdeen; Bangor; Leeds; London (RH).

Offers to applicants repeating A-Levels: Higher Leicester; **Possibly higher** Nottingham; **Same** Bangor, Birmingham, Leeds, London (RH), Sheffield.

Probable vacancies from June 2001 and in Clearing (see Ch.4): Most universities are worth trying for this subject.

NEW GRADUATE DESTINATIONS AND EMPLOYMENT (1999 HESA) (see **Ch.4**)

Out of 82 graduates in the survey, 28 secured full-time employment, 28 entered further study and 10 were seeking employment after six months.

BUILDING (including **Building Services Engineering, Building Surveying, Construction Management** and **Facilities Management**; for **Architectural Technology** see **Architecture**)

NB The information supplied by the universities and colleges this year varies considerably and the offers listed below should be used as a first source of reference only. Many institutions will accept combinations of Advanced (AL), Advanced Subsidiary (AS) and Vocational Advanced (VA) level qualifications to achieve the required points total, but applicants must check web sites and prospectuses for full details of all offers. Grades and points totals shown should be regarded as the minimum levels to be achieved, but offers may be adjusted downwards when results are known. The points totals shown to the left of the institutions are for ease of reference only. It must not be assumed that tariff points are always used by institutions or that they can be substituted for an offer in grades. The level of an offer is not necessarily indicative of the quality of a course. To calculate your offers see Chapter 4 and the inside fold of the back cover.

Special subject requirements/preferences: A-Level: Mathematics may be required. **GCSE:** English, mathematics and science usually required.

300 pts   **Edinburgh** – BBB–CCC (Civ Eng/Constr Mgt)
              UMIST – 300 pts 18u – BBB/300 pts **or** BB/200 pts+bb (inc AL maths+phys); (not gs) (Bld Serv Eng)
260 pts   **Brunel** – BCC (Mech Eng/Bld Serv)
              Glamorgan – 260–240 pts (Bld Path; Bld Surv; Archit Bld Cons)
              Kingston – 260 pts (Bld Surv courses; Constr Econ; Prop Plan Dev; Prop St)
              Loughborough – 260 pts 18u – 2ALs+ALs/2ASs **or** VAs; (not gs) (Constr Eng Mgt)
              Reading – BCC/AB (Bld Constr Mgt; Costr Mgt Eng/Surv)
              Salford – BCC (Bld Surv; Constr Mgt)
              Strathclyde – BCC (BBB – 2nd yr entry) (Bld Des Eng)
              Ulster – BCC (Archit Tech/Mgt)
              UMIST – 260 pts 18u – BCC (260 pts) **or** BC/180 pts+cc; (not gs) (Commer Mgt/Qty Surv; Constr Mgt)
240 pts   **Bristol UWE** – 240–180 pts 18u pref/12u – ALs **or** ALs+ASs **or** VAs+/-ALs/ASs; (Bus Constr KN21)
              Central Lancashire – 240 pts 12u (inc AL maths); gs; (Bld Serv Eng; Bld Surv)
              De Montfort (Leicester) – 240 pts – ALs; gs; (Bld Surv)
              Heriot-Watt – 240–220 pts 18u – CCC; gs; (Constr Mgt; Bld Serv Constr Mgt; Bld Surv; Env Serv Mgt/Eng)
              Liverpool – 240 pts (Constr Proj Mgt)
              London (UCL) – CCC **or** 3ALs+AS/VA; (Constr Mgt)
              UMIST – 240 pts approx (Bld Serv Eng; Constr Mgt)
220 pts   **Anglia** – 220 pts 12u – 2ALs **or** ALs+ASs **or** VA12u AB; gs; (Constr Econ/Mgt; Bld Surv)
              Bristol UWE – 220 pts 12u – ALs **or** ALs+ASs **or** VAs+/-ALs/ASs; gs; (Constr Mgt K252)
              Central Lancashire – 220 pts 12u; gs; (Constr Proj Mgt)
              Greenwich – 220 pts approx (Bld Surv; Bld courses)
              Kingston – 220 pts 2x6u (Bld Surv)
              Liverpool John Moores – 220–140 pts (inc 2ALs **or** VAs) – ALs **or** ALs+ASs **or** VAs+/-ALs/ASs; (Bld Surv; Bld Des Tech/Mgt; Bld Mntnce/Mgt; Constr Mgt)
              Luton – 220–180 pts approx (Bld Surv; Constr St; Constr Mgt)
              Napier – CCD (Bld Eng/Mgt; Bld Mntnce Mgt)
              Nottingham – CCD–CDD (Bld Env Eng)
              Plymouth – 220–200 pts approx (Bld Surv Env; Constr Mgt Env)
              Sheffield hallam – 220–200 pts (Bld Surv; Constr Mgt)
              Teesside – 220–180 pts approx (Constr Eng)
              Ulster – CCD–CDD (Constr Eng/Mgt)
              Wolverhampton – 220 pts 12u – CCD/BB **or** BB+ASs **or** VA12u BB; gs; (CAD/Constr; Constr Mgt; Blt Env; Bld Surv)
200 pts   **Bristol UWE** – 200–160 pts 12u – ALs **or** ALs+ASs **or** VAs+/-ALs/ASs; (Blt Env St)
              Central England – 200 pts 12u – CCE/BB; (Constr Mgt/Econ)
              Central England – 200 pts approx (Bld Surv)
              Coventry – 200 pts approx (Bld Surv; Constr Mgt)
              Glasgow Caledonian – CCE (Bld Contr; Bld Surv; Constr Mgt)
              Northumbria – 200 pts approx (Bld Surv; Bld Des Mgt; Bld Proj Mgt; Constr Mgt)
              Nottingham Trent – 200 pts approx (Bld (Cons) (Eng); Bld Surv; Constr Mgt)
              Portsmouth – 200 pts – ALs **or** ALs+ASs **or** VAs; (Constr Eng Mgt; Constr Tech)
              South Bank – 200–180 pts approx (Bld courses)

180 pts   **Anglia** – 180 pts 12u – 2ALs **or** ALs+ASs **or** VA12u BC; gs; (Constr Eng)
           Brighton – 180 pts approx (Bld Surv; Bld St)
           Dundee – 180 pts approx (Civ Eng/Bld)
           Oxford Brookes – DDD/CC–CD (Bld courses)
           Robert Gordon – 180 pts approx (Bld Surv; Constr Mgt)
160 pts   **Anglia** – 160 pts 12u – 2ALs **or** ALs+ASs **or** VA12u CC; gs; (Constr Mgt;
              Constr Facil Mgt; Constr Comm Mgt; Prop Mgt)
           Bell (CT) – DDE/CD (Costr Mgt; Facil Mgt; Prem Mgt)
           Brighton – 160 pts approx (Constr Mgt)
           Derby – 160 pts approx (Constr Mgt)
           Glamorgan – 160 pts (Comb Hons: Bld Econ; Bld Mgt)
           South Bank – 160–140 pts approx (Blt Env St; Bld Serv)
           Staffordshire – CC **or** CD+AS(40 pts) **or** VAs; gs; (Constr Mgt)
           Westminster – CC (Bld Surv; Bld Eng)
140 pts   **Abertay Dundee** – CD (Constr Mgt)
           Kingston – 140 pts (inc 2x6u or equiv) **or** VAs (Eng/Constr); gs (up to 60 pts);
              (Constr Mgt)
           Paisley – CD (Constr Eng; Constr Mgt; Constr Env Mgt; Prop St)
120 pts   **Bolton (IHE)** – 120 pts approx (Constr Mgt; Bld Surv)
           Westminster – DD (Bld courses except under **160 pts**; Constr Mgt)
100 pts   **and below**
           Bristol UWE – 100 pts 6u – ALs **or** ALs+ASs **or** VAs+/-ALs/ASs (60 pts min
              from 6u/12u awards); (Fdn Blt Env St)
           Glasgow Caledonian – DE (Bld Serv Eng)
           Nescot – EE (Constr Mgt; Facil Mgt)
           Southampton (Inst) – (Constr courses)
           Swansea (IHE) – (Proj Constr Mgt)

           Leeds Met – (contact university)

Diploma of Higher Education courses
     Abertay Dundee.

Higher National Diploma courses
120 pts   **and below**
     Anglia; Bell (CT); Barking (Coll); Blackburn (Coll); Blackpool & Fylde (Coll); Bolton
     (IHE); Bradford (Coll); Brighton; Bromley (Coll) gs; Cardiff (UWI); Central England;
     Central Lancashire EEE/DD; Cheltenham & Glos (CHE); Colchester (Inst);
     Crawley (Coll) gs; De Montfort; Derby; Doncaster (Coll); Dudley (CT); Fife (CFHE);
     Glamorgan; Glasgow (CBP); Glasgow Caledonian; Greenwich (West Kent Coll);
     Gloucestershire (CAT); Grimsby (Coll); Guildford (CFHE); Hammersmith & West
     London (Coll); Hastings (Coll); Hertfordshire (Build Surv); Huddersfield; Liverpool
     John Moores; Llandrillo (Coll) (Build Serv); Luton; Manchester (CAT) (HNC);
     Manchester Met; Mid Kent (CHFE); Motherwell (Coll); Napier EE; Nescot;
     Newport (UWCN); North East London (Coll) (HNC); Northampton (UC);
     Northumbria; Nottingham Trent; Oldham (Coll); Oxford Brookes; Pembrokeshire
     (Coll); Plymouth; Portsmouth; Preston (Coll); Robert Gordon; Rycotewood (Coll)
     (Constr Plant Eng); St Helens (Coll); Salford; Sheffield Hallam; Solihull (Coll);
     Somerset (CAT); South Bank; South Devon (Coll); South East Essex (Coll);
     Stockport (CFHE); Stoke on Trent (Coll); Swansea (IHE); UHI (Perth); Wigan &
     Leigh (Coll); Willesden (CT); Wirral Met (Coll); Wolverhampton.

College Diploma courses
  40 pts   **or equivalent**
     Glasgow Caledonian (Bld Surv); Northumbria.

Alternative Offers:

IB offers: Bath 28 pts H5 maths; Brighton 24 pts inc 12 pts Highers 3 subjects; Bristol
UWE 26 pts (Bld Surv); Central Lancashire 26pts; Heriot-Watt 32 pts; Sheffield IA; UMIST
28 pts inc H55.

Irish offers: Brighton CCCC; Bristol UWE CCCC.

Scottish Qualifications: Abertay Dundee BCC; Dundee BBBB; Edinburgh (Civ Eng/Cons) BBBB; Glasgow (CB) BBB; Glasgow Caledonian BBCC/CCC; Heriot-Watt BBBC; Paisley BBC; Robert Gordon BBCC; Strathclyde CCCC.

Overseas applicants: Sheffield Hallam Courses available in language and study skills.

CHOOSING YOUR COURSE (See also **Ch.1**)

> **Subject information:** These Building and Construction courses involve the techniques and management methods employed in the building industry. Building Services courses cover heating, lighting, air conditioning (shortage of applicants). See also references to Environmental Engineering under **Civil Engineering**. Similar subject areas are covered in Civil and Structural Engineering courses, Architecture, Estate Management and Quantity Surveying. See also **Appendix 1**.

Special features: Central Lancashire Courses also offered include Facilities and Utilities Management and Building Surveying. **Liverpool John Moores** Building Maintenance Management is the only course of its kind in the UK. **South Bank** After a common first year the decision is made to take a degree in construction or surveying. **Wolverhampton** (Bld Surv) Bias towards residential and domestic property. *NOW CHECK PROSPECTUSES AND WEB SITES.*

Top universities and colleges (Teaching Quality) (see Ch.4): Coventry; Kingston; Liverpool John Moores; Loughborough; Luton; North West London (Coll); Napier; Northumbria; Nottingham Trent; Oxford Brookes; Plymouth; Reading; Southampton (Inst); UMIST; Westminster; not all institutions assessed

Top universities and colleges (Research) (see Ch.4): Built Environment (this category includes **Architecture** and **Surveying**) Cambridge; Cardiff; Heriot-Watt; London (UCL); Loughborough; Newcastle; Nottingham; Reading; Salford; Strathclyde; Ulster.

Study opportunities abroad: Anglia; Bolton (IHE); Central Lancashire; Coventry; De Montfort; Glamorgan; Glasgow Caledonian; Huddersfield; Liverpool John Moores (Bld Surv); Middlesex; Northumbria (Bld Serv Eng); Nottingham Trent; Paisley; Robert Gordon; Sheffield Hallam; Strathclyde; UMIST; Wolverhampton.

Work opportunities abroad: Abertay Dundee; Brighton; Central Lancashire; Coventry; Glasgow Caledonian; Glamorgan; Kingston; Liverpool John Moores; Loughborough; Northumbria; Robert Gordon; Salford; South Bank; Westminster.

ADMISSIONS INFORMATION

Number of applicants per place (approx): Anglia 6; Bristol UWE (Constr Mgt) 5; Central Lancashire (Bld Mgt) 5; Coventry 9; De Montfort (Bld Surv) 5, (Constr Tech) 5; Derby 5; Glamorgan 3; Glasgow Caledonian 6; Greenwich 13; Heriot-Watt 6; Kingston 4; Liverpool John Moores 15; London (UCL) 4; Loughborough (Constr Eng Mgt) 1; Napier 8; Northumbria 6; Nottingham (Bld Serv) 8; Nottingham Trent 5; Plymouth (CFE) 1; Salford (Bld Surv) 6, (Bld) 4; Sheffield Hallam (Bld Surv) 7; Staffordshire 5; Strathclyde 5; UMIST 8; Wolverhampton 6.

Planning your UCAS personal statement (see Ch.4): Details of work experience with any levels of responsibility should be included. Make contact with any building organisation to arrange a meeting with staff to discuss careers in building. Building also covers civil engineering, surveying, quantity surveying etc and these areas should also be explored. **Salford** Personal achievement in technological areas, work experience. **South Bank** (Bld Surv) Knowledge of the profession. See also **Appendix 1**.

Selection interviews (see Ch.4): Abertay Dundee (No); Brighton; Bristol UWE (No); Brunel; Coventry (No); De Montfort; Derby; Glamorgan; Glasgow Caledonian; Greenwich; Kingston; Liverpool John Moores; Loughborough; Napier (No); Northampton (UC) (No); Nottingham (No); Paisley (No); Plymouth (W); Portsmouth (No); Robert Gordon; Salford; Sheffield Hallam; Staffordshire; Westminster; Wolverhampton (No).

Interview questions (see Ch.4): Work experience in the building and civil engineering industries is important and you could be expected to describe any building project you have seen. A knowledge of the range of activities to be found on a building site will be expected, for example quantity and land surveyors and the various building trades.

Reasons for rejection (non-academic): Inability to communicate. Lack of motivation. Indecisiveness about reasons for choosing the course.

GAP YEAR ADVICE

Glamorgan (No). **Greenwich** Delays professional qualifications. **Loughborough** (Constr Eng Mgt) Fully sponsored course – see sponsor.

Institutions willing to defer entry after A-Levels: Anglia; Bolton (IHE); Brighton; Central Lancashire; De Montfort; Derby; Glamorgan; Greenwich; Heriot-Watt; Hertfordshire; Huddersfield; Kingston; London (UCL) (No); Luton; Northumbria; Nottingham (after discussion); Nottingham Trent; Robert Gordon (Bld Surv); Salford; Sheffield Hallam; Swansea (IHE); UMIST; Wolverhampton.

AFTER RESULTS ADVICE

Institutions which may accept the same points score after A-Levels: Bolton (IHE); Brighton; Bristol UWE; Coventry; De Montfort; Derby; Glamorgan; Glasgow Caledonian; Heriot-Watt; Hertfordshire; Huddersfield; Kingston; Liverpool John Moores; London (UCL) (No); Loughborough; Northampton (UC); Northumbria; Nottingham; Nottingham Trent; Paisley; Salford; Sheffield Hallam; Staffordshire; Strathclyde; Swansea (IHE); UMIST; Westminster; Wolverhampton.

Institutions which may accept lower grades/points score after A-Levels: Bolton (IHE); Brighton; Coventry; Derby; Heriot-Watt; Hertfordshire; Huddersfield; London (UCL); Northumbria; Reading; Robert Gordon; Salford; Swansea (IHE); UMIST; Westminster; Wolverhampton.

Offers to applicants repeating A-Levels: Higher Liverpool John Moores, Strathclyde; **Possibly higher** Bristol UWE; **Same** Bolton (IHE), Brighton, Coventry, De Montfort, Heriot-Watt, Huddersfield, Kingston, London (UCL), Northumbria, Robert Gordon.

Probable vacancies from June 2001 and in Clearing (see Ch.4): Take your pick – choose your university! Almost all of them are expected to have vacancies. Building Services Engineering should not be overlooked since these courses offer a more specialised type of training and many vacancies are again likely.

NEW GRADUATE DESTINATIONS AND EMPLOYMENT (1999 HESA) (see **Ch.4**)

In a survey of 1677 graduates, 1355 obtained full-time employment, 87 went on to further study and 67 were believed to be unemployed.

BUSINESS COURSES (Section A: Business and Management Courses;
Section B: International and European Business and Management Courses, Business and Management Courses with Languages; **Section C:** Specialised Business and Management Courses including Advertising, E-Commerce, Entrepreneurship, Health Services Management, Human Resources Management and Retail Management; see also **Hospitality, Hotel and Catering Management, Marketing** and **Tourism**)

NB The information supplied by the universities and colleges this year varies considerably and the offers listed below should be used as a first source of reference only. Many institutions will accept combinations of Advanced (AL), Advanced Subsidiary (AS) and Vocational Advanced (VA) level qualifications to achieve the required points total, but applicants must check web sites and prospectuses for full details of all offers. Grades and points totals shown should be regarded as the minimum levels to be achieved, but offers may be adjusted downwards when results are known. The points totals shown to the left of the institutions are for ease of reference only. It must not be assumed that tariff points are always used by institutions or that they can be substituted for an offer in grades. The level of an offer is not necessarily indicative of the quality of a course. To calculate your offers see Chapter 4 and the inside fold of the back cover.

Special subject requirements/preferences: A-Level: Mathematics (or AS-Level) required or preferred by some universities. Foreign language/s required for some European or international courses. **East Anglia** (Maths/Mgt St) Mathematics preferred. **Exeter** Mathematics grade B.

GCSE: Mathematics and English often at grade A or B required. **Belfast (Queen's)**, **Birmingham, Brighton, Central England** (Bus Decn Analys), **City, Dundee, East Anglia, Huddersfield, Lancaster, Leeds, London Guildhall, Loughborough, Napier, Oxford Brookes, Portsmouth, Sheffield, Sheffield Hallam** (or grade C at A-Level), **Southampton, Swansea** and **Warwick** All require mathematics at grade A or B. **Kingston** Prefer mathematics grade B or higher. **Aberdeen, Dundee, Edinburgh, Glasgow** English, mathematics or science and a foreign language. **Bangor** Average of grade Bs. **Buckingham** Five grade Bs (minimum). **De Montfort** Four subjects grade A–B. **European (Bus Sch London)** Five subjects at grade A preferred. **Exeter** Majority of subjects grade A*, A or B. **Hull** Three Grade As, three grade Bs, three grade Cs preferred. **London (LSE)** Grades A and B.

Section A: BUSINESS AND MANAGEMENT COURSES

(refer to **Section B** and **Section C** for other Business courses)

360 pts **and above**
  Bath – 430–400 pts 24u – AAB+90–60 pts **or** 3ALs+2ASs; (not gs) (Bus Admin)
  London (UCL) – AAA–AAB **or** 3ALs+AS/VA; (Maths Mgt St)
  Oxford – Offers vary between candidates (Mgt courses)
  Southampton – 370 pts 21u (inc 220 pts from 2ALs); GCSE B maths; (not gs) (Mgt Sci; Mgt Sci/Acc)
  Warwick – AAA–BBB (Bus St/Mgt courses; Maths/Bus St)
350 pts **York** – 350–300 pts 21–18u – BBB **or** BBB+b **or** BB+bb **or** VAs (check with univ); (Mgt/Inf Tech/Lang)
340 pts **Birmingham** – AAB (Law/Bus St)
  Lancaster – AAB (Org St/USA/Can; Bus St/USA/Can; Mgt Sci/USA/Can; Ops Mgt/USA/Can)
  London (Imp) – AAB–BBB (Mgt/Elec Electron Eng)
  London (King's) – AAB+b **or** AA+bbb **or** VA12u AA+AL(B)+AS(b) **or** VA6u+ALs/ASs; (Bus Mgt)
  London (LSE) – AAB–BBB (Bus Maths/Stats; Mgt Sci)
320 pts **Bath** – ABB–BBB (Bus courses; Inf Mgt/Modn Lang)
  Belfast (Queen's) – ABB (Management)

City – 3x6u – ABB; VAs (contact univ); (not gs) (Mgt/Sys; Bus St)
Durham – ABB (Soc Sci Mgt St)
Edinburgh – ABB (1 sitting); (not gs) (Bus St courses)
Leeds – ABB **or** AB+bb (VAs contact univ); (not gs) (Mgt St/Law; Mgt St/Psy)
Leeds – 18u – AB+B/2ASs (not gs) (Mgt St)
London (Imp) – ABB (Maths/Mgt)
London (RH) – ABB (Mgt/Econ)
London (UCL) – ABB–BBC **or** 3ALs+AS/VA; (Mgt courses except under **360 pts**)
Loughborough – 18u – AB+B/bb **or** VA12u AB+AL(B)/2ASs; (Mgt Sci)
Nottingham – ABB–BBB (Mgt St courses)
St Andrews – ABB (Mgt/Psy)
Sheffield – 320 pts approx (Bus St)
UMIST – ABB–BBB (Mgt courses)
Warwick – ABB (Mgt Sci)

300 pts   **Aston** – 18u – BBB; gs; (Mgt/Admin St)
Birmingham – BBB–BBC (BCom Bus St courses except under **340 pts**)
Bradford – 300 pts 12u; gs; (Bus St/Law)
Brunel – 300–280 pts 2x6u – ALs **or** ALs+ASs **or** VAs+/-ALs/ASs; (Bus Mgt courses)
Cardiff – 300–280 pts approx (Bus Admin courses)
Durham – ABC (Mgt St/Chin/Jap)
East Anglia – BBB–CCC (Mgt courses except under **280 pts**)
Exeter – 300 pts 18u – BBB **or** BB+bb **or** VA6u B+BB; (not gs) (Bus/Acc courses; Bus/Mgt courses)
Keele – BBB–BBC **or** equiv AS accepted; gs; (Business courses)
Kent – 300 pts approx (Bus Admin; Bus Admin/Econ/Pol)
Lancaster – BBB–BCC (Bus St; Org St courses except under **340 pts**)
Leeds – 18u – BB+B/2ASs (not gs) (Mgt/Trans St)
Leeds – BBB–BCC (Mgt St/Stats; Mgt St/Maths; Mgt St/Phil)
London (Imp) – BBB–BBC (Mgt courses except under **340/320/240 pts**)
London (King's) – 300–260 pts approx (Pharmacol/Mgt)
London (RH) – BBB (Mgt courses except under **320 pts**)
Manchester – BBB (Comp Sci/Bus/Mgt; Eng Bus; Mat Sci/Bus/Mgt)
Newcastle – BBB (Bus Mgt; Chem/Mgt; Econ Bus Mgt)
Nottingham Trent – 300 pts approx (Bus Mgt – 3 yrs)
Reading – BBB (Mgt/Bus Admin; Acc/Mgt)
St Andrews – BBB (Mgt courses except under **320 pts**)
Sheffield – 300 pts approx (Mgt/Maths; Bus St/Econ)
Surrey – BBB–CCC (Bus St courses)
Sussex – BBB–BCD (Mgt St courses)
Swansea – 300 pts 18u – BBB/BCC **or** ALs+ASs **or** VAs+/-AL/ASs; (Bus St courses)

280 pts   **Bradford** – 280–260 pts 12u; gs; (Bus Mgt St)
Durham (Stockton) – BBC (Bus Fin)
East Anglia – BBC (2ASs max); gs; (BSc Bus Mgt)
Essex – 280 pts 21u – BB+AL/2ASs **or** VA12u BB+AL; gs; (Bus Mgt)
Glasgow – BBC–BCC (Mgt St courses)
Hull – BBC/AB (BA Mgt courses)
Kent – 280 pts approx/AB (Mgt Sci/Bus Admin)
Leeds, Trinity & All Saints (Coll) – BBC/BC (Mgt/Psy)
Liverpool – 280 pts approx (Mgt Comb Hons; Bus St; Maths/Mgt)
Oxford Brookes – BBC–CCC–CCD (offer varies with 2nd subj) (Bus Admin/Mgt)
Stirling – BBC–BCC (Mgt Sci courses)
Strathclyde – BBC (Bus courses)
Ulster – BBC–BCC (Bus St courses)
Westminster – BBC–CCC (Bus courses)

260 pts   **Aston** – 18u – 3ALs **or** ALs+ASs **or** VAs+/-ALs/ASs; gs; (Bus Admin Comb Hons)
      Belfast (Queen's) – BCC (BA Inf Mgt)
      De Montfort (Leicester) – 260 pts – ALs **or** ALs+ASs **or** VA12u+/-ALs/ASs; (Bus St sandwich courses)
      Dundee – BCC (Bus Econ/Mark)
      Exeter – 260 pts 18u – BCC **or** BC+cd (inc AL maths/stats) **or** VA6u B+CC; gs; (Mgt/Stats; Mgt/Stats Euro)
      Gyosei (Int Coll) – BCC (Bus St)
      Heriot-Watt – 260 pts 18u – BCC; gs; (Bus Mgt; Bus Admin; Mgt courses)
      Hull – BCC (Bus St joint courses)
      Kent – BCC/BB (Mgt Sci; Mgt Sci/Comp)
      Leeds, Trinity & All Saints (Coll) – BCC–CCD (Mgt St courses except under 280 pts)
      Leicester – 260 pts 18u – BCC; (Mgt St; Chem/Mgt)
      Liverpool – 260 pts approx (Mgt/Eng; Bus Econ)
      London (Imp) – 260 pts approx (Mgt/Mat)
      Loughborough (Peterborough) – BC+C/cc **or** VA12u BC+AL(B)/2ASs (Bus St)
      Manchester – 260 pts approx (Bus/Eng; Bus/Mgt Mat Sci; Bus Mgt/Phys)
      Northumbria – BCC (Bus St)
      Nottingham Trent – BCC (Bus St)
      Salford – BCC–CCC (Bus Mgt and Joint courses)
      Sussex – BCC–BCD (Mgt Sci courses)
250 pts   **Buckingham** – 250 pts 21u – 3ALs **or** 3ALs+AS; (Bus St courses)
240 pts   **Aberdeen** – CCC (Mgt courses)
      Aberystwyth – 240–220 pts approx (Bus St courses)
      Aston – 240 pts approx (Trans Mgt; Log)
      Bangor – 240 pts; gs; (Bus St/Econ; Bus St/Fin; Bus St/Mark; Bus St/Modn Lang; Mgt/Acc; Mgt/Welsh; Agric/Bus Mgt)
      Belfast (Queen's) – CCC/BB (Bus Admin)
      Bell (CT) – 240–120 pts approx (Bus courses)
      Bournemouth – 240 pts – BCD **or** VAs; (not gs) (Bus St)
      Bradford – 240 pts 12u; gs; (Euro St/Mgt; Bus Comp))
      Brighton – 240 pts approx (Business courses)
      Bristol UWE – 240–200 pts 18u pref/12u – ALs **or** ALs+ASs **or** VAs+/-ALs/ASs; (not gs) (Bus St; Bus St Tour)
      De Montfort (Leicester) – 240–180 pts – 2ALs **or** VAs+/-ALs/ASs; (Mgt Sci)
      Durham (Stockton) – 240–220 pts approx (Bus Fin)
      Glamorgan – 240 pts approx (Law/Bus)
      Glasgow Caledonian – CCC/BC; gs; (Bus St)
      Hertfordshire – 240 pts approx (Bus courses)
      Kent – 240 pts approx (Phys/Mgt Sci)
      Kingston – 240 pts (inc 2x6u) – ALs **or** ALs+ASs **or** VAs+/-AL/ASs; (not gs) (Bus St)
      Lincolnshire & Humberside – 240–160 pts (E-Commerce)
      Liverpool John Moores – 240–180 pts (soc sci subj pref) – ALs **or** ALs+ASs **or** VAs+/-ALs/ASs; (Bus/Econ)
      London (Imp) – CCC–CCD (Agric Bus Mgt courses)
      London (QM) – 240 pts approx (Bus St courses)
      Manchester Met (Crewe) – 240 pts; (Bus Ent)
      Napier – CCC (Bus Inf Mgt)
      Portsmouth – 240 pts – ALs **or** ALs+ASs **or** VAs; gs; (Bus St; Econ/Bus Pol; Bus/Sociol; Bus Admin; E-Bus)
      Robert Gordon – CCC/BB (Bus St; Bus Admin)
      Sheffield Hallam – 240 pts approx (Bus St courses)
      Sunderland – 240 pts approx (Bus St; Bus/Mark; Bus Admin; Bus/Hum Res Mgt; Bus/Mgt St; Bus Leg St)
      UMIST – BCD (Mgt Chem Sci)
      Warrington (CI) – 240–200 pts approx (Bus Mgt; Bus Mgt/Media St)

220 pts   **Bournemouth** – 220 pts (inc AL sci) **or** VAs; (not gs) (Bus Decn Mgt)
        Bradford – CCD/BB (Pharm Mgt)
        Bristol UWE – 220–180 pts 18u pref/12u – ALs **or** ALs+ASs **or** VAs+/-
        ALs/ASs; (not gs) (Bus Admin courses; Bus/St Comb Sci (inc 6u sci))
        Central England – 220 pts – 2ALs **or** ALs+ASs **or** VAs+/-ALs/ASs; gs;
        (Business courses except under **200 pts**)
        Central Lancashire – 220 pts 12u; gs; (Bus St; Bus/Mark/Law; Mgt courses
        except under **200 pts**)
        Cheltenham & Glos (CHE) – 220–180 pts approx (Bus Mgt; Hum Res Mgt
        courses)
        Chester (Coll) – 220 pts – ALs (200–180 pts inc C bus subj)+AS(40+ pts) **or**
        VA (200–180 pts inc C bus subj)+ASs(40+ pts); (Bus St Spec Prog)
        Cranfield – CDD (Bus Mgt Env)
        De Montfort (Leicester) – 220 pts – ALs **or** ALs+ASs **or** VA12u+/-AL/ASs;
        (Bus St joint courses; Bus Admin)
        De Montfort (Leicester) – 220 pts – 2ALs **or** VA12u+/-AL/ASs; (Mgt St joint
        courses)
        Greenwich – 220–200 pts approx (Bus St; Bus Admin; Mgt Sci; Bus/Law)
        Huddersfield – CCD–CDD/BC (Mgt/Acc; Mgt/Sci; Bus St courses)
        Kent – 220 pts approx (Chem/Mgt Sci)
        King Alfred's Winchester (Coll) – 220 pts 12u; gs; (Bus Mgt/Bus courses;
        Comb courses)
        Kingston – 220–180 pts approx (Bus Mgt Hons courses)
        Liverpool John Moores – 220 pts (inc ALs+VA6 160 pts – ALs **or** ALs+ASs **or**
        VAs+/-ALs/ASs; (Bus Admin; Bus St; Bus Econ)
        Luton – 220–180 pts approx (Mod Bus courses)
        Middlesex – 220–180 pts approx (Bus courses; Hum Res Mgt)
        Nottingham Trent – 220–180 pts approx (Bus courses except under **260 pts**)
        Paisley – CCD/BB (Bus Mgt)
        Plymouth – 220–200 pts approx (Bus St courses; Bus Admin courses; Marit
        Bus)
        Sheffield Hallam – 220 pts approx (Bus St courses)
        South East Essex (Coll) – 220–180 pts (Business)
        Staffordshire – CCD **or** CCE+AS(40 pts); gs; (Bus Admin; Bus St courses;
        Mgt courses)
        Swansea – CCD/BC–CC **or** ALs+ASs **or** VAs+/-ALs/ASs; (Welsh Bus St)
        Wolverhampton – 220 pts 12u – CCD/BC/AC/BCE **or** BC+c **or** VA12u BB **or**
        VA6u B+AL; gs; (Bus courses)
200 pts   **Bangor** – 200 pts; ALs only; gs; (Bus/Soc Admin)
        Bradford – 200 pts 12u; gs; (Manuf Mgt; Mat Tech Mgt; Tech Mgt; Med Hlthcr
        Res Mgt)
        Central England – 200 pts – 2ALs **or** ALs+ASs **or** VAs+/-AL/ASs; gs; (BSc
        Mgt)
        Central Lancashire – 200 pts 12u; gs; (Bus/Econ; Bus/Bus Inf Sys; Mgt/Bus
        Inf Sys)
        Chester (Coll) – 200 pts – ALs (180 pts C bus subj)+AS **or** VAs (180 pts C
        bus subj)+AS; (Bus Admin)
        Coventry – 200–160 pts approx (Bus St courses)
        Derby – 200 pts 12u – CDD **or** CD+dd **or** VA12u CD+AL(D); gs; (Bus St; Mgt
        courses)
        East London – 200–180 pts approx (Bus St courses)
        Heriot-Watt – CDD (BBC 2nd yr entry) (Bus/Econ)
        Lampeter – 200 pts approx (Bus Mgt courses)
        Liverpool John Moores – 200 pts (inc AL+VA6u 160 pts) – ALs **or** ALs+ASs
        or VAs+/-ALs/ASs; (Bus Admin; Bus Inf)
        South Bank – CDD/CC (Bus St; Bus Admin)
        Stranmillis (UC) – 200–160 pts approx (Herit/Mgt St)
        Sunderland – 200 pts approx (Bus Comb St)

Warrington (CI) – 200–180 pts approx (Bus Mgt courses)

Westminster – CDD/CC (Bus St courses)

190 pts **North London** – 190 pts (inc 2ALs 160 pts) **or** VAs+/-AL/ASs; (Bus St; Bus Admin; Bus Ops Mgt; Entre; Mgt courses)

180 pts **Barnsley (Coll)** – 180 pts 12u; gs; (Bus/Mgt)

Buckinghamshire Cilterns (UC) – 180–140 pts approx (Business courses)

Cardiff (UWI) – 180 pts approx (Bus St courses)

Cornwall & Duchy (Coll) – 180 pts approx (Bus Ad)

Cranfield – 180 pts approx (Bus Inf Sys; Inf Sys Mgt)

Doncaster (Coll) – 180 pts approx (Bus Mgt Acc/Bus Mark)

Dundee – 180 pts approx (Mgt/Eng courses)

Farnborough (CT) – 180–160 pts approx (Bus Admin)

Glamorgan – 180 pts approx (Bus St courses)

Glasgow Caledonian – BC (Bus Inf Mgt)

Liverpool Hope (Coll) – 180 pts approx (Bus Commun Ent courses)

London Guildhall – DDD/CD (Bus courses)

Napier – 180–140 pts approx (Bus courses except under **240 pts**)

Northumbria – 180 pts approx (Bus Admin)

Norwich City (Coll) – 180 pts approx (Bus St – optnl Lang)

Nottingham Trent – 180 pts approx (Bus Tech)

Royal (CAg) – 180 pts approx (Bus Mgt courses)

St Martin's (Coll) – 180–160 pts approx (Bus Mgt St courses)

St Mary's (Coll) – 180–140 pts approx (Mgt St courses)

Southampton (Inst) – 180–160 pts approx (Bus St)

Surrey Roehampton – 180 pts approx – ALs **or** ALs+ASs **or** VAs+/-ALs/ASs; (Bus St)

Swansea (IHE) – 180 pts approx (Bus St; Bus Admin)

Thames Valley – 180–140 pts approx (Bus St courses; Hum Res Mgt courses)

Teesside – 180–160 pts approx (Bus courses)

Wirral Met (Coll) – 180–160 pts approx (Bus St)

160 pts **Abertay Dundee** – CC (Bus St)

Anglia – 160 pts 12u – 2ALs **or** ALs+ASs **or** VA12u CC; gs; (Bus Admin; Bus St)

Bath Spa (UC) – CC **or** ALs+ASs **or** VAs+/-ALs/ASs; (not gs) (Bus St)

Bolton (IHE) – 160 pts approx (Bus St courses)

Canterbury Christ Church (UC) – CC (Bus St courses)

De Montfort (Bedford) – 160 pts – ALs **or** ALs+ASs **or** VA12u+/-ALs/ASs; (Bus St courses)

Doncaster (Coll) – 160 pts – CC **or** ALs+ASs **or** VAs+/-AL/ASs; gs; ((Business courses)

Edge Hill (CHE) – CC (Bus/Mgt St; Org/Mgt St)

Glasgow Caledonian – DDE/CD (Mgt Sci)

Heriot-Watt (Scottish Borders) – CC (Qual Mgt; Bus Mgt)

Huddersfield – 160 pts 12u – 2ALs **or** AL+ASs **or** VAs+/-ALs/ASs (40 pts max from 3u awards); gs; (Bus Mgt)

Hull (Scarborough) – 160–140 pts approx (Bus Mgt)

Kingston – 160–140 pts approx (Chem Bus Mgt)

Lincolnshire & Humberside – 160 pts (Bus courses; Mgt courses)

Manchester Met (Crewe) – 160 pts – CC; (Bus Mgt)

Newport (UWCN) – 160–140 pts – ALs **or** ALs+ASs **or** VAs+/-ALs/ASs; (Bus/Ent; Bus/Leg St; Bus Admin)

North East Wales (IHE) – 160–80 pts approx (Bus courses)

Northampton (UC) – 160–140 pts approx (Bus courses)

Ripon & York (Coll) – 160 pts approx (Mgt courses)

Sheffield Hallam – 160–140 pts approx (Bus/Tech; Comp/Mgt Sci)

South Bank – 160–140 pts approx (Mgt Comb Hons; Bus St; Bus Admin)

West Suffolk (Coll) – 160 pts 12u – 2ALs **or** ALs+ASs **or** VAs+/-ALs/ASs; gs; (Bus Admin)

Management *and* Business Opportunities

All our standard courses have a Management theme with the Higher Diploma as the outcome of stage one and the degree award as stage two. This means that you can specialise in a practical area where interests can be pursued both with academic studies and hands-on vocational skills.

Would you like skills in catering, running a pub, managing the renovation of a classic car, then our Higher programmes can develop these interests. If you choose accounting you can be on your way to Chartered status: if law then Legal Executive status. New Foundation Degrees (2 years) are planned for Vocational Management and Tourism.

You may decide to seek employment with those practical skills, perhaps with a Sports Centre management focus or marketing in a retail environment or managing people in a voluntary organisation.

What is a wonderful opportunity is to be able to mix this practical skills approach with the BA Business Management degree outcome (Exeter University award). Ordinary degree possibilities are at year three and honours possibility at year 4.

Exeter College

Exeter Business School is situated in the heart of the attractive provincial city of Exeter in the pleasant countryside of England's West Country. The School works in Partnership with the Universities of Exeter and Plymouth. Students may apply for the Exeter Halls of Residence or seek self-contained flats in the city itself. Exeter Business School offers a variety of Higher Education courses in Business and Management in a modern, purpose built complex and specialises in professional and vocational linked programmes.

Exeter Business School

BA Business Management	HND Business
HND Management	HND Business Information Technology
HND Legal Practice	HND with Marketing, Personnel or Finance
HND Applied Art	HND Professional Accounting

HND Sports & Recreation Management, Sports Science, Leisure & Tourism and Countryside Management Pathways

Foundation Degree (Vocational Management)*

BA Foundation (for overseas)

*Subject to validation

Exeter Business School, Brittany House, New North Road, Exeter, Devon EX4 4EP, UK
Telephone: +44(0)1392 205581   Fax: 01392 279972   email: busschool@exe-coll.ac.uk

Writtle (Coll) – 160 pts approx (Agric Eng/Bus Mgt; Bus Mgt; Hort/Bus Mgt)

140 pts **Abertay Dundee** – CD (Management)

Bath Spa (UC) – CD **or** ALs+ASs **or** VAs+/-ALs/ASs; (not gs) (Bus St Comb Hons)

Bradford (Coll) – 140 pts approx (Business courses)

Derby – 140 pts 12u – CD **or** DE+ee **or** VA12u CD **or** VA6u C+AL(D); (Bus Comb Hons courses)

Exeter (Coll) – 140–120 pts approx (Bus Mgt)

Harper Adams (UC) – 140 pts 18u – CD **or** DE+e **or** VAs+/-ALs/ASs; gs; (Bus Ent; Bus Mgt/Mark; Bus Mgt Mark/Agric; Bus Mgt Mark/Fd Ind)

Manchester Met (Crewe) – 140 pts 12u; (BA Bus Mgt)

120 pts **Colchester (Inst)** – DD (Bus courses)

Croydon (Coll) – 120 pts approx (Business courses)

Greenwich – 120 pts approx (Mgt Sci)

London (Inst) – 120 pts approx (Mark Adv)

Nescot – DD (Bus St)

Worcester (UC) – DD **or** ALs+ASs **or** VAs+/-AL/ASs; gs; (Bus Mgt courses)

York (CFHE) – (Bus Mgt)

100 pts **and below**

Bell (CT) – (Bus courses)

Blackpool & Fylde (Coll) – (Business courses)

Chichester (UC) – (Bus St extended – mainly for overseas students)

Crawley (Coll) – 80 pts (Bus St)

Gyosei Int (Coll) – 40 pts approx (Business courses)

Holborn (Coll) – (Bus Admin)

North East Wales (IHE) – (Bus courses)

Northbrook (Coll) – (Business courses)

Suffolk (Coll) – DE–EE (Bus Mgt courses)

Swansea (IHE) – (Bus St)

UHI (Inverness/Lews Castle/Moray/North Highland/Orkney) – (Bus Admin via DipHE, HND, HNC)

Warrington (CI) – not AS only; gs (Bus Mgt courses)

West Herts (Coll) – (Bus Admin)

West Thames (Coll) – (Bus Travel Tour)

Wolverhampton – (Bus Mgt Sys – also part-time course for mature students)

Leeds Met – (contact university)

Section B: INTERNATIONAL AND EUROPEAN BUSINESS AND MANAGEMENT COURSES, BUSINESS AND MANAGEMENT COURSES WITH LANGUAGES

(refer to **Section A** and **Section C** for other Business courses)

360 pts **and above**

Bath – 370 pts 21u – 2ALs (100 pts ea)+AL (Fr 120 pts) **or** ALs (Fr 120 pts)+ASs **or** VAs (check with univ); (not gs) (Int Mgt/Fr)

Southampton – 370 pts 21u (2ALs 220 pts inc Fr/Ger; GCSE maths B); (Mgt Sci/Fr/Ger/Span)

350 pts **Bath** – 350 pts 21u – 3ALs **or** ALs+ASs (350 pts – Ger/Span 100 pts) **or** VAs (check with univ); (not gs) (Int Mgt/Ger/Span)

340 pts **Lancaster** – AAB (Int Bus Econ/USA/Can)

Warwick – AAB–ABB (Int Bus/Fr/Ger; Law/Bus)

320 pts **Edinburgh** – ABB (1 sitting) (not gs) (Bus/Fr/Ger/Span; Int Bus/Lang)

Exeter – 320–280 pts (Bus Mgt Euro)

Lancaster – ABB (Euro Mgt with Fr/Ger/Ital/Span)

Nottingham – ABB (Mgt St with Fr/Ger/Span/Port/E Euro St)

UMIST – ABB (Int Mgt/Am Bus St; Int Mgt/Fr)

York – 320 pts approx (Mgt Inf Tech/Lang)

300 pts **Aston** – 18u – BBB–BBC **or** ALs+ASs **or** VAs+/-ALs/ASs; (Int Bus Fr/Ger) (Int Bus/Bus Fr/Ger/Euro)

Belfast (Queen's) – BBB (Mgt with Fr/Ger/Ital/Span/Euro Area St)
Birmingham – BBB–BBC (Bus St with Fr/Ger/Hisp St/Ital/Jap/Port/Russ)
Cardiff – BBB–BCC (Bus Admin with Fr/Span/Jap)
Keele – BBB–BBC **or** equiv AS accepted; gs; (Hum Res Mgt and Bus St with Fr/Ger/Russ)
London (RH) – BBB (Mgt with Fr/Ger/Ital/Jap/Span)
Loughborough – 18u – BB+B/bb **or** VA12u BB+AL(B)/2ASs **or** VA6u+2ASs; (not gs) (Int Bus; Bus/Lang)
Manchester – BBB–BBC (Int Bus Fin Econ)
Newcastle – BBB; (not gs) (Int Bus Mgt; Euro Bus Mgt)
Reading – BBB–BCC (Int Mgt with Fr/Ger/Ital)
St Andrews – BBB (Mgt/Fr/Ger/Ital/Russ/Span)
Sheffield – BBB–BBC (Bus St with Fr/Ger/Hisp/Jap/Russ/Span/Chin/Inf Mgt)
Stirling – BBB–CCC (Bus St courses with Fr/Ger/Jap/Span)
Surrey – BBB (Bus Euro)
Swansea – 300 pts 18u – BBB–BBC **or** ALs+ASs **or** VAs+/-ALs/ASs; (Am Mgt Sci; Euro Bus St; Euro Mgt Sci with Fr/Ger/Ital/Span/Russ/Welsh; Bus St with yr abroad)

280 pts **Bradford** – 280 pts 12u (inc AL French); gs; (Int Mgt Fr)
Durham – BBC (Chin/Mgt; Jap/Mgt)
Durham (Stockton) – BBC (Bus Fin)
East Anglia – BBC–BCC (Lang Bus – Fr/Ger/Dan)
Glasgow – BBC (Mgt St with Celtic/Czech/Fr/Ger/Ital/Polish/Russ)
Heriot-Watt – 280 pts 18u – BBB **or** ALs+ASs; gs; (Int Bus Lang/Fr/Ger/Russ/Span)
Hull – BBC/BB (Bus St with Fr/Ger/Ital/Scand/Span/Dutch)
Kent – BBC/AB (Euro Mgt Sci/Fr/Ger/Ital/Span)
Kingston – BBC (C lang) (Bus St with Fr/Ger/Span)
Lancaster – BBC (Int Bus Econ)
Leeds – BBC (Mgt St with Arab/Fr/Ger/Ital/Span/Russ/Port/ Jap/Chin)
Liverpool – 280 pts – ALs **or** ALs+ASs **or** VAs+/-ALs/ASs; (Euro Bus St/Ger/Fr/Hisp St)
London (King's) – BBC (Fr/Mgt)
London (SOAS) – 280–260 pts approx (Mgt with Af/As Lang)
London (UCL) – BBC **or** 3ALs+AS/VA; (Mgt St/Dutch/Ger/Ital)
Oxford Brookes – BBC–CCD (Bus Admin/Lang – offer varies with subj choice)
Salford – 280 pts approx (Euro Bus St)
Strathclyde – BBC/AB (Int Bus/Modn Lang)
UMIST – BBC (Int Mgt/Ger)

260 pts **Aberystwyth** – 260 pts approx (Bus St with Fr/Ger/Ital/Span/Welsh)
Bradford – 260 pts approx (C lang) (Int Mgt with Ger/Span)
Bristol UWE – 260–240 pts; gs; (Int Bus Econ)
De Montfort (Leicester) – 260 pts – ALs **or** ALs+ASs **or** VA12u+/-ALs/ASs; (Euro Bus St/Fr/Ger)
Heriot-Watt – BCC (BBB 2nd yr entry) (Int Mgt)
Leeds, Trinity & All Saints (Coll) – BCC–CCD (Fr/Mgt; Span/Mgt)
Ulster – BCC (Int Bus St)

240 pts **Aberdeen** – CCC (Bus St/Fr/Ger/Hisp; Euro Mgt St)
Bangor – CCC–CCD (Mgt with Ger/Welsh/Fr; Bus St courses)
Bournemouth – 240 pts – 3ALs **or** 200 pts from 2ALs; (Int Rtl Mgt)
Bristol UWE – 240–200 pts 18u pref/12u – ALs **or** ALs+ASs (inc lang) **or** VAs+/-ALs/ASs; (not gs) (Int Bus St courses) (Int Bus St/Tour; Int Bus St with named Lang)
Glasgow Caledonian – CCC (Euro Bus St)
Hertfordshire – 240 pts approx (Int Bus St Fr/Ger/Span; As Pacif Bus/Chin/Jap)
Kingston – 240 pts 3x6u (inc AL lang 60 pts min); (Bus St/Fr/Ger/Span)
London (QM) – 240 pts approx (Bus St with Fr/Ger/Hisp/Russ)

Manchester Met – 240 pts approx (Int Bus; Int Bus/Fr/Ger/Ital/Span)
Northumbria – 240 pts approx (Int Bus St – Fr/Ger/Span)
Nottingham Trent – CCC–CCE (Euro Bus/Fr/Ger/Span)
Portsmouth – 240 pts – ALs **or** ALs+ASs **or** VAs; gs; (Euro Bus; Int Trade/Fr/Ger/Ital/Port/Span)
Robert Gordon – CCC/BC (Euro Bus St – Fr/Ger; Bus St; Bus Admin)
Sunderland – 240 pts approx (Int Bus/Fr/Ger/Span)
Ulster – CCC (Int Bus Comm)

220 pts **Brighton** – 220 pts approx (Int Bus)
Bristol UWE – 220–180 pts approx (Int Bus St/Tour; Int Bus St with Lang)
Central England – 220 pts – ALs **or** ALs+ASs **or** VAs+/-ALs/ASs; gs; (Int Bus courses Fr/Ger/Span)
Central Lancashire – 220–180 pts 12u; gs; (Int Bus courses)
Coventry – 220 pts approx (Bus St with Fr/Ger/Span/Ital/Port/Russ)
Greenwich – 220 pts approx (Int Bus E Euro; Int Bus/Ger/Fr/Span; Pers Mgt; Herit Mgt; Ops Mgt)
Huddersfield – 220 pts approx (Int Bus/Fr/Ger/Span; Bus/Lang)
Middlesex – 220 pts approx (Int Mgt)
Oxford Brookes – CCD/BB (Euro Bus St with Fr/Ger)
Plymouth – CCD (Int Bus with Fr/Ger/Ital/Span; Euro Bus)
Sheffield Hallam – 220 pts approx (Int Bus with Fr/Ger/Ital/Span)
Staffordshire – CCD **or** CCE+40 pts **or** VAs+/-ALs/ASs; gs; (Int Bus; Int Fin/Bus)
Surrey Roehampton – 220–200 pts approx (Bus/Fr/Ger/Span)
Wolverhampton – 220 pts approx (Euro Bus Admin; Bus with Fr/Ger/Russ/Span)

200 pts **Cardiff (UWI)** – 200–180 pts approx (Int Bus/Fr/Ger/Ital/Port/Russ/Span)
Cheltenham & Glos (CHE) – 200–180 pts approx (Int Bus Mgt)
Chester (Coll) – 200 pts – ALs (180 pts inc C bus subj)+AS **or** VAs (180 pts inc C bus subj)+AS; AS(20+ pts); Fr/Ger GCSE C; (Bus Admin/Fr/Ger/Span)
Coventry – 200 pts approx (Euro Bus Tech – Fr/Ger/Span; Bus Admin; Bus Decn Mthds)
Derby – 200 pts 12u – CDD **or** CD+dd **or** VA12u CD+AL(D); gs; (Int Bus/Fr/Ger/Span)
East London – 200 pts approx (Bus St/Fr/Ger/Span)
European Bus Sch London – 200 pts approx (Int Bus/Modn Lang)
Lampeter – 200 pts approx (Mgt/Fr/Welsh)
Liverpool John Moores – 200 pts (inc AL lang 80 pts); (Int Bus St/Chin/Fr/Ger/Span/Jap/Ital)
London Guildhall – CDD/CC (Bus St; Fr/Bus; Ger/Bus)
Nottingham Trent – 200 pts approx (Bus with Fr/Ger/Span)
Portsmouth – 200–180 pts approx (Int Bus/Fr/Ger/Ital/Port/Russ/Span)

190 pts **North London** – 190 pts (inc 2ALs 160 pts) **or** VAs; (Int Bus)

180 pts **Anglia** – 180–160 pts approx (Euro Bus; Bus/Fr/Ger/Ital/Span)
Buckinghamshire Chilterns (UC) – 180 pts approx (Bus Admin with Fr/Ger/Ital/Span)
Central Lancashire – 180–160 pts 12u (inc B in main lang); gs; (Lang/Bus)
Glamorgan – 180 pts approx (Euro Int Bus)
Glasgow Caledonian – BC (Bus/Lang)
Liverpool Hope (Coll) – 180 pts approx (Bus Commun Ent/Lang)
Luton – 180–160 pts approx (Bus Sys with Fr/Ger/Ital/Jap/Span; Int Bus)
Napier – BC (Publishing)
North London – 180 pts approx (Int Bus with Fr/Ger/Span; Euro Bus St)
Regents Bus Sch London – 180 pts approx (Int Bus courses)
Royal (CAg) – 180 pts approx (Int Bus Mgt)
South Bank – 180 pts approx (Mgt/Span)
South Kent (Coll) – 180 pts approx (Bus St)
Southampton (Inst) – 180–160 pts approx (Bus/Fr/Ger/Span)

Teesside – 180 pts approx (Bus St/Fr/Ger/Span)
Westminster – BC (Euro Mgt; Int Bus)
160 pts **Abertay Dundee** – CC (inc Engl or lang); (Euro Bus Mgt)
Canterbury Christ Church (UC) – CC (Bus/Fr)
Doncaster (Coll) – CC **or** ALs+ASs **or** VAs+/-ALs/ASs; gs; (Bus/Fr/Ger; Int Bus)
East London – 160 pts approx (Int Bus)
Heriot-Watt (Scottish Borders) – CC (Int Tex Mgt/Mark)
Hull (Scarborough) – 160 pts approx (Bus/Mgt courses)
Lincolnshire & Humberside – 160 pts (Int Bus; Euro Bus)
Napier – CC/C (Lang/Export Mgt with Fr/Ger/Span)
Newport (UWCN) – 160–140 pts – ALs **or** ALs+ASs **or** VAs+/-AL/ASs; (Bus St/Modn Lang)
Northampton (UC) – 160 pts approx (Bus Admin with Fr/Ger/Ital/Span)
Southampton (Inst) – 160 pts approx (Bus St/Fr/Ger/Span)
140 pts **and below**
Bell (CT) – DD (Lang/Bus)
Bolton (IHE) – CD (Bus St with Hum Res Mgt Fr/Ger)
Bradford (Coll) – (Law/Euro Bus)
Gyosei Int (Coll) – 40 pts approx (Bus/Lang)
Suffolk (Coll) – 80 pts approx (Bus Mgt/Euro Bus)
Thames Valley – 140 pts approx (Bus St/Fr/Ger/Span)

Leeds Met – (contact university)

Section C: SPECIALISED BUSINESS STUDIES COURSES including;

Advertising, Air Transport Management, Arts Management, Quality Management, Consumer and Product Management, E-Commerce, Enterprise, Events Management, Fashion Management, Health Service Management, Heritage Management, Human Resources Management, Industrial Relations, Marine Business, Pharmacy Management, Public Relations, Publishing, Quality Management, Retail Management, Risk Management, Trading Standards, Transport Management, Wastes Management, Welsh Business Studies.

(Refer to **SECTION A** and **SECTION B** for other Business courses)

320 pts **Lancaster** – ABB (Adv/Mark)
London (LSE) – ABB (Ind Rel/Hum Res Mgt)
Ulster – ABB (Comm/Adv/Mark)
300 pts **Aston** – 300 pts 18u – BBB **or** VA12u BB+AL(B) **or** VA6u B+ALs(BB); gs; (Hum Res Mgt)
Bournemouth – 300 pts – ABC **or** VAs; (PR)
Lancaster – BBB (Adv/Econ/Mark)
Loughborough – 18u – BB+B/bb **or** VA12u BB+AL(B) **or** VA6u+2ASs; (Rtl Mgt courses)
280 pts **Bournemouth** – 280 pts – BBC; (Adv/Mark Comm)
Central Lancashire – 280–240 pts 12u; gs; (PR; PR/Mgt/Mark)
Keele – BBC–BCC **or** equiv AS accepted; gs; (Hum Res Mgt)
Loughborough – 280 pts approx/AB (Ind Rel courses except under **300 pts**)
Oxford Brookes – BBC–CCC (offer varies with second subj) (Rtl Mgt)
Stirling – BBC–BCC (Rtl Mgt; Hum Res Mgt courses)
260 pts **Brunel** – BCC (Hlth Serv Admin)
Kent – 260 pts approx (Ind Rel with Econ/Pol/Soc/Acc)
Loughborough – 260 pts (Air Trans Mgt)
Manchester Met – BCC–CCC/AA (Rtl Mark)
Northumbria – BCC (Hum Res Mgt)
240 pts **Bell (CT)** – CCC/CC (Quality)
Bournemouth – 240 pts – 3ALs **or** 200 pts from 2ALs; (Int Rtl Mgt; Rtl Mgt)

Bradford – 240 pts 12u; gs; (Pharm Mgt)
Central England – 240 pts approx (Fash Rtl Mgt)
Hertfordshire – 240 pts approx (Hum Res)
Kent – CCC/BB (Ind Rel/Hum Res Mgt)
Lincolnshire & Humberside – 240–160 pts (PR)
Nottingham Trent – 240 pts approx (Fash Tex Mgt)
Oxford Brookes – BCD–CCC (Bus Op Mgt; Bus Rtl Mgt)
Oxford Brookes – CCC (offers vary with 2nd subj) (Publishing Joint Hons)
Strathclyde – CCC (Hum Res Mgt)
Surrey – 240 pts 18u – ALs or ALs+ASs or VAs (depends on subj)+/-ALs/AS; (not gs) (Rtl Mgt)
UMIST – CCC or CC+cc or VAS+/-ALs/ASs; gs; (Fash/Tex Rtl; Tex Tech/Mgt/Modn Lang; Mgt (Mark))
Warrington (CI) – 240–180 pts approx (Hum Res Mgt)

220 pts   **Central Lancashire** – 220–200 pts; gs; (Hum Res Mgt; Rtl Mgt courses)
Central Lancashire – 220 pts 12u; gs; (Entre courses except under **200 pts**)
De Montfort (Leicester) – 220–200 pts – ALs or ALs+ASs or VAs+/-ALs/ASs; (Arts Mgt courses; Hum Res Mgt)
Greenwich – 220–200 pts approx (Arts Mgt; Herit Mgt; Ops/Pers Mgt)
Huddersfield – 220 pts approx (Hum Res Mgt)
Liverpool (LIPA) – 220 pts approx (Perf Arts Mgt)
Luton – 220–180 pts approx (Rtl Mgt; Hum Res Mgt)
Middlesex – 220–180 pts approx (Hum Res Mgt; Pblc Art)
Nottingham Trent – CCD (Bus Qual St)
Plymouth – CCD/BB (Perfum Bus; Pers Mgt; Marit Bus courses)
St Mark & St John (Coll) – 220–160 pts approx (PR)
South East Essex (Coll) – 220–180 pts (Hum Res Mgt)
Staffordshire – CCD or CCE+AS(40 pts) or VAs+/-ALs/ASs; gs; (Hum Res Mgt)
Staffordshire – 220 pts (Leg St/Intnet Commer; Mgt Entre)
Surrey Roehampton – 220 pts approx – ALs (inc C) or ALs+ASs or VAs B+/-AL/ASs; (Rtl Mgt/Mark; Hum Res Mgt)
Swansea – CCD/BC–CC (Welsh Bus St)
Wolverhampton – 220 pts 12u – CCD/BCE/BB/AC or BC+ASs or VA12u BB or VA6u B+AL; gs; (Hum Res Mgt; e-commer)

200 pts   **Bournemouth** – 200 pts – 3ALs or 180 pts from 2ALs; Lic Rtl Mgt)
Central England – 200 pts – ALs or ALs+ASs or VAs+/-ALs/ASs; (not gs) (e-commer)
Central Lancashire – 200–180 pts 12u; gs; (Entre/Des St; Entre/Fash Prom St)
Dartington (CA) – 200 pts approx (Arts Mgt)
Derby – 200 pts 12u – CDD or CD+dd or VA12u CD+AL; gs; (Int Bty Hlth Spa Mgt; Hum Res Mgt)
Glamorgan – 200 pts approx (Hum Res Mgt; Bus Inf Mgt; Ent Small Bus; Purch Sply Chn Mgt)
King Alfred's Winchester (Coll) – 200 pts approx (Pblc Serv Mgt)
North London – 200–180 pts approx (Arts Mgt; Rtl Mgt; Hum Res Mgt)
Sunderland – 200–180 pts approx (Hum Res Mgt)

190 pts   **North London** – 190 pts (inc 2ALs 160 pts) or VAs; (Arts Mgt; Evnt Mgt; Hum Res St; Rtl Mgt; Facil Mgt)

180 pts   **Abertay Dundee** – DDD (Retail Mgt)
Birmingham (CFCTS) – 180–160 pts approx (Fd/Rtl Mgt)
Bradford (Coll) – 180 pts approx (Hum Res Mgt)
Brighton – 180 pts approx (Rtl Mgt)
Cardiff (UWI) – 180 pts approx (Rtl Mgt)
Cheltenham & Glos (CHE) – 180–160 pts approx (Hum Res Mgt; Prof Media – Adv))
Coventry – 180 pts approx (Hum Res Mgt)
Doncaster (Coll) – 180 pts approx (Bus/Pers)
Glasgow Caledonian – BC (Risk Mgt)

Hertfordshire – 180 pts approx (Bus Stats; Bus Decn Sci)
London (Inst) – 180–160 pts approx (Rtl Mgt; Fash Mgt; Bus Comm Ent)
Manchester Met – 180 pts approx (Consum Prot)
Napier – BC (Tour Mgt/Entre)
Northumbria – 180 pts approx (Hum Res Mgt)
Norwich City (Coll) – 180 pts approx (Hum Res Mgt)
Portsmouth – 180 pts – ALs **or** ALs+ASs **or** VAs; gs; (Leis Res Mgt; Hum Res Mgt)
Royal (CAg) – 180 pts approx (Rtl Mgt)
Salford – 180 pts approx (Qual Mgt)
South Bank – 180 pts approx (Arts Mgt)
Staffordshire – DDD (Bus Comm Tech; Internet Comm)
Teesside – 180 pts approx (Hum Res Dev)
Thames Valley – 180–140 pts approx (Rtl Mgt; Adv)

160 pts **Anglia** – 160 pts 12u – ALs **or** ALs+ASs **or** VA12u CC; gs; (Optical Mgt; Hum Res Mgt)
Birmingham (CFTCS) – 12u (inc 1 6u) – CC (Lic Rtl Mgt)
Bradford (Coll) – CC (Mgt/Org)
Cardiff (UWI) – 160 pts approx (Tr Stand)
Glasgow Caledonian – CC (Rtl Mgt)
Heriot-Watt (Scottish Borders) – 160 pts 12u; CC; gs; (Tex Fash Des Mgt)
Huddersfield – 160 pts 12u; gs; (Hum Res Mgt)
Hull (Scarborough) – 160 pts approx (Bus Mgt; Bus Mgt Inf Tech)
Lincolnshire & Humberside – 160 pts (Hum Res Mgt; Adv)
Liverpool John Moores – CC (Consum St; Pblc Serv Mgt; Bus/Prod Des)
Napier – 160–120 pts approx (Trans St)
Robert Gordon – DDE/CD (Pblc Admin; Rtl Mgt)
Salford – 160 pts approx (Fd Ind Mgt)
South Bank – 160 pts approx (Hum Res Mgt)
Southampton (Inst) – 160 pts approx (Hum Res Mgt)
Thames Valley – 160–140 pts approx (Hum Res Mgt courses)
West Herts (Coll) – 160–140 pts approx (Adv Mark)

140 pts **Chichester (UC)** – 140 pts approx (Hlth/Mgt)
Dartington (CA) – 140 pts approx + portfolio/auditions (Mgt courses)

120 pts **and below**
Bournemouth (AI) – 80 pts 12u – EE **or** VA6u+AL(D); (not gs) (Arts/Event Prod)
Cumbria (CAD) – (Herit Mgt courses)
North East Wales (IHE) – (Hum Res Mgt)
Northampton (UC) – (Wastes Mgt)
Queen Margaret (UC) – (Rtl Bus; Cons St)
Robert Gordon – DD (Consum Prod Mgt)
Wolverhampton – 120–110 pts – DD **or** ccd **or** VA12u DD; gs; (Euro Ofce Admin/Comm)

Derby – 140 pts 12u – CD **or** DE+ee **or** VA12u C+AL(D); (Comb Hons courses)

Leeds Met – (contact university)

Diploma of Higher Education courses
80 pts Anglia (Corp Admin); Barking (Coll); Bath Spa (UC); Bell (CT); Cheltenham & Glos (CHE); East London; Glasgow (CC); Manchester Met; Paisley (Qual Mgt); UHI; Wolverhampton CC (Lang for Bus).

Higher National Diploma courses
140 pts **and below**
Aberdeen (Coll); Abertay Dundee; Aberystwyth (Bus/Eqn St; Bus/Agric); Anglia; Askham Bryan (Coll); Ayr (Coll); Barking (Coll); Barnsley (Coll); Bath; Batley (SA); Bell (CT); Blackburn (Coll); Blackpool & Fylde (Coll); Bolton (IHE); Boston (Coll); Bradford (Coll); Bridgwater (Coll); Brighton; Bromley (Coll) gs; Brooklands (Coll); Brunel; Canterbury Christ Church (UC); Cardiff (UWI); Carlisle (Coll);

Carmarthenshire (Coll); Central England; Central Lancashire; Cheltenham & Glos (CHE); Chester (Coll); Chesterfield (Coll); Chichester (CAST); City of Birmingham (Coll); City of Bristol (Coll); City Coll Manchester (CFHE); Clydebank (Coll); Colchester (Inst); Cornwall & Duchy (Coll); Coventry; Cranfield; Craven (Coll); Crawley (Coll); Croydon (Coll); Cumbria (CAD); De Montfort; Dearne Valley (Coll); Derby; Dewsbury (Coll); Doncaster (Coll); Dudley (CT); Dumfries & Galloway (CT); Durham New (Coll); East London; Enfield (Coll); Exeter (Coll); Farnborough (CT); Fife (CFHE); Filton (Coll); Glamorgan; Glasgow Caledonian; Glasgow (CC); Gloucestershire (CAT); Greenwich; Grimsby (Coll); Guildford (CFHE); Halton (Coll); Hammersmith & West London (Coll); Harper Adams (UC); Herefordshire (CT); Heriot-Watt; Hertfordshire; High Peak (Coll); Highbury (Coll); Huddersfield; Inverness (Coll); Isle of Wight (Coll); Kilmarnock (Coll); King Alfred's Winchester (Coll); Kingston; Lews Castle (Coll); Lincolnshire & Humberside; Liverpool John Moores; Liverpool (CmC); Llandrillo (Coll); London (Coll/Dist Tr); London (CP); London (Inst); London (Guildhall); Loughborough (CT); Lowestoft (Coll); Luton; Manchester (CAT); Manchester Met; Matthew Boulton (CFHE); Mid Cheshire (Coll) 80 pts (not gs); Mid Kent (CHFE); Motherwell (Coll); Napier; Nescot; Newcastle (Coll); Newport (UWCN); North Down & Ards (IFHE); North East Wales (IHE); North East Worcestershire (Coll); North Herts (CFE); North Highland (Coll); North Lincolnshire (Coll); North London; North Oxfordshire (Coll); North Tyneside (Coll); North West Kent (Coll); Northampton (UC); Northbrook (Coll); Northumbria; Norwich City (Coll); Nottingham Trent; Oldham (Coll); Oxford Brookes; Park Lane (Coll); People's (Coll); Plymouth; Plymouth (CFE); Portsmouth; Preston (Coll); Reading (SAD); Reid Kerr (Coll); Richmond-on-Thames (Coll) DE–E; St Helens (Coll); Salford; Salisbury (Coll); Sandwell (Coll); Sheffield (Coll); Sheffield Hallam; Shrewsbury (CAT); Solihull (Coll) (Retail); Somerset (CAT); South Bank; South Devon (Coll); South Kent (Coll); Southampton (Inst); Southport (Coll); Southwark (Coll); Staffordshire; Stevenson (Coll); Stockport (CFHE); Stoke on Trent (Coll); Stratford on Avon (Coll); Suffolk (Coll); Sunderland; Sutton Coldfield (Coll); Swansea (IHE); Tameside (Coll); Teesside; Thames Valley; Thanet (Coll); Tresham (Inst); UHI (Adv/PR); UMIST; Walsall (Coll); Warrington (CI); Warwickshire (Coll); West Herts (Coll); West Suffolk (Coll); West Thames (Coll); Westminster (Coll); Wigan & Leigh (Coll); Wiltshire (Coll); Wirral Met (Coll); Wolverhampton DE; Worcester (CT); Worcester (UC); Writtle (Coll); Wulfrun (Coll); York (CFHE); Yorkshire Coast (CFHE).

College Diploma courses
140 pts West Herts (Coll) (Adv).
40 pts Kingston (Personnel Mgt); Robert Gordon (Commer).

International Foundation Diploma
Holborn (Coll) (Bus Admin).

Alternative Offers:

EB offers: Aston 72%; Lancaster 70%; Manchester Met 70%; UMIST 70%.

IB offers: Aberdeen 30 pts; Aberystwyth 30 pts; Aston 31 pts; Bangor 28 pts; Bath 30 pts inc or H66; Birmingham 33 pts; Birmingham (CFTCS) 26 pts min; Bournemouth 24 pts; Bradford (Bus Mgt St) 32–30 pts, H 16 pts H5 Eng S5 maths, (Mgt St/Lang) 32 pts, H6 Fr/German H5 Span, S5 maths; Brighton 28 pts; Bristol UWE 24 pts with 12 pts 3 Highers; Brunel 28 pts; Buckingham 26 pts; Buckinghamshire Chilterns (UC) 27 pts; Cardiff 30 pts, H655 + 14 pts; Central England H555; Central Lancashire 28 pts; City H655 S555 – 34 pts overall, (Mgt/Sys) 26 pts min; Coventry 24 pts; Cranfield 27 pts; De Montfort 32–28 pts; Essex 28 pts inc 10 pts 2 Highers; European Bus Sch 28 pts; Exeter 32 pts; Glamorgan 26 pts; Greenwich 26 pts; Heriot-Watt 30 pts; Hertfordshire 28–26 pts; Hull 28 pts; Keele 28–27 pts; Kent 30 pts; Kingston 29 pts; Lancaster 32–30 pts; Leeds 30 pts; Liverpool John Moores 25 pts; London (LSE) 37 pts H766, (RH) 30 pts; London Guildhall 24 pts; Manchester Met 30 pts; Newcastle 32 pts; Northumbria 30–24 pts;

Oxford Brookes 28 pts; Plymouth 21 pts; Portsmouth 24 pts plus mathematical ability, lang at H level for Bus/Lang; St Andrews 30 pts; St Martin's (Coll) 28 pts; Salford 30 pts; Southampton 32–30 pts, 14/14 at H; Surrey (Rtl Mgt) 34 pts; Swansea 32 pts, H 16 pts; UMIST 30 pts inc 15 pts Highers, (Int Mgt) 35 pts; Warwick 34–32 pts; Westminster 30 pts inc 15 pts Highers.

Irish offers: Aberdeen BBBB; Bradford BBBBC; Brighton BBBCC; Bristol UWE CCCC; London Guildhall CCCCC; Sheffield ABBBB; Sunderland BCCC; Teesside CCCC; UMIST AABBBC; Warwick AAAAB.

Scottish Qualifications: Aberdeen BBBB; Abertay Dundee BBCC; Bell (CT) CCC; Dundee (Bus Econ/Mark) BBCC; Edinburgh BBBBB; Glasgow (Mgt St) ABBB; Glasgow Caledonian BBCC/BBB; Heriot-Watt (Mgt) ABBB; Napier BBCC; Paisley BBBC–BCCC; Queen Margaret (UC) (Inf Mgt) BCC; Robert Gordon BBBC; St Andrews (Mgt) BBBB; Stirling ABBB–BBBB; Strathclyde ABBB.

Overseas applicants: Competence in written and spoken English essential at **Northumbria, Nottingham Trent, Manchester Met, Staffordshire. Buckinghamshire Chilterns (UC)** Interview essential. **Hull** Living expenses 30% lower than in London. **North London** Induction course available. **Sheffield Hallam** Orientation programme and English tuition available. **Tile Hill (CFE)** and **Warwick** Offer one year preparatory course for international students who have failed to obtain the right entry grades. Details from the International Office, Warwick University.

CHOOSING YOUR COURSE (See also **Ch.1**)

Subject information: These are very popular courses which usually attract more applicants than any other subject. However, many other degree courses also lead to management careers. Other appropriate courses include Accountancy, Financial Services, Banking, Insurance, Public Administration, Hospitality Management, Tourism, Transport Management, Estate Management, Teaching and Textile Management.

At HND level many institutions offer Business courses with specialist streams such as: accountancy, advertising, broadcasting/media, business administration, company secretaryship, computer studies, distribution, European business and marketing, fashion, food, health, horticulture, journalism, languages, law, leisure, marketing, media, personnel, printing, publicity, purchasing and tourism. Full details in the *Compendium of Higher Education*, available from the Laser Advisory Council, 232 Vauxhall Bridge Road, London SW1V 1AV.

Special features: Aberdeen A unique course in Entrepreneurship is offered. **Anglia** The European Business course offers European programmes in Clermont Ferrand, Berlin and Madrid. **Bath** Language options include Mandarin Chinese and Japanese. **City** The courses in Business and Management and Systems can lead to the degree of Master of European Business following placements abroad. **Coventry** The American Business Administration course enables some second year students to take modules in the USA. **Durham** Management Studies is offered as part of the Combined Studies programme in Social Sciences. Business Finance is available at the Stockton campus. **Greenwich** The course includes options for placements in Finland, Germany, Hungary, Poland or Russia. **Hertfordshire** Asia Pacific Business is available with Chinese or Japanese. **Kingston** Links have been arranged with European and American universities. **Liverpool John Moores** The Consumer Studies degree focuses on food, textiles and domestic appliances. **London Guildhall** (Bus Admin) Two core specialisms in human resource management or information technology. **Loughborough** A course is offered in Air Transport Management. **Manchester Met** A unique degree is offered in Consumer Protection leading to qualification as a Trading Standards Officer. **Newcastle** Business Management can be taken withh Japanese or Korean. **Northumbria** A degree is available in Logistics and Supply Chain Management. **Nottingham Trent** (Bus Mgt 3 yr) Innovative new course aimed at high calibre students with strong management potential. Limited number of places (20). **Oxford Brookes** International Management students are placed in a partner institution for one term in Europe or the USA. **Plymouth** Courses are available in Maritime Business, Sports Management and Perfumery. **South Bank** There is a course in Arts Management covering technology, performance and visual arts. **Surrey** Specialist options in the Retail Mangement course include fashion, food and nutritional and small business management. **Westminster** A three-year degree in Fashion Merchandising is available. *NOW CHECK PROSPECTUSES AND WEB SITES*.

Top universities and colleges (Teaching Quality) (see Ch.4): Bath; City; De Montfort; Edinburgh; Glamorgan; Kingston; Lancaster; Liverpool John Moores; Llandrillo (Coll); London (Imp), (LSE); Loughborough; Manchester; Northumbria; Nottingham; Nottingham Trent; Pembrokeshire (Coll); Strathclyde; Surrey; Swansea (IHE); UMIST; Warwick; not all institutions assessed.

Top universities and colleges (Research) (see Ch.4): Aston; Bath; Birmingham; Bradford; Cardiff; City; Cranfield; Edinburgh; Glasgow; Keele; Lancaster; Leeds; London (Imp), (LSE); Manchester; Nottingham; Reading; St Andrews; Sheffield; Southampton; Strathclyde; UMIST; Warwick.

Study opportunities abroad: Aberystwyth; Anglia; Aston; Bath; Birmingham; Bolton (IHE); Bournemouth; Bradford; Brighton; Bristol UWE; Brunel; Buckinghamshire Chilterns (UC); Cardiff; Cardiff (UWI); Central England; Central Lancashire; Cheltenham & Glos (CHE); Chester (Coll); City; Coventry; De Montfort; Derby; East London; European Bus Sch London; Exeter; Glamorgan; Glasgow Caledonian; Greenwich; Harper Adams (UC); Hertfordshire; Huddersfield; Hull; Keele; King Alfred's Winchester (Coll); Kingston; Lancaster; Leeds; Liverpool John Moores; London (King's), (RH); London Guildhall; Loughborough; Luton; Manchester Met; Middlesex; Napier; Nescot; Newcastle; North London; Northampton (UC); Northumbria; Norwich City (Coll); Nottingham Trent; Oxford Brookes; Plymouth; Portsmouth; Queen Margaret (UC) (Inf Mgt); Reading; Robert Gordon; Salford; Sheffield; Sheffield Hallam; South Bank; Southampton (Inst); Staffordshire; Stirling; Strathclyde; Suffolk (Coll); Sunderland; Surrey Roehampton; Swansea (IHE); Teesside; Thames Valley; Westminster; Wolverhampton; Worcester (UC).

Work opportunities abroad: Aston; Bath; Bournemouth (PR); Bradford; Brighton; Bristol UWE; Brunel; Buckinghamshire Chilterns (UC); Canterbury Christ Church (UC); Cardiff (UWI) (Tourism); Central England; Cheltenham & Glos (CHE); City; Coventry; Cranfield; De Montfort; Dearne Valley (Col); Derby; Glamorgan; Glasgow Caledonian; Greenwich (Int Mark); Harper Adams (UC); Hertfordshire; Huddersfield; Hull; Kingston; Lancaster; Lincolnshire & Humberside; Liverpool Hope (Coll); Liverpool John Moores; London Guildhall; Loughborough; Manchester Met; Middlesex; Napier; Northumbria; Nottingham Trent; Oxford Brookes; Plymouth; Portsmouth; Queen Margaret (UC) (Inf Mgt); Robert Gordon; Royal (CAg); Salford; Sheffield; Sheffield Hallam; Staffordshire; Sunderland; Surrey Roehampton; Swansea; Teesside; Ulster; Warwick; Wolverhampton.

ADMISSIONS INFORMATION

Number of applicants per place (approx): Abertay Dundee (Bus St) 4; Anglia 9; Aston 6; Bangor 4; Bath (Bus Admin) 10, (Int Mgt Lang) 9; Birmingham 7; Birmingham (CFTCS) 5, (Tour Mgt) 30; Bolton (IHE) 3; Bournemouth 36, (Adv) 20, (Retail Mgt) 8, (PR) 10; Bradford 12; Bristol UWE 5–10; Brunel 12; Buckingham 13; Buckinghamshire Chilterns (UC) (Euro Bus St) 11; Canterbury Christ Church (UC) 20; Cardiff 12; Central England 25; Central Lancashire 15; City (Bus St) 17, (Mgt/Sys) 6; Colchester (Inst) 2; Coventry 20; Cranfield 3; De Montfort (Bus St) 17, (Bus Admin) 10, (Mgt Sci) 3; Derby 3; Doncaster (Coll) 10; East Anglia (Bus/Fin) 18; East London 11; Edge Hill (CHE) 4; Glamorgan 5; Glasgow Caledonian 18; Greenwich 24; Hertfordshire 10, (Euro Bus St) 8; Heriot-Watt 8; Huddersfield 21, (Mgt) 6; Hull (Bus St) 19, (Mgt Sci) 10; Hull (Scarborough) 3; Kent 30; Kingston 50; Leeds 27; Leeds, Trinity & All Saints (Coll) 3; Lincolnshire & Humberside (Tourism) 10; Liverpool John Moores 21; London (LSE) (Mgt) 24, (Mgt Sci) 11, (Ind Rel) 13, (RH) 9; London Guildhall 20; Manchester Met (Bus St) 26, (Retail Mark) 10, (Int Bus) 8; Mid Kent (CFHE) 2; Middlesex 12; Napier (Publishing) 7; Nescot 6; Newcastle 27, (Euro Bus Mgt) 54, (Int Bus Mgt) 25, (Bus Mgt) 40; North London 15; Northumbria 10;

Nottingham Trent 35; Oxford Brookes 40, (Retail Mgt) 11; Portsmouth 10; Paisley 5; Plymouth 4; Queen Margaret (UC) (Inf Mgt) 3; Robert Gordon 5; Salford (Bus St) 9; Sheffield Hallam 22; South Bank 4; Southampton (Inst) 30; Staffordshire 9; Strathclyde 12, (Int Bus/Lang) 6; Sunderland 20; Surrey (Retail Mgt) 12; Surrey Roehampton 7; Swansea 10; Swansea (IHE) 7; Teesside (Bus St) 4; Thames Valley 4; UMIST (Int Mgt) 16, (Mgt Sci) 6; Warwick 22; Westminster 12; Wolverhampton 20, (Maths Bus Analys) 2.

Planning your UCAS personal statement (see Ch.4): There are many different kinds of businesses and any work experience is useful. This should be described on the UCAS form in detail: for example, size of firm, turnover, managerial problems, sales and marketing aspects, customers' attitudes. Any special interests in business management should also be included, for example, personnel work, purchasing, marketing. Give details of travel or work experience abroad for international courses and examples of leadership and organising skills. Reference can be made to any particular business topics you have studied in the *Financial Times*, the *Economist* and the business sections in the weekend press. **Bournemouth** (Adv Mark Comm) Focus required on marketing. **Leeds** Refer to your interests and ambitions. **Manchester Met** Experience in retailing essential. Questionnaire and essay on retailing to supplement UCAS form. **Salford** Why this course? What are my academic strengths? What are my personal strengths and interests? Further information could be obtained from the Institute of Public Relations, the Chartered Institute of Marketing and the Institute of Personnel and Development. (See **Appendix 1**.) Some employment information on administration can be obtained from the Civil Service Commission, Room 707, Alencon Link, Basingstoke, Hants RG21 1JB. See also **Accountancy**.

Selection interviews (see Ch.4): Abertay Dundee; Aberystwyth; Anglia (No); Bangor (No); Bath (No); Bath Spa (UC) (No); Birmingham (No); Bournemouth (No); Bradford; Brighton (some); Brunel (No); Buckingham; Cardiff (No); Cardiff (UWI); Carmarthenshire (CTA); Central England; City (some); Cornwall & Duchy (Coll) (No); Coventry; Cranfield; De Montfort (some); Derby (No); Doncaster (Coll); East Anglia (No); Edge Hill (CHE); European Bus Sch London; Exeter (No); Glamorgan (T); Glasgow Caledonian; Greenwich (some); Hertfordshire (No); Huddersfield; Hull; Hull (Scarborough) (No); Kent (mature and Access students); Kingston (No); Lampeter; Lincolnshire & Humberside; Liverpool John Moores (Int Bus) (No); London Guildhall (No); Loughborough (No); Manchester Met (some); Middlesex; Napier (No); Nescot (No); Newcastle (No); Newport (UWCN) (No); North London; Northumbria; Norwich City (Coll) (No); Nottingham Trent; Oxford Brookes (No); Paisley (No); Plymouth; Portsmouth (No); Queen Margaret (UC) (Inf Mgt) (some); Robert Gordon (T); St Martin's (Coll) (No); Salford (T, Maths test for mature applicants); Sheffield (No); Sheffield Hallam; South Kent (Coll); Southampton (No); Staffordshire (some); Stirling (No); Strathclyde; Suffolk (Coll) (No); Sunderland (No); Surrey Roehampton; Swansea; Teesside; Thames Valley; Warwick; West Thames (Coll).

Interview questions (see Ch.4): Any work experience you describe on the UCAS form probably will be the focus of questions which could include topics covering marketing, selling, store organisation and management and customer problems. Personal qualities are naturally important in a career in business, so be ready for such questions as: What qualities do you have which are suitable and important for this course? Describe your strengths and weaknesses. Why should we give you a place on this course? Is advertising fair? What qualities does a person in business require to be successful? What makes a good manager? What is a cash-flow system? What problems can it cause? How could supermarkets improve customer relations?

Reasons for rejection (non-academic): Poor written English. Lack of communication skills. Limited commercial interest. Weak on numeracy and problem-solving. Lack of interview preparation (no questions). Lack of outside interests. Inability to cope with a year abroad. The candidate brought his parent who answered all the questions. **Bournemouth** The Business Studies course is very popular. UCAS applicants may be offered an alternative course. See also **Marketing**.

GAP YEAR ADVICE

Relevant experience recommended by most universities. **Buckinghamshire Chilterns (UC)** Applicants taking a gap year get a lower offer! **London Guildhall** Prefers gap year to be spent gaining work experience.

Institutions willing to defer entry after A-Levels: Abertay Dundee; Aston; Bath; Birmingham (No); Birmingham (CFTCS); Bournemouth; Bradford; Brighton; Bristol UWE (No); Brunel; Buckingham; Cardiff; Central England; Central Lancashire; Cheltenham & Glos (CHE) (Prof Media); Chester (Coll); City; Colchester (Inst); Coventry; Cranfield; De Montfort; Derby; East Anglia; East London; Edge Hill (CHE); European Bus Sch London; Farnborough (CT); Glamorgan (HRM) (No); Glasgow Caledonian (No); Harper Adams (UC); Heriot-Watt; Hertfordshire; Hull; Huddersfield; Kent; Kingston; Lancaster; Leeds; Lincolnshire & Humberside; Liverpool John Moores; London (RH); Luton; Manchester; Manchester Met; Nescot; Newcastle; Newport (UWCN); Northumbria; Nottingham; Nottingham Trent (No); Oxford Brookes; Paisley; Plymouth; Portsmouth; Queen Margaret (UC) (Inf Mgt); Robert Gordon (No); Royal (CAg); St Andrews; St Helens (Coll); Salford; Sheffield; Sheffield Hallam (Bus Tech); Southampton; Staffordshire; Surrey; Surrey Roehampton; Swansea (IHE); Thames Valley; UMIST; Westminster (Deferred entry only rarely); Wolverhampton; Worcester (UC); York (CFHE).

AFTER RESULTS ADVICE

Institutions which may accept the same points score after A-Levels: Abertay Dundee (No); Aston; Bangor; Bath; Belfast (Queen's); Birmingham (No); Bradford (Bus Mgt St); Brighton; Bristol UWE; Brunel; Buckingham; Cardiff; City; Cranfield; East Anglia; East London; Edge Hill (CHE); Glamorgan; Glasgow Caledonian (No); Greenwich (Int Mark) (No); Heriot-Watt; Hertfordshire; Hull; Huddersfield; Kingston; Lancaster (Mark) (No); Leeds (No); Liverpool John Moores; London (RH); London Guildhall; Loughborough (varies); Luton; Manchester Met; Middlesex; Napier; Newcastle; North London; Northumbria; Nottingham Trent; Oxford Brookes; Plymouth; Portsmouth; Queen Margaret (UC) (Inf Mgt); Robert Gordon; St Andrews (No); Salford; Staffordshire; Stirling (No); Strathclyde (No); Sunderland; Surrey (Rtl Mgt); Swansea; Ulster; UMIST; Warwick (Mgt Sci) (No); Wolverhampton.

Institutions which may accept lower grades/points score after A-Levels: Aston; Bath; Birmingham (No); Bournemouth; Bradford; Brighton; Brunel; Buckingham; Cardiff; Central England; Chester (Coll); Coventry; Cranfield; De Montfort; Derby; East Anglia; Edge Hill (CHE); Edinburgh; Farnborough (CT); Harper Adams (UC); Hertfordshire; Heriot-Watt; Huddersfield; Hull (overseas students 240–220 pts); Kingston; Leeds (No); Leeds, Trinity & All Saints (Coll); London (RH); Luton; Manchester Met; Nescot; Oxford Brookes; Plymouth (No); Portsmouth; Queen Margaret (UC) (Inf Mgt); Robert Gordon; Royal (CAg); St Andrews; Sheffield Hallam; Staffordshire; Surrey Roehampton; Thames Valley; Westminster; Worcester (UC). Check with other institutions.

Offers to applicants repeating A-Levels: Higher Bradford, Bristol UWE, Brunel, Cardiff, Central England, East Anglia (2 pts), Greenwich, Hertfordshire, Huddersfield, Kingston, Lancaster, Leeds, Liverpool, Manchester Met, Oxford Brookes, St Andrews, Sheffield, Strathclyde, Swansea, Teesside, West Glamorgan (IHE); **Same** Aston, Bath, Bournemouth, Cardiff (UWI), Central England, Cheltenham & Glos (CHE), Chester (Coll), De Montfort, Derby, Greenwich (Int Mark), Harper Adams (UC), Huddersfield, Hull, Lincolnshire & Humberside, Loughborough, Manchester Met, Northumbria, Oxford Brookes, Robert Gordon, Royal (CAg), Salford (Bus Op/Contr), Sheffield Hallam, Surrey Roehampton, Thames Valley, Ulster, UMIST, Worcester (UC); **Rare** Lancaster (Mark), Queen Margaret (UC) (Inf Mgt), Staffordshire, Warwick.

Probable vacancies from June 2001 and in Clearing (see Ch.4): A large number of universities had vacancies last year, mostly for joint courses. Contact all universities. It is likely that there will be a large number of vacancies for specialised courses in Human Resource Management and Industrial Relations courses.

NEW GRADUATE DESTINATIONS AND EMPLOYMENT (1999 HESA) (see **Ch.4**)

In a survey of 10,815 graduates, 7756 entered full-time employment, 869 went into further study and 680 were believed to be unemployed. In a survey of 290 industrial relations graduates, 210 entered full-time employemnt, 24 went on to further research and 18 were reported to be unemployed.

CHEMISTRY (including **Applied Chemistry**)

NB The information supplied by the universities and colleges this year varies considerably and the offers listed below should be used as a first source of reference only. Many institutions will accept combinations of Advanced (AL), Advanced Subsidiary (AS) and Vocational Advanced (VA) level qualifications to achieve the required points total, but applicants must check web sites and prospectuses for full details of all offers. Grades and points totals shown should be regarded as the minimum levels to be achieved, but offers may be adjusted downwards when results are known. The points totals shown to the left of the institutions are for ease of reference only. It must not be assumed that tariff points are always used by institutions or that they can be substituted for an offer in grades. The level of an offer is not necessarily indicative of the quality of a course. To calculate your offers see Chapter 4 and the inside fold of the back cover.

Special subject requirements/preferences: A-level: Chemistry and another science usually required. **GCSE: Birmingham** Nine subjects grades A/B; also A/B in appropriate modern langauge. **Bradford** (Chem/Pharm Foren Sci) Grade A or B in mathematics or combined science. **Cambridge, Oxford** Grade As in most subjects preferred. **Cardiff** Good range of subjects including humanities. **Exeter** Mainly grade As and Bs. **London (King's)** English and mathematics required. **Sheffield** Mathematics at grade A or above if not offered at A-level; (Chem/Euro) A language at grade A or above if not at A-level. **Surrey** Four-five grades A, the rest grade B, preferred. **Swansea** Grade B in all subjects preferred.

360 pts **and above**
    Bristol – AAA–AAB **or** AAB+b-ABB+b **or** AB+aab-AB+bbb(AL chem); (not gs) (Chem/Law)
    Cambridge – Offers, mainly in grades, vary between colleges (Nat Sci – Chem)
    Oxford – Offers vary between candidates (Chemistry)
350 pts **Southampton** – 350 pts 21u (inc 200 pts in 2 subjs B chem+maths/sci); (MChem: Chem/Comp Sci; Chem/Env Sci; Chem/Geol; Chem/Mgt; Chem/Maths; Chem/Ocean; Chem/Maths)
340 pts **Birmingham** – AAB–ABB inc chem, maths (Chem MNat Sci)
    Durham – AAB (Nat Sci (Chem))
320 pts **Bristol** – ABB–BBB (inc chem); (not gs) (Chem courses except under **360 pts**)
    London (King's) – ABB+AS **or** AAC+AS **or** AB+aaa (inc B chem+A maths); VAs considered; (Chem/Maths)
    Manchester – ABB (Chem/Pat Law)
    Sheffield – ABB (A chem or maths) (Chem/USA; Chem/Jap; Chem/Aus)
    Southampton – 320 pts 21u (inc 180 pts in 2 subjs inc chem+sci/maths); (Chem courses except under **350 pts**)
    Strathclyde – ABB (MSci Chem for 2nd yr sitting; Foren Analyt Chem)
    UMIST – ABB (inc maths, phys) **or** 2ALs+ASs; (MChem Biol Chem)
300 pts **Bradford** – BBB (Chem/Pharm Foren Sci)
    East Anglia – BBB (inc chem+maths/phys/biol); gs; (Chem/N Am; BSc Chem Phys)
    Exeter – 300–260 pts 18u – BBB–BCC **or** BB+bb-BC+cc **or** VA6u B+BB **or** VA6u B+BC; (not gs) (Chem/N Am (300 pts); Chem/Law)
    Hertfordshire – 300–200 pts 1x12u **or** 2x6u – 2ALs **or** AL+2ASs **or** VA12u; gs; (Comb Hons Mod)

Leicester – BBB (Chem USA)

London (Imp) – BBB (Chem courses)

London (UCL) – BBB–BCC **or** 3ALs+AS/VA; (MSci Chem; Chem with Mgt St/Maths/Euro Lang; MSci Med Chem)

Newcastle – BBB–BCC (BChem: Chem/Euro; Chem/N Am; MChem Chem)

Sheffield – BBB (B in chem, maths/lang) (Chem/Euro; Chem/Maths; MChem Biol Chem)

Sussex – BBB (Chem/Law)

Warwick – BBB (Chem/Mgt)

UMIST – ABC/BBB (inc maths, phys) **or** ALs+ASs; (Mgt Chem/Ind Exp; Chem/Chem Eng)

280 pts   **Bangor** – 280–260 pts approx (MChem)

Birmingham – BBC–BCC (Chem/Biorg Chem; Chem/Env Chem; Chem/Analyt Sci; Chem/Bus St; Chem/Fr; Chem/Euro)

Durham – 280 pts – BBB (B chem) **or** 2ALs+2ASs; (not gs) (MSc/BSc Chem courses)

East Anglia – BBC (inc chem+maths/phys/biol); gs; (MChem; Chem/Ind; Chem/Euro; BSc Chem)

Glasgow – BBC–CCC (Chem courses)

Kent – BBC (Chem/Phys/Ind; Chem/Mgt Sci/Ind)

Leeds – BBC (Chem/Maths; Chem/Fr; Chem/Ger)

London (King's) – BBC+AS **or** BB+ccc **or** BC+bbc (or equiv) (inc B chem + 1–2 sci AS b) **or** VA12u BC+B(chem)+AS **or** VA6u+ALs/ASs; (Chem courses except under **320 pts**)

Nottingham – 280 pts 18u – ALs (C chem) **or** VAs+/-ALs/ASs; (not gs) (MSc Chem/Mat)

Salford – 280 pts approx/AB (Chem/N Am)

Sheffield – 280 pts approx (MChem Chem Ind; MChem Chem Phys; BSc Biol Chem)

Swansea – 280 pts 18u – BBC **or** ALs+ASs **or** VAs+/-ALs/ASs; (MChem courses; Double Hons BSc Chem))

UMIST – BBC (inc Maths, phys) **or** 2ALs+ASs; (Mgt Chem Sci; Chem/Ind Exp; Chem/Fr/Ger/Span; Chem/Ppr Sci)

York – 280 pts 21–18u – BCC/CCC **or** CCC+c **or** VAs (check with univ); gs; (Chemistry)

260 pts   **Bangor** – 260–200 pts approx (Chem; Env Chem; Mar Chem; Ind Chem Exd; Chem/Euro)

Bangor – 260–180 pts approx (Chem/PE; Chem/Spo Sci)

Bath – BCC (B chem); (not gs) (MChem; Chem Mgt)

Belfast (Queen's) – BCC–CCC (Chem courses)

Bradford – 260 pts 12u (inc AL chem); gs; (Chem/Pharm Foren Sci)

Cardiff – BCC (MChem)

East Anglia – BCC (Env Chem; Chem/Mgt; Chem/Analyt Sci; Biol/Med Chem; Chem/Maths))

Exeter – 260 pts 18u – BCC **or** BC+cc **or** VA6u B+CC; (not gs) (MChem: Chem/Ind; Chem/Euro)

Hertfordshire – 260–220 pts 1x12u **or** 2x6u – 2ALs (inc biol, chem) **or** AL+2ASs **or** VA12u; gs; (Chem courses)

Leeds – BCC (B chem) **or** 2ALs (inc chem)+AS; VAs (contact univ); (not gs) (Col Chem; Col/Poly Chem; App Chem)

Leeds – BCC (Joint Hons Chem courses except under **280/220 pts**)

Leicester – BCC (Chem courses except under **300 pts**)

London (UCL) – 3ALs+AS/VA; (Chem/Phys)

Manchester – BCC (Chem courses except under **320 pts**)

Nottingham Trent – 260 pts – ALs (2 inc chem, sci pref) **or** ALs+ASs **or** VAs+/-ALs/ASs; (Chem; Env Chem/Acc Fin)

Oxford Brookes – BCC (Chem; Anth/Env Chem)

St Andrews – BCC–CCC (Chem courses)

Salford – BCC/BB (App Chem; Chem/Euro; Chem/Bus St)
Salford – 260–240 pts (Chem/Chem/Med Chem courses)
Sheffield – 260 pts approx (BSc Chem; Chem Phys)
Sheffield Hallam – 260–240 pts approx (MChem/BSc Chem/USA)
Surrey – 260 pts 18u – BCC–CCC (inc chem) **or** ALs+ASs **or** VAs (depends on subj)+/-ALs/ASs; (not gs) (Chemistry)
Sussex – BCC–BCD (Chem/N Am)
Swansea – 260 pts 18u – BCC–CCC/AB **or** ALs+ASs **or** VAs+/-ALs/ASs; (Chem/Phys; BSc Chem; Chem Comb Hons)
UMIST – BCC (inc maths, phys) **or** 2ALs+ASs; (BSc Chem; Chem/Poly Sci/Tech; Med Chem; Analyt Chem; MChem: Chem/Poly Sci/Tech (4 yr))
Warwick – BCC (All courses except under **300 pts**)
240 pts **Aberdeen** – CCC–CCD/BC (Chem courses)
Aston – 240–200 pts – 3ALs **or** ALs+ASs **or** VAs+/-ALs/ASs; gs; (Chem; App Chem; Comb Hons)
Bangor – 240–200 pts approx (Chem/Mgt)
Bradford – 240 pts 12u (inc AL chem); gs; (Chem; Pharm Mgt)
Bristol – CCC (Chem courses except under **320 pts**)
De Montfort (Leicester) – 240 pts – 2ALs min (200 pts) **or** VAs (240 pts); (not gs) (MChem)
Exeter – 240 pts 18u – CCC **or** CC+cc **or** VA6u C+CC; (not gs) (Chemistry courses except under **300/260 pts**)
Heriot-Watt – 240 pts 18u – CCC (DDD 1st yr entry); gs; (Chem courses; Brew/Dist)
Hull – 240 pts approx (Chem courses)
Keele – BCD–CCC/BC–CC **or** equiv AS accepted; gs; (Chem courses)
Lancaster – BCD–CCD (Chem courses)
Leeds – CCC **or** CC+cc; VAs (contact univ); (not gs) (Env Chem)
Liverpool – 240 pts – ALs **or** ALs+ASs **or** VAs+/-ALs/ASs; (Chem courses)
London (QM) – CCC approx – ALs **or** ALs+ASs; (Chem courses)
London (UCL) – 240 pts **or** 3ALs+AS/VA (Chem; Chem Euro Lang; Med Chem)
Loughborough – 240 pts 18u – B (chem)+AL+AL/2ASs **or** VA12u+AL **or** VA6u+2ALs; (not gs) (Chem/PE/Spo Sci; MChem courses)
Manchester – CCC/BB (Chem courses except under **320 pts**)
Manchester Met – 240–140 pts offer varies with subject (Chem Comb)
Newcastle – CCC (Chemistry courses except under **300 pts**)
Nottingham – 240 pts 18u – ALs(C chem) **or** VAs+/-ALs/ASs; (not gs) (BSc Chem Mat)
Oxford Brookes – CCC–DDD (offer varies with 2nd subj) (Env Chem/Bus Stats; Env Chem/Wtr Res)
Paisley – CCC–EE (Chem courses)
Reading – CCC (Chem courses inc Env Geochem)
Salford – 240–200 pts approx (Chem/Med Chem)
Strathclyde – CCC (Chem; App Chem; for 2nd yr entry)
Sussex – BCD (Chem courses except under **300/260 pts**)
220 pts **Bradford** – 220 pts 12u (inc 2AL sci); gs; (Chem Proc)
Edinburgh – CCD/BB (Chem courses)
Kent – 240 pts approx (Biol Chem; Chem; Chem/Comp Sci/ Chem/Mgt Sci)
Leeds – 18u – CCD **or** ALs+ASs **or** VAs+/-ALs/ASs; (not AL gs) (Fuel Combust Sci)
Loughborough – 220 pts 18u – C(chem)+AL+AL/2ASs **or** VA12u+AL **or** VA6u+2ALs; (not gs) (BSc Chem)
Loughborough – 220 pts approx (Chemistry courses except under **240 pts**)
Nottingham Trent – 220 pts – ALs (inc chem, sci pref) **or** ALs+ASs **or** VAs+/-ALs/ASs; (Chem Euro; Med Chem)

Robert Gordon – CCD (Pharm Sci)
Sheffield – 220 pts approx (Chem Fdn)
Stirling – CCD/BC (1st yr entry) BCC (2nd yr entry) (Chemistry)
200 pts **Bangor** – 200 pts approx (D in chem) (Chem/Bioch)
Bristol UWE – 200–160 pts 12u – ALs **or** ALs+ASs **or** VAs+/-ALs/ASs (inc chem 6u 60 pts min); (Biol/Chem; Biomed Sci/Chem; Chem/Env Sci; Chem/IT)
De Montfort (Leicester) – 200 pts – 2ALs min (160 pts) **or** VAs (200 pts); (not gs) (Chem; Analyt Chem; App Chem; Biol/Chem; Env Chem; Foren Chem; Pharm Chem; Chem Bus St)
Dundee – CDD/BC (Chem courses)
Glasgow Caledonian – CDD/CC (App Chem/Mgt; Chem/Inf Tech Instr)
Hertfordshire – 200 pts approx (Chem courses)
Manchester Met – 200–140 pts offer varies with subject (Chem courses except under **240/180 pts**)
Nottingham Trent – 200 pts – ALs (inc chem, sci pref) **or** ALs+ASs **or** VAs+/-ALs/ASs; (Chem; App Chem)
Salford – 200–180 pts approx (Chem Ind; Env Chem; Chem)
Sheffield Hallam – 200 pts approx (Chem courses except under **120 pts**)
Strathclyde – CDD (1st yr entry) (App Chem)
Teesside – 200–180 pts approx (Chem; Chem Tech; Chem/Med Sci)
180 pts **Brighton** – 180 pts approx (Chem/Phys; Pharm/Chem Sci)
Bristol UWE – 180–140 pts 12u – ALs **or** ALs+ASs **or** VAs+/-ALs/ASs (inc biochem); (App Chem Sci; Env Chem)
Coventry – 180 pts approx (App Chem/Chem courses; Pharm Chem)
Derby – 180 pts 12u – CDD **or** CC+ee **or** VA12u BC; (Foren Sci)
Glamorgan – 180 pts approx (Foren Sci)
Greenwich – 180–140 pts approx (Chem courses)
Kingston – 180 pts (inc AL chem+sci); (MChem Chem/Bus)
Liverpool John Moores – 180 pts approx (inc AL chem+1 subj) – ALs **or** ALs+ASs **or** VAs+/-ALs/ASs; (not gs) (Chem; App Chem courses)
Manchester Met – 180–160 pts approx (Chem Euro)
Northumbria – 180 pts approx (App Chem courses; Chem courses)
Portsmouth – 180 pts approx (App Chem)
Staffordshire – 180 pts approx (Chem courses
Sunderland – 180 pts – ALs **or** ALs+ASs **or** VAs+/-ALs/ASs; gs (Chem/Pharm Sci; Chem Comb Hons)
160 pts **Abertay Dundee** – 160 pts – DDE (inc chem); (App Chem)
Huddersfield – 160 pts 12u – 2ALs **or** AL+2ASs **or** VA12u; gs; (Chem courses; Foren Sci)
Kingston – 160–140 pts (inc AL chem+sci); (Chem; App Chem; Med Chem)
Plymouth – CC (Chem courses; App Chem; Env Chem)
South Bank – 160 pts approx (Foren Sci)
Sunderland – 160 pts approx (Chem; Pharm Sci)
140 pts **Derby** – 140 pts 12u – CD **or** DD+dd **or** VAs C/D+/-ALs/ASs; (Chem; Chem/Herit Cons; Chem/Geol)
Sheffield Hallam – 140 pts approx (Chem Comb Hons)
120 pts **Anglia** – 120 pts 12u (ino D chem) – ALs or ALs+ASs **or** VA12u DD (inc chem); gs; (Chem; Med Chem)
Bell (CT) – DD–DE (Chem; Instr Analyt)
Liverpool – 120 pts – 2ALs; (Chem Sci 4 yr)
North London – 120 pts 1x12u **or** 2x6u; (Chem; Chem Sci; Biol/Med Chem; Herb Med Chem)
Ulster – 120 pts approx (Sci Chem/Biol)
120 pts **and below**
De Montfort – 80 pts 12u – ALs **or** ALs+ASs **or** VAs+/-ALs/ASs; (not gs) (Chem Ext courses)

Glamorgan – (Chem courses)
Halton (Coll) – (Sci (Chem))
Liverpool – 60 pts; (Fdn Chem Sci)
Northampton (UC) – (Lea Tech; Chem courses)
Robert Gordon – DE (Chem; App Chem courses)
Salford/North East Wales (IHE) – DE (2x2 Chem courses)
Stockport (CFHE) – (Chem courses)

Diploma of Higher Education courses
Abertay Dundee.

Higher National Diploma courses
100 pts Abertay Dundee; Bangor (Access courses); Bell (CT); Bradford (Coll); Cardiff (UWI) (Med Lab Tech); Cordwainers (Coll) (Saddlery Tech); Coventry; De Montfort (Pharm Sci; Chem; Cos); Falkirk (CFHE); Fife (CFHE); Glasgow Caledonian; Greenwich; Halton (Coll); Heriot-Watt (Scottish Borders); Hertfordshire; Huddersfield; Kingston; Luton; Manchester Met; Napier; North East Wales (IHE); North London; Northampton (UC) (Lea Tech); Nottingham Trent 11–5 pts (BSc/HND programme); Portsmouth; People's (Coll); Robert Gordon; Salford; Sheffield Hallam; Stockport (CFHE); Sunderland (Chem Pharm Sci); Teesside; Ulster; Westminster (Med Lab Tech).

Note:
Eligible students on BTEC HND courses in Science (Chemistry) may elect to take an additional paper for Graduate Membership Part I of the Royal Society of Chemistry.

Alternative Offers:
EB offers: Aston 70%; East Anglia (Chem) 60%; Edinburgh Grades 7 or 8 in 3 relevant subjects; Hertfordshire 60%.

IB offers: Aberdeen 26 pts; Aston 30 pts; Belfast (Queen's) H555 S555; Bangor 28 pts; Bath 32 pts, H5 chem; Birmingham 36–32 pts; Bradford 26 pts; Bristol (Chem/Law) 34 pts H655, (Chem) 30 pts H555; Cardiff 25 pts H6 chem; Coventry 24 pts; De Montfort 24 pts; Dundee H554; Durham 29 pts H5 chem; East Anglia (Chem) 28 pts inc 15 pts Highers, (Chem USA) 32 pts, (Euro Chem) 30 pts; Edinburgh 28 pts inc 5 or 6 in relevant subjects; Exeter 28 pts; Heriot-Watt 28 pts; Hertfordshire 24 pts; Hull 27 pts; Keele 26 pts; Kent 25 pts, H 11 pts; Leeds 26 pts; London Guildhall 28 pts 7 subjects, 24 pts 6 subjects; Newcastle H6 chem + H55; North London 24 pts inc H444; Northumbria 24 pts inc H444; Nottingham 30–28 pts H555; Nottingham Trent 30 pts; St Andrews 28 pts; Salford 30 pts; Sheffield 26 pts inc H655; South Bank 24 pts; Southampton 30–28 pts; Surrey 36–30 pts; Swansea 30–28 pts; UMIST 30 pts; Warwick 30–28 pts; York 27 pts H555.

Irish offers: Aberdeen BBCC/BCCCC; Aston BBBBBB; Bangor BBCCC; Bradford ABBCCC; Brighton CCC; Coventry CCCC; East Anglia (Chem) BBBC; Edinburgh BBBB; Hertfordshire DDD; Keele BBBCC; Liverpool John Moores CCC; Newcastle BBBCCC; St Andrews BBCC/BBB; Sheffield BBBCC; South Bank CCCC; Sunderland BCCC; UMIST ABBBBC; Warwick BBBBB; York BBBCC.

Scottish Qualifications: Aberdeen BBBC; Abertay Dundee BBC; Dundee BBCC; Edinburgh BBBC; Glasgow BBBB; Glasgow Caledonian BBCC/BBB; Heriot-Watt BBCC; Paisley BBC; Robert Gordon BCC; Scottish (CText) DD; St Andrews BBBC; Stirling BBCC; Strathclyde (Foren Analyt Chem) AABB, (Chem courses) BBBB/ABB.

Overseas applicants: East Anglia, Language courses are available; **Hertfordshire** Foundation science course offered; **Huddersfield** Two-week induction course (write for information pack); **Surrey** English proficiency required; **UMIST** 25% overseas students; **York** Some scholarships available.

CHOOSING YOUR COURSE (See also **Ch.1**)

Subject information: There is a considerable shortage of applicants for Chemistry which has very many career applications. These include oceanography (marine chemistry), agricultural and environmental work, colour chemistry, chemical engineering, medical chemistry, medicine, genetics, microbiology, biochemistry, pharmacy, pharmacology and polymer science. Refer to tables covering these subjects. See also **Appendix 1**.

Special features: Aston Transfers to Chemical Engineering and Applied Chemistry possible. **Bangor** Industrial placement and a 'European experience' course with a third year abroad is offered. **Brighton** Energy Studies is also offered with industrial experience. **Cardiff** The Chemistry and Chemistry with Industrial Experience degrees have the same content. **Coventry** Biochemistry, Management or Polymer Science are specialisms in years 2 and 3 of the Applied Chemistry course. **De Montfort** A course is offered in the Chemistry of Food Packaging. **Huddersfield** Options include business studies or environmental science. **Loughborough** Chemistry is offered with Forensic Analysis. **Manchester Met** A flexible programme with Chemistry offered with study in industry or in Europe, environmental, medicinal and applied chemistry. **Sheffield** Most students enrol for the MChem course. The Chemical Physics course offers opportunities to study in Europe, Australia, Japan or the the USA. **South Bank** The degree in Forensic Science is offered covering scientific methods, identifying scientific evidence, legal systems and criminal law. *NOW CHECK PROSPECTUSES AND WEB SITES.*

Top universities and colleges (Teaching Quality) (see Ch.4): Abertay Dundee; Bangor; Bristol; Cambridge; Cardiff; Durham; Glasgow; Glasgow Caledonian; Hull; Leeds; Leicester; London (Imp); Manchester; Nottingham; Nottingham Trent; Oxford; Robert Gordon; St Andrews; Southampton; Strathclyde; not all institutions assessed.

Top universities and colleges (Research) (see Ch.4): Bath; Birmingham; Bristol; Cambridge; Cardiff; Durham; Edinburgh; Exeter; Hull; Leeds; Leicester; Liverpool; London (Imp), (UCL); Manchester; Nottingham; Oxford; Reading; St Andrews; Sheffield; Southampton; Strathclyde; Sussex; UMIST; York.

Study opportunities abroad: Aberdeen; Aston; Bangor; Belfast (Queen's); Birmingham; Bradford; Bristol; Cardiff; City; Coventry; De Montfort; Derby; Dundee; Durham (MSc); East Anglia; Edinburgh; Exeter; Greenwich; Heriot-Watt; Hertfordshire; Huddersfield; Hull; Kent; Kingston; Leeds; Leicester; London (Imp), (King's), (QM), (UCL); Manchester Met; Napier; Newcastle; Northumbria; Nottingham Trent; Oxford Brookes; Plymouth; Reading; Robert Gordon; St Andrews; Salford; Sheffield; Sheffield Hallam; Southampton; Stirling; Strathclyde; Surrey; Sussex; Swansea; Teesside; UMIST; York.

Work opportunities abroad: Aston; Cardiff; City; Coventry; Durham; Heriot-Watt; Hull; Kingston; Leeds; Liverpool John Moores; London (Imp); Loughborough; Napier; Northumbria; Nottingham Trent; Oxford Brookes; Portsmouth; Robert Gordon; Salford; South Bank; Southampton; Strathclyde; Surrey; Teesside; UMIST; Warwick; York.

ADMISSIONS INFORMATION

Number of applicants per place (approx): Abertay Dundee 25; Anglia 3; Aston 6; Bangor (Mar Chem) 3, (Chem) 6; Bath 9; Birmingham 5; Bradford (Chem Pharm/Foren Sci) 10; Bristol (Chem/Law) 4, (Chem) 20; Bristol UWE 2; Cardiff 5; Coventry 8; De Montfort (Chem/Bus) 3, (App Chem) 4; Dundee 9; Durham 4; East Anglia 7; Edinburgh 5; Exeter 4; Glamorgan 12; Glasgow Caledonian 4; Greenwich 10, (App Geochem) 3; Hertfordshire 11; Heriot-Watt 6; Huddersfield 12; Hull 7; Keele 9; Kent 6; Kingston 4; Leeds 3; Leicester 4; Liverpool John Moores 7; London (Imp) 3, (QM) 4, (UCL) 5; Loughborough 9; Manchester Met 5; Napier 4; Newcastle 5; North London 3; Northampton (UC) 1; Northumbria 8; Nottingham (Chem/Mol Phys) 20, (Chem) 8; Nottingham Trent 20; Oxford 1.5; Oxford Brookes 8; Portsmouth 5, (App Chem) 4; Reading 5; Salford 7; Sheffield 6; Sheffield Hallam 3; South Bank 5; Southampton 7; Strathclyde 6; Surrey 3; Swansea 6; Teesside 3; UMIST 7; York 7.

Planning your UCAS personal statement (see Ch.4): Extend your knowledge by reading scientific journals and keeping abreast of scientific developments in the news. Scientific interests should also be developed outside the examination syllabus and mentioned on the UCAS form, together with reports of any visits to chemical firms and laboratories, for example, pharmaceutical, food science, rubber and plastic, paper, photographic, environmental health. **St Andrews** Reasons for choosing the course and evidence of interest. Sport/extra-curricular activities, positions of responsibility. **Southampton** We value the individuality of students. The style of personal statement should reflect this. **Surrey** Work experience, language skills, travel, computing, business experience. Career information can also be obtained from the Schools Liaison Section, Civil Service Commission, Alencon Link, Basingstoke, Hants RG21 1JB. See also **Appendix 1**.

Selection interviews (see Ch.4): Abertay Dundee (No); Anglia (No); Aston; Bangor; Bath; Brighton (No); Bristol (No); Bristol UWE (No); Brunel; Cambridge; Cardiff (some); Coventry; De Montfort; Derby (No); Durham (some); East Anglia; Exeter; Glasgow Caledonian; Greenwich; Huddersfield; Hull; Keele (mature students only); Kent; Kingston; Leeds (No); Liverpool John Moores (No); London (UCL); London Guildhall; Loughborough; Newcastle; Northumbria; Nottingham Trent; Oxford; Oxford Brookes; Paisley (No); Portsmouth (App Chem); Robert Gordon (No); St Andrews (No); Salford; Sheffield; Sheffield Hallam; South Bank; Southampton; Stirling; Sunderland (No); Surrey; Swansea; Teesside (No); UMIST; Warwick.

Interview questions (see Ch.4): Be prepared for questions on your chemistry syllabus and the aspects which you enjoy the most. In the past a variety of questions have been asked, for example: Why is carbon a special element? Discuss the nature of forces between atoms with varying intermolecular distances. Describe recent practicals. What is acid rain? What other types of pollution are caused by the human race? What is an enzyme? What are the general properties of benzene? Why should sciences be less popular among girls at school? What can a mass spectrometer be used for? What would you do if a river turned bright blue and you were asked how to test a sample? What would be the difference between metal and non-metal pollution?

Reasons for rejection (non-academic): Didn't attend interview. Rude and unco-operative. Arrived under influence of drink. Poor attitude and poor commitment to chemistry. **Southampton** Applicants called for interview are not normally rejected.

GAP YEAR ADVICE

Relevant experience in the chemical industry useful. **Heriot-Watt** Some revision desirable during the year. Intensive courses available in some subjects a month before starting course. **London (QM)** Take up some worthwhile employment, learn a language, VSO etc. **UMIST** Try to keep in touch with chemistry if year is not spent on scientific pursuits. **York** Have a definite plan. Apply for deferred entry.

Institutions willing to defer entry after A-levels: Aston; Bangor; Bath (providing decision is made early on); Birmingham; Bradford; Brighton; Bristol; Bristol UWE; Cardiff; Coventry; De Montfort; Derby; Dundee; Durham; Glamorgan; Greenwich; Heriot-Watt; Hertfordshire; Huddersfield; Hull; Kent; Kingston; Leeds; London (UCL) (No); Leicester; Manchester; Manchester Met; Newcastle; Northampton (UC); Northumbria; Nottingham; Nottingham Trent; Oxford Brookes; Plymouth; Portsmouth; Robert Gordon; St Andrews; Salford; Sheffield; Sheffield Hallam; South Bank; Surrey; Sussex; Swansea; Teesside; UMIST (good reasons needed); Warwick; York.

AFTER RESULTS ADVICE

Institutions which may accept the same points score after A-levels: Abertay Dundee; Aston; Bangor; Bath; Birmingham (No); Bradford; Brighton; Bristol; Bristol UWE; Cardiff; Coventry; De Montfort; East Anglia; Edinburgh; Exeter; Greenwich; Heriot-Watt; Hertfordshire; Hull; Keele; Kent; Kingston (No); Leeds; Leicester; Liverpool John Moores; London (UCL) (No); Loughborough; Manchester Met; Napier; Newcastle (provided offer was firmly accepted and at least D in chemistry); North London; Northampton (UC);

Northumbria; Nottingham; Oxford Brookes; Plymouth; Portsmouth; St Andrews (No); Salford; Sheffield; Sheffield Hallam; South Bank; Strathclyde; Sunderland; Surrey; Swansea; Teesside; UMIST; Warwick (No); most other institutions.

Institutions which may accept lower grades/points score after A-levels: Brighton; Cardiff; Coventry; De Montfort; Derby; Durham; Heriot-Watt; Hertfordshire; Hull; Kent; Kingston; Leeds; Leicester; Manchester Met; Northampton (UC); Nottingham Trent; Oxford Brookes; Portsmouth; St Andrews; Sheffield (some); South Bank; Surrey; UMIST; Warwick; most other institutions.

Offers to applicants repeating A-levels: Higher Bangor, Dundee, Hull, Kingston, Leeds, Liverpool John Moores, Loughborough, Northumbria, Nottingham, St Andrews, Sheffield Hallam, Swansea, UMIST, Warwick; **Possibly higher** Coventry, East Anglia, Edinburgh, Newcastle; **Same** Aston, Bath, Bristol (no offer if first-time grades are low), Derby, Durham, Exeter, Greenwich, Heriot-Watt, Huddersfield, Keele, Kingston, London (UCL), Manchester, North London, Oxford Brookes, Robert Gordon, Salford, Sheffield, South Bank, Surrey.

Probable vacancies from June 2001 and in Clearing (see Ch.4): Vacancies are almost certain in most universities in this undersubscribed subject. Some offers could be quite low.

NEW GRADUATE DESTINATIONS AND EMPLOYMENT (1999 HESA) (see **Ch.4**)

Out of 2641 graduates surveyed, 1195 went into full-time employment, 1059 went on to further study and 151 were reported unemployed.

CHINESE (including **Korean**)

NB The information supplied by the universities and colleges this year varies considerably and the offers listed below should be used as a first source of reference only. Many institutions will accept combinations of Advanced (AL), Advanced Subsidiary (AS) and Vocational Advanced (VA) level qualifications to achieve the required points total, but applicants must check web sites and prospectuses for full details of all offers. Grades and points totals shown should be regarded as the minimum levels to be achieved, but offers may be adjusted downwards when results are known. The points totals shown to the left of the institutions are for ease of reference only. It must not be assumed that tariff points are always used by institutions or that they can be substituted for an offer in grades. The level of an offer is not necessarily indicative of the quality of a course. To calculate your offers see Chapter 4 and the inside fold of the back cover.

Special subject requirements/preferences: A-level: Foreign language/s. **GCSE: Cambridge, Oxford** Grade As in most subjects preferred. **Edinburgh** English, mathematics or science and a foreign language. **Leeds** Grade B in language. **Sheffield** Mathematics grade B for Chin St/Bus St.

360 pts **and above**
    Cambridge – Offers, mainly in grades, vary between colleges (Oriental St)
    Oxford – Offers vary between candidates (Oriental St)
340 pts **Edinburgh** – AAB–BBB (Chinese; Hist Art/Chin St)
    Leeds – AAB (Law – Chinese)
300 pts **Durham** – 300 pts 18u – BBB; gs; (Chinese courses; Korean courses)
    London (SOAS) – BBB–BBC/AB (Chinese courses)
    Newcastle – ABC–BBB (Comb St (Chin); Ling/Chin; Ling/Kor; Chin/Kor; Comb Kor St; Bus Mgt/Kor)
280 pts **Leeds** – BBC (As/Pacif/Chin courses; Chinese courses except under **340 pts**)
    Sheffield – BBC (Kor St courses; Chin St; Chin St/Bus St)
180 pts **Central Lancashire** – 180 pts 12u (in AL modn lang); gs; (Chin/Bus)
    European (Bus Sch) – 180 pts (Int Bus Mgt St/Mndrn Chin)
160 pts **Westminster** – CC (Chin/Crim; Chin/Int Rel)

Alternative Offers:

EB offers: Leeds 70%.

IB offers: Leeds 31 pts.

Scottish Qualifications: Edinburgh BBBB.

Overseas applicants: Leeds English tuition, some scholarships.

CHOOSING YOUR COURSE (See also **Ch.1**)

> **Subject information:** Chinese is not a language to be studied for its novelty! An interest in, and appreciation of, the Chinese, their lives and culture are important considerations in selection. Those students interested in languages should note that they also have a wide range of African, Middle Eastern and South East Asian languages from which to choose. See also **Appendix 1** under **Modern Languages**.

Special features: Leeds Intensive language study and year 2 placement in China or Japan for joint courses. **London (SOAS)** Offered as a joint course with other Asian languages and nine other subjects. *NOW CHECK PROSPECTUSES AND WEB SITES.*

Study opportunities abroad: Leeds; Sheffield; most other universities.

Work opportunities abroad: Leeds.

ADMISSIONS INFORMATION

Number of applicants per place (approx): Leeds 3, (Chin/Jap) 5; London (SOAS) 8; Westminster 18.

General Studies acceptable: Leeds.

Planning your UCAS personal statement (see Ch.4): It will be necessary to demonstrate a knowledge of China, its culture, political and economic background. Visits to the Far East should be mentioned, with reference to any features which have influenced you in your choice of degree course. See also **Appendix 1** under **Modern Languages**.

Selection interviews (see Ch.4): Cambridge; Edinburgh (No); Leeds; London (SOAS); Oxford (W); Sheffield (Chin St/Bus St) (No) applications welcomed.

Interview questions (see Ch.4): You will naturally be expected to convince the admissions tutor why you wish to study the language. Your knowledge of Chinese culture, politics and society in general and the problems being faced will also be tested.

GAP YEAR ADVICE

Institutions willing to defer entry after A-levels: Leeds; Sheffield.

AFTER A-LEVELS ADVICE

Institutions which may accept lower grades/points score after A-levels: Leeds; Sheffield.

Offers to applicants repeating A-levels: Higher Leeds.

Probable vacancies from June 2001 and in Clearing (see Ch.4): Universities should be contacted. Offers could range between 260 and 220 pts.

NEW GRADUATE DESTINATIONS AND EMPLOYMENT (1999 HESA) (see **Ch.4**)

Of 54 graduates surveyed, 27 went into full-time employment, 15 went on to further study and five were believed to be unemployed.

CHIROPRACTIC (see also **Health Sciences/Studies** and **Osteopathy**)

NB The information supplied by the universities and colleges this year varies considerably and the offers listed below should be used as a first source of reference only. Many institutions will accept combinations of Advanced (AL), Advanced Subsidiary (AS) and Vocational Advanced (VA) level qualifications to achieve the required points total, but applicants must check web sites and prospectuses for full details of all offers. Grades and points totals shown should be regarded as the minimum levels to be achieved, but offers may be adjusted downwards when results are known. The points totals shown to the left of the institutions are for ease of reference only. It must not be assumed that tariff points are always used by institutions or that they can be substituted for an offer in grades. The level of an offer is not necessarily indicative of the quality of a course. To calculate your offers see Chapter 4 and the inside fold of the back cover.

Special subject requirements/preferences: A-level: Science subjects (contact institutions).

300 pts Glamorgan – 300–260 pts (Chiropractic)
200 pts Bournemouth (Anglo Euro Coll) – 200 pts approx (Chiropractic; apply direct – not in UCAS scheme)

CHOOSING YOUR COURSE (See also **Ch.1**)

> **Subject information:** Chiropractic is an alternative medicine which aims at healing by manipulation, mainly in the spinal region. Alternative courses are Physiotherapy, Osteopathy, Sports Science/Injuries, Exercise and Health Science. See **Appendix 1**.

Special features: Bournemouth (Anglo Euro Coll) After graduating, further clinical training takes place for one year leading to the award of a postgraduate diploma. Finally, after an extra year of supervised clinical practice, graduates will be eligible for registration as chiropractors.

ADMISSIONS INFORMATION

Planning your UCAS personal statement (see Ch.4): Give evidence of talking to a chiropractor and details of any work using your hands.

Interview questions (see Ch.4): It is very important that applicants should have discussed this career with a practising chiropractor. Interview questions are likely to arise from this and will test the applicant's understanding of chiropractic, including the differences between the work of chiropractors, osteopaths and physiotherapists.

AFTER RESULTS ADVICE

Probable vacancies from June 2001 and in Clearing (see Ch.4): Contact the institutions.

NEW GRADUATE DESTINATIONS AND EMPLOYMENT (1999 HESA) (see **Ch.4**)

No data available.

CLASSICAL STUDIES/CLASSICAL CIVILISATION

NB The information supplied by the universities and colleges this year varies considerably and the offers listed below should be used as a first source of reference only. Many institutions will accept combinations of Advanced (AL), Advanced Subsidiary (AS) and Vocational Advanced (VA) level qualifications to achieve the required points total, but applicants must check web sites and prospectuses for full details of all offers. Grades and points totals shown should be regarded as the minimum levels to be achieved, but

offers may be adjusted downwards when results are known. The points totals shown to the left of the institutions are for ease of reference only. It must not be assumed that tariff points are always used by institutions or that they can be substituted for an offer in grades. The level of an offer is not necessarily indicative of the quality of a course. To calculate your offers see Chapter 4 and the inside fold of the back cover.

Special subject requirements/preferences: A-level: Aberdeen, Bristol, London (RH) A foreign language (required or preferred), check with university. **Birmingham** Ancient Greek. **Bristol** Ancient history. **London (King's)** Ancient history or classical civilisation. **GCSE: Bristol** Ancient or modern language. **Edinburgh, Glasgow, St Andrews** English, mathematics, foreign language. **Leeds** Grade B in five subjects or better.

340 pts   **Birmingham** – AAB–ABB (Class Lit Civ/Mus)
320 pts   **Durham** – ABB (Class St/Engl Lit)
300 pts   **Birmingham** – BBB–BBC (Class Lit Civ courses except under **340 pts**)
        Edinburgh – BBB (Class St)
        Liverpool – 300–260 pts – ALs **or** ALs+ASs **or** VAs+/-ALs/ASs; (Class St)
        Warwick – BBB (Phil/Class Civ)
280 pts   **Bristol** – BBC/BCC; (not gs) (Class St courses)
        Durham – BBC (Class St; Class St/Phil)
        Glasgow – BBC (Class Civ courses)
        Kent – 280–260 pts approx (Class St courses)
        Leeds – BBC (Gk/Rom Civ courses; Class Lit courses; Class Civ)
        London (King's) – BBC+AS **or** BB+bb (or equiv) (AL/AS class civ/anc hist pref; some courses req lang/Fr/Lat/Gk); (Class St; Class St/Fr; Class St/Port; Class St/App Comp; Class St/Engl; Class St/War St; Class St/Film; Class St/Gk)
        London (RH) – 280–260 pts approx (Class St courses)
        London (UCL) – BBC–BCC **or** 3ALs+AS/VA; (Anc World St)
        Nottingham – BBC–BCC (Class Civ with Engl/Phil/Theol)
        St Andrews – BBC (Class St courses)
        Swansea – 280 pts 18u – BBC–BCC/BB **or** ALs+ASs **or** VAs+/-ALs/ASs; (Gk Rom St; Class Civ courses)
        Warwick – BBC–BCC (Class Civ; Class Civ/Phil)
260 pts   **Belfast (Queen's)** – BCC–CCC (Class St courses)
        Exeter – BCC (Gk Rom St)
        Manchester – BCC (Class St)
        Newcastle – 260 pts (Class St)
        Nottingham – BCC (Class Civ; Class As Civ)
        Reading – BCC (Class St courses)
220 pts   **Lampeter** – 220 pts approx/CC (Class St courses)
160 pts   **St Mary's (Coll)** – 12u – CC–DD; gs; (Class St courses)

Alternative Offers:

EB offers: Keele 60%.

IB offers: Bristol 32–30 pts H655; Durham 31 pts; Edinburgh H665; Keele 26 pts; Kent 25 pts, H 11 pts; Lampeter 28 pts; London (RH) 28 pts; St Andrews 28 pts; Warwick 30 pts.

Irish offers: Keele BBBCC; St Andrews BBBB; Warwick BBBBC.

Scottish Qualifications: Edinburgh BBBB; Glasgow BBBB; St Andrews BBBB.

CHOOSING YOUR COURSE (See also **Ch.1**)

> **Subject information:** Classical Studies and Classical Civilisation cover the literature, history, philosophy and archaeology of Ancient Greece and Rome. A knowledge of classical languages is not necessary for many courses. Ancient History, History of Art, Architecture, Archaeology and Philosophy may also be of interest as alternative courses.

Special features: Bristol Emphasis on literature and philosophy, not archaeology or history. Gives access to study of classical literature and culture without previous knowledge of ancient languages. **Lampeter** Options in art, archaeology and philosophy. **Leeds** Modular, no language requirement, flexibility and ability to change course. Department caters for a wide range of students with differing interests in the ancient world. **London (RH)** Wide range of options covering classical literature, history, philosophy, art and archaeology. **Newcastle** Wide choice of courses covering literature, history, philosophy, science, art and archaeology. Study of Latin and Greek for each entrant. **Nottingham** Latin or Greek not required for entry. **Swansea** Course offered in Classical Civilisation and Egyptology – one of the few universities offering this course. *NOW CHECK PROSPECTUSES AND WEB SITES.*

Top universities and colleges (Research) (see Ch.4): Bristol; Durham; Leeds; London (RH), (UCL); Nottingham; Swansea; Warwick.

Study opportunities abroad: Bristol; Durham; Edinburgh; Kent; Leeds; London (King's), (UCL); Newcastle; Nottingham; St Andrews.

ADMISSIONS INFORMATION

Number of applicants per place (approx): Birmingham 5; Bristol 11; Durham 15; Exeter 12; Lampeter 2; Leeds 7; London (RH) 4; Manchester 6; Newcastle 8; Nottingham 26; Reading 10; St Mary's (Coll) 3; Warwick 23.

Planning your UCAS personal statement (see Ch.4): Interests will develop through A-level work, supplemented by museum visits. These, and any first-hand knowledge and interest in Greek or Roman architecture and antiquities, should be described fully. **St Andrews** Reasons for choosing course. Evidence of interest. Sport/extra-curricular activities. Posts of responsibility.

Selection interviews (see Ch.4): Bristol (No); Durham (no subject interviews); Kent; Lampeter; Leeds (No); London (RH), (UCL); Manchester (No); Newcastle; Nottingham; Swansea; Warwick.

Interview questions (see Ch.4): What special interests do you have in Classical Studies/Classics? Have you visited Greece, Rome or any other classical sites or museums and what were your impressions? These are the types of questions to expect along with those to explore your knowledge of the culture, theatre and architecture of the period.

GAP YEAR ADVICE

London (RH) We send a reading list and also advise attendance at a summer school in Latin or Greek.

Institutions willing to defer entry after A-levels: Birmingham; Bristol; Kent; Lampeter; Leeds; London (RH); Manchester; Newcastle; Nottingham; St Mary's (Coll); Warwick.

AFTER RESULTS ADVICE

Institutions which may accept the same points score after A-levels: Birmingham; Bristol; Durham; Keele; Kent; Leeds (No); London (RH); Manchester; Newcastle (No); Nottingham (No); St Andrews (No); St Mary's (Coll); Warwick (No).

Institutions which may accept lower grades/points score after A-levels: Durham; Keele; Kent; Lancaster; Leeds; London (RH); St Andrews; St Mary's (Coll); Warwick.

Offers to applicants repeating A-levels: Higher Nottingham, St Andrews, Warwick; **Same** Bristol, Durham, Leeds, London (RH), Newcastle.

Probable vacancies from June 2001 and in Clearing (see Ch.4): A small number of places were advertised last year; universities could be contacted from June onwards.

NEW GRADUATE DESTINATIONS AND EMPLOYMENT (1999 HESA) (see **Ch.4**)

See under **Classics**.

CLASSICS (see also Greek and Latin)

NB The information supplied by the universities and colleges this year varies consider-ably and the offers listed below should be used as a first source of reference only. Many institutions will accept combinations of Advanced (AL), Advanced Subsidiary (AS) and Vocational Advanced (VA) level qualifications to achieve the required points total, but applicants must check web sites and prospectuses for full details of all offers. Grades and points totals shown should be regarded as the minimum levels to be achieved, but offers may be adjusted downwards when results are known. The points totals shown to the left of the institutions are for ease of reference only. It must not be assumed that tariff points are always used by institutions or that they can be substituted for an offer in grades. The level of an offer is not necessarily indicative of the quality of a course. To calculate your offers see Chapter 4 and the inside fold of the back cover.

Special subject requirements/preferences: A-level: Latin or Greek usually required. (0) no classical language required, (1) one classical language required, (2) two classical languages required. **Bristol, Durham, Exeter, Leeds** Courses available for applicants without Latin. **Manchester** Students taking only Greek or Latin A-levels must take the four-year version of the course. **Oxford** (Classics) A-level Latin and/or Greek recom-mended. (Classics/Engl/Modn Lang) English or modern language at A-level essential. **GCSE: Cambridge, Oxford** Grade As in most subjects preferred. **Durham** Four grade A*, three grade A. **Edinburgh, St Andrews** English, mathematics and a foreign language. **Swansea** Greek if not at A-level, five grade A*, five grade B.

360 pts and above
  Cambridge – Offers, mainly in grades, vary between colleges (1) (Class; Class/Modn Lang)
  Oxford – Offers vary between candidates (0 or 1) (Class; Class/Modn Lang)
300 pts Birmingham – BBB–BBC (1) (Classics)
  Durham – 300 pts (Gk Rom Civ; Latin courses(
  Edinburgh – BBB (1) (Classics courses)
  Leeds – BBB–BBC (Class Lit/Hist)
  Liverpool – 300–260 pts – ALs **or** ALs+ASs **or** VAs+/-ALs/ASs; (Classics)
280 pts Birmingham – BBC–BCC (Class/Class Arch)
  Bristol – BBC–BCC (1 inc gk/lat+modn lang for Euro course); (not gs) (Class; Class Euro)
  Durham – BBC (1 or 2) (Class; Class St)
  London (King's) – BBC+AS **or** BB+bb (or equiv) (AL Lat/Gk pref); (Classics)
  London (RH) – BBC/BB (Classics)
  London (UCL) – BBC (1) **or** 3ALs+AS/VA; (Classics)
  Nottingham – BBC–BCC (1) (Classics)
  St Andrews – BBC (Classics)
260 pts Exeter – 260 pts 18u – BCC **or** BC+cc **or** VAs (contact univ); (not gs) (Classics)
  Leeds – BCC (1) (AL language B) (Class; Class Lit)
  Manchester – BCC (Class/Anc Hist)
  Newcastle – BCC (1) (Classics)
  Reading – BCC (1) (Classics)
  Swansea – 260 pts 18u – BCC/BB (1) **or** ALs+ASs **or** VAs+/-ALs/ASs; (Classics courses)
240 pts Belfast (Queen's) – CCC (1) (Classics courses)
200 pts Lampeter – 220–180/CC approx (0–1) (Classics)

Alternative Offers:

IB offers: Bristol 32–30 pts H655; Durham 31 pts; Exeter 30 pts; Kent 25 pts, H 11 pts; St Andrews 30 pts; Swansea 28 pts.

Irish offers: St Andrews BBBB.

Scottish Qualifications: Edinburgh BBBB; St Andrews BBBB.

CHOOSING YOUR COURSE (See also **Ch.1**)

Subject information: Classics covers the study of the classical languages – Greek and Latin – but it may also include topics related to drama, philosophy and art and architecture. See also **Classical Studies**.

Special features: Durham One of the largest departments in the United Kingdom offering a wide range of courses. **Edinburgh** Study of Greek and Roman civilisations with equal amounts of Greek and Latin. **London (UCL)** Topics for detailed study include Greek philosophy, sculpture, drama and history, Roman Britain, law and history and Latin satire, elegy, late and medieval Latin, art and architecture. **Nottingham** Emphasis on literature for students with a good knowledge of Latin. **Oxford** The Honours School of Literae Humaniores provides a unique combination of classics, philosophy and ancient history. **Reading** Latin literature to Middle Ages and medieval, vernacular language. **Swansea** Emphasis on language and literature. *NOW CHECK PROSPECTUSES AND WEB SITES.*

Top universities and colleges (Research) (see Ch.4): (including Ancient History and Modern Greek Studies) Birmingham; Bristol; Cambridge; Durham; Edinburgh; Exeter; Glasgow; Leeds; Liverpool; London (King's), (RH), (UCL); Manchester; Newcastle; Oxford; Reading; St Andrews; Swansea; Warwick.

Study opportunities abroad: Birmingham; Edinburgh; Leeds; Manchester; Newcastle; Nottingham; St Andrews.

Work opportunities abroad: Leeds.

ADMISSIONS INFORMATION

Number of applicants per place (approx): Birmingham 33; Bristol 14; Cambridge 1.5; Durham 15; Lampeter 5; Leeds 4; London (RH) 6; Manchester 6; Newcastle 14; Nottingham 22; Oxford 1.4; Swansea 10.

Planning your UCAS personal statement (see Ch.4): See under **Classical Studies**.

Selection interviews (see Ch.4): Birmingham; Cambridge (W); Durham (No); Exeter; Lampeter; Leeds (No); London (RH), (UCL); Manchester; Newcastle; Oxford (W – Test designed to test linguistic ability) (T); St Andrews (No); Swansea.

Interview questions (see Ch.4): See under **Classical Studies**.

GAP YEAR ADVICE

Institutions willing to defer entry after A-levels: Birmingham; Bristol; Lampeter; Leeds; London (RH), (UCL) (No); Manchester; Newcastle; Nottingham; St Andrews; Swansea.

AFTER RESULTS ADVICE

Institutions which may accept the same points score after A-levels: Bristol; Durham (No); Leeds (some); London (RH), (UCL) (No); Manchester; Newcastle (some flexibility); Nottingham (No); St Andrews (No); Swansea.

Institutions which may accept lower grades/points score after A-levels: Durham; Lampeter; Leeds; Liverpool; London (RH), (UCL); St Andrews.

Offers to applicants repeating A-levels: Higher Leeds, Nottingham, St Andrews; **Same** Birmingham, Durham, Newcastle.

Probable vacancies from June 2001 and in Clearing (see Ch.4): Joint courses with Classics often will have vacancies, with offers up to 280 pts at the most popular universities.

NEW GRADUATE DESTINATIONS AND EMPLOYMENT (1999 HESA) (see **Ch.4**)

In a survey of 430 graduates, 195 went into full-time employment, 128 went on to further study and 27 were believed to be unemployed.

COMMUNICATION STUDIES (see also **Art and Design (General), Film, Radio, Video & TV Studies, Media Studies, Publishing** and **Speech Pathology/Sciences/Therapy**)

NB The information supplied by the universities and colleges this year varies considerably and the offers listed below should be used as a first source of reference only. Many institutions will accept combinations of Advanced (AL), Advanced Subsidiary (AS) and Vocational Advanced (VA) level qualifications to achieve the required points total, but applicants must check web sites and prospectuses for full details of all offers. Grades and points totals shown should be regarded as the minimum levels to be achieved, but offers may be adjusted downwards when results are known. The points totals shown to the left of the institutions are for ease of reference only. It must not be assumed that tariff points are always used by institutions or that they can be substituted for an offer in grades. The level of an offer is not necessarily indicative of the quality of a course. To calculate your offers see Chapter 4 and the inside fold of the back cover.

Special subject requirements/preferences: A-level: Leicester Communications, media studies and sociology required. **Paisley** (Comm Tech) Mathematics. **GCSE:** English and mathematics grade A–C may be required. **Bangor** Welsh grade C or above.

340 pts   **Birmingham** – AAB–ABB (Media Cult Soty/Mus)
320 pts   **Brunel** – 320–280 pts 2x6u – ALs **or** ALs+ASs **or** VAs+/-ALs/ASs; (not gs) (Comm/Media St)
            Leeds – ABB (Communications)
            Liverpool – ABB (Comm St/Engl; Comm St/Pol)
            Ulster – ABB (Comm Adv Mark)
300 pts   **Birmingham** – BBB (Media Cult Soty courses)
            Bradford – 300–280 pts 12u; gs; (Electron Imag/Media Comm)
            Lancaster – BBB–BBC (Cult Media Comm)
            Leicester – BBB (Comm/Soty)
            Liverpool – 300 pts – ALs **or** ALs+ASs **or** VAs+/-ALs/ASs; (Comm/Bus St)
            London (Gold) – BBB/BB+work experience for mature candidates (Media Comm)
280 pts   **Aberystwyth** – 280–260 pts 21–18u – CCC **or** CC+ASs; gs; (Comm/Learn)
            Bournemouth – 280 pts from 3ALs (BBC) **or** 240 pts from 2ALs (pref ALs Engl/comm st/psy) **or** VAs; (Communication)
            Cardiff – BBC–BCC (Lang/Comm; Comm)
            De Montfort – 280 pts approx (Multim Des)
            London (Gold) – BBC/BC +work experience for mature candidates; (Comm St/Sociol; Comm St/Cult St; Anth/Comm St)
            London Guildhall – BBC (Comm Audio Vis Prod – Early Specialist)
            Loughborough – 280 pts 18u – 2ALs **or** ALs/2ASs **or** VAs+/-ALs/ASs; (Comm/Media St)
            Manchester – BBC–BCC (Lang, Lit, Comm)
            Nottingham Trent – BBC (Comm St)
            Sheffield – BBC (Hum Comm Disorders)
260 pts   **Central England** – 260 pts approx (Media/Comm)
            Coventry – 260–240 pts approx (Comm Cult Media)
            Coventry – 260–160 pts (Comm Auth Des)
            Glasgow Caledonian – BCC (Comm/Mass Media)
            Leeds, Trinity & All Saints (Coll) – 260 pts approx (Comm Cult St)
            Loughborough – 260 pts approx (Pol Comm Media St)
            Newcastle – BCC (App Comm/Engl/Mgt/Soc Pol)
            Oxford Brookes – BCC–DDD/BB (offer varies with subj) (Publishing courses)
            Sheffield Hallam – BCC/AA (Comm St courses)
            Sunderland – 260 pts; gs; (Comm Cult Media St)
            Ulster – BCC (Comm St)
240 pts   **Central England** – 240 pts approx (Vis Comm)
            London Guildhall – BCD (Comm Joint Hons; Comm Aud Vis Prod – deferred)

Nottingham Trent – 240–180 pts approx (Comm St/Ling/Med St; Med Cult St courses)
St Mark & St John (Coll) – 240 pts approx (Hum Comm St)
Sheffield Hallam – 240 pts approx (Comm St Comb Hons)
Wolverhampton – 240 pts approx; gs; (Comm St courses)
220 pts **Bangor** – 220 pts – ALs; (not gs) (PP34; PP36: Welsh medium only)
Glamorgan – 220 pts (Media Comm)
Huddersfield – 220 pts approx (Comm/Cult)
Lincolnshire & Humberside – 220 pts (Communucations)
Middlesex – 220–180 pts approx (Comm St courses)
Napier – CCD (Communication)
200 pts **Anglia** – 200 pts approx (Comm St courses)
Bournemouth – 200 pts from 2ALs (eg comp/media) **or** VAs; (Multim courses)
Bradford – 200–180 pts 12u; gs; (Fdn Electron Imag/Media Comm)
Cheltenham & Glos (CHE) – 200–180 pts approx (Media/Comm courses)
Luton – 200 pts approx (Adv Mark Comm)
Manchester Met – CDD (Hum Comm; Inf Comm courses)
Robert Gordon – CDD/CC (Comm courses; Pub St)
Southampton (Inst) – 200 pts approx (Corp Comm)
190 pts **Buckingham** – 190 pts 21u – 3ALs **or** 3ALs+AS; (Comm/EFL)
180 pts **Cheltenham & Glos (CHE)** – 180–160 pts approx (Comm St)
East London – 180 pts approx (Comm St)
Greenwich – BC (Media Comm)
Napier – BC (Publishing)
Queen Margaret (UC) – BC (Corp Comm; Comm St)
Wolverhampton – 180 pts approx (Deaf St; Media Comm St)
160 pts **Doncaster (Coll)** – 160 pts – CC **or** ALs+ASs **or** VAs+/-ALs/ASs; (not gs) (Cult/Comm)
Edge Hill (CHE) – CC (Comm Media courses)
North London – 160 pts – 2ALs **or** VAs6u/12u; (Mass Comm)
Ravensbourne (CDC) – CC (Comm/Tech)
Ripon & York (Coll) – CC (Comm Arts/Drama/Dance/Mus)
140 pts **and below**
Bath Spa (UC) – 140 pts approx (Media Comm)
Glasgow Caledonian – CD (Mark Comm)
London (Inst) – (Des Comm)
Paisley – DE (Comm Tech)
Ripon & York (Coll) – (Comm Arts/Mus)
Warrington (CI) – 200 pts (Media courses)

Leeds Met – (contact university)

Higher National Diploma courses
100 pts **and below**
Aberdeen (Coll); Abertay Dundee; Bell (CT); Bournemouth (AI) (Publishing); Cheltenham & Glos (CHE); Falkirk (CFHE); Falmouth (CA) (Adv); Fife (CFHE); Glasgow (CC); Greenwich (Adv Des); London Inst (Adv); Motherwell (Coll); Napier EE (also HND Journal); Northumberland (Coll); Queen Margaret (UC); Ravensbourne (CDC) (Des (Comm)); Reid Kerr (Coll); Robert Gordon; Southampton (Inst) (Des Comm); UHI; Wolverhampton; Worcester (CT) (Des).

Alternative Offers:

EB offers: Coventry 60%.

IB offers: Bangor 28 pts; Bradford 27 pts; Cardiff 30 pts; Coventry 24 pts; Glamorgan 26 pts; Glasgow Caledonian 28 pts; Leeds 32 pts; Leicester 32 pts; Sheffield Hallam IA; Sunderland 26 pts 6 subjects inc 3 Highers.

Irish offers: London Guildhall CCCCC.

Scottish Qualifications: Glasgow Caledonian (Comm/Mass Media) BBBB; Napier BBBCC; Paisley BCC; Queen Margaret (UC) BBBC; Robert Gordon BBCC.

Overseas applicants: Glamorgan Proficiency in English required.

CHOOSING YOUR COURSE (See also **Ch.1**)

Subject information: Communications Studies courses are not necessarily a training for the media (see **Media Studies**) but many cover management, international communications and psychology. Some courses focus on human communications, for example what are the physical signs of stress? Would you talk to your boss as you would to a friend? Why do some people react strongly to accents? See also **Media Studies** and **Film, Radio, Video and TV Studies**.

Special features: Brunel (Comm/Media St) Covers sociology, psychology, anthropology and video production. Not a practical course leading to media production. **Central England** Course 50% academic, 50% vocational. **Coventry** (Comm Auth Des) English test at interview. Course leads to a career in writing and designing information. **De Montfort** (Multim Des) Modules in animation, video, sound, interactive games, software development. **Edge Hill (CHE)** Audio-visual studies, radio, film, photography, electronic publishing. **Huddersfield** Communication arts core with English, theatre or modern language. **Leeds** The course works in co-operation with the BBC covering practical, professional and academic aspects of communications. There is a foreign language option. **Leicester** (Comm/Soty) Main focus on mass communication and modules in sociology. TV element in year 2 leading to production on Leicester Cable TV. **London (Gold)** Course 50% practical in fields of TV, film, radio, journalism and photography. **Manchester Met** (Hum Comm) Not a media course. Covers psychology, liguistics, sociology, physiology. **Nottingham Trent** Focus on cultures and 20th century society. (Comm St) Course is primarily theoretical although there are practical media options at each level. **Sheffield Hallam** Human communication with particular reference to role of language in British society; not a course in media training. **Southampton (Inst)** Three main themes – communications, business and design. Access to media production facilities. *NOW CHECK PROSPECTUSES AND WEB SITES.*

Top universities and colleges (Teaching Quality) (see Ch.4): Bournemouth (AI); Central Lancashire; Chichester (UC); East Anglia; Glamorgan; Leeds; Liverpool John Moores; London (Gold); Oxford Brookes; Ravensbourne (CDC); Sunderland; Sussex; Warwick; Westminster; not all institutions assessed.

Top universities and colleges (Research) (see Ch.4): See under **Media Studies**.

Study opportunities abroad: Brunel; Cheltenham & Glos (CHE); Coventry; Glamorgan; Glasgow Caledonian; Leicester; Lincolnshire & Humberside; London (Gold); London Guildhall; Napier; Nottingham Trent; Ravensbourne (CDC); Robert Gordon; Sheffield Hallam; Sunderland.

Work opportunities abroad: Cheltenham & Glos (CHE); Glamorgan; London Guildhall; Queen Margaret (UC); Ravensbourne (CDC); Robert Gordon.

ADMISSIONS INFORMATION

Number of applicants per place (approx): Anglia 21; Bangor 3; Birmingham 41; Bradford 7; Brunel 9; Cardiff 8; Coventry 28; De Montfort 13; Edge Hill (CHE) 5; Glamorgan 7; Glasgow Caledonian 26; Leeds 27; Leeds, Trinity & All Saints (Coll) 46; Leicester 23; London (Gold) 7; London Guildhall 20; Manchester Met 7; Middlesex 15; Napier 17; North London 10; Nottingham Trent 17; St Mark & St John (Coll) 6; Sheffield Hallam 11; Sunderland 20.

Planning your UCAS personal statement (see Ch.4): Applicants should be able to give details of any work/work shadowing/discussions they have had in the media, including, for example, in newspaper offices, advertising agencies, local radio stations or film companies (see also under **Media Studies**). **London (Gold)** Interest in a study in depth of media theory plus some experience in media practice. For Comm/Sociol equal interest in both fields. **Manchester Met** Motivation more important than grades.

Selection interviews (see Ch.4): Anglia (some); Bangor; Bournemouth (Al) (No); Brunel; Cardiff; Coventry; Edge Hill (CHE) (No); Glamorgan (T); Glasgow Caledonian; Leicester; London (Gold) (mature applicants only); London Guildhall; Manchester Met; Middlesex; Nottingham Trent (No); Paisley (No); Robert Gordon (No); Sheffield (No); Sheffield Hallam (mature students only); Southampton (Inst); Sunderland (No); Ulster.

Interview questions (see Ch.4): Courses vary in this subject and, depending on your choice, the questions will focus on the type of course, either biased towards the media, or towards human communication by way of language, psychology, sociology or linguistics. See also under separate subject tables.

Reasons for rejection (non-academic): Unlikely to work well in groups. Poor writing. Misguided application, for example more practical work wanted. Poor motivation. Inability to give reasons for choosing the course (Comm/Sociol) or to articulate connections between sociology and the media. More practice needed in academic writing skills.

GAP YEAR ADVICE

Coventry Deferred applicants not normally considered; applicants should apply during the gap year. No interviews so students abroad are not at a disadvantage.

Institutions willing to defer entry after A-levels: Anglia; Brunel; Cardiff; Cheltenham & Glos (CHE); De Montfort; Edge Hill (CHE); Glamorgan; Glasgow Caledonian (No); Leeds; Leicester; Lincolnshire & Humberside; Loughborough; Manchester; Manchester Met; Queen Margaret (UC); Robert Gordon; St Mark & St John (Coll); Sheffield Hallam.

AFTER RESULTS ADVICE

Institutions which may accept the same points score after A-levels: Bangor; Birmingham; Bournemouth (No); Brunel; Cardiff; Cheltenham & Glos (CHE); Edge Hill (CHE); Glasgow Caledonian; Leeds, Trinity & All Saints (Coll); Leicester; Lincolnshire & Humberside; London (Gold) (No); Loughborough; Manchester Met; Middlesex; Robert Gordon; Sheffield Hallam; Southampton (Inst).

Institutions which may accept lower grades/points score after A-levels: Bournemouth; Brunel; Cheltenham & Glos (CHE); Edge Hill (CHE); Leeds, Trinity & All Saints (Coll); Leicester; Lincolnshire & Humberside; Loughborough; Robert Gordon; Sheffield Hallam.

Offers to applicants repeating A-levels: Possibly higher Coventry; **Same** Brunel; Nottingham Trent, Robert Gordon, Sheffield Hallam.

Probable vacancies from June 2001 and in Clearing (see Ch.4): Vacancies are likely to be declared by a number of universities with moderately low offers.

NEW GRADUATE DESTINATIONS AND EMPLOYMENT (1999 HESA) (see **Ch.4**)

Of 887 graduates surveyed, 562 entered full-time employment, 92 went into further study and 60 were believed to be unemployed.

COMMUNITY STUDIES (see also **Health Sciences/Studies** and **Nursing & Midwifery**)

NB The information supplied by the universities and colleges this year varies considerably and the offers listed below should be used as a first source of reference only. Many institutions will accept combinations of Advanced (AL), Advanced Subsidiary (AS) and Vocational Advanced (VA) level qualifications to achieve the required points total, but applicants must check web sites and prospectuses for full details of all offers. Grades and points totals shown should be regarded as the minimum levels to be achieved, but offers may be adjusted downwards when results are known. The points totals shown to

the left of the institutions are for ease of reference only. It must not be assumed that tariff points are always used by institutions or that they can be substituted for an offer in grades. The level of an offer is not necessarily indicative of the quality of a course. To calculate your offers see Chapter 4 and the inside fold of the back cover.

Special subject requirements/preferences: A-level: Chester (Coll) Biology plus another science subject preferred. **GCSE:** English and mathematics grade A–C may be required at some institutions. **Other: North East Wales (IHE)** Minimum age 19 plus youth work experience.

330 pts   **Southampton** – 330 pts 21u (inc 180 pts from 2ALs); (App Soc Sci (Commun/Vol Sect) St)
   Southampton (New Coll) – 330 pts (inc 2ALs 180 pts); gs; (Hum Sci)
260 pts   **Reading** – BBD–CCC (Commun/Yth St courses – Contact Admissions Tutor)
220 pts   **Ulster** – CCD (Commun Yth Wk)
200 pts   **Plymouth** – 200 pts (Commun Wk/Soc Pol/Admin)
180 pts   **Anglia** – 180 pts approx (Family Commun Hist)
   Teesside – 180–160 pts approx (Yth St)
160 pts   **Birmingham (Westhill)** – 160 pts 12u (inc C); ALs **or** ALs+ASs **or** VAs (contact univ); gs; (Commun Play/Yth St)
   Central Lancashire – CC (Commun St/Soc Wk courses)
   Edge Hill (CHE) – CC–CD (Disab Commun St courses)
   Edinburgh – CC (Commun Educ)
   Liverpool John Moores – 160 pts – ALs **or** ALs+ASs **or** VAs+/-ALs/ASs; (App Commun St)
   Luton – 160–120 pts approx (Commun Mgt)
   Manchester Met – 160 pts approx; (Yth Commun Wk St; App Commun St)
   St Mark & St John (Coll) – 160 pts approx (Commun St courses)
   Strathclyde – CC (Commun Arts)
   Strathclyde – 160 pts approx (Commun Educ)
140 pts   **Bolton (IHE)** – CD (Commun St courses)
   Bradford (Coll) – 140 pts approx (Commun St; Educ/Commun St; Couns/Psy Commun Set)
   Huddersfield – 140–120 pts approx (Commun Educ)
   Newport (UWCN) – 140–120 pts – ALs **or** ALs+ASs **or** VAs+/-ALs/ASs; (Commun St; Commun Just)
   Sunderland – 140 pts – ALs **or** ALs+ASs **or** VAs+/-ALs/ASs; gs; BTEC accepted; (Perf Arts St)
120 pts   **and below**
   Cardiff (UWI) – (Commun St courses – min age 20 via DipHE)
   Derby – 80 pts 12u – EE **or** E+ee **or** VAs; (App Commun/Yth St; App Commun Wk/Soc Care St)
   Durham – (Chbd Commun/Yth Wk St; Commun Yth Wk)
   Liverpool (LIPA) – unconditional offer after successful audition/interview (Perf Arts (Commun Arts))
   North East Wales (IHE) – (Commun Wk)

Diploma of Higher Education courses
   Birmingham (Westhill) (Cummun Play/Yth St); Bradford (Coll); Bristol UWE; Durham; Greenwich; Liverpool John Moores; London (Gold); Manchester Met; Newman (CHE); North East Wales (IHE); Sunderland; Ulster; Wigan & Leigh (Coll).

Higher National Diploma courses
   Truro (Coll).

Certificate courses
   Five GCSE (grades A–C) Manchester Met; Newman (CHE).

College Diploma courses
80–40 pts or equivalent
Edinburgh; Strathclyde (Jordanhill).

Alternative Offers:

IB offers: Chester (Coll) 24 pts.

Scottish Qualifications: Edinburgh (Commun Educ) BBB; Strathclyde BBB–BBC.

Overseas applicants: St Mark & St John (Coll) Strong multi-cultural policy. English as a Foreign Language teaching offered.

CHOOSING YOUR COURSE (See also **Ch.1**)

Subject information: These courses cover aspects of social problems, for example housing, food, health, the elderly, welfare rights and counselling. Work experience is very important. Most courses will give professional qualifications. Refer also to Social Administration, Social Policy, Social Studies and Sociology courses. See also **Appendix 1**.

Special features: Birmingham (Westhill) Practical work placement. **Bradford (Coll)** Course covers housing, deviance, leisure, food, nutrition, community arts. **Cardiff (UWI)** Options in learning disabilities or social work. **Derby** Course attracts good students without formal academic qualifications. (App Commun/Youth St) Mature students with at least one or two years' experience with some academic ability but not necessarily with formal qualifications. **Edge Hill (CHE)** Can be taken as a joint or minor Honours degree subject with a strong race relations element. **Newport (UWCN)** Six pathways: Youth, Community, Voluntary Sector, Community Education, Professional Education, Social and Labour Studies. **Reading** (Commun St) For those with one year in field work before applying. *NOW CHECK PROSPECTUSES AND WEB SITES.*

Top universities and colleges (Teaching Quality) (see Ch.4): Edge Hill (CHE); not all institutions assessed.

Study opportunities abroad: Edinburgh; Northern (Coll); Strathclyde; Teesside.

Work opportunities abroad: Liverpool John Moores; Plymouth; Strathclyde.

ADMISSIONS INFORMATION

Number of applicants per place (approx): Bradford (Coll) 5; Chester (Coll) 3; Edge Hill (CHE) 5; Edinburgh 3; Liverpool John Moores 3; Manchester Met 8; Northern (Coll) 6; St Mark & St John (Coll) 7; Strathclyde 6.

Planning your UCAS personal statement (see Ch.4): You should describe any work you have done dealing with people, particularly in a caring capacity, such as social work, or with the elderly, experience with young children in schools, nursing, hospital work, youth work, community or charity work. See also **Appendix 1**. **Derby** Experience and the ability to express oneself in written and spoken form. **Sunderland** Minimum age 19 plus one year's experience (paid or voluntary) in community work.

Selection interviews (see Ch.4): Birmingham (Westhill); Bradford (Coll); Derby (T); Durham; Edinburgh; Huddersfield (groups); Manchester Met; Strathclyde; most institutions interview for this subject.

Interview questions (see Ch.4): This subject has a vocational emphasis and work experience, or even full-time work in the field, will be expected. Community problems vary considerably so depending on your experiences, you could be asked how you would solve such problems.

Reasons for rejection (non-academic): Insufficient experience. Lack of understanding of community and youth work. Uncertain career aspirations. Incompatibility with values, methods and aims of the course. No work experience.

GAP YEAR ADVICE

Aim to get paid or voluntary experience in health or community care work.

Institutions willing to defer entry after A-levels: Bolton (IHE); Chester (Coll); Derby; Huddersfield; Luton; Manchester Met; Teesside.

AFTER RESULTS ADVICE

Institutions which may accept the same points score after A-levels: Bolton (IHE); Chester (Coll) (No); Derby; Huddersfield; Luton; Manchester Met; Strathclyde.

Institutions which may accept lower grades/points score after A-levels: Derby; Teesside.

Offers to applicants repeating A-levels: Higher Chester (Coll); **Same** Bradford (Coll), St Mark & St John (Coll), Teesside.

Probable vacancies from June 2001 and in Clearing (see Ch.4): Applicants are in short supply for these degree courses and mature students are usually in demand. Institutions can be contacted from June onwards.

NEW GRADUATE DESTINATIONS AND EMPLOYMENT (1999 HESA) (see **Ch.4**)

See **Social Work**.

COMPUTER COURSES (including **Business Information Science** and **Technology Systems**)

NB The information supplied by the universities and colleges this year varies considerably and the offers listed below should be used as a first source of reference only. Many institutions will accept combinations of Advanced (AL), Advanced Subsidiary (AS) and Vocational Advanced (VA) level qualifications to achieve the required points total, but applicants must check web sites and prospectuses for full details of all offers. Grades and points totals shown should be regarded as the minimum levels to be achieved, but offers may be adjusted downwards when results are known. The points totals shown to the left of the institutions are for ease of reference only. It must not be assumed that tariff points are always used by institutions or that they can be substituted for an offer in grades. The level of an offer is not necessarily indicative of the quality of a course. To calculate your offers see Chapter 4 and the inside fold of the back cover.

Special subject requirements/preferences: A-level: Bristol, Bristol UWE, Cambridge, Leeds, Leicester (grade C), **London (Imp), (King's), (QM), (RH), (UCL), Loughborough, Manchester, Nottingham, Oxford, Sheffield, Southampton, Sussex, Swansea, Warwick** (for GIGN/GIG5 see under **Mathematics**), **York** Mathematics required. Check other universties for change in requirements. **Oxford** A full A-level in mathematics is essential with a further science or further mathematics recommended. **GCSE: Aston, Belfast (Queen's), Essex** (Psy/Art Intel) **Sheffield Hallam, Staffordshire, UMIST, Warwick** Mathematics grade A or B. **Brunel** Nine subjects at grade A–C. **Cambridge, Oxford** Grade As in most subjects preferred. **Exeter** Top seven GCSEs to equal 40 pts (see **Ch.4 – Special subject requirements**) with grade B in mathematics. **Hull** Three subjects Grade A, three subjects grade B, three subjects grade C average preferred. **Kingston** Grade A or B in English, mathematics preferred. **London (King's)** Mathematics grade B. **Surrey** Eight subjects at grade B or better. **Warwick** Grade A/B in mathematics if not at A-level, B in English, seven subjects at grade B or better. **York** Six subjects at grade A.

360 pts and above
Bath – 21u – ABB+addit units; (Comp Soft Theor; Comp Inf Sys)
Cambridge – Offers, mainly in grades, vary between colleges (Comp Sci)

Leeds – AAA (Analys Bus Comm IT)
London (Imp) – AAA (Comp courses)
Oxford – Offers vary between candidates (Comp courses)
Southampton – 370 pts 21u (inc 220 pts 2ALs inc maths, phys); (Comp Sci courses; Soft Eng)
Warwick – AAA–AAB (Maths/Comp)
York – 390–340 pts 18–12u – AAB+b; (Comp Sci courses)

340 pts
Birmingham – AAB–ABB (Comp St/Mus; Artif Intel/Mus)
Bristol – AAB; (not gs) (Comp Sci; Comp Sci/Maths/Euro)
Manchester – AAB (MEng Comp Sci)
Nottingham – AAB (Comp Sci/Maths)
Warwick – AAB–BBB (Comp Sci; Comp/Bus; Comp/Mgt Sci)

320 pts
Bath – 18u – ABB or VA12u+AL(maths); (Comp Sci)
Brunel – 320 pts 2x6u – ALs or ALs+ASs or VAs+/-ALs/ASs; (Inf Sys; Comp Sci)
London (King's) – ABB+AS or AAC+AS or AB+bb+As (or equiv) (inc AL maths/comp sci/electron/stats/phys) or VA12u BB (sci/eng/IT)+AL(A) or VA6u+ALs/ASs; (Comp Sci; Comp Sci/Mgt)
London (UCL) – ABB or 3ALs+AS/VA; (Comp Sci)
Nottingham – ABB–BBC (Comp Sci/Mgt St)

310 pts
Aberystwyth – 310 pts 21u/260 pts 18u; gs; (Comp Sci; Comp Sci/Artif Intel; Soft Eng)

300 pts
Aberystwyth – 300 pts 18u – 3ALs; gs; (MEng Soft Eng)
Aston – 18u – BBB or 2ALs+ASs or VAs+/-ALs/ASs; gs; (Bus Comp/IT)
Bangor – BBB (MEng Electron Eng/Comp Sys Eng)
Belfast (Queen's) – BBB–BCC (Comp Sci courses)
Birmingham – BBB–BBC (Artif Intel/Comp Sci)
Bournemouth – 300 pts from 3ALs (BBB) pref ALs art+maths; (Comp Vis Animat)
Bradford – 300 pts 12u; gs; (Comp Animat; Interact Sys/Vid Gms Des; Media Tech/Prod; Intnet Prod Des; MEng Intnet Comp; Comp/Perf Eng; MEng Soft Eng)
Brunel – 300 pts 2x6u – ALs or ALs+ASs or VAs+/-ALs/ASs; (Multim Tech/Des)
Cardiff – 300 pts approx/BB (Comp Sci)
City – BBB/AB (Bus Comp Sys; Comp)
East Anglia – 300 pts 18u min – BBB or BBB+c(B maths); flexible policy for new quals (Comp Sci/N Am; App Comp/N Am; Bus Inf Sys)
Hertfordshire – 300–200 pts 1x12u or 2x6u; gs; (Bus Decn Sci; Comb Hons Mod)
Kent – BBB/AB (Comp/Soc Psy)
Leeds – BBB (inc maths) or BB (inc maths)+bb; VAs (contact univ); (Inf Sys; Comp Sci; Comp)
London (QM) – 300 pts – ALs; (Comp Sci courses)
London (RH) – BBB–BBC/BB (Comp Sci courses except under **280 pts**; Mgt Inf Sys)
London (UCL) – BBB or 3ALs+AS/VA; (Inf Mgt)
Loughborough – 300 pts 18u – 2ALs (inc maths subj)+AL/2ASs or VA12u+AL; (not gs) (Comp/Mgt; MComp courses)
Manchester – BBB (Artif Intel courses; Soft Eng courses; Comp Inf Sys courses; Comp Sci courses except under **340 pts**)
Nottingham – BBB–BBC (Comp Sci; Artif Intel courses)
Reading – 300–260 pts approx (Comp Sci courses)
Sheffield – BBB (All Comp Sci courses)
Southampton – 300–280 pts approx (BSc Comp Sci)
Surrey – 300 pts 18u – ALs or ALs+ASs or VAs (depends on subj)+/-ALs/ASs; (not gs) (MSc Comp: Comp Model Simu; Comp Inf Tech)
Sussex – BBB (Artif Intel; Comp Sci; Comp Sci/Artif Intel; Comp Sci/Euro St; Coimp Sci/Mgt St; Artif Intel/Euro St; Artif Intel/Mgt St)

Swansea – 300 pts 18u – BBB–BCC/AB–BB **or** ALs+ASs **or** VAs+/-ALs/ASs; (Comp courses)

UMIST – 300 pts 18u – BBB **or** BB+bb **or** VA12u BB+AL(B); gs; (Comp Sci; Comp/Geog; Artif Intel; Comput)

280 pts **Aberdeen** – BBC–CCD (Comp Sci courses – MA)

Abertay Dundee – BBC (Comp Gms Tech (inc maths); Comp Arts (inc art/mus+interview))

Cardiff – 280–260 pts approx (Comp/Maths; Comp/Phys)

De Montfort – 280 pts (Multim Des)

Durham – 280 pts approx (Comp Sci; Artif Intel; Inf Sys Mgt)

East Anglia – 280 pts 18u min – BBC **or** BBC+c (B maths for Comp/Maths); flexible policy for new quals; (Comp Sci Sys; Comp Comp Graph; Artif Intel/Maths; Comp Sci; App Comp)

Essex – 280–260 pts 21u – BB–BC+AL/2ASs **or** VA12u BB–BC (inc sci/IT)+AL **or** VA6u+2ALs; gs; (Comp Sci)

Exeter – 280 pts 18u – BBC **or** BB+cc **or** BC+bb **or** VA6u B+BC; gs; (Comp Sci; Comp Sci/Euro; Comp Sci/Maths (inc AL maths)))

Glasgow – BBC (MA Comp Sci courses)

Heriot-Watt – 280 pts 18u – BBC **or** ALs+ASs **or** VAsB+/-AL/ASs; gs; (Comp Sci courses except under **260 pts**)

Kent – 280 pts 21u – BC(C maths)+AL+ASs **or** VA12u BB+AL+ASs; gs; (Comp courses except under **300 pts**; Multim courses)

Lancaster – BBC–BCC (Comp Sci/Ling; Comp Sci/Maths; Comp Sci/Euro Lang)

Liverpool – 280 pts – ALs **or** ALs+ASs **or** VAs+/-ALs/ASs; (Comp Electron/Robot Sys; Comp/Microelec Sys)

London (QM) – BBC–BCC/BB (Comp/Ling; Comp/Bus)

London (RH) – BBC(B phys, maths) **or** BB+cc; gs (Comp Sci/Phys)

Loughborough – 280 pts 18u – 2ALs (inc maths subj)+AL/2ASs **or** VA12u+AL; (not gs) (BSc Comp)

Newcastle – BBC (Soft Eng)

Surrey – 280 pts 18u – ALs **or** ALs+ASs **or** VAs (depends on subj)+/-ALs/ASs; (not gs) (BSc Comp)

Sussex – BBC (Inf Tech Sys)

Warwick – 280–260 pts approx (Comp Biol)

260 pts **Aston** – 260–240 pts 18u – 3ALs **or** 2ALs+ASs **or** VAs+/-ALs/ASs; gs; (Comp courses except under **300 pts**)

Bradford – 260 pts 12u (inc AL maths+sci); gs; (Med Cyber; Cyber courses)

Edinburgh – BCC (Comp Sci Maths)

Heriot-Watt – 260 pts 18u – BCC **or** ALs+ASs **or** VAsB+/-AL/ASs; gs; (Comp/Electron; Inf Tech)

Hull – BCC–BCD (Comp Sci courses (not G501); Inf Mgt)

Keele – BCC–CCD **or** equiv AS accepted; gs; (Comp Sci courses)

Lancaster – BCC (Comp Sci courses except under **280 pts**)

Leeds, Trinity & All Saints (Coll) – BCC–CCC (Dig Media Cult)

Leicester – 260 pts approx/BC (Comp Sci)

Liverpool – 260 pts – ALs **or** ALs+ASs **or** VAs+/-ALs/ASs; (Comp Inf Sys; Comp Sci; Comp Sci/Lang)

Newcastle – BCC (Comp Sci; Inf Sci)

Nottingham Trent – 260 pts 15u – BBC **or** BB+dd **or** VA12u BB+/-ALs/ASs; (not gs) (Comp St; Comp Sys)

St Andrews – BCC–CCC (Comp Sci courses)

Salford – BCC–CCD (Inf Tech courses; Comp Sci/Arbc)

Teesside – 260–220 pts approx (Vis; Vrtl Rlty; Interact Comp Ent; Comp Animat; Crea Vis; Comp Games Des)

Ulster – BCC–CCC (Comp courses except under **200 pts**)

UMIST – 260 pts approx (Comput Ling)

250 pts   **Staffordshire** – 250 pts (inc 200 pts from 2ALs); gs; (Comp Sci; Comp; Comp Electron/Inf Tech; Bus/Inf Tech; Soft Eng/Inf Sys courses)

240 pts   **Aberdeen** – CCC–CCD/BC (Comp Sci courses except under **280 pts**)

Bangor – 240 pts – ALs **or** ALs+ASs; (Comp Sci; see also **Engineering (Computer, Control, Software & Systems)**

Bournemouth – 240–220 pts – ALs **or** ALs+ASs **or** VAs+/-ALs/ASs; (Comp; Bus Inf Tech; Soft Eng Mgt)

Bradford – 240 pts 12u; gs; (Comp Sci; Comp Inf Sys; Intnet Comp; Comp/Mgt; Bus Comp; Multim Comp; E-commer; Intnet Law/Soty; BEng Comp Perf Eng; BEng Soft Eng)

Brighton – 240 pts approx (Comp Sci; Comp St; Comp Inf Sys; Comp/OR; Comp/Stats)

Bristol UWE – 240–200 pts 18u pref/12u – ALs **or** ALs+ASs **or** VAs+/-ALs/ASs; (not gs) (Comp Sci; Inf Sys Analys; Inf Sys/Sociol; Comp Real Time Sys; Bus Inf Sys; Comp Inf Sys)

Brunel – 240 pts 2x6u (inc A in sci/comp/eng subj) – ALs **or** ALs+ASs **or** VAs+/-ALs/ASs; (Inf Tech/Ind Sys; Comp/Mech Eng)

Central Lancashire – 240–180 pts 12u; gs; (Web Multim courses)

Cranfield – CCC/BC (Cmnd Contr Comm Inf Sys – CIS)

De Montfort (Leicester/Milton Keynes) – 240–140 pts – ALs **or** ALs+ASs; VAs+/-ALs/ASs; (Comp Sci; Comp/Inf Sys; Comp; Comp joint courses; Bus Inf Sys; Bus Comp; Soft Eng; Multim Comp)

Dundee – 240–200 pts approx (App Comp courses)

Edinburgh – CCC/BB (Comp Sci courses except under **260 pts**)

Glasgow – CCC–CCD/BC (Comp Sci courses except under **280 pts**)

Greenwich – 240 pts approx (Comp courses; Inf Sys courses; Multim Tech)

Hertfordshire – 240–180 pts approx (Comp Sci courses; Bus Inf Sys)

Hull – BCD/BB (Comp Sci courses; Comp Graph Math Model)

Kingston – 240 pts from 2x6u (inc 160 pts in IT/sci/eng) **or** VA12u+80 pts; (not gs) (Comp Sci courses)

Leicester – BCD (Maths/Comp)

Lincolnshire & Humberside – 240–160 pts (Inf Sys; E-comm)

Liverpool – 240 pts – ALs **or** ALs+ASs **or** VAs+/-ALs/ASs; (Inf Tech Mgt; E-bus)

Liverpool John Moores – 240–160 pts (inc 2ALs); Soft Eng; Multim Sys; Inf Sys; Comp St)

London (Gold) – CCC/BB (Comp Inf Sys)

Manchester Met – 240–180 pts approx (offers varies with 2nd subj) (Comp Sci/Comp Tech)

Napier – CCC (Bus Inf Tech)

Newcastle – BCD (Comp Sci/Phys; Geog Inf Sci; Inf Sys)

Northumbria – 240–180 pts approx (Comp Sci courses)

Nottingham Trent – CCC **or** ALs+ASs **or** VAs+/-ALs/ASs; (not gs) (Bus Inf Sys)

Oxford Brookes – CCC–CCD (Comp courses)

Plymouth – 240 pts approx (Psy/Comp; Robot Auto Sys; Intnet Tech)

Portsmouth – 240 pts – ALs **or** ALs+ASs **or** VAs; gs; (Comp Tech; Comp Aid Prod Des; Comp; Comp Sci; Bus Inf Tech; Intnet Tech)

St Andrews – CCC (Comp Sci)

Salford – 240/200–180 pts approx (Comp Sci courses)

Staffordshire – CCC **or** CCD+AS(40 pts); gs; (BSc courses: Bus Comm Tech; Comp/Electron IT; Interact Ent Tech; Sim/Vrtl Rlty)

Stirling – CCC/BC (Soft Eng; Comp Sci courses)

Strathclyde – CCC–CCD (Comp Sci courses)

UMIST – CCC/BB (Comp Ling/Fr; Comp Ling/Ger)

Warrington (CI) – 240–180 pts approx (Inf Sys Mgt)

220 pts   **Bristol UWE** – 220–180 pts 12u – ALs (inc maths) **or** ALs+ASs **or** VAs+/-ALs/ASs (maths 80 pts 6u); (not gs) (Comp/Stats; Comp/Maths)

Brunel – CCD (Comp Sci – Integ Deg scheme)
Central England – 220 pts – CCD **or** ALs+ASs **or** VAs+/-ALs/ASs; (not gs) (Multim Tech)
Central Lancashire – 220 pts 12u; gs; (Bus Comp Comp/Psy; Comb Hons Comp)
City – CCD/BC (Comp Sys Eng)
Derby – CCD **or** CC+dd **or** VA12u CC **or** VA6u C+2AL(CD); gs; (Comp St; Inf Sys courses)
Glasgow Caledonian – CCD/CC (Comp courses)
Hertfordshire – 220 pts approx (Multim Tech)
Huddersfield – 220 pts 12u; gs; (Soft Dev courses; Bus Comp courses; Comp/Stats; Comp/Bus Analys; Comp/Mgt; Comp/Sci)
Kingston – 220 pts (inc 2x6u) – ALs **or** ALs+ASs **or** VAs+/-ALs/ASs; (not gs) (Bus Inf Tech)
Kingston – 220 pts (inc 2x6u **or** AL geog pref) – ALs **or** ALs+ASs **or** VAs+/-ALs/ASs; gs; (Geog Inf Sys courses)
Lampeter – 220–200 pts approx (Inf Tech courses)
Liverpool – 220 pts – ALs **or** ALs+ASs **or** VAs+/-ALs/ASs; (Comp Multim Sys)
Luton – 220–180 pts approx (Comp Sci Mod courses)
Manchester Met – 220–160 pts approx (Bus Inf Tech; Comp; Inf Sys)
Middlesex – 220–180 pts approx (Comp courses)
Plymouth – 220 pts approx (Bus Inf Mgt Sys; Comp Sys Net; Comp Inform)
Salford – CCD/BC (Phys/Inf Tech)
South Bank – 220–180 pts approx (Comp; Bus Inf Tech courses)
South East Essex (Coll) – 220–180 pts (Inf Sys/Glob Intnet Comm; Soft Eng; E-comm; Media; Multim Tech)
Surrey Roehampton – 220 pts approx – ALs **or** ALs+ASs **or** VAs+/-ALs/ASs; (Bus Comp)
Teesside – 220–180 pts approx (Comp Sci; Comp St; Inf Soc; Soft Eng; Comp/Maths; Comp/Stats; Multim; Inform; Inf Tech; Bus Comp)
Wolverhampton – 220 pts 12u – CCD **or** CC+dd **or** VA12u BC–CC; gs; (Computing)
Wolverhampton – 220 pts 12u – CCD **or** CC+dd; gs; (Comp Sci; Virt Rlty Des)

210 pts **Aberystwyth** – 210 pts 21u/180 pts 18u; gs; (Intnet Comp)
Buckingham – 210 pts 21u – 3ALs **or** 3ALs+AS; (Inf Sys courses)

200 pts **Bournemouth** – 200 pts – ALs **or** ALs+ASs **or** VAs+/-ALs/ASs; (Bus Comm Sys)
Central England – 200 pts – CDD **or** ALs+ASs **or** VAs+/-ALs/ASs; (not gs) (Computer courses except under **220/120 pts**)
Central England – 200 pts approx (Comp and Bus Inf Tech courses except under **180 pts**)
Central Lancashire – 200–180 pts 12u; gs; (Comp; Comp/Acc; Comp/Maths(C); Media Tech; Bus Sys Inf courses)
Chester (Coll) – 200 pts – ALs (180 pts inc C maths, comp subjs)+AS **or** VA (180 pts inc C maths, comp subjs)+AS; AS(20+ pts); gs; (Comp Sci courses)
Hull – 200–180 pts approx (Intnet Comp)
Kingston – 200–180 pts (inc 2ALs) (Intnet Comp; Comp/Bus; Comp)
Lincolnshire & Humberside – 200–160 pts (Inf Tech)
Liverpool John Moores – 200 pts (inc AL+VA6u 160 pts) – ALs **or** ALs+ASs **or** VAs+/-ALs/ASs; (Bus Inf Sys)
Northumbria – 200–180 pts approx (Bus Inf Tech; Comp Net Tech)
Sheffield Hallam – 200 pts approx (Comp courses)
Southampton – BB (Comp/Modn Lang)
Ulster – CDD (Comp Sci)

190 pts **North London** – 190 pts; inc 160 pts from 2ALs or VAs; (E-commer)
180 pts **Bournemouth** – 180 pts approx (Bus Inf Sys Mgt; Bus Dec Mgt; Comp; Soft Eng Mgt)

Brighton – 180 pts approx (Soft Eng; Comp St; Comp with Maths/Inf Sys)

Central England – 180 pts approx (Comp; Bus Inf Sys)

Central Lancashire – 180 pts approx (Bus Inf Sys Comb)

Cheltenham & Glos (CHE) – 180–140 pts approx (Bus Inf Tech; Bus Comp Sys)

Coventry – 180 pts approx (Comp Sci; Comp Sys; Multim Comp; Net Comp; Bus Inf Tech courses)

Cranfield – 180 pts 18u – BC **or** B+ccc **or** VA12u (Comm Tech/Soft Eng) BC; (not gs) (M61 Comp; Bus Inf Sys; Inf Sys Mgt)

East London – 180 pts approx (Comp courses; Bus Inf Tech; Soft Eng)

Glamorgan – 180–160 pts approx (All courses except under **140 pts**)

Huddersfield – 2ALs (160 pts) **or** ALs+ASs (180 pts) **or** VAs+/-ALs/ASs (160 pts); (not gs) (Multim Des; Multim Tech; Vrtl Rlty Des; Vrtl Rlty Sys; E-comm/Multim)

Hull – DDD/CC (Soft Eng G701; Comp Sci G501; Comp Graph joint courses; Comp Sci; Intnet Sci)

Liverpool Hope (Coll) – 180–160 pts approx (Inf Tech courses; Bus Inf Mgt)

Manchester Met – 180–40 pts approx (Inf Tech; Inf Tech Soc)

Mid Kent (CFHE) – 180 pts approx (Soft Eng)

Napier – DDD/CD (Multim Sys)

Newman (CHE) – 180 pts approx (Inf Tech BA QTS)

Portsmouth – 180 pts approx (Comp Tech)

Queen Margaret (UC) – DDD/CC (Inf Mgt)

St Martin's (Coll) – 180 pts approx (Multim Prod/App Imag)

Salford – DDD/CC (Soft Eng)

Sunderland – 180 pts – ALs **or** ALs+ASs **or** VAs+/-ALs/ASs; gs; (Comp courses)

Thames Valley – 180–140 pts approx (Inf Mgt; Inf Sys; Multim Comp; Dig Arts/Multim Comp)

Wolverhampton – 180–160 pts 12u – DDD–DDE/CC **or** CC+ASs **or** VA12u CC; gs; (Comp Comb Hons)

160 pts **Abertay Dundee** – CC (Computing)

Anglia – 160 pts 12u; gs; (Comp Sci courses; Intnet Tech)

Buckinghamshire Chilterns (UC) – 160–120 pts approx (Bus Inf Tech; Comp courses)

Canterbury Christ Church (UC) – CC–DD (Inf Tech courses)

Cardiff (UWI) – 160–140 pts approx (Bus Inf Sys courses)

Dundee – 160 pts approx (App Comp)

Edge Hill (CHE) – CC–CD (Inf Sys courses)

Glasgow Caledonian – DDE/CD (Comp St)

Hull – 160 pts approx (Inf Comm Tech)

Lincolnshire & Humberside – 160 pts (Computing)

Newport (UWCN) – 160–140 pts – ALs **or** ALs+ASs **or** VAs+/-ALs/ASs; (Inf Tech Hum; Comp; E-commer; Ind Inf Tech)

North East Wales (IHE) – 160–80 pts approx (Bus Inf Sys; Comp Sci/Comp St courses)

North London – 160 pts 1x12u **or** 2x6u; (Comp Sci; Multim Comp Comb; Multim Tech)

Northumbria – 160 pts approx (Comp St)

Paisley – CC (Comp Sci courses; Soft Eng; Inf Sys)

Salford – 160–140 pts approx (Soft Dev; Comp courses 2+2)

Southampton (Inst) – 160–140 pts approx (Comp Sci; Bus Inf Tech)

Trinity Carmarthen (Coll) – CC–EE (Inf Sys Tech)

Warrington (CI) – 160 pts not ASs only; gs; (Comp Sci/Bus Mgt; Inf Sys Mgt)

Westminster – CC–CD (Comp Sci; Bus Inf Tech courses)

Writtle (Coll) – 160 pts approx (Bus Inf Sys)

140 pts **Abertay Dundee** – CD (Inf Tech; Bus Comp; Inf Mgt)
Bolton (IHE) – CD (Bus Inf Sys courses; Comp courses)
Bradford (Coll) – 140 pts approx (Bus Sys Mgt)
Cumbria (CAD) – CD (Dig Animat)
Derby – 140 pts 12u – CD **or** DD+ee **or** VA12u CD **or** VA6u C+AL(D); gs;
(Comp/OR; Comp Comb courses)
Liverpool John Moores – 140 pts 1x6u – ALs **or** ALs+ASs **or** VA12u/6u+/-
ALs/ASs; approx (App Comp Tech)
London Guildhall – CD–DD (Comp; Bus Inf Tech courses)
Napier – CD (Soft Eng)
Paisley – CD (Bus Inf Tech courses)
Robert Gordon – CD (Artif Intel/Rob)
120 pts **Bangor** – DD (Comp Sys Eng – wide entry)
Barnsley (Coll) – 120 pts 12u – ALs **or** ALs+ASs **or** VAS+/-AL/ASs; (Crea Mus
Tech)
Bradford – 120 pts 9u; gs; (Fdn Comp; Cyber)
Central England – 120 pts – ALs **or** ALs+ASs **or** VAs+/-ALs/ASs; (Fdn Comp
Tech)
Colchester (Inst) – DD (Bus Sys courses)
Farnborough (CT) – 120 pts approx (Computing)
Glamorgan – DD (Bus Inf Mgt; Inf Tech)
Nescot – DD (Comp St; Dig Imag)
North London – 120 pts – 2ALs **or** VA6u/12u; (Comp Net; Microcomp Sys
Tech)
Oxford Brookes – DD (Comp Maths)
South Bank – DD (Comp Prod Des Fdn; all other Comp courses except under
220 pts)
Worcester (UC) – 120 pts 12u – DD **or** ALs+ASs; gs; (Inf Tech)
100 pts **and below**
Anglia – (Bus Inf Sys; Inf Sys Dev; Inf Sys)
Bell (CT) – (Comp courses)
Bournemouth & Poole (Coll) – (Fdn Comp)
Brighton – (Fdn Comp Sci)
Bristol UWE – (Fdn Comp)
Cheltenham & Glos (CHE) – (Bus Comp Sys/Env Pol)
Crawley (Coll) – 80 pts (Comp Sci)
Hertford Regional (Coll) – (Comb Mod Inf Sci)
London (Gold) – (Comp Sci courses except under **240 pts**)
Napier – (Comp Inf Sys; App Phys Comp)
Northampton (UC) – (Inf Sys courses)
Northbrook (Coll) – (Inf Tech/Bus)
Paisley – DE (Comp Net; Comp Tech; Media Tech; Multim Sys)
Robert Gordon – (Comp courses except under **140 pts**)
St Helens (Coll) – (Multim Prod)
St Mark & St John (Coll) – (Inf Tech courses)
Suffolk (Coll) – (Inf Tech courses)
Sunderland – 80 pts approx (Bus Inf Tech)
Swansea (IHE) – (Soft Eng; Bus Inf Tech; Comp Inf Sys)
UHI (Inverness/Lews Castle/Moray/Orkney/Perth/Shetland – (Comp via
DipHE, HND, HNC)
Wigan & Leigh (Coll) – (Inf Tech)

Leeds Met – (contact university)

Diploma of Higher Education courses
80 pts Abertay Dundee; Canterbury Christ Church (UC); Craven (Coll); Filton (Coll);
Glamorgan; London Guildhall; Northumbria; Peterborough Regional (Coll); St
Martin's (Coll) (Imag Sci); Saltash (Coll); South Devon (Coll); Southwark (Coll);
Staffordshire (Coll); Ulster; UHI; Wolverhampton.

Higher National Diploma courses
120 pts   and below

Aberdeen (Coll); Abertay Dundee; Anglia; Ayr (Coll); Barnsley (Coll); Bell (CT); Birmingham City (Coll); Blackburn (Coll); Blackpool & Fylde (Coll); Bolton (IHE); Boston (Coll); Bournemouth & Poole (Coll); Bournville (Coll); Bradford (Coll); Bridgwater (Coll); Brighton; Brunel; Buckinghamshire Chilterns (UC); Burnley (Coll); Cardiff (UWI); Carlisle (Coll); Central England; Central Lancashire; Cheltenham & Glos (CHE); Chesterfield (Coll); Cornwall & Duchy (Coll); Coventry; Crawley (Coll) gs; De Montfort; Derby; Doncaster (Coll); Dudley (Coll); Durham New (Coll); East London; Exeter; Falkirk (CFHE); Falmouth (CA); Farnborough (CT); Fife (CFHE); Glamorgan; Glasgow Caledonian; Glasgow (Coll); Glasgow (CBP); Gloucestershire (CAT); Greenwich; Grimsby (Coll); Guildford (CFHE); Hastings (CT); Herefordshire (CT); Heriot-Watt (Scottish Borders); Hertfordshire; Huddersfield; Kilmarnock (Coll); Kingston; Llandrillo (Coll); Lincolnshire & Humberside; Liverpool John Moores; Loughborough (Coll); Manchester (CAT); Manchester Met; Mid Cheshire (Coll); Mid Kent (CHFE); Middlesex; Motherwell (Coll); Napier; Nescot; Newcastle (Coll); Newport (UWCN); North East Wales (IHE); North Lincolnshire (Coll); North London; North Oxfordshire (Coll); North West Kent (Coll); Northampton (UC); Northbrook (Coll); Northumbria; Norwich City (Coll); Nottingham Trent; Oxford Brookes; Oldham (Coll); Park Lane (Coll); People's (Coll); Plymouth; Portsmouth; Preston (Coll); Reid Kerr (Coll); Robert Gordon; St Helens (Coll); Salford; Sheffield Hallam; Solihull (Coll); South Bank; South Kent (Coll); South Thames (Coll); Southampton (Inst); Staffordshire; Stevenson (Coll); Stoke-on-Trent (Coll) (mature students only); Sunderland; Sutton Coldfield (Coll); Swansea (IHE); Teesside; Thames Valley; Thanet (Coll); Truro (Coll); UHI (Perth); Ulster; Warwickshire (Coll); West Herts (Coll); West Suffolk (Coll); West Thames (Coll) (Bus Inf Tech); Westminster; Wigan & Leigh (Coll); Wiltshire (Coll); Wirral Met (Coll); Wolverhampton; Worcester (UC); Worcester (CT); York (CFHE) C+cc **or** VA CC; gs; Yorkshire Coast (CFHE).

Alternative Offers:

IB offers: Aberdeen 30 pts (Arts), 26 pts (Sci); Aberystwyth 30 pts; Aston 30 pts; Bradford 30 pts inc H5 maths; Brighton 27 pts; Bristol 32 pts H6 maths; Brunel 32 pts H5 maths, (Inf Tech/Ind Sys; Comp/Mech Eng) 24 pts; Buckingham 26 pts; Cardiff 30 pts; Cheltenham & Glos (CHE) 24 pts; City 31 pts inc 16 pts Highers; De Montfort 30 pts; Dundee H554; Durham 28 pts; Essex H765; Exeter 30 pts; Greenwich 24 pts; Hertfordshire 20 pts; Heriot-Watt 24 pts; Hull 28 pts inc 16 pts Highers; Keele 26 pts; Kent 28 pts, H 12 pts; Lancaster 30 pts; Leeds 30 pts H 15 pts; London (QM) 24 pts, (RH) 30 pts, (UCL) 34 pts; London Guildhall 28 pts 7 subjects, 24 pts 6 subjects; Newcastle 30 pts; Portsmouth 28 pts; St Andrews 28 pts; Staffordshire 24 pts; Stirling 28 pts; Surrey 32 pts; Surrey Roehampton 26 pts; Swansea 28 pts inc H 13 pts; UMIST 28 pts H655; Warwick 36–34 pts; Westminster 26 pts; York 32 pts in 6 subjects inc H6 maths + physics.

Irish offers: Aberdeen BBBB (Arts) BBCC/BCCCC (Sci); Aston BBBBC; Bradford BBBCCC; Brighton BBCCC; Central Lancashire CCCD; Glamorgan CCCC; Paisley BCC; Robert Gordon BBBB; St Andrews BBCC/BBB; Sheffield BBBBC; Sunderland CCCC; Surrey BBBB; Teesside (Comp Sci) BBB, (Inf Tech) CCC; Warwick AAAAB.

Scottish Qualifications: Aberdeen BBBB–BBBC; Abertay Dundee BBC; Bell (CT) CCC; Dundee BBBC; Edinburgh BBBB; Glasgow BBBB; Glasgow Caledonian BBC/BBB; Heriot-Watt BBBC; Napier BBC; Paisley BCCC–BCC; Robert Gordon BBC/BCCC; St Andrews AABB, (Intnet Comp) BBBC; Stirling BBCC; Strathclyde BBBB.

Overseas applicants: Coventry Good English required. **Glamorgan** Induction and English as a Foreign Language courses offered. **Hull** Living costs 30% lower than in London. **Nottingham Trent** A-level course advised + GCSE maths and English. **Sheffield Hallam** Introductory and English programme – 1300 overseas students. **Teesside** English GCSE grades A–C required.

CHOOSING YOUR COURSE (See also **Ch.1**)

Subject information: Computing courses are extremely popular with good career opportunities. Programming languages, data processing, systems analysis, artificial intelligence, graphics, software and hardware are all aspects of these courses. Several institutions offer courses with European languages and placements. Artificial Intelligence courses cover psychology, philosophy, logic, linguistics and neurobiology. Several of these subjects are offered as degree courses in their own right and these, along with Electrical, Electronic and Systems Engineering, could also be considered. See also **Appendix 1**.

Special features: Bangor Computer Systems available with Business Studies, French, German, Mathematics and Psychology. **Bristol UWE** The four-year Computer Science course has placements in Europe and the USA. **Cardiff** Routes are available for candidates with or without mathematics. **Cranfield** Business Information Systems and Software Engineering is offered to civilian students at the Royal Military College at Shrivenham in Essex. **Essex** Modular course with eight Foundation units in year 1 leading to a choice of degrees chosen from Computer Science, Artificial Intelligence, Robotics or Software. **Lampeter** The Information Technology course emphasises how computers are used rather than how they work. **Nottingham Trent** A flexible course with four routes after a common first year. **South Bank** A course in Internet Computing is available. **Teesside** The Computer Science course offers two main themes – computer applications and computer science. Other degrees are offered in Visualisation, the Information Society and Multimedia. **York** Course involves both hardware and software aspects. *NOW CHECK PROSPECTUSES AND WEB SITES.*

Top universities and colleges (Teaching Quality) (see Ch.4): Cambridge; Edinburgh; Exeter; Glasgow; Heriot-Watt; Kent; London (Imp); Manchester; Oxford; Southampton; Teesside; Warwick; York; not all institutions assessed.

Top universities and colleges (Research) (see Ch.4): Aberdeen; Aberystwyth; Aston; Bath; Belfast (Queen's); Birmingham; Bristol; Cambridge; Cardiff; Dundee; Durham; East Anglia; Edinburgh; Essex; Exeter; Glasgow; Heriot-Watt; Hertfordshire; Kent; Lancaster; Leeds; London (Imp), (QM), (RH), (UCL); Loughborough; Manchester; Newcastle; Nottingham; Oxford; Reading; St Andrews; Sheffield; Southampton; Sussex; Swansea; UMIST; Warwick; York.

Study opportunities abroad: Aberdeen; Aberystwyth; Anglia; Aston; Belfast (Queen's); Birmingham; Brighton; Bristol; Bristol UWE; Brunel; Buckingham; Central England; Central Lancashire; Cheltenham & Glos (CHE); Chester (Coll); City; Coventry; De Montfort; Dundee; Durham; East Anglia; Edinburgh; Exeter; Glamorgan; Glasgow; Glasgow Caledonian; Greenwich; Hertfordshire; Huddersfield; Hull; Kent; Leeds; Liverpool Hope (Coll); Liverpool John Moores; London (QM), (Imp), (RH); Luton; Manchester; Manchester Met; Middlesex; Napier; Newcastle; North London; Northumbria; Nottingham; Nottingham Trent; Oxford Brookes; Paisley; Plymouth; Portsmouth; Salford; Sheffield; Staffordshire; Sunderland; Surrey Roehampton; Teesside; Wolverhampton; York.

Work opportunities abroad: Aberystwyth; Anglia; Bangor; Birmingham; Brighton; Bristol; Bristol UWE; Brunel; Central England; Central Lancashire; Cheltenham & Glos (CHE); Chester (Coll); City; Coventry; Cranfield; De Montfort; Derby; Dundee; Glamorgan; Huddersfield; Hull; Kingston; Leeds; Liverpool John Moores; London (RH); Loughborough; Northumbria; Oxford Brookes; Plymouth; Portsmouth; Queen Margaret (UC); Robert Gordon; Salford; Sheffield Hallam; South Bank; Staffordshire; Sunderland; Surrey; Teesside; Worcester (UC); York.

ADMISSIONS INFORMATION

Number of applicants per place (approx): Abertay Dundee 2; Aberystwyth 8; Aston 10; Bath 10; Birmingham 12; Bournemouth 8; Bradford 13; Bristol 15; Bristol UWE 4; Brunel 10; Buckingham 6; Buckinghamshire Chilterns (UC) 2; Cambridge 3.4; Canterbury Christ

Church (UC) 15; Cardiff 4; Central Lancashire 10; Cheltenham & Glos (CHE) 8; Chester (Coll) 7; City 7; Coventry 10; Cranfield 2; De Montfort 9; Derby 5; Durham 13; East Anglia (Comp/Maths) 7; East London 7; Edinburgh 4; Essex 2; Exeter 14; Glamorgan 3; Glasgow Caledonian 8; Greenwich 15; Hertfordshire 8; Heriot-Watt 6; Hull (Comp Sci) 6, (Comp/Elect Eng) 12, (Comp/Maths) 12; Kent 8; Kingston 10; Lampeter 1; Lancaster 5; Leeds 10; Leicester 22; Lincolnshire & Humberside 5; Liverpool John Moores 18; London (Imp) 6, (QM) 15, (RH) 5; London Guildhall 7; Loughborough (CT) 2; Manchester (Comp Inf Sys) 30, (Artif Intel) 20, (Comp Sci) 10; Manchester Met 10, (Bus Inf Tech) 8; Nescot 2; Newcastle 7; North East Wales (IHE) 3; Northampton (UC) 1; Northumbria 4; Nottingham Trent 4; Oxford 2.3; Oxford Brookes 18; Paisley 8; Plymouth 12; Portsmouth 6; Queen Margaret (UC) 3; Robert Gordon 3; Sheffield Hallam 5; South Bank 7; Southampton 9; Staffordshire 5; Stirling 6; Strathclyde 16; Suffolk (Coll) 1; Sunderland 10; Surrey (Comp Inf Tech) 15; Surrey Roehampton 3; Swansea 8; Teesside 4; Trinity Carmarthen (Coll) 2; UMIST 4; Warwick 11; Westminster 5; Wolverhampton 6; Worcester (UC) 4; York 12.

Planning your UCAS personal statement (see Ch.4): Any experience with computers, programming etc outside school or college should be described. It is also useful to give details of any visits, work experience and work shadowing relating to industrial or commercial organisations and their computer systems. See also **Appendix 1**. **De Montfort** (Multim Comp) Interest in hardware and software. Prior experience using multimedia packages. Knowledge of computer usage and programming. **Portsmouth** Evidence needed that applicants can work with people. Contact the British Computer Society for information. **Queen Margaret (UC)** Outgoing personality. Mature students welcome. **St Andrews** Reasons for choosing the course and evidence of interest. Sport/extra curricular activities, positions of responsibility.

Selection interviews (see Ch.4): Abertay Dundee; Aberystwyth (some); Bath; Bradford; Bradford (Coll) (No); Brighton (No); Bristol (No); Bristol (UWE); Brunel; Buckingham; Cambridge; Cardiff; Central England (No); Central Lancashire (No); City; Coventry (T); Cranfield; De Montfort (No); Durham (No); East Anglia; Edinburgh; Exeter (No); Glamorgan; Greenwich (No); Hertfordshire; Hull; Kent (No); Kingston; Leeds (No); Liverpool Hope (Coll); Liverpool John Moores (No); London (Gold), (QM) (T), (RH) (No), (UCL) (No); Loughborough; Manchester (No); Manchester Met (some); Napier (some); Newcastle; Newport (UWCN); North London (some); Northampton (UC); Northbrook (Coll); Nottingham; Nottingham Trent (No); Oxford (W) (T); Oxford Brookes (No); Paisley (No); Plymouth; Portsmouth; St Andrews (No); Sheffield Hallam; South Bank (W) (T); Southampton; Staffordshire (No); Stirling (No); Suffolk (Coll) (No); Sunderland (No); Surrey; Swansea; Teesside (No); Thames Valley; UMIST; Warwick; Wigan & Leigh (Coll); Wolverhampton (No); York.

Interview questions (see Ch.4): Whilst A-level computer studies or other examinations are not essential for the applicant, you will be questioned on your computer experience and aspects of the subject which interest you. Some applicants expected Information Technology and not Computer Science.

Reasons for rejection (non-academic): Little practical interest in computers/electronics. Inability to work as part of a small team. Mismatch between referee's description and performance at interview. Unsatisfactory English. Can't communicate. Inability to convince interviewer of the candidate's worth. Incoherent, unmotivated, arrogant and without any evidence of good reason. **Southampton** Lack of motivation in chosen topic of engineering. Incoherence. Carelessness.

GAP YEAR ADVICE

Cheltenham & Glos (CHE) Relevant experience can count instead of a year's industrial placement.

Institutions willing to defer entry after A-levels: Aberystwyth; Anglia; Aston; Bell (CT); Birmingham; Bournemouth; Bradford; Brighton; Bristol; Bristol UWE; Brunel; Buckingham; Cardiff; Central Lancashire; Chester (Coll); City; Coventry; Cranfield; De Montfort; Derby; Dundee; Edge Hill (CHE); Glamorgan; Glasgow Caledonian; Heriot-Watt; Hertfordshire; Huddersfield; Hull; Inverness (Coll); Kingston; Lampeter; Lancaster; Leicester; Lincolnshire

& Humberside; Liverpool John Moores; London (RH), (UCL) (No); Luton; Manchester Met; Nescot; Newcastle; Northampton (UC); Northumbria; Nottingham; Oxford Brookes; Paisley; Plymouth; Portsmouth; Robert Gordon; St Andrews (No); Sheffield; Sheffield Hallam; South Bank; Southampton; Staffordshire; Sunderland (No); Surrey; Surrey Roehampton; Sussex; Swansea; Teesside; Thames Valley; Trinity Carmarthen (Coll); UMIST; Wolverhampton; Warwick; York.

AFTER RESULTS ADVICE

Institutions which may accept the same points score after A-levels: Abertay Dundee; Aberystwyth; Aston; Bath (No); Bournemouth; Bradford; Brighton; Bristol; Bristol UWE; Brunel; Buckingham; Buckinghamshire Chilterns (UC); Canterbury Christ Church (UC); Central Lancashire; City; Coventry (reduced points in some cases); Cranfield; De Montfort; Derby; Dundee; Durham; East Anglia; East London; Edinburgh; Farnborough (CT); Glamorgan; Glasgow Caledonian; Heriot-Watt; Hertfordshire (No); Huddersfield; Hull; Inverness (Coll); Kent; Kingston; Lampeter (perhaps); Leeds; Leicester; Lincolnshire & Humberside; Liverpool John Moores; London (RH); Loughborough (No); Manchester Met; Nescot; Newcastle; North East Wales (IHE); Northampton (UC); Nottingham Trent; Oxford Brookes; Paisley; Plymouth; Portsmouth; St Andrews (No); Salford (Inf Tech); Sheffield (usually); Sheffield Hallam; South Bank; Staffordshire; Stirling (No); Strathclyde; Sunderland; Surrey; Surrey Roehampton; Swansea; Teesside; Thames Valley; Trinity Carmarthen (Coll); UMIST; Warwick (No); Westminster; Worcester (UC); Wolverhampton; York.

Institutions which may accept lower grades/points score after A-levels: Aberystwyth; Anglia; Aston (Elec/Comp Sci); Bournemouth; Bradford; Brighton; Bristol UWE; Brunel; Buckinghamshire Chilterns (UC); Cheltenham & Glos (CHE); Chester (Coll); City; Cranfield; De Montfort; Derby; Farnborough (CT); Heriot-Watt; Hertford Regional (Coll); Hertfordshire; Huddersfield; Hull (overseas students 18–16 pts); Inverness (Coll); Kent; Lampeter; Leicester; Lincolnshire & Humberside; Liverpool John Moores; London (RH), (UCL); Manchester Met; Newcastle; North East Wales (IHE); Northumbria; Oxford Brookes (No); Paisley; Plymouth (No); Portsmouth; Robert Gordon; St Andrews; Salford (Inf Tech); Sheffield; Sheffield Hallam; South Bank; Staffordshire; Sunderland; Surrey; Surrey Roehampton; Thames Valley; Trinity Carmarthen (Coll); UMIST; Warwick; Wolverhampton; York (No); most institutions and colleges consider applicants who have missed their offer by one or two points.

Offers to applicants repeating A-levels: Higher Brighton, De Montfort, Greenwich, Kingston, St Andrews, Salford, Surrey, Sussex, Teesside, Warwick, Wolverhampton; **Possibly higher** Bath, Bristol UWE, Durham, East Anglia, Edinburgh, Lancaster, Leeds, Newcastle, Oxford Brookes, Portsmouth, Sheffield, Sunderland, Teesside; **Same** Anglia, Aston, Brunel, Chester (Coll), City, Cranfield, Derby, Dundee, Farnborough (CT), Huddersfield, Hull, Kent, Liverpool, Loughborough, London (RH), (UCL), Manchester Met, Northumbria, Robert Gordon, Salford (Inf Tech), Sheffield, Sheffield Hallam, South Bank, Thames Valley, Ulster; Worcester (UC).

Probable vacancies from June 2001 and in Clearing (see Ch.4): Most universities are likely to have vacancies on Computer, Information Science and Artificial Intelligence courses from June onwards, particularly on joint courses.

NEW GRADUATE DESTINATIONS AND EMPLOYMENT (1999 HESA) (see **Ch.4**)

Of 6791 graduates surveyed, 5174 obtained full-time employment, 465 went on to further study and 544 were believed to be unemployed.

CONSUMER STUDIES (including **Home Economics**; see also **Food Science/Studies & Technology** and **Hospitality, Hotel and Catering Management**)

NB The information supplied by the universities and colleges this year varies considerably and the offers listed below should be used as a first source of reference only. Many institutions will accept combinations of Advanced (AL), Advanced Subsidiary (AS) and Vocational Advanced (VA) level qualifications to achieve the required points total, but applicants must check web sites and prospectuses for full details of all offers. Grades and points totals shown should be regarded as the minimum levels to be achieved, but offers may be adjusted downwards when results are known. The points totals shown to the left of the institutions are for ease of reference only. It must not be assumed that tariff points are always used by institutions or that they can be substituted for an offer in grades. The level of an offer is not necessarily indicative of the quality of a course. To calculate your offers see Chapter 4 and the inside fold of the back cover.

Special subject requirements/preferences: A-level: Cardiff (UWI), **Manchester Met**, **North London** Home economics desirable plus a science subject.

280 pts	**Harper Adams (UC)** – 280–140 pts (Fd Consum St)
240 pts	**Ulster** – CCC (Consum St)
180 pts	**Manchester Met** – 180 pts approx (Consum Prot; Consum Prod Mark Tech)
160 pts	**Liverpool John Moores** – 160 pts – ALs **or** ALs+ASs **or** VAs+/-ALs/ASs; (Consum St; Home Econ)
	North London – 160 pts – 2ALs **or** VAs6u/12u; (Consum Bhv)
	Salford – 160 pts approx (App Consum St)
	Sheffield Hallam – 160 pts approx (Fd Consum St)
140 pts	**Cardiff (UWI)** – CD (Consum Sci/Fd St)
	Glasgow Caledonian – CD–DD (Consum Tr Stand; Consum/Mgt St)
120 pts	**and below**
	Abertay Dundee – DD (Fd/Consum Sci)
	Birmingham (CFTCS) – (Fd/Consum Mgt)
	North London – 120 pts – 2ALs **or** VAs6u/12u; (Consum St; Home Econ)
	North London – 2ALs **or** ALs+ASs **or** VAs+/-ALs/ASs; (Consum St courses)
	Queen Margaret (UC) – EE (Consum Affrs; Consum St)

Higher National Diploma courses
100 pts and below
Aberdeen (Coll); Birmingham (CFTCS); Croydon (Coll); Fife (CFHE); Manchester Met; Motherwell (Coll); North London; Salford; Sheffield Hallam; UHI.

Alternative Offers:

IB offers: Birmingham (CFTCS) 24 pts; Cardiff (UWI) 28 pts; Dundee 27 pts; Manchester Met 24 pts.

Irish offers: Dundee BBC.

Scottish Qualifications: Abertay Dundee BCC; Dundee BBC; Glasgow Caledonian BBC; Queen Margaret (UC) BCC.

CHOOSING YOUR COURSE (See also **Ch.1**)

Subject information: Consumer Studies courses involve food and nutrition, shelter, clothing, community studies and consumer behaviour and marketing. Alternative courses could include Health Science, Health Studies, Housing, Urban Studies, Dietetics, Nutrition, Community Studies and Hospitality, Hotel and Catering Management.

Special features: Cardiff (UWI) Part I covers home and consumer studies, food studies and textile studies. Part II extends to energy, environmental physics, ergonomics, communications studies, nutrition and health promotion. **Glasgow Caledonian** Three routes – Fashion and Business, Home Economics or the General route. **Manchester Met** Core studies throughout the course cover food, shelter and clothing studies with the emphasis on consumer studies, marketing, management services and lifestyles. **Salford** Two pathways from four from Food Production, Applied Consumer Studies, Hospitality Management and Leisure Management. **Sheffield Hallam** Options in food preparation, selection or commodities and vegetarian. *NOW CHECK PROSPECTUSES AND WEB SITES.*

Study opportunities abroad: Cardiff (UWI); Manchester Met; Sheffield Hallam.

Work opportunities abroad: Liverpool John Moores; Manchester Met.

ADMISSIONS INFORMATION

Number of applicants per place (approx): Bath Spa (UC) 6; Birmingham (CFTCS) 2; Cardiff (UWI) 5; Dundee 3; Glasgow Caledonian 12; Liverpool John Moores (BA) 7; Manchester Met 4; North London 5; Salford 2; Sheffield Hallam 5.

Planning your UCAS personal statement (see Ch.4): Relevant work experience/shadowing in, for example, restaurants, cafes, schools meals service, would be useful and should be described. Visits to food factories should be mentioned. (See also **Hospitality, Hotel and Catering Management** and **Dietetics**.) Details may be obtained from the Institute of Home Economics. See **Appendix 1**.

Selection interviews (see Ch.4): Bath Spa (UC); Salford; Sheffield Hallam.

Interview questions (see Ch.4): Questions will stem from your special interests in this subject, for example: What new developments are taking place in cookery techniques? What are the advantages and disadvantages? What is a home economist? What advice would you give to the designers of cookers? Why do you want to teach? What is ergonomics? What interests you in current affairs? What world or national news has annoyed, pleased or upset you? What relevance do textiles and dress have to home economics? How would you react in a room full of fools?

GAP YEAR ADVICE

Institutions willing to defer entry after A-levels: Birmingham (CFTCS); Cardiff (UWI); Dundee; Glasgow Caledonian; Leeds, Trinity & All Saints (Coll); Manchester Met; Queen Margaret (UC); Salford; Sheffield Hallam.

AFTER RESULTS ADVICE

Institutions which may accept the same points score after A-levels: Birmingham (CFTCS); Cardiff (UWI); Dundee; Liverpool John Moores; Manchester Met; Sheffield Hallam.

Institutions which may accept lower grades/points score after A-levels: Bath Spa (UC); Cardiff (UWI); Liverpool John Moores; Manchester Met.

Offers to applicants repeating A-levels: Possibly higher Manchester Met (BSc); **Same** Bath Spa (UC), Liverpool John Moores, Ulster.

Probable vacancies from June 2001 and in Clearing (see Ch.4): A number of institutions advertised vacancies last year on single and joint courses.

NEW GRADUATE DESTINATIONS AND EMPLOYMENT (1999 HESA) (see **Ch.4**)

See under **Hospitality, Hotel and Catering Management**.

DANCE/DANCE STUDIES (see also Drama (Performing Arts))

NB The information supplied by the universities and colleges this year varies considerably and the offers listed below should be used as a first source of reference only. Many institutions will accept combinations of Advanced (AL), Advanced Subsidiary (AS) and Vocational Advanced (VA) level qualifications to achieve the required points total, but applicants must check web sites and prospectuses for full details of all offers. Grades and points totals shown should be regarded as the minimum levels to be achieved, but offers may be adjusted downwards when results are known. The points totals shown to the left of the institutions are for ease of reference only. It must not be assumed that tariff points are always used by institutions or that they can be substituted for an offer in grades. The level of an offer is not necessarily indicative of the quality of a course. To calculate your offers see Chapter 4 and the inside fold of the back cover.

Special subject requirements/preferences: GCSE: **Laban Centre** Five subjects grade C+. **Surrey** Seven subjects grades A–C. **Other:** Practical dance experience required.

300 pts **Birmingham** – BBB (Dance courses)
280 pts **Surrey** – 280 pts 18u – BBC **or** ALs+ASs **or** VAs (depends on subj); gs; (Dance Cult)
220 pts **King Alfred's Winchester (Coll)** – 220 pts 12u – ALs **or** ALs+ASs **or** VAs+/ -ALs/ASs; gs; (Dance St)
　　　　　Middlesex – 220–200 pts approx (Dance)
200 pts **Chester (Coll)** – ALs (180 pts inc C)+AS **or** VAs (180 pts inc C)+AS; AS(20+ pts); gs; (Dance Comb Hons)
　　　　　Derby – 200 pts approx (Arts Thera)
　　　　　Wolverhampton – 200 pts 12u – DDD/CDE/BD/CC **or** VA12u CC; gs; (Dance)
180 pts **Cheltenham & Glos (CHE)** – 180 pts approx (Perf Arts)
　　　　　Coventry – 180 pts approx (Dance Prof Prac)
　　　　　De Montfort (Leicester) – 180 pts – ALs **or** ALs+ASs **or** VAs (Art Des)+/- ALs/ASs; audition; (not gs) (Dance)
　　　　　St Martin's (Coll) – CDE/CC (Perf Arts (Dance))
160 pts **Bath Spa (UC)** – 160–120 pts 12u – CD **or** VA12u CD; (not gs) (Dance)
　　　　　Brunel – 160 pts 2x6u – ALs **or** ALs+ASs **or** VAs+/-ALs/ASs; (Ballet/Contemp Dance)
　　　　　Chichester (UC) – 160 pts (inc C); interview; (Dance)
　　　　　De Montfort (Bedford) – 160 pts – Als **or** ALs+ASs **or** VAs (Art Des)+/- ALs/ASs; audition; (Dance)
　　　　　Hull (Scarborough) – 160 pts approx (Dance courses)
　　　　　Leeds (Bretton Hall) – CC (Dance)
　　　　　Liverpool John Moores – 160 pts – ALs **or** ALs+ASs **or** VAs+/-ALs/ASs; (Dance; Dance/Drama)
　　　　　Manchester Met – CC (Dance courses; Contemp Arts)
　　　　　Ripon & York (Coll) – CC (Dance; Perf/Comm Arts)
　　　　　Surrey Roehampton – 160 pts inc 2 ALs **or** VA; (Dance St)
140 pts **Derby** – 140 pts 12u – CD **or** DE+ee **or** VA6u C+AL(D); gs; experience in dance; (Dance Comb Hons)
　　　　　Sunderland – 140 pts – ALs **or** ALs+ASs **or** VAs+/-ALs/ASs; gs; BTEC accepted; (Perf Arts St)
80 pts **and below**
　　　　　Brighton – (Dance/Vis Prac)
　　　　　Laban Centre – 80 pts approx (Dance Thea – apply early)
　　　　　Liverpool (LIPA) – unconditional after successful audition (Perf Arts (Dance))
　　　　　Northern (Sch Contemp Dance) – (Dance)

Higher National Diploma courses
100 pts **and below**
　　　　　Chichester (UC) (Perf Arts); Liverpool (CmC); Newcastle (Coll); Northbrook (Coll); Northern (Sch Contemp Dance); Oldham (Coll); Plymouth; Salford; Stratford on Avon (Coll); Wigan & Leigh (Coll).

Diploma
      Laban Centre – (Dance Thea – full/part-time courses, apply early).

Alternative Offers:

IB offers: St Martin's (Coll) 28 pts; Surrey H555 30–28 pts; Surrey Roehampton 30 pts.

CHOOSING YOUR COURSE (See also **Ch.1**)

> **Subject information:** Be prepared for theoretical, educational, historical and social aspects of dance as well as practical studies. Performance Arts, Drama and Human Movement courses should also be considered. See also **Appendix 1**.

Special features: Chichester (UC) Dance criticism and analysis. Focus on choreography, dance and the National Curriculum. Contacts with dance profession, companies, administrators, promoters, agents, associations, Arts Council. **De Montfort** Current, innovative contemporary dance practice and choreography. **Laban Centre** (independent institution) Technical excellence in contemporary dance and choreography. Academic and practical studies. Versatility, inventiveness and individuality required. **Leeds (Bretton Hall)** Performance-based course covering dance, theatre, performance and dance in the community. **Liverpool (LIPA)** Applicants must apply on a separate LIPA form. **Middlesex** Fifteen modules including jazz, Tai-chi and choreography. **Surrey** Training for a career in the dance profession (community dance, dance company education, dance and disability, education management, notation/reconstruction). National Resource Centre for Dance and Labanotation Institute on site for teaching. **Surrey Roehampton** Opportunity to study dance in relation to other art forms. *NOW CHECK PROSPECTUSES AND WEB SITES.*

Top universities and colleges (Research) (see Ch.4): See under **Drama**.

Study opportunities abroad: Cheltenham & Glos (CHE); Chester (CHE); King Alfred's Winchester (Coll); Surrey Roehampton.

Work opportunities abroad: Cheltenham & Glos (CHE).

ADMISSIONS INFORMATION

Number of applicants per place (approx): Birmingham 12; Chichester (UC) 6; De Montfort 6; Derby 12; Hull (Scarborough) 2; Laban Centre 4; Middlesex 12, (Perf Arts) 23; Northern (Sch Contemp Dance) 6; Ripon & York (Coll) 3; Surrey 6; Surrey Roehampton 17.

Planning your UCAS personal statement (see Ch.4): Full details should be given of examinations taken and practical experience in contemporary dance or ballet. Refer to visits you have made to the theatre and your impressions. See also **Appendix 1**.

Selection interviews (see Ch.4): All institutions will organise auditions. The following scheme required by Liverpool (LIPA) may act as a guideline:

1) Write a short essay (500 words) on your own views and experience of dance. You should take into account the following:

a) Your history and how you have developed physically and intellectually in your run-up to applying to LIPA.

b) Your main influences and what inspires you.

c) What you want to gain from training as a dancer.

d) Your ideas on health and nutrition as a dancer, taking into account sex and physicality.

2) All candidates must prepare **two** practical audition pieces:

a) The first piece must be a dance piece choreographed by the candidate. You are free to create whatever you like, in whatever style you wish as long as the piece does not exceed two minutes (please note: panel will stop anyone exceeding this time-limit). There will be no pianist at this part of the session, so if you're using music please bring it with you on a cassette tape. This devised piece should be created through means that you feel comfortable with and that *expresses something personal about you*. You should wear your regular practice clothes for your presentation.

b) You must prepare a song of your own choice. An accompanist is provided, but you must provide the sheet music for your song, fully written out for piano accompaniment and in the key you wish to sing (the accompanist will **not** transpose at sight). **Important:** Do NOT choreograph your song. You should expect to sit on a high stool or stand when singing for the audition.

3) Additionally, all candidates will participate in a class given on the day of audition. Please ensure that you are dressed appropriately for class with clothing you are comfortable in but allow your movement to be seen.

In preparing the practical elements of the audition, please remember that audition panels are not looking for a 'polished' performance. The panel will be looking for candidates' ability to make a genuine emotional and physical connection with the material that they are presenting which shows clear intent and focus.

Remember that it is in your best interest to prepare thoroughly. Nerves inevitably play a part in any audition and can undermine even the best-prepared candidate. Your best defence is to feel confident in your preparation.

Reasons for rejection (non-academic): Surrey Perhaps looking for a vocational course in Dance Performance or joint degrees rather than Single honours. Inadequate dance background. Had not seen/read about/done any dance.

GAP YEAR ADVICE

Chichester (UC) Continue with some practical dance work and study performances. **Surrey Roehampton** Advisable to give reasons and information on intended activities.

Institutions willing to defer entry after A-levels: Birmingham (No); Cheltenham & Glos (CHE); De Montfort; Derby; King Alfred's Winchester (Coll); Laban Centre; Liverpool John Moores; St Martin's (Coll); Surrey; Surrey Roehampton (No).

AFTER RESULTS ADVICE

Institutions which may accept lower grades/points score after A-levels (see Ch.4): Surrey Roehampton.

Probable vacancies from June 2001 and in Clearing (see Ch.4): Almost all institutions are likely to have vacancies in Dance.

NEW GRADUATE DESTINATIONS AND EMPLOYMENT (1999 HESA) (see **Ch.4**)

See **Drama**.

DENTISTRY (including **Dental Technology**)

NB The information supplied by the universities and colleges this year varies considerably and the offers listed below should be used as a first source of reference only. Many institutions will accept combinations of Advanced (AL), Advanced Subsidiary (AS) and Vocational Advanced (VA) level qualifications to achieve the required points total, but applicants must check web sites and prospectuses for full details of all offers. Grades and points totals shown should be regarded as the minimum levels to be achieved, but offers may be adjusted downwards when results are known. The points totals shown to the left of the institutions are for ease of reference only. It must not be assumed that tariff points are always used by institutions or that they can be substituted for an offer in grades. The level of an offer is not necessarily indicative of the quality of a course. To calculate your offers see Chapter 4 and the inside fold of the back cover.

Special subject requirements/preferences: A-level: Preference given to three subjects from science/mathematics. Chemistry usually essential. **London Dental Schools** Chemistry and biology must be included at least one at A-level and the other at AS-level. Non-science subjects chosen from humanities and social sciences are welcome. General studies not acceptable. Mathematics and further mathematics cannot be offered as separate subjects. **London (QM)** There is a growing trend towards biology becoming a compulsory A-level for Dentistry, since first year non-biology students have difficulty with the course. We now specify that chemistry is compulsory and biology is highly desirable. **Manchester Met** (Dental Tech) One science subject required, art or CDT preferred. **GCSE: Birmingham** Five subjects grade A/B including mathematics and English. **Bristol** Six subjects grade A. **Cardiff (UWCM)** Double award science grades BB; **Leeds** Grade A science subjects, grade A/B English language. **London Dental Schools** Grade B in English, mathematics, physics and biology or double award or combined science. **London (King's)** Six subjects at grade A/B (see also under **Medicine**). **Manchester** All B grades and five A grades preferred (As in science subjects). **Sheffield** Grade A in English, chemistry, mathematics, biology and physics (dual science accepted). **Other: Cardiff (UWCM), Leeds and most dental schools**. Evidence of non-infectivity or hepatitis-B immunisation required. Completion of a criminal record disclaimer required and consent to a police record check.

360 pts   and above
> **Cardiff (UWCM)** – 360 pts 12u – ABB+c **or** AA+aa **or** VA12u AA/AB+AL(A); (not gs); (Dentistry)
> **Liverpool** – 360 pts – ALs **or** ALs+ASs **or** VAs+/-ALs/ASs; (Dentistry)
> **London (King's)** – ABB+b **or** AB+aaa (inc min AL chem/biol but not for Nat Sci); VAs considered; (Dentistry; Fdn Nat Sci)
> **London (QM)** – AAAb – 3ALs+AS (inc 2ALs inc sci+chem/biol or with chem/biol AS min b); (Dentistry)

340 pts   Belfast (Queen's) – AAB (Dentistry)
> **Bristol** – AAB (5 yr course inc chem; 6 yr course inc 2 non-sci subjs min); (not gs) (Dentistry)

320 pts   Birmingham – ABB (also pre-dental year) AAA/AAB 2nd attempt (Dentistry)
> **Dundee** – ABB (not VAs or gs) (Dentistry)
> **Glasgow** – ABB (Dentistry)
> **Leeds** – 21u – 3ALs+AS **or** 2ALs+3ASs (inc A/B range inc AL chem and AL/AS biol) (Dentistry)
> **Manchester** – ABB (also pre-dental yr) **or** VA12u AL (Dentistry courses)
> **Newcastle** – ABB (not VAs) (Dental Surgery)
> **Sheffield** – ABB (Dentistry) (2nd yr entry AL sci+2ASs A/B)

160 pts   and below
> **Cardiff (UWI)** – (Dental Tech)
> **Manchester Met** – (Dental Tech)

Higher National Diploma courses
100 pts   Cardiff (UWI) – (Dental Tech)

Alternative Offers:

EB offers: Cardiff (UWCM) 73% overall; London (King's) 80% overall + 80% in each science (written papers).

IB offers: Belfast (Queen's) H666 S555; Birmingham 36 pts; Bristol 32 pts inc H766; Cardiff (UWCM) 32 pts, H666; Dundee 32 pts; Glasgow 34 pts; Leeds 32 pts inc H666 in science subjs; Liverpool 32 pts; London (QM) 34–32 pts inc H655; London (King's) H665; Manchester H665; Newcastle 34–32 pts; Sheffield 33 pts.

Irish offers: Birmingham AAAAB; Cardiff AAABBB; London (King's) not acceptable; Sheffield BBBBBB.

Scottish Qualifications: Dundee AAAAB–ABBBB; Glasgow AAAAB.

Overseas applicants: Cardiff (UWCM) EU and foreign students must be available for interview (two places only for foreign students). **London (King's)** Maximum four places available for overseas (non-EU) students. Must meet normal entry requirements and be available for interview in UK. **Sheffield** Three students taken per year – interviews not held (intake 45).

CHOOSING YOUR COURSE (See also **Ch.1**)

Subject information: Courses cover basic medical sciences, human disease, clinical studies and clinical dentistry. Amount of contact with patients varies. Work shadowing or experience of this career beyond that of the ordinary patient is important. Possible alternative courses are Medicine, Pharmacy, Speech Therapy, Radiography, Physiotherapy, Nursing, Chemistry, Biochemistry, Biological Sciences, Anatomy and Physiology. Intercalated courses with other science degrees are offered by most dental schools. **NB** Candidates should not apply for both Dentistry and Medicine courses. For applicants to Dentistry (also Medicine and Veterinary Science/Medicine) a maximum of four choices is allowed (see **Chapter 3**. See also **Appendix 1**.)

Mature students: A-level standard necessary. Graduates require 2:1 degree plus A-level grades close to the normal requirement.

Special features: Belfast (Queen's) Clinical dentistry starts in year 3. **Birmingham** Recently revised curriculum; emphasis on preparation for present-day dental practice and future changes. **Bristol** Emphasis on concept of whole-patient care through clinical teaching and early experience of clinical procedures. **Cardiff (UWCM)** Teaching based on whole-patient care; newly equipped areas for children and adult dentistry. **Dundee** Practical experience in hospital begins in the second professional year. **Leeds** Clinical dentistry starts in year 2. **London (King's)** Opportunity for intercalated BSc degree, and Foundation course for those without science A-levels. **Newcastle** New integrated five-term course in basic sciences. Opportunity for intercalated degree. New six-term course in human disease. **Sheffield** Students treat patients, under supervision, from year 3 onwards. *NOW CHECK PROSPECTUSES AND WEB SITES.*

Top universities and colleges (Teaching Quality) (see Ch.4): Cardiff (UWCM); Dundee; Glasgow; not all institutions assessed.

Top universities and colleges (Research) (see Ch.4): Bristol; Leeds; London (King's), (QM), (UCL); Manchester.

Study opportunities abroad: Birmingham; Bristol; Cardiff (UWCM); Dundee; Glasgow; Manchester; Sheffield.

ADMISSIONS INFORMATION

Number of applicants per place (approx): Belfast (Queen's) 5; Birmingham 15; Bristol 13; Cardiff (UWCM) (6 yr course) 15, (5 yr course) 11; Dundee 18, (Pre-dental) 5; Glasgow 5; Leeds 18; Liverpool 15; London (QM) 18, (King's) 20 (non-EU) 25; Manchester 25, (Pre-dental) 40; Manchester Met 16; Newcastle 12; Sheffield 16. **Foreign applicants** Birmingham 129 (no quota); Manchester 6.

Planning your UCAS personal statement (see Ch.4): UCAS applications listing four choices only should be submitted by 15 October. Show evidence of manual dexterity, work experience, evidence of paid or voluntary employment in any field, preferably dealing with people in an environment widely removed from your home or school etc. Details must be provided of discussions with dentists and work-shadowing in dental surgeries. Discuss any specialised fields of dentistry in which you might be interested. See also **Appendix 1**. **Cardiff (UWCM), Manchester** Expect students to have had work experience. **Cardiff (UWCM)** Evidence of, and potential for, high acdemic achievement; a caring and committed attitude towards people; an understanding of the demands of dental training and practice; the ability to communicate effectively; a willingness to accept responsibility; evidence of broad, social, cultural or sporting interests, good manual dexterity.

Selection interviews (see Ch.4): Birmingham (400–450 applicants – only 50% of applicants get through the initial sort); Bristol; Cardiff (UWCM); Dundee; Glasgow; Leeds; London (King's), (QM); Manchester; Newcastle; Sheffield.

Interview questions (see Ch.4): Work shadowing in a dental surgery is essential and as a result, questions will be asked on your reactions to the work and your understanding of the different types of treatment which a dentist can offer. In the past questions at interview have included: What is conservative dentistry? What does integrity mean? Do you think the first year syllabus is a good one? What qualities are required by a dentist? What are prosthetics, periodontics, orthodontics? What causes tooth decay? **Leeds** The interview assesses personality, verbal and communication skills and knowledge of dentistry.

Reasons for rejection (non-academic): Lack of knowledge of dentistry and lack of evidence of a firm commitment to dentistry. Lack of breadth of interests. Lack of motivation for a health care profession. Unprofessional attitude. Poor manual dexterity. Poor communication skills. Poor English. Lack of evidence of ability to work in groups. Not for the faint-hearted!

GAP YEAR ADVICE

Cardiff (UWCM) Explain your reasons on UCAS application.

Institutions willing to defer entry after A-levels: Birmingham (No); Cardiff (UWCM) (No); Dundee; London (King's); Manchester; Newcastle; Sheffield.

AFTER RESULTS ADVICE

Institutions which may accept the same points score after A-levels: Birmingham; Bristol; Cardiff (UWCM) (some); Dundee (No); Glasgow (No); Leeds (No); Liverpool (varies); London (King's) only under exceptional circumstances; Manchester (No); Newcastle (in most cases); Sheffield (No).

Institutions which may accept lower grades/points score after A-levels: Birmingham (No); Cardiff (UWCM) (some); Dundee (No); London (King's) perhaps; Newcastle.

Offers to applicants repeating A-levels: Higher Bristol (AAB), Cardiff (UWCM) (preference given to students who previously applied), Leeds (Very few – AAB); **Same** Belfast (Queen's); **Resits not acceptable** Birmingham, Dundee, London (King's).

Probable vacancies from June 2001 and in Clearing (see Ch.4): No vacancies were advertised last year, but students with good A-levels should contact the universities to which they previously applied. There were some vacancies in Dental Technology.

NEW GRADUATE DESTINATIONS AND EMPLOYMENT (1999 HESA) (see **Ch.4**)

Of 676 graduates surveyed, 639 entered full-time employment, five went into further study and three were seeking employment.

DEVELOPMENT STUDIES (see also **Agricultural Sciences/ Agriculture** and **Town & Country Planning**)

NB The information supplied by the universities and colleges this year varies considerably and the offers listed below should be used as a first source of reference only. Many institutions will accept combinations of Advanced (AL), Advanced Subsidiary (AS) and Vocational Advanced (VA) level qualifications to achieve the required points total, but applicants must check web sites and prospectuses for full details of all offers. Grades and points totals shown should be regarded as the minimum levels to be achieved, but

offers may be adjusted downwards when results are known. The points totals shown to the left of the institutions are for ease of reference only. It must not be assumed that tariff points are always used by institutions or that they can be substituted for an offer in grades. The level of an offer is not necessarily indicative of the quality of a course. To calculate your offers see Chapter 4 and the inside fold of the back cover.

Special subject requirements/preferences: GCSE: Mathematics, English and a foreign language may be required.

300 pts	**St Andrews** – BBB (Dev St)
	Sussex – BBB–BBC (Dev St courses)
280 pts	**Bradford** – 280 pts 12u; gs; (Dev/Peace St)
	East Anglia – 280 pts 18u – BBC **or** BB+cc; gs; (Dev St/Ovrs St; Dev St/Lang; Dev St (Econ Pol Soc Pol p/t)
	Hull – BBC (Sociol/Soc Anth/Dev St)
	Leeds – 18u – BBC **or** BB+cc; gs; (Dev St)
	London (SOAS) – 280 pts (Dev St courses)
260 pts	**Swansea** – 260 pts 18u – BCC/BB **or** ALs+ASs **or** VAs+/-ALs/ASs; (Dev St courses)
220 pts	**Coventry** – 220 pts approx (Dev St)
	Kingston – 220–200 pts approx (Dev St)
200 pts	**Central Lancashire** – 200–180 pts 12u; gs; (Dev St courses)
180 pts	**Coventry** – 180 pts approx (Thrd Wrld Dev St)
	East London – 180 pts approx (Thrd Wrld Dev St; Dev St)
	St Mark & St John (Coll) – 180–160 pts approx (Dev St courses)
	St Mary's (Coll) – 12u – BC–CC **or** VA12u CC–DD **or** VA6u+AL/ASs; gs; (Dev St)
140 pts	**Derby** – 140 pts 12u – CD **or** DD+cc **or** VAs C/D; gs; (Thrd Wrld Dev)
	Portsmouth – CD (Lat Am Dev St)
120 pts	**London Guildhall** – 120 pts approx (Dev St courses)

Open Access:
Hertfordshire – (Contemp St)

Alternative Offers:

IB offers: Bradford 30 pts; East Anglia 31 pts; Leeds 28 pts; Swansea 30 pts.

Scottish Qualifications: St Andrews BBB.

Overseas applicants: East Anglia Competence in English required.

CHOOSING YOUR COURSE (See also **Ch.1**)

> **Subject information:** Development Studies is a multi-disciplinary subject covering, for example, economics, sociology, social anthropology, politics, natural resources, environment policy analysis with special reference to countries overseas. Several of these subjects can be studied as degree courses in their own right and could also be considered as alternative subject choices.

Special features: East Anglia Interdisciplinary programme covering social anthropology, natural resources, economics, sociology and politics. This is the only dedicated course in Development Studies. **Leeds** Joint course in combination with Economics, Geography, Politics and Sociology concentrating on past and present relationships between industrialised nations and poorer developing countries. **London (SOAS)** Regional specialisms covering Asia and Africa. **Swansea** Single Honours course has compulsory field-work (part-subsidised). *NOW CHECK PROSPECTUSES AND WEB SITES.*

Top universities and colleges (Research) (see Ch.4): East Anglia.

Study opportunities abroad: Derby; East Anglia; East London; Leeds; Swansea.

Work opportunities abroad: Derby.

ADMISSIONS INFORMATION

Number of applicants per place (approx): Bradford 6; East Anglia 8; East London 8; Kent 7; Leeds 8; Swansea 5.

Planning your UCAS personal statement (see Ch.4): Discuss aspects of development studies which interest you, for example in relation to geography, economics, politics. Interests in Third World countries should be mentioned. **St Andrews** Reasons for choosing the course and evidence of interest. Sport/extra-curricular activities, positions of responsibility.

Selection interviews (see Ch.4): East London; Kent; St Andrews (No); Swansea.

Interview questions (see Ch.4): Since this is a multidisciplinary subject questions will vary considerably. Initially they will stem from your interests and the information given on your UCAS form and your reasons for choosing the course. In the past questions at interview have included: Define a third world country. What help does the United Nations provide in the third world? Could it do too much? What problems have the United Nations faced in their work throughout the world?

GAP YEAR ADVICE

Institutions willing to defer entry after A-levels: Derby; East Anglia; Leeds; Swansea.

AFTER RESULTS ADVICE

Institutions which may accept the same points score after A-levels: East Anglia; Swansea.

Institutions which may accept lower grades/points score after A-levels (see Ch.4): East Anglia; St Mary's (Coll).

Probable vacancies from June 2001 and in Clearing (see Ch.4): Contact all universities since vacancies are almost certain.

NEW GRADUATE DESTINATIONS AND EMPLOYMENT (1999 HESA) (see **Ch.4**)

No data available.

DIETETICS (see also **Food Science/Studies & Technology** and **Nutrition**)

NB The information supplied by the universities and colleges this year varies considerably and the offers listed below should be used as a first source of reference only. Many institutions will accept combinations of Advanced (AL), Advanced Subsidiary (AS) and Vocational Advanced (VA) level qualifications to achieve the required points total, but applicants must check web sites and prospectuses for full details of all offers. Grades and points totals shown should be regarded as the minimum levels to be achieved, but offers may be adjusted downwards when results are known. The points totals shown to the left of the institutions are for ease of reference only. It must not be assumed that tariff points are always used by institutions or that they can be substituted for an offer in grades. The level of an offer is not necessarily indicative of the quality of a course. To calculate your offers see Chapter 4 and the inside fold of the back cover.

Special subject requirements/preferences: A-level: Chemistry and another science usually essential. **GCSE:** English and mathematics.

260 pts   London (King's) – BCC (Nutr/Diet)
Surrey – BCC–CCC (Nutrition courses)

240 pts **Coventry** – 240 pts approx (Dietetics)
          Ulster – CCC (Hum Nutr)
220 pts **North London** – 220 pts (Hum Nutr/Diet)
200 pts **Cardiff (UWI)** – 200 pts approx (App Hum Nutr (Diet))
160 pts **Glasgow Caledonian** – CC (Hum Nutr/Diet)
140 pts **Queen Margaret (UC)** – CD (Dietetics)
          Robert Gordon – CD (Nutr/Diet/SR)

          Leeds Met – (contact university)

Alternative Offers:

Scottish Qualifications: Glasgow Caledonian BBCC; Queen Margaret (UC) BBC.

CHOOSING YOUR COURSE (See also **Ch.1**)

Subject information: This subject includes scientific and medical topics, and some courses lead to state registration in Dietetics (check prospectuses and web sites). Work experience (usually in hospitals) is very important prior to submitting your application. Alternative course choices will depend on whether your interest lies in food or medical aspects, for example, Food Science, Home Economics, Consumer Studies or paramedical courses such as Speech Therapy or Occupational Therapy. See also **Appendix 1.**

Special features: Queen Margaret (UC) Course covers biological science, nutrition, food science and social sciences. *NOW CHECK PROSPECTUSES AND WEB SITES.*

ADMISSIONS INFORMATION

Number of applicants per place (approx): Cardiff (UWI) 10; Glasgow Caledonian 11; Queen Margaret (UC) 5.

Planning your UCAS personal statement (see Ch.4): Discuss the work with a hospital dietitian and describe fully any work experience gained in hospital dietetics departments or with the schools meals services. See also **Appendix 1**.

Selection interviews (see Ch.4): All institutions.

Interview questions (see Ch.4): Your knowledge of a career in dietetics will be fully explored and questions will be asked on your work experience and how you reacted to it.

GAP YEAR ADVICE

Most institutions accept a gap year.

Institutions willing to defer entry after A-levels: Queen Margaret (UC).

AFTER RESULTS ADVICE

Offers to applicants repeating A-levels: Higher Cardiff (UWI); **Possibly higher** Glasgow Caledonian.

Probable vacancies from June 2001 and in Clearing (see Ch.4): Contact all universities and colleges since many vacancies are likely.

NEW GRADUATE DESTINATIONS AND EMPLOYMENT (1999 HESA) (see **Ch.4**)

No data available.

DRAMA (including **Performing Arts, Theatre Arts**, **Theatre Studies** and **Theatre Design**; see also **Art & Design (General)**)

NB The information supplied by the universities and colleges this year varies considerably and the offers listed below should be used as a first source of reference only. Many institutions will accept combinations of Advanced (AL), Advanced Subsidiary (AS) and Vocational Advanced (VA) level qualifications to achieve the required points total, but applicants must check web sites and prospectuses for full details of all offers. Grades and points totals shown should be regarded as the minimum levels to be achieved, but offers may be adjusted downwards when results are known. The points totals shown to the left of the institutions are for ease of reference only. It must not be assumed that tariff points are always used by institutions or that they can be substituted for an offer in grades. The level of an offer is not necessarily indicative of the quality of a course. To calculate your offers see Chapter 4 and the inside fold of the back cover.

Special subject requirements/preferences: A-level: English, theatre studies, drama, a foreign language and history are relevant for some courses. **Aberystwyth** English or a modern language preferred. **Manchester, Warwick** English. **GCSE:** English usually essential; mathematics may be required. **De Montfort** English grade B. **Exeter** Majority (60%) of A* and A grades. **London (RH)** Good passes in English, mathematics and a foreign language. **Welsh (CMus/Dr)** Three subjects at grade C.

360 pts **and above**
  London (QM) – 370 pts 21u; (Drama courses)
350 pts **Brunel** – 350–290 pts 2x6u (inc AL B thea st/drama/perf arts) – ALs **or**
  ALs+ASs **or** VAs+/-ALs/ASs; (Modn Drama St)
320 pts **Birmingham** – ABB (Drama/Thea Arts; Drama courses)
  Bristol UWE – 320–260 pts 18u pref/12u – ALs **or** ALs+ASs (thea st/arts/soc
  sci subj pref) **or** VAs+/-ALs/ASs (200 pts from 6/12u awards); (Drama;
  Drama/Cult Media St; Drama/Engl)
  Brunel – 320–280 pts 2x6u (inc AL B thea st/drama/perf arts) – ALs **or**
  ALs+ASs **or** VAs+/-ALs/ASs; (Modn Drama St joint courses)
  Exeter – 320 pts 18u – ABB **or** AB+ab **or** VAs (contact univ); (not gs) (Drama)
  Hull – ABB–BBC (Drama; Drama/Engl)
  Leeds – ABB (Engl Lit/Thea St)
  London (RH) – ABB (not gs) (Drama/Thea St; Int Thea (Fr))
  Manchester – ABB (Drama/Engl)
300 pts **Bristol** – BBB–BCC (inc B modn lang for Lang courses) (not gs) (Drama;
  Drama/Fr/Ger/Ital/Port/Span)
  Bristol UWE – 300–240 pts 18u pref/12u – ALs **or** ALs+ASs (thea st/arts/soc
  sci subj pref) **or** VAs+/-ALs/ASs (200 pts from 6/12u awards); (Drama/Hist;
  Film TV St/Drama)
  East Anglia – 300 pts 18u – ABB+addit units/BBB **or** AB+bb (VA as 3rd AL);
  (not gs) (Drama)
  Hull – BBB–BBC (Drama)
  Kent – 300–280 pts approx (Drama/Thea St)
  King Alfred's Winchester (Coll) – 300–260 pts 15u – ALs or ALs+ASs or
  VAs+/-ALs/ASs; gs; (Drama/Thea/TV St)
  Lancaster – BBB–BBC (Thea St/Engl)
  Manchester – BBB (Drama/Scrn St; Drama)
  Reading – BBB–BBC (Drama courses)
  Sussex – BBB (Euro Drama/Fr/Ger/Ital)
  Warwick – BBB (Thea/Perf St)
280 pts **Bristol** – BBC(inc B Engl) (not gs) (Drama/Engl)
  Cambridge (Hom) – BBC–BCD (Drama Engl/Educ St)
  Essex – 280 pts 21u – BB+AL/2ASs **or** VA12u BB (perf arts)+AL; gs; (Acting
  (East 15, Loughton **see Ch.2**); Drama (Colchester (Inst)))
  Glasgow – BBC (Theatre Studies courses)

Hull – BBC (Drama joint courses (B in Fr/Mus))
Lancaster – BBC–BCC (Thea St; Thea St/Engl/Fr/Span St)
London (Gold) – BBC (Drama/Thea Arts)
London (QM) – 280–260 pts approx (Modn Lang/Drama courses)
Loughborough – 280 pts 18u – 2ALs+AL/2ASs **or** VA12u+AL **or** VA6u+2AL/2AS; (not gs) (Drama courses)

260 pts **Aberystwyth** – BCC/BB (Drama courses)
Brunel – BCC (Film TV St/Drama)
Central (Sch Sp/Dr) – BCC (Drama/Educ)
De Montfort (Leicester) – 260 pts – ALs **or** ALs+ASs **or** VAs+/-ALs/ASs; (not gs) (Theatre)
King Alfred's Winchester (Coll) – 260 pts 15u; gs; (Drama)
Queen Margaret (UC) – BCC (Drama courses)
Ripon & York (Coll) – BCC/BB (Thea Film TV)
Surrey Roehampton – 260–240 pts (inc CC in thea st/soc sci/hum; Single Hons courses B thea st pref); VA B; (Drama Thea St)

240 pts **Brighton** – 240 pts approx (Thea Vis Art)
Central England – 240 pts approx (Perf Des/Comm)
Chester (Coll) – ALs (220–200 pts inc C drama/thea st/perf arts)+AS **or** VAs (220–200 pts inc C drama subj)+AS; AS(20–40+ pts) (Drama courses)
Durham – 240 pts approx (Performing Arts)
King Alfred's Winchester (Coll) – 240 pts 12u; gs; (Drama St)
Liverpool John Moores – 240 pts – 3ALs (inc B drama/thea st/perf st) **or** VA A (Perf Arts); (Drama/Thea St)
Plymouth – BCD (Theatre Perf/Engl)
Rose Bruford (Coll) – 240 pts approx (Acting; Actor Mus; Dir; Stg Mgt; Ltg Des)
Ulster – CCC (Thea St; Hum (Thea St))
Welsh (CMus/Dr) – 240–140 pts (Actg; Stg Mgt; Des)

220 pts **Bangor** – 220 pts – ALs; (not gs) (Welsh medium) (Astudiaethau Theatr a'r Cyfryngau)
Kingston – 220 pts (inc 2x6u or equiv); gs; (Drama)
Middlesex – 220 pts approx (Perf Arts (Drama); Tech Thea Arts)
Wolverhampton – 220–160 pts 12u – DDD/CDE/BD/CC **or** DD+bb **or** VA12u CC; gs; (Drama)

200 pts **Bristol** – BB (Drama/Engl)
Dartington (CA) – BB–CD (Perf Thea; Perf Writ; Arts Mgt courses)
De Montfort (Leicester) – 200 pts; (not gs) (Perf/Arts)
Glamorgan – 200 pts approx (Drama courses)
Huddersfield – 200 pts 12u – ALs (inc C relevant subj) **or** ALs+ASs **or** VAs+/-ALs/ASs; gs; (Thea St courses)
King Alfred's Winchester (Coll) – 220 pts approx (Drama St Tour Herit Mgt)
Leeds (Bretton Hall) – 200–160 pts approx (Drama/Arts Educ; Thea courses)
Staffordshire – 200 pts (inc CC)+/-ASs **or** VA12u CC; gs; (Drama/Thea Arts)

180 pts **Central Lancashire** – 180 pts 12u; audition; gs; (Contemp Perf Arts)
Cheltenham & Glos (CHE) – 180 pts minimum (Performance Arts)
Coventry – 180 pts approx (Thea Prof Prac)
Hull (Scarborough) – 180 pts approx (Theatre Studies courses)
Liverpool Hope (Coll) – 180 pts approx (Drama courses)
London Inst (CFash) – 180 pts approx (Cost/Mk-up Perf Arts)
Manchester Met – 180–160 pts approx; (Drama courses; Contemp Arts)
Northampton (UC) – 180–160 pts approx (Drama courses)
Northumbria – BC (Drama)
Ripon & York (Coll) – 180 pts approx (Dance (Perf Comm Arts); Drama (Perf Comm Arts))
St Martin's (Coll) – CDE/CC (Perf Arts/Drama)
St Mary's (Coll) – 12u – BC–CC **or** VAs; gs; (Drama)
South Bank – 180 pts approx (Wrld Thea courses)

160 pts **Birmingham (Westhill)** – CC (Hum Crea Arts – Dance)

        Bishop Grosseteste (Coll) – CC (inc C drama/thea st/perf arts/media) **or** C+c or VA12u CC; (Drama)

        Central (Sch Sp/Dr) – CC (Theatre courses)

        Chichester (UC) – 160 pts (inc C); (Thea/Scrn St)

        Cumbria (CAD) – 160 pts – CC **or** ASs (contact coll) **or** VA; (Perf St)

        De Montfort (Bedford) – 160 pts; ALs **or** ALs+ASs **or** VAs+/-ALs/ASs; gs; (Theatre joint courses)

        Derby – 160 pts 12u – CC **or** DD+ee **or** VA12u CC **or** VA6u C+AL(D); gs; (Perf Media Arts)

        Edge Hill (CHE) – CC (Drama courses)

        North London – 160 pts 1x12u **or** 2x6u (AL applicants to inc C Engl/thea st/film st/media st/dance/drama); (Perf Arts; Thea St; Thea St Comb Hons)

        Warrington (CI) – CC not ASs only; gs (Perf Arts/Bus Mgt; Perf Arts)

140 pts **Bolton (IHE)** – 140 pts approx (Theatre Studies courses)

        Bromley (Coll) – 140 pts 12u; gs; (Comb St Perf Arts)

        Derby – 140 pts 12u – CD **or** DE+ee **or** VA12u CD **or** VA6u+AL(D); gs; (Thea St Comb)

        Sunderland – 140 pts – 2ALs **or** ALs+ASs **or** VA12u+/-AL/ASs; gs; BTEC accepted; (Perf Arts St)

        Worcester (UC) – 140 pts 12u – CD **or** ALs+ASs; gs; (Drama)

120 pts **Barnsley (Coll)** – 120 pts approx (Perf Arts Comb St)

        Bishop Grosseteste (Coll) – DD (inc AL pref thea st/perf arts/drama) **or** D+dd **or** VA12u (Perf Arts); (Drama/Commun)

        North London – 120 pts 1x12u **or** 2x6u; (Int Perf Arts/Tech; Perf Arts Tech)

100 pts **and below**

        Bath Spa (UC) – (Drama/Engl)

        Birmingham (Sch Sp/Dr) – (Acting; Acting (Mus Thea))

        Central (Sch Sp/Dr) – Audition (Acting)

        Cumbria (CAD) – (Thea St)

        Doncaster (Coll) – 100 pts – ALs **or** ALs+ASs **or** VAs+/-ALs/ASs; gs; (Theatre)

        Greenwich (Central Sch) – EE (Speech and Drama BEd)

        Guildford (Sch Acting) – Audition (Actg/Mus Thea)

        Laban Centre – (Dance; Theatre)

        Liverpool (LIPA) – unconditional after successful audition (All Perf Arts courses inc Snd Tech)

        London Drama Centre – Audition only (Acting)

        London Mountview – Audition (Mus Thea)

        Manchester Met – Audition (Acting)

        Paisley (Craigie) – (Drama QTS)

        Plymouth – Audition – offer varies (Thea/Perf St)

        Queen Margaret (UC) – (Stg Mgt Thea Prod)

        Royal Scottish (AMD) – (Drama)

        Southampton (Inst) – (Media Cult St)

        Swansea (IHE) – 60 pts approx (Engl St Drama Media St)

        Trinity Carmarthen (Coll) – (Thea St)

        Wimbledon (SA) – portfolio assess (Thea Des; Thea-Tech Arts Des; Thea Cost Des/Interp)

Diploma of Higher Education courses

  80 pts Birmingham (Sch Sp/Dr); Central (Sch Sp/Dr) (Stg Mgt; Des); Liverpool (LIPA) (Prod Perf Tech); Manchester Met.

Higher National Diploma courses

100 pts Birmingham City (Coll); Blackpool & Fylde (Coll); Buckinghamshire Chilterns (UC); Chichester (UC); Coventry; Crawley (Coll) gs; De Montfort; Doncaster (Coll); Dudley (CT); Glasgow (Coll); Gloucestershire (CAT); Great Yarmouth (Coll); Hertfordshire; Kidderminster (Coll); Liverpool (CmC); Llandrillo (Coll); Nescot;

Newcastle (Coll); Northbrook (Coll); Oldham (Coll); St Helens (Coll); Salford; Salisbury (Coll); Somerset (CAT); South Devon (Coll); South East Essex (Coll); Southwark (Coll); Suffolk (Coll); Tameside (Coll); Thames (Coll) (Perf Arts); Trinity Carmarthen (Coll); Wigan & Leigh (Coll); Yorkshire Coast (Coll).

Other Diploma courses:

Birmingham (Sch Sp/Dr); Guildford (Sch Acting); London Academy of Music and Dramatic Art (LAMDA) (Stg Mgt Tech Thea 2 yrs) (Class Actg 1 yr) (Actg 3 yrs); London Mountview (Acad Thea Arts) (Actg; Mus Thea; Stg Mgt Tech Des); Manchester Met; Middlesex; Queen Margaret (UC) (Actg; Stg Mgt); Rose Bruford (Coll); Royal Scottish (AMD) (Dr Art; Stg Mgt); Welsh (CMus/Dr).

Alternative Offers:

IB offers: Aberystwyth 30 pts; Birmingham 33 pts; Bristol 28 pts inc 5 in Engl/history or other appropriate subject; Brunel 32 pts; Exeter 30 pts; Hull Average of 5; Kent 32 pts, H 13 pts; Lancaster 32–30 pts; London (RH) 30 pts; Loughborough 30 pts; Plymouth 26 pts; St Martin's (Coll) 28 pts; Surrey Roehampton (Comb St) 30 pts; Warwick 34–32 pts.

Scottish Qualifications: Glasgow BBBB; Queen Margaret (UC) ABBCC

Overseas applicants: Leeds (Bretton Hall) Offers one, two or three-year diploma courses which provide an individually designed programme of study and do not require standard entry requirements. These give an opportunity for overseas students to work alongside Honours Degree students in a very rich arts context.

CHOOSING YOUR COURSE (See also **Ch.1**)

Subject information: Drama is an increasingly popular subject amongst women (approximately 6000 women are on courses compared with about 2500 men). Your choice of course will depend on your interests and preferences. For example, how much theory or practice do you want? It is worth remembering that by choosing a different degree course your interest in drama can be maintained by joining amateur drama groups. Performance Arts and English courses could also be considered as well as courses offered by the stage schools. See also **Appendix 1**.

Special features: Bangor The course is taught in Welsh. **Birmingham (Sch Sp/Dr)** (Acting; Acting Musical Theatre) A three-year fully vocational degree course in acting with a pathway for musical theatre in years 2 and 3. The first year shares a common year with students opting, if they meet the required standard in singing and movement, for the musical theatre pathway which provides a greater emphasis on singing, dance and musical performance. This is not a separate course as the students share a number of classes and productions with the Acting students. Funding possible through Dance and Drama Award Scheme. **Brunel** The course focuses on 20th century theory and has a strong practical experience. **Coventry** The Arts Practice and Cultural Policy course brings together competency in performance or visual arts with administration. **Luton** Drama Studies offers a theoretical overview of dramatic writing in English and American Literature. **Manchester** Not primarily an acting course. **Manchester Met** The Contemporary Arts course provides opportunities for creative practice and academic studies in dance, drama, live arts, music, visual arts and writing. **South Bank** A degree in Acting is taught at the Italia Conti Academy which includes stage management. *NOW CHECK PROSPECTUSES AND WEB SITES.*

Top universities and colleges (Teaching Quality) (see Ch.4): Including Dance and Performing Arts and Film: Bournemouth; Bristol; Brunel; Canterbury Christ Church (UC); Central (Sch Sp/Dr); Chichester (UC); Dartington (CA); De Montfort; Exeter; Hull; Hull (Scarborough); Kent; Lancaster; Leeds (Bretton Hall); London (Gold), (RH); Loughborough; Manchester Met; Middlesex; North London; Northern (Sch Contemp Dance); Northumbria; Ulster; Warwick; not all institutions assessed.

Top universities and colleges (Research) (see Ch.4): Including Dance and Performing Arts: Birmingham; Bristol; Exeter; Glasgow; Hull; Kent; Lancaster; London (Gold), (RH); Reading; Surrey; Surrey Roehampton (Dance); Warwick.

Study opportunities abroad: Aberystwyth; Birmingham; Cheltenham & Glos (CHE); East Anglia; Glasgow; Hull; Kent; King Alfred's Winchester (Coll); Lancaster; Liverpool John Moores; London (Gold), (RH); Manchester; Manchester Met; North London; Plymouth; Surrey Roehampton; Warwick.

ADMISSIONS INFORMATION

Number of applicants per place (approx): Aberystwyth 10; Birmingham 29; Bishop Grosseteste (Coll) 4; Bournemouth 3; Bristol 44; Brunel 9; Cambridge (Hom) 4; Central (Sch Sp/Dr) 21; Cheltenham & Glos (CHE) 7; Chester (Coll) 14; Dartington (CA) 8; De Montfort (Perf Arts) 33; East Anglia 20; Edge Hill (CHE) 8; Exeter 20; Glamorgan 6; Huddersfield 4; Hull 16; Hull (Scarborough) 2; Kent 24; King Alfred's Winchester (Coll) 15; Lancaster 18; Leeds (Bretton Hall) 10; Liverpool (LIPA) 12 average; London Drama Centre 33; London (Gold) 28, (RH) 10; London Mountview (Tech/Des) 3, (Mus Thea) 8; Loughborough 16; Manchester 30; Manchester Met 48; Middlesex 26; North London 20; Northumbria 25; Queen Margaret (UC) 4; Reading 17; Ripon & York (Coll) 9; St Martin's (Coll) 11; Surrey Roehampton 6; Warwick 18; Welsh (CMus/Dr) 37; Wimbledon (SA) (Thea Des) 2, (Thea Arts) 3, (Thea Cost) 3; Worcester (UC) 4.

Admissions Tutor's advice: Bristol Assesses each case on its merits, paying attention to candidate's educational and cultural opportunities. Particularly interested in applicants who have already shown some evidence of commitment in their approach to drama in practical work, theatre-going, film viewing or reading. One fifth of applicants are called for interview and take part in practical sessions. They may present any art work, photography or similar material. (London Board Practical Music not acceptable for Drama/Music unless offered with theoretical music + one other A-level.) **Brunel** All applicants to whom an offer may be made will be auditioned, involving a practical workshop, voice, movement improvisation and a short prepared speech. Offers unlikely to be made to those with less than a grade B in drama or theatre studies. **De Montfort** Emphasis on practical work – no written exams. **East Anglia** Looks for candidates with a sound balance of academic and practical skills. **Hull** Interviews two groups of 18 for whole day which presents a mini-version of the course, with entire staff and number of current students present. Offers then made to about half. Selection process is all-important. More applicants for the Joint Honours courses with English, Theology, Classical Studies, American Studies or Modern Language who have a conventional half-hour interview. Drama/English is the most popular combination and the offer includes a B in English. **Kent** No Single Honours candidate accepted without interview. Emphasis equally on academic and practical abilities. **Lancaster** (Thea St) Candidates invited for interview and should be prepared to take part in a workshop with other candidates. We are just as interested in backstage people as actors and now have an arts administration option. **Liverpool (LIPA)** Candidates prepare a brief (500 words) review of a live theatre performance or film they have seen. Two practical audition pieces and a song follow. The first piece must be devised by the candidate, the second is selected from a list of Shakespeare pieces. **London (RH)** At interview we look for students who are mentally agile and versatile who enjoy reading as well as taking part in productions. **Loughborough** Offers in terms of A-levels not set. Candidates judged as individuals. Applicants with unconventional subject combinations and mature students considered. Final selection based on interview and audition. Applicants ought to show experience of practical drama, preferably beyond school plays. **Middlesex** (Perf Arts) Audition important; ability to perform in more than one discipline essential. A-levels not required but the following add weight to an application: for Dance, A-level dance; for Drama, A-levels in theatre studies, drama or English literature; for Music, A-level music. **Warwick** Interview is important to assess academic potential and particularly commitment to, and suitability for, teaching; offers therefore variable.

Planning your UCAS personal statement (see Ch.4): Full details of any practical experience must be given (preferably outside school or college) with the names of the productions, dates etc. Visits to the theatre should also be mentioned, describing the range of productions you have seen and reviewing the acting/production etc, giving your preferences. Visits to the cinema and background reading are also important, as is any back-stage experience. A scrapbook of theatre reviews taken from the national press could be a useful reference source. **De Montfort** A keen interest in 20th century theatre and dance. See also **Appendix 1**.

Selection interviews (see Ch.4): Bristol (1 in 5); Brunel (popular course – highly selective); Central (Sch Sp/Dr) (W); Central Lancashire (W) (T); De Montfort (W) (T); Liverpool (LIPA); London (RH) (W); London Mountview (voice, movement and singing sessions plus acting pieces); Welsh (CMus/Dr) (T); All institutions, usually with auditions which will usually involve solo and group tests.

Interview questions (see Ch.4): All applicants are auditioned either individually or in workshops with other applicants. In some cases there may be written tests. See under **Admissions Tutor's advice**.

Reasons for rejection (non-academic): Lack of general education, dedication or talent. Immaturity. Lack of flexibility and ability to respond to a challenge. Lacking in interpersonal skills, therefore unsuitable for group activities. Poor ambition. Wrong expectations of the course. Several students clearly want a drama school acting training rather than a degree course. Not enough background reading.

GAP YEAR ADVICE

Bristol We prefer applications in the year of entry but candidates must be available for interview between December and March; **Glasgow** No; **Loughborough** Cannot consider deferred options; **Manchester Met** Prefers a gap year.

Institutions willing to defer entry after A-levels: Aberystwyth; Birmingham; Brunel; Cheltenham & Glos (CHE); Chester (Coll); Dartington (CA); De Montfort; Derby; East Anglia (some); Glamorgan; Huddersfield; Hull; Kent; Lancaster; Liverpool John Moores; London (RH); Manchester Met (Acting) (No); North London; Northumbria; Plymouth; Rose Bruford (Coll) (No – prefers to interview candidates during the year immediately prior to entry); Surrey Roehampton; Warwick; Welsh (CMus/Dr).

AFTER RESULTS ADVICE

Institutions which may accept the same points score after A-levels: Aberystwyth; Birmingham; Bradford; Bristol; Brunel; Central (Sch Sp/Dr); Cheltenham & Glos (CHE); Derby; East Anglia (some); Huddersfield; Hull; Lancaster (No); Leeds (Bretton Hall); London (RH); Loughborough; Manchester; Manchester Met; Middlesex; Ripon & York (Coll); Rose Bruford (Coll); Surrey Roehampton; Warwick (No).

Institutions which may accept lower grades/points score after A-levels: Aberystwyth; Bristol; Brunel; Cambridge (Hom); Cheltenham & Glos (CHE); Chester (Coll); Derby; East Anglia (some); Exeter; Glasgow; Liverpool Hope (Coll); Liverpool John Moores (No); Loughborough; Manchester Met; Rose Bruford (Coll); Surrey Roehampton; Warwick.

Offers to applicants repeating A-levels: Higher Hull, Warwick; **Possibly higher** Cambridge (Hom), London (RH); **Same** Brunel, East Anglia, Leeds (Bretton Hall) (further audition required), Liverpool Hope (Coll), Liverpool John Moores, Loughborough, Surrey Roehampton.

Probable vacancies from June 2001 and in Clearing (see Ch.4): Despite the popularity of this subject, vacancies were declared in the majority of universities and colleges in Clearing last year, a pattern likely to be repeated. Many universities are likely to have vacancies in Theatre Studies.

NEW GRADUATE DESTINATIONS AND EMPLOYMENT (1999 HESA) (see **Ch.4**)

Of 1802 graduates surveyed, 993 entered full-time employment, 272 went on to further study and 94 were believed to be unemployed.

ECONOMICS

NB The information supplied by the universities and colleges this year varies considerably and the offers listed below should be used as a first source of reference only. Many institutions will accept combinations of Advanced (AL), Advanced Subsidiary (AS) and Vocational Advanced (VA) level qualifications to achieve the required points total, but applicants must check web sites and prospectuses for full details of all offers. Grades and points totals shown should be regarded as the minimum levels to be achieved, but offers may be adjusted downwards when results are known. The points totals shown to the left of the institutions are for ease of reference only. It must not be assumed that tariff points are always used by institutions or that they can be substituted for an offer in grades. The level of an offer is not necessarily indicative of the quality of a course. To calculate your offers see Chapter 4 and the inside fold of the back cover.

Special subject requirements/preferences: A-level: Exeter Mathematics leads to lower offer. **Swansea** Economics and mathematics. **Bristol, Leicester, Warwick** Mathematics (for LG11 see under **Mathematics**). **London (SOAS)** Offers below are for applicants without mathematics. **Oxford** Full A-level in mathematics recommended. **Warwick** Business studies **and** economics not accepted as two A-levels. **GCSE:** Mathematics and occasionally English and a foreign language required. **Aberystwyth** 50% grade A or B. **Bangor** Average grade B. **Bath** Majority of A or B grades. **Bristol** Grade A or B in all subjects. **Cambridge, Oxford** Grade As in most subjects preferred. **Durham** Minimum three As and four Bs. Mathematics grade A if not taken at A-level. **Essex** Eight As or Bs including mathematics and English. **Exeter** Mathematics/English at grade B or above plus a majority of As and Bs. **Hull** Three subjects grade A, three subjects grade B, three subjects grade C average preferred. **Leicester** (Econ/Law) Six subjects grade A or B. **London (RH)** A high proportion of As and Bs, mathematics grade B. **Nottingham** Six subjects at grade A including mathematics A or B. **City, Portsmouth, Surrey** Grade A or B in mathematics if not taken at A-level. **London (LSE)** Grade A or B for most subjects. **Southampton** Good mathematics (grade B) and science. Remaining subjects at grade A or B preferred. A good range of As and Bs. **Aberdeen, Dundee, Edinburgh, Glasgow, St Andrews** English, mathematics and a foreign language. **Warwick** For LG11 see under **Mathematics**. **York** Mainly As and Bs including mathematics.

360 pts **and above**
        Cambridge – Offers, mainly in grades, vary between colleges (Econ)
        Oxford – Offers vary between candidates (Pol Phil Econ; Econ/Mgt; Econ)
350 pts **Southampton** – 350 pts 21u (inc 220 pts from subjs inc B lang for some
        courses); (Econ courses)
340 pts **Bristol** – AAB–ABB (inc maths Lang/Euro courses); (not gs) (Econ; Econ/Euro;
        Econ/Economet)
        Bristol – AAB–ABC (inc maths); (not gs) (Econ/Fin; Econ/Pol; Econ/Maths;
        Econ/Mgt)
        Lancaster – AAB (Econ/USA/Can)
        London (LSE) – AAB (if no AL maths)-ABB (Econ; Econ/Econ Hist)
        London (UCL) – AAB **or** 3ALs+AS/VA; (Economics)
        Nottingham – AAB gs (Econ courses except under **320 pts**)
        St Andrews – AAB (Econ/Int Rel)
        Warwick – AAB (Econ courses)
320 pts **Bristol** – ABB–BBC (inc maths); (not gs) (Econ/Sociol; Econ/Econ Hist;
        Econ/Acc)
        Durham – 320 pts 18u – ABB **or** AB+bb **or** BB+dd (not gs) (Econ; Bus Econ;
        Econ/Fr)
        Edinburgh – ABB (1 sitting) (Econ courses)
        Kent – ABB (Econ/Law; Econ/Sociol)
        London (LSE) – ABB (Economet Maths Econ)
        London (RH) – 320–300 pts – ABB–BBB; (not gs) (Econ; Fin Bus Econ)
        London (UCL) – ABB **or** 3ALs+AS/VA; (Econ)

Nottingham – ABB (Ind Econ)
Sheffield – 320 pts approx (Bus Geog; Econ/Geog)

300 pts **Aston** – BBB (Int Bus/Econ)
Bath – BBB (not gs) (Econ; Econ/Pol; Econ/Int Dev)
Birmingham – BBB–BBC (Econ; Econ/Lang; Econ/Modn Econ Hist)
Brunel – 300–260 pts 2x6u; (not gs) (Econ; Econ/Bus Fin; Econ/Mgt; Fin/Acc; Bus Econ)
Cardiff – BBC–BCC (Econ courses except under **280 pts**)
East Anglia – 300–280 pts 18u – BBB–BBC **or** BB+cc **or** BBC+e **or** VA12u (280 pts **or** 200 pts+C); gs; (Econ courses; Bus Econ)
Exeter – 300 pts 18u – BBB–BBC **or** BB+bb/bc **or** VAs (contact univ); (not gs) (Econ courses except under **260 pts**)
Hull – BBB (Pol Phil Econ)
Lancaster – 300 pts approx (Econ; Econ/OR; Econ/Maths)
Leeds – BBB (Econ with Maths/Stats/Pol/Soc Pol/Sociol/Mgt St)
Liverpool – 300 pts – ALs **or** ALs+ASs **or** VAs+/-ALs/ASs; (Econ/Econ Hist; Econ/Maths)
London (UCL) – BBB–BBC **or** 3ALs+AS/VA; (Econ/Geog)
Manchester – ABC–BBC (BEcon Sci)
Manchester – BBB–BBC (BA Econ courses)
Newcastle – BBB–BBC (Econ Bus Mgt; Econ/Acc)
St Andrews – BBB (Econ courses except under **340 pts**)
Sheffield – BBB (Econ; Econ/Pol; Econ Maths; Econ Stats)
Sussex – BBB (Econ courses)
York – 21–18u – BBB **or** BB+bb **or** VAs (contact univ); (Econ courses)

280 pts **Aberdeen** – BBC (Econ courses)
Aberystwyth – 280–220 pts 18u – 3ALs **or** ALs+ASs **or** VAs+/-ALs/ASs; gs; (Econ; Econ/Acc Fin; Econ/Mark; Econ/Int Pol)
Belfast (Queen's) – BBC (BSc Econ courses except under **240 pts**)
Birmingham – BBC (Maths Econ; Econ Stats)
Cardiff – BBC (Econ/Mgt St; Econ/Phil; Econ/Soc Phil/App Eth)
City – BBC/AB (Econ/Acc)
Essex – 280 pts 3x6u – BBC; VAs (contact univ); (not gs) (Econ courses)
Glasgow – BBC (Econ courses)
Hertfordshire – 280–240 pts 1x12u **or** 2x6u; gs; (Econ; Bus Econ; Econ/Fin; Int Econ)
Keele – 280 pts **or** equiv AS accepted; gs; (Econ courses)
Kent – 280 pts approx/AB (Econ Euro; Econ courses except under **320 pts**; Econ/Comp)
Leeds – BBC (Econ; Econ Modn Lang)
Leicester – 18u – BBC **or** ALs+ASs **or** VAs+/-ALs/ASs; gs; (BA Econ; Econ/Law)
London (QM) – 280 pts – 3x6u **or** 2x6u (AL maths pref); (Econ courses)
London (SOAS) – 280 pts approx (Econ courses)
Loughborough – 18u – BB+C/cc **or** VA12u BB+AL(C) **or** VA6u+2ASs; (not gs) (Econ courses except below)
Loughborough – 18u – B+C (lang)+B/bb **or** VA12u BB+AL(C) **or** VA6u CC+2ASs; (not gs) (Econ/Fr/Ger/Span)
Newcastle – BBC (Econ courses except under **300 pts**)
Reading – BBC–BCC (Econ courses except under **220 pts**)
Sheffield – BBC (Econ; Econ/Economet; Econ/Sociol; Econ/Soc Phil; Econ/Jap St; Econ/Kor St; Russ/Econ)
Stirling – BBC (Bus St/Econ; Econ/Fin St; Econ)
Surrey – 280 pts 18u – ALs **or** ALs+ASs **or** VAs (depends on subj)+/-ALs/ASs; (not gs) (Economics)
Swansea – 280 pts 18u – BBC/AA–AB **or** ALs+ASs **or** VAs+/-ALs/ASs; (Econ courses)
Ulster – BBC (Law/Econ)

260 pts **Bradford** – 260 pts 12u; gs; (Econ; Econ/Hist; Econ/Pol; Econ/Sociol; Econ/Soc Psy)
Bristol UWE – 260–240 pts gs (Econ courses)
City – BCC/BB (Econ)
Exeter – 260 pts 18u – BCC **or** BB+bc **or** VAs (contact univ) gs; (Econ Pol Dev; Econ/Stats courses; Econ Pol Dev Euro)
Hull – BCC/BB (BSc Econ; Econ joint courses)
Leicester – 18u – BCC **or** 2ALs+ASs (inc C maths); gs; (BSc Econ; Bus Econ)
Liverpool – 260 pts – ALs **or** ALs+ASs **or** VAs+/-ALs/ASs; (Econ; Bus Econ/Comp Sci; Bus Econ)
London (UCL) – BCC **or** 3ALs+AS/VA; (Econ/Stats; Econ Bus/E Euro St)
Salford – BCC–CCC (Econ; Bus Econ; Bus Econ/Gam St)
Stirling – BCC–CCC/BC (Econ courses except under **280 pts**)
Surrey – 260 pts 18u – BBC **or** ALs+ASs **or** VAs (depends on subj)+/- ALs/ASs; (not gs) (Bus Econ/Comp)
Surrey – BCC (Econ with Int Bus; Econ/Fr; Econ/Ger; Econ/Span; Econ/Swed; Econ/Sociol)
240 pts **Aberystwyth** – 240–200 pts approx (Econ courses except under **280 pts**)
Bangor – 240 pts; gs; (Econ courses except under **220 pts**)
Belfast (Queen's) – CCC/BB (Agric Econ – GCSE or AS maths reqd)
Bristol UWE – 240–200 pts 18u pref/12u – ALs **or** ALs+ASs **or** VAs+/- ALs/ASs; (Econ; Int Bus Econ)
Coventry – 240–180 pts approx (Econ courses)
Dundee – CCC/BB (Econ; Fin Econ 3 yr BSc)
Glasgow Caledonian – CCC/BC (Bus Econ)
Heriot-Watt – 240 pts 18u – CCC **or** VAs; gs; (Econ courses)
Kent – CCC/BB (Econ/Fr/Ger; Econ/Economet)
Liverpool John Moores – 240–180 pts (inc 2ALs soc sci pref **or** VA) – ALs **or** ALs+ASs **or** VAs+/-ALs/ASs; (Econ courses)
London (Gold) – BCD/BC (Econ/Soc Pol; Econ Pol; Econ Pol Pblc Pol)
Manchester Met – 240 pts; (Econ courses)
Nottingham Trent – 240 pts 18u – CCC **or** ALs+ASs **or** VAs+/-AL/ASs; gs (AL only); (Econ; Bus Econ; Econ/Fin Serv; Euro Econ)
Portsmouth – 240–220 pts approx (Bus Econ; Econ)
Salford – CCC (Pol Econ)
South Bank – 240–180 pts approx (Econ courses)
Sunderland – CCC (Acc/Econ)
Ulster – CCC (Econ; Econ/Govt)
230 pts **Buckingham** – 230 pts 21u – 3ALs **or** 3ALs+AS; (Econ courses)
220 pts **Bangor** – 220 pts; gs; (Econ/Fr/Ger)
De Montfort (Leicester) – 220 pts – 2ALs **or** VA12u; (Bus Econ)
Edinburgh – CCD (Agric Env Econ)
Kingston – 220–180 pts 2x6u; (Econ courses)
Middlesex – 220–180 pts approx (Econ courses)
Oxford Brookes – 220–140 pts approx (Econ courses offer varies with 2nd subject)
Plymouth – 220–200 pts approx (Econ courses)
Reading – CCD/BB (Agric Econ)
200 pts **Central England** – 200 pts 12u – BB **or** CC+c **or** VA12u (200 pts); gs; (Econ; Bus Econ)
Central Lancashire – 200–180 pts 12u; (Econ/Bus)
Central Lancashire – 200 pts 12u; (Econ/Geog; Econ/Int Bus; Econ/Law; Econ/Mark)
Derby – 200 pts 12u – CDD **or** CD+dd **or** VA12u CD+AL(D); gs; (Fin Econ)
Dundee – CDD (Econ; Fin Econ 4 yr BSc)
Glamorgan – 200–180 pts approx (Econ courses)
Huddersfield – 200 pts approx (Econ courses)
London Guildhall – CDD (Econ; Fin Econ; Bus Econ; Glob Econ)

Manchester Met – CDD/CC **or** ALs+ASs **or** VAs+/-ALs/ASs; (Hum/Soc St (Econ))
Northumbria – 200–180 pts approx (Econ courses)
Paisley – CDD (App Econ; Bus Econ)
Portsmouth – 200 pts – ALs **or** ALs+ASs **or** VSs; gs; (Econ; Bus Econ; Int Bus Econ)
Sunderland – 200 pts approx (Bus Econ; Econ Comb St)
Westminster – 200 pts approx (Economics)
Wolverhampton – 200–180 pts approx; gs (Econ courses)

190 pts **North London** – 160 pts inc 160 pts from 2ALs **or** VAs; (Econ courses)
180 pts **Anglia** – 180 pts approx (Econ courses)
Central England – BC–CC (Bus Econ; Econ)
East London – 180 pts approx (Econ courses)
Greenwich – 180 pts approx (Econ courses)
Teesside – 180–160 pts approx (Econ courses)
160 pts **Doncaster (Coll)** – 160 pts – CC **or** ALs+ASs **or** VAs +/- AL/ASs; gs; (Econ/Leg St)
Lincolnshire & Humberside – 160 pts (Econ/Fd St; Econ Foren Sci; Econ/Journal)
Napier – DDE (Bus Econ courses)
Northampton (UC) – 160 pts approx (Econ Comb)
Staffordshire – CC **or** CD+AS(40 pts); gs; (Econ; Bus/Fin Econ; Euro Econ; Leis Econ)
Sunderland – 160 pts approx (Econ courses except under **200 pts**)
140 pts **Abertay Dundee** – CD (Econ courses)
Bolton (IHE) – CD (Bus Econ courses)
Buckinghamshire Chilterns (UC) – 140 pts approx (Econ courses)
Derby – 140 pts 12u – CD **or** DE+ee **or** VA12u CD **or** VA6u C+AL(D); (Econ Comb Hons)
London Guildhall – CD (Econ St)
Northampton (UC) – 140 pts approx (Econ courses except under **160 pts**)
Strathclyde – CD (Maths/Stats/Econ)
120 pts **and below**
Coventry – (Am/Euro Econ – mainly for overseas students)
Suffolk (Coll) – (Econ courses)

Leeds Met – (contact university)

Diploma of Higher Education courses
80 pts Oxford Brookes.

Alternative Offers:

EB offers: Aberystwyth 70%; Bath 70%; De Montfort 60%; Keele 65%; Lancaster 70%; Surrey 70%.

IB offers: Aberdeen 30 pts; Aberystwyth 26 pts; Anglia 28 pts; Bangor 32 pts; Bath 32 pts inc H666; Birmingham 32 pts inc 16 pts H; Bristol 34–32 pts inc H665 inc maths; Brunel 30 pts; Buckingham 26 pts; Cambridge H777; Cardiff H655 + 14 pts; City 28 pts min H655 S655; Dundee 29 pts H 15 pts; East Anglia 30 pts; Essex 30 pts; Exeter 33–30 pts; Greenwich 24 pts; Heriot-Watt 28 pts; Hull 28 pts; Keele 27 pts; Kent 28 pts, H 13 pts; Kingston 30–28 pts; Lancaster 32–30 pts; Leeds 30 pts inc 15 pts Highers; Leicester (Econ) 30 pts; London (LSE) 38 pts H666 (39 pts if no A-level maths), (RH) 30 pts, (UCL) 32 pts; London Guildhall 28 pts 7 subjects 24 pts 6 subjects; Loughborough 30–28 pts inc H555; Manchester Met 24 pts; Newcastle 30 pts min; Nottingham H655; Oxford H777; Plymouth 24 pts; St Andrews 28 pts; Salford 30 pts; Southampton 30–28 pts; Staffordshire 24 pts; Stirling 28 pts; Surrey 28 pts; Sussex 15 pts Highers; Swansea 32–30 pts; Warwick 36–34 pts; York 30 pts inc H5 maths.

Irish offers: Aberdeen BBBB; Aberystwyth BBBCC; Bangor BBBCC; Brunel AAAABB; East Anglia BBBCC; Greenwich CCCCC; Keele BBBCC; Leeds ABB; London Guildhall CCCCC; Sunderland BCCC; Surrey BBBBC; Warwick AAAAB; York BBBC.

Scottish Qualifications: Aberdeen BBBB; Dundee BBCC; Edinburgh ABBBC; Glasgow ABBB; Glasgow Caledonian BBCC; Heriot-Watt BBBC; Napier (Bus Econ) BCCC; Paisley BCC; St Andrews BBBC; Stirling BBCC; Strathclyde BBBB.

Overseas applicants: East Anglia Far Eastern, Nigerian and Cypriot students. **De Montfort** Induction courses available. **Hull** Living costs 30% lower than in London. **Leeds, East Anglia,** and **Newcastle** English courses available.

CHOOSING YOUR COURSE (See also **Ch.1**)

Subject information: Applicants without a background of economics at A-level should be prepared for study involving some mathematics, statistics and, depending on which course you choose, economic and social history, industrial policies, the British economy and labour history, money, banking and regional economics. Business Studies, Accountancy, Estate Management, Financial Services, Banking and Insurance and Quantity Surveying degree courses might also be considered. Suitability for employment is an important factor in selection: interviews for sandwich courses are designed, in part, to test the applicant's suitability for work experience. See also **Appendix 1** under **Accountancy, Actuarial Work, Banking, Business**.

Special features: Aberdeen Students choose between Economic Science with a mathematical bias or Political Economy. **Aberystwyth** Complementary subjects such as law, politics and geography can be taken. **Bristol UWE** Economics, politics and sociology are taken by all students in year 1 with additional modules in other subjects. Thereafter students follow a choice of pathways. **Central England** In addition to Economics there is a wide choice of optional subjects including banking, labour economics, public sector economics and business forecasting. **Hertfordshire** The Business Economics degree has an optional year in industry. **Kent** The Economics course has a strong European emphasis with the opportunity to spend a year in France, Germany, Greece or Spain. **Lancaster** There is a USA/Canada route with year 2 abroad. **Leicester** The BSc degree places greater emphasis on statistics, mathematics and computer applications. **London Guildhall** Economics can be taken as a joint or minor subject. **Nottingham** All Economics degrees have a common first year followed by specialist studies. **Salford** Courses are offered in Chinese and Economics. **Warwick** Options in languages, business studies, politics and international relations. *NOW CHECK PROSPECTUSES AND WEB SITES.*

Top universities and colleges (Teaching Quality): Aberdeen; Abertay Dundee; St Andrews; Staffordshire; Stirling; not all institutions assessed.

Top universities and colleges (Research): Aberdeen; Birmingham; Bristol; Cambridge; Dundee; East Anglia; Edinburgh; Essex; Exeter; Glasgow; Keele; Kent; Leicester; Liverpool; London (LSE), (QM), (UCL); Loughborough; Manchester; Newcastle; Nottingham; Oxford; Reading; St Andrews; Southampton; Stirling; Strathclyde; Surrey; Sussex; Swansea; Warwick; York.

Study opportunities abroad: Abertay Dundee; Aberystwyth; Bangor; Bristol; Brunel; Buckingham; Cardiff; Central England; City; Dundee; East Anglia; East London; Exeter; Greenwich; Heriot-Watt; Hull; Keele; Kingston; Lancaster; Leicester; Leeds; Liverpool John Moores; London (LSE), (QM), (RH); London Guildhall; Loughborough; Manchester; Manchester Met; Middlesex; Nottingham Trent; Plymouth; Portsmouth; Reading; Salford; Sheffield; Southampton; Staffordshire; Sunderland; Teesside; Surrey; Warwick; Westminster; Wolverhampton; York.

Work opportunities abroad: Bangor; Bath; Bristol; Brunel; City; Greenwich; Leeds; Manchester Met; Newcastle; Staffordshire; York.

ADMISSIONS INFORMATION

Number of applicants per place (approx): Abertay Dundee 3; Aberystwyth 4; Anglia 10; Bangor 4; Bath 12; Belfast (Queen's) 10; Birmingham 9, (Econ/Stats) 6; Bradford 5; Bristol average 11; Brunel 15; Buckingham 4; Cambridge 4; Cardiff 8; Central England 16; Central

Lancashire 5; City 18, (Econ/Acc) 12, (Econ/Comp) 3; Coventry 10; Derby 3; Durham 13; East Anglia 15; Essex 10; Exeter 12; Greenwich 8; Heriot-Watt 4; Huddersfield 6; Hull 15; Kent 11; Kingston 9; Lancaster 14; Leeds 11; Leicester 10; London (LSE) (Econ) 9, (Econ/Maths Econ) 12, (RH) (Econ Soc Pol) 10, (Econ/Pblc Admin) 10, (UCL) 12; London Guildhall 9; Loughborough 15; Manchester 12; Manchester Met 5; Middlesex (Econ) 8, (Bus Econ) 10; Newcastle 11, (Econ/Bus Mgt) 27, (Fin Bus Econ) 16; North London 15; Northampton (UC) 8; Northumbria 16; Nottingham 15; Nottingham Trent 7; Oxford (Econ/Mgt) 13, (PPE) 3; Oxford Brookes 51; Paisley 7; Plymouth 4; Portsmouth 4; Salford 6; Sheffield 10; Southampton (Econ Act) 5; Staffordshire 4; Stirling 6; Sunderland 8; Surrey (Bus Econ; Econ) 9; Swansea 7; Teesside 2; Warwick 16; Wolverhampton 9; York 9.

Planning your UCAS personal statement (see Ch.4): Visits, work experience, work shadowing in banks, insurance companies, accountants' offices etc should be described. Keep up-to-date with economic issues by reading *The Economist*, *Financial Times* and find other sources of information. Describe any particular aspects of economics which interest you – and why. **Hull** Interests and ambitions. **St Andrews** Evidence of interest and reasons for choosing the course. Sport/extra-curricular activities. Positions of responsibility. **Southampton** Clearly written statement of academic and non-academic strengths and interests. See also under **Subject information**.

Selection interviews (see Ch.4): Abertay Dundee (No); Aberystwyth; Bangor (some); Bath (No); Birmingham (No); Bradford (No); Bristol UWE; Brunel; Buckingham; Cambridge (T); Cardiff (No); Central England (No); City (No); Coventry; Derby (No); Dundee (No); Durham (No); East Anglia (No); East London; Edinburgh; Essex; Exeter (No); Greenwich (No); Huddersfield; Hull (No); Keele; Kent (some); Leeds; Leicester (No); Lincolnshire & Humberside (No); London (LSE) (some), (RH), (UCL); London Guildhall (mature students); Loughborough (No); Manchester; Manchester Met; Middlesex; Newcastle (No); North London; Nottingham Trent (No); Oxford (W – (Econ/Mgt) one-hour test to assess reasoning and language accuracy. No prior knowledge of philosophy, politics or economics required) (T); Paisley (No); Portsmouth (No); St Andrews (No); Salford (No); Sheffield (No); Southampton (Econ Act) (interviews influence level of offer); Staffordshire (No); Stirling (No); Sunderland (No); Surrey (W) (T); Swansea; Teesside; UMIST; Warwick (No); York (No).

Interview questions (see Ch.4): If you have studied economics at A-level or in other examinations, expect to be questioned on aspects of the subject. This is a subject which is constantly in the news, so keep abreast of developments and be prepared to be asked questions such as: What is happening to sterling at present? What is happening to the dollar? How relevant is economics today? What are your views on government economic policy? Do you think that the family is declining as an institution? Discuss Keynesian economics. Is the power of the Prime Minister increasing? What is a recession? How would you get the world out of recession? What causes a recession?

Reasons for rejection (non-academic): Lack of knowledge about the course offered and the subject matter.

GAP YEAR ADVICE

Use it constructively; paid or voluntary work and travel recommended. **Brunel** Tell us when you apply; **Newcastle** (Econ/Acc) Summarise your plan on your UCAS form.

Institutions willing to defer entry after A-levels: Abertay Dundee; Aberystwyth; Bangor; Birmingham (No); Bradford; Brunel; Buckingham; Central Lancashire; City; Coventry; Derby; Dundee; Durham; East Anglia; East London; Heriot-Watt; Hull; Hertfordshire; Kent; Lancaster; Leeds; Leicester; London (Gold), (RH), (UCL) (No); London Guildhall; Manchester Met; Napier; Newcastle; Northumbria; Nottingham; Paisley; Plymouth; Portsmouth; St Andrews; Salford; Sheffield; Staffordshire; Surrey; Sussex; Swansea; Teesside; Warwick; Westminster (No); Wolverhampton; York.

AFTER RESULTS ADVICE

Institutions which may accept the same points score after A-levels: Aberystwyth; Bangor; Bath (No); Belfast (Queen's); Birmingham; Bradford; Brunel; Buckingham; City

(No); Dundee; Durham (No); East Anglia; Essex; Exeter; Hull; Kent; Lancaster (No); Leeds (possibly); Leicester; London (RH); London Guildhall; Loughborough (Econ/Minor) (No); Manchester Met; Middlesex; Napier; Newcastle (No); Nottingham (No); Salford; Sheffield; Surrey; Swansea; UMIST; Warwick (No); York.

Institutions which may accept lower grades/points score after A-levels: Aberystwyth; Bangor; Bath; Birmingham; Bradford; Brunel; Buckingham; City; Coventry; Derby; Dundee; East Anglia; East London; Glasgow; Heriot-Watt; Hertfordshire; Hull (overseas students 18–14 pts); Lancaster; Leeds (some); Leicester; London (RH), (UCL); London Guildhall; Loughborough; Manchester Met; Napier; Newcastle; Paisley; Plymouth; Portsmouth; St Andrews; Salford; Sheffield; Staffordshire; Surrey; Swansea; Teesside; Warwick; Wolverhampton; York (No).

Offers to applicants repeating A-levels: Higher Aberystwyth, Belfast (Queen's), Bradford, Central England, City, Derby, East Anglia, Essex, Hull, Leeds (2 pts), Liverpool, Newcastle, Northumbria, Nottingham, St Andrews, Staffordshire, Swansea, Warwick, York; **Possibly higher** Bradford, Brunel, Durham, Lancaster, Nottingham Trent, Oxford Brookes, Surrey; **Same** Bangor, Bath, Coventry, Dundee, East London, Heriot-Watt, Hull, Kingston, London (RH), London Guildhall, Loughborough, Napier, Salford, Sheffield, Surrey, Teesside, Ulster.

Probable vacancies from June 2001 and in Clearing (see Ch.4): While many universities are likely to have vacancies prior to, and in Clearing, most will be for Combined and Joint Honours courses.

NEW GRADUATE DESTINATIONS AND EMPLOYMENT (1999 HESA) (see **Ch.4**)

Of 2715 graduates surveyed, 1794 secured full-time employment, 441 went on to further study and 132 were believed to be unemployed.

EDUCATION

NB The information supplied by the universities and colleges this year varies considerably and the offers listed below should be used as a first source of reference only. Many institutions will accept combinations of Advanced (AL), Advanced Subsidiary (AS) and Vocational Advanced (VA) level qualifications to achieve the required points total, but applicants must check web sites and prospectuses for full details of all offers. Grades and points totals shown should be regarded as the minimum levels to be achieved, but offers may be adjusted downwards when results are known. The points totals shown to the left of the institutions are for ease of reference only. It must not be assumed that tariff points are always used by institutions or that they can be substituted for an offer in grades. The level of an offer is not necessarily indicative of the quality of a course. To calculate your offers see Chapter 4 and the inside fold of the back cover.

The following table is divided into two sections: **Education Studies** and **Teacher Training Courses** (including Childhood Studies: see also **Social Sciences**).

EDUCATION STUDIES

Special subject requirements/preferences: A-level: In chosen major subjects. **GCSE:** English, mathematics and a science subject for those born after 1 September 1979. **Anglia** Grade B or higher in English. **Cambridge (Hom)** (BA) Grade A in the majority of subjects. **London (Gold)** Grade A or B in a design-related subject. **Warwick** Eight subjects grade A–C.

360 pts and above
    Cambridge (Hom) – AAA–AAB (BA courses – Biol Sci/Educ St; Engl Drama/Educ St; Engl/Educ St; Geog/Educ St; Hist/Educ St; Maths/Educ St; Mus/Educ St; Relig/Educ St)
320 pts Cardiff – ABB (Educ/Engl Lit)

300 pts **Aberystwyth** – 300–180 pts (offer depends on subjs) – ALs **or** ALs+ASs; gs (varies) (Educ joint courses)

Cardiff – BBB (Educ/Psy)

Keele – BBB **or** equiv AS accepted; gs; (Cond Educ)

280 pts **Cardiff** – BBC (Educ/Phil; Educ/Hist Ideas; Educ/Fr)

De Montfort (Bedford) – 280–220 pts – ALs **or** ALs+ASs **or** VAs+/-ALs/ASs; (Educ courses)

Keele – BBC–BCC **or** equiv AS accepted; gs; (Educ courses)

Leeds – 280 pts; (Child St)

Lancaster – BBC (Educ St/Psy; Educ St/Hist)

York – 280–240 pts 18–12u – CCC (Educ St)

260 pts **Bristol** – BCC **or** BB+cc **or** VA6u+AL(C); gs; (Early Child St)

Bristol – BCC (Deaf St)

Cardiff – BCC–CCC (Sociol/Educ; Lang St/Educ; Welsh/Educ; Educ)

Lancaster – BCC (Educ St/Sociol)

Swansea – BCC (Early Child St)

240 pts **Cardiff** – CCC/BB (Education)

Hertfordshire – 240–200 pts 1x12u **or** 2x6u; gs; Educ St courses)

Lancaster – CCC (Educ St; Educ St/Relig St; Educ St/App Soc Sci; Crim/Educ St)

230 pts **Brunel** – 230–220 pts 2x6u – ALs **or** ALs+ASs **or** VAs+/-ALs/ASs; (Educ St)

220 pts **Bangor** – 220 pts – ALs **or** VAs+/-ALs/ASs; (Child St Single/Joint Hons courses)

Bangor – CCD/BC (Education (Addysgcyd anrhydedd) Welsh medium only)

Durham (Stockton) – 220 pts approx (Child/Arts)

King Alfred's Winchester (Coll) – 220 pts 12u; gs; (Educ St courses)

Liverpool John Moores – 220–180 pts – ALs **or** ALs+Ass **or** VAs+/-ALs/ASs; (Out/Env Educ)

Plymouth – CCD (Educ St/Comb Hons)

200 pts **Central Lancashire** – 200–180 pts 12u (inc AL Engl lang/hum subj); gs; (Educ/Pol; Educ/Engl)

Sunderland – 200–180 pts approx (Educ Trg Comb St)

Warrington (CI) – 200 pts approx (Prof St Educ)

180 pts **Central Lancashire** – 180–160 pts 12u; gs; (Educ/Hist; Educ/Pol)

Derby – 180 pts 12u – DD+dd **or** VAs+/-ALs/ASs; (Early Child St)

Liverpool John Moores – 180–160 pts approx – ALs **or** ALs+ASs **or** VAs+/-ALs/ASs; (Child St)

Northumbria – 180 pts approx (CarEd Disab St; Disab St/Child St; Child St)

Oxford Brookes – DDD/CC (Educ St)

Suffolk (Coll) – 180 pts approx (Early Child St)

Surrey Roehampton – 180 pts – ALs **or** ALs+ASs (inc C/AL 80 pts) **or** VAs BC+/-ALs/ASs; (Early Child St)

160 pts **Bath Spa (UC)** – 160–120 pts 12u – BD **or** VA12u BD (not gs) (Int Educ courses; Educ Comb Hons)

Birmingham (Westhill) – 160 pts 12u – ALs **or** C+ASs **or** VAs+/-ALs/ASs; gs; (Hum (Educ))

Chichester (UC) – 160 pts (inc AL) (Child St)

Newman (CHE) – 160 pts 12u – CC **or** ALs+ASs **or** VA12u CC; (not gs) (Early Yrs Educ St)

North London – 160 pts 1x12u **or** 2x6u; (Educ St courses)

St Mary's (Coll) – 12u – CC–DD **or** ALs+ASs **or** VAs+/-ALs/ASs; gs; (Educ/Emp courses)

Strathclyde – CC (Commun Educ; Outdoor Educ Commun)

Surrey Roehampton – 160 pts – ALs **or** ALs+ASs (inc C/AL 80 pts) **or** VAs CC+/-ALs/ASs; (Educ courses)

West Suffolk (Coll) – 160 pts 12u – 2ALs **or** AL+AL/2AS **or** VA12u CC; gs; (Child/Yth St)

Worcester (UC) – 160 pts 12u – CC **or** ALs+ASs; gs; (Early Child St)

140 pts   **Derby** – 140 pts 12u – CD **or** DE+ee **or** VAs+/-ALs/ASs; (Educ St Comb Hons)
  Sunderland – 140 pts approx (Early Child St)
  Warrington (CI) – 140–120 pts – ALs **or** ALs+ASs **or** VAs+/-ALs/ASs; gs; (Educ)
120 pts   **Worcester (UC)** – 120 pts 12u – DD **or** ALs+ASs; gs; (Educ St)
  UHI (Inverness/Lews Castle/Moray/North Highland/Perth) – (Child Yth St
    via DipHE, HNC)

TEACHER TRAINING COURSES

Special subject requirements/preferences: A-levels: In chosen major subjects. **GCSE:** English and mathematics. Applicants for Initial Teacher Training courses born after 1 September 1979 and who are candidates for entry from September 1998 are required to hold GCSE grades A to C (or equivalent standard) in English language, mathematics and **a science subject. Cambridge (Hom)** Majority of grade As. **Chichester (UC)** (Art/Educ) Grade A or B in art. **Durham** English and mathematics at grade A or B. **London (Gold)** Grade A or B in design related subject. **Worcester (UC)** Grade A in at least one curriculum subject.

Subjects attracting the most applicants include Drama, History, Physical Education, Social Science, English and Art. Subjects attracting the least applicants include Modern Languages, Sciences, Craft Design and Technology, Music, Religious Education, Mathematics and Home Economics. The choice of subject will affect the level of the offer made. See also under separate subject tables.

Abbreviations: P – Primary Teaching; S – Secondary Teaching; N – Nursery Teaching; QTS – Qualified Teacher Status.

300 pts   **Cardiff** – BBB–CCC (Educ/Sociol)
  Keele – BBB **or** equiv AS accepted; gs; (Psy/Cond Educ)
  Warwick – ABC–BBB (BA QTS P Engl)
  York – ABC–BBC (Biol/Educ)
280 pts   **Cambridge (Hom)** – BBC–BCD (4 yr QTS courses – Educ with Biol
    Sci/Drama/Engl/Geog/Hist/Maths/Mus/Relig St)
  London (King's) – BB (2 langs)C/D (Modn Lang/Educ)
  Stirling – BBC–CCC (Educ Comb Hons courses – BA/BSc P/S)
260 pts   **Bath** – 260 pts approx (Biol/Educ BSc)
  De Montfort (Bedford) – 260–200 pts – ALs **or** ALs+ASs **or** VAs+/-ALs/ASs;
    (BEd P)
  Durham – BCC **or** ALs+ASs **or** VAs+/-ALs/ASs; (ITT)
  Hull – 260–240 pts approx (Educ with Biol/Chem/Maths BSc S)
  London (Gold) – BCC–CCC/BC–CC (Educ BA P with QTS)
  Sheffield – 260 pts approx (P Early Yrs Engl)
  Surrey – 260 pts approx (Chem with ITT)
250 pts   **Brunel** – 250–240 pts 2x6u (inc AL C spo st/PE) – ALs **or** ALs+ASs **or** VAs+/-
    ALs/ASs; (BA P)
240 pts   **Bath** – 240 pts approx (Chem/Educ; Phys/Educ BSc)
  Exeter – CCC/DD (Educ St BA/BSc P/S)
  Hertfordshire – CCC (Engl Lit/Lang BEd P)
  Hertfordshire – 240 pts approx (BEd P Engl)
  Leeds, Trinity & All Saints (Coll) – 240 pts (PE BA P)
  Manchester Met – 240 pts approx; gs; (BA/BSc S PE)
  St Andrew's (Coll) – CCC–CCD (Educ BEd P; BTheol S)
  Sheffield Hallam – 240 pts approx (Early Child St; Spo Dev/Coach)
  Warwick – CCC (BA QTS Science/Maths)
230 pts   **Brunel** – 230–220 pts 2x6u (inc 1/2ALs from Engl/maths/sci/IT) – ALs **or**
    ALs+ASs **or** VAs+/-ALs/ASs; (BSc PE)
220 pts   **Anglia** – 220 pts approx (BEd P/S)
  Bangor – 220–200 pts; gs (BSc Des Tech (QTS) S)
  King Alfred's Winchester (Coll) – 220 pts 12u: ALs **or** ALs+ASs (AL D in
    relevant subject); (BA P)

Kingston – 220–200 pts approx (P QTS; Engl/Drama; Hist/Geog; Maths IT/Music; Sci)
Nottingham Trent – 220 pts approx (Educ BA P QTS/S)
Paisley – CCD/BB (Educ BEd P)
Ripon & York (Coll) – CCD (Engl St BA P)
Worcester (UC) – 220 pts approx (Early/Later Yrs BA QTS)

200 pts   **Central Lancashire** – 200 pts approx (Deaf St; Educ St)
Cheltenham & Glos (CHE) – 200 pts approx (inc AL from Engl, maths, sci & AL from art, geog hist IT, PE, music, relig st) (BEd P)
Chester (Coll) – 200 pts approx (BEd)
Leeds, Trinity & All Saints (Coll) – 200 pts approx (Educ BA/BSc P)
Liverpool John Moores – 200 pts (inc 100 pts lang); (BA/TESOL)
Middlesex – 200 pts approx (Educ BA P/S)
Newport (UWCN) – 200–160 pts – ALs or ALs+/-ASs or VAs+/-ALs/ASs; (BA P)
Sheffield Hallam – 200 pts approx (BSc Sci QTS)
Sunderland – 200 pts approx (BA Early Yrs Educ 3–8; Jnr Yrs Educ 7–11)
Wolverhampton – 200 pts 12u – DDD/CDE/CC or DD+b or VA12u CC; gs; (All Educ courses inc Cond Educ)

180 pts   **Brighton** – 180 pts approx (BA P Educ with Maths/Sci/Engl/Des Tech/Relig St; PE; Modn Lang BA P; Educ Maths/Sci; Bus Educ/Inf Tech QTS S)
Bristol UWE – 180–140 pts 12u – ALs (80 pts 6u in (Engl/biol/art/maths/hist/geog) or ALs+ASs or VAs+/-ALs/ASs (QTS courses Art/Biol Sci/Engl/Geog/Hist/Maths)
Cardiff (UWI) – 180 pts approx (Drama S; Educ QTS P)
Central Lancashire – 180 pts approx (Comb Hons)
Chichester (UC) – 180 pts approx + interview (N; P; S Maths, S PE)
Chichester (UC) – 180 pts approx (Child St)
Coventry – 180 pts approx (Modn Lang QTS)
Derby – 180 pts 12u – BC or DD+dd or VA12u BC or VA6u B+AL(C); (BEd P)
Greenwich – 180–160 pts approx (BEd/BA/BSc P/S)
Hertfordshire – 180 pts approx (BEd P/S: Relig St; Geog/Env St)
Kingston – 180 pts (inc 2x6u and AL 80 pts in spec subj) or VA12u (160 pts); (BA P QTS)
Liverpool Hope (Coll) – 180 pts approx (BEd P)
Liverpool John Moores – 180 pts – ALs or ALs+ASs or VAs+/-ALs/ASs; (BA P Ed QT)
London (Gold) – DDD (Des Tech; PE; Maths BA S)
Loughborough – CDE/CC (Des Tech BA/BSc)
Manchester Met – 180 pts approx; gs; (BA P; BEd P; BA/BSc S)
Newman (CHE) – BC–CC (BEd/BA S Engl QTS)
North East Wales (IHE) – 180 pts approx (BA P; BEd S)
Northampton (UC) – 180 pts approx (BA P)
Nottingham Trent – 180 pts approx (Des Tech Educ)
Oxford Brookes – DDD/CC (BA QTS)
Oxford Brookes (Westminster) – 180 pts approx (BEd P Engl; Fr; Maths; Relig St)
Plymouth – CDE/CC (Lang/Lit P)
Reading – BC (B main subj) (BA Ed P)
Ripon & York (Coll) – 180–160 pts approx (Geog BA/BSc Int Tech; Theol/Relig St P)
St Mark & St John (Coll) – 180 pts approx (Engl BEd P)
St Martin's (Coll) – 180 pts approx (Engl BA/BSc)
Sheffield Hallam – DDD/CC (BA P)
Strathclyde – DDD/CD (BEd P/S)
Sunderland – 180 pts approx (BA Engl (7–18) Relig St (11–18) Inf Tech (7–14))
Surrey Roehampton – 180 pts – ALs or ALs+ASAs (inc C/AL 80 pts from relevant subj area) or VA BC; (BA P)

Swansea (IHE) – 180 pts – ALs **or** ALs+ASs; gs (AL only); (BA Educ P)
Trinity Carmarthen (Coll) – 180–160 pts approx (BEd P)
Warwick – CDE/CC (Biol/Geog/Music BA P)

160 pts **Bath** – 160 pts approx (BEd P)
Birmingham (Westhill) – CC (BA QTS)
Bishop Grosseteste (Coll) – CC (inc AL pref Engl/maths or art/drama/geog/hist/mus/relig st/sci/PE/CDT) **or** C+cc **or** VA12u CC; (BA P)
Canterbury Christ Church (UC) – CC (BA P joint courses)
Central England – 160 pts 12u – 2ALs **or** 2ALs+3ASs **or** VAs+/-ALs/ASs; (not gs); AL/VA subj chosen in spec subj area; (BA P with QTS)
Chichester (UC) – 160 pts (inc AL); (BA P/S; Maths S/PE; BA Engl Lang (B Engl))
Edge Hill (CHE) – CC–DD (BA/BSc P)
Edinburgh – CC (Educ P)
Hertfordshire – 160 pts approx (BEd P Maths/Sci)
Hull (Scarborough) – 160 pts approx (BA/BSc P)
Leeds (Bretton Hall) – CC–CD (Educ BA P)
Liverpool John Moores – 160–120 pts – ALs **or** ALs+ASs **or** VAs+/-ALs/ASs; (BA/BSc up QTS)
London (King's) – BD (Maths/Educ)
Manchester Met – 160 pts approx (BEd S Maths)
Newman (CHE) – CC **or** ALs+ASs **or** VA12u+/-AL/ASs; (not gs) (BA/BEd P S)
North London – 160 pts 1x12u **or** 2x6u; (BEd P QTS)
Northern (Coll) – 160 pts approx (BEd P/S – contact the admissions tutor)
St Mark & St John (Coll) – 160–140 pts approx (Maths/Geog/Hist BEd P)
St Martin's (Coll) – 160 pts approx (BA/BSc P)
St Mary's (Coll) – CC **or** ALs+ASs **or** VAs+/-ALs/ASs; gs; (BA QTS P)
Sheffield Hallam – 160 pts approx (BA S)
South Bank – 160 pts approx (BEd P)
Worcester (UC) – 160 pts 12u – C+AL/2ASs **or** VA6u; not gs; (P Art/Biol/Engl/PE with QTS; 3 yr QTS)

140 pts **Bath Spa (UC)** – 140–120 pts – CD **or** VA12u CD; (not gs) (Educ/PGCE P)
Bradford (Coll) – 140 pts approx (BA P)
Central (Sch Sp/Dr) – 140 pts approx (BA S)
Edinburgh – 140 pts approx (BEd/DTech P/S)
Huddersfield – 140 pts approx (BEd Mus/Sci; Commun Educ)
Leeds, Trinity & All Saints (Coll) – 140 pts approx (Maths BA/BSc P/S)
Northern (Coll) – 140 pts approx (Commun Educ)
Plymouth – 140 pts approx (BEd P)
Ripon & York (Coll) – CD (Des Tech Maths)
Sheffield Hallam – 140 pts approx (BA P)
Sunderland – 140 pts approx (BA/BSc Des Tech (11–18))
Swansea (IHE) – 140 pts approx (BA S)
Warwick – CD (BA S Maths)
Welsh (CMus/Dr) – 140 pts approx (BA S)

120 pts **and below**
Crawley (Coll) – 80 pts; gs (BA Engl/Educ)
Greenwich – (Des Tech)
London (King's) – DD (Phys/Educ)
Plymouth – Steiner (Waldorf) Educ – subject to interview)
Reading – (Thea Arts; Educ; Deaf – contact department)
Ripon & York (Coll) – DD (Music QTS P)
Stockport (CFHE) – 80 pts 6u; (Prof St; Learn Diff; Early Child St)
Sunderland – 120 pts – 2ALs **or** ALs+ASs **or** VA12u+/-AL/ASs; gs; (Des Tech)

Leeds Met – (contact university)

Diploma of Higher Education courses
40 pts Manchester Met; Oxford Brookes (Westminster).

Higher National Diploma courses (Child St and other courses)
100 pts   and below

Barnsley (Coll); Birmingham (CFTCS); Bridgwater (Coll); Burnley (Coll); Central Lancashire; City of Bristol (Coll); Derby; Doncaster (Coll); Exeter (Child St); Fife (CHFE) (Spec Educ); Guildford (CFHE); Hopwood Hall (Coll); Liverpool (CmC); Llandrillo (Coll); North Down & Ards (IFHE); Northbrook (Coll); Norwich City (Coll); Oldham (Coll); St Austell (Coll) (Playwk); Shrewsbury (Coll) (Early Child St); Stockport (CFHE); Stratford on Avon (Coll); Truro (Coll) (Out Educ); Warwickshire (Coll) (Early Child St); Wigan & Leigh (Coll); Wiltshire (Coll) (Early Child St); Worcester (UC); Yorkshire Coast (CFHE).

Alternative Offers:

IB offers: Aberystwyth 30–28 pts; Anglia 26 pts; Bangor 30–28 pts; Bristol 30–28 pts H555/4; Brunel 28–25 pts; Cambridge (Hom) (BA) 36 pts inc H7 in main subject, (BEd) 33 pts; Cardiff 26 pts; Durham 25 pts; Exeter 30 pts; Kingston 24 pts; Lancaster 30 pts; Manchester Met 28 pts; Oxford Brookes H444; Oxford Brookes (Westminster) 26 pts; Surrey Roehampton 24 pts; Warwick 30–28 pts, (English) 34 pts;

Irish offers: Aberystwyth BBCCC; Bangor BBCCC; Brighton BBCCC/CCCC; Cardiff BBBCCC; De Montfort (Bedford) CCCC; Durham BBCCC; Newman (CHE) CCC + maths and English at pass (Ordinary level); Oxford Brookes (Westminster) BBCC; Warwick BBBBC, (English) AABB.

Scottish Qualifications: Aberdeen (Lang/Educ) BBBB; Edinburgh (Out Educ) BBBB; Northern (Coll) (Commun Educ) CCC; Paisley BBBB; Stirling (Adult Educ) BBCC; Strathclyde BBB–BCC.

Overseas applicants: English language ability crucial in all cases. **Brunel** GCSE maths and English grades A–C or British Council test of 6–5. **Surrey Roehampton** No Foundation course.

CHOOSING YOUR COURSE (See also **Ch.1**)

Subject information: There are two types of degree courses in Education – those which cover the history, philosophy and theory of education but which are not necessarily teacher training courses, and those which prepare the student for a career in the teaching profession. Read prospectuses carefully. For the latter, candidates should be well-motivated towards teaching and education – interview is important. Interview panels look for candidates with confidence in their own ability, a lively personality, patience and optimism. Experience of working with children important. Students planning to follow a degree with a Postgraduate Certificate in Education (PGCE) are advised that problems may arise if their first degree subject is not a National Curriculum subject. Teacher training courses are offered in the following subject areas: Art/Design (P); Biology (P/S); Business Studies (S); Chemistry (P/S); Childhood (P); Computer Education (P); Creative/Performing Arts (P); Dance (P/S); Design/Technology (P/S); Drama (P/S); English (P/S); Environmental Science (P/S); Environmental Studies (P); French (P/S); General Primary; Geography (P/S); History (P/S); Home Economics (P/S); Maths (P/S); Music (P/S); Physical Education/Movement Studies (P/S); Religious Studies (P); Science (P/S); Sociology (P); Textile Design (P); Welsh (P). See also **Appendix 1**.

Two-year BEd courses are also offered for holders of HND or equivalent qualifications (minimum age in some cases 23–25) in the following subject areas: Business Studies (S); Chemistry (S); Design and Technology (S); English (P); French (S); General Primary; German (S); Home Economics (S); Language Studies (P); Mathematics (S); Music (S); Physics (S); Science (S); Spanish (S); Welsh (S). For further information on teaching as a career write to the Teacher Training Agency or the General Teaching Council for Scotland (see **Appendix 1** for contact details). Over 50 taster courses are offered each year to those considering teaching as a career.

Special features: Some courses offer the opportunity to study abroad including **Brighton, Liverpool Hope (Coll)** and **Manchester Met. Bangor** (Educ) Course taught in Welsh. (Sport, Health & PE) Practical and theoretical studies covering sport and exercise psychology, human development, health promotion, counselling and physical education. **Bath** Concurrent sandwich degree and certificate courses in Biological Science, Chemistry, Chemical, Electrical or Mechanical Engineering, Materials Science or Physics. **Bristol** (Child St) Covers psychology, sociology, social policy and child health. (Deaf St) Many course options taught in sign language. **Brunel** 70% of course covers design; degree confers design and teaching qualifications. **Cardiff** British Psychological Society recognition for selected options. **Chichester (UC)** Early Years route – ages 3–7; two new courses for 1999; 2+2 subject + Education Structure for PQTS course; special 2 year conversion route for S Maths; special extra route at Crawley for mature students. **Loughborough** Years 1 and 2 Joint BEd common with single Honours specialist subject courses; years 3 and 4 have substantial education component, with teaching practice leading to degree and teaching qualification. **Manchester Met** (Maths) Two-year course for mature students. **Newman (CHE)** Three and four-year options on all initial teacher training courses. **Plymouth** BA in Steiner (Waldorf) Education offered mainly targeted at mature applicants. **Sheffield Hallam** Exchange scheme with Ohio University, USA; design and technology option available. **Stirling** Subject can be studied to minor, subsidiary or major level in Part I. *NOW CHECK PROPECTUSES AND WEB SITES*.

Top universities, colleges and education departments (Teaching Quality) (see Ch.4): Smithers/Robinson Teacher Training Index League: Oxford; Cambridge (Hom); Cambridge; Bishop Grosseteste (Coll); East Anglia; Sheffield; Bristol; Birmingham; York; Canterbury Christ Church (UC); Liverpool; Leicester; Warwick; Central England; Sussex; Ripon & York (Coll); Exeter; Nottingham; Liverpool Hope (Coll); Manchester Met; not all institutions assessed.

Top universities and colleges (Research) (see Ch.4): Aberdeen; Bath; Belfast (Queen's); Birmingham; Bristol; Cambridge; Cardiff; Durham; East Anglia; Edinburgh; Exeter; Lancaster; Leeds; London (Gold), (King's); Manchester; Newcastle; Nottingham; Oxford; Reading; Sheffield; Southampton; Stirling; Sussex; Ulster; Warwick; York.

Study opportunities abroad: Bath; Brighton; Cambridge (Hom); Canterbury Christ Church (UC); Cardiff (UWI); Central Lancashire; Cheltenham & Glos (CHE); Chester (Coll); Chichester (UC); De Montfort; Durham; Dundee; Edge Hill (CHE); Edinburgh; Glasgow; King Alfred's Winchester (Coll); Kingston; Lancaster; Liverpool Hope (UC); London (Gold); Manchester Met; Newman (CHE); North East Wales (IHE); Northampton (UC); Oxford Brookes; Oxford Brookes (Westminster); Plymouth Steiner (Waldorf) (Educ); Ripon & York (Coll); St Mark & St John (Coll); St Mary's (Coll); Sheffield Hallam; South Bank; Worcester (UC); York.

Work opportunities abroad: Brighton; Chester (Coll); Chichester (UC); Greenwich; Kingston; North East Wales (IHE); Oxford Brookes (Westminster); Plymouth Steiner (Waldorf) (Educ); St Mary's (Coll).

ADMISSIONS INFORMATION

Number of applicants per place (approx): Aberystwyth 6; Anglia 3; Bangor 9; Bath Spa (UC) 5; Bishop Grosseteste (Coll) 12; Bristol 16; Bristol UWE 20; Brunel (PE) 5, (P/S) 17; Cambridge (Hom) 9 (average per course); Canterbury Christ Church (UC) 15; Cardiff (Educ) 8; Cardiff (UWI) 3; Central Lancashire 5; Cheltenham & Glos (CHE) 20; Chester (Coll) 25; De Montfort 10; De Montfort (Bedford) 4; Derby 13; Durham 8; Edge Hill (CHE) 17; Edinburgh (P) 3, (PE) 4; Exeter 10, (Sec/PE) 13; Greenwich 3; Hertfordshire 18; Hull 7; Hull (Scarborough) 4; Kingston 9; Leeds (Bretton Hall) 4; Liverpool Hope (Coll) 5; London (Gold) 5, (Des/Tech) 4; Loughborough (Educ/Maths) 3; Manchester Met 23, (Maths) 4; Middlesex 7; Newman (CHE) (Engl) 15; North East Wales (IHE) 15; Northumbria 8; Nottingham Trent 3; Oxford Brookes 6; Oxford Brookes (Westminster) 5; Paisley 7; Plymouth 14; Ripon & York (Coll) (Music) 6, (Maths) 10, (Biol) 10, Engl) 23, (Relig St) 20, (French) 12, (Des Tech) 10; St Mark & St John (Coll) 5; St Martin's (Coll) 5; St Mary's

(Coll) 19; Sheffield Hallam 7, (PE) 60; South Bank 8; Strathclyde 7; Sunderland 10; Surrey Roehampton 6; Swansea (IHE) 10; Trinity Carmarthen (Coll) 10; Wolverhampton 13; Worcester (UC) 21, (Engl) 51; York 8.

Planning your UCAS personal statement (see Ch.4): Any application for teacher training courses requires candidates to have had experience of observation in schools and with children relevant to the choice of age range. Describe what you have learned from this experience. Any work with young people should be described in detail, indicating any problems which you may have encountered which children create for the teacher. Applicants are strongly advised to have had some teaching practice prior to interview. Evidence of time spent in primary school. Evidence of analysis of activity undertaken with children. Music qualifications, if any. **Kingston** Precise, succinct, well-reasoned, well-written (no mistakes!). **Newman (CHE)** Be prepared for hard work throughout the course. See also **Appendix 1**.

Selection interviews (see Ch.4): Bangor (W); Bishop Grosseteste (Coll); Bristol; Bristol UWE; Cambridge (Hom) (W); Cardiff (W); Derby; Kingston (MTeach) (W); London (Gold); Manchester Met (T) (group interviews. We look for an ability to express personal views, to listen and respond to others appropriately and the ability to call on personal experience); Nottingham Trent (T); Oxford Brookes (W); Paisley (some); Plymouth (W); Ripon & York (Coll); South Bank (W); Stockport (CFHE); Worcester (UC) (T); York (some). All institutions for teacher training courses usually interview. It is a requirement by the Department for Education and Employment that all candidates for teacher education are interviewed. Additionally, candidates are asked to compose a short written statement on a given topic at interview in order to ensure an acceptable standard of written English.

Interview questions (see Ch.4): Questions will invariably focus on why you want to teach and your experiences in the classroom. In some cases you may be asked to write an essay on these topics. Questions in the past have included: What do you think are important issues in education at present? Discussion of course work will take place for Art applicants. **Bath Spa (UC)** Short essay on an aspect of education. **Brighton** 200 word essay. **Derby** Applicants are asked about an aspect of education. **Nottingham Trent** English test. **Ripon & York (Coll)** A short piece of written work is set on arrival for interview. **Worcester (UC)** Interviewees are asked to write a statement concerning their impressions of the interview.

Reasons for rejection (non-academic): Poor communication skills. Lack of commitment. Insufficient experience of working with people/children. Lacking in confidence and maturity. Not sufficiently out-going. Lack of interest in, or potential for, teaching. Mismatch between application form and interview revelations. Problems with written English/grammar. Inarticulate at interview. Attitudes not consistent with student culture/racist/prejudiced. Poor spelling. Inability to discuss educational issues. Not reliable or punctual. **Hertfordshire** Failed English test.

GAP YEAR ADVICE

Plan a well-organised programme involving some work with children/young people.

Institutions willing to defer entry after A-levels: Most institutions; Bangor (No); Bishop Grosseteste (Coll); Brighton; Brunel (No); Cambridge (Hom) (No); Canterbury Christ Church (UC); Cardiff; Central Lancashire; Cheltenham & Glos (CHE); Chester (Coll); Derby; Durham; Edge Hill (CHE); Edinburgh; Hertfordshire; King Alfred's Winchester (Coll); Kingston; Lancaster; Liverpool Hope (Coll); Manchester Met; Newman (CHE); North East Wales (IHE); Oxford Brookes; Plymouth; Ripon & York (Coll) (No); St Mark & St John (Coll) (Yes but not preferred); Sheffield Hallam; South Bank; Strathclyde (No); Surrey Roehampton; Swansea (IHE); Warwick; Wolverhampton; Worcester (UC); York.

AFTER RESULTS ADVICE

Institutions which may accept the same points score after A-levels: Brighton; Bristol; Bristol UWE; Cambridge (Hom) (Educ St possibly), (BEd No); Canterbury Christ Church

(UC); Cardiff; Chester (Coll) (No); Derby; Edge Hill (CHE); Exeter; Hertfordshire; Hull (Scarborough) (No); Manchester Met; Newman (CHE) (No); Nottingham Trent (No); Oxford Brookes (No); Ripon & York (Coll) (No); Surrey Roehampton; Warwick (No); York.

Institutions which may accept lower grades/points score after A-levels: Bangor; Brighton; Brunel; Derby; Durham (No); Hertfordshire; Manchester Met, Newman (CHE); Oxford Brookes; Surrey Roehampton; Warwick. Some institutions will consider applicants whose A-level results do not quite match the offer made. Check with admissions tutor at the time of the offer. (Two A-level passes and English and mathematics at GCSE (grades A–C) are the minimum requirements.)

Offers to applicants repeating A-levels: Higher Oxford Brookes, Warwick; **Possibly higher** Cambridge (Hom), Ripon & York (Coll), St Martin's (Coll); **Same** Bangor, Bishop Grosseteste (Coll), Brunel, Canterbury Christ Church (UC), Derby, Durham, Liverpool Hope (Coll), Liverpool John Moores, London (Gold), Loughborough (Educ/Maths), Newman (CHE), North London, Northumbria, Oxford Brookes, St Mary's (Coll), Surrey Roehampton, Wolverhampton, Worcester (UC); **Not considered** Chester (Coll), Kingston.

Probable vacancies from June 2001 and in Clearing (see Ch.4): Most institutions are worth contacting since vacancies are likely in Educational Studies and Teacher Training courses covering general education subjects for infants, juniors and middle school and secondary teaching.

NEW GRADUATE DESTINATIONS AND EMPLOYMENT (1999 HESA) (see **Ch.4**)

Academic Study of Education; *Teacher Training* No data available.

ENGINEERING/ENGINEERING SCIENCES (including Extended Courses)

NB The information supplied by the universities and colleges this year varies consider-ably and the offers listed below should be used as a first source of reference only. Many institutions will accept combinations of Advanced (AL), Advanced Subsidiary (AS) and Vocational Advanced (VA) level qualifications to achieve the required points total, but applicants must check web sites and prospectuses for full details of all offers. Grades and points totals shown should be regarded as the minimum levels to be achieved, but offers may be adjusted downwards when results are known. The points totals shown to the left of the institutions are for ease of reference only. It must not be assumed that tariff points are always used by institutions or that they can be substituted for an offer in grades. The level of an offer is not necessarily indicative of the quality of a course. To calculate your offers see Chapter 4 and the inside fold of the back cover.

> **The following statement has been provided by the Engineering Council:**
>
> **Professional Engineering Degrees** Due to recent developments in the profession, there are now **two** different types of degree courses available for those wishing to become Professional Engineers:
>
> Chartered Engineers (CEng) create tomorrow's technology and systems. It is possible to take a 4-year MEng degree, or 3-year BEng (Hons) degree supplemented by one year of further learning. Guideline admission standards for these degree courses are as follows: **MEng** (GCE A-levels) ABC/BBB; (SQA Highers) AABB; (SQA Advanced Highers) ABC/BBB; (IB) 30 pts; (Irish Leaving) AABB. **BEng (Hons)** (GCE A-levels) CCC/BCD; (SQA Highers) BBBC; (SQA Advanced Highers) CCC/BCD; (IB) 26 pts; (Irish Leaving) BBBC. **Applicants should check the offer for MEng/BEng/BSc courses in each of the Engineering tables unless otherwise stated.**
>
> Incorporated Engineers (IEng) are expert in present day technology and its applications. The degree for an Incorporated Engineer will be an appropriate 3-year engineering degree. Guideline admission standards for these degree courses are as follows: (GCE

A-levels) CD/CEE/DDE; (SQA Highers) BCC/CCCC; (IB) 24 pts; (Irish Leaving) BCC/CCC.

For the smooth progression of your career it is important to confirm with universities whether their courses are accredited for CEng or IEng by relevant professional engineering Institutions. There are 23 degree-awarding Institutions that work in partnership with the Engineering Council.

Training for Professional Engineers A Chartered or Incorporated Engineer also needs appropriate training and experience, usually arranged in employment after graduation but especially valuable if gained, in part, during the degree course itself by a 'sandwich' placement in industry. Later in their careers, both Chartered and Incorporated Engineers occupy positions of responsibility, often as team leaders and with key roles in middle management. In recent years salaries have increased by more than inflation. Chartered Engineers have an average salary of £42,159, and the top 10% of them earn over £60,000. Incorporated Engineers have an average salary of £31,152 and the top 6% of them earn over £50,000.

Special subject requirements/preferences: A-level: Mathematics and physics usually essential (except for Foundation courses). **Bradford** (Tech Mgt) Mathematics/science subjects are not required. **Oxford** Full A-levels in mathematics and physics are essential. **GCSE:** Grade A–C may be required in English, chemistry or language for some courses. Mathematics essential. **Bath** Three subjects at grade A including mathematics; grade A/B in language for French and German courses. **Brunel** (Spec Eng Prog) Grade A in mathematics and English, other subjects grade B. Other courses grade B in mathematics and English. **Cambridge, Oxford** Grade As in most subjects preferred. **De Montfort** CDT preferred. **Manchester Met, Portsmouth** Mathematics grade A or B; language grade B for Euro course.

360 pts　**and above**
　　　　Cambridge – Offers, mainly in grades, vary between colleges (Engineering)
　　　　Oxford – Offers vary between candidates (Engineering)
　　　　Southampton – 390 pts 21u – 2ALs (220 pts inc maths, phys)+ALs/ASs/VA as 3rd AL; (MEng Interd)
　　　　Southampton – 370 21u (inc 220 pts AL maths+phys); (Integ Eng; Eng/Euro St)
350 pts　**Southampton** – 350 pts 21u; (Fdn Eng)
340 pts　**Bath** – AAB (MEng Innov Eng Des)
　　　　Bristol – AAB (inc AA maths+phys) **or** AA (maths+phys)+cc; (not gs) (MEng Eng Des)
320 pts　**Brunel** – 320–300 pts – ALs **or** ALs+ASs **or** VAs+/-ALs/ASs; (Spec Eng Prog (SEP); SEP/Fr; SEP/Ger)
　　　　Cardiff – 320–300 pts approx (MEng Integ Eng; Med Eng)
　　　　Durham – 320 pts – ABB/AAC (inc maths); (not gs) (MEng Eng courses)
　　　　London (UCL) – ABB–BBC (Eng Bus Fin)
300 pts　**Bradford** – 300 pts 12u (inc 2AL sci subjs); gs; (MEng Med Eng)
　　　　Bristol – BBB (Eng Maths)
　　　　City – BBB/AB (MEng Eng Ext courses)
　　　　Exeter – 300 pts 18u (inc AL maths) – BBB **or** BB+bb **or** VAs (contact univ); (not gs) (MEng courses)
　　　　Hull – 300–260 pts approx (B/A maths) (MEng Integ Eng)
　　　　Hull – BBB (MEng Eng Des/Manuf)
　　　　Lancaster – BBB (Eng – Comb Sci/USA/Can)
　　　　Leeds – BBB/AA (Maths/Eng)
　　　　Leicester – AAD/ABC/BBB **or** BB/AC+bb/ac (AL maths+phys) **or** VA12u (grades as ALs)+AL; gs (AL only); (MEng courses)
　　　　London (QM) – 300 pts – ALs **or** ALs+ASs **or** VAs+/-ALs/ASs; (MEng Med Eng)
　　　　Loughborough – 300 pts 18u – CC(maths, phys)+AL/2AS **or** VAs+/-ALs/ASs; gs; (MEng Eng Sci/Tech)
　　　　Manchester – BBB (MEng Eng/Bus; Eng Des Simul Mdl)

Nottingham – 300 pts – 3ALs (inc maths, phys) **or** 2ALs (maths, phys)+2ASs; (not gs) (Integ Eng)
Strathclyde – BBB (MEng courses)

280 pts **Bath** – BBC (BSc/BEng courses)
Birmingham – BBC–CCC (Eng with Fdn Yr; Eng/Bus)
Cardiff – 280–240 pts approx (BEng Integ Eng; Med Eng)
Durham – 280 pts – 3ALs (inc maths); (not gs) (BEng Eng courses)
Reading – BBC (MEng Integ Eng)

260 pts **Aston** – 260–240 pts 18u – 3ALs **or** ALs+ASs **or** VAs+/-ALs/ASs; gs; (Eng Mgt)
Bradford – 260 pts 12u (inc 2AL sci subjs); gs; (BEng Med Eng)
Coventry – 260 pts approx (Ind Prod Des)
Lancaster – BCC (Eng courses)
Liverpool – 260 pts – ALs **or** ALs+ASs **or** VAs+/-ALs/ASs; (Integ Eng courses except under **180 pts**)
Loughborough – 260 pts approx (Ind Des Tech)
Loughborough – 260 pts 18u – CC(maths, phys)+AL/2AS **or** VAs+/-AL/ASs; gs; (MEng Eng Sci/Tech)
Warwick – BCC (BEng Eng Des Appr Tech; Gen Eng; Eng/Bus St)

240 pts **Bath** – CCC **or** CC+cc; VAs (contact univ); (not gs) (Fdn Eng)
Brighton – 240 pts approx (Eng; Prod Des)
Brunel – 240 pts 2x6u (inc AL maths C+pref tech/eng sci) – ALs **or** ALs+ASs **or** VAs+/-ALs/ASs; (Integ Eng courses)
Cardiff – CCC (Eng with Fdn Yr)
City – 3x6u – BCD–CCD; ASs/VAs (contact univ); (not gs) (Eng/Ener Mgt)
Coventry – 240 pts approx (Euro Eng St)
Edinburgh – CCC (Engineering)
Exeter – 240 pts 18u (inc AL maths) – CCC **or** CC+cc **or** VAs (contact univ); (not gs) (BEng Eng; Eng/Bus St; BSc Eng)
Glasgow – 240 pts approx (Prod Des Eng)
Greenwich – 240 pts approx (BEng Integ Eng)
Heriot-Watt – 240 pts 18u – CCC **or** ALs+ASs **or** VAs B+/-AL/ASs; gs; (Eng; Eng Mgt; Int Prod Des)
Hull – 240–220 pts approx (BEng Integ Eng)
Leeds – 240 pts approx (Eng with Fdn Yr)
Leicester – 240 pts 18u – BBE/CCC/BCD (inc maths+phys) **or** CC/BD (inc maths+phys)+cc/bd **or** VA12u (grades as ALs); gs (AL only); (BEng courses)
Lincolnshire & Humberside – 240–160 pts (Engineering)
London (QM) – 240 pts – ALs **or** ALs+ASs **or** VAs+/-ALs/ASs; (BEng Eng Sci courses)
Manchester – CCC (BEng Eng/Bus; Eng Des Sim Mdl; BSc Eng Bus Mgt) maths)
Portsmouth – 240 pts – ALs **or** ALs+ASs **or** VA; (Eng; Eng Des Mats; Eng Sys Mecha)
Reading – CCC/BCD (BEng Integ Eng)
Staffordshire – CCC **or** CCD+AS(40 pts) **or** VAs+/-ALs/ASs; gs; (Eng Des)
Strathclyde – CCC (4 yr BEng; Eng/Bus Mgt Euro St; Pros/Orthot)
Sussex – CCC (Gen Eng)
Ulster – CCC (Engineering)

220 pts **Bradford** – 220 pts 12u (inc AL maths+sci); gs; (Med Sys Eng)
Central England – 220 pts approx (BSc Hons Eng Prod Des)
Brunel – 220 pts 2x6u (inc AL maths D pref sci or VA sci) – ALs **or** ALs+ASs **or** VAs+/-ALs/ASs; (Eng Sci Tech courses; Eng Mgt)
Hertfordshire – 220 pts approx (Eng Mgt)
Leeds – CCD (Eng Tech)
Liverpool John Moores – 220–180 pts approx (BEng Integ Eng)
Luton – 220–180 pts approx (Integ Eng)
South East Essex (Coll) – 220–180 pts (Engineering)
Swansea – CCD (Engineering)
Teesside – 220 pts approx (Gen Eng; Des Eng)

200 pts   **Bradford** – 200 pts 12u; gs; (Ind Eng (inc AL maths); (Mat Des Prod)
Bristol UWE – 200/180–160 pts 12u – ALs **or** ALs+ASs **or** VAs+/-ALs/ASs (6u maths+sci/tech subj); (BSc Eng)
Brunel – 200–160 pts 2x6u (pref AL maths D or VA Eng) – ALs **or** ALs+ASs **or** VAs+/-ALs/ASs; (Fdn Eng)
Central England – 200 pts approx (Eng/Bus St; Eng Sys Mgt; Bus Sys Eng)
Central England – C (art/des) DD **or** ALs+ASs **or** VAs+/-ALs/ASs; (not gs) (Eng Prod Des)
Coventry – 200 pts approx (Int Disas Eng Mgt)
De Montfort – 200 pts – CC (inc art subj)+AL/2ASs **or** VAs+/-ALs/ASs; (not gs) (Ind Des (Eng))
East London – 200 pts approx (Integ Eng)
Robert Gordon – CDD/CC (Eng Des)
Liverpool John Moores – 200 pts approx (Prod Des Eng)
Salford – 200 pts approx (Pros/Orthot)

180 pts   **Aberdeen** – BC (BBB 2nd yr entry) (MEng courses)
Anglia – 180 pts approx (Eng Mgt)
Bournemouth – 180 pts (pref ALs maths/phys) **or** VAs; (Des Eng)
Bournemouth – 180 pts approx (Eng Bus Dev)
Dundee – 180 pts approx (Eng/Lang)
Greenwich – 180 pts approx (Eng/Bus Mgt)
Huddersfield – 180–160 pts approx (Eng/Tech Mgt)
Liverpool (IoM Coll) – 180 pts – ALs **or** ALs+ASs **or** VAs+/-ALs/ASs; (Fdn Integ Eng Bus; Integ Eng)
Napier – DDD/CD (Eng Mgt)
Northumbria – 180 pts approx (Eng/Bus)
Nottingham Trent – 180 pts approx (BSc Integ Eng)
Swansea – DDD (Fdn Eng)

160 pts | See Engineering Council statement at the beginning of this table |

Aberdeen – CC (BBC 2nd yr entry) (BEng)
Coventry – 160 pts approx (Eng Fdn; Euro Bus Tech Eng)
Glasgow Caledonian – CC (Eng/Env)
Leicester – CC (Fdn Int Eng)
Liverpool John Moores – DDE/DD (Fdn Eng/Tech)
Manchester Met – 160 pts approx (App Eng; Eng; Eng Des)
Sheffield Hallam – 160–140 pts approx (Env Eng; Eng Des Innov)
Southampton (Inst) – 160–120 pts approx (Eng Bus)

140 pts   **Bristol UWE** – 140–100 pts 6u – ALs **or** ALs+ASs **or** VAs+/-ALs/ASs; (Fdn Eng)
Derby – 140 pts 12u – CD **or** DD+ee **or** VA12u CD **or** VA6u+AL(D); gs; (Prod Des Eng)
Liverpool – 140 pts – ALs **or** ALs+ASs **or** VAs+/-ALs/ASs; (Fdn Eng)
Salford – 140 pts approx (Unif Eng)
Westminster – 140 pts approx (Ind Sys/Bus Mgt)

120 pts   **Aberdeen** – DD (Eng/Fdn St)
Bournemouth – 120 pts – ALs; (Fdn Des Eng)
Bradford – 120 pts 9u; gs; (Fdn Ind Eng)
Central England – 120 pts; (Fdn Eng)
Huddersfield – 120 pts approx 6u min; (not gs) (Fdn Eng)
Oxford Brookes – DD (Fdn Eng)
Warwickshire (Coll) – 120 pts 12u (Engineering)
Wolverhampton – 120 pts 12u – DEE/DD **or** DE+d **or** VA12u DD; gs; (Eng/Tech Mgt; Eng/Lang/Law)

100 pts   **and below**
Barnsley (Coll) – (Fdn Eng Ext)
Blackburn (Coll) – 80 pts approx (BEng)
Cornwall & Duchy (Coll) – (Fdn Eng)
Greenwich – (Ind Auto Ext)

Hertfordshire – (Ext Eng)
Nottingham Trent – (Ext Eng)
Plymouth – (Eng Sys; Ext Eng)
Portsmouth – (Ext Eng)
Reading (CSAD) – (Engineering)
Southampton (Inst) – E (Fdn Eng Bus)
Staffordshire – EE; gs; (Ext Eng)
Sunderland – (Fdn Eng)
Teesside – (Ext Eng)

Leeds Met – (contact university)

Diploma of Higher Education courses
Abertay Dundee; Sheffield Hallam (Ind St)

Higher National Diploma courses
100 pts and below
Abertay Dundee; Anglia; Bell (CT); Blackburn (Coll); Blackpool & Fylde (Coll); Bolton (IHE); Boston (Coll); Bradford (Coll); Brighton; Brooklands (Coll); Central Lancashire; Coventry; Crawley (Coll) 40 pts, gs; Derby; Durham New (Coll); Epping Forest (Coll); Falkirk (CFHE); Fife (CFHE); Glamorgan; Greenwich; Halton (Coll); Huddersfield; Inverness (Coll); James Watt (Coll); Kingston; Liverpool John Moores; Liverpool (CmC); Mid Cheshire (Coll); Motherwell (Coll); Napier; Newport (UWCN); Northampton (UC); Northbrook (Coll); Nottingham Trent; Park Lane (Coll); Robert Gordon; St Helens (Coll); Sheffield Hallam; Solihull (Coll); South East Essex (Coll); Staffordshire; Stratford on Avon (Coll); Swansea (IHE); UHI (Perth); West Suffolk (Coll); Wiltshire (Coll); Wolverhampton; Worcester (CT).

Alternative Offers:

IB offers: Aberdeen 24 pts; Aston 30 pts; Bath 32 pts maths H6, phys H5; Brighton 26 pts; Brunel 25 pts; Cambridge H777; Cardiff 28 pts H5 maths; City 26 pts; Coventry 24 pts; Durham 30 pts H666; Exeter 29 pts; Hull 28 pts H55 in maths and physics; Lancaster 30 pts; Leicester 26 pts, (Integ Eng) 24 pts; London (QM) 30 pts; Loughborough H66 in maths and physics; Oxford H777; Portsmouth 28 pts; Sheffield Hallam 26 pts; Staffordshire 24 pts; UMIST 30 pts; Warwick 32–28 pts.

Irish offers: Aberdeen ABBBB; Aston BBCCC; Bradford BBBBC; Brunel AABBB; Liverpool BCCCC; Warwick AABBB–BBBBC.

Scottish Qualifications: Aberdeen BBBC; Abertay Dundee BC; Edinburgh BBBB; Glasgow BBBB; Glasgow Caledonian BBC; Napier CCC; Paisley BCC; Robert Gordon BBC/BCCC; Stirling BBBC; Strathclyde (Eng Bus Mgt courses) AAAAB–ABBBB.

Overseas applicants: Warwick and **Coventry (TC)** offer a one-year preparatory course for international students who do not have the right entry grades. Details from the International Office at Warwick University.

CHOOSING YOUR COURSE (See also **Ch.1**)

Subject information: These courses provide the opportunity to study two, three or four engineering specialisms and enable students to delay their choice of specialism. Mathematics and physics provide the foundation of engineering subjects. Several universities and colleges offer one-year Foundation courses for applicants with non-science A-levels. Many sponsorships are available in engineering subjects. (Applicants at interview for scholarships should be aware that they are being judged as potential employees as well as suitable academic candidates for degree courses.) Alternative courses to Engineering include Materials Science, Metallurgy, Computer Science, Technology courses as well as Mathematics, Physics and Applied Physics. See also **Appendix 1**.

Special features: Aberdeen Level 3 specialisms in Civil, Electrical, Electronic, Manufacturing, Mechanical or Software Engineering. **Bath** Engineering offered with French or German. Choice between Aeronautical, Mechanical or Manufacturing Engineering can be delayed until year 2. **Bradford** Choice of nine engineering options following the Foundation course. **Bristol** For BEng, MEng, BSc, MSc applicants decide on a first choice subject and then will be considered automatically for other courses. **Brunel** (SEP) Broad-based programme covering mechanical, electrical and manufacturing engineering with a significant management content. All students sponsored by one of 50 companies. **Cambridge** Two extra years of study are required for the Production and Chemical Engineering Tripos examination. **Cardiff** (Integ Eng) Embraces mechanical, electrical and manufacturing engineering. Common first year for all. **Central England** First year involves electrical, mechanical, electronic and manufacturing engineering together with computer programming. **Coventry** A modular course with a choice which includes mechanical, electrical, manufacturing and building services engineering, design, management and language. **Durham** Common course for first five terms; in final four terms students specialise in Civil or Mechanical or Electrical or Electronic Engineering. **Edinburgh** Common first year with later specialism in one of 11 engineering subjects. **Exeter** Core course in year 1, then BEng or BSc in General Engineering or Chemical, Civil, Electrical, Electronic or Mechanical Engineering. **Glasgow** Common first and second year. Specialisms in years 3 and 4 in Aeronautical or Mechanical Engineering, Naval Architecture and Ocean Engineering. **Hull** After year 1 students qualify for entry to courses in Physics, Computing and Engineering. **Lancaster** Choice in year 2 from Civil, Environmental, Electronic, Mechanical, Mechatronic Engineering. **London (QM)** Flexible programme leading to options in mechanical, aeronautical. **Loughborough** (Eng Sci/Tech) Final year options in Mechanical, Electronic and Electrical and Manufacturing Engineering. **Newcastle** Course includes electronic and mechanical subjects with computer technology and business management. **Northumbria** Integrated degree course allows transfer between courses covering communication, microelectronics, electrical, electronic, opto-electronic, manufacturing, materials and mechanical engineering at the end of the first semester (February). **Nottingham Trent** (Integ Eng) Covers electrical and electronic, mechanical and manufacturing engineering. **Portsmouth** All courses share a common first year. French or German language option. **Reading** Course tailored to achieve balanced approach between mechanical, electrical and electronic engineering. **Salford** (Pros/Orthot) Artificial limbs, braces, splint technology. **Southampton** Foundation year feeds all Engineering courses and Physics. **UMIST** (Integ Eng) An integrated engineering course with second year options covering building, mechanical, civil, chemical or electrical/electronic engineering. **Warwick** Course comprises common first year followed by two-year programmes in each of Civil, Mechanical, Electrical and General Engineering. *NOW CHECK PROSPECTUSES AND WEB SITES.*

Top universities and colleges (Teaching Quality) (see Ch.4): Bristol; Brunel; Cambridge; Cranfield; Durham; Hertfordshire; Kingston; Lancaster; London (Imp); Loughborough; Nottingham; Oxford; Southampton; not all institutions assessed.

Top universities and colleges (Research) (see Ch.4): Aston; Cambridge; Cranfield; Dundee; Durham; Keele; Lancaster; Leicester; Liverpool John Moores; London (Imp); Oxford; Southampton; Sussex; Warwick.

Study opportunities abroad: Aberdeen; Birmingham; Brunel; Central England; City; Coventry; Exeter; Hull; Lancaster; Leeds; Leicester; London (QM); Napier; Portsmouth (SEP); Strathclyde; Ulster; UMIST; Warwick; Wolverhampton.

Work opportunities abroad: Bournemouth; Birmingham; Bradford; Brighton; Brunel; Cardiff; Central England; Huddersfield; Hull; Leicester; Napier; Nottingham Trent; Oxford Brookes; Plymouth; Portsmouth; Sheffield Hallam; Strathclyde; Ulster; UMIST; Warwick.

ADMISSIONS INFORMATION

Number of applicants per place (approx): Aberdeen 6; Abertay Dundee 2; Aston 8; Bath 15; Birmingham 6; Blackburn (Coll) 1; Bournemouth 5; Brunel 4; Cambridge 3.2;

Cardiff (Int Eng) 5; City 3; Coventry 6, (Fdn) 2; De Montfort 5, (Ind Des Eng) 3; Durham 9; Edinburgh 5; Exeter 6; Glasgow Caledonian 10; Hertfordshire 2; Hull 6; Kingston 5; Lancaster 15; Leicester 12; London (UCL) 5; Loughborough 9; Manchester Met 2; Nottingham Trent 3; Oxford 2.6; Robert Gordon 2; Salford (Pros/Orthot) 3; Sheffield Hallam 6; South Bank 5; Strathclyde 5; UMIST 4; Warwick 10.

Planning your UCAS personal statement (see Ch.4): Details of careers in the various engineering specialisms should be obtained from the relevant engineering institutions. This will enable you to describe the interests you have in various aspects of engineering. Contact any engineers to discuss their work with them. Try to arrange a visit to an engineering firm relevant to your choice of specialism. **Bristol** (Eng Maths) Skills, work experience. **Manchester** Talk to the local planning office and planning, landscape and environmental professionals. See also **Appendix 1**.

Selection interviews (see Ch.4): Abertay Dundee (No); Aston (No); Bath (No); Brighton (No); Bristol (Eng Maths); Bristol UWE (No); Brunel; Cambridge (W); Cardiff; Central Lancashire (No); City (No); Coventry (T); Durham; Exeter (No); Hertfordshire (No); Hull (No); Lancaster; Leeds; Leicester; Liverpool John Moores (No); London (QM), (UCL); Loughborough; Manchester; Manchester Met; Nottingham Trent; Oxford (W – optional); Oxford Brookes (English test for overseas students); Portsmouth; Robert Gordon; Salford; Sheffield Hallam; South Bank; Staffordshire (No); Strathclyde; Warwick (No); UMIST (some).

Interview questions (see Ch.4): Since mathematics and physics are important subjects, it is probable that you will be questioned on the applications of these subjects to, for example, the transmission of electricity, nuclear power, aeronautics, mechanics etc. Past questions have included: Explain the theory of an arch; what is its function? What is the connection between distance and velocity and acceleration and velocity? How does a car ignition work? See also under separate Engineering tables.

Reasons for rejection (non-academic): Salford (Pros/Orthot) Lack of sympathy with people with disabilities.

GAP YEAR ADVICE

South Bank Learn to use a computer; Gap year students should try to get engineering experience.

Institutions willing to defer entry after A-levels: Aston; Bath (but give notice before April); Birmingham; Brighton; Brunel; Cardiff; Coventry; De Montfort; Derby; Exeter; Heriot-Watt; Hertfordshire; Huddersfield; Hull; Kingston; Leeds; Leicester; Liverpool; London (UCL) (No); Luton; Manchester Met; Napier; Nottingham Trent; Plymouth; Robert Gordon; Salford; Sheffield Hallam; South Bank; Staffordshire (No); Sussex; Swansea; UMIST; Warwick; Westminster.

AFTER RESULS ADVICE

Institutions which may accept the same points score after A-levels: Birmingham (No); Brighton; Brunel (SEP) (No); Cardiff; Coventry; De Montfort; Derby; Durham (No); Exeter; Heriot-Watt; Hertfordshire; Leeds; Leicester; London (UCL) (No); Manchester Met; Napier; Stirling (No); Strathclyde (No); UMIST; Warwick (No). Most universities and colleges.

Institutions which may accept lower grades/points score after A-levels: Most universities and colleges including Brighton; Brunel; Derby; Hertfordshire; Hull; Leeds; Leicester; London (UCL); Napier; UMIST; Warwick.

Offers to applicants repeating A-levels: Higher Loughborough, Manchester Met, Warwick; **Possibly higher** Coventry, De Montfort, Durham, Edinburgh, Lancaster, Manchester Met, Robert Gordon, Sheffield Hallam; **Same** Brunel (Good reasons needed for repeating), Central England, Derby, Exeter, Heriot-Watt, Huddersfield, Hull, Leeds, Liverpool, London (UCL), Napier, South Bank, UMIST.

Probable vacancies from June 2001 and in Clearing (see Ch.4): This is an undersubscribed subject field and most universities are expected to have some vacancies from

June onwards. Several universities offering Engineering with Business courses are likely to have vacancies.

NEW GRADUATE DESTINATIONS AND EMPLOYMENT (1999 HESA) (see **Ch.4**)

Of 1109 General Engineering graduates surveyed, 754 went into full-time employment, 140 went into further study and 84 were believed to be unemployed.

ENGINEERING (ACOUSTICAL)

NB The information supplied by the universities and colleges this year varies consider-ably and the offers listed below should be used as a first source of reference only. Many institutions will accept combinations of Advanced (AL), Advanced Subsidiary (AS) and Vocational Advanced (VA) level qualifications to achieve the required points total, but applicants must check web sites and prospectuses for full details of all offers. Grades and points totals shown should be regarded as the minimum levels to be achieved, but offers may be adjusted downwards when results are known. The points totals shown to the left of the institutions are for ease of reference only. It must not be assumed that tariff points are always used by institutions or that they can be substituted for an offer in grades. The level of an offer is not necessarily indicative of the quality of a course. To calculate your offers see Chapter 4 and the inside fold of the back cover.

Engineering Council Statement: See **Engineering/Engineering Sciences**.

Special subject requirements/preferences: See **Engineering/Engineering Sciences**.

360 pts **and above**
    Southampton – 370 pts 21u (inc 220 pts AL maths+phys); (MEng Acoust Eng; Acoust Eng/Mus)
350 pts **Southampton** – 350 pts 21u (inc 220 pts AL maths+phys); BEng Acoust Eng)
240 pts **Bristol UWE** – 240 pts approx (Mus Sys Eng)
    Salford – CCC/BB (Acoustics)
220 pts **Salford** – 220 pts approx (Aud Vid Sys; Audtech)

160 pts	See **Engineering Council statement under Engineering/Engineering Sciences**

    Anglia – 160 pts approx (Audiotechnology)

Diploma in Higher Education courses
    Liverpool (LIPA) (Perf Arts – Acoust)

Higher National Diploma courses
100 pts **and below**
    Salford; Sandwell (Coll)

CHOOSING YOUR COURSE (See also **Ch.1**)

Subject information: Courses in Acoustics cover the measurement of sound, hearing, environmental health and legal aspects of acoustics and vibration. Acoustics topics are also included in some music courses. Electrical and Electronic Engineering and Music courses with electronics are alternative courses. See also **Appendix 1**.

Special features: Salford (Aud Vid Sys) Covers architectural and music acoustics, creative studio techniques and music production techniques. **Southampton** Vibration and sound engineering, musical and underwater acoustics. *NOW CHECK PROSPECTUSES AND WEB SITES.*

Top universities and colleges (Teaching Quality) (see Ch.4): Southampton; not all institutions assessed.

Top universities and colleges (Research) (see Ch.4): Southampton.

Work opportunities abroad: Salford.

ADMISSIONS INFORMATION

Number of applicants per place (approx): Salford 4.

Planning your UCAS personal statement (see Ch.4): See under **Engineering/ Engineering Sciences**. See also **Appendix 1**.

Selection interviews: Southampton.

Interview questions (see Ch.4): What interests you about this subject? What career do you have in mind on graduating?

GAP YEAR ADVICE

Institutions willing to defer entry after A-levels: Anglia; Salford.

AFTER RESULTS ADVICE

Institutions which may accept the same points score after A-levels (see Ch.4): Salford.

Institutions which may accept lower grades/points score after A-levels (see Ch.4): Salford.

Probable vacancies from June 2001 and in Clearing (see Ch.4): Contact universities since vacancies are likely.

NEW GRADUATE DESTINATIONS AND EMPLOYMENT (1999 HESA) (see **Ch.4**)

No data available.

ENGINEERING (AERONAUTICAL & AEROSPACE)

NB The information supplied by the universities and colleges this year varies consider- ably and the offers listed below should be used as a first source of reference only. Many institutions will accept combinations of Advanced (AL), Advanced Subsidiary (AS) and Vocational Advanced (VA) level qualifications to achieve the required points total, but applicants must check web sites and prospectuses for full details of all offers. Grades and points totals shown should be regarded as the minimum levels to be achieved, but offers may be adjusted downwards when results are known. The points totals shown to the left of the institutions are for ease of reference only. It must not be assumed that tariff points are always used by institutions or that they can be substituted for an offer in grades. The level of an offer is not necessarily indicative of the quality of a course. To calculate your offers see Chapter 4 and the inside fold of the back cover.

Engineering Council Statement: See **Engineering/Engineering Sciences**.

Special subject requirements/preferences: See also **Engineering/Engineering Sciences**. **GCSE: Bath** Three subjects at grade A including mathematics. French/German grade A for long course. **Bristol** (Aero Eng/Euro) Grade A language. **Cranfield** Four subjects at grade A including mathematics. **London (QM)** Grade A or B in mathematics and science. **Salford** Six to eight grades A–C.

360 pts and above
      Cambridge – Offers, mainly in grades, vary between colleges (Aero Eng)
      Southampton – 390 pts 21u (inc 220 pts AL maths+phys); (MEng Aerosp Eng courses)

350 pts **Southampton** – 350 pts 21u (inc 200 pts AL maths+phys); (BEng Aerosp Eng)
340 pts **Bath** – 3/2ALs (AA maths+phys+AL B); (not gs) (MEng Aerosp Eng; Aerosp
Eng/Fr; Aerosp Eng/Ger)
Bristol – AAB (inc maths+phys) (not gs) (MEng Aero Eng; Aero Eng/Euro)
London (Imp) – AAB (B maths) (Aero Eng; Aero Eng Euro)
Loughborough – 340 pts 18u – BB maths, phys)+AL/2ASs **or** VAs+/-ALs/ASs;
(not gs) (MEng Aero Eng)
320 pts **Bristol** – ABB (inc maths+phys) (not gs) (Avion Sys courses)
City – 3x6u – ABB–BBB (inc maths+phys); ASs/VAs (contact univ); (not gs)
(MEng Aero Eng; Air Trans Eng)
Hertfordshire – 320–300 pts 1x12u **or** 2x6u – ALs **or** ALs+ASs **or** VA6u
(sci/tech/eng)+AL(C maths); gs; (MEng Aerosp Eng; Aerosp Sys Eng)
Sheffield – ABB (BB maths+phys) (MEng Aero Eng)
Strathclyde – ABB (Mech Eng/Aero)
300 pts **Belfast (Queen's)** – BBB–BCC (Aero Eng; Aero Ext)
Glasgow – BBB (MEng Aero Eng)
Kingston – 300 pts 18u (inc 3x6u inc AL maths+2 sci); (Aerosp Eng)
Liverpool – 300 pts – ALs **or** ALs+ASs **or** VAs+/-ALs/ASs; (Aerosp Eng
courses)
London (QM) – 300 pts – ALs **or** ALs+ASs **or** VAs+/-ALs/ASs; (MEng Aerosp
Eng courses)
Loughborough – 300 pts 18u – CC(maths, phys)+AL/2ASs **or** VAs+/-ALs/ASs;
(not gs) (BEng Aero Eng)
Manchester – BBB (Aerosp Eng courses; Aerosp Eng/Euro; Avion/Aerosp Sys)
Salford – 300 pts approx (MEng Aero Eng)
Surrey – 300–240 pts approx (Aerosp Mech Sat Eng)
UMIST – BBB **or** ALs+ASs(AL maths+phys) (not gs) (Aerosp Eng)
York – BBB/BB (Aero Avionics)
280 pts **City** – 3x6u – BBC–BCC (inc maths+phys); ASs/VAs (contact univ); (not gs)
(BEng Aero Eng; Air Trans Ops)
Cranfield – 280 pts – BBC **or** BB+cc (B maths+phys); (not gs) (Aeromech Sys
Eng)
Salford – BBC/BB (Aero Eng)
260 pts **Bristol UWE** – 260–200 pts 18u pref/12u – ALs **or** ALs+ASs VAs+/-ALs/ASs
(min 80 pts 6u maths+sci/tech); (not gs) (MEng Aerosp Manuf Eng)
Brunel – 260 pts approx (Mech Eng/Aero)
City – 3x6u – BCC–CCC (inc maths+phys); ASs/VAs (contact univ); (not gs)
(BEng Air Trans Eng)
London (Imp) – BCC (Aerosp Mat)
London (QM) – BCC–CCD (BEng Aerosp Eng; Avion)
240 pts **Bristol UWE** – 240 pts – ALs **or** ALs+ASs **or** VAs+/-ALs/ASs; (Aero/Aerosp
Eng)
Bristol UWE – 240–220 pts 18u pref/12u – AL **or** ALs+ASs **or** VAs+/-ALs/ASs
(min 80 pts 6u maths+sci/tech subj); (not gs) (BEng Aerosp Sys Eng)
Coventry – 240 pts approx (Aerosp Sys Eng; Avion Sys Eng)
Hertfordshire – 240 pts approx (BEng Aerosp Eng)
Lincolnshire & Humberside – 240 pts approx (Avion; Air Struct Eng)
London (QM) – 240 pts – ALs **or** ALs+ASs **or** VAs+/-ALs/ASs; (Avionics)
220 pts **Brighton** – 220 pts approx (Mech Aero Des Eng)
Glasgow – CCD (1st yr entry) ABC (2nd yr entry) (BEng Avion (Electron))
200 pts **Hertfordshire** – 200 pts approx (Aerosp Tech Mgt)
Salford – 200 pts approx (Aerosp Bus Sys)
180 pts **Staffordshire** – 180 pts approx (Des Tech/Aero)

160 pts | See Engineering Council statement under Engineering/Engineering Sciences |

and below
City – 2x6u – ALs (maths/phys pref); ASs/VAs (contact univ); (not gs) (Fdn Air
Trans Eng)

Coventry – 160 pts approx (Fdn Aerosp Sys Eng)
Farnborough (CT) – 160 pts approx (Aero Eng)
Kingston – 120 pts 21u; (Fdn Aerosp Eng)
North East Wales (IHE) – (Avion; Aero Mech Eng; Sp Tech)
Stockport (CFHE) – (Aero Eng)

Higher National Diploma courses
100 pts   and below

Belfast (IFHE); Brooklands (CFHE); City of Bristol (Coll); Coventry; Crawley (Coll) 40 pts; gs; Ealing (CT); Farnborough (CT); Hertfordshire; Lincolnshire & Humberside; North East Wales (IHE); Northbrook (Coll); Norwich City (Coll); Stockport (CFHE); UHI.

Alternative Offers:

IB offers: Bath 30 pts maths/phys H6/5; Belfast (Queen's) H655 S555; Bristol 34 pts H66 maths/phys; Bristol UWE 26 pts; City (BEng) 28 pts, (MEng) 30 pts inc H555, (Air Trans Eng) 31 pts inc H655; Coventry 24 pts; Cranfield 28 pts H655; Kingston 25 pts; Liverpool 32 pts; London (QM) 26 pts; Loughborough 24 pts; Salford 28 pts; Southampton 34 pts; UMIST 32 pts inc H66 maths/phys; York 30 pts.

Irish offers: Liverpool BCCCCC.

Scottish Qualifications: Glasgow ABBBB–BBBBC; Strathclyde (Mech Eng/Aero) AAAAB.

CHOOSING YOUR COURSE (See also **Ch.1**)

> **Subject information:** Courses cover the manufacture of military and civil aircraft, theories of mechanics, thermodynamics, electronics, computing and engine design and manufacture. Alternative courses include Physics and Applied Physics, Mathematics and Materials Science. Aircraft design is also very similar to the design of sea-going vessels in a number of aspects so Naval Architecture or Ship Science could also be considered. See also **Appendix 1**.

Special features: Bath Choice between Aeronautical, Mechanical and Manufacturing Engineering can be delayed until year 2. Language options. **Belfast (Queen's)** Course covers manufacture and operation of civil and military aircraft. **Bristol** (Aero Eng/Euro) Year 3 in Europe. Course includes languages and European Studies. **City** (Aero Eng) Year 1 common with Air Transport and Mechanical Engineering. **Cranfield** Common year 1 with Mechanical and Electronic Systems Engineering. Transfers possible before year 2. Final year based around aircraft design project. Helicopter aerodynamics part of the course. Cranfield flight test course included in final year. Scholarships available for well-qualified candidates. **Glasgow** Course shares similar subjects in years 1 and 2 with Mechanical Engineering, Naval Architecture and Ocean Engineering. **Hertfordshire** Common year 1 with Mechanical and Vehicle Engineering. Emphasis on design and computer simulation. Most able students can transfer to MEng in year 2. **London (Imp)** Broadly-based courses in engineering science, combined with specialist study of aerodynamics and advanced structural mechanics. Optional year in Europe. **London (QM)** Course unit system allows flexible choice of subjects studied within the Aeronautical and Electronics Departments. **Loughborough** Year 1 common with Automobile Engineering; transfers possible. **Manchester** British Aerospace plc designated centre of excellence. Choice of 3 or 4-year courses can be made during the first 2 years. **Southampton** Design, technology, social and economic aspects. Aerospace materials, languages, industrial law are options in year 3. *NOW CHECK PROSPECTUSES AND WEB SITES.*

Top universities and colleges (Teaching Quality) (see Ch.4): See **Engineering/ Engineering Sciences**.

Top universities and colleges (Research) (see Ch.4): See under **Engineering (Mechanical)**.

Study opportunities abroad: Bath; Bristol; City; Coventry; Hertfordshire; London (Imp), (QM); Manchester; Salford.

Work opportunities abroad: Bath; Coventry; Lincolnshire & Humberside; Loughborough; London (Imp); Salford; Staffordshire.

ADMISSIONS INFORMATION

Number of applicants per place (approx): Bath 13, (MEng) 18; Belfast (Queen's) 6; Bristol 12; Bristol UWE 4; City 17; Coventry 7; Cranfield 10; Farnborough (CT) 7; Hertfordshire 17; Kingston 9; London (Imp) 7, (QM) 8; Loughborough 18; Manchester 10; North East Wales (IHE) 5; Salford 6; Southampton 13; UMIST 10.

Planning your UCAS personal statement (see Ch.4): Bristol Interest in engineering and aerospace. Work experience in engineering. Flying experience. Personal attainments. **London (QM)** Practical experience. Relevant hobbies. Membership of Air Training Corps. See also under **Engineering/Engineering Sciences**. See also **Appendix 1**.

Selection interviews (see Ch.4): Bath (No); Bristol; Cambridge; City (No); Cranfield; Farnborough (CT); Hertfordshire; Kingston; London (QM); Loughborough; Manchester; Salford; Southampton; Staffordshire (No).

Interview questions (see Ch.4): Why Aeronautical Engineering? Questions about different types of aircraft and flight principles of helicopters.

Reasons for rejection (non-academic): Poor work ethic. Lack of motivation towards the subject area. Better suited to a less specialised engineering/science course. Failure to attend interview.

GAP YEAR ADVICE

Bath and **Liverpool** Preferably for industrial training; **London (QM)** Apply for a sponsorship to British Aerospace plc; **Loughborough** Seek sponsorship for the 1:3:1 scheme. See under **Engineering (Mechanical)**.

Institutions willing to defer entry after A-levels: Bath (but give notice before April); Bristol; City; Coventry; Cranfield (No); Farnborough (CT); Hertfordshire; Kingston; Leicester; Loughborough; North East Wales (IHE); Salford; Southampton; Staffordshire; UMIST; York.

AFTER RESULTS ADVICE

Institutions which may accept the same points score after A-levels: Bath (No); Belfast (Queen's) (No); Bristol (No); City; Coventry; Cranfield; Hertfordshire (No); Kingston; Loughborough; Manchester; North East Wales (IHE); Salford; Southampton (No); Staffordshire; UMIST.

Institutions which may accept lower grades/points score after A-levels: Bath; Belfast (Queen's); Bristol; City; Coventry; Cranfield; Farnborough (CT); Hertfordshire; Lincolnshire & Humberside; Loughborough; North East Wales (IHE); Sheffield (No); Southampton; UMIST.

Offers to applicants repeating A-levels: Higher Belfast (Queen's), Bristol; **Possibly higher** Hertfordshire; **Same** Bath, City, Cranfield, Farnborough (CT), Kingston, Liverpool, Loughborough, Southampton, Staffordshire.

Probable vacancies from June 2001 and in Clearing (see Ch.4): Several universities are likely to have vacancies with offers in popular institutions ranging from 300 to 240 pts.

NEW GRADUATE DESTINATIONS AND EMPLOYMENT (1999 HESA) (see **Ch.4**)

Out of a survey of 504 graduates, 337 graduates entered full-time employment, 96 went on to further study and 35 were believed to be unemployed.

ENGINEERING (AGRICULTURAL) (see also Agricultural Sciences/Agriculture)

NB The information supplied by the universities and colleges this year varies considerably and the offers listed below should be used as a first source of reference only. Many institutions will accept combinations of Advanced (AL), Advanced Subsidiary (AS) and Vocational Advanced (VA) level qualifications to achieve the required points total, but applicants must check web sites and prospectuses for full details of all offers. Grades and points totals shown should be regarded as the minimum levels to be achieved, but offers may be adjusted downwards when results are known. The points totals shown to the left of the institutions are for ease of reference only. It must not be assumed that tariff points are always used by institutions or that they can be substituted for an offer in grades. The level of an offer is not necessarily indicative of the quality of a course. To calculate your offers see Chapter 4 and the inside fold of the back cover.

> **Engineering Council Statement: See Engineering/Engineering Sciences.**

Special subject requirements/preferences: See Engineering/Engineering Sciences.
Other: Harper Adams (UC) Farming experience prior to entry recommended.

300 pts and above
    Harper Adams (UC) – 300 pts 18u – BBB **or** BB+bb **or** VAs+/-ALs/ASs; (not gs) (MEng: Agric Eng; OffRd Veh Des)
    Writtle (Coll) – 300 pts approx (MEng Agric Eng)
240 pts Harper Adams (UC) – 240 pts 18u – CCC **or** CC+cc **or** VAs+/-AL/ASs; (not gs) (BEng Agric Eng)
220 pts Writtle (Coll) – 220 pts approx (BEng Agric Eng)

160 pts | See Engineering Council statement under Engineering/Engineering Sciences

    Harper Adams (UC) – 160 pts 18u – CC **or** C+cc **or** VA CC; (not gs) (BSc: Eng Des Dev; BSc Agric Eng; OffRd Veh Des)
    Royal (CAg) – 160 pts 12u – CC/CEE/DDE **or** CE+c **or** DD+c **or** VA CC; gs; (Farm Mech/Mgt; Farm Mech/Euro Lang)
    Writtle (Coll) – 160 pts approx (Agric Eng; Agric Eng Bus Mgt; Agric Mech)

Higher National Diploma courses
100 pts and below
    Bell (CT); Central Lancashire; Rycotewood (Coll); Scottish (CAg); Wiltshire (Coll); Writtle (Coll).

CHOOSING YOUR COURSE (See also **Ch.1**)

> **Subject information:** This is a study of agricultural, food or environmental engineering systems. Forestry and Agroforestry could also be considered as alternative courses. See also **Appendix 1**.

Special features: Harper Adams (UC) The course includes Engineering Design, Machine Mechanisms, modules in Management and Marketing, and options in Product Development, Building Design and Environmental Engineering. **Writtle (Coll)** The BEng Agricultural Engineering course includes Agricultural Machine Technology, Engineering Communications, Land and Water Engineering, Soil Mechanics, Mathematics and Statistics. *NOW CHECK PROSPECTUSES AND WEB SITES.*

ADMISSIONS INFORMATION

Number of applicants per place (approx): Newcastle 7; Writtle (Coll) 2.

Interview questions (see Ch.4): What kind of work are you interested in after completing your degree course? What do you already know about agricultural engineering? Have you visited any agricultural shows in the past year? What did you find of interest?

GAP YEAR ADVICE

Institutions willing to defer entry after A-levels: Writtle (Coll).

AFTER RESULTS ADVICE

Institutions which may accept the same points score after A-levels: Newcastle. Most universities and colleges.

Probable vacancies from June 2001 and in Clearing (see Ch.4): Contact all institutions since vacancies are likely.

NEW GRADUATE DESTINATIONS AND EMPLOYMENT (1999 HESA) (see **Ch.4**)

No data available.

ENGINEERING (CHEMICAL)

NB The information supplied by the universities and colleges this year varies considerably and the offers listed below should be used as a first source of reference only. Many institutions will accept combinations of Advanced (AL), Advanced Subsidiary (AS) and Vocational Advanced (VA) level qualifications to achieve the required points total, but applicants must check web sites and prospectuses for full details of all offers. Grades and points totals shown should be regarded as the minimum levels to be achieved, but offers may be adjusted downwards when results are known. The points totals shown to the left of the institutions are for ease of reference only. It must not be assumed that tariff points are always used by institutions or that they can be substituted for an offer in grades. The level of an offer is not necessarily indicative of the quality of a course. To calculate your offers see Chapter 4 and the inside fold of the back cover.

Engineering Council Statement: See **Engineering/Engineering Sciences**.

Special subject requirements/preferences: See **Engineering/Engineering Sciences**. **A-level:** Chemistry with mathematics and possibly physics. Check biology for some university courses. **GCSE: Bath** Physics grade C (if not at A-level) or double science grade B. **Swansea** Three subjects grade A, three subjects grade B.

360 pts **and above**
 Cambridge – Offers, mainly in grades, vary between colleges (Chem Eng)
 Oxford – Offers vary between candidates (Chem Eng)
320 pts **London (Imp)** – ABB–BBB (MEng Chem Eng; Petrol Eng)
 London (UCL) – ABB–BBB or 3ALs+AS/VA; (Chem Eng courses; Biochem Eng courses)
300 pts **Aston** – 300 pts 18u – 3ALs or ALs+ASs or VAs+/-ALs/ASs; gs; (MEng Chem Eng/App Chem)
 Bath – 300 pts 18u – ALs (inc maths, chem: 100 pts each) or ALs (inc maths, chem 100 pts each)+2ASs; (not gs) (MEng Bioch Eng; Env Chem Eng; Chem Eng)
 Belfast (Queen's) – BBB–BCC (Chem Eng courses)
 Bradford – BBB (MEng Chem Eng)
 Edinburgh – BBB–CCC (MEng/BEng Chem Eng courses)
 Leeds – 18u – BBB(B maths) or ALs+ASs or VAs+/-ALs/ASs; gs (AL only); (MEng Sfty Eng; Ener Eng; Fire Eng; Env Ener Eng)
 Leeds – 18u – BBB or BB+bb; VAs (contact dept); (not gs) (Med Mech Eng)
 Loughborough – 300 pts 18u – 2ALs (maths, sci)+AL/2ASs (sci) or VAs+/-ALs/ASs; (not gs) (MEng/BEng Chem Eng)
 Manchester – BBB (MEng Ener Sys)
 Newcastle – BBB/300 pts approx (MEng Chem Proc Eng)
 Nottingham – BBB–BBC (Chem Eng)

Sheffield – 300 pts approx (MEng Chem Proc Eng/Fuel Tech; Chem Eng/Lang; Chem Eng/Env Biotech; Chem Proc Eng)

Surrey – 300 pts 18u – BBB **or** ALs+ASs **or** VAs (depends on subj)+/-ALs/ASs (inc AL maths); (not gs) (MEng: Chem Eng; Chem Eng Env)

Swansea – 300 pts 18u – 300 pts **or** ALs+ASs **or** VAs+/-ALs/ASs; (MEng Chem Eng)

UMIST – 300 pts (Chem Eng courses)

280 pts **Birmingham** – BBC (Chem Eng courses except under **240 pts**)

Sheffield – 280 pts approx (MEng Chem Proc Eng Fdn)

Swansea – 280 pts 18u – BBC–BCC/BB **or** ALs+ASs **or** VAs+/-ALs/ASs; (Chem Eng courses except under **300/200 pts**)

260 pts **Belfast (Queen's)** – BCC (Chem Eng; Chem/Food Eng)

Glasgow Caledonian – BCC (Fire Risk Eng)

Leeds – BCC (Env Chem Eng; Chem Eng)

Newcastle – BCC/BC (BEng Chem/Proc Eng)

Surrey – 260 pts 18u – BCC **or** ALs+ASs **or** VAs (depends on subj)+/-ALs/ASs(inc AL maths); (not gs) (BEng Chem Eng; Chem Proc Eng)

240 pts **Aston** – 240 pts 18u – 3ALs **or** ALs+ASs **or** VAs+/-ALs/ASs; gs; (BEng Chem Eng)

Birmingham – 240 pts approx (Chem Eng Fdn)

Bradford – CCC/BB (BEng Chem Eng)

Central Lancashire – 240 pts 12u (inc AL maths+sci); gs; (Fire Eng)

City – 240 pts 3x6u – CCC (inc C maths/sci); ASs/VAs (contact univ); (not gs) (Biomed Eng/App Phys)

Heriot-Watt – 240 pts 18u – CCC **or** ALs+ASs **or** VAs B+/-ALs/ASs; gs; (Chem Eng courses; Brew/Distil Tech)

Leeds – 18u – CCC(C maths) **or** ALs+ASs **or** VAs+/-ALs/ASs; gs (AL only); (BEg Sfty Eng; Ener Eng; Fire Eng; Fire Sci; Env Ener Eng)

Loughborough – 240 pts 18u – 2ALs (maths, sci)+AL/2ASs (sci) **or** VAs+/-ALs/ASs; (not gs) (Chem Eng/Env Prot)

Manchester – CCC (Ener Sys)

Newcastle – CCC; (not gs) (Fdn Chem/Proc Eng)

South Bank – 240 pts (Chem Eng)

220 pts **Bradford** – CCD (Chem Proc)

Leeds – 18u – CCD **or** ALs+ASs **or** VAs+/-AL/ASs; gs; (Sfty Eng; Fire Sfty/Mgt; Fuel Combus Sci)

South Bank – 220–140 pts (Chem Eng Des)

Strathclyde – CCD (BCC 2nd yr entry) (Chem Eng)

Swansea – 220 pts 18u – CCD/CC **or** ALs+ASs **or** VAs+/-ALs/ASs; (Chem Eng Integ; Bioch Integ)

Teesside – 220–180 pts approx (Chem Eng)

200 pts **Northumbria** – 200 pts (Chem/Chem Eng)

Swansea – 200 pts 18u – CDD/DD **or** ALs+ASs **or** VAs+/-ALs/ASs; (Bioch Eng Int; Chem Eng 2+2)

Teeside – 200–180 pts (Chem Eng/Fd Tech)

180 pts **Heriot-Watt** – DDD (CCC 2nd yr entry) (Brew/Distil Tech)

Huddersfield – 180 pts approx (Chem/Chem Eng)

Staffordshire – 180 pts approx (Des Tech/Renew Ener; Med Eng)

160 pts | See Engineering Council statement under Engineering/Engineering Sciences |

Central Lancashire – 160 pts 12u; gs; (Fire Sfty Mgt)

120 pts **North London** – 120 pts – 2ALs **or** VAs; (Poly Eng courses)

Paisley – DD (Chem Eng)

Higher National Diploma courses
100 pts **and below**

Central Lancashire (Fire Sfty); Dudley (CT); Farnborough (CT) (Ener Mgt); Fife (CFHE); Glamorgan; Halton (Coll); Huddersfield; South Bank; Teesside; Wirral Met (Coll).

Biochemical Engineering - the challenge to numerate sixth formers in creating health and wealth from new life science discoveries

The discovery of penicillin was a momentous achievement. However, it took 15 years and an international effort to find a way to produce it in the quantities needed for medical treatment. The subsequent realisation of the lives lost as a result of this delay from discovery to availability set the scene for the birth of the discipline of biochemical engineering.

The medicines of the future — human proteins, therapeutic vaccines and human tissue for repair — are vastly more complex than penicillin. They are addressing previously intractable conditions and generating opportunities even more exciting than e-commerce. Many disciplines are now involved in the initial discoveries. However, it is those who are numerate and have gained engineering, team and leadership skills that are translating these sensitively into the new medicines. It is also such people who are managing the billions of pounds of investment needed to achieve the outcome and who are dealing with the social and environmental issues that all big endeavours must address.

Those seeking a professional career in a subject that is demanding, and who want a life at the cutting edge that is highly rewarded, should consider the excitement of biochemical engineering as a degree option.

Information on courses can be found in UCAS guides both under biochemical engineering and chemical engineering and more information is on the web. Visits can be arranged to explore in more detail the A level requirements, the courses and the careers available.

Alternative Offers:

IB offers: Aston 32 pts; Bath 30 pts inc H6 chem; Belfast H655 S555; Birmingham 30 pts; Brighton 24 pts; Edinburgh BBBB; Exeter 30 pts; Heriot-Watt 26 pts; Leeds 28 pts; London (UCL) 30 pts; Loughborough 25 pts H555; Newcastle 28 pts H555; Staffordshire 24 pts; Surrey 28 pts inc H555 in maths, phys, chem; Swansea 28 pts; Teesside 24 pts H555; UMIST 32–31 pts.

Irish offers: Bradford BBCCC; Sheffield BBBBB; Swansea BBBBBB.

Scottish Qualifications: Edinburgh ABBB–BBBB; Glasgow Caledonian BBCC; Heriot-Watt (1st yr) BBBB; Napier BBB; Paisley BBC; Strathclyde AAAB–BBBB.

Overseas applicants: Bath One month remedial English course. **Birmingham, Leeds, UMIST** Foundation courses available.

CHOOSING YOUR COURSE (See also **Ch.1**)

> **Subject information:** Chemical Engineering courses are based on maths, physics and chemistry and lead on to studies in energy resources, nuclear energy, pollution, petroleum engineering, bio-process engineering and biotechnology. Several of these topics such as environmental engineering or engineering or science courses and biochemistry are also offered as degree courses and could be considered as alternatives. See also **Appendix 1**.

Special features: Aston Easy transfer between Chemical Engineering and Applied Chemistry in year 1. **Bath** Flexible course choice in year 3, graduating in Chemical Engineering or Chemical and Bioprocess Engineering. **Bradford** Thin sandwich courses; 50% of students have at least one placement in France, Germany or Belgium. French and German language taken in early semesters. Process control, management available as specialisms. **Leeds** Strong chemistry content. (Fuel Combus Sci) Course covers all aspects of energy supply and conservation including major fuels, coal, oil, gas and nuclear as well as alternative sources such as solar, biomass, wind, wave etc. **London (Imp)** Years 3 and 4 options include management, nuclear chemical engineering, energy fuels and pollution biotechnology. Language options include Japanese. **Loughborough** All courses have common years 1 and 2; transfers possible up to end of year 2. Emphasis on plant safety, loss prevention, environmental protection, food and other bioprocessing. **Newcastle** (Chem/Proc Eng) Modular course, language tuition available. Deferred choice for sandwich until year 2. **Nottingham** Options in languages, management, accountancy, patents and licensing. **Sheffield** Options in nuclear, fuel and energy and environmental engineering and modern languages. **Teesside** Subjects covered include biotechnology, separation processes and process and systems design. **UMIST** A range of Chemical Engineering courses with French, German, Spanish, Biotechnology or Environmental Technology options. *NOW CHECK PROSPECTUSES AND WEB SITES.*

Top universities and colleges (Teaching Quality) (see Ch.4): Cambridge; London (Imp); Loughborough; Sheffield; UMIST; not all institutions assessed. See also **Engineering/ Engineering Science**.

Top universities and colleges (Research) (see Ch.4): Bath; Birmingham; Cambridge; Edinburgh; Leeds; London (Imp), (UCL); Loughborough; UMIST.

Study opportunities abroad: Aston; Bath; Birmingham; Bradford; Exeter; Heriot-Watt; Huddersfield; Leeds; London (Imp), (UCL); Loughborough; Napier; Newcastle; Sheffield; Strathclyde; Swansea; Teesside; UMIST.

Work opportunities abroad: Aston; Bath; Birmingham; Bradford; Leeds; London (UCL); Loughborough; Napier; Newcastle; North London; South Bank; Surrey; Swansea; Teesside.

ADMISSIONS INFORMATION

Number of applicants per place (approx): Aston 6; Bath 6; Bradford (all courses) 5; Birmingham 5; Heriot-Watt 8; Huddersfield 7; Leeds 9; London (Imp) 4, (MEng) 4 (UCL)

8; Loughborough 7; Newcastle (MEng/BEng) 6; Nottingham 10; Sheffield 14; South Bank 5; Strathclyde 6; Surrey 4; Swansea 5; Teesside 5; UMIST 9.

Selection interviews (see Ch.4): Aston; Bath; Bradford; Cambridge; Leeds; London (UCL); Napier; Newcastle; Nottingham; Oxford; Paisley (No); Sheffield (No); South Bank; Staffordshire (No); Surrey; Swansea; Teesside; UMIST.

Interview questions (see Ch.4): Discuss some industrial applications of chemistry. How would you justify the processing of radioactive waste to people living in the neighbourhood? What is public health engineering? What is biochemical engineering? What could be the sources of fuel and energy in the year 2101?

Reasons for rejection (non-academic): No contribution of any sort is made to the project discussion during the UCAS visit. Poor interview preparation.

GAP YEAR ADVICE

Aston Discuss sandwich placements with admissions tutor; **Bradford** If working with a chemical firm discuss your arrangements with admissions tutor; **Loughborough** Take a job in the process industry; **South Bank** Not acceptable; **UMIST** Year out in the process industry is valuable.

Institutions willing to defer entry after A-levels: Anglia; Aston; Birmingham; Coventry; Heriot-Watt; Leeds (No); London (UCL) (No); Loughborough; Napier; Newcastle; Northampton (UC); Nottingham; Sheffield; Surrey; Swansea; UMIST.

AFTER RESULTS ADVICE

Institutions which may accept the same points score after A-levels: Aston; Bath; Birmingham; Bradford; Heriot-Watt; Leeds; London (UCL) (No); Loughborough; Napier; Newcastle; Nottingham (No); Sheffield (No); South Bank; Strathclyde; Surrey; Swansea; Teesside; UMIST. Most universities and colleges.

Institutions which may accept lower grades/points score after A-levels: Bath; Belfast (Queen's); Birmingham; Bradford; Leeds; Loughborough; Napier; Newcastle; Surrey; Swansea; Teesside; UMIST. Most universities and colleges.

Offers to applicants repeating A-levels: Higher Swansea, UMIST; **Possibly higher** Bath, Belfast, Leeds, South Bank; **Same** Aston, Birmingham, Bradford, Exeter, Loughborough, Napier, Newcastle, Nottingham, Sheffield, Surrey, Swansea, Teesside, Ulster.

Probable vacancies from June 2001 and in Clearing (see Ch.4): 260–200 pts are expected to be considered by several of the more competitive universities.

NEW GRADUATE DESTINATIONS AND EMPLOYMENT (1999 HESA) (see **Ch.4**)

In a survey of 637 graduates, 413 entered full-time employment, 137 opted for further study and 45 were believed to be unemployed.

ENGINEERING (CIVIL) (including Environmental Engineering)

NB The information supplied by the universities and colleges this year varies considerably and the offers listed below should be used as a first source of reference only. Many institutions will accept combinations of Advanced (AL), Advanced Subsidiary (AS) and Vocational Advanced (VA) level qualifications to achieve the required points total, but applicants must check web sites and prospectuses for full details of all offers. Grades and points totals shown should be regarded as the minimum levels to be achieved, but offers may be adjusted downwards when results are known. The points totals shown to the left of the institutions are for ease of reference only. It must not be assumed that tariff points are always used by institutions or that they can be substituted for an offer in grades. The level of an offer is not necessarily indicative of the quality of a course. To calculate your offers see Chapter 4 and the inside fold of the back cover.

> **Engineering Council Statement:** See **Engineering/Engineering Sciences.**

Special subject requirements/preferences: See **Engineering/Engineering Sciences.**
GCSE: Aston (Euro courses) Grade A or B in French or German if not at A-level. **Bath** Grades A and B in all subjects plus double science if no A-level in physics. **Bristol** Grade As in mathematics/sciences. Grade A or B in languages for Euro courses. **Durham** Minimum of five A* or A grades. **Newcastle** (Civ Env Eng) Sciences if not offered at A-level. **Surrey** Grade A–B including mathematics, physics, science and English language. **Swansea** Mathematics grade B or higher. **Warwick** Grade A or B in physics or combined/dual science.

360 pts **and above**
 Cambridge – Offers, mainly in grades, vary between colleges (Engineering)
 Oxford – Offers vary between candidates (Engineering)
 Southampton – 390 pts 21u – 2ALs (220 pts AL maths+phys)+ALs/ASs/VA as 3rd AL; (MEng Civ Eng/Euro St)
 Southampton – 370 pts 21u (inc 220 pts AL maths+phys); (MEng Civ Eng courses except above; Env Eng courses)

350 pts **Bath** – 350 pts – ALs **or** 2ALs+2ASs(AL maths); (not gs) (MEng Civ/Archit Eng)
 Southampton – 350 pts 21u (inc 200 pts AL maths+phys); (BEng Civ Eng; Wtr Mgt/Eng; Env Eng courses)

320 pts **UMIST** – 350–300 pts (inc maths+phys) – ABB–BBB; (not gs) (MEng courses)
 Cardiff – 320–300 pts approx (MEng Civ Eng courses; Archit Eng; Civ Env Eng)
 London (Imp) – ABB (A/B for lang courses) (Civ Eng courses)
 Nottingham – 320–260 pts 18u – ABB–BCC (not gs) (Civ Eng; Env Eng/Fr/Ger)
 Strathclyde – ABB (Env Eng 2nd yr entry)
 UMIST – 320 pts 18u – ABB **or** AB+bb(AL maths, phys); (not gs) (MEng Civ Eng/N Am St)
 Warwick – ABB (MEng Civ Eng; Civ Eng Euro)

310 pts **Southampton** – 310 pts – 2ALs (180 pts maths, phys)+ALs/ASs/VA as 3rd AL; (BEng Civ Eng; Env Eng)

300 pts **Aberdeen** – BBB (Civ Eng)
 Bath – 300 pts(inc AL maths) – ALs **or** 2ALs+2ASs **or** VA+AL(maths); (not gs) (BEng Civ Eng)
 Belfast (Queen's) – BBB–BCC (Civ Eng courses)
 Birmingham – BBB–BBC (Civ/Env Eng courses)
 Brighton – 300 pts approx (MEng Archit Struct)
 Bristol – BBB/ABC (inc maths, phys) (not gs) (Civ Eng courses)
 City – 3x6u – ABC; ASs/VAs (contact univ); (not gs) (MEng Civ Eng)
 Cranfield – 300 pts 18u – BBB **or** BB+bb(B maths, phys); (not gs) (MEng Civ Eng)
 Dundee – 300 pts approx (MEng Civ Eng)
 East London – 300–160 pts approx (Civ Eng courses)
 Edinburgh – BBB–CCC (MEng/BEng Civ Eng)
 Exeter – 300 pts 18u (inc AL maths) – BBB **or** BB+bb **or** VAs (contact univ); (not gs) (MEng Civ Eng courses)
 Kingston – 300 pts approx (MEng Civ Eng)
 Loughborough – 300 pts (MEng Civ Eng)
 Manchester – BBB (MEng Civ Eng; Struct Eng/Archit with Euro/Jap)
 Liverpool John Moores – 300 pts – ALs **or** ALs+ASs **or** VAs+/-ALs/ASs; (MEng Civ Eng)
 London (UCL) – BBB **or** 3ALs+AS/VA (MEng Civ Eng; Civ/Env Eng)
 Loughborough – 300 pts – C(maths)+AL+AL/2ASs **or** VAs+/-ALs/ASs; (not gs) (MEng Civ Eng)
 Newcastle – 300 pts approx/BBB; (not gs) (MEng Civ Eng; Civ Struct Eng; Civ Env Eng with Fdn Yr)
 Portsmouth – 300 pts (inc 2x6u) – ALs **or** ALs+ASs **or** VAs; (MEng Civ Eng; Civ Eng/Euro)

Salford – BBB (MEng Civ Eng courses)
Sheffield – BBB (Civ Eng courses)
Strathclyde – BBB (MEng Civ Eng courses)
Surrey – 300 pts 18u – BBB **or** ALs+ASs **or** VAs (depends on subj)+/-ALs/ASs (inc AL maths); (not gs) (MEng Civ Eng)
Swansea – 300 pts 18u – BBB **or** ALs/ASs **or** VAs+/-ALs/ASs; (MEng Civ Eng)
UMIST – 300–250 pts (inc maths+phys) – BBB–BBC (BEng courses)
UMIST – 300 pts 18u – BBB **or** BB+bb (AL maths, phys); (not gs) (MEng Civ/Struct Eng/Fr/Ger; MEng/BEng Civ Eng; Env Eng)

280 pts **Birmingham** – BBC–BCC (Civ Eng; Env Eng courses)
Cardiff – 280–240 pts approx (BEng Civ Eng; Archit Eng)
Durham – 280 pts approx (Civ Eng)
London (UCL) – BBC **or** 3ALs+AS/VA (BEng Civ Eng; Civ/Env Eng; Struct Eng)
Strathclyde – BBC–CCC (BEng Civ Eng courses; Env Hlth)
Swansea – 280 pts 18u – BBC/AA **or** ALs+ASs **or** VAs+/-ALs/ASs; (MEng Env Eng)

260 pts **Belfast (Queen's)** – BCC (BEng Civ Eng)
Birmingham – BCC (Fdn Civ Eng)
Edinburgh – BCC (Civ Eng; Civ Env Eng)
Greenwich – 260 pts approx (Euro Civ Eng)
Liverpool – 260 pts – ALs **or** ALs+ASs **or** VAs+/-ALs/ASs; (Civ Eng courses)
London (UCL) – BCC **or** 3ALs+AS/VA (BEng Civ Eng with Fdn Yr)
Loughborough – 260 pts – ALs+ALs/2ASs **or** VAs+/-ALs/ASs; (not gs) (Archit Eng/Des Mgt)
Newcastle – BCC–CCC; (not gs) (BEng Civ Eng/Civ Struct Eng; Civ Env Eng; Fdn Yr)
Nottingham – BCC (Env Eng)
Surrey – 260 pts 18u – BCC **or** ALs+ASs **or** VAs (depends on subj)+/-ALs/ASs; (not gs) (BEng Civ Eng)
Swansea – 260 pts 18u – BCC–CCC (C maths) **or** ALs+ASs **or** VAs+/-ALs/ASs; (Civ Eng/Fr; Civ Eng/Span; Civ Eng/Ger; Civ Eng/Ital)
Ulster – BCC (BEng Civ Eng courses; Env Eng)
Warwick – BCC (BEng Civ Eng)

240 pts **Aston** – 18u – CCC/AB **or** ALs+ASs **or** VAs+/-ALs/ASs; gs; (BEng Civ Eng courses)
Bradford – CCC/BB (Civ Eng; Comp Aid Struct Eng; Env Mgt/Tech)
Brighton – CCC/BC (Env Eng; Civ Eng)
Bristol UWE – 240–220 pts approx (Env Eng)
Central Lancashire – 240 pts approx (Env Eng)
City – 3x6u – CCC; ASs/VAs (contact univ); (not gs) (BEng Civ Eng)
Cranfield – 240 pts 18u – CCC **or** CC+cc(C maths, phys); (not gs) (BEng Civ Eng)
Dundee – 240 pts approx/CC (BEng 3 yr Civ Eng)
Exeter – 240 pts 18u (inc AL maths) – CCC **or** CC+cc **or** VAs (contact univ); (not gs) (BEng Civ Eng)
Greenwich – 240 pts (Civ Eng/Wtr Env Mgt)
Heriot-Watt – 240 pts 18u – CCC **or** ALs+ASs **or** VAs B+/-ALs/ASs; gs; (Civ Eng; Struct Eng courses; Off Eng)
Hertfordshire – 240–200 pts 1x12u **or** 2x6u – (Civ Eng courses H200/H250)
Kingston – 240 pts inc 2x6u (inc 40 pts AL maths or 20 pts AS maths); gs; (Civ Eng)
Leeds – 18u – CCC **or** 2ALs+2ASs (AL maths); VAs (contact univ); (Civ Eng/Archit; Civ Eng; Archit Eng; Civ Eng Euro)
Liverpool John Moores – 240 pts – ALs **or** ALs+ASs **or** VAs+/-ALs/ASs; (BEng Civ Eng)
Loughborough – 240 pts – C(maths)+AL+AL/2ASs **or** VAs+/-ALs/ASs; (not gs) (BEng; Civ Eng)

Manchester – CCC/BB (BEng Civ Eng; Struct Eng/Archit; Struct Eng/Euro/Jap)
Newcastle – CCC/BC–CC; (not gs) (Off Eng)
Nottingham Trent – 240 pts approx (Civ Eng courses)
Oxford Brookes – CCC (Civ Eng courses)
Paisley – CCC (MEng Civ/Struct Eng courses)
Plymouth – 240 pts approx (MEng Civ Eng; Civ Coast Eng)
South Bank – 240 pts (Civ Eng)
Surrey – CCC/AB (BEng Civ Eng courses)

220 pts   **Glasgow** – CCD (Civ Eng; Civ Eng/Geol)
Greenwich – 220 pts approx (Civ Eng; Civ Eng Wtr Env Mgt; Civ Eng/Proj Mgt; Civ Eng/Euro Lang)
Sheffield Hallam – 220 pts approx (Civ Eng)
South Bank – 220–140 pts (Civ Env Eng; Civ Eng; Blt Env St; Constr Eng)

200 pts   **City** – 200 pts (Civ Eng/Surv)
Coventry – 200 pts approx (Int Disas Resp Eng Mgt; Int Disas Eng/Mgt)
Paisley – CDD/BC (BEng Civ Eng)
Plymouth – 200 pts approx (BEng Civ Eng; Civ Coast Eng; Eng Des Mgt; BSc Civ Eng)
Portsmouth – 200 pts (inc 2x6u) – ALs **or** ALs+ASs **or** VAs; (BEng Civ Eng; Civ Eng Euro)
Portsmouth – 200 pts – ALs **or** ALs+ASs **or** VAs; gs; (Disas Risk Mgt)
Wolverhampton – 200 pts approx; gs (BSc Civ Eng Surv; Civ Eng Mgt; Civ Eng Euro St)

180 pts   **Coventry** – 180–160 pts approx (Civ Eng Fdn; Civ Eng Constr; Civ Eng Constr Euro St; Civ Eng Des)
Dundee – DDD/CC (BEng 4 yr Civ Eng; Civ Eng/Mgt; Civ Eng/Bld)
Glamorgan – DDD/CC (BEng Civ Eng)
Staffordshire – 180 pts approx (Env Eng)
Teesside – 180 pts (Civ Eng St)
Ulster – DDD (BEng Civ Eng)

160 pts | **See Engineering Council statement under Engineering/Engineering Sciences** |

Anglia – 160 pts 12u – 2ALs **or** ALs+ASs **or** VA12u CC; gs; (Civ Eng courses)
Coventry – 160 pts approx (Civ Eng Constr; Civ Eng Des/Env St)
Doncaster (Coll) – CC (Qry Rd Surf Eng)
Napier – CC (Civ/Trans Eng)
Napier – DDE/CD (BSc Civ Eng)
Paisley – DDE/CD (BSc Civ Eng)

140 pts   **Bradford** – 140 pts approx (Fdn Civ/Struct Eng)
Glamorgan – 140 pts approx (BSc Civ Eng)
Napier – CD (Ener/Env Eng)
Newport (UWCN) – 140–120 pts – ALs **or** ALs+ASs **or** VAs+/-ALs/ASs; (Civ/Constr Eng)
Portsmouth – 140 pts approx (Env Ass)

120 pts   **Kingston** – 120 pts 21u; (Fdn Civ Eng)
Oxford Brookes – 120 pts approx (Fdn Civ Eng)
Salford – EEE (Civ Eng Tech; Civ Eng Euro 4 yrs)
South Bank – DD–DE (Fdn Civ Eng Des)

100 pts   **and below**
City – contact univ; (not gs) (Fdn Civ Eng)
Glasgow Caledonian – DE (Env Civ Eng)
Liverpool John Moores – EE (Fdn)
Sheffield Hallam – (Env Eng/Dipl-Ing Entsorgungstechnik)
Staffordshire – 80 pts approx (Env Eng Ext – for over 21s + experience)
Stockport (CFHE) – (Civ Eng)
Leeds Met – (contact university)

Diploma of Higher Education courses
Abertay Dundee

Higher National Diploma courses
100 pts and below
Abertay Dundee; Anglia; Bell (CT); Bradford (Coll); Coventry; Derby; East London; Fife (CFHE); Glamorgan; Gloucestershire (CAT); Greenwich; Kingston; Liverpool John Moores; Mid Kent (CHFE); Napier; Nescot; Newport (UWCN); Northampton (UC); Nottingham Trent; Oxford Brookes; Plymouth; Portsmouth; St Helens (Coll); Sheffield Hallam; Somerset (CAT); South Bank; Stockport (CFHE); Swansea (IHE); Teesside; Wigan & Leigh (Coll); Wiltshire (Coll); Wolverhampton.

Alternative Offers:

IB offers: Aberdeen 24 pts; Aston 29 pts; Bath 32–30 pts H7–5 maths; Belfast H655 S555; Birmingham 30 pts; Bradford 24 pts H655; Brighton 30–26 pts; Bristol 30 pts H66 in maths and physics; Cardiff 28 pts H555; City (MEng) 30 pts, (BEng) 28 pts; Cranfield 30 pts inc H 15 pts; Durham 30 pts H666; Exeter 30 pts; Hertfordshire 24 pts; Heriot-Watt 30 pts; Kingston 24 pts; Leicester (MEng) 36 pts, (BEng) 30 pts; Liverpool 28–24 pts; London (UCL) 32–30 pts; Loughborough 30 pts inc 15 pts Highers 5 pts in maths; Nottingham Trent 30 pts; Portsmouth 28 pts; Sheffield 30 pts inc 5 in maths; Southampton (MEng) 33–32 pts, (BEng) 28 pts; Staffordshire 24 pts; Surrey 26 pts H66; Swansea 30–28 pts; Teesside 24 pts; UMIST H666; Warwick 28 pts.

Irish offers: Aberdeen BBCCC/BCCCC; Bradford BBCCC; Brighton BBCC; Bristol BBBCCC; Glamorgan CCCDD; Sheffield BBBCC inc English.

Scottish Qualifications: Aberdeen AABB–BBBC; Abertay Dundee BBBC; Bell (CT) CC; Dundee AABB–BBBB; Edinburgh ABBB–BBBB; Glasgow BBBB; Glasgow Caledonian BCCC; Heriot-Watt ABBB; Napier BBCC–CCCC; Paisley BBBC; Robert Gordon (Env Eng) BCCC; Strathclyde ABBB/BBBBC.

Overseas applicants: Bath Competence in written and spoken English required. **Brighton** Two-week English language course available. **Liverpool John Moores, Newcastle** Foundation course offered. **City, Sheffield, Liverpool, Brighton** and many other institutions: direct access possible to year 2 for some students. **Southampton** 1 ELTS 6.5.

CHOOSING YOUR COURSE (See also **Ch.1**)

Subject information: Specialist courses in Civil Engineering may cover traffic and highway engineering, water and waste engineering, construction management, explosives and public health engineering. Essential elements in all courses include surveying, project design (for example, from the Channel Tunnel to suspension bridges) and building technology. Aesthetic design may also play a part in the design of some structures, for example, motorway bridges. (Environmental Engineering) These courses vary in content and often cover aspects of biology and chemistry, for example, at **Newcastle** waste, water treatment, solid and hazardous waste, at **Portsmouth** and **Brunel** air and water pollution and at **Edinburgh** fire hazards; **Napier** Energy and waste management. As alternatives to Civil Engineering, students could consider Architecture, Building, Surveying and Town and Country Planning and Environmental Engineering. See also **Appendix 1**.

Special features: Aston Options in water resources, highway engineering, remote sensing and GIS materials, French and German. **Bath** Two six-month placements in years 2 and 3; emphasis on project work. **Birmingham** Language options in French, German, Spanish, Japanese and Russian. **Bradford** Strong emphasis on business, communication and design. **Brighton** (Civ Eng) Options in transportation, water, public health, river and coastal engineering, applied ecology. **Bristol** Third stage includes 'The Engineer in Society' as one of the core subjects with a range of options which may include water resources, traffic engineering, concrete technology, coastal engineering and French. **Dundee** Courses with management or building available. Common years 1 and 2; choice in years 3 and 4. **Heriot-Watt** (Off Eng) Common years 1 and 2 with Chemical, Civil, Electrical and Mechanical Engineering. **London (Imp)** Unique in the number of options available including languages, management, earthquake engineering and water technology. **Loughborough** Common year 1 with Building Sevices Engineering, option to transfer in year 2. **Southampton** A wide subject choice including environmental topics. **Strathclyde** Third year includes public health, traffic and highway engineering and the fourth year, practical design projects. **Swansea** Civil engineering courses are offered with German, Italian or Spanish. *NOW CHECK PROSPECTUSES AND WEB SITES.*

Top universities and colleges (Teaching Quality) (see Ch.4): Bath; Belfast (Queen's); Birmingham; Bristol; Kingston; London (Imp); Loughborough; Plymouth; Southampton (Inst); Surrey; UMIST; not all institutions assessed. See also **Engineering/Engineering Sciences**.

Top universities and colleges (Research) (see Ch.4): (See also **Building**) Belfast (Queen's); Birmingham; Bradford; Bristol; Cardiff; City; Dundee; Edinburgh; Glasgow (inc Naval Archit); Heriot-Watt; Liverpool; London (Imp), (UCL); Loughborough; Manchester; Newcastle; Nottingham; Sheffield; Southampton; Swansea; Warwick.

Study opportunities abroad: Aston; Bath; Birmingham; Brighton; Bristol; Cardiff; City; Coventry; Doncaster (Coll); Dundee; Glamorgan; Glasgow; Heriot-Watt; Hertfordshire; Kingston; Leeds; Liverpool John Moores; London (Imp), (UCL); Loughborough; Manchester; Napier; Newcastle; Nottingham; Oxford Brookes; Paisley; Plymouth; Reading; Salford; Sheffield; Sheffield Hallam; Southampton; Strathclyde; Surrey; Swansea; Warwick; Wolverhampton.

Work opportunities abroad: Aston; Bath; Birmingham; Brighton; Cardiff; City; Coventry; Doncaster (Coll); Dundee; Glamorgan; Greenwich; Leeds; Loughborough; Napier; Newcastle; Nottingham Trent; Oxford Brookes; Salford; South Bank; Surrey; Warwick.

ADMISSIONS INFORMATION

Number of applicants per place (approx): Abertay Dundee 8; Aston 10; Bath 8; Belfast (Queen's) 6; Birmingham 9; Bradford (BEng) 5; Bristol 10; Brunel 4; Cardiff 9; City 11; Coventry 10, (Civ Eng) 11; Cranfield 4; Dundee 12; Durham 8; East London 5; Glamorgan 6; Glasgow Caledonian 4; Greenwich 11; Hertfordshire 8; Heriot-Watt 7; Kingston 8; Leeds 10; Liverpool John Moores 16; London (Imp) 4, (UCL) 5; Loughborough 8, (Civ Eng/Ger) 3; Manchester 4; Napier 4; Newcastle 11, (Off Eng) 9; Nottingham 10; Nottingham Trent 11; Oxford Brookes 16; Paisley 4; Plymouth 3; Salford 5; Sheffield 7; Sheffield Hallam 20; South Bank 5; Southampton 5; Strathclyde 4; Surrey 5; Swansea 8; Teesside 6; UMIST 4; Wolverhampton 3.

Planning your UCAS personal statement (see Ch.4): Aston Reason for taking a gap year if relevant; **Portsmouth** Evidence of mathematical skills. See **Engineering/ Engineering Sciences**. Also read the magazine *The New Civil Engineer* and discuss articles which interest you on the form. See also **Appendix 1**.

Selection interviews (see Ch.4): Abertay Dundee (No); Aston; Bath; Belfast (Queen's); Bradford; Brighton; Bristol; Bristol UWE (No); Brunel; Cambridge; Cardiff; City (No); Coventry; Cranfield; Dundee; Durham; Glamorgan; Greenwich; Heriot-Watt; Kingston; Leeds; Liverpool John Moores (No); London (UCL); Loughborough; Manchester; Napier; Newcastle; Nottingham; Nottingham Trent (No); Oxford; Oxford Brookes; Paisley (No); South Bank; Southampton; Staffordshire (No); Surrey; Swansea; UMIST (No); Warwick; Wolverhampton (No).

Interview questions (see Ch.4): Why have you chosen Civil Engineering? Have you written to the Institution of Civil Engineers? How would you define the difference between the work of a civil engineer and the work of an architect? What would happen to a concrete beam if a load was applied? Where would it break and how could it be strengthened? The favourite question: Why do you want to be a civil engineer? What would you do if you were asked to build a concrete boat? Do you know any civil engineers? What problems have been faced in building the Channel Tunnel?

Reasons for rejection (non-academic): Lack of vitality. Lack of interest in buildings, the built environment or in civil engineering. Poor communication skills.

GAP YEAR ADVICE

Students are strongly recommended to try to get some work in industry.

Institutions willing to defer entry after A-levels: Aston; Bath; Birmingham; Bradford; Brighton; Cardiff; City; Coventry; Cranfield; Dundee; Durham; East London; Glamorgan; Glasgow Caledonian; Heriot-Watt; Hertfordshire; Leeds; Leicester; London (UCL) (No); Newcastle; North East Wales (IHE); Nottingham; Nottingham Trent; Oxford Brookes; Plymouth; Salford; Sheffield Hallam; South Bank, Strathclyde; Surrey, Swansea; Teesside; UMIST; Warwick.

AFTER RESULTS ADVICE

Institutions which may accept the same points score after A-levels: Aston; Bath (No); Belfast (Queen's) (No); Birmingham (No); Bradford (BSc – No); Brighton; Bristol; Cardiff; City; Coventry; Cranfield; Dundee; Durham (No); East London; Glamorgan; Greenwich; Heriot-Watt; Hertfordshire; Kingston; Liverpool John Moores; London (UCL) (No); Loughborough (usually); Manchester; Manchester Met; Napier; Newcastle; North East Wales (IHE); Nottingham; Nottingham Trent; Oxford Brookes; Plymouth; Salford; Sheffield; Sheffield Hallam; South Bank; Southampton (No); Strathclyde; Surrey; Swansea; Teesside; UMIST; Warwick (No).

Institutions which may accept lower grades/points score after A-levels: Aberdeen; Aston; Bath; Belfast (Queen's); Birmingham; Bradford; Brighton; City; Dundee; East London (12 pts min); Glamorgan; Heriot-Watt; Hertfordshire; Leeds; Liverpool John Moores; London (UCL); Loughborough; Newcastle; North East Wales (IHE); Nottingham; Oxford Brookes; Salford; Sheffield; Southampton; Strathclyde; Surrey (perhaps); Swansea; Teesside; UMIST; Warwick; Most universities and colleges.

Offers to applicants repeating A-levels: Higher Belfast (Queen's), East London, Kingston, Liverpool John Moores, Nottingham, Oxford Brookes, Teesside, Warwick; **Possibly higher** Durham, Portsmouth, Southampton, UMIST; **Same** Aston, Bath, Birmingham, Bradford, Brighton, Bristol, City, Coventry, Greenwich, Heriot-Watt, Leeds, London (UCL), Loughborough, Newcastle, Sheffield, South Bank, Southampton, Swansea; **Not considered** Loughborough.

Probable vacancies from June 2001 and in Clearing (see Ch.4): Most universities are likely to have vacancies, with the more popular institutions asking up to 240 pts. Also, there are likely to be vacancies in Offshore Engineering.

NEW GRADUATE DESTINATIONS AND EMPLOYMENT (1999 HESA) (see **Ch.4**)

Of 1645 graduates surveyed, 1212 entered full-time employment, 188 went into further study and 82 were believed to be unemployed.

ENGINEERING (COMMUNICATIONS) (see also Engineering (Electrical & Electronic))

NB The information supplied by the universities and colleges this year varies consider-ably and the offers listed below should be used as a first source of reference only. Many institutions will accept combinations of Advanced (AL), Advanced Subsidiary (AS) and Vocational Advanced (VA) level qualifications to achieve the required points total, but applicants must check web sites and prospectuses for full details of all offers. Grades and points totals shown should be regarded as the minimum levels to be achieved, but

offers may be adjusted downwards when results are known. The points totals shown to the left of the institutions are for ease of reference only. It must not be assumed that tariff points are always used by institutions or that they can be substituted for an offer in grades. The level of an offer is not necessarily indicative of the quality of a course. To calculate your offers see Chapter 4 and the inside fold of the back cover.

Engineering Council Statement: See **Engineering/Engineering Sciences**.

Special subject requirements/preferences: See **Engineering/Engineering Sciences**.

360 pts   **and above**
      Leeds – 18u – AAA (maths reqd; f.maths+phys desr) (Analys Bus Comm IT)
320 pts   **Bath** – ABB (maths+phys or electron pref); (not gs) (MEng Comm Eng/Psy;
      Electron/Comm Eng)
      Birmingham – ABB–BCC (Comm Sys Eng)
      Bristol – ABB (AB maths/phys any order); (not gs) (MEng Comm/Multim
      Eng)
      Sheffield – ABB (Electron Eng (Comm))
      Surrey – 320 pts approx (MEng Telecomm Sys)
      UMIST – 320–300 pts – ABB–BBB (inc maths+phys); (not gs) (MEng Comm
      Contr Eng courses)
300 pts   **Bradford** – BBB (MEng Electron Telecomm/Comp Eng)
      Essex – 300 pts 12u – BB(maths, sci)+AL/2ASs **or** VA12u BB+AL **or**
      VA6u+2ALs; gs; (MEng Telecomm Eng)
      Hull – BBB/300 pts approx (MEng Electron Comm Eng 4 yr)
      Lancaster – 300 pts approx (MEng Comm Eng 4 yr)
      Leeds – 18u – BBB **or** 2ALs+2ASs (B maths/phys); (Comm IT Eng)
      London (King's) – BBB+AS **or** BB+bb+AS (or equiv) (inc A maths reqd, B
      phys pref) **or** VA12u/6u+ALs/ASs; (Telecomm Eng courses)
      London (QM) – 300 pts – ALs **or** ALs+ASs **or** VAs+/-ALs/ASs; (MEng Comm
      Eng)
      Loughborough – 300 pts approx (Comm Eng)
      UMIST – 300–250 pts – BBB–BCC (inc maths+phys); (not gs) (BEng courses)
280 pts   **Aberdeen** – BBC (Electron/Comm)
      Bath – BBC (maths+phys or electron pref); (not gs) (BEng Comm Eng/Psy;
      Electron/Comm Eng)
260 pts   **Aberystwyth** – 260–240 pts approx (Interact Multim Eng)
      Aston – 260–220 pts 18u – 3ALs (C maths or sci) **or** ALs+ASs **or** VAs+/-
      ALs/ASs; VAs; gs; (Comm Eng)
      Edinburgh – BCC (Electron/Comm)
      Heriot-Watt – 260 pts 18u – BCC **or** ALs+ASs **or** VAs B+/-ALs/ASs; gs;
      (Comm Sys)
      Hertfordshire – 260–240 pts 1x12u **or** 2x6u – ALs **or** ALs+ASs **or** VA12u **or**
      VA6u (sci/tech eng)+AL(C maths); gs; (Comm Sys)
      Hull – BCC/BB (Electron Comm Eng; Mbl Telecomm Tech)
      Lancaster – 260 pts approx (Electron Comm Eng; MEng Comm/Comp Sys;
      Comm Eng)
240 pts   **Bradford** – CCC/BB (BEng Electron Comm/Comp Eng)
      City – 240 pts 3x6u – CCC (inc maths+phys); ASs/VAs (contact univ); (not gs)
      (BEng Media Comm Sys)
      Essex – 240 pts 12u – CC (maths, sci)+AL/2ASs **or** VA12u CC+AL **or**
      VA6u+2ALs; gs; (BEng Telecomm Eng)
      London (QM) – 240 pts – ALs **or** ALs+ASs **or** VAs+/-ALs/ASs; (BEng Electron
      Eng; Telecomm)
      Plymouth – 240–220 pts approx (Comm Eng; Robot Auto Eng; Dig Sys Eng;
      Mbl Comm; Broad Eng)
      Portsmouth – 240 pts (inc 2x6u) – ALs **or** ALs+ASs **or** VAs; (MEng Comm Sys
      Eng)

Robert Gordon – CCC (Electron/Comm Eng)
Staffordshire – CCC **or** CCD+AS(40 pts); VA; gs; (Comm/Contr Eng)
Sussex – CCC (Broad Eng)
200 pts **Central England** – 200 pts approx (Comm Net Eng)
Liverpool John Moores – 200–160 pts (inc 1x6u maths/phys 60 pts) – ALs **or** ALs+ASs **or** VA12u/6u+/-ALs/ASs; (Comm/Comp Eng)
180 pts **Coventry** – 180 pts approx (Comm Sys Eng)
Cranfield – BC (Electron Sys Eng)
Oxford Brookes – 180 pts approx (Telecomm courses)
Portsmouth – 180 pts (inc 2x6u) – ALs **or** ALs+ASs **or** VAs; (BEng Comm Eng)
Sunderland – 180 pts approx (Dig Comm Tech)

160 pts | See Engineering Council statement under Engineering/Engineering Sciences |

Cranfield – CC approx (Inf Sys Mgt; Cmnd Contr Comm Inf Sys)
Derby – 160 pts approx (Comm Sys Tech)
Luton – 160–120 pts approx (Comm Sys Des; Artif Intel)
Manchester Met – 160 pts approx (Comm/Electron Eng)
Napier – CC (Electron/Comm Eng)
South Bank – CC (Multim Eng)
140 pts **and below**
Abertay Dundee – DD (Intnet/Comm Tech)
Anglia – (Telecomm Eng)
Glasgow Caledonian – CD (Telecomm Eng)
Lincolnshire & Humberside – 180 pts (Eng (Electron Comm))
Napier – DD (Electron/Comm Sys)
North London – 120 pts 1x12u **or** 2x6u; (Comm Sys)
Northumbria – CD (Comm/Electron Eng)

Higher National Diploma courses
100 pts **and below**
Blackburn (Coll); Blackpool & Fylde (Coll); Cardiff (UWI); Central England; East London; Glasgow (Coll); Kingston; Liverpool John Moores; Luton; Newport (UWCN); Norwich City (Coll); Plymouth; Ravensbourne (CDC); UHI.

Alternative Offers:

IB offers: Aston 29 pts; City 28 pts; Kent 29 pts, H 13 pts.

Irish offers: Aston BBBBB.

Scottish Qualifications: Aberdeen BBCC; Edinburgh (Electron/Comm) BBBB; Glasgow Caledonian BBC; Heriot-Watt (Electron/Comm) BBBC; Napier BBB; Robert Gordon BBCC.

CHOOSING YOUR COURSE (See also **Ch.1**)

Subject information: Communications Engineering varies in content depending on the chosen course but usually it focuses on telecommunications and the design of systems. See also **Engineering (Electrical & Electronic)** for alternative courses. See also **Appendix 1.**

Special features: Anglia Part of course at Cable & Wireless College in Coventry. **Cranfield** Common first year with Information Systems Management. **London (QM)** (Comm Eng) Combines electronics, telecommunications and computers. **Northumbria** Transfers possible to Electrical/Electronic Engineering at end of year 1. *NOW CHECK PROSPECTUSES AND WEB SITES.*

Study opportunities abroad: Coventry; Kent; London (QM); Plymouth.

Work opportunities abroad: Coventry; Loughborough; Plymouth.

ADMISSIONS INFORMATION

Number of applicants per place (approx): Bradford 9; Coventry 7; Cranfield 3; Hull 8; North London 5; Northumbria 7; North London 8; Plymouth 4; South Bank 3.

Planning your UCAS personal statement (see Ch.4): See **Engineering (Electrical & Electronic)**. See also **Appendix 1**.

Selection interviews (see Ch.4): Aston; Bradford; Coventry (No); Cranfield; Hertfordshire; Kent; Liverpool John Moores (No); North London; Sheffield (No); South Bank; Sunderland.

Interview questions (see Ch.4): See **Engineering (Electrical & Electronic)**.

GAP YEAR ADVICE

Institutions willing to defer entry after A-levels: Aston; Coventry; Cranfield; Hull; Loughborough; Northumbria; Plymouth.

AFTER RESULTS ADVICE

Institutions which may accept the same points score after A-levels: Aston; Bradford; Coventry; Cranfield; Kent; Loughborough; North London.

Offers to applicants repeating A-levels: Same Loughborough.

Probable vacancies from June 2001 and in Clearing (see Ch.4): Many vacancies are likely on these courses, with offers of 220 pts and below.

NEW GRADUATE DESTINATIONS AND EMPLOYMENT (1999 HESA) (see **Ch.4**)

See **Engineering (Electrical & Electronic)**.

ENGINEERING (COMPUTER, CONTROL, SOFTWARE & SYSTEMS) (see also **Computer Courses**)

NB The information supplied by the universities and colleges this year varies consider-ably and the offers listed below should be used as a first source of reference only. Many institutions will accept combinations of Advanced (AL), Advanced Subsidiary (AS) and Vocational Advanced (VA) level qualifications to achieve the required points total, but applicants must check web sites and prospectuses for full details of all offers. Grades and points totals shown should be regarded as the minimum levels to be achieved, but offers may be adjusted downwards when results are known. The points totals shown to the left of the institutions are for ease of reference only. It must not be assumed that tariff points are always used by institutions or that they can be substituted for an offer in grades. The level of an offer is not necessarily indicative of the quality of a course. To calculate your offers see Chapter 4 and the inside fold of the back cover.

Engineering Council Statement: See **Engineering/Engineering Sciences**.

Special subject requirements/preferences: See **Engineering/Engineering Sciences**. **A-level.** Cranfield Mathematics not required. **Oxford** A-level in mathematics and physics essential. **GCSE:** Grade A or B mathematics. **Huddersfield** French grade A–C, mathematics grade A–B. **Hull** Physics and chemistry grade A–C. **Manchester** Grade A in mathematics if not taken at A-level. **York** English grade B.

360 pts   and above
        Cambridge – Offers, mainly in grades, vary between colleges (Engineering)
        Oxford – Offers vary between candidates (Eng/Comp Sci)
        Southampton – 370 pts 21u (inc 220 pts AL maths+phys); (MEng Comp Eng; Soft Eng)

350 pts **Southampton** – 350 pts 21u (inc 200 pts AL maths+phys); (BEng Comp Eng; Soft Eng)
UMIST – 350–300 pts (inc maths+phys) – ABB–BBB; (not gs) (MEng Comp Sys Eng)

320 pts **Bath** – ABB (maths+phys or electron pref); (not gs) (MEng Comp Electron Comm)
Birmingham – ABB–BCC (Electron Soft Eng; Comp Comm Sys Eng)
Bristol – ABB (inc maths, phys); (not gs) (Comp Sys Eng; Comp Sys/Euro)
London (Imp) – ABB (Inf Sys Eng)
Newcastle – ABB; (not gs) (MEng Microelec/Soft Eng)
Sheffield – ABB (Electron Eng (Comp))
Warwick – ABB–BBB (Comp Sys Eng)
York – 320 pts approx (A maths, expmt sci) (Electron Comp Eng; Comp Sys Eng)

310 pts **Aberystwyth** – 310 pts 21u/260 pts 18u – ALs **or** ALs+ASs **or** VAs+/-ALs/ASs; gs; (Soft Eng; Intnet Comp; Interact Multim Eng)

300 pts **Aberdeen** – BBB (Electron Comp Eng)
Bangor – BBB (MEng/BEng Comp Sys Eng)
Bradford – BBB (MEng Electron Telecomm Comp Eng)
Bradford – 300 pts approx (MEng Soft Eng)
Brighton – 300 pts approx (MEng Elec Comp/Elec)
Dundee – 300 pts (Electron Eng/Microcomp Sys)
Durham – 300 pts approx (Inf Sys Eng)
East Anglia – 300 pts 18u – BBB **or** BBB+c (B maths); flexible policy for new quals; (Comp Sys Eng/N Am)
Essex – 300 pts 21u – 2ALs (maths, sci)+AL/2ASs **or** VA12u BB+AL; gs; (MEng Comp Eng)
Huddersfield – 300 pts 12u; gs; (MEng Soft Eng)
Hull – BBB/300 pts (MEng Electron Contr Robot Eng; Comp Sys Eng)
Kent – 300 pts 21u – BB (maths+phys)+AL+AS; gs; (MEng Comp Sys Eng courses)
Lancaster – 300–260 pts approx (Comp Sys Eng)
Leicester – 300–280 pts approx (Electron/Soft Eng)
London (King's) – BBB+AS **or** BB+bb (or equiv) (inc B maths reqd, B phys pref) **or** VA12u/6u+ALs/ASs; (Comp Sys Electron courses)
London (QM) – 300 pts – ALs **or** ALs+ASs **or** VAs+/-ALs/ASs; (MEng Comp Eng courses)
London (UCL) – BBB **or** 3ALs+AS/VA; (Comp Sci/Electron Eng)
Loughborough – 300–240 pts (Electron Comp Eng)
Manchester – BBB (Comp Eng courses; Soft Eng courses)
Newcastle – 300 pts; (not gs) (Microelec/Soft Eng)
Nottingham – BBB–BBC (Comp Sys Eng)
Portsmouth – 300 pts (inc 2x6u) – ALs **or** ALs+ASs **or** VAs; (MEng Comp Eng)
Reading – 300–260 pts approx (Cybernetics courses)
Sheffield – BBB–BBC/BB (Comp Sys Eng; Fdn Soft Eng; MEng Soft Eng courses; Contr Sys Eng courses)
Strathclyde – BBB–CCD (Comp Electron Sys)
Surrey – 300 pts 18u – BBB **or** ALs+ASs **or** VAs (depends on subj)+/-ALs/ASs (AL maths reqd); (MEng Inf Sys Eng)
Sussex – BBB (Robot Cyber Proc Auto; Comp Sys Eng)
Swansea – 300 pts 18u – BBB–BCC **or** ALs+ASs **or** VAs+/-ALs/ASs; (Comp Sci yr abroad)
UMIST – 300–250 pts (inc maths+phys) – BBB–BBC; (not gs) (BEng courses)
UMIST – 300 pts 18u – BBB **or** BB+ASs (AL maths/phys) **or** VA12u BB+AL (B maths/phys); gs; (Soft Eng; Comp Sys Eng)
UMIST – 300 pts 18u – BBB **or** BB+bb **or** VA12u BB+AL(B); gs; (Inf Sys Eng courses)

280 pts **Aberdeen** – BBC (Comp Eng)

Bath – BBC (maths+phys or electron pref); (not gs) (BEng Comp Electron Comm)
Cardiff – 280–240 pts approx (Comp Sys Eng)
East Anglia – 280 pts 18u – BBC **or** BBC+c(B maths); flexible policy for new quals; (Comp Sys/Inf Sys courses; Media Eng)
Edinburgh – BBC (Electron/Comp Sci)
Glasgow – BBC (Electron/Soft Eng)
Liverpool – 280 pts approx (Comp/Microelec Sys)
London (QM) – BBC (Comp Eng)

260 pts **Aberystwyth** – 260–200 pts approx (BEng Soft Eng)
Aston – 260–220 pts 18u – 3ALs **or** 2ALs+ASs **or** VAs+/-ALs/ASs; gs; (Elect Eng/Comp Sci)
Belfast (Queen's) – BCC (Electron/Soft Eng)
Bradford – 260 pts approx (Comp Aid Struct Eng)
Bristol UWE – 260–200 pts 18u pref/12u – ALs **or** ALs+ASs **or** VAs+/-ALs/ASs (min 80 pts 6u maths+sci/tech subj); (not gs) (MEng Dig Sys Eng)
Brunel – 260 pts 2x6u (inc sci/eng pref maths) – ALs **or** ALs+ASs **or** VAs+/-ALs/ASs; (Intnet Eng; Comp Sys Eng)
Essex – 260–240 pts 21u – BC–CC(maths, sci)+AL/2ASs **or** VA12u BC–CC+AL; gs; (BEng Comp Eng; Intnet Eng; Comp Gms Tech)
Essex – BCC/BB (Inf Mgt Sys)
Glasgow – BCC (Electron Soft Eng; Microcomp Sys Eng)
Heriot-Watt – 260 pts 18u – BCC **or** ALs+/-ASs **or** VAs B+/-ALs/ASs; gs; (Inf Sys Eng; Autom Sys; Soft Eng)
Hertfordshire – 260–240 pts 1x12u **or** 2x6u – ALs **or** ALs+ASs **or** VA12u (sci/tech/eng) **or** VA6u+AL(C maths); gs; (Comp Aid Eng; Dig Sys)
Hull – BCC/BB (BEng Comp Sys Eng; Comp Sys Eng/Fr/Ger/Jap)
Hull – 260 pts approx (Soft Eng; Soft Eng/Ind Exp; Soft Eng/St Abrd; BSc Soft Eng)
Kent – 260 pts 21u – CC (maths+phys)+AL/ASs **or** VA12u CC+AL/ASs; gs; (BEng Comp Sys Eng courses except under **160** pts)
Leeds – BCC (Electron/Comp Eng)
Plymouth – 260–220 pts (Computing)
Surrey – 260 pts 18u – BCC **or** ALs+ASs **or** VAs (depends on subj)+/-ALs/ASs (AL maths reqd); (BEng Inf Sys Eng)
Sussex – 260 pts (Robot Auto Manuf)
Ulster – BCC (Soft Eng)
UMIST – 260 pts 18u – BCC (inc maths+phys) **or** ALs+ASs; gs (AS only); (Manuf Sys Eng)

240 pts **Bangor** – 240 pts; (Comp Sys Eng; Comp Sys/Bus/Fr/Psy)
Bolton (IHE) – 240 pts approx (MEng Electron Comp Eng)
Bournemouth – 240–220 pts approx (Soft Eng Mgt/Comp)
Bradford – 240 pts approx (BEng Electron Telecomm Comp Eng; Cyber/Auto Electron; Soft Eng; Cyber/Virt Wrld)
Brighton – 240 pts approx (BEng Electron/Comp Eng; Soft Eng)
Bristol UWE – 240–200 pts 18u pref/12u – ALs **or** ALs+ASs **or** VAs+/-ALs/ASs (comp/maths/IT/sci subjs reqd); (Soft Eng)
City – 3x6u (inc maths/comp/phys pref); ASs/VAs (contact univ); (MEng Comp Sys Eng)
Coventry – 240 pts approx (Comp Hard/Soft Eng)
Cranfield – 240 pts 18u – CD **or** BC+cc(B maths) **or** VA12u BC+AL(C); (not gs) (Comp Sys Eng)
Edinburgh – CCC/BB (Comp Sci; Artif Intel/Soft Eng)
Greenwich – 240 pts approx (Comp Sys/Soft Eng; Contr Instr Eng)
Huddersfield – 240 pts – ALs **or** ALs+ASs **or** VAs+/-ALs/ASs; (MEng Comp Aid Eng)
Hull – 240 pts (Inf Comp Contr Tech; Comp Sys Eng)
Kingston – 240 pts approx (Soft Eng)
Kingston – 240 pts approx (Comp Sci (Dig Microelec))

Nottingham Trent – 240 pts approx (Electron/Comp)
Oxford Brookes – CCC (Comp Sci/Sys offer varies with 2nd subject)
Plymouth – 240–220 pts approx (Comp Eng)
Portsmouth – 240 pts approx (Electron Comp Eng)
Robert Gordon – CCC (Electron Comp Eng)
Staffordshire – CCC or CCD+AS(40 pts); VAs; gs; (Comp Aid Eng)

220 pts **Bristol UWE** – 220–180 pts 12u – ALs or ALs+ASs or VAs+/-ALs/ASs (min 80 pts 6u maths+sci/tech subj); (Dig Sys Eng)
City – CCD/BC (BEng Comp Sys Eng)
Derby – 220–200 pts approx (Comp St (Soft Eng))
East Anglia – 220 pts 18u – CCD or CCD+e; flexible policy for new quals; (Comp Sys Eng inc Fdn yr)
Manchester Met – 220 pts approx (Comp Electron Eng)
Salford – 220 pts approx (Comp Sys Telecomm)
Stirling – CCD/BC (Soft Eng)
Ulster – CCD (Electron/Comp)

200 pts **Central Lancashire** – 200 pts approx (Soft Eng)
Dundee – 200 pts (App Comp/Dig Microelec)
Liverpool John Moores – 200–160 pts (inc 1x6u 60 pts maths/phys) – ALs or ALs+ASs or VA12u/6u+/-ALs/ASs; (Comp Eng; Comp Aid Eng)
Plymouth – 200–160 pts approx (Comp Sys Eng)
Portsmouth – 200 pts (inc 2x6u) – ALs or ALs+ASs or VAs; (BEng Comp Eng)
Sheffield Hallam – 200 pts approx (Bus Net Eng; Comp Eng)
South Bank – 200–120 pts (Intnet Eng)

180 pts **Bolton (IHE)** – 180 pts (Electron Comp Eng)
Central England – 180 pts approx (Soft Eng)
Cranfield – 180 pts 18u – BC or B+ccc or VA12u (eng, IT, comm tech) BC; (not gs); (Soft Eng; Inf Sys Mgt)
Glamorgan – 180 pts approx (Soft Eng; Comp Sys Eng))
Luton – 180–120 pts approx (Comp App; Comp Sys Eng)
Staffordshire – 180 pts (Microelec Comp Eng; Soft Eng)
Westminster – 180 pts (Soft Eng)
Wolverhampton – 180–160 pts 12u – DDD/CC or CD+cd or VA12u BB; (not gs) (Comp Aid Eng Des)

160 pts | See Engineering Council statement under Engineering/Engineering Sciences |

Buckinghamshire Chilterns (UC) – 160–140 pts (Comp Eng Euro)
City – 3x6u – DDE (inc maths+sci); ASs/VAs (contact univ); (BSc Comp Sys Eng)
Cranfield – 160 pts 12u – CC or ALs+ASs; (not gs) (Cmnd Contr Comm Inf Sys; Comm Soft Eng)
Huddersfield – 160 pts 12u – ALs (160 pts inc maths) or ALs+ASs (180 pts inc AL maths) or VA (160 pts)+/-AL/ASs; (not gs) (Comp Contr Sys; Comp Aid Eng)
Kent – 160 pts 12u – ALs or ALs+ASs or VAs+/-ALs/ASs; gs; (Fdn Comp Sys Eng)
Manchester Met – 160–140 pts approx (Comm Electron Eng)
Paisley – CC (Soft Eng)
Sheffield Hallam – 160–140 pts approx (Inf Eng Tech)
Teesside – 160 pts approx (Instr/Contr Eng; Soft Eng; Comp Eng Microelec)
Westminster – CC (C in maths) (Contr/Comp Eng)
Wolverhampton – 160 pts approx; gs (Soft Eng)

140 pts **Abertay Dundee** – CD (Intnet Comm Tech)
Glasgow Caledonian – DEE (Computing)
Napier – CD (Soft Eng)
Paisley – CD (Comp Eng)
Wolverhampton – 140–120 pts – DEE/DD or DE+d or VA12u DD; (Dig Des Tech)

120 pts   and below
Abertay Dundee – DD (Intnet Tech)
Anglia – (Comm Comp Sci Electron)
Central England – 100 pts approx (Fdn Comp Tech)
City – 2x6u – EE (inc maths); ASs/VAs (contact univ); (Fdn Comp Sys Eng)
Glamorgan – DD (Electron/IT St)
Greenwich – 120 pts approx (Ext Comp Sys Soft Eng)
Napier – DD–EE (Comp Electron Eng)
Swansea (IHE) – EE (Soft Eng Sys)

Diploma of Higher Education courses
UHI.

Higher National Diploma courses
120 pts   Manchester Met.
 80 pts   **and below**
Anglia; Blackpool & Fylde (Coll); Bolton (IHE); Bournemouth; Bromley (CFHE) gs; Cardiff (UWI); Central Lancashire; Coventry; Derby; Doncaster (Coll); Dumfries & Galloway (CT); Farnborough (CT); Gateshead (Coll); Glamorgan; Glasgow Caledonian; Hertfordshire; Huddersfield; Isle of Man (Coll); Lincolnshire & Humberside; Liverpool John Moores; Llandrillo (Coll); Luton; Mid Kent (CHFE); Napier; Newcastle (Coll); Newport (UWCN); North East Wales (IHE); North East Worcs (Coll); North London; Northumbria; Norwich City (Coll); Nottingham Trent; People's (Coll); Plymouth; Portsmouth; Salford; Sandwell (Coll) (Eng); St Helens (Coll); Sheffield Hallam; South Bank; Staffordshire; Swansea (IHE); Teesside; Thames Valley; UHI; West Herts (Coll); Westminster; Wigan & Leigh (Coll).

Alternative Offers:

IB offers: Aston 29 pts; Bangor 28 pts; Bath 32 pts; Birmingham 30 pts H5 in maths and another science; Brighton 24 pts; Bristol 30 pts H65 maths/phys; Brunel 28 pts; City 28 pts; Cranfield 22 pts; Derby 26 pts; Heriot-Watt 28 pts; Huddersfield 24 pts; Hull 28 pts; Kent 27 pts, H 12 pts; Kingston 26 pts; Lancaster 30 pts H5 in maths; Manchester Met 26 pts; Newcastle H665 (MEng) grades 5 (BEng); Oxford Brookes 24 pts; South Bank 24 pts; Staffordshire 24 pts; Stirling 28 pts; UMIST 30 pts H65 maths/phys; Warwick 32 pts; York 32 pts H6 maths.

Irish offers: Aston BBBBB; Edinburgh BBBB; Sheffield BBBBB–BBCCC; South Bank CCCC; Warwick AAAAB.

Scottish Qualifications: Aberdeen AABB–BBBC; Abertay Dundee BCC; Dundee AABB–BBBC; Edinburgh ABBB–BBBB; Glasgow BBBBC; Heriot-Watt BBBB; Napier BCC; Paisley BCCC–BBC; Robert Gordon BBCC; Strathclyde AAAA–ABBBB.

Overseas applicants: Surrey Sponsorship difficult. **East Anglia**, **Coventry** Language tuition available.

CHOOSING YOUR COURSE (See also **Ch.1**)

Subject information: The design and application of modern computer systems is fundamental to all these courses which will also include electronic engineering, software engineering and computer-aided engineering. Several universities offer sufficient flexibility to enable final course decisions to be made in the second year. Applied Physics, Computer Science, Electrical and Electronic Engineering and Telecommunications and Microelectronics could be considered as alternative courses. See also **Appendix 1**.

Special features: Aston Equal mix of software and hardware. Easy transfer between related disciplines at the end of year 1. **Bristol** (Comp Sys Eng) Course covers micro-electronics, software design, communications, mathematics and computer architecture.

City Emphasis on engineering design and management. **Coventry** At the end of year 1 transfers are possible to Electrical and Electronic Engineering or Information Systems Engineering. **Kent** Three/four-year sandwich variants available. **Liverpool John Moores** (Comp Aid Eng) The emphasis is on design and computer integrated manufacture. Management, business and applied industrial studies are included. **London (Imp)** During the third and fourth years special emphasis is on the principles and practice of software engineering. **London (QM)** Course intended for students aiming for a career in the electronics industry dealing with digital and microprocessor-based systems. **Manchester Met** (Soft Eng) Common first year with Computer and Information Systems allowing transfer. **Reading** (Cyber/Contr Eng) Control and communication of information (not information technology or computer science). Covers psychology, automation, robotics and artificial intelligence. **Sheffield** (Soft Eng) First year is common with other courses and transfers are possible up to the end of that year. **Surrey** Transfers possible to the Electrical/ Electronic Engineering course. French and German offered as subsidiary subjects. **UMIST** Common first year with other courses. Transfers possible. **York** (Comp Sys/Soft Eng) Course involves both hardware and software aspects. *NOW CHECK PROSPECTUSES AND WEB SITES.*

Top universities and colleges (Teaching Quality) (see Ch.4): See **Computer Courses** and **Engineering/Engineering Sciences**.

Top universities and colleges (Research) (see Ch.4): See **Computer Courses**.

Study opportunities abroad: Bangor; Bristol; Buckinghamshire Chilterns (UC); City; Glasgow Caledonian; Napier; Newcastle; Sheffield; Staffordshire; Strathclyde; Teesside.

Work opportunities abroad: Aberystwyth; Coventry; East Anglia; Huddersfield; Napier; Plymouth; Salford; Sheffield; Swansea (IHE); Teesside; York.

ADMISSIONS INFORMATION

Number of applicants per place (approx): Aberystwyth 6; Aston 5; Bangor 5; Bournemouth 3; Bradford 6; Bristol 11; Bristol UWE 12; Central England 6; Central Lancashire 12; Coventry 2; Cranfield 1; Durham 6; East Anglia 4; Edinburgh 3; Huddersfield 2; Kent 5; Lancaster 12; London (Imp) 5; Loughborough 17; Manchester 15; Sheffield 10; Sheffield Hallam 8; South Bank 3; Staffordshire 5, (Comp Aid Eng) 6; Stirling 7; Strathclyde 7; Suffolk (Coll) 1; Surrey (MEng, BEng) 3; Swansea (IHE) 4; Teesside 3; UMIST 6; Warwick 6; Westminster 5.

Planning your UCAS personal statement (see Ch.4): See **Computer Courses** and **Engineering (Electrical & Electronic)**. See also **Appendix 1**.

Selection interviews (see Ch.4): Aberystwyth (some); Aston; Bath; Bradford; Brighton (No); Bristol (No); Bristol UWE (No); Brunel; Cardiff; Central Lancashire (No); City (No); Coventry (No); Cranfield; Derby (No); Durham; East Anglia; Glamorgan; Greenwich (No); Hertfordshire; Huddersfield; Hull (No); Kent; Liverpool John Moores; Manchester (some); Manchester Met (No); Nottingham Trent; Oxford Brookes (No); Paisley (No); Sheffield (No); Sheffield Hallam; South Bank; Staffordshire (No); Stirling (No); Suffolk (Coll) (No); Swansea (IHE) Teesside (No); Warwick; Westminster; York.

Interview questions (see Ch.4): See **Computer Courses** and **Engineering (Electrical & Electronic)**.

Reasons for rejection (non-academic): Lack of understanding that the course involves engineering. See also **Computer Courses** and **Engineering (Electrical & Electronic)**.

GAP YEAR ADVICE

Institutions willing to defer entry after A-levels: Aston; Coventry; Cranfield; Durham; East Anglia; Glamorgan; Heriot-Watt; Hull; Lancaster; Luton; North East Wales (IHE); Plymouth; Portsmouth; Salford; Sheffield Hallam; South Bank; Staffordshire; Surrey; Sussex; Swansea (IHE); Teesside; UMIST; Warwick; Westminster; York.

AFTER RESULTS ADVICE

Institutions which may accept the same points score after A-levels: Aberystwyth; Aston; Birmingham; Bournemouth; Bradford; Bristol; Central England; Central Lancashire; City; Coventry; Cranfield; Durham; Huddersfield; Hull; Kent; Liverpool John Moores; Manchester; North East Wales (IHE); Plymouth; Sheffield; Sheffield Hallam; South Bank; Staffordshire; Swansea (IHE); Teesside; UMIST; Westminster (No); York. Most other universities and colleges.

Institutions which may accept lower grades/points score after A-levels: Aberystwyth; Aston; Bangor; Birmingham; Bournemouth; Central England; Coventry; East Anglia; Heriot-Watt; Huddersfield; Hull; Liverpool John Moores; North East Wales (IHE); Plymouth; Salford; Sheffield; South Bank; Southampton; Staffordshire; Strathclyde; Teesside; UMIST; Warwick; York. Most other universities and colleges.

Offers to applicants repeating A-levels: Higher Bristol, Strathclyde, Warwick, York; **Possibly higher** City, Huddersfield, Sheffield; **Same** Aston, Bath, Birmingham, Coventry, East Anglia, Huddersfield, Lancaster, Liverpool John Moores, Salford, South Bank, Teesside, Ulster, UMIST.

Probable vacancies from June 2001 and in Clearing (see Ch.4): A good choice of courses and universities is likely in this subject field.

NEW GRADUATE DESTINATIONS AND EMPLOYMENT (1999 HESA) (see **Ch.4**)

See **Computer Courses**.

ENGINEERING (ELECTRICAL & ELECTRONIC) (including Microelectronics)

NB The information supplied by the universities and colleges this year varies considerably and the offers listed below should be used as a first source of reference only. Many institutions will accept combinations of Advanced (AL), Advanced Subsidiary (AS) and Vocational Advanced (VA) level qualifications to achieve the required points total, but applicants must check web sites and prospectuses for full details of all offers. Grades and points totals shown should be regarded as the minimum levels to be achieved, but offers may be adjusted downwards when results are known. The points totals shown to the left of the institutions are for ease of reference only. It must not be assumed that tariff points are always used by institutions or that they can be substituted for an offer in grades. The level of an offer is not necessarily indicative of the quality of a course. To calculate your offers see Chapter 4 and the inside fold of the back cover.

Engineering Council Statement: See **Engineering/Engineering Sciences**.

Special subject requirements/preferences: See **Engineering/Engineering Sciences**. **A-levels: Oxford** A-levels in mathematics and physics essential. **GCSE: Manchester** MEng Elec/Comp Sys) Five subjects at grade B including mathematics, English language, science. **Surrey** (European courses) Grade A in language. **Swansea** (European courses) Grade B in language. **Warwick** Grade A or B physics, combined science, plus French for French options. **York** Majority grades A and B.

360 pts and above
    Cambridge – Offers, mainly in grades, vary between colleges (Engineering)
    Oxford – Offers vary between candidates (Engineering)
    Southampton – 370 pts 21u (inc 220 pts AL maths+phys); (MEng Electron Eng; Elec Eng; Electromech Eng courses)
    York – 370–320 pts 21–18u – ABB+b; (Electron courses)
350 pts   **Southampton** – 350 pts 21u (inc 200 pts AL maths+phys); (BEng Electron/Elec Eng/Electromech courses)

UMIST – 350–300 pts (inc maths+phys); ABB–BBB; (not gs) (MEng Elec/
Electron Eng courses)

340 pts   **Durham** – AAB (Nat Sci(Electron Eng))

London (Imp) – AAB–BBB (Elec/Electron Eng 3/4 yr courses; Elec/Electron
Eng Euro)

London (UCL) – AAB–ABB **or** 3ALs+AS/VA/; (MEng/BEng Electron Elec Eng;
Electron Eng with Med Electron; Electron Eng/Comm Eng; Electron
Eng/Comp Sci; Electron Eng/Mgt St; Electron Eng/Euro)

Manchester – AAB (MEng Electron Comp Sys)

320 pts   **Bath** – 320 pts (maths+phys or electron pref); (not gs) (MEng Elec/App
Electron Eng; Elec/Electron Eng)

Bristol – ABB (A/B maths/phys any order); (not gs) (Elec/Electron Eng;
Elec/Electron Eng Euro; MEng/BEng Electron Comm Eng)

London (QM) – 320 pts (inc AL maths) – ALs **or** ALs+ASs **or** VAs+/-ALs/ASs;
(MEng Elec Eng)

Newcastle – ABB; (not gs) (MEng Microelectron/Soft Eng; Electron Eng;
Electron/Elec Eng)

Sheffield – ABB (MEng Elec Eng/Electron Eng courses)

Warwick – ABB (MEng Elec/Electron Eng courses)

300 pts   **Aberdeen** – BBB (Elec/Electron Eng Contr; Elec/Electron Eng)

Aston – 300 pts 18u – BBB–ABC **or** ALs+ASs **or** VAs+/-ALs/ASs; gs; (MEng
Electron Sys Eng courses; Electromech Eng)

Bangor – 300 pts; (Electron Eng H601)

Belfast (Queen's) – BBB (MEng Elec/Electron Eng)

Birmingham – BBB–BCC (Electron/Elec Eng courses)

Bradford – 300 pts 12u (inc AL maths+2 sci subjs); gs; (MEng Elec/Electron
Eng; Electron Telecomm Comp Eng)

Brighton – 300 pts (MEng Electron Eng)

Cardiff – 300 pts approx (MEng/BEng Elec/Electron Eng; Electron Eng)

Dundee – 300 pts approx (MEng Electron Eng/Microcomp Sys)

Durham – 300 pts (Electron Eng; Elec Eng)

Edinburgh – BBB–CCC (MEng Electron; Electron Elec Eng; Elec Eng)

Essex – 300 pts 21u – BB(maths, sci)+AL/2AS **or** VA12u (eng/sci) BB+AL **or**
VA6u+2ALs; gs; (MEng Electron Eng)

Exeter – 300 pts 18u (inc AL maths) – BBB **or** BB+bb **or** VAs (contact univ);
(not gs) (MEng Electron Eng courses)

Hertfordshire – 300–200 pts 1x12u **or** 2x6u – inc 2ALs **or** AL+2ASs **or** VA12u;
gs; (Electron Comb Eng; Electron Contr Robot Eng)

Hull – BBB/300 pts (MEng Electron Microelec Sys Eng; Optoel Sys Eng; Env
Electron)

Kent – 300 pts 21u – BB (maths, phys)+AL+ASs; gs; (MEng Electron
Eng)

Kingston – 300 pts approx (Dig Microelectron (Comp Sci))

Lancaster – 300–260 pts approx (Mecha; Electron Eng; Electron Eng)

Leeds – BBB **or** BB+bb (B maths reqd+B phys pref); VAs (contact dept); gs;
(MEng/BEng Electron Elec Eng; Electron Eng; Mechatron)

Leicester – 300 pts – AAD/ABC/BB(BB maths, phys) **or** BB/AC+bb/cc **or**
VA12u+AL; gs (AL only); (MEng Elec/Electron Eng courses)

London (King's) – BBB+AS **or** BB+bb+AS or equiv) (inc B maths reqd, B phys
pref) **or** VA12u/6u+ALs/ASs; (Electron Eng courses)

Loughborough – 300 pts – BB(maths, phys)+AL/2ASs **or** VA12u+AL/2ASs;
(MEng Elec/Electron; Sys Eng)

Manchester – BBB (Electron/Comp Sys; Electron Comp Sys Ind Exp)

Nottingham – BBB–BCC (Electron Eng joint courses)

Portsmouth – 300–240 pts (inc 2x6u) – ALs **or** ALs+ASs **or** VAs; (MEng
Elec/Electron Eng; Electron/Comp Eng)

Reading – 300–260 pts approx (MEng/BEng courses)

Robert Gordon – BBB–ABC (MEng Elec Electron Eng)

Sheffield – BBB–BCC (Electron Contr Sys Eng; Electron Eng; Elec Eng; Fdn Sys Eng)

Surrey – 300 pts 18u – BBB **or** ALs+ASs **or** VAs (depends on subj)+/-AL/ASs(maths AL only); (not gs) (MEng Electron Eng)

Sussex – BBB–CCC (Elec/Electron Eng; Electron Comm Eng)

Sussex – BBB (Elec/Electron Eng courses except above and in **240 pts**)

Swansea – 300 pts 18u – BBB **or** ALs+ASs **or** VAs+/-AL/ASs; (MEng courses in Electron Comm; Electron Comp Sci; Elec/Electron Eng; Elec/Electron Eng/Euro/Aust/N Am/Ind)

UMIST – 300–250 pts (inc maths+phys); BBB–BBC; (not gs) (BEng courses)

280 pts **Bath** – BBC (maths+phys or electron pref) (not gs) (BEng Elec Eng/App Electron; Elec/Electron Eng)

Cardiff – 280–240 pts approx (BEng Elec/Electron Eng; Electron Eng)

City – 3x6u – BBC (inc maths+phys); ASs/VAs (contact univ); (not gs) (MEng Elec/Electron Eng)

East Anglia – BBC (MEng Electron Eng/N Am; Electron Sys Eng; Media Eng)

Glasgow – BBC–CCC (Elec/Electron Eng courses)

Liverpool – 280 pts – ALs **or** ALs+ASs **or** VAs+/-ALs/ASs; (Elec/Electron Eng courses except under **180 pts**; Med Electron Instr)

Strathclyde – BBC (Elec Mech Eng)

Surrey – BBC–BCC (BEng Elec/Electron courses)

Swansea – 280 pts 18u – BBC/BC **or** ALs+ASs **or** VAs+/-ALs/ASs; (BEng 4 yr courses – Electron Elec Eng; Electron Comp Sci; Electron Comm/Euro/Aust/N Am/Ind)

260 pts **Aston** – 260–240 pts approx (Elec/Electron Eng; Electron Eng/Mgt St; Electron Sys Eng; Electromech Eng; Electron Eng/Comp Sci; Eng Prod Des Telecomm)

Belfast (Queen's) – BCC (Elec/Electron Eng; Electron Soft Eng – BEng/BSc)

Bristol UWE – 260–200 pts 18u pref/12u – ALs **or** ALs+ASs **or** VAs+/-ALs/ASs (min 80 pts 6u maths+sci/tech subj); (not gs) (MEng Elec/Electron Eng courses; Mus Sys Eng)

Brunel – 260 pts 2x6u (inc AL maths B or eng subj C) – ALs **or** ALs+ASs **or** VAs+/-ALs/ASs; (Electron/Elec Eng courses; Electron/Microelectron Eng)

Heriot-Watt – 260 pts 18u – BCC **or** ALs+ASs **or** VAs B+/-ALs/ASs; gs; (Elec/Electron Eng; Elec/Electron Eng (Autom Sys); (Power Eng); Electron/Microelect Manuf Eng)

Hertfordshire – 260–240 pts 1x12u **or** 2x6u – ALs **or** ALs+ASs **or** VA12u (sci/tech/eng) **or** VA6u+AL (C maths); gs; (BEng Electron/Elec courses)

Hull – BCC/BB (Optoelec Sys Eng; Env Electron; Mecha; Electron Contr Robot Eng; Electron Eng)

Kent – 260 pts 21u – CC (maths+phys)+AL+ASs; gs; (BEng Electron Eng courses)

London (QM) – 260 pts (inc AL maths) – ALs **or** ALs+ASs **or** VAs+/-ALs/ASs; (BEng Elec Eng)

Newcastle – BCC–CCC; (not gs) (BEng Elec/Electron Eng)

Nottingham – BCC–CCC (Elec/Electron courses except **300 pts**)

Oxford Brookes – BCC/DD (Elec/Electron Eng courses – offer varies with 2nd subject)

Plymouth – 260–220 pts approx (Mgt Electron Comm Sys)

Surrey – 260 pts 18u – BBC **or** ALs+ASs **or** VAs (depends on subj)+/-AL/ASs(AL maths reqd); (not gs) (BEng Electron Eng)

Swansea – 260 pts 18u – BCC/BC **or** ALs+ASs **or** VAs+/-ALs/ASs; (BEng 3 yr courses – Elec Electron Eng; Electron Comp Sci; Electron Comm)

Warwick – BCC (BEng Elec/Electron Eng courses)

240 pts **Aston** – 240 pts 18u – 3ALs **or** ALs+ASs **or** VAs+/-ALs/ASs; gs; (Electromech Eng; Electromech Eng/Euro St)

Bangor – 240 pts; (Electron Eng H600)

Bradford – 240 pts 12u (inc AL maths); gs; BEng Electron/Telecomm/Comp Eng; Elec/Electron Eng; Auto Electron)

Brighton – 240 pts approx (BEng Elec/Electron Eng; Electron/Broad Eng; Electron/Comp Eng)

Central England – 240 pts inc maths – CCC (inc maths) **or** ALs+ASs **or** VAs+/-ALs/ASs; (Electron Sys)

Central Lancashire – 240 pts 12u (inc AL maths+phys) – ALs **or** ALs+ASs; gs; (Electron Eng)

Coventry – 240 pts (Electron Eng)

Cranfield – 240 pts 18u – BC+AL **or** BC+cc(AL maths, phys) **or** VA12u(Eng) BC+AL(C); (not gs) (Elec Eng; Electron Eng Sys; Elec Eng/Mgt)

De Montfort (Leicester) – 240–180 pts (inc AL maths/phys) **or** VA (Eng/Sci); (Electron Eng)

Derby – 240 pts approx (BEng Elec/Electron Eng)

Edinburgh – CCC/BB (Elec/Electron Eng courses; Microelec)

Essex – 240 pts 21u – CC (maths, sci)+AL/2AS; **or** VA12u (eng/sci)+AL **or** VA6u+2ALs; gs; (BEng Electron Eng)

Exeter – 240 pts 18u (inc AL maths) – CCC **or** CC+cc **or** VAs (contact univ); (not gs) (BEng Electron Eng)

Leicester – 240 pts 18u – BBE/CCC/BCD (B maths, phys) **or** CC/BD+cc/bd (B maths, phys) **or** VA12u+AL; gs (AL only); (BEng courses except Euro course)

Leicester – 240 pts 18u – BBE/CCC/BCD (inc maths, phys, modn lang) **or** VA12u+AL; (not gs); (BEng Elec/Electron/Euro)

Lincolnshire & Humberside – 240 pts approx (Eng (Elec/Electron) (Electron Comm Sys) (Electron Contr) (Mech Elec))

Loughborough – 240 pts 18u – CC(maths, phys)+AL/2ASs **or** VA12u+AL/2ASs; (not gs) (BEng Elec/Electron; Comm Eng; Electron/Soft; Electron/Comp Sys Eng)

Northumbria – 240–180 pts approx (Elec/Electron Eng courses)

Nottingham Trent – 240 pts 18u – CCC **or** 240 pts with 120 pts maths+sci/tech **or** 2ALs+3ASs **or** VAs+/-AL/ASs (inc maths); gs; (BEng Electron/Comm Eng; Elec/Electron Eng; Electron; Electron Comp)

Plymouth – 240–220 pts approx (Elec Electron Eng; Electron Eng; Robot Auto)

Reading – 240 pts (BEng Electron Eng)

Robert Gordon – CCC–BCD (BEng Electron Comm Eng; Elec/Electron Eng)

Sheffield Hallam – 240 pts approx (Elec Electron Sys)

Staffordshire – CCC **or** CCD+AS(40 pts); VAs; gs; (Microelectron Comp Eng; Electron Eng; Elec Eng; Mecha)

Sussex – CCC (Electromech Eng; Electron Eng/Comp Sci; Electron Comm Eng/Bus Mgt)

Swansea – 240 pts 18u – CCC/CC **or** ALs+ASs **or** VAs+/-ALs/ASs; (Electron Mgt/Entre)

Ulster – CCC–CCD (BEng Hons Electron Soft Sys; Electron Comp)

220 pts Bristol UWE – 220–180 pts 12u – ALs **or** ALs+ASs **or** VAs+/-ALs/ASs (80 pts min 6u maths+sci/tech subj) (BEng Elec/Electron courses)

City – 3x6u – CCD (inc maths+phys); ASs/VAs (contact univ); (not gs) (BEng Elec/Electron Eng)

East Anglia – CCD/BC (Electron courses except under **280 pts**)

East London – 220 pts approx (Elec Electron Eng)

Huddersfield – 220 pts 18u – ALs (200 pts inc maths) **or** ALs+ASs (220 pts inc AL maths) **or** VAs (200 pts)+/-ALs/ASs; (not gs) (MEng Electron Eng; Electron/Comm Eng; Electron Eng/Comp Sci; Electron Contr Eng)

Manchester Met – 220 pts (Elec/Electron Eng; Electron Eng/Mgt; Mecha; Media Tech)

Portsmouth – 220 pts (inc 2x6u) – ALs **or** ALs+ASs **or** VAs; (BEng Elec/Comp Eng; Elec/Electron Eng; Electron)

Salford – 220 pts approx (Electron Eng courses)

South Bank – 220–140 pts (Elec/Electron Eng)
Strathclyde – CCD (BEng Comp Electron Sys courses)
Teesside – 220–180 pts approx (BEng Elec Eng; Electron Eng; BSc Electron
    Sys Eng with Lang/Law/Bus St/Env Tech)
200 pts   **Bradford** – 200 pts 12u(inc AL sci); gs; (Med Electron)
Central England – 200 pts inc maths – CDD (inc maths) **or** ALs+ASs **or**
    VAs+/-ALs/ASs; (Electron Eng)
Dundee – 200 pts (Dig Microelec/Maths)
Greenwich – 200 pts approx (Electron Eng)
Heriot-Watt – CDD (Elec/Electron Eng courses)
Liverpool John Moores – 200–160 pts (inc 1x6u maths/phys 60 pts) – ALs **or**
    ALs+ASs **or** VA12u/6u+/-ALs/ASs; (Elec/Electron Eng; Electron/Comm Eng;
    Electron/Contr Sys Eng)
Plymouth – 200–180 pts approx (Electron Comm Sys; Elec Electron Sys)
180 pts   **Bangor** – 180 pts; (Electron Eng H605)
Bournemouth – 180 pts – ALs **or** ALs+ASs **or** VAs+/-ALs/ASs;
    (Comp/Electron; Electron Sys Des; Med Electron Des)
Central Lancashire – 180 pts approx (Media Tech)
Coventry – 180–160 pts approx (Electron Tech)
Dundee – 180 pts (Electron Elec Eng; Electron Eng/Mgt; Electron Eng/Phys)
East London – 180 pts approx (Electron Eng)
Heriot-Watt – DDD/CC (Optoel Las Eng)
Hull – 180 pts/CC (BEng Electron Yr 1 frchd)
Lincolnshire & Humberside – 180 pts (Electron/Commer Telecomm Tech;
    Electron Comm; Electron Contr)
Liverpool – 180 pts – ALs **or** ALs+ASs **or** VAs+/-ALs/ASs; (Fdn Elec/Electron)
Luton – 180 pts approx (Electron Sys Des courses)
South Kent (Coll) – 180–160 pts approx (BEng Electron)
Sunderland – 180 pts – ALs **or** ALs+ASs **or** VAs+/-ALs/ASs; gs; (Elec/Electron
    Eng)
Ulster – DDD (BTech Elec/Electron Eng)

160 pts | See Engineering Council statement under Engineering/Engineering Sciences |

Aberdeen – CC (Elec/Electron Eng)
Anglia – 160 pts 12u – 2 ALs **or** ALs+ASs **or** VA12u CC; gs; (Electron)
Bolton (IHE) – 160–80 pts approx (Electron Eng)
Derby – 160 pts 12u – CC **or** DD+ee **or** VA12u CC **or** VA6u C+AL(C);
    (Elec/Electron Eng)
Glamorgan – 160 pts (Elect/Electron Eng courses)
Glasgow Caledonian – CC (Electron Eng; Elec Pwr Eng)
Greenwich – 160 pts approx (BSc Elec/Electron Eng)
Huddersfield – 160 pts 12u – ALs (160 pts inc maths) **or** ALs+ASs (180 pts
    inc AL maths) **or** VAs (160 pts)+/-ALs/ASs; (not gs) (BEng Electron Eng;
    Elec/Electron Eng; Electron/Comm Eng; Electron Eng/Contr Eng; Electron
    Eng/Comp Sys)
Kent – 160 pts 21u – ALs+ASs **or** VAs+/-ALs/ASs; (Fdn Electron Eng)
North London – 160 pts 1x12u **or** 2x6u; (Electron Eng; Electron/Comm Eng)
Oxford Brookes – CC (BSc Electron)
Sheffield Hallam – 160 pts (Electron Eng)
Southampton (Inst) – 160 pts (Electron Eng)
Swansea – 160 pts 18u – CC **or** ALs+ASs **or** VAs+/-ALs/ASs; (Integ BEng
    Elec/Electron Eng)
Westminster – CC (Electron Eng)
140 pts   **Bell (CT)** – CD (Elec/Electron Eng)
Liverpool John Moores – 140 pts 1x6u (inc comp/IT/maths/phys/dtech/eng) –
    ALs **or** ALs+ASs **or** VA12u/6u+/-ALs/ASs; (App Electron)
Newport (UWCN) – 140–120 pts – ALs **or** ALs+ASs **or** VAs+/-ALs/ASs; (Elec
    Instr Sys)

Paisley – CD (Elec/Electron Eng)
Robert Gordon – CD (Elec/Electron Eng)
120 pts   and below
Abertay Dundee – DE (Electron; Mecha)
Bangor – 120 pts; (Electron Eng H602)
Bournemouth – 120 pts – ALs; (Comp/Electron Fdn)
Bradford – 120 pts 9u; gs; (Fdn Elec/Electron)
Cardiff (UWI) – EE (Electron Des)
City – EE (Fdn Elec/Electron Eng)
Falkirk (CFHE) – (Mechatronics)
Greenwich – 100 pts (Ext Eng)
Inverness (Coll) – (Elec/Electron Eng)
Napier – DD (Electron Comp Eng)
North East Wales (IHE) – 120–80 pts(Elec/Electron courses)
North London – 120 pts 2x6u **or** VAs; (Electron Prod Tech)
Northumbria – DD (Optoel Eng)
Paisley – DD (Media; Media Tech)
UHI (Inverness/Moray/North Highland/Perth/Shetland – E (Elect Eng – via
    DipHE, HND)
Stockport (CFHE) – (Elec/Electron Eng)
Wolverhampton – DD; gs; (Media courses)

Leeds Met – (contact university)

Diploma of Higher Education courses:
    Greenwich; Paisley; UHI.

Higher National Diploma courses
100 pts   and below
    Abertay Dundee; Anglia (Audio; Electron); Bedford (Coll); Bell (CT); Blackburn
    (Coll); Blackpool & Fylde (Coll); Bolton (IHE); Bournemouth; Brighton; Bromley
    (CT) gs; Brooklands (Coll); Cardiff (UWI); Carlisle (Coll); Central England; Central
    Lancashire; Chesterfield (Coll); Coventry; Crawley (Coll); De Montfort; Derby;
    Doncaster (Coll); Dudley (CT); Dumfries & Galloway (CT); Durham (Stockton);
    East London; Exeter; Falkirk (CFHE); Farnborough (CT); Fife (CFHE); Glamorgan;
    Glasgow Caledonian; Glasgow (Coll); Greenwich; Hastings (CT); Hertfordshire;
    Huddersfield; Inverness (Coll); James Watt (Coll); Kilmarnock (Coll); Kingston;
    Lincolnshire & Humberside; Liverpool John Moores; Loughborough (Coll); Luton;
    Manchester Met; Napier; Newport (UWCN); North East Wales (IHE); North
    Highland (Coll); North Lincolnshire (Coll); North London; North West Kent (Coll);
    Northampton (UC); Northumbria; Norwich City (Coll); Nottingham Trent; Oldham
    (Coll); Oxford Brookes; People's (Coll); Plymouth; Portsmouth; Robert Gordon;
    St Helens (Coll); Salford; Salisbury (Coll); Sheffield Hallam; Shrewsbury (CAT);
    Solihull (Coll); Somerset (CAT); South Bank; South Devon (CAT); Southall (CT);
    Southampton (Inst); Staffordshire; Stevenson (Coll); Stockport (CFHE); Stoke on
    Trent (Coll); Sunderland; Swansea (IHE); Swindon (Coll); Teesside; Thames Valley;
    UHI; Warwickshire (Coll); Westminster; Wigan & Leigh (Coll); Willesden (CT); York
    (CFHE); Yorkshire Coast (CFHE).

Alternative Offers:

EB offers: Aston 70%; Liverpool 70%

IB offers: Aberdeen 26 pts; Aston 29 pts; Bath (MEng) 32–30 pts inc H665, (BEng) 28
pts inc H555; Belfast (Queen's) H666 S555; Birmingham 33 pts; Bradford 24 pts; Bristol
32 pts inc H66 in maths, phys; Brunel 28 pts; Cardiff 30–28 pts; City 30–26 pts; Cranfield
27 pts; Derby 24 pts; Durham H666; Essex 30 pts inc H655; Exeter 30 pts; Glamorgan
24 pts; Heriot-Watt 28 pts; Hertfordshire 24 pts; Huddersfield 24 pts; Hull 27 pts inc H5
maths; Kent 27 pts; Kingston 24 pts; Lancaster 31–29 pts inc H55 maths + phys; Leeds
30 pts; Leicester (MEng) 30 pts, (BEng) 26 pts; London (UCL) 34 pts; Loughborough

H766; Manchester Met 24 pts; Newcastle (BEng) 31 pts Grades 5, (MEng) Grades 6; North London 29 pts with 14 pts Highers; Portsmouth 28 pts inc 14 pts Highers; Reading 30 pts; Southampton 32–28 pts; Staffordshire 24 pts; Strathclyde 36 pts; Swansea 30–28 pts; UMIST 30 pts H65 in maths/phys; Warwick 28 pts; Wirral Met (Coll); York 30 pts + H66 maths/phys; Yorkshire Coast (CFHE).

Irish offers: Aberdeen BBCCC; Aston BBBBB; Bangor BBCCC; Bradford CCCCC; Liverpool BBCCC.

Scottish Qualifications: Aberdeen AABB–BBBC; Abertay Dundee BCC; Dundee AABB–BBBC; Edinburgh ABBB–BBBB; Glasgow BBBBC; Glasgow Caledonian BBBC; Heriot-Watt BBBC; Napier BBC–CCC; Paisley BBC; Robert Gordon ABBB–BBCC; Strathclyde AAAA–AABB.

Overseas applicants: Aston Direct entry to year 2 considered. **Bath** Competence in English required. **East Anglia, Leeds, Sheffield Hallam** Language courses available. **Heriot-Watt** Some Norwegian scholarships available. **Hull** Living costs 30% lower than in London. **Newcastle** Foundation year offered. **Surrey** Direct entry to year 2 sometimes possible. Sponsorships can be difficult to arrange.

CHOOSING YOUR COURSE (See also **Ch.1**)

> **Subject information:** Options to specialise should be considered when choosing courses, so read the prospectuses carefully. Many of these courses have common first years with other similar courses, allowing transfer in year 2. In this field options include optoelectronics and optical communication systems, microwave systems, radio frequency engineering and circuit technology. Degree courses are also offered in the associated subject areas of Microelectronics, Control, Systems and Telecommunications Engineering. Computer Science courses and Aeronautical Engineering could all be considered as alternative courses. See also **Appendix 1**.

Special features: Aston STEPS Foundation course available for students without the right qualifications. **Bangor** First year common with Electronic, Computer Systems and Electrical Engineering. Opportunity to transfer in year 2. **Bath** The final year options allow specialisms in electronics, communications control engineering, electrical machines and power systems. **Belfast** Common first year with software and systems engineering. **Birmingham** Options in French, German, Spanish, Russian or Japanese. **Bradford** Programmes include a European Studies option with language training and placement abroad. **Bristol** Final year specialisations include communications, industrial economics and computer architecture. **Brunel** Choice of specialisation in communication, control and instrumentation, power and electronic systems. **City** First and second years are taken in common with other Engineering subjects and transfers are possible at the end of the first year. **Cranfield** (Electron Eng) Broad-based electrical/mechanical electronic engineering course with bias towards land and aerial vehicle systems. **Essex** A flexible approach with options to transfer between degrees. **Hull** Special Honours course covers mathematics, computer science, engineering management and business finance in addition to electronics. **Kent** Specialisation in medical or digital electronics available. Direct entry to year two possible for suitably qualified applicants. **Kingston** Non-engineering subjects include business, foreign language, software applications, information systems. **Leicester** Common first year for all courses; degree specialisation at the end of semester three. **London (RH)** Options in digital, audio and video and/or computer engineering and/or telecommunications and networks. **Loughborough** Common first year with choice to transfer to other subjects. **Manchester** Industrial placement and overseas programmes available. **Newcastle** Common first year for MEng/BEng students. MEng courses specially related to BT sponsorship. **Northumbria** Option of a European route with a year abroad for all courses. **Southampton** Separate specialist departments of Electrical Engineering and Electronics and Computer Science. **Surrey** Two main subject streams – Electrical and Electronic Engineering and Information Systems Engineering. *NOW CHECK PROSPECTUSES AND WEB SITES.*

Top universities and colleges (Teaching Quality) (see Ch.4): Belfast (Queen's); Birmingham; Bristol; Cardiff; Edinburgh; Essex; Glamorgan; Huddersfield; Hull; Leeds; London (Imp), (UCL); Loughborough; Manchester; North London; Nottingham; Reading; Sheffield; Southampton; Strathclyde; Surrey; Swansea; York; not all institutions assessed. See also **Engineering/Engineering Science.**

Top universities and colleges (Research) (see Ch.4): Aston; Bath; Belfast (Queen's); Birmingham; Bristol; Cardiff; Edinburgh; Essex; Glasgow; Heriot-Watt; Kent; Liverpool; London (Imp), (King's), (QM), (UCL); Loughborough; Newcastle; Sheffield; Southampton; Strathclyde; Surrey; Swansea; UMIST; York.

Study opportunities abroad: Aston; Bangor; Bath; Birmingham; Bournemouth; Brighton; Bristol; Brunel; Cardiff; Central England; Central Lancashire; City; Coventry; De Montfort; Derby; Dundee; East Anglia; East London; Glamorgan; Glasgow; Heriot-Watt; Huddersfield; Hull; Kent; Leeds; Liverpool John Moores; London (Imp), (QM), (UCL); Loughborough; Manchester; Manchester Met; Newcastle; Nottingham; Nottingham Trent; Oxford Brookes; Paisley; Portsmouth; Robert Gordon; Salford; Sheffield; Sheffield Hallam; South Bank; Staffordshire; Strathclyde; Surrey; Sussex; Swansea; Teesside; York.

Work opportunities abroad: Aston; Bath; Bournemouth; Brighton; Bristol; Brunel; Central England; Central Lancashire; Coventry; Dundee; De Montfort; East Anglia; Glamorgan; Hertfordshire; Huddersfield; Hull; Leicester; Lincolnshire & Humberside; London (UCL); Loughborough; Nottingham Trent; Oxford Brookes; Plymouth; Salford; Sheffield; Sheffield Hallam; South Bank; Surrey; Swansea; Teesside; Warwick; York.

ADMISSIONS INFORMATION

Number of applicants per place (approx): Abertay Dundee 3; Aston 7; Bath 10; Birmingham 7; Bolton (IHE) 3; Bournemouth 3; Bradford (Electron Eng) 8; Bristol 20; Bristol UWE 8; Brunel 10; Cardiff 7; Central England 11; Central Lancashire 4, (Media Tech) 7; City 10; Coventry 8; De Montfort 1; Derby 8; Dundee 9; Falkirk (CFHE) 1; Glamorgan 2; Glasgow Caledonian 5; Greenwich 10; Hertfordshire 7; Heriot-Watt 6; Huddersfield 5; Hull 8; Inverness (Coll) 1; Kent 7; Kingston 8; Leeds 15; Lancaster 7; Leicester 15; Lincolnshire & Humberside 8; Liverpool John Moores 9; London (UCL) 9; Manchester 12; Manchester Met 5; Napier 8; Newcastle 9; Newport (UWCN) 1; North East Wales (IHE) 3; North London 3; Northumbria 7; Nottingham 12, (Fdn courses) 6, (BEng/MEng) 8; Nottingham Trent 6; Plymouth 22; Portsmouth 6; Robert Gordon 3; Salford 5; Sheffield 15; Sheffield Hallam 2; South Bank 5; Staffordshire 7; Strathclyde 7; Sunderland 11; Surrey (BEng) 6, (MEng) 3; Swansea 5; Teesside 4; UMIST 5; Westminster 5; Warwick 8; York 9.

Planning your UCAS personal statement (see Ch.4): See **Engineering/Engineering Sciences.** See also **Appendix 1.**

Selection interviews (see Ch.4): Aberdeen (No); Abertay Dundee; Aston; Bangor (Electron Eng only); Bath; Belfast (Queen's); Bournemouth; Bradford (T); Brighton; Bristol; Bristol UWE; Brunel; Cambridge; Cardiff; Central Lancashire; City (No); Coventry (No); Cranfield; De Montfort; Derby; Dundee; Durham; East Anglia (Electron Eng) (T); Essex; Falkirk (CHFE); Glamorgan (No); Greenwich (No); Heriot-Watt; Hertfordshire; Huddersfield; Hull; Kent; Kingston; Lancaster; Leeds (No); Leicester (some); Liverpool; London (UCL); Loughborough; Manchester; Manchester Met (No); Newcastle; Newport (UWCN); Nottingham; Nottingham Trent (No); Oxford; Paisley (No); Plymouth; Portsmouth; Robert Gordon (No); Sheffield (No); South Bank; South Kent (Coll); Southampton; Staffordshire (No); Strathclyde; Sunderland; Surrey (W) (T); Swansea (none rejected at interview); UMIST; Warwick (No); Westminster; York.

Interview questions (see Ch.4): How does a combustion engine work? How does a trumpet work? Why, being female, did you choose to study Electrical Engineering? What type of position do you hope to reach in five to ten years' time? Could you sack an employee? What was your last physics practical? What did you learn from it? What are the methods of transmitting information from a moving object to a stationary observer?

Wire bending exercise – you are provided with an accurate diagram of a shape that could be produced by bending a length of wire in a particular way. You are supplied with a pair of pliers and the exact length of wire required and you are given 10 minutes to reproduce as accurately as possible the shape drawn. How does a transistor work? A three-minute talk had to be given on one of six subjects (topics given several weeks before the interview); for example, the best is the enemy of the good. Is there a lesson here for British industry? 'I was asked to take my physics file and discuss some of my conclusions in certain experiments.' Explain power transmission through the National Grid. How would you explain power transmission to a friend who hasn't done physics?

Reasons for rejection (non-academic): Poor English. Inability to communicate. Frightened of technology or mathematics. Poor motivation and work ethic. Better suited to a less specialised engineering/science course. Some foreign applicants do not have adequate English. **Surrey** Can't speak English (it has happened!).

GAP YEAR ADVICE

Aston Welcomed, particularly if relevant. **Bournemouth** Prefers not – year 3 in industry; **Bradford** Work experience in gap year is unlikely to be counted towards industrial training; **De Montfort** Could be in danger of losing motivation; **Hull** Apply as normal and request deferred entry; **London (QM)** Students advised to work in industry; **Loughborough** Should be informed as soon as possible to confirm that you do not wish to take up your place; **Salford** Some courses require applicant to select a relevant employer beforehand. Check with admissions tutor.

Institutions willing to defer entry after A-levels: Abertay Dundee; Aston; Bath; Bell (CT); Birmingham; Bournemouth; Bolton (IHE); Bradford; Brighton; Bristol UWE; Brunel; Cardiff; Coventry; Cranfield; Derby; Durham; Dundee; Glamorgan; Glasgow Caledonian; Heriot-Watt; Huddersfield; Hull; Inverness (Coll); Kingston; Leeds (Mechatronics); Leicester; Lincolnshire & Humberside; London (UCL); Loughborough; Manchester Met; Newcastle; North East Wales (IHE); Northumbria; Nottingham; Nottingham Trent; Oxford Brookes; Plymouth; Portsmouth; Robert Gordon; Sheffield Hallam; South Bank; Southampton; Staffordshire; Strathclyde; Surrey; Sussex; Swansea; Teesside; UMIST; Warwick; York.

AFTER RESULTS ADVICE

Institutions which may accept the same points score after A-levels: Abertay Dundee; Aberdeen (No); Aston; Bangor; Bath; Belfast (Queen's) (No); Birmingham; Bolton (IHE); Bournemouth; Brighton; Bristol; Bristol UWE (No); Brunel; Cardiff (No for MEng); Central Lancashire; Coventry; De Montfort; Derby; Dundee; Durham; East Anglia; Essex; Glamorgan (provided maths is D or better); Glasgow (No); Glasgow Caledonian; Greenwich (No); Heriot-Watt; Hertfordshire; Huddersfield; Hull; Kingston; Kent; Leeds; Lincolnshire & Humberside; Liverpool John Moores; London (UCL) (No); Loughborough (No); Manchester; Manchester Met (inc maths grade E); Newcastle (Yes for Fdn, No for MEng); North London (No); Northumbria; Nottingham; Oxford Brookes; Plymouth; Portsmouth; Robert Gordon; Salford; Sheffield Hallam; South Bank; Staffordshire; Strathclyde; Surrey; Swansea; UMIST (No); Warwick (No); Westminster (No); York.

Institutions which may accept lower grades/points score after A-levels: Abertay Dundee; Aston; Bangor; Bath; Birmingham; Bolton (IHE); Bournemouth; Bradford; Brighton; Bristol UWE; Brunel; Cardiff; Central Lancashire; City (Wide Access and Fdn courses); Coventry; Derby; Dundee; Glamorgan; Glasgow Caledonian; Hertfordshire; Hull (overseas students 18–16 pts); Huddersfield; Inverness (Coll); Kingston; Leeds; Lincolnshire & Humberside; Liverpool John Moores; London (UCL); Loughborough; Manchester Met; Newcastle; North East Wales (IHE); Nottingham Trent; Oxford Brookes; Plymouth; Salford; Sheffield; Sheffield Hallam; South Bank; Strathclyde; Surrey; Swansea; Teesside; Warwick; Westminster; York.

Offers to applicants repeating A-levels: Higher Belfast (Queen's), Brighton, Central Lancashire, Greenwich, Huddersfield, Kingston, Newcastle, Northumbria, South Bank, Staffordshire, Strathclyde, Swansea, Warwick; **Possibly higher** Aston, City, De Montfort,

Derby, Glasgow, Hertfordshire, Manchester, North London, Portsmouth, Sheffield; **Same** Bangor, Bath, Birmingham, Bolton (IHE), Bradford, Brunel, Coventry, Derby, Huddersfield, Hull, Kent, Leeds, Liverpool, Loughborough, Newport (UWCN), Northumbria, Nottingham (usually), Nottingham Trent, Robert Gordon, Salford, South Bank, Southampton, Surrey, UMIST.

Probable vacancies from June 2001 and in Clearing (see Ch.4): Vacancies are very likely in most universities for these subjects. Offers from the most popular institutions are expected in the 240–220 pts range, but applicants with lower grades are likely to be offered places.

NEW GRADUATE DESTINATIONS AND EMPLOYMENT (1999 HESA) (see **Ch.4**)

Of 2353 graduates surveyed, 1630 obtained full-time employment, 275 went on to further study and 274 graduates were believed to be unemployed.

ENGINEERING (MANUFACTURING) (including Production Engineering)

NB The information supplied by the universities and colleges this year varies considerably and the offers listed below should be used as a first source of reference only. Many institutions will accept combinations of Advanced (AL), Advanced Subsidiary (AS) and Vocational Advanced (VA) level qualifications to achieve the required points total, but applicants must check web sites and prospectuses for full details of all offers. Grades and points totals shown should be regarded as the minimum levels to be achieved, but offers may be adjusted downwards when results are known. The points totals shown to the left of the institutions are for ease of reference only. It must not be assumed that tariff points are always used by institutions or that they can be substituted for an offer in grades. The level of an offer is not necessarily indicative of the quality of a course. To calculate your offers see Chapter 4 and the inside fold of the back cover.

Special subject requirements/preferences: See **Engineering/Engineering Sciences**. **A-level:** Physics may be required, check prospectuses. **Oxford** Mathematics and physics essential. **GCSE: Brunel** Grade A or B in mathematics and English. **Paisley** Three subjects at grade A/B. **Portsmouth** Grade A or B mathematics. **Salford** Six to eight subjects at grade A–C. **Strathclyde** Grade A or B mathematics and physics. **Swansea** Mathematics grade B or above.

Engineering Council Statement: See **Engineering/Engineering Sciences**.

---

360 pts	**and above**
	Cambridge – Offers, mainly in grades, vary between colleges (Engineering)
	Oxford – Offers vary between candidates (Engineering)
340 pts	**Bath** – 3ALs (AA maths+phys)+B; (not gs) (MEng Manuf courses)
320 pts	**Loughborough** – 320 pts 18u – B (maths)B+AL/2ASs **or** VAs; gs; (MEng Manuf/Eng Mgt; Prod Des/Manuf; Spo Tech)
	Strathclyde – ABB (MEng Manuf Eng/Mgt)
	Warwick – ABB (Manuf Sys Eng)
300 pts	**Belfast (Queen's)** – BBB (MEng Mech Manuf Eng)
	Bradford – 300 pts 12u (inc AL maths+2 sci subjs); gs; (MEng Manuf Eng)
	Cardiff – 300–240 pts approx (MEng Manuf Eng courses)
	Durham – 300 pts (Manuf Eng Mgt)
	Hertfordshire – 300–200 pts 1x12u **or** 2x6u; (Manuf Sys Comb Mod)
	Nottingham – 300–260 pts (Manuf Eng courses; Ital/Prod Ops Mgt)
	UMIST – BBB (MEng 4 yr Enhanced Eng Manuf/Mgt)
280 pts	**Birmingham** – BBC (Manuf Eng; Fdn courses)
	Cardiff – 280–240 pts approx (BEng Manuf Eng)
	Hertfordshire – 280–200 pts (Manuf Sys Eng)
	Leeds – BBC/BB (Mech Manuf Eng Mgt)

London (King's) – BBC+AS **or** BC+bb+AS (or equiv) (inc B maths, AL/AS phys B or des tech) **or** VA12u BB+AL(B maths) **or** VA6u+ALs/ASs; (Manuf Sys Eng; Manuf Sys Eng/Mgt)

Strathclyde – BBC (Manuf Eng/Mgt; Manuf Sys Eng; Prod Des Eng)

260 pts **Aston** – 18u – 3ALs **or** ALs+ASs **or** VAs; gs; (Eng Prod Des)

Belfast (Queen's) – BCC (Manuf Eng)

Central Lancashire – 260 pts approx (MEng Des Manuf)

Loughborough – 260 pts 18u – C (maths)C+AL/2ASs **or** VAs; (BEng Manuf Eng/Mgt; Prod Des Manuf)

Sussex – BCC (Robot/Auto Manuf)

Swansea – 260 pts 18u – BCC **or** ALs+ASs **or** VAs+/-ALs/ASs; (Prod Des Manuf)

UMIST – 260 pts 18u – BCC (inc maths+phys) **or** ALs+ASs; gs (AS only); (Manuf Sys Eng)

Warwick – BCC (BEng Manuf Sys Eng)

240 pts **Bradford** – 240 pts 12u (inc AL maths); gs; (BEng Manuf Sys/Mgt; Manuf Sys/Mech Eng)

Brighton – 240 pts approx (Manuf Sys)

Brunel – 240 pts 2x6u (inc AL maths C+pref tech/eng sci or VA Eng) – ALs **or** ALs+ASs **or** VAs+/-ALs/ASs; (Manuf Eng; Manuf Eng/Mgt; Manuf Eng/Bus St; Ind Des Eng)

Cardiff – CCC/BB (Manuf Eng courses except under **300 pts**; Tech Mgt)

Derby – 240–200 pts maths/phys (Mech/Manuf Eng)

Greenwich – 240 pts approx (BEng Manuf Sys Eng)

Hull – CCC/BC (Eng Des/Manuf)

Liverpool – 240 pts – ALs **or** ALs+ASs **or** VAs+/-ALs/ASs; (Manuf Eng/Mgt)

Northumbria – 240 pts (Manuf Sys Eng)

220 pts **Heriot-Watt** – CCD (Eng/Mgt)

Luton – 220–180 pts (Manuf Mgt/Qual Sys courses)

Manchester Met – 220 pts (Manuf Sys Eng)

200 pts **Bradford** – 200 pts 12u; gs; (Manuf Sys Mgt; Ind Eng; Mat/Des/Prod)

Bristol UWE – 200 pts (Manuf Sys Eng)

Central England – CDD (inc maths) **or** ALs+ASs **or** VAs (200 pts inc maths); (Mgt/Manuf Sys; Eng Prod Des)

East London – 200 pts (Manuf Sys Eng courses; Manuf Eng Tech)

Glasgow – CDD (Prod Des Eng)

Huddersfield – 200 pts (Manuf Ops Mgt; Prod Innov Des Dev; Auto Des Tech; Comp Aid Des)

Liverpool John Moores – 200–160 pts (inc 1x6u 60 pts) – ALs **or** ALs+ASs **or** VAs+/-ALs/ASs; (Manuf Sys Eng)

Salford – 200 pts approx (Manuf Bus Sys)

180 pts **Lincolnshire & Humberside** – 180 pts (Eng (Mech Manuf))

Staffordshire – 180 pts approx (Manuf Eng/Bus)

Westminster – 180 pts approx (Prod Des Eng)

160 pts | **See Engineering Council statement under Engineering/Engineering Sciences** |

Coventry – 160 pts approx (Manuf Sys Tech; Manuf Mgt)

Glasgow Caledonian – CC (Bus Manuf Sys Eng; Manuf Sys Eng)

Plymouth – 160–120 pts (Mech Des Manuf; Manuf Mech Des)

Robert Gordon – CC–EE (Des Eng)

140 pts **Kingston** – 140 pts 2x6u (inc AL maths+sci) **or** VA(Eng); (Manuf Sys Eng Tech)

Liverpool John Moores – 140 pts 1x6u – ALs **or** ALs+ASs **or** VAs+/-ALs/ASs; (Robot/Manuf Sys)

Newport (UWCN) – 140–120 pts – ALs **or** ALs+ASs **or** VAs+/-ALs/ASs; (Integ Manuf Tech)

Portsmouth – 140 pts (Mech Manuf Sys Eng)

South Bank – 140 pts (Eng Prod Des)

Wolverhampton – 140 pts; gs; (Comp Aid Des/Manuf; Manuf Eng)

120 pts **Bell (CT)** – 120 pts (Manuf Eng Mgt)
Wolverhampton – 120 pts 12u – DEE/DD **or** DE+d **or** VA12u DD; gs; (Vrtl Rlty Manuf)
100 pts **and below**
Cardiff (UWI) – 40 pts (Manuf Eng)
Glamorgan – (Mech/Manuf Eng)
Glasgow Caledonian – (Fdn Eng Mgt)
Kingston – 80 pts 2x6u (inc AL maths+sci) **or** VA(eng); Manuf Sys Eng St)
North East Wales (IHE) – (Mech Manuf Eng courses)
Staffordshire **– 80 pts approx (Ext Eng)**
Stockport (CFHE) – (Mech Eng; Manuf Eng)

Leeds Met – (contact university)

Diploma of Higher Education courses
UHI.

Higher National Diploma courses
100 pts Abertay Dundee; Bedford (Coll); Bell (CT); Blackpool & Fylde (Coll); Brighton; Brighton (CT); Cardiff (UWI); Carlisle (Coll); Central England; Coventry; Crawley (Coll) gs; Derby; Dudley (CT); Farnborough (CT); Gateshead (Coll); Glamorgan; Hertfordshire; Huddersfield; Kingston; Lincolnshire & Humberside; Liverpool John Moores; Luton; Manchester Met; Newbury (CFE); Newport (UWCN); North East Wales (IHE); Norwich City (Coll); Nottingham Trent; Portsmouth; Reading (CSAD); St Helens (Coll); Salisbury (Coll); Scottish (CAg); Sheffield Hallam; Somerset (CAT); Southampton (IHE) (Yacht Manuf Mgt); Staffordshire; Stockport (CFHE); Stoke on Trent (Coll); Swansea (IHE); Teesside; UHI; Warwickshire (Coll); Wigan & Leigh (Coll); Wirral Met (Coll).

Alternative Offers:

IB offers: Bath H55 overall 30 pts; Birmingham 30–28 pts; Bradford 24 pts; Brighton 26 pts; Brunel 25 pts; Cardiff 554 + 13 pts; Central England 24 pts; Loughborough H766-H655; Manchester Met 30 pts; UMIST 32–30 pts; Warwick 28 pts.

Irish offers: Brighton ABBBB–CCCCC; Bristol UWE CCCC.

Scottish Qualifications: Glasgow Caledonian BBBC; Heriot-Watt (Eng Mgt) BBBB; Napier BBB; Strathclyde BBBBC.

Overseas applicants: Hull Living costs 30% lower than London.

CHOOSING YOUR COURSE (See also **Ch.1**)

Subject information: Manufacturing Engineering is sometimes referred to as Production Engineering. It is a branch of the subject concerned with management aspects of engineering such as industrial organisation, purchasing and the planning and control of operations. At the same time it provides an overview of engineering design systems. Several courses have first years common with Mechanical Engineering, allowing transfers in year 2. This is a shortage area – out of 18,000 applicants for Engineering, around 350 applied for Manufacturing Engineering. Business Studies and Technology courses could also be considered as alternatives. See also **Appendix 1**.

Special features: Bath Choice between Aeronautical, Mechanical or Manufacturing Engineering made at the end of year 1. Study in USA and language options available. **Bradford** Common first year with Mechanical Engineering. **Cardiff** A Manufacturing Engineering course with Japanese Business Studies includes language study and an option for placement in Japan. **Central England** (Eng Prod Des) Optional schemes cover advanced manufacture, information technology, business management and a foreign language. **Hull** (Eng Des/Manuf) This is a broad course covering engineering science, materials, manufacturing processes and business management. **Nottingham Trent** Emphasis on computer-aided manufacturing. Joint degree with Fachhochschule, Karlsruhe. *NOW CHECK PROSPECTUSES AND WEB SITES.*

Top universities and colleges (Teaching Quality) (see Ch.4): See **Engineering/ Engineering Sciences**.

Top universities and colleges (Research) (see Ch.4): See under **Engineering (Mechanical)**.

Study opportunities abroad: Bath; Birmingham; Brunel; Derby; Hertfordshire; Leeds; Liverpool John Moores; Nottingham Trent; Salford; Strathclyde; Warwick; Wolverhampton.

Work opportunities abroad: Bath; Birmingham; Bradford; Brunel; Cardiff; Central England; Coventry; Derby; East London; Hertfordshire; Huddersfield; Leeds; Lincolnshire & Humberside; Liverpool John Moores; Nottingham Trent; Salford; UMIST; Warwick.

ADMISSIONS INFORMATION

Number of applicants per place (approx): Bath 18; Birmingham 3; Bradford 4; Bristol UWE 3; Brunel 3; Cardiff 6; Central Lancashire 3; Coventry 3; Derby 4; Hertfordshire 1; Huddersfield 1; Kingston 3; Loughborough 6; Manchester Met 2; North East Wales (IHE) 2; Northumbria 4; Nottingham 6; Nottingham Trent 3; Portsmouth 6; Salford 5; Sheffield Hallam 3, (Euro) 1; Strathclyde 8; Teesside 4; UMIST 9; Warwick 8.

Planning your UCAS personal statement (see Ch.4): Experience in industry should be mentioned. See **Engineering/Engineering Sciences**. See also **Appendix 1**.

Selection interviews (see Ch.4): Bath (No); Bradford; Brighton (No); Brunel (T); Cambridge; Cardiff; Coventry; Hertfordshire; Hull; Leeds; Loughborough; Manchester Met; Newport (UWCN); Nottingham; Nottingham Trent; Oxford; Portsmouth; Sheffield Hallam (No); South Bank; Staffordshire (No); Strathclyde; Warwick (No).

Interview questions (see Ch.4): What is the function of an engineer? Describe something interesting you have recently done in your A-levels. What do you know about careers in engineering? Discuss the role of women engineers in industry. Why is a disc brake better than a drum brake? Would you be prepared to make people redundant to improve the efficiency of a production line?

Reasons for rejection (non-academic): Mature students failing to attend interview are rejected. One applicant produced a forged reference and was immediately rejected.

GAP YEAR ADVICE

Institutions willing to defer entry after A-levels: Bath (but advise before April); Birmingham; Bradford; Brunel; Cardiff; Derby; Durham; Hertfordshire; Kingston; Leeds (Manuf Sys/Mech Eng); Manchester Met; North East Wales (IHE); Northumbria; Nottingham Trent; Portsmouth; Salford; South Bank; Strathclyde; UMIST; Westminster.

AFTER RESULTS ADVICE

Institutions which may accept the same points score after A-levels: Bath (No); Birmingham (No); Bradford; Brunel; Cardiff; Coventry; Derby; Durham; Hertfordshire; Huddersfield; Hull; Loughborough (Manuf Eng); Manchester Met; North East Wales (IHE); Northumbria; Nottingham; Nottingham Trent; Portsmouth; Salford; Sheffield Hallam; Strathclyde; UMIST (No). Most other universities and colleges.

Institutions which may accept lower grades/points score after A-levels: Birmingham; Brunel; Cardiff; Hertfordshire; Huddersfield; Hull (overseas students 240–220 pts); North East Wales (IHE); Northumbria; Portsmouth; Strathclyde; most other universities and colleges.

Offers to applicants repeating A-levels: Higher Strathclyde; **Possibly higher** Brunel, Hertfordshire; **Same** Huddersfield, Nottingham, Nottingham Trent, Salford.

Probable vacancies from June 2001 and in Clearing (see Ch.4): Many vacancies are likely in this subject area.

NEW GRADUATE DESTINATIONS AND EMPLOYMENT (1999 HESA) (see **Ch.4**)

Of 1477 graduates surveyed, 1033 entered full-time employment, 138 went on to further study and 103 were seeking employment six months after graduating.

ENGINEERING (MARINE) (see also Naval Architecture)

NB The information supplied by the universities and colleges this year varies considerably and the offers listed below should be used as a first source of reference only. Many institutions will accept combinations of Advanced (AL), Advanced Subsidiary (AS) and Vocational Advanced (VA) level qualifications to achieve the required points total, but applicants must check web sites and prospectuses for full details of all offers. Grades and points totals shown should be regarded as the minimum levels to be achieved, but offers may be adjusted downwards when results are known. The points totals shown to the left of the institutions are for ease of reference only. It must not be assumed that tariff points are always used by institutions or that they can be substituted for an offer in grades. The level of an offer is not necessarily indicative of the quality of a course. To calculate your offers see Chapter 4 and the inside fold of the back cover.

Engineering Council Statement: See **Engineering/Engineering Sciences**.

Special subject requirements/preferences: A-level: Two A-levels in mathematics/science subjects.

280 pts **Newcastle** – BBC–BCC/BB–BC; (not gs) (MEng Mar Tech; Mar Eng; Off Eng; Small Craft Tech)
260 pts **Liverpool** – 260 pts approx (MEng Civ Marit Eng)
     Newcastle – BCC–CCC/BB; (not gs) (BEng Mar Tech; Mar Eng 3 yr; Off Eng; Small Craft Tech)
240 pts **Newcastle** – CCC–CCD/CC; (not gs) (Mar Eng 4 yr)
220 pts **Liverpool John Moores** – 220–160 pts (Mech/Mar Eng; Marit Eng; Marit Tech)
200 pts **Plymouth** – 200 pts approx (Mar Tech courses)
180 pts **Southampton (Inst)** – 180–140 pts approx (Mar Tech; Yacht/Pwrcft Des)

Higher National Diploma courses
100 pts and below
     Glamorgan; Liverpool John Moores; Southampton (Inst) (Yacht Des Op; Yacht Manuf Mgt).

CHOOSING YOUR COURSE (See also **Ch.1**)

Subject information: There is a shortage of applicants for these courses which cover all aspects of the marine industry, including offshore engineering, small craft technology and naval architecture (a subject in its own right). See also **Appendix 1**.

Special features: Liverpool Maritime Engineering is offered with Civil Engineering and involves work in estuary, port and offshore projects. **Liverpool John Moores** Final year projects include ship technology, marine propulsion systems and ship technology and design. **Newcastle** Marine Technology courses cover six degree options including engineering, naval architecture, offshore engineering and small craft technology. **Plymouth** Options in the Marine Technology course include marine navigation, maritime history, maritime law and commercial practice. *NOW CHECK PROSPECTUSES AND WEB SITES.*

Study opportunities abroad: Newcastle.

ADMISSIONS INFORMATION

Number of applicants per place (approx): Newcastle 8.

General Studies acceptable: Newcastle (No).

Planning your UCAS personal statement (see Ch.4): See **Engineering/Engineering Sciences**. See also **Appendix 1**.

Interview questions (see Ch.4): Why do you want to study Marine Engineering? What future career are you considering? Shipping world-wide is on the decrease: do you see this situation changing?

Reasons for rejection (non-academic): Confusion or misunderstanding about what courses offer.

AFTER RESULTS ADVICE

Probable vacancies from June 2001 and in Clearing (see Ch.4): Contact all institutions since vacancies are likely.

NEW GRADUATE DESTINATIONS AND EMPLOYMENT (1999 HESA) (see **Ch.4**)

185 students graduated from courses in Maritime Technology of whom 119 entered full-time employment, 27 went on to further study and 14 were believed to be unemployed.

ENGINEERING (MECHANICAL)

NB The information supplied by the universities and colleges this year varies considerably and the offers listed below should be used as a first source of reference only. Many institutions will accept combinations of Advanced (AL), Advanced Subsidiary (AS) and Vocational Advanced (VA) level qualifications to achieve the required points total, but applicants must check web sites and prospectuses for full details of all offers. Grades and points totals shown should be regarded as the minimum levels to be achieved, but offers may be adjusted downwards when results are known. The points totals shown to the left of the institutions are for ease of reference only. It must not be assumed that tariff points are always used by institutions or that they can be substituted for an offer in grades. The level of an offer is not necessarily indicative of the quality of a course. To calculate your offers see Chapter 4 and the inside fold of the back cover.

> **Engineering Council Statement:** See **Engineering/Engineering Sciences**.

Special subject requirements/preferences: See **Engineering/Engineering Sciences**. **A-level: Loughborough** Grade A in mathematics and physics. **Oxford** Mathematics and physics essential. **Swansea** Grade C French/German/Italian/Spanish required for Mech Eng/Euro course. **GCSE: Bradford** Grade A or B in physics and mathematics. **Cardiff** Grade A–B in science and mathematics. **Warwick** Grade A or B in physics, combined/dual sciences.

360 pts **and above**
 Bristol – AAA–BBB (inc maths+phys); (not gs) (Mech Eng courses)
 Brunel – 360–300 pts 2x6u (inc AL maths+phys **or** VA B(Eng)) – ALs **or** ALs+ASs **or** VAs+/-ALs/ASs; (MEng Mech Eng courses)
 Cambridge – Offers, mainly in grades, vary between colleges (Engineering)
 Oxford – Offers vary between candidates (Engineering)
 Southampton – 370 pts 21u (inc 220 pts AL maths+phys); (MEng Mech Eng)
350 pts Southampton – 350 pts 21u (inc 200 pts maths+phys); (BEng Mech Eng)
 UMIST – 350–300 pts (inc maths+phys) – ABB–BBB (not gs) (MEng Mech Eng courses)

School of Mechanical & Materials Engineering | University of Surrey

Why should you choose the University of Surrey?

The University of Surrey provides:

- Top-rated accredited degrees
- The best graduate employment record of any UK University
- An attractive location 30 minutes from London and 10 minutes from the countryside
- A compact, friendly campus
- Dedicated and supportive staff who are professional engineers
- On-site accommodation guaranteed for all first-year and overseas students.

Bachelor of Engineering degrees: 3 or 4 year programmes
Master of Engineering degrees: 4, 6 year programmes

- Aerospace *(MEng/BEng)*
- Bio-Materials *(BEng)*
- Engineering for the Environment *(MEng/BEng)*
- Engineering with Business Management *(MEng/BEng)*
- Materials Science and Engineering *(MEng/BEng)*
- Mechanical Engineering *(MEng/BEng)*
- Mechanical Engineering with Mechatronics *(BEng)*
- Mechanical and Satellite Engineering *(MEng)*
- Mechanical and Bio-Medical Engineering *(MEng/BEng)*
- Metallurgy *(BEng)*
- Science of Materials *(BSc)*

Second-year entry to the BEng and MEng programmes may be possible for suitably qualified applicants. All programmes can be taken with a European Language or an Integrated Foundation Year.

How to contact us

Undergraduate Admissions
School of Mechanical
& Materials Engineering
University of Surrey
Guildford
Surrey
GU2 7XH

Tel: 01483 876270
Fax: 01483 306039
e-mail: mme.ugrad@surrey.ac.uk
http://www.surrey.ac.uk/MME/

Please see the Materials Science/Metallurgy section for details of entry requirements for our Materials Science/Metallurgy programmes

340 pts   **Bath** – 3ALs (AA maths+phys)+AL(B) (not gs) (Auto Eng; Mech Eng; Mech Eng/Lang)

              Cardiff – 340–320 pts (C maths) (MEng Mech Eng)

              London (Imp) – AAB (MEng Mech Eng)

              Loughborough – 340 pts 18u – BB(maths, phys)+AL/2ASs **or** VAs+/-ALs/ASs; gs; (MEng Auto Eng)

              Strathclyde – AAB (MEng Mech Eng)

320 pts   **City** – 3x6u – ABB–BBB (inc maths+phys); ASs/VAs (contact univ); (not gs) (MEng Mech Eng)

              Hertfordshire – 320 pts 1x12u **or** 2x6u – ALs **or** ALs+ASs **or** VA12u **or** VA6u (sci/tech/eng)+AL(C maths); gs; (Mech Eng)

              Nottingham – ABB–BBB (Mech Eng courses)

              Sheffield – ABB (MEng Mech Eng courses except under **300 pts**)

              Warwick – ABB–BCC (MEng Mech Eng; Mech Eng/Euro)

300 pts   **Aberdeen** – BBB (Mech Eng)

              Aston – 300 pts – 3ALs **or** ALs+ASs; (MEng Mech Eng)

              Birmingham – BBB–BCC (Mech Eng courses)

              Bradford – 300 pts 12u (inc AL maths+2 sci subjs); (not gs) (MEng Mech Eng)

              Brighton – 300–240 pts (MEng/BEng Mech Eng)

              Brunel – 300–240 pts 2x6u (inc AL maths+phys **or** VA B (Eng)) – ALs **or** ALs+ASs **or** VAs+/-ALs/ASs; (BEng Mech Eng courses)

              Durham – 300 pts (Mech Eng)

              Edinburgh – BBB–BCC (Mech Eng courses)

              Exeter – 300 pts 18u (inc AL maths) – BBB **or** BB+bb **or** VAs (contact univ); (not gs) (MEng Mech Eng courses)

              Glasgow – BBB–CCC (Mech Eng courses)

              Hertfordshire – 300 pts 1x12u **or** 2x6u – ALs **or** ALs+ASs **or** VA6u(sci/tech/eng)+AL(C maths); gs; (Auto Eng courses)

              Hull – BBB/300 pts (MEng Mech Eng)

              Kingston – 300 pts 18u (3x6u) (AL maths+2 sci); (MEng Mech Eng)

              Lancaster – 300–260 pts approx (MEng/BEng Mech Eng; Mecha)

              Leeds – 18u – BBB **or** BB+bb; VAs (contact dept); (not gs) (MEng/BEng Auto Eng; Math Eng)

              Leicester – 300 pts 18u – AAD/ABC/BBB **or** BB/AC+bb/ac (AL maths+phys) **or** VAs (grades as ALs)+AL/ASs; gs (AL only); (MEng courses)

              London (QM) – 300 pts – ALs **or** ALs+ASs **or** VAs+/-ALs/ASs; (MEng Mech Eng courses; Mech Eng Sys)

              London (UCL) – BBB–BCC **or** 3ALs+AS/VA; (Mech Eng)

              Loughborough – 300 pts 18u – CC(maths, phys)+AL/2ASs **or** VAs+/-ALs/ASs; gs; (MEng Mech Eng; BEng Auto Eng)

              Manchester – BBB (MEng Mech Eng; Mech Eng (Int Euro))

              Newcastle – BBB; (not gs) (MEng Mech Eng courses)

              Portsmouth – 300 pts (inc 2x6u) – ALs **or** ALs+ASs **or** VAs; (MEng Mech Eng)

              Reading – BBB (MEng Mech Eng)

              Robert Gordon – BBB/ABC (MEng Mech Eng)

              Salford – 300 pts (MEng Mech Eng)

              Sheffield – BBB–BCC (Mech Sys Eng; Fdn Mech Eng)

              Strathclyde – BBB (BEng Mech Eng)

              Surrey – 300 pts 18u; BBB **or** ALs+ASs **or** VAs (depends on subj)+/-ALs/ASs; (not gs) (MEng Mech Eng)

              Sussex – BBB (MEng Mech Eng)

              Swansea – 300 pts 18u – BBB **or** ALs+ASs **or** VAs+/-ALs/ASs; (MEng courses)

              UMIST – 300–250 pts (inc maths+phys) – BBB–BCC; (not gs) (MEng/BEng Mech Eng courses)

280 pts   **Cardiff** – 280 pts (Mech Eng/Fr/Ger/Span)

              Cranfield – 280 pts 18u – BBC **or** BB+cc (inc AL maths+phys); (not gs) (Mech Eng; Mech Eng/Mgt)B (Mech Eng; Mech Eng/Mgt)

Leeds – 18u – BBC **or** BB+cc; VAs (contact dept); (not gs) (MEng/BEng; Mgt/Mech Manuf Eng; Mech Eng)

Liverpool – 280 pts – ALs **or** ALs+ASs **or** VAs+/-ALs/ASs; (Mech Eng courses)

London (King's) – BBC+AS **or** BC+bb+AS (or equiv) (inc B maths, AL/AS phys B or des tech) **or** VA12u BB+AL(B maths) **or** VA6u+ALs/ASs; (Mecha courses)

Strathclyde – BBC (Elec Mech Eng)

260 pts **Belfast (Queen's)** – BCC (Mech Eng; Mech Fd Eng)

Bristol UWE – 260–220 pts 18u pref/12u – ALs **or** ALs+ASs **or** VAs+/-ALs/ASs (min 80 pts 6u maths+sci/tech subjs); (not gs) (MEng Mech Eng)

Coventry – 260 pts (MEng Auto Eng; Auto Eng Des; BEng Auto Eng Des)

London (UCL) – BCC–CCC **or** 3ALs+AS/VA; (Mech Eng/Bioeng)

Loughborough – 260 pts 18u – CC(maths, phys)+AL/2ASs **or** VAs+/-ALs/ASs; gs; (BEng Mech Eng)

Newcastle – BCC; (not gs) (BEng Mech Eng courses)

Nottingham – 260 pts – 3ALs (inc maths, phys) **or** 2ALs (maths, phys)+2ASs; (not gs) (Mech Des Mat Manuf)

Surrey – 260 pts 18u – BBC **or** ALs+ASs **or** VAs (depends on subj)+/-ALs/ASs; (not gs) (BEng Mech Eng)

Surrey – 260–240 pts (Fdn Mech Eng)

Sussex – BCC (Prod Des)

Swansea – 260 pts 18u – BCC/BB **or** ALs+ASs **or** VAs+/-ALs/ASs; (BEng Mech Eng courses/N Am/Euro)

Warwick – BCC (Mech Eng H300)

240 pts **Aston** – 240 pts (Mech Eng; ElecMech Eng; Eng Prod Des)

Bradford – 240 pts 12u; gs; (BEng Mech Eng; Mech/Auto Eng; Mech Eng/Mgt (inc AL maths); Med/Tech/Spo (inc AL sci))

Brighton – 240 pts (BEng Mech Aero Des Eng; Mech Eng; Mech Env Eng)

Central Lancashire – 240 pts (Mech Eng; Mecha; Mtr Spo)

City – 3x6u – BCD–CCD (inc maths/phys pref); ASs/VAs (contact univ); (not gs) (BEng Mech Eng)

Coventry – 240 pts (Mech Eng)

De Montfort – 240–180 pts (inc 2ALs maths/phys) **or** VA (eng/sci); (Mech Eng)

Exeter – 240 pts 18u (inc AL maths) – CCC **or** CC+cc **or** VAs (contact univ); (not gs) (BEng Mech Eng)

Glasgow – CCC (Mech Des Eng)

Greenwich – 240 pts approx (MEng Mech Eng; Mecha)

Heriot-Watt – 240 pts 18u – CCC **or** ALs+ASs **or** VAs B+/-ALs/ASs; gs; (Mech Eng courses)

Huddersfield – CCC (MEng Mech Eng; Auto Des; Mech Auto Des; Precsn Eng)

Hull – CCC/240 pts (Mech Des)

Kingston – 240 pts 18u (3x6u) (AL maths+sci) **or** VA(eng); (BEng Mech Eng)

Leicester – 240 pts 18u min – BBE/CCC/BCD **or** CC/BD+cc/bd (inc AL maths+phys) **or** VAs (grades as AL)+ALs/ASs; gs (AL only) (BEng courses except Euro)

Leicester – 240 pts 18u – BBE/CCC/BCD (inc maths+phys+modn lang); (not gs) (Mech Eng/Euro)

London (QM) – 240 pts – ALs **or** ALs+ASs **or** VAs+/-ALs/ASs; (BEng Mech Eng)

Manchester – CCC/220 pts (BEng Mech Eng courses)

Northumbria – 240–160 pts (Mech Eng)

Nottingham Trent – 240 pts approx (BEng Mech Eng)

Oxford Brookes – 240 pts approx (Mech Eng)

Paisley – CCC (BEng Mech Eng)

Plymouth – 240 pts (Mech Eng)

Portsmouth – 240 pts (inc 2x6u) – ALs **or** ALs+ASs **or** VAs; (BEng Mech Eng courses; Mech/Manuf Eng)

Reading – 240 pts (BEng Mech Eng)

Robert Gordon – CCC (BEng Mech Eng)
Salford – 240 pts (MEng Mech Eng)
Sheffield Hallam – 240 pts (Mech Comp Aid Eng)
Staffordshire – CCC **or** CCD+AS(40 pts) **or** VAs+/-ALs/ASs; gs; (Mech Eng)
Sussex – CCC (Mech Eng/Bus Mgt; Electromech Eng; Mecha)

220 pts **Bristol UWE** – 220–180 pts 12u – ALs **or** ALs+ASs **or** VAs+/-AL/ASs (min 80 pts 6u maths+sci/tech subjs); (BEng Mech Eng)
Manchester Met – 220 pts (Mech Eng)
Ulster – CCD (BEng Mech Eng)
Wolverhampton – 220 pts 12u – CCD/BB **or** CC+b; gs; (Mech Eng; Auto Sys Eng; Mecha)

210 pts **Wolverhampton** – 210–180 pts 12u – DDD/CC **or** CD+cd **or** VA12u BB; (not gs) (Spec Veh Des)

200 pts **Central England** – 200 pts inc maths – CDD (inc maths) **or** ALs+ASs **or** VAs+/-ALs/ASs; (Mech Eng; Auto Eng; Mech Eng Sys)
Dundee – 200 pts (MEng/BEng Mech Eng)
Greenwich – 200–160 pts approx (BEng Mech Eng courses)
Liverpool John Moores – 200–160 pts (inc 1x6u 60 pts) – ALs **or** ALs+ASs **or** VAs+/-ALs/ASs; (Mech Eng; Mech/Mar Eng)
Teesside – 200 pts (Mech Eng)

180 pts **Huddersfield** – 180–160 pts 12u – ALs (160 pts inc maths/phys) **or** ALs+ASs (inc 180 pts maths/phys); (not gs) (BEng Mech/Auto Manuf/Tech courses)
Lincolnshire & Humberside – 180 pts approx (Mech Eng)
Sheffield Hallam – 180 pts approx (Mech Eng)
Sunderland – 180 pts; gs; (Auto Tech; Mech Eng)

160 pts | **See Engineering Council statement under Engineering/Engineering Sciences** |

Bolton (IHE) – 160–100 pts (Mech Eng; Mech/Manuf Eng; Auto Eng)
Bradford – 160 pts 12u (inc AL maths); gs; (Mech/Auto Eng Sys; Mech Eng Sys)
Buckinghamshire Chilterns (UC) – 160–140 pts (Mech Eng Des)
Coventry – 160 pts (BSc Mech Eng; Fdn Mech Eng; Mech Tech)
Doncaster (Coll) – CC (Min/Mech Eng)
Glasgow Caledonian – CC (Mech Electron Sys Eng)
Greenwich – 160 pts (BSc Mech Eng)
Napier – CC (Mech Eng)
Plymouth – 160 pts approx (Mech Des Manuf)
Robert Gordon – CEE/CD (BSc Mech Eng)

140 pts **Derby** – 140 pts 12u – CD **or** DD+ee **or** VAs+/-ALs/ASs (AL maths/phys/des tech reqd); gs; (Mech/Manuf Eng)
Glamorgan – 140 pts approx (Mech Eng; Mecha Eng)
Hull – 140 pts approx (Mech Eng frchd 4 yr)
Kingston – 140 pts inc 2x6u (inc AL maths+sci) **or** VA(Eng); (BEng Mech Eng Tech; Mtrcycl Eng Tech)

120 pts **Bell (CT)** – DD (Manuf Eng/Mgt; Auto Eng)
Bradford – 120 pts 9u (inc AL maths); gs; (Fdn Mech Eng Sys)
City – 2x6u (contact univ); (not gs) (Fdn Mech Eng)
Greenwich – 120 pts approx (Ext Eng)
Kingston – 120 pts 12u; (Fdn Mech Eng)
Paisley – DD (Prod Des Dev; Mecha)

100 pts **and below**
Abertay Dundee – DE (Mechatronics)
Bell (CT) – (Auto Eng)
Kingston – 80 pts inc 2x6u (inc AL maths+sci) **or** VA(eng); (Mech Eng St; Biomed Eng; BEng Mtrcycl Eng St)
North East Wales (IHE) – 80 pts approx (Mech Eng)
St Helens (Coll) – (Mechatronics)
Southampton (Inst) – 100–80 pts (Mech Des)

Staffordshire – (Ext Eng)
Stockport (CFHE) – (Mech Eng)
Swansea (IHE) – (Auto Electron Eng)
UHI (Inverness/Lews Castle/Moray/North Highland/Perth) – (Mech Eng via DipHE, HND, HNC)
Westminster – (Mech Eng)

Diploma of Higher Education courses:
Greenwich.

Higher National Diploma courses
100 pts and below
Abertay Dundee; Anglia; Bedford (Coll); Belfast (IHE); Bell (CT); Blackburn (CT); Blackpool & Fylde (Coll); Bolton (IHE); Bournemouth; Brighton; Bromley (Coll) gs; Brooklands (CFHE) (Auto; Mecha; Motor Spo); Burton on Trent (TC); Cardiff (UWI); Carlisle (Coll); Central England; Cheltenham & Glos (CHE); Chesterfield (Coll); Chippenham (TC); Coventry; Coventry (CT); Crawley (Coll) gs; De Montfort; Derby (Motor Spo); Doncaster (Coll); Dudley (Coll); Ealing (TerC); Exeter (CSM); Farnborough (CT); Fife (CFHE); Furness (Coll); Glamorgan; Gloucester (CAT); Glasgow Caledonian (Mechatronics); Greenwich; Grimsby (Coll); Guildford (CT); Hastings (CT); Hertfordshire; Huddersfield; Kingston; Lincolnshire & Humberside; Liverpool John Moores; Llandrillo (Coll) (Motor Veh); Loughborough (Coll); Luton; Manchester Met; Mid Kent (CHFE); Myerscough (Coll) (Motor Spo); Newcastle (Coll); Newport (UWCN); North East Wales (IHE); North East Worcestershire (Coll); North Herts (Coll); North Highland (Coll); Northampton (UC); Northbrook (Coll); Northumbria; Norwich City (Coll); Nottingham Trent; Oldham (CT); Oxford Brookes; People's (Coll); Plymouth; Portsmouth; Reading (CT); Robert Gordon; Rycotewood (Coll) (Veh Restor Cons Tech); St Helens (Coll); Sheffield Hallam; Shrewsbury (CAT); Solihull (Coll); Somerset (CAT) (Auto Eng); South Cheshire (Coll); Southampton (Inst); Staffordshire; Stevenson (Coll) (Auto); Stockport (CFHE); Stoke on Trent (CT) (Motor Veh Mgt); Suffolk (Coll) (Auto); Sunderland; Swansea (IHE); Teesside; Warrington (CI); Warwickshire (Coll); West Herts (Coll); Westminster; Wigan & Leigh (Coll); Willesden (CT); Wirral Met (Coll); Yorkshire Coast (CFHE).

Alternative Offers:

EB offers: Aston 69%; Glamorgan 60%; Liverpool 70%; Surrey 65%; UMIST 65%.

IB offers: Aberdeen 24 pts; Aston 29 pts; Bath 30 pts Highers maths 5, phys 6; Belfast (Queen's) 655+555; Birmingham 33–30 pts; Bradford 30–24 pts; Brighton 24 pts; Bristol 32 pts H66 maths/phys; Brunel (MEng) 30 pts, (BEng) 26 pts; Cardiff 28 pts; City (MEng) 30 pts, (BEng) 28 pts; Coventry 24 pts; Cranfield 28 pts H655; Dundee 24 pts; Durham 666; Exeter 30 pts; Hertfordshire 26 pts; Lancaster 30 pts; Leeds 26 pts; Leicester (MEng) 36 pts, (BEng) 30 pts; London (QM) 30 pts; Loughborough 6 maths 6 physics 30 pts total; Manchester Met 24 pts; Northumbria 28 pts; Salford 28 pts; Southampton 32–28 pts; Surrey 28 pts + H555; UMIST 30 pts; Warwick 28 pts.

Irish offers: Aberdeen BBCCC; Aston BBCCC; Bradford BBCCC; Brunel BBCCC; Lancaster BBBBC; Liverpool BBCCC; Paisley BCC; Salford BBCC; Sunderland CCC; Westminster DDD.

Scottish Qualifications: Aberdeen ABBB–BBBB–BBBC; Abertay Dundee BCC; Dundee BBBC–BCCC; Edinburgh ABBB–BBBB; Glasgow ABBB–BBBB; Glasgow Caledonian BBBC; Heriot-Watt BBBC; Napier BCC; Paisley ABBB; Robert Gordon AABB–BBBB; Strathclyde AAAAB–ABBBB.

Overseas applicants: Some applicants (with appropriate qualifications) may be accepted for second year courses. **Hull** Living costs 30% lower than in London; **Loughborough** English language tuition pre-sessional or concurrent with courses.

CHOOSING YOUR COURSE (See also **Ch.1**)

Subject information: All courses involve the design, installation and maintenance of equipment used in industry. Thermodynamics, computer-aided design, fluid mechanics and materials science are subjects fundamental to this branch of engineering. Many universities offer students the opportunity to transfer to other Engineering courses in year 2. Alternative courses include Agricultural, Automobile, Manufacturing, Marine and Textile Engineering, and Building Services Engineering (heating, ventilation and refrigeration), Environmental Engineering (see **Engineering (Civil)**). Mathematics and Physics courses also could be considered. See also **Appendix 1**.

Special features: Aston Year 1 transfer possible between Mechanical or Electro-mechanical Engineering. **Bath** Common first year with Aeronautical and Manufacturing Engineering. Study in USA and language options available. **Bradford** Year 1 common with Manufacturing Engineering, transfers possible. A wide range of options including automotive engineering and languages. **Brighton** Option in forensic engineering. Final year options in either engineering production technology or mechanical engineering and design. **Bristol** End of first year transfers possible to Civil or Aeronautical Engineering, Engineering Mathematics or Manufacturing Systems Engineering. Language options and modules in Engineering, Business Management and Management Studies. **Brunel** Five specialist courses including automotive design, building services and biomedical applications. **Cardiff** Common first year with Civil, Mechanical, Environmental and Architectural Engineering; course decision at 16 weeks. **Coventry** (Auto Eng) Design studio-based course targeted at the automotive industry. **Cranfield** Includes weapons systems and land vehicle systems. **Dundee** First year is common with Manufacturing Engineering, Electrical and Electronic Engineering. **Glasgow** Common course is taken by all students initially opting for Aeronautical and Mechanical Engineering and Naval Architecture and Ocean Engineering. Specialisation then follows in the third and fourth years. **Heriot-Watt** The first year is taken in common with Energy Resource and Mechanical Engineering. Flexibility between Mechanical Engineering and Energy Resource Engineering. Possible specialisation in computer aided engineering in later years. Final year language option. **London (UCL)** A modern language is an optional subject in the third year. **Loughborough** Common first year then choice between Mechanical, Aeronautical and Systems Engineering. **Portsmouth** Computer-aided engineering is included in all areas of the course. **Salford** Special emphasis is placed on the business and commercial aspects of manufacturing. **Southampton** Multi-disciplinary approach to the MEng course. **Sussex** Specialised topics including robotics, computer-aided design, thermal power and microprocessors. Engineering management is studied throughout the second and third years. **Swansea** European Engineering courses are offered with French, German, Italian and Spanish (grade C at A-level in these languages is required). **UMIST** In the first two years it is possible to choose as an option one topic from modern languages (German or French) or history of science and technology. *NOW CHECK PROSPECTUSES AND WEB SITES.*

Top universities and colleges (Teaching Quality) (see Ch.4): Bath; Bristol; Cardiff; Coventry; Cranfield; Manchester; Manchester Met; Nottingham; Reading; Sheffield; Strathclyde; not all institutions assessed. See also **Engineering/Engineering Sciences**.

Top universities and colleges (Research) (see Ch.4): (Engineering including Aeronautical and Manufacturing Engineering) Bath; Belfast (Queen's); Bradford; Bristol; Brunel; Cardiff; Cranfield; Glasgow (Aero); Heriot-Watt; Leeds; Liverpool; London (Imp), (King's), (QM), (UCL); Loughborough; Manchester; Nottingham; Sheffield; Southampton; Strathclyde; Swansea; UMIST.

Study opportunities abroad: Abertay Dundee; Bath; Belfast (Queen's); Birmingham; Brighton; Bristol; Brunel; Cardiff; Central England; City; Coventry; De Montfort; Dundee; Edinburgh; Glamorgan; Glasgow; Glasgow Caledonian; Hertfordshire; Huddersfield; Leeds; Leicester; London (Imp), (QM), (UCL); Loughborough; Manchester; Manchester Met; Napier; Newcastle; Northumbria; Nottingham; Nottingham Trent; Oxford Brookes; Paisley;

Plymouth; Portsmouth; Robert Gordon; Salford; Sheffield; Sheffield Hallam; South Bank; Southampton; Staffordshire; Strathclyde; Sunderland; Surrey; Sussex; Swansea; Teesside; Warwick.

Work opportunities abroad: Abertay Dundee; Aston; Bath; Birmingham; Brighton; Bristol; Brunel; Central England; Coventry; Cranfield; De Montfort; Glamorgan; Hertfordshire; Huddersfield; Leicester; Lincolnshire & Humberside; London (UCL); Loughborough; Manchester Met; Napier; Northumbria; Oxford Brookes; Plymouth; Portsmouth; Salford; Sheffield; South Bank; Staffordshire; Strathclyde; Sunderland; Surrey; Swansea; Teesside; UMIST; Warwick.

ADMISSIONS INFORMATION

Number of applicants per place (approx): Abertay Dundee 4; Aston 8; Bath (MEng) 13; Birmingham 7; Bradford 4; Brighton 10; Bristol 13; Bristol UWE 17; Brunel 12; Cardiff 8; Coventry 8; City 13; Cranfield 3; Dundee 7; Durham 8; Glamorgan 6; Hertfordshire 10; Heriot-Watt 9; Huddersfield 1; Hull 11; Kingston 8; Lancaster 8; Leeds 15; Leicester 11; Liverpool John Moores (Mech Eng) 10; London (QM) 6; Loughborough (Mech Eng) 12, (Auto Eng) 5; Manchester 10; Manchester Met 6, (Mecha) 2, (Mech Eng) 6; Newcastle 10; North East Wales (IHE) 4; Northumbria 4; Nottingham 18; Nottingham Trent 4; Paisley 2; Plymouth 6; Portsmouth 6; Salford 7; Sheffield 10; South Bank 4; Staffordshire 6; Strathclyde 6; Surrey 9; Swansea 6; Teesside 7; UMIST 8; Warwick 8; Westminster 11.

Planning your UCAS personal statement (see Ch.4): Cardiff Work experience; hands-on skills; self-starter. See **Engineering/Engineering Sciences**. See also **Appendix 1**.

Selection interviews (see Ch.4): Abertay Dundee (No); Aston; Bath (No); Belfast (Queen's); Birmingham; Bolton (IHE); Bradford; Brighton (No); Bristol; Bristol UWE (No); Brunel; Cambridge; Cardiff; City (No); Cranfield; Durham; Greenwich (No); Hertfordshire; Huddersfield; Hull (No); Kingston; Lancaster; Leeds; Leicester; Liverpool John Moores; London (QM), (UCL) (No); Loughborough; Manchester; Manchester Met; Newcastle; Nottingham; Nottingham Trent; Oxford; Paisley (No); Salford; Sheffield; Sheffield Hallam; South Bank; Staffordshire (No); Strathclyde; Sunderland; Surrey; Swansea; UMIST.

Interview questions (see Ch.4): What mechanical objects have you examined and/or tried to repair? How do you see yourself in five years' time? What do you imagine you would be doing (production, management or design engineering)? What engineering interests do you have? What qualities are required to become a successful mechanical engineer? Do you like sixth form work? Describe the working of parts on an engineering drawing. How does a fridge work? **Hertfordshire** All interviewees receive a conditional offer. See also **Engineering/Engineering Sciences**.

Reasons for rejection (non-academic): Lack of enthusiasm/drive.

GAP YEAR ADVICE

Aston Welcomed, particulary if relevant; **Bradford** If you are working in industry you will be visited by a member of our staff; **Brunel** Not recommended: the four-year thin sandwich course is a better investment of time; **London (QM)** For a list of industrial contacts and sponsors write to the Department of Mechanical Engineering; **Manchester Met** and **Newcastle** Seek sponsorship or relevant experience; **Surrey** Year in Industry scheme useful.

Institutions willing to defer entry after A-levels: Aston; Birmingham; Bradford; Brighton; Cardiff; Central Lancashire; City; Coventry; Cranfield (No); Derby; Dundee; Durham; Glamorgan (No); Heriot-Watt; Hertfordshire; Huddersfield; Hull; Leeds; Leicester; Lincolnshire & Humberside; London (UCL) (No); Loughborough; Manchester Met; Napier; North East Wales (IHE); Northumbria; Nottingham (relevant experience preferred); Oxford Brookes; Plymouth; Robert Gordon; Salford; Sheffield; Southampton; Strathclyde; Surrey; Sussex; Swansea; Teesside; UMIST; Warwick.

AFTER RESULTS ADVICE

Institutions which may accept the same points score after A-levels: Abertay Dundee; Aston; Bath (MEng) (No); Belfast (Queen's) (No); Birmingham (No); Bradford; Brighton; Bristol (No); Brunel; Cardiff; Central Lancashire (No); City; Coventry; Cranfield (No); De Montfort; Derby; Dundee; Durham (No); Heriot-Watt; Hertfordshire; Huddersfield; Hull; Kingston; Lancaster; Leeds; Leicester; Lincolnshire & Humberside; Liverpool; Liverpool John Moores; London (UCL) (No); Loughborough; Manchester; Manchester Met; Napier; Newcastle; Northumbria; Nottingham (No); Oxford Brookes; Plymouth; Portsmouth; Salford; Sheffield (No); Sheffield Hallam; South Bank; Staffordshire; Strathclyde; Sunderland; Surrey; Swansea; Teesside; UMIST (No); Warwick (No).

Institutions which may accept lower grades/points score after A-levels: Dundee; Hertfordshire; Hull (overseas students 18–16 pts); Lincolnshire & Humberside; Napier; Oxford Brookes; Salford; Sheffield; Sheffield Hallam; Southampton; Staffordshire; Strathclyde; Warwick. Most institutions consider candidates who do not achieve target offers.

Offers to applicants repeating A-levels: Higher Belfast (Queen's), Brighton, Dundee, Kingston, Loughborough, Newcastle, Swansea, Warwick; **Possibly higher** City, Durham, Huddersfield; **Same** Aston, Bath, Bradford, Bristol, Brunel, Coventry, Derby, East London, Heriot-Watt, Leeds (usually), Lincolnshire & Humberside, Liverpool, Liverpool John Moores, Manchester Met, Napier, Northumbria, Nottingham, Oxford Brookes, Salford, Sheffield, Sheffield Hallam, South Bank, Southampton, Staffordshire, Surrey, Teesside, UMIST.

Probable vacancies from June 2001 and in Clearing (see Ch.4): Most universities can be contacted since vacancies are almost certain in this subject area.

NEW GRADUATE DESTINATIONS AND EMPLOYMENT (1999 HESA) (see **Ch.4**)

Of 1927 graduates surveyed, 1307 were full-time employed, 278 went on to further study and 130 were believed to be unemployed.

ENGINEERING (MINING) (see also Geology/Geological Sciences)

NB The information supplied by the universities and colleges this year varies considerably and the offers listed below should be used as a first source of reference only. Many institutions will accept combinations of Advanced (AL), Advanced Subsidiary (AS) and Vocational Advanced (VA) level qualifications to achieve the required points total, but applicants must check web sites and prospectuses for full details of all offers. Grades and points totals shown should be regarded as the minimum levels to be achieved, but offers may be adjusted downwards when results are known. The points totals shown to the left of the institutions are for ease of reference only. It must not be assumed that tariff points are always used by institutions or that they can be substituted for an offer in grades. The level of an offer is not necessarily indicative of the quality of a course. To calculate your offers see Chapter 4 and the inside fold of the back cover.

Engineering Council Statement: See **Engineering/Engineering Sciences**.

Special subject requirements/preferences: As for **Engineering/Engineering Sciences**.

300 pts **Exeter** – 300 pts 18u (inc 2ALs sci from maths/phys/chem) – BBB **or** BB+bb **or** VAs (contact univ); (not gs) (MEng Min Eng)
London (Imp) – 300 pts (Min Eng; Env Min Eng; Petrol Eng; Env Earth Res Eng)

240 pts **Exeter** – 240 pts 18u (inc 2ALs sci from maths/phys/chem); CCC **or** CC+cc **or** VAs (contact univ) (not gs) (BEng Min Eng; Miner Eng courses)
Leeds – CCC/BB (MEng/BEng Miner Eng; Min Eng)
Nottingham – CCC–CDD/BC (Min Eng; Mining Miner Eng)

180 pts   Leeds – DDD (BSc Ind Min Tech)
160 pts   Glamorgan – 160 pts approx (Min Surv courses)

140 pts | See Engineering Council statement under Engineering/Engineering Sciences |
  and below
  Doncaster (Coll) – 80 pts – ALs+/-VA6u; (Min/Elec Eng; Min/Mech Eng;
    Qry/Road Eng)
  Doncaster (Coll) – offer varies (Qry Rd Surf Eng)

Diploma of Higher Education
  Leeds (Ind Min Tech).

Higher National Diploma courses
100 pts   and below
  Doncaster (Coll); Exeter; Fife (CFHE); Glamorgan (Min Surv); Sheffield Hallam.

Alternative Offers:

EB offers: Exeter 60%.

IB offers: Exeter 26–24 pts.

CHOOSING YOUR COURSE (See also **Ch.1**)

Subject information: Mining Engineering covers geology, surveying and mineral processing and gives access to careers in petroleum engineering as well as coal and metalliferous mining. New career opportunities are now opening up using engineering techniques to clean up the environment. See also **Geology**. Quarry Engineering may be of particular interest to students of geography and geology. See also **Appendix 1**.

Special features: Exeter International reputation. Minerals and Mining/Quarrying Engineering students have a common first year; opportunities for vacation work in the minerals and mining industries at home and abroad. Financial and general management techniques are included on these courses opening the way to various managerial courses. **Leeds** Minerals and Mining students have separate programmes with some common modules. **London (Imp)** Third-year students work at least 500 hours in industry during summer vacations in UK or abroad. (Petrol Eng) Choice between Petroleum Engineering and Mining Engineering at end of first or second years. Optional sandwich placements. Quarry Engineering option on the Mining Engineering course. **Nottingham** Options enable students to specialise in petroleum engineering as well as coal and metalliferous mining. *NOW CHECK PROSPECTUSES AND WEB SITES.*

Top universities and colleges (Research) (see Ch.4): Exeter; Leeds; London (Imp); Nottingham.

Study opportunities abroad: Birmingham; Doncaster (Coll); Exeter; Nottingham.

Work opportunities abroad: Doncaster (Coll); Exeter; Leeds.

ADMISSIONS INFORMATION

Number of applicants per place (approx): Exeter 3; Leeds (Mining) 2, (Mineral) 1; Nottingham 5.

Planning your UCAS personal statement (see Ch.4): Visits to mines and quarries are essential to understand the basic facts about this career. Discuss these interests fully on your UCAS form. Information about school projects, visits etc should also be given. See also **Engineering/Engineering Sciences**. See also **Appendix 1**.

Selection interviews (see Ch.4): Exeter; Leeds; Nottingham.

Examples of interview questions (see Ch.4): Have you visited any mines? Describe them. Have you any relatives in the mining industry? What problems are there at present for the mining unions? Where are the largest coalfields in Britain? What other products are mined in Britain? What products are mined in other parts of the world?

GAP YEAR ADVICE

Institutions willing to defer entry after A-levels: Exeter; Glamorgan; Leeds; Nottingham (some experience in an extractive industry preferred).

AFTER RESULTS ADVICE

Institutions which may accept the same points score after A-levels: Exeter; Leeds; Nottingham.

Institutions which may accept lower grades/points score after A-levels: Exeter; Leeds. Most institutions consider applicants who have failed to achieve target A-levels.

Offers to applicants repeating A-levels: Same Leeds.

Probable vacancies from June 2001 and in Clearing (see Ch.4): Almost all institutions are likely to have vacancies with offers averaging 240–220 pts.

NEW GRADUATE DESTINATIONS AND EMPLOYMENT (1999 HESA) (see **Ch.4**)

In a survey of 104 graduates who had followed courses in Minerals Technology, 79 entered full-time employment, five went on to further study and four were reported to be unemployed.

ENGLISH

NB The information supplied by the universities and colleges this year varies considerably and the offers listed below should be used as a first source of reference only. Many institutions will accept combinations of Advanced (AL), Advanced Subsidiary (AS) and Vocational Advanced (VA) level qualifications to achieve the required points total, but applicants must check web sites and prospectuses for full details of all offers. Grades and points totals shown should be regarded as the minimum levels to be achieved, but offers may be adjusted downwards when results are known. The points totals shown to the left of the institutions are for ease of reference only. It must not be assumed that tariff points are always used by institutions or that they can be substituted for an offer in grades. The level of an offer is not necessarily indicative of the quality of a course. To calculate your offers see Chapter 4 and the inside fold of the back cover.

Special subject requirements/preferences: A-level: English, usually the highest grade shown in the offers below. **Oxford** (Engl) A-level expected + modern language or history either at A or AS-level; (Engl/Modn Lang) English and modern language essential at A-level. **GCSE:** A foreign language may be preferred. **Aberdeen, Dundee, Edinburgh, Glasgow, St Andrews** Mathematics and foreign language required. **Birmingham** Five-six grades A*, A or B plus decent grade in mathematics (not applicable to mature students). **Birmingham (Westhill)** Three subjects minimum including English. **Cardiff** No fixed target, the higher the better. **Leeds** Good GCSEs sought. **Liverpool** Grade Bs are important. **Newman (CHE)** Five subjects grades A–C. **Reading** Seven subjects at grade A–C. **South Bank** Five subjects minimum at grade A–C. **Swansea (IHE)** Three subjects minimum at grade A–C. **Warwick** Ten subjects. **York** A good grade in another language.

360 pts   and above
    Cambridge – Offers, mainly in grades, vary between colleges (English; Anglo-Saxon)
    London (QM) – 370 pts 21 (inc B Engl); (English courses)
    Oxford – Offers vary between candidates (Engl Lang/Lit)
    Southampton – 370 pts 21u (inc 220 pts 2ALs inc B Engl); (Engl; Engl/Film St)
    York – 390–340 pts 21–18u – AAB+b; (Engl courses except under **320 pts**)
350 pts   Southampton – 350 pts 21u (inc 220 pts inc E or e Engl) (check with univ); (English courses except under **360 pts** above)

340 pts   **Birmingham** – AAB–ABB (Engl; Engl/Mus)
    Bristol – AAB–ABB (A Engl) (Engl; Engl/Phil)
    Cambridge (Hom) – AAB–ABB (Engl/Educ St (BA); Engl/Dr/Educ St (BA))
    Durham – AAB/AA+2ASs (Engl Lit)
    Edinburgh – AAB–BBB (Engl Lang/Lit courses)
    Leeds – 18u – A (Engl) AB; (not gs) (English)
    London (UCL) – AAB or 3ALs+AS/VA; (Engl; Engl/Ger; Engl/Hist Art)
    Manchester – AAB (Engl Lang/Lit; Engl with Am St)
    Sheffield – A (Engl) AB (Engl Lit)
    Warwick – AAB (Engl Lit; Engl/Am Lit; Engl/Euro Lit; Engl Lit/Crea Writ)

330 pts   **Southampton** – 330 pts 21u (inc 180 pts from 2ALs); (Hum courses)
    Southampton (New Coll) – 330 pts (inc 180 pts from 2ALs) (AS b Engl/hist min); gs; (Hum (Engl St); Hum (Engl St/Hist St)

320 pts   **Bristol UWE** – 320–260 pts (200–180 pts from 6u/12u awards) 18u pref/12u – 6u award Engl/lit; ALs or ALs+ASs or VAs+/-AL/ASs; (Engl; Engl/Hist)
    Cardiff – ABB/AA (Engl Lit Joint Hons; Engl Lit)
    Durham – ABB (Engl Lit/Lat; Engl Lit/Phil; Engl Lit/Ling)
    East Anglia – 320 pts 18u: ABB (VA as 3rd AL) or AB+bb; (not gs) (Engl Lit/Compar Lit; Engl Lit/Crea Writ)
    Exeter – 320 pts 18u (inc AL Engl); (Engl/Fine Art)
    Keele – ABB–BBB or equiv AS accepted; gs; (Engl/Am St; Engl Russ Hist Cult; Engl/Law; Engl/Psy)
    Kent – 320–280 pts (single/joint courses English)
    Leeds – ABB (Engl with Hist/Hist Art/Ling/Phil)
    Leicester – 320 pts 18u – ABB or ALs+ASs(ALs min B) or VA12uAB; (English)
    Liverpool – ABB (Engl Lang/Lit; Engl/Comm St)
    London (King's) – ABB+AS (inc A Engl) or VA6u+ALs/ASs; (Engl Lang/Lit; Engl/Film St)
    Manchester – ABB (Engl/Lang)
    Newcastle – A (Engl) BB (Engl Lang/Lit; Engl Lit)
    St Andrews – ABB (MA English)
    Sheffield – ABB–BBB (Engl and Fr/Phil/Hist/Engl Lit)
    Sussex – ABB (English courses except under **300 pts**)
    Warwick – ABB (Engl/Thea St)
    York – BBC+c or BB+ccc; gs; (Engl Lang/Ling)

300 pts   **Aberystwyth** – 300–200 pts – 3ALs (inc Engl A/B) or ALs+ASs; gs; (Engl; Writ Engl)
    Birmingham – BBB (English courses except under **340 pts**)
    Bristol UWE – 300–240 pts approx (EFL and Euro St courses)
    Brunel – 300–220 pts 2x6u (inc AL Engl or VA (Media/Comm) B) – ALs or ALs+ASs or VAs+/-ALs/ASs; (English courses)
    Durham – ABC (Engl Lit/Mus)
    East Anglia – 300 pts 18u – ABB+addit units or BBB (VA as 3rd AL) or AB+bb; (not gs) (Engl/Am Lit; Engl Lit courses)
    Edinburgh – BBB (Scot Lit)
    Exeter – 300 pts 18u (inc AL lang for joint Lang courses+AL Engl) – BBB or BB+bb or VAs (contact univ); (not gs) (Engl courses except under **320/280/240 pts**)
    Essex – 300–280 pts 12u – BB+AL/2ASs; gs; (Engl Lang/Lit/US Lit)
    Glasgow – BBB (Engl/Film TV St)
    Hull – ABC (Engl/Dr)
    Hull – BBB–BBC/BC (Engl courses except above)
    Keele – BBB–BBC/AB–BC or equiv AS accepted; gs; (English courses except under **320 pts**)
    Lancaster – BBB–BBC (Engl Lit; Engl Lang Lit courses)
    Liverpool – BBB–BBC (English courses except under **320 pts**)
    London (King's) – BBB or AB+bb (or equiv) (inc B Engl lang/lit/modn lang); (Engl Lang/Comm)

London (RH) – A(Engl)BC (English courses except under **280 pts**)

London (UCL) – ABC **or** 3ALs+AS/VA; (Engl/Ger)

Loughborough – 300 pts 18u – B(Engl)+AL+AL/2ASs **or** VAs+/-AL/ASs; gs; (Engl/PE)

Manchester – BBB–BBC (Engl/Russ/Ital/Span/Fer/Fr)

Nottingham – ABC (not gs) (Engl St; Engl/Phil)

Oxford Brookes – BBB/AB (Engl St)

Reading – BBB–BBC (BC for mature students) (English courses)

St Andrews – BBB (English courses except under **320 pts**)

Sheffield – BBB (Engl with Russ/Mus/Ger/Hisp St/Ling/Mediev Lit)

Sussex – BBB (Engl Lang courses)

Swansea – 300 pts 18u – BBB/AB–BB **or** ALs+ASs **or** VAs+/-AL/ASs; (Engl Lit; Engl/Am St) BBB–BBC (English Joint courses)

Warwick – BBB (Engl/Span Am Lit; Engl/Fr; Engl/Lat Lit)

280 pts **Aberdeen** – BBC (English courses)

Bristol – BBC–BCC (B Engl lit/Lat); (not gs) (Engl/Latin)

Cambridge (Hom) – BBC–BCD (Engl/Educ BEd)

Cardiff – BBC–BCC (Engl Lang St; Lang/Comm)

Exeter – 280 pts 18u (inc AL Engl); BBC **or** BB+cc **or** VAs (contact univ); (not gs) (Engl Gk Rom St)

Falmouth (CA) – BBC (Engl/Media St)

Glasgow – BBC (English courses except under **300 pts**)

Lancaster – BBC (Engl Lit/Ling; Engl/Mus; Engl/Phil; Engl/Relig St)

Leeds – BBC/BB (English courses except under **340/320 pts**)

London (Gold) – BBC–BCC/BB (Engl; Engl with Hist/Hist Art/Thea Arts)

London (RH) – BBC/BB (Engl/Ital/Class St/Lat/Ger)

Loughborough – BBC (Pub/Engl)

Newcastle – 280 pts approx (Engl Lang/Ger)

Northumbria – BBC (Engl St; Engl/Film St)

Nottingham – 280 pts – 3ALs(B Engl) (English)

Nottingham Trent – BBC/BB (English)

Reading – BBC (BC for mature students) (English courses except under **300/260 pts**)

Salford – BBC–BCC/AA–AB (English courses)

Sheffield – BBC (Engl/Sociol)

Sheffield Hallam – 280 pts (Engl St)

Stirling – BBC–CCC (English courses except under **240 pts**)

Surrey Roehampton – 280 pts – ALs **or** ALs+ASs (inc C Engl lit); (Engl Lit)

Swansea – 280 pts 18u – BBC–BCC/BB **or** ALs+ASs **or** VAs+/-AL/ASs; (Engl Lang schemes)

Warwick – BBC (Engl/Ger Lit)

260 pts **Aberystwyth** – 260 pts approx (B lang/lit)/BB (English courses)

Bangor – 260 pts approx (Engl Crea Writ)

Belfast (Queen's) – BCC (English courses)

Bristol UWE – 260 pts approx (Engl/Hist)

Brunel – BCC (Film TV St/Engl)

Dundee – BCC/BB (English courses)

Hertfordshire – 260–220 pts 1x12u **or** 2x6u; (Engl Lit; Modn Engl Lit; Lit)

Kent – 260 pts approx (single Hons Lit St)

Leeds, Trinity & All Saints (Coll) – BCC–CCD (Engl/Media)

Leicester – BCC (Engl Comb Arts)

Liverpool John Moores – 260 4ALs; 220 pts 3ALs; 160 pts 2ALs (nc C Engl) **or** VA C (Media/Comm Prod)+C (Engl) (English courses; Engl Lit/Cult Hist; Imgntv Writ)

London (QM) – 260 pts approx (Engl courses)

Loughborough – 260 pts 18u – B(Engl)+AL+AL/2ASs **or** VAs+/-ALs/ASs; gs; (Engl; Engl/Hist Art)

Manchester – BCC (Engl/Gk; Engl/Lat)

Manchester Met – BCC/BC (Engl St)
Northumbria – BCC/BB (Engl/Hist; Engl/Wmns Cult)
Oxford Brookes – 260–220 pts average offer (English offer varies with 2nd subject)
Reading – BCC (BC for mature students) (Engl/Lat; Engl/Class St)
Salford – BCC/AA (Engl/Modn Lang)
Sheffield Hallam – 260 pts (Film/Lit; Engl; Engl St)
Sunderland – 260 pts (Engl St/Media)
Ulster – BCC–CCC (English)
Wolverhampton – 260–200 pts 12u – C(Engl)CD/BB **or** CD+cc **or** VA12u AB/BB; gs; (English)

240 pts   **Bangor** – 240 pts 18u; gs; (Engl/Crim)
Blackburn (Coll) – 240 pts approx (Engl Lang/Lit)
Bradford – 240 pts 12u; gs; (English)
Central Lancashire – 240 pts 12u (inc B Engl lit or comb lit/lang); gs; (Engl/Am Lit; Engl Lit St)
De Montfort (Leicester) – 240 pts (inc C Engl) – ALs; (English)
Exeter (Truro) – 240 pts (inc AL Engl) – CCC **or** CC+cc **or** VAs (contact univ); gs; (English)
Glamorgan – 240 pts approx (Engl/Law)
Huddersfield – 240 pts 18u – CCC (inc Engl C, hist) **or** CC+cc **or** VA6u B+C/cc; gs; (Engl/Media/Hist)
King Alfred's Winchester (Coll) – 240 pts 18u (AL Engl); gs; (English)
Lampeter – 240–220 pts approx (B Engl) (English courses)
London Guildhall – 240–200 pts approx (English courses)
Plymouth – BCD (English courses)
Sheffield Hallam – 240 pts approx (BEd Engl; English Comb; Engl/Hist)
South Bank – 240–220/200–180 pts (English courses)
Stirling – CCC (Engl St/Fr/Ger/Span)
Strathclyde – CCC (BBD 2nd yr entry) (English)
Ulster – CCC (Humanities)

220 pts   **Anglia** – 220–200 pts approx (English)
Bangor – 220 pts approx (Engl Lang; Ling)
Central England – 220–180 pts approx (Engl Lang Lit)
Central Lancashire – 220 pts 12u (inc A Engl lit or comb lit/lang); gs; (Engl/Thea St)
Central Lancashire – 220 pts 12u (inc C Engl lit or comb lit/lang); gs; (Engl Lang/Lit; Engl Lang St)
Chester (Coll) – 220–200 pts – ALs (180 pts inc C Engl)+AS **or** VA (180 pts C in 1 subj)+ASs; gs; (Engl courses)
Glamorgan – 220 pts approx (B Engl)/BC (English)
Hertfordshire – 220–200 pts approx (English courses)
Huddersfield – 3/2ALs (inc C Engl) **or** CC+dd **or** C+bbc VAs (contact dept); gs; (Engl/Crea Writ)
Kingston – 220–180 pts 2x6u (inc 100 pts AL Engl lit); gs; (Engl Lit courses
Lincolnshire & Humberside – 220 pts (English)
Luton – 220–180 pts approx (Engl St joint courses Mod)
Middlesex – 220–180 pts approx (English courses)
Nottingham Trent – 220–180 pts approx (Humanities)
Portsmouth – 220 pts – ALs **or** ALs+ASs **or** VAs; gs; (Engl Lang/Lit; Engl Lit; Engl joint courses)
St Mark & St John (Coll) – 220–180 pts approx (English courses)

200 pts   **Anglia** – C Engl+120 pts approx (English courses except under **220 pts**)
Bangor – 200 pts; gs; (Engl Lit)
Bath Spa (UC) – 200 pts 12u – BB (inc Engl) **or** VA12u BB; (not gs) (English)
Blackburn (Coll) – 200 pts approx – ALs (inc C Engl) **or** ALs+ASs; gs; (Engl Lang/Lit)
Bristol – BB (Engl/Drama)

Central Lancashire – 200–180 pts 12u (inc AL Engl lang/lit); gs; (Engl/Educ St/Hist)
De Montfort (Leicester) – 200 pts (inc C Engl) – ALs; (English joint courses)
Derby – 200 pts 12u – CDD **or** CD+dd **or** VA12u (grades as AL)+/-AL/ASs; gs; (English)
Leeds (Bretton Hall) – BB–CC (English courses)
Manchester Met – CDD/CC (Hum/Soc St)
Newman (CHE) – 200–180 pts approx (English courses)
Northampton (UC) – 200–160 pts (English courses)
Ripon & York (Coll) – 200–180 pts approx (English courses)
St Martin's (Coll) – 200–160 pts approx (English)
Staffordshire – 200 pts – CC+ASs **or** VA12u CC; gs; (Engl courses)
Teesside – 200–180 pts approx (English courses)

190 pts **Buckingham** – 190 pts 21u – 3ALs **or** 3ALs+AS; (Engl Lit courses)

180 pts **Anglia** – 180 pts 12u (inc CC in Engl lit/lit lang/lang); gs; (English)
Blackpool & Fylde (Coll) – 180 pts approx (Engl Lang Lit Writ)
Buckinghamshire Chilterns (UC) – 180–140 pts approx (English courses)
Canterbury Christ Church (UC) – B(Engl)C (English courses)
Cheltenham & Glos (CHE) – 180 pts approx (C Engl) (Engl St courses)
Chester (Coll) – 180 pts approx (English courses)
Colchester (Inst) – 180 pts approx (English courses)
Coventry – 180 pts aprox (Engl/Fr/Ger/Ital/Russ/Span)
Dartington (CA) – BC (Perf Writ)
De Montfort (Bedford) – 180–160 pts – ALs **or** ALs+ASs **or** VAs+/-ALs/ASs; (English single/joint courses)
East London – 180 pts approx (C Engl) (Lit courses)
Glamorgan – 180 pts approx (Engl St/Media St; Engl/Phil)
Greenwich – 180 pts approx (English courses)
Hull (Scarborough) – 180 pts/DDD (Engl Cult St)
Liverpool Hope (Coll) – 180 pts approx (English courses)
Newcastle – BC (Engl Lit/Lat)
Norwich City (Coll) – 180 pts approx (English courses)
Oxford Brookes (Westminster) – 180 pts approx (Engl QTS)
St Mary's (Coll) – 12u – BC–CC **or** ALs+ASs **or** VA12u BC–CD; gs; (English)
Sunderland – 180 pts; gs; (Engl; Engl Comb St; Comp Lit Comb St)

160 pts **Bath Spa (UC)** – 160–120 pts 12u – B(Engl or related subj)D **or** VA12u BD; (not gs) (Crea Engl Comb)
Birmingham (Westhill) – 160 pts 12u (inc C); ALs **or** ALs+ASs **or** VAs (contact univ); gs; (Humanities)
Bishop Grosseteste (Coll) – CC (inc AL Engl) **or** C+cc **or** VA12u+AL; (not gs) (English)
Bolton (IHE) – 160 pts approx (English)
Chichester (UC) – 160 pts (inc C Engl); (English)
Cumbria (CAD) – 160 pts – CC **or** ASs (contact coll) **or** VA; (Crea Writ)
Doncaster (Coll) – 160 pts – CC **or** ALs+ASs **or** VAs+/-AL/ASs; (Engl Lit/Lang)
Edge Hill (CHE) – CC (English courses)
Hull (Scarborough) – 160 pts approx (English with QTS)
Manchester Met – CC (English Comb)
Newport (UWCN) – 160–140 pts – ALs **or** ALs+ASs **or** VAs+/-AL/ASs; (Engl; Engl Hum)
North London – 160 pts 2x6u **or** 1x12u + 2 poems/prose/crea writ for Crea Writ course; (Crea Writ; Engl)
Southampton City (Coll) – 160 pts approx (Engl/Art/Pol/Psy/Soc)
Surrey Roehampton – 160 pts 15u inc 12u ALs **or** VA12u; (Engl Lang/Ling)
Trinity Carmarthen (Coll) – CC–EE (English courses)
Westminster – CC (English courses)
Worcester (UC) – 160 pts 12u – CC **or** ASs **or** VA12u CC; gs; (Engl/Lit St)

140 pts **Barnsley (Coll)** – 140 pts 12u; gs (AL only); (Engl/Drama)
Bishop Grosseteste (Coll) – CD (inc C Engl) **or** C+dd **or** VA12u; (Engl Lit)

Derby – 140 pts 12u – CD **or** DE+ee **or** VAs (grades as ALs)+/-AL/ASs; gs; (Engl Comb; Crea Writ)

Middlesex – CD approx (Engl Mod)

120 pts and below

Anglia – 120 pts 12u (inc 2ALs); ALs+ASs(or equiv); (Engl/Lang St for foreign students + ELTS)

Coventry – (English courses for non-native English speakers)

Doncaster (Coll) – (Engl Comb)

North East Wales (IHE) – (English courses)

Rose Bruford (Coll) – (Engl Thea)

Solihull (Coll) – EE (Cult St)

Surrey Roehampton – 80 pts – Camb Advnc Cert Engl grade C or 6.0 IELTS or 213 TOEFL or GCSE grade C (EFL)

Swansea (IHE) – 100 pts approx (Engl St with Art/Drama/Media/Soc St)

Leeds Met – (contact university)

Diploma of Higher Education courses
80 pts and below

Bath Spa (UC); Liverpool John Moores; Manchester Met; Oxford Brookes; Oxford Brookes (Westminster); Worcester (UC).

Higher National Diploma courses

North West Kent (Coll) (Prof Writ); Plymouth (Writ).

Alternative Offers:

IB offers: Aberdeen 30 pts; Aberystwyth 30 pts; Anglia 28 pts; Bangor 28 pts H5 Engl; Birmingham 32 pts 6 in English; Bristol 33 pts H7 Engl; Bristol UWE 30 pts; Brunel 32 pts; Buckingham 24 pts; Cardiff 32 pts H66 incl English; H555 S444; Central England 30–28 pts H5 English; De Montfort 30 pts; Dundee 29 pts; Durham H665; Edinburgh H665; Essex 30 pts; Exeter 32 pts; Hull 30 pts; Kent 34–30 pts; King Alfred's Winchester (Coll) 24 pts; Kingston 32–30 pts; Lampeter 30–28 pts; Lancaster 32–30 pts; Leeds 33 pts inc H7 English 6; Liverpool 34 pts; London (Gold) 28 pts, (King's) 34–32 pts, (QM) H655; Loughborough 28 pts Highers 14 pts; Portsmouth 24 pts; St Andrews 30 pts; St Martin's (Coll) 28 pts; Sheffield 33 pts; South Bank 24 pts; Southampton 32 pts; Warwick 34–32 pts; Swansea 30 pts; York 32 pts H766 inc 6 in English.

Irish offers: Bangor BBBCC (B English); Lampeter BBBCC; St Andrews BBBB; Sheffield ABBBC; South Bank CCCC; Southampton AABBBB; York AABB.

Scottish Qualifications: Aberdeen BBBB; Dundee BBBC; Edinburgh (Lang) BBBB, (Lit) ABBB; Glasgow BBBB; St Andrews AABB; Stirling BBBB; Strathclyde BBBB.

Overseas applicants: Hull Living costs 30% lower than in London; **Liverpool** Limited places: English language competence essential. **Oxford Brookes** International Foundation Programme available for overseas students.

CHOOSING YOUR COURSE (See also **Ch.1**)

> **Subject information:** Applications for English courses are still increasing with approximately seven applicants for each place. These courses are an extension of school studies in literature and language and may cover topics ranging from Anglo-Saxon literature to the present day. Most courses, however, will focus on certain areas such as the Medieval or Renaissance periods of literature or English language studies. Admissions tutors will expect students to have read widely outside their A-level syllabus. (Sunday newspapers' book reviews will give a useful introduction to modern literature.) Alternative courses depend on special interests. A preference for literature can apply to language courses, for example French, German, Spanish and to Drama. An interest in English language can lead to Linguistics, Communication and Media Studies courses.

Special features: Aberystwyth Options include creative writing. **Bristol UWE** Additional modules are offered in history, media studies, women's studies, modern languages and American literature. There is an optional second year in the USA. **Buckingham** A two-year course is offered and also an English language programme for overseas students. **Essex** Strong emphasis on Film Studies in the literature course. **Glasgow** Specialist options include dialectology and Scots language. **Huddersfield** The English Studies course covers language, literature and writing. **Kingston** Emphasis on 19th and 20th century Anglo-American literature and women's writing. Opportunity to study in Europe and America. **Loughborough** Subsidiary subjects include publishing, marketing, art history and politics. **Northumbria** Level 3 options include contemporary or creative writing and American literature and cinema. **South Bank** The degree covers literatures spanning African, American, Australian, British and Caribbean texts, film and detective fiction. *NOW CHECK PROSPECTUSES AND WEB SITES.*

Top universities and colleges (Teaching Quality) (see Ch.4): Aberdeen; Aberystwyth; Anglia; Bath Spa (UC); Belfast (Queen's); Birmingham; Bristol; Bristol UWE; Cambridge; Cardiff; Chester (Coll); Dundee; Durham; East London; Exeter; Glamorgan (Crea Writ); Glasgow; Kingston; Lancaster; Leeds; Leicester; Liverpool; London (Birk), (QM), (UCL); Newcastle; North London; Northumbria; Nottingham; Oxford; Oxford Brookes; Sheffield; Sheffield Hallam; Southampton; Stirling; Strathclyde; Sussex; Warwick; York; not all institutions assessed.

Top universities and colleges (Research) (see Ch.4): Birmingham; Bristol; Cambridge; Cardiff; Durham; East Anglia; Edinburgh; Essex; Lancaster; Leeds; Leicester; Liverpool; London (King's), (QM), (RH), (UCL); Manchester; Nottingham; Oxford; Reading; St Andrews; Sheffield; Southampton; Sussex; Warwick; York.

Study opportunities abroad: Aberdeen; Aberystwyth; Bangor; Belfast (Queen's); Bristol; Central England; Cheltenham & Glos (CHE); Coventry; Dundee; Durham; East Anglia; Edinburgh; Exeter; Glasgow; Hull; King Alfred's Winchester (Coll); Lampeter; Lancaster; Leeds; Leeds (Bretton Hall); Leicester; London (UCL); Manchester; Manchester Met; Newcastle; North London; Northumbria; Plymouth; Salford; Sheffield; Sheffield Hallam; Southampton; Staffordshire; Swansea; York.

Work opportunities abroad: Aberystwyth; Leeds; Salford; Sheffield; Sheffield Hallam; Worcester (UC).

ADMISSIONS INFORMATION

Number of applicants per place (approx): Aberystwyth 7; Anglia 6; Bangor 5; Bath Spa (UC) 8; Birmingham 12; Bristol 33; Bristol UWE 4; Brunel 10; Buckingham 2; Cambridge 4; Cambridge (Hom) 4 (All BEd courses); Cardiff (Engl/Psy) 12, (Engl Lit) 6; Central England 9; Central Lancashire 10; Cheltenham & Glos (CHE) 35; Chester (Coll) 20; Chichester (UC) 7; De Montfort 18; Derby 3; Durham 15; East Anglia 20; Edge Hill (CHE) 4; Exeter 13; Glamorgan 8; Huddersfield 5; Hull 14; Hull (Scarborough) 1; Kingston 6; Lampeter 4; Lancaster 12; Leeds 12, (Engl/Thea St) 19; Leeds (Bretton Hall) 4; Leeds, Trinity & All Saints (Coll) 7; Leicester 7; London (Gold) 9, (King's) 15, (QM) 9, (RH) 9 average, (UCL) 13; Loughborough (Engl) 11, (Engl/PE/Spo Sci) 18, (Engl/Drama) 40; Manchester (Engl) 14, (Engl/Am Lit) 33, (Engl/Ital) 10; Manchester Met 7; Middlesex 8; North East Wales (IHE) 2; North London 5; Nottingham 30; Nottingham Trent 21; Oxford 3.7; Oxford Brookes 15 average; Portsmouth 11; Reading 11; Ripon & York (Coll) 3; St Martin's (Coll) 24; Salford 12; Sheffield 12; Sheffield Hallam 10; South Bank 5; Southampton 10; Stirling 9; Sunderland 10; Surrey Roehampton 5; Swansea 5; Swansea (IHE) 4; Teesside 5; Warwick 15, (Engl/Thea) 26; Worcester (UC) (BEd) 5; York 20.

Planning your UCAS personal statement (see Ch.4): Applicants should read outside their subject. Details of any writing should be provided. Theatre visits and play readings are also important. Keep up to date by reading literary and theatre reviews in the national newspapers (keep a scrapbook of reviews for reference). Evidence is needed of a good writing style. **Birmingham** Independence of mind, wit! **Bristol UWE** Favourite authors, spare-time reading. **Cardiff** (Engl Lit) Ability to write lucidly, accurately and succinctly.

Evidence of literary enthusiasm. Ability to spell, punctuate and write in paragraphs. **Durham** Background reading about linguistics essential. **London (Gold)** Some interests should reflect chosen course. **London (QM)** Evidence of commitment to literature, also for drama, dramatic arts, acting, production experience. **Nottingham Trent** Ability to write accurately and clearly. **St Andrews** Evidence of interest and reasons for choosing the course. Sport/extra-curricular activities. Posts of responsibility. **Stirling** What has the student done between school and university? Literary and linguistic interests. **Swansea** (Engl Lang) Self-assessment of language competence. **Warwick** Oxbridge decisions awaited before offers made. Reading beyond the syllabus. (Engl/Thea) Synopsis of theatre experience (viewing and/or practical).

Selection interviews (see Ch.4): Aberystwyth (some); Anglia (W); Bangor (mature students); Bath Spa (UC); Birmingham (No); Birmingham (Westhill) (No); Blackburn (Coll) (some); Bristol UWE (No); Brunel; Buckingham (No); Cambridge (W) (T); Cambridge (Hom); Canterbury Christ Church) (UC); Cardiff (No) (W); Central England (No); Cheltenham & Glos (CHE); Chester (Coll) (No); Derby (No); Dundee (No); Durham (Engl/Mus) (No); East Anglia; Edge Hill (CHE) (No); Edinburgh (No); Exeter; Greenwich (No); Huddersfield; Hull; Hull (Scarborough); Kent (No); Kingston; Lampeter; Lancaster; Leeds (mature students only); Leeds, Trinity & All Saints (Coll); Leicester (No); Liverpool (Engl Lit/Fr); London (Gold), (King's) (some), (RH); Loughborough; Manchester (No); Manchester Met (No); Middlesex; Newcastle (T); Newman (CHE) (No); Newport (UWCN); North London (some); Nottingham (No); Oxford (W) Candidates advised before interview) (T); Portsmouth; Reading (T); Ripon & York (Coll) (No); St Andrews (No); Salford (W) (T); Sheffield (No); Sheffield Hallam (No); Solihull (Coll); South Bank (T); Southampton (some); Stirling (No); Sunderland (No); Surrey Roehampton; Swansea; Swansea (IHE) (not usually); Warwick; Worcester (UC) (No); York (No).

Interview questions (see Ch.4): Questions will almost certainly be asked on set A-level texts. You will also be expected to have read outside your A-level subjects, your favourite authors, poets, dramatists etc. Questions in the past have included: Do you think that class discussion plays an important part in your English course? What is the value of studying a text in depth rather than just reading it for pleasure? What is the difference between satire and comedy? Are books written by women different from those written by men? Why would you go to see a production of Hamlet? What are your views on the choice of novels for this year's Booker Prize? Short verbal tests and a précis may be set. **Warwick** We may ask students to sight-read or to analyse a text.

Reasons for rejection (non-academic): Some are well-informed about English literature – others are not. Inability to respond to questions about their current studies. Lack of enthusiasm for the challenge of studying familiar subjects from a different perspective. (One admissions tutor preferred to think positively: 'We look for interviewees who respond positively to ideas and can think on their feet, who can intelligently engage with critical issues and sustain an argument. If they don't evince any of these we reject them!') Must be able to benefit from the course. Little interest in how people communicate with each other. They don't know a single thing about our course. **Bangor** We reject those who decline interviews. **Reading** None. If they have reached the interview we have already eliminated all other factors.

GAP YEAR ADVICE

Buckingham Not appropriate; **London (QM)** Keep in touch with admissions tutor during gap year.

Institutions willing to defer entry after A-levels: Aberystwyth; Anglia; Bangor; Bath Spa (UC) (No); Birmingham; Blackburn (Coll) (No); Bristol; Brunel; Buckingham; Canterbury Christ Church (UC) (No); Cardiff; Central Lancashire; Cheltenham & Glos (CHE); Chester (Coll); Dartington (CA); De Montfort; Dundee; Durham (No); Edge Hill (CHE); Glamorgan; Huddersfield; Hull; Kent; King Alfred's Winchester (Coll); Lampeter; Lancaster; Leeds; Leicester; Liverpool Hope (Coll); London (RH), (UCL) (No); Loughborough; Luton; Manchester Met; Newcastle (prefer not); Newport (UWCN); North East Wales (IHE); Northumbria; Nottingham; Nottingham Trent; Oxford Brookes; Plymouth; Portsmouth;

Ripon & York (Coll) (No); St Andrews; St Martin's (Coll); Salford; Sheffield (No); Sheffield Hallam; Southampton; Staffordshire; Surrey Roehampton; Sussex; Swansea; Teesside; Warwick; Wolverhampton; York (Possibly).

AFTER RESULTS ADVICE

Institutions which may accept the same points score after A-levels: Aberystwyth (including B in English); Anglia; Bangor; Blackburn (Coll); Bristol (No); Brunel; Canterbury Christ Church (UC); Cardiff (No); Central England; Central Lancashire; Cheltenham & Glos (CHE); Chester (Coll) (No); Dartington (CA); Derby; Dundee (No); Durham (No); East Anglia (No); Edge Hill (CHE); Exeter; Glamorgan (No); Huddersfield; Hull (No); Kent (No); Kingston; Lampeter; Leeds (No); Leeds (Bretton Hall); Leicester; London (Gold) (No), (RH); London Guildhall (No); Loughborough (No); Manchester (No); Manchester Met (No); Middlesex (No); Newcastle (No); North East Wales (IHE); Northumbria (No); Nottingham (No); Oxford Brookes; Ripon & York (Coll); Salford; Sheffield; Sheffield Hallam; South Bank; Southampton (No); Staffordshire (No); Sunderland (No); Surrey Roehampton; Swansea; Teesside; Warwick (No); Worcester (UC) (No); York (No).

Institutions which may accept lower grades/points score after A-levels: Aberystwyth; Anglia; Bangor; Blackburn (Coll); Brunel; Cambridge (Hom); Central England; Central Lancashire; Chester (Coll); Chichester (UC); Durham (No); East Anglia; Edge Hill (CHE); Exeter; Glasgow; Hull (overseas students 16–14 pts) Keele; Kent; Lampeter; Lancaster; Leicester (grade B English); Liverpool Hope (Coll); London (Gold), (RH); Loughborough; Manchester Met (No); Newport (UWCN); North East Wales (IHE); Nottingham; Sheffield; Surrey Roehampton; Swansea; Ulster; Warwick.

Offers to applicants repeating A-levels: Higher Aberystwyth, Leeds, Newcastle (varies), Sheffield Hallam, Southampton (varies), Warwick; **Possibly higher** Cambridge (Hom), Lancaster, Newcastle, Oxford Brookes; **Same** Anglia, Bangor, Bristol, Chichester (UC), Durham, East Anglia, Edge Hill (CHE), Hull, Lampeter, Leeds (Bretton Hall), Leeds, Trinity & All Saints (Coll), Liverpool, London (Gold), (RH), Loughborough (varies), Manchester Met, Newport (UWCN), Nottingham, Portsmouth, St Martin's (Coll), Salford, Sheffield, Surrey Roehampton, Swansea, Ulster, York.

Probable vacancies from June 2001 and in Clearing (see Ch.4): Most vacancies will be on combined courses. The more competitive universities will make offers in the 280 to 240 pts range.

NEW GRADUATE DESTINATIONS AND EMPLOYMENT (1999 HESA) (see **Ch.4**)

In a survey of 4820 graduates, 2290 secured full-time employment (mainly in business administration, managerial, manufacturing and community service work), 1484 went on to further study and 264 were believed to be unemployed.

ENVIRONMENTAL SCIENCE/STUDIES (including Environmental Health)

NB The information supplied by the universities and colleges this year varies considerably and the offers listed below should be used as a first source of reference only. Many institutions will accept combinations of Advanced (AL), Advanced Subsidiary (AS) and Vocational Advanced (VA) level qualifications to achieve the required points total, but applicants must check web sites and prospectuses for full details of all offers. Grades and points totals shown should be regarded as the minimum levels to be achieved, but offers may be adjusted downwards when results are known. The points totals shown to the left of the institutions are for ease of reference only. It must not be assumed that tariff points are always used by institutions or that they can be substituted for an offer in grades. The level of an offer is not necessarily indicative of the quality of a course. To calculate your offers see Chapter 4 and the inside fold of the back cover.

Special subject requirements/preferences: A-level: Sciences, biology and chemistry usually preferred. Geography may be required or optional at **Aberdeen, Bangor,**

Birmingham, East Anglia, Leeds, London (QM), Northumbria, Reading, Ripon & York (Coll), Sheffield, Staffordshire, Ulster. Bradford Science/mathematics may attract lower offers. **GCSE:** English, mathematics and a science (often chemistry) usually required. **Surrey** Grade A in chemistry or combined science if not at A-level. **York** Mathematics A or B.

360 pts   **and above**
        Cambridge – Offers, mainly in grades, vary between colleges (Nat Sci – Ecol)
        Nottingham – AAA–BBB (Env Eng
350 pts   **York** – 350–300 pts 21–18u – ABB/BBB/ABC **or** ALs+ASs; VAs (contact univ);
        gs; (Env Econ/Ecol)
340 pts   **East Anglia** – AAB; (not gs) (Env Sci/N Am; Env Sci/Euro)
        Edinburgh – AAB–BBB (Env Sci courses; Env St courses)
330 pts   **Southampton** – 330–310 pts 21u (inc 200–180 pts from AL geog+sci); (Env
        Sci)
300 pts   **Cardiff** – 300 pts approx (Ecol/Env Mgt)
        De Montfort (Bedford) – 300–220 pts inc 2ALs **or** VAs+/-ALs/ASs; (Env/Dev)
        Lancaster – BBB (Env Sci/USA Can; Pollut Sci)
        London (Imp) – 300–260 pts (Env/Earth Sci courses)
        London (LSE) – BBB (Env Pol/Econ; Env Mgt Pol)
        London (UCL) – BBB–BCC **or** 3ALs+AS/VA; (Env courses)
        Sussex – BBB (Env Sci/Law)
        York – BBB (Ecol Cons Env)
280 pts   **East Anglia** – BBC **or** BB+bc; (not gs) (Env Sci/Maths)
        Glasgow – BBC (Env St)
        Harper Adams (UC) – 280–140 pts approx (Rur Env Prot)
        Kent – 280 pts approx (Env Soc Sci)
        London (RH) – 280 pts 18u – BBC–BCC **or** 2ALs+2ASs; (not gs) (Env Biol)
        London (RH) – BBC–CCC (Env courses)
        Reading – 280 pts (Env Sci Earth Atmos)
        St Andrews – BBC (Env Biol)
        Ulster – BBC (Env Hlth)
270 pts   **Kingston** – 270 pts 2x6u **or** VA12u (inc sci/maths/geog); (M Env Sci)
260 pts   **Aston** – 260–240 pts 18u – 3ALs **or** ALs+ASs **or** VAs+/-ALs/ASs; gs; (Env Sci
        Tech)
        Bangor – BCC (inc chem or biol 70 pts); (not gs) (Env Sci)
        Belfast (Queen's) – BCC (Env Plan)
        Birmingham – BCC (Env Sci; Env Mgt)
        Bournemouth – 260–220 pts – ALs (pref sci/geog) **or** VAs; (Env Prot)
        Keele – BCC **or** equiv AS accepted; gs; (Env Mgt/App Env Sci courses)
        Lancaster – BCC (Env Mgt; Env Sci; Env Sys Eng)
        Leeds – 18u – BCC **or** BC+cc (inc AL sci+maths/geog) **or** VAs (contact univ);
        gs (not AL); (Env Sci; Env Geol; Atmos Sci; Env Mgt; Env /Chem/Env
        Biogeosci)
        Leicester – BCC (Env Biol)
        London (King's) – BCC+AS **or** BC+cc+AS (or equiv) (inc C biol+sci); VAs
        considered; (Env Sci)
        Loughborough – BCC (Env Sci courses)
        Manchester – 260 pts approx (Env Sci; Env Mgt; Env St)
        Nottingham – BCC–CCC (Env Eng Res Mgt; Env Tech)
        Reading – BCC–CCC (Env Earth Sci)
        Salford – 260–220/180 pts (App Env/Res Sci; App Env/Res Sci/Euro/China)
        Sheffield – BCC (Nat Env Sci)
        Sussex – BCC (Env Sci/N Am St)
        Swansea – 260 pts 18u – BCC–CCC **or** ALs+ASs **or** VAs+/-ALs/ASs; (Env Biol)
240 pts   **Aberystwyth** – 240 pts 21u – CCC **or** CC+cc **or** VAs; gs; (Env Biol)
        Bangor – CCC; (not gs) (Ocean Sci)
        Belfast (Queen's) – CCC (Env Biol; Env Chem)

Bradford – 240 pts 12u; gs; (Env Sci; Env Mgt/Sust (inc AL sci); Geog/Env Sci; Phys/Env Geog (inc AL geog/sci); App Ecol/Cons (inc AL biol/sci); Env Pollut Mgt (inc AL chem/sci); Env Mgt/Tech; Hlth/Sfty Mgt (inc AL sci))

Bristol UWE – 240–180 pts approx (Env Qual/Res Mgt; Env Health)

Brunel – CCC–CCD (Env Geosci)

Cornwall & Duchy (Coll) – CCC (Env Res Mgt)

De Montfort (Bedford) – 240–180 pts inc 2ALs **or** VAs+/-ALs/ASs; (Env St)

Durham (Stockton) – CCC–CCD **or** ALs+ASs **or** VAs+/-AL/ASs; gs; (Env Mgt; Env Dev)

Essex – 240 pts 21u – CC (inc biol, sci)+AL/2ASs **or** VA12u CC+AL; gs; (Env Sci)

Exeter – 240 pts 18u (inc 2 AL sci/AL+AS sci subjs) – CCC **or** CC+cc **or** VAs (contact univ); (not gs) (Env Sci/Tech)

Glamorgan – 240 pts (Ener Env Tech)

Heriot-Watt – 240 pts 18u – CCC **or** ALs+ASs **or** VAs B+/-ALs/ASs; gs; (Env Mgt Tech; Env Serv Eng)

Hertfordshire – 240–200 pts 1x12u **or** 2x6u; gs; (Env St; Env/Pollut Sci/ Mgt Bus)

Lampeter – 240 pts approx (Arch Env)

Leeds – 18u – CCC **or** ALs+ASs **or** VA6u+AL; (AL gs only) (Env Sci/Env Mgt)

Lancaster – CCC (Env; Env Mgt)

Liverpool – 240 pts approx (Env Phys Sci)

London (Imp) – CCC (Env courses)

London (King's) – CCC **or** CC+cc+AS (or equiv) (inc AL sci); VAs considered; (Env Hlth)

London (QM) – 240 pts (Env Sci)

London (RH) – 240–220 pts approx (Env Earth Sci; Env Geol; Env Geochem)

Newcastle – CCC (Env Sci/Agric Ecol; Ecol Res Mgt)

Nottingham – CCC/BC (Env Sci)

Oxford Brookes – CCC–DD (Env Sci courses – offer varies with subj choices)

Plymouth – 240–180 pts approx (Env Sci)

Southampton (Inst) – 240–200 pts (Mar Env/Sci courses)

Staffordshire – 240 pts inc 2x6u; gs; (Env Sci; Env St)

Stirling – CCC/BC (Env Sci courses; Cons Mgt)

Strathclyde – CCC–BCD (2nd yr entry) (Env Health; Env Sci courses)

Surrey – CCC (Env Microbiol)

Sussex – BCD (Env Sci courses except under **300/260 pts**)

Ulster – CCC–CCD (Env Sci courses)

UMIST – BCD (Env Sci courses)

220 pts **Aberdeen** – CCD (Env Sci)

Aberystwyth – 220 pts 18u – 3ALs **or** ALs+ASs (AL sci pref inc geog); (Env Earth Sci; Env Sci)

Bangor – CCD (Rur Res Mgt)

Bristol UWE – 220–180 pts 12u (6u sci award 60 pts min) – ALs **or** ALs+ASs **or** VAs+/-ALs/ASs; (Env Hlth courses; Env Qual/Res Mgt; Env Sci courses)

Central England – 220 pts approx (Geog Env Mgt)

Kent – 220 pts approx (Chem Env Sci)

Lampeter – CCD/200 pts approx (C env subj) (Env Mgt/Res Dev)

Middlesex – 220–180 pts approx (Hlth Env)

Nottingham Trent – 220–200 pts approx (Env Hlth)

Portsmouth – 220 pts (Mar Env Sci)

Salford – 220–180 pts approx (Env Sci)

South Bank – 220–140 pts approx (Prod Des/Env)

Southampton – 220–200 pts (Coast Cons Mgt)

200 pts **Central Lancashire** – 200–180 pts 12u; gs; (Env Mgt/Law/Ecotour)

Cornwall & Duchy (Coll) – CDD (Env Sci)

Coventry – 200 pts approx (Int Disas Res Eng Mgt)

Derby – 200 pts 12u – CCE **or** CC+e **or** VAs (grades as ALs)+/-AL/ASs; gs; (Env St)

Dundee – CDD/BC (Env Mgt; Env Sci)

Dundee – 200 pts (Env Sci 3 yr)

King Alfred's Winchester (Coll) – 200 pts approx (Bus Env Mgt)

Portsmouth – 200 pts – ALs **or** ALs+ASs (inc 2 sci subjs) **or** VAs; gs; (Env Res; Env Haz; Env Sci)

Sheffield Hallam – 200 pts (BSc Env Sci/Tech; Env Cons)

Scottish (CAg) – 200 pts(pref inc AL biol+chem) – CDD; (Env Prot Mgt)

Sunderland – 200 pts; gs; (Env St/Env Sci)

Surrey Roehampton – 200 pts approx – ALs **or** ALs+ASs **or** VAs+/-Als/ASs; (Env St/Sci; Nat Res St)

180 pts   **Anglia** – 180–160 pts (Env Ass Pol; Env Tox; Env Plan; Env Plan/Law)

Brighton – 180 pts approx (Env Sci; Urb Cons Env Mgt)

Bristol UWE – 180–160 pts approx (Comb Sci)

Central Lancashire – 180 pts 12u; gs; (Env Mgt; Env Mgt/Dev St; Env Mgt/Geog; Env Sci)

Chester (Coll) – ALs (160 pts inc C biol/geog/env sci)+AS **or** VAs (160 pts inc C sci)+AS; AS(20+ pts); gs; (Env Sci)

Coventry – 180 pts approx (Env Monit Ass)

East London – 180 pts approx (Env Sci courses)

Greenwich – 180 pts approx (Earth Env Sci; Env Geol)

Kingston – 180 pts – 2x6u **or** VA12u (inc sci/mnaths/geog); (BSc Env Sci)

Lincolnshire & Humberside – 180 pts (Env St; Env Sci)

Liverpool Hope (Coll) – 180–160 pts approx (Env St courses)

Luton – 180 pts approx (Env Sci/Mgtcourses)

Manchester Met – 180 pts approx (Env Mgt; Env Prot; Env St)

Middlesex – 180 pts (Env Sci)

North East London (Coll) – 180 pts approx (Env Hlth)

Northampton (UC) – 180 pts approx (Env Mgt)

Northumbria – 180–160 pts approx (Env courses)

Norwich City (Coll) – 180–120 pts approx (Env Hlth; Env Biol)

Nottingham Trent – ALs (inc biol/chem) (Env Sci)

South Bank – 180 pts approx (Env Prod Des)

160 pts   **Canterbury Christ Church (UC)** – CC–DD (Env Sci)

Cheltenham & Glos (CHE) – 160 pts average (Env Pol courses; Nat Res)

Chichester (UC) – 160 pts(inc AL) (Env St Comb)

Glamorgan – CC (Env Pollut Sci/Miner Surv Sci; Ener Mgt)

Huddersfield – 160 pts 12u; (not gs) (Env Prot; Env Sci; Env/Geog; Env Hum Hlth; Env Analys)

Manchester Met (Crewe) – 160 pts – CC **or** ALs+ASs **or** VAs+/-ALs/ASs; gs (AL only); (Joint Hons)

Newport (UWCN) – 160–140 pts – ALs **or** ALs+ASs **or** VAs+/-ALs/ASs; (Env St; Soc Env St)

North East Wales (IHE) – 160–100 pts approx (Env St)

Otley (Coll) – 160 pts approx (Cons Mgt)

Swansea (IHE) – 160 pts – 2ALs **or** VA12u; gs; (Env Cons)

Trinity Carmarthen (Coll) – CC–EE (Env courses)

Westminster – CC (Env Sci Bus Mgt)

Writtle (Coll) – 160 pts approx (Env Ass; Cons Env; Env St)

140 pts   **Abertay Dundee** – CD (Env Sci Tech)

Bath Spa (UC) – 140 pts 12u – CD **or** VA12u CD; (Env Sci; Env Cult Sci)

Bolton (IHE) – 140 pts approx (Env St courses)

Cardiff (UWI) – CD (Env Risk Mgt)

Derby – 140 pts 12u – CD **or** DD+d **or** VAs CD+/-AL/ASs; gs; (Env Sci courses)

Glasgow Caledonian – CD–DD (Env Tox; Env)

Hull – 140 pts (Env Sci)

Imperial College
T H Huxley School of Environment, Earth Sciences & Engineering

MSc Programmes

The T H Huxley School is the largest, most prestigious multidisciplinary Environmental Research Department in Europe with campuses at South Kensington, London, Ascot, Berkshire and Wye, in Kent. It offers the following Masters Degree courses for the coming academic year:

- **MSc in Environmental Technology** – provides training in environmental science, economics, law, policy, health and technology.
- **MSc in Environmental Diagnosis** – gives students the practical skills necessary to analyse and assess the extent of environmental contamination.
- **MSc in Environmental Management** – This new degree will provide a sound training in environmental appraisal, planning and management to a professional and consultancy level, emphasizing the transdisciplinary nature of environmental issues.
- **MSc in Sustainable Agriculture and Rural Development (SARD)** – The principles of sustainability against a background of changes in agricultural policy and increasing concerns over environmental, agro-bio-diversity and food safety issues have formed the basis for this new MSc.
- **Agricultural Economics and Business Management** – The five MScs in economics and business at Wye is based upon policy-relevant research and strong links with agriculture, the food industry, government agencies, and other professional groups.
- **MSc in Mineral Deposit Evaluation** – offers the employment skills required for the wide range of technical, financial and legal requirements of the minerals and financial services industries.
- **MSc in Petroleum Geoscience** – provides the advanced training needed for the full spectrum of petroleum exploration and production activities.
- **MSc in Petroleum Engineering** – trains candidates to understand the work-flow concepts now prevailing in the oil and gas industry and fully prepares them for work on a multidisciplinary basis.
- **MSc in Petroleum Production Management** – Petroleum Engineering MSc modules are supplemented by those on economics, finance and management, taught at the College of Petroleum and Energy Studies in Oxford.
- **MSc in Remote Sensing** – administered jointly by University College London and Imperial College, this programme includes core modules on the principles and practical techniques of digital image processing and GIS for earth science and related environmental applications.

The teaching quality on our MSc Programmes has recently been rated the best of its kind by the Higher Education Funding Council of England and Wales. Our 3, 800 plus graduates have been highly successful in gaining Degree-related employment. PhD research programmes in the above fields are also available.

Some courses are generously supported by the European Social Fund, the ESRC, the EPSRC, NERC, the British Council, industrial sponsors and a favourable loan facility.

For further details contact:
The Assistant Registrar (Admissions), Imperial College of Science, Technology and Medicine, London SW7 2AZ.
E-mail: f.mchugh@ic.ac.uk
Tel: +44 171 594 8046 Fax: +44 171 594 8004.
Web-site: http://www.huxley.ic.ac.uk/

Hull (Scarborough) – 140 pts approx (Env Sci)
Liverpool John Moores – 140–120 pts (inc AL sci 80–60 pts) – ALs **or**
    ALs+ASs **or** VAs+/-ALs/ASs; (Env Sci)
Ripon & York St John (Coll) – CD (Env Sci/Educ)
Sunderland – 140 pts approx (Fdn Env Sci; Fdn Wtr Res Env Mgt)
Wolverhampton – 140 pts 12u – CD **or** VAs+/-ALs/ASs; gs; (Env Sci)
Worcester (UC) – 140 pts 12u – EE/ASs **or** VAs+/-ALs/ASs; (Env Sci courses)

120 pts   **Bell (CT)** – DD (App Env Sci; Env Sci Env Mgt)
      Bournemouth – DD (Fdn Cons Sci)
      Edge Hill (CHE) – DD (Earth Env Sci)
      Napier – DD (Env Tox)
      North London – 120 pts 2x6u **or** VAs; (Env Sci; Env Mgt)
      Paisley – DD (Env Sci/Tech; Wtr Env Mgt)

100 pts   **and below**
      Bridgwater (Coll) – (Env Sci yr 1)
      Farnborough (CT) – DE (Env Mgt/Bus; Env Prot (Cons Mgt) (Pollut Contr)
        (Sust Dev)
      Robert Gordon – DE (Env Sci Tech; Env Sci Mgt)
      Salford – (Env Health – part-time)
      Staffordshire – (Ext Env Sci)
      UHI (Inverness) – (App Env Sci via DipHE, HND,HNC)
      UHI (North Highland) – (Env Herit St via DipHE, HND,HNC)
      UHI (Orkney) – (Sust Dev Env Mgt viaDipHE, HND, HNC)

      Leeds Met – (contact univerity)

Diploma of Higher Education courses
80 pts   Abertay Dundee; Askham Bryan (Coll); Bath Spa (UC); Canterbury Christ Church
      (UC); Cornwall & Duchy (Coll); Doncaster (Coll); King Alfred's Winchester (Coll);
      Manchester Met; Middlesex; Otley (Coll); Oxford Brookes; UHI; Wolverhampton;
      Worcester (UC).

Higher National Diploma courses
100 pts   **and below**
      Askham Bryan (Coll); Bournemouth (Env Con); Canterbury Christ Church (UC);
      Central Lancashire (Newton Rigg) (Game/Wildlife Mgt); Cornwall (Coll) (Wildlife);
      Coventry; De Montfort; Derby; Exeter; Falmouth (Coll)Farnborough (CT); Fife
      (CFHE); Glamorgan; Glasgow (CFood); Halton (Coll); Isle of Wight (Coll);
      Manchester Met; Nescot; North Highland (Coll); North London (Coll) HNC, Env
      Health (HND); Park Lane (Coll) gs; Plymouth (Seale Hayne); Queen Margaret
      (UC); Robert Gordon; Rodbaston (Coll); St Helens (Coll); Salford (Env Health);
      Scottish (CAg) (Rur Res; Env Prot Mgt); Staffordshire (Env Sci); Stevenson (Coll);
      Teesside; UHI (Perth); West Herts (Coll); Wigan & Leigh (Coll); Wiltshire (Coll);
      Wirral Met (Coll); Worcester (UC) (Forest); Writtle (Coll) (Rur Mgt).

Professional Diploma courses: (Environmental Health)
      Nottingham Trent.

Alternative Offers:

EB offers: Aberystwyth 75%; East Anglia 70%; London (RH) 75%; Sheffield 65%.

IB offers: Aberdeen 26 pts; Aberystwyth 30–28 pts; Bath Spa (UC) 24 pts; Bradford 28
pts; Brighton 24 pts; Cardiff 26 pts H12 pts; Coventry 24 pts; De Montfort 26 pts; East
Anglia H555 inc 28 pts; Essex 28 pts inc 10 pts Highers chem, biol; Hertfordshire 24
pts; Huddersfield 26 pts; Kent 30–28 pts; Lancaster 30 pts; Leicester 30 pts; London
(LSE) 35 pts H655, (RH) 25 pts; Manchester Met 24 pts; Nottingham 28 pts 7 subjects
24 pts 6 subjects; Oxford Brookes 26 pts; Ripon & York (Coll) 27 pts; Sheffield H555;
Staffordshire 24 pts; Stirling 28 pts; Surrey Roehampton 26 pts; Swansea 28 pts;
Worcester (UC) 24 pts; York 28 pts.

Irish offers: Aberdeen BBCC/BCCCC; Aberystwyth BBBCC; Bell (CT) CCC; Bradford BBBBCC; Brighton BBCC; Dundee (Env Mgt) BCCC; East Anglia BBBBB; Glasgow Caledonian BBC; Harper Adams (UC) CCCC; London (RH) BBCCC; St Andrews BBBC; Sheffield BBBCC; South Bank CCCC.

Scottish Qualifications: Aberdeen BBBC; Abertay Dundee BBC; Bell (CT) CCC; Dundee BBBC; Edinburgh ABBBC–BBBC; Glasgow BBBB; Glasgow Caledonian BCC; Heriot-Watt BBBB; Napier BCC; Paisley BBC–BCC; Robert Gordon BCC; St Andrews BBBB; Scottish (CAg) BCCC; Stirling BBBC; Strathclyde ABBC/BBBB.

CHOOSING YOUR COURSE (See also **Ch.1**)

Subject information: Environmental Science/Studies courses need to be considered with care as, depending on their content and specialisms, they lead to very different careers. Environmental Health courses usually lead to qualifying as an environmental health officer. Environmental Science, however, covers a range of subjects with options which may include biology, geography, geology, oceanography, chemistry, legal, social and political issues. Biology, Biological Sciences, Applied Chemistry, Geography, Geology, Environmental and Occupational Health, even Town and Country Planning and Urban Studies, could be considered as alternative courses. See also **Appendix 1.** (See also references to Environmental Engineering under **Engineering (Civil)**.)

Special features: Anglia The course focuses on ecology and earth science. **Birmingham** Specialisation in five pathways takes place in biological, atmospheric, physical and water environments and environmental science and policy. **Bournemouth** The Environmental Protection degree covers river/water/waste management, health and industrial safety and coastal protection. **Greenwich** The degree in Environmental Health (also similar degrees in other universities) lead to professional status and work as an environmental health officer. **Hull** Environmental Resource Management covers geography, management and policy studies. The Environmental Science course focuses on biology, chemistry, geography and physics. **Kent** Eco-systems, social sciences, climate changes, tourism and population studies are all covered in the degree in Biodiversity, Conservation and Environmental Management. **Liverpool John Moores** Environmental Studies covers biology, chemistry and earth science. **Luton** Both scientific and social aspects are covered on the Environmental Studies course. **Portsmouth** The course offers industrial place-ments and the opportunity to train and qualify as sports or advanced diver. **Southampton** Seven pathways – physical, chemical, biodiversity and ecology, scientific management, water, global and human. *NOW CHECK PROSPECTUSES AND WEB SITES.*

Top universities and colleges (Teaching Quality) (see Ch.4: Bangor (Ocean Sci); Bath Spa (UC); Cardiff; East Anglia; Greenwich; Hertfordshire; Lancaster; Liverpool; Liverpool Hope (Coll); London (QM); Newcastle; Plymouth (Ocean Sci); Reading; Southampton (Ocean Sci); Stirling; Writtle (Coll); not all institutions assessed.

Top universities and colleges (Research) (see Ch.4): See under **Geology**.

Study opportunities abroad: Abertay Dundee; Aberystwyth; Bangor; Birmingham; Chester (Coll); Coventry; Derby; Dundee; East Anglia; Farnborough (CT); Greenwich; Hertfordshire; Huddersfield; Kingston; Lancaster; Lincolnshire & Humberside; Liverpool Hope (Coll); Luton; Manchester Met; Middlesex; Napier; North East Wales (IHE); Norwich City (Coll); Nottingham; Oxford Brookes; Salford; Staffordshire; Strathclyde; Surrey; Ulster; UMIST; Wolverhampton; Worcester (UC).

Work opportunities abroad: Aberystwyth; Aston; Bangor; Bristol UWE; Chester (Coll); Coventry; Derby; Farnborough (CT); Greenwich (Earth Sci); Hertfordshire; Huddersfield; Kingston; Lincolnshire & Humberside; Liverpool John Moores; Manchester Met; Napier; Oxford Brookes; Plymouth; Salford; South Bank; Staffordshire; Scottish (CAg); Surrey; Worcester (UC).

ADMISSIONS INFORMATION

Number of applicants per place (approx): Abertay Dundee 5; Aberystwyth 4; Bangor 10; Bath Spa (UC) 4; Birmingham 7; Bournemouth 4; Bradford 3; Bristol UWE 1, (Env Hlth) 7; Cardiff (Env Geosci) 5; Cardiff (UWI) 5; Central Lancashire 10; Cheltenham & Glos (CHE) 11; Coventry 9; De Montfort 9; Dundee 6; Durham (Stockton) 5; East Anglia 8; East London 4; Edinburgh 1; Essex 3; Farnborough (CT) 2; Glamorgan 1; Glasgow Caledonian 1; Greenwich 2; Harper Adams (UC) 5; Hertfordshire 5; Hull 8; Kingston 3; Lampeter 3; Lancaster 11; Leeds 5; Liverpool John Moores 4; London Guildhall 3; London (LSE) 8, (RH) 8, (Wye) 6; Manchester Met (Env Mgt) 16, (Env Health) 6, (Env Sci) 5; Middlesex (Env Hlth) 6; Nescot 1; Newcastle (Nat Res) 6; North East Wales (IHE) 3; Northampton (UC) 3; Northumbria 8; Nottingham Trent (Env Hlth) 8; Oxford Brookes 13; Plymouth 8; Portsmouth 5; Ripon & York (Coll) (Env Mgt) 6, (ELHM) 2; Salford 8; Sheffield Hallam 8; Staffordshire 4; Stirling 10; Strathclyde 1; Sunderland 10; Surrey Roehampton 3; Trinity Carmarthen (Coll) 2; Ulster 16; Westminster 3; Wolverhampton 10; Worcester (UC) 7; York 10.

Planning your UCAS personal statement (see Ch.4): 'We want doers, not just thinkers'. Describe any field courses which you have attended; make an effort to visit one of the National Park centres. Discuss these visits and identify any particular aspects which impressed you. Outline travel interests. Give details of work as a conservation volunteer and other outside school activities. **Cardiff** (Env Geosci) Interests in outdoor activities or work experience in earth sciences. **Leeds** Outside activities, career interests. **Manchester** Talk to local planning officers, environment and landscape professionals. **Salford** (Env Sci) For Environmental Health option, knowledge of environmental health officer's work. Read scientific and geographical magazines and describe any special areas of study which impress you. See also **Appendix 1**.

Selection interviews (see Ch.4): Abertay Dundee (No); Aberystwyth (No); Bangor (No); Bath Spa (UC) (some); Bradford; Bridgwater (Coll); Brighton (No); Bristol UWE; Cardiff (No); Cheltenham & Glos (CHE); Coventry; Derby (Ecol Des) (W) (T); Dundee (No); Durham (Stockton) (some); East Anglia; Farnborough (CT) (No); Glamorgan; Greenwich; Harper Adams (UC) (advisory); Hertfordshire; Huddersfield; Kent (No); Kingston; Lampeter; Leeds (No); Liverpool John Moores (No); London Guildhall; London (RH); Manchester Met; Newcastle; Newport (UWCN); Norwich City (Coll); Nottingham; Otley (Coll); Oxford Brookes; Paisley (No); Plymouth; Portsmouth (No); Ripon & York (Coll) (No); Salford; Sheffield (No); Sheffield Hallam; South Bank; Southampton (No); Staffordshire (No); Strathclyde; Suffolk (Coll) (No); Sunderland; Surrey; Surrey Roehampton (No); Sussex; Warwick; Worcester (UC) (No); York (No).

Interview questions (see Ch.4): Environmental issues are constantly in the news, so keep abreast with developments. You could be asked to discuss any particular environmental problems in the area in which you live and to justify your stance on any environmental issues on which you have strong opinions.

GAP YEAR ADVICE

Environmentally related experience preferred.

Institutions willing to defer entry after A-levels: Aberystwyth (contact Admissions Tutor as soon as possible); Bangor; Birmingham; Bolton (IHE); Bradford; Brighton; Bristol UWE; Canterbury Christ Church (UC); Cheltenham & Glos (CHE); Coventry (positively encouraged); De Montfort; Derby; Dundee (Env Mgt); Edinburgh; Exeter; Glamorgan; Glasgow Caledonian; Harper Adams (UC); Hertfordshire; Kingston; Lampeter; Lancaster; Leeds; Lincolnshire & Humberside; Liverpool Hope (Coll); London (RH); Manchester Met; Nescot; Newcastle; Newport (UWCN); North East Wales (IHE); Northampton (UC); Northumbria; Nottingham (relevant experience preferred); Nottingham Trent; Plymouth; Robert Gordon; Salford; Scottish (CAg); Sheffield Hallam; South Bank; Staffordshire; Surrey; Surrey Roehampton; Sussex; Swansea (last minute deferrals discouraged); Westminster; York.

AFTER RESULTS ADVICE

Institutions which may accept the same points score after A-levels: Aberystwyth; Bangor; Bolton (IHE); Bradford; Brighton; Bristol UWE; Central Lancashire; Cheltenham & Glos (CHE); Coventry; Derby; East Anglia; Essex; Glamorgan (No); Greenwich; Harper Adams (UC); Hertfordshire; Kingston; Lampeter; Lancaster; Leeds; Lincolnshire & Humberside; Liverpool Hope (Coll); London Guildhall; London (RH); Manchester Met; Nescot; North East Wales (IHE); Northampton (UC); Northumbria; Nottingham; Plymouth (perhaps); Ripon & York (Coll); Salford; Sheffield Hallam; South Bank; Southampton (No); Stirling (No); Strathclyde; Sunderland; Surrey; Surrey Roehampton; Swansea; Ulster; Worcester (UC) (No); York (No).

Institutions which may accept lower grades/points score after A-levels: Aberystwyth; Bangor; Bolton (IHE); Bradford; Brighton; Bristol UWE; Derby; East Anglia; Harper Adams (UC); Hertfordshire; Lampeter; Lancaster; Leeds; Lincolnshire & Humberside; Liverpool Hope (Coll); London (RH); Manchester Met; Nescot; Newport (UWCN); North East Wales (IHE); Northampton (UC); Northumbria; Nottingham (Env Biol); Plymouth (perhaps); Salford; Scottish (CAg); Sheffield Hallam; Stirling; Surrey; Surrey Roehampton; Swansea; Ulster.

Offers to applicants repeating A-levels: Higher Dundee (Env Mgt), Greenwich, Lancaster, Nottingham, Strathclyde, Swansea; **Possibly higher** Aberystwyth, Bradford, Northumbria; **Same** Bangor, Cardiff (UWI), East Anglia, London (RH), Manchester Met, Scottish (CAg), South Bank, Ulster.

Probable vacancies from June 2001 and in Clearing (see Ch.4): Over 100 universities and colleges went into Clearing last year in this subject area covering Environmental Science, Health and Management.

NEW GRADUATE DESTINATIONS AND EMPLOYMENT (1999 HESA) (see **Ch.4**)

Of 1980 graduates surveyed, 1067 obtained full-time employment, 397 went to further study and 181 were believed to be unemployed.

EUROPEAN STUDIES (see also Business Courses and Modern Languages)

NB The information supplied by the universities and colleges this year varies considerably and the offers listed below should be used as a first source of reference only. Many institutions will accept combinations of Advanced (AL), Advanced Subsidiary (AS) and Vocational Advanced (VA) level qualifications to achieve the required points total, but applicants must check web sites and prospectuses for full details of all offers. Grades and points totals shown should be regarded as the minimum levels to be achieved, but offers may be adjusted downwards when results are known. The points totals shown to the left of the institutions are for ease of reference only. It must not be assumed that tariff points are always used by institutions or that they can be substituted for an offer in grades. The level of an offer is not necessarily indicative of the quality of a course. To calculate your offers see Chapter 4 and the inside fold of the back cover.

Special subject requirements/preferences: A-level: Two/three appropriate languages. **GCSE:** English for all courses and possibly mathematics. **Aberdeen, Dundee, Edinburgh, Glasgow** English, mathematics or science, grade B in languages. **Bangor** Grade A* or A in chosen language. **Bradford** Grades A and B preferred; B in languages. **Leeds** Grade A*, A or B in eight-ten subjects.

360 pts and above
        Aberystwyth – 360–300 pts 21u – 3ALs (300–220 pts) **or** ALs (200 pts)+ASs (total 360–300 pts) **or** VAs (200 pts)+/-AL/ASs; gs; (ALs in Fr/Ger/Span highly desirable) (Euro St courses)
350 pts Southampton – 350 pts 21u (inc 200 pts from 2ALs, C in 1 of langs to be studied); (Contemp Euro)

320 pts **London (King's)** – ABB+AS **or** AB+aaa (or equiv) (inc B lang); VAs considered; (Euro St)
London (UCL) – ABB–BBB **or** 3ALs+AS/VA; (Modn Euro St)
Manchester – ABB–BBB (Euro St/Modn Lang (Fr/Ger/Ital/Span))

300 pts **Birmingham** – BBB (Euro St)
Bristol UWE – 300–200 pts approx (Euro St courses with Modn Lang/EFL)
Cardiff – BBB–BBC (EU St)
Durham – BBB (Modn Euro Langs/Mus)
Edinburgh – BBB (EU St/Modn Euro Langs)
Nottingham – BBB–BBC (Modn Euro St)
Sussex – BBB (Euro Drama/Fr/Ger/Ital)

280 pts **Aston** – 280 pts 18u – BBC–BCC **or** ALs+ASs **or** VAs+/-ALs/ASs; gs; (Euro St courses)
Bangor – BBC–CCD (Euro Lang courses)
East Anglia – ACC–BCC (Euro Cult St; Contemp Euro St; Euro St courses)
Hull – BBC–BCC (Euro St courses)
Kent – 280–260 pts (Euro St single/joint courses)
Leeds – BBC (B modn Euro lang) (Euro St; EU St)
Newcastle – BBC (Chem/Euro St/Lang)
Oxford Brookes – BBC–CCC–CD (Euro St courses)
Reading – BBC (Euro St)
Salford – BBC (Contemp Euro St/Arbc)
Swansea – BBC (Geog/Euro St)

260 pts **Belfast (Queen's)** – BCC (Euro Area St)
Dundee – BCC (Contemp Euro St courses)
Durham (Stockton) – BCC **or** ALs/ASs **or** VAs+/-ALs/ASs; gs; (Euro St)
Essex – 260 pts 21u – BC+AL/2ASs; gs; (Euro St)
Keele – BCC **or** equiv AS accepted; gs; (Euro St courses)
Lancaster – BCC (Euro St)
Leicester – BCC (Euro St)
Stirling – BCC (Euro St)
Surrey – 260–240 pts approx (Euro St/Fr/Ger/Russ)

240 pts **Aberdeen** – CCC (European courses)
Bradford – 240 pts 12u; gs; (Euro St(inc AL lang); Euro Area St; Euro St/Law/Mgt)
Hertfordshire – 240–200 pts approx (Euro St courses)
Hull – CCC–CCD (Dutch courses)
Liverpool John Moores – 240–180 pts (from 2ALs) – ALs **or** ALs+ASs **or** VAs+/-ALs/ASs; (Euro St)
London (Gold) – BCD (Euro Lang Cult Soc)
London (QM) – 240 pts/BC (Euro St courses)
London (UCL) – CCC/CC **or** 3ALs+AS/VA; (Contemp East Euro St)
Loughborough – C(Fr/Ger/Span)+AL+AL/2ASs **or** VAs+/-ALs/ASs; gs; (Modn Euro St)
Plymouth – 240 pts (Euro St courses)
Portsmouth – 240 pts – ALs **or** ALs+ASs **or** VAs; gs; (Euro St; Euro St with Engl/Fr/Ger/Ital/Port/Russ/Span)
Strathclyde – CCC (BBD 2nd yr entry) (Euro St (Arts/Soc Sci))
Ulster – CCC (Euro St Hum)

220 pts **Kingston** – 220–200 pts approx (Euro St)
Liverpool John Moores – 220 pts (inc AL lang C) – ALs **or** ALs+ASs **or** VAs+/-ALs/ASs; (Euro St with Fr/Ger/Span/Ital)
Manchester Met – 220 pts (Euro St/Inf Sys)
South Bank – 220 pts (Euro St)
Sunderland – 220–180 pts approx (Euro St courses)

200 pts **Central Lancashire** – 200 pts approx (Euro St Sociol)
Coventry – 200 pts approx (Euro St 3 yr; Euro St/Lang)
Derby – 200 pts 12u- CDD **or** CD+dd **or** VA CD+/-ALs/ASs; gs; (Euro St)

Manchester Met – 200 pts (Euro St/Bus Econ)
Northumbria – 200 pts approx (Euro St/Fr/Ger/Span)
Nottingham Trent – 200–180 pts approx (Euro St courses)
180 pts **Buckinghamshire Chilterns (UC)** – 180–140 pts (Euro St/Hum Res Mgt; Mark/Euro St)
East London – 180 pts (Euro St courses)
Liverpool Hope (Coll) – 180 pts approx (Euro St Comb)
London Guildhall – CDD–CCC (Euro St courses)
Luton – 180 pts approx (Euro Lang St)
Manchester Met – CDD (Euro St/Hist; Euro St/Inf Comm)
Sheffield Hallam – CCC–AB (Euro Pol Pol)
Staffordshire – 180 pts (Euro Econ)
Thames Valley – 180 pts approx (Adv Langs)
Wolverhampton – 180 pts 12u – DDD/CC **or** CD+de **or** VA12u CC; gs; (Euro St)
160 pts **Abertay Dundee** – CC (Euro Bus Law; Mark/Lang)
Doncaster (Coll) – 160 pts – CC **or** ALs/ASs **or** VAs+/-ALs/ASs; gs; (Euro St)
Edge Hill (CHE) – CC (Modn Euro St courses)
Lincolnshire & Humberside – 160 pts (Comb St)
Newport (UWCN) – 160–140 pts – ALs **or** ALs+ASs **or** VAs+/-ALs/ASs; (Euro St Hum)
North London – 160 pts 1x12u **or** 2x6u; (Euro St courses)
140 pts **Derby** – 140 pts 12u – CD **or** DE+ee **or** VAs CD+/-ALs/ASs; (Euro St Comb)
Liverpool Hope (Coll) – 140 pts approx (Euro St Single Hons)
120 pts **Wolverhampton** – 120 pts 6u – DD **or** ccd **or** VA12u DD; gs; (Euro Offce Admin/Comm)
100 pts **Swansea (IHE)** – 100 pts approx (Euro Bus/Lang; Euro St/Env Cons)

Diploma in Higher Education courses
Bath Spa (UC); Thames Valley; York (CFHE).

Alternative Offers:

EB offers: Aston 72%; North London 60%.

IB offers: Aberdeen 30 pts; Aberystwyth 32–30 pts; Aston 31–29 pts; Bradford 24 pts H4 lang; Derby 24 pts; Dundee 29 pts H 15 pts; Durham (Stockton) 26–24 pts; East Anglia 29 pts; Essex 28 pts; Hull 32 pts; Kent 27 pts, H 12 pts; Lancaster 32–30pts; Leeds 32 pts; Leicester 30 pts; London (Gold) 24 pts, (LSE) H766, (RH) 30–28 pts, (UCL) 31 pts; Northumbria 24 pts; St Andrews 30 pts; Sheffield Hallam 26 pts; Staffordshire 27 pts; Stirling 31 pts; Wolverhampton 24 pts.

Irish offers: Bradford BBBCC; Sunderland BCCC.

Scottish Qualifications: Aberdeen BBBB; Dundee BBBC; Edinburgh BBBB; Heriot-Watt BBBB; Paisley BBB–BBCC; St Andrews BBBB; Stirling BBBC; Strathclyde BBBB.

CHOOSING YOUR COURSE (See also **Ch.1**)

Subject information: European Studies is an increasingly popular subject and offers the language student an opportunity to study modern languages within the context of a European country (for example, economics, politics, legal, social and cultural aspects). In these courses there is usually a strong emphasis on the written and spoken word. A European language is often also involved in Economics, Politics and Law courses and these might also be considered along with History, International Relations, Sociology, Development Studies and Business Studies.

Special features: Bath Degree programmes involve French, German, Italian and Russian with year 3 spent abroad. **Bradford** Three and four-year courses are offered, the latter allowing a combined study of either politics, history, economics, sociology or geography with a modern language. **Bristol UWE** The degree covers history, politics, economics. **Central Lancashire** There are opportunities to spend a semester in France, Denmark, Germany or Spain. There is also a non-language route. **Essex** The Social Science scheme involves politics, law, economics or sociology. The Humanities scheme covers literature, film, history, philosophy or the history of art. *NOW CHECK PROSPECTUSES AND WEB SITES.*

Top universities and colleges (Research) (see Ch.4): Aston; Bath; Belfast (Queen's); Birmingham; Bradford; Cardiff; Glasgow; Heriot-Watt; Hull; London (UCL); Loughborough; Portsmouth; Salford; Strathclyde; Surrey.

Study opportunities abroad: All institutions are able to make arrangements. Aberdeen; Aston; Birmingham; Bradford; Cardiff (UWI); Coventry; Derby; Dundee; East Anglia; East London; Essex; Hull; Kent; Lancaster; Leicester; Liverpool Hope (Coll); Liverpool John Moores; London (QM), (RH), (UCL); Manchester; North London; Northumbria; Nottingham; Plymouth; Salford; Southampton; Staffordshire; Surrey; Sussex; Teesside; Thames Valley; Wolverhampton; Worcester (UC).

Work opportunities abroad: Aston; Derby; Hull; Salford; Wolverhampton.

ADMISSIONS INFORMATION

Number of applicants per place (approx): Aberystwyth 10; Bradford 5; Cardiff (EUS) 5; De Montfort 3; Durham (Stockton) 2; East Anglia 11; East London 6; Edge Hill (CHE) 5; Hull 6; Kent 11; Lancaster 9; Leicester 15; London (RH) 6, (UCL) 2; Loughborough 10; Manchester (Euro St/Fr) 8; North London 4; Northumbria 7; Nottingham 23; Nottingham Trent 12; Plymouth 9; Portsmouth 5; Salford 8; South Bank 6; Thames Valley 5; Wolverhampton 7.

Planning your UCAS personal statement (see Ch.4): Try to identify an interest you have in the country relevant to your studies. Visits to that country should be described. Read the national newspapers and magazines and keep up to date with political and economic developments. Interest in the culture and civilisation of Europe as a whole. **Leeds** Motivation for choosing the course; personal achievements; future career plans, if any; travel. **Portsmouth** International awareness and perspective. **St Andrews** Evidence of interest and reasons for choosing course. Sport/extra-curricular activities. Posts of responsibility.

Selection interviews (see Ch.4): Bangor; Bradford; Cardiff (No); Central Lancashire (No); Coventry; Dundee (No); Durham (Stockton) (No); East Anglia; Hull; Kent (not usually); Leeds (No); London (Gold), (UCL); Loughborough (mature students); Manchester (No); North London; Nottingham (No); Portsmouth (some); St Andrews (No); South Bank (W) (T); Stirling; Sunderland (No); Surrey; Sussex; Swansea (IHE) (No); Thames Valley.

Interview questions (see Ch.4): Whilst your interest in studying a language may be the main reason for applying for this subject, the politics, economics and culture of European countries are constantly in the news. You should keep up-to-date on any such topics concerning your chosen country and be prepared for questions. A language test may occupy part of the interview.

Reasons for rejection (non-academic): Poor powers of expression. Lack of ideas on any issues. Lack of enthusiasm.

GAP YEAR ADVICE

The general advice is to travel and preferably to spend part of the year in a country where you can use your interest in its language and culture.

Institutions willing to defer entry after A-levels: Aberystwyth (Prefers not); Aston; Bradford; Coventry; De Montfort; Derby; Dundee; Edge Hill (CHE); Hull; Kent; Leicester; Liverpool Hope (Coll); London (RH), (UCL) (No); Luton; Newport (UWCN); Northumbria; Nottingham; Plymouth; Portsmouth; Salford; Sheffield Hallam; South Bank (No); Sussex; Thames Valley.

AFTER RESULTS ADVICE

Institutions which may accept the same points score after A-levels: Aberystwyth; Aston; Bradford; Buckingham; Derby; Durham; Hull; Leicester; London (UCL) (No); Manchester (No); Nottingham (No); Portsmouth; Salford; South Bank (perhaps); Thames Valley; Wolverhampton.

Institutions which may accept lower grades/points score after A-levels: Aston; Bradford; Brighton; Derby; Hull; Kent; Leicester; Liverpool Hope (Coll); London (UCL); Loughborough; Middlesex; North London; Newport (UWCN); Salford; South Bank; Thames Valley; Wolverhampton.

Offers to applicants repeating A-levels: Higher Aberystwyth, East Anglia; **Same** Aston, Bradford, Derby, Liverpool Hope (Coll), Loughborough, Newport (UWCN), North London, South Bank, Wolverhampton.

Probable vacancies from June 2001 and in Clearing (see Ch.4): A good selection of course vacancies can be expected from June onwards covering European Studies, Business and Marketing.

NEW GRADUATE DESTINATIONS AND EMPLOYMENT (1999 HESA) (see **Ch.4**)

See under separate languages.

FILM, RADIO, VIDEO & TV STUDIES (see also **Communication Studies, Media Studies** and **Photography**)

NB The information supplied by the universities and colleges this year varies consider-ably and the offers listed below should be used as a first source of reference only. Many institutions will accept combinations of Advanced (AL), Advanced Subsidiary (AS) and Vocational Advanced (VA) level qualifications to achieve the required points total, but applicants must check web sites and prospectuses for full details of all offers. Grades and points totals shown should be regarded as the minimum levels to be achieved, but offers may be adjusted downwards when results are known. The points totals shown to the left of the institutions are for ease of reference only. It must not be assumed that tariff points are always used by institutions or that they can be substituted for an offer in grades. The level of an offer is not necessarily indicative of the quality of a course. To calculate your offers see Chapter 4 and the inside fold of the back cover.

Special subject requirements/preferences: A-level: Brunel All A-levels from media studies/film studies/communications studies. **Liverpool John Moores** One A-level at least from English lit/lang, media studies, film studies, history or sociology. **North London** Applicants not offering film studies, English or theatre studies should contact the admis-sions tutor. **GCSE:** English usually required. Courses vary, check prospectuses. **Bournemouth** Grade A/B profile. **Warwick** Grade B English literature. **Ancient Scottish universities** English, mathematics and foreign language.

350 pts   **Southampton** – 350 pts 21u (inc 200 pts AL inc Engl/Span); (Film St with/ Engl/Span/Fr)

340 pts   **Warwick** – AAB (not AL gs, des/tech) (Film/Lit; Film TV)

320 pts   **East Anglia** – 320 pts 12u – ABB (+addlt subj) -BBB **or** AB+bb; VA as 3rd AL; (not gs) (Film and Engl/Am St)

        Kent – 320 pts approx (Film St Single Hons)

300 pts   **Bournemouth** – 300 pts from 3ALs (ABC) **or** 240 pts from 2ALs (AB); (Script Film/TV; TV Vid Prod)

        Bradford – 300–280 pts 12u; gs; (Electron Imag/Media courses; Media Tech/Prod; Interact Sys/Vid Gms Des)

        Bristol UWE – 300–260 pts 18u pref/12u (180 pts from 6u/12u awards); ALs **or** ALs+ASs **or** VAs+/-ALs/ASs (subjs pref- media/arts/soc sci); (Film St courses)

          Glasgow – BBB (Film/TV courses)
          Kent – 300–280 pts (Film St Joint Hons)
          Liverpool – 300 pts – ALs **or** ALs+ASs **or** VAs+/-ALs/ASs; (Euro Film St/Modn Lang)
          Manchester – BBB (Drama/Screen St)
          Newcastle – ABC–BBB (Film St; Film – Comb St)
280 pts **Brunel** – 280–250 pts 2x6u – ALs **or** ALs+ASs **or** VAs+/-ALs/ASs; (Film/TV St)
          Cardiff – BBC (Jrnl Film Broad)
          Essex – 280 pts 21u – BB+AL/2ASs; (Film St)
          Exeter – 280 pts 18u – BCC **or** BB+dd **or** BC+cc **or** VAs (contact univ); (not gs) (Film St)
          London (QM) – 280 pts – 3ALs; (Film St/Hist)
          Salford – BBC/BC (TV Rad)
          Stirling – BBC (Film Media St courses)
          Surrey Roehampton – 280 pts (inc BB) – ALs **or** ALs+ASs; (Film/TV St)
          Warwick – BBC (Ital Film St)
260 pts **Aberystwyth** – 260 pts (Film/TV St courses)
          Bangor – 260 pts approx (Engl/Film St)
          Brunel – 260–240 pts 2x6u – ALs **or** ALs+ASs **or** VAs+/-ALs/ASs; (Film/TV St joint courses)
          Northumbria – BCC (Engl/Film St)
          Reading – BCC (Ital Film St)
          Sheffield Hallam – BCC/BB (Film St (Film Prod) (Hist/Crit) (Photo); Film/Lit)
          Sunderland – 260 pts; gs; (Film Media St)
240 pts **Aberdeen** – CCC (Film St courses)
          De Montfort (Leicester) – 240 pts; (not gs) (Photo/Vid Prod courses)
          Derby – 240 pts 12u – CCC **or** CC+cc **or** VA12u AB+AL/ASs; gs; portfolio; (Film/Vid)
          Heriot-Watt – 240 pts approx (Vis Comm (Film/TV) (Photo))
          King Alfred's Winchester (Coll) – 240 pts approx (Media/Film St)
          Southampton (Inst) – 240 pts approx (Film St)
          Staffordshire – 240 pts (inc 2ALs)+/-ASs **or** VA12u CC; gs; (Film/TV/Rad St)
          Staffordshire – CCC **or** CCD+AS(40 pts) **or** VAs+/-AL/ASs; gs; (Film Prod Tech)
220 pts **Central Lancashire** – 220 pts 12u; (Film/Hist/Media St)
          Cheltenham & Glos (CHE) – 220–160 pts (Film St courses)
          Falmouth (CA) – 220 pts approx (Film St)
          Lincolnshire & Humberside – 220 pts (TV/Film Des)
          Middlesex – 220–180 pts approx (Film St courses)
          Surrey Roehampton – 220 pts (inc 2ALs) – ALs **or** ALs+ASs; (Film/TV St Comb courses)
          Warrington (CI) – 220 pts approx (Media St (Rad Prod)/Bus/IT; Media St (TV Prod)/Mgt/It)
200 pts **Anglia** – 200–180 pts approx (Film St courses)
          Bradford – 200–180 pts 12u; gs; (Fdn Electron Imag)
          Central England – 200 pts – CDD **or** ALs+ASs **or** VAs+/-ALs/ASs; (not gs) (TV Tech Prod)
          Central Lancashire – 200–180 pts 12u (pref AL art/des or art fdn); gs; (Film/Aud Vis Media St)
          Liverpool John Moores – BB **or** VA A (bus/IT/media/comm prod/perf arts); (Screen St courses)
          Manchester Met – 200 pts approx (Film TV St courses)
          Salford – CDD (Aud Vid Broad Eng)
180 pts **Buckinghamshire Chilterns (UC)** – 180–140 pts approx (Film courses)
          East London – 180 pts (Film Hist)
          Kingston – 180 pts 2x6u; gs; (Film St)
          Napier – BC+portfolio+essay; (Phot/Film/TV)
          North London – 180 pts 1x12u **or** 2x6u; (Flim St)

Portsmouth – 180 pts – ALs **or** ALs+ASs **or** VAs; gs; (Film St/Lang; Film St; Mov Imag)

Westminster – BC–CC (Film TV; Photo Dig Arts)

Wolverhampton – 180–160 pts 12u – DDD/CC **or** CD+e **or** VA12u CC; gs; (Film St)

160 pts **Anglia** – 160 pts approx (Aud Tech courses)

Canterbury Christ Church (UC) – CC (Film/Rad/TV courses)

Cumbria (CAD) – 160 pts – CC **or** ASs (contact coll) **or** VA; (Film St courses)

Derby – 160 pts 12u – CC **or** DD+dd **or** VAs CC+/-ALs/ASs; gs; (Film/TV)

Newport (UWCN) – 160–140 pts approx (Film/Vid; Doc Photo; Photo Art)

North London – 160 pts 1x12u **or** 2x6u; (Film St Comb courses)

Ravensbourne (CDC) – 160 pts approx (Prof Broad)

140 pts **and below**

Bolton (IHE) – CD (Film TV St courses)

Bournemouth (AI) – 80 pts 12u; portfolio; (not gs) (Film Animat Prod)

Derby – VAs (CD approx)+/-ALs/ASs; portfolio; (Film+Video; Film TV Comb)

Edinburgh (CA) – 140 pts approx – 2ALs **or** AL+2ASs (inc Engl+art des) **or** via fdn art course/HNC; (Film/TV)

Northbrook (Coll) – (Film Vid Media Soty)

Salisbury (Coll) – 120 pts approx (Prof Comm)

Surrey (IAD/UC) – 120 pts approx (Film Video)

West Herts (Coll) – 140 pts approx (TV/Vid Prod)

Higher National Diploma courses
100 pts **and below**

Bournemouth (AI) (Film/TV); Cleveland (CAD); Manchester Met (TV); Newport (UWCN); North East Wales (IHE) (TV/Film Graph); Northumberland (CFE); Plymouth (CAD) (Film/TV; Mov Image; Animat Prod); Ravensbourne (CDC); St Helens (Coll); Salford (Aud Vid Tech); Salisbury (Coll); Stevenson (Coll); UHI; Walsall (Coll).

Alternative Offers:

IB offers: Aberystwyth 30 pts; Bournemouth 34–32 pts; Central Lancashire 28 pts; East Anglia 28 pts; Kent 34 pts (Joint courses); Staffordshire 27 pts; Stirling 35 pts; Warwick 32 pts.

Irish offers: Aberystwyth BBBCC; Warwick AAAAB; Westminster CCCCC.

Scottish Qualifications: Aberdeen BBBB; Glasgow AABB; Napier BCC; Stirling ABBB–BBBC.

CHOOSING YOUR COURSE (See also **Ch.1**)

Subject information: Many of these courses are mainly theoretical and historical in approach but may cover practical aspects, TV studies, the media in general and video work. See also **Media Studies** and **Communications Studies**. See also **Appendix 1** for contact details of relevant professional organisations.

Special features: Aberdeen Film Studies is available as the minor component in a number of major/minor honours programmes. **Bournemouth** (TV Vid Prod) 50% practical, 50% theory. **East Anglia** Theoretical and practical approaches to film complemented by cultural studies. **Kent** (Film St) Mainly theory, some practical work. **Southampton (Inst)** 60% theory, 40% practical. **Staffordshire** Not a practical course. **Warwick** This course has a strong literary component. *NOW CHECK PROSPECTUSES AND WEB SITES.*

Top universities and colleges (Teaching Quality) (see Ch.4): See **Drama**.

Top universities and colleges (Research) (see Ch.4): Warwick.

Study opportunities abroad: Aberystwyth; Staffordshire; Surrey Roehampton.

ADMISSIONS INFORMATION

Number of applicants per place (approx): Bournemouth 30; Brunel 10; Canterbury Christ Church (UC) 50; Cardiff 11; Central Lancashire 5; Derby 24; East Anglia 50; Kent 30; Liverpool John Moores 17; North London 7; Ravensbourne (CDC) 9; Salford 19; Sheffield Hallam 60; Southampton (Inst) 7; Staffordshire (Film) 31, (Media) 11; Stirling 12; Warwick 18; Westminster 41.

Planning your UCAS personal statement (see Ch.4): Any experience in film-making (beyond home videos) should be described in detail. Knowledge and preferences of types of films and the work of some producers should be included on the UCAS form. Read film magazines and other appropriate literature to keep informed of developments. See also **Appendix 1**.

Selection interviews (see Ch.4): Most institutions will interview some applicants in this subject. Aberystwyth (No); Anglia (some); Bournemouth (W); Brunel; Canterbury Christ Church (UC) (TV); Central England (No); Cumbria (CAD) (some); Derby (No); Kent (No); Liverpool John Moores; Newport (UWCN); Salford (W); Staffordshire (No); Stirling (No); Surrey Roehampton (No).

Interview questions (see Ch.4): Questions will focus on your chosen field. In the case of films be prepared to answer questions not only on your favourite films but on the work of one or two directors you admire and early Hollywood examples. **Bournemouth** (Script Film TV) Successful applicants will be required to submit a 20 page screenplay; (TV/Video Prod) A good applicant will have the ability to discuss media issues in depth, to have total commitment to TV and Video productions and will have attempted to make programmes.

Reasons for rejection (non-academic): Not enough drive or ambition. No creative or original ideas. Preference for production work rather than practical work. Inability to artic-ulate the thought process behind the work in the applicant's portfolio. Insufficient knowledge of media affairs.

GAP YEAR ADVICE

Practical experience in the industry excellent.

Institutions willing to defer entry after A-levels: Aberystwyth; Bournemouth; Bradford; Brunel; Cardiff; Central Lancashire; Cheltenham & Glos (CHE); Derby; Liverpool John Moores; Newport (UWCN); Nottingham; North London; Nottingham; Salford; Sheffield Hallam; Staffordshire; Warwick.

AFTER RESULTS ADVICE

Institutions which may accept the same points score after A-levels: Aberystwyth; Bournemouth; Cheltenham & Glos (CHE); Derby; East Anglia (No); Liverpool John Moores (No); Sheffield Hallam (No); Staffordshire; Warwick (No).

Probable vacancies from June 2001 and in Clearing (see Ch.4): Despite the apparent popularity of these subjects, vacancies in Film Studies were declared in Clearing last year at more than 20 universities and colleges.

NEW GRADUATE DESTINATIONS AND EMPLOYMENT (1999 HESA) (see **Ch.4**)

Out of 586 graduates surveyed who were completing courses in Cinematics, 339 entered full-time employment, 64 were believed to be unemployed and 51 went into further study. See also **Media Studies**.

FOOD SCIENCE/STUDIES & TECHNOLOGY (see also **Agricultural Sciences/Agriculture, Consumer Studies, Dietetics** and **Nutrition**)

NB The information supplied by the universities and colleges this year varies considerably and the offers listed below should be used as a first source of reference only. Many institutions will accept combinations of Advanced (AL), Advanced Subsidiary (AS) and Vocational Advanced (VA) level qualifications to achieve the required points total, but applicants must check web sites and prospectuses for full details of all offers. Grades and points totals shown should be regarded as the minimum levels to be achieved, but offers may be adjusted downwards when results are known. The points totals shown to the left of the institutions are for ease of reference only. It must not be assumed that tariff points are always used by institutions or that they can be substituted for an offer in grades. The level of an offer is not necessarily indicative of the quality of a course. To calculate your offers see Chapter 4 and the inside fold of the back cover.

Special subject requirements/preferences: A-level: Sciences, usually including chemistry. **GCSE:** English, mathematics and a science. **Bournemouth** English, mathematics and double science at grade A–C. **Newcastle** Chemistry or dual science if not at A-level. **Surrey** (Fd Sci/Microbiol) Grades A or B in sciences if not offered at A-level.

280 pts	**Harper Adams (UC)** – 280–140 pts (Fd Consum St; Bus Mgt Mark/Fd Ind)
260 pts	**Belfast (Queen's)** – BCC (Mech Fd Eng)
	Leeds – BCC (Fd Sci (Biol) (Bioch))
	Newcastle – BCC (Fd Mark; Fd Mark/Mgt)
240 pts	**Cardiff (UWI)** – 240 pts (Psy Nutr)
	Heriot-Watt – 240 pts 18u – CCC **or** ALs+ASs **or** VAs+/-ALs/ASs; gs; (Fd Sci Tech/Mgt)
	Huddersfield – 240–200 pts approx (Fd Sply Chn Mgt)
	Newcastle – CCC (Fd/Hum Nutr)
	Nottingham – BCD; (not gs) (Fd Sci)
	Oxford Brookes – CCC (Fd SCi Nutr/Wtr Res)
	Reading – 240 pts (Fd Manuf Mgt Mark; Fd Tech; Fd Sci)
	Staffordshire – CCC (Fd Sci)
	Surrey – CCC/BB (Nutr/Fd Sci; Fd Sci/Microbiol)
	Ulster – CCC (Fd Tech Mgt; Hum Nutr)
220 pts	**Belfast (Queen's)** – CCD (Fd Sci; Fd Tech)
	Leeds – CCD (Fd Sci)
	Reading – CCD (Fd Mark Econ)
	South Bank – 220–140 pts (Fd Nutr Hlth; Fd Sci Tech; Fd Chc Des)
200 pts	**Harper Adams (UC)** – 200 pts 18u – CC (inc 1 sci AL) **or** DD+c (inc 1 sci AL) **or** VAs+/-ALs/ASs; (not gs) (Fd/Consum St)
	Leeds – CDD (Fd Prod Proc Mark)
	Nottingham – CDD/CC (Nutrition)
	Sheffield Hallam – 200 pts (Nutr Hlth Life)
	Teesside – 200–180 pts approx (Fd Sci Nutr; Fd Tech; Chem Eng/Fd Tech)
	Wolverhampton – 200–160 pts 12u – DDD/DDE/CC **or** CC+dd/de **or** VA12u CC; gs; (Fd Biol)
180 pts	**Bournemouth** – 180–140 pts (inc sci/home econ); (Fd Prod/Dev Rtl)
	Chester (Coll) – 180 pts – ALs (160 pts inc D biol/chem/home econ)+AS/ks **or** VAs (160 pts inc D HlthSC/sci)+AS; AS(20+ pts); gs; (Fd Nutr Hlth)
	Heriot-Watt – DDD (CCC 2nd yr entry) (Fd Sci Tech Mgt)
	Lincolnshire & Humberside – 180 pts (Fin Fd St)
	Manchester Met – 180 pts approx (Fd Mark; Fd Nutr)
	Northumbria – 180 pts approx (Fd Sci Nutr; Biol Fd Sci)
	Nottingham Trent – ALs (inc sci) (Fd Sci Tech; Fd Sfty Mgt)
	Sheffield Hallam – 180 pts (Fd Mark Mgt; Fd Consum St)
160 pts	**Bath Spa (UC)** – 160–120 pts 12u – CD **or** VA12u CD; (not gs) (Fd St Comb; Des/Tech (Fd) Comb)

Birmingham (CFTCS) – 12u(inc 1 × 6u) – CC **or** ALs+ASs **or** VAs+/-ALs/ASs; (Fd Rtl Mgt; Fd Consum Mgt)
Cardiff (UWI) – 160–140 pts approx (Fd St courses)
Central Lancashire – 160 pts 12u (inc AL biol/chem/env sci); gs; (Fd Nutr)
Manchester Met – 160 pts approx (Fd Tech Mgt)
Plymouth – 160–140 pts approx (Fd Qual Mgt; Fd Qual Prod Dev Nutr)
Scottish (CAg) – 160 pts (inc AL sci) – CC; (Fd Tech)
South Bank – CC–CD (Nutr)

140 pts **Abertay Dundee** – CD (Fd Consum Sci; Fd Prod Des)
Bath Spa (UC) – 140 pts 12u – CD **or** ALs+ASs **or** VAs+/-ALs/ASs; (Fd Nutr Consum Prot)
Harper Adams (UC) – 140 pts 12u – CD **or** DD+e **or** VA CD; gs; (Fd Rtl Mgt)
Queen Margaret (UC) – CD (Fd Mark; Hum Nutr; Pblc Hlth Nutr)
Staffordshire – 140 pts approx (Fd Proc Tech Ext)

120 pts **and below**
Abertay Dundee – 120 pts (Fd Consum Sci)
Glasgow Caledonian – DD (Fd Prod Des/Mgt)
Liverpool John Moores – 120 pts – ALs **or** ALs+ASs **or** VAs+/-ALs/ASs; (Fd/Nutr)
North London – 120 pts – 2ALs **or** VA12u **or** VA6u+AL; (Fd courses; Fd Consum St; Home Econ)
Robert Gordon – DD (Nutr Prod)
Suffolk (Coll) – EE (Fd Prod courses)

Diploma of Higher Education courses
Bath Spa (UC); Suffolk (Coll).

Higher National Diploma courses
100 pts **and below**
Birmingham (CFTCS); Blackpool & Fylde (Coll); Brackenhurst (Coll); Brighton (Wine St); Cannington (Coll); Cardiff (UWI); Cheshire (CAg); Glasgow (CFood); Lincolnshire & Humberside; Loughry (CAg); Manchester Met; Northumbria; Nottingham Trent; Plumpton (Coll) (Wine St); Robert Gordon; Salford; Scottish (CAg); Truro (Coll); Wolverhampton; Worcester (UC).

Alternative Offers:

EB offers: Nottingham 60% (sci); South Bank 70%.

IB offers: Bournemouth 24 pts; Brighton 24 pts; Dundee 27 pts; Leeds 27 pts; Nottingham 24 pts (sci); South Bank 24 pts; Surrey 28 pts.

Irish offers: Dundee BBC; Manchester Met CCCC/DDDD; Nottingham CCCCC1; South Bank CCCC.

Scottish Qualifications: Aberdeen BBBC; Abertay Dundee BBC; Dundee BBC; Glasgow Caledonian CCC; Nottingham BBBB (first sitting); Strathclyde BBB.

CHOOSING YOUR COURSE (See also **Ch.1**)

Subject information: Biochemistry, microbiology, dietetics, human nutrition, food processing and technology are components of these courses as well as degree courses in their own right (and appropriate alternative courses). The study depends for its understanding on a secure foundation of several pure sciences – chemistry and two subjects from physics, mathematics, biology, botany or zoology. Only students offering such a combination can be considered. Food Technology covers the engineering aspects of food processing and management. See also **Appendix 1**.

Special features: Bournemouth The course in Food Production Development and Retailing covers management, quality assurance, science and technology. **Heriot-Watt** The Food Science Technology and Management course combines biochemistry, microbiology, nutrition, human resources, health and safety and marketing. A degree in Brewing and Distilling is also offered. **Nottingham** opportunity for a major research project. *NOW CHECK PROSPECTUSES AND WEB SITES.*

Top universities and colleges (Teaching Quality) (see Ch.4): Belfast; Harper Adams (UC); Liverpool John Moores; Newcastle; Nottingham; Nottingham Trent; Reading; not all institutions assessed.

Top universities and colleges (Research) (see Ch.4): Belfast (Queen's); Heriot-Watt; Leeds; Newcastle; Nottingham; Reading; Surrey.

Study opportunities abroad: Bath Spa (UC); Brighton; Dundee; Leeds; Lincolnshire & Humberside; Newcastle; Nottingham; Reading; Sheffield Hallam; Surrey.

Work opportunities abroad: Lincolnshire & Humberside; Liverpool John Moores; Manchester Met; Newcastle; Reading; Sheffield Hallam; Scottish (CAg); South Bank; Surrey; Teesside.

ADMISSIONS INFORMATION

Number of applicants per place (approx): Bath Spa (UC) 4; Belfast (Queen's) 10; Blackpool & Fylde (Coll) 1; Bournemouth 5; Dundee 3; Huddersfield (Fd/Nutr) 4; Leeds 5; Manchester Met 7; Newcastle 13; North London 5; Nottingham 7; Oxford Brookes 20; Robert Gordon 4; Sheffield Hallam 4; Strathclyde 2; South Bank 3; Surrey 17.

Planning your UCAS personal statement (see Ch.4): Visits, work experience or work shadowing in any food manufacturing firm or visits to laboratories should be described on your UCAS form. Keep up-to-date with developments by reading journals relating to the industry. See also **Appendix 1.**

Selection interviews (see Ch.4): Abertay Dundee (No); Bath Spa (UC) (No); Belfast (Queen's); Brighton; Dundee; Leeds; Manchester Met; Nottingham (depending on application); Reading; Sheffield Hallam (No); South Bank; Staffordshire (No); Surrey.

Interview questions (see Ch.4): This is a specialised field and admissions tutors will want to know your reasons for choosing the subject. You will be questioned on any experience you have had in the food industry. More general questions may cover the reasons for the trends in the popularity of certain types of food, the value of junk food and whether scientific interference with food is justifiable.

Reasons for rejection (non-academic): Too immature. Unlikely to integrate well. Lack of vocational commitment.

GAP YEAR ADVICE

Institutions willing to defer entry after A-levels: Bath Spa (UC) (No); Bournemouth; Brighton; Dundee; Glamorgan; Leeds; Lincolnshire & Humberside; Manchester Met; Newcastle; North London; Northumbria; Nottingham; Robert Gordon; Sheffield Hallam; South Bank; Surrey; Teesside.

AFTER RESULTS ADVICE

Institutions which may accept the same points score after A-levels: Belfast (Queen's); Brighton; Dundee; Leeds; Lincolnshire & Humberside; Manchester Met; Newcastle; Nottingham (No); Oxford Brookes; Robert Gordon; Sheffield Hallam; South Bank; Strathclyde (No); Scottish (CAg) (No); Surrey; Teesside.

Institutions which may accept lower grades/points score after A-levels: Brighton; Leeds; Lincolnshire & Humberside; Manchester Met; Newcastle; Sheffield Hallam; South Bank; Scottish (CAg); Surrey; Teesside.

Offers to applicants repeating A-levels: Higher Leeds, Nottingham; **Possibly higher** Manchester Met; **Same** Belfast (Queen's), Sheffield Hallam, Surrey.

Probable vacancies from June 2001 and in Clearing (see Ch.4): A large number of universities declared vacancies in Clearing last year in both Food Science and Food Marketing.

NEW GRADUATE DESTINATIONS AND EMPLOYMENT (1999 HESA) (see **Ch.4**)

Of 380 graduates surveyed, 270 were employed full-time, further study accounted for a further 36, whilst 15 were believed to be unemployed.

FORESTRY (including **Wood Science** and **Forest Products Technology**; see also **Agricultural Sciences/Agriculture**)

NB The information supplied by the universities and colleges this year varies considerably and the offers listed below should be used as a first source of reference only. Many institutions will accept combinations of Advanced (AL), Advanced Subsidiary (AS) and Vocational Advanced (VA) level qualifications to achieve the required points total, but applicants must check web sites and prospectuses for full details of all offers. Grades and points totals shown should be regarded as the minimum levels to be achieved, but offers may be adjusted downwards when results are known. The points totals shown to the left of the institutions are for ease of reference only. It must not be assumed that tariff points are always used by institutions or that they can be substituted for an offer in grades. The level of an offer is not necessarily indicative of the quality of a course. To calculate your offers see Chapter 4 and the inside fold of the back cover.

Special subject requirements/preferences: A-level: Mathematics or science subjects; check prospectuses. **GCSE:** Mathematics usually required.

240 pts **Bangor** – 240 pts – ALs or VAs CC+/-ALs/ASs; inc sci subj at AL/VA; (not gs) (Frsty; Frsty/Frsty Prod; Agrofor)
      Edinburgh – CCC/BB (Forestry)
200 pts **Aberdeen** – CDD/BC (Arbor Amen Frsty; Frsty Mgt; Frsty Sci)
160 pts **Buckinghamshire Chilterns (UC)** – 160–140 pts approx (Frsty Prod Tech/Frsty)
120 pts **Central Lancashire** – 120 pts (Frsty Wdlnd Mgt; Arboricult)
      De Montfort (Grantham) – 120 pts – ALs or ALs+ASs or VAs+/-ALs/ASs; gs; (Forestry)
80 pts **and below**
      UHI (Inverness) – (Frsty Cons – via DipHE, HND, HNC)

Diploma of Higher Education courses
      UHI.

Higher National Diploma courses
      De Montfort; Durham New (Coll); Inverness (Coll); Myerscough (Coll); Newton Rigg (Coll) (Forestry); Oaklands (Coll); Plumpton (Coll); Sparsholt (Coll); UHI; Warwickshire (Coll); Worcester (UC).

Alternative Offers:

IB offers: Bangor 28 pts.

Scottish Qualifications: Aberdeen BBBC; Edinburgh BBBB.

Overseas applicants: Bangor Good proportion of overseas students on course.

CHOOSING YOUR COURSE (See also **Ch.1**)

> **Subject information:** Forestry is concerned with the establishment and management of forests for timber production, environmental, conservation and amenity purposes. There are several Agriculture courses which could provide alternatives for study, in addition to Biology and the Biological Sciences. See also **Appendix 1**.

Special features: Aberdeen Two programmes – Arboriculture (production of oriental trees/shrubs and seed nursery production) and Amenity Forestry or forest management.

Bangor (Frsty) Forest management, timber production, conservation. **Buckinghamshire Chilterns (UC)** Sponsorships offered. (Frsty Prod Tech/Frsty) A study of the harvesting, processing and uses of wood-based products. *NOW CHECK PROSPECTUSES AND WEB SITES.*

Top universities and colleges (Teaching Quality) (see Ch.4): Bangor; not all institutions assessed.

Study opportunities abroad: Aberdeen; Bangor; Buckinghamshire Chilterns (UC).

Work opportunities abroad: Aberdeen.

ADMISSIONS INFORMATION

Number of applicants per place (approx): Bangor 5; Edinburgh 9.

Planning your UCAS personal statement (see Ch.4): Contact the Forestry Training Council and Commission and try to arrange visits to forestry centres and nature trails. Discuss the work with forest officers and learn about future plans for specific forest areas and describe any visits made. See also **Appendix 1.**

Selection interviews (see Ch.4): Most institutions.

Interview questions (see Ch.4): Work experience or field courses attended are likely to be discussed and questions asked such as: What is arboriculture? On a desert island how would you get food from wood? How do you see forestry developing in the next hundred years? What aspects of forestry are the most important?

GAP YEAR ADVICE

Institutions willing to defer entry after A-levels: Bangor.

AFTER RESULTS ADVICE

Institutions which may accept the same points score after A-levels: Bangor.

Probable vacancies from June 2001 and in Clearing (see Ch.4): Most universities are expected to have some vacancies from June onwards.

NEW GRADUATE DESTINATIONS AND EMPLOYMENT (1999 HESA (see **Ch.4**)

In a survey of 68 graduates, 49 entered employment, 10 went into further study and six were seeking employment six months after graduation.

FRENCH (see also **European Studies** and **Modern Languages**)

NB The information supplied by the universities and colleges this year varies consider-ably and the offers listed below should be used as a first source of reference only. Many institutions will accept combinations of Advanced (AL), Advanced Subsidiary (AS) and Vocational Advanced (VA) level qualifications to achieve the required points total, but applicants must check web sites and prospectuses for full details of all offers. Grades and points totals shown should be regarded as the minimum levels to be achieved, but offers may be adjusted downwards when results are known. The points totals shown to the left of the institutions are for ease of reference only. It must not be assumed that tariff points are always used by institutions or that they can be substituted for an offer in grades. The level of an offer is not necessarily indicative of the quality of a course. To calculate your offers see Chapter 4 and the inside fold of the back cover.

Special subject requirements/preferences: A-level: French usually the highest grade shown in the offers below. **Oxford** Full A-levels expected. **GCSE: Aberdeen, Dundee, Edinburgh, Glasgow, St Andrews** English, mathematics or science. **Bangor** Grade A* or A in French. **Exeter** As and Bs preferable in most subjects. **Hull** French grade A–B plus a range of As and Bs in other subjects. **Leeds** Grade A in languages. **Nottingham** French grade A–B. **Oxford** and **Cambridge** Usually majority of grade As. **Portsmouth** Three A grades, three B grades. **Sheffield** (Fr/Bus) Mathematics grade B. **Swansea** Grade A in three subjects, grade B in three subjects. **UMIST** Grade B mathematics.

360 pts **and above**
> **Cambridge** – Offers, mainly in grades, vary between colleges (Modn Lang)
> **Oxford** – Offers vary between candidates (Modn Lang)

350 pts **Southampton** – 350 pts 21u (inc 200 pts inc B/C Fr or b (check with univ)); French courses)

340 pts **Birmingham** – AAB (Fr/Law)
> **Bristol** – AAB–BBC (POl/Fr)
> **Edinburgh** – AAB (Engl Lit/Fr; Law/Fr)
> **Manchester** – AAB (MML French with Ital/Span/Ger/Russ)
> **Nottingham** – AAB (Fr/Law)
> **St Andrews** – AAB (Fr/Int Rel)
> **Sheffield** – AAB (Law/Fr)

320 pts **Bath** – 320 pts (Int Mgt Modn Lang)
> **Belfast (Queen's)** – ABB (Law/Fr; Acc/Fr)
> **Bristol** – ABB–BBB (inc Fr/Ger); (not gs) (Fr/Ger; Fr/Ital; Fr/Span; Fr/Port)
> **Cardiff** – ABB (Engl Lit/Fr)
> **Durham** – ABB (Hist/Fr; Econ/Fr)
> **Kent** – 320 pts approx (Fr Maitrise)
> **Lancaster** – ABB (Euro Mgt (Fr))
> **Leeds** – ABB (Law/Fr; Engl/Fr)
> **Leicester** – 320 pts (Law/Fr Law/Lang)
> **Liverpool** – 320 pts – ALs or ALs+ASs or VAs+/-ALs/ASs; (Fr/Hisp St)
> **London (British Inst in Paris)** – ABB (French St)
> **London (King's)** – ABB+AS or AAC+AS (inc A maths/Fr); VAs considered inc A maths, B Fr; (Fr/Maths)
> **London (RH)** – ABB–BBB (Econ/Fr)
> **Manchester** – ABB–BBC (Engl/Fr; Euro St/Fr)
> **Newcastle** – ABB (Law/Fr)
> **Nottingham** – ABB (Econ/Fr; Fr/Mech Eng)
> **Nottingham** – AAC (Fr/Hist; Fr/Pol; Fr/Ger)
> **Sheffield** – ABB (Engl/Fr)
> **UMIST** – ABB (Int Mgt/Fr)
> **York** – BBC+c or BB+ccc; gs; (Fr/Ger)
> **York** – ABB (Hist/Fr)

300 pts **Aston** – 18u – BBB–BBC or ALs+ASs or VAs+/-ALs/ASs; gs; (Int Bus/Fr/Ger)
> **Belfast (Queen's)** – BBB–BCC (French courses except under **320 pts**)
> **Birmingham** – BBB (French courses except under **340 pts**)
> **Bristol** – BBB–BBC (inc B French) (Fr/Russ)
> **Bristol UWE** – 300–280 pts (Fr/Euro St; Fr/Inf Sys; Fr/Bus Sys; Euro St/Fr/Ger; Euro St/Fr/Span; Euro St/EFL/Fr)
> **Brunel** – BBB–BCC (French courses)
> **Durham** – BBB (French Comb Arts)
> **East Anglia** – ABC (Fr St)
> **Edinburgh** – BBB (French)
> **Hull** – BBB–BBC/AB–BB (French Joint courses)
> **Leeds** – BBB (Fr/Span; Fr/Ger; Fr/Mgt St; Fr/Phil)
> **Liverpool** – 300 pts – ALs or ALs+ASs or VAs+/-ALs/ASs; (French courses except under **320 pts**)
> **London (King's)** – BBB+AS or BB+bbb (inc B Fr; B Engl for FR/Engl course); VAs considered inc B Fr; (Fr 3 yr course; Fr/Phil; Fr/Engl; Fr/Mgt)
> **London (RH)** – 300 pts 18u – ABC(B French) or AB(B French)+cc; (not gs) (French)
> **London (UCL)** – BBB–BBC or 3ALs+AS/VA; (Fr/Hist Art; Fr/Phil; Fr/Span; French)

Manchester – BBB (French courses except under **340/320 pts**)
Nottingham – BBB–BBC (French courses except under **340/320/280/260 pts**)
St Andrews – BBB (French courses)
Salford – BBB–CCC (French courses)
Sheffield – BBB–BBC (French courses except under **340/320/280 pts**)
Swansea – 300 pts 18u – BBB **or** ALs+ASs **or** VAs+/-ALs/ASs; (Fr/Law)
UMIST – BBB–BCC (French courses except under **320 pts**)

280 pts **Aberdeen** – BBC (French courses)
Aberystwyth – BBC (Law/French)
Aston – 280–260 pts – 3ALs **or** ALs+ASs **or** VAs+/-ALs/ASs; gs; (French; Modn Lang Transl)
Bath – BBC (French courses except under **320 pts**)
Bradford – 280 pts 12u (inc AL Fr); gs; (Int Mgt/Fr)
Bristol – BBC (inc B Fr+Lat) (Fr; Fr/Lat)
Bristol – BBC–BCC (Drama/Fr)
Cardiff – BBC/AB (B French) (French courses except under **320 pts**)
Dundee – BBC (Law/Fr)
Durham – BBC (Modn Lang/Ling; Modn Lang/Mus)
East Anglia – BBC (Interp/Transl/Langs)
Exeter – 280 pts 18u (inc AL Fr) – BBC **or** BB+cc **or** BC+bb **or** VAs (contact univ); gs; (French courses except under **260 pts**)
Glasgow – BBC (French courses)
Heriot-Watt – BBC (BB langs) (App Lang/Transl)
Keele – BBC–BCC **or** equiv AS accepted; gs (French courses)
Kent – BBC–BCC/AB (French courses)
Lancaster – BBC–BCC (French courses except under **320 pts**)
Leeds – 280 pts 18u – B(French)BC **or** B(French)B+AS(80 pts); (not gs) (French)
London (King's) – BBC+AS **or** BB+bbc (or equiv) (inc B Fr plus B Span/Ger for Fr/Span/Ger course); VAs considered inc B Fr; (French 4 yr course; Fr with Span/Gk/Port/Ger/Comp/Film)
London (QM) – 280 pts approx (Fr/Drama)
London (UCL) – BBC **or** 3ALs+AS/VA; (Fr with Af/As Lang/Russ)
Manchester Met – BBC–BCC (Bus Euro; Law/Fr)
Newcastle – BBC (French courses except under **320 pts**)
Nottingham – BBC (Fr/Russ)
Plymouth – BBC (Psy/Fr)
Reading – BBC–BCC (B French) (French courses)
Sheffield – BBC (Fr St; Fr/Russ)
Swansea – 280 pts 18u – BBC–BCC/BB **or** ALs+ASs **or** VAs+/-ALs/ASs; (French courses except under **300 pts**)
Warwick – BBC–BCC (French courses)
Westminster – BBC (Law/Fr)

260 pts **Aston** – 260 pts approx (French Comb Hons)
Bangor – 260 pts – ALs, VAs(enquire); gs; (Triple Lang courses from Fr/Ger/Ital/Span)
Bradford – 260 pts 12u (inc AL Fr); gs; (French; Fr/Ger/Span)
Dundee – BCC–CCC (French courses except under **280 pts**)
East Anglia – 260 pts (French St)
Exeter – 260 pts 18u(inc AL Fr) – BCC **or** BC+cc **or** BB+dd **or** VAs (contact univ); gs; (Fr/Arbc; Fr/Gk Rom St; Fr/Russ)
Heriot-Watt – 260–220 pts approx (French courses)
Hull – BCC–CCC (French courses)
Leicester – BCC–BCD (French courses except under **320 pts**)
London (QM) – 260–240 pts approx (French courses except under **280 pts**)
Nottingham – BCC (Fr/Class Civ)
Oxford Brookes – BCC–CCD/BB–DD (French Joint courses – offer varies with 2nd subject)

Portsmouth – 260 pts – ALs (inc Fr) **or** ALs+ASs **or** VAS; gs; (Fr St; Fr/Ital)
Sunderland – 260 pts (Fr/Media St)
Surrey – 260 pts 18u (B lang) – ALs **or** ALs+ASs **or** VAs+AL lang; gs; (Fr/Bus/Euro St/Law/Econ)
Sussex – BCC/BB (French Joint courses)

240 pts **Aberystwyth** – CCC (French courses except under **280 pts**)
Bangor – 240 pts – ALs, VAs (enquire); gs; (French joint courses except under **260/220 pts**)
Bradford – 240 pts 12u; gs; (Pol/Fr; Hist/Fr)
Central Lancashire – 240 pts 12u; gs; (Fr/Pblc Rel)
Durham – 240 pts approx (Euro St/Fr)
Loughborough – 240 pts – 2ALs+AL/2ASs **or** VA12u+AL **or** VA6u+ASs; gs; (Fr/Pol; Fr/Ger)
Nottingham Trent – 240–200 pts approx (Euro Bus/Fr)
Plymouth – 240 pts (Fr/Euro St; Geog/Fr; Int Bus/Fr)
Robert Gordon – CCC (Euro Bus Admin/Fr)
Stirling – CCC/BC (French courses)
Strathclyde – CCC/BC (BBD 2nd yr entry) (French)
Ulster – CCC/BC (Hum (Fr))

220 pts **Bangor** – 220 pts – ALs, VAs (enquire); gs; (Fr/Wmns St)
Buckingham – 220–160 pts approx (French courses)
Central England – 220 pts (Mark/Fr)
Cheltenham & Glos (CHE) – 220–140 pts (French courses)
Coventry – 220 pts approx (French courses with QTS option)
Greenwich – 220 pts (Archit/Fr; Land Archit/Fr)
Huddersfield – 220 pts approx (French courses)
Kingston – 220–180 pts 2x6u (inc 80 pts AL Fr); gs; (French)
Liverpool John Moores – 220 pts approx (Fr/Chin; Fr/Jap)
Luton – 220–160 pts approx (French)
Middlesex – 220–180 pts approx (French courses)
Nottingham Trent – 220–180 pts approx (French courses except under **240 pts**)
Plymouth – 220–200 pts approx (Fr/App Stats)
Sheffield Hallam – CCD (Int Bus Fr)
South Bank – 220–180 pts approx (French courses)
Wolverhampton – 220–160 pts 12u – DDD/CC **or** CD+e **or** VA12u CC; gs; (French courses)

200 pts **Brighton** – 200 pts approx (Lang St/Bus; Lang St/Ling)
Central England – 200 pts approx (Bus Admin Fr)
Dundee – 2000 pts (Phys/Fr)
European (Bus Sch) – 200 pts (Int Bus St/Fr; Euro Bus Admin)
Greenwich – 200–160 pts approx (Mark/Fr; Pers Mgt/Fr)
Kingston – 200 pts approx (Fr/Psy)
Lampeter – 200 pts (French courses)
Liverpool John Moores – 200 pts approx (French with Ger/Ital/Span/Jap/Russ)
London Guildhall – CDD–DDD/DD (French courses)
Manchester Met – CDD/CC (Hum/Soc St)
Plymouth – 200 pts (Fr/Geol; Crim Just St/Fr)
Staffordshire – 200 pts (inc CC) **or** VA12u CC; gs; (French courses)
Sunderland – 200–180 pts approx (French courses except under **260 pts**)
Teesside – 200–160 pts approx (French courses)

180 pts **Chester (Coll)** – 180 pts – ALs (160 pts inc C)+AS **or** VAs (160 pts inc C)+AS (20–40 pts); gs; (French Comb)
De Montfort (Leicester) – 180 pts – ALs (inc Fr pref); (not gs) (French)
East London – 180 pts approx (French courses)
Glamorgan – 180 pts approx (Joint Hons Fr inc FR/Welsh)
Greenwich – 180 pts (Pharm Sci/Fr)
Leeds, Trinity & All Saints (Coll) – 180 pts approx (Fr/Media; Fr/Mgt; Fr/Mark)

Manchester Met – BC (inc B lang) (Modn Lang Fr)
Surrey Roehampton – 160 pts (inc AL Fr 80 pts or AS Fr 60 pts+AL); (French)
160 pts **Anglia** – 160 pts 12u (inc C lang) – ALs **or** ALs+ASs **or** VAs+/-ALs/ASs; gs; (French courses)
Buckinghamshire Chilterns (UC) – 160–140 pts approx (French courses)
Canterbury Christ Church (UC) – CC (French courses)
Greenwich – 160 pts approx (Biol/Fr)
North London – 160 pts 1x12u **or** 2x6u; (French courses)
Northampton (UC) – 160 pts approx (Fr/Ger; Fr/Econ)
Northumbria – CC–CD (Fr/Pol; Fr/Econ)
Southampton (Inst) – 160 pts (Bus Fr)
Westminster – CC (Fr/Inf Tech; Fr/Crim; Fr/Sociol)
140 pts **Derby** – 140 pts 12u – CD **or** DE+ee **or** VAs CD+/-ALs/ASs; (French Comb)
Greenwich – 140 pts approx (Chem/Fr)

Leeds Met – (contact university)

Diploma of Higher Education courses
100 pts London Guildhall; Manchester Met; Middlesex; Oxford Brookes; Westminster (Ofce Inf Tech/Fr).

Higher National Diploma courses (with Business Studies)
80 pts **and below**
Glamorgan; Lincolnshire & Humberside; Loughborough (CT); Manchester Met; Newport (UWCN); Northumbria; Norwich City (Coll); Plymouth; Salford; Stockport (CFHE); Swansea (IHE).

Alternative Offers:

EB offers: Keele 65%; Leeds 65%; Surrey 60%; Swansea 65–60%.

IB offers: Aberdeen 30 pts; Aston 31–29 pts; Birmingham 33 pts; Bradford 24 pts; Bristol 32–30 pts inc H655; Buckingham 26 pts; Canterbury Christ Church (UC) 24 pts; Derby 26 pts; East Anglia 30–28 pts inc 15 pts Highers; Exeter 24–22 pts; Heriot-Watt 34 pts; Huddersfield 24 pts; Hull 30 pts; Kent 30–28 pts; Kingston 30–28 pts; Lancaster 32 pts; Leeds 28 pts inc H6(Fr)+7 pts; Leicester 28 pts; London (QM) 24 pts, (RH) 30–28 pts, (UCL) 32 pts; London Guildhall 28 pts 7 subjs, 24 pts 6 subjs; North London H555; Oxford Brookes 27 pts; St Andrews 30 pts; Sheffield 33–30 pts; Staffordshire 26 pts; Surrey 28 pts; Swansea 30–27 pts; Warwick 30 pts; York 30 pts.

Irish offers: Aberdeen BBBB; Aston AAABB; Bristol UWE CCCC; Keele BBBCC; Liverpool BBBCC; London Guildhall CCCCC; Manchester Met ABBBB; Newcastle BBCCC; St Andrews BBBB; Sheffield BBBBB; Surrey BBBCC; Warwick BBBBB; York BBBC.

Scottish Qualifications: Aberdeen BBBB; Dundee BBBC; Edinburgh ABBB–BBBB; Glasgow ABBB–BBBB; Robert Gordon BBBC–BBCC; St Andrews BBBB; Stirling BBBC; Strathclyde BBBB.

Overseas applicants: North London French nationals accepted (essays written in French and English). **Sheffield** Applicants should state if French is their first language. **Surrey** High level of competence in French required.

CHOOSING YOUR COURSE (See also **Ch.1**)

> **Subject information:** Courses could include an emphasis on literature and linguistics, the written or spoken word, or a wider study of France and its culture, as in European Studies courses. Check prospectuses before choosing courses. See also **Appendix 1** under **Modern Languages**.

Special features: Bangor Options include French commercial language and business practice. **Bradford** French may be offered with subsidiary languages (Italian, Dutch, Greek, Portuguese). **Bristol** Students take subsidiary subject from 10 options in first and second years. Traditional literary or historical emphasis. **Durham** (Comb Arts – French) The first year covers the study of language, translation and history, phonetics and medieval and 17th century literature. **East Anglia** The subject has an emphasis on linguistic proficiency. **Exeter** Year 2 French based on the commercial language, for example, banking, business correspondence. **Hull** Communication skills, modern French culture (including literature) art, music, drama, film covered in course. Wide range of topics include literature, lexicology, linguistics, politics, sociology and new technology. Other languages or additional subjects as options in years 1/2/4. **Kent** The Maitrise programme includes two years in France. Business French courses are available. Extensive use of modern technology. **Lampeter** Flexible structure offering students opportunity to tailor own course (linguistic, literary, contemporary society, history of ideas). **Lancaster** Emphasis on practical language work. **Leeds** Option-based flexible course with few compulsory subjects. Practical language teaching. All tuition in French. **Leicester** (Fr/Ital) Italian can be studied from scratch. **London (British Inst in Paris)** Study of contemporary French language, literary/business studies option. Course taught in French. **London (RH)** All areas of French literature, institutions and computer-assisted language learning. Wide range of options, linguistic, literary, political, economic. **London Guildhall** Delayed specialisation possible in the modular degree programme. **Newcastle** Emphasis on oral and aural skills including interpreting and translation. **Portsmouth** This is a course with a strong bias towards modern French and modern France. (Fr/St) Emphasis on contemporary politics and economics. **Sheffield** Two other subjects taken in first year. **Swansea** (French/Bus St) Common core of post A/AS-level general language plus specialised business language courses. Study of political, social, economic, life of France plus other options. *NOW CHECK PROSPECTUSES AND WEB SITES.*

Top universities and colleges (Teaching Quality) (see Ch.4): Aberdeen; Aston; Cambridge; De Montfort; Durham; Exeter; Glasgow; Leeds; Liverpool; London (QM); Newcastle; Northumbria; Oxford Brookes; Portsmouth; South Bank; Staffordshire; Sussex; Westminster; not all institutions assessed.

Top universities and colleges (Research) (see Ch.4): Aberdeen; Belfast (Queen's); Birmingham; Bristol; Cambridge; Cardiff; Durham; Edinburgh; Exeter; Glasgow; Hull; Keele; Leeds; Leicester; Liverpool; London (King's), (QM), (RH), (UCL); Manchester; Newcastle; Nottingham; Oxford; Reading; St Andrews; Sheffield; Southampton; Stirling; Sussex; Warwick.

Study opportunities abroad: Institutions offering four-year courses usually arrange study placements abroad for students.

Work opportunities abroad: Aston; Birmingham; Bradford; Cardiff; Leeds; London (RH); Manchester; Sheffield; Surrey; Surrey Roehampton; Swansea. Also most other universities.

ADMISSIONS INFORMATION

Number of applicants per place (approx): Anglia 7; Aston 6 pts; Bangor 4; Birmingham 8; Bradford 3; Bristol 11; Bristol UWE 13; Cardiff 6; Central Lancashire 5; Durham 8; Edge Hill (CHE) 5; Exeter 8; Huddersfield 3; Hull 12; Kent 10; Kingston 4; Lampeter 3; Lancaster 7; Leeds 6; Leeds, Trinity & All Saints (Coll) 3; Leicester (Fr/Pol) 6, (Fr/Ital) 5; Liverpool 5; London (RH) 5, (UCL) (Fr/Phil) 7, (Fr/Span) 8, (Fr/Ital) 4, (Fr/Hist Art) 8; London (British Inst in Paris) 9; Manchester Met 13; Middlesex 6; Newcastle (Fr) 17, (Fr/Minor) 16, (Fr/Span) 22, (Fr/Ger) 20; North London 5; Nottingham 16; Oxford Brookes 8; Portsmouth 20; Surrey 10; Surrey Roehampton 5; Swansea 5; UMIST 5; Warwick 7; York 8.

Planning your UCAS personal statement (see Ch.4): Visits to France (including exchange visits) should be described with reference to any particular cultural or geographical features of the region visited. Contacts with pen friends and experience in speaking the language are also important. Willingness to work/live/travel abroad. Interests in French life and culture. Read French newspapers and magazines and keep up-to-date with news stories etc. **Hull** We look for dynamism – students looking for a challenge. **St Andrews** Evidence of interest and reasons for choosing the course. Sport/extra-curricular activities. Posts of responsibility. Career information *Using Languages* can be obtained from the Schools Liaison Section. Room 707, Civil Service Commission, Alencon Link, Basingstoke, Hants RG21 1JB. See also **Appendix 1**.

Selection interviews (see Ch.4): Aberystwyth (No); Aston (No); Bangor; Birmingham; Bradford; Bristol (No); Cambridge; Canterbury Christ Church (UC); Cardiff (No); De Montfort (No); Durham; East Anglia (after offer); Edinburgh (No); Essex; Exeter; Heriot-Watt; Huddersfield; Hull; Kingston; Lampeter; Lancaster; Leeds (mature students and non-standard applicants) (T); Leeds, Trinity & All Saints (Coll); Leicester (No); Liverpool (T); Liverpool John Moores (T); London (Gold), (RH) (T), (UCL); London Guildhall; Newcastle (No); ; Nottingham (No); Oxford (W) (T); Oxford Brookes (No); Portsmouth; Reading; St Andrews (No); Sheffield (No); South Bank; Southampton (No); Staffordshire (No); Stirling (No); Surrey (T); Surrey Roehampton (No); Sussex; Swansea; Warwick; York (No).

Interview questions (see Ch.4): Questions will almost certinly be asked on your A-level texts in addition to any reading you do outside the syllabus – books, magazines, newspapers etc. Part of the interview may be conducted in French and written tests may be involved.

Reasons for rejection (non-academic): Unstable personality. Known alcoholism. Poor motivation. Candidate unenthusiastic, unmotivated, ill-informed about the nature of the course (had not read the prospectus).

GAP YEAR ADVICE

Most universities recommend part or all of the year in a French-speaking environment.

Institutions willing to defer entry after A-levels: Aberystwyth; Anglia; Aston; Bangor; Birmingham; Bradford; Bristol UWE; Cardiff; Edge Hill (CHE); Hull; Kent; Lampeter; Lancaster; Leeds; Leicester; London (UCL); London (British Inst in Paris); Luton; Manchester; Newcastle; North London; Northampton (UC); Northumbria; Nottingham; Portsmouth; Sheffield; South Bank (Prefers not); Staffordshire; Surrey; Surrey Roehampton; Sussex; Swansea; UMIST; Warwick; Wolverhampton; York.

AFTER RESULTS ADVICE

Institutions which may accept the same points score after A-levels: Aberystwyth; Aston; Birmingham; Bradford; Bristol; Bristol UWE; Cardiff; Durham; East Anglia; Edge Hill (CHE); Hull; Kent (No); Lampeter; Lancaster; Leeds (B in French); Leicester (No); Liverpool; Liverpool John Moores (No); London (RH); London Guildhall (No); Newcastle (varies); North London; Nottingham (Fr/Ger), (Fr/Russ), (Fr/Lat) (No); Oxford Brookes; Portsmouth; Southampton (No); Staffordshire; Stirling (No); Surrey; Surrey Roehampton; Swansea (but actual grade in French); UMIST; Warwick (No); York (grade B in French).

Institutions which may accept lower grades/points score after A-levels: Aberystwyth; Aston; Belfast (Queen's); Birmingham; Bradford; Bristol UWE; Durham; East Anglia; Edge Hill (CHE); Essex; Exeter; Glasgow; Hull; Kent; Lampeter; Lancaster; Leeds; Leicester; Liverpool; London (RH), (UCL); Nottingham; Portsmouth; Reading; Sheffield; Staffordshire; Surrey; Surrey Roehampton; Swansea; UMIST; Warwick; York.

Offers to applicants repeating A-levels: Higher Aberystwyth (1 pt), Bristol (Fr), Leeds, Oxford Brookes, Warwick; **Possibly higher** Aston (Fr; Fr/Ger); **Same** Aston, Bradford, Bristol (Fr/Phil; Fr/Lat), Durham, East Anglia, Lampeter (most), Lancaster, Liverpool, London (RH), Newcastle, North London, Nottingham (Fr/Ger; Fr; Fr/Lat), Sheffield, Surrey Roehampton, Sussex, Swansea, Ulster.

Probable vacancies from June 2001 and in Clearing (see Ch.4): Vacancies are expected to be mainly in the 'new' university sector for Single and Joint Honours courses. The more competitive universities are likely to ask for 260 or 240 pts.

NEW GRADUATE DESTINATIONS AND EMPLOYMENT (1999 HESA) (see **Ch.4**)

In a survey of 871 graduates, 487 went into full-time employment, 209 went on to further study and 37 were believed to be unemployed.

GENETICS (see also Biological Sciences)

NB The information supplied by the universities and colleges this year varies considerably and the offers listed below should be used as a first source of reference only. Many institutions will accept combinations of Advanced (AL), Advanced Subsidiary (AS) and Vocational Advanced (VA) level qualifications to achieve the required points total, but applicants must check web sites and prospectuses for full details of all offers. Grades and points totals shown should be regarded as the minimum levels to be achieved, but offers may be adjusted downwards when results are known. The points totals shown to the left of the institutions are for ease of reference only. It must not be assumed that tariff points are always used by institutions or that they can be substituted for an offer in grades. The level of an offer is not necessarily indicative of the quality of a course. To calculate your offers see Chapter 4 and the inside fold of the back cover.

Special subject requirements/preferences: A-Level: Biology and chemistry usually required plus GCSE mathematics. **Curriculum 2000: Oxford** At least one science at full A-Level. **GCSE: Birmingham** Average of Bs in five relevant subjects. **Cambridge, Oxford** Usually a majority of As.

360 pts and above
    Cambridge – Offers, mainly in grades, vary between colleges (Nat Sci (Genet))
    Oxford – Offers vary between candidates (Hum Sci (Genet))
350 pts   **York** – 350–300 pts 21–18u – ABB/BBB/BBC **or** ALs+ASs **or** VAs (contact univ); gs; (Genetics)
340 pts   **Nottingham** – AAB **or** AAB+AS **or** VAs(see Ad Tutor); (not gs) (Genet; Hum Genet)
320 pts   **Liverpool** – 320–280 pts – ALs **or** ALs+ASs **or** VAs+/-ALs/ASs; (Genet: App Genet)
    London (UCL) – ABB–BBB **or** 3ALs+AS/VA; (Genet; Hum Genet)
300 pts   **Cardiff** – BBB–BCC (Genetics)
    Leeds – BBB (Genet; Hum Genet)
    London (King's) – BBB+AS **or** BB+bb+AS (or equiv) (inc C chem+sci) **or** VA12uBB+AL(C chem)+AS; (Mol Genet)
    London (QM) – 300–250 pts – ALs **or** ALs+ASs **or** VAs+/-ALs/ASs; (Genet; Genet/Microbiol)
280 pts   **Birmingham** – BBC (Biol Sci (Genet))
    Edinburgh – BBC (Genetics)
    Glasgow – BBC–CCC/BC (Genetics courses)
    Lancaster – BBC (Bioch/Genet)
    Leeds – BBC (Genet-Microbiol; Bioch-Genet)
    Leicester – BBC **or** BB+2ASs **or** VA12u+AL; gs (at AL if only 2ALs offered); (Genetics)
    Manchester – BBC (Genetics courses)
    Newcastle – BBC–BCC (Genet; Hum Genet)
    Sheffield – BBC (Genetics courses)
    Swansea – 280 pts 18u – BBC–BCC/AB–BB **or** ALs+ASs **or** VAs+/-ALs/ASs; (Genetics)
260 pts   **Brunel** – 260 pts approx (Med Genet)
    London (RH) – BCC (Mol Biol (Genet))
    Sussex – BCC (Mol Genet Biotech courses)
240 pts   **Aberystwyth** – 240 pts 21u – CCC **or** CC+cc **or** VAs; gs; (Genet; Genet/Bioch)
    Belfast (Queen's) – CCC/BB (Genetics)
220 pts   **Aberdeen** – CCD/BC (Genet; Genet (Immun))
200 pts   **Dundee** – 200 pts (Mol Genet)
    Wolverhampton – 200–160 pts 12u – DDD–DDE/CC **or** CC+dd/de **or** VA12u CC; gs; (Genet Mol Biol)

Alternative Offers:

IB offers: Aberdeen 26 pts; Aberystwyth 27 pts; Birmingham 30 pts; Leeds 26 pts H5 biol; Liverpool 30 pts; Nottingham 34 pts; Swansea 26 pts; York 32–30 pts.

Irish offers: Aberdeen BBCC; Liverpool BBCCC.

Scottish Qualifications: Aberdeen BBBC; Dundee BBCC; Edinburgh BBBB; Glasgow BBBB; St Andrews BBCC.

CHOOSING YOUR COURSE (See also **Ch.1**)

Subject information: Genetics is an appropriate course of study for those aiming for careers in such areas as biological and medical research, biotechnology, plant or animal breeding. Biological Science, Biotechnology and Microbiology courses should also be considered. See also **Appendix 1** under **Biological Sciences**.

Special features: Aberystwyth Biology, biochemistry and a computer science option. Strong research base in plant genetics. **Cardiff** Seven biological degrees served by the same first-year course. Students have free choice of major honours subject in year 2. **Manchester** Studies in the School of Biological Sciences with flexibility to transfer within the School to other modules. **Newcastle** Twelve modules taken in each year. Genetics specialisation in second and third years. Course covers organisms from virus to man. **Nottingham** Options can also be taken from subjects within biochemistry and life sciences. **York** Flexible choice of options. Language courses available. *NOW CHECK PROSPECTUSES AND WEB SITES.*

Top universities and colleges (Research) (see Ch.4): Cambridge; Glasgow; Leicester; Nottingham.

Study opportunities abroad: Aberystwyth; Birmingham; Leeds; Leicester; Manchester; Swansea.

Work opportunities abroad: Aberystwyth; Brunel; Cardiff; Leeds.

ADMISSIONS INFORMATION

Number of applicants per place (approx): Cardiff 8; Leeds 7; Leicester (for all Biol Sci) 10; Newcastle 8; Nottingham 13; Swansea 7; York 12.

Planning your UCAS personal statement (see Ch.4): See **Biological Sciences**.

Selection interviews (see Ch.4): Aberystwyth (No); Cambridge; Cardiff (No); Kingston; Leeds (No); Leicester (No); Liverpool; Manchester; Newcastle (No); Nottingham (No); Oxford; Sheffield (No); Swansea; York (some).

Interview questions (see Ch.4): Likely questions will focus on your A-Level science subjects, particularly biology, why you wish to study genetics and on careers in genetics.

GAP YEAR ADVICE

Most universities suggest working in a related area if possible.

Institutions willing to defer entry after A-Levels: Aberystwyth; Birmingham; Cardiff; London (UCL) (No); Newcastle (No); Nottingham; Sussex; Swansea; York.

AFTER RESULTS ADVICE

Institutions which may accept the same points score after A-Levels: Aberystwyth; Cardiff; Leeds; Liverpool; London (UCL) (No); Manchester; Swansea; York.

Institutions which may accept lower grades/points score after A-Levels: Aberdeen; Cardiff; Lancaster; Leeds; Liverpool; London (UCL); Newcastle; Swansea.

Offers to applicants repeating A-Levels: Higher Aberystwyth, Leeds, Newcastle, Nottingham, Swansea, York (1 pt); **Same** London (UCL), Swansea.

Probable vacancies from June 2001 and in Clearing (see Ch.4): In Clearing last year about 20 universities declared vacancies, with offers in the range of 260 to 200 pts.

NEW GRADUATE DESTINATIONS AND EMPLOYMENT (1999 HESA) (see **Ch.4**)

In a survey of 348 graduates, 153 went into full-time employment, mainly into managerial, administrative or professional work, 137 went on to further study and 25 were believed to be unemployed.

GEOGRAPHY

NB The information supplied by the universities and colleges this year varies considerably and the offers listed below should be used as a first source of reference only. Many institutions will accept combinations of Advanced (AL), Advanced Subsidiary (AS) and Vocational Advanced (VA) level qualifications to achieve the required points total, but applicants must check web sites and prospectuses for full details of all offers. Grades and points totals shown should be regarded as the minimum levels to be achieved, but offers may be adjusted downwards when results are known. The points totals shown to the left of the institutions are for ease of reference only. It must not be assumed that tariff points are always used by institutions or that they can be substituted for an offer in grades. The level of an offer is not necessarily indicative of the quality of a course. To calculate your offers see Chapter 4 and the inside fold of the back cover.

Special subject requirements/preferences: A-Level: Geography usually the highest grade shown in the offers below. One or more science subjects may be required for BSc courses. **Oxford** Full A-Level recommended in geography. **GCSE:** Mathematics often required for BSc courses. **Aberdeen, Dundee, Edinburgh, Glasgow, Nottingham, St Andrews** English, mathematics and a foreign language. **Bristol** (BSc), **Cambridge, Oxford** Usually a majority of grade As. **Durham** Grade A*, A and very few grade Cs. **Exeter** Good range of grade A*, A or Bs. **Hull** (BSc) Grade B in geography and one science. **London (LSE)** Grade A*, A or Bs, grade C in mathematics preferred. **London (QM)** (BSc) Seven grade As. **London (RH)** (BSc) Three grade As, six grade Bs. **Swansea** Balance of Grade As. Most other universities will require English and mathematics.

360 pts and above
    Cambridge – Offers, mainly in grades, vary between colleges (Geography)
    Oxford – Offers vary between candidates (Geography)
    Southampton – 370 pts 21u (inc 220 pts from 2ALs inc geog); (Geog courses)
340 pts **Bristol** – AAB–BBB; (not gs) (Geog courses)
    Cambridge (Hom) – AAB–ABB (BA Geog/Educ St)
    Durham – AAB (Nat Sci (Geog))
    East Anglia – AAB (Meteor Ocean/USA/Euro)
    London (SOAS) – 340 pts (Geog/Soc Anth)
320 pts **Durham** – ABB–ABC–BBB (BA/BSc Geog; Geog (Geog Euro St)
    Edinburgh – ABB (1 sitting) (not gs) (Geog courses)
    Leeds – ABB (not gs) (Geog/Trans Plan; Geog; Geog Mgt St)
    Liverpool – 320–280 pts – ALs **or** ALs+ASs **or** VAs+/-ALs/ASs; (Geog; Geog/Biol)
    London (UCL) – ABB–BBC **or** 3ALs+AS/VA; (Geog courses)
    Nottingham – ABB–BBC (Geog courses)
    St Andrews – ABB–BBC (Geog courses)
    Sheffield – 320 pts approx (Geog F800/L800)
    Sheffield – ABB/320 pts (Geog; Geog/Maths; Geog/Econ; Geog/Sociol)
310 pts **Southampton** – 310 pts – 2ALs (180 pts)+AL **or** BCC+b **or** BC+bbd; (gs as 1 of 3ALs, not 1 of 2ALs) (Pop Sci)
300 pts **Birmingham** – BBB–BCC (Geog courses)
    Brunel – 300–260 pts 2x6u (inc C geog/geol/env sci) – ALs **or** ALs+ASs **or** VAs+/-ALs/ASs; (Hum Geog courses)
    Cardiff – BBB (Hum Geog/Plan)
    Leeds – BBB–BBC (not gs) (Geog; Geog/Econ; Geog/Stats; Geog/Pol; Geog/Sociol)

Liverpool – 300–260 pts – ALs or ALs+ASs or VAs+/-ALs/ASs; (Geog/Arch)

London (King's) – BBB+AS or BB+bbc or equiv) (inc AL geog); VAs considered + B hist for Geog/Hist course; (Geog; Geog/Hist/War St)

London (LSE) – BBB (Geog/Econ; Geog/Pop St; Geog)

London (QM) – 300–240 pts 18u; (Geog courses)

London (SOAS) – 300 pts (Geog/Chin; Geog/Jap)

Loughborough – 300 pts 18u – C (geog)+AL+AL/2AS or VA12u+/-AL/ASs; (not gs) (Geog/PE/Spo Sci)

Manchester – BBB–BBC (Geog; Geog/Arch)

Oxford Brookes – BBB–DDD (Geog courses)

280 pts Belfast (Queen's) – BBC–BCC (BA Geog courses)

Cambridge (Hom) – BBC–BCD (BEd Geog/Educ)

Glasgow – BBC–CCC (Geog courses)

Lancaster – BBC–CCC (Geog courses)

Leeds – BBC (Geog/Ital; Geog/Maths; Geog/Geol)

Leicester – 280 pts 18u – BBC–BCC or ALs+ASs; gs; (BSc/BA Geog)

London (RH) – 280 pts – BBC (B geog pref) (Geog courses)

London (SOAS) – 260 pts approx (Geog/Arbc; Geog/Af St)

Loughborough – 280 pts 18u – C(geog)+AL+AL/2AS or VA12u+/-AL/ASs; (not gs) (Geog; Geog/Econ; Geog/Recr Mgt)

Newcastle – BBC–CCC (Geog courses except under **240 pts**)

Reading – BBC (B geog) (Geog courses; Meteor)

Sheffield – BBC (Geog/Arch Sci)

Sussex – BBC–BCD (Geog courses)

Swansea – 280 pts 18u – BBC/AB or ALs+ASs or VAs+/-ALs/ASs; (Geography)

260 pts Aberystwyth – 260 pts 18u – ALs or ALs+ASs (geog 80 pts min); (BSc/BA Geog)

Aston – 260–240 pts 18u – 3ALs or ALs+ASs or VAs+/-ALs/ASs; gs; (Geog Inf Sys)

Bristol UWE – 260–200 pts 18u pref/12u – ALs (inc geog) or ALs+ASs or VA12u (land env/bus/IT/sci); (not gs if offering 12u) (Geog; Geog/Env Mgt)

Brunel – 260–240 pts 2x6u – ALs or ALs+ASs or VAs+/-ALs/ASs; (Geography)

Cardiff – BCC–CCC (Mar Geog)

Dundee – 260 pts approx (Geog courses BSc 3 yr)

Durham (Stockton) – BCC(B geog) or VA12u+AL; (not gs) (Geog courses)

East Anglia – BCC (BSc Meteor/Ocean)

Exeter – 260 pts 18u (inc AL geog+lang (for Euro course)) – BBC or BB+bb/bc or VAs (contact univ); (not gs) (BA: Geog/Euro; Geog)

Hull – BCC/BB (Geog courses except below)

Hull – BCC (inc sci); (Phys Geog)

Keele – BCC/BB or equiv AS accepted; gs; (Geog courses)

Leicester – 260 pts 18u – BCC or ALs+ASs; (Geog (Soc Sci))

Leicester – BCC or 2ALs+2ASs or VAs+/-ALs/ASs; (Geog/Geol)

Manchester – BCC (Geog/Geol)

Manchester Met – 260 pts (Geog/Spo)

Newcastle – BCC (Geog/Maths; Geog/Stats; Geog/Surv Map Sci)

Oxford Brookes – BCC–DDD (Geog courses)

Plymouth – 260 pts (Geog/Law)

Salford – BCC–ccd (Geog/Biol; Geog/Econ)

240 pts Aberdeen – CCC–CCD (Geog courses)

Bradford – 240 pts 12u (inc AL geog/sci); gs; (Geog/Env Sci; Phys/Env Geog)

Exeter – 240 pts 18u (inc AL geog) – BCC or BC+bc or VAs (contact univ); (not gs) (BSc Geog)

Glamorgan – CCC (Spo Sci/Phys Geog)

Hertfordshire – 240–200 pts 1x12u or 2x6u; (Geog; Geog/Geol)

Lampeter – BCD (B Engl) (Australian Studies)

Leicester – CCC or ALs+ASs; (Geog/Econ Soc Hist)

Geography at Portsmouth

The Department of Geography at the University of Portsmouth is recognised as one of the leading departments in the University sector and is strongly committed to high quality teaching and research. Our aim is to develop understanding in an increasingly inter-connected world and central to this commitment is the idea of learning in a research environment. Three key national achievements demonstrate these beliefs:

- The quality of geography education at Portsmouth was rated excellent by the Higher Education Funding Council for England.

- The Department's high quality research was judged to be of national and international significance by the most recent national Research Assessment Exercise.

- Portsmouth is one of just 25 geography departments in the UK to achieve the ESRC's highest recognition for its postgraduate training.

"The Geography degree is well thought out and meets its objectives of genuine student centred learning... There is a strong commitment to teaching... Staff are strongly committed to students in a major way both in stretching them intellectually and through strong personal support mechanisms".

At the undergraduate level, three broad degree pathways, and a number of joint programmes are offered. Each pathway provides a foundation offering maximum flexibility while allowing scope for future specialisation as the degree progresses. Our undergraduate programme leads into an exciting range of courses at the Masters level, reflecting our teaching expertise and research strengths.

Our current main undergraduate degree pathways are:

BA (Hons) Geography
BSc (Hons) Geographical Science
BA (Hons) Human Geography

If you would like more information on our courses, the Department, the Faculty of the Environment, the University of Portsmouth and the City of Portsmouth, visit our website at:

http://www.port.ac.uk

We also offer a series of open days when you can see both the University and the Department, with the opportunity to talk to both students and staff.

For further information contact:

Dianne Claxton
Department of Geography
University of Portsmouth
Buckingham Building
Lion Terrace
Portsmouth
PO1 3HE

tel: (023) 9284 2506
fax: (023) 9284 2512
email: dianne.claxton@port.ac.uk

University of **Portsmouth**

Liverpool John Moores – 240–180 pts – ALs **or** ALs+ASs **or** VAs+/-ALs/ASs; (Geog; Hum Geog)
Manchester Met – 240 pts (Geog/Phys)
Newcastle – CCC (Geog Inf Sci)
Oxford Brookes – CCC (Cartography courses)
Plymouth – 240 pts approx (Geog courses except under **260/220 pts**)
Staffordshire – 240 pts inc 2ALs **or** VA12u; gs; (Geog courses)
Strathclyde – CCC (1st yr entry) BBD (2nd yr entry) (Geog courses)
Ulster – CCC–CCD (Geog courses)
Westminster – 240 pts (Hum Geog)

220 pts **Brighton** – 220 pts approx (Geog courses except under **180 pts**)
Central Lancashire – 220–180 pts 12u (pref AL geog); gs; (Geog courses)
Coventry – 220–200 pts approx (Geog courses)
Kingston – 220 pts 2x6u (inc 80 pts AL Geog) **or** VA (constr/blt env) 160 pts min; gs; (Geog courses)
Kingston – 220 pts (inc 2x6u **or** AL geog pref) – ALs **or** ALs+ASs **or** VAs+/-ALs/ASs; gs; (Geog Inf Sys courses)
Lampeter – 220 pts approx (C geog) (Geog courses)
Luton – 220–180 pts approx (Geog courses)
Manchester Met – 220 pts (Geog/Inf Sys)
Middlesex – 220–180 pts approx (Geog courses)
Northumbria – 220 pts (Geog/Spo St)
Nottingham Trent – 220 pts – ALs (160 pts inc C geog) (Hum Geog)
Plymouth – 220 pts (Crim Just St/Geog)
Portsmouth – 220 pts – ALs **or** ALs+ASs **or** VAS; gs; (Hum Geog; Geog; Geog Sci; Geog Inf Sys; Phys Geog)
Sheffield Hallam – 220 pts (Urb Reg Geog; Euro Urb Reg St)
South Bank – 220–180 pts approx (Geog courses)
Southampton (Inst) – 220–200 pts (Mar Geog)
Surrey (Roehampton) – 220 pts approx (inc 2ALs) – ALs **or** ALs+ASs **or** VAs+/-ALs/ASs; (Geog; Hum Geog)

200 pts **Bangor** – 200 pts – ALs **or** VAs+/-ALs/ASs; (AL gs only) (Geog)
Bournemouth – 200 pts from 2ALs (BC) (pref ALs geog/sci) **or** VAs; (App Geog; Land/Geog Sci)
Cheltenham & Glos (CHE) – 200–140 pts approx (Geog courses)
Chester (Coll) – ALs (160 pts C geog/geol/env sci)+AS **or** VA (160 pts+C sci/land mgt)+AS (20–40 pts); gs; (Geog courses)
De Montfort (Bedford) – 200 pts – ALs; gs; (Hum Geog; Geog Dev)
Derby – 200 pts 12u – CCE **or** CC+A Ss **or** VAs (AL grades)+/-ALs/ASs; (MSci Geog)
Dundee – 200 pts (Geog BSc 4 yr)
Huddersfield – 200 pts 12u (inc 40 pts min AL geog) – ALs **or** ALs+ASs **or** VAs+/-ALs/ASs; gs; (Geog courses)
Manchester Met – 200 pts (Geog courses except under **260/240/220 pts**)
Newman (CHE) – 200–140 pts approx (Geog courses)
Northampton (UC) – 200–160 pts (Geog courses)
Ripon & York St John (Coll) – 200–180 pts approx (Geog St courses)
St Martin's (Coll) – BDE–BC (Geog/Engl)

180 pts **Anglia** – 180 pts approx (Geography)
Brighton – 180 pts approx (Geog/Geol; Biogeog)
Central England – 180 pts 12u min; (Geog/Env Mgt)
East London – 180 pts approx (Geog Inf Sys)
Glamorgan – 180 pts approx (Geog Inf Sys/Hum Geog)
Greenwich – 180 pts approx (Geog; Geog Inf Sys/Rem Sens)
Liverpool Hope (Coll) – 180–160 pts (Geog courses)
North East Wales (IHE) – 180–160 pts (Geog courses)
St Martin's (Coll) – CDE/CC (Geog courses)
Sheffield Hallam – 180 pts approx (P Geog QTS)

Wolverhampton – 180 pts 12u – DDD/CC **or** DD+c/ee **or** VA12u CC; gs; (Geog; Hum Geog)

160 pts   **Bath Spa (UC)** – 160–120 pts 12u – BD **or** VA12u BD; (not gs) (Geog Comb)

Bishop Grosseteste (Coll) – CC (inc C geog) **or** C+cc **or** VA12u+C (geog); (not gs) (Geography)

Canterbury Christ Church (UC) – 160 pts approx (Geog Mod courses)

Chichester (UC) – 160 pts (inc C); (Geography)

Derby – 160–140 pts approx (Geog courses except under **200 pts**; BSc Geog)

Glamorgan – CC (Geol Sci/Phys Geog; Hum Geog/Psy; Phys Geog/Env Sci)

Liverpool John Moores – 160–120 pts (inc AL geog/geol 80 pts) – ALs **or** ALs+ASs **or** VAs+/-ALs/ASs; (Phys Geog)

Newport (UWCN) – 160–140 pts – ALs **or** ALs+ASs **or** VAs+/-ALs/ASs; (Geog courses)

St Mary's (Coll) – 160 pts 12u – CC–DD **or** ALs+ASs **or** VA12u CC–DD; gs; (Geography)

Stirling – CC (Env Sci (Geog))

Sunderland – 160 pts – 2ALs **or** ALs+ASs **or** VA12u+/-AL/ASs; (Geography)

Trinity Carmarthen (Coll) – CC–EE (Geog courses)

140 pts   **Bath Spa (UC)** – 140 pts 12u – CD **or** VA12u CD; (not gs) (Geography)

Derby – 140 pts 12u – CD **or** DD+dd **or** VA CD+/-AL/ASs; (All Geog courses except under **200 pts**)

North London – 140 pts 1x12u **or** 2x6u – (Hum Geog)

Wolverhampton – 140 pts 12u – CD **or** VAs+/-ALs/ASs; gs; (Phys Geog)

120 pts   **Edge Hill (CHE)** – DD (Geography)

Hull (Scarborough) – DD (Geog Sci)

100 pts   **Barnsley (Coll)** – 100 pts (Geog St courses)

80 pts   **Worcester (UC)** – 80 pts 12u – EE **or** ALs+ASs **or** VAs+/-ALs/ASs; gs; (Geography)

Leeds Met – (contact university)

Diploma of Higher Education courses
80 pts   Bath Spa (UC); London Guildhall; Manchester Met; Middlesex; Oxford Brookes; Worcester (UC).

Higher National Diploma courses
Bournemouth; Derby; Kingston.

Alternative Offers:

EB offers: Aberystwyth 75%; Keele 70%; Sheffield 60%.

IB offers: Aberdeen (Arts) 30 pts, (Sci) 26 pts; Aberystwyth 30–28 pts; Bath Spa (UC) 24 pts; Birmingham 33 pts; Bristol 34 pts H665; Brunel 26 pts; Cardiff – H665 S555; Cheltenham & Glos (CHE) 26 pts; Durham 35–32 pts inc Geog H6; East Anglia 29 pts; Edinburgh 32 pts; Exeter 30 pts; Guildhall 24 pts; Huddersfield 26 pts; Hull 28 pts; Kent 28 pts, H 12 pts; Lampeter 24 pts; Lancaster 30 pts; Leeds 32–30 pts; Leicester 32–30 pts; Liverpool 30 pts inc 5/6 in 2 science subjects; London (King's) 34 pts, (LSE) 35 pts, (QM) 30 pts, (RH) 30 pts, (UCL) 34 pts; London Guildhall 24 pts; Newcastle 24 pts; Nottingham H655; Nottingham Trent 27 pts; Oxford Brookes 26 pts; Ripon & York St John (Coll) 30 pts; St Andrews 28 pts; St Martin's (Coll) 28 pts; Salford 35 pts inc 16 pts Highers; Sheffield (BA) H655, (BSc) 555 overall 24 pts; South Bank 24 pts; Southampton 30 pts, (Pop St) 28 pts; Staffordshire 26 pts; Swansea (BSc) 28 pts H 17 pts; Worcester (UC) 24 pts.

Irish offers: Aberdeen (Arts) BBBB, (Sci) BBCC; Aberystwyth BBBBC; Brighton (BSc) BBCC; Edge Hill (CHE) BBBB; Edinburgh ABBB; Keele BBBCC; Liverpool BBCCC; London (RH) BBBCC; London Guildhall CCCCC; Oxford Brookes CCCCC; Plymouth BCCCC; St Andrews BBBB; Sheffield BBBCC; South Bank CCC.

Scottish Qualifications: Aberdeen BBBB; Dundee BBBC; Edinburgh ABBBC–ABBB; Glasgow BBBB; St Andrews BBBB; Strathclyde BBBB **or** AABB.

Overseas applicants: Durham Interview essential. **Oxford Brookes** Orientation course prior to autumn and spring terms.

CHOOSING YOUR COURSE (See also **Ch.1**)

Subject information: Geography courses cover the human, physical, economic and social aspects of geography. Each institution offers its own particular emphasis. Check the prospectuses for all courses, with particular attention to the specialist options in the second and third years. For those with a geographical interest, courses in Development Studies, Geology, Environmental Studies, Estate Management and Surveying, Town and Country Planning and Urban Studies should also be considered.

Special features: Dundee The BSc course includes the study of two science subjects in years 1 and 2. **Glamorgan** Geographical Information Systems and Human Geography are offered as one degree course. **Greenwich** Sandwich course students are offered work placement in industry or commerce in year 3. **Hertfordshire** A broad degree offering both human and physical geography; also offered as a sandwich course. **Kingston** A range of options covering both human and physical geography include exchange arrangements in Europe and the USA. **Lancaster** Human and physical; geography and geographical techniques are taken by all students in year 1, with environmental themes developing in years 2 and 3. **Leicester** Supplementary subjects are offered such as archaeology, computer science, history and politics. **London (LSE)** The Geography course covers the environment, economy and society in year 1 and focuses on environmental themes in years 2 and 3. **Manchester Met** The course can include work experience with full-time placements in the UK, Western Europe or further afield in the summer term of year 2. **Wolverhampton** The BSc course includes topics in soil management, pollution and the alpine environment. *NOW CHECK PROSPECTUSES AND WEB SITES.*

Top universities and colleges (Teaching Quality) (see Ch.4): Aberdeen; Birmingham; Bristol; Cambridge; Canterbury Christ Church (UC); Cheltenham & Glos (CHE); Coventry; Dundee; Durham; East Anglia; Exeter; Glasgow; Lancaster; Leeds; Liverpool Hope (Coll); London (King's), (QM), (UCL); Manchester; Nottingham; Oxford; Oxford Brookes; Plymouth; Portsmouth; Reading; St Andrews; Sheffield; Southampton; Strathclyde; not all institutions assessed.

Top universities and colleges (Research) (see Ch.4): Aberystwyth; Birmingham; Bristol; Cambridge; Durham; East Anglia; Edinburgh; Exeter; Hull; Lancaster; Leeds; Liverpool; London (LSE), (QM), (RH), (UCL); Loughborough; Manchester; Newcastle; Nottingham; Oxford; Sheffield; Southampton; Swansea.

Study opportunities abroad: Aberdeen; Aberystwyth; Aston; Belfast (Queen's); Birmingham; Bristol; Brunel; Cardiff (Mar Geog); Cheltenham & Glos (CHE); Chester (Coll); Chichester (UC); Coventry; Dundee; Durham; East Anglia; Edinburgh; Exeter; Glasgow; Greenwich; Hull; Keele; Kingston; Lampeter; Lancaster; Leeds; Leicester; Liverpool; Liverpool Hope (Coll); Liverpool John Moores; London Guildhall; London (King's), (LSE), (QM), (UCL); Manchester; Middlesex; Nottingham; Oxford Brookes; Plymouth; Portsmouth; St Andrews; Salford; Sheffield; South Bank; Southampton; Staffordshire; Surrey Roehampton; Swansea; Ulster; Worcester (UC).

Work opportunities abroad: Aberystwyth; Aston; Cardiff; Chester (Coll); Coventry; Brunel; Leicester; London (RH); Plymouth; Worcester (UC).

ADMISSIONS INFORMATION

Number of applicants per place (approx): Aberystwyth 7; Anglia 10; Birmingham 12; Bristol 24; Bristol UWE 10; Brunel 5; Cambridge 2.5; Cambridge (Hom) 4; Cardiff 5; Central Lancashire 15; Cheltenham & Glos (CHE) 40; Chester (Coll) 10; Chichester (UC) 1; Coventry 12; De Montfort 7; Durham 8; Edinburgh (Geog Sci) 8; Edge Hill (CHE) 8; Exeter 10; Glamorgan 5; Greenwich 2; Huddersfield 22; Hull 10; Kent 15; Kingston 7; Lampeter 4; Lancaster 13; Leeds 12 average; Leicester (BA) 19, (BSc) 17; Liverpool (BA)

10, (BSc) 8; Liverpool John Moores 4; London (King's) 7, (LSE) 7, (QM) 5, (RH) 7, (SOAS) 8; Loughborough 17; Luton 4; Manchester 17; Middlesex 10; Newcastle 14, (Geog/Surv Map Sci) 6; Newman (CHE) 15; North London 4; Northampton (UC) 8; Northumbria 16; Nottingham 13; Oxford 2.6; Oxford Brookes (Cart) 9; Plymouth 10; Portsmouth (Geog) 5; St Martin's (Coll) 5, (Comb) 10, (QTS) 11; St Mary's (Coll) 4; Salford 3; Sheffield (BA) 13, (BSc) 10; South Bank 6; Southampton 17, (Pop St) 2; Staffordshire 10; Strathclyde 8; Surrey Roehampton 6; Swansea 8; Worcester (UC) 5.

Planning your UCAS personal statement (see Ch.4): Visits/field courses to any specific geographical region should be fully described. Study your own locality in detail and get in touch with the area Town and Country Planning Office to learn about any future developments. Read geographical magazines and describe any special interests you have – and why. **London (King's)** Awareness of world issues. **St Andrews** Reasons for choosing course and evidence of interest. Sport/extra-curricular activities. Posts of responsibility. **Swansea** (Topog Sci) Most applicants fail to state why they have chosen this course.

Selection interviews: Aberystwyth; Anglia (No); Bath Spa (UC) (No); Birmingham; Bristol; Bristol UWE; Brunel; Cambridge (W); Cambridge (Hom); Cardiff (No); Central Lancashire; Coventry; Dundee (No); Durham; East Anglia; Edge Hill (CHE); Exeter (No); Greenwich; Huddersfield; Hull (No); Kingston; Lampeter; Leeds (No); Leicester (No); Liverpool; Liverpool Hope (Coll) (No); Liverpool John Moores (No); London (King's), (LSE) (No), (QM), (RH), (SOAS), (UCL); London Guildhall; Loughborough; Manchester (No); Manchester Met; Middlesex; Newcastle (50%); Newman (CHE) (No); Northumbria; Nottingham (some); Nottingham Trent (No); Oxford (W); Oxford Brookes (No); Plymouth; Portsmouth (No); Ripon & York St John (Coll) (No); St Andrews (No); St Martin's (Coll) (No); Salford (No); South Bank; Southampton (No); Staffordshire (No); Strathclyde (No); Sunderland (No); Surrey Roehampton; Swansea; Warwick (BA QTS); Worcester (UC) (No).

Interview questions: Geography is a very broad subject and applicants can expect to be questioned on their syllabus and those aspects which they find of special interest. Some questions in the past have included: What fieldwork have you done? What are your views on ecology? What changes in the landscape have you noticed on the way to the interview? Explain in simple meteorological terms today's weather. Why are earthquakes almost unknown in Britain? What is the value of practical work in geography to primary school children? (BEd course). What do you enjoy about geography and why? Are there any articles of geographical importance in the news at present? Discuss the current economic situation in Britain and give your views. Questions on the third world, on world ocean currents and drainage and economic factors world-wide. Expect to comment on local geography and on geographical photographs and diagrams. **Oxford** No written tests at interview. Questions may be based on written work previously submitted.

Reasons for rejection (non-academic): Lack of awareness of the content of the course. Failure to attend interview. Poor general knowledge. Lack of geographical awareness. **Hull** (BSc) Usually insufficient science background.

GAP YEAR ADVICE

Birmingham Reading list available.

Institutions willing to defer entry after A-Levels: Aberystwyth; Birmingham; Bristol; Bristol UWE; Brunel; Central Lancashire; Cheltenham & Glos (CHE); Chester (Coll); Coventry; De Montfort; Durham (inform univ at interview); Edge Hill (CHE); Glamorgan; Kingston; Lampeter; Lancaster; Leeds (No); Leicester; Liverpool Hope (Coll); London (RH); London Guildhall; Manchester Met; Newcastle (Geog/Surv Map Sci: Yes); Newport (UWCN); North London; Northumbria; Nottingham (for 'improving' activities); Plymouth (No); Portsmouth; St Andrews; St Mary's (Coll); Salford; Sheffield Hallam; South Bank; Southampton; Staffordshire; Surrey Roehampton; Sussex; Swansea; Wolverhampton; Worcester (UC).

AFTER RESULTS ADVICE

Institutions which may accept the same points score after A-Levels: Aberystwyth; Anglia (No); Birmingham (No); Bristol UWE (No); Cardiff; Central Lancashire; Cheltenham & Glos (CHE); Chester (Coll); Chichester (UC); Coventry; Dundee (No); Durham (No); East Anglia (No); Edge Hill (CHE); Edinburgh; Huddersfield; Hull; Kingston; Lampeter; Leicester (varies); Liverpool; London (RH), (SOAS) (No); Loughborough; Manchester Met; Middlesex; Newcastle; Newman (CHE); North London; Northumbria; Nottingham (No); Oxford Brookes; Plymouth (Grade C in geog); Portsmouth; St Andrews (No); St Martin's (Coll); Salford; Sheffield; South Bank; Southampton; Staffordshire; Surrey Roehampton (No); Swansea; Wolverhampton; Worcester (UC).

Institutions which may accept lower grades/points score after A-Levels: Aberdeen; Aberystwyth (1 pt); Belfast (Queen's); Bristol; Cambridge (Hom); Durham (very few); Edinburgh; Edge Hill (CHE); Exeter; Glasgow; Hull; Huddersfield; Kingston; Lampeter; Leicester; Liverpool; London (RH), (SOAS); Loughborough; Luton; Manchester Met; Newcastle (Geog/Surv Map Sci); Newport (UWCN); Plymouth; Portsmouth; St Andrews; Salford; South Bank; Southampton; Staffordshire; Surrey Roehampton; Swansea; Wolverhampton; Worcester (UC).

Offers to applicants repeating A-Levels: Higher Bournemouth, Durham, Hull, Kingston, Leeds, London (Gold), Nottingham, St Andrews, Sussex (Geog/Lang); **Possibly higher** Aberystwyth, Edinburgh, Plymouth; **Same** Birmingham, Bristol, Coventry, Edge Hill (CHE), Huddersfield, Lampeter, Lancaster, Leeds (applicants consider which A-Levels to resit for the BSc course), Liverpool, London (RH), (SOAS), Loughborough, Manchester Met, Newcastle, Newport (UWCN), North London, Northumbria, Oxford Brookes, St Martin's (Coll), Salford, South Bank, Southampton, Staffordshire, Surrey Roehampton, Swansea, Ulster.

Probable vacancies from June 2001 and in Clearing (see Ch.4): A large number of universities are expected to have vacancies from June onwards although most of these will be for joint courses, many combined with less popular subjects. Several vacancies are likely in Cartography.

NEW GRADUATE DESTINATIONS AND EMPLOYMENT (1999 HESA) (see **Ch.4**)

In a survey of 3971 graduates, 2185 went into a wide range of full-time occupations, 1016 went on to further study and 161 were believed to be unemployed.

GEOLOGY/GEOLOGICAL SCIENCES (including **Earth Sciences**; see also **Engineering (Mining)** and **Geophysics**)

NB The information supplied by the universities and colleges this year varies considerably and the offers listed below should be used as a first source of reference only. Many institutions will accept combinations of Advanced (AL), Advanced Subsidiary (AS) and Vocational Advanced (VA) level qualifications to achieve the required points total, but applicants must check web sites and prospectuses for full details of all offers. Grades and points totals shown should be regarded as the minimum levels to be achieved, but offers may be adjusted downwards when results are known. The points totals shown to the left of the institutions are for ease of reference only. It must not be assumed that tariff points are always used by institutions or that they can be substituted for an offer in grades. The level of an offer is not necessarily indicative of the quality of a course. To calculate your offers see Chapter 4 and the inside fold of the back cover.

Special subject requirements/preferences: A-Level: Two to three subjects in science/mathematics usually required. **Oxford** Full A-Levels in mathematics, physics or chemistry expected with a second of these subjects and further mathematics, geology, geography, biology at A/AS-Levels. **GCSE:** English and mathematics required. **Anglia** Four grade As, four grade Bs. **Bristol** Majority of grades A and B. **Cambridge** Usually a majority of grade As.

360 pts **and above**
    Cambridge – Offers, mainly in grades, vary between colleges (Nat Sci; Geol Sci)
    Leeds – AAA (Geol N Am)
    Oxford – Offers vary between candidates (Earth Sci; Geol)
340 pts **East Anglia** – AAB (Geophys Sci)
320 pts **Durham** – ABB (Nat Sci (Earth Sci))
    Liverpool – 320 pts – ALs **or** ALs+ASs **or** VAs+/-ALs/ASs; (MSci Geol; Geol/Euro Lang)
310 pts **Southampton** – 310 pts 21u (inc 180 pts from 2ALs – subj reqs vary); (not gs) (Geol courses; Mar Geosci)
300 pts **St Andrews** – BBB (Geosci – Mgt; Geosci – Mgt Sci)
280 pts **Birmingham** – BBC–CCC (Geol; Res App Geol; Geol/Biol; Env Geosci)
    Bristol – BBC; (not gs) (Geol; Geol/Biol; Env Geosci; Geol/Arch)
    Cardiff – 280 pts approx (MSc Earth Sci)
    Durham – BBC (Env Geosci; Geol Sci; Geol; Geol/Geophys; Geophys)
    East Anglia – BBC **or** BB+bc; (not gs) (Env Earth Sci)
    Glasgow – BBC–CCC (Earth Sci; Env Biogeochem)
    Leeds – BBC (Geog/Geol)
    Liverpool – 280 pts – ALs **or** ALs+ASs **or** VAs+/-ALs/ASs; (Geol/Geophys; Geol/Geog; BSc Geol)
    London (RH) – 280 pts 18u – BBC–BCC **or** 2ALs+2ASs; (not gs) (Geol/Biol)
    Manchester – BBC (Geol/Biol)
    St Andrews – BBC (Env Biol/Geosci; Comp Sci – Geosci)
270 pts **Kingston** – 270 pts inc ALs or VAs with 1 subj from sci/maths/geog; interview; (Earth Sci courses; Geol courses)
260 pts **Birmingham** – BCC/AB (Geol/Geog)
    Birmingham – BCC (Geol/Arch)
    Cardiff – 260 pts approx (Geol; Env Geosci; Explor Geol)
    Durham – BCC (Earth Sci)
    Keele – BCC **or** equiv AS accepted; gs; (Geol courses)
    Leeds – BCC (Geol Sci; Env Geol)
    London (Imp) – 260 pts approx (Env Geol; Geol Sci; Geol; Petrol Geol)
    London (RH) – BCC (inc BC phys+maths) **or** BC+cc and/or gs; (Geol/Astrophys)
    London (UCL) – 260 pts **or** 3ALs+AS/VA; (Geol; Env Geosci; Earth/Space Sci; Planet Sci)
    Manchester – 260 pts approx (Geol; Geol/Geog)
    Reading – 260 pts approx (Env Geol)
    St Andrews – BCC (Geosci; Chem/Geosci)
240 pts **Aberystwyth** – 240–220 pts (Env Earth Sci)
    Bangor – CCC (Geol Ocean)
    Brunel – 240–200 pts 2x6u (inc C geog/geol/env sci) – ALs **or** ALs+ASs **or** VAs+/-ALs/ASs; (Env Geosci; Earth Sci)
    Edinburgh – CCC (Geol courses)
    Exeter – 240 pts 18u (inc 2ALs sci or AL+AS sci or AL geol) – CCC **or** CC+cc **or** VAs (contact univ); (not gs) (App Geol; Eng Geol/Geotech)
    Greenwich – 240 pts approx (MSci Geol)
    Hertfordshire – 240–200 pts 1x12u **or** 2x6u; gs; (Eng Geol)
    Leicester – 240 pts 18u – CCC **or** 2ALs+ASs **or** VAs+/-ALs/ASs; gs; (Geol; App Env Geol)
    Manchester – CCC (Earth Sci; Env Res Geol; Geochem; Geol)
    Oxford Brookes – CCC (Geol/Comp Sci; Geol/Bus Stats)
    Plymouth – 240 pts (Geol/Geog)
    Staffordshire – 240 pts (inc 2x6u); gs; (Geol courses)
220 pts **Aberdeen** – CCD/BC (Geol courses)
    Hertfordshire – 220–200 pts (Env Geol/Euro; Geol/Astro; Econ/Geol)
    Plymouth – 220 pts (Geol/Bus; Geol/Ocean Sci)

200 pts   **Derby** – 200 pts 12u – CCE **or** CC+e **or** VAs+/-ALs/ASs; gs; (MSci Geol)

           Huddersfield – 200 pts 12u (inc min AL sci eg. geog/geol/env sci) – ALs **or** ALs+ASs **or** VAs+/-ALs/ASs; (Earth Sci)

           Northampton (UC) – 200–160 pts (Earth Sci/Foss; Ecol/Foss)

           Portsmouth – 200 pts – ALs **or** ALs+ASs **or** VAs; gs; (Earth Sci; Geol; Geol Haz; Geol/Geog Sci; Eng Geol/Geol)

180 pts   **Cheltenham & Glos (CHE)** – 180–140 pts (Geol courses)

           Derby – 180–160 pts (App Env Earth Sci)

           Glamorgan – 180–160 pts – CC (inc sci/maths); (not gs) (Geol; App Earth Sci)

           Nottingham Trent – 180 pts (Geol Eng)

           Plymouth – 180 pts approx (Geol Comp; Earth Sci; Geol/Chem)

           Sunderland – 180 pts; gs; (Geol courses)

160 pts   **Exeter** – CC (Ind Geol)

           Liverpool John Moores – 160–120 pts (inc VA Sci) **or** 140–120 pts (from 2ALs inc geog/geol 80–60 pts) – ALs **or** ALs+ASs **or** VAs+/-ALs/ASs; (Earth Sci; Geol)

           Luton – 160–120 pts approx (Geol – Mod)

           Oxford Brookes – CC–DD (Geol Map Cart Sci; Geol/Trans Trav)

140 pts   **Derby** – 140 pts 12u – CD **or** DD+dd **or** VAs CD+/-ALs/ASs; gs; (Geol courses except under **200 pts**)

           Liverpool – 140 pts – ALs **or** ALs+ASs **or** VAs+/-ALs/ASs; (Fdn Earth Sci)

           Wolverhampton – 140 pts 12u – CD **or** VAs+/-ALs/ASs; gs; (App Env Geol; Ecol/Earth Sci)

120 pts   **Bath Spa (UC)** – DD (Rem Sens Geog Inf Sys/Geog)

           Paisley – DD (Geol courses)

 80 pts   **Staffordshire** – EE (Geol Fdn)

Diploma of Higher Education courses
 80 pts   London Guildhall; Oxford Brookes.

Higher National Diploma courses
100 pts   **and below**
           Exeter (Ind Geol); Luton (Geol Tech).

Alternative Offers:

EB offers: London (RH) 70%.

IB offers: Aberdeen 26 pts; Birmingham 30 pts; Brighton 26 pts; Bristol 28 pts; Brunel 26 pts; Cardiff 26 pts H 12 pts; Cheltenham & Glos (CHE) – 26 pts; Durham H555; East Anglia 33–29 pts; Exeter 30 pts; Kingston (Earth Sci) H555 13 pts in subsids inc maths 5; Liverpool H555 30 pts average; London (RH) 27 pts, (UCL) 30 pts; Northampton (UC) 24 pts inc 12 pts Highers; Oxford Brookes 26 pts; Plymouth 26 pts; Portsmouth 12 pts Highers; Southampton 28 pts; Staffordshire 26 pts.

Irish offers: Aberdeen BBCC/BCCCC; Edinburgh BBBBC; Leeds BBBCC; Liverpool BBCCC; London (RH) BBBCC.

Scottish Qualifications: Aberdeen BBBC; Edinburgh BBBB; Glasgow BBBB; Paisley BBC; St Andrews BBCC.

Overseas applicants: Leeds Solid maths and science background required.

CHOOSING YOUR COURSE (See also **Ch.1**)

Subject information: Topics in Geology courses include the physical and chemical constitution of the earth, exploration geophysics, oil and marine geology (oceanography) and seismic interpretation. Earth Sciences cover geology, environmental science, physical geography and can also include business studies and language modules. Civil and Mining Engineering, Soil Science and Environmental Science could also be considered as alternative courses. See also **Appendix 1**.

Special features: Aberystwyth The degree in Environmental Earth Studies covers Earth Science and Physical Geography. **Birmingham** Courses are also offered in Resource and Applied Geology (including Water Resource Management) and Environmental Geoscience (pollution and hazards). **East Anglia** The Geophysical Science course applies mathematics and physics to a range of natural phenomena such as floods, earthquakes and other weather systems. **Huddersfield** The course in Earth Science has optional supervised work experience. **Nottingham Trent** Geological Engineering has a common first year with Civil Engineering and Surveying courses. **Plymouth** The degrees in Applied and Environmental Geology and Geological Science follow the same course in years 1 and 2 after which different specialisms are chosen. **Staffordshire** There is a broad introduction in minerology, petrology and geographical map interpretation. Links with industry are encouraged in years 2 and 3. *NOW CHECK PROSPECTUSES AND WEB SITES.*

Top universities and colleges (Teaching Quality) (see Ch.4): Aberystwyth (Earth Sci); Birmingham; Cambridge; Cardiff (Earth Sci); Derby; Durham; Edinburgh; Glasgow; Kingston; Leeds; Liverpool; London (Imp), (RH), (UCL); Newcastle; Oxford; Plymouth; Reading; Southampton; not all institutions assessed.

Top universities and colleges (Research) (see Ch.4): (including Earth Sciences and Environmental Sciences) Bristol; Cambridge; Cardiff; Durham; Edinburgh; Leeds; Leicester; Liverpool; London (Imp), (RH), (UCL); Manchester; Newcastle; Oxford; Reading (Earth Sci).

Study opportunities abroad: Aberystwyth; Brunel; Cardiff; Cheltenham & Glos (CHE); Greenwich; London (RH); Southampton; Staffordshire; Surrey.

Work opportunities abroad: Aberystwyth; Bristol; Brunel; Cardiff; Cheltenham & Glos (CHE); Exeter; Greenwich; Hull; London (Imp), (RH); Plymouth; Portsmouth (Eng Geol/Geotech).

ADMISSIONS INFORMATION

Number of applicants per place (approx): Bangor 4; Birmingham 6; Bristol 8; Brunel 6; Cardiff 7; Cheltenham & Glos (CHE) 11; Derby 6; Durham 4; East Anglia 4; Edinburgh 5; Exeter 5; Greenwich 2; Hertfordshire 5; Kingston 19; (Earth Sci) 3; Leeds 8; Liverpool 5; London (Imp) 5, (RH) 5, (UCL) 6; Luton 4; Northampton (UC) 7; Oxford 1.2; Oxford Brookes 9; Plymouth 7; Portsmouth (Eng Geol/Geotech) 5, (Geol) 15; Southampton 5; Staffordshire 4.

Planning your UCAS personal statement (see Ch.4): Visits to any outstanding geological sites and field courses should be described in detail. Apart from geological formations, you should also be aware of how geology has affected humankind in specific areas in the architecture of the region and artefacts used. Evidence of social skills could be given. See also **Appendix 1**.

Selection interviews (see Ch.4): Birmingham; Brighton (No); Bristol (No); Brunel; Cambridge; Cardiff (No); Cheltenham & Glos (CHE); Derby; Durham; East Anglia; Edinburgh; Exeter; Greenwich; Kingston; Liverpool; London (RH); London Guildhall; Manchester; Oxford; Oxford Brookes; Paisley (No); Portsmouth (No); Southampton; Staffordshire (No); Sunderland; Swansea.

Interview questions (see Ch.4): A previous knowledge of the subject will be expected and applicants could be questioned on specimens of rocks and their origins. Past interviews have included: Questions on the field courses attended, and the geophysical methods of exploration in the detection of metals. How would you determine the age of this rock (sample shown)? Can you integrate a decay curve function and would it help you to determine the age of rocks? How many planes of crystallisation could this rock have? What causes a volcano? What is your local geology? **Oxford** (Earth Sci) Candidates may be asked to comment on specimens of a geological nature, based on previous knowledge of the subject.

Reasons for rejection (non-academic): Misconceptions about the course. **Exeter** Outright rejection uncommon but some applicants advised on other programmes.

GAP YEAR ADVICE

Cardiff and **Greenwich** Discuss your plans with the admissions tutor beforehand.

Institutions willing to defer entry after A-Levels: Birmingham; Bristol; Cheltenham & Glos (CHE); Exeter; Hertfordshire; Kingston; Leeds; London (RH), (UCL); Luton; Northampton (UC); Plymouth (Earth Sci); Portsmouth; Southampton.

AFTER RESULTS ADVICE

Institutions which may accept the same points score after A-Levels: Bristol; Cardiff; Cheltenham & Glos (CHE); Derby; Durham; Exeter; Hull (No); Kingston; Leeds; Liverpool; London (RH); London Guildhall (No); Northampton (UC); Plymouth; St Andrews (No); Southampton; Swansea.

Institutions which may accept lower grades/points score after A-Levels: Aberdeen; Birmingham; Cardiff; Cheltenham & Glos (CHE); Derby; Durham; Exeter; Keele; Leeds; Leicester; Liverpool; London (RH); Luton; Plymouth; Portsmouth; St Andrews; Southampton; Swansea.

Offers to applicants repeating A-Levels: Higher Bristol, St Andrews, Swansea; **Possibly higher** Derby, Portsmouth; **Same** Birmingham (BBC–CCC), Durham, East Anglia, Leeds, London (RH), Southampton.

Probable vacancies from June 2001 and in Clearing (see Ch.4): Most universities are likely to have vacancies in Earth Science and Geology. Competitive universities are expected to ask for 240–200 pts.

NEW GRADUATE DESTINATIONS AND EMPLOYMENT (1999 HESA) (see **Ch.4**)

Of 935 graduates surveyed, 464 went into full-time employment, with most geologists going into business, finance and retail work. Approximately 80 went into subject-related work, further study accounted for 285, and 51 were believed to be unemployed.

GEOPHYSICS/GEOPHYSICAL SCIENCES (see also
Geology/Geological Sciences and **Physics**)

NB The information supplied by the universities and colleges this year varies consider-ably and the offers listed below should be used as a first source of reference only. Many institutions will accept combinations of Advanced (AL), Advanced Subsidiary (AS) and Vocational Advanced (VA) level qualifications to achieve the required points total, but applicants must check web sites and prospectuses for full details of all offers. Grades and points totals shown should be regarded as the minimum levels to be achieved, but offers may be adjusted downwards when results are known. The points totals shown to the left of the institutions are for ease of reference only. It must not be assumed that tariff points are always used by institutions or that they can be substituted for an offer in grades. The level of an offer is not necessarily indicative of the quality of a course. To calculate your offers see Chapter 4 and the inside fold of the back cover.

Special subject requirements/preferences: A-Level: Mathematics and physics usually required.

360 pts	**and above**
	Leeds – AAA (Geophys Sci/N Am)
	Liverpool – 360–340 pts – ALs **or** ALs+ASs **or** VAs+/-ALs/ASs; (Geophys (Phys))
340 pts	**East Anglia** – AAB+interview (not gs) (Geophys/N Am)
320 pts	**East Anglia** – ABB; (not gs) (Geophys/Euro)
310 pts	**Southampton** – 310 pts 21u (inc 180 pts AL maths+phys); (not gs) (Geophys Sci)

300 pts   **Liverpool** – 300 pts – ALs **or** ALs+ASs **or** VAs+/-ALs/ASs; (Geophys/Lang)

280 pts   **Durham** – BBC (Geol/Geophys; Geophys; Geophys Sci)

         East Anglia – BBC **or** BB+bc (not gs) (Geophys Sci)

         London (UCL) – BBC–BCC **or** 3ALs+AS/VA; (Explor Geophys; Geophys; Env Geophys)

260 pts   **Edinburgh** – BCC/BB (Geophysics)

         Leeds – BCC/BB (Geophys Sci; Geophys Sci Comb Hons)

         Liverpool – 260–240 pts – ALs **or** ALs+ASs **or** VAs+/-ALs/ASs; (Geophys/Geol)

         St Andrews – BCC (Geoscience)

240 pts   **Lancaster** – CCC/AB (Geophys Sci)

         Leicester – CCC **or** 2ALs+2ASs **or** VAs (C ave)+/-ALs/ASs; gs; (Geophysics courses)

220 pts   **Aberdeen** – CCD (Geoscience)

Alternative Offers:

IB offers: East Anglia H555; Liverpool H555.

Scottish Qualifications: Aberdeen BBBC; Edinburgh ABBB; St Andrews BBCC.

CHOOSING YOUR COURSE (See also **Ch.1**)

> **Subject information:** Geophysics/Geophysical Scioences is a study of the techniques of physics and mathematics relating to earth systems which include meteorology, oceanography, climatic change, hydrology and sedimentology, the first two of which are degree courses in their own right. These could be considered as alternative courses together with Physical Geography, Earth Sciences, Geology, Applied Physics, Astronomy and Astrophysics. See also **Appendix 1**.

Special features: East Anglia Study of atmosphere, oceans and solid earth; wide range of specialist subjects. Good contacts with leading oil companies, the Meteorological Office, water authorities and environmental consultants. **Edinburgh** Very flexible course – years 1, 2 & 3 curricula compatible with Mathematics, Physics, Geology and Astronomy courses. **Leicester** Two thirds geology, one third physics. **Southampton** Core units in physics, maths and earth materials. Options cover astronomy, electronics and oceanography. *NOW CHECK PROSPECTUSES AND WEB SITES.*

Top universities and colleges (Teaching Quality) (see Ch.4): East Anglia; not all institutions assessed.

ADMISSIONS INFORMATION

Number of applicants per place (approx): East Anglia 7; Edinburgh 4; Lancaster 6; Liverpool 9; Southampton 9.

Planning your UCAS personal statement (see Ch.4): See **Geology/Geological Sciences** and **Physics**. See also **Appendix 1**.

Selection interviews (see Ch.4): Southampton.

Interview questions (see Ch.4): Why do you want to study Geophysics? Explain what you think a study of Geophysics will involve. What future career do you have in mind? What other careers could geophysicists consider?

GAP YEAR ADVICE

Institutions willing to defer entry after A-Levels: Lancaster; Leeds; Southampton.

AFTER RESULTS ADVICE

Institutions which may accept the same points score after A-Levels: Edinburgh; Lancaster; Liverpool; Southampton.

Institutions which may accept lower grades/points score after A-Levels: Lancaster; Southampton.

Offers to applicants repeating A-Levels: Same East Anglia, Southampton.

Probable vacancies from June 2001 and in Clearing (see Ch.4): Most universities can be contacted since vacancies are likely.

NEW GRADUATE DESTINATIONS AND EMPLOYMENT (1999 HESA) (see **Ch.4**)

See **Geology/Geological Sciences**.

GERMAN (see also **European Studies** and **Modern Languages**)

NB The information supplied by the universities and colleges this year varies consider-ably and the offers listed below should be used as a first source of reference only. Many institutions will accept combinations of Advanced (AL), Advanced Subsidiary (AS) and Vocational Advanced (VA) level qualifications to achieve the required points total, but applicants must check web sites and prospectuses for full details of all offers. Grades and points totals shown should be regarded as the minimum levels to be achieved, but offers may be adjusted downwards when results are known. The points totals shown to the left of the institutions are for ease of reference only. It must not be assumed that tariff points are always used by institutions or that they can be substituted for an offer in grades. The level of an offer is not necessarily indicative of the quality of a course. To calculate your offers see Chapter 4 and the inside fold of the back cover.

Special subject requirements/preferences: A-Level: German at A-Level usually the highest grade in the offers below. **Oxford** Full A-Levels expected. **GCSE: Aberdeen, Dundee, Edinburgh, Glasgow, St Andrews** English, mathematics or science and a foreign language. **Birmingham** German grade A–B. **London (Gold)** Three subjects at grade A–B. **Portsmouth** Three grade As, three grade Bs. Other universities require English and a foreign language.

360 pts **and above**
  Cambridge – Offers, mainly in grades, vary between colleges (Modn Lang)
  Oxford – Offers vary between candidates (Modn Lang)
350 pts **Southampton** – 350 pts 21u (inc 200 pts 2ALs inc C Ger or VAs (check with univ)); (German courses)
340 pts **Bath** – AAB (Ger/Law; Ger St/Mus)
  Birmingham – AAB (Law/Ger; Ger/Mus)
  Bristol – AAB–BBB (Pol/Ger; Ger/Span; Ger/Port; Ger/Russ; Ger/Ital)
  Edinburgh – AAB (Ger/Law)
  Edinburgh – AAB–BBB (German)
  London (King's) – AAB+AS **or** AA+abb (or equiv) (inc A mus, B Ger); VAs considered; (Ger/Mus)
  Manchester – AAB (MML Ger/Span; Ger/Ital)
  Nottingham – AAB (Econ/Ger)
  St Andrews – AAB–ABB (Int Rel/Ger; Psy/Ger; Phil/Ger)
  Sheffield – AAB (Law/Ger)
320 pts **Belfast (Queen's)** – ABB (Acc/Ger; Mgt/Ger)
  Bristol – ABB/AB (Ger/Law; Ger/Fr)
  Cardiff – ABB (Cult Crit/Ger; Engl Lit/Ger)
  Durham – ABB (Hist/Ger)
  Glasgow – ABB (Law/Ger)
  Lancaster – ABB (Euro Mgt/Ger)
  London (King's) – ABB+AS **or** AB+bbb (or equiv) (inc A Ger, B hist) **or** VA6u+ALs/ASs; (Ger/l list)
  London (RH) – ABB (Econ/Ger; Engl/Ger; Ger/Jap St; Ger/Mgt)

London (UCL) – ABB **or** 3ALs+AS/VA; (Engl/Ger)
Nottingham – ABB–ACC (Law/Ger; Fr/Ger; Ger/Mgt St)
St Andrews – ABB (Engl/Ger; Ger/Mgt; Ger/Psy)
York – 18u – BBC+c **or** BB+ccc; gs; (Ger/Ling; Ger/Fr)

300 pts **Aston** – 18u – BBB–BBC **or** ALs+ASs **or** VAs+/-ALs/ASs; gs; (Int Bus/Ger)
Bath – BBB (Ger courses except under **340/280 pts**)
Belfast (Queen's) – BBB (Fin Ger)
Birmingham – BBB/AB (Ger St; Ger/Bus St; Econ/Ger; Ger St/Hist; Ger
    St/Phil; Ger St/Hisp St; Money Bank Fin/Ger)
Bristol – BBB(B Ger); (not gs) (Ger; Ger/Ital/Port/Russ/Span)
Bristol UWE – 300–280 pts (Ger/Bus Sys; Ger/Euro St; Ger/Law; Euro St EFL
    Ger; Euro St Fr Ger; Euro St Ger Span)
Brunel – BBB–BCC (German courses)
Durham – 300 pts approx (German)
East Anglia – ABC–BBB (Ger/Interp Transl)
Edinburgh – BBB (Celtic/Ger; Ger/Ling)
Glasgow – BBB–BBC (Ger courses except under **320 pts**)
Hull – BBB (Ger Lang Law/Law)
Kingston – BBB (Ger St/Law)
Leeds – BBB (Comp/Ger; Stats/Ger; Engl/Ger; Ger/Span)
London (King's) – BBB+AS **or** BB+bbb (or equiv) (inc B Ger); VAs considered
    inc B Ger; (Ger/Phil)
London (QM) – BBB (Law/Ger)
London (RH) – ABC–BBB(B Ger); (not gs) (Ital/Ger)
London (RH) – BBB (German courses except under **320 pts**)
Manchester – BBB/BB (German courses except under **340/280 pts**)
Newcastle – ABC–BBB (Ger Comb St)
Reading – 300 pts (Ger Inform)
St Andrews – BBB (Ger/Bib St; Ger/Art Hist)
Sheffield – 300 pts/BBB–BBC (German courses except under **340/280 pts**)
Southampton – BBB (Acc/Ger; Econ/Ger; Mgt Sci/Ger)
Sunderland – 300–260 pts approx (Ger/Media St)
Surrey – 300 pts (Ger/Law)
UMIST – BBB–CCC (Civ Eng/Ger)
Warwick – BBB (Ger Bus St)

280 pts **Aberystwyth** – BBC (Law with Ger)
Aberystwyth – 280–220 pts (German courses except **above** and under **240
    pts**)
Bath – BBC (Ger/Int St)
Belfast (Queen's) – 280 pts (Econ/Ger)
Bristol – BBC/BB (Ger/Phil; Ger/Russ; Ger; Ger/Hist Art)
Cardiff – BBC–BCC/AB–BB (German courses except under **320 pts**)
East Anglia – 280 pts – BBC (Ger St 3 yrs)
Exeter – 280 pts 18u (inc AL lang) – BBC **or** BB+cc **or** BC+bb **or** VAs (contact
    univ); gs; (Ger; Ger/Ital/Span)
Heriot-Watt – BBC (inc BB langs) (Ger/Interp/Transl courses)
Kent – 280–260 pts approx (German joint courses)
Lancaster – BBC–BCC (German courses except under **240 pts**)
Leeds – BBC–BCC (German courses except under **300 pts**)
Liverpool – 280 pts; ALs **or** ALs+ASs **or** VAs+/-ALs/ASs; (Ger/Hisp St)
London (King's) – BBC+AS **or** BB+bbc (or equiv) (inc B Ger+Span for
    Ger/Hisp St course; VAs considered; (Ger/Class St/Hisp
    St/Gk/Port/Engl/Film St/Ling)
London (QM) – 280 pts approx (Ger/Drama)
London (UCL) – BBC **or** 3ALs+AS/VA; (German; Ger/Hist; Ger/Ital; Ger/Scand
    St; Ger/Russ)
Manchester – BBC (Ger St)
Newcastle – BBC–BCC (German courses except under **300 pts**)

Nottingham – BBC–BCC (German courses except under **340/320 pts**)
Oxford Brookes – BBC–DDD/CD offer varies with 2nd subject (German courses)
Plymouth – BBC–BCC (Law/Ger; Psy/Ger)
Reading – BBC–BCC (German courses except under **300 pts**)
St Andrews – BBC (Ger/Maths; Ger/Russ; Ger/Comp Sci)
Sheffield – BBC (Ger/Mus; Ger/Hisp St; Ger/Pol St)
Surrey – BBC (Ger/Comp)
Swansea – 280 pts 18u – BBC–BCC **or** ALs+ASs **or** VAs+/-ALs/ASs; (German courses)
Warwick – BBC–BCC (Engl Ger Lit)

260 pts   **Aston** – 260 pts 18u – 3ALs **or** ALs+ASs **or** VAs+/-ALs/ASs; gs; (German courses except under **300 pts**)
Bangor – 260 pts – ALs **or** VAs (enquire); gs; (Triple Lang courses from Ger/Fr/Ital/Span)
Belfast (Queen's) – BCC (German courses except under **320/300/280 pts**)
Birmingham – BCC (Ger St)
Bradford – 260 pts 12u (inc AL lang); gs; (Ger; Ger/Span; Fr/Ger)
Coventry – 260 pts (Ger Law/Ger)
Dundee – BCC–CCC (Hist/Ger; Geog/Ger; Am St/Ger)
Durham – BCC (Ger/Euro St)
East Anglia – 260 pts – BCC (Ger St 4 yrs)
Exeter – 260 pts 18u (inc AL lang) – BCC **or** BC+cc **or** BB+dd **or** VAs (contact univ); gs; (Ger/Russ)
Heriot-Watt – BCC (Acc/Ger)
Hull – BCC–CCC (Ger/Scand St; Ger/Span; Ger/Dutch St)
Keele – BCC/BB–BC **or** equiv AS accepted; gs; (German courses)
Kent – 260–220 pts approx (German)
Liverpool – 260 pts – ALs **or** ALs+ASs **or** VAs+/-ALs/ASs; (German)
London (King's) – BCC+AS **or** BB+bcc (or equiv) (inc B Ger); VAs considered inc B Ger; (German; Ger/App Comp)
London (QM) – 260–240 pts approx (Ger courses except under **300/280 pts**)
London (UCL) – BCC **or** 3ALs+AS/VA; (Ger/Jew St)
Manchester Met – BCC–CCC (Bus Euro – Ger)
Plymouth – 260 pts (Law/Ger)
Portsmouth – 260 pts (Inf Tech/Ger; Ger Fr St)
Salford – BCC ave (German courses)
Stirling – BCC (Ger Lang/Acc)
Strathclyde – BCC (German)
Surrey – 260 pts 18u – ALs **or** ALs+ASs **or** VAs+A (B Ger); gs; (Ger/Econ/Int Bus; Ger/Euro St; Ger/Law)
Sussex – BCC (German courses)
UMIST – 260 pts (Ger Lang St)
Warwick – 260 pts approx (Ger St; Ger St/Ital; Ger/Fr; Ger/Int St)

240 pts   **Aberdeen** – CCC (German courses)
Aberystwyth – CCC (Cymraeg gydag Almaeneg)
Bangor – 240 pts – ALs **or** VAs (enquire); gs; (German joint courses)
Bradford – 240 pts 12u; gs; (Hist/Ger; Pol/Ger)
Dundee – CCC (Fin Econ/Ger)
Hull – CCC/BCD (Ger/Chem)
Lancaster – CCC (Ger St)
Leicester – BCD/BC (B German) (Ger; Ger with Fr/Ital/Span)
Loughborough – 240 pts 18u – 2ALs+AL/2ASs; (Ger/Pol)
Nottingham Trent – 240 pts (Ger/Euro Bus)
Portsmouth – 240 pts – ALs **or** ALs+ASs **or** VAs; gs; (German courses except under **260/220 pts**)
Robert Gordon – CCC (Euro Bus Admin/Ger)

Stirling – CCC (German courses except under **260 pts**)
Ulster – CCC (German Hum)
220 pts **Bangor** – 220 pts – ALs **or** VAs (enquire); gs; (Ger/Wmns St)
Cardiff (UWI) – 220 pts (Ger/Tour)
Central England – 220–200 pts approx (Bus/Ger; Mark/Ger; Int Bus/Ger)
Central Lancashire – 220 pts 12u; GCSE german; gs; (Ger/Mark)
Coventry – 220 pts approx (Geog/Ger)
De Montfort – CCD (Ger/Psy)
Greenwich – 220 pts approx (Law/Ger; Archit Ger)
Heriot-Watt – CCD (Chem/Ger)
Hertfordshire – 220–200 pts (German courses)
Huddersfield – 220 pts (German courses)
Liverpool John Moores – 220–200 pts approx (German courses)
Manchester Met – CCD/CD (Hum/Soc Sci Ger)
Middlesex – 220–180 pts approx (German courses)
Nottingham Trent – 220–180 pts approx (German courses except under **240 pts**)
Portsmouth – 220 pts approx (Ger St)
Sheffield Hallam – CCD (Int Bus/Ger)
200 pts **Coventry** – 200 pts approx (German courses except under **220 pts**)
Dundee – 200 pts approx (Phys/Ger)
European (Bus Sch) – 200–180 pts approx (German courses)
Greenwich – 200 pts approx (Arts Mgt/Ger; Bus/Ger)
North London – 200–180 pts (German courses)
Northampton (UC) – 200–160 pts approx (German courses)
Northumbria – 200 pts (Euro St/Ger)
Plymouth – 200 pts approx (German courses except under **280/260 pts**)
St Martin's (Coll) – BDE–CDE (German courses)
Staffordshire – 200 pts – ALs (inc CC) **or** CC+AS(40 pts) **or** VA CC+AS(40 pts); gs; (German courses except under **180 pts**)
Teesside – 200–160 pts approx (German courses)
180 pts **Buckingham** – 180 pts approx (German courses)
Buckinghamshire Chilterns (UC) – 180–140 pts approx (Euro Bus Ger; Ger/Law; Hum Res Mgt/Ger)
Chester (Coll) – 180 pts – ALs (160 pts inc C)+AS **or** VAs (160 pts inc C)+AS; AS(20–40 pts); gs; (German courses)
De Montfort (Leicester) – 180 pts – ALs (inc Ger pref); (not gs) (German)
Doncaster (Coll) – 180 pts (Ger/Bus St)
East London – 180 pts approx (German courses)
Glamorgan – 180 pts approx (German courses)
Kingston – 180 pts 2x6u (inc 80 pts AL Ger); gs; (German)
Kingston – 180 pts approx (Ger/Pol; Ger/Hist; Ger/Engl)
Manchester Met – BC (inc B lang) (Modn Lang Ger)
Staffordshire – BC (Ger/Journal)
Sunderland – 180–140 pts (German courses except under **300 pts**)
Wolverhampton – 180 pts approx; gs; (Ger Comb)
160 pts **Anglia** – 160 pts 12u (inc C lang) – ALs **or** ALs+ASs; gs; (German courses)
Canterbury Christ Church (CHE) – CC (Ger/Bus St)
Derby – 160 pts approx (German)
London Guildhall – CC–CD (German courses)
Luton – 160–120 pts approx (Ger Mod)
Northumbria – CC–CD (German courses except under **200 pts**)
Southampton (Inst) – 160 pts (Ger/Bus)
Westminster – CC (German courses)
140 pts **Derby** – 140 pts 12u – CD **or** DE+ee **or** VAs CD+/-ALs/ASs; (German Comb)
Durham – CD (Euro St/Ger; Urb St/Ger)

Leeds Met – (contact university)

Diploma of Higher Education courses
80 pts   London Guildhall; Oxford Brookes.

Higher National Diploma courses (with Business Studies)
100 pts   and below
Loughborough (CT); Northumbria; Norwich City (Coll); Salford; Swansea (IHE).

Alternative Offers:

IB offers: Aberdeen 30 pts; Aston 31 pts; Birmingham 33 pts; Bradford 24 pts; Bristol 26 pts; Central Lancashire 24 pts; Durham H555; East Anglia 29 pts; Exeter 31–30 pts; Heriot-Watt 34 pts; Kent 30–28 pts; Lancaster 30–28 pts; Leicester 30–28 pts; London (QM) 30–28 pts, (RH) 30–28 pts, (UCL) 30 pts; Oxford Brookes 27 pts; Reading 30–29 pts; St Andrews 30 pts; Staffordshire 26 pts; Stirling 31 pts; Surrey 28 pts H5 German; Swansea 30–28 pts H645; UMIST 30 pts; Warwick 32–29 pts; York 30 pts.

Irish offers: Aberdeen BBBB; Keele BBBCC; Liverpool BBBB; London (RH) BBBCC; St Andrews BBBB; Surrey BBBCC; Warwick ABBBB; York BBBC.

Scottish Qualifications: Aberdeen BBBB; Edinburgh AAAAB–BBBB; Glasgow AAAAB–BBBB; Heriot-Watt AABB inc AA in languages + interview; Robert Gordon BBBC–BBCC; St Andrews BBBB; Stirling BBBB–BBBC; Strathclyde BBBB.

CHOOSING YOUR COURSE (See also **Ch.1**)

Subject information: Language, literature, practical language skills or a broader study of Germany and its culture (European Studies) are alternative study approaches. See also **Appendix 1** under **Modern Languages**.

Special features: Bangor Dutch for beginners is offered as an option in years 2 and 4. **Birmingham** One of the largest departments in the country. **Bristol** A subsidiary subject is taken in the first two years. **Bradford** Emphasis on interpreting and translating options in politics, economics, literature. Dutch with *ab initio* Russian or Spanish. **Cardiff** Course decisions finalised at end of first year. Options include emphasis on present-day language. **Hull** Practical language course including commercial German. **Leeds** Study of main features of German political, social and economic life. **Leicester** Balance between language, literature and society. All students take a supplementary subject for two years. **London (QM)** Students also take a subsidiary subject, for example, English, French, Latin, Russian, Spanish, history, geography, economics or politics. **Newcastle** Wide range of final year German options including business German. **Nottingham** Second language possible through three years. **Sheffield** Special options are available in Dutch and Swedish. **Surrey** German plus a subsidiary language plus a combined subject. Focus on language in its socio-cultural context. Work placements. *NOW CHECK PROSPECTUSES AND WEB SITES.*

Top universities and colleges (Teaching Quality) (see Ch.4): Aberdeen; Belfast (Queen's); De Montfort; Derby; Durham; Exeter; Glasgow; Heriot-Watt; Leeds; London (QM), (UCL); Newcastle; Northumbria; Nottingham; Oxford; Portsmouth; St Andrews; Staffordshire; Strathclyde; Sunderland; Swansea; Warwick; not all institutions assessed.

Top universities and colleges (Research) (see Ch.4): Birmingham; Cambridge; Edinburgh; Exeter; Lancaster; Leicester; Liverpool; London (King's), (QM), (UCL); Manchester; Nottingham; Oxford; St Andrews; Sheffield; Southampton; Sussex; Swansea; Warwick.

Study opportunities abroad: Institutions offering four-year courses usually arrange study placements abroad for students.

Work opportunities abroad: Aston; Birmingham; Bradford; Cardiff; Leeds; Reading; Surrey; Warwick.

ADMISSIONS INFORMATION

Number of applicants per place (approx): Aston 4; Bangor 6; Birmingham 6; Bradford 6; Bristol 5; Cardiff 6; Central Lancashire 2; Durham 4; East Anglia 4; Exeter 4; Heriot-Watt 10; Hull 12; Kent 10; Lancaster 7; Leeds 6; Leicester 4, (Ger/Pol) 4; London (QM) 6, (RH) 5, (UCL) 4; Manchester 6; Middlesex 2; Newcastle 6; Nottingham 14; Oxford Brookes 4; Portsmouth 8; Salford 5; Staffordshire 5; Stirling 6; Surrey 3; Swansea 5; UMIST 5; Warwick (Ger/Bus) 16, (Ger) 8; York 6.

Planning your UCAS personal statement (see Ch.4): Describe visits to Germany or a German-speaking country and the particular cultural and geographical features of the region. Contact with pen friends and language experience should also be mentioned. Bilingual experience. Read German newspapers and magazines and keep up-to-date with national news. **Nottingham** We are looking for a high degree of competence in using and understanding German; a genuine determination to develop skills in linguistic comprehension and analysis; a love of literature and an imaginative approach to it and a keen interest in German affairs. **Portsmouth** Experience of German-speaking countries not necessary. **St Andrews** Evidence of interest and reasons for choosing the course. Information on careers *Using Languages* can be obtained from the Schools Liaison Section, Room 707, Civil Service Commission, Alencon Link, Basingstoke, Hants RG21 1JB.

Selection interviews (see Ch.4): Bangor; Birmingham (short conversation in German); Bradford; Bristol (No); Cambridge; Cardiff (No); Durham; East Anglia; Edinburgh (No); Exeter; Heriot-Watt; Huddersfield; Hull; Kingston; Leeds (No); Leicester (No); Liverpool; Liverpool John Moores (T); London (RH), (UCL); Manchester; Middlesex (No); Newcastle; Oxford (W) (T); Oxford Brookes (No); Portsmouth (some) (W) (T); St Andrews (No); Sheffield; Southampton; Staffordshire (No); Surrey (always); Sussex; Swansea; UMIST; York (No).

Interview questions (see Ch.4): Questions asked on A-level syllabus. Part of the interview may be in German. What foreign newspapers and/or magazines do you read? Questions on German current affairs, particularly politics and re-unification problems, books read outside the course, etc. **Aston** Audio-visual test. **Liverpool John Moores** Written and oral tests.

Reasons for rejection (non-academic): Unstable personality. Poor motivation. Insufficient commitment. Unrealistic expectations.

GAP YEAR ADVICE

Most institutions will accept a gap year and prefer students to spend some time in a German-speaking country.

Institutions willing to defer entry after A-Levels: Aberystwyth; Aston; Bradford; Bristol; Bristol UWE; Central Lancashire; Heriot-Watt; Lancaster; Leeds; Leicester; London (RH); Luton; Newcastle; North London; Nottingham (encouraged, if a substantial period will be spent in a German-speaking country); St Andrews; Staffordshire; Surrey; Swansea; UMIST; Warwick; York.

AFTER RESULTS ADVICE

Institutions which may accept the same points score after A-Levels: Aberystwyth; Aston; Bangor; Birmingham; Bradford; Bristol (No); Bristol UWE; Dundee (No); Durham; East Anglia; Exeter; Heriot-Watt; Huddersfield; Kent (No); Kingston; Lancaster; Leicester; London (RH) (No); London Guildhall (No); Manchester; Middlesex; Newcastle; Nottingham (No); Oxford Brookes; Reading; Salford; Southampton (No); Staffordshire; Stirling (No); Surrey (incl grade B German); Swansea; UMIST; Warwick (No); York (grade B in German).

Institutions which may accept lower grades/points score after A-Levels: Aberystwyth; Aston; Birmingham; Bristol UWE; Durham; Exeter; Glasgow; Heriot-Watt; Hull; Kent; Leeds; Leicester; London (RH); St Andrews; Staffordshire; Surrey; Swansea; UMIST; Warwick; York.

Offers to applicants repeating A-Levels: Higher Birmingham, Leeds, Oxford Brookes, Warwick; **Same** Aston, Bradford, Durham, East Anglia, London (RH), Newcastle (not always), Nottingham, Surrey, Swansea, Ulster, York.

Probable vacancies from June 2001 and in Clearing (see Ch.4): German is one of the less popular language subjects and many vacancies are likely. Many universities declared vacancies in Clearing last year.

NEW GRADUATE DESTINATIONS AND EMPLOYMENT (1999 HESA) (see **Ch.4**)

In a survey of 306 graduates, 181 entered full-time employment in a range of occupations, mainly in business and finance; 60 went on to further study and eight were believed to be unemployed.

GOVERNMENT (see also **Politics**)

NB The information supplied by the universities and colleges this year varies considerably and the offers listed below should be used as a first source of reference only. Many institutions will accept combinations of Advanced (AL), Advanced Subsidiary (AS) and Vocational Advanced (VA) level qualifications to achieve the required points total, but applicants must check web sites and prospectuses for full details of all offers. Grades and points totals shown should be regarded as the minimum levels to be achieved, but offers may be adjusted downwards when results are known. The points totals shown to the left of the institutions are for ease of reference only. It must not be assumed that tariff points are always used by institutions or that they can be substituted for an offer in grades. The level of an offer is not necessarily indicative of the quality of a course. To calculate your offers see Chapter 4 and the inside fold of the back cover.

Special subject requirements/preferences: GCSE: Mathematics usually required. **London (LSE)** Grade A*, A or Bs, mathematics grade B or better.

320 pts	**London (LSE)** – ABB (Gov; Gov/Econ; Gov/Hist)
	Manchester – ABB (Gov/Law)
300 pts	**London (LSE)** – BBB (Soc Pol/Gov)
	Manchester – BBB–BBC (Gov)
280 pts	**Newcastle** – BBC/AB–BB (Gov EU St)
	Ulster – BBC (Gov/Law)
180 pts	**Central Lancashire** – 180 pts approx (Gov/Pol)

Alternative Offers:

IB offers: London (LSE) 38 pts; Newcastle 30 pts.

CHOOSING YOUR COURSE (See also **Ch.1**)

> **Subject information:** The history of political thought, analysis and institutions covering major foreign countries and also British politics and government will be covered on government courses. Other courses which could be considered are Development Studies, Economics, Economic History, International Relations, History, Public Administration, Politics and Public and Social Policy.

Special features: Newcastle Language element essential from French, German, Spanish or Portuguese. Options in European law, economics and agricultural policy. Year 3 abroad. *NOW CHECK PROSPECTUSES AND WEB SITES.*

Top universities and colleges (Research) (see Ch.4): See under **Politics**.

Study opportunities abroad: Newcastle.

ADMISSIONS INFORMATION

Number of applicants per place (approx): Central England 9; London (LSE) (Gov) 14, (Gov/Econ) 10, (Gov/Hist) 2; Newcastle 9.

Planning your UCAS personal statement (see Ch.4): Study the workings of government in the UK and abroad. Describe visits to the House of Commons/Lords and the debates taking place. Extend your knowledge to local affairs. Attend council meetings at county, district – even village level. Describe these visits and the agendas. Know your local area and the developments planned and taking place – and any objections by the public.

Selection interviews (see Ch.4): London (LSE) (some).

Interview questions (see Ch.4): Questions are likely to be asked on your study of this subject at A-Level and your general knowledge could be tested on current affairs. Courses in this subject vary and you could expect questions related to your chosen university course.

GAP YEAR ADVICE

Institutions willing to defer entry after A-Levels: Newcastle.

AFTER RESULTS ADVICE

Offers to applicants repeating A-Levels: Same Newcastle.

Probable vacancies from June 2001 and in Clearing (see Ch.4): See **Politics**.

NEW GRADUATE DESTINATIONS AND EMPLOYMENT (1999 HESA) (see **Ch.4**)

See under **Politics**.

GREEK (see also **Classical Studies/Classical Civilisation** and **Classics**)

NB The information supplied by the universities and colleges this year varies considerably and the offers listed below should be used as a first source of reference only. Many institutions will accept combinations of Advanced (AL), Advanced Subsidiary (AS) and Vocational Advanced (VA) level qualifications to achieve the required points total, but applicants must check web sites and prospectuses for full details of all offers. Grades and points totals shown should be regarded as the minimum levels to be achieved, but offers may be adjusted downwards when results are known. The points totals shown to the left of the institutions are for ease of reference only. It must not be assumed that tariff points are always used by institutions or that they can be substituted for an offer in grades. The level of an offer is not necessarily indicative of the quality of a course. To calculate your offers see Chapter 4 and the inside fold of the back cover.

Special subject requirements/preferences: A-Level: Edinburgh A-Level foreign language. **Leeds, London (UCL), Newcastle** Greek. Courses requiring A-Level Greek = (G) or Latin = (L). **GCSE:** Mathematics usually required. **Edinburgh, Glasgow, St Andrews** English, mathematics or science and a foreign language. **Lampeter** Five to six subjects at grade A or B. **London (King's)** English, history, foreign language. **London (RH)** Good grade in Greek. **Oxford, Cambridge** Mostly grade As/Bs. **Swansea** Five A* or A, five Bs.

360 pts and above
        Cambridge – Offers, mainly in grades, vary between colleges (L or G) (Classics)
        Oxford – Offers vary between candidates (L or G) (Classics)
320 pts **Leeds** – ABB (Engl – Gk Civ)
300 pts **Edinburgh** – BBB (Greek courses)
        London (King's) – BBB+AS **or** BB+bbb (or equiv) (inc AL/AS anc Gk); VAs considered; (Gk/Phil)
        Newcastle – ABC–BBB (Gk (New Testmt))

280 pts **Birmingham** – BBC (Modn Gk St courses)
Bristol – BBC–BCC (inc AL lang); (not gs) (Gk/Phil)
Glasgow – BBC (Greek courses)
Leeds – BBC (Gk Civ/Gk)
London (King's) – BBC+AS **or** BB+bbc (or equiv) (inc B Engl+anc Gk for Gk/Engl course); VAs considered; (Gk/Engl; Modn Gk/Port)
London (RH) – BBC/BB (G) (Greek)
London (UCL) – BBC (G) **or** 3ALs+AS/VA; (Gk/Lat)
Manchester – BBC (Gk/Arch)
Nottingham – BBC–BCC (Class (Gk/Lat))
St Andrews – BBC (Greek)
Swansea – 280 pts 18u – BBC–BCC/BB(G some courses) **or** ALs+ASs **or** VAs+/-ALs/ASs; (Greek courses)
260 pts **Belfast (Queen's)** – BCC (Greek courses)
Exeter – 260 pts 18u (inc AL lang or GCSE Ital): BCC **or** BC+cc **or** BB+dd **or** VAs (contact univ); gs; (Gk/Rom St/Ital)
London (King's) – BCC+AS **or** BC+cc (or equiv); VAs considered; (Modn Gk St; Modn Gk/App Comp; Modn Gk/Engl; Modn Gk/Ling)
Manchester – BCC (G) (Greek; Gk/Engl
Newcastle – BCC/260 pts (Greek (with Latin))
Reading – BCC (Gk/Engl Lit; Gk/Phil)
240 pts **Lampeter** – 240–220 pts approx (Greek Joint Hons)

Alternative Offers:

IB offers: Bristol 32 pts; Exeter 30 pts; Lampeter 28 pts; St Andrews 28 pts; Swansea 28 pts.

Irish offers: St Andrews BBBB.

Scottish Qualifications: Aberdeen BBBB; Edinburgh BBBB; Glasgow BBBB; St Andrews BBBB.

CHOOSING YOUR COURSE (See also **Ch.1**)

> **Subject information:** Courses are offered in Ancient and Modern Greek covering the language and literature from ancient times to present day. Archaeology, Ancient History, Classical Civilisation and Classical Studies courses could also be considered.

Special features: Durham, **Edinburgh** and **Leeds** Greek for beginners. **Leeds** Subsidiary subject in first year. **London (RH)** Options include art and archaeology, philosophy and history. **Swansea** Possibility of deferring decisions on some courses to second year. Departmental travel grants. *NOW CHECK PROSPECTUSES AND WEB SITES.*

Top universities and colleges (Research) (see Ch.4): See **Classics**.

Study opportunities abroad: Birmingham; Leeds; London (RH); Swansea.

ADMISSIONS INFORMATION

Number of applicants per place (approx): Birmingham 10; Bristol 5, (Gk/Phil) 10; Lampeter 1; Leeds 2; Manchester 4; Newcastle 20; Swansea 7.

Planning your UCAS personal statement (see Ch.4): See **Classical Studies/Classical Civilisation**.

Selection interviews (see Ch.4): Birmingham; Edinburgh (No); Exeter; Lampeter; London (RH); Manchester; Newcastle; St Andrews (No); Swansea.

Interview questions (see Ch.4): Questions asked on A-level syllabus. Why do you want to study Greek? What aspects of this course interest you? (Questions will develop from answers.)

Reasons for rejection (non-academic): Poor language ability.

GAP YEAR ADVICE

Institutions willing to defer entry after A-Levels: Lampeter; Leeds; St Andrews; Swansea.

AFTER RESULTS ADVICE

Institutions which may accept the same points score after A-Levels: Birmingham; Leeds (No); London (RH); Manchester; Newcastle (flexible); St Andrews (No); Swansea.

Institutions which may accept lower grades/points score after A-Levels: Exeter; St Andrews.

Offers to applicants repeating A-Levels: Higher Leeds, St Andrews; **Same** Birmingham, Bristol, Leeds, Newcastle.

Probable vacancies from June 2001 and in Clearing (see Ch.4): A small number of vacancies are likely, particularly on joint courses. Offers from 260–220 points are expected.

NEW GRADUATE DESTINATIONS AND EMPLOYMENT (1999 HESA) (see **Ch.4**)

No data available; see **Classics.**

HEALTH SCIENCES/STUDIES (see also **Chiropractic, Community Studies, Environmental Science/Studies, Life Sciences, Nursing & Midwifery, Optometry, Osteopathy, Physiotherapy, Podiatry** and **Radiography**)

NB The information supplied by the universities and colleges this year varies considerably and the offers listed below should be used as a first source of reference only. Many institutions will accept combinations of Advanced (AL), Advanced Subsidiary (AS) and Vocational Advanced (VA) level qualifications to achieve the required points total, but applicants must check web sites and prospectuses for full details of all offers. Grades and points totals shown should be regarded as the minimum levels to be achieved, but offers may be adjusted downwards when results are known. The points totals shown to the left of the institutions are for ease of reference only. It must not be assumed that tariff points are always used by institutions or that they can be substituted for an offer in grades. The level of an offer is not necessarily indicative of the quality of a course. To calculate your offers see Chapter 4 and the inside fold of the back cover.

Special subject requirements/preferences: A-Level: Central Lancashire, Liverpool John Moores. Social sciences required. **Chester (Coll), Manchester Met** Sciences. **De Montfort** Sciences not required. **GCSE:** Mathematics and a science usually preferred. **Bournemouth, Sunderland** Grade B mathematics.

320 pts **Hertfordshire** – 320–280 pts 1x12u **or** 2x6u; gs; (Paramed Sci)
300 pts **Bradford** – 300 pts 12u (inc AL maths+sci); gs; (MEng (Med Eng))
          Hull – BBB–BCC (Biomed Sci)
          Leeds – BBB (Med Sci)
          London (King's) – BBB (Biomed Sci)
          York – 300–260 pts 21–18u – BCC+c; (Hlth Sci)
280 pts **Brunel** – 280–240 pts 3x6u (inc pref AL psy/sociol/biol/hum biol **or** VA (hlthsc)) – ALs **or** ALs+ASs **or** VAs+/-ALs/ASs; (Hlth St; Hlth Prom; Hlth Serv Mgt/ Admin; Hlth Cre Law/Eth)
          Glasgow – BBC–CCC (Spo Med)
          Swansea – 280 pts 18u – BBC **or** ALs+ASs **or** VAs+/-ALs/ASs; (Med Sci/Hum)
260 pts **Aston** – 260–240 pts 18u – 3ALs **or** ALs+ASs **or** VAs+/-ALs/ASs; gs; (Hlth Sfty Mgt; Comb Hlth courses)
          Bangor – 260 pts approx (Spo Hlth Phys Educ)
          Bradford – 260 pts 12u (inc AL maths+sci); gs; (Med Cyber; Med Eng)
          Essex – 260 pts 12u – BC+AL/2ASs **or** VA12u BC+AL; gs; (Hlth/Soc Care)
          London (King's) – BCC (Clin Sci)

Sheffield – BCC (Paramed St; Hlth Sci)

Swansea – 260 pts 18u – BCC **or** ALs+ASs **or** VAs+/-ALs/ASs; (Hlth Pol Eth)

240 pts **Bradford** – 240 pts 12u (inc AL sci); gs; (Med Tech/Spo; Hlth Sfty Mgt)

Coventry – CCC/BC (Hlth Sci)

Durham (Stockton) – 240 pts (Hlth Hum Sci)

Middlesex – 240 pts approx (Herb Med; Trad Chin Med)

Salford – CCC/BB (Spo Rehab)

Strathclyde – CCC (Pros Orthot)

220 pts **Aberdeen** – CCD/BC (Hlth Sci)

Bradford – 220 pts 12u (inc AL biol/chem); gs; (Med Microbiol; Med Sys Eng; Biomed Sci; Cell Path)

British Coll (Natur/Ost) – 220 pts approx (Inc B/C); (Ost Med; Naturop Med)

Central Lancashire – 220 pts 12u; gs; (Herb Med; Hom Med)

Middlesex – CCD/BC (Hlth St)

Portsmouth – 220 pts – ALs **or** ALs+ASs **or** VAs; gs; (Exer Hlth Sci; Hlth Sci/Nutr; Hlth Cre)

Salford – CCD/BB (Pros/Orthot)

Staffordshire – 220 pts (Exer Hlth)

Teesside – CCD/AB–BB (Hlth Sci)

Wolverhampton – 220 pts 18u – 3ALs **or** ALs+ASs **or** VAs(B overall)+/-ALs/ASs; (Occ Hlth Sfty)

Wolverhampton – 220–200 pts (Hlth Sci)

200 pts **Anglia** – 200 pts (Osteopathy)

Bournemouth – 200–180 pts (AL biol pref); (Hlth Commun Dev; Hlth Sci)

Bournemouth (Anglo Euro Coll) – 200 pts approx (Chiropractic) (Apply direct – not in UCAS scheme)

Bradford – 200 pts 12u (inc AL sci); gs; (Med Electron)

Central Lancashire – 200–180 pts 12u; gs; (Hlth Sci/Complem Med; Hlth St; Hlth St with Psy/Soc Pol/Sociol)

Manchester Met – 200 pts approx (Hlth St; Env Hlth)

Nescot – BB (Ost Med)

Sheffield Hallam – 200 pts approx (Hlth St)

Wolverhampton – 200 pts 12u – CCD/BB **or** CC+b **or** VA BB+/-AL/ASs; gs; (Pblc Hlth)

Wolverhampton – 200–160 pts – CCD **or** CD+cc **or** VA12u AA–CD; gs; (Hlth St Comb)

180 pts **Chester (Coll)** – 180 pts – ALs (160 pts inc C)+AS **or** VA (160 pts inc C)+AS; AS(20 pts); gs; (Hlth Sci Comb; Hlth St Comb)

East London – 180 pts approx (Hlth St; Hlth/Prom; Hlth/Serv Mgt)

Farnborough (CT) – 180 pts approx (Sci Mgt Exer Hlth)

Greenwich – 180 pts approx (Pblc Hlth; Hlth Comb courses)

Lincolnshire & Humberside – 180 pts (Hlth St; Biomed Sci)

Liverpool Hope (Coll) – 180 pts approx (Hlth Spo Recr/Phys Educ; Hlth Comb courses)

Liverpool John Moores – 180–160 pts – ALs **or** ALs+ASs **or** VAs+/-ALs/ASs; (Hlth; Pblc Hlth)

Luton – 180 pts approx (Hlth Exer Bhv courses)

Northumbria – 180 pts approx (Hlth Dev St)

Oxford Brookes – DDD/CC (Exer/Hlth offer varies with 2nd subject)

Queen Margaret (UC) – BC (Hlth Prom)

St Martin's (Coll) – CDE/CC (Hlth St courses)

Staffordshire – 180 pts approx (Hlth Sys Des; Hlth St; Hlth Tech)

Sunderland – 180 pts; gs; (Hlth St)

Thames Valley – 180 pts (Spo Hlth Fit Mgt)

160 pts **Bath Spa (UC)** – 160–120 pts 12u – CD **or** VA12u CD; (not gs) (Hlth St Comb)

Canterbury Christ Church (UC) – CC (Hlth Sci; Phyl/Hlth Sci)

Central England – 160 pts approx (Hlth St)

Chichester (UC) – 160 pts (inc AL); (Biokin; Hlth Sci; Child Hlth/Exer)

Derby – 160 pts 12u – CC **or** DD+ee **or** VAsCC+/-ALs/ASs; gs; (Complem Thera/Hol Med)

European (Sch Ost) – 160 pts – CC **or** cccc **or** VA12u CC; (not gs) (Osteopathy)

Huddersfield – 160 pts 12u; (Hlth/Env; Hum Hlth)

St Mary's (Coll) – 12u – CC–DD **or** ALs+ASs **or** VA12u CC–DD; gs; (Hlth/Hum Biol/Spo Rehab; Spo Rehab/Spo Sci)

Salford – 160 pts (Complem Med Prac)

Trinity Carmarthen (Coll) – CC–EE (Hlth Env)

140 pts   **Abertay Dundee** – CD (Hlth/Bhv Sci)

Barnsley (Coll) – 140 pts 12u – ALs (D min) **or** ALs+ASs **or** VAs (120 pts)+/-ALs/ASs; gs; (Hlth St)

De Montfort – 140 pts – ALs **or** ALs+ASs **or** VAs+/-ALs/ASs; (Hlth St)

Derby – 140 pts 12u – CD **or** DE+ee **or** VAs CD+/-AL/ASs; gs; (Heal Arts)

Huddersfield – 140 pts 12u – DEE **or** D+cc **or** VA12u CC; gs; (Hlth/Spo St)

Napier – CD (Hlth Sci courses)

North London – 140 pts 1x12u **or** 2x6u; (Hlth St)

Surrey Roehampton – 140 pts approx – ALs **or** ALs+ASs; (Hlth St courses; Hlth Soc Cre)

120 pts   **and below**

Huddersfield – 100 pts 12u; gs; (Hlth/Commun St)

London (Inst) – (Cos Sci)

North London – 120 pts; 2ALs **or** VAs; (Hlth Sci; Hlth Prom; Complem Med)

UHI (Lews Castle/Perth) – (Rur Hlth St via DipHE)

Worcester (UC) – 80 pts 12u – EE **or** ALs+ASs **or** VAs+/-ALs/ASs; gs; (Hlth St courses)

Leeds Met – (contact university)

Diploma of Higher Education

Barnsley (Coll); Bath Spa (UC); Canterbury Christ Church (UC); Cheltenham & Glos (CHE) (Commun Hlth); Manchester Met (Commun Hlth)

Higher National Diploma courses

Birmingham (CFTCS); Brooklands (Coll) gs (Couns); Bromley (Coll) gs (Couns); Cardiff (UWCM) (Disab St); City of Bristol (Coll); Cornwall & Duchy (Coll); Crawley (Coll) (Bty Thera); Derby (Spo Mgt); Dudley (Coll); Farnborough (CT); Glasgow (Coll) (Hlth Fitness); Grantham (Coll); Llandrillo (Coll); Reid Kerr (Coll); Salford (Env Hlth St); Somerset (CAT); South East Essex (Coll) (Hlth Complem Thera); Stockport (CFHE); UHI; Walsall (Coll); Wigan & Leigh (Coll); Worcester (UC). *Beauty courses are offered by:* Bradford (Coll); City (Coll); Gloucestershire (CAT); London (Inst); Middlesex; Newcastle (Coll); St Austell (Coll); Saltash (Coll); Tile Hill (Coll); Warwickshire (Coll); Wolverhampton; Worcester (UC).

Alternative Offers:

IB offers: Canterbury Christ Church (UC) 24 pts; Liverpool Hope (Coll) 28 pts; St Martin's (Coll) 28 pts.

Scottish Qualifications: Aberdeen BBBB; Abertay Dundee BBC; Glasgow (Spo Med) BBBB; Napier BBC; Queen Margaret (UC) (Hlth Prom) BBBC.

CHOOSING YOUR COURSE (See also **Ch.1**)

> **Subject information:** Health Sciences and Studies courses cover different aspects of health and may include human biology, stress and prevention in health care. There is an overlap into Sport and Exercise Science, Chiropractic, Community Studies, Osteopathy, Nursing and Life Science courses which should also be considered.

Special features: Brunel Several courses are offered by way of the modular health related degree programme. These cover health promotion, health information science, ethico-legal issues, health service administration and community health development. **Central England** The Combined Health Studies degree provides a broad-based education in health and covers biology, psychology and sociology. **Central Lancashire** The Health Studies degree covers politics, sociology, economics, philosophy and history as well as a focus on health service provision. **Liverpool John Moores** The School of Health is a major provider of health care education, courses mainly covering childhood studies and health. **Oxford Brookes** A range of courses are also offered including Health Care and Management, Gerontology (care of the elderly), Clinical Aromatherapy and Osteopathy: check with admissions tutors. **Swansea** The new Health Science course commenced in October 1999 offering a broad range of subjects related to health care planning and delivery. **Westminster** Several courses in Complementary Therapies are available. *NOW CHECK PROSPECTUSES AND WEB SITES.*

Top universities and colleges (Teaching Quality) (see Ch.4): Glasgow Caledonian; Hull; Liverpool John Moores; Robert Gordon; not all institutions assessed.

Study opportunities abroad: Greenwich (Occ Hlth/Sfty); Liverpool Hope (Coll); Northumbria; Oxford Brookes; Salford; Surrey Roehampton; York.

Work opportunities abroad: Coventry; Derby; Liverpool Hope (Coll); Salford.

ADMISSIONS INFORMATION

Number of applicants per place (approx): Barnsley (Coll) 2; Bournemouth 4; Bournemouth (Anglo Euro Coll) 1; Central Lancashire 6; Chester (Coll) 6; Chichester (UC) 5; De Montfort 2; Durham (Stockton) 3; Huddersfield 5; Manchester Met 10; Middlesex 4; North London 7; Portsmouth 12; St Martin's (Coll) 4; Salford 8; Surrey Roehampton 10; Worcester (UC) 3.

Planning your UCAS personal statement (see Ch.4): You should describe any work you have done dealing with people, particularly in a caring capacity, for example, working with the elderly, nursing, hospital work. Give evidence of why you wish to study this subject. **Durham (Stockton)** Demonstrate an interest in medical anthropology.

Selection inteviews (see Ch.4): Barnsley (Coll); Bradford (Coll) (No); Brunel (No); Canterbury Christ Church (UC) (some); Central Lancashire; Coventry; De Montfort (W); Durham (Stockton) (W); Glamorgan; Huddersfield (No); Hull (No); Manchester Met (No); Middlesex; Nottingham Trent; Oxford Brookes (No); Portsmouth; Sunderland; Swansea; Worcester (UC); York (No).

Interview questions (see Ch.4): Courses vary considerably and you are likely to be questioned on your reasons for choosing the course at that university or college. If you have studied biology then questions are possible on the A-level syllabus and you could also be asked to discuss any work experience you have had.

Reasons for rejection (non-academic): Some students are mistakenly looking for a professional qualification in, for example, occupational therapy, nursing. **Coventry** Inadequate mathematics.

GAP YEAR ADVICE

Aim to get paid or voluntary experience in health or community care work.

Institutions willing to defer entry after A-Levels: Aston; Bournemouth (preferred); Bournemouth (Anglo Euro Coll); Central Lancashire; Chester (Coll); Coventry; De Montfort; Derby; Farnborough (CT); Huddersfield; Hull; Liverpool Hope (Coll); Luton; North London; Northumbria; Oxford Brookes; St Martin's (Coll); Salford; Surrey Roehampton; Teesside; Thames Valley; Worcester (UC).

AFTER RESULTS ADVICE

Institutions which may accept the same points score after A-Levels: Central Lancashire; Chester (Coll) (No); Hull; Manchester Met; Middlesex; Oxford Brookes; Salford; Sheffield (No); Worcester (UC) (No).

Institutions which may accept lower grades/points score after A-Levels: Coventry; De Montfort; Farnborough (CT); Hull; Liverpool Hope (Coll); Surrey Roehampton.

Offers to applicants repeating A-Levels: Higher Chester (Coll); **Same** Surrey Roehampton.

Probable vacancies from June 2001 and in Clearing (see Ch.4): At least 16 universities declared vacancies last year. See also **Environmental Science/Studies**.

NEW GRADUATE DESTINATIONS AND EMPLOYMENT (1999 HESA) (see **Ch.4**)

See **Chiropractic, Dentistry, Medicine, Nursing & Midwifery, Nutrition, Optometry, Osteopathy, Physiotherapy, Podiatry** and **Radiography**.

HEBREW (see also Near & Middle East Studies)

NB The information supplied by the universities and colleges this year varies considerably and the offers listed below should be used as a first source of reference only. Many institutions will accept combinations of Advanced (AL), Advanced Subsidiary (AS) and Vocational Advanced (VA) level qualifications to achieve the required points total, but applicants must check web sites and prospectuses for full details of all offers. Grades and points totals shown should be regarded as the minimum levels to be achieved, but offers may be adjusted downwards when results are known. The points totals shown to the left of the institutions are for ease of reference only. It must not be assumed that tariff points are always used by institutions or that they can be substituted for an offer in grades. The level of an offer is not necessarily indicative of the quality of a course. To calculate your offers see Chapter 4 and the inside fold of the back cover.

Special subject requirements/preferences: GCSE: Foreign language usually required. **Cambridge** Majority of grade As usually required. **London (Sch Jewish St)** (Jew St/Educ) English, mathematics and science preferred.

360 pts and above
   Cambridge – Offers, mainly in grades, vary between colleges (Oriental St (Hebrew))
   Oxford – Offers vary between candidates (Hebrew; Jew St)
320 pts London (SOAS) – 320 pts (Law/Heb)
   St Andrews – ABB (Heb – Fr)
300 pts St Andrews – BBB (Heb/Maths)
280 pts London (SOAS) – BBC–BCC/BB–BC (Hebrew courses except under **320 pts** inc Smtc Langs)
   St Andrews – BBC (Bib St – Heb)
240 pts London (Sch Jewish St) – CCC/CC (Jew St/Heb; Jew St; Jew St/Educ)
   London (UCL) – CCC **or** 3ALs+AS/VA; (Hebrew)
220 pts and below
   Lampeter – (Jew St courses)
   Leo Baeck (Coll) – by interview (Heb Jew St)

Alternative Offers:

IB offers: London (Sch Jewish St) 4–5 subjects at B–C; St Andrews 28 pts.

Scottish Qualifications: St Andrews BBBB.

CHOOSING YOUR COURSE (See also **Ch.1**)

Subject information: Hebrew attracts the occasional student of languages. It is often a useful preparation for Biblical Studies courses which, along with Theology, Ancient History and Archaeological courses focusing on the Middle East, might also be considered.

Special features: St Andrews (Bib St – Heb) Language and grammar of classical Hebrew; later topics include Aramaic, prophetic literature and worship. *NOW CHECK PROSPECTUSES AND WEB SITES.*

ADMISSIONS INFORMATION

Number of applicants per place (approx): London (SOAS) 1.5.

Planning your UCAS personal statement (see Ch.4): Describe the reasons for wishing to follow these courses and how your interests have developed. **St Andrews** Reasons for choosing the course. Evidence of interest.

Selection interviews: London (Sch Jewish St); London (UCL); St Andrews (No).

Interview questions (see Ch.4): Discuss your interest in Hebrew. What are your reasons for choosing this course? What do you hope to do at the end of the course?

Reasons for rejection (non-academic): Insufficient background knowledge.

AFTER RESULTS ADVICE

Institutions which may accept the same points score after A-Levels: London (SOAS) (No), (UCL) (No).

Probable vacancies from June 2001 and in Clearing (see Ch.4): London (UCL) may have vacancies at about 240 pts.

NEW GRADUATE DESTINATIONS AND EMPLOYMENT (1999 HESA) (see **Ch.4**)

No data available.

HISTORY (including **Heritage Management** and **Medieval Studies**; see also **History (Ancient), (Economic & Social)** and **History of Art**)

NB The information supplied by the universities and colleges this year varies considerably and the offers listed below should be used as a first source of reference only. Many institutions will accept combinations of Advanced (AL), Advanced Subsidiary (AS) and Vocational Advanced (VA) level qualifications to achieve the required points total, but applicants must check web sites and prospectuses for full details of all offers. Grades and points totals shown should be regarded as the minimum levels to be achieved, but offers may be adjusted downwards when results are known. The points totals shown to the left of the institutions are for ease of reference only. It must not be assumed that tariff points are always used by institutions or that they can be substituted for an offer in grades. The level of an offer is not necessarily indicative of the quality of a course. To calculate your offers see Chapter 4 and the inside fold of the back cover.

Special subject requirements/preferences: A-Level: History, usually the highest grade in offers below. **Oxford** (Anc Hist/Modn Hist) Full A-Level in history recommended. Classical language at A/AS-Level considered. **GCSE: Aberdeen, Dundee, Edinburgh, Glasgow, Nottingham** (also IT preferred), **St Andrews** English, mathematics or science and a foreign language. **Birmingham, Durham** (mostly grades A* and A), **Exeter, Leicester, London (QM), (RH), (UCL), Manchester, Southampton, Sussex, Ulster** GCSE foreign language required. **Birmingham** (Econ Soc Hist), **Sheffield Hallam** mathematics grade A–C. **London (Gold)** Six subjects grade A–C. **Manchester Met** Five subjects A–C minimum). **Oxford, Cambridge** Majority of grade As preferred.

360 pts   and above

          Cambridge – Offers, mainly in grades, vary between colleges (History)
          Oxford – Offers vary between candidates (Anc Modn Hist; Modn Hist)
          York – 370–320 pts 21–18u – ABB+c; (History courses)

350 pts **London (King's)** – BBB+b or BB+bbb for Hist/Port (inc AL hist) or VA12u
BB+AL(B hist)+b AS arts); (Hist; Hist/Port/Braz St)

Southampton – 350 pts 21u (inc 200 pts from 2ALs inc hist); (History courses
with Fr/Ger/Span – AS b; Jew Hist courses approx offer)

340 pts **Cambridge (Hom)** – AAB–ABB (Hist/Educ St BA)

Edinburgh – AAB (Hist/Engl Lang; Soc Anth/Soc Hist)

Manchester – AAB–BBC (Hist; Mediev St; Modn Hist/Econ; Hist Sociol)

330 pts **Southampton (New Coll)** – 330 pts (inc 180 pts from 2ALs); gs; (Hum (Hist
St))

320 pts **Birmingham** – ABB (Mediev/Modn Hist)

Bristol – ABB–BCC (inc Ger for Lang course); (not gs) (Hist; Hist/Ger)

Durham – ABB (not gs) (Hist; Hist/Fr/Ger; joint courses)

East Anglia – ABB–BCC; gs; (History courses except under **300 pts**)

Exeter – 320–300 pts 18u – ABB–BBB or AB+ab or BB+aa or VAs (contact
univ); (History courses except under **300/280 pts**)

Liverpool – 320 pts – ALs or ALs+ASs or VAs+/-ALs/ASs; (Hist; Hist/Hisp St;
Modn Hist/Pol)

London (LSE) – ABB (Hist; Int Rel Hist)

London (UCL) – ABB or 3ALs+AS/VA; (Hist; Law/Hist)

Manchester – ABB–BBB (History)

Newcastle – ABB–BBB (History)

Nottingham – 21u – ABB+AS (contrasting) or VA+AL (B hist); (not gs) (History)

Sheffield – ABB (History courses except under **300/280 pts**)

Warwick – ABB–BBB (Hist/Pol; Hist)

300 pts **Birmingham** – BBB–BBC (Mediev St)

Cardiff – 300–260 pts (Mediev St)

Edinburgh – BBB (Hist; Scot Hist St; Sociol Econ Hist; Hist/Scot Hist St; Scot
Hist; Scot Ethnol/Scot Hist St)

East Anglia – 300 pts 18u – BBB (VA as 3rd AL) or BB+bb; (not gs) (Hist
Engl/Am)

East Anglia – BBB–BCC (Hist; Euro Hist/Fr/Ger; Hist/Land Arch; Hist Art Hist;
Modn Hist; Hist/Pol)

Essex – 300–260 pts – BBB–BC+AL/2ASs; gs; (History courses)

Exeter – 300 pts 18u (inc AL lang for Lang courses) – BBB or BB+bb or
AC+ac or VAs (contact univ); gs (not AL); (Hist with Fr/Ger/Ital; Hist Econ
Cult; Hist/Span)

Hull – BBB–BCC (Hist/Pol; Hist/Engl; Hist/Fr)

Kent – 300–280 pts approx (History single/joint courses)

Leeds – BBB–BBC (History courses)

Leicester – 300 pts – BBB or ALs+ASs or VA12u (inc AL hist); gs; (Hist St)

Liverpool – 300 pts – ALs or ALs+ASs or VAs+/-ALs/ASs; (Hist/Ger)

London (RH) – ABC–BBB/BB (History courses)

London (UCL) – BBB or 3ALs+AS/VA; (Hist/Euro Lang)

Manchester – BBB (Mediev St)

Nottingham – BBB–BBC (History courses except under **320/260 pts**)

St Andrews – BBB (History courses; Scot St)

Sheffield – BBB (Hist/Hisp St)

Sussex – BBB (History courses except under **280 pts**)

Swansea – 300 pts 18u – BBB–BBC/AB or ALs+ASs or VAs+/-ALs/ASs; (Hist;
Mediev St; Medit Modn Hist)

Warwick – BBB–BBC (Hist/Sociol)

280 pts **Aberystwyth** – 280–240 pts (History courses)

Birmingham – BBC (E Medit Hist; Hist/Soc Sci)

Bradford – BBC/BB (Peace St)

Bristol UWE – 280–220 pts 18u pref/12u (180 min pts at 6u/12u awards); ALs
or ALs+ASs or VAs+/-ALs/ASs; (History courses; Cult Media St)

Brunel – 280–220 pts 2x6u (inc AL hist or rel subj C) – ALs or ALs+ASs or
VAs+/-ALs/ASs; (History courses)

Cambridge (Hom) – BBC–BCD (Hist/Educ BEd)
Cardiff – BBC/AB (History)
Exeter – 280 pts 18u – BBC **or** BC+bb **or** VAs (contact univ); gs; (Hist/Russ; Hist/Soty)
Glasgow – BBC (History courses)
Keele – BBC–BCC **or** equiv AS accepted; gs; (History courses)
Lancaster – BBC (History courses)
Leicester – 280 pts – BBC **or** BC+bb; gs; (Contemp Hist)
Liverpool – 280 pts – ALs **or** ALs+ASs **or** VAs+/-ALs/ASs; (Hist/Fr)
London (QM) – 280 pts from 3ALs (inc B hist); (History courses)
London (UCL) – BBC **or** 3ALs+AS/VA; (Hist/Hist Art)
Manchester – BBC (Modn Mid E Hist)
Reading – BBC–BCC (History courses)
Salford – BBC (Hist/Engl)
Sheffield – BBC (Modn Hist/Jap)
Sussex – BBC (Intlctl Hist courses)

260 pts **Aberystwyth** – 260–240 pts (Modn Welsh Hist)
Belfast (Queen's) – BCC–CCC (History courses)
Bristol UWE – BCC (History; Engl/Hist; Cult Media St/Hist)
Cardiff – BCC (Hist Id/Welsh Hist)
Dundee – BCC (History courses)
Hertfordshire – 260–220 pts 1x12u **or** 2x6u; gs; (Hum Mod)
Hull – BCC (Hist; Hist/Ital; Scand St/Hist)
Kent – 260 pts 12u – BC+AL+ASs **or** VA12u+AL+ASs; gs; (Hist/Arch)
London (Gold) – BCC/BC (Hist/Sociol; Engl/Hist; Hist/Pol)
London (UCL) – BCC–CCC/BC–CC **or** 3ALs+AS/VA; (Hist; Hist/Jew St)
Manchester Met – BCC (History)
Northumbria – BCC (History courses)
Nottingham – BCC (Hist/Russ)
Oxford Brookes – BCC (Modn Hist)
Stirling – BCC–CCC/BB (History courses)
Sunderland – 260–160 pts approx offer varies with second subject (Hist courses)

240 pts **Aberdeen** – CCC (History courses)
Bangor – 240 pts 18u – ALs; (History courses except under **220/200 pts**)
Bradford – 240 pts 12u; gs; (Hist; Hist with Phil/Fr/Ger/Span)
Huddersfield – 240 pts 12u; ALs (inc C hist); gs; (Hist; Hist/Herit; Hist/Sociol)
Liverpool John Moores – 240–180 pts (inc 2ALs **or** VAs) – ALs **or** ALs+ASs **or** VAs+/-ALs/ASs; (History)
London (UCL) – CCC **or** 3ALs+AS/VA; (Jew Hist)
Oxford Brookes – CCC offer varies with 2nd subject (History joint Hons)
Salford – CCC (Contemp Mltry Int Hist)
Sheffield Hallam – 240–180 pts approx (Hist Comb St)
Strathclyde – CCC/BC (BBD 2nd yr entry) (History courses; Arts Soc Sci; Soc Sci – Econ Soc Hist)
Strathclyde – CCC/BB (Hist – Bus Sch)
Ulster – CCC (Irish Hist Pol; Hum (Hist); Modn Contemp Hist)
Wolverhampton – 240–180 pts – CDD–CCE **or** CC+e **or** CEE+e **or** VA12u BC; gs; (History)

220 pts **Bangor** – 220 pts; gs; (Welsh Hist/Soc Pol)
Central Lancashire – 220 pts 12u; gs; (Soc Cult Hist; Hist; Herit Mgt; Hist/Law; Modn Wrld Hist)
De Montfort (Leicester) – 220 pts; 200 pts for joint/comb courses (inc C) – ALs **or** ALs+ASs **or** VAs+/-ALs/ASs; (not gs) (History courses)
King Alfred's Winchester (Coll) – 220 pts 12u – 3/2ALs **or** ALs+ASs **or** VAS+/-ALs/ASs; gs; (Hist Prac; Hist)
Kingston – 220–180 pts 2x6u (inc 200 pts in 2x6u awards); gs; (History)
Lampeter – 220 pts approx (Hist; Mediev St courses; Vict St)

Lincolnshire & Humberside – 220 pts (History)
London Guildhall – 220 pts approx (Modn Hist)
Luton – 220–180 pts approx (Modn Hist courses)
Nottingham Trent – 220 pts – 2ALs (inc C hist); (History)
Middlesex – 220–180 pts approx (Cul Intlctl Hist; Hist)
Plymouth – CCD/BC (Herit/Hist; Hist Media Arts; Hist/Euro Langs/Cult)
Portsmouth – 220 pts – ALs **or** ALs+ASs **or** VAs; gs; (History courses; Herit Mgt)
Teesside – 220–200 pts approx (Hist; Cult St/Hist; Modn Contemp Euro Hist)

200 pts **Anglia** – 200–160 pts approx (Hist; Euro Hist/Pol; Herit)
Bangor – 200 pts – ALs **or** ALs+ASs; (Herit Mgt)
Bangor – 200 pts; gs (AL only); (History)
Bournemouth – 200–180 pts from 2ALs (inc geog/hist/arcaeol/biol pref); (Herit Cons)
Central Lancashire – 200–180 pts 12u; gs; (History courses except under **220/180 pts**)
Chester (Coll) – 200 pts; ALs (180 pts inc C hist)+AS **or** VA (180 pts inc C 1 subj)+AS; AS(20+ pts); (History; Hist/Herit Mgt)
Coventry – 200 pts approx (History courses)
De Montfort (Leicester) – 200 pts (not gs); (History joint courses)
Derby – 200 pts 12u – CDD **or** CD+dd **or** VAs (AL grades)+/-ALs/ASs; gs; (History)
Glamorgan – 200 pts approx (History courses)
Greenwich – 200 pts approx (Herit Mgt courses)
Lampeter – 200 pts approx (Ch Hist)
Leeds, Trinity & All Saints (Coll) – 200 pts (Hist/Mgt)
Manchester Met – CDD/CC (Hum/Soc St; Hist)
Nottingham Trent – 200/180 pts approx (Hist/Int Rel)
Ripon & York (Coll) – 200–180 pts approx (Hist Am St; Hist; App Soc Sci – Hist; Hist/Engl; Hist/Geog; Hist/Ital; Hist/Wmns St)
Staffordshire – 200 pts – ALs (inc CC) **or** CC+AS(40 pts) **or** VA CC+AS(40 pts); gs; (History courses)

190 pts **Buckingham** – 190 pts 21u – 3ALs **or** 3ALS+AS; (History courses)
180 pts **Central Lancashire** – 180–160 pts 12u; gs; (Hist/Pol; Hist/Race Eth St)
Cheltenham & Glos (CHE) – 180–160 pts approx (History courses)
Chester (Coll) – 180 pts approx (Hist Herit Mgt)
Colchester (Inst) – 180 pts approx (History courses)
De Montfort (Bedford) – 180 pts; 160 pts joint/comb courses; (not gs) (History courses)
East London – 180 pts approx (History)
Greenwich – 180 pts approx (History courses)
Leeds, Trinity & All Saints (Coll) – BC (Hist Mgt; Hist Media)
Liverpool Hope (Coll) – 180 pts approx (History courses)
London (SOAS) – BC (History courses)
Newman (CHE) – DDD/CC (BEd Hist; Hist/PE; Hist/Engl; Hist/Theol)
Norwich City (Coll) – 180 pts approx (History courses)
St Mark & St John (Coll) – 180 pts approx (C hist) (History courses)
St Martin's (Coll) – CDE/CC (History)
Trinity Carmarthen (Coll) – 180–140 pts approx (History courses; Herit Cons)
Westminster – BC (Modn Hist)

160 pts **Bath Spa (UC)** – 160–120 pts 12u – BD **or** ALs+ASs **or** VA12u DD; (not gs) (History Comb Hons)
Birmingham (Westhill) – 160 pts 12u (inc C) – ALs **or** ALs+ASs; VAs (contact univ); (Hum Hist)
Bishop Grosseteste (Coll) – CC **or** C+cc **or** VA12u+AL(C); (History)
Bolton (IHE) – 160 pts approx (History courses)
Brighton – CC (Cult Hist St; Modn Hist)
Canterbury Christ Church (UC) – CC (History courses)

Chichester (UC) – 160 pts (inc C); (History)
Cumbria (CAD) – 160 pts – CC **or** ASs contact coll) **or** VA; (Hist; Herit)
De Montfort – 160 pts – ALs **or** ALs+ASs **or** VAs+ALs/ASs; (Musm/Mat Cult)
Edge Hill (Coll) – CC (History P Educ)
Hull (Scarborough) – CC (Herit Mgt)
Leeds, Trinity & All Saints (Coll) – CC (Hist P Educ)
London (Inst) – CC (Conservation)
Newport (UWCN) – 160–140 pts – ALs **or** ALs+ASs **or** VAs+/-AL/ASs; (Hum Hist)
North East Wales (IHE) – 160 pts approx (History courses)
North London – 160 pts 1x12u **or** 2x6u – (Hist; Hist Comb courses)
St Martin's (Coll) – CEE/CD (Hist QTS)
St Mary's (Coll) – 12u – CC–DD **or** ALs+ASs **or** VAs+/-ALs/ASs; gs; (History; Herit)
Sunderland – 160 pts – 2ALs **or** ALs+ASs **or** VA12u+/-ALs/ASs; (History)
Surrey Roehampton – 160 pts – ALs **or** ALs+ASs **or** VAs+/-ALs/ASs; (History)

140 pts **Buckinghamshire Chilterns (UC)** – 140 pts approx (Herit St)
Derby – CD **or** DD+dd **or** VAs CD+/-ALs/ASs; (Hist; Herit CAMS; Lcl Hist CAMS)
Derby – CD **or** DE+ee **or** VAs CD+/-ALs/ASs; (Hist/Herit Comb courses)
London Guildhall – CD (Modn Hist)
Northampton (UC) – CD (History courses)

120 pts **Bath Spa (UC)** – 120 pts – DD **or** ALs+ASs **or** VA12u DD; (not gs) (History Single Hons)
Bishop Grosseteste (Coll) – DD **or** D+dd **or** VA12u; (Herit St)
Southampton (Inst) – 120 pts – ALs **or** ALs+ASs; (Ant (Hist/Cllct)
Worcester (UC) – 120 pts 12u – DD **or** ASs **or** VAs; gs; (Hist; Herit St)

100 pts **and below**
Barnsley (Coll) – (Hum Hist))
Edge Hill (CHE) – (Hist Urb Pol St)
London Guildhall – (Restor Cons)
St Mary's (Coll) – (Hist QTS)
Sheffield Hallam – (Hist QTS)

Leeds Met – (contact university)

Diploma of Higher Education courses
80 pts Bath Spa (UC); Bradford (Coll); East London; Edge Hill (CHE); London Guildhall; Manchester Met; Middlesex; Oxford Brookes; Worcester (UC).

Higher National Diploma courses
Cornwall & Duchy (Coll) (Herit/Vstr Mgt); Cumbria (CAD) (Herit Mgt); Derby (Herit).

Alternative Offers:

EB offers: Aberystwyth 65% overall or 70% in 2 specified subjects; Lampeter 60%; Manchester Met 65%.

IB offers: Aberdeen 30 pts; Aberystwyth 28 pts H555; Bangor 30–28 pts; Birmingham 34 pts; Bradford (Peace St) 30 pts; Brighton 24 pts; Bristol 33 pts; Brunel 32 pts; Buckingham 24 pts; Cardiff 28 pts; De Montfort 28 pts H/S 5/6; Dundee 29 pts H 15 pts; Durham 30 pts H666; East Anglia 30 pts; Exeter 30 pts; Glamorgan 26 pts; Huddersfield 28 pts; Hull 28 pts; Kent 30–28 pts; Kingston 30–28 pts; Lampeter 30–28 pts; Lancaster 32–30 pts; Leeds 30 pts inc H77; Leicester 28 pts; London (Gold) 24 pts, (King's) 32 pts hist 6, (LSE) 36 pts H666, (QM) 32 pts, (RH) 34–32 pts, (UCL) 30 pts; Manchester Met 28 pts; Newcastle 30 pts; Nottingham 32 pts hist 6; Ripon & York (Coll) 30 pts; St Andrews 30 pts; St Martin's (Coll) 28 pts; Staffordshire 27 pts; Stirling 30 pts; Surrey Roehampton 28 pts; Swansea 30 pts H 14 pts; Warwick 32–29 pts H655; York 32 pts H6 hist.

Irish offers: Aberdeen BBBB; Aberystwyth BBCC; Keele BBBCC; Lampeter BBBCC; Manchester Met BBBB; North London CCCC; St Andrews BBBB; Sheffield ABBB; Warwick AAABB.

Scottish Qualifications: Aberdeen BBBB; Dundee BBBC; Edinburgh BBBB; Glasgow ABBB/BBBB; St Andrews BBBB; Stirling BBBC; Strathclyde BBBB.

Overseas applicants: Oxford Brookes Access course and English language teaching available.

CHOOSING YOUR COURSE (See also **Ch.1**)

Subject information: History is a very broad popular subject, with most courses covering British and European history. There is, however, a wide range of specialist topics on offer, for example American, Scottish, East European and Far Eastern History. International Relations, Politics, Ancient, Economic and Social History could also be considered as degree courses in their own right, together with Biblical Studies, Archaeology, History of Art, Anthropology and the History of Science.

Special features: Aberdeen Topics include religious wars, plagues, poisons and persecution. **Bristol UWE** Complementary modules are offered in such subjects as philosophy, psychology, sociology and modern languages. **Central Lancashire** Options include science and medicine, war and society and international relations. **Durham** A minor subject can be taken as a third of the degree. **Essex** Opportunity to spend a year in Belgium, France, Germany or Spain or a term in Rotterdam. **Glasgow** The course covers medieval, modern and Scottish history. **Kent** The course in British and European History offers a year in France or Germany. The History and Heritage degree includes the preservation of old buildings and documents. **London (UCL)** There is a degree in Jewish History and a unique course in Viking Studies. **Salford** A new degree in Contemporary Military and International History covers the period from World War I to the present day. **Sheffield Hallam** The History course concentrates on the 19th and 20th centuries. Options include a foreign language and another subject in the School of Cultural Studies. Non-standard entry encouraged; the major focus is on modern history and includes a number of post-1945 courses. *NOW CHECK PROSPECTUSES AND WEB SITES.*

Top universities and colleges (Teaching Quality) (see Ch.4): Aberdeen; Belfast (Queen's); Birmingham; Brunel; Cambridge; Canterbury Christ Church (UC); Durham; East London; Edinburgh; Exeter; Glasgow; Hull; Lancaster; Leicester; Liverpool; London (King's), (LSE), (RH), (UCL); Oxford; St Andrews; Sheffield; Strathclyde; Warwick; York; not all institutions assessed.

Top universities and colleges (Research) (see Ch.4): Aberystwyth; Belfast (Queen's); Birmingham; Bristol; Cambridge; Cardiff; Durham; East Anglia; Edinburgh; Essex; Exeter; Hull; Keele; Kent; Lancaster; Leeds; Leicester; Liverpool; London (Gold), (King's), (LSE), (QM), (RH), (SOAS), (UCL); London Guildhall; Manchester; Newcastle; Nottingham; Oxford; Oxford Brookes; Reading; St Andrews; Sheffield; Sheffield Hallam; Southampton; Stirling; Strathclyde; Sussex; Swansea; Ulster; Warwick; York.

Study opportunities abroad: Aberdeen; Aberystwyth; Bangor; Bristol; Cardiff; Cheltenham & Glos (CHE); Chester (Coll); Chichester (UC); De Montfort; Dundee; Durham; East Anglia; Edinburgh; Essex; Exeter; Hull; King Alfred's Winchester (Coll); Lampeter; Lancaster; Leeds; Leicester; Liverpool; Liverpool Hope (Coll); London (QM), (RH); Manchester; Manchester Met; Middlesex; North London; Nottingham; Portsmouth; Reading; St Andrews; Sheffield; Sheffield Hallam; Southampton; Staffordshire; Sunderland; Surrey Roehampton; Sussex; Swansea; Teesside; Warwick; Worcester (UC); York (E).

ADMISSIONS INFORMATION

Number of applicants per place (approx): Aberystwyth 6; Anglia 4; Bangor 6; Bath Spa (UC) 6; Birmingham 12, (Mediev St) 5, (E Medt Hist) 3; Bournemouth (Herit Cons) 3; Bristol 18; Bristol UWE 6; Brunel 6; Buckingham 10; Cambridge 2.8; Cardiff 9; Central

Lancashire 5; Cheltenham & Glos (CHE) 26; Chichester (UC) 3; De Montfort 17; Durham 15; East Anglia 8; Edge Hill (CHE) 8; Exeter 9; Huddersfield 4; Hull 9; Kent 12; Kingston 6; Lampeter 6; Lancaster 11; Leeds 12; Leeds, Trinity & All Saints (Coll) 14; Leicester 16; Liverpool 15; London Guildhall 2; London (Gold) 6, (King's) 11, (LSE) 11, (QM) 3, (RH) 9, (UCL) 13; Manchester Met 8; Middlesex 10; Newcastle 13; Newman (CHE) 10; North East Wales (IHE) 2; Northampton (UC) 8; Nottingham 20; Oxford 3; Oxford Brookes 25; Portsmouth 5; St Mark & St John (Coll) 3; St Martin's (Coll) 5; St Mary's (Coll) 5; Sheffield Hallam 21; Southampton 10; Staffordshire 8; Stirling 16; Surrey Roehampton 3; Swansea 8; Teesside 4; York 11.

Planning your UCAS personal statement (see Ch.4): Visits to places of interest should be mentioned, together with any particular features which impressed you. Read historical books and magazines outside your A-level syllabus. Mention these and describe any special areas of study which interest you. (Check that these areas are covered in the courses for which you are applying!) **Bangor** Clear commitment to history/archaeological studies work experience. Travel. **Birmingham** An interest in the past above and beyond school work. **London (King's)** History books read and enjoyed – why? **Nottingham** Active engagement with history and enthusiasm for the subject. **Portsmouth** Write clearly and concisely. **St Andrews** Reasons for choosing the course. Evidence of interest.

Selection interviews (see Ch.4): Aberystwyth (No); Anglia (No); Bangor (No); Bath Spa (UC) (No); Birmingham (Mediev Modn Hist) (No), (Mediev St) (all), E Medit Hist); Bishop Grosseteste (CHE); Brighton; Bristol; Brunel; Buckingham; Cambridge (W, T); Cardiff (No); Cheltenham & Glos (CHE) (No); Cumbria (CAD) (some); De Montfort (No); Durham (No); East Anglia (No); Edge Hill (CHE); Edinburgh (No); Essex; Exeter (some); Glamorgan (No); Hertfordshire; Huddersfield (some); Hull; Kent (No); Kingston (No); Lampeter (some); Lancaster; Leeds, Trinity & All Saints (Coll); Leicester (No); Liverpool; Liverpool Hope (Coll) (No); London (Inst) (W); London (Gold) (No), (King's), (LSE) (rarely), (QM), (RH), (UCL); London Guildhall; Manchester (No); Manchester Met (mature students only); Middlesex; Newcastle (No); Newman (CHE) (No); Nottingham (No); Nottingham Trent (No); Oxford (W – short test lasting no more than one hour; candidates advised beforehand); Oxford Brookes; Portsmouth; Ripon & York (Coll) (No); St Andrews (No); Sheffield (No); Sheffield Hallam (some); South Bank; Southampton (some); Staffordshire; Stirling (No); Surrey Roehampton; Sussex; Swansea (50%); Warwick (Oxbridge decisions awaited before offer); Worcester (UC) (No); York (No).

Interview questions (see Ch.4): Questions are almost certain to be asked on those aspects of the history A-level syllabus which interest you. Examples of questions in previous years have included: Why did Imperialism happen? If a Martian arrived on Earth what aspect of life would you show him/her to sum up today's society? Has the role of class been exaggerated by Marxist historians? What is the difference between power and authority and between patriotism and nationalism? Did Elizabeth I have a foreign policy? What is the relevance of history in modern society? Who are your favourite monarchs? How could you justify your study of history to the taxpayer?

Reasons for rejection (non-academic): Lack of commitment and enthusiasm. Lack of clear reason for choice of course. Lack of understanding of history. Absence or narrowness of intellectual pursuits. Deception or concealment on the UCAS form. **Birmingham** Commitment level insufficient to sustain interest over three years. **London (King's)** Inability to think analytically and comparatively. **Nottingham** No discrimination against Oxbridge applicants.

GAP YEAR ADVICE

Birmingham (E Medit Hist) Improve your knowledge of one foreign language and of the modern Middle East; **Bournemouth** (Herit Cons) Department can advise on relevant experience; **Buckingham** Master another language; **Manchester Met** Apply for your place during the gap year; **Swansea** Request reading lists. Early decision preferable.

Institutions willing to defer entry after A-Levels: Aberystwyth; Bangor; Birmingham; Bournemouth (Herit Cons); Bradford; Brighton; Bristol UWE; Buckingham; Cardiff; Central

Lancashire; Cheltenham & Glos (CHE); De Montfort; Dundee; East Anglia; Edge Hill (CHE); Huddersfield; Hull; Kent; King Alfred's Winchester (Coll); Lampeter; Lancaster; Leeds; Leicester; Liverpool Hope (Coll); London (Gold), (RH); London Guildhall; Luton; Manchester Met (No); Newcastle; Newport (UWCN); North East Wales (IHE); North London; Northumbria; Nottingham; Portsmouth; Ripon & York (Coll) (No); St Andrews; St Mark & St John (Coll); St Mary's (Coll); Salford; Sheffield Hallam; Southampton (some); Sunderland; Surrey Roehampton; Sussex; Swansea; Warwick; Wolverhampton; Worcester (UC); York.

AFTER RESULTS ADVICE

Institutions which may accept the same points score after A-Levels: Aberystwyth; Anglia; Bangor; Birmingham; Brighton; Bristol; Bristol UWE (No); Buckingham; Cardiff; Cheltenham & Glos (CHE); Chichester (UC); De Montfort; Durham (varies); East Anglia (varies); Edge Hill (CHE); Essex; Exeter; Hull; Kent; Kingston (No); Lampeter; Lancaster; Leeds (No); Leeds, Trinity & All Saints (Coll); Leicester (No); Liverpool; London (Gold), (RH), (SOAS) (No); London Guildhall; Manchester Met; Middlesex; Newcastle (in some cases); Newman (CHE); North East Wales (IHE); Nottingham (No); Oxford Brookes; Portsmouth (No); Ripon & York (Coll); St Andrews (No); St Martin's (Coll); Sheffield Hallam; Stirling (No); Surrey Roehampton; Swansea; Warwick (No); Wolverhampton; Worcester (UC) (No); York (varies).

Institutions which may accept lower grades/points score after A-Levels: Aberystwyth; Bangor; Birmingham; Bradford; Brighton; Bristol; Cheltenham & Glos (CHE); Chichester (UC); East Anglia; Edge Hill (CHE); Essex; Exeter; Glasgow; Hull; Kent: Lampeter; Lancaster; Leeds, Trinity & All Saints (Coll); Liverpool (Modn Hist/Pol); Liverpool Hope (Coll); London (Gold), (RH), (SOAS); Manchester Met; Newcastle; Newport (UWCN); North East Wales (IHE); Portsmouth; St Andrews; St Martin's (Coll); Sheffield Hallam; Surrey Roehampton; Swansea; Warwick; Wolverhampton.

Offers to applicants repeating A-Levels: Higher East Anglia, Exeter, Lampeter, Leeds, Liverpool, St Andrews, Swansea, Warwick; **Possibly higher** Aberystwyth, Birmingham, Cambridge (Hom), Durham, Portsmouth, York; **Same** Anglia, Bangor, Bristol, Edge Hill (CHE), Hull, Lancaster, London (RH), (SOAS), Newcastle, Newport (UWCN), Oxford Brookes, St Martin's (Coll); Surrey Roehampton.

Probable vacancies from June 2001 and in Clearing (see Ch.4): There is likely to be a good selection of vacancies, particularly on joint courses.

NEW GRADUATE DESTINATIONS AND EMPLOYMENT (1999 HESA) (see **Ch.4**)

In a survey of 4508 graduates, 2092 obtained full-time employment (the majority going into business activities, community and social services and finance), 1442 went on to further study and 240 were believed to be unemployed.

HISTORY (ANCIENT) (see also History)

NB The information supplied by the universities and colleges this year varies consider-ably and the offers listed below should be used as a first source of reference only. Many institutions will accept combinations of Advanced (AL), Advanced Subsidiary (AS) and Vocational Advanced (VA) level qualifications to achieve the required points total, but applicants must check web sites and prospectuses for full details of all offers. Grades and points totals shown should be regarded as the minimum levels to be achieved, but offers may be adjusted downwards when results are known. The points totals shown to the left of the institutions are for ease of reference only. It must not be assumed that tariff points are always used by institutions or that they can be substituted for an offer in grades. The level of an offer is not necessarily indicative of the quality of a course. To calculate your offers see Chapter 4 and the inside fold of the back cover.

Special subject requirements/preferences: A-Level: History, ususally the highest grade in offers below. **London (King's)** Ancient history/classical civilisation. **Oxford** Full A-Levels desirable. **GCSE: Birmingham, Durham, Liverpool, London (King's), (RH), (UCL)** A foreign language or classical language required. **Cardiff** Evidence of linguistic ability an advantage. **Durham** Four or five A* grades, three or four As. **Lampeter** Five or six subjects at grade A or B. **Oxford** Majority of grade As preferred. **Scottish universities** See under **History. Swansea** Five A* or As, five Bs.

360 pts **and above**
Oxford – Offers vary between candidates (Anc Modn Hist)
320 pts **Durham** – ABB (Anc Mediev Mod Hist)
Edinburgh – ABB–BBB (Anc Hist courses)
300 pts **Birmingham** – BBB/24 pts (Hist E Medit Hist)
Liverpool – 300 pts – ALs **or** ALs+ASs **or** VAs+/-ALs/ASs; (Anc Hist/Arch)
London (RH) – ABC–BBB/AB–BB (Anc Mediev Hist)
London (RH) – BBB (Anc Hist)
London (UCL) – BBB **or** 3ALs+AS/VA (Anc Hist)
Manchester – BBB (Anc Hist/Arch)
St Andrews – BBB (Anc Hist)
Swansea – 300 pts 18u – BBB–BBC/BC **or** ALs+ASs **or** VAs+/-ALs/ASs; (Anc/Mediev Hist)
280 pts **Birmingham** – BBC (Anc Hist/Arch/E Medit Hist)
Bristol – BBC–BCC (inc anc hist/hist/class civ); (not gs) (Anc Hist)
Durham – BBC (Anc Hist/Arch; Anc Hist)
London (King's) – BBC+AS **or** BB+bb (inc AL/AS hist); (Anc Hist)
London (UCL) – BBC **or** 3ALs+AS/VA; (Anc Hist with Egypt/Soc Anth; Anc Wrld St)
Manchester – BBC/AB–BB (Anc Hist/Class)
Swansea – 280 pts 18u – BBC–BCC/BB **or** ALs+ASs **or** VAs+/-ALs/ASs; (Anc Hist; Anc Hist/Welsh)
Warwick – BBC–BCC (Anc Hist/Class Arch)
260 pts **Belfast (Queen's)** – BCC–CCC (Anc Hist courses; Byz St joint courses)
Cardiff – BCC/AB–BB (Anc Hist; Anc Mediev Hist)
Exeter – 260 pts 18u – BCC **or** BC+cc **or** VAs (contact univ); (not gs) (Anc Hist courses)
Leicester – BCC/BB (Anc Hist/Arch)
Newcastle – BCC (Anc Hist; Anc Hist/Arch)
Nottingham – BCC (Anc Hist)
Reading – BCC (Anc Hist/Arch; Anc Hist)
Warwick – BCC (Anc Hist/Class Arch)
240 pts **Leeds** – CCC/BB (Lat/Anc Hist)
220 pts **Lampeter** – 220 pts approx (Anc Hist; Anc Hist/Arch)
Reading – CCD (Anc Hist/Sociol)

Alternative Offers:

IB offers: Birmingham 33 pts; Bristol H655; Cardiff 28 pts; Durham 36–31 pts; Exeter 30 pts; Lampeter 28 pts; London (RH) 30 pts; St Andrews 28 pts; Swansea 30 pts.

Irish offers: St Andrews BBBB.

Scottish Qualifications: Edinburgh BBBB; St Andrews BBBB.

CHOOSING YOUR COURSE (See also **Ch.1**)

Subject information: Ancient History covers the Greek and Roman world and the social, religious, political and economic changes which took place in the Byzantine period and the medieval era which followed. Other relevant courses include Archaeology, Classical Studies or Civilisation, Classics and the History of Art and Architecture.

Special features: See also **History. Exeter** Greek and Roman history, also sociology, politics, philosophy and religion. **Lampeter** Study of Early Greek, Roman Republic, Roman Empire and also Egypt and Asia Minor. **Leicester** No ancient languages studied after first year (not included in degree assessment). **London (RH)** and **Reading** Includes archaeological aspects of Greece and Rome. **Newcastle** (Anc Hist) 50% assessment through submitted work. Offer made with invitation to visit the department. *NOW CHECK PROSPECTUSES AND WEB SITES.*

Top universities and colleges (Teaching Quality) (see Ch.4): See **History.**

Top universities and colleges (Research) (see Ch.4): See **Classics.**

Study opportunities abroad: Cardiff; Leicester.

ADMISSIONS INFORMATION

Number of applicants per place (approx): Birmingham (Anc/Mediev Hist) 8; Bristol 15; Cardiff 4; Durham 15; Lampeter 6; Leicester 32; London (RH) 3; Newcastle 10; Oxford 2; Swansea 5.

Planning your UCAS personal statement (see Ch.4): Any information about experience of excavation or museum work should be given. Visits to Greece and Italy to study architectural sites should be described. See also **History.**

Selection interviews (see Ch.4): Birmingham; Cardiff (some); Durham; Edinburgh (No); Lampeter (only special cases); Leeds; London (RH) (T); Newcastle (some); Oxford (T) (W – short 1 hour test may be set; candidates will be advised beforehand); St Andrews (No); Swansea.

Interview questions (see Ch.4): See **History.**

GAP YEAR ADVICE

Birmingham Practical archaeological experience and foreign language study useful; **Cardiff** Secure university place before taking gap year.

Institutions willing to defer entry after A-Levels: Bristol (No); Cardiff; Durham; Lampeter; Leicester (not usually); Newcastle (Anc Hist/Arch); Nottingham; Swansea.

AFTER RESULTS ADVICE

Institutions which may accept the same points score after A-Levels: Birmingham; Durham; Leeds; Leicester; Newcastle (No); Nottingham (No); Swansea.

Institutions which may accept lower grades/points score after A-Levels: Durham; Leeds; Swansea.

Offers to applicants repeating A-Levels: Same Birmingham, Durham, Newcastle, Swansea.

Probable vacancies from June 2001 and in Clearing (see Ch.4): Most universities could be contacted since vacancies are likely.

NEW GRADUATE DESTINATIONS AND EMPLOYMENT (1999 HESA) (see **Ch.4**)

See **History.**

HISTORY (ECONOMIC & SOCIAL) (see also History)

NB The information supplied by the universities and colleges this year varies considerably and the offers listed below should be used as a first source of reference only. Many institutions will accept combinations of Advanced (AL), Advanced Subsidiary (AS) and Vocational Advanced (VA) level qualifications to achieve the required points total, but applicants must check web sites and prospectuses for full details of all offers. Grades and points totals shown should be regarded as the minimum levels to be achieved, but offers may be adjusted downwards when results are known. The points totals shown to the left of the institutions are for ease of reference only. It must not be assumed that tariff points are always used by institutions or that they can be substituted for an offer in grades. The level of an offer is not necessarily indicative of the quality of a course. To calculate your offers see Chapter 4 and the inside fold of the back cover.

Special subject requirements/preferences: A-Level: History usually the highest grade in offers below. **Manchester** B in history. **GCSE:** Mathematics usually required. **London (LSE)** Grades A/B. **Manchester** A foreign language. **Scottish universities** See under **History**. **York** Spread of As and Bs.

340 pts	**and above**
	London (LSE) – AAB–BBB (Econ Hist/Econ)
	Manchester – AAB–BBC (Econ Hist/Econ)
	Warwick – AAB (Econ/Econ Hist)
320 pts	**Bristol** – ABB–BCC; (not gs) (Econ Soc Hist)
	Edinburgh – ABB (1 sitting) (not gs) (Econ Hist courses)
	London (LSE) – ABB (Econ Hist; Econ Hist/Pop St)
	York – ABB (Hist/Econ; Hist/Sociol)
300 pts	**East Anglia** – ABC–BCC (Econ/Soc Hist)
	Kent – 300 pts approx (Hist/Herit St)
	Leeds – BBB (Econ Soc Hist (Pol))
	Liverpool – 300 pts – ALs **or** ALs+ASs **or** VAs+/-ALs/ASs; (Hist Soc/Econ)
	London (RH) – ABC–BBB/AB–BB (Modn Hist Econ Hist/Pol)
	Manchester – BBB–BBC (Econ Soc Hist)
	Manchester Met – BBB–BBC (Econ Soc Econ Hist)
	Sussex – BBB (Econ Soc Hist courses)
280 pts	**Birmingham** – BBC (Econ Soc Hist; Hist/Soc Sci)
	Bristol – BBC–BCC/BB–BC (Econ/Econ Hist)
	Exeter – BBC–CCC (Hist/Econ/Cult)
	Glasgow – BBC (Econ Soc Hist courses)
	Lancaster – BBC (Soc Hist)
	Leeds – BBC–BCC (Econ Soc Hist (Geog) (Soc Pol) (Sociol))
	Sheffield – BBC (Soc Hist)
	Swansea – BBC (Econ Hist/Econ)
260 pts	**Aberystwyth** – 260–240 pts (Econ/Soc Hist Comb)
	Belfast (Queen's) – BCC (BSSc/BA Econ Soc Hist; Econ Hist)
	Leicester – 260 pts 18u – BCC; gs; (Econ Soc Hist courses)
240 pts	**Aberdeen** – CCC (Econ Hist)
	Bradford – 240 pts 12u; gs; (Econ/Hist; Econ/Pol; Econ/Sociol; Econ/Soc Psy)
	Hull – BCD–CCD/BC–CC (Econ/Soc Hist)
220 pts	**Manchester Met** – CCD/CC (Hum/Soc St)
	Swansea – 220 pts 18u – CCD/BC **or** ALs+ASs **or** VAs+/-ALs/ASs; (Econ Hist/ Russ St; Econ/Soc Hist)
200 pts	**Portsmouth** – 200 pts (Econ Soc Hist)
	Wolverhampton – 200 pts approx; gs (Soc Pol Hist)

Alternative Offers:

IB offers: Aberdeen 30 pts; Aberystwyth 30 pts; Bristol 32–30 pts; East Anglia 30 pts; Exeter 30 pts; Hull 28 pts inc scores of 5; Kent 32 pts; London (LSE) 36 pts H666.

Irish offers: St Andrews BBBB.

Scottish Qualifications: Aberdeen BBBB; Edinburgh BBBB; Glasgow ABBB–BBBB; St Andrews BBBB.

CHOOSING YOUR COURSE (See also **Ch.1**)

Subject information: Economic and Social History students will follow courses covering economics and the historical changes in Britain, Europe and other major powers. Degree courses in Economics, Politics, Government, International Relations and European/East European Studies could also be considered.

Special features: See **History**. **Belfast (Queen's)** Covers Irish and US social history in first year followed by European, British and Canadian topics. **Edinburgh** Specialisms in Eastern Europe, Latin America, India and Russia. **Glasgow** Study of wealth creation and improvement of social welfare and standard of life in Western Europe since 1700. **Hull** Large choice of options in second and third years covering economic and/or social history and a range of countries (Germany, Soviet Union, USA, India). **Kent** Unique course in Social History and Heritage Studies. **Leeds** Covers British economy and industrialisation in Europe. Subsidiary subject taken in year 1. **Leicester** Two additional supplementary subjects taken in first year from economics, geography, politics and sociology etc. Similar arrangements at **Liverpool**. **Portsmouth** Language options in French and German. Similarly at **Swansea** and also in Italian, Russian and Spanish. *NOW CHECK PROSPECTUSES AND WEB SITES.*

Top universities and colleges (Teaching Quality) (see Ch.4): See **History**.

Top universities and colleges (Research) (see Ch.4): Belfast (Queen's); Birmingham; Edinburgh; Glasgow; Hull; Leicester; London (LSE).

ADMISSIONS INFORMATION

Number of applicants per place (approx): Birmingham 10; Bristol 9; East Anglia 10; Hull 4; Leeds 7; Leicester 5; Liverpool 3; London (LSE) (Econ Hist) 5, (Econ Hist/Econ) 8, (Econ Hist/Pop St) 11; Portsmouth 10; York 8.

Planning your UCAS personal statement (see Ch.4): See **History**.

Selection interviews (see Ch.4): Aberystwyth; Birmingham; Bristol; Exeter (No); Leicester; Liverpool; Portsmouth (No); Sheffield; Warwick; York (No).

Interview questions (see Ch.4): See **History**.

GAP YEAR ADVICE

Institutions willing to defer entry after A-Levels: Bristol (No); Kent; Leeds.

AFTER RESULTS ADVICE

Institutions which may accept the same points score after A-Levels: Birmingham; Exeter; Hull; Kent; Leicester; Liverpool; Portsmouth; Warwick (No); York (No).

Offers to applicants repeating A-Levels: Higher Portsmouth, Warwick, York; **Possibly higher** Liverpool; **Same** Exeter, Hull.

Probable vacancies from June 2001 and in Clearing (see Ch.4): Several universities are likely to have vacancies in this subject. Offers are likely to average 240 pts.

NEW GRADUATE DESTINATIONS AND EMPLOYMENT (1999 HESA) (see **Ch.4**)

In a survey of 263 graduates, 147 went into full-time employment (mainly in business, public administration and finance), 58 went on to further study and 11 were believed to be unemployed.

HISTORY OF ART

NB The information supplied by the universities and colleges this year varies consider-ably and the offers listed below should be used as a first source of reference only. Many institutions will accept combinations of Advanced (AL), Advanced Subsidiary (AS) and Vocational Advanced (VA) level qualifications to achieve the required points total, but applicants must check web sites and prospectuses for full details of all offers. Grades and points totals shown should be regarded as the minimum levels to be achieved, but offers may be adjusted downwards when results are known. The points totals shown to the left of the institutions are for ease of reference only. It must not be assumed that tariff points are always used by institutions or that they can be substituted for an offer in grades. The level of an offer is not necessarily indicative of the quality of a course. To calculate your offers see Chapter 4 and the inside fold of the back cover.

Special subject requirements/preferences: A-Level: History of art at A-Level is not necessarily a requirement for these courses. **Sheffield Hallam** Prefers English, history and history of art. **GCSE: Cambridge** Usually grade As; **East Anglia** Modern language grade A–C preferred; **York** Good spread of A/B grades.

360 pts **and above**
Cambridge – Entry to History of Art takes place after successful completion of Part 1 of another course
350 pts **Southampton** – 350 pts 21u (inc 200 pts from 2ALs inc Fr/Ger/Span; AS b); (Hist Art Des with Fr/Ger/Span)
340 pts **St Andrews** – AAB (Art Hist – Int Rel)
330 pts **Southampton** – 330 pts 21u (inc 180 pts from hum subj); (Hist Art Des)
320 pts **Edinburgh** – ABB (1 sitting); (not gs) (Soc Archit Hist)
Edinburgh – ABB (Hist Art/Engl Lit)
Leeds – ABB (Engl/Hist Art)
St Andrews – ABB (Art Hist – Psy)
York – 320–280 pts 21–18u – BBC+b; (Hist Art)
300 pts **Birmingham** – BBB (Hist Art courses)
Edinburgh – BBB (Archit Hist)
Kent – 300–260 pts; gs; (Hist/Theor Art)
Leeds – BBB (Hist/Hist Art)
Liverpool – BBB–ABC (Hist Art/Archit)
London (UCL) – BBB **or** 3ALs+AS/VA; (Hist Art/Mat St)
Newcastle – BBB (Hist Art Comb courses)
Sussex – BBB (Hist Art courses)
Warwick – BBB–BBC (Hist Art)
Winchester (SA) – ABC (Hist Art/Modn Lang; Hist Art Des)
280 pts **Bristol** – BBC(inc B Fr/Ger or modn lang for Lang courses); (not gs) (Hist Art; Hist Art/Fr/Ger/Ital/Port/Russ/Span)
East Anglia – BBC/BB (Hist Art courses)
Edinburgh – BBC (Hist Art/Scand St)
Essex – 280–260 pts 21u – BB–BC+AL/2ASs **or** VA12u BB–BC (art)+AL; gs; (Hist Art)
Glasgow – BBC (Hist Art)
Lancaster – BBC–BCC (Art Hist/Art)
Leeds – BBC (Hist Art – Mus)
Leicester – BBC–BCC/BB (Hist Art except under **260 pts**)
London (Court) – BBC (Hist Art)
London (UCL) – BBC **or** 3ALs+AS/VA; (Hist Art)
Manchester – BBC (Hist Modn Art; Hist Art/Archit; Art Arch Anc Wrld)
Nottingham – BBC (Art Hist courses)
Reading – BBC (Art Hist courses)
St Andrews – BBC (Hist Art)
260 pts **Aberystwyth** – 260 pts (Art Hist with Drama/Film TV St, Maths, Geog)
Belfast (Queen's) – BCC (Hist Art courses)

Leicester – BCC–CCC (Art Hist Comb)
London (Gold) – BCC (Art/Art Hist; Hist Art)
London (SOAS) – 260 pts approx (Hist Art As, Af, Euro)
Loughborough – BCC (Engl/Hist Art Des)
Oxford Brookes – BCC offer varies with 2nd subject (Hist Art Joint Hons)

240 pts **Aberdeen** – CCC (Hist Art courses)
Aberystwyth – 240 pts approx (Art Hist/Art and Art Hist courses except under 260 pts)
Brighton – 240 pts approx (Vis Cult)
Central England – 240 pts approx (Hist Mgt Vis Arts)
De Montfort (Leicester) – 240 pts – ALs **or** ALs+ASs **or** VAs+/-ALs/ASs; (Cons/Restor)
Northumbria – CCC (Hist Modn Art)
Sheffield Hallam – 240 pts approx (Hist Art/Des Film Comb)
Staffordshire – 240 pts approx (Hist Art Des/Law; Hist Art Des/Leg St)

220 pts **Falmouth (CA)** – 220 pts (Hist Modn Art Des)
Glamorgan – 220–140 pts approx offers vary with 2nd subject (Art Hist Comb)
Kingston – 220–180 pts (inc 2x6u); gs; (Art/Archit/Des Hist)
Kingston – 220 pts approx (B Engl) (Hist Art Archit Des/Engl Lit)
Middlesex – 220–180 pts approx (Hist Theor Media Art Des; Art Des Hist)
Portsmouth – 220 pts – ALs **or** ALs+ASs **or** VAs; gs; (Art Hist/Vis Cult)
Sheffield Hallam – 220 pts approx (Hist Art Des Film)

210 pts **Buckingham** – 210 pts 21u – 3ALs **or** 3ALs+AS; (Hist Art courses)

200 pts **Chester (Coll)** – 200–180 pts – ALs (160 pts inc C 1 subj)+AS **or** VAs (160 pts inc C 1 subj)+AS; AS(20–40 pts); (Art Hist Comb)
Northampton (UC) – 200–160 pts approx (Hist/Hist Art)
Plymouth – CDD (Art Hist courses)
Sunderland – 200–180 pts approx (Hist Art courses)

180 pts **Buckinghamshire Chilterns (UC)** – 180–140 pts (Art Hist courses)
East London – 180 pts approx offers vary with 2nd subj (Hist Art Des Film)
London Inst (Camberwell) – 180 pts approx (Hist Art; Hist/Theory)
Manchester Met – 189 pts approx (Hist Art Des; Hist/Film Photo/Graph Media)
Staffordshire – 180 pts approx (Hist Art Des/Inf Sys)
Surrey Roehampton – 180 pts (pref ALs in hist/anc hist/econ hist/class hist/Engl); (Art Hist)

160 pts **Anglia** – 160 pts 12u – CC/DD/BE **or** ALs+ASs; gs; (Art Hist courses)
Brighton – CC (Des Cult Soty; Hist Decr Arts/Crafts)
Cumbria (CAD) – CC (Art Hist joint courses)
De Montfort (Leicester/Lincoln) – 160 pts – ALs **or** ALs+ASs **or** VAs+/-ALs/ASs; (not gs) (Hist Art/Des; Hist Archit/Des)
De Montfort (Leicester) –160 pts –ALs **or** ALs+ASs **or** VAs+/-ALs/ASs; (Art Hist)
Liverpool John Moores – 160 pts – ALs (inc art/des subj); (Art Hist St)
Loughborough – Art Fdn reqd (Hist Art Des/Studio Prac)

140 pts **Derby** – 140 pts 12u – CD **or** DE+ee **or** VAs CD+/-ALs/ASs; (Hist/Theor Art Des/Photo courses)
Oxfordshire (SAD) – 140 pts approx (Fine Art/Hist Art Des)

100 pts **and below**
Staffordshire – (Hist Art Des)

Higher National Diploma courses
Somerset (CAT) (Ant Restor).

Alternative Offers:

IB offers: Aberdeen 30 pts; Anglia 28 pts; Brighton 24 pts inc H 12 pts; Bristol 30 pts inc H6; Buckingham 24 pts; De Montfort (Comb) 30–26 pts; East Anglia H444 (min); Edinburgh BBBB; Glamorgan 24 pts; Leeds 30 pts; Leicester 30–28 pts; London (Court) 28 pts inc H 16 pts, (UCL) 30 pts; Plymouth 28 pts; St Andrews 28 pts; Southampton 25 pts; Staffordshire 24 pts; Warwick 30 pts; York 32 pts.

Irish offers: Aberdeen BBBB; Brighton BCCC; London Guildhall CCCCC; Warwick BBBBB.

Scottish Qualifications: Aberdeen BBBB; Edinburgh BBBB; Glasgow BBBB; St Andrews BBBB.

CHOOSING YOUR COURSE (See also **Ch.1**)

Subject information: History of Art and Design courses vary slightly between universities although most will focus on the history and appreciation of European art and architecture from the 14th to 20th centuries. Some courses will also cover the Egyptian, Greek and Roman periods and, in the case of London (SOAS), Asian, African and European Art. The history of all aspects of design and film can also be studied in some courses (see also **Appendix 1**).

Special features: Aberystwyth Practical art and art history with year abroad, possibly in USA. Facilities for painting, graphic arts and photography. **Anglia** Studio work and history or art history on its own; course in Visual Studies covers drawing, printmaking, typography, photography and video work. **East Anglia** (Hist Art) Programme built around two separate periods in history of art, selected from wide variety of subjects which range from antiquity to present day. **Edinburgh** (Fine Art) Course takes five years and combines the history of art and practical art with (in years 1 & 2) a second subject. **Essex** (Hist Art) Third year includes art theory, practical criticism, an extended essay and two options from European art, 20th century art, Latin American art and architecture, Russian art, art in USA or Spanish art and architecture. Studio or practical work is not included. **London (Court)** Covers arts and architecture of Europe from classical antiquity to present day (no practical courses for artists/designers). **London (Gold)** Emphasis on contemporary and modern art. **London (Inst)** (Conservation) International reputation in paper conservation; course involves study of art, science, history, hand skills. Textile conservation also offered. **London (UCL)** (Fine Art) Practical study in Slade School of Fine Art; major part of course devoted to practical work with some course work in the history of art. **Manchester Met** (Hist Film Photo Graph Media) Option of 25% of studio work. Placements in museums, galleries etc in year 2 (no previous graphical experience necessary). (Hist Art Des) Students may choose optional units of practical work as 25% of their course (no previous experience necessary). **Newcastle** (Fine Art) Four-year course in the history of European art and architecture, with studio work in painting, sculpture or design. **Nottingham** (Art Hist) Topics range from the Greek and Roman periods to modern art. Practical work possible but not compulsory. **Oxford** (Fine Art) Full-time study of drawing, painting, printmaking, sculpture, history of art and anatomy. **Sheffield Hallam** (Hist Art Des Film) One of the few degrees in which history of art can be studied alongside film history and media studies. **Sotheby's (Inst)** (Fine/Decr Art) Approved by the University of Manchester. Regular visits to art galleries, museums, historic houses and Sotheby's auction rooms. **Staffordshire** (Hist Art Des) Students select six options: history of ceramics and glass, graphic design, architecture of the industrial society, history of painting and sculpture, film studies, history of fashion. **Warwick** (Hist Art) History of European art and architecture with practical work options. Research-led training. Good geographical base for architecture and art and gallery visits. *NOW CHECK PROSPECTUSES AND WEB SITES.*

Top universities and colleges (Teaching Quality) (see Ch.4): Birmingham; Brighton; Cambridge; East Anglia; Essex; Kent; Leicester; London (Birk), (Court), (SOAS), (UCL); Manchester; Manchester Met; Middlesex; Northumbria; Nottingham; Oxford Brookes; Reading; St Andrews; Warwick; not all institutions assessed.

Top universities and colleges (Research) (see Ch.4): See **Architecture**.

Study opportunities abroad: Aberystwyth; Brighton; Dundee; East Anglia; Kingston; Leicester; London (Inst); London (Court); Manchester Met; Newcastle; Staffordshire; York.

Work opportunities abroad: Aberystwyth; Manchester Met.

ADMISSIONS INFORMATION

Number of applicants per place (approx): Aberystwyth 9; Birmingham 20; Brighton 8; De Montfort 5; Derby 4; East Anglia 7; Glamorgan 3; Kent 12; Kingston 4; Leeds 29; Leicester 10; Liverpool John Moores 2; London (Court) 8, (Gold) 10, (SOAS) 4; London (Inst) 2; Loughborough 7; Manchester Met 10; Middlesex (Hist Art) 16; Newcastle 23; Portsmouth 8; Sheffield Hallam 15; Staffordshire 7; York 20.

Planning your UCAS personal statement (see Ch.4): Applicants for History of Art courses should have made extensive visits to art galleries, particularly in London, and be familiar with the main European schools of painting. Evidence of lively interest required. Discuss your preferences and say why you prefer certain types of work or particular artists. You should also describe any visits to museums and any special interests in furniture, pottery or other artifacts (see also **Appendix 1**). **Aberystwyth** Attendance at evening classes in Art History (if not at A-level). Related hobbies and interests, for example, reading, literature, music, cinema. **London (Gold)** Art enthusiasms, influences, passions. **St Andrews** Reasons for choosing the course and evidence of interest. Sport/extra-curricular activities and positions of responsibility.

Selection interviews (see Ch.4): Aberystwyth (No); Brighton; Buckingham (T); Cambridge; Central England; Cumbria (CAD); De Montfort; East Anglia (majority); Kent; Leicester (No); London (Court) (T), (UCL); Manchester Met; Newcastle (also portfolio); St Andrews (No); Sheffield Hallam; Staffordshire; Warwick; York (No).

Interview questions (see Ch.4): Some universities set slide tests on painting and sculpture. Those applicants who have not taken history of art at A-level will be questioned on their reasons for choosing the subject, their visits to art galleries and museums and their reactions to the art work which has impressed them.

Reasons for rejection (non-academic): Poorly presented practical work. Students who do not express any interest or enthusiasm in contemporary visual arts are rejected.

GAP YEAR ADVICE

Travel and visits to art galleries and museums strongly recommended by many universities and colleges.

Institutions willing to defer entry after A-Levels: Aberystwyth (considered individually); Birmingham; Brighton; Buckingham; De Montfort; Derby; Dundee (No); East Anglia; Leicester; London (UCL); Luton; Manchester Met (No); Newcastle (No); St Andrews; Sheffield Hallam (No); Staffordshire; Sussex; Warwick; Wolverhampton.

AFTER RESULTS ADVICE

Institutions which may accept the same points score after A-Levels: Aberystwyth; Anglia (No); Brighton; Brunel; Cheltenham & Glos (CHE); Chester (Coll); De Montfort; Derby; East Anglia; Leeds; Leicester; Liverpool John Moores; London (Court) (No), (SOAS) (No); Manchester Met; Newman (CHE); Northampton (UC); Nottingham Trent; Oxford Brookes; St Andrews (No); Sheffield Hallam; Staffordshire; Warwick (No); Wolverhampton.

Institutions which may accept lower grades/points score after A-Levels: Aberystwyth; Brighton; De Montfort; Derby; East Anglia; Glasgow; Kent; Leeds; Loughborough; Manchester Met; St Andrews; Warwick; most institutions.

Offers to applicants repeating A-Levels: Possibly higher Loughborough, Oxford Brookes, St Andrews; **Same** Aberystwyth, Derby, Leeds, Newcastle, Warwick.

Probable vacancies from June 2001 and in Clearing (see Ch.4): Vacancies are likely – contact institutions for further information.

NEW GRADUATE DESTINATIONS AND EMPLOYMENT (1999 HESA) (see **Ch.4**)

In a survey of 741 graduates, 367 obtained full-time employment and 63 part-time employment, 160 went on to further study and 52 were believed to be unemployed.

HORTICULTURE (including Garden Design)

NB The information supplied by the universities and colleges this year varies considerably and the offers listed below should be used as a first source of reference only. Many institutions will accept combinations of Advanced (AL), Advanced Subsidiary (AS) and Vocational Advanced (VA) level qualifications to achieve the required points total, but applicants must check web sites and prospectuses for full details of all offers. Grades and points totals shown should be regarded as the minimum levels to be achieved, but offers may be adjusted downwards when results are known. The points totals shown to the left of the institutions are for ease of reference only. It must not be assumed that tariff points are always used by institutions or that they can be substituted for an offer in grades. The level of an offer is not necessarily indicative of the quality of a course. To calculate your offers see Chapter 4 and the inside fold of the back cover.

Special subject requirements/preferences: A-Level: Science subjects required – biology and chemistry usually preferred. **GCSE:** Mathematics usually required.

260 pts **London (Imp)** – 260 pts approx (App Nat Sci/Mgt (Hort Sci))
240 pts **Central England** – 240 pts approx (Gard Des)
 Nottingham – CCD–BC; (not gs) (Horticulture)
200 pts **Reading** – CDD/BC (Horticulture)
180 pts **Royal (CAg)** – 180 pts approx (Hort (Prod Mgt) (Crop Mgt) (Amen Mgt))
160 pts **Bishop Burton (CAg)** – 160 pts approx (Gard Des)
 Harper Adams (UC) – 160 pts 12u – CC/CEE/DDE **or** CE+c **or** DD+c **or** VA CC; gs; (Hort Crop Mgt; Hort/Prod Mgt; Hort/Amen Mgt)
 Scottish (CAg) – 160 pts (inc AL sci) – CC; (Horticulture)
 Writtle (Coll) – 160 pts approx (Hort Crop Prod; Hort; Hort/Bus Mgt; Gard Land Des; Int Hort)
140 pts **and below**
 Central Lancashire (Myerscough) – DD (Hort courses)
 Greenwich – 140 pts approx (Hort; Gard Des St)
 Worcester (UC) – 120 pts 12u – DD **or** ALs+ASs **or** VAs+/-ALs/ASs; gs; (Horticulture)

 Leeds Met – (contact university)

Higher National Diploma courses (England & Wales)
100 pts **and below**
 Askham Bryan (Coll); Cannington (Coll) (Golf Course Mgt); Capel Manor (Coll); Central England; Central Lancashire (Newton Rigg) (Amen/Land Des); De Montfort (Floristry); Greenwich (Gard Des; Hort); Hadlow (Coll); Harper Adams (UC) (Golf Course Mgt); Lackham (Coll) (Hort/Gard Mgt; Gard Plan Des; Orgnc Crop Prod); Myerscough (Coll) (Commer Floral Des; Hort; Turf Sci; Gard Des); Pershore (Coll); Rycotewood (Coll); Scottish (CAg); Warwickshire (Coll); Worcester (UC); Writtle (Coll) (Amen/Commer/Rtl/Nursy Hort).

Alternative Offers:

IB offers: London (Imp) 25 pts; Nottingham 24 pts (sci).

Scottish Qualifications: Nottingham BBBB (first sitting); Scottish (CAg) BCC.

CHOOSING YOUR COURSE (See also **Ch.1**)

> **Subject information:** Horticulture is a broad subject area which covers commercial horticulture and the provision of recreational and leisure facilities (amenity horticulture). The subject also overlaps into Agriculture, Botany and Landscape Architecture; degree courses in these subjects could also be considered. See also **Botany**. See also **Appendix 1**.

Special features: Central Lancashire (Myerscough) (Horticulture) Strong links with horticultural industry through research and development work. **London (Imp)** Covers crop science, business management and fresh produce production. **Nottingham** Opportunity for a major research project. **Writtle (Coll)** Industrial placement year. Specialisms in landscape and amenity and crop technology management. *NOW CHECK PROSPECTUSES AND WEB SITES.*

Top universities and colleges (Research) (see Ch.4): London (Imp) (Biol Sci); Nottingham.

Study opportunities abroad: Askham Bryan (Coll) (HND); Bath; Central Lancashire (Myerscough); London (Imp); Nottingham; Reading; Worcester (UC); Writtle (Coll).

Work opportunities abroad: Bath; Royal (CAg); Scottish (CAg); Writtle (Coll).

ADMISSIONS INFORMATION

Number of applicants per place (approx): Central Lancashire (Myerscough) 7; Scottish (CAg) 1; Writtle (Coll) 3.

Planning your UCAS personal statement (see Ch.4): Practical experience is important and visits to botanical gardens (the Royal Botanic Gardens, Kew or Edinburgh, and the Royal Horticultural Society gardens at Wisley) could be described. Contact your local authority offices for details of work in Parks and Gardens Departments. See also **Appendix 1**.

Selection interviews (see Ch.4): Nottingham; Scottish (CAg); Worcester (UC).

Interview questions (see Ch.4): How did you become interested in horticulture? How do you think this course will benefit you? Could you work in all weathers? What career are you aiming for? Are you interested in gardening? Describe your garden. What plants do you grow? How do you prune rose trees and fruit trees? Are there any EU policies at present affecting the horticulture industry? Topics relating to the importance of science and horticulture.

GAP YEAR ADVICE

Institutions willing to defer entry after A-Levels: Harper Adams (UC); London (Imp); Nottingham; Royal (CAg); Writtle (Coll).

AFTER RESULTS ADVICE

Institutions which may accept the same points score after A-Levels: Royal (CAg); Scottish (CAg); Worcester (UC).

Institutions which may accept lower grades/points score after A-Levels: London (Imp); Nottingham; Royal (CAg); Scottish (CAg).

Offers to applicants repeating A-Levels: Possibly higher Nottingham; **Same** Royal (CAg); Scottish (CAg).

Probable vacancies from June 2001 and in Clearing (see Ch.4): All universities and colleges can be contacted since vacancies are likely from June onwards.

NEW GRADUATE DESTINATIONS AND EMPLOYMENT (1999 HESA) (see **Ch.4**)

No data available for this subject area. See **Agricultural Sciences/Agriculture**.

HOSPITALITY, HOTEL AND CATERING MANAGEMENT (including Institutional Management; see also Consumer Studies and Leisure & Recreational Studies)

NB The information supplied by the universities and colleges this year varies considerably and the offers listed below should be used as a first source of reference only. Many institutions will accept combinations of Advanced (AL), Advanced Subsidiary (AS) and Vocational Advanced (VA) level qualifications to achieve the required points total, but applicants must check web sites and prospectuses for full details of all offers. Grades and points totals shown should be regarded as the minimum levels to be achieved, but offers may be adjusted downwards when results are known. The points totals shown to the left of the institutions are for ease of reference only. It must not be assumed that tariff points are always used by institutions or that they can be substituted for an offer in grades. The level of an offer is not necessarily indicative of the quality of a course. To calculate your offers see Chapter 4 and the inside fold of the back cover.

Special subject requirements/preferences: GCSE: English and mathematics usually required, plus a foreign language for International Management courses. **Bournemouth** Average grades B. **Salford** Five subjects grades A–C including English and mathematics.

260 pts **Oxford Brookes** – BCC–DDD/BC–CC offers vary with 2nd subject (Hspty Mgt courses; Htl Rstrnt Mgt)

240 pts **Barnfield (Coll)** – 240 pts (Hspty Mgt)
Manchester Met – 240–200 pts approx (Hspty Mgt)
Napier – CCC (Hspty Mgt courses)
Surrey – 240 pts 18u – ALs **or** ALs+ASs **or** VAs (depends on subj)+/-ALs/ASs; (not gs) (Htl Cat Mgt; Int Hspty Tour Mgt)
Ulster – CCC–CCD (Htl/Tour Mgt; Hspty Mgt)

220 pts **Central Lancashire** – 220 pts 12u; gs; (Hspty Mgt; Int Hspty Mgt)
Portsmouth – 220 pts – ALs **or** ALs+ASs **or** VAs; gs; (Hspty/Herit; Hspty Mgt; Hspty Mgt/Tour)
Sheffield Hallam – 220–200 pts approx (Htl Tour Mgt)
South East Essex (Coll) – 220–180 pts (Serv Ind Mgt)

200 pts **Bournemouth** – 200 pts from 3ALs **or** 180 pts from 2ALs **or** VAs; (Int Hspty Mgt; Int Culn Arts Mgt)
Derby – CDD **or** CD+dd **or** VAs (AL grades)+/-ALs/ASs; gs; (Hspty Mgt; Prof Culn Arts)
Sheffield Hallam – 200 pts approx (Htl/Cat Mgt)
Strathclyde – CDD (Htl Cat Mgt)

190 pts **North London** – 190 pts inc 160 pts from 2ALs **or** VAs; (Hspty Mgt; Int Hspty Mgt)

180 pts **Brighton** – 180 pts approx (Hspty Mgt; Int Hspty Mgt)
Buckingham – 180 pts approx (Bus St/Int Htl Mgt)
Cardiff (UWI) – 180 pts approx (Int Hspty Mgt; Hspty Mgt; Recr/Leis Mgt; Cat Mgt)
Cheltenham & Glos (CHE) – 180 pts approx (Hspty Mgt courses)
Huddersfield – DDD/CC (Hspty Mgt/Lang)
Luton – 180 pts approx (Hspty Mgt – Mod)
Sheffield Hallam – 180 pts approx (Food Consum St)
Wolverhampton – 180 pts 12u – DDD–CDE/BD–CC **or** DD+b **or** VA12u CC; gs; (Hspty Mgt; Hspty/Lic Rtl Mgt)

160 pts **Abertay Dundee** – CC (Hspty Mgt)
Birmingham (CFTCS) – 12u (inc 1x6u) – CC **or** ALs+ASs **or** VAs+/-ALs/ASs; (Hspty Bus Mgt; Hspty/Fd Mgt; Hspty/Leis Mgt; Hspty/Tour Mgt; Lic Rtl Mgt)
Cheltenham & Glos (CHE) – 160–140 pts approx (Hspty Mgt (Cat) courses)
Glasgow Caledonian – CC (Hspty Mgt)
Huddersfield – CC **or** C+cc **or** VA12u CC; gs; (Cat Mgt Food Sci; Cat Mgt Nutr; Hspty Mgt; Hspty Lic Hous Mgt)
Napier – 160 pts (Hspty Mgt; Hspty Tour Mgt)
Plymouth (Seale Hayne) – 160 pts approx (Hspty Mgt)
Salford – 160 pts approx (Hspty Tour Mgt)
South Bank – CC (Int Hspty Tour Mgt; Hspty Mgt)

140 pts **Blackpool & Fylde (Coll)** – 140 pts approx (Hspty Mgt; Int Htl Mgt; Hspty Mgt/Tour)
Middlesex – CD (Htl Mgt)
Queen Margaret (UC) – CD (Hspty Tour Mgt)

120 pts   and below
> **Colchester (Inst)** – DD (Hspty courses)
> **Norwich City (Coll)** – 120 pts approx (Hspty Tour Mgt courses)
> **Robert Gordon** – DD (Tour/Hspty Mgt; Htl Hspty Mgt)
> **UHI (Moray/North Highland/Perth)** – (Hspty Mgt – via DipHE, HND, HNC)
>
> **Leeds Met** – (contact university)

Diploma of Higher Education courses
> UHI; Ulster.

Higher National Diploma courses
> Bell (CT); Birmingham (CFTCS); Blackpool & Fylde (Coll) gs; Bournemouth; Bradford (Coll); Brighton (CT); Brooklands (Coll); Canterbury Christ Church (UC); Carlisle (Coll); Cheltenham & Glos (CHE); Christchurch/Thanet (Coll); Colchester (Inst); Cornwall & Duchy (Coll); Craven (Coll); Croydon (Coll); Derby; Doncaster (Coll); Farnborough (CT); Fife (CFHE); Glasgow (CFood); Glasgow Caledonian; Greenwich; Guildford (CFE); Grimsby (Coll); Henley (Coll); Herefordshire (Coll); Huddersfield; Leicester (Coll); Lincolnshire & Humberside; Liverpool (CmC); Llandrillo (Coll); Loughborough (Coll); Manchester Met (Htl Mgt/Tour Mgt); Mid Cheshire (Coll); Mid Kent (Coll); Middlesex; Napier; Nescot; Newcastle (Coll); North East Worcs (Coll); North Lincolnshire (Coll); North London 8 pts; North West Kent (Coll); Norwich City (Coll); Nottingham Trent; Oxford Brookes (Westminster); Peterborough (Reg Coll); Plymouth (CFE); Portsmouth (Highbury Coll); Preston (Coll); Queen Margaret (UC); Reading (Coll); Reid Kerr (Coll); Robert Gordon; St Helens (Coll); Salford; Salisbury (Coll); Sheffield Hallam; Shrewsbury (CAT); Somerset (CAT; South Devon (Coll); Southampton (Inst); Stafford (Coll); Stoke on Trent (Coll); Stratford upon Avon (Coll); Suffolk (Coll); Swansea (IHE); UHI; Ulster; Walsall (Coll); West Herts (Coll); Wigan & Leigh (Coll); Wirral Met (Coll); Wolverhampton; York (CFHE); Yorkshire Coast (CFHE).

Professional courses
80 pts   and below
> Glasgow Caledonian; Middlesex; Napier; Norwich City (Coll); Oxford Brookes; Queen Margaret (UC); Robert Gordon.

Alternative Offers:

IB offers: Birmingham (CFTCS) 24 pts; Bournemouth 24 pts; Brighton 24 pts; Buckingham 24 pts; Central England 24 pts; Cheltenham & Glos (CHE) 26 pts; Dundee 27 pts; Manchester Met 28 pts; Oxford Brookes 26 pts; Plymouth (Seale Hayne) 21 pts; Portsmouth 24 pts; Sheffield Hallam 28 pts; South Bank 24 pts; Surrey 30 pts.

Irish offers: Brighton BBCC; Dundee BBCC/BBB; Glasgow Caledonian CCC; Huddersfield CCCC; Plymouth (Seale Hayne) CCC; Sheffield Hallam CCCC; Surrey BBBBB.

Scottish Qualifications: Abertay Dundee BBCC; Glasgow Caledonian BBCC/BBB; Napier BBCC; Queen Margaret (UC) BBC; Robert Gordon BBC; Strathclyde BBCC.

Overseas applicants: Bournemouth, Central England, Middlesex, North London Ability required in spoken and written English. **Central England** Interviews usually in home country. **Central Lancashire** English as a Foreign Language (EFL) provision available. **Huddersfield** English language teaching available.

CHOOSING YOUR COURSE (See also **Ch.1**)

> **Subject information:** All courses provide a comprehensive preparation for entry into hotel, catering, tourism and leisure industries. Alternative courses could include Consumer Studies, Food Science, Dietetics, Nutrition, Tourism Studies, Environmental Health Studies and Health and Business Studies. See also **Appendix 1**.

Special features: Brighton (Int Hspty Mgt) Six months is spent on placements abroad in Europe, USA, Far East or Australia. **Cheltenham & Glos (CHE)** Major joint or minor courses offered. **Leeds** The sandwich course covers all aspects of the industry – food and accommodation studies, management and human resource studies, finance, law and business policy. **Manchester Met** (Int Hspty Mgt) Relevant work experience desirable. Language electives from French, German or Spanish. **Portsmouth** The course covers catering and accommodation studies, behavioural science, personnel work, law, marketing and finance. **Sheffield Hallam** (Htl Tour Mgt) French, German, Spanish, Italian options. **Surrey** There are four main areas of study in the first two years – management studies, quantitative studies (accounting), food and beverage management and business studies. French and German language study available. *NOW CHECK PROPECTUSES AND WEB SITES.*

Study opportunities abroad: Bournemouth; Brighton; Cardiff (UWI); Cheltenham & Glos (CHE); Dundee; Huddersfield; Manchester Met; Napier; Oxford Brookes; Plymouth (Seale Hayne); Sheffield Hallam; South Bank; Strathclyde.

Work opportunities abroad: Birmingham (CFTCS); Bournemouth; Brighton; Central England; Central Lancashire; Cheltenham & Glos (CHE); Dundee; Huddersfield; Manchester Met; Middlesex; Napier; Plymouth (Seale Hayne); Portsmouth; Queen Margaret (UC) Robert Gordon; Sheffield Hallam; South Bank; Strathclyde; Surrey.

ADMISSIONS INFORMATION

Number of applicants per place (approx): Blackpool & Fylde (Coll) 9; Bournemouth 9; Buckingham 25; Central England 8; Central Lancashire 8; Dundee 10; Glasgow Caledonian 16; Manchester Met (Hspty Mgt) 12, (Hspty Mgt Tour) 20; Middlesex 4; Napier 17; North London 10; Norwich City (Coll) 3; Oxford Brookes 9; Plymouth (Seale Hayne) 5; Portsmouth 10; Robert Gordon 5; Sheffield Hallam 15; South Bank 6; Strathclyde 8; Surrey 12.

Planning your UCAS personal statement (see Ch.4): Experience in dealing with members of the public is an important element in this work which, coupled with work experience in cafes, restaurants or hotels, should be described fully. See also **Appendix 1**.

Selection interviews (see Ch.4): Blackpool & Fylde (Coll) (No); Bournemouth (No); Brighton; Cheltenham & Glos (CHE) (No); Colchester (Inst); Dundee; Glasgow Caledonian; Manchester Met; Napier (No); Oxford Brookes (No); Portsmouth; Robert Gordon; Salford (No); Sheffield Hallam (No); South Bank; Surrey.

Interview questions (see Ch.4): What books do you read? What do you know about hotel work and management? What experience have you had? What kind of job do you have in mind when you have qualified? How did you become interested in this course? Do you eat in restaurants? What types of restaurants? Discuss examples of good and bad restaurant organisation. What qualities do you have which make you suitable for management? All applicants are strongly recommended to obtain practical experience in catering or hotel work.

Reasons for rejection (non-academic): Lack of suitable work experience or practical training. Inability to communicate. Lack of awareness of work load, for example shift working, weekend work. **Oxford Brookes** Lack of commitment to the hotel and restaurant industry.

GAP YEAR ADVICE

Oxford Brookes Be in the UK the following August to receive enrolment package.

Institutions willing to defer entry after A-Levels: Birmingham (CFTCS); Brighton; Bournemouth; Buckingham; Central Lancashire; Cheltenham & Glos (CHE); Dundee; Glasgow Caledonian; Huddersfield; Luton; Manchester Met (but clarify your intentions as soon as possible); Nottingham Trent; Oxford Brookes; Plymouth (Seale Hayne); Portsmouth; Queen Margaret (UC); Robert Gordon; Sheffield Hallam; Strathclyde; Surrey (No).

AFTER RESULTS ADVICE

Institutions which may accept the same points score after A-Levels: Bournemouth; Brighton; Central England; Cheltenham & Glos (CHE); Dundee; Glasgow Caledonian; Huddersfield; Manchester Met; Napier (No); North London; Norwich City (Coll); Plymouth (Seale Hayne); Portsmouth; Queen Margaret (UC); Robert Gordon; Sheffield Hallam; South Bank; Strathclyde; Surrey.

Institutions which may accept lower grades/points score after A-Levels: Birmingham (CFTCS); Bournemouth; Brighton; Central England; Cheltenham & Glos (CHE); Glasgow Caledonian; Manchester Met; North London; Plymouth (Seale Hayne); Portsmouth; Queen Margaret (UC); Robert Gordon; Sheffield Hallam.

Offers to applicants repeating A-Levels: Higher Bournemouth, Huddersfield, Oxford Brookes, Surrey; **Same** Brighton, Dundee, Manchester Met, South Bank, Strathclyde, Surrey (BSc Ord), Ulster.

Probable vacancies from June 2001 and in Clearing (see Ch.4): There is likely to be a reasonable choice of institutions with vacancies from June.

NEW GRADUATE DESTINATIONS AND EMPLOYMENT (1999 HESA) (see **Ch.4**)

Of 2395 graduates surveyed, 1796 entered full-time employment, of whom 869 went directly into the hotel and restaurant industry, with the remainder going into other business areas, in many cases associated with their training. A further 141 went on to further study and 110 were believed to be unemployed.

HOUSING (see also **Community Studies**, **Consumer Studies**, **Town & Country Planning** and **Urban Studies**)

NB The information supplied by the universities and colleges this year varies considerably and the offers listed below should be used as a first source of reference only. Many institutions will accept combinations of Advanced (AL), Advanced Subsidiary (AS) and Vocational Advanced (VA) level qualifications to achieve the required points total, but applicants must check web sites and prospectuses for full details of all offers. Grades and points totals shown should be regarded as the minimum levels to be achieved, but offers may be adjusted downwards when results are known. The points totals shown to the left of the institutions are for ease of reference only. It must not be assumed that tariff points are always used by institutions or that they can be substituted for an offer in grades. The level of an offer is not necessarily indicative of the quality of a course. To calculate your offers see Chapter 4 and the inside fold of the back cover.

Special subject requirements/preferences: GCSE: English and mathematics usually required.

260 pts	**Cardiff** – BCC (City Reg Plan)
240 pts	**South Bank** – 240–200 pts approx (Housing)
	Ulster – CCC (Housing)
200 pts	**Bristol UWE** – 200–160 pts 12u – ALs **or** ALs+ASs **or** VAs+/-ALs/ASs; (Hous Pol Mgt)
	Greenwich – 200 pts approx (Hous St)
	Northumbria – 200 pts approx (Housing)
	Wolverhampton – 200 pts approx; gs (Hous Dev Mgt)
180 pts	**Central England** – 180–140 pts 12u; gs; (Housing)
	Liverpool John Moores – 180 pts – ALs **or** ALs+ASs **or** VAs+/-ALs/ASs; (Hous St)
	Salford – 180 pts approx (Hous Hlth Env)
	Sheffield Hallam – 180 pts approx (Hous St; Hous Soty)

160 pts **Anglia** – 160 pts 12u (inc 2ALs) – ALs **or** ALs+ASs **or** VA12u CC; gs; (Housing)
Cardiff (UWI) – 160–140 pts approx (Hous St)
140 pts **Westminster** – DD (Hous Mgt Dev)

Higher National Diploma courses
100 pts **and below**
Sheffield Hallam.

Alternative Offers:

Irish offers: Bristol UWE BC–CC.

CHOOSING YOUR COURSE (See also **Ch.1**)

> **Subject information:** More applicants are sought for Housing courses, which provide a preparation for careers involving housing management which are allied to social needs and also to economic and political considerations. Topics covered will include housing law, planning policy, finance and construction. Courses in Home Economics and Consumer Studies may also involve a study of housing problems. From a different angle, accommodation problems also feature largely in hospitality management courses. See also **Appendix 1**.

Special features: Anglia A blend of human geography, economics and sociology. **Cardiff (UWI)** Final options include housing design, environmental risk, housing in Europe and North America. **Sheffield Hallam** A study of the rural and urban environment in terms of housing, living conditions, financing and residential segregation in city development. *NOW CHECK PROSPECTUSES AND WEB SITES.*

Study opportunities abroad: Sheffield Hallam.

Work opportunities abroad: South Bank.

ADMISSIONS INFORMATION

Number of applicants per place (approx): Anglia 2; Bristol UWE 4; Greenwich 5; Northumbria 1; Sheffield Hallam 2.

Planning your UCAS personal statement (see Ch.4): An interest in people, housing problems, social affairs and the built environment are important for this course. Contacts with local housing managers (through local authority offices or housing associations) are important. Describe any such contacts and your knowledge of the housing types and needs in your area. The Town and Country Planning Office in your area will also be able to provide information on the various types of developments taking place in your locality and how housing needs have changed during the past 50 years. See also **Appendix 1**.

Selection interviews (see Ch.4): Liverpool John Moores; Salford; Wolverhampton (No).

Interview questions (see Ch.4): Since the subject is not studied at school, questions will be asked on reasons for choosing this degree. Other related questions include: What is a housing association? Why were housing associations formed? In which parts of the country would you expect private housing to be expensive and by comparison, cheap? What is the cause of this? Have estates of multi-storey flats fulfilled their original purpose? If not, why not? What causes a slum? What is an almshouse? **Sheffield Hallam** An informal discussion of the course focusing on the student's interest in housing and any experience of working with the public.

Reasons for rejection (non-academic): Lack of awareness of current social policy issues.

GAP YEAR ADVICE

Institutions willing to defer entry after A-Levels: Northumbria; Sheffield Hallam; South Bank (prefer not).

AFTER RESULTS ADVICE

Institutions which may accept the same points score after A-Levels: Bristol UWE; Sheffield Hallam; South Bank.

Probable vacancies from June 2001 and in Clearing (see Ch.4): Institutions can be contacted since vacancies are almost certain. The highest offers are likely to be in the 240–220 pts range.

NEW GRADUATE DESTINATIONS AND EMPLOYMENT (1999 HESA) (see **Ch.4**)

No data available for this subject area.

HUMAN SCIENCES/HUMAN STUDIES

NB The information supplied by the universities and colleges this year varies consider-ably and the offers listed below should be used as a first source of reference only. Many institutions will accept combinations of Advanced (AL), Advanced Subsidiary (AS) and Vocational Advanced (VA) level qualifications to achieve the required points total, but applicants must check web sites and prospectuses for full details of all offers. Grades and points totals shown should be regarded as the minimum levels to be achieved, but offers may be adjusted downwards when results are known. The points totals shown to the left of the institutions are for ease of reference only. It must not be assumed that tariff points are always used by institutions or that they can be substituted for an offer in grades. The level of an offer is not necessarily indicative of the quality of a course. To calculate your offers see Chapter 4 and the inside fold of the back cover.

Special subject requirements/preferences: A-Level: Sciences. **GCSE:** Mathematics usually required. **Oxford** Usually grade As.

360 pts	**and above**
	London (UCL) – AAB–ABB **or** 3ALs+AS/VA; (Hum Sci)
	Oxford – Offers vary between candidates (Hum Sci)
300 pts	**Loughborough** – 300 pts 18u – 2ALs+AL/2ASs **or** VAs+/-ALs/ASs; gs; (Psy/Ergon)
	Sussex – 300 pts – BBB; (Hum Sci)
240 pts	**Bradford** – 240 pts 12u; gs; (Interd Hum St)
	Durham (Stockton) – CCC **or** ALs+ASs **or** VAs+/-ALs/ASs; gs; (Hum Sci)
	Loughborough – 240 pts 18u – 2ALs+AL/2ASs **or** VAs+/-ALs/ASs; gs; (Ergonomics)
	Nottingham Trent – 240–200 pts approx (Hum Sci)
220 pts	**Surrey (Roehampton)** – 220 pts approx (inc 2ALs) – ALs **or** ALs+ASs **or** VAS+/-ALs/ASs; (Hum Sci)
200 pts	**Liverpool John Moores** – 200 pts approx (Hum Sci)
160 pts	**Norwich City (Coll)** – 160 pts approx (Hum Life Sci/Psy; Hum Life Sci)
140 pts	**and below**
	Derby – CD **or** DD+dd **or** VAs CD+/-ALs/ASs; gs; (Hum Sci)
	Suffolk (Coll) – (Hum Sci)

Alternative Offers:

IB offers: Bradford 27 pts; London (UCL) 34 pts.

CHOOSING YOUR COURSE (See also **Ch.1**)

Subject information: Human Sciences is a multi-disciplinary study relating to biological and social sciences. Topics range from genetics and evolution to health, disease, social behaviour and industrial societies. Consequently, alternative courses could include Community Studies, Environmental Health, Life Sciences, Sociology, Psychology, Human Biology, Genetics and Physiology. See also **Appendix 1.**

Special features: Bradford The course covers communication studies, human nature, human society and logic and thought. **Loughborough** (Ergonomics) Covers psychology, anatomy, design, information technology. *NOW CHECK PROSPECTUSES AND WEB SITES.*

ADMISSIONS INFORMATION

Number of applicants per place (approx): Bradford 7; Oxford 2.

Planning your UCAS personal statement (see Ch.4): See **Biology** and **Anthropology**. See also **Appendix 1.**

Selection interviews (see Ch.4): Durham (Stockton); London (UCL).

Interview questions (see Ch.4): What do you expect to get out of a degree in Human Sciences? Why are you interested in this subject? What problems do you think you will be able to tackle after completing the course?

GAP YEAR ADVICE

Institutions willing to defer entry after A-Levels: Bradford; Surrey Roehampton.

AFTER RESULTS ADVICE

Institutions which may accept the same points score after A-Levels: Bradford.

Probable vacancies from June 2001 and in Clearing (see Ch.4): Most institutions are likely to have vacancies. See also **Health Sciences/Studies**.

NEW GRADUATE DESTINATIONS AND EMPLOYMENT (1999 HESA) (see **Ch.4**)

No data available for this subject area.

INTERNATIONAL RELATIONS (see also Politics)

NB The information supplied by the universities and colleges this year varies considerably and the offers listed below should be used as a first source of reference only. Many institutions will accept combinations of Advanced (AL), Advanced Subsidiary (AS) and Vocational Advanced (VA) level qualifications to achieve the required points total, but applicants must check web sites and prospectuses for full details of all offers. Grades and points totals shown should be regarded as the minimum levels to be achieved, but offers may be adjusted downwards when results are known. The points totals shown to the left of the institutions are for ease of reference only. It must not be assumed that tariff points are always used by institutions or that they can be substituted for an offer in grades. The level of an offer is not necessarily indicative of the quality of a course. To calculate your offers see Chapter 4 and the inside fold of the back cover.

Special subject requirements/preferences: GCSE: English and mathematics usually required, also foreign language for language courses. **London (LSE)** A and B grades.

360 pts **Aberystwyth** – 360–300 pts 21u – 3ALs (200 pts min)+ASs (360–300 pts total) **or** VAs+/-ALs/ASs (300–220 pts); gs; (Int Rel)
350 pts **London (King's)** – BBB+b **or** BB+bbb (inc AL Fr/geog/Ger/hist for joint courses); VAs considered; (War St; War St with Class) St/Fr/Geog/Ger/Hist/ Gk/Phil/Port/Theol/App Comp)
340 pts **St Andrews** – AAB (MA Int Rel courses)
320 pts **London (LSE)** – ABB (Int Rel; Int Rel/Hist)
Warwick – ABB–BBC (Int St courses)
300 pts **Birmingham** – BBB (Int St/Econ; Int St/Pol Sci)
Essex – 300–280 pts 21u – BB+AL/2ASs; gs; (Int Rel)
Liverpool – 300–260 pts – ALs **or** ALs+ASs **or** VAs+/-ALs/ASs; (Int Dev)
Sussex – BBB (Int Rel courses)

280 pts **Bradford** – 280 pts 12u; gs; (Peace St; Int Rel/Secur St; Cnflct Resoln)
Birmingham – BBC (B lang) (Int St/Fr/Ger/Span)
Hull – BBC–BCC/AB (Int Rel/Int Pol Econ)
Kent – BBC/AB (Int Rel/Lang)
Leeds – BBC **or** BB+cc; VAs (contact univ); gs; (Int St)
Swansea – 280 pts 18u – BBC **or** ALs+ASs **or** VAs+/-ALs/ASs; (Int Rel courses)

260 pts **Keele** – BCC (Int Rel courses)
Lancaster – BCC (Int Rel/Strat St; Int Rel/Hist; Peace St/Int Rel)
Plymouth – 260 pts approx (Int Rel/Law)
Portsmouth – 260 pts – ALs **or** ALs+ASs **or** VAs; gs; (Int Rel/Lang)
Reading – BCC/BB (Int Rel/Sociol)

240 pts **Aberdeen** – CCC (Int Rel courses)
Coventry – 240 pts approx (Int Rel; Int Rel/Law)
Ulster – CCC (Int St; Cnflct St)

220 pts **Lincolnshire & Humberside** – 220 pts (Int Rel/Crim)
Nottingham Trent – 220 pts – 2ALs (inc C in relevant subj (pol/hist/econ/geog)); (Int Rel)
Nottingham Trent – 220–180 pts approx (Int St joint courses)
Wolverhampton – 220–160 pts 12u – DDD–CDE **or** CC/CD+d/e **or** VA12u CC; gs; (Int Rel; War St)

200 pts **De Montfort (Leicester)** – 200 pts – ALs **or** ALs+ASs **or** VAs+/-ALs/ASs; (Int Rel courses)
Glamorgan – 200–180 pts approx (Int St)
Plymouth – 200 pts approx (Int Rel with Geog/Comp/Bus/App Econ/Langs/Soc Pol)
Staffordshire – 200 pts – ALs (inc CC) **or** CC+AS(40 pts); **or** VA CC; gs; (Int Rel courses)

180 pts **Bolton (IHE)** – DDD/CD (Peace/War St courses)
Kingston – 180 pts 2x6u; gs; (Int St)
Lincolnshire & Humberside – 180 pts (Int Rel; Int Rel/Econ)

160 pts **London Guildhall** – CC–CD (Int Rel courses)

Alternative Offers:

IB offers: Birmingham 33 pts; Bradford 30 pts; Kent 29 pts H 12 pts; Leeds 32 pts; London (LSE) 36 pts H666; Reading 28 pts; St Andrews 36 pts; Staffordshire 26 pts.

Irish offers: Aberdeen BBBB; St Andrews ABBB.

Scottish Qualifications: St Andrews AAAB.

CHOOSING YOUR COURSE (See also **Ch.1**)

Subject information: A strong interest in international affairs is a prerequisite for these courses which often allow students to specialise in a geographical area such as African, Asian, West European politics. Other appropriate courses include Development Studies, Economics, Politics and Government.

Special features: Aberdeen (Int Rel courses) Cover Europe, USA, Britain, politics and the history of international relations. **Aberystwyth** Includes House of Commons placement scheme with students working for an MP for one semester. **Birmingham** Core courses in international politics, history, economics, law and a language (French, German, Spanish, Russian, Greek). **Bradford** (Peace St) Focus on contemporary issues of peace, conflict and conflict resolution. Specialisms in international relations, defence and security. 30% are mature students. **London (LSE)** Philosophy, sociology, politics, public and international law. **Staffordshire** Options from international history, geography, sociology, world economy, psychology, computing, statistics, French, German and Spanish. *NOW CHECK PROSPECTUSES AND WEB SITES.*

Top universities and colleges (Research) (see Ch.4): See **Politics**.

Study opportunities abroad: Aberdeen; Birmingham; Kent; London (LSE); Nottingham Trent; Plymouth; Staffordshire; Sussex; Warwick.

ADMISSIONS INFORMATION

Number of applications per place (approx): Aberystwyth 6; Birmingham 13; Leeds 13; London (King's) 11, (LSE) (Int Rel) 15, (Int Rel/Hist) 15; Reading 5; Staffordshire 6.

Planning your UCAS personal statement (see Ch.4): Describe any special interests you have in the affairs of any particular country. Contact embassies for information on cultural, economic and political developments. Follow up international events through newspapers and magazines. Give details of any voluntary work you have done. **London (King's)** Substantial experience in some area of direct relevance to War Studies. **St Andrews** Reasons for choice of course. Evidence of interest.

Selection interviews: Birmingham; De Montfort (No); Hull (No); Kent (some); London (King's), (LSE) (No); London Guildhall; Nottingham Trent; Portsmouth (No); St Andrews (No); Staffordshire (No).

Interview questions (see Ch.4): Applicants are likely to be questioned on current international events and crises between countries. **Nottingham Trent** Be prepared to be challenged on your existing views!

GAP YEAR ADVICE

Institutions willing to defer entry after A-Levels: Aberystwyth; Birmingham; Bradford; Leeds; Plymouth; St Andrews; Staffordshire; Warwick.

AFTER RESULTS ADVICE

Institutions which may accept the same points score after A-Levels: Aberystwyth; Birmingham (No); Leeds; Plymouth; Staffordshire; Warwick.

Institutions which may accept lower grades/points score after A-Levels: Aberystwyth; Birmingham (No); Leeds; Plymouth; Staffordshire; Warwick.

Probable vacancies from June 2001 and in Clearing (see Ch.4): Several universities are likely to have vacancies, with offers at the 'old' universities ranging between 280 and 240 pts.

NEW GRADUATE DESTINATIONS AND EMPLOYMENT (1999 HESA) (see **Ch.4**)

See **Politics**.

ITALIAN (see also **Modern Languages**)

NB The information supplied by the universities and colleges this year varies considerably and the offers listed below should be used as a first source of reference only. Many institutions will accept combinations of Advanced (AL), Advanced Subsidiary (AS) and Vocational Advanced (VA) level qualifications to achieve the required points total, but applicants must check web sites and prospectuses for full details of all offers. Grades and points totals shown should be regarded as the minimum levels to be achieved, but offers may be adjusted downwards when results are known. The points totals shown to the left of the institutions are for ease of reference only. It must not be assumed that tariff points are always used by institutions or that they can be substituted for an offer in grades. The level of an offer is not necessarily indicative of the quality of a course. To calculate your offers see Chapter 4 and the inside fold of the back cover.

Special subject requirements/preferences: A-Level: Modern language usually required. **Leeds**, **London (RH)** Italian preferred. **Oxford** Full A-Levels expected. **GCSE:** English and a foreign language usually required. **Edinburgh** and **Glasgow** English, mathematics or science and foreign language required. **London (RH)** Two subjects grade A, four subjects grade B, two subjects grade C. **Oxford, Cambridge** Majority of grade As usually required.

360 pts **and above**
    Cambridge – Offers, mainly in grades, vary between colleges (Modn Lang)
    Oxford – Offers vary between candidates (Modn Lang)
340 pts **Birmingham** – AAB–BBB (Ital/Phil)
    Manchester – AAB (Ital/Russ; Ital/Span)
    St Andrews – AAB (Int Rel/Ital; Ital/Mgt)
320 pts **Cardiff** – ABB (Ital/Cult Crit)
    Edinburgh – ABB–BBB (Italian courses)
    St Andrews – ABB (Engl/Ital)
300 pts **Birmingham** – BBB (Ital courses except under **280 pts**)
    Bristol – BBB(B relevant lang); (not gs) (Ital/Russ/Span/Port)
    Cardiff – BBB–BBC (Ital/Law)
    Durham – BBB–BBC (Arts Comb)
    Hull – 300–280 pts approx (Ital courses except under **260/240 pts**)
    Liverpool – BBB–BBC (Ital Comb Hons)
    London (RH) – ABC(B lang) **or** AB+cc; (not gs) (Ital courses)
    London (UCL) – BBB **or** 3ALs+AS/VA; (Ital/Hist Art)
    Manchester – BBB (Ital/Hist Ant)
    Nottingham – 300–260 pts (Ital/Manuf Eng/Mgt; Ital/Prod Ops Mgt)
    St Andrews – BBB (Ital courses except under **340/320 pts**)
280 pts **Bath** – 280 pts (Fr/Ital; Ger/Ital)
    Birmingham – BBC (Ital St)
    Bristol – BBC (Drama/Ital)
    Glasgow – BBC (Ital courses)
    Kent – 280–260 pts approx (Ital joint hons)
    Lancaster – BBC–BCC (Ital courses except under **260 pts**)
    Leeds – BBC–BCC B in lang/Latin (Ital courses)
    London (UCL) – BBC–BCC **or** 3ALs+AS/VA; (Ital/Ling; Ital/Lat; Ital/Des;
        Ital/Bus St; Ital/Jew St)
    Reading – BBC–BCC (Ital courses)
    Swansea – 280 pts 18u – BBC–BCC/BB–BC **or** ALs+ASs **or** VAs+/-ALs/ASs;
        (Ital courses)
    Warwick – BBC–BCC (Ital/Fr; Ital/Ger; Ital/Film St; Ital/Int St; Ital/Thea St;
        Ital/Euro Lit)
260 pts **Bangor** – 260 pts – ALs; VAs (enquire); (Ital/Span/Fr; Ital/Span/Ger)
    Bristol – BCC (inc modn lang); (not gs) (Italian)
    Cardiff – BCC (Italian)
    Coventy – 260–180 pts approx (Ital courses)
    Exeter – 260 pts 18u (inc lang) – BCC **or** BC+cc **or** BB+dd **or** VAs (contact
        univ); gs; (Italian courses)
    Hull – BCC (Ital/Span)
    Lancaster – 260 pts (Ital St/Maths)
    Leicester – BCC (Ital Comb Arts)
    Leicester – BCC–BCD (Ital/Span/Ger/Fr)
    London (UCL) – BCC **or** 3ALs+AS/VA; (Italian 4 yrs)
    Manchester Met – BCC (Bus Euro (Ital))
    Portsmouth – 260–240 pts approx (Ital courses)
    Salford – BCC ave (Ital courses)
    Strathclyde – BCC (Italian)
    Sussex – BCC (Ital courses)
240 pts **Bradford** – CCC (Pol/Ital)
    Hull – CCC (Italian)
    Oxford Brookes – CCC–CDD/BC (Ital courses)
    Plymouth – CCC–CDD (Ital/Euro St; Ital/Bus St; Ital/Int Rel)

220 pts **Liverpool John Moores** – 220–200 pts approx (Int Bus/Ital)
Luton – 220–180 pts approx (Ital – Mod)
Nottingham Trent – 220–180 pts approx (Ital courses)
Sheffield Hallam – CCD (Int Bus Ital)
Wolverhampton – 220–160 pts – DDD–CDE/CC or CD+e **or** VA12u CC; gs; (Ital St)
200 pts **European (Bus Sch)** – 200 pts approx (Ital/Bus)
Manchester Met – CDD/CD (Hum/Soc St)
Northampton (UC) – 200–160 pts approx (Ital courses)
180 pts **Buckinghamshire Chilterns (UC)** – 180–140 pts approx (Ital courses)
Central Lancashire – 180 pts 12u pref (inc AL modn lang) – ALs **or** ALs+ASs **or** VAs+/-ALs/ASs; gs; (Ital/Bus)
East London – 180 pts approx (Ital courses)
Manchester Met – BC (inc for lang) (Modn Lang Ital)
160 pts **Anglia** – 160 pts 12u (inc C lang) – ALs **or** ALs+ASs **or** VAs+/-ALs/ASs; gs; (Italian courses)
Westminster – CC–CD (Ital courses)

Higher National Diploma courses (with Business Studies)
100 pts **and below**
South Bank.

Alternative Offers:

IB offers: Birmingham 33 pts; Bristol 32 pts; Cardiff 30 pts, H 15 pts; Hull 30–28 pts; Kent 30–28 pts; Lancaster 28 pts; Leeds 28 pts; Leicester 28 pts; London (RH) 28 pts; St Andrews 28 pts; Warwick 29 pts.

Scottish Qualifications: Edinburgh BBBB; Glasgow BBBB; Strathclyde BBBB; St Andrews BBBB.

CHOOSING YOUR COURSE (See also **Ch.1**)

> **Subject information:** The language and literature of Italy will feature strongly on most Italian courses. The majority of applicants have no knowledge of Italian. They will need to give convincing reasons for their interest and to show that they have the ability to assimilate language quickly. See also **Appendix 1** under **Modern Languages**.

Special features: Bristol Equal emphasis on art history, language and literature. **Cardiff** Opportunity to start beginners' course in Italian in first year. **Hull** Emphasis on language skills; options in second and third years. Intensive beginners' course. Erasmus agreements with eight universities in Italy. **Leeds** Broad-based course covering literature and society. Extra year for beginners in Italian. **London (RH)** Wide choice of subjects available in new course system. Single, combined, major or minor options. *NOW CHECK PROSPECTUSES AND WEB SITES.*

Top universities and colleges (Teaching Quality) (see Ch.4): Cambridge; Exeter; Hull; London (QMW); Oxford; Oxford Brookes; not all institutions assessed.

Top universities and colleges (Research) (see Ch.4): Cambridge; Exeter; Lancaster; Leeds; London (RH), (UCL); Oxford; Reading; Sussex; Westminster.

Study opportunities abroad: Institutions offering four-year courses usually arrange study placements abroad for students.

Work opportunities abroad: Leeds.

ADMISSIONS INFORMATION

Number of applicants per place (approx): Anglia 6; Birmingham 4; Bristol 6; Cardiff 3; Coventry 28; Hull 8; Lancaster 8; Leeds 3; London (RH).

Planning your UCAS personal statement (see Ch.4): Describe any visits to Italy and experience of speaking the language. Interest in Italian art, literature, culture, society and architecture could also be mentioned. Read Italian newspapers and magazines. Bilingual background. **St Andrews** Evidence of interest. Reasons for choosing the course. See also **Appendix 1** under **Modern Languages**.

Selection interviews (see Ch.4): Birmingham (majority receive offers); Cambridge; Cardiff (No); Edinburgh (No); Exeter (No); Hull (No); Kent (No); Leeds (No); Leicester (No), London (RH); Manchester (No); Oxford; St Andrews (No); Westminster.

Interview questions (see Ch.4): Why do you want to learn Italian? What foreign newspapers or magazines do you read (particularly if the applicant has taken A-level Italian)? Have you visited Italy? What do you know of the Italian people, culture, art?

GAP YEAR ADVICE

Try to spend some time in Italy.

Institutions willing to defer entry after A-Levels: Anglia; Birmingham; Bristol; Cardiff; Central Lancashire; Leeds; London (RH), (UCL) (No); Sussex; Swansea; Warwick.

AFTER RESULTS ADVICE

Institutions which may accept the same points score after A-Levels: Birmingham (usually); Cardiff; Exeter; Hull; Lancaster; Leeds; London (UCL) (No); Swansea.

Institutions which may accept lower grades/points score after A-Levels: Cardiff; Glasgow; Hull; Kent; Leeds; London (RH), (UCL); Swansea; Warwick.

Offers to applicants repeating A-Levels: Higher Birmingham, Warwick; **Same** Hull, Leeds.

Probable vacancies from June 2001 and in Clearing (see Ch.4): A number of universities are likely to have vacancies from June onwards. Popular universities are likely to make offers in the range of 260–220 pts.

NEW GRADUATE DESTINATIONS AND EMPLOYMENT (1999 HESA) (see **Ch.4**)

In a survey of 89 graduates, 62 entered full-time employment (mainly in business activities), 10 went on to further study and none were believed to be unemployed.

JAPANESE (see also **Modern Languages**)

NB The information supplied by the universities and colleges this year varies considerably and the offers listed below should be used as a first source of reference only. Many institutions will accept combinations of Advanced (AL), Advanced Subsidiary (AS) and Vocational Advanced (VA) level qualifications to achieve the required points total, but applicants must check web sites and prospectuses for full details of all offers. Grades and points totals shown should be regarded as the minimum levels to be achieved, but offers may be adjusted downwards when results are known. The points totals shown to the left of the institutions are for ease of reference only. It must not be assumed that tariff points are always used by institutions or that they can be substituted for an offer in grades. The level of an offer is not necessarily indicative of the quality of a course. To calculate your offers see Chapter 4 and the inside fold of the back cover.

Special subject requirements/preferences: A-Level: Modern language usually required. **GCSE: Durham** A/B grades in languages. **Edinburgh** English, mathematics or science or a foreign language. **Oxford, Cambridge** Usually a majority of grade As. English often required at other universities, also mathematics for some joint courses.

360 pts   and above
> **Cambridge** – Offers, mainly in grades, vary between colleges (Oriental St (Jap))
> **Oxford** – Offers vary between candidates (Oriental St (Jap))

320 pts	**Leeds** – ABB (Law/Jap St)
	London (RH) – ABB (Jap St/Econ; Jap St/Hist; Jap St/Mgt)
300 pts	**Cardiff** – BBB (Law/Jap)
	Durham – 300 pts 18u – BBB; (not gs) (Japanese courses)
	Edinburgh – BBB (Japanese)
	Leeds – BBB–BBC (Japanese courses except under **320 pts**)
	London (RH) – BBB–BCC (Japanese courses except under **320 pts**)
	London (SOAS) – 300 pts (Japanese courses)
	Newcastle – ABC–BBB (Jap/Bus Mgt; Jap/Ling; Jap Comb St)
	Nottingham – 300–260 pts (Mech Eng Mgt/Jap)
	Reading – BBB (Int Mgt/Jap)
280 pts	**Cardiff** – BBC–BCC (Japanese courses except under **300 pts**)
	Sheffield – BBC (Japanese courses)
260 pts	**Oxford Brookes** – BCC–CDD/BC–DD (Japanese courses)
	Reading – BCC (Ger/Jap)
	Stirling – BCC/BC (Jap St/Bus St)
240 pts	**Nottingham** – CCC (Manuf Eng Mgt/Jap)
	Stirling – CCC (Jap St courses except under **260 pts**)
	Sunderland – 240 pts approx (Int Bus/Jap)
	Ulster – CCC (Jap St Hum Comb)
220 pts	**Liverpool John Moores** – 220–200 pts approx (Japanese courses)
180 pts	**Central Lancashire** – 180 pts 12u (pref inc AL modn lang) – ALs **or** ALs+ASs **or** VAs+/-ALs/ASs; gs; (Jap/Bus)
	European Bus (Sch) – 180 pts approx (Int Bus St/Jap)
	Wolverhampton – 180 pts approx; ALs; gs (Jap St)

Alternative Offers:

EB offers: Sheffield 75% average.

IB offers: Leeds 17 pts at Highers; London (SOAS) 34 pts; Sheffield 33 pts.

Irish offers: Sheffield AABBB; Stirling.

Scottish Qualifications: Edinburgh BBBB; Stirling BBBC.

CHOOSING YOUR COURSE (See also **Ch.1**)

> **Subject information:** A strong interest in Japan and its culture is expected of applicants. A number of four-year joint courses are now offered, all of which include a period of study in Japan. Potential employers are showing an interest in Law/Japanese. Students report that 'it is not a soft option'. They are expected to be firmly dedicated to a Japanese degree (for example, by listing only Japanese on the UCAS application form), to have an interest in using their degree in employment and to be prepared for a lot of hard work. See also **Appendix 1** under **Modern Languages**.

Special features: Durham Offered with Management Studies. **London (RH)** Minor field offered with year 2 in Tokyo. **Sheffield** Japanese can be taken only as one half of a four-year dual degree course with the first year given entirely to an intensive study of basic Japanese grammar and the writing system. *NOW CHECK PROSPECTUSES AND WEB SITES.*

ADMISSIONS INFORMATION

Number of applicants per place (approx): Cardiff 8; Durham 11; London (SOAS) 9; Sheffield 10; Stirling 7.

Planning your UCAS personal statement (see Ch.4): Discuss your interest in Japan and your reasons for wishing to study the language. Know Japan, its culture and background history. Discuss any visits you have made or contacts with Japanese nationals. See also **Appendix 1** under **Modern Languages**.

Selection interviews (see Ch.4): Durham; Edinburgh (No); Oxford (W); Stirling; most institutions.

Interview questions (see Ch.4): Japanese is an extremely demanding subject and applicants are most likely to be questioned on their reasons for choosing this degree. In addition they will be expected to have some knowledge of Japanese culture, history and current affairs.

Reasons for rejection (non-academic): Insufficient evidence of genuine motivation.

AFTER RESULTS ADVICE

Institutions which may accept the same points score after A-Levels: Durham (No); Leeds; Sheffield (No).

Probable vacancies from June 2001 and in Clearing (see Ch.4): Vacancies in this subject usually will exist only on joint courses. Each university should be contacted.

NEW GRADUATE DESTINATIONS AND EMPLOYMENT (1999 HESA) (see **Ch.4**)

In a survey of 47 graduates, 31 went into full-time employment (mostly in business and finance), six went on to further study and three were believed to be unemployed.

LANDSCAPE ARCHITECTURE (including **Landscape Design and Management** and **Garden Design**; see also **Art and Design (Industrial/Product Design)** and **Horticulture**)

NB The information supplied by the universities and colleges this year varies considerably and the offers listed below should be used as a first source of reference only. Many institutions will accept combinations of Advanced (AL), Advanced Subsidiary (AS) and Vocational Advanced (VA) level qualifications to achieve the required points total, but applicants must check web sites and prospectuses for full details of all offers. Grades and points totals shown should be regarded as the minimum levels to be achieved, but offers may be adjusted downwards when results are known. The points totals shown to the left of the institutions are for ease of reference only. It must not be assumed that tariff points are always used by institutions or that they can be substituted for an offer in grades. The level of an offer is not necessarily indicative of the quality of a course. To calculate your offers see Chapter 4 and the inside fold of the back cover.

Special subject requirements/preferences: A-Level: Art, biology, geography may be required. **Manchester Met** Two subjects from art, biology, geography or geology. Requirements may vary from year to year. **GCSE:** English and art almost certainly required, also a science.

320 pts	**Kingston** – 320 pts (inc 280 pts from 3x6u); (not gs) (Land Archit)
260 pts	**Manchester** – BCC (Land Plan Mgt)
	Manchester Met – 260 pts (Land Archit)
	Sheffield – BCC (Land Des courses)
240 pts	**Central England** – 240 pts approx (Land Archit)
	Edinburgh (CA) – CCC (art/maths/Engl/geog/biol pref); (Land Archit)
220 pts	**Greenwich** – 220 pts approx (Land Archit; Gard Des)
200 pts	**Cheltenham & Glos (CHE)** – 200–160 pts approx (AL art/geog/biol) (Land Archit)
180 pts	**Central England** – 180 pts approx (Gard Des)
160 pts	**Bishop Burton (CAg)** – 160 pts approx (Gard Des)
	Capel Manor (Coll) – CC (Gard Des)
	Otley (Coll) – 160 pts approx (Land Des Cons)
	Scottish (CAg) – 160 pts – CC; (Land Mgt)
	Writtle (Coll) – 160 pts approx (Land Amen Mgt; Land/Gard Des)
100 pts	**Suffolk (Coll)** – DE (Land Gard Des)

80 pts   Central Lancashire (Myerscough) – EE (Gard Des)

   Leeds Met – (contact university)

For these courses a portfolio of art work must be presented at interview.

Diploma of Higher Education courses
   Suffolk (Coll).

Higher National Diploma courses
   Bournemouth (Land Cons); Brackenhurst (Coll); Central Lancashire (Myerscough), (Newton Rigg) (Amen/Land Des); Glamorgan (Land Sci); Hadlow (Coll) (Land Mgt; Gard Des); Kingston; Myerscough (Coll); Scottish (CAg); Writtle (Coll).

Alternative Offers:

IB offers: Edinburgh (CA) 30 pts; Greenwich 24 pts inc 12 pts Highers; Kingston 28 pts.

Irish offers: Edinburgh (CA) ABBCC; Sheffield BBBBC.

Scottish Qualifications: Edinburgh (CA) ABBB + interview.

Overseas applicants: Cheltenham & Glos (CHE) Fluency in English required. **Manchester Met** Some interviews held in Malaysia. English courses available.

CHOOSING YOUR COURSE (See also **Ch.1**)

> **Subject information:** Landscape architecture is a specialised branch of architecture for which an ability in art and design is sought. It focuses on the design of the environment surrounding buildings. (It should not be confused with the work of a garden centre.) Other alternative courses might include Architecture and Horticulture. See also **Appendix 1**.

Special features: Central England Includes history, science, technology, plant science and graphics. **Edinburgh (CA)** Course covers design, rural land use, ecology, horticulture and construction. **Greenwich** Includes French and German options. (Gard Des) Integrated HND/BA course. **Sheffield** Science, ecology and environmental geography and design. Options in plant science or archaeology in second and third years. *NOW CHECK PROSPECTUSES AND WEB SITES.*

Top universities and colleges (Research) (see Ch.4): Cheltenham & Glos (CHE).

Study opportunities abroad: Central England; Cheltenham & Glos (CHE); Greenwich; Manchester Met.

Work opportunities abroad: Central England; Edinburgh (CA); Manchester Met.

ADMISSIONS INFORMATION

Number of applicants per place (approx): Cheltenham & Glos (CHE) 9; Edinburgh (CA) 7; Greenwich 3; Kingston 4; Manchester Met 9; Writtle (Coll) 5.

Planning your UCAS personal statement (see Ch.4): Knowledge of the work of landscape architects is important. Arrange a visit to a landscape architect's office and try to organise some work experience. Read up on historical landscape design and visit country house estates with examples of outstanding designs. Describe these visits in detail and your preferences. Membership of the National Trust could be useful. **Sheffield** Portfolio of work required. A-level art not necessary. See also **Appendix 1**.

Selection interviews (see Ch.4): Cheltenham & Glos (CHE); Greenwich; Manchester Met; Suffolk (Coll); Writtle (Coll).

Interview questions (see Ch.4): Applicants will be expected to have had some work experience and are likely to be questioned on their knowledge of the career and the subject. Historical examples of good landscaping could also be asked for.

Reasons for rejection (non-academic): Lack of historical knowledge and awareness of current developments. Poor portfolio.

GAP YEAR ADVICE

Travel, sketch, but preferably work in a landscape architect's office or similar.

Institutions willing to defer entry after A-Levels: Central England; Cheltenham & Glos (CHE); Edinburgh (CA); Greenwich; Manchester Met (No); Sheffield.

AFTER RESULTS ADVICE

Institutions which may accept the same points score after A-Levels: Central England; Cheltenham & Glos (CHE); Edinburgh (CA) (No); Greenwich; Manchester Met; Sheffield (No).

Institutions which may accept lower grades/points score after A-Levels: Central England; Cheltenham & Glos (CHE); Manchester Met; Sheffield.

Offers to applicants repeating A-Levels: Possibly higher Manchester Met; **Same** Edinburgh (CA), Greenwich.

Probable vacancies from June 2000 and in Clearing (see Ch.4): Contact all institutions since some vacancies are likely.

NEW GRADUATE DESTINATIONS AND EMPLOYMENT (1999 HESA) (see **Ch.4**)

See **Architecture**.

LATIN (see also **Classical Studies/Classical Civilisation** and **Classics**)

NB The information supplied by the universities and colleges this year varies considerably and the offers listed below should be used as a first source of reference only. Many institutions will accept combinations of Advanced (AL), Advanced Subsidiary (AS) and Vocational Advanced (VA) level qualifications to achieve the required points total, but applicants must check web sites and prospectuses for full details of all offers. Grades and points totals shown should be regarded as the minimum levels to be achieved, but offers may be adjusted downwards when results are known. The points totals shown to the left of the institutions are for ease of reference only. It must not be assumed that tariff points are always used by institutions or that they can be substituted for an offer in grades. The level of an offer is not necessarily indicative of the quality of a course. To calculate your offers see Chapter 4 and the inside fold of the back cover.

Special subject requirements/preferences: A-Level: Latin usually required, the highest grade of offer below. Course requiring A-Level Latin = (L), Greek = (G). **GCSE: Edinburgh, Glasgow, St Andrews** English, mathematics or science and a foreign language. **Lampeter** Five/six subjects at grade A or B. **London (RH)** Good grade in Latin (Latin/Anc Hist). **Oxford, Cambridge** Usually grade As.

360 pts and above
    Cambridge – Offers, mainly in grades, vary between colleges (L or G) (Classics)
    Oxford – Offers vary between candidates (L or G) (Classics)
320 pts **London (RH)** – ABB (Lat/Engl)
300 pts **Birmingham** – BBB (L) (Latin courses)
    Durham – 300 pts (Lat/Mus)
    Edinburgh – BBB (Latin courses)
    Leeds – ABC (Lat – Engl)
    London (RH) – BBB (Lat with Fr/Ger)
    Newcastle – ABC–BBB (Lat Comb St)

St Andrews – BBB–BBC (Latin courses)
Warwick – BBB (L) (Engl/Lat Lit)
280 pts **Belfast (Queen's)** – BBC–BCC (Latin courses)
Bristol – BBC (Fr/Lat; Engl/Lat)
Durham – BBC (Latin)
Glasgow – BBC (Latin courses)
Leeds – BBC (L some courses) (Latin)
London (King's) – BBC+AS **or** BB+bbc (inc B Engl+AL Lat pref); (Lat/Engl)
London (RH) – BBC (Latin)
London (UCL) – BBC–BCC (L) **or** 3ALs+AS/VA; (Latin courses)
Manchester – BBC/AB (L) (Lat/Arch)
Newcastle – BBC (Lat/Engl Lit)
Nottingham – BBC–BCC (Latin courses except under **260 pts**)
Swansea – 280 pts 18u – BBC–BCC/BB (L) **or** ALs+ASs **or** VAs+/-ALs/ASs;
  (Latin)
260 pts **Exeter** – 260 pts 18u – BCC **or** BC+cc **or** VAs (contact univ); (not gs) (Latin)
Manchester – BCC (Latin courses except under **280 pts**)
Nottingham – 260 pts (Latin)
Reading – BCC (Latin courses)
220 pts **Lampeter** – 220 pts approx (L) (Latin courses)

Alternative Offers:

IB offers: Birmingham 32 pts; Bristol H665/655; Exeter 30 pts; Lampeter 28 pts; London (RH) 28 pts; St Andrews 30 pts; Swansea 28 pts.

Scottish Qualifications: Edinburgh BBBB; Glasgow BBBB; St Andrews BBBB.

CHOOSING YOUR COURSE (See also **Ch.1**)

> **Subject information:** Latin courses provide a study of the language, art, religion and history of the Roman world. This table should be read in conjunction with the **Classical Studies/Classical Civilisation** and **Classics** tables.

Special features: Belfast (Queen's) and **Leeds** The study of Latin is not restricted to the ancient world but extends into the history of Latin in medieval and Renaissance periods. **Birmingham** Funded study tour in second year vacation. Includes medieval and Renaissance Latin. **Edinburgh** and **Leeds** One course is available for beginners. **St Andrews** See under **Arts**. *NOW CHECK PROSPECTUSES AND WEB SITES.*

Top universities and colleges (Teaching Quality) (see Ch.4): See **Classics**.

Top universities and colleges (Research) (see Ch.4): See **Classics**.

Study opportunities abroad: Birmingham; Leeds.

ADMISSIONS INFORMATION

Number of applicants per place (approx): Birmingham 4; Lampeter 3; Leeds 2.

Planning your UCAS personal statement (see Ch.4): See **Classical Studies/Classical Civilisation**.

Selection interviews (see Ch.4): Birmingham; Cambridge; Durham; Edinburgh (No); Exeter; Hull; Lampeter; London (RH), (UCL); Manchester (No); Newcastle; Nottingham; Oxford; Reading; St Andrews (No); Swansea.

Interview questions (see Ch.4): See **Classical Studies/Classical Civilisation**.

GAP YEAR ADVICE

London (RH) Reading list available.

Institutions willing to defer entry after A-Levels: Birmingham; Lampeter; Leeds; London (UCL) (No); Newcastle; St Andrews; Swansea; Warwick.

AFTER RESULTS ADVICE

Institutions which may accept the same points score after A-Levels: Birmingham; Durham; Leeds (No); London (RH), (UCL) (No); Newcastle (flexible); St Andrews (No); Swansea; Warwick (No).

Institutions which may accept lower grades/points score after A-Levels: Birmingham; Leeds; London (RH); St Andrews; Swansea; Warwick.

Offers to applicants repeating A-Levels: Higher Durham, Leeds, St Andrews, Warwick; **Same** Newcastle, Swansea.

Probable vacancies from June 2001 and in Clearing (see Ch.4): A small number of vacancies were declared last year with offers averaging 240 pts.

NEW GRADUATE DESTINATIONS AND EMPLOYMENT (1999 HESA) (see **Ch.4**)

In a survey of 12 graduates, five went into full-time employment (mainly into business), three went on to further study and two were unemployed.

LATIN-AMERICAN STUDIES (including **Hispanic Studies**; see also **American Studies** and **Spanish**)

NB The information supplied by the universities and colleges this year varies considerably and the offers listed below should be used as a first source of reference only. Many institutions will accept combinations of Advanced (AL), Advanced Subsidiary (AS) and Vocational Advanced (VA) level qualifications to achieve the required points total, but applicants must check web sites and prospectuses for full details of all offers. Grades and points totals shown should be regarded as the minimum levels to be achieved, but offers may be adjusted downwards when results are known. The points totals shown to the left of the institutions are for ease of reference only. It must not be assumed that tariff points are always used by institutions or that they can be substituted for an offer in grades. The level of an offer is not necessarily indicative of the quality of a course. To calculate your offers see Chapter 4 and the inside fold of the back cover.

Special subject requirements/preferences: A-Level: English or history preferred by **London (King's)**. Spanish required by **Leeds, Manchester, Newcastle. GCSE: Aberdeen** English, mathematics or science and a foreign language. English and a foreign language required by most universities.

340 pts **and above**
    London (UCL) – AAB **or** 3ALs+AS/VA; (Hisp Law/Law)
    Nottingham – AAB–ABB (Hisp St/Econ

320 pts **London (King's)** – ABB–BCC (Hisp St courses; Hisp Port St; Port/Braz St)

300 pts **Birmingham** – BBB (Am St/Hisp St; Hisp St/Comp St)
    Glasgow – BBB–BBC (Hisp St courses)
    Liverpool – 300–260 pts – ALs **or** ALs+ASs **or** VAs+/-ALs/ASs; (Lat Am St)
    London (King's) – BBB (Port/War St)
    Sheffield – BBB–BBC (Hisp St courses)
    Southampton – ABC (Lat Am courses)

280 pts **Cardiff** – BBC–BCC (Hisp St)
    Essex – 280–260 pts 21u – BB–BC+AL/2ASs **or** VA12u BB–BC+AL; gs; (Lat Am St)
    Leeds – BBC (Hisp St/Lat Am St)
    London (King's) – BBC (Hisp St joint courses except under **320/300 pts**)
    London (QM) – BBC–BCD (Hisp St Ling/Comp Sci)
    London (UCL) – BBC **or** 3ALs+AS/VA; (Hisp St; Mod Iber/Lat Am Reg St)
    Manchester – BBC (Hisp St)
    Newcastle – BBC–BCC (Lat Am St)
    Nottingham – BBC (Lat Am St/Am St)

260 pts   **Bristol** – BCC (Hisp St)
240 pts   **Aberdeen** – CCC (Hisp St courses)
          London (Gold) – BCD (Span/Lat Am St)
          London (QM) – CCC (Hisp St)
          Portsmouth – 240 pts – ALs **or** ALs+ASs **or** VAs; gs; (Lat Am St; Lat Am Dev St)
220 pts   **Middlesex** – 220–180 pts approx (Lat Am St)
          Wolverhampton – 220–160 pts 12u – DDD–CDE/CC or CD+d/e **or** VA12u CC; gs; (Lat Am St)

Alternative Offers:

IB offers: Aberdeen 30 pts; Essex 28 pts inc 10 pts 2 Highers; Portsmouth 24 pts.

Scottish Qualifications: Aberdeen BBBB/AAB; Glasgow BBBB.

CHOOSING YOUR COURSE (See also **Ch.1**)

Subject information: In Latin American courses there will be an emphasis on the study of Spanish and of Latin-American republics, covering both historical and present-day conditions and problems. Normally a year is spent in Latin America. Courses in Spanish, Hispanic Studies, which cover Spanish, Catalan, Portuguese and Latin-American Studies, and degree courses in American Studies could also be considered.

Special features: Essex Year 3 in Colombia, Brazil, Mexico or Venezuela. **Glasgow** No knowledge of Spanish or Portuguese necessary. **Portsmouth** Course options can lead to humanities or social science or to spending year 2 in Latin-America or to starting Spanish *ab initio* or adding Portuguese from year 3. *NOW CHECK PROSPECTUSES AND WEB SITES.*

Top universities and colleges (Research) (see Ch.4): Birmingham; Bristol.

Study opportunities abroad: Liverpool; Newcastle; Portsmouth.

ADMISSIONS INFORMATION

Number of applicants per place (approx): Essex 3; Liverpool 3; Newcastle 25; Portsmouth 5.

Planning your UCAS personal statement (see Ch.4): Visits and contacts with Spain and Latin-American countries should be described. An awareness of the economic, historical and political scene of these countries is also important. Information may be obtained from respective embassies.

Selection interviews (see Ch.4): Newcastle; Portsmouth (some) (W) (T).

Interview questions (see Ch.4): Why are you interested in studying this subject? What countries related to the degree course have you visited? What career are you planning when you finish your degree? Applicants taking Spanish are likely to be asked questions on their syllabus and should also be familiar with some Spanish newspapers and magazines.

GAP YEAR ADVICE

Institutions willing to defer entry after A-Levels: Newcastle.

AFTER RESULTS ADVICE

Institutions which may accept the same points score after A-Levels: Essex; Newcastle (No); Portsmouth.

Offers to applicants repeating A-Levels: Higher Essex; **Same** Newcastle, Portsmouth.

Probable vacancies from June 2001 and in Clearing (see Ch.4): Vacancies are likely at a small number of universities. Offers on Single Honours courses are likely to average 240 pts.

NEW GRADUATE DESTINATIONS AND EMPLOYMENT (1999 HESA) (see **Ch.4**)

Of 57 graduates surveyed, 32 entered full-time employment (evenly balanced across most occupations), nine went on to further study and four were believed to be unemployed.

LAW (including **Criminal Justice/Criminology**)

NB The information supplied by the universities and colleges this year varies considerably and the offers listed below should be used as a first source of reference only. Many institutions will accept combinations of Advanced (AL), Advanced Subsidiary (AS) and Vocational Advanced (VA) level qualifications to achieve the required points total, but applicants must check web sites and prospectuses for full details of all offers. Grades and points totals shown should be regarded as the minimum levels to be achieved, but offers may be adjusted downwards when results are known. The points totals shown to the left of the institutions are for ease of reference only. It must not be assumed that tariff points are always used by institutions or that they can be substituted for an offer in grades. The level of an offer is not necessarily indicative of the quality of a course. To calculate your offers see Chapter 4 and the inside fold of the back cover.

Special subject requirements/preferences: A-Level: Good grades in languages for foreign language courses. **Hull** Law at grade B when taken. **Manchester Met** Art or art history not acceptable. **Oxford** A/AS-Levels considered in arts/science subjects; (Law/Euro) French, German or Italian at A-Level essential. **Strathclyde** A-Level English required. **GCSE: Aberdeen, Dundee, Edinburgh, Glasgow** English, mathematics or science and a foreign language. **Birmingham** Grade A in approximately five subjects with grade A or B in English. **Bristol UWE** Eight subjects with some at grade A and B. **Brunel** Minimum of six subjects at grade A–C. **Exeter** Four subjects at grade A* or A, usually none below B. **Hull** Six subjects (minimum), four As or Bs. **Kingston** Seven subjects, not more than two at grade C. **Leeds** Six subjects at grade B or above. **London (LSE)** A and B grades. **Manchester Met** Grade A or B in French or German for foreign language options. **Oxford** (mathematics required), **Cambridge** Majority of grade As. **Robert Gordon** Six to eight subjects with grade A or B. **Swansea (IHE)** Three subjects at grades A–C minimum.

360 pts and above
 Cambridge – Offers, mainly in grades, vary between colleges (Law)
 East Anglia – AAA; (not gs) (Law/Am Leg St)
 Liverpool – 390–340 pts – ALs **or** ALs+ASs **or** VAs+/-ALs/ASs; (Law)
 London (King's) – 390 pts – AAB+b **or** ABB+b **or** AA+bbb **or** AB+aab (inc B Ger for Engl/Ger Law course); VAs considered; (Law; Engl/Fr Law; Engl/Ger Law)
 London (UCL) – AAA **or** 3ALs+AS/VA; (Law)
 Oxford – Offers vary between candidates (Law)
 Southampton – 360 pts 21u (inc 220 pts from 2ALs); (Law)
350 pts **Kingston** – 350 pts 21u **or** 370 pts 24u; (Law; Law/Bus; Law/Euro St)
 Southampton – 350 pts 21u (inc 200 pts from 2ALs); (Law/Pol)
340 pts **Belfast (Queen's)** – AAB (Law/Acc)
 Birmingham – AAB same sitting (Law; Law/Bus St; Law/Fr; Law/Ger)
 Bristol – AAB–ABB (Law courses)
 Durham – AAB (Law; Law/Econ; Law/Sociol)
 Edinburgh – AAB (Law courses except under **320 pts**)
 Leeds – AAB **or** AA+bb; gs; (Law; Law/Fr/Chin/Jap)
 Leicester – 3ALs **or** 3ALs+2ASs (340 pts reqd) **or** VAs (340 pts)+/-ALs/ASs; gs; (Law)
 London (LSE) – AAB–BBB (Law; Law/Fr Law)
 London (UCL) – AAB **or** 3ALs+AS/VA; (Law/Advnc St; Law/Hisp Law; Law with Ital Law/Ger Law/Fr Law)

Manchester – AAB (A Fr) (Engl Law/Fr Law)
Manchester – AAB (Law)
Newcastle – AAB (Law/Fr)
Nottingham – AAB **or** ABB+2ASs (not gs) (Law)
Sheffield – AAB/AA (Law; Law/Fr; Law/Ger; Law/Span; Law/Crim)
Warwick – AAB (Euro Law; Law)

330 pts **Kingston** – 330 pts 21u **or** 350 pts 24u (inc min 80 pts lang); (Law/Fr Law;
Law/Fr St; Law/Ger Law; Law/Ger St; Law/Span St)
Southampton – 330 pts 21u (inc 180 pts from 2ALs); (App Soc Sci/Crim)

320 pts **Belfast (Queen's)** – ABB (Law courses except under **340 pts**)
Cardiff – ABB (Law; Law/Crim)
East Anglia – ABB; (not gs) (Law; Law Euro Sys; Law/Fr Law/Lang; Law/Ger
Law/Lang)
Edinburgh – ABB (Law/Bus St; Law/Soc Pol)
Essex – 320–280 pts – AA–BB+AL/2ASs **or** VA12u AA–BB+AL; gs; (Law courses)
Exeter – 320 pts 18u – ABB **or** AB+bb **or** BB+aa **or** VAs (contact univ); gs;
(Law; Law Euro; Law Euro St)
Glasgow – ABB (Law courses)
Kent – 320 pts (Law)
Lancaster – ABB–BBC/AB (BB–CC mature students) (Law; Euro Leg St)
Leeds – ABB (AB for mature entry) (Acc/Law)
Leicester – 18u – ABB **or** ALs+ASs(A/B Fr) **or** VAs+AL (A/B Fr); gs; (Law/Fr
Law/Lang)
London (SOAS) – 320 pts (Law courses)
Manchester – ABB (Pat Law/Chem)
Newcastle – ABB (Law)
Northumbria – ABB (Law; Law/Fr Law)
Nottingham – ABB (Law/Pol)
Oxford Brookes – ABB (Law)
Reading – ABB–ABC (Law courses)
Sheffield – ABB (Law/Crim)
Strathclyde – ABB (Euro Law)
Sussex – ABB (Law courses)
Warwick – ABB (Law; Law/Sociol; Law/Bus St)

300 pts **Aberdeen** – BBB (Law)
Bradford – 300 pts 12u; gs; (Bus St/Law)
Bristol UWE – BBB–BBC **or** ALs+ASs **or** VAs+/-ALs/ASs; (not gs) (Law
courses except under **240 pts**)
Brunel – 300 pts 2x6u pref 3x6u (inc B Fr/Ger) – ALs **or** ALs+ASs **or** VAs+/-
ALs/ASs; (Law; Bus/Fin Law; Law/Fr; Law/Ger; Law (Crim Just))
Cardiff – BBB (Crim/Soc Pol)
City – 3x6u – BBB **or** ASs/VAs (contact univ); (not gs) (Law)
Exeter – 300 pts 18u – BBB **or** BB+bb **or** VAs (contact univ); gs; (Law Soty)
Hull – BBB–BBC (Law)
Hull – BBB (Law/Ger; Law/Fr (Law & Lang))
Keele – BBB **or** equiv AS accepted; gs; (Law courses)
Kent – 300 pts approx (Euro Legal St; Law (Ind Rel/Hum Res Mgt))
Leicester – BBB (Law/Econ)
Liverpool – 300 pts; (Leg/Bus St)
London (LSE) – BBB (Law/Anth)
London (QM) – BBB; (Law courses)
Oxford Brookes – BBB (Law Pub)
Reading – ABC (Law/Fr Law)
Strathclyde – BBB (Law Comp Sci)
Surrey – 300 pts 18u – BBB **or** ALs+ASs(B lang) **or** VAs+/-ALs/ASs (contact
univ); gs; (Law courses)
Sussex – BBB (Law/Lang; Maths/Law)
Swansea – 300 pts 18u – BBB/AB **or** ALs+ASs **or** VAs+/-ALs/ASs; (Law
courses)

280 pts   **Aberystwyth** – BBC (Law courses)

         Buckingham – 280 pts 21u – 3ALs **or** 3ALs+AS; (Law courses)

         De Montfort (Leicester) – 280 pts (inc 2ALs inc lang for Fr/Ger courses) – ALs **or** ALs+ASs **or** VAs+/-ALs/ASs; (Law; Law/Fr; Law/Ger)

         Dundee – BBC (Scots Law; Engl Law; Law/Acc)

         Hertfordshire – 280–260 pts approx (Law courses)

         Liverpool John Moores – BBC–BCC **or** ALs+ASS **or** VA+AL(B); (Law; Bus Law)

         Manchester Met – BBC (Law; Law/Fr)

         Nottingham Trent – 280 pts approx (C French/German) (Law Euro Fr/Ger)

         Ulster – BBC (Law/Econ; Law/Gov)

         Westminster – BBC approx (Law)

260 pts   **Bangor** – 260–240 pts approx (Crim/Crim Just; Crim/Wmns St)

         Bournemouth – 260 pts – BCC; (Law courses)

         Brunel – 260–180 pts (Eth Leg Iss Hlth Cre)

         Coventry – 260 pts (Law/Euro Langs)

         Heriot-Watt – BCC (Mgt/Bus Law)

         London Guildhall – BCC/BC (Bus Law)

         Northumbria – BBD (Crim/Sociol; Crim Soc Res)

         Plymouth – BCC (Crim Just/Law)

         Plymouth – 260 pts approx (Law)

         Sheffield Hallam – 260–240 pts; gs; (Law courses)

         Staffordshire – 260 pts (inc 220 pts from 2x6u); gs; (Law/Am St)

         Staffordshire – 260 pts approx (Crim/Foren Sci)

         Stirling – BCC (Bus Law)

         Wolverhampton – 260 pts 12u – CCC/AB **or** CC+bc **or** VA12u BB; gs; (Law)

240 pts   **Bradford** – 240 pts 12u – gs; (Pol/Law; Euro St/Law)

         Brighton – 240 pts approx (Acc/Law; Bus/Law; Bus Admin/Law)

         Bristol UWE – 240 pts – ALs **or** ALs+ASs **or** VAs+/-ALs/ASs; gs; (Euro Lang/Law)

         Central England – 240–220 pts approx (Law; Law with Pol/Psy/Sociol; Crim Just/Plcg)

         Central Lancashire – CCC (Law)

         Derby – CCC **or** CC+cc **or** VAs CC+/-ALs/ASs; gs; (Law; Law with Euro St/Pol/Lang)

         East London – 240–200 pts approx (Law courses)

         Glamorgan – 240 pts approx (Law courses)

         Greenwich – 240–160 pts approx (Law courses)

         Huddersfield – CCC/BB (BCC 2 sittings) (Law; Law/Bus; Law/Euro Leg St)

         Lancaster – CCC (Criminology courses)

         Lincolnshire & Humberside – 240 pts (Law)

         Middlesex – 240 pts (Law)

         Napier – CCC (Law)

         North London – 240 pts 1x12u **or** 2x6u; (Law; Law Comb; Bus Law)

         Portsmouth – 240 pts – ALs **or** ALs+ASs **or** VAs; gs; (Law courses; Crim courses)

         Staffordshire – CCC (Law)

         Sunderland – 240 pts approx (Bus Leg St; Law/Psy; Law/Bus St; Law)

         Wolverhampton – 240 pts 12u – DDEE/DDD/CC **or** CD+dd **or** VA12u CC; gs; (Law/Bus Law; Crim Just/Hum Rights + 2nd subj)

220 pts   **Blackburn (Coll)** – 220 pts 12u – BCD/CCC/AB **or** BB+aa **or** C+bbc **or** BC+c **or** aaac **or** aabb **or** bbccc **or** VA6u B; gs; (Law)

         Bradford – 220 pts 12u; gs; (App Crim Just St)

         Bradford (Coll) – 220 pts approx (Law)

         Central Lancashire – CCD (inc Fr/Ger); gs; (Law/Fr/Ger)

         Central Lancashire – 220 pts 12u – ALs **or** ALs+ASs **or** VAs+/-ALs/ASs; gs; (Law/Bus; Law/Crim; Law/Engl; Law/Pol; Law/Psy)

         Glamorgan – 220 pts (Crim Just)

Huddersfield – 220 pts approx (Law/Acc)
Lincolnshire & Humberside – 200 pts (Criminology courses)
Liverpool John Moores – 220 pts approx (Crim Just/Pol)
London Guildhall – CCD–CDD/BB–CC (Law courses except under **260 pts** – offers depend on combinations)
Luton – 220–180 pts approx (Law)
South Bank – 220–180 pts (Law)
South Bank – 220–140 pts (Crim Comb)
Teesside – 220 pts approx (Crim; Foren Invstg)

200 pts   **Anglia** – 200 pts approx (Law)
Buckinghamshire Chilterns (UC) – 200–180 pts approx (Crim courses)
Buckinghamshire Chilterns (UC) – 200–140 pts (Law courses)
De Montfort (Leicester) – 200 pts (inc 2ALs) – ALs **or** ALs+ASs **or** VAs+/- ALs/ASs; gs; (Law joint courses)
Derby – 200 pts approx (Law Comb)
Glasgow Caledonian – CCE/BC (Law Admin St)
Northampton (UC) – 200–160 pts approx (Law Comb courses; Crim Comb courses)
Plymouth – 200 pts approx (Crim Just/FR)
Southampton (Inst) – 200 pts (Criminology)
Sunderland – 200–180 pts approx (Bus Law Math Sci; Bus Law/Comp St; Crim Comb)
Teesside – 200 pts (Law)

180 pts   **Anglia** – 180 pts approx (Bus Law)
Sunderland – 180 pts (Criminology courses)

160 pts   **Abertay Dundee** – CC–DD (inc Engl); (Law; Euro Bus Law)
Croydon (Coll) – CC (Law)
Edge Hill (CHE) – CC–CD (Criminology courses)
Manchester Met – 160 pts/CC (Crim/Sociol)
Newport (UWCN) – 160–140 pts approx (Leg St courses)
Paisley – CC (Euro Bus Law)
Robert Gordon – DDE/CD (Law/Mgt)
Southampton (Inst) – 160 pts approx (Bus Law)

140 pts   **and below**
Abertay Dundee – CD (Conv Ex Law)
Bell (CT) – (Leg St)
Bolton (IHE) – (Law)
Derby – CD **or** ALs+ASs **or** VA CD+/-AL/ASs; (Law Comb)
Glasgow Caledonian – 140 pts (Leg St)
Holborn (Coll) – (Law (LLB) London Ext/Wolverhampton – check tuition fees)
Lansdowne (Coll) – 80 pts approx (Law courses)
Nottingham Trent – Access (Law – part-time)
Swansea (IHE) – EE (Law)
Thames Valley – 140 pts approx (Law courses)
Wolverhampton – ALs **or** VAs; gs (Law – part-time course for mature students)

Leeds Met – (contact university)

Diploma of Higher Education courses
80 pts   **and below**
East London; London Guildhall.

Higher National Diploma courses
140 pts   **and below**
Aberdeen (Coll) (Leg Serv) Abertay Dundee; Bell (CT); Blackburn (Coll); Central England; Exeter (leg St); Farnborough (CT); Glamorgan; Glasgow Caledonian; Glasgow (Coll); Llandrillo (Coll) (Leg St); Mid Kent (CFHE); Napier EE; Newport (UWCN); North East Wales (IHE); Suffolk (Coll); Truro (Coll) (Leg St).

Alternative Offers:

EB offers: Aston 72%; East Anglia 70%; Edinburgh 80%; Glamorgan 75%; Keele 70%; Lancaster 75%; Leeds 70%; Surrey 70%.

IB offers: Aberdeen 34 pts; Aberystwyth 30 pts; Anglia 28 pts; Aston 31 pts; Bangor 24 pts; Belfast (Queen's) H666 S555; Birmingham 36 pts; Bournemouth 26 pts; Brighton 24 pts; Bristol 34 pts H665; Bristol UWE 26 pts; Brunel 31 pts; Buckingham 27 pts; Cardiff H 17 pts S 14 pts; Derby 30 pts; Dundee 28 pts; Durham H7 average; East Anglia 30 pts; Essex 30 pts inc 11 pts 2 Highers; Exeter 33 pts; Hull 30–28 pts, 18 at Highers; Kent 33 pts, H 16 pts; Kingston 33 pts; Lancaster 32 pts; Leeds 33 pts inc H66; Leicester 30 pts inc H66; London (LSE) 36 pts, (QM) H655, (UCL) 36 pts; London Guildhall 24 pts; Manchester Met 30 pts; Middlesex 30 pts; Newcastle 34 pts; Plymouth 30 pts; Reading 30 pts; Robert Gordon (Leg/Admin St) 24 pts; Southampton 32 pts H 16 pts; Staffordshire 26 pts min; Surrey 28 pts; Warwick 36–34 pts; Wolverhampton 31 pts.

Irish offers: Aberdeen BBBB; Abertay Dundee CCC; Aberystwyth BBBBCC; Birmingham AAABB; Brighton BBBB; Bristol UWE CCCC; Brunel AABBB; East Anglia ABBBB; Edinburgh AAAAB; Holborn (Coll) BBBCC; Hull BBBCC; Keele BBBBCC; Leeds AAABBB; London Guildhall CCCCC; Middlesex BBBCC; Napier BBCC; Warwick AAAB.

Scottish Qualifications: Aberdeen ABBBBB; Abertay Dundee BBC; Bell (CT) CCC; Dundee ABBBC; Edinburgh AAAAB; Glasgow AAAAB, AAABBB at 2 sittings; Glasgow Caledonian BBBC; Napier BBCC; Robert Gordon (Law/Mgt) BBCC; Stirling (Bus Law) BBBB; Strathclyde AAABB.

Overseas applicants: Bournemouth Good command of English required. **Brunel** Intermediate London External LLB may enable direct entry to year 2. **Glamorgan** Fluency in English required. **Hull** Living costs 30% lower than in London. **Leeds** Some scholarships available. **Manchester Met** Stay in touch with us by fax. **Middlesex** No Foundation course. **Newcastle** Intensive pre-sessional English course. **Surrey** Pre-sessional English course.

CHOOSING YOUR COURSE (See also **Ch.1**)

> **Subject information:** Law courses are usually divided into two parts. Part I occupies the first year and introduces the student to criminal and constitutional law and the legal process. Thereafter many different specialised topics can be studied in the second and third years. The course content is very similar for most courses. Students interested in Law could also consider such courses as Government, Politics and International Relations. Criminology courses bridge law and social studies. It should be noted that a small number of universities prefer students not to offer law at A-level. Applicants are advised to check with universities as to their current policies, in particular Belfast (Queen's), Brunel, Cambridge (colleges), Central England, De Montfort, Edinburgh, Greenwich, Kingston, London (LSE), (QM), (UCL), Newcastle and Oxford (colleges). See also **Appendix 1**.

Special features: Aberystwyth The LLB scheme is offered for students wishing to concentrate entirely on law whilst the broader BA degree offers a major in Law and a minor in another subject. **Bristol** Optional units include criminology, women and the law, law and medicine and ethics and the law. **Buckingham** This is a two-year course with the opportunity to take a year out at universities in Canada or the USA. **Essex** Exemption from the common professional exam of the Law Society and Bar. **Hertfordshire** Law is also offered on the modular scheme with other subjects ranging from computer science to psychology. **Leicester** Students on the LLB scheme take certain options which are guaranteed to gain them a place at the College of Law. **Liverpool John Moores** Students taking the BA in Criminal Justice will not receive exemptions from the legal profession first stage examination. **London Guildhall** The Legal and Economics Studies degree is offered in connection with the Universite Rene Descartes in Paris. *NOW CHECK PROSPECTUSES AND WEB SITES.*

Top universities and colleges (Teaching Quality) (see Ch.4): Aberdeen; Belfast (Queen's); Bristol; Bristol UWE; Cambridge; Durham; East Anglia; Edinburgh; Essex; Glasgow; Leicester; Liverpool; London (King's), (LSE), (SOAS), (UCL); Manchester; Northumbria; Nottingham; Oxford; Oxford Brookes; Sheffield; Warwick; not all institutions assessed.

Top universities and colleges (Research) (see Ch.4): Aberdeen; Belfast (Queen's); Birmingham; Bristol; Brunel; Cambridge; Cardiff; Durham; Edinburgh; Essex; Glasgow; Keele; Kent; Leeds; Leicester; London (King's), (LSE), (QM), (UCL); Manchester; Nottingham; Oxford; Sheffield; Southampton; Strathclyde; Warwick.

Study opportunities abroad: Aberdeen; Abertay Dundee; Aberystwyth; Anglia; Aston; Bangor; Belfast (Queen's); Birmingham; Bristol; Brunel; Cardiff; Central England; Central Lancashire; Coventry; De Montfort; Derby; Dundee; Durham; East Anglia; East London; Edinburgh; Exeter; Glamorgan; Glasgow; Hull; Kingston; Lancaster; Leeds; Leicester; London (QM), (UCL); Manchester Met; Napier; Newcastle; Nottingham; Nottingham Trent; Oxford; Oxford Brookes; Sheffield; Sheffield Hallam; South Bank; Southampton; Southampton (Inst); Staffordshire; Strathclyde; Surrey; Sussex; Thames Valley; Warwick; Westminster; Wolverhampton; York.

Work opportunities abroad: Brighton; Brunel; Cardiff; Central England; Exeter; Leeds; London (UCL); Warwick; Wolverhampton.

ADMISSIONS INFORMATION

Number of applicants per place (approx): Abertay Dundee 3; Aberystwyth 7; Anglia 10; Aston 10; Bangor 10; Birmingham 15; Bournemouth (Bus Law) 9; Bristol 19; Bristol UWE 27; Brunel 12; Buckingham 3; Cambridge 4.7; Cardiff 13; Central England 20; Central Lancashire 36; City 14; Coventry 15; De Montfort 25; Derby 7; Dundee 7; Durham 20; East Anglia 14; East London 13; Edinburgh 5; Essex 26; Exeter 15; Glamorgan 3; Glasgow 8; Glasgow Caledonian 10; Holborn (Coll) no quotas; Huddersfield 10; Hull 15; Kent 11; Kingston 25; Lancaster 26; Leeds 17; Leicester 14; Liverpool 10; Liverpool John Moores 10; London (LSE) 15, (QM) 17, (UCL) 17; London Guildhall 13; Manchester 17; Manchester Met 21; Middlesex 25; Napier 7; Newcastle 13; North London 27; Northumbria 12; Nottingham 25; Nottingham Trent 15, (Crim) 16; Oxford 3.5; Oxford Brookes 18; Plymouth 14; Robert Gordon 4; Sheffield 16; Sheffield Hallam 18; South Bank 22; Southampton 6; Southampton (Inst) 5; Staffordshire 12; Strathclyde (Euro Law) 12, (Law) 10; Swansea 3; Swansea (IHE) 2; Teesside 3; Thames Valley 18; Warwick 20; Westminster 29; Wolverhampton 12.

Planning your UCAS personal statement (see Ch.4): Visit the law courts and take notes on cases heard. Follow leading legal arguments in the press. Read the law sections in *The Independent*, *The Times* and *The Guardian*. Discuss the career with lawyers and, if possible, obtain work shadowing in lawyers' offices. Describe these visits and experiences and indicate any special areas of law which interest you. (Read *Learning the Law* by Glanville Williams.) **Oxford Brookes** Work experience very important, particularly for mature students. **Southampton** Evidence that the applicant has given serious thought to the career; reading, work experience, court visits. See also **Appendix 1**.

Selection interviews (see Ch.4): Abertay Dundee (No); Aberystwyth (T); Anglia (No); Bangor; Belfast (Queen's); Birmingham; Blackburn (Coll) (No); Bournemouth (No); Brighton (No); Bristol; Bristol UWE; Brunel (No); Buckingham; Cambridge; Cardiff (No); Central England (No); Central Lancashire; Coventry; De Montfort (No); Derby (No); Dundee; Durham (No); East Anglia (No); East London; Essex; Exeter (some); Glamorgan (No); Glasgow; Huddersfield (No); Hull (No); Kent (mature/Access students); Kingston (No); Lancaster; Leeds (No); Leicester (No); Liverpool; Liverpool John Moores (T); London (UCL) (W); London Guildhall (No); Manchester (No); Mid Kent (CFHE) (T); Napier; Newcastle (No); Northampton (UC) (No); Northumbria; Nottingham (T); Nottingham Trent (mature students) (T); Oxford (T – An unseen legal dispute aptitude test may be set); Oxford Brookes (all mature applicants); Robert Gordon (No); Sheffield (No); Sheffield Hallam (No); South Bank; Southampton (mature students only); Southampton (Inst); Staffordshire (No); Surrey; Swansea (No); Teesside; Warwick.

Interview questions (see Ch.4): This is a highly competitive subject and applicants will be expected to have a basic knowledge of aspects of law and to have gained some work experience, on which they are likely to be questioned. It is almost certain that a legal question will be asked at interview and applicants will be tested on their reponses. Questions in the past have included: What interests you in the study of law? What would you do to overcome the problem of prison overcrowding if you were (a) a judge (b) a prosecutor (c) the Prime Minister? What legal cases have you read about recently? What is jurisprudence? What are the causes of violence in society? A friend bought a bun which, unknown to him, contained a stone. He gave it to you to eat and you broke a tooth. Could you sue anyone? Have you visited any law courts? What cases did you see? A person arrives in England unable to speak the language. He lights a cigarette in a non-smoking compartment of a train. Can he be charged and convicted? What should be done in the case of an elderly person who steals a bar of soap? What, in your opinion, would be the two basic laws in Utopia? Describe, without using your hands, how you would do the butterfly stroke. What would happen if there were no law? Should we legalise euthanasia? If you could change any law, what would it be? How would you implement the changes? If a person tries to kill someone using black magic, are they guilty of attempted murder? If a jury uses a ouija board to reach a decision, is it wrong? If so, why? **Nottingham Trent** Mature students have a timed essay.

Reasons for rejection (non-academic): 'Dreams' about being a lawyer! Poorly informed about the subject. Badly drafted application. Under-estimate of work load. Poor communication skills.

GAP YEAR ADVICE

Institutions willing to defer entry after A-Levels: Aberdeen; Abertay Dundee; Aberystwyth; Birmingham; Bournemouth; Brighton; Brunel (only with a good reason); Buckingham; Cardiff; Central England; Central Lancashire; City; Coventry; De Montfort; Derby; Dundee; East Anglia; East London; Glamorgan (No); Glasgow Caledonian; Hertfordshire; Hull; Kent; Lancaster (No); Leicester; Lincolnshire & Humberside; London (UCL) (No); London Guildhall; Manchester Met (generally No); Newcastle; North London; Northumbria; Plymouth; Robert Gordon; Sheffield Hallam; South Bank (Prefer not); Staffordshire; Surrey; Sussex; Swansea (IHE); Teesside (No); Thames Valley; Warwick; Wolverhampton.

AFTER RESULTS ADVICE

Institutions which may accept the same points score after A-Levels: Aberdeen; Abertay Dundee; Aberystwyth; Anglia; Bangor; Belfast (Queen's); Birmingham; Brighton; Bristol UWE (perhaps); Brunel (usually); Buckingham; Cardiff; Central England; Central Lancashire; City; Coventry; De Montfort; Derby; Dundee; Durham (No); East Anglia; East London; Essex; Glamorgan; Glasgow; Glasgow Caledonian; Holborn (Coll); Huddersfield; Hull; Kent (No); Kingston (No); Lancaster; Leeds; Leicester (varies); Liverpool; Liverpool John Moores; London Guildhall; Luton; Middlesex; Napier; Newcastle (No); North London (No); Northampton (UC); Nottingham (No); Nottingham Trent; Oxford Brookes; Plymouth; Sheffield (No); Sheffield Hallam; South Bank; Southampton (No); Southampton (Inst); Staffordshire; Strathclyde; Surrey; Swansea (IHE); Teesside; Thames Valley; Warwick (No); Wolverhampton.

Institutions which may accept lower grades/points score after A-Levels: Aberdeen; Abertay Dundee; Aberystwyth (perhaps); Anglia; Brighton; Bristol UWE (perhaps); Brunel; Buckingham; Cardiff (perhaps); Central Lancashire; City; Coventry; De Montfort; Derby; Dundee; East London; Essex; Exeter; Holborn (Coll); Huddersfield; Hull (overseas applicants 18 pts); Kingston; Lancaster; Leicester; Liverpool; Luton; Manchester Met; Sheffield Hallam; South Bank; Staffordshire; Teesside; Thames Valley; Warwick; Wolverhampton.

Offers to applicants repeating A-Levels: Higher Aberystwyth, Belfast (Queen's), Birmingham, Bristol UWE, Coventry, Essex, Glamorgan, Glasgow, Hull, Leeds, Liverpool (unlikely), London Guildhall, Manchester Met, Newcastle, North London, Nottingham,

Oxford Brookes, Sheffield, Staffordshire, Strathclyde, Warwick; **Possibly higher** Cardiff, Durham; **Same** Brighton, Bristol, Brunel, De Montfort, Holborn (Coll), Huddersfield, Kingston, Liverpool John Moores, Northumbria, Surrey, Wolverhampton.

Probable vacancies from June 2001 and in Clearing (see Ch.4): Over 60 universities declared vacancies last year, many on joint courses. For entry to careers as solicitors and barristers, always check that joint courses in Law cover the core subjects required by the Law Society. Vacancies are likely at several universities for Criminology and Criminal Justice.

NEW GRADUATE DESTINATIONS AND EMPLOYMENT (1999 HESA) (**see Ch.4**)

Of 6510 graduates surveyed, 1808 went into permanent employment (mainly into business, finance and public administration), 3879 into further study (with 3211 aiming for Law Society and Bar examinations) and 190 graduates were believed to be unemployed.

LEISURE & RECREATIONAL STUDIES (see also **Sports Studies** and **Tourism**)

NB The information supplied by the universities and colleges this year varies considerably and the offers listed below should be used as a first source of reference only. Many institutions will accept combinations of Advanced (AL), Advanced Subsidiary (AS) and Vocational Advanced (VA) level qualifications to achieve the required points total, but applicants must check web sites and prospectuses for full details of all offers. Grades and points totals shown should be regarded as the minimum levels to be achieved, but offers may be adjusted downwards when results are known. The points totals shown to the left of the institutions are for ease of reference only. It must not be assumed that tariff points are always used by institutions or that they can be substituted for an offer in grades. The level of an offer is not necessarily indicative of the quality of a course. To calculate your offers see Chapter 4 and the inside fold of the back cover.

Special subject requirements/preferences: GCSE: Normally English and mathematics grade A–C. **Portsmouth** Subjects grade A–C including English and mathematics.

300 pts **Loughborough** – 300 pts (Spo Leis Mgt)
280 pts **Brunel** – 280 pts approx (Leis Mgt/Acc; Leis Mgt/Comp St; Leis Mgt/Spo Sci)
De Montfort (Bedford) – 280–200 pts (inc 2ALs **or** VA12u) – ALs **or** ALs+ASs **or** VAs+/-ALs/ASs; gs; (Leis Recr St; Advntr Recr)
Loughborough – 280 pts (Recr Mgt)
Manchester – BBC–CCC (Leis Mgt)
240 pts **Bournemouth** – 240–220 pts approx (Leis Mark)
Brighton – 240 pts approx (Leis/Spo St; Leis/Spo Mgt)
Ulster – CCC (Spo Exer Leis St)
220 pts **Cheltenham & Glos (CHE)** – 220–200 pts approx (Leis Mgt; Leis Mark courses)
Coventry – 220–200 pts approx (Leis Mgt courses)
King Alfred's Winchester (Coll) – 220 pts 12u – 2ALs (min); gs; (Leis Mgt Comb courses)
Kingston – 220 pts 2x6u; (Leis Plan Dev)
Sheffield Hallam – 220 pts approx (Recr Mgt)
Staffordshire – 220 pts approx (Spo Leis Mgt)
200 pts **Bangor** – 200 pts; gs; (Leisure courses)
Cardiff (UWI) – 200–180 pts approx (Recr/Leis Mgt courses)
Derby – 200 pts 12u – CDD **or** CD+dd **or** VAs (AL grades)+/-ALs/ASs; gs (Leis Mgt)
Glasgow Caledonian – CCE–CC (Leis Fac Mgt; Leis Mgt)
Luton – 200–160 pts approx (Leis St)
Portsmouth – 200 pts – ALs **or** ALs+ASs **or** VAs; gs; (Leis Res Mgt; Leis/Lang)

Sheffield Hallam – 200 pts approx (Out Leis/Mgt)
Surrey Roehampton – 200 pts (inc AL) – ALs **or** ALs+ASs **or** VAs+/-ALs/ASs; (Leis Mgt)
Teesside – 200–160 pts approx (Leis Mgt)
Warrington (CI) – CDD/CC; not AS only; gs (Leisure courses)
Westminster – 200–160 pts approx (Leis Dev Strat Mgt)
Writtle (Coll) – 200 pts approx (Leis Mgt/Herit Mgt)

190 pts **North London** – 190 pts inc 160 pts from 2ALs **or** VAs; (Leis St; Leis/Tour Mgt; Int Leis/Tour Mgt)

180 pts **Anglia** – 180 pts approx (Leis/Tour/Env)
Farnborough (CT) – 180 pts approx (Leis Mgt)
Glamorgan – 180 pts approx (Leis Tour Mgt; Leis Recr Mgt)
Liverpool John Moores – 180 pts approx (Leis Tour)
Salford – 180–160 pts approx (Leis Mgt; Leis Tour Mgt)
Staffordshire – 180 pts approx (Leis Econ)
Wolverhampton – 180 pts 12u – DDD–CDE **or** CC/BD/DD+b **or** VA12u CC; gs (Leis Mgt)

160 pts **Birmingham (CFTCS)** – 12u (inc 1x6u) – CC **or** ALs+ASs **or** VAs+/-ALs/ASs; (Leis Mgt)
Blackburn (Coll) – 160 pts 12u – DDE **or** DD+ee **or** aac **or** VA6u C; gs; (Leis Mgt)
Blackpool & Fylde (Coll) – 160 pts approx (Leis Ent Mgt)
Buckinghamshire Chilterns (UC) – 160–140 pts approx (Leis Mgt courses)
Edge Hill (CHE) – CC (Leis Mgt St)
Glasgow Caledonian – CC (Leis Mgt)
Hull (Scarborough) – 160–140 pts (Leis Tour Mgt)
Manchester Met – CC (Bus Leis)
Plymouth (Seale Hayne) – 160 pts approx (Tour Hspty Mgt)
Ripon & York (Coll) – CC (Leis/Tour Mgt)
Scottish (CAg) – 160 pts – CC (Rur Recr/Tour Mgt)
South Bank – CC (Leis Mgt)
Southampton (Inst) – CC (Marit Leis Mgt)

140 pts **and below**
Bell (CT) – DD (Leis Mgt)
Bolton (IHE) – CD (Leis Mgt)
Bradford (Coll) – (Leis Recr Commun St)
Colchester (Inst) – (Leis St courses)
De Montfort (Lincoln) – 120 pts – ALs **or** ALs+ASs **or** VAs+/-ALs/ASs; (Recr Mgt: Golf option reqs single handicap)
Herefordshire (CT) – DD (Leis Mgt/Spo Recr Out Act)
Suffolk (Coll) – EE (Leis Mgt/Spo St)
Swansea (IHE) – 2ALs **or** ALs+ASs **or** VAs+/-ALs/ASs; gs (AL only) (Leis Mgt courses)

Leeds Met – (contact university)

Diploma in Higher Education
Askham Bryan (CAgH); Bell (CT); Cheltenham & Glos (CHE).

Higher National Diploma courses (in Business Studies)
100 pts **and below**
Barking (Coll); Barnsley (Coll); Bedford (Coll); Bell (CT); Birmingham (CFTCS); Bishop Burton (CAg); Blackburn (Coll); Blackpool & Fylde (Coll); Bradford (Coll); Bromley (Coll); Brooklands (Coll); Buckinghamshire Chilterns (UC); Cardiff (UWI); Carlisle (Coll); Colchester (Inst); Cornwall & Duchy (Coll); Crawley (Coll) gs; Cumbria (CAD) (Herit Mgt); De Montfort; Derby; Doncaster (Coll); Edge Hill (CHE); Farnborough (CT); Filton (Coll); Gloucestershire (CAT); Guildford (CT); Herefordshire (CT); High Peak (Coll); King Alfred's Winchester (Coll); Lincolnshire & Humberside; Liverpool (CmC); Loughborough (Coll); Manchester City (Coll),

Manchester Met; Myerscough (Coll); Nescot; Newcastle (Coll); North Down & Ards (IFHE); North East Wales (IHE); North East Worcestershire (Coll) gs; North Lincolnshire (Coll); North London; North West Kent (Coll); Norwich City (Coll); Park Lane (Coll); Reid Kerr (Coll); Salford; Solihull (Coll); Somerset (CAT); Southampton (Inst); Scottish (CAg) (Leis Mgt; Country/Recr/Cons); Sparsholt (Coll); Suffolk (UC); Sutton Coldfield (Coll); Swansea (IHE); Teesside; UHI; Warrington (CI); West Herts (Coll); West Thames (Coll); Warwickshire (Coll); Wigan & Leigh (Coll); Wirral Met (Coll); Worcester (UC); Writtle (Coll); Yorkshire Coast (CFHE).

Alternative Offers:

IB offers: Brighton 24 pts; Loughborough 30 pts; Portsmouth 24 pts; Sheffield Hallam 24 pts.

Irish offers: Brighton BBCCC.

Scottish Qualifications: Aberdeen BBBB; Bell (CT) CCC; Glasgow Caledonian BBCC; Scottish (CAg) BCC.

CHOOSING YOUR COURSE (See also **Ch.1**)

Subject information: The courses cover various aspects of leisure and recreation. Specialist options include recreation management, tourism, countryside management, all of which are offered as individual degree courses in their own right. There is also an obvious link with Sports Studies and Physical Education courses. See also **Appendix 1.**

Special features: Coventry (Leis Mgt) Offered with a study in Europe. **Loughborough** (Recr Mgt) Course includes accountancy and financial management and sociology of sport. **Manchester** (Leis Mgt) Course covers financial studies, sociology, psychology, law and marketing. **Scottish (CAg)** Course includes outdoor education, consumer studies and management. **Teesside** (Leis Mgt) Course offers specialist studies in hospitality, sport or tourism and can include languages. **Westminster** (Leis Dev/Strat Mgt) Course focuses on investment, valuation and management. *NOW CHECK PROSPECTUSES AND WEB SITES.*

Study opportunities abroad: Brighton; Cheltenham & Glos (CHE); Liverpool John Moores; Loughborough; Oxford Brookes; Ripon & York (Coll); Sheffield Hallam; Surrey Roehampton.

Work opportunities abroad: Brighton; Cheltenham & Glos (CHE); Hereford (CT); Liverpool John Moores; Scottish (CAg); Sheffield Hallam.

ADMISSIONS INFORMATION

Number of applicants per place (approx): Bangor 5; Bournemouth 8; Brighton 10; Brunel 8; Cheltenham & Glos (CHE) 7; Coventry 14; Farnborough (CT) 6; Glasgow Caledonian 10; Herefordshire (CT) 1; Hull (Scarborough) 3; Loughborough 25; Manchester 22; North London 11; Portsmouth 3; Sheffield Hallam 20; Scottish (CAg) 4; Swansea (IHE) 8; Warrington (CI) 3; Writtle (Coll) 8.

Planning your UCAS personal statement (see Ch.4): Work experience, visits to leisure centres and national park centres and any interests you have in particular aspects of leisure should be described, for example, art galleries, museums, countryside management, sport. See also **Appendix 1.**

Selection interviews (see Ch.4): Anglia (No); Bournemouth (No); Brighton (No); Coventry; Glasgow Caledonian (No); Liverpool John Moores (No); Manchester (No); Portsmouth (No); Ripon & York (Coll) (No); Sheffield Hallam (No); Staffordshire (No); Surrey Roehampton (No); Writtle (Coll);

Interview questions (see Ch.4): In addition to sporting or other related interests (eg history for Heritage Studies courses) applicants will be expected to have had some work experience and can expect to be asked to discuss their interests.

Reasons for rejection (non-academic): Poor communication or presentation skills. Relatively poor sporting background or knowledge.

GAP YEAR ADVICE

Loughborough Use your time for general enrichment, travel etc, rather than spend it gaining relevant experience as, for example, swimming pool attendant.

Institutions willing to defer entry after A-Levels: Bangor; Bournemouth; Brighton; Cheltenham & Glos (CHE); Colchester (Inst); Coventry; Farnborough (CT); Herefordshire (CT); North London; Ripon & York (Coll); Scottish (CAg); Sheffield Hallam; Swansea (IHE); Warrington (CI).

AFTER RESULTS ADVICE

Institutions which may accept the same points score after A-Levels: Bangor; Bournemouth; Brighton; Cheltenham & Glos (CHE); Coventry; Glasgow Caledonian; Herefordshire (CT); Manchester; Ripon & York (Coll); Scottish (CAg); Sheffield Hallam; Surrey Roehampton.

Institutions which may accept lower grades/points score after A-Levels: Brighton; Cheltenham & Glos (CHE); Farnborough (CT); Herefordshire (CT); Scottish (CAg); Surrey Roehampton.

Probable vacancies from June 2001 and in Clearing (see Ch.4): Most institutions are expected to have vacancies from June onwards.

NEW GRADUATE DESTINATIONS AND EMPLOYMENT (1999 HESA) (see **Ch.4**)
No specific data for this subject area.

LIBRARY MANAGEMENT/STUDIES AND INFORMATION MANAGEMENT

NB The information supplied by the universities and colleges this year varies considerably and the offers listed below should be used as a first source of reference only. Many institutions will accept combinations of Advanced (AL), Advanced Subsidiary (AS) and Vocational Advanced (VA) level qualifications to achieve the required points total, but applicants must check web sites and prospectuses for full details of all offers. Grades and points totals shown should be regarded as the minimum levels to be achieved, but offers may be adjusted downwards when results are known. The points totals shown to the left of the institutions are for ease of reference only. It must not be assumed that tariff points are always used by institutions or that they can be substituted for an offer in grades. The level of an offer is not necessarily indicative of the quality of a course. To calculate your offers see Chapter 4 and the inside fold of the back cover.

Special subject requirements/preferences: A-Level: Subject requirements may apply to joint courses. **GCSE:** English, mathematics and occasionally a foreign language.

300 pts **London (UCL)** – BBB–BBC **or** 3ALs+AS/VA; (Inf Mgt)
   Sheffield – 300 pts approx (Inf Mgt/Bus St; Inf Mgt/Acc Fin Mgt; Inf Mgt)
280 pts **Loughborough** – 280 pts 18u – 2ALs+AL/2ASs; gs; (Inf Mgt/Comp; Inf Mgt/Bus St)
260 pts **Loughborough** – 260 pts 18u – 2ALs+AL/ASs; gs; (Lib Inf Mgt)
240 pts **Aberystwyth** – 240–180 pts 21–18u; gs; (Inf/Lib St; Inf Mgt)
   Brighton – 240 pts approx (Inf/Mgt)
   Napier – CCC (Inf Mgt/Bus St)
200 pts **Aberystwyth** – 200 pts approx (Inf/Lib St; Inf Mgt)
   Brighton – 200 pts (Inf/Lib St)
   Lampeter – 200 pts approx (Arch Inf Mgt)
   Wolverhampton – 200 pts approx; gs (Bus Inf Mgt)

180 pts Manchester Met – 180–160 pts – ALs; (Inf/Comm courses; Inf Mgt; Inf Lib Mgt)
160 pts Central England – 160 pts – EE or above; gs; (Inf/Lib St)
North London – CC (Inf Tech courses)
Northumbria – CC (Inf St courses)
140 pts Abertay Dundee – CD (Inf Mgt)
Liverpool John Moores – 140 pts – ALs **or** ALs+ASs **or** VAs+/-ALs/ASs; (Inf Serv Mgt)
Queen Margaret (UC) – CD (Inf Mgt)
Thames Valley – 140 pts approx (Inf Sys/Inf Knw Mgt)

Leeds Met – (contact university)

Higher National Diploma courses
Bell (CT); Gloucester (CAT).

Diploma of Higher Education courses
80 pts Loughborough (CT) – EE

Alternative Offers:

IB offers: Aberystwyth 30–28 pts; Brighton 27 pts inc H 12 pts; London (UCL) 30 pts; Sheffield 32 pts.

Irish offers: Brighton BCCCC; Sheffield ABBBB.

Scottish Qualifications: Abertay Dundee BBC; Bell (CT) CC; Napier BBCC; Queen Margaret (Coll) BBC.

Overseas applicants: Manchester Met, Queen Margaret (Coll) Good command of written and spoken English required.

CHOOSING YOUR COURSE (See also **Ch.1**)

Subject information: Library and Information Management covers the very wide field of information. Its organisation, retrieval, indexing, computer and media technology, classification and cataloguing are all included in these courses. Information means communication so degree courses in this subject should also be considered. Other alternatives would be Media Studies, English, and Information Systems courses in the sphere of computer science. See also **Appendix 1**.

Special features: Aberystwyth BLib degree now changed to BA, BSc or BSc (Econ) depending on other half of Information and Library Studies degree. Extensive computer support for retrieval systems and word processing. Course decisions can be delayed until start of second year. **Brighton** Course has large computing, media and communications element. **Central England** Four specialisms available: business information, information management, libraries in education, public libraries. **Loughborough** Options include the study of a foreign language (French or German) and a minor subject from a wide range which includes geography, English, drama, ergonomics and accounting. There is an optional sandwich year or a six-week placement. **Manchester Met** Exams and continuous assessment; two periods fieldwork placement; information management skills in third year. **Northumbria** Students follow own pathway (no compulsory subjects in third year). Options in second year: French, German, Russian, Spanish *ab initio*. Strengths in information technology, work with young people and history of the book/archive. **Queen Margaret (Coll)** Optional second year in the USA and industrial placement in part of year 3. Routes include multi-media computing, business information, healthcare informatics and library and information management. Focus on electronic information, for example the Internet. *NOW CHECK PROSPECTUSES AND WEB SITES.*

Top universities and colleges (Teaching Quality) (see Ch.4): (inc Information Management) Aberystwyth; not all institutions assessed.

Top universities and colleges (Research) (see Ch.4): City; Loughborough; Salford; Sheffield; Strathclyde.

Study opportunities abroad: Aberystwyth; Manchester Met; Napier; Northumbria; Queen Margaret (UC); Sheffield.

Work opportunities abroad: Aberystwyth; Manchester Met; Queen Margaret (UC).

ADMISSIONS INFORMATION

Number of applicants per place (approx): Aberystwyth 4; Central England 6; Liverpool John Moores 4; London (UCL) 7; Loughborough 7; Manchester Met 4; Northumbria 5; North London 4; Queen Margaret (UC) 3; Sheffield 30; Thames Valley 3.

Planning your UCAS personal statement (see Ch.4): Work experience/shadowing in local libraries is important but remember that reference libraries provide a different field of work. Visit university libraries and major reference libraries and discuss the work with librarians. Describe your experiences on the form. See also **Appendix 1**.

Selection interviews (see Ch.4): Aberystwyth (No); Brighton (No); Central England (No); Liverpool John Moores; London (UCL); Loughborough; Manchester Met; North London (T); Northumbria; Queen Margaret (UC) (some); Sheffield (No); Thames Valley.

Interview questions (see Ch.4): What is it about librarianship which interests you? Why do you think you are suited to be a librarian? What does the job entail? What is the role of the library in school? What is the role of the public library? What new developments are taking place in libraries? Which books do you read? How often do you use a library? What is the Dewey number for the history section in the library? (*Applicant studying A-level History*).

GAP YEAR ADVICE

Most institutions will accept a gap year. Experience in library or information centre useful.

Institutions willing to defer entry after A-Levels: Aberystwyth; Brighton; Manchester Met; Napier; Queen Margaret (UC); Sheffield; Thames Valley.

AFTER RESULTS ADVICE

Institutions which may accept the same points score after A-Levels: Aberystwyth; Brighton; Central England; Liverpool John Moores; Loughborough; Manchester Met; Napier; North London; Northumbria; Queen Margaret (UC); Sheffield; Thames Valley.

Institutions which may accept lower grades/points score after A-Levels: Aberystwyth; Central England; Liverpool John Moores; Loughborough; Manchester Met; Napier; Northumbria; Queen Margaret (UC); Sheffield.

Offers to applicants repeating A-Levels: Higher Central England; **Same** Liverpool John Moores, Loughborough, Napier, North London; Northumbria; Queen Margaret (UC), Sheffield.

Probable vacancies from June 2001 and in Clearing (see Ch.4): All universities can be contacted from June, since vacancies are almost certain.

NEW GRADUATE DESTINATIONS AND EMPLOYMENT (1999 HESA) (see **Ch.4**)

Out of 362 surveyed, 212 graduates in librarianship and information sciences entered full-time employment; further study accounted for 64 graduates and 29 were believed to be unemployed.

LIFE SCIENCES (see also **Biological Sciences**, **Biology** and **Health Sciences/Studies**)

NB The information supplied by the universities and colleges this year varies considerably and the offers listed below should be used as a first source of reference only. Many institutions will accept combinations of Advanced (AL), Advanced Subsidiary (AS) and Vocational Advanced (VA) level qualifications to achieve the required points total, but applicants must check web sites and prospectuses for full details of all offers. Grades and points totals shown should be regarded as the minimum levels to be achieved, but offers may be adjusted downwards when results are known. The points totals shown to the left of the institutions are for ease of reference only. It must not be assumed that tariff points are always used by institutions or that they can be substituted for an offer in grades. The level of an offer is not necessarily indicative of the quality of a course. To calculate your offers see Chapter 4 and the inside fold of the back cover.

Special subject requirements/preferences: A-Level: 2–3 science/mathematics subjects usually required. Check universities since course requirements vary. **GCSE: Manchester** Mathematics grade A–C.

320 pts	**Liverpool** – 320 pts – ALs **or** ALs+ASs **or** VAs+/-ALs/ASs; (Life Sci/Lang)
280 pts	**Manchester** – BBC (Life Sci; Life Sci/Ind Exp; Life Sci Modn Lang)
240 pts	**Aberystwyth** – 240 pts 21u – CCC **or** CC+cc **or** VAs; gs; (Life Sci)
220 pts	**Aberdeen** – CCD/BC (Hum Life Sci)
	Salford – 220 pts approx (Pros/Orthot)
180 pts	**Northumbria** – 180 pts approx (App Life Sci)
140 pts	**and below**
	Aberystwyth – (Fdn year – students without A-Levels considered)
	North London – 120 pts; 2ALs **or** VAs; (Hum Life Sci)

Higher National Diploma courses
Cardiff (UWI).

Diploma of Higher Education courses
80 pts   and below
Westminster.

Alternative Offers:

Irish offers: South Bank CCCC.

Scottish Qualifications: Aberdeen BBBB.

CHOOSING YOUR COURSE (See also **Ch.1**)

Subject information: Life Sciences is a field of considerable breadth and may include biochemistry, biology, biological and environmental sciences (these are good alternative degree options). Students are advised to check each course and select the emphasis they seek. The prosthetist/orthotist requires a wide range of theoretical and practical knowledge and skills. Prospective students for the Prosthetics and Orthotics course are rarely strong in all of the relevant subjects, so weeks 2–5 of the course are dedicated to balancing studies which comprise fundamentals of mathematics, fundamentals of life sciences and introductory workshop practice. This allows students who are weak in any of these areas to quickly bring themselves up to the standard required at the start of the course itself. See also **Anatomy/Anatomical Science**, **Physiology**, **Nursing and Midwifery**, **Speech Pathology/Science**, **Occupational Therapy**, **Radiography** and **Physiotherapy**. See also **Appendix 1**.

Special features: Liverpool Course unit system. Options for degrees made in year 2.
NOW CHECK PROSPECTUSES AND WEB SITES.

ADMISSIONS INFORMATION

Number of applicants per place (approx): Manchester 9; Southampton 1.

Planning your UCAS personal statement (see Ch.4): See **Biology** and **Biological Sciences**. See also **Appendix 1**.

Selection interviews (see Ch.4): Manchester; Southampton.

Interview questions (see Ch.4): See **Biological Sciences**.

GAP YEAR ADVICE

Institutions willing to defer entry after A-Levels: Northumbria; Salford.

AFTER RESULTS ADVICE

Institutions which may accept the same points score after A-Levels: Manchester.

Probable vacancies from June 2001 and in Clearing (see Ch.4): Contact all institutions.

NEW GRADUATE DESTINATIONS AND EMPLOYMENT (1999 HESA) (see **Ch.4**)

There is no specific data for this subject area.

LINGUISTICS (see also **English**)

NB The information supplied by the universities and colleges this year varies considerably and the offers listed below should be used as a first source of reference only. Many institutions will accept combinations of Advanced (AL), Advanced Subsidiary (AS) and Vocational Advanced (VA) level qualifications to achieve the required points total, but applicants must check web sites and prospectuses for full details of all offers. Grades and points totals shown should be regarded as the minimum levels to be achieved, but offers may be adjusted downwards when results are known. The points totals shown to the left of the institutions are for ease of reference only. It must not be assumed that tariff points are always used by institutions or that they can be substituted for an offer in grades. The level of an offer is not necessarily indicative of the quality of a course. To calculate your offers see Chapter 4 and the inside fold of the back cover.

Special subject requirements/preferences: A-Level: A modern language may be required. **East Anglia**, **Newcastle** English and a foreign language preferred. **GCSE: Lancaster**, **UMIST** Mathematics and foreign language grade A–B. **Sussex** Language grade A–B.

320 pts	**Durham** – ABB–BBB (Engl/Ling)
	Edinburgh – ABB–BBB (Ling courses)
	Leeds – ABB–BCC (Ling courses)
	Manchester – ABB–BCC (Ling courses)
	St Andrews – ABB–BBC (Ling courses)
	York – 320–280 pts 21–18u – BBC+c; (Lang/Ling Sci)
300 pts	**London (SOAS)** – 300–220 pts approx (Ling courses)
	Reading – BBB (Ling courses)
	Sheffield – BBB (Engl Lang/Ling; Fr/Ling)
	Sheffield – BBB–BCC (Ling with Jap/Ger/Russ/Kor St/Hisp St)
	UMIST – 300 pts (Comp Ling)
280 pts	**Bristol UWE** – 280–220 pts approx (Joint Ling courses)
	Essex – 280–260 pts 21u – BB–BC+AL/2ASs; gs; (Linguistics)
	Lancaster – BBC–BCC (Ling courses)
	London (UCL) – BBC **or** 3ALs+AS/VA; (Ling; Ling Cog Sci)
	Newcastle – BBC/BB (Ling; Ling/Chin/Jap/Kor) courses)
	Sussex – BBC–BCC (Ling courses)

260 pts	**East Anglia** – 260 pts – BCC; (Ling; Ling/Lang; Ling/Phil)
	London (QM) – 260–240 pts approx (Ling courses)
	UMIST – 260 pts (Comput Ling)
240 pts	**Aberdeen** – CCC (Lang Lit Scot)
	Hertfordshire – 240–200 pts 1x12u **or** 2x6u; gs; (Hum Mod; Ling)
	Ulster – CCC (Ling Sci)
220 pts	**Bangor** – CCD/BB (Ling courses)
	Brighton – 220 pts approx (Lang St/Ling)
	Luton – 220 pts approx (Linguistics)
	Nottingham Trent – 220–180 pts approx (Lang/Ling courses)
	Wolverhampton – 220–160 pts 12u – DDD–CDE **or** CC/CD+d/e **or** VA12u CC; gs; (Linguistics)
200 pts	**Central Lancashire** – 200–160 pts 12u – ALs **or** ALs+ASs **or** VAs+/-ALs/ASs; gs; (Ling/Deaf St; Ling/Fr)
180 pts	**East London** – 180 pts (Ling courses)
160 pts	**Westminster** – CC (Ling courses)

Diploma of Higher Education courses
80 pts Bradford (Coll); Central Lancashire; East London; Ripon & York (Coll).

Alternative Offers:

EB offers: UMIST 70%

IB offers: Bangor 32–28 pts; Essex 28 pts; Lancaster 30 pts; Leeds 26 pts; UMIST 28 pts 7 subjects 24 pts 6 subjects; York 30 pts.

Irish offers: UMIST BBBBC; York BBBC.

Scottish Qualifications: Aberdeen BBBB; Edinburgh ABBB–BBBB; St Andrews BBBB.

CHOOSING YOUR COURSE (See also **Ch.1**)

> **Subject information:** Linguistics covers the study of language in general and also includes areas such as children's language, slang, language handicap, advertising language, styles of language and the learning of foreign languages. Speech Science and language courses as well as degree courses in languages should also be considered. See also **Appendix 1**.

Special features: Bangor Focus on language in society. Emphasis on assessment by practical course work rather than examinations. Course includes 'learning to talk', authors' styles, women's and men's language. Scholarship offered. **Edinburgh** Links with sociology, social anthropology, psychology and philosophy. **Newcastle** Variety of exam arrangements; possibility of studying more than one foreign language including Chinese, Korean, Sanskrit or Japanese. **Reading** Wide range of joint courses with modern languages. *NOW CHECK PROSPECTUSES AND WEB SITES.*

Top universities and colleges (Teaching Quality) (see Ch.4): Central Lancashire; Durham; Lancaster; London (QM), (UCL); Newcastle; Sheffield; Sussex; York; not all institutions assessed.

Top universities and colleges (Research) (see Ch.4): Edinburgh; Essex; Lancaster; London (QM), (SOAS), (UCL); Manchester; Newcastle; York.

Study opportunities abroad: Bangor; Edinburgh; Essex; Lancaster; London (UCL); Manchester; Newcastle; Reading; Westminster; York.

ADMISSIONS INFORMATION

Number of applicants per place (approx): Bangor 3; Central Lancashire 3; East London 3; Essex 1; Lancaster 12; Leeds 12; UMIST 11; York 11.

Planning your UCAS personal statement (see Ch.4): See under separate language headings. See also **Appendix 1** under **Modern Languages**.

Selection interviews (see Ch.4): Bangor (No) (T) mature applicants; Brighton; East London; Edinburgh (No); Essex; Lancaster; Leeds (No); Liverpool; Newcastle; Reading.

Interview questions (see Ch.4): Why do you want to study Linguistics? What does the subject involve? What do you intend to do at the end of your degree course? What answer do you give to your parents or friends when they ask why you want to study the subject? How and why does language vary according to sex, age, social background and regional origins?

Reasons for rejection (non-academic): Lack of knowledge of linguistics.

GAP YEAR ADVICE

Most institutions will accept a gap year and recommend that time is spent abroad.

Institutions willing to defer entry after A-Levels: Bangor; Leeds; Luton; Newcastle (Prefer not); Sheffield (No); UMIST; York.

AFTER RESULTS ADVICE

Institutions which may accept the same points score after A-Levels: Bangor; Brighton; East London; Essex; Leeds; Newcastle (No); Sheffield; UMIST; York.

Institutions which may accept lower grades/points score after A-Levels: Bangor; Essex; Leeds; Sheffield; UMIST; York.

Offers to applicants repeating A-Levels: Higher Essex, Sussex; **Same** Brighton, East Anglia, Leeds, Newcastle, UMIST, York.

Probable vacancies from June 2001 and in Clearing (see Ch.4): Almost all universities are expected to have vacancies, particularly on joint courses.

NEW GRADUATE DESTINATIONS AND EMPLOYMENT (1999 HESA) (see **Ch.4**)

There were 392 graduates in this survey; 207 went into full-time employment, 20 were believed to be unemployed and 96 went on to further study.

LITERATURE (including **Literary Studies**; see also **English**)

NB The information supplied by the universities and colleges this year varies considerably and the offers listed below should be used as a first source of reference only. Many institutions will accept combinations of Advanced (AL), Advanced Subsidiary (AS) and Vocational Advanced (VA) level qualifications to achieve the required points total, but applicants must check web sites and prospectuses for full details of all offers. Grades and points totals shown should be regarded as the minimum levels to be achieved, but offers may be adjusted downwards when results are known. The points totals shown to the left of the institutions are for ease of reference only. It must not be assumed that tariff points are always used by institutions or that they can be substituted for an offer in grades. The level of an offer is not necessarily indicative of the quality of a course. To calculate your offers see Chapter 4 and the inside fold of the back cover.

Special subject requirements/preferences: A-Level: Required in named subject courses eg English, French, German etc, normally the highest grade in the offers below.

320 pts   **East Anglia** – ABB (Engl Compar Lit)
   Warwick – ABB–BBC (Lit courses)
300 pts   **East Anglia** – 300–280 pts 18u – BBB or BB+cc or BBC+e or VA12u 200
   pts+C; gs; (Lit/Cult/Pol)
   Edinburgh – 300 pts/BBB (Scot Lit)
   Essex – 300–260 pts (Lit courses)

280 pts	**East Anglia** – BBC–BCD (Lit/Lang – Dan/Fr/Ger/Norw/Swed)
	Glasgow – BBC (Lit courses)
	Stirling – BBC (Scot Lit)
260 pts	**Kent** – 260 pts approx (Compar Lit St)
240 pts	**East Anglia** – CCC/CC (Lit/Lang double Hons)
	Hertfordshire – 240–200 pts 1x12u **or** 2x6u; gs; (Hum Mod; Lit)
	Portsmouth – CCC (Engl Compar Lit)
220 pts	**Lampeter** – 220 pts/CC (Australian St)
	Liverpool John Moores – 220–180 pts approx (Lit/Life Tht courses)
180 pts	**Derby** – 180 pts approx (Literature)
	East London – 180 pts approx (Literature)
	Luton – 180 pts (Lit St)
	St Mark & St John (Coll) – 180–160 pts approx (Engl Lit St)
	Staffordshire – B(Engl)C (Lit St)
	Sunderland – 180–160 pts approx (Compar Lit)
160 pts	**Northampton (UC)** – CC (Lit Cult St)
	Staffordshire – CC (Lit Comb)
140 pts	**Bolton (IHE)** – CD (Lit courses)
	Suffolk (Coll) – CD (Lit St/Hist)

Diploma of Higher Education courses
80 pts Bradford (Coll); Doncaster (Coll); Edge Hill (CHE); Lincolnshire & Humberside.

Alternative Offers:

IB offers: Bradford 27 pts; Essex 28 pts inc 10 pts 2 Highers; Kent 32–28 pts.

Scottish Qualifications: Aberdeen BBBB; Edinburgh ABBB BBBB; Glasgow BBBB; Stirling BBBB.

CHOOSING YOUR COURSE (See also **Ch.1**)

Subject information: This is a very broad subject which introduces many aspects of the study of literature and aesthetics. Courses will vary in content. Degree courses in English and foreign languages will also include a study of literature.

Special features: Glasgow Scottish poetry and fiction – Middle Ages to the present day. **Liverpool John Moores** Study of literature covering gender, sexuality, class, race, working class writing, women's writing. **Portsmouth** (Lit St) Covers poetry, narrative, creative writing and practical drama workshops. *NOW CHECK PROSPECTUSES AND WEB SITES.*

ADMISSIONS INFORMATION

Number of applicants per place (approx): Bradford 7; East Anglia 12; Essex 4; Liverpool John Moores (Lit/Life Tht) 2; Portsmouth 7; Staffordshire 8.

Planning your UCAS personal statement (see Ch.4): See **English**.

Selection interviews (see Ch.4): Lampeter.

Interview questions (see Ch.4): See **English**.

AFTER RESULTS ADVICE

Institutions which may accept the same points score after A-Levels: Staffordshire.

Probable vacancies from June 2001 and in Clearing (see Ch.4): Several universities are likely to have vacancies particularly in Comparative Literature.

NEW GRADUATE DESTINATIONS AND EMPLOYMENT (1999 HESA) (see **Ch.4**)

In a survey of 240 graduates, 73 went into full-time employment, 86 went on to further study and 24 were believed to be unemployed.

MARINE/MARITIME STUDIES (see also **Engineering (Marine)** and **Oceanography**)

NB The information supplied by the universities and colleges this year varies considerably and the offers listed below should be used as a first source of reference only. Many institutions will accept combinations of Advanced (AL), Advanced Subsidiary (AS) and Vocational Advanced (VA) level qualifications to achieve the required points total, but applicants must check web sites and prospectuses for full details of all offers. Grades and points totals shown should be regarded as the minimum levels to be achieved, but offers may be adjusted downwards when results are known. The points totals shown to the left of the institutions are for ease of reference only. It must not be assumed that tariff points are always used by institutions or that they can be substituted for an offer in grades. The level of an offer is not necessarily indicative of the quality of a course. To calculate your offers see Chapter 4 and the inside fold of the back cover.

Special subject requirements/preferences: A-Level: Science, mathematics, geography required for some universities. **GCSE:** Mathematics and science subjects for several courses.

350 pts	**Southampton** – 350 pts 21u (inc 200 pts from 2ALs); (Mar Sci)
310 pts	**Southampton** – 310 pts 21u (inc 180 pts from 2ALs sci+AS sci); (Mar Sci/Fr)
300 pts	**Newcastle** – BBB; (not gs) (MEng Mar Tech)
280 pts	**Glasgow** – 280 pts approx (Mar Des)
260 pts	**Cardiff** – BCC–CCC/BB (Mar Geog)
	Newcastle – BCC–CCC (Mar courses except under **300 pts**)
240 pts	**Bangor** – CCC–CCD (Mar courses)
	Heriot-Watt – 240 pts 18u CCC; gs; (Mar Biol; Mar Biotech)
	Southampton (Inst) – 240 pts 12u – ALs (80 pts maths+40 pts phys/dtech etc); (not gs) (Yacht/Pwr Des)
220 pts	**Plymouth** – 220 pts approx (Fish Sci; Hydrog; Undwtr St courses; Mar Tech; Mar Navig courses; Marit Bus courses)
200 pts	**Portsmouth** – 200 pts – ALs **or** ALs+ASs **or** VAs; gs; (Mar Biol; Mar Env Sci)
	Southampton (Inst) – 200–180 pts approx (Marit St; Ship Ops)
160 pts	**Southampton (Inst)** – 160 pts – 2ALs **or** ALs+ASs **or** VA12u; gs; (Yacht Manuf/Surv; Marit Bus; Mar Env Sci)
140 pts	**Liverpool John Moores** – 140 pts 2x6u or 2x6u or 1x12u – ALs **or** ALs+ASs **or** VAs+/-ALs/ASs; (Marit Int Modl Trans; Marit Tech; Naut Sci; Marit St; Marit Bus Mgt; Mar Ops)

Diploma of Higher Education courses
UHI.

Higher National Diploma courses
Cornwall & Duchy (Coll); Falmouth (CA); Glasgow; Liverpool John Moores.

Alternative Offers:

IB offers: Cardiff 30 pts; Newcastle 35 pts.

Scottish Qualifications: Glasgow CCC.

CHOOSING YOUR COURSE (See also **Ch.1**)

Subject information: Marine and Maritime Studies can involve a range of subjects such as marine business, technology, navigation, nautical studies, underwater rescue and transport. Transport Management courses which cover sea transport could also be considered. See also **Appendix 1**.

Special features: Cardiff (Mar Geog) There is a large marine resource management unit in the department. **Liverpool John Moores** (Marit St) A business studies course in shipping. **Newcastle** (Mar Tech) Common first year allows choice of options in marine engineering, naval architecture, offshore engineering or small craft technology. **Plymouth** The Department of Marine Sciences offers over 110 combinations in their modular programme based on major and minor pathways. The main subject options cover fisheries science, hydrography, marine technology, maritime business, ocean science, transport and underwater studies. Minor pathways include astronomy, marine navigation, maritime law and maritime history. **Southampton (Inst)** Common first year allows year 2 specialisms in maritime technology, leisure activities, navigation, marine vehicle surveying. *NOW CHECK PROSPECTUSES AND WEB SITES.*

ADMISSIONS INFORMATION

Number of applicants per place (approx): Glasgow 2; Liverpool John Moores 3.

Planning your UCAS personal statement (see Ch.4): This is a specialised field and in many cases applicants will have experience of marine activities. Describe these experiences, for example, sailing, snorkelling, fishing. See also **Appendix 1**.

Interview questions (see Ch.4): Most applicants will have been stimulated by their studies in science or will have strong interests or connections with marine activities and are likely to be questioned on their reasons for choosing the course.

GAP YEAR ADVICE

Institutions willing to defer entry after A-Levels: Cardiff; Glasgow; Newcastle; Plymouth.

AFTER RESULTS ADVICE

Probable vacancies from June 2001 and in Clearing (see Ch.4): Contact all universities since vacancies are likely.

NEW GRADUATE DESTINATIONS AND EMPLOYMENT (1999 HESA) (see **Ch.4**)

In a survey of 185 graduates in Maritime Technology, 119 went into full-time employment, 30 on to further study and 14 were believed to be unemployed.

MARKETING (see also **Art & Design (Fashion)** and **Business Courses**)

NB The information supplied by the universities and colleges this year varies considerably and the offers listed below should be used as a first source of reference only. Many institutions will accept combinations of Advanced (AL), Advanced Subsidiary (AS) and Vocational Advanced (VA) level qualifications to achieve the required points total, but applicants must check web sites and prospectuses for full details of all offers. Grades and points totals shown should be regarded as the minimum levels to be achieved, but offers may be adjusted downwards when results are known. The points totals shown to the left of the institutions are for ease of reference only. It must not be assumed that tariff points are always used by institutions or that they can be substituted for an offer in grades. The level of an offer is not necessarily indicative of the quality of a course. To calculate your offers see Chapter 4 and the inside fold of the back cover.

Special subject requirements/preferences: A-Level: A-Levels in the appropriate language (normally the highest grade in the offers below) for Marketing and Language. **GCSE:** English and mathematics required in all cass. **Glasgow Caledonian** English grade B. **Lancaster** Mathematics grade A or B.

340 pts **Lancaster** – AAB (Mark/USA Can)
320 pts **Lancaster** – ABB (Marketing)
300 pts **Aston** – 18u – BBB **or** ALs+ASs **or** VAs+/-ALs/ASs; gs; (Marketing)
       Bradford – 300 pts 12u (inc GCSE maths C); gs; (Marketing)
       Keele – BBB–BBC **or** equiv AS accepted; gs; (Marketing courses)

Lancaster – BBB–BBC (Marketing courses except under **340/320 pts**)
Newcastle – ABC/BBB (Mark/Mgt)
280 pts **Harper Adams (UC)** – 280–140 pts (Agri-Fd Prod Mark Mgt)
Oxford Brookes – BBC (Joint Hons Mark Mgt)
Salford – BBC (Mark St/Modn Lang)
Stirling – BBC (Marketing)
260 pts **Heriot-Watt** – BCC (Mgt Mark)
Hertfordshire – 260–240 pts (Marketing)
Northumbria – BCC (Marketing)
Plymouth – 260 pts approx (Marketing)
Ulster – BCC (Comp Mark)
UMIST – BCC (Mark Mgt Tex)
250 pts **Buckingham** – 250 pts 21u – 3ALs **or** 3ALs+AS; (Marketing)
240 pts **Aberystwyth** – 240–220 pts (Marketing courses)
Bangor – 240 pts; gs; (Mark/Comp St; Mark/Modn Lang)
Bournemouth – 240 pts – CCC (inc Fr/Ger/Span); tests in numeracy +
   language; interview; (Int Mark Mgt)
Brighton – 240 pts approx (Bus St Mark)
Bristol UWE – 240–200 pts 18u pref/12u – ALs **or** ALs+ASs **or** VAs+/-
   ALs/ASs; (not gs) (Marketing courses)
Central Lancashire – 240–220 pts 12u; gs; (Marketing courses)
Coventry – 240 pts approx (Mark Mgt)
Dundee – CCC (Bus Econ/Mark)
Liverpool John Moores – 240 pts (inc 180 pts ALs from media/comm
   st/Engl/soc/hist) – ALs **or** ALs+ASs **or** VA6u+/-ALs/ASs; (Marketing)
Manchester Met – 240 pts approx (Rtl Mark; Mark Mgt)
Portsmouth – 240 pts – ALs **or** ALs+ASs **or** VAs; gs; (Mark/Lang/Bus; Mark)
220 pts **Central England** – 220 pts – 2ALs **or** ALs+ASs **or** VAs+/-ALs/ASs; gs; (Mark;
   Mark/Fr/Ger)
De Montfort – 220 pts (inc 2ALs **or** VA12u) – ALs **or** ALs+ASs **or** VAs+/-
   ALs/ASs; (Mark courses)
Derby – 220 pts 12u – CCD **or** CC+dd **or** VAs(AL grade level)+/-ALs/ASs; gs;
   (Intnet Mark; Mark)
Middlesex – 220–180 pts approx (Marketing courses)
South East Essex (Coll) – 220–180 pts (Marketing)
Staffordshire – CCD **or** CCE+AS(40 pts) **or** VAs; gs; (Mark; Mark/Mgt)
Wolverhampton – 220 pts 12u – CCD/BB/AC **or** BC+c **or** VA12u BB; gs;
   (Marketing)
200 pts **Greenwich** – 200 pts approx (Mark/Comm; Mark; Int Mark/Fr/Ger/Span)
Huddersfield – 200–180 pts approx (Mark; Mark/Lang; Mark/Invn; Mark Rtl
   Dist)
Luton – 200–160 pts approx (Marketing – Mod)
Northampton (UC) – 200 pts approx (Marketing courses)
Teesside – 200–160 pts approx (Marketing)
190 pts **North London** – 190 pts inc 160 pts from 2ALs **or** VAs; (Mark; Mark/Bus
   Mgt)
180 pts **Brighton** – 180 pts (Rtl Mark)
Cheltenham & Glos (CHE) – 180 pts approx (Mark Mgt courses)
Doncaster (Coll) – 180 pts approx (Bus Mark)
East London – 180 pts approx (Marketing courses)
Glamorgan – 180 pts approx (Mark; Mark/Lang)
London Guildhall – DDD/CC (Marketing courses)
Manchester Met – 180 pts approx (Int Fash Mark)
North East Wales (IHE) – 180–140 pts approx (Bus St/Mark)
Norwich City (Coll) – 180 pts approx (Marketing)
Regent (Bus Sch London) – DDD/CC (Int Mark)
Sheffield Hallam – 180 pts approx (Fd Mark Mgt)
Thames Valley – 180–140 pts approx (Marketing courses)

160 pts   **Abertay Dundee** – CC (Mark; Mark/Rtl Mgt/Lang (inc Fr/Ger/Span))
　　　　　Anglia – 160 pts 12u – 2ALs; ASs/VAs (contact univ); (Marketing)
　　　　　Canterbury Christ Church (UC) – CC (Marketing courses)
　　　　　Farnborough (CT) – 160 pts approx (Marketing)
　　　　　Lincolnshire & Humberside – 160 pts (Marketing)
　　　　　Napier – CC (Mark courses)
　　　　　Paisley – CC (Mark/Int Mark)
　　　　　Surrey Roehampton – 160 pts (inc C/AL Fr 80 pts) – ALs **or** ALs+ASs (inc AS
　　　　　　　Fr 60 pts) **or** VAs+/-ALs/ASs; (Mark; Mark/Fr/Span)
　　　　　Warrington (CI) – 160 pts – ALs or ALs+ASs (not ASs only) **or** VAs+/-ALs/ASs;
　　　　　　　gs; (Mark Mgt)
　　　　　Writtle (Coll) – 160 pts (Mark Sply Chn Mgt)
140 pts   **Bolton (IHE)** – CD (Marketing courses)
　　　　　Buckinghamshire Chilterns (UC) – 140 pts approx (Marketing courses)
　　　　　Derby – 140 pts 12u – CD **or** DE+ee **or** VA CD+/-ALs/ASs; (Mark Comb)
　　　　　Glasgow Caledonian – CD (Mark Comm)
120 pts   **Hull (Scarborough)** – DD (Marketing courses)
　　　　　Queen Margaret (UC) – DD–DE (Mark Joint Hons; Fd/Mark)
100 pts   **and below**
　　　　　London (Inst) – (Mark Adv – part-time courses available)
　　　　　Northbrook (Coll) – (Mark/Des Bus)
　　　　　Teesside – portfolio (Des Mark)

Higher National Diploma courses (in Business Studies)
140 pts   **and below**
　　　　　Blackburn (Coll); Blackpool & Fylde (Coll); Bolton (IHE); Bradford (Coll); Brighton;
　　　　　Buckinghamshire Chilterns (UC); Central Lancashire; Cheltenham & Glos (CHE);
　　　　　Coventry; Croydon (Coll); Dudley (CT); Farnborough (CT); Glasgow (Coll); Harper
　　　　　Adams (UC) 4 pts; Huddersfield; Lincolnshire & Humberside; Liverpool John
　　　　　Moores; London Guildhall; London (Inst); Luton; Motherwell (Coll); Napier;
　　　　　Newport (UWN); North East Wales (IHE); North London; North Worcestershire
　　　　　(Coll); Northampton (UC); Northbrook (Coll); Northumbria; Norwich City (Coll);
　　　　　Oxford Brookes; Plymouth; Portrush (HCC); Reading (CSAD); St Helens (Coll);
　　　　　Salford; Sandwell (Coll); Sheffield Hallam; South Bank; Southampton (Inst);
　　　　　Staffordshire; Stockport (CFHE); Swansea (IHE); Swindon (Coll); Tameside (Coll);
　　　　　Teesside; West Herts (Coll); Wigan & Leigh (Coll).

Alternative Offers:

IB offers: Aston 31 pts; Bournemouth 26 pts; Central Lancashire 30–28 pts; Greenwich
25 pts; Lancaster 32 pts; Plymouth H554; Surrey Roehampton 28 pts.

Irish offers: Harper Adams (UC) CCCC.

Scottish Qualifications: Abertay Dundee BBBC; Dundee BBCC; Glasgow Caledonian
BBCC; Heriot-Watt ABBB–BBC; Napier BBCC; Paisley BCCC; Queen Margaret (UC) BCC;
Stirling BBBB.

CHOOSING YOUR COURSE (See also **Ch.1**)

> **Subject information:** Marketing courses are very popular and applications should
> include some evidence of work experience or shadowing. Marketing is a subject also
> covered by most Business Studies courses and by specialist (and equally relevant)
> courses such as Textile Marketing and Food Marketing for which lower offers are often
> made. Most courses offer the same subject content. In addition to Business Studies
> courses, Advertising could also be considered. See also **Appendix 1**.

Special features: Aston Compulsory sandwich year of industrial placement. **Central
England** Strong foundation in business administration. **Central Lancashire** Options in
public relations and market research. **Greenwich** Options in French, German and Spanish.

Huddersfield Covers retail, travel, tourism, leisure marketing, consumer behaviour and foreign language options including Japanese. **North London** Covers theoretical and practical aspects of marketing including international and media dimensions. *NOW CHECK PROSPECTUSES AND WEB SITES.*

Top universities and colleges (Teaching Quality) (see Ch.4): Glasgow Caledonian; Manchester Met; not all institutions assessed.

Top universities and colleges (Research) (see Ch.4): Aston.

Study opportunities abroad: Aberystwyth; Aston; Bournemouth; Central England; Cheltenham & Glos (CHE); Derby; Farnborough (CT); Glamorgan; Harper Adams (UC); Huddersfield; Keele; Lancaster; Oxford Brookes; Plymouth; Staffordshire; Surrey Roehampton; Teesside.

Work opportunities abroad: Central England; Cheltenham & Glos (CHE); Derby; Farnborough (CT); Harper Adams (UC); Northumbria; Plymouth; Surrey Roehampton.

ADMISSIONS INFORMATION

Number of applicants per place (approx): Abertay Dundee 6; Aston 10; Bournemouth 10; Central England 15; Central Lancashire 13; Derby 5; Glasgow Caledonian 15; Harper Adams (UC) 3; Huddersfield 7; Lancaster 28; Lincolnshire & Humberside 3; North London 10; Northumbria 8; Plymouth 12; Sheffield Hallam 9; Staffordshire 6; Stirling 10; Teesside 3.

Planning your UCAS personal statement (see Ch.4): See **Business Courses.** See also **Appendix 1**.

Selection interviews (see Ch.4): Bournemouth (No); Buckingham; Central Lancashire (No); De Montfort (No); Greenwich (No); Harper Adams (UC) (advisory); Huddersfield (No); Manchester Met (No); Middlesex; Napier (No); Northbrook (Coll); Norwich City (Coll); Paisley (No); Staffordshire (No); Stirling (No); Surrey Roehampton (No); Warrington (CI) (No); Writtle (Coll).

Interview questions (see Ch.4): What is marketing? Why do you want to take a Marketing degree? Is sales pressure justified? How would you feel if you had to market a product which you considered to be inferior?

Reasons for rejection (non-academic): Little thought of reasons for deciding on a Marketing degree. Weak on numeracy and problem-solving. Limited commercial awareness. Poor inter-personal skills. Lack of leadership potential. No interest in widening their horizons either geographically or intellectually. 'We look at appearance and motivation and the applicant's ability to ask questions.' Not hungry enough.

GAP YEAR ADVICE

Improve your command of language (French/German/Spanish) and widen your business experience.

Institutions willing to defer entry after A-Levels: Aston; Canterbury Christ Church (CHE); Central Lancashire; Cheltenham & Glos (CHE); Farnborough (CT); Glamorgan (No); Harper Adams (UC); Huddersfield; Lancaster (No); Lincolnshire & Humberside; Luton; North London; Northumbria; Plymouth; Surrey Roehampton.

AFTER RESULTS ADVICE

Institutions which may accept the same points score after A-Levels: Bournemouth; Central Lancashire; Cheltenham & Glos (CHE); Harper Adams (UC); Lincolnshire & Humberside; Middlesex; Surrey Roehampton.

Probable vacancies from June 2001 and in Clearing (see Ch.4): There were vacancies in more than 60 universities and colleges last year and these institutions should be contacted this year. Several universities are expected to have vacancies in International and European Marketing (see also **Food Science**).

NEW GRADUATE DESTINATIONS AND EMPLOYMENT (1999 HESA) (see **Ch.4**)

Of 1196 graduates surveyed, 875 went into full-time employment and 48 into part-time work, 86 went on to further study and 62 were believed to be unemployed.

MATERIALS SCIENCE/METALLURGY (including **Polymer Science**)

NB The information supplied by the universities and colleges this year varies considerably and the offers listed below should be used as a first source of reference only. Many institutions will accept combinations of Advanced (AL), Advanced Subsidiary (AS) and Vocational Advanced (VA) level qualifications to achieve the required points total, but applicants must check web sites and prospectuses for full details of all offers. Grades and points totals shown should be regarded as the minimum levels to be achieved, but offers may be adjusted downwards when results are known. The points totals shown to the left of the institutions are for ease of reference only. It must not be assumed that tariff points are always used by institutions or that they can be substituted for an offer in grades. The level of an offer is not necessarily indicative of the quality of a course. To calculate your offers see Chapter 4 and the inside fold of the back cover.

Special subject requirements/preferences: A-Level: Two–three science/mathematics subjects required for most courses. **Oxford** Full A-Levels expected in chemistry or physics or mathematics. A second mathematics or science recommended at A-Level. **GCSE:** Science/mathematics subjects. **Brunel** Grade A–C in physics and chemistry if not offered at A-level. **Swansea** Eight A*, A and B grades.

360 pts **and above**
    Cambridge – Offers, mainly in grades, vary between colleges (Nat Sci (Mat Sci/Metal))
    Oxford – Offers vary between candidates (Metal; Metal Sci Mat; Eng Mat)
300 pts **Bath** – 300–240 pts approx (Mat Sci)
    Birmingham – BBB (Spo Mat Sci)
    Leeds – BBB (Mat Sci Eng; Metal)
    London (Imp) – 300 pts (Aero Mat)
    London (QM) – 300 pts approx (Env Mat Eng; Mat Eng Med)
    Loughborough – 300 pts 18u – 2ALs (from maths, phys, chem)+AL/2ASs; (not gs) (MEng (Mat Eng) (Auto) Mat)
    Manchester – BBB (MEng Mat Sci courses)
    Newcastle – 300 pts (MEng Mech Mat Eng)
    Surrey – 300–220 pts approx (Bio Mat Eng; Mat Sci Eng courses; Sci Mat)
    UMIST – 300 pts 18u – BBB **or** BB+ASs(ALs from maths, phys, chem or other subj); VAs (indiv basis); (not gs) (Mat Sci/Eng; Mat Sci Eng/Metals/Poly/Ceram/Ind Exp; Mat Sci/Bus; Biomed Mat Sci courses)
280 pts **Birmingham** – BBC–BCC (Mech/Mat Eng)
    Liverpool – 280 pts (Mat Eng)
    Nottingham – 280 pts 18u (inc C chem); (not gs) (MSc Med Mat Sci; Chem/Mat)
    Sheffield – BBC–BCC (Mat Chem; Med Mat Sci/Eng; Mat Sci Eng/Lang; Metal Sci Eng/Lang; Glass Sci Eng/Lang; Ceram Eng/Lang; Poly Sci Eng);
    UMIST – BBC (Ppr Science)
260 pts **Birmingham** – BCC (Biomed Mat Sci)
    Liverpool – 260 pts (inc C maths) – ALs **or** ALs+ASs **or** VAs+/-ALs/ASs; (Mat Sci; Mat Eng; Mat Des Manuf)
    Liverpool – 260 pts (Clin Eng/Mat Sci)
    London (Imp) – 260 pts (Mat Mgt; Mat Sci/Eng)
    London (QM) – 260 pts (Biomed Mat Sci Eng)
    Nottingham – BBD (Chem Mat)
240 pts **Belfast (Queen's)** – CCC (Phys/Mat Sci)
    Birmingham – CCC (Mat Sci Tech/Mat Eng courses)

Hull – CCC (Mech/Mat Eng)
Leeds – CCC (Ceram Sci/Eng)
Liverpool – 240 pts – ALs **or** ALs+ASs **or** VAs+/-ALs/ASs; (Mat Chem)
London (QM) – 240 pts approx (Phys Mat Sci)
Loughborough – 240 pts 18u – 2ALs (from maths,phys, chem)+AL/2ASs; (not gs) (BEng Mat Eng; Mat Eng/Mgt; Auto Mat)
Manchester – CCC (BEng Biomed Mat Sci; Mat Sci Eng;Chem/Poly Sci)
Northumbria – 240–180 pts approx (Mat Eng)
Plymouth – 240–220 pts approx (Cmpst Mat Eng)
Swansea – 240 pts 18u – 240 pts **or** ALs+ASs **or** VAs+/-ALs/ASs; (Mat Sci Eng; Mat Sci Eng/N Am; BSc Mat Eng/Bus Mgt)

220 pts **Aberdeen** – CCD (Chem/New Mat Tech)
Liverpool – 220 pts – ALs **or** ALs+ASs **or** VAs+/-ALs/ASs; (Mat Sci/Mgt)
Manchester Met – 220–160 pts approx (Mat Sci courses)
Sheffield Hallam – 220 pts approx (Foren Eng)

200 pts **Bradford** – 200 pts 12u; gs; (Mat Tech/Mgt; Mat Des Prod)
Teesside – 200–180 pts approx (Mat Sys Eng with Law/Mark/IT)

180 pts **Heriot-Watt (Scottish Borders)** – DDD (Biomed Mat)
Liverpool – 180 pts – ALs **or** ALs+ASs **or** VAs+/-ALs/ASs; (Fdn Mat Sci)
Staffordshire – 180 pts approx (Des Tech Ceram Manuf)

160 pts **Surrey** – CC (Sci Metals) (Arts AL+1 sci acceptable) (Fdn)
Sheffield Hallam – 160–140 pts approx (Mat Eng)

140 pts **North London** – 140 pts approx (Poly Eng)
Wolverhampton – 140 pts; gs (Mat Qual Eng; Des Tech Mat Tech)

120 pts **and below**
Napier – DD (Poly Eng)
North London – 120 pts 1x12u **or** 2x6u; (Poly Comb Hons; Poly Eng)
Northampton (UC) – EE (Lea Tech)

Higher National Diploma courses
100 pts **and below**
Bell (CT); Bradford (Coll); Capel Manor (Coll) (Leather); Chesterfield (Coll); London (Inst) (Ppr Con); Manchester Met; North East Wales (IHE); North London; Sandwell (Coll); Sheffield Hallam; Staffordshire; Trowbridge (Coll).

Alternative Offers:

EB offers: Newcastle 70%.

IB offers: Bath 30–28 pts inc H555; Birmingham 30–28 pts; Leeds 28 pts; Manchester 26 pts; Newcastle 26 pts, 5 maths, 5 phys or chem; Northumbria 28 pts; Sheffield Hallam 26 pts; Surrey 28 pts; Swansea 30–28 pts; UMIST 28 pts.

Irish offers: Liverpool BBCCC; Swansea CCCCC; UMIST ABBBBC.

Scottish Qualifications: Aberdeen BBBC; Heriot-Watt BBCC; Napier BBC.

Overseas applicants: Bath English course available. **Newcastle** Foundation courses available. **Swansea** Foundation course essential.

CHOOSING YOUR COURSE (See also **Ch.1**)

Subject information: Materials Science is a subject which covers physics, chemistry and engineering (which could also be considered as degree course choices) at one and the same time! From its origins in metallurgy, materials science has now moved into the processing, structure and properties of materials – ceramics, polymers, composites and electrical materials. Materials science and metallurgy are perhaps the most misunderstood of all careers and applications for degree courses are low with very reasonable offers. Valuable bursaries (one at each university) are offered by the Institute of Materials (£1000 for students with at least BBB) through certain universities (check with Institute – see **Appendix 1**). Polymer Science is a branch of materials science and is often studied in conjunction with Chemistry and covers such topics as polymer properties and processing relating to industrial applications with, for example, plastics, paints, adhesives. As with other careers in which there is a short-fall of applicants, graduate employment and future prospects are good. Other related degree subjects include Biomedical Materials, Photographic Technology, Textile and Wood Science. Paper Science degree courses are offered by only one university in the United Kingdom – UMIST – which has a broad base of general science and provides all graduates for the paper industry. It is well worth considering by all those interested in sciences: there is a great shortage of applicants. See also **Appendix 1.**

Special features: Birmingham Courses are offered in Materials Engineering and Metallurgy with specialisms associated with biomedical studies and sport. **London (QM)** Students are encouraged to gain practical experience during summer vacations in the UK and abroad. The course covers polymers, biomaterials, metals and ceramics. **Nottingham** A course is offered in Medical Materials Science with specialisms in cell biology and pharmaceutical applications. **Sheffield** Courses are offered in Metal Science, Ceramic Science, Glass Science, Medical Materials Science and Polymer Science. **Sheffield Hallam** (Foren Eng) The only course of its kind in the UK focusing on materials failures. *NOW CHECK PROSPECTUSES AND WEB SITES.*

Top universities and colleges (Teaching Quality) (see Ch.4): Bath; Bolton (IHE) (Text); Cambridge; Cranfield; Exeter; London (Imp); Loughborough; Manchester; Manchester Met; Northampton (UC) (Lea Tech); Nottingham; Oxford; Sheffield; Surrey; not all institutions assessed.

Top universities and colleges (Research) (see Ch.4): Bath; Birmingham; Cambridge; Leeds (also Textiles); Liverpool; London (Imp), (QM); Loughborough; Manchester; Nottingham; Oxford; Sheffield, Surrey; Swansea; UMIST (Crsn Sci; Ppr Sci; Text).

Study opportunities abroad: Bath; Birmingham; Leeds; London (Imp); Newcastle; Nottingham; Sheffield; Swansea; UMIST.

Work opportunities abroad: Bath; Birmingham; Sheffield; Swansea; Trowbridge (Coll).

ADMISSIONS INFORMATION

Number of applicants per place (approx): Bath 4; Birmingham; Leeds 4; Liverpool 3; London (Imp) 3; Manchester Met 7; Newcastle 4; Northumbria 2; Nottingham 7; Oxford 1; Sheffield Hallam 1; Surrey 4; Swansea 4; UMIST 6.

Planning your UCAS personal statement (see Ch.4): Read scientific and engineering journals and describe any special interests you may have. Try to visit chemical or technological installations (rubber, plastics, glass etc) describing any such visits. See also **Appendix 1.**

Interview questions (see Ch.4): Questions will be based on A/AS-Level science subjects. Recent examples include: Why did you choose Materials Science? How would you make each part of this table lamp (on the interviewer's desk)? Identify this piece of material. How was it manufactured? How has it been treated? (Questions related to metal and polymer samples.) What would you consider the major growth area in materials science?

GAP YEAR ADVICE

See the world and try to get some industrial experience. Take time to plan a gap year and use it constructively.

Institutions willing to defer entry after A-Levels: Leeds; Manchester Met; Northumbria; Surrey; Swansea; UMIST.

AFTER RESULTS ADVICE

Institutions which may accept the same points score after A-Levels: Bath; Birmingham; Leeds; Liverpool; Manchester; Manchester Met; North East Wales (IHE); Nottingham; Sheffield Hallam; UMIST.

Institutions which may accept lower grades/points score after A-Levels: Bath; Leeds; Manchester Met; Newcastle; Northumbria; North East Wales (IHE); Surrey; UMIST.

Offers to applicants repeating A-Levels: Higher Swansea; **Same** Birmingham, Leeds, Liverpool, Manchester Met, Surrey, Trowbridge (Coll).

Probable vacancies from June 2001 and in Clearing (see Ch.4): This is one of the less popular subjects and almost certainly there will be vacancies in most universities from June onwards.

NEW GRADUATE DESTINATIONS AND EMPLOYMENT (1999 HESA) (see **Ch.4**)

Out of 792 students surveyed, 519 graduates went into full-time employment, another 119 went into research and further study and 43 were believed to be unemployed.

MATHEMATICS (including **Applied Mathematics**)

NB The information supplied by the universities and colleges this year varies considerably and the offers listed below should be used as a first source of reference only. Many institutions will accept combinations of Advanced (AL), Advanced Subsidiary (AS) and Vocational Advanced (VA) level qualifications to achieve the required points total, but applicants must check web sites and prospectuses for full details of all offers. Grades and points totals shown should be regarded as the minimum levels to be achieved, but offers may be adjusted downwards when results are known. The points totals shown to the left of the institutions are for ease of reference only. It must not be assumed that tariff points are always used by institutions or that they can be substituted for an offer in grades. The level of an offer is not necessarily indicative of the quality of a course. To calculate your offers see Chapter 4 and the inside fold of the back cover.

Special subject requirements/preferences: A-Level: Mathematics subjects, normally the highest grade in the offers below. **Cambridge** Two mathematics A-Levels (only a very tiny minority are accepted with a single A-Level in mathematics. No distinction is made between A-Level syllabi). **Warwick** Students encouraged to take a special or STEP paper in addition to mathematics or further mathematics. Preference is given to students taking four A-Levels, excluding general studies. **Curriculum 2000: Oxford** (Maths/Phil) Full A-Levels expected in mathematics and recommended in further mathematics. **GCSE:** English often required. **Aberdeen, Edinburgh, St Andrews** English and a foreign language required. **Birmingham (Westhill)** Grade B double science, grade B mathematics, grade C English. **Brunel** (Fin Maths) English/mathematics at grades A or B; (Maths/Lang) French or German at grades A or B. **City** Two subjects at grade A, three subjects at grade B, grade A mathematics, grade B English. **London (LSE)** A*, A and B grades. **Oxford,**

Cambridge Usually grade As. **Strathclyde** (Maths Stats Acc) English language and literature grades AA–BB. **Warwick** A* mathematics plus five As.

360 pts and above

Bath – 21u – ABB+addit us **or** VA12u+AL(maths); (MMaths; BSc Maths; Maths Sci; Maths/Comp; Maths/Stats)

Cambridge – Offers, mainly in grades, vary between colleges (Mathematics)

London (UCL) – AAA–ABB **or** 3ALs+AS/VA; (MSc Maths; Maths with Euro Lang/Mgt/Econ/Stats Sci/Comp Sci/Theor Phys/Phys/Astron)

Oxford – Offers vary between candidates (Mathematics)

Southampton – 370 pts 21u (inc 220 pts from 2ALs inc maths); (MMaths courses)

Warwick – AAA–AAB (A maths or further maths) (Maths courses except under **340 pts**)

350 pts **Southampton** – 350 pts 21u (inc 200 pts from 2ALs inc maths); (Maths; Ind/App Maths)

York – 21–18u – ABC **or** AB+cc **or** AB+ccc **or** VAs (contact univ); gs; (Maths courses)

340 pts **Bristol** – AAB (A maths); (not gs) (BSc Maths; Maths with Stats/Euro/Phys)

Liverpool – 340 pts – ALs **or** ALs+ASs **or** VAs+/-ALs/ASs; (Math Phys courses)

London (Imp) – AAB (Maths courses)

London (LSE) – AAB–BBB (Bus Maths)

Nottingham – AAB–ABB (Maths courses)

Warwick – AAB (A maths) (MMaths/Stats; Maths/OR/Stats/Econ; Maths/Phys)

330 pts **Southampton** – 330 pts 21u (inc 200 pts from 2ALs inc maths); (Maths courses except under **360/350 pts**)

320 pts **Bath** – 3ALs (inc A maths, B phys); (not gs) (Maths/Phys)

Bristol – ABB (from maths/phys/eng sci/f.maths); (not gs) (Maths/Intel Sys; Comp Exp Maths; Eng Maths)

Brunel – 320 pts 2x6u pref 3x6u (inc AL maths B) – ALs **or** ALs+ASs **or** VAs+/-ALs/ASs; (Fin Maths)

Durham – ABB (A maths+phys); (not gs) (MSc Maths; Maths/Phys)

East Anglia – 320 pts (inc AB) – ABB **or** AB+bb (A maths; for Biomaths B biol); (MMaths courses)

Edinburgh – ABB–BBC (Maths courses)

Exeter – 320 pts 18u (inc AL maths) – ABB **or** AB+bb **or** VAs (contact univ); gs; (MMaths)

London (King's) – ABB+AS **or** AAC+AS (inc A maths) **or** VA12u AA+AL (A maths)+AS **or** VA6u+ALs/ASs; (Maths; Maths with Comp Sci/Educ/Mgt/Phil/Phys/Astro)

London (LSE) – ABB (Maths/Econ)
London (RH) – ABB (Maths/Econ; Maths/Mgt; Maths)
Manchester – ABB–BBC (Maths/Phys)
St Andrews – ABB–BBC (Maths/Psy)
UMIST – 320 pts – 3ALs (320 pts, A maths) **or** ALs (A maths)+ASs; gs; (Maths/Mgt)

300 pts **Bangor** – BBB (MMaths)
Birmingham – BBB (Maths/Spo Sci; Maths/Psy; Maths Eng)
Birmingham – ABC (Maths/Euro; MSc Maths Sci)
Brunel – 300 pts 2x6u pref 3x6u (inc AL maths B) – ALs **or** ALs+ASs **or** VAs+/-ALs/ASs; (Maths/Eng)
East Anglia – 300 pts 12u (inc BB) – BBB **or** BB+bb; (not gs) (Maths courses except under **320 pts**)
Essex – 300–260 pts – B (maths)B+AL/2ASs-B (maths)C+AL/2ASs; gs; (Maths courses)
Exeter – 300 pts 18u (inc AL maths) – BBB **or** BB+bb **or** VAs (contact univ); gs; (Maths courses except under **320/280 pts**)
Heriot-Watt – 300 pts 18u – BBB **or** ALs+ASs **or** VAs+/-ALs/ASs; gs; (Act Maths; Fin Maths)
Kent – 300–260 pts approx (Maths courses)
Lancaster – 300–260 pts approx (Maths courses)
Leeds – 300 pts 18u (inc 12u ALs, B maths); (Mathematics)
Leicester – 300 pts 18u – B (maths)BB **or** B (maths)B+bb; gs; (MMaths Comp Maths)
Liverpool – 300–260 pts – ALs **or** ALs+ASs **or** VAs+/-ALs/ASs; (Maths courses except under **340/140 pts**)
London (RH) – BBB (Maths/Fr; Maths/Geol; Maths/Mus)
Manchester – BBB (Maths/Comp Sci; Maths Engl)
Newcastle – BBB–CCC (Maths/Psy)
Reading – ABC (Maths Meteor)
St Andrews – BBB–BBC (Maths courses except under **320/280 pts**)
Sheffield – 300 pts approx/AB (Maths Astron; Maths with Econ/Comp Sci/Chem)
Surrey – 300 pts 18u – BBB **or** ALs+ASs **or** VAs+AL/ASs (maths); (MMaths)
Sussex – BBB–BCC (Maths courses)
Swansea – 300 pts 18u – BBB/AB **or** ALs+ASs **or** VAs+/-ALs/ASs; (OR)
UMIST – 300 pts – 3ALs (300 pts, A maths) **or** ALs(A maths)+ASs; gs; (Maths; Maths with Lang/Soft Eng/Euro/Astro)

280 pts **Aston** – 280 pts – BBC **or** VAs (inc B maths)+/-ALs/ASs; gs; (Inf Maths)
Bangor – 280 pts – 3ALs **or** VAs+/-ALs/ASs; gs; (Maths/Phys Educ)
Belfast (Queen's) – BBC–CCC (Maths courses)

Birmingham – BBC (BSc Maths Sci)
Birmingham – ACC (Maths/Artif Intel; Maths/Comp Sci)
Brunel – 280 pts 2x6u pref 3x6u (inc AL maths B) – ALs **or** ALs+ASs **or** VAs+/-ALs/ASs; (Maths courses)
Cambridge (Hom) – BBC–BCD (Maths/Educ BEd)
Cardiff – BBC–BCC/BB(B maths) (P Maths; P Maths/Comp; P Maths/Fr/Ger; P Maths/Educ; P Maths/Mus; P Maths/Phil; P Maths/Relig St; P Maths/Welsh)
Coventry – 280–200 pts approx (Maths courses)
East Anglia – BBC (Maths/Meteor)
Exeter – 280 pts 18u (inc AL maths+lang/phys) – BBC **or** BB+cc **or** VAs (contact univ); not gs for Maths/Phys; (Maths/Fr/Ger/Phys)
Glasgow – BBC–CCC (Maths courses)
Hull – BBC–BCC (Maths courses)
Leeds – 280 pts (Maths St)
Leicester – 280 pts 18u – B(maths)BC **or** B(maths)B+cc; gs; (BSc Comp Maths)
London (QM) – BBC (Maths/Bus St; Maths/Comp; Maths; Maths Sci Bus Ind Fin; Dscrt Maths)
London (RH) – BBC (BB maths, phys) **or** BB+cc (inc gs); (Maths/Phys)
Loughborough – 280 pts – B(maths)+AL+AL/2ASs **or** VAs+/-ALs/ASs; (Maths courses except under **260 pts**)
Newcastle – 280 pts (Math Sci)
Reading – BBC (Maths/Psy)
Strathclyde – BBC (Maths/Stats/Acc)
Swansea – 280 pts 18u – BBC–BCC/BB **or** ALs+ASs **or** VAs+/-ALs/ASs; (Maths)

260 pts **Aston** – 260–240 pts 18u – 3ALs **or** ALs+ASs **or** VAs+/-ALs/ASs; gs; (Maths Comb)
Cardiff – BCC (Phil P Maths; Maths Phys)
City – 3x6u – BCC (inc B maths); ASs/VAs (contact univ); (not gs) (MMaths courses)
Dundee – BCC (Env Sci Maths; Engl/Maths; Fin Econ/Maths)
Heriot-Watt – 260 pts 18u – BCC **or** ALs+ASs **or** VAs B+/-ALs/ASs; gs; (Maths courses except under **300 pts**)
Hull – BCC–BCD (Maths; Maths/Phil; Maths Fin; P Maths; Maths/Span)
Keele – BCC/BB **or** equiv AS accepted; gs; (Maths courses)
Leicester – B(maths)CC **or** B(maths)C+cc; gs; (Maths; Maths/USA/Euro; Maths/Comp Sci (Euro); MMaths courses; Maths/Astron courses)
London (QM) – BCC (Maths/Astro)
Loughborough – 260 pts – B(maths)+AL+AL/2ASs **or** VAs+/-ALs/ASs; (Maths/Eng)

Newcastle – BCC (Maths/Comp Sci; Maths/Geog)
Oxford Brookes – BCC–CCC (Maths courses)
Portsmouth – 260 pts – ALs **or** ALs+ASs **or** VAs; gs; (Maths courses)
Reading – BCC (Maths; Comp Maths; Maths Econ)
Salford – BCC–CCD (Biol/Maths; Bus Decn Analys)
Stirling – BCC (Acc/Maths)
Strathclyde – BCC (Maths Biol)
Surrey – 260 pts 18u – BCC **or** ALs+ASs **or** VAs+AL/AS(maths); (BSc Maths)
Swansea – 260 pts 18u – BCC **or** ALs+ASs **or** VAs+/-ALs/ASs; (Maths/Phys; Maths courses except under **280 pts**)
Ulster – BCC (Maths Stats Comp)
UMIST – BCC (Maths/Phys)

240 pts **Aberdeen** – CCC–CCD (Maths courses)
De Montfort – 240–200 pts approx (Maths courses)
Liverpool John Moores – 240 pts (inc 2ALs **or** VAs) – ALs **or** ALs+ASs **or** VAs+/-ALs/ASs; (Maths/Stats/Comp; Bus/Maths)
Manchester Met – 240–200 pts approx (Maths courses)
Newcastle – BCD (Maths/Chem; Maths Surv Map Sci)

220 pts **Brighton** – 220 pts approx (Maths courses)
Bristol UWE – 220–180 pts 18u (inc 6u maths 80 pts min); ALs **or** ALs+ASs **or** VAs+/-ALs/ASs; (not gs) (Maths Sci; Maths courses)
Greenwich – 220 pts approx (Maths/Law)
Hertfordshire – 220–200 pts 1x12u **or** 2x6u – ALs(D maths); gs; (Maths; Comp Maths; Maths Bus; Maths QTS)
Huddersfield – 220 pts approx (Maths courses)
Nottingham Trent – 220–180 pts approx (Maths courses)
Plymouth – C+140 pts approx (Maths)
Stirling – CCD (Maths courses except under **260 pts**)

200 pts **Bangor** – 200 pts gs (AL only); (Maths courses except under **300/280 pts**)
Central Lancashire – 200–160 pts 12u (C maths for Maths/Psy/Stats); gs; (Maths courses)
Chester (Coll) – 200–180 pts – ALs (160 pts, C maths or AS maths)+AS **or** VA (160 pts, C maths subj)+AS; AS(20–40 pts); (Maths Comb/Comp; Comp Maths)
Coventry – 200–160 pts approx (Maths/Sci)
Dundee – 200 pts approx (Maths/Chem; App Maths; Maths/Acc)
Kingston – 200–180 pts (inc 2ALs inc maths); (Maths courses)
Luton – 200–160 pts approx (Maths – Mod)
Northampton (UC) – 200–160 pts approx (Maths courses)
Reading – CDD (Maths St)
Sheffield Hallam – 200–180 pts approx (Maths courses)
Sunderland – 200–180 pts approx (Maths Comb)
Ulster – CDD (Maths Stats Comp)

180 pts **Edge Hill (CHE)** – BC (Maths/Spo St)
Glamorgan – 180 pts approx (MMaths; Maths; Maths Acc Fin)
Liverpool Hope (Coll) – 180–160 pts approx (Maths Comb)
Northumbria – 180–140 pts approx (Maths Bus Admin)
Staffordshire – 180 pts approx (Maths courses)

160 pts **Anglia** – 160 pts 12u – 2ALs **or** ALs+ASs; VAs (contact univ); gs; (Maths Sci; Bus Maths; Maths/Comp)
Bath Spa (UC) – 160 pts approx (App Maths BA/BSc QTS)
Birmingham (Westhill) – 160 pts 12u (inc C) – ALs **or** ALs+ASs; VAs (contact univ); gs; (Maths Sci/Educ; Maths Sci/Psy)
Bishop Grosseteste (Coll) – CC (inc C maths) **or** C+cc **or** VA12u+C(maths); (Maths/Tech)
Canterbury Christ Church (UC) – CC–CD (Maths courses)
Chichester (UC) – 160 pts (inc C); (Maths; Maths/Educ QTS)
Coventry – 160 pts (Maths/Chem)

Glasgow Caledonian – DDE/CD (Comp Maths; Fin Maths; Maths Bus Analys)
Greenwich – 160–140 pts approx (Maths/Comp)
Middlesex – 160–140 pts approx (Maths courses; Maths/Bus)
Napier – CC (Maths courses)
North London – 160 pts 1x12u **or** 2x6u; (Maths Educ)
Westminster – CC (Maths courses)
Wolverhampton – 160 pts approx; gs (Maths Sci)

140 pts **Bolton (IHE)** – CD–DD (Maths courses)
Derby – 140 pts 12u – CD **or** DD+ee **or** VAs CD+/-ALs/ASs; gs; (App Maths/Comp; Maths Stats; Maths with Comp/Educ/Lang/Comb)
Edge Hill (CHE) – CD–DD (Maths; App Soc Sci/Maths; Maths/Educ St; Maths/Geog; Maths/Inf Sys)
Liverpool – 140 pts – ALs **or** ALs+ASs **or** VAs+/-ALs/ASs; (Fdn Maths Sci)
London Guildhall – CD–DD (Maths courses)
Manchester Met – 140 pts approx (App Maths – part–time)
St Martin's (Coll) – DEE/DD (Maths QTS)
Strathclyde – CD (Sci St/Maths courses)
Wolverhampton – 140 pts 12u – DEE **or** DE+c; (Maths Bus Analys)

120 pts **and below**
Bath Spa (UC) – EE (App Maths Comb)
Bolton (IHE) – DD (App Maths Fdn)
Hull – (Maths/Phil 4 yr – for non-traditional entrants)
Hull (Scarborough) – DD (Maths QTS)
London (Gold) – DD (Maths courses)
North London – 120 pts 1x12u **or** 2x6u; (Maths; Maths Sci; Maths Sci Comb)
Ripon & York (Coll) – DD (Maths QTS)
Sheffield Hallam – (P Educ QTS)

Diploma of Higher Education courses
80 pts Bath Spa (UC); East London; Hertfordshire; Manchester Met; Westminster (IEd).

Higher National Diploma courses
140 pts **and below**
Bell (CT); Blackburn (Coll); Brighton; Coventry; De Montfort; Greenwich; Kingston; North London; Portsmouth; Sheffield Hallam.

Alternative Offers:

EB offers: Brunel 70%; Sheffield 70%.

IB offers: Aberdeen (Arts) 30 pts; (Sci) 26 pts; Anglia (MS) 28 pts; Bath 32 pts; Belfast (Queen's) H666; Birmingham 32–30 pts; Brighton 27 pts inc 12 pts Highers; Bristol 30 pts inc H644; Brunel 29 pts H6 maths; Cardiff 28 pts; East Anglia 32 pts; Essex 28 pts; Exeter 33–30 pts; Glasgow H555; Heriot–Watt H554; Kent 32–28 pts; Lancaster 30 pts; Leeds 32 pts maths H6; Leicester 28 pts; Liverpool H655/555; London (LSE) 36 pts H766, (RH) 28 pts, (UCL) 30 pts; Newcastle 28 pts, 24 pts for 4 yr courses; Portsmouth 24 pts; Ripon & York (Coll) 27 pts; St Andrews 28 pts; St Martin's (Coll) 28 pts; Sheffield H6 (maths) 55 or 555; Southampton 30 pts; Stirling 28 pts; Surrey 28 pts; Sussex 15 pts Highers; Swansea 28 pts; UMIST 30 pts H 16 pts; Warwick 36–32 pts; York 30 pts H6 maths.

Irish offers: Aberdeen (Arts) BBBB, (Sci) BCCCC; Aberystwyth ABBBC; Bangor BBCCC; Brighton CCCCC; Brunel BBBCCC; Coventry BBB; Edinburgh ABBC; Glamorgan CCCC; Glasgow BBB; Keele BBBCC; Leeds AAAA; Liverpool BBCCC; London Guildhall CCCCC; North London BCCC; St Andrews BBBB; Sheffield BBBB; South Bank CCCC; Warwick AAABB.

Scottish Qualifications: Aberdeen BBBB–BBBC; Dundee BBBC; Edinburgh ABBBC; Glasgow BBBB; Glasgow Caledonian BBC; Heriot–Watt BBBC; Napier BBC (B maths); Paisley DBC; St Andrews BBBB; Stirling BBCC; Strathclyde AAABB–BBBC.

Overseas applicants: Coventry Fluency in oral and written English required. **Newcastle** Preliminary course available. **Sheffield** Foundation course available.

CHOOSING YOUR COURSE (See also **Ch.1**)

> **Subject information:** Mathematics at degree level is an extension of A-Level mathematics covering pure and applied mathematics, statistics, computing, mathematical analysis and mathematical applications. Alternative courses such as Operational Research, Statistics, Accountancy, Astronomy and Astrophysics, Computer Science, Management Science and Actuarial Studies could also be considered. See also **Appendix 1**.

Special features: Aberystwyth Possibility to transfer to a joint course at the end of first year. **Bangor** Broad flexible course leaving final choices between pure maths, applied maths and computing until third year. Electives in IT, psychology and accounting. **Bath** Common first year for all Maths degrees. **Bristol** Modular course. Flexible course structure during second and third years. Transfer possible between various Honours schools and from Joint Honours to Single Honours at end of first or second year. Students can spend one third of time on subjects outside department in either or both of second or third years. **Brunel** Sandwich course – work placements included. **Cardiff** Options to specialise in pure maths, applied maths or statistics. **City** Option to change maths course in second year. **East Anglia** (Deferred course choice) Transfer to Physics/Maths/Physics and Maths programme expected after first year. **Heriot-Watt** Degrees cover 75 per cent maths and 25 per cent of course from other departments. **Leeds** Possibility of studying non-maths modules. Option to study in Europe or USA. **London (RH)** First-year tutorials in groups of three. Wide range of options and a course unit system. **Manchester Met** Emphasis on applied maths in second and third years. **Newcastle** Transfer between courses possible up to end of second year. **Salford** Optional one-year sandwich placement. Two years' accommodation guaranteed. **Surrey** Strong links with industry and commerce. **UMIST** (Maths) Course options include mathematics with French or German or study in Spain. **Warwick** (Maths/OR/Stats/Econ) An Honours degree involving mathematics, statistics, economics and the Warwick Business School. Maths and Applied Maths have a very flexible option structure. **York** Flexibility in changing course options. *NOW CHECK PROSPECTUSES AND WEB SITES.*

Top universities and colleges (Teaching Quality) (see Ch.4): Aberdeen; Abertay Dundee; Brighton; Brunel; Derby; Dundee; Durham; Edinburgh; Exeter; Glasgow; Glasgow Caledonian; Hertfordshire; Lancaster; Leeds; Leicester; St Andrews; Stirling; Strathclyde; UMIST; York; not all institutions assessed.

Top universities and colleges (Research) (see Ch.4): (P=Pure; A=Applied) Aberystwyth; Bath (PA); Birmingham (PA); Bristol (PA); Brunel (A); Cambridge (PA); Cardiff (P); Dundee (P); Durham (PA); East Anglia (PA); Edinburgh (PA); Exeter (A); Glasgow (PA); Heriot-Watt; Hull (P); Keele (A); Leeds (PA); Liverpool (PA); London (Imp) (PA), (King's) (PA), (QM) (PA), (RH) (PA), (UCL); Loughborough (A); Manchester (PA); Newcastle (A); Nottingham (PA); Oxford (PA); St Andrews (P); Sheffield (A); Southampton (A); Strathclyde (A); Sussex (PA); Swansea (P); UMIST (PA); Warwick (P); York (P).

Study opportunities abroad: Aberystwyth; Bangor; Birmingham; Brighton; Bristol; Bristol UWE; Brunel; Chester (Coll); City; Coventry; Dundee; Durham; East Anglia; Edinburgh; Essex; Glamorgan; Hertfordshire; Hull; Kent; Kingston; Lancaster; Leeds; Leicester; Liverpool; Liverpool John Moores; London (QM), (Imp); Manchester; Manchester Met; Nottingham; Nottingham Trent; Plymouth; St Andrews; Sheffield; Southampton; Strathclyde; Sussex; Swansea; UMIST; Warwick; York.

Work opportunities abroad: Aberystwyth; Birmingham; Brunel; Chester (Coll); Coventry; De Montfort; Kingston; Leeds; Liverpool John Moores; Loughborough; Napier; Nottingham Trent; Sheffield.

ADMISSIONS INFORMATION

Number of applicants per place (approx): Aberystwyth 8, (App Maths) 5; Anglia 6; Bangor 4; Bath 10; Birmingham 5; Bristol 12; Brunel 5; Cambridge 2.2; Cambridge (Hom) 4 (All BEd courses); Cardiff 3; Central Lancashire 7; City 6; Coventry 8; De Montfort 5; Derby 4; Dundee 12; Durham 5; East Anglia 8; East London 2; Edinburgh 4; Exeter 6; Glamorgan 3; Greenwich 2; Hertfordshire 9; Heriot–Watt 5; Hull 8; Kent 8; Lancaster 12; Leeds 7; Leicester 8; Liverpool 8; London (Gold) 5, (King's) 5 average, (LSE) (Maths/Econ) 7, (Bus Maths) 6, (QM) 5, (RH) 8, (UCL) 8; Loughborough (Maths Eng) 5, (Maths Educ) 3; Manchester Met 3; Middlesex 5; Newcastle 7; Newman (CHE) 5; North London 3; Northumbria 7; Nottingham 15; Oxford 2; Oxford Brookes 21; Plymouth 3, (Maths/Eng) 6; Portsmouth 9; Ripon & York (Coll) 10; St Martin's (Coll) 9; Salford 10; Sheffield 5; Sheffield Hallam 3; Southampton 8; Strathclyde 6; Surrey 7; Swansea 6; UMIST 6; Warwick 6; Westminster 3; York 9.

Planning your UCAS personal statement (see Ch.4): Any interests you have in careers requiring mathematical ability could be mentioned – for example, engineering, computers (hardware and software) and business applications. **Bristol** (Eng Maths) Skills, work experience, positions of responsibility. **St Andrews** Reasons for course choice. Evidence of interest. See also **Appendix 1**.

Selection interviews (see Ch.4): Aberystwyth; Bangor; Bath; Birmingham; Bishop Grosseteste (Coll) (T); Bristol; Bristol UWE; Brunel; Cambridge; Cardiff; Central Lancashire; City; Coventry; De Montfort (No); Derby (No); Durham; East Anglia (No); East London; Edinburgh (No); Essex; Exeter; Glamorgan; Greenwich (some); Heriot-Watt; Hull; Kent; Kingston; Lancaster; Leeds; Leicester (No); Liverpool; Liverpool John Moores; London (Gold), (King's), (LSE) (rarely), (RH), (UCL); London Guildhall; Loughborough (some); Manchester Met; Newcastle; Newman (CHE); North London; Northampton (UC); Northumbria; Nottingham; Oxford (W – overseas applicants; (T – Maths; Maths/Phil; Maths/Comp) Test lasting 2.5 hrs; details of questions available from colleges); Oxford Brookes (No); Paisley (No); Portsmouth (No); Reading; St Andrews (No); Salford; Sheffield; Sheffield Hallam; Southampton (Maths Act St); Stirling (No); Surrey (No); Sussex; Swansea; UMIST; Warwick; York.

Interview questions (see Ch.4): Questions are likely to be asked arising from the statement made in your UCAS form and in your stated interests in the subjects. Questions in recent years have included: How many ways are there of incorrectly setting up the back row of a chess board? A ladder on a rough floor leans against a smooth wall – describe the forces acting on the ladder and give the maximum angle of inclination possible. There are three articles connected by a string, the middle one is made to move – describe the subsequent motion of the particles. What mathematics books have you read outside your syllabus? Why does a ball bounce? Discuss the work of any renowned mathematician. Balance a pencil on your index fingers and then try to move both towards the centre of the pencil. Explain what is happening in terms of forces and friction.

Reasons for rejection (non-academic): Usually academic reasons only. Lack of motivation.

GAP YEAR ADVICE

Some institutions will accept a gap year, but many universities feel that the break can be detrimental. Keep up your maths and revise your A–level course at the end of the gap year.

Institutions willing to defer entry after A-Levels: Aston; Bangor; Bath; Birmingham; Brighton; Bristol (Maths/Phys); Brunel; Cardiff; Chester (Coll); Coventry; De Montfort; Derby; Dundee; East Anglia; East London; Edge Hill (CHE); Glamorgan; Glasgow Caledonian; Heriot–Watt; Hertfordshire; Hull; Hull (Scarborough) (No); Kingston; Leeds; Leicester; London (Gold), (RH), (UCL) (No); Luton; Newcastle; North London; Northumbria; Nottingham (academic revision recommended during gap year); Nottingham Trent; Plymouth; Salford (No); Southampton; Surrey; Sussex; Swansea; UMIST; Warwick; Westminster; Wolverhampton; York.

AFTER RESULTS ADVICE

Institutions which may accept the same points score after A-Levels: Aberystwyth; Aston (No); Bangor; Bath (depends on distribution of points); Birmingham; Brighton (No); Bristol; Brunel (maths grade B); Cardiff; Central Lancashire; Chichester (UC); City; Coventry; De Montfort; Dundee (No); Durham; East Anglia (perhaps); East London; Essex; Glamorgan; Heriot–Watt; Hertfordshire; Hull; Kent; Lancaster (B maths); Leeds; Liverpool; London (Gold), (RH), (UCL) (No); Loughborough (Math Eng); Manchester Met; Napier; Newcastle; Newman (CHE); North London; Northampton (UC); Northumbria; Nottingham (No); Nottingham Trent (No); Salford; Sheffield Hallam; Sheffield; Southampton (No); Strathclyde; Surrey; Swansea; UMIST; Warwick (No); York (No).

Institutions which may accept lower grades/points score after A-Levels: Aston; Bangor; Brighton; Brunel; Cardiff; Chester (Coll); Chichester (UC); De Montfort; Glamorgan; Hertfordshire; Leicester; Manchester Met; Newcastle; North London; Northumbria; Nottingham Trent; Surrey; UMIST; Warwick.

Offers to applicants repeating A-Levels: Higher Birmingham, Brighton, Coventry, De Montfort, Essex, Leeds, Liverpool, North London, Salford, Strathclyde, Swansea, Surrey, Warwick; **Possibly higher** Cambridge (Hom), Durham, Lancaster, Leeds, Loughborough (Maths Eng), Newcastle, Sheffield; **Same** Aberystwyth, Aston, Bangor, Bath, Brunel, East Anglia, Hull, London (RH), Loughborough (usually), Manchester Met, Nottingham, Nottingham Trent, Oxford Brookes, Southampton, Ulster, UMIST, York.

Probable vacancies from June 2001 and in Clearing (see Ch.4): There are always vacancies at most universities in this subject area from June and in Clearing.

NEW GRADUATE DESTINATIONS AND EMPLOYMENT (1999 HESA) (see **Ch.4**)

Of 2945 graduates surveyed, 1682 went into full-time employment, 795 went into further study and 165 were believed to be unemployed.

MEDIA STUDIES (including **Broadcasting** and **Journalism**; see also **Art & Design (General)**, **Communications Studies**, **Computer Courses** and **Film, Radio, Video and TV Studies**)

NB The information supplied by the universities and colleges this year varies considerably and the offers listed below should be used as a first source of reference only. Many institutions will accept combinations of Advanced (AL), Advanced Subsidiary (AS) and Vocational Advanced (VA) level qualifications to achieve the required points total, but applicants must check web sites and prospectuses for full details of all offers. Grades and points totals shown should be regarded as the minimum levels to be achieved, but offers may be adjusted downwards when results are known. The points totals shown to the left of the institutions are for ease of reference only. It must not be assumed that tariff points are always used by institutions or that they can be substituted for an offer in grades. The level of an offer is not necessarily indicative of the quality of a course. To calculate your offers see Chapter 4 and the inside fold of the back cover.

Special subject requirements/preferences: A-Level: Language requirement for appropriate language course. **GCSE:** English and mathematics often required. **Bangor** Grade C in Welsh. **Bradford** Grade C in mathematics, combined science, physics and English. **Cardiff** Grade A or B in English. **Nottingham Trent** Majority grades A/B. **Sheffield Hallam** Majority of grades A and B; grade B minimum in double science, mathematics, English; (Media Sci) Double sci and mathematics at grade B. **Ravensbourne (CDC)** Average eight subjects grade A–C. **South Bank** Two subjects grade A, two at grade B, English grade A or B.

340 pts   Birmingham – AAB–ABB (Media Cult Soty/Mus)
Warwick – AAB (Crea Writ/Engl Lit)

320 pts **Leeds** – ABB (Broadcasting)
Sheffield – 320–300 pts approx (Journal St)
300 pts **Birmingham** – BBB (Media Cult St courses except under **340 pts**)
Bournemouth – 300 pts – BBB (New Media Prod)
Bradford – 300–280 pts 12u; gs; (Electron Imag/Media Comm; Intnet Prod Des)
Bristol UWE – 300–260 pts 18u pref/12u – (200 pts reqd in 12u/6u awards) ALs **or** ALs+ASs **or** VAs+/-ALs/ASs (media st/soc sci subjs pref); (Cult Media St)
Central Lancashire – 300–280 pts approx (Journalism)
Lancaster – BBB–BBC (Cult Media Comm)
Leeds – BBB (Broad Journal)
Leeds, Trinity & All Saints (Coll) – 300–240 pts (Media (Spo Hlth Leis))
London (Gold) – BBB (Media Comm)
Nottingham Trent – 350 pts 18u – BBB **or** ALs (300 pts min) **or** VA12u (240 pts)+AL (100 pts); (Broad Journal)
280 pts **Bournemouth** – 280 pts – BBC; (Multim Journal)
Cardiff – BBC (Journal Film Broad; Journal Film Broad/Sociol; Journal Film Broad/Soc Pol)
City – 3x6u – BBC; ASs/VAs (contact univ); (Journal with Econ/Psy/Sociol; Journal/Contemp Hist (AL hist pref))
Leeds, Trinity & All Saints (Coll) – BBC–CCC (Media Mgt; Media/Psy)
Liverpool John Moores – 280 pts 4ALs; 240 pts 3ALs; 180 pts 2ALs **or** VA E (Media/Comm Prod)+2ALs (C in Engl/comm st/media/hist/sociol); (Media Cult St courses)
London (QM) – 280 pts – 3ALs; (Journal/Contemp Hist)
London (RH) – 280 pts – BBC–BCC **or** 2ALs+2ASs; (Sci/Media)
Loughborough – 280 pts approx (Comm/Media St)
Nottingham Trent – 2ALs (inc BB) **or** VA12u (inc B); (Media/Cult St)
Sheffield Hallam – BBC (Media St)
Staffordshire – 280 pts – CCC(min) **or** CCC+AS(40 pts) **or** VA12u CC+AL(C); gs; (Journal Single Hons)
Stirling – BBC–CCC (Film/Media St courses)
Sussex – BBC (Multim Dig Sys)
Warrington (CI) – 280 pts approx (Media (Consum Mus Prod))
Westminster – BBC (Media St courses)
Wolverhampton – 280–220 pts 12u – CCC–CCD **or** CC+cc **or** VA12u AB; gs; (Media/Comm St)
260 pts **Bangor** – 260 pts (Engl/Journal)
Bristol UWE – BCC; gs (Cult Media St Hist)
Central England – 260 pts; gs; (Media/Comm)
Central Lancashire – 260 pts (Journalism)
Coventry – 260–220 pts approx (Comm Cult Media)
Coventry – 260–160 pts (Comm Auth Des)
De Montfort (Leicester) – 260 pts – ALs **or** ALs+ASs **or** VAs+/-ALs/ASs; (not gs) (Media St)
Glasgow Caledonian – BCC (Comm Mass Media)
Huddersfield – BCC (Media/Engl)
Leeds, Trinity & All Saints (Coll) – BCC–CCD (Media Sociol; Media/Span)
Liverpool – BCC **or** 3ALs **or** BC (2ALs **or** VA C (media /comm prod or inf comm tech)) – ALs **or** ALs+ASs **or** VAs+/-ALs/ASs; (Journal; Int Journal)
Napier – BCC (Journal)
Southampton (Inst) – 260 pts approx (Journal)
Sunderland – 260 pts – ALs **or** ALs+ASs **or** VA12u+AL+AS; (Journal; Media Prod (TV Rad))
Surrey Roehampton – 260–220 pts approx (Film TV courses)
Wolverhampton – 260–220 pts 12u – CCD–CDD/BB **or** CD+cc **or** VA12u AB; gs; (Media Cult St)

Wolverhampton – 260 pts 12u – CCC/AB **or** BC+b **or** VA12u AA; gs; (Journal/Edit Des)

240 pts **Brighton** – 240 pts approx (Inf Media St; Comp Media)

Central Lancashire – 240 pts approx (Media Tech; Media Tech/Journal)

De Montfort (Leicester) – 240 pts – ALs **or** ALs+ASs **or** VAs+/-ALs/ASs; (Broad Tech; Media Tech)

Falmouth (CA) – 240 pts (Media St/Engl)

Huddersfield – 240 pts 18u – CCC **or** CC+cc **or** VA6u B+C/cc; gs; (Media St)

King Alfred's Winchester (Coll) – 240 pts 12u; gs; (Media/Film St)

Lincolnshire & Humberside – 240 pts (Media Prod; Journal; Media Prod/Foren Sci)

Nottingham Trent – 240 pts 18–12u – CCC **or** ALs+ASs **or** VAs+/-ALs/ASs; gs; (Multim Prod; Media St)

Portsmouth – 240 pts – ALs **or** ALs+ASs **or** VAs; gs; (Media St; Media/Lang; Euro Media St)

Sheffield Hallam – 240 pts approx (Media St Comb courses)

South Bank – 240 pts approx (Media Soty)

Southampton (Inst) – 240 pts; ALs **or** ALs+ASs **or** VAs+/-ALs/ASs; gs; (Media Writ)

Staffordshire – 240 pts (inc CC) – 2ALs+AS **or** VA CC; gs; (Journal Joint Hons)

Staffordshire – 240 pts – CCC **or** CCD+AS(40 pts) **or** VA; gs; (Media Tech; Broad Tech) approx (Journal Single Hons)

Sunderland – 240 pts – ALs **or** ALs+ASs **or** VA12u+AL+AS; (Joint courses)

Ulster – CCC (Media St Comb Hons)

Warrington (CI) – 240–220 pts approx (Media St/Bus Mgt/IT; Multim Journal; Media Radio/TV Prod; Media St courses)

220 pts **Bristol UWE** – 220 pts (Sci Soty Media)

Central Lancashire – 220–200 pts approx (Film/Media St)

Cheltenham & Glos (CHE) – 220–140 pts approx + Fdn for some pathways (Media courses)

Falmouth (CA) – 220 pts approx (Broad St; Journal St)

Glamorgan – 220–200 pts approx (Media Prac; Media Comm; Media St/Thea Media Dr)

Lampeter – 220–200 pts approx (Media Cult St)

Luton – 220–180 pts approx (Media courses)

Manchester Met – 220 pts approx (Media Tech)

Middlesex – 220–180 pts (Media Cult St; Journal)

Oxford Brookes – 220–180 pts approx (Media Tech)

Sheffield Hallam – 220 pts approx (Media Sci)

South East Essex (Coll) – 220–180 pts (Media Prod/Tech)

Sunderland – 220–200 pts (Media St courses)

Surrey (IAD/UC) – 220 pts approx (Journal)

200 pts **Bradford** – 200–180 pts 12u; gs; (Fdn Electron Imag)

Bretton Hall – BB–BC (Media Arts/Engl)

Buckinghamshire Chilterns (UC) – 200–180 pts approx (Media courses)

Central Lancashire – 200 pts approx (Aud-Vis Media Tech)

Chester (Coll) – 200 pts – ALs (180 pts inc C 1 subj)+AS **or** VAs (180 pts inc C in 1 subj)+AS; AS(20 pts); gs; (Media/Perf Comb courses)

De Montfort (Leicester) – 200 pts – ALs **or** ALs+ASs **or** VAs+/-ALs/ASs; (not gs) (Media St Joint/Comb Hons)

East London – 200–180 pts approx (Media St courses)

Farnborough (CT) – 200 pts approx (Media Tech – Prod)

Huddersfield – CCE **or** CE+cc (AL lang) **or** VA6u B+C/cc; gs; (Media/Lang; Interact Media)

Liverpool John Moores – BB; 2ALs **or** VA A (media/comm prod/bus)+AL (C in media st/comm st/sociol/Engl); (Media Prof St)

Northumbria – 200 pts approx (Multim Des; Media St/Pol)

St Mark & St John (Coll) – 200–160 pts approx (Media St courses)

Teesside – 200 pts approx (Multim; Media St)

180 pts   **Cheltenham & Glos (CHE)** – 180–140 pts (Multimedia)

Colchester (Inst) – 180 pts approx (Comm/Media St courses)

Glamorgan – 180 pts (Media St/Engl St; Media St/Cult St; Media St/Psy)

Greenwich – 180 pts approx (Media/Soty)

Lincolnshire & Humberside – 180 pts (Interact Des Media Tech; Media Tech courses)

North East Wales (IHE) – 180–140 pts approx (Media courses)

Northampton (UC) – 180–160 pts approx (Media courses)

Queen Margaret (UC) – BC (Media Cult St)

Thames Valley – 180–140 pts approx (Journal; Media courses)

Wolverhampton – 180–170 pts – DDD/CC or CD+d or VAs CC; gs; (Dig Media courses; Multim courses)

160 pts   **Barnsley (Coll)** – 160 pts – DD or ALs+ASs or VAs (160 pts)+/-ALs/ASs; (Journal Comb; Media Comb)

Bath Spa (UC) – 160–120 pts 12u – DD or ALs+ASs or VA12u DD; (not gs); (Media Comm Comb)

Canterbury Christ Church (UC) – CC (Media St courses)

Chichester (UC) – 160 pts (inc C) (Media St courses)

Cumbria (CAD) – 160 pts – CC or ASs (contact coll) or VA; (Media Prod; New Journal)

Doncaster (Coll) – 160 pts – CC or ASs or VA6u+AS; gs; (Screen Writ)

Edge Hill (CHE) – CC (Media courses)

Lincolnshire & Humberside – 160 pts (Media Tech)

Manchester Met – 160 pts approx (Media Tech – Fdn course may be pref)

North London – 160 pts 1x12u or 2x6u; (Dig Media)

Paisley – CC (Media Theor/Prod)

St Mary's (Coll) – 12u – CC or ALs+ASs or VA12u CC or VA6u C+AL(C); gs; (Media Arts)

South Bank – CC–CD (Media Spec Efcts; Media St)

Trinity Carmarthen (Coll) – CC (Media St courses)

140 pts   **Liverpool John Moores** – 140 pts (inc 1x6u or 2x6u or 1x12u inc sci/tech subj) – ALs or ALs+ASs or VAs+/-ALs/ASs; (Broad Tech)

Thames Valley – 140 pts approx (Multim Comp)

120 pts   **Glamorgan** – DD (Media Tech courses)

Newport (UWCN) – 120 pts approx (Media/Vis Cult; Multim)

Worcester (UC) – 120 pts 12u – DD or ALs+ASs or VAs+/-ALs/ASs; (not gs) (Media/Cult St)

100 pts   **and below**

Central England – 80 pts approx (Media Tech Fdn)

London Inst (Central Saint Martins) – (Media Graph Des – contact Admissions Tutor)

Paisley – 100 pts (Media Tech)

Paisley (Ayr) – DE (Media Theor/Prod)

SAE (CT) – (Multim Arts; Recr Arts)

Southampton (Inst) – 100–80 pts (Fdn Media Tech)

Suffolk (Coll) – D (Media St)

Wirral Met (Coll) – (Media St)

Leeds Met – (contact university)

Higher National Diploma courses

140 pts   **and below**

Aberdeen (Coll); Barking (Coll); Barnsley (Coll) (Media; Journal); Bath (Media Prod); Bell (CT) (Journal); Central England; City of Bristol (Coll); Cornwall & Duchy (Coll) (Journal; Media); Crawley (Coll) can inc gs (Multim); Derby; Doncaster (Coll); Dudley (CT); Durham New (Coll) (Multim); Falkirk (CFHE); Farnborough (CT) (Media Prod); Glasgow (CBP); Gloucestershire (CAT) (NCJT course); Grimsby (Coll); Halton (Coll); Henley (Coll); Huddersfield; Kidderminster (Coll); Leeds (CAD); Liverpool (CmC) (Journal); Llandrillo (Coll) (Media Tech); London (Inst) (Journal); Luton; Manchester (CAT); Manchester City (Coll); Mid Cheshire (Coll); Mid Kent (CFHE); Middlesex (Journal); Newcastle (Coll); North Oxfordshire (Coll); North Worcestershire (Coll); Norwich City (Coll); Oldham (Coll); Oxfordshire (SAD); Plymouth (CAD) (Multim); Ravensbourne (CDC); St Helens (Coll); Salisbury (Coll); Solihull (Coll); Stevenson (Coll); Stratford on Avon (Coll); Surrey (IAD/UC); Sutton Coldfield (Coll); Teesside; Thames Valley (Media Tech); Truro (Coll); UHI (Perth); Warrington (CI) 120 pts; Warwickshire (Coll); West Herts (Coll) (Adv; Media); Wigan & Leigh (Coll); Wiltshire (Coll); Worcester (UC); Yorkshire Coast (CFHE).

One-year Journalism courses

Central Lancashire; Harlow (Coll); Highbury (Coll) (also Radio Journal); London (Inst) (Prdcl Journal); Stradbroke (Coll).

Alternative Offers:

IB offers: Birmingham 30 pts; Bournemouth 34–32 pts; Brighton 28 pts; Bristol UWE 30 pts; De Montfort H666 S554; Leeds 35–32 pts; London (RH) 32 pts; Surrey Roehampton 30 pts.

Irish offers: Cardiff ABBBCC.

Scottish Qualifications: Bell (CT0 (Journal) BCC; Glasgow Caledonian BBBB; Napier BBBB; Paisley BBB–BCC; Queen Margaret (UC) BBBC; Stirling ABBB.

Overseas applicants: Bournemouth Fluency in written and spoken English required.

CHOOSING YOUR COURSE (See also **Ch.1**)

Subject information: Intending Media applicants need to check course details carefully since this subject area can involve graphic design, illustration and other art courses as well as the media in the fields of TV, radio and journalism. See also **Communications Studies** and **Film, Radio, Video and TV Studies**. See also **Appendix 1**.

Special features: Aberystwyth A degree course in Film and TV Studies can be combined in year 1 with another subject. Years 2 and 3 focus on practical studies including scriptwriting. **Central England** The Media and Communications course covers theory and practice and involves two four-week placements in industry. **Coventry** The course in Communications, Culture and Media offers modules in film, TV, photography, journalism, public relations and video. **Huddersfield** The Media degree leads to specialisms chosen from radio journalism, print journalism or TV production. **Leicester** The Communications and Society course covers all aspects of the media with modules in radio and TV production. **Lancaster** The course in Culture, Media and Communication is largely theoretical with such topics as anthropology, language, visual representation, media and marketing. **London (Gold)** The media element of the course involves TV, radio, journalism, video graphics and animation, photography, creative and script writing. **Warwick** Film and Television Studies covers history, Hollywood and the silent cinema and TV studies. *NOW CHECK PROSPECTUSES AND WEB SITES.*

Top universities and colleges (Teaching Quality) (see Ch.4): Bournemouth; Bristol UWE; Brunel; Central England; Central Lancashire; Chichester (UC); City; East Anglia; Glamorgan; Glasgow Caledonian; Leeds; Liverpool John Moores; London (Gold); Luton; Napier; Northampton (UC); Nottingham Trent; Oxford Brookes; Sunderland; Ulster; Wolverhampton; not all institutions assessed. See also **Communications Studies**.

Top universities and colleges (Research) (see Ch.4): (including Communication and Cultural Studies) Birmingham; Bristol UWE; East Anglia; East London; London (Gold), (RH); Stirling; Sussex; Warwick; Westminster.

Study opportunities abroad: Central England; City; Liverpool John Moores; Middlesex; Plymouth; Staffordshire; Stirling; Ulster.

Work opportunities abroad: Bournemouth; Bradford; City; Farnborough (CT); Plymouth.

ADMISSIONS INFORMATION

Number of applicants per place (approx): Birmingham 57; Bournemouth (Media Prod) 24, (Journal) 30; Bradford 13; Bristol UWE 20; Canterbury Christ Church (CHE) 23; Cardiff 10; Central Lancashire 33; Cheltenham & Glos (CHE) 25; City 50; De Montfort 50; East London 27; Greenwich 12; Lincolnshire & Humberside 4; London (Gold) 13, (RH) 11; Newport (UWCN) 12; Northumbria 14; Nottingham Trent 50; Paisley 6; St Mark & St John (Coll) 33; Sheffield Hallam 56; South Bank 11; Southampton (Inst) (Journal) 20, (Media Tech) 6; Staffordshire 13; Surrey (IAD/UC) 3; Swansea (IHE) 5; Teesside 33; Warrington (CI) 25; Westminster 44.

Planning your UCAS personal statement (see Ch.4): Work experience/shadowing is important. Contact local newspaper offices to meet journalists and to discuss their work. Contact local radio stations and advertising agencies, read newspapers (all types) and be able to describe the different approaches of newspapers. Watch TV coverage of news stories and the way in which the interviewer deals with politicians or members of the public. Give your opinions on the various forms of media. School magazine and/or any published work should be mentioned. **Nottingham Trent** (Broad Journal) Some experience of journalism. See also **Communications Studies**. See also **Appendix 1**.

Selection interviews (see Ch.4): Bournemouth (W); Brunel; Cardiff (some); City (T); East Anglia; Glamorgan; Huddersfield; Liverpool John Moores; London (Gold), (RH); Nottingham Trent (No); Portsmouth (W) (T); St Mark & St John (Coll) (W); St Martin (UC); Sheffield Hallam; Solihull (Coll) (W); South Bank (W); Staffordshire (No); Surrey (IAD/UC); Swansea (IHE); Thames Valley; Warrington (CI) (No); most institutions interview some applicants.

Interview questions (see Ch.4): Which newspapers do you read? Discuss the main differences between the national daily newspapers. Which radio programmes do you listen to each day? Which television programmes do you watch? Why do you think that ITV needs to spend £2 million advertising itself? Should the BBC broadcast advertisements? What do you think are the reasons for the popularity of *East Enders*? **Bournemouth** 250 word essay. **City** Spelling, punctuation, grammar, general knowledge tests and an essay assignment.

Reasons for rejection (non-academic): No clear commitment (to broadcast journalism) plus no evidence of experience (now proving to be essential). Mistaken expectations of the nature of the course. Can't write and doesn't work well in groups. Too specific and narrow areas of media interest, for example, video or script-writing. Lack of knowledge of current affairs. **Nottingham Trent** (Broad Journal) Voice quality.

GAP YEAR ADVICE

Most institutions will accept a gap year except City and Westminster. Work experience in the media is very useful (see above).

Institutions willing to defer entry after A-Levels: Birmingham; Bournemouth; Central Lancashire; Cheltenham & Glos (CHE); City (No); De Montfort; East London (No); Farnborough (CT); Leeds; Lincolnshire & Humberside; London (RH); Luton; Napier; Northumbria (No); Nottingham Trent; Plymouth; Staffordshire; Sussex; Warrington (CI); Westminster (Contemp Media Prac).

AFTER RESULTS ADVICE

Institutions which may accept the same points score after A-Levels: Bradford (No); Central England (No); Central Lancashire; De Montfort; South Bank.

Probable vacancies from June 2001 and in Clearing (see Ch.4): Vacancies are likely in Media Studies and Media Production courses at many universities and colleges.

NEW GRADUATE DESTINATIONS AND EMPLOYMENT (1999 HESA) (see **Ch.4**)

Of 1072 Media Studies graduates surveyed, 709 entered full-time employment, 88 went on to further study and 75 were believed to be unemployed. In addition, a survey of 374 Journalism graduates revealed that 278 had entered permanent employment, 16 went on to further study and 14 were seeking full-time employment six months after graduation.

MEDICINE (see also Medical Sciences under **Health Sciences/Studies**)

NB The information supplied by the universities and colleges this year varies considerably and the offers listed below should be used as a first source of reference only. Many institutions will accept combinations of Advanced (AL), Advanced Subsidiary (AS) and Vocational Advanced (VA) level qualifications to achieve the required points total, but applicants must check web sites and prospectuses for full details of all offers. Grades and points totals shown should be regarded as the minimum levels to be achieved, but offers may be adjusted downwards when results are known. The points totals shown to the left of the institutions are for ease of reference only. It must not be assumed that tariff points are always used by institutions or that they can be substituted for an offer in grades. The level of an offer is not necessarily indicative of the quality of a course. To calculate your offers see Chapter 4 and the inside fold of the back cover.

Applicants for places in Medicine may select only four universities or medical schools.

Special subject requirements/preferences: The A/AS-Level and GCSE requirements are given for each medical school (see below). Two AS-Levels are usually acceptable instead of one A-Level, with AS chemistry accepted by some medical schools; general studies is not normally acceptable as an A-Level subject. Applicants wishing to offer art or music as a third A-Level should contact the medical school of choice. If biology or physics or mathematics are not offered at A-Level then a high grade is normally required in the appropriate subject at AS-Level (or in the double science paper) in the GCSE. **London Medical Schools** The minimumn GCSE requirement is grade B in English, mathematics and biology, double award or combined science and in some schools, physics. Normally grade B is also expected in other subjects.

360 pts   and above

Belfast (Queen's) – AAA–AAB (Medicine) (**A-Level** chem+2 from biol (rcmd) phys or maths or 1 other subj; **GCSE** biol, phys, maths, dsci if not at A-Level)

Cambridge – AAA (Med Sci) (**MVAT; A-Level** min chem + 1 from biol, phys or maths; **GCSE** grade A most subjs)

Cardiff (UWCM) – 370 pts 21u – ABB+b **or** AAB+d **or** AAA+e **or** VA12uAA+AL(A)+AS/ks; (not gs) (Medicine) (**A-Level** chem + 1 from biol (pref) or phys + sci, or non-sci subj if biol or phys or dsci passed at GCSE or AS-Level; **GCSE** normally 5 As or A*s, dsci at grades AA or 3 sci subjs grades AAB, Engl or Welsh grade A + maths grade B)

Durham – (new Medical School with Newcastle) ABB+b (Medicine) (offers to be confirmed) (**A-Level** chem or biol reqd; **AS** grade a chem/biol)

Edinburgh – AAA+b **or** AAB+a; VAs contact dept; (not gs) (Medicine) (**A-Level** chem + 2 from biol, phys or maths (biol at least at AS biol); **GCSE** chem, biol (or dsci) maths, Engl, for lang – all at grade B)

Leeds – 390 pts – AAB+b **or** AA+bbb **or** AB+aab; (Medicine) (**A-Level** chem +1 subj; **GCSE** biol, phys, maths grade B min if not offered at A-Level)

Liverpool – 390 pts – ALs **or** ALs+ASs **or** VAs+/-ALs/ASs; (Medicine) (**A-Level** chem +1 or 2 from biol, maths, phys, zool or 1 non-sci subj; **GCSE** 6 subjs inc Engl and maths grades A*, A or B)

London (Imp) – 390 pts – AAB+a **or** AAB+b **or** ABB; (not gs) (Medicine) (**A-Level** chem or phys sci + 1–2 subjs or 1 non-sci subj; **GCSE** see above)

London (King's) – 370 pts – ABB+b **or** AB+aaa (Medicine; Nat Sci Fdn) (**A-Level** chem+biol (1 at AS but not for Nat Sci course); **GCSE** see above)

London (QM) – AAAB **or** 3ALs+AS (inc 2ALs inc sci+chem/biol or with chem/biol AS min b); (Medicine) (**A-Level** chem + 1 sci subj, biol pref; **AS-Level** grade b in chem or biol if not at A-Level; **GCSE** see above)

London (St George's HMS) – AAA–ABB (Medicine) (**A-Level** chem + biol min; **AS-Level** chem or biol grade a, other subjs grade b (not gs); **GCSE** see above)

Manchester – 360 pts – ABB+c **or** ABB; (not gs) (Medicine) (**A-Level** chem + at least 1 from biol, phys or maths; **GCSE** 6 subjs grade A or A* (pref), biol, phys grade B min if not offered at A/AS-Level)

Oxford – AAA–AAB **or** AA+ab; (not gs) (Medicine) (**A-Level** Full A-Levels expected in chem, with maths or biol or phys, hum subj considered at A or AS-Level; **GCSE** grade A in most subjs, biol, phys, or dsci + maths if not at A-Level)

Southampton – 370 pts 21u – ABB **or** ABB+b; (not gs) (Medicine) (**A-Level** chem + 2 subjs; **GCSE** 7 subjs at A*, A or B)

340 pts   **Birmingham** – AAB (Medicine) (**A-Level** chem + 2 from biol, phys or maths or 1 non-sci subj, hum biol or zool accepted but not with biol; **GCSE** mainly grade As, some A*s and none less than grade C, Engl grade B, biol, phys, maths grade A if not at A-Level)

Bristol – AAB (inc chem for A106 or non-sci subjs for A104); (not gs) (Medicine) (**A-Level** chem + 2 apprv subjs which can incl 1 non-sci subj; **GCSE** 6 subjs at grade A or A*)

Dundee – AAB (Medicine pre-med yr) (**A-Level** usually non-sci subjs, 1 sci acceptable)

East Anglia – (new Medical School – first entry 2002; (Medicine) (application details and offers to be confirmed)

Glasgow – AAB; (not gs) (Medicine) (**A-Level** chem + biol, phys or maths min; **GCSE** biol, phys or maths (rcmd) if not offered at A-Level)

Keele – (new Medical School) AAB (inc chem) (Medicine) (offers to be confirmed) (**AS** grade accepted chem/biol) (subj reqs see Manchester)

Leicester Warwick – (new combined Medical School – first entry 2002); AAB **or** VA12u AB+AL (A chem); (not gs) (Medicine) (**A-Level** chem + 1 sci + 1 sci, arts or soc sci subj)

London (UCL) – AAB–ABB **or** 3ALs+AS/VA; (not gs) (Medicine) (**A-Level** 3 subjs inc chem at grade A or AS-Level; **GCSE** see above)

Newcastle – AAB; (not gs) (Medicine) (**A-Level** chem or biol or hum biol; **GCSE** grades AAAAB inc Engl lang, maths, biol, chem, phys, dsci grade A)

Nottingham – 340 pts – AAB; (not gs) (Medicine) (**A-Level** chem, biol + 1 approv academic subj; **GCSE** 6 subjs grade A or A*)

Exeter Plymouth (Peninsular Medical School) – (new Medical School) 340 pts – AAB (inc 120 pts chem or IB 36 pts inc 6 H chem) (Medicine) (**A-Level** chem+sci; **GCSE** 7 subjs inc grade A/B inc Engl, maths, biol (unless AL biol offered)

320 pts   **Aberdeen** – ABB (Medicine) (**A-Level** chem + 2 from biol, phys or maths or non-sci subj)

Barnsley (Coll)/Sheffield – 320 pts (Fdn Medicine)

Dundee – ABB (Medicine) (**A-Level** (min) chem + 1 other sci subj – hum biol or soc biol accepted as an alt to biol)

St Andrews – ABB (Medicine) (**A-Level** chem + phys or maths; **GCSE** grades A*, A or B)

Sheffield – ABB (Medicine) (**A-Level** chem + 1 from biol, phys or maths; **GCSE** 4 subjs grades A* or A min)

Alternative Offers:

EB offers: Cardiff (UWCM) 77%; Glasgow 80%; London (King's) overall 80% + 80% in each sci option); Sheffield 80%.

IB offers: Aberdeen 36, pts average of 6 at Higher and Subsid; Belfast (Queen's) 35 pts H766 S555; Birmingham 36 pts; Bristol 34 pts inc H766; Cambridge 36 pts approx; Cardiff (UWCM) 34 pts H6 chem; Dundee 34 pts H766; Edinburgh 37 pts inc H766; Glasgow 36 pts average of grade 6 but not less than 6 in chem; Leeds 36 pts inc H666; Leicester 34 pts inc H666 S666; Liverpool 36 pts H666; London (Imp) chem H6+55 S555, (King's) 35 pts H665, (QM) 34 pts H666, (St George's HMS) H665 32 pts overall, (UCL) 36 pts H766; Manchester 34 pts; Newcastle 35 pts; Nottingham 32 pts H666; Oxford 36 pts; St Andrews 36–34 pts; Sheffield 33 pts H666 S555; Southampton 33 pts H666.

Irish offers: Birmingham AAAAB; Cardiff (UWCM) AAAABB; Glasgow AAABBB; London (King's) not acceptable; St Andrews AAABB; Sheffield ABBBBB.

Scottish Qualifications: Aberdeen AAAAB; Dundee AAAAB; Edinburgh AAAAB; Glasgow AAAAB; St Andrews AAABB.

CHOOSING YOUR COURSE (See also **Ch.1**)

Subject information: All courses offer the same components leading to a qualification and career in medicine. Many medical schools are moving away from an emphasis on lectures and factual learning to a system based on acquiring appropriate skills and understanding as well as knowledge. This system is referred to as the 'New Curriculum' which introduces communication, problem-solving and more directed self-learning. Whilst there is a core curriculum of knowledge, the first three years integrate scientific and clinical experience, and there are fewer formal lectures than before and more group and individual work. For outstanding students without science A-Levels, some pre–medical courses are available. Thereafter for all, a period of pre–clinical studies leads on to clinical studies. Intercalated courses of one year leading to a BSc are also offered and elective periods abroad in the final years can sometimes be taken. All courses are very similar in course content. Other courses in the medical field include Dentistry, Nursing, Pharmacy and Pharmacology, Biological Sciences, Microbiology, Genetics, Anatomy, Physiology, Medical Sciences (a branch of biological science), Physiotherapy, Occupational Therapy, Osteopathy, Chiropractic and Radiography. See also **Appendix 1**.

Top universities and colleges (Teaching Quality) (see Ch.4): Excellent Aberdeen; Cardiff; Dundee; Edinburgh; Glasgow; Leicester; Manchester; St Andrews; not all Medical Schools assessed.

Top universities and colleges (Research) (see Ch.4): Birmingham; Bristol; Cambridge; Cardiff (UWCM); London (King's), (St George's HMS); Newcastle; Nottingham; Oxford; Southampton.

Study opportunities abroad: Bristol; Cardiff (UWCM); Leeds; Leicester; Liverpool; Manchester; short elective periods abroad are available in most medical schools.

Work opportunities abroad: Bristol; Edinburgh. All students have an elective period in the final clinical year which the majority spend abroad (most medical schools operate similar arrangements).

ADMISSIONS INFORMATION

Attitudes towards overseas (non–EU) applicants: Aberdeen 12 places available. **Aberdeen, Cardiff (UWCM), Glasgow, Nottingham** Preference given to applicants from countries unable to provide a medical training. **Bristol** Encourages overseas applicants; 12 places available. **Cardiff** 14 places available. No offers without interview. English language qualification required. **Edinburgh** Will normally only consider applicants who present A-Levels or IB; 10 places available. **Glasgow** Limited number of places. **Leeds** 15 places available. Overseas students re-sitting are not usually considered. **London (King's)** 12 places approx available. **London (St George's HMS)** 6 places available; preference for applicants from countries with inadequate facilities for training in Medicine. **London (Imp)** 5 places available. Preference given to those from countries

unable to offer a medical education. **Nottingham** 15 places available. **Southampton** 12 places available.

Number of applicants per place (approx): Aberdeen 6; Belfast (Queen's) 5; Birmingham 11; Bristol 15; Cambridge 4; Cardiff (UWCM) 14; Dundee 8, (pre-med) 17; Edinburgh 9, (6 yr course) 40; Glasgow 4; Leeds 15; Leicester 14; Liverpool 9; London (Imp) 21, (King's) 21, (QM) 12, (St George's HMS) 14; Manchester 9; Newcastle 10, (pre-med) 27; Nottingham 15; Oxford 5; St Andrews 8; Sheffield 15; Southampton 15. **Foreign applicants:** Aberdeen 15; Birmingham 21; Cardiff (UWCM) 16; Edinburgh no quota; Leeds 25; London (King's) 15, (UCL) 27; Newcastle 14; Nottingham 15; Southampton 15.

Age at entry: The minimum age for entry is usually 18 on 30 September, although some medical schools will accept 17 yrs 6 mths, and one or two 17 yrs although these (exceptional) students would probably be advised to take a gap year. Cambridge, Edinburgh (minimum age 17.6 yrs on 30 September of year of entry). Leeds minimum age at entry 17 yrs. London University regulations state 17 yrs. Check with medical schools.

Admissions Tutors' advice: Bristol Nine places available on the pre-medical course. **Cambridge** All applicants must take the Medical and Veterinary Admissions Test (MVAT), see **Chapter 3** under **Admissions to Cambridge University. Cardiff (UWCM)** Integrated course; great emphasis placed on applicant's evidence of a caring nature, of exposure to the hospital/medical environment (for example, voluntary work in hospitals or residential homes). Considers applicants with two science A–levels (including chemistry) and one other A-Level provided they have good science background at GCSE or AS-Level. **Glasgow** It is sometimes assumed that all candidates must meet the 'going rate' at the first attempt. In fact, if a candidate just misses, s/he may be allowed to come on the basis of re–sits, although s/he would be expected to pass at the 'going rate'. English candidates wrongly assume that Glasgow is biased against anyone not from the west of Scotland. **Leeds** Consider your motivation carefully – we do. We look for evidence of it, together with broadly-ranging interests and academic capacity. Decisions made at any time between November and March. Applications cannot be considered from applicants who have commenced another degree course. **London (Imp)** We look for resourceful men and women with wide interests and accomplishments, practical concern for others and those who will make a contribution to the life of school and hospital. Academic ability, motivation, character and depth of interests are all assessed. **London (King's)** Referee's assessment, academic ability, work experience which demonstrates a commitment to a caring profession, and other outside interests are all taken into account when deciding which applicants are called for interview. There are approximately 300 applications each year for the Foundation course in Natural Sciences/Medicine, 10 places are available. We operate an equal opportunities policy for student admissions and welcome applications from enterprising and well-motivated candidates from a wide variety of backgrounds. Academic ability, personal qualities, interests and accomplishments all taken into account when selecting candidates for interview. Prospective students very welcome to attend annual Open Days in May. We admit the largest number of medical and dental students in London, and the innovative courses emphasise development of communication skills, early contact with patients, flexibility of study and self-directed learning. **Newcastle** The typical A-Level requirement is AAB including chemistry or biology/human biology but excluding general studies. We accept two AS-Levels in place of one A-Level. Candidates are also required to have AAAAB at GCSE including English language, mathematics, biology, chemistry and physics (or dual award science at grade A). Candidates with Scottish qualifications are typically asked for AAAAB at Higher Grade including chemistry or biology at grade A as well as English language and mathematics. The Pre-medical programme is designed for students who do not possess the prerequisite scientific background for Stage 1 entry. We have 14 overseas places available at Newcastle ewach year and overseas students form approximately five per cent of the student body. **St Andrews** Linked to the medical programme at Manchester University with guaranteed place. **Sheffield** Students without A or AS physics take short course in medical physics in first year.

Planning your UCAS form and personal statement (see Ch.4): See also **Admissions Tutors' advice**. Four medical choices only may be listed on the UCAS form, which must

Understanding How To Make The New Medicines — 5th/6th UCAS Choices

The discovery of penicillin was a momentous achievement. However, it took 15 years and an international effort to find a way to produce it in the quantities needed for medical treatment. The subsequent realisation of the lives lost as a result of this delay from discovery to availability set the scene for the birth of the discipline of biochemical engineering.

The medicines of the future — human proteins, therapeutic vaccines, human cells and tissue for repair — are vastly more complex than penicillin. Even the new, small molecule medicines have a far higher degree of complexity. The challenges to biochemical engineers in understanding how to bring the new discoveries to fruition have therefore never been greater, nor the prospects more exciting.

All who apply for a medical place through UCAS are asked to choose additional fifth and sixth places in other fields. Those seeking a professionally recognised qualification in a subject that is demanding, and who want a life at the cutting edge that is highly rewarded, should consider the excitement of biochemical engineering as a degree option.

Details of courses can be found in UCAS guides, or on the web and visits can be arranged to explore in more detail the A level requirements, the courses and the careers available.

be submitted by 15 October. Admissions tutors obviously look for certain personal qualities and these will emerge in your personal statement, at the interview and on your school or college reference. There should be evidence of scientific interest, commitment, enthusiasm, determination, stability, self-motivation, ability to organise your own work, interest in the welfare of others, communication skills, modesty (arrogance and over-confidence could lead to rejection!), breadth of interest, leadership skills, stamina, good physical and mental health. Medical schools require all students to have their immunity status for Hepatitis B, tuberculosis and rubella checked on entry. All offers are usually made subject to satisfactory health screening for Hepatitis B. In line with advice from the General Medical Council, students will not be admitted to courses who are found to be e-antigen positive when screened within the first week of the course. Candidates accepting offers should assure themselves of their immunity status.

Some kind of first-hand experience in a medical setting is almost obligatory for those applying for Medicine, actual practice and experience of caring being important factors. Depending on your personal contacts in the medical profession, this could include observing operations (for example, orthopaedic surgery) working in hospitals and discussing the career with your GP. You should also remember that the elderly, people with learning difficulties or who are blind or deaf may also present medical conditions, and any social visits you do in this context, or visits to old people's homes could also be described. Read medical and scientific magazines and keep up-to-date with important current issues, for example, AIDS, euthanasia, abortion. Community work, clubs, societies, school and social activities should be mentioned. Show that you have an understanding of the role of health professionals in society and the social factors which influence health and disease. All institutions seek some evidence of motivation in candidates applying for medical training. The following medical schools say that they make a conscious effort to assess this quality, and in some cases, will 'test' it: Aberdeen; Birmingham; Bristol; Cambridge; Edinburgh; Glasgow; Leeds; Liverpool, London (Imp), (King's), (QM), (St George's HMS), (UCL); Newcastle; Nottingham; Oxford; Sheffield. **Cardiff (UWCM)** Evidence of, and potential for, high academic achievement, a caring and commited attitude towards people, an understanding of the demands of medical training and practice; the ability to communicate effectively, a willingness to accept responsibility; evidence of broad, social, cultural or sporting interests. **Edinburgh** Describe plans if applying for deferred entry. **London (St George's HMS)** Did they use their own initiative in organising work experience? How have they benefited from it? See also **Appendix 1**.

Selection interviews (see Ch.4): Most medical schools will shortlist a percentage of their applicants for interview. **Birmingham** Performance at interview is very important. No offers are made without an interview. **Bristol** 70% of those interviewed receive offers. **Cambridge** A short exercise or set of problems are set before interview, which may be used as a basis of discussion. **Dundee** Does not usually interview. **Edinburgh** Unusual to interview – special cases and short-listed graduates. **Leeds** 20% of all applicants interviewed. **London (King's)** No offers are made without interview. **London (St George's HMS)** (W) Short essay on understanding of medicine as a career plus a questionnaire. **Oxford** (T) short written test but 50% are interviewed by admissions tutors seeking evidence of initiative, breadth, dedication, compassion and good communication skills. **St Andrews** No interviews; **Southampton** No interviews for school leavers.

Interview questions (see Ch.4): Questions will vary considerably and may focus on the applicant's A/AS-Level choice of subjects, their work experience, the medical activities they have experienced and medical issues in the news. The following questions which have been asked in recent years provide a good example of the variety of topics: Should doctors be allowed to test patients for AIDS without their consent? What can you do with a brick? Why do you want to study Medicine? What qualities are needed to be a good doctor? What qualities would your friends say that you possess? Do you agree with the concept of Trust Hospitals? Would you treat lung cancer patients who refuse to give up smoking? What do you understand by 'gene therapy'? Can you give any examples? Should we pay for donor organs? What area of medicine is of special interest to you? What are your views on vivisection? Why should we offer you a place rather than giving it to another candidate? What are your views on private and NHS medicine? How is rejection prevented in transplants? How do they choose a transplant donor? Are heart transplants worth the money? What advance in medicine has impressed you the most? What does an ECG measure? How does the heart work? Are doctors paid well? What satisfaction do you think a GP gets from his/her work? Do you think your lifestyle will be affected by the course? What will you do if you fail to get into Medicine? If you were Health Secretary what changes would you make? What are your views on euthanasia? What has been the most important advance in biology in the last 50 years? What was the last non-technical book you read? What is your favourite piece of classical music and why?

Reasons for rejection (non-academic): Insufficient vocation demonstrated. No steps taken to gain practical experience relevant to medicine. Doubts as to the ability to cope with the stress of a medical career. Inability to communicate effectively. Not enough awareness about the career. Lack of knowledge about the course. Applicant appears dull and lacking in enthusiasm and motivation. Lacking in a caring, committed attitude towards people. No evidence of broad social, cultural, sporting interests or teamwork. Poor communication skills. Uncaring attitude. Arrogance.

GAP YEAR ADVICE

Most institutions are willing to accept a gap year.

Institutions willing to defer entry after A-Levels: Aberdeen (only in exceptional circumstances); Birmingham; Cardiff; Dundee (No); Edinburgh; Leeds; London (St George's HMS), (UCL) (No); Manchester; Sheffield; Southampton (No).

Attitude towards a year out: *Acceptable:* Birmingham; Bristol; Cardiff (UWCM); Dundee; Leicester; Liverpool; London (Imp), (QM), *Acceptable for positive reasons:* Cambridge; Edinburgh; Glasgow; Liverpool; London (King's); Manchester; Nottingham (constructive experience expected, eg travel or work in a medical field); Oxford; St Andrews; Sheffield. *Not encouraged:* Aberdeen; Newcastle.

AFTER RESULTS ADVICE

Medical schools policies on the same points score after A-Levels: Aberdeen (No); Birmingham (possibly); Bristol (No); Cardiff (UWCM) (No); Dundee (No); Edinburgh (perhaps); Glasgow (No); Leeds (No); Leicester (in special circumstances); Liverpool; London (Imp) (E grades not acceptable), (King's) (No), (QM) (every candidate failing to meet exact offer automatically reconsidered to see if strengths likely to balance weaknesses), (St George's HMS) (ABD only), (UCL) (No); Manchester (No); Newcastle (No); Nottingham (No); Sheffield (possibly); Southampton (No).

Medical Schools which may accept under–achieving applicants after A-Levels: Aberdeen (No); Birmingham; Cardiff (UWCM) not usually, only for very good interviewees if place available; Dundee (No); Edinburgh (in special circumstances); Glasgow; Leeds (No); Leicester (rarely); London (King's), (QM), (St George's HMS) only in exceptional non–academic circumstances, (UCL); Manchester (No); St Andrews; Sheffield and Southampton (only in special circumstances).

Attitudes towards applicants repeating A-Levels: Those wishing to re-apply should be aware that because of the very large number of applicants for medicine, places are scarce and in the majority of cases preference will be given to first-time applicants who achieve the required grades and who impress at interview. Some medical schools will stipulate a minimum grade achievement at the first sitting (probably BBB) and others will consider candidates who applied the previous year. The following medical schools will only consider those who failed to achieve the required grades due to exceptional circumstances, for example bereavement, illness (documentary evidence will be required): Birmingham; Bristol; Cambridge; Cardiff; Dundee; Edinburgh; Leeds; London (Imp), (King's), (QM); St Andrews, Southampton. (Check with medical schools before applying.)

Attitudes towards second applications to the same Medical Schools (check before applying): *Acceptable:* Bristol (ABB grades); Cardiff (UWCM); London (St George's HMS); Manchester.

Probable vacancies from June 2000 and in Clearing (see Ch.4): No vacancies are advertised. Students with very high grades (AAA–AAB) and no offers should telephone medical schools to which they originally applied.

ADVICE FOR MATURE STUDENTS

Medical schools usually accept a small number of mature students each year. However, several, if not the majority, reject applicants over 30 years of age. Some medical schools accept non-graduates although A-level passes at high grades are usually stipulated. The majority of applicants accepted are likely to be graduates with a first or upper second Honours degree. **Birmingham, Bristol, Leeds** Maximum age at entry is 30 years. **Leeds** Applicants to hold the required A-Level grades or a high class science degree; 15–20 places.

Percentage of mature students: Cardiff (UWCM) 5 (12 places available); Leeds 10; Leicester 10; Manchester 10; Sheffield 10.

NEW GRADUATE DESTINATIONS AND EMPLOYMENT (1999 HESA) (see **Ch.4**)

In a survey of 3538 graduates, 3498 went into full-time employment, 14 went into research, and four were reported to be unemployed.

MICROBIOLOGY (see also **Biological Sciences** and **Biology**)

NB The information supplied by the universities and colleges this year varies considerably and the offers listed below should be used as a first source of reference only. Many institutions will accept combinations of Advanced (AL), Advanced Subsidiary (AS) and Vocational Advanced (VA) level qualifications to achieve the required points total, but applicants must check web sites and prospectuses for full details of all offers. Grades and points totals shown should be regarded as the minimum levels to be achieved, but offers may be adjusted downwards when results are known. The points totals shown to the left of the institutions are for ease of reference only. It must not be assumed that tariff points are always used by institutions or that they can be substituted for an offer in grades. The level of an offer is not necessarily indicative of the quality of a course. To calculate your offers see Chapter 4 and the inside fold of the back cover.

Special subject requirements/preferences: A-Level: Chemistry and one or two other science subjects. **GCSE:** English and mathematics; **Leicester** English, mathematics and chemistry at grade A–C if not at A/AS-Level. **Newcastle** Five subjects at grade A, five at grade B or C. **Surrey** Grade A in chemistry or combined science if not offered with A-Levels.

320 pts **Liverpool** – 320–280 pts – ALs **or** ALs+ASs **or** VAs+/-ALs/ASs; (Microbiol; Microbial Biotech)
      London (Imp) – ABB (Microbiol; Biol/Microbiol)
300 pts **Bristol** – BBB (inc chem+sci) **or** BB+bbb(AL chem/biol/maths); (not gs) (Microbiol; Vet – Pathogen)
      Cardiff – BBB–BBC (Microbiology)
      Leeds – 18u – BBB; gs (AL only); (Microbiol/Immun)
      London (QM) – 300–260 pts (Microbiol/Bioch; Microbiol/Genet)
280 pts **Birmingham** – BBC–BCC (Microbiol courses)
      Edinburgh – BBC (Med Microbiol; Microbiol; Virol)
      Glasgow – BBC–CCC/BB–BC (Microbiol; Virol)
      Kent – 280–240 pts 21–18u – BBC–CCC **or** BC–CC+AS; gs; (Microbiology)
      Leeds – 18u – BBC; gs (AL only) (Med Microbiol; Microbiol)
      Leicester – 18u – BBC **or** BB+2ASs **or** VA12u+AL; gs (as 3rd AL); (Microbiology)
      London (King's) – BBC+AS **or** BB+bc (inc B chem+sci) **or** VA12u BB+AL (C chem)+AS; (Microbiol courses)

Manchester – BBC (Microbiol; Microbiol/Biotech; Microbiol/Ind Exp; Microbiol/Modn Lang)

Sheffield – BBC (Microbiol/Bioch; Microbiol/Genet; Microbiol)

Strathclyde – BBC (Microbiol/Bioch; Microbiol/Immun)

260 pts **East Anglia** – BCC/BB (Microbiology)

Hertfordshire – 260–220 pts 1x12u **or** 2x6u – ALs **or** AL+2ASs **or** VA12u; gs; (Microbiology)

Lancaster – BCC (Bioch/Microbiol)

Newcastle – BCC (Microbiol; Med Microbiol)

Reading – 260 pts (Microbiology)

Surrey – BCC–CCC (Med Microbiol; Fd Sci/Microbiol; Mol Microbiol; Microbiol (Biotech))

Warwick – BCC (Microbiol/Virol)

240 pts **Aberystwyth** – 240 pts 21u – CCC **or** CC+cc **or** VAs; gs; (Microbiology)

Belfast (Queen's) – CCC/BB (Microbiology)

Heriot-Watt – 240 pts 18u – CCC; gs; (Microbiology)

Huddersfield – 240–160 pts approx (Microbiol Sci)

Nottingham – BCC–CCC; (not gs) (Microbiology)

Plymouth – CCC (Microbiol/Mar Biol)

Staffordshire – 240–180 pts approx (App Microbiol; Microbiol/Bioch)

220 pts **Aberdeen** – CCD (Microbiol courses)

Bradford – 220 pts 12u (inc AL biol/chem); gs; (Med Microbiol)

Bristol UWE – 220–180 pts 12u (6u sci subj) – ALs **or** ALs+ASs **or** VAs+/- ALs/ASs (chem reqd); (App Microbiol)

Central Lancashire – 220 pts 12u (inc AL chem+sci); gs; (App Microbiol/ Bus)

Wolverhampton – 220–160 pts 12u – DDD–DDE/CC **or** CC+dd/de **or** VA12u CC; gs; (Microbiology)

200 pts **Central Lancashire** – 200–180 pts 12u (inc AL chem+sci); gs; (App Microbiol/ Env Mgt/Fr/Ger)

Dundee – 200 pts approx (Microbiology)

Portsmouth – 200 pts – ALs **or** ALs+ASs **or** VAs; gs; (App Microbiol)

180 pts **East London** – 180 pts approx (Microbiology)

Heriot–Watt – DDD (1st yr entry) CCC (2nd yr entry) (Microbiology)

Lincolnshire & Humberside – 180 pts (App Microbiol)

Liverpool John Moores – 180–120 pts (inc AL biol/chem) – ALs **or** ALs+ASs **or** VAs+/-ALs/ASs; (App Microbiol)

Sunderland – 180 pts approx (App Microbiol; Immun/Med Microbiol)

Teesside – 180–160 pts approx (Microbiology)

160 pts **Anglia** – 160 pts approx (Microbiology)

Central Lancashire – 160 pts 12u (inc AL biol/chem/env sci); gs; (Microbiology)

Huddersfield – 160 pts 12u; gs; (Microbiol Sci)

Nottingham Trent – 160 pts approx (Microbiol/Bioch; Fd Sfty Mgt)

Plymouth – CC (Microbiol/Chem; Microbiol/Maths)

Westminster – CC (Bioch/Microbiol; Microbiol)

140 pts **Napier** – CD (App Microbiol/Biotech)

South Bank – DEE/DD (Microbiology)

Sunderland – 140 pts approx (Microbiol Hum Res Mgt)

120 pts **and below**

Nescot – DD–EE (Microbiology)

North London – 120 pts 1x12u **or** 2x6u; (Microbiol courses)

Paisley – DD (Microbiol/Immun; Microbiol/Bioch)

Staffordshire – EE (Ext Bioch/Microbiol)

Higher National Diploma courses

Hertfordshire; Truro (Coll).

Alternative Offers:

EB offers: Bradford 65%; East Anglia 70%; Nottingham 60% (sci).

IB offers: Aberdeen 26 pts; Aberystwyth 28 pts and above; Birmingham 30 pts; Bradford 24 pts, 5 pts min in biol, chem, maths; Bristol 32–30 pts with 5 or 6 in relevant subjects; Cardiff 30 pts; Glasgow H555; Heriot–Watt 28 pts; Hertfordshire 24 pts; Leeds 26 pts; Leicester 30 pts; Liverpool 30 pts inc H555; Newcastle 26 pts inc 5 chem; Nottingham 24 pts (sci); Surrey 32 pts H55 biol/chem; Swansea 28 pts; Warwick 30–28 pts.

Irish offers: Aberdeen BBCC/BCCCC; Aberystwyth BBBCC; Bradford BBBB; East Anglia BBBCCC; Glasgow BBB; Leeds BBBCC; Liverpool BBCCC; Nottingham CCCCC1; Warwick BBBBB.

Scottish Qualifications: Aberdeen BBBC; Dundee BBCC; Edinburgh BBBB; Glasgow BBBB; Heriot–Watt BBB; Napier BCC; Nottingham BBBB (first sitting); Paisley BBC; Strathclyde BBC.

CHOOSING YOUR COURSE (See also **Ch.1**)

Subject information: Microbiology is a branch of biological science specialising in a study of micro–organisms: bacteria, viruses and fungi. The subject covers the relationship between these organisms and disease and such industrial applications as food and drug production, waste-water treatment as well as future biochemical uses. Other courses for consideration include Genetics, Biochemistry, Biology and Physiology. See also **Appendix 1**.

Special features: Bradford Broad-based course in first and second years in subjects allied to medicine. Optional year out in industry. Final year specialisation. **Bristol** Second year course units cover medical and food bacteriology. Strong research areas in genetics and virology. Close collaboration with Pathology course with shared options and possibility of transfer. Transfer available to four-year course with year of study in industry. **Cardiff** Seven degrees in biological sciences. Common first year. Free choice of specialisation in second year. Sandwich placement option. **Heriot-Watt** Transfer between courses possible. Specialist options from other related biological areas. **Kent** Specialisation possible in microbiology with biotechnology or cell biology or medical biosciences. **Newcastle** Six half-units taken in first year subjects then degree subjects chosen for entry to second year. **Nottingham** Opportunity to carry out major research project. **Swansea** Specialisation possible in aquatic microbiology, genetic engineering of micro-organisms, biotechnology and immunology. **Warwick** Common first year in Biological Sciences. *NOW CHECK PROSPECTUSES AND WEB SITES.*

Top universities and colleges (Teaching Quality) (see Ch.4): See **Biology**.

Top universities and colleges (Research) (see Ch.4): See **Biological Sciences**.

Study opportunities abroad: Aberystwyth; Birmingham; Heriot-Watt; Kent; Leeds; Leicester; Manchester; Napier; Nottingham; Sheffield; Staffordshire; Surrey; Swansea.

Work opportunities abroad: Aberystwyth; East London; Hertfordshire; Leeds; Liverpool John Moores; Napier; Staffordshire; Surrey.

ADMISSIONS INFORMATION

Number of applicants per place (approx): Aberystwyth 11; Bradford 6; Bristol 10; Cardiff 4; East London 2; Hertfordshire 10; Kent 9; Leeds 7; Liverpool 3; Newcastle 6; Strathclyde 10; Surrey 6; Swansea 5.

Planning your UCAS personal statement (see Ch.4): Relevant experience, particularly for mature students. See **Biological Sciences**. See also **Appendix 1**.

Selection interviews (see Ch.4): Aberystwyth; Bristol; Bristol UWE (No); Cardiff (No); Central Lancashire (No); East London; Kent; Leeds (No); Leicester (No); Liverpool John Moores (No); Manchester; Newcastle; Nottingham (depends on application); Paisley (No); Portsmouth (No); Sheffield (No); South Bank; Staffordshire (No); Sunderland (No); Surrey; Swansea.

Interview questions (see Ch.4): Examples of past questions include: Is money spent on the arts a waste? How much does the country spend on research and on the armed forces? Discuss reproduction in bacteria. What do you particularly like about your study of biology? What would you like to do after your degree? Do you have any strong views on vivisection? Discuss the differences between the courses you have applied for. What important advances have been made in the biological field recently? How would you describe microbiology? Do you know anything about the diseases caused by micro-organisms? What symptoms would be caused by which particular organisms?

GAP YEAR ADVICE

Most institutions will accept a gap year although **East London** stresses that a year out is built into the course. Apply before taking year out so that you can visit the universities of your choice. Consider carefully before you interrupt your studies. Have a positive reason: don't just take a break.

Institutions willing to defer entry after A-Levels: Aberystwyth (contact admissions tutor); Bristol; Cardiff (only if previously agreed); Heriot-Watt; Huddersfield; Leeds; Newcastle; North London; Nottingham (relevant work experience recommended); Portsmouth; Sheffield; Swansea (discouraged); Warwick.

AFTER RESULTS ADVICE

Institutions which may accept the same points score after A-Levels: Aberystwyth; Bradford; Cardiff; East Anglia; East London; Kent; Leeds; Liverpool; Liverpool John Moores; Manchester; Newcastle; Sheffield; Strathclyde; Swansea; Surrey.

Institutions which may accept lower grades/points score after A-Levels: Aberystwyth; Bradford; Bristol; East Anglia; Liverpool; Liverpool John Moores; Newcastle; Nottingham; Sheffield (No); Strathclyde; Surrey; Swansea; Warwick.

Offers to applicants repeating A-Levels: Higher Bristol, Strathclyde, Swansea, Warwick; **Possibly higher** Aberystwyth, East Anglia, Leeds, Newcastle; Nottingham; **Same** Bradford, Leeds, Liverpool.

Probable vacancies from June 2001 and in Clearing (see Ch.4): Most universities are likely to have some vacancies in this subject.

NEW GRADUATE DESTINATIONS AND EMPLOYMENT (1999 HESA) (see **Ch.4**)

In a survey of 504 graduates, 245 were in full-time employment (the majority in laboratory occupations), 174 went on to further study and 27 were believed to be unemployed.

MODERN LANGUAGES (see also **French, German, Greek, Italian, Japanese, Portuguese, Russian, Spanish**)

NB The information supplied by the universities and colleges this year varies considerably and the offers listed below should be used as a first source of reference only. Many institutions will accept combinations of Advanced (AL), Advanced Subsidiary (AS) and Vocational Advanced (VA) level qualifications to achieve the required points total, but applicants must check web sites and prospectuses for full details of all offers. Grades and points totals shown should be regarded as the minimum levels to be achieved, but offers may be adjusted downwards when results are known. The points totals shown to the left of the institutions are for ease of reference only. It must not be assumed that tariff points are always used by institutions or that they can be substituted for an offer in grades. The level of an offer is not necessarily indicative of the quality of a course. To calculate your offers see Chapter 4 and the inside fold of the back cover.

Special subject requirements/preferences: A-Level: Appropriate language studies, normally the highest grade in the offers below. **Oxford** Full A-Levels expected. **GCSE:**

English. **Bath** French or German at grade B. **Durham** Range of A* to B grades. **Cambridge, Oxford** Grade As in most subjects. **Oxford Brookes** Grade A in a language allows entry to a second language.

This table is provided as a general guide to modern language courses, often offering two or more languages in combination. Check separate language tables for offers.

360 pts **and above**
    Cambridge – Offers, mainly in grades, vary between colleges (Modn/Mediev Lang)
    Oxford – Offers vary between candidates (Class Modn Lang; Modn Langs)
350 pts **Liverpool** – 350 pts – ALs **or** ALs+ASs **or** VAs+/-ALs/ASs; (Modn Euro Lang)
320 pts **Manchester** – ABB–BBC (Euro St/Modn Lang courses)
300 pts **Birmingham** – BBB–BBC (Comb Hons Modn Lang)
    Bristol UWE – 300–240 pts approx (Modn Lang with EFL/Law/Euro St/Bus Sys/Inf Sys)
    London (UCL) – BBB–BBC **or** 3ALs+AS/VA; (Dutch/Scand St)
    Nottingham – ABC (Modn Lang St)
    St Andrews – BBB (Modn Langs)
    Salford – ABC–BBC (Modn Lang/Mark St)
    Sheffield – BBB (Modn Langs)
    Surrey – 300–240 pts approx (Modn Lang Comb with Fr/Ger/Russ)
280 pts **Aston** – BBC–BCC **or** ALs+ASs **or** VAs+/-ALs/ASs; gs; (Modn Lang courses except under **260 pts**)
    Bath – BBC–BCC **or** ALs+ASs; (not gs) (Modn Lang/Euro St)
    Bradford – 280 pts 12u (inc AL Fr); (Int Mgt/Fr; Peace St/Span)
    Durham – BBC (Modn Lang/Mus; Modn Lang/Ling)
    East Anglia – 280 pts – ACC (Modn Lang 3yr; Lang/Mgt St 3yr)
    Essex – 280–260 pts 21u – BB–BC+AL/2ASs **or** VA12u BB–BC+AL; gs; (Modn Lang)
    Exeter – BBC–BCC (Comb Lang courses – approx offer)
    Heriot-Watt – 280 pts 18u – BBC **or** ALs+ASs; gs; (Interp Trans; App Lang; Lang Int Teach(Fr/Ger/Russ/Span reqd))
    Hull – BBC (Lang Comb Hons)
    Lancaster – BBC–BCC (Modn Lang/Mark)
    Leeds – BBC–BCC/AA (Modn Lang – 4+ joint schemes)
    London (UCL) – BBC (Dutch)
    Newcastle – BBC–BCC (Modn Lang courses)
    Salford – BBC–BCC (Modn Lang/Engl; Modn Lang)
    Salford – BBC (Modn Lang/Contemp Euro St)
    Sheffield – BBC (Modn Lang/Educ)
    Strathclyde – BBC (BBD 2nd yr entry) (Modn Lang)
    Swansea – 280 pts 18u – BBC–BCD/BB–BC **or** ALs+ASs **or** VAs+/-ALs/ASs; (Most Modn Lang/Bus St courses)
    York – BBC/BB (Modn Lang/Ling)
260 pts **Aston** – 3ALs **or** ALs+ASs **or** VAs+/-ALs/ASs; gs; (Ger/Fr Comb courses)
    Bradford – 260 pts 12u (inc AL Fr/lang); gs; (French; German; Spanish; Fr/Ger/Span; Ger/Span)
    East Anglia – 260 pts – BCC (Modn Lang)
    Hull – BCC–BCD (Dutch St courses except under **220 pts**)
    Leicester – BCC/BC (Modn Lang St – 3 yr course)
    London (QM) – 260 pts approx – 3ALs **or** 2ALs+2ASs (pref B lang); (Modn Lang)
    Wolverhampton – 260–160 pts 12u – CDE–DDD/CC/CD+de **or** VA12u CC; gs; (Lang/Bus)
240 pts **Aberystwyth** – 240 pts 18u – CCC **or** CC+cc; gs; (Fr/Span/Euro Lang; Modn Lang/Bus St; Comb)
    Bangor – 240 pts – ALs; VAs (enquire); gs; (Modn Lang with Tour/Acc/Econ; Lang/Tour)

Bournemouth – 240–220 pts approx (Langs/Bus St)

Bradford – 240 pts 12u (inc AL lang); gs; (Euro St courses; Hist/Fr/Ger/Span; Pol/Fr/Ger/Span)

Leicester – BCD/BC (Modn Lang St courses)

Napier – CCC (Langs/Hspty Mgt)

Plymouth – 240–220 pts approx (Modn Lang courses)

Portsmouth – 240 pts – ALs **or** ALs+ASs **or** VAs; gs; (Lang/Int Trade; App Lang; Lang Intnet)

Southampton – CCC–CC (Expo Mgt; Langs Mark Mgt; Langs/Hspty Mgt)

Ulster – CCC (App Lang)

Wolverhampton – 240–180 pts – CDD–CDE/CC/CC+e/CEE+e **or** VA12u BC; gs; (Interpret)

220 pts   **Bristol UWE** – 220–180 pts 18u pref/12u – ALs **or** ALs+ASs **or** VAS+/-ALs/ASs; (Modn Lang courses)

Hull – CCD (Dutch St)

Liverpool John Moores – 220 pts (inc B Fr/Ger/Span) – ALs **or** ALs+ASs; (App Lang Euro)

Manchester Met – 220–180 pts approx (Langs courses)

Nottingham Trent – 220 pts – ALs (inc 120 pts fron 2ALs inc D lang; AS lang considered) (Modn Lang)

South Bank – 220–140 pts (Int Bus/Modn Lang)

200 pts   **Derby** – 200–180 pts approx (Modn Lang)

Huddersfield – ALs **or** ALs+ASs (AL Fr/Ger/Span) **or** VAs (check with univ); (not gs) (Modn Langs)

Oxford Brookes – CDD/BC (Lang for Bus)

180 pts   **Central Lancashire** – 180–160 pts 12u (inc C main lang); gs; (Modn Lang; Lang/Tour)

Kingston – 180 pts – 2x6u (inc 80 pts AL lang); gs; (App Euro Lang)

Lincolnshire & Humberside – 180 pts (Modn Lang courses)

Liverpool John Moores – 180 pts (inc 80 pts lang) – ALs **or** ALs+ASs **or** VAs+/-ALs/ASs; (Modn Lang St (Fr/Ger/Ital/Span/Chin/Jap))

Manchester Met – BC (inc for lang) (Modn Lang Fr/Ger/Ital/Span)

Thames Valley – 180–140 pts approx (Lang courses)

Wolverhampton – 180 pts approx – ALs **or** ALs+ASs; (Lang; Lang Comb Hons)

160 pts   **Newport (UWCN)** – 160–140 pts – ALs **or** ALs+ASs **or** VAs+/-ALs/ASs; (Modn Lang)

Napier – CC (Langs courses except under **240 pts**)

Surrey Roehampton – 160 pts – ALs (inc Fr 80 pts) **or** ALs+ASs (AS Fr 60 pts) **or** VAs+/-ALs/ASs; (Modn Lang; Modn Lang/Mark)

Westminster – CC (Modn Lang)

Leeds Met – (contact university)

Higher National Diploma courses

Aberdeen (Coll) (Lang/Bus); Glamorgan (Euro Lang/Bus St); Glasgow (Coll) (Lang St); Stevenson (Coll).

For other **DipHE** and **HND** courses see separate language tables.

Alternative Offers:

EB offers: Leeds 60%.

IB offers: Aston 31–29 pts; Bangor 26 pts; Bath 32–30 pts; Birmingham 33–30 pts; Bristol 32 pts (average) with H6 for each lang to be studied; Bristol UWE 26 pts; Derby 24 pts; Durham 33 pts; East Anglia 29 pts; Exeter 30 pts; Lancaster 30–28 pts; Leeds 32–28 pts H555; Manchester Met 28 pts 7 subjects 24 pts 6 subjects; Northumbria 30 pts; Portsmouth 24 pts; St Andrews 30 pts; Sheffield 32 pts; Surrey 28 pts; Swansea 28–26 pts; York H655.

Irish offers: Bradford BBBCCC; Heriot-Watt AABB; Surrey BBBCC.

Scottish Qualifications: Heriot-Watt AABB + interview; Napier BBC; St Andrews BBBB; Strathclyde ABBC.

CHOOSING YOUR COURSE (See also **Ch.1**)

> **Subject information:** Modern Language courses usually offer three main options: a single subject degree usually based on literature and language, a European Studies course, or two-language subjects which can often include languages different from those available at school – for example, Scandinavian Studies, Russian and the languages of Eastern Europe, the Middle and Far East. See also **Appendix 1**.

Special features: Bangor French, German, Italian and Spanish are offered with subsidiary Dutch. One, two and three language courses are available. **Derby** The Modern Language course allows for a study of three out of the four languages offered (French, German, Russian and Spanish). **Durham** French, German, Russian and Spanish are offered post-A-level with beginners' courses in Italian, Russian and Spanish. There are also options in Portuguese and Serbo-Croat, Arabic; Chinese and Japanese are also available. **Liverpool** The Modern European Languages course offers three languages in year 1 from French, German, Spanish and a beginner's language from Catalan, Irish, Italian or Portuguese. **Salford** The Modern Languages programme consists of a choice of two languages from Arabic, French, German, Italian, Spanish or Portuguese which can also be taken with Translation and Interpreting Studies. *NOW CHECK PROSPECTUSES AND WEB SITES.*

Top universities and colleges (Teaching Quality) (see Ch.4): See separate language tables.

Top universities and colleges (Research) (see Ch.4): See separate language tables.

Study opportunities abroad: Most universities offering four-year courses usually arrange for students to be placed in the appropriate country.

Work opportunities abroad: Aston; Bath; Bradford; Bristol; Bristol UWE; Durham; Heriot-Watt; Huddersfield; Plymouth; Salford; South Bank; Southampton; Wolverhampton.

ADMISSIONS INFORMATION

Number of applicants per place (approx): Aston 4; Bangor 5; Bath 10; Birmingham 19; Bradford 3; Brighton 4; Bristol 15; Bristol UWE (Modn Lang/Euro) 4, (Modn Lang/Inf Sys) 2; Cambridge 3.1; Cardiff 6; Durham 10; East Anglia 15; Heriot-Watt 5; Huddersfield 12; Lancaster 10; Leeds 9; Leicester 5; Liverpool John Moores 12; Manchester 8; Manchester Met 7; Newcastle 22; Northumbria 4; Nottingham Trent 4; Oxford 2; Portsmouth 10; Salford 6, (Modn Lang/Mark) 5; Surrey Roehampton 3; Wolverhampton 10.

Planning your UCAS personal statement (see Ch.4): See separate language tables. See also **Appendix 1**.

Selection interviews (see Ch.4): Aston; Bradford (all); Brighton (some); Bristol UWE (some); Cambridge (W, T); Coventry; Durham; East Anglia; Heriot-Watt; Huddersfield; Hull (No); Liverpool John Moores (T); Manchester Met (No); Nottingham (No); Oxford (W 30 min test in the relevant European language) (T); Oxford Brookes (No); Portsmouth (No); St Andrews (No); Salford (No); Sheffield (No); Surrey; Surrey Roehampton; York (No).

Interview questions (see Ch.4): See the specific language subject tables.

Reasons for rejection (non-academic): Lack of commitment to spend a year abroad. Poor references. Poor standard of English. No reasons for why the course has been selected. Poor communication skills.

GAP YEAR ADVICE

Most institutions will accept a gap year and prefer students to have some language experience.

Institutions willing to defer entry after A-Levels: Aston; Bangor; Birmingham; Bournemouth; Bradford; Bristol UWE; Central Lancashire; East Anglia; Heriot-Watt; Leeds; Leicester; Nottingham; Salford; Surrey; Surrey Roehampton; Swansea; Wolverhampton; York.

AFTER RESULTS ADVICE

Institutions which may accept the same points score after A-Levels: Aston; Birmingham (in some cases); Bradford; Bristol (No); Bristol UWE; Coventry (No); Hull (No); Leeds; Leicester; Liverpool John Moores; Manchester Met; Newcastle; Northumbria; Salford; Sheffield (No); Surrey; Surrey Roehampton; York.

Institutions which may accept lower grades/points score after A-Levels: Aston (a few); Birmingham (a few); Bradford; Coventry; Exeter; Newcastle; Salford; Sheffield (No); Wolverhampton; York (a few).

Offers to applicants repeating A-Levels: Higher Bristol UWE; **Possibly higher** Aston; **Same** Birmingham, Bradford, Bristol, Leeds, Newcastle, Salford, York.

Probable vacancies from June 2001 and in Clearing (see Ch.4): A large number of vacancies were declared last year on joint courses, particularly in combinations with less popular subjects. Most universities could be contacted. Fewer vacancies, however, are likely on single Honours courses.

NEW GRADUATE DESINATIONS AND EMPLOYMENT (1999 HESA) (see **Ch.4**)

See separate language tables.

MUSIC

NB The information supplied by the universities and colleges this year varies considerably and the offers listed below should be used as a first source of reference only. Many institutions will accept combinations of Advanced (AL), Advanced Subsidiary (AS) and Vocational Advanced (VA) level qualifications to achieve the required points total, but applicants must check web sites and prospectuses for full details of all offers. Grades and points totals shown should be regarded as the minimum levels to be achieved, but offers may be adjusted downwards when results are known. The points totals shown to the left of the institutions are for ease of reference only. It must not be assumed that tariff points are always used by institutions or that they can be substituted for an offer in grades. The level of an offer is not necessarily indicative of the quality of a course. To calculate your offers see Chapter 4 and the inside fold of the back cover.

Special subject requirements/preferences: A-Level: music usually the highest grade in the offers below. ABRSM grade VIII may be an alternative to A-Level music – check with universities. **Durham** Grade B in music. **Huddersfield, London (RAcMus)** Music grade A. **Leeds** A-Levels not to include music technology or practical music. **Oxford** A-Level music expected. **Surrey** For both courses Associated Board or equivalent grade VII or VIII expected on principal instrument. See also under **Admissions Tutors' advice** and **Examples of interview questions** below. GCSE: **Bangor** Music grade A or B. **Cardiff** Five–eight A grades or above. **Colchester (Inst)** Five subjects at grade A–C. **Edinburgh** Five–eight A–B grades incl foreign language, **Glasgow** English, mathematics or science and a foreign language. **Exeter** Four to eight A–C grades. **Leeds** Eight subjects mostly A*, A or B grades. **London (RH)** A good range of As and Bs preferred. **Oxford, Cambridge** A good range of grades A and B.

360 pts   and above

   Cambridge – Offers, mainly in grades, vary between colleges (Music)
   London (King's) – AAB+AS **or** AA+aab (inc A mus); VAs considered; (Mus; Mus/App Comp)
   Oxford – Offers vary between candidates (Music)

350 pts   **Southampton** – 350 pts 21u (inc 240 pts from 2ALs inc B mus) (Music; Mus Mgt)

340 pts   **Cambridge (Hom)** – AAB–ABB (BA Mus/Educ St)
              London (Imp) – AAB–ABB (Phys/Mus Perf)
              York – 21–18u – ABC+c (Music)

330 pts   **Southampton** – 330 pts 21u (inc 200 pts from 2ALs inc B mus+maths+phys) (Acoust/Mus; Mus/Maths; Mus/Phys)

320 pts   **Birmingham** – ABB + keyboard to ABRSM grade D (Music)
              Leeds – ABB (Mus/Psy)
              Surrey – 320 pts 18u (inc AL maths+phys+mus) – ALs **or** ALs+ASs; (not gs) (Mus/Snd Rec (Tonmeister))

310 pts   **Liverpool** – 310 pts – ALs **or** ALs+ASs **or** VAs+/-ALs/ASs; (Mus; Mus/Pop Mus)

300 pts   **Durham** – ABC (Engl/Mus) (see **Admissions Tutors' advice**)
              Durham – BBB (Modn Euro Langs/Mus)
              Glasgow – BBB–BBC (Music courses)
              Hull – BBB–BCC/BB–BC (Mus; Engl/Mus; Dr/Mus; Fr/Mus)
              Lancaster – BBB–BCC/BB–BC (Music courses)
              Leeds – BBB (Mus/Comp Sci; Mus/Maths)
              Liverpool – 300 pts – ALs **or** ALs+ASs **or** VAs+/-ALs/ASs; (Pop Mus)
              London (RH) – ALs (300 pts+grade VIII on 1st Instr) (not AS music) (not gs) (B Mus)
              London (SOAS) – 300–260 pts approx (Music courses)
              Manchester – BBB/AB + grade VIII instrument/grade VI keyboard (Music)
              Nottingham – ABC (B mus); (not gs) (Music; Mus/Film St)

280 pts   **Bangor** – BBC **or** VA12u BC+AL(B)(mus); gs; (Music courses)
              Belfast (Queen's) – BBC (Mus/Psy)
              Bristol – BBC(B modn lang Fr/Ger); (not gs) (Mus; Mus with Fr/Ger/Ital)
              Brunel – 280–260 pts 2x6u (inc AL mus/perf arts C); grade VIII inst/vocal; (Music courses; Crea Mus Tech)
              Cambridge (Hom) – BBC–BCD (BEd Music/Educ)
              Cardiff – BBC–BCC (Music)
              City – 3x6u – BBC–BCC; ASs/VAs (contact univ); (not gs); Grade VII inst/vocal; (Music)
              Durham – BBC (Lat/Mus; Mus/Theol) (see **Admissions Tutors' advice**)
              East Anglia – BBC–BCC (B music); (not gs) (Music)
              Edinburgh – BBC (Mus; Mus Tech)
              Exeter – 280 pts 18u (inc AL lang+AS mus) – BBC **or** BB+cc **or** BC+bb **or** VAs (contact univ); gs; (Mus with Fr/Ger)
              Hertfordshire – 280–200 pts (Electron Mus courses)
              Keele – BBC–BCC **or** equiv AS accepted; gs; (Music courses)
              Leeds – BBC/AB (Mus/Electron Eng; Mus/Phil; Mus/Theol/Relig St)
              Liverpool John Moores – 280 pts 4ALs; 240 pts 3ALs; 180 pts 2ALs (inc 1/2 C Engl/media st/comm st/hist/sociol) **or** VA E (Media/Comm Prod)+2ALs (C Engl/media st/comm st/hist/sociol); (Pop Mus St – to be validated)
              London (Gold) – BBC (Music)
              Newcastle – BBC/BB (not prac mus grades) (Music)
              Nottingham – BBC (Ger/Mus)
              Reading – BBC (Mus/Engl; Mus Fr)
              Sussex – BBC (Mus; Mus/Media St)

260 pts   **Belfast (Queen's)** – BCC (Music courses except under **280 pts**; Ethnomus)
              Cardiff (WCMD) – 260–180 pts (Music – grade VIII principal instrument; Perf Arts) (Apply direct)
              Durham – BCC (Music – see **Admissions Tutors' advice**))
              Exeter – 260 pts 18u (inc AL mus/lang+AS mus) – BCC **or** BC+cc **or** BB+dd **or** VAs (contact univ); gs; (Music; Mus with Ital/Span/Russ(inc GCSE Russ)
              Hertfordshire – 260–240 pts 1x12u **or** 2x6u; (Electron Mus courses; Mus Tech)

Hull – B(music)+160 pts approx+2 ALs/BB ABRSM grade VIII alternative to A music (Music; see also **300 pts**)

Manchester Met – 260 pts (Mus/Spo)

Oxford Brookes – BCC–DDD (Music joint Hons)

Reading – BCC inc grade VIII in prac mus (Mus Ger; Mus Ital)

Reading – BBD (Mus/Hist Art; Mus)

Salford – BCC (Pop Mus Rec)

Surrey – 260 pts 18u – ALs **or** ALs+ASs; (not gs) (Music)

Ulster – BCC (Music)

240 pts **Bristol UWE** – 240 pts approx (Mus Sys Eng)

De Montfort (Leicester) – 240–200 pts (Mus Single Hons); 200 pts (Mus Joint/Comb Hons) – ALs **or** ALs+ASs **or** VAs+/-ALs/ASs; (not gs) (Mus Tech courses)

Huddersfield – CCC (inc mus/mus tech/sci/maths) **or** CC (inc mus)+cc(inc sci/maths) **or** cccc (inc mus/mus tech+sci/maths) **or** VAs+/-ALs/ASs; (not gs) (Mus Tech)

Plymouth – BCD–CCD (Music courses)

Rose Bruford (Coll) – 240 pts approx (Mus Tech)

Staffordshire – CCC **or** CCD+AS(40 pts) **or** VAs; gs; (Mus Tech courses)

220 pts **Buckinghamshire Chilterns (UC)** – 220–180 pts approx (Mus Ind Mgt courses)

King Alfred's Winchester (Coll) – 220 pts approx (Perf Arts.Theol/Relig St)

London (RAcMus) – AB–BC (BMus Lond)

Middlesex – 220–180 pts approx (Music; Mus/Perf Arts; Jazz; Sonic Arts)

Sunderland – 220–180 pts (Music courses)

Warrington (CI) – 220 pts approx (Commer Mus Prod courses)

200 pts **Bangor** – 200 pts; gs (AL only); (Music)

Central Lancashire – 200 pts+audition; (New Mus Media)

Manchester Met – 200 pts approx (Music courses except under **260 pts**)

Northampton (UC) – 200–160 pts approx (Music courses)

St Martin's (Coll) – BDE–BC (Mus/Engl)

Wolverhampton – 200 pts 12u – DDD–CDE/BD–CC (inc mus) **or** DD+b **or** VA12u CC; gs; (Mus; Pop Mus)

190 pts **North London** – 190 pts inc 160 pts from 2ALs **or** VAs; (Mus/Media Mgt)

180 pts **Anglia** – 180 pts 12u – 2ALs (inc C mus) **or** VA12u BC; grade VII instr/vocal; gs; (Music)

Bath Spa (UC) – 180 pts 12u – B(mus tech)C **or** BA12u BC; (not gs) (Crea Mus Tech)

Chichester (UC) – 180 pts approx/grade VIII + AL C + prac interview (Music)

Derby – 180–160 pts 12u – CC **or** DD+ee (AL grades phys/maths/electron/des tech) **or** VA(eng)+/-ALs/ASs; gs; (Mus Tech; Live Perf)

Derby – 180 pts – CC **or** DD+ee(AL mus tech + mus qual) **or** VA CC+/-ALs/ASs; audition; gs (Pop Mus/Mus Tech)

Kingston – 180 pts 18u (inc 2x6u inc 80 pts AL mus); grade VIII; (Mus; Mus/Tech; Mus/Educ)

Liverpool Hope (Coll) – 180 pts approx (Music courses)

London (RAcMus) – BC possibly lower (Music)

Napier – BC (Music)

Royal Scottish (AMD) – DDD/CC (Mus St)

St Martin's (Coll) – CDE/CC (Music courses except under **200 pts**)

Surrey Roehampton – 180–140 pts (inc for BMus, AL mus 80 pts+grade VII; for BA/BSc, AL mus 60 pts+grade VII); (BMus; BA/BSc Mus)

160 pts **Anglia** – 160 pts 12u – 2ALs **or** VA12u CC; gs; (Aud Tech/Mus courses)

Barnsley (Coll) – 160 pts 12u – 2ALs (min DD) **or** ALs+ASs **or** VAs+/-ALs/ASs; gs; (Pop Mus St; Folk Commun Mus St; Jazz Mus St)

Birmingham (Westhill) – 160 pts 12u (inc C) – ALs **or** ALs+ASs; VAs (contact univ); gs; (Art/Mus Educ)

Bishop Grosseteste (Coll) – CC (inc C mus) **or** C+cc+grade IV piano+grade VII/VIII main instr/voice **or** VA12u; (Music QTS)

Brighton – 160 pts approx (Music Vis Prac – see **Art and Design (General)**)

Canterbury Christ Church (UC) – CC (Music courses) (see **Admissions Tutors' advice**)

Colchester (Inst) – BD (Music)

Coventry – 160 pts approx (Mus courses; Mus Cmpsn/Prof Prac)

Cumbria (CAD) – 160 pts – CC **or** ASs (contact coll) **or** VA; (Pop Mus)

Exeter (Truro) – 160 pts 18u (inc AL mus/mus tech) – DDD **or** DD+cc **or** VAs (contact univ); gs; (Jazz)

Huddersfield – 160 pts 12u – CC (Engl+mus)+Grade VIII **or** CC (inc mus+thea st)/drama/Engl)+Grade VIII; gs; (Mus/Engl; Mus/Thea St)

Leeds (Bretton Hall) – CC (Pop Mus St; Mus)

Leeds (CMus) – CC (Jazz St; Mus)

Newcastle (Coll) – 160 pts – ALs+ASs **or** VAs+/-AL/ASs; gs; grade VIII equiv/written paper/audition; BTEC considered; (Music)

North London – 160 pts 1x12u **or** 2x6u; (Mus Educ)

Strathclyde – CC (App Mus)

Truro (Coll) – 160 pts (Jazz)

140 pts   **Bath Spa (UC)** – 140–120 pts 12u – C(C mus)D **or** VA12u CD+Mus Gr VIII; (not gs) (Music courses)

Colchester (Inst) – 140 pts (Pop Mus)

Dartington (CA) – CD (Music)

Huddersfield – 140 pts 12u – CD(C mus+D chosen lang)+Grade VIII; (Mus/Modn Lang)

St Martin's (Coll) – DEE/DD (Mus QTS)

Salford – CD–E (Band Mus)

Sunderland – 140 pts – ALs **or** ALs+ASs **or** VAs+/-ALs/ASs; gs; BTEC accepted; (Perf Arts St)

120 pts   **Barnsley (Coll)** – 120 pts 12u – 2ALs(min DD) **or** ALs+ASs **or** VAs+/-ALs/ASs; gs; (Crea Mus Tech; Band St)

Huddersfield – 120 pts 12u – 2ALs (C mus)+Grade VIII; gs; (B Mus)

Reading – CE (BEd Music)

Ripon & York (Coll) – DD (Mus QTS; Mus Perf/Comm Arts)

Thames Valley (London CMus/Media) – 120 pts (C mus); grade VIII; portfolio written scores+interview; (Mus (Perf Cmpsn))

100 pts   **and below**

Barnsley (Coll) – 60 pts (Mus Ext)

Birmingham (Sch Sp/Dr) – (Mus Thea – see **Drama**)

Central England/Birmingham (Cons) – 40 pts 6u – E+4xGCSE+audition; (BMus; Jazz; Raga Sangeet)

Colchester (Inst) – (Music)

Edge Hill (CHE) – (Mus QTS)

Glasgow Caledonian – (Mus Tech Electron)

Guildhall (Sch Mus Dr) – (BMus; Mus; Thea)

Hull (Scarborough) – (Comb courses; Mus QTS; Crea Mus Tech; Crea Mus Tech/Bus Mgt)

Liverpool (LIPA) – unconditional offer after successful audition/interview (Perf Arts (Mus); Snd Tech)

London (RCMus) – grades irrelevant (Music)

London (Tr CMus) – no specific grades (Music; Mus Perf Teach (overseas non-EU students))

Manchester (RNCM) – (BA BMus Music)

Newcastle – B (Folk Mus)

Newcastle (Coll) – (Jazz Pop Commer Mus)

Northern (Coll) – (BEd Hons)

Rose Bruford (Coll) – (Act/Mus)

Royal Scottish (AMD) – (Perf; Scot Mus)

UHI (Perth/North Highland) – (Mus Perf via HND, HNC)
Westminster – (Commer Mus)
Worcester (UC) – (Music QTS)

Leeds Met – (contact university)

Diploma of Higher Education courses
80 pts Barnsley (Coll) (Mus Tech); Bath Spa (UC); Edge Hill (CHE); Manchester Met; Middlesex; Northampton (UC); Oxford Brookes; Thames Valley (Pop Mus Perf).

Higher National Diploma courses
140 pts and below
Bournemouth (Pop Mus); Bournemouth & Poole (Coll); City College Manchester (CHFE) (Pop; Mus Tech; Mus); Derby (Electron Mus); Doncaster (Coll) (Mus Tech; Comp Mus St); Great Yarmouth (Coll); London Guildhall (Mus Instr Tech); Nelson & Colne (Coll) 80 pts (not gs) (Pop Mus Perf); Newcastle (Coll); People's (Coll) (Mus Tech); Rycotewood (Coll) (Str Mus; Instr Mak/Restor); Salford (Pop Mus/Rec); South Downs (Coll); South East Essex (Coll); Wakefield (Coll); Wigan & Leigh (Coll) (Pop).

Diploma courses
80 pts and below
Blackpool & Fylde (Coll) (Mus Thea); Cardiff (WCMD); Central England; Chichester (UC); City (Coll) (Mus Mgt); Doncaster (Coll); Guildhall (Sch Mus Dr); Huddersfield; Leeds (CM); Liverpool (CmC); London (RAcMus), (RCMus) (Perf Dip; Grad Dip), (Tr CMus); Manchester (RNCM); Newcastle (CAT); St Helens (Coll); Stevenson (Coll); UHI (Perth) (Rock Mus/Perf); Wigan & Leigh (Coll) (Pop Mus; Mus Tech).

College Diplomas (Scotland)
80 pts and below or equivalent
Napier EE; Royal Scottish (AMD).

Alternative Offers:

EB offers: London (RH) 75%; Oxford Brookes 60%.

IB offers: Bangor 28 pts; Belfast (Queen's) H655 28–27 pts overall; Birmingham 30 pts; Bristol 28 pts H6 music; Cardiff 28 pts H5 in music; Dartington (CA) 30–28 pts; Durham 30 pts; Edinburgh 30 pts; Exeter 30 pts; Hull 28 pts; Keele 28–24 pts H55; Liverpool 30 pts; London (Gold) mus H6 + 1 other H5, (King's) 32 pts 7 in music, (RH) 35 pts; Newcastle 29 pts H6 music; St Martin's (UC) 28 pts H5 music; Surrey 30 pts; Sussex H67; York 30 pts H6 music.

Irish offers: Aberystwyth BBBC; Bangor BBCCC; Bristol BBCCC; Central England CCCCC; Keele BBBCC; London (RH) BBBCC; Manchester BBBBC; Oxford Brookes CCCCC; York BBC.

Scottish Qualifications: Aberdeen BBBB; Edinburgh ABC; Glasgow ABBB (MA), CCC (Mus St); Napier ABB; Strathclyde BBC.

Overseas applicants: Recent written work and casette tape acceptable instead of interview in most cases. Extension degree offered by London (Gold) for overseas students only.

CHOOSING YOUR COURSE (See also **Ch.1**)

Subject information: Theory and practice are combined in most Music courses to a greater or lesser extent. The menu of options is varied – choose with care! See also **Appendix 1**.

Special features: Anglia Study of many types of music: jazz, electronic, ethnic and classical; practical emphasis. **Bangor** Five main study areas: performance and interpretation, technology composition, composition, ethnomusicology, history and analysis. Options include music therapy, recording techniques, studio compositions, jazz, organ and choral; entrance scholarships available. **Bath Spa (UC)** Specialisms in performance, composition, musicology or 'sound and image' (with Fine Art). **Birmingham** Early music to 20th century electro–acoustic music. Continuous assessment in first year. **Bristol** Progressive programme with modularised syllabus. **Brunel** Attention is given to 20th century and contemporary music covering western classical, jazz, rock and pop. **Cambridge (Hom)** Initially emphasis is on free composition, performance and historical studies. Close relationship with Cambridge University music scene – choirs, orchestras etc. **Cardiff** Balance between theory and practice. Free instrumental tuition. **Cardiff (WCMD)** Strong practical emphasis on performance. **City** The course is concerned with music in today's technological and multi-cultural society, bridging the gap between music as an art and a science. **Colchester (Inst)** Special Honours studies in Christian liturgical music, arts administration, composition, performance, education and special needs. Great stress laid on candidates' practical ability (grade VII on at least one instrument or voice). **Durham** An extensive field of interest ranging from medieval music to creative work in the electronic and computer music studios. **East Anglia** Western music (Middle Ages to present day). Personal contacts with employers in most branches of music profession. Options in performance, composition and conducting. **Edinburgh** Two-year course followed by one or two years of chosen options. New electronic stuios for Music Technology courses. Music in the Community options available. Subsidised instrumental tuition. **Exeter** Strengths in early music, classical and romantic periods, 20th century music. **Kingston** Recording facilities on site. **Lancaster** Opportunity to delay course decisions; large amount of course assessment; 25% instrumental tuition free. Combined majors with many other subjects including languages. **Leeds** Balance between practical and academic approaches. **Liverpool** Balance between practical and academic studies. **London (SOAS)** Strong focus on Asian and African music. **Manchester (RNCM)** Strong emphasis on performance. **Newcastle** Recent options include arts administration, conducting, jazz, aesthetics and criticism. **Royal Scottish (AMD)** Emphasis on performance and practical studies. **Salford** (Pop Mus/Rec) Popular music emphasis on music technology (recording, synthesis, electro-acoustics, video-composition, performance), experience and talent important. (Band Mus) Brass, wind, big-band ensembles, composition, conducting, electro-acoustics. **Southampton** Highly flexible curriculum. Music computing, ensemble performance options. Most extensive series of concerts promoted by a UK university. **Strathclyde** (App Mus) Main route – music teaching, community music and music and business. **Surrey** Subject options in second and third year. Specialisation in third year from performance, conducting, composition, dissertation. Broad core of subjects taken with a wide range of options (conducting can be studied as an option). Courses are assessed by a mixture of formal exams, one week 'take away' papers and coursework. Electro-acoustics facilities. (Tonmeister) A unique combination of recording techniques, audio-engineering and practical and academic music. **Surrey Roehampton** Strong choral and orchestral tradition. **York** (Music) Special opportunities for composition, performance, electronic and computer music. Twentieth-century music features on a number of courses as at **Bangor** and **Nottingham**, and Music and Sound Recording (Tonmeister) at **Surrey**. NOW CHECK PROSPECTUSES AND WEB SITES.

Top universities and colleges (Teaching Quality) (see Ch.4): Anglia; Bangor; Belfast (Queen's); Birmingham; Bristol; Cambridge; City; Edinburgh; Exeter; Glasgow; Huddersfield; Keele; Lancaster; Leeds; London (Gold), (King's), (RAcMus), (Tr CMus), (SOAS); Manchester (RNCM); Nottingham; Royal Scottish (AMD); Salford; Southampton; Surrey; Sussex; Ulster; York; not all institutions assessed.

Top universities and colleges (Research) (see Ch.4): Belfast (Queen's); Birmingham; Bristol; Cambridge; Cardiff; City; De Montfort; Durham; Edinburgh; Exeter; Huddersfield; Hull; Keele; Lancaster; Leeds; Liverpool; London (Gold), (King's), (RH), (RAcMus), (RCMus), (SOAS); Manchester; Manchester (RNCM); Nottingham; Oxford; Reading; Southampton; Surrey; Sussex; York.

Study opportunities abroad: Cardiff; Dartington (CA); Durham; Exeter; Lancaster (E); Leeds; London (Gold), (RH); Manchester Met; Surrey Roehampton; Worcester (UC); York.

Work opportunities abroad: Bristol; Hull; Leeds; Surrey.

ADMISSIONS INFORMATION

Number of applicants per place (approx): Aberystwyth 5; Anglia 16; Bangor (BA) 6; Bath Spa (UC) 8; Belfast (Queen's) 6; Birmingham 18; Bristol (Music) 14; Brunel 7; Cambridge 2.8; Cambridge (Hom) 4 (All BEd courses); Cardiff 6; Chichester (UC) 3; City 7; Colchester (Inst) 4; Dartington (CA) 8; Durham 5; East Anglia 12; Edge Hill (CHE) 16; Edinburgh 11; Exeter 12; Glasgow 4; Huddersfield 6; Hull 21; Hull (Scarborough) 3; Kingston 18; Lancaster 8; Leeds 18; Leeds (Bretton Hall) 8; Liverpool 9; London (Gold) 7, (King's) 16, (RH) 7, (RAcMus) 7, (RCMus) 7, (Tr CMus) 4; London Guildhall 10; Manchester 12; Manchester (RNCM) 8; Middlesex 23; Napier 3; Newcastle 24; Northampton (UC) 3; Northern (Coll) 3; Northumbria 12; Nottingham 11; Oxford 2; Oxford Brookes 12; Ripon & York (Coll) 15; Rose Bruford (Coll) 15; Royal Scottish (AMD) 6; St Martin's (Coll) 7; Salford 5, (Pop Music/Rec) 23, (Mus/Acous/Rec) 30; Southampton 3; Strathclyde 15; Surrey (Mus/Snd Rec) 11, (Music) 11; Surrey Roehampton 4; Ulster 8; Worcester (UC) 8; York (Mus/Educ) 15, (Mus Tech) 25.

Admissions Tutors' advice: Anglia In addition to A-Levels, we also require Grade VII (good pass, first study) plus Grade V minimum keyboard standard. **Bangor** Offer depends on proven ability in historical or compositional fields plus acceptable performance standard. Options include music therapy, recording techniques, jazz. **Bath Spa (UC)** Some candidates interviewed. Required to perform and sight-read on main instrument, and given aural and critical listening tests. **Bristol** (Mus/Modn Lang) No in-depth interviews; candidates invited to open days. **Cambridge** At interview candidates may have to undergo some simple keyboard or aural tests (such as harmonisation of an unseen melody or memorisation of a rhythm). More importantly, they will have to comment on some unseen musical extracts from a stylistic and analytical point of view. Candidates are also asked to submit some samples of work before the interview, from the fields of harmony and counterpoint, history, and analysis; they are also encouraged to send any other material such as compositions, programme notes or an independent essay on a subject of interest to the candidate. (Taking the STEP examination is not a requirement for admission.) Above all this, though, the main prerequisite for reading Music at St Catherine's is an *academic* interest in the subject itself. **Cambridge (Hom)** Tests will also include busking accompaniments to children's songs on keyboard. Questions on stylistic features of piece performed. **Canterbury Christ Church (CHE)** AEB examinations in two instruments (or one instrument and voice); keyboard competence essential particularly for the BEd course. **Cardiff (WCMD)** All UK and Eire applicants are called to audition in person; overseas candidates may audition by tape. Candidates are required to perform on their sight reading ability. Candidates who are successful in the audition proceed to interview in which there will be a short aural test. Candidates for the BA (Music) course are required to bring recent examples of harmony, counterpoint and essays. **Colchester (Inst)** Great stress laid on candidate's ability to communicate love of the subject.

Durham We also require Grade VI piano (Associated Board) and a foreign language (GCSE (grade A–C), A-Level music grade B. **East Anglia** Only unusual and mature candidates are interviewed. Applicants are expected to perform music with insight and show genuine intellectual curiosity about music and its cultural background. At interview candidates will be asked to perform on their principal instrument. Those who play orchestral instruments or sing will also be expected to play simple music on the piano. At interview we look for applicants with proficiency in instrumental or vocal performance (preferably at Grade VIII standard or above), range of experience of music of many types and an intelligent attitude towards discussion. **Edinburgh** Most candidates are called for interview although very well qualified candidates may be offered a place without interview. All are asked to submit samples of their work. Associated Board Grade VII on piano is usually expected. **Exeter** Candidates cannot be accepted without interview, which is adapted to individuals. Entrants need not be good keyboard players but must be able to read easy music at the piano. **Glasgow** The BA (Mus Educ) course is for students aiming at a career in school music and is largely keyboard-orientated. The BA (Music Performance) course is for those wanting a career in professional performance (Instrument and Voice). **Hull** Good instrumental grades can improve chances of an offer and of confirmation in August. **Kingston** Associated Board Grade VIII on main instrument is required, with at least Grade IV on a keyboard instrument (where this is not the main instrument). Audition and interview may be required.

Lancaster Grade VIII Associated Board required on an instrument or voice and some keyboard proficiency (grade VI) usually expected. We do not accept candidates without interview. **Leeds** Intending students should follow an academic rather than practical-oriented A-level course. The University is experimenting with abandoning the formal interview in favour of small group open days for those holding offers made on the UCAS information, which focus on a practical exchange of information relevant to the applicant's decision to accept or reject the offer. Grade VIII Associated Board on an instrument is a normal expectation. **Leeds (Bretton Hall)** Great weight placed on achievement at very thorough practical interview/audition. There is also subsidiary interview for Dance, Dramatic Presentation, English or Inter Arts. Good musicianship plus sound academic background required. Ethnic minority candidates welcomed. **Liverpool** At interview each candidate is required to take a piano sight-reading test (Associated Board Grade VI) and a series of simple aural tests. They will be asked to play a prepared piece on the piano or on their main instrument (required standard approximately Grade VIII), and to enter into a musical discussion on a topic of interest to them. Great importance is attached to performing and composing achievement prior to interview and to potential for future development (intellect, motivation and enthusiasm). **Liverpool (LIPA)** Candidates should bring with them a short (about 500 words) review of a piece of music that they have recently heard. This could be music from a film, an advertising jingle, a recording or a live gig, but do not just **describe** the music, try to tell us why and how you think it worked (or not), and what it meant to you. For audition days there will be: (1) a solo interview/audition; (2) an interdisciplinary workshop. Candidates should prepare two pieces of contrasting contemporary music to play on their chosen instrument (maximum of 3 to 4 minutes each). The selection panel will listen to one or both pieces at their discretion. Candidates sometimes do not represent the skills appropriate for the degree course at LIPA if they choose to play only pieces of classical repertoire. Piano accompanists are provided if required. Bring your instrument and a portfolio (as cassette, score, CD for example) of any of your work you would like us to hear and talk about. Candidates who have put 'Songwriting/Composition' as either their first or second choice should have a cassette or CD of their work to play to the panel. The selection panel will listen to up to 3 original pieces, at their discretion. All cassettes (of original material or backing tapes) should be properly cued up and ready to play **before** the audition. Candidates will have access to amplifiers, PA, drums, piano, CD player and a cassette (with vari-speed function) in the audition. **London (Gold)** The interview will include an aural discussion of music and the personal interests of the applicant. **London (Royal Academy of Music)** All candidates are called for audition, and those who are successful are called for a further interview; places are offered later, subject to the minimum GCSE requirements being achieved. **London (Royal College of Music)** All UK and Eire candidates are required to attend for audition in person but tapes are acceptable from overseas applicants. It must be stressed, however, that personal audition is preferable and those students offered places on the basis of a tape audition may be required to take a confirmatory audition on arrival. Candidates are required to perform on the principal study instrument as well as undertaking sight reading aural tests and paperwork. There is also an interview. Potential scholars sometimes proceed to a second audition, usually on the same day. The academic requirement for the BMus (RCM) course is two A-levels at pass grades. Acceptance is ultimately based on the quality of performance at audition, performing experience and perceived potential as a performer. As a guide, applicants should be of at least Grade VIII distinction standard. **London (RH)** Candidates are tested with an aural test, a harmony-counterpoint test, a conceptual essay, and a viva at which they are asked questions and asked to perform. On the basis of the results in these tests we make offers. For strong candidates we offer a place with a C in music and E in another A-Level. For weaker candidates we offer a place with a B in music and a C in another A-Level. There is a tradition of caring for each individual and we strive to give each applicant a fair hearing. Musicality, a good intellect and real enthusiasm are the qualities we look for. **London (SOAS)** Candidates are judged on individual merits. Applicants are expected to have substantial practical experience of musical performance, but not necessarily Western music. **London (Trinity College of Music)** Applicants for the BMus degree must attend an audition and show that they have attained a certain level of competence in their principal and second studies, musical subjects and in musical theory. Grade VIII practical and theory can count as one A-Level, but not if the second A-Level is in music. Overseas applicants may submit a tape recording in the first instance when a place may be offered for one year. Thereafter they will have to undergo a further test. They must also show evidence of good aural perception in musical techniques and musical analysis.

Manchester (RNCM) All applicants are called for audition. Successful applicants proceed to an academic interview which will include aural tests and questions on music theory and history. **Newcastle** We expect a reasonable background knowledge of musical history, basic harmony and counterpoint and keyboard skills of approximately Grade VIII standard: if the main instrument is not piano or organ – Grade V. While practical skills are important, academic ability is the primary requisite. Practical Music or Music Technology accepted in place of Music. **Nottingham** A high standard of aural ability is expected. Interviewees take two short written papers, intellectual enquiry and attainment is looked for, together with a good range of knowledge and sense of enterprise. No places are offered without interview – each offer is 'tailored' to the student at interview. **Nottingham Trent** Music students require Grade VI on two instruments. Candidates submit a marked sample of Harmony and/or Counterpoint and two marked essays on any areas or aspects of music. Candidates may also submit a portfolio of compositions if they wish, but it is not possible to return any copies. Candidates will take the following tests at interview: (i) A one-hour Harmony or Counterpoint written test (candidates will not have access to a piano; there is no composition option); (ii) A 40-minute aural test in three parts: dictation of a bach chorale (bass given)/melodic dictation, and identification of errors heard in a two-part piece; (iii) Performance of a prepared piece on the candidate's principal instrument or voice (organists, percussionists and candidates requiring an accompanist should inform the Faculty in advance of the interview period); (iv) Keyboard skills in three parts: score reading of a string quartet; keyboard harmony; and sight-reading (sight-reading examples will take into account candidates' keyboard proficiency). **Surrey** (Music) Applicants may expect to be questioned in the interview about their musical experience, enthusiasm and any particular compositions they have studied. They will also be asked to perform on their first instrument. (Mus/Snd/Rec) Applicants can expect to be questioned about their recording interests and motivation and show an ability to relate A-level scientific knowledge to simple recording equipment. They may be asked to perform on their first instrument.

Planning your UCAS personal statement (see Ch.4): In addition to your ability and expertise with your chosen musical instrument, it is also important to know your composers and take a critical interest in various kinds of music. Reference should be made to these, visits to concerts listed and any special interests indicated in types of musical activity, for example, opera, ballet. Work with orchestras, choirs and other musical groups should also be included and full details given of any competitions entered and awards obtained. **Surrey** (Tonmeister) Demonstration of motivation towards professional sound recorders. See also **Appendix 1**.

Selection interviews (see Ch.4): Most courses; Bishop Grosseteste (Coll) (W); Cardiff; Colchester (IHE) (W); Derby (W); London Guildhall; Surrey (W) (T); in all other cases except Bath Spa (UC) (some) and Oxford Brookes (Modular). See also **Admissions Tutors' advice**.

Interview requirements:

Key: P = Performance   A = Aural
       K = Keyboard Tests   H = Harmony & Counterpoint (Written)
       E = Essay   X = Extracts for analysis or 'guessing
       S = Sight–Singing   composer, date' etc.

Bangor..........................PAX (bring example)
Barnsley (Coll).......................................A
Bath Spa (UC)....................................PKXA
Birmingham................................PSKHXA
Bristol..PSKHEXA
Cambridge (Hom).........PKE (bring example)
Cardiff...PH
City...PASKE
Colchester (Inst)................................PKSX
Derby...AE
Durham........................PKX (also ear tests)
East Anglia....................................PKHEXA
Edinburgh.......................................PKHEA
Glasgow..........PK (optional) EXH (portfolio)
Huddersfield...PEH
Hull...PSKX
Kingston...PSKE
Lancaster...PAH

Leeds (Bretton Hall)................................PX
Liverpool...PK
Liverpool Hope (UC) (BEd)...................PKH
London (Gold)...PS
London (King's)....................................PASK
London (RAcMus)................................PKHX
London (RCollMus)...........................PKEXH
London (RH)....................................PHEXA
Manchester (RNCM)............................PAX
Newcastle..PHXA
Oxford..HAPK
Salford..PKEH
Southampton..P
Surrey...PH or X
Surrey Roehampton............................PKH
Ulster...P
York..PEKHX

(Examples may include essays, harmony and counterpoint compositions.)

Interview questions (see Ch.4): See under **Admissions Tutors' advice** and **Interview requirements**.

Reasons for rejection: Usually academic (auditions, practical, aural/written test – see **Admissions Tutors' advice**). Dull, unenthusiastic students, ignorant about their subject, showing lack of motivation and imagination. **Coventry** Proforma used prior to interview (some students rejected at this stage). **London (King's)** Apparent lack of interest, performance not good enough, lack of music history knowledge. Foreign students: language skills inadequate.

GAP YEAR ADVICE

Most institutions will accept a gap year. Students should listen critically to as much music as possible and gain as much performing experience as they can. **Cambridge (Hom)**, **Glasgow** Apply as soon as possible stating preference for delayed entry. **Lancaster** Apply in last year at school, not in gap year. **London (RCM)** Subject to negotiation; similarly with **Belfast (Queen's)**. **Salford** We prefer singers to be slightly older than most undergraduates, otherwise please advise us. It might be necessary to re-audition since performance standard may diminish.

Institutions willing to defer entry after A-Levels: Bangor (No); Bath Spa (UC) (No); Bristol; Cardiff; Cardiff (WCM); City; Colchester (Inst); Dartington (CA); Durham; Edinburgh; Huddersfield; Kingston; Leeds (varies); Liverpool (LIPA) (encouraged); London (RAcMus) (No); London (RH); Manchester (RNCM) (No); Newcastle; Northern (Coll) (No); Northumbria; Nottingham; Rose Bruford (Coll); Royal Scottish (AMD) (No); Surrey; Surrey Roehampton; Worcester (UC); York.

AFTER RESULTS ADVICE

Institutions which may accept the same points score after A-Levels: Aberystwyth; Bangor (No); Bath Spa (UC) (No); Birmingham (Mus DD); Bristol; City; Colchester (Inst); Dartington (CA); Durham; East Anglia; Edge Hill (CHE); Huddersfield; Hull; Hull (Scarborough); Kingston (No); Lancaster; Leeds; Liverpool; London (Gold) (No), (RH) (perhaps); London Guildhall (No); Newcastle; Nottingham (No); Rose Bruford (Coll); Surrey; Surrey Roehampton; Ulster; Worcester (UC); York (No).

Institutions which may accept lower grades/points score after A-Levels: Bangor; Belfast (Queen's); Bristol; Cambridge (Hom); Chichester (UC); Colchester (Inst); Dartington (CA); East Anglia; Edinburgh; Exeter; Hull; Leeds (some); Leeds (Bretton Hall); Liverpool; London (RCMus), (RH); Newcastle; Nottingham; Oxford; Rose Bruford (Coll); Surrey; Surrey Roehampton; Ulster; York.

Offers to applicants repeating A-Levels: Higher Aberystwyth, Leeds; **Possibly higher** Cambridge (Hom); **Same** Anglia, Bath Spa (UC), Bristol, City, Colchester (Inst), Durham, East Anglia, Exeter, Hull, Kingston, London (RAcMus), (RH), Nottingham, Rose Bruford (Coll), Surrey, York.

Probable vacancies from June 2001 and in Clearing (see Ch.4): Vacancies are likely at many universities and colleges, particularly on joint courses.

NEW GRADUATE DESTINATIONS AND EMPLOYMENT (1999 HESA) (see **Ch.4**)

Of 1915 graduates surveyed, 808 went into full-time employment, 720 into further study (mainly for professional training and teaching, with over 437 going to teacher training) and 64 were believed to be unemployed.

NATURAL SCIENCES (see also Biological Sciences and Science)

NB The information supplied by the universities and colleges this year varies considerably and the offers listed below should be used as a first source of reference only. Many institutions will accept combinations of Advanced (AL), Advanced Subsidiary (AS) and Vocational Advanced (VA) level qualifications to achieve the required points total, but applicants must check web sites and prospectuses for full details of all offers. Grades and points totals shown should be regarded as the minimum levels to be achieved, but offers may be adjusted downwards when results are known. The points totals shown to the left of the institutions are for ease of reference only. It must not be assumed that tariff points are always used by institutions or that they can be substituted for an offer in grades. The level of an offer is not necessarily indicative of the quality of a course. To calculate your offers see Chapter 4 and the inside fold of the back cover.

Special subject requirements/preferences: A-Level: Two/three science/mathematics subjects. **GCSE: Cambridge** Grade As in most subjects.

360 pts	**and above**
	Cambridge – Offers, mainly in grades, vary between colleges (Nat Sci)
	Durham – AAA–ABB **or** AA+ab **or** AA+bb; (not gs) (Nat Sci)
300 pts	**Bath** – BBB–BCC (2 sci pref); (not gs) (Nat Sci)
	Birmingham – BBB–BBC Nat Sci; Nat Sci Euro)
	East Anglia – BBB (Nat Sci)
	Lancaster – BBB (Nat Sci/USA/Can)
280 pts	**Bath** – 280–260 pts approx inc at least 1 sci (Nat Sci)
260 pts	**Lancaster** – BCC (Nat Sci)
	Sussex – BCC (Nat Sci)
160 pts	**De Montfort** – 160 pts approx (Nat Sci)
	Liverpool John Moores – 160–120 pts (inc AL sci 80 pts) – ALs **or** ALs+ASs **or** VAs+/-ALs/ASs; (Nat Sci)
120 pts	**Canterbury Christ Church (UC)** – DD (Nat Sci courses)

Alternative Offers:

IB offers: Bath 32 pts; Cambridge H777 S777; De Montfort 24 pts; Durham 30 pts.

CHOOSING YOUR COURSE (See also **Ch.1**)

> **Subject information:** Natural Science courses are broad-based covering the main science subjects, with options to specialise at a later stage. See also **Appendix 1**.

Special features: Bath Optional year in study abroad, industrial training or Certificate of Education. **Birmingham** Two courses are offered, one with a year in Continental Europe which includes training in French and German. **Cambridge** First year choice of study includes, for example, biology, chemistry, geology, materials, maths, physiology, physics. Second year choice is as above, together with anatomy, biochemistry, ecology, genetics, history of science, neuroscience, pathology, pharmacology, plant science, psychology and zoology. *NOW CHECK PROSPECTUSES AND WEB SITES.*

ADMISSIONS INFORMATION

Number of applicants per place (approx): Bath 8; Cambridge 3; Durham 6.

Planning your UCAS personal statement (see Ch.4): See **Physics**, **Chemistry** and **Biology**. See also **Appendix 1**.

Selection interviews (see Ch.4): Bath; Cambridge; Durham (No).

Interview questions (see Ch.4): Cambridge Questions are dependent on subject choices and studies at A-level and past questions have included the following: Discuss the setting up of a chemical engineering plant and the probabilities of failure of various components. Questions on the basic principles of physical chemistry, protein structure and functions and physiology. Questions on biological specimens. Comment on the theory of evolution and the story of the Creation in Genesis. What are your weaknesses? Questions on electro-micrographs. What do you talk about with your friends? How would you benefit from a university education? What scientific magazines do you read? Questions on atoms, types of bonding and structures. What are the problems of being tall? What are the differences between metals and non-metals? Why does graphite conduct? Questions on quantum physics and wave mechanics. How could you contribute to life here? What do you see yourself doing in five years' time? Was the Second World War justified? If it is common public belief that today's problems, for example industrial pollution, are caused by scientists, why do you wish to become one? Questions on the gyroscopic motion of cycle wheels, the forces on a cycle in motion and the design of mountain bikes. What do you consider will be the most startling scientific development in the future? What do you estimate is the mass of air in this room?

GAP YEAR ADVICE

Most institutions will accept a gap year.

Institutions willing to defer entry after A-Levels: Bath.

AFTER RESULTS ADVICE

Probable vacancies from June 2001 and in Clearing (see Ch.4): Contact universities since some vacancies are likely.

NEW GRADUATE DESTINATIONS AND EMPLOYMENT (1999 HESA) (see **Ch.4**)

See separate science subjects.

NAVAL ARCHITECTURE (including **Ship Science**; see also **Marine/Maritime Studies**)

NB The information supplied by the universities and colleges this year varies considerably and the offers listed below should be used as a first source of reference only. Many institutions will accept combinations of Advanced (AL), Advanced Subsidiary (AS) and Vocational Advanced (VA) level qualifications to achieve the required points total, but applicants must check web sites and prospectuses for full details of all offers. Grades and points totals shown should be regarded as the minimum levels to be achieved, but offers may be adjusted downwards when results are known. The points totals shown to the left of the institutions are for ease of reference only. It must not be assumed that tariff points are always used by institutions or that they can be substituted for an offer in grades. The level of an offer is not necessarily indicative of the quality of a course. To calculate your offers see Chapter 4 and the inside fold of the back cover.

Special subject requirements/preferences: A-Level: Mathematics and physics.

360 pts and above
Southampton – 370 pts 21u (inc 22 pts AL maths+phys); (MEng Ship Sci; Ship Sci/Advnc Mats; Eng Mgt (Ship Sci))
330 pts **Southampton** – 330 pts 21u (inc 180 pts AL maths+phys); (BEng Ship Sci)
320 pts **London (UCL)** – ABB–BBC **or** 3ALs+AS/VA; (Naval Archit/Mar Eng)
300 pts **Strathclyde** – BBB–BCC (Naval Archit courses)
280 pts **Glasgow** – BBC (Naval Archit courses)
Newcastle – BBC–BCC; (not gs) (MEng Naval Archit; Small Craft Tech)
260 pts **Newcastle** – BCC–CCC/BC; (not gs) (BEng Naval Archit; Small Craft Tech) CCC (4 yr courses)
240 pts **Southampton (Inst)** – 240 pts approx (Yacht/Pwrcft Des)
200 pts **Heriot-Watt** – CDD (Off Eng)
100 pts **Southampton (Inst)** – 100 pts (Fdn Yacht/Pwrcft Des)

Higher National Diploma courses:
100 pts and below
Cornwall & Duchy (Coll); Glamorgan; Southampton (Inst)

Alternative Offers:

EB offers: Newcastle 70%; Southampton (MEng) 75%, (BEng) 70%.

IB offers: Newcastle H555; Southampton H665.

Scottish Qualifications: Glasgow BBBC; Heriot-Watt BBBC; Strathclyde AAAB–BBBB.

CHOOSING YOUR COURSE (See also **Ch.1**)

Subject information: There is a shortage of applicants for Naval Architecture and Ship Science courses. Naval Architecture is also an option at **Newcastle** in the Marine Technology course. Studies involve marine structures, transport and operations, design, propulsion and mathematics. There is a shortage of well-qualified naval archi-tects. Ship design has many similarities with the design of aircraft. Other marine courses include Marine Biology, Commerce, Geography, Technology, Transport, and Nautical Studies. See also **Appendix 1**.

Special features: Southampton (Inst) Twenty years' experience in small craft design; world-wide reputation. **Strathclyde** Course includes business skills. *NOW CHECK PROSPECTUSES AND WEB SITES.*

Top universities and colleges (Research) (see Ch.4): London (UCL); Southampton.

Study opportunities abroad: Glasgow; Newcastle; Southampton; Strathclyde.

ADMISSIONS INFORMATION

Number of applicants per place (approx): Glasgow 7; London (UCL) 8; Newcastle 9; Southampton 6; Strathclyde 7.

Planning your UCAS personal statement (see Ch.4): Special interests in this subject area should be described fully. Visits to shipyards and awareness of ship design from the 'Mary Rose' to modern speed boats should be fully explained and the problems noted. See also **Engineering/Engineering Sciences** and **Marine (Maritime) Studies**. See also **Appendix 1**.

Selection interviews (see Ch.4): Newcastle; Southampton.

Interview questions (see Ch.4): Because of the highly vocational nature of this subject, applicants will naturally be expected to discuss any work experience and to justify their reasons for choosing the course.

GAP YEAR ADVICE

Institutions willing to defer entry after A-Levels: London (UCL) (No); Southampton; Strathclyde.

AFTER RESULTS ADVICE

Institutions which may accept the same points score after A-Levels: Newcastle; Southampton; Strathclyde.

Offers to applicants repeating A-Levels: Higher Newcastle.

Probable vacancies from June 2001 and in Clearing (see Ch.4): Contact all universities offering courses.

NEW GRADUATE DESTINATIONS AND EMPLOYMENT (1999 HESA) (see **Ch.4**)

No data available.

NEAR & MIDDLE EAST STUDIES (see also **Arabic, Asia-Pacific Studies** and **Hebrew**)

NB The information supplied by the universities and colleges this year varies considerably and the offers listed below should be used as a first source of reference only. Many institutions will accept combinations of Advanced (AL), Advanced Subsidiary (AS) and Vocational Advanced (VA) level qualifications to achieve the required points total, but applicants must check web sites and prospectuses for full details of all offers. Grades and points totals shown should be regarded as the minimum levels to be achieved, but offers may be adjusted downwards when results are known. The points totals shown to the left of the institutions are for ease of reference only. It must not be assumed that tariff points are always used by institutions or that they can be substituted for an offer in grades. The level of an offer is not necessarily indicative of the quality of a course. To calculate your offers see Chapter 4 and the inside fold of the back cover.

Special subject requirements/preferences: A-Level: Foreign languages required. **GCSE: Edinburgh, Glasgow** English, mathematics or science and a foreign language. **Oxford, Cambridge** Grade A in most subjects.

360 pts and above
    Cambridge – Offers, mainly in grades, vary between colleges (Oriental St)
    Oxford – Offers vary between candidates (Oriental St)
320 pts **Durham** – ABB (Mid E Islam St)
    Manchester – ABB–BBB (Mid E Langs/Ling)
    St Andrews – ABB–BBC (Arbc courses)
300 pts **Durham** – BBB (Arbc/Econ; Arbc/Sociol/Soc Pol; Arbc/Pol)
    Edinburgh – BBB (Persn Arbc Lang courses)
280 pts **Durham** – BBC (Pol Hist Mid E with/Arbc/Persn/Turk/Islam St)
    Exeter – 280 pts 18u – BBC **or** BB+cc **or** CC+aa **or** VAs (contact univ); gs; (Mid E St/Arbc)
    London (SOAS) – 280 pts (Persn; Arbc courses; Turk courses)
    Manchester – BBC (Mid E St; Mid E St/Modn Euro Langs)
240 pts **Exeter** – 240 pts 18u – CCC **or** CC+cc **or** VAs (contact univ); gs; (Islam St)
160 pts **Birmingham** – CC (Islam St)

Alternative Offers:

Scottish Qualifications: Edinburgh BBBB; St Andrews BBBB.

CHOOSING YOUR COURSE (See also **Ch.1**)

> **Subject information:** Near and Middle East Studies cover the major language cultures of the Middle East such as Arabic, Hebrew, Persian and Turkish.

Special features: Manchester Study of two Middle Eastern languages plus history, literature and culture. *NOW CHECK PROSPECTUSES AND WEB SITES.*

Top universities and colleges (Research) (see Ch.4): (inc African Studies) Birmingham, Cambridge; Durham; Edinburgh; London (SOAS); Manchester; Oxford.

Study opportunities abroad: Durham.

ADMISSIONS INFORMATION

Number of applicants per place (approx): Cambridge (Oriental) 3; London (SOAS) (Persn) 2; Manchester 4.

Planning your UCAS personal statement (see Ch.4): Visits to the countries in these regions should be fully described and an awareness shown of national, historical and economic differences. Contact embassies for further information.

Selection interviews: Durham.

Interview questions (see Ch.4): Applicants are likely to be questioned on the reasons for choosing this subject. Strong interest in the Near and Middle East must be shown at interview.

AFTER RESULTS ADVICE

Probable vacancies from June 2001 and in Clearing (see Ch.4): Contact universities and colleges since some vacancies are possible.

NEW GRADUATE DESTINATIONS AND EMPLOYMENT (1999 HESA) (see **Ch.4**)

See **Arabic**.

NURSING & MIDWIFERY (see also **Community Studies, Health Sciences/ Studies, Life Sciences**)

NB The information supplied by the universities and colleges this year varies considerably and the offers listed below should be used as a first source of reference only. Many institutions will accept combinations of Advanced (AL), Advanced Subsidiary (AS) and Vocational Advanced (VA) level qualifications to achieve the required points total, but applicants must check web sites and prospectuses for full details of all offers. Grades and points totals shown should be regarded as the minimum levels to be achieved, but offers may be adjusted downwards when results are known. The points totals shown to the left of the institutions are for ease of reference only. It must not be assumed that tariff points are always used by institutions or that they can be substituted for an offer in grades. The level of an offer is not necessarily indicative of the quality of a course. To calculate your offers see Chapter 4 and the inside fold of the back cover.

Application details for courses:

For England: Nursing and Midwifery Admissions Service, UCAS, Rosehill, New Barn Lane, Cheltenham, Glos GL50 3LA. **For Wales:** Welsh National Board for Nursing, Midwifery and Health Visiting, 2nd Floor, Golate House, 101 St Mary's Street, Cardiff CF1 1DX. **For Scotland:** National Board for Nursing, Midwifery and Health Visiting for Scotland, 22

Queens Street, Edinburgh EH2 1NT. **For Northern Ireland:** National Board for Nursing, Midwifery and Health Visiting for Northern Ireland, Centre House, 79 Chichester Street, Belfast BT1 4JE.

For applications for training courses in Schools of Nursing, candidates may apply up to two years before the starting date. Students cannot start training until they are 17 and cannot submit applications until they are 16. Check Nursing Schools for the starting dates of courses.

Special subject requirements/preferences: GCSE: English and a science subject. Mathematics required at **Anglia, Bristol UWE, City, Glasgow, Glasgow Caledonian, Hertfordshire, Hull, Liverpool, Manchester, Northumbria, Robert Gordon, Sheffield Hallam, Southampton, Staffordshire, Surrey, Ulster.** All applicants holding firm offers are required to provide documentary evidence that they have not been infected with Hepatitis B.

Abbreviations used in the following table: A Adult; C Child; CN Cancer Nursing; DN District Nursing; FN Forensic Nursing; HV Health Visiting; LD Learning Disability; MH Mental Health; PN Paediatric Nursing; SW Social Work.

310 pts   **Southampton** – 310 pts 21u (inc 180 pts from 2ALs); (Nurs A/CH; Midwif; Paramed Sci)

280 pts   **Edinburgh** – BBC (1 sitting); (not gs) (Nurs A/MH)
     Hertfordshire – 280–240 pts (inc sci subj); gs; (Nurs A/CH; Midwif; Paramed Sci)
     London (King's) – CCC+c **or** BC+ccc (or equiv) (inc C sci) **or** VA12u CC (sci/hlth sc/nurs)+C+c **or** VA6u+ALs/ASs; (Nursing)
     Ulster – BBC (Nurs A)

260 pts   **Bournemouth** – 260 pts – ALs (Clin Nurs A/C/MH)
     De Montfort (Leicester) – 260 pts (inc 2ALs **or** VA12u) – ALs **or** ALs+ASs (60 pts max) **or** VA12u+/-AL/ASs; (Nurs A/C/MH; Midwif)
     East Anglia – BCC (Nurs A/C/LD/M)
     Leeds – BCC (Midwifery)
     Liverpool – 260 pts – ALs **or** ALs+ASs **or** VAs+/-ALs/ASs; (Nurs A/A+HV)
     Manchester – BCC (Nurs A (HV or DN/MH; Midwif)
     Nottingham – BCC (Nurs C/LD/MH)

240 pts   **Birmingham** – CCC (Nurs A/C/MH)
     Bournemouth – 240 pts from 3ALs **or** 220 pts from 2ALs (inc AL sci); (Midwifery)
     Bradford – 240 pts 12u; gs; (Nurs; Midwif)
     Cambridge (Hom) – 240 pts approx (Nurs A/C/MH)
     Cardiff (UWCM) – 240 pts 18u – CC **or** VA12u CC (hlth sc); (not gs) (Nurs A/C/MH)
     Central Lancashire – 240 pts 12u +interview/police clearance; gs; (Midwifery)
     Glamorgan – CCC (Nurs/Midwif)
     Glasgow – CCC (Nurs A)
     Hertfordshire – 280–240–220 pts (Paramed Sci)
     Hull – CCC (Nurs Sci A/LD)
     London (King's) – CCC (Nurs St)
     Northumbria – CCC/BC (Nurs St A/C/LD/MH; Midwif St)
     Oxford Brookes – CCC (inc sci) **or** CC+cc **or** VA12u CC (hlth sc)+AL(C)/cc **or** VA6u C (hlth sc)+AL(C)+cc; (Nursing A)
     Surrey – 240 pts 18u – ALs (inc C in 2 sci); ALs **or** ALs+ASs **or** VAs+/-ALs/ASs; (Nurs St A/C/LD/MH; Midwif)
     Swansea – 240 pts 18u – CCC **or** ALs+ASs **or** VAs+/-ALs/ASs; (Nurs A/C/MH; Midwif)

230 pts   **Kingston** – 230 pts (inc 2x6u **or** 1x12u inc sci or hlth subj) – ALs **or** ALs+ASs **or** VAs+/-ALs/ASs; gs; (Nurs A)

220 pts   **Brighton** – 220 pts approx (Euro Nurs A/MH; Nurs A/LD/MH)
     Buckinghamshire Chilterns (UC) – 220–180 pts approx (Nurs A/C/MH)
     Central England – 220 pts approx (Nurs A/C/LD/MH; Midwif)

Central Lancashire – 220 pts 12u +interview/police clearance; gs; (Nurs A/C/MH)

Huddersfield – CCD (inc C biol/hum biol) **or** VA12u BB+AL (C biol/hum biol); (not gs) (Midwif St)

Middlesex – 220–180 pts approx (Nurs A/C/MH; Midwif)

North East Wales (IHE) – CCD/CC (Nursing)

Queen Margaret (UC) – CCD (Nurs A)

St Martin's (Coll) – CCD/BB (Nurs St)

200 pts **Bangor** – 200 pts approx (Nurs A/C/LD/MH)

City – 18u – ALs **or** ALs+ASs **or** VAs+/-ALs/ASs; (not gs) (Nurs A/CH/MH)

Hertfordshire – 200 pts approx (Nurs/Soc Wk St)

Liverpool John Moores – 200 pts approx – ALs **or** ALs+ASs **or** VAs+/-ALs/ASs; (Nurs A/C/MH; Midwif)

Oxford Brookes – BB (inc sci) **or** B+bb **or** VA12u (Hlth SC) BB (inc sci) **or** VA6u (hlth sc) B+AL(B); (Nurs C; Midwif)

Staffordshire – 200 pts (inc 160 pts from 2x6u); (Nurs; Midwif)

180 pts **Anglia** – 180 pts 12u – 2ALs **or** VA12u BC; gs; interview+health/police clearance; (Nurs A/C/LD/MH; Midwif)

Bristol UWE – 180–160 pts 12u (inc 6u in biol/psy/sociol); ALs **or** ALs+ASs **or** VAs+/-ALs/ASs; (not gs) (Nurs A/C/LD/MH; Midwif)

Robert Gordon – BC (Nurs A/CN/FN/MH)

Wolverhampton – 180 pts 12u – CDE **or** CD+d **or** VA12u BC; gs; (Nurs; Midwif)

160 pts **Canterbury Christ Church (UC)** – CC (Nurs; Midwif)

Huddersfield – CC (inc 1 sci pref) **or** VAs+AL; gs (not AL) (Nurs C/LD/MH)

Salford – CC (Nurs A/C)

Sheffield Hallam – CC (Nurs St A/C/MH)

Worcester (UC) – 160 pts 12u – CC or/with ASs **or** VAs+/-ALs/ASs; (Midwifery)

150 pts **Southampton** – 150 pts 12u (inc 120 pts from ALs); (Nurs Dip)

140 pts **Abertay Dundee** – CD (inc sci); (Nurs A/MH)

Glasgow Caledonian – CD (inc sci subject) (Nurs St A/LD/MH)

Oxford Brookes – CD **or** C+cd **or** VA12u (hlth sc) CC **or** VA6u (hlth sc) C+AL(D)/cd; (Nurs LD/MH)

Thames Valley – 140 pts approx (Nurs C/MH; Midwif)

120 pts **Suffolk (Coll)** – 120 pts approx (Nurs A/C/LD/MH)

Leeds Met – (contact university)

Diploma of Higher Education and Diploma of Nursing courses:

Anglia; Bournemouth (Midwif); Brighton; Bristol UWE (Nurs C; Midwif); Canterbury Christ Church (UC); Central England; Central Lancashire; Chester (Coll) (also Midwif); City; Coventry; De Montfort; East Anglia (Nurs A/C/LD/MH; Midwif); Glamorgan; Greenwich; Hertfordshire; Hull; Keele; King Alfred's Winchester (Coll); Liverpool John Moores (also Midwif); Luton; Manchester (Coll); Middlesex; Napier; Northampton (UC); Nottingham; Plymouth; Robert Gordon; Sheffield; South Bank; Southampton; Staffordshire; Stirling; Suffolk (Coll) (Commun Nurs); Surrey; Teesside (Coll); Thames Valley; Worcester (UC); York (flexible offer).

Alternative Offers:

IB offers: Birmingham 28 pts; Hull 30–26 pts; Surrey 28 pts (5 in chem and biol); Ulster H555 S44; Wales (UWCM) 26 pts H555.

Irish offers: Brighton BCCC; Bristol UWE BBCC; Surrey BBBB.

Scottish Qualifications: Abertay Dundee BBCC; Edinburgh BBBBC; Glasgow BBBC; Glasgow Caledonian BBCC/BBB; Queen Margaret (UC) BBCC; Robert Gordon BBCC.

Overseas applicants: North East Wales (IHE) No foundation courses. **Surrey** EFL course available.

SCHOOL OF NURSING AND MIDWIFERY

"Qualify for Life"

At UEA we offer Degree and Diploma courses – alongside Professional Registration to practice as a Nurse or Midwife.

We provide a very supportive learning environment and we maintain close links with practice areas.

For specific course information, or to arrange a visit, please contact the Admissions Office:

Norwich campus - 01603 421419
King's Lynn campus - 01553 613917
E-Mail - NAM.Admissions@uea.ac.uk
Website - www.uea.ac.uk/nam

CHOOSING YOUR COURSE (See also **Ch.1**)

Subject information: Nursing and Midwifery courses, usually covering the social sciences and biological and medical studies, lead to state registration. Alternative course choices could include Environmental Health, Community Studies and the para-medical courses and careers of Occupational or Speech Therapy, Physiotherapy or Radiography. See also **Health Sciences/Studies**. See also **Appendix 1**.

Special features: Bangor Emphasis on health promotion within education with complementary strands of information technology and counselling. **Birmingham** Overseas elective and European language option. **Cardiff (UWCM)** Four-year degree follows Project 2000 format. First and second years share a common foundation, specialising in adult, child or mental health nursing. Two-year degree for diploma qualified nurses. **City** Course covers psychology, sociology, philosophy, ethics, physiology, pathology and microbiology in addition to nursing studies. **Edinburgh** Third year options in general or mental health nursing. **Liverpool** Final year electives in clinical nursing research, district nursing or health visiting. **Nottingham** Branch programmes in adult and child nursing, mental health problems and people with learning disabilities. **Oxford Brookes** (Midwif) 50% practice placement under supervision. **Surrey** Integrated teaching of nursing and applied sciences with a final year choice of nursing courses. *NOW CHECK PROSPECTUSES AND WEB SITES.*

Top universities and colleges (Teaching Quality) (see Ch.4): Edinburgh; Glasgow Caledonian; Huddersfield; Liverpool John Moores; Staffordshire; Worcester (UC); not all institutions assessed.

Top universities and colleges (Research) (see Ch.4): London (King's); Manchester; Surrey.

Study opportunities abroad: Central England; East London; Edinburgh; Glamorgan; Middlesex; Oxford Brookes; Queen Margaret (UC); St Martin's (Coll); Sheffield Hallam.

Work opportunities abroad: North London (Health St).

ADMISSIONS INFORMATION

Number of applicants per place (approx): Abertay Dundee 10; Anglia 10; Bangor 10; Birmingham 5; Bournemouth 9; Brighton 3; Bristol UWE 27; Cardiff (UWCM) 12, (Non-EU) 6; Central England 15; Central Lancashire (Midwif) 14; City 21; De Montfort 26; Glasgow Caledonian 12; Hull 10; Leeds (Midwif) 12; Manchester 17; Middlesex 10; North East Wales (IHE) 4; Northumbria 16; St Martin's (Coll) 8; Sheffield Hallam 36; South Bank 16; Surrey 3.

Planning your UCAS personal statement (see Ch.4): Nursing experience – for example in hospitals, old people's homes, children's homes – is important. Describe these experiences and what you have learned from them. Read nursing journals in order to be aware of new developments in the treatment of illnesses. Note, in particular, the various needs of patients and the problems they experience. Try to compare different nursing approaches with, for example children, people with learning disabilities, old people and terminally ill people. If you under-performed at GCSE, provide mitigating circumstances if possible. See also **Appendix 1**.

Selection interviews (see Ch.4): Birmingham (T – essay); Bournemouth (Midwif); Cardiff (UWCM) (T); City (T); Hertfordshire; Sheffield Hallam (T). All institutions interview for this subject since personal qualities and motivation are particularly important.

Interview questions (see Ch.4): Past questions have included: Why do you want to be a nurse? What experience have you had in nursing? What do you think of the nurses' pay situation? Should nurses go on strike? What are your views on abortion? What branch of nursing most interests you? How would you communicate with a foreigner who can't speak English? What is the nurse's role in the community? How should a nurse react in an emergency? How would you cope with telling a patient's relative that the patient was dying? **South Bank** What do you understand by equal opportunities?

Reasons for rejection (non-academic): Insufficient awareness of the roles and responsibilities of a midwife or nurse. Lack of motivation. Poor communication skills. Lack of awareness of nursing departments through the media. (Detailed knowledge of the NHS or nursing practice not usually required.) Failed medical. Unsatisfactory health record. Not fulfilling the Hepatitis B requirements or police check requirements. **Birmingham** No work experience.

GAP YEAR ADVICE

Some institutions will accept a gap year but check with admissions tutor. Work related to health or nursing important. **Bournemouth** Not applicable; offers have to be limited because of clinical placement contracts with NHS Trusts. Offers have to be made subject to occupational health clearance which must be close to the start date. **Northumbria** Gap year not acceptable.

Institutions willing to defer entry after A-Levels: Abertay Dundee; Birmingham; Bournemouth; Cardiff; De Montfort; Glasgow Caledonian; Hertfordshire; Hull; North East Wales (IHE); Northumbria (No); Nottingham; St Martin's (Coll); Sheffield Hallam; South Bank (Prefers not); Surrey.

AFTER RESULTS ADVICE

Institutions which may accept the same points score after A-Levels: Abertay Dundee; Bournemouth; Brighton; Bristol UWE; Cardiff (UWCM); Central England (No); Central Lancashire (No); City; De Montfort; Glasgow Caledonian; Hertfordshire; Hull (No); North East Wales (IHE); Nottingham (No); Queen Margaret (UC); Sheffield Hallam; South Bank; Surrey; Swansea.

Institutions which may accept lower grades/points score after A-Levels: Cardiff (UWCM); De Montfort; Glasgow Caledonian; Hertfordshire; Hull; North East Wales (IHE); Queen Margaret (UC); Sheffield Hallam; Surrey.

Offers to applicants repeating A-Levels: Higher Bristol UWE, Cardiff (UWCM) (BBB), Hull; **Same** South Bank, Surrey.

Probable vacancies from June 2001 and in Clearing (see Ch.4): Some vacancies are likely with offers ranging from 260–160 pts.

NEW GRADUATE DESTINATIONS AND EMPLOYMENT (1999 HESA) (see **Ch.4**)

Of 2210 graduates surveyed, 1812 entered full-time employment, 38 went on to further study and 29 were believed to be unemployed.

NUTRITION (see also Dietetics and Food Science/Studies & Technology)

NB The information supplied by the universities and colleges this year varies considerably and the offers listed below should be used as a first source of reference only. Many institutions will accept combinations of Advanced (AL), Advanced Subsidiary (AS) and Vocational Advanced (VA) level qualifications to achieve the required points total, but applicants must check web sites and prospectuses for full details of all offers. Grades and points totals shown should be regarded as the minimum levels to be achieved, but offers may be adjusted downwards when results are known. The points totals shown to the left of the institutions are for ease of reference only. It must not be assumed that tariff points are always used by institutions or that they can be substituted for an offer in grades. The level of an offer is not necessarily indicative of the quality of a course. To calculate your offers see Chapter 4 and the inside fold of the back cover.

Special subject requirements/preferences: A-Level: Two/three science subjects at A-Level. **GCSE:** Mathematics and a science subject. Chemistry and biology may be required or preferred. **Surrey** Good grade in science required.

330 pts   **Southampton** – 330 pts 21u (inc 200 pts from 2ALs sci pref inc chem); (not gs) (Nutr Sci)

320 pts   **Oxford Brookes** – ABB–CCD; offers depends on 2nd subj; (Nutr/Fd Sci; Pblc Hth Nutr)

280 pts   **Glasgow** – BBC–CCC (Physiol Spo Sci Nutr)

            London (King's) – BBC+AS **or** BB+ccc (or equiv) (inc AL chem+biol pref); VAs considered; (Nutr/Diet)

260 pts   **London (King's)** – BCC+AS **or** BC+ccc (or equiv) (inc AL chem+biol pref); VAs considered; (Nutrition)

            Surrey – BCC (Nutr/Diet)

240 pts   **Glasgow Caledonian** – CCC (Hum Nutr/Fd Sci; Hum Nutr/Diet)

            Newcastle – CCC (Fd/Hum Nutr)

            Nottingham – CCC–CCD; (not gs) (Nutrition)

            Surrey – CCC (Nutr; Nutr/Fd Sci)

            Ulster – CCC/BB (Hum Nutr)

220 pts   **Liverpool John Moores** – 220–180 pts (inc AL biol/chem) – ALs **or** ALs+ASs **or** VAs+/-ALs/ASs; (Nutrition courses)

            South Bank – 220–140 pts approx (Nutrition courses)

            Surrey Roehampton – 220–160 pts approx (inc 2ALs) – ALs **or** ALs+ASs **or** VAs+/-ALs/ASs; (Nutr/Hlth)

200 pts   **Cardiff (UWI)** – 200 pts approx (App Hum Nutr; Diet)

            Greenwich – 200 pts approx (Hum Nutr)

            Kingston – 200 pts 2x6u (inc AL 80 pts chem/biol); (not gs) (Nutrition)

            North London – 200 pts – 3ALs **or** VA12u **or** VA6u (Hum Nutr/Diet)

            Sheffield Hallam – 200 pts approx (Nutr Hlth Lif)

            Teesside – 200–180 pts approx (Fd Sci/Nutr)

180 pts   **Chester (Coll)** – 180 pts approx (Fd Nutr Hlth)

            Manchester Met – 180 pts approx (Fd/Nutr)

            Nottingham Trent – 180 pts (inc sci) (Hum Nutr/Prod Dev)

            Teeside – 180–160 pts (Nutr Hlth Sci)

160 pts   **Central Lancashire** – 160 pts 12u (inc AL biol/chem/env sci); gs; (Fd Nutr)

            Glasgow Caledonian – CC (Hum Nutr/Diet)

            Huddersfield – CC **or** C+cc **or** VA12u CC; gs; (Fd Nutr/Hlth)

            Huddersfield – 160 pts approx (Cat Mgt Nutr)

            Oxford Brookes – CC (Pblc Hlth Nutr)

            Plymouth (Seale Hayne) – 160 pts approx (Fd Qual/Prod Dev Nutr)

140 pts   **Abertay Dundee** – CD (Fd Nutr Hlth)

            Queen Margaret (UC) – CD (Hum Nutr)

            Robert Gordon – CD (Nutr; Nutr/Diet)

120 pts   **North London** – 120 pts – 2ALs **or** VA12u **or** VA6u; (Nutrition)

            Leeds Met – (contact university)

Diploma of Higher Education courses
 80 pts   Oxford Brookes.

Higher National Diploma courses
        Manchester Met.

Alternative Offers:

IB offers: Nottingham 24 pts (sci); South Bank 24 pts; Surrey 28 pts overall.

Irish offers: Nottingham CCCCC1; South Bank CCCC.

Scottish Qualifications: Abertay Dundee BBC; Glasgow BBBB; Glasgow Caledonian BBCC; Nottingham BBBB (first sitting); Queen Margaret (UC) BBC; Robert Gordon BBC.

CHOOSING YOUR COURSE (See also **Ch.1**)

Subject information: This is a study of nutrition in health and disease combined with related subjects such as food science, dietetics, biochemistry, microbiology which could also be considered as separate subjects. See also **Appendix 1** under **Dietetics**.

Special features: Cardiff (UWI) Covers biochemistry, food studies, nutrition, physiology and computing. **Huddersfield** The course covers the basic chemical and biological sciences leading to the study of metabolism, nutrition and food science, as well as catering technology and management. **Nottingham** opportunity for a major research project. **Oxford Brookes** All students take courses in biochemistry, physiology, food chemistry and microbiology. Options include human and clinical nutrition, food science and technology, food microbiology and fermentation and dairy science. **Robert Gordon** Emphasis on applied nutrition, computer applications and management. Course decision can be delayed until end of second year. Course contains elements of business studies. **Surrey** Modular degree programme gives students opportunity to follow interests within discipline. *NOW CHECK PROSPECTUSES AND WEB SITES.*

Top universities and colleges (Research) (see Ch.4): London (King's); Nottingham; Southampton; Surrey.

Study opportunities abroad: Glasgow Caledonian; Huddersfield; Northumbria; Nottingham; Robert Gordon; Southampton; Surrey Roehampton.

Work opportunities abroad: Glasgow Caledonian; Robert Gordon; Sheffield Hallam; Surrey; Teesside; Ulster.

ADMISSIONS INFORMATION

Number of applicants per place (approx): Cardiff (UWI) 5; Glasgow Caledonian 8; Newcastle 5; North London 9; Robert Gordon 4; South Bank 5; Surrey 7.

Planning your UCAS personal statement (see Ch.4): See **Dietetics**. See also **Appendix 1**.

Selection interviews (see Ch.4): Leeds (No); North London; Nottingham (depends on application); Robert Gordon; Sheffield Hallam (No); South Bank; Surrey.

Interview questions (see Ch.4): Past questions have focused on scientific A-level subjects studied – syllabi and aspects of subjects enjoyed by the applicants. Questions then arise from answers. Extensive knowledge expected of nutrition as a career and candidates should have talked to people involved in this type of work, for example dietitians. They will also be expected to discuss wider problems such as food supplies in developing countries and nutritional problems resulting from famine.

GAP YEAR ADVICE

Most institutions will accept a gap year and prefer some work experience related to nutrition.

Institutions willing to defer entry after A-Levels: North London; Nottingham; Queen Margaret (UC); Robert Gordon; Surrey (No preferences; most students change direction as a result of a gap year).

AFTER RESULTS ADVICE

Institutions which may accept the same points score after A-Levels: Cardiff (UWI); Newcastle; North London; Nottingham; Robert Gordon (No); South Bank; Surrey (No); Surrey Roehampton.

Offers to applicants repeating A-Levels: Possibly higher Nottingham; **Same** Surrey, Surrey Roehampton.

Probable vacancies from June 2001 and in Clearing (see Ch.4): Vacancies are likely with offers ranging from 240 to 140 pts.

NEW GRADUATE DESTINATIONS AND EMPLOYMENT (1999 HESA) (see **Ch.4**)

In a survey of 245 graduates, 184 went into full-time employment, 20 went on to further study, and 12 were believed to be unemployed.

OCCUPATIONAL THERAPY

NB The information supplied by the universities and colleges this year varies considerably and the offers listed below should be used as a first source of reference only. Many institutions will accept combinations of Advanced (AL), Advanced Subsidiary (AS) and Vocational Advanced (VA) level qualifications to achieve the required points total, but applicants must check web sites and prospectuses for full details of all offers. Grades and points totals shown should be regarded as the minimum levels to be achieved, but offers may be adjusted downwards when results are known. The points totals shown to the left of the institutions are for ease of reference only. It must not be assumed that tariff points are always used by institutions or that they can be substituted for an offer in grades. The level of an offer is not necessarily indicative of the quality of a course. To calculate your offers see Chapter 4 and the inside fold of the back cover.

Special subject requirements/preferences: A-Level: Biology may be preferred by a number of institutions. **Brunel** Preferred subjects – biology, human biology, psychology, sociology. **GCSE:** English, mathematics and a science, grade A–C. **Brunel** At least four subjects including biology, human biology, chemistry, art and design **Cardiff (UWCM)** Five subjects minimum grade A–C at one sitting including English and mathematics. **Coventry** Five subjects grades A–B.

300 pts   **Brunel** – 300–260 pts 3x6u (inc AL hum sci subj C pref psy/sociol/hum biol **or** VA (hlth subj) B – ALs **or** ALs+ASs **or** VAs+/-ALs/ASs; (not gs) (Occ Thera)
         Ulster – BBB (Occ Thera)
280 pts   **Robert Gordon** – BBC (Occ Thera)
         Southampton – 280 pts 21u (inc 160 pts in 2 sci subjs); (Occ Thera)
270 pts   **Cardiff (UWCM)** – 270 pts 21u – BCD **or** bbcc **or** VA12u (HlthSC) BB; (not gs) (Occ Thera)
260 pts   **St Martin's (Coll)** – BCC/AA (Occ Thera)
         Southampton – BCC (Occ Thera)
240 pts   **Coventry** – CCC/BC (Occ Thera)
         Derby – 240 pts 18u – C(hum biol)CC **or** VAs(HlthSC) CC+/-AL/ASs; gs; (Occ Thera) (Occ Thera)
         East Anglia – 240 pts 18u – CCC; (not gs) (Occ Thera)
         Liverpool – 240 pts – ALs **or** ALs+ASs **or** VAs+/-ALs/ASs; (Occ Thera)
         Northumbria – 240 pts approx (Occ Thera)
         Oxford Brookes – CCD+AS (Occ Thera)
         Ripon & York (Coll) – CCC/BB (Occ Thera)
         Sheffield Hallam – CCC (Occ Thera)
         Teesside – CCC (Occ Thera)
220 pts   **Northampton (UC)** – 220 pts approx (Occ Thera)
200 pts   **Canterbury Christ Church (UC)** – BB (Occ Thera)
160 pts   **Glasgow Caledonian** – CC; gs; (Occ Thera)
         Queen Margaret (UC) – CC (Occ Thera)
         St Loyes (SOT) – CC (Occ Thera)
         Salford – CC (Occ Thera)
140 pts   **and below approx**
         Bristol UWE – (Occ Thera: p/t in-service)

Higher National Diploma courses
         Stevenson (Coll).

Alternative Offers:

IB offers: East Anglia 32 pts; Oxford Brookes 24 pts; Salford 35 pts; Ulster 32 pts.

Scottish Qualifications: Glasgow Caledonian BBCC; Queen Margaret (UC) BBB; Robert Gordon BBCC.

CHOOSING YOUR COURSE (See also **Ch.1**)

Subject information: Occupational Therapy is not an art career although art and craft-work may be involved as a therapeutic exercise. Occupational therapists (who work mostly in hospital departments) are involved in the rehabilitation of those who have required medical treatment and involve the young, aged and, for example, people with learning difficulties. Most courses include psychology, sociology and psychiatry. Selectors look for maturity, initiative, enterprise, tact, sound judgement and organising ability. Other paramedical courses for consideration include Radiography, Osteopathy, Physiotherapy and Podiatry, as well as Psychology, Community Studies and Nursing. See also **Appendix 1**.

Special features: Cardiff (UWCM) Students investigate aspects of the work in community and social services. **Liverpool** The department has a history of accepting students from overseas. Special provision made for disabled students – similarly at **Northampton (UC)**. *NOW CHECK PROSPECTUSES AND WEB SITES.*

Study opportunities abroad: Brunel; Cardiff (UWCM); Coventry; Derby; Oxford Brookes; Queen Margaret (UC); Ripon & York (Coll); Salford.

Work opportunities abroad: Salford.

ADMISSIONS INFORMATION

Number of applicants per place (approx): Brunel 9; Canterbury Christ Church (UC) 5; Cardiff (UWCM) 10; Coventry 15; Derby 17; East Anglia 15; Glasgow Caledonian 40; Northampton (UC) 4; Northumbria 4; Oxford Brookes 12; Queen Margaret (UC) 7; Ripon & York (Coll) 14; Robert Gordon 6; St Martin's (Coll) 20; Salford 16; Sheffield Hallam 23; Southampton 11; Teesside 12; Ulster 13.

Planning your UCAS personal statement (see Ch.4): Contact your local hospital and discuss this career with the occupational therapists. Try to obtain work shadowing experience and make notes of your observations. Describe any such visits in full (see **Reasons for rejection** below). **Brunel** Breadth and nature of health-related work experience. Also skills, interests for example, sports, design. **Ripon & York (Coll)** Contact with the profession essential; very competitive course. **Sheffield Hallam** Applicants should have a high standard of communication skills and experience of working with people with disabilities. See also **Appendix 1**.

Selection interviews (see Ch.4): Brunel; Cardiff (UWCM) (T: Essay set plus problem-solving group); Derby; East Anglia; Oxford Brookes (W); Queen Margaret (UC) (T); Ripon & York (Coll); Robert Gordon; Salford (T); Sheffield Hallam; Southampton (T) (mature students: essay on their life experience).

Interview questions (see Ch.4): Since this a vocational course, work experience is almost essential and applicants are likely to be questioned on the types of work involved and the career.

Reasons for rejection (non-academic): Poor communication skills. Lack of knowledge of occupational therapy. Little evidence of working with people. Applicants are expected to have visited at least two occupational therapy departments, one in a physical or social services setting, one in the mental health field. Uncertain about their future career. Lack of maturity. Indecision regarding the profession. **Salford** Failure to function well in groups and inability to perform practical tasks.

GAP YEAR ADVICE

Some institutions will accept a gap year. Check with admissions tutors. **Coventry** Sometimes; **Northumbria** Does not accept a gap year; **Robert Gordon** Encourages a gap year.

Institutions willing to defer entry after A-Levels: Cardiff (possibly); Derby; Glasgow Caledonian; Northampton (UC); Northumbria; Queen Margaret (UC); Ripon & York (Coll) (No); Robert Gordon; St Martin's (Coll); Salford; Sheffield Hallam; Southampton.

AFTER RESULTS ADVICE

Institutions which may accept the same points score after A-Levels: Cardiff (UWCM); Coventry; East Anglia (in principle); Oxford Brookes; Southampton.

Institutions which may accept lower grades/points score after A-Levels: East Anglia (in principle); Oxford Brookes; Ripon & York (Coll); Southampton.

Probable vacancies from June 2001 and in Clearing (see Ch.4): Some vacancies are possible. Contact your university or college of choice.

NEW GRADUATE DESTINATIONS AND EMPLOYMENT (1999 HESA) (see **Ch.4**)

See **Physiotherapy**.

OCEANOGRAPHY (see also **Marine/Maritime Studies**)

NB The information supplied by the universities and colleges this year varies considerably and the offers listed below should be used as a first source of reference only. Many institutions will accept combinations of Advanced (AL), Advanced Subsidiary (AS) and Vocational Advanced (VA) level qualifications to achieve the required points total, but applicants must check web sites and prospectuses for full details of all offers. Grades and points totals shown should be regarded as the minimum levels to be achieved, but offers may be adjusted downwards when results are known. The points totals shown to the left of the institutions are for ease of reference only. It must not be assumed that tariff points are always used by institutions or that they can be substituted for an offer in grades. The level of an offer is not necessarily indicative of the quality of a course. To calculate your offers see Chapter 4 and the inside fold of the back cover.

Special subject requirements/preferences: A-Level: Check prospectuses, usually science and mathematics subjects. **GCSE:** Science/mathematics subjects.

350 pts **Southampton** – 350 pts 21u (inc 200 pts in 2 ALs sci); (not gs) Oceanography)
340 pts **East Anglia** – AAB+interview; (not gs) (Meteor/Ocean/N Am)
320 pts **East Anglia** – ABB; (not gs) (Meteor/Ocean/Euro)
310 pts **Southampton** – 310 pts 21u (inc 180 pts 2ALs sci inc biol); (not gs) (Ocean; Ocean with Biol/Maths/Phys Geog)
290 pts **Southampton** – 290 pts 21u (inc 160 pts 2ALs+AS sci); (not gs) (Ocean with Geol/Phys)
280 pts **Bangor** – 280 pts – BBC (inc biol+1 sci) **or** VA12u(sci)+AL(biol 80 pts); (not gs) (Mar Biol; App Mar Biol)
　　　　 East Anglia – BBC **or** BB+bc; (not gs) (Meteor/Ocean)
240 pts **Bangor** – 240 pts – CCC (inc biol+1 sci) **or** VA12u(sci)+AL(biol); (not gs) (Mar Biol/Ocean; Mar Biol/Zool)
　　　　 Liverpool – 240 pts – ALs **or** ALs+ASs **or** VAs+/-ALs/ASs; (Ocean/Chem; Ocean/Earth Sci))
　　　　 Plymouth – 240 pts approx (Ocean Sci/Geog; Undwtr St)
220 pts **Plymouth** – 220 pts (Ocean Sci/Chem; Ocean Sci; Surf Sci/Tech)

Diploma of Higher Education courses
80 pts   Plymouth.

Alternative Offers:

IB offers: Bangor 28 pts; Liverpool H555.

CHOOSING YOUR COURSE (See also **Ch.1**)

Subject information: Oceanography includes the dynamics and mathematical modelling of ocean circulation, waves, tides and turbulence; problems of ocean engineering related to oil and gas exploration are covered, together with studies of pollution, marine food production and aquaculture. See also **Marine/Maritime Studies**.

Special features: Bangor Multi-disciplinary marine science course. Strong practical content with work at sea. Heavy continuous assessment. *NOW CHECK PROSPECTUSES AND WEB SITES.*

Top universities and colleges (Teaching Quality) (see Ch.4): Bangor; Plymouth; Southampton; not all institutions assessed.

Top universities and colleges (Research) (see Ch.4): Bangor; Southampton.

Study opportunities abroad: Southampton.

ADMISSIONS INFORMATION

Number of applicants per place (approx): Bangor (All courses) 5; Liverpool 3; Plymouth 5.

Planning your UCAS personal statement (see Ch.4): See **Marine/Maritime Studies**.

Selection interviews (see Ch.4): Bangor; Liverpool.

Interview questions (see Ch.4): Past questions asked on applicants' reasons for choosing Oceanography or Marine Sciences and on A-level science subjects studied. Be prepared to be asked about aspects of the A-level subjects you enjoy since questions are likely to arise from this.

GAP YEAR ADVICE

Institutions willing to defer entry after A-Levels: Bangor.

AFTER RESULTS ADVICE

Probable vacancies from June 2001 and in Clearing (see Ch.4): Contact all universities since vacancies are likely.

NEW GRADUATE DESTINATIONS AND EMPLOYMENT (1999 HESA) (see **Ch.4**)

Of 95 graduates surveyed, 46 obtained full-time employment, 23 went on to further study and eight were unemployed.

OPERATIONAL RESEARCH (see also **Business Courses** and **Mathematics**)

NB The information supplied by the universities and colleges this year varies considerably and the offers listed below should be used as a first source of reference only. Many institutions will accept combinations of Advanced (AL), Advanced Subsidiary (AS) and Vocational Advanced (VA) level qualifications to achieve the required points total, but applicants must check web sites and prospectuses for full details of all offers. Grades and points totals shown should be regarded as the minimum levels to be achieved, but offers may be adjusted downwards when results are known. The points totals shown to the left of the institutions are for ease of reference only. It must not be assumed that tariff points are always used by institutions or that they can be substituted for an offer in grades. The level of an offer is not necessarily indicative of the quality of a course. To calculate your offers see Chapter 4 and the inside fold of the back cover.

Special subject requirements/preferences: A-Level: Mathematics usually required. **GCSE: Swansea** Grade B mathematics.

360 pts and above
       Warwick – AAA–AAB (Maths/OR/Stats/Econ)
300 pts Lancaster – 300 pts approx (OR courses)
       Swansea – 300 pts 18u – BBB/AB **or** ALs+ASs **or** VAs+/-ALs/ASs; (OR)
280 pts Essex – 280–260 pts 21u – BB–BC(B maths)+AL/2ASs; gs; (OR)

Alternative Offers:

IB offers: Lancaster 30 pts; Swansea 32 pts; Warwick 32 pts.

CHOOSING YOUR COURSE (See also **Ch.1**)

> **Subject information:** Operational Research involves mathematical programming, management and statistics leading to applications in production, marketing, distribution and information systems. This is a branch of business studies and management science and these degrees could also be considered. *NOW CHECK PROSPECTUSES AND WEB SITES.*

Study opportunities abroad: Lancaster.

ADMISSIONS INFORMATION

Number of applicants per place (approx): Lancaster 7; Swansea 20.

Planning your UCAS personal statement (see Ch.4): See **Business Courses**.

Interview questions (see Ch.4): This is a highly specialised subject and applicants will be expected to have a knowledge of this field and the types of work done.

AFTER RESULTS ADVICE

Probable vacancies from June 2001 and in Clearing (see Ch.4): Most universities can be contacted for vacancies from June onwards.

NEW GRADUATE DESTINATIONS AND EMPLOYMENT (1999 HESA) (see **Ch.4**)

Out of 59 graduates surveyed, 40 went into full-time employment, one went on to further study and four were believed to be unemployed.

OPTOMETRY (OPHTHALMIC OPTICS) (including Ophthalmic Dispensing, Ophthalmic Management and Orthoptics)

NB The information supplied by the universities and colleges this year varies considerably and the offers listed below should be used as a first source of reference only. Many institutions will accept combinations of Advanced (AL), Advanced Subsidiary (AS) and Vocational Advanced (VA) level qualifications to achieve the required points total, but applicants must check web sites and prospectuses for full details of all offers. Grades and points totals shown should be regarded as the minimum levels to be achieved, but offers may be adjusted downwards when results are known. The points totals shown to the left of the institutions are for ease of reference only. It must not be assumed that tariff points are always used by institutions or that they can be substituted for an offer in grades. The level of an offer is not necessarily indicative of the quality of a course. To calculate your offers see Chapter 4 and the inside fold of the back cover.

Special subject requirements/preferences: A-Level: Mathematics/science subjects. **GCSE:** English usually required. **Bradford** A*, A and B grades

340 pts	**Aston** – 18u – AAB–ABB **or** ALs+ASs **or** VAs+/-ALs/ASs; gs; (Optometry)
	Cardiff – AAB (Optometry)
	City – 2x6u – AAB–ABB (inc 2 sci from maths/biol/phys/chem); ASs/VAs (contact univ); (not gs); (Optometry)
	Ulster – AAB (Optometry)
320 pts	**Anglia** – 320 pts approx (Optometry)
	Bradford – 320 pts 12u (inc 2ALs sci); gs; (Optometry)
	Glasgow Caledonian – ABB; (not gs) (Optometry)
	UMIST – ABB (Optometry)
310 pts	**Liverpool** – 310–300 pts – ALs **or** ALs+ASs **or** VAs+/-ALs/ASs; (Orthoptics)
300 pts	**Glasgow Caledonian** – BBB (Optometry)
280 pts	**Sheffield** – BBC (Orthoptics)
180 pts	**Anglia** – 180–160 pts approx (Oph Disp courses)
160 pts	**Anglia** – 160 pts approx (Opt Mgt)
120 pts	**Glasgow Caledonian** – DD; (not gs) (Oph Disp)
80 pts	**Bradford (Coll)** – 80 pts approx (Oph Disp/Mgt)

Diploma of Higher Education
  Glasgow Caledonian (Oph Disp)

Higher National Diploma courses
  Bradford (Coll)

Alternative Offers:

IB offers: Aston 32 pts; Cardiff H655 + 14 pts; City H655.

Scottish Qualifications: Glasgow Caledonian BBBBB.

CHOOSING YOUR COURSE (See also **Ch.1**)

Subject information: Optometry courses lead to qualification as an optometrist (previously known as an ophthalmic optician). Courses provide training in detecting defects and diseases in the eye and prescribing treatment with, for example, spectacles, contact lenses and other appliances to correct or improve vision. Applied Physics might also be considered as an alternative subject as well as courses related to other medical careers. **Orthoptics** includes the study of general anatomy, physiology and normal child development and leads to a career as an orthoptist. This involves the investigation, diagnosis and treatment of binocular vision and other eye conditions. Most of orthoptists' work is with children and the elderly in areas of public health and education. The main components of degree courses include the study of the eye, the use of diagnostic and measuring equipment and treatment of eye abnormalities. See also **Appendix 1**.

Special features: Anglia (Opt Mgt) The course is a preparation for entry to a career as a dispensing optician. Language option in year 3. **Aston** One-week period of hospital experience. **Bradford** Students have opportunity to work in four eye hospitals on this very clinically oriented course. Special emphasis on the detection of abnormal eye diseases. **City** Tuition in small groups. Modular course in second and third years. Attendance at Moorfields Eye Hospital as part of course. **UMIST** Optometry can be studied with business management, optical instrumentation or clinical neuroscience. *NOW CHECK PROSPECTUSES AND WEB SITES.*

Top universities and colleges (Teaching Quality) (see Ch.4): Aston; Cardiff; not all institutions assessed.

Top universities and colleges (Research) (see Ch.4): Aston; Bradford.

ADMISSIONS INFORMATION

Number of applicants per place (approx): Aston 11; Bradford 12; Cardiff 14; City 11; Glasgow Caledonian 15; UMIST 15.

Planning your UCAS personal statement (see Ch.4): Contact with optometrists is essential, either work shadowing or gaining some work experience. Make notes of your experiences and the work done and report fully on the UCAS form on why the career interests you. See also **Appendix 1**.

Selection interviews (see Ch.4): Aston (No); Bradford; Cardiff (some); City; Glasgow Caledonian; UMIST.

Interview questions (see Ch.4): A competitive subject requiring the applicant to have had some work experience on which they will be questioned.

GAP YEAR ADVICE

Institutions willing to defer entry after A-Levels: Aston; City (submit request in writing); Glasgow Caledonian; UMIST.

AFTER RESULTS ADVICE

Institutions which may accept the same points score after A-Levels: Aston; Bradford; Cardiff; City (No); Glasgow Caledonian; UMIST.

Institutions which may accept lower grades/points score after A-Levels: Bradford; City; UMIST.

Offers to applicants repeating A-Levels: Higher Aston, City; **Same** UMIST.

Probable vacancies from June 2001 and in Clearing (see Ch.4): Only a small number of vacancies are likely.

NEW GRADUATE DESTINATIONS AND EMPLOYMENT (1999 HESA) (see **Ch.4**)

There were 469 graduates surveyed of whom 443 obtained full-time employment. 12 went on to further study and four were believed to be seeking employment.

OSTEOPATHY/OSTEOPATHIC MEDICINE (see also **Chiropractic** and **Health Sciences/Studies**)

NB The information supplied by the universities and colleges this year varies considerably and the offers listed below should be used as a first source of reference only. Many institutions will accept combinations of Advanced (AL), Advanced Subsidiary (AS) and Vocational Advanced (VA) level qualifications to achieve the required points total, but applicants must check web sites and prospectuses for full details of all offers. Grades and points totals shown should be regarded as the minimum levels to be achieved, but offers may be adjusted downwards when results are known. The points totals shown to the left of the institutions are for ease of reference only. It must not be assumed that tariff points are always used by institutions or that they can be substituted for an offer in grades. The level of an offer is not necessarily indicative of the quality of a course. To calculate your offers see Chapter 4 and the inside fold of the back cover.

Special subject requirements/preferences: A-Level: One or two sciences usually required. **European (Sch Ost)** Two sciences inc physics if not taken at GCSE. Check institutions. **GCSE:** English and mathematics.

240 pts	**British Coll (Natur/Ost)** – 240–220 pts approx (inc B/C); (Ost Med; Naturop Med)
200 pts	**Anglia** – 200 pts approx (Osteopathy)
	Nescot – BB (Ost Med)

160 pts **European (Sch Ost)** – 160 pts – CC **or** cccc **or** VA12u CC; (not gs)
(Osteopathy)
80 pts **minimum**
British School of Osteopathy – (College diploma – contact admissions tutor)

CHOOSING YOUR COURSE (See also **Ch.1**)

> **Subject information:** Osteopathy is a system of manipulation which, by correcting joint and tissue abnormalities to restore physical and mental well-being, makes it easier for a patient's body to function normally and use its own recuperative powers more effectively. In short, it helps to restore harmony within the body's mechanism. Naturopathic, or holistic, osteopathy focuses on more than diagnosing and treating the structural and mechanical problems of the body. It lays emphasis on wholeness and health. It does this by linking the mental make-up, the body's structure and its biochemistry (nutrition). Alternative courses include Physiotherapy, Chiropractic, Sports Science/Injuries, Exercise and Health Science, Sports Rehabilitation. See **Appendix 1**.

Special features: British School of Osteopathy Largest training establishment in Europe. Third and fourth year students assist clinical staff with treatments of outpatients. Average cost of training is £5600.

ADMISSIONS INFORMATION

Planning your UCAS personal statement (see Ch.4): Evidence of talking to an osteopath and any work using your hands.

Interview questions (see Ch.4): It is very important that applicants should have discussed this career with a practising osteopath. Interview questions are likely to arise from this and will test the applicant's understanding of osteopathy, including the differences between the work of osteopaths, chiropractors and physiotherapists.

AFTER RESULTS ADVICE

Probable vacancies from June 2001 and in Clearing (see Ch.4): Contact the institutions.

NEW GRADUATE DESTINATIONS AND EMPLOYMENT (1999 HESA) (see **Ch.4**)

No data available.

PATHOLOGY (see also **Biological Sciences**, **Biology** and **Microbiology**)

NB The information supplied by the universities and colleges this year varies considerably and the offers listed below should be used as a first source of reference only. Many institutions will accept combinations of Advanced (AL), Advanced Subsidiary (AS) and Vocational Advanced (VA) level qualifications to achieve the required points total, but applicants must check web sites and prospectuses for full details of all offers. Grades and points totals shown should be regarded as the minimum levels to be achieved, but offers may be adjusted downwards when results are known. The points totals shown to the left of the institutions are for ease of reference only. It must not be assumed that tariff points are always used by institutions or that they can be substituted for an offer in grades. The level of an offer is not necessarily indicative of the quality of a course. To calculate your offers see Chapter 4 and the inside fold of the back cover.

Special subject requirements/preferences: A-Level: Three science/mathematics subjects. **GCSE:** Grade A mathematics.

300 pts   **Bristol** – BBB (inc chem+sci) **or** BB+bbb (AL chem/biol/maths); (not gs)
           (Path/Microbiol; Cell/Mol Path)
220 pts   **Bradford** – 220 pts 12u (inc AL biol/chem); gs; (Cell Path)

Alternative Offers:

IB offers: Bradford 24 pts; Bristol 34 pts.

CHOOSING YOUR COURSE (See also **Ch.1**)

> **Subject information:** This subject is concerned with the study of disease processes and their underlying cellular and molecular mechanisms. Most courses are research-based and students normally undertake their own final year original research projects. Appropriate alternative courses include Anatomy, Physiology, Genetics and Microbiology. See also **Appendix 1** under **Biology**.

Special features: Bristol (Pathology) Emphasis on cancer biology; immunology and virology at cellular and molecular level. This is a strong science-based course with emphasis on research. *NOW CHECK PROSPECTUSES AND WEB SITES.*

ADMISSIONS INFORMATION

Planning your UCAS personal statement (see Ch.4): Describe your interest in this subject. Read scientific and medical journals to increase your awareness of its importance. Discuss the work with hospital staff working in pathology departments. See also **Appendix 1** under **Biology**.

Interview questions (see Ch.4): Applicants are likely to be tested on their motivation for choosing a degree course in Pathology. Questions are often asked about their A/AS-Level subjects, particularly on work relating to the biological sciences.

AFTER RESULTS ADVICE

Probable vacancies from June 2001 and in Clearing (see Ch.4): Contact universities.

NEW GRADUATE DESTINATIONS AND EMPLOYMENT (1999 HESA) (see **Ch.4**)

No data available.

PEACE STUDIES (see also **Social Studies/Science**)

NB The information supplied by the universities and colleges this year varies considerably and the offers listed below should be used as a first source of reference only. Many institutions will accept combinations of Advanced (AL), Advanced Subsidiary (AS) and Vocational Advanced (VA) level qualifications to achieve the required points total, but applicants must check web sites and prospectuses for full details of all offers. Grades and points totals shown should be regarded as the minimum levels to be achieved, but offers may be adjusted downwards when results are known. The points totals shown to the left of the institutions are for ease of reference only. It must not be assumed that tariff points are always used by institutions or that they can be substituted for an offer in grades. The level of an offer is not necessarily indicative of the quality of a course. To calculate your offers see Chapter 4 and the inside fold of the back cover.

Special subject requirements/preferences: A-Level: Any two subjects. **Bradford** History preferred.

300 pts   **Bradford** – BBC/BB (Peace St courses; Int Rel/Secur St; Cnflct Resoln)
260 pts   **Lancaster** – BCC–CCC (Peace St/Int Rel)

Alternative Offers:

IB offers: Bradford 28 pts.

CHOOSING YOUR COURSE (See also **Ch.1**)

Subject information: Peace Studies is a very specialised subject which can be described as a joint study of politics and sociology covering international relations, conflict, democracy, Third World politics, peace and security. Politics, Government, Sociology and Development Studies courses can be considered separately.

Special features: Bradford Focus on contemporary issues of peace, conflict and conflict resolution; specialisms include conflict, international relations, defence and security; 30% of students are mature. *NOW CHECK PROSPECTUSES AND WEB SITES.*

ADMISSIONS INFORMATION

General Studies acceptable: Bradford.

Planning your UCAS personal statement (see Ch.4): Maintain a constant update on news reports of national and international affairs. On your UCAS form explain your interests in the subject and any particular aspects which you feel are important. Give details of any voluntary work you have done.

Examples of interview questions (see Ch.4): Applicants should be fully aware of the course content. They should also have read widely outside the subject and be familiar with national, international, social and political problems relating to it.

AFTER RESULTS ADVICE

Probable vacancies from June 2001 and in Clearing (see Ch.4): Vacancies are almost certain.

NEW GRADUATE DESTINATIONS AND EMPLOYMENT (1999 HESA) (see **Ch.4**)

No data available.

PHARMACOLOGY (including **Pharmaceutical Science** and **Toxicology**; see also **Biological Sciences** and **Health Sciences/Studies**)

NB The information supplied by the universities and colleges this year varies considerably and the offers listed below should be used as a first source of reference only. Many institutions will accept combinations of Advanced (AL), Advanced Subsidiary (AS) and Vocational Advanced (VA) level qualifications to achieve the required points total, but applicants must check web sites and prospectuses for full details of all offers. Grades and points totals shown should be regarded as the minimum levels to be achieved, but offers may be adjusted downwards when results are known. The points totals shown to the left of the institutions are for ease of reference only. It must not be assumed that tariff points are always used by institutions or that they can be substituted for an offer in grades. The level of an offer is not necessarily indicative of the quality of a course. To calculate your offers see Chapter 4 and the inside fold of the back cover.

Special subject requirements/preferences: A-Level: Two–three science subjects. Chemistry usually required. **GCSE:** English and mathematics. **Cambridge** Grade A in most subjects preferred. **Portsmouth** Chemistry essential, biology preferred.

360 pts   and above
        Cambridge – Offers, mainly in grades, vary between colleges (Nat Sci – Pharmacology)
330 pts   Southampton – 330 pts 21u (inc 200 pts 2ALs sci pref inc chem) (Pharmacology)

300 pts **Bath** – BBB or ALs+ASs (inc AL chem+biol/maths/phys); (not gs)
(Pharmacology)
Bristol – BBB (inc chem+1 sci); (not gs) (Pharmacology)
London (King's) – BBB+AS or BB+ab+AS or AC+ab+AS (inc 2ALs
chem/biol/sci) or VA12u BB+AL(B)+AS; (Pharmacol/Mgt)
London (UCL) – BBB–BBC or 3ALs+AS/VA; (Pharmacol; Physiol/Pharmacol)
Middlesex – 300–240 pts (Trad Chin Med)
Newcastle – BBB–BCC; (not gs) (Pharmacology)
Sheffield – 300 pts approx (Pharmacol/Physiol)
Strathclyde – BBB (Pharm Sci)
280 pts **Aberdeen** – BBC (Pharmacol Biomed Sci)
Cardiff – BBC (Pharmacology)
Edinburgh – BBC (Pharmacology)
Glasgow – BBC–CCC (Pharmacology courses)
Leeds – BBC (Pharmacology)
Leeds – 280 pts approx (Pharmacol/Physiol; Pharmacol/Mgt St;
Pharmacol/Chem; Pharmacol/Euro)
London (King's) – BBC+AS or BB+bb+AS or AC+bb+AS (inc 2ALs
chem/biol/sci) or VA12u BB+AL(C)+AS or VA6u+ALs/ASs; (Pharmacol;
Pharmacol/Euro; Pharmacol/Tox)
Manchester – BBC (Pharmacol courses)
Sheffield – BBC (Pharmacology)
Strathclyde – BBC (Pharmacol Bioch; Immun/Pharmacol)
260 pts **Hertfordshire** – 260–220 pts 1x12u or 2x6u – 2ALs or ALs+ASs or VA12u; gs;
(Pharmacol; Pharm Sci)
Surrey – BCC–CCC (Biochem (Pharmacol))
Wolverhampton – 260 pts 18u – BCC or CC+e or VA12u AA; gs; (Pharmacol
Comb Hons)
240 pts **Liverpool** – 240 pts – ALs or ALs+ASs or VAs+/-ALs/ASs; (Pharmacology)
Liverpool John Moores – CCC–CDD (inc AL chem+2 sci biol pref) or
ALs+ASs or VA+AL (chem); (not gs) (Pharm Chem Sci)
North London – 240 pts approx (Pharm Sci)
Sunderland – 240 pts – ALs or VA12u+/-AL/ASs; (Pharmacology)
220 pts **Aberdeen** – CCD (Pharmacology)
Bradford – 220 pts 12u (inc AL biol/chem); gs; (Pharmacology)
Brighton – 220 pts (Herb Med; Hom Med)
Bristol UWE – 220 pts approx (App Physiol/Pharmacol)
Central Lancashire – CCD (Physiol/Pharmacol)
Luton – 220 pts approx (Pharmacology)
Middlesex – 220–180 pts approx (Herb Med)
Portsmouth – 220 pts – ALs or ALs+ASs or VAs; gs; (Pharmacol; Pharm
Sci)
200 pts **Brighton** – 200 pts approx (Pharm Chem Sci)
Dundee – 200 pts approx/CDD (Pharmacology courses)
Kingston – 200–160 pts (inc AL chem/biol); (MPharm Sci)
Robert Gordon – CDD (Pharm Sci)
180 pts **Coventry** – 180 pts approx (Pharm Sci courses)
De Montfort (Leicester) – 180 pts – ALs or ALs+ASs or VAs+/-ALs/ASs;
(Pharm Sci courses)
East London – 180–120 pts approx (Pharmacology courses)
Greenwich – 180 pts approx (Pharm Sci)
Kingston – 180–160 pts (inc AL chem/biol); (BSc Pharm Sci)
Nottingham Trent – 180 pts approx (Physiol/Pharmacol)
160 pts **Anglia** – 160 pts approx (Env Tox)
Huddersfield – 160 pts 12u – 2ALs or AL+2ASs or VAs+/-ALs/ASs; gs;
(Pharm Sci)
140 pts **Napier** – CD (Tox; Immun)
Sunderland – CD (Fdn Pharmacol)

120 pts and below
Barnsley (Coll) – (Sci Fdn – Pharmacol)
Nescot – DD (Pharmacology)
North London – 120 pts 1x12u **or** 2x6u; (Pharm Sci)

Higher National Diploma courses
Hertfordshire; Kingston; Wolverhampton.

Alternative Offers:

EB offers: Bradford 65% (Pass with minimum 6s in biol/chem + 5 Engl).

IB offers: Aberdeen 26 pts; Bath 32 pts; Birmingham 30 pts; Bradford 24 pts; Bristol 30 pts H66 inc 2 sci; Cardiff 28 pts; Glasgow H555; Leeds 26; Liverpool 30 pts H555; Portsmouth H555; Sheffield 28 pts inc H6 chem.

Irish offers: Aberdeen BBCC/BCCCC; Bradford BBBB; Glasgow BBB; Liverpool BBCCC; Sheffield BBBBC inc chemistry.

Scottish Qualifications: Aberdeen BBBC; Dundee BBCC; Edinburgh BBBB; Glasgow BBBB; Napier (Tox) CD; Robert Gordon (Pharm Sci) BCC; Strathclyde BBC.

CHOOSING YOUR COURSE (See also **Ch.1**)

Subject information: Pharmacology is the study of drugs and medicine in which courses focus on physiology, biochemistry, toxicology, immunology, microbiology and chemotherapy. Pharmacologists are not qualified to work as pharmacists. Toxicology involves the study of the adverse effects of chemicals on living systems. Note that 'Pharmaceutical Science' is not a pharmacy qualification although it is a subject which covers chemistry, biochemistry and pharmacology. Other scientific/medical courses include Anatomy, Genetics, Human Sciences, Life Sciences which could also be considered. See also **Appendix 1** under **Pharmacy**.

Special features: Bath Majority of students follow sandwich courses. High level of practical project work. **Birmingham** Options in anatomy, pharmacology, physiology. **Bristol** Subjects studied include chemistry, anatomy and biochemistry. Emphasis on neuropharmacology. **Cardiff** Specialist services (clinical trials unit, poisons information and adverse drug reaction) allow for a broad-based course and provide excellent individual research projects in final year. **Edinburgh** Biology and physiology are taken by all students specialising in Pharmacology. **Leeds** Pharmacology is taken with physiology and biochemistry in the first year. **Middlesex** (Herbal Medicine) Four-year course leading to full qualification membership of the National Institute of Medical Herbalists (includes clinical training). **Portsmouth** Pharmacology taken in all three years. Industrial placement option between second and third years. **Sheffield** Close contacts with two pharmaceutical companies, one giving financial support to department; paid vacation employment arranged with this company. *NOW CHECK PROSPECTUSES AND WEB SITES.*

Top universities and colleges (Research) (see Ch.4): Bristol; Cambridge; Dundee; Edinburgh; Leicester; Liverpool; London (Royal Free HSM), (UCL); Newcastle.

Study opportunities abroad: Dundee; East London; Kingston; Leeds; Manchester.

Work opportunities abroad: Bath; Hertfordfshire; Kingston; Leeds; Manchester.

ADMISSIONS INFORMATION

Number of applicants per place (approx): Bath 12; Birmingham 8; Bradford 20; Bristol 12; Cardiff 6; East London 4; Hertfordshire 10; Leeds 7; Liverpool 8; Manchester 27; Nescot 8; Portsmouth 7; Sheffield 12; Strathclyde 10; Sunderland 12.

Planning your UCAS personal statement (see Ch.4): Contact with the pharmaceutical industry is important in order to be aware of the range of work undertaken. Read pharmaceutical journals (although note that Pharmacology and Pharmacy courses lead to different careers). **Bath** Interests outside A-level studies. Evidence that there is more to the student than A-level ability. See also **Pharmacy**.

Selection interviews (see Ch.4): Bath; Cardiff; Liverpool John Moores; Manchester; Newcastle; Portsmouth (No); Sheffield (No); Strathclyde (No); Sunderland.

interview questions (see Ch.4): Why do you want to do Pharmacology? Why not Pharmacy? Why not Chemistry? How are pharmacologists employed in industry? What are the issues raised by anti-vivisectionists on animal experimentation? Questions relating to the A-level syllabus in chemistry and biology.

Reasons for rejection (non-academic): Confusion between Pharmacology and Pharmacy. One university rejected two applicants because they had no motivation or understanding of the course (one had A-Levels at AAB!). Insurance against rejection for Medicine.

GAP YEAR ADVICE

Institutions willing to defer entry after A-Levels: Bath; Birmingham; Bradford; Bristol; Cardiff; Leeds; London (UCL) (No); Portsmouth.

AFTER RESULTS ADVICE

Institutions which may accept the same points score after A-Levels: Bath; Bradford; Bristol; Cardiff; Leeds; Liverpool; London (UCL) (No); Manchester; Portsmouth; Sheffield (C chem); Strathclyde (No); Sunderland.

Institutions which may accept lower grades/points score after A-Levels: Bath; Bradford.

Offers to applicants repeating A-Levels: Higher Bristol, Leeds; **Possibly higher** Bath, Sheffield; **Same** Bradford, Portsmouth.

Probable vacancies from June 2001 and in Clearing (see Ch.4): Most institutions had vacancies, but, again, do not confuse Pharmacology with Pharmacy (the pharmacologist cannot work as a pharmacist). Highest offers 260–240 pts.

NEW GRADUATE DESTINATIONS AND EMPLOYMENT (1999 HESA) (see **Ch.4**)

Out of 510 graduates surveyed, 251 entered full-time employment (mainly in pharmaceuticals but also in managerial, clerical and sales occupations), 40 were believed to be unemployed and 173 went into research.

PHARMACY

NB The information supplied by the universities and colleges this year varies considerably and the offers listed below should be used as a first source of reference only. Many institutions will accept combinations of Advanced (AL), Advanced Subsidiary (AS) and Vocational Advanced (VA) level qualifications to achieve the required points total, but applicants must check web sites and prospectuses for full details of all offers. Grades and points totals shown should be regarded as the minimum levels to be achieved, but offers may be adjusted downwards when results are known. The points totals shown to the left of the institutions are for ease of reference only. It must not be assumed that tariff points are always used by institutions or that they can be substituted for an offer in grades. The level of an offer is not necessarily indicative of the quality of a course. To calculate your offers see Chapter 4 and the inside fold of the back cover.

Special subject requirements/preferences: A-Level: Two–three science subjects. Chemistry usually required. **GCSE:** English, mathematics and a science subject. **Aston** Ideally, grade A in English, mathematics and a science. **Bath** Grade A or B in mathematics preferred and at least grade C in English. **Cardiff** A*, A and Bs in chemistry, a biological subject and mathematics. **Robert Gordon** Grade A–C in English. **Strathclyde** School leavers from England and N Ireland only admitted into year 1.

350 pts **London (King's)** – BBB+b **or** ABC+b **or** BB+bbb **or** AB+bbc (inc AL chem+sci+AS or AL/AS maths pref); (Pharmacy)
340 pts **Belfast (Queen's)** – AAB–ABB (Pharmacy)
          Cardiff – 340 pts approx (B chem) (Pharmacy)
          Nottingham – AAB–ABB (Pharmacy)
320 pts **Bath** – ABB (inc chem+sci) **or** ALs+ASs (check with dept); (not gs) (Pharmacy)
          London (Sch Pharm) – ABB–BBB; (not gs) (Pharmacy)
          Manchester – ABB–BBB (Pharmacy)
300 pts **Aston** – 18u – BBB **or** ALs+ASs **or** VAs+/-ALs/ASs; gs; (Pharmacy)
          Brighton – 300–260 pts approx (B chem) (Pharmacy)
          De Montfort (Leicester) – BBB–BBC (inc chem) **or** ALs+ASs **or** VAs+/-ALs/ASs; (not gs) (Pharmacy)
          Liverpool John Moores – 300–240 pts approx (inc AL chem+2 sci biol pref) – ALs **or** ALs+ASs **or** VA (Sci)+AL (chem); (Pharmacy)
          Strathclyde – BBB (Pharmacy)
          Sunderland – 300 pts – ALs **or** ALs+ASs **or** VAs+/-ALs/ASs; gs; (Pharmacy)
280 pts **Bradford** – 280 pts 12u (inc AL chem+sci); ((MPharm) Pharmacy)
260 pts **Portsmouth** – 260 pts – ALs **or** ALs+ASs **or** VAs; (Pharmacy)
          Robert Gordon – BCC (Pharmacy)
240 pts **Bradford** – 240 pts 12u (inc AL sci); gs; (Pharm Mgt)

Alternative Offers:

IB offers: Aston 32 pts; Bath 32 pts; Belfast (Queen's) H766; Bradford 30 pts; Brighton 28 pts H6 chem; Cardiff H665 chem, biol, phys or maths; De Montfort 30 pts.

Irish offers: Bradford AABBB; Brighton ABB.

Scottish Qualifications: Robert Gordon BBBB; Strathclyde BBBB.

Overseas applicants: De Montfort Introductory courses available. **Robert Gordon** No foundation course.

CHOOSING YOUR COURSE (See also **Ch.1**)

> **Subject information:** All Pharmacy courses are very similar and lead to qualification as a pharmacist who may then work in hospitals or private practice. Alternative courses include Biochemistry, Biological Sciences, Chemistry, Pharmacology or Pharmaceutical Sciences and the wide range of medical courses. **Note** All courses leading to MPharm are now four years. See also **Appendix 1**.

Special features: Aston Introductory courses available for students without A-Levels in mathematics. **Bath** Final year compulsory courses in infectious diseases, chemotherapy, medicinal chemistry, the practice of pharmacy, computer-aided learning, clinical pharmacy and therapeutics. Students taught by practising pharmacists. Assistance and encouragement given in obtaining vacation employment and pre-registration placements. **Bradford** (Pharmacy) Two six-month sandwich periods. (Pharm Mgt) The course covers pharmaceutical science, management and a language but is not a qualification as a pharmacist. (Pharm) Unique sandwich course. **Brighton** Work experience in hospital and community pharmacy. **Robert Gordon** Course has a blend of pharmaceutical sciences and patient-focused teaching. *NOW CHECK PROSPECTUSES AND WEB SITES.*

Top universities and colleges (Teaching Quality) (see Ch.4): Aston; Cardiff; not all institutions assessed.

Top universities and colleges (Research) (see Ch.4): Bath; Cardiff; London (King's); (Sch Pharm); Manchester; Nottingham; Strathclyde.

Study opportunities abroad: Aston; Bath; Bradford; De Montfort; London (Sch Pharm); Portsmouth; Sunderland.

ADMISSIONS INFORMATION

Number of applicants per place (approx): Aston 14; Bath 12; Bradford 10; Brighton 24 (apply early); Cardiff 15; De Montfort 14; Liverpool John Moores 20; London (Sch Pharm) 13; Nottingham 11; Portsmouth 20; Robert Gordon 11; Strathclyde 10; Sunderland 20.

Planning your UCAS personal statement (see Ch.4): Work experience/shadowing with a retail and/or hospital pharmacist is important. Read pharmaceutical journals, extend your knowledge of well-known drugs and antibiotics. Read up on the history of drugs. Attendence at open days or careers conference. See also **Appendix 1**.

Selection interviews (see Ch.4): Aston; Bath; Bradford; Brighton; Cardiff (T); De Montfort; Liverpool John Moores (T); London (Sch Pharm); Nottingham; Portsmouth (No); Robert Gordon; Strathclyde; Sunderland.

Interview questions (see Ch.4): Work experience is essential for applicants for this degree course and relevant questions could include: Why do you want to study Pharmacy? What types of work do pharmacists do? What interests you about the Pharmacy course? What branch of pharmacy do you want to enter? Name a drug – what do you know about it (formula, use etc)? Name a drug from a natural source and its use. Can you think of another way of extracting a drug? Why do fungi destroy bacteria? What is an antibiotic? Can you name one and say how it was discovered? What is insulin? What is its source and function? What is diabetes? What type of insulin is used in its treatment? What is a hormone? What drugs are available over the counter without prescription? What is the formula of aspirin? What is genetic engineering? **Bath** 400 approx selected for interview – very few rejected at this stage. **Cardiff** Interviews cover both academic and vocational aspects; candidates must gain a satisfactory level in both areas. **Liverpool John Moores** Aptitude test.

Reasons for rejection (non-academic): Poor communication skills. Poor knowledge of Pharmacy and the work of a pharmacist.

GAP YEAR ADVICE

Most institutions are willing to accept a gap year. **Liverpool John Moores** Applicants must confirm in writing their intention to join the course at least six weeks before it starts.

Institutions willing to defer entry after A-Levels: Aston; Bath; Bradford; Brighton; De Montfort (No); London (Sch Pharm); Portsmouth (No); Robert Gordon (No); Strathclyde.

AFTER RESULTS ADVICE

Institutions which may accept the same points score after A-Levels: Aston; Bath; Bradford; Brighton; De Montfort; Liverpool John Moores (No); London (Sch Pharm) (No); Portsmouth; Robert Gordon; Strathclyde (No); Sunderland.

Institutions which may accept lower grades/points score after A-Levels: De Montfort.

Offers to applicants repeating A-Levels: Higher Bath (depending upon various factors), Belfast (Queen's), Bradford, Cardiff, De Montfort, Liverpool John Moores, London (Sch Pharm), Nottingham (offers rarely made), Portsmouth; Strathclyde, Sunderland; **Possibly higher** Aston, Robert Gordon; **Same** Brighton.

Probable vacancies from June 2001 and in Clearing (see Ch.4): A number of universities usually declare vacancies.

NEW GRADUATE DESTINATIONS AND EMPLOYMENT (1999 HESA) (see **Ch.4**)

Of 1238 graduates surveyed, 1186 entered full-time employment (mainly retail or hospital pharmacies and a small number in the pharmaceutical industry), 13 went into research, and only five were reported to be unemployed.

PHILOSOPHY

NB The information supplied by the universities and colleges this year varies consider-ably and the offers listed below should be used as a first source of reference only. Many institutions will accept combinations of Advanced (AL), Advanced Subsidiary (AS) and Vocational Advanced (VA) level qualifications to achieve the required points total, but applicants must check web sites and prospectuses for full details of all offers. Grades and points totals shown should be regarded as the minimum levels to be achieved, but offers may be adjusted downwards when results are known. The points totals shown to the left of the institutions are for ease of reference only. It must not be assumed that tariff points are always used by institutions or that they can be substituted for an offer in grades. The level of an offer is not necessarily indicative of the quality of a course. To calculate your offers see Chapter 4 and the inside fold of the back cover.

Special subject requirements/preferences: A-Level: Oxford (PPE) One or more from A-Level science/mathematics recommended. (Phil/Theol) A-Level religious studies con-sidered. **GCSE:** English and mathematics. **Aberdeen, Dundee, Edinburgh, Glasgow, St Andrews** English, mathematics or science and a foreign language. **London (LSE)** Grades A*, A or B, grade C or better in mathematics. **Oxford, Cambridge** Grade A in most subjects preferred. **Sussex** Grade B in foreign language. **Swansea** Grades AA BBB CC.

360 pts **and above**
    Cambridge – Offers, mainly in grades, vary between colleges (Philosophy courses)
    Oxford – Offers vary between candidates (Philosophy courses)
    Southampton – 370–330 pts 21u (inc 200 pts from 2ALs inc econ/maths for Joint Hons courses); (Phil; Phil with Econ/Maths/Pol/Sociol)
340 pts **Bristol** – AAB (inc A maths subj); (not gs) (Phil; Phil with Fr/Maths/Pol)
    Bristol – AAB–BBC (Philosophy courses except **above**)
    Edinburgh – AAB–BBB (Philosophy courses)
    Nottingham – AAB–BBC (Philosophy courses)
    St Andrews – AAb-BBC (Philosophy courses)
    Sheffield – AAB (Phil/Psy)
    Warwick – AAB–ABB (Phil/Pol; Phil/Lit)
    York – 18–12u – BBB+c-BBC+c; (Philosophy)
320 pts **Birmingham** – ABB (Philosophy courses)
    Bristol – ABB–BBC (check subj reqs); (not gs); (Phil with Econ/Ger/Ital/Port/Psy/Russ/Span)
    Cardiff – ABB–BCC (Philosophy courses)
    Durham – ABB (Phil/Engl Lit; Phil/Psy)
    Exeter – 320–300 pts 18u (inc AL lang for Euro course) – ABB–BBB **or** AB+ab **or** BB+aa **or** VAs (contact univ); (not gs) (Phil/Hist/Euro St; Phil/Hist)
    London (LSE) – ABB (Phil; Phil Econ)
    London (UCL) – ABB **or** 3ALs+AS/VA; (Philosophy; Phil/Hist Art; Phil/Econ; Phil/Gk; Phil/Ling)
    Manchester – ABB–BBB (Philosophy courses)
    Sheffield – ABB (Phil/Engl)
    Warwick – 320 pts approx (Phil; Phil/Comp Sci; Phil/Class Civ; Phil/Psy)
300 pts **Durham** – BBB (Phil/Pol)
    East Anglia – 300–280 pts 18u (inc AL BB) – BBC–BCC **or** BBC+e **or** BB+cc **or** VA BB+AL(C); gs; (Philosophy courses; PPE)
    Hull – BBB–BCC (Philosophy courses)
    Keele – BBB–BCC **or** equiv AS accepted; gs; (Philosophy courses)
    Kent – 300 pts approx (Philosophy)
    Leeds – 18u – BBB **or** BB+bb; VAs (contact univ); gs; (Philosophy courses)
    Liverpool – 300 pts – ALs **or** ALs+ASs **or** VAs+/-ALs/ASs; (Phil/Pol; Phil)

London (King's) – BBB+AS or BB+bbb; VAs considered; (Phil; Phil with Hisp St/Theol/Gk)

Newcastle – ABC–BBB (Phil St courses)

Reading – BBB–BCC (Philosophy courses except under **260 pts**)

Sheffield – BBB (Phil; Phil/Mus; Phil/Pol; Phil/Ger; Phil/Hisp St)

Sussex – BBB (Philosophy courses)

280 pts **Durham** – BBC (Jap/Phil; Phil/Chin; Phil)

Essex – 280–260 pts 21u – BB–BC+AL/2ASs or VA12u BB–BC+AL; gs; (Philosophy courses)

Exeter – 280 pts 18u – BBC or BB+bb or VAs (contact univ); gs; (Philosophy courses except under **320 pts**)

Glasgow – BBC (Philosophy courses)

Lancaster – BBC–BCC (Philosophy courses)

Liverpool – 280 pts – ALs or ALs+ASs or VAs+/-ALs/ASs; (Phil/Lang courses)

London (Hey) – 280–260 pts approx (Phil; Phil/Theol)

Sheffield – BBC (Phil/Russ)

Stirling – BBC–CCC (Philosophy courses)

Swansea – 280 pts 18u – BBC–BCC/AB or ALs+ASs or VAs+/-ALs/ASs; (Philosophy courses)

260 pts **Belfast (Queen's)** – BCC (Philosophy courses)

Dundee – BCC (Philosophy courses except under **280 pts**)

Hull – BCC–CCC (Phil/Theol; Fr/Phil)

Reading – 260 pts approx (Phil Comp Sci)

240 pts **Aberdeen** – CCC (Philosophy)

Bradford – 240 pts 12u; gs; (Phil; Hist/Phil)

Hertfordshire – 240–200 pts 1x12u or 2x6u; gs; (Phil Hum Mod)

Ulster – CCC/BC (Philosophy; Hum Comb courses)

220 pts **Greenwich** – 220–160 pts approx (Philosophy courses)

Kingston – 220 pts approx (Hist Ideas courses except under **200 pts**)

Lampeter – 220 pts approx (Phil St; Phil)

Manchester Met – CDD (Phil/Ital; Phil/Span; Phil/Soc Econ Hist)

Manchester Met – 220–200 pts approx (Philosophy)

Middlesex – 220–180 pts approx (Phil; Phil/Span)

Wolverhampton – 220–160 pts 12u – DDD–CDE/CC or CD+d/e or VA12u CC; gs; (Philosophy)

200 pts **Central Lancashire** – 200–160 pts 12u – gs; (Philosophy courses)

Kingston – 200–180 pts 2x6u; gs; (Hist Ideas)

Northampton (UC) – 200–160 pts approx (Philosophy courses)

Staffordshire – 200 pts – ALs (inc CC) or CC+AS(40 pts) or VA CC; gs; (Philosophy courses)

Sunderland – 200–180 pts approx (Phil Comb)

Surrey Roehampton – 200 pts approx (inc AL) – ALs or ALs+ASs; (Philosophy)

Teesside – CDD (Cult St)

180 pts **Anglia** – 180 pts approx (C Engl/phil) (Euro Phil/Lit)

Glamorgan – 180 pts approx (Philosophy courses)

London Guildhall – DDD–CD (Phil Pol Econ)

160 pts **Brighton** – CC (Hum Phil)

Newport (UWCN) – 160–140 pts – ALs or ALs+ASs or VAs+/-ALs/ASs; (Phil/Relig St; Phil St)

North London – 160 pts 1x12u or 2x6u; (Philosophy courses; Ethics)

140 pts **and below**

Bolton (IHE) – CD (Philosophy courses)

St Mark & St John (Coll) – (Theol/Phil)

Diploma of Higher Education courses

80 pts Manchester Met; Middlesex.

Alternative Offers:

EB offers: Keele 60%; Sheffield 65%.

IB offers: Aberdeen 30 pts; Birmingham 33 pts; Bradford 27 pts; Anglia 30 pts; Essex 28 pts inc 10 pts in 2 Highers; Hull 28 pts; 28 pts; Lancaster 30 pts; Leeds 32 pts; London (LSE) 30 pts, Andrews 30 pts; Staffordshire 24 pts; Stirling 28 pts; Swansea ...pts; York 27 pts.

Irish offers: Aberdeen BBBB; East Anglia CCCCC; Keele BBBCC; Warwick AABBB.

Scottish Qualifications: Aberdeen BBBB; Dundee BBBC; Edinburgh ABBB–BBBB; Glasgow BBBB; St Andrews BBBC; Stirling BBBC.

Overseas applicants: East Anglia Pre-sessional courses in English and study skills.

CHOOSING YOUR COURSE (See also **Ch.1**)

> **Subject information:** Contemporary Philosophy covers political, educational, psychological, linguistic, aesthetic and religious issues. Some reading of the works of the leading philosophers is recommended prior to applying for these courses. Psychology, Religious Studies, Sociology and the Social Sciences in general could also be considered as alternative courses.

Special features: Anglia (Euro Phil/Lit) Languages included. **Bradford** Studies include psychology, sociology and literature. **Bristol** Language option offered. **Cardiff** No previous knowledge of philosophy is required by the student who is introduced to the practical relevance of political and moral philosophy and the theory of knowledge in part I. **Durham** Three study options (a) 50% of a Joint Honours degree with either English, politics, psychology or theology; (b) 33% of a Combined Honours degree in arts, social sciences or natural sciences; (c) Single Honours degree. **Essex** Covers anthropology, psychopathology, mind and action, history and society and justice. Options in ethics, justice, human rights, metaphysics and anthropology. **Hull** The first two terms introduce the subject, its history, methods and problems. Over the next six terms courses are taken in epistemology (theory of knowledge), moral philosophy and metaphysics. **Leeds, St Andrews** Two subjects taken in first year. **York** Advanced options are also offered in certain specialised areas (classical philosophy, modern European philosophy, political philosophy, the philosophy of science and the philosophy of religion). (Phil/Ling) Language options. *NOW CHECK PROSPECTUSES AND WEB SITES.*

Top universities and colleges (Teaching Quality) (see Ch.4): Aberdeen; Cambridge; Cardiff; Edinburgh; Glasgow; Oxford; St Andrews; Stirling; York; not all institutions assessed.

Top universities and colleges (Research) (see Ch.4): Birmingham; Bradford; Bristol; Cambridge; Durham; Essex; Hull; Leeds; Liverpool; London (King's), (LSE), (UCL); Oxford; Reading; St Andrews; Sheffield; Stirling; Sussex; Warwick.

Study opportunities abroad: Aberdeen; Belfast (Queen's); Bristol; Cardiff; Dundee; Edinburgh; Hull; Keele; Lancaster; Leeds; Liverpool; London (Hey); Manchester; North London; Nottingham; Reading; St Andrews; Teesside; Warwick; York.

Work opportunities abroad: Bristol.

ADMISSIONS INFORMATION

Number of applicants per place (approx): Birmingham 9; Bradford 7; Bristol 10; Cambridge 4; Cardiff 5; Durham 14 (all courses); East Anglia 6; Hull 19; Kent 9; Lampeter 4; Lancaster 6; Leeds 10; Liverpool 5; London (Hey) 4, (LSE) 9; Middlesex 8; North London 3; Nottingham 11; Oxford 2.5, (Phil Pol Econ) 3, (Psy Phil Physiol) 3.6; Sheffield 6; Southampton 6; Staffordshire 8; Swansea 4; Warwick 9; York 17.

your UCAS personal statement (see Ch.4): Read Bertrand Russell's *Problems osophy*. Refer to any particular aspects of philosophy which interest you (check these are offered on the courses for which you are applying). Since philosophy is ot a school subject then selectors will expect applicants to have read widely on the subject. **Bristol** Reasons for studying the subject carefully considered. **Lampeter** Books which have influenced you. **Swansea** Interests in English language and literature.

Selection interviews (see Ch.4): Bangor; Birmingham; Bristol (mature students); Cambridge; Durham; East Anglia (No); Edinburgh (No); Hull (some); Kent (No); Kingston; Lampeter; Lancaster; Leeds (T); Liverpool; London (Hey), (LSE) (rare), (UCL) (T); Manchester (No); Newcastle; Oxford (PPE) (W) (T); Southampton; Staffordshire; Stirling (No); Swansea; Warwick (T); York (some).

Interview questions (see Ch.4): Philosophy is a very wide subject and initially applicants will be asked for their reasons for their choice and their special interests in the subject. Questions in recent years have included: Is there a difference between being tactless and being insensitive? Can you be tactless and thin-skinned? Define the difference between knowledge and belief. Was the vertical distortion of El Greco's paintings a product of a vision defect? What is the point of studying philosophy? What books on philosophy have you read? Discuss the work of a renowned philosopher. What is a philosophical novel? Who has the right to decide your future – yourself or another? What do you want to do with your life? What is a philosophical question? John is your husband, and if John is your husband then necessarily you must be his wife; if you are necessarily his wife then it is not possible that you could not be his wife; so it was impossible for you not to have married him – you were destined for each other. Discuss. What is the difference between a man's entitlements, his deserts and his attributes? What are morals? A good under-standing of philosophy is needed for entry to degree courses, and applicants are expected to demonstrate this if they are called to interview. As one admissions tutor stated, 'If you find Bertrand Russell's *Problems of Philosophy* unreadable – don't apply!' **Leeds** 500 word essay. **London (UCL)** Written test at interview. **Oxford** (Phil Pol Econ) A one-hour test at Interview. No prior knowledge of philosophy required. (Psy Phil Physiol) One-hour mathematics test. **Warwick** Aptitude test may be set.

Reasons for rejection (non-academic): Evidence of severe psychological disturbance, criminal activity, drug problems (evidence from referees' reports). Lack of knowledge of philosophy.

GAP YEAR ADVICE

Institutions willing to defer entry after A-Levels: Birmingham; Bristol (usually, until one-third of places are committed); Cardiff; Dundee; East Anglia; Hull; Kent; Lampeter; Lancaster; Leeds; London (Hey); Nottingham; Southampton; Staffordshire; Sussex; Swansea; Warwick; York.

AFTER RESULTS ADVICE

Institutions which may accept the same points score after A-Levels: Birmingham; Bristol; Dundee (No); Essex; Hull; Kent; Kingston; Lampeter; Lancaster; Leeds; Leicester (No); Liverpool; London (Hey); Newcastle; Nottingham; Southampton; Staffordshire; Stirling (No); Swansea; Warwick (No); York.

Institutions which may accept lower grades/points score after A-Levels: Essex; Kent; Lampeter; Leeds; Liverpool; Newcastle; Newport (UWCN); North London; Nottingham; Southampton; Swansea; Warwick; York.

Offers to applicants repeating A-Levels: Higher Bristol (Phil/Econ), Essex, Leeds, Nottingham (in some cases), Warwick; **Same** Bangor, Birmingham, Bristol, Hull, Leeds, Newcastle, Newport (UWCN), Nottingham (for previous applicants), Southampton, Swansea, Ulster, York.

Probable vacancies from June 2001 and in Clearing (see Ch.4): Vacancies are likely in many universities with the highest offers in the 260–240 pts range.

NEW GRADUATE DESTINATIONS AND EMPLOYMENT (1999 HESA) (see **Ch.4**)

Out of 695 graduates surveyed, 362 entered full-time employment (occupations equally divided between retail work, financial and property services, community or social and health work and public services, with a small number going into hotel work and manufacturing), 66 went on to further study and 53 were believed to be unemployed.

PHOTOGRAPHY (see also **Film, Radio, Video and TV Studies** and **Media Studies**)

NB The information supplied by the universities and colleges this year varies considerably and the offers listed below should be used as a first source of reference only. Many institutions will accept combinations of Advanced (AL), Advanced Subsidiary (AS) and Vocational Advanced (VA) level qualifications to achieve the required points total, but applicants must check web sites and prospectuses for full details of all offers. Grades and points totals shown should be regarded as the minimum levels to be achieved, but offers may be adjusted downwards when results are known. The points totals shown to the left of the institutions are for ease of reference only. It must not be assumed that tariff points are always used by institutions or that they can be substituted for an offer in grades. The level of an offer is not necessarily indicative of the quality of a course. To calculate your offers see Chapter 4 and the inside fold of the back cover.

Special subject requirements/preferences: A-Level: Arts-based subjects usually preferred. **Napier** Grade A–E mathematics or science. **GCSE:** English usually required. Art portfolio required in many cases.

Applicants should note that there are two pathways for those applying for some of these courses (Route A or Route B or both). See the general notes under **Art and Design (General)** and the UCAS *Directory* for course details.

300 pts **Bradford** – 300–280 pts 12u; gs; (Intnet Sys/Vid Gms; Electron Imag/Media Tech Comm courses)

280 pts **Bournemouth** – 280 pts – BBC **or** AL+AS+Fdn Art; (Photo-media)

240 pts **Central England** – 240 pts approx (Vis Comm (Photo))
   De Montfort (Lincoln) – 240 pts (inc 160 pts ALs or VAs) – ALs **or** ALs+ASs **or** VAs+/-ALs/ASs; (Photo/Video)
   Derby – 240 pts 12u – CCC **or** CC+cc **or** VA12u AA; gs; portfolio; (Photo Fdn)
   Nottingham Trent – 240 pts approx (Photography)

220 pts **Central Lancashire** – 220 pts 12u (inc AL art/des/photo/media/film st); gs; (Photo/Aud Vis Media St; Photo/Journal)

200 pts **Bradford** – 200–180 pts 9u; gs; (Fdn Electron Imag)
   Central Lancashire – 200–180 pts 12u; gs; (Photo/Des St; Photo/Media Tech; Photo/Vis Cult)
   Derby – 200–160 pts approx (Photography)
   Kent (IAD) – 200 pts min +portfolio (Vis Comm (Photomedia); Edit/Adv Photo)
   Southampton (Inst) – 200–100 pts (Photography)
   Wolverhampton – 200–170 pts – DDD/CC or CD+d/e **or** VA12u CC; gs; (Photography)

180 pts **Blackpool & Fylde (Coll)** – 180 pts 12u – gs; (Photo; Wldlf Photo)
   Cheltenham & Glos (CHE) – 180–160 pts approx (Photo (Prof Media))
   Napier – BC+portfolio+essay (Photo/Film/TV)
   Thames Valley – 180–140 pts approx (Photography courses)

160 pts **Anglia** – 160 pts 12u – BB (inc B art) **or** ALs+ASs(B art) **or** VA12(art) CC; gs; (Photo/Dig Media Comb)
   Cumbria (CAD) – 160 pts – CC **or** ASs (contact coll) **or** VA; portfolio; (Edit Photo)
   Falmouth (CA) – CC (Photo Comm)
   Manchester Met – CC (Photography)

Sunderland – CC (Photo/Vid Drg Imag)
Swansea (IHE) – CC +portfolio (Photojournalism)
Westminster – CC (Photo/Dig Arts)
140 pts   **Edinburgh (CA)** – 140 pts approx – 2ALs **or** AL+2ASs (inc Engl+art des) **or** fdn art/HNC; (Photography)
Newport (UWCN) – 140–120 pts – ALs **or** ALs+ASs **or** VAs+/-ALs/ASs; portfolio; (Photo Art)
Sunderland – 140 pts – ALs **or** ALs+ASs **or** VAs+/-ALs/ASs; BTEC accepted; gs; (Photo/Vid Drg)
100 pts   **Westminster** – DE (Dig Photo Imag)
80 pts   **and below**
Bolton (IHE) – (Photography)
Bournemouth (AI) – 80 pts 12u – EE **or** ALs+ASs **or** VAs+/-ALs/ASs; (not gs) (Photography)
Brighton – (Edit Photo – Fdn art required)
Cleveland (CAD) – portfolio (Photography)
Croydon (Coll) – portfolio+Fdn art reqd (Photomedia)
Heriot-Watt – (Vis Comm)
London (Inst) – No standard offer (Photography)
Northbrook (Coll) – (Photo/Media/Soc)
Northumbria – (Contemp Photo Prac – check with Admissions Tutor)
Plymouth (CAD) – portfolio (PhotoMedia)
Portsmouth – 80 pts – ALs **or** ALs+ASs **or** VA; gs; portfolio; (Photography)
Reading (CSAD) – (Photo/Dig Imag)
Staffordshire – EE (Des (Photo))
Stockport (CFHE) – portfolio+interview (Doc Fine Art Photo)
Surrey (IAD/UC) – EE+portfolio (Photo; Film/Video)

Higher National Diploma course
100 pts   and below
Batley (SA); Bournemouth (IA); Bradford (Coll); Carmarthenshire (Coll); Cheltenham & Glos (CHE) (Adv Photo); City of Bristol (Coll); Cleveland (CAD); Falmouth (CA); Filton (Coll); Glasgow (CDP); Great Yarmouth (Coll); Kent (IAD); Leeds (CAD); Leicester South Fields (Coll); Mid Cheshire (Coll); Nescot; Newcastle (Coll); Newport (UWCN); North East London (Coll); North East Wales (IHE); North West Kent (Coll); Plymouth (CAD); St Helens (Coll); Salisbury (Coll); Sandwell (Coll); Solihull (Coll); South East Essex (Coll); Stevenson (Coll); Stockport (CFHE); Swansea (IHE); Tameside (Coll); Truro (Coll).

College awards
40 pts   Manchester Met (Prtg/Photo); Salisbury (Coll).

Overseas applicants: Derby Fluency in written and spoken English important. Portfolio of work essential.

CHOOSING YOUR COURSE (See also **Ch.1**)

> **Subject information:** Photography courses offer a range of specialised studies involving commercial, industrial and still photography, portraiture and film and video work. Increasingly this subject is featuring in Graphic Design courses which could also be considered. See also **Appendix 1**.

Special features: Surrey (IAD/UC) 70% practice, 30% theory. **Swansea (IHE)** 60%/40% Theory/practice or vice versa. **Westminster** (Dig Photo Imag) The course is one of science and technology – not an artistic one. Interest in photographic materials and black & white techniques. *NOW CHECK PROSPECTUSES AND WEB SITES.*

Top universities and colleges (Teaching Quality) (see Ch.4): Swansea (IHE); not all institutions assessed.

ADMISSIONS INFORMATION

Number of applicants per place (approx): Cleveland (CAD) 2; Croydon (Coll) 15; Derby 20; Kent (IAD) 10; London Inst 10; Napier 33; Newport (UWCN) 2; Nottingham Trent 23; Plymouth (CAD) 7; Stockport (CFHE) 6; Surrey (IAD/UC) 10; Swansea (IHE) 12.

Planning your UCAS personal statement (see Ch.4): Discuss your interest in photography and your knowledge of various aspects of the subject, for example, landscape, medical, nature, portrait, industrial, still and cine work. Read photographic journals to keep up-to-date on developments, particularly in photographic technology. **Croydon (Coll)** Broad range of interests. See also **Appendix 1.**

Selection interviews (see Ch.4): Kent (IAD) (T); most institutions will interview applicants and expect to see a portfolio of work.

Interview questions (see Ch.4): Questions relate to the applicant's portfolio of work which, for these courses, is of prime importance.

Reasons for rejection (non-academic): Lack of passion for the subject. Lack of exploration and creativity in practical work.

AFTER RESULTS ADVICE

Institutions which may accept the same points score after A-Levels: Derby (No); Nottingham Trent; Westminster.

Probable vacancies from June 2001 and in Clearing (see Ch.4): All institutions should be contacted.

NEW GRADUATE DESTINATIONS AND EMPLOYMENT (1999 HESA) (see **Ch.4**)

No data available.

PHYSICAL EDUCATION (including **Sports Studies and Education**; see also **Sports Studies**)

NB The information supplied by the universities and colleges this year varies considerably and the offers listed below should be used as a first source of reference only. Many institutions will accept combinations of Advanced (AL), Advanced Subsidiary (AS) and Vocational Advanced (VA) level qualifications to achieve the required points total, but applicants must check web sites and prospectuses for full details of all offers. Grades and points totals shown should be regarded as the minimum levels to be achieved, but offers may be adjusted downwards when results are known. The points totals shown to the left of the institutions are for ease of reference only. It must not be assumed that tariff points are always used by institutions or that they can be substituted for an offer in grades. The level of an offer is not necessarily indicative of the quality of a course. To calculate your offers see Chapter 4 and the inside fold of the back cover.

Special subject requirements/preferences: GCSE: English, mathematics and a science subject.

Abbreviations: P – Primary Teaching; S – Secondary Teaching; QTS – Qualified Teacher Status.

320 pts	**De Montfort (Bedford)** – 320–220 pts (inc 2ALs or VAs) – ALs **or** ALs+ASs **or** VAs+/-ALs/ASs; (BA PE QTS S)
280 pts	**Durham** – BBC (Spo Commun)
	Hull – 280–260 pts (PE/Spo Sci/Mgt; PE/Spo Sci/Scand St)
260 pts	**Hull** – 260–240 pts approx (B/C biol)-CCC (PE/Spo Sci/Biol; PE/Spo Sci/ Maths)
	Manchester Met – 260 pts approx (Educ Ss/Spo)

240 pts   **Hull** – CCC (PE/Spo Sci/Tech)
          Liverpool John Moores – 240 pts – ALs **or** ALs+ASs **or** VA12u+/-AL/ASs; (Physical Education S)
          Sheffield Hallam – 240 pts approx (Spo Dev Coach)

220 pts   **Brighton** – 220 pts approx (Physical Education P/S)
          Brunel – 220 pts approx (PE S; Phys Educ/Engl/Geog)
          Chester (Coll) – 220–160 pts approx (Physical Education P)
          Surrey (Roehampton) – 220–180 pts approx (Spo Exer/Educ St)

200 pts   **Cardiff (UWI)** – BB (Spo PE)
          Leeds, Trinity & All Saints (Coll) – 200 pts approx (Phyusical Education)
          Newman (CHE) – 200–140 pts approx (PE Spo St/Geog)
          Nottingham Trent – 200 pts approx (Spo Sci/Admin/Coach)
          Ripon & York (Coll) – 200–180 pts approx (PE/Geog St; PE/Mgt St; PE/Psy)
          Sheffield Hallam – 200 pts approx (Physical Education S)
          Wolverhampton – 200–180 pts approx; gs (Spo St/Educ St)
          Worcester (UC) – 200 pts approx (QTS Physical Education P)

180 pts   **Greenwich** – 180 pts approx approx (Spo Sci Educ)
          Liverpool Hope (Coll) – 180–160 pts approx (Sport, Recreation PE courses)
          Strathclyde – BC (Spo Commun)

160 pts   **Birmingham (Westhill)** – 160 pts 12u (inc C) – ALs **or** ALs+ASs **or** VAs (contact univ); gs; (PE/Dance/Educ; Spo/PE/Commun St)
          Chichester (UC) – 160 pts (Educ St/Spo St)
          Edge Hill (CHE) – 160 pts (Physical Education courses)
          Ripon & York (Coll) – CC (PE/Commun St)
          St Martin's (Coll) – 160 pts (Physical Education courses)
          Trinity Carmarthen (Coll) – CC–EE (Physical Education P)

140 pts   **Edinburgh** – 140 pts (Physical Education)
          Plymouth – 140 pts approx (Physical Education P)
          St Mary's (Coll) – 140 pts approx (PE St/Spo Sci)

120 pts   **St Mark & St John (Coll)** – DD (Physical Educatio P/S)

          Leeds Met – (contact university)

Diploma of Higher Education courses
 80 pts   Edge Hill (CHE); Ripon & York (Coll).

Alternative Offers:

IB offers: Bangor 28–24 pts; De Montfort 26 pts; Exeter 30 pts; Liverpool 30 pts H655 (6 in biol); Loughborough 30 pts; Ripon & York (Coll) 30 pts; Worcester (UC) 28 pts.

Scottish Qualifications: Edinburgh BBCC.

Overseas applicants: Loughborough Three-week pre-sessional course.

CHOOSING YOUR COURSE (See also **Ch.1**)

> **Subject information:** Physical Education courses are very popular and unfortunately restricted in number. Ability in gymnastics and involvement in sport are obviously important factors. Other course options could also include Sports Studies, Leisure Management, Sports Science, Anatomy and Human Biology. See also **Appendix 1**.

Special features: Bangor Part II (years 2 and 3) includes sports psychology, human development and health promotion and students will pursue sporting excellence in their own field. **Loughborough** In the first year all students take introductory courses in anatomy, biology of physical activity, biomechanics, skill acquisition and psychology plus two other subjects. **Surrey (Roehampton)** Students are not assessed at playing sport. *NOW CHECK PROSPECTUSES AND WEB SITES.*

Top universities and colleges (Research) (see Ch.4): See under **Sports Studies**.

Study opportunities abroad: Brighton; Chester (Coll); Edinburgh; Liverpool; Liverpool Hope (Coll); St Mark & St John (Coll).

ADMISSIONS INFORMATION

Number of applicants per place (approx): Bangor 19; Brunel 12; Cardiff (UWI) 6; Cheltenham & Glos (CHE) 10; Chester (Coll) 25; Chichester (UC) 25; De Montfort 7; Edge Hill (CHE) 40; Leeds, Trinity & All Saints (Coll) 33; Liverpool John Moores 9; Loughborough 20; Newman (CHE) 15; Ripon & York (Coll) 11 average; St Mark & St John (Coll) 18; St Mary's (Coll) 9; Sheffield Hallam 60; Strathclyde 12; Worcester (UC) 31.

Planning your UCAS personal statement (see Ch.4): Ability in gymnastics, athletics and all sports and games is important. Full details should be given on the UCAS form of these activities – for example, teams, dates and awards achieved, assisting in extra-curricular activities. Involvement with local sports clubs, health clubs, summer camps, gap year. Relevant experience in coaching, teaching, community and youth work. **Durham** (Spo Commun) We expect county representative standard or above.

Selection interviews (see Ch.4): All institutions. In most cases applicants will take part in physical education practical tests and games/gymnastics, depending on the course. The results of these tests could affect the level of offers. Brighton (500 word essay).

Interview questions (see Ch.4): The applicants' interests in physical education will be discussed with specific questions on their interests, for example on sportsmanship, refereeing, umpiring and coaching. Questions in the past have also included: What qualities should a good netball goal defence possess? How could you encourage a group of children into believing that sport is fun? Do you think that physical education should be compulsory in schools? Why do you think you would make a good teacher?

Reasons for rejection (non-academic): Poor communication and presentational skills. Relatively poor sporting background or knowledge. Lack of knowledge about the teaching of physical education and the commitment required. Lack of ability in practicalities, for example, gymnastics, dance when relevant. Poor self-presentation. Poor writing skills.

GAP YEAR ADVICE

Institutions willing to defer entry after A-Levels: Brighton (No); Chester (Coll); De Montfort; Leeds, Trinity & All Saints (Coll); Ripon & York (Coll) (No); Strathclyde (No).

AFTER RESULTS ADVICE

Institutions which may accept the same points score after A-Levels: Bangor; Brighton; Cardiff (UWI); Chester (Coll) (No); Hull (No); Loughborough (No); Newman (CHE); St Mark & St John (Coll); Sheffield Hallam; Worcester (UC) (No).

Institutions which may accept lower grades/points score after A-Levels: Bangor; Cardiff (UWI); Chester (Coll); De Montfort; Leeds, Trinity & All Saints (Coll); Loughborough (No).

Offers to applicants repeating A-Levels: Same Cardiff (UWI), Loughborough.

Probable vacancies from June 2001 and in Clearing (see Ch.4): A number of universities and colleges declared vacancies from June and in Clearing. Most institutions are worth contacting.

NEW GRADUATE DESTINATIONS AND EMPLOYMENT (1999 HESA) (see **Ch.4**)

Of 913 graduates surveyed, 542 went into full-time employment (half into teaching, with others going into managerial, clerical and retail occupations), 137 went on to further study and 44 were reported to be unemployed after six months.

PHYSICS (including **Applied Physics**)

NB The information supplied by the universities and colleges this year varies consider-
ably and the offers listed below should be used as a first source of reference only. Many
institutions will accept combinations of Advanced (AL), Advanced Subsidiary (AS) and
Vocational Advanced (VA) level qualifications to achieve the required points total, but
applicants must check web sites and prospectuses for full details of all offers. Grades
and points totals shown should be regarded as the minimum levels to be achieved, but
offers may be adjusted downwards when results are known. The points totals shown to
the left of the institutions are for ease of reference only. It must not be assumed that
tariff points are always used by institutions or that they can be substituted for an offer in
grades. The level of an offer is not necessarily indicative of the quality of a course. To
calculate your offers see Chapter 4 and the inside fold of the back cover.

Special subject requirements/preferences: A-Level: Mathematics and physics usually
required. See prospectuses for Foundation courses. **Oxford** Physics and mathematics
full A-Levels essential; further mathematics at AS-Level considered. **York** Physics and
mathematics. **GCSE:** Grade A–C English. **Belfast, Exeter, Reading, UMIST** Grade B in
French or German for language courses. **Durham** (App Phys) Grade A–C in seven/eight
subjects; (MPhys) (BSc) Grade A in three subjects, grade B in three subjects.
Hertfordshire, Paisley Grade A–C English. **London (QM)** Average of grade B across all
subjects. **London (RH)** Good proportion of grades A and B. **Sheffield Hallam** Five
subjects at grade A–C. **Surrey** Six subjects at grade B or better including science and
mathematics. **Swansea** Three to four grades A* or A, three to four grades B. **York** Grade
B in physics and mathematics.

360 pts **and above**
    Cambridge – Offers, mainly in grades, vary between colleges (Nat Sci (Astro)
      (Phys/Theor Phys))
    Nottingham – AAA–AAB (Math Phys)
    Oxford – Offers vary between candidates (Phys; Phys/Phil)
340 pts **Liverpool** – 340 pts – ALs **or** ALs+ASs **or** VAs+/-ALs/ASs; (Phys/Maths)
    London (Imp) – AAB–ABB (Physics courses)
    Warwick – AAB (Maths/Phys)
320 pts **Bristol** – ABB–BBB (Physics courses)
    Leeds – 18u – AB(maths, phys)B(f.maths); (Phys/Maths)
    London (King's) – ABB+AS **or** AB+bbb (or equiv) (inc A from phys+maths);
      VAs considered; (Phys/Phil)
    London (UCL) – ABB–ABC **or** 3ALs+AS/VA; (Maths/Phys courses)
    Manchester – ABB–BBC (Maths/Phys)
300 pts **Birmingham** – ABC (Theor Phys/App Maths; Phys/Theor Phys)
    Durham – ABC (A/B phys/maths); (not gs) (MSci/BSc Phys; Theor Phys;
      Phys/Astron)
    Durham – ABC–BBC (Physics courses except **above**)
    Glasgow – BBB–CCC (Physics courses)
    Lancaster – ABC (Theor Phys/Maths)
    Lancaster – BBB–BCC (Physics courses except **above**)
    Leeds – BBB (Phys/Hist Phil Sci; Phys/Mus; Phys/Phil)
    Liverpool – 300 pts – ALs **or** ALs+ASs **or** VAs+/-ALs/ASs; Physics courses
      except under **340/170/140 pts**)
    London (King's) – BBB+AS **or** BB+bbb (inc AL phys+maths); VAs considered;
      (Phys; Phys with Astro/Educ/Comp Sci/Fr/Mgt/Med Apps/Phil Sci)
    London (QM) – 300 pts (inc 180 pts maths+phys) – ALs **or** ALs+ASs **or**
      VAs+/-ALs/ASs; (Physics courses)
    London (UCL) – BBB **or** 3ALs+AS/VA; (Phys; Theor Phys; App Phys; Med
      Phys; Chem Phys; Phys/Space Sci)
    London (UCL) – BBB–BBC (Chem Phys 4 yrs)
    Manchester – ABC–BBC (Phys/Bus/Mgt; Phys/Theor Phys; Phys/Technol
      Phys; Phys; Phys/Astro; Phys/Euro)

Newcastle – ABC (MPhys)

Nottingham – 300 pts 24u – AB(min)+ALs/ASs (not gs) (MSc Phys courses)

Reading – 300–260 pts approx (Phys courses except under **260 pts**)

St Andrews – BBB–BCC (Physics courses)

Sheffield – 300 pts approx (Phys/Maths)

Strathclyde – BBB (Biophys; App Phys; Phys/Math Fin; Phys/Vis Sim; Lsr Phys/Optoel; Phys)

Strathclyde – ABC (Phys/Maths)

Sussex – BBB (Phys/Law)

Warwick – ABC (Phys; Phys/Comp; Phys/Bus St)

York – 21–18u – BBC+c; (BSc Phys courses)

280 pts   **Bath** – BBC–CCC/AB (MPhys; Physics and allied subjects)

Belfast (Queen's) – BBC–CCC (Phys/App Phys courses)

Birmingham – BBC (Phys Bus St; Phys/Euro; Phys/Electron; Phys/Biomed Phys)

Cardiff – 280 pts approx (Phys/Astron; MPhys; Astrophys)

Exeter – 280 pts 18u (inc AL maths+phys) – BBC **or** BC+bb **or** VAs (contact univ); (not gs) (Physics courses except under **260 pts**)

Glasgow – BBC–CCC (Physics courses)

Heriot-Watt – 280 pts 18u – BBC **or** ALs+ASs **or** VAsB+/-ALs/ASs; gs; (Phys; Eng Phys; Comp Phys; Optoel/Lsr Eng; App Phys)

Kent – BBC–BCC (Physics courses)

Leeds – BBC (Phys/Maths; Theor Phys; Phys/Fr; Phys/Ger)

Leeds – BBC (BB maths, phys) **or** BB+cc(BB maths, phys); gs; (Phys; Phys/Astro/Electron Ins)

Leicester – 280 pts 18u – BB(maths, phys)C; gs; (MPhys Phys; Phys/Space Sci Tech/Astro)

London (Imp) – BBC–BCC/BB–CC (Phys courses except under **340 pts**)

London (QM) – 280 pts approx (Phys/Electron; Phys/Med Phys)

London (RH) – BBC(BB maths, phys) **or** BB+cc; gs; (MSc Phys; App Phys; Astrophys; Theor Phys)

Loughborough – 280 pts – BBC (maths, phys)+AL/2ASs **or** VAs+/-ALs/ASs; gs; (MPhys)

Loughborough – BBC–BCC (Phys; Eng Phys; Phys/Mgt; Phys/PE/Spo Sci; Phys/Comp)

Manchester – BBC/AB (MPhys Theor Phys)

Newcastle – BBC–CCC (Physics courses except under **300 pts**)

Nottingham – 280 pts 24u – BB(min)+ALs/ASs; (not gs) (BSc Phys courses)

Reading – 280 pts (Phys/Meteor)

Sheffield – BBC (Phys/Phil; Chem Phys)

Strathclyde – BBC (lsr Phys/Optoel; App Phys; Phys)

Surrey – 280 pts 18u (AL maths+phys, AS phys check dept); BBC **or** ALs+ASs **or** VAs+/-ALs/ASs; (not gs) (MPhys courses)

Sussex – BBC (Math Phys)

Swansea – 280 pts 18u – BBC/AB **or** ALs+ASs **or** VAs+/-ALs/ASs; (MPhys Phys)

York – 21–18u – BBC **or** BB+cc **or** VAs (contact univ); gs; (MPhys courses)

260 pts   **Aberystwyth** – 260–240 pts approx (Comp Sci/Phys; Geog/Phys; Phys courses)

Birmingham – BCC (Phys Astro; Phys Space Res)

East Anglia – BCC (Chem Phys)

Exeter – 260 pts 18u (inc AL maths+phys) – BCC **or** BC+bb **or** VAs (contact univ); (not gs) (Phys; Phys/Med Apps; Phys/Med Phys; Phys/Qntm Lsr Tech; Qntm Sci Lsrs)

Hertfordshire – 260–200 pts 1x12u **or** 2x6u; gs; (Physics courses)

Keele – BCC **or** equiv AS accepted; gs; (Physics courses)

Lancaster – BCC–CCE (Phys courses except under **300 pts**)

Liverpool – 260 pts approx (Rdtn Phys/Env Sci)

London (RH) – BCC (BC maths, phys) **or** BC+cc; gs (BSc Phys; Theor Phys; Phys with Mgt/Mus/Astro/Euro/Sci Media)

London (UCL) – BCC **or** 3ALs+AS/VA; (Phys Sci courses)

Loughborough – 260 pts – BC(maths, phys)+AL/2ASs **or** VAs+/-AL/ASs; gs; (Eng Phys; Phys with Maths/Mgt/Comp/PE; Phys)

Reading – BCC (Phys/Maths)

Salford – BCC–CCD (Chem/Phys; Geog/Phys; Phys/Bioch)

Sheffield – BCC (Phys; Theor Phys; Phys/Euro; Phys/Astron; Phys/Med Phys; Phys/Electron)

Southampton – 260 pts 21u; (Physics courses)

Surrey – 260 pts 18u (AL maths+phys, AS phys check dept) – BCC **or** ALs+ASs **or** VAs+/-ALs/ASs; (not gs) (BSc Phys courses)

Sussex – BCC–BCD (Physics courses except under **300/280/140 pts**)

Swansea – 260 pts 18u – BCC–CCC/BB **or** ALs+ASs **or** VAs+/-ALs/ASs; (Physics courses except under **280/240 pts**)

York – 21–18u – BCC **or** BC+cc **or** VAs (contact univ); gs; (BSc Physics courses)

UMIST – 18u – BCC **or** BC+2ASs(AL phys, maths); gs; (MSc/BSc Physics courses)

240 pts **Aberdeen** – CCC–CCD (Physics courses)

Aberdeen – 240 pts approx (Earth Planet Space Sci; Phys/Bus St; Phys/Atmos Phys)

Aberystwyth – 240 pts approx (Phys/Fr; Phys/Atmos Phys; Phys (Inf Lib St))

Bangor – CCC (Comput Phys)

Cardiff – CCC (Phys/Maths; Phys; Phys/Mus; Phys/Astron; Phys/Med Phys)

Edinburgh – CCC (Astro; Phys/Meteor; Phys

Leicester – 240 pts 18u – CC(maths, phys)C; (not gs) (BSc Phys; Phys with Astro/Space Sci Tech/Med Phys)

London (QM) – 240 pts approx (Phys/Env; Theor Phys; Maths/Phys)

Sheffield – CCC (Phys Fdn)

Staffordshire – CCC (Physics courses except under **140 pts**)

Sussex – BCD (Chem Phys Maths Joint courses)

Swansea – 240 pts 18u – CCC **or** ALs+ASs **or** VAs+/-ALs/ASs; (Phys Fdn)

220 pts **Central Lancashire** – CCD (inc AL maths+phys); gs; (Phys; App Phys; Phys/Astron)

Edinburgh – CCD (Chem/Phys)

Hertfordshire – 220–200 pts approx (Phys; App Phys courses)

Hull – CCD–CDD/BC–CC (MPhys/BSc Phys; Phys/Med Tech; Phys/Lsr/Photon; App Phys courses except **below**)

Hull – CCD–CDD (App Phys frchd)

Sheffield Hallam – 220 pts approx (Eng Phys)

200 pts **Central Lancashire** – 200–180 pts 12u (inc AL maths+phys); (App Phys with Mgt/Mark)

Dundee – 200 pts approx (Phys/Phil; Phil/Psy; Phys/App Comp; Phys; Phys/Dig Microelec; Phys/Env Sci)

Nottingham Trent – 200–180 pts approx (Physics courses)

180 pts **Central Lancashire** – 180–160 pts 12u (inc AL maths+phys); (App Phys with Comp/Lang/Maths/Media Tech)

Dundee – 180–160 pts approx (Phys/Electron Eng)

Glasgow Caledonian – DDD/CC (App Phys/Instr)

Reading – DDD (Phys Fdn)

Salford – 180 pts approx (Phys/N Am; Phys/Acoust; Phys/Space Tech; Phys/Comp; Phys/Med Phys)

170 pts **Liverpool** – 170 pts – ALs **or** ALs+ASs **or** VAs+/-ALs/ASs; (Phys/New Tech)

160 pts **Northumbria** – 160 pts approx (App Phys)

140 pts **Liverpool** – 140 pts (inc 2ALs) – ALs **or** ALs+ASs **or** VAs+/-ALs/ASs; (Fdn Phys)

Sheffield Hallam – 140 pts approx (Phys Comb St)

120 pts   and below
   Paisley – DD (Physics courses)
   Robert Gordon – DE (App Phys)
   Staffordshire – EE (Fdn Phys)
   Strathclyde – DD (Sci St Phys)
   Sussex – DD (Phys; Phys Sci)

Diploma of Higher Education courses
140 pts   Glamorgan; Hertfordshire.

Higher National Diploma courses
100 pts   and below
   Bradford (Coll); Bell (CT); Glasgow Caledonian; Kingston; People's (Coll); Portsmouth; Robert Gordon; Sheffield Hallam; Staffordshire; Suffolk (Coll) (Rdtn St).

Alternative Offers:

EB offers: Keele 60%; London (RH) 75%; Salford 60%; UMIST 65%, (Phys/Fr; Comp Phys) 70%.

IB offers: Aberystwyth 24 pts H6 phys H5 maths; Bangor H555; Bath 30–28 pts Gr 5 Phys/Maths; Birmingham 30 pts; Bristol 30–28 pts; Cardiff H555 + 13 pts; Durham H555; Exeter 28 pts; Glasgow H555; Hull 25 pts H55; Kent 26 pts, H 11 pts; Lancaster 28 pts inc maths and physics H; Leeds 30 pts inc maths H5 phys H6; Liverpool 30 pts; London (RH) 30 pts, (UCL) 32–30 pts; Loughborough H555 24 pts; Newcastle H555; Northumbria 24 pts; St Andrews 28 pts; Salford 28 pts; Staffordshire 26 pts; Surrey 28 pts; Swansea 26 pts; UMIST 27 pts; Warwick 32–30 pts; York 28 pts H55 phys maths.

Irish offers: Glasgow BBB; Keele BBCCC; Kent BBBCC; Liverpool BBCCC; London (RH) BBBCC; Loughborough BBCCC; Northumbria CCC inc C maths & phys; St Andrews BBCC; Salford BBCCC; UMIST AABBC; Warwick ABBBB.

Scottish Qualifications: Aberdeen BBBC; Dundee BBCC–BCC; Edinburgh BBBC; Glasgow BBBB; Glasgow Caledonian BBCC/BBB; Heriot-Watt BBBC; Paisley BBC; Robert Gordon BCC; St Andrews BBBC; Strathclyde BBB.

Overseas applicants: Durham Interview essential. **Loughborough** A pre-sessional course of 3 weeks is offered. **UMIST** Foundation courses. **York** English language courses.

CHOOSING YOUR COURSE (See also **Ch.1**)

> **Subject information:** There is a considerable shortage of applicants for Physics courses. Many courses have flexible arrangements to enable students to follow their own interests and specialisations, for example circuit design, microwave devices, cosmology, medical physics, solid state electronics. Possible alternative courses include Astronomy, Astrophysics, Computing, Engineering, Geophysics. See also **Appendix 1.**

Special features: Aberystwyth Specialisation possible in planetary and space physics. **Bath** The final year allows for a choice of specialisms between geophysics, microelectronics, computing or applied physics. Research and development placement year gives work experience and enhances employment prospects. **Bristol** Core of subjects studied in first and second years; students' own choice of specialisms follow in third year. Easy transfers to Chemical Physics, Maths/Physics or Physics/Philosophy. **Cardiff** Great emphasis is laid on practical training with lasers, x-ray sources and electronic devices. (Phys/Astro) 75% physics, 25% astronomy options. **Durham** Second and third year courses develop and allow for specialisation in subjects which include astrophysics and planetary physics, modern optics and nuclear physics. **Heriot-Watt** The first year is common to all seven degrees with elective options in other subjects such as business

or languages. Physics is developed in year 2 with specialist pathways in years 3 and 4. **Hull** Flexible transfer arrangements between courses. Specialisms in electronics, laser technology, medical technology, optoelectronics. **London (RH)** Wide range of third year options; great flexibility to change degree option (for example, Physics to Physics/ Astrophysics or Management). **Loughborough** Choice of Physics, Engineering Physics, Applied Physics made in year 2. **Newcastle** Physics students cover such topics as optics, nuclear physics, thermodynamics, solid state physics, astrophysics and geophysics. **Nottingham** (Physics) Covers medical physics, computing, astronomy, radio and communications. **Sheffield Hallam** Focus on the physics of materials. **Swansea** Options include medical and laser physics, micro-electronics, particle physics and foundations of cosmology. **UMIST** Common first year followed by a choice of six specialisms. **York** Modular course ensures flexibility; communication skills emphasised. *NOW CHECK PROSPECTUSES AND WEB SITES.*

Top universities and colleges (Teaching Quality) (see Ch.4): Cambridge; Dundee; Durham; Edinburgh; Exeter; Glasgow; Glasgow Caledonian; Hertfordshire; Leeds; Leicester; St Andrews; Staffordshire; Strathclyde; Surrey; Swansea; York; not all institutions assessed.

Top universities and colleges (Research) (see Ch.4): Aberystwyth; Bath; Belfast (Queen's); Birmingham; Bristol; Cambridge; Cardiff; Durham; Edinburgh; Exeter; Glasgow; Heriot-Watt; Hertfordshire; Leeds; Leicester; Liverpool; London (Imp), (King's), (QM), (RH), (UCL); Manchester; Newcastle; Nottingham; Oxford; Reading; St Andrews; Sheffield; Southampton; Stirling; Strathclyde; Surrey; Swansea; UMIST; Warwick; York.

Study opportunities abroad: Aberystwyth; Bath; Belfast (Queen's); Birmingham; Bristol; Cardiff; Dundee; Exeter; Glasgow; Heriot-Watt; Hull; Kent; Lancaster; Leeds; Leicester; London (Imp), (QM); Loughborough; Manchester; Newcastle; Northumbria; Nottingham Trent; Oxford; Portsmouth; Reading; Robert Gordon; St Andrews; Salford; Sheffield; Strathclyde; Surrey; Sussex; Swansea; UMIST; Warwick; York.

Work opportunities abroad: Bath; Birmingham; Leicester; Loughborough; Northumbria; Portsmouth; Robert Gordon; Salford; Strathclyde; Surrey; UMIST; Warwick.

ADMISSIONS INFORMATION

Number of applicants per place (approx): Bath 8; Birmingham 6; Bristol 5; Cardiff 4; Dundee 6; Durham 6; Edinburgh 9; Exeter 5; Heriot-Watt 5; Hull 7; Kent 8; Lancaster 8; Leeds 7; Leicester 8; Liverpool 4; London (Imp) 3, (QM) 6, (RH) 9, (UCL) 6; Loughborough 6; Manchester (Phys) 5; Newcastle 7; Nottingham 9; Oxford 2.6; Salford 5; Sheffield Hallam 3; Staffordshire 4; Strathclyde 5; Surrey 5; Swansea 3; UMIST 8; Warwick 8; York 13.

Planning your UCAS personal statement (see Ch.4): Work experience should be mentioned and also interests in maths and physics. Admissions tutors look for potential, enthusiasm and interest in the subject, courses attended, reading interests (not in science fiction). The Institute of Physics can provide information on the work of the physicist. An awareness of the range of careers in which physics is involved should also be mentioned on the UCAS form, and any particular interests explained, books read on physics or mathematics and attendence at open days/courses on physics or engineering. See also **Appendix 1.**

Selection interviews (see Ch.4): Aston; Bath; Birmingham; Cambridge; Cardiff; Durham; Exeter; Heriot-Watt; Hull; Lancaster; Leeds (No); Liverpool; London (QM), (RH); Loughborough; Newcastle; Nottingham; Oxford (T); Paisley (No); St Andrews (No); Salford (travel expenses paid); Sheffield; Sheffield Hallam (No); Strathclyde; Surrey; Swansea; UMIST; Warwick; York.

Interview questions (see Ch.4): Questions will almost certainly focus on those aspects of the physics A/AS-level course which the student enjoys.

GAP YEAR ADVICE

Most institutions will accept a gap year, but students should maintain their mathematical competence.

Institutions willing to defer entry after A-Levels: Aberystwyth; Birmingham; Bristol; Brunel; Cardiff; Durham; Glasgow Caledonian; Heriot–Watt; Hull; Lancaster; Leeds; Leicester; London (RH), (UCL); Loughborough; Newcastle; Nottingham; Portsmouth; Robert Gordon; St Andrews; Salford; Staffordshire; Surrey; Sussex; Swansea; UMIST; Warwick; York.

AFTER RESULTS ADVICE

Institutions which may accept the same points score after A-Levels: Aberystwyth (No); Bath (No); Belfast (Queen's) (No); Birmingham; Bristol (No); Brunel; Dundee; Durham (No); Exeter (No); Heriot-Watt; Hull; Kent; Lancaster; Leeds; Leicester; Liverpool; London (RH); Loughborough; Newcastle; Northumbria; Nottingham; Paisley; St Andrews (No); Sheffield Hallam; Strathclyde (No); Surrey; Swansea; UMIST; Warwick (No); York; most institutions.

Institutions which may accept lower grades/points score after A-Levels: Bath; Birmingham; Brunel; Durham; Exeter; Kent; Lancaster; Leeds; Leicester; Liverpool; London (RH); Loughborough; Newcastle; Northumbria; Nottingham; St Andrews; Salford; Surrey; Swansea; UMIST; Warwick; York.

Offers to applicants repeating A-Levels: Higher St Andrews, UMIST, Warwick; **Possibly higher** Aberystwyth, Hull, Leeds, Loughborough, Newcastle, York; **Same** Birmingham, Lancaster, Leicester, Liverpool, Salford, Swansea.

Probable vacancies from June 2001 and in Clearing (see Ch.4): Most universities will have vacancies. Take your pick!

NEW GRADUATE DESTINATIONS AND EMPLOYMENT (1999 HESA) (see **Ch.4**)

In a survey of 1843 graduates, 877 entered full-time employment (of whom over half went into subject-related occupations), 104 were thought to be seeking employment and 703 graduates went into further study/research (363 in higher degrees).

PHYSIOLOGY (see also **Animal Sciences**)

NB The information supplied by the universities and colleges this year varies considerably and the offers listed below should be used as a first source of reference only. Many institutions will accept combinations of Advanced (AL), Advanced Subsidiary (AS) and Vocational Advanced (VA) level qualifications to achieve the required points total, but applicants must check web sites and prospectuses for full details of all offers. Grades and points totals shown should be regarded as the minimum levels to be achieved, but offers may be adjusted downwards when results are known. The points totals shown to the left of the institutions are for ease of reference only. It must not be assumed that tariff points are always used by institutions or that they can be substituted for an offer in grades. The level of an offer is not necessarily indicative of the quality of a course. To calculate your offers see Chapter 4 and the inside fold of the back cover.

Special subject requirements/preferences: A-Level: Mathematics/sciences. Chemistry usually required. **Oxford** Two subjects from science and mathematics recommended at A-Level. **GCSE:** Science and mathematics at grade A. **Cardiff** Minimum of six grade Bs or above. **Newcastle** Biology and mathematics if not offered at A-Level. Predominance of grade A or above (75%)

360 pts and above
　　　　Cambridge – Offers, mainly in grades, vary between colleges (Nat Sci (Physiol Orgnsms))
　　　　Oxford – Offers vary between candidates (Physiol Sci; Physiol/Phil; Physiol/Psy; Psy Phil Physiol)
330 pts Southampton – 330 pts 21u (inc 200 pts from 2ALs sci inc chem); (not gs) (Physiology courses)

300 pts **Bristol** – BBB (inc 2 sci); (not gs) (Physiol)
Leeds – BBB (Physiol/Spo Sci)
London (King's) – BBB+AS **or** BB+bb+AS **or** AC+ac+AS (inc B min chem/biol) **or** VA12u BB+AL(B sdci)+AS; (Physiol; Physiol/Pharmacol)
Sheffield – 300 pts approx (Physiology)

280 pts **Cardiff** – BBC (Physiol/Psy)
Edinburgh – BBC (Physiology)
Essex – 280–260 pts 21u – BB–BC+AL/2ASs **or** VA12u BB–BC+AL; gs; (Philosophy courses)
Glasgow – BBC–CCC/BC (Physiology courses)
Leeds – BBC (Physiol/Pharmacol)
Leicester – 18u – BBC **or** BB+2ASs **or** VA12u+AL; gs (AL only if 2ALs offered); (Physiology)
London (RH) – 280 pts – BBC–BCC **or** 2ALs+2ASs; (Physiol/Zool)
Manchester – BBC (Physiol; Physiol with Ind Exp/Modn Lang)

260 pts **Cardiff** – BCC (Physiology)
Hertfordshire – 260–220 pts 1x12u **or** 2x6u – 2ALs **or** AL+2ASs **or** VA12u; gs; (Hum Physiol)
Lancaster – BCC (Bioch/Anim Physiol)
London (UCL) – BCC **or** 3ALs+AS/VA; (Physiol; Physiol/Pharmacol)
Newcastle – BCC (Physiol Sci)
Reading – 260 pts approx (Physiol/Bioch)
St Andrews – BCC (Physiology)
Salford – BCC–CDD/AB–BC (Physiol/Bioch; Physiol/Geog)
Wolverhampton – 260 pts 18u – BCC **or** CC+e **or** VAs AA+/-AL/ASs; gs; (Hum Physiol Comb Hons)

240 pts **Belfast (Queen's)** – CCC/BB (Physiology)
Leeds – CCC (Physiology courses)
Liverpool – 240 pts – ALs **or** ALs+ASs **or** VAs+/-ALs/ASs; (Physiology)
Staffordshire – 240–180 pts approx (Physiol/Biochem)

220 pts **Aberdeen** – CCD (Physiology)
Bristol UWE – 220–180 pts 6u sci subj – ALs **or** ALs+ASs **or** VAs+/-ALs/ASs (chem reqd); (App Physiol/Pharmacol)
East London – 220–180 pts approx (Physiology courses)
Sunderland – 220–180 pts approx (Physiology courses except under **180 pts**)
Wolverhampton – 220–180 pts approx; gs; (Physiology courses)

200 pts **Central Lancashire** – 200–160 pts 12u (inc AL chem+biol) – ALs **or** ALs+ASs **or** VAs+/-ALs/ASs; (Physiology courses except under **160 pts**)
Dundee – 200 pts approx (Physiol Sci)
Greenwich – 200–160 pts approx (Physiology courses)

180 pts **Nottingham Trent** – 180 pts approx (inc chem+biol); (Physiol/Pharmacol)
Sunderland – 180 pts approx (Physiol Fdn)

160 pts **Central Lancashire** – 160 pts 12u (inc AL biol/chem/env sci) – ALs **or** ALs+ASs **or** VAs+/-ALs/ASs; gs; Physiol/Pharmacol)
Sunderland – 160 pts approx (Physiol)
Westminster – CC (Physiology courses)

140 pts **and below**
Strathclyde – DD (Physiol Sci St)
Sunderland – 140 pts approx (Physiol Joint courses)

Diploma of Higher Education courses
 80 pts East London.

Alternative Offers:

IB offers: Aberdeen 26 pts; Birmingham 30 pts; Bristol 28–26 pts; Cardiff 24 pts, H 15 pts; Central Lancashire 26 pts; Leeds 26 pts; Leicester 30 pts; Liverpool 30 pts + H55; London (UCL) 32 pts; St Andrews 28 pts; Southampton 28 pts.

Irish offers: Aberdeen BBCC/BCCCC; Dundee BBCC; Edinburgh BBBB; Glasgow BBB; Liverpool BBCCC; Sheffield AABB.

Scottish Qualifications: Aberdeen BBBC; Dundee BBCC; Edinburgh BBBB; Glasgow BBBB; Glasgow Caledonian BBCC; St Andrews BBBC; Stathclyde CCC.

Overseas applicants: Leeds Foundation courses offered.

CHOOSING YOUR COURSE (See also **Ch.1**)

Subject information: Physiology is a study of body function and courses in this wide-ranging subject will cover the central nervous system, special senses and neuro-muscular mechanisms, and body-regulating systems such as exercise, stress and temperature regulation. Anatomy, Medicine, Biological Sciences, Microbiology and Genetics are possible alternative courses.

Special features: Bristol Course primarily related to mammalian physiology. Options include anatomy, psychology, pharmacology, zoology. **Cardiff** Emphasis on neurophysiology (final year specialisation) with a sound background of human physiology. Transfers possible to Physiology, Biochemistry, Pharmacology or joint Honours courses. **Leeds** Covers biochemistry, psychology, microbiology and genetics in year 1. **Manchester** Modular structure in School of Biological Sciences. Easy transfer. **Newcastle** Possibility to change to one of six other biological science subjects at end of first year. Components of physiological biochemistry and biophysics integrated into physiology. *NOW CHECK PROSPECTUSES AND WEB SITES.*

Top universities and colleges (Research) (see Ch.4): Birmingham; Bristol; Cambridge; Liverpool; London (Royal Free), (UCL); Newcastle; Oxford.

Study opportunities abroad: Leicester; Manchester; Oxford; Reading; Salford.

Work opportunities abroad: Bristol; Salford.

ADMISSIONS INFORMATION

Number of applicants per place (approx): Birmingham 9; Bristol 10; Cardiff 6; Leeds 4; Liverpool 10; Newcastle 6; Nottingham Trent 3; Oxford 2; Sheffield 25; Southampton 7.

Planning your UCAS personal statement (see Ch.4): See **Anatomical Science/Anatomy** and **Pathology**.

Selection interviews (see Ch.4): Birmingham; Bristol UWE (No); Cambridge; Cardiff (No); Central Lancashire (No); Leicester (No); Leeds; London (UCL); Manchester; Newcastle; Nottingham Trent; Oxford; St Andrews (No); Sheffield.

Interview questions (see Ch.4): What made you decide to do a Physiology degree? What experimental work have you done connected with physiology? What future career do you have in mind? What is physiology? Why not choose Medicine instead? What practicals do you do at school? **Cardiff** Expect to see outside interests and ability to mix with people as well as an interest in biological sciences.

GAP YEAR ADVICE

Newcastle Indicate on UCAS application how gap year will be spent.

Institutions willing to defer entry after A-Levels: Bristol; Cardiff; Leeds; Leicester; London (UCL) (No); Newcastle; St Andrews; Salford; Sheffield; Westminster.

AFTER RESULTS ADVICE

Institutions which may accept the same points score after A-Levels: Bristol; Cardiff; Leeds; Leicester; Liverpool; London (UCL) (No); Newcastle; Salford; Sheffield (No).

Offers to applicants repeating A-Levels: Higher Bristol, Leeds (BCC), Leicester, Liverpool, Newcastle, St Andrews, Sheffield.

Probable vacancies from June 2001 and in Clearing (see Ch.4): An under-subscribed subject with a good choice of vacancies likely from June and in Clearing.

NEW GRADUATE DESTINATIONS AND EMPLOYMENT (1999 HESA) (see **Ch.4**)

No data available.

PHYSIOTHERAPY

NB The information supplied by the universities and colleges this year varies considerably and the offers listed below should be used as a first source of reference only. Many institutions will accept combinations of Advanced (AL), Advanced Subsidiary (AS) and Vocational Advanced (VA) level qualifications to achieve the required points total, but applicants must check web sites and prospectuses for full details of all offers. Grades and points totals shown should be regarded as the minimum levels to be achieved, but offers may be adjusted downwards when results are known. The points totals shown to the left of the institutions are for ease of reference only. It must not be assumed that tariff points are always used by institutions or that they can be substituted for an offer in grades. The level of an offer is not necessarily indicative of the quality of a course. To calculate your offers see Chapter 4 and the inside fold of the back cover.

Special subject requirements/preferences: A-Level: Biological science subject. **Birmingham** Biology mandatory. **Brighton**, Grade A–C biology. **Cardiff (UWCM)** Grade B biology. **East Anglia** Biol or hum biol desirable. **Northumbria** One science subject. **Southampton** One science award. **GCSE:** English, mathematics and science subjects. **Birmingham** Seven subjects grades A/B including English, mathematics, science taken at one sitting. **Bradford** Seven subjects at good grades taken at one sitting. **Brighton** Eight grade Bs or better at one sitting. **Bristol UWE** Minimum of five subjects grades A–C. **Brunel** Six subjects grades A–C at one sitting. **Cardiff (UWCM)** Seven subjects grades A–C. **Coventry** Seven subjects grades A–C including English, mathematics. **Glasgow Caledonian** Two sciences. **Hertfordshire** Grade B in mathematics, English and sciences. **Huddersfield** Six to eight grades A–C. **Liverpool** Six subjects including two sciences. **London (King's)** At least two-three grade As. **Manchester** Grades A/B in physics and several other subjects. **Northumbria** Six subjects at grades A/B (for applicants under 21 years). **Nottingham** Grades A/B in six-eight subjects. **Robert Gordon** Grades A*/B. **Southampton** Five (minimum) grades A–C. **Ulster** Three sciences.

360 pts and above

    Hertfordshire – 360–320 pts 1x12u **or** 2x6u – BB+160–120 pts **or** VA12u(hlthsc) BB+160–120 pts; gs; (Physiotherapy)

    Kingston – 360 pts (inc 3x6u inc biol/hum biol+AL sci) – ALs **or** ALs+ASs **or** VAs+/-ALs/ASs; (not gs) (Physiotherapy)

    London (King's) – 370 pts – ABB+c **or** AB+abb (inc 2ALs chem/biol/maths/phys) **or** VA12u BB+AL(A sci)+AS c; (Physiotherapy)

350 pts   Bristol UWE – 350–300 pts 18u pref/12u (6u biol/hum biol); ALs **or** ALs+ASs **or** VAs+/-ALs/ASs; (Physiotherapy)

    Brunel – 350–300 pts 3x6u (inc AL biol subj B) – ALs **or** ALs+ASs **or** VAs+/-ALs/ASs; (not gs) (Physiotherapy)

    Southampton – 350 pts 21u (inc 200 pts from 2ALs inc sci); (Physiotherapy)

340 pts   Birmingham – 340–300 pts – 3ALs (or equiv inc 2ALs(B) inc biol); (not gs) (Physiotherapy)

    Ulster – AAB–ABB (Physiotherapy)

320 pts   Queen Margaret (UC) – ABB (Physiotherapy)

    Robert Gordon – ABB (inc 2 sci) (Physiotherapy)

310 pts	**Cardiff (UWCM)** – 310 pts 12u – BB+110 pts min **or** VA12u BB+110 pts; (not gs) (Physiotherapy)
300 pts	**Bradford** – 300 pts 12u (inc AL biol sci); (Physiotherapy)
	Brighton – 300 pts approx (school leavers); AL A/B (mature students) (Physiotherapy)
	Coventry – BBB (Physiotherapy)
	East Anglia – 300 pts 18u – BBB (not gs) (Physiotherapy)
	East London – 300 pts approx (Physiotherapy)
	Keele – BBB **or** equiv AS accepted; gs; (Physiotherapy)
	Liverpool – 300 pts – ALs **or** ALs+ASs **or** VAs+/-ALs/ASs; (Physiotherapy)
	London (St George's HMS) – 300 pts approx (Physiotherapy)
	Manchester – BBB (B biol)+AL+2AS **or** VA AA+AL(B biol); (not gs) (Physiotherapy)
	Nottingham – BBB+ASs (Physiotherapy)
	Oxford Brookes – BBB (inc a biol sci); gs (not AL) (Physiotherapy)
	Salford – BBB; (not gs) (Physiotherapy)
280 pts	**Lincolnshire & Humberside** – 280 pts (Physiotherapy)
	Northumbria – BBC (not gs) (Physiotherapy)
	Sheffield Hallam – BBC (Physiotherapy)
	Teesside – BBC (B biol) (Physiotherapy)
260 pts	**Huddersfield** – BCC/BB (Physiotherapy)
240 pts	**Glasgow Caledonian** – contact univ (Physiotherapy)
220 pts	**East London** – 220 pts approx (Physio – mature students only)
	Leeds Met – (contact university)

Alternative Offers:

IB offers: Birmingham 32 pts H 16 pts; Bradford 28 pts; Brighton 28 pts; Brunel 32 pts; Cardiff (UWCM) 28 pts; East Anglia 35 pts; Hertfordshire 30 pts; Northumbria 32–30 pts; Queen Margaret (UC) 30 pts; Southampton 28 pts.

Irish offers: Birmingham BBBBB minimum; Bradford BBBBBB; Brighton BBBBBB; Northumbria BBBBBB inc sci; Ulster AABBBB.

Scottish Qualifications: Glasgow Caledonian ABBB; Queen Margaret (UC) AAABB; Robert Gordon BBBB.

Overseas applicants: Places for students from overseas are limited and applicants must be able to read, speak and write English fluently. Information on the minimum educational qualifications required by overseas students and details concerning grants and funding are available from the Chartered Society of Physiotherapy (see **Appendix 1**). **Brunel, Glasgow Caledonian** Proficiency in English essential. **Queen Margaret (UC)** Several overseas students recruited each year. **Ulster** Exams and continuous assessment.

CHOOSING YOUR COURSE (See also **Ch 1**)

Subject information: All courses lead to state registration as physiotherapists. The course content is similar in all cases. Competition is intense for the limited number of places available each year (at **Nottingham** 48 applications for each place). Good work experience or work shadowing is necessary prior to application. All six applications for Physiotherapy can be made on the UCAS form. For appropriate alternative courses Medicine, Physical Education, Sports Science, Osteopathy and Chiropractic might also be considered. See also **Appendix 1**.

Special features: Brighton Graduates would normally not be considered until two or three years after obtaining their degree. **East London** A special unit exists for visually impaired students. **North London** Course designed with visually impaired and blind candidates in mind. **Northumbria** Emphasis on small-group teaching. *NOW CHECK PROSPECTUSES AND WEB SITES.*

Top universities and college (Teaching Quality) (see Ch.4): Glasgow Caledonian; Queen Margaret (UC); not all institutions assessed.

Study opportunities abroad: Brunel; Coventry; East London; Glasgow Caledonian; Oxford Brookes; Queen Margaret (UC); Robert Gordon; Teesside.

Work opportunities abroad: Brunel; Huddersfield; Oxford Brookes; Northumbria; Queen Margaret (UC); Robert Gordon; Teesside.

ADMISSIONS INFORMATION

Number of applicants per place (approx): Bath 5; Birmingham 25; Bradford 22; Brighton 30 (6 places for overseas candidates); Bristol UWE 12; Brunel 10; Cardiff (UWCM) 17; Coventry 15; East Anglia 18; East London 10; Glasgow Caledonian 12; Hertfordshire 13; Huddersfield 25; Liverpool 20; London (King's) 10; Manchester 18; Newcastle 8; Northumbria 37; Nottingham 48; Queen Margaret (UC) 20; Robert Gordon 13; Salford 28; Sheffield Hallam 20; Southampton 30; Teesside 33; Ulster 12. **Foreign applicants** Coventry 40; Northumbria 20; Queen Margaret (UC) 7.

Planning your UCAS personal statement (see Ch.4): Visits to, and work experience in, hospital physiotherapy departments are important although many universities publicly state that this is not necessary. However, with the level of competition for this subject I would regard this as doubtful (see **Reasons for rejection** below). Applicants must demonstrate a clear understanding of the nature of the profession. Give details of voluntary work activities. Take notes of the work done and the different aspects of physiotherapy. Explain your experiences fully on the UCAS form. Outside interests and team work are considered important. See also **Appendix 1**.

Selection interviews (see Ch.4): Most institutions; Birmingham (T – mature applicants); Bradford; Brighton; Brunel (mature students); Cardiff (UWCM) (mature students); Coventry (W) (T); East London; Huddersfield; Nottingham; Queen Margaret (UC); Robert Gordon (T); Salford; Sheffield Hallam; Southampton (mature students who are asked to write about life experience).

Interview questions (see Ch.4): Physiotherapy is one of the most popular courses at present and work experience is essential. A sound knowledge of the career, types of treatment and the problems experienced by patients will be expected.

Reasons for rejection (non-academic): Lack of knowledge of the profession. Failure to convince the interviewers of a reasoned basis for following the profession. Failure to have visited a hospital physiotherapy unit. Lack of awareness of the demands of the course. **Birmingham** Poor communication skills. Lack of career insight. **Bristol UWE** Applicants re-sitting A-levels are not normally considered (see **Offers to applicants repeating A-levels**). **Cardiff (UWCM)** Lack of knowledge of physiotherapy; experience of sports injuries only.

GAP YEAR ADVICE

Some institutions will accept a gap year. Check with admissions tutor. Bristol UWE (No); Brunel; London (King's) (Yes); Southampton (Yes).

Institutions willing to defer entry after A-Levels: Birmingham; Bradford; Brighton (No); Brunel (No); Coventry (No); East London (No); Glasgow Caledonian; Hertfordshire; Northumbria; Nottingham; Queen Margaret (UC); Robert Gordon; Sheffield Hallam (No); Southampton.

AFTER RESULTS ADVICE

Institutions which may accept the same points score after A-Levels: Bradford (No); Brighton; Bristol UWE (No); Cardiff (UWCM) (No); Coventry (No); East Anglia (possibly); East London; Hertfordshire; Nottingham (B in biol); Robert Gordon; Sheffield Hallam (No); Southampton.

Institutions which may accept lower grades/points score after A-Levels: Brighton (if candidate improved at interview); Bristol UWE; Brunel; Coventry (No); East Anglia (rare); Northumbria; Nottingham; Queen Margaret (UC); Robert Gordon; Southampton; Teesside (No); Ulster.

Offers to applicants repeating A-Levels: Higher Bristol UWE (candidates who fail at interview will not normally be recommended), East London, Glasgow Caledonian, Teesside; **Same** Coventry, Southampton.

Probable vacancies from June 2001 and in Clearing (see Ch.4): A number of vacancies were declared last year.

NEW GRADUATE DESTINATIONS AND EMPLOYMENT (1999 HESA) (see **Ch.4**)

No data available.

PODIATRY (CHIROPODY)

NB The information supplied by the universities and colleges this year varies considerably and the offers listed below should be used as a first source of reference only. Many institutions will accept combinations of Advanced (AL), Advanced Subsidiary (AS) and Vocational Advanced (VA) level qualifications to achieve the required points total, but applicants must check web sites and prospectuses for full details of all offers. Grades and points totals shown should be regarded as the minimum levels to be achieved, but offers may be adjusted downwards when results are known. The points totals shown to the left of the institutions are for ease of reference only. It must not be assumed that tariff points are always used by institutions or that they can be substituted for an offer in grades. The level of an offer is not necessarily indicative of the quality of a course. To calculate your offers see Chapter 4 and the inside fold of the back cover.

Special subject requirements/preferences: A-Level: One or two science subjects. **GCSE:** Mathematics and science subjects.

280 pts	**Southampton** – 280 pts 12u (inc 160 pts from 2ALs inc 1 sci); (Podiatry)
220 pts	**London (UCL)** – 3ALs (chem pref+sci) **or** ALs+AS; (Podiatry)
180 pts	**Brighton** – 180 pts approx (Podiatry)
	Cardiff (UWI) – 180 pts approx (Podiatry)
	Salford – 180–120 pts – ALs **or** ALs+ASs; (Podiatry)
160 pts	**Huddersfield** – 160 pts 12u – ALs (inc 60 pts biol/pe); (Podiatry)
140 pts	**Northampton (UC)** – 140 pts approx (Podiatry)
120 pts	**Glasgow Caledonian** – DD (Podiatry)
	Queen Margaret (UC) – DD (BSc Podiatry)
80 pts	**Matthew Boulton (CFHE)** – EE (Podiatry)
	Plymouth – EE (Podiatry)

Alternative Offers:

IB offers: London (UCL) 30 pts.

Irish offers: Brighton CCCC.

Scottish Qualifications: Glasgow Caledonian BCC; Queen Margaret (UC) BCC.

CHOOSING YOUR COURSE (See also **Ch.1**)

Subject information: Podiatry is a relatively new term for chiropody. Courses lead to state registration. Some work-shadowing prior to application is preferred by admissions tutors. In addition to the courses listed above, a private Podiatry/Chiropody course is offered by Scholl leading to a Certificate or Diploma but not to state registration. Details are available from Scholl, 40 Upper Street, London N1 0PM. For the many alternative medical careers see **Medicine**. See also **Appendix 1**.

Special features: Cardiff (UWI) School is a self-contained unit with clinics, operating theatre suite, orthotics laboratory. **Northampton (UC)** Clinical experience includes sports injuries, orthopaedics, paediatrics. **Queen Margaret (UC)** Placement in wide variety of clinical settings. *NOW CHECK PROSPECTUSES AND WEB SITES.*

Top universities and colleges (Teaching Quality) (see Ch.4): Cardiff (UWI); not all institutions assessed.

ADMISSIONS INFORMATION

Number of applicants per place (approx): Cardiff (UWI) 2; Huddersfield 4; London (UCL) 6; Matthew Boulton (CFHE) 4; Plymouth 4; Salford 5; Southampton 5.

Planning your UCAS personal statement (see Ch.4): Visit a podiatrist's clinic to gain work experience/work shadowing experience. Discuss your knowledge of the work fully on your UCAS form. See also **Appendix 1**.

Selection interviews (see Ch.4): Southampton; most institutions.

Interview questions (see Ch.4): Have you visited a podiatrist's surgery? What do your friends think about your choice of career? Do you think that being a podiatrist could cause any physical problems? With which groups of people do podiatrists come into contact?

Reasons for rejection (non-academic): Unconvincing attitude; poor communication and inter-personal skills; lack of motivation; medical or physical disabilities which are incompatible with professional practice; no knowledge of chosen profession; lack of work experience.

GAP YEAR ADVICE

Brighton Advise us; **Queen Margaret (UC)** Apply in year of entry.

Institutions willing to defer entry after A-Levels: Brighton; Cardiff (UWI); Huddersfield; London (UCL) (No); Matthew Boulton (CFHE); Northampton (UC) (No); Plymouth; Salford; Southampton; Westminster.

AFTER RESULTS ADVICE

Institutions which may accept the same points score after A-Levels: London (UCL) (No).

Probable vacancies from June 2001 and in Clearing (see Ch.4): Contact all universities and colleges.

NEW GRADUATE DESTINATIONS AND EMPLOYMENT (1999 HESA) (see **Ch.4**)

See **Physiotherapy**.

POLITICS (see also **Government** and **International Relations**)

NB The information supplied by the universities and colleges this year varies considerably and the offers listed below should be used as a first source of reference only. Many institutions will accept combinations of Advanced (AL), Advanced Subsidiary (AS) and Vocational Advanced (VA) level qualifications to achieve the required points total, but applicants must check web sites and prospectuses for full details of all offers. Grades and points totals shown should be regarded as the minimum levels to be achieved, but offers may be adjusted downwards when results are known. The points totals shown to the left of the institutions are for ease of reference only. It must not be assumed that tariff points are always used by institutions or that they can be substituted for an offer in grades. The level of an offer is not necessarily indicative of the quality of a course. To calculate your offers see Chapter 4 and the inside fold of the back cover.

Special subject requirements/preferences: A-Level: Foreign languages for courses with a language option. **Hull** French grade C. **Oxford** AS-Levels considered. **GCSE: Bath** Majority of grade A*, A or B. **Belfast (Queen's), Bristol UWE, London (LSE), Newcastle, Plymouth, South Bank** Mathematics required. **Bristol UWE, Brunel, London Guildhall, South Bank, York** Grade B English required. **Cambridge, Oxford** Grade A in most subjects preferred. **Durham** High proportion of grades A and B and at least one humanities subject at grade A or B. **Glasgow, Lincoln & Humberside, Newcastle, Swansea** (Euro Pol) Foreign language required. **South Bank** Six subjects, majority grade B.

360 pts   and above
Aberystwyth – 360–300 pts 21u – 3ALs (200 pts min)+ASs **or** VAs+/-AL/ASs (300–220 pts); gs; (Int Pol and Intell St/Am/Thrd Wrld/Hist/Strat St; Euro Pol; Pol St)
Cambridge – Offers, mainly in grades, vary between colleges (Soc Pol Sci)
Oxford – Offers vary between candidates (Pol Phil Econ)
York – 21–18u – ABB+b; (Politics courses)

350 pts   Southampton – 350 pts 21u (inc 200 pts from 2ALs); gs; (Pol/Law)
340 pts   Bristol – AAB–BBC; (not gs) (Pol; Pol and Fr/Ital/Ger/Port/Soc/Russ/Span)
St Andrews – AAB (Int Rel courses)

320 pts   Durham – ABB (Pol/Hist; Pol/Econ; Pol/Law)
Edinburgh – ABB (1 sitting) (not gs) (Politics courses)
London (LSE) – ABB (Gov; Int Rel courses)
Manchester – ABB–BBC (Politics courses)
Nottingham – ABB–BBB (Pol; Law/Pol)
Warwick – ABB (Pol; Pol/Fr; Pol/Int St; Pol/Sociol)

310 pts   Southampton – 310 pts (inc 180 pts from 2ALs); gs; (Politics courses except under **350 pts**)

300 pts   Bath – BBB–BBC; (not gs) (Pol/Econ)
Birmingham – BBB–BBC (Pol Sci)
Cardiff – BBB (Pol/Law)
Durham – ABC–BBB (Pol; Pol/Euro)
East Anglia – 300–280 pts 18u – BBC–BCC **or** BB+cc **or** BBC+e **or** VA (280 pts or 200 pts+C); (Politics courses)
Essex – 300–280 pts 21u – BB+AL/2ASs **or** VA12u BB+AL; gs; (Politics courses)
Hull – BBB–BCC (Pol courses)
Kent – 300 pts approx (Pol/Law)
Leeds – BBB **or** BB+bb (VAs contact univ); gs; (Politics courses)
Manchester – BBB–BBC (Gov; Pol/Modn Hist)
Nottingham – BBB (Pol/E Euro St)
Sheffield – BBB/AA (Politics courses)
Stirling – BBB (Pol/Parl St)
Sussex – BBB (Pol/N Am St)

280 pts   Aberdeen – BBC (Politics courses)
Belfast (Queen's) – BBC–BCC (BSc Econ Pol)
Bradford – BBC/BB (Peace St; Pol/Sociol; Int Rel)
Cardiff – BBC (Pol; Pol/Modn Hist; Educ/Pol; Fr/Pol)
Durham – BBC/BB (Pol/Hist Mid East with Arab/Turk/Persn)
Exeter – 280 pts 18u – BBC **or** BB+bb **or** VAs (contact univ); gs; (Politics courses)
Glasgow – BBC (Politics courses)
Keele – BBC–BCC/BB–BC **or** equiv AS accepted; gs; (Politics courses)
Kent – 280 pts approx (Politics courses except under **300/260 pts**)
Lancaster – BBC (Econ/Pol; Hist/Pol; Hist Phil/Pol)
Liverpool – 280 pts – ALs **or** ALs+ASs **or** VAs+/-ALs/ASs; (Pol/Comm St; Pol)
London (QM) – BBC from 3ALs **or** 2ALs+2ASs; (Politics courses)
London (SOAS) – 280–260 pts approx (Politics courses)
London (UCL) – 280 pts **or** 3ALs+ASs/VAs; (Pol/E Euro St)

Newcastle – BBC (Politics courses)
Reading – BBC–BCC (Politics courses)
Salford – BBC (Politics)
Sussex – BBC (Politics courses except under **300 pts**)
Swansea – 280 pts 18u – BBC–BCC/BB **or** ALs+ASs **or** VAs+/-ALs/ASs; (Politics courses)

260 pts **Aston** – 260–240 18u – 3ALs **or** ALs+ASs **or** VAs+/-ALs/ASs; gs; (Politics courses)
Bangor – BCC/BC (Pol Soc Sci)
Belfast (Queen's) – BCC (BSSc/BA Pol)
Cardiff – BCC (Politics with Fr/Span/Ger/Ital/Sociol)
Dundee – BCC/BB (MA Politics courses)
Kent – 260 pts approx (Pol 1 yr in Finland; Euro Pol courses)
Lancaster – BCC (Politics courses except **280 pts**)
Leicester – 260 pts 18u – BCC **or** ALs+ASs **or** VAs+ALs/ASs; gs; (Pol; Pol Econ Soc Hist)
Salford – BCC (Pol Econ)
Stirling – BCC (Pol; Pol Phil Econ)
Strathclyde – BCC/BB (Politics – Bus Sch)
Strathclyde – BCC/BC (Pol; BA Arts Soc Sci)
Ulster – BCC (Politics (Hum))

240 pts **Bradford** – 240 pts 12u; gs; (Politics courses)
Bristol UWE – 240–200 pts 18u pref/12u; ALs **or** ALs+ASs **or** VAs+/-ALs/ASs; (Politics courses)
Brunel – 240 pts 1x6u – ALs **or** ALs+ASs **or** VAs+/-ALs/ASs; (Politics courses)
Kingston – 240 pts approx (Pol/Engl; Pol/Psy)
Liverpool John Moores – 240–180 pts (inc 2ALs) – ALs **or** ALs+ASs **or** VAs+/-ALs/ASs; (Politics courses)
London (Gold) – BCD/BC (Pol/Econ; Pol/Pub Pol)
Loughborough – 240 pts – 2ALs(C lang)+AL/2ASs **or** VAs+/-ALs/ASs; gs; (Pol/Fr/Ger/Span)
Loughborough – 240 pts – 2ALs+AL/2ASs; **or** VAs+/-ALs/ASs; gs; (Pol and Econ/Sociol/Soc Pol/Soc Psy/Geog/Engl St/Comm Media St)
Nottingham Trent – 240 pts 18u – CCC–CCD (VAs check with dept); gs; (Politics)
Oxford Brookes – CCC offer varies with 2nd subject (Politics)

220 pts **Coventry** – 220–200 pts approx (Politics courses)
De Montfort (Leicester) – 220 pts; (200 pts joint/comb courses) – ALs **or** ALs+ASs **or** VAs+/-ALs/ASs; (not gs) (Politics courses)
Hertfordshire – 220–200 pts approx (Politics courses)
Kingston – 220 pts 2x6u (inc 200 pts in 2x6u awards); (Politics)
Luton – 220–180 pts approx (Pol – Mod)
Manchester Met – 220 pts approx (Politics)
Middlesex – 220–180 pts approx (Pol Int St; Pol Int Fdn)
South Bank – 220–140 pts approx (Politics courses)
Sunderland – 220–180 pts approx (Politics courses)
Teesside – 220 pts (Crim/Pol)
Wolverhampton – 220–160 pts 12u – DDD–CDE/CC **or** CD+d/e **or** VA12u CC; gs; (Politics)

210 pts **Buckingham** – 210 pts 21u – 3ALs **or** 3ALs+AS; (Politics courses)
200 pts **Anglia** – 200–180 pts approx (Pol Comb courses)
Central England – 200 pts 12u; (Politics courses)
Glamorgan – 200–180 pts approx (Politics courses)
Huddersfield – 200 pts 12u – ALs (inc D); gs; (Politics courses)
Northumbria – 200 pts approx (Pol; Pol/Media St)
Plymouth – 200 pts approx (Int Rel; Pol courses)
Portsmouth – 200 pts – ALs **or** ALs+ASs **or** VAs; gs; (Pol; Pol Soc)
Sheffield Hallam – 200 pts approx (Euro Pol Pol)

Staffordshire – 200 pts; ALs (inc CC) **or** CC+AS(40 pts); **or** VA CC; gs; (Politics courses)

Sunderland – 200–180 pts approx (Politics courses)

Teesside – 200–160 pts approx (Politics courses except under **220 pts**)

180 pts   **Central Lancashire** – 180–160 pts 12u – gs; (Pol/Hist/Phil)

Cheltenham & Glos (CHE) – 180–160 pts approx (Pol Soty courses)

East London – 180 pts approx (Politics courses)

Lincolnshire & Humberside – 180 pts approx (Politics)

London Guildhall – DDD/CC (Politics courses)

Sunderland – 180–140 pts approx (Pol St courses)

160 pts   **Brighton** – CC (Hum (Pol))

Central Lancashire – 160–140 pts 12u; gs; (Pol/Soc Pol)

Lincolnshire & Humberside – 160 pts (Politics)

Southampton (Inst) – CC (Pol St)

140 pts   **Derby** – 140 pts 12u – CD **or** DE+ee **or** VA CD+/-ALs/ASs; (Pol Comb Hons)

North London – 140 pts 1x12u **or** 2x6u; (Politics courses)

120 pts   **Robert Gordon** – DD (Gov Pol Mgt)

100 pts   **Barnsley (Coll)** – 100 pts approx (Hum (Pol/Hist/Int Rel))

Leeds Met – (contact university)

Diploma of Higher Education courses

80 pts   Bradford (Coll); London Guildhall; Oxford Brookes; Plymouth; Wolverhampton.

Alternative Offers:

EB offers: Brunel 70%; Keele 65%; Lancaster 70%; Liverpool 60%; Newcastle 75%.

IB offers: Aberdeen 30 pts; Aberystwyth 30 pts; Birmingham 33 pts; Bradford (Peace St) 30 pts; Bristol 34–30 pts H665; Brunel 28 pts; Buckingham 28 pts; Central Lancashire 28 pts; De Montfort 26 pts; Durham H666; East Anglia 30 pts; Essex 28 pts; Exeter 32 pts; Hull (PPE) 30 pts; Kent 29 pts; Lancaster 30 pts; Leicester 30–28 pts; Liverpool 28 pts; London (SOAS) 32 pts; Newcastle 30 pts, (Pol/Hist) 33 pts H7 hist; Northumbria 24 pts; Portsmouth 24 pts; Staffordshire 24 pts; Swansea 30–28 pts; Warwick 34–32 pts; York 28 pts.

Irish offers: Aberdeen BBBB; Brunel BBCCC; East Anglia CCCCC; Guildhall London CCCCC; Keele BBBCC; Newcastle ABBBB; Northumbria CCCCC; Warwick AAABB.

Scottish Qualifications: Aberdeen BBBB; Dundee BBBC; Edinburgh ABBBC; Glasgow ABBB/BBBB; Robert Gordon (Gov) BCCC; St Andrews (int Rel) AAAB; Stirling AABB–BBBC; Strathclyde BBBB.

Overseas applicants: East Anglia Pre-sessional courses available in English and study skills. **Hull** Living costs 30% lower than in London.

CHOOSING YOUR COURSE (See also **Ch.1**)

Subject information: Politics courses have become increasingly popular in recent years and usually cover the politics and government of the major powers. Because of the variety of degree courses on offer it is possible to study the politics of almost any country in the world. International Relations, Peace Studies, Social Administration, Development Studies and Economics courses could be considered as alternatives.

Special features: Aberystwyth Second largest Politics department in the United Kingdom. Wide choice of options include strategic studies, political studies in international relations. House of Commons placement scheme. **Birmingham** In the second and third years students take either political theory or political analysis, with a choice of options from British, European, American, Latin-American, Soviet or African politics. **Bristol UWE** The Social Science programme features a common first year allowing delayed choice from 24 different specialist and joint honours degrees. **Brunel** Specialisms include Politics and Policy, European Politics and Politics and Philosophy. **Durham** First year involves two introductory courses: politics and policy-making, and politics and ideas. Two additional subjects are also taken from economics, business studies, geography, psychology, history, sociology, law, anthropology and computing. **Essex** Courses can be selected on a geographical basis. Specialisms in the politics of Britain, Western Europe, USA, Russia, Latin-America and Japan. Options in the politics of Europe, Japan, Russia and Africa **Huddersfield** The course includes European and Third World politics. **Lancaster** Students take two other subjects in year 1, for example law, history, religious studies. **Leeds** Second year subjects cover foreign governments and comparative government in the USA, the former Soviet Union, France, China, India and Pakistan, modern political doctrines and political and social history. **Liverpool John Moores** The course covers the politics of the UK, the European Union, Eastern Europe and South East Asia. **Loughborough** Western European emphasis with French/German available as minor subjects; possibility to transfer within Social Sciences in second year. **Manchester** One of the largest departments in the United Kingdom. Broad course leading to final year specialisms (choice of 50). Other disciplines offered in first and second years including foreign languages. **Newcastle** Government and European Union Studies students have one year in Europe. **Staffordshire** Study visits: first year London, second year Europe, third year Eastern Europe. **York** Wide spectrum of subjects include the major governmental systems of Britain, Western Europe, America, China, Japan and the former Soviet Union. Subject strengths include Third World and British politics and political philosophy. *NOW CHECK PROSPECTUSES AND WEB SITES.*

Top universities and colleges (Teaching Quality) (see Ch.4): Aberystwyth; Strathclyde; not all institutions assessed.

Top universities and colleges (Research) (see Ch.4): Aberdeen; Aberystwyth; Belfast (Queen's); Bradford; Bristol; Edinburgh; Essex; Exeter; Glasgow; Hull; Keele; Leicester; London (King's), (LSE), (QM); Manchester; Newcastle; Oxford; Sheffield; Southampton; Strathclyde; Sussex; Swansea; York.

Study opportunities abroad: Aberystwyth; Bangor; Belfast (Queen's); Bradford; Bristol; Bristol UWE; Brunel; Cardiff; Central England; Cheltenham & Glos (CHE); De Montfort; Dundee; Durham; Edinburgh; Exeter; Huddersfield; Keele; Kent; Lancaster; Leeds; Liverpool; Liverpool John Moores; London Guildhall; Loughborough; Manchester Met; Newcastle; Oxford Brookes; Portsmouth; Salford; Sheffield; Staffordshire; Sunderland; Swansea; Teesside; Warwick; York.

Work opportunities abroad: Brunel; Leeds; London Guildhall; Staffordshire; Swansea.

ADMISSIONS INFORMATION

Number of applicants per place (approx): Aberystwyth 6; Bath 8; Birmingham 13; Bradford 10; Bristol 20; Brunel 5; Buckingham 2; Cambridge 3.8; Cardiff 14; De Montfort 15; Durham 11 (all courses); East Anglia 15; Exeter 8; Hull 11, (PPE) 20; Kent 14; Lancaster 14; Leeds 18; Leicester (Pol/Econ/Soc Hist) 3, (Pol) 10; Liverpool 9; Liverpool John Moores 10; London (QM) 10, (SOAS) 8; London Guildhall 3; Loughborough 7; Newcastle 9, (Pol/Hist) 18; North London 7; Nottingham 12; Oxford (Pol Phil Econ) 3; Oxford Brookes 12; Portsmouth 14; Salford 7; Staffordshire 10; Stirling 9; Swansea 6; Warwick 10; York 15, (Pol/Engl subsid) 6.

Planning your UCAS personal statement (see Ch.4): Read current affairs avidly. Be aware of political developments in the major countries (UK, Europe, USA and the Russian Independent States). Keep abreast of developments in theatres of war. Explain your interests in detail.

Selection interviews (see Ch.4): Bath (mature students); Birmingham; Bristol UWE (No); Brunel (No); Cambridge; Durham (No, except for mature students and for Pol/Arab/Turk/Persn courses); East Anglia (No); Exeter; Huddersfield; Hull; Kingston (No); Leeds (Pol/Parl St); Leicester; Liverpool; Liverpool John Moores; London (Gold) (W) (T), (SOAS); London Guildhall; Loughborough; Manchester (No); Nottingham; Nottingham Trent (No); Oxford (PPE) (W, T); Oxford Brookes (No); Portsmouth; Salford; Sheffield; Sheffield Hallam

(No); South Bank (W) (T); Staffordshire (some); Stirling (No); Swansea; Ulster; Warwick; York.

Interview questions (see Ch.4): Questions may stem from A/AS-Level studies but applicants will also be expected to be up-to-date in their knowledge and opinions of current events. Questions in recent years have included: What constitutes a 'great power'? What is happening at present in the Labour Party? Define capitalism. What is a political decision? How do opinion polls detract from democracy? Is the European Union a good idea? Why? What is the Maastricht Agreement? What are the views of the present government on the European Union? What is a 'spin doctor'? Are politicians hypocrites? **London (Gold)** Essays required from current course.

Reasons for rejection (non-academic): No opinions.

GAP YEAR ADVICE

Institutions willing to defer entry after A-Levels: Aberystwyth; Birmingham; Bradford; Bristol; Bristol UWE; Brunel (No); Buckingham; Cheltenham & Glos (CHE); Coventry; De Montfort; Dundee; Durham; Hull; Kent; Leeds; Leicester; London (Gold); London Guildhall; Luton; Newcastle; Northampton (UC); Northumbria; Nottingham; Plymouth; Portsmouth; Salford; Sheffield (varies); South Bank (Prefers not); Sussex; Swansea; York.

AFTER RESULTS ADVICE

Institutions which may accept the same points score after A-Levels: Birmingham (No); Bristol (No); Bristol (UWE); Cheltenham & Glos (CHE); Durham (No); East Anglia; Essex; Hull; Kent; Lancaster (No); Leeds; Leicester; Liverpool; London (SOAS); London Guildhall; Loughborough; Manchester; Newcastle (No); Northumbria; Nottingham (No); Oxford Brookes; Portsmouth; Salford; South Bank; Staffordshire; Stirling (No); Swansea; Warwick (No); York.

Institutions which may accept lower grades/points score after A-Levels: Aberystwyth; Birmingham; Buckingham (Univ); Cheltenham & Glos (CHE); Durham (No); East Anglia; Essex; Exeter; Hull (overseas applicants 18–16 pts); Leeds; Leicester; London (SOAS); London Guildhall; Northumbria; Portsmouth; Salford; South Bank; Swansea; Warwick; York.

Offers to applicants repeating A-Levels: Higher East Anglia, Essex, Leeds, Newcastle, Nottingham, Warwick; **Possibly higher** Hull, Lancaster, Oxford Brookes, Swansea; **Same** Birmingham, Bristol, Durham, Lancaster, London (SOAS), London Guildhall, Loughborough, Portsmouth, South Bank, Sussex, York.

Probable vacancies from June 2001 and in Clearing (see Ch.4): A large selection of Politics and Government courses could be available, particularly in combination with other subjects.

NEW GRADUATE DESTINATIONS AND EMPLOYMENT (1999 HESA) (see **Ch.4**)

Out of 2200 graduates surveyed, 1261 went into full-time employment (the majority going into managerial and administrative occupations in finance, property and public service areas) and 139 into part-time work; 164 were believed to be unemployed and 482 went into further study.

PORTUGUESE (see also **Latin American Studies** (Hispanic Studies), **Modern Languages** and **Spanish**)

NB The information supplied by the universities and colleges this year varies considerably and the offers listed below should be used as a first source of reference only. Many institutions will accept combinations of Advanced (AL), Advanced Subsidiary (AS) and Vocational Advanced (VA) level qualifications to achieve the required points total, but applicants must check web sites and prospectuses for full details of all offers. Grades and points totals shown should be regarded as the minimum levels to be achieved, but

offers may be adjusted downwards when results are known. The points totals shown to the left of the institutions are for ease of reference only. It must not be assumed that tariff points are always used by institutions or that they can be substituted for an offer in grades. The level of an offer is not necessarily indicative of the quality of a course. To calculate your offers see Chapter 4 and the inside fold of the back cover.

Special subject requirements/preferences: A-Level: English and a foreign language may be stipulated. Check institutions for changing requirements. **GCSE: London (King's)** Three to four grades A*, A or B.

360 pts   and above
    Cambridge – Offers, mainly in grades, vary between colleges (Modn/Mediev Lang (Port))
320 pts   Birmingham – ABB (Portuguese courses)
    Nottingham – ABB (Port St/Mgt)
300 pts   Edinburgh – BBB (Span/Port courses)
    Manchester – BBB (Portuguese courses)
    Newcastle – ABC–BBB (Port Comb St)
    Southampton – ABC (Portuguese courses)
280 pts   Leeds – BBC (Port/Russ; Port/Span)
    Liverpool – BBC–BCC (Port Arts Comb)
    London (King's) – BBC+AS **or** BB+bbc (inc AL lang/hist); VAs considered; (Port/Braz St; Port/Engl; Port/App Comp; Port/Modn Gk; Hisp/Port St)
    Nottingham – BBC (Port/Engl St; Port/Fr; Port/Ger)
240 pts   Portsmouth – 240 pts approx (Euro St/Port)

Alternative Offers:

IB offers: Birmingham 33 pts; London (King's) 30 pts.

Scottish Qualifications: Edinburgh ABBB–BBBB.

CHOOSING YOUR COURSE (See also **Ch.1**)

> **Subject information:** Portuguese may be studied as a language in its own right, but more often is a combined study with another language, or part of a course in Hispanic Studies. See also **Appendix 1** under **Modern Languages**.

Top universities and colleges (Teaching Quality) (see Ch.4): London (King's); not all institutions assessed.

Top universities and colleges (Research) (see Ch.4): London (King's).

ADMISSIONS INFORMATION

Planning your UCAS personal statement (see Ch.4): See **Spanish**.

Selection interviews (see Ch.4): Edinburgh (No); London (King's).

Interview questions (see Ch.4): Past questions have included: Why Portuguese? Have you been to Portugal? What career are you aiming for at the end of the course? (It is important for applicants to be informed about Portugal and its people.) **London (King's)** We are looking for a genuine commitment to the literature and culture of the Portuguese-speaking world, not just the language.

AFTER RESULTS ADVICE

Probable vacancies from June 2001 and in Clearing (see Ch.4): Liverpool and London (King's) declared vacancies last year with offers in the 260–240 pts range.

NEW GRADUATE DESTINATIONS AND EMPLOYMENT (1999 HESA) (see **Ch.4**)

No data available.

PRINTING, PUBLISHING & PACKAGING

NB The information supplied by the universities and colleges this year varies considerably and the offers listed below should be used as a first source of reference only. Many institutions will accept combinations of Advanced (AL), Advanced Subsidiary (AS) and Vocational Advanced (VA) level qualifications to achieve the required points total, but applicants must check web sites and prospectuses for full details of all offers. Grades and points totals shown should be regarded as the minimum levels to be achieved, but offers may be adjusted downwards when results are known. The points totals shown to the left of the institutions are for ease of reference only. It must not be assumed that tariff points are always used by institutions or that they can be substituted for an offer in grades. The level of an offer is not necessarily indicative of the quality of a course. To calculate your offers see Chapter 4 and the inside fold of the back cover.

Applicants should note that there are two pathways for those applying for some of these courses (Route A or Route B or both). See the general notes under **Art and Design (General)** and the *UCAS Directory* for course details.

Special subject requirements/preferences: GCSE: *Printing:* Science may be required. *Publishing:* English usually required. **London (Inst)** (Prtg) Minimum three subjects at grade A or B. (Pub) Minimum three subjects grade A; English and mathematics grade A–C for both courses. **Nottingham Trent** Five subjects at grade A/B.

280 pts	**London (Inst)** – BBC/BB (Publishing)
	Loughborough – 280 pts 18u – AL(B Engl)+AL+AL/2ASs **or** VAs+/-AL/ASs; gs; (Pub/Engl)
260 pts	**Oxford Brookes** – BCC–CCD (Publishing Joint Hons)
240 pts	**London (Inst)** – CCC/CC (Prt Media Mgt)
220 pts	**Middlesex** – 220 pts approx (Writ; Pub/Media)
180 pts	**Napier** – BC (Publishing)
140 pts	**Robert Gordon** – CD/120 pts (Pub St)
120 pts	**and below and other selection criteria**
	Sheffield Hallam – portfolio; (Pack Comm Des)
	West Herts (Coll) – EE (Pub; Pack; Prtg)

Diploma of Higher Education courses
80 pts Oxford Brookes.

Higher National Diploma courses
100 pts and below
Berkshire (CAD) (Prtg); Blackpool & Fylde (Coll) (Pub); Farnborough (CT) (Pub); Glasgow (CBP); Gloucestershire (CAT) (Pub); London (Inst) (Prtg; Pub); Napier (Pub); Newcastle (Coll) (Prtg); Northampton (UC) (Prtg); Nottingham Trent (Prtg Media Mgt); Sheffield (Coll) (Typo); Sheffield Hallam (Pack Des); Stockport (CFHE) (Prtg); West Herts (Coll) (Prtg; Pub; Pack); Wiltshire (Coll) (Pack Des); Wolverhampton (Typo).

Alternative Offers:

Scottish Qualifications: Napier BBB; Robert Gordon BBCC.

CHOOSING YOUR COURSE (See also **Ch.1**)

Subject information: Printing is an undersubscribed area for applications, yet it requires graduates to work at all levels. It is closely related to Publishing which is a specialised branch of business studies. Packaging could be considered particularly by students interested in three dimensional and graphic design. Degree courses in Business Studies, Advertising, Public Relations and Graphics should also be considered alongside these courses. See also **Appendix 1.**

Special features: London Inst (Prt Media/Mgt) Mature students with practical experience but limited academic qualifications are welcome. **West Herts (Coll)** Research at MSc, MPhil and PhD levels. Company consultancy work; strong employer contacts. *NOW CHECK PROSPECTUSES AND WEB SITES.*

Study opportunities abroad: London (Inst).

Work opportunities abroad: West Herts (Coll).

ADMISSIONS INFORMATION

Number of applicants per place (approx): Nottingham Trent 4; Oxford Brookes 16; West Herts (Coll) 2 (Interviews held).

Planning your UCAS personal statement (see Ch.4): Since each of these activities is a career in its own right, work experience is important to understand the range of work (and problems) involved, including work on a school magazine. This awareness should be explained on the UCAS form. See also **Appendix 1**.

Interview questions (see Ch.4): Applicants should have some knowledge of methods of printing and of the printing and publishing industry. This should come from personal contact with printers and publishers. What makes a good book?

GAP YEAR ADVICE

Institutions willing to defer entry after A-Levels: West Herts (Coll).

AFTER RESULTS ADVICE

Probable vacancies from June 2001 and in Clearing (see Ch.4): Contact all institutions since vacancies are likely.

NEW GRADUATE DESTINATIONS AND EMPLOYMENT (1999 HESA) (see **Ch.4**)

Of 46 Publishing graduates surveyed, 34 obtained full-time employment (mainly in managerial and publishing fields), four went into further study and two were unemployed.

PSYCHOLOGY (including Behavioural Science)

NB The information supplied by the universities and colleges this year varies considerably and the offers listed below should be used as a first source of reference only. Many institutions will accept combinations of Advanced (AL), Advanced Subsidiary (AS) and Vocational Advanced (VA) level qualifications to achieve the required points total, but applicants must check web sites and prospectuses for full details of all offers. Grades and points totals shown should be regarded as the minimum levels to be achieved, but offers may be adjusted downwards when results are known. The points totals shown to the left of the institutions are for ease of reference only. It must not be assumed that tariff points are always used by institutions or that they can be substituted for an offer in grades. The level of an offer is not necessarily indicative of the quality of a course. To calculate your offers see Chapter 4 and the inside fold of the back cover.

Special subject requirements/preferences: A-Level: Sciences required for BSc courses as follows: **Aston** (1), **Bristol** (2), **Chester (CHE)** Psychology preferred. **Edinburgh** (1), **Exeter** (1), **Lincolnshire & Humberside** (1), **London (Gold)** (1–2), **(UCL)** (1), **Newcastle** (2), **Nottingham** (3), **Reading** (1); **Curriculum 2000: Oxford** Full A-Levels desirable. **GCSE:** (Science subjects) **Bangor** Biology desirable, **Bristol, Exeter, Glasgow Caledonian, Lancaster,** Biology, **Leicester** Mathematics and biology, **Lincolnshire & Humberside, London (Gold), (RH), (UCL), Manchester Met, Newcastle** Biology. **Other GCSEs:** Most universities require mathematics grade A–C. **Bath** Mainly A* and As. **Birmingham, Derby, Hull, Plymouth, Portsmouth, Swansea, York** English and mathematics grade A–C. **Buckingham** Five grade Bs or Cs minimum. **Greenwich, Nottingham Trent** Mathematics grades A/B. **Leeds** Majority of A*, A or Bs, mathematics grade B. **Northumbria** Mathematics grade B or above, science grade B or above preferred. **Oxford** Seven subjects at grade A. **Portsmouth** Seven subjects grade A–C. **Warwick** Seven subjects grade B or above. **York** Mathematics grade B.

360 pts **and above**
> **Cambridge** – Offers, mainly in grades, vary between colleges (Nat Sci (Psychology))
> **Oxford** – Offers vary between candidates (Psy Phil Physiol; Psy/Physiol; Psy/Phil; Expmt Psy)
> **York** – 21–18u – ABB+b; (Psychology)

350 pts **Southampton** – 350 pts 21u (inc 200 pts from 2ALs); (Psychology)
340 pts **Bristol** – AAB–BBC (Psy/Phil)
> **Exeter** – AAB–BBB (Psychology courses)
> **London (UCL)** – AAB–ABB **or** 3ALs+AS/VA; (Psy; Psy Cog Sci)
> **Sheffield** – AAB/BB (mature applicants only) (Psy/Sociol)

320 pts **Bath** – 320 pts approx (BSc Psychology)
> **Birmingham** – ABB–BBB (Psychology)
> **Brunel** – 320–280 pts 2x6u – ALs **or** ALs+ASs **or** VAs+/-ALs/ASs; (not gs) (Psychology courses)
> **Cardiff** – ABB (Psy/Engl)
> **Cardiff** – ABB–BBC (Psychology)
> **Durham** – ABB–BBB (BA/BSc Psy; Psy/Anth; Psy/Sociol; Psy/Phil)
> **Edinburgh** – ABB (1 sitting); (not gs) (Psychology courses)
> **Exeter** – 320–300 pts 18u – ABB–BBB **or** AB+ab **or** VAs (contact univ); (not gs for Psy) (Psy; Psy/Euro St)
> **Kent** – ABB (App Soc Psy/Clin Psy)
> **Leeds** – ABB (Psychology Joint Hons courses)
> **Manchester** – ABB/AA (Psy; Psy/Euro)
> **Newcastle** – ABB (Psychology)
> **Nottingham** – ABB–BBB (Psychology courses; Bhv Sci)
> **Oxford Brookes** – ABB–CCD (Psychology joint Hons – offer varies with 2nd subject)
> **St Andrews** – ABB (MA Psychology)
> **Sheffield** – ABB/BB (mature applicants only) (Psy/Cog Sci; Psy)
> **Warwick** – ABB–BBC (Psy; Psy Phil)

300 pts **Aston** – 300 pts 18u – 3ALs **or** ALs+ASs **or** VAs+/-ALs/ASs; gs; (Hum Psy courses)
> **Birmingham** – BBB (Psy/Artif Intel)
> **Bristol** – BBB/BB (Psy; Psy/Zool)
> **Cardiff** – BBB (Psychology courses except under **320 pts**)
> **Hertfordshire** – 300–280 pts approx (Psy; Psy Mod)
> **Hull** – BBB–BBC/AA (Psychology courses)
> **Keele** – BBB **or** equiv AS accepted; gs; (Psychology courses)
> **Kent** – 300 pts approx/BBB (Psychology and joint courses except under **320/280 pts**; Soc Psy; App Soc Psy)
> **Kent** – BBB/AB (App Psy)
> **Lancaster** – BBB (Psychology)
> **Leeds** – BBB **or** BB+bb; VAs (contact univ); gs; (Cog Sci)
> **Leicester** – BBB–BBC (inc biol) **or** ALs+ASs(B biol) **or** VAs+/-AL/ASs; gs; (Psy/Neuro; Psy/Sociol)
> **Liverpool** – 300 pts – ALs **or** ALs+ASs **or** VAs+/-ALs/ASs; (Psychology courses)
> **London (RH)** – BBB–BBC; (not gs) (Psychology)
> **London (RH)** – BBB (Cog Sci)
> **Loughborough** – 300 pts – 2ALs+AL/2ASs **or** VA12u+AL **or** VA6u+2ALs; (not gs) (Psy; Psy/Ergon)
> **Newcastle** – BBB–BBC (Psy Stats)

Reading – BBB (Psychology courses)
Surrey – 300 pts 18u; (not gs) (Psychology)
Sussex – BBB (Psychology courses)
Swansea – 300 pts 18u – BBB/AB **or** ALs+ASs **or** VAs+/-ALs/ASs; (Psychology)

280 pts **Anglia** – 280 pts; gs (Bhv Sci)
Aston – 280–260 pts – 3ALs **or** ALs+ASs **or** VAs+/-AL/ASs; gs; (Psy Comb courses)
Bangor – BBC/AB (Psychology (Arts); Psychology (Sci); Psy/Hlth Psy)
Belfast (Queen's) – BBC (Psychology courses)
Birmingham – BBC (Psy/Artif Intel)
Bristol UWE – 280 pts – ALs **or** ALs+ASs; (Psy/Hlth Sci)
City – 3x6u – BBC; ASs/VAs (contact univ); (not gs) (Psy; Psy/Econ; Psy/Sociol)
Durham (Stockton) – BBC **or** VA12u+AL (App Psy)
East Anglia – BBC–BCC/BC (Psysoc St courses)
Essex – 280 pts 12u – BB+AL/2ASs **or** VA12u (Sci/HlthSC) BB+AL; gs (Psychology)
Glasgow – BBC–CCC (Psychology courses)
Leeds, Trinity & All Saints (Coll) – BBC/BB (Psy-Media; Psy-Mgt)
London (Gold) – BBC–BCC (Psy/Euro Lang; Psy/Comp Sci; Psy)
Loughborough – 280 pts 18u – 2ALs+AL/2ASs **or** VA12u+AL; (flexible for mature students only) (Soc Psy)
Manchester – BBC (Psy/Neuro courses)
Nottingham Trent – BBC (Psychology)
Plymouth – BBC/BB (Psychology courses)
Southampton – BBC (Psy/Physiol)
Swansea – 280 pts 18u – BBC/BC **or** ALs+ASs **or** VAs+/-ALs/ASs; (Psy/Law; Psy/Fr; Psy/Ger; Psy/Ital; Psy/Welsh; Psy/Russ; Psy/Span; Psy/Econ; Psy/Sociol; Psy/Anth; Psy/Phil)
Ulster – BBC–CCC (Psy/Soc Psy courses)
Wolverhampton – 280–260 pts – CCC **or** CC+cc **or** VA12u BB; (Psy; Psy Comb)

260 pts **Anglia** – 260 pts 12u – 2ALs; ASs/VAs (contact univ); gs; (Psychology)
Bristol UWE – 260–200 pts 18u pref/12u – (not gs) (Psy; Psy/Hlth Sci)
Dundee – BCC (MA Psychology courses)
Exeter – 260 pts 18u – BCC **or** BC+cc **or** VAs (contact univ); gs; (Cog Sci)
Leicester – BCC (Psychology Comb Sci)
Manchester Met – BCC (Psy/Sp Path)
Portsmouth – 260 pts – ALs (inc sci subj) **or** ALs+ASs **or** VAs; gs; portfolio; (Psy; Psy/Lang)
Sheffield Hallam – BCC/BC (Psychology)
Staffordshire – 260 pts approx; gs; (Psy/Crim; Psy; Psy/Comp)
Staffordshire – BCC (Psy/Foren Sci)
Stirling – BCC/AB (Psychology courses – BA/BSc)
Strathclyde – BCC (Psychology)

240 pts **Aberdeen** – CCC–CCD (Psychology courses)
Bradford – 240 pts 12u; gs; (Psy; Sociol/Soc Psy)
Cardiff (UWI) – 240 pts approx (Psy/Comm; Psy Nutr)
Central Lancashire – 240 pts 12u – CCC; gs; (Psy; Psy/Crim; App Psy; Foren Psy; Neuropsy; Spo Psy)
De Montfort (Leicester) – 240 pts (inc 2ALs **or** VAs) – ALs **or** ALs+ASs **or** VAs+/-ALs/ASs; (Hum Psy)
Derby – 240 pts approx (Psychology)
Hertfordshire – 240–180 pts approx (Cog Sci)
Kingston – 240 pts approx (Psy; Psy/Hist; Psy/Hist Ideas; Psy/Pol; Psy/Sociol)
Lincolnshire & Humberside – 240 pts (Psychology)

Manchester Met – CCC/BB (Psychology)
Middlesex – 240–200 pts approx (Psychology courses)
Northumbria – CCC (Psy; Psy/Spo Sci)
Southampton (Inst) – 240 pts approx (Psychology)
230 pts **Buckingham** – 230 pts 21u – 3ALs **or** 3ALs+AS; (Psychology courses)
220 pts **Bournemouth** – 220–200 pts approx (App Psy/Comp)
Bristol UWE – 220–180 pts 12u (6u sci 60 pts min) – ALs **or** ALs+ASs **or** VAs+/-ALs/ASs; (Psy/Inf sys; Psi/Sci)
Central Lancashire – 220 pts 12u; gs; (Psy/Bus; Psy/Law)
Cheltenham & Glos (CHE) – 220–140 pts approx (Psychology courses)
Glamorgan – 220 pts approx (Psychology)
Glasgow Caledonian – CCD (Psychology)
Greenwich – 220–180 pts approx (Psychology courses)
Huddersfield – 220 pts 18u – CCD **or** CC+cc **or** VA12u CC+ASs(inc c); gs; (Psychology)
King Alfred's Winchester (Coll) – 220–100 pts approx (Psychology courses – offer depends on 2nd subj)
Kingston – 220–180 pts 2x6u (inc 200 pts in 2 6u awards); (Psychology)
Liverpool John Moores – 220–200 pts ALs **or** 240–200 pts VAs (sci) – ALs **or** ALs+ASs **or** VAs+/-ALs/ASs; (Psychology courses)
Luton – 220–120 pts approx (Psychology – Mod)
Northampton (UC) – 220–160 pts approx (Psy; Psy/Crim; Psy/Archit St; Psy/Eqn St)
Nottingham Trent – 220 pts 18u – CCC (Psy;/Soc Sci)
South Bank – 220–140 pts approx (Psychology courses)
Teesside – 220 pts approx (Psy; Psy Crim; Psy/Sociol)
200 pts **Buckinghamshire Chilterns (UC)** – 200–140 pts approx (Psychology courses)
Central Lancashire – 200–180 pts 12u; gs; (Psy/Educ St; Psy/Hlth St; Psy/Physiol; Psy/Stats)
Chester (Coll) – 200–180 pts approx (Psychology courses)
Derby – 200 pts approx (Psychology Comb Hons)
Dundee – 200 pts approx/CDD (Psychology)
Newman (CHE) – 200–140 pts approx (App Psy courses)
Nottingham Trent – 200–180 pts approx (Psy/Educ Dev)
Ripon & York (Coll) – 200 pts approx (Psychology courses except under **160 pts**)
Sunderland – 200–180 pts; gs (Psychology courses)
190 pts **North London** – 190 pts inc 160 pts from 2ALs or VAs; (Bus App Psy)
180 pts **Bolton (IHE)** – 180–160 pts approx (Psychology courses)
Derby – 180 pts approx (Bus Psy)
East London – 180 pts approx (Psychsoc St courses)
Liverpool Hope (Coll) – 180–160 pts approx (Psychology courses; Bhv Sci)
London Guildhall – BC (Psychology)
Napier – CDE (Soc Sci)
Newport (UWCN) – 180–100 pts approx (Psychology courses)
Queen Margaret (UC) – BC (Psychology courses)
St Martin's (Coll) – CDE/CC (App Psy)
St Mary's (Coll) – 180–140 pts approx (Psychology Comb courses)
160 pts **Birmingham (Westhill)** – CC (Psychology (Hum))
Canterbury Christ Church (UC) – CC (Psychology courses)
De Montfort (Leicester) – 160 pts (inc min 160 pts ALs or VA) – Als **or** ALs+ASs **or** VAs+/-ALs/ASs; (Psy major/joint/minor courses)
Huddersfield – 160 pts 18u – DDE **or** DD+AS(6u) **or** VA12u DD+ASs (inc c); gs; (Bhv Sci)
Manchester Met – CC (Psychology part-time course)
North London – 160 pts 1x12u **or** 2x6u; (App Psy)

North London – 160 pts – 2ALs **or** ALs+ASs **or** VA12u **or** VA6u+AL; (Psychology)
Norwich City (Coll) – 160 pts approx (Psychology courses)
Ripon & York (Coll) – CC (Psy/Commun St)
Surrey Roehampton – 160 pts – ALs **or** ALs+ASs; (Psy; Psy/Couns)
Thames Valley – 160–140 pts approx (Psychology courses)
West Suffolk (Coll) – 160 pts – CC/DD+c **or** VA12u CC; gs (Bhv Sci)
Westminster – CC (Psy Sci)
Worcester (UC) – 160 pts 12u – CC **or** ALs+ASs **or** VAs+/-ALs/ASs; gs (Psychology)

140 pts **Abertay Dundee** – CD (Bhv Sci; Psy; Psy/Comp; Psy/Biol (inc biol); Foren Sci (inc biol/chem)
Bath Spa (UC) – 140–120 pts 12u – CD **or** VA12u CD; (not gs) (Psy Comb Hons)
Bradford (Coll) – 140 pts approx (Couns/Psy Commun Stgs; Psy/Mgt)

120 pts **North London** – 120 pts 1x12u **or** 2x6u; (Psybiol)
Paisley – DD (Psy/Biol; Psy/Chem)
Suffolk (Coll) – DD (Psy/Sociol)
Warwickshire (Coll) – 120 pts – 2ALs **or** ALs+ASs; (Psychology)

Leeds Met – (contact university)

Diploma of Higher Education courses
80 pts Bath Spa (UC); Blackburn (Coll) (Couns); East London; Filton (Coll) (Couns); London Guildhall; Middlesex; Oxford Brookes; Stockport (CFHE) (Couns); Wolverhampton; Worcester (UC).

Higher National Diploma courses
Halton (Coll) (Bhv Sci); Truro (Coll) (App Psy).

Alternative Offers:

EB offers: Keele 70%; Plymouth 68%; Sheffield 70%.

IB offers: Aberdeen 30 pts; Aston 31 pts overall; Bangor 30 pts; Bath 30 pts; Birmingham 33 pts; Bradford 32–30 pts; Bristol 32 pts; Brunel 29 pts; Buckingham 24 pts; Cardiff 32 pts; City 28 pts overall H655 S444; Dundee H544; Durham 33 pts; Essex 28 pts; Exeter 32 pts; Glasgow H555 (BSc); Greenwich 24 pts; Hull 32 pts inc scores of 6; Kent 27 pts, H 12 pts; Kingston 32 pts; Lancaster 32–30 pts; Leeds 32–30 pts; Leicester 30 pts; Liverpool 30 pts H65; London (RH) 30 pts, (UCL) 36 pts; Loughborough 28 pts inc H6; Manchester H655 or 30 pts; Manchester Met 24 pts; Newcastle 33 pts; Northumbria 26 pts; Nottingham 34 pts+; Plymouth 30 pts; Portsmouth 30 pts inc H in sci; St Andrews 30 pts; Sheffield 33 pts H666; South Bank 24 pts; Southampton 32 pts; Staffordshire 24 pts; Stirling 32 pts; Surrey 32 pts; Surrey Roehampton 30 pts; Swansea 30 pts; Warwick 34–32 pts; Worcester (UC) 24 pts; York 32 pts.

Irish offers: Aberdeen BBBB; Bangor BBBCC; Brunel BBBCCC; Glasgow BBB (BSc); Keele BBBCC; Liverpool BBCCC; Manchester ABBBB; Northumbria BBCCCCC–CCCCCC; Plymouth BBCC; St Andrews ABBB; Sheffield ABBBB; South Bank CCCC; Warwick AABBB.

Scottish Qualifications: Aberdeen BBBB–BBCC; Abertay Dundee BBC; Dundee BBBC; Edinburgh AABBC; Glasgow (BSc)BBB, (Soc Sci) ABBB, (Arts) BBBB; Glasgow Caledonian BBBCC; Paisley BBC; Queen Margaret (UC) BBBC; St Andrews ABBB; Stirling BBBC; Strathclyde BBBB (Arts), AABB (Bus Sch).

Overseas applicants: Bangor English language courses available. **Manchester Met**, **Northumbria** Fluency in English required. **Oxford Brookes** Access courses available.

CHOOSING YOUR COURSE (See also **Ch.1**)

Subject information: Psychology is an increasingly popular subject with the number of applications rising by 40,000 in the last ten years. The study attracts three times more women than men. It covers studies in development, behaviour, perception, memory, language, learning, personality as well as social relationships and abnormal psychology. Psychology is a science and you will be involved in experimentation and statistical analysis. The degree is offered as a BA or BSc course and there are many similarities between them. The differences are in the elective subjects which can be taken in the second and third years. It is not a training to enable you to psycho-analyse your friends – psychiatry is not the same as psychology! To qualify as a chartered psychologist (for which a postgraduate qualification is required) it is neces-sary to obtain a first degree (or equivalent) qualification which gives eligibility for both Graduate Membership (GM) **and** the Graduate Basis for Registration (GBR) of the British Psychological Society (BPS). However, the Society does not publish a list of accredited degrees and there are several reasons for this.

The majority of degree programmes are modular and students are permitted a wide choice over which options they take from the range on offer. Often, therefore, a degree will be accredited as conferring eligibility for the GBR only if students opt to take a prescribed set of modules. These modules will cover social, biological, developmental and cognitive psychology. It is, therefore, the particular 'pathway' through the degree which is accredited by the Society rather than the degree itself; some pathways through the degree result in an entitlement to obtain GBR as well as GM alone. Enquiries about accreditation by the Society of a particular degree should therefore be addressed to the university or college itself. The institution should be able to tell you exactly which option you need to take in order to gain eligibility for the GBR. You need eligi-bility for both GM and GBR to enter a postgraduate course leading to qualification as a chartered psychologist. Full details about careers in psychology can be obtained from the British Psychological Society (see **Appendix 1**). Behavioural Science covers the study of animal as well as human behaviour and offers an overlap between Zoology, Sociology, Psychology and Biological Sciences (possible alternatives to a Psychology course). Psychology, however, also crosses over into Education, Business Studies (personnel work), Public Relations, Advertising, Artificial Intelligence and Social Studies. See also **Appendix 1**.

Special features: Aston (Psychology) The emphasis is on human psychology, and is pro-vided either as a full-time or as a sandwich course; decision is made in the second year. A course in Ergonomics is also offered. **Bangor** (Psy/Hlth Psy) Child and health psychol-ogy bias. Applied mental health option in second year covering schizophrenia, child abuse, depression, AIDS, addictive behaviour; growing, vigorous development. **Bath** Emphasis on human psychology especially social, health, developmental. Work placements. **Birmingham** Experimental work with animals not compulsory. **Bradford** Strong bias towards physiological and pharmacological aspects of behaviour – emphasis on experi-mental work. **Bristol** Emphasis on both human and animal behaviour; no practical work on animals. **Brunel** Emphasis on mental health and illness including psychoanalysis. **Cardiff** One of the largest Psychology schools in the United Kingdom. Applied Psychology confers membership of the BPS division of Occupational Psychology. **Cheltenham & Glos (CHE)** Includes counselling, clinical, occupational and educational psychology. **City** Emphasis on health and organisational psychology. **Dundee** Strengths in biological psychology and social development. **Durham** In the third year three options are chosen from a list which includes developmental, medical, social and animal psychology. **Essex** Emphasis is on cognitive science, linguistics and social science. Specialist options in abnormal and per-formance psychology, health and language development. **Huddersfield** Multi-disciplinary course combining sociology and psychology. **Hull** Comprehensive course covering clinical and occupational areas. **Kent** In Part II there is an emphasis on practical work and such topics as clinical psychology, psychology and law, occupational psychology. **Leeds** Strong bias towards applied, social, biological, cognitive and clinical psychology. **London (LSE)** Links principally with other social sciences rather than with biological sciences. **London (RH)** Topics include psychometrics, psychopathology, social and developmental psychology, animal behaviour, individual differences and occupational psychology. **Loughborough** Psychology can be studied from a social rather than the more usual biological perspective. **Manchester Met** Emphasis on applied psychology as a vocational preparation at a later stage in the course. Academic qualifications not necessarily the most important factor. **Northumbria** Specialised areas include social psychology, artificial intelligence, behaviour, health and illness, dyslexia and word recognition (no animal experiments). **Nottingham** (Bhv Sci) Covers animal and human behaviour. A mix between zoology and psychology. **Oxford Brookes** Modules allow additional studies in a number of vocational options, for example, personnel work, market research, educational or clinical psychology. **Portsmouth** Options in forensic psychology, ecological psychology, health and disabilities and counselling. **Sheffield** In the first year lectures fall into four groups: psychobiology, personality, social psychology and psychological disorders, cognition and developmental psychology. **Stirling** Part II covers psychological methods, animal behaviour, social psychology, perception and performance, clinical and counselling psychology and occupational psychology. **Surrey Roehampton** Psychology and Counselling course is first of its kind in the country. **Swansea** Options include eating behaviour, sleep, dreams and rhythms. **Warwick** Core courses in second year cover personality, psychopathology, perception, action, memory and language. **York** Emphasis is on psychology as an experiential science and academic discipline avoiding strong bias in favour of or against any specific field. Ten core courses covering major aspects of the subject including the increasingly popular neuropsychology. *NOW CHECK PROSPECTUSES AND WEB SITES.*

Top universities and colleges (Teaching Quality) (see Ch.4): Aston; Bangor; Brunel; Cambridge; Canterbury Christ Church (UC); Cardiff; Derby; Dundee; Durham (Stockton); Edinburgh; Essex; Exeter; Glasgow; Glasgow Caledonian; Hertfordshire; Lancaster; Liverpool John Moores; London (RH); Nottingham Trent; Oxford; Oxford Brookes; Portsmouth; St Andrews; Staffordshire; Stirling; Surrey; Swansea; not all institutions assessed.

Top universities and colleges (Research) (see Ch.4): Aberdeen; Bangor; Birmingham; Bristol; Cambridge; Cardiff; City; Dundee; Durham; Essex; Exeter; Lancaster; Leeds; London (Gold), (RH), (UCL); Loughborough; Manchester; Newcastle; Nottingham; Oxford; Reading; St Andrews; Sheffield; Stirling; Surrey; Swansea; Warwick; York.

Study opportunities abroad: Aberdeen; Aston; Bangor; Birmingham; Brunel; Cardiff; Cheltenham & Glos (CHE); City; Durham; Edinburgh; Essex; Exeter; Glamorgan; Kent; Lancaster; Leeds; London (UCL); Manchester; Manchester Met; Newcastle; Nottingham; Oxford Brookes; Plymouth; Portsmouth; Reading; Sheffield; Stirling; Sunderland; Surrey; Surrey Roehampton; Sussex; Ulster; Warwick; Worcester (UC); York.

Work opportunities abroad: Brunel; Leeds; Loughborough; Plymouth; Surrey.

ADMISSIONS INFORMATION

Number of applicants per place (approx): Abertay Dundee 5; Aston 16; Bangor 11; Birmingham 12; Bolton (IHE) 4; Bournemouth 4; Bradford 14, (Int Hum St) 7; Bristol 45; Bristol UWE 12; Brunel 20; Buckingham 1; Cardiff 12; Cardiff (UWI) 10; Central Lancashire 13; Cheltenham & Glos (CHE) 50; Chester (Coll) 20; City 18; De Montfort 10; Derby 10; Dundee 27; Durham 20; Exeter 12; Glamorgan 6; Glasgow Caledonian 15; Greenwich 8; Hertfordshire 22; Huddersfield 3; Hull 14; Kent 15; Lancaster 20; Leeds 14; Leeds, Trinity & All Saints (Coll) 13; Leicester 22; Liverpool 21; Liverpool John Moores 20; London (LSE) 41, (RH) 7, (UCL) 15; Loughborough 8; Manchester Met 27; Middlesex 10; Newcastle 20; Northampton (UC) 13; Northumbria 25; Nottingham 27; Oxford 3; Oxford Brookes 29; Plymouth 8; Portsmouth 10; Sheffield 19; Sheffield Hallam 11; Staffordshire 20; Stirling 9; Surrey 10; Surrey Roehampton 11; Swansea 6; Teesside 10; Warwick 13; Westminster 6; Worcester (UC) 9; York 8.

Planning your UCAS personal statement (see Ch.4): Contact the Education and Social Services Departments in your local authority office to arrange meetings with psychologists to gain a knowledge of the work. Make notes during any meetings of work experience gained and describe these fully on the UCAS form. **Bangor** Evidence of interest in caring-type work including voluntary or paid experience. **Keele** Reference to introductory reading in psychology (many students have a distorted image of it). **Manchester Met** Use UCAS form section 10 well. (Psy/Sp Path) Observations with speech therapists working with children and adults. **St Andrews** Evidence of interest. Reasons for choosing the course. See also **Appendix 1**.

Selection interviews (see Ch.4): Aberdeen (No); Bangor (some); Bath (No); Birmingham; Bolton (IHE) (T); Bournemouth (No); Bristol (No); Brunel (T) (maths test if no maths at GCSE (grade A–C)); Buckingham; Cambridge; Cardiff (No); Cheltenham & Glos (CHE) (No); De Montfort (Hum Psy) (No); Derby (No); Dundee (No); Durham; Durham (Stockton) (No); Exeter (mature students); Glamorgan; Glasgow Caledonian; Greenwich (No); Huddersfield (mature students); Hull (No); Keele (some); Kent (No); Lancaster (No); Leeds (mature students only); Leeds, Trinity & All Saints (Coll); Liverpool (No); Liverpool Hope (Coll) (No); London (LSE) (rare) (RH) (No), (UCL); London Guildhall; Loughborough (No); Manchester Met (Psy) (No); Middlesex; Newcastle; Northampton (UC); Norwich City (Coll); Nottingham (No); Nottingham Trent (non-standard applicants); Oxford (T) (W); Oxford Brookes; Paisley (No); Plymouth; Portsmouth (No); Sheffield (No); South Bank (Psy/Sp Path) (T); Staffordshire (No); Stirling (No); Surrey; Surrey Roehampton (No); Swansea; Worcester (UC) (No); York (No); most other colleges.

Interview questions (see Ch.4): Although some applicants will have studied the subject at A-level and will have a broad understanding of its coverage, it is still essential to have gained some work experience or to have discussed the career with a professional psychologist. Questions will be asked relevant to this experience and in previous years these have included: What have you read about psychology? What do you expect to gain by studying psychology? What are your parents' and teachers' views on your choice of subject? Are you interested in any particular branch of the subject? Is psychology an art or a science? Do you think you are well suited to this course? Why? Do you think it is possible that if we learn enough about the functioning of the brain we can create a computer which is functionally the same? What is counselling? Is it necessary? Know the differences between the various branches of psychology and discuss any specific interests, for example, in clinical, occupational, educational, criminal psychologists and cognitive, neuro, social or physiological psychology. What influences young children's food choices? What stereotypes do we have of people with mental illness? **Birmingham** (Psy/Artif Intel) May be asked to submit a 500 word essay in relation to artificial intelligence. **Manchester Met** Two essays and a questionnaire. **Oxford** Written assessment to test applicant's comprehension of published psychological material.

Reasons for rejection (non-academic): Lack of background reading and awareness of psychology; poor communication skills; misunderstanding of what is involved in a degree course. **Surrey** Inarticulate; **Warwick** (BSc) Lack of science background.

GAP YEAR ADVICE

Most institutions will accept a gap year and recommend an early application after A-level results are known. Work experience or employment abroad or time spent caring for people recommended.

Institutions willing to defer entry after A-Levels: Abertay Dundee; Aston; Bangor; Birmingham; Bournemouth; Bradford; Bristol; Brunel; Canterbury Christ Church (UC); Cardiff; Central Lancashire; Cheltenham & Glos (CHE); Chester (Coll); City (No); De Montfort; Durham (No); Glamorgan; Glasgow Caledonian; Hertfordshire; Hull; Kent; Lancaster; Leeds; Leeds, Trinity & All Saints (Coll) (prefer not); Leicester; Lincolnshire & Humberside; London (Gold), (RH), (UCL); London Guildhall; Luton; Manchester Met; Middlesex; Newcastle; Northampton (UC); Northumbria; Nottingham (for Bhv Sci higher offers may be made); Portsmouth; Plymouth; Sheffield Hallam; South Bank; Staffordshire (No); Sunderland; Surrey; Surrey Roehampton; Swansea; Teesside; Westminster; Warwick; Worcester (UC); York.

AFTER RESULTS ADVICE

Institutions which may accept the same points score after A-Levels: Aberdeen (No); Abertay Dundee; Aston; Bangor; Birmingham; Bolton (IHE); Bradford; Brunel; Cardiff;

Central Lancashire; Cheltenham & Glos (CHE); Chester (Coll) (No); City; De Montfort; Derby; Dundee (No); Durham (No); Exeter; Glamorgan; Glasgow Caledonian; Hertfordshire; Huddersfield; Hull (No); Lancaster (No); Leeds (No); Leeds, Trinity & All Saints (Coll); Leicester (No); Lincolnshire & Humberside; Liverpool; London (Gold), (RH); Loughborough (some); Manchester Met; Newcastle (BSc No); Northampton (UC); Northumbria; Nottingham (No); Nottingham Trent; Plymouth (perhaps); Portsmouth; Sheffield; Stirling (No); Surrey (No); Surrey Roehampton; Swansea (No); Warwick (No); Worcester (UC); York (No).

Institutions which may accept lower grades/points score after A-Levels: Aston; Bangor; Bolton (IHE); Bradford; Brunel; Cheltenham & Glos (CHE); City; Derby; Essex; Exeter; Hertfordshire; Hull; Kent; Leeds (No); Leeds, Trinity & All Saints (Coll); Lincolnshire & Humberside; Liverpool; London (RH); Manchester Met; Newcastle (possibly by one grade); Northampton (UC); Northumbria; Portsmouth; St Mary's (Coll); Sheffield; Surrey Roehampton; Swansea; Warwick; York (No).

Offers to applicants repeating A-Levels: Higher Aston, Bangor, Birmingham, City, Loughborough, Newcastle, Portsmouth, Swansea, Warwick, York; **Possibly higher** Aston (Hum Psy), Northampton (UC); **Same** Aston (Comb Hons), Bolton (IHE), Brunel, Derby, Huddersfield, Hull, London (RH), Manchester Met, Nottingham, Oxford Brookes, South Bank, Surrey, Surrey Roehampton, Ulster.

Probable vacancies from June 2001 and in Clearing (see Ch.4): Over 70 universities declared vacancies in Clearing last year. Applicants aiming for a career in psychology and choosing joint courses should check whether the necessary core subjects for acceptance by the British Psychological Society are included.

NEW GRADUATE DESTINATIONS AND EMPLOYMENT (1999 HESA) (see **Ch.4**)

Out of 5395 graduates surveyed, 2853 entered full-time employment (539 into part-time work), 1195 went into further study and 314 were thought to be seeking employment.

PUBLIC ADMINISTRATION (including **Public Policy**; see also **Community Studies**)

NB The information supplied by the universities and colleges this year varies considerably and the offers listed below should be used as a first source of reference only. Many institutions will accept combinations of Advanced (AL), Advanced Subsidiary (AS) and Vocational Advanced (VA) level qualifications to achieve the required points total, but applicants must check web sites and prospectuses for full details of all offers. Grades and points totals shown should be regarded as the minimum levels to be achieved, but offers may be adjusted downwards when results are known. The points totals shown to the left of the institutions are for ease of reference only. It must not be assumed that tariff points are always used by institutions or that they can be substituted for an offer in grades. The level of an offer is not necessarily indicative of the quality of a course. To calculate your offers see Chapter 4 and the inside fold of the back cover.

Special subject requirements/preferences: GCSE: English and mathematics grade A–C.

320 pts	**London (RH)** – ABB–BBC (Econ Soc Pol)
310 pts	**Southampton** – 310 pts 21u (inc 180 pts from 2ALs); (Pblc Soc Admin; Soc Pol/Admin)
280 pts	**Birmingham** – BBC (Plan Pblc Pol Govt/Mgt)
	Stirling – BBC (Pblc Mgt)
260 pts	**Aston** – 260–240 pts approx (Pblc Pol/Mgt Comb courses)
	Birmingham – BCC/BB (Pblc Soc Pol Mgt; Plan Soc Pol)
	Durham – BCC (Sociol Soc Pol)
	Kent – 260 pts approx (Soc Pol Pblc Mgt)
240 pts	**Nottingham Trent** – 240 pts approx (Pol Sci)

220 pts   **King Alfred's Winchester (Coll)** – 220 pts 12u – 2ALs **or** ALs+ASs **or** VAs+/
-ALs/ASs; gs; (Pblc Serv Mgt)
Sheffield Hallam – CCD/BC (Pblc Pol Mgt)
200 pts   **Manchester Met** – 200–180 pts (Pblc Pol/Admin)
Paisley – BB (Pblc Mgt Admin)
180 pts   **Glamorgan** – 180 pts approx (Pblc Mgt/Stats; Pol/Pblc Pol)
Liverpool John Moores – 180 pts (inc 140 pts ALs **or** VAs) – ALs **or** ALs+ASs
or VAs+/-ALs/ASs; (Pblc Serv Admin)
Luton – 180–120 pts approx (Pblc Pol/Law)
160 pts   **and below**
Buckingham – (Pol St)
De Montfort (Leicester) – 160 pts – ALs **or** ALs+ASs **or** VAs+/-ALs/ASs; (Pblc
Admin/Mgt St)
Glasgow Caledonian – CC (Pblc Admin)
North London – 140 pts 1x12u **or** 2x6u; (Pblc Admin)

Diploma in Higher Education
Cheltenham & Glos (CHE).

Higher National Diploma courses
100 pts   and below
Barnsley (Coll); Blackburn (Coll); Chesterfield (Coll); Cornwall & Duchy (Coll); De
Montfort; Derby; Glamorgan; Gloucestershire (CAT); Herefordshire (CT);
Lincolnshire & Humberside; Luton; Plymouth (Coll); Sheffield Hallam (also HNC);
Solihull (Coll); South Bank; Stockport (CFHE); Wigan & Leigh (Coll);
Wolverhampton; Worcester (UC).

Alternative Offers:

IB offers: Birmingham 30 pts; Kent 26 pts inc 12 pts H; London (RH) 30 pts.

Scottish Qualifications: Glasgow Caledonian BBB; Paisley BBB; Stirling BBBB.

Overseas applicants: Sheffield Hallam Orientation programme and languages tuition.

CHOOSING YOUR COURSE (See also **Ch.1**)

Subject information: Public Administration is a vocational subject area for those interested in administrative work for agencies providing public services, for example, the
NHS, the Civil Service, local authorities, public corporations and housing associations.
Social Administration, Business Studies and Management Science courses could also
be considered. See also **Appendix 1**.

Special features: Birmingham (Pblc Soc Pol Mgt) Covers economics, sociology,
psychology, law, local government and the European Union. **Glamorgan** Many students
obtain sponsorship through sandwich placement year. **Manchester Met** Opportunity to
study a modern language and for placements in a Western European university through
the ERASMUS scheme. **Nottingham Trent** Course focuses on politics and economics.
NOW CHECK PROSPECTUSES AND WEB SITES.

Study opportunities abroad: De Montfort; Glamorgan; Glasgow Caledonian; Manchester
Met.

ADMISSIONS INFORMATION

Number of applicants per place (approx): Birmingham 8; De Montfort 9; Glamorgan 6;
Glasgow Caledonian 9; Kent 5; Manchester Met 4; Nottingham Trent 13; Sheffield Hallam 3.

Planning your UCAS personal statement (see Ch.4): Contact should be made with
local authority departments (for example, housing, social services) and hospitals to learn
something about administration work. See also **Appendix 1**.

Selection interviews (see Ch.4): Aston (No); Liverpool John Moores; Manchester Met (No); Nottingham Trent (No); Sheffield Hallam (No).

Interview questions (see Ch.4): It is important for applicants to have made the effort to discuss this career with management staff in town halls, hospitals, public utilities etc. Questions are likely to arise from these contacts.

GAP YEAR ADVICE

Very useful, particularly with experience in public sector work. Inform course leader before gap year.

Institutions willing to defer entry after A-levels: Aston; Birmingham; De Montfort; Glamorgan; Kent; London (RH); Luton; Manchester Met; Sheffield Hallam.

AFTER RESULTS ADVICE

Institutions which may accept the same points score after A-Levels: De Montfort; Glamorgan; Glasgow Caledonian; Kent; Manchester Met; Nottingham Trent; Sheffield Hallam (No).

Offers to applicants repeating A-Levels: Same Manchester Met.

Probable vacancies from June 2001 and in Clearing (see Ch.4): Usually there are vacancies from June onwards and in Clearing at many universities and colleges.

NEW GRADUATE DESTINATIONS AND EMPLOYMENT (1999 HESA) (see **Ch.4**)

No data is available for this subject area. See **Business Courses.**

QUANTITY SURVEYING

NB The information supplied by the universities and colleges this year varies considerably and the offers listed below should be used as a first source of reference only. Many institutions will accept combinations of Advanced (AL), Advanced Subsidiary (AS) and Vocational Advanced (VA) level qualifications to achieve the required points total, but applicants must check web sites and prospectuses for full details of all offers. Grades and points totals shown should be regarded as the minimum levels to be achieved, but offers may be adjusted downwards when results are known. The points totals shown to the left of the institutions are for ease of reference only. It must not be assumed that tariff points are always used by institutions or that they can be substituted for an offer in grades. The level of an offer is not necessarily indicative of the quality of a course. To calculate your offers see Chapter 4 and the inside fold of the back cover.

Special subject requirements/preferences: A-Level: Mathematic/physics subjects may be required; check prospectuses. **GCSE:** English and mathematics grade A–C.

280 pts **Loughborough** – 280 pts approx (Commer Mgt/Quant Surv)
260 pts **Glamorgan** – 260 pts approx (Quant Surv)
Kingston – 260 pts (Quant Surv)
Reading – 260 pts approx (Quant Surv)
Salford – 260 pts approx (Quant Surv)
240 pts **Bristol UWE** – 240–200 pts 18u pref/12u – ALs or ALs+ASs or VAs+/-ALs/ASs; (Quant Surv)
UMIST – 240 pts approx (Commer Mgt/Quant Surv)
220 pts **Anglia** – 220 pts 12u – 2ALs or 2ALs+ASs or VA12u AB; gs; (Quant Surv)
Glasgow Caledonian – CCD (Quant Surv)
Heriot–Watt – 220 pts 18u – CCD or ALs+ASs or VAs+/-ALs/ASs; gs; (Bld Econ Quant Surv)
Liverpool John Moores – 220–180 pts (inc 2ALs or VAs) – ALs or ALs+ASs or VAs+/-ALs/ASs; (Quant Surv)

Napier – CCD (Quant Surv)
Northumbria – 220 pts approx; (not gs) (Quant Surv)
Nottingham Trent – 220 pts approx (Quant Surv/Constr Cost Mgt)
Plymouth – 220–200 pts approx (Quant Surv/Env)
Portsmouth – 220 pts – ALs **or** ALs+ASs **or** VAs; gs; (Quant Surv)
Sheffield Hallam – 220 pts approx (Quant Surv)
South Bank – 220–140 pts approx/CC (Quant Surv)
Wolverhampton – 220 pts 12u – CCD/BB **or** CC+b; gs; (Quant Surv)

200 pts   **Central England** – 200 pts 12u – BB/CCE; gs; (Quant Surv)
Greenwich – 200 pts approx (Quant Surv)
Westminster – 200–160 pts approx (Quant Surv)

160 pts   **Bolton (IHE)** – 160–100 pts approx (Quant Surv)
Staffordshire – CC **or** CD+AS(40 pts) **or** VAs+/-ALs/ASs; gs; (Quant Surv)

120 pts   **Abertay Dundee** – DD (Quant Surv)
Nottingham Trent – DD (Quant Surv – part-time)

100 pts   **and below**
Glamorgan – DE (Quant Surv – part–time)
Robert Gordon – EE (Quant Surv)
Salford – (Quant Surv – part-time)
Southampton (Inst) – (Constr Econ – part-time)
Westminster – E (Fdn Quant Surv)

Leeds Met – (contact university)

Higher National Diploma courses
140 pts   **and below**
Abertay Dundee; Anglia; Bell (CT); Brighton; Luton; Northumbria 120 pts; Nottingham Trent; Robert Gordon; UHI; Wigan & Leigh (Coll).

Alternative Offers:

IB offers: Northumbria 24 pts; Portsmouth 24 pts; South Bank 24 pts; UMIST 30 pts.

Irish offers: Northumbria BCCC; South Bank CCCC.

Scottish Qualifications: Abertay Dundee BCC; Bell (CT) CC; Glasgow Caledonian BBCC; Heriot-Watt BBBC; Napier BBCC; Robert Gordon BCC.

Overseas applicants: Northumbria, Westminster Competence in English required.

CHOOSING YOUR COURSE (See also **Ch.1**)

Subject information: Quantity Surveying is a specialised field of surveying which focuses on the costing of the built environment. Students are introduced to construction studies, measurement cost studies, economics and law. The work is similar, in some aspects, to the work of an accountant and requires the same attention to detail. See also **Architecture, Building** and **Surveying** courses. See also **Appendix 1**.

Special features: Bristol UWE Modular scheme – flexible options. UK and European field trips. **Heriot-Watt** In the first two years building technology, mathematics, economics and legal and business studies are included. First and second years with Building and Building Surveying. **Loughborough** All students sponsored by industry. **Northumbria** Option of a European route with a year abroad. **Nottingham Trent** This four-year sandwich course has a particular emphasis on building economics and control of costs of buildings. **Portsmouth** Financial management is an important feature of the course. **Reading** The course's first two years are common with Building Construction and Management and Building Surveying. **Robert Gordon** First year shared with Building Surveying. **Sheffield Hallam** Common first year with Construction and Building Surveying; possibility to transfer. **Staffordshire** After a common first year with Valuation Surveying, specialist studies cover the analysis, construction and documentation techniques needed by the quantity surveyor. *NOW CHECK PROSPECTUSES AND WEB SITES.*

Top universities and colleges (Teaching Quality) (see Ch.4): Kingston; Staffordshire; not all institutions assessed.

Top universities and colleges (Research) (see Ch.4): Salford.

Study opportunities abroad: Central England; Glamorgan; Glasgow Caledonian; Liverpool John Moores; Northumbria; Plymouth; Robert Gordon; Staffordshire; Westminster; Wolverhampton.

Work opportunities abroad: Central England; Kingston; Liverpool John Moores; Northumbria; Plymouth; Robert Gordon; Salford; South Bank; Staffordshire; Wolverhampton.

ADMISSIONS INFORMATION

Number of applicants per place (approx): Abertay Dundee 5; Anglia 2; Bolton (IHE) 4; Bristol UWE 6; Central England 14; Glamorgan 4; Glasgow Caledonian 3; Greenwich 11; Kingston 13; Liverpool John Moores 10; Loughborough 9; Napier 2; Northumbria 11; Nottingham Trent 10; Portsmouth 3; Robert Gordon 5; Salford 16; Sheffield Hallam 7; Staffordshire 5; UMIST 10; Wolverhampton 6.

Planning your UCAS personal statement (see Ch.4): Surveyors work with architects and builders as well as in their own consultancies and these organisations should be approached to discuss quantity surveying or to obtain work experience. Explain your interests fully. Read *The Chartered Quantity Surveyor* magazine. See also **Appendix 1**.

Selection interviews (see Ch.4): Abertay Dundee (No); Anglia (No); Bristol UWE (T); Central England; Glamorgan; Glasgow Caledonian; Greenwich (No); Heriot-Watt; Kingston; Liverpool John Moores; Napier (No); Nottingham Trent; Portsmouth (No); Robert Gordon; South Bank; Staffordshire (No); Ulster; UMIST; Wolverhampton (No).

Interview questions (see Ch.4): Past questions have included: What is quantity surveying? What is the scope of the work? How do you qualify to do this work? Have you spoken to a quantity surveyor or spent any time in a quantity surveyor's office?

GAP YEAR ADVICE

Most institutions accept a gap year. **Portsmouth** Gain experience and maturity dealing with people of all ages. **Salford** Students must inform the department and liaise during the gap year.

Institutions willing to defer entry after A-Levels: Abertay Dundee; Anglia; Bath (No); Bolton (IHE); Brighton; Glamorgan; Glasgow Caledonian; Heriot-Watt; Kingston; Loughborough; Northumbria; Portsmouth; Robert Gordon; Salford; Sheffield Hallam; South Bank; Staffordshire; UMIST (No – because of the need to obtain sponsorship applications); Wolverhampton.

AFTER RESULTS ADVICE

Institutions which may accept the same points score after A-Levels: Anglia (No); Bolton (IHE); Bristol UWE; Central England; Glamorgan; Glasgow Caledonian; Greenwich; Heriot-Watt; Liverpool John Moores; Nottingham Trent; Portsmouth; Salford; Sheffield Hallam; South Bank; Staffordshire; Ulster; UMIST.

Institutions which may accept lower grades/points score after A-Levels: Bolton (IHE); Central England; Glamorgan; Liverpool John Moores; Nottingham Trent; Portsmouth; Salford; UMIST.

Offers to applicants repeating A-Levels: Higher Bolton (IHE), Bristol UWE, Nottingham Trent; **Possibly higher** Glamorgan, Liverpool John Moores; **Same** Salford, South Bank.

Probable vacancies from June 2001 and in Clearing (see Ch.4): Most universities are expected to have vacancies from June and in Clearing.

NEW GRADUATE DESTINATIONS AND EMPLOYMENT (1999 HESA) (see **Ch.4**)

No data is available for this subject area.

RADIOGRAPHY (see also **Health Sciences/Studies**)

NB The information supplied by the universities and colleges this year varies considerably and the offers listed below should be used as a first source of reference only. Many institutions will accept combinations of Advanced (AL), Advanced Subsidiary (AS) and Vocational Advanced (VA) level qualifications to achieve the required points total, but applicants must check web sites and prospectuses for full details of all offers. Grades and points totals shown should be regarded as the minimum levels to be achieved, but offers may be adjusted downwards when results are known. The points totals shown to the left of the institutions are for ease of reference only. It must not be assumed that tariff points are always used by institutions or that they can be substituted for an offer in grades. The level of an offer is not necessarily indicative of the quality of a course. To calculate your offers see Chapter 4 and the inside fold of the back cover.

Details of entry requirements should be obtained from these institutions. Information on courses is available also from the College of Radiographers (see **Appendix 1**).

Special subject requirements/preferences: A-Level: At least one science subject is often required. **GCSE:** Five subjects including English, mathematics and a science subject (usually at one sitting). **Bangor** Grade A or B in English, mathematics and science. **London (St George's HMS)** Six subjects at grade C or higher.

280 pts   **Hertfordshire** – 280–240 pts 1x12u **or** 2x6u (inc sci subj); gs; (Diag Radiog; Ther Radiog)
         Robert Gordon – BBC (Diag Radiog)
         Ulster – BBC (Diag Radiog; Ther Radiog)
240 pts   **Bradford** – 240 pts 12u (inc AL sci); gs; (Diag Radiog)
         Leeds – 240 pts approx (Radiog (Diag; Ther))
         Liverpool – 240 pts – ALs **or** ALs+ASs **or** VAs+/-ALs/ASs; (Radiog Diag)
         St Martin's (Coll) – CCC/AB (Radiog (Diag))
         Salford – 240–200 pts approx (Diag Radiog)
220 pts   **Cardiff (UWCM)** – 220 pts 18u – C(sci)+AL/VA12u (Hlth SC) CC; (not gs) (Radiog Diag/Ther)
         Derby – 220 pts 12u – CCD/BB **or** CD+dd **or** VA (AL grades)+ALs/ASs; (not gs) (Ther Radiog)
         Kingston – 220 pts (inc 2x6u **or** 1x12u inc sci or hlth subj) – ALs **or** ALs+ASs **or** VAs+/-ALs/ASs; (not gs) (Diag/Ther Radiog)
         London (St George's HMS) – 220 pts approx (Ther Radiog)
         South Bank – 220–140 pts approx (Diag Imag (Radiog))
200 pts   **Bangor** – 200 pts approx (Diag Radiog Imag)
         City – 12u – ALs **or** ALs+ASs **or** VAs (contact univ); (not gs) (Radiog (Diag; Ther))
         Portsmouth – 200 pts – ALs **or** ALs+ASs **or** VAs; gs; (Diag/Ther Radiog)
         Teesside – 200–180 pts approx (Diag Radiog)
180 pts   **Bristol UWE** – 180–160 pts 12u (6u sci) – ALs **or** ALs+ASs **or** VAs+/-ALs/ASs; (Diag Imag; Radiog)
         Central England – 180 pts approx (Diag Radiog; Ther Radiog)
160 pts   **Canterbury Christ Church (UC)** – CC (Med Imag (Radiog))
         Cranfield – 160 pts 12u – 2ALs **or** ALs+ASs **or** VAs+/-ALs/ASs; (not gs) (Radiog Ther; Radiog Diag)
         Derby – 160 pts 12u – CC **or** DD+ee **or** VAs CC; (not gs) (Diag Radiog)
         Sheffield Hallam – CC (Diag Radiog)
140 pts   **Queen Margaret (UC)** – CD (Diag Radiog; Ther Radiog)
120 pts   **Glasgow Caledonian** – DD (Radiog (Diag (Ther Radiog))
         Suffolk (Coll) – DD (Diag Radiog; Ther Radiog)

Alternative Offers:

IB offers: Hertfordshire 26 pts; South Bank 24 pts; Southampton 28 pts.

Irish offers: Bradford BBCCCC; South Bank CCCC.

Scottish Qualifications: Glasgow Caledonian BBCC; Queen Margaret (UC) BBC; Robert Gordon BBCC.

CHOOSING YOUR COURSE (See also **Ch.1**)

Subject information: Most institutions offer both Diagnostic and Therapeutic Radiography, but applicants should check this before applying. (Diagnostic Radiography) The demonstration on film (or other imaging materials) of the position and structure of the body's organs using radiation or other imaging media. (Therapeutic Radiography) The planning and administration of treatment for patients suffering from malignant and non-malignant disease using different forms of radiation. Courses lead to state registration. For alternative medical courses see **Medicine, Dentistry, Pharmacy** and **Health Sciences/Studies**. See also **Appendix 1**.

Special features: Bangor Course located in Wrexham Health Care faculty campus. **Bradford, Cardiff (UWCM)** 50% of course is clinical. **Cranfield** 50% of course is clinical. Clinical placements at two different hospitals for 50% of the course. *NOW CHECK PROSPECTUSES AND WEB SITES.*

Study opportunities abroad: Salford.

Work opportunities abroad: Derby; Salford.

ADMISSIONS INFORMATION

Number of applicants per place (approx): Anglia 10; Bangor 7; Bradford 8; Cardiff (UWCM) 3; Central England (Ther) 8, (Diag) 5; Cranfield 8; Derby 9; Glasgow Caledonian 7; Hertfordshire (Diag) 8, (Ther) 50; Leeds 10; Liverpool 13; Portsmouth 10; Salford 10; Sheffield Hallam 15; South Bank 9; Southampton 5; Suffolk (Coll) 6; Teesside 10.

Planning your UCAS personal statement (see Ch.4): Contacts with radiographers and visits to the radiography departments of hospitals should be discussed in full on the UCAS form. **Central England** Evidence of a visit to at least one imaging department or oncology (radiotherapy) department before completing UCAS form. Evidence of good research of career. **Cranfield** Require time spent in an X-ray department plus a successful report. **Liverpool** Decision to choose between Therapeutic and Diagnostic pathways should be made before applying. **Salford** Communication skills, teamwork, work experience in public areas. See also **Appendix 1**.

Selection interviews (see Ch.4): Bangor; Cardiff (UWCM); Central England; City; Cranfield (W); Derby; Hertfordshire; Queen Margaret (UC); Salford (All); Sheffield Hallam; South Bank; most institutions.

Interview questions (see Ch.4): All applicants should have discussed this career with a radiographer and visited a hospital radiography department. Questions follow from these contacts.

Reasons for rejection (non-academic): Lack of interest in people. Poor communication skills. Occasionally students may be unsuitable for the clinical environment, for example, they express a fear of blood and needles; poor grasp of radiography as a career. Unable to meet criteria for employment in the Health Service, for example, health factors, criminal convictions, severe disabilities.

GAP YEAR ADVICE

Most institutions will accept a gap year. Try to gain experience of working with a wide range of people of different age groups. **South Bank** Apply before gap year.

Institutions willing to defer entry after A-Levels: Bangor; Bradford (No); Bristol UWE; Cranfield; Derby; Hertfordshire; Portsmouth; Salford; Sheffield Hallam; South Bank.

AFTER RESULTS ADVICE

Institutions which may accept the same points score after A-Levels: Bangor; Bradford; Bristol UWE; Central England; Hertfordshire; Portsmouth; South Bank.

Institutions which may accept lower grades/points score after A-Levels: Portsmouth; Salford.

Probable vacancies from June 2001 and in Clearing (see Ch.4): Several universities and colleges had vacancies from June onwards last year with the highest offers in the region of 200–180 pts.

NEW GRADUATE DESTINATIONS AND EMPLOYMENT (1999 HESA) (see **Ch.4**)

No data available.

RELIGIOUS STUDIES (including Biblical Studies, Divinity and Divinity)

NB The information supplied by the universities and colleges this year varies consider-ably and the offers listed below should be used as a first source of reference only. Many institutions will accept combinations of Advanced (AL), Advanced Subsidiary (AS) and Vocational Advanced (VA) level qualifications to achieve the required points total, but applicants must check web sites and prospectuses for full details of all offers. Grades and points totals shown should be regarded as the minimum levels to be achieved, but offers may be adjusted downwards when results are known. The points totals shown to the left of the institutions are for ease of reference only. It must not be assumed that tariff points are always used by institutions or that they can be substituted for an offer in grades. The level of an offer is not necessarily indicative of the quality of a course. To calculate your offers see Chapter 4 and the inside fold of the back cover.

Special subject requirements/preferences: A-Level: Religious studies may be preferred; check institutions. **Hull** Religious studies. **London (Sch Jewish St)** Six subjects grades A–C in preferred subjects from biblical Hebrew, history and English. **Oxford** A/AS-Levels considered in religious studies or arts subjects. **GCSE: Aberdeen**, **Edinburgh** English and mathematics or science and a foreign language. *For teacher training:* English, math-ematics and science. **Cambridge, Oxford** Grade A in most subjects preferred. **Cardiff** (Theol) English language plus a foreign language. **London (SOAS)** Six subjects grade A–C minimum.

360 pts **and above**
    Cambridge – Offers, mainly in grades, vary between colleges (Theol/Relig St)
    Oxford – Offers vary between candidates (Theology)
340 pts **Bristol** – AAB–BBC (Theol/Pol)
    Cambridge (Hom) – AAB–ABB (BA Relig St/Educ St)
320 pts **St Andrews** – ABB–BBC (Bib St Joint courses)
300 pts **Birmingham** – BBB (Theology courses)
    Bristol – BBB–CCC (Theol/Relig St)
    Cardiff – ABC–CCC (Relig St courses; Theol; offers vary with second subject)
    Edinburgh – BBB (MA/BA/BD Relig St; Div)
    Hull – BBB–CCD (Theology courses)
    Leeds, Trinity & All Saints (Coll) – 300–180 pts approx (Engl/Theol)
    Manchester – BBB (Compar Relig/Soc Anth)
    Newcastle – ABC–BBB (Bib St (Comb))
    Sheffield – BBB/BC (Bib St/Engl)
290 pts **Durham** – 290 pts – 3ALs/290 pts **or** 2ALs+2ASs **or** VA6u; (Theology)
280 pts **Bangor** – 280 pts – 3ALs **or** VAs+/-ALs/ASs; (Relig St/PE)
    Cambridge (Hom) – BBC–BCD (BEd Relig St/Educ)
    Glasgow – BBC–CCD (Theol/Relig St courses)
    Kent – 280 pts approx (Theol/Drama; Theol/Film St)

Leeds – 18u – ALs **or** ALs+2ASs; VAs (contact univ); gs; (Theol/Relig St)
London (SOAS) – 280 pts approx (St Relig/Heb)
Manchester – BBC–BCC (St Relig/Theol)
St Andrews – BBC (Divinity)
Sheffield – BBC/BC (Bib St with Ger/Phil)

260 pts   **Belfast (Queen's)** – BCC–CCC (Theology courses)
Cardiff – BCC/AA (Relig/Theol St)
Exeter – 260 pts 18u – BCC **or** BC+bc **or** VAs (contact univ); gs; (Theol St)
Kent – 260 pts approx (Theol/Ger; Theol/Compar Lit St)
Lancaster – BCC–BCD (Relig St/Phil)
Leo Baeck (Coll) – BCC (Heb Jew St)
London (Hey) – 260–240 pts approx (Theology)
London (King's) – BCC+AS **or** BC+cc+AS **or** BB+dd+AS **or** VA6u+ALs/ASs; (Relig St; Theol; Bib St)
London (SOAS) – 260 pts approx (Compar Relig; St Relig/Pol)
London (SSEES) – BCC (Jewish St)
Newcastle – BCC (Relig St)
Sheffield – BCC/BC (Bib St with Ling/Mus; Bib St)
Stirling – BCC/BC (Hist/Relig St; Relig St)

240 pts   **Aberdeen** – CCC (Relig St courses; Div courses)
Aberdeen – CCC/CC (Theology courses)
Bangor – 240 pts – 3ALs; VAs (enquire); gs; (Relig St/Ger)
Hertfordshire – 240–200 pts 1x12u **or** 2x6u; gs; (Hum Mod)
Nottingham – CCC; (not gs) (Theology)

220 pts   **King Alfred's Winchester (Coll)** – 220 pts 12u – 2ALs **or** ALs+ASs **or** VAs+/-ALs/ASs; (Theol/Relig St)
Lampeter – 220–200 pts approx (Theol/Class St; Relig/Islam St; Relig/Jew St; Div)
Middlesex – 220–200 pts approx (Relig St)
Sunderland – 220–180 pts approx (Media St/Relig St)
Surrey Roehampton – 220–180 pts (inc AL) – ALs **or** ALs+ASs; (Theol/Relig St)

200 pts   **Bangor** – 200 pts; gs (AL only); (Relig St; Theol; Bib St)
Chester (Coll) – 200 pts – ALs (180 pts inc C theol/relig st)+AS(20 pts); (Theol/Relig St Comb)
Greenwich – 200–160 pts approx (Theol/Educ St)
London (Bible Coll) – CDD/CD (Theol; Chr Life/Mnstry)
London (Oak Hill) – CDD/CC–DD (Theol/Past St)
Newman (CHE) – 200–140 pts approx (Theology courses)
Sunderland – 200–180 pts approx (Relig St/Psy)
Wolverhampton – 200–140 pts 12u – DDE/CD **or** DD+c/d **or** VA12u CD; gs; (App Theol; Relig St)

180 pts   **Chester (Coll)** – 180 pts – ALs (160 pts inc C theol/relig st)+AS(20 pts) **or** VAs (160 pts inc C related subj); gs; (Theology)
Liverpool Hope (Coll) – 180 pts approx (Relig St Comb; Theol courses)
Oxford Brookes (Westminster) – 180–140 pts approx (Theology courses)
Ripon & York (Coll) – 180 pts approx (Theol/Relig St P Educ)
St Martin's (Coll) – CDE/CC (C relig st) (Relig St/Art Des; Chr Min)

160 pts   **Bath Spa (UC)** – 160–120 pts 12u – BD **or** VA12u BD; (not gs) (St Relig Comb)
Birmingham (Westhill) – 160 pts 12u (inc C) – ALs **or** ALs+ASs **or** VAs (contact univ); gs; (Theol St; Hum (Theol) (Islam) (Educ); App Islam St)
Bishop Grosseteste (Coll) – CC **or** C+cc **or** VA12u (HlthSC); (not gs) (Relig St)
Canterbury Christ Church (UC) – CC–CD (Relig St courses)
Cheltenham & Glos (CHE) – 160–140 pts approx (Pol Soty/Relig St; Relig St/Theol; Theol courses)
Chichester (UC) – 160 pts (inc C); (St Rel; Theol)

Derby – 160 pts 12u – CC **or** DD+ee **or** VAs CC+/-ALs/ASs; gs; (St Relig)
Leeds, Trinity & All Saints (Coll) – CC (Theol; Theol – Media)
St Mary's (Coll) – CC–DD **or** ALs+ASs **or** VA12u CC–DD **or** VA6u C/D+AL(C/D); (Theol/Relig St)
Trinity Carmarthen (Coll) – CC–EE (Relig St)
Sunderland – 160 pts approx (Relig St/Mus; Relig St/Sociol)

140 pts **Cheltenham & Glos (CHE)** – 140 pts approx (Relig St QTS)
Derby – 140 pts 12u – CD **or** DE+ee **or** VAs CD+/-ALs/ASs; (Relig/Cult Comb)
St Mark & St John (Coll) – 140–80 pts approx (Theol/Phil)

120 pts **and below**
Aberystwyth – EE (Div; Theol)
Bath Spa (UC) – 120 pts 12u – DD **or** VA12u DD; (not gs) (St Relig single Hons)
UHI (Highland Theol Coll) – (Theol St – via DipHE)

Diploma of Higher Education courses
80 pts   Bath Spa (UC); Edge Hill (CHE); Middlesex; Oxford Brookes (Westminster); Ripon & York (Coll); UHI.

Diploma courses
Edinburgh (Scot Church Coll); London (Bible Coll).

Alternative Offers:

IB offers: Bangor 28 pts; Birmingham 33 pts; Birmingham (Westhill) 28 pts; Bristol 32–28 pts; Cheltenham & Glos (CHE) 26 pts; Exeter 30 pts; Kent 30–28 pts; Lampeter 24 pts; Lancaster 28 pts; Leeds 22 pts; St Andrews 28 pts; St Martin's (Coll) 28 pts.

Irish offers: St Andrews BBB.

Scottish Qualifications: Aberdeen BBBB; Edinburgh BBBC; Glasgow BBBB; Napier CCC; St Andrews BBBB; Stirling BBBC.

CHOOSING YOUR COURSE (See also **Ch.1**)

> **Subject information:** Religious Studies courses cover four degree course subjects: Religious Studies, Divinity, Theology and Biblical Studies. The subject content of these courses varies and students should check prospectuses carefully. They are not intended as training courses for the church ministry; an adherence to a particular religious persuasion is not a necessary qualification for entry. (Religious studies is an acceptable second or third A-Level for any non–scientific degree course.) Alternative courses could include Study of Religions, History, Community Studies, Philosophy, Psychology and Social Studies.

Special features: Bangor (Relig St) Combines biblical studies with twentieth century Christianity, theological studies and Judaism. Biblical languages compulsory. **Bath Spa (UC)** (St Relig) Different religions – world views both traditional and new (not Theology or Biblical Studies). **Birmingham** A very flexible course enabling students to devise their own programmes. **Bristol** Emphasis on biblical studies. In years 2 and 3 the course also covers inter-faith studies, religion and gender, the New Testament, Judaism, Islam, Buddhism and Hinduism. **Cardiff** (Relig St) Includes the history of the early church, the crusades and religious literature. **Durham** Equal grounding in Old and New Testament, church history, patristics and contemporary theology in years one and two. Wide range of options in Bible, church history, philosophy and modern theology. Optional languages in Hebrew, Latin, Aramaic, Syriac, Ancient Egyptian and Ugric. **Edinburgh** (MA Relig St) Students specialise in one religion from Christianity, Judaism, Islam, Hinduism, Buddhism, Chinese or ancient Near Eastern religions. **Exeter** Mixed traditional aspects of a Theology degree (Biblical Studies, Patristics and Modern Doctrine). Option in philosophy, ethics and world religions. **Hull** Common first year followed by free choice of courses in second and third years; Indian religions a departmental specialism. Second and third years are 'free option' years (students plan own courses). **Kent** Religious Studies and Theology are offered. Topics include applied theology, biblical interpretation, mysticism and religious experience. The faiths of the Jews, Muslims, Hindus and Buddhists are covered and there is a specialist study of Roman Catholic theology. **Lampeter** Modular degree with wide range of options in major world religions. **Leeds** Equal grounding in biblical studies, Christian history, theology and religious studies. **London (Hey)** Individual weekly tutorials for all students. **Manchester** A broad-based course covering the theological, historical anthropological, psychological and philosophical aspects of the subject. **Newcastle** Optional languages – Sanskrit, Greek or Hebrew. **St Andrews** Small group teaching emphasised. **Stirling** Units of study include religion – myth and meaning, religion – ethics and society, religion in the modern world. Advanced courses cover biblical studies, eastern religions and historical and philosophical studies. *NOW CHECK PROSPECTUSES AND WEB SITES.*

Top universities (Teaching Quality) (see Ch.4): Bangor; Edinburgh; Glasgow; Stirling; not all institutions assessed.

Top universities and colleges (Research) (see Ch.4): (including Theology and Divinity) Aberdeen; Bath Spa (UC); Birmingham; Bristol; Cambridge; Cardiff; Durham; Edinburgh; Glasgow; Hull; Lampeter; Lancaster; Leeds; London (King's), (SOAS); Manchester; Nottingham; Oxford; St Andrews; Sheffield; Surrey Roehampton.

Study opportunities abroad: Birmingham; Cheltenham & Glos (CHE); Durham; Edinburgh; Lancaster; London (Hey); London (SOAS); London (Oak Hill); Middlesex; Nottingham; Ripon & York (Coll); Sheffield; Surrey Roehampton.

ADMISSIONS INFORMATION

Number of applicants per place (approx): Bangor 5; Birmingham 10; Birmingham (Westhill) 3; Bristol 11; Cambridge 2.5; Cambridge (Hom) 4 (All BEd courses); Cheltenham & Glos (CHE) 3; Chichester (UC) 6; Durham 6; Edinburgh 4; Exeter 7; Glasgow 4; Greenwich 10; Hull (Theol) 10; Kent 13; Lampeter 7; Lancaster 6; Leeds (Theol/Relig St) 6; Leeds, Trinity & All Saints (Coll) 4; Liverpool Hope (Coll) 6; London (Bible Coll) 3; (London (Hey) 4; London (SOAS) 1; London (Oak Hill) 2; Middlesex 4; Newcastle 8; Nottingham 16; Oxford 1.5; Ripon & York (Coll) (Relig St) 11, (Theol) 3; St Martin's (Coll) 12; Sheffield 7; Surrey Roehampton 2.

Planning your UCAS personal statement (see Ch.4): An awareness of the differences between the main religions is important as is any special research undertaken. Interests in the religious art and architecture of various periods and styles should be noted. **Birmingham (Westhill)** Evidence of interactions with others, for example, homeless children. **St Andrews** Evidence of interest, reasons for choosing the course.

Selection interviews (see Ch.4): Aberystwyth; Bangor (No); Bath Spa (UC) (No); Birmingham; Birmingham (Westhill) (No); Cambridge; Cardiff; Durham; Edinburgh; Exeter (No); Glasgow; Hull; Kent (No); King Alfred's Winchester (Coll) (No); Lampeter; Lancaster; Leeds; Leeds, Trinity & All Saints (Coll); Liverpool Hope (Coll) (No); London (Bible Coll) (T); London (Hey); London (SOAS); London (Oak Hill); Manchester (No); Newcastle; Nottingham; Oxford (T) (W); Oxford Brookes (Westminster); Ripon & York (Coll) (No); St Andrews (No); Sheffield; Sunderland (No); Surrey Roehampton.

Interview questions (see Ch.4): Past questions have included: Why do you want to study Theology/Biblical Studies/Religious Studies? What do you hope to do after obtaining your degree? Questions relating to the A-level syllabus. Questions on current theological topics. Do you have any strong religious convictions? Do you think that your religious beliefs will be changed at the end of the course? Why did you choose Religious Studies rather than Biblical Studies? How would you explain the miracles to a 10-year old? (BEd course). Do you agree with the National Lottery?

Reasons for rejection (non-academic): Students not attending open days may be rejected. Psychological disturbance, criminal activities, drug problems (information supplied on referees' reports). Too religiously conservative. Belief that being religious and never having read anything will get you a place. Failure to interact. Lack of motivation to study a subject which goes beyond A-level. **Cardiff** Insufficiently open to an academic study of religion. **London (SOAS)** Inability to fit into life of the community, bearing in mind that its main aim is to provide educational, personal rabbis for the community.

GAP YEAR ADVICE

Cardiff Contact department well before your month of proposed entry to confirm your intentions.

Institutions willing to defer entry after A-Levels: Aberystwyth; Bangor; Birmingham; Bristol; Cardiff (No); Cheltenham & Glos (CHE); Chester (Coll); Glamorgan; Glasgow; Hull; Kent; Lampeter; Lancaster; Leeds, Trinity & All Saints (Coll); London (Bible Coll); London (SOAS); Newcastle; Newman (CHE); Nottingham; Ripon & York (Coll) (No); St Andrews; St Martin's (Coll); Surrey Roehampton; Westminster (IEd); Wolverhampton.

AFTER RESULTS ADVICE

Institutions which may accept the same points score after A-Levels: Bangor; Birmingham; Durham; Edinburgh; Exeter; Glasgow; Greenwich; Hull; Kent; Lancaster; Leeds; London (Bible Coll); London (SOAS); London (Oak Hill); Newcastle; Nottingham; Ripon & York (Coll); St Andrews (No); Sheffield; Stirling (No); Surrey Roehampton; most other institutions.

Institutions which may accept lower grades/points score after A-Levels: Bangor; Birmingham; Cambridge (Hom); Cheltenham & Glos (CHE); Chester (Coll); Durham; Edinburgh; Exeter; Glasgow; Kent; Lampeter; Lancaster; Leeds; Leeds, Trinity & All Saints (Coll); London (Bible Coll); London (Oak Hill); Newcastle; St Andrews; Sheffield; most other institutions.

Offers to applicants repeating A-Levels: Higher Durham, Hull, Manchester (BCD), St Andrews; **Possibly higher** Cambridge (Hom); **Same** Bangor, Birmingham, Cheltenham & Glos (CHE), Glasgow, Greenwich, Lampeter, Lancaster, Leeds, London (Bible Coll), London (Oak Hill), London (SOAS), Nottingham, Sheffield, Surrey Roehampton.

Probable vacancies from June 2001 and in Clearing (see Ch.4): Vacancies are expected on many Religious Studies and Theology courses.

NEW GRADUATE DESTINATIONS AND EMPLOYMENT (1999 HESA) (see **Ch.4**)

In a survey of 1017 graduates, 385 went into full-time employment (the majority into community and social services, health and social work), 65 into part-time work, 434 went into further training (272 into teacher training and 139 into higher degrees) and 52 were reported to be unemployed.

RUSSIAN (including **East European Studies**; see also **Modern Languages**)

NB The information supplied by the universities and colleges this year varies considerably and the offers listed below should be used as a first source of reference only. Many institutions will accept combinations of Advanced (AL), Advanced Subsidiary (AS) and Vocational Advanced (VA) level qualifications to achieve the required points total, but applicants must check web sites and prospectuses for full details of all offers. Grades and points totals shown should be regarded as the minimum levels to be achieved, but offers may be adjusted downwards when results are known. The points totals shown to the left of the institutions are for ease of reference only. It must not be assumed that tariff points are always used by institutions or that they can be substituted for an offer in grades. The level of an offer is not necessarily indicative of the quality of a course. To calculate your offers see Chapter 4 and the inside fold of the back cover.

Special subject requirements/preferences: A-Level: Edinburgh, Nottingham (beginners' course). **Essex, Manchester, Nottingham, Swansea** Grade A–C in Russian if taken. **Oxford** Modern language at full A-Level expected. **Sheffield** A foreign language. **GCSE: Edinburgh** English, mathematics or science and a foreign language. **London (LSE)** Grades A*, A and B. **Oxford, Cambridge** Grade A in most subjects preferred. **Portsmouth** Grade A or B in five subjects plus a foreign language.

360 pts	**and above**
	Cambridge – Offers, mainly in grades, vary between colleges (Modn/Mediev Lang; Modn Lang)
	Oxford – Offers vary between candidates (Modn/Mediev Lang; Modn Lang)
340 pts	**Manchester** – AAB (MMC Russ/Span)
	Nottingham – AAB–ABB (Econ/Russ)
300 pts	**Bristol** – BBB–BBC(B one relevant lang); (not gs) (Russ/Port)
	Durham – BBB–BBC (Russ/Pol; Russ; Hist/Russ)
	Edinburgh – BBB (Russ St/Bus St; Russ/Ling; Russ/Euro Hist)
	London (LSE) – BBB (Russ St)
	Manchester – BBB (Russ/Port)
280 pts	**Bath** – 280–260 pts approx (Russ/Ger; Russ/Fr)
	Glasgow – BBC (Russ/Czech; Mgt St/Russ Lang)
	Heriot-Watt – BBC (Russian (Interp/Transl courses))
	London (QM) – 280 pts approx (Russ/Drama)
	London (UCL) – BBC–BCC/BB–BC **or** 3ALs+AS/VA; (Russian courses; Bulg; Czech; Slov; Finn; Hung; Polh; Romn; Serb; Cro; Ukr)
	Nottingham – BBC–BCC (Engl St/Russ; Hisp St/Russ)
	St Andrews – BBC (Russ/Art Hist)
	Sheffield – BBC (Russ/Pol; Russ/E As St/Bus St; Russ/Econ)
	Swansea – 280 pts 18u – BBC–BCC/BB **or** ALs+ASs **or** VAs+/-ALs/ASs; (Russian courses)
260 pts	**Bristol** – BCC (inc modn lang); (not gs) (Russian)
	Essex – 260 pts 21u – BC+AL/2ASs **or** VA12u BC+AL; gs; (Russian)
	Exeter – 260 pts 18u (inc AL Span, GCSE Russ) – BCC **or** BC+cc **or** BB+dd **or** VAs (contact univ); gs; (Russ/Span)
	London (QM) – BCC (Russ/Econ)
	Nottingham – BCC (Russ/E Euro Area St)
	Sheffield – BCC (Russ/Polish; Russ/Czech; Russ/Hisp St; Russ Bus St)
	Strathclyde – BCC (Russian)
	Surrey – 260 pts 18u – ALs **or** ALs+ASs **or** VAs+AL (B lang); (not gs) (Russ/Econ/Int Bus; Russ/Law; Russ/Euro St)
	Sussex – BCC (E Euro St/Russ; Russ/Ling)
240 pts	**Bradford** – CCC/CC (Hist/Russ)
	Bradford – CCC (Russ; Russ/Fr; Russ/Span; Russ/Ger)
	Leeds – 3ALs (C Russ+2ALs – R800) CCC (R805) (Russian)
	Nottingham – CCC–CDD (Russ St; Russ/Serbo-Croat; Russ St – beginners)
	Portsmouth – 240 pts – ALs **or** ALs+ASs **or** VAs; gs; (Russian courses)
220 pts	**Nottingham** – CCD (Russ/Serb-Cro)
	Wolverhampton – 220–160 pts 12u – DDD–CDE/CC or CD+e **or** VA12u CC; gs; (Russian courses)
200 pts	**Coventry** – 200 pts approx (Russ Euro St)
	Euro Bus (Sch) – 200 pts approx (Russian courses)
160 pts	**Westminster** – CC–CD (Russian courses)

Alternative Offers:

EB offers: Surrey 70%.

IB offers: Bristol 30–28 pts; Essex 28 pts inc 10 pts in 2 Highers; Leeds 30–28 pts; London (LSE) 36 pts H655, (UCL) 30–28 pts; Newcastle 32–30 pts; Portsmouth 24 pts; St Andrews 28 pts; Surrey 28 pts, (Russ/Law) 30 pts; Swansea 28 pts H55.

Irish offers: St Andrews BBB; Surrey BBBCC.

Scottish Qualifications: Edinburgh BBBB; Glasgow ABBB/BBBB; Heriot-Watt AABB; St Andrews BBBB; Strathclyde BBBB.

Overseas applicants: Surrey, Leeds Fluent English important.

CHOOSING YOUR COURSE (See also **Ch.1**)

> **Subject information:** Studies in Russian language and literature are the main features of most courses. East European Studies involves language options such as Bulgarian, Czech, Hungarian, Polish and Romanian. Their applications in the world of commerce could now be on the increase. See also **Appendix 1** under **Modern Languages**.

Special features: Bradford Can be studied post A-level or *ab initio*. Options include economics, politics, literature and interpreting. **Bristol** Subsidiary subject must be taken in first and second years from 11 options; nineteenth and twentieth century literature. Fluency in language emphasised. Czech options in third year. **Durham** (Russian) Includes literature and history with options including Czech or Croation language. (Russian with Central and East European Area Studies) Includes business studies. Work opportunities exist in Russia and the Czech Republic for the students' year abroad. **Essex** Written and spoken Russian politics and history. **Leeds** Computer-assisted learning and word processing in English and Cyrillic. **Nottingham** Two visits to Russia. Options in Serbo-Croat or Slovene. **Surrey** Beginners in Russian accepted; two periods of three months in Russia. **Swansea** Options include business Russian, politics, economics and history. Three subjects taken in first year; final course choice can be delayed until end of first year. Most universities offer courses for beginners. *NOW CHECK PROSPECTUSES AND WEB SITES.*

Top universities and colleges (Teaching Quality) (see Ch.4): Cambridge; London (QM), (UCL); Oxford; Sheffield; Wolverhampton; not all institutions assessed.

Top universities and colleges (Research) (see Ch.4): Bristol; Cambridge; Leeds; London (QM), (UCL); Nottingham; Oxford; Portsmouth; St Andrews; Sheffield; Surrey; Sussex; Swansea.

Study opportunities abroad: Leeds; Manchester; Sheffield; Surrey; Swansea. Most institutions have contacts in Russia.

Work opportunities abroad: Leeds; Swansea.

ADMISSIONS INFORMATION

Number of applicants per place (approx): Bradford 3; Bristol 3; Durham 7; Leeds 5; London (LSE) (Russ) 9, (UCL) (Bulg) 1; Portsmouth (Russ/Ger) 10, (Russ/Sov St) 2; Surrey 5; Swansea 7.

Planning your UCAS personal statement (see Ch.4): Visits to Russian-speaking states must be mentioned, supported by your special reasons for wishing to study the language. A knowledge of the cultural, economic and political scene would also be important. **Portsmouth** Evidence of self-motivation, for example music qualifications, Duke of Edinburgh award. **St Andrews** Evidence of interest, reasons for choosing the course. See also **Appendix 1** under **Modern Languages**.

Selection interviews (see Ch.4): Bradford; Bristol; Cambridge; Durham; Edinburgh (No); Essex; Exeter; London (UCL); Nottingham (some); Oxford; Portsmouth (No); St Andrews (No); Surrey (T); Swansea (some).

Interview questions (see Ch.4): Since many applicants will not have taken Russian at A-level, questions often focus on the reasons for choosing a Russian degree, and the candidate's knowledge of, and interest in, Russia. Those taking A-level Russian are likely to be questioned on the course and on any reading done outside A-level work. East European Studies applicants will need to show some knowledge of their chosen country/ countries and any specific reasons why they wish to follow the course.

Reasons for rejection (non-academic): Lack of perceived commitment for a demanding *ab initio* subject.

GAP YEAR ADVICE

Surrey Experience involving Russian an asset.

Institutions willing to defer entry after A-Levels: Bradford; Cardiff (rarely); Leeds; Newcastle; Nottingham; Portsmouth; St Andrews; Sussex; Swansea; Wolverhampton.

AFTER RESULTS ADVICE

Institutions which may accept the same points score after A-Levels: Bradford; Bristol; Durham; Essex; Hull; Leeds; Nottingham (No); Portsmouth; St Andrews (No); Surrey; Swansea.

Institutions which may accept lower grades/points score after A-Levels: Bradford; Bristol; Essex; Exeter; Leeds; St Andrews; Swansea.

Offers to applicants repeating A-Levels: Higher Bradford, Essex, St Andrews, Surrey (if candidate is re-sitting 2 A-Levels), Swansea; **Possibly higher** Portsmouth; **Same** Bristol, Durham, Leeds.

Probable vacancies from June 2001 and in Clearing (see Ch.4): A reasonable selection of vacancies is likely. Popular universities normally make offers in the 260–220 pts range.

NEW GRADUATE DESTINATIONS AND EMPLOYMENT (1999 HESA) (see **Ch.4**)

In a survey of 82 graduates, 46 entered full-time employment (the majority into business fields), further research and study accounted for 14, and seven were reported to be seeking employment. Twenty-two students graduated in Slavonic and East European languages and culture, of whom eight went into full-time employment and 10 on to further study.

SCANDINAVIAN STUDIES

NB The information supplied by the universities and colleges this year varies considerably and the offers listed below should be used as a first source of reference only. Many institutions will accept combinations of Advanced (AL), Advanced Subsidiary (AS) and Vocational Advanced (VA) level qualifications to achieve the required points total, but applicants must check web sites and prospectuses for full details of all offers. Grades and points totals shown should be regarded as the minimum levels to be achieved, but offers may be adjusted downwards when results are known. The points totals shown to the left of the institutions are for ease of reference only. It must not be assumed that tariff points are always used by institutions or that they can be substituted for an offer in grades. The level of an offer is not necessarily indicative of the quality of a course. To calculate your offers see Chapter 4 and the inside fold of the back cover.

Special subject requirements/preferences: A-Level: A foreign language usually preferred; check institutions. **GCSE:** Foreign language preferred for all courses. **Cambridge** Grade A in most subjects preferred. **East Anglia** Mathematics and foreign language preferred. **Edinburgh** English, mathematics or science and a foreign language preferred.

360 pts	**and above**
	Cambridge – Offers, mainly in grades, vary between colleges (Anglo Saxon, Norse and Celtic)
340 pts	**Edinburgh** – AAB (Scand St/Law)
300 pts	**Edinburgh** – BBB (Celt/Scand St; Engl Lang/Scand St; Scot Ethnol/Scand St)
	London (UCL) – BBB–BBC **or** 3ALs+AS/VA; (Ger/Scand St)
280 pts	**East Anglia** – 280 pts – ACC; (Scand St 3 yr course)
	Edinburgh – BBC (Scand St/Euro Hist; Scand St/Hist Art; Scand St/Ling)
260 pts	**Hull** – BCC (Scand St/Drama; Scand/Hist)

240 pts **East Anglia** – 240 pts – CCC (Scand St 4 yr course)
Hull – CCC (Scand St/Ital; Scand St/Span)
London (UCL) – CCC or 3ALs+AS/VA; (Ice; Scand St; Scand St/Mgt St; Viking St)
160 pts **Hull** – CC (Scand St)

Alternative Offers:

IB offers: Edinburgh H665; Hull 28 pts.

Scottish Qualifications: Edinburgh ABBB–BBBB.

CHOOSING YOUR COURSE (See also **Ch.1**)

> **Subject information:** Scandinavian Studies are usually offered as an option on modern language courses and provide a useful second language for linguists looking towards careers abroad.

Special features: East Anglia Students interested in Scandinavian Studies can opt for a more literature-based course, or one with a stronger language component, or for a combined language/literature/history course. In all cases students specialise in one Scandinavian language (Danish, Norwegian or Swedish) but acquire a working knowledge of the other two. **Hull** Wide range of topics covered, including Nordic history, philosophy and literature. Danish or Swedish can be taken as specialist languages. *NOW CHECK PROSPECTUSES AND WEB SITES.*

Top universities and colleges (Teaching Quality) (see Ch.4): London (UCL); not all institutions assessed.

Top universities and colleges (Research) (see Ch.4): See **German**.

Study opportunities abroad: East Anglia; Edinburgh; Hull; London (UCL); most universities can arrange placements in Scandinavia.

ADMISSIONS INFORMATION

Number of applicants per place (approx): East Anglia 5; Hull 11; London (UCL) 3.

Planning your UCAS personal statement (see Ch.4): Visits to Scandinavian countries could be the source of an interest in studying these languages. You should also be aware of cultural, political, geographical and economic aspects of Scandinavian countries. Such information should be included on the form.

Selection interviews (see Ch.4): Cambridge; Edinburgh (No).

Interview questions (see Ch.4): Applicants in the past have been questioned on why they have chosen this subject area, on any visits to Scandinavia and on their knowledge of the country/countries and their people. Future career plans are likely to be discussed.

Reasons for rejection (non-academic): No formal background in a foreign language. Don't know the difference between a noun and a verb.

GAP YEAR ADVICE

Institutions willing to defer entry after A-Levels: London (UCL) (No).

AFTER RESULTS ADVICE

Probable vacancies from June 2001 and in Clearing (see Ch.4): Contact each university since some may have vacancies.

NEW GRADUATE DESTINATIONS AND EMPLOYMENT (1999 HESA) (see **Ch.4**)

In a survey of 33 graduates, 22 entered full-time employment, four went on to further study and one graduate was reported to be unemployed.

SCIENCE (including **Combined** and **General Science**; see also **Biological Sciences**)

NB The information supplied by the universities and colleges this year varies considerably and the offers listed below should be used as a first source of reference only. Many institutions will accept combinations of Advanced (AL), Advanced Subsidiary (AS) and Vocational Advanced (VA) level qualifications to achieve the required points total, but applicants must check web sites and prospectuses for full details of all offers. Grades and points totals shown should be regarded as the minimum levels to be achieved, but offers may be adjusted downwards when results are known. The points totals shown to the left of the institutions are for ease of reference only. It must not be assumed that tariff points are always used by institutions or that they can be substituted for an offer in grades. The level of an offer is not necessarily indicative of the quality of a course. To calculate your offers see Chapter 4 and the inside fold of the back cover.

Special subject requirements/preferences: A-Levels: Two–three science subjects.
GCSE: Science/mathematics subjects. *Teacher Training courses:* English, mathematics.
Cambridge Grade A in most subjects preferred. **Cranfield** Predominantly As and Bs.

360 pts	**and above**
	Cambridge – Offers, mainly in grades, vary between colleges (Nat Sci)
	Oxford – Offers vary between candidates (Hum Sci)
340 pts	**Durham** – AAB (Nat Sci)
	London (UCL) – AAB–ABB (Hum Sci)
320 pts	**Liverpool** – 320–280 pts; (Comb Hons)
300 pts	**Bath** – 300–260 pts approx (Nat Sci)
	Birmingham – BBB–BBC (Nat Sci courses)
	East Anglia – BBB (Nat Sci)
	Lancaster – BBB (Comb Sci USA)
	Lancaster – BBB–CCC (Comb Sci courses; Nat Sci)
	Newcastle – 300–240 pts approx (BSc Comb St)
280 pts	**Glasgow** – BBC–CCC (Gen Sci)
	London (RH) – 280 pts 18u – BBC–BCC **or** 2ALs+2ASs; (not gs) (Sci Media)
	London (UCL) – BBC **or** 3ALs+AS/VA; (Sci Comm Pol)
260 pts	**London (UCL)** – BCC **or** 3ALs+AS/VA; (Phys Sci)
	Sussex – BCC (Nat Sci)
240 pts	**Barnsley (Coll)** – 240 pts – ALs **or** ALs+ASs **or** VAs+/-ALs/ASs; gs; (Sci Ext)
	Bath – 240 pts approx (Fdn Sci Eng)
	Cranfield – CCC/AB (App Sci)
	London (RH) – CCC/BC–CC (Fdn Sci)
	Paisley – CCC–EE (Sci Tech)
	St Andrews – CCC (Fac Sci courses General Degree)
220 pts	**Aberdeen** – CCD (Science)
	Bristol UWE – 220–120 pts – ALs **or** ALs+ASs **or** VAs+/-ALs/ASs; (Comb Sci)
	Bristol UWE – 220–180 pts 12u – ALs **or** ALs+ASs **or** VAs+/-ALs/ASs; (Sci/Soty/Media)
	De Montfort – 220–180 pts approx (Comb Hons – Mod)
	Leeds – 220–180 pts approx (Interd Sci Fdn)
	Salford – 220–200 pts approx/CC (Comb Sci courses)
200 pts	**Anglia** – 200–160 pts approx (Comb Sci)
	Surrey Roehampton – 200–180 pts approx (Hum Sci)
	Teesside – 200–180 pts approx (Comb Sci; App Sci)
180 pts	**Chester (Coll)** – 180 pts – AL (160 pts inc C)+AS(20 pts) **or** VAs (160 pts inc C)+AS(20 pts); Hist/Sci Comb)
	Durham (Stockton) – 180–140 pts approx (Sci Soc)
	Edge Hill (CHE) – BC (Sci/Spo St)
	Heriot-Watt – 180 pts 18u – DDD **or** ALs+ASs **or** VAsB+/-ALs/ASs; gs (BSc Comb St)

North London – 180–140 pts approx (Sci/Eng Comb Awards)
Norwich City (Coll) – 180 pts approx (Comb Sci)
St Martin's (Coll) – CDE/CC (Sci Tech courses)

160 pts **Bishop Grosseteste (Coll)** – CC (inc C sci pref/biol) **or** C+cc **or** VA12u+AL (C biol); (not gs) (Science QTS)
Canterbury Christ Church (CHE) – CC (Sci/Am St)
Derby – 160–140 pts approx (Comb Sci)
Glamorgan – 160 pts approx (Sci/Sci Fctn)
Huddersfield – 160 pts 12u; (App Sci)
Kingston – DDE–DEE/CD–DD (Science joint Hons)
Liverpool John Moores – 160–120 pts approx (Nat Sci)
Loughborough – 160 pts 12u – 2ALs **or** VA12u **or** VA6u+AL; (not gs) (Sci/Eng Fdn)
Sheffield Hallam – 160–140 pts approx (Sci Tech)

140 pts **Bath Spa (UC)** – CD (Combined Awards)
Bolton (IHE) – CD (Sci Soty Env)
Bradford (Coll) – 140 pts approx (Fdn Sci)
Glasgow Caledonian – CD (Science)
Greenwich – 140 pts (Hum Sci Soc)
Wolverhampton – 140 pts 12u – CD **or** VAs+/-ALs/ASs; gs; (App Sci)

120 pts **Bradford** – 120 pts 9u; gs; (Fdn Sci)
Brunel – 120 pts 2x6u – ALs **or** ALs+ASs **or** VAs+/-ALs/ASs; (Sci Fdn)
Oxford Brookes – DD (Comb Sci courses)
South Bank – DD (Sci Fdn)
Strathclyde – DD (Sci St)

100 pts **and below**
Bristol UWE – ALs **or** ALs+ASs **or** VAs+/-ALs/ASs; (Sci Fdn)
Cornwall & Duchy (Coll) – (Ext Sci Fdn)
East London – 100 pts approx (Sci Ext)
Edge Hill (CHE) – (Sci QTS)
Glamorgan – E (Fdn Sci)
Hertfordshire – 100 pts approx (Comb Mod Sci)
Huddersfield – 80 pts 6u; (Sci Fdn)
Kingston – (Sci Joint Hons Fdn)
Leeds, Trinity & All Saints (Coll) – EE (Sci/Educ)
London (QM) – E (Eng Sci Fdn courses)
Luton – (Sci Fdn)
Newport (UWCN) – (Science)
Oxford Brookes – EE (Ext Sci)
Sheffield Hallam – E (Comb Sci courses; Sci Fdn)
Somerset (CAT) – 80 pts approx (Ext Sci)
Teesside – 100 pts approx (Ext Sci)
UHI (Perth) – (App Sci)
West Herts (Coll) – (Sci Fdn course)

Diploma of Higher Education courses
80 pts Boston (Coll); Brooklands (Coll); East London; Oxford Brookes; Paisley.

Higher National Diploma courses
100 pts **and below**
Bristol UWE; Cardiff (UWI); Coventry; Derby; Halton (Coll); North Down & Ards (IHE); Paisley; Portsmouth; Robert Gordon; South Bank; Stockport (CFHE).

Foundation or Extended Science courses for those without the normal A-Level or equivalent qualifications are available as follows:
Bristol UWE; Coventry; De Montfort; East London; Glamorgan; North London; Northumbria; Oxford Brookes; Portsmouth; South Bank; Teesside; Wirral Met (Coll).

Alternative Offers:

EB offers: Keele 60%; Lancaster 65%; Newcastle 70–65%; St Andrews 65%.

IB offers: Aberdeen 26 pts; Birmingham 28 pts; Brunel 25 pts; Cheltenham & Glos (CHE) 27 pts; Glasgow 36–30 pts; Lancaster 28 pts; Leeds 32–30 pts; London (UCL) 32 pts; Loughborough 28 pts; Newcastle 29 pts inc H5 in relevant subject; St Andrews 28 pts; Salford H555; South Bank 24 pts; Warwick 25 pts.

Irish offers: Aberdeen BBBC; Glasgow BBB; St Andrews BBBB–BBCC.

Scottish Qualifications: Aberdeen BBBC; Glasgow BBB; Glasgow Caledonian BBC; St Andrews BBBB/BBCC.

Overseas applicants: St Andrews Pre-sessional English course available.

CHOOSING YOUR COURSE (See also **Ch.1**)

> **Subject information:** These courses, which have a considerable shortage of appli-
> cants, cover various scientific subjects in combination. For studies in the history and
> philosophy of sciences, A-levels in science subjects are not always required. Check
> other science courses. See also **Appendix 1** under separate **Sciences**.

Special features: (Combined and joint courses) **Bristol UWE** Two subjects chosen from six. **Cranfield** (App Sci) Broad course in applied physics, maths and materials science; specialisation in two of these after first year. **De Montfort** Three subjects chosen in first year from 15. Degree in one or two subjects. **Lancaster** Three subjects in first year (science and another course or a non-science subject from 20 subjects). **Newcastle** Choice of course units. **St Andrews** Three science classes or half classes from 32 options. **Salford** Three subjects taken in first year from nine subjects. Two taken in second and third years. *NOW CHECK PROSPECTUSES AND WEB SITES.*

Study opportunities abroad: Aberdeen; Cranfield; Glasgow; Salford; Teesside.

Work opportunities abroad: Salford; Teesside; Wolverhampton.

ADMISSIONS INFORMATION

Number of applicants per place (approx): Brighton 6; Bristol UWE 3; Chester (Coll) 4; Coventry 2; Cranfield 1; De Montfort 3; Durham (Stockton) 50; East London 8; Glamorgan 9; Greenwich 7; Heriot-Watt 2; Hertfordshire 8; Kingston 4; Lancaster 7; Leeds 10; Luton 4; Loughborough (Ergon) 4; Newcastle (Nat Res) 2; North East Wales (IHE) 2; Paisley 4; Salford 5; Worcester (UC) 12.

Planning your UCAS personal statement (see Ch.4): See under **Biology, Biological Sciences, Chemistry, Physics**. See also **Appendix 1**.

Selection interviews (see Ch.4): Bishop Grosseteste (Coll) (T); Bristol UWE; Cambridge; Cranfield; Derby (No); Hertfordshire; Leeds (T); London (UCL).

Interview questions (see Ch.4): Past applicants have been questioned on their A-level work and aspects they particularly enjoyed. **Leeds** 500-word essay is set.

Reasons for rejection (non-academic): (Mainly academic.) Lack of an active interest in scientific issues.

GAP YEAR ADVICE

Institutions willing to defer entry after A-Levels: Bristol UWE; Cheltenham & Glos (CHE); Cranfield; Edge Hill (CHE); Glamorgan; Glasgow (only for good academic reason); Heriot-Watt; Lancaster; Leeds, Trinity & All Saints (Coll); London (UCL) (No); Newcastle; North East Wales (IHE); St Andrews; Salford; South Bank.

AFTER RESULTS ADVICE

Institutions which may accept the same points score after A-Levels: Bristol UWE; Coventry; Cranfield; Glamorgan; Glasgow; Hertfordshire; Leeds; Luton; Newcastle; North East Wales (IHE); St Andrews (No); Wolverhampton; most institutions.

Institutions which may accept lower grades/points score after A-Levels: Coventry; Glasgow; Hertfordshire; Leeds; Newcastle; North East Wales (IHE); St Andrews; Worcester (UC).

Offers to applicants repeating A-Levels: Higher Hertfordshire, Leeds, Newcastle; **Possibly higher** Coventry; **Same** De Montfort, Glasgow, North London, Ulster, Wolverhampton.

Probable vacancies from June 2001 and in Clearing (see Ch.4): Most universities should be contacted since these courses invariably have vacancies throughout the year.

NEW GRADUATE DESTINATIONS AND EMPLOYMENT (1999 HESA) (see **Ch.4**)

No data available.

SOCIAL POLICY AND ADMINISTRATION (see also **Community Studies** and **Social Work**)

NB The information supplied by the universities and colleges this year varies consider-ably and the offers listed below should be used as a first source of reference only. Many institutions will accept combinations of Advanced (AL), Advanced Subsidiary (AS) and Vocational Advanced (VA) level qualifications to achieve the required points total, but applicants must check web sites and prospectuses for full details of all offers. Grades and points totals shown should be regarded as the minimum levels to be achieved, but offers may be adjusted downwards when results are known. The points totals shown to the left of the institutions are for ease of reference only. It must not be assumed that tariff points are always used by institutions or that they can be substituted for an offer in grades. The level of an offer is not necessarily indicative of the quality of a course. To calculate your offers see Chapter 4 and the inside fold of the back cover.

Special subject requirements/preferences: GCSE: English and mathematics normally required. **London (LSE)** A* to B grades, mathematics grade C or better. **London (RH)** Six subjects grade A* to C. **Southampton** Grade B mathematics.

320 pts **London (RH)** – ABB (Soc Pol/Econ; Soc Pol Mgt)
300 pts **Bristol** – ABC–BBC; (not gs) (Soc Pol/Pol)
Edinburgh – BBB (1 sitting); (not gs) (Soc Pol courses)
Hull – BBB (Soc Pol/Sociol)
London (LSE) – BBB (Soc Pol; Soc Pol with Admin; Soc Pol/Gov; Soc/Pop St; Soc Pol/Soc Psy; Soc Pol/Sociol)
London (RH) – BBB (Soc Pol/Fr; Soc Pol/Ger; Soc Pol/Mus)
Manchester – BBB–BBC (BA Econ Soc Pol)
Newcastle – ABC–BBB (Soc Pol Comb St)
York – 21–18u – BCC+c; (Soc Pol courses)
290 pts **Southampton** – 290 pts 21u (inc 180 pts from 2ALs inc B); (Soc Pol/Admin)
280 pts **Bangor** – 280–260 pts – BBC **or** VA12u AA; gs; (Soc Pol/Psy C 184)
Belfast (Queen's) – BBB (BSc Econ Soc Pol)
Bristol – BBC–BCC (Soc Pol; Soc Admin courses)
Essex – 280 pts 21u – BB+AL/2ASs **or** VA12u (hlth sc) BB+AL; gs; (Soc/Pblc Pol)
Kent – 280 pts approx (Soc Pol/Pblc Mgt; Soc Pol; Soc Pol/Comp; Soc Pol/Acc Fin)
London (RH) – BBC (Soc Pol; Urb St/Soc Pol)

Newcastle – BBC–BCC/BB (Econ/Soc Pol; Sociol)
Nottingham – BBC (Soc Pol/Admin)
Sheffield – BBC (Soc Pol/Sociol; Soc Pol/Econ; Soc Pol/Crim)
Sussex – BBC (Soc Pol)
Swansea – 280 pts 18u – BBC–BCC **or** ALs+ASs **or** VAs+/-ALs/ASs; (Soc Pol)
260 pts **Bath** – BCC+AS; gs; (Soc Pol/Admin)
Belfast (Queen's) – BCC (Soc Pol/Sociol; Soc Pol/Wmns St)
Birmingham – BCC (Plan Pblc Pol Gov Mgt; Pblc Soc Pol Mgt; Soc Pol)
Bradford – BCC/AA (App Soc)
Bristol – BCC; (not gs) (Soc Pol/Sociol)
Brunel – BCC (Soc Pol courses)
Cardiff – BCC/BB (Soc Pol; Soc Pol/Crim; Soc Pol/Soc Rsch Meth)
Durham – BCC (Sociol/Soc Pol)
Glasgow – BCC (MA Soc Sci CQSW; Soc/Urb Pol courses)
Hull – 260–240 pts approx (Soc Pol)
Kent – 260 pts approx (Euro St (Soc Pol))
Leeds – BCC **or** BC+cc; gs; (Soc Pol/Admin; Soc Pol/Sociol)
Liverpool – BCC (Sociol/Soc Pol)
Manchester – BCC (BSoc Sci; Soc Pol)
Plymouth – BCC (Soc Pol Admin/Psy; Soc Pol Admin/Law)
Stirling – BCC (Soc Pol/Sociol)
Warwick – BCC (Sociol/Soc Pol)
240 pts **Bangor** – 240–220 pts – 3ALs; gs; (Soc Pol/Hist)
Bristol – CCC; (not gs) (Soc Pol/Plan)
Coventry – 240 pts approx (Law/Soc Pol)
London (Gold) – BCD/CC (Soc Pol; Soc Pol/Econ; Soc Pol/Pol)
Loughborough – 240 pts 18u – 2ALs+AL/2ASs **or** VAs; gs; (Soc Pol)
Nottingham Trent – 240 pts 18u – CCC (Pol Sci)
Sheffield Hallam – CCC (Soc Pol)
Ulster – CCC (Soc Admin/Pol; Comb Soc Pol)
220 pts **Bangor** – ALs **or** VAs+/-ALs/ASs; gs; (Soc Pol joint courses except under
280/240 pts)
Bradford – 220 pts 12u; gs; (Soc Pol Admin; Soc Welf St; App Crim Just St;
Gndr St/Soc Pol)
Buckingham – 220 pts approx (Pol St)
De Montfort (Leicester) – 220 pts (inc 2ALs **or** VA12u) – ALs **or** ALs+ASs **or**
VAs+/-ALs/ASs; Pblc Pol)
Hertfordshire – 220–200 pts approx (Euro St/Soc Pol; Soc Pol; Soc Pol/Econ;
Soc Pol/Pol; Soc Pol/Sociol)
Middlesex – 220–180 pts approx (Soc Pol)
South Bank – 220–140 pts approx (Soc Pol courses)
Teesside – 220 pts approx (Crim/Soc Pol)
200 pts **Anglia** – 200 pts approx (Crim/Soc Pol; Euro Phil Lit Soc Pol)
Brighton – 200 pts approx (Soc Pol Admin)
Central England – 200 pts 12u – ALs **or** ALs+ASs **or** VAs+/-ALs/ASs;
(Soc/Pol St)
Luton – 200–120 pts approx (Soc Pol)
Plymouth – 200 pts approx (Soc Pol Admin/App Econ; Soc Pol Admin/Crim
Just)
Salford – 200 pts approx (Soc Pol; Soc Pol/Couns)
180 pts **Buckinghamshire Chilterns (UC)** – 180 pts approx (Soc Welf/Soc Pol)
East London – 180 pts approx (Soc Pol courses)
Portsmouth – 180 pts – ALs **or** ALs+ASs **or** VAs; gs; (Soc Pol courses)
Queen Margaret (UC) – BC (Sociol/Soc Pol)
Wolverhampton – DDD/DDEE/CC **or** CD+d/e **or** VA12u CC; gs; (Soc Pol)
160 pts **Central Lancashire** – 160 pts 12u – ALs **or** ALs+ASs **or** VAs+/-ALs/ASs; gs;
(Soc Pol Admin)
Coventry – BD–CC (Soc Pol Int Rel)

Lincolnshire & Humberside – 160 pts (Soc Pol)
London Guildhall – CC (Comm Soc Pol/Mgt)
North London – 160 pts approx (Pblc Admin/Soc Pol)
Paisley – CC (Euro Pol St)
140 pts **Napier** – CD (Hlth Prom/Hlth Sci)
North London – 140 pts 1x12u **or** 2x6u; (Soc Pol; Soc Des)
Suffolk (Coll) – CD–EE (Soc Pol courses)
120 pts **Surrey Roehampton** – 120 pts (inc 2ALs) – ALs **or** ALs+ASs **or** VAs+/-ALs/
ASs; (Soc Pol/Admin)

Leeds Met – (contact university)

Alternative Offers:

IB offers: Bangor 30 pts; Bath 32 pts; Birmingham 30 pts; Bradford 24 pts; Bristol 30–28 pts; Cardiff 28 pts; Durham H666 S555; Exeter 30 pts; Kent 28 pts; Lancaster 32–30 pts; London (LSE) 36 pts, (RH) 30 pts; Loughborough 28 pts; Swansea 30 pts; York 28 pts.

Irish offers: Bangor BBBCC; Bradford BBCCC; Loughborough BBCCC.

Scottish Qualifications: Abertay Dundee (Soc Hlth Sci – Dip) BC; Dundee BBBC; Edinburgh BBBBC; Glasgow ABBB; Napier BCC; Paisley BBB; Queen Margaret (UC) BBBC; Stirling BBBC.

Overseas applicants: Hull Living costs 30% lower than in London; **Leeds** English language package available; **Loughborough** Proficiency in English important; **Plymouth** Fluency in English important – no EFL facilities.

CHOOSING YOUR COURSE (See also **Ch.1**)

Subject information: Social Policy is mainly concerned with those aspects of people's welfare which are affected by government policy, for example, unemployment, education, health, housing, social services. Alternative courses therefore could include Education, Nursing, Housing, Social Administration, Social Work, Health Studies and Community Studies (see **Appendix 1**).

Special features: Anglia (Euro Phil Lit Soc Pol) Chance to live and study abroad, with English as the language of instruction, and to spend time working in/observing European health and welfare agencies. **Bangor** Modules in NHS, housing, health care and poverty. **Birmingham** Course includes health care, housing, social work, criminology. **Bristol** Strong emphasis on international dimensions. Role of the European Union. Research skills. (Soc Pol/Plan) Covers history, law, philosophy, economics and sociology. **Cardiff** Students must take six first year courses: social welfare and social change, and social welfare in Britain, as well as four options in the social sciences. Later studies cover poverty, housing, crime, the care of the elderly, health and welfare agencies. **Hull** Option courses include health, education, crime and housing – 10-week placement in second year. **Leeds** Third year options include gender, sexuality, social security, housing, sociology of medicine, race relations and the family. **London (Gold)** Foundation course includes government, politics and economics. **Loughborough** (Soc Pol) Options include voluntary euthanasia, mental illness, child abuse. **Portsmouth** High percentage of mature students. Specialist areas: health, education, housing; French and German offered. **Stirling** Closely related to Sociology. **Sussex** Pathways in Health Studies, Housing, Social Welfare and Criminal Justice. **Swansea** Strengths in health policy, disability, politics of welfare, family and community care, race relations. *NOW CHECK PROSPECTUSES AND WEB SITES.*

Top universities and colleges (Teaching Quality) (see Ch.4): Bath; Brunel; Durham; Edinburgh; Glasgow; Hull; Kent; London (LSE); London Guildhall; Newcastle; Sheffield; Ulster; York; not all institutions assessed.

Top universities and colleges (Research) (see Ch.4): Bath; Bangor; Birmingham; Bristol; Brunel; Edinburgh; Glasgow; Hull; Keele; Kent; Lancaster; London (LSE); Manchester; Middlesex; Sheffield; South Bank; Ulster; York.

Study opportunities abroad: Anglia; Bangor; Bath; Bradford; Brighton; Bristol; Glasgow; Leeds; London (RH); London Guildhall; North London; Plymouth; Sheffield; Surrey Roehampton; Swansea; Teesside.

Work opportunities abroad: Bath; Brighton; Plymouth; Teesside.

ADMISSIONS INFORMATION

Number of applicants per place (approx): Bangor 6; Bath 8; Birmingham 10; Bristol 8; Cardiff 4; Central Lancashire 6; Durham 8; Exeter 7; Hull 9; Kent 5; Lancaster 12; Leeds 10; London (LSE) 4, (RH) 4; Loughborough 13; Middlesex 12; Newcastle 8; North London 3; Nottingham 21; Plymouth 4; Portsmouth 6; Sheffield Hallam 33; Southampton 8; Stirling 11; Surrey Roehampton 4; Swansea 10; York 8.

Planning your UCAS personal statement (see Ch.4): Social work careers are covered by this subject; consequently a good knowledge of these occupations and contacts with the social services should be discussed fully on your UCAS form. Gain work experience if possible. **York** Work experience including voluntary work relevant to Social Policy. Further information from the Central Council for Education and Training in Social Work. See also under **Social Work** and **Appendix 1**.

Selection interviews (see Ch.4): Bangor (No); Bath (No); Birmingham; Bradford (No); Brighton (No); Cardiff (some); Central Lancashire (No); Durham; Hull (No); Kent (some); Lancaster; Leeds (mature students); London (Gold) (some) (W) (T), (LSE), (RH); Loughborough; Manchester (No); Newcastle (No); North London; Nottingham (No); Portsmouth (No); Sheffield (No); Sheffield Hallam (No); Stirling (No); Suffolk (Coll) (No); Surrey Roehampton (No); Swansea; York (No).

Interview questions (see Ch.4): Past questions have included: What relevance has history to social administration? What qualities are needed to be a social worker? What use do you think you will be to society as a social worker? Why should money be spent on prison offenders? Your younger brother is playing truant, and mixing with bad company. Your parents don't know. What would you do? What do you understand by 'public policy'? What advantage do you think studying Social Science gives when working in policy fields? How could the image of public management of services be improved? Applicants should be fully aware of the content and the differences between all the courses on offer, why they want to study the subject and their career objectives. **London (LSE)** Essays required from current course.

Reasons for rejection (non-academic): Some universities **require** attendance when they invite applicants to open days (check). Lack of awareness of current social issues. See also **Social Work**.

GAP YEAR ADVICE

Work experience in management, welfare or social care an advantage.

Institutions willing to defer entry after A-Levels: Bangor; Bath; Birmingham; Bristol; Central Lancashire; London (Gold), (RH); London Guildhall; Luton; North London; Nottingham; Plymouth; Portsmouth; Sheffield (No); Sheffield Hallam; Surrey Roehampton; Swansea.

AFTER RESULTS ADVICE

Institutions which may accept the same points score after A-Levels: Aston; Bangor; Birmingham; Bradford; Brighton; Bristol; Central Lancashire; Durham (No); Essex; Kent; Leeds (No); London (RH); Loughborough; Newcastle; North London; Nottingham (No); Plymouth; Surrey Roehampton; Swansea (but very low grades, for example E in 1–2 subjects, not accepted); York.

Institutions which may accept lower grades/points score after A-Levels: Bradford; Durham; Essex; Hull (overseas applicants 18–16 pts); Kent; London (RH); Newcastle; North London; Plymouth; Salford; Surrey Roehampton; York.

Offers to applicants repeating A-Levels: Higher East Anglia, Leeds, Newcastle; **Same** Birmingham, Brighton, Durham, Loughborough, North London, Surrey Roehampton, Ulster, York.

Probable vacancies from June 2001 and in Clearing (see Ch.4): Several universities and colleges declared vacancies last year. Contact all institutions.

NEW GRADUATE DESTINATIONS AND EMPLOYMENT (1999 HESA) (see **Ch.4**)

Out of 989 graduates surveyed, 548 entered full-time employment (evenly divided across health, social work and public administration business activities and finance) 124 into part-time work, 163 went on to further study and 70 were believed to be unemployed.

SOCIAL STUDIES/SCIENCE (including **Applied Social Studies**); see also
under specific subjects in the Social Science field (**Anthropology, Politics, Social Policy and Administration** and **Sociology** etc)

NB The information supplied by the universities and colleges this year varies considerably and the offers listed below should be used as a first source of reference only. Many institutions will accept combinations of Advanced (AL), Advanced Subsidiary (AS) and Vocational Advanced (VA) level qualifications to achieve the required points total, but applicants must check web sites and prospectuses for full details of all offers. Grades and points totals shown should be regarded as the minimum levels to be achieved, but offers may be adjusted downwards when results are known. The points totals shown to the left of the institutions are for ease of reference only. It must not be assumed that tariff points are always used by institutions or that they can be substituted for an offer in grades. The level of an offer is not necessarily indicative of the quality of a course. To calculate your offers see Chapter 4 and the inside fold of the back cover.

Special subject requirements/preferences: GCSE: Usually English and mathematics; a science may be required. **Bristol** 35 pts (see **Ch.4**). **Durham** Science grade A or B.

360 pts   and above
   Cambridge – Offers, mainly in grades, vary between colleges (Soc Pol Sci)
330 pts   Southampton (New Coll) – 330 pts (inc 2ALs 180 pts); gs; (App Soc Sci
      (Crim/Pst St))
320 pts   Durham – ABB/AB (Soc Sci Comb courses)
   Leeds – 18u – ABB **or** AB+bb; gs; (Crim Just St)
300 pts   Bangor – 300 pts – 3ALs **or** VAs+/-ALs/ASs; gs; (Crim/Psy)
   Essex – 300–280 pts 21u – BB+AL/2ASs; gs (Hum Rts)
   Hull – BBB–BCC (Gndr St)
   Newcastle – ABC–BBC (Soc St Comb St)
   York – 300–260 pts 21–18u – BCC **or** BC+cc **or** VAs (contact univ); gs; (App
      Soc Sci)
280 pts   Bradford – 280 pts 12u; gs; (Int Rel/Secur St; Peace St)
   Bristol – BBC–BCC (Early Child St)
   City – 3x6u – BBC; ASs/VAs (contact univ); (not gs) (Soc Sci)
   East Anglia – BBC; gs; (Psychosoc St)
   Glasgow – BBC (Fac Soc Sci)
   Nottingham – BBC (Soc/Cult St)
   Sheffield – BBC (Soc Pol St)
260 pts   Bangor – 260 pts – 3ALs **or** VAs+/-ALs/ASs; gs; (Crim/Crim Just)
   Bath – BCC+AS; gs; (Soc Sci; App Soc St/Soc Wk)
   Belfast (Queen's) – BCC (Wmns St)
   Bristol UWE – 260–240 pts (Soc Sci courses)
   Essex – 260 pts 21u – BC+AL/2ASs **or** VA12u (Hlth SC) BC+AL; gs; (Soc Sci)
   Keele – BCC **or** equiv AS accepted; gs; (App Soc St courses)
   Lancaster – BCC (Wmns St courses)

Liverpool – 260 pts – ALs **or** ALs+ASs **or** VAs+/-ALs/ASs; (Crim/Soc)
Northumbria – BBD (Soc Sci; Crim/Sociol)
Strathclyde – BCC/BC (Arts/Soc Sci)
Swansea – 260 pts 18u – BCC–CCC/BB **or** ALs+ASs **or** VAs+/-ALs/ASs; (Early Child St)

240 pts **Aberdeen** – CCC (Fac Soc Sci courses)
Anglia – 240 pts approx (Wmns St – joint)
Bangor – 240 pts – 3ALs **or** VAs+/-ALs/ASs; gs; (Crim/Hist; Crim/Relig St; Crim Wmns St)
Bradford – 240 pts 12u; gs; (Interd Hum St)
Bristol – CCC; (not gs) (Deaf St)
Bristol UWE – 240–220 pts 12u – ALs **or** ALs+ASs **or** VAs+/-ALs/ASs; (Soc Sci courses)
Brunel – 240 pts approx (Soc Welf St)
Central England – 240 pts 12u – ALs+ASs **or** VAs+/-ALs/ASs; (Crim Just)
Hertfordshire – 240–220 pts 1x12u **or** 2x6u; VAs (contact univ); gs; (App Soc St)
Kent – CCC (Soc Sci)
Kingston – 240 pts (inc 2x6u **or** 1x12u) – ALs **or** ALs+ASs **or** VAs+/-ALs/ASs; (not gs) (Commun Care Mgt; Crim Just St)
Lancaster – CCC (App Soc Sci)
Liverpool John Moores – 240–180 pts (inc 2ALs **or** VA) – ALs **or** ALs+ASs **or** VAs+/-ALs/ASs; (Wmns St courses)
Nottingham Trent – 240 pts 18u – CCC (VAs contact univ) (Hum Serv; Soc Sci; Crim)
Sheffield Hallam – CCC (App Soc St)

220 pts **Bangor** – 220 pts – 3ALs **or** VAs+/-ALs/ASs; gs; (Wmns St except under **240 pts**)
Bradford – 220 pts 12u; gs; (Soc Welf St; Gndr St/Soc Pol; App Crim Just St)
Central Lancashire – 220–180 pts 12u; gs; (Crim courses)
Coventry – 220 pts (Thrd Wrld Dev St)
Glasgow Caledonian – CCD (Soc Sci)
King Alfred's Winchester (Coll) – 220 pts approx (Soc Cr St)
Liverpool John Moores – 220 pts 3ALs; 200 pts 2ALs – ALs **or** ALs+ASs **or** VA+AL(C); (App Soc St; Crim Just courses)
Middlesex – 220–180 pts approx (Gndr/Wmns St; Soc Sci)
Salford – CCD (Soc Sci)
South East Essex (Coll) – 220–180 pts (Soc Sci)
Sunderland – 220–180 pts approx (Gndr St courses)
Teesside – 220–160 pts approx (Soc Sci courses)
Wolverhampton – 220–160 pts 12u – DDD–CDE/CC **or** CD+d **or** VA12u CC; gs; (Wmns St)

200 pts **Buckinghamshire Chilterns (UC)** – 200–160 pts approx (Crimt/Sociol)
Central England – 200 pts approx (Soc Pol St)
Central Lancashire – 200–180 pts 12u; gs; (Deaf St courses; Race Eth St)
Cheltenham & Glos (CHE) – 200–140 pts approx (Wmns St courses)
Chester (Coll) – 200 pts approx (D psy/sociol/geog) (Soc Sci)
Hertfordshire – 200–160 pts approx (Soc Sci)
Kingston – 200–180 pts 2x6u; gs; (Wmns St; Soc Welf)
London Guildhall – 200–180 pts approx (Soc Pol Mgt)
Luton – 200 pts approx (App Soc St)
Manchester Met – CDD/CC **or** ALs+ASs **or** VAs+/-ALs/ASs; (Hum/Soc St; App Soc St/Spo)
Manchester Met – CDD/CC(inc C); Crim/Sociol)
Plymouth – 200 pts approx (Soc Rsch courses)
Salford – 200 pts approx (Sociol Econ)
Staffordshire – 200 pts (inc 160 pts from 2x6u); gs; (App Soc St; Crim/Dvnc/Soty)

180 pts	**Chichester (UC)** – 180 pts (inc AL) (Child St; Soc St)
	Coventry – 180 pts approx (Wmns St/Soc Pol; Wmns St/Sociol; Wmns St/Hum Res Mgt)
	Derby – 180 pts approx (Soc Cult St; Sociol)
	East London – 180 pts approx (Soc Sci)
	Huddersfield – 180–160 pts approx (App Soc St)
	Napier – CDE/CC (Soc Sci; Soc/Mgt Sci)
	Northumbria – 180–160 pts approx (Child St Prof Prac)
	Paisley – DDD/CC (Soc Sci; App Soc St)
	Queen Margaret (UC) – BC (Soc Sci Hlth)
	St Martin's (Coll) – CDE/CC (App Soc Sci/Soc Eth)
	St Mary's (Coll) – 180–140 pts approx (Irish St)
160 pts	**Birmingham (CFTCS)** – 12u (inc 1x6u) – CC; (Child Care)
	Birmingham (Westhill) – CC (Race Eth St)
	Canterbury Christ Church (UC) – CC–DD (Soc Sci courses; Early Child St courses)
	De Montfort – 160 pts (inc 2ALs or VA12u) – ALs or ALs+ASs or VAs+/- ALs/ASs; (App Soc St)
	Derby – 160 pts 12u – CC or DD+ee or VAs CC+/-ALs/ASs; gs; (Soc/Cult St)
	Doncaster (Coll) – CC or VA12u CC (Soc Leg St; Crim St; App Soc Sci)
	Leeds (Bretton Hall) – CC–CD (Soc St)
	Lincolnshire & Humberside – 160 pts (App Soc Sci)
	Manchester Met – CC (inc Fr for Int St) (Crim Sociol; Int St/Soc Sci; Soc Sci)
	North London – 160 pts 1x12u or 2x6u; (Wmns St)
	Southampton (Inst) – 160 pts (Soc Commun St; Soc Sci)
	Westminster – CC (Soc Sci)
140 pts	**Abertay Dundee** – CD (Soc Sci)
	East London – CD–DD (Thrd Wrld St; Wmns St courses)
	Edge Hill (CHE) – CC–DD (App Soc Sci; Wmns St/Modn Euro St; Commun Race Rel)
	Newport (UWCN) – 140–120 pts – ALs or ALs+ASs or VAs+/-ALs/ASs; (Commun Just; Comm St; Soc Welf)
	Robert Gordon – CD (App Soc Sci)
	Sunderland – CD; gs; (Soc Sci; App Soc Sci)
	Swansea – 140 pts – ALs or ALs+ASs or VAs+/-ALs/ASs; (1) (Fdn Soc St overseas students)
	Warrington (CI) – 140 pts (not AS only); gs; (App Soc St)
120 pts	**Bath Spa (UC)** – DD (Soc Sci)
	Bath Spa (UC) – DD–EE (Irish St – Comb)
	Edge Hill (CHE) – DD (App Soc Sci; Disab Commun St/App Soc Sci)
	Surrey Roehampton – 120 pts approx – ALs or ALs+ASs; (Wmns St; Child/Soty)
100 pts	**and below**
	Barnsley (Coll) – 100 pts 12u – 2ALs or ALs+ASs or VAs+/-AL/ASs; gs; (Soc St Comb)
	Bell (CT) – DE (Soc Sci)
	Solihull (Coll) – EE (Cult St)
	South Devon (Coll) – (Soc Sci)
	Swansea (IHE) – 100 pts approx (Soc St Comb)
	UHI (Inverness/Moray/Perth) – (Soc Sci via DipHE, HND, HNC)
	Worcester (UC) – 80 pts 12u – EE or ALs+ASs or VAs; gs; (Wmns St)
	Leeds Met – (contact university)

Diploma of Higher Education courses
Barnsley (Coll); Blackburn (Coll); Burnley (Coll) (Child St); City of Bristol (Coll); East London; Edge Hill (CHE); Manchester Met; Northumbria 200 pts; Nottingham Trent; Oxford Brookes (Westminster); UHI; Wiltshire (Coll); Wolverhampton.

Higher National Diploma courses
> Aberdeen (Coll); Barnsley (Coll) (Care Prac); Bell (CT); Dewsbury (Coll); Plymouth; Somerset (CAT); UHI (Perth); Worcester (UC); Yorkshire Coast (CFHE).

Alternative Offers:

IB offers: Aberdeen 30 pts; Birmingham (Westhill) 28 pts; Bradford (Peace St) 30 pts; City H655 S655; East Anglia 30 pts; Edinburgh 32–30 pts; Lampeter 24 pts; Sheffield Hallam 24 pts; Strathclyde 28 pts.

Irish offers: Aberdeen BBBB; Bradford BBBBCC; Bristol UWE CCCC; East Anglia CCCCC; Kingston CCCC; Manchester Met CCCCC; Nottingham Trent BBCCC; Sheffield Hallam BBCC.

Scottish Qualifications: Aberdeen BBBB; Edinburgh AAAA–BBBB; Glasgow BBBB/AAB; Glasgow Caledonian BBBC/BBB; Paisley BBB; Strathclyde (5th yr) BBBB, (6th yr) BBBBB.

Overseas applicants: East Anglia Pre-sessional courses in English and study skills. **Robert Gordon** High standard of English required.

CHOOSING YOUR COURSE (See also **Ch.1**)

> **Subject information:** Most Social Sciences/Studies courses will take a broad-brush view of aspects of society, for example, economics, politics, history, social psychology and urban studies. Applied Social Studies usually focuses on practical and theoretical preparation for a career in social work. Peace Studies covers politics, sociology, international relations, conflict and democracy, Third World politics, peace and security, some of which are degree subjects in their own right (see relevant tables). Women's Studies courses cover women's experiences, achievements and gender relationships. These courses are particularly popular with mature students, and some universities and colleges offer shortened degree courses for those with relevant work experience (for example, Brunel University with its Applied Social Studies and Social Welfare courses).

Special features: Bradford In second and third years modules can be selected from Economics or up to 25% content from other science subjects or languages. **Bristol UWE** Common first year allowing for delayed choice from 24 different programmes. **City** (Soc Sci) Unit degree schemes with students specialising in a single subject – economics, psychology or sociology or a combination from these and others, for example philosophy, media studies, health, accountancy. **Coventry** Other modules include employment and industrial studies, health studies, European studies and equal opportunities. **Durham** (Comb Hons) Three or four subjects taken from a choice of 11 subjects including management studies, politics, economics, archaeology and psychology. **Glasgow** Six subjects taken in first and second years; degree choice in third and fourth years. **Newcastle** Course covers sociology, anthropology, politics, economics and psychology. **Nottingham** (Soc/Cult St) Social science core with opportunities to take Arts Faculty modules. **Nottingham Trent** Four disciplines are initially studied – economics, psychology, politics and sociology. In second and third years students specialise within these disciplines. **Plymouth** First year offers a Foundation course or a combination of two or three subjects. In second year students embark on pathways leading to a Single Honours degree in Politics, Sociology or Social Policy. A language option is available. **Sheffield Hallam** (App Soc St) Course covers sociology, psychology, social work, health studies, equal opportunities; career related options in third year. Social work qualification in fourth year. **Strathclyde** Five subjects in first year; two subjects in second year. Specialisations in third and fourth years. Faculty, not subject, admission. *NOW CHECK PROSPECTUSES AND WEB SITES.*

Top universities and colleges (Teaching Quality) (see Ch.4): Edinburgh; Lancaster; not all institutions assessed.

Top universities and colleges (Research) (see Ch.4): Bradford.

Study opportunities abroad: Bradford; Bristol UWE; Cheltenham & Glos (CHE); Derby; Edinburgh; Essex; Glasgow Caledonian; Hertfordshire; Hull; Kingston; Lancaster; Leeds (Child St); London Guildhall; Manchester Met; Robert Gordon; Salford; Strathclyde; Sunderland; Surrey Roehampton; Teesside; Westminster; Wolverhampton; Worcester (UC).

Work opportunities abroad: Bradford; Derby; Hull; King Alfred's Winchester (Coll); Leeds (Child St); Manchester Met; Robert Gordon; Salford.

ADMISSIONS INFORMATION

Number of applicants per place (approx): Abertay Dundee 1; Aston 5; Bangor 10; Bath Spa (UC) 4; Bradford 15, (Peace St) 5; Bristol (Early Child St) 13; Bristol UWE 5; Cambridge 3.8; City 9; Cornwall & Duchy (Coll) 2; Coventry 7; De Montfort 1; Durham 3; East London 10; Edge Hill (CHE) 5; Glasgow Caledonian 9; Hertfordshire 6; Hull 5; Kingston 5; Liverpool 13; Manchester Met 10; Middlesex 26; Nottingham 16; Nottingham Trent 5, (Hum/Educ) 2, (App Soc St) 15; Paisley 5; St Martin's (Coll) 4; Salford 12; Sheffield Hallam 33; South Bank 3; Staffordshire 1; Strathclyde 9; Sunderland 11; Surrey Roehampton 6; Swansea 8; Westminster 14.

Planning your UCAS personal statement (see Ch.4): The Social Sciences/Studies subject area covers several topics (see above under **Subject information**). Focus on these (or some of these) stating your main areas of interest when completing your UCAS form. Work experience, personal goals, motivation to follow the course. See under separate subject headings, for example, **Social Policy and Administration**, **Sociology**, **Geography**, **Economics**, **Politics** for further information. **Birmingham (Westhill)** Work with children. Understanding of multi-cultural environments. Evidence of commitment to study, especially developing personal reading of 'good fiction'. **Bristol** Evidence of a bright, lively mind.

Selection interviews (see Ch.4): Aberdeen (No); Anglia; Bangor (No); Birmingham; Birmingham (Westhill); Bradford (No); Bristol UWE (No); Brunel; City (No); Coventry (W) (T); De Montfort (No); Doncaster (Coll) (W) (T); Durham; East London; Edge Hill (CHE); Essex; Glasgow Caledonian; Hertfordshire (No); Hull; Kingston (T); Lampeter; Manchester Met (some); Napier (No); Newcastle; Newport (UWCN); Nottingham Trent (No); Paisley (No); Robert Gordon (some); St Martin's (Coll); Salford; Sheffield (No); Sheffield Hallam (No); South Bank (W) (T); Staffordshire; Sunderland; Surrey Roehampton; Westminster; Worcester (UC) (No); York (some).

Interview questions (see Ch.4): Past questions have included: How do you think religion should be presented to people? Define democracy. What is the role of the Church in nationalistic aspirations? Does today's government listen to its people? Questions on current affairs. How would you change the running of your school? What are the faults of the Labour Party/Conservative Party? Do you agree with the National Lottery? Is money from the National Lottery being well spent? Give examples of how the social services have failed. **Cambridge (Robinson)** 'The main interview is to assess potential. Achievement is measured far more by school reports and the details on the Preliminary Application Form. The interview consists of three main elements. Firstly, the applicant is asked to think about issues which raise questions relating to the four topics in Part I of the course. He or she has to think about and discuss a current political issue, an anthropological question about ritual or how psychology experiments are carried out, for example. The applicant's views are not assessed, merely their ability to discuss their views in a serious and academic way. Next, the applicant is asked to discuss an unfamiliar and difficult text – handed out prior to interview – in order that interpretation and comprehension skills may be assessed. Lastly, we ask the applicant to bring with them an appropriate school essay.'

Reasons for rejection (non-academic): Stated preference for other institutions. Incompetence in answering questions.

GAP YEAR ADVICE

Some institutions will accept a gap year; check with the admissions tutor. **Kingston** Not recommended; **Manchester Met** Not encouraged; **Swansea** Consult us first.

Institutions willing to defer entry after A-Levels: Aston; Bradford; Bristol UWE; Canterbury Christ Church (UC); Cheltenham & Glos (CHE); Coventry; East London; Edge Hill (UC); Glasgow Caledonian; Hertfordshire; King Alfred's Winchester (Coll); Kingston; Lancaster; Lincolnshire & Humberside; London Guildhall; Luton; Manchester Met; Newport (UWCN); North London; Nottingham; Paisley; Robert Gordon; Sheffield Hallam; South Bank (prefer not); Sunderland; Surrey Roehampton; Swansea.

AFTER RESULTS ADVICE

Institutions which may accept the same points score after A-Levels: Aberdeen (No); Anglia (No); Bradford; Bristol UWE; Central Lancashire; Coventry; Durham; East London; Edge Hill (CHE); Essex; Hertfordshire; Hull (No); Kent (No); Kingston; Leeds; Lincolnshire & Humberside; Liverpool; Liverpool John Moores (No); Manchester Met; Newcastle; North London; Nottingham Trent (No); Sheffield Hallam (perhaps); South Bank; Staffordshire; Sunderland; Surrey Roehampton; Westminster.

Institutions which may accept lower grades/points score after A-Levels: Bristol UWE; Cheltenham & Glos (CHE); Coventry; Durham (2 pts); East London; Hertfordshire; Leeds; Lincolnshire & Humberside; London Guildhall; Newport (UWCN); Paisley; Sheffield Hallam (perhaps); Surrey Roehampton.

Offers to applicants repeating A-Levels: Higher Aston, Bristol UWE, City, Essex, Salford (possibly), Swansea; **Same** Anglia, Bath Spa (UC), Bradford, Cheltenham & Glos (CHE), Coventry, Durham, Leeds, Liverpool, London Guildhall, Manchester Met, Newport (UWCN), Nottingham Trent, St Martin's (Coll), South Bank, Surrey Roehampton.

Probable vacancies from June 2001 and in Clearing (see Ch.4): A large number of universities and colleges declared vacancies last year on single and joint Honours courses.

NEW GRADUATE DESTINATIONS AND EMPLOYMENT (1999 HESA) (see **Ch.4**)

See also **Social Policy and Administration, Social Work** and **Sociology**. Of 315 graduates taking combined courses, 158 went into full-time employment, 58 went on to further study and 32 were believed to be unemployed.

SOCIAL WORK (including **Social Welfare**; see also **Community Studies** and **Social Policy and Administration**)

NB The information supplied by the universities and colleges this year varies considerably and the offers listed below should be used as a first source of reference only. Many institutions will accept combinations of Advanced (AL), Advanced Subsidiary (AS) and Vocational Advanced (VA) level qualifications to achieve the required points total, but applicants must check web sites and prospectuses for full details of all offers. Grades and points totals shown should be regarded as the minimum levels to be achieved, but offers may be adjusted downwards when results are known. The points totals shown to the left of the institutions are for ease of reference only. It must not be assumed that tariff points are always used by institutions or that they can be substituted for an offer in grades. The level of an offer is not necessarily indicative of the quality of a course. To calculate your offers see Chapter 4 and the inside fold of the back cover.

Special subject requirements/preferences: GCSE: English and mathematics usually required.

300 pts	**Hull** – 300–260 pts (Soc Wk/Soc Pol incl DipSW)
	Ulster – BBB (Soc Wk inc DipSW)
290 pts	**Southampton** – 290 pts – 2ALs (160 pts min)+ALs/ASs **or** VAs+/-AL/ASs; (not gs) (Soc Wk St/Soc Pol)
280 pts	**Bradford** – 280 pts 12u; gs; (App Soc Sci+Dip SW)

260 pts	**Bath** – 260 pts approx (Soc Wk/App Soc St)
	Bristol – BCC **or** BB+cc **or** VA12u BC+AL(C); gs; (Soc Wk/Soc Welf inc DipSW)
	Brunel – 260–20 pts 2x6u (inc 2 yrs exp) – ALs **or** ALs+ASs **or** VAs+/- ALs/ASs; (Soc Wk)
	Dundee – BCC/BB (Soc Wk)
	Edinburgh – BCC (1 sitting); (not gs) (Soc Wk)
	Lancaster – BCC (Soc Wk inc DipSW)
	Stirling – BCC (Soc Wk)
240 pts	**Hertfordshire** – 240–220 pts 1x12u **or** 2x6u – VAs (contact univ); gs; (Soc Wk inc DipSW)
	Nottingham Trent – 240 pts 18u – CCC; gs; min age 19 yrs 3 mths (Soc Wk inc DipSW)
220 pts	**King Alfred's Winchester (Coll)** – 220 pts 12u – 2ALs **or** ALs+ASs **or** VAs+/ -ALs/ASs; gs; (Soc Care St)
	Middlesex – 220–180 pts approx (Soc Sci inc DipSW)
	Teesside – 220 pts approx (Soc Wk/Learn Disab)
	Warrington (CI) – 220–200 pts approx (Prof St (Soc Wk))
200 pts	**Kingston** – 200 pts approx (Commun Care Mgt; Crim Just St; Fam Child Care St; Soc Wk)
	Northumbria – 200 pts approx (Soc Wk) M
	Plymouth – 200 pts approx (Soc Wk/Soc Pol inc DipSW)
	Staffordshire – 200 pts (inc 160 pts from 2x6u); gs; Soc Wk Dip)
180 pts	**Anglia** – 180 pts approx (Soc Wk)
	Bournemouth – 180 pts – ALs **or** VA (hlth sc); (Soc Wk + DipSW/Dip/HE)
	Lincolnshire & Humberside – 180 pts (Soc Wk; Soc Wk/Soc Welf)
	Luton – 180 pts approx (Commun Mgt)
	St Mark & St John (Coll) – 180 pts approx (Commun St courses)
160 pts	**Central England** – CC (Soc Wk)
	Central Lancashire – 160 pts 12u (plus interview+police clearance) – ALs **or** ALs+ASs **or** VAs+/-ALs/ASs; gs; (Soc Wk courses)
	Chichester (UC) – 160 pts (inc AL) (Soc Wk St)
	Coventry – CC–BD (Soc Wk inc DipSW; Soc Wk; Soc Welf)
	Glasgow Caledonian – CC; (not gs) (Soc Wk)
	Manchester Met – 160 pts approx (App Commun St)
	North London – 160 pts 1x12u **or** 2x6u; (Soc Wk)
	Sheffield Hallam – CC (Soc Wk St)
140 pts	**Bolton (IHE)** – CD (Commun St courses)
	Newport (UWCN) – 140 pts approx (Soc Welf courses)
	Robert Gordon – CD (Soc Wk)
	Sunderland – 140 pts; gs; (Soc Welf)
120 pts	**and below**
	Bradford (Coll) – (Soc Commun Care courses; Commun Youth Commun Dev)
	Buckinghamshire Chilterns (UC) – (Soc Wk St min age 20 – contact Admissions Tutor)
	Derby – 80 pts 12u – EE **or** EE+ee **or** VAs+/-ALs/ASs; (App Soc Wk)
	Edge Hill (CHE) – DD (Soc Wk St)
	Huddersfield – EE **or** E+ee **or** VA12u **or** VA6u; wk exp/min age 19; (Soc Wk)
	Cardiff (UWI) – (Commun St (Soc Wk) – contact Admissions Tutor)
	Leeds Met – (contact university)
	Liverpool John Moores – (Yth Commun Dev – contact Admissions Tutor)
	Reading – (Commun/Yth St – contact Admissions Tutor)
	Salford – EE (Soc Wk inc DipSW)
	Strathclyde – DD (BA+DipSW)
	Warrington (CI) – 80 pts- ALs+ASs (not ASs only); gs; Soc Wk)
	Warwickshire (Coll) – 40 pts 6u; (Fdn Soc Wk/Welf)

Diploma of Higher Education courses
    Birmingham; De Montfort (Soc Wk); Northumbria; Suffolk (Coll).

Higher National Diploma courses (England)

Bradford (Coll); Brooklands (Coll) (Care; Couns); Bromley (Coll) (Couns) gs; Buckinghamshire Chilterns (UC); Cardiff (UWI); Cheltenham & Glos (CHE); Colchester (Inst) (Hlth Soc Care); Cornwall & Duchy (Coll); Crawley (Coll); De Montfort; Dewsbury (Coll) (Soc Care); Dudley (CT); Durham; Gloucestershire (CAT); King Alfred's Winchester (Coll); Liverpool (CmC); North West Kent (Coll); North Worcestershire (Coll); Northern (Coll) contact admissions tutor; Northumbria; Oldham (Coll); Oxford Brookes; Plymouth; St Helens (Coll); Somerset (CAT); Stockport (CFHE) (Soc Care); West Herts (Coll); Wigan & Leigh (Coll); Worcestershire (CHE); Yorkshire Coast (CFHE).

Alternative Offers:

Scottish Qualifications: Dundee BBBC; Edinburgh BBBCC; Glasgow Caledonian BBB; Robert Gordon BCC; Stirling BBBC; Strathclyde CCC.

CHOOSING YOUR COURSE (See also **Ch.1**)

Subject information: Social Work courses which lead to careers in social work overlap those in Applied Social Studies, Social Policy and Administration and Community Studies and Health Studies (see also these tables) which should also be considered. Check for possible future changes in training for social work careers with the Central Council for Education and Training in Social Work (see **Appendix 1**). Full details of all qualifying Social Work courses and the method of application can be obtained from the Social Work Admissions System (SWAS), UCAS, Rosehill, New Barn Lane, Cheltenham, Glos GL52 3LA. See also **Appendix 1**.

Special features: Cardiff (UWI) (Commun St (Soc Wk)) Minimum age for applicants 20. **Coventry** Specialisms in child care and community care. **Liverpool John Moores** Covers social work practice, probation, educational welfare, child psychology, voluntary agencies. **North London** (Soc Wk) Minimum age 21. *NOW CHECK PROSPECTUSES AND WEB SITES.*

Top universities and colleges (Research) (see Ch.4): Bristol; East Anglia; Edinburgh; Huddersfield; Keele; Lancaster; Leicester; Stirling; Swansea; Warwick; York.

ADMISSIONS INFORMATION

Numbers of applicants per place (approx): Bath 11; Bradford 10; Central Lancashire 8; Coventry 22; North London 27; Sheffield Hallam 9.

Planning your UCAS personal statement (see Ch.4): This should show motivation for social work, relevant work experience, awareness of the demands of social work and give relevant personal information, for example disabilities. Previous relevant experience in Social Work preferred in most cases. See also **Social Policy and Administration**. See also **Appendix 1**.

Selection interviews (see Ch.4): Bradford (W); Coventry (W); Sheffield Hallam; most courses.

Interview questions (see Ch.4): See **Social Policy and Administration**.

GAP YEAR ADVICE

Since qualified social workers are not able to practise until they are 22, institutions actively encourage a year out.

AFTER RESULTS ADVICE

Institutions which may accept the same points score after A-Levels: Coventry; Hertfordshire.

Institutions which may accept lower grades/points score after A-Levels: Bath (No); Hertfordshire.

Probable vacancies from June 2001 and in Clearing (see Ch.4): Contact all universities and colleges since some vacancies are likely.

NEW GRADUATE DESTINATIONS AND EMPLOYMENT (1999 HESA) (see **Ch.4**)

In a survey of 1266 graduates, 849 were in full-time employment (with over 400 in professional work, health, social services and public administration) and 140 in part-time work, 82 went into further study and 65 were reported to be unemployed.

SOCIOLOGY (see also **Social Studies/Science**)

NB The information supplied by the universities and colleges this year varies considerably and the offers listed below should be used as a first source of reference only. Many institutions will accept combinations of Advanced (AL), Advanced Subsidiary (AS) and Vocational Advanced (VA) level qualifications to achieve the required points total, but applicants must check web sites and prospectuses for full details of all offers. Grades and points totals shown should be regarded as the minimum levels to be achieved, but offers may be adjusted downwards when results are known. The points totals shown to the left of the institutions are for ease of reference only. It must not be assumed that tariff points are always used by institutions or that they can be substituted for an offer in grades. The level of an offer is not necessarily indicative of the quality of a course. To calculate your offers see Chapter 4 and the inside fold of the back cover.

Special subject requirements/preferences: A-Level: Sociology is not necessarily a requirement at A-Level. **GCSE:** English and mathematics usually required. **Bath** Majority of A*, A and B grades. **London (LSE)** A*, A and B grades.

360 pts and above
  Cambridge – Offers, mainly in grades, vary between colleges (Soc Pol Sci)
  Oxford – Offers vary between candidates (Hum Sci (Sociol))
320 pts Bristol – ABB–BCC; (not gs) (Sociol/Phil)
  Brunel – 320–280 pts 2x6u – ALs **or** ALs+ASs **or** VAs+/-ALs/ASs – (not gs) (Sociol; Sociol/Psy; Sociol/Soc Anth; Sociol/Comm)
  Durham – ABB (Law/Sociol; Soc Sci Comb; Sociol/Hist; Sociol; Econ/Sociol)
300 pts Bristol – BBB; (not gs) (Sociol; Sociol/Euro)
  Cardiff – BBB/AA (Sociol/Psy)
  Durham – BBB (Pol/Sociol)
  East Anglia – 300–280 pts 18u (inc BB/200 pts+C) – ALs **or** ALs+ASs **or** VAs+/-ALs/ASs; gs (Sociology courses)
  Edinburgh – BBB (1 sitting) (not gs) (Sociology courses)
  Essex – 300–280 pts 18u – BB+AL/2ASs **or** VA12u (hlth sc) BB; gs; (Sociology)
  Leeds – BBB **or** BB+bb; gs; (Sociology courses)
  London (LSE) – 300 pts approx (Sociology)
  London (RH) – BBB (Sociol/Econ; Sociol/Euro Lang)
  Manchester – BBB–BBC (Sociology courses)
  Sussex – BBB–BCC (Sociology courses)
  York – 300–260 pts 21–18u – BBC+c **or** BCC+c; (Sociol; Pol/Sociol; Phil/Sociol; Econ/Sociol)
290 pts Southampton – 290 pts 21u (inc 180 pts ALs); (Sociology courses)
280 pts Bangor – 280–260 pts – BBC **or** VA12u AA; gs; (Sociol/Psy; Sociol/Phys Educ)
  Birmingham – BBC (Sociology)
  Cardiff – BBC/AB (Sociol/Ind Rel; Sociol/Econ; Sociol/Law)

Durham – BBC (Sociol/Anth)
Exeter – 280 pts 18u – BBC **or** BB+cc **or** BC+bb **or** VAs (contact univ); gs;
(Soc with Ital/Span/Ger/Fr)
Glasgow – BBC (Sociology courses)
Hull – BBC–CCC (Sociology courses)
Kent – 280pts approx (Sociology)
Newcastle – BBC–BCC (Sociology)
Nottingham – BBC **or** BB+cc; gs; (Sociology courses)
Oxford Brookes – BBC (Sociol/Telecomm)
Sheffield – BBC (Sociol/Jap St; Sociol/Soc Pol)
Swansea – 280 pts 18u – BBC–BCC **or** ALs+ASs **or** VAs+/-ALs/ASs;
(Sociology courses)
York – BBC–BCC (Sociology courses)

260 pts **Aston** – 260–240 pts approx (Sociology Comb Hons)
Bath – BCC+AS; gs; (Sociology courses)
Belfast (Queen's) – BCC (BSc Econ Sociology)
Cardiff – BCC/BB (Sociol; Sociol/Soc Pol; Sociol/Educ)
Durham – BCC (Sociol/Law; Sociol/Soc Pol)
Exeter – 260 pts 18u – BCC **or** BC+bc **or** VAs (contact univ); gs; (Sociol;
Sociol/Russ (GCSE Russ reqd)/Euro St
Keele – BCC/BB–BC **or** equiv AS accepted; gs; (Sociol/Soc Anth/HR Mgt)
Lancaster – 260 pts approx (Sociology)
Leeds, Trinity & All Saints (Coll) – BCC–CCD (Sociology courses)
Leicester – 260 pts 18u – BCC; gs; (Sociology)
Liverpool – 260 pts – ALs **or** ALs+ASs **or** VAs+/-ALs/ASs; (App Sociol; Sociol/
Soc Pol)
London (Gold) – BCC (Sociology courses)
Loughborough – 260 pts approx (Sociology)
Northumbria – BBD (Crim/Sociol)
Oxford Brookes – BCC–DD (Sociol Stats)
Reading – BCC (Sociology)
Stirling – BCC/BB (Sociol/Mgt Sci)
Strathclyde – BCC (Sociology)
Surrey – 260 pts 18u – BCC **or** ALs+ASs **or** VAs (depends on subj); (not gs)
(Sociol; App Psy/Sociol)
Ulster – BCC (Sociology)

240 pts **Aberdeen** – CCC (Sociology courses)
Bradford – 240 pts 12u; gs; (Sociol; Sociol/Soc Psy)
Bristol UWE – 240–200 pts 18u pref/12u – ALs **or** ALs+ASs **or** VAs+/-ALs/
ASs; (Sociology courses)
City – 3x6u – CCC; ASs/VAs (contact univ); (not gs) (Sociol; Sociol/Econ;
Sociol/Media St; Sociol/Psy)
Hertfordshire – 240–200 pts 1x12u **or** 2x6u; gs; (Hum Mod)
Kingston – 240 pts approx (Sociol/Engl Lit; Sociol/Psy)
Liverpool John Moores – 240–180 pts (inc 2ALs **or** VAs) – ALs **or** ALs+ASs
or VAs+/-ALs/ASs; (Sociology courses)
Loughborough – 240 pts 12u – 2ALs+AL/2ASs **or** VAs+/-ALs/ASs; gs;
(Sociology)
Portsmouth – 240–200 pts – ALs **or** ALs+ASs **or** VAs; gs; (Sociol courses)
Sheffield Hallam – CCC (Sociology)
Warwick – 240 pts approx (Sociology)
Westminster – 240 pts approx (Sociology courses)

220 pts **Bangor** – 220 pts; 3/2ALs **or** VAs+/-ALs/ASs; (Sociology courses except under
280 pts)
Central Lancashire – 220 pts 12u; gs; (Sociol/Crim/Law)
Kingston – 220–180 pts 2x6u; gs; (Sociology courses)
Luton – 220–180 pts approx (Sociology courses)
Middlesex – 220–180 pts approx (Sociology)

South Bank – 220–180 pts approx (Sociology courses)
Teesside – 220 pts approx (Psy/Sociol)
Wolverhampton – 220–160 pts 12u – DDEE/CC–DD or CD+d/e **or** VA12u CC; gs; (Sociology)
200 pts **Central England** – 200 pts 12u – 2ALs **or** ALs+ASs **or** VAs+/-ALs/ASs; (Sociol; Sociol/Law; Sociol/Pol St; Sociol/Law; Sociol/Psy)
Central Lancashire – 200–180 pts 18u; gs; (Sociol; Sociol/Hist; Sociol/Pol; Sociol/Soc Pol)
Cheltenham & Glos (CHE) – 200–180 pts approx (Sociol St courses)
Kingston – 200 pts approx (Sociol; Sociol/Econ; Sociol/Hist; Sociol/Hist Ideas; Sociol/Pol; Sociol/Wmns St)
Manchester Met – CDD/CC (Sociol/Soc Econ Hist; Sociol/Engl St; Crim Soc; Sociol/Ital)
Northampton (UC) – 200–160 pts approx (Sociol Comb courses)
Plymouth – 200 pts approx (Sociology)
Staffordshire – 200 pts (inc CC) **or** CC+AS(40 pts) **or** VA CC; gs; (Sociology courses)
180 pts **Anglia** – 180–160 pts approx (Sociology courses)
Buckinghamshire Chilterns (UC) – 180–140 pts approx (Sociology courses)
Colchester (Inst) – 180 pts approx (Sociology courses)
De Montfort (Bedford) – 180–160 pts – ALs **or** ALs+ASs **or** VAs+/-ALs/ASs; gs; (Sociology courses)
East London – 180 pts apoprox (Sociology courses)
Glamorgan – 180 pts approx (Sociology courses)
Greenwich – 180 pts approx (Hlth/Sociol courses)
Liverpool Hope (Coll) – 180 pts approx (Sociol Comb courses)
North East Wales (IHE) – 180–120 pts (Sociology courses)
Northumbria – BC (Sociology)
Queen Margaret (UC) – BC (Sociol/Soc Pol/Psy)
160 pts **Bath Spa (UC)** – 160–120 pts 12u – BD **or** ALs+ASs **or** VA12u BD; (not gs) (Sociology Comb)
Coventry – BD–CC (Sociology courses)
Derby – 160 pts 12u – CC **or** DD+ee **or** VAs CC+/-AL/ASs; gs; (Sociology)
Huddersfield – 160 pts 12u – DDE **or** DD+2ASs **or** VAs DD+/-ALs/ASs; gs; (Sociology)
London Guildhall – CC–CD (Sociology courses)
Napier – CC (App Stats/Sociol)
Norwich City (Coll) – 160 pts approx (Sociol Comb courses)
St Mary's (Coll) – 12u – CC–DD **or** VA CC–DD; gs; (Sociology)
Staffordshire – CC (Sociology)
140 pts **Abertay Dundee** – CD (Sociology)
Bolton (IHE) – CD (Sociology courses)
Derby – 140 pts 12u – CD **or** DE+ee **or** VAs CD+/-ALs/ASs; gs; (Sociol Comb Hons)
North London – 140 pts 1x12u **or** 2x6u; (Sociology)
Robert Gordon – CD (App Soc Sci)
St Mark & St John (Coll) – 140 pts approx (Sociology courses)
Sunderland – 140 pts; gs; (Sociology)
120 pts **Bath Spa (UC)** – 120 pts 12u – DD **or** ALs+ASs **or** VA12u DD; (not gs) (Sociology)
Surrey Roehampton – 120 pts (inc 2ALs) – ALs **or** ALs+ASs; (Sociology)
Worcester (UC) – 120 pts 12u – DD **or** ALs+ASs **or** VA12u+/-AL/ASs; gs; (Sociology)

Leeds Met – (contact university)

Diploma of Higher Education courses
80 pts Bath Spa (UC); East London; Greenwich; London Guildhall; Middlesex; Oxford Brookes; Plymouth; Worcester (UC).

Alternative Offers:

EB offers: Liverpool 60%; Northumbria 64%.

IB offers: Aberdeen 30 pts; Aberystwyth 30 pts; Bangor 30 pts; Bath H665 30 pts overall; Birmingham 33–32 pts; Bradford 27 pts; Bristol 28 pts inc 15 pts Highers; Cardiff 30 pts; Cheltenham & Glos (CHE) 26 pts; City H655 S655; Durham 28 pts inc H15 pts; East Anglia 30 pts; Essex 28 pts inc 10 pts in 2 Highers; Exeter 29 pts; Hull 27 pts inc H65; Kent H554; Lancaster 30 pts; Leicester 28 pts; Liverpool 28 pts; London Guildhall 28–24 pts; Loughborough 28 pts; Northumbria 24 pts; Nottingham H554; Sheffield H665 inc English or H665 + S6 English; Surrey 32 pts; Swansea 28 pts; Warwick 34–32 pts; York 28 pts.

Irish offers: Aberdeen BBBB; Bangor BBBCC; Bath BBBB; Brunel BBBCC; East Anglia CCCCC; Keele BBBCC; Liverpool BBCCC; London Guildhall CCCCC; Northumbria BCCCC; Warwick ABBBC.

Scottish Qualifications: Aberdeen BBBB; Abertay Dundee BBC; Bell (CT) (Soc Sci) CC; Edinburgh AABBC–BBBBC; Glasgow ABBB; Glasgow Caledonian (Soc Sci) BBBC; Napier (Maths/Soc) BBC; Paisley (Soc Sci) BBB; Queen Margaret (UC) BBBC; Robert Gordon (App Soc Sci) BCC; Stirling BBBC; Strathclyde BBBB.

Overseas applicants: East Anglia Pre-sessional study skills and English courses available. **Northumbria** Fluency in English required.

CHOOSING YOUR COURSE (See also **Ch.1**)

> **Subject information:** Sociology is the study of societies in general, both in Britain and abroad. Elective subjects offered often include industrial behaviour, crime and deviance, health and illness. Other related degree courses include Anthropology, History, Social Studies, Social Administration, Social Work, Government and Politics.

Special features: Aston A course is offered in the Sociology and Politics of Business course which includes industrial relations, personnel management and management problems. **Bangor** Course covers criminology and penology, law and social policy, health services, community studies, Northern Ireland and gender. Separate scheme for Welsh speakers. **Bath** Subsidiary subjects include psychology, history, politics, philosophy and economics, with elective subjects covering social work, industrial relations and sociology of health, illness, crime, deviance and education. **Brunel** Course covers psychology and social anthropology as well as sociology. **Central England** A modular course is offered in which students select subjects in areas of psychology, law, government and policy studies. **Durham** (Sociol Law) No exemptions from professional training in Law. **Edinburgh** Introduction covers social inequality, social order and deviant behaviour. **Essex** Specialist courses in globalisation, gender, crime, race and health. **Hull** Social anthropolgy is part of the first year course. **Lancaster** In first year the introductory course includes two options from the sociology of class and gender, criminal law, culture and the media. In second and third years subjects include deviance and social control, education and society, health and illness, the sociology of sport, popular culture and race. **Leeds** Sociological theory, sociology of modern Britain, developing countries, methods and gender. **London (RH)** Three main disciplines – social policy, sociology, social administration. **Newcastle** Teaching strengths in contemporary culture, analysis, feminism and equal opportunities. Research strengths in criminal justice system, trade union studies. Six-month placement arranged for those taking Social Research (four-year degree). **Northumbria** Specialisms in criminal justice, information technology and a modern European language. **Portsmouth** Options include psychology, criminology and criminal justice, race and society, social work and society. **Sheffield Hallam** A study of national and international issues. *NOW CHECK PROSPECTUSES AND WEB SITES.*

Top universities and colleges (Teaching Quality) (see Ch.4): Aberdeen; Bath Spa (UC); Birmingham; Bristol; Bristol UWE; Brunel; Cheltenham & Glos (CHE); Durham; Edinburgh; Essex; Exeter; Glasgow; Glasgow Caledonian; Greenwich; Keele; Kent; Kingston;

Lancaster; Liverpool; Liverpool Hope (Coll); London (Gold), (LSE); Loughborough; Manchester; Manchester Met; Oxford Brookes; Reading; St Mark & St John (Coll); Sheffield; Sheffield Hallam; Stirling; Strathclyde; Sussex; Warwick; Worcester (UC); York; not all institutions assessed.

Top universities and colleges (Research) (see Ch.4): Aberdeen; Belfast (Queen's); Birmingham; Bristol UWE; Brunel; Cambridge; Cardiff; City; Edinburgh; Essex; Glasgow; Greenwich; Keele; Lancaster; Leeds; Leicester; London (Gold), (LSE); Loughborough; Manchester; North London; Oxford; Reading; Salford; Sheffield Hallam; Southampton; Stirling; Surrey; Sussex; Warwick; York.

Study opportunities abroad: Aberdeen; Bangor; Bath; Belfast (Queen's); Birmingham; Bristol; Bristol UWE; Central England; Cheltenham & Glos (CHE); City; Coventry; East Anglia; Edinburgh; Glasgow; Greenwich; Huddersfield; Kingston; Lancaster; Leeds; Leicester; London (Gold); London Guildhall; Manchester; Manchester Met; Oxford Brookes; Portsmouth; Salford; Sheffield; Staffordshire; Surrey; Surrey Roehampton; Sussex; Swansea; Teesside; Warwick; Worcester (UC); York.

Work opportunities abroad: Bath; Birmingham; Brunel; Central England; Plymouth; Surrey.

ADMISSIONS INFORMATION

Number of applicants per place (approx): Bangor 6; Bath 9; Birmingham 10; Bristol 12; Brunel 24; Cardiff 5; Central England 12; Cheltenham & Glos (CHE) 8; City 11; De Montfort 6; Durham 13; East Anglia 15; East London 8; Exeter 5; Greenwich 5; Hull 11; Kent 10; Kingston 9; Lancaster 12; Leeds (Psy/Sociol) 35, (Geog/Sociol) 11, (Sociol) 14; Leeds, Trinity & All Saints (Coll) 5; Leicester 6; Liverpool 9; London (Gold) 5, (LSE) 7, (RH) 6; Loughborough 10; Northampton (UC) 10; Northumbria 18; Nottingham 30; Plymouth 9; Portsmouth 12; St Mark & St John (Coll) 13; Southampton 9; Staffordshire 10; Sunderland 5; Surrey 6; Surrey Roehampton 4; Swansea 8; Warwick 20; Worcester (UC) 5; York 12.

Planning your UCAS personal statement (see Ch.4): See **Social Studies/Science**.

Selection interviews (see Ch.4): Aston; Bangor (No); Bath; Bristol; Brunel; Central England; City; Derby; Durham (some); East Anglia (No); East London; Exeter (W); Greenwich (No); Hull; Kent (some); Kingston (No); Lancaster; Leeds; Leeds, Trinity & All Saints (Coll); Leicester; Liverpool; Liverpool Hope (Coll); Liverpool John Moores (No); London (Gold); London Guildhall (No); Loughborough; Newcastle; Nottingham; Portsmouth; St Mary's (Coll); Sheffield Hallam (No); Stirling (No); Sunderland (No); Surrey; Swansea; Warwick (T); York.

Interview questions (see Ch.4): Past questions have included: Why do you want to study Sociology? What books have you read on the subject? How do you see the role of women changing in the next 20 years? **Leeds** Copy of written work requested.

Reasons for rejection (non-academic): Evidence of difficulty with written work. Non-attendance at open days (find out from your universities if your attendance will affect their offers). In the middle of an interview for Sociology a student asked us if we could interview him for Sports Studies instead! **Durham** No evidence of awareness of what the course involves. See also **Social Policy and Administration**.

GAP YEAR ADVICE

Bristol Inform us when you apply; **Cardiff** Apply before departure asking for deferred entry; **Greenwich** Maintain reading; **Kingston** Contact admissions tutor; **Salford** Try to maintain some contact with academic work; **Surrey** Do not apply for deferred entry.

Institutions willing to defer entry after A-Levels: Bangor; Bath; Birmingham; Bradford; Bristol; Bristol UWE; Brunel; Cardiff; Cheltenham & Glos (CHE); Coventry; Derby; Greenwich; Humberside; Kingston (contact Admissions Tutor); Lancaster; Leeds; Leeds, Trinity & All Saints (Coll); Leicester; London (Gold); London Guildhall; Northampton (UC);

Northumbria; Nottingham; Plymouth; Salford; Sheffield (No); Staffordshire (No); Surrey Roehampton; Swansea; Teesside; Warwick; Worcester (UC); York.

AFTER RESULTS ADVICE

Institutions which may accept the same points score after A-Levels: Aberystwyth; Aston; Bangor; Bath; Birmingham; Bradford; Bristol; Brunel; Central England; City; Coventry; Derby; Durham (No); East Anglia; East London; Essex; Exeter; Greenwich; Hull; Kent; Kingston (No); Lancaster; Leeds (No); Leicester; Liverpool; London (Gold); London Guildhall (No); Loughborough; Newcastle; Northampton (UC); Nottingham (No); Portsmouth; Sheffield; Stirling (No); Surrey; Surrey Roehampton; Warwick (No); Worcester (UC); York.

Institutions which may accept lower grades/points score after A-Levels: Bangor; Birmingham; Bristol; Brunel; Cheltenham & Glos (CHE); City; Coventry; Derby; Durham; Essex; Exeter; Leeds, Trinity & All Saints (Coll); Leicester; Liverpool; London (RH); Nottingham; Surrey Roehampton; Swansea; Warwick; York.

Offers to applicants repeating A-Levels: Higher Brunel, East London, Essex, Hull, London Guildhall, Newcastle, Swansea, Warwick; **Possibly higher** Aston, Leeds, Liverpool, Portsmouth, Salford, York; **Same** Bangor, Bath, Bristol, Central England, Cheltenham & Glos (CHE), Coventry, Derby, Durham, Kingston, Lancaster, London (RH), Loughborough, Northumbria, Surrey Roehampton.

Probable vacancies from June 2001 and in Clearing (see Ch.4): A large number of universities and colleges declared vacancies last year in this subject in Clearing. Most institutions are likely to have places.

NEW GRADUATE DESTINATIONS AND EMPLOYMENT (1999 HESA) (see **Ch.4**)

In a survey of 3252 graduates, 1809 secured full-time employment in a wide range of occupations (there were 352 in part-time work), 583 went on to further study or career training and 218 were believed to be unemployed.

SPANISH (see also **Latin-American Studies** and **Modern Languages**)

NB The information supplied by the universities and colleges this year varies considerably and the offers listed below should be used as a first source of reference only. Many institutions will accept combinations of Advanced (AL), Advanced Subsidiary (AS) and Vocational Advanced (VA) level qualifications to achieve the required points total, but applicants must check web sites and prospectuses for full details of all offers. Grades and points totals shown should be regarded as the minimum levels to be achieved, but offers may be adjusted downwards when results are known. The points totals shown to the left of the institutions are for ease of reference only. It must not be assumed that tariff points are always used by institutions or that they can be substituted for an offer in grades. The level of an offer is not necessarily indicative of the quality of a course. To calculate your offers see Chapter 4 and the inside fold of the back cover.

Special subject requirements/preferences: A-Level: Spanish is required at the following universities with the asking grade shown in brackets: **Bristol** (B), **Leeds** (B) *Ab initio* students accepted but may not progress to single Honours Spanish, **London (Gold)** (B), **(UCL)** (B), **Newcastle** (B), **Southampton** (B), **Stirling** (B), **Swansea** (B). **Curriculum 2000:** Oxford Full A-levels expected. **GCSE: Edinburgh, St Andrews** English, mathematics or science and a foreign language. **London (Gold)** Grade A–B in three subjects. **Oxford, Cambridge** Grade A in most subjects usually preferred.

360 pts   and above
  Cambridge – Offers, mainly in grades, vary between colleges (Modn/Mediev Langs)
  Oxford – Offers vary between candidates (Modn Langs)

350 pts **Southampton** – 350 pts 21u (inc 200 pts inc C Span); (Spanish courses)
340 pts **Belfast (Queen's)** – AAB–BCC (Spanish courses)
　　　　　Bristol – AAB (Pol/Span)
　　　　　Edinburgh – AAB–BBB (Spanish courses)
　　　　　Manchester – AAB (Fr/Span; Ital/Span)
　　　　　St Andrews – AAB–ABB (Spanish courses)
320 pts **Cardiff** – ABB (Cult Crit/Span)
　　　　　Cardiff – ABB–BCC (Spanish courses)
　　　　　Lancaster – ABB–BCC (Spanish courses)
　　　　　Leeds – ABB–BBC (Spanish courses)
　　　　　London (RH) – ABB–BBB (Spanish courses)
　　　　　Nottingham – ABB (Span/Mgt)
　　　　　Sheffield – ABB (Law/Span)
300 pts **Birmingham** – BBB–BBC (Spanish courses)
　　　　　Bristol – BBB–BBC(B in relevant lang); (not gs) (Span/Port; Span/Russ)
　　　　　Bristol UWE – 300–240 pts – (Spanish courses)
　　　　　Durham – 300 pts approx (Arts Comb (Span))
　　　　　Hull – BBB–CCC/BB–BC (Spanish courses)
　　　　　Leicester – 300–260 pts approx (Spanish courses)
　　　　　London (UCL) – BBB–BBC **or** 3ALs+AS/VA; (Hisp St; Span courses)
　　　　　Newcastle – ABC–BBB (Span/Lat Am St (Comb St))
　　　　　Nottingham – BBB–BBC (Hisp St)
　　　　　Sheffield – BBB/AB (Hisp St courses)
280 pts **Aberystwyth** – BBC (Law/Span)
　　　　　Essex – 280–260 pts approx (Lat Am St courses)
　　　　　Exeter – 280 pts 18u – BBC **or** BB+cc **or** BC+bb **or** VAS (contact univ); gs;
　　　　　　(Spanish)
　　　　　Glasgow – BBC (Hisp St courses)
　　　　　Heriot-Watt – BBC (Span/Fr (App Lang/Transl); Span/Ger (Interp Transl))
　　　　　Kent – 280–260 pts – gs; (Spanish courses)
　　　　　Leeds – BBC–BCC (Spanish courses)
　　　　　Liverpool – 280 pts – ALs **or** ALs+ASs **or** VAs+/-ALs/ASs; (Hisp St)
　　　　　London (King's) – BBC+AS **or** BB+bcc (or equiv) (inc B Span); (Hisp St)
　　　　　Loughborough – 280–240 pts approx (Spanish courses)
　　　　　Manchester – 280–260 pts approx (Spanish courses except under **340 pts**;
　　　　　　Hisp St)
　　　　　Newcastle – BBC (Spanish courses except under **300 pts**)
　　　　　Oxford Brookes – BBC–CDD (offer varies with 2nd subject) (Spanish
　　　　　　courses)
　　　　　St Andrews – BBC (Span/Econ)
　　　　　Salford – BBC (Modn Lang/Transl (Spanish courses))
　　　　　Swansea – 280 pts 18u – BBC–BCC/BB **or** ALs+ASs **or** VAs+/-AL/ASs;
　　　　　　(Spanish courses)
　　　　　UMIST – BBC (Span/Chem)
　　　　　Westminster – BBC (Span/Law)
260 pts **Aberystwyth** – 260–220 pts approx (Span/Comp Sci)
　　　　　Bradford – 260 pts 12u (inc AL lang); gs; (Spanish courses)
　　　　　Bristol – BCC (inc modn lang); (not gs) (Hisp St; Spanish courses except
　　　　　　under **300 pts**)
　　　　　Dundee – BCC–CCC (Spanish courses)
　　　　　Greenwich – 260–160 pts approx (Spanish courses)
　　　　　Heriot-Watt – BCC–CCD (Span/Acc; Span/Chem)
　　　　　Stirling – BCC–CCC (Spanish courses)
　　　　　Strathclyde – BCC (Arts/Soc Sci Span)
240 pts **Aberdeen** – CCC (Span/Phys; Span/Theol)
　　　　　Aberystwyth – 240 pts approx (Span; Span/Art Hist; Span/Welsh)
　　　　　Bangor – 240 pts – ALs; VAs (enquire); gs; (Span/Ital)
　　　　　Bradford – CCC/CC (Span/Fr; Span/Pol; Span)

Hertfordshire – 240–200 pts 1x12u **or** 2x6u; gs; (Hum Mod)
London (Gold) – BCD/BC (Span/Lat Am St)
Manchester Met – 240 pts (Acc Fin Euro/Span)
Nottingham Trent – 240 pts approx (Span/Euro Bus St)
Plymouth – 240 pts approx (Span/Int Bus)
South Bank – 240–200 pts approx (Span/Media St courses)
Ulster – CCC (Hum Spanish)
220 pts **Bangor** – 220 pts approx (Fr/Span; Ger/Span)
Cardiff (UWI) – 220 pts approx (Tour/Span)
Central England – 220–200 pts approx (Int Bus Mgt/Span; Mark/Span)
Luton – 220–180 pts approx (Spanish)
Middlesex – 220–180 pts approx (Spanish courses)
Nottingham Trent – 220–180 pts approx (Spanish courses except under **240 pts**)
Sheffield Hallam – CCD (Int Bus/Span)
Sunderlaand – 220–180 pts approx (Span St courses)
200 pts **Buckingham** – 200 pts (Spanish courses)
Chester (Coll) – 200–180 pts – ALs (160 pts inc C)+AS(40–20 pts) **or** VAs (160 pts inc C); gs; (Spanish Comb courses)
Coventry – 200 pts approx (Spanish courses)
Liverpool John Moores – 200 pts approx (Span/Fr; Span/Ger)
London Guildhall – CDD–DD (Spanish courses)
Northampton (UC) – 200–160 pts approx (Spanish courses)
Plymouth – 200 pts approx (Span/Bus Econ; Geog Span)
Portsmouth – 200 pts – ALs **or** ALs+ASs **or** VAs; gs; (Span St; Span/Lat Am St; Span/Ital)
Salford – CDD (Span Arbc)
Salford – 200 pts approx (Span/Sociol; Span/Pol; Span/Ital)
Staffordshire – 200 pts (inc CC) **or** CC+AS(40 pts) **or** VA CC; gs; (Spanish courses)
180 pts **Buckinghamshire Chilterns (UC)** – 180–140 pts approx (Spanish courses)
Central Lancashire – 180 pts (inc GCSE Span) – ALs **or** ALs+ASs **or** VAs+/ -ALs/ASs; gs; (Span/Bus)
De Montfort (Leicester) – 180 pts (inc AL lang pref) – ALs **or** ALs+ASs **or** VAs+/-ALs/ASs; (not gs) (Hisp St)
East London – 180 pts approx (Spanish courses)
European Bus Sch (London) – 180 pts approx (Span/Int Bus)
Kingston – 180 pts 2x6u (inc AL Span 80 pts; (Spanish courses)
Leeds, Trinity & All Saints (Coll) – 180–160 pts approx (Span/Mgt; Span/Media)
Manchester Met – BC (Spanish)
Surrey Roehampton – 180 pts 12u (inc 2ALs) – ALs **or** ALs+ASs; (Spanish)
Wolverhampton – 220–160 pts 12u – DDD–CDE/CC **or** CD+e **or** VA12u CC; gs; Spanish courses)
160 pts **Anglia** – 160 pts 12u (inc C lang); gs; (Span Comb)
North London – 160 pts 1x12u **or** 2x6u; (Span/Lat Am Comb St)
Northumbria – CC (Span/Fr; Span/Ger; Span/Inf St)
Westminster – CC (Spanish courses except under **280 pts**)
140 pts **Derby** – CD **or** DE+ee **or** VAs CD+/-ALs/ASs; (Spanish Comb)
Southampton (Inst) – 140 pts approx (Antiq/Hist/Cllct/Span; Bus/Span)
Thames Valley – 140 pts approx (Spanish courses)

Diploma of Higher Education courses
 80 pts Middlesex.

Higher National Diploma courses (with Bus St)
140 pts **and below**
Northumbria; Sheffield Hallam; Southampton (Inst); Thames Valley.

Alternative Offers:

IB offers: Aberdeen 30 pts; Aberystwyth 32 pts; Bradford 24 pts; Bristol 32 pts; Cardiff 30 pts, H 15 pts; Edinburgh H655; Exeter 31 pts; Heriot-Watt 34 pts; Hull 28 pts; Kent 30–28 pts; Kingston 28 pts; Leeds 28 pts; London (Gold) 24 pts, (RH) 30 pts, (UCL) 32 pts; Liverpool 28 pts inc 15 pts Highers; Portsmouth 25 pts; St Andrews 28 pts; Sheffield H665; Swansea 28 pts.

Scottish Qualifications: Aberdeen BBBB; Dundee BBBC–BBCC; Edinburgh ABBB–BBBB; Glasgow BBBB; Heriot-Watt AABB; St Andrews BBBB; Stirling BBBC; Strathclyde BBBB.

CHOOSING YOUR COURSE (See also **Ch.1**)

Subject information: Spanish can be studied by focusing on the language and literature of Spain, although broader courses in Hispanic Studies are available which also include Portuguese and Latin American studies. See also **Appendix 1** under **Modern Languages**.

Special features: Bradford Can be studied with or without A-level Spanish. Options include economics, literature, film or interpreting. **Bristol** Opportunity to learn three languages – Spanish, Portuguese and Catalan. **Cardiff** Spanish and Portuguese fully integrated in School of European Studies which also offers politics, culture and society. **Leeds** Innovative approaches to language teaching. Integrated area studies course, comprising study of language, culture, history or geography of Iberian Peninsula and Latin America including Portuguese-speaking countries. Subsidiary subject taken in first year. **Newcastle** Emphasis on language skills. **Sheffield** Emphasis on communication skills and contemporary Spanish and South American affairs. Wide range of options. **Swansea** (Span/Bus St) The Business element occupies one third of the degree. *NOW CHECK PROSPECTUSES AND WEB SITES.*

Top universities and colleges (Teaching Quality) (see Ch.4): Birmingham; Bristol; Cambridge; Hull; Leeds; London (King's), (QM); Newcastle; Northumbria; Nottingham Trent; Oxford; Oxford Brookes; South Bank; Staffordshire; Swansea; not all institutions assessed.

Top universities and colleges (Research) (see Ch.4): (Iberian and Latin American Languages) Aberdeen; Aberystwyth; Belfast (Queen's); Birmingham; Bristol; Cambridge; Cardiff; Edinburgh; Exeter; Glasgow; Hull; Leeds; Liverpool; London (King's), (QM), (UCL); Nottingham; Oxford; St Andrews; Sheffield; Southampton; Swansea.

Study opportunities abroad: Most institutions can arrange placements in Spain or Spanish-speaking countries.

Work opportunities abroad: Most universities and colleges offering four-year courses.

ADMISSIONS INFORMATION

Number of applicants per place (approx): Birmingham 6; Bradford 3; Bristol 7; Cardiff 3; Durham 5; Exeter 5; Hull 14; Leeds 10; Leeds, Trinity & All Saints (Coll) 2; Liverpool 6; London (Gold) 6, (QM) 5, (UCL) 6; Middlesex 2; Newcastle 12; Nottingham 16; Portsmouth 4; Salford 5.

Planning your UCAS personal statement (see Ch.4): Visits to Spanish-speaking countries should be discussed. Study the geography, culture, literature and politics of Spain (or Portugal) and discuss your interests in full. Further information could be obtained from embassies in London. **St Andrews** Evidence of interest. Reasons for choosing the course. See also **Appendix 1** under **Modern Languages**.

Selection interviews (see Ch.4): Bradford; Cambridge; Cardiff (No); De Montfort (No); Durham; Edinburgh (No); Huddersfield; Hull; Kent (No); Kingston; Leeds; Leeds, Trinity & All Saints (Coll); Liverpool; London (Gold) (T), (RH), (UCL); Newcastle (No); Nottingham; Oxford (W 30 mins) (T); Portsmouth (No) (T); St Andrews (No); Sheffield (No); South Bank; Southampton (No); Staffordshire (No); Sunderland (No); Surrey Roehampton (No); Swansea.

Interview questions (see Ch.4): Candidates offering A-level Spanish are likely to be questioned on their A-Level work, their reasons for wanting to take the subject and on their knowledge of Spain and its people. Interest in Spain important for all applicants. **Durham** Looks particularly for evidence of wide reading (outside the syllabus), curiosity and intellectual initiative. **London (Gold)** Diagnostic language tests. **Oxford** A short written test of 30 minutes will be set.

GAP YEAR ADVICE

Bradford Special tutorial assistance is available for deferred entry students; **Cardiff** Spend some time in a Spanish-speaking country.

Institutions willing to defer entry after A-Levels: Aberystwyth; Birmingham; Bradford; Bristol (No); Heriot-Watt; Huddersfield; Hull; Lancaster; Leeds; London (Gold), (UCL); Luton; Newcastle; Nottingham (lengthy stay in a Spanish-speaking country preferred); Portsmouth; South Bank (prefer not); Sussex; Swansea; York.

AFTER RESULTS ADVICE

Institutions which may accept the same points score after A-Levels: Aberdeen; Aberystwyth (Not in the language); Bradford; Durham; Hull; Leeds; Liverpool; Newcastle (No); Nottingham (No); Portsmouth; Sheffield; Stirling (No); Strathclyde; Swansea.

Institutions which may accept lower grades/points score after A-Levels: Aberystwyth; Bradford; Durham; Exeter; Kent; Liverpool; Newcastle; Surrey Roehampton.

Offers to applicants repeating A-Levels: Same Durham, Hull, Leeds, London (RH), Newcastle, Nottingham, Surrey Roehampton, Swansea.

Probable vacancies from June 2001 and in Clearing (see Ch.4): Many single and joint course vacancies were declared last year.

NEW GRADUATE DESTINATIONS AND EMPLOYMENT (1999 HESA) (see **Ch.4**)

Out of 207 graduates surveyed, 103 secured full-time employment (mainly in a variety of business activities), 53 went into further study or career training and 11 were believed to be unemployed.

SPEECH PATHOLOGY/SCIENCES/THERAPY

NB The information supplied by the universities and colleges this year varies considerably and the offers listed below should be used as a first source of reference only. Many institutions will accept combinations of Advanced (AL), Advanced Subsidiary (AS) and Vocational Advanced (VA) level qualifications to achieve the required points total, but applicants must check web sites and prospectuses for full details of all offers. Grades and points totals shown should be regarded as the minimum levels to be achieved, but offers may be adjusted downwards when results are known. The points totals shown to the left of the institutions are for ease of reference only. It must not be assumed that tariff points are always used by institutions or that they can be substituted for an offer in grades. The level of an offer is not necessarily indicative of the quality of a course. To calculate your offers see Chapter 4 and the inside fold of the back cover.

Special subject requirements/preferences: A-Level: London (UCL), **Newcastle** Biology preferred. **Ulster** One subject from English, geography, psychology or a science or mathematics. **GCSE: Central England** At least five subjects at grade A or B. **Manchester Met** Biology grade A–C.

320 pts   **Manchester** – ABB–BBC/AB–BB (Sp Lang Thera)
        Newcastle – ABB–BBB (Sp Lang Sci)
        Sheffield – ABB (Sp Sci)

300 pts **City** – 18u – BBB (inc sci) **or** 2ALs+2ASs **or** VA12u (Hlth SC)+AL; (not gs) (Sp Lang Thera)
London (UCL) – BBB–BBC **or** 3ALs+AS/VA; (Sp Sci; Sp Comm)
Ulster – BBB (Sp Lang Thera)

280 pts **Queen Margaret (UC)** – BBC (Sp Path Thera)
Reading – BBC/CC (Ling/Lang Path)
Strathclyde – BBC (Sp Lang Path)

260 pts **Cardiff (UWI)** – 260 pts approx (Sp Lang Thera)
Central England – 260 pts approx (Sp Lang Thera)
De Montfort (Leicester) – 260–240 pts (inc 2ALs **or** VA12u) – ALs **or** ALs+ASs **or** VA+/-AL/ASs; (Sp Thera)
Manchester – 260 pts approx (Ling/Clin Lang St)
Manchester Met – BCC/BB (Sp Path Thera; Psy/Sp Path)
Reading – BCC (Ling Clin Lang St)

Leeds Met – (contact university)

Alternative Offers:

IB offers: City H655 S555; London (UCL) 32 pts; Manchester Met 28 pts inc biol.

Irish offers: Manchester Met BBBBB.

Scottish Qualifications: Queen Margaret (UC) BBBBB.

Overseas applicants: Manchester Met Good English required because of placement periods.

CHOOSING YOUR COURSE (See also **Ch.1**)

Subject information: Speech Pathology/Sciences/Therapy is the study of speech defects which may be caused by accident, disease or psychological trauma. Courses lead to qualification as a speech therapist. This is one of many medical courses. See also **Medicine** (Subject information). See also **Appendix 1**.

Special features: Cardiff (UWI) Strong emphasis on practical work. **Central England** Knowledge of processes underlying speech and language behaviour in both normal and pathological states. **Newcastle** Multidisciplinary department, substantial clinical practice, active in research, some medical school teaching. **Queen Margaret (UC)** Clinical placements and research projects. Course covers clinical education, linguistics, disordered speech and language, severe learning difficulties, cerebral palsy, stroke. **Strathclyde** Strong community and management areas of study. Practical studies in sport included. *NOW CHECK PROSPECTUSES AND WEB SITES.*

Top universities and colleges (Teaching Quality) (see Ch.4): Cardiff (UWI); not all institutions assessed.

Top universities and colleges (Research) (see Ch.4): London (UCL); Manchester.

Study opportunities abroad: Cardiff (UWI); Central England; London (UCL); Sheffield.

Work opportunities abroad: Queen Margaret (UC); Sheffield.

ADMISSIONS INFORMATION

Number of applicants per place (approx): Cardiff (UWI) 10; Central England 28; City 16; De Montfort 15; London (UCL) 9; Manchester 29; Manchester Met 21; Newcastle 23; Queen Margaret (UC) 12.

Planning your UCAS personal statement (see Ch.4): Contact with speech therapists and visits to their clinics would be an essential part of the preparation for this career. Discuss these contacts in full, together with details of any work experience/shadowing you may have done. **Manchester Met** Observations with speech therapists working with children and adults. See also **Appendix 1**.

Selection interviews (see Ch.4): All institutions. City (No); De Montfort (W) (T – listening ability); London (UCL); Manchester Met (T); Queen Margaret (UC) (T); Sheffield.

Interview questions (see Ch.4): Have you visited a speech therapy clinic? What made you want to become a speech therapist? What type of speech problems are there? What type of person would make a good speech therapist? Interviews often include an ear test (test of listening ability). **Manchester Met** Two essays and a questionnaire.

Reasons for rejection (non-academic): Insufficient knowledge of speech and language therapy. Lack of maturity. Poor communication skills. Written language problems.

GAP YEAR ADVICE

Institutions willing to defer entry after A-Levels: City; De Montfort; London (UCL) (No); Manchester Met; Queen Margaret (UC).

AFTER RESULTS ADVICE

Institutions which may accept the same points score after A-Levels: Central England; City; De Montfort; Manchester Met (No); Newcastle (No); Ulster.

Institutions which may accept lower grades/points score after A-Levels: Central England; City; Sheffield.

Offers to applicants repeating A-Levels: Higher Bradford, Central England; **Possibly higher** Manchester Met; **Same** City, Newcastle, Ulster.

Probable vacancies from June 2001 and in Clearing (see Ch.4): Few vacancies are likely although it is worthwhile contacting all institutions.

NEW GRADUATE DESTINATIONS AND EMPLOYMENT (1999 HESA) (see **Ch.4**)

No data available.

SPORTS STUDIES (including **Sport & Recreational Studies, Sports Science**; see also **Physical Education**)

NB The information supplied by the universities and colleges this year varies considerably and the offers listed below should be used as a first source of reference only. Many institutions will accept combinations of Advanced (AL), Advanced Subsidiary (AS) and Vocational Advanced (VA) level qualifications to achieve the required points total, but applicants must check web sites and prospectuses for full details of all offers. Grades and points totals shown should be regarded as the minimum levels to be achieved, but offers may be adjusted downwards when results are known. The points totals shown to the left of the institutions are for ease of reference only. It must not be assumed that tariff points are always used by institutions or that they can be substituted for an offer in grades. The level of an offer is not necessarily indicative of the quality of a course. To calculate your offers see Chapter 4 and the inside fold of the back cover.

Special subject requirements/preferences: A-Level: For Sports Science courses a science subject may be required: (S) in the table below indicates courses in which a science subject or subjects are stipulated. **Bangor** Grade C mathematics. **Coventry** One subject from human biology, biology, PE or sports studies/science. **GCSE:** English and mathematics and often a science subject; check prospectuses. **Bath** Grade B in English, mathematics and science. **Leeds** Mainly grade Bs or better. Minimum grade B in mathematics, science and English.

340 pts   **Bath** – 340 pts 18u – AAB (120 pts in sci subj); (not gs) (Spo/Exer Sci)

              Hertfordshire – 340–300 pts 1x12u **or** 2x6u – ALs (biol+1/2 other sci pref) **or** ALs+ASs **or** VAs (inc A biol); (Spo Thera)

              Loughborough – 340 pts 18u – 2ALs+AL/2ASs **or** VAs+/-ALs/ASs; (not gs) (Spo Leis Mgt)

320 pts   **Bath** – ABB (inc maths+phys) **or** BB (maths+phys)+2ASs; (MEng Spo Eng)
        De Montfort (Bedford) – 320–260 pts (inc 2ALs **or** VA12u) – ALs **or** ALs+ASs **or** VAs+/-ALs/ASs; gs; (Spo St courses)
        Oxford Brookes – ABB–CCC (S) (Exer Hlth courses offer depends on 2nd subject)

310 pts   **Hertfordshire** – 310–280 pts 1x12u **or** 2x6u – ALs (inc 2 sci) **or** ALs+ASs **or** VAs (inc AL biol); gs; (Spo Sci)

300 pts   **Bath** – BBB (from maths/phys/chem/biol); (not gs) (Spo Tech; BEng Spo Eng)
        Birmingham – BBB (Spo/Mat Sci; Spo Exer St)
        Leeds – BBB (S) (Spo Sci/Physiol; Spo Sci; Out Actv)
        Leeds, Trinity & All Saints (Coll) – BBB–CCC (Spo Hlth Exer Nutr)
        Loughborough – 300 pts 18u – B(maths)+AL+AL/2ASs **or** VAs+/-ALs/ASs; gs; (Spo Tech)

280 pts   **Bangor** – 280 pts – ALs; VAs (enquire); gs; (Sports courses)
        Durham (Stockton) – 280 pts 18u – BBC **or** 2ALs+2ASs **or** VA+AL; (not gs) (Spo Commun)
        Essex – 280–240 pts 21u – BC–CC (inc biol + chem/PE/spo st/psy/maths/phys)+AL/2ASs **or** VA12u BB–CC(sci)+AL; gs; (Spo Sci)
        Exeter – 280 pts 18u – BBC **or** BB+bb **or** VAs (contact univ); (not gs) (Exer Spo Sci)
        Glasgow – BBC–CCC (S) (Spo Sci/Spo Med courses)
        Hull – 280–240 pts approx (Spo Exer Sci)
        Liverpool John Moores – BBC–BCC (inc AL sci) **or** ALs+ASs **or** VAs+/-ALs/ASs; (Spo Sci; Spo Sci/Ftbl; Coach Sci)
        Sheffield Hallam – 280 pts approx (Spo Exer Sci)
        Stirling – BBC–CCC (Spo St courses)
        Swansea – 280 pts 18u – BBC/AB (S) **or** ALs+ASs **or** VAs+/-ALs/ASs; (Sports Science)
        Ulster – BBC (Spo Exer Leis)

260 pts   **Brighton** – 260–240 pts approx (Spo Exer Sci; Spo Tech)
        Durham (Stockton) – 260 pts 18u – BCC **or** 2ALs+2ASs **or** VA+AL; (not gs) (Spo Hlth Exer)
        Edinburgh – BCC (App Spo Sci)
        Teesside – 260 pts approx (Spo Thera)
        Wolverhampton – BCC **or** CC+e **or** VA12u AA+/-AL/ASs; gs; (Exer Sci Comb courses; Spo St; Exer Sci)

240 pts   **Bournemouth** – 240 pts – 3ALs (inc spo/sci subj); (Spo Dev Coach Sci; Spo Mgt Golf)
        Bradford – 240 pts 12u (inc AL sci); gs; (Med Tech Spo)
        Brighton – 240 pts approx (Leis/Spo Mgt; Leis/Spo St)
        Bristol UWE (Hartpury) – 240 pts; gs; (Spo Sci)
        Brunel – 240 pts 2x6u (inc AS sci/soc sci) – ALs **or** ALs+ASs **or** VAs+/-ALs/ASs; (Spo Sci; Spo Sci/Bus St; Spo Sci/Admin; Spo Sci/Coach; Spo Sci/Exer; Spo Sci/Fit)
        Central Lancashire – 240–220 pts 12u (inc AL maths/sci); gs; (Mtr Spo; Spo Sci; Spo Mgt)
        Glamorgan – CCC (S) (Spo Sci courses)
        Heriot-Watt – 240 pts 18u – CCC **or** ALs+ASs **or** VAs B+/-ALs/ASs; gs; (Spo Exer Sci; Spo Sci/Psy; Spo Exer Sci/Mgt)
        Liverpool John Moores – ALs 240–180 pts **or** VA12u 220–180 pts – ALs **or** ALs+ASs **or** VAs+/-ALs/ASs; (Spo Dev/PE)
        Northumbria – CCC (Spo St)
        Nottingham Trent – 240–220 pts; (not gs) (Spo Exer Sci/Biol; Spo Exer Sci/Comp)
        Plymouth – 240 pts approx (Spo Mgt)
        Portsmouth – 240 pts – ALs **or** ALs+ASs **or** VAs; gs; (Spo Sci; Spo Tech; Spo Dev)
        Salford – CCC/CC (S) some courses (Spo Rehab)

Sheffield Hallam – 240 pts approx (Spo Dev Coach)

Staffordshire – 240 pts (inc 200 pts from ALs); gs; (Spo Sci courses; Spo St; Spo Exer Sci; Spo Leis St courses; Spo Recr Tour; Spo Exer Sci)

Staffordshire – CCC **or** CCD+AS(40 pts) **or** VAs; gs; (Spo Tech/Mgt; Spo Tech)

Wolverhampton – 240–180 pts 12u – DDD–CDE/BD–CC **or** DD+d **or** VA12u CC; gs; (Spo St)

220 pts **Aberdeen** – CCD (S) (Spo Exer Sci)

Cheltenham & Glos (CHE) – 220–180 pts approx (S) some courses (Spo Sci courses)

Chester (Coll) – 220–180 pts approx (S) some courses (PE/Spo Sci courses)

Greenwich – 220 pts approx (S) (Spo St Prof Tns Coach)

Huddersfield – 220–180 pts approx (Hlth Spo St)

King Alfred's Winchester (Coll) – 220 pts 12u – 2/3ALs **or** ALs+ASs **or** VAs+/-ALs/ASs; gs; (Spo St; Spo Dev)

Luton – 220–160 pts approx (Exer Physiol; Spo Exer Sci; Spo Fit St)

Middlesex – 220–180 pts approx (Spo Perf Thera)

Northampton (UC) – 220–160 pts approx (S) some courses (Spo St – Comb courses)

St Mark & St John (Coll) – 220–100 pts approx (Sports Sci courses)

Sheffield Hallam – 220–200 pts approx (S) some courses (Spo Soty; Spo Mgt; Spo Equip Dev)

South Bank – 220–140 pts approx (Spo Exer St; Spo Sci courses; Spo Prod Des)

South East Essex (Coll) – 220–180 pts (Spo St)

Sunderland – 220 pts approx (Spo Sci courses; Spo Exer Dev)

Teesside – 220–180 pts approx (Spo Sci courses; Spo St courses)

200 pts **Cardiff (UWI)** – BB (S) (Spo Exer Sci; Spo Coach; Spo Dev)

Coventry – 200 pts approx (Eqn/Hum Spo Sci; Spo Sci HR Mgt)

Derby – 200 pts 12u – CDD **or** CD+dd **or** VA CD+/-AL/ASs; gs; (Spo St; Out Actvts Mgt)

Kingston – 200 pts 2x6u (inc 80 pts from AL biol/spo sci); (Spo Sci)

Manchester Met – BB (S) (Spo courses)

North London – 200 pts – 3ALs **or** VA12u+AL (inc biol/pe/sci); (Spo Thera)

Ripon & York (Coll) – 200 pts approx (Spo/Exer Sci; Spo St/PE)

St Martin's (Coll) – BDE–CC (Spo St courses)

Salford – 200 pts approx (Exer/Hlth St)

Solihull (Coll) – 200 pts approx (Spo Sci/Hlth with Coventry Univ)

Strathclyde – BB–BC (Spo Exer Sci; Spo Commun)

Surrey Roehampton – 200 pts – ALs **or** ALs+ASs **or** VAs+/-AL/ASs; (Sci/Spo/Exer; Soc Sci/Spo; Spo Exer Sci)

Sunderland – 200 pts; gs; (Spo St; Spo Exer Dev)

Warrington (CI) – CDD/CC (not AS only); gs; (Spo St courses)

190 pts **North London** – 190 pts inc 160 pts from 2ALs **or** VAs; (Spo Mgt)

180 pts **Buckinghamshire Chilterns (UC)** – 180–140 pts approx (Leis Mgt; Spo St courses)

Edge Hill (CHE) – BC–CC (S) some courses (Spo Sci courses)

Greenwich – 180 pts approx (S) (Fit Sci)

Liverpool Hope (Coll) – 180–160 pts approx (Spo Recr PE courses)

North East Wales (IHE) – 180–80 pts approx (Spo Sci courses)

St Mary's (Coll) – 12u – BC(B biol) **or** VAs+/-ALs/ASs; gs; (Spo Rehab)

Thames Valley – 180 pts approx (Spo Hlth Fit Mgt)

160 pts **Anglia** – 160 pts approx (S) (Spo Sci courses)

Birmingham (Westhill) – 160 pts 12u (inc C) – ALs **or** ALs+ASs; VAs (contact univ); gs; (Spo/PE/Commun St)

Canterbury Christ Church (UC) – CC–DD (Spo Sci courses)

Chichester (UC) – 160 pts (inc C); (Advntr Educ; Spo Sci; Spo Thera; Spo St; Spo Sci Fdn)

Lincolnshire & Humberside – 160 pts (Spo Sci)
Newport (UWCN) – 160–140 pts – ALs **or** ALs+ASs **or** VAs+/-AL/ASs; (Spo St)
North London – 160 pts – 3ALs **or** VAs; (Spo Sci)
St Mary's (Coll) – 12u – CC **or** VAs+/-ALs/ASs; gs; (Spo Sci)
Trinity Carmarthen (Coll) – CC–EE (Spo St courses)
Westminster – CC (Spo Exer Sci)
Worcester (UC) – 160 pts 12u – CC **or** ALs+ASs **or** VAs+/-ALs/ASs; gs; (Spo St; Spo/Exer St)

140 pts and below
Bolton (IHE) – CD (S) (Spo Exer Sci)
Sunderland – (Spo Sci Fdn)
UHI (Inverness/Moray/Perth) – (Out Adv Purs Mgt via DipHE)
Warwickshire (Coll) – 40 pts 6u; (Spo Sci/Hlth Sci)

Leeds Met – (contact university)

Diploma of Higher Education courses
80 pts Manchester Met; North London; South Bank; UHI.

Higher National Diploma courses
140 pts and below
Anglia; Barnsley (Coll) (Leis Spo); Basingstoke (Coll); Bedford (Coll); Bell (CT); Blackburn (Coll); Blackpool & Fylde (Coll); Bolton (Coll); Bridgwater (Coll); Carmarthenshire (Coll); Central Lancashire; Colchester (Inst); Cornwall & Duchy (Coll) (Srf Sci/Tech; Golf Mgt); Coventry; Craven (Coll); Crawley (Coll); De Montfort (Golf); Derby; Doncaster (Coll); Durham New (Coll); Exeter (Out Educ); Falmouth (CA); Farnborough (CT); Glamorgan; Glasgow (Coll) (Spo Thera); Halton (Coll); Harper Adams (UC); Hartpury (Coll) gs; Hastings (Coll); Llandrillo (Coll); Loughborough (CT); Mid Cheshire (Coll); Middlesex; Moulton (Coll); Myerscough (Coll) (Golf); Nescot; Newcastle (Coll); Nottingham Trent; Park Lane (Coll); Pembrokeshire (Coll); Rodbaston (Coll); St Helens (Coll); Sheffield (Coll); Sheffield Hallam; Shrewsbury (Coll); Solihull (Coll); Somerset (CAT); Southwark (Coll); Staffordshire; Stockport (Coll); Sutton Coldfield (Coll); Swansea; Truro (Coll); UHI; Wakefield (Coll); Warwickshire (Coll); Wigan & Leigh (Coll); Wiltshire (Coll); Wirral Met (Coll); Worcester (UC); Writtle (Coll); York (CFHE); Yorkshire Coast (CFHE).

Alternative Offers:

IB offers: Bath 32 pts; Birmingham 33–32 pts; Durham 30 pts; Kingston 30 pts; Leeds 30–28 pts; Loughborough 32–31 pts; Manchester Met 28 pts; Nottingham Trent 30 pts; St Martin's (Coll) 30 pts; Staffordshire 28 pts; Surrey Roehampton 26 pts; Swansea 30–28 pts.

Irish offers: Brighton BBCCC; Liverpool John Moores CCCCC; Nottingham Trent BBC.

Scottish Qualifications: Aberdeen BBBC; Edinburgh BBBB; Glasgow BBBB; Napier BCC; Robert Gordon BBBB; St Andrews BBBB; Stirling BBBB; for other universities and colleges refer to **Chapter 4** under **Alternative Offers**.

CHOOSING YOUR COURSE (See also **Ch.1**)

> **Subject information:** In addition to the theory and practice of many different sporting activities, Sports Studies students will also cover the psychological aspects of sport and business administration. The geography, economics and sociology of recreation may also be included. These subjects, and Physical Education, Leisure and Recreation Management, could also be considered as alternative degree courses. See also **Appendix 1**.

Special features: Bangor The SHAPE course covers sport psychology, health promotion, information technology and counselling. It is a 'theory' and 'practice' course. **Brighton** The courses in Sports and Exercise Science have a common first year with specialisms following in years 2 and 3. **Central Lancashire** The Sports Science degree covers biomechanics, physiology and information technology. **Essex** Options in sports psychology, sports medicine and coaching. **Hertfordshire** The course covers psychology, physiotherapy, sports injuries and treatment. **Salford** A Sports Rehabilitation programme is offered dealing with sports injuries with hospital and overseas placements. *NOW CHECK PROSPECTUSES AND WEB SITES.*

Top universities and colleges (Research) (see Ch.4): Bangor; Birmingham; Glasgow; Liverpool John Moores; Loughborough; Manchester Met; Nottingham.

Study opportunities abroad: Bangor; Bath; Brighton; Cardiff (UWI); Cheltenham & Glos (CHE); Coventry; Edinburgh; Kingston; Leeds, Trinity & All Saints (Coll); Liverpool Hope (Coll); Manchester Met; Northumbria; Nottingham; Nottingham Trent; Ripon & York (Coll); Surrey Roehampton.

Work opportunities abroad: Brighton; Coventry.

ADMISSIONS INFORMATION

Number of applicants per place (approx): Bangor 15; Bath 25; Birmingham 22; Brunel 4; Canterbury Christ Church (UC) 30; Cardiff (UWI) 10; Cheltenham & Glos (CHE) 8; Chichester (UC) 30; De Montfort 11; Durham 6; Edge Hill (CHE) 13; Edinburgh 11; Exeter 23; Kingston 13; Leeds 25; Leeds, Trinity & All Saints (Coll) 35; Liverpool John Moores 33; Manchester Met 16; Northumbria 30; Nottingham Trent 8; Portsmouth 12; St Martin's (Coll) 14, (Spo Sci) 6; St Mary's (Coll) 4; Salford 30; Staffordshire 12; Stirling 10; Strathclyde 28; Surrey Roehampton 8; Teesside 15; Worcester (UC) 10.

Planning your UCAS personal statement (see Ch.4): Liverpool John Moores (Coach Sci) Coaching experience necessary. See **Physical Education**. See also **Appendix 1**.

Selection interviews (see Ch.4): Bangor (No); Bath, Birmingham (No); Birmingham (Westhill); Brighton (No); Bristol UWE; Brunel (No); Durham; Durham (Stockton); Edinburgh; Exeter (No); Hertfordshire (No); Hull (No); King Alfred's Winchester (Coll); Kingston (No); Leeds; Leeds, Trinity & All Saints (Coll); Liverpool Hope (Coll) (No); Liverpool John Moores; Loughborough (No); Manchester Met (No); Northumbria (No); Nottingham Trent (No); Portsmouth (No); St Martin's (Coll); Salford; Sheffield Hallam (some); Staffordshire (No); Stirling (No); Sunderland (No); Surrey Roehampton; Swansea; Thames Valley (No); Warrington (CI); Worcester (UC) (No).

Interview questions (see Ch.4): Applicants' interests in sport and their sporting activities discussed at length. **Loughborough** A high level of sporting achievement is expected.

Reasons for rejection (non-academic): Not genuinely interested in outdoor activities. Poor sporting background or knowledge. Personal appearance. Inability to apply their science to their specialist sport. Illiteracy. Using the course as a second option to physiotherapy. Arrogance. Expectation that they will be playing sport all day.

GAP YEAR ADVICE

Chichester (UC) Apply before taking a gap year. **Liverpool John Moores** Preliminary reading required during the year out. **Manchester Met** Gain relevant experience to strengthen your application.

Institutions willing to defer entry after A-Levels: Birmingham; Brighton (No); Cheltenham & Glos (CHE); Glamorgan; Leeds; Luton; Manchester Met (possibly); Northampton (UC); Northumbria; Nottingham Trent; St Martin's (Coll); St Mary's (Coll); Staffordshire; Surrey Roehampton; Worcester (UC).

AFTER RESULTS ADVICE

Institutions which may accept the same points score after A-Levels: Brighton; Cardiff (UWI); Chichester (UC); Manchester Met (No); Northumbria; Nottingham Trent; Portsmouth; St Mary's (Coll); Sunderland; Surrey Roehampton; Worcester (UC); York.

Institutions which may accept lower grades/points scores after A-Levels: Brighton; Cheltenham & Glos (CHE); Liverpool John Moores; Nottingham Trent; Staffordshire.

Probable vacancies from June 2001 and in Clearing (see Ch.4): More than 50 universities and colleges declared vacancies in Clearing last year.

NEW GRADUATE DESTINATIONS AND EMPLOYMENT (1999 HESA) (see **Ch.4**)

No data available for this subject area but see **Physical Education**.

STATISTICS

NB The information supplied by the universities and colleges this year varies considerably and the offers listed below should be used as a first source of reference only. Many institutions will accept combinations of Advanced (AL), Advanced Subsidiary (AS) and Vocational Advanced (VA) level qualifications to achieve the required points total, but applicants must check web sites and prospectuses for full details of all offers. Grades and points totals shown should be regarded as the minimum levels to be achieved, but offers may be adjusted downwards when results are known. The points totals shown to the left of the institutions are for ease of reference only. It must not be assumed that tariff points are always used by institutions or that they can be substituted for an offer in grades. The level of an offer is not necessarily indicative of the quality of a course. To calculate your offers see Chapter 4 and the inside fold of the back cover.

Special subject requirements/preferences: A-Level: Mathematics subjects usually required. **GCSE:** English and mathematics. **Exeter** Reasonable spread of grades A*, A and B. **Greenwich, Kingston, Sheffield Hallam** Mathematics grade A or B.

360 pts   and above
       Warwick – AAA–AAB (Maths OR Stats Econ (MORSE))
340 pts   Bristol – AAB (Maths/Stats)
       London (Imp) – AAB (Statistics courses)
       London (LSE) – AAB–BBB (Bus Maths/Stats)
320 pts   Bath – 21u – ABB–ABC **or** VAs+2ALs/ASs; (Statistics)
       Edinburgh – ABB–BBC (Statistics courses)
       Oxford Brookes – ABB (Psy/Stats)
300 pts   Bath – 300 pts approx (A maths/AB) (BSc Stats courses)
       Birmingham – BBB (Math Econ/Stats)
       Edinburgh – BBB (Stats/Bus St)
       Heriot-Watt – 300 pts 18u – BBB **or** ALs+ASs **or** VAs+/-ALs/ASs; gs;
          (Statistics courses)
       Lancaster – 300 pts approx (Stats/USA)
       Lancaster – 300–260 pts approx (Statistics courses)
       Leeds – BBB (Statistics courses)
       London (RH) – BBB (Stats/Maths)
       London (UCL) – ABC–BCC **or** 3ALs+AS/VA (Stats/OR/Mgt St;
          Stats/OR/Econ/Comp; Stats/OR/Econ/Euro Lang; Maths/Stat Sci)
       Newcastle – BBB (B maths) (Statistics courses)
       St Andrews – BBB–BBC (MA Statistics; App Stats)
       Sheffield – 300 pts approx (Econ/Stats)
       Sheffield – BBB–BCC (Statistics courses)
       Sussex – BBB–BCC (Statistics courses)

UMIST – 300 pts approx (Maths/Stats)
York – 300 pts approx (Maths/Stats)

280 pts **Brunel** – BBC–BCC/BB (Stats/Maths)
Cardiff – 280 pts approx (MORS)
Exeter – BBC (B maths) (Math/Stats/OR)
Glasgow – BBC–CCC (Statistics courses)
Glasgow Caledonian – BBC–CCC (Statistics courses)
Hertfordshire – 280–200 pts approx (Stats Comb)
Liverpool – 280 pts approx (Math/Stats)
London (QM) – 280 pts approx (Statistics)
Manchester – 280 pts approx (Statistics)
St Andrews – BBC (Stats (Arts) (Sci))
Southampton – BBC (Maths/Stats)
Swansea – 280 pts 18u – BBC/AB **or** ALs+ASs **or** VAs+/-ALs/ASs; (Statistics courses)

260 pts **Aberystwyth** – 260–220 pts approx (App Maths/Stats)
East Anglia – BCC (Maths/Stats)
Essex – 260 pts 12u – B(maths)C+AL/2ASs; gs; (Statistics)
Exeter – 260 pts approx (Mgt/Stats)
Hull – 260–240 pts approx (Stat Econ)
Keele – BCC–CCC/BB–CC **or** equiv AS accepted; gs; (Statistics Joint Hons)
Kent – 260 pts approx (Statistics courses)
Manchester – BCC (Geog/Stats; Chem/Stats; Comb St Stats)
Oxford Brookes – BCC–CCD/CC–DD (Statistics courses)
Reading – 260 pts approx (Stats; App Stats)
Strathclyde – BCC (Statistics 2nd yr entry; Maths/Stats)
Surrey – 260 pts approx (Maths/Stats)

240 pts **Aberdeen** – CCC–CCD (Statistics courses)
City – 240 pts approx (B maths) (Math Sci Stats)
De Montfort (Leicester) – 240–160 pts (inc 2ALs **or** VA12u) – ALs **or** ALs+ASs **or** VAs+/-ALs/ASs; (Statistics Joint courses)
Heriot-Watt – 240–220 pts approx (Statistics courses)

220 pts **Brighton** – 220 pts approx (Statistics courses)
Bristol UWE – 220–180 pts 12u – ALs (inc 6u maths 80 pts) **or** ALs+ASs **or** VAs+/-ALs/ASs; (not gs) (Stats; Stats/Inf Sys)
Coventry – 220–180 pts approx (Statistics courses)
Greenwich – 220 pts approx (Statistics courses)
Hertfordshire – 220–200 pts approx (Bus Stats)
Huddersfield – 220 pts approx (Statistics courses)
Luton – 220–180 pts approx (App Stats)
Plymouth – 220–180 pts approx (Statistics courses)

200 pts **Central Lancashire** – 200–180 pts 12u – ALs **or** ALs+ASs **or** VAs+/-ALs/ASs; gs; (Stats/Mark/Psy)
Dundee – 200 pts approx (Stats/Maths)
Glamorgan – 200–140 pts approx (Statistics courses)
Kingston – 200–180 pts (inc 2ALs+AS maths min); (Statistics courses)
Sheffield Hallam – 200 pts approx (App Stats)

180 pts **Central Lancashire** – 180–140 pts 12u – ALs **or** ALs+ASs **or** VAs+/-ALs/ASs; gs; (Statistics courses except under **200 pts**)
Chester (Coll) – 180 pts – ALs (160 pts inc C)+AS(20 pts) **or** VAs (160 pts inc C); gs; (App Stats Comb)
Glamorgan – 180 pts approx (Stats/Psy)

160 pts **Anglia** – 160 pts 12u – 2ALs **or** ALs+ASs **or** VAs+/-ALs/ASs; (Statistics courses)
Canterbury Christ Church (CHE) – CC (Statistics courses)
Liverpool John Moores – 160 pts approx (App Stats/Comp; Maths/Stats/Comp)
Middlesex – 160 pts approx (Statistics Joint Hons)

Napier – CC (App Stats courses)
Paisley – CC (Comp Sci/Stats/OR)
Westminster – CC (Statistics courses)

140 pts **Bolton (IHE)** – CD (Statistics courses)
Derby – 140 pts 12u – CD **or** DE+ee **or** VAs CD+/-AL/ASs; (Stats Comb Hons)

120 pts **London (Gold)** – DD (Statistics courses)
North London – 120 pts 2x6u **or** 1x12u; (Stats; App Stats)
Strathclyde – DD (Stats; Stats/Comp)
Ulster – DD (Math St)

Higher National Diploma courses
100 pts and below
Blackburn (Coll); Cheltenham & Glos (CHE); Coventry; De Montfort; Glamorgan; Greenwich; Hertfordshire; Leeds Met; Manchester Met; North London; Sheffield Hallam; Ulster.

Alternative Offers:

IB offers: Aberdeen (Arts) 30 pts, (Sci) 26 pts; Bath 32 pts H6 maths; Birmingham 32 pts; Brighton 24 pts; Brunel 29 pts; Central Lancashire 24 pts; Exeter 30 pts; Glasgow H555; Heriot-Watt 24 pts inc H7 maths; Hertfordshire 26–24 pts; Kent 27 pts, H 12 pts; Lancaster 30 pts; Liverpool H555; London (UCL) 30 pts; Newcastle 28 pts; St Andrews 30 pts; Swansea 28 pts.

Irish offers: Aberdeen (Arts) BBBB, (Sci) BCCCC; Brunel BBCCC; Heriot-Watt BBBBC; Keele BBBCC; London Guildhall CCCCC; Sheffield Hallam BBBBB.

Scottish Qualifications: Aberdeen BBBB–BBBC; Dundee BBBC–BBCC; Edinburgh ABBC; Glasgow BBBB; Glasgow Caledonian BBC; Heriot-Watt ABBC; Napier BBC; Paisley BCCC; St Andrews BBBB; Strathclyde BBBC.

Overseas applicants: Sheffield Hallam English language programme possible.

CHOOSING YOUR COURSE (See also **Ch.1**)

Subject information: Statistics is a challenging branch of mathematics which, currently, has a shortage of applicants. Management Sciences, Mathematics and Operational Research are possible alternative courses. See also **Appendix 1**.

Special features: Bristol UWE Options in economics, marketing, modern languages. **Heriot-Watt** Common first year with Actuarial Maths and Statistics; opportunity to change course at end of second year. **Liverpool John Moores** Course covers computing, operational research and business information systems. **Newcastle** See **Mathematics**. **Sheffield Hallam** Experimental design, surveys, applied probability covered in course. Active links with public and private sectors via the final year student project programme; also a modern language course placement in Europe. **Warwick** (MORSE) A three-year degree involving maths, economics, statistics and the Warwick Business School. **York** The degree is Economic Statistics. *NOW CHECK PROSPECTUSES AND WEB SITES.*

Top universities and colleges (Research) (see Ch.4): Including Operational Research. Bath; Birmingham; Bristol; Brunel; Cambridge; Edinburgh; Glasgow; Lancaster; London (Imp), (QM), (UCL); Newcastle; Oxford; Salford; Warwick.

Study opportunities abroad: Brighton; Bristol UWE; Brunel; City; Exeter; Kent; Leeds; London (LSE); Napier; Nottingham; Oxford Brookes; St Andrews; Sheffield; Sheffield Hallam; Southampton (inc OR); Strathclyde; Surrey; Swansea.

ADMISSIONS INFORMATION

Number of applicants per place (approx): Bath 10; Bristol UWE 2; Brunel 3; Cardiff 3; Central Lancashire 5; Coventry 3; East London 3; Exeter 5; Heriot-Watt 6; Lancaster 11;

Liverpool John Moores 6; London (UCL) 9; Newcastle 5; Northumbria 3; Sheffield Hallam 2; Staffordshire 1; UMIST 2; York 5.

Planning your UCAS personal statement (see Ch.4): See **Mathematics**. See also **Appendix 1**.

Selection interviews (see Ch.4): Anglia (No); Bath; Birmingham; Brighton (No); Bristol UWE (No); Brunel; Canterbury Christ Church (UC); Exeter; Greenwich (some); Hertfordshire (No); Hull (No); Liverpool; Liverpool John Moores; London (UCL); Newcastle; St Andrews (No); Sheffield; Sheffield Hallam; Solihull (Coll); Sussex; Swansea (No); UMIST.

Interview questions (see Ch.4): Questions could be asked on your A-level syllabus (particularly in mathematics). The applicant's knowledge of statistics and his/her interest in the subject are likely to be tested. Application of statistics in commerce and industry. **St Andrews** Evidence of interest. Reasons for choosing course.

GAP YEAR ADVICE

Most institutions will accept a gap year but students are recommended to keep their A-level maths knowledge up to standard.

Institutions willing to defer entry after A-Levels: Birmingham; Bristol UWE; Brunel; Central Lancashire; Coventry; Heriot-Watt; Hertfordshire; Leeds; Newcastle; Northumbria; Plymouth; Sheffield Hallam; Sussex; Swansea.

AFTER RESULTS ADVICE

Institutions which may accept the same points score after A-Levels: Birmingham; Brunel; Cardiff; Central Lancashire; Greenwich; Hertfordshire; Kent (No); Leeds; Liverpool; Liverpool John Moores; Newcastle; North London; Northumbria; Sheffield Hallam; Ulster; UMIST.

Institutions which may accept lower grades/points score after A-Levels: Birmingham; Brunel; Exeter; Hertfordshire; Newcastle.

Offers to applicants repeating A-Levels: Higher Kent, Leeds, Liverpool, Liverpool John Moores, Newcastle, Swansea; **Same** Birmingham, Brunel.

Probable vacancies from June 2001 and in Clearing (see Ch.4): Most universities declared vacancies in Clearing last year, many on joint courses. The most competitive universities are likely to expect grades in the 280–240 pts range.

NEW GRADUATE DESTINATIONS AND EMPLOYMENT (1999 HESA) (see **Ch.4**)

A survey of 229 graduates showed that 163 entered full-time employment (mainly into managerial and professional employment, with the majority into finance), 43 went into research or career training and seven were believed to be unemployed.

SURVEYING (including **Estate, Land and Valuation Surveying** and **Countryside Management**; see also **Building Surveying** (under **Building**), **Housing** and **Quantity Surveying**)

NB The information supplied by the universities and colleges this year varies considerably and the offers listed below should be used as a first source of reference only. Many institutions will accept combinations of Advanced (AL), Advanced Subsidiary (AS) and Vocational Advanced (VA) level qualifications to achieve the required points total, but applicants must check web sites and prospectuses for full details of all offers. Grades and points totals shown should be regarded as the minimum levels to be achieved, but offers may be adjusted downwards when results are known. The points totals shown to the left of the institutions are for ease of reference only. It must not be assumed that tariff points are always used by institutions or that they can be substituted for an offer in grades. The level of an offer is not necessarily indicative of the quality of a course. To calculate your offers see Chapter 4 and the inside fold of the back cover.

Special subject requirements/preferences: GCSE: English and mathematics required, and for some institutions a science subject (for Chartered Surveyor registration). **Newcastle** (Comp Sci Surv Map Sci) Mathematics grade B. **Nottingham Trent** Two subjects grade A, three subjects grade B, three subjects grade C including mathematics and English language.

360 pts   **Cambridge** – Offers mainly in grades vary between colleges (Land Econ)
280 pts   **Reading** – BBC (Land Mgt)
260 pts   **Bristol UWE** – 260–200 pts 18u pref/12u – ALs **or** ALs+ASs **or** VAs+/-AL/ASs;
                   (Bus Prop; Val/Est Mgt; Bld Surv)
                   Glamorgan – 260 pts approx (Plan Dev Surv)
                   Newcastle – BCC–CCC/BB–BC; (not gs) (Country Mgt; Comp Sci Surv Map
                   Sci; Map Inf Sci)
                   Salford – 260 pts approx (Bld Surv)
240 pts   **Aberdeen** – CCC (Land Econ; (Rur Surv))
                   Bradford – 240 pts 12u; gs; (Env Mgt)
                   De Montfort (Leicester) – 240 pts (inc 2ALs **or** VA12u) – ALs **or** ALs+ASs **or**
                   VAs+/-ALs/ASs; (Bus Prop Mgt; Plan/Dev; Land Mgt)
                   Exeter – 240 pts 18u (inc 2ALs sci or AL+AS sci) – CCC **or** CC+cc **or** VAS
                   (contact univ); (not gs) (Miner Surv courses; Surv/Env Mgt)
220 pts   **Anglia** – 220 pts 12u (inc 2ALs) – ALs **or** ALs+ASs **or** VA12u AB; gs; (Real Est
                   Mgt; Prop Mgt; Plan Dev Surv)
                   Greenwich – 220–200 pts approx (Est Mgt; Urb Env St; Prop Mgt)
                   Heriot–Watt – CCD/CC (BCC 2nd yr entry) (Est Mgt)
                   Kingston – 220 pts (inc 6u awards); (Prop Plan/Dev; Est Mgt courses; Env
                   Real Est)
                   Napier – CCD (Est Mgt; Plan Dev Surv)
                   Northumbria – 220 pts approx (Est Mgt; Plan Dev Surv)
                   Nottingham Trent – 220 pts approx (Prop Surv)
                   Portsmouth – 220 pts approx (Real Est Mgt; Prop Dev)
                   Reading – CCD (Rur Res Mgt)
                   Sheffield Hallam – 220–180 pts approx (Urb St; Bus Prop DEv Mgt; Prop Dev;
                   Resid Dev)
                   Wolverhampton – 220 pts 12u – CCD/BB or CC+b **or** VA12u BB; gs; (Bld
                   Surv)
200 pts   **Bristol UWE** – 200–160 pts; ALs **or** ALs+ASs **or** VAs+/-ALs/ASs; (Real Est;
                   Real Est/Leis Mgt; House Pol Mgt)
                   Central England – 200 pts 12u; gs; (Est Mgt)
                   Liverpool John Moores – 200 pts approx – ALs **or** ALs+ASs **or** VAs+/-
                   ALs/ASs; (Urb Est Mgt)
                   Scottish (CAg) – CDD (Rur Res Mgt)
                   Sheffield Hallam – 200 pts approx (Country Mgt Comb)
                   Westminster – 200–160 pts approx (Urb Est Mgt)
                   Wolverhampton – 200 pts approx (Prop Asst Mgt)
180 pts   **Aberystwyth** – 180 pts approx (Country Mgt; Rur Res Mgt)
                   Central England – 180–140 pts 12u; gs; (Housing)
                   Central England – DDD/CC (Bus St/Prop)
                   East London – 180 pts approx (Prop Plan Inform; Geog Land Inf Mgt)
                   Harper Adams (UC) – 180 pts 12u – CC/CEE/DDE **or** CE+c **or** DD+c **or** VA
                   CC; gs (AL only); (Rur Land Mgt)
                   Reading – DDD/CD (Est Mgt – for external students)
                   South Bank – 180 pts approx (Est Mgt) (also part–time course)
160 pts   **Anglia** – 160 pts 12u (inc 2ALs) – ALs **or** ALs+ASs **or** VA12u CC; gs; (Surv;
                   Prop Surv)
                   Bangor – 160 pts approx (Env Plan Mgt)
                   Cheltenham & Glos (CHE) – 160 pts approx (Country Plan)
                   De Montfort (Lincoln) – 160 pts – ALs **or** ALs+ASs **or** VAs+/-ALs/ASs;
                   (Val/Auct)

Glasgow Caledonian – CC (Prop Mgt/Dev)
North East Wales (IHE) – 160 pts approx (Est Mgt Surv Val)
Staffordshire – CC/CD+AS (40 pts) **or** VAs; gs; (Surv courses; Prop courses)
140 pts **Central Lancashire** – 140 pts approx (Prop Surv)
Glamorgan – 140 pts approx (Min Surv)
120 pts **Paisley** – DD (Prop St)
80 pts **and below**
Glamorgan – 80 pts approx (Surv/Resid Dev)
Manchester (CAT) – 80 pts approx (Surveying)
Northampton (UC) – E (Country Mgt)
Royal (CAg) – 80 pts approx (Rur Est Mgt)
South Bank – 80 pts approx (Fdn)
Southampton (Inst) – 80 pts – ALs **or** ALs+ASs; (Fine Arts Val; Real Est Val)
Trinity Carmarthen (Coll) – EE (Rur Env St)
Welsh (CAg) – 80 pts approx (Country Mgt)

Diploma of Higher Education courses
Abertay Dundee.

Higher National Diploma courses
160 pts Royal (CAg).
140 pts **and below**
Aberystwyth; Anglia; Broomfield (Coll) (Land Mgt); Central England; Central Lancashire (Myerscough Coll) (Land Mgt); De Montfort; Derby; Doncaster (Coll) (Min Surv); Durham New (Coll); East London; Exeter; Glamorgan (Min Surv); Hertfordshire; Lincolnshire & Humberside; Luton; Manchester (CAT); North East Wales (IHE); Northampton (UC); Northumbria; Nottingham Trent; Park Lane (Coll); Plymouth; Robert Gordon (Build Surv); Sheffield Hallam (Land Admin); Shirecliffe (Coll); South Bank; Southampton (Inst); Stoke on Trent (CT); Writtle (Coll).

Other Diploma courses
Royal (CAg) (Rur Est Mgt).

Alternative Offers:

IB offers: Newcastle 30 pts.

Scottish Qualifications: Aberdeen BBBB; Glasgow Caledonian BBCC; Heriot-Watt BBCC; Napier BBCC; Paisley BBBB; Robert Gordon BBBC.

Overseas applicants: Newcastle List of alumni available. **Oxford Brookes** Written and spoken English must be good. **Sheffield Hallam** (Min Est Surv) Induction and language course available.

CHOOSING YOUR COURSE (See also **Ch.1**)

Subject information: Surveying is a very broad subject (and career) which includes several specialisms, for example building surveying, quantity surveying, land valuation surveying and architecture which could also be considered as alternative courses. Most courses cover very similar topics and lead to professional qualifications. See also **Appendix 1**.

Special features: Bristol UWE Transfer to Quantity Surveying possible in first year. **Central England** Main emphasis on legal aspects of property valuation, property development and management. **Exeter** Courses offered include languages and placement abroad. Substantial fieldwork. (Surv/Env Mgt) Leads to careers in environmental control and waste management. **Glamorgan** Computer applications to valuation and appraisal are electives in the final year. **Newcastle** Subject of interest to students interested in mapping, engineering, geography and computing. (Surv/Map Sci) The course covers land surveying and mapping. First year maths course necessary for those without A-level maths. Course relies on computer technology but includes fieldwork, map appreciation and management. **Northumbria** Common first year course with Quantity and Building Surveying. Full-time or sandwich course choice made in second year. Option of a European route with a year abroad in conservation or European property studies management. Emphasis on live project work. **Nottingham Trent** Opportunities for sandwich placement. Core study areas include investment, management and property management. **Staffordshire** Common first year for all surveying, building and property students. Strong business management theme to the course. *NOW CHECK PROSPECTUSES AND WEB SITES.*

Top universities and colleges (Teaching Quality) (see Ch.4): Bristol UWE; Cambridge; De Montfort; Harper Adams (UC); Kingston; Liverpool John Moores; Northumbria; Oxford Brookes; Plymouth; Reading; Southampton (Inst); not all institutions assessed.

Study opportunities abroad: Aberdeen; Central England; Liverpool John Moores; Plymouth; Reading.

Work opportunities abroad: Central England; Kingston.

ADMISSIONS INFORMATION

Number of applicants per place (approx): Bristol UWE 11, (Real Est) 5; Cambridge 2.9; Central England 28; City 20; De Montfort 20, (Land Mgt) 2; Glamorgan 6, (Surv/Res Dev) 1; Greenwich 9; Harper Adams (UC) 4; Heriot-Watt 6; Kingston 22; Liverpool John Moores 15; Newcastle 6; North East Wales (IHE) 3; Northumbria 17; Nottingham Trent 10; Portsmouth 4; Royal (CAg) 3; Salford 3; Sheffield Hallam 5; Staffordshire 8; Westminster 10.

Planning your UCAS personal statement (see Ch.4): There are different specialisms in this field, for example, building, land, quantity, hydrographic and agricultural as well as general practice surveying. If you have any special interests list and discuss them. Give details of all the contacts you have made, especially with surveying practices in your locality. Discuss the careers with surveyors and try to arrange work experience/shadowing. See also **Appendix 1**.

Selection interviews (see Ch.4): Bristol UWE (T); Cambridge; Central Lancashire (No); De Montfort; East London (some); Exeter; Glamorgan; Greenwich; Harper Adams (UC); Heriot-Watt; Liverpool John Moores (No); Napier (No); Newcastle; Nottingham Trent (No); Paisley (No); Plymouth (Seale Hayne) (No); Portsmouth (No); Royal (CAg); Staffordshire (No); Wolverhampton (No).

Interview questions (see Ch.4): Some work experience will be expected and questions will be asked on why the applicant wishes to pursue this course and career.

GAP YEAR ADVICE

Gain work experience if possible. **Liverpool John Moores** Gap year not recommended.

Institutions willing to defer entry after A-Levels: Bristol UWE; De Montfort; Glamorgan; Harper Adams (UC); Kingston; Newcastle (Surv/Map Sci) Prefers applications after A-Level results known; North East Wales (IHE); Northumbria; Nottingham Trent; Oxford Brookes (No); Portsmouth; Salford; Sheffield Hallam; Staffordshire; Stoke on Trent (CT).

AFTER RESULTS ADVICE

Institutions which may accept the same points score after A-Levels: Bristol UWE; Central England; City; De Montfort; East London; Glamorgan; Greenwich; Liverpool John Moores; Newcastle (Surv/Map Sci); North East Wales (IHE); Northumbria; Nottingham Trent; Plymouth; Portsmouth; Sheffield Hallam; South Bank; Ulster; Westminster.

Institutions which may accept lower grades/points score after A-Levels: North East Wales (IHE).

Probable vacancies from June 2001 and in Clearing (see Ch.4): Vacancies are expected from June onwards in Estate Management with offers from 180 pts and lower.

NEW GRADUATE DESTINATIONS AND EMPLOYMENT (1999 HESA) (see **Ch.4**)

Of 277 graduates surveyed in land and property management, 209 obtained full-time employment, 16 went into further training and 20 were believed to be unemployed.

TECHNOLOGY (see also Education (Design Technology), Engineering/Engineering Sciences and Science)

NB The information supplied by the universities and colleges this year varies considerably and the offers listed below should be used as a first source of reference only. Many institutions will accept combinations of Advanced (AL), Advanced Subsidiary (AS) and Vocational Advanced (VA) level qualifications to achieve the required points total, but applicants must check web sites and prospectuses for full details of all offers. Grades and points totals shown should be regarded as the minimum levels to be achieved, but offers may be adjusted downwards when results are known. The points totals shown to the left of the institutions are for ease of reference only. It must not be assumed that tariff points are always used by institutions or that they can be substituted for an offer in grades. The level of an offer is not necessarily indicative of the quality of a course. To calculate your offers see Chapter 4 and the inside fold of the back cover.

Special subject requirements/preferences: A-Level: Mathematics and science subjects required. **GCSE:** English and mathematics.

320 pts   **Brunel** – 320 pts 2x6u (inc AL maths B+sci (pref phys) **or** VA (Sci/Eng)) – ALs **or** ALs+ASs **or** VAs+/-ALs/ASs; (Tech/Innov/Bus Ent)

300 pts   **Lancaster** – BBB (Comb Tech/USA/Can)

280 pts   **Strathclyde** – BBC–CCC (Tech/Bus St courses)

260 pts   **Lancaster** – BCC (Comb Tech)

240 pts   **De Montfort (Leicester)** – 240–160 pts (inc 2ALs) – ALs **or** ALs+ASs **or** VAs+/-ALs/ASs; (Technology)

       Portsmouth – 240 pts – ALs **or** ALs+ASs **or** VAs; gs; (Tech Mgt courses; Sust Tech; Crea Tech)

220 pts   **Glasgow Caledonian** – CCD/CC (Media Tech Mgt)

       Oxford Brookes – CCD (Tech Mgt)

200 pts   **Bradford** – 200 pts 12u; gs; (Tech Mgt; Pers/Tech; Mat Tech Mgt; Manuf Mgt/ Tech; Env Mgt Tech; Inf Tech Mgt)

       Glasgow Caledonian – CDD (Med Tech)

       Huddersfield – 200 pts approx (Tech Bus Mgt)

180 pts   **East London** – 180 pts approx (New Tech courses)

160 pts   **Blackburn (Coll)** – 160–120 pts – ALs **or** ALs+ASs **or** VAs+/-ALs/ASs
(sci/maths)   pref); gs; (Fdn Tech)

       Sheffield Hallam – 160 pts approx (Bus Tech)

       Staffordshire – CC/CD+AS(40 pts); gs; (App Tech Innov)

140 pts   **Derby** – 140 pts 12u – CD **or** DD+ee **or** VAs CD+/-ALs/ASs; gs; (Tech Mgt/ Innov/Mark; Tech Mgt/Innov/HR Mgt)

       Liverpool John Moores – 140 pts (inc 1x6u) – ALs **or** ALs+ASs **or** VAs+/- ALs/ASs; (Tech Mgt)

120 pts   **Paisley** – DD (Qual Mgt/Tech)

       Peterborough Reg (Coll) – DD (Comb St Integ Tech)

100 pts   **Napier** – DE (Ind Tech Bus)

Diploma of Higher Education courses

80 pts   Doncaster (Coll) (Tech/Soty); Manchester Met; Swansea (IHE).

Higher National Diploma courses
Bradford (Coll); Burnley (Coll); Lincolnshire & Humberside; Sheffield Hallam; Staffordshire (App Tech).

Alternative Offers:

IB offers: Bradford 24 pts; Staffordshire 27 pts.

Scottish Qualifications: Glasgow Caledonian BBCC/BBB; Napier BBC; Paisley BBC; Strathclyde BBBC.

CHOOSING YOUR COURSE (See also **Ch.1**)

Subject information: Technology courses are broad courses and cover various aspects of technology. They overlap into Manufacturing, Production Engineering and Business Studies degree courses which should also be considered in their own right.

Special features: Bradford (Tech Mgt) Covers management science, mechanical and electrical technology. **Oxford Brookes** (Tech Mgt) Management, business studies, automation, mechanical and electronic processes. *NOW CHECK PROSPECTUSES AND WEB SITES.*

Study opportunities abroad: Staffordshire.

Work opportunities abroad: Huddersfield; Staffordshire.

ADMISSIONS INFORMATION

Number of applicants per place (approx): Paisley 1.

Planning your UCAS personal statement (see Ch.4): See **Engineering** courses and **Physics**.

Interview questions (see Ch.4): See **Engineering/Engineering Sciences**.

GAP YEAR ADVICE

Institutions willing to defer entry after A-Levels: Bradford; Paisley; Staffordshire.

AFTER RESULTS ADVICE

Institutions accepting the same points score after A-Levels: Bradford.

Probable vacancies from June 2001 and in Clearing (see Ch.4): This is one of the less popular subjects. All universities and colleges could be contacted.

NEW GRADUATE DESTINATIONS AND EMPLOYMENT (1999 HESA) (see **Ch.4**)

No data available. See **Engineering/Engineering Sciences**.

TEXTILE COURSES (Design/Management/Marketing/ Technology) (see also **Art and Design (Fashion)** and **Consumer Studies** including Home Economics)

NB The information supplied by the universities and colleges this year varies considerably and the offers listed below should be used as a first source of reference only. Many institutions will accept combinations of Advanced (AL), Advanced Subsidiary (AS) and Vocational Advanced (VA) level qualifications to achieve the required points total, but applicants must check web sites and prospectuses for full details of all offers. Grades and points totals shown should be regarded as the minimum levels to be achieved, but offers may be adjusted downwards when results are known. The points totals shown to the left of the institutions are for ease of reference only. It must not be assumed that tariff points are always used by institutions or that they can be substituted for an offer in grades. The level of an offer is not necessarily indicative of the quality of a course. To calculate your offers see Chapter 4 and the inside fold of the back cover.

Applicants should note that for some of these courses there are two application pathways (Route A or B) or both. See the general notes under **Art and Design (General)** and refer to the UCAS *Directory* for course details. **NB** Textile Design courses will usually require a portfolio inspection.

Special subject requirements/preferences: A–level: Art and mathematics/science subjects may be required. **GCSE:** English and mathematics usually required. **Nottingham Trent** Foundation course preferred.

240 pts   **Central England** – 240 pts approx (Tex Des)
          Leeds – CCC (Tex Mgt; Tex/Manuf; Tex Des; Tex St (Options))
          UMIST – 240 pts 18u – 3ALs **or** 2ALs+2ASs **or** AL+4ASs **or** VA12u+AL **or**
          VA6u+2ALs; gs; (Tex Des/Des Mgt courses; Tex Sci/Tech courses; Fbe
          Proc/Prod Des courses; Des Mgt/Fash Rtl; Cloth Eng/Mgt courses; Tex
          Tech/Mgt courses)
          UMIST – 240–220 pts approx (Mgt/Mark Tex; Tex Des/Des Mgt; Tex Tech
          Mgt/Lang/Ind Exp; Tex Sci; Tex Sci/Tech with Lang/Ind Exp; Cloth Eng
          Mgt/Lang)

200 pts   **Nottingham Trent** – 200 pts approx + portfolio (Fash Tex Des)
180 pts   **East London** – 180 pts approx (Prtd Tex Surf Decr/Span)
          Huddersfield – 180–140 pts approx (Tex Des (Fdn Art course))
          Manchester Met – 180–140 pts approx (Grmnt Tech Mgt; Cloth Prod Dev)

160 pts   **Bolton (IHE)** – 160 pts approx (Tex (Tech Des))
          De Montfort (Leicester) – 160 pts (inc 2ALs) – ALs **or** ALs+ASs **or** VAs+/
          -ALs/ASs; (Tex Des/Prod; Tex Mgt; Tex Rtl Mark; Cloth Des/Prod)
          Heriot-Watt (Scottish Borders) – 160 pts 12u – CC **or** ALs+ASs **or** VAs C+/
          -ALs/ASs; gs; (Int Tex Mark; Tex/Fash Des Mgt; Tex Tech Manuf; Cloth Des
          Manuf; Biomed Mat)

140 pts   **Bath Spa (UC)** – CD (Tex Des)
          London Guildhall – CD (Tex Furn Des Manuf)

80 pts   **and below and other selection criteria**
          Bolton (IHE) (Tex); Bristol UWE (Fash/Tex Des); Central Lancashire (Fash; Fash
          Prom); Derby (Tex Des); London Inst (Chelsea) (Tex); Loughborough; Manchester
          Met (Tex; Fash); Newport (UWCN) (Fash/Tex); North East Wales (IHE) (Fash/Tex);
          Fash/Tex Comb); North Warwickshire/Hinckley (Coll) (Fash/Tex); Northampton
          (UC) (Fash/Tex; Lea Tech); Northbrook (Coll) (Tex); Norwich (SAD) (Tex);
          Nottingham Trent (Tex Des; Knit); Portsmouth (Tex/Fash); Ravensbourne (CDC)
          (Fash/Tex); Shrewsbury (CAT) (Tex); Somerset (CAT) (Fash/Tex; Surf Tex);
          Southampton (Winchester); Staffordshire (Surf Patt); Surrey (IAD/UC) (Fash);
          Sutton Coldfield (Coll) (Fash/Tex); Teesside (Tex Surf Patt; Des Tex); Ulster
          (Tex/Fash).

Diploma of Higher Education courses
80 pts   Bath Spa (UC) (Tex Des); Huddersfield (Tex Des); UHI.

Higher National Diploma courses
100 pts   **and below**
          Barnsley (Coll); Batley (SA); Bath Spa (UC); Blackburn (Coll); Bolton (IHE);
          Buckinghamshire Chilterns (UC); Carmarthenshire (Coll); Central England;
          Clarendon (Coll); Cleveland (CA); De Montfort; Derby; Glamorgan; Handsworth
          (Coll); Heriot-Watt (Scottish Borders); Huddersfield; Llandrillo (Coll); Leeds (CAD);
          Liverpool (CmC); London (CFash) (Beauty Thera); London (Inst); Manchester
          Met; Mid Cheshire (Coll); Newcastle (Coll); North Warwickshire/Hinckley (Coll);
          Northbrook (Coll); Nottingham Trent; Shrewsbury (CAT); Solihull (Coll); Southwark
          (Coll); Stockport (CFHE); Ulster; Wigan & Leigh (Coll).

Alternative Offers:

Irish offers: De Montfort CCCCC; UMIST ABBBBC.

Scottish Qualifications: Heriot-Watt (Scottish Borders) BBC.

CHOOSING YOUR COURSE (See also **Ch.1**)

> **Subject information:** Textile technologists and managers are in short supply and these courses offer students interested in applied science or management an opportunity to gain the necessary skills and knowledge. Low grades are usually acceptable. Retail Management courses, Marketing and Journalism are also appropriate alternative courses which could lead to the fashion industry. See also **Appendix 1.**

Special Features: Bolton (IHE) Recognised centre of excellence for textiles. Close ties with national employers who frequently sponsor students. Options in colour science, design appreciation, marketing etc. **De Montfort** (Tex Des) Modular course – study routes in textile design, management, clothing design and production. **Heriot-Watt (Scottish Borders)** (Tex Fash Des Mgt) Gives commercial design, management, product development, retail buying or own business. **UMIST** (Cloth/Eng Mgt) Combined course with Manchester Metropolitan University. Five main areas – science and engineering, clothing materials, garment construction, garment manufacture and support subjects in management and design. *NOW CHECK PROSPECTUSES AND WEB SITES.*

Top universities and colleges (Teaching Quality) (see Ch.4): Dundee; Glasgow (SA); Heriot-Watt (Scottish Borders); Manchester Met; Robert Gordon; not all institutions assessed.

Top universities and colleges (Research) (see Ch.4): See **Materials Science/Metallurgy**.

Study opportunities abroad: Bolton (IHE); De Montfort; Heriot-Watt (Scottish Borders); Huddersfield; Leeds; Loughborough; Manchester Met; Nottingham Trent; UMIST.

Work opportunities abroad: Heriot-Watt (Scottish Borders); Huddersfield; Manchester Met.

ADMISSIONS INFORMATION

Number of applicants per place (approx): Bolton (IHE) 2; De Montfort (Tex Des) 3; Heriot-Watt (Scottish Borders) (Tex/Fash Des Mgt) 5; Huddersfield (Tex Des) 4; Leeds 6, (Tex Mgt) 8; Manchester Met 6; UMIST 7 approx for all courses.

General Studies acceptable: De Montfort (2); Heriot-Watt (Scottish Borders); Huddersfield (JMB); Leeds; Manchester Met; UMIST.

Planning your UCAS personal statement (see Ch.4): Contact textile firms and, if possible, textile designers to learn about the scope of this career field. Visit art galleries and museums with textile exhibits. **UMIST** Students must show evidence of good art/design work (grade A/B or equivalent or Foundation Art course). See also **Appendix 1.**

Selection interviews (see Ch.4): Bath Spa (UC); Central England; De Montfort; Derby; Dundee; Huddersfield; Manchester Met (No); UMIST (No); Winchester (SA).

Interview questions (see Ch.4): Applicants should be very familiar with the content of their chosen Textile course and be able to discuss reasons for their choices and their career interests. Questions on properties of different fabrics.

Reasons for rejection (non-academic): Poor design ability. Inability to communicate effectively.

GAP YEAR ADVICE

Work in textiles useful. Keep up the drawing. A Foundation course in Art and Design would be useful but not essential. Talk to admissions tutors.

Institutions willing to defer entry after A-Levels: Bolton (IHE); De Montfort; Heriot-Watt (Scottish Borders); Manchester Met (Fash Des/Tech); UMIST.

AFTER RESULTS ADVICE

Institutions which may accept the same points score after A-Levels: Bolton (IHE); De Montfort; Heriot-Watt (Scottish Borders); Huddersfield; Leeds (all courses); Manchester Met; UMIST.

Institutions which may accept lower grades/points score after A-Levels: De Montfort; UMIST.

Offers to applicants repeating A-Levels: Same Heriot-Watt (Scottish Borders), Leeds (Tex Mgt).

Probable vacancies from June 2001 and in Clearing (see Ch.4): Contact all universities and colleges since vacancies will definitely exist.

NEW GRADUATE DESTINATIONS AND EMPLOYMENT (1999 HESA) (see **Ch.4**)

TOURISM (see also **Business Courses, Hospitality, Hotel & Catering Management** and **Leisure & Recreational Studies**)

NB The information supplied by the universities and colleges this year varies considerably and the offers listed below should be used as a first source of reference only. Many institutions will accept combinations of Advanced (AL), Advanced Subsidiary (AS) and Vocational Advanced (VA) level qualifications to achieve the required points total, but applicants must check web sites and prospectuses for full details of all offers. Grades and points totals shown should be regarded as the minimum levels to be achieved, but offers may be adjusted downwards when results are known. The points totals shown to the left of the institutions are for ease of reference only. It must not be assumed that tariff points are always used by institutions or that they can be substituted for an offer in grades. The level of an offer is not necessarily indicative of the quality of a course. To calculate your offers see Chapter 4 and the inside fold of the back cover.

Special subject requirements/preferences: GCSE: English and mathematics required. For some courses a foreign language may be required.

260 pts **Hertfordshire** – 260–240 pts approx (Mark Tour; Tour Mgt)
Surrey – 260 pts 18u – ALs **or** ALs+ASs **or** VAs (depends on subj); (not gs) (Tour Mgt)
240 pts **Aberystwyth** – 240–200 pts 18–12u – 3/2ALs **or** ALs+ASs; (Tour Mgt)
Bangor – 240 pts (inc ELTS 6.0) (Tour/EFL)
Birmingham (CFCTS) – 12u (inc 1x6u) – CCC; (Tour Mgt)
Bournemouth – 240–200 pts approx (Tour St)
Bristol UWE – 240–220 pts approx (Int Bus St/Tour; Bus Admin/Tour)
Manchester Met – 240–200 pts approx (Hspty Mgt/Tour)
Napier – CCC (Lang/Tour Mgt; Tour Mgt)
North London – 240 pts approx (Int Leis Tour Mgt)
Northumbria – 240 pts approx (Trav/Tour Mgt)
Ulster – 240 pts approx (Htl Tour Mgt)
220 pts **Aberystwyth** – 220–190 pts 18–12u – 3/2ALs **or** ALs+ASs **or** VAs+/-ALs/ASs; (Country Recr Tour)
Bangor – 220 pts (Tour/Lang)
Cardiff (UWI) – 220–160 pts approx (Tourism courses)
Central Lancashire – 220–180 pts 12u; gs; (Tour/Leis; Tour Leis Comb St; Ecotour; Lang/Tour; Int Tour)

Cheltenham & Glos (CHE) – 220–200 pts offer varies with subjects (Tour Mgt courses)

Coventry – 220–200 pts approx (Tour Mgt)

King Alfred's Winchester (Coll) – 220 pts 12u – 3/2ALs **or** 2ALs+ASs; gs; (Tour/Herit Mgt)

Oxford Brookes – CCD/BC (Tourism Joint Hons)

St Mark & St John (Coll) – 220–160 pts approx (Leis/Tour courses)

Sheffield Hallam – 220–200 pts approx (Tourism courses)

South Bank – 220–140 pts approx (Tourism courses)

Staffordshire – 220 pts approx (Spo Recr Tour)

Warrington (CI) – 220–180 pts approx (Tour/Leis courses)

200 pts **Birmingham (CFTCS)** – 200–180 pts approx (Tour Bus Mgt)

Brighton – 200 pts approx (Int Tour Mgt; Tour Mgt; Trav Mgt)

Buckingham – 200 pts approx (Bus St/Tour)

Chester (Coll) – 200 pts – ALs (180 pts inc C)+AS(20 pts) **or** VAs (180 pts inc C)+AS(20 pts); gs; (Tourism courses)

Coventry – 200–180 pts approx (Tourism courses)

Derby – 200 pts 12u – CDD **or** CD+dd **or** VAsCD+/-AL/ASs; gs; (Tourism)

Greenwich – 200 pts approx (C lang) (Tour Mgt; Tour Mgt with Fr/Ger/Span)

Liverpool John Moores – 200 pts (inc C lang) – ALs **or** ALs+ASs **or** VAs+AL(C lang); (Tour/Leis with Chin/Fr/Ger/Ital/Span)

Luton – 200 pts approx (Trav/Tour; Spo Tour; Int Tour Mgt)

Westminster – 200–180 pts approx (Tour Plan)

Wolverhampton – 200–160 pts 12u – DDD–CDE/BD–CC **or** DD+b **or** VA12u CC; gs; (Tourism)

190 pts **North London** – 190 pts (inc 160 pts from 2ALs **or** VAs; (Tour St; Trav St)

180 pts **Buckinghamshire Chilterns (UC)** – 180–140 pts approx (Tourism courses)

Glamorgan – 180 pts approx (Leis/Tour Mgt)

Plymouth – 180 pts approx (Bus Tour; Cult Tour)

St Martin's (Coll) – CDE (Tour Leis Recr)

160 pts **Anglia** – 160 pts 12u (inc 2ALs) – ALs **or** ALs+ASs **or** VA12u BC; gs; (Tour Leis Geog; Tour Leis/Herit Mgt; Sust Tour Dev)

Birmingham (CFTCS) – 12u (inc 1x6u); CC; (Tour Bus Mgt; Advntr Tour Mgt)

Canterbury Christ Church (UC) – CC–EE (Tourism courses)

Chichester (UC) – 160 pts (inc C); (Tour/Leis)

Glasgow Caledonian – CC (Tour Mgt; Int Tour/Inf Sys))

Huddersfield – 160 pts approx (Geog/Tour Leis St)

Hull (Scarborough) – 160–140 pts approx (Leis Tour Mgt)

Lincolnshire & Humberside – 160 pts (Tourism)

Paisley – CC (Leis/Tour)

Scottish (CAg) – 160 pts – CC (Rur Recr/Tour Mgt)

Sunderland – 160 pts; ALs **or** ALs+ASs; (Tour Dev St)

Trinity Carmarthen (Coll) – 160–80 pts approx (Tourism courses)

140 pts **Abertay Dundee** – CD (Tourism)

Bath Spa (UC) – 140 pts 12u – CD **or** ALs+ASs **or** VA12uCD; (not gs) (Tour Mgt)

Blackpool & Fylde (Coll) – 140 pts approx (Hspty Mgt/Tour)

Bolton (IHE) – CD (Tourism courses)

Cumbria (CAD) – CD (Tour Perf St)

Derby – 140 pts 12u – CD **or** DE+ee **or** VAs CD+/-ALs/ASs; (Tour Comb Hons)

Herefordshire (CT) – 140 pts approx (Leis Mgt (Advntr Tour courses))

London (Inst) – 140 pts approx (Int Trav Tour Mgt)

Queen Margaret (UC) – CD (Hspty Tour Mgt; Tour Comb St)

Thames Valley – 140 pts approx (Tour Mgt courses)

Warrington (CI) – 140 pts – ALs **or** ALs+ASs (not AS only) **or** VAs+/-ALs/ASs; gs; (Leis/Tour)

120 pts **and below**

Bradford (Coll) – (Tourism courses)

Colchester (Inst) – DD minimum (Bus Admin Tour)
Herefordshire (CT) – 120 pts – ALs **or** ALs+ASs **or** VAs+/-ALs/ASs; (Tour Mgt)
Robert Gordon – DD (Tour Hspty Mgt)
Solihull (Coll) – (Tourism)
Southampton (Inst) – (Tourism)
Suffolk (Coll) – CE–EE (Tourism courses)
UHI (Moray/North Highland/Perth) – (Tourism via DipHE, HND, HNC)

Leeds Met – (contact university)

Diploma of Higher Education courses
200 pts and below
East Devon (Coll)(Euro Tour Mgt; Tour Mgt); UHI.

Higher National Diploma courses
120 pts and below
Aberystwyth (Welsh Inst Rur St); Barking (Coll); Barnsley (Coll); Bedford (Coll); Bell (CT); Birmingham (CFTCS); Blackburn (Coll); Blackpool & Fylde (Coll); Bournemouth & Poole (Coll); Bradford (Coll); Brighton (CT); Buckinghamshire Chilterns (UC); Cardiff (UWI); Central Lancashire; City College Manchester (CHFE) (Tour Mgt; Leis Mgt; Advntr Tour Mgt); Cornwall & Duchy (Coll); Craven (Coll); Croydon (Coll); Cumbria (CAD); Derby; Doncaster (Coll); Dudley (CT); East Devon (Coll); Farnborough (CT); Filton (Coll); Glasgow (Coll); Gloucestershire (CAT); Greenwich; Herefordshire (CT); Hertfordshire; High Peak (Coll); King Alfred's Winchester (Coll); Llandrillo (Coll); Lincolnshire & Humberside; Loughborough (Coll); Manchester Met; Newcastle (Coll); North East Wales (IHE); North East Worcestershire (Coll); North Highland (Coll); Northbrook (Coll); Norwich City (Coll); Oaklands (Coll); Oldham (Coll); Park Lane (Coll); Plymouth; Portrush (HCC); Portsmouth; St Helens (Coll); Salford; Salisbury (Coll); Scottish (CAg); Sheffield (Coll); Shrewsbury (CAT); Solihull (Coll); Somerset (CAT); South Devon (Coll); South Downs (Coll); Southampton (Inst); Southport (Coll); Stockport (CFHE); Suffolk (Coll); Sutton Coldfield (Coll); Teesside; Thames Valley; UHI; West Herts (Coll); West Thames (Coll); Westminster (IEd); Wigan & Leigh (Coll); Wirral Met (Coll); Yorkshire Coast (CFHE).

Alternative Offers:

IB offers: Brighton 24 pts inc 12 pts H; Buckinghamshire Chilterns (UC) 27 pts; Hertfordshire 29–26 pts; Northumbria 26 pts.

Scottish Qualifications: Abertay Dundee BBC; Bell (CT) CC; Glasgow Caledonian BBCC; Napier BBCC/BBC; Paisley BBB; Queen Margaret (UC) BBC; Robert Gordon BBC; Scottisg (CAg) BCC; Stirling BBBB; Strathclyde BBBB.

CHOOSING YOUR COURSE (See also **Ch.1**)

Subject information: Tourism and Travel courses are becoming very popular; some are combined with Hospitality Management which provide students with specialisms in two areas. Courses involve business studies and a detailed study of tourism and travel. Industrial placements are frequently involved and language options are often included. See also **Appendix 1**.

Special features: Birmingham Offered through the Birmingham College of Food, Tourism and Creative Studies (CFTCS). **Bournemouth** Business studies and a language with a study of aspects of tourism, tourists and destinations. Visits to places in UK and Europe, currently Cyprus or Portugal. *NOW CHECK PROSPECTUSES AND WEB SITES.*

Study opportunities abroad: Birmingham (CFTCS); Brighton; Canterbury Christ Church (UC); Cardiff (UWI); Cheltenham & Glos (CHE); Chester (Coll); Coventry; Derby; Glasgow Caledonian; King Alfred's Winchester (Coll); Liverpool John Moores; Oxford Brookes; Plymouth; Thames Valley; Wolverhampton.

Work opportunities abroad: Brighton; Cheltenham & Glos (CHE); Chester (Coll); Coventry; Derby; Herefordshire (CT); King Alfred's Winchester (Coll); Liverpool John Moores; Northumbria; Plymouth; Robert Gordon; Thames Valley.

ADMISSIONS INFORMATION

Number of applicants per place (approx): Birmingham (CFTCS) 10; Bournemouth 16; Derby 4; Glamorgan 8; Glasgow Caledonian 30; Northumbria 18; Sheffield Hallam 12; Sunderland 2.

Planning your UCAS personal statement (see Ch.4): Work experience in the travel and tourism industry is important – in agencies or hotels. This work could be described in detail. Any experience with people in sales work, dealing with the public – their problems and complaints – should also be included. Travel should be outlined, detailing places visited. Genuine interest in travel, diverse cultures and people. Good communication skills required. See also **Appendix 1**.

Selection interviews (see Ch.4): Bournemouth (No); Brighton; Derby; Glasgow Caledonian; Greenwich (No); Paisley (No); Sheffield Hallam (No); Sunderland.

Interview questions (see Ch.4): Past questions have included: What problems have you experienced when travelling? Questions on places visited. Experiences of air, rail and sea travel. What is marketing? What special qualities do you have that will be of use in the travel industry?

GAP YEAR ADVICE

Relevant experience, particularly involving travel or the hotel industry, is recommended by most universities.

Institutions willing to defer entry after A-Levels: Bournemouth; Cheltenham & Glos (CHE); Derby; Glamorgan; Herefordshire (CT); Hertfordshire; Luton.

AFTER RESULTS ADVICE

Institutions which may accept the same points score after A-Levels: Birmingham (CFTCS); Derby.

Probable vacancies from June 2001 and in Clearing (see Ch.4): Almost all universities and colleges are expected to have vacancies. Offers could range from 240–180 pts.

NEW GRADUATE DESTINATIONS AND EMPLOYMENT (1999 HESA) (see **Ch.4**)

See **Business Courses**.

TOWN & COUNTRY PLANNING (see also **Development Studies**, **Environmental Science/Studies** and **Urban Studies**)

NB The information supplied by the universities and colleges this year varies considerably and the offers listed below should be used as a first source of reference only. Many institutions will accept combinations of Advanced (AL), Advanced Subsidiary (AS) and Vocational Advanced (VA) level qualifications to achieve the required points total, but applicants must check web sites and prospectuses for full details of all offers. Grades and points totals shown should be regarded as the minimum levels to be achieved, but offers may be adjusted downwards when results are known. The points totals shown to the left of the institutions are for ease of reference only. It must not be assumed that tariff points are always used by institutions or that they can be substituted for an offer in grades. The level of an offer is not necessarily indicative of the quality of a course. To calculate your offers see Chapter 4 and the inside fold of the back cover.

Special subject requirements/preferences: A-Level: Economics and geography are appropriate. **GCSE:** English and mathematics.

300 pts **Birmingham** – BBB–BCC (Planning courses)
Liverpool – 300 pts – ALs **or** ALs+ASs **or** VAs+/-ALs/ASs; (Town Plan)
260 pts **Belfast (Queen's)** – BCC (Env Plan)
Bristol UWE – 260–200 pts 18u pref/12u – ALs **or** ALs+ASs **or** VAs+/-ALs/ASs; (Town/Country Plan; Plan Dev)
Cardiff – BCC (City Reg Plan)
Edinburgh (CA) – BCC (Engl/geog pref); (Town Plan)
London (UCL) – BCC–CCC **or** 3ALs+AS/VA; (Town/Country Plan)
Manchester – BCC (Town/Country Plan; Land Plan Mgt)
Newcastle – BCC/BB (Town Plan; Env Plan Soty)
Sheffield – BCC (Urb St/Plan; Land Des Plan)
240 pts **Aberdeen** – CCC (Land Econ (Plan))
Bradford – 240 pts 12u (inc AL sci); gs; (Env Mgt)
Bristol UWE – 240–180 pts 18u pref/12u – ALs **or** ALs+ASs **or** VAs+/-ALs/ASs; (Plan/Leis; Plan/Trans)
220 pts **Central England** – 220 pts; (Env Plan/Geog; Town/Country Plan)
Sheffield Hallam – 220 pts approx (Plan St/Town Plan)
Strathclyde – CCD/BC (Env Plan)
200 pts **Bangor** – 200 pts; gs; (Env Plan Mgt)
De Montfort – 200–160 pts approx (Plan Dev)
Dundee – CDD/BC (Town Reg Plan)
Westminster – 200–160 pts approx (Town Plan)
180 pts **Cheltenham & Glos (CHE)** – 180–140 pts approx (Env Mgt/Urb Des courses)
Coventry – 180 pts approx (Plan Econ)
Liverpool Hope (Coll) – 180 pts approx (Cits/Commun/Regn Plan)
Liverpool John Moores – 180 pts – ALs **or** ALs+ASs **or** VAs+/-ALs/ASs; (Urb Plan)
Oxford Brookes – DDD/CC (Plan St joint Hons)
160 pts **Anglia** – 160 pts 12u (inc 2ALs) – ALs **or** ALs+ASs **or** VA12u BC; gs; (Env Plan)

Leeds Met – (contact university)

Higher National Diploma courses
100 pts **and below**
Sheffield Hallam.

Alternative Offers:

EB offers: Newcastle 60%.

IB offers: Belfast (Queen's) H655 S555; Cardiff 26 pts; Newcastle 30 pts; Sheffield Hallam 30–25 pts; South Bank 24 pts.

Irish offers: Bristol UWE CCCC; Dundee CCCCC; Heriot-Watt BBBC; Newcastle CCCCC; Sheffield CCCCC; South Bank CCCC; Westminster CCCCC.

Scottish Qualifications: Aberdeen (Land Econ) BBBC; Dundee BBBC; Napier BBCC; Strathclyde BBBC.

Overseas applicants: Oxford Brookes, **South Bank** Good spoken English essential.

CHOOSING YOUR COURSE (See also **Ch.1**)

Subject information: Town and Country Planning courses are all very similar and some lead to qualification or part of a qualification as a member of the Royal Town Planning Institute (RTPI). Further information from the RTPI (see **Appendix 1**). Alternative course choices include Architecture, Development Studies, Geography, Surveying, Environmental Studies, Law, Countryside Management, Urban Studies and Public Administration.

Special Features: Cardiff A large university planning school with widest range of specialist options, for example, housing, developing countries, transport, information systems. **De Montfort** The Planning and Development degree has a strong emphasis on practical assignments and visits. **Dundee** Final year options include housing policy, minerals planning, employment, agriculture and forestry, countryside planning and urban design. **Newcastle** Options include housing, landscape, European property development. Employer contact in project work. Professional practice placements; 100% employment record over 15 years. **Oxford Brookes** Pathways in Urban Policy, Transport, Environment and Design, Countryside Planning. **Sheffield** The three major subjects studied in the first year are urban studies, the design of urban areas and one from economics, social history, geography, politics or sociology and social policy. **Westminster** Four main themes of this three-year course cover the environment and society, public intervention, policy and skills for planning. Later studies include social housing, housing and transport policy. *NOW CHECK PROSPECTUSES AND WEB SITES.*

Top universities and colleges (Teaching Quality) (see Ch.4): Belfast (Queen's); Bristol UWE; Cardiff; Cheltenham & Glos (CHE); De Montfort; Kingston; Leeds Met; Liverpool; London (UCL); Newcastle; Oxford Brookes; Reading; Sheffield; Sheffield Hallam; South Bank; not all institutions assessed.

Top universities and colleges (Research) (see Ch.4): Aberdeen; Cardiff; Cheltenham & Glos (CHE); Glasgow; Leeds; Liverpool; London (UCL); Loughborough; Newcastle; Oxford Brookes; Reading; Sheffield.

Study opportunities abroad: Belfast (Queen's); Bristol UWE; Central England; Dundee; Manchester; Newcastle; Strathclyde.

ADMISSIONS INFORMATION

Number of applicants per place (approx): Bristol UWE 6; Cardiff 2; Central England 8; Cheltenham & Glos (CHE) 20; Dundee 10; London (UCL) 6; Newcastle 9; Sheffield Hallam 6; South Bank 3; Strathclyde 5.

Planning your UCAS personal statement (see Ch.4): Visit your local planning office and discuss the career with planners. Know the plans and proposed developments in your area and any objections to them. Study the history of town planning worldwide and the development of new towns in the United Kingdom during the 20th century, for example Bourneville, Milton Keynes, Port Sunlight, Welwyn Garden City, Cumbernauld, and the advantages and disadvantages which became apparent. See also **Appendix 1**.

Selection interviews (see Ch.4): Bristol UWE; Cardiff; Central England; Coventry (No); Dundee; London (UCL); Newcastle (T); South Bank.

Interview questions (see Ch.4): Since town planning is a vocational course, work experience in a planning office is relevant and questions are likely to be asked on the type of work done and the problems faced by planners. Questions in recent years have included: If you were re-planning your home county for the future, what points would you consider? How are statistics used in urban planning? How do you think the problem of inner cities can be solved? Have you visited your local planning office?

Reasons for rejection (non-academic): Lack of commitment to study for a professional qualification in town planning.

GAP YEAR ADVICE

Most institutions will accept a gap year, recommending work experience in a planning office.

Institutions willing to defer entry after A-Levels: Cardiff; Cheltenham & Glos (CHE) (prefer not); Dundee; London (UCL) (No); Luton; Newcastle (No); Oxford Brookes; Sheffield Hallam; South Bank.

AFTER RESULTS ADVICE

Institutions which may accept the same points score after A-Levels: Bristol UWE; Cardiff; Central England; Cheltenham & Glos (CHE); Dundee (No); Newcastle; South Bank.

Institutions which may accept lower grades/points score after A-Levels: Bristol UWE; Cheltenham & Glos (CHE); Newcastle; South Bank.

Offers to applicants repeating A-Levels: Higher Bristol UWE, Central England, East Anglia, Newcastle; **Same** Oxford Brookes, South Bank.

Probable vacancies from June 2001 and in Clearing (see Ch.4): Most institutions are worth contacting. Offers could average 200–160 pts.

NEW GRADUATE DESTINATIONS AND EMPLOYMENT (1999 HESA) (see **Ch.4**)

In a survey of 959 graduates, 593 entered full-time employment (the great majority into property services and public administration), 27 were believed to be unemployed and 220 went into further study (112 into professional training) or research.

TRANSPORT MANAGEMENT & PLANNING (see also **Business Courses** and **Engineering/Engineering Sciences**)

NB The information supplied by the universities and colleges this year varies considerably and the offers listed below should be used as a first source of reference only. Many institutions will accept combinations of Advanced (AL), Advanced Subsidiary (AS) and Vocational Advanced (VA) level qualifications to achieve the required points total, but applicants must check web sites and prospectuses for full details of all offers. Grades and points totals shown should be regarded as the minimum levels to be achieved, but offers may be adjusted downwards when results are known. The points totals shown to the left of the institutions are for ease of reference only. It must not be assumed that tariff points are always used by institutions or that they can be substituted for an offer in grades. The level of an offer is not necessarily indicative of the quality of a course. To calculate your offers see Chapter 4 and the inside fold of the back cover.

Special subject requirements/preferences: GCSE: English and mathematics.

260 pts	**Bradford** – 260 pts 12u (inc AL maths); gs; (Cyber/Trans Sys)
	Loughborough – 260 pts approx (Trans Mgt Plan; Air Trans Mgt; Log)
240 pts	**Aston** – 240 pts 18u – 3ALs **or** ALs+ASs **or** VAs+/-AL/ASs; gs; (Trans Mgt; Log courses)
	Bristol UWE – 240–180 pts 18u pref/12u – ALs **or** ALs+ASs **or** VAs+/-ALs/ASs; (Plan/Trans)
220 pts	**Bristol UWE** – 220–180 pts approx (Trans/Env Mgt)
200 pts	**Huddersfield** – 200 12u – CDD **or** ALs+ASs **or** VAs+/-ALs/ASs; gs; (Trans/Log Mgt; Log Sply Chn Mgt; Fd Sply Chn Mgt; Euro Log Mgt)
	Oxford Brookes – CDD/CC (Trans Trav courses)
160 pts	**Nottingham Trent** – CC (Fd Sply Chn Mgt)
	Swansea (IHE) – 160 pts approx (Trans Mgt)
	Ulster – CC (Trans Log)
140 pts	**Liverpool John Moores** – 140 pts (inc 1x6u **or** 2x6u **or** 1x12u) – ALs **or** ALs+ASs **or** VAs+/-ALs/ASs; (Transport)
120 pts	**Napier** – DD (Trans Eng)
80 pts	**Coventry** – portfolio (Trans Des)

Diploma of Higher Education courses
80 pts Plymouth.

Higher National Diploma courses (in Business Studies)
100 pts and below
Glamorgan; North East Worcestershire (Coll); Northumbria (Bus Trans Mgt); Plymouth; Swansea (IHE) (Trans).

Alternative Offers:

Scottish Qualifications: Napier BBCC.

CHOOSING YOUR COURSE (See also **Ch.1**)

Subject information: Transport Management and Planning is a specialised branch of business studies with many applications on land, sea and air. It is not as popular as the less specialised Business Studies courses but just as relevant and will provide the student with an excellent introduction to management and its problems. Civil Engineering, Town and Country Planning, Urban Studies and Marine Transport courses could also be considered. See also **Appendix 1**.

Special Features: Aston Course covers road, rail, air, maritime transport, inland waterways and pipeline transport (passenger and freight movements). Three or four-year sandwich programme. **Huddersfield** Emphasis on road freight transport and distribution. Excellent employment record. *NOW CHECK PROSPECTUSES AND WEB SITES.*

Top universities and colleges (Teaching Quality) (see Ch.4): not all institutions assessed.

Study opportunities abroad: Aston; Huddersfield; Loughborough; Napier; Swansea (IHE).

Work opportunities abroad: Huddersfield.

ADMISSIONS INFORMATION

Number of applicants per place (approx): Aston 4; Coventry 5; Huddersfield 5; Loughborough 11; Oxford Brookes 4.

Planning your UCAS personal statement (see Ch.4): Air, sea, road and rail transport are the main specialist areas. Contacts with those involved and work experience/shadowing should be described in full. See also **Appendix 1**.

Selection interviews (see Ch.4): Aston (No); Huddersfield (T); Loughborough.

Interview questions (see Ch.4): A sound knowledge of the transport industry (land, sea and air) is likely to be important at interview. Reading around the subject is also important, as are any contacts with management staff in the industries. Past questions have included: What developments are taking place to reduce the number of cars on the roads? What transport problems exist in your own locality? How did you travel to your interview? What problems did you encounter? How could they have been overcome?

GAP YEAR ADVICE

Institutions willing to defer entry after A-Levels: Aston; Huddersfield.

AFTER RESULTS ADVICE

Institutions which may accept the same points score after A-Levels: Aston.

Offers to applicants repeating A-Levels: Same Aston.

Probable vacancies from June 2001 and in Clearing (see Ch.4): Contact universities since some vacancies are likely.

NEW GRADUATE DESTINATIONS AND EMPLOYMENT (1999 HESA) (see **Ch.4**)

Of 280 graduates surveyed, 186 went into full-time employment (mainly transport areas), 29 went on to further research and training and 17 were believed to be unemployed.

URBAN STUDIES (see also **Development Studies** and **Town & Country Planning**)

NB The information supplied by the universities and colleges this year varies considerably and the offers listed below should be used as a first source of reference only. Many institutions will accept combinations of Advanced (AL), Advanced Subsidiary (AS) and Vocational Advanced (VA) level qualifications to achieve the required points total, but applicants must check web sites and prospectuses for full details of all offers. Grades and points totals shown should be regarded as the minimum levels to be achieved, but offers may be adjusted downwards when results are known. The points totals shown to the left of the institutions are for ease of reference only. It must not be assumed that tariff points are always used by institutions or that they can be substituted for an offer in grades. The level of an offer is not necessarily indicative of the quality of a course. To calculate your offers see Chapter 4 and the inside fold of the back cover.

Special subject requirements/preferences: GCSE: English and mathematics.

280 pts	**Kent** – 280 pts approx (Urb St (Sociol); Urb St Soc Pol)
	Oxford Brookes – BBC–DDD (Planning Studies courses)
260 pts	**Belfast (Queen's)** – BCC (Env Plan)
	Sheffield – BCC (Urb St Plan)
240 pts	**Bradford** – 240 pts 12u (inc AL sci); gs; (Env Mgt)
	Liverpool – CCC (Env Plan; MPlan)
	Westminster – 240 pts approx (Urb Des Plan)
200 pts	**Cheltenham & Glos (CHE)** – 200–180 pts approx (Urb Des courses)
	Sheffield Hallam – 200 pts approx (Urb Reg Pol)
	Westminster – 200–160 pts approx (Urb Des)
180 pts	**Brighton** – 180 pts approx (Urb Cons Env Mgt)
	Coventry – 180 pts approx (Plan/Econ)
	Glamorgan – 180 pts approx (Urb St)
	Liverpool John Moores – 180 pts approx (Urb Plan)
	Nottingham Trent – 180 pts approx (Plan Dev)
	Sheffield Hallam – 180 pts approx (Urb St)
	South Bank – 180 pts approx (Urb Env Plan)
	Leeds Met – (contact university)

Alternative Offers:

IB offers: Kent 28 pts; Sheffield Hallam 30–25 pts

CHOOSING YOUR COURSE (See also **Ch.1**)

> **Subject information:** Urban Studies is a broad study of the social, economic and political processes underlying contemporary problems in towns and cities. See also **Town & Country Planning** (Subject information). See also **Appendix 1**.

Special Features: Kent Urban Studies is offered with pathways in geography, economics, sociology and social policy. **Liverpool John Moores** Urban society, countryside, planning policy, British and world cities. *NOW CHECK PROSPECTUSES AND WEB SITES.*

Top universities and colleges (Teaching Quality) (see Ch.4): Sheffield; not all institutions assessed.

Top universities and colleges (Research) (see Ch.4): Kent; Sheffield Hallam.

Study opportunities abroad: Coventry; North London; Sheffield; Sheffield Hallam.

Work opportunities abroad: Coventry.

ADMISSIONS INFORMATION

Number of applicants per place (approx): Central England 8; Coventry 10; Kent 15; Liverpool John Moores 10; Middlesex 2; North London 4; Nottingham 10; Sheffield Hallam 4; Westminster 5.

Planning your UCAS personal statement (see Ch.4): See **Town & Country Planning.**

Selection interviews (see Ch.4): Kent (No).

Interview questions (see Ch.4): See **Town & Country Planning**.

GAP YEAR ADVICE

Institutions willing to defer entry after A-Levels: Kent; Sheffield Hallam.

AFTER RESULTS ADVICE

Probable vacancies from June 2001 and in Clearing (see Ch.4): A good selection of vacancies is likely from June onwards.

NEW GRADUATE DESTINATIONS AND EMPLOYMENT (1999 HESA) (see **Ch.4**)

See **Town & Country Planning.**

VETERINARY SCIENCE/MEDICINE

NB The information supplied by the universities and colleges this year varies consider-ably and the offers listed below should be used as a first source of reference only. Many institutions will accept combinations of Advanced (AL), Advanced Subsidiary (AS) and Vocational Advanced (VA) level qualifications to achieve the required points total, but applicants must check web sites and prospectuses for full details of all offers. Grades and points totals shown should be regarded as the minimum levels to be achieved, but offers may be adjusted downwards when results are known. The points totals shown to the left of the institutions are for ease of reference only. It must not be assumed that tariff points are always used by institutions or that they can be substituted for an offer in grades. The level of an offer is not necessarily indicative of the quality of a course. To calculate your offers see Chapter 4 and the inside fold of the back cover.

For places in Veterinary Science/Medicine, applicants may select only four universities.

Special subject requirements/preferences: A-Level: Three subjects in mathematics/science subjects, chemistry essential. **Bristol, Glasgow, London** Biology required. **Edinburgh** Grade A in chemistry, grade A or B from biology, mathematics, physics. **Middlesex** (Vet Nurs) Sciences not required for the degree course. **GCSE: Bristol, Glasgow** Grade A or B in physics. **Bristol** Grade A in five–six subjects.

It is likely that most universities will set standards similar to those listed above.

360 pts and above
> **Cambridge** – Offers, mainly in grades, vary between colleges and will include the Medical and Veterinary Admission Test (Vet Med)
> **London (RVC)** – AAA (Vet Med)

340 pts **Bristol** – AAB (chem/biol/phys/maths); (not gs) (Vet Sci)
> **Edinburgh** – AAB (Vet Med)
> **Glasgow** – AAB (Vet Sci)
> **Liverpool** – 340 pts – ALs **or** ALs+ASs **or** VAs+/-ALs/ASs; (Vet Sci)

300 pts **Bristol** – BBB (chem+sci) **or** BB+bbb (AL chem/biol/maths); (not gs) (Vet Pathgen)

240 pts **Middlesex** – 240 pts approx (Vet Nurs)

160 pts **Bristol** – CC **or** ALs+ASs **or** VA6u C+AL(C); (not gs) (Vet Nurs/Prac Admin)

Higher National Diploma courses
Bicton (CAg); Bristol UWE (Hartpury); Central Lancashire (Vet Prac Mgt); Moulton (Coll); Plymouth 120 pts approx (Vet Nurs).

Alternative Offers:

IB offers: Bristol 33 pts inc H776 inc chem/biol; Edinburgh 34 pts inc 6/7 in science subjects; Glasgow H766; Liverpool H666; London (RVC) H777–H666; Middlesex 28 pts.

Scottish Qualifications: Edinburgh AAABB; Glasgow AAABB.

Author's note: Veterinary Science/Medicine is the most intensely competitive subject and, as in the case of Medicine, one or two offers and three rejections are not uncommon. As a result the Royal College of Veterinary Surgeons has raised a number of points which are relevant to applicants and advisers:

(a) Every candidate for a veterinary degree course should be advised to spend a suitable period with a veterinarian in practice.

(b) A period spent in veterinary work may reveal a hitherto unsuspected allergy or sensitivity following contact with various animals.

(c) Potential applicants should be under no illusions about the difficulty of the task they have set themselves . . . five applicants for every available place . . . with no likelihood of places being increased at the present time.

(d) There are so many candidates who can produce the necessary level of scholastic attainment that other considerations have to be taken into account in making the choice. In most cases the number of grade As in the GCSE will be crucial. This is current practice. Headteachers' reports and details of applicants' interests, activities and background are very relevant and are taken fully into consideration . . . applicants are reminded to include details of periods of time spent with veterinary surgeons.

(e) Any applicant who has not received an offer but who achieves the grades required for admission ought to write as soon as the results are known to the schools and enquire about the prospects of entry at the Clearing stage. All courses cover the same subject topics. **Cambridge** All applicants must take the Medical and Veterinary Admissions Test (MVAT). See **Chapter 3 – Admission to Cambridge University**.

CHOOSING YOUR COURSE (See also **Ch.1**)

These are very popular and academically demanding courses for which some work experience prior to application is essential. Courses have much the same content, but check with prospectuses for all courses. Animal Science courses are the obvious alternative, although many students also turn to Medicine and related courses. See also **Appendix 1**.

Top universities and colleges (Teaching Quality) (see Ch.4): Edinburgh; Glasgow; not all institutions assessed.

Top universities and colleges (Research) (see Ch.4): Bristol; Cambridge; Edinburgh; Glasgow; Liverpool; London (RVC).

Study opportunities abroad: Glasgow; London (RVC).

ADMISSIONS INFORMATION

Number of applicants per place (approx): Bristol 25; Cambridge 8; Edinburgh 15; Glasgow 15; Liverpool 17; London (RVC) 20.

Planning your UCAS personal statement (see Ch.4): Applicants for Veterinary Science must limit their choices to four universities and submit their applications by 15 October. Work experience is essential for all applicants. Discuss experiences in full with information on the size and type of practice and the type of work in which you were involved. **Bristol** Evidence of wide veterinary animal experience. Initiative. See also **Appendix 1**.

Selection interviews (see Ch.4): Bristol; Cambridge (T); Edinburgh; Glasgow.

Interview questions (see Ch.4): Past questions have included: Why do you want to be a vet? Have you visited a veterinary practice? What did you see? Do you think there should be a Vet National Health Service? What are your views on vivisection? What are your views on intensive factory farming? How can you justify thousands of pounds of taxpayers' money being spent on training you to be a vet when it could be used to train a civil engineer? When would you feel it your responsibility to tell battery hen farmers that they were being cruel to their livestock? What are your views on vegetarians? How does aspirin stop pain? Why does it only work for a certain length of time? Do you eat beef? Outline the BSE problem and European attitudes. Questions on A-level science syllabus.

Reasons for rejection (non-academic): Failure to demonstrate motivation. Lack of basic knowledge or understanding of ethical and animal issues.

GAP YEAR ADVICE

Check universities for information on gap year applications.

Institutions willing to defer entry after A-Levels: Bristol.

AFTER RESULTS ADVICE

Liverpool All hopeful candidates, with or without the required grades in August, should contact the faculty office for advice about future prospects.They should do this before accepting an alternative course.

Institutions which may accept the same points score after A-Levels: Bristol (No); Edinburgh; Glasgow; Liverpool; London (RVC).

Offers to applicants repeating A-Levels: Higher London (RVC); **Unlikely** Liverpool; **Not acceptable** Edinburgh, Glasgow.

Probable vacancies from June 2001 and in Clearing (see Ch.4): No vacancies are likely in this subject area. Applicants not placed but who achieve very high grades however, could contact veterinary schools in Clearing.

NEW GRADUATE DESTINATIONS AND EMPLOYMENT (1999 HESA) (see **Ch.4**)

Of 440 graduates surveyed, 337 had entered full-time employment, 65 went into further study and 19 graduates reported that they were unemployed.

WELSH (CYMRAEG) & CELTIC STUDIES (including Irish Studies)

NB The information supplied by the universities and colleges this year varies consider-ably and the offers listed below should be used as a first source of reference only. Many institutions will accept combinations of Advanced (AL), Advanced Subsidiary (AS) and Vocational Advanced (VA) level qualifications to achieve the required points total, but applicants must check web sites and prospectuses for full details of all offers. Grades and points totals shown should be regarded as the minimum levels to be achieved, but offers may be adjusted downwards when results are known. The points totals shown to the left of the institutions are for ease of reference only. It must not be assumed that tariff points are always used by institutions or that they can be substituted for an offer in grades. The level of an offer is not necessarily indicative of the quality of a course. To calculate your offers see Chapter 4 and the inside fold of the back cover.

Special subject requirements/preferences: A-Level: *Celtic courses* Irish or Gaelic is required. *Welsh courses* Welsh may be required or preferred.

360 pts   and above
        Cambridge – Offers, mainly in grades, vary between colleges (Anglo–Saxon, Norse and Celtic)
340 pts   Edinburgh – AAB (Law/Celtic)

320 pts **Cardiff** – ABB–CCC (Welsh courses)
300 pts **Edinburgh** – BBB (Celtic courses except under **320 pts**)
280 pts **Glasgow** – BBC (Celtic courses)
      Liverpool – BBC (Irish St Comb Hons)
260 pts **Belfast (Queen's)** – BCC (Celtic courses)
      Liverpool – BCC (Irish St)
      Swansea – 260 pts 18u – BCC–CCC **or** ALs+ASs **or** VAs+/-ALs/ASs; (Welsh courses)
240 pts **Aberdeen** – CCC (Celtic St; Gaelic St)
      Aberystwyth – CCC–CCD/BC (Celtic St; Welsh)
      Lampeter – 240–160 pts approx (Welsh; Welsh St)
      Ulster – CCC (Irish St courses)
220 pts **Bangor** – 220 pts – CCD **or** BDD (Welsh 2nd lang); gs; (Welsh courses except under **200 pts**)
200 pts **Bangor** – 200 pts; gs (AL only); (Welsh)
180 pts **Glamorgan** – 180 pts approx (Welsh courses)
      North East Wales (IHE) – 180–120 pts approx (Welsh St/Hist courses)
      North London – 180 pts approx (Irish St; Irish St/Pol)
      UHI – 180 pts approx (Gaelic)
160 pts **Bath Spa (UC)** – 160–120 pts 12u – CD **or** VA12u CD; (not gs) (Irish St)
      St Mary's (Coll) – 12u – CC–DD **or** VAs CC–DD+/-AL/ASs; gs; (Irish St)
      Trinity Carmarthen (Coll) – CC–EE (Dyniaethau; Welsh; Welsh St)
      UHI (Lews Castle/Sabhal Mor Ostaig) – (Gaelic Lang/Cult St/N Atlantic St)
140 pts **St Mary's (Coll)** – 140–80 pts approx (Irish St Comb)

Diploma of Higher Education courses
    Ulster.

Alternative Offers:

IB offers: Aberdeen 30 pts; Lampeter 24 pts.

Irish offers: Aberdeen BBBB; Aberystwyth BBBCC.

Scottish Qualifications: Aberdeen BBBB; Edinburgh BBBB; Glasgow BBBB.

CHOOSING YOUR COURSE (See also **Ch.1**)

Subject information: There are five living Celtic languages – Irish, Scottish, Gaelic, Welsh and Breton – but this subject area also covers the extinct languages – Manx, Cornish, Gaulish and Celtiberian – and also the history and civilisation of the Celtic peoples. As alternative courses, Ancient History and Anthropology could be appropriate.

Special features: Aberystwyth Beginners' course available with options in Breton and Irish. **Bangor** Offered jointly with 14 other subjects. **Belfast (Queen's)** Course includes Scottish, Gaelic, Manx and Cornish. **Cardiff** Medieval Welsh literature and linguistics of modern Welsh; course in Welsh and the media. **Lampeter** Prize-winning department in innovative teaching. *NOW CHECK PROSPECTUSES AND WEB SITES.*

Top universities and colleges (Teaching Quality) (see Ch.4): Aberystwyth; Bangor; not all institutions assessed.

Top universities and colleges (Research) (see Ch.4): Aberystwyth; Belfast (Queen's); Cardiff; Edinburgh; Glasgow; Swansea; Ulster.

Study opportunities abroad: Aberdeen; Aberystwyth; Belfast (Queen's); Edinburgh; Glasgow; Swansea.

ADMISSIONS INFORMATION

Number of applicants per place (approx): Aberystwyth 4; Bangor 8; Cambridge 2.3; Cardiff 2; Lampeter 3; St Mary's (Coll) 3; Swansea 7.

Planning your UCAS personal statement (see Ch.4): Interests in this field largely develop through literature, museum visits or archaeology which should be fully described in the UCAS form.

Selection interviews (see Ch.4): Aberystwyth; Bath Spa (UC) (No); Lampeter; Swansea.

Interview questions (see Ch.4): Past questions have included: Why do you want to study this subject? What specific areas of Celtic culture interest you? What do you expect to gain by studying unusual subjects?

GAP YEAR ADVICE

Most institutions will accept a gap year.

Institutions willing to defer entry after A-levels: Aberystwyth; Bangor; Cardiff; Lampeter; Swansea.

AFTER RESULTS ADVICE

Institutions which may accept the same points score after A-Levels: Aberystwyth; Bangor; Cardiff; Lampeter; Swansea.

Institutions which may accept lower grades/points score after A-Levels: Aberystwyth; Cardiff; Lampeter.

Probable vacancies from June 2001 and in Clearing (see Ch.4): A number of universities are expected to have vacancies on both Single and Joint Honours courses. Offers in the more competitive universities will probably range between 240 and 200 pts.

NEW GRADUATE DESTINATIONS AND EMPLOYMENT (1999 HESA) (see **Ch.4**)

Of the 128 graduates in Celtic languages and culture surveyed, 38 obtained employment (mainly in education, community and social work) within six months, 67 went on to further study (professional or teacher training courses) and two were unemployed.

ZOOLOGY (see also **Agricultural Sciences/Agriculture, Animal Sciences** and **Biology**)

NB The information supplied by the universities and colleges this year varies considerably and the offers listed below should be used as a first source of reference only. Many institutions will accept combinations of Advanced (AL), Advanced Subsidiary (AS) and Vocational Advanced (VA) level qualifications to achieve the required points total, but applicants must check web sites and prospectuses for full details of all offers. Grades and points totals shown should be regarded as the minimum levels to be achieved, but offers may be adjusted downwards when results are known. The points totals shown to the left of the institutions are for ease of reference only. It must not be assumed that tariff points are always used by institutions or that they can be substituted for an offer in grades. The level of an offer is not necessarily indicative of the quality of a course. To calculate your offers see Chapter 4 and the inside fold of the back cover.

Special subject requirements/preferences: A-Level: Three subjects from mathematics/science. **Bangor** Biology plus another science. **GCSE: Bristol** Grade A or B in chemistry and mathematics if not at A-Level. **Swansea** Majority of grade Bs or better.

360 pts   and above
Cambridge – Offers, mainly in grades, vary between colleges (Nat Sci Zoology)
Nottingham – AAA–BBB (Zoology)
330 pts   Southampton – 330 pts 12u (inc 2ALs inc biol/zool/bot/hum biol) (Zoology)
320 pts   Bristol – ABB–BBB(inc biol+sci); (not gs) (Zoology)
Liverpool – 320–280 pt – ALs **or** ALs+ASs **or** VAs+/-ALs/ASs; (Zoology)
London (Imp) – ABB (Zoology)

300 pts **Cardiff** – BBB–BCC (Zoology)
Durham – B(biol)B(sci)+B/bb; (not gs) (Zoology)
Leeds – BBB (Zoology)
London (QM) – 300–250 pts – ALs or ALs+ASs or VAs+/-ALs/ASs; (Zoology)
280 pts **Bangor** – 280 pts – ALs (inc biol); (Zool/Anim Ecol; Zool; Zool/Mar Biol)
Birmingham – BBC (Biol Sci (Anim Biol))
Edinburgh – BBC (Zoology)
Glasgow – BBC–CCC (Zoology)
Leeds – BBC (App Zool; Microbiol (Zool); Bioch (Zool))
Leicester – 18u – BBC or BB+2ASs or VA12u+AL; gs (AL only if only 2ALs offered) (Zoology)
London (RH) – 280 pts – BBC–BCC or 2ALs+2ASs; (Zoology courses)
Manchester – BBC (Zoology courses)
Newcastle – BBC–BCC (Zoology)
Reading – 280 pts approx (Zoology)
Sheffield – BBC (Zool Genet)
Swansea – 280 pts 18u – BBC–BCC/AB–BB or ALs+ASs or VAs+/-ALs/ASs; (Zoology)
240 pts **Aberystwyth** – 240 pts 21u – CCC or CC+cc or VAs; gs; (Zool; Zool/Microbiol)
Belfast (Queen's) – CCC/BB (Zoology)
220 pts **Aberdeen** – CCD–CCD/BC (Zool; Maths/Zool)
Dundee – 220 pts approx (Zoology)
Surrey Roehampton – 220–180 pts approx (inc 2ALs) – ALs or ALs+ASs or VAs+/-ALs/ASs; (Zoology)
200 pts **Liverpool John Moores** – 180–160 pts (inc AL biol 80 pts) or 200–160 pts VA – ALs or ALs+ASs or VAs+/-ALs/ASs; (App Zool)
140 pts **Derby** – 140 pts 12u – CD or DD+dd or VAs CD+/-ALs/ASs; gs; (Zoology)

Higher National Diploma courses
St Austell (Coll)/Newquay Zoo (Zool Cons Mgt).

Alternative Offers:

EB offers: Bangor 65%; Birmingham 30 pts; London (RH) 70%; Newcastle 65%.

IB offers: Aberdeen 26 pts; Aberystwyth 28 pts and above; Bangor 28 pts H655 S555; Bristol 32 pts inc H6 (biol) 55; Durham 28 pts; Glasgow H555; Leeds 30–28 pts; Liverpool 30 pts; London (RH) 27 pts; Newcastle 30 pts; Swansea 26 pts.

Irish offers: Aberdeen BBBC; Aberystwyth BBBCC; Bangor BBCCC; Dundee BBCC; Edinburgh BBBB; Glasgow BBB; Liverpool BBCC; London (RH) BBBCC; Newcastle BBCC.

Scottish Qualifications: Aberdeen BBBC; Dundee BBCC; Glasgow BBBB.

Overseas applicants: Newcastle English language courses offered.

CHOOSING YOUR COURSE (See also **Ch.1**)

Subject information: Zoology courses have a biological science foundation and could cover animal ecology, marine and fisheries biology, animal population development and behaviour and, on some courses, wildlife management and fisheries. There is a shortage of applicants. Veterinary Science and Animal Science courses are alternatives but the range of Biological Science courses should be considered.

Special features: Aberdeen Several named subject degrees are offered within this subject. **Bangor** Three Zoology courses are offered. **Cardiff** For Single Honours students the theme of the course is the animal in its environment in which students study the behaviour, physiology and ecology of animals and special topics on cell and marine biology. **Liverpool** Zoology courses include animal diversity, ecology, freshwater biology and animal behaviour. **Newcastle** Degree based on ecology and behaviour. Flexible first year; course based on ecology and neurobiology. New psychology modules in each year of course. Practical work a major element. **Southampton** Common first year for Biology, Applied Biology, Botany and Zoology students. Specialist studies follow in years 2 and 3. **Swansea** Modular course. Variety of marine and terrestrial habitats. See also under **Agricultural Sciences/Agriculture**, **Animal Sciences** and **Biology**. *NOW CHECK PROSPECTUSES AND WEB SITES.*

Top universities and colleges (Teaching Quality) (see Ch.4): See **Biology**.

Top universities and colleges (Research) (see Ch.4): Cambridge; Leicester; Nottingham.

Study opportunities abroad: Aberdeen; Aberystwyth; Bangor; Leeds; Leicester; London (QM); Manchester; Reading; Sheffield; Swansea.

Work opportunities abroad: Swansea.

ADMISSIONS INFORMATION

Number of applicants per place (approx): Aberystwyth 8; Bangor 6; Bristol 13; Cardiff 8; Durham 11; Leeds 7; London (RH) 6, (UCL) 8; Manchester 17; Newcastle 15; Nottingham 7; Swansea 11.

Planning your UCAS personal statement (see Ch.4): Interests in animals should be described, together with any first-hand experience gained. Visits to zoos, farms, fish farms etc should be described with any special points of interest which you noted.

Selection interviews (see Ch.4): Aberdeen (No); Aberystwyth; Cambridge; Cardiff (No); Durham; Hull; Leeds (No); Liverpool; London (RH); Manchester; Newcastle; Nottingham (No); Surrey Roehampton (No); Swansea.

Interview questions (see Ch.4): Past questions have included: Specimens may be given to identify. Why do you want to study Zoology? What career do you hope to follow on graduation? Questions asked on the A-level subjects.

GAP YEAR ADVICE

Try to gain experience in the biological field.

Institutions willing to defer entry after A-Levels: Aberystwyth (contact admissions tutor); Bangor; Bristol; Cardiff (providing deferred entry has been previously agreed); Durham; Leeds; London (RH), (UCL); Newcastle; Nottingham; Swansea (discouraged).

AFTER RESULTS ADVICE

Institutions which may accept the same points score after A-Levels: Aberdeen (No); Bangor; Bristol; Durham; Hull; Leeds; Liverpool; London (RH (No); Manchester; Newcastle; Nottingham (No); Swansea.

Institutions which may accept lower grades/points score after A-Levels: Aberystwyth; Bangor; Bristol; Leeds; Liverpool; London (RH); Newcastle; Surrey Roehampton; Swansea.

Offers to applicants repeating A-Levels: Higher Aberystwyth; Bristol, Hull, Leeds, Swansea; **Same** Durham, Leeds, Liverpool, London (RH) Surrey Roehampton.

Probable vacancies from June 2001 and in Clearing (see Ch.4): A number of universities can be contacted as vacancies are expected with offers ranging from 240–160 pts.

NEW GRADUATE DESTINATIONS AND EMPLOYMENT (1999 HESA) (see **Ch.4**)

Of 669 graduates surveyed, 297 successfully secured full-time employment, 192 went on to further study and 54 were believed to be unemployed.

APPENDIX 1 PROFESSIONAL ASSOCIATIONS

Professional associations vary in size and function and many offer examinations to provide members with vocational qualifications. However, many of the larger bodies do not conduct examinations but accept evidence provided by the satisfactory completion of appropriate degree and diploma courses. When applying for courses in vocational subjects therefore, it is important to check whether your chosen course is accredited by a professional association, since membership of such bodies is usually necessary for advancement in your chosen career after graduation.

Further information about careers in the following subjects which can be used as background information for your UCAS form can be obtained from the associations listed below under the subject table headings of **Chapter 5**. Full details of their examinations and the degree courses accredited to them are published in *British Qualifications* (see **Appendix 2, Booklist**).

Accountancy

The Institute of Chartered Accountants in England and Wales, Gloucester House, 399 Silbury Boulevard, Central Milton Keynes MK9 2HL. Tel 01908 248100; www.icaew.co.uk

The Institute of Chartered Accountants of Scotland, 27 Queen Street, Edinburgh EH2 1LA. Tel 0131 347 0100; www.icas.org.uk

The Institute of Chartered Accountants in Ireland, 11 Donegal Square South, Belfast BT1 5JE. Tel 028 9032 1600; www/icai.ie

The Chartered Association of Certified Accountants, 29 Lincoln's Inn Fields, London WC2A 3EE. Tel 020 7396 5751; www.acca.org.uk

The Chartered Institute of Public Finance and Accountancy, 3 Robert Street, London WC2N 6BH. Tel 020 7424 3419; www.cipfa.org.uk

The Chartered Institute of Management Accountants, 63 Portland Place, London W1N 4AB. Tel 020 7637 2311; www.cima.org.uk

Actuarial Work

The Faculty of Actuaries, 40 Thistle Street, Edinburgh EH2 1AQ. Tel 0131 240 1300; www.actuaries.org.uk

The Institute of Actuaries, Napier House, 4 Worcester Street, Oxford OX1 2AW. Tel 01865 268200; www.actuaries.org.uk

Agriculture

Royal Agricultural Society, Stoneleigh, Kenilworth, Warwickshire CV8 2LX. Tel 024 7669 6969; www.rasf.org.uk

Animal Science

Animal Care and Equine National Training Organisation (ACETO), Second Floor, The Burgess Building, The Green, Stafford ST17 4BL. Tel 01785 227399; www.aceto.co.uk

The British Horse Society, Stoneleigh, Kenilworth, Warwickshire CV8 2LR.
Tel 08701 202244; www.bhs.or.uk

Archaeology

The Council for British Archaeology, Bowes Morrell House, 11 Walmgate, York
YO1 9WA. Tel 01904 671417; www.britarch.ac.uk

The Institute of Field Archaeologists, University of Reading, 2 Earley Gate,
PO Box 239, Reading, Berkshire RG6 6AU. Tel 0118 931 6446;
www.archaeologists.net

Architecture

The Royal Institute of British Architects, 66 Portland Place, London W1N 4AD.
Tel 020 7580 5533; www.riba.org.uk

British Institute of Architectural Technologists, 397 City Road, London EC1V 1NE.
Tel 020 7278 2206; www.biat.org.uk

Art and Design

The Chartered Society of Designers, Ist Floor, 32 Saffron Hill, London EC1N 8FH.
Tel 020 7357 8088.

The Crafts Council, 44a Pentonville Road, London N1 9BY. Tel 020 7278 7700;
www.craftscouncil.org.uk

The Association of British Picture Restorers, Station Avenue, Kew, Surrey
TW9 3QA. Tel 020 8948 5644; www.abpr.co.uk

The Design Council, 34 Bow Street, London WC2E 7DL. Tel 020 7420 5200;
www.designcouncil.org.uk

National Society for Education in Art and Design (NSEAD), The Gatehouse,
Corsham Court, Corsham, Wiltshire SN13 0BZ. Tel 01249 714825;
www.nsead.org

Arts

The Arts Council of England, Education and Training Department, 14 Great Peter
Street, London SW1P 3NQ. Tel 020 7333 0100; www.artscouncil.org.uk

Astronomy

Royal Astronomical Society, Burlington House, Piccadilly, London W1V 0NL.
Tel 020 7734 4582; www.ras.org.uk

Institute of Astronomy, Madingley Road, Cambridge CB3 0HA. Tel 01223 337548;
www.ast.cam.ac.uk

Banking (and Insurance)

The Chartered Institute of Bankers, 90 Bishopsgate, London EC2N 4AS.
Tel 020 7444 7111; www.ciob.org.uk

Chartered Institute of Bankers in Scotland, 19 Rutland Square, Edinburgh
EH1 2DE. Tel 0131 473 7777; www.ciobs.org.uk

The Chartered Insurance Institute, 20 Aldermanbury, London EC2V 7HY.
Tel 020 8989 8464; www.cii.co.uk

Biochemistry (see under Chemistry)

Biological Sciences
The Institute of Biology, 20 Queensbury Place, London SW7 2DZ. Tel 020 7581 8333; www.iob.org

Biology (see under Biological Sciences)

Biophysics (see under Physics)

Biotechnology (see under Biological Sciences)

Botany (see under Biological Sciences)

Building
The Chartered Institute of Building, Englemere, King's Ride, Ascot, Berkshire SL5 8BJ. Tel 01344 630700; www.ciob.org.uk

The Chartered Institution of Building Services Engineers, Delta House, 222 Balham High Road, London SW12 9BS. Tel 020 8675 5211; www.cibse.org

Business Studies
Chartered Institute of Personnel and Development, IPD House, 35 Camp Road, London SW19 4UX. Tel 020 8971 9000; www.cipd.co.uk

Communications, Advertising and Marketing Education Foundation (CAM Foundation), Abford House, 15 Wilton Road, London SW1V 1NJ. Tel 020 7828 7506; www.cm.uk.com

Institute of Chartered Secretaries and Administrators, 16 Park Crescent, London W1N 4AH. Tel 020 7580 4741; www.icsa.org.uk

Institute of Export, Export House, Minerva Business Park, Lynch Wood, Peterborough PE2 6FT. Tel 01733 404400; www.export.org.uk

Institute of Management, Management House, Cottingham Road, Corby, Northamptonshire NN17 1TT. Tel 01536 204222; www.inst-mgt.org.uk

The Institute of Public Relations, The Old Trading House, 15 North Burgh Street, London EC1V 0PR. Tel 020 7253 5151; www.ipr.org.uk

The Institute of Sales and Marketing Management (ISMM), Romeland House, Romeland Hill, St Albans, Hertfordshire AL3 4ET. Tel 01727 812500; www.ismm.co.uk

Chemistry
The Royal Society of Chemistry, Burlington House, Piccadilly, London W1J 0BA. Tel 020 7437 8656; www.rsc.org

Computing
British Computer Society, 1 Sandford Street, Swindon, Wiltshire SN1 1HJ. Tel 01793 417424; www.bsc.org.uk

The Institution of Analysts and Programmers, Charles House, 36 Culmington Road, Ealing, London W13 9NH. Tel 020 8567 2118; www.iap.org.uk

Consumer Studies
Institute of Consumer Sciences, 21 Portland Place, London W1B 1PY. Tel 020 7436 5677; www.institute-consumer-sciences.co.uk

Dance

The British Ballet Organisation, 39 Lonsdale Road, Barnes, London SW13 9JP. 020 8748 1241.

Council for Dance Education and Training, Studio 8, The Glasshouse, 49a Goldhawk Road, London W12 8QP. Tel 020 8746 0076; www.cdet.org.uk

Dentistry

British Dental Association, 64 Wimpole Street, London W1M 8AL. www.bda-dentistry.org.uk

The General Dental Council, 37 Wimpole Street, London W1M 8DQ. Tel 020 7887 3800; www.gdc-uk.org

Dietetics

The British Dietetic Association, 7th Floor, Elizabeth House, 22 Suffolk Street, Queensway, Birmingham B1 1LS. Tel 0121 616 4900; www.bda.uk.com

Drama

National Council for Drama Training, 5 Tavistock Place, London WC1H 9SS. Tel 020 7387 3650; www.ncdt.co.uk

Education

The Department for Education and Employment, Sanctuary Buildings, Great Smith Street, London SW1P 3BT. Tel 0870 001 2345; www.dfee.gov.uk

The General Teaching Council for Scotland, Clerwood House, 96 Cleriston Road, Edinburgh EH1 6UT. Tel 0131 314 6000; www.gtcs.org.uk

Teacher Training Agency, PO Box 3210, Chelmsford, Essex CM1 3WA. Tel 01245 454454; www.teach-tta.gov.uk

Welsh Office, Education Department, Cathays Park, Cardiff CF1 3NQ. Tel 01222 826010.

Engineering/Engineering Science

The Engineering Council, 10 Maltravers Street, London WC2R 3ER. Tel 020 7240 7891; www.engc.org.uk

Engineering (Acoustical)

Institute of Acoustics, 77a St Peter's Street, St Albans, Hertfordshire AL1 3BN. Tel 01727 848195; www.ioa.org.uk

Engineering (Aeronautical)

Royal Aeronautical Society, 4 Hamilton Place, London W1V 0BQ. Tel 020 7670 4300; www.aersociety.com

Engineering (Agricultural)

Institution of Agricultural Engineers, West End Road, Silsoe, Bedfordshire MK45 4DU. Tel 01525 861096; www.iagre.org.uk

Engineering (Chemical)

The Institution of Chemical Engineers, 165–189 Railway Terrace, Rugby CV21 3HQ. Tel 01788 578214; www.whynotchemeng.com

Institution of Nuclear Engineers, 1 Penerley Road, London SE6 2LQ. Tel 020 8698 1500; www.inuce.org.uk

Institute of Energy, 18 Devonshire Street, London W1N 2AV. Tel 020 7580 7124; www.instenergy.org.uk

Engineering (Civil)

The Institution of Civil Engineers, 1 Great George Street, London SW1P 3AA. Tel 020 7222 7722; www.ice.org.uk

Engineering (Electrical/Electronic)

The Institution of Electrical Engineers, Savoy Place, London WC2R 0BL. Tel 020 7240 1871; www.iee.org.uk

Institution of Electronics and Electrical Incorporated Engineers, Savoy Place, London WC2R 0BL. Tel 020 7240 1871; www.iee.org.uk

Engineering (Manufacturing)

Institute of Manufacturing, 58 Clarendon Avenue, Royal Leamington Spa, Warwickshire CV32 4SA. Tel 01926 855498.

Engineering (Marine)

The Institution of Marine Engineers, 76 Mark Lane, London EC2R 1JN. Tel 020 7382 2600; www.imare.org.uk

Engineering (Mechanical)

The Institution of Mechanical Engineers, 1 Birdcage Walk, Westminster, London SW1H 9JJ. Tel 020 7222 7899; www.imeche.org.uk

Engineering (Mining)

The Institution of Mining & Metallurgy, Danum House, South Parade, Doncaster DN1 2DY. Tel 01302 320486; www.imm.org.uk

Environmental Science

Chartered Institute of Environmental Health, Chadwick Court, Hatfields, London SE1 8DJ. Tel 020 7928 6006; www.cieh.org.uk

Film Studies

British Film Institute, 21 Stephen Street, London W1P 1PL. Tel 020 7255 1444; www.bfi.org.uk

Food Science and Technology

The Institute of Food Science and Technology, 5 Cambridge Court, Shepherds Bush Road, London W6 7NJ. Tel 020 7603 6316; www.ifst.org

Forestry

The Royal Forestry Society of England, Wales and Northern Ireland, 102 High Street, Tring, Hertfordshire HP23 4AF. Tel 01442 822028; www.rfs.org.uk

Institute of Chartered Foresters, 7A Colme Street, Edinburgh EH3 6AA. Tel 0131 225 2705; www.charteredforesters.org

Institute of Wood Science, Stocking Lane, Hughenden Valley, High Wycombe, Buckinghamshire HP14 4NU. Tel 01494 565374; www.iwsc.org.uk

Geology

The Geological Society, Burlington House, Piccadilly, London W1V 0JU.
Tel 020 7434 9944; www.geolsoc.org.uk

Home Economics and Consumer Studies

Institute of Consumer Sciences, 21 Portland Place, London W1N 3AF.
Tel 020 7436 5677; www.institute-consumer-sciences.co.uk

Hospitality Training Foundation, International House, High Street, Ealing, London W5 5DB. Tel 020 8579 2400; www.htf.org.uk

Horticulture

The Institute of Horticulture, 14 Belgrave Square, London SW1X 8PS.
Tel 020 7246 6943; www.horticulture.org.co.uk

Hotel Management

Hotel and Catering International Management Association, 191 Trinity Road, London SW17 7HN. Tel 020 8772 7400; www.hcima.org.uk

Housing

The Chartered Institute of Housing, Octavia House, Westwood Way, Coventry CV4 8JP. Tel 024 7685 1700; www.cih.org

Journalism

National Council for the Training of Journalists, Latton Bush Centre, Southern Way, Harlow, Essex CM18 7BL. Tel 01279 430009; www.nctj.com

Landscape Architecture

The Landscape Institute, 6 Barnard Mews, London SW11 1QU. Tel 020 7350 5200; www.l-i.org.uk

Law

The Law Society, Ipsley Court, Berrington Close, Redditch, Worcestershire B98 0TD. Tel 01527 517141; www.lawsociety.org.uk

The General Council of the Bar, 2–3 Cursitor Street, London EC4A 1NE.
Tel 020 7440 4000; www.barcouncil.org.uk

The Law Society of Scotland, 26 Drumsheugh Gardens, Edinburgh EH3 7YR.
Tel 0131 226 7411; www.lawscot.org.uk

Faculty of Advocates, Parliament House, Edinburgh EH1 1RF.

The Law Society of Northern Ireland, Law Society House, 98 Victoria Street, Belfast BT1 3JZ. Tel 028 9023 1614; www.lawsoc-ni.org

Leisure and Recreation Studies

Institute of Leisure and Amenity Management, ILAM House, Lower Basildon, Reading, Berkshire RG8 9NE. Tel 01491 874800; www.ilam.co.uk

Library Management and Information Management

Institute of Information Scientists, 39–41 North Road, London N7 9DP.
Tel 020 7619 0624; www.iis.org.uk

The Library Association, 7 Ridgmount Street, London WC1E 7AE. Tel 020 7255 0500; www.la-hq.org.uk

Marine Studies

The Nautical Institute, 202 Lambeth Road, London SE1 7LQ. Tel 020 7928 1351; www.nautinst.org

Marketing

The Chartered Institute of Marketing, Moor Hall, Cookham, Maidenhead, Berkshire SL6 9QH. Tel 01628 427500; www.cim.co.uk

Materials Science

The Institute of Materials, 1 Carlton House Terrace, London SW1Y 5DB. Tel 020 7451 7300; www.instmat.co.uk

Mathematics

The Institute of Mathematics and its Applications, Catherine Richards House, 16 Nelson Street, Southend-on-Sea, Essex SS1 1EF. Tel 01702 354020; www.ima.ork.uk

The Mathematical Association, 259 London Road, Leicester LE2 3BE. Tel 0116 221 0013; www.m-a.org.uk

Media Studies

National Council for the Training of Journalists, Latton Bush Centre, Southern Way, Harlow, Essex CM18 7BL. Tel 01279 430009; www.nctj.com

British Broadcasting Corporation Recruitment Services, PO Box 7000, London W12 9GJ. Tel 0845 988 3883; www.bbc.co.uk/jobs

Medicine

General Medical Council, 178 Great Portland Street, London W1N 6JE. Tel 020 7580 7642; www.gmc-uk.org

Microbiology (See under Biological Sciences)

Modern Languages

Institute of Linguists, Saxon House, 48 Southwark Street, London SE1 1UN. Tel 020 7940 3100; www.iol.org.uk

Music

Incorporated Society of Musicians, 10 Stratford Place, London W1C 1AA. Tel 020 7629 4413; www.ism.org

Naval Architecture

Royal Institution of Naval Architects, 10 Upper Belgrave Street, London SW1X 8BQ. Tel 020 7235 4622; www.rina.org.uk

Nursing

English National Board for Nursing, Midwifery and Health Visiting, PO Box 2EN, London W1A 2EN. Tel 020 7788 3131; www.enb.org.uk

National Board for Nursing, Midwifery and Health Visiting in Scotland, PO Box 21, Queen Street, Edinburgh EH2 1NT. Tel 0131 226 7371; www.nbs.org.uk

National Board for Nursing, Midwifery and Health Visiting in Northern Ireland, RAC House, 79 Chichester Street, Belfast BT1 4JE. Tel 028 9033 3298.

Welsh National Board for Nursing, Midwifery and Health Visiting, Floor 13, Pearl Assurance House, Greyfriars Road, Cardiff CF1 3AG. Tel 029 2026 1400; www.wnb.org.uk

Nutrition (see under **Dietetics**)

Occupational Therapy
British Association of Occupational Therapists, College of Occupational Therapists, 106–114 Borough High Street, London SE1 1LB. Tel 020 7357 6480; www.cot.co.uk

Optometry
British Orthoptic Society, Tavistock House North, Tavistock Square, London WC1H 9HX. Tel 020 7387 7992; www.orthoptics.org.uk

College of Optometrists, 42 Craven Street, London WC2N 5NG. Tel 020 7839 6000; www.college-optometrists.org

General Optical Council, 41 Harley Street, London W1N 2DJ. Tel 020 7580 3898; www.optical.org

Osteopathy
General Osteopathic Council, Osteopathy House, 176 Tower Bridge Road, London SE1 3LU. Tel 020 7357 6655; www.osteopathy.org.uk

Pharmacology (see under **Pharmacy**)

Pharmacy
The Royal Pharmaceutical Society of Great Britain, 1 Lambeth High Street, London SE1 7JN. Tel 020 7735 9141; www.rpsgb.org.uk

Photography
British Institute of Professional Photography, Fox Talbot House, Ware, Hertfordshire SG12 9HN. Tel 01920 464011; www.bipp.com

Royal Photographic Society, The Octagon, Milsom Street, Bath BA1 1DN. Tel 01225 462841; www.rps.org

Physical Education (see under **Education**)

Physics
Institute of Physics, 76 Portland Place, London W1B 1NT. Tel 020 7470 4800; www.iop.org

Physiotherapy
Chartered Society of Physiotherapists, 14 Bedford Row, London WC1R 4ED. Tel 020 7306 6666; www.csp.org.uk

Podiatry
The Society of Chiropodists and Podiatrists, 1 Fellmonger's Path, Tower Bridge Road, London SE1 3LY. Tel 020 7234 8620; www.feetforlife.org

Polymer Science
School of Polymer Technology, University of North London, Holloway Road, London N7 8DB. Tel 020 7753 5128; www.unl.ac.uk

Printing

Institute of Printing and Graphic Communications, The Mews, Hill House, Tunbridge Wells, Kent TN1 1NU.
Tel 01892 538118; www.globalprint.com/uk/iop

Psychology

British Psychological Society, 48 Princess Road East, Leicester LE1 7DR.Tel 0116 254 9568; www.bps.org.uk

Quantity Surveying (see under Surveying)

Radiography

The Society of Radiographers 207 Providence Square, Mill Street, London NW1 1BU. Tel 020 7740 7200; www.sor.org

Secretarial

Institute of Qualified Private Secretaries, First Floor, 6 Bridge Avenue, Maidenhead, Berkshire SL6 1RR. Tel 01628 625007; www.iqps.org.uk

Social Work

Central Council for the Education and Training in Social Work (CCETSW), London Office, 4th Floor, Caledonian House, 223–231 Pentonville Road, London N1 9NG. Tel 020 7278 2455; www.ccetsw.org.uk

Speech Pathology/Therapy

Royal College of Speech and Language Therapists, 2–3 White Hart Yard, London SE1 1NX. Tel 020 7378 1200; www.rcslt.org

Sports Studies

English Sports Council (Sport England), 16 Upper Woburn Place, London WC1H 0QP. Tel 020 7273 1500; www.english.sports.gov.uk

The Institute of Sport and Recreation Management, 36 Sherrard Street, Melton Mowbray, Leicestershire LE13 1XJ. Tel 01664 565531; www.isrm.co.uk

Scottish Sports Council, Caledonia House, South Gyle, Edinburgh, Scotland EH12 9DQ. Tel 0131 317 7200.

Statistics

Royal Statistical Society, 12 Errol Street, London EC1X 8LX. Tel 020 7638 8998; www.rss.org.uk

Surveying

Royal Institution of Chartered Surveyors, Education and Training Department, Surveyor Court, Westwood Way, Coventry CV4 8JE. Tel 020 7222 7000; www.rics.org.uk

Textiles

The Textile Institute, 4th Floor, St James's Buildings, Oxford Street, Manchester M1 6FQ. Tel 0161 237 1188; www.texi.org

Tourism

Institute of Travel and Tourism, 113 Victoria Street, St Albans, Hertfordshire AL1 3TJ. Tel 01727 854395; www.itt.co.uk

The Travel Training Company, The Cornerstone, The Broadway, Woking, Surrey GU21 5AR. Tel 01483 727321.

Town Planning

Royal Town Planning Institute, 26 Portland Place, London W1N 4BE. Tel 020 7636 9107; www.rtpi.org.uk

Toxicology

British Toxicology Society, Institute of Biology, 20–22 Queensberry Place, London SW7 2DZ. Tel 020 7581 8333.

Transport Management

Chartered Institute of Transport in the UK, 80 Portland Place, London W1N 4DP. Tel 020 7467 9425; www.citrans.org.uk

Urban Studies (see under Town Planning)

Veterinary Science/Nursing

Royal College of Veterinary Surgeons, Belgravia House, 62 Horseferry Road, London SW1P 2AF. Tel 020 7222 2001; www.rcvs.org.uk

British Veterinary Nursing Association, Level 15, Terminus House, Terminus Street, Harlow, Essex CM20 1XA. Tel 01279 450567; www.bnva.org.uk

APPENDIX 2 BOOKLIST

Standard Reference Books

British Qualifications Kogan Page Ltd, 120 Pentonville Road, London N1 9JN.

British Vocational Qualifications Kogan Page Ltd, 120 Pentonville Road, London N1 9JN.

Laser Compendium of Higher Education Butterworth Heinemann, Linacre House, Jordan Hill, Oxford OX2 8DP. Published annually.

COSHEP Entrance Guide to Higher Education in Scotland, UCAS, Rosehill, New Barn Lane, Cheltenham, Glos GL52 3LA.

Further Education Colleges in Scotland SFEU, University of Strathclyde, Jordanhill Campus, 76 South Brae Drive, Glasgow G13 1PP.

The UCAS Directory 2002 Entry UCAS, Rosehill, New Barn Lane, Cheltenham, Glos GL52 3LA. Published annually.

UCAS The Big Guide – University and College Entrance UCAS, Rosehill, New Barn Lane, Cheltenham, Glos GL52 3LA.

Other Books

The Best in University and College Courses Brian Heap. Trotman and Company Ltd, 2 The Green, Richmond, Surrey TW9 1PL.

Choosing Your Degree Course and University Brian Heap. Trotman and Company Ltd, 2 The Green, Richmond, Surrey TW9 1PL.

The Complete Parents' Guide to Higher Education Trotman and Company Ltd, 2 The Green, Richmond, Surrey TW9 1PL.

Discretionary Awards Survey and *Welfare Manual* (Both are published by the National Union of Students and can be consulted in Student Union offices in universities and colleges.)

Financial Support for Higher Education Department for Education, Student Finance, Rathgoel House, Balloo Road, Bangor, County Down BT19 2PR.

First Destinations Higher Education Statistics Agency Services, 18 Royal Crescent, Cheltenham, Glos GL50 3DA.

Socrates-Erasmus: UK Guide for Students Entering Higher Education ISCO Publications, 12a Princess Way, Camberley, Surrey GU15 3SP.

The Student Book Klaus Boehm & Jenny Lees-Spalding. Trotman and Company Ltd, 2 The Green, Richmond, Surrey TW9 1PL.

The Student Guide Students' Award Agency for Scotland, Gyleview, 3 Redheugh Riggs, South Gyle, Edinburgh EH12 9AH.

Students' Money Matters Trotman and Company Ltd, 2 The Green, Richmond, Surrey TW9 1PL.

Surfing Your Career Hilary Nickell. How To Books Ltd, 3 Newtec Place, Magdalen Road, Oxford OX4 1RE.

Taking a Year Off Val Butcher. Trotman and Company Ltd, 2 The Green, Richmond, Surrey TW9 1PL.

University Scholarships and Awards Brian Heap. Trotman and Company Ltd, 2 The Green, Richmond, Surrey TW9 1PL.

APPENDIX 3 KEY SKILLS PREFERENCE TABLES

Major reforms to the qualifications for 16–19 year-old students in full-time education and training were introduced in September 2000. These included the introduction of a teaching programme covering key skills which is now offered by some schools and colleges. The programme focuses on three main units – Application of Number, Communication and Information Technology – and will lead to a Key Skills Certificate. However, it is unlikely that the Certificate will be required as an entry qualification for admission to degree courses in 2002 although universities will recognise the achievement of the main key skills units at levels 2, 3 and 4 when included on the UCAS application form. In addition, however, students may also acquire key skills through the subjects they take at GCE and VCE AS- and A-levels as well as through part-time employment or out-of-school activities, which applicants can list in their personal statement.

Whilst schools and colleges are preparing their students in key skills, universities and colleges are following similar programmes with their undergraduates to prepare them for employment after a degree. In so doing, three further key skills, not yet being examined, are also considered by universities and colleges who regard them as equally important for their degree courses. These cover Study Skills, Problem Solving and Working with Others and the acquisition of these by the university applicant will considerably enhance the chances of a place on a degree course.

The importance of these six key skills in different degree course subjects varies considerably depending on the context of the course in question but as yet there is little published information. However, for this year's edition of *Degree Course Offers* an attempt has been made to obtain opinions from admissions tutors on the importance of key skills in their respective degree subjects: they have been asked to consider each of the six skills and identify those which they regard as the most or least important for their subject on a scale of 1–6. The results are set out in the tables below. Because of the large number of returns in most subject areas and because of the individual differences between courses the information provided can only aim to represent an average of all returns in each subject. In certain subjects, the information given will be self-evident. However, the following tables may help students and advisers to be aware of the level of importance attached by admissions tutors to specific key skills. It may also provide a prompt for discussion in exploring possible future careers.

Abbreviations:
>**Application of Number** – No
>**Communication** – Comm
>**Information Technology** – IT
>**Study Skills** – SS
>**Problem Solving** – PS
>**Working with Others** – WO

The key skills are arranged in order of importance:

Accountancy – No/Comm/PS=SS/IT/WO
Agriculture – Comm/SS/PS/WO/No/IT

American Studies – Comm/SS/IT/PS/WO/No
Animal Science – No/SS/Comm/IT/PS/WO
Anthropology – Comm/SS=WO/IT/PS/No
Archaeology – SS/Comm=PS/WO/No/IT
Architecture – IT=PS/Comm/No=WO/SS
Art & Design (General) – Comm/SS=PS/WO/IT/No
Art & Design (Fashion) – Comm/PS/SS/WO/IT/No
Art & Design (Fine Art) – Comm/SS/PS/WO/IT/No
Art & Design (Graphic Design) – Comm/PS/SS/IT/WO/No
Art & Design (Industrial Design) – Comm/PS/SS/IT/WO/No
Art & Design (Three-Dimensional Design) – Comm/SS=PS/IT=WO/No

Biochemistry – No/PS=Comm/SS=IT/WO
Biological Sciences – No/PS/Comm/SS/IT/WO
Building – Comm/PS/No/IT/SS=WO
Business Studies – Comm/IT/PS/WO=SS/No

Chemistry – No=Comm/SS=PS/IT/WO
Communication Studies – Comm/SS=IT/WO=PS/No
Community Studies – WO=Comm/PS/SS/No=IT
Computer Science – No/IT=PS/Comm/SS/WO

Dance – Comm/WO=SS/IT=PS=No
Dentistry – Comm/No=IT/WO=PS=SS
Drama – Comm/WO/SS/PS/IT/No

Economics – No/Comm=IT=PS/SS/WO
Education – Comm/WO/SS/IT/No/PS
Engineering (General) – PS/No/SS/Comm=WO/IT
Engineering (Aeronautical) – No=PS/IT=SS/Comm/IT
Engineering (Chemical) – PS=No/SS/Comm=IT=WO
Engineering (Civil) – No/PS/SS/Comm=IT=WO
Engineering (Computer) – No/PS/IT/SS/Comm/WO
Engineering (Electrical/Electronic) – No/PS=IT/Comm/SS/WO
Engineering (Manufacturing) – No/IT=PS/Comm=SS/WO
Engineering (Mechanical) – No/PS/IT/Comm/SS/WO
English – Comm/SS/WO/IT/PS/No
Environmental Science – Comm/No/SS=PS/IT=WO

Film/Video/Radio – Comm/SS/WO=IT/PS/No
Forestry – Comm/No/PS/IT=SS=WO
French – Comm/SS/IT/WO/PS/No

Geography – SS=PS/Comm/IT=No/WO
Geology – PS/SS/Comm/No=IT/WO

Health Studies – Comm/WO/SS/PS/IT/No
History – Comm/SS/WO/IT=PS/No
Horticulture – Comm/IT/No/SS=PS=WO
Hotel Management – Comm/WO/PS/No=IT/SS

Law – Comm/SS/PS/IT=WO/No
Leisure Studies – Comm/WO/IT/PS/No/SS
Librarianship – Comm=IT/SS=WO/PS/No

Marine Studies – Comm/SS=No/IT/PS/WO
Marketing – No=Comm/IT/PS/WO/SS

Materials Science – No/PS/SS/Comm=IT/WO
Mathematics – No/PS/SS/Comm=IT/WO
Media Studies – Comm/IT/PS/WO/SS/No
Medicine – Comm/No/SS=PS/IT/WO
Microbiology – No/Comm/SS=PS/IT/WO
Music – Comm/WO/IT/PS/SS/No

Nursing – Comm/No/WO/PS/IT/SS

Occupational Therapy – Comm/WO/PS/IT=SS/No
Oceanography – No/Comm/SS/PS/IT/WO

Photography – Comm/PS=WO/SS/IT/No
Physiotherapy – Comm/PS/WO=SS/IT/No
Politics – Comm/PS/IT=SS/WO/No
Psychology – SS/PS/Comm/No/WO/It

Radiography – Comm/WO/No/PS/IT=SS
Religious Studies – Comm/SS/WO/PS/IT/No

Social Policy – SS/PS/WO/Comm=IT/No
Social Studies – Comm/SS/PS/WO/IT/No
Social Work – WO/Comm/PS/SS/IT/No
Sociology – Comm/WO/SS=PS/IT/No
Sports Studies – Comm/WO/SS/IT/PS/No
Surveying – Comm/SS/PS/WO/IT=No

Tourism – Comm/WO/PS/SS/No/IT

COURSE INDEX

INDEX OF ADVERTISERS